FOR REFERENCE

Do Not Take From This Room

Morrison's
Sound-It-Out
Speller

a Phonic Key to English

Morrison's
Sound-It-Out
Speller

a Phonic Key to English

edited
and expanded by
Penelope Kister McRann

compiled by
Marvin L. Morrison and Penelope Kister McRann

originated by
Marvin L. Morrison

COMPLETE EDITION

Published by
Stone Cloud Phonics
Hope Mills, NC & La Mesa, CA
USA

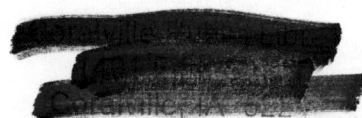

Publisher's Cataloging-in-Publication
  (Provided by Quality Books, Inc.)

Morrison's sound-it-out speller : a phonic key to English /
edited and expanded by Penelope Kister McRann ; compiled
by Marvin L. Morrison and Penelope Kister McRann ;
originated by Marvin L. Morrison. -- 1st ed. Expanded
ed.
  p. cm.
  ISBN : 0-9678068-0-1

  1. English language--Phonetic transcriptions.
  2. English language--Phonetics. 3. English language--
Orthography and spelling--Dictionaries.   I. Morrison,
Marvin.   II. Kister, Penelope A.

PE1135.M67 2000   421'.5
                          QBI00-265

Morrison's Sound-It-Out Speller is an expanded edition of Word Finder: the Phonic Key to the
Dictionary last published in 1993. Morrison's Sound-It-Out Speller's principle copyright is
1981, and is based on The Phonetic Finder.

www.Sound-It-Out.com

Book design and typography by Marvin L. Morrison

Made in the USA

Contents

Acknowledgements

With deepest appreciation to our sons, Spencer and Chad Morrison and Ian Dillon, whose quick grasp and grateful usage of the system made it impossible for us to quit; to Laurence Urdang, who first mentioned that the book might help dyslexics and offered suggestions that were incorporated into the system; to Ken Kister (no relation to Penelope Kister McRann), for his encouragement and suggestion that we demonstrate the book's principle —the omission of vowels—on its cover; to Audrey McRann, whose tireless efforts improved our hints immeasurably; to Wood Smethurst, for recognizing the usefulness of this system and writing two powerful Introductions in previous editions; to a host of wonderful educators, including Dr. Ginger Hovenic, Casey Zawacki, Becky Ritter and Cathryn Weiss, for their words of praise and for letting us know how much their students loved our system; to Alice Koontz for introducing *Word City* and *Word Finder* to so many people; to Helen Ignas, who minded the business while we were away; to "Cosmic" Carla Marks and Greg Sindewald, for the bookstore gig and more; to Jilly Eggerton, for showing us what persistence is all about; and to Bob McRann, without whose guidance and support this expanded and revised edition might never have been completed.

Editor's Notes

This Complete Edition includes accepted spellings for almost all of the words generally listed in standard collegiate dictionaries, with some exceptions. Entries listed after the word "or" in most dictionaries (i.e., lambaste *or* lambast) are included, but entries listed after the word "also" in most dictionaries (i.e., peddler *also* pedlar) are omitted. Archaic words have been excluded. Legal, scientific and medical terms are included as well as many common chemicals along with many widely known locations and historical figures. My sincere apologies for any word(s) that may have been overlooked.

The generally accepted practices of dictionary listings for plurals and verbs are used in this book:

- Words should be looked up in their singular forms. Plurals have been spelled out whenever they involve more than simply adding an *s*.
- Unusual plurals that do not end in an *s* sound (i.e., *oxen* as the plural of *ox*) have their own entries.
- Whenever a verb has an irregular form (as *cry* does) all of the verb forms are spelled out (*cries, cried, crying*).

The italicized words immediately following entries are *hints*. They are provided to help confirm that the proper word has been found. Hints are not intended to be complete definitions and only cover the most common meanings. Words that have a large number of meanings are given an asterisk (*) to indicate that additional common meanings exist.

Words with only vowel sounds (i.e., *oh, awe, eye*, etc.) are listed alphabetically on page 1 along with their hints.

British spellings and usages are identified by the notation (Br).

When there is more than one standard pronunciation for a word, each pronunciation will have a locator (i.e., the word *often* is listed at **FTN** and **FN**). Words like *link* that have an **NG** sound (ling-k) are listed with and without the **NG** sound (**LNGK** and **LNK**). When a pronunciation allows for either the **T** or **D** sound, both are used (*butter* is listed at **BTR** and **BDR**). In the same way, both **ZH** and **SH** can be used to describe the sound in *vision* (**VZHN** or **VSHN**). And to help avoid confusion, anytime the "*see*," "*gee*" and "*cue*" syllables are heard, the **C**, **G** and **Q** letters can be used (i.e., the word *scene* is listed at **SN** and **CN**, the word *ecology* is listed at **KLJ** and **KLG** and the word *cube* is listed at **KB**, **KYB** and **QB**).

Penelope Kister McRann
San Diego, California
January 20, 2000

Originator's Comments

I have always been a poor speller and have experienced many long, frustrating dictionary searches that have ended without the needed word. Finding the word meant taking the time to find and read text where there was a good chance the word would be used. And even then there was no guarantee. Committing the the hard-to-spell words to memory didn't help much because they were forgotten in a few days. Only familiar words stayed in my memory for long. I'm very glad the problem has lessened with age.

My children probably inherited my less-than-perfect visual memory for word forms. They were constantly interrupting at crucial times during the Sunday afternoon pro football games to ask me to spell words they knew—but couldn't look up easily. They would hear the familiar "Look it up" come back from the direction of the TV. About the fifth grade they began to respond, "But Dad, how can I look it up if I can't spell it?" You have to try and try again. And while showing them how not to give up, I too sometimes failed to find the word. After a while, this got to be very embarrassing.

About the time my children reached middle school, I set out to find an easy way to look up words. After about three months I gave up, but somehow the project lived on. From time to time the issue would show up without any invitation at all.

While I was looking out of a train window one cold and gray winter morning in 1981, the issue came up one more time. After wrestling with it for a while, I became very angry at the vowels. And, all of a sudden, lightning struck. Kick them out? Consonants became heavier objects like stones and vowels became lighter objects like clouds that could easily be swept out of the away. I watched as the problem solved itself.

I relate this story because the usual question is "How did this book come about?" Thank you for your indulgence.

Penelope Kister McRann, my partner and editor of this new edition, brought her ideas and her attention to detail and applied them to my original work, enlarging it and making it easier to understand and use.

To do this she eliminated my somewhat strict set of rules that were part of the first two editions and expanded the system by making sure *every* entry had a hint, adding many more entries and alternate locators, and by bringing all of the consonant letters into play.

A good example of her work is how she uses the letters **C**, **G** and **Q**. The **C** is used as part of the **CH** symbol as would be expected but also when the *"see"* sound is heard. She gives a similar treatment to **G**, and the letter **Q** may be used for the **KY** *and* **KW** sounds. So, in this new edition, the word *psychology* can be found at **SKLJ** as well as **SKLG**, and the word *sequence* can be found at **CKWNS**, **SKWNS**, **CQNS**, **SQNS**, **CKWNTS**, **SKWNTS**, **CQNTS**, and **SQNTS**.

Her insight, thoroughness, and hard work come out and meet you.

Thank you, Penny, for your many ideas and for making them real.

Marvin L. Morrison
Hope Mills, NC
January 2000

How to Use This Book

Using this book is easy when you listen carefully.

To find a word, try not to picture how it is spelled. Instead, focus on sound and use what you hear to create a spelling *locator* which will lead you to the word you want.

Creating a *locator*:

Sound the word out............................	**KOR US**
Omit the vowels....................................	**K_R_S**
Look up the *locator* that remains	**KRS**
...and find the word and its hint.	**chorus** *music*

Things to remember:

When constructing a *locator*, always use letters to indicate what you actually hear instead of letters you think might be in the correct spelling. In order to help relax the visual memory...

— Never use **C** when **S** or **K** is what you hear.
     (**SRKL circle**) (**SKL cycle**)

— Use **J** when you hear the sound that begins *jag* and *gem*.
     (**JG jag**) (**JM gem**)

— Use **W** and **Y** only when you hear them as consonant sounds.
     (**WD widow**) (**YRL yearly**)

— Never double a consonant to represent a single sound.
     (to find **valley** use **VL** not **VLL**)

Going through the examples on the next page should help you to master the system quickly.

Examples

Sound the word out.	Omit the vowels.	Look up the locator.	Find the word and hint.
SIR KUL	S_RK_L	**SRKL**	circle *enclose, ring*
NA CHUR	N_CH_R	**NCHR**	nature *creation, type*
E ZE	_Z_	**Z**	easy *simple*
A BIL A DE	_B_L_D_	**BLD**	ability *skill*
A BIL A TE	_B_L_T_	**BLT**	ability *skill*
SIN IK	S_N_K	**SNK**	cynic *doubter*
SU	S_	**S**	Sioux *Native American*
FA ZEK	F_Z_K	**FZK**	physique *body shape*
OR DERV	_RD_RV	**RDRV**	hors d'oeuvre *appetizer*
SA PE NA	S_P_N_	**SPN**	subpoena *legal summons*
NIF	N_F	**NF**	knife *blade, slice*
NU MA DIK	N_M_D_K	**NMDK**	pneumatic *compressed air*
NU MA TIK	N_M_T_K	**NMTK**	pneumatic *compressed air*
LAF	L_F	**LF**	laugh *happy sound*
KWIK	KW_K	**KWK**	quick *fast*
QUIK	Q_ _K	**QK**	quick *fast*
WUNS	W_NS	**WNS**	once *one time, formerly*
WUNTS	W_NTS	**WNTS**	once *one time, formerly*
O PAK	_P_K	**PK**	opaque *milky*

Abbreviations

(abbr) .... abbreviation
(adj) .... adjective
(adv) .... adverb
(Br) .... British spelling or usage
(conj) .... conjunction
(f) .... feminine
(interj) .... interjection
(m) .... masculine
(n) .... noun
(pl) .... plural
(prep) .... preposition
(pron) .... pronoun
(s) .... singular
(v) .... verb

aah (or) aaahh *(interj) relief, pleasure**

ah *(interj) satisfaction, surprise**

aw *(interj) regret*

awe *(v) inspire wonder* awed awing

awe *(n) wonderment*

aye *yes*

eh *(interj) question*

ewe *sheep*

eye *(v) look at* eyed eyeing (or) eying

eye *(n) vision tool, center*

I *(pron) me*

i *alphabet letter* i's (or) is

i.e. *(Latin abbr) that is*

Io *volcanic moon*

o *alphabet letter* o's (or) os

oh *(interj) surprise, fear** oh's

ooh *(interj) pleasure, satisfaction** oohs

ow *(interj) pain*

owe *be indebted to* owed owing

uh *(interj) uncertainty, hesitation*

uh-oh *(interj) mistake*

you *(pron) not me*

B

B aba *fabric*

B abbé *title*

B abbey *monastery* abbeys

B baa *bleat* baaed baaing

B bah *(interj) contempt*

B bay *(v) howl, pursue (n) horse, compartment, laurel**

B bayou *creek*

B be *exist*

B beau *boyfriend* beaux (or) beaus

B bee *insect, letter B,*

gathering

B boa *snake, scarf*

B boo *(interj) frighten*

B bough *branch*

B bow *(v) bend (n) ship, arrow, knot*

B boy *male child*

B buoy *float*

B buy *purchase* bought buying buys

B by *near*

B bye *farewell*

B ebb *go back*

B hautboy (or) hautbois *oboe* hautboys (or) hautbois

B obe**ah** sor*cery*

B obey *comply*

B obi *sash*

B oboe *music*

BB babe *baby*

BB babu *Hindu gentleman*

BB baby *(v) coddle* babied babying babies

BB baby *(n) infant* babies

BB bawbee *coin*

BB bib *(v) drink* bibbed bibbing

BB bib *(n) apron*

BB bob *(v) bounce, cut short* bobbed bobbing

BB bob *(n) weight, shilling, hairdo**

BB bobby *(Br) policeman* bobbies

BB boo-boo *mistake, injury* boo-boos

BB boob *simpleton*

BB booby *bird, dunce* boobies

BB bub *fellow*

BB bubo *swelling* buboes

BB bulb *flower, light*

BB bye-bye *farewell*

BBB baobab *tree*

BBBL baby blue *color*

BBBM baby boom *birthrate*

BBBMR baby boomer *post-war baby*

BBDST baptist *religion (often capitalized)*

BBDSTR baptistery *church part* baptisteries

BBGN BB gun *pellet gun*

BBGRN baby grand *piano*

BBGRND baby grand *piano*

BBHCH booby hatch *asylum, storage area*

BBHD babyhood *infancy*

BBHWT bobwhite *bird*

BBK buyback *repurchase*

BBKK bibbcock *faucet*

BBKT bobcat *lynx*

BBL abubble *boiling*

BBL babble *talk* babbled babbling

BBL Babel *tower*

BBL bauble *trinket*

BBL bibelot *ornament* bibelots

BBL bible *official book*

BBL Bible *sacred book*

BBL bobble *fumble* bobbled bobbling

BBL bubble *(n) hollow globule*

BBL bubble *(v) gurgle, effervesce* bubbled bubbling

BBL bubbly *with bubbles* bubblier bubbliest

BBLBLT Bible Belt (the) *region*

BBLDS Bibb lettuce *vegetable*

BBLFL bibliophile *book lover*

BBLGM bubble gum (or) bubblegum *(n) gum, rock music* bubblegum *(adj)*

BBLGRF bibliography *book list* bibliographies

BBLGRFR bibliographer *compiler*

BBLKL biblical *of the Bible*

BBLN Babylon *city*

BBLNGK bobolink *bird*

BBLNK bobolink *bird*

BBLNN Babylonian *of Babylon*

BBLNYN Babylonian *of Babylon*

BBLPL bibliopole (or) bibliopolist *book dealer*

BBLPLST bibliopolist (or) bibliopole *book dealer*

BBLR babbler *talker*
BBLR bubbler *fountain*
BBLR bubblier *more bubbles*
BBLS bibulous *absorbent*
BBLSNS bibulousness
absorbency
BBLST bubbliest *most
bubbles*
BBLT bulblet *small bulb*
BBLTHK bibliotheca *library*
bibliothecas (or)
bibliothecae
BBLTHRP bibliotherapy
reading
BBLTS Bibb lettuce
vegetable
BBLYFL bibliophile *book
lover*
BBLYGRF bibliography *book
list* bibliographies
BBLYGRFR bibliographer
compiler
BBLYPL bibliopole (or)
bibliopolist *book dealer*
BBLYPLST bibliopolist (or)
bibliopole *book dealer*
BBLYR bubblier *more bubbles*
BBLYST bubbliest *most
bubbles*
BBLYTHK bibliotheca
library bibliothecas (or)
bibliothecae
BBLYTHRP bibliotherapy
reading
BBN baboon *ape*
BBN bobbin *sewing*
BBNK bubonic *swollen*
BBNKPLG bubonic plague
disease
BBNT bobbinet *machine*
BBP bebop *dance*
BBPN bobby pin *clip*
BBPR bebopper *dancer*
BBPRZ booby prize *last
place*
BBR bayberry *myrtle*
bayberries
BBR bibber *drinker*
BBR bobber *floater*
BBRD beebread *pollen*
BBS babassu *palm*
BBSBRTH baby's breath

plant
BBSDR baby-sitter *childcare
worker*
BBSH babyish *youthful*
BBSH bobeche *candle*
BBSHK babushka *scarf*
BBSKS bobby socks (or)
bobby sox *stockings*
BBSKSR bobby-soxer
teenager
BBSLD bobsled *vehicle*
BBSLDNG bobsledding
sport
BBST baby-sit *child care*
baby-sat baby-sitting
BBST bobstay *rope*
BBSTR baby-sitter *childcare
worker*
BBSX bobby socks (or)
bobby sox *stockings*
BBSXR bobby-soxer
teenager
BBT Babbitt *conformist*
BBT babbitt *alloy*
BBTB boob tube *television*
BBTK baby talk *babble*
BBTL bobtail *(n) animal*
BBTL bobtail (or) bobtailed
(adj) short tail
BBTLD bobtailed (or)
bobtail (adj) *(adj) short tail*
BBTRP booby trap *pitfall*
BBTRPT booby-trapped
pitfall
BBTST baptist *(often
capitalized) religion*
BBTSTR baptistery *church
part* baptisteries
BBTTH baby tooth *milktooth*
BBTZ baptize *initiate*
baptized baptizing
BBTZM baptism *water ritual*
BBTZML baptismal *water
ritual*
BBTZR baptizer *initiator*
BBWR barbed wire *fence*
BBWT bobwhite *bird*
BBWYR barbed wire *fence*
BBYLS bibulous *absorbent*
BBYLSNS bibulousness
absorbency
BBYSH babyish *youthful*

BBZBRTH baby's breath
plant
BC abbacy *abbot* abbacies
BC Boise *city*
BC bossy *(adj) dictatorial*
bossier bossiest
BC bossy *(n) cow* bossies
BCCH beseech *implore*
beseeched (or) besought
beseeching
BCDRN abecedarian *learner*
BCDRYN abecedarian
learner
BCH bach *live alone*
BCH batch *amount* batches
BCH beach *seashore*
beaches
BCH beachy *sandy*
BCH beech *tree* beeches
(or) beech
BCH bitch *dog* bitches
BCH bitchy *angry* bitchier
bitchiest
BCH boccie (or) bocci (or)
bocce *game*
BCH botch *ruin*
BCH botchy *messy*
BCH butch *mannish* butches
BCHB beachboy *attendant*
BCHBG beach buggy *car*
BCHBL beach ball *inflatable
ball*
BCHD beachhead *foothold*
BCHDP botched up *ruined*
BCHFRNT beachfront
shoreline
BCHGR beachgoer *shore
visitor*
BCHGWR beachgoer *shore
visitor*
BCHHD beachhead *foothold*
BCHKMR beachcomber
shell seeker
BCHL bitchily *angrily*
BCHLN botulin *toxin*
BCHLR bachelor *unmarried
man*
BCHLRHD bachelorhood
unmarried
BCHLRSBTN bachelor's
button *flower*
BCHLRT bachelorette

unmarried woman
BCHLRZBTN bachelor's button *flower*
BCHLZM botulism *disease*
BCHNS bitchiness *anger*
BCHNT beechnut *edible nut*
BCHP botch up *ruin*
BCHR batcher *mixer*
BCHR bitchier *angrier*
BCHR butcher *meat cutter*
BCHR butchery *meat market* butcheries
BCHR obituary *death notice* obituaries
BCHRBRD butcher-bird *bird*
BCHSD beachside *shoreline*
BCHST bitchiest *angriest*
BCHTP botched up *ruined*
BCHWR beachwear *clothing*
BCHWR obituary *death notice* obituaries
BCHYR bitchier *angrier*
BCHYST bitchiest *angriest*
BCJ besiege *surround, beset* besieged besieging
BCJR besieger *surround, beset*
BCKWS obsequious *subservient*
BCKWSL obsequiously *subservient*
BCKWSNS obsequiousness *subservience*
BCKWYS obsequious *subservient*
BCKWYSL obsequiously *subservient*
BCKWYSNS obsequiousness *subservience*
BCN obscene *lewd*
BCNL obscenely *lewdly*
BCNSS biocenosis (or) biocoenosis *ecology* biocenoses
BCQS obsequious *subservient*
BCQSL obsequiously *subservient*
BCQSNS obsequiousness *subservience*

BCQYS obsequious *subservient*
BCQYSL obsequiously *subservient*
BCQYSNS obsequiousness *subservience*
BCR bossier *dominating*
BCST bossiest *dominating*
BCYR bossier *dominating*
BCYST bossiest *dominating*
BCZ bases (pl) *foundation* basis
BD abide *endure* abode (or) abided abiding
BD abode *house*
BD aubade *music*
BD bad *evil, foul* worse worst
BD baddie (or) baddy *evil one* baddies
BD bade *(v-past) bid*
BD batty *crazy* battier battiest
BD baud *speed*
BD bawd *prostitute*
BD bawdy *lewd* bawdier bawdiest
BD bead *tiny ball, droplet*
BD beady *small and shiny* beadier beadiest
BD beauty *pretty one* beauties
BD bed *(v) put to sleep, base (n) sleep area, foundation, heap* bedded bedding
BD bedew *wet*
BD beta *Greek letter*
BD betta *fish*
BD bid *(v) command, offer* bade (or) bid bidding bidden
BD bid *(n) attempt*
BD biddy *hen* biddies
BD bide *stay* bode (or) bided biding
BD bidet *toilet*
BD biota *life*
BD bitty *tiny*
BD bod *(slang) body*
BD bode *foretell* boded boding
BD body *(n) trunk, main part*

bodies
BD body *(v) give shape to* bodied bodying bodies
BD bootee (or) bootie *slipper*
BD booty *prize* booties
BD boughed *branched*
BD bowed *bent*
BD bud *sprout* budded budding
BD Buddha *enlightened one*
BD buddy *(n) friend* buddies
BD buddy *(v) be friendly* buddied buddying buddies
BD buteo *hawk* buteos
BDB Abu Dhabi *city*
BDB bedaub *spot*
BDBG bedbug *insect*
BDBG body bag *container*
BDBL biddable (adj) *docile* biddably (adv)
BDBL body blow *punch*
BDBLD bad blood *resentment*
BDBLD biddability *docility*
BDBLDN bodybuilding *muscles*
BDBLDNG bodybuilding *muscles*
BDBLDR bodybuilder *muscles*
BDBLKR beta-blocker *heart drug*
BDBLT biddability *docility*
BDBRD bed board *support*
BDCHK bed check *report*
BDCHK body check (n) *shove* bodycheck (v)
BDCHL Botticelli *artist*
BDCHMBR bedchamber *bedroom*
BDD beaded *decoration*
BDD bedded *sleep*
BDDN butadiene *gas*
BDF beat off *(vulgar) masturbate*
BDF beatify *sanctify* beatified beatifying beatifies
BDF beautify *make pretty* beautified beautifying beautifies

BDFL beautiful (adj) *lovely* beautifully (adv)

BDFL bedfellow *associate*

BDFS bedfast *in bed*

BDFST bedfast *in bed*

BDG bodega *saloon*

BDGRD bodyguard *protector*

BDGRDBL biodegradable *digestible*

BDHS bawdy house *bordello*

BDK abduct *kidnap*

BDK abiotic *not living*

BDK bedeck *adorn*

BDK biotic *living*

BDK boat hook *pole*

BDK buttock *rump*

BDKBL abdicable *resign*

BDKDR abdicator *one who resigns*

BDKDR abductor *kidnapper*

BDKL abiotically *not living*

BDKLTHZ bedclothes *sheets*

BDKLZ bedclothes *sheets*

BDKN bodkin *needle*

BDKNT body count *number*

BDKRTN beta-carotene *plant isomer*

BDKSHN abdication *resignation*

BDKSHN abduction *kidnapping*

BDKT abdicate *resign* abdicated abdicating

BDKT abduct *kidnap*

BDKT body count *number*

BDKTR abdicator *one who resigns*

BDKTR abductor *kidnapper*

BDL badly *poorly*

BDL battle *fight* battled battling

BDL bawdily *lewdly*

BDL beau ideal *model* beau ideals

BDL beetle *insect*

BDL betel *plant*

BDL bodily *flesh*

BDL bottle (v) *confine* bottled bottling

BDL bottle (n) *container*

BDL buddleia *shrub*

BDL butyl *chemical*

BDLD bottled *confined*

BDLDD butylated *combined*

BDLFL battlefield *war arena*

BDLFL bottleful *container*

BDLFLD battlefield *war arena*

BDLFTG battle fatigue *war exhaustion*

BDLGRN battleground *war arena*

BDLGRND battleground *war arena*

BDLJS Betelgeuse *star*

BDLJZ Betelgeuse *star*

BDLKR battle cry *war yell* battle cries

BDLKS battle-ax *tool,* woman battle-axes

BDLM bedlam *asylum, confusion*

BDLMNT battlement *parapet*

BDLN abutilon *plant*

BDLN bottling *containers*

BDLN butylene *chemical*

BDLNDZ badlands *hilly region*

BDLNG bottling *containers*

BDLNGGWJ body language *gestures*

BDLNGWJ body language *gestures*

BDLNK bottleneck *narrow part*

BDLNZ badlands *hilly region*

BDLR battler *fighter*

BDLR Baudelaire *poet*

BDLR bottler *containers*

BDLRL battle royal *struggle* battles royal

BDLRYL battle royal *struggle* battles royal

BDLRZ bowdlerize *abridge* bowdlerized bowdlerizing (Br) bowdlerise

BDLRZSHN bowdlerization *abridge* (Br) bowdlerisation

BDLS abuttals *boundaries*

BDLS Beatles *musicians*

BDLS bodiless *without form*

BDLS body louse *insect*

BDLSHP battleship *war ship*

BDLTD butylated *combined*

BDLWGN battlewagon *war ship*

BDLX battle-ax *tool, woman* battle-axes

BDLY buddleia *shrub*

BDLZ Beatles *musicians*

BDM bottom *buttocks, base*

BDMD bottomed *ended*

BDMLN bottom line (n) *main point*

BDMLN bottom-line (adj) *profits*

BDMLND bottomland *low-lying*

BDMLS bottomless *unlimited*

BDMN abdomen *stomach*

BDMNL abdominal (adj) *stomach* abdominally (adv)

BDMNTN badminton *sport*

BDMST bottommost *deepest*

BDMT bedmate *partner*

BDMTH bad-mouth *criticize*

BDMTN badminton *sport*

BDN abiding *enduring*

BDN batten (n) *thin strip* (v) *fasten*

BDN beading *decoration*

BDN bedding *foundation, sheets*

BDN bedouin (or) beduin *nomad* bedouin (or) bedouins (or) beduin (or) beduins

BDN bidden (v-past) *bid*

BDN boding *omen*

BDN budding *early stage*

BDN button (v) *fasten* (n) *fastener*

BDNBL buttonball *plane*

BDNBSH buttonbush *shrub*

BDNDN button-down *conservative, collar*

BDNDP buttoned-up *reserved*

BDNDRFN beta-endorphin *pituatary*

BDNG abiding *enduring*

BDNG bating *excepting*

BDNG batting *action,*

material
BDNG beading *decoration*
BDNG beating *defeat, whipping*
BDNG bedding *foundation, sheets*
BDNG betting *wager*
BDNG biting *sharp*
BDNG boating *ship*
BDNG budding *early stage*
BDNGGLSH body English *motion*
BDNGL abidingly *enduringly*
BDNGLSH body English *motion*
BDNGVRJ batting average *statistic*
BDNHK buttonhook *fastener, football play*
BDNHL buttonhole *(n) opening (v) detain*
BDNHLR buttonholer *(n) opening (v) detain*
BDNJ badinage *banter*
BDNR buttoner *fastener*
BDNRSH Baton Rouge *city*
BDNRZH Baton Rouge *city*
BDNS abidance *compliance*
BDNS badness *evil*
BDNS battiness *craziness*
BDNS bawdiness *lewdness*
BDNS obedience *dutifulness*
BDNSH badinage *banter*
BDNSK buttinsky *meddler* buttinskies
BDNT obedient *dutiful*
BDNTL obediently *dutifully*
BDNTS abidance *compliance*
BDNTS obedience *dutifulness*
BDNZH badinage *banter*
BDP beat up *(v) pummel*
BDP beat-up *(adj) damaged*
BDPLR beauty parlor *salon* (Br) beauty parlour
BDPN bedpan *waste vessel*
BDPRLR beauty parlor *salon* (Br) beauty parlour
BDPST bedpost *bed fixture*
BDPST Budapest *city*
BDR abater *lessen*

BDR abettor (or) abetter *aide*
BDR abider *endurer*
BDR abutter *toucher*
BDR badder *(slang) better*
BDR batter *(n) hitter, food mixture, slope (v) bombard, coat food*
BDR battery *(n) energy source, guns, array** batteries
BDR battier *crazier*
BDR bawdier *lewd*
BDR bayadere *fabric*
BDR beadier *smaller and shinier*
BDR beater *hitter, mixer*
BDR bedder *plant*
BDR bee-eater *bird*
BDR better *improved, gambler*
BDR bettor (or) better *wagerer*
BDR bidder *offer*
BDR bider *tolerate*
BDR biter *teeth*
BDR bitter *taste*
BDR boater *ship*
BDR budder *plant*
BDR butter *food*
BDR buttery *creamy*
BDRBL butterball *chubby one*
BDRBN butter bean *vegetable*
BDRBRSH bitterbrush *shrub*
BDRC obduracy *stubborn* obduracies
BDRD battered *beaten, coated*
BDRDKD obiter dicta (pl) *opinion* obiter dictum
BDRDKDM obiter dictum *opinion* obiter dicta
BDRDKT obiter dicta (pl) *opinion* obiter dictum
BDRDKTM obiter dictum *opinion* obiter dicta
BDRDN bedridden *confined*
BDRF better-off *comfortable*
BDRFL butterfly *insect* butterflies
BDRFNGGRD

butterfingered *clumsy*
BDRFNGGRS butterfingers *clumsy*
BDRFNGGRZ butterfingers *clumsy*
BDRFNGRD butterfingered *clumsy*
BDRFNGRS butterfingers *clumsy*
BDRFNGRZ butterfingers *clumsy*
BDRFSH butterfish *fish*
BDRFT butterfat *milk fat*
BDRGL bedraggle *wet* bedraggled bedraggling
BDRGLD bedraggled *wet and limp*
BDRK bedrock *foundation*
BDRKP buttercup *flower*
BDRKSHNL bidirectional *two directions*
BDRL bedroll *bedding*
BDRM bedroom *sleep area*
BDRMLK buttermilk *beverage*
BDRMNT betterment *improvement*
BDRN bedridden *confined*
BDRND bitter end *conclusion*
BDRNF butter knife *utensil*
BDRNG battering *attacking*
BDRNGRM battering ram *metal bar*
BDRNRM battering ram *metal bar*
BDRNT butternut *tree*
BDRS bitters *flavoring*
BDRS obduracy *stubborn* obduracies
BDRSKCH butterscotch *candy, color*
BDRSPDR beta-receptor *nerve cell*
BDRSPTR beta-receptor *nerve cell*
BDRST bed rest *illness*
BDRSWT bittersweet *(adj) taste, feeling (n) plant*
BDRT bitterroot *herb*
BDRT obdurate *stubborn*
BDRTL obdurately *stubborn*

Letters aren't doubled for single sounds: to find alley use **L** not **LL**. Use **Y** and **W** as hard sounds only: to find yellow use **YL**. (Br)=British spelling or usage. * See dictionary.

BDRTNS obdurateness *stubborn*
BDRWD bitterweed (or) butterweed *plant*
BDRWRT butterwort *herb*
BDS badass *(vulgar)* mean one *(vulgar)*
BDS beauteous *lovely*
BDS boathouse *shelter*
BDS bodice *dress*
BDSD bedside *by a bed*
BDSHP beauty shop *salon*
BDSHP body shop *car repair*
BDSHRT body shirt *blouse*
BDSHS bodacious *remarkable*
BDSHSL bodaciously *remarkably*
BDSHT bedsheet *bedding*
BDSLN beauty salon *personal care shop*
BDSPRD bedspread *cover*
BDSPRNG bedspring *mattress*
BDSR bedsore *ulcer*
BDSRF bodysurf *ride waves*
BDSRFR bodysurfer *ride waves*
BDST baddest *(slang) best*
BDST battiest *craziest*
BDST bawdiest *lewd*
BDST beadiest *smallest and shiniest*
BDST bodysuit *attire*
BDSTD bedstead *framework*
BDSTKNG body stocking *hosiery*
BDSTR bedstraw *herb*
BDSTV bodhisattva *deity*
BDTBL bed table *lap board*
BDTD beatitude *blissful state*
BDTM bedtime *time to sleep*
BDTMPRD bad-tempered *irate*
BDTRN betatron *accelerator*
BDTYD beatitude *blissful state*
BDVL bedevil *annoy*
BDVLMNT bedevilment *annoyance*
BDVRSD biodiversity *different species*

BDVRST biodiversity *different species*
BDVRZZ bed of roses *good situation*
BDW boudoir *bedroom*
BDWN bedouin (or) beduin *nomad* bedouin (or) bedouins (or) beduin (or) beduins
BDWR boudoir *bedroom*
BDWRK beadwork *decoration*
BDWRM budworm *insect*
BDWV beta wave *brain wave*
BDY buteo *hawk* buteos
BDYNS obedience *dutifulness*
BDYNT obedient *dutiful*
BDYNTL obediently *dutifully*
BDYNTS obedience *dutifulness*
BDYR battier *crazier*
BDYR bawdier *lewd*
BDYR beadier *smaller and shinier*
BDYRC obduracy *stubborn* obduracies
BDYRS obduracy *stubborn* obduracies
BDYRT obdurate *stubborn*
BDYRTL obdurately *stubborn*
BDYRTNS obdurateness *stubborn*
BDYS beauteous *lovely*
BDYST battiest *craziest*
BDYST bawdiest *lewd*
BDYST beadiest *smallest and shiniest*
BDZL bedazzle *enchant* bedazzled bedazzling
BDZLMNT bedazzlement *enchantment*
BDZM Buddhism *religion*
BF abaft *behind*
BF beef *meat* beefs (or) beeves
BF beefy *meaty, sturdy* beefier beefiest
BF boff (or) boffo *laugh, smash hit* boffs (or) boffos

BF buff *(v) shine (n) nude, enthusiast, color (adj) coloring*
BF buffet *meal*
BF buffo *clown* buffi (or) buffos
BFBRGNN beef bourguignon *food*
BFBRGNYN beef bourguignon *food*
BFDBK biofeedback *mental control*
BFDL befuddle *confuse* befuddled befuddling
BFDLD befuddled *confused*
BFDLMNT befuddlement *confusion*
BFDNG befitting *proper*
BFDR beefeater *guard*
BFG befog *mist*
BFKK beefcake *male physique*
BFKL bifocal *two lenses*
BFKLS bifocals *two lenses*
BFL baffle *(v) perplex* baffled baffling
BFL baffle *(n) wall*
BFL beefalo *animal* beefalos (or) beefaloes
BFL befall *happen to* befell befallen
BFL befool *trick*
BFL befoul *dirty*
BFL Buffalo *city*
BFL buffalo *(n) animal* buffalo (or) buffaloes
BFL buffalo *(v) baffle* buffaloed buffaloing buffaloes
BFLHD bufflehead *duck*
BFLMNT bafflement *frustration*
BFLN befallen *happened to*
BFLR baffler *frustrate*
BFN buffoon *clown*
BFNB Baffin Bay *body of water*
BFNR buffoonery *clown*
BFNSH buffoonish *clown*
BFNT bouffant *puffed*
BFR beefier *meatier, sturdier*
BFR before *sooner*

Use letters that best describe the sounds you hear and omit the vowels. Use **S** or **K** instead of **C**: to find circle use **SRKL**. Use **J** to find joy, **JM** to find gem and **G** to find go.

BFR buffer *protect, go-between*
BFRDSKL Beaufort scale *wind force*
BFRHN beforehand *sooner*
BFRHND beforehand *sooner*
BFRKT bifurcate *divide* bifurcated bifurcating
BFRN befriend *acquaint*
BFRN boyfriend *sweetheart*
BFRND befriend *acquaint*
BFRND boyfriend *sweetheart*
BFRNT bowfront *curved*
BFRTSKL Beaufort scale *wind force*
BFSKT obfuscate *confuse* obfuscated obfuscating
BFST beefiest *meatiest, sturdiest*
BFSTK beefsteak *meat*
BFSTRGNF beef Stroganoff *food*
BFSTRGNV beef Stroganoff *food*
BFT abaft *behind*
BFT befit *be proper* befitted befitting
BFT buffet *strike*
BFTL befuddle *confuse* befuddled befuddling
BFTLD befuddled *confused*
BFTLMNT befuddlement *confusion*
BFTN befitting *proper*
BFTNG befitting *proper*
BFTR beefeater *guard*
BFYR beefier *meatier, sturdier*
BFYSKT obfuscate *confuse* obfuscated obfuscating
BFYST beefiest *meatiest, sturdiest*
BFZKS biophysics *science*
BFZSST biophysicist *scientist*
BFZX biophysics *science*
BG bag (v) *catch, put in pouch* bagged bagging
BG bag (n) *purse, suitcase*
BG baggy *loose* baggier baggiest
BG beg *ask* begged begging

BG big *large* bigger biggest
BG bigeye *fish*
BG biggie *(slang) large item*
BG bog (v) *impede* bogged bogging
BG bog (n) *marsh*
BG bogey (v) *golf* bogeyed bogeying
BG bogey (n) *phantom* bogeys
BG boggy *wet*
BG boogie *dance* boogied boogying boogies
BG bougie *candle*
BG bug (v) *pester* bugged bugging
BG bug (n) *insect*
BG bugeye *boat*
BG buggy (n) *carriage* buggies
BG buggy (adj) *insects* buggier buggiest
BGB bugaboo *fear* bugaboos
BGBN Big Ben *clock*
BGBN bugbane *plant*
BGBNG big bang *creation theory*
BGBR bugbear *problem*
BGBRTHR Big Brother *fictional watcher*
BGD biggety (or) biggity *conceited*
BGD Bogota *city*
BGD bug-eyed (adj) *protruding*
BGDD Baghdad *city*
BGDN begotten *born*
BGDN bogged down *stuck*
BGFL bagful *amount*
BGFT Bigfoot *fictional creature*
BGHD bighead *conceited one*
BGHDD bigheaded *conceited*
BGHRDD bighearted *kind*
BGHRTD bighearted *kind*
BGHS bughouse *(slang) asylum*
BGHWL big wheel *bigwig*
BGJ baggage *luggage*
BGL abigail *maid*
BGL bagel *food*

BGL baggily *loosely*
BGL beagle *dog*
BGL beguile *charm* beguiled beguiling
BGL boggle *confuse* boggled boggling
BGL bugle *music* bugled bugling
BGLD bag lady *woman*
BGLG big league (n) *sport* big-league (adj)
BGLGR big leaguer *sport*
BGLMNT beguilement *charm*
BGLN beguiling *charming*
BGLNG beguiling *charming*
BGLR beguiler *charmer*
BGLR bugler *musician*
BGM begum *Muslim woman*
BGM big game *animals*
BGM bigamy *two spouses*
BGMN backgammon *game*
BGMN bagman *money* bagmen
BGMN bogeyman *ogre*
BGMS bigamous *two spouses*
BGMST bigamist *two spouses*
BGMTH bigmouthed *loud*
BGMTHD bigmouthed *loud*
BGN began (v-past) *begin* beginning begun
BGN begin *start* began beginning begun
BGN begone *depart*
BGN begonia *flower*
BGN beguine *dance*
BGN begun (v-past) *begin* beginning begun
BGN bygone *past*
BGNK biogenic *from living*
BGNN beginning *start*
BGNN bignonia *plant*
BGNNG beginning *start*
BGNNY bignonia *plant*
BGNR beginner *inexperienced one*
BGNRSLK beginner's luck *good fortune*
BGNRZLK beginner's luck *good fortune*

Letters aren't doubled for single sounds: to find alley use **L** not **LL**. Use **Y** and **W** as hard sounds only: to find yellow use **YL**. (Br)=British spelling or usage. * See dictionary.

BGNS bagginess *looseness*
BGNS biogenous *from living*
BGNV bougainvillea *plant*
BGNVL bougainvillea *plant*
BGNVLY bougainvillea *plant*
BGNVY bougainvillea *plant*
BGNY begonia *flower*
BGNZ bygones *past*
BGPL Big Apple (the) (nickname) *New York City*
BGPP bagpipe *music*
BGPPR bagpiper *musician*
BGR bagger *one who bags*
BGR baggier *loose*
BGR beggar *pauper*
BGR beggary *poverty* beggaries
BGR begorra *oath*
BGR bigger *larger*
BGR bugger *(n) rascal (v)* damn, *(vulgar)* sodomize
BGR buggery *(vulgar)* sodomy
BGR buggier *insects*
BGRD bigarade *sauce*
BGRF biography *life history* biographies
BGRFR biographer *writer*
BGRJ begrudge *disapprove* begrudged begrudging
BGRL beggarly *poor*
BGRLNS beggarliness *poverty*
BGRSLS beggar's-lice *plant*
BGRZLS beggar's-lice *plant*
BGS bagasse *residue*
BGS biggest *largest*
BGS bogus *false*
BGSH biggish *large*
BGSHT big shot *important one*
BGST baggiest *loosest*
BGST biggest *largest*
BGST buggiest *insects*
BGT baguette *food, gem*
BGT beget *birth* begot begetting begotten
BGT biggety (or) biggity *conceited*
BGT bigot *prejudice*
BGT Bogota *city*
BGTKT big-ticket *expensive*

BGTL bagatelle *trifle, game*
BGTM big time (n) *top rank* big-time (adj)
BGTN begotten *born*
BGTP big top *tent*
BGTR bigotry *prejudice* bigotries
BGVDGD Bhagavad Gita *Hindu book*
BGVDGT Bhagavad Gita *Hindu book*
BGWG bigwig *important one*
BGWG boogie-woogie *dance*
BGWL big wheel *bigwig*
BGWRM bagworm *insect*
BGYL beguile *charm* beguiled beguiling
BGYLMNT beguilement *charm*
BGYLN beguiling *charming*
BGYLNG beguiling *charming*
BGYLR beguiler *charmer*
BGYR baggier *loose*
BGYR buggier *insects*
BGYST baggiest *loosest*
BGYST buggiest *insects*
BH Bahai *religion*
BH bohea *tea*
BHD behead *decapitate*
BHD boyhood *youthful time*
BHF behalf *benefit*
BHKLFRN Baja California *peninsula*
BHKLFRNY Baja California *peninsula*
BHLD behold *see beheld* beholding
BHLDN beholden *indebted*
BHM Bohemia *region*
BHMN Bahamian *islander*
BHMN bohemian *(often capitalized) gypsy*
BHMTH behemoth *giant*
BHMY Bohemia *region*
BHMYN Bahamian *islander*
BHMYN bohemian *(often capitalized) gypsy*
BHMZ Bahamas (the) *islands*
BHN behind (prep) *to the rear* (adj, adv) *late* (n) *buttocks*
BHND behind (prep) *to the*

rear, (adj, adv) *late* (n) *buttocks*
BHNDHND behindhand *arrears*
BHNDTHCNS behind-the-scenes *secret*
BHNDTHCNZ behind-the-scenes *secret*
BHNDTHSNS behind-the-scenes *secret*
BHNDTHSNZ behind-the-scenes *secret*
BHNGK bohunk *(slang) Central European*
BHNHND behindhand *arrears*
BHNK bohunk *(slang) Central European*
BHNTHCNS behind-the-scenes *secret*
BHNTHCNZ behind-the-scenes *secret*
BHNTHSNS behind-the-scenes *secret*
BHNTHSNZ behind-the-scenes *secret*
BHR abhor *hate* abhorred abhorring
BHRNS abhorrence *hatred*
BHRNT abhorrent *hated*
BHRNTS abhorrence *hatred*
BHRR abhorrer *hater*
BHS Bauhaus *architecture*
BHST behest *command*
BHV beehive *honey, hairdo*
BHV behave *act* behaved behaving
BHV behoove *benefit* behooved behooving (Br) behove
BHVR behavior *actions* (Br) behaviour
BHVRL behavioral *actions* (Br) behavioural
BHVYR behavior *actions* (Br) behaviour
BHVYRL behavioral *actions* (Br) behavioural
BHY bohea *tea*
BHYZM Bahaism *religion*
BHZM Bahaism *religion*
BHZRD biohazard *life*

Use letters that best describe the sounds you hear and omit the vowels. Use **S** or **K** instead of **C**: to find circle use **SRKL**. Use **J** to find joy, **JM** to find gem and **G** to find go.

threatener
BJ badge *emblem*
BJ beige *color*
BJ bijou *jewel* bijous (or)
　bijoux
BJ bougie *candle*
BJ budge *move* budged
　budging
BJ budgie *bird*
BJDR bijouterie *ornaments*
BJDR objet d'art *curio*
　objets d'art
BJDRT objet d'art *curio*
　objets d'art
BJK abject *hopeless*
BJK object *(n) thing (v)*
　oppose
BJKDF objectify *give form*
　objectified objectifying
　objectifies
BJKDR objector *opposer*
BJKDV objective *(n) goal,*
　intention (adj) material,
　word, fair
BJKDVL objectively *fairly*
BJKDVNS objectiveness
　fairness
BJKDVST objectivist *realist*
BJKDVZM objectivism
　realism
BJKL abjectly *hopelessly*
BJKNS abjectness
　hopelessness
BJKSHN abjection
　hopelessness
BJKSHN objection
　opposition
BJKSHNBL objectionable
　(adj) *offensive*
　objectionably (adv)
BJKT abject *hopeless*
BJKT object *(n) thing (v)*
　oppose
BJKTF objectify *give form*
　objectified objectifying
　objectifies
BJKTL abjectly *hopelessly*
BJKTNS abjectness
　hopelessness
BJKTR objector *opposer*
BJKTV objective *(n) goal,*
　intention (adj) material,

word, fair
BJKTVD objectivity *fairness*
BJKTVL objectively *fairly*
BJKTVNS objectiveness
　fairness
BJKTVST objectivist *realist*
BJKTVT objectivity *fairness*
BJKTVZM objectivism
　realism
BJL Beaujolais *wine*
　Beaujolais
BJL bejewel *gems*
BJLD bejeweled (or)
　bejewelled *gems*
BJMN bigeminy *2 beats*
BJMNL bigeminal *2 beats*
BJNDK biogenetic *from*
　living
BJNDKL biogenetically *from*
　living
BJNG Beijing *city*
BJNK biogenic *from living*
BJNRK bigeneric *hybrid*
BJNS biogenous *from living*
BJNSS abiogenesis *from*
　non-living
BJNSS biogenesis *from*
　living
BJNST abiogenist *scientist*
BJNTK biogenetic *from*
　living
BJNTKL biogenetically *from*
　living
BJR abjure *swear* abjured
　abjuring
BJR badger *(v) pester (n)*
　animal
BJRGR budgerigar *bird*
BJRGSHN objurgation
　quarrel
BJRGT objurgate *quarrel*
　objurgated objurgating
BJRGTR objurgatory
　quarrelsome
BJRR abjurer *swearer*
BJRSHN abjuration *oath*
BJST beau geste *gesture*
　beaux gestes (or) beau
　gestes
BJT budget *finances*
BJTR bijouterie *ornaments*
BJTR budgetary *financial*

BJTR budgeteer *accountant*
BJWL bejewel *gems*
BJWLD bejeweled (or)
　bejewelled *gems*
BK abaca *hemp*
BK aback *unawares*
BK Bacchae *women*
BK Bach *composer*
BK back *(v) reverse, support*
BK back *(n) side, spine*
BK bake *cook* baked baking
BK balk *stop*
　(Br) baulk
BK balky *contrary* balkier
　balkiest
　(Br) baulky
BK beak *bird's bill, nose* (Br)
　headmaster
BK beaucoup *many*
BK beck *summons*
BK bike *bicycle* biked biking
BK bock *beer*
BK book *writing*
BK bookie *wager*
BK bouquet *flowers, aroma*
BK buck *(v) resist (n) male*
　animal, dollar
BK buckeye *plant*
BK bucko *cowboy* buckoes
BKBDNG backbiting
　gossiping
BKBDR backbiter *gossiper*
BKBL bookable *bets*
BKBLKS backblocks
　boondocks
BKBLX backblocks
　boondocks
BKBN backbone *spine*
BKBN buckbean *food*
BKBNCH backbench *rank-*
　and-file members
BKBNCHR backbencher
　rank-and-file member
BKBRD backboard
　basketball
BKBRD buckboard *wagon*
BKBRKN backbreaking
　oppressive
BKBRKNG backbreaking
　oppressive
BKBRKR backbreaker
　oppressor

Letters aren't doubled for single sounds: to find alley use **L** not **LL**. Use **Y** and **W** as hard
sounds only: to find yellow use **YL**. (Br)=British spelling or usage. * See dictionary.

BKBRNR back burner *inactive*
BKBT backbeat *rhythm*
BKBT backbite *gossip* backbit backbiting backbitten
BKBTN backbiting *gossiping*
BKBTNG backbiting *gossiping*
BKBTR backbiter *gossiper*
BKC boxy *square* boxier boxiest
BKCH Boccaccio *author*
BKCHY Boccaccio *author*
BKCL abaxial *central*
BKCL biaxial (adj) *double axis* biaxially (adv)
BKCR boxier *square*
BKCST boxiest *square*
BKCT backseat *rear position*
BKCT box seat *good position*
BKCYL abaxial *central*
BKCYL biaxial (adj) *double axis* biaxially (adv)
BKCYR boxier *square*
BKCYST boxiest *square*
BKD beaked *nose or bill*
BKDBK back-to-back *consecutive*
BKDBR abracadabra *magic*
BKDLSK baked Alaska *dessert*
BKDN back down *withdraw*
BKDR backdoor *rear*
BKDR boycotter *avoider*
BKDRP backdrop *background*
BKDT backdate *earlier date*
BKDV back dive *backward*
BKF back off *retreat*
BKFL backfield *football*
BKFL backfill *refill*
BKFL backflow *water*
BKFLD backfield *football*
BKFR backfire *retort, fire* backfired backfiring
BKFS back-office *internal*
BKFVR buck fever *excitement*
BKFYR backfire *retort, fire* backfired backfiring
BKGMN backgammon *game*

BKGRN background *setting*
BKGRND background *setting*
BKH backhoe *tool*
BKHN backhand *tennis stroke*
BKHND backhand *tennis stroke*
BKHNDD backhanded *devious*
BKHNDDL backhandedly *deviously*
BKJKT book jacket *cover*
BKK bacchic *(often capitalized) Bacchus*
BKK backache *pain*
BKL bouclé (or) boucle *fabric*
BKL buccal (adj) *mouth* buccally (adv)
BKL buckle *fasten, bend* buckled buckling
BKLB book club *organization*
BKLCHRL bicultural *two cultures*
BKLCHRLZM biculturalism *two cultures*
BKLD becloud *muddle*
BKLG backlog *accumulation*
BKLK bucolic *rural*
BKLKL bucolically *rural*
BKLM becalm *quiet*
BKLMD becalmed *quieted*
BKLR bicolor (or) bicolored *two-tone* (Br) bicolour
BKLR buckler *shield*
BKLRD bicolored (or) bicolor *two-tone* (Br) bicoloured
BKLRNN book learning *education*
BKLRNNG book learning *education*
BKLRT baccalaureate *bachelor's degree*
BKLRYT baccalaureate *bachelor's degree*
BKLS backless *attire*
BKLSH backlash *adverse reaction*

BKLST backlist *books*
BKLT booklet *small book*
BKLTH backcloth *(Br) backdrop*
BKLTRL bicultural *two cultures*
BKLTRLZM biculturalism *two cultures*
BKLV baklava *dessert*
BKM becalm *quiet*
BKM become *change* became becoming
BKMBL bookmobile *library*
BKMCH book-match *flame*
BKMD becalmed *quieted*
BKMDR back matter *book text*
BKMKL biochemical (adj) *organisms* biochemically (adv)
BKMKR bookmaker *bets*
BKMN becoming *attractive*
BKMN bookman *seller*
BKMNG becoming *attractive*
BKMPLKS B complex *vitamins*
BKMPLX B complex *vitamins*
BKMRK bookmark (or) bookmarker *place holder*
BKMRKR bookmarker (or) bookmark *place holder*
BKMRL bicameral *two chambers*
BKMRLZM bicameralism *two chambers*
BKMST biochemist *scientist*
BKMSTR biochemistry *organisms*
BKMTR back matter *book text*
BKMV become of *happen to*
BKN backing *support*
BKN bacon *meat*
BKN beacon *light*
BKN beckon *gesture*
BKN bikini *bathing suit*
BKN bookend *holder*
BKN booking *reservation*
BKND bikinied (adj) *bathing suit*
BKND bookend *holder*

Use letters that best describe the sounds you hear and omit the vowels. Use **S** or **K** instead of **C**: to find circle use **SRKL**. Use **J** to find joy, **JM** to find gem and **G** to find go.

BKNFRTH back and forth (adv) *motion* back-and-forth (n)
BKNG backing *support*
BKNG booking *reservation*
BKNL bacchanal *orgy*
BKNL bacchanalia *orgy* bacchanalia
BKNLN bacchanalian *orgy*
BKNLY bacchanalia *orgy* bacchanalia
BKNLYN bacchanalian *orgy*
BKNR buccaneer *pirate*
BKNT bacchant *orgy* bacchants (or) bacchantes
BKNT bacchante *priestess*
BKNTR backcountry *remote area*
BKP back up (v) *support* backup (n)
BKPDL backpedal *retreat*
BKPK backpack *(v)* hike (n) *hiking equipment*
BKPLT bookplate *identification*
BKPN bookkeeping *accountant*
BKPNG bookkeeping *accountant*
BKPR beekeeper *apiarist*
BKPR bookkeeper *accountant*
BKPSN buck-passing *avoiding*
BKPSNG buck-passing *avoiding*
BKPSR buck passer *avoider*
BKR baccarat *game*
BKR backer *supporter*
BKR baker *cook*
BKR bakery *market* bakeries
BKR balkier *contrary* (Br) baulkier
BKR beaker *container*
BKR bicker *argue*
BKR biker *cyclist*
BKR buckaroo *cowboy* buckaroos
BKR bucker *striver*
BKRBNT bicarbonate *chemical*

BKRM back room *(n)* meeting place
BKRM backroom *(adj)* inconspicuous
BKRM buckram *fabric*
BKRN background *setting*
BKRN bicorne *hat*
BKRND background *setting*
BKRR bickerer *arguer*
BKRS backcross *hybrid*
BKRST backrest *support*
BKRST Bucharest *city*
BKRT baccarat *game*
BKRT backcourt *basketball*
BKRTMN backcourtman *basketball*
BKRV book review *criticism*
BKRVY book review *criticism*
BKS abacus *calculator* abaci (or) abacuses
BKS Bacchus (or) Dionysus *Greek god*
BKS bookcase *furniture*
BKS box *(v)* hit, enclose
BKS box *(n)* container boxes
BKS boxy *square* boxier boxiest
BKS bucksaw *tool*
BKS ibex *animal* ibex (or) ibexes
BKSBRD boxboard *cardboard*
BKSD backside *rear*
BKSDK bauxitic *mineral*
BKSFS box office *theater*
BKSH bookish *literate*
BKSH buckshee *money*
BKSHL bookishly *literately*
BKSHLF bookshelf *display area*
BKSHNS bookishness *literacy*
BKSHP bakeshop *sweets*
BKSHP bookshop *bookstore*
BKSHSH baksheesh *payment*
BKSHT buckshot *ammunition*
BKSKN buckskin *leather*
BKSKND buckskinned *attired*

BKSKR box score *sports*
BKSKR boxcar *train*
BKSKT box kite *toy*
BKSL abaxial *away from axis*
BKSL biaxial (adj) *double axis* biaxially (adv)
BKSLD backslide *lapse* backslid (or) backslidden backsliding
BKSLDR backslider *lapser*
BKSLNCH box lunch *food* box lunches
BKSLR bookseller *retailer*
BKSM buxom *full-bosomed*
BKSMNS buxomness *full-bosomed*
BKSN boxing *sport, casing*
BKSNG boxing *sport, casing*
BKSPD bicuspid *tooth, two points*
BKSPN backspin *motion*
BKSPRNG box spring *bed*
BKSPS backspace *keyboard* backspaced backspacing
BKSR boxer *dog, fighter*
BKSR boxier *square*
BKSST boxiest *square*
BKST backseat *rear position*
BKST balkiest *contrary* (Br) baulkiest
BKST bauxite *mineral*
BKST box seat *good position*
BKSTCH backstitch *sewing* backstitches
BKSTJ backstage *private*
BKSTK bauxitic *mineral*
BKSTP backstop *screen*
BKSTR bookstore *bookshop*
BKSTRCH backstretch *racecourse*
BKSTRK backstroke *swimming*
BKSTRZ backstairs *secret*
BKSWNG backswing *motion*
BKSYL abaxial *away from axis*
BKSYL biaxial (adj) *double axis* biaxially (adv)
BKSYR boxier *square*
BKSYST boxiest *square*
BKT back out *withdraw*

Letters aren't doubled for single sounds: to find alley use **L** not **LL**. Use **Y** and **W** as hard sounds only: to find yellow use **YL**. (Br)=British spelling or usage. * See dictionary.

BKT beaked *nose or bill*
BKT becket *fastener*
BKT bhakti *devotion*
BKT boycott *avoid*
BKT bucket *pail*
BKTBK back-to-back *consecutive*
BKTBRGD bucket brigade *firemen*
BKTCT bucket seat *separate seat*
BKTFL bucketful *amount* bucketfuls (or) bucketsful
BKTHRN buckthorn *tree*
BKTK back talk *sass*
BKTLSK baked Alaska *dessert*
BKTR bacteria (pl) *germ* bacterium
BKTR boycotter *avoider*
BKTRK backtrack *retrace steps*
BKTRL abacterial *no germs*
BKTRL bacterial *germs*
BKTRLG bacteriology *germ science*
BKTRLJ bacteriology *germ science*
BKTRLJST bacteriologist *germ scientist*
BKTRM bacterium *germ* bacteria
BKTRR bacteriuria *urine germs*
BKTRRY bacteriuria *urine germs*
BKTRY bacteria (pl) *germ* bacterium
BKTRYL bacterial *germs*
BKTRYLG bacteriology *germ science*
BKTRYLJ bacteriology *germ science*
BKTRYLJST bacteriologist *germ scientist*
BKTRYM bacterium *germ* bacteria
BKTRYR bacteriuria *urine germs*
BKTRYRY bacteriuria *urine germs*
BKTSHP bucket shop

saloon
BKTST bucket seat *separate seat*
BKTTH bucktooth *projecting tooth* buckteeth
BKTTHD bucktoothed *projecting tooth*
BKTTHT bucktoothed *projecting tooth*
BKVL book value *assessment*
BKVLY book value *assessment*
BKWD ubiquity *widespread*
BKWDR backwater *inlet, isolated place*
BKWDS ubiquitous *widespread*
BKWDSL ubiquitously *widespread*
BKWDSNS ubiquitousness *widespread*
BKWDZ backwoods *remote area*
BKWDZMN backwoodsman *isolated one* backwoodsmen
BKWRD backward (adj) *shy, retarded*
BKWRD backward (or) backwards (adv) *reverse*
BKWRDL backwardly *shyly*
BKWRDNS backwardness *shyness*
BKWRDS backwards (or) backward (adv) *reverse*
BKWRDZ backwards (or) backward (adv) *reverse*
BKWRM bookworm *studious one*
BKWSH backwash *aftermath* backwashes
BKWST bequest *legacy*
BKWT buckwheat *grain*
BKWT ubiquity *widespread*
BKWTH bequeath *transmit*
BKWTHL bequeathal *transmittal*
BKWTR backwater *inlet, isolated place*
BKWTS ubiquitous *widespread*
BKWTSL ubiquitously

widespread
BKWTSNS ubiquitousness *widespread*
BKYR balkier *contrary* (Br) baulkier
BKYRD backyard *rear of house*
BKYST balkiest *contrary* (Br) baulkiest
BKZ because *since*
BL abelia *plant*
BL able *skillful* abler ablest
BL ably *with skill*
BL aboil *bubbly*
BL abulia *indecision*
BL Baal *deity* Baals (or) Baalim
BL bail (n) *payment* (v) *empty*
BL bailee *receiver of bail*
BL bailey *wall* baileys
BL bald *no hair*
BL bale (v) *wrap* baled baling
BL bale (n) *bundle*
BL Bali *country*
BL ball (n) *sphere, party* (v) *contract*
BL ballet *dance*
BL bawl *cry*
BL bel *ratio*
BL belay *hold, stop*
BL belie *contradict* belied belying belies
BL bell *ringer*
BL belle *lady*
BL bellow *roar*
BL belly (v) *sit close* bellied bellying bellies
BL belly (n) *stomach* bellies
BL below *under*
BL bile *acid*
BL bill (n) *invoice, jaws* (v) *invoice, caress*
BL billow *sail*
BL billy *club, pot* billies
BL blah *nonsense*
BL blew (v-past) *blow*
BL blow (v) *move air, gasp* blew blowing blown
BL blow (n) *hit, storm*
BL blowy *windy*
BL blue (v) *dye* blued

Use letters that best describe the sounds you hear and omit the vowels. Use **S** or **K** instead of **C**: to find circle use **SRKL**. Use **J** to find joy, **JM** to find gem and **G** to find go.

blueing (or) bluing

BL blue *(adj) color, sad mood* bluer bluest

BL blue *(n) sky, dye*

BL boil *bubble*

BL bola *rope*

BL boldly *confidently*

BL bole *color, tree*

BL boll *seed pod*

BL bolo *knife* bolos

BL boulle *inlay*

BL bowel *intestine*

BL bowl *(v) surprise, roll a ball (n) dish, stadium, game*

BL buhl *style*

BL bull *animal, decree*

BL bulla *blister* bullae

BL bully *intimidate* bullied bullying bullies

BL bylaw (or) byelaw *legislation*

BL eyeball *(n) sense organ (v) watch*

BL obeli (pl) *symbol* obelus

BL obelia *hydra*

BLB Balboa *explorer*

BLB balboa *money*

BLB ball boy *tennis*

BLB bell buoy *ocean*

BLB bellboy *porter*

BLB blab *talk* blabbed blabbing

BLB blob *splotch* blobbed blobbing

BLB blub *(Br) cry*

BLB bulb *flower, light*

BLBB blue baby *color*

BLBBL blow-by-blow *detailed*

BLBD bilobed *two lobes*

BLBDD able-bodied *fit*

BLBDL bluebottle *blowfly*

BLBDM bell-bottom *trousers*

BLBK blue book *register*

BLBL bailable *able to be released*

BLBL bilabial *two lips*

BLBL billable *invoice*

BLBL boilable *bubble*

BLBLD blue blood *royalty*

BLBLDD blue-blooded *elite*

BLBLT bulblet *small bulb*

BLBN bail bond *payment*

BLBN bellyband *girth*

BLBND bail bond *payment*

BLBND bellyband *girth*

BLBNG billabong *backwater*

BLBNT bluebonnet *cap, plant*

BLBR belabor *attack, explain* (Br) belabour

BLBR blabber *talk foolishly*

BLBR blubber *(v) cry (n) fat* (Br) blub

BLBR blubbery *fat*

BLBR blueberry *food* blueberries

BLBR bulbar *protruding*

BLBRD billboard *advertising*

BLBRD Bluebeard *pirate*

BLBRD bluebird *bird*

BLBRMTH blabbermouth *talk foolishly*

BLBRN ball bearing *machine part*

BLBRNG ball bearing *machine part*

BLBS bouillabaisse *stew*

BLBS bulbous *round*

BLBTL bluebottle *blowfly*

BLBTM bell-bottom *trousers*

BLBW Balboa *explorer*

BLBW balboa *money*

BLBW bell buoy *ocean*

BLBYL bilabial *two lips*

BLBZ bouillabaisse *stew*

BLCH belch *burp* belches

BLCH bleach *whiten* bleaches

BLCH blotch *spot* blotches

BLCH blotchy *spotted*

BLCHBL bleachable *whiten*

BLCHL blotchily *spottily*

BLCHP blue chip (n) *finest stock* blue-chip (adj)

BLCHR blucher *shoe*

BLCHRS bleachers *seating*

BLCHRZ bleachers *seating*

BLCHZ blue cheese *food*

BLD ability *skill* abilities

BLD bald *no hair*

BLD ballad *song*

BLD ballade *verse*

BLD billet-doux *love letter*

billets-doux

BLD blade *knife, grass*

BLD bleed *lose blood or color* bled bleeding

BLD blood *body liquid*

BLD bloody *(adj) cruel, gory* bloodier bloodiest

BLD bloody *(v) make gory* bloodied bloodying bloodies

BLD blue-eyed *eye color*

BLD bold *confident*

BLD build *erect* built building

BLD build *(n) body shape*

BLDBNGK blood bank *storage*

BLDBNK blood bank *storage*

BLDBRTHR blood brother *kin*

BLDBTH bloodbath *slaughter*

BLDD belated *late*

BLDD bloated *swelled*

BLDDL belatedly *late*

BLDDNS belatedness *lateness*

BLDFS boldface *(n) type*

BLDFST bald-faced *obvious*

BLDFST boldfaced (or) bold-faced *(adj) impudent, type*

BLDG bulldog *(v) steer throw* bulldogger bulldogging

BLDG bulldog *(n) dog (adj) tenacious*

BLDGL bald eagle *bird*

BLDGN bulldogging *steer throwing*

BLDGNG bulldogging *steer throwing*

BLDGR bulldogger *steer thrower*

BLDGRP blood group *type*

BLDHD baldhead *hairless one*

BLDHDD baldheaded *hairless*

BLDHN bloodhound *dog*

BLDHND bloodhound *dog*

BLDK balletic *dance*

BLDK Baltic *region*

BLDKC Baltic Sea *body of*

Letters aren't doubled for single sounds: to find alley use **L** not **LL**. Use **Y** and **W** as hard sounds only: to find yellow use **YL**. (Br)=British spelling or usage. * See dictionary.

water

BLDKN baldachin (or) baldachino *canopy* baldachins (or) baldachinos

BLDKNT blood count *measurement*

BLDKRDLN bloodcurdling *horrible*

BLDKRDLNG bloodcurdling *horrible*

BLDKS Baltic Sea *body of water*

BLDKS belowdecks *ship*

BLDKT blood count *measurement*

BLDL belittle *disparage* belittled belittling

BLDL boldly *confidently*

BLDLDN bloodletting *bleeding*

BLDLDNG bloodletting *bleeding*

BLDLK bladelike *like a knife*

BLDLMNT belittlement *disparagement*

BLDLR belittler *disparager*

BLDLTN bloodletting *bleeding*

BLDLTNG bloodletting *bleeding*

BLDM beldam (or) beldame *old woman*

BLDMN blood money *payment*

BLDMR Baltimore *city*

BLDMR Bloody Mary *drink*

BLDN balding *hairless*

BLDN belladonna *plant*

BLDN bleeding *(Br) bloody*

BLDN building *structure*

BLDN bulletin *notification*

BLDNBRD bulletin board *public notice*

BLDNG balding *hairless*

BLDNG belting *strapping*

BLDNG bleeding *(Br) bloody*

BLDNG building *structure*

BLDNGHRT bleeding heart *plant, sympathetic one*

BLDNHRT bleeding heart *plant, sympathetic one*

BLDNS baldness *no hair*

BLDNS boldness *confidence*

BLDP build up (v) *develop* buildup (n)

BLDPRSHR blood pressure *measurement*

BLDPT baldpate *hairless*

BLDPZNN blood poisoning *septicemia*

BLDPZNNG blood poisoning *septicemia*

BLDR balladeer *singer*

BLDR balladry *songs*

BLDR bladder *sac*

BLDR bleeder *hemophiliac (Br) bloke*

BLDR bloater *fish*

BLDR bloodier *gory*

BLDR blotter *paper*

BLDR bolder *confident*

BLDR bolter *fastener, runner*

BLDR Boulder *city*

BLDR boulder *rock*

BLDR builder *erector*

BLDRD blood-red *color*

BLDRD blow-dried *hair*

BLDRDR obliterator *remover*

BLDRDSH balderdash *nonsense*

BLDRDV obliterative *removed*

BLDRK baldric *belt*

BLDRL bilateral (adj) *two sides* bilaterally (adv)

BLDRLK bladderlike *saclike*

BLDRNT bladdernut *shrub*

BLDRR blow-dryer *appliance*

BLDRSHN obliteration *removal*

BLDRT obliterate *remove* obliterated obliterating

BLDRTR obliterator *remover*

BLDRTV obliterative *removed*

BLDRWRT bladderwort *plant*

BLDRYR blow-dryer *appliance*

BLDS boletus *mushroom* boletus (or) boleti

BLDSHD bloodshed *slaughter*

BLDSHT bloodshot *red*

BLDSKR bloodsucker *leech*

BLDSL blood cell *circulatory system*

BLDST bloodiest *gory*

BLDSTN bloodstain *spot*

BLDSTRM bloodstream *circulatory system*

BLDT blot out *destroy*

BLDTHRSD bloodthirsty *eager to kill*

BLDTHRSDNS bloodthirstiness *eagerness to kill*

BLDTHRST bloodthirsty *eager to kill*

BLDTHRSTNS bloodthirstiness *eagerness to kill*

BLDTS blood test *test for disease*

BLDTST blood test *test for disease*

BLDV ablative (n, adj) *grammatical case (adj) removal*

BLDVL ablatively *removal*

BLDWRM bloodworm *animal*

BLDX belowdecks *ship*

BLDYR bloodier *gory*

BLDYST bloodiest *gory*

BLDZ bulldoze *move dirt, bully* bulldozed bulldozing

BLDZHR bulldozer *machine*

BLDZR bulldozer *machine*

BLF bailiff *law*

BLF bay leaf *plant*

BLF belief *tenet*

BLF bluff (n) *cliff, deception* (v) *deceive*

BLFDL bull fiddle *music*

BLFDR bullfighter *entertainer*

BLFL baleful (adj) *sad* balefully (adv)

BLFL bellyful *maximum*

BLFL billfold *wallet*

BLFL blowfly *insect*

BLFL bowlful *full bowl*

BLFLD billfold *wallet*

Use letters that best describe the sounds you hear and omit the vowels. Use **S** or **K** instead of **C**: to find circle use **SRKL**. Use **J** to find joy, **JM** to find gem and **G** to find go.

BLFLP belly flop *dive*
BLFLR bellflower *herb*
BLFLWR bellflower *herb*
BLFNCH bullfinch *bird*
BLFNTN bluefin tuna *fish*
BLFR belfry *tower* belfries
BLFR bill of fare *menu*
BLFR bluffer *deceiver*
BLFRG bullfrog *animal*
BLFRPLSD blepharoplasty
 surgery
BLFRPLST blepharoplast
 cell
BLFRPLST blepharoplasty
 surgery
BLFRSPZM blepharospasm
 blink
BLFS boldface *(n) type*
BLFSH blowfish *bloated fish*
BLFSH bluefish *fish*
BLFST bald-faced *obvious*
BLFST Belfast *city*
BLFST boldfaced (or) bold-
 faced *(adj) impudent,*
 print
BLFT bullfight *arena spectacle*
BLFTL bull fiddle *music*
BLFTR bullfighter *entertainer*
BLG beluga *caviar*
BLG biology *science*
BLG bowleg *bent leg*
BLG obligee *bonded one*
BLGD bowlegged *bent legs*
BLGD obbligato *necessary*
 obbligatos
BLGDS bill of goods *fraud*
BLGDZ bill of goods *fraud*
BLGL bluegill *fish*
BLGM ball game *sports*
BLGN blowgun *weapon*
BLGR beleaguer *pester*
BLGR Bulgaria *country*
BLGR bulgur *wheat*
BLGRD beleaguered
 pestered
BLGRD Belgrade *city*
BLGRD blackguard *rude*
 person
BLGRL ball girl *tennis*
BLGRN belowground
 underground
BLGRN Bulgarian *of*

 Bulgaria
BLGRND belowground
 underground
BLGRS bluegrass *plant,*
 music
BLGRY Bulgaria *country*
BLGRYN Bulgarian *of*
 Bulgaria
BLGSHN obligation
 commitment
BLGT billy goat *animal*
BLGT obbligato *necessary*
 obbligatos
BLGT obligate *(v) commit*
 obligated obligating
BLGT obligate *(adj) essential*
BLGTL obligately *essential*
BLGTR obligatory *required*
BLGTRL obligatorily
 required
BLH ballyhoo *noise*
 ballyhoos
BLHD baldhead *hairless one*
BLHD bullhead *fish*
BLHDD baldheaded *hairless*
BLHDD bullheaded *obstinate*
BLHDDL bullheadedly
 obstinately
BLHDDNS bullheadedness
 obstinancy
BLHL blowhole *nostril*
BLHP bellhop *porter*
BLHRD blowhard *braggart*
BLHRN bullhorn *loudspeaker*
BLHWP bullwhip *lash*
 bullwhipped bullwhipping
BLJ bilge *worthless, water*
BLJ biology *science*
BLJ blue jay *bird*
BLJ bulge *protrude* bulged
 bulging
BLJ bulgy *protruding*
BLJ oblige *force, put in debt*
 obliged obliging
BLJ obligee *bonded one*
BLJK biologic (or) biological
 (adj) *living* biologically
 (adv)
BLJKL biological (or)
 biologic (adj) *living*
 biologically (adv)
BLJM Belgium *country*

BLJN Belgian *of Belgium*
BLJN bludgeon *weapon,*
 attack
BLJN obliging *helpful*
BLJNG obliging *helpful*
BLJNGL obligingly *helpfully*
BLJNGNS obligingness
 helpfulness
BLJNL obligingly *helpfully*
BLJNS blue jeans *trousers*
BLJNS obligingness
 helpfulness
BLJNZ blue jeans *trousers*
BLJR bell jar *covered dish*
BLJR bludger *loafer*
BLJR obliger *forcer*
BLJRNS belligerence
 aggression belligerency
BLJRNT belligerent
 aggressive
BLJRNTS belligerence
 aggression belligerency
BLJST biologist *scientist*
BLJWDR bilgewater *waste*
BLJWTR bilgewater *waste*
BLK abulic *indecisive*
BLK balk *stop*
 (Br) baulk
BLK balky *contrary* balkier
 balkiest
 (Br) baulky
BLK bellyache *complain*
 bellyached bellyaching
BLK bilk *cheat*
BLK black *color*
BLK black eye *bruise, ugly*
 mark
BLK bleak *barren*
BLK bloc *group*
BLK block *(v) hinder (n)*
 square
BLK blocky *square* blockier
 blockiest
BLK bloke *(Br) man*
BLK bulk *mass*
BLK bulky *massive* bulkier
 bulkiest
BLK bullock *animal*
BLK oblique *tilted, tricky*
BLKBK black book *addresses*
BLKBKS black box *airplane*
BLKBL blackball *exclude*

Letters aren't doubled for single sounds: to find alley use **L** not **LL**. Use **Y** and **W** as hard
sounds only: to find yellow use **YL**. (Br)=British spelling or usage. * See dictionary.

BLKBLT black belt *karate*
BLKBR blackberry *fruit* blackberries
BLKBRD blackbird *bird*
BLKBRD blackboard *slate*
BLKBSDN blockbusting *property*
BLKBSDNG blockbusting *property*
BLKBSDR blockbuster *bomb, property, success*
BLKBSTN blockbusting *property*
BLKBSTNG blockbusting *property*
BLKBSTR blockbuster *bomb, property, success*
BLKBX black box *airplane*
BLKC Biloxi *city*
BLKC Black Sea *body of water*
BLKD blackhead *pimple*
BLKD blockade *obstruct* blockaded blockading
BLKDP black-eyed pea *vegetable*
BLKDR blockader *obstructor*
BLKDRNR blockade-runner *infiltrator*
BLKDSZN black-eyed Susan *flower*
BLKFLG black flag (n) *pirate* black-flag (v)
BLKFT Blackfoot *Native American*
BLKGL black gold *oil*
BLKGLD black gold *oil*
BLKHD blackhead *pimple*
BLKHD blockhead *idiot*
BLKHD bulkhead *ship*
BLKHL black hole *space region*
BLKHRT blackheart *disease*
BLKHS blockhouse *building*
BLKJ blockage *obstruction*
BLKJK blackjack *card game*
BLKL bleakly *barrenly*
BLKL bulkily *massive*
BLKL obliquely *tilted, tricky*
BLKLB ball club *sports*
BLKLB billy club *weapon*
BLKLDR black alder

winterberry
BLKLNG black lung *disease*
BLKLR blue-collar *working class*
BLKLST blacklist *disapprove*
BLKLSTR blacklister *disapprover*
BLKLT black light *ultraviolet*
BLKLV balaclava *cap*
BLKMJK black magic *voodoo*
BLKML blackmail *extortion*
BLKMLR blackmailer *extortionist*
BLKMRKDR black marketer (or) black marketeer *illicit trader*
BLKMRKT black market (n) *illicit trade* black-market (v)
BLKMRKTR black marketer (or) black marketeer *illicit trader*
BLKMZLM Black Muslim *Islamic*
BLKN balcony *porch* balconies
BLKN bel canto *singing*
BLKN bellyaching *complaining*
BLKN blacken *make black, sully*
BLKN blacking *substance*
BLKNBL black-and-blue *bruise*
BLKND blackened *made black*
BLKNDBL black-and-blue *bruise*
BLKNDTKL block and tackle *pulley*
BLKNDWT black and white (n) *writing*
BLKNDWT black-and-white (adj) *monochrome, clear-cut*
BLKNG bellyaching *complaining*
BLKNG blacking *substance*
BLKNS bleakness *barrenness*
BLKNS bulkiness *massiveness*

BLKNS obliqueness *tilted, tricky*
BLKNT bel canto *singing*
BLKNTKL block and tackle *pulley*
BLKNWT black and white (n) *writing*
BLKNWT black-and-white (adj) *monochrome, clear-cut*
BLKNZ Balkans (the) *region*
BLKP bulk up *gain weight*
BLKPL blackpoll *bird*
BLKPNTHR Black Panther *militant*
BLKR balkier *contrary* (Br) baulkier
BLKR bellyacher *complainer*
BLKR blocker *football*
BLKR blockier *squarer*
BLKR blucher *shoe*
BLKR bulkier *massive*
BLKRR ballcarrier *football*
BLKRSR black racer *snake*
BLKRT black rot *fungus*
BLKRT blackheart *disease*
BLKRV bell curve *statistics*
BLKRYR ballcarrier *football*
BLKS bellicose *angry*
BLKS Biloxi *city*
BLKS Black Sea *body of water*
BLKS bollix *bungle*
BLKSD bellicosity *anger*
BLKSH bleakish *barren*
BLKSH blockish *square*
BLKSHN bilocation *two places*
BLKSHN by-election *vote*
BLKSHP black sheep *discredited one*
BLKSHRT Blackshirt *fascist*
BLKSMTH blacksmith *iron worker*
BLKSNK blacksnake *reptile*
BLKSPLTSHN blaxploitation *movies*
BLKST balkiest *contrary* (Br) baulkiest
BLKST bellicosity *anger*
BLKST blockiest *squarest*
BLKST bulkiest *massive*
BLKT black out (v) *faint,*

Use letters that best describe the sounds you hear and omit the vowels. Use **S** or **K** instead of **C**: to find circle use **SRKL**. Use **J** to find joy, **JM** to find gem and **G** to find go.

darken
BLKT black-tie *formal*
BLKT blackout *(n) dark, fainting spell*
BLKT bluecoat *Union officer, policeman*
BLKTHRN blackthorn *fruit*
BLKTP blacktop *surface*
BLKTRK bioelectric *plants and animals*
BLKTRST bioelectricity *plants and animals*
BLKW obloquy *abuse* obloquies
BLKWD black widow *spider*
BLKWD obliquity *double-dealing* obliquities
BLKWLNT black walnut *nut*
BLKWT obliquity *double-dealing* obliquities
BLKWTR blackwater *disease*
BLKYR balkier *contrary* (Br) baulkier
BLKYR blockier *squarer*
BLKYR bulkier *massive*
BLKYST balkiest *contrary* (Br) baulkiest
BLKYST blockiest *squarest*
BLKYST bulkiest *massive*
BLL blue law *moral code*
BLLDN bill of lading *listing*
BLLDNG bill of lading *listing*
BLLF belly laugh *humor*
BLLK balalaika *music*
BLLN belly-land *without landing gear*
BLLN blue line *printing, hockey*
BLLND belly-land *without landing gear*
BLLNDN belly landing *without landing gear*
BLLNDNG belly landing *without landing gear*
BLLTNG bill of lading *listing*
BLM abloom *flowering*
BLM Baalim (pl) *deity* Baal
BLM balm *salve*
BLM balmy *warm* balmier balmiest
BLM blame *fault* blamed

blaming
BLM bloom *flower*
BLM bulimia *eating disorder*
BLMBL blamable *reprehensible*
BLMDR bolometer *thermometer*
BLMFL blameful *reprehensible*
BLMK bulimic *eating disorder*
BLML balmily *warmly*
BLMN bellman *porter* bellmen
BLMN blooming *(Br) complete*
BLMNG blooming *(Br) complete*
BLMNJ blancmange *dessert*
BLMNS balminess *warmness*
BLMNSNS bioluminescence *light*
BLMNSNT bioluminescent *light*
BLMNSNTS bioluminescence *light*
BLMNT bailment *payment*
BLMP blimp *airship*
BLMR balmier *warmer*
BLMR blamer *faulter*
BLMR bloomer *flower*
BLMRL balmoral *boot*
BLMRZ bloomers *trousers*
BLMSH blemish *imperfection* blemishes
BLMST balmiest *warmest*
BLMSTF bullmastiff *dog*
BLMTR bolometer *thermometer*
BLMTRK bolometric *thermometer*
BLMTRKL bolometrically *thermometer*
BLMWRTH blameworthy *faulty*
BLMY bulimia *eating disorder*
BLMYR balmier *warmer*
BLMYST balmiest *warmest*
BLN abalone *shellfish*
BLN abelian *commutative*
BLN Abilene *city*
BLN baleen *whale*
BLN balloon *(n) globe (v)*

expand
BLN baloney *food, worthless talk*
BLN beeline *direct route*
BLN billing *advertising, business*
BLN billion *number*
BLN blain *soreness*
BLN bland *tasteless*
BLN blend *mix*
BLN blenny *fish*
BLN blind *no sight*
BLN blond (m) (or) blonde (f) *hair color*
BLN blown *windswept*
BLN blown *(v-past)* blow
BLN Boleyn (Anne) *queen*
BLN bologna (or) boloney *sausage*
BLN Boolean *mathematics*
BLN bouillon *soup*
BLN bowline *ship*
BLN bowling *sport*
BLN byline *name*
BLNCH blanch *bleach* blanches
BLNCLT oblanceolate *leaf*
BLNCYLT oblanceolate *leaf*
BLND bland *tasteless*
BLND blend *mix*
BLND blind *no sight*
BLND blond (m) (or) blonde (f) *hair color*
BLNDD blended *mixed*
BLNDFL blindfold *eye cover*
BLNDFLD blindfold *eye cover*
BLNDL blind alley *pathway*
BLNDMNZBF blindman's buff *game*
BLNDMNZBLF blindman's buff *game*
BLNDR blender *mixer*
BLNDR blinder *eye flap*
BLNDR blunder *error*
BLNDRBS blunderbuss *gun, erroneous one*
BLNDRR blunderer *erroneous one*
BLNDSD blind side *(n) side without sight*
BLNDSD blindside *(v)*

Letters aren't doubled for single sounds: to find alley use **L** not **LL**. Use **Y** and **W** as hard sounds only: to find yellow use **YL**. (Br)=British spelling or usage. * See dictionary.

surprise blindsided blindsiding
BLNDSH blandish *coax*
BLNDSH blondish *color*
BLNDSHMNT blandishment *allurement*
BLNDSHR blandisher *coaxer*
BLNDSPT blind spot *vision*
BLNDT blind date *engagement*
BLNDTRST blind trust *assets*
BLNF blown off *ignored*
BLNFL blindfold *eye cover*
BLNFLD blindfold *eye cover*
BLNG belong *suitable, attached*
BLNG billing *advertising, business*
BLNG boiling *bubbly*
BLNG bowling *sport*
BLNG oblong *shape*
BLNGGWL bilingual (adj) *two languages* bilingually (adv)
BLNGGWLZM bilingualism *two languages*
BLNGGYWL bilingual (adj) *two languages* bilingually (adv)
BLNGK blank *featureless, bullet*
BLNGK blink *wink*
BLNGKCHK blank check *freedom*
BLNGKL blankly *emptily*
BLNGKMNJ blancmange *dessert*
BLNGKNS blankness *no expression, empty*
BLNGKR blinker *signal, hood*
BLNGKRD blinkered *narrow-minded*
BLNGKT blanket *cover*
BLNGKT blanquette *stew*
BLNGKVRS blank verse *poetry*
BLNGL bowling alley *place to bowl*
BLNGN belonging *possession*
BLNGNG belonging *possession*

BLNGNGS belongings *possessions*
BLNGNGZ belongings *possessions*
BLNGNS belongings *possessions*
BLNGNZ belongings *possessions*
BLNGPNT boiling point *temperature*
BLNGWL bilingual (adj) *two languages* bilingually (adv)
BLNGWLZM bilingualism *two languages*
BLNK blank *featureless, bullet*
BLNK blink *wink*
BLNKCHK blank check *freedom*
BLNKD bullnecked *strong*
BLNKL blankly *emptily*
BLNKMNJ blancmange *dessert*
BLNKNS blankness *no expression, empty*
BLNKR blinker *signal, hood*
BLNKRD blinkered *narrow-minded*
BLNKT blanket *cover*
BLNKT blanquette *stew*
BLNKT bullnecked *strong*
BLNKVRS blank verse *poetry*
BLNL bowling alley *place to bowl*
BLNMNZBF blindman's buff *game*
BLNMNZBLF blindman's buff *game*
BLNN ballooning *expanding, ascending*
BLNNG ballooning *expanding, ascending*
BLNPNT boiling point *temperature*
BLNR bilinear *two lines*
BLNR billionaire *wealthy one*
BLNS balance (v) *stabilize, compute* balanced balancing
BLNS balance (n) *remainder, stability*

BLNS baldness *no hair*
BLNS boldness *confidence*
BLNS ebullience *enthusiasm* ebulliency
BLNSD blind side (n) *side without sight*
BLNSD blindside (v) *surprise* blindsided blindsiding
BLNSHT balance sheet *tally*
BLNSHWL balance wheel *stabilizer*
BLNSLT oblanceolate *leaf*
BLNSN balancing *stabilizing*
BLNSNG balancing *stabilizing*
BLNSPT blind spot *vision*
BLNSR balancer *stabilizer*
BLNSSHT balance sheet *tally*
BLNST balloonist *balloon rider*
BLNSWL balance wheel *stabilizer*
BLNSYLT oblanceolate *leaf*
BLNT blue note *jazz*
BLNT blunt *dull, direct*
BLNT ebullient *excited*
BLNTCLT oblanceolate *leaf*
BLNTCYLT oblanceolate *leaf*
BLNTH billionth *number*
BLNTL bluntly *dull, direct*
BLNTNS bluntness *dull, direct*
BLNTRST blind trust *assets*
BLNTS balance (v) *stabilize, compute* balanced balancing
BLNTS balance (n) *remainder, stability*
BLNTS blintze (or) blintz *pancake*
BLNTS ebullience *enthusiasm* ebulliency
BLNTSHT balance sheet *tally*
BLNTSHWL balance wheel *stabilizer*
BLNTSLT oblanceolate *leaf*
BLNTSN balancing *stabilizing*
BLNTSNG balancing

Use letters that best describe the sounds you hear and omit the vowels. Use **S** or **K** instead of **C**: to find circle use **SRKL**. Use **J** to find joy, **JM** to find gem and **G** to find go.

stabilizing
BLNTSR balancer *stabilizer*
BLNTSSHT balance sheet
tally
BLNTSWL balance wheel
stabilizer
BLNTSYLT oblanceolate
leaf
BLNTZ blintze (or) blintz
pancake
BLNVR blown over *passed*
BLNW blown away *killed,*
impressed
BLNYR bilinear *two lines*
BLNZ Balinese *of Bali*
BLNZ bluenose *moralist*
BLP belly up *dead*
BLP bleep *noise*
BLP blip *radar* blipped
blipping
BLP blowup (n) *enlarge* blow
up (v)
BLPK belle époque (or)
belle époque *artistic*
period
BLPL bellpull *rope*
BLPLR ballplayer *sportsman*
BLPLYR ballplayer
sportsman
BLPN ball-peen *hammer*
BLPN bull pen *prison,*
baseball
BLPNSL blue pencil (n) *edit*
blue-pencil (v)
BLPNT ballpoint *pen*
BLPNT blue point *cat*
BLPNT bluepoint *oyster*
BLPNTSL blue pencil (n)
edit blue-pencil (v)
BLPPR bell pepper *vegetable*
BLPR blooper *mistake*
BLPRK ballpark *baseball,*
range
BLPRNT blueprint *plan*
BLPT baldpate *hairless*
BLQ obloquy *abuse*
obloquies
BLQD obliquity *double-*
dealing obliquities
BLQT obliquity *double-*
dealing obliquities
BLQTR blackwater *disease*

BLR abler *skillful*
BLR bailer *bucket*
BLR bailor (or) bailer
deliverer
BLR baler *wrapper*
BLR bawler *cryer*
BLR belier *contradict*
BLR biller *invoice*
BLR blare *sound* blared
blaring
BLR blear *(v, adj) dim,*
obscure
BLR bleary *(adj) dim, tired*
BLR blower *device, braggart*
BLR bluer *more blue, sadder*
BLR blur *smear* blurred
blurring
BLR blurry *smeared* blurrier
blurriest
BLR boiler *heater*
BLR bolero *dance, jacket*
boleros
BLR bowler *person bowling,*
hat
BLRB blurb *short ad*
BLRBN blue ribbon *(n)*
award
BLRBN blue-ribbon *(adj)*
outstanding
BLRD billiard *ball*
BLRD bleary-eyed *tired*
BLRD bollard *post*
BLRDZ billiards *pool game*
BLRG bullyrag *pester*
BLRL blearily *dim, tired*
BLRM ballroom *dance area*
BLRM boiler room *heating,*
sales
BLRMKR boilermaker
worker, whiskey
BLRN ballerina *dancer*
BLRN blarney *nonsense*
BLRNG bullring *arena*
BLRNS bleariness *dim, tired*
BLRNS blurriness *smeared*
BLRNSTN Blarney stone
myth
BLRPLT boilerplate *standard*
text
BLRR blurrier *smeared*
BLRSH bull rush *intimidate*
bull rushes

BLRSH bulrush *plant*
BLRST blurriest *smeared*
BLRT blurt *utter*
BLRTS bill of rights *(often*
capitalized) constitution
BLRYD bleary-eyed *tired*
BLRYR blurrier *smeared*
BLRYST blurriest *smeared*
BLS balsa *wood*
BLS Belize *country*
BLS bilious *peevish, illness*
BLS bless *sanctify* blessed
(or) blest blessing
BLS bliss *happiness*
BLS blouse *(n) shirt*
BLS blouse *(v) billow*
bloused blousing
BLS bolus *pill* boluses
BLS bowels *intestines*
BLS bullous *blister*
BLS obelus *symbol* obeli
BLSBK blesbok *animal*
BLSCHL blastula *embryo*
blastulas (or) blastulae
BLSCHLSHN blastulation
embryo
BLSD blessed *holy*
BLSDCL blastocoel (or)
blastocoele *cell*
BLSDCLK blastocoelic *cell*
BLSDD blasted *damaged*
BLSDF blast off (v) *take off*
blast-off (n)
BLSDK ballistic *motion*
BLSDKL ballistically *motion*
BLSDKS ballistics *motion*
BLSDMKSS blastomycosis
infection
BLSDMR blastomere *cell*
BLSDPR blastopore *opening*
BLSDR baluster *rail*
BLSDR blaster *explosive*
BLSDR blister *bulge*
BLSDR bluster *blowing*
BLSDR blustery *windy*
BLSDR bolster *(n) pillow (v)*
add support
BLSDRN blistering *intense*
BLSDRNG blistering *intense*
BLSDRNGL blusteringly
noisily
BLSDRNL blusteringly

Letters aren't doubled for single sounds: to find alley use **L** not **LL**. Use **Y** and **W** as hard sounds only: to find yellow use **YL**. (Br)=British spelling or usage. * See dictionary.

noisily

BLSDRR blusterer *blower*

BLSDRS blusterous *windy*

BLSDSL blastocoel (or) blastocoele *cell*

BLSDSLK blastocoelic *cell*

BLSDSPR blastospore *fungus*

BLSDSST blastocyst *cell*

BLSDX ballistics *motion*

BLSFL blissful (adj) *happy* blissfully (adv)

BLSFLNS blissfulness *happiness*

BLSFM blaspheme *revile* blasphemed blaspheming

BLSFM blasphemy *contempt* blasphemies

BLSFMR blasphemer *reviler*

BLSFMS blasphemous *profane*

BLSH abolish *destroy*

BLSH bluish *blue color*

BLSH blush *redden*

BLSH bullish *optimistic*

BLSHBL abolishable *able to be destroyed*

BLSHL bullishly *optimisticly*

BLSHMNT abolishment *destruction*

BLSHN ablation *removal*

BLSHN ablution *wash*

BLSHN abolition *destruction*

BLSHN ebullition *boil*

BLSHN oblation *offer*

BLSHNGL blushingly *redden*

BLSHNL blushingly *redden*

BLSHNR ablutionary *washed*

BLSHNR abolitionary *destructive*

BLSHNS bullishness *optimism*

BLSHNST abolitionist *anti-slavery*

BLSHNZM abolitionism *anti-slavery*

BLSHR abolisher *destroyer*

BLSHR blusher *cosmetic*

BLSHT bullshit (vulgar) *nonsense*

BLSHT bullshot *drink*

BLSHVK Bolshevik *communist*

BLSHVST Bolshevist *communist*

BLSHVZM bolshevism *communism*

BLSHVZSHN Bolshevization *communization*

BLSK blue-sky *visionary*

BLSK obelisk *pillar*

BLSL bill of sale *receipt*

BLSM balsam *resin*

BLSM blossom *flower*

BLSM blossomy *flowery*

BLSMK balsamic *resinous*

BLSMN bailsman *payer*

BLSN blessing *approval, grace*

BLSNG blessing *approval, grace*

BLSNS biliousness *peevishness*

BLSSHN bull session *discussion*

BLST ablest *skillful*

BLST ballast *stabilizer*

BLST ballista *warfare* ballistae

BLST blast *explosion*

BLST blessed *holy*

BLST bluest *most blue, saddest*

BLSTCL blastocoel (or) blastocoele *cell*

BLSTCLK blastocoelic *cell*

BLSTD blasted *damaged*

BLSTF blast off (v) *take off* blast-off (n)

BLSTK ballistic *motion*

BLSTKL ballistically *motion*

BLSTKN bluestocking *intellectual*

BLSTKNG bluestocking *intellectual*

BLSTKS ballistics *motion*

BLSTL blastula *embryo* blastulas (or) blastulae

BLSTLSHN blastulation *embryo*

BLSTM bluestem *grass*

BLSTMKSS blastomycosis *infection*

BLSTMR blastomere *cell*

BLSTPR blastopore *opening*

BLSTR baluster *rail*

BLSTR blaster *explosive*

BLSTR blister *bulge*

BLSTR bluster *blowing*

BLSTR blustery *windy*

BLSTR bolster (n) *pillow* (v) *add support*

BLSTRD balustrade *barrier*

BLSTRK blue streak *words*

BLSTRN blistering *intense*

BLSTRNG blistering *intense*

BLSTRNGL blusteringly *noisily*

BLSTRNL blusteringly *noisily*

BLSTRR blusterer *blower*

BLSTRS blusterous *windy*

BLSTSL blastocoel (or) blastocoele *cell*

BLSTSLK blastocoelic *cell*

BLSTSPR blastospore *fungus*

BLSTSST blastocyst *cell*

BLSTX ballistics *motion*

BLSTYL blastula *embryo* blastulas (or) blastulae

BLSTYLSHN blastulation *embryo*

BLT ability *skill* abilities

BLT ablate *remove* ablated ablating

BLT ablaut *sound*

BLT bail out *leave, remove water*

BLT bailout (n) *rescue*

BLT ballot *vote*

BLT belt (n) *strap* (v) *strap, sing, hit*

BLT billet *berth*

BLT blat *blurt* blatted blatting

BLT bleat *cry*

BLT blight *disease*

BLT bloat *swelling*

BLT blot *spot* blotted blotting

BLT blow out (v) *defeat, extinguish*

BLT blowout (n) *big party,*

Use letters that best describe the sounds you hear and omit the vowels. Use **S** or **K** instead of **C**: to find circle use **SRKL**. Use **J** to find joy, **JM** to find gem and **G** to find go.

victory, or eruption
BLT bluet *flower*
BLT boleti (pl) *fungus*
　boletus
BLT bolo tie *necktie*
BLT bolt *(n) fastener,*
　lightning (v) run, fasten
BLT built *well-formed*
BLT bullet *cartridge, dot,*
　fastball
BLT eyebolt *hardware*
BLT oblate *(adj) flattened (n)*
　layman
BLT oubliette *dungeon*
BLTBKS ballot box *vote*
　ballot boxes
BLTBX ballot box *vote* ballot
　boxes
BLTD abluted *washed*
BLTD belated *late*
BLTD bloated *swelled*
BLTDL belatedly *late*
BLTDNS belatedness
　lateness
BLTH blithe *merry* blither
　blithest
BLTHL bolt-hole *(Br) refuge*
BLTHR blather *talk*
BLTHR blither *merrier*
BLTHRN blithering *babbling*
BLTHRNG blithering
　babbling
BLTHSM blithesome *merry*
BLTHSML blithesomely
　merrily
BLTHST blithest *merriest*
BLTK balletic *dance*
BLTK Baltic *region*
BLTK bluetick *dog*
BLTKC Baltic Sea *body of*
　water
BLTKS Baltic Sea *body of*
　water
BLTKSHN bolt-action
　firearm
BLTL belittle *disparage*
　belittled belittling
BLTLMNT belittlement
　disparagement
BLTLR belittler *disparager*
BLTLS beltless *no strap*
BLTMR Baltimore *city*

BLTN belting *strapping*
BLTN built-in *construction*
BLTN bulletin *notification*
BLTNBRD bulletin board
　public notice
BLTNC blatancy *brazen*
　blatancies
BLTNG belting *strapping*
BLTNG bluetongue *sheep*
　virus
BLTNS blatancy *brazen*
　blatancies
BLTNT blatant *brazen*
BLTNTC blatancy *brazen*
　blatancies
BLTNTS blatancy *brazen*
　blatancies
BLTP built-up *developed*
BLTPRF bulletproof *no*
　passage through
BLTR belles-lettres *literature*
BLTR bladder *sac*
BLTR blatter *talk*
BLTR bleater *cry*
BLTR bloater *fish*
BLTR blotter *paper*
BLTR bolter *fastener, runner*
BLTRCH blowtorch *flame*
　blowtorches
BLTRDR obliterator *remover*
BLTRDV obliterative *removed*
BLTRL bilateral (adj) *two*
　sides bilaterally (adv)
BLTRLK bladderlike *saclike*
BLTRN bullet train
　transportation
BLTRNT bladdernut *shrub*
BLTRR bullterrier *dog*
BLTRSDK belletristic
　writing
BLTRSHN obliteration
　removal
BLTRST belletrist *writer*
BLTRSTK belletristic *writing*
BLTRT obliterate *remove*
　obliterated obliterating
BLTRTR obliterator *remover*
BLTRTV obliterative *removed*
BLTRWRT bladderwort
　plant
BLTRYR bullterrier *dog*
BLTS blitz *air raid* blitzes

BLTS boletus *mushroom*
　boletus (or) boleti
BLTSKRG blitzkrieg *war*
BLTT blot out *destroy*
BLTV ablative *(n, adj)*
　grammatical case (adj)
　removal
BLTVL ablatively *removal*
BLTW beltway *highway*
BLTZ blitz *air raid* blitzes
BLTZKRG blitzkrieg *war*
BLV believe *trust* believed
　believing
BLV Bolivia *country*
BLVBL believable (adj)
　plausible believably (adv)
BLVD beloved *loved one*
BLVDR belvedere *view*
　structure
BLVFR bill of fare *menu*
BLVGDS bill of goods *fraud*
BLVGDZ bill of goods *fraud*
BLVL bi-level *two levels*
BLVLDN bill of lading *listing*
BLVLDNG bill of lading
　listing
BLVLTNG bill of lading
　listing
BLVN oblivion *unknown*
BLVR believer *truster*
BLVR blow over *pass* blew
　over blown over
BLVR bolivar *money*
　bolivares (or) bolivars
BLVRD boulevard *street*
BLVRDR boulevardier *man-*
　about-town
BLVRDY boulevardier *man-*
　about-town
BLVRTS bill of rights *(often*
　capitalized) constitution
BLVS oblivious *inattentive*
BLVSL bill of sale *receipt*
BLVSL obliviously *inattentive*
BLVSNS obliviousness
　inattention
BLVY Bolivia *country*
BLVYN oblivion *unknown*
BLVYS oblivious *inattentive*
BLVYSL obliviously
　inattentive
BLVYSNS obliviousness

Letters aren't doubled for single sounds: to find alley use **L** not **LL**. Use **Y** and **W** as hard sounds only: to find yellow use **YL**. (Br)=British spelling or usage. * See dictionary.

inattention
BLW billowy *waving*
BLW blowy *windy*
BLWD blue-eyed *eye color*
BLWD blueweed *sunflower*
BLWF blow off *ignore* blew off blown off
BLWK bailiwick *domain*
BLWL blue whale *animal*
BLWP blowup (n) *enlarge* blow up (v)
BLWP bullwhip *lash* bullwhipped bullwhipping
BLWR blower *device, braggart*
BLWR bluer *more blue, sadder*
BLWRK bulwark *seawall*
BLWRM bollworm *insect*
BLWRT bellwort *herb*
BLWSH bluish *blue color*
BLWST bluest *most blue, saddest*
BLWT blow out (v) *defeat, extinguish*
BLWT blowout (n) *big party, victory, or eruption*
BLWT bluet *flower*
BLWTHR bellwether *leader*
BLWVL boll weevil *insect*
BLWVR blow over *pass* blew over blown over
BLWW blow away *kill, impress* blew away blown away
BLX Biloxi *city*
BLX Black Sea *body of water*
BLX bollix *bungle*
BLXMTH blacksmith *iron worker*
BLXNK blacksnake *reptile*
BLXPLTSHN blaxploitation *movies*
BLY abelia *plant*
BLY abulia *indecision*
BLY obelia *hydra*
BLYBS bouillabaisse *stew*
BLYBZ bouillabaisse *stew*
BLYK bellyache *complain* bellyached bellyaching
BLYKN bellyaching *complaining*

BLYKNG bellyaching *complaining*
BLYKR bellyacher *complainer*
BLYN abelian *commutative*
BLYN billion *number*
BLYN Boolean *mathematics*
BLYN bouillon *soup*
BLYN bullion *metal*
BLYNR billionaire *wealthy one*
BLYNS ebullience *enthusiasm* ebulliency
BLYNT ebullient *excited*
BLYNTH billionth *number*
BLYNTS ebullience *enthusiasm* ebulliency
BLYP belly up *dead*
BLYR belier *contradict*
BLYRD billiard *ball*
BLYRDZ billiards *pool game*
BLYS bilious *peevish, illness*
BLYSNS biliousness *peevishness*
BLYT oubliette *dungeon*
BLZ ablaze *on fire*
BLZ ballsy *(vulgar) courageous* ballsier ballsiest
BLZ Belize *country*
BLZ bellows *blower*
BLZ blasé *casual*
BLZ blaze *fire* blazed blazing
BLZ blouse (v) *billow* bloused blousing
BLZ blouse (n) *shirt*
BLZ blousy *shirt-like*
BLZ blowsy *sloppy*
BLZ blues *sadness*
BLZ bluesy *melancholy* bluesier bluesiest
BLZ bowels *intestines*
BLZ bull's-eye *target*
BLZBB Beelzebub *devil*
BLZMN bailsman *payer*
BLZMN bluesman *jazz* bluesmen
BLZN blazing *outstanding*
BLZN blazon *proclaim*
BLZNG blazing *outstanding*
BLZNGL blazingly

outstandingly
BLZNL blazingly outstandingly
BLZNNG blazoning *display*
BLZNR blazoner *announcer*
BLZNR blazonry *display*
BLZR ballsier *(vulgar) more courage*
BLZR blazer *coat, one that blazes*
BLZR bluesier *sadder*
BLZRD blizzard (n) *storm* blizzardy (adj)
BLZRDL blizzardly *stormy*
BLZST ballsiest *(vulgar) most courage*
BLZST bluesiest *saddest*
BLZYR ballsier *(vulgar) more courage*
BLZYR bluesier *sadder*
BLZYST ballsiest *(vulgar) most courage*
BLZYST bluesiest *saddest*
BM A-bomb *weapon*
BM abeam *side*
BM ABM *(abbr) Antiballistic Missile*
BM balm *salve*
BM balmy *warm* balmier balmiest
BM beam *ray, support*
BM bema *altar*
BM biome *ecological community*
BM bomb (v) *bombard, fail* (n) *weapon, flop*
BM bombe *dessert*
BM boom *sound, fast growth*
BM bum (v) *beg* bummed bumming
BM bum (n) *vagrant* (Br) *buttocks*
BMB bamboo *reed* bamboos
BMB bimbo *nitwit* bimbos
BMB Bombay *city*
BMB bombe *furniture*
BMBDR bombardier *bomber*
BMBKS boom box *radio*
BMBL bumble *buzz, blunder* bumbled bumbling
BMBLB bumblebee *insect*
BMBLR bumbler *blunderer*

Use letters that best describe the sounds you hear and omit the vowels. Use **S** or **K** instead of **C**: to find circle use **SRKL**. Use **J** to find joy, **JM** to find gem and **G** to find go.

BMBN bambino *baby* bambinos (or) bambini
BMBRD bombard *(n) cannon (v) attack*
BMBRDMNT bombardment *attack*
BMBRDR bombardier *bomber*
BMBRSHT bumbershoot *umbrella*
BMBSDK bombastic *pompous*
BMBSDKL bombastically *pompously*
BMBST bombast *speech*
BMBSTK bombastic *pompous*
BMBSTKL bombastically *pompously*
BMBX boom box *radio*
BMBZL bamboozle *deceive* bamboozled bamboozling
BMBZLMNT bamboozlement *deception*
BMD beamed *supported*
BMD bombed *drunk*
BMD Burmuda *island*
BMDKL biomedical *medicine*
BMDL bimodal *two modes*
BMDLD bimodality *two modes*
BMDLT bimodality *two modes*
BMDLZM bimetallism *two metals*
BMDSN biomedicine *science*
BMDT bummed out *(slang) depressed*
BMKN bumpkin *oaf, spar*
BMKNKL biomechanical (adj) *muscles* biomechanically (adv)
BMKNKS biomechanics *muscles*
BMKNX biomechanics *muscles*
BML balmily *warmly*
BMLKLR bimolecular *two molecules*
BMLKYLR bimolecular *two molecules*

BMLNL bimillennial (or) bimillenary *2000 years*
BMLNR bimillenary (or) bimillenial *2000 years*
BMLNYL bimillennial (or) bimillenary *2000 years*
BMLQLR bimolecular *two molecules*
BMN bemoan *whine*
BMN booming *growing*
BMN bowman *archer* bowmen
BMNBL abominable (adj) *detestable* abominably (adv)
BMND beau monde *high society* beau mondes (or) beaux mondes
BMNDR abominator *hater*
BMNG booming *growing*
BMNL bimanual (adj) *two hands* bimanually (adv)
BMNS balminess *warmness*
BMNSHN abomination *loathing*
BMNT abominate *detest* abominated abominating
BMNT Beaumont *city*
BMNTHL bimonthly *every two months* bimonthlies
BMNTR abominator *hater*
BMNWL bimanual (adj) *two hands* bimanually (adv)
BMNYL bimanual (adj) *two hands* bimanually (adv)
BMNYWL bimanual (adj) *two hands* bimanually (adv)
BMP bump *(n) swelling (v) nudge*
BMP bumpy *lumps* bumpier bumpiest
BMPKN bumpkin *oaf, spar*
BMPL bumpily *lumps*
BMPNS bumpiness *lumps*
BMPR bumper *cushion*
BMPR bumpier *lumps*
BMPRDBMPR bumper-to-bumper *line of cars*
BMPRF bombproof *safe*
BMPRTBMPR bumper-to-bumper *line of cars*

BMPSHS bumptious *aggressive*
BMPSHSNS bumptiousness *aggressiveness*
BMPST bumpiest *lumps*
BMPYR bumpier *lumps*
BMPYST bumpiest *lumps*
BMR balmier *warmer*
BMR bemire *dirty* bemired bemiring
BMR bomber *airplane*
BMR boomer *growth*
BMR bummer *disappointment*
BMRNG boomerang *returning club*
BMS abomasa (pl) *stomach* abomasum
BMSH beamish *optimistic*
BMSHL bombshell *stunning one*
BMSHS bumptious *aggressive*
BMSHSNS bumptiousness *aggressiveness*
BMSL abomasal *stomach*
BMSM abomasum *stomach* abomasa
BMST balmiest *warmest*
BMST bombsight *target*
BMSTR bum steer *bad advice*
BMT boehmite *mineral*
BMTLK bimetallic *two metals*
BMTLZM bimetallism *two metals*
BMTN boomtown *growing town*
BMTR biometry *statistics*
BMTRKS biometrics *statistics*
BMTRX biometrics *statistics*
BMYD Bermuda *islands*
BMYD Burmuda *island*
BMYDSHRTS Bermuda shorts *attire*
BMYR balmier *warmer*
BMYST balmiest *warmest*
BMYZ bemuse *bewilder* bemused bemusing
BMYZD bemused *bewildered*

Letters aren't doubled for single sounds: to find alley use **L** not **LL**. Use **Y** and **W** as hard sounds only: to find yellow use **YL**. (Br)=British spelling or usage. * See dictionary.

BMYZDL bemusedly *bewildered*

BMYZMNT bemusement *bewilderment*

BMZ bemuse *bewilder* bemused bemusing

BMZD bemused *bewildered*

BMZDL bemusedly *bewildered*

BMZMNT bemusement *bewilderment*

BN abound *be prevalent*

BN ban (*v*) *prevent* banned banning

BN ban (*n*) *prohibition*

BN band *circle, group*

BN bane *ruin*

BN bean *food*

BN beanie *hat*

BN been (*v-past*) *to be*

BN being (*n*) *entity* (*v*) *existing*

BN bend (*n*) *turn* (*v*) *curve, subdue** bent bending

BN Benét *poet*

BN benny (*slang*) *stimulant* bennies

BN biennia (pl) *two years* biennium

BN bin *container* binned binning

BN bone *skeleton* boned boning

BN Bonn *city*

BN bonne *maid*

BN bonny *pleasing* bonnier bonniest

BN bony *skinny* bonier boniest

BN boon *good*

BN bound (*v-past*) *bind, jump, sure**

BN bounty *generosity* bounties

BN bun *bread, hairdo, buttocks*

BN bunny *animal* bunnies

BN ebon *black*

BN ebony *tree, dark* ebonies

BNB bamboo *reed* bamboos

BNB by and by (adv) *soon* by-and-by (n)

BNBG beanbag *toy, furniture*

BNBKS bandbox *luggage* bandboxes

BNBL beanball *high pitch*

BNBLK bone black *residue*

BNBLT obnubilate *make unclear* obnubilated obnubilating

BNBN bonbon *candy*

BNBR baneberry *herb*

BNBRTH B'nai B'rith *Jewish organization*

BNBX bandbox *luggage* bandboxes

BNC bouncy *springy* bouncier bounciest

BNC buoyancy *float*

BNCH bench (*n*) *seat, court* (*v*) *sit down* benches

BNCH bunch *group* bunches

BNCH bunchy *close together*

BNCHBR bunchberry *herb*

BNCHGRS bunchgrass *plant*

BNCHL bunchily *grouped*

BNCHMRK bench mark (or) benchmark *reference point*

BNCHN bone china *porcelain*

BNCHPRS bench press (n) *weights* bench-press (v)

BNCHT bunched *grouped* bunch

BNCHWRNT bench warrant *crime*

BNCR bouncier *springy*

BNCST bounciest *springy*

BNCYR bouncier *springy*

BNCYST bounciest *springy*

BND abound *be prevalent*

BND band *circle, group*

BND bandeau *hair, bra* bandeaux

BND bandy (*v*) *bat, toss* bandied bandying bandies

BND bandy (*adj*) *bowed legs* (*n*) *game*

BND banned (*v-past*) *ban*

BND bend (*n*) *turn* (*v*) *curve, subdue** bent bending

BND bendy *curved*

BND bind (*v*) *tie, combine, hinder** bound binding

BND bond *unity*

BND bonito *fish* bonitos (or) bonito

BND bound (*v-past*) *bind, jump, sure**

BNDB by and by (adv) *soon* by-and-by (n)

BNDBKS bandbox *luggage* bandboxes

BNDBL bendable *curve*

BNDBL bondable *trustworthy*

BNDBX bandbox *luggage* bandboxes

BNDD Band-Aid (*trademark*) *bandage*

BNDD banded *with bands*

BNDD benighted *unenlightened*

BNDD bonded *two layers, united*

BNDGL boondoggle *waste*

BNDHLDR bondholder *investor*

BNDJ bandage *wound dressing* bandaged bandaging

BNDJ bondage *slavery*

BNDK benedict *married man*

BNDKDR benedictory *blessing*

BNDKS boondocks *rural area*

BNDKSHN benediction *blessing*

BNDKSLSHN Benedict's solution *chemical*

BNDKT bandicoot *animal*

BNDKT benedict *married man*

BNDKTN Benedictine *monk*

BNDKTR benedictory *blessing*

BNDL bundle (*v*) *wrap, hurry* bundled bundling

BNDL bundle (*n*) *package, band*

BNDLDR bandleader

Use letters that best describe the sounds you hear and omit the vowels. Use **S** or **K** instead of **C**: to find circle use **SRKL**. Use **J** to find joy, **JM** to find gem and **G** to find go.

musician

BNDLGD bandy-legged *bowlegged*

BNDLR bandolier (or) bandoleer *belt*

BNDLR bundler *wrapper*

BNDLS boundless *unlimited*

BNDLSL boundlessly *unlimited*

BNDLSNS boundlessness *unlimited*

BNDLSTF bindle stiff *hobo*

BNDMSTR bandmaster *musician*

BNDN abandon *leave*

BNDN bandanna (or) bandana *scarf*

BNDN binding *restraint*

BNDND abandoned *forsaken*

BNDNG binding *restraint*

BNDNMNT abandonment *surrender, withdrawal*

BNDNR abandoner *deserter*

BNDNS abundance *wealth*

BNDNT abundant *ample*

BNDNTL abundantly *amply*

BNDNTS abundance *wealth*

BNDPPR bond paper *stationery*

BNDR banderilla *dart*

BNDR bandore (or) bandora *music*

BNDR bender *drunken spree*

BNDR binder *notebook, one who binds*

BNDR bindery *books binderies*

BNDR bone-dry *arid*

BNDR boundary *limit boundaries*

BNDR bounder *cad*

BNDRL banderilla *dart*

BNDRL banderole (or) banderol *flag*

BNDRLR banderillero *dart thrower banderilleros*

BNDRLY banderilla *dart*

BNDRY banderilla *dart*

BNDRYR banderillero *dart thrower banderilleros*

BNDS band saw *tool*

BNDSHL band shell

bandstand

BNDSMN bandsman *music* bandsmen

BNDSMN bondsman *surety* bondsmen

BNDSTN bandstand *stage*

BNDSTND bandstand *stage*

BNDT bandit *outlaw*

BNDTR banditry *robbery*

BNDWDTH bandwidth *frequency range*

BNDWGN bandwagon *trend*

BNDX boondocks *rural area*

BNDZ bends *deep sea*

BNDZ bounds *limits*

BNDZMN bondsman *surety* bondsmen

BNF bowie knife *tool*

BNFD bona fide *(adj) real*

BNFDS bona fides *(n) sincerity*

BNFDZ bona fides *(n) sincerity*

BNFKDR benefactor *donator*

BNFKSHN benefaction *donation*

BNFKTR benefactor *donator*

BNFKTRS benefactress *donator (f)*

BNFL baneful *harmful*

BNFL bountiful *(adj) generous* bountifully *(adv)*

BNFR bonfire *flame*

BNFS benefice *estate*

BNFS boniface *proprietor*

BNFSH bonefish *animal*

BNFSH bony fish *class of fish*

BNFSHL beneficial *(adj) for the better* beneficially *(adv)*

BNFSHR beneficiary *receiver* beneficiaries

BNFSHYR beneficiary *receiver* beneficiaries

BNFSNS beneficence *kindness*

BNFSNT beneficent *kind*

BNFSNTS beneficence *kindness*

BNFT benefit *advantage* benefited (also) benefitted benefiting

(also) benefitting

BNFYR bonfire *flame*

BNG bang *noise*

BNG being *(n) entity (v) existing*

BNG bhang *marijuana*

BNG bingo *game* bingos

BNG bong *sound, pipe*

BNG bongo *drum* bongos

BNG bung *cork*

BNG Ubangi *African*

BNGDR abnegator *relinquisher*

BNGG bingo *game* bingos

BNGG bongo *drum* bongos

BNGG Ubangi *African*

BNGGL bangle *ornament*

BNGGL Bengal *region*

BNGGL Bengali *of Bengal*

BNGGL bungalow *house*

BNGGL bungle *fail* bungled bungling

BNGGLDSH Bangladesh *country*

BNGGLNL bunglingly *failure*

BNGGLR bungler *failure*

BNGGR Bangor *city*

BNGHL bunghole *cask*

BNGK bank *money, slope*

BNGK bunco (or) bunko *scheme* buncos (or) bunkos

BNGK bunk *nonsense, bed*

BNGKBK bankbook *ledger*

BNGKBL bankable *profitable*

BNGKBLD bankability *profit*

BNGKBLT bankability *profit*

BNGKHS bunkhouse *building*

BNGKK Bangkok *city*

BNGKK bangkok *hat*

BNGKKNT bank account *money*

BNGKKT bank account *money*

BNGKM bunkum *nonsense*

BNGKN banking *money*

BNGKNG banking *money*

BNGKNT banknote *currency*

BNGKR banker *money, fisherman, bench*

BNGKR bunker *fort*

Letters aren't doubled for single sounds: to find alley use **L** not **LL**. Use **Y** and **W** as hard sounds only: to find yellow use **YL**. (Br)=British spelling or usage. * See dictionary.

BNG

BNGKRD bungee cord *rope*
BNGKRL bankroll *(v) fund (n) money*
BNGKRLR bankroller *funder*
BNGKRP bankrupt *no assets*
BNGKRPC bankruptcy *no assets* bankruptcies
BNGKRPS bankruptcy *no assets* bankruptcies
BNGKRPT bankrupt *no assets*
BNGKRPTC bankruptcy *no assets* bankruptcies
BNGKRPTS bankruptcy *no assets* bankruptcies
BNGKRS bonkers *crazy*
BNGKRZ bonkers *crazy*
BNGKS banksia *tree*
BNGKS bunkhouse *building*
BNGKSHT bank shot *basketball*
BNGKSY banksia *tree*
BNGKT banquette *sidewalk, bench*
BNGKWT banquet *feast*
BNGKWTR banqueter *feaster*
BNGL bangle *ornament*
BNGL Bengal *region*
BNGL Bengali *of Bengal*
BNGL bungalow *house*
BNGL bungle *fail* bungled bungling
BNGLDSH Bangladesh *country*
BNGLR bungler *failure*
BNGND benignity *kindness*
BNGNNC benignancy *kindness*
BNGNNS benignancy *kindness*
BNGNNT benignant *kind*
BNGNNTC benignancy *kindness*
BNGNNTS benignancy *kindness*
BNGNT benignant *kind*
BNGNT benignity *kindness*
BNGP bang-up *excellent*
BNGQT banquet *feast*
BNGQTR banqueter *feaster*
BNGR Bangor *city*

BNGSHN abnegation *relinquishment*
BNGT abnegate *relinquish* abnegated abnegating
BNGTL bangtail *racehorse*
BNGTR abnegator *relinquisher*
BNGX banksia *tree*
BNGXY banksia *tree*
BNGZ bangs *hair*
BNGZDZZ Bang's disease *abortion*
BNHD bonehead *numskull*
BNHDD boneheaded *numskull*
BNHDDNS boneheadedness *stupidity*
BNHLDR bondholder *investor*
BNHM bonhomie *good humor*
BNHMS bonhomous *good humor*
BNHNTR bounty hunter *finds outlaws*
BNJ banjo *music* banjos
BNJ binge *overdo* binged binging
BNJKRD bungee cord *rope*
BNJNRN bioengineering *biotechnology*
BNJNRNG bioengineering *biotechnology*
BNJR binger *overdoer*
BNJST banjoist *musician*
BNJWST banjoist *musician*
BNK bank *money, slope*
BNK bannock *cake*
BNK bionic *robot*
BNK bunco (or) bunko *scheme* buncos (or) bunkos
BNK bunk *nonsense, bed*
BNKBK bankbook *ledger*
BNKBL bankable *profitable*
BNKBLD bankability *profit*
BNKBLT bankability *profit*
BNKHS bunkhouse *building*
BNKK Bangkok *city*
BNKK bangkok *hat*
BNKKNT bank account

money
BNKKT bank account *money*
BNKL binnacle *box*
BNKLRS binoculars *two eyes, magnifier*
BNKLRZ binoculars *two eyes, magnifier*
BNKLT binucleate *two centers*
BNKLYT binucleate *two centers*
BNKM bunkum *nonsense*
BNKN banking *money*
BNKNG banking *money*
BNKNR bean counter *(slang) accountant*
BNKNT banknote *currency*
BNKNTR bean counter *(slang) accountant*
BNKR banker *money, fisherman, bench*
BNKR bunker *fort*
BNKRD bean curd *tofu*
BNKRL bankroll *(v) fund (n) money*
BNKRLR bankroller *funder*
BNKRP bankrupt *no assets*
BNKRPC bankruptcy *no assets* bankruptcies
BNKRPS bankruptcy *no assets* bankruptcies
BNKRPT bankrupt *no assets*
BNKRPTC bankruptcy *no assets* bankruptcies
BNKRPTS bankruptcy *no assets* bankruptcies
BNKRS bonkers *crazy*
BNKRZ bonkers *crazy*
BNKS banksia *tree*
BNKS bionics *robotics*
BNKS bunkhouse *building*
BNKSHS obnoxious *offensive*
BNKSHSL obnoxiously *offensively*
BNKSHSNS obnoxiousness *offensiveness*
BNKSHT bank shot *basketball*
BNKSY banksia *tree*
BNKT banquette *sidewalk,*

Use letters that best describe the sounds you hear and omit the vowels. Use **S** or **K** instead of **C**: to find circle use **SRKL**. Use **J** to find joy, **JM** to find gem and **G** to find go.

bench

BNKWT banquet *feast*

BNKWTR banqueter *feaster*

BNKYLRS binoculars *two eyes, magnifier*

BNKYLRZ binoculars *two eyes, magnifier*

BNL banal (adj) *trite* banally (adv)

BNL biannual (adj) *two per year* biannually (adv)

BNL biennial (adj, n) *two years* biennially (adv)

BNL bonnily *pleasing*

BNLD banality *triteness* banalities

BNLDR bandleader *musician*

BNLS boundless *unlimited*

BNLSL boundlessly *unlimited*

BNLSNS boundlessness *unlimited*

BNLT banality *triteness* banalities

BNM bantam *rooster*

BNM benumb *no feeling*

BNM biennium *two years* bienniums (or) biennia

BNM bon mot *witticism* bons mots

BNM bonhomie *good humor*

BNMKS bionomics *ecology*

BNML binomial *number*

BNML bonemeal *feed*

BNMR bain-marie *pan* bains-marie

BNMS bonhomous *good humor*

BNMSTR bandmaster *musician*

BNMWT bantamweight *118 or 119 pounds*

BNMX bionomics *ecology*

BNMYL binomial *number*

BNN banana *fruit* bananas

BNN benign *kind, harmless*

BNN Benin *country*

BNNG bunting *bird, fabric*

BNNL benignly *kindly*

BNNZ bananas *(slang) crazy*

BNNZ bonanza *large and*

rich

BNPL beanpole *rod, tall thin one*

BNPPR bond paper *stationery*

BNPRT Bonaparte *noble family*

BNQLRS binoculars *two eyes, magnifier*

BNQLRZ binoculars *two eyes, magnifier*

BNQT banquet *feast*

BNQTR banqueter *feaster*

BNR banner *flag*

BNR banter *talk*

BNR beanery *diner* beaneries

BNR binary *math* binaries

BNR boner *mistake*

BNR bonier *skinnier*

BNR bonnier *pleasing*

BNRJTK bioenergetic *energy exchange*

BNRJTKS bioenergetics *energy exchange*

BNRJTX bioenergetics *energy exchange*

BNRL binaural (adj) *two ears* binaurally (adv)

BNRML abnormal (adj) *unusual* abnormally (adv)

BNRMLD abnormality *exception* abnormalities

BNRMLT abnormality *exception* abnormalities

BNRSTR binary star *two stars*

BNRT banneret *knight*

BNS abeyance *lapse*

BNS band saw *tool*

BNS bonsai *tree* bonsai

BNS bonus *extra* bonuses

BNS bounce *rebound* bounced bouncing

BNS bouncy *springy* bouncier bounciest

BNS bounteous *generous*

BNS buoyancy *float*

BNSDR banister *handrail*

BNSDR bonesetter *doctor*

BNSH ab initio *beginning*

BNSH banish *exile*

BNSH banshee *wild man*

BNSHL band shell *bandstand*

BNSHMNT banishment *exile*

BNSHNL binational *two countries*

BNSHR banisher *exiler*

BNSK banausic *practical*

BNSMN bondsman *surety* bondsmen

BNSN bouncing *lively*

BNSNBRNR Bunsen burner *(trademark) gas flame*

BNSNG bouncing *lively*

BNSPL bonspiel *tournament*

BNSPRTS bean sprouts *vegetable*

BNSR bouncer *guard*

BNSR bouncier *springy*

BNSRZ Buenos Aires *city*

BNSST bounciest *springy*

BNST boniest *skinniest*

BNST bonniest *pleasing*

BNSTN bandstand *stage*

BNSTND bandstand *stage*

BNSTR banister *handrail*

BNSTR bonesetter *doctor*

BNSYR bouncier *springy*

BNSYST bounciest *springy*

BNT Bantu *language* Bantu (or) Bantus

BNT bayonet *knife*

BNT bent *(v-past) bend* (adj) *curved*

BNT bonito *fish* bonitos (or) bonito

BNT bonnet *hat*

BNT bounty *generosity* bounties

BNT bowknot *tie*

BNT bunt *baseball*

BNTC bouncy *springy* bouncier bounciest

BNTC buoyancy *float*

BNTCR bouncier *springy*

BNTCST bounciest *springy*

BNTCYR bouncier *springy*

BNTCYST bounciest *springy*

BNTD benighted *unenlightened*

BNTFL bountiful (adj)

Letters aren't doubled for single sounds: to find alley use **L** not **LL**. Use **Y** and **W** as hard sounds only: to find yellow use **YL**. (Br)=British spelling or usage. * See dictionary.

generous bountifully (adv)
BNTGRS bent grass *plant*
BNTH beneath *under*
BNTHNTR bounty hunter *finds outlaws*
BNTLN buntline *sail*
BNTM bantam *rooster*
BNTMWT bantamweight *118 or 119 pounds*
BNTN bon ton *fashionable*
BNTN bunting *bird, fabric*
BNTNG bunting *bird, fabric*
BNTR ab intra *beginning*
BNTR banter *talk*
BNTR bunter *baseball*
BNTRNGL banteringly *chiding*
BNTRR banterer *chider*
BNTS abeyance *lapse*
BNTS bounce *rebound bounced bouncing*
BNTS bouncy *springy bouncier bounciest*
BNTS bounteous *generous*
BNTS buoyancy *float*
BNTSN bouncing *lively*
BNTSNBRNR Bunsen burner *(trademark) gas flame*
BNTSNG bouncing *lively*
BNTSR bouncer *guard*
BNTSR bouncier *springy*
BNTSST bounciest *springy*
BNTSYR bouncier *springy*
BNTSYST bounciest *springy*
BNTWD bentwood *curved wood*
BNTYS bounteous *generous*
BNVLNS benevolence *kindness*
BNVLNT benevolent *kind*
BNVLNTL benevolently *kindly*
BNVLNTS benevolence *kindness*
BNVVN bon vivant *cultivated one* bons vivants
BNVVNT bon vivant *cultivated one* bons vivants
BNVWSH bon voyage *farewell*

BNVWYSH bon voyage *farewell*
BNVWYZH bon voyage *farewell*
BNVWZH bon voyage *farewell*
BNVYJ bon voyage *farewell*
BNVYSH bon voyage *farewell*
BNVYZH bon voyage *farewell*
BNWDTH bandwidth *frequency range*
BNWGN bandwagon *trend*
BNWL biannual (adj) *two per year* biannually (adv)
BNX banksia *tree*
BNX bionics *robotics*
BNXY banksia *tree*
BNY biennia (pl) *two years* biennium
BNYBLT obnubilate *make unclear* obnubilated obnubilating
BNYKLT binucleate *two centers*
BNYKLYT binucleate *two centers*
BNYL biannual (adj) *two per year* biannually (adv)
BNYL biennial (adj) *two years* biennially (adv)
BNYM biennium *two years* bienniums (or) biennia
BNYN banyan *tree*
BNYN bunion *foot sore*
BNYR bonier *skinnier*
BNYR bonnier *pleasing*
BNYRD boneyard *(slang) cemetery*
BNYS bounteous *generous*
BNYST boniest *skinniest*
BNYST bonniest *pleasing*
BNYWL biannual (adj) *two per year* biannually (adv)
BNZ banns *wedding*
BNZ banzai *cry*
BNZ bends *deep sea*
BNZ bonsai *tree* bonsai
BNZ boonies *(slang) outback*
BNZDRN Benzedrine *(trademark) amphetamine*

BNZK banausic *practical*
BNZL benzol *benzene*
BNZL benzyl *toluene*
BNZLDHD benzaldehyde *chemical*
BNZMN bandsman *music* bandsmen
BNZMN bondsman *surety* bondsmen
BNZN benzene *type of hydrocarbon*
BNZN benzine *class of hydrocarbons*
BNZN benzoin *resin*
BNZT benzoate *acid*
BNZWN benzoin *resin*
BNZWT benzoate *acid*
BP beep *sound*
BP bop *dance, hit* bopped bopping
BPC biopsy *test* biopsies
BPD biped *two feet*
BPD bipod *two legs*
BPDL bipedal (adj) *two feet* bipedally (adv)
BPL byplay *side action*
BPLN biplane *aircraft*
BPLR bipolar *two poles*
BPR beeper *alarm*
BPR bopper *dancer*
BPRDK by-product *result*
BPRDKT by-product *result*
BPRDSN bipartisan *two parties*
BPRDZN bipartisan *two parties*
BPRFN ibuprofen *drug*
BPRTSHN bipartition *two parts*
BPRTSN bipartisan *two parties*
BPRTT bipartite *two parts*
BPRTZN bipartisan *two parties*
BPS biopsy *test* biopsies
BPS bypass (v) *go around* (n) *detour* bypasses
BPTH bypath *side road*
BPTST baptist *(often capitalized) religion*
BPTSTR baptistery *church part* baptisteries

Use letters that best describe the sounds you hear and omit the vowels. Use **S** or **K** instead of **C**: to find circle use **SRKL**. Use **J** to find joy, **JM** to find gem and **G** to find go.

BPTZ baptize *initiate* baptized baptizing

BPTZM baptism *water ritual*

BPTZML baptismal *water ritual*

BPTZR baptizer *initiator*

BQD ubiquity *widespread*

BQDR backwater *inlet, isolated place*

BQDS ubiquitous *widespread*

BQDSL ubiquitously *widespread*

BQDSNS ubiquitousness *widespread*

BQDZ backwoods *remote area*

BQDZMN backwoodsman *isolated one* backwoodsmen

BQRD backward *(adj) shy, retarded*

BQRD backward (or) backwards *(adv) reverse*

BQRDL backwardly *shyly*

BQRDNS backwardness *shyness*

BQRDS backwards (or) backward *(adv) reverse*

BQRDZ backwards (or) backward *(adv) reverse*

BQRM bookworm *studious one*

BQSH backwash *aftermath* backwashes

BQST bequest *legacy*

BQT buckwheat *grain*

BQT ubiquity *widespread*

BQTH bequeath *transmit*

BQTHL bequeathal *transmittal*

BQTR backwater *inlet, isolated place*

BQTS ubiquitous *widespread*

BQTSL ubiquitously *widespread*

BQTSNS ubiquitousness *widespread*

BR abhor *hate*

BR bar *(v) prevent, exclude* barred barring

BR bar *(n) rod, tavern, court**

BR bare *(v) uncover* bared baring

BR bare *(adj) minimal, nude* barer barest

BR barre *handle*

BR barrio *ghetto* barrios

BR barrow *cart*

BR bear *(v) birth, put up with, possess* bore bearing borne

BR bear *(n) large animal*

BR beer *drink*

BR beery *like beer* beerier beeriest

BR beret *hat*

BR berry *(v) produce berries* berried berrying berries

BR berry *(n) fruit* berries

BR bier *platform*

BR birr *money*

BR boar *male pig*

BR Boer *South African*

BR boor *rude one*

BR bora *wind*

BR bore *(v) dig, tire* bored boring

BR bore *(n) hole, tiresome one*

BR borough *town*

BR borrow *adopt, acquire*

BR bower *shelter*

BR bowery *farm, bar district* boweries

BR bra *brassiere*

BR bray *howl*

BR brew *(n) concoction (v) cook*

BR Brie *cheese*

BR brio *vigor*

BR brow *forehead*

BR bureau *dresser, agency* bureaus

BR burr (or) bur *bristle*

BR burro *donkey* burros

BR burrow *(n) hole (v) dig*

BR burry *rough edge* burrier burriest

BR bury *conceal, inter* buried burying buries

BR buyer *purchaser*

BR eyebrow *facial hair*

BR Iberia *peninsula*

BRB barb *hook*

BRB bribe *offer* bribed bribing

BRBBL bribable *influenced*

BRBCHRT barbiturate *drug*

BRBCHT barbiturate *drug*

BRBCHWT barbiturate *drug*

BRBD barbed *sarcastic, hooked*

BRBDS Barbados *island*

BRBDWR barbed wire *fence*

BRBK barbecue *grill* barbecued barbecuing

BRBK bareback *no saddle*

BRBKD barbecued *grilled*

BRBKN barbican *tower*

BRBKWR barbecuer *cook*

BRBKY barbecue *grill* barbecued barbecuing

BRBKYD barbecued *grilled*

BRBKYWR barbecuer *cook*

BRBL barbel *fish*

BRBL barbell *weight*

BRBL barbule *feather*

BRBL bearable (adj) *tolerable* bearably (adv)

BRBL brabble *quarrel* brabbled brabbling

BRBL burble *gurgle* burbled burbling

BRBLD bearability *support, birth*

BRBLN beurre blanc *sauce*

BRBLNGK beurre blanc *sauce*

BRBLNK beurre blanc *sauce*

BRBLR burbler *gurgler*

BRBLT bearability *support, birth*

BRBN bourbon *whiskey*

BRBND beribboned *adorned*

BRBNZ bare bones (n) *minimal* bare-bones (adj)

BRBQ barbecue *grill* barbecued barbecuing

BRBQD barbecued *grilled*

BRBQR barbecuer *cook*

BRBQWR barbecuer *cook*

BRBR barber *haircut*

BRBR Berber *African*

BRBR beriberi *disease*

BRBR briber *influencer*

BRBR bribery *crime*

BRBRD barbarity *wildness*

Letters aren't doubled for single sounds: to find alley use **L** not **LL**. Use **Y** and **W** as hard sounds only: to find yellow use **YL**. (Br)=British spelling or usage. * See dictionary.

barbarities
BRBRD bowerbird *bird*
BRBRK barbaric *wild*
BRBRKL barbarically *wildly*
BRBRKST Barbary Coast
region
BRBRN barbarian *wild*
BRBRS barbarous *wild*
BRBRSHP barbershop *hair
salon*
BRBRSL barbarously *wildly*
BRBRSNS barbarousness
wildness
BRBRT barbarity *wildness*
barbarities
BRBRYN barbarian *wild*
BRBRYNZM barbarianism
wildness
BRBRZ barbarize *make wild*
barbarized barbarizing
BRBRZM barbarism
wildness
BRBT barbet *bird*
BRBT barbette *platform*
BRBT browbeat *nag*
browbeat browbeating
browbeaten
BRBTN browbeaten *nagged*
BRBTRT barbiturate *drug*
BRBTYRT barbiturate *drug*
BRBWR barbed wire *fence*
BRBWYR barbed wire *fence*
BRBYL barbule *feather*
BRC brassy *color, bold*
brassier brassiest
BRCD bar code *price*
BRCH abroach *astir*
BRCH birch *tree*
BRCH breach *gap, break,
leap* breaches
BRCH breccia *rock*
BRCH breech *buttocks, pants*
breeches
BRCH broach *(v) open up,
veer (n) tool*
BRCH brooch *pin* brooches
BRCHBLK breechblock
firearm
BRCHKLTH breechcloth
loincloth
BRCHL braciola (or)
braciole *meat*

BRCHN breeching *harness,
fur*
BRCHNG breeching *harness,
fur*
BRCHS breeches *pants*
breech
BRCHSHN brecciation
breakage
BRCHT brecciate *break*
brecciated brecciating
BRCHY breccia *rock*
BRCHYL braciola (or)
braciole *meat*
BRCHYSHN brecciation
breakage
BRCHYT brecciate *break*
brecciated brecciating
BRCHZ breeches *pants*
breech
BRCHZB breeches buoy
seat
BRCHZBW breeches buoy
seat
BRCR brassier *color, bolder*
BRCST brassiest *color,
boldest*
BRCYR brassier *color, bolder*
BRCYST brassiest *color,
boldest*
BRD aboard *on*
BRD abrade *scrape away*
abraded abrading
BRD abroad *away*
BRD bard *poet*
BRD barred *with bands*
BRD beard *facial hair*
BRD berried *with fruit*
BRD bird *feathered animal*
BRD birdie *golf* birdied
birdieing
BRD biretta *cap*
BRD board *wood, get on*
BRD Bordeaux *wine region*
BRD boride *mineral*
BRD brad *nail* bradded
bradding
BRD braid *intertwine*
BRD bratty *unruly*
BRD bread *food*
BRD bred *(v-past) breed*
BRD breed *(v) reproduce*
bred breeding

BRD breed *(n) bloodline*
BRD bride *wedding*
BRD broad *wide*
BRD brood *(n) animals (v)
ponder (adj) breeding*
BRD broody *breed, moody*
BRD burrito *food* burritos
BRD byroad *side path*
BRDBL abradable *scrape
away*
BRDBN broad bean *food*
BRDBN broadband *signal*
BRDBND broadband *signal*
BRDBRD breadboard
cutting, testing
BRDBRN birdbrain *idiot*
BRDBRND birdbrained
stupid
BRDBSKT breadbasket
farm region
BRDBTH birdbath *basin*
BRDCD birdseed *food*
BRDD aberrated *deviant*
BRDD bearded *with hair*
BRDD borated *with borate*
BRDFRT breadfruit *tree*
BRDFSHNT abortifacient
drug
BRDFT board foot *lumber*
BRDG bird dog *(n) animal*
BRDG bird-dog *(v) watch,
follow*
BRDGJ broad gauge (n)
wide broad-gauge (adj)
BRDGJD broad-gauged (or)
broad-gauge (adj) *wide*
BRDGJT broad-gauged (or)
broad-gauge (adj) *wide*
BRDGM board game
amusement
BRDGN bird-dogging *steal
one's date*
BRDGNG bird-dogging *steal
one's date*
BRDGRM bridegroom
husband
BRDHS birdhouse *aviary*
BRDJMP broad jump *sport*
BRDK burdock *herb*
BRDKL birdcall *device*
BRDKLTH broadcloth *fabric*
BRDKRD bradycardia *heart*

Use letters that best describe the sounds you hear and omit the vowels. Use **S** or **K**
instead of **C**: to find circle use **SRKL**. Use **J** to find joy, **JM** to find gem and **G** to find go.

BRDKRDY bradycardia *heart*

BRDKS broadax (or) broadaxe *tool* broadaxes

BRDKSDNG broadcasting *transmitting*

BRDKSDR broadcaster *transmitter*

BRDKST broadcast *transmit* broadcast broadcasting

BRDKSTN broadcasting *transmitting*

BRDKSTNG broadcasting *transmitting*

BRDKSTR broadcaster *transmitter*

BRDL barred owl *animal*

BRDL bordello *residence* bordellos

BRDL bridal *wedding*

BRDL bridle *horse restraint* bridled bridling

BRDL brittle *stiff* brittler brittlest

BRDL broadly *widely*

BRDL brutal (adj) *savage* brutally (adv)

BRDLF broad-leaf (or) broadleaved *no needles*

BRDLM broadloom *fabric*

BRDLN breadline *free food*

BRDLPTH bridle path *trail*

BRDLR brittler *stiffer*

BRDLST brittlest *stiffest*

BRDLTR bardolater *Shakespeare lover*

BRDLTR bardolatry *Shakespeare study*

BRDLVD broad-leaved (or) broadleaf *plant*

BRDLZ bordelaise *sauce*

BRDLZ brutalize *savage* brutalized brutalizing (Br) brutalise

BRDLZSHN brutalization *violence* (Br) brutalisation

BRDM boredom *no interest*

BRDMNDD broad-minded *tolerant*

BRDN Aberdeen *city, cow*

BRDN braiding *intertwined material*

BRDN breeding *ancestry, reproducing*

BRDN broaden *widen*

BRDN burden *load*

BRDNBDR bread and butter (n) *basic sustenance* bread-and-butter (adj)

BRDNBTR bread and butter (n) *basic sustenance* bread-and-butter (adj)

BRDNDBDR bread and butter (n) *basic sustenance* bread-and-butter (adj)

BRDNDBTR bread and butter (n) *basic sustenance* bread-and-butter (adj)

BRDNG braiding *intertwined material*

BRDNG breeding *ancestry, reproducing*

BRDNGHS boardinghouse *lodging*

BRDNGL broodingly *contemplation*

BRDNGSKL boarding school *lodging*

BRDNHS boardinghouse *lodging*

BRDNL broodingly *contemplation*

BRDNS brattiness *misbehavior*

BRDNS broadness *width*

BRDNS broodiness *contemplation*

BRDNSKL boarding school *lodging*

BRDNSM burdensome *heavy*

BRDPRDS bird of paradise *bird*

BRDPRDS bird-of-paradise *plant*

BRDR aborter *terminator*

BRDR abrader *scrape away*

BRDR barter *trade*

BRDR boarder *guest*

BRDR border (v) *abut* (n) *edge*

BRDR breeder *one who breeds*

BRDR brooder *animal, ponderer*

BRDRKL Border collie *dog*

BRDRLN borderland *country*

BRDRLN borderline *edge*

BRDRLND borderland *country*

BRDRM boardroom *conference area*

BRDRR barterer *trader*

BRDRTRR Border terrier *dog*

BRDRTRYR Border terrier *dog*

BRDSD birdseed *food*

BRDSD broadside *width*

BRDSH brattish *misbehaving*

BRDSH British *from Britain*

BRDSH brutish *savage*

BRDSHKLMB British Columbia *province*

BRDSHKLMBY British Columbia *province*

BRDSHT broadsheet (Br) *newspaper*

BRDSKL broadscale *wide-ranging*

BRDSMD bridesmaid *attendant*

BRDSNG birdsong *chirp*

BRDSNSP bird's nest soup *food*

BRDSNSTSP bird's nest soup *food*

BRDSPKTRM broad-spectrum *wide range*

BRDSRD broadsword *weapon*

BRDSWRD broadsword *weapon*

BRDTH breadth *width*

BRDTL broadtail *lamb*

BRDV abortive *fruitless*

BRDVL abortively *fruitlessly*

BRDVNS abortiveness *fruitlessness*

BRDVPRDS bird of paradise *bird*

BRDVPRDS bird-of-paradise *plant*

BRDW Broadway *theater*

Letters aren't doubled for single sounds: to find alley use **L** not **LL**. Use **Y** and **W** as hard sounds only: to find yellow use **YL**. (Br)=British spelling or usage. * See dictionary.

street
BRDWCHN bird-watching *observing*
BRDWCHNG bird-watching *observing*
BRDWCHR bird-watcher *observer*
BRDWK boardwalk *beach*
BRDWNR breadwinner *wage earner*
BRDX broadax (or) broadaxe *tool* broadaxes
BRDZ bird's-eye *close up*
BRDZMD bridesmaid *attendant*
BRF barf *vomit*
BRF brief *(v, n) report* briefs
BRF brief *(adj) short*
BRFDD barefooted (or) barefoot *no shoes*
BRFDK bryophytic *plant*
BRFKS briefcase *carrying case*
BRFL barfly *pub dweller* barflies
BRFL briefly *shortly*
BRFLM bryophyllum *plant*
BRFN briefing *report*
BRFNG briefing *report*
BRFNS briefness *conciseness*
BRFR briefer *coach*
BRFST barefaced *open*
BRFT barefoot (or) barefooted *no shoes*
BRFT bereft (or) bereaved *lonely*
BRFT bryophyte *plant*
BRFTD barefooted (or) barefoot *no shoes*
BRFTK bryophytic *plant*
BRG bargee *(Br) bargeman*
BRG berg *iceberg*
BRG brag *boast* bragged bragging
BRG brig *jail*
BRG brogue *speech*
BRG burg *town*
BRG burgee *flag*
BRG burgoo *food* burgoos
BRGD brigade *troops*
BRGDC braggadocio *boaster*
BRGDCH braggadocio

boaster
BRGDCHY braggadocio *boaster*
BRGDCY braggadocio *boaster*
BRGDR brigadier *officer*
BRGDS braggadocio *boaster*
BRGDSH braggadocio *boaster*
BRGDSHY braggadocio *boaster*
BRGDSY braggadocio *boaster*
BRGL Brueghel (or) Breughel *artist*
BRGL burgle *rob* burgled burgling
BRGLR burglar *thief*
BRGLR burglary *crime* burglaries
BRGLRPRF burglarproof *secure*
BRGLRZ burglarize *rob* burglarized burglarizing
BRGMT bergamot *orange, mint*
BRGN bargain *(v) haggle (n) agreement*
BRGN brigand *bandit*
BRGN brogan *shoe*
BRGNBSMNT bargain-basement (adj) *cheap* bargain basement (n)
BRGND brigand *bandit*
BRGND burgundy *wine, color* burgundies
BRGNDJ brigandage *bandits*
BRGNDN brigandine *armor*
BRGNN bourguignonne (or) bourguignon *sauce*
BRGNR bargainer *haggler*
BRGNTN brigantine *ship*
BRGNYN bourguignonne (or) bourguignon *sauce*
BRGR bragger *boaster*
BRGR burger *food*
BRGR burgher *citizen*
BRGRF bar graph *picture*
BRGRF barograph *air pressure*
BRGRM barogram *air*

pressure
BRGRT braggart *boaster*
BRGSHN abrogation *nullification*
BRGT abrogate *nullify* abrogated abrogating
BRHDD bareheaded *no hat*
BRHH brouhaha *uproar*
BRHL borehole *well*
BRHNDD bare-handed *without gloves*
BRHP barhop *visit pubs*
BRHPN barhopping *visiting pubs*
BRHPNG barhopping *visiting pubs*
BRJ abridge *cut short* abridged abridging
BRJ auberge *inn*
BRJ barge *(v) thrust oneself* barged barging
BRJ barge *(n) ship*
BRJ bargee *(Br) bargeman*
BRJ barrage *(n) dam*
BRJ barrage *(v) outpouring* barraged barraging
BRJ borage *plant*
BRJ bridge *span* bridged bridging
BRJ burgee *flag*
BRJBL bridgeable *span*
BRJHD bridgehead *fortification*
BRJMN bargeman *deckhand*
BRJMNT abridgment *shortened form*
BRJMNT abridgment (or) abridgement *short form*
BRJMP broad jump *sport*
BRJN aborigine *(often capitalized) native*
BRJN aubergine *eggplant*
BRJN burgeon *grow*
BRJNL aboriginal (adj, n) *(often capitalized) native* aboriginally (adv)
BRJR abridger *shortener*
BRJS burgess *citizen*
BRJWRK bridgework *dental*
BRK bark *(n) tree, boat, growl (v) growl*
BRK barky *tree* barkier

Use letters that best describe the sounds you hear and omit the vowels. Use **S** or **K** instead of **C**: to find circle use **SRKL**. Use **J** to find joy, **JM** to find gem and **G** to find go.

barkiest
BRK baroque (*often capitalized*) *style*
BRK barrack (*Br*) *jeer*
BRK Baruch (Bernard) *businessman*
BRK bract *seed*
BRK brake *stop* braked braking
BRK break (*v*) *smash, suspend, violate* broke breaking broken
BRK break (*n*) *pause, dash, chance**
BRK brick *clay* bricks (or) brick
BRK brock (*Br*) *badger*
BRK broke (*v-past*) *break, no money*
BRK brook *stream*
BRK burke *suppress* burked burking
BRKBL breakable *fragile*
BRKBN breakbone *fever*
BRKBRK bric-a-brac *curios* bric-a-brac
BRKBT brickbat *part of a brick*
BRKD bar code *price*
BRKD barracuda *fish* barracuda (or) barracudas
BRKD barricade *block* barricaded barricading
BRKD brocade *material*
BRKDBR abracadabra *magic*
BRKDD bracketed *braced*
BRKDD brocaded *material*
BRKDL bracteole *seed*
BRKDN break down (*v*) *collapse, decompose, fail*
BRKDN breakdown (*n*) *failure, classification, dance*
BRKDNS break-dance *acrobatics*
BRKDNSN break dancing *acrobatics*
BRKDNSNG break dancing *acrobatics*
BRKDNSR break-dancer *acrobatics*

BRKDNTS break-dance *acrobatics*
BRKDNTSNG break dancing *acrobatics*
BRKDNTSR break-dancer *acrobatics*
BRKDYL bracteole *seed*
BRKF break off *end*
BRKFL brickfield (*Br*) *brickyard*
BRKFLD brickfield (*Br*) *brickyard*
BRKFRNT breakfront *furniture*
BRKFS breakfast *meal*
BRKFST breakfast *meal*
BRKJ breakage *pieces*
BRKJ brockage *coin*
BRKL Berkeley *city*
BRKL brachial *throat*
BRKL broccoli *vegetable*
BRKLM berkelium *element*
BRKLN Brooklyn *New York*
BRKLR bricklayer *worker*
BRKLT brooklet *stream*
BRKLYM berkelium *element*
BRKLYR bricklayer *worker*
BRKMN brakeman *train* brakemen
  (Br) brakesman
BRKN barchan *dune*
BRKN barracoon *slave house*
BRKN bracken *fern*
BRKN break in (v) *forced entry* break-in (n)
BRKN broken *smashed*
BRKN broking (*Br*) *stocks*
BRKNDN broken-down *worn-out*
BRKNFL broken-field *running style*
BRKNFLD broken-field *running style*
BRKNG broking (*Br*) *stocks*
BRKNHRDD brokenhearted *grieving*
BRKNHRTD brokenhearted *grieving*
BRKNK breakneck *fast*
BRKNTN barkentine *ship*
BRKP barkeep *bartender*
BRKP break up (v) *split*

breakup (n)
BRKPD brachiopod *invertebrate*
BRKPDRS brachypterous *winged*
BRKPR barkeeper *bartender*
BRKPTRS brachypterous *winged*
BRKR barker *seller*
BRKR breaker *wave*
BRKR broker *stocks*
BRKRC bureaucracy *ruling group* bureaucracies
BRKRD brick red *color*
BRKRD brokered *arranged*
BRKRDK bureaucratic *official*
BRKRDKL bureaucratically *officially*
BRKRDZSHN bureaucratization *make official*
  (Br) bureaucratisation
BRKRJ brokerage *stocks*
BRKRL barcarole (or) barcarolle *song*
BRKRN brokering *arranging*
BRKRNG brokering *arranging*
BRKRS bureaucracy *ruling group* bureaucracies
BRKRT bureaucrat *official*
BRKRTK bureaucratic *official*
BRKRTKL bureaucratically *officially*
BRKRTZ bureaucratize *make official* bureaucratized bureaucratizing
  (Br) bureaucratise
BRKRTZSHN bureaucratization *make official*
  (Br) bureaucratisation
BRKS barracks *residence*
BRKS borax *mineral*
BRKSD boric acid *kills roaches*
BRKSFLK brachiocephalic *blood vessel*
BRKSH brackish *salty*

BRKSHN abreaction *verbalization*

BRKSHNS brackishness *saltiness*

BRKSHR Berkshire *hills, county*

BRKSHRS Berkshires *hills*

BRKSHRZ Berkshires *hills*

BRKSMN brakesman (Br) *brakeman* brakesmen

BRKT abreact *therapy*

BRKT bracket *brace*

BRKT bract *seed*

BRKT break out (v) *leave, emerge, produce**

BRKT breakout (n) *emergence*

BRKT briquette (or) briquet *charcoal*

BRKT brocket *deer*

BRKTD bracketed *braced*

BRKTHR breakthrough *shatter*

BRKTL bracteole *seed*

BRKTYL bracteole *seed*

BRKVN breakeven (n) *no gain or loss* break-even (adj)

BRKW break away (v) *detach, depart*

BRKW breakaway (n,adj) *departure, speed, made to break off*

BRKWDR breakwater *wall*

BRKWN break wind *emit gas* broke wind breaking wind

BRKWND break wind *emit gas* broke wind breaking wind

BRKWRK brickwork *arrangement*

BRKWTR breakwater *wall*

BRKYL brachial *throat*

BRKYPD brachiopod *invertebrate*

BRKYRD brickyard *factory*

BRKYSFLK brachiocephalic *blood vessel*

BRL aboral (adj) *mouth* aborally (adv)

BRL barely *small margin*

BRL barley *cereal*

BRL barlow *knife*

BRL barrel (v) *speed* barreled (or) barrelled barreling (or) barrelling

BRL barrel (n) *container*

BRL beryl *mineral*

BRL birl *spin*

BRL boreal *north*

BRL brail *sail*

BRL braille *(often capitalized) type for sightless*

BRL Braille *blind teacher*

BRL brawl *fight*

BRL brill *fish*

BRL broil *grill*

BRL burial *tomb*

BRL burl *knot*

BRL burley *tobacco (often capitalized)*

BRL burly *strong* burlier burliest

BRLCHSDD barrel-chested *broad*

BRLCHSTD barrel-chested *broad*

BRLD burled *swirled*

BRLF bas-relief *projection*

BRLFL barrelful *amount* barrelfuls (or) barrelsful

BRLHD barrelhead *flat end*

BRLHS barrelhouse *pub*

BRLJ barrelage *amount*

BRLKRN barleycorn *grain*

BRLM beryllium *element*

BRLN Berlin *city*

BRLNS burliness *strength*

BRLP burlap *fabric*

BRLR brawler *fighter*

BRLR broiler *cooker*

BRLR burlier *stronger*

BRLRDR braillewriter *machine*

BRLRGN barrel organ *music*

BRLRL barrel roll *spin*

BRLRTR braillewriter *machine*

BRLS braless *no brassiere*

BRLSK burlesque *ridicule, comedy and dancing show* burlesqued burlesquing

BRLSKR burlesquer

ridiculer

BRLST braillist *type*

BRLST burliest *strongest*

BRLT briolette *gem*

BRLYM beryllium *element*

BRLYNS brilliance *glitter, keenness* brilliancy

BRLYNT brilliant *glittery, keen*

BRLYNTN brilliantine *fabric*

BRLYNTS brilliance *glitter, keenness* brilliancy

BRLYR burlier *stronger*

BRLYST burliest *strongest*

BRM barium *element*

BRM barm *foam*

BRM barmy *frothy* barmier barmiest

BRM barroom *pub*

BRM berm *mound*

BRM Brahma *Hindu god*

BRM bream *fish* bream (or) breams

BRM brim *rim* brimmed brimming

BRM bromo *seltzer* bromos

BRM broom *sweep*

BRM brougham *sedan*

BRM brume *vapor*

BRM Burma *country*

BRMB brumby *horse* brumbies

BRMBL bramble *shrub*

BRMBL brambly *prickly*

BRMBL broomball *game*

BRMD barmaid *waitress*

BRMD Bermuda *islands*

BRMD bromide *sedative*

BRMD Burmuda *island*

BRMDR barometer *air pressure*

BRMDSHRTS Bermuda shorts *attire*

BRMFL brimful *to the brim*

BRMG Oberammergau *city*

BRMJM brummagem *phony*

BRMLD bromeliad *plant*

BRMLYD bromeliad *plant*

BRMN barman *bartender* barmen

BRMN Brahman (or) Brahmin *Hindu*

BRMN bromine *element*
BRMND barramundi *fish*
BRMNGHM Birmingham *city*
BRMNGM Birmingham *city*
BRMNHM Birmingham *city*
BRMNK Brahmanic *Hindu*
BRMNKL Brahmanical *Hindu*
BRMR barmier *frothier*
BRMR brimmer *cup*
BRMRG Oberammergau *city*
BRMS brumous *foggy*
BRMST barmiest *frothiest*
BRMSTK broomstick *handle*
BRMSTN brimstone *sulfur*
BRMT bromate *chemical*
BRMTR barometer *air pressure*
BRMTR barometry *air pressure*
BRMTRK barometric *air pressure*
BRMTRKL barometrically *air pressure*
BRMTSV bar mitzvah *Jewish ritual*
BRMTZV bar mitzvah *Jewish ritual*
BRMYD Bermuda *islands*
BRMYD Burmuda *island*
BRMYDSHRTS Bermuda shorts *attire*
BRMYR barmier *frothier*
BRMYST barmiest *frothiest*
BRMZ Brahms *composer*
BRMZ Burmese *of Burma*
BRN auburn *color*
BRN Bahrain (or) Bahrein *country*
BRN barn *farm building*
BRN baron *title*
BRN barony *domain* baronies
BRN barren *fruitless*
BRN barring *except*
BRN baryon *particle*
BRN bearing *direction, posture*
BRN Bern *city*
BRN boring *dull*

BRN born *birth*
BRN borne *carried*
BRN Borneo *country*
BRN boron *element*
BRN borrowing *thing acquired*
BRN brain *organ for thinking*
BRN brainy *smart* brainier brainiest
BRN bran *food*
BRN brand *name*
BRN brand-new *unused*
BRN brawn *strength*
BRN brawny *strong* brawnier brawniest
BRN brine *salt* brined brining
BRN briny *salty* brinier briniest
BRN brown *color*
BRN brownie *Scout, cookie*
BRN bruin *bear*
BRN Brunei *country*
BRN bryony *vine* bryonies
BRN burin *tool*
BRN burn *flame, cheat, anger** burned (or) burnt burning
BRNBD brown Betty *dessert*
BRNBG brown-bag (v or adj) *carry liquor or lunch*
BRNBGNG brown bagging *lunch or liquor carrying*
BRNBGR brown bagger *lunch or liquor carrier*
BRNBR brown bear *animal*
BRNBRD brown bread *wheat*
BRNBRNR barn burner *exciting*
BRNBT brown Betty *dessert*
BRNC Barents Sea *body of water*
BRNC Bering Sea *body of water*
BRNCH branch (n) *limb, division* branches
BRNCH branch (v) *diverge, extend*
BRNCH brunch *meal* brunches
BRNCHL brainchild *imagination*

BRNCHLD brainchild *imagination*
BRNCHLN branchline *railroad*
BRNCHLT branchlet *small arm*
BRND bran *food*
BRND brand *name*
BRND brandy (n) *liquor* brandies
BRND brandy (v) *flavor* brandied brandying brandies
BRND burned (v-past) *burn*
BRNDD branded *named*
BRNDD brandied *flavored*
BRNDL brindle *color* brindled
BRNDLD brindled *color*
BRNDN brand-new *unused*
BRNDNM brand name (n) *trade name* brand-name (adj)
BRNDNS barn dance *social*
BRNDNTS barn dance *social*
BRNDNY brand-new *unused*
BRNDSH brandish *wave*
BRNDSZN brown-eyed Susan *with brown eyes*
BRNDWRF brown dwarf *star*
BRNG barong *knife*
BRNG barring *except*
BRNG bearing *direction, posture*
BRNG boring *dull*
BRNG borrowing *thing acquired*
BRNG bring *carry* brought bringing
BRNGC Bering Sea *body of water*
BRNGK barranca (or) barranco *gulley* barrancas (or) barrancos
BRNGK brink *edge*
BRNGK bronc (or) bronco *horse* broncos
BRNGK bronchi- (or) bronchio- (prefix) *lungs*
BRNGK bronchi (pl) *lungs*

Letters aren't doubled for single sounds: to find alley use **L** not **LL**. Use **Y** and **W** as hard sounds only: to find yellow use **YL**. (Br)=British spelling or usage. * See dictionary.

bronchus

BRNGKBSDR broncobuster *cowboy*

BRNGKBSTR broncobuster *cowboy*

BRNGKDS bronchitis *disease*

BRNGKL branchial *gills*

BRNGKL bronchial (adj) *lungs* bronchially (adv)

BRNGKL bronchiole *lung branch*

BRNGKLR bronchiolar *lungs*

BRNGKMNSHP brinkmanship *strategy*

BRNGKNMN bronchopneumonia *disease*

BRNGKNMNY bronchopneumonia *disease*

BRNGKPD branchiopod *crustacean*

BRNGKS bronchus *lungs* bronchi

BRNGKS Bronx *New York borough*

BRNGKSCHR Bronx cheer *rude noise*

BRNGKSMNSHP brinksmanship *strategy*

BRNGKTS bronchitis *disease*

BRNGKY bronchi- (or) bronchio- *(prefix) lungs*

BRNGKYL branchial *gills*

BRNGKYL bronchial (adj) *lungs* bronchially (adv)

BRNGKYL bronchiole *lung branch*

BRNGKYLR bronchiolar *lungs*

BRNGKYNMN bronchopneumonia *disease*

BRNGKYNMNY bronchopneumonia *disease*

BRNGKYPD branchiopod *crustacean*

BRNGL boringly *dully*

BRNGN born-again *revived*

BRNGN Bren gun *weapon*

BRNGNS boringness *dullness*

BRNGS Bering Sea *body of water*

BRNGSTRT Bering Strait *body of water*

BRNGX Bronx *New York borough*

BRNGXCHR Bronx cheer *rude noise*

BRNGXMNSHP brinksmanship *strategy*

BRNHRT Bernhardt (Sarah) *actress*

BRNJ baronage *nobility*

BRNK barranca (or) barranco *gulley* barrancas (or) barrancos

BRNK boronic *element*

BRNK brink *edge*

BRNK bronc (or) bronco *horse* broncos

BRNK bronchi- (or) bronchio- *(prefix) lungs*

BRNK bronchi (pl) *lungs* bronchus

BRNKBSDR broncobuster *cowboy*

BRNKBSTR broncobuster *cowboy*

BRNKDS bronchitis *disease*

BRNKL bare-knuckle *fist*

BRNKL barnacle *mollusk*

BRNKL branchial *gills*

BRNKL bronchial (adj) *lungs* bronchially (adv)

BRNKL bronchiole *lung branch*

BRNKLD barnacled *mollusk*

BRNKLR bronchiolar *lungs*

BRNKMNSHP brinkmanship *strategy*

BRNKNMN bronchopneumonia *disease*

BRNKNMNY bronchopneumonia *disease*

BRNKPD branchiopod *crustacean*

BRNKS bronchus *lungs*

bronchi

BRNKS Bronx *New York borough*

BRNKSCHR Bronx cheer *rude noise*

BRNKSMNSHP brinksmanship *strategy*

BRNKTS bronchitis *disease*

BRNKY bronchi- (or) bronchio- *(prefix) lungs*

BRNKYL branchial *gills*

BRNKYL bronchial (adj) *lungs* bronchially (adv)

BRNKYL bronchiole *lung branch*

BRNKYLR bronchiolar *lungs*

BRNKYNMN bronchopneumonia *disease*

BRNKYNMNY bronchopneumonia *disease*

BRNKYPD branchiopod *crustacean*

BRNL barn owl *bird*

BRNL baronial *titled*

BRNL barrenly *without fruit*

BRNL brawnily *strong*

BRNLK barnlike *large*

BRNLNG brown lung *disease*

BRNLS brainless *stupid*

BRNLSL brainlessly *stupidly*

BRNLSNS brainlessness *stupidity*

BRNM brand name (n) *trade name* brand-name (adj)

BRNN burn in *(v) etch*

BRNN burn-in *(n) test*

BRNN burning *intense*

BRNNG burning *intense*

BRNNS braininess *intelligence*

BRNNS brawniness *strength*

BRNNS brininess *salty*

BRNPR brainpower *intellect*

BRNPWR brainpower *intellect*

BRNR brainier *smarter*

BRNR brawnier *stronger*

BRNR briner *use salt*

BRNR brinier *saltier*

BRNR burner *fire*

Use letters that best describe the sounds you hear and omit the vowels. Use **S** or **K** instead of **C**: to find circle use **SRKL**. Use **J** to find joy, **JM** to find gem and **G** to find go.

BRNRT brown rot *fungus*
BRNRZN barn raising *building*
BRNRZNG barn raising *building*
BRNS aberrance *deviation* aberrancy
BRNS abhorrence *hatred*
BRNS Barents Sea *body of water*
BRNS baroness *title*
BRNS barrenness *fruitless*
BRNS Bering Sea *body of water*
BRNS burnoose (or) burnous *cloak*
BRNSH burnish *polish*
BRNSHD burnished *polished*
BRNSHGR brown sugar *sweetener*
BRNSHN burnishing *polish*
BRNSHNG burnishing *polish*
BRNSHR burnisher *polisher*
BRNSHRT Brownshirt *Nazi*
BRNSHT burnished *polished*
BRNSRS brontosaurus *dinosaur*
BRNST brainiest *smartest*
BRNST brawniest *strongest*
BRNST briniest *saltiest*
BRNST burnoosed *cloaked*
BRNSTN brownstone *townhouse*
BRNSTRM barnstorm *travel, pilot*
BRNSTRM brainstorm *idea*
BRNSTRMR barnstormer *traveller*
BRNSTRST brains trust *(Br) advisors*
BRNSTRT Bering Strait *body of water*
BRNT aberrant *not typical*
BRNT abhorrent *hated*
BRNT baronet *title*
BRNT brant *goose* (Br) brent
BRNT brownout *power failure*
BRNT brunet (or) brunette *hair color*
BRNT brunt *burden*

BRNT burnout (n) *wear out, cease* burn out (v)
BRNT burnt (or) burned *(v-past)* burn
BRNTC Barents Sea *body of water*
BRNTC baronetcy *rank*
BRNTJ baronetage *rank*
BRNTL aberrantly *not typically*
BRNTRST brain trust *advisors* (Br) brains trust
BRNTRT brown trout *fish*
BRNTS aberrance *deviation* aberrancy
BRNTS abhorrence *hatred*
BRNTS Barents Sea *body of water*
BRNTS baronetcy *rank*
BRNTSR brainteaser *puzzle*
BRNTSRS brontosaurus *dinosaur*
BRNTZR brainteaser *puzzle*
BRNWL barn owl *bird*
BRNWSH brainwash *indoctrinate*
BRNWSHN brainwashing *indoctrination*
BRNWSHNG brainwashing *indoctrination*
BRNWV brain wave *idea*
BRNX Bronx *New York borough*
BRNXCHR Bronx cheer *rude noise*
BRNXMNSHP brinksmanship *strategy*
BRNY Borneo *country*
BRNY brand-new *unused*
BRNYL baronial *titled*
BRNYR brainier *smarter*
BRNYR brawnier *stronger*
BRNYR brinier *saltier*
BRNYRD barnyard *farm*
BRNYST brainiest *smartest*
BRNYST brawniest *strongest*
BRNYST briniest *saltiest*
BRNZ béarnaise *sauce*
BRNZ bronze *metal* bronzed bronzing
BRNZ bronzy *like bronze*

BRNZJ Bronze Age *era*
BRNZN bronzing *tanning*
BRNZNG bronzing *tanning*
BRNZR bronzer *tanner*
BRNZTRST brains trust *(Br) advisors*
BRP abrupt *unexpected*
BRP bear up *support*
BRP burp *belch*
BRPGN burp gun *weapon*
BRPL abruptly *unexpectedly*
BRPNS abruptness *curtness*
BRPSHN abruption *break off*
BRPT abrupt *unexpected*
BRPTL abruptly *unexpectedly*
BRPTNS abruptness *curtness*
BRQDR breakwater *wall*
BRQN break wind *emit gas* broke wind breaking wind
BRQND break wind *emit gas* broke wind breaking wind
BRQRK brickwork *arrangement*
BRQTR breakwater *wall*
BRR abhorrer *hater*
BRR barrier *shield*
BRR bearer *carrier*
BRR beerier *like beer*
BRR borer *driller*
BRR borrower *adopt, acquire*
BRR brayer *one who howls, ink roller*
BRR brewer *beer maker*
BRR brewery *beer factory* breweries
BRR briar *bush*
BRR brier *thorn*
BRR briery *thorny*
BRR burrier *bristle*
BRR burrower *digger*
BRRD briard *dog*
BRRF barrier reef *coral*
BRRLN barrier island *protector*
BRRLND barrier island *protector*
BRS brace (v) *reinforce, prepare, freshen* braced

Letters aren't doubled for single sounds: to find alley use **L** not **LL**. Use **Y** and **W** as hard sounds only: to find yellow use **YL**. (Br)=British spelling or usage. * See dictionary.

bracing

BRS brace (n) pair, teeth, bracket braces

BRS brass metal

BRS brassy color, bold brassier brassiest

BRS bursa sac bursas (or) bursae

BRS burse purse

BRSBN breastbone sternum

BRSDR barrister lawyer

BRSDS bursitis swelling

BRSFD breast-feed mother's milk breast-fed

BRSH auberge inn

BRSH barouche carriage

BRSH barrage (v) outpouring barraged barraging

BRSH bearish gruff

BRSH boarish brute

BRSH boorish rude

BRSH borscht soup

BRSH brash impudent

BRSH brioche bread

BRSH brush device, touch brushes

BRSH brushy hairy brushier brushiest

BRSHBK brushback (n) fastball brush back (v)

BRSHD brushed bushy, polished

BRSHF brush-off (n) dismissal

BRSHFR brushfire flames

BRSHFYR brushfire flames

BRSHKT brush cut haircut

BRSHL bearishly gruffly

BRSHL biracial two races

BRSHL boorishly rudely

BRSHL brashly impudently

BRSHLN brushland meadow

BRSHLND brushland meadow

BRSHLSM biracialism two races

BRSHLZM biracialism two races

BRSHN aberration deviation

BRSHN abortion termination

BRSHN abrasion cut

BRSHN aubergine eggplant

BRSHNKF Baryshnikov dancer

BRSHNKV Baryshnikov dancer

BRSHNL aberrational deviating

BRSHNS bearishness gruffness

BRSHNS boorishness rudeness

BRSHNS brashness impudence

BRSHNST abortionist pregnancy terminator

BRSHNV Brezhnev USSR president

BRSHP brush up renew

BRSHR brazier brass worker, grill

BRSHR brochure leaflet

BRSHR brushier hairier

BRSHST brushiest hairiest

BRSHT borscht soup

BRSHT brass hat rank

BRSHT brochette skewer

BRSHT brushed bushy, polished

BRSHW bourgeois capitalist bourgeoise (fem)

BRSHWD brushwood thicket

BRSHWRK brushwork paint

BRSHWZ bourgeoisie middle class

BRSHYR brushier hairier

BRSHYST brushiest hairiest

BRSK brisk quick

BRSK brusque abrupt

BRSKL briskly quickly

BRSKL brusquely abrupt

BRSKN bearskin fur

BRSKNS briskness quickness

BRSKNS brusqueness abrupt

BRSKP borescope optical

BRSKT brisket beef

BRSL Brasilia city

BRSL brassily boldly

BRSL bristle anger, hair bristled bristling

BRSL bristly angry, hairy bristlier bristliest

BRSL brucella bacteria brucellae

BRSLN Barcelona city

BRSLNG brisling fish

BRSLNS bristliness anger, hairiness

BRSLR bristlier angrier, hairier

BRSLS Brussels city

BRSLSPRT brussels sprout vegetable

BRSLSS brucellosis disease brucelloses

BRSLST bristliest angriest, hairiest

BRSLT bracelet band

BRSLY Brasilia city

BRSLYR bristlier angrier, hairier

BRSLYST bristliest angriest, hairiest

BRSLZ Brussels city

BRSN bracing vigorous

BRSNG bracing vigorous

BRSNKLS brass knuckles weapon

BRSNS brassiness boldness

BRSPLT breastplate armor

BRSR bracer archery

BRSR bracero laborer braceros

BRSR brasserie cafe

BRSR brassier color, bolder

BRSR bursar treasurer

BRSR bursary treasury

BRSRD brassard band

BRSRK berserk crazy

BRSST brassiest color, boldest

BRST abreast side-by-side

BRST beeriest like beer

BRST breast chest

BRST burriest bristle

BRST burst explode burst bursting

BRSTBN breastbone sternum

BRSTFD breast-feed mother's milk breast-fed

BRSTKS brass tacks details

Use letters that best describe the sounds you hear and omit the vowels. Use **S** or **K** instead of **C**: to find circle use **SRKL**. Use **J** to find joy, **JM** to find gem and **G** to find go.

BRSTN buhrstone *millstone*
BRSTPLT breastplate *armor*
BRSTR barrister *lawyer*
BRSTRK breaststroke
 swimming
BRSTS bursitis *swelling*
BRSTSTRK breaststroke
 swimming
BRSTWRK breastwork
 fortification
BRSTX brass tacks *details*
BRSV abrasive *irritating*
BRSVL abrasively
 irritatingly
BRSVNS abrasiveness
 irritation
BRSWRK breastwork
 fortification
BRSYR brassier *color, bolder*
BRSYST brassiest *color,*
 boldest
BRSZ berceuse *lullaby*
 berceuses
BRT abort *terminate*
BRT barrette *hairpin*
BRT bear out *prove*
BRT Beirut *city*
BRT berate *scold* berated
 berating
BRT biretta *cap*
BRT borate *mineral*
BRT bort *diamond*
BRT brat *unruly child*
BRT bratty *unruly*
BRT bright *sparkling, clever*
BRT brit *sea creatures*
BRT brought *(v-past) bring*
BRT brut *wine*
BRT brute *beast*
BRT burette *tube*
BRT burrito *food* burritos
BRTD aberrated *deviant*
BRTD borated *with borate*
BRTFSHNT abortifacient
 drug
BRTH barathea *fabric*
BRTH berth *space,*
 accommodation
BRTH bertha *collar*
BRTH birth *born*
BRTH breadth *width*
BRTH breath *air*

BRTH breathe *take in air*
 breathed breathing
BRTH breathy *panting*
 breathier breathiest
BRTH broth *soup* broths
BRTHBL breathable *porous*
BRTHD birthday *anniversary*
BRTHKNTRL birth control
 contraception
BRTHL breathily *panting*
BRTHL brothel *house*
BRTHLS breathless *panting*
BRTHLZR Breathalyzer
 (trademark) alcohol test
BRTHMRK birthmark
 blemish
BRTHN breathing *language*
 mark, respiration
BRTHNG breathing *language*
 mark, respiration
BRTHNS breathiness
 panting
BRTHPLS birthplace *origin*
BRTHR breather *rest*
BRTHR breathier *panting*
BRTHR brother *sibling*
BRTHRHD brotherhood
 fraternity
BRTHRL brotherly
 affectionate
BRTHRLNS brotherliness
 affection
BRTHRN brethren *brothers*
BRTHRN Brethren *Dunkers*
BRTHRNL brother-in-law
 relative brothers-in-law
BRTHRSNL brothers-in-law
 relatives
BRTHRT birthrate *number*
BRTHRT birthright *heritage*
BRTHRZNL brothers-in-law
 relatives
BRTHSRTFKT birth
 certificate *record*
BRTHST breathiest *panting*
BRTHSTFKT birth
 certificate *record*
BRTHSTN birthstone *gem*
BRTHTKN breathtaking
 exciting
BRTHTKNG breathtaking
 exciting

BRTHWRT birthwort *herb*
BRTHY barathea *fabric*
BRTHYR breathier *panting*
BRTHYST breathiest
 panting
BRTL brightly *sparkling,*
 clever
BRTL brittle *stiff* brittler
 brittlest
BRTL broadtail *lamb*
BRTL brutal (adj) *violent*
 brutally (adv)
BRTLD brutality *violence*
BRTLR brittler *stiffer*
BRTLST brittlest *stiffest*
BRTLT brutality *violence*
BRTLZ brutalize *savage*
 brutalized brutalizing
 (Br) brutalise
BRTLZSHN brutalization
 violence
 (Br) brutalisation
BRTN baritone *between bass*
 and tenor
BRTN Breton *of Brittany*
BRTN brighten *lighten*
BRTN Britain *island,*
 commonwealth
BRTN Britannia *Britain*
BRTN Briton *Englishman*
BRTN Brittany *dog* Brittanys
BRTN Brittany (or) Bretagne
 region
BRTNDR bartender *pub*
 worker
BRTNL baritonal *between*
 bass and tenor
BRTNR brightener *lightener*
BRTNS brattiness
 misbehavior
BRTNS brightness *light*
BRTNY Britannia *Britain*
BRTR aborter *terminator*
BRTR barrator *seller of rights*
BRTR barratry *sale of rights*
 barratries
BRTR barter *trade*
BRTRR barterer *trader*
BRTSH brattish *misbehaving*
BRTSH British *from Britain*
BRTSH brutish *savage*
BRTSHKLMB British

Letters aren't doubled for single sounds: to find alley use **L** not **LL**. Use **Y** and **W** as hard
sounds only: to find yellow use **YL**. (Br)=British spelling or usage. * See dictionary.

Columbia *province*
BRTSHKLMBY British
Columbia *province*
BRTV abortive *fruitless*
BRTVL abortively *fruitlessly*
BRTVNS abortiveness
fruitlessness
BRTWRST bratwurst
sausage
BRV bereave *mourn*
bereaved (or) bereft
bereaving
BRV brave *(v) risk* braved
braving
BRV brave *(adj) courageous*
braver bravest
BRV bravo *(n) villain, shout*
bravos (or) bravoes
BRV bravo *(v) applaud*
bravoed bravoing
BRV breve *symbol*
BRVD bereaved (or) bereft
mourning
BRVD bravado *foolhardy*
bravadoes (or) bravados
BRVD brevity *shortness*
brevities
BRVDR abbreviator
shortener
BRVL bravely *courageously*
BRVMNT bereavement
mourning
BRVR braver *courage*
BRVR bravery *courage*
braveries
BRVR bravura *skill*
BRVR breviary *book*
breviaries
BRVSHN abbreviation *short
form*
BRVST bravest *courage*
BRVT abbreviate *cut short*
abbreviated abbreviating
BRVT brevity *shortness*
brevities
BRVTR abbreviator
shortener
BRVYDR abbreviator
shortener
BRVYR bravura *skill*
BRVYR breviary *book*
breviaries

BRVYSHN abbreviation
short form
BRVYT abbreviate *cut short*
abbreviated abbreviating
BRVYTR abbreviator
shortener
BRWN borrowing *thing
acquired*
BRWN bruin *bear*
BRWNG borrowing *thing
acquired*
BRWR barware *glasses*
BRWR Boer War *South
Africa*
BRWR borrower *adopt,
acquire*
BRWR brewer *beer maker*
BRWR brewery *beer factory*
breweries
BRWR burrower *digger*
BRX barracks *residence*
BRX borax *mineral*
BRXMN brakesman (Br)
brakeman brakesmen
BRY barrio *ghetto* barrios
BRY brio *vigor*
BRY Iberia *peninsula*
BRYFDK bryophytic *plant*
BRYFLM bryophyllum *plant*
BRYFT bryophyte *plant*
BRYFTK bryophytic *plant*
BRYK abreact *therapy*
BRYKSHN abreaction
verbalization
BRYKT abreact *therapy*
BRYL boreal *north*
BRYL broil *grill*
BRYL burial *tomb*
BRYLR broiler *cooker*
BRYLT briolette *gem*
BRYM barium *element*
BRYN baryon *particle*
BRYN bryony *vine* bryonies
BRYNS brilliance *glitter,
keenness* brilliancy
BRYNT brilliant *glittery, keen*
BRYNTN brilliantine *fabric*
BRYNTS brilliance *glitter,
keenness* brilliancy
BRYR barrier *shield*
BRYR beerier *like beer*
BRYR brayer *one who howls,*

ink roller
BRYR briar *bush*
BRYR brier *thorn*
BRYR briery *thorny*
BRYR burrier *bristle*
BRYRD briard *dog*
BRYRF barrier reef *coral*
BRYRLN barrier island
protector
BRYRLND barrier island
protector
BRYSH brioche *bread*
BRYST beeriest *like beer*
BRYST burriest *bristle*
BRZ borzoi *dog*
BRZ braise *cook* braised
braising
BRZ breeze *air* breezed
breezing
BRZ breezy *windy* breezier
breeziest
BRZ browse *look over, graze*
browsed browsing
BRZ bruise *sore spot* bruised
bruising
BRZH auberge *inn*
BRZH barrage *(v)
outpouring* barraged
barraging
BRZHN abrasion *cut*
BRZHN aubergine *eggplant*
BRZHNKF Baryshnikov
dancer
BRZHNKV Baryshnikov
dancer
BRZHNV Brezhnev *USSR
president*
BRZHR brazier *brass worker,
grill*
BRZHW bourgeois *capitalist*
bourgeoise (fem)
BRZHWZ bourgeoisie
middle class
BRZL Brasilia *city*
BRZL Brazil *country*
BRZL breezily *airy,
nonchalant*
BRZLN brisling *fish*
BRZLNG brisling *fish*
BRZLY Brasilia *city*
BRZN brazen *brass, defiant*
BRZNS breeziness *airiness,*

Use letters that best describe the sounds you hear and omit the vowels. Use **S** or **K** instead of **C**: to find circle use **SRKL**. Use **J** to find joy, **JM** to find gem and **G** to find go.

nonchalance
BRZNS brisance *explosive*
BRZNT brisant *explosive*
BRZNTS brisance *explosive*
BRZR brassiere *garment*
BRZR brazier *brass worker, grill*
BRZR breezier *airy, nonchalant*
BRZR browser *look over, graze*
BRZR bruiser *big man*
BRZRK berserk *crazy*
BRZRKR berserker *warrior*
BRZST breeziest *airy, nonchalant*
BRZV abrasive *irritating*
BRZVL abrasively *irritatingly*
BRZVNS abrasiveness *irritation*
BRZW breezeway *passage*
BRZYR breezier *airy, nonchalant*
BRZYST breeziest *airy, nonchalant*
BS abaci (pl) *calculator* abacus
BS abase *lower* abased abasing
BS abbacy *abbot* abbacies
BS abbess *convent* abbesses
BS abuse (n) *misuse, invective* abuses
BS abyss *pit*
BS base (v) *locate, reason* based basing
BS base (adj) *vile* baser basest
BS base (n) *foundation, chemical, number** bases
BS bass *fish, voice* bass (or) basses
BS basso *singer* bassos (or) bassi
BS BC (or) B.C. *(abbr) Before Christ*
BS bias *slant* biased (or) biassed biasing (or) biassing
BS bis *twice*

BS Boise *city*
BS boss (v) *give orders* (n) *authority* bosses
BS bossy (adj) *dictatorial* bossier bossiest
BS bossy (n) *cow* bossies
BS bus (n) *vehicle* buses (or) busses
BS bus (v) *transport* bused (or) bussed busing (or) bussing
BS buss *kiss* busses
BS buzz saw *tool*
BS ibis *bird* ibis (or) ibises
BS obese *fat*
BSB best boy *assistant*
BSB busboy *waiter*
BSBL baseball *sport*
BSBRD baseboard *molding*
BSBRN baseborn *ignoble*
BSCH beseech *implore* beseeched (or) besought beseeching
BSCHL bestial (adj) *brutal, beasts* bestially (adv)
BSCHLD bestiality *beasts*
BSCHLT bestiality *beasts*
BSCHLZ bestialize *brutalize* bestialized bestializing
BSCHN bastion *fort*
BSCHND bastioned *fortified*
BSCHR bestiary *animal book* bestiaries
BSCHYL bestial (adj) *brutal, beasts* bestially (adv)
BSCHYLD bestiality *beasts*
BSCHYLT bestiality *beasts*
BSCHYR bestiary *animal book* bestiaries
BSD beastie *monster*
BSD beside *next to*
BSD biased *slanted*
BSD bustier (n) *garment* (adj) *bosomy*
BSD busty *bosom* bustier bustiest
BSD obesity *fat*
BSDD besotted *infatuated*
BSDD busted *no money*
BSDKL obstacle *barrier*
BSDL bastille *(often capitalized) jail*

BSDN obsidian *glass*
BSDNG basting *thread, liquid*
BSDNG besetting *obsessive*
BSDR baster *sew, moisten*
BSDR boaster *braggart*
BSDR booster *shot, supporter*
BSDR bustier (n) *garment* (adj) *bosomy*
BSDRD bastard *illegitimate one*
BSDRD bastardy *illegitimacy* bastardies
BSDRD bustard *bird*
BSDRDZ bastardize *make illigitimate* bastardized bastardizing (Br) bastardise
BSDRDZSHN bastardization *made illigitimate* (Br) bastardisation
BSDRM bass drum *music*
BSDRN abecedarian *learner*
BSDRS boisterous *loud*
BSDRSL boisterously *loudly*
BSDRSNS boisterousness *loudness*
BSDRYN abecedarian *learner*
BSDS besides *except*
BSDST bustiest *bosom*
BSDY bustier (n) *garment* (adj) *bosomy*
BSDYN obsidian *glass*
BSDYR bustier (n) *garment* (adj) *bosomy*
BSDYST bustiest *bosom*
BSDZ besides *except*
BSF basify *make alkaline* basifed basifying basifies
BSFDL bass fiddle *music*
BSFKSHN basification *make alkaline*
BSFL basophil (or) basophile *cell*
BSFL boastful (adj) *brag* boastfully (adv)
BSFLK basophilic *cell*
BSFLNS boastfulness *brag*
BSFLY basophilia *cell*

Letters aren't doubled for single sounds: to find alley use **L** not **LL**. Use **Y** and **W** as hard sounds only: to find yellow use **YL**. (Br)=British spelling or usage. * See dictionary.

BSFR biosphere *habitable area*
BSGD spaghetti *food*
BSGT spaghetti *food*
BSH abash *embarrass*
BSH bash *hit, party*
BSH beige *color*
BSH bijou *jewel* bijous (or) bijoux
BSH Bosch (Hieronymus) *artist*
BSH bosh *nonsense*
BSH bouchée *food*
BSH bougie *candle*
BSH boyish *male*
BSH bush *shrub* bushes
BSH bushy *overgrown* bushier bushiest
BSHD abashed *embarrassed*
BSHD bushed *tired*
BSHDMR bêche-de-mer *language* bêche-de-mer (or) bêches-de-mer
BSHDR bijouterie *ornaments*
BSHDR objet d'art *curio* objets d'art
BSHDRT objet d'art *curio* objets d'art
BSHFL bashful (adj) *shy* bashfully (adv)
BSHFLNS bashfulness *shyness*
BSHL abbatial *abbey*
BSHL Beaujolais *wine* Beaujolais
BSHL boyishly *male*
BSHL bushel *dry measure*
BSHLG bush league (n) *amateur* bush-league (adj)
BSHLGR bush leaguer *amateur*
BSHML béchamel *sauce*
BSHMN bushman *woodsman* bushmen
BSHMNT abashment *embarrassment*
BSHMSDR bushmaster *snake*
BSHMSTR bushmaster *snake*
BSHN bushing *lining*
BSHNFRZ bichon frise *dog*

bichons frises
BSHNG Beijing *city*
BSHNG bushing *lining*
BSHNS boyishness *maleness*
BSHNS bushiness *overgrown*
BSHP bishop *clergyman*
BSHPRK bishopric *district*
BSHR basher *hitter*
BSHR bushier *overgrown*
BSHRN bass horn *music*
BSHRNJN bushranging *woodsman*
BSHRNJNG bushranging *woodsman*
BSHRNJR bushranger *woodsman*
BSHST beau geste *gesture* beaux gestes (or) beau gestes
BSHST bushiest *overgrown*
BSHT abashed *embarrassed*
BSHT base hit *baseball*
BSHT bushed *tired*
BSHTR bijouterie *ornaments*
BSHTT bushtit *bird*
BSHW bourgeois *capitalist* bourgeoise (fem)
BSHWK bushwhack *ambush*
BSHWKR bushwhacker *ambusher*
BSHWZ bourgeoisie *middle class*
BSHYR bushier *overgrown*
BSHYST bushiest *overgrown*
BSJ besiege *surround, beset* besieged besieging
BSJR besieger *surround, beset*
BSK basic *fundamental*
BSK BASIC *computer language*
BSK bask *lie in*
BSK Basque *region*
BSK basque *bodice*
BSK bisect *divide*
BSK bisque *soup, odds, china*
BSK bosk (or) bosque *woods*
BSK bosky *woodsy*
BSKCHL bisexual (adj) *both sexes* bisexually (adv)
BSKCHWL bisexual (adj)

both sexes bisexually (adv)
BSKD spaghetti *food*
BSKDR bisector *divider*
BSKJ boscage *thicket*
BSKL bascule *seesaw*
BSKL basically *fundamentally*
BSKL bicycle *vehicle* bicycled bicycling
BSKLF bass clef *staff*
BSKLR bicycler *rider*
BSKLST bicyclist *rider*
BSKN abscond *leave and hide*
BSKN buskin *boot, drama*
BSKND abscond *leave and hide*
BSKNDR absconder *leave and hide*
BSKNGSHRK basking shark *animal*
BSKR busker *(Br) musician*
BSKR obscure *(v) darken, conceal* obscured obscuring
BSKR obscure *(adj) dark, vague*
BSKRD obscurity *darkness, vagueness* obscurities
BSKRL obscurely *dark, vague*
BSKRNS obscureness *dark, vague*
BSKRNT obscurant *cloud*
BSKRT obscurity *darkness, vagueness* obscurities
BSKS basics *fundamentals*
BSKSHL bisexual (adj) *both sexes* bisexually (adv)
BSKSHN bisection *division*
BSKSHNL bisectional *division*
BSKSHWL bisexual (adj) *both sexes* bisexually (adv)
BSKT basket *container*
BSKT biscuit *food*
BSKT bisect *divide*
BSKT bosquet *thicket*
BSKT boy scout *troop member*
BSKT spaghetti *food*
BSKTBL basketball *sport*

Use letters that best describe the sounds you hear and omit the vowels. Use **S** or **K** instead of **C**: to find circle use **SRKL**. Use **J** to find joy, **JM** to find gem and **G** to find go.

BSKTFL basketful *amount* basketfuls

BSKTKS basket case *incapacitated*

BSKTR basketry *craft*

BSKTR bisector *divider*

BSKTRNN basic training *military*

BSKTRNNG basic training *military*

BSKTWRK basketwork *containers*

BSKTWV basket weave *pattern*

BSKW obsequy *funeral* obsequies

BSKWS obsequious *subservient*

BSKWSL obsequiously *subservient*

BSKWSNS obsequiousness *subservience*

BSKWYS obsequious *subservient*

BSKWYSL obsequiously *subservient*

BSKWYSNS obsequiousness *subservience*

BSKYL bascule *seesaw*

BSKYR obscure *(v) darken, conceal* obscured obscuring

BSKYR obscure *(adj) dark, vague*

BSKYRD obscurity *darkness, vagueness* obscurities

BSKYRL obscurely *dark, vague*

BSKYRNS obscureness *dark, vague*

BSKYRNT obscurant *cloud*

BSKYRT obscurity *darkness, vagueness* obscurities

BSL abseil *rappel*

BSL abyssal *deep*

BSL bacilli *(pl) bacteria* bacillus

BSL basal *(adj) fundamental* basally *(adv)*

BSL basil *herb*

BSL beastly *disagreeable*

beastlier beastliest

BSL bustle *(n) clothing*

BSL bustle *(v) hurry* bustled bustling

BSLDK basaltic *rock*

BSLDST absolutist *despot*

BSLDV absolutive *grammar*

BSLDZM absolutism *despotism*

BSLFD bisulfide *disulfide*

BSLFT bisulfate *acid sulfate*

BSLFT bisulfite *acid sulfite*

BSLK basilica *church*

BSLN baseline *out of bounds*

BSLN best-selling *popular*

BSLNG best-selling *popular*

BSLNS beastliness *disagreeableness*

BSLR basilar *basic*

BSLR beastlier *more disagreeable*

BSLR best seller *popular item*

BSLS bacillus *bacteria* bacilli

BSLS baseless *no foundation*

BSLS obsolesce *out of date* obsolesced obsolescing

BSLSHN absolution *removal of guilt*

BSLSK basilisk *reptile*

BSLSNS obsolescence *out of date*

BSLSNT obsolescent *out of date*

BSLSNTS obsolescence *out of date*

BSLST beastliest *most disagreeable*

BSLT absolute *ultimate*

BSLT basalt *rock*

BSLT obsolete *out of date*

BSLTK basaltic *rock*

BSLTL absolutely *ultimately*

BSLTL obsoletely *out of date*

BSLTNS absoluteness *perfection*

BSLTNS obsoleteness *out of date*

BSLTST absolutist *despot*

BSLTSTK absolutistic *despotic*

BSLTV absolutive *grammar*

BSLTZ absolutize *perfect* absolutized absolutizing

BSLTZM absolutism *despotism*

BSLV absolve *remove guilt* absolved absolving

BSLVR absolver *guilt remover*

BSLYR beastlier *more disagreeable*

BSLYST beastliest *most disagreeable*

BSMD basmati *rice*

BSMN baseman *baseball* basemen

BSMN basement *bottom floor*

BSMN best man *wedding*

BSMNT abasement *lowering*

BSMNT basement *bottom floor*

BSMR besmear *smear*

BSMRCH besmirch *sully*

BSMRPRSS Bessemer process *steel*

BSMT basmati *rice*

BSMTSV bas mitzvah *Jewish ritual*

BSMTZV bas mitzvah *Jewish ritual*

BSN basin *sink*

BSN bassoon *music*

BSN bison *animal*

BSN boatswain *sailor*

BSN bos'n *(or)* bo's'n *(or)* bosun *(or)* bo'sun *boatswain*

BSN boson *particle*

BSN obscene *lewd*

BSNBLZ base on balls *baseball*

BSNCS byssinoses *(pl) disease* byssinosis

BSNCZ byssinoses *(pl) disease* byssinosis

BSND obscenity *indecency* obscenities

BSNG basenji *dog*

BSNJ basenji *dog*

BSNL obscenely *lewdly*

BSNN Abyssinian *cat*

BSNS absence *lack*

Letters aren't doubled for single sounds: to find alley use **L** not **LL**. Use **Y** and **W** as hard sounds only: to find yellow use **YL**. (Br)=British spelling or usage. * See dictionary.

BSNS obeisance *bowing*
BSNSMT boatswain's mate *sailor*
BSNSS biocenosis (or) biocoenosis *ecology* biocenoses
BSNSS byssinosis *disease* byssinoses
BSNST bassoonist *musician*
BSNT absent *not present*
BSNT absentee *not present*
BSNT bassinet *cradle*
BSNT obeisant *bowing*
BSNT obscenity *indecency* obscenities
BSNTH absinthe *liqueur*
BSNTHSS biosynthesis *chemical*
BSNTL obeisantly *bowing*
BSNTMNDD absentminded *preoccupied*
BSNTMNDDL absentmindedly *preoccupied*
BSNTMNDDNS absentmindedness *preoccupied*
BSNTNL bicentennial *two hundred years*
BSNTNR bicentenary *two hundred years*
BSNTNYL bicentennial *two hundred years*
BSNTS absence *lack*
BSNTS obeisance *bowing*
BSNTYZM absenteeism *not present*
BSNTZM absenteeism *not present*
BSNYN Abyssinian *cat*
BSNZMT boatswain's mate *sailor*
BSP base pay *salary*
BSPK bespeak *address, signify* bespoke bespoken bespeaking
BSPK bespoke (or) bespoken *custom-made, engaged*
BSPKN bespoken (or) bespoke *custom-made, engaged*

BSPL bias-ply *tire*
BSPRFND basso profundo *deep voice* basso profundos
BSPRT bowsprit *spar*
BSPS biceps *muscles* biceps
BSQ obsequy *funeral* obsequies
BSQL bascule *seesaw*
BSQR obscure *(v) darken, conceal* obscured obscuring
BSQR obscure *(adj) dark, vague*
BSQRD obscurity *darkness, vagueness* obscurities
BSQRT obscurity *darkness, vagueness* obscurities
BSQS obsequious *subservient*
BSQSL obsequiously *subservient*
BSQSNS obsequiousness *subservience*
BSQYS obsequious *subservient*
BSQYSL obsequiously *subservient*
BSQYSNS obsequiousness *subservience*
BSR baser *more common*
BSR bossier *dominating*
BSRB absorb *take in*
BSRBBL absorbable *take in*
BSRBBLD absorbability *take in*
BSRBBLT absorbability *take in*
BSRBN absorbing *engrossing*
BSRBNC absorbency (or) absorbancy *take in* absorbencies (or) absorbancies
BSRBNG absorbing *engrossing*
BSRBNGL absorbingly *engrossingly*
BSRBNL absorbingly *engrossingly*
BSRBNS absorbance *radiation*

BSRBNS absorbency (or) absorbancy *take in* absorbencies (or) absorbancies
BSRBNT absorbent *taking in*
BSRBNTC absorbency (or) absorbancy *take in* absorbencies (or) absorbancies
BSRBNTS absorbance *radiation*
BSRBNTS absorbency (or) absorbancy *take in* absorbencies (or) absorbancies
BSRBR absorber *one that takes in*
BSRBSHN absorption *take in, intercept, engross*
BSRBTNS absorptance *energy ratio*
BSRBTNTS absorptance *energy ratio*
BSRD absurd *meaningless*
BSRDD absurdity *meaninglessness* absurdities
BSRDL absurdly *unreasonably*
BSRDNS absurdness *meaninglessness*
BSRDSM absurdism *philosophy*
BSRDST absurdist *philosopher*
BSRDT absurdity *meaninglessness* absurdities
BSRDZM absurdism *philosophy*
BSRK berserk *crazy*
BSRLF bas-relief *projection*
BSRNN baserunning *baseball*
BSRNNG baserunning *baseball*
BSRNR base runner *baseball*
BSRPSHN absorption *take in, intercept, engross*
BSRPTNS absorptance *energy ratio*

Use letters that best describe the sounds you hear and omit the vowels. Use **S** or **K** instead of **C**: to find circle use **SRKL**. Use **J** to find joy, **JM** to find gem and **G** to find go.

BSRPTNTS absorptance *energy ratio*

BSRPTVT absorptivity *radiation* absorptivities

BSRV observe *watch, remark* observed observing

BSRVSHN observation *watch, remark, record*

BSS abscess *pus* abscesses

BSS abscissa *axis* abscissas (also) abscissae

BSS basis *foundation* bases

BSS byssus *cloth, filament* byssuses (or) byssi

BSS obsess *preoccupy*

BSSD abscessed *with pus*

BSSHN abscission *removal*

BSSHN obsession *fixation*

BSSHNL obsessional (adj) *overwhelming* obsessionally (adv)

BSSKSD abscisic acid *inhibitor*

BSSN abscisin *inhibitor*

BSST abscessed *with pus*

BSST basest *common*

BSST bassist *musician*

BSST bossiest *dominating*

BSSV obsessive *overwhelming*

BSSVKMPLSV obsessive-compulsive *neurotic*

BST bast *phloem*

BST baste *sew, moisten* basted basting

BST beast *animal*

BST beastie *monster*

BST beset *harass* beset besetting

BST besot *infatuate* besotted besotting

BST besought *asked*

BST best *superior*

BST bestow *give*

BST biased *slanted*

BST boast *brag*

BST boost *push up*

BST bust *(v)* break, arrest busted busting

BST bust *(n) upper torso, spree, arrest*

BST bust (or) busted *(adj) bankrupt*

BST bustier *(n) garment (adj) bosomy*

BST busty *bosomy* bustier bustiest

BST obesity *fat*

BST oboist *musician*

BSTB best boy *assistant*

BSTD besotted *infatuated*

BSTD busted (or) bust *(adj) bankrupt*

BSTDTRK obstetric (or) obstetrical (adj) *birth* obstetrically (adv)

BSTDTRKL obstetrical (or) obstetric (adj) *birth* obstetrically (adv)

BSTDTRKS obstetrics *birth*

BSTDTRX obstetrics *birth*

BSTFL boastful (adj) *brag* boastfully (adv)

BSTFLNS boastfulness *brag*

BSTHN basset hound *dog*

BSTHND basset hound *dog*

BSTKL obstacle *barrier*

BSTL bastille *(often capitalized) jail*

BSTL beastly *disagreeable* beastlier beastliest

BSTL bestial (adj) *brutal, beasts* bestially (adv)

BSTL bestowal *gift*

BSTLD bestiality *beasts*

BSTLNS beastliness *disagreeableness*

BSTLR beastlier *more disagreeable*

BSTLST beastliest *most disagreeable*

BSTLT bestiality *beasts*

BSTLYR beastlier *more disagreeable*

BSTLYST beastliest *most disagreeable*

BSTMN best man *wedding*

BSTMNT besetment *harassment*

BSTMS abstemious *restrained*

BSTMYS abstemious *restrained*

BSTN abstain *refrain*

BSTN basting *thread, liquid*

BSTN besetting *obsessive*

BSTN Boston *city*

BSTNC obstinacy *stubborn* obstinacies

BSTNCHN abstention *refrain from*

BSTNCHS abstentious *refraining*

BSTND bastinado (or) bastinade *beating* bastinadoes (or) bastinades

BSTNDR bystander *spectator*

BSTNG basting *thread, liquid*

BSTNG bee-stung *swollen*

BSTNG besetting *obsessive*

BSTNNC obstinacy *stubbornness* obstinacies

BSTNNS abstinence *denial*

BSTNNS obstinacy *stubbornness* obstinacies

BSTNNT abstinent *denial*

BSTNNT obstinate *stubborn*

BSTNNTC obstinacy *stubbornness* obstinacies

BSTNNTL abstinently *denial*

BSTNNTL obstinately *stubborn*

BSTNNTNS obstinateness *stubborn*

BSTNNTS abstinence *denial*

BSTNNTS obstinacy *stubbornness* obstinacies

BSTNR abstainer *refrainer*

BSTNS abstinence *denial*

BSTNS obstinacy *stubborn* obstinacies

BSTNSHN abstention *refrain from*

BSTNSHS abstentious *refraining*

BSTNT abstinent *denial*

BSTNT obstinate *stubborn*

BSTNTC obstinacy *stubborn* obstinacies

BSTNTL abstinently *denial*

BSTNTL obstinately *stubborn*

BSTNTNS obstinateness

stubborn

BSTNTS abstinence *denial*

BSTNTS obstinacy *stubborn*
obstinacies

BSTR baster *sew, moisten*

BSTR bestir *arouse* bestirred
bestirring

BSTR bistro *pub* bistros

BSTR boaster *braggart*

BSTR booster *shot, supporter*

BSTR buster *wind, fellow*

BSTR bustier *(n) garment
(adj) bosomy*

BSTRD bastard *illegitimate
one*

BSTRD bastardy *illegitimacy*
bastardies

BSTRD bustard *bird*

BSTRDZ bastardize *make
illigitimate* bastardized
bastardizing
(Br) bastardise

BSTRDZSHN bastardization
*made illigitimate
(Br)* bastardisation

BSTRK abstract *(n) idea (v)
remove, (adj) theoretical*

BSTRK obstruct *block*

BSTRKDBL abstractable
removable

BSTRKDD abstracted
preoccupied

BSTRKDDL abstractedly
preoccupied

BSTRKDR abstractor (or)
abstracter *remover*

BSTRKDR obstructor
blocker

BSTRKDV abstractive
separate, art

BSTRKDV obstructive
blocking

BSTRKDVNS
obstructiveness *blocking*

BSTRKL abstractly
theoretically

BSTRKNS abstractness
preoccupation

BSTRKSHN abstraction
idea, removal

BSTRKSHN obstruction
blockage

BSTRKSHNL abstractional
separate, preoccupied

BSTRKSHNSDK
obstructionistic
interference

BSTRKSHNST
abstractionist *separator,
artist*

BSTRKSHNST
obstructionist *interference*

BSTRKSHNSTK
obstructionistic
interference

BSTRKSHNZM
abstractionism *art*

BSTRKSHNZM
obstructionism
interference

BSTRKT abstract *(n) idea,
summary (v) remove (adj)
theoretical*

BSTRKT obstruct *block*

BSTRKTBL abstractable
removable

BSTRKTD abstracted
preoccupied

BSTRKTDL abstractedly
preoccupied

BSTRKTL abstractly
theoretically

BSTRKTNS abstractness
preoccupation

BSTRKTR abstractor (or)
abstracter *remover*

BSTRKTR obstructor *blocker*

BSTRKTV abstractive
separate, art

BSTRKTV obstructive
blocking

BSTRKTVNS
obstructiveness *blocking*

BSTRNG bowstring *cord*

BSTRPRS obstreperous
unruly

BSTRPRSL obstreperously
unruly

BSTRPRSNS
obstreperousness
unruliness

BSTRS abstruse *obscure*

BSTRS boisterous *loud*

BSTRSL abstrusely

obscurely

BSTRSL boisterously *loudly*

BSTRSN bacitracin
antibiotic

BSTRSNS abstruseness
obscureness

BSTRSNS boisterousness
loudness

BSTRST abstrusity *obscurity*
abstrusities

BSTRT Bass Strait *body of
water*

BSTRT bystreet *side lane*

BSTRZM boosterism
support

BSTSLN best-selling
popular

BSTSLNG best-selling
popular

BSTSLR best seller *popular
item*

BSTST bustiest *bosom*

BSTTRK obstetric (or)
obstetrical (adj) *birth*
obstetrically (adv)

BSTTRKL obstetrical (or)
obstetric (adj) *birth*
obstetrically (adv)

BSTTRKS obstetrics *birth*

BSTTRSHN obstetrician
birth

BSTTRX obstetrics *birth*

BSTVBRDN beast of
burden *pack animal*

BSTWL bestowal *gift*

BSTY bustier *(n) garment
(adj) bosomy*

BSTYL bestial (adj) *brutal,
beasts* bestially (adv)

BSTYLD bestiality *beasts*

BSTYLT bestiality *beasts*

BSTYR bustier *(n) garment
(adj) bosomy*

BSTYST bustiest *bosom*

BSV absolve *remove guilt*
absolved absolving

BSV abusive *damaging*

BSVL abusively *damaging*

BSVL bass viol *music*

BSVR absolver *guilt remover*

BSWD basswood *linden*

BSX basics *fundamentals*

Use letters that best describe the sounds you hear and omit the vowels. Use **S** or **K**
instead of **C**: to find circle use **SRKL**. Use **J** to find joy, **JM** to find gem and **G** to find go.

BSYR bossier *dominating*
BSYST bossiest *dominating*
BSZ abscise *cut* abscised abscising
BSZ bases (pl) *foundation* basis
BSZ besides *except*
BSZHN abscission *removal*
BSZKSD abscisic acid *inhibitor*
BT abate *lessen* abated abating
BT abbot *monk*
BT abet *incite* abetted abetting
BT about *regarding, near*
BT abut *touch* abutted abutting
BT baddie (or) baddy *evil one* baddies
BT baht *money* baht
BT bait *lure, torment*
BT bat (v) *hit, wave* batted batting
BT bat (n) *animal, club*
BT bate *restrain* bated bating
BT bateau *boat* bateaux
BT battu *ballet*
BT battue *hunt*
BT batty *crazy* battier battiest
BT beady *small and shiny* beadier beadiest
BT beat (v) *pound, defeat, cheat** beat beating beaten
BT beat (adj) *tired* (n) *rhythm, area, tack**
BT beaut *excellent*
BT beauty *pretty one* beauties
BT beet *vegetable*
BT bet *wager* bet betting
BT beta *Greek letter*
BT betta *fish*
BT biddy *hen* biddies
BT bight *curve*
BT biota *life*
BT bit (v) *bridle* bitted bitting
BT bit (n) *tool, bridle, piece**
BT bite *chew* bit bitten biting

BT bitt (v) *fasten* (n) *post*
BT bitty *tiny*
BT boat *ship*
BT boot *shoe*
BT bootee (or) bootie *slipper*
BT booty *prize* booties
BT bota *bottle*
BT bought (v-past) *buy*
BT bout *fight*
BT bow tie *neckwear*
BT Btu (abbr) *British thermal unit* Btu
BT Buddha *enlightened one*
BT buddy (n) *friend* buddies
BT buddy (v) *be friendly* buddied buddying buddies
BT but *except that*
BT buteo *hawk* buteos
BT butt *ram, end*
BT Butte *city*
BT butte *mountain*
BT buyout (n) *purchase* buy out (v)
BT byte *computer*
BT obit *obituary*
BT U-boat *ship*
BTBL bed table *lap board*
BTBL biddable (adj) *docile* biddably (adv)
BTBLD biddability *docility*
BTBLK bootblack *polish*
BTBLKR beta-blocker *heart drug*
BTBLT biddability *docility*
BTC bitsy *small*
BTCHL Botticelli *artist*
BTD beaded *decoration*
BTD bedded *sleep*
BTD betide *befall, happen*
BTD ebb tide *ocean*
BTDN butadiene *gas*
BTF beat off (vulgar) *masturbate*
BTF beatify *sanctify* beatified beatifying beatifies
BTF beautify *make pretty* beautified beautifying beautifies
BTFK beatific *blissful*
BTFKL beatifically *blissfully*

BTFL batfowl *catch birds*
BTFL beautiful (adj) *lovely* beautifully (adv)
BTFS about-face *turn around* (Br) about-turn
BTFSH batfish *animal*
BTH bath *tub* baths
BTH bathe *wash* bathed bathing
BTH booth *enclosure* booths
BTH both *two*
BTHDK bathetic *trite*
BTHDKL bathetically *tritely*
BTHHS bathhouse *dressing room*
BTHK boat hook *pole*
BTHKS bioethics *medical research*
BTHL bathyal *ocean depth*
BTHL bethel *chapel*
BTHLN biathlon *ski and shoot*
BTHLT biathlete *ski and shoot*
BTHMT bath mat *rug*
BTHMTR bathymetry *depth measure*
BTHMTRK bathymetric *depth measure*
BTHMTRKL bathymetrically *depth measure*
BTHN bathing *wash, swim*
BTHNG bathing *wash, swim*
BTHNGK bethink *recall* bethought bethinking
BTHNGKP bathing cap *head cover*
BTHNGST bathing suit *swim attire*
BTHNK bethink *recall* bethought bethinking
BTHNKP bathing cap *head cover*
BTHNST bathing suit *swim attire*
BTHR bather *swimmer, washer*
BTHR bother *annoy*
BTHRB bathrobe *attire*
BTHRM bathroom *toilet*
BTHRSM bothersome

Letters aren't doubled for single sounds: to find alley use **L** not **LL**. Use **Y** and **W** as hard sounds only: to find yellow use **YL**. (Br)=British spelling or usage. * See dictionary.

annoying

BTHS bathhouse *dressing room*

BTHS bathos *trite*

BTHS boathouse *shelter*

BTHSFR bathysphere *submersible*

BTHSKF bathyscaphe (or) bathyscaph *submersible*

BTHT bethought *recalled*

BTHTB bathtub *washing area*

BTHTK bathetic *trite*

BTHTKL bathetically *tritely*

BTHWDR bathwater *warm tub water*

BTHWTR bathwater *warm tub water*

BTHX bioethics *medical research*

BTHYL bathyal *ocean depth*

BTJK bootjack *device*

BTK abiotic *not living*

BTK batik *fabric*

BTK biotech *science*

BTK biotic *living*

BTK boat hook *pole*

BTK boutique *shop*

BTK buttock *rump*

BTKL abiotically *not living*

BTKMP boot camp *army*

BTKN betoken *presage*

BTKNLG biotechnology *human engineering*

BTKNLJ biotechnology *human engineering*

BTKNLJKL biotechnological *human engineering*

BTKNLJST biotechnologist *human engineering*

BTKRTN beta-carotene *plant isomer*

BTL battle *fight* battled battling

BTL beetle *insect*

BTL betel *plant*

BTL bottle (v) *confine* bottled bottling

BTL bottle (n) *container*

BTL buddleia *shrub*

BTL butyl *chemical*

BTLD boatload *amount*

BTLD bottled *confined*

BTLDD butylated *combined*

BTLFL battlefield *war arena*

BTLFL bottleful *container*

BTLFLD battlefield *war arena*

BTLFTG battle fatigue *war exhaustion*

BTLG bootleg *make liquor illegally* bootlegged bootlegging

BTLGR bootlegger *make liquor illegally*

BTLGRN battleground *war arena*

BTLGRND battleground *war arena*

BTLJS Betelgeuse *star*

BTLJZ Betelgeuse *star*

BTLKR battle cry *war yell* battle cries

BTLKS battle-ax *tool, woman* battle-axes

BTLMNT battlement *parapet*

BTLN abutilon *plant*

BTLN bottling *containers*

BTLN botulin *toxin*

BTLN butylene *chemical*

BTLNG bottling *containers*

BTLNK bottleneck *narrow part*

BTLR battler *fighter*

BTLR bottler *containers*

BTLR butler *manservant*

BTLRL battle royal *struggle* battles royal

BTLRYL battle royal *struggle* battles royal

BTLS abuttals *boundaries*

BTLS Beatles *musicians*

BTLS bootlace *string*

BTLSHP battleship *war ship*

BTLTD butylated *combined*

BTLWGN battlewagon *war ship*

BTLX battle-ax *tool, woman* battle-axes

BTLYN battalion *army*

BTLZ Beatles *musicians*

BTLZM botulism *disease*

BTM bottom *buttocks, base*

BTMD bottomed *ended*

BTMLN bottom line (n) *main point*

BTMLN bottom-line (adj) *profits*

BTMLND bottomland *low-lying*

BTMLS bottomless *unlimited*

BTMN batman *sport* batmen

BTMN bitumen *coal*

BTMN boatman *sailor* boatmen

BTMNS bituminous *coal*

BTMNT abatement *lessening*

BTMNT abetment *encouragement*

BTMNT abutment *bridge*

BTMST bottommost *deepest*

BTMTSV bat mitzvah *Jewish ritual*

BTMTZV bat mitzvah *Jewish ritual*

BTMZ betimes *early*

BTN Bataan *peninsula*

BTN baton *wand*

BTN batten (n) *thin strip* (v) *fasten*

BTN batting *action, material*

BTN beaten *whipped*

BTN beating *defeat, whipping*

BTN betting *wager*

BTN Bhutan *country*

BTN bidden (v-past) *bid*

BTN biotin *vitamin B*

BTN biting *sharp*

BTN bitten (v-past) *bite*

BTN botany *science*

BTN butane *chemical*

BTN button (v) *fasten* (n) *fastener*

BTN obtain *attain*

BTNBL buttonball *plane*

BTNBL obtainable *attainable*

BTNBLD obtainability *attainment*

BTNBLT obtainability *attainment*

BTNBSH buttonbush *shrub*

BTNDN button-down *conservative, collar*

BTNDP buttoned-up *reserved*

Use letters that best describe the sounds you hear and omit the vowels. Use **S** or **K** instead of **C** to find circle use **SRKL**. Use **J** to find joy, **JM** to find gem and **G** to find go.

BTNDRFN beta-endorphin *pituatary*

BTNDSWTCH bait and switch *deceive*

BTNG bating *excepting*

BTNG batting *action, material*

BTNG beading *decoration*

BTNG beating *defeat, whipping*

BTNG bedding *foundation, sheets*

BTNG betting *wager*

BTNG biting *sharp*

BTNG boating *ship*

BTNG budding *early stage*

BTNGVRJ batting average *statistic*

BTNHK buttonhook *fastener, football play*

BTNHL buttonhole (n) *opening* (v) *detain*

BTNHLR buttonholer (n) *opening* (v) *detain*

BTNK beatnik *rebel*

BTNKL botanical (adj) *plant* botanically (adv)

BTNMNT obtainment *attainment*

BTNR boutonniere *flower*

BTNR buttoner *fastener*

BTNR obtainer *attainer*

BTNRSH Baton Rouge *city*

BTNRZH Baton Rouge *city*

BTNS battiness *craziness*

BTNSK buttinsky *meddler* buttinskies

BTNST botanist *scientist*

BTNSWTCH bait and switch *deceive*

BTNVRJ batting average *statistic*

BTNWR bête noire *hated one* bêtes noires

BTNYR boutonniere *flower*

BTNZ botanize *collect plants* botanized botanizing (Br) botanise

BTP beat up (v) *pummel*

BTP beat-up (adj) *damaged*

BTP biotype *ecology*

BTPLR beauty parlor *salon*

(Br) beauty parlour

BTPRLR beauty parlor *salon* (Br) beauty parlour

BTR abater *lessen*

BTR abettor (or) abetter *aide*

BTR abutter *toucher*

BTR badder (slang) *better*

BTR batter (n) *hitter, food mixture, slope* (v) *bombard, coat food*

BTR battery (n) *energy source, guns, array** batteries

BTR battier *crazier*

BTR beadier *smaller and shinier*

BTR beater *hitter, mixer*

BTR bedder *plant*

BTR bee-eater *bird*

BTR betray *reveal, show treachery*

BTR better *improved, gambler*

BTR bettor (or) better *wagerer*

BTR bidder *offer*

BTR biter *teeth*

BTR bitter *taste*

BTR bo tree *Buddha*

BTR boater *ship*

BTR budder *plant*

BTR butter *food*

BTR buttery *creamy*

BTR obituary *death notice* obituaries

BTRBL butterball *chubby one*

BTRBN butter bean *vegetable*

BTRBRSH bitterbrush *shrub*

BTRD battered *beaten, coated*

BTRD obtrude *interfere* obtruded obtruding

BTRDKD obiter dicta (pl) *opinion* obiter dictum

BTRDKDM obiter dictum *opinion* obiter dicta

BTRDKT obiter dicta (pl) *opinion* obiter dictum

BTRDKTM obiter dictum *opinion* obiter dicta

BTRDL botryoidal *grapes*

BTRDR obtruder *interferer*

BTRF better-off *comfortable*

BTRFL butterfly *insect* butterflies

BTRFNGGRD butterfingered *clumsy*

BTRFNGGRS butterfingers *clumsy*

BTRFNGGRZ butterfingers *clumsy*

BTRFNGRD butterfingered *clumsy*

BTRFNGRS butterfingers *clumsy*

BTRFNGRZ butterfingers *clumsy*

BTRFSH butterfish *fish*

BTRFT butterfat *milk fat*

BTRK butyric *butter*

BTRKP buttercup *flower*

BTRL betrayal *treachery*

BTRMLK buttermilk *beverage*

BTRMNT betterment *improvement*

BTRN about-turn (Br) *about-face*

BTRN bitter end *conclusion*

BTRN bittern *bird, brine*

BTRN boat train *cargo*

BTRND bitter end *conclusion*

BTRNF butter knife *utensil*

BTRNG battering *attacking*

BTRNGRM battering ram *metal bar*

BTRNRM battering ram *metal bar*

BTRNT butternut *tree*

BTRR betrayer *treacherous one*

BTRS bitters *flavoring*

BTRS buttress *support* buttresses

BTRSD buttressed *supported*

BTRSHN obtrusion *interference*

BTRSKCH butterscotch *candy, color*

BTRSPDR beta-receptor *nerve cell*

BTRSPTR beta-receptor *nerve cell*

Letters aren't doubled for single sounds: to find alley use **L** not **LL**. Use **Y** and **W** as hard sounds only: to find yellow use **YL**. (Br)=British spelling or usage. * See dictionary.

BTRST buttressed *supported*
BTRSV obtrusive *interfering*
BTRSVL obtrusively *interfering*
BTRSVNS obtrusiveness *interference*
BTRSWT bittersweet *(adj) taste, feeling (n) plant*
BTRT beetroot *(Br) vegetable*
BTRT bitterroot *herb*
BTRTH betroth *promise to marry*
BTRTHD betrothed *engaged one*
BTRTHL betrothal *promise to marry*
BTRWD bitterweed (or) butterweed *plant*
BTRWRT butterwort *herb*
BTRYDL botryoidal *grapes*
BTRYL betrayal *treachery*
BTRYR betrayer *treacherous one*
BTRZ bitters *flavoring*
BTRZHN obtrusion *interference*
BTRZV obtrusive *interfering*
BTRZVL obtrusively *interfering*
BTRZVNS obtrusiveness *interference*
BTS beauteous *lovely*
BTS bitsy *small*
BTS boathouse *shelter*
BTS obtuse *dull* obtuser obtusest
BTSHN beautician *cosmetologist*
BTSHP beauty shop *salon*
BTSLN beauty salon *personal care shop*
BTSMN batsman *hitter* batsmen
BTSPRSKN bits-per-second *speed*
BTSPRSKND bits-per-second *speed*
BTSPRSKNT bits-per-second *speed*
BTSR obtuser *duller*
BTSST obtusest *dullest*
BTST baddest *(slang) best*

BTST batiste *fabric*
BTST battiest *craziest*
BTST beadiest *smallest and shiniest*
BTSWN Botswana *country*
BTTD beatitude *blissful state*
BTTRN betatron *accelerator*
BTTYD beatitude *blissful state*
BTVN Beethoven *composer*
BTWKS betwixt *between*
BTWKST betwixt *between*
BTWN between *in the middle*
BTWNG bitewing *x-ray*
BTWNTMS betweentimes *during intervals*
BTWR abattoir *slaughterhouse*
BTWR obituary *death notice* obituaries
BTWV beta wave *brain wave*
BTWX betwixt *between*
BTWXT betwixt *between*
BTY battu *ballet*
BTY battue *hunt*
BTY Btu *(abbr) British thermal unit* Btu
BTY buteo *hawk* buteos
BTYMN bitumen *coal*
BTYMNS bituminous *coal*
BTYN battalion *army*
BTYR battier *crazier*
BTYR beadier *smaller and shinier*
BTYS beauteous *lovely*
BTYS obtuse *dull* obtuser obtusest
BTYSR obtuser *duller*
BTYSST obtusest *dullest*
BTYST battiest *craziest*
BTYST beadiest *smallest and shiniest*
BTZ bêtise *stupidity* bêtises
BTZM Buddhism *religion*
BV above *over*
BV bevy *group* bevies
BVBRD aboveboard *openly*
BVD bovid *animal*
BVD obovoid *shape*
BVGRN aboveground *surface*
BVGRND aboveground

surface
BVL above all *topmost*
BVL bevel *edge* beveled (or) bevelled beveling (or) bevelling
BVLNT bivalent *pair*
BVLV bivalve *shell*
BVN bovine *cow, ox*
BVR Bavaria *region*
BVR beaver *animal*
BVRBRD beaverboard *fiberboard*
BVRJ beverage *drink*
BVRN Bavarian *of Bavaria*
BVRS obverse *opposite*
BVRSL obversely *opposite*
BVRY Bavaria *region*
BVRYN Bavarian *of Bavaria*
BVS beeves (pl) *meat* beef
BVS obvious *evident*
BVSL obviously *evidently*
BVSNS obviousness *evidence*
BVT obovate *shape*
BVT obviate *prevent* obviated obviating
BVWK bivouac *camp* bivouacked bivouacking
BVYS obvious *evident*
BVYSL obviously *evidently*
BVYSNS obviousness *evidence*
BVYT obviate *prevent* obviated obviating
BVZ beeves (pl) *meat* beef
BW boa *snake, scarf*
BW buoy *float*
BW byway *side road*
BWCH bewitch *enchant* bewitched bewitching
BWCHNGL bewitchingly *enchantingly*
BWCHNL bewitchingly *enchantingly*
BWCHT bewitched *enchanted*
BWDL beau ideal *model* beau ideals
BWKL biweekly *every two weeks* biweeklies
BWL bewail *cry*
BWL bowel *intestine*

Use letters that best describe the sounds you hear and omit the vowels. Use **S** or **K** instead of **C**: to find circle use **SRKL**. Use **J** to find joy, **JM** to find gem and **G** to find go.

BWLDR bewilder *perplex* bewildered bewildering

BWLDRMNT bewilderment *puzzlement*

BWLKTRK bioelectric *plants and animals*

BWLKTRKL bioelectrical *plants and animals*

BWLKTRSD bioelectricity *plants and animals*

BWLKTRST bioelectricity *plants and animals*

BWLS bowels *intestines*

BWLZ bowels *intestines*

BWN bwana *boss*

BWND bay window *flat glass*

BWND bow window *curved glass*

BWNF bowie knife *tool*

BWNJNRN bioengineering *biotechnology*

BWNJNRNG bioengineering *biotechnology*

BWNRJDK bioenergetic *energy exchange*

BWNRJDKS bioenergetics *energy exchange*

BWNRJDX bioenergetics *energy exchange*

BWNRJTK bioenergetic *energy exchange*

BWNRJTKS bioenergetics *energy exchange*

BWNRJTX bioenergetics *energy exchange*

BWNSRZ Buenos Aires *city*

BWR beware *watch out*

BWR bower *shelter*

BWR bowery *farm, bar district* boweries

BWRBRD bowerbird *bird*

BWRD byword *proverb*

BWRM bollworm *insect*

BWSKRD bewhiskered *facial hair*

BWST oboist *musician*

BWTHKS bioethics *medical research*

BWTHX bioethics *medical research*

BWVL boll weevil *insect*

BWW bowwow *dog*

BX box *(v) hit, enclose*

BX box *(n) container* boxes

BX boxy *square* boxier boxiest

BX bucksaw *tool*

BX ibex *animal* ibex (or) ibexes

BXBRD boxboard *cardboard*

BXD backside *rear*

BXDK bauxitic *mineral*

BXFS box office *theater*

BXKN buckskin *leather*

BXKND buckskinned *attired*

BXKR box score *sports*

BXKR boxcar *train*

BXKT box kite *toy*

BXL abaxial *away from axis*

BXL biaxial (adj) *double axis* biaxially (adv)

BXLD backslide *lapse* backslid (or) backslidden backsliding

BXLDR backslider *lapser*

BXLNCH box lunch *food* box lunches

BXLR bookseller *retailer*

BXM buxom *full-bosomed*

BXMNS buxomness *full-bosomed*

BXN boxing *sport, casing*

BXNG boxing *sport, casing*

BXPN backspin *motion*

BXPRNG box spring *bed*

BXPS backspace *keyboard* backspaced backspacing

BXR boxer *dog, fighter*

BXR boxier *square*

BXST boxiest *square*

BXT backseat *rear position*

BXT bauxite *mineral*

BXT box seat *good position*

BXTCH backstitch *sewing* backstitches

BXTJ backstage *private*

BXTK bauxitic *mineral*

BXTP backstop *screen*

BXTR bookstore *bookshop*

BXTRCH backstretch *racecourse*

BXTRK backstroke *swimming*

BXTRZ backstairs *secret*

BXWNG backswing *motion*

BXYL abaxial *away from axis*

BXYL biaxial (adj) *double axis* biaxially (adv)

BXYR boxier *square*

BXYST boxiest *square*

BY bayou *creek*

BY obeah *sorcery*

BYB bubo *swelling* buboes

BYBB baobab *tree*

BYBNK bubonic *swollen*

BYBNKPLG bubonic plague *disease*

BYBS bouillabaisse *stew*

BYBZ bouillabaisse *stew*

BYCNSS biocenosis (or) biocoenosis *ecology* biocenoses

BYD beauty *pretty one* beauties

BYD biota *life*

BYD buteo *hawk* buteos

BYDDN butadiene *gas*

BYDF beatify *sanctify* beatified beatifying beatifies

BYDF beautify *make pretty* beautified beautifying beautifies

BYDFL beautiful (adj) *lovely* beautifully (adv)

BYDGRDBL biodegradable *digestible*

BYDK abiotic *not living*

BYDK biotic *living*

BYDKL abiotically *not living*

BYDL butyl *chemical*

BYDLDD butylated *combined*

BYDLN abutilon *plant*

BYDLN butylene *chemical*

BYDLTD butylated *combined*

BYDPLR beauty parlor *salon* (Br) beautyparlour

BYDPRLR beauty parlor *salon* (Br) beauty parlour

BYDR bayadere *fabric*

BYDS beauteous *lovely*

BYDSHP beauty shop *salon*

BYDSLN beauty salon

personal care shop
BYDTD beatitude *blissful state*
BYDTYD beatitude *blissful state*
BYDVRSD biodiversity *different species*
BYDVRST biodiversity *different species*
BYDY buteo *hawk* buteos
BYDYS beauteous *lovely*
BYFDBK biofeedback *mental control*
BYFZKS biophysics *science*
BYFZSST biophysicist *scientist*
BYFZX biophysics *science*
BYGL bugle *music* bugled bugling
BYGLR bugler *musician*
BYGNK biogenic *from living*
BYGNS biogenous *from living*
BYGRF biography *life history* biographies
BYGRFR biographer *writer*
BYHZRD biohazard *life threatener*
BYJNDK biogenetic *from living*
BYJNDKL biogenetically *from living*
BYJNK biogenic *from living*
BYJNS biogenous *from living*
BYJNSS abiogenesis *from non-living*
BYJNSS biogenesis *from living*
BYJNST abiogenist *scientist*
BYJNTK biogenetic *from living*
BYJNTKL biogenetically *from living*
BYKCL biaxial (adj) *double axis* biaxially (adv)
BYKCYL biaxial (adj) *double axis* biaxially (adv)
BYKLK bucolic *rural*
BYKLKL bucolically *rural*
BYKMKL biochemical *organisms*

BYKMST biochemist *scientist*
BYKMSTR biochemistry *organisms*
BYKRST Bucharest *city*
BYKSL biaxial (adj) *double axis* biaxially (adv)
BYKSYL biaxial (adj) *double axis* biaxially (adv)
BYL aboil *bubbly*
BYL abulia *indecision*
BYL bile *acid*
BYL boil *bubble*
BYL boulle *inlay*
BYLBL boilable *bubble*
BYLG biology *science*
BYLJ biology *science*
BYLJK biologic (or) biological (adj) *living* biologically (adv)
BYLJKL biological (or) biologic (adj) *living* biologically (adv)
BYLJST biologist *scientist*
BYLK abulic *indecisive*
BYLKSHN by-election *vote*
BYLKTRK bioelectric *plants and animals*
BYLKTRKL bioelectrical *plants and animals*
BYLKTRSD bioelectricity *plants and animals*
BYLKTRST bioelectricity *plants and animals*
BYLKTRZD bioelectricity *plants and animals*
BYLKTRZT bioelectricity *plants and animals*
BYLM bulimia *eating disorder*
BYLMK bulimic *eating disorder*
BYLMNSNS bioluminescence *light*
BYLMNSNT bioluminescent *light*
BYLMNSNTS bioluminescence *light*
BYLMY bulimia *eating disorder*
BYLN boiling *bubbly*
BYLNG boiling *bubbly*
BYLNGPNT boiling point

temperature
BYLNPNT boiling point *temperature*
BYLR boiler *heater*
BYLRM boiler room *heating, sales*
BYLRMKR boilermaker *worker, whiskey*
BYLRPLT boilerplate *standard text*
BYLY abulia *indecision*
BYLZBB Beelzebub *devil*
BYM biome *ecological community*
BYMDKL biomedical *medicine*
BYMDSN biomedicine *science*
BYMKNKL biomechanical (adj) *muscles* biomechanically (adv)
BYMKNKS biomechanics *muscles*
BYMKNX biomechanics *muscles*
BYMTR biometry *statistics*
BYMTRKS biometrics *statistics*
BYMTRX biometrics *statistics*
BYN being (n) *entity* (v-*present*) to be
BYN beyond *farther out*
BYN biennia (pl) *two years* biennium
BYN billion *number*
BYN bouillon *soup*
BYN bullion *metal*
BYNC buoyancy *float*
BYND beyond *farther out*
BYNG being (n) *entity* (v) *existing*
BYNJNRN bioengineering *biotechnology*
BYNJNRNG bioengineering *biotechnology*
BYNK bionic *robot*
BYNKS bionics *robotics*
BYNL biannual (adj) *two per year* biannually (adv)
BYNL biennial (adj) *two years* biennially (adv)

Use letters that best describe the sounds you hear and omit the vowels. Use **S** or **K** instead of **C**: to find circle use **SRKL**. Use **J** to find joy, **JM** to find gem and **G** to find go.

BYNM biennium *two years* bienniums (or) biennia
BYNMKS bionomics *ecology*
BYNMX bionomics *ecology*
BYNR billionaire *wealthy one*
BYNRJTK bioenergetic *energy exchange*
BYNRJTKS bioenergetics *energy exchange*
BYNRJTX bioenergetics *energy exchange*
BYNS abeyance *lapse*
BYNS buoyancy *float*
BYNT abeyant *lapsed*
BYNT bayonet *knife*
BYNT buoyant *floating*
BYNTC buoyancy *float*
BYNTH billionth *number*
BYNTS abeyance *lapse*
BYNTS buoyancy *float*
BYNWL biannual (adj) *two per year* biannually (adv)
BYNX bionics *robotics*
BYNY biennia (pl) *two years* biennium
BYNYL biannual (adj) *two per year* biannually (adv)
BYNYL biennial (adj) *two years* biennially (adv)
BYNYM biennium *two years* bienniums (or) biennia
BYNYWL biannual (adj) *two per year* biannually (adv)
BYPC biopsy *test* biopsies
BYPRFN ibuprofen *drug*
BYPS biopsy *test* biopsies
BYR bureau *dresser, agency* bureaus
BYR buyer *purchaser*
BYRD billiard *ball*
BYRDZ billiards *pool game*
BYRKRC bureaucracy *ruling group* bureaucracies
BYRKRDK bureaucratic *official*
BYRKRDKL bureaucratically *officially*
BYRKRDZSHN bureaucratization *make official* (Br) bureaucratisation

BYRKRS bureaucracy *ruling group* bureaucracies
BYRKRT bureaucrat *official*
BYRKRTK bureaucratic *official*
BYRKRTKL bureaucratically *officially*
BYRKRTZ bureaucratize *make official* bureaucratized bureaucratizing (Br) bureaucratise
BYRKRTZSHN bureaucratization *make official* (Br) bureaucratisation
BYRL biyearly *every two years*
BYRN burin *tool*
BYRNZ béarnaise *sauce*
BYRT burette *tube*
BYS abuse *(n) misuse, invective* abuses
BYS bias *slant* biased (or) biassed biasing (or) biassing
BYSBL abusable *damage*
BYSD biased *slanted*
BYSFR biosphere *habitable area*
BYSH boyish *male*
BYSHL boyishly *male*
BYSHNS boyishness *maleness*
BYSNSS biocenosis (or) biocoenosis *ecology* biocenoses
BYSNTHSS biosynthesis *chemical*
BYSPL bias-ply *tire*
BYST biased *slanted*
BYSV abusive *damaging*
BYSVL abusively *damaging*
BYT beaut *excellent*
BYT beauty *pretty one* beauties
BYT biota *life*
BYT buteo *hawk* buteos
BYT Butte *city*
BYT butte *mountain*
BYT buyout (n) *purchase* buy

out (v)
BYTDN butadiene *gas*
BYTF beatify *sanctify* beatified beatifying beatifies
BYTF beautify *make pretty* beautified beautifying beautifies
BYTFK beatific *blissful*
BYTFKL beatifically *blissfully*
BYTFL beautiful (adj) *lovely* beautifully (adv)
BYTHKS bioethics *medical research*
BYTHLN biathlon *ski and shoot*
BYTHLT biathlete *ski and shoot*
BYTHX bioethics *medical research*
BYTK abiotic *not living*
BYTK biotech *science*
BYTK biotic *living*
BYTKL abiotically *not living*
BYTKNLG biotechnology *human engineering*
BYTKNLJ biotechnology *human engineering*
BYTKNLJKL biotechnological *human engineering*
BYTKNLJST biotechnologist *human engineering*
BYTL butyl *chemical*
BYTLDD butylated *combined*
BYTLN abutilon *plant*
BYTLN butylene *chemical*
BYTLTD butylated *combined*
BYTN biotin *vitamin B*
BYTN butane *chemical*
BYTP biotype *ecology*
BYTPLR beauty parlor *salon* (Br) beauty parlour
BYTPRLR beauty parlor *salon* (Br) beauty parlour
BYTRK butyric *butter*
BYTS beauteous *lovely*
BYTSHN beautician *cosmetologist*

Letters aren't doubled for single sounds: to find alley use **L** not **LL**. Use **Y** and **W** as hard sounds only: to find yellow use **YL**. (Br)=British spelling or usage. * See dictionary.

BYTSHP beauty shop *salon*
BYTSLN beauty salon
personal care shop
BYTTD beatitude *blissful
state*
BYTTYD beatitude *blissful
state*
BYTY buteo *hawk* buteos
BYTYS beauteous *lovely*
BYWLKTRK bioelectric
plants and animals
BYWLKTRKL bioelectrical
plants and animals
BYWLKTRSD bioelectricity
plants and animals
BYWLKTRST bioelectricity
plants and animals
BYWNJNRN bioengineering
biotechnology
BYWNJNRNG
bioengineering
biotechnology
BYWNRJDK bioenergetic
energy exchange
BYWNRJDKS bioenergetics
energy exchange
BYWNRJDX bioenergetics
energy exchange
BYWNRJTK bioenergetic
energy exchange
BYWNRJTKS bioenergetics
energy exchange
BYWNRJTX bioenergetics
energy exchange
BYWTHKS bioethics *medical
research*
BYWTHX bioethics *medical
research*
BYXL biaxial (adj) *double axis*
biaxially (adv)
BYXYL biaxial (adj) *double
axis* biaxially (adv)
BYZ abuse *(v) maltreat,
revile* abused abusing
BYZBL abusable *damage*
BYZR abuser *damager*
BYZV abusive *damaging*
BYZVL abusively *damaging*
BZ abuse *(v) maltreat, revile*
abused abusing
BZ abuzz *busy*
BZ baiza *money* baiza (or)
baizas
BZ baize *fabric*
BZ biz *(slang) business*
BZ Bizet *composer*
BZ Boise *city*
BZ booze *liquor* boozed
boozing
BZ boozy *drunk*
BZ bozo *clown* bozos
BZ busy *(adj) diligent,
occupied* busier busiest
BZ busy *(v) occupy* busied
busying busies
BZ buzz *sound* buzzes
BZB busby *hat* busbies
BZBD busybody *gossip*
busybodies
BZBL abusable *damage*
BZBM buzz bomb *missile*
BZH beige *color*
BZH bijou *jewel* bijous (or)
bijoux
BZH bougie *candle*
BZHDR bijouterie *ornaments*
BZHDR objet d'art *curio*
objets d'art
BZHDRT objet d'art *curio*
objets d'art
BZHL Beaujolais *wine*
Beaujolais
BZHNG Beijing *city*
BZHST beau geste *gesture*
beaux gestes (or) beau
gestes
BZHTR bijouterie *ornaments*
BZHW bourgeois *capitalist*
bourgeoise (fem)
BZHWZ bourgeoisie *middle
class*
BZK bazooka *gun*
BZK bezique *card game*
BZK bouzouki *music*
bouzoukis
BZKT buzz cut *haircut*
BZL basal (adj) *fundamental*
basally (adv)
BZL basil *herb*
BZL bezel *facet*
BZL busily *occupied*
BZLR basilar *basic*
BZLV absolve *remove guilt*
absolved absolving
BZLVR absolver *guilt
remover*
BZM abysm *pit*
BZM besom *broom*
BZM bosom *breast*
BZM bosomy *big-breasted*
BZMD basmati *rice*
BZML abysmal (adj)
unfathomable abysmally
(adv)
BZMRK Bismarck *chancellor*
BZMT basmati *rice*
BZMTH bismuth *element*
BZMTHK bismuthic *element*
BZMYTHK bismuthic
element
BZN bison *animal*
BZN boson *particle*
BZNBR boysenberry *fruit*
boysenberries
BZNS business *(n) trade,
right, affair** businesses
BZNS busyness *occupied*
BZNSLK businesslike
serious
BZNSMN businessman
executive businessmen
BZNSPRSN
businessperson *executive*
BZNSWMN
businesswoman *executive*
businesswomen
BZNT bezant *disk*
BZNTN Byzantine *of
Byzantium*
BZR abuser *damager*
BZR bazaar *market*
BZR beaux arts *art*
BZR bizarre *strange*
BZR boozer *drunk*
BZR busier *occupied*
BZR buzzer *sound*
BZRB absorb *take in*
BZRBBL absorbable *take in*
BZRBBLD absorbability *take
in*
BZRBBLT absorbability *take
in*
BZRBN absorbing
engrossing
BZRBNC absorbency (or)
absorbancy *take in*

absorbencies (or)
absorbancies
BZRBNG absorbing *engrossing*
BZRBNGL absorbingly *engrossingly*
BZRBNL absorbingly *engrossingly*
BZRBNS absorbance *radiation*
BZRBNS absorbency (or) absorbancy *take in* absorbencies (or) absorbancies
BZRBNT absorbent *taking in*
BZRBNTC absorbency (or) absorbancy *take in* absorbencies (or) absorbancies
BZRBNTS absorbance *radiation*
BZRBNTS absorbency (or) absorbancy *take in* absorbencies (or) absorbancies
BZRBR absorber *one that takes in*
BZRBSHN absorption *take in, intercept, engross*
BZRBTNS absorptance *energy ratio*
BZRBTNTS absorptance *energy ratio*
BZRD buzzard *bird*
BZRK berserk *crazy*
BZRKR berserker *warrior*
BZRPSHN absorption *take in, intercept, engross*
BZRPTNS absorptance *energy ratio*
BZRPTNTS absorptance *energy ratio*
BZRPTVT absorptivity *radiation* absorptivities
BZRV observe *watch, remark* observed observing
BZRVBL observable (adj) *seen* observably (adv)
BZRVBLD observability *watch*
BZRVBLT observability

watch
BZRVNS observance *rite, watch*
BZRVNTS observance *rite, watch*
BZRVR observer *watch, remark*
BZRVSHN observation *watch, remark, record*
BZRVTR observatory *view* observatories
BZS buzz saw *tool*
BZSGNL busy signal *telephone*
BZST busiest *occupied*
BZV absolve *remove guilt* absolved absolving
BZV abusive *damaging*
BZVL abusively *damaging*
BZVNT observant *watchful*
BZVNTL observantly *watchful*
BZVR absolver *guilt remover*
BZWKS beeswax *honeycomb*
BZWRD buzzword *trendy word*
BZWRK busywork *occupation*
BZWX beeswax *honeycomb*
BZYR busier *occupied*
BZYST busiest *occupied*

C

C aecia (pl) *fungus* aecium
C Aussie *of Australia*
C cee *letter C*
C icy *frozen* icier iciest
C sea *ocean*
C see *(v) view, understand, escort** saw seen seeing
C see *(n) authority*
CB ceiba *tree*

CB Seabee *Navy*
CBD seabed *ocean*
CBG seabag *luggage*
CBM sebum *fat*
CBRD seabird *bird*
CBRD seaboard *coast*
CBRN seaborne *ocean*
CBRZ sea breeze *wind*
CBS sea bass *fish*
CCD secede *pull out* seceded seceding
CCDR seceder *pull out*
CCH seiche *wave*
CD acedia *apathy*
CD cede *grant, give up* ceded ceding
CD seed *(n) embryo, ranking (v) plant* seed (or) seeds
CD seedy *run-down* seedier seediest
CDBD seedbed *soil*
CDC acey-deucey *card game*
CDF acetify *sour* acetifies acetified acetifying
CDFKSHN acetification *sour*
CDK acetic *acid*
CDK sea duck *bird*
CDKDRS seductress *enticer (f)* seductresses
CDKDV seductive *enticing*
CDKK seedcake *food*
CDKSD acetic acid *vinegar*
CDKSHN seduction *enticement*
CDKTRS seductress *enticer (f)* seductresses
CDKTV seductive *enticing*
CDL acetal *aldehyde*
CDL acetyl *acid*
CDL cedilla *mark*
CDL Seattle *city*
CDL seedily *run-down*
CDLDV acetylative *with acetyl*
CDLKLN acetylcholine *neurotransmitter*
CDLKLNSTRS acetylcholinesterase *enzyme*
CDLKLNSTRZ acetylcholinesterase *enzyme*

Letters aren't doubled for single sounds: to find alley use **L** not **LL**. Use **Y** and **W** as hard sounds only: to find yellow use **YL**. (Br)=British spelling or usage. * See dictionary.

CDLN seedling *plant*

CDLNG seedling *plant*

CDLSHN acetylation *adding acetyl*

CDLT acetylate *chemical* acetylated acetylating

CDLTV acetylative *with acetyl*

CDM sedum *herb*

CDMD acetamide *chemical*

CDMNFN acetaminophen *pain reliever*

CDN sedan *vehicle*

CDNG seating *chairs*

CDNS seediness *run-down*

CDPD seedpod *sac*

CDR cedar *tree*

CDR ceder *yielder*

CDR seater *sitting space*

CDR seder *(often capitalized) feast*

CDR seeder *planter*

CDR seedier *run-down*

CDRBRD cedarbird *waxwing*

CDRWD cedarwood *lumber*

CDS acetous *sour*

CDS acey-deucey *card game*

CDS seduce *entice* seduced seducing

CDSHN sedation *relaxation*

CDSMNT seducement *enticement*

CDSR seducer *enticer*

CDST seediest *run-down*

CDT sedate *quiet* sedated sedating

CDTM seedtime *season*

CDY acedia *apathy*

CDYC acey-deucey *card game*

CDYR seedier *run-down*

CDYS acey-deucey *card game*

CDYS seduce *entice* seduced seducing

CDYSMNT seducement *enticement*

CDYSR seducer *enticer*

CDYST seediest *run-down*

CFD seafood *food*

CFRN seafaring *ocean*

CFRNG seafaring *ocean*

CFRNT seafront *shoreline*

CFRR seafarer *sailor*

CG sego *lily*

CGL sea gull *bird*

CGN seagoing *ocean*

CGNG seagoing *ocean*

CGWN seagoing *ocean*

CGWNG seagoing *ocean*

CH aitch *alphabet letter (H)*

CH chaw *tobacco*

CH chew *eat*

CH cholla *cactus*

CH chow *food, dog*

CH ciao *greeting*

CH each *every*

CH etch *engrave*

CH h *alphabet letter* h's (or) hs

CH itch *irritation, desire* itches

CH itchy *irritated, desirous*

CH ouch *(interj) hurt*

CHB Chevy *Chevrolet* Chevies

CHB chub *fish* chub (or) chubs

CHB chubby *husky* chubbier chubbiest

CHBL chewable *eat*

CHBL chubbily *huskily*

CHBM H-bomb *weapon*

CHBN aitchbone *hipbone*

CHBNS chubbiness *huskiness*

CHBR chubbier *huskier*

CHBST chubbiest *huskiest*

CHBYR chubbier *huskier*

CHBYST chubbiest *huskiest*

CHCH cha-cha *dance*

CHCH chow chow *(often capitalized) dog*

CHCH chowchow *relish*

CHD Chad *country*

CHD chatty *talkative* chattier chattiest

CHD cheetah *animal*

CHD chide *tease* chided chiding

CHDL chattel *slave*

CHDL chattily *talkative*

CHDNG Chattanooga *city*

CHDNS chattiness *talkative*

CHDR chatter *talk*

CHDR chattier *talkative*

CHDR cheater *swindler*

CHDR cheddar *cheese*

CHDR chowder *soup*

CHDRBKS chatterbox prattler chatterboxes

CHDRBX chatterbox *prattler* chatterboxes

CHDRR chatterer *prattler*

CHDST chattiest *talkative*

CHDYR chattier *talkative*

CHDYST chattiest *talkative*

CHF chafe *rub* chafed chafing

CHF chaff *(n) debris (v) banter*

CHF chief *principal*

CHF chuff *boor, sound*

CHF UHF *(abbr) Ultra High Frequency*

CHFD chuffed *proud*

CHFDN chieftain *tribal leader*

CHFJSDS chief justice *judge*

CHFJSTS chief justice *judge*

CHFN chafing *dish, rubbing*

CHFNG chafing *dish, rubbing*

CHFR chafer *beetle*

CHFR chaffer *chatter, bargain*

CHFRR chafferer *haggler*

CHFT chuffed *proud*

CHFTN chieftain *tribal leader*

CHFVSTF chief of staff *advisor*

CHFVSTT chief of state *national head*

CHG chug *engine sound, guzzle* chugged chugging

CHGLG chugalug *guzzle* chugalugged chugalugging

CHGR chigger *insect*

CHGR chugger *move along*

CHK chalk *mineral*

CHK chalky *powdery*

CHK check *(n) mark, stop, investigation* (v) verify, restrain, brake** (Br) cheque

---

Use letters that best describe the sounds you hear and omit the vowels. Use **S** or **K** instead of **C**: to find circle use **SRKL**. Use **J** to find joy, **JM** to find gem and **G** to find go.

CHK cheek *facial feature, boldness*
CHK cheeky *bold* cheekier cheekiest
CHK chick *bird*
CHK chock *block*
CHK choke *strangle* choked choking
CHK chook *(Au) chicken*
CHK chuck *(v) toss (n) pat, beef*
CHK chukka *boot*
CHK Czech *Slavic*
CHKBK checkbook *banking*
CHKBLK chockablock *full*
CHKBN cheekbone *face*
CHKBRD chalkboard *blackboard*
CHKCHR chokecherry *fruit* chokecherries
CHKD chickadee *bird*
CHKF check off *(v) eliminate*
CHKF checkoff *(n) deduction*
CHKFL chock-full (or) chockful *to the limit*
CHKFSG Tchaikovsky *composer*
CHKFSK Tchaikovsky *composer*
CHKHL chuckhole *pothole*
CHKHLK chocoholic *crave chocolate*
CHKL cheekily *boldly*
CHKL chicle *gum*
CHKL chuckhole *pothole*
CHKL chuckle *laugh* chuckled chuckling
CHKLD chocolaty (or) chocolatey *like or with cocoa*
CHKLST checklist *listing*
CHKLT chocolate *food, color*
CHKLT chocolaty (or) chocolatey *like or with cocoa*
CHKLTR chocolatier *candy maker or seller*
CHKMRK check mark *writing*
CHKMT checkmate *stop, frustrate*
CHKN check in (v) *register*

check-in (n)
CHKN Chicano *Mexican* Chicanos
CHKN chicken *(v) coward (n) bird*
CHKN choking *strangling, indistinct*
CHKNFD chicken feed *small sum*
CHKNG choking *strangling, indistinct*
CHKNHK chicken hawk *bird*
CHKNHRDD chickenhearted *timid*
CHKNHRTD chickenhearted *timid*
CHKNLVRD chicken-livered *cowardly*
CHKNPKS chicken pox *disease*
CHKNPX chicken pox *disease*
CHKNS cheekiness *boldness*
CHKNWR chicken wire *fencing*
CHKNWYR chicken wire *fencing*
CHKP chalk up *note*
CHKP checkup *examination*
CHKP chickpea *garbanzo*
CHKPNT checkpoint *inspection*
CHKR chakra *energy*
CHKR checker *(v) vary, mark* (Br) chequer
CHKR checker *(n) game piece, one who checks* (Br) chequer
CHKR cheekier *bolder*
CHKR chicory *herb* chicories
CHKR choker *jewelry*
CHKR chukar *bird*
CHKRBRD checkerboard *game*
CHKRD checkered *varied, squares*
CHKRM checkroom *parcels*
CHKRN checkrein *harness*
CHKRZ checkers *game*
CHKSLVK Czechoslovakia

country
CHKSLVKY Czechoslovakia *country*
CHKST cheekiest *boldest*
CHKT check out *(v) total, vacate*
CHKT checkout *(n) time, test*
CHKT Choctaw *Native American*
CHKTK chalk talk *lecture*
CHKTR acciaccatura *musical note*
CHKV Chekhov *writer*
CHKVSG Tchaikovsky *composer*
CHKVSK Tchaikovsky *composer*
CHKWD chickweed *plant*
CHKWGN chuck wagon *food*
CHKWL chuckwalla (or) chuckawalla *lizard*
CHKWLZWD chuck-will's-widow *bird*
CHKYR cheekier *bolder*
CHKYST cheekiest *boldest*
CHL cello *music* cello
CHL challis *fabric* challises
CHL child *toddler* children
CHL Chile *country*
CHL chili (or) chile (or) chilli *food* chilies (or) chiles (or) chillies
CHL chill *cool*
CHL chilly *cool* chillier chilliest
CHL cholla *cactus*
CHLBD childbed *pregnancy*
CHLBLN chilblain *sore*
CHLBRN childbearing *birth*
CHLBRNG childbearing *birth*
CHLBRTH childbirth *birth process*
CHLD child *toddler* children
CHLDBD childbed *pregnancy*
CHLDBRN childbearing *birth*
CHLDBRNG childbearing *birth*

CHLDBRTH childbirth *birth process*

CHLDHD childhood *early period*

CHLDLK childlike *innocent*

CHLDLS childless *no offspring*

CHLDLSNS childlessness *no offspring*

CHLDRN children *kids*

CHLDSH childish *simple*

CHLDSPL child's play *simple task*

CHLDZPL child's play *simple task*

CHLHD childhood *early period*

CHLK childlike *innocent*

CHLKNKRN chili con carne *food*

CHLM chillum *pipe*

CHLN Cellini *goldsmith*

CHLNJ challenge *question, dare, invite** challenged challenging

CHLNJN challenging *fascinating*

CHLNJNG challenging *fascinating*

CHLNJR challenger *question, dare, invite**

CHLNS chilliness *coolness*

CHLR chiller *refrigerant*

CHLR chillier *cooler*

CHLRND accelerando *tempo* accelerandos

CHLS chalice *cup*

CHLS challis *fabric* challises

CHLS childless *no offspring*

CHLSD celesta (or) celeste *music*

CHLSDN chalcedony *quartz* chalcedonies

CHLSDNK chalcedonic *quartz*

CHLSNS childlessness *no offspring*

CHLSPL child's play *simple task*

CHLSS chili sauce *food*

CHLST celesta (or) celeste *music*

CHLST cellist *music*

CHLST chilliest *coolest*

CHLYR chillier *cooler*

CHLYST chilliest *coolest*

CHLZPL child's play *simple task*

CHM chime *ring* chimed chiming

CHM chum *pal* chummed chumming

CHM chummy *friendly* chummier chummiest

CHM HMO *health insurance*

CHMBL cembalo *music* cembali (or) cembalos

CHMBR chamber *(v) house* chambered chambering

CHMBR chamber *(n) room, compartment*

CHMBRD chambered *compartments*

CHMBRLN chamberlain *attendant*

CHMBRMD chambermaid *maid*

CHMCHNG chimichanga *food*

CHMCHNGG chimichanga *food*

CHML chummily *friendly*

CHMN chimney *fireplace* chimneys

CHMN chow mein *food*

CHMNPT chimney pot *pipe*

CHMNS chumminess *friendliness*

CHMNSWFT chimney swift *bird*

CHMNSWP chimney sweep *cleaner*

CHMP champ *winner*

CHMP chimp *ape*

CHMP chomp *bite*

CHMP chump *fool*

CHMPN champion *(n) hero (v) advocate*

CHMPNSHP championship *contest*

CHMPNYN champignon *mushroom*

CHMPNZ chimpanzee *ape*

CHMPRD champerty *law*

CHMPRT champerty *law*

CHMPYN champion *(n) hero (v) advocate*

CHMPYNSHP championship *contest*

CHMR chimer *ringer*

CHMR chummier *friendlier*

CHMSMN chum salmon *fish*

CHMST chummiest *friendliest*

CHMYR chummier *friendlier*

CHMYST chummiest *friendliest*

CHN chain *linkage*

CHN chin *(v) raise oneself* chinned chinning

CHN chin *(n) jaw*

CHN China *country*

CHN china *tableware*

CHN chine *backbone* chined chining

CHN chino *fabric* chinos

CHN etching *engraving*

CHNBN chinbone *jaw*

CHNBR chinaberry *tree* chinaberries

CHNC chancy *risky* chancier chanciest

CHNCHBG chinch bug *insect*

CHNCHL chinchilla *animal*

CHNCNS chanciness *risk*

CHNCR chancier *riskier*

CHNCST chanciest *riskiest*

CHNCYR chancier *riskier*

CHNCYST chanciest *riskiest*

CHNDLR chandler *candle maker*

CHNDLR chandlery *candle store* chandleries

CHNG Ching (or) Ch'ing *dynasty*

CHNG etching *engraving*

CHNG I Ching *book*

CHNGGM chewing gum *chicle*

CHNGK chink *small bit*

CHNGK chunk *hunk, sound*

CHNGK chunky *stocky, lumpy* chunkier chunkiest

CHNGKL chunkily *stocky, lumps*

Use letters that best describe the sounds you hear and omit the vowels. Use **S** or **K** instead of **C**: to find circle use **SRKL**. Use **J** to find joy, **JM** to find gem and **G** to find go.

CHNGKNS chunkiness *stocky, lumps*
CHNGKPN chinquapin (or) chinkapin *tree*
CHNGKR chunkier *stocky, lumps*
CHNGKSHK Chiang Kai-shek *Chinese president*
CHNGKST chunkiest *stocky, lumps*
CHNGKYR chunkier *stocky, lumps*
CHNGKYST chunkiest *stocky, lumps*
CHNGM chewing gum *chicle*
CHNGNG chain gang *prisoner*
CHNJ change (*v*) *switch, alter* changed changing
CHNJ change (*n*) *alteration, money*
CHNJBL changeable (*adj*) *fickle* changeably (*adv*)
CHNJBLD changeability *fickleness*
CHNJBLT changeability *fickleness*
CHNJLN changeling *child*
CHNJLNG changeling *child*
CHNJLS changeless *constant*
CHNJP change-up *pitch*
CHNJR changer *converter*
CHNJVR changeover *conversion*
CHNK chink *small bit*
CHNK chunk *hunk, sound*
CHNK chunky *stocky, lumpy* chunkier chunkiest
CHNKL chunkily *stocky, lumps*
CHNKLS Auchincloss *writer*
CHNKNS chunkiness *stocky, lumps*
CHNKPN chinquapin (or) chinkapin *tree*
CHNKR chunkier *stocky, lumps*
CHNKSHK Chiang Kai-shek *Chinese president*
CHNKST chunkiest *stocky, lumps*

CHNKYST chunkiest *stocky, lumps*
CHNL channel (*v*) *convey* channeled (or) channelled channeling (or) channelling
CHNL channel (*n*) *strait, conduit, groove*
CHNL Chou En-lai *Chinese leader*
CHNLDR chain letter *mail*
CHNLLNZ Channel Islands *land masses*
CHNLR chandler *candle maker*
CHNLR chandlery *candle store* chandleries
CHNLR channeler *spiritualist*
CHNLS chinless *no jaw*
CHNLTR chain letter *mail*
CHNLZ channelize *convey, straighten* channelized channelizing
CHNLZSHN channelization *convey, straighten*
CHNML chain mail *armor*
CHNMN Chinaman (*vulgar*) *native of China*
CHNP chin-up *raise oneself*
CHNR chanter *singer*
CHNRKSHN chain reaction *series of events*
CHNRKT chain-react *series of events*
CHNRYKSHN chain reaction *series of events*
CHNRYKT chain-react *series of events*
CHNRZ China rose *flower*
CHNS chain saw (*n*) *cutting tool* chainsaw (*v*)
CHNS chance (*v*) *risk* chanced chancing
CHNS chance (*n*) *luck, opportunity, possibility*
CHNS chancy *risky* chancier chanciest
CHNS itchiness *irritation, desire*
CHNSL chancel *church*
CHNSLR chancellery (or)

chancellory *position* chancelleries (or) chancellories
CHNSLR chancellor *person*
CHNSMK chain-smoke *continuous*
CHNSMKR chain-smoker *continuous smoker*
CHNSNS chanciness *risk*
CHNSR chancery *law* chanceries
CHNSR chancier *riskier*
CHNSST chanciest *riskiest*
CHNSTCH chain stitch *sewing*
CHNSTR chain store *retail*
CHNSYR chancier *riskier*
CHNSYST chanciest *riskiest*
CHNT chant *sing*
CHNT chantey (or) chanty *song* chanteys (or) chanties
CHNTCNS chanciness *risk*
CHNTCR chancier *riskier*
CHNTCST chanciest *riskiest*
CHNTCYR chancier *riskier*
CHNTCYST chanciest *riskiest*
CHNTKLR chanticleer *rooster*
CHNTN Chinatown *city area*
CHNTR chanter *singer*
CHNTR chantry *endowment* chantries
CHNTS chance (*v*) *risk* chanced chancing
CHNTS chance (*n*) *luck, opportunity, possibility*
CHNTS chintz *fabric*
CHNTS chintzy *cheap* chintzier chintziest
CHNTSL chancel *church*
CHNTSLR chancellery (or) chancellory *position* chancelleries (or) chancellories
CHNTSLR chancellor *person*
CHNTSNS chanciness *risk*
CHNTSR chancery *law* chanceries
CHNTSR chancier *riskier*
CHNTSR chintzier *cheaper*

Letters aren't doubled for single sounds: to find alley use **L** not **LL**. Use **Y** and **W** as hard sounds only: to find yellow use **YL**. (Br)=British spelling or usage. * See dictionary.

CHNTSST chanciest *riskiest*
CHNTSST chintziest *cheapest*
CHNTSYR chancier *riskier*
CHNTSYR chintzier *cheaper*
CHNTSYST chanciest *riskiest*
CHNTSYST chintziest *cheapest*
CHNTZ chintz *fabric*
CHNTZ chintzy *cheap* chintzier chintziest
CHNTZR chintzier *cheaper*
CHNTZST chintziest *cheapest*
CHNTZYR chintzier *cheaper*
CHNTZYST chintziest *cheapest*
CHNWR chinaware *dinnerware*
CHNZ Chinese *of China*
CHP chap *(v) dry out* chapped chapping
CHP chap *(n) fellow*
CHP cheap *not costly* cheaper cheapest
CHP cheep *peep*
CHP chip *(v) break, hit a ball* chipped chipping
CHP chip *(n) piece, money*
CHP chop *(v) cut* chopped chopping
CHP chop *(n) blow, meat, wave*
CHP choppy *rough* choppier choppiest
CHPBRD chipboard *paperboard*
CHPCHP chop-chop *quickly*
CHPD chapped *rough and dry*
CHPDR chapter *division*
CHPHS chophouse *restaurant*
CHPK Capek *writer*
CHPL chapel *church*
CHPL cheaply *not costly*
CHPL choppily *roughly*
CHPLJK choplogic *argument*
CHPLN chaplain *clergyman*
CHPLNC chaplaincy *clergy*

CHPLNS chaplaincy *clergy*
CHPMNGK chipmunk *animal*
CHPMNK chipmunk *animal*
CHPN cheapen *devalue*
CHPN chip in *contribute*
CHPN cioppino *food*
CHPNS cheapness *stingy*
CHPNS choppiness *roughness*
CHPR cheaper *less costly*
CHPR chipper *well*
CHPR chopper *cutter, helicopter*
CHPR choppier *rougher*
CHPS chaps *leggings, fellows*
CHPS Cheops (or) Khufu *pyramid builder*
CHPS chop suey *food*
CHPS chophouse *restaurant*
CHPS chops *chin*
CHPSKT cheapskate *miser*
CHPST cheapest *least costly*
CHPST choppiest *roughest*
CHPSTK chopstick *utensil*
CHPSW chop suey *food*
CHPT chapped *rough and dry*
CHPTR chapter *division*
CHPYR choppier *rougher*
CHPYST choppiest *roughest*
CHQD chickweed *plant*
CHQGN chuck wagon *food*
CHQL chuckwalla (or) chuckawalla *lizard*
CHQLZWD chuck-will's-widow *bird*
CHR chair *(n) seat (v) preside*
CHR char *burn* charred charring
CHR chary *cautious* charier chariest
CHR cheer *(n) gaity (v) shout*
CHR cheerio *(Br) greeting*
CHR cheery *gay* cheerier cheeriest
CHR cherry *fruit* cherries
CHR chewer *eater*
CHR chirr *sound*
CHR chore *job*
CHR etcher *engraver*

CHRB cherub *angel* cherubim
CHRBK cherubic *angelic*
CHRBKL cherubically *angelic*
CHRBM cherubim (pl) *angel* cherub
CHRCH church *religion* churches
CHRCHGN churchgoing *religion*
CHRCHGNG churchgoing *religion*
CHRCHGR churchgoer *religion*
CHRCHGWN churchgoing *religion*
CHRCHGWNG churchgoing *religion*
CHRCHGWR churchgoer *religion*
CHRCHMN churchman *clergy* churchmen
CHRCHWRDN churchwarden *officer, pipe*
CHRCHYRD churchyard *cemetery*
CHRD chard *beet*
CHRD charity *mercy* charities
CHRDBL charitable (adj) *generous* charitably (adv)
CHRDL chortle *chuckle* chortled chortling
CHRDLR chortler *chuckle*
CHRDR charter *contract*
CHRDSH czardas *dance* czardas
CHRDST chartist *analyst, map maker*
CHRFL cheerful (adj) *happy* cheerfully (adv)
CHRJ charge *(n) thrill, obligation, supervision**
CHRJ charge *(v) restore energy, attack, pay** charged charging
CHRJBL chargeable *credit, restorable*
CHRJD charged *emotional, energized*
CHRJDFR chargé d'affaires

Use letters that best describe the sounds you hear and omit the vowels. Use **S** or **K** instead of **C**: to find circle use **SRKL**. Use **J** to find joy, **JM** to find gem and **G** to find go.

diplomat chargés d'affaires

CHRJKNT charge account *credit card*

CHRJKT charge account *credit card*

CHRJR charger *dish, battery, horse*

CHRK Cherokee *Native American* Cherokee (or) Cherokees

CHRKL charcoal *burnt wood, gray*

CHRL charily *cautious*

CHRL churl *peasant*

CHRLDR cheerleader *enthusiast*

CHRLF chairlift *conveyer*

CHRLFT chairlift *conveyer*

CHRLHRS charley horse *muscle pain*

CHRLS cheerless *bleak*

CHRLSH churlish *vulgar acting*

CHRLSHL churlishly *vulgar manner*

CHRLSHNS churlishness *vulgarity*

CHRLSNS cheerlessness *bleakness*

CHRLSTN Charleston *city, dance*

CHRM charm (v) *fascinate, compel* (n) *amulet, attraction*

CHRM cherimoya *fruit*

CHRMBL tremble *shake* trembled trembling

CHRMD charmed *quantum theory**

CHRMN chairman *leader* chairmen

CHRMN charming *pleasing*

CHRMNDS tremendous *huge*

CHRMNDSL tremendously *huge*

CHRMNDSNS tremendousness *huge*

CHRMNG charming *pleasing*

CHRMNSHP chairmanship *leadership*

CHRMR charmer *fascinator*

CHRMR tremor *shake*

CHRMY cherimoya *fruit*

CHRN churn (v) *agitate* (n) *vessel*

CHRNCH trench (n) *ditch* (v) *carve* trenches

CHRNL charnel *bone site*

CHRNS cheeriness, *happiness*

CHRP chirp *sound*

CHRP chirpy *happy*

CHRPRSN chairperson *leader*

CHRR charier *cautious*

CHRR cheerier *happy*

CHRS sea horse *animal*

CHRSH cherish *appreciate*

CHRSHDFR chargé d'affaires *diplomat* chargés d'affaires

CHRST chariest *cautious*

CHRST cheeriest *happy*

CHRSTN cherrystone *clam*

CHRT chariot *vehicle*

CHRT charity *mercy* charities

CHRT chart *graph*

CHRT eye chart *test*

CHRTBL charitable (adj) *generous* charitably (adv)

CHRTL chortle *chuckle* chortled chortling

CHRTLR chortler *chuckle*

CHRTR charioteer *driver*

CHRTR charter *contract*

CHRTST chartist *analyst, map maker*

CHRVL chervil *herb*

CHRWMN chairwoman *leader* chairwomen

CHRWMN charwoman *cleaning woman* charwomen

CHRY cheerio (Br) *greeting*

CHRYR charier *cautious*

CHRYR cheerier *happy*

CHRYST chariest *cautious*

CHRYST cheeriest *happy*

CHRYT chariot *vehicle*

CHRYTR charioteer *driver*

CHRZ cheers *a toast*

CHRZ chorizo *food* chorizos

CHRZHDFR chargé d'affaires *diplomat* chargés d'affaires

CHS chase (v) *follow* chased chasing

CHS chase (n) *groove, frame*

CHS chassé *dance* chasséd chasséing

CHS chassis *frame* chassis

CHS chess *game*

CHS chest *box, bosom*

CHS choice *option*

CHSBL chasuble *garment*

CHSBRD chessboard *game*

CHSD chesty *proud, bosom* chestier chestiest

CHSDD chastity *purity, no sex*

CHSDDRRZ chest of drawers *dresser*

CHSDDRWRZ chest of drawers *dresser*

CHSDR chestier *prouder, bosom*

CHSDRDRRZ chest of drawers *dresser*

CHSDRDRWRZ chest of drawers *dresser*

CHSDST chestiest *proudest, bosom*

CHSDT chastity *purity, no sex*

CHSDYR chestier *prouder, bosom*

CHSDYST chestiest *proudest, bosom*

CHSHBL chasuble *garment*

CHSHRKT Cheshire cat *grin*

CHSL chastely *purely*

CHSMN chessman *game piece* chessmen

CHSN chasten *punish* chastened chastening

CHSNR chastener *punisher*

CHSNS chasteness *modesty*

CHSNT chestnut *color, nut*

CHSPK Chesapeake *city, bay*

CHSR chaser *drink, tool, worker*

Letters aren't doubled for single sounds: to find alley use **L** not **LL**. Use **Y** and **W** as hard sounds only: to find yellow use **YL**. (Br)=British spelling or usage. * See dictionary.

CHSS chassis *frame* chassis
CHSSK Ceausescu *Romanian president*
CHSSKY Ceausescu *Romanian president*
CHSSQ Ceausescu *Romanian president*
CHST chaste *pure* chaster chastest
CHST chest *box, bosom*
CHST chesty *proud, bosom* chestier chestiest
CHSTD chastity *purity, no sex*
CHSTL chastely *purely*
CHSTNS chasteness *modesty*
CHSTNT chestnut *color, nut*
CHSTR chaster *purer*
CHSTR chestier *prouder, bosom*
CHSTRDRWRZ chest of drawers *dresser*
CHSTRDRZ chest of drawers *dresser*
CHSTST chastest *purest*
CHSTST chestiest *proudest, bosom*
CHSTT chastity *purity, no sex*
CHSTVDRRZ chest of drawers *dresser*
CHSTVDRWZ chest of drawers *dresser*
CHSTYR chestier *prouder, bosom*
CHSTYST chestiest *proudest bosom*
CHSTZ chastise *punish* chastised chastising
CHSTZMNT chastisement *punishment*
CHSTZR chastiser *punisher*
CHSZ chassis *frame* chassis
CHT chat *(v) talk* chatted chatting
CHT chat *(n) talk, bird*
CHT chatty *talkative* chattier chattiest
CHT chayote *fruit*
CHT cheat *swindle*
CHT cheetah *animal*

CHT chit *voucher, child*
CHTCHT chitchat *talk*
CHTHR each other *mutual*
CHTL chattel *slave*
CHTL chattily *talkative*
CHTLNS chitterlings (or) chitlins *food*
CHTLNZ chitterlings (or) chitlins *food*
CHTN chutney *relish*
CHTNG Chattanooga *city*
CHTNS chattiness *talkative*
CHTR chatter *talk*
CHTR chattier *talkative*
CHTR cheater *swindler*
CHTR cheddar *cheese*
CHTRBKS chatterbox *prattler* chatterboxes
CHTRBX chatterbox *prattler* chatterboxes
CHTRR chatterer *prattler*
CHTST chattiest *talkative*
CHTYR chattier *talkative*
CHTYST chattiest *talkative*
CHV achieve *accomplish* achieved achieving
CHV Chevy *Chevrolet* Chevies
CHV chive *onion*
CHV chivy (or) chivvy *annoy* chivied (or) chivvied chivying (or) chivvying chivies (or) chivvies
CHV HIV *virus*
CHVBL achievable *accomplishable*
CHVMNT achievement *accomplishment*
CHVR achiever *accomplisher*
CHVR echeveria *plant*
CHVRY echeveria *plant*
CHW chewy *pliable*
CHWBL chewable *eat*
CHWNGGM chewing gum *chicle*
CHWNGM chewing gum *chicle*
CHWNL Chou En-lai *Chinese leader*
CHWR chewer *eater*
CHWW Chihuahua *city*
CHY cholla *cactus*

CHYPS Cheops (or) Khufu *pyramid builder*
CHYT chayote *fruit*
CHZ chaise *carriage, chair*
CHZ cheese *food*
CHZ cheesy *like cheese, cheap* cheesier cheesiest
CHZ choose *select* chose choosing chosen
CHZ choosy (or) choosey *fussy* choosier choosiest
CHZ chose *(v-past) choose*
CHZBL chasuble *garment*
CHZBRGR cheeseburger *food*
CHZHBL chasuble *garment*
CHZKK cheesecake *dessert*
CHZKLTH cheesecloth *fabric*
CHZL chisel *(v) cut, cheat* chiseled (or) chiselled chiseling (or) chiselling
CHZL chisel *(n) tool*
CHZLD chiseled (or) chiselled *well-formed*
CHZLNG chaise longue *chair* chaise longues
CHZLNJ chaise longue *chair* chaise longues
CHZLR chiseler (or) chiseller *cheater*
CHZM chasm *gap*
CHZN chosen *picked*
CHZNS cheesiness *food, cheapness*
CHZR cheesier *food, cheaper*
CHZR chooser *selector*
CHZR choosier *fussy*
CHZST cheesiest *food, cheapest*
CHZST choosiest *fussy*
CHZYR cheesier *food, cheaper*
CHZYR choosier *fussy*
CHZYST cheesiest *food, cheapest*
CHZYST choosiest *fussy*
CJ siege *capture*
CK acequia *canal*
CK ceca (pl) *pouch* cecum
CK seek *look for* sought seeking

Use letters that best describe the sounds you hear and omit the vowels. Use **S** or **K** instead of **C**: to find circle use **SRKL**. Use **J** to find joy, **JM** to find gem and **G** to find go.

CK Seiko (trademark) watch
CK sequoia tree
CK Sequoya (or) Sequoyah (or) Sequoia Cherokee scholar
CK Sikh Indian
CKL cecal (adj) pouch cecally (adv)
CKLD seclude isolate secluded secluding
CKLDD secluded private
CKLMP C-clamp tool
CKLSHN seclusion privacy
CKLSV seclusive private
CKLSVL seclusively private
CKLSVNS seclusiveness private
CKLZHN seclusion privacy
CKLZV seclusive private
CKLZVL seclusively private
CKLZVNS seclusiveness private
CKM cecum pouch ceca
CKNT secant line
CKR secure (v) make safe, effect, ensure* secured securing
CKR secure (adj) safe, dependable securer securest
CKR seeker searcher
CKRC secrecy hiding secrecies
CKRD secured safe, locked
CKRD security safety securities
CKRDR secretor blood
CKRDV secretive silent
CKRDVL secretively silent
CKRDVNS secretiveness silence
CKRMNT securement safe, locked
CKRR securer safe, locked
CKRS secrecy hiding secrecies
CKRSHN secretion concealment, elimination
CKRST securest safe, locked
CKRT secret hidden
CKRT secrete hide, form and give off secreted

secreting
CKRT security safety securities
CKRTBLT secret ballot vote
CKRTN secretin hormone
CKRTR secretor blood
CKRTR secretory form and give off
CKRTSRVS secret service (often capitalized) Presidential guard
CKRTV secretive silent
CKRTVL secretively silent
CKRTVNS secretiveness silence
CKST seacoast shoreline
CKW acequia canal
CKW sequoia tree
CKW Sequoya (or) Sequoyah (or) Sequoia Cherokee scholar
CKWL sequel subsequent
CKWN sequin ornament
CKWNCHL sequential (adj) in order sequentially (adv)
CKWND sequined (or) sequinned ornaments
CKWNS sequence order sequenced sequencing
CKWNSHL sequential (adj) in order sequentially (adv)
CKWNTS sequence order sequenced sequencing
CKWSDR sequester separate
CKWSHS sequacious servile
CKWSTR sequester separate
CKWSTRM sequestrum bone sequestrums
CKWSTRSHN sequestration custody
CKWY acequia canal
CKWY sequoia tree
CKWY Sequoya (or) Sequoyah (or) Sequoia Cherokee scholar
CKY acequia canal
CKYR secure (v) make safe, effect, ensure* secured securing
CKYR secure (adj) safe, dependable securer

securest
CKYRD secured safe, locked
CKYRD security safety securities
CKYRMNT securement safe, locked
CKYRR securer safe, locked
CKYRST securest safe, locked
CKYRT security safety securities
CL seal (n) animal, emblem, closure (v) secure
CLGS sea legs walking
CLGZ sea legs walking
CLK celiac cavity
CLK select choose, excellent
CLKD selectee chosen one
CLKDBL selectable chosen, excellent
CLKDR selector chooser
CLKDV selective specific
CLKDVL selectively specific
CLKDVNS selectiveness specific
CLKMN selectman administrator
CLKSHN selection choice
CLKT select choose, excellent
CLKT selectee chosen one
CLKTBL selectable chosen, excellent
CLKTMN selectman administrator
CLKTR selector chooser
CLKTV selective specific
CLKTVD selectivity specific
CLKTVL selectively specific
CLKTVNS selectiveness specific
CLKTVT selectivity specific
CLM coelom space coeloms (or) coelomata
CLMD coelomata (pl) space coelom
CLMK coelomic with space
CLMT acoelomate one cavity
CLMT coelomata (pl) space coelom
CLMT coelomate with space
CLN ceiling cover

Letters aren't doubled for single sounds: to find alley use **L** not **LL**. Use **Y** and **W** as hard sounds only: to find yellow use **YL**. (Br)=British spelling or usage. * See dictionary.

CLN sea lion *animal*
CLN sea-lane *route*
CLNG ceiling *cover*
CLNT sealant *glue*
CLR sealer *glue*
CLSKN sealskin *fur*
CLVL sea level *altitude*
CLYK celiac *cavity*
CLYN sea lion *animal*
CM aecium *fungus* aecia
CM seam *sew*
CM seamy *wicked* seamier seamiest
CM seem *appear*
CM seme *sign*
CMDK semiotic *symbols*
CMDK Semitic *Jew*
CMDSST semioticist *symbols*
CML seemly *attractive, fit* seemlier seemliest
CMLG semiology *signs*
CMLJ semiology *signs*
CMLJKL semiological (adj) *signs* semiologically (adv)
CMLJST semiologist *signs*
CMLNS seemliness *attractive, fit*
CMLR seemlier *attractive, fit*
CMLS seamless *smooth*
CMLSL seamlessly *smooth*
CMLSNS seamlessness *smooth*
CMLST seemliest *attractive, fit*
CMLYR seemlier *attractive, fit*
CMLYST seemliest *attractive, fit*
CMM sememe *sign*
CMMK sememic *sign*
CMN seaman *sailor* seamen
CMN seeming *evident*
CMN semen *sperm*
CMNG seeming *evident*
CMNK semantic *language*
CMNKL semantically *language*
CMNKS semantics *language*
CMNS seaminess *wickedness*
CMNSHP seamanship

sailing
CMNSST semanticist *language*
CMNT cement (n) *concrete* (v) *unite*
CMNTK semantic *language*
CMNTKL semantically *language*
CMNTKS semantics *language*
CMNTR cementer *concrete, unify*
CMNTSHN cementation *concrete, unity*
CMNTSHS cementitious *concrete*
CMNTSST semanticist *language*
CMNTX semantics *language*
CMNX semantics *language*
CMNZ siemens *electricity* siemens
CMR seamier *wicked*
CMSS semiosis *signing process*
CMST seamiest *wicked*
CMSTRS seamstress *sewing* seamstresses
CMT Semite *Jew*
CMTK semiotic *symbols*
CMTK Semitic *Jew*
CMTSHN semiotician *symbols*
CMTSM Semitism *Jews*
CMTSST semioticist *symbols*
CMTST Semitist *Jews*
CMTZM Semitism *Jews*
CMYDK semiotic *symbols*
CMYDSST semioticist *symbols*
CMYLG semiology *signs*
CMYLJ semiology *signs*
CMYLJKL semiological (adj) *signs* semiologically (adv)
CMYLJST semiologist *signs*
CMYR seamier *wicked*
CMYSS semiosis *signing process*
CMYST seamiest *wicked*
CMYTK semiotic *symbols*

CMYTSHN semiotician *symbols*
CMYTSST semioticist *symbols*
CN acini (pl) *sac* acinus
CN cine *movie*
CN Essene *monk*
CN oscine *bird*
CN ossein *collagen*
CN scene *view, stage*
CN seeing *inasmuch as*
CN seen (v-past) *see*
CN seine *net* seined seining
CN Seine *river*
CN sienna *pigment*
CNBDK cenobitic *monastic*
CNBT cenobite *monk*
CNBTK cenobitic *monastic*
CNG seeing *inasmuch as*
CNGRF scenography *theater*
CNGRFK scenographic *theater*
CNGRFR scenographer *theater*
CNK scenic *pretty view*
CNKDTD senectitude *senior*
CNKL scenically *pretty view*
CNKTTD senectitude *senior*
CNL senile *confused*
CNLD senility *confusion*
CNLT senility *confusion*
CNR scenario *plot* scenarios
CNR scenery *view* sceneries
CNR seigneur *lord*
CNR seigneury *estate* seigneuries
CNR seigniory (or) seignory *territory* seigniories (or) seignories
CNR seiner *boat, person*
CNR senary *six*
CNR senior *superior, eldest*
CNR senor (or) senor *Spanish man* senors (or) senores
CNR senora (or) senora *Spanish woman* senoras
CNR signor *Italian man* signors (or) signori
CNR signora *Italian woman* signoras (or) signore
CNRD seniority *position,*

Use letters that best describe the sounds you hear and omit the vowels. Use **S** or **K** instead of **C**: to find circle use **SRKL**. Use **J** to find joy, **JM** to find gem and **G** to find go.

superior

CNRD senorita (or) senorita *Spanish girl* senoritas

CNRJ seigniorage (or) seignorage *revenue*

CNRN signorina *Italian girl* signorinas (or) signorine

CNRST scenarist *writer*

CNRT seniority *position, superior*

CNRT senorita (or) senorita *Spanish girl* senoritas

CNRY scenario *plot* scenarios

CNS acinous *(adj) with sacs*

CNS acinus *(n) sac* acini

CNS iciness *frigid*

CNSDK coenocytic *protoplasm*

CNSNS senescence *growth*

CNSNT senescent *growth*

CNSNTS senescence *growth*

CNSPSHZ cenospecies *related*

CNST coenocyte *protoplasm*

CNSTK coenocytic *protoplasm*

CNYR seigneur *lord*

CNYR seigneury *estate* seigneuries

CNYR seigniory (or) seignory *territory* seigniories (or) seignories

CNYR senior *superior, eldest*

CNYR senor (or) senor *Spanish man* senors (or) senores

CNYR senora (or) senora *Spanish woman* senoras

CNYR signor *Italian man* signors (or) signori

CNYR signora *Italian woman* signoras (or) signore

CNYRD seniority *position, superior*

CNYRD senorita (or) senorita *Spanish girl* senoritas

CNYRJ seigniorage (or) seignorage *revenue*

CNYRN signorina *Italian girl*

signorinas (or) signorine

CNYRT seniority *position, superior*

CNYRT senorita (or) senorita *Spanish girl* senoritas

CNZK Cenozoic *geologic era*

CNZWK Cenozoic *geologic era*

CP seep *ooze*

CP sepia *brown*

CP sepoy *Indian soldier*

CPJ seepage *ooze*

CPL sepal *flower*

CPLD sepaloid *leaf*

CPLN seaplane *airplane*

CPR sea power *navy*

CPRT seaport *ships*

CPWR sea power *navy*

CPY sepia *brown*

CQ acequia *canal*

CQL sequel *subsequent*

CQN sequin *ornament*

CQNCHL sequential (adj) *in order* sequentially (adv)

CQND sequined (or) sequinned *ornaments*

CQNS sequence *order* sequenced sequencing

CQNSHL sequential (adj) *in order* sequentially (adv)

CQNTS sequence *order* sequenced sequencing

CQSDR sequester *separate*

CQSTR sequester *separate*

CQSTRM sequestrum *bone* sequestrums

CQSTRSHN sequestration *custody*

CQY acequia *canal*

CR cere *wrap* cered cering

CR cere *(n) nodule*

CR ciré (or) cire *fabric*

CR cirri (pl) *arm, cloud* cirrus

CR icier *frozen*

CR sear *burn*

CR seer *prophet* seers (or) seer

CR sera (pl) *drug* serum

CR sere *(adj) dry (n) ecology*

CR sierra *mountains, fish*

CRCHN sea urchin *sea*

animal

CRFSHS scire facias *law*

CRGRF serigraph *silk-screen*

CRGRF serigraphy *silk-screen*

CRGRFR serigrapher *silk-screen*

CRK serac *ice*

CRKLCHR sericulture *silk*

CRKLCHRL sericultural *silk*

CRKLCHRST sericulturist *silk*

CRKLTR sericulture *silk*

CRKLTRL sericultural *silk*

CRKLTRST sericulturist *silk*

CRKMK seriocomic *serious and comic*

CRL cereal *grain*

CRL seral *ecology*

CRL serial *series*

CRLG serology *serum*

CRLJ serology *serum*

CRLJK serologic (or) serological (adj) *serum* serologically (adv)

CRLJKL serological (or) serologic (adj) *serum* serologically (adv)

CRLJST serologist *serum*

CRLN Sierra Leone *country*

CRLST serialist *writer*

CRLYN Sierra Leone *country*

CRLZ serialize *arrange* serialized serializing (Br) serialise

CRLZM serialism *music*

CRM serum *drug* serums (or) sera

CRN sierran *(often capitalized) mountains*

CRS cirrus *arm, cloud* cirri

CRS scirrhous *tumor*

CRS serious *solemn, earnest*

CRS serosa *membrane*

CRS serous *watery*

CRSKR seersucker *fabric*

CRSL seriously *earnest, severe*

CRSMNDD serious-minded *solemn, earnest*

CRSN sericin *protein*

Letters aren't doubled for single sounds: to find alley use **L** not **LL**. Use **Y** and **W** as hard sounds only: to find yellow use **YL**. (Br)=British spelling or usage. * See dictionary.

CRSNS seriousness *solemn, earnest*

CRSS cirrhosis *liver disease* cirrhoses

CRT seriate *arrange* seriated seriating (Br) serialise

CRTP serotype *antigens*

CRYKMK seriocomic *serious and comic*

CRYL cereal *grain*

CRYL serial *series*

CRYLST serialist *writer*

CRYLZ serialize *arrange* serialized serializing (Br) serialise

CRYLZM serialism *music*

CRYS serious *solemn, earnest*

CRYSL seriously *earnest, severe*

CRYSMNDD serious-minded *solemn, earnest*

CRYSNS seriousness *solemn, earnest*

CRYT seriate *arrange* seriated seriating (Br) serialise

CRZ series *set, group* series

CRZ serosa *membrane*

CRZL serosal *membrane*

CS cease *stop* ceased ceasing

CS osseous *bony*

CS seesaw *(v) move up and down (n) plank*

CSD seaside *coastal area*

CSD siesta *nap*

CSFR cease-fire *no shooting*

CSFYR cease-fire *no shooting*

CSH seiche *wave*

CSHL seashell *mollusk*

CSHLZ Seychelles *islands*

CSHR seashore *beach*

CSHR seizure *grasp, spasm*

CSK seasick *nausea*

CSKNS seasickness *nausea*

CSKP seascape *view*

CSKT Sea Scout *youth*

CSKWRT sea squirt *sea animal*

CSLG sea slug *sea animal*

CSLS ceaseless *constant*

CSLSL ceaselessly *constantly*

CSLSNS ceaselessness *without pause*

CSNDSST cease and desist *stop*

CSNK sea snake *serpent*

CSPR aeciospore *fungus*

CSQRT sea squirt *sea animal*

CSRN Caesarean *birth*

CSRNSKSHN Caesarean section *birth*

CSRPNT sea serpent *creature*

CSRYN Caesarean *birth*

CSRYNSKSHN Caesarean section *birth*

CST iciest *frozen*

CST siesta *nap*

CSTR sea star *starfish*

CSTRN seastrand *seashore*

CSTRND seastrand *seashore*

CT seat *chair*

CT seta *bristle* setae

CTBLT seat belt *restraint*

CTF acetify *sour* acetifies acetified acetifying

CTFKSHN acetification *sour*

CTH seethe *churn* seethed seething

CTHN seething *hot, churning*

CTHNG seething *hot, churning*

CTHR see-through *transparent*

CTK acetic *acid*

CTKSD acetic acid *vinegar*

CTL acetal *aldehyde*

CTL acetyl *acid*

CTL Seattle *city*

CTLDHD acetaldehyde *chemical*

CTLDV acetylative *with acetyl*

CTLG cetology *whale study*

CTLJ cetology *whale study*

CTLJST cetologist *whale study*

CTLKLN acetylcholine • *neurotransmitter*

CTLKLNSTRS acetylcholinesterase *enzyme*

CTLKLNSTRZ acetylcholinesterase *enzyme*

CTLSHN acetylation *adding acetyl*

CTLSLSLKSD acetylsalicylic acid *acid salt*

CTLSLSLT acetylsalicylate *acid salt*

CTLT acetylate *chemical* acetylated acetylating

CTLTV acetylative *with acetyl*

CTM seedtime *season*

CTMD acetamide *chemical*

CTMNFN acetaminophen *pain reliever*

CTN seating *chairs*

CTNG seating *chairs*

CTR seater *sitting space*

CTS acetous *sour*

CTS setose *bristly*

CTSHN cetacean *animal*

CTSHS cetaceous *marine animal*

CTSHS setaceous *bristly*

CVBN sieva bean *vegetable*

CVJPN Sea of Japan *body of water*

CW seaway *route*

CWD seaweed *plant*

CWDR seawater *ocean*

CWL seawall *levee*

CWRD seaward *toward the sea*

CWRTH seaworthy *afloat*

CWRTHNS seaworthiness *afloat*

CWTR seawater *ocean*

CY aecia (pl) *fungus* aecium

CYDL Seattle *city*

CYM aecium *fungus* aecia

CYN ossein *collagen*

CYN seeing *inasmuch as*

CYN sienna *pigment*

CYNG seeing *inasmuch as*

CYR icier *frozen*

CYR seer *prophet* seers (or)

Use letters that best describe the sounds you hear and omit the vowels. Use **S** or **K** instead of **C**: to find circle use **SRKL**. Use **J** to find joy, **JM** to find gem and **G** to find go.

seer
CYR sierra *mountains, fish*
CYRCHN sea urchin *sea animal*
CYRLN Sierra Leone *country*
CYRLYN Sierra Leone *country*
CYRN sierran *(often capitalized) mountains*
CYS osseous *bony*
CYSD siesta *nap*
CYSPR aeciospore *fungus*
CYST iciest *frozen*
CYST siesta *nap*
CYTL Seattle *city*
CZ cease *stop* ceased ceasing
CZ oases (pl) *water* oasis
CZ seize *grasp* seized seizing
CZFR cease-fire *no shooting*
CZFYR cease-fire *no shooting*
CZHR seizure *grasp, spasm*
CZLS ceaseless *constant*
CZLSL ceaselessly *constantly*
CZLSNS ceaselessness *without pause*
CZM cesium *element* (Br) caesium
CZN season *(v)* spice *(n) time of year*
CZN seizing *rope*
CZNBL seasonable (adj) *well-timed* seasonably (adv)
CZNBLNS seasonableness *good timing*
CZNDSST cease and desist *stop*
CZNG seizing *rope*
CZNL seasonal (adj) *time of year* seasonally (adv)
CZNLD seasonality *time of year*
CZNLS seasonless *any time*
CZNLT seasonality *time of year*
CZNN seasoning *spices*
CZNNG seasoning *spices*

CZNR seasoner *spices*
CZR Caesar *Roman ruler*
CZRN Caesarean *birth*
CZRNSKSHN Caesarean section *birth*
CZRYN Caesarean *birth*
CZRYNSKSHN Caesarean section *birth*
CZYM cesium *element* (Br) caesium

D

D A.D. *(abbr) Anno Domini*
D à deux *two people*
D ad *advertisement*
D add *sum*
D adieu *goodbye* adieus (or) adieux
D ado *commotion*
D aid *assist*
D aide *assistant*
D audio *sound*
D auto *car* autos
D awed *amazed*
D daw *bird*
D day *time*
D dew *moisture*
D dey *ruler*
D dhow *boat*
D die *death* died dying
D do *(v) accomplish* did doing done does
D do *(n) musical tone, hairstyle, action* dos (or) do's
D doe *female deer* does (or) doe
D dough *paste, money*
D doughlike *pasty*
D doughy *pasty, plump* doughier doughiest
D doux *sweet*
D Dow *stock market*

D due *(adj) owed, appropriate, scheduled (n) debt (adv) directly*
D duo *twosome* duos
D dye *color* dyed dyeing
D eddy *whirlpool* eddied eddying eddies
D eighty *number (80)* eighties
D eta *Greek letter*
D eye-to-eye *agreement*
D eyed *watched*
D I.D. (or) ID *(abbr) identification*
D I'd *(contr) I had (or) I would (or) I should*
D id *psychology*
D idea *thought*
D iota *tiny bit*
D odd *not even, unusual*
D ode *poem*
D odea (pl) *theater* odeum
D oidia (pl) *fungus* oidium
D out of *depleted, beyond*
D outdo *(v) best* outdid outdone outdoing outdoes
D Tao *philosophy*
D you'd *(contr) you would, you had*
DB adobe *brick*
DB adobo *food* adobos
DB attaboy *(interj) approval*
DB dab *spot* dabbed dabbing
DB daub *smear*
DB deb *debutante*
DB debut *introduce*
DB dobby *weave* dobbies
DB dub *voice over* dubbed dubbing
DBC Debussy *composer*
DBCH debauch *corrupt*
DBCH debauchee *corrupt one*
DBCH debouch *appear*
DBCHMNT debouchment *appearance*
DBCHR debaucher *corrupter*
DBCHR debauchery *corruption* debaucheries

Letters aren't doubled for single sounds: to find alley use **L** not **LL**. Use **Y** and **W** as hard sounds only: to find yellow use **YL**. (Br)=British spelling or usage. * See dictionary.

DBD daybed *couch*
DBD dubiety *doubt* dubieties
DBD out-of-body *spiritual*
DBDBL debatable *discuss*
DBDBL dubitable *questionable*
DBDK diabetic *disease*
DBDR debater *discuss*
DBDS diabetes *disease*
DBDZ diabetes *disease*
DBF oeil-de-boeuf *eye* oeils-de-boeuf
DBG debug *remove insects or errors or microphones* debugged debugging
DBGR debugger *remove insects or errors or microphones*
DBGRF autobiography *personal history* autobiographies
DBGRFK autobiographic *of oneself*
DBGRFKL autobiographical (adj) *of oneself* autobiographically (adv)
DBGRFR autobiographer *writer*
DBK daybook *diary*
DBK dieback *plants*
DBK Dubuque *city*
DBKL debacle *rout*
DBL addable (or) addible *sum*
DBL audible (adj) *heard* audibly (adv)
DBL dabble *experiment* dabbled dabbling
DBL dibble *(v) make holes* dibbled dibbling
DBL dibble *(n) tool*
DBL doable *possible*
DBL double *times two* doubled doubling
DBL double-u *the letter W*
DBL doubly *twice*
DBL dyeable *color*
DBL eatable *food*
DBL edible *fit to eat*
DBL oddball *eccentric*
DBLBLN double-blind *experiment*

DBLBLND double-blind *experiment*
DBLBRLD double-barreled *twofold*
DBLBRSDD double-breasted *garment*
DBLBRSTD double-breasted *garment*
DBLBS double bass *music*
DBLCHK double-check (v) *examine* double check (n)
DBLD debility *weakness* debilities
DBLD dyeability *color*
DBLD edibility *fit to eat*
DBLDJT double-digit *10 or more*
DBLDKR double-decker *two layers*
DBLDLN double-dealing *deceiving*
DBLDLNG double-dealing *deceiving*
DBLDLR double-dealer *deceiver*
DBLDPR double-dipper *two salaries*
DBLDRBL double dribble *basketball*
DBLDT double-date (v) *social engagement* double date (n)
DBLFCHR double feature *two films*
DBLFLT double-fault (v) *tennis* double fault (n)
DBLFSD double-faced *hypocritical*
DBLFST double-faced *hypocritical*
DBLFTR double feature *two films*
DBLHDR doubleheader *baseball*
DBLHLKS double helix *two strands*
DBLHLX double helix *two strands*
DBLJD double-edged *two aspects*
DBLJND double-jointed *flexible*

DBLJNTD double-jointed *flexible*
DBLJPRD double jeopardy *trial*
DBLJT double-edged *two aspects*
DBLK adobelike *clay*
DBLK diabolic *evil*
DBLKL diabolical (adj) *evil* diabolically (adv)
DBLKLCH double-clutch *shift gears*
DBLKRP double-crop *farming*
DBLKRS double-cross (v) *betray* double cross (n)
DBLKRSR double-crosser *betrayer*
DBLKWK double-quick *soon*
DBLN dabbling *experimenting*
DBLN doubloon *money*
DBLN Dublin *city*
DBLNG dabbling *experimenting*
DBLNT double knit *fabric*
DBLNTN double entendre *two meanings* double entendres
DBLNTND double entendre *two meanings* double entendres
DBLNTNDR double entendre *two meanings* double entendres
DBLP double up *share, bend*
DBLPL double play *baseball*
DBLPRK double-park *car*
DBLQK double-quick *soon*
DBLR dabbler *experimenter*
DBLR doubler *two*
DBLRD double reed *woodwind*
DBLSPK doublespeak *language*
DBLSPS double-space *type*
DBLT debility *weakness* debilities
DBLT doublet *jacket, two parts*
DBLT dyeability *color*
DBLT edibility *fit to eat*

Use letters that best describe the sounds you hear and omit the vowels. Use **S** or **K** instead of **C**: to find circle use **SRKL**. Use **J** to find joy, **JM** to find gem and **G** to find go.

DBLTK double take *reaction*
DBLTK double-talk *nonsense*
DBLTM double-time (v) *fast* double time (n)
DBLTN doubleton *cards*
DBLTNG double-tongue *musician*
DBLTSHN debilitation *weaken*
DBLTT debilitate *weaken* debilitated debilitating
DBLWD double-wide *mobile home*
DBLY double-u *the letter W*
DBLZ diabolize *make evil* diabolized diabolizing
DBLZM diabolism *devil worship*
DBN Audubon *birds, artist*
DBN autobahn *highway*
DBN dobbin *horse*
DBN dubbin *leather*
DBNCHR debenture *bond*
DBNGK debunk *expose as false*
DBNK debunk *expose as false*
DBNR debonair *smooth*
DBNRL debonairly *smoothly*
DBNTR debenture *bond*
DBNTYR debenture *bond*
DBR dabber *pad*
DBR dauber *applier*
DBR debar *stop, hinder*
DBR debris *trash* debris
DBR dewberry *fruit* dewberries
DBR dubber *voice over*
DBRF debrief *question*
DBRFN debriefing *questioning*
DBRFNG debriefing *questioning*
DBRK daybreak *dawn*
DBRK debark *leave*
DBRKSHN debarkation *leaving*
DBRMN Doberman *dog*
DBRMNPNCHR Doberman pinscher *dog*
DBRMNPNSHR Doberman pinscher *dog*
DBRMNPNSR Doberman pinscher *dog*
DBRMNPNTSR Doberman pinscher *dog*
DBRMNT debarment *stoppage*
DBS D-base *computer*
DBS debase *cheapen* debased debasing
DBS Debussy *composer*
DBS dibs *claim*
DBS dubious *questionable*
DBSH debauchee *corrupt one*
DBSH debouch *appear*
DBSHMNT debouchment *appearance*
DBSL dubiously *questionable*
DBSMNT debasement *cheapen*
DBSNFL dobsonfly *insect* dobsonflies
DBSNS dubiousness *questionable*
DBSR debaser *cheapen*
DBT debate *discuss* debated debating
DBT debit *subtract*
DBT dubiety *doubt* dubieties
DBTBL debatable *discuss*
DBTBL dubitable *questionable*
DBTK diabetic *disease*
DBTNT debutant (m or f) society entrant debutante (f)
DBTR debater *discuss*
DBTS diabetes *disease*
DBTZ diabetes *disease*
DBY debut *introduce*
DBY double-u *the letter W*
DBYC Debussy *composer*
DBYD dubiety *doubt* dubieties
DBYGRF autobiography *personal history* autobiographies
DBYGRFK autobiographic *of oneself*
DBYGRFKL autobiographical (adj) *of oneself* autobiographically (adv)

DBYGRFR autobiographer *writer*
DBYK Dubuque *city*
DBYS Debussy *composer*
DBYS dubious *questionable*
DBYSL dubiously *questionable*
DBYSNS dubiousness *questionable*
DBYT dubiety *doubt* dubieties
DBYTNT debutant (m or f) *society entrant* debutante (f)
DBZ dibs *claim*
DC idiocy *stupidity* idiocies
DC odyssey *journey* odysseys
DCDNT decedent *dead one*
DCH dacha *house*
DCH ditch *(n) gulley (v-slang) throw away* ditches
DCH duce *fascist*
DCH duchy *domain* duchies
DCH Dutch *Netherlands*
DCHDGR ditchdigger *laborer*
DCHDR Dutch door *divided door*
DCHMN dutchman *hiding device*
DCHMRK Deutschemark *money*
DCHNGKL Dutch uncle *stern one*
DCHNKL Dutch uncle *stern one*
DCHR dowitcher *bird*
DCHS duchess *rank* duchesses
DCHTRT dutch treat *pay for oneself*
DCR dicier *risky*
DCS decease *death*
DCS diocese *church* dioceses
DCSD deceased *dead*
DCST deceased *dead*
DCST diciest *risky*
DCT deceased *dead*
DCT deceit *trick*
DCTFL deceitful (adj)

Letters aren't doubled for single sounds: to find alley use **L** not **LL**. Use **Y** and **W** as hard sounds only: to find yellow use **YL**. (Br)=British spelling or usage. * See dictionary.

dishonest deceitfully (adv)
DCTFLNS deceitfulness *dishonesty*
DCV deceive *trick* deceived deceiving
DCVBL deceivable *dishonesty*
DCVNGL deceivingly *trick*
DCVNL deceivingly *trick*
DCVR deceiver *trick*
DCYR dicier *risky*
DCYST diciest *risky*
DCZ decease *death*
DCZ diocese *church* dioceses
DCZ disease *illness*
DD adyta (pl) *sanctum* adytum
DD aoudad *animal*
DD D-day *war*
DD dad *father*
DD Dada *art*
DD daddy *father* daddies
DD dado (n) *pedestal* dadoes
DD dado (v) *groove* dadoed dadoing
DD data (s) or (pl) *information* datum (s)
DD dead *not alive*
DD deadeye *aim*
DD deed (n) *action, contract* (v) *transfer*
DD deity *god* deities
DD dewy-eyed *innocent*
DD did (v-past) *do*
DD dido *prank* didoes (or) didos
DD diode *electricity*
DD ditto *same, copy* dittos
DD ditty *song* ditties
DD dodo *bird, moron* dodoes (or) dodos
DD doe-eyed *innocent*
DD dotty *crazy* dottier dottiest
DD doughty *brave* doughtier doughtiest
DD dowdy *shabby* dowdier dowdiest
DD dud *failure*
DD dude (v) *dress up* duded duding

DD dude (n) *dandy*
DD duty *obligation* duties
DD dyad *pair*
DD iodide *chemical*
DD oddity *peculiarity* oddities
DDBG ditty bag *luggage*
DDBL auditable *check*
DDBL datable *appointment*
DDBL dutiable *obliging*
DDBL editable *correct*
DDBLT dead bolt *lock*
DDBS database *computer*
DDBT deadbeat *bum*
DDC Dead Sea *body of water*
DDD dated *old, day*
DDD day-to-day *everyday*
DDD doodad *thing*
DDFL deadfall *trap*
DDFL dutiful (adj) *obliging* dutifully (adv)
DDFR duty-free *no tax*
DDHD deadhead (n) *dullard* (v) *return trip, trim*
DDHT dead heat *tie race*
DDJ dotage *senility*
DDK dead duck *doomed*
DDK deduct *subtract, conclude*
DDK didact *teacher*
DDK dyadic *mathematics*
DDK eidetic *recall*
DDK idiotic *stupid*
DDKDBL deductible *subtracted*
DDKDBLD deductibility *subtract*
DDKDBLT deductibility *subtract*
DDKDD dedicated *devoted*
DDKDK didactic *teaching*
DDKDKL didactical (adj) *teaching* didactically (adv)
DDKDKS didactics *education*
DDKDR dedicator *devote*
DDKDSZM didacticism *teaching*
DDKDV deductive *inferred*
DDKDVL deductively *inferred*
DDKDX didactics *education*

DDKGN dodecagon *shape*
DDKHDR dodecahedra (pl) *shape* dodecahedron
DDKHDRN dodecahedron *shape* dodecahedrons (or) dodecahedra
DDKL dyadically *mathematics*
DDKL eidetically *recall*
DDKL idiotically *stupid*
DDKMP aide-de-camp *assistant* aides-de-camp
DDKSHN dedication *devotion*
DDKSHN deduction *subtraction, conclusion*
DDKT dedicate *devote* dedicated dedicating
DDKT dedicatee *honoree*
DDKT deduct *subtract, conclude*
DDKT didact *teacher*
DDKTBL deductible *subtracted*
DDKTBLD deductibility *subtract*
DDKTBLT deductibility *subtract*
DDKTD dedicated *devoted*
DDKTK didactic *teaching*
DDKTKL didactical (adj) *teaching* didactically (adv)
DDKTKS didactics *education*
DDKTR dedicator *devote*
DDKTR dedicatory *devoted*
DDKTSZM didacticism *teaching*
DDKTV deductive *inferred*
DDKTVL deductively *inferred*
DDKTX didactics *education*
DDL daedal *complicated*
DDL dawdle *loiter* dawdled dawdling
DDL deadly *lethal, unerring, extreme* deadlier deadliest
DDL diddle *waste, fool, toy* diddled diddling
DDL doodle *scribble* doodled doodling
DDL dottle *tobacco*
DDL dowdily *shabby*

Use letters that best describe the sounds you hear and omit the vowels. Use **S** or **K** instead of **C**: to find circle use **SRKL**. Use **J** to find joy, **JM** to find gem and **G** to find go.

DDLBG doodlebug *insect, device, bomb*
DDLDR dead letter *mail*
DDLFT dead lift (n) *weight lifting* deadlift (v)
DDLK deadlock *standstill*
DDLN deadline *time*
DDLNS deadliness *lethal, unerring, extreme*
DDLR dawdler *loiterer*
DDLR deadlier *lethal, unerring, extreme*
DDLR diddler *waste, fool, toy*
DDLR doodler *scribbler*
DDLS Daedalus *Greek myth*
DDLSKWT diddly-squat *(slang) small amount*
DDLSKWT doodley-squat (or) doodly-squat *(slang) small amount*
DDLSQT diddly-squat *(slang) small amount*
DDLSQT doodley-squat (or) doodly-squat *(slang) small amount*
DDLST deadliest *lethal, unerring, extreme*
DDLTR dead letter *mail*
DDLYR deadlier *lethal, unerring, extreme*
DDLYST deadliest *lethal, unerring, extreme*
DDM adytum *sanctum* adyta
DDM datum *information* data (or) datums
DDM diadem *crown*
DDMRCH dead march *funeral*
DDN dead end (n) *terminal* dead-end (adj, v)
DDN deaden *kill pain*
DDN didn't *(contr) did not*
DDN duodena (pl) *intestine* duodenum
DDND dead end (n) *terminal* dead-end (adj, v)
DDNL duodenal *intestine*
DDNM duodenum *intestine* duodena (or) duodenums
DDNNG deadening *killing pain*
DDNNGL deadeningly

killing pain
DDNR deadener *pain killer*
DDNS deadness *no life*
DDNS dottiness *craziness*
DDNS dowdiness *shabby*
DDNT didn't *(contr) did not*
DDNTHWL dyed-in-the-wool *thorough*
DDPN deadpan *straight-faced*
DDR auditor *account verifier*
DDR daughter *female child*
DDR dead air *silence*
DDR debtor *person who owes*
DDR dieter *weight loss*
DDR dodder *(v) tremble (n) vine*
DDR doter *carer, senile one*
DDR dotter *marker*
DDR dottier *crazier*
DDR doubter *disbeliever*
DDR doughtier *braver*
DDR dowdier *shabbier*
DDR editor *writer*
DDRD dotard *senility*
DDRKNN dead reckoning *guesswork*
DDRKNNG dead reckoning *guesswork*
DDRL dotterel *bird*
DDRLS daughterless *no female child*
DDRM daydream *vision*
DDRMR daydreamer *visionary*
DDRN doddering *feeble*
DDRNCH dude ranch *resort*
DDRNG doddering *feeble*
DDRNL daughter-in-law *son's wife*
DDRNP deuteranope *color-blind person*
DDRNP deuteranopia *color blindness*
DDRNPY deuteranopia *color blindness*
DDRNT deodorant *destroy odor*
DDRP dewdrop *water*
DDRR dodderer *trembler*
DDRZ deodorize *destroy odor* deodorized

deodorizing
DDRZ out-of-doors *open air*
DDRZR deodorizer *destroy odor*
DDS Dead Sea *body of water*
DDS deduce *conclude* deduced deducing
DDS duteous *obliging*
DDSBL deducible *conclude*
DDSH dudish *dandy*
DDSML duodecimal *twelves*
DDSPS dead space *lungs*
DDST dottiest *craziest*
DDST doughtiest *bravest*
DDST dowdiest *shabbiest*
DDSTK dadaistic *(often capitalized) art*
DDT out-of-date *obsolete*
DDV additive *ingredient*
DDV dative *grammar*
DDWD deadwood *useless material*
DDWT deadweight *inert mass*
DDYBL dutiable *obliging*
DDYR dottier *crazier*
DDYR doughtier *braver*
DDYR dowdier *shabbier*
DDYS deduce *conclude* deduced deducing
DDYS duteous *obliging*
DDYSBL deducible *conclude*
DDYST dottiest *craziest*
DDYST doughtiest *bravest*
DDYST dowdiest *shabbiest*
DDZ duds *clothing*
DDZM dadaism *(often capitalized) art*
DF daffy *crazy* daffier daffiest
DF deaf *unable to hear*
DF defy *go against* defied defying defies
DF deify *god* deified deifying deifies
DF doff *take off*
DF duff *(n) fruit, waste, rump (adj) worthless*
DF edify *instruct* edified edifying edifies
DFBRLDR defibrillator *heart rhythm*

Letters aren't doubled for single sounds: to find alley use **L** not **LL**. Use **Y** and **W** as hard sounds only: to find yellow use **YL**. (Br)=British spelling or usage. * See dictionary.

DFBRLSHN defibrillation *heart rhythm*

DFBRLT defibrillate *heart rhythm* defibrillated defibrillating

DFBRLTR defibrillator *heart rhythm*

DFDL daffodil *flower*

DFDNS diffidence *shyness*

DFDNT diffident *shy*

DFDNTS diffidence *shyness*

DFDST defeatist *resignation*

DFDZM defeatism *resignation*

DFG defog *remove fog* defogged defogging

DFGR defogger *remove fog*

DFK defect (n) *blemish* (v) *leave*

DFK edaphic *soil*

DFKD de facto *actual*

DFKDR defector *deserter*

DFKDV defective *faulty*

DFKDVL defectively *faulty*

DFKDVNS defectiveness *faulty*

DFKL edaphically *soil*

DFKLD difficulty *problem* difficulties

DFKLT difficult *not easy*

DFKLT difficulty *problem* difficulties

DFKS idée fixe *obsession*

DFKSHN defecation *feces*

DFKSHN defection *desertion*

DFKSHN deification *god*

DFKSHN edification *instruction*

DFKT de facto *actual*

DFKT defecate *feces* defecated defecating

DFKT defect (n) *blemish* (v) *leave*

DFKTR defector *deserter*

DFKTV defective *faulty*

DFKTVL defectively *faulty*

DFKTVNS defectiveness *faulty*

DFL audiophile *sound*

DFL daffily *crazily*

DFL defile *dirty* defiled defiling

DFL deftly *skillful*

DFL dewfall *moisture*

DFL duffel (or) duffle *supplies*

DFLBG duffel bag *luggage*

DFLD defilade *fortify* defiladed defilading

DFLDK diphyletic *decandance*

DFLDR defaulter *failure*

DFLDR deflator *reducer*

DFLDR defoliator *kill leaves*

DFLGRSHN deflagration *burning*

DFLGRT deflagrate *burn* deflagrated deflagrating

DFLK deflect *turn away*

DFLKDBL deflectable *turn away*

DFLKDR defalcator *embezzler*

DFLKDR deflector *turn away*

DFLKDV deflective *turn away*

DFLKSHN defalcation *embezzlement*

DFLKSHN deflection *turn away*

DFLKT defalcate *embezzle* defalcated defalcating

DFLKT deflect *turn away*

DFLKT duffle coat (or) duffel coat *clothing*

DFLKTBL deflectable *turn away*

DFLKTR defalcator *embezzler*

DFLKTR deflector *turn away*

DFLKTV deflective *turn away*

DFLNT defoliant *kill leaves*

DFLR deflower *take virginity*

DFLRSHN defloration *hymen rupture*

DFLSHN deflation *reduction*

DFLSHN defoliation *kill leaves*

DFLSHNR deflationary *reduction*

DFLT default *fail*

DFLT deflate *reduce, release*

air deflated deflating

DFLT defoliate *kill leaves* defoliated defoliating

DFLTK diphyletic *decendance*

DFLTR defaulter *failure*

DFLTR deflator *reducer*

DFLTR defoliator *kill leaves*

DFLWR deflower *take virginity*

DFLYDR defoliator *kill leaves*

DFLYNT defoliant *kill leaves*

DFLYSHN defoliation *kill leaves*

DFLYT defoliate *kill leaves* defoliated defoliating

DFLYTR defoliator *kill leaves*

DFM defame *slander* defamed defaming

DFMNZ defeminize *make masculine* defeminized defeminizing (Br) defeminise

DFMNZSHN defeminization *make masculine* (Br) defeminisation

DFMR defamer *slanderer*

DFMSHN defamation *slander*

DFMT deaf-mute *unable to hear or speak*

DFMTR defamatory *slandering*

DFMYT deaf-mute *unable to hear or speak*

DFN daphne *shrub*

DFN daphnia *animal*

DFN dauphin (m) *royalty* dauphine (f)

DFN deafen *no hearing*

DFN defend *safeguard*

DFN define *distinguish, separate* defined defining

DFNBK dieffenbachia *plant*

DFNBKY dieffenbachia *plant*

DFNBL definable (adj) *distinguish, separate* definably (adv)

DFND defend *safeguard*

DFNDBL defendable *safeguard*

DFNDNT defendant (n) *legal*

Use letters that best describe the sounds you hear and omit the vowels. Use **S** or **K** instead of **C**: to find circle use **SRKL**. Use **J** to find joy, **JM** to find gem and **G** to find go.

contestant *(adj)* defending
DFNDR defender *guard*
DFNDV definitive *conclusive*
DFNDVL definitively
conclusive
DFNDVNS definitiveness
conclusive
DFNG defang *make harmless*
DFNGKSHNL difunctional
chemistry
DFNGKT defunct *dead*
DFNKSHNL difunctional
chemistry
DFNKT defunct *dead*
DFNN deafening *loud*
DFNND definienda (pl)
expression definiendum
DFNNDM definiendum
expression definienda
DFNNG deafening *loud*
DFNR definer *distinguish,*
separate
DFNS daftness *craziness*
DFNS defense *safeguard*
(Br) defence
DFNS defiance *challenge*
DFNS deftness *skill*
DFNS diaphanous *thin*
DFNSBL defensible
protection
DFNSHN definition *meaning,*
outline
DFNSLS defenseless
unprotected
DFNSLSL defenselessly
unprotected
DFNSLSNS
defenselessness
unprotected
DFNSTRSHN
defenestration *throw out a*
window
DFNSTRT defenestrate
throw out a window
defenestrated
defenestrating
DFNSV defensive *protection*
DFNSVL defensively
protection
DFNSVNS defensiveness
protection
DFNT defiant *challenging*

DFNT definite *sure*
DFNTD definitude *precision*
DFNTL defiantly *challenging*
DFNTL definitely *surely*
DFNTNS definiteness *surety*
DFNTS defense *safeguard*
(Br) defence
DFNTS defiance *challenge*
DFNTSBL defensible
protection
DFNTSLS defenseless
unprotected
DFNTSLSL defenselessly
unprotected
DFNTSLSNS
defenselessness
unprotected
DFNTSV defensive
protection
DFNTSVL defensively
protection
DFNTSVNS defensiveness
protection
DFNTV definitive *conclusive*
DFNTVL definitively
conclusive
DFNTVNS definitiveness
conclusive
DFNTYD definitude *precision*
DFNY daphnia *animal*
DFNYND definienda (pl)
expression definiendum
DFNYNDM definiendum
expression definienda
DFNYNSH definientia (pl)
definition definiens
DFNYNZ definiens *definition*
definientia
DFR daffier *crazier*
DFR defer *delay* deferred
deferring
DFR defier *dare, disregard*
DFR defray *pay*
DFR differ *not alike*
DFR duffer *peddler, clumsy*
one
DFRBL deferrable *delay*
DFRBL defrayable *payable*
DFRD defraud *cheat*
DFRDR defrauder *cheater*
DFRK defrock *priest*
DFRK diffract *break apart*

DFRKSHN diffraction *light*
DFRKT diffract *break apart*
DFRL deferral *delay*
DFRL defrayal *payment*
DFRM deform *twist, warp*
DFRM diaphragm *membrane*
DFRMBL deformable *twist,*
warp
DFRMD deformed *distorted*
DFRMD deformity *distortion*
deformities
DFRMDV deformative
distortion
DFRMLZ deformalize *make*
casual deformalized
deformalizing
(Br) deformalise
DFRMNT deferment *delay*
DFRMSHN deformation
distortion
DFRMSHNL deformational
distortion
DFRMT deformity *distortion*
deformities
DFRMTV deformative
distortion
DFRNCH differentia
distinguishing trait
differentiae
DFRNCHL deferential (adj)
respectful deferentially
(adv)
DFRNCHL differential *(n)*
math, gear
DFRNCHL differential (adj)
difference differentially
(adv)
DFRNCHSHN differentiation
difference
DFRNCHT differentiate
discriminate differentiated
differentiating
DFRNCHYSHN
differentiation *difference*
DFRNCHYT differentiate
discriminate differentiated
differentiating
DFRNS deference *honor*
DFRNS difference *not alike*
DFRNSH differentia
distinguishing trait
differentiae

DFRNSHL deferential (adj) *respectful* deferentially (adv)
DFRNSHL differential *(n) math, gear*
DFRNSHL differential (adj) *difference* differentially (adv)
DFRNSHSHN differentiation *difference*
DFRNSHT differentiate *discriminate* differentiated differentiating
DFRNSHYSHN differentiation *difference*
DFRNSHYT differentiate *discriminate* differentiated differentiating
DFRNT deferent *respectful*
DFRNT different *not alike*
DFRNTS deference *honor*
DFRNTS difference *not alike*
DFRR deferrer *delayer*
DFRSDR defroster *refrigerator*
DFRSDSHN deforestation *remove trees*
DFRST deforest *remove trees*
DFRST defrost *refrigerator*
DFRSTR defroster *refrigerator*
DFRSTSHN deforestation *remove trees*
DFRYBL defrayable *payable*
DFRYL defrayal *payment*
DFS deface *mar* defaced defacing
DFS diffuse *(adj) wordy*
DFS doofus *(slang) fool* doofuses
DFS edifice *building*
DFSHN diffusion *spread*
DFSHNC deficiency *lack* deficiencies
DFSHNS deficiency *lack* deficiencies
DFSHNST diffusionist *culture*
DFSHNT deficient *lacking*
DFSHNTC deficiency *lack* deficiencies
DFSHNTL deficiently *lacking*

DFSHNTS deficiency *lack* deficiencies
DFSHNZM diffusionism *culture*
DFSMNT defacement *injury*
DFSR defacer *injurer*
DFST daffiest *craziest*
DFST deficit *lack*
DFSV diffusive *spreading*
DFSVD diffusivity *spread*
DFSVL diffusively *spread*
DFSVNS diffusiveness *spread*
DFSVT diffusivity *spread*
DFT daft *crazy*
DFT defat *remove fat*
DFT defeat *conquer*
DFT deft *skillful*
DFTHNG diphthong *vowel sound*
DFTHR diphtheria *disease*
DFTHRY diphtheria *disease*
DFTL deftly *skillful*
DFTNS daftness *craziness*
DFTNS deftness *skill*
DFTST defeatist *resignation*
DFTZM defeatism *resignation*
DFX idée fixe *obsession*
DFYL defile *dirty* defiled defiling
DFYNS defiance *challenge*
DFYNT defiant *challenging*
DFYNTL defiantly *challenging*
DFYNTS defiance *challenge*
DFYR daffier *crazier*
DFYR defier *dare, disregard*
DFYS diffuse *(adj) wordy*
DFYSHN diffusion *spread*
DFYSHNST diffusionist *culture*
DFYSHNZM diffusionism *culture*
DFYST daffiest *craziest*
DFYSV diffusive *spreading*
DFYSVD diffusivity *spread*
DFYSVL diffusively *spread*
DFYSVNS diffusiveness *spread*
DFYSVT diffusivity *spread*
DFYZ defuse *remove a threat*

defused defusing
DFYZ diffuse *(v) spread* diffused diffusing
DFYZBL diffusible *spread*
DFYZHN diffusion *spread*
DFYZHNST diffusionist *culture*
DFYZHNZM diffusionism *culture*
DFYZR diffuser *spreader*
DFYZV diffusive *spreading*
DFYZVD diffusivity *spread*
DFYZVL diffusively *spread*
DFYZVNS diffusiveness *spread*
DFYZVT diffusivity *spread*
DFZ defuse *remove a threat* defused defusing
DFZ diffuse *(v) spread* diffused diffusing
DFZBL defeasible *defeat*
DFZBL diffusible *spread*
DFZBLD defeasibility *defeat*
DFZBLT defeasibility *defeat*
DFZHN diffusion *spread*
DFZHNST diffusionist *culture*
DFZHNZM diffusionism *culture*
DFZNS defeasance *defeat*
DFZNTS defeasance *defeat*
DFZR diffuser *spreader*
DFZT deficit *lack*
DFZV diffusive *spreading*
DFZVD diffusivity *spread*
DFZVL diffusively *spread*
DFZVNS diffusiveness *spread*
DFZVT diffusivity *spread*
DG dago *(vulgar) Italian or Spanish* dagos (or) dagoes
DG dig *burrow, appreciate* dug digging
DG dodgy *(Br) tricky, risky*
DG dog *(v) follow* dogged dogging
DG dog *(n) animal*
DG doggy (or) doggie *dog* doggies
DG dogie *calf*
DGBG doggie bag (or)

Use letters that best describe the sounds you hear and omit the vowels. Use **S** or **K** instead of **C**: to find circle use **SRKL**. Use **J** to find joy, **JM** to find gem and **G** to find go.

doggy bag *leftover food*
DGBN dogbane *plant*
DGD dogged *obstinate*
DGDL doggedly *obstinate*
DGDNS doggedness
obstinacy
DGDR do-gooder *kind
person*
DGDZ dog days *summer*
DGFSH dogfish *shark*
DGFT dogfight *contest*
DGHS doghouse *shelter*
DGJ dégagé *casual*
DGKCHR dogcatcher
animal control
DGL Day-Glo *(trademark)
paint*
DGL dayglow *brightness*
DGL de Gaulle *French
president*
DGLCSHN deglaciation *ice
sheet*
DGLCYSHN deglaciation *ice
sheet*
DGLG dogleg *bend*
DGLSHSHN deglaciation *ice
sheet*
DGLSHYSHN deglaciation
ice sheet
DGLSRD diglyceride
chemical
DGLSSHN deglaciation *ice
sheet*
DGLSYSHN deglaciation *ice
sheet*
DGLTSHN deglutition
swallowing
DGLZ deglaze *remove glaze,
dissolve* deglazed
deglazing
DGM digamy *second
marriage* digamies
DGM dogma *belief* dogmas
DGMDK dogmatic *bossy*
DGMDKL dogmatically
bossy
DGMTK dogmatic *bossy*
DGMTKL dogmatically
bossy
DGMTST dogmatist *believer*
DGMTZ dogmatize *assert
beliefs* dogmatized

dogmatizing
DGMTZM dogmatism *belief*
DGMTZR dogmatizer *assert
beliefs*
DGN doggone (or)
doggoned *damn*
DGND dignity *honor*
dignities
DGND doggoned (or)
doggone *damn*
DGNF dignify *ennoble*
dignified dignifying
dignifies
DGNFD dignified *noble*
DGNG dugong *animal*
DGNGZ diggings *ore (Br)
lodging*
DGNL diagonal (n, adj)
slanted line diagonally
(adv)
DGNP dognap *steal dogs*
dognapped (or)
dognaped dognapping
(or) dognaping
DGNPR dognapper (or)
dognaper *steal dogs*
DGNS diagnose *analyze*
diagnosed diagnosing
DGNSBL diagnosable
analysis
DGNSDK diagnostic
analytic
DGNSDKL diagnostically
analytic
DGNSS diagnosis *analysis*
diagnoses
DGNSTK diagnostic *analytic*
DGNSTKL diagnostically
analytic
DGNSTSHN diagnostician
analysis
DGNT dignity *honor* dignities
DGNTR dignitary *noble rank*
dignitaries
DGNZ diagnose *analyze*
diagnosed diagnosing
DGNZ diggings *ore (Br)
lodging*
DGNZBL diagnosable
analysis
DGPDL dog paddle (n) *swim*
dog-paddle (v)

DGPTL dog paddle (n) *swim*
dog-paddle (v)
DGR dagger *knife*
DGR degree *angle, diploma*
DGR digger *miner, soldier*
DGRD degrade *demote, break
down* degraded
degrading
DGRD degree-day
temperature
DGRD degreed *angle,
diploma*
DGRD dog-eared *bent page*
DGRDBL degradable *break
down*
DGRDD degraded *reduced*
DGRDDV degradative
decline
DGRDNG degrading *reduced*
DGRDNGL degradingly
reduced
DGRDNL degradingly
reduced
DGRDR degrader *reducer*
DGRDSHN degradation
demotion, breakdown
DGRDTV degradative
decline
DGRF autograph *signature*
DGRF digraph *sound*
DGRF ideograph *symbol*
ideography
DGRFK autographic *self-
written*
DGRFK digraphic *sound*
DGRFK ideographic *symbol*
DGRFK idiographic *concept*
DGRFKL ideographically
symbol
DGRL doggerel *trivial, verse*
DGRLK daggerlike *like a
knife*
DGRM audiogram *hearing*
DGRM diagram *picture*
diagrammed (or)
diagramed diagramming
(or) diagraming
DGRM ideogram *symbol*
DGRMBL diagrammable
picture
DGRMDK diagrammatic
picture

Letters aren't doubled for single sounds: to find alley use **L** not **LL**. Use **Y** and **W** as hard
sounds only: to find yellow use **YL**. (Br)=British spelling or usage. * See dictionary.

DGRMDK ideogrammatic *symbol*
DGRMDKL diagrammatically *picture*
DGRMK ideogramic (or) ideogrammic *symbol*
DGRMTK diagrammatic *picture*
DGRMTK ideogrammatic *symbol*
DGRMTKL diagrammatically *picture*
DGRS degrease *remove oil* degreased degreasing
DGRS digress *wander*
DGRSHN digression *wander*
DGRSHNL digressional *wander*
DGRSHNR digressionary *wander*
DGRSR degreaser *remove oil*
DGRSV degressive *downward*
DGRSV digressive *wander*
DGRSVL degressively *downward*
DGRSVL digressively *wander*
DGRSVNS digressiveness *wander*
DGRTP daguerreotype *photograph* daguerreotypy
DGRTPST daguerreotypist *photographer*
DGS degauss *neutralize*
DGS digs *living quarters*
DGSDSHN degustation *taste*
DGSH dégagé *casual*
DGSH doggish *canine, stylish*
DGSLD dogsled *vehicle*
DGSR degausser *neutralizer*
DGST degust *taste*
DGSTSHN degustation *taste*
DGT dugout *shelter*
DGTDG dog-eat-dog *competitive*
DGTG dog tag *identification*
DGTRT dogtrot *gait*
DGTTH dogtooth *dental, ornament* (Br) houndstooth

check
DGWCH dogwatch *night shift*
DGWD dogwood *tree*
DGZ digs *living quarters*
DGZH dégagé *casual*
DGZR degausser *neutralizer*
DH Idaho *US State*
DHBRD dihybrid *breeding*
DHDRDR dehydrator *remove water*
DHDRL dihedral *angle*
DHDRSHN dehydration *remove water*
DHDRT dehydrate *remove water* dehydrated dehydrating
DHDRTR dehydrator *remove water*
DHK ad hoc *improvised*
DHK doohickey *thing* doohickeys
DHMDF dehumidify *remove moisture* dehumidified dehumidifying dehumidifies
DHMDFKSHN dehumidification *remove moisture*
DHMDFR dehumidifier *remove moisture*
DHMDFYR dehumidifier *remove moisture*
DHMNM ad hominem *emotional*
DHMNZ dehumanize *remove human elements* dehumanized dehumanizing
DHMNZSHN dehumanization *remove human elements*
DHPNDK autohypnotic *self-induced trance*
DHPNSS autohypnosis *self-induced trance*
DHPNTK autohypnotic *self-induced trance*
DHR adhere *stick* adhered adhering
DHRD die-hard (adj) *determined* diehard (n)

DHRN dehorn *no horns*
DHRNS adherence *attachment*
DHRNT adherent *follower*
DHRNTL adherently *connected*
DHRNTS adherence *attachment*
DHS dehisce *split* dehisced dehiscing
DHS outhouse *toilet*
DHSHN adhesion *attachment*
DHSHNL adhesional *attachment*
DHSNS dehiscence *split*
DHSNT dehiscent *split*
DHSNTS dehiscence *split*
DHSV adhesive *glue*
DHSVL adhesively *glue*
DHSVNS adhesiveness *attachment*
DHYMDF dehumidify *remove moisture* dehumidified dehumidifying dehumidifies
DHYMDFKSHN dehumidification *remove moisture*
DHYMDFR dehumidifier *remove moisture*
DHYMDFYR dehumidifier *remove moisture*
DHYMNZ dehumanize *remove human elements* dehumanized dehumanizing
DHYMNZSHN dehumanization *remove human elements*
DHZHN adhesion *attachment*
DHZHNL adhesional *attachment*
DHZV adhesive *glue*
DHZVL adhesively *glue*
DHZVNS adhesiveness *attachment*
DJ adage *saying*
DJ adagio *slow, ballet* adagios
DJ deejay (or) DJ *disc jockey*

Use letters that best describe the sounds you hear and omit the vowels. Use **S** or **K** instead of **C**: to find circle use **SRKL**. Use **J** to find joy, **JM** to find gem and **G** to find go.

DJ dodge *(v) avoid* dodged dodging
DJ dodge *(n) trick*
DJ dodgy *(Br) tricky, risky*
DJ dojo *school* dojos
DJ étagère *(or)* etagere *furniture*
DJ outage *loss, interruption*
DJDL digital *(adj) numbers, limbs* digitally *(adv)*
DJDLZ digitalize *drug* digitalized digitalizing
DJDLZSHN digitalization *drug*
DJKBL educable *learning*
DJKBLD educability *learning*
DJKBLT educability *learning*
DJKD dejecta *feces*
DJKDD dejected *depressed*
DJKDD educated *skilled*
DJKDDL dejectedly *depressed*
DJKDDNS dejectedness *depression*
DJKDR educator *teacher*
DJKDV educative *instructive*
DJKSHN dejection *depression*
DJKSHN education *study*
DJKSHNL educational *(adj) teaching* educationally *(adv)*
DJKSHNST educationist *learning*
DJKT deject *make depressed*
DJKT dejecta *feces*
DJKT educate *teach* educated educating
DJKTD dejected *depressed*
DJKTD educated *skilled*
DJKTDL dejectedly *depressed*
DJKTDNS dejectedness *depression*
DJKTR educator *teacher*
DJKTV educative *instructive*
DJN dudgeon *offense*
DJNK autogenic *from within*
DJNRC degeneracy *corruption* degeneracies
DJNRDV degenerative

deterioration
DJNRS degeneracy *corruption* degeneracies
DJNRSHN degeneration *deterioration*
DJNRT degenerate *(v) deteriorate* degenerated degenerating
DJNRT degenerate *(n) corrupt one (adj) corrupted, simplified*
DJNRTL degenerately *corruptly, simply*
DJNRTNS degenerateness *corruption, simplification*
DJNRTV degenerative *deterioration*
DJNS dodginess *(Br) tricky, risky*
DJNZ Diogenes *philosopher*
DJNZ Dow Jones *stock market*
DJR de jure *lawful*
DJR dodger *avoider*
DJR dodgery *trickery* dodgeries
DJR dowager *woman*
DJR du jour *of the day*
DJSCHN digestion *absorption*
DJSDBL digestible *absorb*
DJSDBLD digestibility *absorb*
DJSDBLT digestibility *absorb*
DJSDR digester *summarizer, container*
DJSDV digestive *absorption*
DJST digest *(n) summation (v) absorb*
DJSTBL digestible *absorb*
DJSTBLD digestibility *absorb*
DJSTBLT digestibility *absorb*
DJSTR digester *summarizer, container*
DJSTV digestive *absorption*
DJT digit *number, limb*
DJTL digital *(adj) numbers, limbs* digitally *(adv)*
DJTLN digitalin *chemical*
DJTLS digitalis *heart drug*
DJTLZ digitalize *drug*

digitalized digitalizing
DJTLZSHN digitalization *drug*
DJTT digitate *divided*
DJTZ digitize *convert to digital* digitized digitizing
DJTZR digitizer *convert to digital*
DJV déjà vu *memory*
DJY adagio *slow, ballet* adagios
DK addict *one who needs*
DK attic *upper room*
DK Dacca *(or)* Dhaka *city*
DK decay *rot*
DK deck *(v) decorate, knock down (n) floor, cards, recording*
DK decoy *lure*
DK dick *(slang) fellow, detective*
DK dickey *(or)* dicky *collar* dickeys *(or)* dickies
DK dike *dam* diked diking *(Br)* dyke
DK doc *doctor*
DK dock *(v) park a ship, reduce* docked docking
DK dock *(n) wharf, court*
DK duck *(v) bird (v) avoid, dip* ducks
DK ducky *fine* duckier duckiest
DK duct *opening*
DK duke *(v) fight* duked duking
DK duke *(n) nobleman, fist*
DK dyke *(n) (vulgar) lesbian* dykey *(adj)*
DK etic *no structure*
DK odic *verse*
DK Utica *city*
DKBL duckbill *animal*
DKBL educable *learning*
DKBLD duck-billed *broad and flat bill*
DKBLD educability *learning*
DKBLT educability *learning*
DKBRD duckboard *flooring*
DKC Dixie *region*
DKC doxy *mistress* doxies
DKCHL ductule *small duct*

Letters aren't doubled for single sounds: to find alley use **L** not **LL**. Use **Y** and **W** as hard sounds only: to find yellow use **YL**. (Br)=British spelling or usage. * See dictionary.

DKCHR deck chair *furniture*
DKCL adaxial *axis*
DKCLN Dixieland *region*
DKCLND Dixieland *region*
DKCYL adaxial *axis*
DKD Dakota *Native American* Dakotas
DKD decade *ten years*
DKD decode *solve* decoded decoding
DKD dicta (pl) *opinion* dictum
DKDD addicted *habitual need*
DKDK deictic *words*
DKDK dichotic *sound*
DKDK dik-dik *bird* dik-diks (or) dik-dik
DKDL dactyl *verse*
DKDL ductal *opening*
DKDL ductile *easily led*
DKDLDN dicotyledon *plant*
DKDLDNS dicotyledonous *plant*
DKDM dichotomy *division* dichotomies
DKDM dictum *opinion* dicta
DKDM dukedom *domain*
DKDMS dichotomous *divided*
DKDMZ dichotomize *divide* dichotomized dichotomizing
DKDMZSHN dichotomization *division*
DKDNG ducting *tubes*
DKDNS decadence *decline*
DKDNT decadent *decline*
DKDNTS decadence *decline*
DKDR adductor *draw together*
DKDR decoder *solver*
DKDR doctor *(v) heal, repair* doctored doctoring
DKDR doctor *(n) healer, PhD*
DKDR educator *teacher*
DKDR eductor *ejector*
DKDRL doctoral *heal, PhD*
DKDRM docudrama *theater*
DKDRN doctrine *dogma*
DKDRT doctorate *degree*
DKDTRL dictatorial (adj)

autocratic dictatorially (adv)
DKDTRYL dictatorial (adj) *autocratic* dictatorially (adv)
DKDV addictive *habitual need*
DKDV adductive *drawn together*
DKDV educative *instructive*
DKDVDR deactivator *make ineffective*
DKDVSHN deactivation *make ineffective*
DKDVT deactivate *make ineffective* deactivated deactivating
DKDVTR deactivator *make ineffective*
DKF decaf *no caffeine*
DKFNDD decaffeinated *no caffeine*
DKFNTD decaffeinated *no caffeine*
DKGN decagon *10 sides*
DKGRM dekagram *measure*
DKHN deckhand *sailor*
DKHN dockhand *longshoreman*
DKHND deckhand *sailor*
DKHND dockhand *longshoreman*
DKHS deckhouse *ship*
DKJ dockage *fee, parking*
DKL decal *emblem*
DKL deckle *frame*
DKL declaw *remove claws*
DKL dewclaw *hoof*
DKL ducal *duke*
DKLDR decaliter (or) dekaliter *measure* (Br) decalitre (or) dekalitre
DKLG Decalogue *Ten Commandments*
DKLJ deckle edge *rough edge*
DKLJD deckle-edged *rough edge*
DKLM declaim *speak*
DKLMR declaimer *speaker*
DKLMSHN declamation

speech
DKLMTR declamatory *speech*
DKLN decline *slope, refuse* declined declining
DKLN duckling *bird*
DKLN eau de cologne *perfume* eaux de cologne
DKLNBL declinable *angle, turn aside*
DKLNCHN declension *word, slope*
DKLNG duckling *bird*
DKLNN declining *deteriorating*
DKLNNG declining *deteriorating*
DKLNR decliner *slope, refuse*
DKLNS diclinous *fertilization*
DKLNSHN declension *word, slope*
DKLNSHN declination *angle, turn aside*
DKLR declare *announce* declared declaring
DKLRBL declarable *announce*
DKLRDV declarative *announcement*
DKLRR declarer *announcer*
DKLRSHN declaration *announcement*
DKLRTR declaratory *announcement*
DKLRTV declarative *announcement*
DKLRZ decolorize *remove color* decolorized decolorizing (Br) decolourize
DKLRZR decolorizer *remove color* (Br) decolourizer
DKLRZSHN decolorization *remove color* (Br) decolourization
DKLS declassé *low status*
DKLS ductless *no opening*
DKLSF decalcify *bone loss* decalcified decalcifying
DKLSF declassify *remove rating* declassified

Use letters that best describe the sounds you hear and omit the vowels. Use **S** or **K** instead of **C**: to find circle use **SRKL**. Use **J** to find joy, **JM** to find gem and **G** to find go.

declassifying declassifies
DKLSFD declassified
remove rating
DKLSFKSHN
decalcification *bone loss*
DKLSFKSHN
declassification *remove*
rating
DKLSHN decollation *behead*
DKLT decollate *behead*
decollated decollating
DKLT décolleté *neckline*
DKLTJ décolletage *neckline*
DKLTR decaliter (or)
dekaliter *measure*
(Br) decalitre (or)
dekalitre
DKLTSH décolletage
neckline
DKLTZH décolletage
neckline
DKLV autoclave *pressure*
device
DKLVD declivity *slope*
declivities
DKLVDS declivitous *steep*
DKLVT declivity *slope*
declivities
DKLVTS declivitous *steep*
DKMBNT decumbent
reclining
DKMDR decameter (or)
dekameter *verse*
DKMNL documental *factual*
DKMNR documentary
factual documentaries
DKMNR documenter
reporter
DKMNT document *(n)*
writing (v) provide facts
DKMNTL documental
factual
DKMNTR documentary
factual documentaries
DKMNTR documenter
reporter
DKMNTSHN
documentation *facts*
DKMNTSHNL
documentational *facts*
DKMP aide-de-camp
assistant aides-de-camp

DKMP decamp *depart*
DKMPMNT decampment
departure
DKMPRS decompress
release pressure
DKMPRSHN
decompression *release*
pressure
DKMPZ decompose *rot,*
separate decomposed
decomposing
DKMPZBL decomposable
rot, separate
DKMPZBLD
decomposability *rot,*
separate
DKMPZBLT
decomposability *rot,*
separate
DKMPZR decomposer
organism
DKMPZSHN decomposition
rot, separation
DKMSDR dockmaster
marina
DKMSHN decommission
remove from service
DKMSTR dockmaster
marina
DKMTR decameter (or)
dekameter *verse*
(Br) decametre (or)
dekametre
DKMTRK dekametric
measure
DKN daikon *radish*
DKN deacon *clergy*
DKN deckhand *sailor*
DKN decking *floor*
DKN dockhand
longshoreman
DKND deckhand *sailor*
DKND dockhand
longshoreman
DKNDR dichondra *plant*
DKNG decking *floor*
DKNJSCHN decongestion
remove blockage
DKNJST decongest *remove*
blockage
DKNJSTNT decongestant
remove blockage

DKNJSTV decongestive
remove blockage
DKNR deaconry *church*
deaconries
DKNR decanter *container*
DKNS deaconess *clergy (f)*
deaconesses
DKNS dickens *devil*
DKNSTRK deconstruct
interpret
DKNSTRKDR
deconstructor
interpretation
DKNSTRKDV
deconstructive
interpretation
DKNSTRKSHN
deconstruction
interpretation
DKNSTRKSHNST
deconstructionist
interpretation
DKNSTRKT deconstruct
interpret
DKNSTRKTR
deconstructor
interpretation
DKNSTRKTV
deconstructive
interpretation
DKNT decant *pour*
DKNTMNDR
decontaminator *remove*
impurity
DKNTMNNT
decontaminant *remove*
impurity
DKNTMNSHN
decontamination *remove*
impurity
DKNTMNT decontaminate
remove impurity
decontaminated
decontaminating
DKNTMNTR
decontaminator *remove*
impurity
DKNTR decanter *container*
DKNTRL decontrol *end*
control
DKNZ dickens *devil*
DKP da capo *repeat*

Letters aren't doubled for single sounds: to find alley use **L** not **LL**. Use **Y** and **W** as hard sounds only: to find yellow use **YL**. (Br)=British spelling or usage. * See dictionary.

DKPD decapod *10 arms*
DKPJ découpage (or) decoupage *cutout art*
DKPL decouple *separate* decoupled decoupling
DKPL decuple *groups of 10*
DKPN duckpin *bowling*
DKPSH découpage (or) decoupage *cutout art*
DKPTDR decapitator *behead*
DKPTSHN decapitation *behead*
DKPTT decapitate *behead* decapitated decapitating
DKPTTR decapitator *behead*
DKPZH découpage (or) decoupage *cutout art*
DKR daiquiri *drink* daiquiris
DKR day care *children*
DKR decare *area measure*
DKR décor (or) decor *furnishings*
DKR decree *announce* decreed decreeing
DKR decry *belittle* decried decrying decries
DKR dicker *bargain*
DKR diker *dam*
DKR docker *longshoreman*
DKR ducker *avoider*
DKR duckier *happier*
DKR duiker *antelope*
DKRBNSHN decarbonation *remove carbon dioxide or carbonic acid*
DKRBNT decarbonate *remove carbon dioxide or carbonic acid* decarbonated decarbonating
DKRBNZ decarbonize *remove carbon* decarbonized decarbonizing
DKRDK autocratic *dictatorial*
DKRDK diacritic *phonetic*
DKRDKL autocratically *dictatorially*
DKRDKL diacritical *phonetic*
DKRDL decretal *decree*
DKRDR decorator *designer*

DKRDV decorative *ornamental*
DKRDV decretive *announced*
DKRM decorum *correctness*
DKRMNLZ decriminalize *repeal a ban* decriminalized decriminalizing
DKRMNLZSHN decriminalization *repeal a ban* (Br) decriminalisation
DKRMNT decrement *reduction*
DKRMNTL decremental *reduction*
DKRN Dacron *(trademark) fabric*
DKRP decrypt *decode*
DKRPD decrepit *weak*
DKRPSHN decryption *decode*
DKRPT decrepit *weak*
DKRPT decrypt *decode*
DKRPTD decrepitude *weakness*
DKRPTSHN decrepitation *weak, crackle*
DKRPTT decrepitate *make weak, crackle*
DKRPTYD decrepitude *weakness*
DKRR decreer *announcer*
DKRR decrier *belittler*
DKRS autocross *race*
DKRS decorous *correct*
DKRS decrease *reduce* decreased decreasing
DKRSHN decoration *ornament*
DKRSHND decrescendo *music* decrescendos
DKRSL decorously *correctly*
DKRSNGL decreasingly *reduce*
DKRSNL decreasingly *reduce*
DKRSNS decorousness *correctness*
DKRSNT decrescent *waning*
DKRT autocrat *dictator*

DKRT decorate *ornament* decorated decorating
DKRT Descartes *philosopher*
DKRT out-of-court *law*
DKRTK autocratic *dictatorial*
DKRTK diacritic *phonetic*
DKRTKL autocratically *dictatorially*
DKRTKL diacritical *phonetic*
DKRTL decretal *decree*
DKRTR decorator *designer*
DKRTR decretory *announced*
DKRTV decorative *ornamental*
DKRTV decretive *announced*
DKRYR decreer *announcer*
DKRYR decrier *belittler*
DKS addax *animal* addaxes
DKS deckhouse *ship*
DKS Dixie *region*
DKS doxy *mistress* doxies
DKS dukes *(slang) fists*
DKSD dioxide *chemical*
DKSD dockside *shore*
DKSDR dexter *right side*
DKSDRD dexterity *skill* dexterities
DKSDRL dextral *right-handed*
DKSDRN Dexedrine *(trademark) drug*
DKSDRS dexterous *skillful*
DKSDRT dexterity *skill* dexterities
DKSDZ deoxidize *remove oxygen* deoxidized deoxidizing
DKSDZR deoxidizer *remove oxygen*
DKSHN addiction *habitual need*
DKSHN adduction *drawn together*
DKSHN dachshund *dog*
DKSHN diction *speech*
DKSHN education *study*
DKSHN eduction *brought out*
DKSHND dachshund *dog*
DKSHNL educational (adj) *teaching* educationally (adv)

Use letters that best describe the sounds you hear and omit the vowels. Use **S** or **K** instead of **C**: to find circle use **SRKL**. Use **J** to find joy, **JM** to find gem and **G** to find go.

DKSHNR dictionary *word book* dictionaries
DKSHNST educationist *learning*
DKSHNT dachshund *dog*
DKSJNSHN deoxygenation *remove oxygen*
DKSJNT deoxygenate *remove oxygen*
DKSL adaxial *axis*
DKSL duxelles *mushrooms*
DKSLG doxology *praise* doxologies
DKSLJ doxology *praise* doxologies
DKSLN Dixieland *region*
DKSLND Dixieland *region*
DKSN dachshund *dog*
DKSN dioxane *solvent*
DKSN dioxin *herbicide*
DKSND dachshund *dog*
DKSP duck soup *easy to do*
DKSS deixis *words*
DKSSHN decussation *cross*
DKSSL dickcissel *bird*
DKST audiocassette *tape*
DKST decussate *cross* decussated decussating
DKST duckiest *happiest*
DKSTR dexter *right side*
DKSTRD dexterity *skill* dexterities
DKSTRL dextral *right-handed*
DKSTRS dexterous *skillful*
DKSTRS dextrose *sugar*
DKSTRT dexterity *skill* dexterities
DKSYL adaxial *axis*
DKT addict *one who needs*
DKT adduct *draw together*
DKT Dakota *Native American* Dakotas
DKT dicot *plant*
DKT dicta (pl) *opinion* dictum
DKT docket *agenda*
DKT ducat *money*
DKT duct *opening*
DKT edict *law*
DKT educate *teach* educated educating

DKT etiquette *manners*
DKTD addicted *habitual need*
DKTDN dictating *speak, command*
DKTDNG dictating *speak, command*
DKTDR dictator *autocrat*
DKTDRSHP dictatorship *autocratic*
DKTHLN decathlon *contest*
DKTHLT decathlete *contestant*
DKTK deictic *words*
DKTK dichotic *sound*
DKTL dactyl *verse*
DKTL ducktail *hairdo*
DKTL ductal *opening*
DKTL ductile *easily led*
DKTL ductule *small duct*
DKTLD ductility *easily led*
DKTLDN dicotyledon *plant*
DKTLDNS dicotyledonous *plant*
DKTLK dactylic *verse*
DKTLS ductless *no opening*
DKTLT ductility *easily led*
DKTM dichotomy *division* dichotomies
DKTM dictum *opinion* dicta
DKTMS dichotomous *divided*
DKTMZ dichotomize *divide* dichotomized dichotomizing
DKTMZSHN dichotomization *division*
DKTN ducting *tubes*
DKTNG ducting *tubes*
DKTP duct tape *adhesive*
DKTR adductor *draw together*
DKTR doctor *(v) heal, repair* doctored doctoring
DKTR doctor *(n) healer, PhD*
DKTR educator *teacher*
DKTR eductor *ejector*
DKTRL doctoral *heal, PhD*
DKTRN doctrine *dogma*
DKTRNL doctrinal (adj) *dogma* doctrinally (adv)
DKTRNR doctrinaire *(n) theorizer (adj) obstinate*

DKTRT doctorate *degree*
DKTSHN dictation *speech*
DKTT dictate *speak, command* dictated dictating
DKTTN dictating *speak, command*
DKTTNG dictating *speak, command*
DKTTR dictator *autocrat*
DKTTRL dictatorial (adj) *autocratic* dictatorially (adv)
DKTTRSHP dictatorship *autocratic*
DKTTRYL dictatorial (adj) *autocratic* dictatorially (adv)
DKTV addictive *habitual need*
DKTV adductive *drawn together*
DKTV educative *instructive*
DKTVDR deactivator *make ineffective*
DKTVSHN deactivation *make ineffective*
DKTVT deactivate *make ineffective* deactivated deactivating
DKTVTR deactivator *make ineffective*
DKTWRK ductwork *tubes*
DKTYL ductule *small duct*
DKWC adequacy *sufficiency* adequacies
DKWD duckweed *plant*
DKWK duckwalk *squatting*
DKWRK ductwork *tubes*
DKWRKR dockworker *longshoreman*
DKWS adequacy *sufficiency* adequacies
DKWT adequate *sufficient*
DKWTL adequately *sufficiently*
DKWTNS adequateness *sufficiency*
DKYDRM docudrama *theater*
DKYMNL documental *factual*
DKYMNR documentary

factual documentaries
DKYMNR documenter *reporter*
DKYMNT document *(n) writing (v) provide facts*
DKYMNTL documental *factual*
DKYMNTR documentary *factual documentaries*
DKYMNTR documenter *reporter*
DKYMNTSHN documentation *facts*
DKYMNTSHNL documentational *facts*
DKYPL decuple *groups of 10*
DKYR duckier *happier*
DKYRD dockyard *shipyard*
DKYST duckiest *happiest*
DL addle *spoil* addled addling
DL aedile *official*
DL at all *none, never*
DL audile *sound*
DL dahlia *flower*
DL daily *every day* dailies
DL dal (or) dahl *food*
DL dale *valley*
DL Dalí *artist*
DL dally *play* dallied dallying dallies
DL deal *trade, give cards* dealt dealing
DL delay *postpone*
DL dele *remove* deled deleing
DL Delhi *city*
DL deli *eatery* delis
DL dell *wooded valley*
DL dhole *animal*
DL dial *(n) numbered face (v) telephone* dialed (or) dialled dialing (or) dialling
DL dill *herb*
DL dilly *remarkable* dillies
DL doily *lace* doilies
DL dole *(v) distribute* doled doling
DL dole *(n) welfare*
DL doll *toy*
DL dolly *(v) move a wheeled platform* dollied dollying

dollies
DL dolly *(n) doll, instrument, wheeled platform* dollies
DL dual *two*
DL duel *combat* dueled (or) duelled dueling (or) duelling
DL dull *(adj) blunt, cloudy, stupid* dully *(adv)*
DL duly *properly*
DL ideal *(n) model, (adj) perfect* ideally *(adv)*
DL idle *(v) move slowly* idled idling
DL idle *(adj) inactive* idler idlest
DL idly *(adv) inactively*
DL idol *false god, ideal*
DL idyll *tale*
DL it'll *(contr) it will, it shall*
DL Italy *country*
DL oddly *unusual*
DL utile *useful* (Br) utilisable
DLB ad lib *(adv) as desired*
DLB ad-lib *(v, adj) improvise* ad-libbed ad-libbing
DLB Dolby *(trademark) stereo*
DLBDM ad libitum *as desired*
DLBRDV deliberative *consideration*
DLBRDVL deliberatively *consideration*
DLBRDVNS deliberativeness *consideration*
DLBRR day laborer *worker* (Br) day labourer
DLBRSHN deliberation *consideration*
DLBRT deliberate *voluntary* deliberated deliberating
DLBRTL deliberately *voluntarily*
DLBRTNS deliberateness *voluntary*
DLBRTV deliberative *consideration*
DLBRTVL deliberatively *consideration*
DLBRTVNS deliberativeness

consideration
DLBTM ad libitum *as desired*
DLCH dolce *music*
DLD delude *deceive* deluded deluding
DLD dildo *(vulgar) sex device* dildos
DLD duality *two* dualities
DLDBL dilatable *expand*
DLDD delighted *elated*
DLDD dilated *expanded*
DLDDL delightedly *elated*
DLDDNS delightedness *elated*
DLDK autolytic *self-destructive*
DLDKSHN delayed-action *postponed*
DLDL dillydally *dawdle*
DLDR adulator *adorer*
DLDR adultery *extramarital sex* adulteries
DLDR day letter *telegram*
DLDR deluder *deceiver*
DLDR dilator *expander*
DLDR diluter (or) dilutor *thinner*
DLDR idolater (or) idolator *worship*
DLDRDR adulterator *mixer*
DLDRMZ doldrums *inactivity*
DLDRNT adulterant *impurity*
DLDRR adulterer *extramarital sex (m)*
DLDRSHN adulteration *impurity*
DLDRSL adulterously *extramarital sex*
DLDRT adulterate *make impure* adulterated adulterating
DLDRTR adulterator *mixer*
DLDSH doltish *stupid*
DLDV dilative *expanded*
DLDV dilutive *thin, weaken*
DLF delft *ceramic ware*
DLFK delphic *(often capitalized) hidden*
DLFKL delphically *hidden*
DLFL doleful *(adj) sad*

dolefully (adv)
DLFLNS dolefulness *sadness*
DLFN dolphin *animal*
DLFNM delphinium *plant*
DLFNYM delphinium *plant*
DLFSH dealfish *fish*
DLFT delft *ceramic ware*
DLG audiology *sound*
DLG dialogue *discuss*
  dialogued dialoguing
DLG etiology *cause*
  etiologies
DLG ideologue *theorist*
DLG ideology *concept*
  ideologies
DLGBL delegable *assigned*
DLGC delegacy *board*
  delegacies
DLGDR delegator *assign*
DLGS delegacy *board*
  delegacies
DLGSHN delegation
  representatives
DLGT delegate *(v) assign*
  delegated delegating
DLGT delegate *(n)*
  representative
DLGT delegatee
  representative
DLGTR delegator *assign*
DLHS dollhouse *toy house*
DLJ audiology *sound*
DLJ deluge *flood* deluged
  deluging
DLJ etiology *cause* etiologies
DLJ ideology *concept*
  ideologies
DLJK etiologic *cause*
DLJKL ideological (adj)
  concept ideologically (adv)
DLJNS diligence *care*
DLJNT diligent *careful*
DLJNTL diligently *carefully*
DLJNTS diligence *care*
DLJST audiologist *sound*
DLJST etiologist *cause*
DLJST ideologist *concept*
DLJZ ideologize *interpret*
  ideologized ideologizing
DLK delict *illegal*
DLK dialect *speech*
DLK idyllic *artistic*

DLKC delicacy *food*
  delicacies
DLKDBL delectable (adj)
  pleasing delectably (adv)
DLKDBLD delectability
  pleasure delectabilities
DLKDBLT delectability
  pleasure delectabilities
DLKDK dialectic *logic*
DLKL idyllically *artistic*
DLKLZ delocalize *position*
  change delocalized
  delocalizing
  (Br) delocalise
DLKLZSHN delocalization
  position
  (Br) delocalisation
DLKR Delacroix *artist*
DLKS delicacy *food*
  delicacies
DLKS deluxe *superior*
DLKT delicate *fragile*
DLKT delict *illegal*
DLKT dialect *speech*
DLKTBL delectable (adj)
  pleasing delectably (adv)
DLKTBLD delectability
  pleasure delectabilities
DLKTBLT delectability
  pleasure delectabilities
DLKTK dialectic *logic*
DLKTL delicately *fragile*
DLKTRK dielectric *current*
DLKTSHN delectation
  delight
DLKTSHN dialectician *logic,*
  speech
DLKTSN delicatessen *food*
  store
DLKW Delacroix *artist*
DLKWS deliquesce *melt*
  deliquesced deliquescing
DLKWSNS deliquescence
  melting, branching
DLKWSNT deliquescent
  melting, branching
DLKWSNTS deliquescence
  melting, branching
DLL daylily *flower* daylilies
DLL Delilah *Samson's*
  betrayer
DLLM Dalai Lama *spiritual*

  leader
DLM bdellium *resin*
DLM dilemma *choice*
DLM dolma *food* dolmas (or)
  dolmades
DLMDK dalmatic *robe*
DLMDK dilemmatic *choice*
DLMDK dolomitic *mineral*
DLMDR delimiter *fix*
  boundaries
DLMDZ dolmades (pl) *food*
  dolma
DLMDZSHN dolomitization
  mineral
DLMN dolman *sleeve*
DLMN dolmen *tomb*
DLMNSHN delamination
  layers
DLMNT delaminate *layers*
DLMSHN Dalmatian *dog*
DLMT delimit *fix boundaries*
DLMT dolomite *mineral*
DLMTHZ dolmades (pl) *food*
  dolma
DLMTK dalmatic *robe*
DLMTK dilemmatic *choice*
DLMTK dolomitic *mineral*
DLMTR delimiter *fix*
  boundaries
DLMTSHN delimitation *fix*
  boundaries
DLMTZSHN dolomitization
  mineral
DLN dealing *trading, giving*
  cards
DLNDR delineator *describer*
DLNDV delineative
  descriptive
DLNG daylong *all day*
DLNG dealing *trading,*
  giving cards
DLNGKWNC delinquency
  illegal, overdue
  delinquencies
DLNGKWNS delinquency
  illegal, overdue
  delinquencies
DLNGKWNT delinquent
  illegal, overdue
DLNGKWNTC delinquency
  illegal, overdue
  delinquencies

Letters aren't doubled for single sounds: to find **alley** use **L** not **LL**. Use **Y** and **W** as hard sounds only: to find **yellow** use **YL**. (Br)=British spelling or usage. * See dictionary.

DLNGKWNTL delinquently *illegal, overdue*
DLNGKWNTS delinquency *illegal, overdue* delinquencies
DLNGQNC delinquency *illegal, overdue* delinquencies
DLNGQNS delinquency *illegal, overdue* delinquencies
DLNGQNT delinquent *illegal, overdue*
DLNGQNTC delinquency *illegal, overdue* delinquencies
DLNGQNTL delinquently *illegal, overdue*
DLNGQNTS delinquency *illegal, overdue* delinquencies
DLNGS dealings *transactions or relations*
DLNKWNC delinquency *illegal, overdue* delinquencies
DLNKWNS delinquency *illegal, overdue* delinquencies
DLNKWNT delinquent *illegal, overdue*
DLNKWNTC delinquency *illegal, overdue* delinquencies
DLNKWNTL delinquently *illegal, overdue*
DLNKWNTS delinquency *illegal, overdue* delinquencies
DLNQNC delinquency *illegal, overdue* delinquencies
DLNQNS delinquency *illegal, overdue* delinquencies
DLNQNT delinquent *illegal, overdue*
DLNQNTC delinquency *illegal, overdue* delinquencies
DLNQNTL delinquently *illegal, overdue*

DLNQNTS delinquency *illegal, overdue* delinquencies
DLNS dalliance *play*
DLNS dealings *transactions or relations*
DLNS dullness (or) dulness *blunt*
DLNS idleness *inactive*
DLNSHN delineation *description*
DLNT delineate *describe* delineated delineating
DLNTR delineator *describer*
DLNTS dalliance *play*
DLNTV delineative *descriptive*
DLNYDR delineator *describer*
DLNYDV delineative *descriptive*
DLNYSHN delineation *description*
DLNYT delineate *describe* delineated delineating
DLNYTR delineator *describer*
DLNYTV delineative *descriptive*
DLP dewlap *fold*
DLP doll up *dress up*
DLP dollop *portion*
DLPDDD dilapidated *ruined*
DLPDSHN dilapidation *ruin*
DLPDT dilapidate *ruin* dilapidated dilapidating
DLPDTD dilapidated *ruined*
DLPRPS dual-purpose *two uses*
DLQ Delacroix *artist*
DLQS deliquesce *melt* deliquesced deliquescing
DLQSNS deliquescence *melting, branching*
DLQSNT deliquescent *melting, branching*
DLQSNTS deliquescence *melting, branching*
DLR dallier *player*
DLR dealer *trader, giver of cards*
DLR delayer *postponer*
DLR dialer *device, person*

DLR dollar *money*
DLR dolor *sorrow* (Br) dolour
DLR dueler (or) dueller *fighter*
DLR idler *inactive*
DLRD dullard *stupid one*
DLRM delirium *madness*
DLRMTRMNS delirium tremens *alcoholic tremors*
DLRMTRMNZ delirium tremens *alcoholic tremors*
DLRNGGLG otolaryngology *ear, nose and throat*
DLRNGGLJ otolaryngology *ear, nose and throat*
DLRNGGLJST otolaryngologist *ear, nose and throat*
DLRNGLG otolaryngology *ear, nose and throat*
DLRNGLJ otolaryngology *ear, nose and throat*
DLRNGLJKL otolaryngological *ear, nose and throat*
DLRNGLJST otolaryngologist *ear, nose and throat*
DLRS delirious *mad*
DLRS dolorous *sad* (Br) dolourous
DLRSHP dealership *point of sale*
DLRSL deliriously *madly*
DLRSNS deliriousness *madness*
DLRYM delirium *madness*
DLRYMTRMNS delirium tremens *alcoholic tremors*
DLRYMTRMNZ delirium tremens *alcoholic tremors*
DLRYS delirious *mad*
DLRYSL deliriously *madly*
DLRYSNS deliriousness *madness*
DLS Dallas *city*
DLS delouse *remove lice* deloused delousing
DLS dulse *seaweed*
DLS utilize *use* utilized utilizing

Use letters that best describe the sounds you hear and omit the vowels. Use **S** or **K** instead of **C**: to find circle use **SRKL**. Use **J** to find joy, **JM** to find gem and **G** to find go.

(Br) utilise
DLSDK dualistic *two*
DLSDK idealistic *perfection*
DLSDKL dualistically *two*
DLSDKL idealistically
perfection
DLSH deluge *flood* deluged
deluging
DLSH dollish *pretty*
DLSH dullish *blunt*
DLSHL dollishly *prettily*
DLSHN adulation *adoration*
DLSHN deletion *removal*
DLSHN delusion *false belief*
DLSHN dilation *expansion*
DLSHN dilution *thin, weaken*
DLSHN etiolation *whiten*
DLSHNL delusional *insane*
DLSHNR delusionary *insane*
DLSHNS dollishness *beauty*
DLSHS delicious *tasty*
DLSHSL deliciously *tasty*
DLSHSNS deliciousness
tasty
DLSK odalisque *slave (f)*
DLSM dolesome *sad*
DLSMR dulcimer *music*
DLSN dal segno *music*
DLSNS adolescence *teenage*
DLSNT adolescent *(n)*
teenager (adj) immature
DLSNTL adolescently
immature
DLSNTS adolescence
teenage
DLSNY dal segno *music*
DLSR delusory *misleading*
DLSS dialysis *separation*
dialyses
DLST delist *remove name*
DLST duelist (or) duellist
fighter
DLST dulcet *sweet*
DLST idealist *perfectionist*
DLST idlest *inactive*
DLSTK dualistic *two*
DLSTK idealistic *perfection*
DLSTKL dualistically *two*
DLSTKL idealistically
perfection
DLSV delusive *misleading*
DLSVL dullsville *boredom*

DLT adulate *adore* adulated
adulating
DLT adult *mature*
DLT daylight *time*
DLT dealt *(v-past) deal*
DLT delete *erase* deleted
deleting
DLT delight *elate*
DLT delta *river, Greek letter*
DLT dilate *expand* dilated
dilating
DLT dilute *thin, weaken*
diluted diluting
DLT dole out *distribute*
doled out doling out
DLT dolt *stupid one*
DLT duality *two* dualities
DLT etiolate *whiten* etiolated
etiolating
DLTBL dilatable *expand*
DLTD adulthood *maturity*
DLTD delighted *elated*
DLTD deltoid *triangle, muscle*
DLTD deltoidei (pl)
triangular deltoideus
DLTD dilated *expanded*
DLTDL delightedly *elated*
DLTDNS delightedness
elated
DLTDS deltoideus *triangular*
deltoidei
DLTDYS deltoideus
triangular deltoidei
DLTFL delightful (adj)
pleasing delightfully (adv)
DLTFNS delightfulness
pleasing
DLTH Duluth *city*
DLTH otolith *ear*
DLTHD adulthood *maturity*
DLTHK otolithic *ear*
DLTK autolytic *self-
destructive*
DLTK deltaic *triangular*
DLTL adultly *maturely*
DLTMDR dilatometer
expansion
DLTMTR dilatometer
expansion
DLTMTR dilatometry
expansion
DLTMTRK dilatometric

expansion
DLTN dial tone *telephone*
DLTNC dilatancy *sticky*
DLTNS adultness *maturity*
DLTNS dilatancy *sticky*
DLTNS diluteness *thin,
weaken*
DLTNT dilatant *sticky*
DLTNT dilettante *dabbler*
dilettantes (or) dilettanti
DLTNTC dilatancy *sticky*
DLTNTS dilatancy *sticky*
DLTNTSH dilettantish *dabble*
DLTNTZM dilettantism
dabble
DLTR adulator *adorer*
DLTR adulatory *adoring*
DLTR adultery *extramarital
sex* adulteries
DLTR day letter *telegram*
DLTR dilator *expander*
DLTR dilatory *tardy*
DLTR diluter (or) dilutor
thinner
DLTR idolater (or) idolator
worship
DLTR idolatry *worship*
idolatries
DLTRDR adulterator *mixer*
DLTRN adulterine *illegal*
DLTRNT adulterant *impurity*
DLTRR adulterer
extramarital sex (m)
DLTRS adulteress
extramarital sex (f)
adulteresses
DLTRS adulterous
extramarital sex
DLTRS deleterious *hurtful*
DLTRS idolatrous *pagan*
DLTRSHN adulteration
impurity
DLTRSL adulterously
extramarital sex
DLTRSL idolatrously *pagan*
DLTRSNS idolatrousness
pagan
DLTRT adulterate *make
impure* adulterated
adulterating
DLTRTR adulterator *mixer*
DLTRYS deleterious *hurtful*

Letters aren't doubled for single sounds: to find alley use **L** not **LL**. Use **Y** and **W** as hard
sounds only: to find yellow use **YL**. (Br)=British spelling or usage. * See dictionary.

DLTS daylights *wits*
DLTSH doltish *stupid*
DLTSHL doltishly *stupidly*
DLTSHN dilatation *expansion*
DLTSHNL dilatational *expansion*
DLTSHNS doltishness *stupidity*
DLTV dilative *expanded*
DLTV dilutive *thin, weaken*
DLTWNG delta wing *airplane*
DLTWV delta wave *brain*
DLTYK deltaic *triangular*
DLV delve *dig* delved delving
DLVL diluvial (or) diluvian *flood*
DLVN diluvian (or) diluvial *flood*
DLVR deliver *hand over, set free, produce**
DLVR delivery *package, birth, speech** deliveries
DLVR delver *digger*
DLVRBL deliverable *hand over, set free, produce**
DLVRBLD deliverability *hand over, set free, produce**
DLVRBLT deliverability *hand over, set free, produce**
DLVRNS deliverance *hand over, set free, produce**
DLVRNTS deliverance *hand over, set free, produce**
DLVRR deliverer *hand over, set free, produce**
DLVS edelweiss *herb*
DLVYL diluvial (or) diluvian *flood*
DLVYN diluvian (or) diluvial *flood*
DLWR Delaware *US State*
DLX deluxe *superior*
DLY dahlia *flower*
DLYJ deluge *flood* deluged deluging
DLYM bdellium *resin*
DLYNS dalliance *play*
DLYNTS dalliance *play*
DLYR dallier *player*
DLYR delayer *postponer*
DLYSH deluge *flood* deluged

deluging
DLYZH deluge *flood* deluged deluging
DLZ autolyze *self-destruct* autolyzed autolyzing (Br) autolyse
DLZ delouse *remove lice* deloused delousing
DLZ dialyze *separate* dialyzed dialyzing
DLZ idealize *perfect* idealized idealizing (Br) idealise
DLZ idolize *worship* idolized idolizing
DLZ oodles *many*
DLZ utilize *use* utilized utilizing (Br) utilise
DLZBL utilizable *useful* (Br) utilisable
DLZH deluge *flood* deluged deluging
DLZHN delusion *false belief*
DLZHNL delusional *insane*
DLZHNR delusionary *insane*
DLZM dualism *two*
DLZM idealism *perfection*
DLZR idealizer *perfect* (Br) idealiser
DLZR idolizer *worship*
DLZR utilizer *user* (Br) utiliser
DLZSHN idealization *perfection* (Br) idealisation
DLZSHN idolization *worship*
DLZSHN utilization *use* (Br) utilisation
DLZVL dullsville *boredom*
DM atom *particle*
DM autumn *Fall season*
DM daimyo *baron* daimyo (or) daimyos
DM dam *block* dammed damming
DM dame *woman*
DM damn *condemn* damned damning
DM deem *consider*
DM demo *demonstration* demos

DM dim *(v) darken, reduce* dimmed dimming
DM dim *(adj) dark, dull* dimmer dimmest
DM dime *money*
DM dome *round top* domed doming
DM doom *(n) fate, ruin (v) condemn*
DM Dumas *writer*
DM dumb *silent, stupid*
DM dummy *(n) puppet, mock-up (Br) pacifier (adj) artificial* dummies
DM dummy *(v) mock-up* dummied dummying dummies
DM edema *swelling* (Br) oedema
DM etyma *(pl) word* etymon
DM idiom *expression*
DM item *article*
DM odeum *theater* odea
DM odium *hatred*
DM oidium *fungus* oidia
DMBB dim bulb *dimwit*
DMBL automobile *car*
DMBL dumbbell *stupid one, weight*
DMBLB dim bulb *dimwit*
DMBLZ demobilize *disband* demobilized demobilizing (Br) demobilise
DMBLZSHN demobilization *disband* (Br) demobilisation
DMBM atom bomb *nuclear weapon*
DMBRDV adumbrative *suggestive*
DMBRDVL adumbratively *suggestively*
DMBRSHN adumbration *suggestion*
DMBRT adumbrate *suggest* adumbrated adumbrating
DMBRTV adumbrative *suggestive*
DMBRTVL adumbratively *suggestively*
DMCN damascene *(v) ornament* damascened

Use letters that best describe the sounds you hear and omit the vowels. Use **S** or **K** instead of **C**: to find circle use **SRKL**. Use **J** to find joy, **JM** to find gem and **G** to find go.

damascening
DMCN Damascene *(n) of*
Damascus
DMD damned *cursed,*
extraordinary damneder
damnedest (or)
damndest
DMD démodé *out of style*
DMD dimity *fabric* dimities
DMDD automated
mechanized
DMDDL admittedly
acknowledged
DMDJLDR demodulator
signal changer
DMDJLSHN demodulation
signal change
DMDJLT demodulate *change*
signal demodulated
demodulating
DMDK automatic *mechanical*
DMDK idiomatic *expression*
DMDKL automatically
mechanically
DMDKL idiomatically
expression
DMDLDR demodulator
signal changer
DMDLSHN demodulation
signal change
DMDLT demodulate *change*
signal demodulated
demodulating
DMDM dum-dum *idiot*
DMDM dumdum *bullet*
DMDN dumb down *make*
easier
DMDNS admittance
entrance
DMDNTS admittance
entrance
DMDR audiometer *sound*
DMDR diameter *circle*
DMDR dimeter *verse*
DMDR odometer *mileage*
DMDS edematous *swollen*
(Br) oedematous
DMDST damnedest (or)
damndest *funniest*
DMDV automotive *car*
DMDYLDR demodulator
signal changer

DMDYLSHN demodulation
signal change
DMDYLT demodulate
change signal
demodulated
demodulating
DMDYLTR demodulator
signal changer
DMFL doomful (adj) *ominous*
doomfully (adv)
DMFNDD dumbfounded
(or) dumfounded *puzzled*
DMFSZ de-emphasize *play*
down de-emphasized de-
emphasizing
(Br) de-emphasise
DMGD demigod *hero*
DMGDS demigoddess
heroine
DMGG demagogue (or)
demagog *false promises*
DMGG demagogy *false*
promises
DMGGK demagogic *false*
promises
DMGGR demagoguery *false*
promises
DMGGYR demagoguery
false promises
DMGJ demagogy *false*
promises
DMGJK demagogic *false*
promises
DMGNTZ demagnetize
remove magnet
demagnetized
demagnetizing
(Br) demagnetise
DMGNTZR demagnetizer
remove magnet
(Br) demagnetiser
DMGNTZSHN
demagnetization *remove*
magnet
(Br) demagnetisation
DMGRF demography
statistics
DMGRFK demographic
statistics
DMGRFKL demographically
statistics
DMGRFKS demographics

statistics
DMGRFR demographer
statistics
DMGRFX demographics
statistics
DMGTS demigoddess
heroine
DMJ damage *injure*
damaged damaging
DMJBLD damageability
injury
DMJBLT damageability
injury
DMJLDR demodulator
signal changer
DMJLSHN demodulation
signal change
DMJLT demodulate *change*
signal demodulated
demodulating
DMJLTR demodulator *signal*
changer
DMJN damaging *hurtful*
DMJN demijohn *bottle*
DMJNG damaging *hurtful*
DMJR damager *injury*
DMKF dummkopf *stupid one*
DMKN dumbcane *plant*
DMKPF dummkopf *stupid*
one
DMKR automaker *car*
producer
DMKRC democracy *social*
equality democracies
DMKRDK democratic *social*
equality
DMKRDKL democratically
social equality
DMKRDZSHN
democratization *social*
equality
DMKRS democracy *social*
equality democracies
DMKRT democrat *social*
equality
DMKRTK democratic *social*
equality
DMKRTKL democratically
social equality
DMKRTZ democratize *make*
social equality
democratized

Letters aren't doubled for single sounds: to find alley use **L** not **LL**. Use **Y** and **W** as hard
sounds only: to find yellow use **YL**. (Br)=British spelling or usage. * See dictionary.

democratizing

DMKRTZR democratizer
make social equality

DMKRTZSHN
democratization *social
equality*

DMKS admix *mix*

DMKSCHR admixture *mix*

DMKSTR admixture *mix*

DML dumbly *stupid, silent*

DMLDRZ demilitarize *no
military* demilitarized
demilitarizing
(Br) demilitarise

DMLG etymology *word
source* etymologies

DMLJ etymology *word
source* etymologies

DMLJKL etymological (adj)
word source
etymologically (adv)

DMLJST etymologist *word
source*

DMLJZ etymologize *word
source* etymologized
etymologizing
(Br) etomologise

DMLSH demolish *destroy*
demolished demolishing

DMLSHD demolished
destroyed

DMLSHN demolition
destruction

DMLSHNST demolitionist
explosives

DMLSHR demolisher
destroyer

DMLSHT demolished
destroyed

DMLSNT demulcent
soothing

DMLTRZ demilitarize *no
military* demilitarized
demilitarizing
(Br) demilitarise

DMLTRZSHN
demilitarization *no
military*
(Br) demilitarisation

DMMND demimonde
mistress

DMMNDN demimondaine

mistress

DMN adman *advertising*
admen

DMN autoimmune *disease-
fighting*

DMN damning *ruinous*

DMN demand *ask*

DMN demean *lower*
demeaned demeaning

DMN demesne *domain*

DMN demon (or) daemon
devil

DMN Des Moines *city*

DMN diamond *gem, shape,
field*

DMN domain *realm*

DMN domino *gamepiece*
dominoes (or) dominos

DMN etymon *word* etyma

DMN ottoman *footstool*

DMN Ottoman *Empire*

DMNBL damnable (adj)
detestable damnably (adv)

DMNBLNS damnableness
detestable

DMNC adamancy *obstinacy*
adamance

DMNCH dementia *insanity*

DMNCHN dimension *size,
aspect, math*

DMNCHNL dimensional
(adj) *size, aspect, math*
dimensionally (adv)

DMNCHNLD dimensionality
size, aspect, math

DMNCHNLS dimensionless
size, aspect, math

DMNCHNLT dimensionality
size, aspect, math

DMND demand *ask*

DMND demented *insane*

DMND diamond *gem, shape,
field*

DMNDBL demandable
request

DMNDL dementedly *insane*

DMNDN demanding
exacting

DMNDNG demanding
exacting

DMNDNS dementedness
insanity

DMNDPL demand-pull
economics

DMNDR demander *asker*

DMNDR dominator
controller

DMNDV diminutive (adj)
small (n) word

DMNDVNS diminutiveness
small

DMNG damning *ruinous*

DMNK demoniac *possessed
by demons*

DMNK demonic *fiendish*

DMNK dominique *fowl*

DMNKL demoniacally
possessed by demons

DMNKL demonically
fiendish

DMNKL dominical *Lord*

DMNKN Dominican *friar*

DMNKNRPBKL Dominican
Republic *country*

DMNLG demonology *evil
spirits*

DMNLJ demonology *evil
spirits*

DMNLJST demonologist
evil spirits

DMNND diminuendo *music*

DMNNS dominance *control*

DMNNT dominant *supreme*

DMNNTS dominance *control*

DMNR domineer *oppress*

DMNRLZ demineralize
remove or lose minerals
demineralized
demineralizing

DMNRLZSHN
demineralization *remove
or lose minerals*

DMNRN domineering
oppressing

DMNRNG domineering
oppressing

DMNS adamance *obstinacy*
adamancy

DMNS dimness *dullness,
darkness*

DMNSDR administer
manage, dispense
administered
administering

Use letters that best describe the sounds you hear and omit the vowels. Use **S** or **K** instead of **C**: to find circle use **SRKL**. Use **J** to find joy, **JM** to find gem and **G** to find go.

DMNSH admonish *reprove*
DMNSH dementia *insanity*
DMNSH diminish *decrease*
DMNSHBL diminishable
decrease
DMNSHL demential
madness
DMNSHMNT
admonishment *reproof*
DMNSHMNT diminishment
decrease
DMNSHN admonition
reproof
DMNSHN damnation *curse*
DMNSHN dimension *size,
aspect, math*
DMNSHN diminution
decrease
DMNSHN domination *power*
DMNSHNGL admonishingly
reprove
DMNSHNL dimensional
(adj) *size, aspect, math*
dimensionally (adv)
DMNSHNLD dimensionality
size, aspect, math
DMNSHNLS dimensionless
size, aspect, math
DMNSHNLT dimensionality
size, aspect, math
DMNSHR admonisher
reprover
DMNSTR administer
manage, dispense
administered
administering
DMNSTRBL administrable
manageable
DMNSTRBL demonstrable
evident
DMNSTRDR administrator
manager
DMNSTRDR demonstrator
show, protest
DMNSTRDV administrative
management
DMNSTRDV demonstrative
display
DMNSTRDVL
administratively *executive*
DMNSTRNT administrant
manager

DMNSTRSHN
administration
management
DMNSTRSHN
demonstration *show,
protest*
DMNSTRT administrate
manage administrated
administrating
DMNSTRT demonstrate
show, protest
demonstrated
demonstrating
DMNSTRTR administrator
manager
DMNSTRTR demonstrator
show, protest
DMNSTRTRCZ
administratrices (pl)
manager (f) administratrix
DMNSTRTRKS
administratrix *manager (f)*
administratrices
DMNSTRTRSZ
administratrices (pl)
manager (f) administratrix
DMNSTRTRX administratrix
manager (f)
administratrices
DMNSTRTV administrative
management
DMNSTRTV demonstrative
display
DMNSTRTVL
administratively *executive*
DMNT adamant *hard*
DMNT autoimmunity *disease-
fighting*
DMNT demount *get down*
DMNT diamanté *decoration*
DMNT dominate *exert power*
dominated dominating
DMNT oddment *remnant,
freak*
DMNTBL demountable *get
down*
DMNTC adamancy
obstinacy adamance
DMNTD demented *insane*
DMNTDL dementedly
insane
DMNTDNS dementedness

insanity
DMNTL adamantly
obstinately
DMNTN adamantine *hard*
DMNTN Edmonton *city*
DMNTR admonitory
warning
DMNTR damnatory *curse*
DMNTR dominator *controller*
DMNTRCZ dominatrices
(pl) *controller (f)*
dominatrix
DMNTRKS dominatrix
controller (f) dominatrices
DMNTRL admonitorily
warning
DMNTRSZ dominatrices (pl)
controller (f) dominatrix
DMNTRX dominatrix
controller (f) dominatrices
DMNTS adamance *obstinacy*
adamancy
DMNTV diminutive *(adj)
small (n) word*
DMNTVNS diminutiveness
small
DMNTZ demonetize *money*
demonetized
demonetizing
DMNTZSHN
demonetization *money*
DMNWND diminuendo
music
DMNYDV diminutive *(adj)
small (n) word*
DMNYDVL diminutively
small
DMNYDVNS diminutiveness
small
DMNYK demoniac *possessed
by demons*
DMNYKL demoniacally
possessed by demons
DMNYN dominion *domain*
DMNYND diminuendo
music
DMNYSHN diminution
decrease
DMNYTV diminutive *(adj)
small (n) word*
DMNYTVL diminutively
small

Letters aren't doubled for single sounds: to find alley use **L** not **LL**. Use **Y** and **W** as hard
sounds only: to find yellow use **YL**. (Br)=British spelling or usage. * See dictionary.

DMNYTVNS diminutiveness *small*

DMNYWND diminuendo *music*

DMNZ demonize *make evil* demonized demonizing

DMNZ Des Moines *city*

DMP damp *(adj, n) moist (v) diminish, wet*

DMP dummy up *say nothing*

DMP dump *(v) dispose of (n) place of disposal*

DMP dumpy *short and fat* dumpier dumpiest

DMPL damply *moisture*

DMPL dimple *dent* dimpled dimpling

DMPL dimply *indented*

DMPL dumpily *short and fat*

DMPLN dumpling *food*

DMPLNG dumpling *food*

DMPN dampen *diminish, wet*

DMPN dumping *selling cheap*

DMPNG dumping *selling cheap*

DMPNR dampener *diminish, wet*

DMPNS dampness *moisture*

DMPNS dumpiness *short and fat*

DMPR damper *valve, block, shock absorber(Br) bread*

DMPR dumper *disposer*

DMPR dumpier *short and fat*

DMPSH dampish *moist*

DMPSH dumpish *sad*

DMPST dumpiest *short and fat*

DMPYR dumpier *short and fat*

DMPYST dumpiest *short and fat*

DMR admire *regard highly* admired admiring

DMR damar (or) dammar *resin*

DMR daymare *nightmare*

DMR demur *protest* demurred demurring

DMR demure *coy*

DMR dimmer *(adj) dull, dark*

(n) light switch

DMRBL admirable (adj) *worthy of praise* admirably (adv)

DMRBLD admirability *worthy of praise*

DMRBLNS admirableness *worthy of praise*

DMRBLT admirability *worthy of praise*

DMRFK idiomorphic *shape*

DMRFZM automorphism *similarity*

DMRJ demiurge *deity*

DMRJ demurrage *detention fee*

DMRJK demiurgic *deity*

DMRKDD demarcated *separate, limit*

DMRKSHN demarcation *separate, limit*

DMRKT demarcate *separate, limit* demarcated demarcating

DMRKTD demarcated *separate, limit*

DMRL admiral *rank*

DMRL Demerol *(trademark) drug*

DMRL demurely *coyly*

DMRL demurral *protest*

DMRLT admiralty *authority*

DMRLZ demoralize *weaken morale* demoralized demoralizing *(Br)* demoralise

DMRLZNGL demoralizingly *weaken morale* *(Br)* demoralisingly

DMRLZNL demoralizingly *weaken morale* *(Br)* demoralisingly

DMRLZR demoralizer *weaken morale* *(Br)* demoraliser

DMRLZSHN demoralization *weaken morale*

DMRN demeanor *bearing* *(Br)* demeanour

DMRNGL admiringly *with high regard*

DMRNL admiringly *with*

high regard

DMRNS demureness *coyness*

DMRR admirer *respecter*

DMRR demurrer *protester*

DMRSH démarche (or) demarche *maneuver*

DMRSHN admiration *high regard*

DMRT demerit *fault*

DMS admass *(Br) advertising*

DMS Dumas *writer*

DMSBL admissible *allowed*

DMSBLD admissibility *permission*

DMSBLT admissibility *permission*

DMSDF demystify *remove mystery* demystified demystifying

DMSDFKSHN demystification *remove mystery*

DMSDK domestic *(adj) tame, native (n) maid*

DMSHN admission *entrance, allowance*

DMSHN automation *mechanization*

DMSHN demission *resignation*

DMSHN demotion *lower rank*

DMSK damask *fabric*

DMSKS Damascus *city*

DMSL damsel *lady*

DMSL domicile *home* domiciled domiciling

DMSLFL damselfly *insect* damselflies

DMSLFSH damselfish *fish*

DMSM dim sum *food*

DMSN damascene *(v) ornament* damascened damascening

DMSN Damascene *(n) of Damascus*

DMSPL Adam's apple *throat*

DMSR doomsayer *foreteller*

DMST dimmest *dull, dark*

DMSTF demystify *remove*

Use letters that best describe the sounds you hear and omit the vowels. Use **S** or **K** instead of **C**: to find circle use **SRKL**. Use **J** to find joy, **JM** to find gem and **G** to find go.

mystery demystified demystifying

DMSTFKSHN demystification *remove mystery*

DMSTK domestic *(adj)* tame, *native (n)* maid

DMSTKSHN domestication *taming*

DMSTKT domesticate *tame* domesticated domesticating

DMSTR dime store *(n) discount store*

DMSTR dime-store *(adj) cheap*

DMSTRK dumbstruck *silence*

DMSTSD domesticity *tamed* domesticities

DMSTST domesticity *tamed* domesticities

DMSV admissive *entrance, allowance*

DMSYR doomsayer *foreteller*

DMT adamant *hard*

DMT admit *allow* admitted admitting

DMT Automat *(trademark) cafeteria*

DMT automate *mechanize* automated automating

DMT demote *lower rank* demoted demoting

DMT demount *get down*

DMT dimity *fabric* dimities

DMT dimout *darken*

DMTBL demountable *get down*

DMTD automated *mechanized*

DMTDL admittedly *acknowledged*

DMTHL dimethyl *chemical*

DMTHLJZ demythologize *remove myth* demythologizer demythologizing

DMTHLJZR demythologizer *remove myth*

DMTK automatic *mechanical*

DMTK idiomatic *expression*

DMTKL automatically *mechanically*

DMTKL idiomatically *expression*

DMTL adamantly *obstinately*

DMTNS admittance *entrance*

DMTNTS admittance *entrance*

DMTR audiometer *sound*

DMTR audiometry *sound*

DMTR diameter *circle*

DMTR dimeter *verse*

DMTR odometer *distance*

DMTRK audiometric *sound*

DMTRK diametric (or) diametrical *center line, opposite* diametrically (adv)

DMTRKL diametrical (or) diametric (adj) *center line, opposite* diametrically (adv)

DMTRLZ dematerialize *disappear* dematerialized dematerializing (Br) dematerialise

DMTRLZSHN dematerialization *disappearance* (Br) dematerialisation

DMTRYLZ dematerialize *disappear* dematerialized dematerializing (Br) dematerialise

DMTRYLZSHN dematerialization *disappearance* (Br) dematerialisation

DMTS demitasse *small cup*

DMTS edematous *swollen* (Br) oedematous

DMTV automotive *car*

DMVRT duumvirate *two rulers*

DMWDD dim-witted *foolish*

DMWDDL dim-wittedly *foolish*

DMWDDNS dim-wittedness *foolish*

DMWDR dumbwaiter *elevator*

DMWRLD demiworld *subclass*

DMWT dimwit *stupid one*

DMWTD dim-witted *foolish*

DMWTDL dim-wittedly *foolish*

DMWTDNS dim-wittedness *foolish*

DMWTR dumbwaiter *elevator*

DMWZL demoiselle *lady, damselfly, damselfish*

DMX admix *mix*

DMXCHR admixture *mix*

DMXTR admixture *mix*

DMY daimyo *baron* daimyo (or) daimyos

DMYN autoimmune *disease-fighting*

DMYNT autoimmunity *disease-fighting*

DMYP dummy up *say nothing*

DMYR demure *coy*

DMYRJ demiurge *deity*

DMYRJK demiurgic *deity*

DMYRL demurely *coyly*

DMYRNS demureness *coyness*

DMZ atomize *spray* atomized atomizing (Br) atomise

DMZ demise *death* demised demising

DMZ itemize *list* itemized itemizing (Br) itemise

DMZD doomsday *judgement day*

DMZDR doomsdayer *foreteller*

DMZDYR doomsdayer *foreteller*

DMZHR admeasure *apportion* admeasured admeasuring

DMZHRMNT admeasurement *portion*

DMZL damsel *lady*

DMZLFL damselfly *insect* damselflies

DMZLFSH damselfish *fish*

Letters aren't doubled for single sounds: to find alley use **L** not **LL**. Use **Y** and **W** as hard sounds only: to find yellow use **YL**. (Br)=British spelling or usage. * See dictionary.

DMZN damson *fruit*
DMZPL Adam's apple *throat*
DMZR atomizer *sprayer*
  (Br) atomiser
DMZSHN itemization *list*
  (Br) itemisation
DN addend *number*
DN aedine *mosquito*
DN dainty *(adj) delicate*
  daintier daintiest
DN dainty *(n) food* dainties
DN Dane *from Denmark*
DN dawn *sunrise*
DN dean *college*
DN deign *stoop, see fit*
DN den *room, hideout, Cub*
  Scouts
DN deny *disclaim* denied
  denying denies
DN didn't *(contr) did not*
DN din *noise* dinned dinning
DN dine *eat* dined dining
DN doing *action*
DN don *(n) title*
DN don *(v) put on* donned
  donning
DN doña *title (f)*
DN done *finished*
DN donee *receiver*
DN down *(adv) below (prep)*
  on, into (v) defeat (n)
  feather, play (adj) lower,
  *depressed**
DN downy *soft* downier
  downiest
DN duenna *chaperon*
DN dun *pester* dunned
  dunning
DN dune *sand hill*
DN dyeing *coloring*
DN dying *death*
DN dyne *force*
DN iodine *element*
DN outdone *bested*
DNB Danube *river*
DNBG dune buggy *vehicle*
DNBL deniable *rejection*
DNBLD deniability *rejection*
DNBLST odontoblast *dentin*
DNBLT deniability *rejection*
DNBRK donnybrook *brawl*
DNBT downbeat *music,*

  gloomy
DNCHLS dentulous *with*
  teeth
DNCHLS edentulous
  toothless
DNCHR denature *modify*
  denatured denaturing
DNCHR denture *teeth*
DNCHRLZ denaturalize
  make unnatural, deprive of
  rights denaturalized
  denaturalizing
  (Br) denaturalise
DNCHRLZSHN
  denaturalization *made*
  unnatural, deprivation of
  rights
  (Br) denaturalisation
DNCHRNT denaturant
  modifier
DNCHRSHN denaturation
  modification
DNCM ad nauseam *to excess*
DND addend *number*
DND addenda (pl) *addition*
  addendum
DND adenoid *gland*
DND dandy *(n) well-dressed*
  man, excellent thing
  dandies
DND dandy *(adj) foppish,*
  first-rate dandier dandiest
DND denude *strip* denuded
  denuding
DND duende *attraction*
DND dynode *electron*
DND identity *name* identities
DNDF dandify *make excellent*
  dandified dandifying
  dandifies
DNDFKSHN dandification
  foppish, first-rate
DNDK dunitic *rock*
DNDL adenoidal *glandular*
DNDL dandle *pet* dandled
  dandling
DNDLN dandelion *plant*
DNDLYN dandelion *plant*
DNDM addendum *addition*
  addenda
DNDMNT denudement
  stripping

DNDR dander *anger*
DNDR dandier *foppish, first-*
  rate
DNDRD dendroid *branching*
DNDRDK dendritic *branch*
DNDRF dandruff *(n) scalp*
DNDRF dandruffy *(adj) flaky*
DNDRF downdraft *air*
DNDRFT downdraft *air*
DNDRHD dunderhead
  stupid one
DNDRLG dendrology *trees*
DNDRLJ dendrology *trees*
DNDRLJKL dendrological
  trees
DNDRLJST dendrologist
  trees
DNDRT dendrite *branch*
DNDRTH down-to-earth
  practical
DNDRTK dendritic *branch*
DNDS adenitis *gland*
  inflammation
DNDSH dandyish *(adj)*
  foppish, first-rate
DNDSHN denudation
  stripping
DNDST dandiest *foppish,*
  first-rate
DNDSTRLZ deindustrialize
  remove industry
  deindustrialized
  deindustrializing
  (Br) deinstitutionalisation
DNDSTRLZSHN
  deindustrialization *remove*
  industry
  (Br) deinstitutionalisation
DNDSTRYLZ deindustrialize
  remove industry
  deindustrialized
  deindustrializing
  (Br) deinstitutionalisation
DNDSTRYLZSHN
  deindustrialization *remove*
  industry
  (Br) deinstitutionalisation
DNDTHWR down-to-the-
  wire (adj) *suspenseful*
DNDYR dandier *foppish,*
  first-rate
DNDYSH dandyish *(adj)*

Use letters that best describe the sounds you hear and omit the vowels. Use **S** or **K** instead of **C**: to find circle use **SRKL**. Use **J** to find joy, **JM** to find gem and **G** to find go.

foppish, first-rate
DNDYST dandiest *foppish, first-rate*
DNF identify *name* identified identifying identifies
DNFBL identifiable (adj) *name* identifiably (adv)
DNFKSHN identification *name*
DNFL downfall *loss of power*
DNFNDM ad infinitum *forever*
DNFNTM ad infinitum *forever*
DNFR identifier *name*
DNFRS dentifrice *toothpaste*
DNFYBL identifiable (adj) *name* identifiably (adv)
DNFYR identifier *name*
DNG dengue *fever*
DNG ding *noise, dent*
DNG dinghy *small boat* dinghies
DNG dingo *dog* dingoes
DNG dingy *dirty* dingier dingiest
DNG doing *action*
DNG dong *(vulgar) penis*
DNG dung *feces*
DNG dyeing *coloring*
DNG dying *death*
DNG eating *food*
DNG outing *trip, disclosure*
DNGBT dingbat *nitwit*
DNGDNG dingdong *sound*
DNGFVR dengue fever *disease*
DNGG dengue *fever*
DNGG dingo *dog* dingoes
DNGGFVR dengue fever *disease*
DNGGL dangle *hang* dangled dangling
DNGGL dingle *valley*
DNGGLBR dingleberry *clot* dingleberries
DNGGLR dangler *hanger*
DNGGR dungaree *denim*
DNGGRZ dungarees *blue jeans*
DNGGS dingus *doodad*
DNGHL dunghill *feces*

DNGK dank *dark and wet*
DNGK dinky *small* dinkier dinkiest
DNGK donkey *animal* donkeys
DNGK dunk *dip*
DNGKNS dankness *dark and wet*
DNGKR dinkier *smaller*
DNGKST dinkiest *smallest*
DNGKYR dinkier *smaller*
DNGKYST dinkiest *smallest*
DNGL dangle *hang* dangled dangling
DNGL dingle *valley*
DNGLBR dingleberry *clot* dingleberries
DNGLNG ding-a-ling *nitwit*
DNGLR dangler *hanger*
DNGLSM odontoglossum *orchid*
DNGR dinger *home run*
DNGR dingier *dirtier*
DNGR dungaree *denim*
DNGRD downgrade *(v) minimize* downgraded downgrading
DNGRD downgrade *(n) slope*
DNGRDR denigrator *belittle, defame*
DNGRSHN denigration *belittle, defame*
DNGRT denigrate *belittle, defame* denigrated denigrating
DNGRTR denigrator *belittle, defame*
DNGRTR denigratory *belittle, defame*
DNGRZ dungarees *blue jeans*
DNGS dingus *doodad*
DNGSHN denegation *denial*
DNGST dingiest *dirtiest*
DNGYR dingier *dirtier*
DNGYST dingiest *dirtiest*
DNHL downhill *slope*
DNHM down-home *simple*
DNHRDD downhearted *sad*
DNHRDDL downheartedly *sadly*

DNHRDDNS downheartedness *sadness*
DNHRTD downhearted *sad*
DNHRTDL downheartedly *sadly*
DNHRTDNS downheartedness *sadness*
DNJ dingy *dirty* dingier dingiest
DNJ dunnage *padding, baggage* ·
DNJN dungeon *prison*
DNJNSKRB Dungeness crab *animal*
DNJR danger *risk*
DNJR dingier *dirtier*
DNJRS dangerous *risky*
DNJRSL dangerously *risky*
DNJRSNS dangerousness *risk*
DNJST dingiest *dirtiest*
DNJYR dingier *dirtier*
DNJYST dingiest *dirtiest*
DNK dank *dark and wet*
DNK dinky *small* dinkier dinkiest
DNK donkey *animal* donkeys
DNK dunk *dip*
DNK identic *same*
DNKHD Don Quixote *idealist*
DNKHT Don Quixote *idealist*
DNKL denticle *tooth*
DNKL identical (adj) *same* identically (adv)
DNKNS dankness *dark and wet*
DNKR dinkier *smaller*
DNKRT downcourt *basketball*
DNKS adnexa *associated*
DNKSL adnexal *associated*
DNKST dinkiest *smallest*
DNKST downcast *dejected*
DNKYR dinkier *smaller*
DNKYST dinkiest *smallest*
DNL daintily *delicately*
DNL denial *rejection*
DNL dental *teeth*
DNLD download *transfer*
DNLDBL downloadable

Letters aren't doubled for single sounds: to find alley use **L** not **LL**. Use **Y** and **W** as hard sounds only: to find yellow use **YL**. (Br)=British spelling or usage. * See dictionary.

transfer
DNLN dunlin *bird* dunlins (or) dunlin
DNLNGK downlink *transmission*
DNLNK downlink *transmission*
DNM adenoma *tumor* adenomas (or) adenomata
DNM denim *fabric*
DNM dynamo *generator* dynamos
DNMD adenomata (pl) *tumor* adenoma
DNMDR dynamiter *exploder*
DNMDR dynamotor *generator*
DNMK autonomic *involuntary*
DNMK dynamic *(adj) forceful (n) cause of change*
DNMKL autonomically *involuntarily*
DNMKL dynamically *forcefully*
DNMKS dynamics *mechanics*
DNMMDR dynamometer *force measure*
DNMMTR dynamometer *force measure*
DNMMTR dynamometry *science*
DNMN denouement *outcome*
DNMNDR denominator *number, standard*
DNMNDV denominative *noun or adjective*
DNMNSHN denomination *name, religion*
DNMNSHNL denominational *name, religion*
DNMNT denominate *name*
DNMNT denouement *outcome*
DNMNTR denominator *number, standard*
DNMNTV denominative *noun or adjective*
DNMRK Denmark *country*

DNMRKT down-market *low income*
DNMSDK dynamistic *force*
DNMST dynamist *force*
DNMSTK dynamistic *force*
DNMT adenomata (pl) *tumor* adenoma
DNMT dynamite *explosive* dynamited dynamiting
DNMTR dynamiter *exploder*
DNMTR dynamotor *generator*
DNMTS adenomatous *tumorous*
DNMX dynamics *mechanics*
DNMZM dynamism *force*
DNN dining *eating*
DNNCDV denunciative *condemnation*
DNNCSHN denunciation *condemnation*
DNNCTV denunciative *condemnation*
DNNCYDV denunciative *condemnation*
DNNCYSHN denunciation *condemnation*
DNNCYTV denunciative *condemnation*
DNNDR down under *Australia*
DNNDT down-and-out *destitute*
DNNDTR down-and-outer *destitute*
DNNG dining *eating*
DNNGL denyingly *disclaim*
DNNL denyingly *disclaim*
DNNS daintiness *delicateness*
DNNS denounce *accuse* denounced denouncing
DNNSDV denunciative *condemnation*
DNNSMNT denouncement *accusation*
DNNSR denouncer *accuser*
DNNSSHN denunciation *condemnation*
DNNSTV denunciative *condemnation*
DNNSYDV denunciative *condemnation*

DNNSYSHN denunciation *condemnation*
DNNSYTV denunciative *condemnation*
DNNT down-and-out *destitute*
DNNTHMTH down in the mouth (adj) *dejected*
DNNTR down-and-outer *destitute*
DNNTS denounce *accuse* denounced denouncing
DNNTSMNT denouncement *accusation*
DNNTSR denouncer *accuser*
DNPL downplay *de-emphasize*
DNPMNT down payment *money*
DNPP downpipe *(Br) spout*
DNPR downpour *rain*
DNR Adenauer *German chancellor*
DNR daintier *delicate*
DNR deanery *office* deaneries
DNR denarii (pl) *coin* denarius
DNR denier *one who rejects, yarn*
DNR dinar *gold coin*
DNR diner *eatery*
DNR dinner *meal*
DNR donor *giver*
DNR downer *depressant, unpleasant news*
DNR downier *softer*
DNRM ad interim *temporary*
DNRNJ downrange *far from launch*
DNRS denarius *coin* denarii
DNRSR day nursery *child care*
DNRT downright *outright*
DNRTM dinnertime *meal*
DNRVR downriver *nearer river's mouth*
DNRVT denervate *cut a nerve* denervated denervating
DNRYS denarius *coin* denarii

Use letters that best describe the sounds you hear and omit the vowels. Use **S** or **K** instead of **C**: to find circle use **SRKL**. Use **J** to find joy, **JM** to find gem and **G** to find go.

DNS Adonis *Greek god*
DNS audience *crowd*
DNS dance *move rhythmically* danced dancing
DNS dense *thick, stupid* denser densest
DNS dunce *stupid one*
DNSBL danceable *rhythmic*
DNSD density *thickness* densities
DNSD downside *negative*
DNSD dynasty *same descent* dynasties
DNSDK dynastic *same descent*
DNSDKL dynastically *same descent*
DNSH Danish *of Denmark*
DNSH donnish *collegiate*
DNSHF downshift *gears*
DNSHFT downshift *gears*
DNSHM ad nauseam *to excess*
DNSHN adnation *growth*
DNSHN donation *contribution*
DNSHNLZ denationalize *remove from national control* denationalized denationalizing (Br) denationalise
DNSHNLZSHN denationalization *remove from national control* (Br) denationalisation
DNSKL downscale *cut back* downscaled downscaling
DNSL densely *thick, stupid*
DNSLD downslide *movement*
DNSLP downslope *descent*
DNSM ad nauseam *to excess*
DNSNDRM Down's syndrome *disease*
DNSNS denseness *thick, stupid*
DNSPT downspout *pipe*
DNSR dancer *performer*
DNSR danseur *ballet (m)*
DNSR denser *thick, stupid*
DNSR dinosaur *animal*

DNSS Dionysus (or) Bacchus *Greek god*
DNSST densest *thick, stupid*
DNST daintiest *delicate*
DNST density *thickness* densities
DNST dentist *teeth*
DNST down east *Maine*
DNST downiest *softest*
DNST dynast *same descent*
DNST dynasty *same descent* dynasties
DNSTJ downstage *theater*
DNSTK dynastic *same descent*
DNSTKL dynastically *same descent*
DNSTR dentistry *teeth*
DNSTR down-easter *(often capitalized) Maine native*
DNSTRK downstroke *movement*
DNSTRM downstream *later*
DNSTRZ downstairs *lower floor*
DNSTT downstate *south*
DNSTTSHNLZ deinstitutionalize *mental patients, reform* deinstitutionalized deinstitutionalizing (Br) deinstitutionalise
DNSTTSHNLZSHN deinstitutionalization *mental patients, reform* (Br) deinstitutionalisation
DNSTTYSHNLZ deinstitutionalize *mental patients, reform* deinstitutionalized deinstitutionalizing (Br) deinstitutionalise
DNSTTYSHNLZSHN deinstitutionalization *mental patients, reform* (Br) deinstitutionalisation
DNSWNG downswing *trend*
DNSYR danseur *ballet (m)*
DNSYZ danseuse *ballet (f)*
DNSZ danseuse *ballet (f)*
DNSZ downsize *make smaller* downsized

downsizing
DNT adnate *growth*
DNT dainty *(adj) delicate* daintier daintiest
DNT dainty *(n) food* dainties
DNT daunt *subdue, dismay*
DNT denote *mean*
DNT dent *tooth, hollow*
DNT dinette *furniture*
DNT dint *force*
DNT don't *(contr) do not*
DNT donate *give* donated donating
DNT donut (or) doughnut *pastry*
DNT doughnut *food, circular mark*
DNT dunite *rock*
DNT identity *name* identities
DNT odonate *insect*
DNTBLST odontoblast *dentin*
DNTCHLS edentulous *toothless*
DNTCHRLZ denaturalize *make unnatural, deprive of rights* denaturalized denaturalizing (Br) denaturalise
DNTCHRLZSHN denaturalization *made unnatural, deprivation of rights* (Br) denaturalisation
DNTD odontoid *vertebra*
DNTF identify *name* identified identifying identifies
DNTFBL identifiable (adj) *name* identifiably (adv)
DNTFKSHN identification *name*
DNTFR identifier *name*
DNTFRS dentifrice *toothpaste*
DNTFYBL identifiable (adj) *name* identifiably (adv)
DNTFYR identifier *name*
DNTGLSM odontoglossum *orchid*
DNTHN do-nothing *lazy one*
DNTHNG do-nothing *lazy*

Letters aren't doubled for single sounds: to find alley use **L** not **LL**. Use **Y** and **W** as hard sounds only: to find yellow use **YL**. (Br)=British spelling or usage. * See dictionary.

one
DNTHS dianthus *pink*
DNTK dunitic *rock*
DNTK identic *same*
DNTKL denticle *tooth*
DNTKL identical (adj) *same*
identically (adv)
DNTKLSHN denticulation
saw-toothed
DNTKLT denticulate (or)
denticulated *saw-toothed*
DNTKLTD denticulated (or)
denticulate *saw-toothed*
DNTKSKSHN
autointoxication *self-poisoning*
DNTKYLSHN denticulation
saw-toothed
DNTKYLT denticulate (or)
denticulated *saw-toothed*
DNTKYLTD denticulated
(or) denticulate *saw-toothed*
DNTL daintily *delicate*
DNTL dental *teeth*
DNTL dentil *molding*
DNTLG deontology *morality*
DNTLJ deontology *morality*
DNTLS dauntless *fearless*
DNTLS dentulous *with teeth*
DNTLS edentulous *toothless*
DNTLSL dauntlessly
fearlessly
DNTLSNS dauntlessness
fearlessness
DNTM downtime *not able to
work*
DNTN dentin (or) dentine
tooth
DNTN downtown *city*
DNTNGL dauntingly *subdue,
dismay*
DNTNL dentinal *tooth*
DNTNS daintiness
delicateness
DNTQLDD denticulated (or)
denticulate *saw-toothed*
DNTQLSHN denticulation
saw-toothed
DNTQLT denticulate (or)
denticulated *saw-toothed*
DNTQLTD denticulated (or)

denticulate *saw-toothed*
DNTR daintier *delicate*
DNTR denature *modify*
denatured denaturing
DNTR denture *teeth*
DNTRDN downtrodden
oppressed
DNTRL day-neutral *light
periods*
DNTRLZ denaturalize *make
unnatural, deprive of rights*
denaturalized
denaturalizing
(Br) denaturalise
DNTRLZSHN
denaturalization *made
unnatural, deprivation of
rights*
(Br) denaturalisation
DNTRM ad interim
temporary
DNTRN downturn *decline*
DNTRN dynatron *tube*
DNTRND downtrend *decline*
DNTRNT denaturant
modifier
DNTRSHN denaturation
modification
DNTRTH down-to-earth
practical
DNTS adenitis *gland
inflammation*
DNTS audience *crowd*
DNTS dance *move
rhythmically* danced
dancing
DNTS dense *thick, stupid*
denser densest
DNTS dunce *stupid one*
DNTSBL danceable
rhythmic
DNTSD density *thickness*
densities
DNTSHN denotation
meaning
DNTSHN dentition *teeth*
DNTSL densely *thick, stupid*
DNTSNS denseness *thick,
stupid*
DNTSR dancer *performer*
DNTSR denser *thick, stupid*
DNTSST densest *thick,*

stupid
DNTST daintiest *delicate*
DNTST density *thickness*
densities
DNTST dentist *teeth*
DNTSTR dentistry *teeth*
DNTT dentate *with teeth*
DNTT edentate *toothless*
DNTT identity *name*
identities
DNTTHHLS down-at-the-
heels (adj) *shabby*
DNTTHWR down-to-the-
wire (adj) *suspenseful*
DNTXKSHN
autointoxication *self-poisoning*
DNTYLS dentulous *with
teeth*
DNTYLS edentulous
toothless
DNTYR daintier *delicate*
DNTYRLZ denaturalize
*make unnatural, deprive of
rights* denaturalized
denaturalizing
(Br) denaturalise
DNTYRLZSHN
denaturalization *made
unnatural, deprivation of
rights*
(Br) denaturalisation
DNTYST daintiest *delicate*
DNWN downwind *detectable*
DNWND downwind
detectable
DNWR Adenauer *German
chancellor*
DNWRD downward (or)
downwards *not up*
DNWRDS downwards (or)
downward *not up*
DNWRDZ downwards (or)
downward *not up*
DNWSH downwash
airstream
DNX adnexa *associated*
DNXL adnexal *associated*
DNY doña *title (f)*
DNYB Danube *river*
DNYBL deniable *rejection*
DNYBLD deniability *rejection*

Use letters that best describe the sounds you hear and omit the vowels. Use **S** or **K**
instead of **C**: to find circle use **SRKL**. Use **J** to find joy, **JM** to find gem and **G** to find go.

DNYBLT deniability *rejection*
DNYD denude *strip* denuded denuding
DNYDMNT denudement *stripping*
DNYDSHN denudation *stripping*
DNYL denial *rejection*
DNYNGL denyingly *disclaim*
DNYNL denyingly *disclaim*
DNYR daintier *delicate*
DNYR denier *one who rejects, yarn*
DNYR downier *softer*
DNYST daintiest *delicate*
DNYST downiest *softest*
DNZHM ad nauseam *to excess*
DNZHYM ad nauseam *to excess*
DNZLST dean's list *scholarship*
DNZM ad nauseam *to excess*
DNZN denizen *inhabitant*
DNZYM ad nauseam *to excess*
DP adapt *adjust*
DP adept *skillful*
DP adopt *keep*
DP deep *not shallow*
DP depot *station*
DP dip *(v) scoop, drench, curve** dipped dipping
DP dip *(n) scoop, drop, sauce**
DP dippy *foolish* dippier dippiest
DP dopa *amino acid*
DP dope *(v) drug, plan* doped doping
DP dope *(n) drug, information, dullard*
DP dopey *drugged, stupid* dopier dopiest
DP dupe *fool* duped duping
DPC deep-sea *ocean*
DPCDD deep-seated *established*
DPCTD deep-seated *established*
DPD deputy *second in command* deputies
DPD dipody *two feet*

dipodies
DPD dopehead *addict*
DPDBL adaptable *changeable*
DPDBL adoptable *acceptable*
DPDBLD adaptability *change*
DPDBLD adoptability *acceptance*
DPDBLT adaptability *change*
DPDBLT adoptability *acceptance*
DPDDNS adaptedness *adjustment*
DPDK dipodic *two feet*
DPDK diptych *tablet*
DPDR adapter *changer*
DPDR adopter *keeper*
DPDR diopter *lens*
DPDR diptera (pl) *fly* dipteron
DPDRN dipteran *like a fly*
DPDRS dipterous *fly*
DPDSH deep-dish *dessert*
DPDV adaptive *able to change*
DPDV adoptive *acquired*
DPDVL adaptively *able to change*
DPDVNS adaptiveness *able to change*
DPFR deep-fry *cook*
DPFRR deep fryer *cooker*
DPFRYR deep fryer *cooker*
DPFRZ deep freeze *(n) cold storage*
DPFRZ deep-freeze *(v) ice* deep-froze deep-freezing deep-frozen
DPFRZ Deepfreeze *(trademark) freezer*
DPHD dopehead *addict*
DPK depict *describe*
DPKDR depicter *describer*
DPKSHN depiction *description*
DPKT deep pocket *wealth*
DPKT depict *describe*
DPKT out-of-pocket *expense*
DPKTR depicter *describer*
DPL adeptly *skillfully*
DPL dapple *pattern* dappled dappling

DPL deeply *intense, depth*
DPL deploy *spread out, use*
DPL diploe *skull*
DPL dipole *two poles*
DPL duopoly *two sellers or rulers* duopolies
DPL duple *two beats*
DPLBL deployable *spread out, use*
DPLD dappled *spotty*
DPLD diploid *doubled*
DPLDBL depletable *empty, exhaust*
DPLDKS diplodocus *dinosaur*
DPLFZ diplophase *life cycle*
DPLG diplegia *paralysis*
DPLGNGR doppelgänger (or) doppelganger *double*
DPLGY diplegia *paralysis*
DPLJ diplegia *paralysis*
DPLJY diplegia *paralysis*
DPLKDR duplicator *copier*
DPLKKS diplococcus *bacteria*
DPLKS duplex *double* duplexes
DPLKSHN duplication *copy*
DPLKSR duplexer *switch*
DPLKT duplicate *copy* duplicated duplicating
DPLKTR duplicator *copier*
DPLM diploma *certificate* diplomas
DPLMC diplomacy *tact*
DPLMDK diplomatic *tactful*
DPLMDKL diplomatically *tactfully*
DPLMNT deployment *spread, use*
DPLMS diplomacy *tact*
DPLMT diplomat *tactful one*
DPLMT diplomate *doctor*
DPLMTK diplomatic *tactful*
DPLMTKL diplomatically *tactfully*
DPLN deplane *disembark* deplaned deplaning
DPLP diplopia *vision*
DPLPD diplopod *millipede*
DPLPY diplopia *vision*
DPLR deplore *regret*

Letters aren't doubled for single sounds: to find alley use **L** not **LL**. Use **Y** and **W** as hard sounds only: to find yellow use **YL**. (Br)=British spelling or usage. * See dictionary.

deplored deploring

DPLR Doppler *physicist*

DPLRBL deplorable (adj) *regrettable* deplorably (adv)

DPLRFK Doppler effect *physics*

DPLRFKT Doppler effect *physics*

DPLRNGL deploringly *regrettably*

DPLRNL deploringly *regrettably*

DPLRR deplorer *regretter*

DPLRZ depolarize *remove poles* depolarized depolarizing (Br) depolarise

DPLRZR depolarizer *remove poles* (Br) depolariser

DPLRZSHN depolarization *remove poles* (Br) depolarisation

DPLSD duplicity *contradiction* duplicities

DPLSDK duopolistic *two sellers or rulers*

DPLSDS duplicitous *contradiction*

DPLSHN depilation *remove hair*

DPLSHN depletion *emptiness, exhaustion*

DPLST duplicity *contradiction* duplicities

DPLSTK duopolistic *two sellers or rulers*

DPLSTS duplicitous *contradiction*

DPLT autopilot *guidance system*

DPLT depilate *remove hair* depilated depilating

DPLT deplete *empty, exhaust* depleted depleting

DPLTBL depletable *empty, exhaust*

DPLTN diplotene *development*

DPLTR depilatory *remove hair* depilatories

DPLTSZ depoliticize *remove politics* depoliticized depoliticizing (Br) depoliticise

DPLTSZSHN depoliticization *remove politics* (Br) depoliticise

DPLX duplex *double* duplexes

DPLXR duplexer *switch*

DPLYBL deployable *spread out, use*

DPMN dopamine *brain chemical*

DPN deepen *make deep*

DPND depend *trust, be based on, hang down*

DPNDBL dependable *reliant*

DPNDNC dependency *adjunct unit* dependencies

DPNDNS dependence *reliance*

DPNDNS dependency *adjunct unit* dependencies

DPNDNT dependent *adjunct, hanging, contingent**

DPNDNTC dependency *adjunct unit* dependencies

DPNDNTS dependence *reliance*

DPNDNTS dependency *adjunct unit* dependencies

DPNNT deponent *verb*

DPNS adeptness *skill*

DPNS deepness *intense, depth*

DPNS dopiness *sluggishness, stupidity*

DPNT deponent *verb*

DPNT dew point *moisture*

DPPLSHN depopulation *killing off*

DPPLT depopulate *kill off* depopulated depopulating

DPPYLSHN depopulation *killing off*

DPPYLT depopulate *kill off* depopulated depopulating

DPR dapper *stylish*

DPR diaper *fabric, pattern, baby garment*

DPR dipper *spoon, bird*

DPR dippier *foolish*

DPR doper *addict*

DPR dopier *sluggish, stupid*

DPR dupery *trick* duperies

DPRCHR departure *leave, deviate*

DPRCT depreciate *devalue* depreciated depreciating

DPRCYT depreciate *devalue* depreciated depreciating

DPRD deportee *one sent away*

DPRDBL deportable *send away*

DPRDD deep-rooted *established*

DPRDD departed *dead, gone*

DPRDDR depredator *plunder*

DPRDSHN depredation *plunder*

DPRDT depredate *plunder* depredated depredating

DPRDTR depredator *plunder*

DPRFL dipperful *amount*

DPRGRM deprogram *advise against* deprogrammed deprogramming

DPRGRMR deprogrammer *advise against*

DPRKSHN deprecation *belittlement*

DPRKT deprecate *belittle* deprecated deprecating

DPRKTR deprecatory *belittle*

DPRKTRL deprecatorily *belittle*

DPRL dapperly *stylishly*

DPRNS dapperness *stylishness*

DPRS depress *sadden, press down* depressed

Use letters that best describe the sounds you hear and omit the vowels. Use **S** or **K** instead of **C**: to find circle use **SRKL**. Use **J** to find joy, **JM** to find gem and **G** to find go.

depressing
DPRSBL depressible
sadden, press down
DPRSD depressed *sad, flat*
DPRSHBL depreciable
devalue
DPRSHDR depreciator
devalue
DPRSHN depression *sorrow,*
lowering
DPRSHRZ depressurize
release pressure
depressurized
depressurizing
(Br) depressurise
DPRSHRZSHN
depressurization *release*
pressure
(Br) depressurisation
DPRSHSHN depreciation
devalue
DPRSHT depreciate *devalue*
depreciated depreciating
DPRSHTR depreciator
devalue
DPRSHTR depreciatory
devalue
DPRSHYDR depreciator
devalue
DPRSHYSHN depreciation
devalue
DPRSHYT depreciate
devalue depreciated
depreciating
DPRSHYTR depreciator
devalue
DPRSN depressing
saddening
DPRSNG depressing
saddening
DPRSNLZ depersonalize
remove identity
depersonalized
depersonalizing
(Br) depersonalise
DPRSNLZSHN
depersonalization *no*
identity
(Br) depersonalisation
DPRSNT depressant *sadden*
DPRSR depressor *muscle,*
device, nerve

DPRST depreciate *devalue*
depreciated depreciating
DPRST depressed *sad, flat*
DPRSV depressive *sorrow*
DPRSVL depressively
sorrow
DPRSYT depreciate *devalue*
depreciated depreciating
DPRT depart *go away*
DPRT deport *send away*
DPRT deportee *one sent*
away
DPRTBL deportable *send*
away
DPRTD deep-rooted
established
DPRTD departed *dead, gone*
DPRTMNLZ
departmentalize *divide*
departmentalized
departmentalizing
DPRTMNLZSHN
departmentalization
divide
DPRTMNT department *area*
DPRTMNT deportment
conduct
DPRTMNTLZ
departmentalize *divide*
departmentalized
departmentalizing
DPRTMNTLZSHN
departmentalization
divide
DPRTR departure *leave,*
deviate
DPRTSHN deportation *send*
away
DPRV deprave *slander,*
corrupt depraved
depraving
DPRV deprive *take away*
deprived depriving
DPRVD depraved *corrupt*
DPRVD depravity *corruption*
depravities
DPRVD deprived *needy*
DPRVDL depravedly
corruptly
DPRVDNS depravedness
corruption
DPRVR depraver *slanderer,*

corrupter
DPRVSHN depravation
corruption
DPRVSHN deprivation *loss*
DPRVT depravity *corruption*
depravities
DPS adipose *fat*
DPS deep-sea *ocean*
DPS depths (pl) *deepest part*
depth
DPS dipso *alcoholic* dipsos
DPS Oedipus *Greek king*
DPSD adiposity *fattiness*
DPSDD deep-seated
established
DPSHN adoption
acquirement
DPSHNST adoptionist *(often*
capitalized) doctrine
DPSHNZM adoptionism (or)
adoptianism *(often*
capitalized) doctrine
DPSK deep-sky *beyond our*
solar system
DPSKMPLKS Oedipus
complex *psychology*
DPSKMPLX Oedipus
complex *psychology*
DPSKS deep-six (v) *discard*
deep six (n)
DPSMN dipsomania
alcoholism
DPSMNK dipsomaniac
alcoholic
DPSMNY dipsomania
alcoholism
DPSMNYK dipsomaniac
alcoholic
DPSN diapason *sound*
DPSPS deep space *beyond*
the moon
DPST adipocyte *fat cell*
DPST adiposity *fattiness*
DPST dippiest *foolish*
DPST dopiest *sluggish,*
stupid
DPSTD deep-seated
established
DPSTK dipstick *oil*
DPSTR dopester *forecaster*
DPSX deep-six (v) *discard*
deep six (n)

Letters aren't doubled for single sounds: to find alley use **L** not **LL**. Use **Y** and **W** as hard
sounds only: to find yellow use **YL**. (Br)=British spelling or usage. * See dictionary.

DPT adapt *adjust*
DPT adept *skillful*
DPT adopt *keep*
DPT adoptee *one kept*
DPT depute *delegate* deputed deputing
DPT deputy *second in command* deputies
DPTBL adaptable *changeable*
DPTBL adoptable *acceptable*
DPTBLD adaptability *change*
DPTBLD adoptability *acceptance*
DPTBLT adaptability *change*
DPTBLT adoptability *acceptance*
DPTDNS adaptedness *adjustment*
DPTH depth *abyss, intensity* depths
DPTHK idiopathic *primary*
DPTHKL idiopathically *primary*
DPTHNG diphthong *vowel sound*
DPTHR diphtheria *disease*
DPTHRT deep throat *informant*
DPTHRY diphtheria *disease*
DPTK dipodic *two feet*
DPTK diptych *tablet*
DPTL adeptly *skillfully*
DPTNS adeptness *skill*
DPTR adapter *changer*
DPTR adopter *keeper*
DPTR diopter *lens*
DPTR diptera (pl) *fly* dipteron
DPTRK dioptric *lens*
DPTRN dipteran *like a fly*
DPTRN dipteron *fly* diptera
DPTRS dipterous *fly*
DPTSHN adaptation *adjustment*
DPTSHN deputation *appointment*
DPTSHNL adaptational (adj) *adjust* adaptationally (adv)
DPTV adaptive *able to change*
DPTV adoptive *acquired*
DPTVD adaptivity *ability to change*
DPTVL adaptively *able to change*
DPTVNS adaptiveness *able to change*
DPTVT adaptivity *ability to change*
DPTZ deputize *appoint deputy* deputized deputizing
DPTZSHN deputization *appoint deputy*
DPWDR deepwater *port*
DPWTR deepwater *port*
DPYD deputy *second in command* deputies
DPYR dippier *foolish*
DPYR dopier *sluggish, stupid*
DPYST dippiest *foolish*
DPYST dopiest *sluggish, foolish*
DPYT depute *delegate* deputed deputing
DPYT deputy *second in command* deputies
DPYTSHN deputation *appointment*
DPYTZ deputize *appoint deputy* deputized deputizing
DPYTZSHN deputization *appoint deputy*
DPZ depose *remove, testify* deposed deposing
DPZDR depositor *placed*
DPZL deposal *removal, testimony*
DPZN diapason *sound*
DPZSHN deposition *removal, testimony*
DPZT deposit (v) *place* (n) *payment, accumulation*
DPZTR depositor *placed*
DPZTR depository *safe place* depositories
DQC adequacy *sufficiency* adequacies
DQD duckweed *plant*
DQDRM docudrama *theater*
DQK duckwalk *squatting*
DQMNL documental *factual*
DQMNR documentary

factual documentaries
DQMNR documenter *reporter*
DQMNT document (n) *writing* (v) *provide facts*
DQMNTL documental *factual*
DQMNTR documentary *factual* documentaries
DQMNTR documenter *reporter*
DQMNTSHN documentation *facts*
DQMNTSHNL documentational *facts*
DQPL decuple *groups of 10*
DQRK ductwork *tubes*
DQRKR dockworker *longshoreman*
DQS adequacy *sufficiency* adequacies
DQT adequate *sufficient*
DQTL adequately *sufficiently*
DQTNS adequateness *sufficiency*
DR adder *snake*
DR adore *worship* adored adoring
DR dairy *cow* dairies
DR dare *risk* dared daring
DR dear (adj) *loved, costly* (n) *loved one*
DR deer *animal* deer
DR dhurrie *rug*
DR diarrhea *feces*
DR diary *journal* diaries
DR dire *dreadful* direr direst
DR direr *dreadful*
DR doer *active one*
DR door *gate*
DR dory *boat* dories
DR dour *stern*
DR dower *estate*
DR dowry *marriage goods* dowries
DR draw (v) *sketch, pull, receive* drew drawing drawn
DR draw (n) *pull, tie score, cards*
DR drawee *payer*
DR dray *cart*

Use letters that best describe the sounds you hear and omit the vowels. Use **S** or **K** instead of **C**: to find circle use **SRKL**. Use **J** to find joy, **JM** to find gem and **G** to find go.

DR dry *(v) remove moisture* dried drying dries

DR dry *(adj) not wet, ironic, not sweet* drier driest

DR dry *(n) political party* drys

DR duro *hog* duros

DR durra *grain*

DR dyer *tinter*

DR eater *one who eats*

DR eatery *diner*

DR eider *duck*

DR oater *western*

DR odor *smell* (Br) odour

DR otter *aquatic animal* otters

DR outdoor *open air*

DR outdraw *attract, gun* outdrew outdrawn outdrawing

DR outer *external*

DR udder *teat*

DR uteri *(pl) womb* uterus

DR utter *(v) speak (adj) total*

DRB derby *hat, race* derbies

DRB drab *(adj) dull* drabber drabbest

DRB drab *(v) prostitute* drabbed drabbing

DRB drab *(n) prostitute, color, amount*

DRB drub *defeat* drubbed drubbing

DRBK draw back *(v) avoid*

DRBK drawback *(n) disadvantage*

DRBL adorable *(adj) cute, sacred* adorably *(adv)*

DRBL doorbell *ringer*

DRBL drabble *wet and muddy* drabbled drabbling

DRBL dribble *drip, bounce a ball* dribbled dribbling

DRBL dryable *no moisture*

DRBL durable *(adj) sturdy* durably *(adv)*

DRBL utterable *spoken*

DRBLD adorability *cuteness, sacredness*

DRBLD durability *sturdiness*

DRBLNS adorableness *cuteness, sacredness*

DRBLR dribbler *drip, bounce a ball*

DRBLS durables *goods*

DRBLT adorability *cuteness, sacredness*

DRBLT driblet *drip*

DRBLT durability *sturdiness*

DRBLZ durables *goods*

DRBNGKS Outer Banks *islands*

DRBNGX Outer Banks *islands*

DRBNKS Outer Banks *islands*

DRBNX Outer Banks *islands*

DRBR deerberry *plant* deerberries

DRBR drabber *dull*

DRBR drubber *winner*

DRBRJ drawbridge *passageway*

DRBRN Dearborn *city*

DRBST drabbest *dull*

DRC addressee *receiver*

DRC dressy *formal* dressier dressiest

DRC drossy *scummy*

DRCR dressier *formal*

DRCST dressiest *formal*

DRCYR dressier *formal*

DRCYST dressiest *formal*

DRCZ diaereses *(pl) symbol, verse* diaeresis

DRD deride *ridicule* derided deriding

DRD dirty *(v) soil, foul* dirtied dirtying dirties

DRD dirty *(adj) soiled, lewd* dirtier dirtiest

DRD do-or-die *final*

DRD dread *fear*

DRD droughty *dry*

DRD druid *wizard*

DRD dry-eyed *no tears*

DRD dryad *nymph*

DRD odored *smelly* (Br) odoured

DRDDR door-to-door *each house*

DRDFL dreadful *(adj) fearful,* extreme dreadfully *(adv)*

DRDFLNS dreadfulness *fear*

DRDK autoerotic *self-stimulating*

DRDK diuretic *more urine*

DRDK druidic (or) druidical *magical*

DRDK dry dock *(n) ships* dry-dock *(v)*

DRDKC Adriatic Sea *body of water*

DRDKL druidical (or) druidic *magical*

DRDKS Adriatic Sea *body of water*

DRDL dirtily *soiled*

DRDL dreidel *toy*

DRDLK dreadlock *hair*

DRDN drawdown *(n) deplete* draw down *(v)*

DRDN eiderdown *goose feathers*

DRDNS dirtiness *soiled*

DRDNS droughtiness *dryness*

DRDNT dreadnought *battleship, garment*

DRDP dried-up *shriveled*

DRDR darter *fish*

DRDR derider *ridiculer*

DRDR dirtier *soiled, lewd*

DRDST dirtiest *soiled, lewd*

DRDSZM autoeroticism (or) autoerotism *self-stimulation*

DRDV iterative *repetition*

DRDVL daredevil *bold one*

DRDYR dirtier *soiled, lewd*

DRDYST dirtiest *soiled, lewd*

DRDZM autoerotism (or) autoeroticism *self-stimulation*

DRDZM druidism *religion*

DRF draft *(v) select, prepare (n) wind, outline, demand** (Br) draught

DRF drift *(v) wander (n) flow, tendency, clump*

DRFD draftee *army*

DRFD drafty *windy* draftier draftiest

DRFD drifty *piled*

Letters aren't doubled for single sounds: to find alley use **L** not **LL**. Use **Y** and **W** as hard sounds only: to find yellow use **YL**. (Br)=British spelling or usage. * See dictionary.

DRFDNS draftiness *breeze*
DRFDR draftier *breezier*
DRFDR drifter *wanderer*
DRFDST draftiest *breeziest*
DRFDYR draftier *breezier*
DRFDYST draftiest *breeziest*
DRFL deerfly *insect* deerflies
DRFL direful (adj) *dreadful*
   direfully (adv)
DRFNT drift net *fishing*
DRFRS odoriferous *stinky*
   (Br) odouriferous
DRFRSL odoriferously
   stinky
   (Br) odouriferously
DRFRSNS odoriferousness
   stinky
   (Br) odouriferousness
DRFS draughts *(Br) checkers*
DRFSMN draftsman *sketch*
   draftsmen
   (Br) draughtsman
DRFT adrift *loose*
DRFT draft *(v) select, prepare
   (n) wind, outline, demand**
   (Br) draught
DRFT draftee *army*
DRFT drafty *windy* draftier
   draftiest
DRFT drift *(v) wander (n)
   flow, tendency, clump*
DRFT drifty *piled*
DRFTNS draftiness *breeze*
DRFTNT drift net *fishing*
DRFTR draftier *breezier*
DRFTR drifter *wanderer*
DRFTS draughts *(Br)
   checkers*
DRFTSMN draftsman *sketch*
   draftsmen
   (Br) draughtsman
DRFTST draftiest *breeziest*
DRFTWD driftwood *floating
   branch*
DRFTYR draftier *breezier*
DRFTYST draftiest *breeziest*
DRFWD driftwood *floating
   branch*
DRG drag *pull* dragged
   dragging
DRG dragee *nut, ball*
DRG draggy *slow* draggier

draggiest
DRG dreggy *leavings*
DRG drogue *funnel*
DRG drug *(v) stupefy,
   medicate* drugged
   drugging
DRG drug *(n) medicine*
DRG druggie *drug user*
   druggies
DRGDV derogative *mocking*
DRGDZ dry goods *textiles*
DRGL draggle *trail* draggled
   draggling
DRGLN dragline *rope*
DRGLTL draggle-tail *slattern*
DRGMN dragoman
   interpreter dragomans (or)
   dragomen
DRGN dragon *serpent*
DRGN dragoon *soldier*
DRGNFL dragonfly *insect*
   dragonflies
DRGNHD dragonhead *plant*
DRGNLD dragon lady *tyrant*
DRGNT dragnet *trapping
   device*
DRGNT dragonet *fish*
DRGR de rigueur *proper*
DRGR dragger *boat*
DRGR draggier *slower*
DRGRS drag race *cars*
DRGRSN drag racing *cars*
DRGRSNG drag racing *cars*
DRGSHN derogation
   detraction
DRGST draggiest *slowest*
DRGST druggist *pharmacist*
DRGSTR dragster *car*
DRGSTR drugstore
   pharmacy
DRGSTRP drag strip
   raceway
DRGT derogate *detract*
   derogated derogating
DRGT drugget *fabric*
DRGTR derogatory *mocking*
DRGTRL derogatorily
   mockingly
DRGTV derogative *mocking*
DRGYR de rigueur *proper*
DRGYR draggier *slower*
DRGYST draggiest *slowest*

DRGZ dregs *leavings*
DRHN deerhound *dog*
DRHND deerhound *dog*
DRJ dirge *lament*
DRJ dragee *nut, ball*
DRJ drayage *fee*
DRJ dredge *deepen* dredged
   dredging
DRJ drudge *work* drudged
   drudging
DRJBL dirigible *(n) airship
   (adj) steering*
DRJLNG Darjeeling (or)
   Darjiling *city*
DRJM doorjamb *side*
DRJR dredger *scoop*
DRJR drudger *worker*
DRJR drudgery *work*
   drudgeries
DRJST dirigiste *planning*
DRJZM dirigisme *planning*
DRK dark *no light, evil,
   obscure*
DRK derrick *crane, frame*
DRK direct *(v) supervise,
   show (adj, adv) straight,
   natural**
DRK dirk *knife*
DRK dork *(slang) jerk, nerd*
DRK dorky *(slang) jerk, nerd*
   dorkier dorkiest
DRK drake *duck*
DRK dreck *trash*
DRK duroc *hog*
DRK dyarchy *two rulers*
   dyarchies
DRKDD directed *supervised,
   shown*
DRKDK ataractic (or)
   ataraxic *tranquilizer*
DRKDL dairy cattle *cow*
DRKDR director *supervisor*
DRKDR directory *listing*
   directories
DRKDRSHP directorship
   supervisor
DRKDRT directorate *board*
DRKDV directive *guide, order*
DRKHRS dark horse
   contender
DRKJZ Dark Ages *time of
   decline*

Use letters that best describe the sounds you hear and omit the vowels. Use **S** or **K** instead of **C**: to find circle use **SRKL**. Use **J** to find joy, **JM** to find gem and **G** to find go.

DRM

DRKL darkle *become dim* darkled darkling
DRKL directly *soon, straight*
DRKL douroucouli *monkey*
DRKLN darkling *in the dark*
DRKLN dry-clean *clothing*
DRKLNBL dry-cleanable *clothing*
DRKLNG darkling *in the dark*
DRKLNN dry cleaning *clothing*
DRKLNN dry-cleaning *clothing*
DRKLNNG dry cleaning *clothing*
DRKLNNG dry-cleaning *clothing*
DRKLNR dry cleaner *clothing*
DRKM drachma *money* drachmas (or) drachmai (or) drachmae
DRKN darken *obscure*
DRKNN draconian *cruel*
DRKNS directness *straightforward*
DRKNYN draconian *cruel*
DRKPR doorkeeper *attendant*
DRKR dorkier *(slang) jerk, nerd*
DRKRM darkroom *photography*
DRKSHN direction *guidance, route, trend*
DRKSHNL directional *route*
DRKSHNLD directionality *route*
DRKSHNLT directionality *route*
DRKSK ataraxic (or) ataractic *tranquilizer*
DRKST dorkiest *(slang) jerk, nerd*
DRKT direct *(v) supervise, show (adj, adv) straight, natural**
DRKTD directed *supervised, shown*
DRKTK ataractic (or) ataraxic *tranquilizer*

DRKTL dairy cattle *cow*
DRKTL directly *soon, straight*
DRKTNS directness *straightforward*
DRKTR director *supervisor*
DRKTR directory *listing* directories
DRKTRL directorial *supervisory*
DRKTRSHP directorship *supervisor*
DRKTRT directorate *board*
DRKTRYL directorial *supervisory*
DRKTV directive *guide, order*
DRKYR dorkier *(slang) jerk, nerd*
DRKYST dorkiest *(slang) jerk, nerd*
DRL dearly *heartfelt, costly*
DRL derail *off rails, frustrate*
DRL direly *dreadful*
DRL dourly *sternly*
DRL drawl *speech* drawly *(adj)*
DRL drill *(n) tool, ape, exercise (v) bore, sow, repeat**
DRL droll *humorous*
DRL drolly *humorously*
DRL drool *saliva*
DRL dryly *without moisture, ironic*
DRL utterly *completely*
DRLBL drillable *bore, sow, repeat**
DRLBLD drillability *bore, sow, repeat**
DRLBLT drillability *bore, sow, repeat**
DRLK derelict *(adj) negligent (n) hobo*
DRLKSHN dereliction *fault, abandonment*
DRLKT derelict *(adj) negligent (n) hobo*
DRLMSDR drillmaster *instructor*
DRLMSTR drillmaster *instructor*
DRLN darling *loved one*
DRLN drilling *fabric*
DRLNG darling *loved one*

DRLNG drilling *fabric*
DRLNS drollness *humor*
DRLPRS drill press *machine* drill presses
DRLR derailleur *gears*
DRLR drawler *speaker*
DRLR driller *tool user*
DRLR drollery *humor* drolleries
DRLS odorless *no smell* (Br) odourless
DRM dayroom *living area*
DRM dharma *Hindu law*
DRM diorama *scene*
DRM dirham *money*
DRM dorm *dormitory*
DRM dram *amount*
DRM drama *theater*
DRM dream *sleep, imagine* dreamed (or) dreamt dreaming
DRM dreamy *pleasing, vague* dreamier dreamiest
DRM drum *(v) beat, throb* drummed drumming
DRM drum *(n) music, barrel*
DRM durum *wheat*
DRMBT dreamboat *(slang) desired one*
DRMBT drumbeat *rhythm*
DRMD dairymaid *milk*
DRMD dramedy *theater*
DRMDK dramatic *theatrical*
DRMDKL dramatically *theatrical*
DRMDKS dramatics *theater*
DRMDR dromedary *camel* dromedaries
DRMDX dramatics *theater*
DRMDZSHN dramatization *adapt for stage* (Br) dramatisation
DRMFR drumfire *barrage*
DRMFYR drumfire *barrage*
DRMHD drumhead *skin*
DRMJR drum major *band*
DRML dermal *skin*
DRML dreamily *vague, ideal*
DRMLK dreamlike *vague*
DRMLN dreamland *sleep*
DRMLND dreamland *sleep*
DRMLS dreamless *no*

dreams
DRMMN Dramamine *(trademark) drug*
DRMN dairyman *milk* dairymen
DRMN doorman *attendant*
DRMN drayman *hauler* draymen
DRMNC dormancy *sleep*
DRMNS dormancy *sleep*
DRMNS dreaminess *vague, ideal*
DRMNT dormant *asleep*
DRMNTC dormancy *sleep*
DRMNTS dormancy *sleep*
DRMPT dreamt *(v-past) dream*
DRMR dormer *room*
DRMR dreamer *idealist*
DRMR dreamier *vague, ideal*
DRMR drummer *musician*
DRMRL drumroll *music*
DRMS deer mouse *white-footed rodent*
DRMS dermis *skin*
DRMS dormouse *squirrel-like rodent* dormice
DRMST dreamiest *vague, ideal*
DRMST outermost *external*
DRMST uttermost *complete, extreme*
DRMSTK drumstick *music, fowl's leg*
DRMT doormat *wiper*
DRMT dreamt *(v-past) dream*
DRMTDS dermatitis *skin ailment*
DRMTK dramatic *theatrical*
DRMTKL dramatically *theatrical*
DRMTKS dramatics *theater*
DRMTLG dermatology *skin*
DRMTLJ dermatology *skin*
DRMTLJK dermatologic (or) dermatological *skin*
DRMTLJKL dermatological (or) dermatologic *skin*
DRMTLJST dermatologist *skin*
DRMTM dreamtime *sleep*
DRMTR dormitory *room*

dormitories
DRMTRG dramaturgy *theater*
DRMTRJ dramaturge (or) dramaturg *theater*
DRMTRJ dramaturgy *theater*
DRMTRJK dramaturgic (or) dramaturgical (adj) *theater* dramaturgically (ad)
DRMTRJKL dramaturgical (or) dramaturgic (adj) *theater* dramaturgically (ad)
DRMTSS dermatosis *skin disease* dermatoses
DRMTST dramatist *playwright*
DRMTTS dermatitis *skin ailment*
DRMTX dramatics *theater*
DRMTZ dramatize *adapt for stage* dramatized dramatizing (Br) dramatise
DRMTZBL dramatizable *adapt for stage*
DRMTZSHN dramatization *adapt for stage* (Br) dramatisation
DRMWRLD dreamworld *illusion*
DRMYR dreamier *vague, ideal*
DRMYST dreamiest *vague, ideal*
DRN adorn *decorate*
DRN daring *boldness*
DRN darn *sew, damn*
DRN drain *(v) deplete (n) pipe*
DRN drawing *sketch*
DRN drawn *(v-past) draw (adj) haggard*
DRN drone *hum* droned droning
DRN drown *submerge, overwhelm*
DRN during *same time*
DRN outdrawn *attract, gun*
DRN uterine *womb*
DRNB doorknob *latch*
DRNBRD drawing board *table*

DRNCH drench *wet* drenches
DRND darned *(adj, adv) damned*
DRND derring-do *daring*
DRNDKS Adirondacks *mountains*
DRNDL dirndl *skirt*
DRNDX Adirondacks *mountains*
DRNF drawknife *tool* drawknives
DRNG daring *boldness*
DRNG drawing *sketch*
DRNG during *same time*
DRNGBRD drawing board *table*
DRNGD derring-do *daring*
DRNGK drink *(v) swallow a beverage* drank drunk drinking
DRNGK drink *(n) beverage, body of water*
DRNGKBL drinkable *beverage*
DRNGKN drinking *beverage*
DRNGKN drunken *intoxicated*
DRNGKNG drinking *beverage*
DRNGKNS drunkenness *intoxication*
DRNGKR drinker *one who swallows a beverage*
DRNGKRD drunkard *alcoholic*
DRNGL adoringly *lovingly*
DRNGL daringly *boldly*
DRNGRM drawing room *reception*
DRNJ derange *disturb* deranged deranging
DRNJ drainage *depletion*
DRNJMNT derangement *disturbance*
DRNJR derringer *gun*
DRNK drink *(v) swallow a beverage* drank drunk drinking
DRNK drink *(n) beverage, body of water*
DRNKBL drinkable *beverage*

Use letters that best describe the sounds you hear and omit the vowels. Use **S** or **K** instead of **C**: to find circle use **SRKL**. Use **J** to find joy, **JM** to find gem and **G** to find go.

DRNKN drinking *beverage*
DRNKN drunken *intoxicated*
DRNKNG drinking *beverage*
DRNKNS drunkenness *intoxication*
DRNKR dernier cri *fashion*
DRNKR drinker *one who swallows a beverage*
DRNKRD drunkard *alcoholic*
DRNKRDKL adrenocortical *glandular*
DRNKRTKL adrenocortical *glandular*
DRNKRTKSTRD adrenocorticosteroid *drug*
DRNL adrenal *gland*
DRNL darnel *grass*
DRNL diurnal (adj) *daytime* diurnally (adv)
DRNL doornail *hardware*
DRNLKDM adrenalectomy *surgery*
DRNLKDMZD adrenalectomized *surgery*
DRNLKTM adrenalectomy *surgery*
DRNLKTMZD adrenalectomized *surgery*
DRNLN Adrenalin *(trademark) drug*
DRNLN adrenaline *epinephrine*
DRNLRNGGLG otorhinolaryngology *ear, nose and throat*
DRNLRNGGLJ otorhinolaryngology *ear, nose and throat*
DRNLRNGGLJKL otorhinolaryngological *ear, nose and throat*
DRNLRNGGLJST otorhinolaryngologist *ear, nose and throat*
DRNLRNGLG otorhinolaryngology *ear, nose and throat*
DRNLRNGLJ otorhinolaryngology *ear, nose and throat*
DRNLRNGLJKL

otorhinolaryngological *ear, nose and throat*
DRNLRNGLJST otorhinolaryngologist *ear, nose and throat*
DRNMNT adornment *decoration*
DRNN darning *stitching*
DRNNG darning *stitching*
DRNPP drainpipe *plumbing*
DRNR darner *stitcher*
DRNR drainer *depletion*
DRNR droner *hummer*
DRNRJK adrenergic *like adrenaline*
DRNRJKL adrenergically *like adrenaline*
DRNRM drawing room *reception*
DRNRS dry nurse (n) *caregiver* dry-nurse (v)
DRNS dearness *love, cost*
DRNS direness *dread*
DRNS dourness *sternness*
DRNS dryness *without water, irony*
DRNS utterance *speech*
DRNT odorant *added smell* (Br) odourant
DRNTS utterance *speech*
DRNWRK drawnwork *fabric*
DRNYKR dernier cri *fashion*
DRP drape (v) *arrange in folds* draped draping
DRP drape (n) *curtain*
DRP drip (v) *spill* dripped dripping
DRP drip (n) *liquid, jerk*
DRP drippy *rainy* drippier drippiest
DRP droop *hang down*
DRP droopy *hanging* droopier droopiest
DRP drop (v) *fall, write, dismiss** dropped dropping
DRP drop (n) *decline, liquid, advantage**
DRP drupe *fruit*
DRPBL drapable *arrange in folds*
DRPBLD drapability *arrange*

in folds
DRPBLT drapability *arrange in folds*
DRPC dropsy *swelling*
DRPD drophead *(Br) convertible*
DRPD dropped *lower*
DRPDD drop-dead *impressive*
DRPDR drip-dry *fabric*
DRPF drop off (v) *sleep*
DRPF drop-off (n) *descent*
DRPFRJ drop-forge *metal work*
DRPFRJR drop forger *metal worker*
DRPFRNT drop front *cover*
DRPHD drophead *(Br) convertible*
DRPKK dropkick (n) *kick* drip-kick (v)
DRPKKR drop-kicker *sports*
DRPKLTH drop cloth *cover*
DRPKR draw poker *card game*
DRPKRTN drop curtain *stage*
DRPL draw play *football*
DRPLF drop leaf *table*
DRPLT doorplate *name*
DRPLT drawplate *wires*
DRPLT droplet *liquid*
DRPLT droplight *illuminate*
DRPLT drupelet *berry*
DRPN drop in (v) *visit*
DRPN drop-in (n) *visitor*
DRPN dropping *dung*
DRPNG dropping *dung*
DRPNGS drippings *juice*
DRPNGZ drippings *juice*
DRPNS drippings *juice*
DRPNZ drippings *juice*
DRPR draper *cloth dealer*
DRPR drapery *curtains* draperies
DRPR dripper *moisture*
DRPR drippier *wetter*
DRPR droopier *hanging*
DRPR dropper *dispenser*
DRPR eyedropper *dispenser*
DRPRZ door prize *winner*
DRPS dropsy *swelling*

Letters aren't doubled for single sounds: to find alley use **L** not **LL**. Use **Y** and **W** as hard sounds only: to find yellow use **YL**. (Br)=British spelling or usage. * See dictionary.

DRPS eyedrops *medicine*
DRPSHS drupaceous *fruit*
DRPSHT drop shot *sports*
DRPSKL dropsical *swollen*
DRPST doorpost *side*
DRPST drippiest *wettest*
DRPST droopiest *hanging*
DRPSTN dripstone *stalactite or stalagmite*
DRPT drop out (v) *quit* dropout (n)
DRPT dropped *lower*
DRPVL drop volley *sports*
DRPYR drippier *wetter*
DRPYR droopier *hanging*
DRPYST drippiest *wettest*
DRPYST droopiest *hanging*
DRPZN drop zone *target*
DRR adorer *worshiper*
DRR darer *bold one*
DRR derrière (or) derriere *rump*
DRR direr *dreadful*
DRR drawer *draftsman, sliding box*
DRR drear *cheerless*
DRR dreary *cheerless* drearier dreariest
DRR drier *(adj) without water*
DRR dryer *(n) moisture extractor*
DRRFL drawerful *furniture*
DRRL drearily *cheerless*
DRRN dry run *rehearsal*
DRRNS dreariness *cheerless*
DRRR drearier *cheerless*
DRRST dreariest *cheerless*
DRRT dry-rot (v) *decay* dry rot (n)
DRRYR drearier *cheerless*
DRRYST dreariest *cheerless*
DRRZ drawers *underwear*
DRS address *(n) place of residence (v) speak to*
DRS addressee *receiver*
DRS daresay *agree*
DRS dorsa (pl) *back* dorsum
DRS dress *garment* dresses
DRS dressy *formal* dressier dressiest
DRS dross *waste*
DRS drossy *scummy*

DRS dry ice *coolant*
DRS duress *force*
DRS odorize *scent* odorized odorizing (Br) odourize
DRS odorous *smelly* (Br) odourous
DRS outdress *clothing*
DRS uterus *womb* uteri
DRSBL addressable *decoder*
DRSBLD addressability *decoder*
DRSBLT addressability *decoder*
DRSD dorsad *back*
DRSDK drastic *severe*
DRSDKL drastically *severe*
DRSDN dress down *scold, dress casually*
DRSFL drosophila *fly*
DRSH dragee *nut, ball*
DRSHK droshky *carriage* droshkies
DRSHLD dress shield *underarm*
DRSHN adoration *worship*
DRSHN derision *ridicule*
DRSHN duration *time*
DRSHN iteration *repetition*
DRSHRT dress shirt *with necktie*
DRSHST dirigiste *planning*
DRSHZM dirigisme *planning*
DRSJ dressage *horses*
DRSKD dress code *rules*
DRSKN deerskin *leather*
DRSL doorsill *entry*
DRSL dorsal (n, adj) *back* dorsally (adv)
DRSL dressily *formal*
DRSL dry cell *battery*
DRSLDRL dorsolateral *back and sides*
DRSLTRL dorsolateral *back and sides*
DRSM dorsum *back* dorsa
DRSMKN dressmaking *clothing*
DRSMKNG dressmaking *clothing*
DRSMKR dressmaker *clothing*

DRSN dressing *sauce, ointment*
DRSNDN dressing-down *scolding*
DRSNG dressing *sauce, ointment*
DRSNGDN dressing-down *scolding*
DRSNGK dry sink *cabinet*
DRSNK dry sink *cabinet*
DRSNS dressiness *formal*
DRSNSHN deracination *uproot*
DRSNT deracinate *uproot* deracinated deracinating
DRSP dress up *fancy clothes*
DRSPS outer space *universe*
DRSR addresser *(n) speaker, sender, director**
DRSR derisory *ridicule*
DRSR dresser *bureau, one that dresses*
DRSR dressier *formal*
DRSRKL dress circle *seats*
DRSS diaeresis *symbol, verse* diaereses
DRSS diuresis *urine* diureses
DRSSH dressage *horses*
DRSSHLD dress shield *underarm*
DRSSHRT dress shirt *with necktie*
DRSST dressiest *formal*
DRST diarist *writer*
DRST direst *dreadful*
DRST driest *without water*
DRSTK drastic *severe*
DRSTKL drastically *severe*
DRSTKR deerstalker *hat*
DRSTN drystone *(Br) no mortar*
DRSTP doorstep *entry*
DRSTP doorstop *holding device*
DRSTRNG drawstring *closure*
DRSV derisive *ridicule*
DRSVL derisively *ridicule*
DRSVNS derisiveness *ridicule*

Use letters that best describe the sounds you hear and omit the vowels. Use **S** or **K** instead of **C**: to find circle use **SRKL**. Use **J** to find joy, **JM** to find gem and **G** to find go.

DRSVNTRL dorsoventral (adj) *back and front* dorsoventrally (adv)
DRSYR dressier *formal*
DRSYST dressiest *formal*
DRSZ diaereses (pl) *symbol,* verse diaeresis
DRSZH dressage *horses*
DRT adroit *clever*
DRT dart (n) *missile* (v) *move quickly*
DRT dirt *soil*
DRT dirty (v) *soil, foul* dirtied dirtying dirties
DRT dirty (adj) *soiled, lewd* dirtier dirtiest
DRT drat *damn* dratted dratting
DRT droit *right*
DRT drought *scarcity*
DRT droughty *dry*
DRT iterate *repeat* iterated iterating
DRTBG dirtbag *bum*
DRTBK dirt bike *vehicle*
DRTBRD dartboard *game*
DRTCHP dirt cheap *inexpensive*
DRTDR door-to-door *each house*
DRTFRMR dirt farmer *crops*
DRTH dearth *lack*
DRTHRS druthers *preference*
DRTHRZ druthers *preference*
DRTK autoerotic *self-stimulating*
DRTK deer tick *insect*
DRTK diuretic *more urine*
DRTKC Adriatic Sea *body of water*
DRTKS Adriatic Sea *body of water*
DRTL adroitly *cleverly*
DRTL dirtily *soiled*
DRTNS adroitness *cleverness*
DRTNS dirtiness *soiled*
DRTNS droughtiness *dryness*
DRTPR dirt-poor *poverty*
DRTR darter *fish*
DRTR dirtier *soiled*
DRTS darts *game*

DRTST dirtiest *soiled*
DRTSZM autoeroticism (or) autoerotism *self-stimulation*
DRTV iterative *repetition*
DRTYR dirtier *soiled*
DRTYST dirtiest *soiled*
DRTZM autoerotism (or) autoeroticism *self-stimulation*
DRV derive *obtain* derived deriving
DRV drive (v) *direct, force, operate a vehicle** drove driving driven
DRV drive (n) *ambition, ride, roadway**
DRV drove (n) *crowd* (v-past) drive
DRVBL derivable *obtain, originate*
DRVBL drivable *move, propel*
DRVBLD drivability *move, propel*
DRVBLT drivability *move, propel*
DRVDV derivative *product*
DRVDVL derivatively *product*
DRVDVNS derivativeness *product*
DRVL drivel (v) *drool, chatter* driveled (or) drivelled driveling (or) drivelling
DRVL drivel (n) *nonsense*
DRVLR driveler *drool, chatter*
DRVN drive-in *theater, restaurant*
DRVN driven *pushed*
DRVN driving *direct, force, car**
DRVNG driving *direct, force, car**
DRVR deriver *source*
DRVR driver *direct, force, car**
DRVR drover *cowboy*
DRVSH dervish *Muslim*
DRVSHFT driveshaft *vehicle*
DRVSHN derivation *source*
DRVT derivate *obtain, originate*
DRVTM drive time *rush hour*

radio
DRVTRN drivetrain *vehicle*
DRVTV derivative *product*
DRVTVL derivatively *product*
DRVTVNS derivativeness *product*
DRVTZ derivatize *convert* derivatized derivatizing
DRVTZSHN derivatization *conversion*
DRVW driveway *private road*
DRW doorway *opening*
DRW drawee *payer*
DRWD druid *wizard*
DRWDK druidic (or) druidical *magical*
DRWDKL druidical (or) druidic *magical*
DRWDZM druidism *religion*
DRWL dry well *drainage*
DRWL drywall *construction*
DRWN drawing *sketch*
DRWNG drawing *sketch*
DRWR outerwear *clothing*
DRXK ataraxic (or) ataractic *tranquilizer*
DRY diarrhea *feces*
DRYBL dryable *no moisture*
DRYD dry-eyed *no tears*
DRYD dryad *nymph*
DRYDKC Adriatic Sea *body of water*
DRYDKS Adriatic Sea *body of water*
DRYJ drayage *fee*
DRYR derrière (or) derriere *rump*
DRYR drier (adj) *without water*
DRYR dryer (n) *moisture extractor*
DRYRD deeryard *herd area*
DRYRD dooryard *area*
DRYS dry ice *coolant*
DRYST driest *without water*
DRYTKC Adriatic Sea *body of water*
DRYTKS Adriatic Sea *body of water*
DRZ drowse *sleep* drowsed drowsing
DRZ drowsy *sleepy* drowsier

Letters aren't doubled for single sounds: to find alley use **L** not **LL**. Use **Y** and **W** as hard sounds only: to find yellow use **YL**. (Br)=British spelling or usage. * See dictionary.

drowsiest

DRZ Druze (or) Druse *Muslim*

DRZ odorize *scent* odorized odorizing (Br) odourize

DRZ outdoors *open air*

DRZH dragee *nut, ball*

DRZHN derision *ridicule*

DRZHST dirigiste *planning*

DRZHZM dirigisme *planning*

DRZL drizzle *rain* drizzled drizzling

DRZL drizzly *rainy*

DRZL drowsily *sleepy*

DRZNS drowsiness *sleepy*

DRZR derisory *ridicule*

DRZR drowsier *sleepier*

DRZST drowsiest *sleepiest*

DRZYR drowsier *sleepier*

DRZYST drowsiest *sleepiest*

DS adduce *cite* adduced adducing

DS adios *goodbye*

DS AIDS *(abbr) acquired immunodeficiency syndrome*

DS dais *platform*

DS deice *thaw* deiced deicing

DS deuce *(v) tennis, damn* deuced deucing

DS deuce *(n) two, tie score, devil*

DS dice *(v) cut into cubes, gamble* diced dicing

DS dice *(pl) (n) gamble, game cube* die (singular)

DS dicey *risky* dicier diciest

DS dis *(v-slang) disrespect* dissed dissing

DS dose *(v) give medicine* dosed dosing

DS dose *(n) portion*

DS dossier *file*

DS douse *wet* doused dousing

DS educe *bring out* educed educing

DS ides *date*

DS idiocy *stupidity* idiocies

DS odds *wager*

DS odious *hateful*

DS odyssey *journey* odysseys

DS otiose *vain*

DS outhouse *toilet*

DSB disobey *fail to comply* disobeyed disobeying

DSBB Addis Ababa *city*

DSBDNS disobedience *fail to comply*

DSBDNT disobedient *fail to comply*

DSBDNTS disobedience *fail to comply*

DSBDYNS disobedience *fail to comply*

DSBDYNT disobedient *fail to comply*

DSBDYNTS disobedience *fail to comply*

DSBL decibel *sound*

DSBL disable *break* disabled disabling

DSBL dishabille *dress*

DSBL dust bowl *drought*

DSBL educible *bring out*

DSBLD disability *handicap* disabilities

DSBLD disabled *handicapped*

DSBLF disbelief *question*

DSBLJ disoblige *inconvenience* disobliged disobliging

DSBLMNT disablement *handicap*

DSBLT disability *handicap* disabilities

DSBLV disbelieve *question* disbelieved disbelieving

DSBLVR disbeliever *questioner*

DSBN disband *break up*

DSBN dustbin *trashcan*

DSBND disband *break up*

DSBNDMNT disbandment *breakup*

DSBNMNT disbandment *breakup*

DSBR disbar *expel*

DSBR disobeyer *no compliance*

DSBRMNT disbarment *expulsion*

DSBRS disburse *distribute* disbursed disbursing

DSBRSBL disbursable *distribute*

DSBRSMNT disbursement *distribute*

DSBRSR disburser *distribute*

DSBYR disobeyer *no compliance*

DSBYZ disabuse *correct* disabused disabusing

DSBZ disabuse *correct* disabused disabusing

DSCBL dissociable *separate*

DSCDV dissociative *separate*

DSCHRJ discharge *(v) shoot, unload, cancel** discharged discharging

DSCHRJ discharge *(n) release, flow*

DSCHRJR discharger *shoot, unload, cancel**

DSCSHN dissociation *separation*

DSCT dissociate *separate* dissociated dissociating

DSCTV dissociative *separate*

DSCYBL dissociable *separate*

DSCYDV dissociative *separate*

DSCYSHN dissociation *separation*

DSCYT dissociate *separate* dissociated dissociating

DSCYTV dissociative *separate*

DSD audacity *boldness* audacities

DSD dayside *light*

DSD decide *determine, resolve* decided deciding

DSD deuced *confused*

DSD do-si-do *square-dance* do-si-dos

DSD dusty *with dust* dustier dustiest

DSD otiosity *in vain*

DSDBL decidable *decision*

Use letters that best describe the sounds you hear and omit the vowels. Use **S** or **K** instead of **C**: to find circle use **SRKL**. Use **J** to find joy, **JM** to find gem and **G** to find go.

DSDD decided *no doubt*
DSDDL decidedly *no doubt*
DSDDNS decidedness *no doubt*
DSDF distaff *female, rod* distaffs
DSDK distich *two lines*
DSDKS distichous *two rows*
DSDL distal (adj) *away from* distally (adv)
DSDL distill *brew* distilled distilling
DSDLSHN distillation *brew*
DSDLT distillate *brew*
DSDN deciding *decisive*
DSDN destine *predetermine* destined destining
DSDN destiny *fate* destinies
DSDN disdain *despise*
DSDNFL disdainful (adj) *despise* disdainfully (adv)
DSDNFNS disdainfulness *despise*
DSDNG deciding *decisive*
DSDNS dissidence *disagreement*
DSDNS distance *(v) keep away, outstrip* distanced distancing
DSDNT decedent *dead one*
DSDNT dissident *disagreer*
DSDNT distant *far-off*
DSDNTS dissidence *disagreement*
DSDNTS distance *(v) keep away, outstrip* distanced distancing
DSDR decider *determine, resolve*
DSDR duster *crop sprayer, garment, cleaner*
DSDR dustier *with dust*
DSDRB disturb *interrupt, alarm*
DSDRBD disturbed *mentally ill*
DSDRBNGL disturbingly *alarmingly*
DSDRBNL disturbingly *alarmingly*
DSDRBNS disturbance *disorder*

DSDRBNTS disturbance *disorder*
DSDRBR disturber *interrupt, alarm*
DSDRD dastard *coward*
DSDRDL dastardly *cowardly*
DSDRDR distorter *misrepresent*
DSDRSHN distortion *misrepresentation*
DSDRT distort *misrepresent* distorted distorting
DSDRTR distorter *misrepresent*
DSDSF dissatisfy *displease* dissatisfied dissatisfying dissatisfies
DSDSFD dissatisfied *displeasure*
DSDSFKDR dissatisfactory *displeasure*
DSDSFKSHN dissatisfaction *displeasure*
DSDSFKTR dissatisfactory *displeasure*
DSDST dustiest *with dust*
DSDTSHN destitution *need*
DSDTT destitute *needy*
DSDTYSHN destitution *need*
DSDTYT destitute *needy*
DSDVL dust devil *whirlwind*
DSDVNJ disadvantage *harm* disadvantaged disadvantaging
DSDVNJD disadvantaged *lacking*
DSDVNJT disadvantaged *lacking*
DSDVNTJ disadvantage *harm* disadvantaged disadvantaging
DSDVNTJD disadvantaged *lacking*
DSDVNTJS disadvantageous *belittling*
DSDVNTJSL disadvantageously *belittling*
DSDVNTJSNS disadvantageousness *belittling*

DSDYR dustier *with dust*
DSDYST dustiest *with dust*
DSFG dysphagia *swallowing*
DSFGR disfigure *maim* disfigured disfiguring
DSFGRMNT disfigurement *maim*
DSFGY dysphagia *swallowing*
DSFGYR disfigure *maim* disfigured disfiguring
DSFGYRMNT disfigurement *maim*
DSFJ dysphagia *swallowing*
DSFJY dysphagia *swallowing*
DSFK disaffect *rebel, estrange*
DSFKDD disaffected *rebellious, estranged*
DSFKSHN disaffection *rebellious, estranged*
DSFKT disaffect *rebel, estrange*
DSFKTD disaffected *rebellious, estranged*
DSFN dysphonia *voice*
DSFNGKSHN dysfunction *damage*
DSFNGKSHNL dysfunctional *damaged*
DSFNGSHN dysfunction *damage*
DSFNGSHNL dysfunctional *damaged*
DSFNKSHN dysfunction *damage*
DSFNKSHNL dysfunctional *damaged*
DSFNY dysphonia *voice*
DSFR decipher *decode*
DSFR dysphoria *illness*
DSFRBL decipherable *decode*
DSFRK dysphoric *ill*
DSFRM disaffirm *contradict*
DSFRMNS disaffirmance *contradiction*
DSFRMNT decipherment *decode*
DSFRMNTS disaffirmance *contradiction*

Letters aren't doubled for single sounds: to find alley use **L** not **LL**. Use **Y** and **W** as hard sounds only: to find yellow use **YL**. (Br)=British spelling or usage. * See dictionary.

DSFRNCHZ disfranchise *no vote*
DSFRR decipherer *decoder*
DSFRY dysphoria *illness*
DSFSH dysphasia *swallowing*
DSFSHY dysphasia *swallowing*
DSFVR disfavor *disproval*
DSFZH dysphasia *swallowing*
DSFZHY dysphasia *swallowing*
DSFZK dysphasic *swallowing*
DSGJSCHN autosuggestion *hypnosis*
DSGNK dysgenic *defective*
DSGR disagree *differ* disagreed disagreeing
DSGRBL disagreeable (adj) *offensive* disagreeably (adv)
DSGRD discard *get rid of*
DSGRDBL discardable *get rid of*
DSGRGSHN desegregation *stop separation*
DSGRGT desegregate *stop separation* desegregated desegregating
DSGRJ disgorge *vomit* disgorged disgorging
DSGRM decigram *measure of mass*
DSGRMNBL discriminable (adj) *distinguish* discriminably (adv)
DSGRMNBLD discriminability *distinguish* discriminabilities
DSGRMNBLT discriminability *distinguish* discriminabilities
DSGRMNDNG discriminating *reasonable*
DSGRMNDR discriminator *judge, circuit*
DSGRMNDV discriminative *reasonable*

DSGRMNNT discriminant *math*
DSGRMNT disagreement *quarrel*
DSGRMNT discriminate *distinguish* discriminated discriminating
DSGRMNTN discriminating *reasonable*
DSGRMNTNG discriminating *reasonable*
DSGRMNTR discriminator *judge, circuit*
DSGRMNTR discriminatory *reasonable*
DSGRMNTRL discriminatorily *reasonably*
DSGRMNTV discriminative *reasonable*
DSGRNL disgruntle *make unhappy* disgruntled disgruntling
DSGRNLD disgruntled *unhappy*
DSGRNLMNT disgruntlement *unhappiness*
DSGRNTL disgruntle *make unhappy* disgruntled disgruntling
DSGRNTLD disgruntled *unhappy*
DSGRNTLMNT disgruntlement *unhappiness*
DSGRPNC discrepancy *variance* discrepancies
DSGRPNS discrepancy *variance* discrepancies
DSGRPNT discrepant *variant*
DSGRPNTC discrepancy *variance* discrepancies
DSGRPNTL discrepantly *variant*
DSGRPNTS discrepancy *variance* discrepancies
DSGRS disgrace *shame* disgraced disgracing
DSGRSFL disgraceful (adj) *shame* disgracefully (adv)
DSGRSFLNS

disgracefulness *shame*
DSGRSHN discretion *caution, choice*
DSGRSHNR discretionary *caution, choice*
DSGRSR disgracer *shame*
DSGRT discreet *prudent*
DSGRT discrete *separate*
DSGRTL discreetly *prudent*
DSGRTL discretely *separately*
DSGRTNS discreetness *prudence*
DSGRTNS discreteness *separation*
DSGRYBL disagreeable (adj) *offensive* disagreeably (adv)
DSGS discus *disk* discuses
DSGS discuss *talk* discussed discussing
DSGSBL discussable (or) discussible *talk*
DSGSDD disgusted *sickened or offended*
DSGSDDL disgustedly *sickened or offended*
DSGSDN disgusting *sickening or offending*
DSGSDNG disgusting *sickening or offending*
DSGSHN discussion *dialogue*
DSGSNT discussant *speaker*
DSGSR discusser *speaker*
DSGST disgust *sicken or offend*
DSGSTD disgusted *sickened or offended*
DSGSTDL disgustedly *sickened or offended*
DSGSTFL disgustful (adj) *sickening or offending* disgustfully (adv)
DSGSTN disgusting *sickening or offending*
DSGSTNG disgusting *sickening or offending*
DSGZ disguise *conceal* disguised disguising
DSGZMNT disguisement *conceal*

Use letters that best describe the sounds you hear and omit the vowels. Use **S** or **K** instead of **C**: to find circle use **SRKL**. Use **J** to find joy, **JM** to find gem and **G** to find go.

DSGZR disguiser *conceal*

DSH adagio *slow, ballet* adagios

DSH attaché *diplomat*

DSH dash (*v*) *run, strike* (*n*) *small amount, punctuation mark* dashes

DSH dashi *broth*

DSH dish (*n*) *plate, food* (*v*) *serve*

DSH dishy *attractive* dishier dishiest

DSH douche *rinse* douched douching

DSH êtagêre (or) etagere *furniture*

DSHBL dishabille *dress*

DSHBRD dashboard *vehicle panel*

DSHD dashed *with dashes, ruined*

DSHD dished *concave*

DSHK dashiki *garment*

DSHKLTH dishcloth *towel*

DSHKS attaché case *briefcase*

DSHMRK Deutschemark *money*

DSHN addition *supplement*

DSHN audition *tryout*

DSHN dashing *striking*

DSHN Duchenne *disease*

DSHN edition *book*

DSHN ideation *thought*

DSHNG dashing *striking*

DSHNGL dashingly *striking*

DSHNL additional (adj) *added* additionally (adv)

DSHNL dashingly *striking*

DSHPN dishpan *sink*

DSHR dasher *runner, mixer*

DSHR dishier *attractive*

DSHR dozer *bulldozer*

DSHR du jour *of the day*

DSHR dysuria *urine*

DSHRG dishrag *towel*

DSHRMN disharmony *discord*

DSHRMNS disharmonious *discord*

DSHRMNYS disharmonious *discord*

DSHRTN dishearten *lose spirit*

DSHRY dysuria *urine*

DSHS audacious *bold*

DSHS autoecious *in one place*

DSHS dioecious *separated sexes*

DSHSL audaciously *boldly*

DSHSL autoeciously *in one place*

DSHSNS audaciousness *boldness*

DSHST dishiest *attractive*

DSHT dashed *with dashes, ruined*

DSHT dish out *dispense*

DSHT dished *concave*

DSHV déjà vu *memory*

DSHVL dishevel *mess up* disheveled (or) dishevelled disheveling (or) dishevelling

DSHVLD disheveled (or) dishevelled *messed up*

DSHWDR dishwater *wash water*

DSHWR dishware *tableware*

DSHWSHR dishwasher *appliance*

DSHWTR dishwater *wash water*

DSHY adagio *slow, ballet* adagios

DSHYR dishier *attractive*

DSHYR dysuria *urine*

DSHYRY dysuria *urine*

DSHYST dishiest *attractive*

DSJ decidua *uterus* deciduae

DSJ dosage *amount*

DSJK disc jockey *radio*

DSJKT dust jacket *book cover*

DSJL decidual *uterus*

DSJN disjoin *detach*

DSJND disjointed *rambling or confused*

DSJNDL disjointedly *rambling or confused*

DSJNDNS disjointedness *rambling or confused*

DSJNGCHR disjuncture *separation*

DSJNGDV disjunctive *separated*

DSJNGDVL disjunctively *separated*

DSJNGK disjunct *separated*

DSJNGKCHR disjuncture *separation*

DSJNGKDV disjunctive *separated*

DSJNGKDVL disjunctively *separated*

DSJNGKSHN disjunction *separation*

DSJNGKSHR disjuncture *separation*

DSJNGKT disjunct *separated*

DSJNGKTV disjunctive *separated*

DSJNGKTVL disjunctively *separated*

DSJNGSHR disjuncture *separation*

DSJNGT disjunct *separated*

DSJNGTV disjunctive *separated*

DSJNGTVL disjunctively *separated*

DSJNK disjunct *separated*

DSJNK dysgenic *defective*

DSJNKCHR disjuncture *separation*

DSJNKDV disjunctive *separated*

DSJNKDVL disjunctively *separated*

DSJNKSHN disjunction *separation*

DSJNKSHR disjuncture *separation*

DSJNKT disjunct *separated*

DSJNKTV disjunctive *separated*

DSJNKTVL disjunctively *separated*

DSJNT disjoint *separate*

DSJNTD disjointed *rambling or confused*

DSJNTDL disjointedly *rambling or confused*

DSJNTDNS disjointedness

Letters aren't doubled for single sounds: to find alley use **L** not **LL**. Use **Y** and **W** as hard sounds only: to find yellow use **YL**. (Br)=British spelling or usage. * See dictionary.

rambling or confused
DSJS deciduous *seasonal*
DSJSCHN autosuggestion
hypnosis
DSJSNS deciduousness
seasonal
DSJT deciduate *uterus*
DSJW decidua *uterus*
deciduae
DSJWL decidual *uterus*
DSJWS deciduous *seasonal*
DSJWSNS deciduousness
seasonal
DSJWT deciduate *uterus*
DSK desk *furniture*
DSK disco *dance* discos
DSK disk (or) disc *circle*
DSK dissect *cut apart*
DSK dusk *evening*
DSK dusky *dark* duskier
duskiest
DSKD discoid *disk*
DSKDD dissected *cut apart*
DSKDL discoidal *disk*
DSKDNG dissecting *cut
apart*
DSKDR desiccator *dry*
DSKDR dissector *cut apart*
DSKDV desiccative *dry*
DSKGRF discography
records discographies
DSKGRFKL discographical
records
DSKGRFR discographer
records
DSKJK disc jockey *radio*
DSKL day school *education*
DSKL duskily *darkly*
DSKLM disclaim *deny*
DSKLMR disclaimer *denial*
DSKLR discolor *change hue*
(Br) discolour
DSKLSHN de-escalation
slow down
DSKLSHR disclosure
exposure
DSKLT de-escalate *slow
down* de-escalated de-
escalating
DSKLTR de-escalatory *slow
down*
DSKLZ disclose *reveal*

disclosed disclosing
DSKLZHR disclosure
exposure
DSKLZN disclosing *stain*
DSKLZNG disclosing *stain*
DSKLZR discloser *reveal*
DSKMBBLSHN
discombobulation *upset*
DSKMBBLT
discombobulate *upset*
discombobulated
discombobulating
DSKMBBYLSHN
discombobulation *upset*
DSKMBBYLT
discombobulate *upset*
discombobulated
discombobulating
DSKMD discommode
trouble discommoded
discommoding
DSKMFCHR discomfiture
embarrassment
DSKMFRT discomfort
annoyance
DSKMFT discomfit
embarrass
DSKMFTR discomfiture
embarrassment
DSKMPSHR discomposure
disturbance
DSKMPZ discompose
disturb
DSKMPZHR discomposure
disturbance
DSKN doeskin *leather*
DSKNBL discountable
devalue
DSKNDK dyskinetic *spasms*
DSKNK disconnect *detach*
DSKNKDD disconnected
detached
DSKNKDDL disconnectedly
detached
DSKNKDDNS
disconnectedness
detached
DSKNKSHN disconnection
detachment
DSKNKT disconnect *detach*
DSKNKTD disconnected
detached

DSKNKTDL disconnectedly
detached
DSKNKTDNS
disconnectedness
detached
DSKNR discounter *devaluer*
DSKNS duskiness *darkness*
DSKNSH dyskinesia *spasms*
DSKNSLSHN
disconsolation *dejection*
DSKNSLT disconsolate
dejected
DSKNSLTL disconsolately
dejected
DSKNSLTNS
disconsolateness
dejection
DSKNSRDNG
disconcerting *disturbing*
DSKNSRDNGL
disconcertingly *disturbing*
DSKNSRT disconcert
disturb
DSKNSRTMNT
disconcertment
disturbance
DSKNSRTN disconcerting
disturbing
DSKNSRTNG disconcerting
disturbing
DSKNSRTNGL
disconcertingly *disturbing*
DSKNSRTNL
disconcertingly *disturbing*
DSKNT descant *melody*
DSKNT desiccant *dry*
DSKNT discount *devalue*
DSKNTBL discountable
devalue
DSKNTK dyskinetic *spasms*
DSKNTN discontinue *stop*
discontinued
discontinuing
DSKNTND discontented
dissatisfied
DSKNTND discontinuity *gap*
DSKNTNDL discontentedly
dissatisfied
DSKNTNNS discontinuance
stop
DSKNTNNS
discountenance

embarrassment
DSKNTNNTS
discontinuance *stop*
DSKNTNNTS
discountenance
embarrassment
DSKNTNS discontinuous
with gaps
DSKNTNT discontent
dissatisfaction
DSKNTNT discontinuity *gap*
DSKNTNTD discontented
dissatisfied
DSKNTNTDL
discontentedly *dissatisfied*
DSKNTNTMNT
discontentment
dissatisfied
DSKNTNTS
discountenance
embarrassment
DSKNTNWD discontinuity
gap
DSKNTNWNS
discontinuance *stop*
DSKNTNWNTS
discontinuance *stop*
DSKNTNWS discontinuous
with gaps
DSKNTNWT discontinuity
gap
DSKNTNY discontinue *stop*
discontinued
discontinuing
DSKNTNYD discontinuity
gap
DSKNTNYNS
discontinuance *stop*
DSKNTNYNTS
discontinuance *stop*
DSKNTNYS discontinuous
with gaps
DSKNTNYT discontinuity
gap
DSKNTNYWD discontinuity
gap
DSKNTNYWNS
discontinuance *stop*
DSKNTNYWNTS
discontinuance *stop*
DSKNTNYWS
discontinuous *with gaps*

DSKNTNYWT discontinuity
gap
DSKNTR discounter
devaluer
DSKNZH dyskinesia *spasms*
DSKR descry *discover*
descried descrying
descries
DSKR duskier *darker*
DSKRB describe *represent*
described describing
DSKRBBL describable
represent
DSKRBR describer *represent*
DSKRD disaccord *disagree*
DSKRD discard *get rid of*
DSKRD discord *conflict*
DSKRDBL discardable *get*
rid of
DSKRDC discourtesy
rudeness discourtesies
DSKRDDBL discreditable
(adj) *disgraceful*
discreditably (adv)
DSKRDNC discordancy
conflict discordancies
DSKRDNS discordance
clash
DSKRDNS discordancy
conflict discordancies
DSKRDNT discordant
conflicting
DSKRDNTC discordancy
conflict discordancies
DSKRDNTS discordance
clash
DSKRDNTS discordancy
conflict discordancies
DSKRDR desecrater (or)
desecrator *violator*
DSKRDS discourteous *rude*
DSKRDS discourtesy
rudeness discourtesies
DSKRDSL discourteously
rudely
DSKRDSNS
discourteousness
rudeness
DSKRDT discredit *disbelieve,*
disgrace
DSKRDTBL discreditable
(adj) *disgraceful*

discreditably (adv)
DSKRDYS discourteous
rude
DSKRDYSL discourteously
rudely
DSKRDYSNS
discourteousness
rudeness
DSKRJ discourage
dishearten discouraged
discouraging
DSKRJBL discourageable
dishearten
DSKRJMNT
discouragement
dishearten
DSKRJN discouraging
disheartening
DSKRJNG discouraging
disheartening
DSKRJR discourager
dishearten
DSKRMNBL discriminable
(adj) *distinguish*
discriminably (adv)
DSKRMNBLD
discriminability
distinguish
discriminabilities
DSKRMNBLT
discriminability
distinguish
discriminabilities
DSKRMNDN discriminating
reasonable
DSKRMNDNG
discriminating *reasonable*
DSKRMNDR discriminator
judge, circuit
DSKRMNDV discriminative
reasonable
DSKRMNNT discriminant
math
DSKRMNSHN
discrimination *judgment*
DSKRMNT discriminate
distinguish discriminated
discriminating
DSKRMNTN discriminating
reasonable
DSKRMNTNG
discriminating *reasonable*

Letters aren't doubled for single sounds: to find alley use **L** not **LL**. Use **Y** and **W** as hard sounds only: to find yellow use **YL**. (Br)=British spelling or usage. * See dictionary.

DSKRMNTR discriminator
judge, circuit

DSKRMNTR discriminatory
reasonable

DSKRMNTRL
discriminatorily *reasonably*

DSKRMNTV discriminative
reasonable

DSKRPDR descriptor
representation

DSKRPDV descriptive
representative

DSKRPNC discrepancy
variance discrepancies

DSKRPNS discrepancy
variance discrepancies

DSKRPNT discrepant
variant

DSKRPNTC discrepancy
variance discrepancies

DSKRPNTL discrepantly
variant

DSKRPNTS discrepancy
variance discrepancies

DSKRPSHN description
representation

DSKRPTR descriptor
representation

DSKRPTV descriptive
representative

DSKRS discourse *speech*
discoursed discoursing

DSKRS disgrace *shame*
disgraced disgracing

DSKRSFL disgraceful (adj)
shame disgracefully (adv)

DSKRSFLNS
disgracefulness *shame*

DSKRSHN desecration
violation

DSKRSHN discretion
caution, choice

DSKRSHNR discretionary
caution, choice

DSKRSR discourser *speaker*

DSKRSR disgracer *shame*

DSKRSV discursive
rambling

DSKRSVL discursively
rambling

DSKRSVNS discursiveness
rambling

DSKRT Descartes
philosopher

DSKRT desecrate *violate*
desecrated desecrating

DSKRT discreet *prudent*

DSKRT discrete *separate*

DSKRTC discourtesy
rudeness discourtesies

DSKRTL discreetly *prudent*

DSKRTL discretely
separately

DSKRTNS discreetness
prudence

DSKRTNS discreteness
separation

DSKRTR desecrater (or)
desecrator *violator*

DSKRTS discourteous *rude*

DSKRTS discourtesy
rudeness discourtesies

DSKRTSL discourteously
rudely

DSKRTSNS
discourteousness
rudeness

DSKRTYS discourteous
rude

DSKRTYSL discourteously
rudely

DSKRTYSNS
discourteousness
rudeness

DSKS discus *disk* discuses

DSKS discuss *talk*
discussed discussing

DSKSBL discussable (or)
discussible *talk*

DSKSDD disgusted *sickened
or offended*

DSKSDDL disgustedly
sickened or offended

DSKSDN disgusting
sickening or offending

DSKSDNG disgusting
sickening or offending

DSKSHN desiccation *dry*

DSKSHN discussion
dialogue

DSKSHN dissection *cut
apart*

DSKSMKN deus ex
machina *device*

DSKSMSHN deus ex
machina *device*

DSKSNT discussant *speaker*

DSKSR discusser *speaker*

DSKST disgust *sicken or
offend*

DSKST duskiest *darkest*

DSKSTD disgusted *sickened
or offended*

DSKSTDL disgustedly
sickened or offended

DSKSTFL disgustful (adj)
sickening or offending
disgustfully (adv)

DSKSTN disgusting
sickening or offending

DSKSTNG disgusting
sickening or offending

DSKT desiccate *dry*
desiccated desiccating

DSKT discount *devalue*

DSKT diskette *computer*

DSKT dissect *cut apart*

DSKTBL discountable
devalue

DSKTD dissected *cut apart*

DSKTK discothèque (or)
discotheque *dance*

DSKTN dissecting *cut apart*

DSKTNG dissecting *cut
apart*

DSKTNNS discountenance
embarrassment

DSKTNNTS
discountenance
embarrassment

DSKTNTS discountenance
embarrassment

DSKTP desktop *table size,
computer*

DSKTR desiccator *dry*

DSKTR dissector *cut apart*

DSKTV desiccative *dry*

DSKVR discover *learn, find*
discovered discovering

DSKVR discovery *find*
discoveries

DSKVR dustcover *cloth*

DSKVRBL discoverable
learn, find

DSKVRR discoverer *learn,
find*

Use letters that best describe the sounds you hear and omit the vowels. Use **S** or **K** instead of **C**: to find circle use **SRKL**. Use **J** to find joy, **JM** to find gem and **G** to find go.

DSKWLF disqualify *make ineligible* disqualified disqualifying disqualifies
DSKWLFKSHN disqualification *ineligible*
DSKWLFR disqualifier *ineligible*
DSKWLFYR disqualifier *ineligible*
DSKWT disquiet *anxiety*
DSKWTD disquietude *anxiety*
DSKWTN disquieting *anxious*
DSKWTNG disquieting *anxious*
DSKWTYD disquietude *anxiety*
DSKWYT disquiet *anxiety*
DSKWYTD disquietude *anxiety*
DSKWYTN disquieting *anxious*
DSKWYTNG disquieting *anxious*
DSKWYTYD disquietude *anxiety*
DSKWZSHN disquisition *discourse*
DSKYR duskier *darker*
DSKYST duskiest *darkest*
DSKZ disguise *conceal* disguised disguising
DSKZMNT disguisement *conceal*
DSKZR disguiser *conceal*
DSL diesel *fuel*
DSL disallow *bar*
DSL docile *tame*
DSL docilely *tamely*
DSL odiously *hatefully*
DSLBL dissoluble *separable*
DSLD docility *tameness*
DSLDNGL desolatingly *forsaken*
DSLDNL desolatingly *forsaken*
DSLDR deciliter *liquid measure*
DSLDR desolater *forsake*
DSLJ dislodge *force out* dislodged dislodging

DSLJMNT dislodgment (or) dislodgement *forced out*
DSLK dislike *disapprove* disliked disliking
DSLKBL dislikable *disapproved*
DSLKC dyslexia *language impairment*
DSLKCY dyslexia *language impairment*
DSLKR disliker *disapprover*
DSLKS dyslexia *language impairment*
DSLKSHN dislocation *displacement*
DSLKSK dyslexic *language impairment*
DSLKSY dyslexia *language impairment*
DSLKT dislocate *displace* dislocated dislocating
DSLL disloyal (adj) *faithless* disloyally (adv)
DSLLD disloyalty *no faith* disloyalties
DSLLT disloyalty *no faith* disloyalties
DSLN decillion *number*
DSLNDR desalinator *remove salt*
DSLNT desalinate *remove salt* desalinated desalinating
DSLNTR desalinator *remove salt*
DSLNZ desalinize *remove salt* desalinized desalinizing
DSLNZSHN desalinization *remove salt*
DSLRDR decelerator *slow down*
DSLRSHN deceleration *slow down*
DSLRT decelerate *slow down* decelerated decelerating
DSLRTR decelerator *slow down*
DSLSHN desolation *grief, ruin*
DSLSHN disillusion *remove*

faith
DSLSHN dissolution *decay, death*
DSLSHNMNT disillusionment *no faith*
DSLT desolate *forsake* desolated desolating
DSLT dissolute *no restraint*
DSLT docility *tameness*
DSLTL desolately *forsaken*
DSLTNGL desolatingly *forsaken*
DSLTNL desolatingly *forsaken*
DSLTNS desolateness *forsaken*
DSLTR deciliter *liquid measure*
DSLTR desolater *forsake*
DSLTR desultory *sluggish, random*
DSLTRL desultorily *sluggish, random*
DSLTRNS desultoriness *sluggish, random*
DSLV dissolve *melt, destroy* dissolved dissolving
DSLVNT dissolvent *melt, destroy*
DSLWNS disallowance *denial*
DSLWNTS disallowance *denial*
DSLX dyslexia *language impairment*
DSLXK dyslexic *language impairment*
DSLXY dyslexia *language impairment*
DSLYBL dissoluble *separable*
DSLYL disloyal (adj) *faithless* disloyally (adv)
DSLYLD disloyalty *no faith* disloyalties
DSLYLT disloyalty *no faith* disloyalties
DSLYN decillion *number*
DSLZHN disillusion *remove faith* disillusioned disillusioning
DSLZHND disillusioned *no faith*

Letters aren't doubled for single sounds: to find alley use **L** not **LL**. Use **Y** and **W** as hard sounds only: to find yellow use **YL**. (Br)=British spelling or usage. * See dictionary.

DSL

DSLZHNMNT
disillusionment *no faith*
DSM dismay *alarm*
DSMBD disembody *no body*
DSMBDD disembodied *no body*
DSMBL disembowel *remove organs*
DSMBL dissemble *take apart* dissembled dissembling
DSMBLMNT
disembowelment *remove organs*
DSMBLR dissembler *take apart*
DSMBR December *month*
DSMBRK disembark *leave*
DSMBRKSHN
disembarkation *leave*
DSMBRST Decembrist *Russian revolutionary*
DSMBWL disembowel *remove organs*
DSMBWLMNT
disembowelment *remove organs*
DSMDR decimeter *measure*
DSMDRK dissymmetric *no balance*
DSML decimal (adj, n) *number system* decimally (adv)
DSMLDR dissimulator *take apart*
DSMLR dissimilar *not alike*
DSMLRD dissimilarity *not alike* dissimilarities
DSMLRT dissimilarity *not alike* dissimilarities
DSMLSHN dissimilation *word sounds*
DSMLSHN dissimulation *take apart*
DSMLT dissimulate *take apart* dissimulated dissimulating
DSMLTD dissimilitude *not alike*
DSMLTR dissimulator *take apart*
DSMLTYD dissimilitude *not alike*

DSMLZ decimalize *convert to ten* decimalized decimalizing
DSMLZSHN decimalization *conversion*
DSMMBR dismember *cut up*
DSMMBRMNT
dismemberment *cut up*
DSMN dustman *(Br) trash collector* dustmen
DSMNDD disseminated *spread*
DSMNDR disseminator *spread*
DSMNL dismantle *take apart* dismantled dismantling
DSMNLMNT dismantlement *take apart*
DSMNSHN dissemination *spread*
DSMNT dismount *get down*
DSMNT disseminate *spread* disseminated disseminating
DSMNTD disseminated *spread*
DSMNTL dismantle *take apart* dismantled dismantling
DSMNTLMNT
dismantlement *take apart*
DSMNTR disseminator *spread*
DSMP dust mop *dry mop*
DSMS dismiss *discharge, reject* dismissed dismissing
DSMSHN decimation *one tenth, destroy*
DSMSHN dismission *discharge, reject*
DSMSL dismissal *discharge, reject*
DSMSV dismissive *discharge, reject*
DSMSVL dismissively *discharge, reject*
DSMT decimate *one tenth, destroy* decimated decimating
DSMT dismount *get down*

DSMTR decimeter *measure*
DSMTR dissymmetry *no balance*
DSMTRK dissymmetric *no balance*
DSMYLDR dissimulator *take apart*
DSMYLSHN dissimulation *take apart*
DSMYLT dissimulate *take apart* dissimulated dissimulating
DSMYLTR dissimulator *take apart*
DSN descend *go down*
DSN disown *denounce*
DSN dissing *(slang) disrespecting*
DSN dyspnea *breath* (Br) dyspnoea
DSNC decency *order, propriety* decencies
DSNCHN dissension *discord*
DSNCHNR disenchanter *no illusions*
DSNCHNT disenchant *no illusions*
DSNCHNT dissentient *disagree*
DSNCHNTMNT
disenchantment *no illusions*
DSNCHNTN disenchanting *no illusions*
DSNCHNTNG
disenchanting *no illusions*
DSNCHNTNGL
disenchantingly *no illusions*
DSNCHNTNL
disenchantingly *no illusions*
DSNCHNTR disenchanter *no illusions*
DSNCHS dissentious *disagree*
DSND descend *go down*
DSND disunity *division*
DSNDBL descendible *go down*
DSNDNT descendant (or) descendent *downward,*

Use letters that best describe the sounds you hear and omit the vowels. Use **S** or **K** instead of **C**: to find circle use **SRKL**. Use **J** to find joy, **JM** to find gem and **G** to find go.

heir *

DSNDR descender *letter*

DSNFK disinfect *cleanse*

DSNFKDNT disinfectant
cleanser

DSNFKSHN disinfection
cleaning

DSNFKT disinfect *cleanse*

DSNFKTNT disinfectant
cleanser

DSNFLSHN disinflation
decrease

DSNFLSHNR disinflationary
decrease

DSNFRMSHN
disinformation *untruth*

DSNFRNCHZ
disenfranchise *no vote*
disenfranchised
disenfranchising

DSNFRNCHZMNT
disenfranchisement *no
vote*

DSNFST disinfest *rid of pests*

DSNFSTNT disinfestant *rid
of pests*

DSNFSTSHN disinfestation
rid of pests

DSNG dissing *(slang)*
disrespecting

DSNGJ disengage *withdraw*
disengaged disengaging

DSNGKLNSHN
disinclination *aversion*

DSNGKRC idiosyncrasy
peculiarity idiosyncrasies

DSNGKRDK idiosyncratic
peculiar

DSNGKRDKL
idiosyncratically *peculiar*

DSNGKRS idiosyncrasy
peculiarity idiosyncrasies

DSNGKRTK idiosyncratic
peculiar

DSNGKRTKL
idiosyncratically *peculiar*

DSNGRDR disintegrator
break apart

DSNGRDV disintegrative
break apart

DSNGRSHN disintegration
break apart

DSNGRT disintegrate *break
apart* disintegrated
disintegrating

DSNGRTR disintegrator
break apart

DSNGRTV disintegrative
break apart

DSNHRDNS disinheritance
deprivation

DSNHRDNTS
disinheritance *deprivation*

DSNHRT disinherit *deprive*

DSNHRTNS disinheritance
deprivation

DSNHRTNTS disinheritance
deprivation

DSNJNS disingenuous
calculating

DSNJNSL disingenuously
calculating

DSNJNSNS
disingenuousness
calculating

DSNJNWS disingenuous
calculating

DSNJNWSL disingenuously
calculating

DSNJNWSNS
disingenuousness
calculating

DSNJNYS disingenuous
calculating

DSNJNYSL disingenuously
calculating

DSNJNYSNS
disingenuousness
calculating

DSNJNYWS disingenuous
calculating

DSNJNYWSL
disingenuously
calculating

DSNJNYWSNS
disingenuousness
calculating

DSNKLND disinclined
reluctant

DSNKLNSHN disinclination
aversion

DSNKRC idiosyncrasy
peculiarity idiosyncrasies

DSNKRDK idiosyncratic

peculiar

DSNKRDKL
idiosyncratically *peculiar*

DSNKRS idiosyncrasy
peculiarity idiosyncrasies

DSNKRTK idiosyncratic
peculiar

DSNKRTKL
idiosyncratically *peculiar*

DSNL decennial *10 years*

DSNM decennium *10 years*

DSNN disunion *separation*

DSNNG dissenting *disagree*

DSNNS dissonance
disharmony

DSNNT dissonant
disharmonic

DSNNTS dissonance
disharmony

DSNR dishonor *shame*
(Br) dishonour

DSNR dissenter *disagree*

DSNRBL dishonorable (adj)
shameful dishonorably
(adv)
(Br) dishonourable,
dishonourably

DSNRBLNS
dishonorableness
shameful
(Br) dishonourableness

DSNRR dishonorer *shame*
(Br) dishonourer

DSNRST disinterest
indifference

DSNRSTD disinterested
indifferent

DSNRSTDL disinterestedly
indifferent

DSNS decency *order,
propriety* decencies

DSNS odiousness *evil*

DSNSD dishonesty *fraud*

DSNSHN dissension *discord*

DSNSHNT dissentient
disagree

DSNSHS dissentious
disagree

DSNSNTV disincentive
deterrent

DSNSNV disincentive
deterrent

Letters aren't doubled for single sounds: to find alley use **L** not **LL**. Use **Y** and **W** as hard
sounds only: to find yellow use **YL**. (Br)=British spelling or usage. * See dictionary.

DSNST dishonest *untruthful*
DSNST dishonesty *fraud*
DSNSTZ desensitize *lessen feeling* desensitized desensitizing (Br) desensitise
DSNSTZR desensitizer *lessen feeling* (Br) desensitiser
DSNSTZSHN desensitization *lessen feeling* (Br) desensitisation
DSNT decent *acceptable, chaste*
DSNT descent *lineage, go down*
DSNT dissent *(v) disagree* dissented dissenting
DSNT dissent *(n) discord*
DSNT disunite *divide*
DSNT disunity *division*
DSNT docent *teacher*
DSNTC decency *order, propriety* decencies
DSNTDL disentitle *no claim* disentitled disentitling
DSNTGRDR disintegrator *break apart*
DSNTGRDV disintegrative *break apart*
DSNTGRSHN disintegration *break apart*
DSNTGRT disintegrate *break apart* disintegrated disintegrating
DSNTGRTR disintegrator *break apart*
DSNTGRTV disintegrative *break apart*
DSNTHRL disenthrall *liberate*
DSNTL decently *acceptable, chaste*
DSNTN dissenting *disagree*
DSNTNG dissenting *disagree*
DSNTNGGL disentangle *unravel* disentangled disentangling
DSNTNGL disentangle *unravel* disentangled disentangling

DSNTR disinter *dig up*
DSNTR dissenter *disagree*
DSNTR dysentery *diarrhea* dysenteries
DSNTRK dysenteric *diarrhea*
DSNTRLZ decentralize *spread widely* decentralized decentralizing (Br) decentralise
DSNTRLZSHN decentralization *spread* (Br) decentralisation
DSNTRMNT disinterment *dig up*
DSNTRST disinterest *indifference*
DSNTRSTD disinterested *indifferent*
DSNTRSTDL disinterestedly *indifferent*
DSNTRSTDNS disinterestedness *indifferent*
DSNTS decency *order, propriety* decencies
DSNTTL disentitle *no claim* disentitled disentitling
DSNVSMNT disinvestment *remove capital*
DSNVST disinvest *remove capital*
DSNVSTMNT disinvestment *remove capital*
DSNVT disinvite *no invitation* disinvited disinviting
DSNY dyspnea *breath* (Br) dyspnoea
DSNYL decennial *10 years*
DSNYM decennium *10 years*
DSNYN disunion *separation*
DSPCH dispatch *(v) send, kill (n) message*
DSPCHR dispatcher *sender, killer*
DSPDBL disputable (adj) *debatable* disputably (adv)
DSPDD dissipated *scattered*
DSPDDL dissipatedly *scatter*
DSPDDNS dissipatedness *scatter*

DSPDK despotic *harsh ruler*
DSPDKL despotically *harsh ruler*
DSPDNT disputant *debater*
DSPDR disputer *debater*
DSPDR dissipater *scatterer*
DSPDV deceptive *misleading*
DSPKBL despicable (adj) *vile* despicably (adv)
DSPL despoil *ruin*
DSPL disciple *follower*
DSPL dispel *scatter* dispelled dispelling
DSPL display *show* displayed displaying
DSPLN discipline *(v) punish* disciplined disciplining
DSPLN discipline *(n) punishment, study*
DSPLND disciplined *controlled*
DSPLNR disciplinary *(adj) punishment, study*
DSPLNR discipliner *punish*
DSPLNRN disciplinarian *punishment*
DSPLNRYN disciplinarian *punishment*
DSPLR despoiler *ruiner*
DSPLS displace *move, expel* displaced displacing
DSPLSBL displaceable *move, expel*
DSPLSDK dysplastic *structure*
DSPLSH dysplasia *growth*
DSPLSHN despoliation *ruin*
DSPLSHR displeasure *offense*
DSPLSMNT displacement *movement, expulsion*
DSPLSTK dysplastic *structure*
DSPLYSHN despoliation *ruin*
DSPLZ displease *offend* displeased displeasing
DSPLZH dysplasia *growth*
DSPLZHR displeasure *offense*
DSPN dustpan *sweep*
DSPN dyspnea *breath*

Use letters that best describe the sounds you hear and omit the vowels. Use **S** or **K** instead of **C**: to find circle use **SRKL**. Use **J** to find joy, **JM** to find gem and **G** to find go.

(Br) dyspnoea

DSPND despond *become hopeless*

DSPND disappointed *let down, frustrated*

DSPNDNS despondence *hopelessness* despondency

DSPNDNT despondent *hopeless*

DSPNDNTS despondence *hopelessness* despondency

DSPNS dispense *distribute, discard* dispensed dispensing

DSPNSBL dispensable *distribute, discard*

DSPNSBLD dispensability *distribute, discard*

DSPNSBLT dispensability *distribute, discard*

DSPNSR dispensary *medical* dispensaries

DSPNSR dispenser *distribute, discard*

DSPNSSHN dispensation *authorization, exemption*

DSPNSSHNL dispensational *authorization, exemption*

DSPNSTR dispensatory *pharmacy* dispensatories

DSPNT disappoint *let down, frustrate* disappointed disappointing

DSPNTD disappointed *let down, frustrated*

DSPNTMNT disappointment *frustration*

DSPNTN disappointing *less than expected*

DSPNTNG disappointing *less than expected*

DSPNTS dispense *distribute, discard* dispensed dispensing

DSPNTSR dispenser *distribute, discard*

DSPNY dyspnea *breath* (Br) dyspnoea

DSPPDK dyspeptic *indigestion*

DSPPDKL dyspeptically *indigestion*

DSPPS dyspepsia *indigestion*

DSPPSH dyspepsia *indigestion*

DSPPSY dyspepsia *indigestion*

DSPPTK dyspeptic *indigestion*

DSPPTKL dyspeptically *indigestion*

DSPR despair *hopelessness*

DSPR Diaspora *Jews*

DSPR diaspore *mineral*

DSPR disappear *vanish*

DSPRBSHN disapprobation *condemnation*

DSPRD desperado *outlaw* desperadoes (or) desperados

DSPRD disparity *difference* disparities

DSPRDD dispirited *saddened*

DSPRDDL dispiritedly *saddened*

DSPRDDNS dispiritedness *sadness*

DSPRF disproof *evidence*

DSPRJ disparage *degrade* disparaged disparaging

DSPRJMNT disparagement *degrade*

DSPRJN disparaging *degrading*

DSPRJNG disparaging *degrading*

DSPRJNGL disparagingly *degrading*

DSPRJNL disparagingly *degrading*

DSPRJR disparager *degrader*

DSPRNS disappearance *vanish*

DSPRNTS disappearance *vanish*

DSPRPRSHN disproportion *difference*

DSPRPRSHNL disproportional (adj) *different* disproportionally

(adv)

DSPRPRSHNT disproportionate *different*

DSPRPRSHNTL disproportionately *differently*

DSPRS disperse *scatter* dispersed dispersing

DSPRSBL dispersible *scatter*

DSPRSHN desperation *hopelessness*

DSPRSHN dispersion *scatter*

DSPRSL dispersal *scatter*

DSPRSNT dispersant *scatterer*

DSPRSR disperser *scatterer*

DSPRSV dispersive *scatter*

DSPRSVNS dispersiveness *scatter*

DSPRT desperate *hopeless*

DSPRT disparate *different*

DSPRT disparity *difference* disparities

DSPRT dispirit *sadden*

DSPRT disport *frolic*

DSPRTD dispirited *saddened*

DSPRTDL dispiritedly *saddened*

DSPRTDNS dispiritedness *sadness*

DSPRTL desperately *hopeless*

DSPRTL disparately *different*

DSPRTMNT disportment *frolic*

DSPRTNS disparateness *difference*

DSPRV disapprove *reject* disapproved disapproving

DSPRV disprove *refute* disproved disproving

DSPRVBL disprovable *refute*

DSPRVL disapproval *censure*

DSPRVNGL disapprovingly *rejection*

DSPRVNL disapprovingly

Letters aren't doubled for single sounds: to find alley use **L** not **LL**. Use **Y** and **W** as hard sounds only: to find yellow use **YL**. (Br)=British spelling or usage. * See dictionary.

rejection
DSPRVR disapprover *reject*
DSPRZHN dispersion *scatter*
DSPRZV dispersive *scatter*
DSPRZVNS dispersiveness *scatter*
DSPSHN deception *trick*
DSPSHN dispassion *fairness*
DSPSHN dissipation *scatter*
DSPSHNT dispassionate *fair*
DSPSHNTL dispassionately *fair*
DSPT despite *in spite of*
DSPT despot *harsh ruler*
DSPT dispute *debate* disputed disputing
DSPT dissipate *scatter* dissipated dissipating
DSPTBL disputable (adj) *debatable* disputably (adv)
DSPTD dissipated *scattered*
DSPTDL dissipatedly *scatter*
DSPTDNS dissipatedness *scatter*
DSPTK despotic *harsh ruler*
DSPTKL despotically *harsh ruler*
DSPTNT disputant *debater*
DSPTR disputer *debater*
DSPTR dissipater *scatterer*
DSPTSHN disputation *debate*
DSPTSHS disputatious *controversial*
DSPTV deceptive *misleading*
DSPTZM despotism *harsh ruler*
DSPYDBL disputable (adj) *debatable* disputably (adv)
DSPYDNT disputant *debater*
DSPYDR disputer *debater*
DSPYL despoil *ruin*
DSPYLR despoiler *ruiner*
DSPYT dispute *debate* disputed disputing
DSPYTBL disputable (adj) *debatable* disputably (adv)
DSPYTNT disputant *debater*
DSPYTR disputer *debater*
DSPYTSHN disputation

debate
DSPYTSHS disputatious *controversial*
DSPZ despise *hate* despised despising
DSPZ dispose *throw away* disposed disposing
DSPZBL disposable *throw away*
DSPZL disposal *throw away*
DSPZR despiser *hater*
DSPZR disposer *throw away*
DSPZS dispossess *expel*
DSPZSD dispossessed *expelled*
DSPZSHN disposition *mood, control*
DSPZSHN dispossession *expulsion*
DSPZSR dispossessor *expell*
DSPZST dispossessed *expelled*
DSQLF disqualify *make ineligible* disqualified disqualifying disqualifies
DSQLFKSHN disqualification *ineligible*
DSQLFR disqualifier *ineligible*
DSQLFYR disqualifier *ineligible*
DSQT disquiet *anxiety*
DSQTD disquietude *anxiety*
DSQTN disquieting *anxious*
DSQTNG disquieting *anxious*
DSQTYD disquietude *anxiety*
DSQYT disquiet *anxiety*
DSQYTD disquietude *anxiety*
DSQYTN disquieting *anxious*
DSQYTNG disquieting *anxious*
DSQYTYD disquietude *anxiety*
DSQZSHN disquisition *discourse*
DSR adducer *analyzer*
DSR deicer *thaw*

DSR dicer *cutter, gambler*
DSR dicier *risky*
DSR disarray *mess*
DSR douceur *gift*
DSR douser *water*
DSR dysuria *urine*
DSRB adsorb *take in*
DSRB disrobe *remove clothing* disrobed disrobing
DSRBBL adsorbable *take in*
DSRBNT adsorbent *substance*
DSRBR adsorber *holder*
DSRBT adsorbate *substance held*
DSRDR disorder *disturb*
DSRDRD disordered *disturbed*
DSRDRL disorderly *disturbed*
DSRGNZ disorganize *destroy system* disorganized disorganizing (Br) disorganise
DSRGNZD disorganized *no system* (Br) disorganised
DSRGNZSHN disorganization *no system* (Br) disorganisation
DSRGRD disregard *neglect* disregarded disregarding
DSRGRDFL disregardful *neglect*
DSRM disarm *win over, remove weapons*
DSRMMNT disarmament *remove weapons*
DSRMN disarming *win over, remove weapons*
DSRMN disharmony *discord*
DSRMNG disarming *win over, remove weapons*
DSRMNS disharmonious *discord*
DSRMNYS disharmonious *discord*
DSRMR disarmer *win over, remove weapons*
DSRN discern *detect*

Use letters that best describe the sounds you hear and omit the vowels. Use **S** or **K** instead of **C**: to find circle use **SRKL**. Use **J** to find joy, **JM** to find gem and **G** to find go.

DSRNBL discernible (adj) *detect* discernibly (adv)
DSRNMNT discernment *understanding difference*
DSRNN discerning *understanding difference*
DSRNNG discerning *understanding difference*
DSRNR discerner *detector*
DSRNT disorient *confuse* disoriented disorienting
DSRNTSHN disorientation *confusion*
DSRP disrupt *interrupt*
DSRPDBL disreputable (adj) *disgraced* disreputably (adv)
DSRPDNG disrupting *interrupt*
DSRPDR disrupter *interrupt*
DSRPDV disruptive *interruption*
DSRPDVL disruptively *interruption*
DSRPDVNS disruptiveness *interruption*
DSRPR disrepair *ruin*
DSRPSHN adsorption *taken in*
DSRPSHN disruption *interruption*
DSRPT disrepute *disgrace*
DSRPT disrupt *interrupt*
DSRPTBL disreputable (adj) *disgraced* disreputably (adv)
DSRPTN disrupting *interrupt*
DSRPTNG disrupting *interrupt*
DSRPTR disrupter *interrupt*
DSRPTV adsorptive *taken in*
DSRPTV disruptive *interruption*
DSRPTVL disruptively *interruption*
DSRPTVNS disruptiveness *interruption*
DSRPYDBL disreputable (adj) *disgraced* disreputably (adv)
DSRPYT disrepute *disgrace*

DSRPYTBL disreputable (adj) *disgraced* disreputably (adv)
DSRSPK disrespect *no esteem*
DSRSPKDBL disrespectable *no esteem*
DSRSPKFL disrespectful (adj) *no esteem* disrespectfully (adv)
DSRSPKFLNS disrespectfulness *no esteem*
DSRSPKT disrespect *no esteem*
DSRSPKTBL disrespectable *no esteem*
DSRSPKTFL disrespectful (adj) *no esteem* disrespectfully (adv)
DSRSPKTFLNS disrespectfulness *no esteem*
DSRT desert (*n*) *barren land,* reward (*v*) *abandon* (adj) *dry*
DSRT dessert *food*
DSRTDR dissertator *doctorate*
DSRTHM dysrhythmia *bad rhythm*
DSRTHMK dysrhythmic *bad rhythm*
DSRTHMY dysrhythmia *bad rhythm*
DSRTN dishearten *lose spirit*
DSRTSHN dissertation *doctorate*
DSRTT dissertate *doctorate* dissertated dissertating
DSRTTR dissertator *doctorate*
DSRV disserve *harm*
DSRVS disservice *harm*
DSRY dysuria *urine*
DSRYNT disorient *confuse*
DSRYNTSHN disorientation *confusion*
DSS decease *death*
DSS diesis *symbol* dieses
DSS diocese *church* dioceses

DSS disuse *not used*
DSS Odysseus *Greek myth*
DSSBL dissociable *separate*
DSSCSHN disassociation *detachment*
DSSCT disassociate *detach* disassociated disassociating
DSSCYSHN disassociation *detachment*
DSSCYT disassociate *detach* disassociated disassociating
DSSD deceased *dead*
DSSDBLSH disestablish *no status*
DSSDBLSHMNT disestablishment *no status*
DSSDR disaster *ruin*
DSSDRS disastrous *ruinous*
DSSDRSL disastrously *ruin*
DSSDV dissociative *separate*
DSSHBL dissociable *separate*
DSSHN decision *conclusion*
DSSHT dissociate *separate* dissociated dissociating
DSSHYBL dissociable *separate*
DSSHYT dissociate *separate* dissociated dissociating
DSSMBL disassemble *take apart* disassembled disassembling
DSSMBL disassembly *scattering*
DSSN diocesan *church*
DSSSHN dissociation *separation*
DSSSHSHN disassociation *detachment*
DSSSHT disassociate *detach* disassociated disassociating
DSSSHYSHN disassociation *detachment*
DSSSHYT disassociate *detach* disassociated disassociating
DSSSSHN disassociation *detachment*

Letters aren't doubled for single sounds: to find alley use **L** not **LL**. Use **Y** and **W** as hard sounds only: to find yellow use **YL**. (Br)=British spelling or usage. * See dictionary.

DSSST disassociate *detach*
disassociated
disassociating
DSSSYSHN disassociation
detachment
DSSSYT disassociate *detach*
disassociated
disassociating
DSST deceased *dead*
DSST desist *stop*
DSST diciest *risky*
DSST dissociate *separate*
dissociated dissociating
DSST otocyst *organ*
DSSTBLSH disestablish *no*
status
DSSTBLSHMNT
disestablishment *no*
status
DSSTBLSHMNTRN
disestablishmentarian *no*
status
DSSTBLSHMNTRYN
disestablishmentarian *no*
status
DSSTNS desistance *stop*
DSSTNTS desistance *stop*
DSSTR disaster *ruin*
DSSTRS disastrous *ruinous*
DSSTRSL disastrously *ruin*
DSSTV dissociative *separate*
DSSV decisive *conclusive*
DSSVL decisively *conclusive*
DSSVNS decisiveness
conclusive
DSSYBL dissociable
separate
DSSYDV dissociative
separate
DSSYSHN dissociation
separation
DSSYT dissociate *separate*
dissociated dissociating
DSSYTV dissociative
separate
DST audacity *boldness*
audacities
DST deceased *dead*
DST deceit *trick*
DST deist *philosopher*
DST deuced *confused*
DST dissed *(slang)*

disrespected
DST dust *speck*
DST dusty *with dust* dustier
dustiest
DST odist *poet*
DST otiosity *in vain*
DST out-of-sight *(slang)*
superior
DST Taoist *philosophy*
DSTBL dust bowl *drought*
DSTBLZ destabilize *make*
unsteady destabilized
destabilizing
DSTBLZSHN destabilization
make unsteady
DSTBN dustbin *trashcan*
DSTDNT day student
education
DSTDVL dust devil
whirlwind
DSTF distaff *female, rod*
distaffs
DSTF dyestuff *coloring*
DSTFL deceitful (adj)
dishonest deceitfully (adv)
DSTFLNS deceitfulness
dishonesty
DSTFSK Dostoyevsky *writer*
DSTJKT dust jacket *book*
cover
DSTK distich *two lines*
DSTKS distichous *two rows*
DSTKVR dustcover *cloth*
DSTL de Stijl *art style*
DSTL diastole *heart*
DSTL distal (adj) *away from*
distally (adv)
DSTL distill *brew* distilled
distilling
DSTL dustily *with dust*
DSTLK diastolic *heart*
DSTLR distiller *brewer*
DSTLR distillery *brewery*
distilleries
DSTLSHN distillation *brew*
DSTLT distillate *brew*
DSTMN dustman *(Br) trash*
collector dustmen
DSTMP dust mop *dry mop*
DSTMPR distemper *disease,*
bad humor
DSTN destain *remove color*

DSTN destine *predetermine*
destined destining
DSTN destiny *fate* destinies
DSTN disdain *despise*
DSTN distend *expand*
DSTNCHN distention
expansion
DSTND distend *expand*
DSTNFL disdainful (adj)
despise disdainfully (adv)
DSTNFLNS disdainfulness
despise
DSTNGG distingué *different*
DSTNGGWSH distinguish
discern distinguished
distinguishing
DSTNGGWSHBL
distinguishable (adj)
discernment
distinguishably (adv)
DSTNGGWSHD
distinguished *famous*
DSTNGGWSHT
distinguished *famous*
DSTNGK distinct *separate,*
notable
DSTNGKDV distinctive
different
DSTNGKDVL distinctively
differently
DSTNGKDVNS
distinctiveness *difference*
DSTNGKL distinctly *different*
DSTNGKNS distinctness
difference
DSTNGKSHN distinction
difference, honor
DSTNGKT distinct *separate,*
notable
DSTNGKTL distinctly
different
DSTNGKTNS distinctness
difference
DSTNGKTV distinctive
different
DSTNGKTVL distinctively
differently
DSTNGKTVNS
distinctiveness *difference*
DSTNGWSH distinguish
discern distinguished
distinguishing

Use letters that best describe the sounds you hear and omit the vowels. Use **S** or **K**
instead of **C**: to find circle use **SRKL**. Use **J** to find joy, **JM** to find gem and **G** to find go.

DSTNGWSHBL
distinguishable (adj)
discernment
distinguishably (adv)
DSTNGWSHD
distinguished *famous*
DSTNGWSHT distinguished
famous
DSTNK distinct *separate,*
notable
DSTNKDV distinctive
different
DSTNKDVL distinctively
differently
DSTNKDVNS
distinctiveness *difference*
DSTNKL distinctly *different*
DSTNKNS distinctness
difference
DSTNKSHN distinction
difference, honor
DSTNKT distinct *separate,*
notable
DSTNKTL distinctly *different*
DSTNKTNS distinctness
difference
DSTNKTV distinctive
different
DSTNKTVL distinctively
differently
DSTNKTVNS
distinctiveness *difference*
DSTNS distance (v) *keep*
away, outstrip distanced
distancing
DSTNS dustiness *with dust*
DSTNSBL distensible
expand
DSTNSBLT distensibility
expansion
DSTNSHN destination *place*
DSTNSHN distention
expansion
DSTNT distant *far-off*
DSTNTS distance (v) *keep*
away, outstrip distanced
distancing
DSTNTS distance (n)
separation, length
DSTNTSBL distensible
expand
DSTNTSBLT distensibility

expansion
DSTNTSHN distention
expansion
DSTPN dustpan *sweep*
DSTR daystar *sun*
DSTR destroy *ruin*
DSTR diester *chemical*
DSTR duster *crop sprayer,*
garment, cleaner
DSTR dustier *with dust*
DSTRB disturb *interrupt,*
alarm
DSTRBD disturbed *mentally*
ill
DSTRBDD distributed *doled*
out
DSTRBDR distributor
wholesaler, engine
DSTRBDV distributive *share,*
math
DSTRBNGL disturbingly
alarmingly
DSTRBNL disturbingly
alarmingly
DSTRBNS disturbance
disorder
DSTRBNTS disturbance
disorder
DSTRBR disturber *interrupt,*
alarm
DSTRBSHN distribution
circulation, marketing
DSTRBT distribute *dole out*
distributed distributing
DSTRBT distributee *receiver*
DSTRBTD distributed *doled*
out
DSTRBTR distributor
wholesaler, engine
DSTRBTV distributive *share,*
math
DSTRBYDD distributed
doled out
DSTRBYDR distributor
wholesaler, engine
DSTRBYDV distributive
share, math
DSTRBYSHN distribution
circulation, marketing
DSTRBYT distribute *dole out*
distributed distributing
DSTRBYT distributee

receiver
DSTRBYTD distributed
doled out
DSTRBYTR distributor
wholesaler, engine
DSTRBYTV distributive
share, math
DSTRD autostrada *highway*
autostradas (or)
autostrade
DSTRD dastard *coward*
DSTRDL dastardly *cowardly*
DSTRDR distorter
misrepresent
DSTRF dystrophy *nutrition*
dystrophies
DSTRFK dystrophic
nutrition
DSTRK district *area*
DSTRKDBL destructible
ruin
DSTRKDBL distractible
confused
DSTRKDD distracted
confused
DSTRKDDL distractedly
confused
DSTRKDV destructive *ruin*
DSTRKDV distractive
confused
DSTRKSHN destruction
ruin
DSTRKSHN distraction
pastime
DSTRKT distract *divert*
distracted distracting
DSTRKT district *area*
DSTRKTBL destructible
ruin
DSTRKTBL distractible
confused
DSTRKTD distracted
confused
DSTRKTDL distractedly
confused
DSTRKTV destructive *ruin*
DSTRKTV distractive
confused
DSTRKTVD destructivity
ruin
DSTRKTVT destructivity
ruin

Letters aren't doubled for single sounds: to find alley use **L** not **LL**. Use **Y** and **W** as hard
sounds only: to find yellow use **YL**. (Br)=British spelling or usage. * See dictionary.

DSTRM dust storm *whirlwind*
DSTRR destroyer *ruiner*
DSTRS distress *upset* distressed distressing
DSTRSFL distressful (adj) *miserable* distressfully (adv)
DSTRSFL distrustful (adj) *wary* distrustfully (adv)
DSTRSFLNS distressfulness *misery*
DSTRSHN distortion *misrepresentation*
DSTRST distrust *no faith*
DSTRSTFL distrustful (adj) *wary* distrustfully (adv)
DSTRT distort *misrepresent* distorted distorting
DSTRT distraught *upset*
DSTRTR distorter *misrepresent*
DSTRYR destroyer *ruiner*
DSTSF dissatisfy *displease* dissatisfied dissatisfying dissatisfies
DSTSFD dissatisfied *displeasure*
DSTSFKDR dissatisfactory *displeasure*
DSTSFKSHN dissatisfaction *displeasure*
DSTSFKTR dissatisfactory *displeasure*
DSTSFL distasteful (adj) *offensive* distastefully (adv)
DSTSFLNS distastefulness *offensive*
DSTSH dystocia *childbirth*
DSTSHS adscititious *derived*
DSTSHY dystocia *childbirth*
DSTST distaste *aversion*
DSTST dustiest *with dust*
DSTSTFL distasteful (adj) *offensive* distastefully (adv)
DSTSTFLNS distastefulness *offensive*
DSTTSHN destitution *need*
DSTTT destitute *needy*
DSTTYSHN destitution *need*

DSTTYT destitute *needy*
DSTVSK Dostoyevsky *writer*
DSTYFSK Dostoyevsky *writer*
DSTYR dustier *with dust*
DSTYST dustiest *with dust*
DSTYVSK Dostoyevsky *writer*
DSV deceive *trick* deceived deceiving
DSV disavow *deny*
DSV dissolve *melt, destroy* dissolved dissolving
DSVBL deceivable *dishonesty*
DSVNGL deceivingly *trick*
DSVNL deceivingly *trick*
DSVR deceiver *trick*
DSVR dissever *cut*
DSVRMNT disseverment *cut*
DSVRNS disseverance *cut*
DSVRNTS disseverance *cut*
DSVWBL disavowable *denial*
DSVWL disavowal *denial*
DSWD dissuade *advise against* dissuaded dissuading
DSWDR dissuader *advise against*
DSWSHN dissuasion *advise against*
DSWSV dissuasive *advise against*
DSWSVNS dissuasiveness *advise against*
DSWTD desuetude *disuse*
DSWTYD desuetude *disuse*
DSWZHN dissuasion *advise against*
DSWZV dissuasive *advise against*
DSWZVNS dissuasiveness *advise against*
DSXMKN deus ex machina *device*
DSXMSHN deus ex machina *device*
DSY dossier *file*
DSYN decillion *number*

DSYND disunity *division*
DSYNN disunion *separation*
DSYNT disunite *divide*
DSYNT disunity *division*
DSYNYN disunion *separation*
DSYR dicier *risky*
DSYR dysuria *urine*
DSYRY dysuria *urine*
DSYS disuse *not used*
DSYS Odysseus *Greek myth*
DSYST diciest *risky*
DSZ decease *death*
DSZ diocese *church* dioceses
DSZ disease *illness*
DSZHN decision *conclusion*
DSZM autoecism *in one place*
DSZV decisive *conclusive*
DT adit *entrance*
DT adyta (pl) *sanctum* adytum
DT audit *check*
DT data (s) or (pl) *information* datum (s)
DT date (v) *day, social engagement* dated dating
DT date (n) *day, fruit, social engagement*
DT debt *owed*
DT deity *god* deities
DT dhoti *garment* dhotis
DT diet *food*
DT dit *code*
DT ditto *same, copy* dittos
DT ditty *song* ditties
DT dot *mark* dotted dotting
DT dote *fawn over, become senile* doted doting
DT dotty *crazy* dottier dottiest
DT doubt *disbelief*
DT doughty *brave* doughtier doughtiest
DT duet *two*
DT duty *obligation, task, tax* duties
DT edit *correct*
DT ideate *think* ideated ideating
DT idiot *moron*
DT iodate *salt*

Use letters that best describe the sounds you hear and omit the vowels. Use **S** or **K** instead of **C**: to find circle use **SRKL**. Use **J** to find joy, **JM** to find gem and **G** to find go.

DT oddity *peculiarity* oddities
DTBG ditty bag *luggage*
DTBL auditable *check*
DTBL datable *appointment*
DTBL dutiable *obliging*
DTBL editable *correct*
DTBS database *computer*
DTC ditsy (or) ditzy *eccentric* ditsier (or) ditzier ditsiest (or) ditziest
DTCH detach *disengage*
DTCHBL detachable *disengage*
DTCHD detached *separate*
DTCHMNT detachment *separation*
DTCHT detached *separate*
DTCR ditsier (or) ditzier *eccentric*
DTCST ditsiest (or) ditziest *eccentric*
DTCYR ditsier (or) ditzier *eccentric*
DTCYST ditsiest (or) ditziest *eccentric*
DTD attitude *position, state of mind*
DTD dated *old, day*
DTD day-to-day *everyday*
DTDK dietetic *special food*
DTDKS dietetics *nutrition*
DTDNL attitudinal (adj) *position, state of mind* attitudinally (adv)
DTDNZ attitudinize *pose* attitudinized attitudinizing (Br) attitudinise
DTDX dietetics *nutrition*
DTFL doubtful (adj) *unsure* doubtfully (adv)
DTFL dutiful (adj) *obliging* dutifully (adv)
DTFLNS doubtfulness *unsure*
DTFR duty-free *no tax*
DTH death *not alive*
DTH eightieth *of number 80*
DTHBD deathbed *bed, last hours*
DTHBL deathblow *killing*

stroke
DTHKMP death camp *concentration camp*
DTHKP death cap *mushroom*
DTHL deathly *fatal*
DTHMSK death mask *plaster cast*
DTHR death row *prison*
DTHR dither *tremble, sway*
DTHRM dithyramb *poem* dithyrambs
DTHRMBK dithyrambic *poem*
DTHRMBKL dithyrambically *poem*
DTHRN dethrone *depose* dethroned dethroning
DTHRR ditherer *tremble, sway*
DTHSD death's-head *skull*
DTHSHD death's-head *skull*
DTHSKWD death squad *vigilante group*
DTHSQD death squad *vigilante group*
DTHTRP death trap *weak structure*
DTHVL Death Valley *desert*
DTHW out-of-the-way *hidden*
DTHWCH deathwatch *vigil*
DTHWRNT death warrant *execution*
DTHWSH death wish *desire to die*
DTJ dotage *senility*
DTK detect *discover*
DTK dyadic *mathematics*
DTK eidetic *recall*
DTK idiotic *stupid*
DTKDBL detectable *discovery*
DTKDBLD detectability *discovery*
DTKDBLT detectability *discovery*
DTKDR detector *finder*
DTKDV detective *discoverer*
DTKL dyadically *mathematics*
DTKL eidetically *recall*

DTKL idiotically *stupid*
DTKSF detoxify *remove poison* detoxified detoxifying detoxifies
DTKSFKSHN detoxification *remove poison*
DTKSHN detection *discovery*
DTKT detect *discover*
DTKTBL detectable *discovery*
DTKTBLD detectability *discovery*
DTKTBLT detectability *discovery*
DTKTR detector *finder*
DTKTV detective *discoverer*
DTL detail *(n) item (v) specify*
DTL diddle *waste, fool, toy* diddled diddling
DTL dotal *dowry*
DTL dottle *tobacco*
DTLD detailed *specific*
DTLN dateline *time*
DTLR detailer *specifier*
DTLR diddler *waste, fool, toy*
DTLS dateless *timeless*
DTLS doubtless *surely*
DTLSKWT diddly-squat *(slang) small amount*
DTLSL doubtlessly *surely*
DTLSNS doubtlessness *sureness*
DTLSQT diddly-squat *(slang) small amount*
DTM adytum *sanctum* adyta
DTM datum *information* data (or) datums
DTM daytime *not night*
DTM diatom *plankton*
DTMSNS detumescence *deflate*
DTMSNT detumescent *deflate*
DTMSNTS detumescence *deflate*
DTN Dayton *city*
DTN detain *hold*
DTN detainee *person held*
DTN detinue *recovery*
DTN dittany *plant* dittanies
DTNCHN detention *hold*

Letters aren't doubled for single sounds: to find alley use **L** not **LL**. Use **Y** and **W** as hard sounds only: to find yellow use **YL**. (Br)=British spelling or usage. * See dictionary.

DTNDBL detonatable *explode*
DTNDR detonator *explode*
DTNDV detonative *explode*
DTNGL dotingly *care, senility*
DTNK diatonic *music*
DTNKL diatonically *music*
DTNL dotingly *care, senility*
DTNR detainer *holder*
DTNR out-of-towner *foreigner*
DTNS dottiness *craziness*
DTNSHN detention *hold*
DTNSHN detonation *explode*
DTNT detent *holder*
DTNT détente (or) detente *policy*
DTNT detonate *explode* detonated detonating
DTNTBL detonatable *explode*
DTNTR detonator *explode*
DTNTV detonative *explode*
DTNY detinue *recovery*
DTP audiotape *recording*
DTR auditor *account verifier*
DTR auditory *sound*
DTR datura *plant*
DTR daughter *female child*
DTR debtor *person who owes*
DTR deter *hold back* deterred deterring
DTR detour *bypass*
DTR dietary *food*
DTR dieter *weight loss*
DTR dodder *(v) tremble (n) vine*
DTR doter *carer, senile one*
DTR dotter *marker*
DTR dottier *crazier*
DTR doubter *disbeliever*
DTR doughtier *braver*
DTR editor *writer*
DTRB diatribe *criticism*
DTRBL deterrable *prevention*
DTRBLD deterrability *prevention*
DTRBLT deterrability *prevention*
DTRD dotard *senility*
DTRDS detritus *rubbish*

detritus
DTRF autotroph *organism*
DTRF autotrophy *self-nourishment*
DTRFK autotrophic *self-nourishing*
DTRFKL autotrophically *self-nourishing*
DTRJ deterge *cleanse*
DTRJNT detergent *cleanser*
DTRK detract *lessen*
DTRKDR detractor *lessen*
DTRKSHN detraction *lessen*
DTRKT detract *lessen*
DTRKTR detractor *lessen*
DTRL dotterel *bird*
DTRL editorial (adj) *opinion* editorially (adv)
DTRLS daughterless *no female child*
DTRLZ editorialize *offer opinion* editorialized editorializing
DTRLZR editorializer *offer opinion*
DTRLZSHN editorialization *opinion*
DTRM auditorium *hall* auditoriums (or) auditoria
DTRM deuterium *element*
DTRMN determine *decide, discover* determined determining
DTRMNBL determinable *decided*
DTRMNC determinacy *exactness* determinacies
DTRMND determined *resolved*
DTRMNDR determinator *decision*
DTRMNL detrimental (adj) *harmful* detrimentally (adv)
DTRMNNT determinant *identifier*
DTRMNR determiner *decider*
DTRMNS determinacy *exactness* determinacies
DTRMNSDK deterministic *fate*
DTRMNSDKL

deterministically *fate*
DTRMNSHN determination *decision*
DTRMNST determinist *fate*
DTRMNSTK deterministic *fate*
DTRMNSTKL deterministically *fate*
DTRMNT determent *restraint*
DTRMNT determinate *limited*
DTRMNT detriment *harm*
DTRMNTL detrimental (adj) *harmful* detrimentally (adv)
DTRMNTR determinator *decision*
DTRMNZM determinism *fate*
DTRN doddering *feeble*
DTRNG doddering *feeble*
DTRNL daughter-in-law *son's wife*
DTRNP deuteranope *color-blind person*
DTRNP deuteranopia *color blindness*
DTRNPY deuteranopia *color blindness*
DTRNS deterrence *prevention*
DTRNT deterrent *prevention*
DTRNTS deterrence *prevention*
DTRP date rape *crime*
DTRPR day-tripper *traveler*
DTRR dodderer *trembler*
DTRRSHN deterioration *fall apart*
DTRRT deteriorate *fall apart* deteriorated deteriorating
DTRT Detroit *city*
DTRTL detrital *debris*
DTRTS detritus *rubbish* detritus
DTRYL editorial (adj) *opinion* editorially (adv)
DTRYLZ editorialize *offer opinion* editorialized editorializing
DTRYLZR editorializer *offer*

Use letters that best describe the sounds you hear and omit the vowels. Use **S** or **K** instead of **C**: to find circle use **SRKL**. Use **J** to find joy, **JM** to find gem and **G** to find go.

opinion
DTRYLZSHN
editorialization *opinion*
DTRYM auditorium *hall*
auditoriums (or) auditoria
DTRYM deuterium *element*
DTRYRSHN deterioration
fall apart
DTRYRT deteriorate *fall*
apart deteriorated
deteriorating
DTS deutzia *shrub*
DTS ditsy (or) ditzy *eccentric*
ditsier (or) ditzier ditsiest
(or) ditziest
DTS ditz *eccentric*
DTS duteous *obliging*
DTSDBL detestable (adj)
hated detestably (adv)
DTSDR detester *hater*
DTSHN dietitian *nutrition*
DTSR ditsier (or) ditzier
eccentric
DTSST ditsiest (or) ditziest
eccentric
DTST detest *hate* detested
detesting
DTST dottiest *craziest*
DTST doughtiest *bravest*
DTSTBL detestable (adj)
hated detestably (adv)
DTSTR detester *hater*
DTSY deutzia *shrub*
DTSYR ditsier (or) ditzier
eccentric
DTSYST ditsiest (or) ditziest
eccentric
DTTK dietetic *special food*
DTTKS dietetics *nutrition*
DTTX dietetics *nutrition*
DTV additive *ingredient*
DTV dative *grammar*
DTVD additivity *sum*
DTVT additivity *sum*
DTXF detoxify *remove poison*
detoxified detoxifying
detoxifies
DTXFKSHN detoxification
remove poison
DTYBL dutiable *obliging*
DTYD attitude *position, state*
of mind

DTYDNL attitudinal (adj)
position, state of mind
attitudinally (adv)
DTYDNZ attitudinize *pose*
attitudinized
attitudinizing
(Br) attitudinise
DTYMSNS detumescence
deflate
DTYMSNT detumescent
deflate
DTYMSNTS detumescence
deflate
DTYR datura *plant*
DTYR dottier *crazier*
DTYR doughtier *braver*
DTYRSLF do-it-yourself
self-made
DTYS duteous *obliging*
DTYST dottiest *craziest*
DTYST doughtiest *bravest*
DTZ deutzia *shrub*
DTZ ditsy (or) ditzy *eccentric*
ditsier (or) ditzier ditsiest
(or) ditziest
DTZR ditsier (or) ditzier
eccentric
DTZST ditsiest (or) ditziest
eccentric
DTZY deutzia *shrub*
DTZYR ditsier (or) ditzier
eccentric
DTZYST ditsiest (or) ditziest
eccentric
DV debut *introduce*
DV diva *opera prima donna*
divas (or) dive
DV dive *drop, swim* dived (or)
dove diving
DV divvy *share* divvied
divvying
DV dove *bird, peaceful one (v-*
past) dive
DV duvet *bedspread*
DV eau-de-vie *brandy* eaux-
de-vie
DV out of *depleted, beyond*
DVBD out-of-body *spiritual*
DVBM dive-bomb *airplane*
DVD devoid *empty*
DVD divide *separate* divided
dividing

DVDBL dividable *separate*
DVDD devoted *caring*
DVDD divided *separated*
DVDDL dividedly *separated*
DVDDNS devotedness
caring
DVDDNS dividedness
separation
DVDLZ devitalize *impair*
devitalized devitalizing
DVDN dividend *share*
DVDND dividend *share*
DVDR deviator *turn*
DVDR divider *separator*
DVDRZ out-of-doors *open*
air
DVDT out-of-date *obsolete*
DVGSHN divagation
swerving
DVGT divagate *swerve*
divagated divagating
DVKC advocacy *support*
DVKDR advocator *supporter*
DVKDV advective *movement*
DVKDV advocative *support*
DVKRT out-of-court *law*
DVKS advocacy *support*
DVKSHN advection
movement
DVKSHN advocation
support
DVKT advect *move*
DVKT advocate *(v)* support
advocated advocating
DVKT advocate *(n)* defender
DVKT dovecote *coop*
DVKTR advocator *supporter*
DVKTV advective *movement*
DVKTV advocative *support*
DVL devalue *lose value*
devalued devaluing
DVL devil *(n)* demon, fellow
DVL devil *(v)* annoy, season
deviled (or) devilled
deviling (or) devilling
DVLFSH devilfish *ray*
DVLJ divulge *reveal* divulged
divulging
DVLJNS divulgence
revelation
DVLJNTS divulgence
revelation

Letters aren't doubled for single sounds: to find alley use **L** not **LL**. Use **Y** and **W** as hard
sounds only: to find yellow use **YL**. (Br)=British spelling or usage. * See dictionary.

DVLMKR devil-may-care *carefree*

DVLP develop *make clear, evolve* developed developing

DVLPBL developable *make clear, evolve*

DVLPD developed *made clear, evolved*

DVLPMNL developmental (adj) *experimental* developmentally (adv)

DVLPMNT development *result, housing*

DVLPMNTL developmental (adj) *experimental, evolving* developmentally (adv)

DVLPN developing *not fully evolved*

DVLPNG developing *not fully evolved*

DVLPR developer *chemical, real estate*

DVLPT developed *made clear, evolved*

DVLR devilry (or) deviltry *mischief* devilries (or) deviltries

DVLRM ad valorem *value percentage*

DVLSFDKK devil's food cake *dessert*

DVLSH devilish *evil, mischievous, extreme*

DVLSHN devaluation *lose value*

DVLSHN devolution *deterioration*

DVLT devaluate *lose value* devaluated devaluating

DVLTR deviltry (or) devilry *mischief* deviltries (or) devilries

DVLV devolve *deteriorate* devolved devolving

DVLWSHN devaluation *lose value*

DVLWT devaluate *lose value* devaluated devaluating

DVLY devalue *lose value* devalued devaluing

DVLYSHN devaluation *lose*

value

DVLYT devaluate *lose value* devaluated devaluating

DVLYWSHN devaluation *lose value*

DVLYWT devaluate *lose value* devaluated devaluating

DVN devein *clean shrimp*

DVN devon *cattle*

DVN divan *sofa*

DVN divine *(v) foresee, find water* divined divining

DVN divine *(adj) godlike* diviner divinest

DVNCH da Vinci (Leonardo) *artist*

DVNCHR adventure *risk* adventured adventuring

DVNCHRR adventurer *risk taker (m)*

DVNCHRS adventuress *(n) risk taker (f)*

DVNCHRS adventurous *(adj) risky*

DVNCHRSL adventurously *(adj) risky*

DVNCHRSM adventuresome *taking risks*

DVNCHRSNS adventurousness *riskiness*

DVND divinity *god divinities*

DVNG diving *under water*

DVNJ advantage *benefit* advantaged advantaging

DVNN divining *find water*

DVNNG divining *find water*

DVNPRT davenport *desk, sofa*

DVNR diviner *foresee, find water*

DVNS advance *(v) go forward, give* advanced advancing

DVNS advance *(adj) forward (n) progress, money*

DVNS deviance *difference* deviancy

DVNSD advanced *more developed*

DVNSHN divination *foresee*

DVNSMNT advancement *improvement*

DVNSR advancer *raiser, giver*

DVNST advanced *more developed*

DVNT Advent *prayer season*

DVNT advent *coming*

DVNT deviant *different*

DVNT divinity *god* divinities

DVNTGS advantageous *beneficial*

DVNTGSL advantageously *beneficially*

DVNTJ advantage *benefit* advantaged advantaging

DVNTJS advantageous *beneficial*

DVNTJSL advantageously *beneficially*

DVNTJSNS advantageousness *benefit*

DVNTR adventure *risk* adventured adventuring

DVNTR divinatory *foresee*

DVNTRR adventurer *risk taker (m)*

DVNTRS adventuress *(n) risk taker (f)*

DVNTRSL adventurously *(adj) risky*

DVNTRSM adventuresome *taking risks*

DVNTRSNS adventurousness *riskiness*

DVNTS advance *(v) go forward, give* advanced advancing

DVNTS advance *(adj) forward (n) progress, money*

DVNTS deviance *difference* deviancy

DVNTSH adventitia *tissue*

DVNTSHL adventitial *tissue*

DVNTSHS adventitious *not inborn*

DVNTSHSL adventitiously *not inborn*

DVNTSMNT advancement *improvement*

DVNTSR advancer *raiser,*

giver

DVNTST advanced *more developed*
DVNTV adventive *not inborn*
DVNV adventive *not inborn*
DVPKT out-of-pocket *expense*
DVR devour *eat up* devoured devouring
DVR diver *swimmer*
DVR Dover *city*
DVRB adverb *modifier*
DVRBL adverbial (adj) *modifying* adverbially (adv)
DVRBM ad verbum *verbatim*
DVRBYL adverbial (adj) *modifying* adverbially (adv)
DVRC divorcée (f) *end marriage* divorce (m)
DVRDNT advertent *attentive*
DVRDNTL advertently *attentively*
DVRDSMNT advertisement *public notice* (Br) advertizement
DVRJ diverge *disagree* diverged diverging
DVRJNS divergence *disagreement*
DVRJNT divergent *disagreeing*
DVRJNTS divergence *disagreement*
DVRR devourer *eater*
DVRS adverse *hostile*
DVRS diverse *not alike*
DVRS divorce *end marriage, separate* divorced divorcing
DVRS divorcée (f) *end marriage* divorce (m)
DVRSD adversity *harm* adversities
DVRSD diversity *variety* diversities
DVRSDV adversative *against*
DVRSDVL adversatively *against*
DVRSF diversify *vary* diversified diversifying

diversifies

DVRSFKSHN diversification *variety*
DVRSFR diversifier *variety*
DVRSFYR diversifier *variety*
DVRSHN diversion *pastime, pretence*
DVRSHNR diversionary *pretence*
DVRSHNST diversionist *pastime, pretence*
DVRSL adversely *hostilely*
DVRSL diversely *not alike*
DVRSMNT divorcement *end marriage, separate*
DVRSNS adverseness *harm*
DVRSNS diverseness *not alike*
DVRSR adversary *enemy* adversaries
DVRSRL adversarial *enemy*
DVRSRNS adversariness *enemy*
DVRSRYL adversarial *enemy*
DVRST adversity *harm* adversities
DVRST diversity *variety* diversities
DVRSTV adversative *against*
DVRSTVL adversatively *against*
DVRT advert *refer*
DVRT divert *turn* diverted diverting
DVRTKL diverticula (pl) *pocket* diverticulum
DVRTKLDS diverticulitis *swelling*
DVRTKLM diverticulum *pocket* diverticula
DVRTKLR diverticular *pocket*
DVRTKLSS diverticulosis *swelling*
DVRTKLTS diverticulitis *swelling*
DVRTKYL diverticula (pl) *pocket* diverticulum
DVRTKYLDS diverticulitis *swelling*
DVRTKYLM diverticulum *pocket* diverticula
DVRTKYLR diverticular

pocket

DVRTKYLSS diverticulosis *swelling*
DVRTKYLTS diverticulitis *swelling*
DVRTNC advertency *attention* advertencies
DVRTNS advertence *attention*
DVRTNS advertency *attention* advertencies
DVRTNT advertent *attentive*
DVRTNTC advertency *attention* advertencies
DVRTNTL advertently *attentively*
DVRTNTS advertence *attention*
DVRTNTS advertency *attention* advertencies
DVRTQL diverticula (pl) *pocket* diverticulum
DVRTQLDS diverticulitis *swelling*
DVRTQLM diverticulum *pocket* diverticula
DVRTQLR diverticular *pocket*
DVRTQLSS diverticulosis *swelling*
DVRTQLTS diverticulitis *swelling*
DVRTRL advertorial *sponsored editorial*
DVRTRYL advertorial *sponsored editorial*
DVRTSMN divertissement *diversion* divertissements
DVRTSMNT divertissement *diversion* divertissements
DVRTZ advertise *make public* advertised advertising (Br) advertize
DVRTZMNT advertisement *public notice* (Br) advertizement
DVRTZN advertising *announcements* (Br) advertizing
DVRTZNG advertising *announcements*

(Br) advertizing

DVRTZR advertiser *sponsor*
(Br) advertizer

DVRZ divers *various*

DVRZHN diversion *pastime,
pretence*

DVRZHNR diversionary
pretence

DVRZHNST diversionist
pastime, pretence

DVS advice *helpful words*

DVS device *tool*

DVS devious *sly*

DVSDCHR divestiture
transfer, disposal

DVSDK atavistic *throwback*

DVSDKL atavistically
throwback

DVSDTR divestiture *transfer,
disposal*

DVSHL audiovisual *seen and
heard*

DVSHN deviation *difference*

DVSHN devotion *loving
attention*

DVSHN division *separate*

DVSHNL devotional *(adj)
loving (n) prayer*

DVSHNL divisional *separate*

DVSHWL audiovisual *seen
and heard*

DVSMNT divestment
transfer, disposal

DVST divest *take away*

DVST out-of-sight *(slang)
superior*

DVSTCHR divestiture
transfer, disposal

DVSTDNGL devastatingly
destroy

DVSTDR devastator
destroyer

DVSTK atavistic *throwback*

DVSTKL atavistically
throwback

DVSTMNT divestment
transfer, disposal

DVSTSHN devastation
destruction

DVSTT devastate *destroy*
devastated devastating

DVSTTNGL devastatingly

destroy

DVSTTR devastator
destroyer

DVSTTR divestiture *transfer,
disposal*

DVSV divisive *disunity*

DVSVNS divisiveness
disunity

DVT davit *crane*

DVT deviate *turn* deviated
deviating

DVT devote *love, give*
devoted devoting

DVT devotee *lover*

DVT devout *serious*

DVT divot *grass*

DVTD devoted *caring*

DVTDNS devotedness
caring

DVTHW out-of-the-way
hidden

DVTL dovetail *joint*

DVTLZ devitalize *impair*
devitalized devitalizing

DVTN duvetyn *fabric*

DVTNR out-of-towner
foreigner

DVTR deviator *turn*

DVV devolve *deteriorate*
devolved devolving

DVWR devoir *duty*

DVWR devour *eat up*
devoured devouring

DVWRR devourer *eater*

DVY debut *introduce*

DVYDR deviator *turn*

DVYNS deviance *difference*
deviancy

DVYNT deviant *different*

DVYNTS deviance *difference*
deviancy

DVYS devious *sly*

DVYSHN deviation *difference*

DVYT deviate *turn* deviated
deviating

DVYTR deviator *turn*

DVZ advise *counsel* advised
advising

DVZ advisee *person helped*

DVZ devise *invent* devised
devising

DVZ devisee *inventor*

DVZBL advisable *suitability*

DVZBL advisable (adj)
suitable, prudent advisably
(adv)

DVZBL devisable *invented*

DVZBL divisible *separate*

DVZBLD advisability
suitability

DVZBLD divisibility *separate*

DVZBLNS advisableness
prudence

DVZBLT advisability
suitability

DVZBLT divisibility *separate*

DVZD advised *considered*

DVZDL advisedly *considered*

DVZHL audiovisual *seen and
heard*

DVZHN division *separate*

DVZHNL divisional *separate*

DVZHWL audiovisual *seen
and heard*

DVZM atavism *throwback*

DVZMNT advisement
consideration

DVZR adviser *person helping*

DVZR advisory *report*
advisories

DVZR deviser *inventor*

DVZR devisor *legacy*

DVZV divisive *disunity*

DVZVNS divisiveness
disunity

DW dewy *moist* dewier
dewiest

DW doughy *pasty, plump*
doughier doughiest

DW duo *twosome* duos

DW eye-to-eye *agreement*

DW Ottawa *Native American*
Ottawas (or) Ottawa

DWB dweeb *(slang) jerk,
nerd*

DWBL doable *possible*

DWCHR dowitcher *bird*

DWD dewy-eyed *innocent*

DWD doe-eyed *innocent*

DWD dyewood *wood*

DWDN duodena (pl)
intestine duodenum

DWDNL duodenal *intestine*

DWDNM duodenum

Use letters that best describe the sounds you hear and omit the vowels. Use **S** or **K**
instead of **C**: to find circle use **SRKL**. Use **J** to find joy, **JM** to find gem and **G** to find go.

intestine duodena (or) duodenums

DWDSML duodecimal *twelves*

DWJR dowager *woman*

DWL dowel *round tool* dowelled dowelling

DWL dual *two*

DWL duel *combat* dueled (or) duelled dueling (or) duelling

DWL dwell *reside* dwelled (or) dwelt dwelling

DWLD duality *two* dualities

DWLN dwelling *residence*

DWLNG dwelling *residence*

DWLP Atahuallpa (or) Atahualpa *Inca king*

DWLPRPS dual-purpose *two uses*

DWLR dueler (or) dueller *fighter*

DWLR dweller *resider*

DWLSDK dualistic *two*

DWLSDKL dualistically *two*

DWLST duelist (or) duellist *fighter*

DWLSTK dualistic *two*

DWLSTKL dualistically *two*

DWLT duality *two* dualities

DWLT dwelt (or) dwelled *resided*

DWLZM dualism *two*

DWMN autoimmune *disease-fighting*

DWMNT autoimmunity *disease-fighting*

DWMVRT duumvirate *two rulers*

DWMYN autoimmune *disease-fighting*

DWMYNT autoimmunity *disease-fighting*

DWN doing *action*

DWN duenna *chaperon*

DWND duende *attraction*

DWNDL dwindle *decrease* dwindled dwindling

DWNG doing *action*

DWNS doughiness *pastiness*

DWNTKSKSHN autointoxication *self-*

poisoning

DWNTXKSHN autointoxication *self-poisoning*

DWP doo-wop *music*

DWPL duopoly *two sellers or rulers* duopolies

DWPLSDK duopolistic *two sellers or rulers*

DWPLSTK duopolistic *two sellers or rulers*

DWR dewier *moist*

DWR doer *active one*

DWR doughier *pastier*

DWR dour *stern*

DWR dower *estate*

DWR dowry *marriage goods* dowries

DWRD do-or-die *final*

DWRDK autoerotic *self-stimulating*

DWRDSZM autoeroticism (or) autoerotism *self-stimulation*

DWRDZM autoerotism (or) autoeroticism *self-stimulation*

DWRF dwarf *(n, adj) small one (v) stunt* dwarfs

DWRFZM dwarfism *stunted growth*

DWRKR autoworker *car maker*

DWRL dourly *sternly*

DWRM dew worm *night crawler*

DWRNS dourness *sternness*

DWRTK autoerotic *self-stimulating*

DWRTSZM autoeroticism (or) autoerotism *self-stimulation*

DWRTZM autoerotism (or) autoeroticism *self-stimulation*

DWSHS autoecious *in one place*

DWSHSL autoeciously *in one place*

DWST dewiest *moist*

DWST doughiest *pastiest*

DWST Taoist *philosophy*

DWSZM autoecism *in one place*

DWT duet *two*

DWTYRSLF do-it-yourself *self-made*

DWYD dewy-eyed *innocent*

DWYN doyen (m) *senior member* doyenne (f)

DWYR dewier *moist*

DWYR doughier *pastier*

DWYST dewiest *moist*

DWYST doughiest *pastiest*

DWZM Taoism *philosophy*

DX addax *animal* addaxes

DX Dixie *region*

DX doxy *mistress* doxies

DX dukes *(slang) fists*

DXD dioxide *chemical*

DXD dockside *shore*

DXDR dexter *right side*

DXDRD dexterity *skill* dexterities

DXDRL dextral *right-handed*

DXDRN Dexedrine *(trademark) drug*

DXDRS dexterous *skillful*

DXDRT dexterity *skill* dexterities

DXDZ deoxidize *remove oxygen* deoxidized deoxidizing

DXDZR deoxidizer *remove oxygen*

DXHN dachshund *dog*

DXHND dachshund *dog*

DXHNT dachshund *dog*

DXJNSHN deoxygenation *remove oxygen*

DXJNT deoxygenate *remove oxygen*

DXL adaxial *axis*

DXL duxelles *mushrooms*

DXLG doxology *praise* doxologies

DXLJ doxology *praise* doxologies

DXLN Dixieland *region*

DXLND Dixieland *region*

DXN dachshund *dog*

DXN dioxane *solvent*

DXN dioxin *herbicide*

DXND dachshund *dog*

Letters aren't doubled for single sounds: to find alley use **L** not **LL**. Use **Y** and **W** as hard sounds only: to find yellow use **YL**. (Br)=British spelling or usage. * See dictionary.

DXP duck soup *easy to do*
DXS deixis *words*
DXSL dickcissel *bird*
DXTR dexter *right side*
DXTRD dexterity *skill*
dexterities
DXTRL dextral *right-handed*
DXTRS dexterous *skillful*
DXTRS dextrose *sugar*
DXTRT dexterity *skill*
dexterities
DXYL adaxial *axis*
DY à deux *two people*
DY adieu *goodbye* adieus (or)
adieux
DY audio *sound*
DY dew *moisture*
DY due *(adj) owed,*
appropriate, scheduled (n)
debt (adv) directly
DY duo *twosome* duos
DY idea *thought*
DY odea (pl) *theater* odeum
DY oidia (pl) *fungus* oidium
DYBD dubiety *doubt*
dubieties
DYBDBL dubitable
questionable
DYBDK diabetic *disease*
DYBDS diabetes *disease*
DYBDZ diabetes *disease*
DYBL dyeable *color*
DYBLD dyeability *color*
DYBLK diabolic *evil*
DYBLKL diabolical (adj) *evil*
diabolically (adv)
DYBLT dyeability *color*
DYBLZ diabolize *make evil*
diabolized diabolizing
DYBLZM diabolism *devil*
worship
DYBR dewberry *fruit*
dewberries
DYBS dubious *questionable*
DYBSL dubiously
questionable
DYBSNS dubiousness
questionable
DYBT dubiety *doubt*
dubieties
DYBTBL dubitable
questionable

DYBTK diabetic *disease*
DYBTS diabetes *disease*
DYBTZ diabetes *disease*
DYBYD dubiety *doubt*
dubieties
DYBYS dubious *questionable*
DYBYSL dubiously
questionable
DYBYSNS dubiousness
questionable
DYBYT dubiety *doubt*
dubieties
DYC idiocy *stupidity* idiocies
DYCS diocese *church*
dioceses
DYCZ diocese *church*
dioceses
DYD deity *god* deities
DYD dewy-eyed *innocent*
DYD diode *electricity*
DYD dude *(n) dandy*
DYD dude *(v) dress up*
duded duding
DYD duty *obligation, task, tax*
duties
DYD dyad *pair*
DYDBL dutiable *obliging*
DYDFL dutiful (adj) *obliging*
dutifully (adv)
DYDFR duty-free *no tax*
DYDK dyadic *mathematics*
DYDK idiotic *stupid*
DYDKL dyadically
mathematics
DYDKL idiotically *stupid*
DYDM diadem *crown*
DYDN duodena (pl) *intestine*
duodenum
DYDNL duodenal *intestine*
DYDNM duodenum *intestine*
duodena (or) duodenums
DYDR dieter *weight loss*
DYDRNCH dude ranch
resort
DYDRNP deuteranope
color-blind person
DYDRNP deuteranopia *color*
blindness
DYDRNPY deuteranopia
color blindness
DYDRNT deodorant *destroy*
odor

DYDRP dewdrop *water*
DYDRZ deodorize *destroy*
odor deodorized
deodorizing
DYDRZR deodorizer *destroy*
odor
DYDS duteous *obliging*
DYDSH dudish *dandy*
DYDSML duodecimal
twelves
DYDYBL dutiable *obliging*
DYDYS duteous *obliging*
DYF deify *god* deified
deifying deifies
DYFKSHN deification *god*
DYFL audiophile *sound*
DYFL dewfall *moisture*
DYFNS diaphanous *thin*
DYFRM diaphragm
membrane
DYGNL diagonal (n, adj)
slanted line diagonally
(adv)
DYGNS diagnose *analyze*
diagnosed diagnosing
DYGNSBL diagnosable
analysis
DYGNSDK diagnostic
analytic
DYGNSDKL diagnostically
analytic
DYGNSS diagnosis *analysis*
diagnoses
DYGNSTK diagnostic
analytic
DYGNSTKL diagnostically
analytic
DYGNSTSHN diagnostician
analysis
DYGNZ diagnose *analyze*
diagnosed diagnosing
DYGNZBL diagnosable
analysis
DYGRF ideograph *symbol*
ideography
DYGRFK ideographic
symbol
DYGRFK idiographic
concept
DYGRFKL ideographically
symbol
DYGRM audiogram *hearing*

Use letters that best describe the sounds you hear and omit the vowels. Use **S** or **K** instead of **C**: to find circle use **SRKL**. Use **J** to find joy, **JM** to find gem and **G** to find go.

DYGRM diagram *picture* diagrammed (or) diagramed diagramming (or) diagraming
DYGRM ideogram *symbol*
DYGRMBL diagrammable *picture*
DYGRMDK diagrammatic *picture*
DYGRMDK ideogrammatic *symbol*
DYGRMDKL diagrammatically *picture*
DYGRMK ideogramic (or) ideogrammic *symbol*
DYGRMTK diagrammatic *picture*
DYGRMTK ideogrammatic *symbol*
DYGRMTKL diagrammatically *picture*
DYJNZ Diogenes *philosopher*
DYK duke *(v) fight* duked duking
DYK duke *(n) nobleman, fist*
DYKBL educable *learning*
DYKBLD educability *learning*
DYKBLT educability *learning*
DYKDD educated *skilled*
DYKDK deictic *words*
DYKDM dukedom *domain*
DYKDR educator *teacher*
DYKDV educative *instructive*
DYKDVDR deactivator *make ineffective*
DYKDVSHN deactivation *make ineffective*
DYKDVT deactivate *make ineffective* deactivated deactivating
DYKDVTR deactivator *make ineffective*
DYKL dewclaw *hoof*
DYKL ducal *duke*
DYKRDK diacritic *phonetic*
DYKRDKL diacritical *phonetic*
DYKRTK diacritic *phonetic*
DYKRTKL diacritical *phonetic*

DYKS dukes *(slang) fists*
DYKSD dioxide *chemical*
DYKSDZ deoxidize *remove oxygen* deoxidized deoxidizing
DYKSDZR deoxidizer *remove oxygen*
DYKSHN education *study*
DYKSHNL educational (adj) *teaching* educationally (adv)
DYKSHNST educationist *learning*
DYKSJNSHN deoxygenation *remove oxygen*
DYKSJNT deoxygenate *remove oxygen*
DYKSN dioxane *solvent*
DYKSN dioxin *herbicide*
DYKSS deixis *words*
DYKST audiocassette *tape*
DYKT educate *teach* educated educating
DYKTD educated *skilled*
DYKTK deictic *words*
DYKTR educator *teacher*
DYKTV educative *instructive*
DYKTVDR deactivator *make ineffective*
DYKTVSHN deactivation *make ineffective*
DYKTVT deactivate *make ineffective* deactivated deactivating
DYKTVTR deactivator *make ineffective*
DYL dial *(n) numbered face (v) telephone* dialed (or) dialled dialing (or) dialling
DYL doily *lace* doilies
DYL dual *two*
DYL duel *combat* dueled (or) duelled dueling (or) duelling
DYL duly *properly*
DYL ideal *(n) model, (adj) perfect* ideally (adv)
DYLD duality *two* dualities
DYLDR adulator *adorer*
DYLG audiology *sound*
DYLG dialogue *discuss*

dialogued dialoguing
DYLG etiology *cause* etiologies
DYLG ideologue *theorist*
DYLG ideology *concept* ideologies
DYLJ audiology *sound*
DYLJ etiology *cause* etiologies
DYLJ ideology *concept* ideologies
DYLJK etiologic *cause*
DYLJKL ideological (adj) *concept* ideologically (adv)
DYLJST audiologist *sound*
DYLJST etiologist *cause*
DYLJST ideologist *concept*
DYLJZ ideologize *interpret* ideologized ideologizing
DYLK dialect *speech*
DYLKDK dialectic *logic*
DYLKDKL dialectical (adj) *logical* dialectically (adv)
DYLKT dialect *speech*
DYLKTK dialectic *logic*
DYLKTKL dialectical (adj) *logical* dialectically (adv)
DYLKTRK dielectric *current*
DYLKTSHN dialectician *logic, speech*
DYLP dewlap *fold*
DYLPRPS dual-purpose *two uses*
DYLR dialer *device, person*
DYLR dueler (or) dueller *fighter*
DYLSDK dualistic *two*
DYLSDK idealistic *perfection*
DYLSDKL dualistically *two*
DYLSDKL idealistically *perfection*
DYLSHN adulation *adoration*
DYLSHN etiolation *whiten*
DYLSS dialysis *separation* dialyses
DYLST duelist (or) duellist *fighter*
DYLST idealist *perfectionist*
DYLSTK dualistic *two*
DYLSTK idealistic *perfection*
DYLSTKL dualistically *two*
DYLSTKL idealistically

Letters aren't doubled for single sounds: to find alley use **L** not **LL**. Use **Y** and **W** as hard sounds only: to find yellow use **YL**. (Br)=British spelling or usage. * See dictionary.

perfection
DYLT adulate *adore* adulated
adulating
DYLT duality *two* dualities
DYLT etiolate *whiten*
etiolated etiolating
DYLTN dial tone *telephone*
DYLTR adulator *adorer*
DYLTR adulatory *adoring*
DYLZ dialyze *separate*
dialyzed dialyzing
DYLZ idealize *perfect*
idealized idealizing
(Br) idealise
DYLZM dualism *two*
DYLZM idealism *perfection*
DYLZR idealizer *perfect*
(Br) idealiser
DYLZSHN idealization
perfection
(Br) idealisation
DYM Dumas *writer*
DYM idiom *expression*
DYM odeum *theater* odea
DYM odium *hatred*
DYM oidium *fungus* oidia
DYMDK idiomatic *expression*
DYMDKL idiomatically
expression
DYMDR audiometer *sound*
DYMDR diameter *circle*
DYMFSZ de-emphasize
play down de-emphasized
de-emphasizing
(Br) de-emphasise
DYMN diamond *gem, shape,*
field
DYMND diamond *gem,*
shape, field
DYMNT diamanté *decoration*
DYMRFK idiomorphic *shape*
DYMS Dumas *writer*
DYMTK idiomatic *expression*
DYMTKL idiomatically
expression
DYMTR audiometer *sound*
DYMTR audiometry *sound*
DYMTR diameter *circle*
DYMTRK audiometric *sound*
DYMTRK diametric (or)
diametrical *center line,*
opposite diametrically

(adv)
DYMTRKL diametrical (or)
diametric (adj) *center line,*
opposite diametrically
(adv)
DYMVRT duumvirate *two*
rulers
DYN doyen (m) *senior*
member doyenne (f)
DYN duenna *chaperon*
DYN dune *sand hill*
DYNBG dune buggy *vehicle*
DYNDSTRLZ
deindustrialize *remove*
industry deindustrialized
deindustrializing
(Br) deinstitutionalisation
DYNDSTRLZSHN
deindustrialization *remove*
industry
(Br) deinstitutionalisation
DYNDSTRYLZ
deindustrialize *remove*
industry deindustrialized
deindustrializing
(Br) deinstitutionalisation
DYNDSTRYLZSHN
deindustrialization *remove*
industry
(Br) deinstitutionalisation
DYNS audience *crowd*
DYNSS Dionysus (or)
Bacchus *Greek god*
DYNSTTSHNLZ
deinstitutionalize *mental*
patients, reform
deinstitutionalized
deinstitutionalizing
(Br) deinstitutionalise
DYNSTTSHNLZSHN
deinstitutionalization
mental patients, reform
(Br) deinstitutionalisation
DYNSTTYSHNLZ
deinstitutionalize *mental*
patients, reform
deinstitutionalized
deinstitutionalizing
(Br) deinstitutionalise
DYNSTTYSHNLZSHN
deinstitutionalization
mental patients, reform

(Br) deinstitutionalisation
DYNTHS dianthus *pink*
DYNTLG deontology
morality
DYNTLJ deontology
morality
DYNTS audience *crowd*
DYP dupe *fool* duped
duping
DYPDR diopter *lens*
DYPL duopoly *two sellers or*
rulers duopolies
DYPL duple *two beats*
DYPLKDR duplicator *copier*
DYPLKS duplex *double*
duplexes
DYPLKSHN duplication
copy
DYPLKSR duplexer *switch*
DYPLKT duplicate *copy*
duplicated duplicating
DYPLKTR duplicator *copier*
DYPLSD duplicity
contradiction duplicities
DYPLSDK duopolistic *two*
sellers or rulers
DYPLSDS duplicitous
contradiction
DYPLST duplicity
contradiction duplicities
DYPLSTK duopolistic *two*
sellers or rulers
DYPLSTS duplicitous
contradiction
DYPLX duplex *double*
duplexes
DYPLXR duplexer *switch*
DYPNT dew point *moisture*
DYPR diaper *fabric, pattern,*
baby garment
DYPR dupery *trick* duperies
DYPSN diapason *sound*
DYPTHK idiopathic *primary*
DYPTHKL idiopathically
primary
DYPTR diopter *lens*
DYPTRK dioptric *lens*
DYPZN diapason *sound*
DYR de jure *lawful*
DYR diarrhea *feces*
DYR diary *journal* diaries
DYR dire *dreadful* direr direst

Use letters that best describe the sounds you hear and omit the vowels. Use **S** or **K**
instead of **C**: to find circle use **SRKL**. Use **J** to find joy, **JM** to find gem and **G** to find go.

DYR direr *dreadful*
DYR dyer *tinter*
DYRBL durable (adj) *sturdy* durably (adv)
DYRBLD durability *sturdiness*
DYRBLS durables *goods*
DYRBLT durability *sturdiness*
DYRBLZ durables *goods*
DYRCZ diaereses (pl) *symbol, verse* diaeresis
DYRDK diuretic *more urine*
DYRFL direful (adj) *dreadful* direfully (adv)
DYRK duroc *hog*
DYRK dyarchy *two rulers* dyarchies
DYRL direly *dreadful*
DYRM diorama *scene*
DYRM durum *wheat*
DYRN during *same time*
DYRNG during *same time*
DYRNL diurnal *daytime*
DYRNS direness *dread*
DYRR direr *dreadful*
DYRS duress *force*
DYRSHN duration *time*
DYRSS diaeresis *symbol, verse* diaereses
DYRSS diuresis *urine* diureses
DYRST diarist *writer*
DYRST direst *dreadful*
DYRSZ diaereses (pl) *symbol, verse* diaeresis
DYRTK diuretic *more urine*
DYRY diarrhea *feces*
DYS adduce *cite* adduced adducing
DYS adios *goodbye*
DYS dais *platform*
DYS deice *thaw* deiced deicing
DYS deuce (v) *tennis, damn* deuced deucing
DYS deuce (n) *two, tie score, devil*
DYS educe *bring out* educed educing
DYS idiocy *stupidity* idiocies
DYS odious *hateful*

DYS otiose *vain*
DYSBL educible *bring out*
DYSD deuced *confused*
DYSHN ideation *thought*
DYSHS dioecious *separated sexes*
DYSKLSHN de-escalation *slow down*
DYSKLT de-escalate *slow down* de-escalated de-escalating
DYSKLTR de-escalatory *slow down*
DYSKSMKN deus ex machina *device*
DYSKSMSHN deus ex machina *device*
DYSL odiously *hatefully*
DYSNGKRC idiosyncrasy *peculiarity* idiosyncrasies
DYSNGKRDK idiosyncratic *peculiar*
DYSNGKRDKL idiosyncratically *peculiar*
DYSNGKRS idiosyncrasy *peculiarity* idiosyncrasies
DYSNGKRTK idiosyncratic *peculiar*
DYSNGKRTKL idiosyncratically *peculiar*
DYSNKRC idiosyncrasy *peculiarity* idiosyncrasies
DYSNKRDK idiosyncratic *peculiar*
DYSNKRDKL idiosyncratically *peculiar*
DYSNKRS idiosyncrasy *peculiarity* idiosyncrasies
DYSNKRTK idiosyncratic *peculiar*
DYSNKRTKL idiosyncratically *peculiar*
DYSNS odiousness *evil*
DYSPR Diaspora *Jews*
DYSPR diaspore *mineral*
DYSR adducer *analyzer*
DYSR deicer *thaw*
DYSS diesis *symbol* dieses
DYSS diocese *church* dioceses
DYSSN diocesan *church*
DYSST otocyst *organ*

DYST deist *philosopher*
DYST deuced *confused*
DYSTL diastole *heart*
DYSTLK diastolic *heart*
DYSTR diester *chemical*
DYSXMKN deus ex machina *device*
DYSXMSHN deus ex machina *device*
DYSZ diocese *church* dioceses
DYT deity *god* deities
DYT diet *food*
DYT duet *two*
DYT duty *obligation, task, tax* duties
DYT ideate *think* ideated ideating
DYT idiot *moron*
DYTBL dutiable *obliging*
DYTDK dietetic *special food*
DYTDKS dietetics *nutrition*
DYTDX dietetics *nutrition*
DYTFL dutiful (adj) *obliging* dutifully (adv)
DYTFR duty-free *no tax*
DYTH eightieth *of number 80*
DYTK dyadic *mathematics*
DYTK idiotic *stupid*
DYTKL dyadically *mathematics*
DYTKL idiotically *stupid*
DYTM diatom *plankton*
DYTNK diatonic *music*
DYTNKL diatonically *music*
DYTP audiotape *recording*
DYTR dietary *food*
DYTR dieter *weight loss*
DYTRB diatribe *criticism*
DYTRM deuterium *element*
DYTRNP deuteranope *color-blind person*
DYTRNP deuteranopia *color blindness*
DYTRNPY deuteranopia *color blindness*
DYTRYM deuterium *element*
DYTS deutzia *shrub*
DYTS duteous *obliging*
DYTSHN dietitian *nutrition*
DYTSY deutzia *shrub*
DYTTK dietetic *special food*

DYTTKS dietetics *nutrition*
DYTTX dietetics *nutrition*
DYTYBL dutiable *obliging*
DYTYS duteous *obliging*
DYTZ deutzia *shrub*
DYTZY deutzia *shrub*
DYV duvet *bedspread*
DYVSHL audiovisual *seen and heard*
DYVSHWL audiovisual *seen and heard*
DYVTN duvetyn *fabric*
DYVZHL audiovisual *seen and heard*
DYVZHWL audiovisual *seen and heard*
DYW dewy *moist* dewier dewiest
DYW duo *twosome* duos
DYWD dewy-eyed *innocent*
DYWDN duodena (pl) *intestine* duodenum
DYWDNL duodenal *intestine*
DYWDNM duodenum *intestine* duodena (or) duodenums
DYWDSML duodecimal *twelves*
DYWL dual *two*
DYWL duel *combat* dueled (or) duelled dueling (or) duelling
DYWLD duality *two* dualities
DYWLPRPS dual-purpose *two uses*
DYWLR dueler (or) dueller *fighter*
DYWLSDK dualistic *two*
DYWLSDKL dualistically *two*
DYWLST duelist (or) duellist *fighter*
DYWLSTK dualistic *two*
DYWLSTKL dualistically *two*
DYWLT duality *two* dualities
DYWLZM dualism *two*
DYWMVRT duumvirate *two rulers*
DYWN duenna *chaperon*
DYWPL duopoly *two sellers or rulers* duopolies

DYWPLSDK duopolistic *two sellers or rulers*
DYWPLSTK duopolistic *two sellers or rulers*
DYWR dewier *moist*
DYWRM dew worm *night crawler*
DYWST dewiest *moist*
DYWT duet *two*
DYWYD dewy-eyed *innocent*
DYWYR dewier *moist*
DYWYST dewiest *moist*
DYX dukes (*slang*) *fists*
DYXD dioxide *chemical*
DYXDZ deoxidize *remove oxygen* deoxidized deoxidizing
DYXDZR deoxidizer *remove oxygen*
DYXJNSHN deoxygenation *remove oxygen*
DYXJNT deoxygenate *remove oxygen*
DYXN dioxane *solvent*
DYXN dioxin *herbicide*
DYXS deixis *words*
DYZ dues *payment*
DYZLDRF Dusseldorf *city*
DYZM deism (*often capitalized*) *philosophy*
DYZPM diazepam *tranquilizer*
DYZPN diazepam *tranquilizer*
DZ adze *tool*
DZ aedes *mosquito* aedes
DZ AIDS (*abbr*) *acquired immunodeficiency syndrome*
DZ daisy *flower* daisies
DZ daze *stun* dazed dazing
DZ disease *illness*
DZ dizzy (*v*) *make giddy* dizzied dizzying dizzies
DZ dizzy (*adj*) *giddy* dizzier dizziest
DZ does *third person singular of "do"*
DZ doozy (or) doozie (*slang*) *exceptional* doozies
DZ dowse *find water*

dowsed dowsing
DZ doze *sleep* dozed dozing
DZ dues *payment*
DZ ides *date*
DZ iodize *with iodine* iodized iodizing (Br) iodise
DZ odds *wager*
DZ outdoes *bests*
DZD diseased *ill*
DZDL dazedly *stun*
DZDNS dazedness *stun*
DZGDK dizygotic *fraternal*
DZGN designee *chosen one*
DZGNDD designated *denoted*
DZGNDL designedly *intended*
DZGNDR designator *denoter*
DZGNSHN designation *indication, appointment*
DZGNT designate *denote* designated designating
DZGNTD designated *denoted*
DZGNTR designator *denoter*
DZGTK dizygotic *fraternal*
DZH adagio *slow, ballet* adagios
DZH étagêre (or) etagere *furniture*
DZHR dozer *bulldozer*
DZHR du jour *of the day*
DZHV déjà vu *memory*
DZHY adagio *slow, ballet* adagios
DZKBN adzuki bean *vegetable*
DZKRT Descartes *philosopher*
DZL dazzle *awe, shine* dazzled dazzling
DZL diesel *fuel*
DZL dizzily *unsteadily*
DZLDRF Dusseldorf *city*
DZLNGL dazzlingly *awe, shine*
DZLR dazzler *awe, shine*
DZLV dissolve *melt, destroy* dissolved dissolving
DZLVBL dissolvable *melt*
DZLVNT dissolvent *melt,*

Use letters that best describe the sounds you hear and omit the vowels. Use **S** or **K** instead of **C**: to find circle use **SRKL**. Use **J** to find joy, **JM** to find gem and **G** to find go.

destroy
DZLVR dissolver *melt, destroy*
DZM deism *(often capitalized) philosophy*
DZM Taoism *philosophy*
DZMKR oddsmaker *wager*
DZML dismal (adj) *bad* dismally (adv)
DZN design *pattern*
DZN doesn't *(contr) does not*
DZN dozen *twelve*
DZN odds-on *favorite*
DZNDNTS do's and don'ts *rules*
DZNGRD dowsing rod *water finding tool*
DZNN designing *crafty*
DZNNDS odds and ends *leftovers*
DZNNG designing *crafty*
DZNNZ odds and ends *leftovers*
DZNR designer *creator*
DZNRD dowsing rod *water finding tool*
DZNS dizziness *unsteadiness*
DZNT doesn't *(contr) does not*
DZPM diazepam *tranquilizer*
DZPN diazepam *tranquilizer*
DZR desire *want* desired desiring
DZR dizzier *giddy*
DZR dowser *water detecter*
DZR dozer *bulldozer*
DZR dysuria *urine*
DZRB adsorb *take in*
DZRBBL adsorbable *take in*
DZRBL desirable *attractive*
DZRBLD desirability *attractiveness*
DZRBLT desirability *attractiveness*
DZRBNT adsorbent *substance*
DZRBR adsorber *holder*
DZRBT adsorbate *substance held*
DZRDR deserter *abandoner*
DZRN discern *detect*
DZRNBL discernible (adj)

detect discernibly (adv)
DZRNMNT discernment *understanding difference*
DZRNN discerning *understanding difference*
DZRNNG discerning *understanding difference*
DZRNR discerner *detector*
DZRPSHN adsorption *taken in*
DZRPTV adsorptive *taken in*
DZRS desirous *wanting*
DZRSHN desertion *abandonment*
DZRT desert *(n) barren place, reward (v) abandon*
DZRT dessert *food*
DZRTHM dysrhythmia *bad rhythm*
DZRTHMK dysrhythmic *bad rhythm*
DZRTHMY dysrhythmia *bad rhythm*
DZRTR deserter *abandoner*
DZRTSPN dessertspoon *utensil*
DZRTSPNFL dessertspoonful *measure*
DZRTWN dessert wine *sweet drink*
DZRV deserve *merit* deserved deserving
DZRVD deserved *merit*
DZRVDL deservedly *merit*
DZRVN deserving *merit*
DZRVNG deserving *merit*
DZRVR deserver *merit*
DZRY dysuria *urine*
DZSDR disaster *ruin*
DZSDRS disastrous *ruinous*
DZSDRSL disastrously *ruin*
DZST desist *stop*
DZST dizziest *giddy*
DZSTNS desistance *stop*
DZSTNTS desistance *stop*
DZSTR disaster *ruin*
DZSTRS disastrous *ruinous*
DZSTRSL disastrously *ruin*
DZTSH dystocia *childbirth*
DZTSHY dystocia *childbirth*
DZV dissolve *melt, destroy* dissolved dissolving

DZVR dissolver *melt, destroy*
DZYR dizzier *giddy*
DZYR dysuria *urine*
DZYRY dysuria *urine*
DZYST dizziest *giddy*
DZYZ diseuse *reciter (f)* diseuses
DZZ disease *illness*
DZZ diseuse *reciter (f)* diseuses
DZZD diseased *ill*

F

F ef *alphabet letter (F)*
F ephah *measure*
F fa *musical note*
F faux *imitation*
F fay *(v) join (n) elf*
F fee *payment*
F feijoa *shrub*
F few *not many*
F fey *doomed, eccentric*
F fie *(interj) disgust*
F foe *enemy*
F if *whether or not*
F iffy *questionable*
F oaf *clumsy one*
F off *not on*
F phooey *(interj) disgust*
F UFO *(abbr) Unidentified Flying Object* UFOs
FB ephebe *youth*
FB ephebi (pl) *Greek youth* ephebus
FB f.o.b. *(abbr) free on board*
FB fib *tell a lie* fibbed fibbing
FB fob *chain*
FB phobia *fear*
FB phoebe *bird*
FBDKP Phi Beta Kappa *honors*
FBK ephebic *youthful*

Letters aren't doubled for single sounds: to find alley use **L** not **LL**. Use **Y** and **W** as hard sounds only: to find yellow use **YL**. (Br)=British spelling or usage. * See dictionary.

FBK phobic *fearful*
FBL affable (adj) *friendly*
    affably (adv)
FBL fable *tale*
FBL feeble *weak* feebler
    feeblest
FBL feebly *weakly*
FBL fibula *bone* fibulae (or)
    fibulas
FBL foible *fault*
FBLD affability *friendliness*
FBLD fabled *famous*
FBLMNDD feebleminded
    stupid
FBLMNDDL feeblemindedly
    stupidly
FBLMNDDNS
    feeblemindedness
    stupidity
FBLR feebler *weaker*
FBLS fabulous *wonderful,*
    fabled
FBLSH feeblish *weak*
FBLSL fabulously *wonderful,*
    fabled
FBLST fabulist *writer, liar*
FBLST feeblest *weakest*
FBLT affability *friendliness*
FBR February *month*
FBR fibber *liar*
FBR fiber *thread*
    (Br) fibre
FBRBRD fiberboard *paper*
    (Br) fibreboard
FBRD fibroid *tumor*
FBRDK fibrotic *tissue*
FBRDW off Broadway
    theater
FBRFJ febrifuge *fever*
    reducer
FBRFYJ febrifuge *fever*
    reducer
FBRGLS fiberglass *(n)*
    material (v) apply material
FBRK fabric *material*
FBRKDR fabricator *creator*
FBRKNT fabricant *creator*
FBRKSHN fabrication
    creation
FBRKT fabricate *create*
    fabricated fabricating
FBRKTR fabricator *creator*

FBRL afebrile *no fever*
FBRL febrile *feverish*
FBRL fibril *thread*
FBRLR fibrillar *thread*
FBRLSHN fibrillation *twitch*
FBRLT fibrillate *twitch*
    fibrillated fibrillating
FBRM fibroma *tumor*
    fibromas
FBRN fibrin *protein*
FBRNJN fibrinogen *protein*
FBRPDK fiber optic
    transmitter fiber optics
FBRPTK fiber optic
    transmitter fiber optics
FBRR February *month*
FBRS fibrous *tough*
FBRSS fibrosis *tissue*
FBRSSDK fibrocystic *tissue*
FBRSSTK fibrocystic *tissue*
FBRTK fibrotic *tissue*
FBRVSKLR fibrovascular
    cells
FBRVSKYLR fibrovascular
    cells
FBRVSQLR fibrovascular
    cells
FBRWR February *month*
FBRZ fiberize *make fibers*
    fiberized fiberizing
FBS ephebus *Greek youth*
    ephebi
FBS Phoebus *Greek god*
FBT offbeat *uncommon*
FBTKP Phi Beta Kappa
    honors
FBWR February *month*
FBY phobia *fear*
FBYL fibula *bone* fibulae (or)
    fibulas
FBYLS fabulous *wonderful,*
    fabled
FBYLSL fabulously
    wonderful, fabled
FBYLST fabulist *writer, liar*
FBYR February *month*
FBYWR February *month*
FC fosse (or) foss *ditch*
FC fussy *neat* fussier
    fussiest
FCH fetch *retrieve*
FCH fitch (or) fitchew *polecat*

FCHD fatuity *stupidity*
    fatuities
FCHN fetching *attractive*
FCHNG fetching *attractive*
FCHR feature *(v) imagine,*
    star featured featuring
FCHR feature *(n)appearance,*
    program
FCHR fetcher *retriever*
FCHR future *yet to come*
FCHRD featured *main part*
FCHRD futurity *yet to come*
futurities
FCHRLG futurology *trends*
FCHRLJ futurology *trends*
FCHRLJKL futurological
    trends
FCHRLJST futurologist
    trends
FCHRLS featureless *bland*
FCHRSDK futuristic *yet to*
    come
FCHRSDKL futuristically *yet*
    to come
FCHRST futurist *predictor*
FCHRSTK futuristic *yet to*
    come
FCHRSTKL futuristically *yet*
    to come
FCHRT featurette *short film*
FCHRT futurity *yet to come*
    futurities
FCHRZM futurism *mechanics*
FCHS fatuous *silly*
FCHSL fatuously *silly*
FCHSNS fatuousness *silly*
FCHT fatuity *stupidity*
    fatuities
FCHT fitchet *polecat*
FCHWD fatuity *stupidity*
    fatuities
FCHWS fatuous *silly*
FCHWSL fatuously *silly*
FCHWSNS fatuousness
    silly
FCHWT fatuity *stupidity*
    fatuities
FCLSS fascioliasis *disease*
    fascioliases
FCLYSS fascioliasis *disease*
    fascioliases
FCND aficionado *fan*

Use letters that best describe the sounds you hear and omit the vowels. Use **S** or **K** instead of **C**: to find circle use **SRKL**. Use **J** to find joy, **JM** to find gem and **G** to find go.

aficionados
FCNS fussiness *neatness*
FCR fussier *neater*
FCSH facetiae *witticism*
FCSHS facetious *witty*
FCSHSL facetiously *wit*
FCSHSNS facetiousness
wit
FCST fussiest *neatest*
FCYLSS fascioliasis *disease*
fascioliases
FCYLYSS fascioliasis *disease*
fascioliases
FCYND aficionado *fan*
aficionados
FCYR fussier *neater*
FCYST fussiest *neatest*
FCZ apheses (pl) *lost vowel*
aphesis
FCZ fasces *emblem*
FCZ fauces *throat*
FCZ feces *dung*
FCZN off-season *less
activity*
FD aphid *insect*
FD fad *style phase*
FD fade *diminish* faded
fading
FD fado *song* fados
FD fatty *(adj) with fat* fattier
fattiest
FD fatty *(n) obese one* fatties
FD fed *(v-past) feed (n)(often
capitalized) government
agent*
FD feed *(v) eat, channel* fed
feeding
FD feed *(n) food*
FD feta *cheese*
FD feud *quarrel*
FD fid *pin*
FD fido *coin* fidos
FD food *nutrient*
FD photo *camera* photos
FDBK feedback *information,
noise*
FDCHN fettuccine (or)
fettuccini (or) fettucine
(or) fettucini *pasta*
FDD fated *destined*
FDD fatted *made fat*
FDD fetid *smelly*

FDD fitted *sized*
FDD footed *with feet*
FDDD fuddy-duddy
conservative fuddy-
duddies
FDFB photophobia
sensitivity to light
FDFBK photophobic
sensitive to light
FDFBY photophobia
sensitivity to light
FDFLD photoflood *lamp*
FDFLJLT phytoflagellate
algae
FDFLSH photoflash *camera*
photoflashes
FDFNSH photo finish *race*
FDFR photophore *spot*
FDFST photo-offset *printing*
FDFZ photophase *cycle*
FDG foo dog *lion-dog*
FDGBL fatigable *tired*
FDGBLD fatigability
tiredness
FDGBLT fatigability *tiredness*
FDGNK photogenic *light,
picture*
FDGNKL photogenically
light, picture
FDGRF photograph *camera*
FDGRFK photographic
camera
FDGRFKL photographically
camera
FDGRVR photogravure
printing
FDGRVYR photogravure
printing
FDHRMN phytohormone
plants
FDJ footage *length*
FDJNK photogenic *light,
picture*
FDJNKL photogenically
light, picture
FDJRNLST photojournalist
pictures
FDJRNLZM
photojournalism *pictures*
FDK euphotic *water plants*
FDK ophitic *rock*
FDK photic *light*

FDKL photically *light*
FDKMKL photochemical
(adj) *light*
photochemically (adv)
FDKMKL phytochemical
(adj) *plants*
phytochemically (adv)
FDKMSDR photochemistry
light
FDKMSTR photochemistry
light
FDKMSTR phytochemistry
plants
FDKNDK photokinetic
motion
FDKNSS photokinesis
motion
FDKNTK photokinetic
motion
FDKP photocopy *duplicate*
photocopied
photocopying
photocopies
FDKPR photocopier
duplicator
FDKPYR photocopier
duplicator
FDKRM phytochrome
protein
FDL fatal (adj) *deadly* fatally
(adv)
FDL fetal *unborn*
(Br) foetal
FDL fettle *health*
FDL feudal (adj) *medieval*
feudally (adv)
FDL fiddle *(v) tinker, cheat,
play violin* fiddled fiddling
FDL fiddle *(n) violin*
FDL fuddle *intoxicate*
fuddled fuddling
FDL futile (adj) *useless* futilely
(adv)
FDLD fidelity *loyalty*
fidelities
FDLDK photolytic *broken
down*
FDLDKL photolytically
broken down
FDLFDL fiddle-faddle
nonsense
FDLKTRK photoelectric

light
FDLN fiddling *petty*
FDLNG fiddling *petty*
FDLNS futileness *uselessness*
FDLR fiddler *violin, cheat*
FDLRKRB fiddler crab
animal
FDLSDK fatalistic
predetermined
FDLSDK feudalistic *medieval*
FDLSDKL fatalistically
predetermined
FDLST fatalist *predetermined*
FDLSTK fatalistic
predetermined
FDLSTK feudalistic *medieval*
FDLSTKL fatalistically
predetermined
FDLSTKS fiddlesticks
nonsense
FDLSTX fiddlesticks
nonsense
FDLT feedlot *livestock*
FDLT fidelity *loyalty* fidelities
FDLTHGRF photolithograph
picture
FDLTHGRF
photolithography *process*
FDLTK photolytic *broken
down*
FDLTKL photolytically
broken down
FDLZ photolyze *break down*
photolyzed photolyzing
FDLZM fatalism
predetermined
FDLZM feudalism *medieval*
FDMDR photometer
brightness
FDMNTJ photomontage
picture
FDMNTSH photomontage
picture
FDMNTZH photomontage
picture
FDMP photomap *atlas*
FDMRL photomural *picture*
FDMSHN photoemission
release
FDMTR photometer
brightness
FDMTR photometry

brightness
FDMTRK photometric
brightness
FDMYRL photomural *picture*
FDN fade-in *visibility*
FDN feeding *eating*
FDN ophidian *snakes*
FDNG feeding *eating*
FDNG fitting *suitable,
adjusting*
FDNG footing *step, base*
FDNGDV photonegative
opposite
FDNGL fittingly *suitable*
FDNGRV photoengrave
printing
FDNGRVNG
photoengraving *printing*
FDNGTV photonegative
opposite
FDNS fattiness *with fat*
FDP fed up *tired*
FDPLNGKDN
phytoplankton *plants*
FDPLNGKTN
phytoplankton *plants*
FDPLNKDN phytoplankton
plants
FDPLNKTN phytoplankton
plants
FDPTHJN phytopathogen
parasite
FDPTHLG phytopathology
parasites
FDPTHLJ phytopathology
parasites
FDPTHLJKL
phytopathological
parasites
FDPZDV photopositive
reactive
FDPZTV photopositive
reactive
FDR after *later than*
FDR ephedra *shrub*
FDR fader *vanish*
FDR fatter *obese*
FDR fattier *with more fat*
FDR fedora *hat*
FDR feeder *tributary,
supplier*
FDR fetter *(v)* restrain *(n)*

chain
FDR fighter *battler*
FDR fitter *tailor, healthier*
FDR fodder *food*
FDRBRNR afterburner *jet
device*
FDRBRTH afterbirth
placenta
FDRDD federated *united*
FDRDK afterdeck *rear*
FDRFK aftereffect *result*
FDRFKT aftereffect *result*
FDRGL afterglow *light*
FDRKLP afterclap *surprise*
FDRKR aftercare *post-
hospital care*
FDRL federal *(adj)
government* federally *(adv)*
FDRLF afterlife *life after
death*
FDRLST federalist *(often
capitalized) government*
FDRLZ federalize *unite*
federalized federalizing
FDRLZM federalism *(often
capitalized) government*
FDRLZSHN federalization
government
FDRMJ afterimage *vision*
FDRMRKT aftermarket
accessories
FDRMST aftermost *rear end*
FDRMTH aftermath *result*
FDRN ephedrine *drug*
FDRNN afternoon *day period*
FDRPS afterpiece *comedy*
FDRRZ after-hours *after
closing time*
FDRS afters *(Br)* dessert
FDRSHK aftershock *tremor*
FDRSHN federation *union*
FDRSHV aftershave *lotion*
FDRSPDR photoreceptor
receiver
FDRSPTR photoreceptor
receiver
FDRT federate *unite*
federated federating
FDRTD federated *united*
FDRTHT afterthought *late
idea*
FDRTKS after-tax *amount*

Use letters that best describe the sounds you hear and omit the vowels. Use **S** or **K** instead of **C**: to find circle use **SRKL**. Use **J** to find joy, **JM** to find gem and **G** to find go.

remaining

FDRTM aftertime *future*

FDRTST aftertaste *persistent flavor*

FDRTX after-tax *amount remaining*

FDRWRD afterward (or) afterwards *later*

FDRWRD afterword *epilogue*

FDRWRDZ afterwards (or) afterward *later*

FDRWRL afterworld *world after death*

FDRWRLD afterworld *world after death*

FDRWRZ after-hours *after closing time*

FDRZ afters *(Br) dessert*

FDS fetus *unborn* (Br) *foetus*

FDSD feticide *fetus death*

FDSFR photosphere *solar surface*

FDSH faddish *style phase*

FDSH fattish *plump*

FDSH fetish *charm, fixation*

FDSHL fiducial (adj) *trust* fiducially (adv)

FDSHNS faddishness *style phase*

FDSHR fiduciary *trust* fiduciaries

FDSHST fetishist *magic, devotion*

FDSHSTK fetishistic *magic, devotion*

FDSHSTKL fetishistically *magic, devotion*

FDSHYR fiduciary *trust* fiduciaries

FDSHZM fetishism *magic, devotion*

FDSKP fetoscope *exam tube*

FDSNSDV photosensitive *light*

FDSNSTV photosensitive *light*

FDSNSTZ photosensitize *light*

FDSNTHDK photosynthetic *plants*

FDSNTHDKL

photosynthetically *plants*

FDSNTHSS photosynthesis *plants*

FDSNTHSZ

photosynthesize *plants* photosynthesized photosynthesizing

FDSNTHTK photosynthetic *plants*

FDSNTHTKL

photosynthetically *plants*

FDST fattest *obese*

FDST fattiest *with most fat*

FDST fittest *healthy*

FDSTF feedstuff *animal food*

FDSTF foodstuff *raw food*

FDSTK feedstock *material*

FDSTMP food stamp *coupon*

FDSTT Photostat (trademark) *copier*

FDSTT photostat *copy*

FDT fade-out *visibility*

FDTKSK phytotoxic *plant killer*

FDTKSSD phytotoxicity *plant killer*

FDTKSST phytotoxicity *plant killer*

FDTR feudatory *allegiance* feudatories

FDTRPK phototropic *stimulus*

FDTRPKL phototropically *stimulus*

FDTXK phytotoxic *plant killer*

FDTXSD phytotoxicity *plant killer*

FDTXST phytotoxicity *plant killer*

FDVD affidavit *statement*

FDVLTK photovoltaic *electricity*

FDVLTYK photovoltaic *electricity*

FDVT affidavit *statement*

FDW fadeaway *baseball*

FDWFST photo-offset *printing*

FDWLKTRK photoelectric *light*

FDWMSHN photoemission *release*

FDWNGRV photoengrave *printing*

FDWNGRVNG

photoengraving *printing*

FDWNGRVR photoengraver *printing*

FDYN ophidian *snakes*

FDYR fattier *with more fat*

FDYSHL fiducial (adj) *trust* fiducially (adv)

FDYSHR fiduciary *trust* fiduciaries

FDYSHYR fiduciary *trust* fiduciaries

FDYST fattiest *with most fat*

FDZ aphides (pl) *insect type* aphis

FDZM faddism *style phase*

FF fief *estate*

FF fife *flute*

FFD fifty *number (50)* fifties

FFDM fiefdom *estate*

FFDTH fiftieth *of number 50*

FFDYTH fiftieth *of number 50*

FFDZ fifties *numbers 50-59*

FFR foofaraw *fuss*

FFT fifty *number (50)* fifties

FFTH fifth *of number 5* fifths

FFTN fifteen *number (15)*

FFTNTH fifteenth *of number 15*

FFTTH fiftieth *of number 50*

FFTYTH fiftieth *of number 50*

FFTZ fifties *numbers 50-59*

FG effigy *image* effigies

FG fag (v) *toil, tire* fagged fagging

FG fag (n) *cigarette, homosexual*

FG faggy *homosexual*

FG fig *fruit*

FG Fiji *islands*

FG fog *blur, mist* fogged fogging

FG foggy *blurred, misty* foggier foggiest

FG fogy *old person* fogies

FG fugu *fish*

FG fugue *music*

FG fuji *silk*

Letters aren't doubled for single sounds: to find alley use **L** not **LL**. Use **Y** and **W** as hard sounds only: to find yellow use **YL**. (Br)=British spelling or usage. * See dictionary.

FGBN fogbound *unable to move*

FGBND fogbound *unable to move*

FGD faggoty *homosexual*

FGDNG faggoting (or) faggotting *embroidery*

FGHRN foghorn *warning*

FGL foggily *blurred*

FGL fugal (adj) *music* fugally (adv)

FGMNT figment *invention*

FGN Afghan *of Afghanistan*

FGN afghan *blanket*

FGN afghani *money*

FGN fagin *(often capitalized) criminal*

FGN Fijian *of Fiji*

FGNM sphagnum *moss*

FGNS fogginess *blurred*

FGNS sphagnous *mossy*

FGNSTN Afghanistan *country*

FGR figure *(n) number, shape*

FGR figure *(v) count, conclude, plan* figured figuring

FGR foggier *blurred*

FGRD figured *portrayed*

FGRDV figurative *symbolic*

FGRDVL figuratively *symbolic*

FGRDVNS figurativeness *symbolism*

FGRHD figurehead *chief*

FGRN figurine *statue*

FGRR figurer *counter, shaper, planner*

FGRSHN figuration *outline*

FGRTV figurative *symbolic*

FGRTVL figuratively *symbolic*

FGRTVNS figurativeness *symbolism*

FGSD fugacity *vapor*

FGSDK phagocytic *cell*

FGSHS fugacious *short-lived*

FGST foggiest *blurred*

FGST fugacity *vapor*

FGST phagocyte *cell*

FGSTDK phagocytotic *cell*

FGSTK phagocytic *cell*

FGSTSS phagocytosis *cell*

FGSTTK phagocytotic *cell*

FGT faggot *homosexual*

FGT faggoty *homosexual*

FGT fagot (or) faggot *bundle*

FGTNG faggoting (or) faggotting *embroidery*

FGTR faggotry *homosexual*

FGYN Fijian *of Fiji*

FGYR figure *(v) count, conclude, plan* figured figuring

FGYR figure *(n) number, shape*

FGYR foggier *blurred*

FGYRD figured *portrayed*

FGYRDV figurative *symbolic*

FGYRDVL figuratively *symbolic*

FGYRDVNS figurativeness *symbolism*

FGYRHD figurehead *chief*

FGYRN figurine *statue*

FGYRR figurer *counter, shaper, planner*

FGYRSHN figuration *outline*

FGYRTV figurative *symbolic*

FGYRTVL figuratively *symbolic*

FGYRTVNS figurativeness *symbolism*

FGYST foggiest *blurred*

FGYZM fogyism *old person*

FGZM fogyism *old person*

FH feijoa *shrub*

FHD fajita *food*

FHN offhand *casual*

FHND offhand *casual*

FHNDD offhanded *casual*

FHNDDNS offhandedness *casual*

FHSN fishing *catch fish*

FHSNG fishing *catch fish*

FHT fajita *food*

FHW feijoa *shrub*

FHWT off-white *color*

FJ effigy *image* effigies

FJ Fiji *islands*

FJ fudge *(v) fake* fudged fudging

FJ fudge *(n) candy, nonsense*

FJ fuji *silk*

FJD fidgety *nervous*

FJDNS fidgetiness *twitch*

FJDV fugitive *(adj) transient (n) escapee*

FJN Fijian *of Fiji*

FJT fidget *twitch*

FJT fidgety *nervous*

FJTNS fidgetiness *twitch*

FJTV fugitive *(adj) transient (n) escapee*

FJYN Fijian *of Fiji*

FK affect *(v) influence, feign (n) emotion*

FK effect *result, appearance, influence**

FK fact *truth*

FK fake *(v) pretend* faked faking

FK fake *(n) imitation*

FK foci *(pl) intersection* focus

FK folk *people* folk (or) folks

FK Foucault *physicist*

FK fuck *(n-vulgar) sex (v-vulgar) cheat, ruin*

FK fyke *net*

FK off-key *music*

FKC efficacy *power* efficacies

FKC folksy *humble* folksier folksiest

FKC foxy *sly* foxier foxiest

FKCH focaccia *food*

FKCHL effectual (adj) *useful* effectually (adv)

FKCHL factual (adj) *true* factually (adv)

FKCHLST factualist *truth*

FKCHLT factuality *truth*

FKCHLZM factualism *truth*

FKCHR facture *making*

FKCHSHN effectuation *cause*

FKCHT effectuate *cause* effectuated effectuating

FKCHWL effectual (adj) *useful* effectually (adv)

FKCHWL factual (adj) *true* factually (adv)

FKCHWLST factualist *truth*

FKCHWLT factuality *truth*

FKCHWLZM factualism *truth*

FKCHWSHN effectuation *cause*
FKCHWT effectuate *cause* effectuated effectuating
FKCHY focaccia *food*
FKCNS foxiness *cleverness*
FKCR folksier *humble*
FKCR foxier *clever*
FKCST folksiest *humble*
FKCST foxiest *clever*
FKCYR folksier *humble*
FKCYR foxier *clever*
FKCYST folksiest *humble*
FKCYST foxiest *clever*
FKD fucoid *rockweed*
FKDBL affectable *influential*
FKDBLD affectability *influence*
FKDBLT affectability *influence*
FKDD affected *pretended, inclined*
FKDDL affectedly *falsely*
FKDDNS affectedness *falseness*
FKDN affecting *moving*
FKDNG affecting *moving*
FKDR effector *enabler*
FKDR factor *(v) calculate (n) ingredient, math, broker**
FKDR factory *manufacturing* factories
FKDRBL factorable *calculate*
FKDRJ factorage *brokerage*
FKDRZSHN factorization *number*
FKDV affective *emotional*
FKDV effective *useful*
FKDV fictive *invented*
FKDVL affectively *emotionally*
FKFNDN fact-finding *examination*
FKFNDNG fact-finding *examination*
FKFNDR fact finder *examiner*
FKL facula *sun* faculae
FKL fecal *dung*
FKL fickle *changeable*
FKL focal *(adj) light, lens* focally *(adv)*

FKLD faculty *ability, teaching* faculties
FKLD fickle *changeable*
FKLDR off-kilter *tilted*
FKLDV faculative *optional*
FKLG phycology *algae*
FKLJ phycology *algae*
FKLJKL phycological *algae*
FKLJST phycologist *algae*
FKLNDLNDZ Falkland Islands *land mass*
FKLNDLNZ Falkland Islands *land mass*
FKLNGKTH focal length *lens*
FKLNGTH focal length *lens*
FKLNKTH focal length *lens*
FKLNLNDZ Falkland Islands *land mass*
FKLNLNZ Falkland Islands *land mass*
FKLNS feculence *dung*
FKLNS fickleness *changeable*
FKLNT feculent *foul*
FKLNTH focal length *lens*
FKLNTS feculence *dung*
FKLR folklore *stories*
FKLR off-color *obscene* (Br) off-colour
FKLS feckless *worthless*
FKLSL fecklessly *worthless*
FKLSNS fecklessness *worthless*
FKLT faculty *ability, teaching* faculties
FKLT Foucault *physicist*
FKLTR off-kilter *tilted*
FKLTV faculative *optional*
FKLZ focalize *concentrate* focalized focalizing
FKMCDS phycomycetous *algae*
FKMCT phycomycete *algae*
FKMCTS phycomycetous *algae*
FKMSDS phycomycetous *algae*
FKMST phycomycete *algae*
FKMSTS phycomycetous *algae*
FKND fecund *fertile*
FKNDD fecundity *fertility*

fecundities
FKNDSHN fecundation *pregnancy*
FKNDT fecundate *impregnate* fecundated fecundating
FKNDT fecundity *fertility* fecundities
FKNR Faulkner *writer*
FKP fuck up (v) *(vulgar) blunder* fuckup (n)
FKR faker *imposter*
FKR fakir *Hindu ascetic*
FKS affix *attach*
FKS efficacy *power* efficacies
FKS fax *transmit document*
FKS ficus *plant* ficus (or) ficuses
FKS fix *(v) mend, arrange, spay (n) dose, predicament** fixes
FKS focus *(v) adjust, concentrate*
FKS focus *(n) adjustment, emphasis* foci
FKS folksy *humble* folksier folksiest
FKS fox *animal* foxes
FKS foxy *sly* foxier foxiest
FKS fucose *sugar*
FKS fucus *algae*
FKSBL affixable *attach*
FKSBL fixable *mend*
FKSBL focusable *adjustment*
FKSCHR fixture *attachment*
FKSD fixity *solidness* fixities
FKSDD fixated *held*
FKSDL fixedly *unmoving*
FKSDNS fixedness *unmoving*
FKSDV fixative *protection*
FKSFR fox fire *light*
FKSFYR fox fire *light*
FKSGRP fox grape *plant*
FKSH focaccia *food*
FKSHL effectual (adj) *useful* effectually (adv)
FKSHL factual (adj) *true* factually (adv)
FKSHL foxhole *ditch*
FKSHLST factualist *truth*

Letters aren't doubled for single sounds: to find alley use **L** not **LL**. Use **Y** and **W** as hard sounds only: to find yellow use **YL**. (Br)=British spelling or usage. * See dictionary.

FKSHLT factuality *truth*
FKSHLZM factualism *truth*
FKSHN affection *love*
FKSHN faction *clique*
FKSHN fiction *invention*
FKSHN foxhound *dog*
FKSHND foxhound *dog*
FKSHNL affectional (adj) *loving* affectionally (adv)
FKSHNL factional (adj) *clique* factionally (adv)
FKSHNL fictional (adj) *invented* fictionally (adv)
FKSHNLD fictionality *invented*
FKSHNLT fictionality *invented*
FKSHNLZ fictionalize *invent* fictionalized fictionalizing (Br) fictionalise
FKSHNLZM factionalism *clique*
FKSHNLZSHN fictionalization *invention*
FKSHNT affectionate *loving*
FKSHNTL affectionately *lovingly*
FKSHNZ fictionize *invent* fictionized fictionizing
FKSHR facture *making*
FKSHS efficacious *effective*
FKSHS factious *dissent*
FKSHSHN effectuation *cause*
FKSHSL efficaciously *effective*
FKSHSNS efficaciousness *effective*
FKSHT effectuate *cause* effectuated effectuating
FKSHWL effectual (adj) *useful* effectually (adv)
FKSHWL factual (adj) *true* factually (adv)
FKSHWLST factualist *truth*
FKSHWLT factuality *truth*
FKSHWLZM factualism *truth*
FKSHWSHN effectuation *cause*
FKSHWT effectuate *cause* effectuated effectuating

FKSHY focaccia *food*
FKSL forecastle *ship area*
FKSL foxhole *ditch*
FKSL foxily *cleverly*
FKSML facsimile *copy*
FKSMNT affixment *attachment*
FKSNG folk song *traditional tune*
FKSNGR folksinger *musician*
FKSNGS fixings *food*
FKSNGZ fixings *food*
FKSNS fixings *food*
FKSNS foxiness *cleverness*
FKSNZ fixings *food*
FKSR fixer *mender*
FKSR focuser *lens*
FKSR folksier *humble*
FKSR foxier *clever*
FKSSHN affixation *attachment*
FKSSHN fixation *obsession*
FKSST folksiest *humble*
FKSST foxiest *clever*
FKST fixate *stare, hold* fixated fixating
FKST fixed *unmoving*
FKST fixity *solidness* fixities
FKST offcast *discarded*
FKSTD fixated *held*
FKSTL foxtail *tail, grass*
FKSTPNT fixed-point *math*
FKSTR fixture *attachment*
FKSTRR fox terrier *dog*
FKSTRT fox-trot *dance music*
FKSTRT Foxtrot *code word*
FKSTRT foxtrot *dance*
FKSTRYR fox terrier *dog*
FKSTV fixative *protection*
FKSYR folksier *humble*
FKSYR foxier *clever*
FKSYST folksiest *humble*
FKSYST foxiest *clever*
FKT affect (v) *influence, feign* (n) *emotion*
FKT effect (n) *result, appearance* (v) *influence**
FKT fact *truth*
FKT fake out *deceive*
FKTBL affectable *influential*
FKTBLD affectability

influence
FKTBLT affectability
influence
FKTD affected *inclined, pretended*
FKTD factoid *invention*
FKTDL affectedly *falsely*
FKTDM factotum *servant*
FKTDNS affectedness *falseness*
FKTDV factitive *verb*
FKTFNDN fact-finding *examination*
FKTFNDNG fact-finding *examination*
FKTFNDR fact finder *examiner*
FKTL effectual (adj) *useful* effectually (adv)
FKTL factual (adj) *true* factually (adv)
FKTL folktale *story*
FKTLD factuality *truth*
FKTLST factualist *truth*
FKTLT factuality *truth*
FKTLZM factualism *truth*
FKTN affecting *moving*
FKTNG affecting *moving*
FKTR effector *enabler*
FKTR factor (v) *calculate* (n) *ingredient, math, broker**
FKTR factory *manufacturing factories*
FKTR facture *making*
FKTRBL factorable *calculate*
FKTRJ factorage *brokerage*
FKTRL factorial *number*
FKTRYL factorial *number*
FKTRZ factorize *number* factorized factorizing
FKTRZSHN factorization *number*
FKTSHN affectation *pose*
FKTSHN effectuation *cause*
FKTSHS factitious *artificial*
FKTSHS fictitious *invented*
FKTSHSL factitiously *artificial*
FKTSHSL fictitiously *invented*
FKTSHSNS factitiousness *artificial*

Use letters that best describe the sounds you hear and omit the vowels. Use **S** or **K** instead of **C**: to find circle use **SRKL**. Use **J** to find joy, **JM** to find gem and **G** to find go.

FKTSHSNS fictitiousness *invented*
FKTT effectuate *cause* effectuated effectuating
FKTTM factotum *servant*
FKTTV factitive *verb*
FKTV affective *emotional*
FKTV effective *useful*
FKTV fictive *invented*
FKTVD affectivity *emotion*
FKTVL affectively *emotionally*
FKTVT affectivity *emotion*
FKTWL effectual (adj) *useful* effectually (adv)
FKTWL factual (adj) *true* factually (adv)
FKTWLD factuality *truth*
FKTWLST factualist *truth*
FKTWLT factuality *truth*
FKTWLZM factualism *truth*
FKTWSHN effectuation *cause*
FKTWT effectuate *cause* effectuated effectuating
FKW folkway *custom*
FKYL facula *sun* faculae
FKYLDV faculative *optional*
FKYLNS feculence *dung*
FKYLNT feculent *foul*
FKYLNTS feculence *dung*
FKYLTV faculative *optional*
FL afield *outside*
FL aphelia (pl) *star path* aphelion
FL awful (adj) *terrible* awfully (adv)
FL eyeful *vision*
FL fail (n) *failure* (v) *weaken, stop, disappoint**
FL faille *fabric*
FL fall (v) *descend, abate, fail** fell fallen falling
FL fall (n) *dropping, season, collapse**
FL fallow (n) *land* (adj) *dormant, color* (v) *plow*
FL feel (v) *sense, believe* felt feeling
FL feel (n) *touch, knowledge*
FL fell (v) *kill, cut down* (v-past) *fall* (n) *skin*, (adj)

*cruel**
FL fellah *laborer* fellahin (or) fellaheen
FL fellow *comrade, peer, man*
FL felly (or) felloe *rim* fellies (or) felloes
FL feyly *doomed, eccentric*
FL field (n) *area* (v) *catch, answer*
FL file (v) *arrange, initiate action, line up** filed filing
FL filé *thickener*
FL file (n) *scraper, folder, line* filed filing
FL filet *lace* (Br) fillet
FL fill (v) *supply, plug, complete** (n) *material*
FL fillet (n) *ribbon, boneless slice* (v) *adorn, cut into strips*
FL filly *horse* fillies
FL filo (or) phyllo *pastry*
FL flaw *mistake*
FL flay *lash*
FL flea *insect*
FL flee *run away* fled fleeing
FL flew (v-past) *fly*
FL floe *ice*
FL flow *stream*
FL flu *illness*
FL flue *chimney*
FL fly (v) *soar, flee, pass* flew flown flying flies
FL fly (n) *insect, closure, flight* flies
FL fly (v) *baseball* flied flying flies
FL foal *horse*
FL foil (n) *thin metal, sword, contrast* (v) *thwart*
FL fold *bend*
FL folio *page, case* folios
FL follow *go after, obey, watch**
FL folly *mistake* follies
FL fool (n) *idiot* (v) *trick*
FL foul (n) *sports* (v) *pollute, block*
FL foul (adj) *not fair, dirty* foully (adv)
FL foully *dirty, indecent*

FL fowl *bird* fowl (or) fowls
FL fuel (v) *stimulate, sustain* fueled (or) fuelled fueling (or) fuelling
FL fuel (n) *energy source*
FL full (adj) *complete* fully (adv)
FL fully *completely*
FL offal *waste*
FL phalli (pl) *penis* phallus
FL phial *bottle*
FL phyla (pl) *division* phylum
FL phyllo *pastry*
FLB flab *loose skin*
FLB flabby *flaccid* flabbier flabbiest
FLB flub *botch* flubbed flubbing
FLB flyboy *pilot*
FLB flyby *low flight* flybys
FLBDD full-bodied *taste, texture*
FLBDM phlebotomy *blood-letting* phlebotomies
FLBDMST phlebotomist *blood-letting*
FLBDS phlebitis *veins*
FLBG fleabag *inferior room*
FLBK fallback (n) *retreat* fall back (v)
FLBK fullback *football*
FLBL fallible (adj) *mistakes* fallibly (adv)
FLBL flabbily *flaccid*
FLBL fly ball *baseball*
FLBL flyable *soar*
FLBL foul ball *bad hit*
FLBLD fallibility *mistakes*
FLBLDD full-blooded *breeding*
FLBLG phlebology *veins*
FLBLJ phlebology *veins*
FLBLN flyblown *seedy*
FLBLN full-blown *total*
FLBLST full blast *capacity*
FLBLT fallibility *mistakes*
FLBN fleabane *plant*
FLBNS flabbiness *flaccid*
FLBNT fly-by-night *shaky*
FLBR flabbier *loose skin*
FLBR Flaubert *writer*
FLBRGSDD flabbergasted

Letters aren't doubled for single sounds: to find alley use **L** not **LL**. Use **Y** and **W** as hard sounds only: to find yellow use **YL**. (Br)=British spelling or usage. * See dictionary.

surprised
FLBRGST flabbergast *surprise*
FLBRGSTD flabbergasted *surprised*
FLBRJ flybridge *boat*
FLBRT filbert *nut*
FLBRT Flaubert *writer*
FLBSDR filibuster *delay*
FLBSDRR filibusterer *delayer*
FLBST flabbiest *loose skin*
FLBSTR filibuster *delay*
FLBSTRR filibusterer *delayer*
FLBT fleabite *pain*
FLBTM phlebotomy *blood-letting* phlebotomies
FLBTMST phlebotomist *blood-letting*
FLBTN flea-bitten *spotted, infested*
FLBTS phlebitis *veins*
FLBYR flabbier *loose skin*
FLBYST flabbiest *loose skin*
FLC fallacy *false idea* fallacies
FLC falsie *imitation*
FLC fleecy *like wool, downy* fleecier fleeciest
FLC flossy *silky, stylish* flossier flossiest
FLCH filch *steal*
FLCH fletch *arrow*
FLCH flitch *bacon, bundle*
FLCHLNS flatulence *gas* flatulency
FLCHLNT flatulent *gas*
FLCHLNTL flatulently *gas*
FLCHLNTS flatulence *gas* flatulency
FLCHNG fletching *feathers*
FLCHR fletcher *arrows*
FLCHRDNG flowcharting *diagram*
FLCHRT flowchart *diagram*
FLCHRTN flowcharting *diagram*
FLCHRTNG flowcharting *diagram*
FLCR fleecier *like wool, downy*
FLCR flossier *silky, stylish*

FLCST fleeciest *like wool, downy*
FLCST flossiest *silky, stylish*
FLCYR fleecier *like wool, downy*
FLCYR flossier *silky, stylish*
FLCYST fleeciest *like wool, downy*
FLCYST flossiest *silky, stylish*
FLD afield *outside*
FLD faulty *imperfect* faultier faultiest
FLD felid *cat*
FLD field *(n) area (v) catch, answer*
FLD fled *(v-past) flee*
FLD flighty *silly* flightier flightiest
FLD flood *surge*
FLD fluid *liquid*
FLD fluty (or) flutey *groove, music, glass*
FLD fold *bend*
FLD off-load *remove*
FLD phyllode *leaf*
FLDBL foldable *bendable*
FLDC felo-de-se *suicide* felones-de-se (or) felos-de-se (pl)
FLDD affiliated *associated*
FLDD fluidity *liquid*
FLDD fluted *grooved*
FLDD foliated *leaf*
FLDGL field goal *sports*
FLDGT floodgate *sluice*
FLDHS field house *sports*
FLDK phyletic *evolution*
FLDKL phyletically *evolution*
FLDL flightily *silly*
FLDL philately *stamps*
FLDLF Philadelphia *city*
FLDLFS philadelphus *plant*
FLDLFY Philadelphia *city*
FLDLK philatelic (adj) *stamps* philatelically (adv)
FLDLST philatelist *stamps*
FLDLT floodlight *(v) illuminate* floodlit floodlighting
FLDLT floodlight *(n) spotlight*

FLDN folding *bendable*
FLDNDR philodendra (pl) *plant* philodendron
FLDNDRM philodendron *plant* philodendrons (or) philodendra
FLDNDRN philodendron *plant* philodendrons (or) philodendra
FLDNG felting *fabric*
FLDNG fleeting *quick*
FLDNG floating *not fixed*
FLDNG fluting *grooves*
FLDNG folding *bendable*
FLDNGL fleetingly *quick*
FLDNS flightiness *silliness*
FLDNS fluid ounce *measure*
FLDNTS fluid ounce *measure*
FLDPLN floodplain *land*
FLDPS fieldpiece *gun*
FLDR aflutter *excited*
FLDR falter *stumble*
FLDR faultier *imperfect*
FLDR fielder *sportsman*
FLDR filter *(v) strain (n) strainer*
FLDR flatter *(v) praise (adj) deflated*
FLDR flattery *praise* flatteries
FLDR flightier *sillier*
FLDR flitter *jerky movement*
FLDR floater *buoy, worker, policy*
FLDR flouter *jeerer*
FLDR fluter *pleater*
FLDR flutter *flap, spasm*
FLDR fluttery *flap, spasm*
FLDR folder *paper holder, device that bends*
FLDR philter (or) philtre *potion*
FLDRBL filterable *strainer*
FLDRBLD filterability *strainer*
FLDRBLT filterability *strainer*
FLDRBRD flutterboard *swimming*
FLDRKK flutter kick *swim*
FLDRL folderol *nonsense*
FLDRM phelloderm *inward cells*

Use letters that best describe the sounds you hear and omit the vowels. Use **S** or **K** instead of **C**: to find circle use **SRKL**. Use **J** to find joy, **JM** to find gem and **G** to find go.

FLDRN flatiron *ironing*
FLDRNGL falteringly *stumble*
FLDRNGL flatteringly *praise*
FLDRNL falteringly *stumble*
FLDRR falterer *stumble*
FLDRR flatterer *praiser*
FLDRS full-dress (adj) *formal* full dress (n)
FLDRTPD filter-tipped *cigarette*
FLDS afflatus *inspiration*
FLDS felo-de-se *suicide* felones-de-se (or) felos-de-se (pl)
FLDSH flattish *overcome, fixed, dull**
FLDSPR feldspar *mineral* (Br) felspar
FLDST faultiest *imperfect*
FLDST flattest *overcome, fixed, dull**
FLDST flautist *flute*
FLDST flightiest *silliest*
FLDSTL faldstool *chair*
FLDSTN fieldstone *rock*
FLDSTRP fieldstrip *take apart*
FLDT flat-out (adj) *completely* flat out (adv)
FLDT fluidity *liquid*
FLDT foldout *book page*
FLDTD flood tide *peak*
FLDTRP field trip *class outing*
FLDTST field-test (v) *trial* field test (n)
FLDW floodway *channel*
FLDW foldaway *bendable*
FLDWDR floodwater *surge*
FLDWRK fieldwork *fort, observation*
FLDWTR floodwater *surge*
FLDYR faultier *imperfect*
FLDYR flightier *sillier*
FLDYST faultiest *imperfect*
FLDYST flightiest *silliest*
FLDZ fluidize *liquid* fluidized fluidizing
FLF falloff (n) *decrease, drop* fall off (v)
FLF fluff (n) *soft material,*

blunder, (v) *botch, plump*
FLF fluffy *airy* fluffier fluffiest
FLFL falafel *food* falafel
FLFL fluffily *airy*
FLFL fulfill (or) fulfil *complete* fulfilled fulfilling
FLFLJD full-fledged *total*
FLFLKR flea-flicker *football*
FLFLMNT fulfillment *completion*
FLFLR fulfiller *complete*
FLFNS fluffiness *airy*
FLFR fluffier *airy*
FLFSH fallfish *animal*
FLFSHN fly-fishing *sport*
FLFSHNG fly-fishing *sport*
FLFST fluffiest *airy*
FLFT fylfot *window*
FLFYR fluffier *airy*
FLFYST fluffiest *airy*
FLG fall guy *dupe*
FLG flag (v) *signal, weaken* flagged flagging
FLG flag (v) *emblem*
FLG flog *whip* flogged flogging
FLGD feel-good *satisfaction*
FLGL field goal *sports*
FLGLHRN flügelhorn (or) fluegelhorn *music*
FLGLT flageolet *flute, bean*
FLGMDK phlegmatic *unemotional*
FLGMDKL phlegmatically *unemotionally*
FLGMN flagman *signal* flagmen
FLGMTK phlegmatic *unemotional*
FLGMTKL phlegmatically *unemotionally*
FLGN flagging *weakening*
FLGN flagon *flask*
FLGNG flagging *weakening*
FLGPL flagpole *display rod*
FLGR filigree (v) *adorn* filigreed filigreeing
FLGR filigree (n) *openwork*
FLGR flogger *whipper*
FLGRNS flagrance *obviousness* flagrancy
FLGRNT flagrant *obvious*

FLGRNT fulgurant *brilliant*
FLGRNTL flagrantly *obvious*
FLGRNTS flagrance *obviousness* flagrancy
FLGRS fulgurous *flashy*
FLGRSHN fulguration *flash*
FLGRT fulgurate *brilliant*
FLGSHP flagship *leader*
FLGSTF Flagstaff *city*
FLGSTF flagstaff *pole*
FLGSTN flagstone *rock*
FLGWVN flag-waving *patriotic*
FLGWVNG flag-waving *patriotic*
FLGWVR flag-waver *patriot*
FLGYRNT fulgurant *brilliant*
FLGYRS fulgurous *flashy*
FLGYRSHN fulguration *flash*
FLGYRT fulgurate *brilliant*
FLHPR fleahopper *insect*
FLHRD foolhardy *rash*
FLHRDL foolhardily *rash*
FLHRDNS foolhardiness *rashness*
FLHRMNK philharmonic *symphony*
FLHS field house *sports*
FLHS full house *crowd*
FLHWL flywheel *machine*
FLJ fledge *feather* fledged fledging
FLJ foliage *leaf*
FLJL flagella (pl) *whip* flagellum
FLJLDD flagellated (or) flagellate *(adj)* whiplike
FLJLM flagellum *whip* flagella
FLJLN flagellin *protein*
FLJLN fledgling *beginner*
FLJLNG fledgling *beginner*
FLJLNT flagellant *whipped one*
FLJLSHN flagellation *whipping*
FLJLT flagellate (v) *whip* flagellated flagellating
FLJLT flagellate (or) flagellated *(adj)* whiplike
FLJLT flageolet *flute, bean*
FLJLTD flagellated (or)

Letters aren't doubled for single sounds: to find alley use **L** not **LL**. Use **Y** and **W** as hard sounds only: to find yellow use **YL**. (Br)=British spelling or usage. * See dictionary.

flagellate (adj) whiplike
FLJN phellogen cork
FLJN phylogeny history
phylogenies
FLJNDK phylogenetic
history
FLJNDKL phylogenetically
history
FLJNS effulgence brilliance
FLJNS fuliginous murky
FLJNSL fuliginously murky
FLJNT effulgent brilliant
FLJNTK phylogenetic
history
FLJNTKL phylogenetically
history
FLJNTS effulgence brilliance
FLK afflict injure
FLK felucca boat
FLK flack publicity
FLK flak guns, criticism
FLK flake chip flaked flaking
FLK flaky layered, wacky
flakier flakiest
FLK fleck tiny bit
FLK flic French police
FLK flick movie
FLK floc fluff
FLK flock (n) group, fiber (v)
gather, decorate
FLK fluke luck, lobe
FLK fluky lucky flukier
flukiest
FLK folic acid
FLK phallic penis
FLKC flaxy texture flaxier
flaxiest
FLKCD flaxseed oil
FLKCHNT fluctuant swing
FLKCHR flycatcher bird
FLKCHSHN fluctuation
swing
FLKCHSHNL fluctuational
swing
FLKCHT fluctuate swing
fluctuated fluctuating
FLKCHWNT fluctuant swing
FLKCHWSHN fluctuation
swing
FLKCHWSHNL
fluctuational swing
FLKCHWT fluctuate swing

fluctuated fluctuating
FLKCR flaxier like linen
FLKCST flaxiest like linen
FLKCYR flaxier like linen
FLKCYST flaxiest like linen
FLKD flokati rug
FLKDR phylactery box,
amulet phylacteries
FLKDV afflictive troublesome
FLKJKT flak jacket garment
FLKL flocculi (pl) mass
flocculus
FLKL follicle sac, hair base
FLKL phallically penis
FLKLDR flocculator fluffer
FLKLDS folliculitis
inflammation
FLKLNT flocculant (n) fluff
FLKLNT flocculent (adj)
fluffy
FLKLR flea collar insecticide
FLKLS flocculus mass
flocculi
FLKLSHN flocculation fluff
FLKLT flocculate fluff
flocculated flocculating
FLKLTR flocculator fluffer
FLKLTS folliculitis
inflammation
FLKN falcon bird
FLKN flacon bottle
FLKN flocking design
FLKNG flocking design
FLKNN falconine bird
FLKNR falconer bird trainer
FLKNR falconry sport
FLKNR Faulkner writer
FLKNS flakiness layers,
wacky
FLKNT falconet bird, cannon
FLKR flaker chipper
FLKR flakier more layers,
wacky
FLKR flicker flutter
FLKR flukier lucky
FLKR fulcra (pl) support
fulcrum
FLKRM fulcrum support
fulcrums (or) fulcra
FLKRNGL flickeringly flutter
FLKS flax linen
FLKS flaxy texture flaxier

flaxiest
FLKS flex bend
FLKS flux fluid, change
FLKS phlox flower phlox (or)
phloxes
FLKSBL flexible (adj) easily
bent flexibly (adv)
FLKSBLD flexibility easily
bent
FLKSBLT flexibility easily
bent
FLKSD flaccid limp
FLKSD flaxseed oil
FLKSDD flaccidity limpness
FLKSDL flaccidly limply
FLKSDNG fly casting fishing
FLKSDT flaccidity limpness
FLKSGRF flexography
printing
FLKSGRFK flexographic
printing
FLKSGRFKL
flexographically printing
FLKSHN affliction ailment
FLKSHN flexion bend
FLKSHN fluxion fluid, change
FLKSHNL fluxional fluid,
change
FLKSHNT fluctuant swing
FLKSHR flexure bend
FLKSHRL flexural bend
FLKSHS flexuous curves
FLKSHSHN fluctuation
swing
FLKSHSHNL fluctuational
swing
FLKSHT fluctuate swing
fluctuated fluctuating
FLKSHWNT fluctuant swing
FLKSHWS flexuous curves
FLKSHWSHN fluctuation
swing
FLKSHWSHNL fluctuational
swing
FLKSHWT fluctuate swing
fluctuated fluctuating
FLKSL flexile easily bent
FLKSN flaxen linen
FLKSR flaxier like linen
FLKSR flexor muscle
FLKSR phylloxera lice
FLKSST flaxiest like linen

Use letters that best describe the sounds you hear and omit the vowels. Use **S** or **K** instead of **C**: to find circle use **SRKL**. Use **J** to find joy, **JM** to find gem and **G** to find go.

FLKST flakiest *most layers, wacky*
FLKST flukiest *lucky*
FLKSTM flextime (or) flexitime *employment*
FLKSTN fly casting *fishing*
FLKSTNG fly casting *fishing*
FLKSYR flaxier *like linen*
FLKSYST flaxiest *like linen*
FLKT afflict *injure*
FLKT falcate *hook* falcated
FLKT flake out *(slang) exhaustion*
FLKT flokati *rug*
FLKTNT fluctuant *swing*
FLKTR phylactery *box, amulet* phylacteries
FLKTSHN fluctuation *swing*
FLKTSHNL fluctuational *swing*
FLKTT fluctuate *swing* fluctuated fluctuating
FLKTV afflictive *troublesome*
FLKTWNT fluctuant *swing*
FLKTWSHN fluctuation *swing*
FLKTWSHNL fluctuational *swing*
FLKTWT fluctuate *swing* fluctuated fluctuating
FLKYL flocculi (pl) *mass* flocculus
FLKYLDR flocculator *fluffer*
FLKYLDS folliculitis *inflammation*
FLKYLNT flocculant *(n) fluff*
FLKYLNT flocculent *(adj) fluffy*
FLKYLS flocculus *mass* flocculi
FLKYLSHN flocculation *fluff*
FLKYLT flocculate *fluff* flocculated flocculating
FLKYLTR flocculator *fluffer*
FLKYLTS folliculitis *inflammation*
FLKYR flakier *more layers, wacky*
FLKYR flukier *lucky*
FLKYST flakiest *most layers, wacky*
FLKYST flukiest *lucky*

FLL filial (adj) *child* filially (adv)
FLL flail *hit, wave*
FLLF flyleaf *book* flyleaves
FLLG philology *language*
FLLJ philology *language*
FLLJKL philological (adj) *language* philologically (adv)
FLLJST philologist *language*
FLLS flawless *no mistakes*
FLLSL flawlessly *no mistakes*
FLLSNS flawlessness *no mistakes*
FLLVZ flyleaves (pl) *book* flyleaf
FLM aflame *on fire*
FLM film *movie, membrane*
FLM filmy *thinly coated, thin* filmier filmiest
FLM flam *drumbeat*
FLM flame *fire* flamed flaming
FLM flume *gorge*
FLM phellem *outward cells*
FLM phlegm *mucus*
FLM phlegmy *like mucus*
FLM phloem *plant tissue*
FLM phyllome *leaf*
FLM phylum *type* phyla (pl)
FLMB flambé *flaming liquor* flambéed flambéing
FLMB flambeau *torch* flambeaux (or) flambeaus
FLMBL flammable *fire*
FLMBLD flammability *fire*
FLMBLT flammability *fire*
FLMBYNS flamboyance *elaborate display* flamboyancy
FLMBYNT flamboyant *elaborate display*
FLMBYNTS flamboyance *elaborate display* flamboyancy
FLMDM filmdom *movies*
FLMDR flowmeter *device*
FLMFLM flimflam *cheat* flimflammed flimflamming
FLMFLMR flimflammer *cheater*

FLMGR filmgoer *audience*
FLMGRF filmography *movies* filmographies
FLMGWR filmgoer *audience*
FLMK filmic *movies*
FLMKL filmically *movies*
FLMKN filmmaking *movies*
FLMKNG filmmaking *movies*
FLMKR filmmaker *movies*
FLMKS flummox *confuse*
FLML filmily *thin*
FLMN flaming *intense*
FLMN full moon *lunar cycle*
FLMNDNG fulminating *explosive*
FLMNG flaming *intense*
FLMNG flamingo *bird* flamingos
FLMNGG flamingo *bird* flamingos
FLMNGK flamenco *dance* flamencos
FLMNGL flamingly *intense*
FLMNK flamenco *dance* flamencos
FLMNN filet mignon *beef* filets mignons
FLMNNT fulminant *censure*
FLMNS filminess *thin*
FLMNSHN fulmination *censure*
FLMNST phillumenist *matchbooks*
FLMNT filament *thread*
FLMNT fulminate *denounce* fulminated fulminating
FLMNTN fulminating *explosive*
FLMNTNG fulminating *explosive*
FLMNTS filamentous *thread*
FLMNWR film noir *dark film*
FLMNYN filet mignon *beef* filets mignons
FLMPRF flameproof *no burn*
FLMPRFT flameproofed *no burn*
FLMR filmier *thinner*
FLMR flamer *burner*
FLMR flummery *dessert, performance* flummeries
FLMR fulmar *bird*

Letters aren't doubled for single sounds: to find alley use **L** not **LL**. Use **Y** and **W** as hard sounds only: to find yellow use **YL**. (Br)=British spelling or usage. * See dictionary.

FLMRKT flea market *open-air shops*
FLMRTRDNT flame-retardant *no burn*
FLMSH Flemish *of Belgium*
FLMST filmiest *thinnest*
FLMSTRP filmstrip *movie*
FLMT flameout *failure*
FLMTHD foulmouthed *indecent*
FLMTHRR flamethrower *fire*
FLMTHRWR flamethrower *fire*
FLMTHT foulmouthed *indecent*
FLMTR flame tree *plant*
FLMTR flowmeter *device*
FLMTS off-limits *forbidden*
FLMX flummox *confuse*
FLMYR filmier *thinner*
FLMYST filmiest *thinnest*
FLMZ flimsy *weak* flimsier flimsiest
FLMZL flimsily *weak*
FLMZNS flimsiness *weak*
FLMZR flimsier *weak*
FLMZST flimsiest *weak*
FLMZYR flimsier *weak*
FLMZYST flimsiest *weak*
FLN aphelion *star path* aphelia
FLN failing *fault*
FLN fall in *line up*
FLN fall line *waterfalls*
FLN fallen *disgraced*
FLN feeling *(n) sense, touch, passion**
FLN feline *cat, sly*
FLN felon *criminal*
FLN felony *crime* felonies
FLN filing *fragment, action*
FLN fill in *(v) add, complete, substitute*
FLN fill-in *(n) short summary, substitute*
FLN filling *fill material*
FLN flan *custard*
FLN flinty *stern, hard* flintier flintiest
FLN flown *(v-past) fly*
FLN flying *aircraft*
FLN foul line *out of bounds*

FLN fouling *deposit*
FLN off-line *not connected*
FLNC flouncy *ruffled*
FLNC fluency *smoothness*
FLNCH flinch *wince* flinches
FLNCHR flincher *wincer*
FLND felinity *cat, sly*
FLNDR flounder *(n) fish* flounder (or) flounders
FLNDR flounder *(v) struggle*
FLNDR philander *flirt*
FLNDRR philanderer *flirt*
FLNDRS flinders *splinters*
FLNDRZ flinders *splinters*
FLNFKS flying fox *bat*
FLNFSH flying fish *animal*
FLNFX flying fox *bat*
FLNG failing *fault*
FLNG feeling *(n) sense, touch, passion**
FLNG filing *fragment, action*
FLNG filling *fill material*
FLNG fling *(v) throw* flung flinging
FLNG fling *(n) brief affair*
FLNG flying *aircraft*
FLNG following *(adj) next (n) disciples*
FLNG fouling *deposit*
FLNGBRJ flying bridge *ship*
FLNGDCHMN Flying Dutchman *ship*
FLNGFKS flying fox *bat*
FLNGFSH flying fish *fish*
FLNGFX flying fox *bat*
FLNGK flank *(n) side (v) attack or place on the side*
FLNGK flunk *fail*
FLNGK flunky (or) flunkey *servant* flunkies (or) flunkeys
FLNGKN flanken *beef*
FLNGKR flanker *football*
FLNGKS phalanx *troops, bone* phalanxes (or) phalanges
FLNGKT flunk out *fail*
FLNGKTH full-length *to the ankles*
FLNGL flowingly *stream*
FLNGL phalangeal *bone*
FLNGSSR flying saucer

space ship
FLNGT falling-out *quarrel* fallings-out (or) falling-outs
FLNGTH full-length *to the ankles*
FLNGX phalanx *troops, bone* phalanxes (or) phalanges
FLNGYL phalangeal *bone*
FLNGZ feelings *emotions*
FLNGZ phalanges (pl) *troops, bone* phalanx
FLNJ flange *edge* flanged flanging
FLNJ phalange *bone*
FLNJL phalangeal *bone*
FLNJR phalanger *mammal*
FLNJST Falangist *fascist*
FLNJYL phalangeal *bone*
FLNJZ phalanges (pl) *troops, bone* phalanx
FLNK flank *(n) side (v) attack or place on the side*
FLNK flunk *fail*
FLNK flunky (or) flunkey *servant* flunkies (or) flunkeys
FLNKN flanken *beef*
FLNKR flanker *football*
FLNKS phalanx *troops, bone* phalanxes (or) phalanges
FLNKT flunk out *fail*
FLNKTH full-length *to the ankles*
FLNL flannel *fabric*
FLNL flintily *stern, hard*
FLNLT flannelette *fabric*
FLNNS flintiness *stern, hard*
FLNR flintier *stern, hard*
FLNS affluence *wealth* affluency
FLNS awfulness *terrible*
FLNS effluence *flow*
FLNS fallowness *neglect*
FLNS felonious *criminal*
FLNS flounce *bounce, trimming* flounced flouncing
FLNS flouncy *ruffled*
FLNS fluency *smoothness*
FLNS foulness *indecency, pollution*

Use letters that best describe the sounds you hear and omit the vowels. Use **S** or **K** instead of **C**: to find circle use **SRKL**. Use **J** to find joy, **JM** to find gem and **G** to find go.

FLNS fullness *complete*
FLNSN flouncing *material*
FLNSNG flouncing *material*
FLNSSR flying saucer *space ship*
FLNST flintiest *stern, hard*
FLNT affluent *(adj) wealthy (n) stream*
FLNT effluent *flow*
FLNT falling-out *quarrel* fallings-out (or) falling-outs
FLNT felinity *cat, sly*
FLNT flaunt *show*
FLNT Flint *city*
FLNT flint *spark*
FLNT flinty *stern, hard* flintier flintiest
FLNT fluent *smooth*
FLNTC flouncy *ruffled*
FLNTC fluency *smoothness*
FLNTH full-length *to the ankles*
FLNTHRP philanthropy *goodwill* philanthropies
FLNTHRPK philanthropic *humanitarian*
FLNTHRPKL philanthropically *humanitarian*
FLNTHRPST philanthropist *humanitarian*
FLNTL flintily *stern, hard*
FLNTL fluently *smooth*
FLNTLK flintlock *weapon*
FLNTNS flintiness *stern, hard*
FLNTR flintier *stern, hard*
FLNTS affluence *wealth* affluency
FLNTS effluence *flow*
FLNTS flounce *bounce, trimming* flounced flouncing
FLNTS flouncy *ruffled*
FLNTS fluency *smoothness*
FLNTSN flouncing *material*
FLNTSNG flouncing *material*
FLNTST flintiest *stern, hard*
FLNTYR flintier *stern, hard*
FLNTYST flintiest *stern, hard*
FLNX phalanx *troops, bone*

phalanxes (or) phalanges
FLNYR flintier *stern, hard*
FLNYS felonious *criminal*
FLNYST flintiest *stern, hard*
FLNZ feelings *emotions*
FLP fill-up (n) *add until full* fill up (v)
FLP fillip *snap*
FLP flap *(v) beat, sway* flapped flapping
FLP flap *(n) fold, airfoil, uproar*
FLP flappy *beating*
FLP flip *(v) turn over, (slang) lose composure* flipped flipping
FLP flip *(n) drink, somersault (adj) flippant*
FLP flippy *flared*
FLP flop *fall, fail* flopped flopping
FLP floppy *(adj) flexible* floppier floppiest
FLP floppy *(n) disk* floppies
FLP follow-up (n, adj) *further action* follow up (v)
FLP foul up (v) *error* foul-up (n)
FLPBL flappable *upset*
FLPDDL flapdoodle *nonsense*
FLPDSK floppy disk *computer*
FLPFLP flip-flop *reversal*
FLPJK flapjack *pancake*
FLPL floppily *flexible*
FLPL foul play *crime*
FLPN Filipina (f) *of the Philippines* Filipinas
FLPN Filipino (m and f) *of the Philippines* Filipinos
FLPN Philippine *island*
FLPNC flippancy *jest* flippancies
FLPNC Philippine Sea *body of water*
FLPNS flippancy *jest* flippancies
FLPNS floppiness *flexibility*
FLPNS Philippine Sea *body of water*
FLPNS Philippines *islands*

FLPNT flippant *jest*
FLPNTB fallopian tube *ovary*
FLPNTC flippancy *jest* flippancies
FLPNTL flippantly *jest*
FLPNTS flippancy *jest* flippancies
FLPNZ Philippines *islands*
FLPPR flypaper *insecticide*
FLPR flapper *dancer*
FLPR flipper *fin, turn over*
FLPR flopper *failure*
FLPR floppier *flexible*
FLPRF foolproof *reliable*
FLPSD flip side *other side*
FLPST floppiest *flexible*
FLPT fleapit *(Br) theater*
FLPYNTB fallopian tube *ovary*
FLPYR floppier *flexible*
FLPYST floppiest *flexible*
FLQL flocculi (pl) *mass* flocculus
FLQLDR flocculator *one that fluffs*
FLQLDS folliculitis *inflammation*
FLQLNT flocculant *(n) fluff*
FLQLNT flocculent *(adj) fluffy*
FLQLS flocculus *mass* flocculi
FLQLSHN flocculation *fluff*
FLQLT flocculate *fluff* flocculated flocculating
FLQLTR flocculator *one that fluffs*
FLQLTS folliculitis *inflammation*
FLR failure *deficiency, decay*
FLR faller *logger*
FLR feeler *sense organ*
FLR filar *thread*
FLR filaria *parasite* filariae
FLR filer *scrape, arrange, initiate action*
FLR filler *material*
FLR flair *knack*
FLR flare *(v) ignite, spread* flared flaring
FLR flare *(n) torch, fire*

Letters aren't doubled for single sounds: to find alley use **L** not **LL**. Use **Y** and **W** as hard sounds only: to find yellow use **YL**. (Br)=British spelling or usage. * See dictionary.

FLR fleer *sneer*
FLR flier *airman*
FLR floor *(n) base, level (v) dumbfound, accelerate*
FLR flora *plants* floras
FLR flour *grain powder*
FLR floury *powdery*
FLR flower *(n) plant (v) bloom, flourish*
FLR flowery *showy*
FLR flurry *(v) hurry* flurried flurrying flurries
FLR flurry *(n) commotion, snowfall* flurries
FLR flyer *advertisement*
FLR follower *disciple*
FLR foolery *folly* fooleries
FLR fuller *hammer*
FLR phyllary *plant* phyllaries
FLRBND floribunda *rose*
FLRBRD floorboard *car*
FLRD florid *blooming*
FLRD Florida *US State*
FLRD flowered *blossoms*
FLRD fluoride *chemical*
FLRD fly rod *fishing*
FLRD foulard *silk*
FLRDD floriated *flowers*
FLRDD floridity *flowers*
FLRDL fleur-de-lis (or) fleur-de-lys *France* fleurs-de-lis (or) fleur-de-lis (or) fleurs-de-lys (or) fleur-de-lys
FLRDL floridly *blooming*
FLRDNS floridness *blooming*
FLRDSHN fluoridation *add fluoride*
FLRDT floridity *flowers*
FLRDT fluoridate *add fluoride* fluoridated fluoridating
FLRFRS floriferous *blooming*
FLRFRSNS floriferousness *blooming*
FLRJN florigen *hormone*
FLRJNK florigenic *hormone*
FLRKLCHR floriculture *flowers*
FLRKLTR floriculture *flowers*
FLRKRBN fluorocarbon *chemical*
FLRL floral *flowers*

FLRLK flowerlike *blossom*
FLRLMP floor lamp *light*
FLRLNGKTH floor-length *to the ankles*
FLRLNGTH floor-length *to the ankles*
FLRLNKTH floor-length *to the ankles*
FLRLNTH floor-length *to the ankles*
FLRLS flourless *no wheat*
FLRMDR fluorometer (or) fluorimeter *light measure*
FLRMNK philharmonic *symphony*
FLRMTR fluorometer (or) fluorimeter *light measure*
FLRMTR fluorometry (or) fluorimetry *science*
FLRN flaring *wide, gaudy*
FLRN flooring *material*
FLRN florin *money*
FLRN fluorine *chemical*
FLRN fullerene *dome*
FLRNG flaring *wide, gaudy*
FLRNG flooring *material*
FLRNG flowering *blooming*
FLRNS floweriness *blossoms, elegance*
FLRNSHN fluorination *add fluorine*
FLRNT fluorinate *add fluorine* fluorinated fluorinating
FLRNTN Florentine *of Florence, with spinach*
FLRP flare up (v) *outburst* flare-up (n)
FLRPT flowerpot *container*
FLRR floorer *worker*
FLRS effloresce *bloom* effloresced efflorescing
FLRS fluoresce *light* fluoresced fluorescing
FLRSH floor show *entertainment*
FLRSH flourish *grow* flourishes
FLRSHN floriation *flowers*
FLRSHR flourisher *grow*
FLRSKP fluoroscope *x-ray* fluoroscoped

fluoroscoping
FLRSKP fluoroscopy *x-ray*
FLRSKPST fluoroscopist *x-ray*
FLRSNS efflorescence *bloom*
FLRSNS florescence *blossom*
FLRSNS fluorescence *light*
FLRSNT florescent *blossom*
FLRSNT fluorescent *light*
FLRSNTS efflorescence *bloom*
FLRSNTS florescence *blossom*
FLRSNTS fluorescence *light*
FLRSR fluorescer *light*
FLRSS fluorosis *flourine*
FLRST florist *flowers*
FLRT flirt *(v) flit, trifle, experiment (n) amorous one*
FLRT floret *bloom*
FLRT fluorite *chemical*
FLRTD floriated *flowers*
FLRTSHN flirtation *flit, trifle, experiment*
FLRTSHS flirtatious *play at love*
FLRTSHSL flirtatiously *play at love*
FLRTSHSNS flirtatiousness *play at love*
FLRWKR floorwalker *overseer*
FLRY filaria *parasite* filariae
FLRYDD floriated *flowers*
FLRYSHN floriation *flowers*
FLRYTD floriated *flowers*
FLRZRTH fuller's earth *clay*
FLS fallacy *false idea* fallacies
FLS false *not true* falser falsest
FLS falsie *imitation*
FLS fleece *(v) cheat* fleeced fleecing
FLS fleece *(n) wool*
FLS fleecy *like wool, downy* fleecier fleeciest
FLS floss *(n) thread (v) clean teeth*
FLS flossy *silky, stylish*

Use letters that best describe the sounds you hear and omit the vowels. Use **S** or **K** instead of **C**: to find circle use **SRKL**. Use **J** to find joy, **JM** to find gem and **G** to find go.

flossier flossiest

FLS phallus *penis* phalli (or) phalluses

FLSD falsetto *voice* falsettos

FLSD falsity *lie* falsities

FLSD felicity *happiness* felicities

FLSD flaccid *limp*

FLSD fleeced *like wool, downy*

FLSDD flaccidity *limpness*

FLSDK felsitic *rock*

FLSDL flaccidly *limply*

FLSDR fluster (v) *upset* (n) *confusion*

FLSDRD flustered *confused*

FLSDT flaccidity *limpness*

FLSF fail-safe *secure*

FLSF falsify *lie* falsified falsifying falsifies

FLSF philosophy *pursuit of wisdom* philosophies

FLSFBL falsifiable *misrepresent*

FLSFBLD falsifiability *misrepresent*

FLSFBLT falsifiability *misrepresent*

FLSFK felicific *joyous*

FLSFK philosophic (or) philosophical (adj) *wise* philosophically (adv)

FLSFKL philosophical (or) philosophic (adj) *wise* philosophically (adv)

FLSFKSHN falsification *misrepresent*

FLSFR falsifier *liar*

FLSFR philosopher *wise one*

FLSFRM falciform *hook*

FLSFYBL falsifiable *misrepresent*

FLSFYBLD falsifiability *misrepresent*

FLSFYBLT falsifiability *misrepresent*

FLSFYR falsifier *liar*

FLSFZ philosophize *explain* philosophized philosophizing (Br) philosophise

FLSFZR philosophizer

explainer (Br) philosophiser

FLSGLD fool's gold *pyrite*

FLSH fellatio *sex act*

FLSH flash *fast, bright*

FLSH flashy *gaudy* flashier flashiest

FLSH flèche *spire*

FLSH flesh *skin*

FLSH fleshy *fat, pulp* fleshier fleshiest

FLSH flush (v) *expose, blush, cleanse* (n) *poker, blush* (adj) *abundant** flushes

FLSH flysch *sandstone*

FLSH foolish *absurd*

FLSHBB flashbulb *camera*

FLSHBK flashback (n) *memory* flash back (v)

FLSHBL flushable *expose, blush, cleanse*

FLSHBLB flashbulb *camera*

FLSHBRD flashboard *dam*

FLSHD falsehood *lie*

FLSHD fleshed *kind of skin*

FLSHDT fleshed-out *enlarged*

FLSHFL flesh fly *insect*

FLSHFLD flash flood *rainfall*

FLSHKB flashcube *camera*

FLSHKRD flash card *learning*

FLSHKYB flashcube *camera*

FLSHL flashily *gaudy*

FLSHL fleshly *worldly*

FLSHLMP flashlamp *camera*

FLSHLT flashlight *illuminator*

FLSHN affiliation *association*

FLSHN filiation *descent*

FLSHN flashing *roofing*

FLSHN foliation *leaf*

FLSHNBLD flesh and blood *real, kin*

FLSHNDBLD flesh and blood *real, kin*

FLSHNG flashing *roofing*

FLSHNGS fleshings *hides*

FLSHNS flashiness *gaudy*

FLSHNS fleshiness *fat, pulp*

FLSHNS flushness *abundance*

FLSHNS foolishness *absurdity*

FLSHNZ fleshings *hides*

FLSHP fellowship *association*

FLSHPNT flash point *ignition*

FLSHPT fleshpot *luxury*

FLSHQB flashcube *camera*

FLSHR flasher *exposer*

FLSHR flashier *gaudy*

FLSHR fleshier *fat, pulp*

FLSHS fallacious *untrue*

FLSHS foliaceous *leaf*

FLSHSL fallaciously *untrue*

FLSHSNS fallaciousness *untrue*

FLSHST flashiest *gaudy*

FLSHST fleshiest *fat, pulp*

FLSHT fléchette *dart*

FLSHT flesh out *enlarge*

FLSHT fleshed *kind of skin*

FLSHT flow sheet *diagram*

FLSHT foul shot *sports*

FLSHTB flashtube *camera*

FLSHTT fleshed-out *enlarged*

FLSHTYB flashtube *camera*

FLSHVR flashover *electricity, flame*

FLSHWND flesh wound *injury*

FLSHY fellatio *sex act*

FLSHYR flashier *gaudy*

FLSHYR fleshier *fat, pulp*

FLSHYST flashiest *gaudy*

FLSHYST fleshiest *fat, pulp*

FLSK flask *bottle*

FLSKL full-scale *total*

FLSKP foolscap *hat, paper*

FLSL falsely *untrue*

FLSL flossily *silky, stylish*

FLSL fuel cell *battery*

FLSM fulsome *abundant*

FLSML fulsomely *abundant*

FLSMNS fulsomeness *abundant*

FLSNS falseness *untrue*

FLSPK flyspeck *waste matter*

FLSPR feldspar *mineral* (Br) felspar

FLSR falser *untrue*

FLSR fleecier *like wool,*

Letters aren't doubled for single sounds: to find alley use **L** not **LL**. Use **Y** and **W** as hard sounds only: to find yellow use **YL**. (Br)=British spelling or usage. * See dictionary.

downy

FLSR flossier *silky, stylish*
FLSRVS full-service *care*
FLSST falsest *untrue*
FLSST fleeciest *like wool, downy*
FLSST flossiest *silky, stylish*
FLST falsetto *voice* falsettos
FLST falsity *lie* falsities
FLST felicity *happiness* felicities
FLST felsite *rock*
FLST fleeced *like wool, downy*
FLSTF Falstaff *fictional rascal*
FLSTFN Falstaffian *fictional rascal*
FLSTFYN Falstaffian *fictional rascal*
FLSTK felsitic *rock*
FLSTN flowstone *calcite*
FLSTN philistine *(often capitalized) materialist*
FLSTR fluster *(v) upset (n) confusion*
FLSTRD flustered *confused*
FLSTRT false start *race*
FLSTS felicitous *apt*
FLSTSHN felicitation *congratulation*
FLSTSL felicitously *aptly*
FLSTSNS felicitousness *aptness*
FLSTT felicitate *congratulate* felicitated felicitating
FLSWDR flyswatter *insect killer*
FLSWRK falsework *construction*
FLSWTR flyswatter *insect killer*
FLSYR fleecier *like wool, downy*
FLSYR flossier *silky, stylish*
FLSYST fleeciest *like wool, downy*
FLSYST flossiest *silky, stylish*
FLSZ full-size *normal*
FLT affiliate *associate* affiliated affiliating

FLT afloat *buoyed*
FLT fall out *(v) quarrel, leave*
FLT fall to *line up*
FLT fallout *(n) aftermath*
FLT fault *(v) blame, err (n) weakness, mistake*
FLT faulty *imperfect* faultier faultiest
FLT fealty *tenant* fealties
FLT fellate *sex act* fellated fellating
FLT felt *(v-past) feel (n) fabric*
FLT fill out *complete*
FLT fillet *(n) ribbon, boneless slice (v) adorn, cut into strips*
FLT flat *(v) music* flatted flatting
FLT flat *(adj) overcome, dead, level* flatter flattest
FLT flat *(n) apartment, tone, box**
FLT fleet *(n) ships (adj) fast*
FLT flight *fly, departure*
FLT flighty *silly* flightier flightiest
FLT flit *twitch* flitted flitting
FLT float *(v) drift upon, negotiate (n) buoy*
FLT floaty *buoyed*
FLT flout *jeer*
FLT flute *(v) music, edge* fluted fluting
FLT flute *(n) music, glass, groove*
FLT folate *folic acid*
FLT foliate *leaf*
FLT foul out *sports*
FLT full-out *totally*
FLTBD flatbed *truck*
FLTBT flatboat *barge*
FLTD affiliated *associated*
FLTD fluted *grooved*
FLTD foliated *leaf*
FLTDK flight deck *ship*
FLTFDD flat-footed *no arches*
FLTFNDN faultfinding *criticizing*
FLTFNDNG faultfinding *criticizing*
FLTFNDR faultfinder *critic*
FLTFSH flatfish *animal*

FLTFT flatfoot *(slang)* policeman flatfoots
FLTFT flatfoot *no arches* flatfeet
FLTFTD flat-footed *no arches*
FLTH filth *dirt*
FLTH filthy *dirty* filthier filthiest
FLTHL filthily *dirty*
FLTHNS filthiness *dirt*
FLTHR filthier *dirtier*
FLTHR follow-through *(n) completion* follow through *(v)*
FLTHST filthiest *dirtiest*
FLTHYR filthier *dirtier*
FLTHYST filthiest *dirtiest*
FLTK phyletic *evolution*
FLTKDK phyllotactic *leaf*
FLTKL phyletically *evolution*
FLTKR flatcar *railroad*
FLTKSS phyllotaxis *leaf*
FLTKTK phyllotactic *leaf*
FLTL faultily *imperfect*
FLTL fleetly *quickly*
FLTL flightily *silly*
FLTL flotilla *ships*
FLTL philately *stamps*
FLTLK philatelic *(adj) stamps* philatelically *(adv)*
FLTLN fault line *geology*
FLTLN flatland *plains*
FLTLND flatland *plains*
FLTLNDR flatlander *plains dweller*
FLTLNS flatulence *gas* flatulency
FLTLNT flatulent *gas*
FLTLNTL flatulently *gas*
FLTLNTS flatulence *gas* flatulency
FLTLS faultless *innocent*
FLTLS flightless *cannot fly*
FLTLSL faultlessly *innocent*
FLTLSNS faultlessness *innocence*
FLTLST philatelist *stamps*
FLTM full-time *(adj) work period* full time *(n)*
FLTMT flatmate *roommate*
FLTN flatten *make level*
FLTN fleeting *quick*

Use letters that best describe the sounds you hear and omit the vowels. Use **S** or **K** instead of **C**: to find circle use **SRKL**. Use **J** to find joy, **JM** to find gem and **G** to find go.

FLTN floating *not fixed*
FLTN fluting *grooves*
FLTNG felting *fabric*
FLTNG fleeting *quick*
FLTNG floating *not fixed*
FLTNG fluting *grooves*
FLTNGL fleetingly *quick*
FLTNS flatness *level*
FLTNS fleetness *speed*
FLTNS flightiness *silliness*
FLTP flattop *haircut*
FLTP foul tip *sports*
FLTPLN flight plan *schedule*
FLTPLN floatplane *airplane*
FLTPTH flight path *airplane*
FLTR aflutter *excited*
FLTR Eiffel Tower *Paris structure*
FLTR falter *stumble*
FLTR faultier *imperfect*
FLTR filter *(v) strain (n) strainer*
FLTR flatter *(v) praise (adj) deflated*
FLTR flattery *praise* flatteries
FLTR flightier *sillier*
FLTR flitter *jerky movement*
FLTR floater *buoy, worker, policy*
FLTR flouter *jeerer*
FLTR fluter *pleater*
FLTR flutter *flap, spasm*
FLTR fluttery *flap, spasm*
FLTR philter (or) philtre *potion*
FLTRBL filterable *strainer*
FLTRBLD filterability *strainer*
FLTRBLT filterability *strainer*
FLTRBRD flutterboard *swimming*
FLTRKK flutter kick *swim*
FLTRN flatiron *ironing*
FLTRNGL falteringly *stumble*
FLTRNGL flatteringly *praise*
FLTRNL falteringly *stumble*
FLTRP field trip *class outing*
FLTRP flytrap *plant*
FLTRR falterer *stumble*
FLTRR flatterer *praiser*
FLTRSHN filtration *spread out*
FLTRT filtrate *material*

FLTRTHR flat-earther *earth is flat*
FLTRTPD filter-tipped *cigarette*
FLTS afflatus *inspiration*
FLTS flattus *gas*
FLTSH flattish *overcome, fixed, dull**
FLTSHN flotation *buoy*
FLTSM flotsam *floating debris*
FLTST faultiest *imperfect*
FLTST field-test (v) *trial field test (n)*
FLTST flattest *overcome, fixed, dull**
FLTST flautist *flute*
FLTST flight-test *airplane*
FLTST flightiest *silliest*
FLTT flat-out (adj) *completely* flat out (adv)
FLTWR Eiffel Tower *Paris structure*
FLTWR flatware *table utensils*
FLTWRK flatwork *laundry*
FLTWRM flatworm *animal*
FLTWZ flatways *flat side down*
FLTWZ flatwise *flat side down*
FLTXS phyllotaxis *leaf*
FLTYR faultier *imperfect*
FLTYR flightier *sillier*
FLTYST faultiest *imperfect*
FLTYST flightiest *silliest*
FLV afoul of *in conflict with*
FLV effluvia (pl) *by-product* effluvium
FLVL fluvial *stream*
FLVM effluvium *by-product* effluvia
FLVN flavin *B vitamin*
FLVN flavine *antiseptic*
FLVN flavone *pigment*
FLVND flavonoid *pigment*
FLVNL flavonol *pigment*
FLVR flavor *taste* (Br) flavour
FLVR flivver *car*
FLVR flyover *low flight (Br) overpass*

FLVRD flavored *taste added* (Br) flavoured
FLVRFL flavorful (adj) *tasty* flavorfully (adv) (Br) flavourful, flavourfully
FLVRLS flavorless *no taste* (Br) flavourless
FLVRN flavoring *taste* (Br) flavouring
FLVRNG flavoring *taste* (Br) flavouring
FLVRSM flavorsome *tasty* (Br) flavoursome
FLVS fulvous *tawny*
FLVY effluvia (pl) *by-product* effluvium
FLVYL fluvial *stream*
FLVYM effluvium *by-product* effluvia
FLW flyaway *light, loose*
FLW flyway *path*
FLWD fluid *liquid*
FLWD fuelwood *tree*
FLWDD fluidity *liquid*
FLWDNS fluid ounce *measure*
FLWDNTS fluid ounce *measure*
FLWDT fluidity *liquid*
FLWDZ fluidize *liquid* fluidized fluidizing
FLWJ flowage *stream*
FLWL flywheel *machine*
FLWM phloem *plant tissue*
FLWN following (adj) *next* (n) *disciples*
FLWNC fluency *smoothness*
FLWNG following (adj) *next* (n) *disciples*
FLWNGL flowingly *stream*
FLWNS affluence *wealth* affluency
FLWNS effluence *flow*
FLWNS fluency *smoothness*
FLWNT affluent (adj) *wealthy* (n) *stream*
FLWNT effluent *flow*
FLWNT fluent *smooth*
FLWNTC fluency *smoothness*
FLWNTL fluently *smooth*
FLWNTS affluence *wealth* affluency

Letters aren't doubled for single sounds: to find alley use **L** not **LL**. Use **Y** and **W** as hard sounds only: to find yellow use **YL**. (Br)=British spelling or usage. * See dictionary.

FLWNTS effluence *flow*
FLWNTS fluency *smoothness*
FLWR flour *grain powder*
FLWR floury *powdery*
FLWR flower *(n) plant (v) bloom, flourish*
FLWR flowery *showy*
FLWR follower *disciple*
FLWRD flowered *blossoms*
FLWRK fieldwork *fort, observation*
FLWRLK flowerlike *blossom*
FLWRLS flourless *no wheat*
FLWRNG flowering *blooming*
FLWRNS floweriness *blossoms, elegance*
FLWRPT flowerpot *container*
FLWRT fleawort *plant*
FLWT flyweight *less than 112 pounds*
FLX flax *linen*
FLX flaxy *texture* flaxier flaxiest
FLX flex *bend*
FLX flux *fluid, change*
FLX phlox *flower* phlox (or) phloxes
FLXBL flexible (adj) *easily bent* flexibly (adv)
FLXBLD flexibility *easily bent*
FLXBLT flexibility *easily bent*
FLXD flaccid *limp*
FLXD flaxseed *oil*
FLXDD flaccidity *limpness*
FLXDL flaccidly *limply*
FLXDT flaccidity *limpness*
FLXGRF flexography *printing*
FLXGRFK flexographic *printing*
FLXGRFKL flexographically *printing*
FLXL flexile *easily bent*
FLXN flaxen *linen*
FLXR flaxier *like linen*
FLXR flexor *muscle*
FLXR phylloxera *lice*
FLXST flaxiest *like linen*
FLXTM flextime (or) flexitime *employment*
FLXYR flaxier *like linen*
FLXYST flaxiest *like linen*

FLY aphelia (pl) *star path* aphelion
FLY folio *page, case* folios
FLYBL flyable *soar*
FLYDD affiliated *associated*
FLYDD foliated *leaf*
FLYJ foliage *leaf*
FLYL filial (adj) *child* filially (adv)
FLYN aphelion *star path* aphelia
FLYN flying *aircraft*
FLYNBRJ flying bridge *ship*
FLYNFKS flying fox *bat*
FLYNFSH flying fish *animal*
FLYNFX flying fox *bat*
FLYNG flying *aircraft*
FLYNGBRJ flying bridge *ship*
FLYNGDCHMN Flying Dutchman *ship*
FLYNGFKS flying fox *bat*
FLYNGFSH flying fish *animal*
FLYNGFX flying fox *bat*
FLYNGSSR flying saucer *space ship*
FLYNSSR flying saucer *space ship*
FLYR failure *deficiency, decay*
FLYR flier *airman*
FLYR flyer *advertisement*
FLYSHN affiliation *association*
FLYSHN filiation *descent*
FLYSHN foliation *leaf*
FLYSHS foliaceous *leaf*
FLYT affiliate *associate* affiliated affiliating
FLYT foliate *leaf*
FLYTD affiliated *associated*
FLYTD foliated *leaf*
FLYVR flyover *low flight (Br) overpass*
FLYW flyaway *light, loose*
FLZ flews *dog lip*
FLZ floozy (or) floozie *lewd woman* floozies
FLZGLD fool's gold *pyrite*
FLZKP foolscap *hat, paper*
FM fame *reputation*
FM FM *(abbr) Frequency*

Modulation
FM foam *bubbles*
FM foamy *with bubbles* foamier foamiest
FM fume *smoke, anger* fumed fuming
FMBL foamable *bubbles*
FMBL fumble *blunder* fumbled fumbling
FMBLR fumbler *blunderer*
FMBR fimbria *fringe* fimbriae
FMBRL fimbrial *fringe*
FMBRSHN fimbriation *fringe*
FMBRTD fimbriated *fringed*
FMBRY fimbria *fringe* fimbriae
FMBRYL fimbrial *fringe*
FMBRYSHN fimbriation *fringe*
FMBRYTD fimbriated *fringed*
FMCH Fu Manchu *villian, mustache*
FMD famed *known*
FMFTL femme fatale *seducer* femmes fatales
FMGDR fumigator *disinfect*
FMGNT fumigant *disinfectant*
FMGSHN fumigation *disinfect*
FMGT fumigate *disinfect* fumigated fumigating
FMGTR fumigator *disinfect*
FMKS euphemics *improvement*
FML family *group* families
FML female *feminine*
FML foamily *bubbles*
FMLL familial *family*
FMLR familiar *known*
FMLRD familiarity *known* familiarities
FMLRT familiarity *known* familiarities
FMLRZ familiarize *make known* familiarized familiarizing (Br) familiarise
FMLRZSHN familiarization *make known*

Use letters that best describe the sounds you hear and omit the vowels. Use **S** or **K** instead of **C**: to find circle use **SRKL**. Use **J** to find joy, **JM** to find gem and **G** to find go.

FMLYL familial *family*
FMLYR familiar *known*
FMLYRD familiarity *known* familiarities
FMLYRT familiarity *known* familiarities
FMLYRZ familiarize *make known* familiarized familiarizing (Br) familiarise
FMLYRZSHN familiarization *make known* (Br) familiarisation
FMN famine *hunger*
FMNC effeminacy *female*
FMNN feminine *female*
FMNND femininity *female*
FMNNT femininity *female*
FMNR fomenter *warm, incite*
FMNS effeminacy *female*
FMNS foaminess *bubbles*
FMNSDK feministic *women's rights*
FMNST feminist *women's rights*
FMNSTK feministic *women's rights*
FMNT effeminate *female*
FMNT foment *warm, incite*
FMNTR fomenter *warm, incite*
FMNTSHN fomentation *warm, incite*
FMNZ feminize *make female* feminized feminizing (Br) feminise
FMNZM feminism *women's rights*
FMNZSHN feminization *make female* (Br) feminisation
FMR ephemera *collectibles* ephemera
FMR femur *bone* femurs (or) femora
FMR foamer *bubbles*
FMR foamier *bubbles*
FMRD ephemerid *mayfly*
FMRDZ ephemerides (pl) *star chart* ephemeris
FMRL ephemeral (adj)

temporary ephemerally (adv)
FMRL femoral *bone*
FMRL fumarole *volcano*
FMRLD ephemerality *temporary* ephemeralities
FMRLT ephemerality *temporary* ephemeralities
FMRS ephemeris *star chart* ephemerides
FMRZ fumarase *enzyme*
FMS famous *known*
FMSDK euphemistic *inoffensive expression*
FMSDKL euphemistically *inoffensive expression*
FMSH famish *hunger*
FMSHD famished *hunger*
FMSHT famished *hunger*
FMSNS famousness *importance*
FMST aftmost *rear*
FMST euphemist *inoffensive expression*
FMST foamiest *bubbles*
FMSTK euphemistic *inoffensive expression*
FMSTKL euphemistically *inoffensive expression*
FMX euphemics *improvement*
FMYL familial *family*
FMYR familiar *known*
FMYR foamier *bubbles*
FMYST foamiest *bubbles*
FMZ euphemize *inoffensive expression* euphemized euphemizing (Br) euphemise
FMZM euphemism *inoffensive expression*
FMZR euphemizer *inoffensive expression* (Br) euphemiser
FN aphonia *whisper*
FN euphony *sound* euphonies
FN fain *willing, gladly*
FN fan (v) *circulate wind, spread, flutter* fanned fanning
FN fan (n) *admirer, cooling*

device
FN fane *church*
FN fanny *buttock* fannies
FN faun *satyr*
FN fauna *animals* faunas
FN fawn (n) *deer* (v) *seek favor*
FN fawny *color*
FN feign *pretend*
FN fiend *monster*
FN fin (v) *add or show flippers* finned finning
FN fin (n) *flipper, (slang) 5-dollar bill*
FN find (v) *encounter, reach, determine** found finding
FN find (n) *discovery*
FN fine (v) *impose a fee, purify* fined fining
FN fine (adj) *precise, small, superior** (n) *payment* (adv) *well* finer finest
FN Finn *person from Finland*
FN finny *fish*
FN fino *wine* finos
FN foehn (or) föhn *wind*
FN fun (n) *amusement, sport, game*
FN fun (v) *joke* funned funning
FN funny (adj) *amusing* funnier funniest
FN funny (n) *joke* funnies
FN offend *hurt*
FN offhand *casual*
FN often *many times*
FN phone *telephone* phoned phoning
FN phony (or) phoney (adj) *false* phonier phoniest phonies (pl)
FN phony (or) phoney (v) *fake* phonied (or) phoneyed phonying (or) phoneying phonies (or) phoneys
FN phony (or) phoney (n) *false one* phonies
FNBN funny bone *elbow*
FNBRBDL phenobarbital *sedative*
FNBRBTL phenobarbital

Letters aren't doubled for single sounds: to find alley use **L** not **LL**. Use **Y** and **W** as hard sounds only: to find yellow use **YL**. (Br)=British spelling or usage. * See dictionary.

sedative

FNC fancy (v) like, imagine, think fancied fancying fancies

FNC fancy (adj) ornate fancier fanciest

FNC fancy (n) love, taste fancies

FNC fantasy dream fantasies

FNCD fantasied imagined

FNCFL fanciful (adj) imaginary fancifully (adv)

FNCFR fancy-free carefree

FNCH finch bird finches

FNCLN fantasyland imagination

FNCPNTS fancy-pants too elegant

FNCR fancier (adj) more ornate (n) lover

FNCST fanciest ornate

FNCWRK fancywork sewing

FNCYR fancier (adj) more ornate (n) lover

FNCYST fanciest ornate

FND affinity closeness affinities

FND effendi gentleman

FND feigned not real

FND fend repel, shift, (Br) support

FND fiend monster

FND find (v) encounter, reach, determine* found finding

FND find (n) discovery

FND fond affectionate

FND fondue food

FND found (v) establish (v-past) find

FND fund money

FND fundi (pl) bottom end fundus

FND offend insult, hurt

FND offhand casual

FNDD offhanded casual

FNDDNS offhandedness casual

FNDK fanatic zealot

FNDK fanatic (or) fanatical (adj) zealous fanatically (adv)

FNDK phenetic biology

FNDK phonetic sound

FNDKL fanatical (or) fanatic (adj) zealous fanatically (adv)

FNDKL phonetically sound

FNDKS phenetics biology

FNDKS phonetics sound

FNDL fondle caress fondled fondling

FNDL fondly affection

FNDLN foundling orphan

FNDLNG foundling orphan

FNDLR fondler caress

FNDMNL fundamental (adj) essential fundamentally (adv)

FNDMNLST fundamentalist literal religious interpretation

FNDMNLZM fundamentalism literal religious interpretation

FNDMNT fundament basis

FNDMNTL fundamental (adj) essential fundamentally (adv)

FNDMNTLST fundamentalist literal religious interpretation

FNDMNTLZM fundamentalism literal religious interpretation

FNDN off and on occasional

FNDNG fandango dance fandangos

FNDNGG fandango dance fandangos

FNDNGS findings results

FNDNGZ findings results

FNDNS fondness affection

FNDNT fondant candy

FNDR fender bumper

FNDR finder locator

FNDR founder (v) collapse (n) establisher

FNDR foundry mill foundries

FNDR offender insult, hurt

FNDRZN fund-raising money

FNDRZNG fund-raising money

FNDRZR fund-raiser money

FNDS fundus bottom end fundi

FNDSH fiendish monster

FNDSHL fiendishly monster

FNDSHN foundation base

FNDSHNL foundational (adj) base foundationally (adv)

FNDSHNLS foundationless no base

FNDSHNS fiendishness monster

FNDSZM fanaticism zealousness

FNDX phenetics biology

FNDX phonetics sound

FNDY fondue food

FNFL fanfold paper

FNFLD fanfold paper

FNFR fanfare display

FNFRM funny farm psychiatry

FNFRND fanfaronade bluster

FNG fungi (pl) plant fungus

FNG fungo fly ball (bat) fungoes

FNG offing future

FNG pfennig money pfennig

FNGG fungo fly ball (bat) fungoes

FNGGL fungal fungus

FNGGR finger (n) hand digit (v) touch, identify

FNGGRBRD fingerboard music

FNGGRD fingered with digits

FNGGRN fingering touching

FNGGRNG fingering touching

FNGGRNL fingernail digit

FNGGRPK fingerpick music

FNGGRPKNG fingerpicking music

FNGGRPNTNG finger-pointing blame

FNGGRPRNT fingerprint identification

FNGGRPST fingerpost guide

FNGGRTP fingertip digit

Use letters that best describe the sounds you hear and omit the vowels. Use **S** or **K** instead of **C**: to find circle use **SRKL**. Use **J** to find joy, **JM** to find gem and **G** to find go.

FNGGRWV finger wave *hair*
FNGGS fungous *(adj) like fungus*
FNGGS fungus *(n) plant fungi*
FNGK fink *(v-slang) inform (n-slang) informer*
FNGK funk *fear, depression*
FNGK funky *foul, quaint, jazzy* funkier funkiest
FNGKNS funkiness *foul, quaint, jazzy*
FNGKR funkier *foul, quaint, jazzy*
FNGKSHN function *(n) purpose, party (v) serve*
FNGKSHNL functional (adj) *useful* functionally (adv)
FNGKSHNLD functionality *usefulness*
FNGKSHNLT functionality *usefulness*
FNGKSHNR functionary *official* functionaries
FNGKST funkiest *foul, quaint, jazzy*
FNGKYR funkier *foul, quaint, jazzy*
FNGKYST funkiest *foul, quaint, jazzy*
FNGL finagle *trick* finagled finagling
FNGL fungal *fungus*
FNGLR finagler *tricker*
FNGR finger *(n) hand digit (v) touch, identify*
FNGRBRD fingerboard *music*
FNGRD fingered *with digits*
FNGRF phonograph *record player*
FNGRF phonography *spelling*
FNGRFK phonographic *record player*
FNGRM phonogram *symbol*
FNGRMK phonogrammic (or) phonogramic *symbol*
FNGRMKL phonogrammically (or) phonogramically *symbol*
FNGRN fingering *touching*

FNGRNG fingering *touching*
FNGRNL fingernail *digit*
FNGRPK fingerpick *music*
FNGRPKNG fingerpicking *music*
FNGRPNTNG finger-pointing *blame*
FNGRPRNT fingerprint *identification*
FNGRPST fingerpost *guide*
FNGRTP fingertip *digit*
FNGRWV finger wave *hair*
FNGS fungous *(adj) like fungus*
FNGS fungus *(n) plant fungi*
FNGSD fungicide *kill fungus*
FNGSDL fungicidal *kill fungus*
FNGSHN function *(n) purpose, party (v) serve*
FNGSHNL functional (adj) *useful* functionally (adv)
FNGSHNLD functionality *usefulness*
FNGSHNLT functionality *usefulness*
FNGSHNR functionary *official* functionaries
FNJ fungi (pl) *plant fungus*
FNJS fungous *like fungus*
FNJSD fungicide *kill fungus*
FNJSDL fungicidal *kill fungus*
FNJT fan-jet *airplane*
FNK aphonic *silent*
FNK euphonic *sound*
FNK fennec *fox*
FNK finicky *exacting*
FNK fink *(v-slang) inform (n-slang) informer*
FNK Finnic *of Finland*
FNK funk *fear, depression*
FNK funky *foul, quaint, jazzy* funkier funkiest
FNK pfennig *money* pfennig
FNK phonic *sound*
FNKL euphonically *sound*
FNKL finical (adj) *exacting* finically (adv)
FNKL funiculi (pl) *cord* funiculus
FNKL phonically *sound*

FNKLR funicular *railway*
FNKLS funiculus *cord* funiculi
FNKNS finickiness *exacting*
FNKNS funkiness *foul, quaint, jazzy*
FNKP phenocopy *variation* phenocopies
FNKR funkier *foul, quaint, jazzy*
FNKR funny car *racer*
FNKRDGRF phonocardiograph *heart*
FNKRDGRM phonocardiogram *heart*
FNKRDYGRF phonocardiograph *heart*
FNKRDYGRM phonocardiogram *heart*
FNKS Phoenix *city*
FNKS phoenix *bird*
FNKS phonics *sound*
FNKSHN function *(n) purpose, party (v) serve*
FNKSHNL functional (adj) *useful* functionally (adv)
FNKSHNLD functionality *usefulness*
FNKSHNLT functionality *usefulness*
FNKSHNR functionary *official* functionaries
FNKST funkiest *foul, quaint, jazzy*
FNKT phenakite (or) phenacite *mineral*
FNKYL funiculi (pl) *cord* funiculus
FNKYLR funicular *railway*
FNKYLS funiculus *cord* funiculi
FNKYR funkier *foul, quaint, jazzy*
FNKYST funkiest *foul, quaint, jazzy*
FNL fennel *herb*
FNL final (adj) *last (n) exam* finally (adv)
FNL finale *last part*
FNL finally (adv) *at last* final (adj)
FNL finely *precisely*

Letters aren't doubled for single sounds: to find alley use **L** not **LL**. Use **Y** and **W** as hard sounds only: to find yellow use **YL**. (Br)=British spelling or usage. * See dictionary.

FNL finial *ornament*
FNL fondly *affection*
FNL funnel *cone*
FNL funnily *in jest*
FNL phenol *disinfectant*
FNL phonily *fake*
FNLD finality *end* finalities
FNLFRM funnelform *cone-shaped*
FNLG phenology *climate*
FNLG phonology *speech*
FNLJ phenology *climate*
FNLJ phonology *speech*
FNLJKL phenological (adj) *climate* phenologically (adv)
FNLJKL phonological (adj) *speech* phonologically (adv)
FNLJST phonologist *speech*
FNLK phenolic *disinfectant, resin*
FNLKTNR phenylketonuria *disease*
FNLKTNRK phenylketonuric *diseased*
FNLKTNRY phenylketonuria *disease*
FNLKTNYR phenylketonuria *disease*
FNLKTNYRK phenylketonuric *diseased*
FNLKTNYRY phenylketonuria *disease*
FNLLNN phenylalanine *amino acid*
FNLN Finland *country*
FNLN foundling *orphan*
FNLND Finland *country*
FNLNG foundling *orphan*
FNLST finalist *contestant*
FNLT fanlight *window*
FNLT finality *end* finalities
FNLZ finalize *end* finalized finalizing (Br) finalise
FNLZSHN finalization *ending* (Br) finalisation
FNM euphonium *music*
FNM Fanny May *Federal National Mortgage*

Association FNMA
FNM phantom *ghost*
FNM phenom *(slang) exceptional person*
FNM phoneme *sound*
FNMBLST funambulist *tightrope*
FNMBLZM funambulism *tightrope*
FNMBYLST funambulist *tightrope*
FNMBYLZM funambulism *tightrope*
FNMK phonemic *sound*
FNMKS phonemics *sound*
FNMLK phantomlike *ghost*
FNMN phenomena (pl) *sensory, exception* phenomenon
FNMNL phenomenal (adj) *remarkable* phenomenally (adv)
FNMNLG phenomenology *consciousness*
FNMNLJ phenomenology *consciousness*
FNMNLJKL phenomenological (adj) *consciousness* phenomenologically (adv)
FNMNLJST phenomenologist *consciousness*
FNMNLSDK phenomenalistic *sensory*
FNMNLSDKL phenomenalistically *sensory*
FNMNLSTK phenomenalistic *sensory*
FNMNLSTKL phenomenalistically *sensory*
FNMNLZM phenomenalism *sensory*
FNMNN phenomenon *sensory, exception* phenomena (or) phenomenons
FNMPN Phnom Penh *city*
FNMX phonemics *sound*
FNN off and on *occasional*

FNN phone-in *telephone*
FNN phonon *energy*
FNNCHL financial (adj) *money* financially (adv)
FNNCR financier *money*
FNNGL fawningly *seeking favor*
FNNHD finnan haddie *food*
FNNHT finnan haddie *food*
FNNL fawningly *seeking favor*
FNNS finance *money* financed financing
FNNS funniness *jest*
FNNS phoniness *fake*
FNNSHL financial (adj) *money* financially (adv)
FNNSN financing *money*
FNNSNG financing *money*
FNNSR financier *money*
FNNT fainéant *idler* faineants
FNNTS finance *money* financed financing
FNNTSN financing *money*
FNNTSNG financing *money*
FNPK fanny pack *wallet*
FNPNCHR affenpinscher *dog*
FNPNSHR affenpinscher *dog*
FNQL funiculi (pl) *cord* funiculus
FNQLR funicular *railway*
FNQLS funiculus *cord* funiculi
FNR fanner *spreader, batter*
FNR feigner *pretender*
FNR finer *small, intricate, superior*
FNR finery *attire* fineries
FNR funnier *amusing*
FNR phonier *fake*
FNRFT phanerophyte *plant*
FNRGM phanerogam *plant*
FNRL funeral *burial*
FNRL funereal (adj) *solemn* funereally (adv)
FNRR funerary *burial*
FNRYL funereal (adj) *solemn* funereally (adv)
FNRZN fund-raising *money*
FNRZNG fund-raising

Use letters that best describe the sounds you hear and omit the vowels. Use **S** or **K** instead of **C**: to find circle use **SRKL**. Use **J** to find joy, **JM** to find gem and **G** to find go.

money

FNRZR fund-raiser *money*

FNS affiance *betroth* affianced affiancing

FNS euphonious *sound*

FNS fancy *(adj) ornate* fancier fanciest

FNS fancy *(n) love, taste* fancies

FNS fancy *(v) like, imagine, think* fancied fancying fancies

FNS fantasy *dream* fantasies

FNS Faunus *mythology*

FNS fence *wall, sword fighting* fenced fencing

FNS feyness *doom, eccentricity*

FNS fiancé *(m) one engaged* fiancée *(f)*

FNS fineness *detail*

FNS finesse *skill, trick* finessed finessing

FNS finis *end*

FNS fondness *affection*

FNS offense *harm, sin*

FNSD fantasied *imagined*

FNSDK faunistic *animals*

FNSDKL faunistically *animals*

FNSFL fanciful (adj) *imaginary* fancifully (adv)

FNSFR fancy-free *carefree*

FNSH finish *(v) end, complete (n) outside coating* finishes

FNSH Finnish *of Finland*

FNSHLN finish line *race*

FNSHN finishing *final*

FNSHN Phoenician *of Phoenicia*

FNSHN phonation *sound*

FNSHNG finishing *final*

FNSHR finisher *completer, ender, closer*

FNSHT finished *ended, completed*

FNSLN fantasyland *imagination*

FNSN fencing *sword fighting, wall*

FNSNG fencing *sword fighting, wall*

FNSPN finespun *detailed*

FNSPNTS fancy-pants *too elegant*

FNSR fancier *(adj) more ornate (n) lover*

FNSR fencer *wall, sword*

FNSR fencerow *land*

FNSST fanciest *ornate*

FNST finest *best*

FNST funniest *comic strip*

FNST phenacite (or) phenakite *mineral*

FNST phoniest *fake*

FNSTK faunistic *animals*

FNSTKL faunistically *animals*

FNSTR fenestra *opening* fenestrae

FNSTRDD fenestrated *openings*

FNSTRSHN fenestration *openings*

FNSTRT fenestrate *openings*

FNSTRTD fenestrated *openings*

FNSV offensive *forceful*

FNSVL offensively *forcefully*

FNSVNS offensiveness *force*

FNSWRK fancywork *sewing*

FNSYR fancier *(adj) more ornate (n) lover*

FNSYST fanciest *ornate*

FNSZ fantasize *imagine* fantasized fantasizing (Br) fantasise

FNSZR fantasizer *imaginer* (Br) fantasiser

FNT affiant *deponent*

FNT affinity *closeness* affinities

FNT faint *(adj) dim, weak (v) lose consciousness*

FNT feint *(n) pretense (v) trick*

FNT finite *limited*

FNT font *type, fountain* (Br) fount

FNT fount *source*

FNT phonate *sound* phonated phonating

FNTC fancy *(v) like, imagine, think* fancied fancying

fancies

FNTC fancy *(adj) ornate* fancier fanciest

FNTC fancy *(n) love, taste* fancies

FNTC fantasy *dream* fantasies

FNTCD fantasied *imagined*

FNTCFL fanciful (adj) *imaginary* fancifully (adv)

FNTCFR fancy-free *carefree*

FNTCHN fantoccine *puppets*

FNTCLN fantasyland *imagination*

FNTCLND fantasyland *imagination*

FNTCPNTS fancy-pants *too elegant*

FNTCR fancier *(adj) more ornate (n) lover*

FNTCST fanciest *ornate*

FNTCWRK fancywork *sewing*

FNTCYR fancier *(adj) more ornate (n) lover*

FNTCYST fanciest *ornate*

FNTD finitude *limited condition*

FNTHRDD fainthearted *timid*

FNTHRDDL faintheartedly *timid*

FNTHRDDNS faintheartedness *timid*

FNTHRTD fainthearted *timid*

FNTHRTDL faintheartedly *timid*

FNTHRTDNS faintheartedness *timid*

FNTK fanatic *zealot*

FNTK phenetic *biology*

FNTK phonetic *sound*

FNTKL fanatical (or) fanatic (adj) *zealous* fanatically (adv)

FNTKL phonetically *sound*

FNTKS phenetics *biology*

FNTKS phonetics *sound*

FNTL faintly *dim, weak*

FNTL fantail *pigeon, rear*

FNTL finitely *limited*

Letters aren't doubled for single sounds: to find alley use **L** not **LL**. Use **Y** and **W** as hard sounds only: to find yellow use **YL**. (Br)=British spelling or usage. * See dictionary.

FNTM phantom *ghost*
FNTMLK phantomlike *ghost*
FNTMS oftentimes (or) ofttimes *repeatedly*
FNTMZ oftentimes (or) ofttimes *repeatedly*
FNTN fan-tan *game*
FNTN fine-tune *adjust*
FNTN Fonteyn, Dame Margot *ballerina*
FNTN fountain *water*
FNTNHD fountainhead *origin*
FNTNL fontanel (or) fontanelle *membrane*
FNTNS faintness *dim, weak*
FNTNS finiteness *limited condition*
FNTP phenotype *variety*
FNTPK phenotypic *variety*
FNTPKL phenotypically *variety*
FNTS affiance *betroth* affianced affiancing
FNTS fancy (v) *like, imagine, think* fancied fancying fancies
FNTS fancy (adj) *ornate* fancier fanciest
FNTS fancy (n) *love, taste* fancies
FNTS fantasy *dream* fantasies
FNTS fence *wall, sword fighting* fenced fencing
FNTS fiancé (m) *one engaged* fiancée (f)
FNTS offense *harm, sin*
FNTSD fantasied *imagined*
FNTSDK fantastic *excellent*
FNTSDKL fantastically *excellent*
FNTSFL fanciful (adj) *imaginary* fancifully (adv)
FNTSFR fancy-free *carefree*
FNTSH fantasia *free form*
FNTSHN phonetician *sound*
FNTSLN fantasyland *imagination*
FNTSLND fantasyland *imagination*
FNTSN fencing *sword*

fighting, wall
FNTSNG fencing *sword fighting, wall*
FNTSPNTS fancy-pants *too elegant*
FNTSR fancier (adj) *more ornate* (n) *love*
FNTSR fencer *wall, sword fence*
FNTSR fencerow *land*
FNTSST fanciest *ornate*
FNTST fantast *visionary*
FNTSTK fantastic *excellent*
FNTSTKL fantastically *excellent*
FNTSV offensive *forceful*
FNTSVL offensively *forcefully*
FNTSVNS offensiveness *force*
FNTSWRK fancywork *sewing*
FNTSYR fancier (adj) *more ornate* (n) *love* .
FNTSYST fanciest *ornate*
FNTSZ fantasize *imagine* fantasized fantasizing (Br) fantasise
FNTSZM fanaticism *zealousness*
FNTSZR fantasizer *imaginer* (Br) fantasiser
FNTTH fine-tooth *comb*
FNTX phenetics *biology*
FNTX phonetics *sound*
FNTYD finitude *definite*
FNTZH fantasia *free form*
FNTZM phantasm *ghost*
FNTZMGR phantasmagoria *illusions*
FNTZMGRY phantasmagoria *illusions*
FNWZ fanwise *shape*
FNX Phoenix *city*
FNX phoenix *bird*
FNX phonics *sound*
FNY aphonia *whisper*
FNYL finial *ornament*
FNYM euphonium *music*
FNYNT fainéant *idler* faineants
FNYR funnier *amusing*

FNYR phonier *fake*
FNYS euphonious *sound*
FNYST funniest *comic strip*
FNYST phoniest *fake*
FNZ funnies *comic strip*
FNZN fanzine *magazine*
FP faux pas *blunder* faux pas
FP fop *dandy*
FPDNG off-putting *resistant*
FPK off-peak *less used*
FPR foppery *folly* fopperies
FPRNT offprint *excerpt*
FPRS off-price *discount*
FPSH foppish *dandy*
FPSHL foppishly *dandy*
FPSHNS foppishness *dandy*
FPTNG off-putting *resistant*
FPZ faux pas (pl) *blunder* faux pas
FQ folkway *custom*
FQL facula *sun* faculae
FQLDV faculative *optional*
FQLNS feculence *dung*
FQLNT feculent *foul*
FQLNTS feculence *dung*
FQLTV faculative *optional*
FR afar *distant*
FR affair *concern, procedure*
FR affray *brawl*
FR afire *on fire*
FR Afro *hairdo, African* Afros
FR euphoria *elation*
FR fair (adj) *clear, just, blond* (n) *exhibition*
FR fairy *mythical being* fairies
FR far *distance* farther (or) further farthest (or) furthest
FR fare (v) *get along, dine, travel* fared faring
FR fare (n) *fee, food*
FR faro *game* faros
FR farrow *birth*
FR fear *fright*
FR ferry *transport* ferried ferrying ferries
FR fewer *not many*
FR fiery *blazing* fierier fieriest
FR fir *tree*
FR fire (v) *ignite, expel from work* fired firing

Use letters that best describe the sounds you hear and omit the vowels. Use **S** or **K** instead of **C**: to find circle use **SRKL**. Use **J** to find joy, **JM** to find gem and **G** to find go.

FR fire *(n) flame*
FR for *(prep) purpose, concerning, goal**
FR foray *raid* forays
FR fore *front*
FR four *number (4)*
FR Frau *wife* Frauen
FR fray *(v) wear out, unravel (n) fight*
FR free *(v) liberate* freed freeing
FR free *(adj, adv) without obligation* freer freest
FR Frey *Norse god*
FR Freya *Norse goddess*
FR fro *from*
FR fry *cook* fried frying fries
FR führer *(or)* fuehrer *dictator*
FR fur *(v) apply fur* furred furring
FR fur *(n) hairy coat*
FR furrow *groove*
FR furry *with hair* furrier furriest
FR fury *rage* furies
FR Fury *Greek myth* Furies
FR off-hour *time*
FR offer *(v) sacrifice, propose (n) proposal, try, bid*
FR pharaoh *(often capitalized) ruler*
FRB euphorbia *plant*
FRB freebie *(or)* freebee *(slang) without charge*
FRBD forbid *prohibit* forbade forbidding forbidden
FRBD forebode *warn*
FRBDN forbidden *prohibited*
FRBDN forbidding *grim*
FRBDN foreboding *omen*
FRBDNG forbidding *grim*
FRBDNG foreboding *omen*
FRBDNS forbiddance *prohibition*
FRBDNTS forbiddance *prohibition*
FRBDR foreboder *warn*
FRBG firebug *arsonist*
FRBGR four-bagger *home run*

FRBKS firebox *furnace* fireboxes
FRBL fair ball *ball in play*
FRBL fireball *flame*
FRBL four-ball *game*
FRBL friable *fragile*
FRBL fribble *trifle* fribbled fribbling
FRBL furbelow *ruffle*
FRBLD friability *fragile*
FRBLT friability *fragile*
FRBM firebomb *explosive*
FRBNGKS Fairbanks *city*
FRBNGX Fairbanks *city*
FRBNKS Fairbanks *city*
FRBNX Fairbanks *city*
FRBR forbear *hold back* forbore forbearing forborne
FRBR forebear *ancestor*
FRBRD freeboard *waterline*
FRBRK firebreak *cleared land*
FRBRK firebrick *furnace*
FRBRN firebrand *agitator*
FRBRN forborne *held back*
FRBRN freeborn *not enslaved*
FRBRND firebrand *agitator*
FRBRNS forbearance *patience*
FRBRNTS forbearance *patience*
FRBRR forbearer *patience*
FRBRTHNG fire-breathing *aggressive*
FRBS freebase *cocaine* freebased freebasing
FRBSH furbish *make over*
FRBSHR furbisher *make over*
FRBSR freebaser *cocaine*
FRBT ferryboat *transport*
FRBT fireboat *put out fires*
FRBX firebox *furnace* fireboxes
FRBY euphorbia *plant*
FRC farci *(or)* farcie *stuffed*
FRC foresee *predict* foresaw foreseeing foreseen
FRC Pharisee *priest*
FRCBL foreseeable *predictable*
FRCBLD foreseeability

predictable
FRCBLT foreseeability *predictable*
FRCH 4-H *club*
FRCH forereach *gain ground*
FRCHD fortuity *chance* fortuities
FRCHN far-reaching *widespread*
FRCHN fortune *luck, fate*
FRCHNG far-reaching *widespread*
FRCHNT fortunate *lucky*
FRCHNTLR fortune-teller *predict*
FRCHR a fortiori *conclusion*
FRCHT fortuity *chance* fortuities
FRCHWD fortuity *chance* fortuities
FRCHWT fortuity *chance* fortuities
FRCN foreseen *predicted*
FRCR foreseer *predict*
FRCYBL foreseeable *predictable*
FRCYBLD foreseeability *predictable*
FRCYBLT foreseeability *predictable*
FRCYR foreseer *predict*
FRCZ aphaereses *(or)* aphereses (pl) *sound loss* aphaeresis *(or)* apheresis
FRD afeard *(or)* afeared *frightened*
FRD afford *provide*
FRD afraid *scared*
FRD far-red *infrared*
FRD farad *capacity*
FRD faraday *unit*
FRD ferrety *animal, searching*
FRD fired *using fuel, job loss*
FRD fjord *inlet*
FRD ford *wade*
FRD foreword *preface*
FRD forty *number (40)* forties
FRD forward *(adj) front, brash (adv) ahead (v) advance (n) sports*
FRD four-eyed *wearing*

Letters aren't doubled for single sounds: to find alley use **L** not **LL**. Use **Y** and **W** as hard sounds only: to find yellow use **YL**. (Br)=British spelling or usage. * See dictionary.

glasses
FRD fraud *deception*
FRD Freud *psychiatrist*
FRD Friday *weekday*
FRD fried *intoxicated*
FRD fruity *like fruit* fruitier fruitiest
FRD furred *hairy*
FRD off-road *vehicle*
FRDBL affordable (adj) *manageable cost* affordably (adv)
FRDBL fordable *wade*
FRDBLD affordability *manageable cost*
FRDBLT affordability *manageable cost*
FRDD fretted *ridged*
FRDD fritted *glass*
FRDD fruited *food-producing*
FRDF fortify *make strong* fortified fortifying fortifies
FRDFD fortified *enriched*
FRDFKSHN fortification *defense*
FRDFR fortifier *strength*
FRDFT phreatophyte *deep roots*
FRDFYR fortifier *strength*
FRDG firedog *andiron*
FRDJ freightage *load*
FRDJ fruitage *food*
FRDK faradic *electricity*
FRDK ferritic *magnet*
FRDK foredeck *ship*
FRDK phreatic *groundwater*
FRDKK friedcake *doughnut*
FRDL fertile (adj) *productive* fertilely (adv)
FRDL forwardly *front, brash*
FRDLKNG forward-looking *future*
FRDLNS fer-de-lance *snake* fer-de-lance
FRDLNS fertileness *productive*
FRDLNS fraudulence *deceit*
FRDLNT fraudulent *deceitful*
FRDLNTL fraudulently *deceitful*
FRDLNTS fer-de-lance *snake* fer-de-lance

FRDLNTS fraudulence *deceit*
FRDLZ fertilize *make productive* fertilized fertilizing
FRDLZBL fertilizable *make productive*
FRDLZR fertilizer *make productive*
FRDLZSHN fertilization *make productive*
FRDM foredoom *predict*
FRDM freedom *liberation*
FRDMN freedman *former slave*
FRDMP firedamp *gas*
FRDN Freudian *psychiatry*
FRDNR affaire d'honneur *matter of honor*
FRDNS forwardness *front, brash*
FRDNS fruitiness *like fruit, crazy*
FRDNZ fraternize *associate* fraternized fraternizing
FRDNZR fraternizer *associate*
FRDR ferreter *searcher*
FRDR fire-eater *performer*
FRDR freighter *ship*
FRDR fritter *(n)* pancake *(v) waste*
FRDR fruitier *like fruit, crazy*
FRDRNR fourdrinier *paper*
FRDRNYR fourdrinier *paper*
FRDRNZ fraternize *associate* fraternized fraternizing
FRDRNZR fraternizer *associate*
FRDRNZSHN fraternization *association*
FRDRR fritterer *waster*
FRDRR fruiterer *merchant*
FRDS fortis *pronunciation*
FRDSHK aphrodisiac *arouser*
FRDSHYK aphrodisiac *arouser*
FRDST fruitiest *like fruit, crazy*
FRDTD fortitude *courage*
FRDTH fortieth *of number 40*
FRDTYD fortitude *courage*

FRDV furtive *secret*
FRDYLNS fraudulence *deceit*
FRDYLNT fraudulent *deceitful*
FRDYLNTL fraudulently *deceitful*
FRDYLNTS fraudulence *deceit*
FRDYN Freudian *psychiatry*
FRDYR fruitier *like fruit, crazy*
FRDYST fruitiest *like fruit, crazy*
FRDYTH fortieth *of number 40*
FRDZ forties *numbers 40-49*
FRDZHK aphrodisiac *arouser*
FRDZHYK aphrodisiac *arouser*
FRDZK aphrodisiac *arouser*
FRDZM faradism *electricity*
FRDZYK aphrodisiac *arouser*
FRF far-off *distant*
FRFCHD far-fetched *improbable*
FRFCHR forfeiture *give up*
FRFCHT far-fetched *improbable*
FRFDBL forfeitable *give up*
FRFDD four-footed *quadruped*
FRFDR firefighter *fireman*
FRFDR forfeiter *give up*
FRFL farfel (or) farfal *noodles*
FRFL fearful (adj) *fright* fearfully (adv)
FRFL firefly *insect* fireflies
FRFL fourfold *times four*
FRFL free fall *drop*
FRFLD fourfold *times four*
FRFLDNG free-floating *without cause*
FRFLN free-flowing *pouring*
FRFLNG far-flung *widespread*
FRFLNG free-flowing *pouring*
FRFLSH four flush (n) *poker* four-flush (v)
FRFLSHR four-flusher

Use letters that best describe the sounds you hear and omit the vowels. Use **S** or **K** instead of **C**: to find circle use **SRKL**. Use **J** to find joy, **JM** to find gem and **G** to find go.

bluffer
FRFLTN free-floating *without cause*
FRFLTNG free-floating *without cause*
FRFLWN free-flowing *pouring*
FRFLWNG free-flowing *pouring*
FRFNGGR forefinger *index*
FRFNGR forefinger *index*
FRFR froufrou *frilly*
FRFRL free-for-all *fight*
FRFRM free-form *irregular*
FRFRNT forefront *face*
FRFRS ferriferous *iron*
FRFT firefight *battle*
FRFT forefoot *paw*
FRFT forfeit *give up*
FRFTBL forfeitable *give up*
FRFTD four-footed *quadruped*
FRFTHR forefather *ancestor*
FRFTR firefighter *fireman*
FRFTR forfeiter *give up*
FRFTR forfeiture *give up*
FRG farrago *mixture* farragoes
FRG forego *precede* forewent foregoing foregone
FRG forgo *give up* forwent forgone forgoes
FRG frig *(vulgar) sex* frigged frigging
FRG frog *amphibian*
FRG frogeye *plant disease*
FRG frug *dance*
FRGDBL forgettable *lose memory*
FRGDN forgotten *no memory*
FRGDR forgetter *lose memory*
FRGL frugal (adj) *sparing* frugally (adv)
FRGLD frugality *spareness* frugalities
FRGLT frugality *spareness* frugalities
FRGMN frogman *scuba diver* frogmen
FRGMNL fragmental (adj) *incomplete* fragmentally

(adv)
FRGMNT fragment *(v) break (n) piece*
FRGMNTL fragmental (adj) *incomplete* fragmentally (adv)
FRGMNTR fragmentary *incomplete*
FRGMNTRL fragmentarily *incomplete*
FRGMNTSHN fragmentation *break*
FRGMNTT fragmentate *break*
FRGMNTZ fragmentize *break* fragmentized fragmentizing
FRGMPLST phragmoplast *plant spindle*
FRGN foregoing *preceding*
FRGN foregone *past*
FRGN forgone *given up*
FRGNG foregoing *preceding*
FRGRN fairground *exhibition place*
FRGRN foreground *front area*
FRGRND fairground *exhibition place*
FRGRND foreground *front area*
FRGRNS fragrance *scent* fragrancy
FRGRNT fragrant *odorous*
FRGRNTL fragrantly *odor*
FRGRNTS fragrance *scent* fragrancy
FRGT forget *lose memory* forgot forgetting forgotten
FRGT frigate *ship*
FRGTBL forgettable *lose memory*
FRGTFL forgetful (adj) *lose memory* forgetfully (adv)
FRGTMNT forget-me-not *flower*
FRGTN forgotten *no memory*
FRGTR forgetter *lose memory*
FRGV forgive *pardon* forgave forgiving forgiven

FRGVBL forgivable (adj) *pardon* forgivably (adv)
FRGVN forgiven *pardoned*
FRGVN forgiving *room for error*
FRGVNG forgiving *room for error*
FRGVNS forgiveness *pardon*
FRGVR forgiver *pardon*
FRGWN foregoing *preceding*
FRGWNG foregoing *preceding*
FRHD forehead *face*
FRHF forehoof *front paw*
FRHL freehold *property*
FRHL frijole *bean* frijoles
FRHLD freehold *property*
FRHLDR freeholder *property*
FRHN forehand *stroke*
FRHN free hand *(n) no force*
FRHN freehand (adj) *drawing*
FRHND forehand *stroke*
FRHND free hand *(n) no force*
FRHND freehand (adj) *drawing*
FRHNDD forehanded *prudent*
FRHNDD freehanded *generous*
FRHNDDL freehandedly *generous*
FRHNDDNS freehandedness *generous*
FRHRD fair-haired *blond*
FRHRDD freehearted *generous*
FRHRTD freehearted *generous*
FRHWL four-wheel *vehicle*
FRHWL freewheel *(n) gear (v) roll freely*
FRHWLN freewheeling *unrestrained*
FRHWLNG freewheeling *unrestrained*
FRHWLR freewheeler *(n) gea, (v) roll freely*
FRJ ferriage *fare*
FRJ forage *(v) search* foraged foraging

Letters aren't doubled for single sounds: to find alley use **L** not **LL**. Use **Y** and **W** as hard sounds only: to find yellow use **YL**. (Br)=British spelling or usage. * See dictionary.

FRJ forage (n) food
FRJ forge (v) copy, form metal forged forging
FRJ forge (n) furnace
FRJ fridge refrigerator
FRJD frigid cold
FRJDD frigidity coldness
FRJDL frigidly cold
FRJDNS frigidness cold
FRJDR Frigidaire (trademark) refrigerator
FRJDT frigidity coldness
FRJJ forejudge expel, prejudge
FRJL fragile frail
FRJLD fragility frailness
FRJLNS fraudulence deceit
FRJLNT fraudulent deceitful
FRJLNTL fraudulently deceitful
FRJLNTS fraudulence deceit
FRJLT fragility frailness
FRJNS ferruginous iron, rusty
FRJR forager searcher
FRJR forger copy, form metal
FRJR forgery crime forgeries
FRJVR frugivore fruit eater
FRJVRS frugivorous fruit eater
FRK Africa continent
FRK euphoric elated
FRK ferric iron
FRK fork (n) untensil (v) split, pay
FRK freak oddity
FRK freaky strange freakier freakiest
FRK frock dress
FRKC fricassee cook fricasseed fricaseeing
FRKCH fair catch ball in play
FRKCHR fracture break fractured fracturing
FRKCHS fructuous fruitful
FRKCHWS fructuous fruitful
FRKD forked split
FRKDF fructify bear fruit fructified fructifying fructifies

FRKDFKSHN fructification plant organs
FRKDL fractal repeating pattern
FRKDS fructose sugar
FRKDT freaked-out (adj) crazy
FRKDV affricative phoneme
FRKDV fricative consonant
FRKFL forkful amount
FRKK free kick sports
FRKL euphorically elated
FRKL fireclay mud
FRKL freckle spot freckled freckling
FRKL freckly with spots
FRKL furcula wishbone furculae
FRKLBR farkleberry fruit farkleberries
FRKLF forklift machine
FRKLFT forklift machine
FRKLK four-o'clock plant
FRKLSHR foreclosure mortgage
FRKLZ foreclose shut out foreclosed foreclosing
FRKLZHR foreclosure mortgage
FRKN African from Africa
FRKN firkin cask
FRKN freaking damned
FRKND fricandeau veal
FRKNG freaking damned
FRKNR Afrikaner European native
FRKNS Afrikaans language
FRKNS freakiness strangeness
FRKNVLT African violet flower
FRKNVYLT African violet flower
FRKNZ Africanize make African Africanized Africanizing (Br) Africanise
FRKNZ Afrikaans language
FRKR Farquhar dramatist
FRKR freakier strange
FRKRKR firecracker fireworks

FRKRT forecourt courtyard, net area
FRKS fracas fight fracases
FRKS fricassee cook fricasseed fricaseeing
FRKSDBL forecastable prediction
FRKSDR forecaster predict
FRKSH freakish strange
FRKSHN fraction portion
FRKSHN friction rub
FRKSHN furcation branch
FRKSHNL fractional (adj) small fractionally (adv)
FRKSHNL frictional (adj) rub frictionally (adv)
FRKSHNLS frictionless no rubbing
FRKSHNLSL frictionlessly no rubbing
FRKSHNLZ fractionalize break fractionalized fractionalizing
FRKSHNLZSHN fractionalization break
FRKSHNSHN fractionation separate
FRKSHNT fractionate separate fractionated fractionating
FRKSHR fracture break fractured fracturing
FRKSHS fractious unruly
FRKSHS fructuous fruitful
FRKSHSL fractiously unruly
FRKSHSNS fractiousness unruly
FRKSHWS fructuous fruitful
FRKSL forecastle ship area
FRKSNL fraxinella herb
FRKST forecast prediction forecast forecasting
FRKST freakiest strange
FRKSTBL forecastable prediction
FRKSTNGGWSHR fire extinguisher put out fire
FRKSTNGWSHR fire extinguisher put out fire
FRKSTR forecaster predict
FRKT affricate phoneme
FRKT forked split

Use letters that best describe the sounds you hear and omit the vowels. Use **S** or **K** instead of **C**: to find circle use **SRKL**. Use **J** to find joy, **JM** to find gem and **G** to find go.

FRKT freak-out (n) *go crazy* freak out (v)
FRKT freaked-out (adj) *crazy*
FRKTF fructify *bear fruit* fructified fructifying fructifies
FRKTFKSHN fructification *plant organs*
FRKTL fractal *repeating pattern*
FRKTR fracture *break* fractured fracturing
FRKTS fructose *sugar*
FRKTS fructuous *fruitful*
FRKTT freaked-out (adj) *crazy*
FRKTV affricative *phoneme*
FRKTV fricative *consonant*
FRKTWS fructuous *fruitful*
FRKWNC frequency *number* frequencies
FRKWNR frequenter *associate*
FRKWNS frequency *number* frequencies
FRKWNS frequentness *repetition*
FRKWNT frequent (adj) *repeated* (v) *associate with*
FRKWNTC frequency *number* frequencies
FRKWNTL frequently *repeatedly*
FRKWNTNS frequentness *repetition*
FRKWNTR frequenter *associate*
FRKWNTS frequency *number* frequencies
FRKWNTSHN frequentation *association*
FRKWR Farquhar *dramatist*
FRKWRDR forequarter *part*
FRKWRTR forequarter *part*
FRKYL furcula *wishbone* furculae
FRKYR Farquhar *dramatist*
FRKYR freakier *strange*
FRKYST freakiest *strange*
FRKYWR Farquhar *dramatist*
FRL Fair Isle *knitting*

FRL fairly *somewhat, honestly*
FRL feral *wild*
FRL ferrule *ring*
FRL ferule *discipline*
FRL frail (adj) *weak* frailly (adv)
FRL freely *without constraint*
FRL frill (n, v) *ruffle* frilly (adj)
FRL furl *wrap*
FRL furlough *absence*
FRLD frailty *weakness* frailties
FRLD freeload *mooch*
FRLDR freeloader *moocher*
FRLDRWRD four-letter word *curse*
FRLG foreleg *front leg*
FRLG vorlage *skiing*
FRLK firelock *gun*
FRLK forelock *hair*
FRLK frolic *dance around* frolicked frolicking
FRLKSM frolicsome *playful*
FRLM forelimb *front limb*
FRLN fairyland *magic place*
FRLN fräulein *woman*
FRLND fairyland *magic place*
FRLNDZ Faeroe Islands *land mass*
FRLNG furlong *length*
FRLNS frailness *weakness*
FRLNS freelance *independent*
FRLNSR freelancer *independent*
FRLNTS freelance *independent*
FRLNTSR freelancer *independent*
FRLNZ Faeroe Islands *land mass*
FRLRN forlorn *alone*
FRLRNL forlornly *alone*
FRLRNS forlornness *alone*
FRLS fearless *not afraid*
FRLS furless *no hair*
FRLT firelight *glow*
FRLT frailty *weakness* frailties
FRLTRWRD four-letter word *curse*
FRLVN free-living *capable of movement*

FRLVNG free-living *capable of movement*
FRLXM frolicsome *playful*
FRM A-frame *structure*
FRM affirm *validate*
FRM farm *crops*
FRM fermi *measure* fermis
FRM firm (adj) *stiff, steady* (n) *company* (v) *tighten, settle*
FRM form (n) *shape, document, type* (v) *shape*
FRM forum *arena* forums
FRM frame (v) *plan, construct, contrive**
framed framing
FRM frame (n) *physique, border, context**
FRM from (prep) *starting point, separation, cause**
FRMBL affirmable *valid*
FRMBL formable *shape*
FRMBL frameable *plan, construct, contrive**
FRMBLD formability *shape*
FRMBLT formability *shape*
FRMBWZ framboise *liqueur*
FRMC pharmacy *drugs* pharmacies
FRMD fermata *music*
FRMDBL formidable (adj) *awesome* formidably (adv)
FRMDBLD formidability *awesome*
FRMDBLNS formidableness *awesome*
FRMDBLT formidability *awesome*
FRMDR formatter *arranger*
FRMDS fremitus *vibration*
FRMDV affirmative *positive*
FRMDV formative *shape*
FRMDVL affirmatively *positive*
FRMFTNG formfitting *snug*
FRMHN farmhand *helper*
FRMHND farmhand *helper*
FRMHS farmhouse *building*
FRMK formic *acid*
FRMK Formica (trademark) *material*
FRMKLG pharmacology

Letters aren't doubled for single sounds: to find alley use **L** not **LL**. Use **Y** and **W** as hard sounds only: to find yellow use **YL**. (Br)=British spelling or usage. * See dictionary.

medicines
FRMKLJ pharmacology
medicines
FRMKLJKL
pharmacological (adj)
medicines
pharmacologically (adv)
FRMKLJST pharmacologist
medicines
FRMKP pharmacopoeia
drugs
FRMKPL pharmacopoeial
drugs
FRMKPY pharmacopoeia
drugs
FRMKPYL pharmacopoeial
drugs
FRMKR formicary *ant nest*
formicaries
FRML firmly *strong or steady*
manner
FRML formal (adj)
methodical, ceremonial
formally (adv)
FRML formula *recipe*
formulas (or) formulae
FRML formyl *acid*
FRMLD formality *ceremony*
formalities
FRMLDHD formaldehyde
preservative
FRMLDR formulator *creator*
FRMLN farmland *crops*
FRMLND farmland *crops*
FRMLNS formalness
ceremony
FRMLRZ formularize *create*
formularized
formularizing
FRMLRZR formularizer
creator
FRMLRZSHN
formularization *recipe*
FRMLS formless *no shape*
FRMLSDK formalistic
custom
FRMLSHN formulation
creation
FRMLSL formlessly *no shape*
FRMLSNS formlessness *no*
shape
FRMLST formalist *custom*

FRMLSTK formalistic
custom
FRMLT formality *ceremony*
formalities
FRMLT formulate *create*
formulated formulating
FRMLTR formulator *creator*
FRMLWN Formula One
racer
FRMLZ formalize *shape,*
approve formalized
formalizing
(Br) formalise
FRMLZ formulize *prepare*
formulized formulizing
FRMLZBL formalizable
shape, approve
FRMLZM formalism *custom*
FRMLZR formalizer *shape,*
approve
(Br) formaliser
FRMLZSHN formalization
shape, approve
(Br) formalisation
FRMM fermium *element*
FRMMNT firmament *world*
FRMN farming *crops*
FRMN fermion *particle*
FRMN ferryman *transporter*
ferrymen
FRMN fireman *firefighter*
firemen
FRMN foreman *supervisor*
foremen
FRMN freeman *citizen*
freemen
FRMN pheromone *scent*
FRMNCHND
aforementioned *said*
before
FRMNDD fair-minded *just*
FRMNFR foraminifer *sea*
organism
FRMNFR foraminifera *sea*
organisms
FRMNFRL foraminiferal *sea*
organism
FRMNG farming *crops*
FRMNL pheromonal *scent*
FRMNR fermenter *enzyme*
FRMNR fermentor *apparatus*
FRMNS affirmance *assertion*

FRMNS firmness *strongness,*
steadiness
FRMNSHND
aforementioned *said*
before
FRMNT ferment *(v) work up*
(n) enzyme, unrest
FRMNTR fermenter *enzyme*
FRMNTR fermentor
apparatus
FRMNTS affirmance
assertion
FRMNTSHN fermentation
breakdown
FRMP frame-up *(n) devise*
falsely
FRMP frump *dowdy*
FRMP off-ramp *highway*
FRMPSH frumpish *dowdy*
FRMR farmer *crops*
FRMR former *once*
FRMR framer *plan,*
*construct, contrive**
FRMRKN Afro-American
African-American
FRMRKTR free-marketeer
economist
FRMRL formerly *before*
FRMRTN freemartin *calf*
FRMS pharmacy *drugs*
pharmacies
FRMSDKL pharmaceutical
(adj) *medicines*
pharmaceutically (adv)
FRMSHN affirmation
validation
FRMSHN formation
structure
FRMSN Freemason *fraternal*
member
FRMSNR freemasonry
(often capitalized)
fellowship
FRMSST pharmacist
medicines
FRMST foremast *ship*
FRMST foremost *important*
FRMSTD farmstead
buildings
FRMSTKL pharmaceutical
(adj) *medicines*
pharmaceutically (adv)

Use letters that best describe the sounds you hear and omit the vowels. Use **S** or **K** instead of **C**: to find circle use **SRKL**. Use **J** to find joy, **JM** to find gem and **G** to find go.

FRMT fermata *music*
FRMT format *layout*
formatted formatting
FRMTR formatter *arranger*
FRMTS fremitus *vibration*
FRMTV affirmative *positive*
FRMTV formative *shape*
FRMTVL affirmatively
positive
FRMWF farmwife *spouse*
FRMWRK farmwork *crops*
FRMWRK formwork *concrete*
FRMWRK framework
structure
FRMWRKR farmworker
helper
FRMYL formula *recipe*
formulas (or) formulae
FRMYLDR formulator
creator
FRMYLRZ formularize *create*
formularized
formularizing
FRMYLRZR formularizer
creator
FRMYLRZSHN
formularization *recipe*
FRMYLSHN formulation
creation
FRMYLT formulate *create*
formulated formulating
FRMYLTR formulator *creator*
FRMYLWN Formula One
racer
FRMYLZ formulize *prepare*
formulized formulizing
FRMYM fermium *element*
FRMYN fermion *particle*
FRMYRD farmyard *barnyard*
FRN fairing *structure, (Br)*
gift
FRN farina *cereal*
FRN fern *plant*
FRN firing *heat, dismissal*
FRN foreign *alien*
FRN forerun *come before*
foreran forerunning
FRN Frauen (pl) *wife* Frau
FRN frena (pl) *membrane*
frenum
FRN Freon *(trademark)*
coolant

FRN friend *pal*
FRN frond *leaf*
FRN frown *wrinkle*
FRN frying *cooking*
FRN offering *gift*
FRNBRD free on board
(abbr) F.O.B.
FRNBRN foreign-born *alien*
FRNBWZ framboise *liqueur*
FRNCH French *of France*
FRNCH french *(often*
capitalized) cut or trim
FRNCHDR French door
glass panes
FRNCHDRSNG French
dressing *food*
FRNCHF frenchify *(often*
capitalized) make French
frenchified frenchifying
frenchifies
FRNCHFR french fry *potato*
french fries
FRNCHGN French Guiana
country
FRNCHGYN French Guiana
country
FRNCHKF French cuff
sleeve
FRNCHKRV french curve
(often capitalized) guide
FRNCHKS French kiss (n)
open-mouth French-kiss
(v)
FRNCHLV French leave
hasty departure
FRNCHPLNSH French
Polynesia *islands*
FRNCHPLNZH French
Polynesia *islands*
FRNCHPRVNCHL French
provincial *style*
FRNCHPRVNSHL French
provincial *style*
FRNCHPSDR French pastry
food
FRNCHPSTR French pastry
food
FRNCHR furniture
equipment
FRNCHRN French horn
music
FRNCHS franchise (v)

license franchised
franchising
FRNCHS franchise (n)
privilege
FRNCHSR franchiser *grant*
or hold a license
FRNCHSR franchisor *grant*
a license
FRNCHTST French toast
food
FRNCHZ franchise (v)
license franchised
franchising
FRNCHZ franchise (n)
privilege
FRNCHZ franchisee *licensee*
FRNCHZR franchiser *grant*
or hold a license
FRNCHZR franchisor *grant*
a license
FRNCM francium *element*
FRNCYM francium *element*
FRNCZ fornices (pl) *arch*
fornix
FRND friend *pal*
FRND frond *leaf*
FRNDF fore-and-aft
lengthwise
FRNDFT fore-and-aft
lengthwise
FRNDK frenetic *frantic*
FRNDKL frenetically *frantic*
FRNDL farandole *dance*
FRNDL friendly *(adj) nice*
friendlier friendliest
FRNDL friendly *(n) native*
friendlies
FRNDLNS friendliness
niceness
FRNDLR friendlier *nice*
FRNDLS friendless *no pals*
FRNDLSNS friendlessness
no pals
FRNDLST friendliest *nice*
FRNDLYR friendlier *nice*
FRNDLYST friendliest *nice*
FRNDSHP friendship
affection
FRNDSZM freneticism
frantic
FRNF fore-and-aft
lengthwise

Letters aren't doubled for single sounds: to find alley use **L** not **LL**. Use **Y** and **W** as hard sounds only: to find yellow use **YL**. (Br)=British spelling or usage. * See dictionary.

FRNFDR fore-and-after *schooner*

FRNFT fore-and-aft *lengthwise*

FRNFTR fore-and-after *schooner*

FRNG fairing *structure, (Br) gift*

FRNG firing *heat, dismissal*

FRNG frying *cooking*

FRNG offering *gift*

FRNGK franc *money*

FRNGK frank *(adj) honest (v) mail (n) stamp, hot dog*

FRNGKBL frankable *mail*

FRNGKFB Francophobe *fear of France*

FRNGKFL Francophile *love of France*

FRNGKFN francophone *language*

FRNGKFRDR frankfurter (or) frankfurt *hot dog*

FRNGKFRT Frankfort *Kansas city*

FRNGKFRT Frankfurt *German city*

FRNGKFRT frankfurt (or) frankfurter *hot dog*

FRNGKFRTR frankfurter (or) frankfurt *hot dog*

FRNGKL frankly *honestly*

FRNGKL furuncle *boil*

FRNGKLN francolin *bird*

FRNGKLN franklin *landowner*

FRNGKLNT franklinite *mineral*

FRNGKLSS furunculosis *boils furunculoses*

FRNGKNS frankness *honesty*

FRNGKNSNS frankincense *incense resin*

FRNGKNSNTS frankincense *incense resin*

FRNGKNSTN Frankenstein *fictional doctor*

FRNGKR franker *mail*

FRNGKS pharynx *throat pharynges*

FRNGKYLSS furunculosis

boils furunculoses

FRNGPN frying pan *utensil*

FRNGQLSS furunculosis *boils* furunculoses

FRNGX pharynx *throat* pharynges

FRNGZ pharynges (pl) *throat* pharynx

FRNHN four-in-hand *vehicle, necktie*

FRNHND four-in-hand *vehicle, necktie*

FRNHT Fahrenheit *thermometer*

FRNJ fringe *border* fringed fringing

FRNJ fringy *border*

FRNJ frontage *land*

FRNJBL frangible *delicate*

FRNJBLD frangibility *delicate*

FRNJBLT frangibility *delicate*

FRNJN fire-engine (adj) *vehicle* fire engine (n)

FRNJPN frangipane *custard*

FRNJPN frangipani *tree* frangipani

FRNJZ pharynges (pl) *throat* pharynx

FRNK franc *money*

FRNK frank *(adj) honest (v) mail (n) stamp, hot dog*

FRNK frantic *anxious*

FRNKBL frankable *mail*

FRNKDR fornicator *adulterer*

FRNKFB Francophobe *fear of France*

FRNKFL Francophile *love of France*

FRNKFN francophone *language*

FRNKFRDR frankfurter (or) frankfurt *hot dog*

FRNKFRT Frankfort *Kansas city*

FRNKFRT Frankfurt *German city*

FRNKFRT frankfurt (or) frankfurter *hot dog*

FRNKFRTR frankfurter (or) frankfurt *hot dog*

FRNKL frankly *honestly*

FRNKL frantically *anxious*

FRNKL furuncle *boil*

FRNKLN francolin *bird*

FRNKLN franklin *landowner*

FRNKLNT franklinite *mineral*

FRNKLSS furunculosis *boils* furunculoses

FRNKNS frankness *honesty*

FRNKNS franticness *anxiety*

FRNKNSNS frankincense *incense resin*

FRNKNSNTS frankincense *incense resin*

FRNKNSTN Frankenstein *fictional doctor*

FRNKR franker *mail*

FRNKS fornix *arch* fornices

FRNKS pharynx *throat* pharynges

FRNKSHN fornication *adultery*

FRNKT fornicate *have sex* fornicated fornicating

FRNKTR fornicator *adulterer*

FRNKYLSS furunculosis *boils* furunculoses

FRNL frenula (pl) *membrane* frenulum

FRNL friendly *(adj) nice* friendlier friendliest

FRNL friendly *(n) native* friendlies

FRNL frontal (adj) *foremost, direct* frontally (adv)

FRNLG phrenology *skull*

FRNLJ foreknowledge *prediction*

FRNLJ phrenology *skull*

FRNLJKL phrenological *skull*

FRNLJST phrenologist *skull*

FRNLM frenulum *membrane* frenula

FRNLNS friendliness *niceness*

FRNLR friendlier *nice*

FRNLS friendless *no pals*

FRNLSNS friendlessness *no pals*

FRNLST friendliest *nice*

FRNLYR friendlier *nice*

FRNLYST friendliest *nice*

Use letters that best describe the sounds you hear and omit the vowels. Use **S** or **K** instead of **C**: to find circle use **SRKL**. Use **J** to find joy, **JM** to find gem and **G** to find go.

FRNM forename *first name*
FRNM frenum *membrane* frenums (or) frena
FRNM pheromone *scent*
FRNML pheromonal *scent*
FRNN forenoon *morning*
FRNND front-end (adj) *beginning, forward* front end (n)
FRNNGL frowningly *angry*
FRNPN frying pan *utensil*
FRNQLSS furunculosis *boils* furunculoses
FRNR fernery *plants* ferneries
FRNR foreigner *alien*
FRNR forerunner *ancestor*
FRNR frowner *angry one*
FRNS fairness *justice*
FRNS fieriness *blazing*
FRNS France *country*
FRNS furnace *oven*
FRNSH furnish *equip*
FRNSHNGS furnishings *equipment*
FRNSHNS furnishings *equipment*
FRNSHNZ furnishings *equipment*
FRNSHP friendship *affection*
FRNSHR furnisher *equip*
FRNSHS farinaceous *cereal*
FRNSK forensic *debate, legal*
FRNSKL forensically *debate, legal*
FRNSKS forensics *debate*
FRNSM francium *element*
FRNSSKN Franciscan *religious order*
FRNSX forensics *debate*
FRNSYM francium *element*
FRNSZ fornices (pl) *arch* fornix
FRNT afferent *toward the center*
FRNT affront *insult*
FRNT efferent *away from center*
FRNT euphoriant *drug*
FRNT fire ant *insect*
FRNT front (n, adj) *foremost area* (v) *face, substitute*

FRNTCM francium *element*
FRNTCYM francium *element*
FRNTJ frontage *land*
FRNTK frantic *anxious*
FRNTK frenetic *frantic*
FRNTKL frantically *anxious*
FRNTKL frenetically *frantic*
FRNTKNS franticness *anxiety*
FRNTL afferently *toward the center*
FRNTL efferently *away from center*
FRNTL frontal (adj) *foremost, direct* frontally (adv)
FRNTLD front-load *costs*
FRNTLD frontality *view*
FRNTLN frontline (adj) *forefront* front line (n)
FRNTLT frontality *view*
FRNTLT frontlet *forehead*
FRNTN fronton *arena*
FRNTND front-end (adj) *beginning, forward* front end (n)
FRNTPJ front-page *news*
FRNTR effrontery *boldness* effronteries
FRNTR frontier *border*
FRNTR furniture *equipment*
FRNTRNR front-runner *contestant*
FRNTRZMN frontiersman *settler* frontiersmen
FRNTS France *country*
FRNTSM francium *element*
FRNTSPS frontispiece *facing area*
FRNTSYM francium *element*
FRNTSZM freneticism *frantic*
FRNX fornix *arch* fornices
FRNX pharynx *throat* pharynges
FRNYL frenula (pl) *membrane* frenulum
FRNYLM frenulum *membrane* frenula
FRNZ frenzy *outburst* frenzies
FRNZD frenzied *frantic*
FRNZDL frenziedly *frantic*

FRNZK forensic *debate, legal*
FRNZKL forensically *debate, legal*
FRNZKS forensics *debate*
FRNZX forensics *debate*
FRP forepaw *foot*
FRP frap *tighten* frapped frapping
FRP frappé *dessert*
FRPL fair play *justice*
FRPL foreplay *warm up*
FRPLG fireplug *hydrant*
FRPLS fireplace *hearth*
FRPR firepower *weapons*
FRPR frippery *finery* fripperies
FRPRF fireproof *no flames*
FRPSDR four-poster *bed*
FRPSTR four-poster *bed*
FRPT firepot *missile, food*
FRPWR firepower *weapons*
FRQL furcula *wishbone* furculae
FRQNC frequency *number* frequencies
FRQNR frequenter *associate*
FRQNS frequency *number* frequencies
FRQNS frequentness *repetition*
FRQNT frequent (adj) *repeated* (v) *associate with*
FRQNTC frequency *number* frequencies
FRQNTL frequently *repeatedly*
FRQNTNS frequentness *repetition*
FRQNTR frequenter *associate*
FRQNTS frequency *number* frequencies
FRQNTSHN frequentation *association*
FRQR Farquhar *dramatist*
FRQRDR forequarter *part*
FRQRTR forequarter *part*
FRR farrier *horseshoes*
FRR fearer *fright*
FRR fierier *blazing*
FRR firer *launcher, dismisser, igniter*

Letters aren't doubled for single sounds: to find alley use **L** not **LL**. Use **Y** and **W** as hard sounds only: to find yellow use **YL**. (Br)=British spelling or usage. * See dictionary.

FRR friar *monk*
FRR friary *monastery* friaries
FRR fryer *cooker, chicken*
FRR führer (or) fuehrer *dictator*
FRR furor *rage* (Br) furore
FRR furrier *fur dealer, hairy*
FRR furriery *fur business*
FRRDN foreordain *predict future*
FRRDNSHN foreordination *predict future*
FRRM firearm *weapon*
FRRM forearm *limb*
FRRNJ free-range *not caged*
FRS farce *mockery*
FRS farci (or) farcie *stuffed*
FRS Farsi *Persian*
FRS ferrous *iron*
FRS fierce *intense* fiercer fiercest
FRS force (*v*) *coerce, strain* forced forcing
FRS force (*n*) *power, group*
FRS foresee *predict* foresaw foreseeing foreseen
FRS furioso *music*
FRS furious *angry, intense*
FRS Pharisee *priest*
FRSBDNG frostbiting *sailing*
FRSBL forcible (adj) *done by power* forcibly (adv)
FRSBL foreseeable *predictable*
FRSBLD foreseeability *predictable*
FRSBLT foreseeability *predictable*
FRSBRN firstborn *eldest*
FRSBS first base *baseball*
FRSBT frostbite *freeze* frostbit frostbiting frostbitten
FRSBTN frostbitten *frozen*
FRSBTNG frostbiting *sailing*
FRSCHL frustule *shell*
FRSD aforesaid *mentioned before*
FRSD farside *other end*
FRSD ferocity *fierceness*
FRSD fireside *hearth*

FRSD forced *unwilling*
FRSD frosty *icy* frostier frostiest
FRSDD farsighted *vision*
FRSDD foresighted *predict*
FRSDD forested *trees*
FRSDD frosted *icy*
FRSDDL foresightedly *predict*
FRSDDNS foresightedness *predict*
FRSDGR first-degree *mild*
FRSDK aphoristic *adage*
FRSDKL aphoristically *adage*
FRSDL frostily *icy*
FRSDN first down *football*
FRSDN frosting *icing*
FRSDNG frosting *icing*
FRSDNS frostiness *icy*
FRSDR forester *ranger*
FRSDR forestry *tree science*
FRSDR frostier *icy*
FRSDST frostiest *icy*
FRSDYR frostier *icy*
FRSDYST frostiest *icy*
FRSFD force-feed *administer* force-fed force-feeding
FRSFL force field *protection*
FRSFL forceful (adj) *strong* forcefully (adv)
FRSFLD force field *protection*
FRSFLNS forcefulness *strength*
FRSFLR first floor *building*
FRSH afresh *anew*
FRSH fairish *large*
FRSH farouche *wild*
FRSH freesia *herb, flower*
FRSH fresh *vigorous, pure, impudent**
FRSH frosh *freshman*
FRSHD foreshadow *predict*
FRSHK fair shake *justice*
FRSHL freshly *vigorous, pure, impudent**
FRSHMN freshman *beginner* freshmen
FRSHN freshen *clean*
FRSHN fruition *realization*
FRSHNR freshener *cleaner*

FRSHNS freshness *vigorous, pure, impudent**
FRSHR a fortiori *conclusion*
FRSHR foreshore *beach*
FRSHR fourragère *cord*
FRSHS ferocious *fierce*
FRSHSL ferociously *fierce*
FRSHSNS ferociousness *fierceness*
FRSHT Fréchette *poet*
FRSHT freshet *stream*
FRSHTN foreshorten *cut*
FRSHWDR freshwater *no salt, unskilled*
FRSHWL Ferris wheel *amusement*
FRSHWTR freshwater *no salt, unskilled*
FRSHY freesia *herb, flower*
FRSHYR a fortiori *conclusion*
FRSK forsake *leave behind* forsook forsaking forsaken
FRSK fresco *art* frescoes
FRSK frisk *check, leap*
FRSK frisky *lively* friskier friskiest
FRSK pharisaic *righteous*
FRSKL farcical (adj) *absurd* farcically (adv)
FRSKL friskily *lively*
FRSKL pharisaical (adj) *righteous* pharisaically (adv)
FRSKLD farcicality *absurdity*
FRSKLS first-class (adj) *best* first class (n)
FRSKLT farcicality *absurdity*
FRSKN foreskin *penis*
FRSKN forsaken *left behind*
FRSKN forsaking *leaving behind*
FRSKNG forsaking *leaving behind*
FRSKNS friskiness *lively*
FRSKP fire escape *ladder*
FRSKR fourscore *eighty*
FRSKR frisker *check, leap*
FRSKR friskier *lively*
FRSKST friskiest *lively*
FRSKT frisket *masking*
FRSKWR foursquare *(adj)*

Use letters that best describe the sounds you hear and omit the vowels. Use **S** or **K** instead of **C**: to find circle use **SRKL**. Use **J** to find joy, **JM** to find gem and **G** to find go.

honest (n) game
FRSKYR friskier *lively*
FRSKYST friskiest *lively*
FRSL fire sale *low prices*
FRSL firstly *before all else*
FRSL foresail *boat*
FRSL furiously *angry, intense*
FRSLD first lady *president's wife*
FRSM fearsome *frightening*
FRSM foursome *four people*
FRSMJR force majeure *act of God*
FRSML fearsomely *frightening*
FRSMNS fearsomeness *frightening*
FRSMSHR force majeure *act of God*
FRSMZHR force majeure *act of God*
FRSN foreseen *predicted*
FRSN frisson *thrill* frissons
FRSNM first name *given name*
FRSNTRK Afrocentric *centered in Africa*
FRSNTRZM Afrocentrism *centered in Africa*
FRSPKN free-spoken *blunt, frank*
FRSPS forceps *instrument* forceps
FRSQR foursquare *(adj) honest (n) game*
FRSR farceur *joker*
FRSR fiercer *intense*
FRSR foreseer *predict*
FRSRN first-run *new*
FRSRT first-rate *best*
FRSS aphaeresis (or) apheresis *sound loss* aphaereses (or) aphereses
FRSST fiercest *intense*
FRST afforest *(v) plant trees*
FRST aphorist *adage*
FRST Far East *region*
FRST ferocity *fierceness*
FRST fieriest *blazing*
FRST first *before all else*
FRST force-out *sports*

FRST forced *unwilling*
FRST foresight *predict*
FRST forest *trees*
FRST forestay *line*
FRST frost *ice*
FRST frosty *icy* frostier frostiest
FRST frusta (pl) *pyramid* frustum
FRST furriest *hairy*
FRSTBDNG frostbiting *sailing*
FRSTBRN firstborn *eldest*
FRSTBS first base *baseball*
FRSTBT frostbite *freeze* frostbit frostbiting frostbitten
FRSTBTN frostbitten *frozen*
FRSTBTNG frostbiting *sailing*
FRSTD farsighted *vision*
FRSTD first aid *medical help*
FRSTD foresighted *predict*
FRSTD forested *trees*
FRSTD frosted *icy*
FRSTDGR first-degree *mild*
FRSTDL foresightedly *predict*
FRSTDN first down *football*
FRSTDNS foresightedness *predict*
FRSTFL foresightful *predict*
FRSTFLR first floor *building*
FRSTH forsooth *indeed*
FRSTH forsythia *shrub*
FRSTHN firsthand *personal*
FRSTHND firsthand *personal*
FRSTHY forsythia *shrub*
FRSTK aphoristic *adage*
FRSTKL aphoristically *adage*
FRSTKLS first-class (adj) *best* first class (n)
FRSTL firstly *before all else*
FRSTL forestall *prevent*
FRSTL freestyle *swim*
FRSTL frostily *icy*
FRSTL frustule *shell*
FRSTLD first lady *president's wife*
FRSTLMNT forestallment *prevention*
FRSTLR forestaller *prevent*

FRSTM frustum *cone* frustums (or) frusta
FRSTN freestone *fruit*
FRSTN frosting *icing*
FRSTNDN freestanding *no support*
FRSTNDNG freestanding *no support*
FRSTNG frosting *icing*
FRSTNM first name *given name*
FRSTNS frostiness *icy*
FRSTP fire-stop *material*
FRSTR forester *ranger*
FRSTR forestry *tree science*
FRSTR four-star *excellent*
FRSTR frostier *icy*
FRSTRDD frustrated *prevented*
FRSTRDNG frustrating *preventing*
FRSTRM firestorm *flames, outburst*
FRSTRN first-run *new*
FRSTRNG first-string *sports*
FRSTRSHN frustration *dissatisfaction*
FRSTRT first-rate *best*
FRSTRT frustrate *prevent* frustrated frustrating
FRSTRTD frustrated *prevented*
FRSTRTN frustrating *preventing*
FRSTRTNG frustrating *preventing*
FRSTSHN afforestation *plant trees*
FRSTSHN forestation *cover with trees*
FRSTST frostiest *icy*
FRSTWRLD first world *developed*
FRSTYL frustule *shell*
FRSTYR frostier *icy*
FRSTYST frostiest *icy*
FRSWL Ferris wheel *amusement*
FRSWR forswear *perjure* forswore forsworn forswearing
FRSWRLD first world

Letters aren't doubled for single sounds: to find alley use **L** not **LL**. Use **Y** and **W** as hard sounds only: to find yellow use **YL**. (Br)=British spelling or usage. * See dictionary.

developed

FRSWRN forsworn *perjury*
FRSYBL foreseeable
  predictable
FRSYBLD foreseeability
  predictable
FRSYBLT foreseeability
  predictable
FRSYK pharisaic *righteous*
FRSYKL pharisaical (adj)
  righteous pharisaically
  (adv)
FRSYR farceur *joker*
FRSYR foreseer *predict*
FRSZ aphaereses (or)
  aphereses (pl) *sound loss*
  aphaeresis (or) apheresis
FRT affright *scare*
FRT afreet (or) afrit *spirit*
FRT effort *try*
FRT far-out *unusual*
FRT fart *(vulgar) gas*
FRT ferret *(n) animal (v)*
  search
FRT ferrety *animal, searching*
FRT ferrite *magnet*
FRT fort *army*
FRT forte *skill, music*
FRT forty *number (40)* forties
FRT frat *fraternity*
FRT fraught *filled*
FRT freight *load*
FRT fret *(v) worry, chafe,*
  decorate fretted fretting
FRT fret *(n) ridge, erosion,*
  network
FRT fright *fear*
FRT frit *glass* fritted fritting
FRT fruit *food*
FRT fruity *like fruit* fruitier
  fruitiest
FRTD fortuity *chance*
  fortuities
FRTD fretted *ridged*
FRTD frittata *omelet*
FRTD fritted *glass*
FRTD fruited *food-producing*
FRTDS fortuitous *lucky*
FRTF fortify *make strong*
  fortified fortifying fortifies
FRTFD fortified *enriched*
FRTFKSHN fortification

defense

FRTFL fretful (adj) *worrisome*
  fretfully (adv)
FRTFL frightful (adj)
  terrifying, extreme
  frightfully (adv)
FRTFL fruit fly *insect*
FRTFL fruitful (adj) *fertile*
  fruitfully (adv)
FRTFLNS fretfulness *worry*
FRTFLNS frightfulness
  terrifying, extreme
FRTFLNS fruitfulness
  fertility
FRTFR fortifier *strength*
FRTFT phreatophyte *deep*
  roots
FRTFYR fortifier *strength*
FRTH firth *inlet*
FRTH forth *forward*
FRTH fourth *of number 4*
FRTH froth *foam* froths
FRTH frothy *foamy* frothier
  frothiest
FRTHKLS fourth class *mail*
FRTHKMN forthcoming
  arriving, responsive
FRTHKMNG forthcoming
  arriving, responsive
FRTHL frothily *foam*
FRTHN farthing *money*
FRTHNG farthing *money*
FRTHNGKNG freethinking
  unbeliever
FRTHNGKR freethinker
  unbeliever
FRTHNKNG freethinking
  unbeliever
FRTHNKR freethinker
  unbeliever
FRTHNS frothiness *foam*
FRTHR farther *distance*
FRTHR free throw *sports*
FRTHR frothier *foam*
FRTHR further *distance*
FRTHRMR furthermore
  besides
FRTHRMST farthermost
  distance
FRTHRMST furthermost
  distance
FRTHRNS furtherance

advancement

FRTHRNTS furtherance
  advancement
FRTHRST furthest *distance*
FRTHRT forthright *frank*
FRTHST farthest *distance*
FRTHST frothiest *foam*
FRTHST furthest *distance*
FRTHSTT Fourth Estate
  press
FRTHT aforethought
  premeditated
FRTHT forethought *plan*
FRTHWL fare-thee-well
  goodbye
FRTHWTH forthwith
  immediately
FRTHYR frothier *foam*
FRTHYST frothiest *foam*
FRTJ freightage *load*
FRTJ fruitage *food*
FRTK ferritic *magnet*
FRTK phreatic *groundwater*
FRTKK fruitcake *food, crazy*
  one
FRTL fairy-tale (adj) *fantasy*
  fairy tale (n)
FRTL fertile (adj) *productive*
  fertilely (adv)
FRTL foretell *predict* foretold
  foretelling
FRTLD fertility *productivity*
FRTLD foretold *predict*
FRTLDRDL Fort Lauderdale
  city
FRTLNS fertileness
  productive
FRTLR foreteller *predict*
FRTLR fritillaria *herb*
FRTLR fritillary *butterfly*
  fritillaries
FRTLRY fritillaria *herb*
FRTLS effortless *easy*
FRTLS fretless *no ridge*
FRTLS fruitless *barren,*
  useless
FRTLSL effortlessly *with*
  ease
FRTLSNS effortlessness
  with ease
FRTLT fertility *productivity*
FRTLT fruitlet *food*

Use letters that best describe the sounds you hear and omit the vowels. Use **S** or **K** instead of **C**: to find circle use **SRKL**. Use **J** to find joy, **JM** to find gem and **G** to find go.

FRTLZ fertilize *make productive* fertilized fertilizing

FRTLZBL fertilizable *make productive*

FRTLZR fertilizer *make productive*

FRTLZSHN fertilization *make productive*

FRTN feuilleton *popular fiction*

FRTN fortune *luck, fate*

FRTN fourteen *number (14)*

FRTN frighten *scare*

FRTNS fruitiness *like fruit, crazy*

FRTNT fortnight *two weeks*

FRTNT fortunate *lucky*

FRTNTL fortnightly *two weeks*

FRTNTLR fortune-teller *predict*

FRTNZ fraternize *associate* fraternized fraternizing

FRTNZR fraternizer *associate*

FRTP ferrotype *photograph*

FRTPN fortepiano (n) *music* forte-piano (adv or adj)

FRTPYN fortepiano (n) *music* forte-piano (adv or adj)

FRTR a fortiori *conclusion*

FRTR ferreter *searcher*

FRTR fire-eater *performer*

FRTR freighter *ship*

FRTR fritter *(n) pancake (v) waste*

FRTR fruitier *like fruit, crazy*

FRTR offertory *(often capitalized) offering* offertories

FRTR phratry *tribe* phratries

FRTRD fair-trade (v, adj) *marketing* fair trade (n)

FRTRD free trade *open to all*

FRTRN FORTRAN (or) Fortran *computer*

FRTRN freight train *transport*

FRTRN fruitarian *diet*

FRTRND fraternity *organization* fraternities

FRTRNL fraternal (adj) *brotherly* fraternally (adv)

FRTRNLZM fraternalism *brotherly*

FRTRNT fraternity *organization* fraternities

FRTRNZ fraternize *associate* fraternized fraternizing

FRTRNZR fraternizer *associate*

FRTRNZSHN fraternization *association*

FRTRP firetrap *apt to burn*

FRTRR fritterer *waster*

FRTRR fruiterer *merchant*

FRTRS fortress *defense* fortresses

FRTRSD fratricide *kill a sibling*

FRTRSDL fratricidal *kill a sibling*

FRTRSTL fratricidal *kill a sibling*

FRTRYN fruitarian *diet*

FRTS fortis *pronunciation*

FRTS fretsaw *tool*

FRTS fritz *broken state*

FRTSM fortissimo *music* fortissimos (or) fortissimi

FRTST foretaste *nibble*

FRTST fruitiest *like fruit, crazy*

FRTT fortuity *chance* fortuities

FRTT frittata *omelet*

FRTTD fortitude *courage*

FRTTH fortieth *of number 40*

FRTTS fortuitous *lucky*

FRTTYD fortitude *courage*

FRTV furtive *secret*

FRTWD fortuity *chance* fortuities

FRTWD fruitwood *tree*

FRTWDS fortuitous *lucky*

FRTWG fright wig *hair*

FRTWRK fretwork *decoration*

FRTWRTH Fort Worth *city*

FRTWT fortuity *chance* fortuities

FRTWTS fortuitous *lucky*

FRTYDS fortuitous *lucky*

FRTYR a fortiori *conclusion*

FRTYR fruitier *like fruit, crazy*

FRTYST fruitiest *like fruit, crazy*

FRTYT fortuity *chance* fortuities

FRTYTH fortieth *of number 40*

FRTYTS fortuitous *lucky*

FRTYWD fortuity *chance* fortuities

FRTYWDS fortuitous *lucky*

FRTYWT fortuity *chance* fortuities

FRTYWTS fortuitous *lucky*

FRTZ forties *numbers 40-49*

FRVD fervid *intense*

FRVDL fervidly *intensely*

FRVDNS fervidness *intensity*

FRVLD frivolity *silliness* frivolities

FRVLS frivolous *unimportant*

FRVLT frivolity *silliness* frivolities

FRVNT fervent *intense*

FRVR fervor *intensity* (Br) fervour

FRVR forever *always*

FRVRMR forevermore *always*

FRVRNS foreverness *always*

FRVRS free verse *no rhyme*

FRVS effervesce *bubble* effervesced effervescing

FRVSNS effervescence *bubbles*

FRVSNT effervescent *bubbles*

FRVSNTS effervescence *bubbles*

FRW fairway *golf*

FRW faraway *distance*

FRW four-way *stop, tie*

FRW freeway *highway*

FRWD fireweed *plant*

FRWD firewood *fuel*

FRWDR firewater *liquor*

FRWL farewell *goodbye*

FRWL fire wall *structure*

FRWL four-wheel *vehicle*

FRWL freewheel *(n) gear (v)*

---

roll freely

FRWL freewill (adj) *voluntary*
free will (n)

FRWLN freewheeling
unrestrained

FRWLNG freewheeling
unrestrained

FRWLR four-wheeler *vehicle*

FRWLR freewheeler *(n) gear*
(v) roll freely

FRWMRKN Afro-American
African-American

FRWN Frauen (pl) *wife* Frau

FRWNG forewing *insect*

FRWNT forewent *preceded*

FRWRD foreword *preface*

FRWRD forward (adj) *front,*
brash (adv) ahead (v)
advance (n) sports

FRWRDL forwardly *front,*
brash

FRWRDLKNG forward-
looking *future*

FRWRDNS forwardness
front, brash

FRWRKS fireworks *display*

FRWRLD free world *(often*
capitalized) not controlled

FRWRN forewarn *alert*

FRWRX fireworks *display*

FRWSHN fruition *realization*

FRWST Far West *region*

FRWTHR fair-weather
during good times

FRWTR firewater *liquor*

FRWZHN Afro-Asian
African-Asian

FRXNL fraxinella *herb*

FRXTNGGWSHR fire
extinguisher *put out fire*

FRXTNGWSHR fire
extinguisher *put out fire*

FRY euphoria *elation*

FRY Freya *Norse goddess*

FRYBL friable *fragile*

FRYBLD friability *fragile*

FRYBLT friability *fragile*

FRYDFT phreatophyte *deep*
roots

FRYDK phreatic
groundwater

FRYJ ferriage *fare*

FRYN Freon *(trademark)*
coolant

FRYN frying *cooking*

FRYNBRD free on board
(abbr) F.O.B.

FRYNG frying *cooking*

FRYNGPN frying pan *utensil*

FRYNPN frying pan *utensil*

FRYNT euphoriant *drug*

FRYR farrier *horseshoes*

FRYR fierier *blazing*

FRYR friar *monk*

FRYR friary *monastery*
friaries

FRYR fryer *cooker, chicken*

FRYR furrier *fur dealer, hairy*

FRYR furriery *fur business*

FRYS furioso *music*

FRYS furious *angry, intense*

FRYSL furiously *angry,*
intense

FRYST fieriest *blazing*

FRYST furriest *hairy*

FRYTFT phreatophyte *deep*
roots

FRYTK phreatic *groundwater*

FRYTN feuilleton *popular*
fiction

FRZ aphorize *make adages*
aphorized aphorizing

FRZ fraise *barrier*

FRZ freesia *herb, flower*

FRZ freeze *ice, chill* froze
freezing frozen

FRZ fries *potatoes*

FRZ frieze *cloth, band*

FRZ frisé *cloth, band*

FRZ frizz *tight curls*

FRZ frizzy *curly* frizzier
frizziest

FRZ frowsy (or) frowzy
dowdy frowsier (or)
frowzier frowsiest (or)
frowziest

FRZ furze *grass*

FRZ furzy *grassy*

FRZ phrase *words* phrased
phrasing

FRZB Frisbee *(trademark)*
toy

FRZDR freeze-dry *process*

FRZDRD freeze-dried

processed

FRZFRM freeze-frame *film*

FRZH freesia *herb, flower*

FRZHN Afro-Asian *African-*
Asian

FRZHR fourragère *cord*

FRZHY freesia *herb, flower*

FRZL frazzle *unnerve*
frazzled frazzling

FRZL frizzle *burn, curl*
frizzled frizzling

FRZL phrasal (adj) *words*
phrasally (adv)

FRZLG phraseology
insincere words
phraseologies

FRZLJ phraseology
insincere words
phraseologies

FRZLJST phraseologist
insincere words

FRZM aphorism *adage*

FRZMCHZ forasmuch as *in*
view of

FRZN freezing *icy*

FRZN frozen *icy*

FRZNG freezing *icy*

FRZNG phrasing *expression*

FRZNL frozenly *icy*

FRZNS frizziness *curls*

FRZNS frozenness *ice*

FRZR freezer *cooler*

FRZR friseur *hairdresser*

FRZR frizzier *curls*

FRZR frowsier (or) frowzier
dowdy

FRZST frizziest *curls*

FRZST frowsiest (or)
frowziest *dowdy*

FRZT freeze-out (n) *exclude*
freeze out (v)

FRZY freesia *herb, flower*

FRZYLG phraseology
insincere words
phraseologies

FRZYLJ phraseology
insincere words
phraseologies

FRZYLJST phraseologist
insincere words

FRZYR frizzier *curls*

FRZYR frowsier (or) frowzier

Use letters that best describe the sounds you hear and omit the vowels. Use **S** or **K**
instead of **C**: to find circle use **SRKL**. Use **J** to find joy, **JM** to find gem and **G** to find go.

dowdy
FRZYST frizziest *curls*
FRZYST frowsiest (or)
frowziest *dowdy*
FS aphis *insect type* aphides
FS efface *rub out* effaced
effacing
FS effuse *pour out* effused
effusing
FS face *(v) confront, make
smooth* faced facing
FS face *(n) front, features,
surface*
FS fess *confess*
FS foci *(pl) intersection* focus
FS fossa *groove* fossae
FS fossa *animal* fossas
FS fosse (or) foss *ditch*
FS fuss *bother* fusses
FS fussy *neat* fussier
fussiest
FS office *work room, function,
rite*
FSBJT fussbudget *neat one*
FSBK fastback *vehicle*
FSBL effaceable *rub out*
FSBL fastball *pitch*
FSBL feasible *(adj) possible*
feasibly (adv)
FSBLD feasibility *possibility*
FSBLT feasibility *possibility*
FSBRK fast break *(n) sports
move* fast-break (v)
FSCHL fistula *passage*
fistulas (or) fistulae
FSCHLS fistulous *passage*
FSCHN fustian *fabric*
FSCHS fastuous *snobbish*
FSCHWS fastuous *snobbish*
FSD facade *front*
FSD fiesta *party* fiestas
FSD fusty *moldy* fustier
fustiest
FSDFS face-to-face *direct*
FSDGSHN fustigation
criticism
FSDGT fustigate *criticize*
fustigated fustigating
FSDK euphuistic *elegant
language*
FSDKFS fisticuffs *boxing*
FSDKL euphuistically

elegant language
FSDL festal *(adj) festive*
festally (adv)
FSDL fustily *moldy*
FSDN facedown *position*
FSDNS fustiness *moldy*
FSDR fester *(n) sore (v) rot,
rankle*
FSDR foster *promote, parent*
FSDR fustier *moldy*
FSDRJ fosterage *parenting*
FSDRR fosterer *promoter,
parent*
FSDRSHN frustration
dissatisfaction
FSDRT frustrate *prevent*
frustrated frustrating
FSDS Faustus (or) Faust
magician
FSDS offsides *sports*
FSDST fustiest *moldy*
FSDV festive *joyous*
FSDVD festivity *party*
festivities
FSDVL festival *party*
FSDVL festively *joyously*
FSDVNS festiveness *joy*
FSDVT festivity *party*
festivities
FSDYR fustier *moldy*
FSDYST fustiest *moldy*
FSDZ offsides *sports*
FSF face-off *confrontation*
FSFD fast food *(n) eating*
fast-food (adj)
FSFLPD phospholipid
lecithin
FSFPRTN phosphoprotein
casein
FSFR phosphor *radiant*
FSFRD fast-forward *tape*
FSFRK phosphoric *acid*
FSFRM fusiform *tapering*
FSFRS phosphoresce *glow*
phosphoresced
phosphorescing
FSFRS phosphorous *(adj)
containing phosphorus*
FSFRS phosphorus *(n)
element*
FSFRSNS
phosphorescence *glow*

FSFRSNT phosphorescent
glow
FSFRSNTS
phosphorescence *glow*
FSFRWRD fast-forward *tape*
FSFT phosphate *phosphoric
acid*
FSFT phosphite *phosphorous
acid*
FSFTZ phosphatize
phosphate
FSH aphasia *no words*
FSH fascia *band* fasciae (or)
fascias
(Br) facia
FSH fiche *microfilm* fiche
FSH fichu *scarf*
FSH fish *animal* fish (or)
fishes
FSH fish-eye *stare*
FSH fishy *smelly, dubious*
fishier fishiest
FSH fuchsia *flower*
FSH oafish *clumsy*
FSH offish *apart*
FSHBL fishbowl *aquarium*
FSHCHL fistula *passage*
fistulas (or) fistulae
FSHCHLS fistulous *passage*
FSHDD fasciated *bundled*
FSHFR fish fry *picnic*
FSHFRM fish farm *hatchery*
FSHK fish hawk *bird*
FSHK fishhook *device*
FSHKK fish cake *food*
FSHL facial *(adj, n) face*
facially (adv)
FSHL fascial *molding*
FSHL faucial *throat*
FSHL oafishly *clumsy*
FSHL official *(adj) legal*
officially (adv)
FSHLDM officialdom *class*
FSHLDR fish ladder
hatchery
FSHLDR officeholder *official*
FSHLK fishlike *aquatic*
FSHLS officialese *language*
FSHLTR fish ladder *hatchery*
FSHLZ officialese *language*
FSHLZM officialism
regulation

Letters aren't doubled for single sounds: to find alley use **L** not **LL**. Use **Y** and **W** as hard
sounds only: to find yellow use **YL**. (Br)=British spelling or usage. * See dictionary.

FSHML fish meal *fertilizer*
FSHMNGGR fishmonger *(Br) seller*
FSHMNGR fishmonger *(Br) seller*
FSHN effusion *poured out*
FSHN fashion *(n) style (v) shape*
FSHN fission *split*
FSHN fusion *melt*
FSHNBL fashionable *(adj) stylish* fashionably *(adv)*
FSHNBL fissionable *split*
FSHNBLT fissionability *split*
FSHNC efficiency *ability* efficiencies
FSHNMNGGR fashionmonger *stylish one*
FSHNMNGR fashionmonger *stylish one*
FSHNPLT fashion plate *stylish one*
FSHNR fashioner *shaper*
FSHNS efficiency *ability* efficiencies
FSHNS Ephesians *Bible*
FSHNS oafishness *clumsy*
FSHNT efficient *able*
FSHNT fishnet *net, fabric*
FSHNT officiant *priest*
FSHNTC efficiency *ability* efficiencies
FSHNTL efficiently *ably*
FSHNTS efficiency *ability* efficiencies
FSHNZ Ephesians *Bible*
FSHPLT fishplate *joint*
FSHPN fishpond *stocked pond*
FSHPND fishpond *stocked pond*
FSHR fisher *fisherman, animal*
FSHR fishery *fishing* fisheries
FSHR fishier *questionable*
FSHR fissure *split* fissured fissuring
FSHR officiary *officer* officiaries
FSHR offshore *ocean*
FSHRMN fisherman *fish*

catcher fishermen
FSHRWMN fisherwoman *fish catcher* fisherwomen
FSHS officious *rude*
FSHSDK fascistic (adj) *(often capitalized) oppressive government*
FSHSDKL fascistically (adv) *(often capitalized) oppressive government*
FSHSHN fasciation *intrigue*
FSHSHN officiation *leader, umpire*
FSHSL officiously *rudely*
FSHSNS officiousness *rudeness*
FSHST fascist *(often capitalized) oppressive government*
FSHST Fascista *Mussolini* Fascisti
FSHST fishiest *questionable*
FSHSTK fascistic (adj) *(often capitalized) oppressive government*
FSHSTK fish stick *food*
FSHSTKL fascistically (adv) *(often capitalized) oppressive government*
FSHSTR fish story *exaggeration*
FSHT officiate *lead, umpire* officiated officiating
FSHT offshoot *branch*
FSHTD fasciated *bundled*
FSHTL fishtail *swing wildly*
FSHWF fishwife *seller, vulgar woman*
FSHY fascia *band* fasciae (or) fascias
FSHYDD fasciated *bundled*
FSHYNT officiant *priest*
FSHYR fishier *questionable*
FSHYR officiary *officer* officiaries
FSHYSHN fasciation *intrigue*
FSHYSHN officiation *leader, umpire*
FSHYST fishiest *questionable*
FSHYT officiate *lead, umpire* officiated officiating

FSHYTD fasciated *bundled*
FSHZ facies *appearance* facies
FSHZM fascism *(often capitalized) oppressive government*
FSK aphasic *no words*
FSK fescue *stick, grass*
FSK fiasco *failure, flask* fiascoes
FSK fossick *search*
FSKL fascicle *bundle*
FSKL fiscal (adj) *finance* fiscally (adv)
FSKLR fascicular *bundle*
FSKLS fasciculus *bundle*
FSKLSHN fasciculation *bundle*
FSKLT fasciculate *bundle*
FSKLTH facecloth *towel*
FSKR fossicker *searcher*
FSKRD face card *jack, queen, king*
FSKRN offscreen *private*
FSKS fuscous *color*
FSKY fescue *stick, grass*
FSKYLR fascicular *bundle*
FSKYLS fasciculus *bundle*
FSKYLSHN fasciculation *bundle*
FSKYLT fasciculate *bundle*
FSL facile *easy*
FSL facilely *easily*
FSL fissile *split*
FSL fossil *remains*
FSL fusil *weapon*
FSL fusilli *pasta*
FSLD facility *structure, aptitude, bathroom* facilities
FSLD fissility *split*
FSLD fusillade *rapid fire*
FSLFRS fossiliferous *with remains*
FSLFT face-lift *surgery*
FSLJ fuselage *airplane*
FSLN fast lane *(n) highway* fast-lane (adj)
FSLND fusulinid *animal*
FSLNS facileness *ease*
FSLR fusilier (or) fusileer *soldier*

Use letters that best describe the sounds you hear and omit the vowels. Use **S** or **K** instead of **C**: to find circle use **SRKL**. Use **J** to find joy, **JM** to find gem and **G** to find go.

FSLS faceless *nondescript*
FSLSH fuselage *airplane*
FSLSS fascioliasis *disease*
  fascioliases
FSLT facility *structure,*
  aptitude, bathroom
  facilities
FSLT fissility *split*
FSLTDR facilitator *make easy*
FSLTDV facilitative *make*
  easy
FSLTSHN facilitation *make*
  easy
FSLTT facilitate *make easy*
  facilitated facilitating
FSLTTR facilitator *make easy*
FSLTTV facilitative *make easy*
FSLYSS fascioliasis *disease*
  fascioliases
FSLZ fossilize *become*
  remains fossilized
  fossilizing
  (Br) fossilise
FSLZH fuselage *airplane*
FSLZSHN fossilization
  become remains
  (Br) fossilisation
FSMNT effacement *erasure*
FSMSK face mask *helmet*
FSN facing *lining*
FSN fasten *secure*
FSND aficionado *fan*
  aficionados
FSNDN fascinating *attractive*
FSNDNG fascinating
  attractive
FSNDR fascinator *attractor*
FSNG facing *lining*
FSNN fastening *attach*
FSNNG fastening *attach*
FSNR fastener *attach*
FSNS fastness *secure,*
  colorfast, speed
FSNS fussiness *neatness*
FSNSHN fascination
  attraction
FSNT fascinate *attract*
  fascinated fascinating
FSNTN fascinating *attractive*
FSNTNG fascinating
  attractive
FSNTR fascinator *attractor*

FSP face up *(v) confront*
FSP faceup *(adv) position*
FSPD off-speed *slower*
FSPLT faceplate *attachment*
FSPRNG offspring *child*
  offspring
FSPT fusspot *neat one*
FSQ fescue *stick, grass*
FSQLR fascicular *bundle*
FSQLS fasciculus *bundle*
FSQLSHN fasciculation
  bundle
FSQLT fasciculate *bundle*
FSR effacer *one who rubs out*
FSR facer *(Br) obstacle*
FSR fussier *neater*
FSR officer *official*
FSS aphesis *lost vowel*
  apheses
FSSH facetiae *witticism*
FSSHS facetious *witty*
FSSHSL facetiously *wit*
FSSHSNS facetiousness *wit*
FSST fussiest *neatest*
FST euphuist *elegant*
  language
FST facet *side*
FST fast *(adv) quickly, deeply*
  (n, v) no food (adj) swift,
  *fixed**
FST faucet *water tap*
FST Faust *(or)* Faustus
  magician
FST feast *meal*
FST feisty *touchy* feistier
  feistiest
FST fiesta *party* fiestas
FST fist *hand*
FST foist *cheat or trick*
FST fusty *moldy* fustier
  fustiest
FST off-site *location*
FST offset *(v) balance* offset
  offsetting
FST offset *(n) shoot, foil,*
  *printing**
FSTBK fastback *vehicle*
FSTBL fastball *pitch*
FSTBRK fast break (n)
  sports move fast-break (v)
FSTDS fastidious *precise*
FSTDSL fastidiously

  precisely
FSTDSNS fastidiousness
  precision
FSTDYS fastidious *precise*
FSTDYSL fastidiously
  precisely
FSTDYSNS fastidiousness
  precision
FSTFD fast food (n) *eating*
  fast-food (adj)
FSTFRD fast-forward *tape*
FSTFRWRD fast-forward
  tape
FSTFS face-to-face *direct*
FSTGSHN fustigation
  criticism
FSTGT fustigate *criticize*
  fustigated fustigating
FSTJ offstage *behind scenes*
FSTK euphuistic *elegant*
  language
FSTK fast-talk *persuade*
FSTKFS fisticuffs *boxing*
FSTKL euphuistically *elegant*
  language
FSTL festal (adj) *festive*
  festally (adv)
FSTL fistula *passage* fistulas
  (or) fistulae
FSTL fustily *moldy*
FSTLN fast lane (n) *highway*
  fast-lane (adj)
FSTLS fistulous *passage*
FSTN festoon *ornament*
FSTNS fastness *secure,*
  colorfast, speed
FSTNS feistiness *touchy*
FSTNS fustiness *moldy*
FSTP f-stop *camera*
FSTR feistier *touchy*
FSTR fester *(n) sore (v) rot,*
  rankle
FSTR foster *promote, parent*
FSTR fustier *moldy*
FSTRDD frustrated
  prevented
FSTRDNG frustrating
  preventing
FSTRJ fosterage *parenting*
FSTRK fast track (n) *race*
  fast-track (v, adj)
FSTRR fosterer *promoter,*

Letters aren't doubled for single sounds: to find alley use **L** not **LL**. Use **Y** and **W** as hard sounds only: to find yellow use **YL**. (Br)=British spelling or usage. * See dictionary.

parent
FSTRSHN frustration
dissatisfaction
FSTRT frustrate *prevent*
frustrated frustrating
FSTRTD frustrated *prevented*
FSTRTN frustrating
preventing
FSTRTNG frustrating
preventing
FSTS fastuous *snobbish*
FSTS Faustus (or) Faust
magician
FSTST feistiest *touchy*
FSTST fustiest *moldy*
FSTV festive *joyous*
FSTVD festivity *party*
festivities
FSTVL festival *party*
FSTVL festively *joyously*
FSTVNS festiveness *joy*
FSTVT festivity *party*
festivities
FSTWS fastuous *snobbish*
FSTYR feistier *touchy*
FSTYR fustier *moldy*
FSTYST feistiest *touchy*
FSTYST fustiest *moldy*
FSV effusive *pouring*
FSVL face value *apparent*
worth
FSVLY face value *apparent*
worth
FSVN face-saving *honor*
FSVNG face-saving *honor*
FSYLSS fascioliasis *disease*
fascioliases
FSYLYSS fascioliasis *disease*
fascioliases
FSYND aficionado *fan*
aficionados
FSYR fussier *neater*
FSYST fussiest *neatest*
FSZ apheses (pl) *lost vowel*
aphesis
FSZ fasces *emblem*
FSZ fauces *throat*
FSZ feces *dung*
FSZN off-season *less activity*
FT afoot *under way*
FT aft *rear*
FT effete *worn out*

FT fat (v) *make obese* fatted
fatting
FT fat (adj) *plump, wealthy*
fatter fattest
FT fat (n) *grease, obesity*
FT fate *destiny* fated fating
FT fatty (adj) *with fat* fattier
fattiest
FT fatty (n) *obese one* fatties
FT feat *act, deed*
FT feet (pl) *measure, lower*
end, appendage foot
FT feta *cheese*
FT fête (or) fete (v) *honor*
fêted (or) feted fêting (or)
feting
FT fête (or) fete (n) *feast*
FT fiat *decree*
FT fight *battle* fought fighting
FT fit (v) *conform, tailor,*
*belong** fitted fitting
FT fit (adj) *suitable, healthy*
fitter fittest
FT fit (n) *spasms*
FT foot (n) *measure, lower*
end, appendage feet
FT foot (v) *pay, dance, move*
FT fought (v-past) *fight*
FT fount *source*
FT oft *often*
FT photo *camera* photos
FTBK fatback *pork*
FTBL football *sports*
FTBRD footboard *platform*
FTBRJ footbridge *pedestrian*
FTBTH footbath *wash*
FTC footsie (or) footsy *game*
FTCHN fettuccine (or)
fettuccini (or) fettucine
(or) fettucini *pasta*
FTD fated *destined*
FTD fatted *made fat*
FTD fatuity *stupidity* fatuities
FTD fetid *smelly*
FTD fitted *sized*
FTD footed *with feet*
FTDD fuddy-duddy
conservative fuddy-
duddies
FTDK fatidic (or) fatidical
prophecy
FTDKL fatidical (or) fatidic

prophecy
FTDRGNG foot-dragging
slowness
FTDT fuddy-duddy
conservative fuddy-
duddies
FTDZM faddism *style phase*
FTFB photophobia
sensitivity to light
FTFBK photophobic
sensitive to light
FTFBY photophobia
sensitivity to light
FTFGS phytophagous *eat*
plants
FTFL fateful (adj) *destiny*
fatefully (adv)
FTFL fitful (adj) *seldom* fitfully
(adv)
FTFL footfall *step*
FTFLD photoflood *lamp*
FTFLJLT phytoflagellate
algae
FTFLNS fatefulness *destiny*
FTFLNS fitfulness *seldom*
FTFLSH photoflash *camera*
photoflashes
FTFLT foot fault (n)
infraction footfault (v)
FTFNSH photo finish *race*
FTFR photophore *spot*
FTFRST feetfirst *lower end*
first
FTFST photo-offset *printing*
FTFZ photophase *cycle*
FTG fatigue *tire* fatigued
fatiguing
FTGBL fatigable *tired*
FTGBLD fatigability *tiredness*
FTGBLT fatigability *tiredness*
FTGNGL fatiguingly *tiring*
FTGNK photogenic *light,*
picture
FTGNKL photogenically
light, picture
FTGNL fatiguingly *tiring*
FTGRF photograph *camera*
FTGRF photography *picture*
taking
FTGRFK photographic
camera
FTGRFKL photographically

Use letters that best describe the sounds you hear and omit the vowels. Use **S** or **K** instead of **C**: to find circle use **SRKL**. Use **J** to find joy, **JM** to find gem and **G** to find go.

camera
FTGRFR photographer
camera
FTGRVR photogravure
printing
FTGRVYR photogravure
printing
FTH faith *belief* faiths
FTH fifth *of number 5* fifths
FTHBKS off-the-books *not
recorded*
FTHBX off-the-books *not
recorded*
FTHD fathead *idiot*
FTHDD fatheaded *idiotic*
FTHDDL fatheadedly *idiotic*
FTHDDNS fatheadedness
idiotic
FTHFL faithful (adj) *loyal*
faithfully (adv)
FTHKF off-the-cuff
unplanned
FTHL foothill *small mountain*
FTHL foothold *step, base*
FTHLD foothold *step, base*
FTHLM ophthalmia
inflammation
FTHLMK ophthalmic *eye*
FTHLMLG ophthalmology
eye
FTHLMLJ ophthalmology
eye
FTHLMLJK ophthalmologic
(or) ophthalmological
(adj) *eye*
ophthalmologically (adv)
FTHLMLJKL
ophthalmological (or)
ophthalmologic (adj) *eye*
ophthalmologically (adv)
FTHLMLJST
ophthalmologist *eye*
FTHLMSKP
ophthalmoscope
instrument
FTHLMSKPK
ophthalmoscopic
instrument
FTHLMY ophthalmia
inflammation
FTHLS faithless *disloyal*
FTHLSL faithlessly *disloyal*

FTHLSNS faithlessness
disloyal
FTHM fathom (v) *probe,
understand* (n) *depth*
FTHMBL fathomable *probe,
understand*
FTHMLG ophthalmology *eye*
FTHMLJ ophthalmology *eye*
FTHMLJK ophthalmologic
(or) ophthalmological
(adj) *eye*
ophthalmologically (adv)
FTHMLJKL
ophthalmological (or)
ophthalmologic (adj) *eye*
ophthalmologically (adv)
FTHMLJST ophthalmologist
eye
FTHMLS fathomless *deep,
mystery*
FTHMLSL fathomlessly
deep, mystery
FTHMLSNS fathomlessness
deep, mystery
FTHMSKP ophthalmoscope
instrument
FTHMSKPK
ophthalmoscopic
instrument
FTHN farthing *money*
FTHNG farthing *money*
FTHR farther *distance*
FTHR father (v) *beget* (n)
sire, priest
FTHR feather (n) *bird plume*
(v) *change angle, blur, add
feathers*
FTHR feathery *light*
FTHRBD feather bed (n)
mattress
FTHRBD featherbed (v, adj)
hire extras
FTHRBDN featherbedding
hiring extras
FTHRBDNG featherbedding
hiring extras
FTHRBRN featherbrain *fool*
FTHRBRND featherbrained
foolish
FTHRBTNG featherbedding
hiring extras
FTHRHD fatherhood *parent*

FTHRJ featheredge *thin
edge*
FTHRK off-the-rack *ready-
made*
FTHRKRD off-the-record
confidential
FTHRL fatherly *parental*
FTHRLN fatherland *country*
FTHRLND fatherland
country
FTHRLNS fatherliness
parental
FTHRLS fatherless *no parent*
FTHRMN phytohormone
plants
FTHRMST farthermost
distance
FTHRN feathering *plumage*
FTHRNG feathering *plumage*
FTHRNL father-in-law
spouse's father fathers-in-
law
FTHRSTCH featherstitch
sewing
FTHRWT featherweight *119-
126 pounds*
FTHRZNL fathers-in-law (pl)
spouse's father father-in-
law
FTHSHLF off-the-shelf *in
stock*
FTHSS phthisis *tuberculosis*
phthises
FTHST farthest *distance*
FTHWL off-the-wall *weird,
unplanned*
FTJ footage *length*
FTJNK photogenic *light,
picture*
FTJNKL photogenically
light, picture
FTJRNLST photojournalist
pictures
FTJRNLZM
photojournalism *pictures*
FTK euphotic *water plants*
FTK ophitic *rock*
FTK photic *light*
FTKL photically *light*
FTKMKL photochemical
(adj) *light*
photochemically (adv)

Letters aren't doubled for single sounds: to find alley use **L** not **LL**. Use **Y** and **W** as hard
sounds only: to find yellow use **YL**. (Br)=British spelling or usage. * See dictionary.

FTKMKL phytochemical (adj) *plants* phytochemically (adv)

FTKMSDR photochemistry *light*

FTKMSTR photochemistry *light*

FTKMSTR phytochemistry *plants*

FTKNDK photokinetic *motion*

FTKNDL foot-candle *light measure*

FTKNSS photokinesis *motion*

FTKNTK photokinetic *motion*

FTKP photocopy *duplicate* photocopied photocopying photocopies

FTKPR photocopier *duplicator*

FTKPYR photocopier *duplicator*

FTKRM phytochrome *protein*

FTKT fat cat (n) *big shot* fat-cat (adj)

FTL effetely *worn out*

FTL fatal (adj) *deadly* fatally (adv)

FTL fetal *unborn* (Br) foetal

FTL fettle *health*

FTL feudal (adj) *medieval* feudally (adv)

FTL fiddle (v) *tinker, cheat, play violin* fiddled fiddling

FTL fiddle (n) *violin*

FTL fuddle *intoxicate* fuddled fuddling

FTL futile (adj) *useless* futilely (adv)

FTLD fatality *death* fatalities

FTLD futility *uselessness* futilities

FTLDK photolytic *broken down*

FTLDKL photolytically *broken down*

FTLFTL fiddle-faddle

nonsense

FTLG fetology *fetus*

FTLJ fetology *fetus*

FTLJST fetologist *fetus*

FTLK fetlock *hair*

FTLKR footlocker *trunk*

FTLKTRK photoelectric *light*

FTLNG fiddling *petty*

FTLNS futileness *uselessness*

FTLR fiddler *violin, cheat*

FTLRKRB fiddler crab *animal*

FTLS footless *no foot*

FTLS footloose *free*

FTLSDK fatalistic *predetermined*

FTLSDKL fatalistically *predetermined*

FTLSS photolysis *breakdown*

FTLST fatalist *predetermined*

FTLSTK fatalistic *predetermined*

FTLSTKL fatalistically *predetermined*

FTLSTKS fiddlesticks *nonsense*

FTLT fatality *death* fatalities

FTLT futility *uselessness* futilities

FTLTHGRF photolithograph *picture*

FTLTHGRF photolithography *process*

FTLTK photolytic *broken down*

FTLTKL photolytically *broken down*

FTLTS footlights *stage*

FTLZ photolyze *break down* photolyzed photolyzing

FTLZM fatalism *predetermined*

FTMDR photometer *brightness*

FTMN footman *servant*

FTMNTJ photomontage *picture* ·

FTMNTSH photomontage *picture*

FTMNTZH photomontage *picture*

FTMP photomap *atlas*

FTMRK footmark *footprint*

FTMRL photomural *picture*

FTMS ofttimes (or) oftentimes *repeatedly*

FTMSHN photoemission *release*

FTMST aftmost *rear*

FTMTR photometer *brightness*

FTMTR photometry *brightness*

FTMTRK photometric *brightness*

FTMYRL photomural *picture*

FTMZ ofttimes (or) oftentimes *repeatedly*

FTN fatten *enlarge*

FTN feuilleton *popular fiction*

FTN fitting *suitable, adjusting*

FTN footing *step, base*

FTN fountain *water*

FTN futon *bed* futons

FTN often *many times*

FTN phaeton *carriage*

FTN photon *particle of light*

FTN phyton *stem*

FTNG fitting *suitable, adjusting*

FTNG footing *step, base*

FTNGDV photonegative *opposite*

FTNGL fittingly *suitable*

FTNGRV photoengrave *printing*

FTNGRVNG photoengraving *printing*

FTNGTV photonegative *opposite*

FTNHD fountainhead *origin*

FTNS effeteness *worn out*

FTNS fattiness *with fat*

FTNS fitness *health*

FTNT footnote *explanation*

FTNTMS oftentimes (or) ofttimes *repeatedly*

FTNTMZ oftentimes (or) ofttimes *repeatedly*

FTPD footpad *thief*

FTPLNGKDN phytoplankton *plants*

FTPLNGKTN phytoplankton

plants
FTPLNKDN phytoplankton *plants*
FTPLNKTN phytoplankton *plants*
FTPN foot-pound *work measure* foot-pounds
FTPND foot-pound *work measure* foot-pounds
FTPRNT footprint *impression*
FTPTH footpath *pedestrians*
FTPTHJN phytopathogen *parasite*
FTPTHLG phytopathology *parasites*
FTPTHLJ phytopathology *parasites*
FTPTHLJKL phytopathological *parasites*
FTPZDV photopositive *reactive*
FTPZTV photopositive *reactive*
FTR after *later than*
FTR ephedra *shrub*
FTR fatter *obese*
FTR fattier *with more fat*
FTR feature *(v) imagine, star* featured featuring
FTR fetter *(v) restrain (n) chain*
FTR fighter *battler*
FTR fitter *tailor, healthier*
FTR fodder *food*
FTR future *yet to come*
FTRBRNR afterburner *jet device*
FTRBRTH afterbirth *placenta*
FTRD featured *main part*
FTRD futurity *yet to come* futurities
FTRDK afterdeck *rear*
FTRFK aftereffect *result*
FTRFKT aftereffect *result*
FTRGL afterglow *light*
FTRK offtrack *wager*
FTRKLP afterclap *surprise*
FTRKR aftercare *post-hospital care*
FTRLF afterlife *life after death*
FTRLG futurology *trends*

FTRLJ futurology *trends*
FTRLJKL futurological *trends*
FTRLJST futurologist *trends*
FTRLS featureless *bland*
FTRMJ afterimage *vision*
FTRMRKT aftermarket *accessories*
FTRMST aftermost *rear end*
FTRMTH aftermath *result*
FTRNN afternoon *day period*
FTRP footrope *sail*
FTRPS afterpiece *comedy*
FTRRZ after-hours *after closing time*
FTRS afters *(Br) dessert*
FTRS footrace *contest*
FTRSDK futuristic *yet to come*
FTRSHK aftershock *tremor*
FTRSHV aftershave *lotion*
FTRSPDR photoreceptor *receiver*
FTRSPTR photoreceptor *receiver*
FTRST footrest *support*
FTRST futurist *predictor*
FTRSTK futuristic *yet to come*
FTRT featurette *short film*
FTRT foot rot *disease*
FTRT futurity *yet to come* futurities
FTRTHT afterthought *late idea*
FTRTKS after-tax *amount remaining*
FTRTM aftertime *future*
FTRTST aftertaste *persistent sensation*
FTRTX after-tax *amount remaining*
FTRWRD afterward (or) afterwards *later*
FTRWRD afterword *epilogue*
FTRWRDZ afterwards (or) afterward *later*
FTRWRL afterworld *world after death*
FTRWRLD afterworld *world after death*
FTRWRZ after-hours *after*

closing time
FTRZ afters *(Br) dessert*
FTRZM futurism *mechanics*
FTS fatso *obese one* fatsoes
FTS fatuous *silly*
FTS fetus *unborn* (Br) foetus
FTS footsie (or) footsy *game*
FTSD feticide *fetus death*
FTSDRL phytosterol *plants*
FTSFR photosphere *solar surface*
FTSH faddish *style phase*
FTSH fattish *plump*
FTSH fetish *charm, fixation*
FTSHNS faddishness *style phase*
FTSHST fetishist *magic, devotion*
FTSHSTK fetishistic *magic, devotion*
FTSHSTKL fetishistically *magic, devotion*
FTSHZM fetishism *magic, devotion*
FTSKP fetoscope *exam tube*
FTSKP fetoscopy *examination* fetoscopies
FTSL fat cell *adipose*
FTSL fatuously *silly*
FTSNSDV photosensitive *light*
FTSNSTV photosensitive *light*
FTSNSTZ photosensitize *light*
FTSNTHDK photosynthetic *plants*
FTSNTHDKL photosynthetically *plants*
FTSNTHSS photosynthesis *plants*
FTSNTHSZ photosynthesize *plants* photosynthesized photosynthesizing
FTSNTHTK photosynthetic *plants*
FTSNTHTKL photosynthetically *plants*
FTSR footsore *pain*
FTST fattest *obese*

Letters aren't doubled for single sounds: to find alley use **L** not **LL**. Use **Y** and **W** as hard sounds only: to find yellow use **YL**. (Br)=British spelling or usage. * See dictionary.

FTST fattiest *with most fat*
FTST fittest *healthy*
FTSTL footstool *support*
FTSTN footstone *grave*
FTSTP footstep *tread*
FTSTRL phytosterol *plants*
FTSTT Photostat *(trademark) copier*
FTSTT photostat *copy*
FTT fatuity *stupidity* fatuities
FTTKSK phytotoxic *plant killer*
FTTKSSD phytotoxicity *plant killer*
FTTKSST phytotoxicity *plant killer*
FTTRPK phototropic *stimulus*
FTTRPKL phototropically *stimulus*
FTTXK phytotoxic *plant killer*
FTTXSD phytotoxicity *plant killer*
FTTXST phytotoxicity *plant killer*
FTVLTK photovoltaic *electricity*
FTVLTYK photovoltaic *electricity*
FTW fatwa *decree*
FTWD fatuity *stupidity* fatuities
FTWD fatwood *fuel*
FTWDD fat-witted *stupid*
FTWFST photo-offset *printing*
FTWLKTRK photoelectric *light*
FTWMSHN photoemission *release*
FTWNGRV photoengrave *printing*
FTWNGRVNG photoengraving *printing*
FTWNGRVR photoengraver *printing*
FTWR footwear *shoes*
FTWRK footwork *movement*
FTWS fatuous *silly*
FTWSL fatuously *silly*
FTWT fatuity *stupidity*

fatuities
FTWTD fat-witted *stupid*
FTYD fatuity *stupidity* fatuities
FTYR fattier *with more fat*
FTYRD futurity *yet to come* futurities
FTYRLJKL futurological *trends*
FTYRLJST futurologist *trends*
FTYRT futurity *yet to come* futurities
FTYST fattiest *with most fat*
FTYT fatuity *stupidity* fatuities
FTYWD fatuity *stupidity* fatuities
FTYWT fatuity *stupidity* fatuities
FTZ futz *(slang) fool around*
FTZK phthisic *tuberculosis*
FTZKL phthisical *tuberculosis*
FV fauve *(often capitalized) art*
FV fava *bean*
FV five *number (5)*
FV fovea *pit, eye* foveae
FVFL fivefold *times five*
FVFLD fivefold *times five*
FVL foveal *pit, eye*
FVNDTN five-and-ten *discount store*
FVNN favonian *mild*
FVNTN five-and-ten *discount store*
FVNYN favonian *mild*
FVR favor *(v) oblige, endow, prefer (n) approval, behalf, token**
(Br) favour
FVR fever *(n) temperature, craze (v) agitate*
FVR fiver *five dollars*
FVRBL favorable *(adj) helpful* favorably *(adv)*
FVRBLNS favorableness *helpfulness*
FVRD favored *helpful*
FVRSH feverish *intense, hot*
FVRSHL feverishly *intense,*

hot
FVRSHNS feverishness *intense, hot*
FVRT favorite *(n) loved one, winner (adj) popular*
FVRTZM favoritism *attraction*
FVRWRT feverwort *herb*
FVST fauvist *(often capitalized) art*
FVSTR five-star *excellent*
FVT foveate *pit, eye*
FVY fovea *pit, eye* foveae
FVYL foveal *pit, eye*
FVYT foveate *pit, eye*
FVZM fauvism *(often capitalized) art*
FVZM favism *allergy*
FW phooey *(interj) disgust*
FWGR foie gras *liver*
FWL foul *(n) sports (v) pollute, block*
FWL foul (adj) *not fair, dirty* foully (adv)
FWL foully *dirty, indecent*
FWL fowl *bird* fowl (or) fowls
FWL fuel *(v) stimulate, sustain* fueled (or) fuelled fueling (or) fuelling
FWL fuel *(n) energy source*
FWLBL foul ball *bad hit*
FWLMTHD foulmouthed *indecent*
FWLMTHT foulmouthed *indecent*
FWLN foul line *out of bounds*
FWLN fouling *deposit*
FWLNG fouling *deposit*
FWLNS foulness *indecency, pollution*
FWLP foul up (v) *error foul-up (n)*
FWLPL foul play *crime*
FWLSHT foul shot *sports*
FWLSL fuel cell *battery*
FWLT foul out *sports*
FWLTP foul tip *sports*
FWLWD fuelwood *tree*
FWR fewer *not many*
FWR off-hour *time*
FWSDK euphuistic *elegant language*

Use letters that best describe the sounds you hear and omit the vowels. Use **S** or **K** instead of **C**: to find circle use **SRKL**. Use **J** to find joy, **JM** to find gem and **G** to find go.

FWSDKL euphuistically *elegant language*
FWST euphuist *elegant language*
FWSTK euphuistic *elegant language*
FWSTKL euphuistically *elegant language*
FWT fouette *ballet*
FWT off-white *color*
FWY foyer *lobby*
FWZM euphuism *elegant language*
FX affix *attach*
FX fax *transmit document*
FX fix *(v) mend, arrange, spay (n) dose, predicament** fixes
FX folksy *humble* folksier folksiest
FX fox *animal* foxes
FX foxy *sly* foxier foxiest
FXBL affixable *attach*
FXBL fixable *mend*
FXCHR fixture *attachment*
FXD fixity *solidness* fixities
FXDD fixated *held*
FXDL fixedly *unmoving*
FXDNS fixedness *unmoving*
FXDV fixative *protection*
FXFR fox fire *light*
FXFYR fox fire *light*
FXGRP fox grape *plant*
FXHN foxhound *dog*
FXHND foxhound *dog*
FXL forecastle *ship area*
FXL foxhole *ditch*
FXL foxily *cleverly*
FXML facsimile *copy*
FXMNT affixment *attachment*
FXNG folk song *traditional tune*
FXNGR folksinger *musician*
FXNGS fixings *food*
FXNGZ fixings *food*
FXNS fixings *food*
FXNS foxiness *cleverness*
FXNZ fixings *food*
FXR fixer *mender*
FXR folksier *humble*
FXR foxier *clever*
FXSHN affixation *attachment*
FXSHN fixation *obsession*

FXST folksiest *humble*
FXST foxiest *clever*
FXT fixate *stare, hold* fixated fixating
FXT fixed *unmoving*
FXT fixity *solidness* fixities
FXTD fixated *held*
FXTL foxtail *tail, grass*
FXTPNT fixed-point *math*
FXTR fixture *attachment*
FXTRR fox terrier *dog*
FXTRT fox-trot *dance music*
FXTRT Foxtrot *code word*
FXTRT foxtrot *dance*
FXTRYR fox terrier *dog*
FXTV fixative *protection*
FXYR folksier *humble*
FXYR foxier *clever*
FXYST folksiest *humble*
FY feijoa *shrub*
FY few *not many*
FY foyer *lobby*
FYCHR future *yet to come*
FYCHRD futurity *yet to come* futurities
FYCHRLG futurology *trends*
FYCHRLJ futurology *trends*
FYCHRLJKL futurological *trends*
FYCHRLJST futurologist *trends*
FYCHRSDK futuristic *yet to come*
FYCHRSDKL futuristically *yet to come*
FYCHRST futurist *predictor*
FYCHRSTK futuristic *yet to come*
FYCHRSTKL futuristically *yet to come*
FYCHRT futurity *yet to come* futurities
FYCHRZM futurism *mechanics*
FYD feud *quarrel*
FYDL feudal (adj) *medieval* feudally (adv)
FYDL futile (adj) *useless* futilely (adv)
FYDLNS futileness *uselessness*
FYDLSDK feudalistic

medieval
FYDLSTK feudalistic *medieval*
FYDLZM feudalism *medieval*
FYDTR feudatory *allegiance* feudatories
FYG fugu *fish*
FYG fugue *music*
FYGL fugal (adj) *music* fugally (adv)
FYGSD fugacity *vapor*
FYGSHS fugacious *short-lived*
FYGST fugacity *vapor*
FYJDV fugitive (adj) *transient (n) escapee*
FYJTV fugitive (adj) *transient (n) escapee*
FYKD fucoid *rockweed*
FYKS fucose *sugar*
FYKS fucus *algae*
FYL faille *fabric*
FYL file (v) *arrange, initiate action, line up** filed filing
FYL file (n) *scraper, folder, line*
FYL foil (n) *thin metal, sword, contrast (v) thwart*
FYL fuel (v) *stimulate, sustain* fueled (or) fuelled fueling (or) fuelling
FYL fuel (n) *energy source*
FYL phial *bottle*
FYLJNS fuliginous *murky*
FYLJNSL fuliginously *murky*
FYLN filing *fragment, action*
FYLNG filing *fragment, action*
FYLR filer *scrape, arrange, initiate action*
FYLSL fuel cell *battery*
FYLT fealty *tenant* fealties
FYLWD fuelwood *tree*
FYM fume *smoke, anger* fumed fuming
FYMGDR fumigator *disinfect*
FYMGNT fumigant *disinfectant*
FYMGSHN fumigation *disinfect*
FYMGT fumigate *disinfect* fumigated fumigating
FYMGTR fumigator *disinfect*

FYMRL fumarole *volcano*
FYMRZ fumarase *enzyme*
FYNKL funiculi (pl) *cord* funiculus
FYNKLR funicular *railway*
FYNKLS funiculus *cord* funiculi
FYNKYL funiculi (pl) *cord* funiculus
FYNKYLR funicular *railway*
FYNKYLS funiculus *cord* funiculi
FYNQL funiculi (pl) *cord* funiculus
FYNQLR funicular *railway*
FYNQLS funiculus *cord* funiculi
FYNRL funeral *burial*
FYNRL funereal (adj) *solemn* funereally (adv)
FYNRR funerary *burial*
FYNRYL funereal (adj) *solemn* funereally (adv)
FYNS affiance *betroth* affianced affiancing
FYNS fiancé (m) *one engaged* fiancée (f)
FYNT affiant *deponent*
FYNTS affiance *betroth* affianced affiancing
FYNTS fiancé (m) *one engaged* fiancée (f)
FYR afire *on fire*
FYR fewer *not many*
FYR fiery *blazing* fierier fieriest
FYR fire (n) *flame*
FYR fire (v) *ignite, expel from work* fired firing
FYR foyer *lobby*
FYR führer (or) fuehrer *dictator*
FYR fury *rage* furies
FYR Fury *Greek myth* Furies
FYRBG firebug *arsonist*
FYRBKS firebox *furnace* fireboxes
FYRBL fireball *flame*
FYRBM firebomb *explosive*
FYRBRK firebreak *cleared land*
FYRBRK firebrick *furnace*

FYRBRN firebrand *agitator*
FYRBRND firebrand *agitator*
FYRBRTHNG fire-breathing *aggressive*
FYRBT fireboat *put out fires*
FYRBX firebox *furnace* fireboxes
FYRD fired *using fuel, job loss*
FYRD fjord *inlet*
FYRDG firedog *andiron*
FYRDMP firedamp *gas*
FYRDR fire-eater *performer*
FYRFDR firefighter *fireman*
FYRFL firefly *insect* fireflies
FYRFT firefight *battle*
FYRFTR firefighter *fireman*
FYRKL fireclay *mud*
FYRKRKR firecracker *fireworks*
FYRKSTNGGWSHR fire extinguisher *put out fire*
FYRKSTNGWSHR fire extinguisher *put out fire*
FYRLK firelock *gun*
FYRLT firelight *glow*
FYRMN fireman *firefighter* firemen
FYRN firing *heat, dismissal*
FYRNG firing *heat, dismissal*
FYRNGKL furuncle *boil*
FYRNGKLSS furunculosis *boils furunculoses*
FYRNGKYLSS furunculosis *boils furunculoses*
FYRNGQLSS furunculosis *boils furunculoses*
FYRNJN fire-engine (adj) *vehicle* fire engine (n)
FYRNKL furuncle *boil*
FYRNKLSS furunculosis *boils furunculoses*
FYRNKYLSS furunculosis *boils furunculoses*
FYRNQLSS furunculosis *boils furunculoses*
FYRNS fieriness *blazing*
FYRNT fire ant *insect*
FYRPLG fireplug *hydrant*
FYRPLS fireplace *hearth*
FYRPR firepower *weapons*
FYRPRF fireproof *no flames*

FYRPT firepot *missile, food*
FYRPWR firepower *weapons*
FYRR fierier *blazing*
FYRR firer *launcher, dismisser, igniter*
FYRR führer (or) fuehrer *dictator*
FYRR furor *rage* (Br) furore
FYRRM firearm *weapon*
FYRS furioso *music*
FYRS furious *angry, intense*
FYRSD fireside *hearth*
FYRSKP fire escape *ladder*
FYRSL fire sale *low prices*
FYRSL furiously *angry, intense*
FYRST fieriest *blazing*
FYRSTP fire-stop *material*
FYRSTRM firestorm *flames, outburst*
FYRTR fire-eater *performer*
FYRTRP firetrap *apt to burn*
FYRWD fireweed *plant*
FYRWD firewood *fuel*
FYRWDR firewater *liquor*
FYRWL fire wall *structure*
FYRWRKS fireworks *display*
FYRWRX fireworks *display*
FYRWTR firewater *liquor*
FYRXTNGGWSHR fire extinguisher *put out fire*
FYRXTNGWSHR fire extinguisher *put out fire*
FYRYR fierier *blazing*
FYRYS furioso *music*
FYRYS furious *angry, intense*
FYRYSL furiously *angry, intense*
FYRYST fieriest *blazing*
FYS effuse *pour out* effused effusing
FYSD fiesta *party*
FYSDK euphuistic *elegant language*
FYSDKL euphuistically *elegant language*
FYSFRM fusiform *tapering*
FYSH fuchsia *flower*
FYSHN effusion *poured out*
FYSHN fusion *melt*
FYSK fiasco *failure, flask*

Use letters that best describe the sounds you hear and omit the vowels. Use **S** or **K** instead of **C**: to find circle use **SRKL**. Use **J** to find joy, **JM** to find gem and **G** to find go.

fiascoes
FYSL fusil *weapon*
FYSL fusilli *pasta*
FYSLD fusillade *rapid fire*
FYSLJ fuselage *airplane*
FYSLND fusulinid *animal*
FYSLR fusilier (or) fusileer
　soldier
FYSLSH fuselage *airplane*
FYSLZH fuselage *airplane*
FYST euphuist *elegant*
　language
FYST fiesta *party*
FYSTK euphuistic *elegant*
　language
FYSTKL euphuistically
　elegant language
FYSV effusive *pouring*
FYT fiat *decree*
FYTL feudal (adj) *medieval*
　feudally (adv)
FYTL futile (adj) *useless*
　futilely (adv)
FYTLD futility *uselessness*
　futilities
FYTLNS futileness
　uselessness
FYTLT futility *uselessness*
　futilities
FYTN feuilleton *popular*
　fiction
FYTRD futurity *yet to come*
　futurities
FYTRLJKL futurological
　trends
FYTRLJST futurologist
　trends
FYTRT futurity *yet to come*
　futurities
FYTYRD futurity *yet to come*
　futurities
FYTYRLJKL futurological
　trends
FYTYRLJST futurologist
　trends
FYTYRT futurity *yet to come*
　futurities
FYW feijoa *shrub*
FYWL fuel (v) *stimulate,*
　sustain fueled (or) fuelled
　fueling (or) fuelling
FYWL fuel (n) *energy source*

FYWLSL fuel cell *battery*
FYWLWD fuelwood *tree*
FYWR fewer *not many*
FYWSDK euphuistic *elegant*
　language
FYWSDKL euphuistically
　elegant language
FYWST euphuist *elegant*
　language
FYWSTK euphuistic *elegant*
　language
FYWSTKL euphuistically
　elegant language
FYWZM euphuism *elegant*
　language
FYZ effuse *pour out* effused
　effusing
FYZ fuse (v) *combine* fused
　fusing
FYZ fuse (n) *electricity,*
　explosive
FYZ fusee *pulley, flare*
FYZBL fusible *combine*
FYZBLD fusibility *combine*
FYZBLT fusibility *combine*
FYZFRM fusiform *tapering*
FYZHN effusion *poured out*
FYZHN fusion *melt*
FYZL fusil *weapon*
FYZLJ fuselage *airplane*
FYZLND fusulinid *animal*
FYZLR fusilier (or) fusileer
　soldier
FYZLZH fuselage *airplane*
FYZM euphuism *elegant*
　language
FYZV effusive *pouring*
FZ effuse *pour out* effused
　effusing
FZ faze *disturb* fazed fazing
FZ fez *hat* fezzes
FZ fizz *bubbles*
FZ fizzy *bubbly*
FZ fuse (v) *combine* fused
　fusing
FZ fuse (n) *electricity,*
　explosive
FZ fusee *pulley, flare*
FZ fuzz *fur, blur*
FZ fuzzy *fur, blur* fuzzier
　fuzziest
FZ phase (v) *adjust,*

　introduce phased phasing
FZ phase (n) *part, cycle*
FZBL feasible (adj) *possible*
　feasibly (adv)
FZBL fusible *combine*
FZBLD feasibility *possibility*
FZBLD fusibility *combine*
FZBLT feasibility *possibility*
FZBLT fusibility *combine*
FZDN phasedown *reduction*
FZFRM fusiform *tapering*
FZGNM physiognomy
　appearances
　physiognomies
FZGRF physiography
　geography
FZGRFK physiographic
　geography
FZGRFR physiographer
　geography
FZH aphasia *no words*
FZHN effusion *poured out*
FZHN fission *split*
FZHN fusion *melt*
FZHNBL fissionable *split*
FZHNBLT fissionability *split*
FZHNS Ephesians *Bible*
FZHNZ Ephesians *Bible*
FZHR fissure *split* fissured
　fissuring
FZK aphasic *no words*
FZK phasic *synchronized*
FZK physic *heal* physicked
　physicking
FZK physique *body shape*
FZKL physical (n) *exam*
FZKL physical (adj) *material,*
　physics physically (adv)
FZKLD physicality *material*
FZKLNS physicalness
　material
FZKLSDK physicalistic
　materialism
FZKLST physicalist
　materialism
FZKLSTK physicalistic
　materialism
FZKLT physicality *material*
FZKLZM physicalism
　materialism
FZKMKL physiochemical
　(adj) *substances*

physiochemically (adv)
FZKS physics *natural science*
FZL fizzle *hiss, weaken*
fizzled fizzling
FZL foozle *bungle* foozled
foozling
FZL fusil *weapon*
FZL fuzzily *fur, blur*
FZLG physiology *functions*
FZLJ fuselage *airplane*
FZLJ physiology *functions*
FZLJK physiologic (or)
physiological (adj)
functioning
physiologically (adv)
FZLJKL physiological (or)
physiologic (adj)
functioning
physiologically (adv)
FZLJST physiologist
function
FZLND fusulinid *animal*
FZLR fusilier (or) fusileer
soldier
FZLZH fuselage *airplane*
FZM euphuism *elegant*
language
FZNM physiognomy
appearances
physiognomies
FZNS fuzziness *fur, blur*
FZNT pheasant *bird*
pheasant (or) pheasants
FZPTHLG physiopathology
function
FZPTHLJ physiopathology
function
FZPTHLJK
physiopathologic (or)
physiopathological
function
FZPTHLJKL
physiopathological (or)
physiopathologic *function*
FZR fuzzier *fur, blur*
FZSHN physician *doctor*
FZSST physicist *natural*
science
FZST fuzziest *fur, blur*
FZT phaseout (n) *stop phase*
out (v)
FZTHRP physiotherapy

treatment physiotherapies
FZTHRPST physiotherapist
treatment
FZTRST physiatrist *doctor*
FZV effusive *pouring*
FZX physics *natural science*
FZYGNM physiognomy
appearances
physiognomies
FZYGRF physiography
geography
FZYGRFK physiographic
geography
FZYGRFR physiographer
geography
FZYKMKL physiochemical
(adj) *substances*
physiochemically (adv)
FZYLG physiology *functions*
FZYLJ physiology *functions*
FZYLJK physiologic (or)
physiological (adj)
functioning
physiologically (adv)
FZYLJKL physiological (or)
physiologic (adj)
functioning
physiologically (adv)
FZYLJST physiologist
function
FZYNM physiognomy
appearances
physiognomies
FZYPTHLG
physiopathology *function*
FZYPTHLJ physiopathology
function
FZYPTHLJK
physiopathologic (or)
physiopathological
function
FZYPTHLJKL
physiopathological (or)
physiopathologic *function*
FZYR fuzzier *fur, blur*
FZYST fuzziest *fur, blur*
FZYTHRP physiotherapy
treatment physiotherapies
FZYTHRPST
physiotherapist *treatment*
FZYTRST physiatrist *doctor*

G

G aggie *marble, agricultural*
G agh (or) agghhh *(interj)*
frustration
G ago *in the past*
G ague *fever*
G edgy *nervous* edgier
edgiest
G egg *fertile cell*
G ego *self-esteem* egos
G g *alphabet letter* g's (or) gs
G Gaea *earth goddess*
G gay *happy, homosexual*
G gee *(interj) wonder*
G ghee (or) ghi *butter*
G go *(v) move, leave, elapse**
went gone going goes
G go *(n) try, game* goes
G goo *mush*
G gooey *sticky*
G goy *Gentile* goyim
G guy *(n) rope, fellow (v)*
ridicule
G ogee *molding*
G ugh *(interj) distaste*
G yuga *Hindu age*
GB gab *talk* gabbed
gabbing
GB gabby *talkative* gabbier
gabbiest
GB gib *cat, metal plate*
GB gob *sailor, lump, (Br)*
mouth
GB gobo *shield* gobos
GB goby *fish* gobies
GB good-bye (or) good-by
farewell
GBDR eggbeater *mixer*
GBFST gabfest *lots of talk*
GBL gabble *talk*
GBL gable *roof*
GBL gobble *eat* gobbled
gobbling
GBLD gabled *roof*

Use letters that best describe the sounds you hear and omit the vowels. Use **S** or **K**
instead of **C**: to find circle use **SRKL**. Use **J** to find joy, **JM** to find gem and **G** to find go.

GBLDGK gobbledygook *jargon*
GBLN goblin *ogre*
GBLR gobbler *turkey*
GBLS Goebbels *propagandist*
GBLT goblet *cup*
GBN gibbon *ape*
GBR gabber *talker*
GBR gabbier *chatty*
GBR goober *peanut*
GBRDN gabardine *fabric*
GBRNTRL gubernatorial *governor*
GBRNTRYL gubernatorial *governor*
GBS gobs *(slang) lots*
GBSN Gibson *drink, hairdo*
GBST gabbiest *chatty*
GBT gobbet *lump*
GBTR eggbeater *mixer*
GBTWN go-between *mediator*
GBYR gabbier *chatty*
GBYST gabbiest *chatty*
GBZ gobs *(slang) lots*
GC gassy *windy* gassier gassiest
GC goosey *nervous* goosier goosiest
GCDP gussied up *overdress*
GCH gaucho *cowboy* gauchos
GCHK Gottschalk *composer*
GCNS gassiness *wind*
GCP gussy up *overdress* gussied up gussying up gussies up
GCR gassier *windy*
GCR goosier *nervous*
GCS gaseous *with gas*
GCST gassiest *windy*
GCST goosiest *nervous*
GCYP gussy up *overdress* gussied up gussying up gussies up
GCYR gassier *windy*
GCYR goosier *nervous*
GCYS gaseous *with gas*
GCYST gassiest *windy*
GCYST goosiest *nervous*
GD agouti *rodent*

GD egad (or) egads *mild oath*
GD gad *(v) wander* gadded gadding
GD gad *(n) chisel*
GD gaiety *joy* gaieties
GD galleta *grass*
GD gaud *trinket*
GD gaudy *(adj) showy* gaudier gaudiest
GD gaudy *(n-Br) dinner* gaudies
GD geode *rock*
GD ghetto *city area* ghettos
GD gid *disease*
GD giddy *lightheaded, dizzy* giddier giddiest
GD goad *prod*
GD god *(often capitalized) deity*
GD good *wholesome, kind, skillful* better best*
GD good day *greeting*
GD goody (or) goodie *treat* goodies
GD Gouda *cheese*
GD guide *(v) lead, direct* guided guiding
GD guide *(n) inform, positioning device*
GDB good-bye (or) good-by *farewell*
GDBK guidebook *handbook*
GDBL guidable *direction*
GDBT gadabout *socialite*
GDC geodesy *math*
GDCHL godchild *baptism*
GDCHLD godchild *baptism*
GDD gaited *step*
GDD gated *door*
GDD guided *directed*
GDDK geodetic *math*
GDDR goddaughter *baptism (f)*
GDF Gadhafi (or) Qadhafi (or) Khadafy *Libyan leader*
GDFL gadfly *insect* gadflies
GDFL god-awful *terrible*
GDFRN God-fearing *devout*
GDFRNG God-fearing *devout*
GDFRNTHN good-for-

nothing *without value*
GDFRNTHNG good-for-nothing *without value*
GDFRSKN godforsaken *desolate*
GDFTHR godfather *sponsor*
GDG guide dog *blind guide*
GDGD goody-goody *proper*
GDHD godhead *divinity*
GDHD godhood *divinity*
GDHMRD good-humored *cheerful* (Br) good-humoured
GDHRDD good-hearted *kind*
GDHRTD good-hearted *kind*
GDHYMRD good-humored *cheerful* (Br) good-humoured
GDK geoduck *clam*
GDL gaudily *showy*
GDL giddily *dizzy*
GDL Godel *mathematician*
GDL godly *divine* godlier godliest
GDL goodly *kind, ample, pleasing* goodlier goodliest
GDLHR Guadalajara *city*
GDLK godlike *all knowing*
GDLKN good-looking *attractive*
GDLKNG good-looking *attractive*
GDLN guideline *rope, outline*
GDLNS godliness *divine*
GDLNS goodliness *kind, ample, pleasing*
GDLP Guadeloupe *islands*
GDLR godlier *divine*
GDLR goodlier *kind, ample, pleasing*
GDLS godless *no divinity*
GDLST godliest *divine*
GDLST goodliest *kind, ample, pleasing*
GDLYR godlier *divine*
GDLYR goodlier *kind, ample, pleasing*
GDLYST godliest *divine*
GDLYST goodliest *kind,*

Letters aren't doubled for single sounds: to find alley use **L** not **LL**. Use **Y** and **W** as hard sounds only: to find yellow use **YL**. (Br)=British spelling or usage. * See dictionary.

ample, pleasing
GDML Guatemala *country*
GDMTHR godmother
sponsor
GDN guidon *flag*
GDNBR good-neighbor (adj)
cooperator
(Br) good-neighbour
GDNCHRD good-natured
cheerful
GDNS gaudiness *showy*
GDNS giddiness *lightheaded,*
dizzy
GDNS goodness *kindness*
GDNS guidance *direction*
GDNSK Gdansk *city*
GDNT good night *farewell*
GDNTRD good-natured
cheerful
GDNTS guidance *direction*
GDP get up (v) *arise, arrange*
GDP getup (n) *outfit*
GDPNDG get-up-and-go
energy
GDPNG get-up-and-go
energy
GDPRCH gutta-percha *latex*
GDPRNT godparent *sponsor*
GDPST guidepost *sign*
GDR gaiter *shoe*
GDR gaudery *finery*
GDR gaudier *showy*
GDR giddier *dizzy*
GDR goiter *gland*
(Br) goitre
GDR guider *leader*
GDR gutter (n) *trough* (v)
channel (adj) *vulgar*
GDRL guttural *throaty*
GDRN guttering *trough*
GDRNG guttering *trough*
GDRS goitrous *gland*
GDRSNP guttersnipe *street*
person
GDS egads (or) egad *mild*
oath
GDS gatehouse *building*
GDS geodesy *math*
GDS goddess *female deity*
goddesses
GDSH goatish *lustful*
GDSK geodesic

construction, line
GDSN godsend *desirable*
event
GDSN godson *baptism* (m)
GDSND godsend *desirable*
event
GDSPD Godspeed *success*
GDSST geodesist *math*
GDST gaudiest *showy*
GDST giddiest *dizzy*
GDSZD goodsized *big*
GDSZT goodsized *big*
GDT godet *inset*
GDTK geodetic *math*
GDTMPRD good-tempered
calm
GDTR goddaughter *baptism*
(f)
GDVL go-devil *device*
GDW getaway *escape*
GDW guideway *track*
GDWL gadwall *duck*
gadwalls (or) gadwall
GDWL goodwill *concern,*
popularity
GDWZ ghettoize *separate*
ghettoized ghettoizing
GDWZSHN ghettoization
separation
GDYR gaudier *showy*
GDYR giddier *dizzy*
GDYST gaudiest *showy*
GDYST giddiest *dizzy*
GDZ egads (or) egad *mild*
oath
GDZ ghettoize *separate*
ghettoized ghettoizing
GDZBRG Gettysburg *city*
GDZKS gadzooks (interj)
oath
GDZSHN ghettoization
separation
GDZX gadzooks (interj) *oath*
GF gaff (n) *spear, ordeal, trick*
(v) *hook, deceive*
GF gaffe *blunder*
GF golf *sport*
GF goof *error*
GF goofy *silly* goofier
goofiest
GF guff *nonsense*
GF guffaw *laugh*

GF gulf *gap, body of water*
GFBL golf ball *sphere*
GFDD gifted *talented*
GFF goof-off (n) *idle* goof off
(v)
GFG geophagy *nutrition*
GFJ geophagy *nutrition*
GFKRS golf course *land*
GFL gleeful (adj) *happy*
gleefully (adv)
GFL goofily *silly*
GFL guileful (adj) *tricky*
guilefully (adv)
GFLNS gleefulness
happiness
GFLTFSH gefilte fish *food*
GFN geophone *vibrations*
GFNS goofiness *silly*
GFR gaffer *old man,* (Br)
foreman
GFR gofer (slang) *servant*
GFR goffer *crimp*
GFR golfer *sportsman*
GFR goofier *silly*
GFR gopher *animal*
GFRP gift wrap *decorate*
GFST goofiest *silly*
GFT geophyte *plant*
GFT gift *present*
GFTD gifted *talented*
GFTRP gift wrap *decorate*
GFTWR giftware *presents*
GFVKB Gulf of Aqaba *body*
of water
GFVLSK Gulf of Alaska *body*
of water
GFVMKSK Gulf of Mexico
body of water
GFVMN Gulf of Oman *body*
of water
GFVMXK Gulf of Mexico
body of water
GFVSWZ Gulf of Suez *body*
of water
GFVSZ Gulf of Suez *body of*
water
GFVTLN Gulf of Thailand
body of water
GFVTLND Gulf of Thailand
body of water
GFWD gulfweed *seaweed*
GFWR giftware *presents*

Use letters that best describe the sounds you hear and omit the vowels. Use **S** or **K**
instead of **C**: to find circle use **SRKL**. Use **J** to find joy, **JM** to find gem and **G** to find go.

GFYR goofier *silly*
GFYST goofiest *silly*
GFZKL geophysical (adj) *earth* geophysically (adv)
GFZKS geophysics *earth*
GFZSST geophysicist *earth*
GFZX geophysics *earth*
GG a-go-go *disco*
GG agog *curious*
GG gag (v) *choke, silence* gagged gagging
GG gag (n) *restraint*
GG gaga *crazy*
GG gewgaw *bauble*
GG gig (v) *spear* gigged gigging
GG gig (n) *boat, job*
GG go-go *disco*
GGBT gigabyte *computer storage*
GGDR go-getter *enthusiast*
GGHRTS gigahertz *frequency*
GGK gagaku *music*
GGL gaggle *flock*
GGL giggle *laugh* giggled giggling
GGL giggly *laughing*
GGL goggle *stare* goggled goggling
GGL googol *number*
GGLD goggle-eyed *stare*
GGLPLKS googolplex *number*
GGLPLX googolplex *number*
GGLR giggler *laugh*
GGLR goggler *stare*
GGLZ goggles *glasses*
GGMN gagman *comedian* gagmen
GGN Gauguin *artist*
GGPLKS googolplex *number*
GGPLX googolplex *number*
GGR gagger *choke, silence*
GGRF geography *earth* geographies
GGRFK geographic (or) geographical *earth*
GGRFKL geographical (or) geographic (adj) *earth* geographically (adv)

GGRFR geographer *earth*
GGRKNR Geiger counter *detector*
GGRKNTR Geiger counter *detector*
GGRKTR Geiger counter *detector*
GGTR go-getter *enthusiast*
GGWT gigawatt *power*
GGWZ goo-goo eyes *affection*
GGZ goo-goo eyes *affection*
GH agh (or) agghhh (interj) *frustration*
GHD egghead *intellectual*
GHD go-ahead *start*
GHDD eggheaded *intellectual*
GHDDNS eggheadedness *intellectual*
GJ gage *pledge*
GJ gauge *measure* gauged gauging
GJ gouge *chisel, poke* gouged gouging
GJD gauged *sized*
GJN gaijin *foreigner* gaijin
GJN gudgeon *pivot, journal, fish*
GJR gauger *measure*
GJR gouger *scoop*
GJT gadget *device*
GK gawk *stare*
GK gawky *clumsy* gawkier gawkiest
GK gecko *lizard* geckos (or) geckoes
GK geek *side show*
GK geeky *nerd*
GK gook (*vulgar*) *Asian*
GKL gawkily *clumsy*
GKM guaiacum *tree*
GKML guacamole *food*
GKNS gawkiness *clumsy*
GKP eggcup *egg holder*
GKR gawkier *clumsy*
GKRM egg cream *drink*
GKRT go-cart *vehicle*
GKS egg case *enclosure*
GKSH gawkish *clumsy*
GKST gawkiest *clumsy*
GKYR gawkier *clumsy*

GKYST gawkiest *clumsy*
GL Aglaia *a Grace*
GL aglow *light*
GL eagle *bird*
GL gaily *with joy*
GL gal *female*
GL gala *party*
GL galah *bird*
GL gale *wind*
GL galea *helmet*
GL gall (n) *bile, swelling* (v) *irritate*
GL galley *ship* galleys
GL galop *dance*
GL ghoul *demon*
GL gill *fish lung,* (Br) *ravine*
GL gillie *shoe*
GL glee *happiness*
GL gley *clay*
GL glia *cell*
GL glow *shine*
GL glue *stick* glued gluing
GL glue *adhesive*
GL gluey *sticky*
GL goal *purpose, score*
GL goalie *player*
GL gold *element, color*
GL golly (interj) *surprise*
GL guile *trickery*
GL gull *bird*
GL gully *ditch* gullies
GL igloo *ice house* igloos
GL ogle *stare* ogled ogling
GL Ugli (trademark) *fruit*
GL ugly *not pretty* uglier ugliest
GLB glebe *soil*
GLB glib *without concern* glibber glibbest
GLB glob *small mass*
GLB globby *blob*
GLB globe *sphere*
GLBD globoid *round*
GLBFLR globeflower *buttercup*
GLBFLWR globeflower *buttercup*
GLBFSH globefish *puffer*
GLBG goldbug *investor*
GLBL glabella *between eyebrows* glabellae
GLBL glibly *without concern*

Letters aren't doubled for single sounds: to find alley use **L** not **LL**. Use **Y** and **W** as hard sounds only: to find yellow use **YL**. (Br)=British spelling or usage. * See dictionary.

GLBL global (adj) *spherical, worldwide* globally (adv)

GLBL globule *droplet*

GLBL gullible (adj) *easily duped* gullibly (adv)

GLBLD gullibility *easily duped*

GLBLDR gallbladder *bile sac*

GLBLN globulin *protein*

GLBLR glabellar *between eyebrows*

GLBLR globular *round*

GLBLSDM glioblastoma *tumor* glioblastomas (or) glioblastomata

GLBLSDMD glioblastomata (pl) *tumor* glioblastoma

GLBLSDMT glioblastomata (pl) *tumor* glioblastoma

GLBLST globalist *worldwide*

GLBLSTM glioblastoma *tumor* glioblastomas (or) glioblastomata

GLBLSTMD glioblastomata (pl) *tumor* glioblastoma

GLBLSTMT glioblastomata (pl) *tumor* glioblastoma

GLBLT gullibility *easily duped*

GLBLTR gallbladder *bile sac*

GLBLZ globalize *make worldwide* globalized globalizing (Br) globalise

GLBLZM globalism *worldwide*

GLBLZSHN globalization *worldwide* (Br) globalisation

GLBN globin *protein*

GLBNS glibness *without concern*

GLBR glibber *without concern*

GLBRK goldbrick (*v*) *swindle* (n) *worthless item, shirker*

GLBRS glabrous *smooth*

GLBRSNT glabrescent *smooth*

GLBRT gilbert *force*

GLBRTLNZ Gilbert Islands *land mass*

GLBST glibbest *without concern*

GLBTRDNG globe-trotting *travelling*

GLBTRDR globe-trotter *traveller*

GLBTRTNG globe-trotting *travelling*

GLBTRTR globe-trotter *traveller*

GLBYL globule *droplet*

GLBYLN globulin *protein*

GLBYLR globular *round*

GLC glassie (or) glassy *(n) marble* glassies

GLC glassy *(adj) dull, clear* glassier glassiest

GLC glossy *(adj) shiny, smooth* glossier glossiest

GLC glossy *(n) photograph* glossies

GLCH glitch *error*

GLCH gulch *ravine* gulches

GLCLG glaciology *ice*

GLCLJ glaciology *ice*

GLCN glycine *amino acid*

GLCNS glossiness *shiny, smooth*

GLCR glacier *ice*

GLCR glassier *dull, clear*

GLCR glossier *shiny, smooth*

GLCSHN glaciation *ice*

GLCST glassiest *dull, clear*

GLCST glossiest *shiny, smooth*

GLCT glaciate *freeze* glaciated glaciating

GLCYLG glaciology *ice*

GLCYLJ glaciology *ice*

GLCYR glacier *ice*

GLCYR glassier *dull, clear*

GLCYR glossier *shiny, smooth*

GLCYSHN glaciation *ice*

GLCYST glassiest *dull, clear*

GLCYST glossiest *shiny, smooth*

GLCYT glaciate *freeze* glaciated glaciating

GLD eagle-eyed *vision*

GLD geld *castrate*

GLD gild *coat with gold*

gilded (or) gilt gilding

GLD gilled *with gills*

GLD glad *happy* gladder gladdest

GLD glade *open space*

GLD glede *bird*

GLD gleyed *clay*

GLD glide *slide* glided gliding

GLD glutei (pl) *muscle* gluteus

GLD gold *element, color*

GLD guild *union*

GLD guilty *blameworthy* guiltier guiltiest

GLDBG goldbug *investor*

GLDBRK goldbrick (*v*) *swindle* (n) *worthless item, shirker*

GLDDR gladiator *warrior*

GLDFL goldfield *mines*

GLDFLD gold-filled *filling*

GLDFLD goldfield *mines*

GLDFNCH goldfinch *bird*

GLDFSH goldfish *animal*

GLDGR gold digger *charmer*

GLDHN glad-hand (v) *welcome* glad hand (n)

GLDHND glad-hand (v) *welcome* glad hand (n)

GLDHNDR glad-hander *welcomer*

GLDJ gilt-edge (or) gilt-edged *gold, best quality*

GLDJD gilt-edged (or) gilt-edge *gold, best quality*

GLDL gladioli (pl) *flower* gladiolus

GLDL gladly *happily*

GLDL glottal *throat*

GLDL gluteal *muscle*

GLDL guiltily *blameworthy*

GLDLF gold leaf *foil*

GLDLS gladiolus *flower* gladioli (or) gladiolus

GLDMN glutamine *chemical*

GLDMT glutamate *chemical*

GLDN gelding *animal*

GLDN gladden *make happy*

GLDN gluten *protein*

GLDN gluttony *greed* gluttonies

Use letters that best describe the sounds you hear and omit the vowels. Use **S** or **K** instead of **C**: to find circle use **SRKL**. Use **J** to find joy, **JM** to find gem and **G** to find go.

GLDN golden *color*
GLDN goldeneye *bird*
GLDN gulden *money*
  guldens (or) gulden
GLDNCL goldenseal *flower*
GLDNG gelding *animal*
GLDNGL gloatingly *brag*
GLDNJ golden age
  prosperity
GLDNJR golden-ager *retiree*
GLDNRD goldenrod *flower*
GLDNS gladness *joy*
GLDNS glutenous *dough*
GLDNS glutinous *gummy*
GLDNS gluttonous *greedy*
GLDNS guiltiness
  blameworthy
GLDNSHN agglutination
  clump
GLDNSL goldenseal *flower*
GLDNT agglutinate *clump*
  agglutinated
  agglutinating
GLDR aglitter *shiny*
GLDR gilder *coat with gold*
GLDR gladder *happy*
GLDR glider *airplane*
GLDR glitter *sparkle*
GLDR glittery *sparkle*
GLDR gloater *braggart*
GLDR guilder *money*
GLDR guiltier *blameworthy*
GLDRD glitterati *celebrities*
GLDRNGL glitteringly
  sparkling
GLDRT glitterati *celebrities*
GLDS glottis *vocal cords*
  glottises (or) glottides
GLDS gluteus *muscle* glutei
GLDSM gladsome *joyful*
GLDSMKSMS gluteus
  maximus *muscle* glutei
  maximi
GLDSMN guildsman
  unionist guildsmen
GLDSMTH goldsmith *dealer*
GLDSMXMS gluteus
  maximus *muscle* glutei
  maximi
GLDST gladdest *happy*
GLDST guiltiest *blameworthy*
GLDSTN gladstone *suitcase*

GLDSTN goldstone *glass*
GLDTR gladiator *warrior*
GLDY glutei (pl) *muscle*
  gluteus
GLDYDR gladiator *warrior*
GLDYL gladioli (pl) *flower*
  gladiolus
GLDYL gluteal *muscle*
GLDYLS gladiolus *flower*
  gladioli (or) gladiolus
GLDYR guiltier *blameworthy*
GLDYS gluteus *muscle* glutei
GLDYSMKSMS gluteus
  maximus *muscle* glutei
  maximi
GLDYSMXMS gluteus
  maximus *muscle* glutei
  maximi
GLDYST guiltiest
  blameworthy
GLDYTR gladiator *warrior*
GLDZMN guildsman
  unionist guildsmen
GLF glyph *symbol*
GLF gold leaf *foil*
GLF golf *sport*
GLF gulf *gap, body of water*
GLF uglify *make ugly* uglified
  uglifying uglifies
GLFBL golf ball *sphere*
GLFK glyphic *symbol*
GLFKRS golf course *land*
GLFKSHN uglification *not*
  pretty
GLFL gallfly *insect* gallflies
GLFL Gallophile *France lover*
GLFL goldfield *mines*
GLFLD gold-filled *filling*
GLFLD goldfield *mines*
GLFLR gillyflower *carnation*
GLFLWR gillyflower
  carnation
GLFR golfer *sportsman*
GLFSH goldfish *animal*
  goldfish
GLFVKB Gulf of Aqaba *body*
  of water
GLFVLSK Gulf of Alaska
  body of water
GLFVMKSK Gulf of Mexico
  body of water
GLFVMN Gulf of Oman *body*

  of water
GLFVMXK Gulf of Mexico
  body of water
GLFVSWZ Gulf of Suez
  body of water
GLFVSZ Gulf of Suez *body*
  of water
GLFVTLN Gulf of Thailand
  body of water
GLFVTLND Gulf of Thailand
  body of water
GLFWD gulfweed *seaweed*
GLG galago *animal* galagos
GLG geology *life history*
  geologies
GLG gulag *labor camp*
GLGD Gielgud (John) *actor*
GLGNT gelignite *dynamite*
GLHD Galahad *knight*
GLJK geologic (or)
  geological *life history*
GLJKL geological (or)
  geologic (adj) *life history*
  geologically (adv)
GLJST geologist *life history*
GLJZ geologize *life history*
  geologized geologizing
GLK Gaelic *Scottish*
GLK Gallic *French*
GLK gallic *acid*
GLKC galaxy *stars* galaxies
GLKDK galactic *galaxy*
GLKGN glucagon *hormone*
GLKJN glycogen *sugar*
GLKK goal kick *sports*
GLKL glycol *chemical*
GLKLDK glycolytic
  breakdown
GLKLK glycolic (or) glycollic
  chemical
GLKLSS glycolysis
  breakdown
GLKLTK glycolytic
  breakdown
GLKM glaucoma *eye disease*
GLKNDK glauconitic
  mineral
GLKNK gluconic *chemical*
GLKNSPL glockenspiel
  music
GLKNT glauconite *mineral*
GLKNT gluconate *acid*

Letters aren't doubled for single sounds: to find alley use **L** not **LL**. Use **Y** and **W** as hard sounds only: to find yellow use **YL**. (Br)=British spelling or usage. * See dictionary.

GLKNTK glauconitic *mineral*
GLKPR goalkeeper *player*
GLKS galax *herb*
GLKS galaxy *stars* galaxies
GLKS glaucous *color*
GLKS glucose *sugar*
GLKSD glucoside *sugar*
GLKSL glycosyl *chemical*
GLKSN gloxinia *flower*
GLKSNS glaucousness *color*
GLKSNY gloxinia *flower*
GLKTK galactic *galaxy*
GLKTR galactorrhea *milk*
GLKTRY galactorrhea *milk*
GLKTS galactose *sugar*
GLKTSL galactosyl *sugar*
GLKZN gloxinia *flower*
GLKZNY gloxinia *flower*
GLL galilee *chapel*
GLL Galilee *region, city*
GLL glial *cell*
GLL uglily *unattractive*
GLM agleam *shiny*
GLM gallium *element*
GLM gleam *light*
GLM glioma *tumor* gliomas (or) gliomata
GLM glom *steal, catch* glommed glomming
GLM gloom *darkness, despair*
GLM gloomy *darkness, despair* gloomier gloomiest
GLM glum *sullen* glummer glummest
GLM golem *blockhead*
GLM guillemet *mark*
GLMD gliomata (pl) *tumor* glioma
GLMF galumph *clumsy tread*
GLMFR gallimaufry *mix* gallimaufries
GLML gloomily *darkness, despair*
GLML glumly *sullen*
GLMN gloaming *dusk*
GLMNG gloaming *dusk*
GLMNS gloominess *darkness, despair*
GLMNS glumness *sullen attitude*

GLMNSTR Gila monster *lizard*
GLMPS glimpse *peek* glimpsed glimpsing
GLMPSR glimpser *peeker*
GLMR glamour (or) glamor *spell, attractive*
GLMR glimmer *spark*
GLMR glomera (pl) *blood* glomus
GLMR gloomier *darkness, despair*
GLMR glummer *sullen*
GLMRL glomerule *flower part*
GLMRL glomeruli (pl) *tuft* glomerulus
GLMRLR glomerular *blood*
GLMRLS glomerulus *tuft* glomeruli
GLMRNG glimmering *spark*
GLMRPS glamour-puss *attractive one*
GLMRS glamorous *stylish*
GLMRSHN agglomeration *mass*
GLMRT agglomerate *mass* agglomerated agglomerating
GLMRYL glomerule *flower part*
GLMRYL glomeruli (pl) *tuft* glomerulus
GLMRYLR glomerular *blood*
GLMRYLS glomerulus *tuft* glomeruli
GLMRZ glamorize *style* glamorized glamorizing (Br) glamorise
GLMRZR glamorizer *style* (Br) glamoriser
GLMS glomus *blood* glomera
GLMST gloomiest *darkness, despair*
GLMST glummest *sullen*
GLMT gliomata (pl) *tumor* glioma
GLMT guillemot *bird*
GLMYR gloomier *darkness, despair*
GLMYST gloomiest

darkness, despair
GLN euglena *algae*
GLN galena *mineral*
GLN galleon *ship*
GLN galling *vexing*
GLN gallon *measure*
GLN galloon *trimming*
GLN gland *bodily organ*
GLN glean *pick up*
GLN glen *valley*
GLN gluon *particle*
GLN goal line *score*
GLNBL gleanable *pick up*
GLND euglenoid *algae*
GLND gland *bodily organ*
GLNDLR glandular *physical*
GLNDR gillnetter *fish net*
GLNDRD glandered *diseased*
GLNDRS glanders *disease*
GLNDRZ glanders *disease*
GLNDYLR glandular *physical*
GLNDZ glandes (pl) *penis* glans
GLNG galling *vexing*
GLNGL galingale *grass*
GLNGL gallingly *vexing*
GLNGL glowingly *shine*
GLNGR glengarry *cap* glengarries
GLNJ gallonage *measure*
GLNJLR glandular *physical*
GLNL gallinule *bird*
GLNL glowingly *shine*
GLNLR glandular *physical*
GLNNGZ gleanings *tidbits*
GLNNZ gleanings *tidbits*
GLNPLD glen plaid *pattern*
GLNPR gallinipper *insect*
GLNR gleaner *pick up*
GLNS glance *touch, peek* glanced glancing
GLNS glans *penis* glandes
GLNS ugliness *not pretty*
GLNSHS gallinaceous *fowl*
GLNSN glancing *indirect*
GLNSNG glancing *indirect*
GLNT gallant *brave, civil*
GLNT gillnet (v) *fish net* gill net (n)
GLNT glint *shine*
GLNTL gallantly *brave, civil*

Use letters that best describe the sounds you hear and omit the vowels. Use **S** or **K** instead of **C**: to find circle use **SRKL**. Use **J** to find joy, **JM** to find gem and **G** to find go.

GLNTN eglantine *sweetbrier*
GLNTR gallantry *courtesy* gallantries
GLNTR gillnetter *fish net*
GLNTS glance *touch, peek* glanced glancing
GLNTSN glancing *indirect*
GLNTSNG glancing *indirect*
GLNYL gallinule *bird*
GLNYLR glandular *physical*
GLNZ glands (pl) *organs*
GLNZ glans *penis* glandes
GLP gallop *run*
GLP galop *dance*
GLP glop *(slang) unattractive stuff*
GLP gloppy *unattractive*
GLP gulp *swallow*
GLPDK glyptic *engraving*
GLPGS Galapagos *islands*
GLPN galloping *increasing*
GLPNG galloping *increasing*
GLPR galloper *runner*
GLPR gulper *swallow*
GLPST goalpost *structure*
GLPTK glyptic *engraving*
GLR galère *group*
GLR galleria *mall*
GLR gallery *showplace* galleries
GLR galore *plentiful*
GLR glair (or) glaire *egg white*
GLR glairy *slimy* glairier glairiest
GLR glare *shine* glared glaring
GLR glary *dazzling* glarier glariest
GLR Gloria *hymn*
GLR glory *(v) rejoice* gloried glorying glories
GLR glory *(n) renown, praise* glories
GLR glower *frown*
GLR gular *throat*
GLR ogler *stare*
GLR uglier *not pretty*
GLRD gaillardia *herb*
GLRD galleried *spectators*
GLRD galliard *dance*
GLRDY gaillardia *herb*

GLRF glorify *praise* glorified glorifying glorifies
GLRFD glorified *praised*
GLRFKSHN glorification *praise*
GLRFR glorifier *praise*
GLRFYR glorifier *praise*
GLRN glaring *obvious*
GLRNG glaring *obvious*
GLRNGL glaringly *obviously*
GLRR glairier *slimy*
GLRR glarier *bright*
GLRS glorious *splendid*
GLRSL gloriously *splendid*
GLRSNS gloriousness *splendid*
GLRST glairiest *slimy*
GLRST glariest *bright*
GLRY galleria *mall*
GLRY Gloria *hymn*
GLRYR glairier *slimy*
GLRYR glarier *bright*
GLRYS glorious *splendid*
GLRYSL gloriously *splendid*
GLRYSNS gloriousness *splendid*
GLRYST glairiest *slimy*
GLRYST glariest *bright*
GLS egoless *without self*
GLS eyeglass *vision aid* eyeglasses
GLS gallows *hanging* gallows (or) gallowses
GLS gallus *suspender* galluses
GLS glacé *glossy, candied*
GLS glacis *incline, buffer* glacis
GLS glass *material, container* glasses
GLS glassie (or) glassy *(n) marble* glassies
GLS glassy *(adj) dull, clear* glassier glassiest
GLS gloss *shine, mask*
GLS glossa *tongue* glossae
GLS glossy *(adj) shiny, smooth* glossier glossiest
GLS glossy *(n) photograph* glossies
GLS guileless *innocent*
GLSBLR glassblower *artist*

GLSBLWN glassblowing *art*
GLSBLWNG glassblowing *art*
GLSBLWR glassblower *artist*
GLSD gallused *suspenders*
GLSD glassy-eyed *intoxicated*
GLSD glissade *glide* glissaded glissading
GLSDR glissader *glide*
GLSFL glassful *quantity*
GLSG Glasgow *city*
GLSH galosh *boot* galoshes
GLSH ghoulish *demon*
GLSH goulash *food*
GLSH guilloche *ornament*
GLSHL ghoulishly *demon*
GLSHL glacial (adj) *ice* glacially (adv)
GLSHLG glaciology *ice*
GLSHLJ glaciology *ice*
GLSHLST glacialist *ice*
GLSHNS ghoulishness *demon*
GLSHR glacier *ice*
GLSHR glazier *glass setter* glaziery
GLSHS galoshes *boots*
GLSHS glasshouse *factory, (Br) greenhouse, prison*
GLSHSHN glaciation *ice*
GLSHT glaciate *freeze* glaciated glaciating
GLSHYLG glaciology *ice*
GLSHYLJ glaciology *ice*
GLSHYSHN glaciation *ice*
GLSHYT glaciate *freeze* glaciated glaciating
GLSHZ galoshes *boots*
GLSK Glasgow *city*
GLSL glassily *dull, clear*
GLSL glycyl *protein*
GLSLG glaciology *ice*
GLSLJ glaciology *ice*
GLSLS glassless *no glass*
GLSMKN glassmaking *production*
GLSMKNG glassmaking *production*
GLSMKR glassmaker *producer*

Letters aren't doubled for single sounds: to find alley use **L** not **LL**. Use **Y** and **W** as hard sounds only: to find yellow use **YL**. (Br)=British spelling or usage. * See dictionary.

GLSMTH goldsmith *dealer*
GLSN glassine *paper*
GLSN glisten *shine*
GLSN glycine *amino acid*
GLSND glissando *music*
  glissandi (or) glissandos
GLSNS glassiness *dull, clear*
GLSNS glossiness *shiny,*
  smooth
GLSNST glasnost *openness*
GLSPPR glasspaper
  sandpaper
GLSR glacier *ice*
GLSR glassier *dull, clear*
GLSR glossary *definitions*
  glossaries
GLSR glossier *shiny, smooth*
GLSRD glyceride *chemical*
GLSRK glyceric *acid*
GLSRL glycerol *solvent*
GLSRL glyceryl *radical*
GLSRN glycerin (or)
  glycerine *sweet*
GLSRNT glycerinate *sweeten*
  glycerinated
  glycerinating
GLSS eyeglasses *vision aid*
GLSSHN glaciation *ice*
GLSST glassiest *dull, clear*
GLSST glossiest *shiny,*
  smooth
GLST gallused *suspenders*
GLST glaciate *freeze*
  glaciated glaciating
GLST ugliest *not pretty*
GLSTN gallstone *obstruction*
GLSTN goldstone *glass*
GLSWR glassware
  containers
GLSWRK glasswork
  manufacture
GLSWRT glasswort *herb*
GLSYD glassy-eyed
  intoxicated
GLSYLG glaciology *ice*
GLSYLJ glaciology *ice*
GLSYR glacier *ice*
GLSYR glassier *dull, clear*
GLSYR glossier *shiny,*
  smooth
GLSYSHN glaciation *ice*
GLSYST glassiest *dull, clear*

GLSYST glossiest *shiny,*
  smooth
GLSYT glaciate *freeze*
  glaciated glaciating
GLSZ eyeglasses *vision aid*
GLSZ gallicize (*often*
  capitalized) French
  gallicized gallicizing
GLSZM gallicism *idiom*
GLT aglet *sheath*
GLT eaglet *bird*
GLT égalité *equality*
GLT Galatea *Greek myth*
GLT galeate *helmet*
GLT gallate *acid*
GLT galliot *ship*
GLT galoot *oaf*
GLT gault (*Br*) *soil*
GLT gilt *gold*
GLT gleet *discharge, pus*
GLT gloat *brag*
GLT glut *excess* glutted
  glutting
GLT glutei (pl) *muscle*
  gluteus
GLT guilt *blame*
GLT guilty *blameworthy*
  guiltier guiltiest
GLT gullet *throat*
GLTDZ glottides (pl) *vocal*
  cords glottis
GLTH Goliath *giant*
GLTJ gilt-edge (or) gilt-
  edged *gold, best quality*
GLTJD gilt-edged (or) gilt-
  edge *gold, best quality*
GLTL glottal *throat*
GLTL gluteal *muscle*
GLTL guiltily *blameworthy*
GLTLS guiltless *no blame*
GLTMK glutamic *chemical*
GLTMN glutamine *chemical*
GLTMT glutamate *chemical*
GLTN gluten *protein*
GLTN glutton *greedy one*
GLTN gluttony *greed*
  gluttonies
GLTN guillotine *behead*
GLTNDNG goaltending *foul*
GLTNDR goaltender *player*
GLTNDV agglutinative
  adhesive

GLTNGL gloatingly *brag*
GLTNJN agglutinogen
  antibody
GLTNJNK agglutinogenic
  antibody
GLTNN agglutinin *adhesive*
GLTNS glutenous *dough*
GLTNS glutinous *gummy*
GLTNS gluttonous *greedy*
GLTNS guiltiness
  blameworthy
GLTNSHN agglutination
  clump
GLTNT agglutinate *clump*
  agglutinated
  agglutinating
GLTNTV agglutinative
  adhesive
GLTR aglitter *shiny*
GLTR gladder *happy*
GLTR glitter *sparkle*
GLTR glittery *sparkle*
GLTR gloater *braggart*
GLTR guiltier *blameworthy*
GLTRD glitterati *celebrities*
GLTRN egalitarian *equality*
GLTRNGL glitteringly
  sparkling
GLTRNZM egalitarianism
  equality
GLTRT glitterati *celebrities*
GLTRYN egalitarian *equality*
GLTRYNZM egalitarianism
  equality
GLTS glitz *glitter*
GLTS glitzy *showy*
GLTS glottis *vocal cords*
  glottises (or) glottides
GLTS gluteus *muscle* glutei
GLTSMKSMS gluteus
  maximus *muscle* glutei
  maximi
GLTSMXMS gluteus
  maximus *muscle* glutei
  maximi
GLTST gladdest *happy*
GLTST guiltiest *blameworthy*
GLTY Galatea *Greek myth*
GLTY glutei (pl) *muscle*
  gluteus
GLTYL gluteal *muscle*
GLTYR guiltier *blameworthy*

Use letters that best describe the sounds you hear and omit the vowels. Use **S** or **K** instead of **C**: to find circle use **SRKL**. Use **J** to find joy, **JM** to find gem and **G** to find go.

GLTYS gluteus *muscle* glutei
GLTYSMKSMS gluteus maximus *muscle* glutei maximi
GLTYSMXMS gluteus maximus *muscle* glutei maximi
GLTYST guiltiest *blameworthy*
GLTZ glitzy *showy*
GLV glove *(v) cover, catch* gloved gloving
GLV glove *(n) mitt*
GLVNK galvanic *electricity*
GLVNKL galvanically *electricity*
GLVNMDR galvanometer *detector*
GLVNMTR galvanometer *detector*
GLVNT gallivant *roam*
GLVNZ galvanize *electrify* galvanized galvanizing (Br) galvanise
GLVNZM galvanism *electricity*
GLVNZR galvanizer *electrifier* (Br) galvaniser
GLVNZSHN galvanization *electricity* (Br) galvanisation
GLVR glover *mitt seller*
GLW gluey *sticky*
GLWG golliwog *doll*
GLWN gluon *particle*
GLWNGL glowingly *shine*
GLWNL glowingly *shine*
GLWR glower *frown*
GLWRM glowworm *animal*
GLX galax *herb*
GLX galaxy *stars* galaxies
GLXN gloxinia *flower*
GLXNY gloxinia *flower*
GLY Aglaia *a Grace*
GLY galea *helmet*
GLY glia *cell*
GLYBLSDM glioblastoma *tumor* glioblastomas (or) glioblastomata
GLYBLSDMD glioblastomata (pl) *tumor*

glioblastoma
GLYBLSDMT glioblastomata (pl) *tumor* glioblastoma
GLYBLSTM glioblastoma *tumor* glioblastomas (or) glioblastomata
GLYBLSTMD glioblastomata (pl) *tumor* glioblastoma
GLYBLSTMT glioblastomata (pl) *tumor* glioblastoma
GLYL glial *cell*
GLYM gallium *element*
GLYM glioma *tumor* gliomas (or) gliomata
GLYMD gliomata (pl) *tumor* glioma
GLYMT gliomata (pl) *tumor* glioma
GLYN galleon *ship*
GLYR uglier *not pretty*
GLYRD galliard *dance*
GLYST ugliest *not pretty*
GLYT galeate *helmet*
GLYT galliot *ship*
GLYTH Goliath *giant*
GLZ gallows *hanging* gallows (or) gallowses
GLZ glaze *(v) fit glass, coat* glazed glazing
GLZ glaze *(n) coating*
GLZD glazed *coated*
GLZG Glasgow *city*
GLZHR glazier *glass setter* glaziery
GLZN glazing *glasswork*
GLZNG glazing *glasswork*
GLZNST glasnost *openness*
GLZR glazier *glass setter* glaziery
GLZYR glazier *glass setter* glaziery
GM gam *(v) chat* gammed gamming
GM gam *(n) leg, whales*
GM gamay *wine*
GM game *(v) gamble* gamed gaming
GM game *(n) animal, amusement*

GM gamma *Greek letter*
GM gammon *(n) win, (Br) ham (v) deceive*
GM gammy *lame*
GM gamy (or) gamey *smelly, racy* gamier gamiest
GM gimme *(slang) give me*
GM gimme, a (n) *(slang) short put* gimmes
GM give me *bestow, confer*
GM Guam *island*
GM guillemet *mark*
GM gum *(v) glue, eat without teeth* gummed gumming
GM gum *(n) sticky substance, tooth bed*
GM gumma *tumor* gummas (or) gummata
GM gummy *sticky* gummier gummiest
GM ogham (or) ogam *alphabet*
GM oogamy *fertilization*
GMB Gambia *river, country*
GMB gumbo *stew, okra, mud* gumbos
GMBD gambado *legging* gambadoes
GMBL gamble *bet* gambled gambling
GMBL gambol *frolic* gamboled (or) gambolled gamboling (or) gambolling
GMBL gimbal *support* gimballed gimballing
GMBLR gambler *bettor*
GMBR gambier *vine*
GMBRL gambrel *hook*
GMBT gambit *strategy*
GMBT gum boot *shoe*
GMBY Gambia *river, country*
GMBYR gambier *vine*
GMD gummata (pl) *tumor* gumma
GMDFDK gametophytic *sex organs*
GMDFR gametophore *branch*
GMDFT gametophyte *sex organs*
GMDFTK gametophytic *sex*

Letters aren't doubled for single sounds: to find alley use **L** not **LL**. Use **Y** and **W** as hard sounds only: to find yellow use **YL**. (Br)=British spelling or usage. * See dictionary.

organs

GMDGNK gametogenic *cell production*

GMDGNS gametogenous *cell production*

GMDJNK gametogenic *cell production*

GMDJNS gametogenous *cell production*

GMDJNSS gametogenesis *cell production*

GMDK gametic *germ cell*

GMDKL gametically *germ cell*

GMDR geometer *mathematician*

GMDRP gumdrop *candy*

GMDST gametocyte *germ cell*

GMGLBLN gamma globulin *blood*

GMGLBYLN gamma globulin *blood*

GMK agamic *asexual*

GMK gimmick *trick*

GMK gimmicky *tricky*

GMKK gamecock *rooster*

GMKPR gamekeeper *animals*

GMKR gimmickry *tricks*

GML gamely *sporting*

GML gamily *smelly, racy*

GMLN gamelan *orchestra*

GMLR gambler *bettor*

GMLT gimlet *(n) tool, drink (v) pierce (adj) piercing*

GMMNN Agamemnon *Greek king*

GMN egomania *selfish*

GMN G-man *FBI* G-men

GMN gamin (m) *child* gamine (f)

GMN gaming *wager*

GMNC geomancy *prophecy*

GMND augmented *made larger*

GMNDV augmentative *supplement*

GMNG gaming *wager*

GMNK egomaniac *selfish*

GMNK geomantic *prophecy*

GMNR augmenter (or)

augmentor *increase*

GMNS gameness *sporting action*

GMNS gaminess *smelly, racy*

GMNS geomancy *prophecy*

GMNS gumminess *sticky*

GMNT augment *supplement*

GMNTC geomancy *prophecy*

GMNTD augmented *made larger*

GMNTK geomantic *prophecy*

GMNTR augmenter (or) augmentor *increase*

GMNTS geomancy *prophecy*

GMNTSHN augmentation *supplement*

GMNTTV augmentative *supplement*

GMNTV augmentative *supplement*

GMNY egomania *selfish*

GMNYK egomaniac *selfish*

GMP gamp *umbrella*

GMP gimp *(v) limp (n) braid, spirit, cripple*

GMP gimpy *crippled*

GMP guimpe *blouse*

GMPSHN gumption *originality, pep*

GMR gamer *player*

GMR gamier *smelly, racy*

GMR gummer *glue*

GMR gummier *sticky*

GMRFK geomorphic *surface*

GMRFLG geomorphology *surface* geomorphologies

GMRFLJKL geomorphological *surface*

GMS gummous *like gum*

GMS oogamous *fertilization*

GMSBK gemsbok *animal*

GMSH gumshoe *detective*

GMSHN gumption *originality, pep*

GMST gamiest *smelly, racy*

GMST gummiest *sticky*

GMSTR gamester *player*

GMT agamete *asexual*

GMT gamete *germ cell*

GMT gamut *range*

GMT gummata (pl) *tumor* gumma

GMT gummite *chemical*

GMTFDK gametophytic *sex organs*

GMTFR gametophore *branch*

GMTFT gametophyte *sex organs*

GMTFTK gametophytic *sex organs*

GMTGNK gametogenic *cell production*

GMTGNS gametogenous *cell production*

GMTJNK gametogenic *cell production*

GMTJNS gametogenous *cell production*

GMTJNSS gametogenesis *cell production*

GMTK gametic *germ cell*

GMTKL gametically *germ cell*

GMTNG gametangia (pl) *cell* gametangium

GMTNGM gametangium *cell* gametangia

GMTNGY gametangia (pl) *cell* gametangium

GMTNGYM gametangium *cell* gametangia

GMTNJ gametangia (pl) *cell* gametangium

GMTNJM gametangium *cell* gametangia

GMTNJY gametangia (pl) *cell* gametangium

GMTNJYM gametangium *cell* gametangia

GMTR geometer *mathematician*

GMTR geometry *math system* geometries

GMTRK geometric (or) geometrical *shapes*

GMTRKL geometrical (or) geometric *shapes*

GMTRKS geometrics *patterns*

GMTRSHN geometrician *shapes*

GMTRX geometrics *patterns*

GMTST gametocyte *germ*

Use letters that best describe the sounds you hear and omit the vowels. Use **S** or **K** instead of **C**: to find circle use **SRKL**. Use **J** to find joy, **JM** to find gem and **G** to find go.

cell
GMWD gumwood *tree*
GMWRDN game warden *official*
GMYR gamier *smelly, racy*
GMYR gummier *sticky*
GMYST gamiest *smelly, racy*
GMYST gummiest *sticky*
GMZBK gemsbok *animal*
GMZMN gamesman *player* gamesmen
GMZMNSHP gamesmanship *winning*
GN Aegean *Greek*
GN again *once more*
GN agon *conflict*
GN agony *pain* agonies
GN Eugene *city*
GN gain *(v) acquire (n) profit*
GN gene *heredity*
GN genie *spirit* genies
GN Ghana *country*
GN gnu *antelope* gnu (or) gnus
GN goanna *lizard*
GN going *(n) movement (adj) working, living, current**
GN going to *intend*
GN gone *(v-past) go*
GN goon *thug*
GN gooney (or) goony *albatross* gooneys (or) goonies
GN gown *dress*
GN guan *bird*
GN guano *waste matter*
GN Guiana *region*
GN Guinea *region*
GN guinea *fowl, money*
GN gun *(v) shoot* gunned gunning
GN gun *(n) weapon*
GN Guyana *country*
GN iguana *animal*
GN oogonia (pl) *germ cell* oogonium
GNBL ignoble (adj) *mean* ignobly (adv)
GNBLD ignobility *mean*
GNBLT ignobility *mean*
GNBT gunboat *ship*
GNC Aegean Sea *body of*

water
GND Gandhi *Indian leader*
GND ganoid *fish scales*
GND gonad *gland*
GND Uganda *country*
GNDBL ignitable *excite, flame*
GNDBLD ignitability *excite, flame*
GNDBLT ignitability *excite, flame*
GNDG gundog *retriever*
GNDK agnatic *paternal*
GNDKDM gonadectomy *surgery* gonadectomies
GNDKTM gonadectomy *surgery* gonadectomies
GNDL gonadal *gland*
GNDL gondola *boat*
GNDLR gondolier *boatman*
GNDN iguanodon *dinosaur*
GNDR gander *goose, look*
GNDR igniter *excite, flame*
GNDTRPK gonadotropic *stimulator*
GNDTRPN gonadotropin *stimulator*
GNF ganef *(slang) thief*
GNFL gainful (adj) *for profit* gainfully (adv)
GNFL guinea fowl *bird*
GNFLN gonfalon *flag*
GNFLNS gainfulness *for profit*
GNFR gunfire *weapon*
GNFR gynophore *flower*
GNFT gunfight *hostility*
GNFWL guinea fowl *bird*
GNFYR gunfire *weapon*
GNG eggnog *beverage*
GNG gang *group*
GNG gangue *ore*
GNG going *(n) movement (adj) working, living, current**
GNG gong *sound, cymbal*
GNGBNGR gangbanger *gang member*
GNGBSTR gangbuster *enforcer*
GNGBSTRZ gangbusters *(adj) excellent*

GNGGL ganglia (pl) *mass* ganglion
GNGGLN ganglion *mass* ganglia
GNGGLNG gangling *lanky*
GNGGLY ganglia (pl) *mass* ganglion
GNGGLYN ganglion *mass* ganglia
GNGGRN gangrene *rot* gangrened gangrening
GNGGRNS gangrenous *rotten*
GNGGSKN Genghis Khan *conqueror*
GNGH gung ho *enthusiastic*
GNGK ginkgo *tree* ginkgoes (or) ginkgos
GNGK gunk *gooey material*
GNGL ganglia (pl) *mass* ganglion
GNGLN gangland *territory*
GNGLN ganglion *mass* ganglia
GNGLND gangland *territory*
GNGLNG gangling *lanky*
GNGLY ganglia (pl) *mass* ganglion
GNGLYN ganglion *mass* ganglia
GNGM gingham *fabric*
GNGP gang up *group*
GNGPLNGK gangplank *bridge*
GNGPLNK gangplank *bridge*
GNGR ganger *(Br) foreman*
GNGRN gangrene *rot* gangrened gangrening
GNGRNS gangrenous *rotten*
GNGSKN Genghis Khan *conqueror*
GNGSTR gangster *racketeer*
GNGVR going-over *scolding, inspection* goings-over
GNGW gangway *aisle, move away*
GNGZ Ganges *river*
GNGZN goings-on *events*
GNHN guinea hen *bird*
GNJ ganja *marijuana*
GNJNDK gynogenetic *fertilization*

Letters aren't doubled for single sounds: to find alley use **L** not **LL**. Use **Y** and **W** as hard sounds only: to find yellow use **YL**. (Br)=British spelling or usage. * See dictionary.

GNJNSS gynogenesis *fertilization*
GNJNTK gynogenetic *fertilization*
GNJZ Ganges *river*
GNK eugenic *breeding*
GNK genic *heredity*
GNK ginkgo *tree* ginkgoes (or) ginkgos
GNK guanaco *animal* guanacos
GNK gunk *gooey material*
GNKD gynecoid *female*
GNKKL gonococcal *bacteria*
GNKKRC gynecocracy *rule by women* gynecocracies
GNKKRDK gynecocratic *rule by women*
GNKKRS gynecocracy *rule by women* gynecocracies
GNKKRTK gynecocratic *rule by women*
GNKKS gonococcus *bacteria* gonococci
GNKL eugenically *breeding*
GNKLG gynecology *female organs* (Br) gynaecology
GNKLJ gynecology *female organs* (Br) gynaecology
GNKLJKL gynecological *female organs* (Br) gynaecological
GNKLJST gynecologist *female organs* (Br) gynaecologist
GNKMST gynecomastia *male breasts*
GNKMSTY gynecomastia *male breasts*
GNKS eugenics *breeding*
GNKTN guncotton *explosive*
GNL agonal *death pain*
GNL genial (adj) *friendly* genially (adv)
GNL gunnel *gunwale, fish*
GNL oogonial *germ cell*
GNLD geniality *friendly*
GNLG genealogy *descent* genealogies
GNLJ genealogy *descent*

genealogies
GNLJKL genealogical (adj) *descent* genealogically (adv)
GNLNDZ Aegean Islands *land masses*
GNLNZ Aegean Islands *land masses*
GNLT geniality *friendly*
GNM oogonium *germ cell* oogonia
GNMD Ganymede *Greek myth*
GNMDL gunmetal *alloy, color*
GNML gun moll *woman*
GNMN gunman *shooter* gunmen
GNMN ignominy *shame* ignominies
GNMNS ignominious *shameful*
GNMNSL ignominiously *shameful*
GNMNSNS ignominiousness *shameful*
GNMNYS ignominious *shameful*
GNMNYSL ignominiously *shameful*
GNMNYSNS ignominiousness *shameful*
GNMTL gunmetal *alloy, color*
GNN guenon *monkey*
GNNDRMRF gynandromorph *both sexes* gynandromorphy
GNNDRMRFK gynandromorphic *both sexes*
GNNDRMRFZM gynandromorphism *both sexes*
GNPDR gunpowder *explosive*
GNPG guinea pig *rodent*
GNPL gene pool *heredity*
GNPL gunplay *shooting*
GNPNT gunpoint *muzzle*
GNR gainer *acquirer*
GNR goner *doomed*
GNR gonorrhea *disease*

GNR gunner *shooter*
GNR gunnery *guns*
GNR ignore *neglect* ignored ignoring
GNRBL ignorable *neglect*
GNRL gonorrheal *disease*
GNRMS ignoramus *fool*
GNRNN gunrunning *arms dealing*
GNRNNG gunrunning *arms dealing*
GNRNR gunrunner *arms dealer*
GNRNS ignorance *no knowledge*
GNRNT ignorant *no knowledge*
GNRNTL ignorantly *no knowledge*
GNRNTS ignorance *no knowledge*
GNRR ignorer *neglect*
GNRY gonorrhea *disease*
GNRYL gonorrheal *disease*
GNS Aegean Sea *body of water*
GNS gainsay *deny* gainsaid gainsaying gainsays
GNS gayness *happiness, homosexuality*
GNS genius *intelligence* geniuses (or) genii
GNS genus *category* genera
GNS goodness *wholesome, kind*
GNS gooeyness *sticky*
GNS igneous *rock*
GNSD gainsaid *denied*
GNSDK agnostic *unsure of God*
GNSDK agonistic *strained*
GNSDKL agonistically *strained*
GNSDR ganister *rock*
GNSH agnosia *brain damage*
GNSH ganache *frosting*
GNSH gun-shy *cautious*
GNSHN ignition *start fire*
GNSHP gunship *helicopter*
GNSHT gunshot *weapon*
GNSK gunnysack *bag*
GNSLNGN gunslinging

Use letters that best describe the sounds you hear and omit the vowels. Use **S** or **K** instead of **C**: to find circle use **SRKL**. Use **J** to find joy, **JM** to find gem and **G** to find go.

shooting
GNSLNGNG gunslinging *shooting*
GNSLNGR gunslinger *shooter*
GNSMTH gunsmith *firearms*
GNSNT ignescent *explosive*
GNSR gainsayer *denyer*
GNSST eugenicist *breeding*
GNST against *not for, upon*
GNST agonist *struggler, muscle*
GNST eugenist *breeding*
GNSTK agnostic *unsure of God*
GNSTK agonistic *strained*
GNSTKL agonistically *strained*
GNSTR ganister *rock*
GNSTSZM agnosticism *unsure of God*
GNSYR gainsayer *denyer*
GNT agnate *paternal kinsman*
GNT gannet *bird* gannets
GNT gaunt *thin*
GNT good night *farewell*
GNT ignite *excite, flame* ignited igniting
GNTBL ignitable *excite, flame*
GNTBLD ignitability *excite, flame*
GNTBLT ignitability *excite, flame*
GNTK agnatic *paternal*
GNTL gauntly *thin*
GNTLT gauntlet *challenge*
GNTNS gauntness *thin*
GNTR gantry *platform* gantries
GNTR igniter *excite, flame*
GNVR going-over *scolding, inspection* goings-over
GNWL gunwale *upper edge*
GNX eugenics *breeding*
GNY gnu *antelope* gnu (or) gnus
GNY oogonia (pl) *germ cell* oogonium
GNYL genial (adj) *friendly* genially (adv)
GNYL oogonial *germ cell*

GNYLD geniality *friendly*
GNYLG genealogy *descent* genealogies
GNYLJ genealogy *descent* genealogies
GNYLJKL genealogical (adj) *descent* genealogically (adv)
GNYLT geniality *friendly*
GNYM oogonium *germ cell* oogonia
GNYS genius *intelligence* geniuses (or) genii
GNYS igneous *rock*
GNZ agonize *suffer, struggle* agonized agonizing (Br) agonise
GNZ gonzo *bizarre*
GNZD agonized *pained* (Br) agonised
GNZH agnosia *brain damage*
GNZN agonizing *painful* (Br) agonising
GNZN goings-on *events*
GNZNG agonizing *painful* (Br) agonising
GNZNGL agonizingly *painfully* (Br) agonisingly
GNZNL agonizingly *painfully* (Br) agonisingly
GP agape (adj, adv) *open* (n) *love*
GP gap *space* gapped gapping
GP gape *yawn* gaped gaping
GP goop *sticky substance*
GP GOP *Republican*
GP guppy *fish* guppies
GPLDKL geopolitical (adj) *policy* geopolitically (adv)
GPLNT eggplant *vegetable*
GPLTKL geopolitical (adj) *policy* geopolitically (adv)
GPLTKS geopolitics *policy*
GPLTX geopolitics *policy*
GPN gaping *open*
GPNG gaping *open*
GPNTHS agapanthus *plant* agapanthus (or) agapanthuses

GPR gaper *clam*
GR agar (or) agar-agar *algae*
GR aggro *(Br) irritation* aggros
GR agora *market* agoras (or) agorae
GR agree *concur* agreed agreeing
GR auger *tool*
GR augur *predict*
GR augury *prediction* auguries
GR eager *keen*
GR edgier *nervous*
GR gaur *animal*
GR gear (v) *adjust* (n) *wheel, goods*
GR gharry *cab* gharries
GR giro *fund transfer*
GR gore (v) *pierce, taper* gored goring
GR gore (n) *tapered piece, blood*
GR gory *bloody* gorier goriest
GR gray (or) grey *color*
GR grew (v-past) *grow*
GR grow *cultivate, increase* grew growing grown
GR guar *legume*
GR guru *wise one* gurus
GR ogre *monster*
GRB garb *attire*
GRB grab (v) *sieze* grabbed grabbing
GRB grab (n) *seizure, clamshell*
GRB grabby (adj) *greedy* grabbier grabbiest
GRB grebe *bird*
GRB grub (v) *dig* grubbed grubbing
GRB grub (n) *food, worm*
GRB grubby *dirty* grubbier grubbiest
GRBG grab bag *receptacle*
GRBJ garbage *trash*
GRBKS gearbox *transmission* gearboxes
GRBL agreeable (adj) *harmonious, pleasing* agreeably (adv)

Letters aren't doubled for single sounds: to find alley use **L** not **LL**. Use **Y** and **W** as hard sounds only: to find yellow use **YL**. (Br)=British spelling or usage. * See dictionary.

GRBL garble *mix up* garbled garbling

GRBL grabble *grope, sprawl* grabbled grabbling

GRBL grubbily *dirty*

GRBLD agreeability *harmony*

GRBLD garibaldi *blouse*

GRBLD Garibaldi *patriot*

GRBLNS agreeableness *pleasantness, harmony*

GRBLR garbler *mix up*

GRBLR grabbler *grope, sprawl*

GRBLS Goebbels *propagandist*

GRBLT agreeability *harmony*

GRBN graben *crust*

GRBNS grubbiness *dirty*

GRBNZ garbanzo *chickpea* garbanzos

GRBR grabber *grasper*

GRBR grabbier *grasping*

GRBR grubber *drudge*

GRBR grubbier *dirty*

GRBRD graybeard *old man*

GRBSNS agribusiness *farm industry*

GRBST grabbiest *grasping*

GRBST grubbiest *dirty*

GRBSTK grubstake *funds*

GRBVR eager beaver *keen one*

GRBX gearbox *transmission* gearboxes

GRBYR grabbier *grasping*

GRBYR grubbier *dirty*

GRBYST grabbiest *grasping*

GRBYST grubbiest *dirty*

GRBZNS agribusiness *farm industry*

GRC grassy *with grass* grassier grassiest

GRC greasy *oily* greasier greasiest

GRCH grouch *grumbler*

GRCH grouchy *angry* grouchier grouchiest

GRCHD gratuity *tip* gratuities

GRCHDS gratuitous *free, voluntary*

GRCHL grouchily *angrily*

GRCHNS grouchiness *anger*

GRCHR grouchier *angrier*

GRCHST grouchiest *angriest*

GRCHT gratuity *tip* gratuities

GRCHTS gratuitous *free, voluntary*

GRCHWD gratuity *tip* gratuities

GRCHWDS gratuitous *free, voluntary*

GRCHWT gratuity *tip* gratuities

GRCHWTS gratuitous *free, voluntary*

GRCHYR grouchier *angrier*

GRCHYST grouchiest *angriest*

GRCR grassier *with grass*

GRCR greasier *oily*

GRCSPN greasy spoon *diner*

GRCST grassiest *with grass*

GRCST greasiest *oily*

GRCYR grassier *with grass*

GRCYR greasier *oily*

GRCYST grassiest *with grass*

GRCYST greasiest *oily*

GRD gird *(v) bind, surround, mock* girded (or) girt girding

GRD gird *(n) remark*

GRD gored *pleated*

GRD gourd *plant*

GRD gourde *money*

GRD grad *graduate*

GRD grade *rate, slope* graded grading

GRD greed *hoggishness*

GRD greedy *hoggish* greedier greediest

GRD grid *grating, football, network*

GRD gritty *sandy* grittier grittiest

GRD grotto *cavern* grottoes

GRD guard *defend*

GRDD guarded *cautious*

GRDDNS guardedness *caution*

GRDF gratify *reward* gratified gratifying gratifies

GRDFKSHN gratification *reward*

GRDFN gratifying *pleasing*

GRDFNG gratifying *pleasing*

GRDFYN gratifying *pleasing*

GRDFYNG gratifying *pleasing*

GRDHS guardhouse *defense*

GRDJ grudge *(v) complain* grudged grudging

GRDJ grudge *(n) spite*

GRDJDD graduated *progressive*

GRDJL gradual *(n) book*

GRDJL gradual (adj) *by degree* gradually (adv)

GRDJN grudging *unwilling*

GRDJNG grudging *unwilling*

GRDJNGL grudgingly *unwillingly*

GRDJNL grudgingly *unwillingly*

GRDJR grudger *complainer*

GRDJSHN graduation *commencement, measure*

GRDJT graduate *(v) receive diploma, divide* graduated graduating

GRDJT graduate *(n) diploma holder, measure*

GRDJTD graduated *progressive*

GRDJWDD graduated *progressive*

GRDJWL gradual *(n) book*

GRDJWL gradual (adj) *by degree* gradually (adv)

GRDJWSHN graduation *commencement, measure*

GRDJWT graduate *(v) receive diploma, divide* graduated graduating

GRDJWT graduate *(n) diploma holder, measure*

GRDJWTD graduated *progressive*

GRDL girdle *(v) encircle* girdled girdling

Use letters that best describe the sounds you hear and omit the vowels. Use **S** or **K** instead of **C**: to find circle use **SRKL**. Use **J** to find joy, **JM** to find gem and **G** to find go.

GRDL girdle *(n) garment*
GRDL Godel *mathematician*
GRDL greedily *hoggish*
GRDL griddle *flat pan*
GRDL grittily *sandy*
GRDLK gridlock *traffic*
GRDLKK griddle cake *food*
GRDLS gradeless *no grade, no slope*
GRDN au gratin *with cheese*
GRDN garden *(v) cultivate (n) yard*
GRDN gardenia *flower*
GRDN Great Dane *dog*
GRDN guardian *custodian*
GRDN gueridon *table*
GRDNG grating *grille*
GRDNG greeting *hello*
GRDNR gardener *landscaper*
GRDNS greediness *hoggish*
GRDNS grittiness *sandy*
GRDNSHP guardianship *custody*
GRDNT Gordian knot *myth*
GRDNT gradient *tilt, change*
GRDNY gardenia *flower*
GRDR garroter *strangler*
GRDR garter *band*
GRDR girder *support*
GRDR grader *leveler, rater, school*
GRDR grater *rasp*
GRDR greater *larger, city and suburbs*
GRDR greedier *hoggish*
GRDR greeter *says hello*
GRDR gridder *football*
GRDR grittier *sandy*
GRDR grouter *mortar worker*
GRDR guarder *defender*
GRDRB garderobe *bedroom*
GRDRL guardrail *barrier*
GRDRM guardroom *prison*
GRDRN gridiron *grating, football, network*
GRDS gratis *free*
GRDSHN aggradation *level grade*
GRDSHN gradation *step*
GRDSMN guardsman *military* guardsmen
GRDSS giardiasis *disease*
giardiases
GRDST greediest *hoggish*
GRDST grittiest *sandy*
GRDTD gratitude *thanks*
GRDTYD gratitude *thanks*
GRDYN guardian *custodian*
GRDYNSHP guardianship *custody*
GRDYNT Gordian knot *myth*
GRDYNT gradient *tilt, change*
GRDYR greedier *hoggish*
GRDYR grittier *sandy*
GRDYRN gridiron *grating, football, network*
GRDYSS giardiasis *disease* giardiases
GRDYST greediest *hoggish*
GRDYST grittiest *sandy*
GRDZMN guardsman *military* guardsmen
GRF agrafe (or) agraffe *clasp*
GRF agrapha *words of Christ*
GRF agraphia *cannot write*
GRF graph *chart*
GRF grief *sorrow*
GRF gruff *harsh, stern*
GRFB agoraphobe *one who fears open places*
GRFB agoraphobia *fear of open places*
GRFBK agoraphobic *fear of open places*
GRFBY agoraphobia *fear of open places*
GRFD graffiti (pl) *writing* graffito
GRFDJ graftage *implantation*
GRFDK graphitic *carbon*
GRFDR grafter *attach*
GRFDR grifter *(slang) thief*
GRFK graphic *(adj) vivid (n) picture*
GRFKL graphically *vivid*
GRFL gruffly *harshly, sternly*
GRFLG graphology *handwriting*
GRFLJ graphology *handwriting*
GRFLJST graphologist *handwriting*
GRFM grapheme *word part*
GRFMK graphemic *word part*
GRFMKL graphemically *word part*
GRFMKS graphemics *word part*
GRFMX graphemics *word part*
GRFN griffin (or) griffon *animal*
GRFNS gruffness *sharpness of tone*
GRFSH garfish *long, thin fish*
GRFSH grayfish *dogfish*
GRFSTRKN grief-stricken *sorry*
GRFT graffiti (pl) *writing* graffito
GRFT graft *(n) unfair gain, plant (v) unite, implant*
GRFT graphite *carbon*
GRFT grift *steal*
GRFTJ graftage *implantation*
GRFTK graphitic *carbon*
GRFTR grafter *attach*
GRFTR grifter *(slang) thief*
GRFY agraphia *cannot write*
GRG garigue *scrubland*
GRG grog *beverage*
GRG groggy *unsteady or sleepy* groggier groggiest
GRGDV aggregative *collective*
GRGDVL aggregatively *collectively*
GRGL gargle *(v) cleanse* gargled gargling
GRGL gargle *(n) mouthwash*
GRGL gargoyle *ugly figure*
GRGL groggily *unsteady or sleepy*
GRGL gurgle *throat noise* gurgled gurgling
GRGN gorgon *(often capitalized) woman*
GRGNCHN gargantuan *huge*
GRGNCHWN gargantuan *huge*
GRGNS grogginess *unsteady or sleepy*

Letters aren't doubled for single sounds: to find alley use **L** not **LL**. Use **Y** and **W** as hard sounds only: to find yellow use **YL**. (Br)=British spelling or usage. * See dictionary.

GRGNTN gargantuan *huge*
GRGNTWN gargantuan *huge*
GRGNZL Gorgonzola *cheese*
GRGR agar-agar (or) agar *algae*
GRGR gris-gris *amulet* gris-gris
GRGR groggier *unsteady or sleepy*
GRGRM grogram *coarse fabric*
GRGRN grosgrain *strong fabric*
GRGRS gregarious *sociable*
GRGRSL gregariously *sociable*
GRGRSNS gregariousness *sociable*
GRGRYS gregarious *sociable*
GRGRYSL gregariously *sociable*
GRGRYSNS gregariousness *sociable*
GRGSHN aggregation *collection*
GRGSHNL aggregational *collected*
GRGSHP grogshop *(Br) bar*
GRGST groggiest *unsteady or sleepy*
GRGT aggregate *total* aggregated aggregating
GRGTV aggregative *collective*
GRGTVL aggregatively *collectively*
GRGYL gargoyle *ugly figure*
GRGYR groggier *unsteady or sleepy*
GRGYST groggiest *unsteady or sleepy*
GRHM graham *wheat*
GRHN greyhound *dog*
GRHND greyhound *dog*
GRJ garage *car storage* garaged garaging
GRJ gorge *(v) overeat* gorged gorging
GRJ gorge *(n) passage*
GRJ grudge *(v) complain* grudged grudging

GRJ grudge *(n) spite*
GRJDD graduated *progressive*
GRJL gradual *(n) book*
GRJL gradual *(adj) by degree* gradually *(adv)*
GRJN grudging *unwilling*
GRJNG grudging *unwilling*
GRJNGL grudgingly *unwillingly*
GRJNL grudgingly *unwillingly*
GRJR gorger *overeat*
GRJR grudger *complainer*
GRJS egregious *outright*
GRJS gorgeous *beautiful*
GRJSHN graduation *commencement, measure*
GRJSL garage sale *household items*
GRJT graduate *(v) receive diploma, divide* graduated graduating
GRJT graduate *(n) diploma holder, measure*
GRJTD graduated *progressive*
GRJWDD graduated *progressive*
GRJWL gradual *(n) book*
GRJWL gradual *(adj) by degree* gradually *(adv)*
GRJWSHN graduation *commencement, measure*
GRJWT graduate *(v) receive diploma, divide* graduated graduating
GRJWT graduate *(n) diploma holder, measure*
GRJWTD graduated *progressive*
GRK agaric *mushroom*
GRK Greek *of Greece*
GRKL grackle *bird*
GRKLCHR agriculture *farming*
GRKLCHRL agricultural *(adj) farming* agriculturally *(adv)*
GRKLCHRLST agriculturalist (or) agriculturist *farmer*

GRKLCHRST agriculturist (or) agriculturalist *farmer*
GRKLTR agriculture *farming*
GRKLTRL agricultural *(adj) farming* agriculturally *(adv)*
GRKLTRLST agriculturalist (or) agriculturist *farmer*
GRKLTRST agriculturist (or) agriculturalist *farmer*
GRKMKL agrochemical *herbicide*
GRKN gherkin *pickle*
GRL eagerly *keenly*
GRL egg roll *food*
GRL girl *female*
GRL girlie *nude women*
GRL gorilla *ape*
GRL Grail *cup*
GRL grill *(v) broil, question (n) bars, food*
GRL grille (or) grill *grating*
GRL growl *rumble*
GRL growly *sound angry* growlier growliest
GRL gruel *cereal*
GRL guerrilla (or) guerilla *fighter*
GRLD garrulity *wordiness*
GRLD grilled *cooked*
GRLFRN girlfriend *pal*
GRLFRND girlfriend *pal*
GRLG greylag *goose*
GRLHD girlhood *age*
GRLJ grillage *framework*
GRLK garlic *food*
GRLK garlicky *flavor*
GRLN garland *flowers*
GRLN growling *sound angry*
GRLN grueling (or) gruelling *difficult*
GRLND garland *flowers*
GRLNG grayling *fish* grayling
GRLNG growling *sound angry*
GRLNG grueling (or) gruelling *difficult*
GRLNGL gruelingly *difficult*
GRLNL gruelingly *difficult*
GRLNS growliness *sound angry*

Use letters that best describe the sounds you hear and omit the vowels. Use **S** or **K** instead of **C**: to find circle use **SRKL**. Use **J** to find joy, **JM** to find gem and **G** to find go.

GRLR griller *broil, question*
GRLR growler *sound angry*
GRLR growlier *sound angry*
GRLRM grillroom *restaurant*
GRLS garrulous *wordy*
GRLS grilse *salmon* grilse
GRLSH girlish *female*
GRLSHL girlishly *female*
GRLSHNS girlishness *female*
GRLSKT Girl Scout
　organization
GRLSNS garrulousness
　wordy
GRLST growliest *sound*
　angry
GRLT garrulity *wordiness*
GRLWRK grillwork *grate*
GRLYR growlier *sound angry*
GRLYST growliest *sound*
　angry
GRM gourami *fish* gourami
　(or) gouramis
GRM gourmet *connoisseur*
GRM graham *wheat*
GRM gram *measure*
　(Br) gramme
GRM Grammy *award*
GRM grandma *grandmother*
GRM grim *sad, fierce*
　grimmer grimmest
GRM grime *dirt*
GRM grimy *dirty* grimier
　grimiest
GRM groom *wedding*
GRMBL grumble *mutter*
　grumbled grumbling
GRMBL grumbly *muttering*
GRMBLNGL grumblingly
　mutter
GRMBLNL grumblingly
　mutter
GRMBLR grumbler *mutter*
GRMDKL grammatical (adj)
　speech grammatically
　(adv)
GRMDR gray matter *brains*
GRMFN gramophone
　phonograph
GRML grimly *sad, fierce*
GRMLKN grimalkin *cat*
GRMLN gremlin *gnome*
GRMN agrimony *herb*

agrimonies
GRMN gourmand *food lover*
GRMND gourmand *food*
　lover
GRMNDZ gormandize
　devour gormandized
　gormandizing
　(Br) gormandise
GRMNDZ gourmandise *food*
　appreciation
GRMNS griminess *dirty*
GRMNS grimness *sad, fierce*
GRMNT agreement *treaty,*
　harmony
GRMNT garment *clothing*
GRMNVRS graminivorous
　grass eater
GRMP gramp (or) gramps
　grandfather gramps
GRMP grandpa *grandfather*
GRMP grump (n) *surly one*
　(v) *sulk*
GRMP grumpy *surly*
　grumpier grumpiest
GRMPL grumpily *surly*
GRMPNS grumpiness *surly*
GRMPR grumpier *surly*
GRMPS gramps (or) gramp
　grandfather gramps
GRMPS grampus *dolphin*
GRMPST grumpiest *surly*
GRMPYR grumpier *surly*
GRMPYST grumpiest *surly*
GRMR grammar *speech*
GRMR grimier *dirty*
GRMR grimmer *sad, fierce*
GRMR groomer *hair stylist*
GRMRN grammarian *speech*
GRMRYN grammarian
　speech
GRMS grimace *show disgust*
　grimaced grimacing
GRMSMN groomsman
　wedding
GRMSR grimacer *show*
　disgust
GRMST grimiest *dirty*
GRMST grimmest *sad, fierce*
GRMT grommet *fastener*
GRMTKL grammatical (adj)
　speech grammatically
　(adv)

GRMTR gray matter *brains*
GRMYR grimier *dirty*
GRMYST grimiest *dirty*
GRN aground *on land*
GRN gearing *wheels*
GRN grain *seed, wood*
GRN grainy *sandy* grainier
　grainiest
GRN grand (adj) *fine* (n)
　thousand
GRN granny (or) grannie
　grandmother grannies
GRN green *color, new*
GRN grin *smile* grinned
　grinning
GRN grind (v) *wear down,*
　rotate, annoy ground
　grinding
GRN grind (n) *labor, rotation,*
　granule
GRN groan *moan*
GRN groin *pelvis, arch*
GRN ground (n) *base, soil* (v)
　base, rely (v-past) grind*
GRN growing *cultivate,*
　increase
GRN grown (v-past) *grow*
GRN Guarani *ethnic group*
　Guarani (or) Guarani
GRN gurney *bed on wheels*
　gurneys
GRNB Green Bay *city*
GRNBB grandbaby *relative*
　grandbabies
GRNBG greenbug *aphid*
GRNBK greenback *dollar*
GRNBL grantable *give,*
　admit
GRNBLT greenbelt *parks*
GRNBN green bean
　vegetable
GRNBR Green Beret *army*
GRNBRKN groundbreaking
　pioneer
GRNBRKNG
　groundbreaking *pioneer*
GRNBRKR groundbreaker
　pioneer
GRNBRR greenbrier *vine*
GRNBRYR greenbrier *vine*
GRNC guernsey (often
　capitalized) *cow* guernseys

Letters aren't doubled for single sounds: to find alley use **L** not **LL**. Use **Y** and **W** as hard sounds only: to find yellow use **YL**. (Br)=British spelling or usage. * See dictionary.

GRNC Guernsey *island*

GRNCH Greenwich *city, time*

GRNCHL grandchild *relative* grandchildren

GRNCHLD grandchild *relative* grandchildren

GRNCHLDRN grandchildren (pl) *relatives* grandchild

GRNCHMNTM Greenwich Mean Time *time standard*

GRNCHR garniture *trimming*

GRND aground *on land*

GRND grand *(adj) fine (n) thousand*

GRND grandee *nobleman*

GRND granita *fruit ice*

GRND green-eyed *envious, eye color*

GRND grenade *weapon*

GRND grind *(v) wear down, rotate, annoy* ground grinding

GRND grind *(n) work, granule, rotation*

GRND ground *(n) base, soil (v) base, rely (v-past)* grind*

GRNDBB grandbaby *relative* grandbabies

GRNDBRKN groundbreaking *pioneer*

GRNDBRKNG groundbreaking *pioneer*

GRNDBRKR groundbreaker *pioneer*

GRNDCHL grandchild *relative* grandchildren

GRNDCHLD grandchild *relative* grandchildren

GRNDCHLDRN grandchildren (pl) *relatives* grandchild

GRNDD granddad (or) grandad *grandfather*

GRNDD granddaddy *grandfather* granddaddies

GRNDDR granddaughter *relative*

GRNDFLR grandiflora *rose*

GRNDFSH groundfish *animal*

GRNDFTHR grandfather *relative*

GRNDHG groundhog *animal*

GRNDJR grand jury *law*

GRNDK granitic *hard*

GRNDKD grandkid *relative*

GRNDKDS grandkids *relative*

GRNDKDZ grandkids *relative*

GRNDKNYN Grand Canyon *gorge*

GRNDLKWNS grandiloquence *language*

GRNDLKWNT grandiloquent *language*

GRNDLKWNTL grandiloquently *language*

GRNDLKWNTS grandiloquence *language*

GRNDLNG groundling *spectator*

GRNDLQNT grandiloquent *language*

GRNDLQNTL grandiloquently *language*

GRNDLQNTS grandiloquence *language*

GRNDLS groundless *no basis*

GRNDM grandam (or) grandame *grandmother*

GRNDM grandma *grandmother*

GRNDML grand mal *siezure*

GRNDMSDR grand master *officer*

GRNDMSTR grand master *officer*

GRNDMTHR grandmother *relative*

GRNDN grenadine *fabric, syrup*

GRNDN grounding *training*

GRNDNF grandnephew *relative*

GRNDNFY grandnephew *relative*

GRNDNG grounding *training*

GRNDNGKL granduncle *relative*

GRNDNGL grindingly *wear down, rotate, annoy*

GRNDNKL granduncle *relative*

GRNDNL grindingly *wear down, rotate, annoy*

GRNDNS grandniece *relative*

GRNDNT grandaunt *relative*

GRNDNT groundnut *peanut*

GRNDP grandpa *grandfather*

GRNDPN grand piano *music*

GRNDPR Grand Prix *race* Grands Prix

GRNDPRNT grandparent *relative*

GRNDPRNTHD grandparenthood *relative*

GRNDPYN grand piano *music*

GRNDQWNS grandiloquence *language*

GRNDR grandeur *splendor*

GRNDR grenadier *soldier, fish*

GRNDR grinder *device*

GRNDR grounder *baseball*

GRNDS grandiose *pompous*

GRNDS grandioso *music*

GRNDS grounds *reasons, land, coffee*

GRNDSKPR groundskeeper *landscaper*

GRNDSL grandiosely *pompously*

GRNDSL groundsel *weed*

GRNDSLM grand slam (n) *tournament* grand-slam (adj)

GRNDSMN groundsman (Br) *landscaper*

GRNDSN grandson *relative*

GRNDSNS grandioseness *pompousness*

GRNDSPD ground speed *velocity*

GRNDSTN grandstand *(n) audience (v) impress*

GRNDSTN grindstone *millstone*

Use letters that best describe the sounds you hear and omit the vowels. Use **S** or **K** instead of **C**: to find circle use **SRKL**. Use **J** to find joy, **JM** to find gem and **G** to find go.

GRNDSTND grandstand (n) audience (v) impress
GRNDSTNDR grandstander show-off
GRNDSWL ground swell wave, growth
GRNDT groundout baseball
GRNDTR granddaughter relative
GRNDWD groundwood pulp
GRNDWDR groundwater wells
GRNDWRK groundwork foundation
GRNDWTR groundwater wells
GRNDYR grandeur splendor
GRNDYS grandiose pompous
GRNDYS grandioso music
GRNDYSL grandiosely pompously
GRNDYSNS grandioseness pompousness
GRNDZ aggrandize enhance aggrandized aggrandizing (Br) aggrandise
GRNDZ grounds reasons, land, coffee
GRNDZKPR groundskeeper landscaper
GRNDZMN groundsman (Br) landscaper
GRNDZMNT aggrandizement enhancement (Br) aggrandisement
GRNDZR aggrandizer enhancer (Br) aggrandiser
GRNF grandnephew relative
GRNFL greenfly insect greenflies
GRNFNCH greenfinch bird
GRNFSH groundfish animal
GRNFTHR grandfather relative
GRNFY grandnephew relative
GRNG gearing wheels
GRNG gringo non-Hispanic

gringos
GRNG growing cultivate, increase
GRNG grungy shabby grungier grungiest
GRNGG gringo non-Hispanic gringos
GRNGJ greengage plum
GRNGR grungier shabbier
GRNGRSR greengrocer (Br) vegetable seller
GRNGST grungiest shabbiest
GRNGYR grungier shabbier
GRNGYST grungiest shabbiest
GRNHD greenhead horsefly
GRNHG groundhog animal
GRNHRN greenhorn newcomer
GRNHRT greenheart tree
GRNHS greenhouse enclosure for plants
GRNHSFK greenhouse effect warming
GRNHSFKT greenhouse effect warming
GRNJ grange farm
GRNJ Greenwich city, time
GRNJ grunge punk
GRNJ grungy shabby grungier grungiest
GRNJMNTM Greenwich Mean Time time standard
GRNJR grand jury law
GRNJR grandeur splendor
GRNJR granger farmer
GRNJR grungier shabbier
GRNJST grungiest shabbiest
GRNJYR grungier shabbier
GRNJYST grungiest shabbiest
GRNKD grandkid relative
GRNKNYN Grand Canyon gorge
GRNKPR greenkeeper (or) greenskeeper golf
GRNKRD green card work permit
GRNKT greenockite mineral
GRNL granola cereal
GRNL granule one piece of grain

GRNL gruntle make agreeable gruntled gruntling
GRNLDD granulated grainy
GRNLDR granulator form grains
GRNLM granuloma inflammation granulomas (or) granulomata
GRNLMD granulomata (pl) inflammation granuloma
GRNLMT granulomata (pl) inflammation granuloma
GRNLN Greenland island
GRNLN greenling fish
GRNLND Greenland island
GRNLNG greenling fish
GRNLNG groundling spectator
GRNLR granular grainy
GRNLRD granularity grainy
GRNLRT granularity grainy
GRNLS granulose grainy
GRNLS groundless no basis
GRNLSHN granulation form grains
GRNLSS granulosis disease granuloses
GRNLT granulate crystallize granulated granulating
GRNLT granulite rock
GRNLT greenlet bird
GRNLTD granulated grainy
GRNLTR granulator form grains
GRNM agronomy crops
GRNM grandma grandmother
GRNMK agronomic crops
GRNMKL agronomically crops
GRNML grand mal siezure
GRNML greenmail stock market
GRNMLR greenmailer stock market
GRNMSDR grand master officer
GRNMST agronomist crops
GRNMSTR grand master officer
GRNMTHR grandmother relative

Letters aren't doubled for single sounds: to find alley use **L** not **LL**. Use **Y** and **W** as hard sounds only: to find yellow use **YL**. (Br)=British spelling or usage. * See dictionary.

GRNN greening *apple*
GRNN grunion *fish*
GRNNG greening *apple*
GRNNS graininess *sandy*
GRNNT granny knot *loose knot*
GRNP grandpa *grandfather*
GRNP grown-up *adult*
GRNPN grand piano *music*
GRNPR Grand Prix *race* Grands Prix
GRNPRNT grandparent *relative*
GRNPRNTHD grandparenthood *relative*
GRNPYN grand piano *music*
GRNR garner *gather*
GRNR grainier *sandy*
GRNR granary *storehouse* granaries
GRNR granter (or) grantor *giver*
GRNR greenery *plants* greeneries
GRNR grinner *smiler*
GRNR groaner *moaner*
GRNRM greenroom *theater*
GRNS eagerness *impatience*
GRNS grandniece *relative*
GRNS greenness *color depth*
GRNS grounds *reasons, land, coffee*
GRNS guernsey *(often capitalized) cow* guernseys
GRNS Guernsey *island*
GRNSH garnish *(v) adorn (n) decoration* garnishes
GRNSH garnishee *withhold wages* garnisheed garnisheeing
GRNSHMNT garnishment *wages*
GRNSHNGK greenshank *bird*
GRNSHNK greenshank *bird*
GRNSK greensick *chlorosis*
GRNSKNS greensickness *chlorosis*
GRNSKPR greenskeeper (or) greenkeeper *golf*
GRNSKPR groundskeeper *landscaper*

GRNSL groundsel *weed*
GRNSLM grand slam (n) *tournament* grand-slam (adj)
GRNSMN groundsman *(Br) landscaper*
GRNSN grandson *relative*
GRNSND greensand *sediment*
GRNSPD ground speed *velocity*
GRNST grainiest *sandy*
GRNSTF greenstuff *vegetation*
GRNSTK greenstick *broken bone*
GRNSTN grandstand (n) *audience* (v) *impress*
GRNSTN greenstone *rock*
GRNSTN grindstone *millstone*
GRNSTND grandstand (n) *audience* (v) *impress*
GRNSTNDR grandstander *show-off*
GRNSWL ground swell *wave, growth*
GRNSWRD greensward *grass*
GRNT garnet *gemstone*
GRNT granita *fruit ice*
GRNT granite *rock*
GRNT grant *(v) give, concede (n) gift*
GRNT grantee *receiver*
GRNT groundnut *peanut*
GRNT grunt *hog sound, fish, soldier**
GRNT guarantee *(v) assure* guaranteed guaranteeing
GRNT guarantee *(n) assurance*
GRNT guaranty *pledge* guaranties
GRNTBL grantable *give, admit*
GRNTD granitoid *hard*
GRNTFRS garnetiferous *gemstone*
GRNTHM green thumb *plant growth*
GRNTK granitic *hard*

GRNTL gruntle *make agreeable* gruntled gruntling
GRNTLK granitelike *hard*
GRNTND grant-in-aid *money gift* grants-in-aid
GRNTR garniture *trimming*
GRNTR granter (or) grantor *giver*
GRNTR guarantor *assurer*
GRNTWR graniteware *dishes*
GRNW greenway *land*
GRNWD greenwood *foliage*
GRNWD groundwood *pulp*
GRNWDR groundwater *wells*
GRNWNG greenwing *bird*
GRNWNGD green-winged *teal*
GRNWRK groundwork *foundation*
GRNWTR groundwater *wells*
GRNYL granule *one piece of grain*
GRNYLDD granulated *grainy*
GRNYLDR granulator *form grains*
GRNYLM granuloma *inflammation* granulomas (or) granulomata
GRNYLMD granulomata (pl) *inflammation* granuloma
GRNYLMT granulomata (pl) *inflammation* granuloma
GRNYLR granular *grainy*
GRNYLRD granularity *grainy*
GRNYLRT granularity *grainy*
GRNYLS granulose *grainy*
GRNYLSHN granulation *form grains*
GRNYLSS granulosis *disease* granuloses
GRNYLT granulate *crystallize* granulated granulating
GRNYLT granulite *rock*
GRNYLTD granulated *grainy*
GRNYLTR granulator *form grains*

Use letters that best describe the sounds you hear and omit the vowels. Use **S** or **K** instead of **C**: to find circle use **SRKL**. Use **J** to find joy, **JM** to find gem and **G** to find go.

GRNYN grunion *fish*
GRNYR grainier *sandy*
GRNYST grainiest *sandy*
GRNZ grounds *reasons, land, coffee*
GRNZ guernsey *(often capitalized) cow* guernseys
GRNZ Guernsey *island*
GRNZKPR greenskeeper (or) greenkeeper *golf*
GRNZKPR groundskeeper *landscaper*
GRNZMN groundsman *(Br) landscaper*
GRP gear up *get ready*
GRP gorp *snack*
GRP grape *fruit*
GRP grappa *brandy*
GRP grip *(v) hold* gripped gripping
GRP grip *(n) suitcase, handle*
GRP gripe *complain* griped griping
GRP grippe *influenza*
GRP grope *feel* groped groping
GRP group *(n) gathering (v) classify*
GRP groupie *rooter*
GRP grow up *mature*
GRPBL groupable *classify*
GRPFRT grapefruit *fruit* grapefruit (or) grapefruits
GRPL grapple *struggle* grappled grappling
GRPL graupel *soft hail*
GRPLK grapelike *clustered*
GRPLN grappling *hook*
GRPLNG grappling *hook*
GRPLR grappler *struggle*
GRPN grouping *set*
GRPNG grouping *set*
GRPNL grapnel *anchor*
GRPR griper *complainer*
GRPR gripper *holder*
GRPR groper *feeler*
GRPR grouper *fish* groupers
GRPSKL groupuscule *activists*
GRPSKYL groupuscule *activists*
GRPSQL groupuscule *activists*

GRPTHNGK groupthink *conformity*
GRPTHNK groupthink *conformity*
GRPVN grapevine *fruit, rumor*
GRR gorier *bloody*
GRR grower *cultivate, increase*
GRR Gruyère *cheese*
GRRN agrarian *farm*
GRRNZM agrarianism *land reform*
GRRYN agrarian *farm*
GRRYNZM agrarianism *land reform*
GRS aggress *quarrel*
GRS egress *go out*
GRS gorse *shrub*
GRS grace *(v) adorn* graced gracing
GRS grace *(n) approval, mercy, charm**
GRS grass *lawn* grasses
GRS grassy *with grass* grassier grassiest
GRS grease *oil* greased greasing
GRS greasy *oily* greasier greasiest
GRS Greece *country*
GRS gross *(adj) out-and-out, coarse (n) 12 dozen, total (v) earn* grosses
GRS grouse *(n) bird* grouse (or) grouses
GRS grouse *(v) complain* groused grousing
GRSBL greaseball *(vulgar) immigrant*
GRSFL graceful *(adj) pleasing* gracefully *(adv)*
GRSFLNS gracefulness *pleasing*
GRSH garage *car storage* garaged garaging
GRSH garish *gaudy*
GRSH grayish *no color*
GRSH groszy *money* groszy
GRSH ogreish *monster*
GRSHF gearshift

transmission
GRSHFT gearshift *transmission*
GRSHL garishly *gaudy*
GRSHN aggression *attack*
GRSHN egression *exit*
GRSHN Grecian *of Greece*
GRSHNS garishness *gaudy*
GRSHPR grasshopper *insect*
GRSHR grazier *rancher*
GRSHR grocery *market* groceries
GRSHRSTR grocery store *market* groceries
GRSHS gracious *polite, merciful*
GRSHSL garage sale *household items*
GRSHSL graciously *politely, mercifully*
GRSHSNS graciousness *manners, mercy*
GRSKP gyroscope *spinner*
GRSKPK gyroscopic *spinner*
GRSKPKL gyroscopically *spinner*
GRSL greasily *oily*
GRSL gristle *cartilage*
GRSL gristly *cartilage* gristlier gristliest
GRSL grossly *coarse, large*
GRSLK grasslike *slender spike*
GRSLN grassland *meadow*
GRSLND grassland *meadow*
GRSLNS gristliness *cartilage*
GRSLR gristlier *cartilage*
GRSLS graceless *clumsy*
GRSLS grassless *no grass*
GRSLS greaseless *dry*
GRSLSL gracelessly *clumsy*
GRSLSNS gracelessness *clumsy*
GRSLST gristliest *cartilage*
GRSLYR gristlier *cartilage*
GRSLYST gristliest *cartilage*
GRSM gruesome *ghastly*
GRSML gristmill *grain*
GRSML gruesomely *ghastly*
GRSMNGK grease monkey

Letters aren't doubled for single sounds: to find alley use **L** not **LL**. Use **Y** and **W** as hard sounds only: to find yellow use **YL**. (Br)=British spelling or usage. * See dictionary.

mechanic

GRSMNK grease monkey *mechanic*

GRSMNS gruesomeness *ghastly*

GRSN garçon *waiter* garçons

GRSN garrison *army*

GRSN greisen *rock*

GRSNS grassiness *with grass*

GRSNS greasiness *oily*

GRSNS grossness *coarse, large*

GRSNT grace note *music*

GRSP grasp *clutch*

GRSPBL graspable *clutch*

GRSPN grasping *greedy*

GRSPNG grasping *greedy*

GRSPNGL graspingly *greedily*

GRSPNL graspingly *greedily*

GRSPNT greasepaint *makeup*

GRSPR grasper *clutch*

GRSPR grasshopper *insect*

GRSPRF greaseproof *waxed*

GRSR aggressor *attacker*

GRSR grassier *with grass*

GRSR greaser *(slang) young man*

GRSR greasier *oily*

GRSR grocer *food seller*

GRSR grocery *market* groceries

GRSR grouser *complainer*

GRSRSTR grocery store *market* groceries

GRSRTS grassroots (adj) *fundamental* grass roots (n)

GRSSPN greasy spoon *diner*

GRSST grassiest *with grass*

GRSST greasiest *oily*

GRST goriest *bloody*

GRST grist *grain*

GRST gross-out (n) *disgust* gross out (v)

GRSTML gristmill *grain*

GRSV aggressive *assertive*

GRSVD aggressivity

assertiveness

GRSVL aggressively *assertively*

GRSVNS aggressiveness *assertiveness*

GRSVT aggressivity *assertiveness*

GRSWD greasewood *shrub*

GRSYR grassier *with grass*

GRSYR greasier *oily*

GRSYST grassiest *with grass*

GRSYST greasiest *oily*

GRT aigrette *feather*

GRT egret *bird*

GRT garret *attic*

GRT garrote (or) garotte *strangle* garroted (or) garotted garroting (or) garotting

GRT girt (or) girded *(v-past)* gird, encircle

GRT Goethe *writer*

GRT grate *(v) irritate* grated grating

GRT grate *(n) grille*

GRT great *very good*

GRT greet *say hello*

GRT grit *sand* gritted gritting

GRT gritty *sandy* grittier grittiest

GRT groat *grain, coin*

GRT grotto *cavern* grottoes

GRT grout *mortar*

GRTBRRF Great Barrier Reef *coral reef*

GRTBRTN Great Britain *island*

GRTBRYRF Great Barrier Reef *coral reef*

GRTD gratuity *tip* gratuities

GRTDN Great Dane *dog*

GRTDS gratuitous *free, voluntary*

GRTF gratify *reward* gratified gratifying gratifies

GRTFKSHN gratification *reward*

GRTFL grateful (adj) *thankful* gratefully (adv)

GRTFLNS gratefulness *thankful*

GRTFN gratifying *pleasing*

GRTFNG gratifying *pleasing*

GRTFRT grapefruit *fruit* grapefruit (or) grapefruits

GRTFYN gratifying *pleasing*

GRTFYNG gratifying *pleasing*

GRTGRNCHL great-grandchild *relative*

GRTGRNCHLD great-grandchild *relative*

GRTGRNDCHL great-grandchild *relative*

GRTGRNDCHLD great-grandchild *relative*

GRTGRNDPRNT great-grandparent *relative*

GRTGRNPRNT great-grandparent *relative*

GRTH garth *enclosure*

GRTH girth *(n) strap (v) encircle*

GRTH Goethe *writer*

GRTH growth *increase, evolution, product*

GRTHRDD greathearted *brave*

GRTHRTD greathearted *brave*

GRTKT greatcoat *overcoat*

GRTL greatly *much, nobly*

GRTL griddle *flat pan*

GRTL grittily *sandy*

GRTLKK griddle cake *food*

GRTLKS Great Lakes *region*

GRTLX Great Lakes *region*

GRTN au gratin *with cheese*

GRTN gratin *crust*

GRTN gratiné (or) gratinée *with cheese* gratinéed

GRTN grating *grille*

GRTN greeting *hello*

GRTNF great-nephew *relative*

GRTNFY great-nephew *relative*

GRTNG grating *grille*

GRTNG greeting *hello*

GRTNGKL great-uncle *relative*

GRTNKL great-uncle *relative*

GRTNS great-niece *relative*

Use letters that best describe the sounds you hear and omit the vowels. Use **S** or **K** instead of **C**: to find circle use **SRKL**. Use **J** to find joy, **JM** to find gem and **G** to find go.

GRTNS greatness *size, nobility, grandeur**
GRTNS grittiness *sandy*
GRTNT great-aunt *relative*
GRTPLNZ Great Plains *region*
GRTR garroter *strangler*
GRTR garter *band*
GRTR grater *rasp*
GRTR greater *larger, city and suburbs*
GRTR greeter *says hello*
GRTR gridder *football*
GRTR grittier *sandy*
GRTR grouter *mortar worker*
GRTS gratis *free*
GRTS grits *food*
GRTSK grotesque *weird*
GRTSKL grotesquely *weirdly*
GRTSKNS grotesqueness *weirdness*
GRTSLTLK Great Salt Lake (the) *body of water*
GRTST grittiest *sandy*
GRTT gratuity *tip* gratuities
GRTTD gratitude *thanks*
GRTTS gratuitous *free, voluntary*
GRTTYD gratitude *thanks*
GRTWD gratuity *tip* gratuities
GRTWDS gratuitous *free, voluntary*
GRTWLVCHN Great Wall of China (the) *structure*
GRTWT gratuity *tip* gratuities
GRTWTS gratuitous *free, voluntary*
GRTYD gratuity *tip* gratuities
GRTYDS gratuitous *free, voluntary*
GRTYR grittier *sandy*
GRTYST grittiest *sandy*
GRTYT gratuity *tip* gratuities
GRTYTS gratuitous *free, voluntary*
GRTYWD gratuity *tip* gratuities

GRTYWDS gratuitous *free, voluntary*
GRTYWT gratuity *tip* gratuities
GRTYWTS gratuitous *free, voluntary*
GRV aggrieve *wrong* aggrieved aggrieving
GRV garvey *boat* garveys
GRV grave *(v) carve, clean* graved graving
GRV grave *(adj) serious* graver gravest
GRV grave *(n) tomb (adj, adv) music*
GRV gravy *sauce* gravies
GRV greave *armor*
GRV grieve *mourn* grieved grieving
GRV groove *(v) fit, enjoy* grooved grooving
GRV groove *(n) rut, niche*
GRV groovy *wonderful* groovier grooviest
GRV grove *trees*
GRVD aggrieved *wronged*
GRVD gravid *pregnant*
GRVD gravida *pregnancy* gravidas (or) gravidae
GRVD gravity *weight, seriousness* gravities
GRVDD aggravated *serious*
GRVDD gravidity *pregnancy*
GRVDL aggrievedly *wronged*
GRVDNG aggravating *annoying*
GRVDR aggravator *annoyer*
GRVDT gravidity *pregnancy*
GRVL gravel *(v) confound, spread rocks* graveled (or) gravelled graveling (or) gravelling
GRVL gravel *(n) rocks*
GRVL gravelly *rocky*
GRVL gravely *seriously*
GRVL grovel *crawl, wallow* groveled (or) grovelled groveling (or) grovelling
GRVLD graveled *with rocks*
GRVLKS gravlax (or) gravlaks *salmon*
GRVLNGL grovelingly *crawl,*

wallow
GRVLNL grovelingly *crawl, wallow*
GRVLR groveler *crawl, wallow*
GRVLX gravlax (or) gravlaks *salmon*
GRVMNT aggrievement *wrong*
GRVN graven *carved*
GRVNMJ graven image *idol*
GRVNS graveness *seriousness*
GRVNS grievance *injustice*
GRVNTS grievance *injustice*
GRVR graver *sculptor, more serious*
GRVR gravure *photograph*
GRVR griever *mourner*
GRVR groover *enjoy, fit*
GRVR groovier *wonderful*
GRVS grievous *serious*
GRVSD graveside *tomb*
GRVSHN aggravation *annoyance*
GRVSL grievously *serious*
GRVSNS grievousness *serious*
GRVST gravest *most serious*
GRVST grooviest *wonderful*
GRVSTN gravestone *tomb*
GRVT aggravate *annoy* aggravated aggravating
GRVT gravity *weight, seriousness* gravities
GRVTD aggravated *serious*
GRVTN aggravating *annoying*
GRVTNG aggravating *annoying*
GRVTR aggravator *annoyer*
GRVTSHN gravitation *move toward*
GRVTT gravitate *move toward* gravitated gravitating
GRVYR gravure *photograph*
GRVYR groovier *wonderful*
GRVYRD graveyard *cemetery*
GRVYS grievous *serious*
GRVYSL grievously *serious*

Letters aren't doubled for single sounds: to find alley use **L** not **LL**. Use **Y** and **W** as hard sounds only: to find yellow use **YL**. (Br)=British spelling or usage. * See dictionary.

GRVYSNS grievousness *serious*
GRVYST grooviest *wonderful*
GRWK graywacke *sandstone*
GRWL growl *sound angry*
GRWL growly *sound angry* growlier growliest
GRWL gruel *cereal*
GRWLN grueling (or) gruelling *difficult*
GRWLNG grueling (or) gruelling *difficult*
GRWLNGL gruelingly *difficult*
GRWN growing *cultivate, increase*
GRWNG growing *cultivate, increase*
GRWP grow up *mature*
GRWR grower *cultivate, increase*
GRYBL agreeable (adj) *harmonious, pleasing* agreeably (adv)
GRYBLD agreeability *harmony*
GRYBLNS agreeableness *pleasantness, harmony*
GRYBLT agreeability *harmony*
GRYLD garrulity *wordiness*
GRYLS garrulous *wordy*
GRYLSNS garrulousness *wordy*
GRYLT garrulity *wordiness*
GRYM graham *wheat*
GRYR gorier *bloody*
GRYR Gruyère *cheese*
GRYSH grayish *no color*
GRYST goriest *bloody*
GRZ graze *eat grass, a scratch* grazed grazing
GRZ greasy *oily* greasier greasiest
GRZBL grazeable (or) grazable *feed, scratch*
GRZH garage *car storage* garaged garaging
GRZHR grazier *rancher*
GRZHSL garage sale *household items*

GRZL greasily *oily*
GRZL grisly *horrid* grislier grisliest
GRZL grizzle (v) *gray, grumble* grizzled grizzling
GRZL grizzly (adj) *gray* grizzlier grizzliest
GRZL grizzly (n) *bear* grizzlies
GRZLBR grizzly bear *animal*
GRZLD grizzled *gray*
GRZLNS grisliness *horrid*
GRZLR grislier *horrid*
GRZLR grizzlier *gray*
GRZLST grisliest *horrid*
GRZLST grizzliest *gray*
GRZLYR grislier *horrid*
GRZLYR grizzlier *gray*
GRZLYST grisliest *horrid*
GRZLYST grizzliest *gray*
GRZN grazing *grass*
GRZNG grazing *grass*
GRZNS greasiness *oily*
GRZR grazer *eater*
GRZR greaser (slang) *young man*
GRZR greasier *oily*
GRZSPN greasy spoon *diner*
GRZST greasiest *oily*
GRZT grisette *woman*
GRZYR greasier *oily*
GRZYST greasiest *oily*
GS gas (v) *talk, supply fuel* gassed gassing
GS gas (n) *fuel* gases
GS gassy *windy* gassier gassiest
GS geese (pl) *goose*
GS goose (n) *bird* geese
GS goose (v) *poke* goosed goosing
GS goosey *nervous* goosier goosiest
GS guess *suppose*
GSBG gasbag *talker*
GSBL guessable *suppose*
GSBMPS goose bumps *skin*
GSBR gooseberry *fruit* gooseberries
GSD Augusta *city*
GSD gassed *drunk*

GSD gusto *enjoyment* gustoes
GSD gusty *windy*
GSDK egoistic *self-centered*
GSDKL egoistically *self-centered*
GSDLT gestalt *pattern* gestalten (or) gestalts
GSDLTN gestalten (pl) *pattern* gestalt
GSDMT guesstimate *estimate*
GSDNG ghosting *image*
GSDNS gustiness *surge*
GSDP gussied up *overdress*
GSDRK gastric *stomach*
GSDRKJS gastric juice *stomach*
GSDRL gastrula *embryo* gastrulas (or) gastrulae
GSDRLR gastrular *embryo*
GSDRLSHN gastrulation *embryo*
GSDRLT gastrulate *embryo*
GSDRPD gastropod *shellfish*
GSDRTRK gastrotrich *animal*
GSDSHN gustation *taste*
GSDTR gustatory *taste*
GSDTRL gustatorily *taste*
GSF gasify *make gas* gasified gasifying gasifies
GSFLSH gooseflesh *skin*
GSFR gasifier *make gas*
GSFSH goosefish *monkfish*
GSFT goosefoot *herb* goosefoots
GSFYR gasifier *make gas*
GSG goose egg *zero*
GSGRS goosegrass *plant*
GSGZLR gas-guzzler *car*
GSH aguish *feverish*
GSH gash *cut*
GSH gauche *crude*
GSH geisha *woman* geisha (or) geishas
GSH gosh (interj) *surprise*
GSH gush *flood*
GSH gushy *sentimental* gushier gushiest
GSHDLT gestalt *pattern* gestalten (or) gestalts

Use letters that best describe the sounds you hear and omit the vowels. Use **S** or **K** instead of **C**: to find circle use **SRKL**. Use **J** to find joy, **JM** to find gem and **G** to find go.

GSHDLTN gestalten (pl) *pattern* gestalt
GSHK goshawk *bird*
GSHL eggshell *egg cover*
GSHL gasohol *fuel*
GSHL gauchely *crude*
GSHL gushily *sentimental*
GSHNGL gushingly *sentimental*
GSHNL gushingly *sentimental*
GSHNS gaucheness *crude*
GSHNS gushiness *sentimental*
GSHR gaucherie *awkward act*
GSHR gusher *flood, oil well*
GSHR gushier *sentimental*
GSHS gaseous *with gas*
GSHST gushiest *sentimental*
GSHTLT gestalt *pattern* gestalten (or) gestalts
GSHTLTN gestalten (pl) *pattern* gestalt
GSHYR gushier *sentimental*
GSHYST gushiest *sentimental*
GSKN gaskin *hind leg*
GSKND gasconade *boast*
GSKNDR gasconader *boaster*
GSKT gasket *fitting*
GSL egg cell *ovum*
GSL gassily *windy*
GSL ghastly *awful* ghastlier ghastliest
GSL ghostly *spirit, pale* ghostlier ghostliest
GSLN gasoline *fuel*
GSLNS ghastliness *awful*
GSLNS ghostliness *spirit, pale*
GSLR ghastlier *awful*
GSLR ghostlier *spirit, pale*
GSLST ghastliest *awful*
GSLST ghostliest *spirit, pale*
GSLT gaslight *(n) flame*
GSLT gaslit *(adj) illuminated*
GSLV Yugoslav *of Yugoslavia*
GSLV Yugoslavia *country*
GSLVY Yugoslavia *country*
GSLYR ghastlier *awful*

GSLYR ghostlier *spirit, pale*
GSLYST ghastliest *awful*
GSLYST ghostliest *spirit, pale*
GSMDR gasometer *measure*
GSMR gossamer *delicate*
GSMSK gas mask *filter*
GSMTR gasometer *measure*
GSNDR goosander *bird*
GSNK gooseneck *flexible*
GSNS gassiness *wind*
GSNS geoscience *earth*
GSNTRK egocentric *selfish*
GSNTRK geocentric *earth as center*
GSNTRKL egocentrically *selfish*
GSNTRKL geocentrically *earth as center*
GSNTRST egocentricity *selfish*
GSNTRZM egocentrism *selfish*
GSNTS geoscience *earth*
GSP gasp *breath*
GSP gossip *rumor*
GSP gossipy *chatty*
GSP gussy up *overdress* gussied up gussying up gussies up
GSPCH gazpacho *soup* gazpachos
GSPL gospel *(often capitalized) good news, truth*
GSPMPLZ goose pimples *skin*
GSPR gasper *(Br) cigarette*
GSPR gossiper *rumor*
GSR gasser *(slang) great*
GSR gassier *windy*
GSR goosier *nervous*
GSR guesser *suppose*
GSRDR ghostwriter *author*
GSRT ghostwrite *author* ghostwrote ghostwritten
GSRTN ghostwritten *authored*
GSRTR ghostwriter *author*
GSS gaseous *with gas*
GSST gassiest *windy*
GSST goosiest *nervous*

GST aghast *shock*
GST August *month*
GST august *dignified*
GST Augusta *city*
GST edgiest *nervous*
GST egoist *self-centered one*
GST G-suit *gravity*
GST gassed *drunk*
GST ghost *spirit*
GST guest *visitor*
GST gusset *insert*
GST gust *surge*
GST gusto *enjoyment* gustoes
GST gusty *windy*
GSTHS guesthouse *visitor*
GSTK egoistic *self-centered*
GSTKL egoistically *self-centered*
GSTL ghastly *awful* ghastlier ghastliest
GSTL ghostly *spirit, pale* ghostlier ghostliest
GSTLNS ghastliness *awful*
GSTLNS ghostliness *spirit, pale*
GSTLR ghastlier *awful*
GSTLR ghostlier *spirit, pale*
GSTLST ghastliest *awful*
GSTLST ghostliest *spirit, pale*
GSTLT gestalt *pattern* gestalten (or) gestalts
GSTLTN gestalten (pl) *pattern* gestalt
GSTLYR ghastlier *awful*
GSTLYR ghostlier *spirit, pale*
GSTLYST ghastliest *awful*
GSTLYST ghostliest *spirit, pale*
GSTMT guesstimate *estimate*
GSTNG ghosting *image*
GSTNS gustiness *surge*
GSTP gestapo *Nazi police* gestapos
GSTP goose-step *(v) marching* goose step *(n)*
GSTR extra *additional*
GSTR gaster *abdomen*
GSTRDR ghostwriter *author*
GSTRDS gastritis *stomach*

Letters aren't doubled for single sounds: to find alley use **L** not **LL**. Use **Y** and **W** as hard sounds only: to find yellow use **YL**. (Br)=British spelling or usage. * See dictionary.

GSTRFK geostrophic *force*
GSTRFKL geostrophically *force*
GSTRK gastric *stomach*
GSTRKDM gastrectomy *stomach* gastrectomies
GSTRKJS gastric juice *stomach*
GSTRKTM gastrectomy *stomach* gastrectomies
GSTRL gastrula *embryo* gastrulas (or) gastrulae
GSTRLR gastrular *embryo*
GSTRLSHN gastrulation *embryo*
GSTRLT gastrulate *embryo*
GSTRNG G-string *bikini*
GSTRNM gastronome *gourmet*
GSTRNM gastronomy *gourmet*
GSTRNMK gastronomic *gourmet*
GSTRNMKL gastronomically *gourmet*
GSTRNMST gastronomist *gourmet*
GSTRNTRDS gastroenteritis *stomach*
GSTRNTRLG gastroenterology *stomach*
GSTRNTRLJ gastroenterology *stomach*
GSTRNTRLJST gastroenterologist *stomach*
GSTRNTRTS gastroenteritis *stomach*
GSTRNTSNL gastrointestinal *stomach*
GSTRNTSTNL gastrointestinal *stomach*
GSTRPD gastropod *shellfish*
GSTRSFGL gastroesophageal *stomach*
GSTRSFJL gastroesophageal *stomach*
GSTRT ghostwrite *author* ghostwrote ghostwritten
GSTRTN ghostwritten authored
GSTRTR ghostwriter *author*
GSTRTRK gastrotrich *animal*
GSTRTS gastritis *stomach*
GSTRWNTRDS gastroenteritis *stomach*
GSTRWNTRLG gastroenterology *stomach*
GSTRWNTRLJ gastroenterology *stomach*
GSTRWNTRLJST gastroenterologist *stomach*
GSTRWNTRTS gastroenteritis *stomach*
GSTRWNTSNL gastrointestinal *stomach*
GSTRWNTSTNL gastrointestinal *stomach*
GSTRWSFGL gastroesophageal *stomach*
GSTRWSFJL gastroesophageal *stomach*
GSTSHN gustation *taste*
GSTTR gustatory *taste*
GSTTRL gustatorily *taste*
GSWRK guesswork *opinion*
GSYNS geoscience *earth*
GSYNTS geoscience *earth*
GSYP gussy up *overdress* gussied up gussying up gussies up
GSYR gassier *windy*
GSYR goosier *nervous*
GSYS gaseous *with gas*
GSYST gassiest *windy*
GSYST goosiest *nervous*
GSZ excise *(v) remove, tax* excised excising
GSZ excise *(n) tax*
GT agate *quartz*
GT agouti *rodent*
GT gaiety *joy* gaieties
GT gait *step*
GT galleta *grass*
GT gate *doorway* gated gating
GT gâteau (or) gateau *cake* gâteaux (or) gateaux
GT get *receive, understand, kill** got getting gotten
GT ghat *stairway*
GT ghetto *city area* ghettos
GT giddy *lightheaded, dizzy* giddier giddiest
GT git *(Br) fool*
GT goat *animal* goats (or) goat
GT goatee *beard*
GT Goethe *writer*
GT gout *disease* gouty
GT gut *intestines* gutted gutting
GT gutta *ornament* guttae
GTC gutsy *couragous*
GTD gaited *step*
GTD gated *door*
GTD goateed *bearded*
GTFL gatefold *foldout*
GTFLD gatefold *foldout*
GTFSH goatfish *mullet*
GTGTHR get-together *social*
GTH Goethe *writer*
GTHK Gothic *medieval* (Br) Gothick
GTHR gather *collect*
GTHRD goatherd *tend goats*
GTHRML geothermal *heat*
GTHRN gathering *crowd*
GTHRNG gathering *crowd*
GTHS gatehouse *building*
GTHSZ gothicize *(often capitalized) medieval* gothicized gothicizing
GTKPR gatekeeper *guard*
GTKRSHR gate-crasher *uninvited*
GTL giddily *dizzy*
GTLG gateleg *furniture*
GTLK goatlike *animal, lustful*
GTLS gutless *cowardly*
GTLSNS gutlessness *cowardice*
GTML Guatemala *country*
GTMR egg timer *clock*
GTN gotten *(v-past) get*
GTN guillotine *behead*
GTNBRG Gutenberg *inventor*
GTNS giddiness *lightheaded, dizzy*

Use letters that best describe the sounds you hear and omit the vowels. Use **S** or **K** instead of **C**: to find circle use **SRKL**. Use **J** to find joy, **JM** to find gem and **G** to find go.

GTP get up (v) arise, arrange
GTP getup (n) outfit
GTPNDG get-up-and-go energy
GTPNG get-up-and-go energy
GTPRCH gutta-percha latex
GTPST gatepost fence
GTR gaiter shoe
GTR giddier dizzy
GTR goiter gland
GTR guitar music
GTR gutter (n) trough (v) channel (adj) vulgar
GTRD goatherd tend goats
GTRFSH guitarfish ray
GTRJN goitrogen substance
GTRJNK goitrogenic substance
GTRL guttural throaty
GTRN gittern guitar
GTRN guttering trough
GTRNCHN gut-wrenching agony
GTRNCHNG gut-wrenching agony
GTRNG guttering trough
GTRP ego trip (n) self-praise ego-trip (v)
GTRPZM geotropism gravity
GTRS goitrous gland
GTRSNP guttersnipe street person
GTRST guitarist musician
GTS gatehouse building
GTS goddess female deity goddesses
GTS gutsy couragous
GTSDK egotistic (or) egotistical conceited
GTSDKL egotistical (or) egotistic conceited egotistically (adv)
GTSH goatish lustful
GTSHK Gottschalk composer
GTSHN guttation water
GTSKN goatskin leather
GTSKR goatsucker bird
GTST egotist conceited one
GTST giddiest dizzy
GTSTK egotistic (or)

egotistical conceited
GTSTKL egotistical (or) egotistic conceited egotistically (adv)
GTTH egg tooth beak
GTW gateway door
GTW getaway escape
GTWTHT get with it be aware
GTWZ ghettoize separate ghettoized ghettoizing
GTWZSHN ghettoization separation
GTYR giddier dizzy
GTYST giddiest dizzy
GTZ ghettoize separate ghettoized ghettoizing
GTZ gutsy couragous
GTZBRG Gettysburg city
GTZM egotism conceit
GTZSHN ghettoization separation
GV agave plant
GV gave (v-past) give
GV give (v) donate, allot, devote* gave giving given
GV guava fruit
GV gyve shackle
GVBK giveback (n) return give back (v)
GVF give off emit
GVHT give a hoot care
GVL gavel hammer gaveled (or) gavelled gaveling (or) gavelling
GVL gavial animal
GVLTFSH gefilte fish food
GVM give me bestow, confer
GVMNT government administration
GVN give in concede
GVN given donated, understood
GVNDTK give-and-take share, meet halfway
GVNM given name first name
GVNR governor authority
GVNRJNRL governor-general authority governors-general (or) governor-generals

GVNTK give-and-take share, meet halfway
GVP give up quit
GVR giver donor
GVRMNL governmental administration
GVRMNT government administration
GVRMNTL governmental administration
GVRN govern control
GVRNBL governable control
GVRNMNL governmental administration
GVRNMNT government administration
GVRNMNTL governmental administration
GVRNNS governance control
GVRNNTS governance control
GVRNR governor authority
GVRNRJNRL governor-general authority governors-general (or) governor-generals
GVRNS governess authority (f), child care governesses
GVT gavotte dance
GVT give out tire, quit
GVW give away (v) donate, betray
GVW giveaway (n) premium
GVYL gavial animal
GW gooey sticky
GWDK geoduck clam
GWDLHR Guadalajara city
GWDLP Guadeloupe islands
GWDML Guatemala country
GWHD go-ahead start
GWKM guaiacum tree
GWKML guacamole food
GWL aiguille rock
GWLT aiguillette cord
GWM Guam island
GWN goanna animal
GWN going (n) movement (adj) working, living, current*
GWN gowan flower
GWN guan bird

Letters aren't doubled for single sounds: to find alley use **L** not **LL**. Use **Y** and **W** as hard sounds only: to find yellow use **YL**. (Br)=British spelling or usage. * See dictionary.

GWN guano *waste matter*
GWN Guiana *region*
GWN iguana *animal*
GWNDN iguanodon *dinosaur*
GWNG going (n) *movement* (adj) *working, living, current**
GWNGVR going-over *scolding, inspection* goings-over
GWNGZN goings-on *events*
GWNK guanaco *animal* guanacos
GWNN guenon *monkey*
GWNS gooeyness *sticky*
GWNVR going-over *scolding, inspection* goings-over
GWNVR Guinevere *queen*
GWNZN goings-on *events*
GWR gaur *animal*
GWR guar *legume*
GWRN Guarani *ethnic group* Guarani (or) Guarani
GWSDK egoistic *self-centered*
GWSDKL egoistically *self-centered*
GWSH aguish *feverish*
GWSH gouache *watercolor*
GWST egoist *self-centered one*
GWSTK egoistic *self-centered*
GWSTKL egoistically *self-centered*
GWTML Guatemala *country*
GWV guava *fruit*
GWYKM guaiacum *tree*
GWYN Guiana *region*
GWZM egoism *self-interest*
GY ague *fever*
GY Gaea *earth goddess*
GYD gaiety *joy* gaieties
GYD galleta *grass*
GYD geode *rock*
GYDC geodesy *math*
GYDDK geodetic *math*
GYDS geodesy *math*
GYDSK geodesic *construction, line*
GYDSST geodesist *math*

GYDTK geodetic *math*
GYFG geophagy *nutrition*
GYFJ geophagy *nutrition*
GYFL guileful (adj) *tricky* guilefully (adv)
GYFN geophone *vibrations*
GYFT geophyte *plant*
GYFZKL geophysical (adj) *earth* geophysically (adv)
GYFZKS geophysics *earth*
GYFZSST geophysicist *earth*
GYFZX geophysics *earth*
GYG gewgaw *bauble*
GYGRF geography *earth* geographies
GYGRFK geographic (or) geographical *earth*
GYGRFKL geographical (or) geographic (adj) *earth* geographically (adv)
GYGRFR geographer *earth*
GYKM guaiacum *tree*
GYL guile *trickery*
GYLG geology *life history* geologies
GYLJK geologic (or) geological *life history*
GYLJKL geological (or) geologic (adj) *life history* geologically (adv)
GYLJST geologist *life history*
GYLJZ geologize *life history* geologized geologizing
GYLS guileless *innocent*
GYM goyim (pl) *Gentile* goy
GYM guillemet *mark*
GYMDR geometer *mathematician*
GYMNC geomancy *prophecy*
GYMNK geomantic *prophecy*
GYMNS geomancy *prophecy*
GYMNTC geomancy *prophecy*
GYMNTK geomantic *prophecy*
GYMNTS geomancy *prophecy*
GYMRFK geomorphic *surface*
GYMRFLG geomorphology

surface geomorphologies
GYMRFLJKL geomorphological *surface*
GYMTR geometer *mathematician*
GYMTR geometry *math system* geometries
GYMTRK geometric (or) geometrical *shapes*
GYMTRKL geometrical (or) geometric *shapes*
GYMTRKS geometrics *patterns*
GYMTRSHN geometrician *shapes*
GYMTRX geometrics *patterns*
GYN Aegean *Greek*
GYN Guiana *region*
GYN Guyana *country*
GYNC Aegean Sea *body of water*
GYNLNDZ Aegean Islands *land masses*
GYNLNZ Aegean Islands *land masses*
GYNS Aegean Sea *body of water*
GYP GOP *Republican*
GYPLDKL geopolitical (adj) *policy* geopolitically (adv)
GYPLTKL geopolitical (adj) *policy* geopolitically (adv)
GYPLTKS geopolitics *policy*
GYPLTX geopolitics *policy*
GYR augury *prediction* auguries
GYR edgier *nervous*
GYRDSS giardiasis *disease* giardiases
GYRDYSS giardiasis *disease* giardiases
GYSH aguish *feverish*
GYSH guilloche *ornament*
GYSNS geoscience *earth*
GYSNTRK geocentric *earth as center*
GYSNTRKL geocentrically *earth as center*
GYSNTS geoscience *earth*
GYST edgiest *nervous*
GYSTRFK geostrophic *force*

Use letters that best describe the sounds you hear and omit the vowels. Use **S** or **K** instead of **C**: to find circle use **SRKL**. Use **J** to find joy, **JM** to find gem and **G** to find go.

GYSTRFKL geostrophically *force*

GYSYNTS geoscience *earth*

GYT gaiety *joy* gaieties

GYT galleta *grass*

GYTHRML geothermal *heat*

GYTN guillotine *behead*

GYTRPZM geotropism *gravity*

GYWSH aguish *feverish*

GZ agaze *looking*

GZ gauze *fabric*

GZ gauzy *thin, sheer*

GZ gaze *look* gazed gazing

GZ goes *moves, is placed (3rd person singular of "go")*

GZ guise *dress, pretext*

GZB gazebo *structure* gazebos

GZBDR exhibitor *displayer*

GZBLG exobiology *life beyond earth*

GZBLJ exobiology *life beyond earth*

GZBLJKL exobiological *life beyond earth*

GZBLJST exobiologist *life beyond earth*

GZBRNS exuberance *profusion, joy*

GZBRNT exuberant *plentiful, joyful*

GZBRNTL exuberantly *plentiful, joyful*

GZBRNTS exuberance *profusion, joy*

GZBRT exuberate *overflow* exuberated exuberating

GZBSHN exhibition *display*

GZBSHNST exhibitionist *exposure*

GZBSHNZM exhibitionism *exposure*

GZBT exhibit *display*

GZBTR exhibitor *displayer*

GZBYLG exobiology *life beyond earth*

GZBYLJ exobiology *life beyond earth*

GZBYLJKL exobiological *life beyond earth*

GZBYLJST exobiologist *life*

beyond earth

GZD exude *ooze* exuded exuding

GZDK exotic *unusual, foreign*

GZDK exotica *unusual items*

GZDKL exotically *foreign, unusual*

GZDKNS exoticness *foreign, unusual*

GZDNSH exodontia *teeth extraction*

GZDNST exodontist *teeth extraction*

GZDNTST exodontist *teeth extraction*

GZDRMS exodermis *outer layer*

GZDS exodus *departure*

GZDSHN exudation *material*

GZDT exudate *material*

GZGCZ exegeses (pl) *explanation* exegesis

GZGM exogamy *marriage* exogamies

GZGMK exogamic *marriage*

GZGMS exogamous *marriage*

GZGS exiguous *scarce*

GZGSS exegesis *explanation* exegeses

GZGSZ exegeses (pl) *explanation* exegesis

GZGT exiguity *scantiness* exiguities

GZGWS exiguous *scarce*

GZGWT exiguity *scantiness* exiguities

GZGYS exiguous *scarce*

GZGYT exiguity *scantiness* exiguities

GZGYWS exiguous *scarce*

GZGYWT exiguity *scantiness* exiguities

GZGZS exegesis *explanation* exegeses

GZHS gaseous *with gas*

GZJCZ exegeses (pl) *explanation* exegesis

GZJDKL exegetical *explanatory*

GZJDST exegetist *explainer*

GZJNC exigency *demand* exigencies

GZJNS exigency *demand* exigencies

GZJNS exogenous *from outside*

GZJNT exigent *demanding*

GZJNTC exigency *demand* exigencies

GZJNTS exigency *demand* exigencies

GZJRDR exaggerator *overstatement*

GZJRDV exaggerative *overstatement*

GZJRSHN exaggeration *overstatement*

GZJRT exaggerate *overstate* exaggerated exaggerating

GZJRTR exaggerator *overstatement*

GZJRTV exaggerative *overstatement*

GZJSS exegesis *explanation* exegeses

GZJSZ exegeses (pl) *explanation* exegesis

GZJTKL exegetical *explanatory*

GZJTST exegetist *explainer*

GZJZS exegesis *explanation* exegeses

GZK exact *(v)* demand *(adj) precise*

GZKD exacta *wager*

GZKDBL executable *kill, perform*

GZKDN exacting *difficult*

GZKDNG exacting *difficult*

GZKDNT executant *performer*

GZKDR executor *administrator*

GZKDTD exactitude *precision*

GZKDTYD exactitude *precision*

GZKDV executive *law, manager*

GZKL exactly *precisely*

GZKRBL execrable (adj)

Letters aren't doubled for single sounds: to find alley use **L** not **LL**. Use **Y** and **W** as hard sounds only: to find yellow use **YL**. (Br)=British spelling or usage. * See dictionary.

wretched execrably (adv)
GZKRBLNS execrableness *wretchedness*
GZKRDR execrator *denouncer*
GZKRDV execrative *denounce*
GZKRN exocrine *secretion*
GZKRP exocarp *outer layer*
GZKRSHN execration *denounce*
GZKRT execrate *denounce* execrated execrating
GZKRTR execrator *denouncer*
GZKRTV execrative *denounce*
GZKSHN execution *kill, perform*
GZKSHNR executioner *killer*
GZKT exact *(v)* demand *(adj) precise*
GZKT exacta *wager*
GZKT execute *kill, perform* executed executing
GZKTBL executable *kill, perform*
GZKTL exactly *precisely*
GZKTN exacting *difficult*
GZKTNG exacting *difficult*
GZKTNT executant *performer*
GZKTR executor *administrator*
GZKTR executory *administrative*
GZKTRCZ executrices (or) executrixes (pl) *administrator (f)* executrix
GZKTRKS executrix *administrator (f)* executrices (or) executrixes
GZKTRSZ executrices (or) executrixes (pl) *administrator (f)* executrix
GZKTRX executrix *administrator (f)* executrices (or) executrixes
GZKTTD exactitude

precision
GZKTTYD exactitude *precision*
GZKTV executive *law, manager*
GZKYDBL executable *kill, perform*
GZKYDNT executant *performer*
GZKYDR executor *administrator*
GZKYDV executive *law, manager*
GZKYSHN execution *kill, perform*
GZKYSHNR executioner *killer*
GZKYT execute *kill, perform* executed executing
GZKYTBL executable *kill, perform*
GZKYTNT executant *performer*
GZKYTR executor *administrator*
GZKYTR executory *administrative*
GZKYTRCZ executrices (or) executrixes (pl) *administrator (f)* executrix
GZKYTRKS executrix *administrator (f)* executrices (or) executrixes
GZKYTRSZ executrices (or) executrixes (pl) *administrator (f)* executrix
GZKYTRX executrix *administrator (f)* executrices (or) executrixes
GZKYTV executive *law, manager*
GZL exile *banish* exiled exiling
GZL gauzily *thin, sheer*
GZL gazelle *animal* gazelles
GZL guzzle *drink* guzzled guzzling
GZLK gauzelike *filmy*
GZLN gasoline *fuel*
GZLNG gosling *goose, fool*

GZLR auxiliary *help, extra* auxiliaries
GZLR guzzler *drink*
GZLRDV exhilarative *stimulated*
GZLRNT exhilarant *enliven*
GZLRSHN exhilaration *stimulation*
GZLRT exhilarate *enliven* exhilarated exhilarating
GZLRTV exhilarative *stimulated*
GZLT exalt *praise*
GZLT exult *rejoice*
GZLTDL exaltedly *elevated*
GZLTNC exultancy *rejoicing* exultance
GZLTNS exultance *rejoicing* exultancy
GZLTNT exultant *rejoicing*
GZLTNTC exultancy *rejoicing* exultance
GZLTNTS exultance *rejoicing* exultancy
GZLTR exalter *praiser*
GZLTSHN exaltation *praise*
GZLTSHN exultation *rejoicing*
GZLYR auxiliary *help, extra* auxiliaries
GZM eczema *skin rash*
GZM egoism *self-interest*
GZM exam *test*
GZM exhume *dig up* exhumed exhuming
GZM gizmo *gadget* gizmos
GZMDS eczematous *skin rash*
GZMN examine *inspect, test* examined examining
GZMN examinee *person tested*
GZMNBL examinable *inspect, test*
GZMNNT examinant *tester*
GZMNR examiner *inspector, tester*
GZMNSHN examination *inspection, test*
GZMP exempt *free*
GZMPL example *model, instance*

Use letters that best describe the sounds you hear and omit the vowels. Use **S** or **K** instead of **C**: to find circle use **SRKL**. Use **J** to find joy, **JM** to find gem and **G** to find go.

GZMPLF exemplify *embody* exemplified exemplifying exemplifies

GZMPLFKSHN exemplification *illustration*

GZMPLGRSH exempli gratia *for example (e.g.)*

GZMPLR exemplar *model*

GZMPLR exemplary *model*

GZMPLRL exemplarily *model*

GZMPLRNS exemplariness *model*

GZMPSHN exemption *freedom*

GZMPT exempt *free*

GZMR exhumer *dig up*

GZMSHN exemption *freedom*

GZMSHN exhumation *dig up*

GZMT exempt *free*

GZMTS eczematous *skin rash*

GZN exine *outer layer*

GZN exon *protein*

GZN gazania *herb*

GZNDHT gesundheit *good health*

GZNHT gesundheit *good health*

GZNMT exanimate *lifeless*

GZNRDV exonerative *forgiving*

GZNRSHN exoneration *forgiveness*

GZNRT exonerate *forgive* exonerated exonerating

GZNRTV exonerative *forgiving*

GZNT exeunt *exit*

GZNTHT gesundheit *good health*

GZNY gazania *herb*

GZPCH gazpacho *soup* gazpachos

GZQDBL executable *kill, perform*

GZQDNT executant *performer*

GZQDR executor

administrator

GZQDV executive *law, manager*

GZQSHN execution *kill, perform*

GZQSHNR executioner *killer*

GZQT execute *kill, perform* executed executing

GZQTBL executable *kill, perform*

GZQTNT executant *performer*

GZQTR executor *administrator*

GZQTR executory *administrative*

GZQTRCZ executrices (or) executrixes (pl) *administrator (f)* executrix

GZQTRKS executrix *administrator (f)* executrices (or) executrixes

GZQTRSZ executrices (or) executrixes (pl) *administrator (f)* executrix

GZQTRX executrix *administrator (f)* executrices (or) executrixes

GZQTV executive *law, manager*

GZR gazar *silk*

GZR gazer *looker*

GZR geezer *old man*

GZR geyser *fountain*

GZRB exurb *outer suburb*

GZRB exurbia *outer suburb*

GZRBDNS exorbitance *excess*

GZRBDNT exorbitant *excessive*

GZRBDNTS exorbitance *excess*

GZRBN exurban *outer suburb*

GZRBNT exurbanite *outer suburb*

GZRBTNS exorbitance *excess*

GZRBTNT exorbitant

excessive

GZRBTNTS exorbitance *excess*

GZRBY exurbia *outer suburb*

GZRD gizzard *grinder*

GZRDTR exhortatory *warning*

GZRL uxorial *wife*

GZRM gisarme *weapon*

GZRP excerpt *extract*

GZRPDR excerptor (or) excerpter *extractor*

GZRPT excerpt *extract*

GZRPTR excerptor (or) excerpter *extractor*

GZRS uxorious *love of wife*

GZRSD uxoricide *wife murder*

GZRSHN exertion *effort*

GZRSKL Exercycle (trademark) *bicycle*

GZRSL uxoriously *love of wife*

GZRSNS uxoriousness *love of wife*

GZRSST exorcist *expel evil*

GZRSZ exercise *(v) exert, use* exercised exercising

GZRSZ exercise *(n) use, exertion, drill*

GZRSZ exorcise *expel evil* exorcised exorcising

GZRSZBL exercisable *exert, use*

GZRSZM exorcism *expel evil*

GZRSZR exerciser *machine*

GZRT exert *put forth effort, wield*

GZRT exhort *warn*

GZRTSHN exhortation *warning*

GZRTTR exhortatory *warning*

GZRTTV exhortative *warning*

GZRYL uxorial *wife*

GZRYS uxorious *love of wife*

GZRYSL uxoriously *love of wife*

GZRYSNS uxoriousness *love of wife*

GZSCHN exhaustion

Letters aren't doubled for single sounds: to find alley use **L** not **LL**. Use **Y** and **W** as hard sounds only: to find yellow use **YL**. (Br)=British spelling or usage. * See dictionary.

depletion
GZSDBL exhaustible
deplete, tired
GZSDBLD exhaustibility
deplete, tired
GZSDBLT exhaustibility
deplete, tired
GZSDV exhaustive *thorough*
GZSFR exosphere
atmosphere
GZSKLTL exoskeletal *outer*
frame
GZSKLTN exoskeleton *outer*
frame
GZSPR exospore *separate*
GZSPRDDL exasperatedly
irritation
GZSPRDNGL
exasperatingly *irritation*
GZSPRDNL exasperatingly
irritation
GZSPRSHN exasperation
irritation
GZSPRT exasperate *irritate*
exasperated
exasperating
GZSPRTDL exasperatedly
irritation
GZSPRTNGL
exasperatingly *irritation*
GZSPRTNL exasperatingly
irritation
GZSRBSHN exacerbation
make worse
GZSRBT exacerbate *make*
worse exacerbated
exacerbating
GZST exhaust *(v)* deplete,
tire *(n)* vapor
GZST exist *live*
GZSTBL exhaustible *deplete,*
tired
GZSTBLD exhaustibility
deplete, tired
GZSTBLT exhaustibility
deplete, tired
GZSTCZ exostoses *(pl)*
outgrowth exotosis
GZSTNCHL existential *(adj)*
experience existentially
(adv)
GZSTNCHLST existentialist

philosopher
GZSTNCHLZM
existentialism *philosophy*
GZSTNS existence *life*
GZSTNSHL existential *(adj)*
experience existentially
(adv)
GZSTNSHLST existentialist
philosopher
GZSTNSHLZM
existentialism *philosophy*
GZSTNT existent *living*
GZSTNTS existence *life*
GZSTSS exocytosis *cell*
fusion exocytoses
GZSTSS exostosis
outgrowth exotoses
GZSTSZ exostoses *(pl)*
outgrowth exotosis
GZSTV exhaustive *thorough*
GZT exit *(v)* leave *(n)*
departure, way out
GZT gazette *journal*
GZTK exotic *foreign, unusual*
GZTK exotica *unusual items*
GZTKL exotically *foreign,*
unusual
GZTKNS exoticness *foreign,*
unusual
GZTR gazetteer *journalist*
GZTRK exoteric *external*
GZTRKL exoterically
external
GZVYR Xavier *Catholic saint*
GZYD exude *ooze* exuded
exuding
GZYDSHN exudation
material
GZYDT exudate *material*
GZYM exhume *dig up*
exhumed exhuming
GZYMR exhumer *dig up*
GZYMSHN exhumation *dig*
up
GZYNT exeunt *exit*

H agh *(or)* agghhh *(interj)*
frustration
H aha *(interj) surprise*
H ahoy *(interj) naval greeting*
H ha *(interj) surprise*
H hao *money* hao
H haw *(n) membrane, berry*
(v) evade, left
H hay *grass*
H he *(pron) that male*
H hew *cut down* hewed
hewed *(or)* hewn hewing
H hey *(interj) attention*
H hi *(interj) hello*
H hie *hurry* hied hying *(or)*
hieing
H high *tall, serious, drugged**
higher highest
H ho *attention (interj)*
H hoe *(v) cultivate* hoed
hoeing
H hoe *(n) tool*
H hooey *nonsense*
H how *in what manner*
H hoy *ship*
H hue *color*
H huh *(interj) question*
H Oahu *island*
H Ohio *US State*
H uh-huh *(interj) agreement*
H who *which person*
HB hautboy *(or)* hautbois
oboe hautboys *(or)*
hautbois
HB highboy *dresser*
HB hob *(v) cut* hobbed
hobbing
HB hob *(n) mischief, hook,*
tool
HB hobby *bird, pastime*
hobbies
HB hobo *transient* hoboes
HB hub *center*

Use letters that best describe the sounds you hear and omit the vowels. Use **S** or **K** instead of **C:** to find circle use **SRKL**. Use **J** to find joy, **JM** to find gem and **G** to find go.

HB hubby *husband* hubbies
HBB hubbub *uproar*
HBCH habitué *customer*
HBCH hibachi *grill*
HBCHL habitual (adj) *usual* habitually (adv)
HBCHSHN habituation *tolerance*
HBCHT habituate *tolerate* habituated habituating
HBCHW habitué *customer*
HBCHWL habitual (adj) *usual* habitually (adv)
HBCHWSHN habituation *tolerance*
HBCHWT habituate *tolerate* habituated habituating
HBDBL habitable *residence*
HBDBLD habitability *residence*
HBDBLT habitability *residence*
HBDS habitus *body build* habitus
HBFRN hebephrenia *mental disorder*
HBFRNK hebephrenic *mental disorder*
HBFRNY hebephrenia *mental disorder*
HBGBLN hobgoblin *ogre*
HBGBZ heebie-jeebies *jitters*
HBHRS hobbyhorse *toy horse*
HBJBZ heebie-jeebies *jitters*
HBKP hubcap *wheel*
HBL habile *able*
HBL highball *drink*
HBL hobble *limp, cripple, restrain* hobbled hobbling
HBLBSH hobblebush *shrub*
HBLR hobbler *crippler*
HBLTSHN habilitation *clothes*
HBLTT habilitate *clothe* habilitated habilitating
HBM high beam *headlight*
HBNB hobnob *associate* hobnobbed hobnobbing
HBNBR hobnobber *associate*

HBNL hobnail *shoe*
HBR Hebrew *language, person*
HBR highbrow *smug*
HBRD highbred *superior*
HBRD hybrid *mixed*
HBRDD hybridity *mixture*
HBRDSHR haberdasher *dealer*
HBRDSHR haberdashery *shop, goods* haberdasheries
HBRDT hybridity *mixture*
HBRDZ hybridize *mix* hybridized hybridizing
HBRDZM hybridism *mixture*
HBRDZR hybridizer *mixer*
HBRDZSHN hybridization *mixture*
HBRK Hebraic *Hebrew*
HBRN highborn *noble*
HBRNDR hibernator *asleep*
HBRNL hibernal *winter*
HBRNSHN hibernation *asleep*
HBRNT hibernate *rest* hibernated hibernating
HBRNTR hibernator *asleep*
HBRS hubris *pride*
HBRSDK hubristic *proud*
HBRSTK hubristic *proud*
HBRYK Hebraic *Hebrew*
HBSH highbush *shrub*
HBSKRPS habeas corpus *restraint*
HBSKS hibiscus *shrub*
HBST hobbyist *pastime*
HBT habit (n) *practice, costume* (v) *clothe*
HBT habitué *customer*
HBT hobbit *fictional creature*
HBT howbeit *although*
HBTBL habitable *residence*
HBTBLD habitability *residence*
HBTBLT habitability *residence*
HBTFRMN habit-forming *addicting*
HBTFRMNG habit-forming *addicting*
HBTL habitual (adj) *usual*

habitually (adv)
HBTS habitus *body build* habitus
HBTSHN habitation *residence*
HBTSHN habituation *tolerance*
HBTT habitat *residence*
HBTT habituate *tolerate* habituated habituating
HBTW habitué *customer*
HBTWL habitual (adj) *usual* habitually (adv)
HBTWSHN habituation *tolerance*
HBTWT habituate *tolerate* habituated habituating
HBYSKRPS habeas corpus *restraint*
HBYST hobbyist *pastime*
HBYT howbeit *although*
HC hissy *tantrum*
HC hussy *lewd female* hussies
HCD hayseed *hillbilly* hayseed (or) hayseeds
HCH hatch (n) *door* (v) *emerge from egg* hatches
HCH hitch (v) *attach, hobble* (n) *jerk, stoppage, connection* hitches
HCH hooch *liquor*
HCH hooch (or) hootch *hut*
HCH hutch *cupboard, coop* hutches
HCHBK hatchback *car*
HCHHK hitchhike *travel* hitchhiked hitchhiking
HCHHKR hitchhiker *travel*
HCHK hitchhike *travel* hitchhiked hitchhiking
HCHKR hitchhiker *travel*
HCHLN hatchling *animal*
HCHLNG hatchling *animal*
HCHN hatching *engraving*
HCHNG hatching *engraving*
HCHPCH hotchpotch *soup*
HCHR hatchery *eggs* hatcheries
HCHR high chair *baby seat*
HCHT hatchet *tool*
HCHTFS hatchet face *thin*

Letters aren't doubled for single sounds: to find alley use **L** not **LL**. Use **Y** and **W** as hard sounds only: to find yellow use **YL**. (Br)=British spelling or usage. * See dictionary.

and sharp

HCHTFST hatchet-faced
thin and sharp

HCHTMN hatchet man
destroyer hatchet men

HCHW hatchway *passage*

HCND hacienda *house*

HCS high seas *ocean*

HCYND hacienda *house*

HCZ high seas *ocean*

HD ahead *in front*

HD had *(v-past) have*

HD Haiti *country*

HD haughty *proud* haughtier
haughtiest

HD he'd *(contr) he had, he
would*

HD head *mind, chief*

HD heady *willful, giddy*
headier headiest

HD heed *take note*

HD heyday *successful time*

HD hide *(v) conceal* hid
hiding hidden

HD hide *(n) skin*

HD hod *tray*

HD hood *covering, thug,
neighborhood*

HD hoodoo *magic* hoodoos

HD howdah *seat*

HD howdy *greeting*

HD hued *colored*

HD who'd *(contr) who had,
who would*

HDBL heatable *warmth*

HDBN headband *hair*

HDBN hidebound *tight*

HDBND headband *hair*

HDBND hidebound *tight*

HDBRD headboard *bed*

HDCHZ headcheese *meat*

HDD headed *going toward*

HDD heated *warm, emotional*

HDD hooded *covered*

HDDL heatedly *warm,
emotional*

HDDNS hoodedness *covered*

HDF head off *block*

HDFL heedful (adj) *attentive*
heedfully (adv)

HDFN headphone *earphones*

HDFRST headfirst *head*

foremost

HDG hot dog *(n) food, show-
off (interj) approval*

HDG hotdog *(v) perform
stunts*

HDGR headgear *hat, harness*

HDGR Heidegger
philosopher

HDGT headgate *irrigation*

HDHL hidey-hole (or) hidy-
hole *hideaway*

HDHNR headhunter
cannibal, recruiter

HDHNTR headhunter
cannibal, recruiter

HDK haddock *fish* haddock

HDK headache *pain*

HDK headachy *painful*

HDKL head cold *sinus*

HDKLD head cold *sinus*

HDKRDR headquarter *reside*

HDKRDRS headquarters
command post

HDKRDRZ headquarters
command post

HDKRTR headquarter *reside*

HDKRTRS headquarters
command post

HDKRTRZ headquarters
command post

HDKWRDR headquarter
reside

HDKWRDRZ headquarters
command post

HDKWRTR headquarter
reside

HDKWRTRZ headquarters
command post

HDL haughtily *proud*

HDL headily *willful, giddy*

HDL hiatal *passage, gap, break*

HDL huddle *bunch* huddled
huddling

HDLG hidalgo *(often
capitalized) nobleman*
hidalgos

HDLK headlock *wrestling*

HDLM hoodlum *thug*

HDLMP headlamp *light*

HDLN headland *peninsula*

HDLN headline *news*
headlined headlining

HDLND headland *peninsula*

HDLNG headlong *headfirst*

HDLNR headliner *star*

HDLR huddler *bunch*

HDLS head louse *insect*
head lice

HDLS headless *no head*

HDLS heedless *careless*

HDLSL heedlessly *carelessly*

HDLSNS heedlessness
carelessness

HDLT headlight *illumination*

HDMN headman *chief*
headmen

HDMSDR headmaster
principal

HDMST headmost *leading*

HDMSTR headmaster
principal

HDMSTRS headmistress
principal

HDN hadn't *(contr) had not*

HDN head-on *head-to-head*

HDN heading *direction*

HDN hidden *concealed*

HDN hoedown *dance*

HDN Houdini *magician*

HDN hoyden *woman*

HDNCK hide-and-seek
game

HDNDCK hide-and-seek
game

HDNDGCK hide-and-go-
seek *game*

HDNDGSK hide-and-go-
seek *game*

HDNDSK hide-and-seek
game

HDNG heading *direction*

HDNGCK hide-and-go-seek
game

HDNGSK hide-and-go-seek
game

HDNK hedonic *pleasure*

HDNS haughtiness *pride*

HDNS headiness *willful,
giddy*

HDNSD high-density *thick*

HDNSDK hedonistic
pleasure

HDNSDKL hedonistically
pleasure

Use letters that best describe the sounds you hear and omit the vowels. Use **S** or **K**
instead of **C**: to find circle use **SRKL**. Use **J** to find joy, **JM** to find gem and **G** to find go.

HDNSK hide-and-seek *game*
HDNST hedonist *pleasure*
HDNST high-density *thick*
HDNSTK hedonistic *pleasure*
HDNSTKL hedonistically *pleasure*
HDNT hadn't *(contr) had not*
HDNT headnote *explanation*
HDNT whodunit *mystery*
HDNTSD high-density *thick*
HDNTST high-density *thick*
HDNZM hedonism *pleasure*
HDPN headpin *bowling*
HDPS headpiece *hat, brains*
HDQRDR headquarter *reside*
HDQRDRZ headquarters *command post*
HDQRTR headquarter *reside*
HDQRTRZ headquarters *command post*
HDR hater *detest*
HDR hatter *hat maker*
HDR haughtier *proud*
HDR header *top, soccer*
HDR headier *willful, giddy*
HDR heater *warmer*
HDR hider *concealer*
HDR hitter *bat, strike*
HDR hooter *owl sound*
HDR hot air *empty talk*
HDR hotter *heat, popular*
HDR hydra *polyp, monster*
HDR hydro *power, (Br) spa* hydros
HDRBLG hydrobiology *water*
HDRBLJ hydrobiology *water*
HDRBLJKL hydrobiological *water*
HDRBLJST hydrobiologist *water*
HDRBYLG hydrobiology *water*
HDRBYLJ hydrobiology *water*
HDRBYLJKL hydrobiological *water*
HDRBYLJST hydrobiologist *water*
HDRCL hydrocele *fluid*
HDRD hydride *chemical*

HDRD hydroid *polyp*
HDRDKC heterodoxy *(n) opinions* heterodoxies
HDRDKS heterodox *(adj) unorthodox*
HDRDKS heterodoxy *(n) opinions* heterodoxies
HDRDN heterodyne *(v) produce a beat* heterodyned heterodyning
HDRDN heterodyne *(n) beat*
HDRDNMK hydrodynamic *fluid motion*
HDRDNMKL hydrodynamically *fluid motion*
HDRDNMKS hydrodynamics *fluid motion*
HDRDNMX hydrodynamics *fluid motion*
HDRDR hydrator *add water*
HDRDX heterodox *(adj) unorthodox*
HDRDX heterodoxy *(n) opinions* heterodoxies
HDRFB hydrophobia *fear of water, rabies*
HDRFBK hydrophobic *fear of water, rabies*
HDRFBY hydrophobia *fear of water, rabies*
HDRFDK hydrophytic *plant*
HDRFL heterophile (or) heterophil *antigen*
HDRFL heterophylly *foliage*
HDRFL hydrofoil *boat*
HDRFLK hydrophilic *water-loving*
HDRFLRK hydrofluoric *etching*
HDRFLS heterophyllous *foliage*
HDRFLSD hydrophilicity *water-loving*
HDRFLST hydrophilicity *water-loving*
HDRFN heterophony *melody* heterophonies
HDRFT hydrophyte *plant*
HDRFTK hydrophytic *plant*

HDRFYL hydrofoil *boat*
HDRGM heterogamy *unlike gametes*
HDRGMS heterogamous *unlike gametes*
HDRGN heterogony *alternate generations*
HDRGND heterogeneity *mixed*
HDRGNS heterogeneous *mixed*
HDRGNT heterogeneity *mixed*
HDRGNYD heterogeneity *mixed*
HDRGNYS heterogeneous *mixed*
HDRGNYT heterogeneity *mixed*
HDRGRF hydrography *chart*
HDRGRFK hydrographic *chart*
HDRGRFR hydrographer *chart*
HDRJN heterogeny *mixed group*
HDRJN hydrogen *element*
HDRJNBM hydrogen bomb *weapon*
HDRJND heterogeneity *mixed*
HDRJNS heterogeneous *mixed*
HDRJNSHN hydrogenation *add hydrogen*
HDRJNT heterogeneity *mixed*
HDRJNT hydrogenate *add hydrogen* hydrogenated hydrogenating
HDRJNYD heterogeneity *mixed*
HDRJNYS heterogeneous *mixed*
HDRJNYT heterogeneity *mixed*
HDRK hydric *needs water*
HDRKC hydroxy *chemical*
HDRKLRK hydrochloric *corrosive*
HDRKNDK hydrokinetic *fluid motion*

Letters aren't doubled for single sounds: to find alley use **L** not **LL**. Use **Y** and **W** as hard sounds only: to find yellow use **YL**. (Br)=British spelling or usage. * See dictionary.

HDRKNTK hydrokinetic *fluid motion*

HDRKRBN hydrocarbon *petroleum*

HDRKRDZN hydrocortisone *steroid*

HDRKRTZN hydrocortisone *steroid*

HDRKS hydroxy *chemical*

HDRKSD hydroxide *chemical*

HDRKSL hydroxyl *chemical*

HDRLDK hydrolytic *decomposition*

HDRLDKL hydrolytically *decomposition*

HDRLG hydrology *water cycle*

HDRLGS heterologous *different*

HDRLGSL heterologously *different*

HDRLJ hydrology *water cycle*

HDRLJK hydrologic (or) hydrological (adj) *water cycle* hydrologically (adv)

HDRLJKL hydrological (or) hydrologic (adj) *water cycle* hydrologically (adv)

HDRLJST hydrologist *water cycle*

HDRLK hydraulic *water*

HDRLKL hydraulically *water*

HDRLKS hydraulics *water in motion*

HDRLKTRK hydroelectric *power*

HDRLKTRKL hydroelectrically *power*

HDRLKTRSD hydroelectricity *power*

HDRLKTRST hydroelectricity *power*

HDRLS hydrolase *enzyme*

HDRLSS hydrolysis *decomposition*

HDRLTK hydrolytic *decomposition*

HDRLTKL hydrolytically *decomposition*

HDRLX hydraulics *water in*

motion

HDRLZ hydrolase *enzyme*

HDRLZ hydrolyze *decompose* hydrolyzed hydrolyzing

HDRLZBL hydrolyzable *decomposition*

HDRM head rhyme *verse*

HDRM headroom *space*

HDRMDR hydrometer *specific gravity*

HDRMDS hydromedusa *polyp* hydromedusae

HDRMKNKL hydromechanical *fluid motion*

HDRMKNKS hydromechanics *fluid motion*

HDRMKNX hydromechanics *fluid motion*

HDRMRFK heteromorphic *deviating*

HDRMRFK hydromorphic *excess water*

HDRMRFZM heteromorphism *deviation*

HDRMS hit-or-miss (adj) *careless* hit or miss (adv)

HDRMTR hydrometer *specific gravity*

HDRMTRK hydrometric *specific gravity*

HDRNG hydrangea *shrub*

HDRNGY hydrangea *shrub*

HDRNJ hydrangea *shrub*

HDRNJY hydrangea *shrub*

HDRNM heteronomy *subjection*

HDRNM heteronym *word*

HDRNT hydrant *faucet*

HDRPDRS heteropterous *insect*

HDRPLD heteroploid *chromosome* heteroploidy

HDRPLN hydroplane *(v)* skim *(n)* boat, seaplane

HDRPNK hydroponic *grown in water*

HDRPNKL hydroponically *grown in water*

HDRPNKS hydroponics

grown in water

HDRPNX hydroponics *grown in water*

HDRPTRS heteropterous *insect*

HDRS headdress *hat* headdresses

HDRS hydrase *enzyme*

HDRS hydrous *water*

HDRSFLK hydrocephalic *brain fluid*

HDRSFLS hydrocephalus *brain fluid*

HDRSFR hydrosphere *atmosphere*

HDRSFRK hydrospheric *atmosphere*

HDRSHN hydration *add water*

HDRSHS heteroecious *different hosts*

HDRSKL heterocycle *atoms*

HDRSKLK heterocyclic *atoms*

HDRSKSHL heterosexual (adj) *opposite sex* heterosexually (adv)

HDRSKSHWL heterosexual (adj) *opposite sex* heterosexually (adv)

HDRSL hydrocele *fluid*

HDRSPR heterospory *spores*

HDRSPRS heterosporous *spores*

HDRSR hadrosaur *dinosaur*

HDRSST heterocyst *cell*

HDRST headrest *support*

HDRSTDKS hydrostatics *pressure*

HDRSTDX hydrostatics *pressure*

HDRSTTKS hydrostatics *pressure*

HDRSTTX hydrostatics *pressure*

HDRSXL heterosexual (adj) *opposite sex* heterosexually (adv)

HDRSXWL heterosexual (adj) *opposite sex* heterosexually (adv)

HDRT hydrate *add water*

Use letters that best describe the sounds you hear and omit the vowels. Use **S** or **K** instead of **C**: to find circle use **SRKL**. Use **J** to find joy, **JM** to find gem and **G** to find go.

hydrated hydrating

HDRTHRML hydrothermal (adj) *hot water* hydrothermally (adv)

HDRTHRP hydrotherapy *treatment* hydrotherapies

HDRTPK heterotypic *different*

HDRTR hydrator *add water*

HDRTRF heterotroph *metabolism* heterotrophy

HDRTRFK heterotrophic *metabolism*

HDRTRFKL heterotrophically *metabolism*

HDRWLKTRK hydroelectric *power*

HDRWLKTRKL hydroelectrically *power*

HDRWLKTRSD hydroelectricity *power*

HDRWLKTRST hydroelectricity *power*

HDRX hydroxy *chemical*

HDRXD hydroxide *chemical*

HDRXL hydroxyl *chemical*

HDRZ hydrase *enzyme*

HDRZGS heterozygous *gene*

HDRZN hydrazine *fuel*

HDRZN hydrozoan *jellyfish*

HDRZWN hydrozoan *jellyfish*

HDS hiatus *passage, gap, break*

HDS hideous *ugly*

HDSHP head shop *drug culture*

HDSHP headship *position*

HDSHRNGKR headshrinker *psychiatrist*

HDSHRNKR headshrinker *psychiatrist*

HDSL headsail *ship*

HDSL hideously *ugly*

HDSMN headsman *executioner*

HDSNB Hudson Bay *body of water*

HDSNS hideousness *ugly*

HDST haughtiest *proud*

HDST headiest *willful, giddy*

HDST headset *earphones*

HDST hottest *heat, popular*

HDSTN headstand *gymnastic*

HDSTN headstone *grave*

HDSTND headstand *gymnastic*

HDSTRM headstream *river*

HDSTRNG headstrong *unruly*

HDSTRT head start *advantage*

HDT hideout *refuge*

HDTD hoity-toity *thoughtless*

HDTT hoity-toity *thoughtless*

HDW headway *progress*

HDW hideaway *secret place*

HDWDR headwaiter *supervisor*

HDWDRZ headwaters *source*

HDWNGK hoodwink *dupe*

HDWNK hoodwink *dupe*

HDWRD headword *heading*

HDWRK headwork *thinking*

HDWTR headwaiter *supervisor*

HDWTRZ headwaters *source*

HDWZM hoodooism *magic*

HDYR haughtier *proud*

HDYR headier *willful, giddy*

HDYS hideous *ugly*

HDYSL hideously *ugly*

HDYSNS hideousness *ugly*

HDYST haughtiest *proud*

HDYST headiest *willful, giddy*

HDZ Hades *hell*

HDZM hoodooism *magic*

HDZMN headsman *executioner*

HF half *one of two parts* halves

HF hi-fi *audio*

HF hoof *paw, (slang) walk* hooves

HF huff *(v) bluster (n) pout*

HF huffy *haughty, irritated* huffier huffiest

HF hypha *fungus* hyphae

HF jefe *chief*

HFBK halfback *sports*

HFBK halfbeak *fish*

HFBKD half-baked *lacking*

HFBKT half-baked *lacking*

HFBLD half-blood (or) half-blooded (adj) *half-breed* half blood (n)

HFBLDD half-blooded (or) half-blood (adj) *half-breed*

HFBRD half-bred *one purebred parent*

HFBRD half-breed *different races*

HFBRTHR half brother *relative*

HFBT hoofbeat *sound*

HFD hefty *bulky* heftier heftiest

HFDL heftily *bulky*

HFDLD high fidelity *reproduction*

HFDLR half-dollar *money*

HFDLT high fidelity *reproduction*

HFDNS heftiness *bulk*

HFDR heftier *bulky*

HFDST heftiest *bulky*

HFDYR heftier *bulky*

HFDYST heftiest *bulky*

HFHCH half hitch *knot*

HFHRD half-hardy *plant*

HFHRDD halfhearted *lacking*

HFHRDDL halfheartedly *lacking*

HFHRDDNS halfheartedness *lacking*

HFHRTD halfhearted *lacking*

HFHRTDL halfheartedly *lacking*

HFHRTDNS halfheartedness *lacking*

HFKKT half-cocked *not prepared*

HFKRT half-court *sports*

HFKST half-caste *different races*

HFL huffily *haughty, irritated*

HFLDNG highfalutin *overbearing*

HFLF half-life *atomic*

HFLN high-flown *exalted*

HFLN high-flying *ambitious*

HFLNG high-flying *ambitious*
HFLNGKTH half-length *portrait*
HFLNGTH half-length *portrait*
HFLNKTH half-length *portrait*
HFLNTH half-length *portrait*
HFLR highflier (or) highflyer *stock*
HFLT half-light *dimness*
HFLTN highfalutin *overbearing*
HFLTNG highfalutin *overbearing*
HFLYN high-flying *ambitious*
HFLYNG high-flying *ambitious*
HFLYR highflier (or) highflyer *stock*
HFMN half-moon *crescent*
HFMST half-mast *below top*
HFN hyphen *divider*
HFNCH hawfinch *bird*
HFNDD hyphenated *mixed*
HFNDHF half-and-half *mixture*
HFNDMTH hoof-and-mouth *disease*
HFNHF half-and-half *mixture*
HFNLSN half nelson *wrestling*
HFNMTH hoof-and-mouth *disease*
HFNS huffiness *haughty, irritated*
HFNSHN hyphenation *division*
HFNT half-knot *tie*
HFNT hyphenate *divide* hyphenated hyphenating
HFNTD hyphenated *mixed*
HFPNS halfpence (pl) *money* halfpenny
HFPNT half-pint *small*
HFPNTS halfpence (pl) *money* halfpenny
HFR half hour *time*
HFR heifer *cow*
HFR hoofer *dancer*
HFR huffier *haughty, irritated*

HFRST half rest *music*
HFSD half-assed (*vulgar*) *weak or poor*
HFSH huffish *sulky*
HFSL half-sole (v) *shoe* half sole (n)
HFSLP half-slip *lingeree*
HFSPS half-space *geometry*
HFSSDR half sister *relative*
HFSSTR half sister *relative*
HFST half-assed (*vulgar*) *weak or poor*
HFST huffiest *haughty, irritated*
HFSTF half-staff *below top*
HFSTP half step *music*
HFT haft *handle*
HFT heft (n) *weight* (v) *hoist*
HFT hefty *bulky* heftier heftiest
HFT hoofed (or) hooved *feet*
HFTL heftily *bulky*
HFTM half-time (adj,adv) *employment*
HFTM halftime (n) *intermission*
HFTN halftone *photograph*
HFTNS heftiness *bulky*
HFTR heftier *bulky*
HFTRK half-track *vehicle*
HFTRTH half-truth *deception*
HFTST heftiest *bulky*
HFTYR heftier *bulky*
HFTYST heftiest *bulky*
HFVR hay fever *allergy*
HFW halfway *midway*
HFWDD half-witted *foolish*
HFWDDNS half-wittedness *foolish*
HFWR half hour *time*
HFWRLD half-world *prostitutes*
HFWT half-wit *fool*
HFWTD half-witted *foolish*
HFWTDNS half-wittedness *foolish*
HFYR huffier *haughty, irritated*
HFYST huffiest *haughty, irritated*
HG hag *old woman*, (Br) *bog*
HG hoagie *sandwich* hoagies

HG hog (v) *cut, take in excess* hogged hogging
HG hog (n) *animal* hogs
HG hug (v) *embrace, stay close* hugged hugging
HG hug (n) *embrace*
HGBK hogback *ridge*
HGD Haggadah *book* Haggadoth
HGDTH Haggadoth (pl) *book* Haggadah
HGFSH hagfish *eel*
HGFSH hogfish *fish*
HGGRF hagiography *biography*
HGGRFR hagiographer *biographer*
HGL haggle *bargain* haggled haggling
HGL higgle *bargain* higgled higgling
HGLDPGLD higgledy-piggledy *confused*
HGLG hagiology *saint list*
HGLJ hagiology *saint list*
HGLJK hagiologic *saint list*
HGLR haggler *bargainer*
HGLR higgler *bargainer*
HGMN hegemony *domination*
HGN hogan *dwelling*
HGN hygiene *health*
HGNK hygienic *healthy*
HGNKL hygienically *healthy*
HGNKS hygienics *health*
HGNST hygienist *health*
HGNX hygienics *health*
HGNZ hognose *snake*
HGR hegira *exodus*
HGR high gear *much activity*
HGR hugger *embrace, stay close*
HGRD haggard (adj) *scrawny* (n) *hawk*
HGRD hagride *torment* hagrode hagridden
HGRD high-grade *prime*
HGRDL haggardly *scrawny*
HGRDN hagridden (v-past) *hagride*
HGRDNS haggardness *scrawny*

Use letters that best describe the sounds you hear and omit the vowels. Use **S** or **K** instead of **C**: to find circle use **SRKL**. Use **J** to find joy, **JM** to find gem and **G** to find go.

HGRMDR hygrometer *humidity*
HGRMTR hygrometer *humidity*
HGRSKPK hygroscopic *hold moisture*
HGRSKPSD hygroscopicity *hold moisture*
HGRSKPST hygroscopicity *hold moisture*
HGS haggis *food*
HGSD hogshead *cask*
HGSH hoggish *selfish*
HGSHD hogshead *cask*
HGSHL hoggishly *selfish*
HGSHNS hoggishness *selfish*
HGT hog-tie *bind*
HGWL hog-wild *crazy*
HGWLD hog-wild *crazy*
HGWSH hogwash *garbage, nonsense*
HGWYL hog-wild *crazy*
HGWYLD hog-wild *crazy*
HGYGRF hagiography *biography*
HGYGRFR hagiographer *biographer*
HGYLG hagiology *saint list*
HGYLJ hagiology *saint list*
HGYLJK hagiologic *saint list*
HGZD hogshead *cask*
HGZHD hogshead *cask*
HH hee-haw *laugh*
HH heigh-ho *(interj) boredom*
HHB jojoba *tree*
HHLS high heels *shoes*
HHLZ high heels *shoes*
HHM ho-hum (adj) *boring* ho hum (interj)
HHNDD high-handed *overbearing*
HHT high hat (or) hi-hat *(n) cymbals*
HHT high-hat *(adj) snobbish*
HJ hajj *pilgrimage*
HJ hajji *pilgrim*
HJ hedge *(v) evade, protect* hedged hedging
HJ hedge *(n) barrier*
HJ huge *enormous* huger hugest

HJGRF hagiography *biography*
HJGRFR hagiographer *biographer*
HJHG hedgehog *animal*
HJHP hedgehop *airplane*
HJHPR hedgehopper *airplane*
HJK hijack *kidnap*
HJKNSDZZ Hodgkin's disease *tumors*
HJKNZDZZ Hodgkin's disease *tumors*
HJKR hijacker *kidnapper*
HJL hugely *enormous*
HJLG hagiology *saint list*
HJLJ hagiology *saint list*
HJLJK hagiologic *saint list*
HJMN hegemony *domination*
HJMNK hegemonic *domination*
HJMP high jump *contest*
HJN hygiene *health*
HJNGKS high jinks *horseplay*
HJNGX high jinks *horseplay*
HJNK hygienic *healthy*
HJNKL hygienically *healthy*
HJNKS high jinks *horseplay*
HJNKS hygienics *health*
HJNS hugeness *enormous*
HJNST hygienist *health*
HJNX high jinks *horseplay*
HJNX hygienics *health*
HJPJ hodgepodge *jumble*
HJR hedger *evader*
HJR hedgerow *shrubs*
HJR hegira *exodus*
HJR huger *enormous*
HJST hugest *enormous*
HJYGRF hagiography *biography*
HJYGRFR hagiographer *biographer*
HJYLG hagiology *saint list*
HJYLJ hagiology *saint list*
HJYLJK hagiologic *saint list*
HK hack *(v) cut, cough* (n) *cabdriver, notch, cough**
HK hackie *cabdriver*
HK haiku *poem* haiku

HK hake *fish*
HK hawk *(v) sell, cough (n) bird*
HK Hawkeye *Iowan*
HK heck *(interj) mild oath*
HK hick *hillbilly*
HK hickey *bruise, gadget* hickeys
HK hike *walk, raise* hiked hiking
HK hock *(n) hind limb, debt (v) pawn*
HK hockey *sport*
HK hoke *fake* hoked hoking
HK hokey *phony*
HK hook *(n) barb (v) sieze, pilfer, curve**
HK hookah *water pipe*
HK hooky (or) hookey *absence*
HKBR hackberry *elm* hackberries
HKD hawkeyed *keen sight*
HKDGRF hectograph *copier*
HKDGRM hectogram *weight*
HKDK hectic *frenzied*
HKDKL hectically *frenzy*
HKDR hector *bully*
HKK haycock *pile of hay*
HKK hoecake *cornmeal*
HKL hackle *(v) comb* hackled hackling
HKL hackle *(n) feather*
HKL heckle *annoy* heckled heckling
HKLBR huckleberry *fruit* huckleberries
HKLR hackler *comb*
HKLR heckler *annoyer*
HKLS high-class *superior*
HKM hakim *Muslim*
HKM hokum *nonsense*
HKM jicama *plant*
HKMND high command *headquarters*
HKMR hackamore *bridle*
HKMTH hawkmoth *insect*
HKN hackney *(n) horse, carriage (adj) for hire (v) make trite* hackneys
HKN hiking *walking*
HKN hook and eye *fastener*

Letters aren't doubled for single sounds: to find alley use **L** not **LL**. Use **Y** and **W** as hard sounds only: to find yellow use **YL**. (Br)=British spelling or usage. * See dictionary.

HKND hackneyed *trite*
HKND hook and eye *fastener*
HKNG hiking *walking*
HKNT high-count *fabric*
HKP hiccup *spasm* hiccuped hiccuping
HKP hook up (v) *connect* hookup (n)
HKR hacker *computer*
HKR hawker *seller*
HKR hickory *tree* hickories
HKR hiker *walker*
HKR hocker *pawn*
HKR hooker *prostitute*
HKRT high court *supreme court*
HKS hacksaw *tool*
HKS hex *curse* hexes
HKS hoax *trick* hoaxes
HKSBL hawksbill *turtle*
HKSDR huckster (n) *peddler* (v) *sell*
HKSDSML hexadecimal *number*
HKSGN hexagon *six angles*
HKSGNL hexagonal (adj) *six angles* hexagonally (adv)
HKSGRM hexagram *star*
HKSH hawkish *warlike*
HKSHDRN hexahedron *six faces* hexahedrons
HKSHP hockshop *pawn*
HKSKLRFN hexachlorophene toothpaste
HKSKRD hexachord *six tones*
HKSL hexyl *petroleum*
HKSMDR hexameter *verse*
HKSMTR hexameter *verse*
HKSN hexane *petroleum*
HKSPD hexapod *six feet, insects*
HKSPKS hocus-pocus *trick* hocus-pocussed (or) hocus-pocused hocus-pocussing (or) hocus-pocusing
HKSPLD hexaploid *chromosome*
HKSR hexarei *witchcraft*

HKSR hoaxer *trick*
HKSTR huckster (n) *peddler* (v) *sell*
HKSTRZM hucksterism *peddling*
HKT high-count *fabric*
HKT hooked *curved, addicted*
HKTGRF hectograph *copier*
HKTGRM hectogram *weight*
HKTK hectic *frenzied*
HKTKL hectically *frenzy*
HKTMDR hectometer *distance*
HKTMTR hectometer *distance*
HKTN high-octane *powerful*
HKTR haute couture *fashion*
HKTR hectare *land measure*
HKTR hector *bully*
HKTYR haute couture *fashion*
HKWD hawkweed *plant*
HKWRK hackwork *commercial*
HKWRM hookworm *parasite*
HKWZN haute cuisine *food*
HKZN haute cuisine *food*
HL eyehole *peephole*
HL hail *icy snow, salute*
HL hale (adj) *healthy*
HL hale (v) *pull* haled haling
HL hall *passage*
HL hallow *venerate*
HL halo *light* halos (or) haloes
HL haole *non-Hawaiian*
HL haul (v) *carry* (n) *load*
HL he'll (contr) *he will*
HL heal *cure*
HL heel *foot*
HL hell *nether world, fun, difficult**
HL hello *greeting* hellos (Br) hullo
HL helo *helicopter* helos
HL Hialeah *city*
HL highly *favorably*
HL hila (pl) *scar* hilum
HL hill *mound*
HL hilly *with mounds* hillier hilliest
HL hold (v) *grasp, restrain,*

last* *held holding*
HL hold (n) *cargo area, grasp, prison**
HL hole (v) *open* holed holing
HL hole (n) *opening, flaw, fix*
HL holey *with holes*
HL hollo (interj) *attention* hollos
HL hollow (adj) *concave, false* hollower hollowest
HL hollow (v) *cut out* (n) *hole, valley*
HL holly *plant* hollies
HL holy *sacred* holier holiest
HL howl *cry*
HL hoyle (often capitalized) *rules*
HL hula *dance*
HL hull (n) *cover, frame* (v) *shuck*
HL hyla *tree frog*
HL jai alai *sport*
HL who'll (contr) *who will*
HL whole *all parts*
HL wholly *entirely*
HLB djellaba *garment*
HLBL hillbilly *backwoods* hillbillies
HLBL hullabaloo *uproar* hullabaloos
HLBNDR hellbender *salamander*
HLBNT hell-bent *reckless*
HLBR hellebore *herb*
HLBRD halberd *weapon*
HLBT halibut *fish* halibut
HLC Holy See *pope*
HLCZ halluces (pl) *toe* hallux
HLCZ helices (pl) *spiral* helix
HLD ahold *hold*
HLD halide *chemical*
HLD hallowed *holy*
HLD hold (v) *grasp, restrain, last** held holding
HLD hold (n) *cargo area, grasp, prison**
HLD holiday *vacation*
HLD hyaloid *glassy*
HLDL holdall (Br) *bag*
HLDN holding (n) *property* (adj) *delaying*

Use letters that best describe the sounds you hear and omit the vowels. Use **S** or **K** instead of **C**: to find circle use **SRKL**. Use **J** to find joy, **JM** to find gem and **G** to find go.

HLDNG halting *unsure*
HLDNG holding *(n) property (adj) delaying*
HLDP holdup (n) *delay, robery* hold up (v)
HLDR halter *strap, blouse*
HLDR holder *container*
HLDRSKLDR helter-skelter *turmoil*
HLDRSKLTR helter-skelter *turmoil*
HLDT hold out *(v) remain, refuse*
HLDT holdout *(n) refuser*
HLDVR holdover (n) *postpone* hold over (v)
HLF whole-life *insurance*
HLFDK holophytic *chlorophyll*
HLFKS Halifax *city*
HLFL halophile *salt*
HLFLK halophilic *salt*
HLFR hellfire *torture*
HLFRSDK holophrastic *phrase*
HLFRSTK holophrastic *phrase*
HLFT halophyte *plant*
HLFT hayloft *barn*
HLFTK holophytic *chlorophyll*
HLFX Halifax *city*
HLFYR hellfire *torture*
HLGN hooligan *hoodlum*
HLGNS halogenous *light*
HLGNZM hooliganism *hoodlum*
HLGRF heliograph *signal*
HLGRF holograph *writing*
HLGRF holography *3-D image*
HLGRFK heliographic *signal*
HLGRFK holographic *3-D image, writing*
HLGRFKL holographically *3-D image*
HLGRFR holographer *3-D image*
HLGRM hologram *3-D image*
HLGST Holy Ghost *Christian deity*

HLHDRL holohedral *symmetry*
HLHG whole hog (n, adv) *completely* whole-hog *(adj)*
HLHK hollyhock *plant*
HLHL hellhole *awful place*
HLHN hellhound *fiend*
HLHND hellhound *fiend*
HLHRDD wholehearted *sincere*
HLHRDDL wholeheartedly *sincere*
HLHRTD wholehearted *sincere*
HLHRTDL wholeheartedly *sincere*
HLHWT whole wheat *grain*
HLJ haulage *fee*
HLJ haylage *feed*
HLJN halogen *light*
HLJNS halogenous *light*
HLK halakah (or) halacha *law*
HLK hillock *mound*
HLK hulk *(n) mass, ship (v) loom*
HLKL heliacal (adj) *sun* heliacally (adv)
HLKL helical (adj) *spiral* helically (adv)
HLKN helicon *tuba*
HLKN hulking *massive*
HLKNG hulking *massive*
HLKPDR helicopter *aircraft*
HLKPTR helicopter *aircraft*
HLKRD hole card *poker*
HLKS hallux *toe* halluces
HLKS helix *spiral* helices
HLKST holocaust *fire, slaughter*
HLKT hellcat *witch*
HLLN Holy Land *region*
HLLND Holy Land *region*
HLLY hallelujah (interj) *joy*
HLM halma *game*
HLM helium *element*
HLM helm *ship*
HLM hilum *scar* hila
HLM holm *island*
HLMLK whole milk *beverage*
HLMN Khomeini *religious*

leader
HLMNSTR Gila monster *lizard*
HLMNT helmet *hat*
HLMNTH helminth *worm*
HLMNTHLG helminthology *worms*
HLMNTHLJ helminthology *worms*
HLMRK hallmark *stamp*
HLMT helmet *hat*
HLMTD helmeted *hat*
HLMTLK helmetlike *hat*
HLMZMN helmsman *steering* helmsmen
HLMZMNSHP helmsmanship *steering*
HLN Halloween *holiday*
HLN Helena *city*
HLN Hellene *Greek*
HLN hellion *brat*
HLN highland *mountain*
HLN Holland *Netherlands*
HLN holland *fabric*
HLN howling *wild*
HLN hyaline (or) hyalin *glassy*
HLND highland *mountain*
HLND Holland *Netherlands*
HLND holland *fabric*
HLNDR highlander *Scot*
HLNDT heel-and-toe *stride*
HLNDZ hollandaise *sauce*
HLNG howling *wild*
HLNK Hellenic *Greek*
HLNMBR whole number *math*
HLNS holiness *sacred*
HLNS wholeness *complete*
HLNT heel-and-toe *stride*
HLNT whole note *music*
HLNTHWL hole-in-the-wall *small place* holes-in-the-wall
HLNZM Hellenism *Greece*
HLP help *assist*
HLP hole up *hide*
HLPD helipad *helicopter*
HLPFL helpful (adj) *useful* helpfully (adv)
HLPFLNS helpfulness *useful*
HLPLS helpless *defenseless*

Letters aren't doubled for single sounds: to find alley use **L** not **LL**. Use **Y** and **W** as hard sounds only: to find yellow use **YL**. (Br)=British spelling or usage. * See dictionary.

HLPLSL helplessly *defenseless*
HLPLSNS helplessness *defenseless*
HLPMT helpmate *spouse*
HLPN helping *serving*
HLPN jalapeño *pepper* jalapeños
HLPNG helping *serving*
HLPNY jalapeño *pepper* jalapeños
HLPR helper *assistant*
HLPRT heliport *helicopter*
HLPS heelpiece *shoe*
HLR haler *money* haleru
HLR hauler *carrier*
HLR healer *curer*
HLR heeler *worker*
HLR heller *brat*
HLR helleri *fish* helleries
HLR hillier *mounds*
HLR holier *sacred*
HLR holler *shout*
HLR hollow (v) *cut out* (n) *hole, valley*
HLR hollow (adj) *concave, false* hollower hollowest
HLR hollower *concave, false*
HLR howler *cryer*
HLR huller *shucker*
HLRD hilarity *humor*
HLRS hilarious *funny*
HLRT hilarity *humor*
HLRT holy writ *(often capitalized) bible*
HLRYS hilarious *funny*
HLRZR hell-raiser *wild one*
HLS Holy See *pope*
HLSD hillside *mound*
HLSDK holistic *the whole*
HLSDKL holistically *the whole*
HLSH hellish *terrible*
HLSHN halation *aura*
HLSHS hellacious *exceptional*
HLSL wholesale *sell in quantity* wholesaled wholesaling
HLSLC Haile Selassie *emperor*
HLSLR wholesaler *sell in*

quantity
HLSLS Haile Selassie *emperor*
HLSM wholesome *healthy*
HLSML wholesomely *healthy*
HLSMNS wholesomeness *healthiness*
HLSN halcyon (n) *bird* (adj) *calm*
HLSNDR hallucinator *imaginer*
HLSNDV hallucinative *delusion*
HLSNGK Helsinki *city*
HLSNJN hallucinogen *drug*
HLSNJNK hallucinogenic *drug*
HLSNK Helsinki *city*
HLSNSHN hallucination *delusion*
HLSNT hallucinate *imagine* hallucinated hallucinating
HLSNTR hallucinator *imaginer*
HLSNTR hallucinatory *delusion*
HLSNTRK heliocentric *sun*
HLSNTV hallucinative *delusion*
HLSPRT Holy Spirit *Christian deity*
HLST hilliest *mounds*
HLST holiest *sacred*
HLST hollowest *concave, false*
HLSTK holistic *the whole*
HLSTKL holistically *the whole*
HLSTN hailstone *icy snow*
HLSTN holstein *cow*
HLSTR holster *gun*
HLSTRM hailstorm *icy snow*
HLSTT heliostat *sunbeam*
HLSYN halcyon (n) *bird* (adj) *calm*
HLSZ halluces (pl) *toe* hallux
HLSZ helices (pl) *spiral* helix
HLT halite *rock salt*
HLT halt *stop*
HLT helot *slave*
HLT highlight *feature,*

illuminate
HLT hilt *sword*
HLTH health *fitness*
HLTH healthy *fit* healthier healthiest
HLTHFL healthful *fit*
HLTHFLNS healthfulness *fitness*
HLTHL healthily *fit*
HLTHNS healthiness *fitness*
HLTHR healthier *fit*
HLTHST healthiest *fit*
HLTHYR healthier *fit*
HLTHYST healthiest *fit*
HLTN halting *unsure*
HLTNG halting *unsure*
HLTP heeltap *shoe*
HLTP hilltop *crest*
HLTP holotype *species*
HLTPK holotypic *species*
HLTR halter *strap, blouse*
HLTR helotry *slavery*
HLTRP heliotrope *herb, color*
HLTRPK heliotropic *sunlight*
HLTRPZM heliotropism *sunlight*
HLTRSKLDR helter-skelter *turmoil*
HLTRSKLTR helter-skelter *turmoil*
HLTSS halitosis *bad breath*
HLV halvah (or) halva *food*
HLV helve *handle*
HLVL high-level *important*
HLW hallway *corridor*
HLWD Hollywood *district*
HLWK Holy Week *before Easter*
HLWN Halloween *holiday*
HLWR hollower *concave, false*
HLWR hollowware (or) holloware *serving dishes*
HLWR holy war *crusade*
HLWST hollowest *concave, false*
HLWT whole wheat *grain*
HLX hallux *toe* halluces
HLX helix *spiral* helices
HLY Hialeah *city*
HLYGRF heliograph *signal*
HLYGRFK heliographic *signal*

Use letters that best describe the sounds you hear and omit the vowels. Use **S** or **K** instead of **C**: to find circle use **SRKL**. Use **J** to find joy, **JM** to find gem and **G** to find go.

HLYKL heliacal (adj) *sun* heliacally (adv)
HLYM helium *element*
HLYN hellion *brat*
HLYR hillier *mounds*
HLYR holier *sacred*
HLYRD halyard *rope*
HLYSNTRK heliocentric *sun*
HLYST hilliest *mounds*
HLYST holiest *sacred*
HLYTRP heliotrope *herb, color*
HLYTRPK heliotropic *sunlight*
HLYTRPZM heliotropism *sunlight*
HLZKMT Halley's comet *meteor*
HM ahem *(interj) attention-getter*
HM ham *(v) overact* hammed hamming
HM ham *(n) thigh, radio, performer**
HM hame *horse collar*
HM hammy *theatrical* hammier hammiest
HM haulm *stem*
HM haymow *cut hay*
HM hem *(v) sew, confine* hemmed hemming
HM hem *(n) cuff*
HM heme *blood*
HM him *(pron) that male*
HM holm *island*
HM home *(v) return* homed homing
HM home *(n) abode*
HM homey *cozy* homier homiest
HM homo *(vulgar) homosexual* homos
HM hum *drone* hummed humming
HM hymn *song*
HM whom *that person*
HMB homeboy *gang*
HMBD homebody *house* homebodies
HMBG humbug *deceive* humbugged humbugging

HMBK humpback *curved back*
HMBK hymnbook *song book*
HMBKD humpbacked *curved back*
HMBKT humpbacked *curved back*
HMBL humble *(v) humiliate* humbled humbling
HMBL humble *(adj) not proud* humbler humblest
HMBL humbly *not proud*
HMBLNS humbleness *modesty*
HMBLP humble pie *modest*
HMBLR humbler *not proud*
HMBLST humblest *not proud*
HMBLT homebuilt *homemade*
HMBN homebound *house*
HMBND homebound *house*
HMBR home brew *alcohol*
HMBRD homebred *native*
HMBRG Hamburg *city*
HMBRG homburg *hat*
HMBRGR hamburger *food*
HMD homemade *created at home*
HMD humid *moist*
HMDD humidity *moisture* humidities
HMDF humidify *add moisture* humidified humidifying humidifies
HMDFKSHN humidification *moisture*
HMDFR humidifier *moisture*
HMDFYR humidifier *moisture*
HMDKRT hematocrit *blood*
HMDLJK hematologic *blood*
HMDLSS hemodialysis *purification*
HMDNGR humdinger *standout*
HMDNMKS hemodynamics *circulation*
HMDNMX hemodynamics *circulation*
HMDR humidor *case*
HMDRM humdrum *dull*
HMDT humidity *moisture*

humidities
HMDYLSS hemodialysis *purification*
HMFB homophobe *fear homosexuals*
HMFB homophobia *fear homosexuals*
HMFBK homophobic *fear homosexuals*
HMFBY homophobia *fear homosexuals*
HMFL hemophilia *disease*
HMFL homophile *gay*
HMFLK hemophiliac *(n) diseased one*
HMFLK hemophilic *(n, adj) diseased*
HMFLY hemophilia *disease*
HMFLYK hemophiliac *(n) diseased one*
HMFN homophone *similar sound*
HMFN homophony *similar sounds*
HMFNK homophonic *similar sound*
HMFNS homophonous *similar sound*
HMFRNT home front *war*
HMFRS home fries *food*
HMFRZ home fries *food*
HMFSDD ham-fisted *clumsy*
HMFSTD ham-fisted *clumsy*
HMGLBN hemoglobin *blood*
HMGM homogamy *mating*
HMGMS homogamous *mating*
HMGND homogeneity *same kind*
HMGNS homogeneous *same kind*
HMGNSL homogeneously *same kind*
HMGNSNS homogeneousness *same kind*
HMGNT homogeneity *same kind*
HMGNYD homogeneity *same kind*
HMGNYS homogeneous *same kind*

Letters aren't doubled for single sounds: to find alley use **L** not **LL**. Use **Y** and **W** as hard sounds only: to find yellow use **YL**. (Br)=British spelling or usage. * See dictionary.

HMGNYSL homogeneously *same kind*

HMGNYSNS homogeneousness *same kind*

HMGNYT homogeneity *same kind*

HMGRF homograph *word*

HMGRFK homographic *word*

HMGRFT homograft *tissue*

HMGRN homegrown *native*

HMHDRL hemihedral *faces*

HMHNDD ham-handed *clumsy*

HMJ homage *tribute*

HMJND homogeneity *same kind*

HMJNS homogeneous *same kind*

HMJNSL homogeneously *same kind*

HMJNSNS homogeneousness *same kind*

HMJNT homogeneity *same kind*

HMJNYD homogeneity *same kind*

HMJNYS homogeneous *same kind*

HMJNYSL homogeneously *same kind*

HMJNYSNS homogeneousness *same kind*

HMJNYT homogeneity *same kind*

HMJNZ homogenize *blend* homogenized homogenizing (Br) homogenise

HMJNZR homogenizer *blend* (Br) homogeniser

HMJNZSHN homogenization *blend* (Br) homogenisation

HMJR homager *vassal*

HMK hammock *bed*

HMK hemic *blood*

HMK hummock *ridge*

HMKDNT humectant *moisture*

HMKMN homecoming *return*

HMKMNG homecoming *return*

HMKR haymaker *punch*

HMKR homemaker *domestic one*

HMKTNT humectant *moisture*

HML hammily *theatrical*

HML hamuli (pl) *hook* hamulus

HML homely *simple, plain* homelier homeliest

HML homily *lecture* homilies

HMLD humility *modesty*

HMLDK hemolytic *blood*

HMLDK homiletic (or) homiletical *preachy*

HMLDK homolytic *decomposition*

HMLDKL homiletical (or) homiletic *preachy*

HMLDKS homiletics *preaching*

HMLDN humiliating *humbling*

HMLDX homiletics *preaching*

HMLG homologue (or) homolog *same genes*

HMLG homology *same genes* homologies

HMLGS homologous *same genes*

HMLGT homologate *allow* homologated homologating

HMLJ homology *same genes* homologies

HMLJKL homological (adj) *same genes* homologically (adv)

HMLK hemlock *herb*

HMLKMNVR Heimlich maneuver *choking*

HMLMF hemolymph *fluid*

HMLN hemline *dress*

HMLN Himalayan *area*

HMLN homeland *country*

HMLND homeland *country*

HMLNS homeliness *simple, plain*

HMLR homelier *simple, plain*

HMLS hamulus *hook* hamuli

HMLS homeless *no residence*

HMLSHN humiliation *shame*

HMLSNS homelessness *no residence*

HMLSS hemolysis *blood*

HMLSS homolysis *decomposition*

HMLST homeliest *simple, plain*

HMLT hamlet *town*

HMLT Hamlet *prince*

HMLT humiliate *shame* humiliated humiliating

HMLT humility *modesty*

HMLTK hemolytic *blood*

HMLTK homiletic (or) homiletical *preachy*

HMLTK homolytic *decomposition*

HMLTKL homiletical (or) homiletic *preachy*

HMLTKS homiletics *preaching*

HMLTN humiliating *humbling*

HMLTX homiletics *preaching*

HMLYDN humiliating *humbling*

HMLYDNG humiliating *humbling*

HMLYN Himalayan *area*

HMLYR homelier *simple, plain*

HMLYSHN humiliation *shame*

HMLYST homeliest *simple, plain*

HMLYT humiliate *shame* humiliated humiliating

HMLYTN humiliating *humbling*

HMLYTNG humiliating *humbling*

HMLYZ Himalayas *mountains*

HMLZ hemolyze *blood* hemolyzed hemolyzing

HMLZ Himalayas *mountains*

Use letters that best describe the sounds you hear and omit the vowels. Use **S** or **K** instead of **C**: to find circle use **SRKL**. Use **J** to find joy, **JM** to find gem and **G** to find go.

HMN he-man *strong he-men*
HMN hominy *corn*
HMN how many *what number*
HMN human *person*
HMN humane *compassionate*
HMN hymen *membrane*
HMN Khomeini *religious leader*
HMNBRD hummingbird *bird*
HMND hominid *humans*
HMND hominoid *humans and apes*
HMND humanity *all persons* humanities
HMND humanoid *like a human*
HMND hymnody *singing*
HMNDD high-minded *pretentious*
HMNDS humanities *human concerns*
HMNDZ humanities *human concerns*
HMNGBRD hummingbird *bird*
HMNGGS humongous *huge*
HMNGKL homunculi (pl) *little man* homunculus
HMNGKLS homunculus *little man* homunculi
HMNGKYL homunculi (pl) *little man* homunculus
HMNGKYLS homunculus *little man* homunculi
HMNGM hemangioma *tumor*
HMNGQL homunculi (pl) *little man* homunculus
HMNGQLS homunculus *little man* homunculi
HMNGS humongous *huge*
HMNGYM hemangioma *tumor*
HMNJM hemangioma *tumor*
HMNJYM hemangioma *tumor*
HMNKL homunculi (pl) *little man* homunculus
HMNKLS homunculus *little man* homunculi
HMNKN humankind *all persons*

HMNKND humankind *all persons*
HMNKYL homunculi (pl) *little man* homunculus
HMNKYLS homunculus *little man* homunculi
HMNL humanely *compassion*
HMNL humanly *of man*
HMNL hymeneal (adj) *marriage* hymeneally (adv)
HMNL hymnal *song book*
HMNLG hymnology *song*
HMNLJ hymnology *song*
HMNM homonym *similar sound*
HMNM homonymy *similar sound*
HMNMK homonymic *similar sound*
HMNPDRN hymenopteran *insect*
HMNPDRS hymenopterous *insect*
HMNPTRN hymenopteran *insect*
HMNPTRS hymenopterous *insect*
HMNQL homunculi (pl) *little man* homunculus
HMNQLS homunculus *little man* homunculi
HMNS hamminess *theatrical*
HMNS homeyness (or) hominess *cozy*
HMNS humaneness *compassion*
HMNS humanize *make human* humanized humanizing
HMNS humanness *of man*
HMNSDK humanistic *life-centered*
HMNSDKL humanistically *life-centered*
HMNSM humanism *life-centered*
HMNSTK humanistic *life-centered*
HMNSTKL humanistically *life-centered*
HMNT humanity *all persons*

humanities
HMNTRN humanitarian *philanthropist*
HMNTRYN humanitarian *philanthropist*
HMNTS humanities *human concerns*
HMNTZ humanities *human concerns*
HMNYL hymeneal (adj) *marriage* hymeneally (adv)
HMNZ humanize *make human* humanized humanizing
HMNZM humanism *life-centered*
HMNZR humanizer *make human*
HMNZSHN hominization *evolution*
HMNZSHN humanization *make human*
HMP hemp *plant*
HMP hump (n) *lump, mound* (v) *work hard*
HMP humpy *lumpy* humpier humpiest
HMPBK humpback *curved back*
HMPBKD humpbacked *curved back*
HMPBKT humpbacked *curved back*
HMPD humped *mound*
HMPDRN homopteran *scale insect*
HMPDRS homopterous *scale insect*
HMPK humpback *curved back*
HMPKD humpbacked *curved back*
HMPKT humpbacked *curved back*
HMPLG hemiplegia *paralysis*
HMPLJ hemiplegia *paralysis*
HMPLJK hemiplegic *paralysis*
HMPLT home plate *baseball*
HMPR hamper (v) *impede* (n) *basket*
HMPR humpier *lumpy*

Letters aren't doubled for single sounds: to find alley use **L** not **LL**. Use **Y** and **W** as hard sounds only: to find yellow use **YL**. (Br)=British spelling or usage. * See dictionary.

HMPRT home port (n) *ship*
homeport (v)
HMPST humpiest *lumpy*
HMPT humped *mound*
HMPTH homeopathy
vaccine
HMPTHK homeopathic
vaccine
HMPTHKL homeopathically
vaccine
HMPTRN hemipteran *insect*
HMPTRN homopteran *scale*
insect
HMPTRS hemipterous
insect
HMPTRS homopterous *scale*
insect
HMPYR humpier *lumpy*
HMPYST humpiest *lumpy*
HMR hammer *(n) tool (v)*
pound
HMR hammier *theatrical*
HMR hemmer *sewer, border*
HMR homer *home run*
HMR homier *cozy*
HMR humeri *(pl) bone*
humerus
HMR hummer *sound*
HMR humor *(n) fun,*
temperament (v) soothe,
indulge
(Br) humour
HMRD hammered *pounded*
HMRD hemorrhoid *swollen*
anal blood vessel
HMRDK homoerotic
homosexual
HMRDL hemorrhoidal
swollen anal blood vessel
HMRDS hemorrhoids
swollen anal blood vessels
HMRDSZM homoeroticism
homosexual
HMRDZ hemorrhoids
swollen anal blood vessels
HMRHD hammerhead *shark*
HMRJ hemorrhage *bleed*
hemorrhaged
hemorrhaging
HMRJK hemorrhagic
bleeding
HMRL home rule

government
HMRL humeral *shoulder*
HMRLK hammerlock
wrestling
HMRLS humorless *no fun*
(Br) humourless
HMRM homeroom *school*
HMRN home run *baseball*
HMRS humerus *bone* humeri
HMRS humorous *funny*
(Br) humourous
HMRSHLD Hammerskjold
UN secretary-general
HMRSK humoresque
fanciful
(Br) humouresque
HMRSL humorously *funny*
(Br) humourously
HMRSNS humorousness
funny
(Br) humourousness
HMRST humorist *funny one*
(Br) humourist
HMRT hammertoe *deformity*
HMRTK homoerotic
homosexual
HMRTSZM homoeroticism
homosexual
HMS ahimsa *doctrine*
HMS high mass *(often*
capitalized) church service
HMS hummus *food*
HMS humus *soil*
HMSD homicide *murder*
HMSDL homicidal (adj)
murder homicidally (adv)
HMSF himself *(pron) that*
male
HMSFR hemisphere *half*
circle, realm
HMSFRK hemispheric (or)
hemispherical *half circle,*
realm
HMSFRKL hemispherical
(or) hemispheric *half*
circle, realm
HMSK homesick *longing*
HMSKL hemicycle *curve*
HMSKSHL homosexual
(adj, n) *prefers same sex*
homosexually (adv)
HMSKSHLD homosexuality

prefers same sex
HMSKSHLT homosexuality
prefers same sex
HMSKSHWL homosexual
(adj, n) *prefers same sex*
homosexually (adv)
HMSKSHWLD
homosexuality *prefers*
same sex
HMSKSHWLT
homosexuality *prefers*
same sex
HMSL hemocoel *cavity*
HMSLF himself *(pron) that*
male
HMSPN homespun *simple*
HMSPNS Homo sapiens
human
HMSPNZ Homo sapiens
human
HMSPYNS Homo sapiens
human
HMSPYNZ Homo sapiens
human
HMST hammiest *theatrical*
HMST hemocyte *blood*
HMST homestay *foreign visit*
HMST homiest *cozy*
HMSTCH hemstitch
needlework hemstitches
HMSTD homestead *house*
HMSTDK hemostatic *stop*
bleeding
HMSTDK homeostatic
balanced
HMSTR hamster *rodent*
HMSTRCH homestretch *last*
part of a race
HMSTRNG hamstring *(v)*
cripple hamstrung
hamstringing
HMSTRNG hamstring *(n)*
tendon
HMSTSS hemostasis *stop*
bleeding
HMSTSS homeostasis
balance
HMSTT hemostat *stop*
bleeding
HMSTTK hemostatic *stop*
bleeding
HMSTTK homeostatic

Use letters that best describe the sounds you hear and omit the vowels. Use **S** or **K** instead of **C**: to find circle use **SRKL**. Use **J** to find joy, **JM** to find gem and **G** to find go.

balanced

HMSVR whomsoever *which person*

HMSWVR whomsoever *which person*

HMT hamate *bone*

HMTFGS hematophagous *blood*

HMTKRT hematocrit *blood*

HMTLG hematology *blood*

HMTLJ hematology *blood*

HMTLJK hematologic *blood*

HMTLJST hematologist *blood*

HMTM hematoma *clot* hematomas (or) hematomata

HMTMD hematomata (pl) *clot* hematoma

HMTMT hematomata (pl) *clot* hematoma

HMTN hometown *city*

HMTR hematuria *blood in urine*

HMTRY hematuria *blood in urine*

HMTT hematite *mineral*

HMTYR hematuria *blood in urine*

HMTYRY hematuria *blood in urine*

HMVR whomever *any person*

HMWRD homeward (or) homewards *toward home*

HMWRDK homoerotic *homosexual*

HMWRDS homewards (or) homeward *toward home*

HMWRDSZM homoeroticism *homosexual*

HMWRDZ homewards (or) homeward *toward home*

HMWRK homework *school*

HMWRTK homoerotic *homosexual*

HMWRTSZM homoeroticism *homosexual*

HMYL hamuli (pl) *hook* hamulus

HMYLS hamulus *hook*

hamuli

HMYPTH homeopathy *vaccine*

HMYPTHK homeopathic *vaccine*

HMYPTHKL homeopathically *vaccine*

HMYR hammier *theatrical*

HMYR homier *cozy*

HMYST hammiest *theatrical*

HMYST homiest *cozy*

HMYSTDK homeostatic *balanced*

HMYSTSS homeostasis *balance*

HMYSTTK homeostatic *balanced*

HMZGS homozygous *genes*

HMZGT homozygote *genes*

HN hand (v) give to (n) *fingers, applause*

HN Hanoi *city*

HN heinie *buttocks*

HN hen *fowl (f)*

HN henna *dye*

HN hewn *cut down*

HN hind *rear, deer* hinds

HN hinny *mule* hinnies

HN hon *honey*

HN hone *sharpen* honed honing

HN honey *sweet* honeys

HN hound (v) harass (n) *dog*

HN Hun *nomad*

HN hyena *animal* hyenas

HN jennet *horse, donkey*

HNB honeybee *insect*

HNBG handbag *purse*

HNBK handbook *manual*

HNBL handball *sport*

HNBL handbill *paper*

HNBL Hannibal *general*

HNBLN handblown *glass*

HNBN henbane *herb*

HNBR handbarrow *frame*

HNBRDTH handbreadth *length*

HNBRN hindbrain *brain*

HNBRTH handbreadth *length*

HNBSKT handbasket *container*

HNCH haunch *leg* haunches

HNCH honcho *boss* honchos

HNCH hunch (n) guess (v) *arch* hunches

HNCHBK hunchback *curved back*

HNCHBKD hunchbacked *curved back*

HNCHBKT hunchbacked *curved back*

HNCHMN henchman *follower* henchmen

HND hand (v) give to (n) *fingers, applause*

HND handy *useful* handier handiest

HND haunted *with ghosts*

HND high-end *upscale*

HND hind *rear, deer* hinds

HND Hindi *language*

HND Hindu *religion*

HND honeydew *melon*

HND hound (v) harass (n) *dog*

HNDBG handbag *purse*

HNDBK handbook *manual*

HNDBL handball *sport*

HNDBL handbill *paper*

HNDBLN handblown *glass*

HNDBR handbarrow *frame*

HNDBRDTH handbreadth *length*

HNDBRN hindbrain *brain*

HNDBRTH handbreadth *length*

HNDBSKT handbasket *container*

HNDD handed *kind, number*

HNDDNS handedness *right or left*

HNDDS hendiadys *expression*

HNDF hand off (v) *throw* handoff (n)

HNDFD hand-feed *use hands* hand-fed hand-feeding

HNDFL handful *quantity* handfuls

HNDGLDN hang gliding *kite sport*

HNDGLDNG hang gliding *kite sport*

Letters aren't doubled for single sounds: to find alley use **L** not **LL**. Use **Y** and **W** as hard sounds only: to find yellow use **YL**. (Br)=British spelling or usage. * See dictionary.

HNDGLDR hang glider *kite*
HNDGN handgun *weapon*
HNDGRND hand grenade
weapon
HNDGRP handgrip *handle*
HNDHLD handheld *portable*
HNDHLD handhold *grip*
HNDHLDNG hand-holding
support
HNDKF handcuff *chains*
HNDKLSP handclasp
handshake
HNDKP handicap *(v)*
disadvantage, rate
handicapped
handicapping
HNDKP handicap *(n)*
disadvantage, race
HNDKPD handicapped
disability
HNDKPR handicapper *rater*
HNDKPT handicapped
disability
HNDKR handcar *railroad*
HNDKRCHF handkerchief
cloth handkerchiefs
HNDKRDR hindquarter *back*
half
HNDKRF handicraft *skill,*
creation
HNDKRFSMN
handcraftsman *creator*
HNDKRFT handcraft *(v, n)*
create, article
HNDKRFT handicraft *skill,*
creation
HNDKRFTSMN
handcraftsman *creator*
HNDKRT handcart *pushcart*
HNDKRTR hindquarter *back*
half
HNDKWRDR hindquarter
back half
HNDKWRTR hindquarter
back half
HNDL handily *convenient*
HNDL handle *(v) manage,*
stand, behave* handled
handling
HNDL handle *(n) grip, name*
HNDL high and low
everywhere

HNDLBL handleable
manageable
HNDLBR handlebar *steer*
HNDLN handling *shipping*
charge
HNDLNG handling *shipping*
charge
HNDLR handler *trainer*
HNDMD handmade *crafted*
HNDMDN hand-me-down
used
HNDMDN handmaiden
servant
HNDMN handyman *odd jobs*
handymen
HNDMST hindmost *last*
HNDMTH hand-to-mouth
basics
HNDNS handiness
convenience
HNDPK handpick *choose*
HNDPKT handpicked *chosen*
HNDPRNT handprint
impression
HNDPRS handpress *squeeze*
HNDQRDR hindquarter *back*
half
HNDQRTR hindquarter *back*
half
HNDR handier *convenient*
HNDR high and dry
abandoned
HNDR hinder *interfere*
HNDR honeyeater *bird*
HNDRD hundred *number*
(100) hundreds (or)
hundred
HNDRDFLD hundredfold
number (100)
HNDRDN handwriting *script*
HNDRDNG handwriting
script
HNDRDTH hundredth *of*
number 100
HNDRDWT hundredweight
100 pounds
HNDRL handrail *support*
HNDRNGNG hand-wringing
worry
HNDRNGR handwringer
guilt
HNDRNS hindrance

stumbling block
HNDRNTS hindrance
stumbling block
HNDRR hinderer *interferer*
HNDRS Honduras *country*
HNDRT handwrite *script*
handwrote handwriting
handwritten
HNDRT handwrought *made*
by hand
HNDRTH hundredth *of*
number 100
HNDRTN handwriting *script*
HNDRTN handwritten *(v-*
past) script
HNDRTNG handwriting
script
HNDS handsaw *tool*
HNDSHK handshake *clasp*
HNDSL handsel *token*
handseled (or)
handselled handseling
(or) handselling
HNDSM handsome
attractive, sizable
handsomer handsomest
HNDSML handsomely
attractive, sizable
HNDSMNS handsomeness
attractive, sizable
HNDSMR handsomer
attractive, sizable
HNDSMST handsomest
attractive, sizable
HNDSPRNG handspring
acrobatics
HNDST handiest *convenient*
HNDST handset *telephone*
HNDST hindsight *perception*
HNDSTN handstand *position*
HNDSTND handstand
position
HNDSTTH houndstooth (or)
hound's-tooth *pattern*
HNDT hand out *(v) give*
HNDT handout *(n) alms,*
paper
HNDTHN hand-to-hand
combat
HNDTHND hand-to-hand
combat
HNDTMTH hand-to-mouth

Use letters that best describe the sounds you hear and omit the vowels. Use **S** or **K** instead of **C**: to find circle use **SRKL**. Use **J** to find joy, **JM** to find gem and **G** to find go.

basics

HNDTRK hand truck *dolly*

HNDVR handover (n) *yield* hand over (v)

HNDWL handwheel *disk*

HNDWRK handiwork *personal product*

HNDWRK handwork *done by hand*

HNDWVN handwoven *loom*

HNDWZM Hinduism *religion*

HNDY honeydew *melon*

HNDYDS hendiadys *expression*

HNDYR handier *convenient*

HNDYRS Honduras *country*

HNDYST handiest *convenient*

HNDZ hounds *ship*

HNDZF hands-off *noninterference*

HNDZM Hinduism *religion*

HNDZN hands-on *personal*

HNDZTNG houndstongue *plant*

HNDZTTH houndstooth (or) hound's-tooth *pattern*

HNFD hand-feed *use hands* hand-fed hand-feeding

HNFL handful *quantity* handfuls

HNG hang *suspend, dangle, delay** hung hanging

HNG hung *(adj) undecided (v-past)* hang

HNGBL hangable *airplane*

HNGDG hangdog *miserable*

HNGGLDN hang gliding *kite sport*

HNGGLDNG hang gliding *kite sport*

HNGGLDR hang glider *kite*

HNGGR hangar *airplane*

HNGGR hanger *holder, (Br) slope*

HNGGR Hungary *country*

HNGGR hunger *craving, appetite*

HNGGR hungry *motivated, craving* hungrier hungriest

HNGGRL hungrily *motivated,*

craving

HNGGRN Hungarian *of Hungary*

HNGGRND hand grenade *weapon*

HNGGRNS hungriness *motivated, craving*

HNGGRR hungrier *motivated, craving*

HNGGRST hungriest *motivated, craving*

HNGGRYN Hungarian *of Hungary*

HNGGRYR hungrier *motivated, craving*

HNGGRYST hungriest *motivated, craving*

HNGK hank *coil*

HNGK hankie (or) hanky *handkerchief* hankies

HNGK honk *horn sound*

HNGK honky (or) honkie *(vulgar) white person* honkies

HNGK hunk *chunk, (slang) man*

HNGKDR hunky-dory *fine*

HNGKNG Hong Kong *city*

HNGKPNGK hanky-panky *mischief*

HNGKR hanker *crave*

HNGKR hunker *crouch*

HNGKRCHF handkerchief *cloth* handkerchiefs

HNGKRDN hunker down *(slang) settle in*

HNGKRS hunkers *haunches*

HNGKRZ hunkers *haunches*

HNGKTNGK honky-tonk *nightclub*

HNGLDN hang gliding *kite sport*

HNGLDNG hang gliding *kite sport*

HNGLDR hang glider *kite*

HNGMN hangman *executioner* hangmen

HNGN handgun *weapon*

HNGN hanging *execution, curtain, jutting*

HNGNG hanging *execution, curtain, jutting*

HNGNL hangnail *finger*

HNGP hang up *(v) disconnect, snag*

HNGP hang-up *(n) problem*

HNGP hung up *delayed, preoccupied*

HNGR hangar *airplane*

HNGR hanger *holder, (Br) slope*

HNGR Honegger *composer*

HNGR Hungary *country*

HNGR hunger *craving, appetite*

HNGR hungry *motivated, craving* hungrier hungriest

HNGRL hungrily *motivated, craving*

HNGRN hanger-on *leech* hangers-on

HNGRN Hungarian *of Hungary*

HNGRND hand grenade *weapon*

HNGRNS hungriness *motivated, craving*

HNGRP handgrip *handle*

HNGRR hungrier *motivated, craving*

HNGRST hungriest *motivated, craving*

HNGRYN Hungarian *of Hungary*

HNGRYR hungrier *motivated, craving*

HNGRYST hungriest *motivated, craving*

HNGRZN hangers-on (pl) *leech* hanger-on

HNGT hang out *(v) droop, reside, display*

HNGT hangout *(n) place*

HNGTG hangtag *attachment*

HNGTM hang time *time in the air*

HNGVR hangover *(n) ailment, remnant*

HNGVR hungover *(adj) ailing*

HNHLD handheld *portable*

HNHLD handhold *grip*

HNHLDNG hand-holding

Letters aren't doubled for single sounds: to find alley use **L** not **LL**. Use **Y** and **W** as hard sounds only: to find yellow use **YL**. (Br)=British spelling or usage. * See dictionary.

support
HNHS henhouse *coop*
HNJ hinge *(n) joint*
HNJ hinge *(v) be subject to, attach* hinged hinging
HNK hank *coil*
HNK hankie (or) hanky *handkerchief* hankies
HNK Hanukkah *holiday*
HNK honk *horn sound*
HNK honky (or) honkie *(vulgar) white person* honkies
HNK hunk *chunk, (slang) man*
HNKDR hunky-dory *fine*
HNKF handcuff *chains*
HNKLSP handclasp *handshake*
HNKM honeycomb *wax*
HNKPNK hanky-panky *mischief*
HNKR handcar *railroad*
HNKR hanker *crave*
HNKR hunker *crouch*
HNKRCHF handkerchief *cloth* handkerchiefs
HNKRDN hunker down *(slang) settle in*
HNKRDR hindquarter *back half*
HNKRFSMN handcraftsman *creator*
HNKRFT handcraft *(v, n) create, article*
HNKRFTSMN handcraftsman *creator*
HNKRPR honeycreeper *bird*
HNKRS hunkers *haunches*
HNKRT handcart *pushcart*
HNKRTR hindquarter *back half*
HNKRZ hunkers *haunches*
HNKTNK honky-tonk *nightclub*
HNKWRDR hindquarter *back half*
HNKWRTR hindquarter *back half*
HNL high and low *everywhere*
HNLL Honolulu *city*

HNLN handling *shipping charge*
HNLNG handling *shipping charge*
HNLR handler *trainer*
HNMD handmade *crafted*
HNMDN hand-me-down *used*
HNMDN handmaiden *servant*
HNMN honeymoon *marriage*
HNMNR honeymooner *marriage*
HNMST hindmost *last*
HNN high noon *12:00 p.m., apex*
HNPK handpick *choose*
HNPK henpeck *nag*
HNPKT handpicked *chosen*
HNPKT henpecked *nagged*
HNPRNT handprint *impression*
HNPRS handpress *squeeze*
HNQRDR hindquarter *back half*
HNQRTR hindquarter *back half*
HNR hennery *poultry farm* henneries
HNR henry *voltage* henrys (or) henries
HNR honer *sharpener*
HNR hunter *searcher*
HNRD hundred *number (100)* hundreds (or) hundred
HNRDFLD hundredfold *number (100)*
HNRDN handwriting *script*
HNRDNG handwriting *script*
HNRDTH hundredth *of number 100*
HNRDWT hundredweight *100 pounds*
HNRG high-energy *speedy*
HNRJ high-energy *speedy*
HNRL handrail *support*
HNRNGNG hand-wringing *worry*
HNRNGR handwringer *guilt*
HNRT handwrite *script* handwrote handwriting

handwritten
HNRT handwrought *made by hand*
HNRTH hundredth *of number 100*
HNRTN handwriting *script*
HNRTN handwritten *(v-past) script*
HNRTNG handwriting *script*
HNS handsaw *tool*
HNS heinous *horrible*
HNS hence *from, therefore*
HNS highness *rank*
HNSFRTH henceforth *from now on*
HNSHK handshake *clasp*
HNSKL honeysuckle *shrub*
HNSL handsel *token* handseled (or) handselled handseling (or) handselling
HNSL heinously *horribly*
HNSM handsome *attractive, sizable* handsomer handsomest
HNSM hansom *carriage*
HNSML handsomely *attractive, sizable*
HNSMNS handsomeness *attractive, sizable*
HNSMR handsomer *attractive, sizable*
HNSMST handsomest *attractive, sizable*
HNSNS heinousness *horribly*
HNSPRNG handspring *acrobatics*
HNST handset *telephone*
HNST hindsight *perception*
HNSTN handstand *position*
HNSTND handstand *position*
HNSTTH houndstooth (or) hound's-tooth *pattern*
HNT haunt *(v) visit (n) ghost*
HNT hint *suggestion*
HNT hunt *search*
HNT junta *council*
HNT junto *group* juntos
HNTD haunted *with ghosts*
HNTHN hand-to-hand *combat*

Use letters that best describe the sounds you hear and omit the vowels. Use **S** or **K** instead of **C**: to find circle use **SRKL**. Use **J** to find joy, **JM** to find gem and **G** to find go.

HNTHND hand-to-hand *combat*

HNTMTH hand-to-mouth *basics*

HNTN hunting *pursuit*

HNTNDPK hunt-and-peck *typing*

HNTNG hunting *pursuit*

HNTNPK hunt-and-peck *typing*

HNTR haunter *ghost*

HNTR honeyeater *bird*

HNTR hunter *searcher*

HNTRK hand truck *dolly*

HNTRLN hinterland *remote area*

HNTRLND hinterland *remote area*

HNTRS huntress *pursuer (f)*

HNTS hence *from, therefore*

HNTSFRTH henceforth *from now on*

HNTSL handsel *token* handseled (or) handselled handseling (or) handselling

HNTSM handsome *attractive, sizable*

HNTSM hansom *carriage*

HNTSML handsomely *attractive, sizable*

HNTSMN huntsman *pursuer* huntsmen

HNTSMNS handsomeness *attractive, sizable*

HNTSMR handsomer *attractive, sizable*

HNTSMST handsomest *attractive, sizable*

HNWL handwheel *disk*

HNWRK handwork *done by hand*

HNWVN handwoven *loom*

HNYDL high and low *everywhere*

HNYDR high and dry *abandoned*

HNYDR honeyeater *bird*

HNYL high and low *everywhere*

HNYTR honeyeater *bird*

HNZ hounds *ship*

HNZBRDTH handsbreadth *length*

HNZBRTH handsbreadth *length*

HNZF hands-off *noninterference*

HNZN hands-on *personal*

HNZTNG houndstongue *plant*

HNZTTH houndstooth (or) hound's-tooth *pattern*

HP hap *chance* happed happing

HP happy *joyful* happier happiest

HP heap *pile*

HP hep *cadence, in the know*

HP hip *(adj) stylish, in the know* hipper hippest

HP hip *(n) bone, roof*

HP hippie (or) hippy *(n) person* hippies

HP hippo *animal* hippos

HP hippy *(adj) large hips*

HP hoop *(n) circle, basketball (v) bind*

HP hoopoe *bird*

HP hop *(v) jump, bounce* hopped hopping

HP hop *(n) dance, trip, grain*

HP hope *wish* hoped hoping

HP Hopi *Native American*

HP hype *promote, deceive* hyped hyping

HP hypo *syringe, chemical* hypos

HPBLST hypoblast *embryo*

HPBN hipbone *skeleton*

HPCHT high-pitched *sound*

HPDK hepatic *liver*

HPDK hepatica *herb*

HPDNS hypotenuse *triangle*

HPDNYS hypotenuse *triangle*

HPDP hopped-up *drugged, excited*

HPDPLD hypodiploid *chromosomes*

HPDRM hippodrome *arena*

HPDRMK hypodermic *injection*

HPDRML hypodermal *beneath skin*

HPDRMS hypodermis *beneath skin*

HPDST hepatocyte *liver cell*

HPFCZ hypophyses (pl) *pituitary* hypophysis

HPFL hopeful (adj) *wishful* hopefully (adv)

HPFLNS hopefulness *wishful*

HPFRNGKS hypopharynx *tongue*

HPFRNGX hypopharynx *tongue*

HPFRNKS hypopharynx *tongue*

HPFRNX hypopharynx *tongue*

HPFSS hypophysis *pituitary* hypophyses

HPFSZ hypophyses (pl) *pituitary* hypophysis

HPG hypogea (pl) *tomb* hypogeum

HPGL hypogeal (or) hypogean (or) hypogeous *underground*

HPGLCM hypoglycemia *less sugar*

HPGLCMK hypoglycemic *less sugar*

HPGLCMY hypoglycemia *less sugar*

HPGLK happy-go-lucky *carefree*

HPGLSM hypoglycemia *less sugar*

HPGLSMK hypoglycemic *less sugar*

HPGLSMY hypoglycemia *less sugar*

HPGM hypogeum *tomb* hypogea

HPGN hypogean (or) hypogeal (or) hypogeous *underground*

HPGN hypogene *molten rock*

HPGS hypogeous (or) hypogeal (or) hypogean *underground*

HPGSDRK hypogastric *abdomen*

Letters aren't doubled for single sounds: to find alley use **L** not **LL**. Use **Y** and **W** as hard sounds only: to find yellow use **YL**. (Br)=British spelling or usage. * See dictionary.

HPGSTRK hypogastric *abdomen*

HPGY hypogea (pl) *tomb* hypogeum

HPGYL hypogeal (or) hypogean (or) hypogeous *underground*

HPGYM hypogeum *tomb* hypogea

HPGYN hypogean (or) hypogeal (or) hypogeous *underground*

HPGYS hypogeous (or) hypogeal (or) hypogean *underground*

HPHD hophead *addict*

HPHP hip-hop *subculture, music*

HPHZRD haphazard *chance*

HPHZRDL haphazardly *randomly*

HPHZRDNS haphazardness *randomness*

HPJ hypogea (pl) *tomb* hypogeum

HPJL hypogeal (or) hypogean (or) hypogeous *underground*

HPJM hypogeum *tomb* hypogea

HPJN hypogean (or) hypogeal (or) hypogeous *underground*

HPJN hypogene *molten rock*

HPJN hypogyny *flower*

HPJNS hypogynous *flower*

HPJS hypogeous (or) hypogeal (or) hypogean *underground*

HPJY hypogea (pl) *tomb* hypogeum

HPJYL hypogeal (or) hypogean (or) hypogeous *underground*

HPJYM hypogeum *tomb* hypogea

HPJYN hypogean (or) hypogeal (or) hypogeous *underground*

HPJYS hypogeous (or) hypogeal (or) hypogean *underground*

HPKC hypoxia *less oxygen*

HPKCM hypoxemia *less oxygen*

HPKCMK hypoxemic *less oxygen*

HPKCMY hypoxemia *less oxygen*

HPKCY hypoxia *less oxygen*

HPKDL hypocotyl *seedling*

HPKLCM hypocalcemia *calcium*

HPKLCMK hypocalcemic *calcium*

HPKLCMY hypocalcemia *calcium*

HPKLRS hypochlorous *acid*

HPKLRT hypochlorite *salt*

HPKLSM hypocalcemia *calcium*

HPKLSMK hypocalcemic *calcium*

HPKLSMY hypocalcemia *calcium*

HPKMP hippocampi (pl) *brain* hippocampus

HPKMPL hippocampal *brain*

HPKMPS hippocampus *brain* hippocampi

HPKNDR hypochondria *imagined ailments*

HPKNDRK hypochondriac *imagined ailments*

HPKNDRKL hypochondriacal (adj) *imagined ailments* hypochondriacally (adv)

HPKNDRSS hypochondriasis *imagined ailments* hypochondriases

HPKNDRY hypochondria *imagined ailments*

HPKNDRYK hypochondriac *imagined ailments*

HPKNDRYKL hypochondriacal (adj) *imagined ailments* hypochondriacally (adv)

HPKNDRYSS hypochondriasis *imagined ailments* hypochondriases

HPKRC hypocrisy *falseness*

hypocrisies

HPKRDKL hypocritical (adj) *falseness* hypocritically (adv)

HPKRDKTH Hippocratic oath *medicine*

HPKRMK hypochromic *anemia*

HPKRS hypocrisy *falseness* hypocrisies

HPKRSDK hypocoristic (or) hypocoristical (adj) *pet names* hypocoristically (adv)

HPKRSDKL hypocoristical (or) hypocoristic (adj) *pet names* hypocoristically (adv)

HPKRSM hypocorism *pet names*

HPKRSTK hypocoristic (or) hypocoristical (adj) *pet names* hypocoristically (adv)

HPKRSTKL hypocoristical (or) hypocoristic (adj) *pet names* hypocoristically (adv)

HPKRT hypocrite *falseness*

HPKRTKL hypocritical (adj) *falseness* hypocritically (adv)

HPKRTKTH Hippocratic oath *medicine*

HPKRZM hypocorism *pet names*

HPKS hypoxia *less oxygen*

HPKSK hypoxic *less oxygen*

HPKSM hypoxemia *less oxygen*

HPKSMK hypoxemic *less oxygen*

HPKSMY hypoxemia *less oxygen*

HPKSY hypoxia *less oxygen*

HPKT hepcat *hipster*

HPKTL hypocotyl *seedling*

HPL haply *by chance*

HPL happily *joyful*

HPL hoi polloi *masses*

HPL hoopla *commotion*

HPL whoopla *merrymaking*

Use letters that best describe the sounds you hear and omit the vowels. Use **S** or **K** instead of **C**: to find circle use **SRKL**. Use **J** to find joy, **JM** to find gem and **G** to find go.

HPLD haploid (adj, n) *cells* haploidy (n)

HPLRJNK hypoallergenic *allergy*

HPLS hapless *unlucky*

HPLS hopeless *despairing*

HPLSL hopelessly *despairing*

HPLSNS hopelessness *despair*

HPMRF hypomorph *mutant gene*

HPMRFK hypomorphic *mutant gene*

HPN halfpenny *money* halfpence (or) halfpennies

HPN happen *occur*

HPN hopping *bouncing*

HPND hypnoid (or) hypnoidal *sleep*

HPNDK hypnotic *trance*

HPNDKL hypnotically *trance*

HPNDL hypnoidal (or) hypnoid *sleep*

HPNG hopping *bouncing*

HPNGJK hypnagogic *drowsiness*

HPNGKF whooping cough *disease*

HPNGKRN whooping crane *disease*

HPNKF whooping cough *disease*

HPNKRN whooping crane *bird*

HPNN happening *event*

HPNNG happening *event*

HPNS halfpence (pl) *money* halfpenny

HPNS happiness *joy*

HPNSS hypnosis *trance* hypnoses

HPNSTNS happenstance *circumstance*

HPNSTNTS happenstance *circumstance*

HPNTH hypanthia (pl) *flower* hypanthium

HPNTHM hypanthium *flower* hypanthia

HPNTHRP hypnotherapy

trance hypnotherapies

HPNTHRPST hypnotherapist *trance*

HPNTHY hypanthia (pl) *flower* hypanthium

HPNTHYM hypanthium *flower* hypanthia

HPNTK hypnotic *trance*

HPNTKL hypnotically *trance*

HPNTS halfpence (pl) *money* halfpenny

HPNTST hypnotist *trance*

HPNTZ hypnotize *put in a trance* hypnotized hypnotizing

HPNTZBL hypnotizable *trance*

HPNTZM hypnotism *trance*

HPPDM hippopotami (pl) *animal* hippopotamus

HPPDMS hippopotamus *animal* hippopotamuses (or) hippopotami

HPPLD hypoploid *fewer*

HPPLSDK hypoplastic *immature*

HPPLSH hypoplasia *immature*

HPPLSTK hypoplastic *immature*

HPPLZH hypoplasia *immature*

HPPRTHRDSM hypoparathyroidism *less hormone*

HPPRTHRDZM hypoparathyroidism *less hormone*

HPPTM hippopotami (pl) *animal* hippopotamus

HPPTMS hippopotamus *animal* hippopotamuses (or) hippopotami

HPR happier *joy*

HPR hipper *stylish*

HPR hopper *bounce, tank*

HPR hyper *extreme*

HPRBL hyperbola *curve* hyperbolas (or) hyperbolae

HPRBL hyperbole *exaggeration*

HPRBLD hyperboloid *shape*

HPRBLDL hyperboloidal *shape*

HPRBLK hyperbolic *exaggeration*

HPRBLKL hyperbolically *exaggeration*

HPRBLST hyperbolist *exaggeration*

HPRBLZ hyperbolize *exaggerate* hyperbolized hyperbolizing

HPRBRK hyperbaric *pressure*

HPRBRKL hyperbarically *pressure*

HPRBRN hyperborean *northern*

HPRBRYN hyperborean *northern*

HPRCHRJ hypercharge *particle*

HPRD high-powered *dynamic*

HPRFG hyperphagia *appetite*

HPRFGY hyperphagia *appetite*

HPRFJ hyperphagia *appetite*

HPRFJK hyperphagic *appetite*

HPRFJY hyperphagia *appetite*

HPRFKL hyperfocal *lens*

HPRFL high profile *noted*

HPRGLCM hyperglycemia *excess sugar*

HPRGLCMK hyperglycemic *excess sugar*

HPRGLCMY hyperglycemia *excess sugar*

HPRGLK hypergolic *ignite*

HPRGLKL hypergolically *ignite*

HPRGLSM hyperglycemia *excess sugar*

HPRGLSMK hyperglycemic *excess sugar*

HPRGLSMY hyperglycemia *excess sugar*

HPRGM hypergamy *marriage* hypergamies

HPRHDRSS hyperhidrosis

sweat

HPRKB hypercube *geometry*

HPRKD hyperacuity
oversensitive

HPRKDLKCZ
hypercatalexes (pl) *verse*
hypercatalexis

HPRKDLKDK
hypercatalectic *verse*

HPRKDLKSS
hypercatalexis *verse*
hypercatalexes

HPRKDLKSZ
hypercatalexes (pl) *verse*
hypercatalexis

HPRKDLKTK
hypercatalectic *verse*

HPRKDLXS hypercatalexis
verse hypercatalexes

HPRKDV hyperactive
overactive

HPRKLCM hypercalcemia
calcium

HPRKLCMK hypercalcemic
calcium

HPRKLCMY hypercalcemia
calcium

HPRKLSM hypercalcemia
calcium

HPRKLSMK hypercalcemic
calcium

HPRKLSMY hypercalcemia
calcium

HPRKLSTRLM
hypercholesterolemia
blood

HPRKLSTRLMK
hypercholesterolemic
blood

HPRKLSTRLMY
hypercholesterolemia
blood

HPRKMPLKS
hypercomplex *numbers*

HPRKMPLX hypercomplex
numbers

HPRKNDK hyperkinetic
activity

HPRKNSH hyperkinesia
activity

HPRKNSS hyperkinesis
activity

HPRKNTK hyperkinetic
activity

HPRKNZH hyperkinesia
activity

HPRKPN hypercapnia *smoke*

HPRKPNK hypercapnic
smoke

HPRKPNY hypercapnia
smoke

HPRKRDK hypercritic
faultfinder

HPRKRDKL hypercritical
(adj) *faultfinding*
hypercritically (adv)

HPRKRDSZM
hypercriticism *nagging*

HPRKRKL hypercorrectly
language

HPRKRKNS
hypercorrectness
language

HPRKRKSHN
hypercorrection *language*

HPRKRKT hypercorrect
language

HPRKRKTL hypercorrectly
language

HPRKRKTNS
hypercorrectness
language

HPRKRTK hypercritic
faultfinder

HPRKRTKL hypercritical
(adj) *faultfinding*
hypercritically (adv)

HPRKRTSZM
hypercriticism *nagging*

HPRKSTNCHN
hyperextension *stretch
out*

HPRKSTND hyperextend
stretch out

HPRKSTNSHN
hyperextension *stretch
out*

HPRKT hyperacuity
oversensitive

HPRKTLKCZ
hypercatalexes (pl) *verse*
hypercatalexis

HPRKTLKDK
hypercatalectic *verse*

HPRKTLKSS hypercatalexis
verse hypercatalexes

HPRKTLKSZ
hypercatalexes (pl) *verse*
hypercatalexis

HPRKTLKTK
hypercatalectic *verse*

HPRKTLXS hypercatalexis
verse hypercatalexes

HPRKTV hyperactive
overactive

HPRKTVD hyperactivity
overactive

HPRKTVT hyperactivity
overactive

HPRKWD hyperacuity
oversensitive

HPRKWT hyperacuity
oversensitive

HPRKYB hypercube
geometry

HPRKYD hyperacuity
oversensitive

HPRKYT hyperacuity
oversensitive

HPRKYWD hyperacuity
oversensitive

HPRKYWT hyperacuity
oversensitive

HPRLPM hyperlipemia *fats*

HPRLPMK hyperlipemic *fats*

HPRLPMY hyperlipemia *fats*

HPRLSDK hyperrealistic
painting

HPRLSM hyperrealism
painting

HPRLST hyperrealist
painting

HPRLSTK hyperrealistic
painting

HPRLZM hyperrealism
painting

HPRM hyperemia *congestion*

HPRMDR hypermeter *verse*

HPRMK hyperemic
congestion

HPRMN hyperimmune
resistance

HPRMND hyperimmunity
resistance

HPRMNSH hypermnesia
memory

Use letters that best describe the sounds you hear and omit the vowels. Use **S** or **K** instead of **C**: to find circle use **SRKL**. Use **J** to find joy, **JM** to find gem and **G** to find go.

HPRMNSK hypermnesic *memory*
HPRMNT hyperimmunity *resistance*
HPRMNZ hypermnesia *memory*
HPRMNZH hypermnesia *memory*
HPRMNZK hypermnesic *memory*
HPRMNZY hypermnesia *memory*
HPRMRKT hypermarket *store*
HPRMTR hypermeter *verse*
HPRMTRP hypermetropia *farsighted*
HPRMTRPY hypermetropia *farsighted*
HPRMY hyperemia *congestion*
HPRMYN hyperimmune *resistance*
HPRMYND hyperimmunity *resistance*
HPRMYNT hyperimmunity *resistance*
HPRN hyperon *particle*
HPRN hyperpnea *breath*
HPRNFLSHN hyperinflation *money value*
HPRNFLSHNR hyperinflationary *money value*
HPRNY hyperpnea *breath*
HPRP hyperopia *farsighted*
HPRPK hyperopic *farsighted*
HPRPLD hyperploid *chromosomes* hyperploidy
HPRPLSDK hyperplastic *excess cells*
HPRPLSH hyperplasia *excess cells*
HPRPLSTK hyperplastic *excess cells*
HPRPLZH hyperplasia *excess cells*
HPRPN hyperpnea *breath*
HPRPNY hyperpnea *breath*
HPRPRKC hyperpyrexia *fever*
HPRPRKCY hyperpyrexia

fever
HPRPRKS hyperpyrexia *fever*
HPRPRKSY hyperpyrexia *fever*
HPRPRTHRDSM hyperparathyroidism *hormone*
HPRPRTHRDZM hyperparathyroidism *hormone*
HPRPRX hyperpyrexia *fever*
HPRPRXY hyperpyrexia *fever*
HPRPTTR hyperpituitary *growth*
HPRPTWTR hyperpituitary *growth*
HPRPTYTR hyperpituitary *growth*
HPRPTYWTR hyperpituitary *growth*
HPRPY hyperopia *farsighted*
HPRQB hypercube *geometry*
HPRQD hyperacuity *oversensitive*
HPRQT hyperacuity *oversensitive*
HPRQWD hyperacuity *oversensitive*
HPRQWT hyperacuity *oversensitive*
HPRRCM hyperuricemia *urine*
HPRRCMY hyperuricemia *urine*
HPRRDBL hyperirritable *response*
HPRRDBLD hyperirritability *response*
HPRRDBLT hyperirritability *response*
HPRRSM hyperuricemia *urine*
HPRRSMY hyperuricemia *urine*
HPRRTBL hyperirritable *response*
HPRRTBLD hyperirritability *response*
HPRRTBLT hyperirritability *response*

HPRSDD hyperacidity *too much acid*
HPRSDS high priestess *leader*
HPRSDT hyperacidity *too much acid*
HPRSHR high-pressure *tension*
HPRSKSHL hypersexual *activity*
HPRSKSHLD hypersexuality *activity*
HPRSKSHLT hypersexuality *activity*
HPRSKSHWL hypersexual *activity*
HPRSKSHWLD hypersexuality *activity*
HPRSKSHWLT hypersexuality *activity*
HPRSNK hypersonic *speed*
HPRSNKL hypersonically *speed*
HPRSNSDV hypersensitive *susceptible*
HPRSNSTV hypersensitive *susceptible*
HPRSNSTVD hypersensitivity *susceptible*
HPRSNSTVT hypersensitivity *susceptible*
HPRSNTSDV hypersensitive *susceptible*
HPRSNTSTV hypersensitive *susceptible*
HPRSNTSTVD hypersensitivity *susceptible*
HPRSNTSTVT hypersensitivity *susceptible*
HPRSPS hyperspace *4th dimension*
HPRST high priest *leader*
HPRSTDK hyperostotic *bone*
HPRSTHDK hyperesthetic *sensitive*
HPRSTHSH hyperesthesia *sensitive*

Letters aren't doubled for single sounds: to find **alley** use **L** not **LL**. Use **Y** and **W** as hard sounds only: to find **yellow** use **YL**. (Br)=British spelling or usage. * See dictionary.

HPRSTHTK hyperesthetic *sensitive*

HPRSTHZH hyperesthesia *sensitive*

HPRSTS high priestess *leader*

HPRSTSS hyperostosis *bone* hyperostoses

HPRSTTK hyperostotic *bone*

HPRTHRDZM hyperthyroidism *metabolism*

HPRTHRM hyperthermia *fever*

HPRTHRMK hyperthermic *fever*

HPRTHRMY hyperthermia *fever*

HPRTKST hypertext *computer*

HPRTN hypertonia *tension*

HPRTNCHN hypertension *blood pressure*

HPRTNK hypertonic *tension*

HPRTNSD hypertonicity *tension*

HPRTNSHN hypertension *blood pressure*

HPRTNST hypertonicity *tension*

HPRTNSV hypertensive *blood pressure*

HPRTNY hypertonia *tension*

HPRTRF hypertrophy *growth* hypertrophied hypertrophying hypertrophies

HPRTRFK hypertrophic *growth*

HPRTXT hypertext *computer*

HPRVDMNSS hypervitaminosis *vitamins* hypervitaminoses

HPRVLSD hypervelocity *speed*

HPRVLST hypervelocity *speed*

HPRVNLSHN hyperventilation *breathe*

HPRVNLT hyperventilate *breathe* hyperventilated hyperventilating

HPRVNTLSHN hyperventilation *breathe*

HPRVNTLT hyperventilate *breathe* hyperventilated hyperventilating

HPRVTMNSS hypervitaminosis *vitamins* hypervitaminoses

HPRXTNCHN hyperextension *stretch out*

HPRXTND hyperextend *stretch out*

HPRXTNSHN hyperextension *stretch out*

HPRYLSDK hyperrealistic *painting*

HPRYLSM hyperrealism *painting*

HPRYLST hyperrealist *painting*

HPRYLSTK hyperrealistic *painting*

HPRYLZM hyperrealism *painting*

HPRYRCM hyperuricemia *urine*

HPRYRCMY hyperuricemia *urine*

HPRYRSM hyperuricemia *urine*

HPRYRSMY hyperuricemia *urine*

HPS eohippus *primitive horse*

HPSK hopsack *fabric*

HPSKCH hopscotch *game*

HPSKLD hypocycloid *curve*

HPSKRT hoopskirt *clothing*

HPSNR hypocenter *earthquake*

HPSNTR hypocenter *earthquake*

HPSNTRL hypocentral *earthquake*

HPST happiest *joy*

HPST hippest *stylish*

HPSTL hypostyle *columns*

HPSTM hypostome *mouth*

HPSTR hipster *aware one*

HPSTRZM hipsterism

awareness

HPSTSS hypostasis *substance* hypostases

HPSTTZ hypostatize *give identity* hypostatized hypostatizing

HPTD heptad *seven*

HPTDS hepatitis *disease* hepatitides

HPTGN heptagon *shape*

HPTGNL heptagonal *shape*

HPTHCZ hypotheses (pl) *theory* hypothesis

HPTHDKL hypothetical (adj) *uncertain* hypothetically (adv)

HPTHKDR hypothecator *pledge*

HPTHKSHN hypothecation *pledge*

HPTHKT hypothecate *pledge* hypothecated hypothecating

HPTHKTR hypothecator *pledge*

HPTHLMK hypothalamic *gland*

HPTHLMS hypothalamus *gland*

HPTHRD hypothyroid *metabolism*

HPTHRDZM hypothyroidism *metabolism*

HPTHRM hypothermia *low temperature*

HPTHRMK hypothermic *low temperature*

HPTHRML hypothermal *ore*

HPTHRMY hypothermia *low temperature*

HPTHSS hypothesis *theory* hypotheses

HPTHSZ hypotheses (pl) *theory* hypothesis

HPTHSZ hypothesize *theorize* hypothesized hypothesizing

HPTHTKL hypothetical (adj) *uncertain* hypothetically (adv)

HPTK hepatic *liver*

Use letters that best describe the sounds you hear and omit the vowels. Use **S** or **K** instead of **C**: to find circle use **SRKL**. Use **J** to find joy, **JM** to find gem and **G** to find go.

HPTK hepatica *herb*
HPTKDM hepatectomy *liver* hepatectomies
HPTKTD hypoeutectoid *melting point*
HPTKTM hepatectomy *liver* hepatectomies
HPTM hepatoma *tumor* hepatomas (or) hepatomata
HPTMD hepatomata (pl) *tumor* hepatoma
HPTMT hepatomata (pl) *tumor* hepatoma
HPTMTR heptameter *verse*
HPTN hypotonia *less tension*
HPTNCHN hypotension *low pressure*
HPTNK hypotonic *less tension*
HPTNS hypotenuse *triangle*
HPTNSHN hypotension *low pressure*
HPTNSV hypotension *low pressure*
HPTNY hypotonia *less tension*
HPTNYS hypotenuse *triangle*
HPTP hopped-up *drugged, excited*
HPTRK heptarchy *seven rulers*
HPTS heptose *sugar*
HPTST hepatocyte *liver cell*
HPTTS hepatitis *disease* hepatitides
HPTZ heptose *sugar*
HPWLRJNK hypoallergenic *allergy*
HPWRD high-powered *dynamic*
HPX hypoxia *less oxygen*
HPXK hypoxic *less oxygen*
HPXM hypoxemia *less oxygen*
HPXMK hypoxemic *less oxygen*
HPXMY hypoxemia *less oxygen*
HPXY hypoxia *less oxygen*
HPYR happier *joy*

HPYST happiest *joy*
HPYTKTD hypoeutectoid *melting point*
HQD hawkweed *plant*
HQRK hackwork *commercial*
HQRM hookworm *parasite*
HQZN haute cuisine *food*
HR gyro *spinner, sandwich* gyros
HR hair *fur, tress*
HR hairy *furry, scary* hairier hairiest
HR hare *rabbit* hare (or) hares
HR harrow *tool*
HR harry *assault, worry* harried harrying harries
HR hear *listen* heard hearing
HR her *(pron) that female*
HR Hera *Greek goddess*
HR here *this place*
HR hero *admired one* heroes
HR higher *tall, serious, drugged**
HR hire *employ, lease* hired hiring
HR hoar *frost, old*
HR hoary *ancient* hoarier hoariest
HR hoer *digger*
HR hooray (or) hurrah (or) hoorah *(interj) joy*
HR hora *dance*
HR Horae *goddess*
HR horror *dread*
HR houri *woman*
HR hurry *rush* hurried hurrying hurries
HR whore *prostitute* whored whoring
HRB herb *plant*
HRB herby *plant*
HRB hereby *by this means*
HRBJ herbage *plant*
HRBL hair ball *cat*
HRBL harebell *herb*
HRBL herbal *plant*
HRBL horrible (adj) *dreadful* horribly (adv)
HRBLK herblike *plant*
HRBLNS horribleness *dreadful*

HRBLST herbalist *healer*
HRBNJR harbinger *forerunner*
HRBR harbor *refuge* (Br) harbour
HRBR herbaria (pl) *plant collection* herbarium
HRBRDTH hairbreadth (or) hairsbreadth *distance*
HRBRJ harborage *refuge*
HRBRM herbarium *plant collection* herbaria
HRBRMSDR harbormaster *dock official* (Br) harbourmaster
HRBRMSTR harbormaster *dock official* (Br) harbourmaster
HRBRND harebrained *foolish*
HRBRR harborer *hider*
HRBRSD harborside *near docks* (Br) harbourside
HRBRTH hairbreadth (or) hairsbreadth *distance*
HRBRY herbaria (pl) *plant collection* herbarium
HRBRYM herbarium *plant collection* herbaria
HRBSD herbicide *kill plants*
HRBSDL herbicidal (adj) *kill plants* herbicidally (adv)
HRBSHS herbaceous *plant*
HRBT hereabout (or) hereabouts *nearby*
HRBTS hereabouts (or) hereabout *nearby*
HRBVR herbivore *eat plants*
HRBVRS herbivorous *eat plants*
HRC heresy *contrary belief* heresies
HRC horsey (or) horsy *like a horse* horsier horsiest
HRCR horsier *like a horse*
HRCST horsiest *like a horse*
HRCYR horsier *like a horse*
HRCYST horsiest *like a horse*
HRD hairdo *style* hairdos
HRD haired *with hair*
HRD hard (adj) *not soft,*

Letters aren't doubled for single sounds: to find alley use **L** not **LL**. Use **Y** and **W** as hard sounds only: to find yellow use **YL**. (Br)=British spelling or usage. * See dictionary.

difficult (adv) fierce, tight
harder hardest

HRD hardy *brave, robust*
hardier hardiest

HRD harried *annoyed*

HRD harried *assaulted, worried*

HRD hayride *wagon ride*

HRD heard *(v-past) hear*

HRD hearty *(n) fellow*
hearties

HRD hearty *(adj) sincere, appetite* heartier heartiest

HRD herd *(n) group (v) gather*

HRD high road *ethical way*

HRD hired *employed*

HRD hoard *reserve*

HRD horde *crowd*

HRD horrid *awful*

HRD hurried *hasty*

HRDBK hardback *book*

HRDBL hard-boil *cook*

HRDBL hardball *sport, tactics*

HRDBL heritable *ancestry*

HRDBLD hard-boiled *tough*

HRDBLD heritability *genetics*

HRDBLT heritability *genetics*

HRDBN hardbound *book*

HRDBND hardbound *book*

HRDBRD hardboard *fiberboard*

HRDBST hartebeest *antelope*

HRDBTN hard-bitten *tough*

HRDBYL hard-boil *cook*

HRDBYLD hard-boiled *tough*

HRDD heredity *genetics*

HRDFR heretofore *until now*

HRDFSDD hardfisted *stingy*

HRDFSTD hardfisted *stingy*

HRDGDS hard goods *durables*

HRDGDZ hard goods *durables*

HRDGRD hurdy-gurdy *music* hurdy-gurdies

HRDGRT hurdy-gurdy *music* hurdy-gurdies

HRDHD hardhead *stubborn*

one

HRDHD hardihood *vigor*

HRDHDD hardheaded *stubborn*

HRDHDDNS hardheadedness *stubborn*

HRDHDNG hard-hitting *effective*

HRDHNDD hardhanded *strict*

HRDHRDD hard-hearted *pitiless*

HRDHRDD hardhearted *no compassion*

HRDHRDDL hardheartedly *not compassionately*

HRDHRDDNS hardheartedness *no compassion*

HRDHRTD hard-hearted *pitiless*

HRDHRTD hardhearted *no compassion*

HRDHRTDL hardheartedly *not compassionately*

HRDHRTDNS hardheartedness *no compassion*

HRDHT hard hat *construction*

HRDHTNG hard-hitting *effective*

HRDJ hard-edge *painting*

HRDJ heritage *family*

HRDJD hard-edged *tough*

HRDK heartache *sorrow*

HRDKL heretical (adj) *contrary belief* heretically (adv)

HRDKLCHR horticulture *plants*

HRDKLCHRL horticultural (adj) *plants* horticulturally (adv)

HRDKLCHRST horticulturist *plants*

HRDKLTR horticulture *plants*

HRDKLTRL horticultural (adj) *plants* horticulturally (adv)

HRDKLTRST horticulturist

plants

HRDKLTYR horticulture *plants*

HRDKLTYRL horticultural (adj) *plants* horticulturally (adv)

HRDKLTYRST horticulturist *plants*

HRDKP hard copy *on paper*

HRDKR hard core *(n) center, (Br) material*
(Br) hardcore

HRDKR hard-core *(adj) confirmed, explicit*

HRDKVR hardcover *book*

HRDL hardily *strong, robust*

HRDL hardly *barely*

HRDL heartily *sincere*

HRDL horridly *awful*

HRDL hurdle *(v) leap* hurdled hurdling

HRDL hurdle *(n) barrier*

HRDL hurtle *fling* hurtled hurtling

HRDLBR hard labor *punishment*
(Br) hard labour

HRDLK herdlike *group*

HRDLKR hard liquor *alcohol*

HRDLN hard-line *unbending*

HRDLNR hard-liner *unbending one*

HRDLR hurdler *leap*

HRDN harden *toughen*

HRDNG hoarding *fence, (Br) billboard*

HRDNGGRS hardinggrass *plant*

HRDNGRS hardinggrass *plant*

HRDNN hardening *arteries*

HRDNNG hardening *arteries*

HRDNR hardener *additive*

HRDNS hardiness *strong, robust*

HRDNS hardness *not soft*

HRDNS heartiness *sincere, appetite*

HRDNS horridness *awful*

HRDNST hard-nosed *stubborn*

HRDNST hardnosed *tough*

Use letters that best describe the sounds you hear and omit the vowels. Use **S** or **K** instead of **C**: to find circle use **SRKL**. Use **J** to find joy, **JM** to find gem and **G** to find go.

HRDNZ hardnose *tough one*
HRDNZD hard-nosed *stubborn*
HRDNZD hardnosed *tough*
HRDP hard up *poor*
HRDPLT hard palate *mouth*
HRDPN hardpan *soil*
HRDPRSD hard-pressed *strained*
HRDPRST hard-pressed *strained*
HRDR harder *(adj) not soft, difficult (adv) fierce, tight*
HRDR hardier *strong, robust*
HRDR heartier *sincere, appetite*
HRDR herder *gather animals*
HRDR heritor *heir*
HRDRSN hairdressing *styling*
HRDRSNG hairdressing *styling*
HRDRSR hairdresser *barber*
HRDSHL hard-shell *fundamentalist, crab*
HRDSHLD hard-shelled *fundamentalist*
HRDSHP hardship *suffering*
HRDSK hard disk *computer*
HRDSKRBL hardscrabble *poor soil*
HRDSL hard sell *maketing*
HRDSS hard sauce *food*
HRDST hardest *(adj) not soft, difficult (adv) fierce, tight*
HRDST hardiest *strong, robust*
HRDST heartiest *sincere, appetite*
HRDT heredity *genetics*
HRDTK hardtack *cracker, tree* hardtack (or) hardtacks
HRDTK heart attack *coronary*
HRDTP hardtop *car*
HRDTR hereditary *genetics*
HRDTR hortatory *advisory*
HRDTRL hereditarily *genetics*
HRDTRN hereditarian

genetics
HRDTRYN hereditarian *genetics*
HRDTV hortative *advisory*
HRDVHRNG hard-of-hearing *deaf*
HRDWD hardwood *tree*
HRDWN hard-won *effort*
HRDWR hardware *tools, fittings*
HRDWRD hardwired *electronic*
HRDWRKN hardworking *industrious*
HRDWRKNG hardworking *industrious*
HRDYR hardier *strong, robust*
HRDYR heartier *sincere, appetite*
HRDYST hardiest *strong, robust*
HRDYST heartiest *sincere, appetite*
HRDZMN herdsman *livestock* herdsmen
HRF horrify *shock* horrified horrifying horrifies
HRFDR hereafter *future*
HRFK horrific *shocking*
HRFKL horrifically *shocking*
HRFN horrifying *shocking*
HRFNGL horrifyingly *shocking*
HRFNT hierophant *priest*
HRFRST hoarfrost *ice*
HRFTR hereafter *future*
HRFYN horrifying *shocking*
HRFYNGL horrifyingly *shocking*
HRFYNL horrifyingly *shocking*
HRGLF hieroglyph *writing*
HRGLFK hieroglyphic *writing*
HRGLFKS hieroglyphics *writing*
HRGLFX hieroglyphics *writing*
HRHN horehound *plant*
HRHND horehound *plant*
HRHS whorehouse *bordello*

HRJN harijan *untouchable*
HRK haricot *bean pod*
HRK hark *listen*
HRK hayrack *feeding rack*
HRK hayrick *haystack*
HRK heroic *brave*
HRK hierarchy *ranking* hierarchies
HRKBS harquebus *gun*
HRKDNG haircutting *style*
HRKDR haircutter *style*
HRKL heroically *brave*
HRKLN Herculean *difficult, powerful*
HRKLTH haircloth *fabric*
HRKLYN Herculean *difficult, powerful*
HRKLZ Hercules *Greek myth*
HRKN harken *return*
HRKN hearken *listen*
HRKN hurricane *storm*
HRKR hara-kiri *suicide*
HRKS hyrax *animal* hyraxes
HRKT haircut *style*
HRKTN haircutting *style*
HRKTNG haircutting *style*
HRKTR haircutter *style*
HRKWBS harquebus *gun*
HRKYLN Herculean *difficult, powerful*
HRKYLYN Herculean *difficult, powerful*
HRKYLZ Hercules *Greek myth*
HRL herald *(v) announce (n) announcer*
HRL hurl *throw*
HRL hurly *uproar*
HRL jurel *fish*
HRLBRL hurly-burly *uproar*
HRLD herald *(v) announce (n) announcer*
HRLDK heraldic *family*
HRLDR heraldry *family* heraldries
HRLG horology *time*
HRLJ horology *time*
HRLJKL horological *time*
HRLJST horologist *time*
HRLKN harlequin *clown*
HRLKND harlequinade *play*
HRLKWN harlequin *clown*

Letters aren't doubled for single sounds: to find alley use **L** not **LL**. Use **Y** and **W** as hard sounds only: to find yellow use **YL**. (Br)=British spelling or usage. * See dictionary.

HRLKWND harlequinade *play*
HRLN hairline *forehead*
HRLN hireling *hatchet man*
HRLN hurling *sport*
HRLNG hireling *hatchet man*
HRLNG hurling *sport*
HRLP harelip *deformity*
HRLQN harlequin *clown*
HRLQND harlequinade *play*
HRLR high roller *big spender, big gambler*
HRLR hurler *sportsman*
HRLS hairless *bald*
HRLSNS hairlessness *bald*
HRLT harlot *prostitute*
HRLTR harlotry *prostitution* harlotries
HRM harem *women*
HRM harm *injure*
HRMDJ hermitage *hideaway*
HRMDK hermetic *solitary, airtight*
HRMDKL hermetically *solitary, airtight*
HRMFL harmful (adj) *injurious* harmfully (adv)
HRMFLNS harmfulness *injury*
HRMFRDDK hermaphroditic *both sexes*
HRMFRDDZM hermaphroditism *both sexes*
HRMFRDT hermaphrodite *both sexes*
HRMFRDTK hermaphroditic *both sexes*
HRMFRDTZM hermaphroditism *both sexes*
HRMJSD Her Majesty *queen*
HRMJST Her Majesty *queen*
HRMLS harmless *not offensive*
HRMN harmony *music* harmonies
HRMN hormone *stimulant*
HRMNDKL hermeneutical (adj) *interpretation* hermeneutically (adv)
HRMNDKS hermeneutics

interpretation
HRMNDX hermeneutics *interpretation*
HRMNGGR whoremonger *pimp*
HRMNGR whoremonger *pimp*
HRMNK harmonic *musical*
HRMNK harmonica *instrument*
HRMNKL harmonically *musical*
HRMNL hormonal (adj) *stimulant* hormonally (adv)
HRMNS harmonious *compatible*
HRMNSNS harmoniousness *compatibility*
HRMNSST harmonicist *instrument*
HRMNTKL hermeneutical (adj) *interpretation* hermeneutically (adv)
HRMNTKS hermeneutics *interpretation*
HRMNTX hermeneutics *interpretation*
HRMNYDKL hermeneutical (adj) *interpretation* hermeneutically (adv)
HRMNYDKS hermeneutics *interpretation*
HRMNYDX hermeneutics *interpretation*
HRMNYS harmonious *compatible*
HRMNYSNS harmoniousness *compatibility*
HRMNYTKL hermeneutical (adj) *interpretation* hermeneutically (adv)
HRMNYTKS hermeneutics *interpretation*
HRMNYTX hermeneutics *interpretation*
HRMNZ harmonize *sing, correspond* harmonized harmonizing (Br) harmonise

HRMNZR harmonizer *singer* (Br) harmoniser
HRMNZSHN harmonization *compatibility* (Br) harmonisation
HRMR harmer *injurer*
HRMSKRM harum-scarum *reckless*
HRMSTR whoremaster *pimp*
HRMT hermit *loner*
HRMTJ hermitage *hideaway*
HRMTK hermetic *solitary, airtight*
HRMTKL hermetically *solitary, airtight*
HRMTZM hermitism *solitude*
HRMZ Hermes *god*
HRN harrowing *vexing*
HRN hearing *listen, meeting*
HRN here and now *present time*
HRN herein *within*
HRN hereon *upon*
HRN hernia *bulge* hernias (or) herniae
HRN heroin *drug*
HRN heroine *hero (f)*
HRN heron *bird* herons
HRN horn *music, antler, land**
HRN horny *sexually excited* hornier horniest
HRN Huron *Native American, lake* Hurons (or) Huron
HRNBFR hereinbefore *preceeding*
HRNBL hereinbelow *after*
HRNBL hornbill *bird*
HRNBLND hornblende *mineral*
HRNBM hornbeam *birch*
HRNBN herringbone *pattern*
HRNBV hereinabove *prior*
HRND hearing aid *device*
HRND horned *antler, tuft*
HRNDL horned owl *bird*
HRNDN here and now *present time*
HRNDR hereunder *according to*
HRNDS horrendous *dreadful*
HRNDTD horned toad *lizard*

Use letters that best describe the sounds you hear and omit the vowels. Use **S** or **K** instead of **C**: to find circle use **SRKL**. Use **J** to find joy, **JM** to find gem and **G** to find go.

HRNFDR hereinafter *following*

HRNFL horn fly *insect* horn flies

HRNFTR hereinafter *following*

HRNG harangue *lecture* harangued haranguing

HRNG harrowing *vexing*

HRNG hearing *listen, meeting*

HRNG herring *fish* herring (or) herrings

HRNG hiring *jobs*

HRNGBN herringbone *pattern*

HRNGD hearing aid *device*

HRNGGR haranguer *lecture*

HRNGR haranguer *lecture*

HRNLS hornless *no antlers*

HRNN horn in *intrude*

HRNNS horniness *hardness*

HRNPP hornpipe *music, dance*

HRNR hornier *hard*

HRNRMS horn-rims *glasses*

HRNRMZ horn-rims *glasses*

HRNS hairiness *furry, scary*

HRNS harness *strap*

HRNS hoariness *old*

HRNSHN herniation *bulge*

HRNST horniest *hard*

HRNSTN hornstone *mineral*

HRNSWGL hornswoggle *hoax* hornswoggled hornswoggling

HRNT herniate *bulge* herniated herniating

HRNT hornet *wasp*

HRNTD horned toad *lizard*

HRNTL horntail *insect*

HRNWRM hornworm *caterpillar*

HRNWRT hornwort *herb*

HRNY hernia *bulge* hernias (or) herniae

HRNYR hornier *hard*

HRNYSHN herniation *bulge*

HRNYST horniest *hard*

HRNYT herniate *bulge* herniated herniating

HRP harp *(n) music (v) nag*

HRP harpy *creature* harpies

HRP higher-up *chief*

HRPDK herpetic *virus*

HRPDLJKL herpetological *reptiles*

HRPN hairpin *fastener, sharp curve*

HRPN harpoon *lance*

HRPN hereupon *on this*

HRPR harper *music, nag*

HRPS hairpiece *wig*

HRPSKRD harpsichord *music*

HRPST harpist *musician*

HRPTK herpetic *virus*

HRPTLG herpetology *reptiles*

HRPTLJ herpetology *reptiles*

HRPTLJKL herpetological *reptiles*

HRPTLJST herpetologist *reptiles*

HRPZ herpes *virus*

HRQBS harquebus *gun*

HRQLN Herculean *difficult, powerful*

HRQLYN Herculean *difficult, powerful*

HRQLZ Hercules *Greek myth*

HRR hairier *furry, scary*

HRR harrier *dog, hawk*

HRR hearer *listen*

HRR hirer *employer*

HRR hoarier *old*

HRR horary *hourly*

HRR horror *dread*

HRR hurrier *fast mover*

HRRK hierarch *leader*

HRRK hierarchy *ranking* hierarchies

HRRKKL hierarchical (adj) *arranged* hierarchically (adv)

HRRSTRK horror-struck *dread*

HRS harass *pester*

HRS hearsay *rumor*

HRS hearse *vehicle*

HRS here's *(contr) here is*

HRS heresy *contrary belief* heresies

HRS hoarse *voice* hoarser

hoarsest

HRS horse *(v) provide a horse* horsed horsing

HRS horse *(n) animal* horses

HRS horsey (or) horsy *like a horse* horsier horsiest

HRSBK horseback *saddle*

HRSBN horsebean *vegetable*

HRSBRG Harrisburg *city*

HRSD horsehide *leather*

HRSDK heuristic *learning*

HRSDKL heuristically *learning*

HRSF herself *she*

HRSFL horsefly *insect* horseflies

HRSFLSH horseflesh *utility*

HRSFTHRS horsefeathers *nonsense*

HRSH harsh *severe*

HRSH horseshoe *hoof, U-shaped*

HRSH whorish *prostitute*

HRSHD horsehide *leather*

HRSHL harshly *severely*

HRSHM Hiroshima *city*

HRSHNS harshness *severeness*

HRSHR horsehair *cloth*

HRSHR horseshoer *blacksmith*

HRSHT horseshit *(vulgar) nonsense*

HRSHWP horsewhip *flog* horsewhipped horsewhipping

HRSHWR horseshoer *blacksmith*

HRSKP horoscope *zodiac*

HRSKR horsecar *vehicle*

HRSL horsily *like a horse*

HRSLF herself *she*

HRSLF horselaugh *guffaw*

HRSLK horselike *similarity*

HRSLS horseless *no horse*

HRSMN horseman *rider, trainer* horsemen

HRSMNSHP horsemanship *rider, trainer*

HRSMNT harassment *bother*

HRSMNT horsemint *herb*

HRSN hoarsen *make harsh*

Letters aren't doubled for single sounds: to find alley use **L** not **LL**. Use **Y** and **W** as hard sounds only: to find yellow use **YL**. (Br)=British spelling or usage. * See dictionary.

HRSNBG horse-and-buggy *bygone era*
HRSNDBG horse-and-buggy *bygone era*
HRSNS horsiness *like a horse*
HRSPCZ haruspices (pl) *seer* haruspex
HRSPKS haruspex *seer* haruspices
HRSPL horseplay *rowdiness*
HRSPLDR hairsplitter *arguer*
HRSPLR horseplayer *bettor*
HRSPLTN hairsplitting *arguing*
HRSPLTNG hairsplitting *arguing*
HRSPLTR hairsplitter *arguer*
HRSPLYR horseplayer *bettor*
HRSPR horsepower *energy*
HRSPRNG hairspring *clock*
HRSPSZ haruspices (pl) *seer* haruspex
HRSPWR horsepower *energy*
HRSPX haruspex *seer* haruspices
HRSR harasser *bother*
HRSR hoarser *voice*
HRSR horsehair *cloth*
HRSR horsier *like a horse*
HRSRDSH horseradish *herb*
HRSRND horse around *play*
HRSSH horseshoe *hoof, U-shaped*
HRSSHR horseshoer *blacksmith*
HRSSHT horseshit *(vulgar) nonsense*
HRSSHWR horseshoer *blacksmith*
HRSST hoarsest *voice*
HRSST horsiest *like a horse*
HRST hairiest *furry, scary*
HRST hirsute *hairy*
HRST hoariest *old*
HRST horst *earth*
HRSTK heuristic *learning*
HRSTKL heuristically *learning*

HRSTL horsetail *plant*
HRSTNS hirsuteness *hairy*
HRSTR herstory *history (f)* herstories
HRSTRK hairstreak *butterfly*
HRSTRK horror-struck *dread*
HRSTZM hirsutism *hairy*
HRSWD horseweed *plant*
HRSWMN horsewoman *rider, trainer* horsewomen
HRSWP horsewhip *flog* horsewhipped horsewhipping
HRSWPR horsewhipper *flogger*
HRSYR horsier *like a horse*
HRSYST horsiest *like a horse*
HRT hart *stag*
HRT heart *center, organ*
HRT hearty *(adj) sincere, appetite* heartier heartiest
HRT hearty *(n) fellow* hearties
HRT hereto *document*
HRT hurt *harm* hurt hurting
HRTBL heritable *ancestry*
HRTBLD heritability *genetics*
HRTBLT heritability *genetics*
HRTBRK heartbreak *grief*
HRTBRKN heartbreaking *difficult, sad*
HRTBRKN heartbroken *sad*
HRTBRKNG heartbreaking *difficult, sad*
HRTBRKR heartbreaker *sorrow*
HRTBRN heartburn *discomfort*
HRTBST hartebeest *antelope*
HRTBT heartbeat *pulse*
HRTCZ heartsease *calmness, flower*
HRTDVL hortatively *advisory*
HRTFL hurtful (adj) *damaging* hurtfully (adv)
HRTFLNS hurtfulness *damage*
HRTFLT heartfelt *sincere*
HRTFR heretofore *until now*
HRTFRD Hartford *city*
HRTGRD hurdy-gurdy *music* hurdy-gurdies

HRTGRT hurdy-gurdy *music* hurdy-gurdies
HRTH hearth *fireplace*
HRTHRT heart-to-heart *intimate*
HRTHSTN hearthstone *fireplace*
HRTJ heritage *family*
HRTK hardtack *cracker, tree* hardtack (or) hardtacks
HRTK heartache *sorrow*
HRTK heretic *contrary belief*
HRTKL heretical (adj) *contrary belief* heretically (adv)
HRTKLCHR horticulture *plants*
HRTKLCHRL horticultural (adj) *plants* horticulturally (adv)
HRTKLCHRST horticulturist *plants*
HRTKLTR horticulture *plants*
HRTKLTRL horticultural (adj) *plants* horticulturally (adv)
HRTKLTRST horticulturist *plants*
HRTKLTYR horticulture *plants*
HRTKLTYRL horticultural (adj) *plants* horticulturally (adv)
HRTKLTYRST horticulturist *plants*
HRTL heartily *sincere*
HRTL hurdle (v) *leap* hurdled hurdling
HRTL hurdle (n) *barrier*
HRTL hurtle *fling* hurtled hurtling
HRTLND heartland *country*
HRTLR hurdler *leap*
HRTLS heartless *cruel*
HRTN hearten *cheer*
HRTNS heartiness *sincere, appetite*
HRTP hardtop *car*
HRTR heartier *sincere, appetite*
HRTR heritor *heir*
HRTRGR hair-trigger (adj)

Use letters that best describe the sounds you hear and omit the vowels. Use **S** or **K** instead of **C**: to find circle use **SRKL**. Use **J** to find joy, **JM** to find gem and **G** to find go.

quick response hair trigger
(n)
HRTRNDN heartrending *sad*
HRTRNDNG heartrending
sad
HRTS hertz *frequency* hertz
HRTSK heartsick *depressed*
HRTST heartiest *sincere,*
appetite
HRTSTRNG heartstring
emotion
HRTSZ heartsease *calmness,*
flower
HRTTHRB heartthrob
sweetheart
HRTTHRT heart-to-heart
intimate
HRTTK heart attack
coronary
HRTTR hortatory *advisory*
HRTTV hortative *advisory*
HRTTVL hortatively *advisory*
HRTWD heartwood *tree*
HRTWRM heartworm
parasite
HRTWRMN heartwarming
cheering
HRTWRMNG heartwarming
cheering
HRTYR heartier *sincere,*
appetite
HRTYST heartiest *sincere,*
appetite
HRV hereof *of this*
HRVSDBL harvestable *reap*
HRVSDR harvester *reaper*
HRVST harvest *(v) reap (n)*
crop
HRVSTBL harvestable *reap*
HRVSTM harvesttime *season*
HRVSTR harvester *reaper*
HRWK heroic *brave*
HRWKL heroically *brave*
HRWN harrowing *vexing*
HRWN heroin *drug*
HRWN heroine *hero (f)*
HRWNG harrowing *vexing*
HRWR harrower *digger*
HRWTH herewith *hereby*
HRWZM heroism *bravery*
HRX hyrax *animal* hyraxes
HRYR hairier *furry, scary*

HRYR harrier *dog, hawk*
HRYR hoarier *old*
HRYR hurrier *fast mover*
HRYST hairiest *furry, scary*
HRYST hoariest *old*
HRZ here's *(contr) here is*
HRZ high-rise *structure*
HRZBRDTH hairsbreadth
(or) hairbreadth *small*
distance
HRZBRTH hairsbreadth (or)
hairbreadth *small distance*
HRZM heroism *bravery*
HRZN hair-raising *scary*
HRZN horizon *junction*
HRZNG hair-raising *scary*
HRZNL horizontal (adj) *level*
horizontally (adv)
HRZNTL horizontal (adj)
level horizontally (adv)
HS hiss *whisper, "s" sound*
hisses
HS hissy *tantrum*
HS house *(n) abode*
HS hussy *lewd female*
hussies
HS Xhosa *African*
HSBND housebound
confined
HSBRK housebreak *tame or*
teach housebroke
housebroken
housebreaking
HSBRKN housebreaking
felony
HSBRKN housebroken *not*
messy
HSBRKNG housebreaking
felony
HSBRKR housebreaker
felon
HSBT houseboat *ship*
HSD hasty *hurried* hastier
hastiest
HSD hayseed *hillbilly*
hayseed (or) hayseeds
HSDL hastily *hurried*
HSDL hostile (adj) *unfriendly*
hostilely (adv)
HSDLD hostility *conflict*
hostilities
HSDLT hostility *conflict*

hostilities
HSDMN histamine *allergy*
HSDMNS histaminase
enzyme
HSDMNZ histaminase
enzyme
HSDN Houston *city*
HSDNG house-sitting
guarding
HSDNS hastiness *hurry*
HSDR hastier *hurried*
HSDR history *record of the*
past histories
HSDR hoister *lift*
HSDR house sitter *guard*
HSDRDM hysterotomy
cesarean section
hysterotomies
HSDRKDM hysterectomy
uterus hysterectomies
HSDRKTM hysterectomy
uterus hysterectomies
HSDRS housedress *clothing*
housedresses
HSDRTM hysterotomy
cesarean section
hysterotomies
HSDST hastiest *hurried*
HSDYR hastier *hurried*
HSDYST hastiest *hurried*
HSF hisself *himself*
HSFL housefly *insect*
houseflies
HSFL houseful *amount*
HSFNCH house finch *bird*
HSFR hausfrau *wife*
HSFRNT housefront *facade*
HSG hoosegow *jail*
HSGST houseguest
company
HSH hash *(n) food, jumble,*
hashish (v) chop, talk
hashes
HSH hush *silence* hushes
HSHHSH hush-hush *secret*
HSHL household *social unit*
HSHLD household *social*
unit
HSHLDR householder
occupant
HSHMRK hash mark
insignia, line

Letters aren't doubled for single sounds: to find alley use **L** not **LL**. Use **Y** and **W** as hard
sounds only: to find yellow use **YL**. (Br)=British spelling or usage. * See dictionary.

HSHN Haitian *of Haiti*
HSHN Hessian *German*
HSHN hessian *burlap*
HSHPP hush puppy *food*
hush puppies
HSHR hachure *shade*
hachured hachuring
HSHR Hoosier *Indiana*
HSHR hosiery *socks*
HSHSH hashish *hemp*
HSHZBN househusband
home duties
HSHZBND househusband
home duties
HSK hassock *stool*
HSK husk *pod*
HSK husky *(adj) hearty,*
hoarse huskier huskiest
HSK husky *(n) dog* huskies
HSKL high school *education*
HSKL house call *home visit*
HSKL huskily *hearty, hoarse*
HSKLN houseclean *tidy*
HSKLNN housecleaning
tidy
HSKLNNG housecleaning
tidy
HSKNS huskiness *hearty,*
hoarse
HSKP housekeep *manage a*
home housekept
housekeeping
HSKPN housekeeping
management
HSKPNG housekeeping
management
HSKPR housekeeper *maid*
HSKR husker *remove husks*
HSKR huskier *hearty, hoarse*
HSKST huskiest *hearty,*
hoarse
HSKT house cat *animal*
HSKT housecoat *clothing*
HSKYR huskier *hearty,*
hoarse
HSKYST huskiest *hearty,*
hoarse
HSL hassle *argue, annoy*
hassled hassling
HSL hustle *hurry, cheat,*
prostitute hustled hustling
HSLF hisself *himself*

HSLR hostler *works with*
horses, trains
HSLR hustler *hurrier, cheater,*
prostitute
HSLTS houselights *theater*
HSMD housemaid *servant*
HSMN houseman *servant*
housemen
HSMS house mouse *animal*
HSMT housemate
companion
HSMTHR housemother
chaperon
HSN hasten *hurry*
HSN high sign *gesture*
HSN housing *shelter, cover*
HSN hyson *tea*
HSND hacienda *house*
HSNDN high-sounding
pompous
HSNDNG high-sounding
pompous
HSNFFR hasenpfeffer *stew*
HSNG housing *shelter, cover*
HSNR hastener *hurry*
HSNTH hyacinth *gem, plant*
HSNTHN hyacinthine *gem,*
plant
HSP hasp *fastener*
HSP hyssop *herb*
HSPD high-speed *fast*
HSPD hispid *bristly*
HSPDBL hospitable (adj)
friendly hospitably (adv)
HSPDL hospital *sickness*
HSPDLZ hospitalize *place a*
patient hospitalized
hospitalizing
(Br) hospitalise
HSPDLZSHN
hospitalization *place a*
patient
(Br) hospitalisation
HSPLNT houseplant *indoors*
HSPNK Hispanic *Latin*
American
HSPNL Hispaniola *island*
HSPNR housepainter *paint*
HSPNTR housepainter *paint*
HSPNYL Hispaniola *island*
HSPRD house party
overnight house parties

HSPRDD high-spirited
energetic
HSPRNT houseparent
resident manager
HSPRT house party
overnight house parties
HSPRTD high-spirited
energetic
HSPS hospice *lodging*
HSPTBL hospitable (adj)
friendly hospitably (adv)
HSPTL hospital *sickness*
HSPTLD hospitality
cordiality hospitalities
HSPTLT hospitality *cordiality*
hospitalities
HSPTLZ hospitalize *place a*
patient hospitalized
hospitalizing
(Br) hospitalise
HSPTLZSHN hospitalization
place a patient
(Br) hospitalisation
HSR hisser *whisper*
HSRGN house organ
periodical
HSRST house arrest
confinement
HSRZN house-raising
building
HSRZNG house-raising
building
HSS high seas *ocean*
HST haste *hurry*
HST hasty *hurried* hastier
hastiest
HST heist *robbery*
HST highest *tall, serious,*
*drugged**
HST hoist *lift*
HST host *(n) provider, group,*
Eucharist (v) emcee,
entertain
HSTJ hostage *person held*
HSTK haystack *pile*
HSTL hastily *hurried*
HSTL haustella (pl) *snout*
haustellum
HSTL hostel *(v) reside*
hosteled (or) hostelled
hosteling (or) hostelling
HSTL hostel *(n) inn*

Use letters that best describe the sounds you hear and omit the vowels. Use **S** or **K** instead of **C**: to find circle use **SRKL**. Use **J** to find joy, **JM** to find gem and **G** to find go.

HSTL hostile (adj) *unfriendly* hostilely (adv)

HSTLD hostility *conflict* hostilities

HSTLG histology *tissue structure* histologies

HSTLJ histology *tissue structure* histologies

HSTLJK histologic (or) histological *tissue structure*

HSTLJKL histological (or) histologic (adj) *tissue structure* histologically (adv)

HSTLJST histologist *tissue structure*

HSTLM haustellum *snout* haustella

HSTLR hosteler (or) hosteller *innkeeper, traveler*

HSTLR hostelry *inn* hostelries

HSTLR hostler *works with horses, trains*

HSTLSS histolysis *breakdown*

HSTLT hostility *conflict* hostilities

HSTMN histamine *allergy*

HSTMNS histaminase *enzyme*

HSTMNZ histaminase *enzyme*

HSTN Houston *city*

HSTNG house-sitting *guarding*

HSTNGS hustings *court*

HSTNGZ hustings *court*

HSTNS hastiness *hurry*

HSTP housetop *roof*

HSTPLZMSS histoplasmosis *disease*

HSTPTHLG histopathology *tissue disease*

HSTPTHLJ histopathology *tissue disease*

HSTPTHLJK histopathologic (or) histopathological (adj) *tissue disease*

histopathologically (adv)

HSTPTHLJKL histopathological (or) histopathologic (adj) *tissue disease* histopathologically (adv)

HSTPTHLJST histopathologist *tissue disease*

HSTR hastier *hurried*

HSTR history *record of the past* histories

HSTR hoister *lift*

HSTR house sitter *guard*

HSTR hysteria *fear, excitability*

HSTRCZ hystereses (pl) *slowing* hysteresis

HSTRD hysteroid *fear, excitability*

HSTRDK hysteretic *slowing*

HSTRDM hysterotomy *cesarean section* hysterotomies

HSTRK ahistoric (or) ahistorical *without history*

HSTRK historic *of history*

HSTRK hysteric *fear, excitability*

HSTRKDM hysterectomy *uterus* hysterectomies

HSTRKL ahistorical (or) ahistoric *without history*

HSTRKL historical (adj) *of history* historically (adv)

HSTRKL hysterical (adj) *fear, excitability* hysterically (adv)

HSTRKS hysterics *fear, excitability*

HSTRKTM hysterectomy *uterus* hysterectomies

HSTRN historian *recorder*

HSTRN house-train *tame*

HSTRNG high-strung *nervous*

HSTRNK histrionic *dramatic*

HSTRNKL histrionically *dramatic*

HSTRNKS histrionics *drama*

HSTRNX histrionics *drama*

HSTRSS hysteresis *slowing*

hystereses

HSTRSST historicist *theorist*

HSTRSZ historicize *record* historicized historicizing

HSTRSZ hystereses (pl) *slowing* hysteresis

HSTRSZM historicism *theory*

HSTRTK hysteretic *slowing*

HSTRTM hysterotomy *cesarean section* hysterotomies

HSTRX hysterics *fit of crying or fear, excitability*

HSTRY hysteria *fear, excitability*

HSTRYN historian *recorder*

HSTRYNK histrionic *dramatic*

HSTRYNKL histrionically *dramatic*

HSTRYNKS histrionics *drama*

HSTRYNX histrionics *drama*

HSTS hostess *entertain* hostesses

HSTST hastiest *hurried*

HSTST histiocyte *cell*

HSTT hastate *triangular*

HSTYR hastier *hurried*

HSTYST hastiest *hurried*

HSTYST histiocyte *cell*

HSVR howsoever *in any way*

HSVR whosoever *any person*

HSWF housewife *woman* housewives

HSWRK housework *cleaning*

HSWRMN housewarming *party*

HSWRMNG housewarming *party*

HSWRS housewares *furnishings*

HSWRZ housewares *furnishings*

HSWVR howsoever *in any way*

HSWVR whosoever *any person*

HSWVZ housewives (pl) *women* housewife

HSYND hacienda *house*

Letters aren't doubled for single sounds: to find alley use **L** not **LL**. Use **Y** and **W** as hard sounds only: to find yellow use **YL**. (Br)=British spelling or usage. * See dictionary.

HSZ high seas *ocean*
HT Haiti *country*
HT hat *head covering* hatted hatting
HT hate *detest* hated hating
HT haughty *proud* haughtier haughtiest
HT heat *warmth, race, estrus**
HT height *altitude*
HT high tea *social event*
HT hit *(v) blow, reach* hit hitting
HT hit *(n, adj) success*
HT hoot *owl sound*
HT hot *(adj) heat, angry, pungent** hotter hottest
HT hot *(v-Br) heat* hotted hotting
HT how-to *instruction*
HT hut *dwelling*
HTB hot tub *jacuzzi*
HTBD hotbed *growth environment*
HTBKS hotbox *bearing* hotboxes
HTBL heatable *warmth*
HTBLDD hot-blooded *passionate*
HTBN hatband *decoration*
HTBND hatband *decoration*
HTBX hotbox *bearing* hotboxes
HTCHK hatcheck *storage*
HTD heated *warm, emotional*
HTD high tide *ocean*
HTDG hot dog *(n) food, show-off (interj) approval*
HTDG hotdog *(v) perform stunts*
HTDL heatedly *warm, emotional*
HTFL hateful *(adj) malicious* hatefully *(adv)*
HTFLSH hot flash *flushing*
HTFT hotfoot *(n) joke (v) hurry* hotfoots
HTH heath *wasteland*
HTH height *altitude*
HTHD hothead *fiery one*
HTHDD hotheaded *fiery*
HTHDDNS hotheadedness *fiery*

HTHN heathen *pagan* heathens *(or)* heathen
HTHNSH heathenish *paganish*
HTHR heather *plant*
HTHR heathery *color*
HTHR hither *near*
HTHRMST hithermost *nearest*
HTHRN hawthorn *shrub*
HTHRT hitherto *until now*
HTHS hothouse *greenhouse*
HTK haddock *fish* haddock
HTK hi-tech *(adj) technology* high tech *(n)*
HTKK hotcake *pancake*
HTKM hot comb *styling*
HTKT hot ticket *rage*
HTKTR haute couture *fashion*
HTKTYR haute couture *fashion*
HTKWZN haute cuisine *food*
HTKZN haute cuisine *food*
HTL haughtily *proud*
HTL hiatal *passage, gap, break*
HTL hightail *leave in a hurry*
HTL hotel *inn*
HTL hotly *emotional*
HTL huddle *bunch* huddled huddling
HTLN hot line *telephone*
HTLR huddler *bunch*
HTLST hit list *targets*
HTLY hotelier *innkeeper*
HTLYR hotelier *innkeeper*
HTMKR hatmaker *creator*
HTMLT hot-melt *sandwich*
HTMN hit man *assassin*
HTN heighten *increase*
HTND high-toned *pompous*
HTNDK hypnotic *trance*
HTNDKL hypnotically *trance*
HTNDRN hit-and-run *accident*
HTNN hootenanny *gadget, folksinging* hootenannies
HTNRN hit-and-run *accident*
HTNS haughtiness *pride*
HTNSHN high-tension *voltage*
HTNSS hypnosis *trance*

hypnoses
HTNTHRP hypnotherapy *trance* hypnotherapies
HTNTHRPST hypnotherapist *trance*
HTNTK hypnotic *trance*
HTNTKL hypnotically *trance*
HTNTST hypnotist *trance*
HTNTZ hypnotize *put in a trance* hypnotized hypnotizing
HTNTZM hypnotism *trance*
HTP high-top *shoes* high-tops
HTPLT hot plate *cooking*
HTPN hatpin *fastener*
HTPNTZBL hypnotizable *trance*
HTPPR hot pepper *plant*
HTPRD hit parade *list*
HTPT hot pot *stew*
HTPTD hot potato *argument*
HTPTT hot potato *argument*
HTQZN haute cuisine *food*
HTR hater *detest*
HTR hatter *hat maker*
HTR haughtier *proud*
HTR hauteur *arrogance*
HTR heater *warmer*
HTR hitter *bat, strike*
HTR hooter *owl sound*
HTR hot air *empty talk*
HTR hotter *heat, popular*
HTRD hatred *loathing*
HTRD hot rod *car*
HTRDKC heterodoxy *(n) opinions* heterodoxies
HTRDKS heterodox *(adj) unorthodox*
HTRDKS heterodoxy *(n) opinions* heterodoxies
HTRDN heterodyne *(v) produce a beat* heterodyned heterodyning
HTRDN heterodyne *(n) beat*
HTRDX heterodox *(adj) unorthodox*
HTRDX heterodoxy *(n) opinions* heterodoxies
HTRFL heterophile *(or)* heterophil *antigen*

Use letters that best describe the sounds you hear and omit the vowels. Use **S** or **K** instead of **C**: to find circle use **SRKL**. Use **J** to find joy, **JM** to find gem and **G** to find go.

HTRFL heterophylly *foliage*
HTRFLS heterophyllous *foliage*
HTRFN heterophony *melody* heterophonies
HTRGM heterogamy *unlike gametes*
HTRGMS heterogamous *unlike gametes*
HTRGN heterogony *alternate generations*
HTRGND heterogeneity *mixed*
HTRGNS heterogeneous *mixed*
HTRGNT heterogeneity *mixed*
HTRGNYD heterogeneity *mixed*
HTRGNYS heterogeneous *mixed*
HTRGNYT heterogeneity *mixed*
HTRJN heterogeny *mixed group*
HTRJND heterogeneity *mixed*
HTRJNS heterogeneous *mixed*
HTRJNT heterogeneity *mixed*
HTRJNYD heterogeneity *mixed*
HTRJNYS heterogeneous *mixed*
HTRJNYT heterogeneity *mixed*
HTRK hat trick *score*
HTRLGS heterologous *different*
HTRLGSL heterologously *different*
HTRMRFK heteromorphic *deviating*
HTRMRFZM heteromorphism *deviation*
HTRMS hit-or-miss (adj) *careless* hit or miss (adv)
HTRNM heteronomy *subjection*
HTRNM heteronym *word*
HTRPDRS heteropterous

insect
HTRPLD heteroploid *chromosome* heteroploidy
HTRPTRS heteropterous *insect*
HTRSHS heteroecious *different hosts*
HTRSKL heterocycle *atoms*
HTRSKLK heterocyclic *atoms*
HTRSKSHL heterosexual (adj) *opposite sex* heterosexually (adv)
HTRSKSHWL heterosexual (adj) *opposite sex* heterosexually (adv)
HTRSPR heterospory *spores*
HTRSPRS heterosporous *spores*
HTRSST heterocyst *cell*
HTRSXL heterosexual (adj) *opposite sex* heterosexually (adv)
HTRSXWL heterosexual (adj) *opposite sex* heterosexually (adv)
HTRTPK heterotypic *different*
HTRTRF heterotroph *metabolism* heterotrophy
HTRTRFK heterotrophic *metabolism*
HTRTRFKL heterotrophically *metabolism*
HTRZGS heterozygous *gene*
HTS hiatus *passage, gap, break*
HTSHBR Haight Ashbury *district*
HTSHT hotshot *talented one*
HTSP chutzpah (or) hutzpah (or) hutzpa *gall*
HTSPRNG hot spring *water*
HTSPT hot spot *interest, heat*
HTST haughtiest *proud*
HTST high-test *octane*
HTST hottest *heat, popular*
HTSTF hot stuff *good*
HTSTRK heatstroke *exhaustion*

HTT Hittite *tribe*
HTTD hoity-toity *thoughtless*
HTTT hoity-toity *thoughtless*
HTWDR hot water *trouble*
HTWR hot-wire *ignition*
HTWTR hot water *trouble*
HTWV heat wave *weather*
HTWYR hot-wire *ignition*
HTYR haughtier *proud*
HTYR hauteur *arrogance*
HTYST haughtiest *proud*
HTZP chutzpah (or) hutzpah (or) hutzpa *gall*
HV halve *divide equally* halved halving
HV have *possess, show, use** had having has
HV heave *toss* heaved (or) hove heaving
HV heavy *(adj) weight* heavier heaviest
HV heavy *(n) villain* heavies
HV hive *bees* hived hiving
HVD hooved (or) hoofed *paw*
HVDD heavy-duty *strong*
HVDT heavy-duty *strong*
HVFDD heavy-footed *slow*
HVFTD heavy-footed *slow*
HVH heave-ho *toss*
HVHNDD heavy-handed *clumsy, cruel*
HVHRDD heavyhearted *sad*
HVHRTD heavyhearted *sad*
HVK havoc *disorder*
HVL heavily *weight*
HVL hovel *shack*
HVLK havelock *hat attachment*
HVLN javelina *boar*
HVN Havana *city*
HVN haven *safe place*
HVN heaven *God's home*
HVNL heavenly *wonderful*
HVNS heaviness *weight*
HVNSNT heavensent *good fortune*
HVNT have-not *poor one* have-nots
HVNTS have-nots *poor ones* have-not
HVNWRD heavenward

Letters aren't doubled for single sounds: to find alley use **L** not **LL**. Use **Y** and **W** as hard sounds only: to find yellow use **YL**. (Br)=British spelling or usage. * See dictionary.

upward
HVR haver *(Br) hesitate*
HVR heaver *toss*
HVR heavier *weight*
HVR hover *hang*
HVR whoever *any person*
HVRD Havarti *cheese*
HVRKRFT hovercraft *vehicle*
HVRSK haversack *bag*
HVRT Havarti *cheese*
HVS halves (pl) *equal share half*
HVST heaviest *weight*
HVST heavyset *obese*
HVWT heavyweight *176 or more pounds*
HVYR heavier *weight*
HVYST heaviest *weight*
HVZ halves (pl) *equal share half*
HVZ heaves *vomit*
HVZ hives *rash*
HW Hawaii *island State*
HW highway *road*
HW hooey *nonsense*
HW whee *(interj) delight*
HW whew *(interj) relief*
HW whey *milk*
HW whoa *stop*
HW why *for what reason* whys
HWCH which *what one*
HWCHMKLT whatchamacallit *gizmo*
HWCHVR whichever *any*
HWD whitey *(slang-often capitalized) white person*
HWD whydah *bird*
HWDF what-if *question*
HWDK white oak *tree*
HWDL wheedle *lure* wheedled wheedling
HWDL whittle *carve* whittled whittling
HWDLFNT white elephant *animal, junk*
HWDLN whittling *carving*
HWDLNG whittling *carving*
HWDLR whittler *carver*
HWDNG whiting *fish*
HWDR high-water *short*
HWDR wheatear *bird*

HWDR whetter *sharpener*
HWDSH white ash *tree*
HWDT whiteout *snow*
HWDVR whatever *anything*
HWDZR howitzer *weapon*
HWF whiff *puff*
HWFL whiffle *air* whiffled whiffling
HWFLTR whiffletree *harness*
HWG Whig *parliament*
HWGR Whiggery *parliament*
HWGSH Whiggish *parliament*
HWH Hawaii *island State*
HWK whack *(v) strike, (Br) defeat (n) blow, portion*
HWKN whacking *very*
HWKNG whacking *very*
HWL awhile *time*
HWL whale *(v) hunt whales, thrash* whaled whaling
HWL whale *(n) animal* whales (or) whale
HWL wheal *welt*
HWL wheel *disk*
HWL wheelie *stunt*
HWL while *(v) pass time* whiled whiling
HWL while *(conj) during*
HWL who'll *(contr) who will*
HWLBN whalebone *baleen*
HWLBR wheelbarrow *cart*
HWLBS wheelbase *length*
HWLBT whaleboat *ship*
HWLCHR wheelchair *vehicle*
HWLD wheeled *movable*
HWLHRS wheelhorse *animal*
HWLHS wheelhouse *ship*
HWLK wheel lock *gun*
HWLK whelk *snail, pustule*
HWLM whelm *engulf*
HWLMN wheelman *driver* wheelmen
HWLN whaling *hunt whales*
HWLN wheeling *riding*
HWLNG whaling *hunt whales*
HWLNG wheeling *riding*
HWLP whelp *young one*
HWLR whaler *hunter, ship*
HWLR wheeler *vehicle*
HWLRDLR wheeler-dealer

shrewd one
HWLRT wheelwright *make or fix wheels*
HWLST whilst *during*
HWLWRK wheelwork *gears*
HWLZMN wheelsman *driver* wheelsmen
HWM wham *hit, sound* whammed whamming
HWM wham (or) whammo *(adv) abruptly*
HWM whammy *curse* whammies
HWM whim *impulse*
HWMN highwayman *robber* highwaymen
HWMPR whimper *whine*
HWMZ whimsy *impulse* whimsies
HWMZKL whimsical (adj) *fanciful* whimsically (adv)
HWMZKLD whimsicality *fanciful*
HWMZKLNS whimsicalness *fanciful*
HWMZKLT whimsicality *fanciful*
HWN Hawaiian *of Hawaii*
HWN when *what time*
HWN whine *complain* whined whining
HWN whinny *neigh* whinnied whinnies
HWN whiny (or) whiney *complaining*
HWNG whang *(n) thong, (Br) chunk (v) beat*
HWNR whiner *complainer*
HWNS whence *what place*
HWNTS whence *what place*
HWNVR whenever *anytime*
HWP whip *lash* whipped whipping
HWP whippy *springy* whippier whippiest
HWP whoop *yell*
HWP whoopee *(interj) exuberance*
HWP whop *hit hard* whopped whopping
HWPDD whoop-de-do (or) whoop-de-doo *activity*

Use letters that best describe the sounds you hear and omit the vowels. Use **S** or **K** instead of **C**: to find circle use **SRKL**. Use **J** to find joy, **JM** to find gem and **G** to find go.

HWPKRD whipcord *rope, fabric*

HWPLSH whiplash *injury* whiplashes

HWPLTR whippletree *harness*

HWPN whipping *beating, fabric, stitch*

HWPN whopping *unbelievable*

HWPNB whipping boy *blamed one*

HWPNG whipping *beating, fabric, stitch*

HWPNG whopping *unbelievable*

HWPNGB whipping boy *blamed one*

HWPNGKF whooping cough *disease*

HWPNGKRN whooping crane *bird*

HWPNKRN whooping crane *bird*

HWPR whippier *springy*

HWPR whooper *crane, one that yells*

HWPR whopper *large thing, lie*

HWPRSNPR whippersnapper *insignificant one*

HWPRWL whippoorwill *bird*

HWPS whipsaw *(n) tool (v) victimize*

HWPS whoops *(interj) mistake*

HWPST whippiest *springy*

HWPSTCH whipstitch *sewing whipstitches*

HWPSTK whipstock *handle*

HWPSTL whip stall *airplane*

HWPT whipped *(slang) tired*

HWPT whippet *dog*

HWPYR whippier *springy*

HWPYST whippiest *springy*

HWR haywire *crazy*

HWR hewer *cut down*

HWR high-wire *tightrope*

HWR hoer *digger*

HWR where *what place*

HWR wherry *boat* wherries

HWR whir *revolve, sound* whirred whirring

HWRB whereby *by what*

HWRBTS whereabouts *what place*

HWRCHZ huaraches *sandals*

HWRF wharf *pier* wharves

HWRFJ wharfage *pier*

HWRFMSTR wharfmaster *manager*

HWRFNGR wharfinger *manager*

HWRFNJR wharfinger *manager*

HWRFR wherefore *why*

HWRL whirl *(n) bustle (v) rotate*

HWRL whorl *swirl*

HWRLBRD whirlybird *helicopter*

HWRLD whorled *swirled*

HWRLGG whirligig *spinner*

HWRLPL whirlpool *vortex*

HWRLWN whirlwind *rush, storm*

HWRLWND whirlwind *rush, storm*

HWRN wherein *in which, how*

HWRPN whereupon *on which*

HWRT whereat *at which*

HWRT whereto *to what end*

HWRV whereof *of which, of whom*

HWRVR wherever *anywhere*

HWRWTH wherewith *how*

HWRWTHL wherewithal *how, resources*

HWRZ whereas *although, since*

HWSH whoosh *rush*

HWSK whisk *brush, mix*

HWSK whiskey *liquor*

HWSKBRM whisk broom *brush*

HWSKR whisker *hair*

HWSKRD whiskered *hair*

HWSL whistle *shrill sound* whistled whistling

HWSLBLR whistle-blower

informer

HWSLBLWR whistle-blower *informer*

HWSLN whistling *hissing*

HWSLNG whistling *hissing*

HWSLR whistler *bird, animal, signal*

HWSLSTP whistle-stop *train station*

HWSPR whisper *(v) speak softly (n) rumor, trace, soft speech*

HWSPRN whispering *hiss, gossip*

HWSPRNG whispering *hiss, gossip*

HWSPRR whisperer *gossip*

HWST whist *(n) game (adj, v) silence*

HWT what *which thing**

HWT wheat *grain*

HWT whet *(v) sharpen* whetted whetting

HWT whet *(n) time, goad, appetizer*

HWT whit *particle*

HWT white *color* whiter whitest

HWT white-tie *(adj) formal* white tie *(n)*

HWT whitey *(slang-often capitalized) white person*

HWTBN white bean *vegetable*

HWTBRCH white birch *tree*

HWTBRD white-bread *(adj) bland*

HWTBRD whitebeard *old one*

HWTBS white bass *fish*

HWTBT whitebait *herring*

HWTCBS white sea bass *fish*

HWTCDR white cedar *tree*

HWTD whited *bleached*

HWTF what-if *question*

HWTFDD white-footed *mouse*

HWTFL whitefly *insect* whiteflies

HWTFLG white flag *surrender*

Letters aren't doubled for single sounds: to find alley use **L** not **LL**. Use **Y** and **W** as hard sounds only: to find yellow use **YL**. (Br)=British spelling or usage. * See dictionary.

HWTFLT white flight *racial bias*

HWTFS whiteface *color, clown*

HWTFSH whitefish *animal*

HWTFST white-faced *face color*

HWTFTD white-footed *mouse*

HWTGDZ white goods *linens, appliances*

HWTGL white gold *mineral*

HWTGLD white gold *metal*

HWTGRB white grub *larva*

HWTHD whitehead *pimple*

HWTHDD white-headed *old*

HWTHNR white hunter *safari*

HWTHNTR white hunter *safari*

HWTHP white hope *contender*

HWTHR whether *if*

HWTHR whither *where*

HWTHRD white-haired *old*

HWTHS White House *US president*

HWTHT white heat *hot*

HWTHT white-hot *earnest*

HWTJRM wheat germ *kernel*

HWTK white oak *tree*

HWTKLR white-collar *worker*

HWTKP whitecap *wave*

HWTKRND white-crowned *sparrow*

HWTL what all *(pron) whatnot*

HWTL white lie *falsehood*

HWTL whitely *color*

HWTL whitetail *deer*

HWTL whitlow *vegetable*

HWTL whittle *carve* whittled whittling

HWTLFNT white elephant *animal, junk*

HWTLN whittling *carving*

HWTLNG whittling *carving*

HWTLR whittler *carver*

HWTLTNN white lightning *liquor*

HWTLTNNG white lightning *liquor*

HWTLVRD white-livered *cowardly*

HWTN wheaten *grain, color*

HWTN whiten *bleach*

HWTNG whiting *fish*

HWTNKL white-knuckle *nervous*

HWTNN whitening *bleach*

HWTNNG whitening *bleach*

HWTNR whitener *bleach*

HWTNS whiteness *pallor*

HWTNT whatnot *miscellany*

HWTNT white knight *rescuer*

HWTNZ white noise *background*

HWTPN white pine *tree*

HWTPPR white paper *report*

HWTPRCH white perch *fish*

HWTR high-water *short*

HWTR wheatear *bird*

HWTR whetter *sharpener*

HWTRM white room *clean area*

HWTRS white rice *grain*

HWTRSH white trash *poor class*

HWTSBS white sea bass *fish*

HWTSDR white cedar *tree*

HWTSH white ash *tree*

HWTSL white cell *blood*

HWTSL white sale *discount*

HWTSND Whitsunday *Pentecost*

HWTSPS white space *no print*

HWTSR howitzer *weapon*

HWTSS whatsis (or) whatsit *gadget*

HWTSS white sauce *food*

HWTST whatsit (or) whatsis *gadget*

HWTSTN whetstone *sharpener*

HWTSVR whatsoever *anything*

HWTSWVR whatsoever *anything*

HWTT white-hot *earnest*

HWTT whiteout *snow*

HWTTHRT whitethroat *bird*

HWTVR whatever *anything*

HWTW white way *theater district*

HWTWD whitewood *tree*

HWTWDR white water (n) *foam* white-water (adj)

HWTWL white whale *animal*

HWTWL whitewall *tire*

HWTWN white wine *drink*

HWTWNG whitewing *uniform*

HWTWSH whitewash *(v) gloss over (n)* lime, defeat

HWTWSHNG whitewashing *lime*

HWTWTR white water (n) *foam* white-water (adj)

HWTZNFNDL white zinfandel *wine*

HWTZR howitzer *weapon*

HWVR however *but, although*

HWVR whoever *any person*

HWY Hawaii *island State*

HWY whew *(interj) relief*

HWYL while *(v) pass time* whiled whiling

HWYL while *(conj) during*

HWYN Hawaiian *of Hawaii*

HWYR haywire *crazy*

HWYR high-wire *tightrope*

HWZ wheeze *hiss* wheezed wheezing

HWZ wheezy *hissing* wheezier wheeziest

HWZ whiz *wizard* whizzes

HWZ whiz (or) whizz *(v) hiss, fly* whizzed whizzing

HWZ whiz (or) whizz *sound* whizzes

HWZBNG whiz-bang (adj) *startling* whizbang (n)

HWZKD whiz kid *clever child*

HWZL wheezily *hissing*

HWZNS wheeziness *hissing*

HWZR wheezier *hissing*

HWZR whizzer *dryer*

HWZST wheeziest *hissing*

HWZYR wheezier *hissing*

HWZYST wheeziest *hissing*

HX hacksaw *tool*

Use letters that best describe the sounds you hear and omit the vowels. Use **S** or **K** instead of **C**: to find circle use **SRKL**. Use **J** to find joy, **JM** to find gem and **G** to find go.

HX hex *curse* hexes
HX hoax *trick* hoaxes
HXBL hawksbill *turtle*
HXDR huckster *(n) peddler (v) sell*
HXDSML hexadecimal *number*
HXGN hexagon *six angles*
HXGNL hexagonal (adj) *six angles* hexagonally (adv)
HXGRM hexagram *star*
HXHDRN hexahedron *six faces* hexahedrons
HXKLRFN hexachlorophene *toothpaste*
HXKRD hexachord *six tones*
HXL hexyl *petroleum*
HXMDR hexameter *verse*
HXMTR hexameter *verse*
HXN hexane *petroleum*
HXPD hexapod *six feet, insects*
HXPLD hexaploid *chromosome*
HXR hexarei *witchcraft*
HXR hoaxer *trick*
HXTR huckster *(n) peddler (v) sell*
HXTRZM hucksterism *peddling*
HY hew *cut down* hewed hewed (or) hewn hewing
HY hoya *shrub*
HY hue *color*
HY Ohio *US State*
HY whew *(interj) relief*
HYBRS hubris *pride*
HYBRSDK hubristic *proud*
HYBRSTK hubristic *proud*
HYD hued *colored*
HYD hyoid *bone*
HYDL hiatal *passage, gap, break*
HYDS hiatus *passage, gap, break*
HYJ huge *enormous* huger hugest
HYJL hugely *enormous*
HYJNS hugeness *enormous*
HYJR huger *enormous*
HYJST hugest *enormous*
HYKTN high-octane

powerful
HYL Hialeah *city*
HYL high yellow *(vulgar) mixed race*
HYL hoyle *(often capitalized) rules*
HYLD hyaloid *glassy*
HYLN hyaline (or) hyalin *glassy*
HYLR high yellow *(vulgar) mixed race*
HYLY Hialeah *city*
HYMD humid *moist*
HYMDD humidity *moisture* humidities
HYMDF humidify *add moisture* humidified humidifying humidifies
HYMDFKSHN humidification *moisture*
HYMDFR humidifier *moisture*
HYMDFYR humidifier *moisture*
HYMDR humidor *case*
HYMDT humidity *moisture* humidities
HYMKDNT humectant *moisture*
HYMKTNT humectant *moisture*
HYMLD humility *modesty*
HYMLDN humiliating *humbling*
HYMLDNG humiliating *humbling*
HYMLSHN humiliation *shame*
HYMLT humiliate *shame* humiliated humiliating
HYMLT humility *modesty*
HYMLTN humiliating *humbling*
HYMLTNG humiliating *humbling*
HYMLYDN humiliating *humbling*
HYMLYDNG humiliating *humbling*
HYMLYSHN humiliation *shame*
HYMLYT humiliate *shame*

humiliated humiliating
HYMLYTN humiliating *humbling*
HYMLYTNG humiliating *humbling*
HYMN human *person*
HYMN humane *compassionate*
HYMND humanity *all persons* humanities
HYMND humanoid *like a human*
HYMNDS humanities *human concerns*
HYMNDZ humanities *human concerns*
HYMNGGS humongous *huge*
HYMNGS humongous *huge*
HYMNKN humankind *all persons*
HYMNKND humankind *all persons*
HYMNL humanely *compassion*
HYMNL humanly *of man*
HYMNS humaneness *compassion*
HYMNS humanness *of man*
HYMNSDK humanistic *life-centered*
HYMNSDKL humanistically *life-centered*
HYMNSM humanism *life-centered*
HYMNSTK humanistic *life-centered*
HYMNSTKL humanistically *life-centered*
HYMNT humanity *all persons* humanities
HYMNTRN humanitarian *philanthropist*
HYMNTRYN humanitarian *philanthropist*
HYMNTS humanities *human concerns*
HYMNTZ humanities *human concerns*
HYMNZ humanize *make human* humanized humanizing

Letters aren't doubled for single sounds: to find alley use **L** not **LL**. Use **Y** and **W** as hard sounds only: to find yellow use **YL**. (Br)=British spelling or usage. * See dictionary.

HYMNZM humanism *life-centered*

HYMNZR humanizer *make human*

HYMNZSHN humanization *make human*

HYMR humeri (pl) *bone* humerus

HYMR humor *(n) fun, temperament (v) soothe, indulge* (Br) humour

HYMRL humeral *shoulder*

HYMRLS humorless *no fun* (Br) humourless

HYMRS humerus *bone* humeri

HYMRS humorous *funny* (Br) humourous

HYMRSK humoresque *fanciful* (Br) humouresque

HYMRSL humorously *funny* (Br) humourously

HYMRSNS humorousness *funny* (Br) humourousness

HYMRST humorist *funny one* (Br) humourist

HYMS humus *soil*

HYN hellion *brat*

HYN hewn *cut down*

HYN hyena *animal* hyenas

HYND high-end *upscale*

HYNRG high-energy *speedy*

HYNRJ high-energy *speedy*

HYR higher *tall, serious, drugged**

HYR hire *employ, lease* hired hiring

HYRD hired *employed*

HYRFNT hierophant *priest*

HYRK hierarchy *ranking* hierarchies

HYRKKL hierarchical (adj) *arranged* hierarchically (adv)

HYRLN hireling *hatchet man*

HYRLNG hireling *hatchet man*

HYRN Huron *Native*

American, lake Hurons (or) Huron

HYRNG hiring *jobs*

HYRP higher-up *chief*

HYRR hirer *employer*

HYRRK hierarch *leader*

HYRRK hierarchy *ranking* hierarchies

HYRRKKL hierarchical (adj) *arranged* hierarchically (adv)

HYRSDK heuristic *learning*

HYRSDKL heuristically *learning*

HYRSTK heuristic *learning*

HYRSTKL heuristically *learning*

HYSDN Houston *city*

HYSNTH hyacinth *gem, plant*

HYSNTHN hyacinthine *gem, plant*

HYST highest *tall, serious, drugged**

HYSTN Houston *city*

HYTL hiatal *passage, gap, break*

HYTS hiatus *passage, gap, break*

HYWR hewer *cut down*

HZ has *possesses (third person singular of "to have")*

HZ hawse *ship*

HZ haze *cloud, heckle* hazed hazing

HZ hazy *cloudy, unclear* hazier haziest

HZ he's *(contr) he is*

HZ his *(pron) that male*

HZ hose *(n) stocking, tube* hose (or) hoses

HZ hose *(v) spray* hosed hosing

HZ house *(v) shelter* housed housing

HZ hussy *lewd female* hussies

HZ huzzah (or) huzza *(interj) joy*

HZ who's *(contr) who is, who has*

HZ whose *belonging to*

HZBN has-been *no longer special*

HZBN husband *(n) spouse (v) conserve*

HZBND husband *(n) spouse (v) conserve*

HZBNDR husbandry *conservation*

HZDNC hesitancy *indecision* hesitancies

HZDNS hesitancy *indecision* hesitancies

HZDNT hesitant *unwilling*

HZDNTC hesitancy *indecision* hesitancies

HZDNTL hesitantly *unwillingly*

HZDNTS hesitancy *indecision* hesitancies

HZHL hawsehole *opening*

HZHR Hoosier *Indiana*

HZHR hosiery *socks*

HZL hawsehole *opening*

HZL hazel *color*

HZL hazily *cloudy, unclear*

HZL hosel *socket*

HZLNT hazelnut *food*

HZN hasn't *(contr) has not*

HZN hazing *torment*

HZN hosanna *praise*

HZN housing *shelter, cover*

HZNG hazing *torment*

HZNG housing *shelter, cover*

HZNS haziness *cloudy, unclear*

HZNT hasn't *(contr) has not*

HZPP hosepipe *(Br) hose*

HZR hawser *rope*

HZR hazer *heckler*

HZR hazier *unclear*

HZR hosiery *socks*

HZR houser *administrator*

HZR hussar *soldier*

HZRD hazard *danger*

HZRDS hazardous *dangerous*

HZST haziest *unclear*

HZTDR hesitater *pause, falter*

HZTNC hesitancy *indecision* hesitancies

Use letters that best describe the sounds you hear and omit the vowels. Use **S** or **K** instead of **C**: to find circle use **SRKL**. Use **J** to find joy, **JM** to find gem and **G** to find go.

HZTNS hesitancy *indecision* hesitancies
HZTNT hesitant *unwilling*
HZTNTC hesitancy *indecision* hesitancies
HZTNTL hesitantly *unwillingly*
HZTNTS hesitancy *indecision* hesitancies
HZTSHN hesitation *pause, falter*
HZTT hesitate *pause, falter* hesitated hesitating
HZTTR hesitater *pause, falter*
HZYR hazier *unclear*
HZYST haziest *unclear*

J

J age *(v) ripen, mature* aged aging
J age *(n) lifetime, period*
J au jus *in juice*
J edge *border* edged edging
J edgy *nervous* edgier edgiest
J g *alphabet letter* g's (or) gs
J Gaea *earth goddess*
J gee *(interj) wonder*
J gee *(v) turn right* geed geeing
J ghee (or) ghi *butter*
J GI *(n) soldier* GIs (or) GI's
J GI *(v) clean up* GI'd GI'ing
J jaw *(n) facial bone (v) talk*
J jay *bird*
J Jew *Hebrew*
J jiao *money*
J jo *dear* joes
J joe *fellow* joes
J joey *kangaroo*
J joy *happiness*
J ogee *molding*
JB gibe *scoff* gibed gibing

JB jab *poke* jabbed jabbing
JB jabot *collar*
JB jib *(v) balk, shift* jibbed jibbing
JB jib *(n) sail, crane*
JB jibe *shift, agree* jibed jibing
JB job *work* jobbed jobbing
JB juba *dance*
JBD Djibouti *country*
JBHPN job-hopping *work*
JBHPNG job-hopping *work*
JBHPR job-hopper *worker*
JBL jubilee *celebration*
JBLNS jubilance *joy*
JBLNT jubilant *joyful*
JBLNTS jubilance *joy*
JBLS jobless *no work*
JBLSHN jubilation *joy*
JBLT jubilate *rejoice* jubilated jubilating
JBLTS giblets *internal organs*
JBM jibboom *spar*
JBN jawbone *facial bone, talk*
JBNN jawboning *pursuasion*
JBNNG jawboning *pursuasion*
JBR gibber *talk*
JBR giber *scoff*
JBR jabber *talk*
JBR jabiru *bird*
JBR jibber *shift, balk*
JBR jobber *wholesale*
JBR jobbery *corruption*
JBRD jaybird *bird*
JBRKR jawbreaker *candy, word*
JBRLDR Gibraltar *city*
JBRLK gibberellic *acid*
JBRLN gibberellin *hormone*
JBRLTR Gibraltar *city*
JBRR jabberer *talk*
JBRSH gibberish *nonsense*
JBS gibbous *swelling*
JBSD gibbosity *swelling* gibbosities
JBST gibbosity *swelling* gibbosities
JBT Djibouti *country*
JBT gibbet *(n) gallows (v) hang*
JBW Ojibwa (or) Ojibway

Native American
JC Jaycee *club*
JC juicy *moist* juicier juiciest
JCNS juiciness *moisture*
JCR juicier *moist*
JCST juiciest *moist*
JCYR juicier *moist*
JCYST juiciest *moist*
JD aged *mature, ripe*
JD edged *bordered*
JD geode *rock*
JD Giotto *artist*
JD jade *(v) tire, dull* jaded jading
JD jade *(n) gemstone, plant*
JD jawed *with jaws*
JD jetty *pier* jetties
JD judo *sport*
JDC geodesy *math*
JDD jaded *dulled*
JDDK geodetic *math*
JDK Judaic *Jew*
JDKCHR judicature *court*
JDKDR adjudicator *judge*
JDKDV adjudicative *judged*
JDKRSCHN Judeo-Christian *Jewish and Christian*
JDKSHN adjudication *settlement*
JDKT adjudicate *settle* adjudicated adjudicating
JDKTR adjudicator *judge*
JDKTR adjudicatory *judgmental*
JDKTR judicatory *court* judicatories
JDKTR judicature *court*
JDKTV adjudicative *judged*
JDKTYR judicature *court*
JDN jotting *note*
JDNC adjutancy *assistant*
JDNG jotting *note*
JDNS adjutancy *assistant*
JDNT adjutant *assistant*
JDNTC adjutancy *assistant*
JDNTS adjutancy *assistant*
JDPRZ jodhpurs *breeches*
JDR jitter *nervous*
JDR jittery *nervous*
JDR judder *(Br) vibrate*
JDRBG jitterbug *dance*

Letters aren't doubled for single sounds: to find alley use **L** not **LL**. Use **Y** and **W** as hard sounds only: to find yellow use **YL**. (Br)=British spelling or usage. * See dictionary.

JDRNS jitteriness *nervous*
JDRZ jitters *nervous condition*
JDS geodesy *math*
JDSHL judicial (adj) *legal* judicially (adv)
JDSHR judiciary *courts* judiciaries
JDSHS judicious *wise*
JDSHSL judiciously *wise*
JDSHSNS judiciousness *wisdom*
JDSHYR judiciary *courts* judiciaries
JDSK geodesic *construction, line*
JDSN jettison *cast off*
JDSPR jeu d'esprit *joke* jeux d'esprit
JDSST geodesist *math*
JDST judoist *sport*
JDT adjutant *assistant*
JDT jadeite *mineral*
JDTK geodetic *math*
JDV adjective *modifier*
JDWST judoist *sport*
JDYK Judaic *Jew*
JDYKRSCHN Judeo-Christian *Jewish and Christian*
JDZM Judaism *Jew*
JF jiff (or) jiffy *instant* jiffies
JFG geophagy *nutrition*
JFJ geophagy *nutrition*
JFL joyful (adj) *happy* joyfully (adv)
JFN geophone *vibrations*
JFRSN Jefferson *US president*
JFSH jewfish *grouper*
JFT geophyte *plant*
JFZKL geophysical (adj) *earth* geophysically (adv)
JFZKS geophysics *earth*
JFZSST geophysicist *earth*
JFZX geophysics *earth*
JG gigot *meat* gigots
JG jag (v) stab *jagged jagging*
JG jag (n) *barb, spree*
JG jaggy *notched*
JG jaygee *rank*

JG jig (v) *dance, fish* jigged jigging
JG jig (n) *dance, trick, device*
JG jog *nudge, run* jogged jogging
JG jug (v) *stew, jail* jugged jugging
JG jug (n) *container, prison*
JG juga (pl) *wing* jugum
JGD jagged *uneven*
JGDL jaggedly *uneven*
JGDNS jaggedness *uneven*
JGL gigolo *male escort* gigolos
JGL jiggle *jerk* jiggled jiggling
JGL joggle (v) *join, shake* joggled joggling
JGL joggle (n) *joint, jog*
JGL juggle *toss and catch, trick* juggled juggling
JGLR joggler *shaker*
JGLR juggler *toss and catch, trick* jugglery
JGLR jugular *vein*
JGM jugum *wing* juga (or) jugums
JGN jogging *running*
JGNG jogging *running*
JGNK gigantic *large*
JGNKL gigantically *large*
JGNTK gigantic *large*
JGNTKL gigantically *large*
JGNTSK gigantesque *large*
JGNTZM gigantism *large size*
JGR jaeger *hunter, bird*
JGR jagger *stab*
JGR jaggery *sugar*
JGR jigger *sail, chigger, measure*
JGR jogger *runner, device*
JGRF geography *earth* geographies
JGRFK geographic (or) geographical *earth*
JGRFKL geographical (or) geographic (adj) *earth* geographically (adv)
JGRFR geographer *earth*
JGRNT juggernaut *campaign*
JGRP age-group *segment*

JGRPKR jiggery-pokery *trick*
JGS jigsaw (n) *tool* (v) *cut* (adj) *puzzle*
JGT gigot *meat* gigots
JGT jugate *paired*
JGWR jaguar *animal*
JGWRND jaguarundi *wildcat*
JGYLR jugular *vein*
JGYWR jaguar *animal*
JHD jihad *crusade*
JHKR jayhawker *(often capitalized) bandit*
JHNSBRG Johannesburg *city*
JHSFT Jehoshaphat *king of Judah*
JHSHFT Jehoshaphat *king of Judah*
JHV Jehovah *God of Old Testament*
JHZFT Jehoshaphat *king of Judah*
JJ adjudge *rule, deem* adjudged adjudging
JJ jaygee *rank*
JJ judge (v) *determine, guess* judged judging
JJ judge (n) *court official*
JJ juju *charm*
JJB jojoba *tree*
JJB jujube *fruit, candy*
JJMDK judgmatic (or) judgmatical (adj) *reasonable, levelheaded* judgmatically (adv)
JJMDKL judgmatically (adv) *reasonable, levelheaded* judgmatic (or) judgmatical (adj)
JJMNT judgment (or) judgement *decision*
JJMTK judgmatic (or) judgmatical (adj) *reasonable, levelheaded* judgmatically (adv)
JJMTKL judgmatically (adv) *reasonable, levelheaded* judgmatic (or) judgmatical (adj)
JJN jejune *dull*
JJNL jejunely *dull*

Use letters that best describe the sounds you hear and omit the vowels. Use **S** or **K** instead of **C**: to find circle use **SRKL**. Use **J** to find joy, **JM** to find gem and **G** to find go.

JJNM jejunum *intestine*
JJNS jejuneness *dull*
JJSHP judgeship *law*
JJTS jujitsu (or) jujutsu *martial arts*
JJTZ jujitsu (or) jujutsu *martial arts*
JK jack *lift*
JK jake *fine*
JK jock *sportsman*
JK jockey (n) *horseman* jockeys
JK jockey (v) *maneuver* jockeyed jockeying
JK joke *jest* joked joking
JK jokey *humorous*
JK juke *deceive* juked juking
JKBKS jukebox *music* jukeboxes
JKBL educable *learning*
JKBLD educability *learning*
JKBLT educability *learning*
JKBN Jacobean *James I*
JKBN jacobean *lily*
JKBN Jacobian *math*
JKBN Jacobin *democrat*
JKBT jackboot *shoe*
JKBT Jacobite *monk, James II*
JKBX jukebox *music* jukeboxes
JKBYN Jacobean *James I*
JKBYN jacobean *lily*
JKBYN Jacobian *math*
JKCH jock itch *rash*
JKCHZ Jack cheese *food*
JKD ejecta *waste*
JKD jackdaw *bird*
JKDD educated *skilled*
JKDR educator *teacher*
JKDR ejector *throw out*
JKDV adjective *modifier*
JKDV educative *instructive*
JKFRT jackfruit *tree, fruit*
JKHMR jackhammer *drill*
JKJNT juke joint *eatery*
JKL jackal *animal*
JKLDR ejaculator *ejector*
JKLG jackleg *amateur*
JKLNDHD Jekyll and Hyde *good and evil*
JKLNHD Jekyll and Hyde

good and evil
JKLNRN jack-o'-lantern *pumpkin*
JKLNTRN jack-o'-lantern *pumpkin*
JKLR jocular *witty*
JKLRD jocularity *wit*
JKLRL jocularly *witty*
JKLRT jocularity *wit*
JKLSHN ejaculation *ejection*
JKLT ejaculate *eject* ejaculated ejaculating
JKLT jacklight *flashlight*
JKLTR ejaculator *ejector*
JKMR jacamar *bird*
JKMR jackhammer *drill*
JKN jacana *bird*
JKND jocund *merry*
JKNDD jocundity *merriment*
JKNDL jocundly *merry*
JKNDT jocundity *merriment*
JKNF jackknife (v) *double up, cut* jackknifed jackknifing
JKNF jackknife (n) *tool, dive*
JKNGL jokingly *humorous*
JKNL jocundly *merry*
JKNL jokingly *humorous*
JKNPS jackanapes *monkey*
JKNT jaconet *fabric*
JKNTHBKS jack-in-the-box *toy* jack-in-the-boxes (or) jacks in the box
JKNTHPLPT jack-in-the-pulpit *herb* jack-in-the-pulpits (or) jacks-in-the-pulpit
JKP jack-up *drill*
JKPN jack pine *tree*
JKPT jackpot *poker, success*
JKR jacquerie (*often capitalized*) *revolt*
JKR joker *jester*
JKRBT jackrabbit *hare*
JKRD jacquard (*often capitalized*) *loom, fabric*
JKRD Jakarta or Djakarta *city, Indonesia*
JKRND jacaranda *tree*
JKRT Jakarta or Djakarta *city, Indonesia*
JKRVL jack crevalle *fish*

JKS Ajax *Greek hero*
JKS jackass *mule* jackasses
JKS jacks *game*
JKS jocose *humor*
JKSD jocosity *humor* jocosities
JKSDPZ juxtapose *side-by-side* juxtaposed juxtaposing
JKSDPZD juxtaposed *side-by-side*
JKSDPZSHN juxtaposition *side-by-side*
JKSDPZSHNL juxtapositional *side-by-side*
JKSHN education *study*
JKSHN ejection *expulsion*
JKSHNL educational (adj) *teaching* educationally (adv)
JKSHNST educationist *learning*
JKSKR jackscrew *lift*
JKSL jocosely *humor*
JKSMLT jacksmelt *fish*
JKSMN jack salmon *fish*
JKSNS jocoseness *humor*
JKST jackstay *rope, rod*
JKST jocosity *humor* jocosities
JKSTN jack stand *car tool*
JKSTND jack stand *car tool*
JKSTPZ juxtapose *side-by-side* juxtaposed juxtaposing
JKSTPZD juxtaposed *side-by-side*
JKSTPZSHN juxtaposition *side-by-side*
JKSTPZSHNL juxtapositional *side-by-side*
JKSTR jackstraw *game*
JKSTRP jockstrap *supporter*
JKT educate *teach* educated educating
JKT eject *throw out*
JKT ejecta *waste*
JKT jacket *garment, cover*
JKTD educated *skilled*
JKTR educator *teacher*

JKTR ejector *throw out*
JKTR jack-tar *(often capitalized) sailor*
JKTTSHN jactitation *twitch*
JKTV adjective *modifier*
JKTV educative *instructive*
JKTVL adjectival (adj) *dependent* adjectivally (adv)
JKVLTRDZ jack-of-all-trades *handyman* jacks-of-all-trades
JKWRD jequirity *bean*
JKWRT jequirity *bean*
JKYLDR ejaculator *ejector*
JKYLR jocular *witty*
JKYLRD jocularity *wit*
JKYLRL jocularly *witty*
JKYLRT jocularity *wit*
JKYLSHN ejaculation *ejection*
JKYLT ejaculate *eject* ejaculated ejaculating
JKYLTR ejaculator *ejector*
JKZ Jacuzzi *bath*
JL age-old *ancient*
JL agile (adj) *spry* agilely (adv)
JL edgily *nervously*
JL gel *(v) set* gelled gelling
JL gel *(n) jelly, semisolid*
JL gelée *cosmetic*
JL jail *prison* (Br) gaol
JL jell *congeal*
JL Jell-O *(trademark) food*
JL jelly *(v) congeal* jellied jellying jellies
JL jelly *(n) food, pulp* jellies
JL jewel *gemstone*
JL jolly *(adj) happy* jollier jolliest
JL jolly *(v) banter* jollied jollying jollies
JL jolly *(n) kicks* jollies
JL joual *language*
JL joule *work unit*
JL jowl *jaw*
JL July *month*
JLB djellaba *garment*
JLBL gelable *set*
JLBN jelly bean *candy*

JLBRD jailbird *prisoner*
JLBRK jailbreak *escape*
JLBT jailbait *girl*
JLBT jolly boat *ship*
JLC jalousie *window*
JLC jealousy *envy* jealousies
JLD age-old *ancient*
JLD agility *spryness* agilities
JLD gelato *ice cream* gelati
JLD gelid *icy*
JLD jollity *humor* jollities
JLDD gelidity *icy*
JLDN gelatin *jelly*
JLDNS gelatinous *jelly*
JLDNZSHN gelatinization *jelly*
JLDR adulator *adorer*
JLDT gelidity *icy*
JLFKSHN jollification *festivity*
JLFSH jellyfish *animal*
JLGNT gelignite *dynamite*
JLHS jailhouse *prison*
JLJ geology *life history* geologies
JLJK geologic (or) geological *life history*
JLJKL geological (or) geologic (adj) *life history* geologically (adv)
JLJST geologist *life history*
JLJZ geologize *life history* geologized geologizing
JLLK jellylike *congealed*
JLN jawline *chin*
JLN Julian *calendar*
JLN julienne *slice* julienned julienning
JLNG agelong *everlasting*
JLNT gellant *thickener*
JLP jalap *root*
JLP jalopy *car* jalopies
JLP julep *drink*
JLR jailer (or) jailor *guard* (Br) gaoler
JLR jeweler *gem merchant* (Br) jeweller
JLR jewelry *gems* (Br) jewellery
JLR jollier *happy*
JLRJR Jolly Roger *flag*
JLRL jelly roll *cake*

JLS ageless *youthful*
JLS jalousie *window*
JLS jawless *no jaws*
JLS jealous *envious*
JLS jealousy *envy* jealousies
JLS joyless *sad*
JLSHN adulation *adoration*
JLSHN gelation *set*
JLSL agelessly *youthful*
JLSL jealously *envious*
JLSNS agelessness *youthful*
JLSNS jealousness *envious*
JLST jolliest *happy*
JLT adulate *adore* adulated adulating
JLT agility *spryness* agilities
JLT gelate *set* gelated gelating
JLT gelato *ice cream* gelati
JLT jilt *drop a lover*
JLT jollity *humor* jollities
JLT jolt *shock*
JLTN gelatin *jelly*
JLTNS gelatinous *jelly*
JLTNZSHN gelatinization *jelly*
JLTR adulator *adorer*
JLTR adulatory *adoring*
JLWD jewelweed *touch-me-not* (Br) jewellery
JLYN Julian *calendar*
JLYN julienne *slice* julienned julienning
JLYR jollier *happy*
JLYST jolliest *happy*
JM gem *(v) bejewel* gemmed gemming
JM gem *(n) jewel*
JM gemma *bud* gemmae
JM gym *gymnasium*
JM jam *(v) pack, block, push* jammed jamming
JM jam *(n) food, music, fix*
JM jamb *door*
JM jimmy *(v) force open* jimmied jimmying jimmies (Br) jemmy
JM jimmy *(n) crowbar* jimmies (Br) jemmy

Use letters that best describe the sounds you hear and omit the vowels. Use **S** or **K** instead of **C**: to find circle use **SRKL**. Use **J** to find joy, **JM** to find gem and **G** to find go.

JMB jumbo *large one* jumbos

JMBL gimbal *support* gimballed gimballing

JMBL jambalaya *food*

JMBL jumble *mix* jumbled jumbling

JMBLY jambalaya *food*

JMBR jamboree *assembly*

JMDND jim-dandy *excellent*

JMJMZ jimjams *jitters*

JMK Jamaica *island*

JMKN gymkhana *sports*

JMKR jim crow *(vulgar-often capitalized) stereotype*

JMKRK gimcrack *gewgaw*

JML gemmule *particle*

JMLG gemology (or) gemmology *jewels*

JMLJ gemology (or) gemmology *jewels*

JMLJKL gemological *jewels*

JMLJST gemologist *jewels*

JMN G-man *FBI* G-men

JMN Gemini *zodiac sign*

JMNC geomancy *prophecy*

JMNK geomantic *prophecy*

JMNL geminal (adj) *atom* geminally (adv)

JMNS geomancy *prophecy*

JMNSDK gymnastic *acrobatic*

JMNSDKL gymnastically *acrobatic*

JMNSDKS gymnastics *acrobatics*

JMNSDX gymnastics *acrobatics*

JMNSFST gymnosophist *ascetic*

JMNSH gymnasia (pl) *sports* gymnasium

JMNSHM gymnasium *sports* gymnasiums (or) gymnasia

JMNSHN gemination *duplicate*

JMNSM gymnasium *sports* gymnasiums (or) gymnasia

JMNSPRM gymnosperm *seed* gymnospermy

JMNSPRMS

gymnospermous *seed*

JMNST gymnast *acrobat*

JMNSTK gymnastic *acrobatic*

JMNSTKL gymnastically *acrobatic*

JMNSTKS gymnastics *acrobatics*

JMNSTX gymnastics *acrobatics*

JMNSYM gymnasium *sports* gymnasiums (or) gymnasia

JMNT geminate *duplicate* geminated geminating

JMNTC geomancy *prophecy*

JMNTK geomantic *prophecy*

JMNTS geomancy *prophecy*

JMNZ gymnasia (pl) *sports* gymnasium

JMNZH gymnasia (pl) *sports* gymnasium

JMNZHM gymnasium *sports* gymnasiums (or) gymnasia

JMNZM gymnasium *sports* gymnasiums (or) gymnasia

JMNZY gymnasia (pl) *sports* gymnasium

JMNZYM gymnasium *sports* gymnasiums (or) gymnasia

JMP jump *leap, start*

JMP jumpy *nervous* jumpier jumpiest

JMPCT jump seat *car*

JMPK jam-pack *crowd*

JMPNS jumpiness *nervousness*

JMPR jumper *dress, (Br) sweater*

JMPR jumpier *nervous*

JMPRKBLZ jumper cables *battery*

JMPRP jump rope *game, cord*

JMPSHT jump shot *basketball*

JMPST jump seat *car*

JMPST jumpiest *nervous*

JMPST jumpsuit *garment*

JMPSTRT jump-start *energize*

JMPYR jumpier *nervous*

JMPYST jumpiest *nervous*

JMR jammer *pack, block, push*

JMRFK geomorphic *surface*

JMRFLJ geomorphology *surface* geomorphologies

JMRFLJKL

geomorphological *surface*

JMSBK gemsbok *animal*

JMSHN gemmation *bud*

JMSNWD jimsonweed *plant*

JMSSHN jam session *music*

JMSTN gemstone *jewel*

JMTR geometry *math system* geometries

JMTRK geometric (or) geometrical *shapes*

JMTRKL geometrical (or) geometric *shapes*

JMTRKS geometrics *patterns*

JMTRSHN geometrician *shapes*

JMTRX geometrics *patterns*

JMYL gemmule *particle*

JMZ jammies *pajamas*

JMZ jimmies *candy*

JMZBK gemsbok *animal*

JN adjoin *abut*

JN Aegean *Greek*

JN edging *border*

JN Eugene *city*

JN gene *heredity*

JN genie *spirit* genies

JN Genoa *city*

JN gin *(v) separate* ginned ginning

JN gin *(n) liquor, card game, machine*

JN Jain *religion*

JN jaunty *lively* jauntier jauntiest

JN jean *cloth, trousers* jeans

JN jenny *donkey, bird* jennies

JN jinni (or) jinn *spirit* jinn (or) jinns

JN john *toilet, client*

JN johnny *fellow, gown* johnnies

JN join *unite*
JN June *month*
JN Juneau *city*
JNBG June bug *insect*
JNBL John Bull *Englishman*
JNBT johnboat *vessel*
JNC Aegean Sea *body of water*
JNC agency *operation, office* agencies
JNC jouncy *bouncy* jouncier jounciest
JNCHR geniture *birth*
JNCHR jointure *joint, estate*
JNCR jouncier *bouncy*
JNCST jounciest *bouncy*
JNCYR jouncier *bouncy*
JNCYST jounciest *bouncy*
JNCZ geneses (pl) *origin* genesis
JND agenda *list, plan*
JND John Doe *unknown name, fellow*
JNDK genetic *heredity*
JNDKL genetically *heredity*
JNDKS genetics *heredity*
JNDL genital (adj) *sexual* genitally (adv)
JNDLS genitals *sex organs*
JNDM agendum *item on list* agenda (or) agendums
JNDR gender *(v) sire (n) sex*
JNDR janitor *cleaner*
JNDR John Dory *fish*
JNDR joinder *conjunction*
JNDRD gendered *sex*
JNDRM gendarme *police*
JNDS jaundice *disease*
JNDSD jaundiced *tainted, diseased*
JNDSST geneticist *heredity*
JNDST jaundiced *tainted, diseased*
JNDV genitive *grammar*
JNDX genetics *heredity*
JNFLK genuflect *kneel*
JNFLKSHN genuflection *kneel*
JNFLKT genuflect *kneel*
JNFR gynophore *flower*
JNG edging *border*
JNG jingo *fanatic patriot*

jingoes
JNGCHR juncture *joint*
JNGG jingo *fanatic patriot* jingoes
JNGGL jangle *quarrel, noise* jangled jangling
JNGGL jangly *clashing*
JNGGL jingle *(v) tinkle* jingled jingling
JNGGL jingle *rhyme, sound* jingly
JNGGL jungle *forest*
JNGGL jungly *dense*
JNGGLJM jungle gym *playground*
JNGGLR jangler *quarrel, noise*
JNGGLR jingler *rhyme, sound*
JNGGSDK jingoistic *fanatic patriot*
JNGGSDKL jingoistically *fanatic patriot*
JNGGSKN Genghis Khan *conqueror*
JNGGST jingoist *fanatic patriot*
JNGGSTK jingoistic *fanatic patriot*
JNGGSTKL jingoistically *fanatic patriot*
JNGGWSDK jingoistic *fanatic patriot*
JNGGWSDKL jingoistically *fanatic patriot*
JNGGWST jingoist *fanatic patriot*
JNGGWSTK jingoistic *fanatic patriot*
JNGGWSTKL jingoistically *fanatic patriot*
JNGGWZM jingoism *fanatic patriotism*
JNGGZM jingoism *fanatic patriotism*
JNGK adjunct *added*
JNGK jink *slip, prank*
JNGK junco *bird* juncos (or) juncoes
JNGK junk *waste*
JNGK junkie *addict*
JNGKBND junk bond *money*

JNGKCHR juncture *joint*
JNGKDV adjunctive *addition*
JNGKFD junk food *bad nutrient*
JNGKL adjunctly *additionally*
JNGKML junk mail *advertising*
JNGKR junker *car*
JNGKS jinx *spell* jinxes
JNGKSHN adjunction *addition*
JNGKSHN junction *intersection*
JNGKSHR juncture *joint*
JNGKT adjunct *added*
JNGKT junket *trip, pudding*
JNGKTL adjunctly *additionally*
JNGKTV adjunctive *addition*
JNGKWL jonquil *flower*
JNGKYRD junkyard *waste*
JNGL jangle *quarrel, noise* jangled jangling
JNGL jangly *clashing*
JNGL jingle *(v) tinkle* jingled jingling
JNGL jingle *rhyme, sound* jingly
JNGL jungle *forest*
JNGL jungly *dense*
JNGLJM jungle gym *playground*
JNGLR jangler *quarrel, noise*
JNGLR jingler *rhyme, sound*
JNGQL jonquil *flower*
JNGSDK jingoistic *fanatic patriot*
JNGSDKL jingoistically *fanatic patriot*
JNGSHN junction *intersection*
JNGSHR juncture *joint*
JNGSKN Genghis Khan *conqueror*
JNGST jingoist *fanatic patriot*
JNGSTK jingoistic *fanatic patriot*
JNGSTKL jingoistically *fanatic patriot*
JNGWSDK jingoistic *fanatic*

patriot
JNGWSDKL jingoistically *fanatic patriot*
JNGWST jingoist *fanatic patriot*
JNGWSTK jingoistic *fanatic patriot*
JNGWSTKL jingoistically *fanatic patriot*
JNGWZM jingoism *fanatic patriotism*
JNGX jinx *spell* jinxes
JNGZM jingoism *fanatic patriotism*
JNHNDKK John Hancock *revolutionary, autograph*
JNHNGKK John Hancock *revolutionary, autograph*
JNHNKK John Hancock *revolutionary, autograph*
JNHNR John Henry *autograph*
JNJMPP Johnny-jump-up *pansy*
JNJR ginger *spice*
JNJR gingery *brown*
JNJRBRD gingerbread *dessert*
JNJRL ginger ale *beverage*
JNJRL gingerly *carefully*
JNJRSNP gingersnap *cookie*
JNJRT gingerroot *spice*
JNJV gingiva *gums* gingivae
JNJVDS gingivitis *gums*
JNJVKDM gingivectomy *surgery* gingivectomies
JNJVKTM gingivectomy *surgery* gingivectomies
JNJVL gingival *gums*
JNJVTS gingivitis *gums*
JNK adjunct *added*
JNK eugenic *breeding*
JNK genic *heredity*
JNK jink *slip, prank*
JNK junco *bird* juncos (or) juncoes
JNK junk *waste*
JNK junkie *addict*
JNKBND junk bond *money*
JNKCHR juncture *joint*
JNKD gynecoid *female*
JNKDV adjunctive *addition*

JNKFD junk food *bad nutrient*
JNKK johnnycake *cornmeal*
JNKKRC gynecocracy *rule by women* gynecocracies
JNKKRDK gynecocratic *rule by women*
JNKKRS gynecocracy *rule by women* gynecocracies
JNKKRTK gynecocratic *rule by women*
JNKL adjunctly *additionally*
JNKL eugenically *breeding*
JNKLDD geniculated (or) geniculate *bent*
JNKLG gynecology *female organs* (Br) gynaecology
JNKLJ gynecology *female organs* (Br) gynaecology
JNKLJKL gynecological *female organs* (Br) gynaecological
JNKLJST gynecologist *female organs* (Br) gynaecologist
JNKLT geniculate (or) geniculated *bent*
JNKLTD geniculated (or) geniculate *bent*
JNKML junk mail *advertising*
JNKMLTL Johnny-come-lately *upstart* Johnny-come-latelies
JNKR junker *car*
JNKS eugenics *breeding*
JNKS jinx *spell* jinxes
JNKSHN adjunction *addition*
JNKSHN junction *intersection*
JNKSHR juncture *joint*
JNKT adjunct *added*
JNKT junket *trip, pudding*
JNKTL adjunctly *additionally*
JNKTR juncture *joint*
JNKTV adjunctive *addition*
JNKWL jonquil *flower*
JNKYLDD geniculated (or) geniculate *bent*
JNKYLT geniculate (or) geniculated *bent*

JNKYLTD geniculated (or) geniculate *bent*
JNKYRD junkyard *waste*
JNL Chou En-lai *Chinese leader*
JNL genial (adj) *friendly* genially (adv)
JNL gentle (v) *raise, placate, pet* gentled gentling
JNL gentle (adj) *kind, easy-going* gentler gentlest
JNL jauntily *lively*
JNLD geniality *friendly*
JNLFK gentlefolk *upper class*
JNLJ genealogy *descent* genealogies
JNLJKL genealogical (adj) *descent* genealogically (adv)
JNLMN gentleman *noble rank* gentlemen
JNLMNL gentlemanly *noble rank*
JNLNDZ Aegean Islands *land masses*
JNLNZ Aegean Islands *land masses*
JNLR gentler *kind, easy-going*
JNLST gentlest *kind, easy-going*
JNLT geniality *friendly*
JNLWMN gentlewoman *noble rank* gentlewomen
JNN adjoining *adjacent*
JNN genuine *authentic*
JNNDRMRF gynandromorph *both sexes* gynandromorphy
JNNDRMRFK gynandromorphic *both sexes*
JNNDRMRFZM gynandromorphism *both sexes*
JNNG adjoining *adjacent*
JNNL genuinely *authentic*
JNNS genuineness *authenticity*
JNNS jauntiness *lively*
JNNTHSPT Johnny-on-the-spot *ready*

Letters aren't doubled for single sounds: to find alley use **L** not **LL**. Use **Y** and **W** as hard sounds only: to find yellow use **YL**. (Br)=British spelling or usage. * See dictionary.

JNPL gene pool *heredity*
JNPR juniper *tree*
JNQL jonquil *flower*
JNQLDD geniculated (or) geniculate *bent*
JNQLT geniculate (or) geniculated *bent*
JNQLTD geniculated (or) geniculate *bent*
JNR genera (pl) *science category* genus
JNR genre *category*
JNR ginner *separator*
JNR January *month*
JNR joiner *unite*
JNR jointer *tool*
JNR junior *younger*
JNRDR generator *power*
JNRDV generative *descent, production*
JNRK generic *general*
JNRKL generically *general*
JNRKNS genericness *general*
JNRKSH jinriksha (or) jinrickisha *cart*
JNRL general (n) *rank* (adj) *whole, universal*
JNRL generally (adv) *usually*
JNRLD generality *statement* generalities
JNRLSHP generalship *leadership*
JNRLSM generalissimo *commander* generalissimos
JNRLT generality *statement* generalities
JNRLZ generalize *draw conclusions* generalized generalizing (Br) generalise
JNRLZBL generalizable *draw conclusions*
JNRLZD generalized *spread throughout* (Br) generalised
JNRLZR generalizer *draw conclusions* (Br) generaliser
JNRLZSHN generalization *draw conclusions*

(Br) generalisation
JNRM gin rummy *card game*
JNRS generous *bighearted*
JNRSD generosity *bighearted* generosities
JNRSHN generation *descent, production*
JNRSHNL generational (adj) *descent, production* generationally (adv)
JNRSL generously *bighearted*
JNRSNS generousness *bighearted*
JNRST generosity *bighearted* generosities
JNRT generate *beget* generated generating
JNRT juniorate *seminary*
JNRTR generator *power*
JNRTRCZ generatrices (pl) *point, line* generatrix
JNRTRKS generatrix *point, line* generatrices
JNRTRSZ generatrices (pl) *point, line* generatrix
JNRTRX generatrix *point, line* generatrices
JNRTV generative *descent, production*
JNRVRSD junior varsity *team*
JNRVRST junior varsity *team*
JNS Aegean Sea *body of water*
JNS agency *operation, office* agencies
JNS edginess *nervousness*
JNS genius *intelligence* geniuses (or) genii
JNS genus *category* genera
JNS jounce *bounce* jounced jouncing
JNS jouncy *bouncy* jouncier jounciest
JNSD genocide *destruction*
JNSDL genocidal *destruction*
JNSFST Janus-faced *two-faced*
JNSHN gentian *herb*

JNSKW je ne sais quoi *mystery*
JNSNG ginseng *herb*
JNSNGRS johnsongrass *sorghum*
JNSQ je ne sais quoi *mystery*
JNSR jouncier *bouncy*
JNSS genesis *origin* geneses
JNSS Genesis *Bible book*
JNSST eugenicist *breeding*
JNSST jounciest *bouncy*
JNST eugenist *breeding*
JNSYR jouncier *bouncy*
JNSYST jounciest *bouncy*
JNSZ geneses (pl) *origin* genesis
JNT adjoint *matrix*
JNT adjutant *assistant*
JNT agent *cause, representative*
JNT genet *animal*
JNT gent *gentleman*
JNT giant (adj) *huge* (n) *huge one*
JNT jaunt *trip*
JNT jaunty *lively* jauntier jauntiest
JNT jennet *horse, donkey*
JNT joint *union, dwelling*
JNT junta *council*
JNT junto *group* juntos
JNTC agency *operation, office* agencies
JNTC jouncy *bouncy* jouncier jounciest
JNTCR jouncier *bouncy*
JNTCST jounciest *bouncy*
JNTCYR jouncier *bouncy*
JNTCYST jounciest *bouncy*
JNTJNRL agent-general *representative* agents-general
JNTK genetic *heredity*
JNTKL genetically *heredity*
JNTKS genetics *heredity*
JNTL genital (adj) *sexual* genitally (adv)
JNTL genitalia *sex organs*
JNTL genteel (adj) *noble* genteelly (adv)

Use letters that best describe the sounds you hear and omit the vowels. Use **S** or **K** instead of **C**: to find circle use **SRKL**. Use **J** to find joy, **JM** to find gem and **G** to find go.

JNTL gentile (*often capitalized*) *non-Jew*

JNTL gentle (*v*) *raise, placate, pet* gentled gentling

JNTL gentle (*adj*) *kind, easy-going* gentler gentlest

JNTL gently (*adv*) *kind, easy-going*

JNTL jauntily *lively*

JNTL jointly *unison*

JNTLD gentility *upper class* gentilities

JNTLFK gentlefolk *upper class*

JNTLK genitalic *sex organs*

JNTLMN gentleman *noble rank* gentlemen

JNTLMNL gentlemanly *noble rank*

JNTLNS genteelness *nobility*

JNTLR gentler *kind, easy-going*

JNTLS genitals *sex organs*

JNTLST gentlest *kind, easy-going*

JNTLT gentility *upper class* gentilities

JNTLWMN gentlewoman *noble rank* gentlewomen

JNTLY genitalia *sex organs*

JNTLZM genteelism *nobility*

JNTNS jauntiness *lively*

JNTP genotype *heredity*

JNTPK genotypic *heredity*

JNTPKL genotypically *heredity*

JNTPRVKTR agent provocateur *sympathizer* agents provocateurs

JNTR geniture *birth*

JNTR gentry *upper class* gentries

JNTR janitor *cleaner*

JNTR jauntier *lively*

JNTR jointer *tool*

JNTR jointure *joint, estate*

JNTRF gentrify *renew* gentrified gentrifying gentrifies

JNTRFKSHN gentrification *renewal*

JNTRFR gentrifier *renewer*

JNTRFYR gentrifier *renewer*

JNTRL janitorial *cleaning*

JNTRNR genitourinary *organs*

JNTRS jointress *woman*

JNTRYL janitorial *cleaning*

JNTS agency *operation, office* agencies

JNTS giantess *huge one (f)*

JNTS jounce *bounce* jounced jouncing

JNTS jouncy *bouncy* jouncier jounciest

JNTSR jouncier *bouncy*

JNTSST geneticist *heredity*

JNTSST jounciest *bouncy*

JNTST jauntiest *lively*

JNTSYR jouncier *bouncy*

JNTSYST jounciest *bouncy*

JNTV genitive *grammar*

JNTVL genitival (adj) *grammar* genitivally (adv)

JNTWRM jointworm *wasp*

JNTX genetics *heredity*

JNTYR geniture *birth*

JNTYR jauntier *lively*

JNTYR jointure *joint, estate*

JNTYRNR genitourinary *organs*

JNTYST jauntiest *lively*

JNTZM giantism *large size*

JNW Genoa *city*

JNWN genuine *authentic*

JNWNL genuinely *authentic*

JNWNS genuineness *authenticity*

JNWR January *month*

JNX eugenics *breeding*

JNX jinx *spell* jinxes

JNYFLK genuflect *kneel*

JNYFLKSHN genuflection *kneel*

JNYFLKT genuflect *kneel*

JNYL genial (adj) *friendly* genially (adv)

JNYLD geniality *friendly*

JNYLG genealogy *descent* genealogies

JNYLJ genealogy *descent* genealogies

JNYLJKL genealogical (adj) *descent* genealogically (adv)

JNYLT geniality *friendly*

JNYN genuine *authentic*

JNYNL genuinely *authentic*

JNYNS genuineness *authenticity*

JNYR January *month*

JNYR jauntier *lively*

JNYR junior *younger*

JNYRT juniorate *seminary*

JNYRVRSD junior varsity *team*

JNYRVRST junior varsity *team*

JNYS genius *intelligence* geniuses (or) genii

JNYST jauntiest *lively*

JNYWN genuine *authentic*

JNYWNL genuinely *authentic*

JNYWNS genuineness *authenticity*

JNYWR January *month*

JNZ jeans (pl) *pants* jean

JNZM Jainism *religion*

JP Egypt *country*

JP GOP *Republican*

JP gyp *cheat* gypped gypping

JP jape *mock* japed japing

JP jeep *vehicle*

JPC gypsy (*often capitalized*) *wanderer* gypsies

JPCS gypseous *clay-like*

JPCYS gypseous *clay-like*

JPDR Jupiter *Roman god, planet*

JPJNT gyp joint *unfair business*

JPLDKL geopolitical (adj) *policy* geopolitically (adv)

JPLTKL geopolitical (adj) *policy* geopolitically (adv)

JPLTKS geopolitics *policy*

JPLTX geopolitics *policy*

JPN Japan *country*

JPN japan *varnish* japanned japanning

JPNKRNT Japan Current *ocean*

JPNZ Japanese *of Japan*

Letters aren't doubled for single sounds: to find alley use **L** not **LL**. Use **Y** and **W** as hard sounds only: to find yellow use **YL**. (Br)=British spelling or usage. * See dictionary.

JPNZ Japanize *make Japanese* Japanized Japanizing
JPNZBDL Japanese beetle *insect*
JPNZBTL Japanese beetle *insect*
JPNZSHN Japanization *Japan*
JPR japer *mock* japery
JPRD jeopardy *peril*
JPRDZ jeopardize *risk* jeopardized jeopardizing (Br) jeopardise
JPRZ jeepers *(interj) oath*
JPS gypsy *(often capitalized) wanderer* gypsies
JPSFL gypsophila *herb*
JPSFRS gypsiferous *clay-like*
JPSHN Egyptian *of Egypt*
JPSM gypsum *mineral*
JPSS gypseous *clay-like*
JPSYS gypseous *clay-like*
JPT Egypt *country*
JPTR Jupiter *Roman god, planet*
JPWD joe-pye weed *herb*
JPZ gypsy *(often capitalized) wanderer* gypsies
JQLDR ejaculator *ejector*
JQLR jocular *witty*
JQLRD jocularity *wit*
JQLRL jocularly *witty*
JQLRT jocularity *wit*
JQLSHN ejaculation *ejection*
JQLT ejaculate *eject* ejaculated ejaculating
JQLTR ejaculator *ejector*
JQRD jequirity *bean*
JQRT jequirity *bean*
JR adjure *judge* adjured adjuring
JR ager *ripener, of age*
JR ajar *open*
JR edger *trimmer*
JR edgier *nervous*
JR giro *fund transfer*
JR gyre *spiral* gyred gyring
JR gyri (pl) *ridge* gyrus
JR gyro *spinner, sandwich* gyros

JR jar *(v) jostle* jarred jarring
JR jar *(n) container, shock*
JR jarrah *eucalyptus*
JR jeer *mock*
JR jewelry *gems*
JR Jewry *Hebrew* Jewries
JR jury *judge* juried jurying juries
JRB jerboa *rodent*
JRBKS jury box *court*
JRBL gerbil *animal*
JRBLD jerry-build *build cheaply* jerry-built jerry-building jerry-builder
JRBLDR jerry-builder *build cheaply*
JRBLT jerry-built *cheap*
JRBM jeroboam *bottle*
JRBW jerboa *rodent*
JRBWM jeroboam *bottle*
JRBX jury box *court*
JRD joyride *reckless drive*
JRDKL juridical *(adj) legal* juridically *(adv)*
JRDM ageratum *herb* ageratum
JRDN Jordan *country*
JRDNR jardinière (or) jardiniere *stand, food*
JRDNYR jardinière (or) jardiniere *stand, food*
JRDSS giardiasis *disease* giardiases
JRDYSS giardiasis *disease* giardiases
JRF giraffe *animal* giraffes (or) giraffe
JRFL jarful *container*
JRFLKN gyrfalcon *bird*
JRGN jargon *language*
JRGN jargoon (or) jargon *zircon*
JRGNZ jargonize *obscure* jargonized jargonizing
JRHD jarhead *marine*
JRJ Georgia *US State, republic*
JRJN Georgian *of Georgia*
JRJT georgette *fabric*
JRK jerk *(v) spasm, preserve meat (n) jolt, (slang) person*
JRK jerky *(adj) spasm,*

senseless jerkier jerkiest
JRK jerky *(n) meat*
JRKF jerk off *(vulgar) masturbate*
JRKL jerkily *spasm, senseless*
JRKMPS gyrocompass *direction*
JRKN jerkin *jacket*
JRKN jerrican (or) jerry can *container*
JRKNS jerkiness *spasm, inane*
JRKR jerkier *spasm, senseless*
JRKST jerkiest *spasm, senseless*
JRKWDR jerkwater *remote*
JRKWTR jerkwater *remote*
JRKYR jerkier *spasm, senseless*
JRKYST jerkiest *spasm, senseless*
JRL jural *law*
JRM germ *bacteria*
JRM Jeremiah *prophet*
JRM jorum *vessel*
JRMD jeremiad *complaint*
JRMFR germfree *no bacteria*
JRMN German *of Germany*
JRMN germane *fitting*
JRMN Germany *country*
JRMNDR germander *plant*
JRMNDR gerrymander *election*
JRMNK Germanic *of Germany*
JRMNL germinal *(adj) creative* germinally *(adv)*
JRMNM germanium *element*
JRMNSHN germination *sprout*
JRMNSHPRD German shepherd *dog*
JRMNT germinate *sprout* germinated germinating
JRMNTV germinative *sprout*
JRMNYN germanium *element*
JRMPRF germproof *no bacteria*
JRMSD germicide *kill bacteria*
JRMSDL germicidal *kill*

Use letters that best describe the sounds you hear and omit the vowels. Use **S** or **K** instead of **C**: to find circle use **SRKL**. Use **J** to find joy, **JM** to find gem and **G** to find go.

bacteria
JRMWRFR germ warfare *chemical*
JRMY Jeremiah *prophet*
JRMYD jeremiad *complaint*
JRN adjourn *suspend*
JRN gerund *word*
JRN journey *trip* journeys
JRND gerund *word*
JRNDL girandole *cluster*
JRNK gerenuk *animal* gerenuk (or) gerenuks
JRNL journal *log*
JRNLSDK journalistic *news*
JRNLSDKL journalistically *news*
JRNLST journalist *news*
JRNLSTK journalistic *news*
JRNLSTKL journalistically *news*
JRNLZ journalese *words*
JRNLZ journalize *write* journalized journalizing
JRNLZM journalism *news*
JRNLZR journalizer *writer*
JRNM geranium *flower*
JRNM Geronimo *Apache leader*
JRNMN journeyman *experienced worker* journeymen
JRNMNT adjournment *suspension*
JRNTK gerontic *old age*
JRNTKRC gerontocracy *rule by elderly* gerontocracies
JRNTKRS gerontocracy *rule by elderly* gerontocracies
JRNTLG gerontology *old age*
JRNTLJ gerontology *old age*
JRNTLJKL gerontological *old age*
JRNTLJST gerontologist *old age*
JRNWRK journeywork *hackwork*
JRNYM geranium *flower*
JRPLN gyroplane *airplane*
JRQDR jerkwater *remote*
JRQTR jerkwater *remote*

JRR juror *law*
JRRG jury-rig *makeshift*
JRRM jury room *court*
JRS gyrase *enzyme*
JRS gyrus *ridge* gyri
JRSDK juristic *law*
JRSDKL juristically *law*
JRSDKSHN jurisdiction *power*
JRSDKSHNL jurisdictional (adj) *power* jurisdictionally (adv)
JRSHN adjuration *oath*
JRSHN gyration *motion*
JRSK Jurassic *Mesozoic era*
JRSKP gyroscope *spinner*
JRSKPK gyroscopic *spinner*
JRSKPKL gyroscopically *spinner*
JRSLM Jerusalem *city*
JRSPRDNS jurisprudence *law*
JRSPRDNSHL jurisprudencial (adj) *law* jurisprudentially (adv)
JRSPRDNT jurisprudent *jurist*
JRSPRDNTS jurisprudence *law*
JRST jurist *judge*
JRSTBLZR gyrostabilizer *motion*
JRSTK juristic *law*
JRSTKL juristically *law*
JRSTKSHN jurisdiction *power*
JRSTKSHNL jurisdictional (adj) *power* jurisdictionally (adv)
JRT gyrate *revolve* gyrated gyrating
JRT jurat *certificate*
JRTKL juridical (adj) *legal* juridically (adv)
JRTM ageratum *herb* ageratum
JRTR adjuratory *oath*
JRTR gyrator (n) *revolver*
JRTR gyratory (adj) *revolving*
JRTRK geriatric *old age*
JRTRKS geriatrics *old age*

JRTRSHN geriatrician *old age*
JRTRX geriatrics *old age*
JRYTRK geriatric *old age*
JRYTRKS geriatrics *old age*
JRYTRSHN geriatrician *old age*
JRYTRX geriatrics *old age*
JRZ jersey *cloth, (often capitalized) cow* jerseys
JRZLM Jerusalem *city*
JS aegis *protection*
JS au jus *in juice*
JS gesso *plaster* gessoes
JS Jaycee *club*
JS jess *strap* jesses
JS joist *support*
JS joss *idol*
JS joyous *happy*
JS juice (v) *extract liquid* juiced juicing
JS juice (n) *fluid, strength*
JS juicy *moist* juicier juiciest
JSCHN egestion *defecation*
JSCHR gesture *motion* gestured gesturing
JSD gessoed *plastered*
JSD jassid *insect*
JSD jessed *strapped*
JSD juiced *drunk*
JSDBL adjustable *adaptable*
JSDBLD adjustability *adaptability*
JSDBLT adjustability *adaptability*
JSDD adjusted *adapted*
JSDF justify *prove, even* justified justifying justifies
JSDFBL justifiable (adj) *excusable* justifiably (adv)
JSDFKSHN justification *support*
JSDFKTR justificatory *supportive*
JSDFR justifier *prove*
JSDFYBL justifiable (adj) *excusable* justifiably (adv)
JSDFYR justifier *prove*
JSDNTM just-in-time *manufacturing*
JSDR adjuster *arranger*
JSDR jester *joker*

Letters aren't doubled for single sounds: to find alley use **L** not **LL**. Use **Y** and **W** as hard sounds only: to find yellow use **YL**. (Br)=British spelling or usage. * See dictionary.

JSDS justice *fairness*

JSDSHN gestation *pregnancy*

JSDSHNL gestational *pregnancy*

JSDT gestate *carry within* gestated gestating

JSDV adjustive *adaptive*

JSF Joseph *husband of Mary*

JSF joseph *cloak*

JSH Jewish *Hebrew*

JSH josh *joke*

JSHD juicehead *(slang) a drunk*

JSHR josher *joker*

JSHRP Jew's harp (or) Jews' harp *music*

JSHT Jesuit *priest*

JSHTR Joshua tree *yucca*

JSHWT Jesuit *priest*

JSHWTR Joshua tree *yucca*

JSL jostle *nudge* jostled jostling

JSL juicily *moist*

JSL justly *fairly*

JSMN jessamine *jasmine*

JSMNL adjustmental *adaptable*

JSMNT adjustment *adaptation*

JSMNTL adjustmental *adaptable*

JSNC adjacency *next to* adjacencies

JSNS adjacency *next to* adjacencies

JSNS geoscience *earth*

JSNS juiciness *moisture*

JSNT adjacent *next to*

JSNTC adjacency *next to* adjacencies

JSNTH jacinth *flower, gem*

JSNTL adjacently *next to*

JSNTRK geocentric *earth as center*

JSNTRKL geocentrically *earth as center*

JSNTS adjacency *next to* adjacencies

JSNTS geoscience *earth*

JSPR jasper *quartz* jaspery

JSPRWR jasperware *pottery*

JSR juicer *extractor*

JSR juicier *moist*

JSRP Jew's harp (or) Jews' harp *music*

JSST juiciest *moist*

JST adjust *settle, adapt*

JST ageist *bigot*

JST edgiest *nervous*

JST egesta *feces*

JST G-suit *gravity*

JST gest (or) geste *adventure*

JST gist *meaning*

JST jessed *strapped*

JST jest *joke*

JST joist *support*

JST joust *combat*

JST juiced *drunk*

JST just *(adv) only, very, exactly**

JST just *(adj) fair, lawful*

JSTBL adjustable *adaptable*

JSTBLD adjustability *adaptability*

JSTBLT adjustability *adaptability*

JSTD adjusted *adapted*

JSTF justify *prove, even* justified justifying justifies

JSTFBL justifiable (adj) *excusable* justifiably (adv)

JSTFKSHN justification *support*

JSTFKTR justificatory *supportive*

JSTFR justifier *prove*

JSTFYBL justifiable (adj) *excusable* justifiably (adv)

JSTFYR justifier *prove*

JSTK joss stick *incense*

JSTK joystick *control*

JSTKLDR gesticulator *gesture*

JSTKLNT gesticulant *gesture*

JSTKLSHN gesticulation *gesture*

JSTKLT gesticulate *gesture* gesticulated gesticulating

JSTKLTR gesticulator *gesture*

JSTKLTR gesticulatory *(adj)*

gesturing

JSTKYLDR gesticulator *gesture*

JSTKYLNT gesticulant *gesture*

JSTKYLSHN gesticulation *gesture*

JSTKYLT gesticulate *gesture* gesticulated gesticulating

JSTKYLTR gesticulator *gesture*

JSTKYLTR gesticulatory *(adj) gesturing*

JSTL justly *fairly*

JSTMNL adjustmental *adaptable*

JSTMNT adjustment *adaptation*

JSTMNTL adjustmental *adaptable*

JSTNTM just-in-time *manufacturing*

JSTQLDR gesticulator *gesture*

JSTQLNT gesticulant *gesture*

JSTQLSHN gesticulation *gesture*

JSTQLT gesticulate *gesture* gesticulated gesticulating

JSTQLTR gesticulator *gesture*

JSTQLTR gesticulatory *(adj) gesturing*

JSTR adjuster *arranger*

JSTR gesture *motion* gestured gesturing

JSTR jester *joker*

JSTRFK geostrophic *force*

JSTRFKL geostrophically *force*

JSTRNG G-string *bikini*

JSTS justice *fairness*

JSTSHBL justiciable *trial*

JSTSHBLD justiciability *trial*

JSTSHBLT justiciability *trial*

JSTSHN gestation *pregnancy*

JSTSHNL gestational *pregnancy*

JSTT gestate *carry within* gestated gestating

Use letters that best describe the sounds you hear and omit the vowels. Use **S** or **K** instead of **C**: to find circle use **SRKL**. Use **J** to find joy, **JM** to find gem and **G** to find go.

JSTV adjustive *adaptive*
JSTYR gesture *motion* gestured gesturing
JSV jussive *command*
JSYNS geoscience *earth*
JSYNTS geoscience *earth*
JSYR juicier *moist*
JSYST juiciest *moist*
JT aged *mature, ripe*
JT Giotto *artist*
JT jet (*v*) *spout, travel* jetted jetting
JT jet (*n*) *airplane, stream*
JT jeté *ballet*
JT jetty *pier* jetties
JT jot (*v*) *write* jotted jotting
JT jot (*n*) *tiny bit*
JT jut *project out* jutted jutting
JT jute *plant*
JTBD jetbead *shrub*
JTBKS jukebox *music* jukeboxes
JTBLK jet-black *ebony*
JTBX jukebox *music* jukeboxes
JTD agitato *music*
JTDD agitated *shaken*
JTDDL agitatedly *shaken*
JTDR agitator *stirrer*
JTDV agitative *disturbing*
JTHRML geothermal *heat*
JTLG jet lag *fatigue*
JTLNR jetliner *airplane*
JTN jitney *bus* jitneys
JTN jotting *note*
JTNC adjutancy *assistant*
JTNG jotting *note*
JTNS adjutancy *assistant*
JTNT adjutant *assistant*
JTNTC adjutancy *assistant*
JTNTS adjutancy *assistant*
JTPRP agitprop *propaganda*
JTPRPLD jet-propelled *speed*
JTPRT jetport *airport*
JTR jitter *nervous*
JTR jittery *nervous*
JTR judder (*Br*) *vibrate*
JTRBG jitterbug *dance*
JTRNS jitteriness *nervous*
JTRPZM geotropism *gravity*

JTRZ jitters *nervous condition*
JTSDNG jet-setting *elite*
JTSDR jet-setter *elite*
JTSHN agitation *disturbance*
JTSHNL agitational *disturbance*
JTSM jetsam *castoff*
JTSN jettison *cast off*
JTST jet set *elite*
JTSTNG jet-setting *elite*
JTSTR jet-setter *elite*
JTSTRM jet stream *wind*
JTT adjutant *assistant*
JTT agitate *stir up* agitated agitating
JTT agitate *shake*
JTT agitato *music*
JTTD agitated *shaken*
JTTDL agitatedly *shaken*
JTTR agitator *stirrer*
JTTV agitative *disturbing*
JTV adjective *modifier*
JTVL adjectival (adj) *dependent* adjectivally (adv)
JV gyve *shackle*
JV Java *island*
JV java *coffee*
JV jayvee *junior varsity*
JV jive (*v*) *tease, dance* jived jiving
JV jive (*n*) *music, slang*
JV Jove *Jupiter*
JV ogive *arch*
JVC Java Sea *body of water*
JVL jovial (adj) *merry* jovially (adv)
JVL ogival *arch*
JVLD joviality *merriment*
JVLN javelin *spear*
JVLT joviality *merriment*
JVN Jovian *Jupiter*
JVNL juvenile *youth*
JVNLD juvenility *youthfulness* juvenilities
JVNLT juvenility *youthfulness* juvenilities
JVNSNS juvenescence *youth*
JVNSNT juvenescent *youth*
JVNSNTS juvenescence

youth
JVNT adjuvant *auxiliary*
JVNZ Javanese *of Java*
JVS Java Sea *body of water*
JVYL jovial (adj) *merry* jovially (adv)
JVYLD joviality *merriment*
JVYLT joviality *merriment*
JVYN Jovian *Jupiter*
JW joey *kangaroo*
JWDVVR joie de vivre *enjoyment*
JWK jaywalk *street*
JWKR jaywalker *street*
JWL jewel *gem*
JWL joual *language*
JWL jowl *jaw*
JWLR jeweler *gem merchant* (Br) jeweller
JWLR jewelry *gems* (Br) jewellery
JWLWD jewelweed *touch-me-not* (Br) jewellery
JWNL Chou En-lai *Chinese leader*
JWSH Jewish *Hebrew*
JWZ edgeways (*Br*) *sideways* (Br) edgeways
JWZ edgewise *sideways* (Br) edgeways
JX Ajax *Greek hero*
JX jacks *game*
JXDPZ juxtapose *side-by-side* juxtaposed juxtaposing
JXDPZD juxtaposed *side-by-side*
JXDPZSHN juxtaposition *side-by-side*
JXDPZSHNL juxtapositional *side-by-side*
JXKR jackscrew *lift*
JXMLT jacksmelt *fish*
JXMN jack salmon *fish*
JXT jackstay *rope, rod*
JXTN jack stand *car tool*
JXTND jack stand *car tool*
JXTPZ juxtapose *side-by-side* juxtaposed juxtaposing

Letters aren't doubled for single sounds: to find alley use **L** not **LL**. Use **Y** and **W** as hard sounds only: to find yellow use **YL**. (Br)=British spelling or usage. * See dictionary.

JXTPZD juxtaposed *side-by-side*

JXTPZSHN juxtaposition *side-by-side*

JXTPZSHNL juxtapositional *side-by-side*

JXTR jackstraw *game*

JXTRP jockstrap *supporter*

JY Gaea *earth goddess*

JY GI *(n) soldier* GIs *(or)* GI's

JY GI *(v) clean* GI'd GI'ing

JY jiao *money*

JYD geode *rock*

JYDC geodesy *math*

JYDDK geodetic *math*

JYDS geodesy *math*

JYDSK geodesic *construction, line*

JYDSST geodesist *math*

JYDTK geodetic *math*

JYFG geophagy *nutrition*

JYFJ geophagy *nutrition*

JYFN geophone *vibrations*

JYFT geophyte *plant*

JYFZKL geophysical (adj) *earth* geophysically (adv)

JYFZKS geophysics *earth*

JYFZSST geophysicist *earth*

JYFZX geophysics *earth*

JYGRF geography *earth* geographies

JYGRFK geographic (or) geographical *earth*

JYGRFKL geographical (or) geographic (adj) *earth* geographically (adv)

JYGRFR geographer *earth*

JYLJ geology *life history* geologies

JYLJK geologic (or) geological *life history*

JYLJKL geological (or) geologic (adj) *life history* geologically (adv)

JYLJST geologist *life history*

JYLJZ geologize *life history* geologized geologizing

JYMNC geomancy *prophecy*

JYMNK geomantic *prophecy*

JYMNS geomancy *prophecy*

JYMNTC geomancy *prophecy*

JYMNTK geomantic *prophecy*

JYMNTS geomancy *prophecy*

JYMRFK geomorphic *surface*

JYMRFLJ geomorphology *surface* geomorphologies

JYMRFLJKL geomorphological *surface*

JYMTR geometry *math system* geometries

JYMTRK geometric (or) geometrical *shapes*

JYMTRKL geometrical (or) geometric *shapes*

JYMTRKS geometrics *patterns*

JYMTRSHN geometrician *shapes*

JYMTRX geometrics *patterns*

JYN Aegean *Greek*

JYNC Aegean Sea *body of water*

JYNLNDZ Aegean Islands *land masses*

JYNLNZ Aegean Islands *land masses*

JYNS Aegean Sea *body of water*

JYNT giant *(adj) huge (n)* huge one

JYNTS giantess *huge one (f)*

JYNTZM giantism *large size*

JYP GOP *Republican*

JYPLDKL geopolitical (adj) *policy* geopolitically (adv)

JYPLTKL geopolitical (adj) *policy* geopolitically (adv)

JYPLTKS geopolitics *policy*

JYPLTX geopolitics *policy*

JYR edgier *nervous*

JYRDSS giardiasis *disease* giardiases

JYRDYSS giardiasis *disease* giardiases

JYS joyous *happy*

JYSNS geoscience *earth*

JYSNTRK geocentric *earth as center*

JYSNTRKL geocentrically

earth as center

JYSNTS geoscience *earth*

JYST edgiest *nervous*

JYSTRFK geostrophic *force*

JYSTRFKL geostrophically *force*

JYSYNS geoscience *earth*

JYSYNTS geoscience *earth*

JYTHRML geothermal *heat*

JYTRPZM geotropism *gravity*

JZ jazz *music, stuff*

JZ jazzy *lively, flashy* jazzier jazziest

JZBL Jezebel *hussy*

JZF Joseph *husband of Mary*

JZF joseph *cloak*

JZHRP Jew's harp (or) Jews' harp *music*

JZHT Jesuit *priest*

JZHWT Jesuit *priest*

JZL jazzily *lively*

JZM ageism *prejudice*

JZMN jasmine *shrub*

JZMN jazzman *musician*

JZNS jazziness *liveliness*

JZR jazzier *lively*

JZRK jazz-rock *music*

JZRP Jew's harp (or) Jews' harp *music*

JZS Jesus *Christ*

JZST jazziest *lively*

JZT Jesuit *priest*

JZWT Jesuit *priest*

JZYR jazzier *lively*

JZYST jazziest *lively*

K

K a.k.a. *also known as*

K A-OK (or) A-Okay *fine*

K ache *(v, n) pain* ached aching

K achy *painful* achier achiest

Use letters that best describe the sounds you hear and omit the vowels. Use **S** or **K** instead of **C**: to find circle use **SRKL**. Use **J** to find joy, **JM** to find gem and **G** to find go.

K akee *tree*
K auk *bird*
K caw *crow sound*
K cay *island*
K coo *dove sound*
K coup *successful act* coups
K cow *(v) intimidate* cowed cowing
K cow *(n) animal* cows
K coy *shy*
K cue *(v) prompt, line up* cued cuing (or) cueing
K cue *(n) hint, line, rod*
K echo *repeat* echoed echoing echoes
K ecu *(often capitalized) European Currency Unit* ecus
K eke *make do* eked eking
K icky *disgusting* ickier ickiest
K k *alphabet letter* k's (or) ks
K kay *the letter K*
K kayo *knock out* kayoed kayoing kayoes
K kea *parrot*
K key *lock, musical pitch, clue**
K koa *tree*
K koi *fish* koi
K oak *tree*
K oca *plant*
K OK (or) okay *approve* OK'd (or) okayed OK'ing (or) okaying Ok's (or) okays
K Okie *of Oklahoma*
K q *alphabet letter* q's (or) qs
K quay (or) quai *pier*
K queue *(v) line up* queued queuing
K queue *(n) line, braid*
K uke *ukulele, music*
KB Aqaba (or) Akaba *city*
KB cab *taxi*
KB cabbie (or) cabby *taxi driver* cabbies
KB cob *corn*
KB cobia *fish*
KB cowboy *ranch hand*
KB cub *young mammal*
KB Cuba *country*
KB cubby *room* cubbies

KB cube *block, math, steak* cubed cubing
KB cubé (or) cube *shrub*
KB Kaaba *Mecca*
KB kobo *money* kobo
KBB cubeb *pepper*
KBB kebab (or) kabob (or) kebob *food*
KBD cuboid *bone, shape*
KBDL caboodle *collection*
KBDL cuboidal *shape*
KBDRVR cabdriver *taxi driver*
KBHL cubbyhole *space*
KBJ cabbage *vegetable*
KBJ cubage *volume*
KBJWRM cabbageworm *insect*
KBK cubic *shape*
KBK Kabuki *drama*
KBK kebbuck (or) kebbock *(Br) cheese*
KBK Quebec *province*
KBKL cubical *(adj) shape* cubically *(adv)*
KBKL cubicle *room*
KBL cabal *intrigue* caballed caballing
KBL cabala (or) caballa (or) caballah *occult*
KBL cable *metal rope, message* cabled cabling
KBL cobble *(v) mend* cobbled cobbling
KBL cobble *(n) stone, (Br) coal*
KBL coble *boat*
KBL cowbell *bell*
KBL cubbyhole *space*
KBL cue ball *billiards*
KBL kibble *(v) grind* kibbled kibbling
KBL kibble *(n) grain*
KBLD cobbled *paved, fixed*
KBLD kobold *gnome*
KBLGRM cablegram *message*
KBLJRNT cobelligerent *ally*
KBLKR cable car *vehicle*
KBLR cobbler *shoemaker, dessert*
KBLST cabalist *occult*

KBLSTK cabalistic *occult*
KBLSTN cobblestone *paving*
KBLT cobalt *element, blue*
KBLYR caballero *horseman* caballeros
KBLZM cabalism *occult*
KBN cabana *beach hut*
KBN cabin *house*
KBN cowbane *plant*
KBN ikebana *flowers*
KBN K-band *radio*
KBND K-band *radio*
KBNKLS cabin class *accommodation*
KBNT cabinet *cupboard*
KBNTMKR cabinetmaker *woodworker*
KBNTWRK cabinetwork *woodwork*
KBNY cabana *beach hut*
KBR cabaret *club*
KBR cabrilla *fish*
KBR cobra *snake*
KBR cowberry *plant* cowberries
KBR cuber *block, math*
KBRD cabretta *leather*
KBRD cowbird *bird*
KBRD cupboard *storage*
KBRD keyboard *piano, type*
KBRL cabrilla *fish*
KBRL cabriole *ballet, furniture*
KBRL cabriolet *carriage*
KBRNSVNN cabernet sauvignon *wine*
KBRNSVNYN cabernet sauvignon *wine*
KBRPS Khyber Pass *trail*
KBRR cupbearer *server*
KBRT cabretta *leather*
KBRT cube root *math*
KBRY cabrilla *fish*
KBRYL cabriole *ballet, furniture*
KBRYL cabriolet *carriage*
KBS caboose *galley, rear car*
KBSH kibosh *stop* (Br) kybosh
KBSHN cabochon *gem*
KBSKTS Cub Scouts *boy's*

Letters aren't doubled for single sounds: to find alley use **L** not **LL**. Use **Y** and **W** as hard sounds only: to find yellow use **YL**. (Br)=British spelling or usage. * See dictionary.

club
KBST cubist *artist*
KBSTK cube steak *meat*
KBSTK cubistic *art*
KBSTN cabstand *taxi*
KBSTND cabstand *taxi*
KBT cubit *length*
KBTJ cabotage *trade*
KBTS kibbutz *farm*
kibbutzim
KBTS kibitz *observe*
KBTSH cabotage *trade*
KBTSM kibbutzim (pl) *farm*
kibbutz
KBTSR kibitzer *observer*
KBTZH cabotage *trade*
KBTZM kibbutzim (pl) *farm*
kibbutz
KBWB cobweb *spider*
filament
KBWB cobwebby *many*
filaments
KBWBD cobwebbed *spider*
filament
KBY cobia *fish*
KBYR caballero *horseman*
caballeros
KBZM cubism *art*
KC oxy *oxygen*
KCD accede *agree* acceded
acceding
KCD exceed *go beyond*
KCDN exceeding
exceptionally
KCDNG exceeding
exceptionally
KCDNGL exceedingly
exceptionally
KCDNL exceedingly
exceptionally
KCDNS accedence
agreement
KCDR exedra *room, seat*
exedrae
KCH catch (v) *sieze, deceive,*
watch* caught catching
KCH catch (n) *fish, game,*
difficulty* catches
KCH catchy *(adj) interesting,*
tricky catchier catchiest
KCH coach (n) *carriage,*
trailer, tutor (v) *prompt*

coaches
KCH couch (v) *rest, phrase*
(n) *sofa, den* couches
KCH ketch *boat* ketches
KCH kitsch *young* kitschy
KCH Quechua *province*
KCHDR actuator *mover*
KCHFRZ catchphrase
expression
KCHK caoutchouc *rubber*
KCHL actual (adj) *real, true*
actually (adv)
KCHL catchall *odds and ends*
KCHLD actuality *fact*
actualities
KCHLT actuality *fact*
actualities
KCHLZ actualize *make real*
actualized actualizing
KCHLZSHN actualization
realization
KCHMN coachman *driver*
coachmen
KCHMNT catchment *holds*
water
KCHN catching
communicable
KCHN eye-catching
attractive
KCHN kachina *doll*
KCHN kitchen *room*
KCHN Quechuan *of Quechua*
KCHNG catching
communicable
KCHNG eye-catching
attractive
KCHNL cochineal *insect, dye*
KCHNT couchant *reclining*
KCHNT kitchenette *small*
room
KCHNWR kitchenware
utensils
KCHNYL cochineal *insect,*
dye
KCHP catch up (v) *achieve*
equality catch-up (n or
adj)
KCHP ketchup *condiment*
KCHR actuary *statistician*
actuaries
KCHR catcher *sieze, grab*
KCHR catchier *interesting,*

tricky
KCHR cochair *leader*
KCHR eye-catcher *attractive*
KCHRL actuarial (adj)
statistical actuarially (adv)
KCHRYL actuarial (adj)
statistical actuarially (adv)
KCHS Cochise *Apache chief*
KCHSHN actuation
movement
KCHST catchiest *interesting,*
tricky
KCHT actuate *move*
actuated actuating
KCHTR actuator *mover*
KCHTR cacciatore *food*
KCHTWNT catch-22
inconsistancy
KCHTWNTT catch-22
inconsistancy
KCHW Quechua *province*
KCHWDR actuator *mover*
KCHWL actual (adj) *real,*
true actually (adv)
KCHWLD actuality *fact*
actualities
KCHWLT actuality *fact*
actualities
KCHWLZ actualize *make real*
actualized actualizing
KCHWLZSHN actualization
realization
KCHWN Quechuan *of*
Quechua
KCHWR actuary *statistician*
actuaries
KCHWRD catchword
expression
KCHWRL actuarial (adj)
statistical actuarially (adv)
KCHWRYL actuarial (adj)
statistical actuarially (adv)
KCHWSHN actuation
movement
KCHWT actuate *move*
actuated actuating
KCHWTR actuator *mover*
KCHYR catchier *interesting,*
tricky
KCHYST catchiest
interesting, tricky
KCHZ Cochise *Apache chief*

KCHZKCHKN catch-as-catch-can *unplanned*
KCK cacique *chief*
KCKNT cosecant *number*
KCL axial (adj) *axis* axially (adv)
KCLG axiology *ethics*
KCLJ axiology *ethics*
KCLJKL axiological (adj) *ethical* axiologically (adv)
KCM axiom *truth*
KCMDK axiomatic *self-evident*
KCMDKL axiomatically *self-evidently*
KCMR oxymora (pl) *contradiction* oxymoron
KCMRN oxymoron *contradiction* oxymora
KCMRNK oxymoronic *contradictory*
KCMRNKL oxymoronically *contradictory*
KCMTKL axiomatically *self-evidently*
KCN axion *particle*
KCN casein *milk*
KCN exine *outer layer*
KCNK auxinic *plant hormone*
KCRSS oxyuriasis *pinworms*
KCRYSS oxyuriasis *pinworms*
KCS caseous *cheesy*
KCSHN caseation *rottenness*
KCT caseate *rot* caseated caseating
KCTSK oxytocic *contraction*
KCTSN oxytocin *hormone*
KCTTRSKLN oxytetracycline *antibiotic*
KCYL axial (adj) *axis* axially (adv)
KCYLG axiology *ethics*
KCYLJ axiology *ethics*
KCYLJKL axiological (adj) *ethical* axiologically (adv)
KCYM axiom *truth*
KCYMDK axiomatic *self-evident*
KCYMDKL axiomatically *self-evidently*
KCYMTKL axiomatically

self-evidently
KCYN axion *particle*
KCYN casein *milk*
KCYRSS oxyuriasis *pinworms*
KCYRYSS oxyuriasis *pinworms*
KCYS caseous *cheesy*
KCYSHN caseation *rottenness*
KCYT caseate *rot* caseated caseating
KCZ axes (pl) *line, partnership* axis
KD Acadia *colony*
KD acuity *sharpness* acuities
KD aikido *self-defense*
KD Akita *dog*
KD CAD *(abbr)* comupter *assisted design*
KD cad *rogue*
KD caddie (or) caddy *golf* caddies caddied caddying
KD Caddo *Native American* Caddo (or) Caddos
KD catty *malicious* cattier cattiest
KD coati *raccoon-like animal*
KD cod *fish*
KD coda *conclusion*
KD code *secret system* coded coding
KD coed *female student*
KD cootie *louse*
KD cotta *surplice*
KD could *(v-past)* can
KD cud *food*
KD cuddy *cabin* cuddies
KD cuddy (or) cuddie *(Br)* blockhead cuddies
KD cutie (or) cutey *pretty one* cuties (or) cuteys
KD kata *exercise* kata (or) katas
KD keto *ketone*
KD khadi (or) khaddar *fabric*
KD kid *(v)* jest, birth kidded kidding
KD kid *(n)* goat, child
KD kiddie (or) kiddy *child* kiddies

KD kitty *cat, fund* kitties
KD kudo *award, praise* kudos
KD kudu *antelope* kudu (or) kudus
KD Kyoto *city in Japan*
KD qaid *leader*
KD Quito *city*
KDBDK katabatic *wind*
KDBK codebook *symbols*
KDBL codable *secret system*
KDBL cuttable *slice*
KDBTK katabatic *wind*
KDC caducei (pl) *symbol* caduceus
KDCH catechu *astringent*
KDCS caduceus *symbol* caducei
KDCYS caduceus *symbol* caducei
KDCZ caudices (pl) *stem* caudex
KDCZ codices (pl) *manuscript* codex
KDD caudad *tail*
KDDD katydid *insect*
KDDRM ectoderm *skin*
KDDRML ectodermal *skin*
KDF codify *classify* codified codifying codifies
KDF cutoff (n) *shortcut, valve* cut off (v)
KDF Gadhafi (or) Qadhafi (or) Khadafy *Libyan leader*
KDFK catafalque *coffin*
KDFKSHN codification *classification*
KDFLK catafalque *coffin*
KDFNDNT codefendant *law*
KDFR cataphora *substitute*
KDFRK cataphoric *substitute*
KDFS cutoffs *shorts*
KDFSH codfish *fish*
KDGLV kid-glove (adj) *consideration* kid glove (n)
KDGN octagon *shape*
KDGR category *type* categories
KDGR coup de grâce (or) coup de grace *finisher* coups de grâce (or) coups de grace

KDGRKL categorical (adj) *absolute* categorically (adv)

KDGRS coup de grâce (or) coup de grace *finisher* coups de grâce (or) coups de grace

KDGRZ categorize *classify* categorized categorizing (Br) categorise

KDGRZSHN categorization *classification* (Br) categorisation

KDHDR octahedra (pl) *eight faces* octahedron

KDHDRN octahedron *eight faces* octahedrons (or) octahedra

KDJ cottage *house*

KDJCHZ cottage cheese *milk product*

KDJR cottager *person*

KDK chaotic *confused*

KDK Kodiak *island*

KDK okey-doke (or) okey-dokey *agree*

KDKL chaotically *without design*

KDKL cuticle *skin*

KDKLZM cataclysm *catastrophe*

KDKLZMK cataclysmic *catastrophic*

KDKLZMKL cataclysmically *catastrophically*

KDKM catacomb *tomb*

KDKMN catechuman *convert*

KDKN catechin *dye*

KDKN katakana *writing*

KDKRNR catercorner *diagonal*

KDKRNR kitty-corner (or) kitty-cornered *diagonal*

KDKRNRD kitty-cornered (or) kitty-corner *diagonal*

KDKRSDK catachrestic *wrong word*

KDKRSDKL catachrestical (adj) *wrong word* catachrestically (adv)

KDKRSS catachresis *wrong*

word catachreses

KDKRSTK catachrestic *wrong word*

KDKRSTKL catachrestical (adj) *wrong word* catachrestically (adv)

KDKS caducous *fall off*

KDKS caudex *stem* caudices (or) caudexes

KDKS codex *manuscript* codices

KDKSHNL coeducational (adj) *both sexes* coeducationally (adv)

KDKSS catechesis *instruction* catecheses

KDKYMN catechuman *convert*

KDKZ catechize *instruct* catechized catechizing

KDKZM catechism *instruction*

KDL cattily *maliciously*

KDL cattle *cows*

KDL caudal *tail*

KDL caudle *drink*

KDL coddle *cook, pamper* coddled coddling

KDL cuddle *snuggle* cuddled cuddling

KDL cuddly *soft* cuddlier cuddliest

KDL kettle *pot*

KDL octal *eight*

KDLBN cuttlebone *shell*

KDLDK catalytic *causing change*

KDLDKL catalytically *causing change*

KDLDN cotyledon *placenta, leaf*

KDLDRM kettledrum *music*

KDLFSH cuttlefish *mollusk*

KDLG catalog (or) catalogue *list* cataloged (or) catalogued cataloging (or) cataloguing

KDLGR cataloger (or) cataloguer *lister*

KDLKCZ catalexes (pl) *incompleteness* catalexis

KDLKDK acatalectic *complete*

KDLKSS catalexis *incompleteness* catalexes

KDLKSZ catalexes (pl) *incompleteness* catalexis

KDLKTK acatalectic *complete*

KDLKTK catalectic *incomplete*

KDLMN cattleman *rancher* cattlemen

KDLPC catalepsy *suspended animation* catalepsies

KDLPDK cataleptic *suspended animation*

KDLPS catalepsy *suspended animation* catalepsies

KDLPTK cataleptic *suspended animation*

KDLR coddler *cook, pamper*

KDLR cuddler *snuggle*

KDLR cuddlier *softer*

KDLS catalase *enzyme*

KDLST catalyst *agent for change*

KDLST cuddliest *softest*

KDLTK catalytic *causing change*

KDLTKL catalytically *causing change*

KDLVRL cod-liver oil *potion*

KDLVRYL cod-liver oil *potion*

KDLXS catalexis *incompleteness* catalexes

KDLXZ catalexes (pl) *incompleteness* catalexis

KDLYR cuddlier *softer*

KDLYST cuddliest *softest*

KDLZ catalase *enzyme*

KDLZ catalyze *bring about* catalyzed catalyzing

KDLZR catalyzer *change agent*

KDM academe *school, pedant*

KDM academia *education*

KDM academy *school* academies

KDMK academic *education*

KDMKL academically

Use letters that best describe the sounds you hear and omit the vowels. Use **S** or **K** instead of **C**: to find circle use **SRKL**. Use **J** to find joy, **JM** to find gem and **G** to find go.

education

KDMM cadmium *element*

KDMN catamenia *menses*

KDMN coup de main *attack* coups de main

KDMNNT codominant *controlling*

KDMNT catamount *cougar*

KDMNY catamenia *menses*

KDMRF ectomorph *slightly built*

KDMRFK ectomorphic *slightly built*

KDMRN catamaran *boat*

KDMSHN academician *educator*

KDMSZM academicism *educator*

KDMT catamount *cougar*

KDMWRD Academy Award *honor*

KDMY academia *education*

KDMYM cadmium *element*

KDMYWRD Academy Award *honor*

KDN Acadian *Cajun*

KDN acting *(n) theater (adj) temporary*

KDN coating *outer layer*

KDN codeine *drug*

KDN couldn't *(contr) could not*

KDN cut-in *(n) interrupt, mix* cut in *(v)*

KDN echidna *animal*

KDN kidding *joking*

KDN kidney *organ* kidneys

KDNBN kidney bean *vegetable*

KDNC cadency *rhythm* cadencies

KDNG acting *(n) theater (adj) temporary*

KDNG coating *outer layer*

KDNG cutting *(n) plant (adj) sharp*

KDNG kidding *joking*

KDNGL cuttingly *intensely*

KDNGL kiddingly *joking*

KDNM code name *identifier*

KDNP kidnap *seize* kidnapped (or) kidnaped

kidnapping (or) kidnaping

KDNPR kidnapper (or) kidnaper *seize*

KDNS cadence *rhythm*

KDNS cadency *rhythm* cadencies

KDNS cattiness *malice*

KDNSTN kidney stone *obstruction*

KDNT cadent *rhythmic*

KDNT couldn't *(contr) could not*

KDNT octant *device, section*

KDNTC cadency *rhythm* cadencies

KDNTS cadence *rhythm*

KDNTS cadency *rhythm* cadencies

KDNZ cadenza *artistic part*

KDP cut up *(v) slice, criticize, clown*

KDP cutup *(n) clown*

KDP octopi *(pl) animal* octopus

KDPD octopod *eight arms*

KDPLD octoploid *genes*

KDPLKC cataplexy *power loss* cataplexies

KDPLKS cataplexy *power loss* cataplexies

KDPLR caterpillar *insect*

KDPLSM cataplasm *poultice*

KDPLSM ectoplasm *outer layer*

KDPLSMK ectoplasmic *outer layer*

KDPLT catapult *launching device*

KDPLX cataplexy *power loss* cataplexies

KDPLZM cataplasm *poultice*

KDPLZM ectoplasm *outer layer*

KDPLZMK ectoplasmic *outer layer*

KDPNDNS codependence *manipulation* codependency

KDPNDNT codependent *manipulator*

KDPNDNTS codependence *manipulation*

codependency

KDPS codpiece *flap, bag*

KDPS octopus *animal* octopuses (or) octopi

KDQMN catechuman *convert*

KDR accoutre (or) accouter *furnish* accoutred (or) accoutered accoutring (or) accoutering

KDR actor *player (m,f)*

KDR cadre *framework*

KDR cater *provide*

KDR cattier *malicious*

KDR cautery *burn* cauteries

KDR coder *secret system*

KDR coterie *group*

KDR cuter *prettier*

KDR cutter *slicer, boat*

KDR khaddar (or) khadi *fabric*

KDR kidder *joker*

KDRFL quatrefoil *4 lobes*

KDRFYL quatrefoil *4 lobes*

KDRK cataract *cloudy vision, flood*

KDRK icteric *jaundice*

KDRKT cataract *cloudy vision, flood*

KDRMNT accoutrement (or) accouterment *equipment*

KDRN catarrhine *primates*

KDRN octoroon *racial*

KDRPLR caterpillar *insect*

KDRPN cotter pin *fastener*

KDRR caterer *provider*

KDRS icterus *jaundice*

KDRWL caterwaul *harsh cry*

KDRZ cauterize *sear* cauterized cauterizing

KDRZSHN cauterization *burn*

KDS caddis *yarn*

KDS caducei *(pl) symbol* caduceus

KDS coitus *intercourse*

KDS cutis *skin* cutes (or) cutises

KDS ictus *rhythm*

KDSD caducity *senility*

KDSDR cadastre *property*

KDSDRL cadastral *property*

Letters aren't doubled for single sounds: to find alley use **L** not **LL**. Use **Y** and **W** as hard sounds only: to find yellow use **YL**. (Br)=British spelling or usage. * See dictionary.

KDSFL caddis fly *insect* caddis flies
KDSH caddish *rude*
KDSH catechu *astringent*
KDSH kaddish (often capitalized) *prayer*
KDSHL caddishly *rudely*
KDSHNS caddishness *rudeness*
KDSKN kidskin *leather*
KDSL codicil *appendix*
KDSLBK octosyllabic *eight sounds*
KDSLBL octosyllable *eight sounds*
KDSS caduceus *symbol* caducei
KDSS ecdysis *molting* ecdyses
KDST caducity *senility*
KDST cattiest *malicious*
KDST cutest *prettiest*
KDSTR cadastre *property*
KDSTRFK catastrophic *failed, tragic*
KDSTRFKL catastrophically *failure, tragedy*
KDSTRL cadastral *property*
KDSYS caduceus *symbol* caducei
KDSZ caudices (pl) *stem* caudex
KDSZ codices (pl) *manuscript* codex
KDT cadet *soldier*
KDT coup d'état (or) coup d'etat *overthrow* coups d'état (or) coups d'etat
KDT cut out (v) *erode, depart, replace*
KDT cutout (n, adj) *piece*
KDTHRP octothorp *symbol* (#)
KDTN catatonia *no movement*
KDTNK catatonic *no movement*
KDTNY catatonia *no movement*
KDTT coup d'état (or) coup d'etat *overthrow* coups d'état (or) coups d'etat

KDV active *lively, busy, in use*
KDV khedive *viceroy*
KDV octave *music, poetry*
KDVDR activator *starter*
KDVL actively *lively, busy, in use*
KDVL khedivial (or) khedival *viceroy*
KDVNS activeness *lively, busy, in use*
KDVR cadaver *corpse*
KDVR cutover *timber*
KDVRMS coat of arms *crest*
KDVRMZ coat of arms *crest*
KDVRS cadaverous *gaunt*
KDVRSL cadaverously *gauntly*
KDVSHN activation *start*
KDVST activist *political worker*
KDVSTK activistic *political action*
KDVT activate *make reactive* activated activating
KDVTR activator *starter*
KDVYL khedivial (or) khedival *viceroy*
KDVZM activism *political action*
KDW cutaway *abbreviated*
KDWK kittiwake *gull*
KDX caudex *stem* caudices (or) caudexes
KDX codex *manuscript* codices
KDY Acadia *colony*
KDYC caducei (pl) *symbol* caduceus
KDYCS caduceus *symbol* caducei
KDYCYS caduceus *symbol* caducei
KDYK Kodiak *island*
KDYKS caducous *fall off*
KDYKSHNL coeducational (adj) *both sexes* coeducationally (adv)
KDYN Acadian *Cajun*
KDYR cattier *malicious*
KDYS caducei (pl) *symbol* caduceus

KDYSD caducity *senility*
KDYSS caduceus *symbol* caducei
KDYST caducity *senility*
KDYST cattiest *malicious*
KDYSYS caduceus *symbol* caducei
KDZ kudzu *vine*
KDZST ecdysiast *stripteaser*
KDZYST ecdysiast *stripteaser*
KF café (or) cafe *restaurant*
KF calf *young cow, leg* calves
KF coffee *bean, beverage*
KF cough *sputter*
KF cuff *hem*
KF kaph *11th Hebrew letter*
KF kef *narcotic*
KF Khufu (or) Cheops *pyramid builder*
KF qoph *19th Hebrew letter*
KFBRK coffee break *rest period*
KFDK kyphotic *curved*
KFDRP cough drop *lozenge*
KFHS coffeehouse *cafe*
KFKK coffee cake *pastry*
KFKLCH coffee klatch *gathering*
KFKLCH kaffeeklatsch *gathering*
KFL cafe au lait *beverage*
KFL coffle *train*
KFLNGKS cuff links *buttons*
KFLNGX cuff links *buttons*
KFLNKS cuff links *buttons*
KFLNX cuff links *buttons*
KFMKR coffeemaker *appliance*
KFML coffee mill *grinder*
KFN caffeine *stimulant*
KFN coffin *corpse box*
KFNR café noir *beverage*
KFNW café noir *beverage*
KFNWR café noir *beverage*
KFPT coffeepot *appliance*
KFR coffer *money box*
KFR kafir *grain*
KFR Kafir *Hindu*
KFR kefir *beverage*
KFRDM cofferdam *enclosure*
KFS kvass *beverage*

Use letters that best describe the sounds you hear and omit the vowels. Use **S** or **K** instead of **C**: to find circle use **SRKL**. Use **J** to find joy, **JM** to find gem and **G** to find go.

KFSH cowfish *fish*
KFSHNT coefficient *number*
KFSHP coffee shop *cafe*
KFSKN calfskin *leather*
KFSS kyphosis *curve*
KFTBL coffee table (n) *furniture* coffee-table (adj)
KFTK kyphotic *curved*
KFTN caftan *garment*
KFTR cafeteria *restaurant*
KFTRM cafetorium *room*
KFTRY cafeteria *restaurant*
KFTRYM cafetorium *room*
KFYL café au lait *beverage*
KG cagey *sly* cagier cagiest
KG cog (v) *defraud* cogged cogging
KG cog (n) *tooth, part*
KG EKG (abbr) *electrocardiogram*
KG keg *cask*
KGHWL cogwheel *gear*
KGL coagula (pl) *clot* coagulum
KGL kugel *pudding*
KGLBL coagulable *clot*
KGLM coagulum *clot* coagula (or) coagulums
KGLNT coagulant *clot*
KGLR kegler *bowler*
KGLSHN coagulation *clot*
KGLT coagulate *clot* coagulated coagulating
KGNSHN cognation *related*
KGNSHN cognition *knowing*
KGNSHNT cognoscente *authority* cognoscenti
KGNT cognate *related*
KGNZBL cognizable (adj) *known* cognizably (adv)
KGNZNS cognizance *knowledge*
KGNZNT cognizant *knowledge*
KGNZNTS cognizance *knowledge*
KGR cagier *slyer*
KGR cougar *animal*
KGRL cowgirl *ranch hand*
KGRLW cog railway *train*
KGST cagiest *slyest*

KGWL cogwheel *gear*
KGYL coagula (pl) *clot* coagulum
KGYLBL coagulable *clot*
KGYLM coagulum *clot* coagula (or) coagulums
KGYLNT coagulant *clot*
KGYLSHN coagulation *clot*
KGYLT coagulate *clot* coagulated coagulating
KGYR cagier *slyer*
KGYST cagiest *slyest*
KGZKDR coexecutor *will*
KGZKTR coexecutor *will*
KGZKYDR coexecutor *will*
KGZKYTR coexecutor *will*
KGZQDR coexecutor *will*
KGZQTR coexecutor *will*
KGZST coexist *live together*
KGZSTNS coexistence *live together*
KGZSTNT coexistent *live together*
KGZSTNTS coexistence *live together*
KH coho *salmon* cohos (or) coho
KHBDNT cohabitant *live together*
KHBT cohabit *live together*
KHBTNT cohabitant *live together*
KHBTSHN cohabitation *live together*
KHD cowhide *leather*
KHL alcohol *ethanol*
KHL keyhole *lock*
KHLK alcoholic *with ethanol, compulsive drinker*
KHLKL alcoholically *with ethanol, compulsive drinker*
KHLZM alcoholism *compulsive drinking*
KHN cowhand *cowboy*
KHN kahuna *witch doctor*
KHND cowhand *cowboy*
KHR cohere *stick* cohered cohering
KHRNS coherence *connection*
KHRNT coherent *understandable*

KHRNTS coherence *connection*
KHRT cohort *group, colleague*
KHSHN cohesion *unity*
KHST cohost *entertainer*
KHSV cohesive *united*
KHT quixote *politeness*
KHTS cahoots *in league with*
KHZHN cohesion *unity*
KHZV cohesive *united*
KJ cadge *beg* cadged cadging
KJ cage (n) *enclosure*
KJ cage (v) *prison* caged caging
KJ cagey *sly* cagier cagiest
KJ EKG (abbr) *electrocardiogram*
KJ kedge *anchor* kedged kedging
KJ quayage *fee, piers*
KJB KGB *secret police*
KJDR coadjutor *assistant*
KJKSHN coeducation *both sexes*
KJKSHNL coeducational (adj) *both sexes* coeducationally (adv)
KJL cagily *slyly*
KJL cajole *persuade* cajoled cajoling
KJLMNT cajolement *persuasion*
KJLR cajoler *persuader*
KJLR cajolery *persuasion* cajoleries
KJN Cajun *Louisiana*
KJNC cogency *truthfulness*
KJNRDR cogenerator *energy*
KJNRSHN cogeneration *energy*
KJNRTR cogenerator *energy*
KJNS caginess *slyness*
KJNS cogency *truthfulness*
KJNT cogent *true*
KJNTC cogency *truthfulness*
KJNTS cogency *truthfulness*
KJPT cajeput *tree*
KJR cadger *beggar*

Letters aren't doubled for single sounds: to find alley use **L** not **LL**. Use **Y** and **W** as hard sounds only: to find yellow use **YL**. (Br)=British spelling or usage. * See dictionary.

KJR cagier *slyer*
KJR codger *old man*
KJR kedgeree *food*
KJST cagiest *slyest*
KJTDV cogitative *thought*
KJTR coadjutor *assistant*
KJTSHN cogitation *thought*
KJTT cogitate *think* cogitated cogitating
KJTTV cogitative *thought*
KJYR cagier *slyer*
KJYST cagiest *slyest*
KK ack-ack *antiaircraft*
KK cacao *bean* cacaos
KK caique *boat*
KK cake *pastry* caked caking
KK cakey *pastry, block*
KK caulk *sealant*
KK coca *cocaine*
KK cocci (pl) *bacteria* coccus
KK cock (n) *rooster, gun hammer, (vulgar) penis*
KK cock (v) *strut, set trigger, tilt*
KK cockeye *squint*
KK cocky *bold* cockier cockiest
KK coco *palm* cocos
KK cocoa *chocolate*
KK coke (v) *make coal residue* coked coking
KK coke (n) *cocaine, coal residue*
KK Coke (trademark) *beverage*
KK cook *prepare food, person*
KK cookie (or) cooky *pastry* cookies
KK cuckoo *bird* cuckoos
KK cuke *cucumber*
KK echoic *repeat*
KK kaka *parrot*
KK kayak *boat*
KK khaki *fabric*
KK kick (v) *boot, rebel, quit* (n) *blow, excitement*
KK kicky *exciting*
KK kook *screwball*
KK kooky *offbeat* kookier kookiest
KK kyack *packsack*

KKBK cookbook *recipes*
KKBK kickback (n) *reaction, money*
KKBKSNG kickboxing *sports*
KKBKSR kickboxer *sports*
KKBR kookaburra *bird*
KKBRD kickboard *swimming*
KKBXNG kickboxing *sports*
KKBXR kickboxer *sports*
KKCHR cowcatcher *frame*
KKCL coaxial *cable*
KKCYL coaxial *cable*
KKD cacti (pl) *plant* cactus
KKD cockade *ornament*
KKD cockeyed *askew*
KKDDLD cock-a-doodle-doo *rooster*
KKDS cactus *plant* cacti (or) cactuses
KKDSH coquettish *flirty*
KKDSHNS coquettishness *flirty*
KKF kick off (v) *start* kickoff (n)
KKFN cacophony *harsh sound* cacophonies
KKFNS cacophonous *harsh sound*
KKFNSL cacophonously *harsh sound*
KKFT cockfight *contest*
KKGRF cacography *bad spelling*
KKHD cokehead *drug addict*
KKKC cachexia *malnutrition*
KKKCY cachexia *malnutrition*
KKKL Coca Cola (trademark) *beverage*
KKKLK cuckoo clock *time*
KKKS cachexia *malnutrition*
KKKSY cachexia *malnutrition*
KKKZ cachexia *malnutrition*
KKKZY cachexia *malnutrition*
KKL cackle *laughing sound* cackled cackling
KKL Coca Cola (trademark) *beverage*

KKL cochlea *ear* cochleas (or) cochleae
KKL cockily *boldly*
KKL cockle *shell, plant, wrinkle*
KKL cuckold *deceived husband*
KKLB key club *private*
KKLBR cocklebur *plant*
KKLD cuckold *deceived husband*
KKLNZ Cook Islands *land mass*
KKLR cackler *laugher*
KKLR cochlear *ear*
KKLRM cockalorum *boast* cockalorums
KKLSHL cockleshell *scallop*
KKLY cochlea *ear* cochleas (or) cochleae
KKLYR cochlear *ear*
KKMBR cucumber *vegetable*
KKMM cockamamy (or) cockamamie *ridiculous*
KKMN kakemono *scroll* kakemonos
KKN caulking *sealant*
KKN cocaine *drug*
KKN cockney *(often capitalized) London, dialect* cocknies
KKN cocoon *shell*
KKN coquina *shellfish*
KKN kuchen *cake* kuchen
KKNBL cock-and-bull *nonsense*
KKNDBL cock-and-bull *nonsense*
KKNG caulking *sealant*
KKNG kayaking *sport*
KKNN cocooning *stay home*
KKNNG cocooning *stay home*
KKNS cockiness *boldness*
KKNS kookiness *offbeat*
KKNSHN cachinnation *laughter*
KKNT cachinnate *laugh* cachinnated cachinnating
KKNT coconut *food*
KKP cockapoo *dog*

Use letters that best describe the sounds you hear and omit the vowels. Use **S** or **K** instead of **C**: to find circle use **SRKL**. Use **J** to find joy, **JM** to find gem and **G** to find go.

KKP kakapo *parrot* kakapos
KKP kick up *(v) provoke*
KKP kickup *(n) quarrel*
KKPT cockpit *airplane*
KKR caulker *sealer*
KKR cocker *dog*
KKR cockier *bolder*
KKR cooker *pot, stove*
KKR cookery *food preparation* cookeries
KKR kayaker *boat*
KKR kicker *surprise*
KKR kookier *offbeat*
KKRCH cockroach *insect*
KKRKLR cocurricular *added study*
KKRKYLR cocurricular *added study*
KKRL cockerel *fowl*
KKRQLR cocurricular *added study*
KKRSPNL cocker spaniel *dog*
KKRSPNYL cocker spaniel *dog*
KKS caucus *group* caucuses
KKS coax *cajole*
KKS cocci (pl) *bacteria* coccus
KKS coccus *bacteria* cocci
KKS cox *sailor* coxes
KKS coxa *limb* coxae
KKSD coccid *insect*
KKSD coccidia (pl) *protozoan* coccidium
KKSDM coccidium *protozoan* coccidia
KKSDSS coccidiosis *disease*
KKSDY coccidia (pl) *protozoan* coccidium
KKSDYM coccidium *protozoan* coccidia
KKSDYSS coccidiosis *disease*
KKSGZ coccyges *bone* coccyx
KKSGZ kok-saghyz (or) kok-sagyz *flower*
KKSHN Caucasian *white race*
KKSHN coaction *interaction*

KKSHR cocksure *overconfident*
KKSJZ coccyges *bone* coccyx
KKSKM cockscomb *plant*
KKSKM coxcomb *fop*
KKSKMKL coxcombical *foppish*
KKSKMR coxcombry *foppery* coxcombries
KKSKS coccyx *bone* coccyges
KKSL coaxial *cable*
KKSN coxswain *sailor*
KKST cockiest *boldest*
KKST kookiest *offbeat*
KKSTND kickstand *bicycle*
KKSTNSV coextensive *same space*
KKSTV cookstove *range*
KKSWN coxswain *sailor*
KKSX coccyx *bone* coccyges
KKSYL coaxial *cable*
KKT cacti (pl) *plant* cactus
KKT cockatoo *bird* cockatoos
KKT cocked *tilted*
KKT cocotte *prostitute, dish*
KKT Cocteau *artist*
KKT cookout *picnic, barbeque*
KKT coquet (or) coquette *flirt* coquetted coquetting
KKTHT cocked hat *hat with brim*
KKTHZ cacoëthes *mania*
KKTL cockatiel *bird*
KKTL cocktail *drink*
KKTR coquetry *flirting* coquetries
KKTSH coquettish *flirty*
KKTSHNS coquettishness *flirty*
KKTSTRF ecocatastrophe *nature destruction*
KKVN coq au vin *food*
KKWK cakewalk *dance*
KKWL coequal (adj) *same as*

coequally (adv)
KKWLD coequality *same as* coequalities
KKWLT coequality *same as* coequalities
KKWTHZ cacoëthes *mania*
KKX cachexia *malnutrition*
KKXY cachexia *malnutrition*
KKYR cockier *bolder*
KKYR kookier *offbeat*
KKYST cockiest *boldest*
KKYST kookiest *offbeat*
KKZHN Caucasian *white race*
KKZKDR coexecutor *will*
KKZKTR coexecutor *will*
KKZKYDR coexecutor *will*
KKZKYTR coexecutor *will*
KKZQDR coexecutor *will*
KKZQTR coexecutor *will*
KKZST coexist *live together*
KKZSTNS coexistence *live together*
KKZSTNT coexistent *live together*
KKZSTNTS coexistence *live together*
KL call *summon, telephone*
KL calla *lily*
KL callow *young*
KL caul *membrane*
KL challah *bread*
KL chyle *lymph*
KL claw *(n) talon (v) scrape, dig*
KL clay *mud*
KL clayey *earthy*
KL clew *thread*
KL Clio *award*
KL cloy *satiate*
KL clue *(n) evidence*
KL clue *(v) give information* clued clueing (or) cluing
KL coal *fuel*
KL coil *spiral*
KL cola *solf drink* colas
KL cola (pl) *intestine, punctuation mark* colon
KL cold *not hot, indifferent, stale**
KL coldly *indifferently*
KL collie *dog*

KL cool (adj) *composed, not warm, (slang) excellent** coolly (adv)

KL coolie *laborer*

KL coulee *gully*

KL coulis *sauce*

KL cowl *hood*

KL coyly *shyly*

KL cull *separate*

KL cully *dupe* cullies

KL éclat *success*

KL kale *vegetable*

KL keel *boat*

KL keyhole *lock*

KL kill (v) *execute, stop* (n) *one killed, creek*

KL kiln *oven*

KL kilo *kilogram* kilos

KL koala *animal*

KL kohl *eye makeup*

KL kolo *dance* kolos

KL oculi (pl) *window* oculus

KLB callboy *bellman*

KLB club (v) *beat, unite* clubbed clubbing

KLB club (n) *weapon, card suit, group**

KLB clubby *sociable* clubbier clubbiest

KLBBL clubbable *sociable*

KLBFT clubfoot *deformity*

KLBHS clubhouse *building, locker room*

KLBK callback *recall*

KLBKR club car *train*

KLBL callable *loan*

KLBLDD cold-blooded *emotionless*

KLBR caliber (or) calibre *measure*

KLBR clabber *curdle*

KLBR clobber *punch*

KLBR clubber *member*

KLBR clubbier *social*

KLBR kilobar *pressure*

KLBRD clapboard *siding*

KLBRD colubrid *snake*

KLBRDR calibrator *measurer*

KLBRDR collaborator *associate*

KLBRN colubrine *snake*

KLBRSHN calibration

measurement

KLBRSHN collaboration *cooperation*

KLBRT calibrate *measure* calibrated calibrating

KLBRT collaborate *cooperate* collaborated collaborating

KLBRTR calibrator *measurer*

KLBRTR collaborator *associate*

KLBS calaboose *jail*

KLBS clubhouse *building, locker room*

KLBSD club soda *beverage*

KLBSH calabash *tree, utensil*

KLBST clubbiest *social*

KLBSTK club steak *meat*

KLBT chalybeate *iron*

KLBT keelboat *riverboat*

KLBT kilobit *1000 bits*

KLBT kilobyte *1024 bytes*

KLBYR clubbier *social*

KLBYST clubbiest *social*

KLBYT chalybeate *iron*

KLC classy *elegant* classier classiest

KLC colossi (pl) *giant* colossus

KLCH caliche *rock*

KLCH clutch (v) *grasp* (n) *group, crucial situation* clutches

KLCH cultch *oyster*

KLCHR cloture *end*

KLCHR culture (v) *grow* cultured culturing

KLCHR culture (n) *customs, growth medium*

KLCHRD culturati *people*

KLCHRD cultured *refined, produced artificially*

KLCHRDV acculturative *adoption of traits*

KLCHRL cultural (adj) *culture* culturally (adv)

KLCHRSHN acculturation *adoption of traits*

KLCHRSHNL accultural *adoption of traits*

KLCHRT acculturate *adopt traits* acculturated acculturating

KLCHRT culturati *people*

KLCHRTV acculturative *adoption of traits*

KLCM calcium *element*

KLCM coliseum *arena*

KLCM Colosseum *Roman arena*

KLCR classier *elegant*

KLCST classiest *elegant*

KLCYM calcium *element*

KLCYM coliseum *arena*

KLCYM Colosseum *Roman arena*

KLCYR classier *elegant*

KLCYST classiest *elegant*

KLCZ calices (pl) *cup* calix

KLCZ calxes (or) calces (pl) *residue* calx

KLCZ calyxes (or) calyces (pl) *flower* calyx

KLD accolade *praise*

KLD chiliad *thousand*

KLD clad *clothe* clad cladding

KLD clod *oaf, lump*

KLD cloud (n) *vapor mass* (v) *obscure*

KLD cloudy (adj) *obscure, vapor mass* cloudier cloudiest

KLD cold *not hot, indifferent, stale**

KLD collide *hit* collided colliding

KLD colloid *suspension*

KLD collude *plot* colluded colluding

KLD Euclid *geometry*

KLD keloid *scar*

KLD kiltie (or) kilty *shoe*

KLD occlude *obstruct, conceal* occluded occluding

KLDBLDD cold-blooded *emotionless*

KLDBRST cloudburst *rain*

KLDD clotted *thick*

KLDFRM cold frame *plant protector*

Use letters that best describe the sounds you hear and omit the vowels. Use **S** or **K** instead of **C**: to find circle use **SRKL**. Use **J** to find joy, **JM** to find gem and **G** to find go.

KLDFRNT cold front *weather*
KLDHPR clodhopper *oaf, shoe*
KLDHRDD coldhearted *unmoved*
KLDHRDDL coldheartedly *unmoved*
KLDHRDDNS coldheartedness *unmoved*
KLDHRTD coldhearted *unmoved*
KLDHRTDL coldheartedly *unmoved*
KLDHRTDNS coldheartedness *unmoved*
KLDK Celtic *Indo-European*
KLDKK coldcock *knock out*
KLDKRM cold cream *cleanser*
KLDKSH cold cash *money*
KLDKSHN claudication *limping*
KLDKTS cold cuts *meat*
KLDL cloudily *murky*
KLDL coldly *indifferently*
KLDL colloidal (adj) *suspension* colloidally (adv)
KLDL keloidal *scar*
KLDLS cloudless *clear*
KLDM caladium *plant*
KLDMNSTR Clytemnestra *Greek myth*
KLDN cladding *metal*
KLDN euclidean *(often capitalized) geometry*
KLDNG cladding *metal*
KLDNN cloud nine *heaven*
KLDNS cloudiness *obscure, vapor mass*
KLDNS coldness *not hot, indifferent, stale**
KLDR caldera *crater*
KLDR chelator *combine with metal*
KLDR clatter *noise*
KLDR cloudier *obscure, vapor mass*
KLDR clutter *mess*
KLDR collator *sorter*

KLDR collider *accelerator*
KLDR killdeer *bird* killdeers (or) killdeer
KLDR kilter *slant*
KLDRDKDM clitoridectomy *surgery* clitoridectomies
KLDRDKTM clitoridectomy *surgery* clitoridectomies
KLDRK clitoric *sex organ*
KLDRL clitoral *sex organ*
KLDRL collateral *(n) payment*
KLDRL collateral (adj) *indirect* collaterally (adv)
KLDRLZ collateralize *secure* collateralized collateralizing
KLDRN cauldron *pot*
KLDRS call letters *radio*
KLDRS clitoris *sex organ* clitorides
KLDS colitis *colon disease*
KLDSDL Clydesdale *horse*
KLDSH cloddish *oaf, lump*
KLDSH coltish *frisky*
KLDSHLDR cold shoulder (n) *ignore* cold-shoulder (v)
KLDSHNS cloddishness *oaf, lump*
KLDSHNS coltishness *frisky*
KLDSK cul-de-sac *blind alley* culs-de-sac
KLDSKP kaleidoscope *patterns*
KLDSKPK kaleidoscopic *patterns*
KLDSL coleslaw *food*
KLDSNP cold snap *weather*
KLDSR cold sore *blister*
KLDST cloudiest *obscure, vapor mass*
KLDSTRJ cold storage *cooler, abeyance*
KLDSWT cold sweat *perspiration*
KLDTD colatitude *complement of latitude*
KLDTRK cold turkey *withdrawal*
KLDVDBL cultivatable *crops*
KLDVDD cultivated *refined*

KLDVDR cultivator *tool*
KLDVSHN cultivation *culture, crops*
KLDVT cultivate *crops, encourage* cultivated cultivating
KLDVTBL cultivatable *crops*
KLDVTD cultivated *refined*
KLDVTR cultivator *tool*
KLDWR Cold War *conflict*
KLDWV cold wave *weather, hair*
KLDYM caladium *plant*
KLDYN euclidean *(often capitalized) geometry*
KLDYR cloudier *obscure, vapor mass*
KLDYST cloudiest *obscure, vapor mass*
KLDZDL Clydesdale *horse*
KLF caliph (or) calif *Muslim*
KLF clef *music*
KLF cleft *divided*
KLF cliff *precipice*
KLF kloof *ravine*
KLFDWLR cliff dweller *resident*
KLFHNGGR cliff-hanger *suspense*
KLFHNGR cliff-hanger *suspense*
KLFKDR calefactory *room* calefactories
KLFKTR calefactory *room* calefactories
KLFL coalfield *deposit region*
KLFLD coalfield *deposit region*
KLFLR cauliflower *vegetable*
KLFLWR cauliflower *vegetable*
KLFN colophon *inscription*
KLFPLT cleft palate *facial fissure*
KLFRM cold frame *plant protector*
KLFRM coliform *bacteria*
KLFRN California *US State*
KLFRNM californium *element*
KLFRNT cold front *weather*
KLFRNY California *US State*

Letters aren't doubled for single sounds: to find alley use **L** not **LL**. Use **Y** and **W** as hard sounds only: to find yellow use **YL**. (Br)=British spelling or usage. * See dictionary.

KLFRNYM californium *element*

KLFSH killifish *animal*

KLFT caliphate *office*

KLFT clef *music*

KLFT cleft *divided*

KLFTPLT cleft palate *facial fissure*

KLG clog *(v) hinder, overload, dance** clogged clogging

KLG clog *(n) hindrance, shoe*

KLG colleague *associate*

KLG collogue *conspire* collogued colloguing

KLG ecology *nature* ecologies

KLG klieg *light*

KLGL collegial (adj) *university* collegially (adv)

KLGM collegium *equal power*

KLGN collegian *student*

KLGR clogger *hindrance, dancer*

KLGRF calligraphy *handwriting*

KLGRFR calligrapher *handwriting*

KLGRFST calligraphist *handwriting*

KLGRL call girl *prostitute*

KLGRM kilogram *mass*

KLGS coal gas *byproduct, heating*

KLGT collegiate *university*

KLGYL collegial (adj) *university* collegially (adv)

KLGYM collegium *equal power*

KLGYN collegian *student*

KLHDD coolheaded *calm*

KLHL keelhaul *torture*

KLHM Oklahoma *city*

KLHRDD coldhearted *unmoved*

KLHRDDL coldheartedly *unmoved*

KLHRDDNS coldheartedness *unmoved*

KLHRTD coldhearted *unmoved*

KLHRTDL coldheartedly *unmoved*

KLHRTDNS coldheartedness *unmoved*

KLHRTS kilohertz *frequency*

KLHRTZ kilohertz *frequency*

KLJ collage *assemblage*

KLJ college *university*

KLJ ecology *nature* ecologies

KLJ killjoy *spoiler*

KLJKL ecological (adj) *nature* ecologically (adv)

KLJL collegial (adj) *university* collegially (adv)

KLJL kilojoule *work unit*

KLJM collegium *equal power*

KLJN collagen *substance*

KLJN collegian *student*

KLJST ecologist *nature*

KLJT collegiate *university*

KLJYL collegial (adj) *university* collegially (adv)

KLJYM collegium *equal power*

KLJYN collegian *student*

KLK calico *fabric, spots* calicoes (or) calicos

KLK caulk *sealant*

KLK clack *sharp sound*

KLK claque *applause*

KLK click *slight sound, fit, succeed*

KLK clique (n) *narrow social circle* cliquey (adj)

KLK cloaca *chamber* cloacae

KLK cloak *coat*

KLK clock *timepiece*

KLK cluck *chicken sound*

KLK colic *pain*

KLK colicky *painful*

KLK collect *gather*

KLK cowlick *hair*

KLK kulak *farmer*

KLK o'clock *time*

KLKCZ calxes (or) calces (pl) *residue* calx

KLKCZ calyxes (or) calyces (pl) *flower* calyx

KLKD Calcutta *city*

KLKDBL collectible (or) collectable *object*

KLKDD collected *calm*

KLKDDNS collectedness *calmness*

KLKDK eclectic *varied*

KLKDKL eclectically *varied*

KLKDR collector *gatherer*

KLKDRZDM collector's item *valued object*

KLKDRZTM collector's item *valued object*

KLKDSZM eclecticism *variety theory*

KLKDV collective *group*

KLKDVZ collectivize *group organization* collectivized collectivizing (Br) collectivise

KLKDVZM collectivism *group control*

KLKDVZSHN collectivization *group organization* (Br) collectivisation

KLKK coldcock *knock out*

KLKL calculi (pl) *math* calculus

KLKL cloacal *chamber*

KLKL colloquial (adj) *informal* colloquially (adv)

KLKLBL calculable *dependable*

KLKLDD calculated *(adj) likely, planned*

KLKLDDL calculatedly *likely*

KLKLDDNS calculatedness *likelihood, planning*

KLKLDN calculating *scheming*

KLKLDNG calculating *scheming*

KLKLDR calculator *math device*

KLKLR kilocalorie *energy unit*

KLKLS calculus *math* calculi

KLKLSHN calculation *math*

KLKLT calculate *figure out* calculated calculating

KLKLTD calculated *(adj) likely, planned*

KLKLTDL calculatedly *likely*

KLKLTDNS calculatedness

Use letters that best describe the sounds you hear and omit the vowels. Use **S** or **K** instead of **C**: to find circle use **SRKL**. Use **J** to find joy, **JM** to find gem and **G** to find go.

likelihood, planning
KLKLTN calculating
scheming
KLKLTNG calculating
scheming
KLKLTR calculator *math*
device
KLKLZM colloquialism
informal speech
KLKM colloquium *meeting*
colloquiums (or)
colloquia
KLKN calcanei (pl) *bone*
calcaneus
KLKN caulking *sealant*
KLKNDGR cloak-and-
dagger *intrigue*
KLKNG caulking *sealant*
KLKNN colcannon *food*
KLKNS calcaneus *bone*
calcanei
KLKNYS calcaneus *bone*
calcanei
KLKR caulker *sealer*
KLKR clacker *bell*
KLKR claqueur *applauder*
KLKRC ochlocracy *mob rule*
ochlocracies
KLKRDK ochlocratic (or)
ochlocratical *mob rule*
KLKRDKL ochlocratical (or)
ochlocratic *mob rule*
KLKRM cloakroom *coats*
KLKRM cold cream *cleanser*
KLKRS ochlocracy *mob rule*
ochlocracies
KLKRT ochlocrat *mob rule*
KLKRTK ochlocratic (or)
ochlocratical *mob rule*
KLKRTKL ochlocratical (or)
ochlocratic *mob rule*
KLKS calix *cup* calices
KLKS calx *residue* calxes
(or) calces
KLKS calyx *flower* calyxes
(or) calyces
KLKS culex *mosquito*
KLKS kolkhoz *farm*
kolkhozy (or) kolkhozes
KLKSH cliquish *narrow*
social circle
KLKSH cold cash *money*

KLKSHL cliquishly *narrow*
social circle
KLKSHN collection *group*
KLKSHN collocation
arrangement
KLKSHN echolocation *bat*
sonar
KLKSHNS cliquishness
narrow social circle
KLKSN Klaxon *(trademark)*
horn
KLKST chalcocite *mineral*
KLKSZ calxes (or) calces
(pl) *residue* calx
KLKSZ calyxes (or) calyces
(pl) *flower* calyx
KLKT Calcutta *city*
KLKT collect *gather*
KLKT collocate *side by side*
collocated collocating
KLKT colocate *share*
facilities
KLKTBL collectible (or)
collectable *object*
KLKTD collected *calm*
KLKTDNS collectedness
calmness
KLKTK eclectic *varied*
KLKTKL eclectically *varied*
KLKTR collector *gatherer*
KLKTRZDM collector's item
valued object
KLKTRZTM collector's item
valued object
KLKTS cold cuts *meat*
KLKTSZM eclecticism
variety theory
KLKTV collective *group*
KLKTVD collectivity *whole*
KLKTVT collectivity *whole*
KLKTVZ collectivize *group*
organization collectivized
collectivizing
(Br) collectivise
KLKTVZM collectivism
group control
KLKTVZSHN
collectivization *group*
organization
(Br) collectivisation
KLKW colloquia (pl) *meeting*
colloquium

KLKW colloquy *conversation*
colloquies
KLKWL colloquial (adj)
informal colloquially (adv)
KLKWLZM colloquialism
informal speech
KLKWM colloquium *meeting*
colloquiums (or)
colloquia
KLKWRK clockwork
precision
KLKWY colloquia (pl)
meeting colloquium
KLKWYL colloquial (adj)
informal colloquially (adv)
KLKWYLZM colloquialism
informal speech
KLKWYM colloquium
meeting colloquiums (or)
colloquia
KLKWZ clockwise
movement
KLKYL calculi (pl) *math*
calculus
KLKYL colloquial (adj)
informal colloquially (adv)
KLKYLBL calculable
dependable
KLKYLDD calculated *(adj)*
likely, planned
KLKYLDDL calculatedly
likely
KLKYLDDNS
calculatedness *likelihood,*
planning
KLKYLDN calculating
scheming
KLKYLDNG calculating
scheming
KLKYLDR calculator *math*
device
KLKYLS calculus *math*
calculi
KLKYLSHN calculation
math
KLKYLT calculate *figure out*
calculated calculating
KLKYLTD calculated *(adj)*
likely, planned
KLKYLTDL calculatedly
likely
KLKYLTDNS

calculatedness *likelihood, planning*

KLKYLTN calculating *scheming*

KLKYLTNG calculating *scheming*

KLKYLTR calculator *math device*

KLKYLZM colloquialism *informal speech*

KLKYM colloquium *meeting* colloquiums (or) colloquia

KLKZ kolkhoz *farm* kolkhozy (or) kolkhozes

KLL callaloo *stew*

KLL echolalia *repeat*

KLL ukulele *music*

KLLDR kiloliter *liquid measure*

KLLK claylike *earthy*

KLLK echolalic *repeat*

KLLL calla lily *flower*

KLLMPR Kuala Lumpur *city*

KLLS clueless *ignorant*

KLLTHSS cholelithiasis *gallstones*

KLLTHYSS cholelithiasis *gallstones*

KLLTR kiloliter *liquid measure*

KLLY echolalia *repeat*

KLM acclaim *praise*

KLM calami (pl) *herb, quill* calamus

KLM calm *serene, quiet*

KLM claim *(v) assert, require (n) title, right*

KLM clam *mollusk* clammed clamming

KLM clammy *cold and damp* clammier clammiest

KLM climb *ascend*

KLM clime *climate*

KLM column *support, line*

KLM coulomb *electricity*

KLM key lime *fruit*

KLM kilim *rug*

KLMB Colombia *country*

KLMB Columbia *district, cape, river*

KLMBK clambake *cookout*

KLMBL claimable *assert, demand*

KLMBL climbable *ascend*

KLMBN columbine *plant*

KLMBR clamber *climb*

KLMBRR clamberer *climber*

KLMBS Columbus *explorer, city*

KLMBY Colombia *country*

KLMBY Columbia *district, cape, river*

KLMCZ chlamyses (pl) *cloak* chlamys

KLMD calamity *disaster* calamities

KLMD chlamydia *bacteria* chlamydiae

KLMD columned *support, line*

KLMDK climatic *weather*

KLMDR coulometer *electricity* coulometry

KLMDR kilometer *distance*

KLMDR oculomotor *nerve*

KLMDS calamitous *disastrous*

KLMDS clematis *plant*

KLMDSL calamitously *disastrously*

KLMDV calmative *serene*

KLMDY chlamydia *bacteria* chlamydiae

KLMDZ acclimatize *adapt to environment* acclimatized acclimatizing (Br) acclimatise

KLMDZ chlamydes (pl) *cloak* chlamys

KLMDZSHN acclimatization *adaptation* (Br) acclimatisation

KLMKDK climactic *culmination*

KLMKS climax *culmination* climaxes

KLMKTK climactic *culmination*

KLMKTRK climacteric *(adj) critical (n) menopause*

KLML calmly *serenely*

KLML calomel *insecticide*

KLML columella *column*

columellae

KLMLR columellar *column*

KLMN calamine *lotion*

KLMN calumny *accusation* calumnies

KLMN Khomeini *religious leader*

KLMNC clemency *forgiveness* clemencies

KLMNDR calumniator *accuser*

KLMNJR Kilimanjaro *mountain*

KLMNNT culminant *fully developed*

KLMNR columnar *support, line*

KLMNS calmness *serenity*

KLMNS calumnious *accusing*

KLMNS clamminess *cold and damp*

KLMNS Clemenceau *French statesman*

KLMNS clemency *forgiveness* clemencies

KLMNSHN calumniation *accusation*

KLMNSHN culmination *climax*

KLMNSL calumniously *accusing*

KLMNST columnist *writer*

KLMNT calumniate *accuse* calumniated calumniating

KLMNT claimant *asserter*

KLMNT clement *lenient*

KLMNT culminate *peak* culminated culminating

KLMNTC clemency *forgiveness* clemencies

KLMNTR calumniator *accuser*

KLMNTS clemency *forgiveness* clemencies

KLMNYDR calumniator *accuser*

KLMNYS calumnious *accusing*

KLMNYSHN calumniation *accusation*

KLMNYSL calumniously *accusing*
KLMNYT calumniate *accuse* calumniated calumniating
KLMNYTR calumniator *accuser*
KLMP clamp *device*
KLMP clump *bunch*
KLMP clumpy *in bunches*
KLMPDN clampdown (n) *restrict* clamp down (v)
KLMR acclaimer *praiser*
KLMR calamari *squid (food)*
KLMR calamary *squid (sea animal)* calamaries
KLMR claimer *asserter, horse*
KLMR clamber *climb*
KLMR clammer *digger*
KLMR clammier *cold and damp*
KLMR clamor *noise* (Br) clamour
KLMR claymore *sword*
KLMR climber *ascend*
KLMRR clamberer *climber*
KLMRS clamorous *noisy* (Br) clamourous
KLMS calamus *herb* calami (pl)
KLMS chlamys *cloak* chlamyses (or) chlamydes
KLMSHL clamshell *mollusk*
KLMSHN acclamation *praise*
KLMSHN acclimation *adjustment*
KLMSHN collimation *straighten*
KLMST clammiest *cold and damp*
KLMST columnist *writer*
KLMSZ chlamyses (pl) *cloak* chlamys
KLMT acclimate *adapt to environment* acclimated acclimating
KLMT calamity *disaster* calamities
KLMT calumet *pipe*
KLMT climate *weather*
KLMT collimate *straighten*

collimated collimating
KLMTK climatic *weather*
KLMTLG climatology *weather*
KLMTLJ climatology *weather*
KLMTLJKL climatological (adj) *weather* climatologically (adv)
KLMTLJST climatologist *weather*
KLMTR coulometer *electricity* coulometry
KLMTR kilometer *distance*
KLMTR oculomotor *nerve*
KLMTRK coulometric *electricity*
KLMTRKL coulometrically *electricity*
KLMTS calamitous *disastrous*
KLMTS clematis *plant*
KLMTSL calamitously *disastrously*
KLMTV calmative *serene*
KLMTZ acclimatize *adapt to environment* acclimatized acclimatizing (Br) acclimatise
KLMTZR acclimatizer *adapt to environment* (Br) acclimatiser
KLMTZSHN acclimatization *adaptation* (Br) acclimatisation
KLMX climax *culmination* climaxes
KLMYR clammier *cold and damp*
KLMYST clammiest *cold and damp*
KLMZ clumsy *awkward* clumsier clumsiest
KLMZ Kalamazoo *city*
KLMZL clumsily *awkward*
KLMZNS clumsiness *awkward*
KLMZR clumsier *awkward*
KLMZST clumsiest *awkward*
KLMZYR clumsier *awkward*
KLMZYST clumsiest *awkward*

KLN Auckland *city*
KLN call loan *money*
KLN call-in (adj) *telephone* call in (v)
KLN calling *work*
KLN choline *chemical*
KLN clan *family*
KLN clean *(adj) tidy (v) scrub*
KLN clone *copy* cloned cloning
KLN clown *jester*
KLN colleen *girl*
KLN Cologne *German city*
KLN cologne *perfume*
KLN Colon *Columbian city*
KLN colon *intestine, punctuation mark* colons (or) cola
KLN colony *group, territory* colonies
KLN cowling *cover*
KLN kaolin *clay*
KLN killing *(n) big gain (adj) difficult*
KLN kiln *oven*
KLN Oakland *city*
KLNBL cleanable *washable*
KLNCH clench *hold tightly* clenches
KLNCH clinch *(n) fastener, embrace (v) settle, win** clinches
KLNCHR clincher *decisive act*
KLND Auckland *city*
KLND colonnade *column*
KLND Oakland *city*
KLNDD colonnaded *columns*
KLNDK Klondike *river*
KLNDR calendar *date list*
KLNDR calender *press*
KLNDR colander *sieve*
KLNDRKL calendrical *date list*
KLNDSDN clandestine *secret*
KLNDSTN clandestine *secret*
KLNG calling *work*
KLNG clang *loud noise*
KLNG cling *hold on, stick*

Letters aren't doubled for single sounds: to find alley use **L** not **LL**. Use **Y** and **W** as hard sounds only: to find yellow use **YL**. (Br)=British spelling or usage. * See dictionary.

clung clinging
KLNG clingy *sticky*
KLNG cloying *sweet*
KLNG clung *(v-past)* cling
KLNG cowling *cover*
KLNG killing *(n)* big gain *(adj)* difficult
KLNGGR clangor *noises* (Br) clangour
KLNGGRS clangorous *noisy* (Br) clangourous
KLNGK clank *loud sound*
KLNGK clink *slight sound, (slang)* jail
KLNGK clunk *thump, dullard*
KLNGK clunky *clumsy* clunkier clunkiest
KLNGK kalanchoe *herb*
KLNGKM collenchyma *plant cells*
KLNGKMTS collenchymatous *plant cells*
KLNGKR clinker *slag, flop*
KLNGKR clunker *dilapidated car*
KLNGKR clunkier *clumsier*
KLNGKST clunkiest *clumsiest*
KLNGKYR clunkier *clumsier*
KLNGKYST clunkiest *clumsiest*
KLNGL cloyingly *sweet*
KLNGLNZ Keeling Islands *land mass*
KLNGR clanger *(Br) blunder* (Br) clangour
KLNGR clangor *noises* (Br) clangour
KLNGR clinger *sticker*
KLNGRS clangorous *noisy* (Br) clangourous
KLNGSTN clingstone *fruit*
KLNHNDD cleanhanded *innocent*
KLNK clank *loud sound*
KLNK clinic *medical*
KLNK clink *slight sound, (slang)* jail
KLNK clonic *spasm*
KLNK clunk *thump, dullard*
KLNK clunky *clumsy*

clunkier clunkiest
KLNK colonic *intestine*
KLNK kalanchoe *herb*
KLNKL clinical (adj) *medical* clinically (adv)
KLNKM collenchyma *plant cells*
KLNKMTS collenchymatous *plant cells*
KLNKR clinker *slag, flop*
KLNKR clunker *dilapidated car*
KLNKR clunkier *clumsier*
KLNKS Kleenex *(trademark) tissue*
KLNKST clunkiest *clumsiest*
KLNKT clean-cut *wholesome*
KLNKYR clunkier *clumsier*
KLNKYST clunkiest *clumsiest*
KLNL cleanly *fastidious* cleanlier cleanliest
KLNL clonal (adj) *copy* clonally (adv)
KLNL colonial (adj) *territory, group* colonially (adv)
KLNLMD clean-limbed *trim*
KLNLNS cleanliness *fastidious*
KLNLNZ Keeling Islands *land mass*
KLNLR cleanlier *fastidious*
KLNLST cleanliest *fastidious*
KLNLYR cleanlier *fastidious*
KLNLYST cleanliest *fastidious*
KLNLZM colonialism *settlers*
KLNMDR clinometer *incline*
KLNMTR clinometer *incline*
KLNNJRK clean and jerk *weight lifting*
KLNP cleanup (adj or n) *wash* clean up (v)
KLNR cleaner *tidy, scrub*
KLNR colinear *same order*
KLNR collinear *straight line*
KLNR culinary *cooking*
KLNRD collinearity *straight line*
KLNRL culinarily *cooking*
KLNRN culinarian *chef*

KLNRT collinearity *straight line*
KLNRYN culinarian *chef*
KLNS clonus *spasm*
KLNS coldness *not hot, indifferent, stale**
KLNS coolness *composed, not warm, (slang) excellence**
KLNSH clannish *family*
KLNSH clownish *boorish*
KLNSHN clinician *practitioner*
KLNSHNS clannishness *family*
KLNSHVN clean-shaven *no beard*
KLNST colonist *settler*
KLNSTRZ cholinesterase *enzyme*
KLNT client *customer*
KLNT coolant *antifreeze*
KLNT kaolinite *mineral*
KLNTL clientele *customers*
KLNX Kleenex *(trademark) tissue*
KLNYL colonial (adj) *territory, group* colonially (adv)
KLNYLZM colonialism *settlers*
KLNYR colinear *same order*
KLNYR collinear *straight line*
KLNYRD collinearity *straight line*
KLNYRT collinearity *straight line*
KLNZ cleanse *wash* cleansed cleansing
KLNZ colonize *settle* colonized colonizing (Br) colonise
KLNZMN clansman *family* clansmen
KLNZR cleanser *cleaning agent*
KLNZR colonizer *settler* (Br) coloniser
KLNZSHN colonization *settlers* (Br) colonisation
KLP call-up (n) *telephone* call

Use letters that best describe the sounds you hear and omit the vowels. Use **S** or **K** instead of **C**: to find circle use **SRKL**. Use **J** to find joy, **JM** to find gem and **G** to find go.

up (v)
KLP Calliope *Greek muse*
KLP calliope *organ*
KLP clap *(v) applaud* clapped clapping
KLP clap *(n) gonorrhea, applause*
KLP clip *(v) cut off, fasten, hit** clipped clipping
KLP clip *(n) fastener, cutting, blow**
KLP clop *hoof sound* clopped clopping
KLP collop *flesh*
KLP kelp *seaweed*
KLP kelpie *dog, sprite*
KLPBL culpable (adj) *blameworthy* culpably (adv)
KLPBLD culpability *blame*
KLPBLNS culpableness *blame*
KLPBLT culpability *blame*
KLPBRD clapboard *siding*
KLPBRD clipboard *write*
KLPD klepto- *theft*
KLPDK ecliptic *obscure, orbit*
KLPDMN kleptomania *theft*
KLPDMNK kleptomaniac *thief*
KLPDMNY kleptomania *theft*
KLPDMNYK kleptomaniac *thief*
KLPDR coleoptera *beetle*
KLPDRS coleopterous *beetle*
KLPDRST coleopterist *beetles*
KLPDS eucalyptus *tree* eucalypti (or) eucalyptuses
KLPDT clapped-out *(Br) tired*
KLPJNT clip joint *overcharge*
KLPK calpac (or) calpack *cap*
KLPN claypan *soil*
KLPN clip-on *fastener*
KLPN clipping *cutting*
KLPNG clipping *cutting*
KLPR caliper *measure* (Br) calliper

KLPR clapper *bell*
KLPR clipper *cutter*
KLPRDR colporteur *book seller*
KLPRS clippers *hair cut*
KLPRT culprit *guilty one*
KLPRTJ colportage *book selling*
KLPRTR colporteur *book seller*
KLPRTSH colportage *book selling*
KLPRTZH colportage *book selling*
KLPRZ clippers *hair cut*
KLPS calypso *nymph, orchid, music* calypsos (or) calypsoes
KLPS collapse *fall* collapsed collapsing
KLPS eclipse *obscure* eclipsed eclipsing
KLPSBL collapsible *fold, break*
KLPSBLD collapsibility *fold, break*
KLPSBLT collapsibility *fold, break*
KLPSHT clipsheet *newspaper*
KLPT eucalypt *tree*
KLPT klepto- *theft*
KLPTK ecliptic *obscure, orbit*
KLPTL eucalyptol *oil*
KLPTMN kleptomania *theft*
KLPTMNK kleptomaniac *thief*
KLPTMNY kleptomania *theft*
KLPTMNYK kleptomaniac *thief*
KLPTR calyptra *hood*
KLPTR Cleopatra *queen*
KLPTR coleoptera *beetle*
KLPTRP claptrap *cheap*
KLPTRS coleopterous *beetle*
KLPTRST coleopterist *beetles*
KLPTS eucalyptus *tree* eucalypti (or) eucalyptuses
KLPTT clapped-out *(Br)*

tired
KLQ colloquia (pl) *meeting* colloquium
KLQ colloquy *conversation* colloquies
KLQL calculi (pl) *math* calculus
KLQL colloquial (adj) *informal* colloquially (adv)
KLQLBL calculable *dependable*
KLQLDD calculated *(adj) likely, planned*
KLQLDDL calculatedly *likely*
KLQLDDNS calculatedness *likelihood, planning*
KLQLDN calculating *scheming*
KLQLDNG calculating *scheming*
KLQLDR calculator *math device*
KLQLS calculus *math* calculi
KLQLSHN calculation *math*
KLQLT calculate *figure out* calculated calculating
KLQLTD calculated *(adj) likely, planned*
KLQLTDL calculatedly *likely*
KLQLTDNS calculatedness *likelihood, planning*
KLQLTN calculating *scheming*
KLQLTNG calculating *scheming*
KLQLTR calculator *math device*
KLQLZM colloquialism *informal speech*
KLQM colloquium *meeting* colloquiums (or) colloquia
KLQRK clockwork *precision*
KLQY colloquia (pl) *meeting* colloquium
KLQYL colloquial (adj) *informal* colloquially (adv)
KLQYLZM colloquialism *informal speech*
KLQYM colloquium *meeting* colloquiums (or)

Letters aren't doubled for single sounds: to find alley use **L** not **LL**. Use **Y** and **W** as hard sounds only: to find yellow use **YL**. (Br)=British spelling or usage. * See dictionary.

colloquia

KLQZ clockwise *movement*

KLR caller *visitor, phoner*

KLR calorie *food energy*

KLR choler *anger*

KLR cholera *disease*

KLR claro *cigar* claros

KLR clear *(adj) transparent, clean, keen (adv) all the way (v) vindicate, explain, approve**

KLR collar *neck*

KLR collier *coal miner*

KLR colliery *coal mine*

KLR color *tint*
(Br) colour

KLR cooler *less warm, container*

KLR éclair *pastry*

KLR killer *murderer*

KLR ocular *eyepiece*

KLRB killer bee *insect*

KLRB kohlrabi *vegetable* kohlrabies

KLRBL colorable (adj) *tint* colorably (adv)
(Br) colourable

KLRBLN color-blind *vision*
(Br) colour-blind

KLRBLND color-blind *vision*
(Br) colour-blind

KLRBLNDNS color blindness *vision*
(Br) colour blindness

KLRBLNS color blindness *vision*
(Br) colour blindness

KLRBN collarbone *clavicle*

KLRC clerisy *intelligentsia*

KLRCHR coloratura *singer*

KLRD chloride *chemical*

KLRD clarity *lucid, clear*

KLRD clear-eyed *vision*

KLRD collard *vegetable*

KLRD Colorado *US State*

KLRD colored *tinted*
(Br) coloured

KLRDN chlordane *chemical*

KLRDS collards *vegetable*

KLRDZ collards *vegetable*

KLRF clarify *clear up* clarified clarifying

clarifies

KLRFK calorific *food energy*

KLRFK colorific *tint*
(Br) colourific

KLRFKSHN clarification *clear up*

KLRFL chlorophyll *plant substance*

KLRFL colorful (adj) *tinted* colorfully (adv)
(Br) colourful, colourfully

KLRFR clarifier *clear up*

KLRFRM chloroform *anesthetic*

KLRFST colorfast *no fading*
(Br) colourfast

KLRFYR clarifier *clear up*

KLRG clergy *church* clergies

KLRGMN clergyman *church* clergymen

KLRGWMN clergywoman *church* clergywomen

KLRHDD clearheaded *sensible*

KLRJ clergy *church* clergies

KLRJMN clergyman *church* clergymen

KLRJWMN clergywoman *church* clergywomen

KLRK caloric *food energy*

KLRK choleric *angry*

KLRK cleric *church*

KLRK clerk *office aide*

KLRKL calorically *food energy*

KLRKL clerical (adj) *church, office* clerically (adv)

KLRKLKLR clerical collar *attire*

KLRKN chloracne *blemish*

KLRKS Clorox *(trademark)* bleach

KLRKST colorcast *television*
(Br) colourcast

KLRKT clear-cut *(adj) distinct (n) forest*

KLRKTL colorectal *bowel*

KLRL chloral *chemical*

KLRL clearly *obviously*

KLRLS collarless *neckline*

KLRLS colorless *no tint*
(Br) colourless

KLRMDR calorimeter *heat measure*

KLRMDR colorimeter *analyzer*
(Br) colourimeter

KLRMTR calorimeter *heat measure*

KLRMTR colorimeter *analyzer*
(Br) colourimeter

KLRMTRK calorimetric *heat measure*

KLRMTRKL calorimetrically *heat measure*

KLRN chlorine *element*

KLRN clarion *trumpet*

KLRN clearing *open area*

KLRN coloring *complexion, bias*
(Br) colouring

KLRNDD chlorinated *add chlorine*

KLRNDR chlorinator *add chlorine*

KLRNDST clarinetist *musician*

KLRNG clearing *open area*

KLRNG coloring *complexion, bias*
(Br) colouring

KLRNGHS clearinghouse *agency*

KLRNGKM chlorenchyma *chlorophyll*

KLRNHS clearinghouse *agency*

KLRNKM chlorenchyma *chlorophyll*

KLRNS clearance *sale, authorization, distance*

KLRNSHN chlorination *add chlorine*

KLRNT chlorinate *add chlorine* chlorinated chlorinating

KLRNT clarinet *music*

KLRNT colorant *tint*
(Br) colourant

KLRNTD chlorinated *add chlorine*

KLRNTR chlorinator *add chlorine*

Use letters that best describe the sounds you hear and omit the vowels. Use **S** or **K** instead of **C**: to find circle use **SRKL**. Use **J** to find joy, **JM** to find gem and **G** to find go.

KLRNTS clearance *sale, authorization, distance*
KLRNTST clarinetist *musician*
KLRPLST chloroplast *cell*
KLRPRMZN chlorpromazine *tranquilizer*
KLRS clerisy *intelligentsia*
KLRSDD clear-sighted *vision*
KLRSDR clerestory *gallery* clerestories
KLRSHN coloration *tint* (Br) colouration
KLRSS chlorosis *anemia*
KLRST colorist *tints* (Br) colourist
KLRST ocularist *glass eye*
KLRSTD clear-sighted *vision*
KLRSTR clerestory *gallery* clerestories
KLRT chlorate *chemical*
KLRT claret *wine*
KLRT clarity *lucid, clear*
KLRTR coloratura *singer*
KLRVNS clairvoyance *extrasensory perception*
KLRVNT clairvoyant *extrasensory perception*
KLRVNTS clairvoyance *extrasensory perception*
KLRVYNS clairvoyance *extrasensory perception*
KLRVYNT clairvoyant *extrasensory perception*
KLRVYNTS clairvoyance *extrasensory perception*
KLRWL killer whale *orca*
KLRWNG clearwing *moth*
KLRX Clorox *(trademark)* bleach
KLRYN clarion *trumpet*
KLRZ colorize *tint* colorized colorizing (Br) colourize
KLRZSHN colorization *tint* (Br) colourization
KLS callous *(adj, v) harden*
KLS callus *(n) skin* calluses
KLS chylous *lymph*

KLS class *(n) type, school, group (v) group** classes
KLS classy *elegant* classier classiest
KLS cloacae (pl) *chamber* cloaca
KLS close *(adj, adv) nearby, intimate* closer closest
KLS coalesce *unite* coalesced coalescing
KLS coleus *herb*
KLS colossi (pl) *giant* colossus
KLS coulisse *hallway*
KLS keyless *no key*
KLS oculus *window* oculi
KLSD callosity *hard and thick* callosities
KLSD chalcid *insect*
KLSDK clastic *rock fragments*
KLSDM colostomy *surgery* colostomies
KLSDN chalcedony *quartz* chalcedonies
KLSDNK chalcedonic *quartz*
KLSDR cloister *monastery, convent*
KLSDR cluster *group*
KLSDR clyster *enema*
KLSDR klister *wax*
KLSDRBM cluster bomb *weapon*
KLSDRD cloistered *sheltered*
KLSDRFB claustrophobe *fear of enclosure*
KLSDRFB claustrophobia *fear of enclosure*
KLSDRFBK claustrophobic *fear of enclosure*
KLSDRFBKL claustrophobically *fear of enclosure*
KLSDRFBY claustrophobia *fear of enclosure*
KLSDRL cholesterol *blood fat*
KLSDRL cloistral *secluded*
KLSF calcify *harden* calcified calcifying calcifies
KLSF classify *arrange, sort*

classified classifying classifies
KLSFBL classifiable *sort, arrange*
KLSFD calcified *hardened*
KLSFD classified *secret, sorted*
KLSFKSHN calcification *hardening*
KLSFKSHN classification *arrangement*
KLSFR classifier *machine, word*
KLSFRL calciferol *vitamin D*
KLSFRS calciferous *vitamin D*
KLSFSTD closefisted *stingy*
KLSFYBL classifiable *sort, arrange*
KLSFYR classifier *machine, word*
KLSGRND close-grained *texture*
KLSH achalasia *tightening*
KLSH calash *carriage, hood*
KLSH calechè (or) caleche *vehicle*
KLSH clash *conflict* clashes
KLSH clayish *mud*
KLSH cliché *trite saying*
KLSH cloche *hat*
KLSH collage *assemblage*
KLSHD clichéd *trite*
KLSHLDR cold shoulder (n) *ignore* cold-shoulder (v)
KLSHN chelation *combine with metal*
KLSHN coalition *union*
KLSHN collation *sort*
KLSHN collision *hit*
KLSHN collusion *plot*
KLSHN occlusion *obstruction, weather*
KLSHR clasher *conflict*
KLSHR closure *end*
KLSHRS clotheshorse *many clothes*
KLSK calcic *lime*
KLSK classic *enduring*
KLSKL classical (adj) *enduring* classically (adv)
KLSKL close call *near miss*

KLSKL kilocycle *unit*
KLSKNCHS class-conscious *status*
KLSKNCHSNS class-consciousness *status*
KLSKNSHS class-conscious *status*
KLSKNSHSNS class-consciousness *status*
KLSKRDRS close quarters *nearby*
KLSKRTRS close quarters *nearby*
KLSKWRDRS close quarters *nearby*
KLSKWRTRS close quarters *nearby*
KLSL callously *hard*
KLSL closely *strictly*
KLSL coleslaw *food*
KLSL colossal (adj) *giant* colossally (adv)
KLSL occlusal *teeth*
KLSM calcium *element*
KLSM coliseum *arena*
KLSM Colosseum *Roman arena*
KLSMN calcimine *plaster wash*
KLSMT classmate *school*
KLSMTHD closemouthed *silent*
KLSMTHT closemouthed *silent*
KLSN keelson *ship*
KLSNCZ calcinoses (pl) *disease* calcinosis
KLSNP cold snap *weather*
KLSNS callousness *hardness*
KLSNS classiness *elegance*
KLSNS closeness *nearness*
KLSNS coalescence *union*
KLSNSS calcinosis *disease* calcinoses
KLSNSZ calcinoses (pl) *disease* calcinosis
KLSNT acaulescent *no stem*
KLSNT coalescent *union*
KLSNTH colocynth *plant*
KLSNTS coalescence *union*
KLSP clasp *fasten, grip*
KLSP close-up *near*

KLSPR clasper *fasten, grip*
KLSQRDRS close quarters *nearby*
KLSQRTRS close quarters *nearby*
KLSR chelicera *fang* chelicerae
KLSR classier *elegant*
KLSR closer *near*
KLSR cold sore *blister*
KLSRDR close order *troops*
KLSRKT closed-circuit *television*
KLSRM classroom *school*
KLSS colossus *giant* colossi
KLSSDDS cholecystitis *gallbladder*
KLSSDKNN cholecystokinin *hormone*
KLSSDTS cholecystitis *gallbladder*
KLSSST classicist *scholar*
KLSST classicist *scholar*
KLSST classiest *elegant*
KLSST classist *prejudiced*
KLSST closest *nearest*
KLSSTDS cholecystitis *gallbladder*
KLSSTKNN cholecystokinin *hormone*
KLSSTTS cholecystitis *gallbladder*
KLST calcite *mineral*
KLST callosity *hard and thick* callosities
KLST clast *rock fragment*
KLST oculist *eye doctor*
KLSTHNK calisthenic *exercise*
KLSTHNKS calisthenics *exercise*
KLSTK clastic *rock fragments*
KLSTM colostomy *surgery* colostomies
KLSTNN calcitonin *hormone*
KLSTR cloister *monestary, convent*
KLSTR cluster *group*
KLSTR clyster *enema*
KLSTR klister *wax*
KLSTRBM cluster bomb *weapon*

KLSTRD cloistered *sheltered*
KLSTRFB claustrophobe *fear of enclosure*
KLSTRFB claustrophobia *fear of enclosure*
KLSTRFBK claustrophobic *fear of enclosure*
KLSTRFBKL claustrophobically *fear of enclosure*
KLSTRFBY claustrophobia *fear of enclosure*
KLSTRJ cold storage *cooler, abeyance*
KLSTRL cholesterol *blood fat*
KLSTRL cloistral *secluded*
KLSTRL colostral *milk*
KLSTRM colostrum *milk*
KLSV collusive *secret*
KLSV occlusive *obstruct, conceal*
KLSWT cold sweat *perspiration*
KLSYM calcium *element*
KLSYM coliseum *arena*
KLSYM Colosseum *Roman arena*
KLSYR classier *elegant*
KLSYST classiest *elegant*
KLSZ calices (pl) *cup* calix
KLSZ calxes (or) calces (pl) *residue* calx
KLSZ calyxes (or) calyces (pl) *flower* calyx
KLSZM classism *prejudice*
KLT acolyte *disciple*
KLT auklet *bird*
KLT calotte *skullcap*
KLT Celt *Indo-European*
KLT chelate *combine with metal* chelated chelating
KLT cleat *shoe spike*
KLT clot *coagulate* clotted clotting
KLT clout *power, hit*
KLT collate *sort* collated collating
KLT collet *collar*
KLT colt *young horse*
KLT culet *armor*
KLT cullet *glass*

KLT culotte *divided skirt* culottes
KLT cult *sect*
KLT kilt *Scottish skirt*
KLT kiltie (or) kilty *shoe*
KLT occult *(n, adj) secret (v) cover*
KLTBL chelatable *combine with metal*
KLTD clotted *thick*
KLTH cloth *fabric* cloths
KLTH clothe *attire* clothed (or) clad clothing
KLTHBND clothbound *book cover*
KLTHN clothing *attire*
KLTHNG clothing *attire*
KLTHR clothier *garment maker or seller*
KLTHYR clothier *garment maker or seller*
KLTHZ clothes *attire*
KLTK Celtic *Indo-European*
KLTMNSTR Clytemnestra *Greek myth*
KLTN kiloton *weight*
KLTNG cladding *metal*
KLTP calotype *photography*
KLTR chelator *combine with metal*
KLTR clatter *noise*
KLTR cloture *end*
KLTR clutter *mess*
KLTR coal tar *distillation*
KLTR collator *sorter*
KLTR coulter *tool*
KLTR culture *(v) grow* cultured culturing
KLTR culture *(n)customs, growth medium*
KLTR kilter *slant*
KLTR kultur *(often capitalized) culture*
KLTRD culturati *people*
KLTRD cultured *refined, produced artificially*
KLTRDKDM clitoridectomy *surgery* clitoridectomies
KLTRDKTM clitoridectomy *surgery* clitoridectomies
KLTRDV acculturative *adoption of traits*

KLTRDZ clitorides (pl) *sex organ* clitoris
KLTRK clitoric *sex organ*
KLTRK cold turkey *withdrawal*
KLTRL clitoral *sex organ*
KLTRL collateral *(n) payment*
KLTRL collateral (adj) *indirect* collaterally (adv)
KLTRL cultural (adj) *culture* culturally (adv)
KLTRLZ collateralize *secure* collateralized collateralizing
KLTRP caltrop *herb*
KLTRS call letters *radio*
KLTRS clitoris *sex organ* clitorides
KLTRSHN acculturation *adoption of traits*
KLTRSHNL acculturational *adoption of traits*
KLTRT acculturate *adopt traits* acculturated acculturating
KLTRT culturati *people*
KLTRTV acculturative *adoption of traits*
KLTS colitis *colon disease*
KLTS culottes *skirt*
KLTS klutz *clumsy* klutzy
KLTSFT coltsfoot *plant* coltsfoots
KLTSH cloddish *oaf, lump*
KLTSH coltish *frisky*
KLTSHN occultation *hidden*
KLTSHNS cloddishness *oaf, lump*
KLTSHNS coltishness *frisky*
KLTSNS klutziness *clumsiness*
KLTST cultist *sect*
KLTST occultist *supernatural*
KLTTD colatitude *complement of latitude*
KLTVBL cultivable *crops*
KLTVDBL cultivatable *crops*
KLTVDD cultivated *refined*
KLTVDR cultivator *tool*
KLTVSHN cultivation *culture, crops*
KLTVT cultivate *crops,*

encourage cultivated cultivating
KLTVTBL cultivatable *crops*
KLTVTD cultivated *refined*
KLTVTR cultivator *tool*
KLTZ klutz *clumsy* klutzy
KLTZM cultism *sect*
KLTZM occultism *supernatural*
KLTZNS klutziness *clumsiness*
KLV cleave *cling* cleaved cleaving
KLV clove *tree, spice*
KLVBL cleavable *split*
KLVD acclivity *slope* acclivities
KLVJ cleavage *split, breasts*
KLVKL clavicle *collarbone*
KLVKLR clavicular *collarbone*
KLVKRD clavichord *music*
KLVKRDST clavichordist *musician*
KLVKYLR clavicular *collarbone*
KLVLN Cleveland *city*
KLVLND Cleveland *city*
KLVLT kilovolt *electricity*
KLVN cloven *two parts*
KLVN Kelvin *scale*
KLVN kelvin *unit*
KLVNSDK Calvinistic *religion*
KLVNST Calvinist *religion*
KLVNSTK Calvinistic *religion*
KLVNZM Calvinism *religion*
KLVQLR clavicular *collarbone*
KLVR calvary *hill* calvaries
KLVR cavalry *horse* cavalries
KLVR clavier *keyboard*
KLVR cleaver *tool*
KLVR clever *smart*
KLVR clover *plant*
KLVR culver *pigeon*
KLVRL cleverly *smartly*
KLVRLF cloverleaf *overpass* cloverleafs (or) cloverleaves
KLVRNS cleverness *smartness*

Letters aren't doubled for single sounds: to find alley use **L** not **LL**. Use **Y** and **W** as hard sounds only: to find yellow use **YL**. (Br)=British spelling or usage. * See dictionary.

KLVRSH cleverish *smart*
KLVRT culvert *drain*
KLVS clevis *shackle*
KLVT acclivity *slope* acclivities
KLVYR clavier *keyboard*
KLW Chloe *lover*
KLWK cloaca *chamber* cloacae
KLWKL cloacal *chamber*
KLWR Cold War *conflict*
KLWR couloir *gorge*
KLWS cloacae (pl) *chamber* cloaca
KLWT kilowatt *electricity*
KLWTR kilowatt-hour *electricity*
KLWTWR kilowatt-hour *electricity*
KLWV cold wave *weather, hair*
KLWZN cloisonné *enamel*
KLX calix *cup* calices
KLX calx *residue* calxes (or) calces
KLX calyx *flower* calyxes (or) calyces
KLX culex *mosquito*
KLXN Klaxon *(trademark) horn*
KLY clayey *earthy*
KLY Clio *award*
KLYBRD colubrid *snake*
KLYBRN colubrine *snake*
KLYD chiliad *thousand*
KLYML columella *column* columellae
KLYMLR columellar *column*
KLYMT calumet *pipe*
KLYNG cloying *sweet*
KLYNGL cloyingly *sweet*
KLYNT client *customer*
KLYNTL clientele *customers*
KLYP Calliope *Greek muse*
KLYP calliope *organ*
KLYPDR coleoptera *beetle*
KLYPDRS coleopterous *beetle*
KLYPDRST coleopterist *beetles*
KLYPTR Cleopatra *queen*
KLYPTR coleoptera *beetle*

KLYPTRS coleopterous *beetle*
KLYPTRST coleopterist *beetles*
KLYR collier *coal miner*
KLYR colliery *coal mine*
KLYS coleus *herb*
KLYSH clayish *mud*
KLZ Achilles *Greek hero*
KLZ chalaza *egg* chalazae (or) chalazas
KLZ clause *words*
KLZ close *(n) conclusion*
KLZ close *(v) shut, end* closed closing
KLZ clothes *attire*
KLZD closed *not open*
KLZDN closed-end *agreement*
KLZDN closedown *operations halt*
KLZDND closed-end *agreement*
KLZDSRKT closed-circuit *television*
KLZH achalasia *tightening*
KLZH collage *assemblage*
KLZHL Achilles' heel *weak spot*
KLZHN collision *hit*
KLZHN collusion *plot*
KLZHN occlusion *obstruction, weather*
KLZHR closure *end*
KLZHRS clotheshorse *many clothes*
KLZL clausal *words*
KLZL occlusal *teeth*
KLZLG ecclesiology *church* ecclesiologies
KLZLJ ecclesiology *church* ecclesiologies
KLZLN clothesline *rope*
KLZMTHD closemouthed *silent*
KLZMTHT closemouthed *silent*
KLZN calzone *food* calzone (or) calzones
KLZN cloisonné *enamel*
KLZN closing *end*
KLZNG closing *end*

KLZPN clothespin *fastener*
KLZPRS clothespress *receptacle*
KLZR closer *salesman*
KLZR kala-azar *disease*
KLZRS clotheshorse *many clothes*
KLZSDK ecclesiastic *clergy*
KLZSDKL ecclesiastical (adj) *clergy* ecclesiastically (adv)
KLZSFSDD closefisted *stingy*
KLZSRKT closed circuit *television*
KLZSTK ecclesiastic *clergy*
KLZSTKL ecclesiastical (adj) *clergy* ecclesiastically (adv)
KLZT close out *(v) exclude, sell, end*
KLZT closeout *(n) sale*
KLZT closet *room, secret*
KLZV collusive *secret*
KLZV occlusive *obstruct, conceal*
KLZYLG ecclesiology *church* ecclesiologies
KLZYLJ ecclesiology *church* ecclesiologies
KLZYSDK ecclesiastic *clergy*
KLZYSDKL ecclesiastical (adj) *clergy* ecclesiastically (adv)
KLZYSTK ecclesiastic *clergy*
KLZYSTKL ecclesiastical (adj) *clergy* ecclesiastically (adv)
KM acme *summit*
KM calm *serene*
KM cam *engine part*
KM came *(v-past) come*
KM camellia *shrub*
KM cameo *pendant, small role* cameos
KM chemo *(abbr) chemotherapy*
KM chyme *digestion*
KM coma *sleep*
KM comb *(n) hair tool, crest*

Use letters that best describe the sounds you hear and omit the vowels. Use **S** or **K** instead of **C**: to find circle use **SRKL**. Use **J** to find joy, **JM** to find gem and **G** to find go.

(v) search, arrange hair
KM combe *valley*
KM come *arrive, happen, extend* came coming
KM comma *punctuation*
KM commie *(often capitalized) communist*
KM cum *(prep) with*
KM cwm *(Br) basin*
KM kame *mound*
KM khoum *money*
KM oakum *caulk*
KMB akimbo *stance*
KMB cambia (pl) *plant layer* cambium
KMB combo *band, mixture* combos
KMBD Cambodia *country*
KMBDN Cambodian *of Cambodia*
KMBDNT combatant *fighter*
KMBDV combative *fighting*
KMBDVNS combativeness *fight*
KMBDY Cambodia *country*
KMBDYN Cambodian *of Cambodia*
KMBK come back *(v) return, regain, retort* came back coming back
KMBK comeback *(n) retort, rally*
KMBM cambium *plant layer* cambiums (or) cambia
KMBN combine *mix* combined combining
KMBNBL combinable *mix*
KMBNDV combinative *mixed*
KMBNR combiner *mixer*
KMBNSHN combination *mixture*
KMBNTV combinative *mixed*
KMBR camber *curve*
KMBR cumber *hinder*
KMBRBN cummerbund *belt*
KMBRBND cummerbund *belt*
KMBRJ Cambridge *city*
KMBRK cambric *fabric*
KMBRN Cambrian *Welsh,*

geologic era
KMBRS cumbrous *heavy*
KMBRSL cumbrously *heavy*
KMBRSM cumbersome *heavy*
KMBRSNS cumbrousness *heavy*
KMBRYN Cambrian *Welsh, geologic era*
KMBSCHN combustion *burn*
KMBSDBL combustible (adj) *burn* combustibly (adv)
KMBSDBLD combustibility *burn*
KMBSDBLT combustibility *burn*
KMBSDR combustor *burn chamber*
KMBST combust *burn*
KMBSTBL combustible (adj) *burn* combustibly (adv)
KMBSTBLD combustibility *burn*
KMBSTBLT combustibility *burn*
KMBSTR combustor *burn chamber*
KMBT combat *fight* combated (or) combatted combating (or) combatting
KMBTNT combatant *fighter*
KMBTV combative *fighting*
KMBTVNS combativeness *fight*
KMBY cambia (pl) *plant layer* cambium
KMBYM cambium *plant layer* cambiums (or) cambia
KMCH kimchi *food*
KMD comedy *funny* comedies
KMD comity *community* comities
KMD committee *group*
KMD commode *cap, toilet*
KMDBL commitable *consign*
KMDBL commutable

changeable
KMDD committed *bound*
KMDD commodity *goods* commodities
KMDDNG accommodating *obliging*
KMDDR accommodator *worker*
KMDDV accommodative *adaptive*
KMDDVNS accommodativeness *adaptivity*
KMDK comedic *funny*
KMDK cometic *meteor*
KMDL committal *agreement*
KMDMN committeeman *member* committeemen
KMDN Camden *city*
KMDN comedian *comic (m)*
KMDN comedienne *comic (f)*
KMDN comedown (n) *descend* come down (v)
KMDN commanding *attention, difficulty*
KMDNG commanding *attention, difficulty*
KMDR commodore *navy*
KMDR commuter *traveler*
KMDS commodious *spacious*
KMDSHN accommodation *lodging, settlement*
KMDSHN accommodation *place, condition*
KMDSHNL accommodational *adaptive*
KMDSHNST accommodationist *adaptive*
KMDT accommodate *fit* accommodated accommodating
KMDT commodity *goods* commodities
KMDTN accommodating *obliging*
KMDTNG accommodating *obliging*
KMDTNGL accommodatingly

Letters aren't doubled for single sounds: to find alley use **L** not **LL**. Use **Y** and **W** as hard sounds only: to find yellow use **YL**. (Br)=British spelling or usage. * See dictionary.

obligingly
KMDTNL accommodatingly *obligingly*
KMDTR accommodator *worker*
KMDTV accommodative *adaptive*
KMDTVNS accommodativeness *adaptivity*
KMDV calmative *serene*
KMDYN comedian *comic (m)*
KMDYN comedienne *comic (f)*
KMDYS commodious *spacious*
KMF comfy *cozy*
KMFLJ camouflage *disguise* camouflaged camouflaging
KMFLSH camouflage *disguise* camouflaged camouflaging
KMFLZH camouflage *disguise* camouflaged camouflaging
KMFR campfire *flame*
KMFR camphor *tree, chemical*
KMFR comfrey *herb* comfreys
KMFRDBL comfortable (adj) *cozy, easy* comfortably (adv)
KMFRDBLNS comfortableness *cozy, easy*
KMFRDNGL comfortingly *consoling*
KMFRDR comforter *bed cover, consoler*
KMFRT comfort *console*
KMFRTBL comfortable (adj) *cozy, easy* comfortably (adv)
KMFRTBLNS comfortableness *cozy, easy*
KMFRTNGL comfortingly *consoling*
KMFRTR comforter *bed*

cover, consoler
KMFT comfit *candy*
KMFYR campfire *flame*
KMGRF kymograph *device*
KMGRM kymogram *record*
KMHTHR come-hither *inviting*
KMJN curmudgeon *miser*
KMK comic *funny, comedian*
KMKBK comic book *magazine*
KMKL chemical *substance*
KMKL chemical (n, adj) *substance* chemically (adv)
KMKL comical (adj) *funny* comically (adv)
KMKLN come clean *confess*
KMKR comaker *agreement*
KMKRDR camcorder *camera*
KMKS commix *mingle* commixes
KMKSCHR commixture *compound*
KMKSTR commixture *compound*
KMKSTRP comic strip *cartoon*
KMKSTYR commixture *compound*
KMKWT kumquat *fruit*
KMKZ kamikaze *suicide pilot*
KML calmly *serenely*
KML camel *animal*
KML camellia *shrub*
KML comely *pretty* comelier comeliest
KML kümmel *liqueur*
KMLD cum laude *with distinction*
KMLDR accumulator *gatherer*
KMLDV accumulative *gathered*
KMLDV cumulative *additional*
KMLF comme il faut *proper*
KMLFLJ camouflage *disguise* camouflaged camouflaging
KMLFLSH camouflage *disguise* camouflaged

camouflaging
KMLFLZH camouflage *disguise* camouflaged camouflaging
KMLHR camel hair *fur*
KMLN chameleon *animal, easily changed*
KMLNK chameleonic *animal, easily changed*
KMLNMBS cumulonimbus *cloud*
KMLNS comeliness *prettiness*
KMLR comelier *prettier*
KMLS cumulous *cloudlike*
KMLS cumulus *cloud*
KMLSHN accumulation *gathering*
KMLSHN cumulation *mass*
KMLST comeliest *prettiest*
KMLT accumulate *gather* accumulated accumulating
KMLT Camelot *imaginary kingdom*
KMLT camlet *fabric*
KMLT cumulate *amass* cumulated cumulating
KMLTR accumulator *gatherer*
KMLTV accumulative *gathered*
KMLTV cumulative *additional*
KMLY camellia *shrub*
KMLYN chameleon *animal, easily changed*
KMLYNK chameleonic *animal, easily changed*
KMLYR comelier *prettier*
KMLYST comeliest *prettiest*
KMMBR Camembert *cheese*
KMML chamomile *herb*
KMMRDR commemorator *observer*
KMMRDV commemorative *remember*
KMMRSHN commemoration *remembrance*
KMMRT commemorate *remember* commemorated

commemorating
KMMRTR commemorator
observer
KMMRTV commemorative
remember
KMN acumen *keenness*
KMN caiman *crocodile*
KMN camion *truck, bus*
KMN coaming *frame*
KMN come on *(v) advance,*
please
KMN come-on *(n) lure*
KMN coming *arriving, soon*
KMN command *order*
KMN commend *praise*
KMN common *everyday*
KMN commune *(v) discuss*
commenced communing
KMN commune *(n)*
community
KMN cowman *ranch hand*
cowmen
KMN cumin *spice*
KMN Khomeini *religious*
leader
KMN kimono *robe* kimonos
KMNCH Comanche *Native*
American
KMND command *order*
KMND commando *soldier*
commandos (or)
commandoes
KMND commend *praise*
KMND community *state,*
fellowship communities
KMND kimonoed *robed*
KMNDBL commandable
order
KMNDBL commendable
(adj) *praise* commendably
(adv)
KMNDMNT commandment
demand
KMNDNT commandant
leader
KMNDPST command post
headquarters
KMNDR commandeer *lead*
KMNDR commander *leader*
KMNDR commandery
district commanderies
KMNDR commender *praiser*

KMNDR komondor *dog*
komondors (or)
komondorok
KMNDRK komondorok (pl)
dog komondor
KMNDRNCHF commander
in chief *supreme leader*
KMNDSHN commendation
citation
KMNDTR commendatory
praiseworthy
KMNG coaming *frame*
KMNG coming *arriving, soon*
KMNGGL commingle
combine commingled
commingling
KMNGL commingle *combine*
commingled
commingling
KMNGS combings *hair*
KMNK communiqué *memo*
KMNKBL communicable
(adj) *able to pass on*
communicably (adv)
KMNKBLD communicability
ability to pass on
KMNKBLT communicability
ability to pass on
KMNKDR communicator
talker
KMNKDV communicative
talkative
KMNKDVL
communicatively *talkative*
KMNKDVNS
communicativeness
talkative
KMNKL ecumenical (adj)
church ecumenically (adv)
(Br) oecumenical
KMNKNT communicant
church, informant
KMNKS ecumenics *church*
KMNKSHN communication
signal, words
KMNKT communicate *make*
known communicated
communicating
KMNKT communicatee
receiver
KMNKTR communicator
talker

KMNKTV communicative
talkative
KMNKTVL communicatively
talkative
KMNKTVNS
communicativeness
talkative
KMNL common-law (adj)
legal common law (n)
KMNL commonly *usually*
KMNL communal (adj)
community communally
(adv)
KMNLD commonality *alike*
commonalities
KMNLNZ Cayman Islands
land mass
KMNLT commonality *alike*
commonalities
KMNLT commonalty *people*
commonalties
KMNLZ communalize *group*
communalized
communalizing
KMNMNT commandment
demand
KMNMRKT Common
Market *Europe*
KMNN communion
sacrament, connection
KMNPLS commonplace
everyday
KMNPST command post
headquarters
KMNR commoner *peasant*
KMNS calmness *serenity*
KMNS combings *hair*
KMNS commence *begin*
commenced
commencing
KMNS commonness
everyday
KMNSHRBL
commensurable (adj)
common measure
commensurably (adv)
KMNSHRSHN
commensuration *equality*
KMNSHRT commensurate
equal
KMNSL commensal (adj)
equally beneficial

Letters aren't doubled for single sounds: to find alley use **L** not **LL**. Use **Y** and **W** as hard sounds only: to find yellow use **YL**. (Br)=British spelling or usage. * See dictionary.

commensally (adv)

KMNSLZM commensalism
equally beneficial

KMNSMNT
commencement
beginning, ceremony

KMNSNS common sense
(n) *sensible* commonsense
(adj)

KMNSNTS common sense
(n) *sensible* commonsense
(adj)

KMNSR commencer
beginner

KMNSRBL commensurable
(adj) *common measure*
commensurably (adv)

KMNSRSHN
commensuration *equality*

KMNSRT commensurate
equal

KMNST communist
collectivist

KMNST ecumenist *church*

KMNSTK communistic
collective

KMNSTKL communistically
collective

KMNT acuminate *tapered*

KMNT comment *observation*

KMNT community *state,
fellowship* communities

KMNTDR commentator
explainer

KMNTR commentary
explanation commentaries

KMNTRN communitarian
social collective

KMNTRNZM
communitarianism *social
collective*

KMNTRYN communitarian
social collective

KMNTRYNZM
communitarianism *social
collective*

KMNTS commence *begin*
commenced
commencing

KMNTSHRBL
commensurable (adj)
common measure

commensurably (adv)

KMNTSHRSHN
commensuration *equality*

KMNTSHRT commensurate
equal

KMNTSL commensal (adj)
equally beneficial
commensally (adv)

KMNTSLZM
commensalism *equally
beneficial*

KMNTSMNT
commencement
beginning, ceremony

KMNTSR commencer
beginner

KMNTSRBL
commensurable (adj)
common measure
commensurably (adv)

KMNTSRSHN
commensuration *equality*

KMNTSRT commensurate
equal

KMNTT commentate *explain*
commentated
commenting

KMNTTR commentator
explainer

KMNWL commonweal
welfare

KMNWLTH commonwealth
republic

KMNX ecumenics *church*

KMNYN communion
sacrament, connection

KMNZ Caymans *islands*

KMNZ communize *make
common* communized
communizing
(Br) communise

KMNZM communism
collectivism

KMNZM ecumenism *church*

KMNZSHN communization
make common
(Br) communisation

KMP camp *tents, cabins*

KMP campo *grassland*
campos

KMP campy *theatrical*

KMP comp *free*

KMP compo *materials*
compos

KMP kemp *fiber*

KMPCH Kampuchea
country

KMPCHY Kampuchea
country

KMPDBL compatible (adj)
harmonious compatibly
(adv)

KMPDBL computable
calculate

KMPDBLD compatibility
harmony

KMPDBLD computability
calculate

KMPDBLNS
compatibleness *harmony*

KMPDBLT compatibility
harmony

KMPDBLT computability
calculate

KMPDD computed
calculated

KMPDDR competitor *rival*

KMPDDV competitive
contest

KMPDDVL competitively
contest

KMPDDVNS
competitiveness *contest*

KMPDNC competency
ability competencies

KMPDNS competence
ability

KMPDNS competency
ability competencies

KMPDNT competent *able*

KMPDNTC competency
ability competencies

KMPDNTS competence
ability

KMPDNTS competency
ability competencies

KMPDR compadre
companion

KMPDR computer *data
device*

KMPDRZ computerese
language

KMPDRZ computerize *data
device* computerized

Use letters that best describe the sounds you hear and omit the vowels. Use **S** or **K** instead of **C**: to find circle use **SRKL**. Use **J** to find joy, **JM** to find gem and **G** to find go.

computerizing
(Br) computerise
KMPDRZD computerized
data device
(Br) computerised
KMPDRZSHN
computerization *data
device*
(Br) computerisation
KMPDTR competitor *rival*
KMPDTV competitive
contest
KMPDTVL competitively
contest
KMPDTVNS
competitiveness *contest*
KMPFR campfire *flame*
KMPFYR campfire *flame*
KMPGRN campground *tent
area*
KMPGRND campground
tent area
KMPK compact *(n) case, car,
agreement (adj) dense (v)
compress*
KMPKDR compactor
compressor
KMPKL compactly *densely*
KMPKNS compactness
density
KMPKSHN compaction
compressed
KMPKT compact *(n) case,
car, agreement (adj) dense
(v) compress*
KMPKTL compactly *densely*
KMPKTNS compactness
density
KMPKTR compactor
compressor
KMPL campily *theatrical*
KMPL compel *force*
compelled compelling
KMPL compile *collect*
compiled compiling
KMPL comply *conform*
complied complying
complies
KMPL Kampala *city*
KMPLBL compellable *force*
KMPLDV completive *finish*
KMPLKC complicacy

difficulty complicacies
KMPLKDD complected *skin*
KMPLKDD complicated
difficult
KMPLKDDL complicatedly
difficult
KMPLKDDNS
complicatedness
difficulty
KMPLKS complex *(adj)
intricate (n) group*
complexes
KMPLKS complicacy
difficulty complicacies
KMPLKSD complexity
details complexities
KMPLKSHN complexion
skin
KMPLKSHN complication
difficulty
KMPLKSHND
complexioned *skin*
KMPLKSL complexly
detailed
KMPLKSNS complexness
difficulty, involvement
KMPLKST complexity
details complexities
KMPLKT complicate *make
difficult* complicated
complicating
KMPLKTD complected *skin*
KMPLKTD complicated
difficult
KMPLKTDL complicatedly
difficult
KMPLKTDNS
complicatedness
difficulty
KMPLMNL complemental
corresponding part
KMPLMNR complementary
completing
KMPLMNR complimentary
praise, free
KMPLMNT complement
corresponding part
KMPLMNT compliment
praise
KMPLMNTL complemental
corresponding part
KMPLMNTR

complementary
completing
KMPLMNTR
complimentary *praise, free*
KMPLN compelling *forceful,
convincing*
KMPLN complain *whine,
accuse*
KMPLNG compelling
forceful, convincing
KMPLNNGL complainingly
whine, accuse
KMPLNNL complainingly
whine, accuse
KMPLNNT complainant
accuser
KMPLNR complainer
whiner, accuser
KMPLNS compliance
conformity compliancy
KMPLNT complaint *outcry,
ailment*
KMPLNT compliant
submissive
KMPLNTL compliantly
submissive
KMPLNTNT complainant
accuser
KMPLNTS compliance
conformity compliancy
KMPLR complier *conformer*
KMPLS accomplice
associate
KMPLSD complicity
association complicities
KMPLSDS complicitous
association
KMPLSH accomplish
perform accomplishes
KMPLSHBL
accomplishable *achievable*
KMPLSHD accomplished
proficient
KMPLSHMNT
accomplishment
achievement
KMPLSHN compellation
address
KMPLSHN compilation
collection
KMPLSHN completion
finish

KMPLSHN compulsion *urge*

KMPLSHR accomplisher *performer*

KMPLSHT accomplished *proficient*

KMPLSNC complacency *satisfaction* complacencies

KMPLSNS complacence *satisfaction*

KMPLSNS complacency *satisfaction* complacencies

KMPLSNS complaisance *friendliness*

KMPLSNT complacent *satisfied*

KMPLSNT complaisant *kindly*

KMPLSNTC complacency *satisfaction* complacencies

KMPLSNTL complacently *satisfied*

KMPLSNTL complaisantly *kindly*

KMPLSNTS complacence *satisfaction*

KMPLSNTS complacency *satisfaction* complacencies

KMPLSNTS complaisance *friendliness*

KMPLSR compulsory *required*

KMPLSRL compulsorily *required*

KMPLST complicit *associated*

KMPLST complicity *association* complicities

KMPLSTS complicitous *association*

KMPLSV compulsive *compelled*

KMPLSVD compulsivity *compelled*

KMPLSVL compulsively *compelled*

KMPLSVNS compulsiveness *compelled*

KMPLSVT compulsivity *compelled*

KMPLT complete (*v*) *end, fulfill* completed completing

KMPLT complete (*adj*) *total, conclude*

KMPLTL completely *totally*

KMPLTNS completeness *totality*

KMPLTV completive *finish*

KMPLX complex (*adj*) *intricate* (*n*) *group* complexes

KMPLXD complexity *details* complexities

KMPLXL complexly *detailed*

KMPLXNS complexness *difficulty, involvement*

KMPLXT complexity *details* complexities

KMPLYNS compliance *conformity* compliancy

KMPLYNT compliant *submissive*

KMPLYNTL compliantly *submissive*

KMPLYNTS compliance *conformity* compliancy

KMPLYR complier *conformer*

KMPLZNS complaisance *friendliness*

KMPLZNT complaisant *kindly*

KMPLZNTL complaisantly *kindly*

KMPLZNTS complaisance *friendliness*

KMPLZR compulsory *required*

KMPLZV compulsive *compelled*

KMPLZVL compulsively *compelled*

KMPLZVNS compulsiveness *compelled*

KMPN accompany *go with* accompanied accompanying accompanies

KMPN campaign *operations*

KMPN company *group, business* companies

KMPN compound (*v*) *combine, augment* (*n*) *combination, buildings*

KMPND compendia (pl) *list* compendium

KMPND compound (*v*) *combine, augment* (*n*) *combination, buildings*

KMPNDBL compoundable *put together*

KMPNDM compendium *list* compendiums (or) compendia

KMPNDR compounder *put together*

KMPNDS compendious *concise*

KMPNDY compendia (pl) *list* compendium

KMPNDYM compendium *list* compendiums (or) compendia

KMPNDYS compendious *concise*

KMPNG kampong *village*

KMPNGKSHN compunction *qualm*

KMPNGSHN compunction *qualm*

KMPNKSHN compunction *qualm*

KMPNL campanile *tower* campaniles (or) campanili

KMPNL campanula *flower*

KMPNLG campanology *bell ringing*

KMPNLJ campanology *bell ringing*

KMPNLT campanulate *bell-shaped*

KMPNMNT accompaniment *association with*

KMPNNT component *part*

KMPNR campaigner *operator*

KMPNS campiness *theatrical*

KMPNS comeuppance *rebuke*

Use letters that best describe the sounds you hear and omit the vowels. Use **S** or **K** instead of **C**: to find circle use **SRKL**. Use **J** to find joy, **JM** to find gem and **G** to find go.

KMPNSBL compensable *payment*
KMPNSBLD compensability *payment*
KMPNSBLT compensability *payment*
KMPNSDR compensator *balance, pay*
KMPNSSHN compensation *balance, pay*
KMPNST accompanist *musician*
KMPNST compensate *balance, pay* compensated compensating
KMPNSTR compensator *balance, pay*
KMPNSTR compensatory *balance, pay*
KMPNT component *part*
KMPNTS comeuppance *rebuke*
KMPNTSBL compensable *payment*
KMPNTSBLD compensability *payment*
KMPNTSBLT compensability *payment*
KMPNYL campanula *flower*
KMPNYLT campanulate *bell-shaped*
KMPNYN companion *comrade*
KMPNYNBL companionable (adj) *sociable* companionably (adv)
KMPNYNSHP companionship *company*
KMPNYNW companionway *stairway*
KMPR camper *tent, vehicle*
KMPR compare *judge* compared comparing
KMPR compeer *equal*
KMPR compere *host* compered (or) compered compering (or) compering
KMPRBL comparable (adj) *alike* comparably
KMPRBLD comparability

alikeness
KMPRBLNS comparableness *alikeness*
KMPRBLT comparability *alikeness*
KMPRDR comparator *measurer*
KMPRDST comparatist *comparison*
KMPRDV comparative *relatively*
KMPRDVL comparatively *relatively*
KMPRGDR compurgator *voucher*
KMPRGSHN compurgation *clearing*
KMPRGTR compurgator *voucher*
KMPRHN comprehend *understand*
KMPRHNCHN comprehension *understanding*
KMPRHND comprehend *understand*
KMPRHNDBL comprehendible *understandable*
KMPRHNSBL comprehensible (adj) *intelligible* comprehensibly (adv)
KMPRHNSBLD comprehensibility *intelligible*
KMPRHNSBLT comprehensibility *intelligible*
KMPRHNSHN comprehension *understanding*
KMPRHNSV comprehensive *inclusive*
KMPRHNSVL comprehensively *inclusive*
KMPRHNSVNS comprehensiveness *inclusion*
KMPRHNTSBL comprehensible (adj)

intelligible
comprehensibly (adv)
KMPRHNTSBLD comprehensibility *intelligible*
KMPRHNTSBLT comprehensibility *intelligible*
KMPRHNTSV comprehensive *inclusive*
KMPRHNTSVL comprehensively *inclusive*
KMPRHNTSVNS comprehensiveness *inclusion*
KMPRMZ compromise *(v)* *adjust, impair* compromised compromising
KMPRMZ compromise *(n)* *settlement*
KMPRMZR compromiser *adjust, impair*
KMPRS compress (n) pad, *machine (v) squeeze* compresses
KMPRSBL compressible *flattened*
KMPRSBLD compressibility *flattened*
KMPRSBLT compressibility *flattened*
KMPRSD compressed *flattened*
KMPRSDL compressedly *flattened*
KMPRSHN compression *flatten*
KMPRSHNL compressional *flatten*
KMPRSN comparison *similarity*
KMPRSR compressor *muscle, machine*
KMPRST compressed *flattened*
KMPRSV compressive *flatten*
KMPRSVL compressively *flatten*
KMPRT comport *behave*

Letters aren't doubled for single sounds: to find alley use **L** not **LL**. Use **Y** and **W** as hard sounds only: to find yellow use **YL**. (Br)=British spelling or usage. * See dictionary.

KMPRTMNL
compartmental *sectioned*
KMPRTMNLZ
compartmentalize *section*
compartmentalized
compartmentalizing
(Br) compartmentalise
KMPRTMNLZSHN
compartmentalization
section
(Br)
compartmentalisation
KMPRTMNT compartment
section
KMPRTMNT comportment
behavior
KMPRTMNTL
compartmental *sectioned*
KMPRTMNTLZ
compartmentalize *section*
compartmentalized
compartmentalizing
(Br) compartmentalise
KMPRTMNTLZSHN
compartmentalization
section
(Br)
compartmentalisation
KMPRTR comparator
measurer
KMPRTST comparatist
comparison
KMPRTV comparative
relatively
KMPRTVL comparatively
relatively
KMPRZ comprise *constitute*
comprised comprising
KMPS campus *college*
campuses
KMPS compass *direction*
compasses
KMPSHN compassion *pity*
KMPSHNT compassionate
sympathetic
KMPSHNTL
compassionately
sympathetic
KMPSHR composure *self-control*
KMPSMNTS compos
mentis *of sound mind*

KMPSN campesino *laborer*
campesinos
KMPST campsite *tent area*
KMPST compost *garbage*
KMPT compete *rival*
competed competing
KMPT compote *food*
KMPT compute *calculate*
computed computing
KMPT kempt *neat*
KMPTBL compatible (adj)
harmonious compatibly
(adv)
KMPTBL computable
calculate
KMPTBLD compatibility
harmony
KMPTBLD computability
calculate
KMPTBLNS
compatibleness *harmony*
KMPTBLT compatibility
harmony
KMPTBLT computability
calculate
KMPTD computed
calculated
KMPTDR competitor *rival*
KMPTDV competitive
contest
KMPTDVL competitively
contest
KMPTDVNS
competitiveness *contest*
KMPTNC competency
ability competencies
KMPTNS competence
ability
KMPTNS competency
ability competencies
KMPTNT competent *able*
KMPTNTC competency
ability competencies
KMPTNTS competence
ability
KMPTNTS competency
ability competencies
KMPTR computer *data*
device
KMPTRLR comptroller
auditor
KMPTRT compatriot

colleague
KMPTRYT compatriot
colleague
KMPTRZ computerese
language
KMPTRZ computerize *data*
device computerized
computerizing
(Br) computerise
KMPTRZD computerized
data device
(Br) computerised
KMPTRZSHN
computerization *data*
device
(Br) computerisation
KMPTSHN competition
contest
KMPTSHN computation
calculation
KMPTSHNL computational
calculation
KMPTTR competitor *rival*
KMPTTV competitive
contest
KMPTTVL competitively
contest
KMPTTVNS
competitiveness *contest*
KMPYDBL computable
calculate
KMPYDBLD computability
calculate
KMPYDBLT computability
calculate
KMPYDD computed
calculated
KMPYDR computer *data*
device
KMPYDRZ computerese
language
KMPYDRZ computerize
data device computerized
computerizing
(Br) computerise
KMPYDRZD computerized
data device
(Br) computerised
KMPYDRZSHN
computerization *data*
device
(Br) computerisation

Use letters that best describe the sounds you hear and omit the vowels. Use **S** or **K** instead of **C**: to find circle use **SRKL**. Use **J** to find joy, **JM** to find gem and **G** to find go.

KMPYL compile *collect* compiled compiling
KMPYT compute *calculate* computed computing
KMPYTBL computable *calculate*
KMPYTBLD computability *calculate*
KMPYTBLT computability *calculate*
KMPYTD computed *calculated*
KMPYTR computer *data device*
KMPYTRZ computerese *language*
KMPYTRZ computerize *data device* computerized computerizing (Br) computerise
KMPYTRZD computerized *data device* (Br) computerised
KMPYTRZSHN computerization *data device* (Br) computerisation
KMPYTSHN computation *calculation*
KMPYTSHNL computational *calculation*
KMPZ compose *form, calm* composed composing
KMPZD composed *cool*
KMPZDL composedly *cool*
KMPZDR compositor *typesetter*
KMPZHR composure *self-control*
KMPZR composer *music writer*
KMPZSHN composition *combination, creation*
KMPZT composite *combination*
KMPZTL compositely *combination*
KMPZTR compositor *typesetter*
KMQT kumquat *fruit*
KMR camera *photograph*
KMR camorra *organization*

KMR chimera *monster*
KMR comber *searcher, wave*
KMR comer *shows promise*
KMR Cymry *Welsh*
KMRBN cummerbund *belt*
KMRBND cummerbund *belt*
KMRD comrade *associate*
KMRDR camaraderie *friendship*
KMRDSHP comradeship *friendship*
KMRJ Khmer Rouge *Cambodia*
KMRK Cymric *Welsh*
KMRKL chimerical (adj) *imaginary* chimerically (adv)
KMRLNDS Comoro Islands *land mass*
KMRLNZ Comoro Islands *land mass*
KMRMN cameraman *photographer* cameramen
KMRN Cameroon *country*
KMRPRSN cameraperson *photographer*
KMRS commerce *business*
KMRSH Khmer Rouge *Cambodia*
KMRSHL commercial (n) *advertisement*
KMRSHL commercial (adj) *business* commercially (adv)
KMRSHLZ commercialize *profit* commercialized commercializing (Br) commercialise
KMRSHLZM commercialism *profit*
KMRSHLZSHN commercialization *profit* (Br) commercialisation
KMRSPDR chemoreceptor *receiver*
KMRSPSHN chemoreception *response*
KMRSPTR chemoreceptor *receiver*
KMRWMN camerawoman *photographer* camerawomen

KMRZH Khmer Rouge *Cambodia*
KMS camise *shirt*
KMS koumiss *beverage*
KMSDBL comestible *edible*
KMSDR chemistry *science* chemistries
KMSH cumshaw *gratuity*
KMSHF camshaft *engine*
KMSHFT camshaft *engine*
KMSHN commission *agency, order*
KMSHN commotion *unrest*
KMSHND commissioned *officer*
KMSHNR commissionaire *doorman*
KMSHNR commissioner *chief*
KMSL camisole *negligee*
KMSN khamsin *wind*
KMSR commissar *official*
KMSR commissary *store* commissaries
KMSRJKL chemosurgical *drug therapy*
KMSRJR chemosurgery *drug therapy*
KMSRL commissarial *official*
KMSRSHN commiseration *grief, pity*
KMSRT commiserate *grieve, pity* commiserated commiserating
KMSRT commissariat *food*
KMSRYL commissarial *official*
KMSRYT commissariat *food*
KMSS ecchymosis *bruise* ecchymoses
KMST chemist *profession*
KMST Comsat *satellite*
KMSTBL comestible *edible*
KMSTR chemistry *science* chemistries
KMSTR Kama Sutra *book*
KMT comet *meteor*
KMT comity *community* comities
KMT commit *consign* committed committing
KMT committee *group*

Letters aren't doubled for single sounds: to find alley use **L** not **LL**. Use **Y** and **W** as hard sounds only: to find yellow use **YL**. (Br)=British spelling or usage. * See dictionary.

KMT commute *travel, exchange* commuted commuting
KMT kempt *neat*
KMTBL commitable *consign*
KMTBL commutable *changeable*
KMTD committed *bound*
KMTDR commutator *motor, number*
KMTHRP chemotherapy *drug therapy*
KMTHRPDK chemotherapeutic *drug therapy*
KMTHRPST chemotherapist *drug therapy*
KMTHRPTK chemotherapeutic *drug therapy*
KMTHRPYDK chemotherapeutic *drug therapy*
KMTHRPYTK chemotherapeutic *drug therapy*
KMTK cometic *meteor*
KMTL committal *agreement*
KMTMN committeeman *member* committeemen
KMTMNT commitment *agreement*
KMTR cometary *meteor*
KMTR commuter *traveler*
KMTRLR comptroller *auditor*
KMTS comatose *unconscious*
KMTSHN commutation *change*
KMTT commutate *reverse* commutated commutating
KMTTR commutator *motor, number*
KMTV calmative *serene*
KMV commove *stir up* commoved commoving
KMX commix *mingle* commixes
KMXCHR commixture *compound*
KMXTR commixture *compound*
KMXTRP comic strip *cartoon*
KMXTYR commixture *compound*
KMY camellia *shrub*
KMY cameo *pendant, small role* cameos
KMYDBL commutable *changeable*
KMYDR commuter *traveler*
KMYLDR accumulator *gatherer*
KMYLDV accumulative *gathered*
KMYLDV cumulative *additional*
KMYLNMBS cumulonimbus *cloud*
KMYLS cumulous *cloudlike*
KMYLS cumulus *cloud*
KMYLSHN accumulation *gathering*
KMYLSHN cumulation *mass*
KMYLT accumulate *gather* accumulated accumulating
KMYLT cumulate *amass* cumulated cumulating
KMYLTR accumulator *gatherer*
KMYLTV accumulative *gathered*
KMYLTV cumulative *additional*
KMYN camion *truck, bus*
KMYN commune *(v) discuss* communed communing
KMYN commune *(n) community*
KMYND community *state, fellowship* communities
KMYNK communiqué *memo*
KMYNKBL communicable *(adj) able to pass on* communicably (adv)
KMYNKBLD communicability *ability to pass on*
KMYNKBLT communicability *ability to pass on*
KMYNKDR communicator *talker*
KMYNKDV communicative *talkative*
KMYNKDVL communicatively *talkative*
KMYNKDVNS communicativeness *talkative*
KMYNKNT communicant *church, informant*
KMYNKSHN communication *signal, words*
KMYNKT communicate *make known* communicated communicating
KMYNKT communicatee *receiver*
KMYNKTR communicator *talker*
KMYNKTV communicative *talkative*
KMYNKTVL communicatively *talkative*
KMYNKTVNS communicativeness *talkative*
KMYNL communal (adj) *community* communally (adv)
KMYNLZ communalize *group* communalized communalizing
KMYNN communion *sacrament, connection*
KMYNST communist *collectivist*
KMYNSTK communistic *collective*
KMYNSTKL communistically *collective*
KMYNT community *state, fellowship* communities
KMYNTRN communitarian *social collective*
KMYNTRNZM communitarianism *social collective*

KMYNTRYN communitarian *social collective*

KMYNTRYNZM communitarianism *social collective*

KMYNYN communion *sacrament, connection*

KMYNZ communize *make common* communized communizing (Br) communise

KMYNZM communism *collectivism*

KMYNZSHN communization *make common* (Br) communisation

KMYT commute *travel, exchange* commuted commuting

KMYTBL commutable *changeable*

KMYTDR commutator *motor, number*

KMYTR commuter *traveler*

KMYTSHN commutation *change*

KMYTT commutate *reverse* commutated commutating

KMYTTR commutator *motor, number*

KMZ camise *shirt*

KMZRSHN commiseration *grief, pity*

KMZRT commiserate *grieve, pity* commiserated commiserating

KN Achaean (or) Achaian *Greek*

KN achene *fruit*

KN aching *sore*

KN acne *blemish*

KN akin *similar*

KN Aquino *Philippine leader*

KN can (v) *ability* could

KN can (v, n) *container* canned canning

KN canaille *riffraff*

KN cane *flog, weave* caned caning

KN Cannes *French city*

KN canny *shrewd* cannier canniest

KN canoe *boat* canoed canoeing

KN cayenne *pepper*

KN coin *money*

KN con (v) *swindle, study* conned conning

KN con (n) *opposition, convict, swindle* (adv) *negative* (adj) *confidence*

KN cone (n) *pine seed, shape, wafer**

KN cone (v) *bevel* coned coning

KN coney *rabbit* coneys

KN coon *raccoon*

KN county *district* counties

KN echini (pl) *sea urchin* echinus

KN icon *image*

KN kana *writing* kana

KN keen (adj) *sharp, eager* (n,v) *lament*

KN ken (v) *know* kenned kenning

KN ken (n) *view*

KN keno *game*

KN khan *title*

KN kin *family*

KN kind (n) *type* (adj) *nice*

KN koan *poem*

KN koine *language*

KN oaken *made of oak*

KN quinoa *grain*

KN quoin *wedge*

KN Yukon *city, territory*

KNBL accountable (adj) *responsible* accountably (adv)

KNBL cannibal *eat one's own kind*

KNBL connubial (adj) *married* connubially (adv)

KNBL countable (adj) *numbers* countably (adv)

KNBLD accountability *responsibility*

KNBLNS accountableness *responsibility*

KNBLSTK cannibalistic *eat one's own kind*

KNBLT accountability *responsibility*

KNBLZ cannibalize *eat one's own kind, salvage parts* cannibalized cannibalizing (Br) cannibalise

KNBLZM cannibalism *eat one's own kind*

KNBR Canberra *city*

KNBR con brio *briskly*

KNBRK canebrake *thicket*

KNBRY con brio *briskly*

KNBS cannabis *marijuana*

KNBYL connubial (adj) *married* connubially (adv)

KNCD concede *admit* conceded conceding

KNCDD conceited *vain*

KNCDR conceder *admitter*

KNCH conch *shell* conchs (or) conches

KNCHLG conchology *shells*

KNCHLJ conchology *shells*

KNCHLJST conchologist *shells*

KNCHNBL conscionable *careful*

KNCHNCHS conscientious *careful*

KNCHNS conscience *moral sense*

KNCHNSHS conscientious *careful*

KNCHNTS conscience *moral sense*

KNCHRD concerto *music* concerti (or) concertos

KNCHRT concerto *music* concerti (or) concertos

KNCHRTN concertino *music* concertinos

KNCHS conscious *awake, aware*

KNCHSL consciously *awake, aware*

KNCHSNS consciousness *awake, aware*

KNCHYNCHS conscientious *careful*

KNCHYNSHS conscientious *careful*

Letters aren't doubled for single sounds: to find alley use **L** not **LL**. Use **Y** and **W** as hard sounds only: to find yellow use **YL**. (Br)=British spelling or usage. * See dictionary.

KNCL conceal *hide*
KNCLBL concealable *hide*
KNCLMNT concealment *hide*
KNCLR concealer *hider*
KNCRJ concierge *residential manager* concierges
KNCRSH concierge *residential manager* concierges
KNCRZH concierge *residential manager* concierges
KNCT conceit *vanity, thought*
KNCTD conceited *vain*
KNCV conceive *imagine, originate, understand* conceived conceiving
KNCVBL conceivable (adj) *imagined* conceivably (adv)
KNCVBLD conceivability *imagined*
KNCVBLT conceivability *imagined*
KNCVR conceiver *imagine, originate, understand*
KNCYRJ concierge *residential manager* concierges
KNCYRSH concierge *residential manager* concierges
KNCYRZH concierge *residential manager* concierges
KND Canada *country*
KND candy *sweet* candied candying candies
KND canned *recorded, drunk, preserved*
KND condo *house* condos
KND echinoid *sea urchin*
KND kendo *sport*
KND kind (n) *type* (adj) *nice*
KND kind of *type*
KNDC candidacy *election* candidacies
KNDD candid *truthful*
KNDD candida *fungus*
KNDD candied *sugared*

KNDDC candidacy *election* candidacies
KNDDS candidacy *election* candidacies
KNDDSS candidiasis *disease*
KNDDT candidate *election*
KNDDYSS candidiasis *disease*
KNDFLS candyfloss *(Br)* cotton candy
KNDGRDN kindergarten *nursery*
KNDGRDNR kindergartner *child, teacher*
KNDGRTN kindergarten *nursery*
KNDGRTNR kindergartner *child, teacher*
KNDHRDD kindhearted *sympathetic*
KNDHRTD kindhearted *sympathetic*
KNDK conduct (n) *actions* (v) *direct*
KNDK kinetic *in motion*
KNDKDBL conductible *transmission*
KNDKDBLT conductibility *transmission*
KNDKDR conductor *transmitter, guide, fare collector*
KNDKDV conductive *transmission*
KNDKL kinetically *motion*
KNDKS kinetics *motion*
KNDKSHN conduction *transmission*
KNDKT conduct (n) *actions* (v) *direct*
KNDKT Connecticut *US State*
KNDKTBL conductible *transmission*
KNDKTBLT conductibility *transmission*
KNDKTNS conductance *electricity*
KNDKTNTS conductance *electricity*
KNDKTR conductor *transmitter, guide, fare collector*
KNDKTV conductive *transmission*
KNDKTVD conductivity *transmission*
KNDKTVT conductivity *transmission*
KNDL candle *egg test* candled candling
KNDL candle *wax with wick*
KNDL condyle *bone*
KNDL kindle *light, arouse, birth* kindled kindling
KNDL kindly *nice* kindlier kindliest
KNDLBR candelabra (or) candelabrum *candles*
KNDLBRM candelabrum (or) candelabra *candles*
KNDLD condyloid *bony*
KNDLDR candlelighter *person, device*
KNDLFSH candlefish *animal*
KNDLHLDR candleholder *device*
KNDLM condyloma *growth* condylomata
KNDLMD condylomata (pl) *growth* condyloma
KNDLMDS condylomatous *growth*
KNDLMS Candlemas *festival*
KNDLMT condylomata (pl) *growth* condyloma
KNDLMTS condylomatous *growth*
KNDLN kindling *wood*
KNDLN kundalini *energy*
KNDLNG kindling *wood*
KNDLNS condolence *sympathy*
KNDLNS kindliness *nice*
KNDLNT candlenut *tree*
KNDLNTS condolence *sympathy*
KNDLPN candlepin *bowling*
KNDLPNS candlepins *bowling*
KNDLPNZ candlepins *bowling*
KNDLPR candlepower

Use letters that best describe the sounds you hear and omit the vowels. Use **S** or **K** instead of **C**: to find circle use **SRKL**. Use **J** to find joy, **JM** to find gem and **G** to find go.

brightness
KNDLPWR candlepower
brightness
KNDLR candler *tester*
KNDLR condoler
sympathizer
KNDLR kindlier *nice*
KNDLST kindliest *nice*
KNDLSTK candlestick
holder
KNDLT candlelight *glow*
KNDLT candlelit (or)
candlelighted *glowing*
KNDLTD candlelighted (or)
candlelit *glowing*
KNDLTR candlelighter
person, device
KNDLTR condolatory
sympathy
KNDLWD candlewood *tree*
KNDLWK candlewick *yarn*
KNDLYR kindlier *nice*
KNDLYST kindliest *nice*
KNDM condemn *doom,*
criticize
KNDM condom *rubber device*
KNDMBL condemnable
doom, criticize
KNDMNBL condemnable
doom, criticize
KNDMNM condominium
abode
KNDMNR condemner (or)
condemnor *doom, criticize*
KNDMNSHN condemnation
doom, criticize
KNDMNT condiment
seasoning
KNDMNTR condemnatory
doom, criticize
KNDMNYM condominium
abode
KNDMR condemner (or)
condemnor *doom, criticize*
KNDN Canadian *of Canada*
KNDN candying *sugaring*
KNDN condign *worthy*
KNDN condone *pardon*
condoned condoning
KNDNBL condonable
pardonable
KNDNG candying *sugaring*

KNDNR condoner *pardoner*
KNDNS condense *reduce*
condensed condensing
KNDNS kindness *niceness*
KNDNSBL condensable
reduction
KNDNSD condensed
reduced
KNDNSHN condonation
pardon
KNDNSR condenser
concentrator
KNDNSSHN condensation
moisture
KNDNST condensate
moisture
KNDNST condensed
reduced
KNDNTS condense *reduce*
condensed condensing
KNDNTSBL condensable
reduction
KNDNTSD condensed
reduced
KNDNTSR condenser
concentrator
KNDNTST condensed
reduced
KNDR candor *honesty*
(Br) candour
KNDR condor *bird* condors
(or) condores
KNDR keynoter *speaker*
KNDRD kindred *(n) relatives*
(adj) like
KNDRGRDN kindergarten
nursery
KNDRGRDNR
kindergartner *child,*
teacher
KNDRGRTN kindergarten
nursery
KNDRGRTNR kindergartner
child, teacher
KNDRK qindarka (pl) *money*
qintar
KNDRM echinoderm *animal*
KNDRMDS
echinodermatous *animal*
KNDRMTS
echinodermatous *animal*
KNDRPLSDK

achondroplastic *dwarfism*
KNDRPLSTK
achondroplastic *dwarfism*
KNDRPLZH achondroplasia
dwarfism
KNDRT achondrite *meteorite*
KNDS candidacy *election*
candidacies
KNDS conduce *lead*
conduced conducing
KNDSHN condition *(v)*
agree, adapt (n) premise,
state of being
KNDSHNL conditional (adj)
dependent conditionally
(adv)
KNDSHNN conditioning
proper state
KNDSHNNG conditioning
proper state
KNDSHNR conditioner *hair*
product, stipulator
KNDSKP kinetoscope *film*
KNDSN condescend
patronize
KNDSNCHN
condescension *patronize*
KNDSND condescend
patronize
KNDSNDN condescending
patronize
KNDSNDNG
condescending *patronize*
KNDSNDNGL
condescendingly
patronize
KNDSNDNL
condescendingly
patronize
KNDSNDNS
condescendence
patronize
KNDSNDNTS
condescendence
patronize
KNDSNS candescence *glow*
KNDSNSHN
condescension *patronize*
KNDSNT candescent
glowing
KNDSNTS candescence
glow

Letters aren't doubled for single sounds: to find alley use **L** not **LL**. Use **Y** and **W** as hard
sounds only: to find yellow use **YL**. (Br)=British spelling or usage. * See dictionary.

KNDSTRPR candy striper *nurse*
KNDSV conducive *promoting*
KNDSVNS conduciveness *promoting*
KNDT candidate *election*
KNDT conduit *tube*
KNDTF candytuft *plant*
KNDTFT candytuft *plant*
KNDV conative *impulse*
KNDV kind of *type*
KNDWT conduit *tube*
KNDX kinetics *motion*
KNDYN Canadian *of Canada*
KNDYN candying *sugaring*
KNDYNG candying *sugaring*
KNDYS conduce *lead* conduced conducing
KNDYSV conducive *promoting*
KNDYSVNS conduciveness *promoting*
KNDYT conduit *tube*
KNDYWT conduit *tube*
KNF confit *meat*
KNF kenaf *fiber*
KNFB confab *chat* confabbed confabbing
KNFBLDR confabulator *chatterer*
KNFBLSHN confabulation *chat*
KNFBLT confabulate *chat* confabulated confabulating
KNFBLTR confabulator *chatterer*
KNFBLTR confabulatory *chatty*
KNFBYLDR confabulator *chatterer*
KNFBYLSHN confabulation *chat*
KNFBYLT confabulate *chat* confabulated confabulating
KNFBYLTR confabulator *chatterer*
KNFBYLTR confabulatory *chatty*
KNFCHR confiture *jam*

KNFD confetti *shredded paper*
KNFD confide *tell* confided confiding
KNFDN confiding *trustful*
KNFDNCHL confidential (adj) *secret* confidentially(adv)
KNFDNCHLD confidentiality *secret*
KNFDNCHLT confidentiality *secret*
KNFDNCHYLD confidentiality *secret*
KNFDNCHYLT confidentiality *secret*
KNFDNG confiding *trustful*
KNFDNS confidence (n) *power, certainty (adj) swindle*
KNFDNSHL confidential (adj) *secret* confidentially (adv)
KNFDNSHLD confidentiality *secret*
KNFDNSHLT confidentiality *secret*
KNFDNSHYLD confidentiality *secret*
KNFDNSHYLT confidentiality *secret*
KNFDNT confidant *trusted one*
KNFDNT confidante *trusted one (f)*
KNFDNT confident *sure*
KNFDNTL confidently *certain*
KNFDNTS confidence (n) *power, certainty (adj) swindle*
KNFDR confider *teller*
KNFDR confiteor *prayer*
KNFDR confuter *arguer*
KNFDRC confederacy *(often capitalized) alliance* confederacies
KNFDRS confederacy *(often capitalized) alliance* confederacies
KNFDRSHN confederation *alliance*
KNFDRT confederate *allied*

confederated
confederating
KNFDYR confiteor *prayer*
KNFGR configure *set up* configured configuring
KNFGRSHN configuration *shape*
KNFGYR configure *set up* configured configuring
KNFGYRSHN configuration *shape*
KNFK kinfolk (or) kinfolks *relatives*
KNFKS kinfolks (or) kinfolk *relatives*
KNFKSHN confection *sweet*
KNFKSHNR confectioner *candy maker or seller*
KNFKSHNR confectionery *candy shop* confectioneries
KNFKT confect *prepare*
KNFLGRNT conflagrant *burning*
KNFLGRSHN conflagration *burning*
KNFLK conflict *fight*
KNFLKCHL conflictual *opposite*
KNFLKCHWL conflictual *opposite*
KNFLKDD conflicted *emotional*
KNFLKDNG conflicting *at odds*
KNFLKDV conflictive *opposite*
KNFLKSHL conflictual *opposite*
KNFLKSHN confliction *opposite*
KNFLKSHWL conflictual *opposite*
KNFLKT conflict *fight*
KNFLKTD conflicted *emotional*
KNFLKTL conflictual *opposite*
KNFLKTN conflicting *at odds*
KNFLKTNG conflicting *at odds*

Use letters that best describe the sounds you hear and omit the vowels. Use **S** or **K** instead of **C**: to find circle use **SRKL**. Use **J** to find joy, **JM** to find gem and **G** to find go.

KNFLKTV conflictive *opposite*
KNFLKTWL conflictual *opposite*
KNFLNS confluence *meeting*
KNFLNT confluent *meeting*
KNFLNTS confluence *meeting*
KNFLSHN conflation *fusion*
KNFLWNS confluence *meeting*
KNFLWNT confluent *meeting*
KNFLWNTS confluence *meeting*
KNFMNS conformance *similarity*
KNFMNTS conformance *similarity*
KNFN confine *restrict* confined confining
KNFN confound *perplex*
KNFND confined *(adj) childbirth (v) restricted*
KNFND confound *perplex*
KNFNDD confounded *confused*
KNFNMNT confinement *childbirth*
KNFNR confiner *limiter*
KNFNS confines *limits*
KNFNZ confines *limits*
KNFR confer *grant, consult* conferred conferring
KNFR conferee *consultant*
KNFR conifer *tree*
KNFRBL conferrable *grant, consult*
KNFRL conferral *grant, consult*
KNFRM confirm *verify*
KNFRM conform *adapt*
KNFRM cuneiform *wedge*
KNFRMBL confirmable *verifiable*
KNFRMBL conformable *(adj) adaptable* conformably *(adv)*
KNFRMD confirmed *persisting*
KNFRMD conformity *sameness* conformities

KNFRML conformal *shape*
KNFRMNT conferment *grant, consult*
KNFRMR conformer *adapter*
KNFRMSHN confirmation *ceremony, agreement*
KNFRMSHN conformation *adaptation, shape*
KNFRMST conformist *adapter*
KNFRMT conformity *sameness* conformities
KNFRMTR confirmatory *provable*
KNFRMZM conformism *adaptability*
KNFRNL confrontal *opposed*
KNFRNR confronter *meeting, conflict*
KNFRNS conference *meeting*
KNFRNSNG conferencing *electronic meeting*
KNFRNT confront *oppose, meet*
KNFRNTL confrontal *opposed*
KNFRNTR confronter *meeting, conflict*
KNFRNTS conference *meeting*
KNFRNTSHN confrontation *meeting, conflict*
KNFRNTSHNL confrontational *opposing*
KNFRNTSHNST confrontationist *opposer*
KNFRNTSNG conferencing *electronic meeting*
KNFRR conferrer *grant, consult*
KNFRR confrere *comrade*
KNFRS coniferous *with cones*
KNFS confess *admit guilt*
KNFSBL confessable *admit guilt*
KNFSDL confessedly *admittedly*
KNFSHN confession *admit guilt*
KNFSHN Confucian *of*

Confucius
KNFSHN confusion *disorder*
KNFSHNL confessional *(adj) autobiographical (n)* church confessionally *(adv)*
KNFSHNZM Confucianism *philosophy*
KNFSHS Confucius *philosopher*
KNFSKBL confiscable *sieze*
KNFSKDBL confiscatable *sieze*
KNFSKDR confiscator *sieze*
KNFSKSHN confiscation *sieze*
KNFSKT confiscate *sieze* confiscated confiscating
KNFSKTBL confiscatable *sieze*
KNFSKTR confiscator *sieze*
KNFSKTR confiscatory *siezed*
KNFSR confessor *priest*
KNFT confetti *shredded paper*
KNFT confute *contradict* confuted confuting
KNFTR confiteor *prayer*
KNFTR confiture *jam*
KNFTR confuter *arguer*
KNFTSHN confutation *contradict*
KNFTYR confiteor *prayer*
KNFTYR confiture *jam*
KNFX kinfolks (or) kinfolk *relatives*
KNFYDR confuter *arguer*
KNFYSHN Confucian *of Confucius*
KNFYSHN confusion *disorder*
KNFYSHNZM Confucianism *philosophy*
KNFYSHS Confucius *philosopher*
KNFYT confute *contradict* confuted confuting
KNFYTR confuter *arguer*
KNFYTSHN confutation *contradict*
KNFYZ confuse *perplex, blur* confused confusing

KNFYZD confused *mixed up*

KNFYZDL confusedly *mixed up*

KNFYZDNS confusedness *mixed up*

KNFYZHN confusion *disorder*

KNFYZNGL confusingly *mixed up*

KNFYZNL confusingly *mixed up*

KNFZ confuse *perplex, blur* confused confusing

KNFZD confused *mixed up*

KNFZDL confusedly *mixed up*

KNFZDNS confusedness *mixed up*

KNFZHN confusion *disorder*

KNFZNGL confusingly *mixed up*

KNFZNL confusingly *mixed up*

KNG aching *sore*

KNG cangue *pillory*

KNG conga *drum*

KNG congé *farewell*

KNG Congo *country, river*

KNG congou *tea*

KNG kanji *writing* kanji

KNG kiang *animal*

KNG king *ruler*

KNGBLT kingbolt *axle*

KNGBRD kingbird *flycatcher*

KNGDM kingdom *realm*

KNGF kung fu *karate*

KNGFSH kingfish *fish*

KNGFSHR kingfisher *bird*

KNGG conga *drum*

KNGG Congo *country, river*

KNGG congou *tea*

KNGGR conger *eel*

KNGGR kangaroo *animal* kangaroos

KNGGRCHLSHNZ congratulations *good wishes*

KNGGRCHLT congratulate *offer good wishes* congratulated congratulating

KNGGRCHLTR

congratulator *well-wisher*

KNGGRCHLTR

congratulatory *good wishes*

KNGGRD congruity *harmony* congruities

KNGGRDJLSHNZ

congratulations *good wishes*

KNGGRDJLT congratulate *offer good wishes* congratulated congratulating

KNGGRDJLTR

congratulator *well-wisher*

KNGGRGSHN congregation *assembly*

KNGGRGSHNL

congregational *communal*

KNGGRGSHNL

Congregational *church*

KNGGRGT congregate *gather* congregated congregating

KNGGRJLSHNZ

congratulations *good wishes*

KNGGRJLT congratulate *offer good wishes* congratulated congratulating

KNGGRJLTR congratulator *well-wisher*

KNGGRJLTR

congratulatory *good wishes*

KNGGRL conger eel *fish*

KNGGRNS congruence *agreement* congruency

KNGGRNT congruent *harmonious*

KNGGRNTL congruently *harmoniously*

KNGGRNTS congruence *agreement* congruency

KNGGRS congress *meeting*

KNGGRS Congress *legislature*

KNGGRS congruous *harmonious*

KNGGRSHNL

congressional (adj) *group*

congressionally (adv)

KNGGRSL congruously *harmoniously*

KNGGRSMN congressman *legislator* congressmen

KNGGRSPRSN

congressperson *legislator* congressmen

KNGGRSWMN

congresswoman *legislator* congresswoman

KNGGRT congruity *harmony* congruities

KNGGRTLDR congratulator *well-wisher*

KNGGRTLSHNZ

congratulations *good wishes*

KNGGRTLTR congratulator *well-wisher*

KNGGRTLTR

congratulatory *good wishes*

KNGGRWD congruity *harmony* congruities

KNGGRWNS congruence *agreement* congruency

KNGGRWNT congruent *harmonious*

KNGGRWNTL congruently *harmoniously*

KNGGRWNTS congruence *agreement* congruency

KNGGRWS congruous *harmonious*

KNGGRWSL congruously *harmoniously*

KNGGRWT congruity *harmony* congruities

KNGK conch *shell* conchs (or) conches

KNGK conk *hit, tire out*

KNGK kink *twist, curl*

KNGK kinky *curly, weird* kinkier kinkiest

KNGKBN concubine *mistress*

KNGKBNJ concubinage *cohabitation*

KNGKBR king cobra *snake*

KNGKDT conked out *tired*

KNGKJ kinkajou *mammal*

KNGKL kinkily *curly, weird*
KNGKLG conchology *shells*
KNGKLJ conchology *shells*
KNGKLJST conchologist *shells*
KNGKNS kinkiness *curl, weirdness*
KNGKP kingcup *plant*
KNGKR canker *sore*
KNGKR chancre *syphilis*
KNGKR coanchor *news*
KNGKR conquer *defeat*
KNGKR kinkier *curlier, weirder*
KNGKRB king crab *crustacean*
KNGKRR conqueror *victor*
KNGKRS cankerous *sore*
KNGKRWRM cankerworm *moth*
KNGKST kinkiest *curliest, weirdest*
KNGKSTDR conquistador *conqueror*
KNGKT conk out *sleep*
KNGKWST conquest *victory*
KNGKWSTDR conquistador *conqueror*
KNGKYBN concubine *mistress*
KNGKYBNJ concubinage *cohabitation*
KNGKYR kinkier *curlier, weirder*
KNGKYST kinkiest *curliest, weirdest*
KNGL congeal *clot*
KNGL kingly *noble* kinglier kingliest
KNGLBL congealable *able to clot*
KNGLBSHN conglobation *round mass*
KNGLBT conglobate *form a round mass* conglobated conglobating
KNGLMNT congealment *clotting*
KNGLMRDR conglomerator *gatherer*
KNGLMRSHN conglomeration *mass*

KNGLMRT conglomerate *gather* conglomerated conglomerating
KNGLMRTR conglomerator *gatherer*
KNGLNS kingliness *nobility*
KNGLR kinglier *noble*
KNGLST kingliest *noble*
KNGLT kinglet *bird*
KNGLTNSHN conglutination *unity*
KNGLTNT conglutinate *unite* conglutinated conglutinating
KNGLYR kinglier *noble*
KNGLYST kingliest *noble*
KNGM con game *swindle*
KNGMKR kingmaker *politics*
KNGNL congenial (adj) *pleasant* congenially (adv)
KNGNLD congeniality *pleasantness*
KNGNLT congeniality *pleasantness*
KNGNYL congenial (adj) *pleasant* congenially (adv)
KNGNYLD congeniality *pleasantness*
KNGNYLT congeniality *pleasantness*
KNGPN kingpin *bowling, chief*
KNGQBN concubine *mistress*
KNGQBNJ concubinage *cohabitation*
KNGQST conquest *victory*
KNGQSTDR conquistador *conqueror*
KNGR conger *eel*
KNGR kangaroo *animal* kangaroos
KNGRCHLSHNZ congratulations *good wishes*
KNGRCHLT congratulate *offer good wishes* congratulated congratulating
KNGRCHLTR congratulator *well-wisher*
KNGRCHLTR

congratulatory *good wishes*
KNGRD congruity *harmony* congruities
KNGRDJLSHNZ congratulations *good wishes*
KNGRDJLT congratulate *offer good wishes* congratulated congratulating
KNGRDJLTR congratulator *well-wisher*
KNGRF iconography *drawings* iconographies
KNGRFK iconographic (or) iconographical (adj) *drawings* iconographically (adv)
KNGRFKL iconographical (or) iconographic (adj) *drawings* iconographically (adv)
KNGRFR iconographer *drawings*
KNGRGDR congregator *gatherer*
KNGRGSHN congregation *assembly*
KNGRGSHNL congregational *communal*
KNGRGSHNL Congregational *church*
KNGRGT congregate *gather* congregated congregating
KNGRGTR congregator *gatherer*
KNGRJLSHNZ congratulations *good wishes*
KNGRJLT congratulate *offer good wishes* congratulated congratulating
KNGRJLTR congratulator *well-wisher*
KNGRJLTR congratulatory *good wishes*
KNGRL conger eel *fish*
KNGRNS congruence *agreement* congruency
KNGRNT congruent

Letters aren't doubled for single sounds: to find alley use **L** not **LL**. Use **Y** and **W** as hard sounds only: to find yellow use **YL**. (Br)=British spelling or usage. * See dictionary.

harmonious
KNGRNTL congruently
harmoniously
KNGRNTS congruence
agreement congruency
KNGRS congress *meeting*
KNGRS Congress *legislature*
KNGRS congruous
harmonious
KNGRSHNL congressional
(adj) *group*
congressionally (adv)
KNGRSL congruously
harmoniously
KNGRSMN congressman
legislator congressmen
KNGRSPRSN
congressperson *legislator*
congressmen
KNGRSWMN
congresswoman *legislator*
congresswoman
KNGRT congruity *harmony*
congruities
KNGRTLDR congratulator
well-wisher
KNGRTLSHNZ
congratulations *good*
wishes
KNGRTLTR congratulator
well-wisher
KNGRTLTR congratulatory
good wishes
KNGRWD congruity
harmony congruities
KNGRWNS congruence
agreement congruency
KNGRWNT congruent
harmonious
KNGRWNTL congruently
harmoniously
KNGRWNTS congruence
agreement congruency
KNGRWS congruous
harmonious
KNGRWSL congruously
harmoniously
KNGRWT congruity
harmony congruities
KNGSD kingside *chess*
KNGSHP kingship *position*
KNGSNK king snake *reptile*

KNGSZ king-size (or) king-
sized *large*
KNGSZD king-sized (or)
king-size *large*
KNGTR conning tower
submarine
KNGTT conked out *tired*
KNGTWR conning tower
submarine
KNGWD kingwood *tree*
KNHN coonhound *dog*
KNHND coonhound *dog*
KNHRDD kindhearted
sympathetic
KNHRTD kindhearted
sympathetic
KNJ coinage *money*
KNJ congé *farewell*
KNJ kanji *writing* kanji
KNJGDD conjugated *united*
KNJGL conjugal (adj)
married conjugally (adv)
KNJGSHN conjugation *verb,*
fusion
KNJGSHNL conjugational
(adj) *verb, fusion*
conjugationally (adv)
KNJGT conjugate (*v*) *verb,*
join conjugated
conjugating
KNJGT conjugate (*adj*)
coupled (*n*) *number*
KNJGTD conjugated *united*
KNJKCHR conjecture
presume conjectured
conjecturing
KNJKCHRL conjectural
(adj) *presumed*
conjecturally (adv)
KNJKCHRR conjecturer
presume
KNJKSHR conjecture
presume conjectured
conjecturing
KNJKSHRL conjectural
(adj) *presumed*
conjecturally (adv)
KNJKSHRR conjecturer
presume
KNJKTR conjecture *presume*
conjectured conjecturing
KNJKTRL conjectural (adj)

presumed conjecturally
(adv)
KNJKTRR conjecturer
presume
KNJL congeal *clot*
KNJLBL congealable *able to*
clot
KNJLMNT congealment
clotting
KNJLSHN congelation
clotting
KNJN conjoin *unite*
KNJNCHR conjuncture
union
KNJNDL congenital (adj)
inbred congenitally (adv)
KNJNGCHR conjuncture
union
KNJNGK conjunct *joined*
KNJNGKCHR conjuncture
union
KNJNGKDV conjunctiva *eye*
membrane conjunctivas
(or) conjunctivae
KNJNGKDV conjunctive
connective
KNJNGKDVDS
conjunctivitis
inflammation
KNJNGKDVTS
conjunctivitis
inflammation
KNJNGKSHN conjunction
combination, word
KNJNGKSHR conjuncture
union
KNJNGKT conjunct *joined*
KNJNGKTR conjuncture
union
KNJNGKTV conjunctiva *eye*
membrane conjunctivas
(or) conjunctivae
KNJNGKTV conjunctive
connective
KNJNGKTVDS
conjunctivitis
inflammation
KNJNGKTVTS
conjunctivitis
inflammation
KNJNGSHR conjuncture
union

Use letters that best describe the sounds you hear and omit the vowels. Use **S** or **K**
instead of **C**: to find circle use **SRKL**. Use **J** to find joy, **JM** to find gem and **G** to find go.

KNJNGT conjunct *joined*
KNJNGTVDS conjunctivitis *inflammation*
KNJNGTVTS conjunctivitis *inflammation*
KNJNKCHR conjuncture *union*
KNJNKDV conjunctiva *eye membrane* conjunctivas (or) conjunctivae
KNJNKDV conjunctive *connective*
KNJNKDVDS conjunctivitis *inflammation*
KNJNKDVTS conjunctivitis *inflammation*
KNJNKSHN conjunction *combination, word*
KNJNKSHR conjuncture *union*
KNJNKT conjunct *joined*
KNJNKTR conjuncture *union*
KNJNKTV conjunctiva *eye membrane* conjunctivas (or) conjunctivae
KNJNKTV conjunctive *connective*
KNJNKTVDS conjunctivitis *inflammation*
KNJNKTVTS conjunctivitis *inflammation*
KNJNL congenial (adj) *pleasant* congenially (adv)
KNJNLD congeniality *pleasantness*
KNJNLT congeniality *pleasantness*
KNJNSHN conjunction *combination, word*
KNJNSHR conjuncture *union*
KNJNT conjoint *united*
KNJNT conjunct *joined*
KNJNTL congenital (adj) *inbred* congenitally (adv)
KNJNTL conjointly *together*
KNJNTV conjunctiva *eye membrane* conjunctivas (or) conjunctivae
KNJNTVDS conjunctivitis *inflammation*

KNJNTVTS conjunctivitis *inflammation*
KNJNYL congenial (adj) *pleasant* congenially (adv)
KNJNYLD congeniality *pleasantness*
KNJNYLT congeniality *pleasantness*
KNJR conjure *summon* conjured conjuring
KNJRP conjure up *summon*
KNJRR conjurer (or) conjuror *wizard*
KNJRSHN conjuration *appeal*
KNJRZ congeries *collection*
KNJSCHN congestion *clog*
KNJSDD congested *clogged*
KNJSDV congestive *clogged*
KNJST congest *clog*
KNJSTD congested *clogged*
KNJSTV congestive *clogged*
KNK Canuck *Canada*
KNK conch *shell* conchs (or) conches
KNK conic *cone-shaped*
KNK conk *hit, tire out*
KNK iconic *symbol*
KNK kink *twist, curl*
KNK kinky *curly, weird* kinkier kinkiest
KNKBN concubine *mistress*
KNKBNJ concubinage *cohabitation*
KNKDBL connectable *join*
KNKDD connected *joined*
KNKDDL connectedly *joined*
KNKDNSHN concatenation *link*
KNKDNT concatenate *link* concatenated concatenating
KNKDR connector *joint*
KNKDT conked out *asleep*
KNKDV connective *joining*
KNKJ kinkajou *mammal*
KNKKDR concoctor *creator*
KNKKS echinococcus *disease* echinococci
KNKKSHN concoction *fabrication*
KNKKT concoct *fabricate*

KNKKTR concoctor *creator*
KNKL canticle *song*
KNKL conical (adj) *cone-shaped* conically (adv)
KNKL iconically *symbol*
KNKL kinkily *curly, weird*
KNKLD conclude *end, infer* concluded concluding
KNKLDR concluder *end, infer*
KNKLG conchology *shells*
KNKLJ conchology *shells*
KNKLJST conchologist *shells*
KNKLS Auchincloss *writer*
KNKLSDK iconoclastic *belief destroyer*
KNKLSDKL iconoclastically *belief destroyer*
KNKLSHN conclusion *end, inference*
KNKLSR conclusory *no evidence*
KNKLST iconoclast *belief destroyer*
KNKLSTK iconoclastic *belief destroyer*
KNKLSTKL iconoclastically *belief destroyer*
KNKLSV conclusive *end, decisive*
KNKLSVL conclusively *end, decisive*
KNKLSVNS conclusiveness *end, decision*
KNKLV conclave *meeting*
KNKLZHN conclusion *end, inference*
KNKLZR conclusory *no evidence*
KNKLZV conclusive *end, decisive*
KNKLZVL conclusively *end, decisive*
KNKLZVNS conclusiveness *end, decision*
KNKMDNS concomitance *accompaniment*
KNKMDNT concomitant *accompanying*
KNKMDNTS concomitance *accompaniment*

Letters aren't doubled for single sounds: to find alley use **L** not **LL**. Use **Y** and **W** as hard sounds only: to find yellow use **YL**. (Br)=British spelling or usage. * See dictionary.

KNKMTNS concomitance *accompaniment*
KNKMTNT concomitant *accompanying*
KNKMTNTS concomitance *accompaniment*
KNKN cancan *dance*
KNKN cannikin *cup*
KNKNS kinkiness *curl, weirdness*
KNKPSNS concupiscence *desire*
KNKPSNT concupiscent *desirous*
KNKPSNTS concupiscence *desire*
KNKR canker *sore*
KNKR chancre *syphilis*
KNKR coanchor *news*
KNKR concur *agree* concurred concurring
KNKR conquer *defeat*
KNKR kinkier *curlier, weirder*
KNKRD Concord *city*
KNKRD concord *agreement*
KNKRDNS concordance *agreement*
KNKRDNT concordant *agreement*
KNKRDNTS concordance *agreement*
KNKRDT concordat *agreement*
KNKRNS concurrence *agreement* concurrency
KNKRNT concurrent *parallel, same time*
KNKRNTL concurrently *parallel, same time*
KNKRNTS concurrence *agreement* concurrency
KNKRR conqueror *victor*
KNKRS cankerous *sore*
KNKRS concourse *meeting place*
KNKRSHN concretion *mass*
KNKRSNS concrescence *fusion*
KNKRSNT concrescent *fused*
KNKRSNTS concrescence *fusion*

KNKRT concrete (*v*) solidify, blend concreted concreting
KNKRT concrete (*n*) cement (adj) real
KNKRTL concretely *tangibly*
KNKRTNS concreteness *tangibility*
KNKRTST concretist *make real*
KNKRTZ concretize *harden* concretized concretizing
KNKRTZM concretism *make real*
KNKRTZSHN concretization *harden*
KNKRWRM cankerworm *moth*
KNKS concuss *stun*
KNKSHN concussion *injury*
KNKSHN connection *link* (Br) connexion
KNKST kinkiest *curliest, weirdest*
KNKSTDR conquistador *conqueror*
KNKSV concussive *injury*
KNKT conk out *tire out*
KNKT connect *join*
KNKTBL connectable *join*
KNKTD connected *joined*
KNKTDL connectedly *joined*
KNKTNSHN concatenation *link*
KNKTNT concatenate *link* concatenated concatenating
KNKTR connector *joint*
KNKTT conked out *tired*
KNKTV connective *joining*
KNKV concave *hollow*
KNKVD concavity *hollow* concavities
KNKVT concavity *hollow* concavities
KNKWST conquest *victory*
KNKWSTDR conquistador *conqueror*
KNKYBN concubine *mistress*
KNKYBNJ concubinage *cohabitation*

KNKYPSNS concupiscence *desire*
KNKYPSNT concupiscent *desirous*
KNKYPSNTS concupiscence *desire*
KNKYR kinkier *curlier, weirder*
KNKYST kinkiest *curliest, weirdest*
KNKZV concussive *injury*
KNL canaille *riffraff*
KNL canal (*v*) dig canaled (or) canalled canaling (or) cannalling
KNL canal (*n*) waterway
KNL cannily *shrewdly*
KNL cannoli *pasta*
KNL cannula *tube* cannulas (or) cannulae
KNL canola *plant, oil*
KNL cantle *portion*
KNL keenly *sharp, eager*
KNL kennel *dog house* kenneled (or) kennelled kenneling (or) kennelling
KNL kindly *nice* kindlier kindliest
KNL quenelle *dumpling*
KNLG iconology *symbols*
KNLJ acknowledge *admit to* acknowledged acknowledging
KNLJ iconology *symbols*
KNLJBL acknowledgeable *admitted*
KNLJD acknowledged *admitted*
KNLJKL iconological *symbols*
KNLJMNT acknowledgment (or) acknowledgement *recognition*
KNLN cannelloni *pasta*
KNLN kindling *wood*
KNLNG kindling *wood*
KNLNGGS cunnilingus *sex*
KNLNGS cunnilingus *sex*
KNLNS kindliness *nice*
KNLP cantaloupe *fruit*
KNLR cannular *tubular*

Use letters that best describe the sounds you hear and omit the vowels. Use **S** or **K** instead of **C**: to find circle use **SRKL**. Use **J** to find joy, **JM** to find gem and **G** to find go.

KNLR kindlier *nice*
KNLSHN cantillation *song*
KNLST kindliest *nice*
KNLT cantillate *sing*
cantillated cantillating
KNLVR cantilever *beam*
KNLYR kindlier *nice*
KNLYST kindliest *nice*
KNLZ canalize *make channels*
canalized canalizing
KNM economy *frugality,*
goods and services
economies
KNMDK kinematic (or)
kinematical (adj) *motion*
kinematically (adv)
KNMDKL kinematical (or)
kinematic (adj) *motion*
kinematically (adv)
KNMDKS kinematics *motion*
KNMDX kinematics *motion*
KNMK economic *thrifty,*
profit
KNMKL economical (adj)
thrifty economically (adv)
KNMKS economics *goods*
and services
KNMN con man *deceiver*
con men
KNMN ichneumon
mongoose, fly
KNMR con amore *tenderly*
KNMSN kanamycin
antibiotic
KNMST economist *goods*
and services
KNMTK kinematic (or)
kinematical (adj) *motion*
kinematically (adv)
KNMTKL kinematical (or)
kinematic (adj) *motion*
kinematically (adv)
KNMTKS kinematics *motion*
KNMTRKL econometrically
statistics
KNMTRKS econometrics
statistics
KNMTRSHN
econometrician *statistics*
KNMTRX econometrics
statistics
KNMTX kinematics *motion*

KNMX economics *goods and*
services
KNMZ economize *save*
economized
economizing
(Br) economise
KNMZR economizer *saver*
(Br) economiser
KNN canine *dog*
KNN cannon *weapon*
cannons (or) cannon
KNN canon *dogma,*
clergyman
KNN cunning *shrewdness*
KNNBL cannonball *missile*
KNND cannonade *artillery*
cannonaded
cannonading
KNNDRM conundrum *riddle*
KNNFDR cannon fodder
soldiers
KNNFTR cannon fodder
soldiers
KNNG accounting *reckoning*
KNNG cunning *shrewdness*
KNNGTR conning tower
submarine
KNNGTWR conning tower
submarine
KNNK canonic *orthodox*
KNNKL canonical (adj)
orthodox canonically (adv)
KNNKLS canonicals
vestments
KNNKLZ canonicals
vestments
KNNL canon law *church*
KNNNL continental (adj)
European, land mass
continentally (adv)
KNNNTL continental (adj)
European, land mass
continentally (adv)
KNNR cannoneer *gunner*
KNNR cannonry *weapons*
cannonries
KNNR canonry *church*
KNNS canniness *shrewdness*
KNNS kindness *niceness*
KNNSD canonicity *orthodox*
KNNST canonicity *orthodox*
KNNST canonist *lawyer*

KNNT accountant *ledger*
keeper
KNNT Canaanite *Semite*
KNNT continent *land mass*
KNNTL continental (adj)
European, land mass
continentally (adv)
KNNTSHP accountantship
ledger keeping
KNNZ canonize *sainthood*
canonized canonizing
KNNZSHN canonization
sainthood
KNP canapé *food*
KNP canopy *cover* canopied
canopying canopies
KNPK canopic *mummy*
KNPRS coin purse *wallet*
KNPSHN conniption *fit*
KNQBN concubine *mistress*
KNQBNJ concubinage
cohabitation
KNQPSNS concupiscence
desire
KNQPSNT concupiscent
desirous
KNQPSNTS concupiscence
desire
KNQST conquest *victory*
KNQSTDR conquistador
conqueror
KNR canary *bird* canaries
KNR caner *chairs*
KNR canner *containers*
KNR cannery *factory*
canneries
KNR cannier *shrewder*
KNR canter *gait, beggar*
KNR cantor *singer*
KNR counter (n) *shelf,*
calculator (v) *oppose*
KNR cunner *fish*
KNRBLNS counterbalance
offset counterbalanced
counterbalancing
KNRBLNTS counterbalance
offset counterbalanced
counterbalancing
KNRBSHN conurbation
cities
KNRCHK counter check
banking

Letters aren't doubled for single sounds: to find alley use **L** not **LL**. Use **Y** and **W** as hard sounds only: to find yellow use **YL**. (Br)=British spelling or usage. * See dictionary.

KNRCHK countercheck
(v,n) restraint
KNRD canard *report*
KNRFNSV counteroffensive
military
KNRFT counterfeit *forgery*
KNRFTR counterfeiter *forger*
KNRK counteract *oppose*
KNRKDV counteractive
opposition
KNRKLCHR counterculture
non-establishment
KNRKLCHRL
countercultural *non-establishment*
KNRKLCHRLST
counterculturalist *non-establishment*
KNRKLKWZ
counterclockwise
direction
KNRKLM counterclaim *legal*
KNRKLQZ
counterclockwise
direction
KNRKLTR counterculture
non-establishment
KNRKLTRL countercultural
non-establishment
KNRKLTRLST
counterculturalist *non-establishment*
KNRKSHN counteraction
opposition
KNRKT counteract *oppose*
KNRKTV counteractive
opposition
KNRMN counterman *clerk*
countermen
KNRMN countermand
revoke
KNRMND countermand
revoke
KNRMSHR countermeasure
opposition
KNRMZHR countermeasure
opposition
KNRNSRJNC
counterinsurgency
military
KNRNSRJNS
counterinsurgency

military
KNRNSRJNT
counterinsurgent *military*
KNRNSRJNTC
counterinsurgency
military
KNRNSRJNTS
counterinsurgency
military
KNRNTLJNS
counterintelligence
spying
KNRNTLJNTS
counterintelligence
spying
KNRPN counterpane
bedspread
KNRPNT counterpoint
melody, opposite
KNRPRDKDV
counterproductive
hindrance
KNRPRDKTV
counterproductive
hindrance
KNRPRT counterpart
complement
KNRPZ counterpoise
balance
KNRS canorous *melodious*
KNRSGNCHR
countersignature *vouch
for*
KNRSGNTR
countersignature *vouch
for*
KNRSL canorously
melodious
KNRSN countersign
signature
KNRSNGK countersink *set
below* countersunk
countersinking
KNRSNK countersink *set
below* countersunk
countersinking
KNRSNS canorousness
melodious
KNRSP counterspy
espionage counterspies
KNRSPNZH
counterespionage *spying*

KNRSPYNJ
counterespionage *spying*
KNRSPYNSH
counterespionage *spying*
KNRSPYNZH
counterespionage *spying*
KNRTK counterattack *fight*
KNRTP countertop *cabinet*
KNRVL countervail *oppose*
KNRVLSHN
counterrevolution
overthrow
KNRVLSHNR
counterrevolutionary *rebel*
counterrevolutionaries
KNRWT counterweight
balancer
KNS achiness *pain*
KNS Cairnes *Australian city*
KNS countess *title*
countesses
KNS coyness *shyness*
KNS echinus *sea urchin*
echini
KNS ickiness *disgusting*
KNS keenness *sharp, eager*
KNS kinase *enzyme*
KNSBSTNSHSHN
consubstantiation *religion*
KNSBSTNSHYSHN
consubstantiation *religion*
KNSD canasta *card game*
KNSD coincide *agree*
coincided coinciding
KNSD concede *admit*
conceded conceding
KNSD iconicity
correspondence
KNSDD conceited *vain*
KNSDNL coincidental (adj)
same time coincidentally
(adv)
KNSDNS coincidence
related event
KNSDNT coincident
harmonious
KNSDNTL coincidental (adj)
same time coincidentally
(adv)
KNSDNTS coincidence
related event
KNSDR canister *container*

KNSDR conceder *admitter*
KNSDR consider *think*
KNSDRBL considerable (adj) *significant* considerably (adv)
KNSDRSHN consideration *thought, regard, payment*
KNSDRT considerate *thoughtful*
KNSFK kinsfolk *relatives*
KNSH congé *farewell*
KNSH knish *food*
KNSHM consume *destroy, engross, use** consumed consuming
KNSHMBL consumable *food*
KNSHMN consuming *eager*
KNSHMNG consuming *eager*
KNSHMR consumer *user*
KNSHMRZM consumerism *user's interests*
KNSHN conation *impulse*
KNSHNBL conscionable *careful*
KNSHNCHS conscientious *careful*
KNSHNS conscience *moral sense*
KNSHNSHS conscientious *careful*
KNSHNTS conscience *moral sense*
KNSHP kinship *relationship*
KNSHR coinsure *joint risk* coinsured coinsuring
KNSHRNS coinsurance *joint risk*
KNSHRNTS coinsurance *joint risk*
KNSHRR coinsurer *joint risk*
KNSHS conscious *awake, aware*
KNSHS Kinshasa *city*
KNSHSL consciously *awake, aware*
KNSHSNS consciousness *awake, aware*
KNSHYM consume *destroy, engross, use** consumed consuming

KNSHYMBL consumable *food*
KNSHYMN consuming *eager*
KNSHYMNG consuming *eager*
KNSHYMR consumer *user*
KNSHYMRZM consumerism *user's interests*
KNSHYNCHS conscientious *careful*
KNSHYNSHS conscientious *careful*
KNSKDV consecutive *in sequence*
KNSKDVL consecutively *in sequence*
KNSKN coonskin *raccoon fur*
KNSKP kinescope *picture tube* kinescoped kinescoping
KNSKRDR consecrator *devotion* consecratory
KNSKRP conscript *recruit*
KNSKRPSHN conscription *draft*
KNSKRPT conscript *recruit*
KNSKRSHN consecration *ceremony*
KNSKRT consecrate *devote* consecrated consecrating
KNSKRTR consecrator *devotion* consecratory
KNSKS kinesics *body language*
KNSKTV consecutive *in sequence*
KNSKTVL consecutively *in sequence*
KNSKWNCHL consequential (adj) *resulting, important* consequentially (adv)
KNSKWNS consequence *result, importance*
KNSKWNSHL consequential (adj) *resulting, important* consequentially (adv)

KNSKWNT consequent *deduction, resulting*
KNSKWNTL consequently *accordingly*
KNSKWNTS consequence *result, importance*
KNSKYDV consecutive *in sequence*
KNSKYDVL consecutively *in sequence*
KNSKYTV consecutive *in sequence*
KNSKYTVL consecutively *in sequence*
KNSL cancel *annul, delete* canceled (or) cancelled canceling (or) cancelling
KNSL conceal *hide*
KNSL console (v) *cheer up* consoled consoling
KNSL console (n) *furniture*
KNSL consul *magistrate*
KNSL council *group*
KNSL counsel *advise* counseled (or) counselled counseling (or) counselling
KNSLBL cancelable *annul, delete*
KNSLBL concealable *hide*
KNSLBL consolable *cheer up*
KNSLDDD consolidated *merged*
KNSLDDR consolidator *merger*
KNSLDNG consulting *advising*
KNSLDNT consultant *advisor*
KNSLDR conciliator *pacifier*
KNSLDR consultor *advisor*
KNSLDSHN consolidation *merger*
KNSLDT consolidate *merge* consolidated consolidating
KNSLDTD consolidated *merged*
KNSLDTR consolidator *merger*
KNSLJNRL consul general

Letters aren't doubled for single sounds: to find alley use **L** not **LL**. Use **Y** and **W** as hard sounds only: to find yellow use **YL**. (Br)=British spelling or usage. * See dictionary.

magistrate consuls
general

KNSLMN councilman
council member
councilmen

KNSLMNT concealment
hide

KNSLN counseling (or)
counselling *advice*

KNSLNG counseling (or)
counselling *advice*

KNSLR canceler (or)
canceller *annul, delete*

KNSLR concealer *hider*

KNSLR conciliar *reconcile*

KNSLR consoler *cheer up*

KNSLR consular *official*

KNSLR councillor (or)
councilor *council member*

KNSLR counselor (or)
counsellor *advisor, lawyer*

KNSLS cancellous *porous*

KNSLSHN cancellation
annulment, deletion

KNSLSHN conciliation
pacification

KNSLSHN consolation *cheer
up*

KNSLSHP consulship *office,
term*

KNSLT conciliate *pacify*
conciliated conciliating

KNSLT consulate *office, term*

KNSLT consult *advise*

KNSLTDV consultative
advice

KNSLTN consulting *advising*

KNSLTNG consulting
advising

KNSLTNT consultant *advisor*

KNSLTR conciliator *pacifier*

KNSLTR conciliatory
pacifying

KNSLTR consolatory *cheer
up*

KNSLTR consultor *advisor*

KNSLTTV consultative
advice

KNSLWMN councilwoman
council member
councilwomen

KNSLYDR conciliator

pacifier

KNSLYR conciliar *reconcile*

KNSLYSHN conciliation
pacification

KNSLYT conciliate *pacify*
conciliated conciliating

KNSLYTR conciliator *pacifier*

KNSLYTR conciliatory
pacifying

KNSM consommé *broth*

KNSM consume *destroy,
engross, use** consumed
consuming

KNSMBL consumable *food*

KNSMDR consummator
completer

KNSMJR Canis Major
constellation

KNSMN consuming *eager*

KNSMN kinsman *family*
kinsmen

KNSMNG consuming *eager*

KNSMNR Canis Minor
constellation

KNSMPDV consumptive
tuberculosis, use

KNSMPSHN consumption
tuberculosis, use

KNSMPTV consumptive
tuberculosis, use

KNSMR consumer *user*

KNSMRZM consumerism
user's interests

KNSMSHN consummation
completion

KNSMT consummate *perfect*
consummated
consummating

KNSMTR consummator
completer

KNSN consign *transfer*

KNSN consignee *receiver*

KNSNBL consignable
transferable

KNSNCHL consensual (adj)
mutual consent
consensually (adv)

KNSNCHWL consensual
(adj) *mutual consent*
consensually (adv)

KNSND concinnity *harmony*
concinnities

KNSNGGWN consanguine
related

KNSNGGWND
consanguinity *kin*

KNSNGGWNS
consanguineous *related*

KNSNGGWNT
consanguinity *kin*

KNSNGGWNYS
consanguineous *related*

KNSNGWN consanguine
related

KNSNGWND consanguinity
kin

KNSNGWNS
consanguineous *related*

KNSNGWNT consanguinity
kin

KNSNGWNYS
consanguineous *related*

KNSNMNT consignment
commitment

KNSNNL consonantal *letter*

KNSNNS consonance
agreement

KNSNNT consonant *(adj)
agreement (n) letter*

KNSNNTL consonantal
letter

KNSNNTS consonance
agreement

KNSNR consenter *agreer*

KNSNR consignor *person
transferring*

KNSNSHL consensual (adj)
mutual consent
consensually (adv)

KNSNSHWL consensual
(adj) *mutual consent*
consensually (adv)

KNSNSS consensus
common consent

KNSNT concinnity *harmony*
concinnities

KNSNT consent *agree*

KNSNT consonant *(adj)
agreement (n) letter*

KNSNTCHL consensual
(adj) *mutual consent*
consensually (adv)

KNSNTCHWL consensual
(adj) *mutual consent*

Use letters that best describe the sounds you hear and omit the vowels. Use **S** or **K** instead of **C**: to find circle use **SRKL**. Use **J** to find joy, **JM** to find gem and **G** to find go.

consensually (adv)
KNSNTL consonantal *letter*
KNSNTR consenter *agreer*
KNSNTRDDL
concentratedly *focus, collect*
KNSNTRDR concentrator *focus, collect*
KNSNTRK concentric *common center*
KNSNTRKL concentrically *common center*
KNSNTRSD concentricity *common center*
KNSNTRSHN concentration *focus, collection*
KNSNTRST concentricity *common center*
KNSNTRT concentrate *focus, collect* concentrated concentrating
KNSNTRTDL
concentratedly *focus, collect*
KNSNTRTR concentrator *focus, collect*
KNSNTSHL consensual (adj) *mutual consent* consensually (adv)
KNSNTSHWL consensual (adj) *mutual consent* consensually (adv)
KNSNTSS consensus *common consent*
KNSP concept *notion*
KNSPCHL conceptual (adj) *ideas* conceptually (adv)
KNSPCHLZ conceptualize *imagine* conceptualized conceptualizing
(Br) conceptualise
KNSPCHLZR
conceptualizer *thinker*
(Br) conceptualiser
KNSPCHLZSHN
conceptualization *thought*
(Br) conceptualisation
KNSPCHWL conceptual (adj) *ideas* conceptually (adv)
KNSPCHWLZ
conceptualize *imagine*

conceptualized
conceptualizing
(Br) conceptualise
KNSPCHWLZR
conceptualizer *thinker*
(Br) conceptualiser
KNSPCHWLZSHN
conceptualization *thought*
(Br) conceptualisation
KNSPKDS conspectus *outline*
KNSPKS conspicuous *obvious*
KNSPKSL conspicuously *obviously*
KNSPKSNS
conspicuousness *obviousness*
KNSPKTS conspectus *outline*
KNSPKWS conspicuous *obvious*
KNSPKWSL conspicuously *obviously*
KNSPKWSNS
conspicuousness *obviousness*
KNSPKYS conspicuous *obvious*
KNSPKYSL conspicuously *obviously*
KNSPKYSNS
conspicuousness *obviousness*
KNSPKYWS conspicuous *obvious*
KNSPKYWSL
conspicuously *obviously*
KNSPKYWSNS
conspicuousness *obviousness*
KNSPQS conspicuous *obvious*
KNSPQSL conspicuously *obviously*
KNSPQSNS
conspicuousness *obviousness*
KNSPQWS conspicuous *obvious*
KNSPQWSL conspicuously *obviously*

KNSPQWSNS
conspicuousness *obviousness*
KNSPR conspire *plot* conspired conspiring
KNSPRC conspiracy *plot* conspiracies
KNSPRDR conspirator *plotter*
KNSPRS conspiracy *plot* conspiracies
KNSPRTR conspirator *plotter*
KNSPRTRL conspiratorial (adj) *plotting* conspiratorially (adv)
KNSPRTRYL conspiratorial (adj) *plotting* conspiratorially (adv)
KNSPSHL conceptual (adj) *ideas* conceptually (adv)
KNSPSHLZ conceptualize *imagine* conceptualized conceptualizing
(Br) conceptualise
KNSPSHLZR
conceptualizer *thinker*
(Br) conceptualiser
KNSPSHLZSHN
conceptualization *thought*
(Br) conceptualisation
KNSPSHN conception *beginning, idea*
KNSPSHWL conceptual (adj) *ideas* conceptually (adv)
KNSPSHWLZ
conceptualize *imagine* conceptualized conceptualizing
(Br) conceptualise
KNSPSHWLZR
conceptualizer *thinker*
(Br) conceptualiser
KNSPSHWLZSHN
conceptualization *thought*
(Br) conceptualisation
KNSPT concept *notion*
KNSPTL conceptual (adj) *ideas* conceptually (adv)
KNSPTLZ conceptualize *imagine* conceptualized

Letters aren't doubled for single sounds: to find alley use **L** not **LL**. Use **Y** and **W** as hard sounds only: to find yellow use **YL**. (Br)=British spelling or usage. * See dictionary.

conceptualizing
(Br) conceptualise

KNSPTLZR conceptualizer *thinker*
(Br) conceptualiser

KNSPTLZSHN
conceptualization *thought*
(Br) conceptualisation

KNSPTWL conceptual (adj)
ideas conceptually (adv)

KNSPTWLZ conceptualize
imagine conceptualized
conceptualizing
(Br) conceptualise

KNSPTWLZR
conceptualizer *thinker*
(Br) conceptualiser

KNSPTWLZSHN
conceptualization *thought*
(Br) conceptualisation

KNSQDV consecutive *in sequence*

KNSQDVL consecutively *in sequence*

KNSQNCHL consequential
(adj) *resulting, important*
consequentially (adv)

KNSQNS consequence
result, importance

KNSQNSHL consequential
(adj) *resulting, important*
consequentially (adv)

KNSQNT consequent
deduction, resulting

KNSQNTL consequently
accordingly

KNSQNTS consequence
result, importance

KNSQTV consecutive *in sequence*

KNSQTVL consecutively *in sequence*

KNSR Cancer *zodiac sign*

KNSR cancer *disease*

KNSR connoisseur *expert*

KNSRDD concerted *in unison*

KNSRDDL concertedly *in unison*

KNSRDDNS concertedness
in unison

KNSRDM consortium

association consortia

KNSRDYM consortium
association consortia

KNSRJ concierge *residential manager* concierges

KNSRN concern (v) *involve* (n) *care, establishment*

KNSRND concerned
interested, anxious

KNSRNMNT concernment
anxiety

KNSRNN concerning *about*

KNSRNNG concerning
about

KNSRS cancerous *diseased*

KNSRSH concierge
residential manager
concierges

KNSRSH consortia (pl)
association consortium

KNSRSHM consortium
association consortia

KNSRT concert *music, together*

KNSRT consort *associate*

KNSRTD concerted *in unison*

KNSRTDL concertedly *in unison*

KNSRTDNS concertedness
in unison

KNSRTM consortium
association consortia

KNSRTMSDR
concertmaster *leader*

KNSRTMSTR
concertmaster *leader*

KNSRTN concertina
accordion

KNSRTYM consortium
association consortia

KNSRV conserve *preserve*
conserved conserving

KNSRVDR conservator
protector

KNSRVDV conservative
traditional

KNSRVDVL conservatively
traditional

KNSRVDZM conservatism
traditional

KNSRVNC conservancy

nature protector
conservancies

KNSRVNS conservancy
nature protector
conservancies

KNSRVNTC conservancy
nature protector
conservancies

KNSRVNTS conservancy
nature protector
conservancies

KNSRVR conserver
preserver

KNSRVSHN conservation
nature protection

KNSRVSHNST
conservationist *nature protection*

KNSRVTR conservator
protector

KNSRVTR conservatory
plants, arts conservatories

KNSRVTV conservative
traditional

KNSRVTVL conservatively
traditional

KNSRVTZM conservatism
traditional

KNSRZH concierge
residential manager
concierges

KNSS concise *brief*

KNSS kinesis *motion*
kineses

KNSSDNC consistency
firmness, persistence
consistencies

KNSSDNS consistence
firmness, persistence

KNSSDNS consistency
firmness, persistence
consistencies

KNSSDNT consistent
unchanging

KNSSDNTC consistency
firmness, persistence
consistencies

KNSSDNTL consistently
regularly

KNSSDNTS consistence
firmness, persistence

KNSSDNTS consistency

Use letters that best describe the sounds you hear and omit the vowels. Use **S** or **K** instead of **C**: to find circle use **SRKL**. Use **J** to find joy, **JM** to find gem and **G** to find go.

firmness, persistence
consistencies
KNSSDR consistory *council*
consistories
KNSSHN concession
admission, lease
KNSSHNR concessionaire
refreshments
KNSSHNR concessionary
admission, lease
KNSSL concisely *briefly*
KNSSNS conciseness
briefness
KNSST consist *composed of*
KNSSTNC consistency
firmness, persistence
consistencies
KNSSTNS consistence
firmness, persistence
KNSSTNS consistency
firmness, persistence
consistencies
KNSSTNT consistent
unchanging
KNSSTNTC consistency
firmness, persistence
consistencies
KNSSTNTL consistently
regularly
KNSSTNTS consistence
firmness, persistence
KNSSTNTS consistency
firmness, persistence
consistencies
KNSSTR consistory *council*
consistories
KNST canasta *card game*
KNST canniest *shrewdest*
KNST canoeist *boater*
KNST choanocyte *collar cell*
KNST conceit *vanity,*
thought
KNST iconicity
correspondence
KNSTBL constable *police*
KNSTBLR constabulary
police constabularies
KNSTBYLR constabulary
police constabularies
KNSTCHNC constituency
people constituencies
KNSTCHNS constituency

people constituencies
KNSTCHNT constituent
element, principal
KNSTCHNTC constituency
people constituencies
KNSTCHNTS constituency
people constituencies
KNSTCHWNC constituency
people constituencies
KNSTCHWNS constituency
people constituencies
KNSTCHWNT constituent
element, principal
KNSTCHWNTC
constituency *people*
constituencies
KNSTCHWNTS
constituency *people*
constituencies
KNSTD conceited *vain*
KNSTHDK kinesthetic
movement
KNSTHDKL kinesthetically
movement
KNSTHSH kinesthesia (or)
kinesthesis *movement*
kinesthesias (or)
kinestheses
KNSTHSS kinesthesis (or)
kinesthesia *movement*
kinestheses (or)
kinesthesias
KNSTHTK kinesthetic
movement
KNSTHTKL kinesthetically
movement
KNSTHZ kinesthesia (or)
kinesthesis *movement*
kinesthesias (or)
kinestheses
KNSTHZH kinesthesia (or)
kinesthesis *movement*
kinesthesias (or)
kinestheses
KNSTLSHN constellation
star pattern
KNSTLT constellate *cluster*
constellated constellating
KNSTNC constancy *loyalty*
constancies
KNSTNNPL Constantinople
city

KNSTNS constancy *loyalty*
constancies
KNSTNT constant *(n) fixed*
quantity (adj) continual
KNSTNTC constancy
loyalty constancies
KNSTNTL constantly
continually
KNSTNTNPL
Constantinople *city*
KNSTNTS constancy *loyalty*
constancies
KNSTPDD constipated *no*
feces, stilted
KNSTPSHN constipation *no*
feces, stilted
KNSTPT constipate *crowd*
together constipated
constipating
KNSTPTD constipated *no*
feces, stilted
KNSTR canister *container*
KNSTR construe *understand*
construed construing
KNSTRBL construable
understandable
KNSTRK constrict *tighten*
KNSTRK construct *(v) build,*
devise (n) concept, form
KNSTRKDR constrictor
tighten
KNSTRKDR constructor
builder
KNSTRKDV constrictive
tight
KNSTRKDV constructive
helpful
KNSTRKDVL constructively
helpfully
KNSTRKSHN constriction
tighten
KNSTRKSHN construction
arrange, build
KNSTRKSHNST
constructionist *law*
KNSTRKT constrict *tighten*
KNSTRKT construct *(v)*
build, devise (n) concept,
form
KNSTRKTR constrictor
tighten
KNSTRKTR constructor

---

builder
KNSTRKTV constrictive *tight*
KNSTRKTV constructive *helpful*
KNSTRKTVL constructively *helpfully*
KNSTRN constrain *hold back*
KNSTRNDL constrainedly *held back*
KNSTRNSHN consternation *dismay*
KNSTRNT consternate *dismay* consternated consternating
KNSTRNT constraint *barrier*
KNSTRWBL construable *understandable*
KNSTTNC constituency *people* constituencies
KNSTTNS constituency *people* constituencies
KNSTTNT constituent *element, principal*
KNSTTNTC constituency *people* constituencies
KNSTTNTS constituency *people* constituencies
KNSTTSHN constitution *nature, laws*
KNSTTSHN Constitution (the) *document*
KNSTTSHNL constitutional (adj) *legal* (n) *walk* constitutionally (adv)
KNSTTSHNLD constitutionality *legality*
KNSTTSHNLT constitutionality *legality*
KNSTTT constitute *establish* constituted constituting
KNSTTWNC constituency *people* constituencies
KNSTTWNS constituency *people* constituencies
KNSTTWNT constituent *element, principal*
KNSTTWNTC constituency *people* constituencies
KNSTTWNTS constituency *people* constituencies
KNSTTYSHN constitution

nature, laws
KNSTTYSHN Constitution (the) *document*
KNSTTYSHNL constitutional (adj) *legal* (n) *walk* constitutionally (adv)
KNSTTYSHNLD constitutionality *legality*
KNSTTYSHNLT constitutionality *legality*
KNSTTYT constitute *establish* constituted constituting
KNSV conceive *imagine, originate, understand* conceived conceiving
KNSVBL conceivable (adj) *imagined* conceivably (adv)
KNSVBLD conceivability *imagined*
KNSVBLT conceivability *imagined*
KNSVR conceiver *imagine, originate, understand*
KNSX kinesics *body language*
KNSYLR consular *official*
KNSYLT consulate *office, term*
KNSYM consume *destroy, engross, use** consumed consuming
KNSYMBL consumable *food*
KNSYMN consuming *eager*
KNSYMNG consuming *eager*
KNSYMR consumer *user*
KNSYMRZM consumerism *user's interests*
KNSYR connoisseur *expert*
KNSYRJ concierge *residential manager* concierges
KNSYRSH concierge *residential manager* concierges
KNSYRZH concierge *residential manager* concierges
KNT account (n) *reckoning*

(v) *explain*
KNT accountant *ledger keeper*
KNT aconite *monkshood*
KNT can't (contr) *cannot*
KNT can't *cannot*
KNT cannot *unable*
KNT cant *slant*
KNT canto *music* cantos
KNT Chianti *wine*
KNT connate *inborn*
KNT connote *imply* connoted connoting
KNT conte *tale*
KNT count (v) *tally* (n) *nobleman, charge*
KNT county *district* counties
KNT cuneate *triangular*
KNT keynote *speaker*
KNT khanate *state*
KNT kyanite *lapis lazuli*
KNTBL accountable (adj) *responsible* accountably (adv)
KNTBL cantabile *music*
KNTBL countable *numbers* countably (adv)
KNTBLD accountability *responsibility*
KNTBLNS accountableness *responsibility*
KNTBLT accountability *responsibility*
KNTD cantata *song*
KNTDN countdown *time remaining*
KNTDV connotative *implying*
KNTGD contiguity *nearness* contiguities
KNTGM contagion *transmission*
KNTGN contagion *transmission*
KNTGS contiguous *adjacent*
KNTGSL contiguously *adjacent*
KNTGT contiguity *nearness* contiguities
KNTGWD contiguity *nearness* contiguities
KNTGWS contiguous

adjacent
KNTGWSL contiguously
adjacent
KNTGWT contiguity
nearness contiguities
KNTGYD contiguity *nearness*
contiguities
KNTGYS contiguous
adjacent
KNTGYSL contiguously
adjacent
KNTGYT contiguity *nearness*
contiguities
KNTGYWD contiguity
nearness contiguities
KNTGYWS contiguous
adjacent
KNTGYWSL contiguously
adjacent
KNTGYWT contiguity
nearness contiguities
KNTH canthi (pl) *angle*
canthus
KNTHKSNTHN
canthaxanthin *food color*
KNTHRDZ cantharides (pl)
aphrodisiac cantharis
KNTHRS cantharis
aphrodisiac cantharides
KNTHS acanthus *herb*
acanthus
KNTHS canthus *angle*
canthi
KNTHSFLN
acanthocephalan *worm*
KNTHXNTHN
canthaxanthin *food color*
KNTJM contagion
transmission
KNTJN contagion
transmission
KNTJS contagious *catching*
KNTJSL contagiously
catching
KNTJSNS contagiousness
catching
KNTK contact *touch*
KNTK eye contact *vision*
KNTK Kentucky *US State*
KNTK kinetic *motion*
KNTKDRB Kentucky Derby
race

KNTKL canticle *song*
KNTKL kinetically *motion*
KNTKS context *setting*
KNTKS kinetics *motion*
KNTKSCHL contextual (adj)
setting contextually (adv)
KNTKSCHWL contextual
(adj) *setting* contextually
(adv)
KNTKSHL contextual (adj)
setting contextually (adv)
KNTKSHWL contextual
(adj) *setting* contextually
(adv)
KNTKST context *setting*
KNTKSTL contextual (adj)
setting contextually (adv)
KNTKSTWL contextual (adj)
setting contextually (adv)
KNTKSTYL contextual (adj)
setting contextually (adv)
KNTKSTYWL contextual
(adj) *setting* contextually
(adv)
KNTKT Connecticut *US
State*
KNTKT contact *touch*
KNTKT eye contact *vision*
KNTL cantala *fiber*
KNTL cantle *portion*
KNTLJ kentledge *ballast*
KNTLP cantaloupe *fruit*
KNTLS countless *many*
KNTLSHN cantillation *song*
KNTLT cantillate *sing*
cantillated cantillating
KNTLVR cantilever *beam*
KNTM contemn *scorn*
KNTMC contumacy *rebellion*
contumacies
KNTMCHS contemptuous
disdainful
KNTMCHSL
contemptuously
disdainfully
KNTMCHWS
contemptuous *disdainful*
KNTMCHWSL
contemptuously
disdainfully
KNTML contumely *harsh
treatment* contumelies

KNTMLS contumelious
abusive
KNTMLYS contumelious
abusive
KNTMNDR contaminator
polluter
KNTMNNT contaminant
impurity
KNTMNR contemner *scorn*
KNTMNSHN contamination
pollution
KNTMNT contaminant
impurity
KNTMNT contaminate *make
impure* contaminated
contaminating
KNTMNTR contaminator
polluter
KNTMP contempt *disdain*
KNTMPCHS contemptuous
disdainful
KNTMPCHSL
contemptuously
disdainfully
KNTMPCHWS
contemptuous *disdainful*
KNTMPCHWSL
contemptuously
disdainfully
KNTMPLDR contemplator
meditate
KNTMPLDV contemplative
meditative
KNTMPLSHN
contemplation *meditation*
KNTMPLT contemplate
meditate contemplated
contemplating
KNTMPLTR contemplator
meditate
KNTMPLTV contemplative
meditative
KNTMPRND
contemporaneity
modernity
KNTMPRNS
contemporaneous
modern
KNTMPRNSL
contemporaneously
modern
KNTMPRNSNS

contemporaneousness
modern

KNTMPRNT
contemporaneity
modernity

KNTMPRNYD
contemporaneity
modernity

KNTMPRNYS
contemporaneous
modern

KNTMPRNYSL
contemporaneously
modern

KNTMPRNYSNS
contemporaneousness
modern

KNTMPRNYT
contemporaneity
modernity

KNTMPRR contemporary
modern contemporaries

KNTMPSHS contemptuous
disdainful

KNTMPSHSL
contemptuously
disdainfully

KNTMPSHWS
contemptuous *disdainful*

KNTMPSHWSL
contemptuously
disdainfully

KNTMPT contempt *disdain*

KNTMPTBL contemptible
(adj) *disdainful*
contemptibly (adv)

KNTMPTS contemptuous
disdainful

KNTMPTSL
contemptuously
disdainfully

KNTMPTWS contemptuous
disdainful

KNTMPTWSL
contemptuously
disdainfully

KNTMR contemner *scorn*

KNTMS contumacy *rebellion*
contumacies

KNTMSHS contemptuous
disdainful

KNTMSHS contumacious

rebellious

KNTMSHSL
contemptuously
disdainfully

KNTMSHSL
contumaciously
rebelliously

KNTMSHWS contemptuous
disdainful

KNTMSHWSL
contemptuously
disdainfully

KNTMT contempt *disdain*

KNTMTBL contemptible
(adj) *disdainful*
contemptibly (adv)

KNTMTS contemptuous
disdainful

KNTMTSL contemptuously
disdainfully

KNTMTWS contemptuous
disdainful

KNTMTWSL
contemptuously
disdainfully

KNTN accounting *reckoning*

KNTN canteen *container,
store*

KNTN cantina *tavern*

KNTN canton *area*

KNTN Canton *city*

KNTN contain *hold*

KNTN contend *assert*

KNTN continue *stay, prolong*
continued continuing

KNTNBL containable *held*

KNTNCHN contention
quarrel, idea

KNTNCHS contentious
quarrelsome

KNTNCHSL contentiously
quarrelsome

KNTNCHSNS
contentiousness *quarrel*

KNTND contained *held*

KNTND contend *assert*

KNTND contented *happy*

KNTND continued *lasting*

KNTND continuity
connection continuities

KNTNDL contentedly *happy*

KNTNDR contender

competitor

KNTNDR continuator *persist*

KNTNG accounting
reckoning

KNTNGKRS cantankerous
difficult

KNTNGKRSL
cantankerously *difficult*

KNTNGKRSNS
cantankerousness
difficulty

KNTNJNC contingency
possibility contingencies

KNTNJNS contingence
possibility

KNTNJNS contingency
possibility contingencies

KNTNJNT contingent
possible, dependent

KNTNJNTC contingency
possibility contingencies

KNTNJNTS contingence
possibility

KNTNJNTS contingency
possibility contingencies

KNTNKRS cantankerous
difficult

KNTNKRSL cantankerously
difficult

KNTNKRSNS
cantankerousness
difficulty

KNTNL continual (adj)
constant continually (adv)

KNTNM continuum *whole*
continua

KNTNMNT containment
holding

KNTNN continuing *lasting*

KNTNNG continuing *lasting*

KNTNNL continental (adj)
European, land mass
continentally (adv)

KNTNNS continence *self-
restraint*

KNTNNS continuance
lasting

KNTNNS countenance (*n*)
appearance

KNTNNS countenance (*v*)
approve countenanced
countenancing

KNTNNT continent *land mass*

KNTNNT continuant *speech, lasting*

KNTNNTL continental (adj) *European, land mass* continentally (adv)

KNTNNTS continence *self-restraint*

KNTNNTS continuance *lasting*

KNTNNTS countenance (n) *appearance*

KNTNNTS countenance (v) *approve* countenanced countenancing

KNTNR container *holder*

KNTNRZ containerize *ship* containerized containerizing (Br) containerise

KNTNRZSHN containerization *shipping* (Br) containerisation

KNTNS contents *something contained*

KNTNS continence *self-restraint*

KNTNS continuous *without pause*

KNTNSHN contention *quarrel, idea*

KNTNSHN continuation *persistence*

KNTNSHS contentious *quarrelsome*

KNTNSHSL contentiously *quarrelsome*

KNTNSHSNS contentiousness *quarrel*

KNTNSL continuously *without pause*

KNTNT accountant *ledger keeper*

KNTNT content (n) *makeup* (adj) *happy*

KNTNT continent *land mass*

KNTNT continuity *connection* continuities

KNTNTD contented *happy*

KNTNTDL contentedly *happy*

KNTNTL continental (adj) *European, land mass* continentally (adv)

KNTNTMNT contentment *happiness*

KNTNTR continuator *persist*

KNTNTS contents *something contained*

KNTNTS continence *self-restraint*

KNTNTSHP accountantship *ledger keeping*

KNTNWD continuity *connection* continuities

KNTNWDR continuator *persist*

KNTNWL continual (adj) *constant* continually (adv)

KNTNWM continuum *whole* continua

KNTNWN continuing *lasting*

KNTNWNG continuing *lasting*

KNTNWNS continuance *lasting*

KNTNWNT continuant *speech, lasting*

KNTNWNTS continuance *lasting*

KNTNWS continuous *without pause*

KNTNWSHN continuation *persistence*

KNTNWSL continuously *without pause*

KNTNWT continuity *connection* continuities

KNTNWTR continuator *persist*

KNTNY continue *stay, prolong* continued continuing

KNTNYD continued *lasting*

KNTNYD continuity *connection* continuities

KNTNYDR continuator *persist*

KNTNYL continual (adj) *constant* continually (adv)

KNTNYM continuum *whole* continua

KNTNYN continuing *lasting*

KNTNYNG continuing *lasting*

KNTNYNS continuance *lasting*

KNTNYNT continuant *speech, lasting*

KNTNYNTS continuance *lasting*

KNTNYS continuous *without pause*

KNTNYSHN continuation *persistence*

KNTNYSL continuously *without pause*

KNTNYT continuity *connection* continuities

KNTNYTR continuator *persist*

KNTNYWD continuity *connection* continuities

KNTNYWDR continuator *persist*

KNTNYWL continual (adj) *constant* continually (adv)

KNTNYWM continuum *whole* continua

KNTNYWN continuing *lasting*

KNTNYWNG continuing *lasting*

KNTNYWNS continuance *lasting*

KNTNYWNT continuant *speech, lasting*

KNTNYWNTS continuance *lasting*

KNTNYWS continuous *without pause*

KNTNYWSHN continuation *persistence*

KNTNYWSL continuously *without pause*

KNTNYWT continuity *connection* continuities

KNTNYWTR continuator *persist*

KNTNZ Cantonese *of Canton*

KNTR canter *gait, beggar*

KNTR cantor *singer*

KNTR contour *shape*

KNTR counter (n) *shelf,*

Letters aren't doubled for single sounds: to find alley use **L** not **LL**. Use **Y** and **W** as hard sounds only: to find yellow use **YL**. (Br)=British spelling or usage. * See dictionary.

calculator (v) oppose
KNTR country (n) land (adj)
   rustic countries
KNTR keynoter speaker
KNTR qintar money qindarka
KNTRBDR contributor giver
KNTRBLNS counterbalance
   offset counterbalanced
   counterbalancing
KNTRBLNTS
   counterbalance offset
   counterbalanced
   counterbalancing
KNTRBN contraband
   smuggling
KNTRBND contraband
   smuggling
KNTRBSHN contribution
   payment, gift
KNTRBT contribute give
   contributed contributing
KNTRBTR contributor giver
KNTRBTR contributory
   given contributories
KNTRBYDR contributor
   giver
KNTRBYSHN contribution
   payment, gift
KNTRBYT contribute give
   contributed contributing
KNTRBYTR contributor
   giver
KNTRBYTR contributory
   given contributories
KNTRCHK counter check
   banking
KNTRCHK countercheck
   (v,n) restraint
KNTRDD contorted twisted
KNTRDK contradict deny
KNTRDKDBL
   contradictable deny
KNTRDKDR contradictor
   deny
KNTRDKDR contradictory
   opposing
KNTRDKDRL
   contradictorily opposite
KNTRDKDRNS
   contradictoriness opposite
KNTRDKSHN contradiction
   true and false

KNTRDKT contradict deny
KNTRDKTBL
   contradictable deny
KNTRDKTR contradictor
   deny
KNTRDKTR contradictory
   opposing
KNTRDKTRL
   contradictorily opposite
KNTRDKTRNS
   contradictoriness opposite
KNTRDSTNGKSHN
   contradistinction contrast
KNTRDSTNGKTV
   contradistinctive contrast
KNTRDSTNKSHN
   contradistinction contrast
KNTRDSTNKTV
   contradistinctive contrast
KNTRFD countrified rustic
KNTRFNSV
   counteroffensive military
KNTRFT counterfeit forgery
KNTRFTR counterfeiter
   forger
KNTRK contract (n)
   agreement (v) shrink, hire,
   incur
KNTRK counteract oppose
KNTRKCHL contractual
   (adj) agreement
   contractually (adv)
KNTRKCHWL contractual
   (adj) agreement
   contractually (adv)
KNTRKDBL contractible
   shrink
KNTRKDL contractile
   shrinking
KNTRKDR contractor build,
   shrink, agree
KNTRKDV counteractive
   opposition
KNTRKLB country club golf
KNTRKLCHR
   counterculture non-
   establishment
KNTRKLCHRL
   countercultural non-
   establishment
KNTRKLCHRLST
   counterculturalist non-

establishment
KNTRKLKWZ
   counterclockwise
   direction
KNTRKLM counterclaim
   legal
KNTRKLQZ
   counterclockwise
   direction
KNTRKLTR counterculture
   non-establishment
KNTRKLTRL
   countercultural non-
   establishment
KNTRKLTRLST
   counterculturalist non-
   establishment
KNTRKSHL contractual
   (adj) agreement
   contractually (adv)
KNTRKSHN contraction
   shrinkage
KNTRKSHN counteraction
   opposition
KNTRKSHWL contractual
   (adj) agreement
   contractually (adv)
KNTRKT contract (n)
   agreement (v) shrink, hire,
   incur
KNTRKT counteract oppose
KNTRKTBL contractible
   shrink
KNTRKTL contractile
   shrinking
KNTRKTL contractual (adj)
   agreement contractually
   (adv)
KNTRKTLD contractility
   shrinking
KNTRKTLT contractility
   shrinking
KNTRKTR contractor build,
   shrink, agree
KNTRKTV counteractive
   opposition
KNTRKTWL contractual
   (adj) agreement
   contractually (adv)
KNTRL contrail vapor trail
KNTRL control manage
   controlled controlling

Use letters that best describe the sounds you hear and omit the vowels. Use **S** or **K** instead of **C**: to find circle use **SRKL**. Use **J** to find joy, **JM** to find gem and **G** to find go.

KNTRLBL controllable *manageable*
KNTRLBLD controllability *manageability*
KNTRLBLT controllability *manageability*
KNTRLN controlling *managing*
KNTRLNG controlling *managing*
KNTRLR comptroller *auditor*
KNTRLR controller *accounting, manager*
KNTRLT contralto *voice* contraltos
KNTRMN counterman *clerk* countermen
KNTRMN countermand *revoke*
KNTRMND countermand *revoke*
KNTRMNS conterminous *shared boundary*
KNTRMSHR countermeasure opposition
KNTRMZHR countermeasure opposition
KNTRNDKSHN contraindication *not advised*
KNTRNDKT contraindicate *not advised*
KNTRNSRJNC counterinsurgency *military*
KNTRNSRJNS counterinsurgency *military*
KNTRNSRJNT counterinsurgent *military*
KNTRNSRJNTC counterinsurgency *military*
KNTRNSRJNTS counterinsurgency *military*
KNTRNTLJNS counterintelligence *spying*
KNTRNTLJNTS

counterintelligence *spying*
KNTRPN counterpane *bedspread*
KNTRPNT counterpoint *melody, opposite*
KNTRPNTL contrapuntal *counterpoint*
KNTRPRDKDV counterproductive *hindrance*
KNTRPRDKTV counterproductive *hindrance*
KNTRPRT counterpart *complement*
KNTRPSHN contraption *gadget*
KNTRPZ counterpoise *balance*
KNTRR contrary *opposite* contraries
KNTRRL contrarily *opposite*
KNTRRNS contrariness *opposite*
KNTRRWZ contrariwise *opposite*
KNTRS contrast *compare*
KNTRSD contrasty *different*
KNTRSD countryside *rural land*
KNTRSDBL contrastable *comparable*
KNTRSDV contrastive *comparative*
KNTRSDVL contrastively *comparatively*
KNTRSGNCHR countersignature *vouch for*
KNTRSGNTR countersignature *vouch for*
KNTRSHN contortion *twist*
KNTRSHN contrition *repentance*
KNTRSHNST contortionist *twister*
KNTRSN countersign *signature*
KNTRSNGK countersink *set below* countersunk

countersinking
KNTRSNK countersink *set below* countersunk countersinking
KNTRSP counterspy *espionage* counterspies
KNTRSPDV contraceptive *preventative*
KNTRSPNJ counterespionage *spying*
KNTRSPNSH counterespionage *spying*
KNTRSPNZH counterespionage *spying*
KNTRSPSHN contraception *prevention*
KNTRSPTV contraceptive *preventative*
KNTRSPYNJ counterespionage *spying*
KNTRSPYNSH counterespionage *spying*
KNTRSPYNZH counterespionage *spying*
KNTRST contrast *compare*
KNTRST contrasty *different*
KNTRSTBL contrastable *comparable*
KNTRSTV contrastive *comparative*
KNTRSTVL contrastively *comparatively*
KNTRT contort *twist*
KNTRT contrite *repent*
KNTRTD contorted *twisted*
KNTRTK counterattack *fight*
KNTRTL contritely *repent*
KNTRTN contretemps *embarrassment* contretemps
KNTRTNS contriteness *repentance*
KNTRTNZ contretemps *embarrassment* contretemps
KNTRTP countertop *cabinet*
KNTRV contrive *create* contrived contriving
KNTRVD contrived *created*
KNTRVL countervail *oppose*
KNTRVLSHN counterrevolution

overthrow
KNTRVLSHNR
counterrevolutionary *rebel*
counterrevolutionaries
KNTRVN contravene *violate*
contravened
contravening
KNTRVNCHN
contravention *violation*
KNTRVNR contravener
violator
KNTRVNS contrivance
device
KNTRVNSHN contravention
violation
KNTRVNTS contrivance
device
KNTRVR contriver *creator*
KNTRVRC controversy
dispute controversies
KNTRVRDBL controvertible
disputed
KNTRVRDR controverter
disputer
KNTRVRS controversy
dispute controversies
KNTRVRSHL controversial
(adj) *disputed*
controversially (adv)
KNTRVRSYL controversial
(adj) *disputed*
controversially (adv)
KNTRVRT controvert
dispute
KNTRVRTBL controvertible
disputed
KNTRVRTR controverter
disputer
KNTRWD countrywide
coast-to-coast
KNTRWT counterweight
balancer
KNTS contuse *bruise*
KNTS countess *title*
countesses
KNTSDBL contestable
dispute
KNTSDNT contestant
competition
KNTSHN connotation
implication
KNTSHN contusion *bruise*

KNTSHNL connotational
implying
KNTSKP kinetoscope *film*
KNTSKWNCHL
consequential (adj)
resulting, important
consequentially (adv)
KNTSKWNS consequence
result, importance
KNTSKWNSHL
consequential (adj)
resulting, important
consequentially (adv)
KNTSKWNT consequent
deduction, resulting
KNTSKWNTL consequently
accordingly
KNTSKWNTS consequence
result, importance
KNTSL cancel *annul, delete*
canceled (or) cancelled
canceling (or) cancelling
KNTSL consul *magistrate*
KNTSL council *group*
KNTSL counsel *advise*
counseled (or)
counselled counseling
(or) counselling
KNTSLBL cancelable *annul,*
delete
KNTSLJNRL consul general
magistrate consuls
general
KNTSLMN councilman
council member
councilmen
KNTSLN counseling (or)
counselling *advice*
KNTSLNG counseling (or)
counselling *advice*
KNTSLR canceler (or)
canceller *annul, delete*
KNTSLR consular *official*
KNTSLR councillor (or)
councilor *council member*
KNTSLR counselor (or)
counsellor *advisor, lawyer*
KNTSLS cancellous *porous*
KNTSLSHN cancellation
annulment, deletion
KNTSLSHP consulship
office, term

KNTSLT consulate *office,*
term
KNTSLTDV consultative
advice
KNTSLTSHN consultation
advice
KNTSLTTV consultative
advice
KNTSLWMN councilwoman
council member
councilwomen
KNTSMDR consummator
completer
KNTSMSHN consummation
completion
KNTSMT consummate
perfect consummated
consummating
KNTSMTR consummatory
completing
KNTSNT consequent
deduction, resulting
KNTSQNCHL
consequential (adj)
resulting, important
consequentially (adv)
KNTSQNS consequence
result, importance
KNTSQNSHL consequential
(adj) *resulting, important*
consequentially (adv)
KNTSQNT consequent
deduction, resulting
KNTSQNTL consequently
accordingly
KNTSQNTS consequence
result, importance
KNTSR Cancer *zodiac sign*
KNTSR cancer *disease*
KNTSRS cancerous *diseased*
KNTST contest (v) *dispute*
(n) *competition*
KNTSTBL contestable
dispute
KNTSTNT contestant
competition
KNTSYLR consular *official*
KNTSYLT consulate *office,*
term
KNTT cantata *song*
KNTTV connotative
implying

Use letters that best describe the sounds you hear and omit the vowels. Use **S** or **K** instead of **C**: to find circle use **SRKL**. Use **J** to find joy, **JM** to find gem and **G** to find go.

KNTV conative *impulse*
KNTX context *setting*
KNTX kinetics *motion*
KNTXCHL contextual (adj) *setting* contextually (adv)
KNTXCHWL contextual (adj) *setting* contextually (adv)
KNTXT context *setting*
KNTXTL contextual (adj) *setting* contextually (adv)
KNTXTWL contextual (adj) *setting* contextually (adv)
KNTXTYL contextual (adj) *setting* contextually (adv)
KNTXTYWL contextual (adj) *setting* contextually (adv)
KNTYMC contumacy *rebellion* contumacies
KNTYML contumely *harsh treatment*
KNTYMLS contumelious *abusive*
KNTYMLYS contumelious *abusive*
KNTYMS contumacy *rebellion* contumacies
KNTYMSHS contumacious *rebellious*
KNTYMSHSL contumaciously *rebelliously*
KNTYS contuse *bruise*
KNTYSHN contusion *bruise*
KNTYZ contuse *bruise*
KNTYZHN contusion *bruise*
KNTZ contuse *bruise*
KNTZHN contusion *bruise*
KNV connive *plan* connived conniving
KNV convey *send*
KNV convoy *escort*
KNVK convict (*n*) prisoner (*v*) find guilty
KNVK convoke *summon* convoked convoking
KNVKDR convector *circulator*
KNVKDV convective *circulative*
KNVKS convex *curved*
KNVKSD convexity *curve*

convexities
KNVKSHN convection *circulation*
KNVKSHN conviction *belief, found guilty*
KNVKSHN convocation *clergy, assembly*
KNVKSHNL convectional *circulation*
KNVKST convexity *curve* convexities
KNVKT convict (*n*) prisoner (*v*) find guilty
KNVKTR convector *circulator*
KNVKTV convective *circulative*
KNVLDD convoluted *twisted*
KNVLS convalesce *recover* convalesced convalescing
KNVLS convulse *shake* convulsed convulsing
KNVLSHN convolution *curved shape*
KNVLSHN convulsion *spasm*
KNVLSNS convalescence *recovery*
KNVLSNT convalescent *recovery*
KNVLSNTS convalescence *recovery*
KNVLSV convulsive *fitful*
KNVLSVL convulsively *fitfully*
KNVLT convolute *twist* convoluted convoluting
KNVLTD convoluted *twisted*
KNVN convene *summon* convened convening
KNVNCHN convention *contract, assembly*
KNVNCHNL conventional (adj) *ordinary* conventionally (adv)
KNVNCHNLD conventionality *ordinary* conventionalities
KNVNCHNLST conventionalist *ordinary*
KNVNCHNLT conventionality *ordinary*

conventionalities
KNVNCHNLZM conventionalism *ordinary*
KNVNCHNLZSHN conventionalization *ordinary*
KNVNCHNR conventioneer *attendee*
KNVNNS convenience *ease, (Br) toilet*
KNVNNT convenient *handy*
KNVNNTL conveniently *handy*
KNVNNTS convenience *ease, (Br) toilet*
KNVNR convener (or) convenor *summoner*
KNVNS connivance *plan*
KNVNS conveyance *movement, vehicle*
KNVNS convince *prove* convinced convincing
KNVNSHN convention *contract, assembly*
KNVNSHNL conventional (adj) *ordinary* conventionally (adv)
KNVNSHNLD conventionality *ordinary* conventionalities
KNVNSHNLST conventionalist *ordinary*
KNVNSHNLT conventionality *ordinary* conventionalities
KNVNSHNLZM conventionalism *ordinary*
KNVNSHNLZSHN conventionalization *ordinary*
KNVNSHNR conventioneer *attendee*
KNVNSN convincing *reasonable*
KNVNSNG convincing *reasonable*
KNVNSNGL convincingly *reasonably*
KNVNSNL convincingly *reasonably*
KNVNSR convincer *prover*
KNVNT convent *religious*

Letters aren't doubled for single sounds: to find alley use **L** not **LL**. Use **Y** and **W** as hard sounds only: to find yellow use **YL**. (Br)=British spelling or usage. * See dictionary.

community
KNVNTL conveniently *handy*
KNVNTS connivance *plan*
KNVNTS conveyance
movement, vehicle
KNVNTS convince *prove*
convinced convincing
KNVNTSN convincing
reasonable
KNVNTSNG convincing
reasonable
KNVNTSNGL convincingly
reasonably
KNVNTSNL convincingly
reasonably
KNVNTSR convincer *prover*
KNVNYNS convenience
ease, (Br) toilet
KNVNYNT convenient
handy
KNVNYNTL conveniently
handy
KNVNYNTS convenience
ease, (Br) toilet
KNVNYT convenient *handy*
KNVNYTL conveniently
handy
KNVR conniver *planner*
KNVR conveyor *mover*
KNVRDBL convertible *(n)*
car (adj) changeable
KNVRDBL convertibly *(adv)*
changeable
KNVRDBLD convertibility
changeable
KNVRDBLT convertibility
changeable
KNVRDR converter (or)
convertor *changer*
KNVRJ converge *meet*
converged converging
KNVRJNS convergence (n)
come together
convergency (n)
KNVRJNT convergent
approaching
KNVRJNTS convergence (n)
come together
convergency (n)
KNVRS converse *(v) talk*
conversed conversing
KNVRS converse *(n, adj)*

reverse order
KNVRSBL conversable *talk*
KNVRSHN conversion
change
KNVRSL conversely *reverse
order*
KNVRSNS conversance
knowledge conversancy
KNVRSNT conversant
knowledge
KNVRSNTS conversance
knowledge conversancy
KNVRSR converser *talker*
KNVRSSHN conversation
talk
KNVRSSHNL
conversational (adj) *talk*
conversationally (adv)
KNVRSSHNLST
conversationalist *talker*
KNVRT convert *change*
KNVRTBL convertible *(n)*
car (adj) changeable
KNVRTBL convertibly *(adv)*
changeable
KNVRTBLD convertibility
changeable
KNVRTBLT convertibility
changeable
KNVRTR converter (or)
convertor *changer*
KNVRZHN conversion
change
KNVS canvas *cover, fabric*
canvased (or) canvassed
canvasing (or)
canvassing
KNVS canvass *solicit*
canvassed canvassing
KNVSR canvasser *solicitor*
KNVVL convivial (adj) *good
company* convivially (adv)
KNVVLD conviviality *good
company* convivialities
KNVVLT conviviality *good
company* convivialities
KNVVYL convivial (adj) *good
company* convivially (adv)
KNVVYLD conviviality *good
company* convivialities
KNVVYLT conviviality *good
company* convivialities

KNVX convex *curved*
KNVXD convexity *curve*
convexities
KNVXT convexity *curve*
convexities
KNVYNS conveyance
movement, vehicle
KNVYNTS conveyance
movement, vehicle
KNVYR conveyor *mover*
KNW Okinawa *island*
KNW quinoa *grain*
KNWST canoeist *boater*
KNY Kenya *country*
KNYBL connubial (adj)
married connubially (adv)
KNYBYL connubial (adj)
married connubially (adv)
KNYFRM cuneiform *wedge*
KNYK cognac *brandy*
KNYL cannula *tube*
cannulas (or) cannulae
KNYLR cannular *tubular*
KNYMN ichneumon
mongoose, fly
KNYN canyon *valley*
KNYR cannier *shrewder*
KNYSHNT cognoscente
authority cognoscenti
KNYST canniest *shrewdest*
KNYT cuneate *triangular*
KNZ Cairnes *Australian city*
KNZ Cannes *French city*
KNZ conenose *insect*
KNZ Keynes *economist*
KNZ kinase *enzyme*
KNZFK kinsfolk *relatives*
KNZH congé *farewell*
KNZJ coon's age *long time*
KNZKS kinesics *body
language*
KNZLG kinesiology
movement
KNZLJ kinesiology
movement
KNZMN kinsman *family*
kinsmen
KNZN Keynesian *economist*
KNZNZM Keynesianism
economist
KNZS Kansas *US State*
KNZX kinesics *body*

Use letters that best describe the sounds you hear and omit the vowels. Use **S** or **K** instead of **C**: to find circle use **SRKL**. Use **J** to find joy, **JM** to find gem and **G** to find go.

language
KNZYLG kinesiology *movement*
KNZYLJ kinesiology *movement*
KNZYN Keynesian *economist*
KNZYNZM Keynesianism *economist*
KP cap *hat, top* capped capping
KP cape *cloak, land*
KP capo *music* capos
KP co-op *share*
KP coop *cage*
KP cop *(n) policeman*
KP cop *(v-slang) steal* copped copping
KP cope *(v) contend, notch, cover* coped coping
KP cope *(n) garment*
KP copy *imitate, duplicate* copied copying copies
KP coupé (or) coupe *automobile*
KP cowpea *herb*
KP cup *holder, curve* cupped cupping
KP eggcup *egg holder*
KP eyecup *optical aid*
KP kappa *Greek letter*
KP keep *(v) maintain, withhold* kept keeping
KP keep *(n) castle, jail*
KP kepi *cap*
KP kept *(v-past) keep*
KP Kewpie *(trademark) doll*
KP kip *(Br) sleep* kipped kipping
KP kip *(n) hide, bed, weight**
KP occupy *fill, reside* occupied occupying occupies
KP okapi *animal*
KP quipu *counter*
KPBK copybook *penmanship*
KPBL capable (adj) *susceptible* capably (adv)
KPBLD capability *potential* capabilities
KPBLNS capableness *ability*
KPBLT capability *potential*

capabilities
KPBR capybara *rodent*
KPBRR cupbearer *server*
KPCHLSHN capitulation *surrender*
KPCHLT capitulate *yield* capitulated capitulating
KPCHN cappuccino *coffee*
KPCHR capture *catch* captured capturing
KPD Cupid *Roman god of love*
KPD keypad *keyboard*
KPDD cupidity *desire* cupidities
KPDGR coup de grâce (or) coup de grace *finisher* coups de grâce (or) coups de grace
KPDGRS coup de grâce (or) coup de grace *finisher* coups de grâce (or) coups de grace
KPDK Coptic *of Egypt*
KPDL capital (adj) *death, excellence (n) money, letter style, city** capitally (adv)
KPDL capitol *building*
KPDLSDKL capitalistically *economic system*
KPDLST capitalist *economic system*
KPDLSTK capitalistic *economic system*
KPDLSTKL capitalistically *economic system*
KPDLZ capitalize *letter style, profit* capitalized capitalizing (Br) capitalise
KPDLZM capitalism *economic system*
KPDLZSHN capitalization *value, letter style* (Br) capitalisation
KPDMN coup de main *attack* coups de main
KPDR captor *catcher*
KPDR copter *helicopter*
KPDSK copy desk *editor*
KPDT cupidity *desire* cupidities

KPDV captive *prisoner*
KPDVDR captivator *charmer*
KPDVSHN captivation *charm*
KPDVT captivate *charm* captivated captivating
KPDVTR captivator *charmer*
KPFL capful *measure* capfuls
KPFL cupful *measure using a cup* cupfuls
KPK cowpoke *ranch hand*
KPK kapok *fiber*
KPK kopeck (or) kopek *money*
KPKK cupcake *pastry*
KPKS cowpox *disease*
KPKT copycat *imitator*
KPL a cappella *singing*
KPL copula *verb*
KPL couple *(v) link* coupled coupling
KPL couple *(n) pair, two*
KPL cupel *strainer* cupelled (or) cupeled cupelling (or) cupeling
KPL cupola *roof*
KPL cupule *cup-shaped*
KPLD cappelletti *pasta*
KPLD cupolaed *roof*
KPLDV copulative *joint*
KPLK Acapulco *city*
KPLN coupling *pairing*
KPLN Keogh plan *retirement*
KPLNG coupling *pairing*
KPLR capillary *blood vessel* capillaries
KPLR coupler *link*
KPLR cupeler *refiner*
KPLRD capillarity *liquid action* capillarities
KPLRT capillarity *liquid action* capillarities
KPLSHN copulation *sex*
KPLSHN cupellation *refinement*
KPLT cappelletti *pasta*
KPLT copilot *airplane*
KPLT copulate *join* copulated copulating
KPLT couplet *poem*
KPLTR copulatory *sex*
KPLTV copulative *joint*

Letters aren't doubled for single sounds: to find alley use **L** not **LL**. Use **Y** and **W** as hard sounds only: to find yellow use **YL**. (Br)=British spelling or usage. * See dictionary.

KPMNT co-payment *insurance*
KPN capon *chicken*
KPN Capone (Al) *gangster*
KPN capping *topping*
KPN captain *leader*
KPN coping *wall, tool*
KPN coupon *ticket*
KPN cow pony *animal* cow ponies
KPN cupping *blood*
KPN keeping *custody*
KPNC occupancy *residents* occupancies
KPNCH keypunch *data entry*
KPNCHR acupuncture *Chinese therapy*
KPNCHR cowpuncher *cowboy*
KPND caponata *relish*
KPNG capping *topping*
KPNG coping *wall, tool*
KPNG cupping *blood*
KPNG keeping *custody*
KPNGCHR acupuncture *Chinese therapy*
KPNGKSHR acupuncture *Chinese therapy*
KPNGS coping saw *tool*
KPNGSHR acupuncture *Chinese therapy*
KPNHGN Copenhagen *city*
KPNKCHR acupuncture *Chinese therapy*
KPNKSHR acupuncture *Chinese therapy*
KPNS coping saw *tool*
KPNS occupancy *residents* occupancies
KPNSHR acupuncture *Chinese therapy*
KPNT caponata *relish*
KPNT occupant *resident*
KPNTC occupancy *residents* occupancies
KPNTS occupancy *residents* occupancies
KPPD copepod *sea animal*
KPR caper *food, leap, prank*
KPR capper *top*
KPR cooper *barrel*
KPR copier *duplicator*

KPR copper *element*
KPR coppery *like copper*
KPR copra *coconut*
KPR keeper *holder*
KPR kipper *fish*
KPR kouprey *animal*
KPRCH capriccio *prank* capriccios
KPRCHY capriccio *prank* capriccios
KPRDBL copyrightable *publishing*
KPRDR cooperator *associate*
KPRDR copywriter *writer*
KPRDV cooperative *(adj)* act together *(n)* shared business
KPRDVL cooperatively *act together*
KPRFG caprifig *fruit*
KPRFG coprophagy *excrement*
KPRFGS coprophagous *excrement*
KPRFJ coprophagy *excrement*
KPRFKSHN caprification *pollination*
KPRFL coprophilia *excrement*
KPRFLK coprophiliac *excrement*
KPRFLS coprophilous *excrement*
KPRFLY coprophilia *excrement*
KPRFLYK coprophiliac *excrement*
KPRFRS cupriferous *copper*
KPRHD copperhead *snake*
KPRKRN Capricorn *zodiac sign*
KPRL capriole *leap*
KPRLDK coprolitic *excrement*
KPRLT coprolite *excrement*
KPRLTK coprolitic *excrement*
KPRN caprine *goat*
KPRNKN Copernican *of Copernicus*
KPRNKS Copernicus *astronomer*
KPRPLT copperplate

engraving
KPRPNTS capri pants *attire*
KPRS caprice *notion*
KPRS cuprous *copper*
KPRSHN cooperation *common effort*
KPRSHR acupressure *massage*
KPRSHS capricious *impulsive*
KPRSHSL capriciously *impulsively*
KPRSHSNS capriciousness *impulsiveness*
KPRSN caparison *adorn*
KPRSNR coparcenary *two owners* coparcenaries
KPRSNR coparcener *two heirs*
KPRSSR coprocessor *computer*
KPRT cooperate *act together* cooperated cooperating
KPRT copyright *publishing*
KPRT cuprite *copper*
KPRTBL copyrightable *publishing*
KPRTR cooperator *associate*
KPRTR copywriter *writer*
KPRTV cooperative *(adj)* act together *(n)* shared business
KPRTVL cooperatively *act together*
KPRYL capriole *leap*
KPS capias *warrant*
KPS Cheops (or) Khufu *pyramid builder*
KPS copious *plentiful*
KPS coppice *(v)* cut back coppiced coppicing
KPS coppice *(n)* thicket
KPS copse *thicket*
KPSD capacity *potential, role, ability* capacities
KPSDK copacetic (or) copasetic *satisfactory*
KPSDNS capacitance *electricity*
KPSDNTS capacitance *electricity*
KPSDR capacitor *device*
KPSH capuche *hood*

Use letters that best describe the sounds you hear and omit the vowels. Use **S** or **K** instead of **C**: to find circle use **SRKL**. Use **J** to find joy, **JM** to find gem and **G** to find go.

KPSHLZ capsulize *make small* capsulized capsulizing
KPSHN caption *subtitle*
KPSHN capuchin *cloak, monkey, religion*
KPSHN occupation *job, seizure*
KPSHNL occupational (adj) *job, seizure* occupationally (adv)
KPSHS capacious *roomy*
KPSHS captious *critical*
KPSHSL capaciously *roomy*
KPSHSNS capaciousness *roomy*
KPSHSNS captiousness *criticism*
KPSK keepsake *memento*
KPSKM capsicum *pepper*
KPSKN capeskin *leather*
KPSL capsule *container* capsuled capsuling
KPSL copiously *plentiful*
KPSLDD capsulated *enclosed*
KPSLR capsular *enclosed*
KPSLTD capsulated *enclosed*
KPSLZ capsulize *make small* capsulized capsulizing
KPSNS copiousness *plentiful*
KPSSRKM Kaposi's sarcoma *disease*
KPST capacity *potential, role, ability* capacities
KPST copyist *imitate, duplicate*
KPSTK copacetic (or) copasetic *satisfactory*
KPSTN capstan *machine*
KPSTN capstone *crown*
KPSTN copestone *crown*
KPSTNS capacitance *electricity*
KPSTNTS capacitance *electricity*
KPSTR capacitor *device*
KPSTSHN capacitation *change*
KPSTT capacitate *change* capacitated capacitating

KPSYL capsule *container* capsuled capsuling
KPSYLDD capsulated *enclosed*
KPSYLR capsular *enclosed*
KPSYLTD capsulated *enclosed*
KPSYLZ capsulize *make small* capsulized capsulizing
KPSZ capsize *overturn* capsized capsizing
KPSZSRKM Kaposi's sarcoma *disease*
KPT cop out (v) *(slang) quit* cop-out (n)
KPT Copt *Egyptian*
KPT cowpat (or) cowpatty *animal feces*
KPT kaput *ruined*
KPT kept *(v-past) keep*
KPTK Coptic *of Egypt*
KPTL capital (adj) *death, excellent (n) money, letter style, city** capitally (adv)
KPTL capitol *building*
KPTLSDKL capitalistically *economic system*
KPTLSHN capitulation *surrender*
KPTLST capitalist *economic system*
KPTLSTK capitalistic *economic system*
KPTLSTKL capitalistically *economic system*
KPTLT capitulate *yield* capitulated capitulating
KPTLZ capitalize *letter style, profit* capitalized capitalizing (Br) capitalise
KPTLZM capitalism *economic system*
KPTLZSHN capitalization *value, letter style* (Br) capitalisation
KPTN Capetown *city*
KPTN captain *leader*
KPTNC captaincy *rank*
KPTNS captaincy *rank*
KPTNTC captaincy *rank*

KPTNTS captaincy *rank*
KPTR captor *catcher*
KPTR copter *helicopter*
KPTSHN capitation *poll tax*
KPTT capitate *form a head*
KPTV captive *prisoner*
KPTVD captivity *confinement*
KPTVDR captivator *charmer*
KPTVSHN captivation *charm*
KPTVT captivate *charm* captivated captivating
KPTVT captivity *confinement*
KPTVTR captivator *charmer*
KPTYLSHN capitulation *surrender*
KPTYLT capitulate *yield* capitulated capitulating
KPVRDLNDZ Cape Verde Islands *country*
KPVRDLNZ Cape Verde Islands *country*
KPWRK capework *bullfight*
KPX cowpox *disease*
KPYL copula *verb*
KPYL cupule *cup-shaped*
KPYLDV copulative *joint*
KPYLSHN copulation *sex*
KPYLT copulate *join* copulated copulating
KPYLTR copulatory *sex*
KPYLTV copulative *joint*
KPYR copier *duplicator*
KPYS capias *warrant*
KPYS copious *plentiful*
KPYSHN capuchin *cloak, monkey, religion*
KPYSL copiously *plentiful*
KPYSNS copiousness *plentiful*
KPYST copyist *imitate, duplicate*
KQL coequal (adj) *same as* coequally (adv)
KQLD coequality *same as* coequalities
KQLT coequality *same as* coequalities
KR acari (pl) *mite* acarus
KR accrue *add up* accrued accruing
KR achier *sorer*

Letters aren't doubled for single sounds: to find alley use **L** not **LL**. Use **Y** and **W** as hard sounds only: to find yellow use **YL**. (Br)=British spelling or usage. * See dictionary.

KR acre *land measure*
KR cahier *pages*
KR Cairo *city*
KR car *vehicle*
KR care *tend* cared caring
KR CARE *organization*
KR carry *tote* carried carrying carries
KR chorea *disease*
KR coheir *inherit*
KR coir *fiber*
KR core *(v) remove center* cored coring
KR core *(n) center, basic*
KR coria *(pl) skin* corium
KR corps *group* corps
KR cower *crouch*
KR cowrie *(or)* cowry *animal* cowries
KR craw *crop, stomach*
KR Cree *Native American* Cree (or) Crees
KR crew *ship, group*
KR crow *(v) gloat* crowed (or) crew *(Br)* crowing
KR Crow *Native American*
KR crow *(n) bird*
KR cry *shout, weep* cried crying cries
KR cur *dog*
KR cure *(v) heal, prepare meat* cured curing
KR curé *priest*
KR cure *(n) remedy*
KR curia *law court* curiae
KR curie *radioactivity*
KR Curie *scientist*
KR curio *curiosity* curios
KR curry *(v) thrash, clean, treat* curried currying curries
KR curry *spice*
KR ecru *beige color*
KR euchre *(v) cheat* euchred euchring
KR euchre *(n) card game*
KR ichor *blood*
KR ickier *disgusting*
KR karoo *(or)* karroo *tableland* karoos *(or)* karroos
KR kauri *tree*

KR kerry *cattle* kerries
KR Korea *country*
KR kouroi *(pl) youth* kouros
KR kuru *disease*
KR kyrie *prayer*
KR occur *happen* occurred occurring
KR ocher *(or)* ochre *yellow color*
KR okra *vegetable*
KRB carabao *buffalo* carabao (or) carabaos
KRB carb *(or)* carbo *(slang)* carbohydrate
KRB carboy *container*
KRB caribou *elk* caribou (or) caribous
KRB carob *bean*
KRB crab *(v) complain, catch* crabs crabbed crabbing
KRB crab *(n) animal, insect*
KRB crabby *grouchy* crabbier crabbiest
KRB crib *bed, cheat* cribbed cribbing
KRB curb *edge* (Br) kerb
KRBB crybaby *complainer* crybabies
KRBD carabid *insect*
KRBD carbide *carbon*
KRBDK acrobatic *gymnastic*
KRBDKL acrobatically *gymnastically*
KRBDKS acrobatics *gymnastics*
KRBDNS crabbedness *sullenness*
KRBDS Charybdis *monster*
KRBDX acrobatics *gymnastics*
KRBGRS crabgrass *weed*
KRBHDRT carbohydrate *food*
KRBJ cribbage *game*
KRBL accruable *adding up*
KRBL corbel *projection* corbeled (or) corbelled corbeling (or) corbelling
KRBL crabbily *grouchy*
KRBL curable *heal, prepare meat*

KRBLG cryobiology *freezing*
KRBLJ cryobiology *freezing*
KRBLK carbolic *phenol*
KRBLKSD carbolic acid *phenol*
KRBMT crabmeat *food*
KRBN carbine *weapon*
KRBN carbon *element*
KRBN Caribbean *region*
KRBN corbina *fish*
KRBN cribbing *material*
KRBNBLK carbon black *soot*
KRBNC Caribbean Sea *body of water*
KRBND carbonado *diamond* carbonados
KRBNDKSD carbon dioxide *gas*
KRBNDT carbon-date *archeology*
KRBNDXD carbon dioxide *gas*
KRBNDYKSD carbon dioxide *gas*
KRBNDYXD carbon dioxide *gas*
KRBNFRS carboniferous *geologic time*
KRBNG cribbing *material*
KRBNGKL carbuncle *inflammation*
KRBNK carbonic *with carbon*
KRBNKL carbuncle *inflammation*
KRBNKP carbon copy *duplicate* carbon copies
KRBNL carbinol *methanol*
KRBNL carbonyl *chemical*
KRBNLSHN carbonylation *add carbon monoxide*
KRBNMNKSD carbon monoxide *poison gas*
KRBNMNXD carbon monoxide *poison gas*
KRBNPPR carbon paper *duplicate*
KRBNR carabineer *(or)* carabinier *soldier*
KRBNR carabiner *hook*
KRBNR carabinero

Use letters that best describe the sounds you hear and omit the vowels. Use **S** or **K** instead of **C**: to find circle use **SRKL**. Use **J** to find joy, **JM** to find gem and **G** to find go.

policeman carabineros
KRBNR carbonara *pasta*
KRBNS Caribbean Sea *body of water*
KRBNS crabbiness *grouchy*
KRBNSHN carbonation *add carbon dioxide*
KRBNSHS carbonaceous *with carbon*
KRBNSTL carbon steel *hard metal*
KRBNT carbonate *add carbon dioxide* carbonated carbonating
KRBNYR carabiniere *policeman* carabinieri
KRBNZ carbonize *char* carbonized carbonizing
KRBNZSHN carbonization *distillation*
KRBPL crab apple *fruit*
KRBR corroboree *festivity*
KRBR crabber *crab catcher, complainer*
KRBR crabbier *grouchy*
KRBR cribber *cheat*
KRBR crowbar *tool*
KRBRDD carbureted *engine*
KRBRDR carburetor *engine*
KRBRDR corroborator *confirmer*
KRBRDV corroborative *confirming*
KRBRFRM cribriform *holes*
KRBRL carbaryl *insecticide*
KRBRN carbarn *bus garage*
KRBRSHN corroboration *confirmation*
KRBRT corroborate *confirm* corroborated corroborating
KRBRTD carbureted *engine*
KRBRTR carburetor *engine*
KRBRTR corroborator *confirmer*
KRBRTR corroboratory *confirming*
KRBRTV corroborative *confirming*
KRBRZ carburize *add carbon* carburized carburizing (Br) carburise

KRBRZSHN carburization *add carbon* (Br) carburisation
KRBST crabbiest *grouchy*
KRBSTN curbstone *edge*
KRBT acrobat *gymnast*
KRBTK acrobatic *gymnastic*
KRBTKL acrobatically *gymnastically*
KRBTKS acrobatics *gymnastics*
KRBTX acrobatics *gymnastics*
KRBWZ crabwise *sideways*
KRBYLG cryobiology *freezing*
KRBYLJ cryobiology *freezing*
KRBYN Caribbean *region*
KRBYNC Caribbean Sea *body of water*
KRBYNS Caribbean Sea *body of water*
KRBYR crabbier *grouchy*
KRBYRDD carbureted *engine*
KRBYRDR carburetor *engine*
KRBYRTD carbureted *engine*
KRBYRTR carburetor *engine* (Br) carburettort
KRBYRZ carburize *add carbon* carburized carburizing (Br) carburise
KRBYRZSHN carburization *add carbon* (Br) carburisation
KRBYST crabbiest *grouchy*
KRC accuracy *correctness* accuracies
KRC curacy *office* curacies
KRCDD cricetid *animal*
KRCF crucify *punish* crucified crucifying crucifies
KRCFKS crucifix *cross*
KRCFKSHN crucifixion *punishment*
KRCFRM cruciform *cross*
KRCFX crucifix *cross*

KRCH caroche *carriage*
KRCH crotch *lap* crotches
KRCH crouch *stoop*
KRCH crutch *support* crutches
KRCH Karachi *city*
KRCHD crotchety *cranky*
KRCHDNS crotchetiness *crankiness*
KRCHF kerchief *cloth square* kerchiefs
KRCHLR cartulary *deed book* cartularies
KRCHR creature *animal*
KRCHT crotchety *cranky*
KRCHTNS crotchetiness *crankiness*
KRCN kerosene (or) kerosine *fuel*
KRCTD cricetid *animal*
KRCZ crises (pl) *critical phase* crisis
KRCZ cruces (pl) *essential part* crux
KRD acarid *mite*
KRD accord *agreement*
KRD acrid *harsh, bitter*
KRD caird *handyman*
KRD card (n) *fiber, game, small rectangle*
KRD cardia *opening* cardiae (or) cardias
KRD -cardia (pl) *heart -* cardium
KRD chord *music*
KRD choroid (or) choroidal *membrane*
KRD cord *rope, wood*
KRD cored *with center*
KRD corrade *wear away* corraded corrading
KRD corrida *bullfight*
KRD corrode *eat away, undermine* corroded corroding
KRD coward *timid one*
KRD credo *belief* credos
KRD creed *belief*
KRD cried *proclaimed, made tears*
KRD crowd *group*
KRD crud *dirt*

KRD cruddy *dirty, low quality*

KRD crude *raw, rude* cruder crudest

KRD curd *milk*

KRD curdy *thick*

KRD karate *martial arts*

KRD Kurd *Turk*

KRD quarto *music* quartos

KRDB Cordoba *province*

KRDB cordoba *money*

KRDBL corps de ballet *ensemble* corps de ballet

KRDBL corrodible *eat away, undermine*

KRDBL credible (adj) *truthful* credibly (adv)

KRDBLD credibility *belief*

KRDBLDGP credibility gap *difference*

KRDBLT credibility *belief*

KRDBLTGP credibility gap *difference*

KRDBRD cardboard *paperboard*

KRDC courtesy *civility* courtesies

KRDC curtesy *estate* curtesies

KRDCZ cortices (pl) *outer layer* cortex

KRDD acridity *harshness, bitterness*

KRDD cardioid *heart shape*

KRDD carotid *artery*

KRDD crawdad *animal*

KRDD crudity *vulgarity* crudities

KRDDBL accreditable *approved*

KRDDBL creditable (adj) *worthy* creditably (adv)

KRDDD accredited *approved*

KRDDNS crowdedness *crush*

KRDDR creditor *debtor*

KRDDSHN accreditation *approval*

KRDFRM cordiform *heart-shaped*

KRDGN cardigan *sweater*

KRDGRF cardiograph *heart machine*

KRDGRF cardiography *heart machine*

KRDGRFK cardiographic *heart machine*

KRDGRFK cartographic *map*

KRDGRFKL cartographically *map*

KRDGRM cardiogram *heart test*

KRDJ cartage *fee*

KRDJ cordage *rope*

KRDK cardiac *heart*

KRDK critic *judge*

KRDK eucritic *rock*

KRDK eukaryotic *organism*

KRDKL cortical (adj) *outer layer* cortically (adv)

KRDKL critical (adj) *fault, crucial* critically (adv)

KRDKLNS criticalness *fault, crucial*

KRDKR cri de coeur *outcry* cris de coeur

KRDKSDR criticaster *petty judge*

KRDKSTR criticaster *petty judge*

KRDKSTRD corticosteroid *drug*

KRDKSTRN corticosterone *metabolism*

KRDL acridly *harshness, bitterness*

KRDL choroidal (or) choroid *membrane*

KRDL cowardly *timid*

KRDL cradle *hold, bed* cradled cradling

KRDL creedal (or) credal *belief*

KRDL curdle *thicken* curdled curdling

KRDLD credulity *belief*

KRDLG cardiology *heart*

KRDLJ cardiology *heart*

KRDLJ cartilage *body tissue*

KRDLJNS cartilaginous *body tissue*

KRDLJST cardiologist *doctor*

KRDLR cordillera *mountains*

KRDLRN cordilleran *mountains*

KRDLS cordless *no cord*

KRDLS corydalis *herb*

KRDLS credulous *believable*

KRDLSNG cradlesong *lullaby*

KRDLT credulity *belief*

KRDLY cordillera *mountains*

KRDLYRN cordilleran *mountains*

KRDM -cardium *heart* -cardia

KRDMM cardamom *fruit*

KRDMN cardamom *fruit*

KRDMPTH cardiomyopathy *disorder* cardiomyopathies

KRDMYPTH cardiomyopathy *disorder* cardiomyopathies

KRDN accordion *music*

KRDN acridine *chemical*

KRDN cardoon *plant*

KRDN carton *box*

KRDN cordon *rope*

KRDN keratin *protein*

KRDNBL cordon bleu *food*

KRDNCHL credential *certificate* credentialed credentialing

KRDNCHLS credentials *knowledge and experience*

KRDNCHLZ credentials *knowledge and experience*

KRDNDD coordinated *matched*

KRDNDR coordinator *manager*

KRDNGL accordingly *thus*

KRDNL accordingly *thus*

KRDNL cardinal (n) *clergy, bird*

KRDNL cardinal (adj) *essential* cardinally (adv)

KRDNLD cardinality *numbers* cardinalities

KRDNLSHP cardinalship *clergy*

KRDNLT cardinalate *office*

KRDNLT cardinality *numbers*

Use letters that best describe the sounds you hear and omit the vowels. Use **S** or **K** instead of **C**: to find circle use **SRKL**. Use **J** to find joy, **JM** to find gem and **G** to find go.

cardinalities
KRDNS accordance *agreement*
KRDNS acridness *harshness, bitterness*
KRDNS credence *truth*
KRDNSHL credential *certificate* credentialed credentialing
KRDNSHLS credentials *knowledge and experience*
KRDNSHLZ credentials *knowledge and experience*
KRDNSHN coordination *smooth function*
KRDNST accordionist *musician*
KRDNT accordant *agreeing*
KRDNT coordinate *(v) manage, harmonize* coordinated coordinating
KRDNT coordinate *(n) intersection, equal, number*
KRDNTD coordinated *matched*
KRDNTL accordantly *agreement*
KRDNTL coordinately *intersection, equal*
KRDNTR coordinator *manager*
KRDNTS accordance *agreement*
KRDNTS credence *truth*
KRDNZ credenza *furniture*
KRDPLMNR cardiopulmonary *heart and lung*
KRDPLR cardplayer *card games*
KRDPLYR cardplayer *card games*
KRDPTH cardiopathy *disease* cardiopathies
KRDR corduroy *fabric*
KRDR corridor *hall*
KRDR courtier *attendant, flatterer*
KRDR crater *pit*
KRDR creator *maker*
KRDR critter *animal*
KRDR cruder *raw, rude*

KRDR curator *caretaker*
KRDR krater *jar*
KRDR quarter *(v) divide, lodge (n) one fourth, area, money**
KRDRBK quarterback *football*
KRDRDK quarterdeck *ship*
KRDRFNL quarterfinal *exam*
KRDRHRS quarter horse *animal*
KRDRJ cartridge *case*
KRDRL quarterly *4 times per year* quarterlies
KRDRMSDR quartermaster *provider*
KRDRMSTR quartermaster *provider*
KRDRNG quartering *right angle*
KRDRPN cotter pin *fastener*
KRDRSN quartersawn *boards*
KRDRSPRTR cardiorespiratory *heart and breath*
KRDRSTF quarterstaff *weapon*
KRDS courteous *civil*
KRDS courtesy *civility* courtesies
KRDS courthouse *law*
KRDS cowardice *fear*
KRDS curtesy *estate* curtesies
KRDSH Kurdish *Turk*
KRDSHRK cardsharp (or) cardsharper *cheater*
KRDSHRP cardsharp (or) cardsharper *cheater*
KRDSHRPR cardsharper (or) cardsharp *cheater*
KRDSL courteously *civilly*
KRDSN courtesan *prostitute*
KRDST crudest *raw, rude*
KRDST karateist *martial arts*
KRDSZ cortices (pl) *outer layer* cortex
KRDSZ criticize *evaluate* criticized criticizing (Br) criticise
KRDSZBL criticizable

evaluate
KRDSZM criticism *evaluation*
KRDSZR criticizer *evaluator* (Br) criticiser
KRDT accredit *approve*
KRDT acridity *harshness, bitterness*
KRDT chordate *backbone*
KRDT cordite *twine*
KRDT credit *belief, account*
KRDT crudités *vegetables*
KRDT crudity *vulgarity* crudities
KRDTBL accreditable *approved*
KRDTBL creditable (adj) *worthy* creditably (adv)
KRDTD accredited *approved*
KRDTNK cardiotonic *heart muscle*
KRDTNN credit union *bank*
KRDTNYN credit union *bank*
KRDTR creditor *debtor*
KRDTSHN accreditation *approval*
KRDTYNN credit union *bank*
KRDTYNYN credit union *bank*
KRDV creative *imaginative*
KRDV curative *healing*
KRDVN cordovan *leather*
KRDVSKLR cardiovascular *heart and blood vessels*
KRDVSKYLR cardiovascular *heart and blood vessels*
KRDVSQLR cardiovascular *heart and blood vessels*
KRDWD cordwood *fireplace*
KRDY cardia *opening* cardiae (or) cardias
KRDY -cardia (pl) *heart -* cardium
KRDYD cardioid *heart shape*
KRDYGRF cardiograph *heart machine*
KRDYGRF cardiography *heart machine*
KRDYGRFK cardiographic *heart machine*
KRDYGRM cardiogram

Letters aren't doubled for single sounds: to find alley use **L** not **LL**. Use **Y** and **W** as hard sounds only: to find yellow use **YL**. (Br)=British spelling or usage. * See dictionary.

heart test
KRDYK cardiac *heart*
KRDYLD credulity *belief*
KRDYLG cardiology *heart*
KRDYLJ cardiology *heart*
KRDYLJST cardiologist
doctor
KRDYLS credulous
believable
KRDYLT credulity *belief*
KRDYM -cardium *heart -
cardia*
KRDYMPTH
cardiomyopathy *disorder*
cardiomyopathies
KRDYMYPTH
cardiomyopathy *disorder*
cardiomyopathies
KRDYN accordion *music*
KRDYNST accordionist
musician
KRDYPLMNR
cardiopulmonary *heart
and lung*
KRDYPTH cardiopathy
disease cardiopathies
KRDYR cordillera *mountains*
KRDYR courtier *attendant,
flatterer*
KRDYRN cordilleran
mountains
KRDYRSPRTR
cardiorespiratory *heart
and breath*
KRDYS courteous *civil*
KRDYSL courteously *civilly*
KRDYTNK cardiotonic *heart
muscle*
KRDYVSKLR
cardiovascular *heart and
blood vessels*
KRDYVSKYLR
cardiovascular *heart and
blood vessels*
KRDYVSQLR
cardiovascular *heart and
blood vessels*
KRDZN cortisone *drug*
KRDZN courtesan *prostitute*
KRF carafe *pitcher*
KRF corf *(Br) mining* corves
KRF coryphée *ballet*

KRF craft *skill, vehicle*
KRF croft *farm*
KRF curfew *time*
KRF kerf *groove*
KRF kraft *paper*
KRFB acrophobe *one who
fears heights*
KRFB acrophobia *fear of
height*
KRFBY acrophobia *fear of
height*
KRFD crafty *shrewd* craftier
craftiest
KRFDL craftily *shrewdly*
KRFDNS craftiness
shrewdness
KRFDR craftier *shrewder*
KRFDR crofter *farmer*
KRFDYR craftier *shrewder*
KRFL careful (adj) *with
attention* carefully (adv)
KRFL carful *automobile load*
KRFLNS carefulness *with
attention*
KRFNN craft union *labor*
KRFNYN craft union *labor*
KRFR carefree *without
worry*
KRFR carfare *payment*
KRFS coryphaeus *chorus
leader* coryphaei
KRFSH crawfish (or)
crayfish *animal*
KRFSMN craftsman *artisan*
craftsmen
KRFSMNSHP
craftsmanship *skill*
KRFSWMN craftswoman
artist craftswomen
KRFT acre-foot *depth
measure*
KRFT craft *skill, vehicle*
KRFT crafty *shrewd* craftier
craftiest
KRFT croft *farm*
KRFT crowfoot *plant*
KRFT kraft *paper*
KRFTL craftily *shrewdly*
KRFTNN craft union *labor*
KRFTNS craftiness
shrewdness
KRFTNYN craft union *labor*

KRFTR craftier *shrewder*
KRFTR crofter *farmer*
KRFTSMN craftsman
artisan craftsmen
KRFTSMNSHP
craftsmanship *skill*
KRFTST craftiest *shrewdest*
KRFTSWMN craftswoman
artist craftswomen
KRFTYNN craft union *labor*
KRFTYNYN craft union
labor
KRFTYR craftier *shrewder*
KRFTYST craftiest *shrewdest*
KRFY curfew *time*
KRFYNN craft union *labor*
KRFYNYN craft union *labor*
KRFYS coryphaeus *chorus
leader* coryphaei
KRG cargo *load* cargoes (or)
cargos
KRG corgi *dog* corgis
KRG crag *rock*
KRG craggy *rugged* craggier
craggiest
KRGDD corrugated
furrowed
KRGL craggily *ruggedly*
KRGM kerygma *salvation*
KRGMDK kerygmatic
salvation
KRGMTK kerygmatic
salvation
KRGN carrageen *moss*
KRGNN carrageenan (or)
carrageenin *moss*
KRGNS cragginess
ruggedness
KRGR craggier *rugged*
KRGRF chirography
handwriting
KRGRF choreography
dancing choreographies
KRGRFK chirographic (or)
chirographical
handwriting
KRGRFK choreographic
dancing
KRGRFKL chirographical
(or) chirographic
handwriting
KRGRFKL

Use letters that best describe the sounds you hear and omit the vowels. Use **S** or **K** instead of **C**: to find circle use **SRKL**. Use **J** to find joy, **JM** to find gem and **G** to find go.

choreographically *dancing*
KRGRFR chirographer *handwriting*
KRGRFR choreographer *dancing*
KRGRN Krugerrand *coin*
KRGRND Krugerrand *coin*
KRGSHN corrugation *furrow*
KRGST craggiest *rugged*
KRGT corrugate *furrow* corrugated corrugating
KRGTD corrugated *furrowed*
KRGVR caregiver *nurse*
KRGYR craggier *rugged*
KRGYST craggiest *rugged*
KRJ acreage *land measure*
KRJ carriage *vehicle*
KRJ corgi *dog* corgis
KRJ courage *no fear*
KRJBL corrigible *set right*
KRJBLD corrigibility *set right*
KRJBLT corrigibility *set right*
KRJKN carjacking *stealing*
KRJKNG carjacking *stealing*
KRJKR carjacker *thief*
KRJL cordial *(n) drink*
KRJL cordial (adj) *gracious* cordially (adv)
KRJLD cordiality *graciousness*
KRJLD credulity *belief*
KRJLS credulous *believable*
KRJLT cordiality *graciousness*
KRJLT credulity *belief*
KRJN cryogen *refrigerant*
KRJN kerogen *shale*
KRJND corrigenda (pl) *error* corrigendum
KRJNDM corrigendum *error* corrigenda
KRJNG kurrajong *tree*
KRJNK cariogenic *tooth decay*
KRJNK cryogenic *freezing*
KRJNKS cryogenics *freezing*
KRJNX cryogenics *freezing*
KRJS courageous *no fear*

KRJSL courageously *no fear*
KRJW carriageway *(Br) road*
KRJYLD cordiality *graciousness*
KRJYLT cordiality *graciousness*
KRK carioca *dance*
KRK choreic *spasmodic*
KRK cork *stopper, bark*
KRK corky *like cork* corkier corkiest
KRK correct *(v) revise, punish (adj) accurate*
KRK crack *(v) split, craze (n) drug, try, fissure**
KRK crake *bird*
KRK creak *squeak*
KRK creaky *squeaky* creakier creakiest
KRK creek *stream*
KRK Creek *Native American*
KRK crick *cramp*
KRK croak *(n) frog noise (v-slang) die*
KRK croc *crocodile*
KRK crock *pot*
KRK crook *outlaw, bend*
KRK croquet *game*
KRK croquis *sketch* croquis
KRK cruck *timber*
KRK karaoke *taped music*
KRK Kerouac *writer*
KRK Krakow *city*
KRKBN carrick bend *knot*
KRKBND carrick bend *knot*
KRKBRN crackbrain *crackpot*
KRKCHR caricature *cartoon* caricatured caricaturing
KRKCHRL caricatural *cartoon*
KRKCHRST caricaturist *cartoonist*
KRKD coracoid *bone*
KRKD cracked *broken, crazy*
KRKD cricoid *larynx*
KRKD crocked *(slang) drunk or high*
KRKD crooked *bent, dishonest*
KRKDBL correctable *revise, punish*

KRKDL crocodile *reptile*
KRKDL crookedly *bent, dishonest*
KRKDLN crocodilian *reptile*
KRKDLYN crocodilian *reptile*
KRKDN crackdown (n) *discipline* crack down (v)
KRKDNS crookedness *bent, dishonest*
KRKDR character *person, letter, reputation**
KRKDR corrector *adjust, punish*
KRKDRSDK characteristic *quality*
KRKDRSDKL characteristically *typically*
KRKDRSTK characteristic *quality*
KRKDRSTKL characteristically *typically*
KRKDRZ characterize *describe* characterized characterizing
KRKDRZSHN characterization *depiction*
KRKDTD correctitude *acceptability*
KRKDTYD correctitude *acceptability*
KRKDV corrective *remedy*
KRKGRD Kierkegaard *philosopher*
KRKJ corkage *fee*
KRKL caracal *cat*
KRKL caracole *turn*
KRKL caracul *fur*
KRKL coracle *boat*
KRKL crackle *(n) sparkle, noise, fissures*
KRKL crackle *(v) sharp sound* crackled crackling
KRKL creakily *squeaky*
KRKL curricula (pl) *education* curriculum
KRKL karakul *sheep*
KRKLM curriculum *education* curricula
KRKLMVD curriculum vitae *career account* curricula vitae

Letters aren't doubled for single sounds: to find alley use **L** not **LL**. Use **Y** and **W** as hard sounds only: to find yellow use **YL**. (Br)=British spelling or usage. * See dictionary.

KRKLMVT curriculum vitae *career account* curricula vitae

KRKLN crackling *sounds, crisp fat*

KRKLNG crackling *sounds, crisp fat*

KRKLR curricular *education*

KRKM currycomb *horse tool*

KRKN corking *good*

KRKN cracking *great*

KRKN kraken *monster*

KRKNG corking *good*

KRKNG cracking *great*

KRKNK crookneck *squash*

KRKNL cracknel *biscuit, crisp fat*

KRKNS corkiness *like cork*

KRKNS correctness *accuracy*

KRKNS creakiness *squeaky*

KRKP crack up *(v) praise, laugh*

KRKP crack-up *(n) collapse, wreck*

KRKPT crackpot *lunatic*

KRKR caracara *hawk*

KRKR corker *excellent one*

KRKR corkier *like cork*

KRKR cracker *food, tool, person*

KRKR creakier *squeakier*

KRKR crockery *pots*

KRKRBRL cracker-barrel *homespun*

KRKRJK crackerjack *excellent*

KRKRS crackers *crazy*

KRKRZ crackers *crazy*

KRKS Caracas *city*

KRKS carcass *body* carcasses (Br) carcase

KRKS crocus *flower* crocuses

KRKS croquis *sketch* croquis

KRKS crux *center* cruxes

KRKSHN correction *revise, punish*

KRKSHNL correctional *penal*

KRKSKR corkscrew *device*

KRKST corkiest *like cork*

KRKST creakiest *squeakiest*

KRKT corked *stopped up*

KRKT correct *(v) revise, punish (adj) accurate*

KRKT cracked *broken, crazy*

KRKT crew cut *hairstyle*

KRKT cricket *insect, sport*

KRKT crocked *(slang) drunk or high*

KRKT crocket *ornament*

KRKT crooked *bent, dishonest*

KRKT croquette *food*

KRKTBL correctable *revise, punish*

KRKTNS correctness *accuracy*

KRKTR caricature *cartoon* caricatured caricaturing

KRKTR character *person, letter, reputation**

KRKTR corrector *adjust, punish*

KRKTRL caricatural *cartoon*

KRKTRSDK characteristic *quality*

KRKTRSDKL characteristically *typically*

KRKTRST caricaturist *cartoonist*

KRKTRSTK characteristic *quality*

KRKTRSTKL characteristically *typically*

KRKTRZ characterize *describe* characterized characterizing

KRKTRZSHN characterization *depiction*

KRKTTD correctitude *acceptability*

KRKTTYD correctitude *acceptability*

KRKTV corrective *remedy*

KRKTYR caricature *cartoon* caricatured caricaturing

KRKTYRL caricatural *cartoon*

KRKTYRST caricaturist *cartoonist*

KRKWS croquis *sketch*

croquis

KRKWZT corequisite *study*

KRKYL curricula (pl) *education* curriculum

KRKYLM curriculum *education* curricula

KRKYLMVD curriculum vitae *career account* curricula vitae

KRKYLMVT curriculum vitae *career account* curricula vitae

KRKYLR curricular *education*

KRKYR corkier *like cork*

KRKYR creakier *squeakier*

KRKYST corkiest *like cork*

KRKYST creakiest *squeakiest*

KRL accrual *accumulation*

KRL carol *music* caroled (or) carolled caroling (or) carolling

KRL carrel *table*

KRL carryall *bag*

KRL choral *chorus*

KRL chorale *hymn, choir*

KRL coral *reef, color*

KRL corolla *flower*

KRL corral *enclosure* corralled corralling

KRL crawl *creep*

KRL crawly *creepy*

KRL creel *basket*

KRL Creole *person, language*

KRL crewel *needlework*

KRL criollo *Spaniard, pony* criollos

KRL cruel *fierce* crueler (or) crueller cruelest (or) cruellest

KRL cruelly *fiercely*

KRL cure-all *remedy*

KRL curl *spiral*

KRL curlew *bird* curlews (or) curlew

KRL curly *spiral* curlier curliest

KRL kraal *pen*

KRL krill *plankton*

KRLBLZ coralbells *plant*

KRLBR coralberry *shrub* coralberries

Use letters that best describe the sounds you hear and omit the vowels. Use **S** or **K** instead of **C**: to find circle use **SRKL**. Use **J** to find joy, **JM** to find gem and **G** to find go.

KRLC Coral Sea *body of water*

KRLD carload *automobile*

KRLD coralloid *reef, color*

KRLD cruelty *fierceness* cruelties

KRLDR correlator *show mutuality*

KRLDV correlative *similar*

KRLDVL correlatively *similarly*

KRLG karyology *cells*

KRLJ karyology *cells*

KRLJKL karyological *cells*

KRLK acrylic *acid, paint*

KRLK curlicue *spiral* curlicued curlicuing

KRLKY curlicue *spiral*

KRLMF karyolymph *sap*

KRLN carillon *music*

KRLN coralline *alga*

KRLN curling *sport*

KRLNG curling *sport*

KRLNR carillonneur *musician*

KRLNS cruelness *meanness*

KRLNS curliness *spirals*

KRLQ curlicue *spiral*

KRLR caroler (or) caroller *singer*

KRLR corollary *result* corollaries

KRLR crawler *one that crawls*

KRLR crueler (or) crueller *fiercer*

KRLR cruller *pastry*

KRLR curler *hair device, sportsman*

KRLR curlier *spiral*

KRLRF coral reef *ocean*

KRLS careless *negligent*

KRLS Coral Sea *body of water*

KRLSHN correlation *similarity*

KRLSL carelessly *negligently*

KRLSNK coral snake *reptile*

KRLSNS carelessness *negligence*

KRLST cruelest (or)

cruellest *fiercest*

KRLST curliest *spiral*

KRLT corollate *flower*

KRLT correlate *correspond* correlated correlating

KRLT cruelty *fierceness* cruelties

KRLT cryolite *ice stone*

KRLTR correlator *show mutuality*

KRLTV correlative *similar*

KRLTVL correlatively *similarly*

KRLWRK crewelwork *needlework*

KRLY criollo *Spaniard, pony* criollos

KRLYR curlier *spiral*

KRLYST curliest *spiral*

KRLZ creolize *speech* creolized creolizing (Br) creolise

KRM carom *billiards*

KRM chrome *metal* chromed chroming

KRM chromo *lithograph* chromos

KRM coremia (pl) *fungus* coremium

KRM corium *skin* coria

KRM corm *tuber*

KRM cram *pack quickly* crammed cramming

KRM cream *milk*

KRM creamy *milky* creamier creamiest

KRM crème (or) creme *liqueur, cream* crèmes (or) cremes

KRM crime *offense*

KRM crumb *piece*

KRM crummy *worthless* crummier crummiest

KRM curium *element*

KRM karma *vibrations*

KRMB corymb *flower* corymbs

KRMB crambo *game* cramboes

KRMBL carambola *starfruit*

KRMBL crumble *flake apart* crumbled crumbling

KRMBL crumbly *flaky* crumblier crumbliest

KRMBLNGS crumblings *flakes*

KRMBLNGZ crumblings *flakes*

KRMBLNS crumbliness *flakiness*

KRMBLNS crumblings *flakes*

KRMBLNZ crumblings *flakes*

KRMBLR crumblier *flakier*

KRMBLST crumbliest *flakiest*

KRMBLYR crumblier *flakier*

KRMBLYST crumbliest *flakiest*

KRMBRL crème brulee *food*

KRMCHZ cream cheese *milk product*

KRMDD chromatid *gene*

KRMDFR chromatophore *cell*

KRMDK achromatic *neutral*

KRMDK chromatic *color*

KRMDKK crème de cacao *liqueur*

KRMDKL achromatically *neutrally*

KRMDKL chromatically *color*

KRMDLKRM crème de la crème *finest*

KRMDMNT crème de menthe *liqueur*

KRMDMNTH crème de menthe *liqueur*

KRMDS achromatous *neutral*

KRMDSZM chromaticism *color*

KRMFRSH crème fraiche *cream*

KRMGL acromegaly *enlargement*

KRMGLK acromegalic *enlargement*

KRMHLTS krummholz *forest* krummholz

KRMHLTZ krummholz *forest* krummholz

Letters aren't doubled for single sounds: to find **alley** use **L** not **LL**. Use **Y** and **W** as hard sounds only: to find **yellow** use **YL**. (Br)=British spelling or usage. * See dictionary.

KRMHRN krummhorn *music*
KRMJN curmudgeon *miser*
KRMK chromic *chromium*
KRMK karmic *vibrations*
KRMKR carmaker *manufacturer*
KRMKRML crème caramel *food*
KRML caramel *candy*
KRML cormel *tuber*
KRML creamily *milky*
KRMLK cromlech *monoliths*
KRMLN kremlin *citadel*
KRMLN Kremlin *Russian statehouse*
KRMLTZ krummholz *forest* krummholz
KRMLZ caramelize *change to caramel* caramelized caramelizing (Br) caramelise
KRMLZ krummholz *forest* krummholz
KRMM chromium *element*
KRMM coremium *fungus* coremia
KRMN accruement *accumulate*
KRMN acrimony *harshness* acrimonies
KRMN carmine *red*
KRMN corpsman *military* corpsmen
KRMN crewman *boat* crewmen
KRMNC chiromancy *palmistry*
KRMNDV carminative *gas reliever*
KRMNGGLZ crème anglaise *food*
KRMNGLZ crème anglaise *food*
KRMNL criminal (adj) *illegal* (n) *offender* criminally (adv)
KRMNLD criminality *offense*
KRMNLG criminology *penal*
KRMNLJ criminology *penal*
KRMNLJKL criminological (adj) *penal* criminologically (adv)

KRMNLJST criminologist *penal*
KRMNLT criminality *offense*
KRMNLZ criminalize *outlaw* criminalized criminalizing
KRMNLZSHN criminalization *outlaw* (Br) criminalisation
KRMNS acrimonious *harsh*
KRMNS chiromancy *palmistry*
KRMNS creaminess *milkiness*
KRMNS cremains *cremation*
KRMNS crumminess *worthlessness*
KRMNSHN crimination *accusation*
KRMNSL acrimoniously *harshly*
KRMNSNS acrimoniousness *harshness*
KRMNSR chiromancer *palmistry*
KRMNT accruement *accumulate*
KRMNT criminate *accuse* criminated criminating
KRMNTC chiromancy *palmistry*
KRMNTS chiromancy *palmistry*
KRMNTSR chiromancer *palmistry*
KRMNTV carminative *gas reliever*
KRMNYS acrimonious *harsh*
KRMNYSL acrimoniously *harshly*
KRMNYSNS acrimoniousness *harshness*
KRMNZ cremains *cremation*
KRMP cramp *pain, confine*
KRMP crimp *curl*
KRMP crimpy *curly* crimpier crimpiest
KRMP crump (v) *crunch* (n) *bomb*
KRMPF cream puff *pastry*
KRMPL crumple *wrinkle*

crumpled crumpling
KRMPL crumply *wrinkled*
KRMPLST chromoplast *pigment*
KRMPNS crampons *hook*
KRMPNZ crampons *hook*
KRMPR crimper *curler*
KRMPR crimpier *curlier*
KRMPST crimpiest *curliest*
KRMPT crumpet *bread*
KRMPYR crimpier *curlier*
KRMPYST crimpiest *curliest*
KRMR crammer *study*
KRMR creamer *milk*
KRMR creamery *producer* creameries
KRMR creamier *milkier*
KRMR crummier *worthless*
KRMR krimmer *fur*
KRMRN krummhorn *music*
KRMRNT cormorant *bird*
KRMS chromous *chromium*
KRMS kermis (or) kermess (or) kermesse *festival*
KRMSHN cremation *burn*
KRMSM chromosome *gene*
KRMSN chromosome *gene*
KRMSN crimson *red*
KRMSS cream sauce *food*
KRMST creamiest *milkiest*
KRMST crummiest *worthless*
KRMT chromate *acid salt*
KRMT cremate *burn* cremated cremating
KRMT crewmate *sailor*
KRMTD chromatid *gene*
KRMTFR chromatophore *cell*
KRMTK achromatic *neutral*
KRMTK chromatic *color*
KRMTKL achromatically *neutrally*
KRMTKL chromatically *color*
KRMTN chromatin *cell*
KRMTR crematoria (pl) *furnace* crematorium
KRMTR crematory *furnace* crematories
KRMTRM crematorium *furnace* crematoriums (or) crematoria
KRMTRY crematoria (pl)

Use letters that best describe the sounds you hear and omit the vowels. Use **S** or **K** instead of **C**: to find circle use **SRKL**. Use **J** to find joy, **JM** to find gem and **G** to find go.

furnace crematorium

KRMTRYM crematorium *furnace* crematoriums (or) crematoria

KRMTS achromatous *neutral*

KRMTSZM chromaticism *color*

KRMTZ achromatize *make neutral*

KRMTZM achromatism *neutrality*

KRMY coremia (pl) *fungus* coremium

KRMYM chromium *element*

KRMYM coremium *fungus* coremia

KRMYR creamier *milkier*

KRMYR crummier *worthless*

KRMYST creamiest *milkiest*

KRMYST crummiest *worthless*

KRMZ chromize *alloy* chromized chromizing

KRMZ kermes *dyestuff*

KRMZN crimson *red*

KRN Acheron *river*

KRN acorn *nut*

KRN Akron *city*

KRN au courant *up-to-date*

KRN cairn *memorial*

KRN careen *swerve*

KRN carina *curve* carinas (or) carinae

KRN carny (or) carney (or) carnie *carnival* carnies (or) carneys

KRN carrion *corpse*

KRN carry on *(v) continue*

KRN carry-on *(adj, n) portable*

KRN chorine *chorus girl*

KRN chorion *placenta*

KRN corn *(n) vegetable, callus, triteness (v) granulate*

KRN cornea *eye*

KRN corny *trite* cornier corniest

KRN corona *halo, flower part*

KRN crane *(n) bird, device*

KRN crane *(v) stretch*

craned craning

KRN cranny *alcove* crannies

KRN crayon *wax marker*

KRN crone *old woman*

KRN crony *pal* cronies

KRN croon *sing*

KRN crown *head, royal*

KRN crying *(adj) offensive*

KRN eccrine *gland*

KRN kern (or) kerne *type*

KRN Koran *sacred book*

KRN Korean *of Korea*

KRN koruna *Czech money* koruny (or) korunas (or) korun

KRN krona *Iceland money* kronur

KRN krona *Swiss money* kronor

KRN krone *Danish money* kroner

KRN krone *Austrian money* kronen

KRN ocarina *music*

KRN Ukraine *country*

KRNB carnauba *palm*

KRNBL cornball *trite*

KRNBLT Corn Belt *region*

KRNBR cranberry *fruit* cranberries

KRNBRD corn bread *food*

KRNC currency *money, recency* currencies

KRNCH acre-inch *depth measure*

KRNCH crunch *(n) sound, critical situation (v) chew* crunches

KRNCH crunchy *hard and dry* crunchier crunchiest

KRNCHBL crunchable *chew, tally*

KRNCHL crunchily *sound*

KRNCHNS crunchiness *sound*

KRNCHP corn chip *food*

KRNCHR cruncher *one that crunches*

KRNCHR crunchier *hard and dry*

KRNCHST crunchiest *hard and dry*

KRNCHYR crunchier *hard and dry*

KRNCHYST crunchiest *hard and dry*

KRND cairned *memorial*

KRND crinoid *echinoderm*

KRND crowned *topped*

KRNDD carinated (or) carinate *curved*

KRNDD crenated (or) crenate *scalloped*

KRNDM corundum *mineral*

KRNDR coriander *herb*

KRNDST cornetist *musician*

KRNFD corn-fed *plump*

KRNFL cornfield *farm*

KRNFLD cornfield *farm*

KRNFLKS cornflakes *cereal*

KRNFLR corn flour *food*

KRNFLR cornflower *blue flower*

KRNFLWR corn flour *food*

KRNFLWR cornflower *blue flower*

KRNFLX cornflakes *cereal*

KRNG crying *(adj) offensive*

KRNG key ring *holder*

KRNGGL cringle *sail*

KRNGK crank *(n) handle, grouch (adj) annoying (v) start up*

KRNGK cranky *(adj) fretful* crankier crankiest

KRNGKL caruncle *growth*

KRNGKL crankily *fretfully*

KRNGKL crinkle *wrinkle* crinkled crinkling

KRNGKL crinkly *wrinkled*

KRNGKNS crankiness *fretfulness*

KRNGKR crankier *fretful*

KRNGKS crankcase *engine*

KRNGKSHF crankshaft *engine*

KRNGKSHFT crankshaft *engine*

KRNGKST crankiest *fretful*

KRNGKYR crankier *fretful*

KRNGKYST crankiest *fretful*

KRNGL cringle *sail*

KRNGN carrying-on *behavior* carryings-on

Letters aren't doubled for single sounds: to find alley use **L** not **LL**. Use **Y** and **W** as hard sounds only: to find yellow use **YL**. (Br)=British spelling or usage. * See dictionary.

KRNGRF coronagraph *telescope*
KRNGRM cairngorm *quartz*
KRNHSKN cornhusking *social*
KRNHSKNG cornhusking *social*
KRNHWSK corn whiskey *bourbon*
KRNJ carnage *slaughter*
KRNJ cringe *shrink* cringed cringing
KRNJL crown jewel *royalty*
KRNJR cringer *shrink*
KRNJWL crown jewel *royalty*
KRNK chorionic *placenta*
KRNK chronic *lasting*
KRNK coronach *dirge*
KRNK crank *(n) handle,* grouch *(adj)* annoying *(v)* start up
KRNK cranky *(adj) fretful* crankier crankiest
KRNK crew neck *collar*
KRNKB corncob *ear of corn*
KRNKL caruncle *growth*
KRNKL chronically *lasting*
KRNKL chronicle *record* chronicled chronicling
KRNKL crankily *fretfully*
KRNKL crinkle *wrinkle* crinkled crinkling
KRNKL crinkly *wrinkled*
KRNKLR chronicler *recorder*
KRNKLZ Chronicles *scripture*
KRNKNS crankiness *fretfulness*
KRNKP cornucopia *horn of plenty*
KRNKPY cornucopia *horn of plenty*
KRNKR crankier *fretful*
KRNKRB corncrib *storage*
KRNKS crankcase *engine*
KRNKS cryonics *freezing*
KRNKSHF crankshaft *engine*
KRNKSHFT crankshaft *engine*
KRNKST crankiest *fretful*

KRNKYR crankier *fretful*
KRNKYST crankiest *fretful*
KRNL carnal (adj) *body* carnally (adv)
KRNL colonel *army rank*
KRNL corn oil *food*
KRNL corneal *eye*
KRNL cornel *dogwood*
KRNL cornily *trite*
KRNL coronal *crown*
KRNL cranial (adj) *head* cranially (adv)
KRNL kernel *grain*
KRNLC colonelcy *army rank*
KRNLD carnality *body*
KRNLDD crenellated (or) creneled *battlement*
KRNLDD crenulated (or) crenulate *wavy*
KRNLG chronology *time* chronologies
KRNLG craniology *head*
KRNLJ chronology *time* chronologies
KRNLJ craniology *head*
KRNLJKL chronological (adj) *time* chronologically (adv)
KRNLJST chronologist *time expert*
KRNLN carnelian *gemstone*
KRNLN crinoline *fabric*
KRNLS colonelcy *army rank*
KRNLS crownless *topless*
KRNLSHN crenelation *battlement*
KRNLT carnality *body*
KRNLT carnallite *mineral*
KRNLT crenulate (or) crenulated *wavy*
KRNLTD crenellated (or) crenelated *battlement*
KRNLTD crenulated (or) crenulate *wavy*
KRNLYN carnelian *gemstone*
KRNM acronym *initials*
KRNM cranium *head*
KRNMDR chronometer *timepiece*
KRNMK acronymic *word composed of initials*
KRNMKL acronymically

word composed of initials
KRNML cornmeal *food*
KRNMTR chronometer *timepiece*
KRNN carrying-on *behavior* carryings-on
KRNN kronen (pl) *Austrian money* krone
KRNN Ukrainian *of Ukraine*
KRNNS corniness *triteness*
KRNPN corn pone *(n) food*
KRNPN cornpone *(adj) down-home*
KRNPRNS crown prince *royalty*
KRNPRNSS crown princess *royalty*
KRNPRNTS crown prince *royalty*
KRNPRNTSS crown princess *royalty*
KRNR corner *(v) catch, turn (n) angle, control, problem**
KRNR cornier *trite*
KRNR cornrow *hairstyle*
KRNR coronary *heart* coronaries
KRNR coroner *investigator*
KRNR crooner *singer*
KRNR kroner (or) kronor (or) kronur (pl) *money* krone (or) krona (or) krone
KRNRBK cornerback *football*
KRNRD cornered *caught*
KRNRSTN cornerstone *foundation*
KRNRWZ cornerwise *diagonal*
KRNS cornice *molding* corniced cornicing
KRNS currency *money,* recency currencies
KRNS occurrence *happening*
KRNSH corniche *road*
KRNSH Cornish *of Cornwall*
KRNSHGR corn sugar *dextrose*
KRNSHN carnation *flower*
KRNSHN coronation *crowning*
KRNSHN crenation *edge*

Use letters that best describe the sounds you hear and omit the vowels. Use **S** or **K** instead of **C**: to find circle use **SRKL**. Use **J** to find joy, **JM** to find gem and **G** to find go.

KRNSLK corn silk *plant fiber*
KRNSRP corn syrup *dextrose*
KRNST corniest *trite*
KRNSTK cornstalk *Indian corn*
KRNSTLK cornstalk *Indian corn*
KRNSTRCH cornstarch *thickener*
KRNT au courant *up-to-date*
KRNT carinate (or) carinated *curved*
KRNT cornet *music*
KRNT coronet *crown*
KRNT craniate *head*
KRNT crenate (or) crenated *scalloped*
KRNT currant *raisin*
KRNT current *(n) flow (adj) at this time*
KRNT kernite *mineral*
KRNTC currency *money,* recency currencies
KRNTD carinated (or) carinate *curved*
KRNTD crenated (or) crenate *scalloped*
KRNTH Corinth *Greek region*
KRNTHN Corinthian *of Corinth*
KRNTHYN Corinthian *of Corinth*
KRNTRR cairn terrier *dog*
KRNTRYR cairn terrier *dog*
KRNTS currency *money,* recency currencies
KRNTS occurrence *happening*
KRNTST cornetist *musician*
KRNVL carnival *festival*
KRNVR carnivore *meat-eater*
KRNVR carnivore *meat-eater*
KRNVRS carnivorous *meat-eating*
KRNVRSL carnivorously *meat-eating*
KRNVRSNS carnivorousness *meat-eating*
KRNWL Cornwall *city*
KRNWSK corn whiskey

bourbon
KRNX cryonics *freezing*
KRNY cornea *eye*
KRNYB carnauba *palm*
KRNYKP cornucopia *horn of plenty*
KRNYKPY cornucopia *horn of plenty*
KRNYL corn oil *food*
KRNYL corneal *eye*
KRNYL cranial (adj) *head* cranially (adv)
KRNYLDD crenulated (or) crenulate *wavy*
KRNYLG craniology *head*
KRNYLJ craniology *head*
KRNYLT crenulate (or) crenulated *wavy*
KRNYLTD crenulated (or) crenulate *wavy*
KRNYM cranium *head*
KRNYN Ukrainian *of Ukraine*
KRNYR cornier *trite*
KRNYST corniest *trite*
KRNYT craniate *head*
KRNYZM cronyism *partiality*
KRNZ Cairnes *Australian city*
KRNZM cronyism *partiality*
KRP carp *(n) fish (v) nag*
KRP carpi *(pl) wrist* carpus
KRP corrupt *(v) rot, debase (adj) tainted, depraved*
KRP crap *(v) dice, (vulgar) defecate* crapped crapping
KRP crap *(v) dice, (vulgar) defecate*
KRP crape *band*
KRP crappie *fish*
KRP crappy *awful* crappier crappiest
KRP creep *crawl* crept creeping
KRP creepy *scary* creepier creepiest
KRP crêpe (or) crepe *rolled pancake, crinkled surface* crêpes (or) crepes
KRP crepey (or) crepy *crinkled*
KRP crop *(v) trim, harvest*

cropped cropping
KRP crop *(n) gullet, product, collection**
KRP croup *sickness, rump*
KRP croupier *dealer*
KRP crypt *tomb*
KRPD chiropody *feet*
KRPD crypto *secret* cryptos
KRPDBL corruptible (adj) *rotten, debased* corruptibly (adv)
KRPDGM cryptogam *plant*
KRPDGNK cryptogenic *unknown source*
KRPDGRM cryptogram *code*
KRPDJNK cryptogenic *unknown source*
KRPDK cryptic *secret*
KRPDKKS cryptococcus *fungus* cryptococci
KRPDKKSS cryptococcosis *disease* cryptococcoses
KRPDKL cryptically *secretly*
KRPDL acropetal *upward* acropetally
KRPDLJKL cryptological *code*
KRPDN carpeting *rug*
KRPDNG carpeting *rug*
KRPDNM cryptonym *code name*
KRPDNT crepitant *crackling*
KRPDR corrupter *rot, debase*
KRPDRKD cryptorchid *testes descent*
KRPDRKDZM cryptorchidism (or) cryptorchism *testes descent*
KRPDRKZM cryptorchism (or) cryptorchidism *testes descent*
KRPDSDR crop duster *airplane*
KRPDSHN crêpe de chine (or) crepe de chine *fabric*
KRPDST chiropodist *foot doctor*
KRPDSTR crop duster *airplane*
KRPDV corruptive *rotting*
KRPDZLG cryptozoology

Letters aren't doubled for single sounds: to find alley use **L** not **LL**. Use **Y** and **W** as hard sounds only: to find yellow use **YL**. (Br)=British spelling or usage. * See dictionary.

animal legends
KRPDZLJ cryptozoology
animal legends
KRPDZLJST
cryptozoologist *animal*
legends
KRPDZWLG cryptozoology
animal legends
KRPDZWLJ cryptozoology
animal legends
KRPDZWLJST
cryptozoologist *animal*
legends
KRPFR carpophore *stalk*
KRPJ creepage *movement*
KRPL car pool (n)
transportation carpool (v)
KRPL carpal *wrist*
KRPL carpel *flower*
KRPL corruptly *tainted*
KRPL creepily *scary*
KRPL cripple *maim* crippled
crippling
KRPLK kreplach *dumpling*
KRPLN cropland *farm*
KRPLND cropland *farm*
KRPLNGL cripplingly *maim*
KRPLNS corpulence *obesity*
corpulency
KRPLNT corpulent *fat*
KRPLNTS corpulence
obesity corpulency
KRPLR carpellary *flower*
KRPLR carpooler
transportation
KRPLR crippler *maim*
KRPLS acropolis *fortress*
KRPLS crapulous *hungover*
KRPLT carpellate *flower*
KRPLTNLSNDRM carpal
tunnel syndrome *wrist*
KRPMRDL crape myrtle *tree*
KRPMRTL crape myrtle *tree*
KRPN carping *critical*
KRPN creeping *crawling*
KRPN crepon *fabric*
KRPNDR carpenter
woodworker
KRPNDR carpentry
woodwork
KRPNDRB carpenter bee
insect

KRPNG carping *critical*
KRPNG creeping *crawling*
KRPNS creepiness *fright*
KRPNTR carpenter
woodworker
KRPNTR carpentry
woodwork
KRPNTRB carpenter bee
insect
KRPPPR crepe paper
crinkled
KRPPR crepe paper *crinkled*
KRPR corpora (pl) *body*
corpus
KRPR crapper *(vulgar)* toilet
KRPR crappier *(vulgar)*
worse
KRPR creeper *crawler*
KRPR creepier *scary*
KRPR cropper *trim, harvest*
KRPR croupier *dealer*
KRPR crupper *saddle*
KRPRD crop-eared *trimmed*
KRPRDLKD corpora delicti
(pl) *crime* corpus delicti
KRPRDLKT corpora delicti
(pl) *crime* corpus delicti
KRPRDV corporative
business
KRPRKDK chiropractic
body adjustment
KRPRKDR chiropractor
body adjustment
KRPRKLS corpora callosa
(pl) *brain* corpus callosum
KRPRKTK chiropractic *body*
adjustment
KRPRKTR chiropractor
body adjustment
KRPRL corporal *rank, body*
KRPRL corporeal (adj)
physical corporeally (adv)
KRPRLD corpora lutea (pl)
ovary corpus luteum
KRPRLD corporality *body*
corporalities
KRPRLD corporeality
existence corporealities
KRPRLDY corpora lutea (pl)
ovary corpus luteum
KRPRLT corpora lutea (pl)
ovary corpus luteum

KRPRLT corporality *body*
corporalities
KRPRLT corporeality
existence corporealities
KRPRLTY corpora lutea (pl)
ovary corpus luteum
KRPRSHN corporation
business
KRPRSR corepressor *gene*
KRPRT carport *garage*
KRPRT corporate *business*
KRPRTST corporatist
business
KRPRTV corporative
business
KRPRTZM corporatism
business
KRPRYL corporeal (adj)
physical corporeally (adv)
KRPRYLD corporeality
existence corporealities
KRPRYLT corporeality
existence corporealities
KRPS carapace *shell*
KRPS carpus *wrist* carpi
KRPS corpse *dead body*
KRPS corpus *body* corpora
KRPS craps *dice*
KRPS croupous *cough*
KRPSDLKD corpus delicti
crime corpora delicti
KRPSDLKT corpus delicti
crime corpora delicti
KRPSHDR crapshooter *dice*
KRPSHN corruption *rot*
KRPSHTR crapshooter *dice*
KRPSKL crepuscule (or)
crepuscle *twilight*
KRPSKLR corpuscular *cell*
KRPSKLR crepuscular *dim*
KRPSKLSM corpus
callosum *brain* corpora
callosa
KRPSKRSD Corpus Christi
city
KRPSKRST Corpus Christi
city
KRPSKYL crepuscule (or)
crepuscle *twilight*
KRPSKYLR corpuscular *cell*
KRPSKYLR crepuscular
dim

Use letters that best describe the sounds you hear and omit the vowels. Use **S** or **K** instead of **C**: to find circle use **SRKL**. Use **J** to find joy, **JM** to find gem and **G** to find go.

KRPSL corpuscle *cell*
KRPSL crepuscle (or) crepuscule *twilight*
KRPSLDM corpus luteum *ovary* corpora lutea
KRPSLDYM corpus luteum *ovary* corpora lutea
KRPSLTM corpus luteum *ovary* corpora lutea
KRPSLTYM corpus luteum *ovary* corpora lutea
KRPSNT corposant *St. Elmo's fire*
KRPSPR carpospore *alga*
KRPSQL crepuscule (or) crepuscle *twilight*
KRPSQLR corpuscular *cell*
KRPSQLR crepuscular *dim*
KRPSS coreopsis *herb* coreopsis
KRPST crappiest *(vulgar) worst*
KRPST creepiest *scary*
KRPSZT crepe suzette *food* crepes suzette (or) crepe suzettes
KRPT carpet *rug*
KRPT corrupt *(v) rot, debase (adj) tainted, depraved*
KRPT crept *(v-past) creep*
KRPT crypt *tomb*
KRPT crypto *secret* cryptos
KRPTBG carpetbag *luggage*
KRPTBGN carpetbagging *meddling*
KRPTBGNG carpetbagging *meddling*
KRPTBGR carpetbagger *outsider*
KRPTBL corruptible (adj) *rotten, debased* corruptibly (adv)
KRPTBM carpet bomb *many bombs*
KRPTGM cryptogam *plant*
KRPTGNK cryptogenic *unknown source*
KRPTGRF cryptography *code*
KRPTGRFK cryptographic *code*
KRPTGRFR cryptographer

code
KRPTGRM cryptogram *code*
KRPTJNK cryptogenic *unknown source*
KRPTK cryptic *secret*
KRPTKKS cryptococcus *fungus* cryptococci
KRPTKKSS cryptococcosis *disease* cryptococcoses
KRPTKL cryptically *secretly*
KRPTL acropetal *upward* acropetally
KRPTL corruptly *tainted*
KRPTLG cryptology *code*
KRPTLJ cryptology *code*
KRPTLJKL cryptological *code*
KRPTLJST cryptologist *code*
KRPTN carpeting *rug*
KRPTN krypton *element*
KRPTNG carpeting *rug*
KRPTNM cryptonym *code name*
KRPTNT crepitant *crackling*
KRPTR corrupter *rot, debase*
KRPTRKD cryptorchid *testes descent*
KRPTRKDZM cryptorchidism (or) cryptorchism *testes descent*
KRPTRKZM cryptorchism (or) cryptorchidism *testes descent*
KRPTSHN crepitation *crackle*
KRPTT crepitate *crackle* crepitated crepitating
KRPTV corruptive *rotting*
KRPTZLG cryptozoology *animal legends*
KRPTZLJ cryptozoology *animal legends*
KRPTZLJST cryptozoologist *animal legends*
KRPTZWLG cryptozoology *animal legends*
KRPTZWLJ cryptozoology *animal legends*
KRPTZWLJST cryptozoologist *animal*

legends
KRPY croupier *dealer*
KRPYLNS corpulence *obesity* corpulency
KRPYLNT corpulent *fat*
KRPYLNTS corpulence *obesity* corpulency
KRPYLS crapulous *hungover*
KRPYR crappier *(vulgar) worse*
KRPYR creepier *scary*
KRPYR croupier *dealer*
KRPYST crappiest *(vulgar) worst*
KRPYST creepiest *scary*
KRPZNT corposant *St. Elmo's fire*
KRQL curricula (pl) *education* curriculum
KRQLM curriculum *education* curricula
KRQLMVD curriculum vitae *career account* curricula vitae
KRQLMVT curriculum vitae *career account* curricula vitae
KRQLR curricular *education*
KRQS croquis *sketch* croquis
KRQZT corequisite *study*
KRR career *job*
KRR carer *nurse*
KRR carrier *transport*
KRR corer *tool*
KRR courier *delivery*
KRR crier *cry, proclaim*
KRR crura (pl) *leg* crus
KRR curare *poison*
KRR curer *healer*
KRR currier *thrash, clean, treat*
KRR curriery *leather*
KRRL crural *leg*
KRRST careerist *advancer*
KRRZM careerism *advancement*
KRS acarus *mite* acari
KRS accuracy *correctness* accuracies
KRS across *crosswise,*

Letters aren't doubled for single sounds: to find alley use **L** not **LL**. Use **Y** and **W** as hard sounds only: to find yellow use **YL**. (Br)=British spelling or usage. * See dictionary.

through
KRS caress *fondle* caresses
KRS carious *cavities*
KRS Caruso (Enrico) *singer*
KRS chorus *music*
KRS coarse *rough* coarser coarsest
KRS coerce *force* coerced coercing
KRS course (v) *flow* coursed coursing
KRS course (n) *golf, lectures, way**
KRS crass *stupid*
KRS crease *bend* creased creasing
KRS cress *plant*
KRS cross (n) *structure* (v) *oppose* crosses
KRS crosse *stick*
KRS crus *leg* crura
KRS Curacao *island*
KRS curacao *liqueur*
KRS curacy *office* curacies
KRS curassow *bird*
KRS curious *inquisitive, strange*
KRS curse *damn* cursed cursing
KRS curse (n) *evil spell*
KRS Icarus *Greek myth*
KRS ichorous *fluid*
KRS kouros *statue* kouroi
KRS kris *dagger*
KRS kurus *money* kurus
KRS ocherous (or) ochreous *yellow*
KRSB crossbow *weapon*
KRSBL coercible *force*
KRSBL crossable *navigable*
KRSBL crossbill *beak*
KRSBL crucible *pot, test*
KRSBLD crossability *breeding*
KRSBLT crossability *breeding*
KRSBNZ crossbones *pirate flag*
KRSBR crossbar *stripe*
KRSBRD crossbreed *fertilize* crossbred crossbreeding

KRSBRR crossbearer *martyr*
KRSCH crosshatch *symbol* (#)
KRSCHF Khrushchev *USSR premier*
KRSCHK cross-check *obstruct, verify*
KRSCHN Christian *religion*
KRSCHN crosshatching *symbol* (#)
KRSCHND Christianity *religion*
KRSCHNG crosshatching *symbol* (#)
KRSCHNSNS Christian Science *religion*
KRSCHNSNTS Christian Science *religion*
KRSCHNSYNS Christian Science *religion*
KRSCHNSYNTS Christian Science *religion*
KRSCHNT Christianity *religion*
KRSCHNZ Christianize *religion* Christianized Christianizing
KRSCHNZR Christianizer *religion*
KRSCHV Khrushchev *USSR premier*
KRSCHYND Christianity *religion*
KRSCHYNT Christianity *religion*
KRSD acaricide *pesticide*
KRSD accursed (or) accurst *damned*
KRSD core city *inner city*
KRSD crista *fold* cristae
KRSD cross-eyed *vision*
KRSD crusade *expedition* crusaded crusading
KRSD crusty *hard and dry, rude* crustier crustiest
KRSD curiosity *interest, curio* curiosities
KRSD cursed *damned*
KRSDD crested *bird*
KRSDD cricetid *animal*
KRSDK acrostic *word*

composition
KRSDK karstic *limestone*
KRSDKL acrostically *word composition*
KRSDL accursedly *damnable*
KRSDL crestal *top*
KRSDL crustal *crust*
KRSDL crustily *rudely*
KRSDL crystal *quartz, clear*
KRSDLD crystalloid *formative*
KRSDLDL crystalloidal *formative*
KRSDLN crystalline *quartz, clear*
KRSDLND crystallinity *quartz, clear*
KRSDLNT crystallinity *quartz, clear*
KRSDLT crystallite *mineral*
KRSDLZ crystallize *become formed* crystallized crystallizing (Br) crystallise
KRSDLZBL crystallizable *become formed* (Br) crystallisable
KRSDLZR crystallizer *become formed* (Br) crystalliser
KRSDLZSHN crystallization *become formed* (Br) crystallisation
KRSDMTH chrestomathy *compilation* chrestomathies chrestomathic
KRSDNG cresting *edging*
KRSDNS accursedness *damnable*
KRSDNS crustiness *rudeness*
KRSDR chorister *music*
KRSDR crustier *hard and dry*
KRSDRS cross-dress *opposite sex attire*
KRSDRSNG cross-dressing *opposite sex attire*
KRSDRSR cross-dresser *opposite sex attire*
KRSDSH crustacea *animal*
KRSDSHN crustacean

Use letters that best describe the sounds you hear and omit the vowels. Use **S** or **K** instead of **C**: to find circle use **SRKL**. Use **J** to find joy, **JM** to find gem and **G** to find go.

animal
KRSDSHS crustaceous
crusty
KRSDSHY crustacea *animal*
KRSDST crustiest *hard and dry*
KRSDYR crustier *hard and dry*
KRSDYST crustiest *hard and dry*
KRSF crucify *punish* crucified crucifying crucifies
KRSFKS crucifix *cross*
KRSFKSHN crucifixion *punishment*
KRSFL cross-file *candidacy*
KRSFLN crestfallen *dejected*
KRSFR cross fire *combat exchange*
KRSFRDLZ cross-fertilize *breed* cross-fertilized cross-fertilizing
KRSFRM cruciform *cross*
KRSFRTLZ cross-fertilize *breed* cross-fertilized cross-fertilizing
KRSFT chrysophyte *alga*
KRSFX crucifix *cross*
KRSFYL cross-file *candidacy*
KRSFYR cross fire *combat exchange*
KRSGRN coarse-grained *rough*
KRSGRND coarse-grained *rough*
KRSGRND cross-grained *diagonal*
KRSGZMN cross-examine *credibility test* cross-examined cross-examining
KRSGZMNR cross-examiner *credibility test*
KRSGZMNSHN cross-examination *credibility test*
KRSH caroche *carriage*
KRSH crash *smash, invade,(slang) sleep*
KRSH crèche *crib*
KRSH Croatia *country*

KRSH crochet *needlework*
KRSH crush *(v) subdue, squeeze (n) crowd, passion* crushes
KRSH currish *ignoble*
KRSH kirsch *brandy*
KRSHBL crushable *squeeze, subdue*
KRSHCH crosshatch *symbol (#)*
KRSHCHN crosshatching *symbol (#)*
KRSHCHNG crosshatching *symbol (#)*
KRSHDV crash dive (n) *submarine* crash-dive (v)
KRSHF Khrushchev *USSR premier*
KRSHL crucial (adj) *important* crucially (adv)
KRSHLMT crash helmet *head protector*
KRSHLN crash-land *airplane*
KRSHLND crash-land *airplane*
KRSHLNDNG crash landing *airplane*
KRSHN accretion *growth*
KRSHN coercion *force*
KRSHN corrasion *worn away*
KRSHN corrosion *decay*
KRSHN crashing (adj) *absolute*
KRSHN creation *making, world*
KRSHN Croatian *of Croatia*
KRSHN Krishna *Hindu deity*
KRSHND crescendo *climax* crescendos (or) crescendoes
KRSHNG crashing (adj) *absolute*
KRSHNGL crashingly *utterly*
KRSHNGL crushingly *severely*
KRSHNL crashingly *utterly*
KRSHNL crushingly *severely*
KRSHNR accretionary *growing*

KRSHNST creationist *Genesis*
KRSHNZM creationism *Genesis*
KRSHPRF crushproof *sturdy*
KRSHR crasher *invader*
KRSHR crocheter *needlework*
KRSHR crosier *staff*
KRSHR crosshair *gun sight*
KRSHR crusher *squeeze, embrace*
KRSHT cruciate *cross*
KRSHV Khrushchev *USSR premier*
KRSHYR crocheter *needlework*
KRSHYT cruciate *cross*
KRSJ corsage *flower*
KRSK carsick *ill*
KRSK crew sock *stocking*
KRSKLCHRL cross-cultural (adj) *multiple cultures* cross-culturally (adv)
KRSKLM cross-claim *legal*
KRSKLTRL cross-cultural (adj) *multiple cultures* cross-culturally (adv)
KRSKN Corsican *of Corsica*
KRSKNS car sickness *nausea*
KRSKNT coruscant *shining*
KRSKNTR cross-country *across land*
KRSKP cryoscope *thermometer*
KRSKP cryoscopy *freezing*
KRSKR chiaroscuro *light and shadow* chiaroscuros
KRSKRNGGL Kriss Kringle *Santa Claus*
KRSKRNGL Kriss Kringle *Santa Claus*
KRSKRNT crosscurrent *conflict*
KRSKRS crisscross *pattern*
KRSKRST chiaroscurist *light and shadow*
KRSKRT crosscourt *opposite side*
KRSKSHN coruscation

Letters aren't doubled for single sounds: to find **alley** use **L** not **LL**. Use **Y** and **W** as hard sounds only: to find **yellow** use **YL**. (Br)=British spelling or usage. * See dictionary.

sparkle, wit

KRSKSHN cross action *law*

KRSKSHN cross section (n) *sample* cross-section (v)

KRSKSMN cross-examine *credibility test* cross-examined cross-examining

KRSKT coruscate *sparkle* coruscated coruscating

KRSKT crosscut *intersect*

KRSKWSCHN cross-question *verify*

KRSKYR chiaroscuro *light and shadow* chiaroscuros

KRSKYRST chiaroscurist *light and shadow*

KRSKZMN cross-examine *credibility test* cross-examined cross-examining

KRSKZMNR cross-examiner *credibility test*

KRSKZMNSHN cross-examination *credibility test*

KRSL carousel *merry-go-round*

KRSL crassly *stupidly*

KRSL curiously *strangely*

KRSLGD cross-legged *sitting position*

KRSLNGK cross-link *connection*

KRSLNGKJ cross-linkage *connection*

KRSLNK cross-link *connection*

KRSLNKJ cross-linkage *connection*

KRSLS chrysalis *growth stage* chrysalides (or) chrysalises

KRSLS creaseless *smooth*

KRSLS crestless *no tuft*

KRSLT corselet (or) corslet (or) corselette *garment*

KRSM karyosome *chromatin*

KRSMC Christmassy (or) Christmasy *like Christmas*

KRSMLD chrysomelid *beetle*

KRSMS Christmas *holiday*

KRSMS Christmassy (or) Christmasy *like Christmas*

KRSMSLN Christmas Island *land mass*

KRSMSLND Christmas Island *land mass*

KRSMSTD Christmastide *season*

KRSMSTM Christmastime *season*

KRSMSV Christmas Eve *holiday*

KRSN christen *baptize*

KRSN coarsen *roughen* coarsened coarsening

KRSN coursing *flowing*

KRSN croissant *pastry* croissants

KRSN crossing *crosswalk*

KRSN kerosene (or) kerosine *fuel*

KRSND carcinoid *tumor*

KRSNDKS cross-index *label*

KRSNDM Christendom *Christianity*

KRSNDX cross-index *label*

KRSNG coursing *flowing*

KRSNG crossing *crosswalk*

KRSNGVR crossing-over *genes*

KRSNJN carcinogen *cancer*

KRSNJNK carcinogenic *cancer*

KRSNJNSD carcinogenicity *cancer*

KRSNJNSS carcinogenesis *cancer*

KRSNJNST carcinogenicity *cancer*

KRSNM carcinoma *tumor* carcinomas (or) carcinomata

KRSNMD carcinomata (pl) *tumor* carcinoma

KRSNMDS carcinomatous *with tumor(s)*

KRSNMT carcinomata (pl) *tumor* carcinoma

KRSNMTS carcinomatous *with tumor(s)*

KRSNMTSS carcinomatosis *tumors*

KRSNN christening *baptism*

KRSNNG christening *baptism*

KRSNRSHP cross-ownership *dual control*

KRSNS crassness *stupidity*

KRSNS curiousness *inquisitive, odd*

KRSNSRKM carcinosarcoma *tumor* carcinosarcomas (or) carcinosarcomata

KRSNSRKMD carcinosarcomata (pl) *tumor* carcinosarcoma

KRSNSRKMT carcinosarcomata (pl) *tumor* carcinosarcoma

KRSNT crescent *shape*

KRSNT croissant *pastry* croissants

KRSNTHMM chrysanthemum *flower*

KRSNTRK acrocentric *not centered*

KRSNVR crossing-over *genes*

KRSP crisp *brittle*

KRSP crispy *brittle* crispier crispiest

KRSPL crisply *brittle*

KRSPLNSHN cross-pollination *fertilization*

KRSPLNT cross-pollinate *fertilization*

KRSPN correspond *match, communicate*

KRSPN crispen *make brittle*

KRSPND correspond *match, communicate*

KRSPNDN corresponding *related*

KRSPNDNG corresponding *related*

KRSPNDNGL correspondingly *related*

KRSPNDNL correspondingly *related*

KRSPNDNS corespondents *divorce*

KRSPNDNS correspondence

Use letters that best describe the sounds you hear and omit the vowels. Use **S** or **K** instead of **C**: to find circle use **SRKL**. Use **J** to find joy, **JM** to find gem and **G** to find go.

similarity, communication
correspondency
KRSPNDNS
correspondents
communicators
KRSPNDNT corespondent
divorce
KRSPNDNT correspondent
(n) communicator *(adj)*
fitting
KRSPNDNTS
corespondents *divorce*
KRSPNDNTS
correspondence
similarity, communication
correspondency
KRSPNDNTS
correspondents
communicators
KRSPNS crispiness
brittleness
KRSPNS crispness
brittleness
KRSPNSV corresponsive
mutual
KRSPR crispier *brittle*
KRSPRPS cross-purpose
contrary
KRSPRZ chrysoprase *gem*
KRSPS crosspiece
horizontal
KRSPST crispiest *brittle*
KRSPYR crispier *brittle*
KRSPYST crispiest *brittle*
KRSQR chiaroscuro *light
and shadow* chiaroscuros
KRSQRST chiaroscurist
light and shadow
KRSQSCHN cross-question
verify
KRSR coarser *rougher*
KRSR corsair *pirate*
KRSR courser *dog, horse*
KRSR creaser *wrinkler*
KRSR crosshair *gun sight*
KRSR cursor *sliding part*
KRSR cursory *hasty*
KRSRD crossroad
intersection
KRSRF crossruff *trump*
KRSRFR cross-refer
notation

KRSRFRNS cross-
reference *notation*
KRSRFRNTS cross-
reference *notation*
KRSRJR cryosurgery
freezing
KRSRL cursorial *running*
KRSRL cursorily *hasty*
KRSRNS cursoriness *haste*
KRSRYL cursorial *running*
KRSS acariasis *disease*
KRSS crisis *critical phase*
crises
KRSS Croesus *rich man*
KRSSH corsage *flower*
KRSST coarsest *roughest*
KRST accursed (or) accurst
damned
KRST Christ *savior*
KRST core city *inner city*
KRST corset *garment*
KRST creosote *tar*
KRST cresset *lantern*
KRST crest *peak, emblem*
KRST crista *fold* cristae
KRST crosstie *railroad*
KRST crust *hard outer layer*
KRST crusty *hard and dry,
rude* crustier crustiest
KRST curiosity *interest, curio*
curiosities
KRST cursed *damned*
KRST Eucharist *communion*
KRST karst *limestone*
KRSTCH cross-stitch
needlework
KRSTD crested *bird*
KRSTD cricetid *animal*
KRSTD croustade *pastry*
KRSTFLN crestfallen
dejected
KRSTHBRD across-the-
board *blanket*
KRSTK acrostic *word
composition*
KRSTK cross talk *noise*
KRSTK karstic *limestone*
KRSTKL acrostically *word
composition*
KRSTL crestal *top*
KRSTL crustal *crust*
KRSTL crustily *rudely*

KRSTL crystal *quartz, clear*
KRSTLD crystalloid
formative
KRSTLDL crystalloidal
formative
KRSTLN crystalline *quartz,
clear*
KRSTLND crystallinity
quartz, clear
KRSTLNT crystallinity
quartz, clear
KRSTLS crestless *no tuft*
KRSTLT crystallite *mineral*
KRSTLZ crystallize *become
formed* crystallized
crystallizing
(Br) crystallise
KRSTLZBL crystallizable
become formed
(Br) crystallisable
KRSTLZR crystallizer
become formed
(Br) crystalliser
KRSTLZSHN crystallization
become formed
(Br) crystallisation
KRSTMTH chrestomathy
compilation
chrestomathies
chrestomathic
KRSTN cresting *edging*
KRSTN crosstown *other side*
KRSTND Christianity
religion
KRSTNG cresting *edging*
KRSTNS accursedness
damnable
KRSTNS crustiness
rudeness
KRSTNT Christianity *religion*
KRSTR chorister *music*
KRSTR corsetiere *merchant*
KRSTR crustier *hard and dry*
KRSTSH crustacea *animal*
KRSTSHN crustacean
animal
KRSTSHS crustaceous
crusty
KRSTSHY crustacea *animal*
KRSTST crustiest *hard and
dry*
KRSTYN Christian *religion*

Letters aren't doubled for single sounds: to find alley use **L** not **LL**. Use **Y** and **W** as hard
sounds only: to find yellow use **YL**. (Br)=British spelling or usage. * See dictionary.

KRSTYND Christianity *religion*

KRSTYNT Christianity *religion*

KRSTYR corsetiere *merchant*

KRSTYR crustier *hard and dry*

KRSTYST crustiest *hard and dry*

KRSV coercive *force*

KRSV corrasive *worn away*

KRSV corrosive *destructive*

KRSV cursive (*n*) *writing* (*adj*) *flowing*

KRSVNS coerciveness *force*

KRSVNS corrosiveness *destruction*

KRSVNS cursiveness *flow*

KRSVR crossover *category*

KRSW crossway *road*

KRSWK crosswalk *pedestrian*

KRSWN crosswind *different direction*

KRSWND crosswind *different direction*

KRSWRD crossword *puzzle*

KRSWZ crossways *diagonal*

KRSWZ crosswise *across*

KRSXMN cross-examine *credibility test* cross-examined cross-examining

KRSXMNR cross-examiner *credibility test*

KRSXMNSHN cross-examination *credibility test*

KRSXZMN cross-examine *credibility test* cross-examined cross-examining

KRSXZMNR cross-examiner *credibility test*

KRSXZMNSHN cross-examination *credibility test*

KRSZ crises (pl) *critical phase* crisis

KRSZ cruces (pl) *essential part* crux

KRSZH corsage *flower*

KRT accrete *accumulate* accreted accreting

KRT accurate *correct*

KRT carat *weight*

KRT caret *mark*

KRT carrot *vegetable*

KRT carryout (n, adj) *take away* carry out (v)

KRT cart *wagon*

KRT court (*n*) *law, sports area* (*v*) *woo, tempt*

KRT cowrite *pen*

KRT crate *box* crated crating

KRT create *make* created creating

KRT cruet *bottle*

KRT curate *organize and oversee* curated curating

KRT curette *scoop* curetted curetting

KRT curt *rude*

KRT eucrite *rock*

KRT eukaryote *organism*

KRT karat *gold*

KRT karate *martial arts*

KRT kart *tiny car*

KRT krait *snake*

KRT kraut *cabbage*

KRT quart *measure*

KRT quarto *music* quartos

KRTBLNCH carte blanche *power* cartes blanches

KRTBLNSH carte blanche *power* cartes blanches

KRTC courtesy *civility* courtesies

KRTC curtesy *estate* curtesies

KRTC curtsy *bend knees* curtsied curtsying

KRTCZ cortices (pl) *outer layer* cortex

KRTD carotid *artery*

KRTD caryatid *column* caryatids (or) caryatides

KRTDDZ keratitides (pl) *cornea* keratitis

KRTDK keratotic *skin*

KRTDS keratitis *cornea* keratitides

KRTGRF cartography *map making*

KRTGRFK cartographic *map*

KRTGRFKL cartographically *map*

KRTGRFR cartographer *map maker*

KRTHRP cryotherapy *cold*

KRTHS courthouse *law*

KRTJ cartage *fee*

KRTJ cortege *procession*

KRTJ curettage *scraping*

KRTK critic *judge*

KRTK critique *review* critiqued critiquing

KRTK eucritic *rock*

KRTK eukaryotic *organism*

KRTKL cortical (adj) *outer layer* cortically (adv)

KRTKL critical (adj) *fault, crucial* critically (adv)

KRTKLNS criticalness *fault, crucial*

KRTKR caretaker *tender*

KRTKS cortex *outer layer* cortices (or) cortexes

KRTKSDR criticaster *petty judge*

KRTKSTR criticaster *petty judge*

KRTKSTRD corticosteroid *drug*

KRTKSTRN corticosterone *metabolism*

KRTL accurately *correctly*

KRTL cartel *combination*

KRTL courtly *elegant, flattering* courtlier courtliest

KRTL curtail *end*

KRTL curtly *rudely*

KRTL quartile *4 parts*

KRTLD cartload *amount*

KRTLJ cartilage *body tissue*

KRTLJNS cartilaginous *body tissue*

KRTLNS courtliness *elegance, flattery*

KRTLR cartulary *deed book* cartularies

KRTLR courtlier *elegant,*

Use letters that best describe the sounds you hear and omit the vowels. Use **S** or **K** instead of **C**: to find circle use **SRKL**. Use **J** to find joy, **JM** to find gem and **G** to find go.

flattering
KRTLST courtliest *elegant, flattering*
KRTLYR courtlier *elegant, flattering*
KRTLYST courtliest *elegant, flattering*
KRTLZ cartelize *combine* cartelized cartelizing (Br) cartelise
KRTLZSHN cartelization *combination* (Br) cartelisation
KRTM Khartoum (or) Khartum *city*
KRTMRSHL court-martial *law*
KRTN carotene *pigment*
KRTN carton *box*
KRTN cartoon *drawing*
KRTN cartoony *drawn*
KRTN cretin *clod*
KRTN cretonne *cloth*
KRTN croton *plant*
KRTN crouton *bread*
KRTN curtain *drapery*
KRTN keratin *protein*
KRTN quartan *4 days, fever*
KRTND carotenoid *pigment*
KRTNFLK keratinophilic *protein*
KRTNKL curtain call *theater*
KRTNLK cartoonlike *drawing*
KRTNNG cartooning *drawing*
KRTNRZR curtain-raiser *play*
KRTNS accurateness *correctness*
KRTNS curtness *rudeness*
KRTNS keratinous *protein*
KRTNSH cartoonish *drawing*
KRTNST cartoonist *artist*
KRTNZ keratinize *protein*
KRTNZM cretinism *hypothyroidism*
KRTNZSHN keratinization *protein*
KRTP carrottop *redhead*
KRTP karyotype *chromosome*

KRTPK karyotypic *chromosome*
KRTR courtier *attendant, flatterer*
KRTR crater *pit*
KRTR creator *maker*
KRTR creature *animal*
KRTR criteria *standards* criterium
KRTR critter *animal*
KRTR curator *caretaker*
KRTR krater *jar*
KRTR quarter *(v) divide, lodge (n) one fourth, area, money**
KRTRBK quarterback *football*
KRTRDK quarterdeck *ship*
KRTRFNL quarterfinal *exam*
KRTRHRS quarter horse *animal*
KRTRJ cartridge *case*
KRTRL quarterly *4 times per year* quarterlies
KRTRM courtroom *law*
KRTRM criterium *standards* criteria (or) criteriums
KRTRMSDR quartermaster *provider*
KRTRMSTR quartermaster *provider*
KRTRN criterion *standard* criteria
KRTRNG quartering *right angle*
KRTRPN cotter pin *fastener*
KRTRSN quartersawn *boards*
KRTRSTF quarterstaff *weapon*
KRTRY criteria *standards* criterium
KRTRYM criterium *standards* criteria (or) criteriums
KRTRYN criterion *standard* criteria
KRTS courteous *civil*
KRTS courtesy *civility* courtesies
KRTS courthouse *law*
KRTS curtesy *estate* curtesies

KRTS curtsy *bend knees* curtsied curtsying
KRTS quartz *rock*
KRTSD courtside *sports*
KRTSH cartouche *frame*
KRTSH cortege *procession*
KRTSHN Cartesian *Descartes*
KRTSHNZM Cartesianism *Descartes*
KRTSHP courtship *engagement*
KRTSHS Cretaceous *geologic era*
KRTSL courteously *civilly*
KRTSN courtesan *prostitute*
KRTSS keratosis *skin* keratoses
KRTSS kurtosis *graph*
KRTSS quartzose *rock*
KRTST karateist *martial arts*
KRTST quartzite *rock*
KRTSZ cortices (pl) *outer layer* cortex
KRTSZ criticize *evaluate* criticized criticizing (Br) criticise
KRTSZBL criticizable *evaluate*
KRTSZM criticism *evaluation*
KRTSZR criticizer *evaluator* (Br) criticiser
KRTT quartet *group of 4*
KRTTDZ keratitides (pl) *cornea* keratitis
KRTTK keratotic *skin*
KRTTS keratitis *cornea* keratitides
KRTV accretive *additional*
KRTV creative *imaginative*
KRTV curative *healing*
KRTVD creativity *imagination*
KRTVT creativity *imagination*
KRTWL cartwheel *handspring*
KRTX cortex *outer layer* cortices (or) cortexes
KRTYLR cartulary *deed book* cartularies
KRTYR courtier *attendant,*

Letters aren't doubled for single sounds: to find alley use **L** not **LL**. Use **Y** and **W** as hard sounds only: to find yellow use **YL**. (Br)=British spelling or usage. * See dictionary.

flatterer
KRTYRD courtyard *enclosure*
KRTYS courteous *civil*
KRTYSL courteously *civilly*
KRTZ Cortes *conqueror*
KRTZ curtsy *bend knees* curtsied curtsying
KRTZH cortege *procession*
KRTZHN Cartesian *Descartes*
KRTZHNZM Cartesianism *Descartes*
KRTZN cortisone *drug*
KRTZN courtesan *prostitute*
KRTZS quartzose *rock*
KRV carve *cut up* carved carving
KRV corvée *labor*
KRV crave *yearn* craved craving
KRV curve *bend* curved curving
KRV curvy *bent*
KRVBL curveball *baseball*
KRVCHR curvature *bend*
KRVG Caravaggio *artist*
KRVGY Caravaggio *artist*
KRVJ Caravaggio *artist*
KRVJY Caravaggio *artist*
KRVL caravel *ship*
KRVL corrival *competitor*
KRVLNR curvilinear *curved lines*
KRVLNYR curvilinear *curved lines*
KRVN caravan *trailer* caravanned (or) caravaned caravanning (or) caravaning
KRVN carven *cut up*
KRVN carving *sculpture*
KRVN corvine *crow*
KRVN craven *cowardly*
KRVN craving *yearning*
KRVNG carving *sculpture*
KRVNG craving *yearning*
KRVNR caravanner (or) caravaner *camper*
KRVNSR caravansary (or) caravanserai *inn* caravansaries (or)

caravanserais (or) caravanserai
KRVR carryover *leftover*
KRVR carver *one who carves*
KRVS crevasse *deep crack or opening*
KRVS crevice *opening*
KRVSHS curvaceous *feminine*
KRVT corvette *ship*
KRVT cravat *necktie*
KRVT curvet *leap* curvetted (or) curveted curvetting (or) curveting
KRVTR curvature *bend*
KRVTYR curvature *bend*
KRVZ corves (pl) *mining* corf
KRW caraway *herb*
KRWBL accruable *adding up*
KRWK Kerouac *writer*
KRWL accrual *accumulation*
KRWL crewel *needlework*
KRWL cruel *fierce* crueler (or) crueller cruelest (or) cruellest
KRWL cruelly *fiercely*
KRWLD cruelty *fierceness* cruelties
KRWLNS cruelness *meanness*
KRWLR crueler (or) crueller *fiercer*
KRWLST cruelest (or) cruellest *fiercest*
KRWLT cruelty *fierceness* cruelties
KRWLWRK crewelwork *needlework*
KRWRN careworn *anxious*
KRWSH car wash *automobile* car washes
KRWSH Croatia *country*
KRWSHN Croatian *of Croatia*
KRWT cruet *bottle*
KRX crux *center* cruxes
KRXKR corkscrew *device*
KRY chorea *spasm*
KRY coria (pl) *skin* corium
KRY criollo *Spaniard, pony* criollos

KRY curia *law court* curiae
KRY curio *curiosity* curios
KRY Korea *country*
KRY kyrie *prayer*
KRYBLG cryobiology *freezing*
KRYBLJ cryobiology *freezing*
KRYBYLG cryobiology *freezing*
KRYBYLJ cryobiology *freezing*
KRYDK eukaryotic *organism*
KRYDR creator *maker*
KRYDV creative *imaginative*
KRYGDD corrugated *furrowed*
KRYGRF choreography *dancing* choreographies
KRYGRFK choreographic *dancing*
KRYGRFKL choreographically *dancing*
KRYGRFR choreographer *dancing*
KRYGSHN corrugation *furrow*
KRYGT corrugate *furrow* corrugated corrugating
KRYGTD corrugated *furrowed*
KRYJN cryogen *refrigerant*
KRYJNK cariogenic *tooth decay*
KRYJNK cryogenic *freezing*
KRYJNKS cryogenics *freezing*
KRYJNX cryogenics *freezing*
KRYK carioca *dance*
KRYK choreic *spasmodic*
KRYK karaoke *taped music*
KRYL carryall *bag*
KRYL Creole *person, language*
KRYL criollo *Spaniard, pony* criollos
KRYLG karyology *cells*
KRYLJ karyology *cells*
KRYLJKL karyological *cells*
KRYLMF karyolymph *sap*
KRYLT cryolite *ice stone*

Use letters that best describe the sounds you hear and omit the vowels. Use **S** or **K** instead of **C**: to find circle use **SRKL**. Use **J** to find joy, **JM** to find gem and **G** to find go.

KRYLZ creolize *speech* creolized creolizing (Br) creolise
KRYM corium *skin* coria
KRYM curium *element*
KRYN carrion *corpse*
KRYN carry on *(v) continue*
KRYN carry-on *(adj, n)* portable
KRYN chorion *placenta*
KRYN crayon *wax marker*
KRYN crying *(adj) offensive*
KRYN Korean *of Korea*
KRYNDR coriander *herb*
KRYNG crying *(adj) offensive*
KRYNGN carrying-on *behavior* carryings-on
KRYNK chorionic *placenta*
KRYNKS cryonics *freezing*
KRYNN carrying-on *behavior* carryings-on
KRYNX cryonics *freezing*
KRYPSS coreopsis *herb* coreopsis
KRYR carrier *transport*
KRYR courier *delivery*
KRYR crier *cry, proclaim*
KRYR currier *thrash, clean, treat*
KRYR curriery *leather*
KRYS carious *cavities*
KRYS curious *inquisitive, strange*
KRYSD curiosity *interest, curio* curiosities
KRYSHN creation *making, world*
KRYSHNST creationist *Genesis*
KRYSHNZM creationism *Genesis*
KRYSKP cryoscope *thermometer*
KRYSKP cryoscopy *freezing*
KRYSL curiously *strangely*
KRYSM karyosome *chromatin*
KRYSNS curiousness *inquisitive, odd*
KRYSRJR cryosurgery *freezing*
KRYSS acariasis *disease*

KRYST creosote *tar* creosoted creosoting
KRYST curiosity *interest, curio* curiosities
KRYT carryout (n, adj) *take away* carry out (v)
KRYT create *make* created creating
KRYT eukaryote *organism*
KRYTD caryatid *column* caryatids (or) caryatides
KRYTHRP cryotherapy *cold*
KRYTK eukaryotic *organism*
KRYTP karyotype *chromosome*
KRYTPK karyotypic *chromosome*
KRYTR creator *maker*
KRYTV creative *imaginative*
KRYTVD creativity *imagination*
KRYTVT creativity *imagination*
KRYVR carryover *leftover*
KRYY criollo *Spaniard, pony* criollos
KRZ caries *decay* caries
KRZ carouse *revel* caroused carousing
KRZ corps (pl) *group* corps
KRZ coryza *common cold*
KRZ craze *fashion, make insane*
KRZ crazy *insane* crazier craziest
KRZ cries *proclaims, makes tears*
KRZ cruise *ship, travel smoothly* cruised cruising
KRZ cruse *pot*
KRZ kersey *wool* kerseys
KRZBN crazy bone *funny bone*
KRZD cruzado *money* cruzados
KRZDBL corps de ballet *ensemble* corps de ballet
KRZFT crow's-foot *wrinkle* crow's-feet
KRZHN coercion *force*
KRZHN corrasion *worn away*

KRZHN corrosion *decay*
KRZHR crosier *staff*
KRZKWLT crazy quilt *jumble*
KRZL carousal *party*
KRZL coryzal *common cold*
KRZL crazily *insanely*
KRZM charisma *charm* charismata
KRZM chrism *oil*
KRZMDK charismatic *charming*
KRZMN corpsman *military* corpsmen
KRZMR kerseymere *wool*
KRZMSHN chrismation *ritual*
KRZMTK charismatic *charming*
KRZNS craziness *insanity*
KRZNST crow's nest *platform*
KRZQLT crazy quilt *jumble*
KRZR carouser *reveler*
KRZR crazier *insane*
KRZR cruiser *ship*
KRZR cruzeiro *money* cruzeiros
KRZR kreuzer *coin*
KRZST craziest *insane*
KRZV coercive *force*
KRZV corrasive *worn away*
KRZV corrosive *destructive*
KRZV cursive *(n) writing* (adj) flowing
KRZVNS coerciveness *force*
KRZVNS corrosiveness *destruction*
KRZWD crazyweed *locoweed*
KRZYR crazier *insane*
KRZYST craziest *insane*
KS acts *deeds*
KS Acts *Bible*
KS Aeacus *Greek myth*
KS ask *request*
KS ax (or) axe *tool* axed axing
KS casa *house*
KS case *cover, watch* cased casing
KS chaos *confusion*
KS cos *lettuce*

Letters aren't doubled for single sounds: to find alley use **L** not **LL**. Use **Y** and **W** as hard sounds only: to find yellow use **YL**. (Br)=British spelling or usage. * See dictionary.

KS cuss *bad words* cusses
KS ex *former*
KS kiss *touch lips* kisses
KS ox *animal* oxen
KS oxeye *daisy*
KS oxy *oxygen*
KS ukase *edict*
KS x *aphabet letter* x's (or) xs
KS x *(v) erase* x-ed x-ing (or) x'ing x-es
KS Xhosa *African*
KSB casaba *melon*
KSB oxbow *yoke*
KSBDR exhibitor *displayer*
KSBK casebook *reference*
KSBL kissable *attractive*
KSBLD oxblood *color*
KSBLG exobiology *life beyond earth*
KSBLJ exobiology *life beyond earth*
KSBLJKL exobiological *life beyond earth*
KSBLJST exobiologist *life beyond earth*
KSBLNGK Casablanca *city*
KSBLNK Casablanca *city*
KSBN X band *radio*
KSBND X band *radio*
KSBNFT cost-benefit *analysis*
KSBRNS exuberance *profusion, joy*
KSBRNT exuberant *plentiful, joyful*
KSBRNTL exuberantly *plentiful, joyful*
KSBRNTS exuberance *profusion, joy*
KSBRT exuberate *overflow* exuberated exuberating
KSBSHN exhibition *display*
KSBSHNST exhibitionist *exposure*
KSBSHNZM exhibitionism *exposure*
KSBT exhibit *display*
KSBTR exhibitor *displayer*
KSBYLG exobiology *life beyond earth*
KSBYLJ exobiology *life beyond earth*

KSBYLJKL exobiological *life beyond earth*
KSBYLJST exobiologist *life beyond earth*
KSCHKR exchequer *treasury*
KSCHNJ exchange *trade* exchanged exchanging
KSCHNJBL exchangeable *trade*
KSCHNJBLD exchangeability *trade* exchangeabilities
KSCHNJBLT exchangeability *trade* exchangeabilities
KSCHNJR exchanger *trader*
KSD accede *agree* acceded acceding
KSD accidie *boredom*
KSD cussed *cursed, obstinate*
KSD exceed *go beyond*
KSD exude *ooze* exuded exuding
KSD oxide *oxygen*
KSD quayside *pier*
KSD quesadilla *food*
KSDBL excitable *arousal*
KSDBLD excitability *arousal*
KSDBLNS excitableness *arousal*
KSDBLT excitability *arousal*
KSDD custody *control* custodies
KŚDD ixodid *tick*
KSDDL custodial *guarding*
KSDDL excitedly *aroused*
KSDDN custodian *guard*
KSDDV oxidative *rust*
KSDDYL custodial *guarding*
KSDDYN custodian *guard*
KSDF cast off (v) *reject* cast-off (adj)
KSDFKDV cost-effective *economical*
KSDFKTV cost-effective *economical*
KSDFSHNT cost-efficient *economical*
KSDGDR castigator *punisher*
KSDGSHN castigation

punishment
KSDGT castigate *punish* castigated castigating
KSDGTR castigator *punisher*
KSDK acoustic (or) acoustical (adj) *sound* acoustically (adv)
KSDK caustic *corrosive*
KSDK ekistic *settlements*
KSDK exotic *foreign, unusual*
KSDK exotica *unusual items*
KSDKL acoustical (or) acoustic (adj) *sound* acoustically (adv)
KSDKL caustically *corrosive*
KSDKL exotically *foreign, unusual*
KSDKNS exoticness *foreign, unusual*
KSDKS ekistics *settlements*
KSDKST coast-to-coast *entire land mass*
KSDL coastal *shoreline*
KSDL cussedly *cursed, obstinately*
KSDM accustom *make familiar*
KSDM custom *practice*
KSDMBLT custom-built *specific*
KSDMD accustomed *usual*
KSDMD custom-made *made to order*
KSDMHS customhouse *duty collection*
KSDMR customary *usual*
KSDMR customer *client*
KSDMRL customarily *usually*
KSDMS customhouse *duty collection*
KSDMZ customize *build or alter* customized customizing (Br) customise
KSDMZ Customs *import tax*
KSDMZN customizing *build or alter* (Br) customising
KSDMZNG customizing

Use letters that best describe the sounds you hear and omit the vowels. Use **S** or **K** instead of **C**: to find circle use **SRKL**. Use **J** to find joy, **JM** to find gem and **G** to find go.

build or alter
(Br) customising

KSDN exceeding
exceptionally

KSDNG casting *(n)* mold,
*toss, acting role**

KSDNG exceeding
exceptionally

KSDNG exciting *stimulating*

KSDNGL exceedingly
exceptionally

KSDNL accidental (adj) *by
chance* accidentally (adv)

KSDNL exceedingly
exceptionally

KSDNL occidental (adj)
western occidentally (adv)

KSDNLNS accidentalness
by chance

KSDNLZ occidentalize *make
western* occidentalized
occidentalizing

KSDNS accedence
agreement

KSDNS accidence *basic
elements*

KSDNS cussedness *cursed,
obstinacy*

KSDNSH exodontia *teeth
extraction*

KSDNST exodontist *teeth
extraction*

KSDNT accident *chance
happening*

KSDNT castanet *music*

KSDNT excitant *arouser*

KSDNT Occident *West*

KSDNT oxidant *rust*

KSDNTL accidental (adj) *by
chance* accidentally (adv)

KSDNTL occidental (adj)
western occidentally (adv)

KSDNTLNS accidentalness
by chance

KSDNTLZ occidentalize
make western
occidentalized
occidentalizing

KSDNTS accidence *basic
elements*

KSDNTST exodontist *teeth
extraction*

KSDR caster (or) castor
sprinkler, wheel

KSDR castor *beaver, wheel*

KSDR Castor *star*

KSDR coaster *mat, ship*

KSDR et cetera *and so forth*

KSDR etcetera *odds and
ends*

KSDR excitor *nerve*

KSDR exedra *room, seat*
exedrae

KSDR keister (or) keester
(slang) buttocks

KSDRD costard *apple*

KSDRD custard *pudding*

KSDRK Costa Rica *country*

KSDRL castor oil *cathartic*

KSDRL kestrel *bird*

KSDRMNGGR
costermonger *(Br)
fruiterer*

KSDRMNGR costermonger
(Br) fruiterer

KSDRMS exodermis *outer
layer*

KSDRPDR extirpator
destroyer

KSDRPSHN extirpation
destruction

KSDRPT extirpate *destroy*
extirpated extirpating

KSDRPTR extirpator
destroyer

KSDRYL castor oil *cathartic*

KSDS exodus *departure*

KSDSHN exudation *material*

KSDSHN oxidation *rust*

KSDT exudate *material*

KSDTR excitatory *arousal*

KSDTV oxidative *rust*

KSDV costive *stingy*

KSDVL costively *stingy*

KSDVNS costiveness *stingy*

KSDW castaway *reject,
shipwreck*

KSDY quesadilla *food*

KSDZ oxidize *mix with
oxygen* oxidized oxidizing

KSDZBL oxidizable *mix
with oxygen*

KSDZR oxidizer *mix with
oxygen*

KSF kiss off (v) *dismiss* kiss-
off (n)

KSFLSHN exfoliation *remove
scales, open leaves*

KSFLT exfoliate *remove
scales, open leaves*
exfoliated exfoliating

KSFLYSHN exfoliation
remove scales, open leaves

KSFLYT exfoliate *remove
scales, open leaves*
exfoliated exfoliating

KSFR ecosphere *habitable
area*

KSFRD Oxford *university*

KSFRD oxford *fabric, shoe*

KSFSH ex officio *office*

KSGCZ exegeses (pl)
explanation exegesis

KSGM exogamy *marriage*
exogamies

KSGMK exogamic *marriage*

KSGMS exogamous
marriage

KSGNK oxygenic *with
oxygen*

KSGNTR cosignatory *joint
signer* cosignatories

KSGRD coast guard *(often
capitalized) navy*

KSGS exiguous *scarce*

KSGSS exegesis *explanation*
exegeses

KSGSZ exegeses (pl)
explanation exegesis

KSGT exiguity *scantiness*
exiguities

KSGWS exiguous *scarce*

KSGWT exiguity *scantiness*
exiguities

KSGYS exiguous *scarce*

KSGYT exiguity *scantiness*
exiguities

KSGYWS exiguous *scarce*

KSGYWT exiguity *scantiness*
exiguities

KSGZS exegesis *explanation*
exegeses

KSH acacia *tree*

KSH cache *(v) hide* cached
caching

KSH cache *(n) hiding place*

Letters aren't doubled for single sounds: to find alley use **L** not **LL**. Use **Y** and **W** as hard
sounds only: to find yellow use **YL**. (Br)=British spelling or usage. * See dictionary.

KSH cachet *seal, approval, prestige*
KSH cachou *astringent*
KSH cash *money*
KSH cashew *nut*
KSH cassia *plant*
KSH cosh *(Br) weapon*
KSH cushaw *squash*
KSH cushy *easy* cushier cushiest
KSH kasha *cereal*
KSH quiche *food*
KSHBK cashbook *record*
KSHD cowshed *barn*
KSHDR actuator *mover*
KSHDR icosahedra (pl) *twenty sides* icosahedron
KSHDRN icosahedron *twenty sides* icosahedrons (or) icosahedra
KSHFL cash flow *money*
KSHK cash cow *profits*
KSHK kishke *sausage*
KSHKRP cash crop *farm*
KSHL actual (adj) *real, true* actually
KSHL casual (adj) *informal* casually (adv)
KSHL cushily *easily*
KSHL exhale *breathe out* exhaled exhaling
KSHLD actuality *fact* actualities
KSHLD casualty *disaster, victim* casualties
KSHLNT exhalant (or) exhalent *outflow*
KSHLRN quiche lorraine *food*
KSHLSHN exhalation *outflow*
KSHLT actuality *fact* actualities
KSHLT casualty *disaster, victim* casualties
KSHLZ actualize *make real* actualized actualizing
KSHLZSHN actualization *realization*
KSHMN accouchement *birth*
KSHMNT accouchement

birth
KSHMR cashmere *soft wool*
KSHMR Kashmir *region*
KSHN action *deed*
KSHN auction *sale*
KSHN cash in *settle*
KSHN caution *care*
KSHN coition *intercourse*
KSHN cushion (n) *pillow* (v) *soften*
KSHN cushiony *soft*
KSHN occasion (n) *event, instance* (v) *bring about*
KSHNBL actionable (adj) *law* actionably (adv)
KSHNDKR cash-and-carry *sales*
KSHNKR cash-and-carry *sales*
KSHNL occasional *specific instance*
KSHNL occasionally *now and then*
KSHNLS actionless *immobile*
KSHNR auctioneer *seller*
KSHNR cautionary *careful*
KSHP cachepot *receptacle*
KSHPT cachepot *receptacle*
KSHR accoucheur *obstetrician*
KSHR actuary *statistician* actuaries
KSHR cashier *money*
KSHR cushier *easier*
KSHR kosher *Jewish*
KSHRDN case-harden *hard cover*
KSHRDND case-hardened *hard cover*
KSHRJSDR cash register *machine*
KSHRJSTR cash register *machine*
KSHRL actuarial (adj) *statistical* actuarially (adv)
KSHRN casuarina *tree*
KSHRT kashruth (or) kashrut *kosher*
KSHRT oxheart *cherry*
KSHRTH kashruth (or) kashrut *kosher*

KSHRYL actuarial (adj) *statistical* actuarially (adv)
KSHS cautious *careful*
KSHSDR case history *record*
KSHSHN actuation *movement*
KSHSL cautiously *carefully*
KSHSNS cautiousness *care*
KSHST casuist *rationalizer*
KSHST cushiest *easiest*
KSHSTK casuistic *rational*
KSHSTR case history *record*
KSHSTR casuistry *rationalism*
KSHT actuate *move* actuated actuating
KSHT x-height *type*
KSHTR actuator *mover*
KSHWDR actuator *mover*
KSHWL actual (adj) *real, true* actually (adv)
KSHWL casual (adj) *informal* casually (adv)
KSHWLD actuality *fact* actualities
KSHWLD casualty *disaster, victim* casualties
KSHWLT actuality *fact* actualities
KSHWLT casualty *disaster, victim* casualties
KSHWLZ actualize *make real* actualized actualizing
KSHWLZSHN actualization *realization*
KSHWR actuary *statistician* actuaries
KSHWRL actuarial (adj) *statistical* actuarially (adv)
KSHWRN casuarina *tree*
KSHWRYL actuarial (adj) *statistical* actuarially (adv)
KSHWSHN actuation *movement*
KSHWST casuist *rationalizer*
KSHWSTK casuistic *rational*
KSHWSTR casuistry *rationalism*
KSHWT actuate *move* actuated actuating
KSHWTR actuator *mover*
KSHY cashew *nut*

Use letters that best describe the sounds you hear and omit the vowels. Use **S** or **K** instead of **C**: to find circle use **SRKL**. Use **J** to find joy, **JM** to find gem and **G** to find go.

KSHY cassia *plant*
KSHYR cushier *easier*
KSHYST cushiest *easiest*
KSJCZ exegeses (pl) *explanation* exegesis
KSJDKL exegetical *explanatory*
KSJDST exegetist *explainer*
KSJN oxygen *element*
KSJNC exigency *demand* exigencies
KSJNK oxygenic *with oxygen*
KSJNLS oxygenless *no oxygen*
KSJNMSK oxygen mask *air supply*
KSJNS exigency *demand* exigencies
KSJNS exogenous *from outside*
KSJNSHN oxygenation *add oxygen*
KSJNT exigent *demanding*
KSJNT oxygenate *add oxygen* oxygenated oxygenating
KSJNTC exigency *demand* exigencies
KSJNTNT oxygen tent *canopy*
KSJNTS exigency *demand* exigencies
KSJRDR exaggerator *overstatement*
KSJRDV exaggerative *overstatement*
KSJRSHN exaggeration *overstatement*
KSJRT exaggerate *overstate* exaggerated exaggerating
KSJRTR exaggerator *overstatement*
KSJRTV exaggerative *overstatement*
KSJSS exegesis *explanation* exegeses
KSJSZ exegeses (pl) *explanation* exegesis
KSJTKL exegetical *explanatory*

KSJTST exegetist *explainer*
KSJZS exegesis *explanation* exegeses
KSK cacique *chief*
KSK cask *container*
KSK casque *helmet*
KSK cassock *garment*
KSK cossack *(often capitalized) horseman*
KSK cusec *unit of flow*
KSK exact *(v) demand (adj) precise*
KSK kiosk *stand*
KSKD cascade *fall* cascaded cascading
KSKD exacta *wager*
KSKDBL executable *kill, perform*
KSKDN exacting *difficult*
KSKDNG exacting *difficult*
KSKDNT executant *performer*
KSKDR executor *administrator*
KSKDTD exactitude *precision*
KSKDTYD exactitude *precision*
KSKDV executive *law, manager*
KSKL exactly *precisely*
KSKLBR Excalibur *sword*
KSKLD exclude *bar, expel* excluded excluding
KSKLDBL excludable (or) excludible *bar, expel*
KSKLDR excluder *bar, expel*
KSKLM exclaim *speak*
KSKLMR exclaimer *speaker*
KSKLMSHN exclamation *sharp utterance*
KSKLMSHNMRK exclamation mark *punctuation*
KSKLMSHNPNT exclamation point *punctuation*
KSKLMTR exclamatory *sharp utterance*
KSKLPSHN exculpation *forgiveness*
KSKLPT exculpate *forgive*

exculpated exculpating
KSKLPTR exculpatory *forgiveness*
KSKLSHN exclusion *bar, expel*
KSKLSHNR exclusionary *bar, expel*
KSKLSHNST exclusionist *bar, expel*
KSKLSV exclusive *(adj) sole, stylish, restricted (n) story, right*
KSKLSVD exclusivity *limitations* exclusivities
KSKLSVL exclusively *sole, stylish, whole*
KSKLSVST exclusivist *limitations*
KSKLSVT exclusivity *limitations* exclusivities
KSKLSVZM exclusivism *limitations*
KSKLV exclave *separation*
KSKLZHN exclusion *bar, expel*
KSKLZHNR exclusionary *bar, expel*
KSKLZHNST exclusionist *bar, expel*
KSKLZV exclusive *(adj) sole, stylish, restricted (n) story, right*
KSKLZVL exclusively *sole, stylish, whole*
KSKLZVST exclusivist *limitations*
KSKMNKDR excommunicator *expeller*
KSKMNKSHN excommunication *expulsion*
KSKMNKT excommunicate *expel* excommunicated excommunicating
KSKMNKTR excommunicator *expeller*
KSKMYNKDR excommunicator *expeller*
KSKMYNKSHN excommunication *expulsion*
KSKMYNKT

Letters aren't doubled for single sounds: to find alley use **L** not **LL**. Use **Y** and **W** as hard sounds only: to find yellow use **YL**. (Br)=British spelling or usage. * See dictionary.

excommunicate *expel*
excommunicated
excommunicating
KSKMYNKTR
excommunicator *expeller*
KSKN ex-con *(slang) former prisoner*
KSKNT cosecant *number*
KSKR cascara *plant*
KSKRBL execrable (adj) *wretched* execrably (adv)
KSKRBLNS execrableness *wretchedness*
KSKRD excreta *waste matter*
KSKRDL cat's cradle *string game*
KSKRDL excretal *waste matter*
KSKRDNT x-coordinate *math*
KSKRDR excreter *discharger*
KSKRDR execrator *denouncer*
KSKRDV execrative *denounce*
KSKRL cascarilla *shrub*
KSKRMNL excremental *feces*
KSKRMNT excrement *feces*
KSKRMNTL excremental *feces*
KSKRMNTSHS excrementitious *feces*
KSKRMSM X chromosome *genes*
KSKRN exocrine *secretion*
KSKRP exocarp *outer layer*
KSKRSHDN excruciating *extreme pain*
KSKRSHDNG excruciating *extreme pain*
KSKRSHN excoriation *chafing*
KSKRSHN excretion *waste matter*
KSKRSHN excursion *trip*
KSKRSHN execration *denounce*
KSKRSHNST excursionist *traveler*
KSKRSHSHN excruciation *torture*

KSKRSHT excruciate *torture*
KSKRSHTN excruciating *extreme pain*
KSKRSHTNG excruciating *extreme pain*
KSKRSHYDN excruciating *extreme pain*
KSKRSHYDNG excruciating *extreme pain*
KSKRSHYSHN excruciation *torture*
KSKRSHYT excruciate *torture*
KSKRSHYTN excruciating *extreme pain*
KSKRSHYTNG excruciating *extreme pain*
KSKRSNC excrescency *blot* excrescence
KSKRSNS excrescence *blot* excrescency
KSKRSNT excrescent *outgrowth*
KSKRSNTC excrescency *blot* excrescence
KSKRSNTL excrescently *outgrowth*
KSKRSNTS excrescence *blot* excrescency
KSKRSV excursive *variation*
KSKRT excoriate *chafe* excoriated excoriating
KSKRT excreta *waste matter*
KSKRT excrete *discharge* excreted excreting
KSKRT execrate *denounce* execrated execrating
KSKRT oxcart *vehicle*
KSKRTL excretal *waste matter*
KSKRTR excreter *discharger*
KSKRTR excretory *discharging*
KSKRTR execrator *denouncer*
KSKRTV execrative *denounce*
KSKRY cascarilla *shrub*
KSKRYSHN excoriation *chafing*
KSKRYT excoriate *chafe*

excoriated excoriating
KSKRZHN excursion *trip*
KSKRZHNST excursionist *traveler*
KSKRZV excursive *variation*
KSKS couscous *food*
KSKS excuse *(n) reason*
KSKSBL excusable (adj) *pardon* excusably (adv)
KSKSHN execution *kill, perform*
KSKSHN exsiccation *dryness*
KSKSHN x-section *cross section*
KSKSHNR executioner *killer*
KSKSS x-axis *math*
KSKSTR excusatory *pardon*
KSKT casket *coffin*
KSKT exact *(v) demand (adj) precise*
KSKT exacta *wager*
KSKT execute *kill, perform* executed executing
KSKT exsiccate *dry* exsiccated exsiccating
KSKTBL executable *kill, perform*
KSKTHDR ex cathedra *position*
KSKTL exactly *precisely*
KSKTN exacting *difficult*
KSKTNG exacting *difficult*
KSKTNT executant *performer*
KSKTR executor *administrator*
KSKTR executory *administrative*
KSKTRCZ executrices (or) executrixes (pl) *administrator (f)* executrix
KSKTRKS executrix *administrator (f)* executrices (or) executrixes
KSKTRSZ executrices (or) executrixes (pl) *administrator (f)* executrix
KSKTRX executrix *administrator (f)*

Use letters that best describe the sounds you hear and omit the vowels. Use **S** or **K** instead of **C**: to find circle use **SRKL**. Use **J** to find joy, **JM** to find gem and **G** to find go.

executrices (or) executrixes

KSKTTD exactitude *precision*

KSKTTYD exactitude *precision*

KSKTV executive *law, manager*

KSKVDR excavator *digger*

KSKVSHN excavation *hole*

KSKVT excavate *dig out* excavated excavating

KSKVTR excavator *digger*

KSKWR chi-square *statistics*

KSKWRDNT x-coordinate *math*

KSKWST exquisite *perfect, acute*

KSKWSTL exquisitely *perfect, acute*

KSKWSTNS exquisiteness *perfect, acute*

KSKWZT exquisite *perfect, acute*

KSKWZTL exquisitely *perfect, acute*

KSKWZTNS exquisiteness *perfect, acute*

KSKYDBL executable *kill, perform*

KSKYDNT executant *performer*

KSKYDR executor *administrator*

KSKYDV executive *law, manager*

KSKYS excuse *(n) reason*

KSKYSBL excusable (adj) *pardon* excusably (adv)

KSKYSHN execution *kill, perform*

KSKYSHNR executioner *killer*

KSKYSTR excusatory *pardon*

KSKYT execute *kill, perform* executed executing

KSKYTBL executable *kill, perform*

KSKYTNT executant *performer*

KSKYTR executor

administrator

KSKYTR executory *administrative*

KSKYTRCZ executrices (or) executrixes (pl) *administrator (f)* executrix

KSKYTRKS executrix *administrator (f)* executrices (or) executrixes

KSKYTRSZ executrices (or) executrixes (pl) *administrator (f)* executrix

KSKYTRX executrix *administrator (f)* executrices (or) executrixes

KSKYTV executive *law, manager*

KSKYZ excuse *(v) pardon* excused excusing

KSKYZBL excusable (adj) *pardon* excusably (adv)

KSKYZR excuser *pardon*

KSKYZTR excusatory *pardon*

KSKZ excuse *(v) pardon* excused excusing

KSKZBL excusable (adj) *pardon* excusably (adv)

KSKZR excuser *pardon*

KSKZTR excusatory *pardon*

KSL axel *jump*

KSL axial (adj) *axis* axially (adv)

KSL axil *leaf*

KSL axilla *armpit* axillae (or) axillas

KSL axle *wheel*

KSL case law *legal*

KSL cassoulet *casserole*

KSL castle *(v) chess move* castled castling

KSL castle *(n) royal abode*

KSL costly *expensive* costlier costliest

KSL excel *surpass* excelled excelling

KSL exhale *breathe out* exhaled exhaling

KSL exile *banish* exiled exiling

KSLD caseload *number of cases*

KSLG axiology *ethics*

KSLJ axiology *ethics*

KSLJKL axiological (adj) *ethical* axiologically (adv)

KSLK oxalic *acid*

KSLN coastline *shore*

KSLNC excellency *title* excellencies

KSLNS costliness *expense*

KSLNS excellence *virtue, best quality*

KSLNS excellency *title* excellencies

KSLNT excellent *first-class*

KSLNT exhalant (or) exhalent *outflow*

KSLNTC excellency *title* excellencies

KSLNTL excellently *first-class*

KSLNTS excellence *virtue, best quality*

KSLNTS excellency *title* excellencies

KSLP cowslip *primrose*

KSLP oxlip *plant*

KSLR axillar *feather*

KSLR axillary *feather* axillaries

KSLR costlier *expensive*

KSLRDNGL acceleratingly *increasingly*

KSLRDR accelerator *speed device*

KSLRDV accelerative *increased*

KSLRDV exhilarative *stimulated*

KSLRMDR accelerometer *speed measure*

KSLRMTR accelerometer *speed measure*

KSLRND accelerando *tempo* accelerandos

KSLRNT accelerant *speed*

KSLRNT exhilarant *enliven*

KSLRSHN acceleration *speed*

KSLRSHN exhilaration *stimulation*

Letters aren't doubled for single sounds: to find alley use **L** not **LL**. Use **Y** and **W** as hard sounds only: to find yellow use **YL**. (Br)=British spelling or usage. * See dictionary.

KSLRT accelerate *speed up* accelerated accelerating

KSLRT exhilarate *enliven* exhilarated exhilarating

KSLRTNGL acceleratingly *increasingly*

KSLRTNL acceleratingly *increasingly*

KSLRTR accelerator *speed device*

KSLRTV accelerative *increased*

KSLRTV exhilarative *stimulated*

KSLS oxalis *plant*

KSLSHN exhalation *outflow*

KSLSHR excelsior *packaging*

KSLSHYR excelsior *packaging*

KSLSR excelsior *packaging*

KSLST costliest *expensive*

KSLSYR excelsior *packaging*

KSLT cassoulet *casserole*

KSLT exalt *praise*

KSLT exult *rejoice*

KSLT oxalate *acid salt*

KSLTDL exaltedly *elevated*

KSLTNC exultancy *rejoicing* exultance

KSLTNS exultance *rejoicing* exultancy

KSLTNT exultant *rejoicing*

KSLTNTC exultancy *rejoicing* exultance

KSLTNTS exultance *rejoicing* exultancy

KSLTR exalter *praiser*

KSLTSHN exaltation *praise*

KSLTSHN exultation *rejoicing*

KSLYR costlier *expensive*

KSLYST costliest *expensive*

KSM axiom *truth*

KSM eczema *skin rash*

KSM exam *test*

KSM exhume *dig up* exhumed exhuming

KSMDK axiomatic *self-evident*

KSMDKL axiomatically *self-evidently*

KSMDS eczematous *skin*

rash

KSMN examine *inspect, test* examined examining

KSMN examinee *person tested*

KSMNBL examinable *inspect, test*

KSMNNT examinant *tester*

KSMNR examiner *inspector, tester*

KSMNSHN examination *inspection, test*

KSMNT casement *fortification*

KSMP exempt *free*

KSMPL example *model, instance*

KSMPLF exemplify *embody* exemplified exemplifying exemplifies

KSMPLFKSHN exemplification *illustration*

KSMPLGRSH exempli gratia *for example (e.g.)*

KSMPLR exemplar *model*

KSMPLR exemplary *model*

KSMPLRL exemplarily *model*

KSMPLRNS exemplariness *model*

KSMPSHN exemption *freedom*

KSMPT exempt *free*

KSMR exhumer *dig up*

KSMR oxymora (pl) *contradiction* oxymoron

KSMRN oxymoron *contradiction* oxymora

KSMRNK oxymoronic *contradictory*

KSMRNKL oxymoronically *contradictory*

KSMS Xmas *Christmas*

KSMSHN exemption *freedom*

KSMSHN exhumation *dig up*

KSMT casemate *fortification*

KSMT exempt *free*

KSMT kismet *fate*

KSMTK axiomatic *self-*

evident

KSMTKL axiomatically *self-evidently*

KSMTS eczematous *skin rash*

KSMTSHN cosmetician *makeup*

KSN auxin *plant hormone*

KSN axion *particle*

KSN axon *neuron*

KSN caisson *vehicle*

KSN casein *milk*

KSN casing *cover*

KSN casino *gambling* casinos

KSN cosign *signature*

KSN cosine *math*

KSN exine *outer layer*

KSN exon *protein*

KSN oxen (pl) *animal* ox

KSNCHL accentual *emphasis*

KSNCHSHN accentuation *emphasis*

KSNCHT accentuate *emphasize* accentuated accentuating

KSNCHWL accentual *emphasis*

KSNCHWSHN accentuation *emphasis*

KSNCHWT accentuate *emphasize* accentuated accentuating

KSNDR Cassandra *prophet*

KSNDTL kiss-and-tell *discuss*

KSNF case knife *tool*

KSNG casing *cover*

KSNK auxinic *plant hormone*

KSNM axoneme *cilium*

KSNML axonemal *cilium*

KSNMT exanimate *lifeless*

KSNMTRK axonometric *drawing*

KSNR cosigner *signature*

KSNRDV exonerative *forgiving*

KSNRSHN exoneration *forgiveness*

KSNRSPT x-intercept *math*

KSNRT exonerate *forgive* exonerated exonerating

KSNRTV exonerative *forgiving*
KSNSHL accentual *emphasis*
KSNSHSHN accentuation *emphasis*
KSNSHT accentuate *emphasize* accentuated accentuating
KSNSHWL accentual *emphasis*
KSNSHWSHN accentuation *emphasis*
KSNSHWT accentuate *emphasize* accentuated accentuating
KSNSTR Cosa Nostra *Mafia*
KSNT accent *inflection, emphasis*
KSNT exeunt *exit*
KSNTL accentual *emphasis*
KSNTL kiss-and-tell *discuss*
KSNTLS accentless *without emphasis, inflection*
KSNTRK eccentric *strange*
KSNTRKL eccentrically *strangely*
KSNTRSD eccentricity *strangeness* eccentricities
KSNTRSPT x-intercept *math*
KSNTRST eccentricity *strangeness* eccentricities
KSNTSHL accentual *emphasis*
KSNTSHN accentuation *emphasis*
KSNTSHT accentuate *emphasize* accentuated accentuating
KSNTSHWL accentual *emphasis*
KSNTSHWT accentuate *emphasize* accentuated accentuating
KSNTT accentuate *emphasize* accentuated accentuating
KSNTWL accentual *emphasis*
KSNTWSHN accentuation *emphasis*
KSNTWT accentuate

emphasize accentuated accentuating
KSNV Casanova *lover*
KSP accept *receive*
KSP Cassiopeia *Greek myth, stars*
KSP cusp *end point*
KSP except *(prep) exclusion (v) exclude, object (conj) unless, only*
KSPBL acceptable *receivable*
KSPBL expiable *amends*
KSPD cusped *pointed*
KSPD cuspid *tooth*
KSPDBL acceptable (adj) *adequate* acceptably (adv)
KSPDBLD acceptability *adequacy*
KSPDBLT acceptability *adequacy*
KSPDD accepted *approved*
KSPDDR expediter *dispatcher*
KSPDL occipital (adj) *bone* occipitally (adv)
KSPDNC expediency *suitability* expedience
KSPDNS acceptance *receptiveness*
KSPDNS expedience *suitability* expediency
KSPDNT acceptant *receptive*
KSPDNT expedient *suitable*
KSPDNTC expediency *suitability* expedience
KSPDNTS acceptance *receptiveness*
KSPDNTS expedience *suitability* expediency
KSPDR accepter (or) acceptor *receiver*
KSPDR accipiter *hawk*
KSPDR cuspidor *spittoon*
KSPDR expiator *atonement*
KSPDSHN expedition *journey, speed*
KSPDSHNR expeditionary *journey*
KSPDSHS expeditious *fast*
KSPDSHSL expeditiously *fast*

KSPDSHSNS expeditiousness *speed*
KSPDT cuspidate *pointed*
KSPDT expedite *speed up* expedited expediting
KSPDTR expediter *dispatcher*
KSPDV acceptive *adequate*
KSPDYNC expediency *suitability* expedience
KSPDYNS expedience *suitability* expediency
KSPDYNT expedient *suitable*
KSPDYNTC expediency *suitability* expedience
KSPDYNTS expedience *suitability* expediency
KSPK expect *look forward, think, await*
KSPKDBL expectable (adj) *look forward, think, await* expectably (adv)
KSPKDDL expectedly *look forward, think, await*
KSPKDNC expectancy *look forward, think, await* expectancies
KSPKDNS expectancy *look forward, think, await* expectancies
KSPKDNT expectant *look forward, think, await*
KSPKDNTC expectancy *look forward, think, await* expectancies
KSPKDNTS expectancy *look forward, think, await* expectancies
KSPKDRNT expectorant *mucus*
KSPKDRSHN expectoration *spit*
KSPKDRT expectorate *spit* expectorated expectorating
KSPKT expect *look forward, think, await*
KSPKTBL expectable (adj) *look forward, think, await* expectably (adv)
KSPKTDL expectedly *look*

forward, think, await

KSPKTDV expectative *look forward, think, await*

KSPKTNC expectancy *look forward, think, await* expectancies

KSPKTNS expectancy *look forward, think, await* expectancies

KSPKTNT expectant *look forward, think, await*

KSPKTNTC expectancy *look forward, think, await* expectancies

KSPKTNTS expectancy *look forward, think, await* expectancies

KSPKTRNT expectorant *mucus*

KSPKTRSHN expectoration *spit*

KSPKTRT expectorate *spit* expectorated expectorating

KSPKTSHN expectation *look forward, think, await*

KSPKTTV expectative *look forward, think, await*

KSPL expel *eject* expelled expelling

KSPL expellee *ejected one*

KSPLBL expellable *eject*

KSPLD explode *burst* exploded exploding

KSPLDBL exploitable *use*

KSPLDD exploded *(adj) diagram*

KSPLDR exploder *burst*

KSPLDR exploiter *user*

KSPLDV expletive *word*

KSPLKBL explicable (adj) *explain* explicably (adv)

KSPLKDV explicative *explanation*

KSPLKSHN explication *explanation*

KSPLKT explicate *explain* explicated explicating

KSPLKTR explicatory *explanation*

KSPLKTV explicative *explanation*

KSPLN explain *clarify*

KSPLNBL explainable *clarify*

KSPLNSHN explanation *clarification*

KSPLNT explant *remove*

KSPLNTR explanatory *clarify*

KSPLNTRL explanatorily *clarify*

KSPLNTSHN explantation *removal*

KSPLR explore *investigate* explored exploring

KSPLR explorer *investigator*

KSPLRDV explorative *investigation*

KSPLRR explorer *investigator*

KSPLRSHN exploration *investigation*

KSPLRTR exploratory *investigation*

KSPLRTV explorative *investigation*

KSPLS cost-plus *price*

KSPLSD explicit *specific*

KSPLSHN explosion *burst*

KSPLSHN expulsion *ejection*

KSPLST explicit *specific*

KSPLSTL explicitly *specifically*

KSPLSTNS explicitness *specific*

KSPLSV explosive *burst*

KSPLSVL explosively *burst*

KSPLSVNS explosiveness *burst*

KSPLT exploit *(n) feat (v) use*

KSPLTBL exploitable *use*

KSPLTDV exploitative *use*

KSPLTDVL exploitatively *use*

KSPLTR expletory *word*

KSPLTR exploiter *user*

KSPLTSHN exploitation *use*

KSPLTTV exploitative *use*

KSPLTTVL exploitatively *use*

KSPLTV expletive *word*

KSPLZHN explosion *burst*

KSPLZV explosive *burst*

KSPLZVL explosively *burst*

KSPLZVNS explosiveness *burst*

KSPN expand *swell*

KSPN expend *spend*

KSPN expound *explain*

KSPNC Caspian Sea *body of water*

KSPNCHN expansion *increase*

KSPNCHNR expansionary *increase*

KSPNCHNST expansionist *more territory*

KSPNCHNZM expansionism *more territory*

KSPND expand *swell*

KSPND expend *spend*

KSPND expound *explain*

KSPNDBL expandable *swelling*

KSPNDBL expendable *easy to replace*

KSPNDBLD expandability *swelling*

KSPNDBLD expendability *easy to replace*

KSPNDBLT expandability *swelling*

KSPNDBLT expendability *easy to replace*

KSPNDCHR expenditure *expense*

KSPNDD expanded *swelled*

KSPNDR expander *increaser*

KSPNDTR expenditure *expense*

KSPNJ expunge *cancel, destroy* expunged expunging

KSPNJR expunger *cancel, destroy*

KSPNNCHL exponential (adj) *rapid increase* exponentially (adv)

KSPNNSHL exponential (adj) *rapid increase* exponentially (adv)

KSPNNT exponent *math symbol, example*

KSPNS Caspian Sea *body of water*

Use letters that best describe the sounds you hear and omit the vowels. Use **S** or **K** instead of **C**: to find circle use **SRKL**. Use **J** to find joy, **JM** to find gem and **G** to find go.

KSPNS expanse *extent*
KSPNS expense *(v) charge*
expensed expensing
KSPNS expense *(n) cost*
KSPNSBL expansible
increase
KSPNSBLD expansibility
increase
KSPNSBLT expansibility
increase
KSPNSHN expansion
increase
KSPNSHNR expansionary
increase
KSPNSHNST expansionist
more territory
KSPNSHNZM
expansionism *more
territory*
KSPNSV expansive *sizable*
KSPNSV expensive *costly*
KSPNSVL expensively
costly
KSPNT excipient *inert base*
KSPNTS expanse *extent*
KSPNTS expense *(v) charge*
expensed expensing
KSPNTS expense *(n) cost*
KSPNTSBL expansible
increase
KSPNTSBLD expansibility
increase
KSPNTSBLT expansibility
increase
KSPNTSV expansive *sizable*
KSPNTSV expensive *costly*
KSPNTSVL expensively
costly
KSPR expire *end, breathe out*
expired expiring
KSPR expiry *end, death*
expiries
KSPRDBL exportable
removal
KSPRDBLD exportability
removal
KSPRDBLT exportability
removal
KSPRDR exporter *wholesaler*
KSPRGDR expurgator
cleanser
KSPRGSHN expurgation

cleansing
KSPRGT expurgate *cleanse*
expurgated expurgating
KSPRGTR expurgator
cleanser
KSPRMNL experimental
(adj) *unproven*
experimentally (adv)
KSPRMNLST
experimentalist *tester*
KSPRMNR experimenter
tester
KSPRMNT experiment *test*
KSPRMNTL experimental
(adj) *unproven*
experimentally (adv)
KSPRMNTLST
experimentalist *tester*
KSPRMNTR experimenter
tester
KSPRMNTSHN
experimentation *testing*
KSPRNCHL experiential
(adj) *questionable*
experientially (adv)
KSPRNS experience *(v)*
undergo experienced
experiencing
KSPRNS experience *(n)*
knowledge, life
KSPRNSD experienced
practiced
KSPRNSHL experiential
(adj) *questionable*
experientially (adv)
KSPRNST experienced
practiced
KSPRNTS experience *(v)*
undergo experienced
experiencing
KSPRNTS experience *(n)*
knowledge, life
KSPRPRDR expropriator
taker
KSPRPRSHN expropriation
taking
KSPRPRT expropriate *take*
expropriated
expropriating
KSPRPRTR expropriator
taker
KSPRPRYDR expropriator

taker
KSPRPRYSHN
expropriation *taking*
KSPRPRYT expropriate *take*
expropriated
expropriating
KSPRPRYTR expropriator
taker
KSPRS espresso *coffee*
KSPRS express *(v) state,
squeeze (n) delivery (adj)
explicit, fast*
KSPRSBL expressible *state,
squeeze*
KSPRSHN expiration *end,
breathe out*
KSPRSHN expression
utterance, symbol
KSPRSHNLS
expressionless *reserved*
KSPRSHNSDK
expressionistic *art*
KSPRSHNSTK
expressionistic *art*
KSPRSHNZM
expressionism *art*
KSPRSJ expressage *fee*
KSPRSL expressly *definitely*
KSPRSMN expressman
delivery expressmen
KSPRSV expressive *show
feeling*
KSPRSVD expressivity *show
feeling, affect*
expressivities
KSPRSVNS expressiveness
show feeling
KSPRSVT expressivity *show
feeling, affect*
expressivities
KSPRSW expressway
highway
KSPRT ex parte *partisan*
KSPRT expert (adj) *proficient*
(n) *master*
KSPRT export *(v) remove (n)
commodity*
KSPRTBL exportable
removal
KSPRTBLD exportability
removal
KSPRTBLT exportability

KSPRTR expiratory *breathe out*

KSPRTR exporter *wholesaler*

KSPRTS expertise *skill*

KSPRTSHN exportation *removal*

KSPRTZ expertise *skill*

KSPRYNCHL experiential (adj) *questionable* experientially (adv)

KSPRYNS experience *(v)* *undergo* experienced experiencing

KSPRYNS experience *(n)* *knowledge, life*

KSPRYNSD experienced *practiced*

KSPRYNSHL experiential (adj) *questionable* experientially (adv)

KSPRYNST experienced *practiced*

KSPRYNTS experience *(v)* *undergo* experienced experiencing

KSPRYNTS experience *(n)* *knowledge, life*

KSPSCHLSHN expostulation *discussion*

KSPSCHLT expostulate *discuss*

KSPSCHLTR expostulatory *discussion*

KSPSFKD ex post facto *after the fact*

KSPSFKT ex post facto *after the fact*

KSPSHN exception *exclusion, objection*

KSPSHN expiation *atonement*

KSPSHNBL exceptionable (adj) *objection* exceptionably (adv)

KSPSHNBLT exceptionability *objection*

KSPSHNL exceptional (adj) *rare* exceptionally (adv)

KSPSHR exposure *no protection*

KSPSHSHN expatiation

KSPSHT expatiate *wander* expatiated expatiating

KSPSHYSHN expatiation *wandering*

KSPSHYT expatiate *wander* expatiated expatiating

KSPSTFKD ex post facto *after the fact*

KSPSTFKT ex post facto *after the fact*

KSPSTLSHN expostulation *discussion*

KSPSTLT expostulate *discuss*

KSPSTLTR expostulatory *discussion*

KSPT accept *receive*

KSPT cuspate *pointed*

KSPT except *(prep) exclusion (v) exclude, object (conj) unless, only*

KSPT expat *exile*

KSPT expiate *make amends* expiated expiating

KSPT occiput *skull* occiputs (or) occipita

KSPTBL acceptable *receivable*

KSPTBL acceptable (adj) *adequate* acceptably (adv)

KSPTBLD acceptability *adequacy*

KSPTBLT acceptability *adequacy*

KSPTD accepted *approved*

KSPTL occipital (adj) *bone* occipitally (adv)

KSPTNGL acceptingly *approving*

KSPTNGNS acceptingness *approval*

KSPTNS acceptance *receptiveness*

KSPTNT acceptant *receptive*

KSPTNTS acceptance *receptiveness*

KSPTR accepter (or) acceptor *receiver*

KSPTR accipiter *hawk*

KSPTR expiator *atonement*

KSPTRN accipitrine *hawklike*

KSPTRSHN expatriation *exile*

KSPTRT expatriate *exile* expatriated expatriating

KSPTRYSHN expatriation *exile*

KSPTRYT expatriate *exile* expatriated expatriating

KSPTSHN acceptation *approval*

KSPTV acceptive *adequate*

KSPY Cassiopeia *Greek myth, stars*

KSPYBL expiable *amends*

KSPYDR expiator *atonement*

KSPYNC Caspian Sea *body of water*

KSPYNS Caspian Sea *body of water*

KSPYNT excipient *inert base*

KSPYR expire *end, breathe out* expired expiring

KSPYSHN expiation *atonement*

KSPYT expiate *make amends* expiated expiating

KSPYTR expiator *atonement*

KSPZ expose *(v) bare* exposed exposing

KSPZ exposé (or) expose *(n) facts*

KSPZD exposed *open*

KSPZDR expositor *commentator*

KSPZHR exposure *no protection*

KSPZR exposer *displayer*

KSPZSHN exposition *essay, display*

KSPZTR expositor *commentator*

KSPZTR expository *explaining*

KSQDBL executable *kill, perform*

KSQDNT executant *performer*

KSQDR executor *administrator*

KSQDV executive *law, manager*

Use letters that best describe the sounds you hear and omit the vowels. Use **S** or **K** instead of **C**: to find circle use **SRKL**. Use **J** to find joy, **JM** to find gem and **G** to find go.

KSQR chi-square *statistics*
KSQS excuse *(n) reason*
KSQSBL excusable (adj)
pardon excusably (adv)
KSQSHN execution *kill,*
perform
KSQSHNR executioner
killer
KSQST exquisite *perfect,*
acute
KSQSTL exquisitely *perfect,*
acute
KSQSTNS exquisiteness
perfect, acute
KSQSTR excusatory *pardon*
KSQT execute *kill, perform*
executed executing
KSQTBL executable *kill,*
perform
KSQTNT executant
performer
KSQTR executor
administrator
KSQTR executory
administrative
KSQTRCZ executrices (or)
executrixes (pl)
administrator (f) executrix
KSQTRKS executrix
administrator (f)
executrices (or)
executrixes
KSQTRSZ executrices (or)
executrixes (pl)
administrator (f) executrix
KSQTRX executrix
administrator (f)
executrices (or)
executrixes
KSQTV executive *law,*
manager
KSQZ excuse *(v) pardon*
excused excusing
KSQZBL excusable (adj)
pardon excusably (adv)
KSQZR excuser *pardon*
KSQZT exquisite *perfect,*
acute
KSQZTL exquisitely *perfect,*
acute
KSQZTNS exquisiteness
perfect, acute

KSQZTR excusatory *pardon*
KSR cusser *curser*
KSR kisser *lips*
KSR X ray (n) *radium* X-ray
(adj) x-ray (v)
KSRB exurb *outer suburb*
KSRB exurbia *outer suburb*
KSRBDNS exorbitance
excess
KSRBDNT exorbitant
excessive
KSRBDNTS exorbitance
excess
KSRBN exurban *outer*
suburb
KSRBNT exurbanite *outer*
suburb
KSRBTNS exorbitance
excess
KSRBTNT exorbitant
excessive
KSRBTNTS exorbitance
excess
KSRBY exurbia *outer suburb*
KSRDD X-rated *offensive*
KSRDSHN x-radiation *X*
rays
KSRDTR exhortatory
warning
KSRDYSHN x-radiation *X*
rays
KSRL casserole *food*
KSRL uxorial *wife*
KSRP excerpt *extract*
KSRPDR excerptor (or)
excerpter *extractor*
KSRPT excerpt *extract*
KSRPTR excerptor (or)
excerpter *extractor*
KSRS uxorious *love of wife*
KSRSD uxoricide *wife*
murder
KSRSHN exertion *effort*
KSRSKL Exercycle
(trademark) bicycle
KSRSL uxoriously *love of*
wife
KSRSNS uxoriousness *love*
of wife
KSRSS oxyuriasis *pinworms*
KSRSST exorcist *expel evil*
KSRSZ exercise *(v) exert,*

use exercised exercising
KSRSZ exercise *(n) use,*
exertion, drill
KSRSZ exorcise *expel evil*
exorcised exorcising
KSRSZBL exercisable *exert,*
use
KSRSZM exorcism *expel evil*
KSRSZR exerciser *machine*
KSRT exert *put forth effort,*
wield
KSRT exhort *warn*
KSRT oxheart *cherry*
KSRTD X-rated *offensive*
KSRTSHN exhortation
warning
KSRTTR exhortatory
warning
KSRTTV exhortative
warning
KSRYL uxorial *wife*
KSRYS uxorious *love of wife*
KSRYSL uxoriously *love of*
wife
KSRYSNS uxoriousness
love of wife
KSRYSS oxyuriasis
pinworms
KSS access *(n) onset, entry*
(v) get at accesses
KSS axis *line, partnership*
axes
KSS caseous *cheesy*
KSS cassis *liqueur*
KSS excess *overage*
excesses
KSSBL accessible (adj)
available accessibly (adv)
KSSBLD accessibility
availability
KSSBLNS accessibleness
availability
KSSBLT accessibility
availability
KSSCHN exhaustion
depletion
KSSDBL exhaustible *deplete,*
tired
KSSDBLD exhaustibility
deplete, tired
KSSDBLT exhaustibility
deplete, tired

KSSDM ecosystem *natural unit*

KSSDV exhaustive *thorough*

KSSFR exosphere *atmosphere*

KSSHN accession *increase, approach*

KSSHN caseation *rottenness*

KSSHN excision *removal*

KSSHNL accessional *increasing, approaching*

KSSKLTL exoskeletal *outer frame*

KSSKLTN exoskeleton *outer frame*

KSSLN oxacillin *antibiotic*

KSSPR exospore *separate*

KSSPRDDL exasperatedly *irritation*

KSSPRDNGL exasperatingly *irritation*

KSSPRDNL exasperatingly *irritation*

KSSPRSHN exasperation *irritation*

KSSPRT exasperate *irritate* exasperated exasperating

KSSPRTDL exasperatedly *irritation*

KSSPRTNGL exasperatingly *irritation*

KSSPRTNL exasperatingly *irritation*

KSSR accessory *adjunct* accessories

KSSRBSHN exacerbation *make worse*

KSSRBT exacerbate *make worse* exacerbated exacerbating

KSSRL accessorial *supplementary*

KSSRYL accessorial *supplementary*

KSSRZ accessorize *add supplement(s)* accessorized accessorizing (Br) accessorise

KSST exhaust *(v) deplete, tire (n) vapor*

KSST exist *live*

KSSTBL exhaustible *deplete, tired*

KSSTBLD exhaustibility *deplete, tired*

KSSTBLT exhaustibility *deplete, tired*

KSSTCZ exostoses (pl) *outgrowth* exotosis

KSSTM ecosystem *natural unit*

KSSTNCHL existential (adj) *experience* existentially (adv)

KSSTNCHLST existentialist *philosopher*

KSSTNCHLZM existentialism *philosophy*

KSSTNS existence *life*

KSSTNSHL existential (adj) *experience* existentially (adv)

KSSTNSHLST existentialist *philosopher*

KSSTNSHLZM existentialism *philosophy*

KSSTNT existent *living*

KSSTNTS existence *life*

KSSTSS exocytosis *cell fusion* exocytoses

KSSTSS exostosis *outgrowth* exotoses

KSSTSZ exostoses (pl) *outgrowth* exotosis

KSSTV exhaustive *thorough*

KSSV excessive *extreme*

KSSVL excessively *extremely*

KSSVNS excessiveness *extremity*

KST accost *approach*

KST achiest *sorest*

KST asked *(v-past)* ask

KST caseate *rot* caseated caseating

KST Cassatt *painter*

KST cassette *tape*

KST cast *(v) toss, discard, mold* cast casting

KST cast *(n) form, tinge, skin*

KST caste *class*

KST coast *(n) seashore (v) glide*

KST coset *math*

KST cosset *pet*

KST cost *price* cost (or) costed costing

KST Cousteau (Jacques) *marine explorer*

KST excite *arouse* excited exciting

KST exit *(v) leave (n) departure, way out*

KST ickiest *disgusting*

KST x-height *type*

KSTBL excitable *arousal*

KSTBLD excitability *arousal*

KSTBLNS excitableness *arousal*

KSTBLT excitability *arousal*

KSTBNFT cost-benefit *analysis*

KSTC ecstasy *rapture* ecstasies

KSTD case study *analysis* case studies

KSTD custody *control* custodies

KSTDK ecstatic *overjoyed*

KSTDKL ecstatically *overjoyed*

KSTDL custodial *guarding*

KSTDL excitedly *aroused*

KSTDN custodian *guard*

KSTDYL custodial *guarding*

KSTDYN custodian *guard*

KSTF cast off *(v) reject* cast-off (adj)

KSTFKDV cost-effective *economical*

KSTFKTV cost-effective *economical*

KSTFSHNT cost-efficient *economical*

KSTGDR castigator *punisher*

KSTGRD coast guard *(often capitalized) navy*

KSTGSHN castigation *punishment*

KSTGT castigate *punish* castigated castigating

KSTGTR castigator *punisher*

Use letters that best describe the sounds you hear and omit the vowels. Use **S** or **K** instead of **C**: to find circle use **SRKL**. Use **J** to find joy, **JM** to find gem and **G** to find go.

KSTH quesadilla *food*
KSTHY quesadilla *food*
KSTK acoustic (or) acoustical (adj) *sound* acoustically (adv)
KSTK caustic *corrosive*
KSTK ekistic *settlements*
KSTK exotic *foreign, unusual*
KSTK exotica *unusual items*
KSTKL acoustical (or) acoustic (adj) *sound* acoustically (adv)
KSTKL caustically *corrosive*
KSTKL exotically *foreign, unusual*
KSTKNS exoticness *foreign, unusual*
KSTKS acoustics *science*
KSTKS ekistics *settlements*
KSTKST coast-to-coast *entire land mass*
KSTL coastal *seashore*
KSTL costly *expensive* costlier costliest
KSTL extol *glorify* extolled extolling
KSTL oxtail *meat*
KSTLMNT extolment *glorification*
KSTLN coastline *shore*
KSTLNS costliness *expense*
KSTLR costlier *expensive*
KSTLR extoller *glorifier*
KSTLST costliest *expensive*
KSTLYR costlier *expensive*
KSTLYST costliest *expensive*
KSTM accustom *make familiar*
KSTM costume *dress* costumed costuming
KSTM custom *practice*
KSTMBLT custom-built *specific*
KSTMD accustomed *usual*
KSTMD custom-made *made to order*
KSTMHS customhouse *duty collection*
KSTMNT excitement *arousal*
KSTMPR extempore *offhand*
KSTMPRNS extemporaneous *offhand*

KSTMPRNSL extemporaneously *offhand*
KSTMPRNT extemporaneity *offhand*
KSTMPRNYS extemporaneous *offhand*
KSTMPRNYSL extemporaneously *offhand*
KSTMPRNYT extemporaneity *offhand*
KSTMPRZ extemporize *compose* extemporized extemporizing (Br) extemporise
KSTMPRZR extemporizer *composer* (Br) extemporiser
KSTMPRZSHN extemporization *composition* (Br) extemporisation
KSTMR costumer *tailor*
KSTMR customary *usual*
KSTMR customer *client*
KSTMRL customarily *usually*
KSTMS customhouse *duty collection*
KSTMZ customize *build or alter* customized customizing (Br) customise
KSTMZ Customs *import tax*
KSTMZN customizing *build or alter* (Br) customising
KSTMZNG customizing *build or alter* (Br) customising
KSTN casting (*n*) *mold, toss, acting role**
KSTN exciting *stimulating*
KSTN extend *unbend, increase bulk, reach out**
KSTN keystone *arch*
KSTNCHN extension *unbend, increase bulk*
KSTNCHNL extensional (adj) *comprehensive* extensionally (adv)

KSTND extend *unbend, increase bulk, reach out**
KSTNDBL extendable *unbend, increase bulk, reach out**
KSTNDBLD extendability *unbend, increase bulk, reach out**
KSTNDBLT extendability *unbend, increase bulk, reach out**
KSTNDD extended *long, intensive*
KSTNDNG extenuating *decreasing*
KSTNDR extender *increaser*
KSTNDR extenuator *one who decreases*
KSTNG casting (*n*) *mold, toss, acting role**
KSTNG exciting *stimulating*
KSTNG oxtongue *plant*
KSTNGGWSH extinguish *quench, nullify*
KSTNGGWSHBL extinguishable *quench, nullify*
KSTNGGWSHMNT extinguishment *quench, nullify*
KSTNGGWSHR extinguisher *quench, nullify*
KSTNGK extinct *not active, not existing*
KSTNGKSHN extinction *not active, not existing*
KSTNGKT extinct *not active, not existing*
KSTNGT extinct *not active, not existing*
KSTNGWSH extinguish *quench, nullify*
KSTNGWSHBL extinguishable *quench, nullify*
KSTNGWSHMNT extinguishment *quench, nullify*
KSTNGWSHR extinguisher *quench, nullify*
KSTNK extinct *not active,*

Letters aren't doubled for single sounds: to find alley use **L** not **LL**. Use **Y** and **W** as hard sounds only: to find yellow use **YL**. (Br)=British spelling or usage. * See dictionary.

not existing

KSTNKSHN extinction *not active, not existing*

KSTNKT extinct *not active, not existing*

KSTNSBL extensible *long, intensive*

KSTNSBLD extensibility *increase*

KSTNSBLT extensibility *increase*

KSTNSHN extension *unbend, increase bulk*

KSTNSHN extenuation *excuse*

KSTNSHNL extensional (adj) *comprehensive* extensionally (adv)

KSTNSL extensile *long, intensive*

KSTNSMDR extensometer *device*

KSTNSMTR extensometer *device*

KSTNSR extensor *muscle*

KSTNSV extensive *considerable*

KSTNSVL extensively *considerably*

KSTNSVNS extensiveness *large size*

KSTNT castanet *music*

KSTNT excitant *arouser*

KSTNT extant *existing*

KSTNT extent *scope*

KSTNT extenuate *decrease* extenuated extenuating

KSTNT extinct *not active, not existing*

KSTNTN extenuating *decreasing*

KSTNTNG extenuating *decreasing*

KSTNTR extenuator *one who decreases*

KSTNTSBL extensible *long, intensive*

KSTNTSBLD extensibility *increase*

KSTNTSBLT extensibility *increase*

KSTNTSL extensile *long,*

intensive

KSTNTSMDR extensometer *device*

KSTNTSMTR extensometer *device*

KSTNTSR extensor *muscle*

KSTNTSV extensive *considerable*

KSTNTSVL extensively *considerably*

KSTNTSVNS extensiveness *large size*

KSTNWDNG extenuating *decreasing*

KSTNWDR extenuator *one who decreases*

KSTNWSHN extenuation *excuse*

KSTNWT extenuate *decrease* extenuated extenuating

KSTNWTN extenuating *decreasing*

KSTNWTNG extenuating *decreasing*

KSTNWTR extenuator *one who decreases*

KSTNYDNG extenuating *decreasing*

KSTNYDR extenuator *one who decreases*

KSTNYSHN extenuation *excuse*

KSTNYT extenuate *decrease* extenuated extenuating

KSTNYTN extenuating *decreasing*

KSTNYTNG extenuating *decreasing*

KSTNYTR extenuator *one who decreases*

KSTNYWDNG extenuating *decreasing*

KSTNYWDR extenuator *one who decreases*

KSTNYWSHN extenuation *excuse*

KSTNYWT extenuate *decrease* extenuated extenuating

KSTNYWTN extenuating *decreasing*

KSTNYWTNG extenuating

decreasing

KSTNYWTR extenuator *one who decreases*

KSTPLS cost-plus *price*

KSTR caster (or) castor *sprinkler, wheel*

KSTR Castor *star*

KSTR castor *beaver, wheel*

KSTR coaster *mat, ship*

KSTR costar *performer* costarred costarring

KSTR et cetera *and so forth*

KSTR etcetera *odds and ends*

KSTR exciter *generator*

KSTR excitor *nerve*

KSTR extra *additional*

KSTR keister (or) keester (slang) *buttocks*

KSTRD castrato *singer* castrati

KSTRD costard *apple*

KSTRD custard *pudding*

KSTRD extrude *push out* extruded extruding

KSTRDDBL extraditable *return for trial*

KSTRDNR extraordinaire *special (used after the noun)*

KSTRDNR extraordinary *special (used before the noun)*

KSTRDNRL extraordinarily *exceptionally*

KSTRDR castrator *geld, spay*

KSTRDR extorter *obtain illegally*

KSTRDR extruder *push out*

KSTRDSHN extradition *return for trial*

KSTRDT extradite *return for trial* extradited extraditing

KSTRDTBL extraditable *return for trial*

KSTRDV extortive *obtain illegally*

KSTRF auxotroph *growth substance* auxotrophy

KSTRFK auxotrophic *growth substance*

KSTRJDSHL extrajudicial

Use letters that best describe the sounds you hear and omit the vowels. Use **S** or **K** instead of **C**: to find circle use **SRKL**. Use **J** to find joy, **JM** to find gem and **G** to find go.

(adj) *private* extrajudicially (adv)

KSTRK Costa Rica *country*

KSTRK exoteric *external*

KSTRK extract *(v) withdraw (n) excerpt*

KSTRK keystroke *typing*

KSTRKBL extricable *disentangle*

KSTRKDBL extractable *withdraw, excerpt*

KSTRKDBLD extractability *withdraw, excerpt*

KSTRKDBLT extractability *withdraw, excerpt*

KSTRKDR extractor *withdraw, excerpt*

KSTRKDV extractive *withdraw, excerpt*

KSTRKL exoterically *external*

KSTRKRKLR extracurricular *after school, sporting*

KSTRKRKYLR extracurricular *after school, sporting*

KSTRKRQLR extracurricular *after school, sporting*

KSTRKSHN extraction *lineage, thing withdrawn*

KSTRKSHN extrication *disentangle*

KSTRKT extract *(v) withdraw (n) excerpt*

KSTRKT extricate *disentangle* extricated extricating

KSTRKTBL extractable *withdraw, excerpt*

KSTRKTBLD extractability *withdraw, excerpt*

KSTRKTBLT extractability *withdraw, excerpt*

KSTRKTR extractor *withdraw, excerpt*

KSTRKTV extractive *withdraw, excerpt*

KSTRL castor oil *catharctic*

KSTRLGL extralegal (adj) *private* extralegally (adv)

KSTRM castoreum *perfume*

KSTRM extreme *(adj) excessive,(n) maximum*

KSTRMD extremity *far point, limb* extremities

KSTRML extremely *excessively*

KSTRMNDR exterminator *destroyer*

KSTRMNGGR costermonger *(Br) fruiterer*

KSTRMNGR costermonger *(Br) fruiterer*

KSTRMNSHN extermination *destruction*

KSTRMNT exterminate *destroy* exterminated exterminating

KSTRMNTR exterminator *destroyer*

KSTRMRDL extramarital *adulterous*

KSTRMRL extramural (adj) *competition* extramurally (adv)

KSTRMRTL extramarital *adulterous*

KSTRMST extremist *beyond the norm*

KSTRMT extremity *far point, limb* extremities

KSTRMYRL extramural (adj) *competition* extramurally (adv)

KSTRMZM extremism *beyond the norm*

KSTRN cast iron (n) *metal* cast-iron (adj)

KSTRNL external (adj) *outside* externally (adv)

KSTRNLD externality *outside*

KSTRNLT externality *outside*

KSTRNLZ externalize *reason* externalized externalizing (Br) externalise

KSTRNLZM externalism *outside*

KSTRNLZSHN externalization *outside* (Br) externalisation

KSTRNS extraneous *outside*

KSTRNSK extrinsic *external*

KSTRNSKL extrinsically *externally*

KSTRNSL extraneously *outside*

KSTRNSNS extraneousness *outside*

KSTRNYS extraneous *outside*

KSTRNYSL extraneously *outside*

KSTRNYSNS extraneousness *outside*

KSTRNZK extrinsic *external*

KSTRNZKL extrinsically *externally*

KSTRPDR extirpator *destroyer*

KSTRPLDR extrapolator *infer*

KSTRPLDV extrapolative *infer*

KSTRPLSHN extrapolation *inferral*

KSTRPLT extrapolate *infer* extrapolated extrapolating

KSTRPLTR extrapolator *infer*

KSTRPLTV extrapolative *infer*

KSTRPSHN extirpation *destruction*

KSTRPT extirpate *destroy* extirpated extirpating

KSTRPTR extirpator *destroyer*

KSTRR exterior *outside*

KSTRRDNR extraordinaire *special (used after the noun)*

KSTRRDNR extraordinary *special (used before the noun)*

KSTRRDNRL extraordinarily *exceptionally*

KSTRRZ exteriorize *make obvious* exteriorized exteriorizing (Br) exteriorise

---

Letters aren't doubled for single sounds: to find alley use **L** not **LL**. Use **Y** and **W** as hard sounds only: to find yellow use **YL**. (Br)=British spelling or usage. * See dictionary.

KSTRSHN castration *geld, spay*

KSTRSHN extortion *obtain illegally*

KSTRSHN extrusion *pushed out*

KSTRSHNR extortioner *obtain illegally*

KSTRSHNST extortionist *obtain illegally*

KSTRSHNT extortionate *excessive*

KSTRSNSR extrasensory *perceptive*

KSTRSNTSR extrasensory *perceptive*

KSTRSV extrusive *pushed out*

KSTRT castrate *geld, spay* castrated castrating

KSTRT castrato *singer* castrati

KSTRT extort *obtain illegally*

KSTRTR castrator *geld, spay*

KSTRTR extorter *obtain illegally*

KSTRTRSCHL extraterrestrial *alien*

KSTRTRSTRL extraterrestrial *alien*

KSTRTRSTRYL extraterrestrial *alien*

KSTRTRTRL extraterritorial *outside*

KSTRTRTRLD extraterritoriality *outside*

KSTRTRTRLT extraterritoriality *outside*

KSTRTRTRYL extraterritorial *outside*

KSTRTRTRYLD extraterritoriality *outside*

KSTRTRTRYLT extraterritoriality *outside*

KSTRTV extortive *obtain illegally*

KSTRVGNS extravagance *excess* extravagancy

KSTRVGNT extravagant *excessive*

KSTRVGNTS extravagance *excess* extravagancy

KSTRVGNZ extravaganza *lavish show*

KSTRVHKLR extravehicular *outside of vehicle*

KSTRVHKYLR extravehicular *outside of vehicle*

KSTRVHQLR extravehicular *outside of vehicle*

KSTRVRSHN extroversion (or) extraversion *outgoing*

KSTRVRT extrovert *outgoing*

KSTRVRZHN extroversion (or) extraversion *outgoing*

KSTRVSKLR extravascular *ouside of vein*

KSTRVSKYLR extravascular *ouside of vein*

KSTRVSQLR extravascular *outside of vein*

KSTRYL castor oil *catharctic*

KSTRYM castoreum *perfume*

KSTRYR exterior *outside*

KSTRYRZ exteriorize *make obvious* exteriorized exteriorizing (Br) exteriorise

KSTRZHN extrusion *pushed out*

KSTRZV extrusive *pushed out*

KSTS ecstasy *rapture* ecstasies

KSTSD causticity *corrosiveness*

KSTSHN acoustician *sound specialist*

KSTSHN excitation *arousal*

KSTSK oxytocic *contraction*

KSTSN oxytocin *hormone*

KSTST causticity *corrosiveness*

KSTT x-ed out *deleted*

KSTTK ecstatic *overjoyed*

KSTTKL ecstatically *overjoyed*

KSTTR excitatory *arousal*

KSTTRSKLN oxytetracycline *antibiotic*

KSTV costive *stingy*

KSTVL costively *stingy*

KSTVNS costiveness *stingy*

KSTW castaway *reject, shipwreck*

KSTWRD coastward *toward shore*

KSTYM costume *dress* costumed costuming

KSTYMR costumer *tailor*

KSTYRN cast iron (n) *metal* cast-iron (adj)

KSV cassava *plant*

KSVYR Xavier *Catholic saint*

KSWR cassowary *bird* cassowaries

KSWRD coastward *toward shore*

KSWRD cussword *swearword*

KSWRK casework *social work*

KSWRKR caseworker *social worker*

KSYD exude *ooze* exuded exuding

KSYDSHN exudation *material*

KSYDT exudate *material*

KSYL axial (adj) *axis* axially (adv)

KSYLG axiology *ethics*

KSYLJ axiology *ethics*

KSYLJKL axiological (adj) *ethical* axiologically (adv)

KSYM axiom *truth*

KSYM exhume *dig up* exhumed exhuming

KSYMDK axiomatic *self-evident*

KSYMDKL axiomatically *self-evidently*

KSYMR exhumer *dig up*

KSYMSHN exhumation *dig up*

KSYMTK axiomatic *self-evident*

KSYMTKL axiomatically *self-evidently*

KSYN axion *particle*

KSYN casein *milk*

KSYNT exeunt *exit*

Use letters that best describe the sounds you hear and omit the vowels. Use **S** or **K** instead of **C**: to find circle use **SRKL**. Use **J** to find joy, **JM** to find gem and **G** to find go.

KSYP Cassiopeia *Greek myth, stars*

KSYPY Cassiopeia *Greek myth, stars*

KSYRSS oxyuriasis *pinworms*

KSYRYSS oxyuriasis *pinworms*

KSYS caseous *cheesy*

KSYSHN caseation *rottenness*

KSYT caseate *rot* caseated caseating

KSZ axes (pl) *line, partnership* axis

KSZ excise *(v) remove, tax* excised excising

KSZ excise *(n) tax*

KSZBL excisable *remove, tax*

KSZHN excision *removal*

KSZPM oxazepam *tranquilizer*

KT account *(n) reckoning (v) explain*

KT act *(n) deed (v) pretend, behave*

KT acuity *sharpness* acuities

KT acute *sharp* acuter acutest

KT Akita *dog*

KT caddie *(or) caddy golf* caddies caddied caddying

KT Caddo *Native American* Caddo (or) Caddos

KT cat *(n) feline animal*

KT cat *(v) search for mate* catted catting

KT catty *malicious* cattier cattiest

KT catty *weight* catties

KT caught *(v-past) catch*

KT coat *(v) layer (n) garment, layer*

KT coati *raccoon-like animal*

KT coot *bird*

KT cootie *louse*

KT cot *bed*

KT cote *coop*

KT cotta *surplice*

KT count *(v) tally (n)* nobleman, charge

KT county *district* counties

KT coyote *dog-like animal* coyotes (or) coyote

KT cuddy *cabin* cuddies

KT cut *trim, cross, divide** cut cutting

KT cute *pretty* cuter cutest

KT cutie *(or) cutey pretty one* cuties (or) cuteys

KT eke out *subsist*

KT K2 *mountain*

KT kata *exercise* kata (or) katas

KT keto *ketone*

KT khadi *(or) khaddar fabric*

KT khat *shrub*

KT kiddie *(or) kiddy child* kiddies

KT kit *(n) set, gear, young animal*

KT kit *(v) outfit* kitted kitting

KT kite *(v) soar, illegal credit* kited kiting

KT kite *(n) bird, sail, flyer*

KT kitty *cat, fund* kitties

KT koto *zither*

KT kowtow *fawn*

KT Kyoto *city in Japan*

KT ocotillo *cactus* ocotillos

KT Quito *city in Equador*

KT quoit *ring*

KTBDK katabatic *wind*

KTBG kit bag *knapsack*

KTBK cutback (n) *trim, lessen* cut back (v)

KTBL countable *numbers* countably (adv)

KTBL cuttable *slice*

KTBLZ catabolize *break down* catabolized catabolizing

KTBLZM catabolism *breakdown*

KTBR October *month*

KTBRD catbird *bird*

KTBRR catbrier *plant*

KTBRYR catbrier *plant*

KTBT catboat *sailboat*

KTBTK katabatic *wind*

KTC cutesy *obnoxious* cutesier cutesiest

KTCH catechu *astringent*

KTCR cutesier *obnoxious*

KTCST cutesiest *obnoxious*

KTCYR cutesier *obnoxious*

KTCYST cutesiest *obnoxious*

KTDD katydid *insect*

KTDK ketotic *disease*

KTDN countdown *time remaining*

KTDRM ectoderm *skin*

KTDRML ectodermal *skin*

KTF cutoff (n) *shortcut* cut off (v)

KTFK catafalque *coffin*

KTFLK catafalque *coffin*

KTFR cataphora *substitute*

KTFRK cataphoric *substitute*

KTFS cutoffs *shorts*

KTFSH catfish *fish*

KTGLS cut glass *decoration*

KTGN octagon *shape*

KTGNL octagonal (adj) *eight sides* octagonally (adv)

KTGR category *type* categories

KTGRKL categorical (adj) *absolute* categorically (adv)

KTGRS cut-grass *bristles*

KTGRZ categorize *classify* categorized categorizing (Br) categorise

KTGRZSHN categorization *classification* (Br) categorisation

KTGT catgut *cord*

KTH couth *polished*

KTH kith *friends*

KTHD cathode *electricity*

KTHDK cathodic *electricity*

KTHDKL cathodically *electricity*

KTHDL cathodal (adj) *electricity* cathodally (adv)

KTHDR catheter *tube*

KTHDR octahedra (pl) *eight faces* octahedron

KTHDRL cathedral *church*

KTHDRN octahedron *eight faces* octahedrons (or) octahedra

KTHDRZ catheterize *tube*

Letters aren't doubled for single sounds: to find alley use **L** not **LL**. Use **Y** and **W** as hard sounds only: to find yellow use **YL**. (Br)=British spelling or usage. * See dictionary.

catheterized
catheterizing
KTHDRZSHN
catheterization *tube*
KTHFGS ichthyophagous
eat fish
KTHFN ichthyofauna *fish*
KTHFNL ichthyofaunal *fish*
KTHKCZ cathexes (pl)
emotion cathexis
KTHKDK cathectic *with*
energy
KTHKSS cathexis *emotion*
cathexes
KTHKSZ cathexes (pl)
emotion cathexis
KTHKTK cathectic *with*
energy
KTHKZS cathexis *emotion*
cathexes
KTHLG ichthyology *fish*
KTHLJ ichthyology *fish*
KTHLJKL ichthyological
(adj) *fish* ichthyologically
(adv)
KTHLJST ichthyologist *fish*
expert
KTHLK catholic *(often*
capitalized) religion,
universal
KTHLSD catholicity
universality catholicities
KTHLST catholicity
universality catholicities
KTHLSZM Catholicism
religion
KTHNDKN kith and kin
friends and relatives
KTHNKN kith and kin
friends and relatives
KTHR coauthor *writer*
KTHR kithara *music*
KTHRDK cathartic *purifying*
KTHRSS catharsis
purification catharses
KTHRTK cathartic *purifying*
KTHS cathouse *bordello*
KTHSR ichthyosaur *dinosaur*
KTHTR catheter *tube*
KTHTRZ catheterize *tube*
catheterized
catheterizing

KTHTRZSHN
catheterization *tube*
KTHXS cathexis *emotion*
cathexes
KTHXZ cathexes (pl)
emotion cathexis
KTHYFGS ichthyophagous
eat fish
KTHYFN ichthyofauna *fish*
KTHYFNL ichthyofaunal *fish*
KTHYLG ichthyology *fish*
KTHYLJ ichthyology *fish*
KTHYLJKL ichthyological
(adj) *fish* ichthyologically
(adv)
KTHYLJST ichthyologist
fish expert
KTHYSR ichthyosaur
dinosaur
KTJ cottage *house*
KTJCHZ cottage cheese
milk product
KTJNRN octogenarian *age*
80-89
KTJNRYN octogenarian *age*
80-89
KTJR cottager *person*
KTK chaotic *confused*
KTKL catcall *shout*
KTKL chaotically *without*
design
KTKL cuticle *skin*
KTKLR cuticular *skin*
KTKLZM cataclysm
catastrophe
KTKLZMK cataclysmic
catastrophic
KTKLZMKL cataclysmically
catastrophically
KTKM catacomb *tomb*
KTKMN catechuman
convert
KTKN catechin *dye*
KTKN catkin *plant*
KTKN katakana *writing*
KTKRNR catercorner
diagonal
KTKRNR kitty-corner (or)
kitty-cornered *diagonal*
KTKRNRD kitty-cornered
(or) kitty-corner *diagonal*
KTKRSDK catachrestic

wrong word
KTKRSDKL catachrestical
(adj) *wrong word*
catachrestically (adv)
KTKRSS catachresis *wrong*
word catachreses
KTKRSTK catachrestic
wrong word
KTKRSTKL catachrestical
(adj) *wrong word*
catachrestically (adv)
KTKSS catechesis
instruction catecheses
KTKYLR cuticular *skin*
KTKYMN catechuman
convert
KTKZ catechize *instruct*
catechized catechizing
KTKZM catechism
instruction
KTL acutely *sharply*
KTL cattail *plant*
KTL cattily *maliciously*
KTL cattle *cows*
KTL coattail *hem*
KTL coddle *cook, pamper*
coddled coddling
KTL cuddle *snuggle* cuddled
cuddling
KTL cuddly *soft* cuddlier
cuddliest
KTL kettle *pot*
KTL ocotillo *cactus* ocotillos
KTL octal *eight*
KTLBN cuttlebone *shell*
KTLDK catalytic *causing*
change
KTLDKL catalytically
causing change
KTLDN cotyledon *placenta,*
leaf
KTLDRM kettledrum *music*
KTLFSH cuttlefish *mollusk*
KTLG catalog (or) catalogue
list cataloged (or)
catalogued cataloging
(or) cataloguing
KTLGR cataloger (or)
cataloguer *lister*
KTLK catlike *stealthy*
KTLKCZ catalexes (pl)
incompleteness catalexis

Use letters that best describe the sounds you hear and omit the vowels. Use **S** or **K** instead of **C**: to find circle use **SRKL**. Use **J** to find joy, **JM** to find gem and **G** to find go.

KTLKDK acatalectic *complete*
KTLKSS catalexis *incompleteness* catalexes
KTLKSZ catalexes (pl) *incompleteness* catalexis
KTLKTK acatalectic *complete*
KTLKTK catalectic *incomplete*
KTLKZS catalexis *incompleteness* catalexes
KTLMN cattleman *rancher* cattlemen
KTLN cotillion *dance*
KTLN octillion *number*
KTLPC catalepsy *suspended animation* catalepsies
KTLPDK cataleptic *suspended animation*
KTLPS catalepsy *suspended animation* catalepsies
KTLPTK cataleptic *suspended animation*
KTLR coddler *cook, pamper*
KTLR cutler *knife maker*
KTLR cutlery *knives*
KTLS catalase *enzyme*
KTLS countless *many*
KTLS cutlass *sword* cutlasses
KTLSS catalysis *reaction* catalyses
KTLST catalyst *agent for change*
KTLT cutlet *slice*
KTLTK catalytic *causing change*
KTLTKL catalytically *causing change*
KTLXS catalexis *incompleteness* catalexes
KTLXZ catalexes (pl) *incompleteness* catalexis
KTLYN cotillion *dance*
KTLYN octillion *number*
KTLZ catalase *enzyme*
KTLZ catalyze *bring about* catalyzed catalyzing
KTLZR catalyzer *change agent*
KTMDR octameter *verse*

KTMN catamenia *menses*
KTMNT catamount *cougar*
KTMNY catamenia *menses*
KTMRF ectomorph *slightly built*
KTMRFK ectomorphic *slightly built*
KTMRN catamaran *boat*
KTMSN actomyosin *chemical*
KTMT catamount *cougar*
KTMTR octameter *verse*
KTMYSN actomyosin *chemical*
KTN accounting *reckoning*
KTN Actaeon *Greek myth*
KTN acting (n) *theater* (adj) *temporary*
KTN chitin *shell*
KTN chiton *mollusk, garment*
KTN coating *outer layer*
KTN cotton (n) *plant fiber* (v) *appreciate*
KTN cottony *soft*
KTN cow town *market*
KTN cut-in (n) *interrupt, mix* cut in (v)
KTN cutin *waxy layer*
KTN cutting (n) *plant* (adj) *sharp*
KTN ecotone *border area*
KTN ketene *gas*
KTN ketone *compound*
KTN kitten (n) *young animal*
KTN kitten (v) *birth cats* kittened kittening
KTN octane *fuel*
KTN Yucatan *peninsula*
KTNBLT Cotton Belt *region*
KTNC cotenancy *roommate*
KTNCD cottonseed *oily seed*
KTNDPST cut-and-paste *piece together*
KTNDRD cut-and-dried *routine*
KTNG accounting *reckoning*
KTNG acting (n) *theater* (adj) *temporary*
KTNG coating *outer layer*
KTNG cutting (n) *plant* (adj) *sharp*
KTNG kidding *joking*

KTNGGLR octangular *eight sides*
KTNGGYLR octangular *eight sides*
KTNGL cuttingly *intensely*
KTNGL kiddingly *joking*
KTNGLR octangular *eight sides*
KTNGYLR octangular *eight sides*
KTNJN cotton gin *machine*
KTNKND cotton candy *food*
KTNL cuttingly *intensely*
KTNM actinium *element*
KTNMCS actinomyces *bacteria genus* actinomyces
KTNMCT actinomycete *bacteria order*
KTNMCTS actinomycetous *bacterial*
KTNMCZ actinomyces *bacteria genus* actinomyces
KTNMKDK actinomycotic *infected*
KTNMKSS actinomycosis *infection*
KTNMKTK actinomycotic *infected*
KTNMRF actinomorphy *symmetry*
KTNMRFK actinomorphic *symmetrical*
KTNMSN actinomycin *antibiotic*
KTNMST actinomycete *bacteria order*
KTNMSTS actinomycetous *bacterial*
KTNMSZ actinomyces *bacteria genus* actinomyces
KTNMTH cottonmouth *snake*
KTNMTR actinometer *gauge*
KTNMTR actinometry *science*
KTNMTRK actinometric *measured*
KTNN actinon *isotope*
KTNNC cotenancy

---

roommate

KTNNS cotenancy *roommate*

KTNNS countenance *(n) appearance*

KTNNT cotenant *roommate*

KTNNTC cotenancy *roommate*

KTNNTLZ cat-o'-nine-tails *whip*

KTNNTS cotenancy *roommate*

KTNNTS countenance *(n) appearance*

KTNP catnap *sleep*

KTNP catnip *plant*

KTNPKN cotton-picking *damned*

KTNPR catnapper *sleeper*

KTNPST cut-and-paste *piece together*

KTNS acuteness *sharpness*

KTNS cattiness *malice*

KTNS chitinous *hard shell*

KTNS cotenancy *roommate*

KTNS countenance *(n) appearance*

KTNS cutaneous *skin*

KTNS cuteness *pretty*

KTNSD cottonseed *oily seed*

KTNSH kittenish *playful*

KTNSHN catenation *link*

KTNT accountant *ledger keeper*

KTNT catenate *link catenated catenating*

KTNT cotenant *roommate*

KTNT octant *device, section*

KTNTC cotenancy *roommate*

KTNTL cottontail *rabbit*

KTNTS cotenancy *roommate*

KTNTS countenance *(n) appearance*

KTNTSHP accountantship *ledger keeping*

KTNWD cottonweed *plant*

KTNWD cottonwood *poplar tree*

KTNYM actinium *element*

KTNYS cutaneous *skin*

KTP cut up *(v) slice, criticize, clown*

KTP cutup *(n) clown*

KTP ecotype *species*

KTP octopi *(pl) animal octopus*

KTP Q-Tip *(trademark) swab*

KTPD octopod *eight arms*

KTPK ecotypic *species*

KTPK ectopic *out of place*

KTPLD octoploid *genes*

KTPLKC cataplexy *power loss cataplexies*

KTPLKS cataplexy *power loss cataplexies*

KTPLR caterpillar *insect*

KTPLSM cataplasm *poultice*

KTPLSM ectoplasm *outer layer*

KTPLSMK ectoplasmic *outer layer*

KTPLT catapult *launching device*

KTPLX cataplexy *power loss cataplexies*

KTPLZM cataplasm *poultice*

KTPLZM ectoplasm *outer layer*

KTPLZMK ectoplasmic *outer layer*

KTPRS cut-price *discount*

KTPRS cutpurse *pickpocket*

KTPS octopus *animal octopuses (or) octopi*

KTQLR cuticular *skin*

KTQMN catechuman *convert*

KTR accoutre *(or) accouter furnish accoutred (or) accoutered accoutring (or) accoutering*

KTR actor *player (m,f)*

KTR acuter *sharper*

KTR catarrh *mucous*

KTR cater *provide*

KTR cattier *malicious*

KTR cautery *burn cauteries*

KTR coterie *group*

KTR couture *clothing*

KTR couturier *(m) fashion couturiere (f)*

KTR cuter *prettier*

KTR cutter *slicer, boat*

KTR khaddar *(or) khadi fabric*

KTR kidder *joker*

KTR Qatar *country*

KTRBLNS counterbalance *offset* counterbalanced counterbalancing

KTRBLNTS counterbalance *offset* counterbalanced counterbalancing

KTRCHK counter check *banking*

KTRCHK countercheck *(v,n) restraint*

KTRFL quatrefoil *4 lobes*

KTRFNSV counteroffensive *military*

KTRFT counterfeit *forgery*

KTRFTR counterfeiter *forger*

KTRFYL quatrefoil *4 lobes*

KTRK cataract *cloudy vision, flood*

KTRK counteract *oppose*

KTRK icteric *jaundice*

KTRKDV counteractive *opposition*

KTRKLCHR counterculture *non-establishment*

KTRKLCHRL countercultural *non-establishment*

KTRKLCHRLST counterculturalist *non-establishment*

KTRKLKWZ counterclockwise *direction*

KTRKLM counterclaim *legal*

KTRKLQZ counterclockwise *direction*

KTRKSHN counteraction *opposition*

KTRKT cataract *cloudy vision, flood*

KTRKT counteract *oppose*

KTRKTV counteractive *opposition*

KTRL catarrhal *(adj) mucous* catarrhally *(adv)*

KTRMN accoutrement *(or)* accouterment *equipment*

KTRMN counterman *clerk* countermen

Use letters that best describe the sounds you hear and omit the vowels. Use **S** or **K** instead of **C**: to find circle use **SRKL**. Use **J** to find joy, **JM** to find gem and **G** to find go.

KTRMN countermand *revoke*

KTRMND countermand *revoke*

KTRMNS coterminous *same boundary*

KTRMNT accoutrement (or) accouterment *equipment*

KTRMSHR countermeasure *opposition*

KTRMZHR countermeasure *opposition*

KTRN catarrhine *primates*

KTRN octoroon *racial*

KTRNSRJNC counterinsurgency *military*

KTRNSRJNS counterinsurgency *military*

KTRNSRJNT counterinsurgent *military*

KTRNSRJNTC counterinsurgency *military*

KTRNSRJNTS counterinsurgency *military*

KTRNTLJNS counterintelligence *spying*

KTRNTLJNTS counterintelligence *spying*

KTRPLR caterpillar *insect*

KTRPN cotter pin *fastener*

KTRPN counterpane *bedspread*

KTRPNT counterpoint *melody, opposite*

KTRPRDKDV counterproductive *hindrance*

KTRPRDKTV counterproductive *hindrance*

KTRPRT counterpart *complement*

KTRPZ counterpoise *balance*

KTRR caterer *provider*

KTRR couturier (m) *fashion* couturiere (f)

KTRS actress *player (f)* actresses

KTRS icterus *jaundice*

KTRSGNCHR countersignature *vouch for*

KTRSM ecotourism *travel*

KTRSN countersign *signature*

KTRSNGK countersink *set below* countersunk countersinking

KTRSNK countersink *set below* countersunk countersinking

KTRSP counterspy *espionage* counterspies

KTRSPNJ counterespionage *spying*

KTRSPNSH counterespionage *spying*

KTRSPNZH counterespionage *spying*

KTRSPYNJ counterespionage *spying*

KTRSPYNSH counterespionage *spying*

KTRSPYNZH counterespionage *spying*

KTRT cut-rate *discount*

KTRTK counterattack *fight*

KTRTP countertop *cabinet*

KTRVL countervail *oppose*

KTRVLSHN counterrevolution *overthrow*

KTRVLSHNR counterrevolutionary *rebel* counterrevolutionaries

KTRWL caterwaul *harsh cry*

KTRWT counterweight *balancer*

KTRY couturier (m) *fashion* couturiere (f)

KTRYR couturier (m) *fashion* couturiere (f)

KTRZ cauterize *sear* cauterized cauterizing

KTRZM ecotourism *travel*

KTRZSHN cauterization *burn*

KTS acts *deeds*

KTS Acts *Bible*

KTS caddis *yarn*

KTS cat's-eye *marble* cat's-eyes

KTS coitus *intercourse*

KTS countess *title* countesses

KTS cutesy *obnoxious* cutesier cutesiest

KTS cutis *skin* cutes (or) cutises

KTS ictus *rhythm*

KTS ketose *sugar*

KTSFL caddis fly *insect* caddis flies

KTSH caddish *rude*

KTSH catechu *astringent*

KTSH kaddish *(often capitalized) prayer*

KTSHL caddishly *rudely*

KTSHNS caddishness *rudeness*

KTSKN CAT scan *medical*

KTSL quetzal *bird* quetzals (or) quetzales

KTSLBK octosyllabic *eight sounds*

KTSLBL octosyllable *eight sounds*

KTSNJMR katzenjammer *distress*

KTSP cat's-paw *wind, dupe, knot, tool* cat's-paws

KTSP catsup *sauce*

KTSR cutesier *obnoxious*

KTSS ketosis *disease*

KTSST cutesiest *obnoxious*

KTST acutest *sharpest*

KTST cattiest *malicious*

KTST cutest *prettiest*

KTSTRF catastrophe *failure, tragedy*

KTSTRFK catastrophic *failed, tragic*

KTSTRFKL catastrophically *failure, tragedy*

KTSYR cutesier *obnoxious*

KTSYST cutesiest *obnoxious*

KTT cut out (v) *erode, depart, replace*

KTT cut out (v) *erode, depart, replace*

Letters aren't doubled for single sounds: to find alley use **L** not **LL**. Use **Y** and **W** as hard sounds only: to find yellow use **YL**. (Br)=British spelling or usage. * See dictionary.

KTT cutout (*n, adj*) piece
KTT octet *eight*
KTTHRP octothorp *symbol* (#)
KTTHRT cutthroat (*n*) *killer* (*adj*) *ruthless*
KTTK ketotic *disease*
KTTN catatonia *no movement*
KTTNK catatonic *no movement*
KTTNY catatonia *no movement*
KTV active *lively, busy, in use*
KTV octave *music, poetry*
KTV octavo *paper size* octavos
KTVD activity *motion, function* activities
KTVDD activated *made reactive*
KTVDR activator *starter*
KTVL actively *lively, busy, in use*
KTVNS activeness *lively, busy, in use*
KTVR cutover *timber*
KTVRMS coat of arms *crest*
KTVRMZ coat of arms *crest*
KTVSHN activation *start*
KTVST activist *political worker*
KTVSTK activistic *political action*
KTVT activate *make reactive* activated activating
KTVT activity *motion, function* activities
KTVTD activated *made reactive*
KTVTR activator *starter*
KTVZM activism *political action*
KTW cutaway *abbreviated*
KTWK catwalk *runway*
KTWK kittiwake *gull*
KTWRK cutwork *lace*
KTWRM cutworm *caterpillar*
KTY ocotillo *cactus* ocotillos
KTYN Actaeon *Greek myth*
KTYN cation *ion*
KTYN cotillion *dance*

KTYN octillion *number*
KTYNK cationic *ion*
KTYR cattier *malicious*
KTYR couture *clothing*
KTYST cattiest *malicious*
KTZ cutes (pl) *skin cutis*
KTZ cutesy *obnoxious* cutesier cutesiest
KTZL quetzal *bird* quetzals (or) quetzales
KTZLKDL Quetzalcoatl *Aztec god*
KTZLKTL Quetzalcoatl *Aztec god*
KTZLKWDL Quetzalcoatl *Aztec god*
KTZLKWTL Quetzalcoatl *Aztec god*
KTZNJMR katzenjammer *distress*
KTZR cutesier *obnoxious*
KTZST cutesiest *obnoxious*
KTZYR cutesier *obnoxious*
KTZYST cutesiest *obnoxious*
KV calve *birth, detach* calved calving
KV cave (*v*) *hollow, submit* caved caving
KV cave (*n*) *underground chamber*
KV cavy *rodent* cavies
KV cove *inlet*
KV covey *flock*
KV kava *shrub*
KV Kiev *city*
KVCH kvetch *gripe* kvetchy
KVD cavity *hole, tooth decay* cavities
KVDS covetous *desire*
KVDWLR cave dweller *prehistoric man*
KVL cavil *carp* caviled (or) cavilled caviling (or) cavilling caviler (or) caviller
KVL coeval *same age*
KVLKD cavalcade *procession*
KVLNS covalence *electrons* covalency
KVLNTS covalence *electrons*
KVLR cavalier *haughty*
KVLR cavalry *horse* cavalries

KVLR caviler (or) caviller *quibbler*
KVMN caveman *prehistoric man* cavemen
KVN cave-in *collapse*
KVN caving *explore caves*
KVN coven *witches*
KVNG caving *explore caves*
KVNNT covenant *agreement*
KVNNT covenantee *person*
KVNNTR Covenanter *Scottish*
KVNNTR covenantor *pledger*
KVNT covenant *agreement*
KVNT covenantee *person*
KVR caviar (or) caviare *food*
KVR cover (*n*) *lid, outer layer, insurance* (*v*) *guard, conceal, treat**
KVRCHRJ cover charge *fee*
KVRDSMT covered smut *disease*
KVRGLS cover glass *microscope*
KVRGRL cover girl *model*
KVRJ coverage *insurance, scope*
KVRKRP cover crop *enricher*
KVRL cover-all (*adj*) *complete*
KVRL coverall (*n*) *garment*
KVRLT coverlet *bedspread*
KVRLZ coveralls *garment*
KVRN cavern *cave*
KVRN covering *lid, outer layer*
KVRNG covering *lid, outer layer*
KVRNS cavernous *spacious*
KVRNS covariance *math*
KVRNT covariant *math*
KVRNTS covariance *math*
KVRP cover-up *mask, garment*
KVRR coverer *guard, conceal*
KVRSLP coverslip *glass*
KVRSTR cover story *magazine*
KVRT cavort *play*
KVRT covert *hidden*
KVRYNS covariance *math*
KVRYNT covariant *math*

Use letters that best describe the sounds you hear and omit the vowels. Use **S** or **K** instead of **C**: to find circle use **SRKL**. Use **J** to find joy, **JM** to find gem and **G** to find go.

KVRYNTS covariance *math*
KVS calves (pl) *baby cow* calf
KVS kvass *beverage*
KVT caveat *warning*
KVT cavity *hole, tooth decay* cavities
KVT covet *desire*
KVT cuvette *test tube*
KVT qiviut *wool*
KVTMPTR caveat emptor *buyer beware*
KVTN cavatina *music*
KVTR cavitary *with holes*
KVTS covetous *desire*
KVTSHN cavitation *with holes*
KVTT cavitate *bubble* cavitated cavitating
KVV qui vive *alert*
KVYR caviar (or) caviare *food*
KVYT caveat *warning*
KVYT qiviut *wool*
KVYTMPTR caveat emptor *buyer beware*
KVYTMTR caveat emptor *buyer beware*
KVZ calves (pl) *baby cow* calf
KW aqua *water, color* aquas (pl, color) aquae (pl, water)
KW equal *(n, adj) same*
KW Kauai *island*
KW keyway *lock*
KW kiwi *fruit, bird*
KW koa *tree*
KW qua *who*
KW quay (or) quai *pier*
KWBK Quebec *province*
KWBL equable (adj) *steady* equably (adv)
KWBL quibble *argue* quibbled quibbling
KWBLD equability *steadiness*
KWBLR quibbler *arguer*
KWBLT equability *steadiness*
KWCH kwacha *money* kwacha
KWD acuity *sharpness* acuities
KWD coati *raccoon-like animal*

KWD coed *female student*
KWD equid *horse family*
KWD equity *law, value* equities
KWD quad *(n) square, BTUs (adj) four*
KWD quad *(v) typeset* quadded quadding
KWD quid *money, wad*
KWD quod *(Br-slang) prison*
KWD quota *share*
KWDBL equitable (adj) *fair* equitably (adv)
KWDBL quotable *repeat*
KWDBLD equitability *fairness*
KWDBLD quotability *repeat*
KWDBLNS equitableness *fairness*
KWDBLT equitability *fairness*
KWDBLT quotability *repeat*
KWDJKSHN coeducation *both sexes*
KWDJKSHNL coeducational (adj) *both sexes* coeducationally (adv)
KWDK aquatic *in water*
KWDK aqueduct *waterway*
KWDKL aquatically *in water*
KWDKS aquatics *water sports*
KWDKSHN coeducation *both sexes*
KWDKSHNL coeducational (adj) *both sexes* coeducationally (adv)
KWDKT aqueduct *waterway*
KWDL acquittal *discharge*
KWDLBT quodlibet *dispute, miscellany*
KWDNNGK quidnunc *busybody*
KWDNNK quidnunc *busybody*
KWDNS acquittance *receipt*
KWDNS quittance *payment*
KWDNTS acquittance *receipt*
KWDNTS quittance *payment*
KWDPRKW quid pro quo *deal, even exchange*

KWDR acquitter *behave, set free*
KWDR cuadrilla *bullfight*
KWDR Ecuador *country*
KWDR equator *midway between poles*
KWDR quitter *defeatist*
KWDR quittor *disease*
KWDRCHR quadrature *stars, math*
KWDRDK quadratic *math*
KWDRFNK quadraphonic *four channels*
KWDRK quadric *math*
KWDRL cuadrilla *bullfight*
KWDRL quadrille *game, dance, square*
KWDRLDRL quadrilateral *4 sides*
KWDRLTRL quadrilateral *4 sides*
KWDRLYN quadrillion *number*
KWDRLYNTH quadrillionth *number*
KWDRMNS quadrumanous *primate*
KWDRMVRT quadrumvirate *group of 4*
KWDRN quadroon *ancestry*
KWDRNGGL quadrangle *square*
KWDRNGGLR quadrangular *square*
KWDRNGGYLR quadrangular *square*
KWDRNGL quadrangle *square*
KWDRNGLR quadrangular *square*
KWDRNGYLR quadrangular *square*
KWDRNL quadrennial (adj) *4 years* quadrennially (adv)
KWDRNM quadrennium *4 years* quadrenniums (or) quadrennia
KWDRNR quaternary *4 units* quaternaries
KWDRNT quadrant *area*
KWDRNYL quadrennial

Letters aren't doubled for single sounds: to find alley use **L** not **LL**. Use **Y** and **W** as hard sounds only: to find yellow use **YL**. (Br)=British spelling or usage. * See dictionary.

(adj) *4 years* quadrennially (adv)

KWDRNYM quadrennium *4 years* quadrenniums (or) quadrennia

KWDRPD quadruped *4 feet*

KWDRPL quadruple *times 4* quadrupled quadrupling

KWDRPLG quadriplegia *paralysis*

KWDRPLGY quadriplegia *paralysis*

KWDRPLJ quadriplegia *paralysis*

KWDRPLJK quadriplegic *paralysis*

KWDRPLJY quadriplegia *paralysis*

KWDRPLKSHN quadruplication *4 copies*

KWDRPLKT quadruplicate *4 copies* quadruplicated quadruplicating

KWDRPLT quadruplet *4 offspring*

KWDRPRTT quadripartite *4 parts*

KWDRSNTNR quatercentenary *400 years*

KWDRSPS quadriceps *muscle*

KWDRT quadrat *rectangle*

KWDRT quadrate *square*

KWDRTK quadratic *math*

KWDRTR quadrature *stars, math*

KWDRTYR quadrature *stars, math*

KWDRVL quadrivial *4 roads*

KWDRVLNT quadrivalent *genes*

KWDRVYL quadrivial *4 roads*

KWDRY cuadrilla *bullfight*

KWDRYN quadrillion *number*

KWDRYNTH quadrillionth *number*

KWDS coitus *intercourse*

KWDS quietus *death*

KWDSDNT equidistant *equal distance*

KWDSTNT equidistant *equal distance*

KWDX aquatics *water sports*

KWDYKSHN coeducation *both sexes*

KWDYKSHNL coeducational (adj) *both sexes* coeducationally (adv)

KWF coif *hairdo* coiffed (or) coifed coiffing (or) coifing

KWF quaff *drink*

KWF quiff *(Br) forelock*

KWFR aquifer *rock*

KWFR coiffeur *hairdresser*

KWFR coiffure *hairstyle*

KWFR quaffer *drinker*

KWFRD coiffured *hairstyle*

KWFRT kiwifruit *gooseberry*

KWFS coiffeuse *hairdresser (f)*

KWFSHNT coefficient *number*

KWFYR coiffeur *hairdresser*

KWFYR coiffure *hairstyle*

KWFYRD coiffured *hairstyle*

KWFYS coiffeuse *hairdresser (f)*

KWFYZ coiffeuse *hairdresser (f)*

KWFZ coiffeuse *hairdresser (f)*

KWG quag *marsh*

KWG quagga *animal*

KWGL coagula (pl) *clot* coagulum

KWGLBL coagulable *clot*

KWGLM coagulum *clot* coagula (or) coagulums

KWGLNT coagulant *clot*

KWGLSHN coagulation *clot*

KWGLT coagulate *clot* coagulated coagulating

KWGMR quagmire *bog, crisis*

KWGYL coagula (pl) *clot* coagulum

KWGYLBL coagulable *clot*

KWGYLM coagulum *clot* coagula (or) coagulums

KWGYLNT coagulant *clot*

KWGYLSHN coagulation *clot*

KWGYLT coagulate *clot* coagulated coagulating

KWGZKDR coexecutor *will*

KWGZKTR coexecutor *will*

KWGZKYDR coexecutor *will*

KWGZKYTR coexecutor *will*

KWGZQDR coexecutor *will*

KWGZQTR coexecutor *will*

KWGZST coexist *live together*

KWGZSTNS coexistence *live together*

KWGZSTNT coexistent *live together*

KWGZSTNTS coexistence *live together*

KWHG quahog *clam*

KWJ quayage *fee, piers*

KWJDR coadjutor *assistant*

KWJKSHN coeducation *both sexes*

KWJKSHNL coeducational (adj) *both sexes* coeducationally (adv)

KWJTR coadjutor *assistant*

KWK echoic *repeat*

KWK quack *(v,n) duck sound (n, adj) fraud*

KWK quake *shake* quaked quaking

KWK quick *(adj) fast, living (n) sensitive area, heart*

KWK quickie *fast motion*

KWKBRD quick bread *food*

KWKCL coaxial *cable*

KWKCYL coaxial *cable*

KWKD aquacade *water exhibition*

KWKFRZ quick-freeze *chill* quick-froze quick-freezing quick-frozen

KWKL quickly *fast*

KWKLCHR aquaculture *farming*

KWKLCHRL aquacultural *farming*

KWKLCHRST aquaculturist *farmer*

Use letters that best describe the sounds you hear and omit the vowels. Use **S** or **K** instead of **C**: to find circle use **SRKL**. Use **J** to find joy, **JM** to find gem and **G** to find go.

KWKLM quicklime *lime*
KWKLM quitclaim *deed*
KWKLTR aquaculture *farming*
KWKLTRL aquacultural *farming*
KWKLTRST aquaculturist *farmer*
KWKN quicken *revive*
KWKNS quickness *fast*
KWKR quackery *pretense* quackeries
KWKR Quaker *Religious Society of Friends*
KWKSDK quixotic *impractical*
KWKSDKL quixotical (adj) *impractical* quixotically (adv)
KWKSHN coaction *interaction*
KWKSL coaxial *cable*
KWKSLVR quicksilver *mercury*
KWKSN quicksand *trap*
KWKSND quicksand *trap*
KWKST quickset *(Br) plants*
KWKST quixote *politeness*
KWKSTK quixotic *impractical*
KWKSTKL quixotical (adj) *impractical* quixotically (adv)
KWKSTNSV coextensive *same space*
KWKSTP quickstep *march*
KWKSTZM quixotism *politeness*
KWKSYL coaxial *cable*
KWKTM quick time *march*
KWKTMPRD quick-tempered *anger*
KWKWDD quick-witted *intelligent*
KWKWDDNS quick-wittedness *intelligence*
KWKWL coequal (n, adj) *same as* coequally (adv)
KWKWLD coequality *same as* coequalities
KWKWLT coequality *same as* coequalities

KWKWTD quick-witted *intelligent*
KWKWTDNS quick-wittedness *intelligence*
KWKZDK quixotic *impractical*
KWKZDKL quixotical (adj) *impractical* quixotically (adv)
KWKZKDR coexecutor *will*
KWKZKTR coexecutor *will*
KWKZKYDR coexecutor *will*
KWKZKYTR coexecutor *will*
KWKZQDR coexecutor *will*
KWKZQTR coexecutor *will*
KWKZST coexist *live together*
KWKZSTNS coexistence *live together*
KWKZSTNT coexistent *live together*
KWKZSTNTS coexistence *live together*
KWKZT quixote *politeness*
KWKZTK quixotic *impractical*
KWKZTKL quixotical (adj) *impractical* quixotically (adv)
KWL cowl *hood*
KWL equal (v) *make the same* equaled (or) equalled equaling (or) equalling
KWL equally (adv) *same*
KWL koala *animal*
KWL quail (n) *bird* (v) *cower*
KWL quale *universal* qualia
KWL qualia (pl) *universal* quale
KWL quell *stop*
KWL quill *feather*
KWLBK quillback *fish*
KWLBR equilibria (pl) *balance* equilibrium
KWLBRDR equilibrator *balance*
KWLBRM equilibrium *balance* equilibriums (or) equilibria
KWLBRNT equilibrant

balance
KWLBRSHN equilibration *balance*
KWLBRST equilibrist *balance*
KWLBRSTK equilibristic *balance*
KWLBRT equilibrate *balance* equilibrated equilibrating
KWLBRTR equilibrator *balance*
KWLBRY equilibria (pl) *balance* eqiilibrium
KWLBRYM equilibrium *balance* equilibriums (or) equilibria
KWLD equality *sameness* equalities
KWLD Quaalude (*trademark*) *drug*
KWLD quality *nature, grade* qualities
KWLDRL equilateral *equal sides*
KWLF qualify *certify, modify* qualified qualifying qualifies
KWLFBL qualifiable *eligible*
KWLFD qualified *eligible*
KWLFKSHN qualification *eligibility*
KWLFR qualifier *eligible*
KWLFYBL qualifiable *eligible*
KWLFYR qualifier *eligible*
KWLLMPR Kuala Lumpur *city*
KWLM qualm *doubt, fear*
KWLMSH qualmish *sick*
KWLMSHL qualmishly *sick*
KWLMSHNS qualmishness *sick*
KWLN aquiline *eagle-like*
KWLND aquilinity *eagles*
KWLNG Aqua-Lung (*trademark*) *scuba gear*
KWLNT aquilinity *eagles*
KWLR queller *stopper*
KWLS coalesce *unite* coalesced coalescing
KWLSHN coalition *union*
KWLSNS coalescence

---

union

KWLSNT coalescent *union*

KWLSNTS coalescence *union*

KWLT equality *sameness* equalities

KWLT quality *nature, grade* qualities

KWLT quilt *(n)* coverlet *(v)* sew

KWLTDV qualitative *characteristic*

KWLTN quilting *fabric, sewing*

KWLTNG quilting *fabric, sewing*

KWLTRL equilateral *equal sides*

KWLTTV qualitative *characteristic*

KWLY qualia (pl) *universal quale*

KWLZ equalize *make equal, (Br) tie score* equalized equalizing *(Br)* equalise

KWLZR equalizer *make equal, (Br) tie score (Br)* equaliser

KWLZSHN equalization *make equal, (Br) tie score (Br)* equalisation

KWM qualm *doubt, fear*

KWMRN aquamarine *color*

KWMSH qualmish *sick*

KWMSHL qualmishly *sick*

KWMSHNS qualmishness *sick*

KWN equine *horse*

KWN koan *poem*

KWN quean *prostitute*

KWN queen *(n)* ruler *(v) dominate, chess*

KWN quoin *wedge*

KWNCH quench *put out, cool, relieve*

KWNCHBL quenchable *put out, cool, relieve*

KWNCHLS quenchless *no relief, no end*

KWNCHR quencher *put out. cool, relieve*

KWND quantity *amount* quantities

KWNDM quondam *former*

KWNDN quinidine *drug*

KWNDR quandary *doubt* quandaries

KWNDSLYN quindecillion *number*

KWNDSYN quindecillion *number*

KWNFBL quantifiable *count*

KWNFKSHN quantification *count*

KWNFKSHNL quantificational (adj) *count* quantificationally (adv)

KWNFR quantifier *count*

KWNFYBL quantifiable *count*

KWNFYR quantifier *count*

KWNGGLR equiangular *same angles*

KWNGGYLR equiangular *same angles*

KWNGKR coanchor *news*

KWNGLR equiangular *same angles*

KWNGYLR equiangular *same angles*

KWNJ coinage *money*

KWNKR coanchor *news*

KWNKS equinox *equal day and night*

KWNKSHL equinoctial *equal day and night*

KWNKWNL quinquennial (adj) *5 years* quinquennially (adv)

KWNKWNYL quinquennial (adj) *5 years* quinquennially (adv)

KWNL queenly *regal* queenlier queenliest

KWNL quenelle *dumpling*

KWNL quiniela (or) quinella *bet*

KWNLNS queenliness *regal*

KWNLR queenlier *regal*

KWNLST queenliest *regal*

KWNLYR queenlier *regal*

KWNLYST queenliest *regal*

KWNM quantum *amount, large quanta*

KWNMD equanimity *balance* equanimities

KWNMT equanimity *balance* equanimities

KWNN quinine *alkaloid*

KWNN quinone *benzene derivative*

KWNNS acquaintance *familiarity, person*

KWNNSHP acquaintanceship *familiarity*

KWNNTS acquaintance *familiarity, person*

KWNPRS coin purse *wallet*

KWNQNL quinquennial (adj) *5 years* quinquennially (adv)

KWNQNYL quinquennial (adj) *5 years* quinquennially (adv)

KWNS Aquinas (Thomas) *Catholic saint*

KWNS Kiwanis *service club*

KWNS quince *fruit*

KWNSD coincide *agree* coincided coinciding

KWNSD queenside *chess*

KWNSDNL coincidental (adj) *same time* coincidentally (adv)

KWNSDNS coincidence *related event*

KWNSDNT coincident *harmonious*

KWNSDNTL coincidental (adj) *same time* coincidentally (adv)

KWNSDNTS coincidence *related event*

KWNSHP acquaintanceship *familiarity*

KWNSHP queenship *rank*

KWNSHR coinsure *joint risk* coinsured coinsuring

KWNSHRNS coinsurance *joint risk*

KWNSHRNTS coinsurance *joint risk*

KWNSHRR coinsurer *joint*

risk

KWNSNCHL quintessential (adj) *pure form* quintessentially (adv)

KWNSNSHL quintessential (adj) *pure form* quintessentially (adv)

KWNSNTNL quincentennial *500 years*

KWNSNTNR quincentenary *500 years*

KWNSNTNYL quincentennial *500 years*

KWNST choanocyte *collar cell*

KWNSTHT Quonset hut *(trademark) shelter*

KWNSZ queen-size *large*

KWNT acquaint *introduce, inform*

KWNT aquanaut *diver*

KWNT quaint *odd, old-fashioned*

KWNT quanta (pl) *amount, large* quantum

KWNT quantity *amount* quantities

KWNT quint *5 offspring*

KWNTD quantity *amount* quantities

KWNTDV quantitative *amount*

KWNTFBL quantifiable *count*

KWNTFKSHN quantification *count*

KWNTFKSHNL quantificational (adj) *count* quantificationally (adv)

KWNTFR quantifier *count*

KWNTFYBL quantifiable *count*

KWNTFYR quantifier *count*

KWNTL quaintly *oddly*

KWNTL quantal *choices*

KWNTL quintal *weight*

KWNTLYN quintillion *number*

KWNTLYNTH quintillionth *number*

KWNTM quantum *amount,*

large quanta

KWNTN quintain *target*

KWNTNS acquaintance *familiarity, person*

KWNTNS quaintness *oddness*

KWNTNSHP acquaintanceship *familiarity*

KWNTNTS acquaintance *familiarity, person*

KWNTPL quintuple *5 times* quintupled quintupling

KWNTPLKT quintuplicate *5 copies* quintuplicated quintuplicating

KWNTPLT quintuplet *5 offspring*

KWNTS acquaintance *familiarity, person*

KWNTS quince *fruit*

KWNTSNCHL quintessential (adj) *pure form* quintessentially (adv)

KWNTSNS quintessence *pure form*

KWNTSNSHL quintessential (adj) *pure form* quintessentially (adv)

KWNTSNTS quintessence *pure form*

KWNTT quantity *amount* quantities

KWNTT quintet *set of 5*

KWNTTDV quantitative *amount*

KWNTTTV quantitative *amount*

KWNTTV quantitative *amount*

KWNTYN quintillion *number*

KWNTYNTH quintillionth *number*

KWNTYPL quintuple *5 times* quintupled quintupling

KWNTYPLKT quintuplicate *5 copies* quintuplicated quintuplicating

KWNTYPLT quintuplet *5 offspring*

KWNTZ quantize *divide* quantized quantizing

KWNTZR quantizer *divider*

KWNTZSHN quantization *division*

KWNX equinox *equal day and night*

KWNYL quiniela (or) quinella *bet*

KWNZ kwanza *money* kwanzas (or) kwanza

KWNZ quinsy *abscess*

KWNZSHN quantization *division*

KWNZTHT Quonset hut *(trademark) shelter*

KWP co-op *share*

KWP equip *furnish* equipped equipping

KWP quip *remark* quipped quipping

KWPJ equipage *carriage*

KWPLN aquaplane *airplane* (Br) hydroplane

KWPLNS equipollence *equal force*

KWPLNT equipollent *equal force*

KWPLNTS equipollence *equal force*

KWPMNT equipment *belongings*

KWPR quipper *remarker*

KWPRDR cooperator *associate* •

KWPRDV cooperative (adj) *act together (n) shared business*

KWPRDVL cooperatively *act together*

KWPRSHN cooperation *common effort*

KWPRT cooperate *act together* cooperated cooperating

KWPRTR cooperator *associate*

KWPRTV cooperative (adj) *act together (n) shared business*

KWPRTVL cooperatively *act together*

Letters aren't doubled for single sounds: to find alley use **L** not **LL**. Use **Y** and **W** as hard sounds only: to find yellow use **YL**. (Br)=British spelling or usage. * See dictionary.

KWPSTR quipster *remarker*
KWPZ equipoise *counterbalance*
KWQL coequal (n, adj) *same as* coequally (adv)
KWQLD coequality *same as* coequalities
KWQLT coequality *same as* coequalities
KWR acquire *gain* acquired acquiring
KWR aquaria (pl) *fish tank* aquarium
KWR choir *singing*
KWR coheir *inherit*
KWR cower *crouch*
KWR cowrie (or) cowry *animal* cowries
KWR equerry *horse caretaker* equerries
KWR kauri *tree*
KWR quarry (v) *dig* quarried quarrying quarries
KWR quarry (n) *stone, prey, pane* quarries
KWR queer (adj) *odd, homosexual* (v) *spoil*
KWR query *ask* queried querying queries
KWR quire *paper*
KWRB choirboy *singer*
KWRBL acquirable *able to be gained*
KWRCTN quercetin *pigment*
KWRD acquired *gained*
KWRD awkward *clumsy*
KWRD coward *timid one*
KWRD keyword *example*
KWRD quarto *music* quartos
KWRDL awkwardly *clumsily*
KWRDL cowardly *timid*
KWRDNDD coordinated *matched*
KWRDNDR coordinator *manager*
KWRDNS awkwardness *clumsiness*
KWRDNSHN coordination *smooth function*
KWRDNT coordinate (v) *manage, harmonize* coordinated coordinating

KWRDNT coordinate (n) *intersection, equal, number*
KWRDNTD coordinated *matched*
KWRDNTL coordinately *intersection, equal*
KWRDNTR coordinator *manager*
KWRDNTS coordinates *clothing*
KWRDR quarter (v) *divide, lodge* (n) *one fourth, area, money**
KWRDRBK quarterback *football*
KWRDRDK quarterdeck *ship*
KWRDRFNL quarterfinal *exam*
KWRDRHRS quarter horse *animal*
KWRDRL quarterly *4 times per year* quarterlies
KWRDRMSDR quartermaster *provider*
KWRDRMSTR quartermaster *provider*
KWRDRN quartering *right angle*
KWRDRNG quartering *right angle*
KWRDRSN quartersawn *boards*
KWRDRSTF quarterstaff *weapon*
KWRDS cowardice *fear*
KWRK quark *particle*
KWRK quirk *twist, trait*
KWRKL quirkily *twist, trait*
KWRKNS quirkiness *twist, trait*
KWRKR coworker *associate*
KWRKSH quirkish *twist, trait*
KWRL aquarelle *watercolor*
KWRL quarrel *fight* quarreled (or) quarrelled quarreling (or) quarrelling
KWRL queerly *odd, homosexual*
KWRLF choir loft *gallery*
KWRLFT choir loft *gallery*

KWRLR quarreler (or) quarreller *fighter*
KWRLS querulous *peevish*
KWRLSL querulously *peevishly*
KWRLSM quarrelsome *hostile*
KWRLSNS querulousness *peevishness*
KWRLST aquarellist *artist*
KWRM aquarium *fish tank* aquariums (or) aquaria
KWRM quorum *majority*
KWRMN quarryman *worker* quarrymen
KWRMNT acquirement *gain*
KWRMSDR choirmaster *director*
KWRMSTR choirmaster *director*
KWRN quern *grinder*
KWRNS queerness *odd, homosexual*
KWRNTN quarantine *separate* quarantined quarantining
KWRR quarrier *worker*
KWRS Aquarius *zodiac sign*
KWRS coerce *force* coerced coercing
KWRS cuirass *armor*
KWRSBL coercible *force*
KWRSH queerish *odd, homosexual*
KWRSHN coercion *force*
KWRST aquarist *fish tank*
KWRST querist *question*
KWRSTN quercetin *pigment*
KWRSTRN quercitron *bark, dye*
KWRSV coercive *force*
KWRSVNS coerciveness *force*
KWRT quart *measure*
KWRT quarto *music* quartos
KWRT quirt *whip*
KWRTL quartile *4 parts*
KWRTN quartan *4 days, fever*
KWRTR quarter (v) *divide, lodge* (n) *one fourth, area, money**

Use letters that best describe the sounds you hear and omit the vowels. Use **S** or **K** instead of **C**: to find circle use **SRKL**. Use **J** to find joy, **JM** to find gem and **G** to find go.

KWRTRBK quarterback *football*

KWRTRDK quarterdeck *ship*

KWRTRFNL quarterfinal *exam*

KWRTRHRS quarter horse *animal*

KWRTRL quarterly *4 times per year* quarterlies

KWRTRMSDR quartermaster *provider*

KWRTRMSTR quartermaster *provider*

KWRTRN quartering *right angle*

KWRTRNG quartering *right angle*

KWRTRSN quartersawn *boards*

KWRTRSTF quarterstaff *weapon*

KWRTS quartz *rock*

KWRTSS quartzose *rock*

KWRTST quartzite *rock*

KWRTT quartet *group of 4*

KWRTZS quartzose *rock*

KWRY aquaria (pl) *fish tank* aquarium

KWRYLS querulous *peevish*

KWRYLSL querulously *peevishly*

KWRYLSNS querulousness *peevishness*

KWRYM aquarium *fish tank* aquariums (or) aquaria

KWRYR quarrier *worker*

KWRYS Aquarius *zodiac sign*

KWRZHN coercion *force*

KWRZV coercive *force*

KWRZVNS coerciveness *force*

KWS acquiesce *agree* acquiesced acquiescing

KWS aqueous *water*

KWS quasi *somewhat*

KWSCHN question (n) *inquiry, issue* (v) *ask*

KWSCHNBL questionable (adj) *doubtful* questionably (adv)

KWSCHNBLNS

questionableness *doubt*

KWSCHNR questioner *inquirer*

KWSCHNR questionnaire *survey*

KWSD cuesta *hill*

KWSD quayside *pier*

KWSDM equisetum *plant* equisetums (or) equiseta

KWSH quash *suppress*

KWSH quassia *drug*

KWSHN coition *intercourse*

KWSHN equation *math*

KWSHNT quotient *number*

KWSHRKR kwashiorkor *disease*

KWSHYRKR kwashiorkor *disease*

KWSN croissant *pastry* croissants

KWSNS acquiescence *agreement*

KWSNS quiescence *inactivity*

KWSNT acquiescent *agreeable*

KWSNT croissant *pastry* croissants

KWSNT quiescent *inactive*

KWSNTL acquiescently *agreeably*

KWSNTS acquiescence *agreement*

KWSNTS quiescence *inactivity*

KWSR quasar *star*

KWST cuesta *hill*

KWST quest *search*

KWSTM equisetum *plant* equisetums (or) equiseta

KWSTRN equestrian (m or f) *horseback rider* equestrienne (f)

KWSTRYN equestrian (m or f) *horseback rider* equestrienne (f)

KWT acquit *discharge* acquitted acquitting

KWT acuity *sharpness* acuities

KWT coati *raccoon-like animal*

KWT equate *make equal* equated equating

KWT equity *law, value* equities

KWT Kuwait *country*

KWT quiet *still*

KWT quit *stop, give up* quit quitting

KWT quite *fully, rather*

KWT quoit *ring*

KWT quota *share*

KWT quote *repeat* quoted quoting

KWTBL equitable (adj) *fair* equitably (adv)

KWTBL quotable *repeat*

KWTBLD equitability *fairness*

KWTBLD quotability *repeat*

KWTBLNS equitableness *fairness*

KWTBLT equitability *fairness*

KWTBLT quotability *repeat*

KWTD quietude *rest*

KWTDN quotidian *common*

KWTDYN quotidian *common*

KWTH quoth *said*

KWTHR coauthor *writer*

KWTK aquatic *in water*

KWTKL aquatically *in water*

KWTKLM quitclaim *deed*

KWTKS aquatics *water sports*

KWTL acquittal *discharge*

KWTL quietly *still*

KWTN quieten *still*

KWTNS acquittance *receipt*

KWTNS quietness *stillness*

KWTNS quittance *payment*

KWTNT aquatint *etching method*

KWTNTS acquittance *receipt*

KWTNTS quittance *payment*

KWTR acquitter *behave, set free*

KWTR equator *midway between poles*

KWTR quitter *defeatist*

KWTR quittor *disease*

KWTRL equatorial *midway between poles*

Letters aren't doubled for single sounds: to find alley use **L** not **LL**. Use **Y** and **W** as hard sounds only: to find yellow use **YL**. (Br)=British spelling or usage. * See dictionary.

KWTRLGN Equatorial Guinea *country*
KWTRN quatrain *verse*
KWTRNN quaternion *4 parts*
KWTRNR quaternary *4 units* quaternaries
KWTRNYN quaternion *4 parts*
KWTRSNTNR quatercentenary *400 years*
KWTRYL equatorial *midway between poles*
KWTRYLGN Equatorial Guinea *country*
KWTS coitus *intercourse*
KWTS quietus *death*
KWTS quits *even terms*
KWTSHN equitation *horseback riding*
KWTSHN quotation *repeat*
KWTSLKDL Quetzalcoatl *Aztec god*
KWTSLKTL Quetzalcoatl *Aztec god*
KWTSLKWDL Quetzalcoatl *Aztec god*
KWTSLKWTL Quetzalcoatl *Aztec god*
KWTX aquatics *water sports*
KWTYD quietude *rest*
KWTZM quietism *religion*
KWVD aqua vitae *liquor*
KWVK equivoque *pun*
KWVKDR equivocator *liar*
· **KWVKL** equivocal (adj) *questionable* equivocally (adv)
KWVKSHN equivocation *lie*
KWVKT equivocate *lie* equivocated equivocating
KWVKTR equivocator *liar*
KWVL coeval *same age*
KWVLNS equivalence *same value* equivalency
KWVLNT equivalent *same value*
KWVLNTL equivalently *same value*
KWVLNTS equivalence *same value* equivalency

KWVR quaver *tremble, trill*
KWVR quavery *tremble, trill*
KWVR quiver *(v)* shake *(n) arrow holder*
KWVRNGL quaveringly *tremble, trill*
KWVT aqua vitae *liquor*
KWXDK quixotic *impractical*
KWXDKL quixotical (adj) *impractical* quixotically (adv)
KWXKDR coexecutor *will*
KWXKTR coexecutor *will*
KWXKYDR coexecutor *will*
KWXKYTR coexecutor *will*
KWXL coaxial *cable*
KWXLVR quicksilver *mercury*
KWXN quicksand *trap*
KWXND quicksand *trap*
KWXQDR coexecutor *will*
KWXQTR coexecutor *will*
KWXST coexist *live together*
KWXSTNS coexistence *live together*
KWXSTNT coexistent *live together*
KWXSTNTS coexistence *live together*
KWXT quickset *(Br) plants*
KWXT quixote *politeness*
KWXTK quixotic *impractical*
KWXTKL quixotical (adj) *impractical* quixotically (adv)
KWXTNSV coextensive *same space*
KWXTP quickstep *march*
KWXTZM quixotism *politeness*
KWXYL coaxial *cable*
KWXZKDR coexecutor *will*
KWXZKTR coexecutor *will*
KWXZKYDR coexecutor *will*
KWXZKYTR coexecutor *will*
KWXZQDR coexecutor *will*
KWXZQTR coexecutor *will*
KWXZST coexist *live together*
KWXZSTNS coexistence

live together
KWXZSTNT coexistent *live together*
KWXZSTNTS coexistence *live together*
KWYJ quayage *fee, piers*
KWYR acquire *gain* acquired acquiring
KWYR choir *singing*
KWYR quire *paper*
KWYRB choirboy *singer*
KWYRBL acquirable *able to be gained*
KWYRD acquired *gained*
KWYRLF choir loft *gallery*
KWYRLFT choir loft *gallery*
KWYRMNT acquirement *gain*
KWYRMSDR choirmaster *director*
KWYRMSTR choirmaster *director*
KWYS acquiesce *agree* acquiesced acquiescing
KWYS aqueous *water*
KWYSNS acquiescence *agreement*
KWYSNS quiescence *inactivity*
KWYSNT acquiescent *agreeable*
KWYSNT quiescent *inactive*
KWYSNTL acquiescently *agreeably*
KWYSNTS acquiescence *agreement*
KWYSNTS quiescence *inactivity*
KWYT quiet *still*
KWYTD quietude *rest*
KWYTL quietly *still*
KWYTN quieten *still*
KWYTNS quietness *stillness*
KWYTYD quietude *rest*
KWYTZM quietism *religion*
KWZ quasi *somewhat*
KWZ queasy *sickened* queasier queasiest
KWZ quiz *test* quizzed quizzing quizzes
KWZDM equisetum *plant* equisetums (or) equiseta

Use letters that best describe the sounds you hear and omit the vowels. Use **S** or **K** instead of **C**: to find circle use **SRKL**. Use **J** to find joy, **JM** to find gem and **G** to find go.

KWZDV acquisitive *covetous*
KWZHN equation *math*
KWZJDSHL quasi-judicial (adj) *law* quasi-judicially (adv)
KWZKL quizzical (adj) *puzzled* quizzically (adv)
KWZLJSLDV quasi-legislative *law*
KWZLJSLTV quasi-legislative *law*
KWZLN quisling *traitor*
KWZLNG quisling *traitor*
KWZMD Quasimodo *Low Sunday, fictional character, poet*
KWZMSDR quizmaster *tester*
KWZMSTR quizmaster *tester*
KWZMT Quasimodo *Low Sunday, fictional character, poet*
KWZN cuisine *food*
KWZNS queasiness *sickened*
KWZPRDK quasiperiodic *unpredictable*
KWZPRDKL quasiparticle *vibration*
KWZPRDSD quasiperiodicity *unpredictable*
KWZPRDST quasiperiodicity *unpredictable*
KWZPRTKL quasiparticle *vibration*
KWZPRYDK quasiperiodic *unpredictable*
KWZPRYDSD quasiperiodicity *unpredictable*
KWZPRYDST quasiperiodicity *unpredictable*
KWZR quasar *star*
KWZR queasier *sickened*
KWZR quizzer *tester*
KWZSHN acquisition *gain*
KWZSHNL acquisitional *gained*
KWZST queasiest *sickened*

KWZTM equisetum *plant* equisetums (or) equiseta
KWZTR acquisitor *gainer*
KWZTV acquisitive *covetous*
KWZTVL acquisitively *covetously*
KWZTVNS acquisitiveness *covetousness*
KWZYR queasier *sickened*
KWZYST queasiest *sickened*
KX coax *cajole*
KX cocci (pl) *bacteria* coccus
KX cox *sailor* coxes
KX coxa *limb* coxae
KXD coccid *insect*
KXD coccidia (pl) *protozoan* coccidium
KXDM coccidium *protozoan* coccidia
KXDSS coccidiosis *disease*
KXDY coccidia (pl) *protozoan* coccidium
KXDYM coccidium *protozoan* coccidia
KXDYSS coccidiosis *disease*
KXGZ coccyges *bone* coccyx
KXGZ kok-saghyz (or) kok-sagyz *flower*
KXJZ coccyges *bone* coccyx
KXKDR coexecutor *will*
KXKM cockscomb *plant*
KXKM coxcomb *fop*
KXKMKL coxcombical *foppish*
KXKMR coxcombry *foppery* coxcombries
KXKS coccyx *bone* coccyges
KXKTR coexecutor *will*
KXKYDR coexecutor *will*
KXKYTR coexecutor *will*
KXL coaxial *cable*
KXN coxswain *sailor*
KXQDR coexecutor *will*
KXQTR coexecutor *will*
KXST coexist *live together*
KXSTNS coexistence *live together*
KXSTNT coexistent *live together*

KXSTNTS coexistence *live together*
KXTND kickstand *bicycle*
KXTNSV coextensive *same space*
KXTV cookstove *range*
KXWN coxswain *sailor*
KXX coccyx *bone* coccyges
KXYL coaxial *cable*
KXZKDR coexecutor *will*
KXZKTR coexecutor *will*
KXZKYDR coexecutor *will*
KXZKYTR coexecutor *will*
KXZQDR coexecutor *will*
KXZQTR coexecutor *will*
KXZST coexist *live together*
KXZSTNS coexistence *live together*
KXZSTNT coexistent *live together*
KXZSTNTS coexistence *live together*
KY cahier *pages*
KY cue (v) *prompt, line up* cued cuing (or) cueing
KY cue (n) *hint, line, rod*
KY ecu (often capitalized) *European Currency Unit* ecus
KY IQ (abbr) *intelligence quotient*
KY kayo *knock out* kayoed kayoing kayoes
KY kea *parrot*
KY q *alphabet letter* q's (or) qs
KY queue (v) *line up* queued queuing
KY queue (n) *line, braid*
KYB Cuba *country*
KYB cube *block, math, steak* cubed cubing
KYB cubé (or) cube *shrub*
KYBB cubeb *pepper*
KYBD cuboid *bone, shape*
KYBDL cuboidal *shape*
KYBJ cubage *volume*
KYBK cubic *shape*
KYBKL cubical (adj) *shape* cubically (adv)
KYBKL cubicle *room*
KYBL cue ball *billiards*

Letters aren't doubled for single sounds: to find alley use **L** not **LL**. Use **Y** and **W** as hard sounds only: to find yellow use **YL**. (Br)=British spelling or usage. * See dictionary.

KYBR cuber *block, math*
KYBRT cube root *math*
KYBST cubist *artist*
KYBSTK cube steak *meat*
KYBSTK cubistic *art*
KYBT cubit *length*
KYBZM cubism *art*
KYD acuity *sharpness*
acuities
KYD cutie (or) cutey *pretty*
one cuties (or) cuteys
KYD kudo *award, praise*
kudos
KYD Kyoto *city in Japan*
KYDK chaotic *confused*
KYDKL chaotically *without*
design
KYDKL cuticle *skin*
KYDR cuter *prettier*
KYDS cutis *skin* cutes (or)
cutises
KYDST cutest *prettiest*
KYJ quayage *fee, piers*
KYK cuke *cucumber*
KYK kayak *boat*
KYK kyack *packsack*
KYKMBR cucumber
vegetable
KYKNG kayaking *sport*
KYKR kayaker *boat*
KYL chyle *lymph*
KYL coil *spiral*
KYL keyhole *lock*
KYL oculi (pl) *window* oculus
KYLKS culex *mosquito*
KYLMDR oculomotor *nerve*
KYLMTR oculomotor *nerve*
KYLN kaolin *clay*
KYLNR culinary *cooking*
KYLNRL culinarily *cooking*
KYLNRN culinarian *chef*
KYLNRYN culinarian *chef*
KYLNT kaolinite *mineral*
KYLR ocular *eyepiece*
KYLRST ocularist *glass eye*
KYLS oculus *window* oculi
KYLST oculist *eye doctor*
KYLT culet *armor*
KYLTS culottes *skirt*
KYLX culex *mosquito*
KYMLDR accumulator
gatherer

KYMLDV accumulative
gathered
KYMLDV cumulative
additional
KYMLNMBS cumulonimbus
cloud
KYMLS cumulous *cloudlike*
KYMLS cumulus *cloud*
KYMLSHN accumulation
gathering
KYMLSHN cumulation *mass*
KYMLT accumulate *gather*
accumulated
accumulating
KYMLT cumulate *amass*
cumulated cumulating
KYMLTR accumulator
gatherer
KYMLTV accumulative
gathered
KYMLTV cumulative
additional
KYMN acumen *keenness*
KYMN cumin *spice*
KYMNKL ecumenical (adj)
church ecumenically (adv)
(Br) oecumenical
KYMNKS ecumenics *church*
KYMNST ecumenist *church*
KYMNT acuminate *tapered*
KYMNX ecumenics *church*
KYMNZM ecumenism
church
KYMYLDR accumulator
gatherer
KYMYLDV accumulative
gathered
KYMYLDV cumulative
additional
KYMYLNMBS
cumulonimbus *cloud*
KYMYLS cumulous *cloudlike*
KYMYLS cumulus *cloud*
KYMYLSHN accumulation
gathering
KYMYLSHN cumulation
mass
KYMYLT accumulate *gather*
accumulated
accumulating
KYMYLT cumulate *amass*
cumulated cumulating

KYMYLTR accumulator
gatherer
KYMYLTV accumulative
gathered
KYMYLTV cumulative
additional
KYN Achaean (or) Achaian
Greek
KYN cayenne *pepper*
KYNDRK qindarka (pl)
money qintar
KYNFRM cuneiform *wedge*
KYNG kiang *animal*
KYNT Chianti *wine*
KYNT cuneate *triangular*
KYNT kyanite *lapis lazuli*
KYNTR qintar *money*
qindarka
KYNYFRM cuneiform *wedge*
KYNYT cuneate *triangular*
KYP Kewpie *(trademark) doll*
KYP occupy *fill, reside*
occupied occupying
occupies
KYPD Cupid *Roman god of*
love
KYPDD cupidity *desire*
cupidities
KYPDT cupidity *desire*
cupidities
KYPL cupel *strainer*
cupelled (or) cupeled
cupelling (or) cupeling
KYPL cupola *roof*
KYPL cupule *cup-shaped*
KYPLD cupolaed *roof*
KYPLN Keogh plan
retirement
KYPLR cupeler *refiner*
KYPLSHN cupellation
refinement
KYPN coupon *ticket*
KYPNC occupancy *residents*
occupancies
KYPNCHR acupuncture
Chinese therapy
KYPNGCHR acupuncture
Chinese therapy
KYPNGKCHR acupuncture
Chinese therapy
KYPNGKSHR acupuncture
Chinese therapy

Use letters that best describe the sounds you hear and omit the vowels. Use **S** or **K** instead of **C**: to find circle use **SRKL**. Use **J** to find joy, **JM** to find gem and **G** to find go.

KYPNGSHR acupuncture *Chinese therapy*
KYPNKCHR acupuncture *Chinese therapy*
KYPNKSHR acupuncture *Chinese therapy*
KYPNS occupancy *residents* occupancies
KYPNSHR acupuncture *Chinese therapy*
KYPNT occupant *resident*
KYPNTC occupancy *residents* occupancies
KYPNTS occupancy *residents* occupancies
KYPRFRS cupriferous *copper*
KYPRS cuprous *copper*
KYPRSHR acupressure *massage*
KYPRT cuprite *copper*
KYPS Cheops (or) Khufu *pyramid builder*
KYPSHN occupation *job, seizure*
KYPSHNL occupational (adj) *job, seizure* occupationally (adv)
KYPYL cupule *cup-shaped*
KYR achier *sorer*
KYR cahier *pages*
KYR coir *fiber*
KYR cure (v) *heal, prepare* cured curing
KYR curé *priest*
KYR cure (n) *remedy*
KYR curia *law court* curiae
KYR curie *radioactivity*
KYR Curie *scientist*
KYR curio *curiosity* curios
KYR ickier *disgusting*
KYRBL curable (adj) *heal, prepare* curably (adv)
KYRC accuracy *correctness* accuracies
KYRC curacy *office* curacies
KYRDR curator *caretaker*
KYRDV curative *healing*
KYRL cure-all *remedy*
KYRM curium *element*
KYRR curare *poison*
KYRR curer *healer*

KYRS accuracy *correctness* accuracies
KYRS Curacao *island*
KYRS curacao *liqueur*
KYRS curacy *office* curacies
KYRS curassow *bird*
KYRS curious *inquisitive, strange*
KYRSD curiosity *interest, curio* curiosities
KYRSKR chiaroscuro *light and shadow*
KYRSKRST chiaroscurist *light and shadow*
KYRSKYR chiaroscuro *light and shadow*
KYRSKYRST chiaroscurist *light and shadow*
KYRSL curiously *strangely*
KYRSNS curiousness *inquisitive, odd*
KYRSQR chiaroscuro *light and shadow*
KYRSQRST chiaroscurist *light and shadow*
KYRST curiosity *interest, curio* curiosities
KYRT accurate *correct*
KYRT curate *organize and oversee* curated curating
KYRT curette *scoop* curetted curetting
KYRTJ curettage *scraping*
KYRTL accurately *correctly*
KYRTNS accurateness *correctness*
KYRTR curator *caretaker*
KYRTV curative *healing*
KYRY curia *law court*
KYRY curio *curiosity* curios
KYRYM curium *element*
KYRYS curious *inquisitive, strange*
KYRYSD curiosity *interest, curio* curiosities
KYRYSL curiously *strangely*
KYRYSNS curiousness *inquisitive, odd*
KYRYST curiosity *interest, curio* curiosities
KYS chaos *confusion*
KYSK cusec *unit of flow*

KYSK kiosk *stand*
KYST achiest *sorest*
KYST ickiest *disgusting*
KYT acuity *sharpness* acuities
KYT acute *sharp* acuter acutest
KYT coyote *dog-like animal* coyotes (or) coyote
KYT cute *pretty* cuter cutest
KYT cutie (or) cutey *pretty one* cuties (or) cuteys
KYT kyat *money*
KYT Kyoto *city in Japan*
KYTC cutesy *obnoxious* cutesier cutesiest
KYTCR cutesier *obnoxious*
KYTCST cutesiest *obnoxious*
KYTCYR cutesier *obnoxious*
KYTCYST cutesiest *obnoxious*
KYTK chaotic *confused*
KYTKL chaotically *without design*
KYTKL cuticle *skin*
KYTKLR cuticular *skin*
KYTKYLR cuticular *skin*
KYTL acutely *sharply*
KYTN cutin *waxy layer*
KYTNS acuteness *sharpness*
KYTNS cutaneous *skin*
KYTNS cuteness *pretty*
KYTNYS cutaneous *skin*
KYTP Q-Tip *(trademark) swab*
KYTQLR cuticular *skin*
KYTR acuter *sharper*
KYTR cuter *prettier*
KYTS cutesy *obnoxious* cutesier cutesiest
KYTS cutis *skin* cutes (or) cutises
KYTSR cutesier *obnoxious*
KYTSST cutesiest *obnoxious*
KYTST acutest *sharpest*
KYTST cutest *prettiest*
KYTSYR cutesier *obnoxious*
KYTSYST cutesiest *obnoxious*
KYTZ cutes (pl) *skin* cutis
KYTZ cutesy *obnoxious* cutesier cutesiest

Letters aren't doubled for single sounds: to find alley use **L** not **LL**. Use **Y** and **W** as hard sounds only: to find yellow use **YL**. (Br)=British spelling or usage. * See dictionary.

KYTZR cutesier *obnoxious*
KYTZST cutesiest *obnoxious*
KYTZYR cutesier *obnoxious*
KYTZYST cutesiest
obnoxious
KYV Kiev *city*
KYVT cuvette *test tube*
KYWD acuity *sharpness*
acuities
KYWT acuity *sharpness*
acuities
KYZ accuse *blame* accused
accusing
KYZD accused *defendant*
accused
KYZDV accusative *blaming*
KYZL accusal *blame*
KYZMS chiasmus *junction*
KYZNGL accusingly *with*
blame
KYZR accuser *blamer*
KYZSHN accusation *blame*
KYZT accused *defendant*
accused
KYZTR accusatory *blaming*
KYZTRL accusatorial (adj)
blaming accusatorially
(adv)
KYZTRYL accusatorial (adj)
blaming accusatorially
(adv)
KYZTV accusative *blaming*
KZ accuse *blame* accused
accusing
KZ cause (*v*) *bring about*
caused causing
KZ cause (*n*) *reason*
KZ coups (pl) *successful act*
coups
KZ coz (*slang*) *cousin*
KZ cozy (*adj*) *snug* cozier
coziest
KZ cozy (*n*) *cover*
KZ kazoo *music* kazoos
KZ oxeye *daisy*
KZ oxy *oxygen*
KZ ukase *edict*
KZB Casbah *fortress*
KZBDR exhibitor *displayer*
KZBLG exobiology *life*
beyond earth
KZBLJ exobiology *life*

beyond earth
KZBLJKL exobiological *life*
beyond earth
KZBLJST exobiologist *life*
beyond earth
KZBRNS exuberance
profusion, joy
KZBRNT exuberant
plentiful, joyful
KZBRNTL exuberantly
plentiful, joyful
KZBRNTS exuberance
profusion, joy
KZBRT exuberate *overflow*
exuberated exuberating
KZBSHN exhibition *display*
KZBSHNST exhibitionist
exposure
KZBSHNZM exhibitionism
exposure
KZBT exhibit *display*
KZBTR exhibitor *displayer*
KZBYLG exobiology *life*
beyond earth
KZBYLJ exobiology *life*
beyond earth
KZBYLJKL exobiological
life beyond earth
KZBYLJST exobiologist *life*
beyond earth
KZD accused *defendant*
accused
KZD exude *ooze* exuded
exuding
KZD oxide *oxygen*
KZDD ixodid *tick*
KZDDV oxidative *rust*
KZDK acoustic (or)
acoustical (adj) *sound*
acoustically (adv)
KZDK exotic *foreign,*
unusual
KZDK exotica *unusual items*
KZDKL exotically *foreign,*
unusual
KZDKNS exoticness *foreign,*
unusual
KZDKS acoustics *science*
KZDNL occidental (adj)
western occidentally (adv)
KZDNLNS accidentalness
by chance

KZDNLZ occidentalize *make*
western occidentalized
occidentalizing
KZDNS accedence
agreement
KZDNS accidence *basic*
elements
KZDNSH exodontia *teeth*
extraction
KZDNST exodontist *teeth*
extraction
KZDNT accident *chance*
happening
KZDNT Occident *West*
KZDNT oxidant *rust*
KZDNTL accidental (adj) *by*
chance accidentally (adv)
KZDNTL occidental (adj)
western occidentally (adv)
KZDNTLNS accidentalness
by chance
KZDNTLZ occidentalize
make western
occidentalized
occidentalizing
KZDNTS accidence *basic*
elements
KZDNTST exodontist *teeth*
extraction
KZDR exedra *room, seat*
exedrae
KZDRMS exodermis *outer*
layer
KZDS exodus *departure*
KZDSHN exudation *material*
KZDSHN oxidation *rust*
KZDT exudate *material*
KZDTV oxidative *rust*
KZDV accusative *blaming*
KZDV causative *reason*
KZDX acoustics *science*
KZDZ oxidize *mix with*
oxygen oxidized oxidizing
KZDZBL oxidizable *mix*
with oxygen
KZDZR oxidizer *mix with*
oxygen
KZGM exogamy *marriage*
exogamies
KZGMK exogamic *marriage*
KZGMS exogamous
marriage

KZGNK oxygenic *with oxygen*

KZGS exiguous *scarce*

KZGSS exegesis *explanation* exegeses

KZGT exiguity *scantiness* exiguities

KZGWS exiguous *scarce*

KZGWT exiguity *scantiness* exiguities

KZGYS exiguous *scarce*

KZGYT exiguity *scantiness* exiguities

KZGYWS exiguous *scarce*

KZGYWT exiguity *scantiness* exiguities

KZGZS exegesis *explanation* exegeses

KZHL casual (adj) *informal* casually (adv)

KZHLT casualty *disaster, victim* casualties

KZHMR cashmere *soft wool*

KZHMR Kashmir *region*

KZHN occasion (n) *event, instance* (v) *bring about*

KZHNL occasional *specific instance*

KZHNL occasionally *now and then*

KZHRN casuarina *tree*

KZHST casuist *rationalizer*

KZHSTK casuistic *rational*

KZHSTR casuistry *rationalism*

KZHWL casual (adj) *informal* casually (adv)

KZHWLT casualty *disaster, victim* casualties

KZHWRN casuarina *tree*

KZHWST casuist *rationalizer*

KZHWSTK casuistic *rational*

KZHWSTR casuistry *rationalism*

KZJDKL exegetical *explanatory*

KZJDST exegetist *explainer*

KZJN oxygen *element*

KZJNC exigency *demand* exigencies

KZJNK oxygenic *with oxygen*

KZJNLS oxygenless *no oxygen*

KZJNMSK oxygen mask *air supply*

KZJNS exigency *demand* exigencies

KZJNS exogenous *from outside*

KZJNSHN oxygenation *add oxygen*

KZJNT exigent *demanding*

KZJNT oxygenate *add oxygen* oxygenated oxygenating

KZJNTC exigency *demand* exigencies

KZJNTNT oxygen tent *canopy*

KZJNTS exigency *demand* exigencies

KZJRDR exaggerator *overstatement*

KZJRDV exaggerative *overstatement*

KZJRSHN exaggeration *overstatement*

KZJRT exaggerate *overstate* exaggerated exaggerating

KZJRTR exaggerator *overstatement*

KZJRTV exaggerative *overstatement*

KZJSS exegesis *explanation* exegeses

KZJTKL exegetical *explanatory*

KZJTST exegetist *explainer*

KZJZS exegesis *explanation* exegeses

KZK exact (v) *demand* (adj) *precise*

KZKD exacta *wager*

KZKDBL executable *kill, perform*

KZKDN exacting *difficult*

KZKDNG exacting *difficult*

KZKDNT executant *performer*

KZKDR executor *administrator*

KZKDTD exactitude

precision

KZKDTYD exactitude *precision*

KZKDV executive *law, manager*

KZKL exactly *precisely*

KZKRBL execrable (adj) *wretched* execrably (adv)

KZKRBLNS execrableness *wretchedness*

KZKRDR execrator *denouncer*

KZKRDV execrative *denounce*

KZKRN exocrine *secretion*

KZKRP exocarp *outer layer*

KZKRSHN execration *denounce*

KZKRT execrate *denounce* execrated execrating

KZKRTR execrator *denouncer*

KZKRTV execrative *denounce*

KZKSHN execution *kill, perform*

KZKSHN exsiccation *dryness*

KZKSHNR executioner *killer*

KZKT exact (v) *demand* (adj) *precise*

KZKT exacta *wager*

KZKT execute *kill, perform* executed executing

KZKT exsiccate *dry* exsiccated exsiccating

KZKTBL executable *kill, perform*

KZKTL exactly *precisely*

KZKTN exacting *difficult*

KZKTNG exacting *difficult*

KZKTNT executant *performer*

KZKTR executor *administrator*

KZKTR executory *administrative*

KZKTRCZ executrices (or) executrixes (pl) *administrator (f)* executrix

KZKTRKS executrix

administrator (f)
executrices (or)
executrixes
KZKTRSZ executrices (or)
executrixes (pl)
administrator (f) executrix
KZKTRX executrix
administrator (f)
executrices (or)
executrixes
KZKTTD exactitude
precision
KZKTTYD exactitude
precision
KZKTV executive law,
manager
KZKYDBL executable kill,
perform
KZKYDNT executant
performer
KZKYDR executor
administrator
KZKYDV executive law,
manager
KZKYSHN execution kill,
perform
KZKYSHNR executioner
killer
KZKYT execute kill, perform
executed executing
KZKYTBL executable kill,
perform
KZKYTNT executant
performer
KZKYTR executor
administrator
KZKYTR executory
administrative
KZKYTRCZ executrices (or)
executrixes (pl)
administrator (f) executrix
KZKYTRKS executrix
administrator (f)
executrices (or)
executrixes
KZKYTRSZ executrices (or)
executrixes (pl)
administrator (f) executrix
KZKYTRX executrix
administrator (f)
executrices (or)
executrixes

KZKYTV executive law,
manager
KZL accusal blame
KZL axel jump
KZL axial (adj) axis axially
(adv)
KZL axil leaf
KZL axilla armpit axillae (or)
axillas
KZL axle wheel
KZL causal (adj) reason
causally (adv)
KZL cozily snugly
KZL exile banish exiled
exiling
KZLD causality reason
causalities
KZLG axiology ethics
KZLJ axiology ethics
KZLJKL axiological (adj)
ethical axiologically (adv)
KZLK oxalic acid
KZLR axillar feather
KZLR axillary feather
axillaries
KZLRDV exhilarative
stimulated
KZLRNT exhilarant enliven
KZLRSHN exhilaration
stimulation
KZLRT exhilarate enliven
exhilarated exhilarating
KZLRTV exhilarative
stimulated
KZLS oxalis plant
KZLSHR excelsior packaging
KZLSHYR excelsior
packaging
KZLSR excelsior packaging
KZLSYR excelsior packaging
KZLT causality reason
causalities
KZLT exalt praise
KZLT exult rejoice
KZLT oxalate acid salt
KZLTDL exaltedly elevated
KZLTNC exultancy rejoicing
exultance
KZLTNS exultance rejoicing
exultancy
KZLTNT exultant rejoicing
KZLTNTC exultancy

rejoicing exultance
KZLTNTS exultance
rejoicing exultancy
KZLTR exalter praiser
KZLTSHN exaltation praise
KZLTSHN exultation
rejoicing
KZM axiom truth
KZM chasm gap
KZM eczema skin rash
KZM exam test
KZM exhume dig up
exhumed exhuming
KZMDK axiomatic self-
evident
KZMDK cosmetic (adj)
superficial (n) makeup
KZMDKL axiomatically self-
evidently
KZMDKL cosmetically
superficially
KZMDS eczematous skin
rash
KZMGN cosmogony origin
of universe cosmogonies
KZMK cosmic universal
KZMKL cosmically universal
KZMKR cosmic ray atoms
KZMLG cosmology nature of
universe cosmologies
KZMLJ cosmology nature of
universe cosmologies
KZMLJKL cosmological
(adj) nature of universe
cosmologically (adv)
KZMLJST cosmologist
nature of universe
KZMN examine inspect, test
examined examining
KZMN examinee person
tested
KZMNBL examinable
inspect, test
KZMNNT examinant tester
KZMNR examiner inspector,
tester
KZMNSHN examination
inspection, test
KZMNT cosmonaut
astronaut
KZMP exempt free
KZMPL example model,

Use letters that best describe the sounds you hear and omit the vowels. Use **S** or **K** instead of **C**: to find circle use **SRKL**. Use **J** to find joy, **JM** to find gem and **G** to find go.

instance

KZMPLDN cosmopolitan *worldly*

KZMPLF exemplify *embody* exemplified exemplifying exemplifies

KZMPLFKSHN exemplification *illustration*

KZMPLGRSH exempli gratia *for example (e.g.)*

KZMPLR exemplar *model*

KZMPLR exemplary *model*

KZMPLRL exemplarily *model*

KZMPLRNS exemplariness *model*

KZMPLTN cosmopolitan *worldly*

KZMPSHN exemption *freedom*

KZMPT exempt *free*

KZMR exhumer *dig up*

KZMR oxymora (pl) *contradiction* oxymoron

KZMRN oxymoron *contradiction* oxymora

KZMRNK oxymoronic *contradictory*

KZMRNKL oxymoronically *contradictory*

KZMS chiasmus *junction*

KZMS cosmos *universe* cosmos

KZMSHN exemption *freedom*

KZMSHN exhumation *dig up*

KZMT exempt *free*

KZMT kismet *fate*

KZMTK axiomatic *self-evident*

KZMTK cosmetic *(adj) superficial (n) makeup*

KZMTKL axiomatically *self-evidently*

KZMTKL cosmetically *superficially*

KZMTLG cosmetology *skin and hair*

KZMTLJ cosmetology *skin and hair*

KZMTLJST cosmetologist *skin and hair*

KZMTS eczematous *skin rash*

KZMTSHN cosmetician *makeup*

KZN auxin *plant hormone*

KZN axion *particle*

KZN axon *neuron*

KZN cousin *relative*

KZN cozen *cheat* cozened cozening

KZN exine *outer layer*

KZN exon *protein*

KZN oxen (pl) *animal* ox

KZNGL accusingly *with blame*

KZNJ cozenage *fraud*

KZNK auxinic *plant hormone*

KZNM axoneme *cilium*

KZNML axonemal *cilium*

KZNMT exanimate *lifeless*

KZNMTRK axonometric *drawing*

KZNR cozener *cheater*

KZNRDV exonerative *forgiving*

KZNRSHN exoneration *forgiveness*

KZNRT exonerate *forgive* exonerated exonerating

KZNRTV exonerative *forgiving*

KZNS coziness *snugness*

KZNSTR Cosa Nostra *Mafia*

KZNT exeunt *exit*

KZNTRSD eccentricity *strangeness* eccentricities

KZNTRST eccentricity *strangeness* eccentricities

KZQDBL executable *kill, perform*

KZQDNT executant *performer*

KZQDR executor *administrator*

KZQDV executive *law, manager*

KZQSHN execution *kill, perform*

KZQSHNR executioner *killer*

KZQT execute *kill, perform* executed executing

KZQTBL executable *kill, perform*

KZQTNT executant *performer*

KZQTR executor *administrator*

KZQTR executory *administrative*

KZQTRCZ executrices (or) executrixes (pl) *administrator (f)* executrix

KZQTRKS executrix *administrator (f)* executrices (or) executrixes

KZQTRSZ executrices (or) executrixes (pl) *administrator (f)* executrix

KZQTRX executrix *administrator (f)* executrices (or) executrixes

KZQTV executive *law, manager*

KZR accuser *blamer*

KZR causer *reason*

KZR cozier *snug*

KZR kaiser *ruler*

KZRB exurb *outer suburb*

KZRB exurbia *outer suburb*

KZRBDNS exorbitance *excess*

KZRBDNT exorbitant *excessive*

KZRBDNTS exorbitance *excess*

KZRBN exurban *outer suburb*

KZRBNT exurbanite *outer suburb*

KZRBTNS exorbitance *excess*

KZRBTNT exorbitant *excessive*

KZRBTNTS exorbitance *excess*

KZRBY exurbia *outer suburb*

KZRDM kaiserdom *emperor*

KZRDTR exhortatory *warning*

Letters aren't doubled for single sounds: to find alley use **L** not **LL**. Use **Y** and **W** as hard sounds only: to find yellow use **YL**. (Br)=British spelling or usage. * See dictionary.

KZRL uxorial *wife*

KZRN casern (or) caserne *barracks*

KZRN kaiserin *ruler's wife*

KZRP excerpt *extract*

KZRPDR excerptor (or) excerpter *extractor*

KZRPT excerpt *extract*

KZRPTR excerptor (or) excerpter *extractor*

KZRS uxorious *love of wife*

KZRSD uxoricide *wife murder*

KZRSHN exertion *effort*

KZRSKL Exercycle *(trademark) bicycle*

KZRSL uxoriously *love of wife*

KZRSNS uxoriousness *love of wife*

KZRSS oxyuriasis *pinworms*

KZRSST exorcist *expel evil*

KZRSZ exercise *(v) exert, use* exercised exercising

KZRSZ exercise *(n) use, exertion, drill*

KZRSZ exorcise *expel evil* exorcised exorcising

KZRSZBL exercisable *exert, use*

KZRSZM exorcism *expel evil*

KZRSZR exerciser *machine*

KZRT exert *put forth effort, wield*

KZRT exhort *warn*

KZRTSHN exhortation *warning*

KZRTTR exhortatory *warning*

KZRTTV exhortative *warning*

KZRYL uxorial *wife*

KZRYS uxorious *love of wife*

KZRYSL uxoriously *love of wife*

KZRYSNS uxoriousness *love of wife*

KZRYSS oxyuriasis *pinworms*

KZRZM kaiserism *emperor*

KZS axis *line, partnership* axes

KZSCHN exhaustion *depletion*

KZSDBL exhaustible *deplete, tired*

KZSDBLD exhaustibility *deplete, tired*

KZSDBLT exhaustibility *deplete, tired*

KZSDV exhaustive *thorough*

KZSFR exosphere *atmosphere*

KZSHN accusation *blame*

KZSHN causation *reason*

KZSHN excision *removal*

KZSKLTL exoskeletal *outer frame*

KZSKLTN exoskeleton *outer frame*

KZSLN oxacillin *antibiotic*

KZSPR exospore *separate*

KZSPRDDL exasperatedly *irritation*

KZSPRDNGL exasperatingly *irritation*

KZSPRDNL exasperatingly *irritation*

KZSPRSHN exasperation *irritation*

KZSPRT exasperate *irritate* exasperated exasperating

KZSPRTDL exasperatedly *irritation*

KZSPRTNGL exasperatingly *irritation*

KZSPRTNL exasperatingly *irritation*

KZSRBSHN exacerbation *make worse*

KZSRBT exacerbate *make worse* exacerbated exacerbating

KZST coziest *snug*

KZST exhaust *(v) deplete, tire (n) vapor*

KZST exist *live*

KZSTBL exhaustible *deplete, tired*

KZSTBLD exhaustibility *deplete, tired*

KZSTBLT exhaustibility *deplete, tired*

KZSTCZ exostoses (pl) *outgrowth* exotosis

KZSTNCHL existential (adj) *experience* existentially (adv)

KZSTNCHLST existentialist *philosopher*

KZSTNCHLZM existentialism *philosophy*

KZSTNS existence *life*

KZSTNSHL existential (adj) *experience* existentially (adv)

KZSTNSHLST existentialist *philosopher*

KZSTNSHLZM existentialism *philosophy*

KZSTNT existent *living*

KZSTNTS existence *life*

KZSTSS exocytosis *cell fusion* exocytoses

KZSTSS exostosis *outgrowth* exotoses

KZSTSZ exostoses (pl) *outgrowth* exotosis

KZSTV exhaustive *thorough*

KZT accused *defendant* accused

KZTK acoustic (or) acoustical (adj) *sound* acoustically (adv)

KZTK exotic *foreign, unusual*

KZTK exotica *unusual items*

KZTKL exotically *foreign, unusual*

KZTKNS exoticness *foreign, unusual*

KZTR accusatory *blaming*

KZTRL accusatorial (adj) *blaming* accusatorially (adv)

KZTRYL accusatorial (adj) *blaming* accusatorially (adv)

KZTV accusative *blaming*

KZTV causative *reason*

KZTX acoustics *science*

KZW causeway *highway*

KZYD exude *ooze* exuded exuding

KZYDSHN exudation *material*

Use letters that best describe the sounds you hear and omit the vowels. Use **S** or **K** instead of **C**: to find circle use **SRKL**. Use **J** to find joy, **JM** to find gem and **G** to find go.

KZYDT exudate *material*
KZYL axial (adj) *axis* axially (adv)
KZYLG axiology *ethics*
KZYLJ axiology *ethics*
KZYLJKL axiological (adj) *ethical* axiologically (adv)
KZYM axiom *truth*
KZYM exhume *dig up* exhumed exhuming
KZYMDK axiomatic *self-evident*
KZYMDKL axiomatically *self-evidently*
KZYMR exhumer *dig up*
KZYMSHN exhumation *dig up*
KZYMTK axiomatic *self-evident*
KZYMTKL axiomatically *self-evidently*
KZYN axion *particle*
KZYNT exeunt *exit*
KZYR cozier *snug*
KZYRSS oxyuriasis *pinworms*
KZYRYSS oxyuriasis *pinworms*
KZYST coziest *snug*
KZZ excise (v) *remove, tax* excised excising
KZZ excise (n) *tax*
KZZBL excisable *remove, tax*
KZZHN excision *removal*
KZZPM oxazepam *tranquilizer*

L

L à la *in the manner of*
L ail *be ill*
L ail *sick, hurt*
L aioli *sauce*

L aisle *pathway*
L ala *wing* alae
L ale *beverage*
L alee *toward shelter*
L all *every*
L Allah *God*
L allay *relieve*
L allee *walkway*
L alley *lane* alleys
L allow *permit*
L alloy *metal*
L ally *associate* allied allying allies
L aloe *plant*
L aloha *greeting*
L alow *below*
L awl *tool*
L eel *animal*
L el *train, letter L*
L ell *extension, measure*
L ilea (pl) *intestine* ileum
L ilia (pl) *bone* ilium
L ill *sick, vicious, evil* worse worst
L isle *island*
L la *musical note*
L law *legal*
L lay (v) *put, bet, calm** laid laying
L lay (n) *lair, plan, price**
L lea (or) ley *pasture*
L lee *sheltered side*
L lei *flowers*
L Leo *zodiac sign*
L lie (v) *fib* lied lying
L lie (v) *position* lay lain lying
L lie (n) *position, untruth*
L lieu *instead (of)*
L lo (interj) *surprise*
L loo (n-Br) *toilet, game* (v) *pay*
L low (adj) *under, soft, depressed** lower lowest
L low (n) *cow sound, depth* (v) *moo*
L luau *feast*
L lye *chemical*
L oil *grease*
L oily *greasy* oilier oiliest
L old *aged*
L olé *bravo*
L oleo *margarine*

L olio *mixture* olios
L olla *pot* ollas
L owl *bird*
L you'll (contr) *you will*
L you-all *all of you*
L yule *Christmas*
LB alb *vestment*
LB alibi *excuse* alibied alibiing
LB Elba *island*
LB elbow *joint*
LB lab *laboratory*
LB labia (pl) *lip* labium
LB lay by (v) *cultivate* lay-by (n)
LB lib (slang) *liberation*
LB Libya *country*
LB lob *high-arching shot* lobbed lobbing
LB lobby (v) *influence* lobbied lobbying lobbies
LB lobby (n) *anteroom* lobbies
LB lobe *projection*
LB lobo *wolf* lobos
LB lowboy *furniture*
LB lube *oil*
LB old boy (often capitalized) *crony*
LBD libido *lust* libidos
LBDM lobotomy *brain surgery* lobotomies
LBDMZ lobotomize *brain surgery* lobotomized lobotomizing (Br) lobotomise
LBDN ill-boding *evil*
LBDN law-abiding *honest*
LBDNG ill-boding *evil*
LBDNG law-abiding *honest*
LBDNL libidinal (adj) *lust* libidinally (adv)
LBDNM labdanum *perfume*
LBDNS libidinous *lustful*
LBDNSL libidinously *lustful*
LBDNSNS libidinousness *lust*
LBDR Labrador *peninsula*
LBDRTRVR Labrador retriever *dog*
LBFRMLCH liebfraumilch *wine*

Letters aren't doubled for single sounds: to find alley use **L** not **LL**. Use **Y** and **W** as hard sounds only: to find yellow use **YL**. (Br)=British spelling or usage. * See dictionary.

LBGRS elbow grease *effort*
LBJB lube job *oil*
LBKDM lobectomy *surgery* lobectomies
LBKR albacore *tuna* albacore (or) albacores
LBKRK Albuquerque *city*
LBKTM lobectomy *surgery* lobectomies
LBL label *tag* labeled (or) labelled labeling (or) labelling
LBL labella (pl) *orchid part, insect part* labellum
LBL labial (adj) *lip* labially (adv)
LBL labile *unstable*
LBL liable *likely, answerable*
LBL libel *slander* libeled (or) libelled libeling (or) libelling
LBL libelee (or) libellee *slandered one*
LBL lobelia *plant*
LBL lobule *bulge*
LBL low blow *punch*
LBL lowball *estimate*
LBLD lability *unstable*
LBLD liability *debt, drawback* liabilities
LBLDD lobulated *bulging*
LBLL loblolly *mire, pine* loblollies
LBLM labellum *orchid part, insect part* labella
LBLR labeler *tagger*
LBLR libeler *slanderer*
LBLR lobular *bulging*
LBLS libelous (or) libellous *slanderous*
LBLST libelist *slanderer*
LBLT lability *unstable*
LBLT liability *debt, drawback* liabilities
LBLTD lobulated *bulging*
LBLY lobelia *plant*
LBM Alabama *US State*
LBM album *collection*
LBM labium *lip* labia
LBM low beam *light*
LBMN albumen *egg white*
LBMN albumin *protein*

LBMNR albuminuria *protein in urine*
LBMNRY albuminuria *protein in urine*
LBMNS albuminous *like protein*
LBMNYRY albuminuria *protein in urine*
LBMRL Albemarle *island, inlet*
LBN Albania *country*
LBN Albany *city*
LBN albino *without pigment* albinos
LBN Libyan *of Libya*
LBNDK albinotic *without pigment*
LBNN Albanian *of Albania*
LBNN Lebanon *country*
LBNSDK albinistic *without pigment*
LBNSTK albinistic *without pigment*
LBNTK albinotic *without pigment*
LBNTS Leibniz *philosopher*
LBNTZ Leibniz *philosopher*
LBNY Albania *country*
LBNYN Albanian *of Albania*
LBNZ Lebanese *of Lebanon*
LBNZM albinism *without pigment*
LBR labor *work* (Br) labour
LBR libber *(slang) for liberation*
LBR Liberia *country*
LBR Libra *zodiac sign*
LBR library *books* libraries
LBR lobar *protrusion*
LBR lobbyer *persuader*
LBR lowbrow *culture*
LBR lubber *clumsy one*
LBRD Alberta *Canadian province*
LBRD ill-bred *rude*
LBRD Labor Day *holiday*
LBRD labored *difficult* (Br) laboured
LBRD lapboard *tray*
LBRD leeboard *sailboat*
LBRD liberty *freedom*

liberties
LBRD libretto *text* librettos (or) libretti
LBRD lowbred *common*
LBRD oilbird *bird*
LBRDD liberated *free*
LBRDR Labrador *peninsula*
LBRDR liberator *one who frees*
LBRDRTRVR Labrador retriever *dog*
LBRDST librettist *opera*
LBRDV elaborative *expand, develop*
LBRKDD lubricated *oiled*
LBRKDR lubricator *oil*
LBRKNT lubricant *oil*
LBRKR lawbreaker *criminal*
LBRKRK Albuquerque *city*
LBRKS lubricous (or) lubricious *lustful, slippery*
LBRKSHN lubrication *oil*
LBRKT lubricate *oil* lubricated lubricating
LBRKTD lubricated *oiled*
LBRKTR lubricator *oil*
LBRL illiberal (adj) *stingy* illiberally (adv)
LBRL liberal (adj) *generous, broad-minded* (n) *politics* liberally (adv)
LBRLD illiberality *stingy* illiberalities
LBRLD liberality *generosity* liberalities
LBRLNS liberalness *generosity*
LBRLSDK liberalistic *freedom*
LBRLSTK liberalistic *freedom*
LBRLT illiberality *stingy* illiberalities
LBRLT liberality *generosity* liberalities
LBRLZ liberalize *make free* liberalized liberalizing (Br) liberalise
LBRLZM liberalism *freedom*
LBRLZSHN liberalization *freedom* (Br) liberalisation

LBRM elbowroom *space*
LBRM Librium *(trademark)*
drug
LBRMRL Albemarle *island, inlet*
LBRN librarian *books*
LBRN lowborn *no status*
LBRNM laburnum *shrub*
LBRNTH labyrinth *maze*
LBRNTHN labyrinthine *complicated*
LBRR laborer *worker*
(Br) labourer
LBRR library *books* libraries
LBRRN librarian *books*
LBRRYN librarian *books*
LBRS laborious *difficult*
(Br) labourious
LBRSD lubricity *lust, slipperiness* lubricities
LBRSHN elaboration *expansion, development*
LBRSHN liberation *freedom*
LBRSHN libration *variation*
LBRSHNL librational *variation*
LBRSHS lubricious (or) lubricous *lustful, slippery*
LBRSHSL lubriciously *lustful, slippery*
LBRST lubricity *lust, slipperiness* lubricities
LBRSVN laborsaving *less work*
(Br) laboursaving
LBRSVNG laborsaving *less work*
(Br) laboursaving
LBRT Alberta *Canadian province*
LBRT elaborate *(v) expand, develop* elaborated elaborating
LBRT elaborate *(adj) complex*
LBRT liberate *free* liberated liberating
LBRT liberty *freedom* liberties
LBRT libretto *text* librettos (or) libretti
LBRTD liberated *free*

LBRTL elaborately *complex*
LBRTN libertine *free one*
LBRTNS elaborateness *complexity*
LBRTNZM libertinism *freedom*
LBRTR laboratory *test area* laboratories
LBRTR liberator *one who frees*
LBRTRN libertarian *freedom*
LBRTRNZM libertarianism *freedom*
LBRTRYN libertarian *freedom*
LBRTRYNZM libertarianism *freedom*
LBRTST librettist *opera*
LBRTV elaborative *expand, develop*
LBRV alla breve *musical notation*
LBRY Liberia *country*
LBRYM Librium *(trademark) drug*
LBRYN librarian *books*
LBRYS laborious *difficult* (Br) labourious
LBSDR alabaster *gypsum*
LBSDR lobster *animal*
LBSDRNG lobstering *catch lobsters*
LBSHN libation *beverage*
LBSHNR libationary *beverage*
LBST lobbyist *persuader*
LBSTR alabaster *gypsum*
LBSTR lobster *animal*
LBSTRN alabastrine *gypsum*
LBSTRNG lobstering *catch lobsters*
LBT albeit *even though*
LBT layabout *lazy one*
LBT libido *lust* libidos
LBT lobate *protrusion*
LBTM lobotomy *brain surgery* lobotomies
LBTMZ lobotomize *brain surgery* lobotomized lobotomizing
(Br) lobotomise
LBTR laboratory *test area*

laboratories
LBTRN libertarian *freedom*
LBTRNZM libertarianism *freedom*
LBTRS albatross *bird* albatross (or) albatrosses
LBTRYN libertarian *freedom*
LBTRYNZM libertarianism *freedom*
LBY labia (pl) *lip* labium
LBY Libya *country*
LBYL labial (adj) *lip* labially (adv)
LBYL lobule *bulge*
LBYLDD lobulated *bulging*
LBYLR lobular *bulging*
LBYLTD lobulated *bulging*
LBYM labium *lip* labia
LBYMN albumen *egg white*
LBYMN albumin *protein*
LBYMNR albuminuria *protein in urine*
LBYMNRY albuminuria *protein in urine*
LBYMNS albuminous *like protein*
LBYMNYR albuminuria *protein in urine*
LBYMNYRY albuminuria *protein in urine*
LBYN Libyan *of Libya*
LBYR lobbyer *persuader*
LBYST lobbyist *persuader*
LBYT albeit *even though*
LC lacy *decorative* lacier laciest
LC lassie *girl*
LC lessee *renter*
LC loci (pl) *point* locus
LCD oilseed *crop*
LCGC loosey-goosey *relaxed*
LCGS loosey-goosey *relaxed*
LCH latch *(n) fastener (v) fasten, seize* latches
LCH leach *draw out*
LCH lech *lecher*
LCH leech *worm* leeches
LCH litchi *fruit*
LCH loach *fish*
LCHBL leachable *draw out*
LCHBLD leachability *draw*

Letters aren't doubled for single sounds: to find alley use **L** not **LL**. Use **Y** and **W** as hard sounds only: to find yellow use **YL**. (Br)=British spelling or usage. * See dictionary.

LCHBLT leachability *draw out*

LCHK latchkey *door*

LCHN lichen *plant, skin disease*

LCHNLG lichenology *plants*

LCHNLJ lichenology *plants*

LCHNLJKL lichenological *plants*

LCHNLJST lichenologist *plants*

LCHNS lichenous *plants*

LCHNT litchi nut *fruit*

LCHP el cheapo *cheap*

LCHR leacher *draw out*

LCHR lecher *corrupter*

LCHR lechery *corruption* lecheries

LCHRS lecherous *corrupt*

LCHRSL lecherously *corruptly*

LCHRSNS lecherousness *corruption*

LCHSTRNG latchstring *door*

LCHT latchet *strap*

LCHW lechwe *animal* lechwe (or) lechwes

LCHZ laches *delay* laches

LCM lyceum *hall*

LCNS laciness *openwork*

LCR lacier *openwork*

LCST laciest *openwork*

LCYM lyceum *hall*

LCYR lacier *openwork*

LCYST laciest *openwork*

LCZ lyses (pl) *decline* lysis

LD a lot of *many*

LD allied *associated*

LD allottee *receiver*

LD allowed *permitted*

LD allude *refer* alluded alluding

LD aloud *sounded*

LD elide *leave out* elided eliding

LD elodea *herb*

LD elude *evade* eluded eluding

LD eyelid *eye cover*

LD Iliad *poem*

LD lad *boy*

LD laddie *boy*

LD lade *load* laded lading laden

LD lady *woman* ladies

LD laid *(v-past)* lay

LD laity *not clergy*

LD laud *praise*

LD lead *(v) go before* led leading

LD lead *(n) vanguard, leash*

LD lead *(v) weight, mix with lead* leaded leading

LD lead *(n) heavy element*

LD lewd *vulgar*

LD lid *cover* lidded lidding

LD lido *beach* lidos

LD load *(n) burden, eyeful (v) burden, bias, insert**

LD lode *ore*

LD lotte *monkfish*

LD lotto *game*

LD loud *noisy*

LD oiled *greased, drunk*

LD old *aged*

LD old lady *wife, mother*

LD oldie *song*

LDB old boy *(often capitalized) crony*

LDBF oeil-de-boeuf *eye* oeils-de-boeuf

LDBG ladybug *insect*

LDBK laid-back *relaxed*

LDBL illaudable (adj) *undeserving* illaudably (adv)

LDBL laudable (adj) *praiseworthy* laudably (adv)

LDCHR literature *books*

LDCZ latices (pl) *rubber* latex

LDD alidade *astrolabe*

LDD elated *overjoyed*

LDD lidded *covered*

LDD loaded *full, ready, drunk, rich*

LDF laid off *employment*

LDF lead off *(v) begin* leadoff (n)

LDFNGGR ladyfinger *cake*

LDFNGR ladyfinger *cake*

LDFSH ladyfish *bonefish*

LDFSHN old-fashioned *outmoded*

LDFSHND old-fashioned *outmoded*

LDG latigo *saddle* latigos

LDGBL litigable *law*

LDGDR litigator *law*

LDGLR Old Glory *flag*

LDGNT litigant *lawsuit*

LDGSHN litigation *law*

LDGT litigate *contest in law* litigated litigating

LDGTHR altogether (adj) *completely (n) nude*

LDGTR litigator *law*

LDHD aldehyde *chemical*

LDHDK aldehydic *chemical*

LDHT old hat *unimportant*

LDK lotic *water*

LDK luetic *syphilis*

LDK lytic *declining*

LDKL lytically *declining*

LDKLR lady-killer *handsome man*

LDKNTR old country *(often capitalized) Europe*

LDKRS ludicrous *laughable*

LDKRSL ludicrously *laughably*

LDKRSNS ludicrousness *laughable*

LDL allowedly *admittedly*

LDL ladle *spoon* ladled ladling

LDL lewdly *vulgar*

LDL little *(adj) small (adv) slightly* littler (or) less (or) lesser littlest (or) least

LDL loudly *noisy*

LDL luteal *ovulation*

LDLD old lady *wife, mother*

LDLDPR Little Dipper *constellation*

LDLG Little League *baseball*

LDLK ladylike *well-bred*

LDLN lead line *depth*

LDLN old-line *traditional*

LDLNGZN auld lang syne *good old times*

LDLNK littleneck *clam*

LDLNZN auld lang syne *good old times*

Use letters that best describe the sounds you hear and omit the vowels. Use **S** or **K** instead of **C**: to find circle use **SRKL**. Use **J** to find joy, **JM** to find gem and **G** to find go.

LDLR littler *smaller*
LDLRK Little Rock *city*
LDLS aldolase *enzyme*
LDLS lidless *no cover*
LDLST littlest *smallest*
LDLV ladylove *sweetheart*
LDLZ aldolase *enzyme*
LDMD old maid *spinster*
LDMN leadman *supervisor*
　leadmen
LDMTH loudmouth *talk*
LDMTHD loudmouthed *talk*
LDMTHT loudmouthed *talk*
LDN Aladdin *fictional hero*
LDN laden *loaded*
LDN lading *cargo*
LDN Latin *language*
LDN lead-in *introduction*
LDN leaden *heavy*
LDN leading *first*
LDN loden *cloth, color*
LDN louden *make noise*
LDN low-down *(adj)*
　revolting
LDN lowdown *(n) facts*
LDN olden *past*
LDNG lading *cargo*
LDNG leading *first*
LDNG lighting *illumination*
LDNGJ leading edge
　forefront
LDNGZN auld lang syne
　good old times
LDNJ leading edge *forefront*
LDNM labdanum *perfume*
LDNM laudanum *opium*
LDNMRK Latin America
　region
LDNS lewdness *vulgarity*
LDNS loudness *noise*
LDNT al dente *cooked*
LDNZ latinize *language*
　latinized latinizing
LDNZSHN latinization
　language
LDP lead-up (n) *prepare the
　way* lead up (v)
LDP let up (v) *ease* letup (n)
LDPLNT leadplant *shrub*
LDPP lead-pipe (adj) *(adj)
　certain*
LDR alder *tree*

LDR allotter *distributor*
LDR altar *worship*
LDR alter *change*
LDR elater *spores*
LDR elder *older*
LDR ladder *step up, scale*
LDR later *after now*
LDR latter *recent*
LDR leader *guide*
LDR letter *alphabet symbol,
　correspondence, renter*
LDR lighter *less weight, flame*
LDR liter *measure*
　(Br) litre
LDR litter *(n) trash, bed (v)
　birth, strew*
LDR loiter *linger*
LDR looter *thief*
LDR lottery *drawing of lots*
　lotteries
LDR older *aged*
LDRB altar boy *aide*
LDRBG litterbag *container*
LDRBG litterbug *strew trash*
LDRBK ladder-back *slats*
LDRBL alterable (adj)
　changeable alterably (adv)
LDRBLD alterability
　changeability
LDRBLT alterability
　changeability
LDRBR elderberry *fruit*
　elderberries
LDRC aliteracy *no desire to
　read*
LDRC illiteracy *unable to read*
　illiteracies
LDRC literacy *read and write*
LDRCHR literature *books*
LDRD latter-day *recent*
LDRD lettered *educated*
LDRD literati *educated class*
LDRDV alliterative *repetitive*
LDRDVL alliteratively
　repetitive
LDRG alter ego *counterpart*
LDRG liturgy *rite* liturgies
LDRHD letterhead *title*
LDRHZN lederhosen *shorts*
LDRJ liturgy *rite* liturgies
LDRKL altar call *appeal*
LDRKRNTS Liederkranz

　(trademark) cheese
LDRKRNZ Liederkranz
　(trademark) cheese
LDRKRR letter carrier
　postman
LDRKRYR letter carrier
　postman
LDRKSHN altercation
　quarrel
LDRKT altercate *wrangle*
　altercated altercating
LDRL altar rail *banister*
LDRL elderly *aged*
LDRL lateral (adj) *sideways*
　laterally (adv)
LDRL latterly *later*
LDRL literal (adj) *actual,
　exact* literally (adv)
LDRL littoral *seashore*
LDRLNS elderliness *aged*
LDRLNS literalness *precision*
LDRLST literalist *realist*
LDRLZ lateralize *one side*
　lateralized lateralizing
LDRLZ literalize *make exact*
　literalized literalizing
LDRLZM literalism *realism*
LDRLZSHN lateralization
　one side
LDRLZSHN literalization
　make exact
LDRMN alderman *magistrate*
　aldermen
LDRMN letterman *athlete*
　lettermen
LDRMNK aldermanic
　magistrate
LDRN lettering *type*
LDRNDNG alternating
　changing
LDRNDR alternator
　generator
LDRNG lettering *type*
LDRNSHN alternation
　succession
LDRNT alternate *change*
　alternated alternating
LDRNT alternate *(adj)
　opposite (n) substitute*
LDRNTN alternating
　changing
LDRNTR alternator

Letters aren't doubled for single sounds: to find alley use **L** not **LL**. Use **Y** and **W** as hard
sounds only: to find yellow use **YL**. (Br)=British spelling or usage. * See dictionary.

generator
LDRPRFK letter-perfect *no mistakes*
LDRPRFKT letter-perfect *no mistakes*
LDRPRS letterpress *printing letterpresses*
LDRPS altarpiece *art*
LDRR alterer *changer*
LDRR literary *well-read*
LDRR loiterer *lingerer*
LDRRNS literariness *bookish*
LDRS aliteracy *no desire to read*
LDRS illiteracy *unable to read illiteracies*
LDRS literacy *read and write*
LDRSHN alliteration *repetition*
LDRSHN alteration *change*
LDRSHP leadership *guidance*
LDRSTN altar stone *relic storage*
LDRT aliterate *no desire to read*
LDRT alliterate *repeat alliterated alliterating*
LDRT illiterate *unable to read*
LDRT literate *read and write*
LDRT literati *educated class*
LDRTHNR lighter-than-air *gas*
LDRTL illiterately *unable to read*
LDRTL literately *well-read*
LDRTNS illiterateness *unable to read*
LDRTNS literateness *well-read*
LDRTR literature *books*
LDRTV alliterative *repetitive*
LDRTVL alliteratively *repetitive*
LDRTYR literature *books*
LDRWMN alderwoman *magistrate alderwomen*
LDS aldose *sugar*
LDS ileitis *inflammation*
LDS lattice *framework*
LDS lettuce *food*
LDS lotus *flower*

LDS luteous *yellow*
LDSD latticed *framework*
LDSH latish *overdue*
LDSH loutish *boorish*
LDSH oldish *aged*
LDSHN laudation *praise*
LDSHP ladyship *rank*
LDSKR leadscrew *rod*
LDSL latosol *soil*
LDSLK latosolic *soil*
LDSLPR lady's slipper *orchid*
LDSPKR loudspeaker *amplifier*
LDST eldest *first born*
LDST latest *most recent*
LDST latticed *framework*
LDST oldest *aged*
LDSTHM lady's thumb *herb*
LDSTN lodestone *magnet*
LDSTR lodestar *guide*
LDSTR oldster *aged one*
LDSTRN aldosterone *steroid*
LDSWRK latticework *frame*
LDSZ latices (pl) *rubber latex*
LDT Luddite *against technology*
LDTD altitude *height*
LDTD latitude *width, freedom*
LDTDNL altitudinal *height*
LDTDNL latitudinal (adj) *width, freedom* latitudinally (adv)
LDTDNS altitudinous *height*
LDTM lead time *notice*
LDTM old-time *ancient*
LDTMR old-timer *veteran*
LDTR laudatory *praise*
LDTSDMNT Old Testament *bible*
LDTSTMNT Old Testament *bible*
LDTV laudative *praise*
LDTYD altitude *height*
LDTYD latitude *width, freedom*
LDTYDNL altitudinal *height*
LDTYDNL latitudinal (adj) *width, freedom* latitudinally (adv)
LDTYDNS altitudinous *height*

LDV a lot of *many*
LDV illative *opinion*
LDVZD ill-advised *unwise*
LDWRK leadwork *made with lead*
LDWRLD Old World (n) *Europe* old-world (adj)
LDY elodea *herb*
LDYL luteal *ovulation*
LDYS luteous *yellow*
LDZ ill at ease *nervous*
LDZ Leeds *city*
LDZM elitism *superiority* (Br) elitism
LDZMN ladies' man *lover*
LDZMN leadsman *depth*
LDZRM ladies' room *bathroom*
LF aleph *Hebrew letter*
LF Alfa *code letter A*
LF aloft *above*
LF aloof *distant*
LF alpha *first Greek letter*
LF elf *tiny person elves*
LF laugh *happy sound*
LF lay off (v) *suspend* layoff (n)
LF leaf *plant, page leaves*
LF leafy *with foliage leafier leafiest*
LF lev *money leva*
LF life *existence lives*
LF loaf (n) *bread unit loaves*
LF loaf (v) *idle loafs loafing*
LF loft (n) *attic (v) propel*
LF loofah *sponge*
LF luff *sail*
LFB life buoy *float*
LFBDK alphabetic *letters*
LFBDKL alphabetical (adj) *in A-Z order* alphabetically (adv)
LFBL laughable (adj) *funny* laughably (adv)
LFBLD lifeblood *strength*
LFBLT life belt (Br) *restraint*
LFBNGK left-bank *(often capitalized) bohemian*
LFBNK left-bank *(often capitalized) bohemian*
LFBT alphabet *letters*
LFBT lifeboat *raft*

Use letters that best describe the sounds you hear and omit the vowels. Use **S** or **K** instead of **C**: to find circle use **SRKL**. Use **J** to find joy, **JM** to find gem and **G** to find go.

LFBTK alphabetic *letters*
LFBTKL alphabetical (adj) *in A-Z order* alphabetically (adv)
LFBTZ alphabetize *put in A-Z order* alphabetized alphabetizing
LFBTZR alphabetizer *in A-Z order*
LFBTZSHN alphabetization *in A-Z order*
LFBW life buoy *float*
LFD leafed *with leaves*
LFD lefty *left-handed* lefties
LFD lofty *high* loftier loftiest
LFDD ill-fated *unfortunate*
LFDF liftoff *takeoff*
LFDK aliphatic *chemistry*
LFDL loftily *high*
LFDNS loftiness *height*
LFDR laughter *happy sound*
LFDR loftier *higher*
LFDSH leftish *liberal*
LFDST leftist *liberal*
LFDST loftiest *highest*
LFDVR leftover *unused*
LFDYR loftier *higher*
LFDYST loftiest *highest*
LFF laugh off *belittle*
LFFRM life-form *organism*
LFGRD lifeguard *swimmer*
LFGT liftgate *car door*
LFGVN life-giving *healthful*
LFGVNG life-giving *healthful*
LFJ leafage *foliage*
LFJKT life jacket *vest*
LFKDMDR olfactometer *smell*
LFKDMTR olfactometer *smell*
LFKDR olfactory *smell*
LFKSHN olfaction *smell*
LFKTMDR olfactometer *smell*
LFKTMTR olfactometer *smell*
LFKTR olfactory *smell*
LFL aloofly *distantly*
LFL lawful (adj) *legal* lawfully (adv)
LFL oil field *region*
LFLD left field *baseball, off*

the path
LFLD oil field *region*
LFLF alfalfa *plant*
LFLK lifelike *animated*
LFLN lifeline *rope, help*
LFLNG lifelong *lasting*
LFLNS lawfulness *legal*
LFLR alfilaria *weed*
LFLRY alfilaria *weed*
LFLS leafless *no leaves*
LFLS lifeless *dead*
LFLSD All Fools' Day *April 1*
LFLT leaflet (v) *hand out* leafletted leafletting
LFLT leaflet (n) *foliage, handout*
LFLTR leafleteer *hand out paper*
LFLZD All Fools' Day *April 1*
LFMRK alphameric *letters and numbers*
LFN allophane *mineral*
LFN allophone *phoneme*
LFN elfin *tiny*
LFN laughing *happy*
LFN olefin *fiber*
LFNDTH life-and-death *critical*
LFNG laughing *happy*
LFNGL laughingly *funny*
LFNGSTK laughingstock *teasing*
LFNK allophonic *phonemic*
LFNK olefinic *fiber*
LFNL laughingly *funny*
LFNMRK alphanumeric *letters and numbers*
LFNMRKL alphanumerical (adj) *letters and numbers* alphanumerically (adv)
LFNMRKS alphanumerics *letters and numbers*
LFNMRX alphanumerics *letters and numbers*
LFNS aloofness *distance*
LFNS leafiness *with leaves*
LFNSHRNS life insurance *death benefit*
LFNSHRNTS life insurance *death benefit*

LFNSTK laughingstock *teasing*
LFNT elephant *animal* elephants
LFNT life net *catcher*
LFNTDS elephantiasis *disease* elephantiases
LFNTN elephantine *massive*
LFNTSS elephantiasis *disease* elephantiases
LFNTTS elephantiasis *disease* elephantiases
LFNTYSS elephantiasis *disease* elephantiases
LFNYMRK alphanumeric *letters and numbers*
LFNYMRKL alphanumerical (adj) *letters and numbers* alphanumerically (adv)
LFNYMRKS alphanumerics *letters and numbers*
LFNYMRX alphanumerics *letters and numbers*
LFPR leafhopper *insect*
LFR alpha ray *atomic*
LFR laugher *happy one*
LFR leafier *with leaves*
LFR lifer *prisoner*
LFR loafer *idler, shoe*
LFRF life raft *boat*
LFRFT life raft *boat*
LFRS all fours *hands and knees*
LFRSK alfresco *outdoor*
LFRSPDR alpha-receptor *nerve*
LFRSPTR alpha-receptor *nerve*
LFRZ all fours *hands and knees*
LFSH elfish *mischievous*
LFSHL elfishly *mischievous*
LFSHN old-fashioned *outmoded*
LFSHND old-fashioned *outmoded*
LFSKL life cycle *stages*
LFSNTR Alpha Centauri *star*
LFSPN life span *existence*
LFSPRT life-support (adj) *medicine* life support (n)
LFST leafiest *with leaves*

Letters aren't doubled for single sounds: to find alley use **L** not **LL**. Use **Y** and **W** as hard sounds only: to find yellow use **YL**. (Br)=British spelling or usage. * See dictionary.

LFSTK leafstalk *stem*

LFSTL lifestyle *way of life*

LFSVN lifesaving *swimming*

LFSVNG lifesaving *swimming*

LFSVR lifesaver *swimmer*

LFSWRK lifework *career*

LFSZ life-size (or) life-sized *same as original*

LFSZD life-sized (or) life-size *same as original*

LFT aloft *above*

LFT leafed *with leaves*

LFT left (*n*) side (*v-past*) leave (*adj*) *radical*

LFT lefty *left-handed* lefties

LFT lift *raise*

LFT loft (*n*) *attic* (*v*) *propel*

LFT lofty *high* loftier loftiest

LFTBNGK left-bank (*often capitalized*) *bohemian*

LFTBNK left-bank (*often capitalized*) *bohemian*

LFTD ill-fated *unfortunate*

LFTF liftoff *takeoff*

LFTFLD left field *baseball, off the path*

LFTGT liftgate *car door*

LFTHN left-hand *side*

LFTHND left-hand *side*

LFTHNDD left-handed *awkward, insincere*

LFTHNDDNS left-handedness *awkward, insincere*

LFTHNDR left-hander *favored side*

LFTK aliphatic *chemistry*

LFTL loftily *high*

LFTM lifetime *existence*

LFTN left-hand *side*

LFTND left-hand *side*

LFTNDD left-handed *awkward, insincere*

LFTNDDNS left-handedness *awkward, insincere*

LFTNDR left-hander *favored side*

LFTNNT lieutenant *rank*

LFTNS loftiness *height*

LFTNT lieutenant *rank*

LFTR laughter *happy sound*

LFTR loftier *higher*

LFTRK laugh track *recording*

LFTSH leftish *liberal*

LFTST leftist *liberal*

LFTST loftiest *highest*

LFTVR leftover *unused*

LFTWNG left-wing (adj) *liberal* left wing (n)

LFTWNGR left-winger *liberal*

LFTWRD leftward *side*

LFTYR loftier *higher*

LFTYST loftiest *highest*

LFVRD ill-favored *ugly*

LFWNG left-wing (adj) *liberal* left wing (n)

LFWNGR left-winger *liberal*

LFWRD leftward *side*

LFWRK lifework *career*

LFWV alpha wave *brain wave*

LFYR leafier *with leaves*

LFYST leafiest *with leaves*

LG alga *plant* algae

LG algae (pl) *plant* alga

LG elegy *lament* elegies

LG eulogy *praise* eulogies

LG lag (*v*) *fall behind, cover, (Br) arrest* lagged lagging

LG lag (*n*) *slowness, interval, (Br) convict (or) ex-convict (adj) last (v) (Br) arrest*

LG league *group* leagued leaguing

LG leg (*v*) *run* legged legging

LG leg (*n*) *limb, pole, distance**

LG leggy *long-legged* leggier leggiest

LG log (*v*) *cut trees, record, achieve* logged logging

LG log (*n*) *tree, record*

LG loggia *gallery* loggias

LG logo *symbol* logos

LG logy *tired* logier logiest

LG lug *drag* lugged lugging

LG lug (*n*) *oaf, nut (Br) ear**

LG oology *bird's eggs*

LG yule log *hearth*

LGBK logbook *record*

LGBRS lugubrious *dismal*

LGBRSL lugubriously *dismal*

LGBRSNS lugubriousness *dismal*

LGBRYS lugubrious *dismal*

LGBRYSL lugubriously *dismal*

LGBRYSNS lugubriousness *dismal*

LGC legacy *inheritance* legacies

LGCHR ligature *binding*

LGD legatee *receiver*

LGD legato *music*

LGD legged *with legs*

LGD logged *heavy*

LGDK logaoedic *rhythm*

LGDR alligator *reptile*

LGDR legator *endower*

LGDRKLP alligator clip *connector*

LGFGS oligophagous *few foods*

LGGRF logograph *symbol*

LGGRF logogriph *puzzle*

LGGRFK logographic *symbol*

LGGRFKL logographically *symbol*

LGGRM logogram *symbol*

LGGRMDK logogrammatic *symbol*

LGGRMTK logogrammatic *symbol*

LGHL leghold *trap*

LGHLD leghold *trap*

LGHRN leghorn *straw, fowl*

LGJ luggage *baggage*

LGJM logjam *snag*

LGK elegiac *poetry*

LGKT oligochaete *earthworm*

LGL algal *plant*

LGL illegal (adj) *not lawful* illegally (adv)

LGL legal (adj) *lawful* legally (adv)

LGL leghold *trap*

LGL ligula *insect part* ligulae

LGL ligule *plant part*

LGLD illegality *unlawful* illegalities

Use letters that best describe the sounds you hear and omit the vowels. Use **S** or **K** instead of **C**: to find circle use **SRKL**. Use **J** to find joy, **JM** to find gem and **G** to find go.

LGLD legal aid *attorney*
LGLD legality *law* legalities
LGLD leghold *trap*
LGLG algology *algae*
LGLGN algolagnia *love of pain*
LGLGNK algolagniac *love of pain*
LGLGNY algolagnia *love of pain*
LGLGNYK algolagniac *love of pain*
LGLJ algology *algae*
LGLJ legal age *adult*
LGLJKL algological *algae*
LGLJST algologist *algae scientist*
LGLR Old Glory *flag*
LGLS legless *no legs*
LGLSDK legalistic *law*
LGLSDKL legalistically *law*
LGLSTK legalistic *law*
LGLSTKL legalistically *law*
LGLT illegality *unlawful* illegalities
LGLT legality *law* legalities
LGLTNDR legal tender *money*
LGLZ legalese *language*
LGLZ legalize *make lawful* legalized legalizing (Br) legalise
LGLZM legalism *law*
LGLZR legalizer *make lawful* (Br) legaliser
LGLZSHN legalization *law* (Br) legalisation
LGM allogamy *reproduction*
LGM legume *bean*
LGMK logomachy *dispute* logomachies
LGMN legman *assistant* legmen
LGMNS leguminous *bean*
LGMNT ligament *tissue band*
LGMRF lagomorph *animal*
LGMS allogamous *reproduction*
LGN Allegheny *mountains* Alleghenies (mountains)
LGN lagan *debris*
LGN lagging *insulation*

LGN lagoon *pond*
LGN legging (or) leggin *tights*
LGN log on *start*
LGNBR loganberry *fruit* loganberries
LGNC elegancy *style* elegancies
LGNDK lignitic *coal*
LGNF lignify *make woody* lignified lignifying lignifies
LGNFKSHN lignification *make woody*
LGNG lagging *insulation*
LGNG legging (or) leggin *tights*
LGNGKWN Algonquian (or) Algonquin (or) Algonkian *Native American*
LGNGKWYN Algonquian (or) Algonquin (or) Algonkian *Native American*
LGNGQN Algonquian (or) Algonquin (or) Algonkian *Native American*
LGNGQYN Algonquian (or) Algonquin (or) Algonkian *Native American*
LGNKN Algonquian (or) Algonquin (or) Algonkian *Native American*
LGNKWN Algonquian (or) Algonquin (or) Algonkian *Native American*
LGNKWYN Algonquian (or) Algonquin (or) Algonkian *Native American*
LGNKYN Algonquian (or) Algonquin (or) Algonkian *Native American*
LGNL lagoonal *pond*
LGNN lignin *cell wall*
LGNQN Algonquian (or) Algonquin (or) Algonkian *Native American*
LGNQYN Algonquian (or) Algonquin (or) Algonkian *Native American*
LGNS elegance *style*
LGNS elegancy *style* elegancies

LGNS legginess *long-legged*
LGNS ligneous *wood*
LGNT elegant *splendid*
LGNT lignite *coal*
LGNTC elegancy *style* elegancies
LGNTK lignitic *coal*
LGNTL elegantly *splendid*
LGNTS elegance *style*
LGNTS elegancy *style* elegancies
LGNYS ligneous *wood*
LGPL leg-pull *hoax*
LGPL oligopoly *market* oligopolies
LGPSN oligopsony *market* oligopsonies
LGPSNSDK oligopsonistic *market*
LGPSNSTK oligopsonistic *market*
LGR Algeria *country*
LGR allegory *story* allegories
LGR allegro *music* allegros
LGR lager *beer*
LGR lagger *idler*
LGR leaguer *member*
LGR leggier *long-legged*
LGR ligure *stone*
LGR logger *trees*
LGR logier *tired*
LGR logorrhea *talk*
LGR lugger *boat*
LGRB algaroba *carob*
LGRD allegretto *music*
LGRD laggard *idle*
LGRD low-grade *poor quality*
LGRF allograph *letter*
LGRGSDZZ Lou Gehrig's Disease *sclerosis*
LGRGZDZZ Lou Gehrig's disease *sclerosis*
LGRHD loggerhead *disagreement, turtle, tool**
LGRK à la grecque *herb sauce*
LGRK logorrheic *talk*
LGRK oligarch *rule by few*
LGRK oligarchy *rule by few* oligarchies
LGRKK oligarchic (or)

Letters aren't doubled for single sounds: to find alley use **L** not **LL**. Use **Y** and **W** as hard sounds only: to find yellow use **YL**. (Br)=British spelling or usage. * See dictionary.

oligarchical *rule by few*
LGRKKL oligarchical (or)
oligarchic *rule by few*
LGRKL allegorical (adj)
symbolic allegorically
(adv)
LGRL logroll *favors*
LGRLN logrolling *favors*
LGRLNG logrolling *favors*
LGRLR logroller *favors*
LGRM legroom *space*
LGRN leghorn *straw, fowl*
LGRNCH lug wrench *tool*
LGRS allegorize *tell a story*
allegorized allegorizing
(Br) allegorise
LGRS eelgrass *plant*
LGRSR allegorizer *storyteller*
(Br) allegoriser
LGRST allegorist *symbolist*
LGRT allegretto *music*
allegrettos
LGRTHM algorithm
mathematics
LGRTHM logarithm *math*
LGRTHMK algorithmic
mathematical
LGRTHMK logarithmic *math*
LGRTHMKL algorithmically
mathematically
LGRTHMKL logarithmically
math
LGRY Algeria *country*
LGRY logorrhea *talk*
LGRYK logorrheic *talk*
LGRZ Algiers *city*
LGRZ allegorize *tell a story*
allegorized allegorizing
(Br) allegorise
LGRZR allegorizer *storyteller*
(Br) allegoriser
LGRZSHN allegorization
representation
(Br) allegorisation
LGS Lagos *city*
LGS legacy *inheritance*
legacies
LGS leges (pl) *law* lex
LGSHN allegation *assertion*
LGSHN legation *trip*
LGSHN ligation *binding*
LGSHR luxury *ease and*

comfort luxuries
LGSHRNS luxuriance
lushness
LGSHRNT luxuriant *lush*
LGSHRNTS luxuriance
lushness
LGSHRS luxurious *lush, rich*
LGSHRT luxuriate *thrive,*
revel luxuriated
luxuriating
LGSHRYNS luxuriance
lushness
LGSHRYNT luxuriant *lush*
LGSHRYNTS luxuriance
lushness
LGSHRYS luxurious *lush,*
rich
LGSHRYT luxuriate *thrive,*
revel luxuriated
luxuriating
LGSKRD oligosaccharide
sweetener
LGSL lugsail *boat*
LGST leggiest *long-legged*
LGST logiest *tired*
LGT leg out *run fast*
LGT legate *bequeath* legated
legating
LGT legatee *receiver*
LGT legato *music*
LGT ligate *bind* ligated
ligating
LGTN ill-gotten *stolen*
LGTP logotype *symbol*
LGTR alligator *reptile*
LGTR legator *endower*
LGTR ligature *binding*
LGTRFK oligotrophic
oxygenated
LGTRKLP alligator clip
connector
LGTS loggets (or) loggats
game
LGVR lawgiver *legislator*
LGWRK legwork *exercise*
LGWRM lugworm *bait*
LGWRMR leg warmer
covering
LGY loggia *gallery* loggias
LGYBRS lugubrious *dismal*
LGYBRSL lugubriously
dismal

LGYBRSNS lugubriousness
dismal
LGYBRYS lugubrious *dismal*
LGYBRYSL lugubriously
dismal
LGYBRYSNS
lugubriousness *dismal*
LGYK elegiac *poetry*
LGYL ligula *insect part*
ligulae
LGYL ligule *plant part*
LGYM legume *bean*
LGYMNS leguminous *bean*
LGYR leggier *long-legged*
LGYR ligure *stone*
LGYR logier *tired*
LGYST leggiest *long-legged*
LGYST logiest *tired*
LGZHR luxury *ease and*
comfort luxuries
LGZHRNS luxuriance
lushness
LGZHRNT luxuriant *lush*
LGZHRNTS luxuriance
lushness
LGZHRS luxurious *lush, rich*
LGZHRT luxuriate *thrive,*
revel luxuriated
luxuriating
LGZHRYNS luxuriance
lushness
LGZHRYNT luxuriant *lush*
LGZHRYNTS luxuriance
lushness
LGZHRYS luxurious *lush,*
rich
LGZHRYT luxuriate *thrive,*
revel luxuriated
luxuriating
LGZNDR Alexander (the
Great) *conqueror*
LGZNDR Alexandria *city*
LGZNDRN Alexandrian *of*
Alexandria
LGZNDRN alexandrine *verse*
LGZNDRT alexandrite
mineral
LGZNDRY Alexandria *city*
LGZNDRYN Alexandrian *of*
Alexandria
LH aloha *greeting*
LH elhi *school*

Use letters that best describe the sounds you hear and omit the vowels. Use **S** or **K**
instead of **C**: to find circle use **SRKL**. Use **J** to find joy, **JM** to find gem and **G** to find go.

LHMBR Alhambra *palace*
LHMRD ill-humored *surly* (Br) ill-humoured
LHS alehouse *pub*
LHT old hat *unimportant*
LHYMRD ill-humored *surly* (Br) ill-humoured
LJ algae (pl) *plant* alga
LJ allege *say* alleged alleging
LJ elegy *lament* elegies
LJ eulogy *praise* eulogies
LJ ledge *shelf*
LJ ledgy *ridged*
LJ liege *loyalty, servant*
LJ lodge *house* lodged lodging
LJ loge *theater box*
LJ loggia *gallery* loggias
LJ luge *sled*
LJ oology *bird's eggs*
LJ ullage *liquid*
LJBL eligible (adj) *entitled* eligibly (adv)
LJBL illegible (adj) *unclear* illegibly (adv)
LJBL legible (adj) *clear* legibly (adv)
LJBLD eligibility *permission*
LJBLD illegibility *unclear*
LJBLD legibility *clearness*
LJBLT eligibility *permission*
LJBLT illegibility *unclear*
LJBLT legibility *clearness*
LJBR algebra *mathematics*
LJBRK algebraic *mathematics*
LJBRKL algebraically *mathematics*
LJBRST algebraist *mathematician*
LJBRYK algebraic *mathematics*
LJBRYKL algebraically *mathematics*
LJBRYST algebraist *mathematician*
LJD algid *cold*
LJD alleged *supposed*
LJDL allegedly *supposed*
LJDMC illegitimacy *not legal*
LJDMC legitimacy *legal*

LJDMDR legitimator *make legal*
LJDMS illegitimacy *not legal*
LJDMS legitimacy *legal*
LJDMSHN legitimation *make legal*
LJDMST legitimist *make legal*
LJDMT illegitimate *not legal*
LJDMT legitimate (v) *make legal* legitimated legitimating
LJDMT legitimate (adj) *legal*
LJDMTL legitimately *legal*
LJDMTR legitimator *make legal*
LJDMTZ legitimatize *make legal* legitimatize legitimatizing
LJDMTZR legitimatizer *make legal*
LJDMZ legitimize *make legal* legitimized legitimizing (Br) legitimise
LJDMZR legitimizer *make legal* (Br) legitimiser
LJDMZSHN legitimization *make legal* (Br) legitimisation
LJK elegiac *poetry*
LJK illogic *senseless*
LJK logic *reason*
LJKL alogical (adj) *beyond reason* alogically (adv)
LJKL illogical (adj) *without reason* illogically (adv)
LJKL logical (adj) *reasonable* logically (adv)
LJKLNS illogicalness *without reason*
LJMNT lodgment (or) lodgement *shelter*
LJN algin *algae*
LJN legend *myth*
LJN legion *many, army*
LJN lodging *residence*
LJND legend *myth*
LJNDR legendary *mythical*
LJNDR legendry *myths*
LJNDRL legendarily *mythical*

LJNG lodging *residence*
LJNR legionary *soldier* legionaries
LJNR legionnaire *soldier*
LJNRZDZZ Legionnaires' disease *pneumonia*
LJNS allegiance *loyalty*
LJNT allegiant *loyal*
LJNTS allegiance *loyalty*
LJR Algeria *country*
LJR ledger *account*
LJR lodger *resident*
LJR luger *sledder*
LJRDMN legerdemain *masterful*
LJRY Algeria *country*
LJRZ Algiers *city*
LJS leges (pl) *law* lex
LJSD algicide (or) algaecide *algae killer*
LJSDK eulogistic *praise*
LJSDK logistic (or) logistical (adj) *reason* logistically (adv)
LJSDKL eulogistically *praise*
LJSDKL logistical (or) logistic (adj) *reason* logistically (adv)
LJSDKS logistics *management*
LJSDX logistics *management*
LJSHN logician *reasoner*
LJSLCHR legislature *lawmakers*
LJSLDR legislator *lawmaker*
LJSLDV legislative *law*
LJSLSHN legislation *law*
LJSLT legislate *make law* legislated legislating
LJSLTR legislator *lawmaker*
LJSLTV legislative *law*
LJST eulogist *praiser*
LJST oologist *bird's eggs*
LJSTK eulogistic *praise*
LJSTK logistic (or) logistical (adj) *reason* logistically (adv)
LJSTKL eulogistically *praise*
LJSTKL logistical (or) logistic (adj) *reason* logistically (adv)
LJSTKS logistics

Letters aren't doubled for single sounds: to find alley use **L** not **LL**. Use **Y** and **W** as hard sounds only: to find yellow use **YL**. (Br)=British spelling or usage. * See dictionary.

management
LJSTSHN logistician *reasoner*
LJSTX logistics *management*
LJT alleged *supposed*
LJT legit *(slang)* legitimate
LJTL allegedly *supposed*
LJTMC illegitimacy *not legal*
LJTMC legitimacy *legal*
LJTMDR legitimator *make legal*
LJTMS illegitimacy *not legal*
LJTMS legitimacy *legal*
LJTMSHN legitimation *make legal*
LJTMST legitimist *make legal*
LJTMT illegitimate *not legal*
LJTMT legitimate *(v) make legal* legitimated legitimating
LJTMT legitimate *(adj) legal*
LJTMTL legitimately *legal*
LJTMTR legitimator *make legal*
LJTMTZ legitimatize *make legal* legitimatize legitimatizing
LJTMTZR legitimatizer *make legal*
LJTMZ legitimize *make legal* legitimized legitimizing *(Br)* legitimise
LJTMZR legitimizer *make legal* *(Br)* legitimiser
LJTMZSHN legitimization *make legal* *(Br)* legitimisation
LJY loggia *gallery* loggias
LJYK elegiac *poetry*
LJZ elegize *lament* elegized elegizing
LJZ eulogize *praise* eulogized eulogizing *(Br)* eulogise
LJZR eulogizer *praiser* *(Br)* eulogiser
LK alack *(interj) regret*
LK alike *similar*
LK elk *deer* elks (or) elk
LK iliac *intestine*
LK ilk *type*

LK lac *resin*
LK lack *need*
LK lackey *servant* lackeys
LK laic (or) laical *(adj) worldly* laically *(adv)*
LK lake *body of water*
LK lakh *money*
LK leak *hole or crack*
LK leaky *not tight* leakier leakiest
LK leek *vegetable*
LK lek *mating ground, money* leks (or) leke
LK lick *tongue*
LK like *(v) prefer, want* liked liking
LK like *(adj) similar (adv) rather (n) equal (prep) similar to (conj) as if**
LK loch *lake*
LK loci *(pl) point* locus
LK lock *(n) hair, key, canal (v) fasten, grapple, interlace**
LK loco *crazy* locos (or) locoes
LK look *(n) glance (v) see, expect, examine**
LK low-key *quiet*
LK luck *fortune*
LK lucky *fortunate* luckier luckiest
LK oleic *fat*
LKBKS lockbox *safe*
LKBL allocable *assigned*
LKBL likable (or) likeable *pleasant*
LKBLD likability *pleasant*
LKBLNS likableness *pleasant*
LKBLT likability *pleasant*
LKBRSHN lucubration *study*
LKBX lockbox *safe*
LKC alexia *unable to read*
LKC look-see *view*
LKCDN leucocidin *bacteria*
LKCHR lecture *sermonize* lectured lecturing
LKCHRR lecturer *sermon*
LKCHSHP lectureship *sermon*
LKCM lexeme *word*
LKCMK lexemic *word*

LKCY alexia *unable to read*
LKCZ lexes (pl) *words* lexis
LKD alcaide (or) alcayde *commander*
LKD alkyd *resin*
LKD Lakota *Native American* Lakota
LKDBL allocatable *rationed*
LKDBL electable *vote*
LKDBL locatable *found*
LKDBLD electability *vote*
LKDBLT electability *vote*
LKDBSLS lactobacillus *bacteria*
LKDGNK lactogenic *milk*
LKDJNK lactogenic *milk*
LKDK lactic *milk*
LKDM leukotomy *surgery* leukotomies
LKDN lockdown *prison*
LKDN locked-in *fixed*
LKDNSHTN Liechtenstein *country*
LKDNSTN Liechtenstein *country*
LKDR allocator *rationer*
LKDR elector *voter*
LKDR lector *reader*
LKDR locator *finder*
LKDRD electrode *circuit*
LKDRDLSS electrodialysis *purification*
LKDRDNMKS electrodynamics *physics*
LKDRDNMX electrodynamics *physics*
LKDRDYLSS electrodialysis *purification*
LKDRF electrify *wire* electrified electrifying electrifies
LKDRFD electrified *wired*
LKDRGRM electrogram *tracing*
LKDRK electric (or) electrical *(adj) shocking, electronic* electrically *(adv)*
LKDRKL electrical (or) electric *(adj) shocking, electronic* electrically *(adv)*
LKDRKMKL electrochemical *(adj)*

Use letters that best describe the sounds you hear and omit the vowels. Use **S** or **K** instead of **C**: to find circle use **SRKL**. Use **J** to find joy, **JM** to find gem and **G** to find go.

chemical currents
electrochemically (adv)
LKDRKMSTR
electrochemistry *chemical currents*
LKDRKNVLSV
electroconvulsive *shock*
LKDRKRDGRF
electrocardiograph *heart instrument*
LKDRKRDGRM
electrocardiogram *heart instrument*
LKDRKRDYGRF
electrocardiograph *heart instrument*
LKDRKRDYGRM
electrocardiogram *heart instrument*
LKDRKSHN electrocution *death by electricity*
LKDRKT electrocute *execute* electrocuted electrocuting
LKDRKYSHN electrocution *death by electricity*
LKDRKYT electrocute *execute* electrocuted electrocuting
LKDRL electoral *vote*
LKDRLDK electrolytic *conductive*
LKDRLDKL electrolytically *conductive*
LKDRLT electrolyte *conductor*
LKDRLTK electrolytic *conductive*
LKDRLTKL electrolytically *conductive*
LKDRLZ electrolyze *remove hair* electrolyzed electrolyzing
LKDRMDV electromotive *force*
LKDRMGNDK
electromagnetic *attractor*
LKDRMGNT electromagnet *attractor*
LKDRMGNTK
electromagnetic *magnet*
LKDRMGNTZM

electromagnetism *magnet*
LKDRMGRF
electromyograph *muscles*
LKDRMGRF
electromyography *muscles*
LKDRMKNKL
electromechanical *converter*
LKDRMTV electromotive *force*
LKDRMYGRF
electromyograph *muscles*
LKDRMYGRF
electromyography *muscles*
LKDRN electron *particle*
LKDRN lectern *book stand*
LKDRNSFLGRF
electroencephalograph *brain instrument*
LKDRNSFLGRM
electroencephalogram *brain instrument*
LKDRPLT electroplate *coating*
LKDRQSHN electrocution *death by electricity*
LKDRQT electrocute *execute* electrocuted electrocuting
LKDRR lecturer *sermon*
LKDRSHK electroshock *electricity*
LKDRSKP electroscope *radiation*
LKDRSTDK electrostatic *electricity*
LKDRSTDKL
electrostatically *electricity*
LKDRSTDKS electrostatics *electricity*
LKDRSTDX electrostatics *electricity*
LKDRSTTK electrostatic *electricity*
LKDRSTTKL
electrostatically *electricity*
LKDRSTTKS electrostatics *electricity*
LKDRSTTX electrostatics *electricity*

LKDRT electorate *voters*
LKDRTHRP electrotherapy *treatment*
LKDRTP electrotype *copy*
LKDSHP lectureship *sermon*
LKDSKL lackadaisical (adj) *sluggish* lackadaisically (adv)
LKDSPLT lickety-split *fast*
LKDV elective *chosen*
LKDZKL lackadaisical (adj) *sluggish* lackadaisically (adv)
LKFRNT lakefront *shoreline*
LKHL alcohol *ethanol*
LKHLK alcoholic *with ethanol, compulsive drinker*
LKHLKL alcoholically *with ethanol, compulsive drinker*
LKHLZM alcoholism *compulsive drinking*
LKHN elkhound *dog*
LKHND elkhound *dog*
LKHRN Lake Huron *body of water*
LKHSDK alkahestic *solvent*
LKHST alkahest *solvent*
LKHSTK alkahestic *solvent*
LKHYRN Lake Huron *body of water*
LKJ leakage *in or out*
LKJ lockjaw *tetanus*
LKL alkali *base* alkalies (or) alkalis
LKL alkyl *compound*
LKL laical (or) laic (adj) *worldly* laically (adv)
LKL leakily *in or out*
LKL likely *probable* likelier likeliest
LKL local (adj) *nearby* locally (adv)
LKL locale *site*
LKL locule *plant cell*
LKL loculi (pl) *chamber* loculus
LKL luckily *fortunate*
LKLD alcalde *official*
LKLD alkaloid *organic base*
LKLD locality *site* localities
LKLDK alkalotic *alkaline blood*

Letters aren't doubled for single sounds: to find alley use **L** not **LL**. Use **Y** and **W** as hard sounds only: to find yellow use **YL**. (Br)=British spelling or usage. * See dictionary.

LKLDL alkaloidal *organic base*

LKLHD likelihood *probability*

LKLK look-alike *double*

LKLMTR alkalimeter *device*

LKLMTR alkalimetry *science*

LKLN alkaline *base (ph of 7+)*

LKLND alkalinity *base (ph of 7+)*

LKLNT alkalinity *base (ph of 7+)*

LKLNT luculent *clear*

LKLNTL luculently *clear*

LKLNZ alkalinize *base (ph of 7+)* alkalinized alkalinizing

LKLNZSHN alkalinization *base (ph of 7+)*

LKLR all clear *signal*

LKLR likelier *probable*

LKLS loculus *chamber* loculi

LKLS luckless *no good fortune*

LKLSDR lackluster *dull* (Br) lacklustre

LKLSHN alkylation *add alkyl*

LKLSS alkalosis *alkaline blood*

LKLST likeliest *probable*

LKLSTR lackluster *dull* (Br) lacklustre

LKLT alkylate *add alkyl* alkylated alkylating

LKLT locality *site* localities

LKLTH laccolith *rock*

LKLTH oilcloth *fabric*

LKLTHK laccolithic *rock*

LKLTK alkalotic *alkaline blood*

LKLYR likelier *probable*

LKLYST likeliest *probable*

LKLZ localize *limit area* localized localizing (Br) localise

LKLZM localism *regional*

LKLZSHN localization *limited area* (Br) localisation

LKM alchemy *transform to gold*

LKM leukemia *disease* (Br) leukaemia

LKMD leukemoid *disease* (Br) leukaemoid

LKMDR locomotor *travel*

LKMDV locomotive *train*

LKMK leukemic *disease* (Br) leukaemic

LKMKL alchemical (adj) *transform to gold* alchemically (adv)

LKMNDD like-minded *same ideas*

LKMNDDNS like-mindedness *same ideas*

LKMSDK alchemistic *transform to gold*

LKMSHGN Lake Michigan *body of water*

LKMSHN locomotion *movement*

LKMST alchemist *transform to gold*

LKMSTK alchemistic *transform to gold*

LKMT locomote *move* locomoted locomoting

LKMTR locomotor *travel*

LKMTV locomotive *train*

LKMY leukemia *disease* (Br) leukaemia

LKMZ alchemize *transform to gold* alchemized alchemizing

LKN alkene *double bond*

LKN alkyne *triple bond*

LKN eulachon *fish* eulachon (or) eulachons

LKN lacuna *gap* lacunae (or) lacunas

LKN lichen *plant, skin disease*

LKN licking *thrashing*

LKN liken *compare*

LKN liking *preference*

LKN look-in *pass, chance*

LKN oilcan *container*

LKNG à la king *cream sauce*

LKNG licking *thrashing*

LKNG liking *preference*

LKNGGLS looking glass *mirror*

LKNGLS looking glass *mirror*

LKNK laconic *brief*

LKNKL laconically *brief*

LKNLG lichenology *plants*

LKNLJ lichenology *plants*

LKNLJKL lichenological *plants*

LKNLJST lichenologist *plants*

LKNS alikeness *similarity*

LKNS leakiness *in or out*

LKNS lichenous *mossy*

LKNS likeness *portrait, resemblance*

LKNS luckiness *fortune*

LKNS lychnis *plant*

LKNT locknut *screw*

LKNTR Lake Ontario *body of water*

LKNTR low country (n) *(often capitalized) land* low-country (adj)

LKNTR old country *(often capitalized) Europe*

LKNTRY Lake Ontario *body of water*

LKP lockup *jail*

LKP lookup (n) *search* look up (v)

LKPD lycopod *moss*

LKPDM lycopodium *moss*

LKPDYM lycopodium *moss*

LKPLST leucoplast *plant cell*

LKPN lycopene *pigment*

LKPR lockkeeper *canal*

LKPRF leakproof *no entry or escape*

LKR lacquer *gloss*

LKR Lake Erie *body of water*

LKR laker *fish*

LKR leaker *in or out*

LKR leakier *not tight*

LKR leukorrhea *discharge*

LKR liqueur *sweet alcohol*

LKR liquor *alcohol*

LKR locker *chest*

LKR looker *(slang) attractive one*

LKR luckier *fortunate*

LKR lucre *money*

LKR Lycra *(trademark) fabric*

LKRD alacrity *promptness*

LKRDS alacritous *prompt*

LKRDV lucrative *profitable*

Use letters that best describe the sounds you hear and omit the vowels. Use **S** or **K** instead of **C**: to find circle use **SRKL**. Use **J** to find joy, **JM** to find gem and **G** to find go.

LKRDVL lucratively *profitable*
LKRDVNS lucrativeness *profitable*
LKRM locker room (n) *sports* locker-room (adj)
LKRMDR lacrimator (or) lachrymator *tear gas*
LKRML lachrymal (or) lacrimal *tears*
LKRMS lachrymose *weeping*
LKRMSD lachrymosity *weeping*
LKRMSHN lacrimation *tears*
LKRMST lachrymosity *weeping*
LKRMTR lacrimator (or) lachrymator *tear gas*
LKRN looker-on *viewer* lookers-on
LKRR lacquerer *gloss*
LKRS lacrosse *sport*
LKRS licorice *candy* (Br) liquorice
LKRSH lickerish *lecherous*
LKRSH licorice *candy* (Br) liquorice
LKRSHS Lucretius *poet*
LKRSN lookers-on (pl) *viewer* looker-on
LKRT à la carte *menu*
LKRT alacrity *promptness*
LKRTS alacritous *prompt*
LKRTV lucrative *profitable*
LKRTVL lucratively *profitable*
LKRTVNS lucrativeness *profitable*
LKRWR lacquerware *decoration*
LKRWRK lacquerwork *decoration*
LKRY leukorrhea *discharge*
LKRZN lookers-on (pl) *viewer* looker-on
LKS alexia *unable to read*
LKS ilex *holly*
LKS lax *loose*
LKS lex *law* leges
LKS locus *point* loci
LKS locust *insect*
LKS look-see *view*
LKS looks *(slang) appearance*

LKS lox *food* lox (or) loxes
LKS lux *candlepower* lux (or) luxes
LKSD lakeside *shoreline*
LKSD laxity *looseness*
LKSDN leucocidin *bacteria*
LKSDV laxative *loosen*
LKSHN allocation *ration*
LKSHN allocution *formal speech*
LKSHN election *vote*
LKSHN elocution *public speaking*
LKSHN lection *lesson*
LKSHN location *site*
LKSHN locution *style of speech*
LKSHNR electioneer *vote*
LKSHNR elocutionary *public speaking*
LKSHNR illocutionary *effect of speech*
LKSHR lakeshore *shoreline*
LKSHR lecture *sermonize* lectured lecturing
LKSHR luxury *ease and comfort* luxuries
LKSHRNS luxuriance *lushness*
LKSHRNT luxuriant *lush*
LKSHRNTS luxuriance *lushness*
LKSHRR lecturer *sermon*
LKSHRS luxurious *lush, rich*
LKSHRT luxuriate *thrive, revel* luxuriated luxuriating
LKSHRYNS luxuriance *lushness*
LKSHRYNT luxuriant *lush*
LKSHRYNTS luxuriance *lushness*
LKSHRYS luxurious *lush, rich*
LKSHRYT luxuriate *thrive, revel* luxuriated luxuriating
LKSHSHP lectureship *sermon*
LKSK lexica (pl) *dictionary* lexicon
LKSKGRF lexicography

dictionary
LKSKGRFKL lexicographical (adj) *dictionary* lexicographically (adv)
LKSKGRFR lexicographer *dictionary*
LKSKL lexical (adj) *words* lexically (adv)
LKSKLD lexicality *words*
LKSKLG lexicology *words*
LKSKLJ lexicology *words*
LKSKLJST lexicologist *words*
LKSKLT lexicality *words*
LKSKLZ lexicalize *give meaning* lexicalized lexicalizing (Br) lexicalise
LKSKLZSHN lexicalization *meaning* (Br) lexicalisation
LKSKN lexicon *dictionary* lexica (or) lexicons
LKSL laxly *loose*
LKSM lexeme *word*
LKSMBRG Luxembourg (or) Luxemburg *province*
LKSMK lexemic *word*
LKSMTH locksmith *keys*
LKSMTHNG locksmithing *keys*
LKSNDR Alexander (the Great) *conqueror*
LKSNDR Alexandria *city*
LKSNDRN Alexandrian *of Alexandria*
LKSNDRN alexandrine *verse*
LKSNDRT alexandrite *mineral*
LKSNDRY Alexandria *city*
LKSNDRYN Alexandrian *of Alexandria*
LKSNGTN Lexington *city*
LKSNS laxness *looseness*
LKSPDL lickspittle *flattery*
LKSPRR Lake Superior *body of water*
LKSPRYR Lake Superior *body of water*
LKSPTL lickspittle *flattery*
LKSR elixir *cure-all*

Letters aren't doubled for single sounds: to find alley use **L** not **LL**. Use **Y** and **W** as hard sounds only: to find yellow use **YL**. (Br)=British spelling or usage. * See dictionary.

LKSS leukosis *disease*
leukoses

LKSS lexis *words* lexes

LKSSHN luxation *dislocation*

LKST laxity *looseness*

LKST leakiest *not tight*

LKST leukocyte *blood*

LKST locust *insect*

LKST luckiest *fortunate*

LKST ulexite *mineral*

LKSTCH lockstitch *sewing*

LKSTP lockstep *marching*

LKSTSS leukocytosis *blood*

LKSTV laxative *loosen*

LKSVT lixiviate *extract*
lixiviated lixiviating

LKSVYT lixiviate *extract*
lixiviated lixiviating

LKSY alexia *unable to read*

LKSZ lexes (pl) *words* lexis

LKT alley cat *animal*

LKT allocate *ration*
allocated allocating

LKT elect *vote*

LKT Lakota *Native American*
Lakota

LKT locate *find* located
locating

LKT locket *necklace*

LKT lockout (n) *bar from
entry* lock out (v)

LKT lookout (n) *watch* look
out (v)

LKTBL allocatable *rationed*

LKTBL electable *vote*

LKTBL locatable *found*

LKTBLD electability *vote*

LKTBLT electability *vote*

LKTBSLS lactobacillus
bacteria

LKTFRS lactiferous *milk*

LKTGNK lactogenic *milk*

LKTJNK lactogenic *milk*

LKTK lactic *milk*

LKTL lacteal *milk*

LKTM leukotomy *surgery*
leukotomies

LKTN lactone *ester*

LKTNK lactonic *ester*

LKTNSHTN Liechtenstein
country

LKTNSTN Liechtenstein

country

LKTR allocator *rationer*

LKTR elector *voter*

LKTR lector *reader*

LKTR lecture *sermonize*
lectured lecturing

LKTR locator *finder*

LKTRD electrode *circuit*

LKTRDLSS electrodialysis
purification

LKTRDNMKS
electrodynamics *physics*

LKTRDNMX
electrodynamics *physics*

LKTRDYLSS electrodialysis
purification

LKTRF electrify *wire*
electrified electrifying
electrifies

LKTRFD electrified *wired*

LKTRFKSHN electrification
wiring

LKTRGRM electrogram
tracing

LKTRK electric (or)
electrical (adj) *shocking,
electronic* electrically (adv)

LKTRKL electrical (or)
electric (adj) *shocking,
electronic* electrically (adv)

LKTRKMKL
electrochemical (adj)
chemical currents
electrochemically (adv)

LKTRKMSTR
electrochemistry *chemical
currents*

LKTRKNVLSV
electroconvulsive *shock*

LKTRKRDGRF
electrocardiograph *heart
instrument*

LKTRKRDGRM
electrocardiogram *heart
instrument*

LKTRKRDYGRF
electrocardiograph *heart
instrument*

LKTRKRDYGRM
electrocardiogram *heart
instrument*

LKTRKSHN electrocution

death by electricity

LKTRKT electrocute *execute*
electrocuted
electrocuting

LKTRKYSHN electrocution
death by electricity

LKTRKYT electrocute
execute electrocuted
electrocuting

LKTRL electoral *vote*

LKTRLDK electrolytic
conductive

LKTRLDKL electrolytically
conductive

LKTRLG electrology *hair
removal*

LKTRLJ electrology *hair
removal*

LKTRLJST electrologist *hair
removal*

LKTRLSS electrolysis *hair
removal*

LKTRLT electrolyte
conductor

LKTRLTK electrolytic
conductive

LKTRLTKL electrolytically
conductive

LKTRLZ electrolyze *remove
hair* electrolyzed
electrolyzing

LKTRMDR electrometer
detector

LKTRMDV electromotive
force

LKTRMGNDK
electromagnetic *attractor*

LKTRMGNT electromagnet
attractor

LKTRMGNTK
electromagnetic *magnet*

LKTRMGNTZM
electromagnetism *magnet*

LKTRMGRF
electromyograph *muscles*

LKTRMGRF
electromyography
muscles

LKTRMKNKL
electromechanical
converter

LKTRMTR electrometer

detector
LKTRMTV electromotive *force*
LKTRMYGRF electromyograph *muscles*
LKTRMYGRF electromyography *muscles*
LKTRN electron *particle*
LKTRN lectern *book stand*
LKTRNK electronic *electricity*
LKTRNKL electronically *electricity*
LKTRNKS electronics *physics*
LKTRNSFLGRF electroencephalograph *brain instrument*
LKTRNSFLGRM electroencephalogram *brain instrument*
LKTRNX electronics *physics*
LKTRPLT electroplate *coating*
LKTRQSHN electrocution *death by electricity*
LKTRQT electrocute *execute* electrocuted electrocuting
LKTRR lecturer *sermon*
LKTRSD electricity *current* electricities
LKTRSHK electroshock *electricity*
LKTRSHN electrician *wirer*
LKTRSKP electroscope *radiation*
LKTRST electricity *current* electricities
LKTRSTDK electrostatic *electricity*
LKTRSTDKL electrostatically *electricity*
LKTRSTDKS electrostatics *electricity*
LKTRSTDX electrostatics *electricity*
LKTRSTTK electrostatic *electricity*
LKTRSTTKL electrostatically *electricity*

LKTRSTTKS electrostatics *electricity*
LKTRSTTX electrostatics *electricity*
LKTRT electorate *voters*
LKTRTHRP electrotherapy *treatment*
LKTRTP electrotype *copy*
LKTS lactase *enzyme*
LKTS lactose *sugar*
LKTSHN lactation *milk*
LKTSHP lectureship *sermon*
LKTSPLT lickety-split *fast*
LKTT lactate *milk* lactated lactating
LKTV elective *chosen*
LKTYL lacteal *milk*
LKV alcove *niche*
LKVD alcoved *niched*
LKWD liquid *fluid*
LKWD locoweed *plant*
LKWDD liquidity *convert, cash*
LKWDDR liquidator *convert, pay*
LKWDL liquidly *fluid*
LKWDNS liquidness *fluidity*
LKWDSHN liquidation *convert, pay*
LKWDT liquidate *convert, pay* liquidated liquidating
LKWDT liquidity *convert, cash*
LKWDTR liquidator *convert, pay*
LKWF liquefy *make fluid* liquefied liquefying liquefies
LKWFD liquefied *made fluid*
LKWFKSHN liquefaction *make fluid*
LKWFR liquefier *make fluid*
LKWFYR liquefier *make fluid*
LKWNS eloquence *expressive speech*
LKWNT eloquent *expressive speech*
LKWNTL eloquently *expressive speech*
LKWNTS eloquence *expressive speech*
LKWRM lukewarm *tepid*

LKWSD loquacity *talkative*
LKWSHN liquation *separation*
LKWSHS loquacious *talkative*
LKWSHSNS loquaciousness *talkative*
LKWSNT liquescent *melting*
LKWST loquacity *talkative*
LKWT aliquot *fraction*
LKWT liquate *separate* liquated liquating
LKWT loquat *fruit*
LKWZ likewise *similarly*
LKYBRSHN lucubration *study*
LKYL locule *plant cell*
LKYL loculi (pl) *chamber* loculus
LKYLNT luculent *clear*
LKYLNTL luculently *clear*
LKYLS loculus *chamber* loculi
LKYN lacuna *gap* lacunae (or) lacunas
LKYR leakier *not tight*
LKYR liqueur *sweet alcohol*
LKYR luckier *fortunate*
LKYSHN allocution *formal speech*
LKYSHN elocution *public speaking*
LKYSHN locution *style of speech*
LKYSHNR elocutionary *public speaking*
LKYSHNR illocutionary *effect of speech*
LKYST leakiest *not tight*
LKYST luckiest *fortunate*
LKZNDR alexander (often *capitalized*) *cocktail*
LKZR alcazar *fortress*
LL allele *gene*
LL alleluia (or) hallelujah (interj) *rejoice*
LL ileal *intestinal*
LL lily *flower* lilies
LL lisle *thread*
LL loll *droop, lounge*
LL lolly (Br) *candy* lollies
LL lowly *humble, base* lowlier

Letters aren't doubled for single sounds: to find alley use **L** not **LL**. Use **Y** and **W** as hard sounds only: to find yellow use **YL**. (Br)=British spelling or usage. * See dictionary.

lowliest

LL loyal (adj) *faithful* loyally (adv)

LL lull (v) *soothe* (n) *calm*

LL lulu (slang) *remarkable one*

LLB lullaby (v) *sing softly* lullabied lullabying lullabies

LLB lullaby (n) *song* lullabies

LLD loyalty *faithfulness* loyalties

LLF low-life (adj) *no status* lowlife (n) lowlifes

LLHWT lily-white *pure*

LLK allelic *gene*

LLK lilac *flower, color*

LLK ololiuqui *vine*

LLLVRD lily-livered *cowardly*

LLMRF allelomorph *gene*

LLMRFK allelomorphic *gene*

LLMRFZM allelomorphism *gene*

LLN lowland *no elevation*

LLND lowland *no elevation*

LLNDR lowlander *inhabitant*

LLNG low-lying *near earth*

LLNS lowliness *humble, base*

LLNT ululant *wailing*

LLP lollop *bob, bound, loll*

LLPD lily pad *leaf*

LLPP lollipop (or) lollypop *candy*

LLPSHN lilliputian (often capitalized) *small*

LLPTH allelopathy *growth suppression*

LLPTHK allelopathic *growth suppression*

LLPYSHN lilliputian (often capitalized) *small*

LLR loller *lax one*

LLR lowlier *humble, base*

LLS lawless *illegal*

LLSHN ululation *wail*

LLST lowliest *humble, base*

LLST loyalist *faithful one*

LLT lilt *song, movement*

LLT lowlight *dim*

LLT loyalty *faithfulness* loyalties

LLT ululate *wail* ululated ululating

LLTN lilting *cheerful*

LLTNG lilting *cheerful*

LLTNGL liltingly *cheerful*

LLTNGNS liltingness *cheerful*

LLVL low-level *unimportant*

LLWT lily-white *pure*

LLY alleluia (or) hallelujah (interj) *rejoice*

LLYK ololiuqui *vine*

LLYNG low-lying *near earth*

LLYR lowlier *humble, base*

LLYST lowliest *humble, base*

LLZM allelism *gene*

LM Alamo (the) *fort in San Antonio*

LM allium *herb*

LM alum *chemical*

LM elemi *resin*

LM elm *tree*

LM ileum *intestine* ilea

LM ilium *bone* ilia

LM lam (v) *thrash, flee* lammed lamming

LM lam (n) *flight*

LM lama *monk*

LM lamb *sheep*

LM lame (v) *disable* lamed laming

LM lamé *fabric*

LM lame (adj) *weak* lamer lamest

LM lame (n) *plate, square*

LM lemma *flower* lemmas (or) lemmata

LM let me *allow me*

LM Lima *city*

LM limb *appendage, branch*

LM lime (v) *smear* limed liming

LM lime (n) *fruit, calcium*

LM limey *sailor* limeys

LM limn *describe* limned limning

LM limo (abbr) *limousine* limos

LM limy *like lime, gummy* limier limiest

LM llama *animal*

LM loam *soil*

LM loamy *soil*

LM loom (n) *frame* (v) *appear large*

LM oleum *oil* olea

LM oleum *corrosive* oleums

LM ulema (or) ulama *mullahs*

LMB limba *tree*

LMB limbo *place of uncertainty, dance* limbos

LMBG lumbago *rheumatism*

LMBK alembic *distill*

LMBK limbic *brain*

LMBLST lambaste (or) lambast *attack*

LMBN lima bean *vegetable*

LMBNC lambency *flickering* lambencies

LMBNS lambency *flickering* lambencies

LMBNT lambent *flickering*

LMBNTC lambency *flickering* lambencies

LMBNTL lambently *flickering*

LMBNTS lambency *flickering* lambencies

LMBR limber *flexible*

LMBR lumbar *back bone*

LMBR lumber (n) *wood* (v) *gait, saw, encumber*

LMBRGR Limburger *cheese*

LMBRJK lumberjack *logger*

LMBRKN lambrequin *scarf*

LMBRMN lumberman *logger* lumbermen

LMBRN lamebrain *bonehead*

LMBRND lamebrained *boneheaded*

LMBRNS limberness *flexibility*

LMBRT lambert *brightness*

LMBRYRD lumberyard *wood*

LMBS limbus *eye*

LMBSKRL lumbosacral *anatomy*

LMBST lambaste (or) lambast *attack*

LMD à la mode *stylish, ice cream*

LMD alameda *park*

LMD almighty *powerful*

LMD lambda *Greek letter*

LMD lamed *Hebrew letter*

LMD lemmata (pl) *heading* lemma

Use letters that best describe the sounds you hear and omit the vowels. Use **S** or **K** instead of **C**: to find circle use **SRKL**. Use **J** to find joy, **JM** to find gem and **G** to find go.

LMD limbed *appendage, branch*
LMD limeade *beverage*
LMD old maid *spinster*
LMDBL illimitable (adj) *without bounds* illimitably (adv)
LMDBL limitable *with bounds*
LMDD limited *restricted*
LMDK lame duck *politics*
LMDN amandine *almonds*
LMDNG limiting *restrictive*
LMDNS almightiness *power*
LMDR limiter *restrict*
LMF lymph *plasma*
LMFD lymphoid *tissue*
LMFDK lymphatic *plasma, sluggish*
LMFM lymphoma *tumor* lymphomas (or) lymphomata
LMFMD lymphomata (pl) *tumor* lymphoma
LMFMT lymphomata (pl) *tumor* lymphoma
LMFND lymph node *tissue*
LMFSDK lymphocytic *blood cell*
LMFST lymphocyte *blood cell*
LMFSTK lymphocytic *blood cell*
LMFSTSS lymphocytosis *infection*
LMFTK lymphatic *plasma, sluggish*
LMJ Limoges *city*
LMKN lawmaking *legislating*
LMKNG lawmaking *legislating*
LMKR lawmaker *legislator*
LMKS lummox *clumsy one* lummoxes
LML lamella *gills* lamellae
LML limuli (pl) *crab* limulus
LMLBRNGK lamellibranch *mollusk* lamellibranchs
LMLBRNK lamellibranch *mollusk* lamellibranchs
LMLFRM lamelliform *plate*
LMLKRN lamellicorn *beetle*

LMLR lamellar *gills*
LMLS limbless *no appendages*
LMLS limulus *crab* limuli
LMLT lamellate *gills*
LMLT limelight *spotlight*
LMMDR alma mater *school*
LMMTR alma mater *school*
LMN alimony *payment* alimonies
LMN allemande *dance*
LMN almond *nut*
LMN alumna *graduate (f)* alumnae
LMN alumni (pl) *graduate (m or f)* alumnus
LMN illumine *enlighten, make clear, decorate* illumined illumining
LMN lamina *layer* laminae (or) laminas
LMN lawman *sheriff* lawmen
LMN layman *non-expert* laymen
LMN lemon *fruit*
LMN lemony *tart*
LMN limen *threshold*
LMN lo mein *food*
LMN lumen *cavity, light unit* lumens
LMN oilman *worker* oilmen
LMNBL lamentable (adj) *unfortunate* lamentably (adv)
LMNC lemnisci (pl) *fiber* lemniscus
LMND allemande *dance*
LMND almond *nut*
LMND almond-eyed *slant-eyed*
LMND Illuminati *intellectuals*
LMND lemonade *beverage*
LMNDD almond-eyed *slant-eyed*
LMNDD laminated *layered*
LMNDD low-minded *base*
LMNDR eliminator *end, expel*
LMNDR illuminator *enlighten, make clear, decorate*
LMNDR laminator *layer*
LMNDT almandite *mineral*

LMNDV eliminative *end, expel*
LMNDV illuminative *light*
LMNFRS luminiferous *light*
LMNG lemming *animal*
LMNG limning *describing*
LMNGRS lemongrass *herb*
LMNK Alemannic *dialect*
LMNK almanac *reference*
LMNKDM laminectomy *surgery* laminectomies
LMNKTM laminectomy *surgery* laminectomies
LMNL elemental (adj) *basic* elementally (adv)
LMNL liminal *perceptible*
LMNL lumenal *cavity, light unit*
LMNM aluminum *metal* (Br) aluminium
LMNN limning *describing*
LMNNG limning *describing*
LMNNS luminance *light*
LMNNT illuminant *light*
LMNNTS luminance *light*
LMNR alimentary *food*
LMNR almoner *beggar*
LMNR elementary *basic*
LMNR limner *describer*
LMNR luminaire *light*
LMNR luminaria *candle* luminarias
LMNR luminary *brilliant one* luminaries
LMNRD ill-mannered *rude*
LMNRNS elementariness *basic*
LMNRY luminaria *candle* luminarias
LMNS aluminous *metal compound*
LMNS alumnus *graduate* alumni
LMNS lemnisci (pl) *fiber* lemniscus
LMNS luminesce *glow* luminesced luminescing
LMNS luminous *light*
LMNSD luminosity *light* luminosities
LMNSHN elimination *end, expel*

Letters aren't doubled for single sounds: to find alley use **L** not **LL**. Use **Y** and **W** as hard sounds only: to find yellow use **YL**. (Br)=British spelling or usage. * See dictionary.

LMNSHN illumination *light*
LMNSHN lamination *layer*
LMNSK lemnisci (pl) *fiber* lemniscus
LMNSKS lemniscus *fiber* lemnisci
LMNSKT lemniscate *curve*
LMNSL luminously *light*
LMNSM illuminism *enlightenment*
LMNSNS luminescence *light*
LMNSNS luminousness *light*
LMNSNT luminescent *light*
LMNSNTS luminescence *light*
LMNST illuminist *enlightenment*
LMNST luminist *painter*
LMNST luminosity *light* luminosities
LMNT ailment *sickness*
LMNT aliment *food*
LMNT aluminate *metal compound*
LMNT element *chemical, ingredient*
LMNT eliminate *end, expel* eliminated eliminating
LMNT illuminate *enlighten, make clear, decorate* illuminated illuminating
LMNT Illuminati *intellectuals*
LMNT lament (v) *regret, wail* (n) *complaint*
LMNT laminate *make layers* laminated laminating
LMNT loment *fruit*
LMNTBL lamentable (adj) *unfortunate* lamentably (adv)
LMNTD laminated *layered*
LMNTL elemental (adj) *basic* elementally (adv)
LMNTR alimentary *food*
LMNTR elementary *basic*
LMNTR eliminator *end, expel*
LMNTR illuminator *enlighten, make clear, decorate*
LMNTR laminator *layer*

LMNTRL elementarily *basic*
LMNTRNS elementariness *basic*
LMNTSHN alimentation *food*
LMNTSHN lamentation *regret, wail*
LMNTV eliminative *end, expel*
LMNTV illuminative *light*
LMNYM aluminium *(Br) aluminum*
LMNZM illuminism *enlightenment*
LMNZM luminism *painting*
LMP lamp *lantern*
LMP limp (v) *walk lamely* (n) *gait* (adj) *weary*
LMP limpa *bread*
LMP lump *mass*
LMP lumpy *with masses* lumpier lumpiest
LMP Olympia *city*
LMPBLK lampblack *soot*
LMPD limpid *clear*
LMPD olympiad *(often capitalized) time interval*
LMPDD limpidity *clearness*
LMPDL limpidly *clear*
LMPDNS limpidness *clearness*
LMPDT limpidity *clearness*
LMPK Olympic *lofty, games*
LMPKDM lumpectomy *surgery* lumpectomies
LMPKGMZ Olympic Games *contests*
LMPKS Olympics *contests*
LMPKTM lumpectomy *surgery* lumpectomies
LMPL limply *weary, not stiff*
LMPL lumpily *with masses*
LMPLT lamplight *illumination*
LMPN lampoon *ridicule*
LMPN Olympian *lofty, games*
LMPNR lampooner *ridicule* lampoonery
LMPNS limpness *weary, not stiff*
LMPNS lumpiness *with masses*
LMPR lamprey *eel* lampreys

LMPR lempira *money*
LMPR lumpier *more masses*
LMPRDNT all-important *vital*
LMPRSTD limp-wristed *effiminate*
LMPRTNT all-important *vital*
LMPS Olympus *mountain*
LMPSH lumpish *with masses*
LMPST lamppost *streetlight*
LMPST lumpiest *most masses*
LMPT limpet *mollusk*
LMPX Olympics *contests*
LMPY Olympia *city*
LMPYD olympiad *(often capitalized) time interval*
LMPYN Olympian *lofty, games*
LMPYR lumpier *more masses*
LMPYST lumpiest *most masses*
LMR lamer *crippled*
LMR lemur *animal*
LMR limier *like lime, gummy*
LMR limner *describer*
LMRF allomorph *word form*
LMRFK allomorphic *word form*
LMRFSM allomorphism *word form*
LMRFZM allomorphism *word form*
LMRJRN oleomargarine *spread*
LMRK limerick *verse*
LMRKN all-American *U.S. best*
LMRT alumroot *herb*
LMSH Limoges *city*
LMSKN lambskin *leather*
LMSN limaçon *curve*
LMSNR eleemosynary *charity*
LMSR lamasery *monastery* lamaseries
LMST almost *nearly*
LMST lamest *crippled*
LMST limiest *like lime, gummy*
LMSTN limestone *rock*

Use letters that best describe the sounds you hear and omit the vowels. Use **S** or **K** instead of **C**: to find circle use **SRKL**. Use **J** to find joy, **JM** to find gem and **G** to find go.

LMT almighty *powerful*
LMT lemmata (pl) *heading* lemma
LMT limit *end*
LMTBL illimitable (adj) *without bounds* illimitably (adv)
LMTBL limitable *with bounds*
LMTD limited *restricted*
LMTDV limitative *restricting*
LMTLS limitless *no bounds*
LMTN limiting *restrictive*
LMTNG limiting *restrictive*
LMTNS almightiness *power*
LMTR limiter *restrict*
LMTSHN limitation *restriction*
LMTTV limitative *restricting*
LMX lummox *clumsy one* lummoxes
LMYL limuli (pl) *crab* limulus
LMYLS limulus *crab* limuli
LMYR limier *like lime, gummy*
LMYST limiest *like lime, gummy*
LMZ alms *charity*
LMZ Lamaze *birth*
LMZH Limoges *city*
LMZN limousine *sedan*
LMZNR eleemosynary *charity*
LN A-line *skirt style*
LN ailing *hurting, sick*
LN alien *foreign*
LN align *straighten*
LN alone *solitary*
LN élan *spirit*
LN eolian *wind*
LN Illinois *US State*
LN island *small land mass*
LN lain *position*
LN Lanai *island*
LN lanai *porch*
LN land (v) *disembark, secure, alight* (n) *country*
LN lane *path*
LN lauan *timber*
LN lawn *grassy area*
LN lean (v) *incline* (adj) *skinny* (n) *muscle*
LN lend *loan* lent lending

LN leno *weave*
LN leone *money* leones (or) leone
LN liana *vine*
LN lie-in *protest*
LN lien *debt*
LN line (v) *draw, align, fill** lined lining
LN line (n) *string, wrinkle, family**
LN lino *linoleum* linos
LN lion *animal* lions
LN llano *plain* llanos
LN loan *borrow*
LN loin *body area*
LN lone *solitary*
LN loon *bird, simpleton*
LN loony *crazy* loonies loonier looniest
LN luna *moon*
LN lune *arc*
LN Lyon *city*
LN old-line *traditional*
LN uhlan *cavalry*
LN ulna *bone*
LNBKNG linebacking *football*
LNBKR linebacker *football*
LNBL alienable *transferable*
LNBL loanable *borrow*
LNBLD alienability *transferability*
LNBLT alienability *transferability*
LNBN loony bin *madhouse*
LNBRD linebred *breeding*
LNBRDN linebreeding *mating*
LNBRDNG linebreeding *mating*
LNBRGR Limburger *cheese*
LNC lunacy *insanity* lunacies
LNCD linseed *flaxseed*
LNCDL linseed oil *flaxseed*
LNCDYL linseed oil *flaxseed*
LNCH launch *take off* launches
LNCH lunch *meal* lunches
LNCH lynch *hang*
LNCHN luncheon *meal*
LNCHNGPD launching pad

rocket
LNCHNPD launching pad *rocket*
LNCHNT luncheonette *diner*
LNCHPD launchpad *rocket*
LNCHPN linchpin *lock*
LNCHR launcher *thrower*
LNCHR lyncher *hangman*
LNCHRD ill-natured *surly*
LNCHRM lunchroom *diner*
LNCHTM lunchtime *noon*
LND eland *animal* eland
LND island *small land mass*
LND land (v) *disembark, secure, alight* (n) *country*
LND landau *carriage*
LND lend *loan* lent lending
LND lenity *mercy*
LND lindy *dance*
LND low-end *cheap*
LND Luanda *city*
LNDD landed *estate*
LNDFL landfall *sighting*
LNDFL landfill *trash*
LNDGRB landgrab *gain*
LNDGRBR land-grabber *acquirer*
LNDHLDN landholding *property*
LNDHLDNG landholding *property*
LNDHLDR landholder *owner*
LNDLBR landlubber *on land*
LNDLD landlady *manager* landladies
LNDLKT landlocked *enclosed*
LNDLRD landlord *manager*
LNDLS landless *without country*
LNDLS lend-lease *goods transfer*
LNDLT landaulet *carriage*
LNDM line item (n) *budget* line-item (adj)
LNDMN land mine *weapon*
LNDMRK landmark *structure*
LNDMS landmass *continent*
LNDN landing *alighting, stairway*
LNDN linden *tree*

Letters aren't doubled for single sounds: to find alley use **L** not **LL**. Use **Y** and **W** as hard sounds only: to find yellow use **YL**. (Br)=British spelling or usage. * See dictionary.

LNDN London *city*

LNDNG landing *alighting, stairway*

LNDNR landowner *property*

LNDPR land-poor *excess acreage*

LNDR alienator *estranger*

LNDR islander *inhabitant*

LNDR lander *vehicle*

LNDR launder *wash*

LNDR laundry *washroom* laundries

LNDR oleander *plant*

LNDRMN laundryman *worker* laundrymen

LNDRMT Laundromat *(trademark) coin laundry*

LNDRN line drawing *sketch*

LNDRNG line drawing *sketch*

LNDRS laundress *woman*

LNDRT launderette *wash*

LNDRV line drive *hit*

LNDSKP landscape *garden* landscaped landscaping

LNDSKPR landscaper *gardener*

LNDSKPST landscapist *painter*

LNDSLD landslide *avalanche, victory* (Br) landslip

LNDSLP landslip *avalanche, victory*

LNDV lenitive *soothing*

LNDWRD landward *toward land*

LNDZMN landsman *countryman* landsmen

LNFL landfall *sighting*

LNFL landfill *trash*

LNFND lymph node *tissue*

LNFSH lionfish *fish*

LNFSR line officer *staff*

LNG ailing *hurting, sick*

LNG along *in tandem*

LNG langue *communication*

LNG lanugo *hair*

LNG ling *fish, plant*

LNG lingo *slang, jargon* lingoes

LNG long *(adj) sizable, extended* longer longest

LNG long *(v) yearn (adv) far, time*

LNG lung *breathe*

LNG lying *fib, position*

LNG oolong *tea*

LNGB longbow *weapon*

LNGBNT langbeinite *mineral*

LNGBT longboat *ship*

LNGDRNT long-drawn-out *extended*

LNGDSDNS long-distance *(adj, adv) faraway* long distance (n)

LNGDSDNTS long-distance *(adj, adv) faraway* long distance (n)

LNGDSTNS long-distance *(adj, adv) faraway* long distance (n)

LNGDSTNTS long-distance *(adj, adv) faraway* long distance (n)

LNGFL lungful *breath*

LNGFSH lungfish *fish*

LNGG lingo *slang, jargon* lingoes

LNGG long-ago *(adj) past* long ago (n)

LNGGLN Long Island *New York*

LNGGLND Long Island *New York*

LNGGN longan *fruit*

LNGGNBR lingonberry *cranberry* lingonberries

LNGGR languor *sluggish*

LNGGR langur *monkey*

LNGGR linger *wait*

LNGGR longer *length, time*

LNGGR longueur *dull section* longueurs

LNGGRNGL lingeringly *slowly*

LNGGRR lingerer *wait*

LNGGRS languorous *sluggish*

LNGGRSL languorously *sluggishly*

LNGGSHN elongation *extension*

LNGGST langouste *lobster*

LNGGST longest *length, time*

LNGGSTN langoustine *lobster*

LNGGT elongate *extend* elongated elongating

LNGGW lingua *tongue* linguae

LNGGWD languid *listless*

LNGGWFRNGK lingua franca *language* lingua francas (or) linguae francae

LNGGWFRNK lingua franca *language*

LNGGWJ language *communication*

LNGGWL lingual (adj) *tongue* lingually (adv)

LNGGWN linguini *food*

LNGGWR longueur *dull section* longueurs

LNGGWSDK linguistic *language*

LNGGWSDKL linguistically *language*

LNGGWSDKS linguistics *language*

LNGGWSDX linguistics *language*

LNGGWSH languish *suffer neglect*

LNGGWSHMNT languishment *pining*

LNGGWSHR languisher *piner*

LNGGWST linguist *language*

LNGGWSTK linguistic *language*

LNGGWSTKL linguistically *language*

LNGGWSTKS linguistics *language*

LNGGWSTX linguistics *language*

LNGHL long-haul (adj) *distance* long haul (n)

LNGHN longhand *writing*

LNGHND longhand *writing*

LNGHR longhair *intellectual, hippie, cat*

LNGHRD longhaired *intellectual, hippie, cat*

Use letters that best describe the sounds you hear and omit the vowels. Use **S** or **K** instead of **C**: to find circle use **SRKL**. Use **J** to find joy, **JM** to find gem and **G** to find go.

LNGHRN longhorn *cattle*
LNGHRND long-horned *antennae, antlers*
LNGHS longhouse *dwelling*
LNGJNZ long johns *underwear*
LNGK elenchi (pl) *refutation* elenchus
LNGK lank *thin, limp*
LNGK lanky *tall and slim* lankier lankiest
LNGK link *connect*
LNGKD lingcod *fish*
LNGKD linked *connected*
LNGKHD lunkhead *dolt*
LNGKJ linkage *connection*
LNGKL lankly *leanly*
LNGKN Lincoln *US President, city*
LNGKNG linking *connecting*
LNGKNS lankiness *tall and slim*
LNGKNS lankness *tall and slim*
LNGKR lankier *tall and slim*
LNGKR lunker *large one*
LNGKS elenchus *refutation* elenchi
LNGKS links *golf course, dunes*
LNGKS lynx *animal* lynx (or) lynxes
LNGKSMN linksman *golfer* linksmen
LNGKST lankiest *tall and slim*
LNGKTH length *dimension* lengths
LNGKTH lengthy *long* lengthier lengthiest
LNGKTHL lengthily *long*
LNGKTHN lengthen *make longer*
LNGKTHNS lengthiness *long*
LNGKTHR lengthier *longer*
LNGKTHST lengthiest *longest*
LNGKTHWZ lengthways *longitudinal*
LNGKTHWZ lengthwise *longitudinal*

LNGKTHYR lengthier *longer*
LNGKTHYST lengthiest *longest*
LNGKYR lankier *tall and slim*
LNGKYST lankiest *tall and slim*
LNGL langley *solar unit* langleys
LNGLN Long Island *New York*
LNGLN longline *fishing*
LNGLND Long Island *New York*
LNGLNG ylang-ylang *tree*
LNGLNNG long-lining *fishing*
LNGLNR long-liner *boat*
LNGLVD long-lived *old*
LNGN longan *fruit*
LNGN longing *craving*
LNGNBR lingonberry *cranberry* lingonberries
LNGNG longing *craving*
LNGPLN long-playing *record*
LNGPLNG long-playing *record*
LNGPLYNG long-playing *record*
LNGR languor *sluggish*
LNGR langur *monkey*
LNGR linger *wait*
LNGR longer *length, time*
LNGR longueur *dull section* longueurs
LNGR lunger *tubercular*
LNGRB landgrab *gain*
LNGRBR land-grabber *acquirer*
LNGRN long-run (adj) *time* long run (n)
LNGRNGL lingeringly *slowly*
LNGRNJ long-range *distance*
LNGRR lingerer *wait*
LNGRS languorous *sluggish*
LNGRSL languorously *sluggishly*
LNGSD alongside *next to*
LNGSDD longsighted *farsighted*
LNGSDDNS

longsightedness *farsighted*
LNGSFRN long-suffering *patient*
LNGSFRNG long-suffering *patient*
LNGSH longish *length*
LNGSHN elongation *extension*
LNGSHR alongshore *coastal*
LNGSHRMN longshoreman *dockworker* longshoremen
LNGSPR longspur *bird*
LNGST langouste *lobster*
LNGST longest *length, time*
LNGSTD longsighted *farsighted*
LNGSTDNS

longsightedness *farsighted*
LNGSTN langoustine *lobster*
LNGSTNDN long-standing *continual*
LNGSTNDNG long-standing *continual*
LNGT elongate *extend* elongated elongating
LNGT linked *connected*
LNGTH length *dimension* lengths
LNGTH lengthy *long* lengthier lengthiest
LNGTHL lengthily *long*
LNGTHN lengthen *make longer*
LNGTHNS lengthiness *long*
LNGTHR lengthier *longer*
LNGTHST lengthiest *longest*
LNGTHWZ lengthways *longitudinal*
LNGTHWZ lengthwise *longitudinal*
LNGTHYR lengthier *longer*
LNGTHYST lengthiest *longest*
LNGTM longtime *lasting*
LNGTN long ton *weight*
LNGTRM long-term *over time*
LNGW lingua *tongue* linguae
LNGWD languid *listless*
LNGWFRNGK lingua franca

Letters aren't doubled for single sounds: to find alley use **L** not **LL**. Use **Y** and **W** as hard sounds only: to find yellow use **YL**. (Br)=British spelling or usage. * See dictionary.

language
LNGWFRNK lingua franca
language
LNGWJ language
communication
LNGWL lingual (adj) tongue
lingually (adv)
LNGWN linguini food
LNGWNDD long-winded
wordy
LNGWNDDL long-windedly
wordy
LNGWNDDNS long-
windedness wordy
LNGWR longueur dull
section longueurs
LNGWRM lungworm
parasite
LNGWRT lungwort plant
LNGWSDK linguistic
language
LNGWSDKL linguistically
language
LNGWSDKS linguistics
language
LNGWSDX linguistics
language
LNGWSH languish suffer
neglect
LNGWSHMNT
languishment pining
LNGWSHR languisher piner
LNGWST linguist language
LNGWSTK linguistic
language
LNGWSTKL linguistically
language
LNGWSTKS linguistics
language
LNGWSTX linguistics
language
LNGX lynx animal lynx (or)
lynxes
LNGXMN linksman golfer
linksmen
LNGZN auld lang syne good
old times
LNHL line-haul transport
LNHLDN landholding
property
LNHLDNG landholding
property

LNHLDR landholder owner
LNHRDD lionhearted brave
LNHRTD lionhearted brave
LNJ alienage status
LNJ linage number of lines
LNJ lineage family
LNJ lounge (v) idle lounged
lounging
LNJ lounge (n) room, couch
LNJ lunge thrust lunged
lunging
LNJJ line judge referee
LNJNS lanuginous downy
LNJR lingerie underwear
LNJR lounger idler, couch
LNJR lunger thruster
LNJRN longeron fuselage
LNJTD longitude vertical line
LNJTDNL longitudinal (adj)
vertical line longitudinally
(adv)
LNJTYD longitude vertical
line
LNJTYDNL longitudinal
(adj) vertical line
longitudinally (adv)
LNJVD longevity lifetime
LNJVT longevity lifetime
LNJWR loungewear clothing
LNK alnico alloy
LNK elenchi (pl) refutation
elenchus
LNK lank thin, limp
LNK lanky tall and slim
lankier lankiest
LNK lentic still waters
LNK link connect
LNKD lingcod fish
LNKD linked connected
LNKHD lunkhead dolt
LNKJ linkage connection
LNKL lankly leanly
LNKL lenticule lens
LNKLR lenticular lens
LNKLSV all-inclusive
complete
LNKLTH loincloth clothing
LNKLZV all-inclusive
complete
LNKN Lincoln US President,
city
LNKNG linking connecting

LNKNS lankiness tall and
slim
LNKNS lankness tall and
slim
LNKR lankier tall and slim
LNKR lunker large one
LNKS elenchus refutation
elenchi
LNKS links golf course, dunes
LNKS lynx animal lynx (or)
lynxes
LNKSMN linksman golfer
linksmen
LNKST lankiest tall and slim
LNKT linecut engraving
LNKT linked connected
LNKT linocut print
LNKTH length dimension
lengths
LNKTH lengthy long
lengthier lengthiest
LNKTHL lengthily long
LNKTHN lengthen make
longer
LNKTHNS lengthiness long
LNKTHR lengthier longer
LNKTHST lengthiest longest
LNKTHWZ lengthways
longitudinal
LNKTHWZ lengthwise
longitudinal
LNKTHYR lengthier longer
LNKTHYST lengthiest
longest
LNKYL lenticule lens
LNKYLR lenticular lens
LNKYR lankier tall and slim
LNKYST lankiest tall and
slim
LNL alanyl chemical
LNL alienly foreign
LNL leanly slender
LNL lentil food
LNL lineal (adj) line lineally
(adv)
LNL lonely solitary lonelier
loneliest
LNL lunule crescent
LNLBR landlubber on land
LNLD landlady manager
landladies
LNLKT landlocked enclosed

Use letters that best describe the sounds you hear and omit the vowels. Use **S** or **K** instead of **C**: to find circle use **SRKL**. Use **J** to find joy, **JM** to find gem and **G** to find go.

LNLM linoleum *flooring* (Br) lino
LNLN lanolin *grease*
LNLNS loneliness *solitary*
LNLR lonelier *solitary*
LNLRD landlord *manager*
LNLS landless *without country*
LNLS lend-lease *goods transfer*
LNLST loneliest *solitary*
LNLYM linoleum *flooring*
LNLYR lonelier *solitary*
LNLYST loneliest *solitary*
LNMN land mine *weapon*
LNMN lineman *wire, football* linemen
LNMNT alignment *position*
LNMNT lineament *feature*
LNMNT liniment *medication*
LNMR lawn mower *grass cutter*
LNMRK landmark *structure*
LNMS landmass *continent*
LNN alanine *amino acid*
LNN El Niño *weather*
LNN leaning *tendency*
LNN leonine *lion*
LNN linen *fabric*
LNN lining *inner surface*
LNNG leaning *tendency*
LNNG lining *inner surface*
LNNGRD Leningrad *city*
LNNS lenience *mercy* leniency
LNNT lenient *merciful*
LNNTL leniently *merciful*
LNNTS lenience *mercy* leniency
LNNY El Niño *weather*
LNP lagniappe *gift*
LNP line up (v) *make a list or row* lineup (n)
LNPR land-poor *excess acreage*
LNQL lenticule *lens*
LNQLR lenticular *lens*
LNR alienor *transferor*
LNR aligner *straightener*
LNR eyeliner *makeup*
LNR lanner *bird*
LNR linear *line, math*

LNR liner *inner surface, ship, lines**
LNR loaner *replacement*
LNR loner *solitary one*
LNR loonier *crazy*
LNR lunar *moon*
LNR ulnar *bone*
LNRBRD linerboard *cardboard*
LNRDDVNCH Leonardo da Vinci *artist*
LNRN lantern *lamp* (Br) lanthorn
LNRT lanneret *bird*
LNRZ linearize *make lines* linearized linearizing (Br) linearise
LNRZSHN linearization *line, math* (Br) linearisation
LNS alienness *foreign*
LNS alliance *bond*
LNS aloneness *solitude*
LNS illness *sickness* illnesses
LNS lance *spear* lanced lancing
LNS leanness *slender*
LNS lenis *speech*
LNS lens *curved glass, eye* lenses
LNS lioness *lion (f)* lionesses
LNS lunacy *insanity* lunacies
LNSD linseed *flaxseed*
LNSDL linseed oil *flaxseed*
LNSDYL linseed oil *flaxseed*
LNSHN alienation *estrangement*
LNSHN lenition *speech*
LNSHN lineation *outline*
LNSHN lunation *moon*
LNSHR lingerie *underwear*
LNSHRK loan shark *lender*
LNSHRKNG loan-sharking *lending*
LNSKP landscape *garden* landscaped landscaping
LNSKPR landscaper *gardener*
LNSKPST landscapist *painter*
LNSKR line score *baseball*

LNSKWL line squall *storm*
LNSL lenticel *pore*
LNSLD landslide *avalanche, victory* (Br) landslip
LNSLP landslip *avalanche, victory*
LNSM lonesome *sad*
LNSMN linesman *referee* linesmen
LNSN alençon *lace*
LNSNG Lansing *city*
LNSNG linsang *animal*
LNSQL line squall *storm*
LNSR lancer *cavalry*
LNST alienist *psychologist*
LNST lancet *knife*
LNST looniest *crazy*
LNSTRM line storm *storm*
LNT alienate *estrange* alienated alienating
LNT all-night *dusk to dawn*
LNT lean-to *shanty* lean-tos
LNT lenity *mercy*
LNT Lent *holy season*
LNT lent *(v-past) lend*
LNT lento *music*
LNT line out *outline, baseball*
LNT linnet *bird*
LNT lint *fuzz*
LNT lunate *(adj) crescent*
LNT lunette *(n) crescent*
LNTH length *dimension* lengths
LNTH lengthy *long* lengthier lengthiest
LNTHL lengthily *long*
LNTHN lengthen *make longer*
LNTHNM lanthanum *element*
LNTHNS lengthiness *long*
LNTHR lengthier *longer*
LNTHRN lanthorn (Br) *lantern*
LNTHS ailanthus *tree*
LNTHST lengthiest *longest*
LNTHWZ lengthways *longitudinal*
LNTHWZ lengthwise *longitudinal*
LNTHYR lengthier *longer*
LNTHYST lengthiest *longest*
LNTK lentic *still waters*

LNTK lunatic *crazy*
LNTKL lenticule *lens*
LNTKLR lenticular *lens*
LNTKYL lenticule *lens*
LNTKYLR lenticular *lens*
LNTL lentil *food*
LNTL lintel *beam*
LNTM line item (n) *budget* line-item (adj)
LNTN lantana *shrub*
LNTNS lawn tennis *sport*
LNTP Linotype *(trademark) typesetter*
LNTQL lenticule *lens*
LNTQLR lenticular *lens*
LNTR alienator *estranger*
LNTR all-nighter *dusk to dawn*
LNTR linter *machine*
LNTRD ill-natured *surly*
LNTRN lantern *lamp* (Br) lanthorn
LNTS alliance *bond*
LNTS lance *spear* lanced lancing
LNTSL lenticel *pore*
LNTSM lentissimo *music*
LNTSNG Lansing *city*
LNTSR lancer *cavalry*
LNTST lancet *knife*
LNTV lenitive *soothing*
LNTVRS lentivirus *disease*
LNWRD landward *toward land*
LNX links *golf course, dunes*
LNX lynx *animal* lynx (or) lynxes
LNXMN linksman *golfer* linksmen
LNYJ lineage *family*
LNYL lineal (adj) *line* lineally (adv)
LNYL lunule *crescent*
LNYNS lenience *mercy* leniency
LNYNT lenient *merciful*
LNYNTL leniently *merciful*
LNYNTS lenience *mercy* leniency
LNYP lagniappe *gift*
LNYR linear *line, math*
LNYR loonier *crazy*

LNYRD lanyard *cord*
LNYRZ linearize *make lines* linearized linearizing (Br) linearise
LNYRZSHN linearization *line, math* (Br) linearisation
LNYSHN lineation *outline*
LNYST looniest *crazy*
LNZ Illinois *US State*
LNZ lens *curved glass, eye* lenses
LNZ lionize *respect, (Br) show sights* lionized lionizing (Br) lionise
LNZ lunes *lunacy*
LNZ lyonnaise *sauce*
LNZHR lingerie *underwear*
LNZMN landsman *countryman* landsmen
LNZMN linesman *referee* linesmen
LNZR lionizer *respect, (Br) show sights* (Br) lioniser
LNZSHN lionization *respect, (Br) show sights* (Br) lionisation
LNZWLZ linsey-woolsey *fabric*
LP alley-oop *basketball*
LP alp *mountain*
LP elope *escape, marry secretly* eloped eloping
LP lap (v) *drink, race, overlap* lapped lapping
LP lap (n) *overlap, frontal area*
LP Lapp *Scandinavian*
LP leap *jump* leaped (or) leapt leaping
LP lip (v) *lick, utter* lipped lipping
LP lip (n) *mouth, back talk, edge*
LP lippy *sassy* lippier lippiest
LP loop *circle*
LP loopy *crazy* loopier loopiest
LP lop *chop* lopped lopping
LP lope *slow gait* loped loping

LP loupe *magnifier*
LPBLT lap belt *seat belt*
LPBRD lapboard *tray*
LPC alopecia *baldness*
LPCS ellipses (pl) *omission, leap* ellipsis
LPCY alopecia *baldness*
LPCZ ellipses (pl) *omission, leap* ellipsis
LPD elapid *snake*
LPD lipid *fat cell*
LPD lipoid (or) lipoidal *fat*
LPD lipped *of lip*
LPD looped *drunk*
LPDG lapdog *animal, dependent*
LPDK elliptic (or) elliptical (adj) *omission, leap* elliptically (adv)
LPDK lipidic *fat cell*
LPDKL elliptical (or) elliptic (adj) *omission, leap* elliptically (adv)
LPDL lipoidal (or) lipoid *fat*
LPDPDR lepidoptera *insect*
LPDPDRLG lepidopterology *insect study*
LPDPDRLJ lepidopterology *insect study*
LPDPDRLJST lepidopterologist *insect study*
LPDPDRN lepidopteran *insect*
LPDPDRS lepidopterous *insect*
LPDPDRST lepidopterist *insect study*
LPDPTR lepidoptera *insect*
LPDPTRLG lepidopterology *insect study*
LPDPTRLJ lepidopterology *insect study*
LPDPTRLJST lepidopterologist *insect study*
LPDPTRN lepidopteran *insect*
LPDPTRS lepidopterous *insect*
LPDPTRST lepidopterist *insect study*

Use letters that best describe the sounds you hear and omit the vowels. Use **S** or **K** instead of **C**: to find circle use **SRKL**. Use **J** to find joy, **JM** to find gem and **G** to find go.

LPDR lapidary *engraving* lapidaries
LPDRN lapidarian *engraver*
LPDRYN lapidarian *engraver*
LPFL lapful *amount* lapfuls
LPFLK lipophilic *fond of fat*
LPFRG leapfrog *game* leapfrogged leapfrogging
LPHL loophole *opening, vagueness*
LPK alpaca *mammal*
LPL lapel *collar*
LPL lapilli (pl) *lava* lapillus
LPL loophole *opening, vagueness*
LPLD lapelled (or) lapeled *collar*
LPLDK lipolytic *fat*
LPLM oil palm *tree*
LPLN Lapland *region*
LPLND Lapland *region*
LPLNDR Lapplander *Scandinavian*
LPLS lapillus *lava* lapilli
LPLS lipless *no edge*
LPLSS lipolysis *fat*
LPLTK lipolytic *fat*
LPM lipoma *tumor* lipomas (or) lipomata
LPM oil palm *tree*
LPMD lipomata (pl) *tumor* lipoma
LPMDS lipomatous *tumor*
LPMNT elopement *escape, marry secretly*
LPMT lipomata (pl) *tumor* lipoma
LPMTS lipomatous *tumor*
LPN alpine *(adj) mountainous (n) plant*
LPN lapin *rabbit*
LPN lipping *bone, music*
LPN lupine *(n) flower (adj) wolfish*
LPN oil pan *receptacle*
LPNG lipping *bone, music*
LPNGL alpenglow *dawn or dusk*
LPNHRN alpenhorn (or) alphorn *music*
LPNST Alpinist *mountain climber*

LPNSTK alpenstock *staff*
LPNZM Alpinism *mountain climbing*
LPPRTN lipoprotein *chemical*
LPR eloper *escape, marry secretly*
LPR leaper *jumper*
LPR leper *diseased one*
LPR lippier *sassy*
LPR looper *caterpillar*
LPR loopier *crazy*
LPR loper *slow gait*
LPR lopper *cutter*
LPRC leprosy *disease*
LPRD leopard *animal*
LPRD lip-read *decipher* lip-read lip-reading
LPRD lop-eared *drooping*
LPRDK leprotic *with leprosy*
LPRDM laparotomy *abdomen* laparotomies
LPRDN lip-reading (v) *decipher* lipreading (n)
LPRDNG lip-reading (v) *decipher* lipreading (n)
LPRDR lip-reader *decipher*
LPRFL all-powerful *mighty*
LPRKN leprechaun *elf*
LPRMTS lepromatous *with leprosy*
LPRPS all-purpose *multiple uses*
LPRS leprosy *disease*
LPRS leprous *with leprosy*
LPRSHR low-pressure *easygoing*
LPRSKP laparoscope *camera*
LPRSKP laparoscopy *examination* laparoscopies
LPRSKPK laparoscopic *camera*
LPRSKPST laparoscopist *surgeon*
LPRTK leprotic *with leprosy*
LPRTM laparotomy *abdomen* laparotomies
LPRZ La Pérouse *explorer*
LPS alopecia *baldness*
LPS Alps *mountains*

LPS El Paso *city*
LPS elapse *pass* elapsed elapsing
LPS ellipse *shape*
LPS lapse *(v) subside, cease, forfeit* lapsed lapsing
LPS lapse *(n) error, interval*
LPS lipase *enzyme*
LPS lupus *disease*
LPSD ellipsoid *shape*
LPSD lapsed *ended*
LPSDD lopsided *unbalanced*
LPSDL ellipsoidal *shape*
LPSH alopecia *baldness*
LPSH Lappish *Scandinavian*
LPSHY alopecia *baldness*
LPSK alopecic *bald*
LPSKSHN liposuction *remove fat*
LPSLSHL lapis lazuli *gemstone*
LPSLZHL lapis lazuli *gemstone*
LPSLZL lapis lazuli *gemstone*
LPSLZYL lapis lazuli *gemstone*
LPSM liposome *drugs*
LPSML liposomal *drugs*
LPSN Lipizzan (or) Lipizzaner *horse*
LPSNGK lip-synch (or) lip-sync (v) *pretend* lip sync (n)
LPSNK lip-synch (or) lip-sync (v) *pretend* lip sync (n)
LPSNR Lipizzaner (or) Lipizzan *horse*
LPSR lapser *subside, cease, forfeit*
LPSRVS lip service *insincerity*
LPSS ellipsis *omission, leap* ellipses
LPST lapsed *ended*
LPST lippiest *sassy*
LPST loopiest *crazy*
LPSTK lipstick *cosmetic*
LPSY alopecia *baldness*
LPSZ ellipses (pl) *omission, leap* ellipsis
LPT eelpout *fish*

Letters aren't doubled for single sounds: to find alley use **L** not **LL**. Use **Y** and **W** as hard sounds only: to find yellow use **YL**. (Br)=British spelling or usage. * See dictionary.

LPT lappet *fold*
LPT leapt (or) leaped (*v- past) leap*
LPT lipped *of lip*
LPT looped *drunk*
LPTK elliptic (or) elliptical (adj) *omission, leap* elliptically (adv)
LPTK lipidic *fat cell*
LPTKL elliptical (or) elliptic (adj) *omission, leap* elliptically (adv)
LPTP laptop *portable*
LPWNG lapwing *bird*
LPWRFL all-powerful *mighty*
LPYR leap year *time*
LPYR lippier *sassy*
LPYR loopier *crazy*
LPYST lippiest *sassy*
LPYST loopiest *crazy*
LPZ La Paz *city*
LPZ lipase *enzyme*
LPZM liposome *drugs*
LPZML liposomal *drugs*
LPZN Lipizzan (or) Lipizzaner *horse*
LPZNR Lipizzaner (or) Lipizzan *horse*
LQBRSHN lucubration *study*
LQD liquid *fluid*
LQDD liquidity *convert, cash*
LQDDR liquidator *convert, pay*
LQDL liquidly *fluid*
LQDNS liquidness *fluidity*
LQDSHN liquidation *convert, pay*
LQDT liquidate *convert, pay* liquidated liquidating
LQDT liquidity *convert, cash*
LQDTR liquidator *convert, pay*
LQF liquefy *make fluid* liquefied liquefying liquefies
LQFD liquefied *made fluid*
LQFKSHN liquefaction *make fluid*
LQFR liquefier *make fluid*
LQFYR liquefier *make fluid*

LQL locule *plant cell*
LQL loculi (pl) *chamber* loculus
LQLNT luculent *clear*
LQLNTL luculently *clear*
LQLS loculus *chamber* loculi
LQN lacuna *gap* lacunae (or) lacunas
LQNS eloquence *expressive speech*
LQNT eloquent *expressive speech*
LQNTL eloquently *expressive speech*
LQNTS eloquence *expressive speech*
LQR liqueur *sweet alcohol*
LQRM lukewarm *tepid*
LQSD loquacity *talkative*
LQSHN allocution *formal speech*
LQSHN elocution *public speaking*
LQSHN liquation *separation*
LQSHN locution *style of speech*
LQSHNR elocutionary *public speaking*
LQSHNR illocutionary *effect of speech*
LQSHS loquacious *talkative*
LQSHSNS loquaciousness *talkative*
LQSNT liquescent *melting*
LQST loquacity *talkative*
LQT aliquot *fraction*
LQT liquate *separate* liquated liquating
LQT loquat *fruit*
LQZ likewise *similarly*
LR alar (or) alary *winglike*
LR allure *entice* allured alluring
LR lair *den*
LR laura *monastery*
LR layer *one thickness, hen*
LR leer *sly look*
LR leery *suspicious*
LR liar *deceiver*
LR lira *money* lire (or) liras (or) liri (or) liroth (or) lirot
LR lore *knowledge*

LR lorry *truck* lorries
LR lory *bird* lories
LR lower (*v*) *let down, frown, humble* (adj) *below* (*n*) *frown*
LR lowery *gloomy*
LR lure (*v*) *tempt* lured luring
LR lure (*n*) *attraction*
LR lyre *music*
LR oiler *person, ship, container*
LR oilier *greasy*
LRBRD larboard *port*
LRBRD lyrebird *bird*
LRCH larch *tree*
LRCH lurch (*v*) *stagger* (*n*) *bad position*
LRCHR lurcher (Br) *dog*
LRD already *previously*
LRD lard *fat*
LRD Laredo *city*
LRD lord *master*
LRD lurid *ghastly*
LRDL lordly *proud* lordlier lordliest
LRDL luridly *ghastly*
LRDLNS lordliness *pride*
LRDLR lordlier *proud*
LRDLST lordliest *proud*
LRDLYR lordlier *proud*
LRDLYST lordliest *proud*
LRDN lardoon (or) lardon *fat*
LRDNS luridness *ghastly*
LRDR larder *pantry*
LRDSHP lordship *title*
LRFB ailurophobe *cat hater*
LRFL ailurophile *cat lover*
LRG allergy *adverse reaction* allergies
LRG largo *music* largos
LRGD larghetto *music*
LRGN larrigan *boot*
LRGT larghetto *music*
LRJ allergy *adverse reaction* allergies
LRJ large (adj) *big, broad* larger largest
LRJ large (*n*) *general*
LRJK allergic *adverse*
LRJL largely *mostly*
LRJN allergen *allergy substance*

Use letters that best describe the sounds you hear and omit the vowels. Use **S** or **K** instead of **C**: to find circle use **SRKL**. Use **J** to find joy, **JM** to find gem and **G** to find go.

LRJNK allergenic *allergy* substance
LRJNSD allergenicity *allergy* substance
LRJNST allergenicity *allergy* substance
LRJR larger *bigger*
LRJS largesse (or) largess *generosity*
LRJSH largish *big*
LRJSKL large-scale *big*
LRJST allergist *doctor*
LRJST largest *biggest*
LRK lark *bird, adventure*
LRK lorica *shell* loricae
LRK lurk *prowl*
LRK lyric *music*
LRKL lyrical (adj) *musical* lyrically (adv)
LRKLNS lyricalness *music*
LRKLS lower class (n) *inferior* lower-class (adj)
LRKN larrikin *hoodlum*
LRKR lurker *prowler*
LRKS lowercase *type*
LRKS lyrics *words*
LRKSPR larkspur *flower*
LRKT lorikeet *bird*
LRL laurel *(n) tree*
LRL laurel *(v) crown* laureled (or) laurelled laureling (or) laurelling
LRL Lorelei *siren*
LRM alarm *signal, fear*
LRMKLK alarm clock *time device*
LRMNT allurement *enticement*
LRMST alarmist *fearful one*
LRMST lowermost *bottom*
LRMZM alarmism *baseless fear*
LRN aileron *wing*
LRN aleurone *protein*
LRN all-around *complete*
LRN learn *discover*
LRN lowering *gloomy*
LRNBL learnable *discover*
LRND all-around *complete*
LRND learned *educated*
LRNDL learnedly *educated*
LRNDNS learnedness

education
LRNG lowering *gloomy*
LRNGGLG laryngology *medicine*
LRNGGLJ laryngology *medicine*
LRNGGSKP laryngoscope *examination* laryngoscopy
LRNGKS larynx *wind pipe* larynges (or) larynxes
LRNGL alluringly *attractively*
LRNGL laryngeal *trachea*
LRNGL leeringly *sly look*
LRNGLG laryngology *medicine*
LRNGLJ laryngology *medicine*
LRNGS larynges (pl) *trachea* larynx
LRNGSKP laryngoscope *examination* laryngoscopy
LRNGX larynx *wind pipe* larynges (or) larynxes
LRNGYL laryngeal *trachea*
LRNGZ larynges (pl) *trachea* larynx
LRNJDS laryngitis *no voice*
LRNJKDM laryngectomee *patient*
LRNJKDM laryngectomy *surgery* laryngectomies
LRNJKDMZD laryngectomized *surgery*
LRNJKTM laryngectomee *patient*
LRNJKTM laryngectomy *surgery* laryngectomies
LRNJKTMZD laryngectomized *surgery*
LRNJL laryngeal *trachea*
LRNJS larynges (pl) *trachea* larynx
LRNJSKP laryngoscope *examination* laryngoscopy
LRNJTS laryngitis *no voice*
LRNJYL laryngeal *trachea*
LRNJZ larynges (pl) *trachea* larynx
LRNKS larynx *wind pipe* larynges (or) larynxes
LRNN learning *knowledge*
LRNNG learning *knowledge*

LRNR learner *discoverer*
LRNT low-rent *cheap*
LRNX larynx *wind pipe* larynges (or) larynxes
LRNYN lorgnon *glasses*
LRNYT lorgnette *glasses*
LRS La Rousse *dictionary author*
LRS loess *loam*
LRS loris *animal* lorises
LRS low-rise *structure*
LRSHFK La Rouchefoucauld *writer*
LRSHFKLD La Rouchefoucauld *writer*
LRSHS largesse (or) largess *generosity*
LRSL loessial *loam*
LRSN larceny *robbery* larcenies
LRSNS larcenous *robbery*
LRSNSL larcenously *robbery*
LRSST lyricist *music*
LRST lyrist *musician*
LRSYL loessial *loam*
LRSZM lyricism *music*
LRT alert *(n,v) alarm* (adj) *watchful*
LRT all right *satisfactory*
LRT lariat *rope*
LRT laureate *(n) honored one*
LRT laureate *(v) crown* laureated laureating
LRTL alertly *watchfully*
LRTNS alertness *watchfulness*
LRV larva *worm* larvae (or)
LRVL larval *worm*
LRVSD larvicide *kill worms*
LRX lyrics *words*
LRXPR larkspur *flower*
LRYT lariat *rope*
LRYT laureate *(v) crown* laureated laureating
LRYT laureate *(n) honored one*
LRZ low-rise *structure*
LRZHS largesse (or) largess *generosity*
LRZN oleoresin *turpentine*
LS Aeolus *Greek myth*
LS alas *(interj) woe*

LS alias *name* aliases
LS also *too*
LS aweless *no fear*
LS else *other*
LS ileus *obstruction*
LS ill-use *abuse*
LS lace (v) *tie, lash* laced lacing
LS lace (n) *openwork, tie*
LS lacy *decorative* lacier laciest
LS Laos *country*
LS lass *girl* lasses
LS lassie *girl*
LS lasso *rope* lassos (or) lassoes
LS lease *rent* leased leasing
LS less *smaller amount*
LS lessee *renter*
LS lice (pl) *insect* louse
LS loci (pl) *point* locus
LS loess *loam*
LS loose (v) *release* loosed loosing
LS loose (adj) *slack, free, unchaste* looser loosest
LS loss *ruin, failure, decrease** losses
LS louse (n) *insect* lice
LS louse (v) *remove lice* loused lousing
LS louse (n) *heel* louses
LS lyse *decline* lysed lysing
LSBK leaseback *rent*
LSBL leasable *rent*
LSD LCD (abbr) *liquid crystal display*
LSD lucid *clear*
LSD lusty *hearty* lustier lustiest
LSD oilseed *crop*
LSDCH last-ditch *final*
LSDD lucidity *clearness*
LSDDR elucidator *explain*
LSDDV elucidative *explanation*
LSDK elastic (adj) *flexible* (n) *rubber band*
LSDL lucidly *clear*
LSDL lustily *heartily*
LSDMR elastomer *rubber*
LSDMRK elastomeric

rubbery
LSDN elastin *protein*
LSDN listing *register*
LSDNG lasting *durable*
LSDNG listing *register*
LSDNS lucidness *clearness*
LSDNS lustiness *heartiness*
LSDP loused up *snarl, mess*
LSDR elicitor *draw forth*
LSDR laster *endure, shape*
LSDR leister *spear*
LSDR lister *plow*
LSDR luster (or) lustre *gleam* lustered (or) lustred lustering (or) lustring (Br) lustre
LSDR lustier *hearty*
LSDRS lustrous *shiny*
LSDRSL lustrously *shiny*
LSDRSNS lustrousness *shine*
LSDRWR lusterware *pottery*
LSDSHN elucidation *explanation*
LSDST lustiest *hearty*
LSDT elucidate *explain* elucidated elucidating
LSDT lucidity *clearness*
LSDTR elucidator *explain*
LSDTV elucidative *explanation*
LSDYR lustier *hearty*
LSDYST lustiest *hearty*
LSFL lustful (adj) *oversexed* lustfully (adv)
LSFLNS lustfulness *oversexed*
LSFR laissez faire *choice* (Br) laisser-faire
LSFR Lucifer *devil*
LSFRN luciferin *heatless light*
LSFRS luciferase *enzyme*
LSFRS luciferous *illuminating*
LSFRZ luciferase *enzyme*
LSGC loosey-goosey *relaxed*
LSGNK lysogenic *bacteria*
LSGNSD lysogenicity *bacteria*
LSGNST lysogenicity *bacteria*
LSGS loosey-goosey *relaxed*

LSH eyelash *hair* eyelashes
LSH lash *whip* lashes
LSH leash *tether* leashes
LSH loge *theater box*
LSH louche *indecent*
LSH luge *sled*
LSH lush (adj) *abundant* (n-slang) *a drunk* lushes
LSH owlish *like an owl*
LSHL lushly *abundantly*
LSHL owlishly *like an owl*
LSHLD leasehold *property*
LSHLDR leaseholder *property*
LSHLT lazulite *mineral*
LSHM Elysium *paradise*
LSHMRZ Alzheimer's *disease*
LSHN Aleutian *island, mountains*
LSHN allusion *reference*
LSHN elation *joy*
LSHN elision *omission*
LSHN elusion *evade*
LSHN elysian (adj) *(often capitalized) heavenly*
LSHN illation *opinion*
LSHN illusion *false idea*
LSHN Laotian *of Laos*
LSHN lashing *binding*
LSHN lesion *skin*
LSHN lotion *salve*
LSHN lotion *liquid*
LSHNG lashing *binding*
LSHNGS lashings (Br) *abundance*
LSHNL illusional *false idea*
LSHNLNS Aleutian Islands *land masses*
LSHNLNZ Aleutian Islands *land masses*
LSHNR illusionary *illusory*
LSHNS lashings (Br) *abundance*
LSHNS lushness *abundance*
LSHNS owlishness *like an owl*
LSHNST illusionist *magician*
LSHNZ lashings (Br) *abundance*
LSHR lasher *bind*
LSHR leisure *free time*
LSHR luger *sledder*

Use letters that best describe the sounds you hear and omit the vowels. Use **S** or **K** instead of **C**: to find circle use **SRKL**. Use **J** to find joy, **JM** to find gem and **G** to find go.

LSHRD leisured *free time*
LSHRL leisurely *free time*
LSHRLNS leisureliness *free time*
LSHRST leisure suit *attire*
LSHS alliaceous *garlic*
LSHS luscious *appealing*
LSHSL lusciously *appealing*
LSHSNS lusciousness *appealing*
LSHWR elsewhere *other place*
LSHYM Elysium *paradise*
LSJ ill-usage *abuse*
LSJN lysogen *bacteria*
LSJND loose-jointed *moveable*
LSJNK lysogenic *bacteria*
LSJNSD lysogenicity *bacteria*
LSJNST lysogenicity *bacteria*
LSJNTD loose-jointed *moveable*
LSJNZ lysogenize *decline* lysogenized lysogenizing (Br) lysogenise
LSK Alaska *US State*
LSKN oilskin *cloth*
LSKNMLMT Alaskan malamute *dog*
LSKNMLMYT Alaskan malamute *dog*
LSKNN loose cannon *uncontrolled*
LSKRTN lace-curtain *middle-class*
LSL lastly *finally*
LSL loessial *loam*
LSL loosely *not tight or exact*
LSLD leasehold *property*
LSLDR leaseholder *property*
LSLF loose-leaf *book*
LSLN Ellis Island *immigration*
LSLND Ellis Island *immigration*
LSLNG low-slung *near ground*
LSLS listless *inactive*
LSLSD All Souls' Day *November 2*

LSLSL listlessly *inactive*
LSLSNS listlessness *inactivity*
LSLVDR El Salvador *country*
LSLZD All Souls' Day *November 2*
LSM alyssum *herb*
LSM Elysium *paradise*
LSM lissome *flexible*
LSM lyceum *hall*
LSML lissomely *flexible*
LSMNS lissomeness *flexibility*
LSMNT last minute *near the end*
LSMRZ Alzheimer's *disease*
LSN elysian (adj) *(often capitalized) heavenly*
LSN lacing *cord*
LSN lessen *decrease*
LSN lesson *study*
LSN leucine *amino acid*
LSN listen *hear*
LSN loosen *release*
LSN lysin *antibody*
LSN lysine *amino acid*
LSNBL listenable *hear*
LSNC licensee *permitted one*
LSNC lucency *clearness*
LSNCHS licentious *unrestrained*
LSNCHSNS licentiousness *unrestrained*
LSND loose end *fragment*
LSNG lacing *cord*
LSNGLS Los Angeles *city*
LSNGP lousing up *snarl, mess*
LSNJ lozenge *diamond, candy*
LSNJLS Los Angeles *city*
LSNJLZ Los Angeles *city*
LSNN Eleusinian *mystical*
LSNN listen in *hear*
LSNN listening *monitoring*
LSNNG listening *monitoring*
LSNP lousing up *snarl, mess*
LSNR listener *audience*
LSNRSHP listenership *audience*
LSNS laciness *openwork*
LSNS license (v) *permit*

licensed licensing
LSNS license (or) licence *(n) permission, document*
LSNS licensee *permitted one*
LSNS lucency *clearness*
LSNSBL licensable *permitted*
LSNSD licensed *permitted*
LSNSHN laciniation *fringe*
LSNSHS licentious *unrestrained*
LSNSHSNS licentiousness *unrestrained*
LSNSPLT license plate *car*
LSNSR licenser (or) licensor *permitter*
LSNST licensed *permitted*
LSNT laciniate *fringed*
LSNT lucent *clear*
LSNTC licensee *permitted one*
LSNTC lucency *clearness*
LSNTL lucently *clear*
LSNTS license (v) *permit* licensed licensing
LSNTS license (or) licence *(n) permission, document*
LSNTS licensee *permitted one*
LSNTS lucency *clearness*
LSNTSBL licensable *permitted*
LSNTSD All Saints' Day *November 1*
LSNTSPLT license plate *car*
LSNTSR licenser (or) licensor *permitter*
LSNYN Eleusinian *mystical*
LSNYSHN laciniation *fringe*
LSNYT laciniate *fringed*
LSP lisp *speech*
LSP louse up *snarl, mess* loused up lousing up
LSPDZ lespedeza *plant*
LSPR lisper *speech*
LSPRDD low-spirited *depressed*
LSPRTD low-spirited *depressed*
LSPS allspice *spice*
LSPS Lhasa apso *dog* Llasa apsos

Letters aren't doubled for single sounds: to find alley use **L** not **LL**. Use **Y** and **W** as hard sounds only: to find yellow use **YL**. (Br)=British spelling or usage. * See dictionary.

LSR illusory *deceptive*
LSR lacer *fastener*
LSR lacier *openwork*
LSR laser *light*
LSR lassoer *roper*
LSR lesser *lower*
LSR lessor *lease*
LSR looser *(adj) slack, free, unchaste*
LSR ulcer *blister*
LSRDD ill-sorted *mismatched*
LSRDV lacerative *cut*
LSRDV ulcerative *blister*
LSRJKSD lysergic acid *drug*
LSRL illusorily *deception*
LSRN also-ran *loser*
LSRN lucerne *(Br) alfalfa*
LSRNS illusoriness *deception*
LSRS allosaurus *dinosaur*
LSRS ulcerous *blister*
LSRSHN laceration *cut*
LSRSHN ulceration *blister*
LSRT lacerate *cut* lacerated lacerating
LSRT ulcerate *blister* ulcerated ulcerating
LSRTD ill-sorted *mismatched*
LSRTV lacerative *cut*
LSRTV ulcerative *blister*
LSS lysis *decline* lyses
LSSHN Alsatian *dog*
LSSM lysosome *saclike*
LSSML lysosomal *saclike*
LSST laciest *openwork*
LSST loosest *(adj) slack, free, unchaste*
LST elicit *draw forth*
LST illicit *unlawful*
LST last *(adj, adv) final (n) form (v) endure*
LST lawsuit *legal*
LST least *slightest*
LST lest *for fear that*
LST leucite *mineral*
LST licit *legal*
LST list *(n) series, roll, tilt (v) cut, register, tilt**
LST lost *mislaid*
LST lowest *beneath*
LST Lucite *(trademark) resin*
LST lust *craving*
LST lusty *hearty* lustier

lustiest
LST oiliest *greasy*
LSTD lassitude *tiredness*
LSTDCH last-ditch *final*
LSTFL lustful (adj) *oversexed* lustfully (adv)
LSTFLNS lustfulness *oversexed*
LSTH Lesotho *country*
LSTHN lecithin *emulsifier*
LSTK elastic *(adj) flexible (n) rubber band*
LSTL illicitly *unlawfully*
LSTL lastly *finally*
LSTL licitly *legal*
LSTL lustily *heartily*
LSTLS listless *inactive*
LSTLSL listlessly *inactive*
LSTLSNS listlessness *inactivity*
LSTMNT last minute *near the end*
LSTMR elastomer *rubber*
LSTMRK elastomeric *rubbery*
LSTN elastin *protein*
LSTN lasting *durable*
LSTN listing *register*
LSTN oilstone *whetstone*
LSTNG lasting *durable*
LSTNG listing *register*
LSTNS lustiness *heartiness*
LSTP loused up *snarl, mess*
LSTR all-star *outstanding*
LSTR elicitor *draw forth*
LSTR laster *endure, shape*
LSTR leister *spear*
LSTR lister *plow*
LSTR luster (or) lustre *gleam* lustered (or) lustred lustering (or) lustring (Br) lustre
LSTR lustier *hearty*
LSTR oldster *aged one*
LSTR oleaster *plant*
LSTR ulster *overcoat*
LSTR Ulster *city*
LSTRD ill-starred *unlucky*
LSTRDR illustrator *demonstrate*
LSTRDV illustrative *demonstrating*

LSTRK allosteric *protein change*
LSTRS illustrious *famous*
LSTRS lustrous *shiny*
LSTRSHN illustration *instance*
LSTRSL illustriously *famous*
LSTRSL lustrously *shiny*
LSTRSNS illustriousness *fame*
LSTRSNS lustrousness *shine*
LSTRSS listeriosis *disease* listerioses
LSTRT illustrate *adorn, demonstrate* illustrated illustrating
LSTRTR illustrator *demonstrate*
LSTRTV illustrative *demonstrating*
LSTRWR lusterware *pottery*
LSTRYS illustrious *famous*
LSTRYSL illustriously *famous*
LSTRYSNS illustriousness *fame*
LSTRYSS listeriosis *disease* listerioses
LSTSD elasticity *flexibility* elasticities
LSTSHN elicitation *draw forth*
LSTST elasticity *flexibility* elasticities
LSTST lustiest *hearty*
LSTSZD elasticized *stretchy*
LSTWZ leastways *at least*
LSTWZ leastwise *at least*
LSTYD lassitude *tiredness*
LSTYR lustier *hearty*
LSTYST lustiest *hearty*
LSV allusive *suggestive*
LSV elusive *evasive*
LSV illusive *deceptive*
LSVGS Las Vegas *city*
LSVL allusively *suggestively*
LSVNS allusiveness *implication*
LSVNS elusiveness *evasion*
LSVNS illusiveness *deceptive*
LSVS lascivious *lewd*

Use letters that best describe the sounds you hear and omit the vowels. Use **S** or **K** instead of **C**: to find circle use **SRKL**. Use **J** to find joy, **JM** to find gem and **G** to find go.

LSVYS lascivious *lewd*
LSWNG lacewing *insect*
LSWR elsewhere *other place*
LSWR lassoer *roper*
LSWRK lacework *fabric*
LSYL loessial *loam*
LSYM Elysium *paradise*
LSYM lyceum *hall*
LSYN elysian (adj) *(often capitalized) heavenly*
LSYR lacier *openwork*
LSYST laciest *openwork*
LSZ laicize *make worldly* laicized laicizing
LSZ lyses (pl) *decline* lysis
LSZM lysozyme *protein*
LT a lot *much*
LT a lot of *many*
LT alate *winged*
LT Aleut *Eskimo*
LT alight *get down*
LT all-out (adj) *total* all out (adv)
LT allot *distribute* allotted allotting
LT allottee *receiver*
LT alto *voice* altos
LT elate *fill with joy* elated elating
LT elite *superior* (Br) elite
LT elute *extract* eluted eluting
LT eyelet *hole*
LT islet *island*
LT laddie *boy*
LT laity *not clergy*
LT late *past due* later latest
LT latte *coffee* lattes
LT lay out (v) *spread* layout (n)
LT layette *baby clothing*
LT let (v) *allow, make, rent** let letting
LT let (n) *replay, obstruction*
LT light (v) *illuminate* lit (or) lighted lighting
LT light (n) *illumination (adj) bright, not heavy, cheerful**
LT lit (v-past) *light (adj) drunk (n-abbr) literature*
LT loot (n) *spoils (v) rob*

LT lot (n) *share, fortune, sort**
LT lot (v) *allot* lotted lotting
LT lota *pitcher*
LT lotte *monkfish*
LT lotto *game*
LT lout *oaf*
LT lute (n) *music, coating*
LT lute (v) *cover* luted luting
LT owlet *bird*
LTBB lightbulb *lamp*
LTBL light table *viewer*
LTBLB lightbulb *lamp*
LTCHR literature *books*
LTCZ latices (pl) *rubber* latex
LTD elated *overjoyed*
LTD lidded *covered*
LTD low tide *ocean*
LTD yuletide *(often capitalized) Christmas*
LTDN let down (v) *fail* letdown (n)
LTFDD light-footed *nimble*
LTFNGGRD light-fingered *stealing*
LTFNGRD light-fingered *stealing*
LTFS lightface *type*
LTFSD lightfaced *type*
LTFSK lutefisk *codfish*
LTFST lightfaced *type*
LTFTD light-footed *nimble*
LTG latigo *saddle* latigos
LTGBL litigable *law*
LTGD light guide *fiber*
LTGDR litigator *law*
LTGNT litigant *lawsuit*
LTGSHN litigation *contest in law*
LTGT litigate *contest in law* litigated litigating
LTGTHR altogether *(adj) completely (n) nude*
LTGTR litigator *law*
LTH although *despite*
LTH eolith *flint*
LTH lath *wood strip* laths (or) lath
LTH lathe *machine* lathed lathing
LTH Lethe *river*
LTH lithe *flexible*
LTH loath (adj) *reluctant*

LTH loathe (v) *hate* loathed loathing
LTHDD light-headed *dizzy*
LTHFT lithophyte *plant*
LTHGRF lithograph *copy*
LTHGRF lithography *copy*
LTHGRFK lithographic *copy*
LTHGRFKL lithographically *copy*
LTHGRFR lithographer *copy*
LTHK Eolithic *geologic age*
LTHK lithic *lithium*
LTHL lethal (adj) *deadly* lethally (adv)
LTHL lithely *flexible*
LTHM lithium *drug*
LTHN Lethean *river*
LTHN Lithuania *country*
LTHN loathing *hatred*
LTHNDD light-handed *skillful*
LTHNG loathing *hatred*
LTHNN Lithuanian *of Lithuania*
LTHNS litheness *flexibility*
LTHNY Lithuania *country*
LTHNYN Lithuanian *of Lithuania*
LTHR lather *foam*
LTHR lathery *foamy*
LTHR leather (n) *tanned hide (v) thrash*
LTHR leathery *like hide*
LTHR lothario *(often capitalized) seducer* lotharios
LTHR luthier *guitar maker*
LTHRBK leatherback *turtle*
LTHRDD lighthearted *gay*
LTHRG lethargy *sluggishness*
LTHRJ lethargy *sluggishness*
LTHRJK lethargic *sluggish*
LTHRJKL lethargically *sluggish*
LTHRLF leatherleaf *shrub*
LTHRLK leatherlike *tanned hide*
LTHRN althorn *alto sax*
LTHRN leathern *like leather*
LTHRN Lutheran *church*
LTHRNK leatherneck *marine*
LTHRR latherer *foam*

Letters aren't doubled for single sounds: to find alley use **L** not **LL**. Use **Y** and **W** as hard sounds only: to find yellow use **YL**. (Br)=British spelling or usage. * See dictionary.

LTHRT leatherette *fabric*
LTHRTD lighthearted *gay*
LTHRWD leatherwood *tree*
LTHRY lothario *(often capitalized) seducer* lotharios
LTHS lighthouse *beacon*
LTHSFR lithosphere *earth*
LTHSM lithesome *flexible*
LTHSM loathsome *hateful*
LTHSML loathsomely *hatefully*
LTHSMNS loathsomeness *hatefulness*
LTHVWT light heavyweight *161-175 pounds*
LTHWN Lithuania *country*
LTHWNN Lithuanian *of Lithuania*
LTHWNY Lithuania *country*
LTHWNYN Lithuanian *of Lithuania*
LTHYM lithium *drug*
LTHYN Lethean *river*
LTHYR luthier *guitar maker*
LTJS litigious *controversial*
LTJSL litigiously *controversially*
LTJSNS litigiousness *controversy*
LTK latke *pancake*
LTK lotic *water*
LTK low-tech *simple*
LTK luetic *syphilis*
LTK lytic *declining*
LTKL lytically *declining*
LTKMLS altocumulus *cloud*
LTKMR latecomer *arrival*
LTKMYLS altocumulus *cloud*
LTKS latex *rubber* latices (or) latexes
LTKYMLS altocumulus *cloud*
LTKYMYLS altocumulus *cloud*
LTL all told *in all*
LTL lately *recently*
LTL lightly *gently*
LTL little *(adj) small (adv) slightly* littler (or) less (or) lesser littlest (or) least

LTL luteal *ovulation*
LTLD all told *in all*
LTLDPR Little Dipper *constellation*
LTLG Little League *baseball*
LTLNK littleneck *clam*
LTLR littler *smaller*
LTLRK Little Rock *city*
LTLST littlest *smallest*
LTM all-time *forever*
LTM lead time *notice*
LTM old-time *ancient*
LTM ultima *end*
LTMC ultimacy *finality* ultimacies
LTMD ultimata (pl) *choice* ultimatum
LTMDM ultimatum *choice* ultimatums (or) ultimata
LTMDR altimeter *height gauge*
LTMNDD light-minded *frivolous*
LTMNT allotment *portion*
LTMPRD ill-tempered *quarrelsome*
LTMR old-timer *veteran*
LTMS litmus *acid-base indicator*
LTMS ultimacy *finality* ultimacies
LTMSPPR litmus paper *acid-base indicator*
LTMT ultimata (pl) *choice* ultimatum
LTMT ultimate *final*
LTMTF leitmotiv (or) leitmotif *theme*
LTMTM ultimatum *choice* ultimatums (or) ultimata
LTMTR altimeter *height gauge*
LTN Aladdin *fictional hero*
LTN lateen *sail*
LTN laten *grow late*
LTN Latin *language*
LTN Latino *heritage* Latinos
LTN latten *alloy*
LTN lighten *relieve, illuminate*
LTN lighting *illumination*
LTN litany *prayer* litanies
LTN lutein *pigment*

LTNC latency *inactivity* latencies
LTNG leading *first*
LTNG lighting *illumination*
LTNGJ leading edge *forefront*
LTNMRK Latin America *region*
LTNN lightning *thunder*
LTNNBG lightning bug *insect*
LTNNC lieutenancy *rank*
LTNNG lightning *thunder*
LTNNGBG lightning bug *insect*
LTNNGRD lightning rod *pole*
LTNNRD lightning rod *pole*
LTNNS lieutenancy *rank*
LTNNT lieutenant *rank*
LTNNTC lieutenancy *rank*
LTNNTS lieutenancy *rank*
LTNR lightener *relieve, illuminate*
LTNS latency *inactivity* latencies
LTNS lateness *past due*
LTNS lightness *illumination, less weight*
LTNSFKSHN latensification *photograph*
LTNST lutenist (or) lutanist *musician*
LTNT latent *inactive*
LTNT lieutenant *rank*
LTNTC latency *inactivity* latencies
LTNTC lieutenancy *rank*
LTNTL latently *inactive*
LTNTS latency *inactivity* latencies
LTNTS lieutenancy *rank*
LTNTSFKSHN latensification *photograph*
LTNZ latinize *language* latinized latinizing
LTNZ luteinize *pigment* luteinized luteinizing
LTNZSHN latinization *language*
LTNZSHN luteinization *pigment*
LTP allotype *antibody*

Use letters that best describe the sounds you hear and omit the vowels. Use **S** or **K** instead of **C**: to find circle use **SRKL**. Use **J** to find joy, **JM** to find gem and **G** to find go.

allotypy
LTP let up (v) *ease* letup (n)
LTPK allotypic *antibody*
LTPKL allotypically *antibody*
LTPLN lightplane *airplane*
LTPRF lightproof *dark*
LTQMLS altocumulus *cloud*
LTQMYLS altocumulus *cloud*
LTR aleatory *by chance*
LTR allotter *distributor*
LTR altar *worship*
LTR alter *change*
LTR elater *spores*
LTR ladder *step up, scale*
LTR later *after now*
LTR latter *recent*
LTR leader *guide*
LTR letter *alphabet symbol, correspondence, renter*
LTR lighter *less weight, flame*
LTR liter *measure* (Br) litre
LTR litter *(n) trash, bed (v) birth, strew*
LTR loiter *linger*
LTR looter *thief*
LTR lottery *drawing of lots* lotteries
LTR luthier *guitar maker*
LTR ultra *extreme*
LTRB altar boy *aide*
LTRBG litterbag *container*
LTRBG litterbug *strew trash*
LTRBK ladder-back *slats*
LTRBL alterable (adj) *changeable* alterably (adv)
LTRBLD alterability *changeability*
LTRBLT alterability *changeability*
LTRBSK ultrabasic *low silica*
LTRC aliteracy *no desire to read*
LTRC illiteracy *unable to read* illiteracies
LTRC literacy *read and write*
LTRCHR literature *books*
LTRCKRT ultrasecret *confidential*
LTRD latter-day *recent*
LTRD leotard *garment*

LTRD lettered *educated*
LTRD literati *educated class*
LTRD ultradry *arid*
LTRDV alliterative *repetitive*
LTRDVL alliteratively *repetitive*
LTRFLTRSHN ultrafiltration *pass through*
LTRFLTRT ultrafiltrate *pass through*
LTRFN ultrafine *soft*
LTRFSH ultrafiche *reduction*
LTRFST ultrafast *quick*
LTRG alter ego *counterpart*
LTRG liturgy *rite liturgies*
LTRH ultrahigh *frequency*
LTRHD letterhead *title*
LTRHMN ultrahuman *superman*
LTRHP ultrahip *stylish*
LTRHT ultrahot *heat*
LTRHYMN ultrahuman *superman*
LTRJ liturgy *rite liturgies*
LTRJKL liturgical (adj) *rite* liturgically (adv)
LTRJKS liturgics *worship*
LTRJST liturgist *worshipper*
LTRJX liturgics *worship*
LTRK aleatoric *by chance*
LTRK Lautrec, Toulouse *artist*
LTRKL altar call *appeal*
LTRKL ultracool *stylish*
LTRKNSRVDV ultraconservative *far right*
LTRKNSRVTV ultraconservative *far right*
LTRKNTMPRR ultracontemporary *new*
LTRKRDKL ultracritical *crucial*
LTRKRR letter carrier *postman*
LTRKRTKL ultracritical *crucial*
LTRKRYR letter carrier *postman*
LTRKSHN altercation *quarrel*
LTRKSKLSV ultraexclusive *elite*

LTRKT altercate *wrangle* altercated altercating
LTRKWT ultraquiet *silent*
LTRKWYT ultraquiet *silent*
LTRL altar rail *banister*
LTRL laetrile *(often capitalized) drug*
LTRL lateral (adj) *sideways* laterally (adv)
LTRL latterly *later*
LTRL light-rail *train*
LTRL literal (adj) *actual, exact* literally (adv)
LTRL littoral *seashore*
LTRL ultralow *frequency*
LTRLBRL ultraliberal *leftist*
LTRLFT ultraleft *liberal*
LTRLNS literalness *precision*
LTRLST literalist *realist*
LTRLT ultralight *(adj) no weight (n) aircraft*
LTRLZ lateralize *one side* lateralized lateralizing
LTRLZ literalize *make exact* literalized literalizing
LTRLZM literalism *realism*
LTRLZSHN lateralization *one side*
LTRLZSHN literalization *make exact*
LTRMDRN ultramodern *new*
LTRMKRSKP ultramicroscope *magnifier*
LTRMKRSKPK ultramicroscopic *tiny*
LTRMKRSKPKL ultramicroscopically *tiny*
LTRMN letterman *athlete* lettermen
LTRMNCHR ultraminiature *tiny*
LTRMNTN ultramontane *authority*
LTRMNTYR ultraminiature *tiny*
LTRMNYCHR ultraminiature *tiny*
LTRMNYTYR ultraminiature *tiny*
LTRMRN ultramarine *color*
LTRN latrine *toilet*
LTRN lettering *type*

Letters aren't doubled for single sounds: to find alley use **L** not **LL**. Use **Y** and **W** as hard sounds only: to find yellow use **YL**. (Br)=British spelling or usage. * See dictionary.

LTRNDNG alternating *changing*
LTRNDR alternator *generator*
LTRNDV alternative *choice*
LTRNDVL alternatively *choice*
LTRNDVNS alternativeness *choice*
LTRNG lettering *type*
LTRNSHN alternation *succession*
LTRNSHNLST ultranationalist *patriotic*
LTRNSHNLZM ultranationalism *patriotism*
LTRNT alternate *change* alternated alternating
LTRNT alternate *(adj)* opposite *(n)* substitute
LTRNTN alternating *changing*
LTRNTNG alternating *changing*
LTRNTR alternator *generator*
LTRNTV alternative *choice*
LTRNTVL alternatively *choice*
LTRNTVNS alternativeness *choice*
LTRP allotrope *two forms*
LTRP allotropy *two forms* allotropies
LTRP light trap *entry, bug trap*
LTRPK allotropic *two forms*
LTRPR ultrapure *clean*
LTRPRFK letter-perfect *no mistakes*
LTRPRFKT letter-perfect *no mistakes*
LTRPRFL ultrapowerful *strong*
LTRPRS letterpress *printing* letterpresses
LTRPS altarpiece *art*
LTRPTRDK ultrapatriotic *nationalistic*
LTRPTRTK ultrapatriotic *nationalistic*
LTRPTRYDK ultrapatriotic *nationalistic*
LTRPTRYTK ultrapatriotic

nationalistic
LTRPWRFL ultrapowerful *strong*
LTRPYR ultrapure *clean*
LTRQT ultraquiet *silent*
LTRQYT ultraquiet *silent*
LTRR alterer *changer*
LTRR literary *well-read*
LTRR loiterer *lingerer*
LTRR ulterior *hidden*
LTRRCH ultrarich *wealthy*
LTRRDKL ultraradical *leftist*
LTRRDST ultrarightist *conservative*
LTRRL ulteriorly *hidden*
LTRRLBL ultrareliable *unchanging*
LTRRLSDK ultrarealistic *rational*
LTRRLST ultrarealist *rational*
LTRRLSTK ultrarealistic *rational*
LTRRLYBL ultrareliable *unchanging*
LTRRLZM ultrarealism *naturalness*
LTRRNS literariness *bookish*
LTRRRR ultrarare *scant*
LTRRRT ultraright *conservative*
LTRRTHDKS ultraorthodox *conventional*
LTRRTHDX ultraorthodox *conventional*
LTRRTKL ultraradical *leftist*
LTRRTST ultrarightist *conservative*
LTRRYLSDK ultrarealistic *rational*
LTRRYLST ultrarealist *rational*
LTRRYLSTK ultrarealistic *rational*
LTRRYLZM ultrarealism *naturalness*
LTRS aliteracy *no desire to read*
LTRS illiteracy *unable to read* illiteracies
LTRS literacy *read and write*
LTRSDK altruistic *benefits others*
LTRSDKL altruistically

benefits others
LTRSF ultrasafe *secure*
LTRSFT ultrasoft *not hard*
LTRSHL altricial *immature*
LTRSHN alliteration *repetition*
LTRSHN alteration *change*
LTRSHN elutriation *purification*
LTRSHP leadership *guidance*
LTRSHRP ultrasharp *pointed*
LTRSHRT ultrashort *not long*
LTRSKRT ultrasecret *confidential*
LTRSL ultraslow *not fast*
LTRSMPL ultrasimple *easy*
LTRSMRT ultrasmart *intelligent*
LTRSMTH ultrasmooth *soft*
LTRSN ultrasound *vibrations*
LTRSND ultrasound *vibrations*
LTRSNGRF ultrasonography *sound*
LTRSNGRFK ultrasonographic *sound*
LTRSNGRFR ultrasonographer *sound*
LTRSNK ultrasonic *frequency*
LTRSNKS ultrasonics *frequency*
LTRSNSDV ultrasensitive *feeling*
LTRSNSTV ultrasensitive *feeling*
LTRSNTRFGL ultracentrifugal *(adj) measured* ultracentrifugally *(adv)*
LTRSNTRFJ ultracentrifuge *scale*
LTRSNTRFYGL ultracentrifugal *(adj) measured* ultracentrifugally *(adv)*
LTRSNTRFYJ ultracentrifuge *scale*
LTRSNX ultrasonics *frequency*
LTRST altruist *benefits others*
LTRST ultraist *extreme measures*

Use letters that best describe the sounds you hear and omit the vowels. Use **S** or **K** instead of **C**: to find circle use **SRKL**. Use **J** to find joy, **JM** to find gem and **G** to find go.

LTRSTK altruistic *benefits others*

LTRSTKL altruistically *benefits others*

LTRSTN altar stone *relic storage*

LTRT aliterate *no desire to read*

LTRT alliterate *repeat* alliterated alliterating

LTRT elutriate *purify* elutriated elutriating

LTRT ill-treat *harm*

LTRT illiterate *unable to read*

LTRT literate *read and write*

LTRT literati *educated class*

LTRTHN ultrathin *not thick*

LTRTHNR lighter-than-air *gas*

LTRTL illiterately *unable to read*

LTRTL literately *well-read*

LTRTMNT ill-treatment *harm*

LTRTNS illiterateness *unable to read*

LTRTNS literateness *well-read*

LTRTR literature *books*

LTRTV alliterative *repetitive*

LTRTVL alliteratively *repetitive*

LTRTYR literature *books*

LTRVLNS ultraviolence *injury*

LTRVLNTS ultraviolence *injury*

LTRVLT ultraviolet *light*

LTRVYLNS ultraviolence *injury*

LTRVYLNTS ultraviolence *injury*

LTRVYLT ultraviolet *light*

LTRWD ultrawide *width*

LTRWSDK altruistic *benefits others*

LTRWSDKL altruistically *benefits others*

LTRWST altruist *benefits others*

LTRWSTK altruistic *benefits others*

LTRWSTKL altruistically

benefits others

LTRWZM altruism *benefit to others*

LTRXKLSV ultraexclusive *elite*

LTRYR ulterior *hidden*

LTRYRL ulteriorly *hidden*

LTRYSHN elutriation *purification*

LTRYT elutriate *purify* elutriated elutriating

LTRZM altruism *benefit to others*

LTRZM ultraism *extreme measures*

LTS ileitis *inflammation*

LTS lattice *framework*

LTS lettuce *food*

LTS lights *lungs*

LTS lots *much, many*

LTS lotus *flower*

LTS luteous *yellow*

LTS lutz *jump*

LTSD latticed *framework*

LTSDMNT Old Testament bible

LTSH latish *overdue*

LTSH loutish *boorish*

LTSHM lutetium *element*

LTSHMRZ Alzheimer's disease

LTSHP lightship *beacon*

LTSHYM lutetium *element*

LTSL latosol *soil*

LTSLK latosolic *soil*

LTST latest *most recent*

LTST latticed *framework*

LTSTMNT Old Testament bible

LTSTRDS altostratus *cloud*

LTSTRTS altostratus *cloud*

LTSWRK latticework *frame*

LTSZ latices (pl) *rubber latex*

LTTD altitude *height*

LTTD latitude *width, freedom*

LTTDNL altitudinal *height*

LTTDNL latitudinal (adj) *width, freedom* latitudinally (adv)

LTTDNS altitudinous *height*

LTTYD altitude *height*

LTTYD latitude *width,*

freedom

LTTYDNL altitudinal *height*

LTTYDNL latitudinal (adj) *width, freedom* latitudinally (adv)

LTTYDNS altitudinous *height*

LTTZ litotes *understatement* litotes

LTV a lot of *many*

LTV illative *opinion*

LTWD lightwood *kindling*

LTWT lightweight *127-135 pounds, not a threat*

LTX latex *rubber* latices (or) latexes

LTYL luteal *ovulation*

LTYN lutein *pigment*

LTYNZ luteinize *pigment* luteinized luteinizing

LTYNZSHN luteinization *pigment*

LTYR light-year *length*

LTYR luthier *guitar maker*

LTYS luteous *yellow*

LTZ ill at ease *nervous*

LTZ lots *much, many*

LTZ lutz *jump*

LTZM elitism *superiority* (Br) elitism

LTZMTH altazimuth *telescope*

LV alive *living*

LV alluvia (pl) *silt* alluvium

LV lava *volcano*

LV lave *wash* laved laving

LV leave *depart* left leaving

LV leave *leaf* leaved leaving

LV levee *ridge* leveed leveeing

LV levy *tax* levied levying levies

LV live (v) *exist* lived living

LV live (adj) *living, vivid, charged*

LV Louvre *museum*

LV love *affection* loved loving

LV olive *tree, color, food*

LV ulva *sea lettuce*

LVB lavabo *ceremony, sink* lavabos

LVBDS love beads *necklace*

LVBDZ love beads *necklace*

LVBG lovebug *fly*

LVBL leviable *tax*
LVBL livable *survival*
LVBL lovable (adj) *attractive*
lovably (adv)
LVBLD lovability *attractive*
LVBLNS livableness *survival*
LVBLT livability *survival*
LVBLT lovability *attractive*
LVBRD lovebird *parrot*
LVBRNCH olive branch
peace
LVCHL love child *illegitimate*
LVCHLD love child
illegitimate
LVCT love seat *couch*
LVD leaved *grew leaves*
LVD levity *laughter*
LVD livid *bruised, enraged*
LVDD elevated *train*
LVDD eluviated *transported soil*
LVDD illuviated *soil*
LVDN lived-in *inhabited*
LVDR alleviator *reliever*
LVDR elevator *lift*
LVDR levator *muscle*
levatores (or) levators
LVDV lovey-dovey *mushy*
LVGSHN levigation *powder*
LVGT levigate *grind*
levigated levigating
LVHNDLS love handles *fat*
LVHNDLZ love handles *fat*
LVJ lavage *washing*
LVJ lovage *herb*
LVK live oak *tree*
LVL alluvial *silt*
LVL alveoli (pl) *cavity*
alveolus
LVL eluvial *transported soil*
LVL illuvial *accumulated soil*
LVL level *(v) even, direct*
leveled (or) levelled
leveling (or) levelling
LVL level *(n) evenness, plane, intensity**
LVL level (adj) *balanced*
levelly (adv)
LVL lively *active* livelier
liveliest
LVL Louisville *city*
LVL lovely *pretty* lovelier

loveliest
LVL olive oil *food*
LVLHD livelihood *work*
LVLHDD levelheaded
sensible
LVLK lavalike *rock*
LVLK lovelock *hair*
LVLNG livelong *whole*
LVLNS levelness *evenness*
LVLNS liveliness *activity*
LVLNS loveliness *pretty*
LVLR alveolar *cavity*
LVLR lavaliere (or) lavalliere
pendant
LVLR leveler (or) leveller
equalizer
LVLR livelier *active*
LVLR lovelier *pretty*
LVLRL alveolarly *cavity*
LVLRN lovelorn *lonely*
LVLS alveolus *cavity* alveoli
LVLS loveless *no affection*
LVLST liveliest *active*
LVLST loveliest *pretty*
LVLT alveolate *pitted*
LVLV lavalava *skirt*
LVLYR livelier *active*
LVLYR lovelier *pretty*
LVLYST liveliest *active*
LVLYST loveliest *pretty*
LVM alluvium *silt* alluvia (or)
alluviums
LVMKN lovemaking
copulation
LVMKNG lovemaking
copulation
LVMN Isle of Man *island*
LVN alevin *salmon*
LVN alluvion *flood*
LVN eleven *number (11)*
LVN elevon *airplane control*
LVN leaven *yeast*
LVN live-in (adj) *inhabit* live
in (v)
LVN liven *activate*
LVN living *alive*
LVN love-in *gathering*
LVN loving *affectionate*
LVN olivine *mineral*
LVNDR lavender *plant, color*
LVNG living *alive*
LVNG loving *affectionate*

LVNGKNDNS loving-
kindness *tenderness*
LVNGKNS loving-kindness
tenderness
LVNGRM living room *salon*
LVNGS leavings *remainder*
LVNHK Leeuwenhoek
naturalist
LVNKNDNS loving-kindness
tenderness
LVNKNS loving-kindness
tenderness
LVNN leavening *yeast*
LVNNG leavening *yeast*
LVNRM living room *salon*
LVNS aliveness *living*
LVNT levant *(Br) run*
LVNT love knot *emblem*
LVNT olivenite *mineral*
LVNTH eleventh *of number 11*
LVNTHR eleventh hour *late*
LVNTHWR eleventh hour
late
LVNTR levanter *wind*
LVNZ leavings *remainder*
LVPL love apple *tomato*
LVR all over (adv) *everywhere*
allover (adj)
LVR allover *(n) fabric (adj)*
whole
LVR aloe vera *plant*
LVR elver *eel*
LVR laver *basin, algae*
LVR lay over (v) *travel stop*
layover (n)
LVR leaver *deserter*
LVR lever *(n) tool (v) pry*
LVR levier *taxer*
LVR liver *organ*
LVR livery *uniform, horses*
liveries
LVR livre *money*
LVR louver (or) louvre *slat*
(Br) louvre
LVR Louvre *museum*
LVR lover *affectionate one*
LVRD liveried *uniformed*
LVRJ leverage *power*
leveraged leveraging
LVRJD leveraged *high debt*
LVRMN liveryman *worker*

Use letters that best describe the sounds you hear and omit the vowels. Use **S** or **K** instead of **C**: to find circle use **SRKL**. Use **J** to find joy, **JM** to find gem and **G** to find go.

liverymen
LVRPL Liverpool *city*
LVRSH liverish *bilious*
LVRSHNS liverishness
bilious
LVRSTBL livery stable
horses
LVRWRST liverwurst *meat*
LVRWRT liverwort *plant*
LVS leaves (pl) *foliage* leaf
LVS lives (pl) *existence* life
LVS loaves (pl) *bread* loaf
LVSH elvish *mischievous*
LVSH lavage *washing*
LVSH lavish *(adj) plentiful (v)*
squander
LVSHL lavishly *plentifully*
LVSHN alleviation *relief*
LVSHN elevation *height*
LVSHN eluviation *transported*
soil
LVSHN illuviation *soil*
LVSHN lavation *wash*
LVSHNS lavishness *plenty*
LVSHS olivaceous *tree, color,*
food
LVSK lovesick *yearning*
LVSKNS lovesickness
yearning
LVST love seat *couch*
LVSTK livestock *animals*
LVT alleviate *relieve*
alleviated alleviating
LVT elevate *raise up*
elevated elevating
LVT levity *laughter*
LVT lovat *tweed*
LVTD elevated *train*
LVTD eluviated *transported*
soil
LVTD illuviated *accumulate*
soil
LVTHN leviathan *monster,*
bureaucracy
LVTKN leave-taking *farewell*
LVTKNG leave-taking
farewell
LVTR alleviator *reliever*
LVTR elevator *lift*
LVTR lavatory *washroom*
lavatories
LVTR levator *muscle*

levatores (or) levators
LVTSHN levitation *lifting*
LVTT levitate *float* levitated
levitating
LVWR live wire *active one*
LVWT Isle of Wight *island*
LVWYR live wire *active one*
LVY alluvia (pl) *silt* alluvium
LVYBL leviable *tax*
LVYDD eluviated *transported*
soil
LVYDD illuviated *accumulate*
soil
LVYDR alleviator *reliever*
LVYL alluvial *silt*
LVYL alveoli (pl) *cavity*
alveolus
LVYL eluvial *transported soil*
LVYL illuvial *accumulate soil*
LVYL olive oil *food*
LVYLR alveolar *cavity*
LVYLRL alveolarly *cavity*
LVYLS alveolus *cavity*
alveoli
LVYLT alveolate *pitted*
LVYM alluvium *silt* alluvia
(or) alluviums
LVYN alluvion *flood*
LVYR levier *taxer*
LVYSHN alleviation *relief*
LVYSHN eluviation
transported soil
LVYSHN illuviation
accumulate soil
LVYT alleviate *relieve*
alleviated alleviating
LVYTD eluviated *transported*
soil
LVYTD illuviated *accumulate*
soil
LVYTHN leviathan *monster,*
bureaucracy
LVYTR alleviator *reliever*
LVZ elves (pl) *mythical being*
elf
LVZ leaves (pl) *foliage* leaf
LVZ Levi's *(trademark) jeans*
LVZ lives (pl) *existence* life
LVZH lavage *washing*
LW alleyway *lane*
LW allow *permit*
LW leeway *space*

LW luau *feast*
LWBDN law-abiding *honest*
LWBDNG law-abiding
honest
LWBL allowable (adj)
permitted allowably (adv)
LWDK luetic *syphilis*
LWDL allowedly *admittedly*
LWDR louis d'or *coin* louis
d'or
LWDR low water *tide*
LWF alewife *pub keeper (f),*
fish alewives
LWL ill will *hatred*
LWL oil well *pump*
LWMN laywoman *non-expert*
laywomen
LWN lauan *timber*
LWND low-end *cheap*
LWND Luanda *city*
LWNHK Leeuwenhoek
naturalist
LWNS allowance *share*
LWNTS allowance *share*
LWR lower *(v) let down,*
frown, humble (adj) below
(n) frown
LWR lowery *gloomy*
LWRD leeward *toward the*
wind
LWRKLS lower class (n)
inferior lower-class (adj)
LWRKS lowercase *type*
LWRLD Old World (n)
Europe old-world (adj)
LWRM eelworm *worm*
LWRMST lowermost *bottom*
LWRN lowering *gloomy*
LWRNG lowering *gloomy*
LWS always *forever*
LWS lewis *hoist*
LWSL loessial *loam*
LWST lowest *beneath*
LWSYL loessial *loam*
LWTK luetic *syphilis*
LWTR low water *tide*
LWVL Louisville *city*
LWW luau *feast*
LWZ always *forever*
LWZ lues *syphilis* lues
LWZN Louisiana *US State*
LWZYN Louisiana *US State*

Letters aren't doubled for single sounds: to find alley use **L** not **LL**. Use **Y** and **W** as hard sounds only: to find yellow use **YL**. (Br)=British spelling or usage. * See dictionary.

LX alexia *unable to read*
LX ilex *holly*
LX lax *loose*
LX lex *law* leges
LX look-see *view*
LX looks *(slang) appearance*
LX lox *food* lox (or) loxes
LX lux *candlepower* lux (or) luxes
LXD lakeside *shoreline*
LXD laxity *looseness*
LXDV laxative *loosen*
LXK lexica (pl) *dictionary* lexicon
LXKGRF lexicography *dictionary*
LXKGRFKL lexicographical (adj) *dictionary* lexicographically (adv)
LXKGRFR lexicographer *dictionary*
LXKL lexical (adj) *words* lexically (adv)
LXKLD lexicality *words*
LXKLG lexicology *words*
LXKLJ lexicology *words*
LXKLJST lexicologist *words*
LXKLT lexicality *words*
LXKLZ lexicalize *give meaning* lexicalized lexicalizing (Br) lexicalise
LXKLZSHN lexicalization *meaning* (Br) lexicalisation
LXKN lexicon *dictionary* lexica (or) lexicons
LXL laxly *loose*
LXM lexeme *word*
LXMBRG Luxembourg (or) Luxemburg *province*
LXMK lexemic *word*
LXMTH locksmith *keys*
LXMTHNG locksmithing *keys*
LXNDR Alexander (the Great) *conqueror*
LXNDR Alexandria *city*
LXNDRN Alexandrian *of Alexandria*
LXNDRN alexandrine *verse*
LXNDRT alexandrite *mineral*

LXNDRY Alexandria *city*
LXNDRYN Alexandrian *of Alexandria*
LXNGTN Lexington *city*
LXNS laxness *looseness*
LXPDL lickspittle *flattery*
LXPTL lickspittle *flattery*
LXR elixir *cure-all*
LXS lexis *words* lexes
LXSHN luxation *dislocation*
LXT laxity *looseness*
LXT ulexite *mineral*
LXTCH lockstitch *sewing*
LXTP lockstep *marching*
LXTV laxative *loosen*
LXVT lixiviate *extract* lixiviated lixiviating
LXVYT lixiviate *extract* lixiviated lixiviating
LXY alexia *unable to read*
LXZ lexes (pl) *words* lexis
LY ilea (pl) *intestine* ileum
LY ilia (pl) *bone* ilium
LY Leo *zodiac sign*
LY oleo *margarine*
LY olio *mixture* olios
LYBL liable *likely, answerable*
LYBLD liability *debt, drawback* liabilities
LYBLT liability *debt, drawback* liabilities
LYBT layabout *lazy one*
LYD Iliad *poem*
LYD laity *not clergy*
LYDS ileitis *inflammation*
LYF lay off (v) *suspend* layoff (n)
LYK iliac *intestine*
LYK laic (or) laical (adj) *worldly* laically (adv)
LYK oleic *fat*
LYKL laical (or) laic (adj) *worldly* laically (adv)
LYL ileal *intestine*
LYL lisle *thread*
LYL loyal (adj) *faithful* loyally (adv)
LYLD loyalty *faithfulness* loyalties
LYLNT ululant *wailing*
LYLSHN ululation *wail*
LYLST loyalist *faithful one*

LYLT loyalty *faithfulness* loyalties
LYLT ululate *wail* ululated ululating
LYM allium *herb*
LYM ileum *intestine* ilea
LYM ilium *bone* ilia
LYM oleum *oil* olea
LYM oleum *corrosive* oleums
LYMNM aluminium *(Br) aluminum*
LYMNYM aluminium *(Br) aluminum*
LYMRJRN oleomargarine *spread*
LYMSNR eleemosynary *charity*
LYMZNR eleemosynary *charity*
LYN aeolian *wind sound*
LYN alien *foreign*
LYN eolian *wind*
LYN leone *money* leones (or) leone
LYN liana *vine*
LYN lie-in *protest*
LYN lion *animal* lions
LYN Lyon *city*
LYNBL alienable *transferable*
LYNDR alienator *estranger*
LYNDR oleander *plant*
LYNFSH lionfish *fish*
LYNG lying *fib, position*
LYNHRDD lionhearted *brave*
LYNHRTD lionhearted *brave*
LYNJ alienage *status*
LYNL alienly *foreign*
LYNN leonine *lion*
LYNR alienor *transferor*
LYNRDDVNCH Leonardo da Vinci *artist*
LYNS alienness *foreign*
LYNS alliance *bond*
LYNS lioness *lion (f)* lionesses
LYNSHN alienation *estrangement*
LYNST alienist *psychologist*
LYNT alienate *estrange* alienated alienating
LYNTR alienator *estranger*
LYNTS alliance *bond*

LYNZ lionize *respect, (Br)* *show sights* lionized lionizing (Br) lionise

LYNZ lyonnaise *sauce*

LYNZR lionizer *respect, (Br)* *show sights* (Br) lioniser

LYNZSHN lionization *respect, (Br) show sights* (Br) lionisation

LYP alley-oop *basketball*

LYR lawyer *attorney*

LYR layer *one thickness, hen*

LYR liar *deceiver*

LYR lyre *music*

LYR oilier *greasy*

LYRBRD lyrebird *bird*

LYRN aleurone *protein*

LYRZN oleoresin *turpentine*

LYS alias *name* aliases

LYS ileus *obstruction*

LYS ill-use *abuse*

LYSHN Laotian *of Laos*

LYSHS alliaceous *garlic*

LYSJ ill-usage *abuse*

LYSNN Eleusinian *mystical*

LYSNYN Eleusinian *mystical*

LYST oiliest *greasy*

LYSTR oleaster *plant*

LYSZ laicize *make worldly* laicized laicizing

LYT laity *not clergy*

LYT lay out (v) *spread* layout (n)

LYT layette *baby clothing*

LYTR aleatory *by chance*

LYTRD leotard *garment*

LYTRK aleatoric *by chance*

LYTRL laetrile *(often capitalized) drug*

LYTS ileitis *inflammation*

LYVR lay over (v) *travel stop* layover (n)

LYW lay away (v) *put aside* layaway (n)

LYZ liaise *bond* liaised liaising

LYZJ ill-usage *abuse*

LYZN liaison *affair*

LZ allies (pl) *(often capitalized) associate* ally

LZ lase *emit light* lased lasing

LZ laze *loaf* lazed lazing

LZ lazy *idle* lazier laziest

LZ lees *sediment*

LZ liaise *bond* liaised liaising

LZ lose *mislay* lost losing

LZ lousy *awful* lousier lousiest

LZ lues *syphilis* lues

LZ lyse *decline* lysed lysing

LZBN lesbian *homosexual (f)*

LZBN Lisbon *city*

LZBNZ lazybones *idler*

LZBNZM lesbianism *homosexual (f)*

LZBTHN Elizabethan *of Elizabeth I*

LZBYN lesbian *homosexual (f)*

LZBYNZM lesbianism *homosexual (f)*

LZFR laissez faire *choice* (Br) laisser-faire

LZH loge *theater box*

LZH luge *sled*

LZHLT lazulite *mineral*

LZHM Elysium *paradise*

LZHMRZ Alzheimer's *disease*

LZHN allusion *reference*

LZHN elision *omission*

LZHN elusion *evasion*

LZHN elysian (adj) *(often capitalized) heavenly*

LZHN illusion *false idea*

LZHN lesion *skin*

LZHNL illusional *false idea*

LZHNR illusionary *illusory*

LZHNST illusionist *magician*

LZHR leisure *free time*

LZHR luger *sledder*

LZHRD leisured *free time*

LZHRL leisurely *free time*

LZHRLNS leisureliness *free time*

LZHRST leisure suit *attire*

LZHYM Elysium *paradise*

LZJ ill-usage *abuse*

LZL lazily *idly*

LZL lousily *awful*

LZLT lazulite *mineral*

LZLZ lose-lose *no winner*

LZM Elysium *paradise*

LZMJST lèse-majesté (or) lese majesty *offense*

LZMRZ Alzheimer's *disease*

LZMSHST lèse-majesté (or) lese majesty *offense*

LZMZHST lèse-majesté (or) lese majesty *offense*

LZN liaison *affair*

LZN Louisiana *US State*

LZNJ lozenge *diamond, candy*

LZNS laziness *idleness*

LZNS lousiness *awfulness*

LZNY lasagna *food*

LZPDZ lespedeza *plant*

LZR laser *light*

LZR lazar *leper*

LZR lazier *idle*

LZR loser *failure*

LZR lousier *awful*

LZRD lazaretto (or) lazaret *quarantine* lazarettos (or) lazarets

LZRD lizard *reptile*

LZRFR laissez faire *choice* (Br) laisser-faire

LZRT lazaretto (or) lazaret *quarantine* lazarettos (or) lazarets

LZST laziest *idle*

LZST lousiest *awful*

LZSZN lazy Susan *tray*

LZT lose out *fail*

LZTNGS lazy tongs *extender*

LZV allusive *suggestive*

LZV elusive *evasive*

LZV illusive *deceptive*

LZVL allusively *suggestively*

LZVNS allusiveness *implication*

LZVNS elusiveness *evasion*

LZVNS illusiveness *deception*

LZYLT lazulite *mineral*

LZYM Elysium *paradise*

LZYN elysian (adj) *(often capitalized) heavenly*

LZYN Louisiana *US State*

LZYR lazier *idle*

LZYR lousier *awful*

LZYST laziest *idle*

LZYST lousiest *awful*

Letters aren't doubled for single sounds: to find alley use **L** not **LL**. Use **Y** and **W** as hard sounds only: to find yellow use **YL**. (Br)=British spelling or usage. * See dictionary.

M

M A.M. (or) a.m. *(abbr) ante meridiem (before noon)*
M aim *(v) point (n) goal*
M am *exist*
M AM *(abbr) amplitude modulation (broadcast wave)*
M ama *diver* amas (or) ama
M amah *nurse*
M ammo *ammunition*
M elm *tree*
M Emmy *award* Emmys
M emu *bird*
M I'm *(contr) I am*
M iamb (or) iambus *poetry* iambs (or) iambuses
M m *alphabet letter* m's (or) ms
M ma *mother*
M maillot *clothing*
M Maui *island*
M maw *mouth*
M May *month*
M may *can* might
M mayo *mayonnaise*
M me *(pron) myself*
M meow *cat sound*
M mew *(n) gull, meow, abode (v) meow, confine*
M mho *electrical unit* mhos
M mi *musical note*
M moa *extinct bird*
M moo *cow sound*
M mot *joke* mots
M moue *pout*
M mow *(v) cut down, kill* mowed mowing mowed (or) mown
M mow *(n) hay, sneer*
M my *of me*
M ohm *electrical unit*

MB amoeba *one-celled animal* amoebas (or) amoebae
MB embay *trap*
MB imbue *penetrate* imbued imbuing
MB maybe *perhaps*
MB mob *crowd* mobbed mobbing
MB mobe (or) mobe *pearl*
MB umbo *projection* umbones (or) umbos
MBB imbibe *drink* imbibed imbibing
MBBR imbiber *drinker*
MBBSHN imbibation *drink*
MBBSHNL imbibational *drink*
MBC embassy *diplomats* embassies
MBD amoeboid *one-celled animal*
MBD embed *enclose* embedded embedding
MBD embody *personify* embodied embodying embodies
MBD embowed *arched*
MBDD embedded *enclosed*
MBDKSTRD ambidexterity *both hands*
MBDKSTRS ambidextrous *both hands*
MBDKSTRSL ambidextrously *both hands*
MBDKSTRT ambidexterity *both hands*
MBDL embattle *fortify* embattled embattling
MBDLD embattled *fighting*
MBDLMNT embattlement *fortification*
MBDMNT embedment *enclosure*
MBDMNT embodiment *personification*
MBDN embedding *enclosure*
MBDNG embedding *enclosure*
MBDR embitter *make bitter*
MBDR embodier *personifier*

MBDSMN ombudsman *investigator* ombudsmen
MBDXTRD ambidexterity *both hands*
MBDXTRS ambidextrous *both hands*
MBDXTRSL ambidextrously *both hands*
MBDXTRT ambidexterity *both hands*
MBDYR embodier *personifier*
MBDZMN ombudsman *investigator* ombudsmen
MBGD ambiguity *uncertainty* ambiguities
MBGS ambiguous *uncertain*
MBGSL ambiguously *uncertainly*
MBGSNS ambiguousness *uncertainty*
MBGT ambiguity *uncertainty* ambiguities
MBGWD ambiguity *uncertainty* ambiguities
MBGWS ambiguous *uncertain*
MBGWSL ambiguously *uncertainly*
MBGWSNS ambiguousness *uncertainty*
MBGWT ambiguity *uncertainty* ambiguities
MBGYD ambiguity *uncertainty* ambiguities
MBGYS ambiguous *uncertain*
MBGYSL ambiguously *uncertainly*
MBGYSNS ambiguousness *uncertainty*
MBGYT ambiguity *uncertainty* ambiguities
MBGYWD ambiguity *uncertainty* ambiguities
MBGYWS ambiguous *uncertain*
MBGYWSL ambiguously *uncertainly*
MBGYWSNS ambiguousness *uncertainty*

Use letters that best describe the sounds you hear and omit the vowels. Use **S** or **K** instead of **C**: to find circle use **SRKL**. Use **J** to find joy, **JM** to find gem and **G** to find go.

MBGYWT ambiguity *uncertainty* ambiguities

MBK amoebic *one-celled animal*

MBK iambic *poetry*

MBKP mobcap *hat*

MBKRC mobocracy *crowd rule* mobocracies

MBKRS mobocracy *crowd rule* mobocracies

MBL amble *saunter* ambled ambling

MBL amiable (adj) *friendly* amiably (adv)

MBL emboli (pl) *clot* embolus

MBL humble (v) *humiliate* humbled humbling

MBL humble (adj) *not proud* humbler humblest

MBL humbly *not proud*

MBL immobile *not moving*

MBL Mobile *city*

MBL mobile (adj) *movable (n) dangling sculpture*

MBL umbel *cluster*

MBLD amiability *friendliness*

MBLD immobility *not movable*

MBLD mobility *movable*

MBLDN embolden *give courage*

MBLFR umbellifer *cluster*

MBLFRS umbelliferous *cluster*

MBLK embolic *clot*

MBLK umbilici (pl) *navel* umbilicus

MBLKDD umbilicated (or) umbilicate *navel*

MBLKDM embolectomy *remove clot* embolectomies

MBLKL umbilical *navel*

MBLKS umbilicus *navel* umbilici (or) umbilicuses

MBLKT umbilicate (or) umbilicated *navel*

MBLKTD umbilicated (or) umbilicate *navel*

MBLKTM embolectomy *remove clot*

embolectomies

MBLM embalm *preserve*

MBLM emblem *symbol*

MBLMDK emblematic *symbolic*

MBLMDKL emblematically *symbolic*

MBLMNT embalmment *preservation*

MBLMR embalmer *preserver*

MBLMTK emblematic *symbolic*

MBLMTKL emblematically *symbolic*

MBLNS ambulance *vehicle*

MBLNS amiableness *friendliness*

MBLNS humbleness *modesty*

MBLNS imbalance *tilt*

MBLNST imbalanced *tilt*

MBLNT ambulant *moving*

MBLNTS ambulance *vehicle*

MBLNTS imbalance *tilt*

MBLNTST imbalanced *tilt*

MBLP amblyopia *lazy eye*

MBLP humble pie *modest*

MBLPK amblyopic *lazy eye*

MBLPY amblyopia *lazy eye*

MBLR ambler *saunterer*

MBLR humbler *not proud*

MBLS embolus *clot* emboli

MBLS umbilici (pl) *navel* umbilicus

MBLSH embellish *decorate, improve* embellishes

MBLSHMNT embellishment *decorate, improve*

MBLSHN ambulation *movement*

MBLSHR embellisher *decorate, improve*

MBLST humblest *not proud*

MBLST myoblast *muscle cell*

MBLT amiability *friendliness*

MBLT immobility *not movable*

MBLT mobility *movable*

MBLT umbellate *cluster*

MBLTR ambulatory (adj) *movable (n) shelter* ambulatories

MBLYP amblyopia *lazy eye*

MBLYPK amblyopic *lazy eye*

MBLYPY amblyopia *lazy eye*

MBLZ emblaze *fire* emblazed emblazing

MBLZ immobilize *not moving* immobilized immobilizing (Br) immobilise

MBLZ mobilize *move* mobilized mobilizing (Br) mobilise

MBLZ umbles *viscera*

MBLZM embolism *clot*

MBLZM immobilism *no change*

MBLZN emblazon *inscribe, praise* emblazoned emblazoning

MBLZNMNT emblazonment *inscription, praise*

MBLZNR emblazoner *inscriber, praiser*

MBLZNR emblazonry *decoration*

MBLZR immobilizer *not moving* (Br) immobiliser

MBLZSHN immobilization *not moving*

MBLZSHN mobilization *movement* (Br) mobilisation

MBM embalm *preserve*

MBMNT embalmment *preservation*

MBMNT embayment *trap*

MBMR embalmer *preserver*

MBNGKMNT embankment *levee*

MBNKMNT embankment *levee*

MBNS ambience (or) ambiance *atmosphere*

MBNT ambient *environment*

MBNTS ambience (or) ambiance *atmosphere*

MBNZ umbones (pl) *projection* umbo

MBR amber *resin, gold color*

MBR ambry *cupboard* ambries

MBR ember *fire*

Letters aren't doubled for single sounds: to find alley use **L** not **LL**. Use **Y** and **W** as hard sounds only: to find yellow use **YL**. (Br)=British spelling or usage. * See dictionary.

MBR embryo *fetus* embryos
MBR hombre *man*
MBR imbrue *stain* imbrued imbruing
MBR ombré *shading*
MBR ombre *game*
MBR umber *brown color*
MBR umbra *shadow* umbras (or) umbrae
MBRDL embrittle *make stiff* embrittled embrittling
MBRDLMNT embrittlement *stiffness*
MBRDR embroider *sew*
MBRDR embroidery *sewing* embroideries
MBRDRR embroiderer *sewing*
MBRFT embryophyte *plant*
MBRG embargo *stop* embargoes embargoed embargoing
MBRGRS ambergris *whale oil*
MBRGS umbrageous *offense, shaded*
MBRGSL umbrageously *offensive, shaded*
MBRGSNS umbrageousness *offense, shade*
MBRGYS umbrageous *offense, shaded*
MBRGYSL umbrageously *offensive, shaded*
MBRGYSNS umbrageousness *offense, shade*
MBRJ umbrage *offense, shadow*
MBRJK amberjack *fish*
MBRJS umbrageous *offense, shaded*
MBRJSL umbrageously *offensive, shaded*
MBRJSNS umbrageousness *offense, shade*
MBRK embark *start, board*
MBRKDR embarcadero *pier*
MBRKMNT embarkment *start, board*

MBRKSHN embarkation *start, board*
MBRKSHN imbrication *overlap*
MBRKT imbricate *overlap* imbricated imbricating
MBRL embroil *make conflict*
MBRL imbroglio *confusion* imbroglios
MBRL umbrella *rain*
MBRLG embryology *fetus*
MBRLJ embryology *fetus*
MBRLJKL embryological (adj) *fetus* embryologically (adv)
MBRLJST embryologist *fetus*
MBRLMNT embroilment *conflict*
MBRLY imbroglio *confusion* imbroglios
MBRNK embryonic *fetal*
MBRNKL embryonically *fetal*
MBRS embarrass *distress*
MBRS embrace *hug* embraced embracing
MBRSBL embarrassable *distress*
MBRSBL embraceable *hug*
MBRSH ambrosia *nectar*
MBRSHL ambrosial *nectar*
MBRSHR embrasure *opening*
MBRSMNT embarrassment *distress*
MBRSNGL embarrassingly *distress*
MBRSNGL embracingly *hug*
MBRSNL embracingly *hug*
MBRSR embracer *hug*
MBRSR embracery *jury tampering* embraceries
MBRSV embracive *inclusive*
MBRTL embrittle *make stiff* embrittled embrittling
MBRTLMNT embrittlement *stiffness*
MBRTP ambrotype *photograph*
MBRY embryo *fetus* embryos

MBRYFT embryophyte *plant*
MBRYL embroil *make conflict*
MBRYLG embryology *fetus*
MBRYLJ embryology *fetus*
MBRYLJKL embryological (adj) *fetus* embryologically (adv)
MBRYLJST embryologist *fetus*
MBRYLMNT embroilment *conflict*
MBRYNK embryonic *fetal*
MBRYNKL embryonically *fetal*
MBRZH ambrosia *nectar*
MBRZHL ambrosial *nectar*
MBRZHR embrasure *opening*
MBS embassy *diplomats* embassies
MBS emboss *raised letters*
MBS iambus (or) iamb *poetry* iambuses (or) iambs
MBS Mobius *strip*
MBSBL embossable *raised letters*
MBSDR ambassador *diplomat*
MBSDR mobster *criminal*
MBSDRL ambassadorial *diplomatic*
MBSDRS ambassadress *diplomat (f)*
MBSDRSHP ambassadorship *diplomat*
MBSDRYL ambassadorial *diplomatic*
MBSH ambush *surprise*
MBSHMNT ambushment *surprise*
MBSHN ambition *aspiration*
MBSHNLS ambitionless *no aspiration*
MBSHR ambusher *surpriser*
MBSHR embouchure *lips*
MBSHS ambitious *aspiring*
MBSHSL ambitiously *aspiring*
MBSHSNS ambitiousness *aspiration*
MBSKD ambuscade *ambush*

Use letters that best describe the sounds you hear and omit the vowels. Use **S** or **K** instead of **C**: to find circle use **SRKL**. Use **J** to find joy, **JM** to find gem and **G** to find go.

MBSKDR ambuscader
ambusher
MBSKSHL ambisexual
either sex
MBSKSHLD ambisexuality
either sex
MBSKSHLT ambisexuality
either sex
MBSKSHWL ambisexual
either sex
MBSKSHWLD
ambisexuality *either sex*
MBSKSHWLT
ambisexuality *either sex*
MBSL imbecile *fool*
MBSLD imbecility *foolishness*
imbecilities
MBSLK imbecilic *foolish*
MBSLT imbecility *foolishness*
imbecilities
MBSMNT embossment
raised letters
MBSR embosser *raised*
letters
MBST amoebocyte *one-*
celled animal
MBSTR ambassador
diplomat
MBSTR mobster *criminal*
MBSTRS ambassadress
diplomat (f)
MBSTRSHP
ambassadorship *diplomat*
MBT ambit *circuit*
MBTD embedded *enclosed*
MBTL embattle *fortify*
embattled embattling
MBTLD embattled *fighting*
MBTLMNT embattlement
fortification
MBTNG embedding
enclosure
MBTR embitter *make bitter*
MBVLNS ambivalence
fluctuation
MBVLNT ambivalent
fluctuating
MBVLNTL ambivalently
fluctuating
MBVLNTS ambivalence
fluctuation
MBY imbue *penetrate*

imbued imbuing
MBYLNS ambulance *vehicle*
MBYLNT ambulant *moving*
MBYLNTS ambulance
vehicle
MBYLSHN ambulation
movement
MBYLTR ambulatory *(adj)*
movable (n) shelter
ambulatories
MBYNS ambience (or)
ambiance *atmosphere*
MBYNT ambient
environment
MBYNTS ambience (or)
ambiance *atmosphere*
MBYS Mobius *strip*
MBZL embezzle *steal*
embezzled embezzling
MBZLMNT embezzlement
stealing
MBZLR embezzler *stealer*
MC amici (pl) *law* amicus
MC emcee *host* emceed
emceeing
MC massé *billiards*
MC messy *dirty* messier
messiest
MC missy *young girl*
MC mossy *with moss*
mossier mossiest
MC mousy (or) mousey
timid, grayish brown
mousier mousiest
MC mussy *messy* mussier
mussiest
MC must-see *good viewing*
MCDZN mycetozoan *slime*
mold
MCDZWN mycetozoan
slime mold
MCH macho *masculine*
machos
MCH match *(n) competition,*
flame, pair (v) compare
matches
MCH mooch *sponge*
MCH much *many* more
most
MCHBK matchbook
container
MCHBKS matchbox

container matchboxes
MCHBL matchable *compare*
MCHBX matchbox *container*
matchboxes
MCHD machete *large knife*
MCHL mutual (adj) *shared*
mutually (adv)
MCHLD mutuality *sharing*
MCHLK matchlock *gun*
MCHLS matchless
unequaled
MCHLT mutuality *sharing*
MCHLZ mutualize *share*
mutualized mutualizing
MCHLZM mutualism
sharing
MCHMKN matchmaking
marriage
MCHMKNG matchmaking
marriage
MCHMKR matchmaker
marriage
MCHPCH Machu Picchu
Inca site
MCHR amateur *not*
professional
MCHR immature *not ripe*
MCHR mature *ripen, age*
matured maturing
MCHR moocher *sponger*
MCHRD immaturity *not ripe*
MCHRD maturity *ripeness*
MCHRL immaturely *unripe*
MCHRSH amateurish
incompetent
MCHRSHL amateurishly
incompetently
MCHRSHN maturation
ripeness
MCHRSHNS
amateurishness
incompetence
MCHRT immaturity *not ripe*
MCHRT maturate *ripen*
maturated maturating
MCHRT maturity *ripeness*
MCHRZM amateurism
incompetence
MCHSTK matchstick *flame*
MCHT machete *large knife*
MCHWL mutual (adj) *shared*
mutually (adv)

Letters aren't doubled for single sounds: to find alley use **L** not **LL**. Use **Y** and **W** as hard
sounds only: to find yellow use **YL**. (Br)=British spelling or usage. * See dictionary.

MCHWLD mutuality *sharing*
MCHWLT mutuality *sharing*
MCHWLZ mutualize *share* mutualized mutualizing
MCHWLZM mutualism *sharing*
MCHZM machismo *power*
MCL mycelia (pl) *fungus* mycelium
MCLM mycelium *fungus* mycelia
MCLY mycelia (pl) *fungus* mycelium
MCLYM mycelium *fungus* mycelia
MCNN Mycenaean *of Mycenae*
MCNYN Mycenaean *of Mycenae*
MCR messier *dirty*
MCR mossier *with moss*
MCR mousier *timid, grayish brown*
MCR mussier *messy*
MCSHN emaciation *thinness*
MCST messiest *dirty*
MCST mossiest *with moss*
MCST mousiest *timid, grayish brown*
MCST mussiest *messy*
MCT emaciate *make thin* emaciated emaciating
MCTFGS mycetophagous *fungus*
MCTM mycetoma *tumor* mycetomas (or) mycetomata
MCTMD mycetomata (pl) *tumor* mycetoma
MCTMT mycetomata (pl) *tumor* mycetoma
MCTZN mycetozoan *slime mold*
MCTZWN mycetozoan *slime mold*
MCYR messier *dirty*
MCYR mossier *with moss*
MCYR mousier *timid, grayish brown*
MCYR mussier *messy*
MCYSHN emaciation *thinness*

MCYST messiest *dirty*
MCYST mossiest *with moss*
MCYST mousiest *timid, grayish brown*
MCYST mussiest *messy*
MCYT emaciate *make thin* emaciated emaciating
MD amid (or) amidst *among*
MD amide *compound*
MD amity *friendship* amities
MD mad *angry, crazy* madder maddest
MD made *(v-past) make*
MD maid *housekeeper*
MD matey *(Br) friendly*
MD May Day *festival*
MD Mayday *distress call*
MD mead *beverage*
MD meadow *grassland*
MD meaty *like flesh* meatier meatiest
MD Medea *enchantress*
MD media *voiced stop, muscle* mediae
MD media *news* medias
MD media (pl) *middle, material* medium
MD métier (or) metier *work*
MD mid *middle*
MD midday *noon*
MD middy *blouse, sailor* middies
MD midi *mid-calf*
MD mighty *powerful* mightier mightiest
MD mode *style*
MD mood *emotion*
MD moody *emotional* moodier moodiest
MD motto *slogan* mottoes
MD mud *(v) dirty* mudded mudding
MD mud *(n) wet dirt*
MD muddy *dirty* muddier muddiest
MDBL imitable *copied*
MDBL immutable (adj) *no change* immutably (adv)
MDBL mutable (adj) *able to change* mutably (adv)
MDBLD immutability *no change*

MDBLD mutability *change*
MDBLK metabolic *cell chemistry*
MDBLKL metabolically *cell chemistry*
MDBLT immutability *no change*
MDBLT mutability *change*
MDBR mud dauber *wasp*
MDBRN midbrain *brain section*
MDC immediacy *urgency* immediacies
MDDR matador *bullfighter*
MDDR mediator *judge*
MDDRDR made-to-order *custom made*
MDF modify *limit, change* modified modifying modifies
MDFKSHN modification *change*
MDFL medfly *(often capitalized) insect* medflies
MDFL mudflow *wet mass*
MDFLD midfield *sports*
MDFLDR midfielder *sports*
MDFLT mudflat *tidal area*
MDFR metaphor *symbol*
MDFR modifier *word*
MDFRK metaphoric (or) metaphorical (adj) *symbolic* metaphorically (adv)
MDFRKL metaphorically (adv) *symbolic* metaphoric (or) metaphorical (adj)
MDFRZ metaphrase *translation*
MDFYR modifier *word*
MDFZ metaphase *growth*
MDFZKL metaphysical (adj) *supernatural* metaphysically (adv)
MDFZKS metaphysics *philosophy*
MDFZSHN metaphysician *philosopher*
MDFZX metaphysics *philosophy*
MDGBL immitigable (adj) *no relief* immitagably (adv)

Use letters that best describe the sounds you hear and omit the vowels. Use **S** or **K** instead of **C**: to find circle use **SRKL**. Use **J** to find joy, **JM** to find gem and **G** to find go.

MDGDR mitigator *reliever*
MDGDV mitigative *relief*
MDGLN Modigliani *artist*
MDGLYN Modigliani *artist*
MDGNSS metagenesis *sex alternation*
MDGRD mudguard *fender*
MDGSHN mitigation *relief*
MDGSKR Madagascar *island*
MDGT mitigate *relieve* mitigated mitigating
MDGTR mitigator *reliever*
MDGTR mitigatory *relieving*
MDGTV mitigative *relief*
MDHS madhouse *asylum*
MDJNSS metagenesis *sex alternation*
MDK emetic *vomit*
MDK mattock *tool*
MDK medic *corpsman, herb*
MDK medico *physician* medicos
MDK meiotic *reduction*
MDKBL medicable *curable*
MDKD medicaid *(often capitalized) insurance*
MDKL emetically *vomit*
MDKL medical (adj) *doctor* medically (adv)
MDKL meiotically *reduction*
MDKM modicum *small portion*
MDKN mod con *(Br) modern convenience*
MDKNDR mitochondria (pl) *cell* mitochondrion
MDKNDRN mitochondrion *cell* mitochondria
MDKNDRY mitochondria (pl) *cell* mitochondrion
MDKNDRYN mitochondrion *cell* mitochondria
MDKP madcap *foolish*
MDKR medicare *(often capitalized) insurance*
MDKR mediocre *ordinary*
MDKRD mediocrity *ordinariness* mediocrities
MDKRLK modacrylic *fiber*
MDKRMDK metachromatic *stain*

MDKRMTK metachromatic *stain*
MDKRPL metacarpal *hand or foot*
MDKRPS metacarpus *hand or foot*
MDKRS midcourse *midway*
MDKRS motocross *race*
MDKRT mediocrity *ordinariness* mediocrities
MDKS meat-ax *cleaver*
MDKSHN medication *substance*
MDKT medicate *give medicine* medicated medicating
MDL madly *angry, crazy*
MDL medal *award*
MDL meddle *interfere* meddled meddling
MDL medial (adj) *average* medially (adv)
MDL medley *mixture* medleys
MDL medulla *marrow* medullas (or) medullae
MDL metal *iron, gold, etc.*
MDL mettle *courage*
MDL middle *center*
MDL mightily *powerfully*
MDL modal (adj) *type* modally (adv)
MDL model *shape, fashion* modeled (or) modelled modeling (or) modelling
MDL module *unit*
MDL moduli (pl) *value* modulus
MDL mottle *spot* mottled mottling
MDL muddily *wet dirt*
MDL muddle *confuse* muddled muddling
MDLBR middlebrow *slightly educated*
MDLD metalloid *like metal*
MDLD modality *form*
MDLDD muddle-headed *confused*
MDLDR modulator *tune, adjust*
MDLDR mutilator *destroyer,*

cutter
MDLF midlife *middle age*
MDLFRS metalliferous *with metal*
MDLGRN middle ground *standpoint*
MDLGRND middle ground *standpoint*
MDLHDD muddle-headed *confused*
MDLJ middle age *age 40-60*
MDLJD middle-aged *age 40-60*
MDLJS Middle Ages *500-1500 AD*
MDLJZ Middle Ages *500-1500 AD*
MDLKLS middle-class (adj) *neither rich nor poor* middle class (n)
MDLMN middleman *dealer* middlemen
MDLN maudlin *sentiment*
MDLN meadowland *grassland*
MDLN Medellin *drug cartel*
MDLN middling *halfway*
MDLN midland *region*
MDLN midline *center line*
MDLN Modigliani *artist*
MDLND meadowland *grassland*
MDLND midland *region*
MDLNG middling *halfway*
MDLNGGWSDK metalinguistic *language*
MDLNGGWSTK metalinguistic *language*
MDLNGWSDK metalinguistic *language*
MDLNGWSTK metalinguistic *language*
MDLR meddler *interferer*
MDLR middle ear *cavity*
MDLR middler *student*
MDLR modeler *shaper*
MDLR modular *standardized*
MDLR mottler *spot*
MDLR muddler *confuser*
MDLRG metallurgy *metal science*
MDLRJ metallurgy *metal*

science

MDLRJKL metallurgical (adj) *metal science* metallurgically (adv)

MDLRJST metallurgist *metal scientist*

MDLRK meadowlark *bird*

MDLS middle C *music*

MDLS modulus *value* moduli

MDLSHN modulation *tune, adjust*

MDLSHN mutilation *destruction*

MDLSKL middle school *grades 5-8 or 6-8*

MDLSM meddlesome *interfering*

MDLSM mettlesome *spirited*

MDLST medalist (or) medallist *award winner*

MDLST Middle East *region*

MDLT modality *form*

MDLT modulate *tune, adjust* modulated modulating

MDLT mutilate *cut up* mutilated mutilating mutilation

MDLTHR muddle through *achieve slowly*

MDLTR modulator *tune, adjust*

MDLTR mutilator *destroyer, cutter*

MDLVNR Medal of Honor *award*

MDLVTHRD middle-of-the-road *neutral*

MDLWR metalware *utensils*

MDLWRK metalwork *art object*

MDLWRKNG metalworking *shaping metal*

MDLWST Middle West *region*

MDLWT middleweight *160 or 165 pounds*

MDLYN medallion *award, portion*

MDLYN Modigliani *artist*

MDLZ metallize *add metal* metallized metallizing

MDM madam *rank, title* madams (or) mesdames

MDM madame *foreign title* mesdames (or) madames

MDM medium (adj) *average* (n) *environment*

MDM modem *computer phone*

MDMN madman *crazy one*

MDMR metamere *segment*

MDMRFK metamorphic *changed*

MDMRFKL metamorphically *changed*

MDMRFS metamorphose *change* metamorphosed metamorphosing

MDMRFSS metamorphosis *change* metamorphoses

MDMRFZ metamorphose *change* metamorphosed metamorphosing

MDMRFZM metamorphism *change*

MDMRK metameric *segmented*

MDMS mittimus *warrant*

MDMST midmost *innermost*

MDMWZL mademoiselle *girl* mademoiselles (or) mesdemoiselles

MDMZL mademoiselle *girl* mademoiselles (or) mesdemoiselles

MDN madden *enrage*

MDN Madonna *Virgin Mary*

MDN maiden *woman*

MDN median *center*

MDN medina *city part*

MDN meeting *assembly, connection*

MDN midden *dunghill*

MDN mitten *glove*

MDN mutiny *rebellion* mutinies

MDNFR metanephroi (pl) *kidney* metanephros

MDNFRS metanephros *kidney* metanephroi

MDNG madding *vexing*

MDNG matting *pad, tangle*

MDNG meeting *assembly,*

connection

MDNGHS meetinghouse *building*

MDNHD maidenhead *hymen*

MDNHD maidenhood *unmarried*

MDNHR maidenhair *fern, tree*

MDNM maiden name *surname*

MDNM metonym *figure of speech*

MDNMK metonymic *figure of speech*

MDNN maddening *vexing*

MDNNG maddening *vexing*

MDNNGL maddeningly *vexing*

MDNNL maddeningly *vexing*

MDNR mutineer *rebel*

MDNRN motoneuron *nerve*

MDNS immittance *electricity*

MDNS madness *craziness*

MDNS mateyness (Br) *friendship*

MDNS mightiness *power*

MDNS muddiness *wet dirt*

MDNS mutinous *rebellious*

MDNSFLN metencephalon *brain*

MDNT mediant *scale tone*

MDNT midnight *12:00 a.m.*

MDNT mutant *changed one*

MDNTS immittance *electricity*

MDNTSN midnight sun *arctic*

MDNYRN motoneuron *nerve*

MDP made-up *invented*

MDPNT midpoint *middle*

MDPP mud puppy *salamander* mud puppies

MDPRND modi operandi (pl) *method* modus operandi

MDR ammeter *ampere gauge*

MDR emitter *give off*

MDR madder *angry, crazy, herb, color*

MDR Madeira *river, islands*

MDR maduro *cigar* maduros

MDR mater *mother*

MDR matter *subject, substance, care**

MDR meatier *fleshy, substantial*

MDR meteor *asteroid*

MDR meter *(n) measure, device (v) measure*
(Br) metre

MDR midair *in the air*

MDR mightier *powerful*

MDR miter *(n) hat, joint (v) join*
(Br) mitre

MDR miter (or) mitre *joint*

MDR moodier *emotional*

MDR motor *engine*

MDR muddier *wet dirt*

MDR mudra *gesture*

MDR muter *silent*

MDR mutter *mumble*

MDR ohmmeter *device*

MDRB midrib *leaf*

MDRBK motorbike *vehicle*

MDRBKS miter box (or) mitre box *handsaw guide* miter boxes (or) mitre boxes

MDRBS motor bus *vehicle*

MDRBT motorboat *boat*

MDRBX miter box (or) mitre box *handsaw guide* miter boxes (or) mitre boxes

MDRC immoderacy *excessive*

MDRD Madrid *city*

MDRD maître d' (or) maitre d' *waiter* maître d's (or) maitre d's

MDRD meteoroid *comet*

MDRD moderato *tempo*

MDRDR made-to-order *custom made*

MDRDR moderator *speaker*

MDRDTL maître d'hotel *headwaiter* maîtres d'hotel

MDRF midriff *diaphragm*

MDRGL madrigal *poem, song*

MDRHM motor home *mobile home*

MDRK meteoric *fast*

MDRKD motorcade *parade*

MDRKR motorcar *vehicle*

MDRKRS motocross *race*

MDRKRT motor court *motel*

MDRLG meteorology *weather*

MDRLJ meteorology *weather*

MDRLJK meteorologic (or) meteorological (adj) *weather* meteorologically (adv)

MDRLJKL meteorological (or) meteorologic (adj) *weather* meteorologically (adv)

MDRLJST meteorologist *weather forecaster*

MDRM mudroom *wet area*

MDRMD meter maid *parking tickets*

MDRMN motorman *driver* motormen

MDRMTH motormouth *talk*

MDRN madrona (or) madrone (or) madrono *tree*

MDRN modern *(adj) up-to-date (n) type, stylish one*

MDRN moderne *art deco*

MDRND modernity *up-to-date*

MDRNS modernize *update* modernized modernizing
(Br) modernise

MDRNSDK modernistic *up-to-date*

MDRNSSHN modernization *updating*
(Br) modernisation

MDRNST modernist *philosopher*

MDRNSTK modernistic *up-to-date*

MDRNT modernity *up-to-date*

MDRNZ modernize *update* modernized modernizing
(Br) modernise

MDRNZM modernism *philosophy*

MDRNZSHN modernization *updating*
(Br) modernisation

MDRPL motor pool *vehicles*

MDRS immoderacy *excessive*

MDRS Madras *city*

MDRS madras *fabric*

MDRSHN immoderation *excess*

MDRSHN moderation *less intensity*

MDRSKDR motor scooter *vehicle*

MDRSKL motorcycle *vehicle*

MDRSKLST motorcyclist *driver*

MDRSKTR motor scooter *vehicle*

MDRST motorist *driver*

MDRT immoderate *excessive*

MDRT meteorite *small asteroid*

MDRT moderate *(v) preside, lessen* moderated moderating

MDRT moderate *(adj) calm, mediocre*

MDRT moderato *tempo*

MDRTL immoderately *excessive*

MDRTL moderately *calm, ordinary*

MDRTNS immoderateness *excessive*

MDRTNS moderateness *calmness, ordinariness*

MDRTR moderator *speaker*

MDRTRK motortruck *vehicle*

MDRVFK matter-of-fact *straightforward*

MDRVFKT matter-of-fact *straightforward*

MDRW motorway *road*

MDRZ mid-rise *structure*

MDRZ motorize *engine* motorized motorizing
(Br) motorise

MDRZSHN motorization *engine*
(Br) motorisation

MDS immediacy *urgency* immediacies

MDS meatus *body passage* meatuses (or) meatus

MDS medusa *jellyfish* medusae
MDS Medusa *Greek myth*
MDS métis *mixed race* (pl) métis
MDS Midas *golden touch*
MDSD immodesty *indecent*
MDSD medusoid *jellyfish*
MDSD miticide *insecticide*
MDSD modesty *dignity*
MDSDRN Mideastern *region*
MDSH modish *stylish*
MDSHN mediation judgement
MDSHPMN midshipman sailor midshipmen
MDSKLG metapsychology mental structure
MDSKLJ metapsychology mental structure
MDSKPR mudskipper *gobie*
MDSKSHN midsection middle
MDSL midsole *shoe*
MDSL mudsill *support*
MDSLNGGR mudslinger offensive one
MDSLNGN mudslinging offensive talk
MDSLNGNG mudslinging offensive talk
MDSLNGR mudslinger offensive one
MDSMR midsummer *middle of summer*
MDSN Madison *US president, city*
MDSN medicine *drug*
MDSN medusan *jellyfish*
MDSNBL medicine ball exercises
MDSNL medicinal (adj) *cure disease* medicinally (adv)
MDSNMN medicine man healer
MDSNR metacenter buoyancy
MDSNSH medicine show entertainment
MDSNTR metacenter buoyancy
MDSPRND modus operandi

method modi operandi
MDSRVNT maidservant helper
MDST amidst (or) amid among
MDST immodest *indecent*
MDST immodesty *indecency*
MDST maddest *angry, crazy*
MDST meatiest *fleshy, substantial*
MDST Mideast *region*
MDST midst *center*
MDST mightiest *powerful*
MDST modest *moderate, chaste*
MDST modesty *dignity*
MDST modiste *fashions*
MDST moodiest *emotional*
MDST muddiest *wet dirt*
MDST mutest *silent*
MDSTL immodestly *indecent*
MDSTN mudstone *shale*
MDSTRM midstream *middle stage*
MDSTRN Mideastern *region*
MDSVVND modus vivendi *way of life* modi vivendi
MDSWT meadowsweet *herb*
MDSZ midsize *medium*
MDT immediate *direct, instant, current*
MDT mediate *judge* mediated mediating
MDTDR meditator *thinker, non thinker*
MDTDV meditative contemplating
MDTDVL meditatively contemplation
MDTDVNS meditativeness contemplation
MDTHRKS metathorax *rear segment*
MDTHRX metathorax *rear segment*
MDTHSS metathesis *transposition* metatheses
MDTL immediately *directly*
MDTN midtown *city*
MDTR mediator *judge*
MDTRDR made-to-order *custom made*

MDTRKS mediatrix *judge (f)*
MDTRM midterm *exam*
MDTRNN Mediterranean *sea, region*
MDTRNYN Mediterranean *sea, region*
MDTRSL metatarsal *bone*
MDTRSS metatarsus *bone*
MDTRX mediatrix *judge (f)*
MDTSHN meditation contemplation
MDTTR meditator *thinker, non thinker*
MDTTV meditative contemplating
MDTTVL meditatively contemplation
MDTTVNS meditativeness contemplation
MDV emotive *feelings*
MDV motive *reason, music*
MDVDR motivator *driver*
MDVL emotively *feelings*
MDVL medieval (or) mediaeval (adj) *Middle Ages* medievally (adv)
MDVLS motiveless unplanned
MDVSHN motivation stimulus
MDVT motivate *compel* motivated motivating
MDVTR motivator *driver*
MDVVND modi vivendi (pl) *way of life* modus vivendi
MDW midway *halfway*
MDWF midwife (v) *birth* midwifed (or) midwived midwifing (or) midwiving
MDWF midwife (n) *nurse* midwives
MDWFR midwifery *birth*
MDWK midweek *weekday*
MDWKL midweekly *weekday*
MDWLNS Midway Islands *Pacific islands*
MDWMN madwoman *insane one* madwomen
MDWNR midwinter *middle of winter*
MDWNTR midwinter *middle of winter*

Use letters that best describe the sounds you hear and omit the vowels. Use **S** or **K** instead of **C**: to find circle use **SRKL**. Use **J** to find joy, **JM** to find gem and **G** to find go.

MDWRT madwort *herb*
MDWST Midwest *region*
MDWSTRN Midwestern *region*
MDWSTRNR Midwesterner *of the Midwest*
MDWVZ midwives (pl) *nurse* midwife
MDWYLNS Midway Islands *Pacific islands*
MDX meat-ax *cleaver*
MDY Medea *enchantress*
MDY media *voiced stop, muscle* mediae
MDY media *news* medias
MDY media (pl) *middle, material* medium
MDY métier (or) metier *work*
MDYC immediacy *urgency* immediacies
MDYDR mediator *judge*
MDYKR mediocre *ordinary*
MDYKRD mediocrity *ordinariness* mediocrities
MDYKRT mediocrity *ordinariness* mediocrities
MDYL medial (adj) *average* medially (adv)
MDYL module *unit*
MDYL moduli (pl) *value* modulus
MDYLDR modulator *tune, adjust*
MDYLR modular *standardized*
MDYLS modulus *value* moduli
MDYLSHN modulation *tune, adjust*
MDYLT modulate *tune, adjust* modulated modulating
MDYLTR modulator *tune, adjust*
MDYM medium *(adj) average (n) environment*
MDYN medallion *award, portion*
MDYN Medellin *drug cartel*
MDYN median *center*
MDYNT mediant *scale tone*
MDYPRND modi operandi

(pl) *method* modus operandi
MDYR meatier *fleshy, substantial*
MDYR meteor *asteroid*
MDYR midyear *calendar*
MDYR mightier *powerful*
MDYR moodier *emotional*
MDYR muddier *wet dirt*
MDYRD meteoroid *comet*
MDYRK meteoric *fast*
MDYRLG meteorology *weather*
MDYRLJ meteorology *weather*
MDYRLJK meteorologic (or) meteorological (adj) *weather* meteorologically (adv)
MDYRLJKL meteorological (or) meteorologic (adj) *weather* meteorologically (adv)
MDYRLJST meteorologist *weather forecaster*
MDYRT meteorite *small asteroid*
MDYS immediacy *urgency* immediacies
MDYS Medusa *Greek myth*
MDYS medusa *jellyfish* medusae
MDYSD medusoid *jellyfish*
MDYSHN mediation *judgement*
MDYSN medusan *jellyfish*
MDYST meatiest *fleshy, substantial*
MDYST mightiest *powerful*
MDYST moodiest *emotional*
MDYST muddiest *wet dirt*
MDYT immediate *direct, instant, current*
MDYT mediate *judge* mediated mediating
MDYTL immediately *directly*
MDYTR mediator *judge*
MDYTRKS mediatrix *judge (f)*
MDYTRX mediatrix *judge (f)*
MDZ mezzo *singer* mezzos
MDZLM metaxylem *plant*

cell
MDZN metazoan *animal*
MDZSPRN mezzo-soprano *singer*
MDZTNT mezzotint *engraving*
MDZWN metazoan *animal*
MF Mafia *criminal*
MF miff *(n) quarrel (v) offend*
MF muff *(v) bungle (n) warmer*
MF oomph *pep*
MFB amphibia *animals*
MFBL amphibole *mineral*
MFBL amphiboly *phrase* amphibolies
MFBLG amphibology *phrase* amphibologies
MFBLJ amphibology *phrase* amphibologies
MFBLT amphibolite *mineral*
MFBN amphibian *water and land*
MFBRK amphibrach *verse*
MFBRL myofibril *muscle*
MFBS amphibious *water and land*
MFBSL amphibiously *water and land*
MFBSNS amphibiousness *water and land*
MFBY amphibia *animals*
MFBYN amphibian *water and land*
MFBYS amphibious *water and land*
MFBYSL amphibiously *water and land*
MFBYSNS amphibiousness *water and land*
MFCM emphysema *lung disease*
MFCMK emphysemic *lung disease*
MFCZ emphases (pl) *stress* emphasis
MFD mufti *jurist, clothing*
MFDK emphatic *forceful*
MFDK mephitic *odor*
MFDKL emphatically *forceful*
MFDKL mephitically *odor*

Letters aren't doubled for single sounds: to find alley use **L** not **LL**. Use **Y** and **W** as hard sounds only: to find yellow use **YL**. (Br)=British spelling or usage. * See dictionary.

MFDMN amphetamine *stimulant*

MFDS mephitis *stench*

MFFL amphiphile *water molecule*

MFFLK amphiphilic *water molecule*

MFK mafic *mineral*

MFL mayfly *insect* mayflies

MFL muffle *suppress* muffled muffling

MFLMNT myofilament *muscle*

MFLR mayflower *plant*

MFLR Mayflower *ship*

MFLR muffler *scarf, silencer*

MFLS omphalos *hub*

MFLSKPSS omphaloskepsis *meditation*

MFLWR mayflower *plant*

MFLWR Mayflower *ship*

MFMKCZ amphimixes (pl) *cell union* amphimixis

MFMKSS amphimixis *cell union* amphimixes

MFMKSZ amphimixes (pl) *cell union* amphimixis

MFMKZZ amphimixes (pl) *cell union* amphimixis

MFMXS amphimixis *cell union* amphimixes

MFN muffin *pastry*

MFPD amphipod *crustacean*

MFPLD amphiploid (adj) *hybrid* amphiploidy (n)

MFR amphora *jar* amphorae (or) amphoras

MFRTN M-14 *weapon*

MFS mafioso *criminal* mafiosi

MFSM emphysema *lung disease*

MFSMK emphysemic *lung disease*

MFSS emphasis *stress* emphases

MFSTFLZ Mephistopheles *devil*

MFSZ emphases (pl) *stress* emphasis

MFSZ emphasize *stress*

emphasized emphasizing (Br) emphasise

MFT mufti *jurist, clothing*

MFTHDR amphitheater *arena* (Br) amphitheatre

MFTHTR amphitheater *arena* (Br) amphitheatre

MFTHYDR amphitheater *arena* (Br) amphitheatre

MFTHYTR amphitheater *arena* (Br) amphitheatre

MFTK emphatic *forceful*

MFTK mephitic *odor*

MFTKL emphatically *forceful*

MFTKL mephitically *odor*

MFTMN amphetamine *stimulant*

MFTRK amphoteric *part of both*

MFTS mephitis *stench*

MFY Mafia *criminal*

MFYS mafioso *criminal* mafiosi

MFZM emphysema *lung disease*

MFZMK emphysemic *lung disease*

MG amigo *friend* amigos

MG imago *insect, image* imagoes (or) imagines

MG maguey *plant, fiber*

MG MiG *airplane*

MG Moog *(trademark) music*

MG mug (v) *pose* mugged mugging

MG mug (n) *cup, face*

MG muggy *warm and moist* muggier muggiest

MG omega *final Greek letter*

MGBKS megabucks *money*

MGBR megabar *pressure*

MGBT megabit *one million bits*

MGBT megabyte *one million bytes*

MGBX megabucks *money*

MGD maggoty *with larvae*

MGDS megadose *large dose*

MGDSH Mogadishu *city*

MGFN megafauna *visible animals*

MGFN megaphone *speaker*

MGFNK megaphonic *speaker*

MGGPN moo goo gai pan *food*

MGHRTS megahertz *frequency*

MGHT megahit *success*

MGL mogul *ski bump, (often capitalized) magnate*

MGLBN myoglobin *blood*

MGLMN megalomania *mental disorder*

MGLMNK megalomaniac *mental disorder*

MGLMNKL megalomaniacal (adj) *mental disorder* megalomaniacally (adv)

MGLMNY megalomania *mental disorder*

MGLMNYK megalomaniac *mental disorder*

MGLMNYKL megalomaniacal (adj) *mental disorder* megalomaniacally (adv)

MGLP megilp *oil*

MGLPLDN megalopolitan *city*

MGLPLS megalopolis *city*

MGLPLTN megalopolitan *city*

MGLTH megalith *monument*

MGLTHK megalithic *monument*

MGM magma *molten rock*

MGM megohm *one million ohms*

MGMDK magmatic *molten rock*

MGMTK magmatic *molten rock*

MGND magneto *generator* magnetos

MGNDGRF magnetograph *instrument*

MGNDK magnetic *attraction*

MGNDKL magnetically

attraction
MGNDPZ magnetopause
boundary
MGNDSFR magnetosphere
orbit
MGNF magnify *enlarge, extol*
magnified magnifying
magnifies
MGNFK magnifico *nobleman*
magnificoes (or)
magnificos
MGNFKSHN magnification
enlargement
MGNFKT magnificat *praise*
MGNFR magnifier *enlarger*
MGNFSNS magnificence
splendor
MGNFSNT magnificent
grand
MGNFSNTL magnificently
grand
MGNFSNTS magnificence
splendor
MGNFYR magnifier *enlarger*
MGNK myogenic *heart*
rhythm
MGNKMLD magna cum
laude *great distinction*
MGNKRD Magna Carta
document
MGNKRT Magna Carta
document
MGNL magnolia *tree*
MGNLKWNS
magniloquence *speech*
MGNLKWNT magniloquent
pompous
MGNLKWNTL
magniloquently *pompous*
MGNLKWNTS
magniloquence *speech*
MGNLQNS magniloquence
speech
MGNLQNT magniloquent
pompous
MGNLQNTL
magniloquently *pompous*
MGNLQNTS
magniloquence *speech*
MGNLY magnolia *tree*
MGNM magnum *1.5 liter*
bottle

MGNMD magnanimity
calmness magnanimities
MGNMPS magnum opus
great work
MGNMT magnanimity
calmness magnanimities
MGNNMD magnanimity
calmness magnanimities
MGNNMS magnanimous
calm
MGNNMSNS
magnanimousnous
calmness
MGNNMT magnanimity
calmness magnanimities
MGNS imagines (pl) *insect,
image* imago
MGNS mugginess *warm and
moist*
MGNSH magnesia *mineral*
MGNSHM magnesium
element
MGNT magnate *ruler*
MGNT magnet *attraction*
MGNT magneto *generator*
magnetos
MGNTD magnitude *quantity*
MGNTGRF magnetograph
instrument
MGNTK magnetic *attraction*
MGNTKL magnetically
attraction
MGNTMDR magnetometer
instrument
MGNTMTR magnetometer
instrument
MGNTN magneton *particle*
MGNTPZ magnetopause
boundary
MGNTRN magnetron *tube*
MGNTSFR magnetosphere
orbit
MGNTT magnetite *mineral*
MGNTYD magnitude
quantity
MGNTZ magnetize *attract*
magnetized magnetizing
(Br) magnetise
MGNTZBL magnetizable
attract
(Br) magnetisable
MGNTZM magnetism

attraction
MGNTZR magnetizer
attraction
(Br) magnetiser
MGNZH magnesia *mineral*
MGNZHM magnesium
element
MGNZM magnesium
element
MGNZYM magnesium
element
MGP magpie *(n) bird (adj)
miscellaneous*
MGR émigré *person
departing*
MGR meager (or) meagre
few
MGR mugger *crocodile,
attacker*
MGR muggier *warm and
moist*
MGRDR migrator *mover*
MGRL meagerly *few*
MGRN migraine *headache*
MGRNS meagerness *few*
MGRNT emigrant *person
departing*
MGRNT immigrant *settler*
MGRNT migrant *moving*
MGRSHN emigration
departing
MGRSHN immigration
entering
MGRSHN migration
movement
MGRT emigrate *depart*
emigrated emigrating
MGRT immigrate *enter*
immigrated immigrating
MGRT migrate *move*
migrated migrating
MGRTR migrator *mover*
MGRTR migratory *moving*
MGS magus *sorcerer, wise
man* magi
MGSHT mug shot *photo*
MGSKL megacycle
frequency
MGSKPK megascopic
observation
MGSKPKL megascopically
observation

Letters aren't doubled for single sounds: to find alley use **L** not **LL**. Use **Y** and **W** as hard
sounds only: to find yellow use **YL**. (Br)=British spelling or usage. * See dictionary.

MGSPRFL megasporophyll *plant cell*

MGST muggiest *warm and moist*

MGSTR megastar *superstar*

MGT maggot *larvae*

MGT maggoty *with larvae*

MGTN megaton *explosives*

MGTNJ megatonnage *explosives*

MGVDMN megavitamin *large dose*

MGVTMN megavitamin *large dose*

MGWMP mugwump *politician*

MGWT megawatt *one million watts*

MGYR Magyar *Hungarian*

MGYR muggier *warm and moist*

MGYST muggiest *warm and moist*

MGZN magazine *warehouse, periodical, chamber**

MH mahoe *tree*

MH Omaha *Native American, city*

MHGN mahogany *tree, color* mahoganies

MHK Mohawk *Native American, hairstyle*

MHL molehill *mound*

MHM mayhem *violence*

MHMD Muhammad *prophet*

MHMDN Muhammadan *Islam*

MHMH mahimahi *fish*

MHN mahonia *shrub*

MHNY mahonia *shrub*

MHR mohair *fur*

MHRJ maharaja (or) maharajah *prince*

MHRN maharani (or) maharanee *princess*

MHRSH maharaja (or) maharajah *prince*

MHRSH maharishi *teacher*

MHRZH maharaja (or) maharajah *prince*

MHT mahout *elephant keeper*

MHTM mahatma *leader*

MHVDZRT Mojave Desert *arid area*

MJ homage *tribute*

MJ image *(v) picture* imaged imaging

MJ image *(n) likeness*

MJ magi (pl) *(often capitalized) sorcerers, wise men* magus

MJ midge *fly*

MJC immediacy *directness* immediacies

MJDN mujahideen (or) mujahedin *fighter*

MJHDN mujahideen (or) mujahedin *fighter*

MJK magic *enchantment*

MJKL magical (adj) *enchanting* magically (adv)

MJL module *unit*

MJL moduli (pl) *value* modulus

MJLDR modulator *tune, adjust*

MJLK majolica *pottery*

MJLN Magellan *explorer*

MJLR modular *standardized*

MJLS modulus *value*

MJLS modulus *value* moduli

MJLSHN modulation *tune, adjust*

MJLT modulate *tune, adjust* modulated modulating

MJLTR modulator *tune, adjust*

MJN imagine *think, fancy, guess* imagined imagining

MJN imaging *picture*

MJN magenta *color*

MJNBL imaginable (adj) *conceivable* imaginably (adv)

MJNDV imaginative *false*

MJNDVL imaginatively *false*

MJNDVNS imaginativeness *false*

MJNG imaging *picture*

MJNG mah-jongg (or) mahjong *game*

MJNK myogenic *heart rhythm*

MJNL imaginal *fanciful, insect*

MJNLN Maginot Line *defense*

MJNR imaginary *fanciful*

MJNRL imaginarily *fanciful*

MJNRNS imaginariness *fanciful*

MJNSHN imagination *idea*

MJNT magenta *color*

MJNTV imaginative *false*

MJNTVL imaginatively *false*

MJNTVNS imaginativeness *false*

MJR homager *vassal*

MJR imager *reflector*

MJR imagery *pictures* imageries

MJR maduro *cigar* maduros

MJR Magyar *Hungarian*

MJR major *greater, rank*

MJRD majority *more than half, age* majorities

MJRDM majordomo *butler* majordomos

MJRK Majorca *island*

MJRL majorly *extremely*

MJRLG major league (n) *sports* major-league (adj)

MJRT majorette *baton twirler*

MJRT majority *more than half, age* majorities

MJS immediacy *directness* immediacies

MJSD majesty *grandeur* majesties

MJSDK majestic *grand*

MJSDKL majestically *grandly*

MJSHN magician *sorcerer*

MJSKL majuscule *capital letter*

MJSKYL majuscule *capital letter*

MJSQL majuscule *capital letter*

MJST imagist *poet*

MJST majesty *grandeur* majesties

MJSTK majestic *grand*

MJSTKL majestically

Use letters that best describe the sounds you hear and omit the vowels. Use **S** or **K** instead of **C**: to find circle use **SRKL**. Use **J** to find joy, **JM** to find gem and **G** to find go.

grandly
MJSTRC magistracy *office* magistracies
MJSTRL magisterial (adj) *arrogant* magisterially (adv)
MJSTRM magisterium *teaching*
MJSTRS magistracy *office* magistracies
MJSTRT magistrate *official*
MJSTRYL magisterial (adj) *arrogant* magisterially (adv)
MJSTRYM magisterium *teaching*
MJT immediate *direct, instant, current*
MJT midget *small*
MJTL immediately *directly*
MJZM imagism *poetry*
MK amici (pl) *law* amicus
MK amok *wild*
MK mac *raincoat*
MK Mac *fellow, computer*
MK Macao (or) Macau *island*
MK macaw *bird*
MK Mach *speed of sound*
MK make (v) *create, appoint, seduce** made making
MK make (n) *brand*
MK mako *shark*
MK maquis *shrub, fighter* maquis
MK mecca *(often capitalized) goal*
MK meek *mild*
MK mica *mineral*
MK Micah *prophet*
MK mike *microphone* miked miking
MK mocha *coffee*
MK mock *ridicule*
MK muck *mire*
MK ohmic *electrical unit*
MK umiak *boat*
MKB macabre *ghastly*
MKBL amicable (adj) *peaceful* amicably (adv)
MKBL makable (or) makeable *possible*

MKBLD amicability *peacefulness*
MKBLNS amicableness *peacefulness*
MKBLT amicability *peacefulness*
MKBLV make-believe *pretend*
MKBR macabre *ghastly*
MKBR Micawber *poor and happy*
MKBTH Macbeth *Scottish general*
MKC maxi *length* maxis
MKC moxie *pep, expertise*
MKCHRSHN micturation *urination*
MKCHRT micturate *urinate* micturated micturating
MKCK Mexico *country*
MKCSLN amoxicillin *drug* (Br) amoxycillin
MKD make-do *makeshift*
MKD mikado *emperor* mikados
MKD mucoid *slimy*
MKDK mycotic *infection*
MKDM macadam *pavement*
MKDM macadamia *nut*
MKDMY macadamia *nut*
MKDMZ macadamize *compact* macadamized macadamizing
MKF make off *steal*
MKFG mycophagy *mushrooms*
MKFGS mycophagous *fungus*
MKFJ mycophagy *mushrooms*
MKFJST mycophagist *mushrooms*
MKFL mycophile *mushrooms*
MKFLR mycoflora *fungus*
MKFN Mickey Finn *drug*
MKFST makefast *fastener*
MKHRK mock-heroic *ridiculous*
MKHRWK mock-heroic *ridiculous*
MKK macaque *monkey*
MKL macula *spot* maculae

MKL macule *spot*
MKL meekly *mildly*
MKL ohmically *electrical unit*
MKLC immaculacy *clean*
MKLDD maculated (or) maculate *spotted*
MKLG mycology *fungus*
MKLJ mycology *fungus*
MKLJKL mycological (adj) *fungus* mycologically (adv)
MKLJST mycologist *fungus*
MKLMS Michaelmas *feast*
MKLNJL Michelangelo *artist*
MKLP mea culpa *fault*
MKLS immaculacy *clean*
MKLSHN maculation *spots*
MKLT immaculate *clean*
MKLT maculate (or) maculated *spotted*
MKLTD maculated (or) maculate *spotted*
MKLTL immaculately *clean*
MKMB macumba *religion*
MKMS Mickey Mouse *cartoon, unimportant*
MKN mackinaw *blanket, coat*
MKN making *batch, material*
MKNBRD mockingbird *bird*
MKNDR machinator *schemer*
MKNG making *batch, material*
MKNG Mekong *river*
MKNGBRD mockingbird *bird*
MKNGL mockingly *ridicule*
MKNGZ makings *materials, potential*
MKNK mechanic *artisan, machinist*
MKNKL mechanical (adj) *machine, spontaneous* mechanically (adv)
MKNKMKL mechanochemical *energy*
MKNKMSTR mechanochemistry *energy*
MKNKS mechanics *science*
MKNL mockingly *ridicule*
MKNRSPDR

mechanoreceptor *neural response*

MKNRSPDV mechanoreceptive *neural response*

MKNRSPSHN mechanoreception *neural response*

MKNRSPTR mechanoreceptor *neural response*

MKNRSPTV mechanoreceptive *neural response*

MKNS meekness *mildness*

MKNSDK mechanistic *machine*

MKNSHN machination *plot*

MKNSHN mechanician *mechanic*

MKNSTK mechanistic *machine*

MKNT machinate *plot* machinated machining

MKNTR machinator *schemer*

MKNTSH mackintosh *raincoat*

MKNTSH McIntosh *apple*

MKNX mechanics *science*

MKNZ makings *materials, potential*

MKNZ mechanize *make automatic* mechanized mechanizing

MKNZM mechanism *machinery, process*

MKNZR mechanizer *make automatic*

MKNZSHN mechanization *machine*

MKP make up *(v) atone, create*

MKP makeup *(n) cosmetic, layout*

MKP mock-up *model*

MKPLZM mycoplasma *parasite* mycoplasmas (or) mycoplasmata

MKPLZMD mycoplasmata (pl) *parasite* mycoplasma

MKPLZMT mycoplasmata (pl) *parasite* mycoplasma

MKR macro *large, computer sequence* macros

MKR maker *creator*

MKR micro *small* micros

MKR mocker *ridiculer*

MKR mockery *ridicule* mockeries

MKRB microbe *germ*

MKRBDK macrobiotic *diet*

MKRBK microbic *germ*

MKRBL microbial *germ*

MKRBLG microbiology *science*

MKRBLJ microbiology *science*

MKRBLJST microbiologist *scientist*

MKRBRK make-or-break *urgent*

MKRBRR microbrewer *beer maker*

MKRBRR microbrewery *beer factory* microbreweries

MKRBRWR microbrewer *beer maker*

MKRBRWR microbrewery *beer factory* microbreweries

MKRBS microbus *vehicle*

MKRBTK macrobiotic *diet*

MKRBYDK macrobiotic *diet*

MKRBYL microbial *germ*

MKRBYLG microbiology *science*

MKRBYLJ microbiology *science*

MKRBYLJST microbiologist *scientist*

MKRBYTK macrobiotic *diet*

MKRCHP microchip *computer*

MKRD makeready *preparation* makereadies

MKRDDS myocarditis *inflammation*

MKRDM myocardium *heart*

MKRDT microdot *tiny copy*

MKRDTS myocarditis *inflammation*

MKRDYM myocardium *heart*

MKRFDK macrophytic *plant*

MKRFJ macrophage *immune cell*

MKRFJ microphage *cell*

MKRFJK macrophagic *immune cell*

MKRFL microphyll *leaf*

MKRFLM microfilm *reduction*

MKRFLMNT microfilament *protein*

MKRFLR microflora *tiny plants*

MKRFM microfilm *reduction*

MKRFN microfauna *unseen animals*

MKRFN microphone *loudspeaker*

MKRFSH microfiche *tiny copy* microfiche (or) microfiches

MKRFSH microphage *cell*

MKRFT macrophyte *plant*

MKRFTK macrophytic *plant*

MKRFTMDR microphotometer *light measure*

MKRFTMTR microphotometer *light measure*

MKRFZH microphage *cell*

MKRFZKL microphysical (adj) *particles* microphysically (adv)

MKRFZKS microphysics *particles*

MKRFZX microphysics *particles*

MKRGRF micrograph *image*

MKRGRM microgram *measure*

MKRGRV microgroove *recording*

MKRK muckrake *expose misconduct* muckraked muckraking

MKRKLCHR microculture *cells*

MKRKLRMDR microcalorimeter *instrument*

MKRKLRMTR

MKRKLTR microculture *cells*

MKRKMPDR
microcomputer *small processor*

MKRKMPTR
microcomputer *small processor*

MKRKMPYDR
microcomputer *small processor*

MKRKMPYTR
microcomputer *small processor*

MKRKNMKS
microeconomics *individual finance*

MKRKNMX
microeconomics *individual finance*

MKRKP microcopy *reduction* microcopies

MKRKR muckraker *expose misconduct*

MKRKRSDL microcrystal *tiny crystal*

MKRKRSTL microcrystal *tiny crystal*

MKRKSM macrocosm *universe*

MKRKSMK macrocosmic *universal*

MKRKSMKL
macrocosmically *universal*

MKRKST microcassette *tape*

MKRKZM macrocosm *universe*

MKRKZM microcosm *little world*

MKRKZMK macrocosmic *universal*

MKRKZMK microcosmic *little world*

MKRKZMKL
macrocosmically *universal*

MKRKZMKL
microcosmically *little world*

microcalorimeter *instrument*

MKRKZMS microcosmos *little world*

MKRL mackerel *fish* mackerel (or) mackerels

MKRL mercurial (adj) *changing* mercurially (adv)

MKRLDR microliter *measure*

MKRLKTRD microelectrode *tiny wire*

MKRLKTRNKS
microelectronics *tiny circuits*

MKRLKTRNX
microelectronics *tiny circuits*

MKRLSK mackerel sky *clouds*

MKRLTR microliter *measure*

MKRM macramé *knotted cord*

MKRMDR micrometer *device, measurement*

MKRMLKL macromolecule *chemistry*

MKRMLKYL
macromolecule *chemistry*

MKRMLQL macromolecule *chemistry*

MKRMN micromini *skirt*

MKRMNJ micromanage *control*

MKRMNJMNT
micromanagement *control*

MKRMR micromere *cell*

MKRMTR micrometer *device, measurement*

MKRN macaroni *pasta* macaronis (or) macaronies

MKRN macaroon *cookie*

MKRN macron *mark*

MKRN micron *unit of length*

MKRN omicron *Greek letter*

MKRNKLS macronucleus *cell*

MKRNKLS micronucleus *cell*

MKRNKLYS macronucleus *cell*

MKRNKLYS micronucleus *cell*

MKRNKPSLT
microencapsulate *enclose*
microencapsulated
microencapsulating

MKRNKPSYLT
microencapsulate *enclose*
microencapsulated
microencapsulating

MKRNLDKL microanalytical *chemistry*

MKRNLSS microanalysis *chemistry*

MKRNLST microanalyst *chemist*

MKRNLTKL microanalytical *chemistry*

MKRNQLS micronucleus *cell*

MKRNSH Micronesia *islands*

MKRNYKLS macronucleus *cell*

MKRNYKLYS
macronucleus *cell*

MKRNZH Micronesia *islands*

MKRPBLSHN
micropublishing *printing*

MKRPBLSHNG
micropublishing *printing*

MKRPBLSHR
micropublisher *printer*

MKRPL micropyle *opening*

MKRPPT micropipette (or) micropipet *small measure*

MKRPR micropore *opening*

MKRPRB microprobe *analyzer*

MKRPRGRM microprogram *computer*

MKRPRGRMN
microprogramming *computer*

MKRPRGRMNG
microprogramming *computer*

MKRPRJKDR
microprojector *enlarger*

MKRPRJKTR
microprojector *enlarger*

MKRPRS microporous *opening*

Letters aren't doubled for single sounds: to find alley use **L** not **LL**. Use **Y** and **W** as hard sounds only: to find yellow use **YL**. (Br)=British spelling or usage. * See dictionary.

MKRPRSD microporosity *opening*

MKRPRSSR microprocessor *computer*

MKRPRST microporosity *opening*

MKRRDR microreader *enlargement*

MKRRGNZM microorganism *tiny plant or animal*

MKRSDK microcytic *blood cell*

MKRSFL microcephaly *small head*

MKRSFLK microcephalic *small head*

MKRSFR microsphere *circle*

MKRSKN microsecond *time unit*

MKRSKND microsecond *time unit*

MKRSKNT microsecond *time unit*

MKRSKP microscope *lens device*

MKRSKP microscopy *lens device*

MKRSKPK macroscopic *large*

MKRSKPK microscopic (or) microscopical (adj) *small* microscopically (adv)

MKRSKPKL macroscopically *large*

MKRSKPKL microscopical (or) microscopic (adj) *small* microscopically (adv)

MKRSKPST microscopist *device user*

MKRSM microsome *cell*

MKRSML microsomal *cell*

MKRSPR microspore *tiny pod*

MKRSPRFL microsporophyll *cell*

MKRSPRST microsporocyte *mother cell*

MKRSRJKL microsurgical *cut apart*

MKRSRJR microsurgery *cut apart*

MKRSRKT microcircuit *electronics*

MKRSRKTR microcircuitry *electronics*

MKRST microcyte *blood cell*

MKRSTK microcytic *blood cell*

MKRSTRKCHR microstructure *cell makeup*

MKRSTRKCHRL microstructural *cell makeup*

MKRSTRKSHR microstructure *cell makeup*

MKRSTRKSHRL microstructural *cell makeup*

MKRSTRKTRL microstructural *cell makeup*

MKRTHYZM McCarthyism *political attitude*

MKRTHZM McCarthyism *political attitude*

MKRTM microtome *cutter*

MKRTN microtone *music*

MKRVLT microvolt *electricity*

MKRVSKLR microvascular *circulation*

MKRVSKYLR microvascular *circulation*

MKRVSQLR microvascular *circulation*

MKRWKNMKS microeconomics *individual finance*

MKRWKNMX microeconomics *individual finance*

MKRWLKTRD microelectrode *tiny wire*

MKRWLKTRNKS microelectronics *tiny circuits*

MKRWLKTRNX microelectronics *tiny circuits*

MKRWNKPSLT
microencapsulate *enclose* microencapsulated microencapsulating

MKRWNKPSYLT microencapsulate *enclose* microencapsulated microencapsulating

MKRWNLDKL microanalytical *chemistry*

MKRWNLSS microanalysis *chemistry*

MKRWNLST microanalyst *chemist*

MKRWNLTKL microanalytical *chemistry*

MKRWRGNZM microorganism *tiny plant or animal*

MKRWT microwatt *electricity*

MKRWV microwave *oven*

MKRWVBL microwavable (or) microwaveable *oven*

MKRYL mercurial (adj) *changing* mercurially (adv)

MKRZ mycorrhiza *association* mycorrhizae (or) mycorrhizas

MKS Amex *(abbr)* American Express

MKS amicus *law* amici

MKS immix *combine*

MKS max *maximum*

MKS maxi *length* maxis

MKS mix *(n) blend (v) blend, confuse, participate* mixes

MKS moxie *pep, expertise*

MKS mucosa *membrane* mucosae (or) mucosas

MKS mucous *(adj) slimy*

MKS mucus *(n) nasal secretion*

MKSBL mixable *blend*

MKSCHR immixture *combine*

MKSCHR mixture *blend*

MKSD mixed *blended*

MKSDM myxedema *disease*

MKSDMDS myxedematous *disease*

MKSDMTS myxedematous *disease*

MKSDP mixed-up *confused*

Use letters that best describe the sounds you hear and omit the vowels. Use **S** or **K** instead of **C**: to find circle use **SRKL**. Use **J** to find joy, **JM** to find gem and **G** to find go.

MKSH mawkish *sentimental*
MKSHF makeshift *substitute*
MKSHFT makeshift *substitute*
MKSHL mawkishly *sentimental*
MKSHNS mawkishness *sentimental*
MKSHS micaceous *mineral*
MKSK Mexico *country*
MKSKN Mexican *of Mexico*
MKSKR amicus curiae *law* amici curiae
MKSKRY amicus curiae *law* amici curiae
MKSKYR amicus curiae *law* amici curiae
MKSKYRY amicus curiae *law* amici curiae
MKSL maxilla *jaw* maxillae (or) maxillas
MKSLFSHL maxillofacial *face*
MKSLPD maxilliped *appendage*
MKSLR maxillary *jaw*
MKSM maxim *truth*
MKSM maxima (pl) *upper limit* maximum
MKSM myxoma *tumor* myxomas (or) myxomata
MKSMCT myxomycete *slime mold*
MKSMD myxomata (pl) *tumor* myxoma
MKSMDS myxomatous *tumor*
MKSML maximal (adj) *upper limit* maximally (adv)
MKSMM maximum *upper limit* maxima (or) maximums
MKSMST myxomycete *slime mold*
MKSMT myxomata (pl) *tumor* myxoma
MKSMTS myxomatous *tumor*
MKSMTSS myxomatosis *virus*
MKSMZ maximize *make the most of* maximized

maximizing (Br) maximise
MKSMZR maximizer *make the most of* (Br) maximiser
MKSMZSHN maximization *make the most of* (Br) maximisation
MKSN moccasin *shoe*
MKSP mix-up *(n) confusion, fight*
MKSQR amicus curiae *law* amici curiae
MKSQRY amicus curiae *law* amici curiae
MKSR mixer *blender, meeting, beverage*
MKSS mycosis *infection* mycoses
MKSSLN amoxicillin *drug* (Br) amoxycillin
MKST max out *(slang) extend to the limit*
MKST mixed *blended*
MKSTP mixed-up *confused*
MKSTR immixture *combination*
MKSTR mixture *blend*
MKSTYR immixture *combination*
MKSVRL myxoviral *influenza*
MKSVRS myxovirus *influenza*
MKSWL maxwell *flux*
MKT make out *complete, get along, neck**
MKT maquette *model*
MKT moquette *carpet*
MKTK mycotic *infection*
MKTRSHN micturation *urination*
MKTRT micturate *urinate* micturated micturating
MKTYRSHN micturation *urination*
MKTYRT micturate *urinate* micturated micturating
MKVLN Machiavellian *cunning*
MKVLYN Machiavellian *cunning*

MKVR makeover (n) *remodel* make over (v)
MKWRK make-work *busy work*
MKYL macula *spot* maculae
MKYL macule *spot*
MKYLC immaculacy *clean*
MKYLDD maculated (or) maculate *spotted*
MKYLS immaculacy *clean*
MKYLSHN maculation *spots*
MKYLT immaculate *clean*
MKYLT maculate (or) maculated *spotted*
MKYLTD maculated (or) maculate *spotted*
MKYLTL immaculately *clean*
MKYRL mercurial (adj) *changing* mercurially (adv)
MKYRYL mercurial (adj) *changing* mercurially (adv)
MKYVLN Machiavellian *cunning*
MKYVLYN Machiavellian *cunning*
MKZM machismo *power*
ML amole *soap*
ML amyl *hydrocarbon*
ML mail *(n) letter, armor (v) post*
ML maile *vine*
ML Malay *of Malasia*
ML male *(adj) masculine (n) man or boy*
ML Mali *country*
ML mall *public area*
ML mallee *shrub*
ML mallow *herb, fruit*
ML maul *(v) injure (n) hammer*
ML meal *food*
ML mealie *corn*
ML mealy *soft* mealier mealiest
ML meld *blend*
ML melee *fight*
ML mellow *mild, laid-back*
ML mewl *meow*
ML mil *1/1000th inch*
ML mildly *gently*
ML mile *5,280 feet*
ML milia (pl) *whitehead*

Letters aren't doubled for single sounds: to find alley use **L** not **LL**. Use **Y** and **W** as hard sounds only: to find yellow use **YL**. (Br)=British spelling or usage. * See dictionary.

milium
ML milieu *background* milieus (or) milieux
ML mill *(n) grinder (v) mix, wander*
ML milo *grain* milos
ML moil *work*
ML mole *burrowing animal, blemish*
ML moll *girlfriend*
ML molly *fish* mollies
ML moly *mythical herb*
ML moola (or) moolah *(slang) money*
ML mule *pack animal, shoe*
ML muley *hornless*
ML mull *(v) ponder, heat (n) fabric, soil*
ML mullah *Muslim official*
MLBDNM molybdenum *element*
MLBG mealybug *insect*
MLBKS mailbox *depository* mailboxes
MLBL mailable *posting*
MLBL malleable *easily molded*
MLBLD mailability *posting*
MLBLD malleability *easily molded*
MLBLST myeloblast *cell*
MLBLT mailability *posting*
MLBLT malleability *easily molded*
MLBR millibar *pressure*
MLBR mulberry *fruit* mulberries
MLBRD moldboard *curved blade*
MLBRN Melbourne *city*
MLBSRPSHN malabsorption *faulty intake*
MLBTST melba toast *food*
MLBX mailbox *depository* mailboxes
MLBZRPSHN malabsorption *faulty intake*
MLCH milch *milk*
MLCH mulch *soil cover* mulches

MLD amyloid *protein*
MLD malady *sickness* maladies
MLD malty *grainy*
MLD meld *blend*
MLD melody *tune* melodies
MLD milady *title* miladies
MLD mild *gentle*
MLD mildew *mold*
MLD mold *(v) shape (n) frame, fungus*
MLD moldy *fungus, wet rot* moldier moldiest
MLD mulatto *mixed race* mulattoes (or) mulattos
MLD multi- *(combined form) many*
MLD myeloid *bone marrow*
MLDBL meltable *soften*
MLDBL moldable *shape*
MLDBLD meltability *soften*
MLDBLT meltability *soften*
MLDBRD moldboard *curved blade*
MLDD malted *beverage*
MLDDMLK malted milk *beverage*
MLDDS myelitides (pl) *inflammation* myelitis
MLDDZ myelitides (pl) *inflammation* myelitis
MLDFLMNT multifilament *many threads*
MLDFNGKSHNL multifunctional *many duties*
MLDFNGSHNL multifunctional *many duties*
MLDFNKSHNL multifunctional *many duties*
MLDFRM multiform *many shapes*
MLDFRS multifarious *different*
MLDFRYS multifarious *different*
MLDFSDD multifaceted *many sides*
MLDFSTD multifaceted *many sides*

MLDHD multihued *many colors*
MLDHYD multihued *many colors*
MLDK melodic *tuneful*
MLDKDR maledictory *curse*
MLDKLCHRL multicultural *different backgrounds*
MLDKLCHRLZM multiculturalism *different backgrounds*
MLDKLRD multicolored *many colors* (Br) multicoloured
MLDKLTRL multicultural *different backgrounds*
MLDKLTRLZM multiculturalism *different backgrounds*
MLDKSHN malediction *curse*
MLDKTR maledictory *curse*
MLDL mildly *gently*
MLDLDRL multilateral (adj) *many sides* multilaterally (adv)
MLDLN multilane *highway*
MLDLNGGWL multilingual (adj) *many languages* multilingually (adv)
MLDLNGWL multilingual (adj) *many languages* multilingually (adv)
MLDLRD multilayered *many levels*
MLDLTRL multilateral (adj) *many sides* multilaterally (adv)
MLDLVL multilevel *many layers*
MLDLYRD multilayered *many levels*
MLDM milldam *pond*
MLDMD multimedia *many technologies*
MLDMDY multimedia *many technologies*
MLDMLYNR multimillionaire *many millions*
MLDMNSDR maladminister *give or rule poorly*
MLDMNSTR maladminister

Use letters that best describe the sounds you hear and omit the vowels. Use **S** or **K** instead of **C**: to find circle use **SRKL**. Use **J** to find joy, **JM** to find gem and **G** to find go.

give or rule poorly
MLDMNSTRSHN
maladministration *give or rule poorly*
MLDMR mal de mer *seasickness*
MLDMYNR multimillionaire *many millions*
MLDN melodeon *organ*
MLDN molding *wood trim*
MLDNG molding *wood trim*
MLDNGPNT melting point *temperature*
MLDNGPT melting pot *ethnic blend*
MLDNML multinomial *number*
MLDNMYL multinomial *number*
MLDNS mildness *gentleness*
MLDNS moldiness *fungus, wet rot*
MLDNSHNL multinational *many nations*
MLDPDD maladapted *poorly suited*
MLDPDV maladaptive *poorly suited*
MLDPL multi-ply *layers*
MLDPL multiple *many*
MLDPL multiply *increase* multiplied multiplies
MLDPLBL multipliable *number*
MLDPLCHS multiple-choice *test*
MLDPLKDV multiplicative *arithmetic*
MLDPLKN multiplicand *number*
MLDPLKND multiplicand *number*
MLDPLKS multiplex *many together*
MLDPLKSHN multiplication *arithmetic*
MLDPLKTV multiplicative *arithmetic*
MLDPLR multiplier *number*
MLDPLR multipolar *poles*
MLDPLSD multiplicity *many* multiplicities

MLDPLSKLRSS multiple sclerosis *disease*
MLDPLST multiplicity *many* multiplicities
MLDPLX multiplex *many together*
MLDPLYBL multipliable *number*
MLDPLYR multiplier *number*
MLDPRD multiparty *politics*
MLDPRPS multipurpose *many uses*
MLDPRT multiparty *politics*
MLDPTD maladapted *poorly suited*
MLDPTSHN maladaptation *poorly suited*
MLDPTV maladaptive *poorly suited*
MLDR emulator *copier*
MLDR immolator *killer*
MLDR molder (v) decay (n) *shaper*
MLDR moldier *fungus, wet rot*
MLDR mule deer *animal*
MLDRM melodrama *theater*
MLDRMDK melodramatic *theater*
MLDRMDKL melodramatically *theater*
MLDRMTK melodramatic *theater*
MLDRMTKL melodramatically *theater*
MLDRS malodorous *bad odor* (Br) malodourous
MLDRSHL multiracial *many races*
MLDRSHLZM multiracialism *many races*
MLDRSL malodorously *bad odor* (Br) malodourously
MLDRSNS malodorousness *bad odor* (Br) malodourously
MLDRST militarist *person*
MLDRT maladroit *awkward*
MLDRTL maladroitly *awkwardly*

MLDRTNS maladroitness *awkwardness*
MLDS melodious *tuneful*
MLDS myelitis *inflammation* myelitides
MLDSNSR multisensory *many senses*
MLDSNTSR multisensory *many senses*
MLDSPD multispeed *gears*
MLDST melodist *singer*
MLDST moldiest *fungus, wet rot*
MLDSTR multistory *highrise*
MLDSTRBSHN maldistribution *uneven placement*
MLDSTRBYSHN maldistribution *uneven placement*
MLDSTRD multistoried *highrise*
MLDTD multitude *crowd*
MLDTDNS multitudinous *crowded*
MLDTLNTD multitalented *many skills*
MLDTRD multitiered *many layers*
MLDTSKNG multitasking *computer*
MLDTYD multitude *crowd*
MLDTYDNS multitudinous *crowded*
MLDVDMN multivitamin *dietary*
MLDVLNS multivalence *values*
MLDVLNTS multivalence *values*
MLDVLNZ Maldive Islands *land mass*
MLDVLTN multivoltine *breeding*
MLDVRSD multiversity *school* multiversities
MLDVRST multiversity *school* multiversities
MLDVTMN multivitamin *dietary*
MLDVZ Maldives *islands*
MLDW mildewy *mold*

Letters aren't doubled for single sounds: to find alley use **L** not **LL**. Use **Y** and **W** as hard sounds only: to find yellow use **YL**. (Br)=British spelling or usage. * See dictionary.

MLDY mildew *mold*
MLDYN melodeon *organ*
MLDYR moldier *fungus, wet rot*
MLDYS melodious *tuneful*
MLDYST moldiest *fungus, wet rot*
MLDYW mildewy *mold*
MLDYZR multiuser *many at one time*
MLDZR multiuser *many at one time*
MLF mollify *pacify* mollified mollifying mollifies
MLFK malefic *evil*
MLFKDR malefactor *criminal*
MLFKSHN malefaction *crime*
MLFKSHN mollification *pacify*
MLFKTR malefactor *criminal*
MLFLNT mellifluent *flowing*
MLFLR millefleur (or) millefleurs *pattern*
MLFLS mellifluous *flowing*
MLFLWNT mellifluent *flowing*
MLFLWS mellifluous *flowing*
MLFN mellophone *horn*
MLFNGKSHN malfunction *failure*
MLFNKSHN malfunction *failure*
MLFRMD malformed *misshapen*
MLFRMSHN malformation *misshape*
MLFSNS maleficence *evil*
MLFSNT maleficent *evil*
MLFSNTS maleficence *evil*
MLFW mille-feuille *pastry*
MLFZNS malfeasance *wrongdoing*
MLFZNTS malfeasance *wrongdoing*
MLG myology *muscles*
MLGM amalgam *alloy*
MLGMDR amalgamator *mixer*
MLGMSHN amalgamation *mixture*
MLGMT amalgamate *mix* amalgamated amalgamating
MLGMTR amalgamator *mixer*
MLGN malaguena *folk tune*
MLGN mulligan *extra try*
MLGND malignity *spite*
MLGNNC malignancy *deadly* malignancies
MLGNNS malignancy *deadly* malignancies
MLGNNT malignant *deadly*
MLGNNTC malignancy *deadly* malignancies
MLGNNTS malignancy *deadly* malignancies
MLGNS myelogenous *bone marrow*
MLGNT malignant *deadly*
MLGNT malignity *spite*
MLGNY malaguena *folk tune*
MLGRM Mailgram (trademark) *letter*
MLGRM milligram *measurement*
MLGTN mulligatawny *soup*
MLGWN malaguena *folk tune*
MLGWNY malaguena *folk tune*
MLHL molehill *mound*
MLHWL mill wheel *grinder*
MLJ mileage *distance*
MLJ millage *tax*
MLJ myology *muscles*
MLJNS myelogenous *bone marrow*
MLJSDD maladjusted *without harmony*
MLJSMNT maladjustment *without harmony*
MLJSTD maladjusted *without harmony*
MLJSTMNT maladjustment *without harmony*
MLK malacca *cane*
MLK malic *acid*
MLK milk (n) *fluid* (v) *draw from*
MLK milky *white* milkier milkiest
MLK Molokai *island*
MLKDL mollycoddle *pamper* mollycoddled mollycoddling
MLKDLR mollycoddler *pamperer*
MLKFSH milkfish *fish*
MLKHS milk house *bottling*
MLKK milchig *dairy*
MLKL molecule *atoms*
MLKLG malacology *mollusks*
MLKLJ malacology *mollusks*
MLKLJKL malacological *mollusks*
MLKLJST malacologist *mollusks*
MLKLR molecular *atoms*
MLKLSHN malocclusion *improper fit*
MLKLZHN malocclusion *improper fit*
MLKMD milkmaid *dairy*
MLKMN milkman *merchant* milkmen
MLKNS milkiness *white*
MLKNTND malcontented *rebellious*
MLKNTNDNS malcontentedness *rebellion*
MLKNTNT malcontent *rebel*
MLKNTNTD malcontented *rebellious*
MLKNTNTDNS malcontentedness *rebellion*
MLKR milker *extractor*
MLKR milkier *whiter*
MLKR millicurie *measurement*
MLKRN milk run *many stops*
MLKS milk house *bottling*
MLKSHK milk shake *beverage*
MLKSNK milk snake *reptile*
MLKSP milksop *unmanly*
MLKST milkiest *whitest*
MLKT malachite *mineral*
MLKT mulct (n) *penalty* (v) *swindle*

MLKTL mollycoddle *pamper* mollycoddled mollycoddling

MLKTLR mollycoddler *pamperer*

MLKTST Milquetoast *timid one*

MLKTTH milk tooth *dental*

MLKW Milky Way *galaxy*

MLKWD milkweed *plant*

MLKWRT milkwort *plant*

MLKYL molecule *atoms*

MLKYLR molecular *atoms*

MLKYR milkier *whiter*

MLKYR millicurie *measurement*

MLKYST milkiest *whitest*

MLKZDK Melchizedek *priest-king*

MLLDR milliliter *measurement* (Br) millilitre

MLLT melilot *clover*

MLLTR milliliter *measurement* (Br) millilitre

MLM milium *whitehead* milia

MLM myeloma *tumor*

MLMDR millimeter *measurement* (Br) millimetre

MLMDS myelomatous *tumor*

MLMN mailman *postman* mailmen

MLMN melamine *resin*

MLMNT emolument *privilege, tip*

MLMPR milliampere *electricity*

MLMT malamute *dog*

MLMTHD mealymouthed *deceitful*

MLMTHT mealymouthed *deceitful*

MLMTR millimeter *measurement* (Br) millimetre

MLMTS myelomatous *tumor*

MLMYT malamute *dog*

MLN mailing *dispatch*

MLN malign *(adj) evil (v)* *defame*

MLN malines *fabric* malines

MLN melon *fruit*

MLN Milan *city*

MLN millennia (pl) *1,000 years* millennium

MLN milling *edge*

MLN moline *symbol*

MLN mullein *herb*

MLN mullion *window*

MLN myelin *nerve sheath*

MLNDD myelinated *nerve sheath*

MLNG mailing *dispatch*

MLNG milling *edge*

MLNGGR malinger *avoid work*

MLNGGRR malingerer *work avoider*

MLNGR malinger *avoid work*

MLNGRR malingerer *work avoider*

MLNJ mélange *mixture*

MLNK myelinic *nerve sheath*

MLNKL melancholia *depression*

MLNKL melancholy *sadness* melancholies

MLNKLK melancholiac *depressed one*

MLNKLK melancholic *depressed*

MLNKLY melancholia *depression*

MLNKLYK melancholiac *depressed one*

MLNM melanoma *tumor* melanomas

MLNM millennium *1,000 years* millennia (or) millenniums

MLNN melanin *pigment*

MLNR millenary *1,000*

MLNR milliner *hat seller*

MLNR millinery *hats*

MLNRN millenarian *1,000 years*

MLNRSHD malnourished *underfed*

MLNRSHT malnourished *underfed*

MLNRYN millenarian *1,000 years*

MLNS maleness *masculine*

MLNS mealiness *softness*

MLNS mildness *gentleness*

MLNSDK melanistic *pigment*

MLNSH Melanesia *islands*

MLNSH mélange *mixture*

MLNST melanocyte *skin cell*

MLNSTK melanistic *pigment*

MLNT emollient *soothing*

MLNTD myelinated *nerve sheath*

MLNTRSHN malnutrition *undernourishment*

MLNY millennia (pl) *1,000 years* millennium

MLNYM millennium *1,000 years* millennia (or) millenniums

MLNYTRSHN malnutrition *undernourishment*

MLNZ melanize *make dark* melanized melanizing

MLNZH Melanesia *islands*

MLNZH mélange *mixture*

MLNZM melanism *pigment*

MLNZSHN melanization *made dark*

MLP milpa *field, corn*

MLPD millipede *insect*

MLPLST amyloplast *plastid*

MLPN millpond *dammed stream*

MLPND millpond *dammed stream*

MLPRKDS malpractice *negligence*

MLPRKTS malpractice *negligence*

MLPRKTSHNR malpractitioner *negligent one*

MLPRP malaprop *misused word(s)*

MLPRP malapropos *inappropriate*

MLPRPZM malapropism *misused word(s)*

MLPRSHND malapportioned *legislation*

Letters aren't doubled for single sounds: to find alley use **L** not **LL**. Use **Y** and **W** as hard sounds only: to find yellow use **YL**. (Br)=British spelling or usage. * See dictionary.

MLPRSHNMNT malapportionment *legislation*
MLPRT malapert *saucy*
MLPRTL malapertly *saucy*
MLPRTNS malapertness *saucy*
MLPST milepost *distance marker*
MLPTH myelopathy *disease*
MLPTHK myelopathic *disease*
MLQD milkweed *plant*
MLQL molecule *atoms*
MLQLR molecular *atoms*
MLQR millicurie *measurement*
MLQRT milkwort *plant*
MLR Mahler *composer*
MLR mailer *sender*
MLR malar *bone*
MLR malaria *disease*
MLR mauler *mangler*
MLR mealier *soft*
MLR miler *racer*
MLR miliaria *prickly heat*
MLR miliary *lumpy*
MLR miller *grinder*
MLR molar *tooth, measure*
MLR Molière *dramatist*
MLR muller *grinder*
MLR Mylar *(trademark) film*
MLRD mallard *duck* mallard (or) mallards
MLRD milord *title*
MLRDR ameliorator *improver*
MLRDR mail-order (adj) *catalog* mail order (n)
MLRDR meliorator *peacemaker*
MLRDV ameliorative *improving*
MLRDV meliorative *soothing*
MLRK malarkey *nonsense*
MLRL malarial *disease*
MLRL miliarial *prickly heat*
MLRNTJN milliroentgen *measurement*
MLRNTSHN milliroentgen *measurement*
MLRS malarious *disease*

MLRS millrace *canal*
MLRSHN amelioration *improvement*
MLRSHN melioration *soothing*
MLRT ameliorate *improve* ameliorated ameliorating
MLRT meliorate *soothe* meliorated meliorating
MLRT millerite *mineral*
MLRT millwright *grinder*
MLRTR ameliorator *improver*
MLRTR amelioratory *improving*
MLRTR meliorator *peacemaker*
MLRTV ameliorative *improving*
MLRTV meliorative *soothing*
MLRY malaria *disease*
MLRY miliaria *prickly heat*
MLRYL malarial *disease*
MLRYL miliarial *prickly heat*
MLRYS malarious *disease*
MLRZM meliorism *become better*
MLS aimless *no purpose*
MLS amylase *enzyme*
MLS amylose *starch*
MLS emulous *copy*
MLS malice *evil*
MLSD emulsoid *solution*
MLSDK myelocytic *cell*
MLSDL emulsoidal *solution*
MLSDR molester *annoyer*
MLSDSHN molestation *bother*
MLSF emulsify *disperse* emulsified emulsifying emulsifies
MLSFKSHN emulsification *dispersion*
MLSFR emulsifier *dispersion*
MLSFYR emulsifier *dispersion*
MLSH Malaysia *country*
MLSH militia *military*
MLSH moulage *impression*
MLSH mulish *stubborn*
MLSHL mulishly *stubbornly*
MLSHMN militiaman *soldier*

militiamen
MLSHN emulation *copy*
MLSHN emulsion *coating, solution*
MLSHN immolation *killing*
MLSHNS mulishness *stubbornness*
MLSHS malicious *evil*
MLSHSL maliciously *evil*
MLSHSNS maliciousness *evil*
MLSK mollusk (or) mollusc *shellfish*
MLSKN moleskin *fabric*
MLSKNR mule skinner *herder*
MLSL aimlessly *no purpose*
MLSL emulously *copy*
MLSM melisma *melody* melismata
MLSMD melismata (pl) *melody* melisma
MLSML millesimal *one of 1,000*
MLSMT melismata (pl) *melody* melisma
MLSNS aimlessness *no purpose*
MLSNS emulousness *copy*
MLSPRR miles per hour *speed*
MLSPRWR miles per hour *speed*
MLSS molasses *syrup*
MLST mealiest *soft*
MLST molest *annoy*
MLST myelocyte *cell*
MLSTK maulstick *handrest*
MLSTK myelocytic *cell*
MLSTN milestone *achievement*
MLSTN millstone *grinder, hindrance*
MLSTR molester *annoyer*
MLSTRM maelstrom *storm*
MLSTRM millstream *river*
MLSTSHN molestation *bother*
MLSZ molasses *syrup*
MLT amulet *charm*
MLT emulate *copy* emulated emulating

Use letters that best describe the sounds you hear and omit the vowels. Use **S** or **K** instead of **C**: to find circle use **SRKL**. Use **J** to find joy, **JM** to find gem and **G** to find go.

MLT immolate *kill* immolated immolating
MLT mallet *hammer*
MLT malt *grain*
MLT Malta *island*
MLT malty *grainy*
MLT melt *(v) soften, blend (n)* spleen, soft mass
MLT millet *grass*
MLT milt *fish sperm*
MLT molt *shed skin*
MLT molto *very much*
MLT mulatto *mixed race* mulattoes (or) mulattos
MLT mullet *fish* mullet (or) mullets
MLT mullite *mineral*
MLT multi- *(combined form)* many
MLT omelette (or) omelet *egg dish*
MLT umlaut *vowel mark*
MLTBL meltable *soften*
MLTBLD meltability *soften*
MLTBLT meltability *soften*
MLTD malted *beverage*
MLTDMLK malted milk *beverage*
MLTDMNSHNL multidimensional *many sides*
MLTDMNTSHNL multidimensional *many sides*
MLTDN meltdown *softening*
MLTDRG multidrug *many drugs*
MLTDRKSHNL multidirectional *many directions*
MLTDS myelitides (pl) *inflammation* myelitis
MLTDSPLN multidiscipline *many fields*
MLTDSPLNR multidisciplinary *many fields*
MLTDZ myelitides (pl) *inflammation* myelitis
MLTFKKTL Molotov cocktail *bomb*
MLTFLMNT multifilament

many threads
MLTFNGKSHNL multifunctional *many duties*
MLTFNGSHNL multifunctional *many duties*
MLTFNKSHNL multifunctional *many duties*
MLTFRM multiform *many shapes*
MLTFRS multifarious *different*
MLTFRYS multifarious *different*
MLTFSDD multifaceted *many sides*
MLTFSTD multifaceted *many sides*
MLTHD multihued *many colors*
MLTHN malathion *insecticide*
MLTHYD multihued *many colors*
MLTHYN malathion *insecticide*
MLTKLCHRL multicultural *different backgrounds*
MLTKLCHRLZM multiculturalism *different backgrounds*
MLTKLRD multicolored *many colors* (Br) multicoloured
MLTKLTRL multicultural *different backgrounds*
MLTKLTRLZM multiculturalism *different backgrounds*
MLTLDRL multilateral (adj) *many sides* multilaterally (adv)
MLTLN multilane *highway*
MLTLNGGWL multilingual (adj) *many languages* multilingually (adv)
MLTLNGWL multilingual (adj) *many languages* multilingually (adv)
MLTLRD multilayered *many levels*

MLTLTRL multilateral (adj) *many sides* multilaterally (adv)
MLTLVL multilevel *many layers*
MLTLYRD multilayered *many levels*
MLTM mealtime *food*
MLTMD multimedia *many technologies*
MLTMDY multimedia *many technologies*
MLTMLYNR multimillionaire *many millions*
MLTMYNR multimillionaire *many millions*
MLTN melton *cloth*
MLTN molten *melted*
MLTNC militancy *fighting*
MLTNGPNT melting point *temperature*
MLTNGPT melting pot *ethnic blend*
MLTNML multinomial *number*
MLTNMYL multinomial *number*
MLTNN melatonin *hormone*
MLTNPNT melting point *temperature*
MLTNPT melting pot *ethnic blend*
MLTNS militancy *fighting*
MLTNSHNL multinational *many nations*
MLTNT militant *fighting*
MLTNTC militancy *fighting*
MLTNTS militancy *fighting*
MLTPL multi-ply *layers*
MLTPL multiple *many*
MLTPL multiply *increase* multiplied multiplies
MLTPLBL multipliable *number*
MLTPLCHS multiple-choice *test*
MLTPLKDV multiplicative *arithmetic*
MLTPLKN multiplicand *number*
MLTPLKND multiplicand *number*

Letters aren't doubled for single sounds: to find alley use **L** not **LL**. Use **Y** and **W** as hard sounds only: to find yellow use **YL**. (Br)=British spelling or usage. * See dictionary.

MLTPLKS multiplex *many together*

MLTPLKSHN multiplication *arithmetic*

MLTPLKTV multiplicative *arithmetic*

MLTPLR multiplier *number*

MLTPLR multipolar *poles*

MLTPLSD multiplicity *many multiplicities*

MLTPLSKLRSS multiple sclerosis *disease*

MLTPLST multiplicity *many multiplicities*

MLTPLX multiplex *many together*

MLTPLYBL multipliable *number*

MLTPLYR multiplier *number*

MLTPRD multiparty *politics*

MLTPRPS multipurpose *many uses*

MLTPRT multiparty *politics*

MLTR emulator *copier*

MLTR immolator *killer*

MLTR military *armed forces military*

MLTR muleteer *herder*

MLTRL militarily *armed forces*

MLTRSDK militaristic *armed forces*

MLTRSHL multiracial *many races*

MLTRSHLZM multiracialism *many races*

MLTRST militarist *person*

MLTRSTK militaristic *armed forces*

MLTRT maltreat *abuse*

MLTRTMNT maltreatment *abuse*

MLTRZ militarize *equip with weapons* militarized militarizing (Br) militarise

MLTRZM militarism *armed forces*

MLTRZSHN militarization *armed forces* (Br) militarisation

MLTS maltase *enzyme*

MLTS Maltese *of Malta*

MLTS maltose *grain sugar*

MLTS myelitis *inflammation* myelitides

MLTSNSR multisensory *many senses*

MLTSNTSR multisensory *many senses*

MLTSPD multispeed *gears*

MLTSTR multistory *highrise*

MLTSTRD multistoried *highrise*

MLTT militate *have effect* militated militating

MLTTD multitude *crowd*

MLTTDNS multitudinous *crowded*

MLTTLNTD multitalented *many skills*

MLTTRD multitiered *many layers*

MLTTSKNG multitasking *computer*

MLTTYD multitude *crowd*

MLTTYDNS multitudinous *crowded*

MLTVDMN multivitamin *dietary*

MLTVKKTL Molotov cocktail *bomb*

MLTVLNS multivalence *values*

MLTVLNTS multivalence *values*

MLTVLTN multivoltine *breeding*

MLTVRSD multiversity *school* multiversities

MLTVRST multiversity *school* multiversities

MLTVTMN multivitamin *dietary*

MLTWDR meltwater *ice*

MLTWTR meltwater *ice*

MLTYZR multiuser *many at one time*

MLTZ maltase *enzyme*

MLTZ Maltese *of Malta*

MLTZR multiuser *many at one time*

MLVLNS malevolence *spite*

MLVLNT malevolent *spiteful*

MLVLNTS malevolence *spite*

MLW Malawi *country*

MLWK Milwaukee *city*

MLWL mill wheel *grinder*

MLWRK millwork *woodwork*

MLWRM mealworm *beetle larva*

MLXP milksop *unmanly*

MLY milia (pl) *whitehead* milium

MLY milieu *background* milieus (or) milieux

MLYBL malleable *easily molded*

MLYBLD malleability *easily molded*

MLYBLT malleability *easily molded*

MLYM milium *whitehead* milia

MLYMNT emolument *privilege, tip*

MLYN million *1,000,000*

MLYN mullion *window*

MLYNR millionaire *wealth*

MLYNRS millionairess *wealth*

MLYNT emollient *soothing*

MLYNTH millionth *1,000,000*

MLYR mealier *soft*

MLYR miliaria *prickly heat*

MLYR miliary *lumpy*

MLYR milieu *background* milieus (or) milieux

MLYR Molière *dramatist*

MLYRD milliard (Br) *1,000,000,000*

MLYRDR ameliorator *improver*

MLYRDR meliorator *peacemaker*

MLYRDV ameliorative *improving*

MLYRDV meliorative *soothing*

MLYRL miliarial *prickly heat*

MLYRSHN amelioration *improvement*

MLYRSHN melioration *soothing*

MLYRT ameliorate *improve* ameliorated ameliorating

MLYRT meliorate *soothe*

Use letters that best describe the sounds you hear and omit the vowels. Use **S** or **K** instead of **C**: to find circle use **SRKL**. Use **J** to find joy, **JM** to find gem and **G** to find go.

meliorated meliorating
MLYRTR ameliorator *improver*
MLYRTR amelioratory *improving*
MLYRTR meliorator *peacemaker*
MLYRTV ameliorative *improving*
MLYRTV meliorative *soothing*
MLYRY miliaria *prickly heat*
MLYRYL miliarial *prickly heat*
MLYRZM meliorism *become better*
MLYST mealiest *soft*
MLZ amylase *enzyme*
MLZ amylose *starch*
MLZ malaise *illness*
MLZH Malaysia *country*
MLZH moulage *impression*
MLZM melisma *melody* melismata
MLZMD melismata (pl) *melody* melisma
MLZMT melismata (pl) *melody* melisma
MM imam *(often capitalized) Muslim leader*
MM ma'am *madam*
MM mahimahi *fish*
MM maim *cripple*
MM mama (or) mamma *mother*
MM mamma *gland* mammae
MM mammy *nurse* mammies
MM mau-mau *(often capitalized) intimidate* mau-maued mau-mauing
MM Maugham (Somerset) *writer*
MM mayhem *violence*
MM memo *note* memos
MM Miami *city*
MM mime *imitate* mimed miming
MM mom *mother*
MM mommy *mother* mommies
MM mum *(v) perform* mummed mumming

MM mum *(adj) silent (n) flower, (Br) mother, beer*
MM mummy *corpse, (Br) mother* mummies
MM muumuu *dress*
MM myoma *tumor* myomas (or) myomata
MMB mamba *snake*
MMB mambo *dance* mambos
MMBJMB mumbo jumbo *rite, doubletalk*
MMBL mumble *mutter* mumbled mumbling
MMBLDPG mumblety-peg *game*
MMBLPG mumblety-peg *game*
MMBLR mumbler *mutterer*
MMBLTPG mumblety-peg *game*
MMBR member *limb, part*
MMBRN membrane *layer*
MMBRNS membranous *thin and pliable*
MMBRSHP membership *status*
MMC malmsey *wine*
MMCHG mummichog *fish*
MMD myomata (pl) *tumor* myoma
MMDK mimetic *imitative*
MMDKL mimetically *imitative*
MMF mummify *embalm* mummified mummifying mummifies
MMFKSHN mummification *embalming*
MMFS Memphis *city*
MMGRF mammography *breast X ray*
MMGRF mimeograph *copy*
MMGRM mammogram *breast X ray*
MMK mimic *copy* mimicked mimicking
MMKR mimicker *copier*
MMKR mimicry *copy* mimicries
MML mammal *animal*
MMLG mammalogy *animals*

MMLJ mammalogy *animals*
MMLJST mammalogist *animals*
MMLN mammalian *animal*
MMLR mammilary *breasts*
MMLYN mammalian *animal*
MMN mammon *wealth*
MMN memento *souvenir* mementos (or) mementoes
MMNM momentum *movement* momenta (or) momentums
MMNS momentous *important*
MMNT memento *souvenir* mementos (or) mementoes
MMNT moment *short period of time*
MMNT momenta (pl) *movement* momentum
MMNTM momentum *movement* momenta (or) momentums
MMNTR momentary *brief*
MMNTRL momentarily *soon*
MMNTS momentous *important*
MMPS mumps *disease*
MMR maimer *crippler*
MMR mammary *gland*
MMR memory *remember* memories
MMR mimer *imitate*
MMR mummer *actor*
MMR mummery *performance* mummeries
MMRB memorabilia *things*
MMRBL memorabilia *things*
MMRBL memorable (adj) *notable* memorably (adv)
MMRBLD memorability *remember*
MMRBLNS memorableness *notable*
MMRBLT memorability *remember*
MMRBLY memorabilia *things*
MMRBY memorabilia *things*
MMRL immemorial (adj)

Letters aren't doubled for single sounds: to find alley use **L** not **LL**. Use **Y** and **W** as hard sounds only: to find yellow use **YL**. (Br)=British spelling or usage. * See dictionary.

ancient immemorially
(adv)
MMRL memorial
commemorative
MMRLD Memorial Day
holiday
MMRLZ memorialize
commemorate
memorialized
memorializing
(Br) memorialise
MMRND memoranda (pl)
note memorandum
MMRNDM memorandum
note memorandums (or)
memoranda
MMRYL immemorial (adj)
ancient immemorially
(adv)
MMRYL memorial
commemorative
MMRYLD Memorial Day
holiday
MMRYLZ memorialize
commemorate
memorialized
memorializing
(Br) memorialise
MMRZ memorize *remember*
memorized memorizing
(Br) memorise
MMRZR memorizer
remember
(Br) memoriser
MMRZSHN memorization
remember
(Br) memorisation
MMS malmsey *wine*
MMS mimosa *tree*
MMT imamate *region*
MMT myomata (pl) *tumor*
myoma
MMTH mammoth *giant*
MMTK mimetic *imitative*
MMTKL mimetically
imitative
MMW memoir *account*
MMWR memoir *account*
MMWRST memoirist *writer*
MMYGRF mimeograph *copy*
MMZ malmsey *wine*
MMZ mumsy *mother*

mumsies
MN almond *nut*
MN amen *so be it*
MN amine *compound*
MN amino *protein*
MN Amman *city*
MN ammine *molecule*
MN ammonia *chemical*
MN amnia (pl) *membrane*
amnion
MN immune *exempt, resistant*
MN main *(adj) principal (n)*
force, pipe, sail
MN Maine *US State*
MN man *(n) adult male,*
person men
MN man *(v) supply with men*
manned manning
MN mane *hair*
MN mania *madness*
MN manna *bread*
MN manta *shawl*
MN many *more than a few*
MN mean *(v) signify, intend*
meant meaning
MN mean *(n) middle (adj)*
average, humble, ignoble*
MN meanie *spiteful one*
meanies
MN menu *food list* menus
MN mesne *intermediate*
MN mien *manner*
MN mind *(n) mental state (v)*
notice, dislike, care*
MN mine *(v) dig* mined
mining
MN mine *(pron) of me (n) pit,*
bomb (v) dig
MN mini *small* minis
MN minnow *bait fish*
minnows
MN moan *groan*
MN money *currency* moneys
(or) monies
MN mono *not stereo,*
mononucleosis
MN monte *game*
MN moon *satellite*
MN mooneye *fish*
MN Moonie *Unification*
Church
MN moony *round, dreamy*

MN mound *hill*
MN Mounty *police* Mounties
MN mown *(v-past) mow*
MN muon *particle*
MN mynah (or) myna *bird*
MN Oman *city*
MN omen *sign*
MNBGLN mind-boggling
overwhelming
MNBGLNG mind-boggling
overwhelming
MNBGS moneybags *wealthy*
one
MNBGZ moneybags *wealthy*
one
MNBK minibike *vehicle*
MNBK money-back
guarantee
MNBL amenable (adj)
willing amenably (adv)
MNBL minable (or)
mineable *dig*
MNBLD amenability
willingness
MNBLN mind-blowing
confusing
MNBLNG mind-blowing
confusing
MNBLT amenability
willingness
MNBLWN mind-blowing
confusing
MNBLWNG mind-blowing
confusing
MNBM moonbeam *light*
MNBNDN mind-bending
confusing
MNBNDNG mind-bending
confusing
MNBRM manubrium
breastbone manubria
MNBRYM manubrium
breastbone manubria
MNBS minibus *vehicle*
MNBS omnibus *(n) book, bus*
(adj) many
MNBTN man-about-town
social one men-about-
town
MNC menisci (pl) *curve*
meniscus
MNCD moonseed *plant*

Use letters that best describe the sounds you hear and omit the vowels. Use **S** or **K** instead of **C**: to find circle use **SRKL**. Use **J** to find joy, **JM** to find gem and **G** to find go.

MNCH munch *chew*
MNCHKN munchkin *midget*
MNCHL man-child *male* men-children
MNCHL Monticello *building*
MNCHLD man-child *male* men-children
MNCHN mansion *house*
MNCHN mention *(n) citation (v) cite*
MNCHNBL mentionable *spoken*
MNCHNJR money changer *dealer, device*
MNCHNL manchineel *tree*
MNCHR Manchuria *region*
MNCHR miniature *tiny*
MNCHR muncher *chewer*
MNCHRY Manchuria *region*
MNCHRZ miniaturize *make small* miniaturized miniaturizing
MNCHRZSHN miniaturization *made small*
MNCHSDR Manchester *city*
MNCHSTR Manchester *city*
MNCHZ munchies *food*
MNCNR monseigneur *French title* messeigneurs
MNCNYR monseigneur *French title* messeigneurs
MNCRZ miniseries *TV episodes*
MNCZ menses *monthly flow*
MND almond *nut*
MND almond-eyed *slant-eyed*
MND amanita *fungus*
MND amend *modify*
MND amenity *comfort* amenities
MND emend *correct*
MND immunity *exemption, resistance* immunities
MND maenad *woman*
MND manned *with humans*
MND mend *fix*
MND mind *(n) mental state (v) notice, dislike, care**
MND monad *unit*
MND Monday *weekday*
MND moneyed *wealthy*

MND moon-eyed *dreamy*
MND mound *hill*
MNDBGLN mind-boggling *overwhelming*
MNDBGLNG mind-boggling *overwhelming*
MNDBL amendable *modify*
MNDBL emendable *correction*
MNDBL mandible *jaw*
MNDBL mendable *fix*
MNDBLN mind-blowing *confusing*
MNDBLNG mind-blowing *confusing*
MNDBLR mandibular *jaw*
MNDBLT mandibulate *jaw*
MNDBLWN mind-blowing *confusing*
MNDBLWNG mind-blowing *confusing*
MNDBNDN mind-bending *confusing*
MNDBNDNG mind-bending *confusing*
MNDBYLR mandibular *jaw*
MNDBYLT mandibulate *jaw*
MNDD almond-eyed *slant-eyed*
MNDD minded *inclined*
MNDDR mandator *director*
MNDFL mindful *(adj) aware* mindfully *(adv)*
MNDFSHNC immunodeficiency *no antibodies*
MNDFSHNS immunodeficiency *no antibodies*
MNDFSHNTC immunodeficiency *no antibodies*
MNDFSHNTS immunodeficiency *no antibodies*
MNDK ammonitic *ammonia*
MNDK amniotic *womb*
MNDKNC mendicancy *begging*
MNDKNS mendicancy *begging*
MNDKNT mendicant *beggar,*

monk
MNDKNTC mendicancy *begging*
MNDKNTS mendicancy *begging*
MNDKSPNDN mind-expanding *hallucinating*
MNDKSPNDNG mind-expanding *hallucinating*
MNDL mandala *pattern*
MNDL mandola *music*
MNDLN mandolin *music*
MNDLN Mendelian *of Mendel*
MNDLNST mandolinist *musician*
MNDLS mindless *heedless*
MNDLSL mindlessly *heedlessly*
MNDLSN Mendelssohn *philosopher*
MNDLSNS mindlessness *heedless*
MNDLYN Mendelian *of Mendel*
MNDMNT amendment *alteration*
MNDMS mandamus *writ*
MNDN amandine *almonds*
MNDN mundane *everyday*
MNDND mundanity *everyday*
MNDNG man-eating *eats humans*
MNDNL mundanely *everyday*
MNDNS mundaneness *everyday*
MNDNT mundanity *everyday*
MNDR amender *modifier*
MNDR emender *correction*
MNDR man-eater *eats humans*
MNDR maunder *grumble, wander*
MNDR meander *(n) path (v) wander*
MNDR mender *fix*
MNDR monitor *(n) device, watcher (v) watch*
MNDRDR mind reader *sixth sense*
MNDRK mandrake *herb*

Letters aren't doubled for single sounds: to find alley use **L** not **LL**. Use **Y** and **W** as hard sounds only: to find yellow use **YL**. (Br)=British spelling or usage. * See dictionary.

MNDRL mandrel *shaft*
MNDRL mandrill *baboon*
MNDRM monodrama *single actor*
MNDRN mandarin *bureaucrat, dialect, orange*
MNDRR maunderer *grumble, wander*
MNDRS meanderous *intricate*
MNDRVN menu-driven *computer*
MNDSD mendacity *dishonesty* mendacities
MNDSHN emendation *correction*
MNDSHS mendacious *dishonest*
MNDSHSL mendaciously *dishonestly*
MNDSHSNS mendaciousness *dishonesty*
MNDST mendacity *dishonesty* mendacities
MNDST mind-set *opinion*
MNDST moondust *soil*
MNDT mandate *order* mandated mandating
MNDTR amendatory *modifying*
MNDTR mandator *director*
MNDTR mandatory *required* mandatories
MNDXPNDN mind-expanding *hallucinating*
MNDXPNDNG mind-expanding *hallucinating*
MNDZ amends *recompense*
MNDZ mind's eye *imagination*
MNF ammonify *add ammonia* ammonified ammonifying ammonifies
MNF minify *lessen* minified minifying minifies
MNFG monophagy *single food*
MNFGS monophagous *single food*
MNFJ monophagy *single food*

MNFK menfolk (or) menfolks *males*
MNFKCHR manufacture *produce* manufactured manufacturing
MNFKCHRR manufacturer *producer*
MNFKDR manufactory *factory* manufactories
MNFKS menfolks (or) menfolk *males*
MNFKSHN ammonification *add ammonia*
MNFKSHR manufacture *produce* manufactured manufacturing
MNFKSHRR manufacturer *producer*
MNFKTR manufactory *factory* manufactories
MNFKTR manufacture *produce* manufactured manufacturing
MNFKTRR manufacturer *producer*
MNFKTYR manufacture *produce* manufactured manufacturing
MNFL manful (adj) *brave* manfully (adv)
MNFL manifold (adj, adv) *many* (v) multiply (n) *pipe fitting, space*
MNFL mindful (adj) *aware* mindfully (adv)
MNFL minefield *weapons*
MNFL monophyly *one ancestor*
MNFLD manifold (adj, adv) *many* (v) multiply (n) *pipe fitting, space*
MNFLD minefield *weapons*
MNFLDK monophyletic *one ancestor*
MNFLNS manfulness *bravery*
MNFLR moonflower *plant*
MNFLTK monophyletic *one ancestor*
MNFLWR moonflower *plant*
MNFN monophony *one melody, one path*

MNFNK monophonic *one melody, one path*
MNFNKL monophonically *one melody, one path*
MNFRM mainframe *computer*
MNFRS omnifarious *all kinds*
MNFRYS omnifarious *all kinds*
MNFS manifest (adj) *evident* (v) show (n) *list*
MNFSD manifesto *declaration* manifestos (or) manifestoes
MNFSH moonfish *sea creature* moonfish (or) moonfishes
MNFSNS munificence *generosity*
MNFSNT munificent *generous*
MNFSNT omnificent *creative*
MNFSNTL munificently *generously*
MNFSNTS munificence *generosity*
MNFST manifest (adj) *evident* (v) show (n) *list*
MNFST manifesto *declaration* manifestos (or) manifestoes
MNFST moonfaced *round*
MNFSTSHN manifestation *evidence*
MNFTHNG monophthong *vowel sound*
MNFTHNGGL monophthongal *vowel sound*
MNFTHNGL monophthongal *vowel sound*
MNFX menfolks (or) menfolk *males*
MNG among *along with*
MNG Managua *city*
MNG mango *fruit* mangoes
MNG mangy *shabby* mangier mangiest
MNG Ming *dynasty*
MNG mounting *mound*

Use letters that best describe the sounds you hear and omit the vowels. Use **S** or **K** instead of **C**: to find circle use **SRKL**. Use **J** to find joy, **JM** to find gem and **G** to find go.

MNGG mango *fruit* mangoes
MNGGL immingle *blend* immingled immingling
MNGGL mangle *wring* mangled mangling
MNGGL mingle *mix* mingled mingling
MNGGL Mongol *of Mongolia*
MNGGL Mongolia *country*
MNGGLD Mongoloid *Asian race*
MNGGLN Mongolian *of Mongolia*
MNGGLR mangler *wringer*
MNGGLY Mongolia *country*
MNGGLYN Mongolian *of Mongolia*
MNGGLZM mongolism *Down's Syndrome*
MNGGNZ manganese *element*
MNGGR monger *(n) dealer (v) peddle*
MNGGRL mongrel *crossbreed*
MNGGRLZ mongrelize *crossbreed* mongrelized mongrelizing
MNGGRV mangrove *tree*
MNGGS mongoose *animal* mongooses
MNGK mink *animal* mink (or) minks
MNGK monk *friar*
MNGK monkey *(n) ape (v) tamper, fool* monkeys
MNGKHD monkhood *friar*
MNGKPD monkeypod *tree*
MNGKR monkery *friar* monkeries
MNGKRNCH monkey wrench *tool*
MNGKS Manx *of the Isle of Man, cat*
MNGKS minx *girl* minxes
MNGKSH monkish *friar*
MNGKSHN monkeyshine *prank*
MNGKWL minke whale *mammal*
MNGL immingle *blend*

immingled immingling
MNGL mangle *wring* mangled mangling
MNGL mingle *mix* mingled mingling
MNGL Mongol *of Mongolia*
MNGL Mongolia *country*
MNGLD Mongoloid *Asian race*
MNGLN Mongolian *of Mongolia*
MNGLR mangler *wringer*
MNGLS meaningless insignificant
MNGLY Mongolia *country*
MNGLYN Mongolian *of Mongolia*
MNGLZM mongolism *Down's Syndrome*
MNGM monogamy *one spouse*
MNGMR Montgomery *city*
MNGMS monogamous *one spouse*
MNGMSL monogamously *one spouse*
MNGMST monogamist *one spouse*
MNGNK immunogenic *antibodies*
MNGNS manginess *shabbiness*
MNGNZ manganese *element*
MNGR mangier *shabby*
MNGR monger *(n) dealer (v) peddle*
MNGRBR money-grubber *greedy one*
MNGRF monograph *one subject*
MNGRL managerial (adj) *supervisory* managerially (adv)
MNGRL mongrel *crossbreed*
MNGRLZ mongrelize *crossbreed* mongrelized mongrelizing
MNGRM monogram *initial* monogrammed monogramming
MNGRMR monogrammer *initials*

MNGRV mangrove *tree*
MNGRYL managerial (adj) *supervisory* managerially (adv)
MNGS mongoose *animal* mongooses
MNGST mangiest *shabby*
MNGW Managua *city*
MNGX Manx *of the Isle of Man, cat*
MNGX minx *girl* minxes
MNGYR mangier *shabby*
MNGYST mangiest *shabby*
MNHD manhood *adult male*
MNHDN menhaden *fish* menhaden
MNHL manhole *opening*
MNHNDL manhandle *treat roughly* manhandled manhandling
MNHNT manhunt *search*
MNHR menhir *tower*
MNHTN Manhattan *island*
MNHWL meanwhile *during*
MNJ manage *control* managed managing
MNJ mange *disease*
MNJ mangy *shabby* mangier mangiest
MNJ mintage *coins*
MNJBL manageable (adj) *controlled* manageably (adv)
MNJBLD manageability *control*
MNJBLT manageability *control*
MNJDS meningitis *brain disease*
MNJMNT management *supervisors*
MNJN immunogen *antibody*
MNJN managing *controlling*
MNJN monogyny *one wife*
MNJNDK monogenetic *single ancestor*
MNJNDKS immunogenetics *antibodies*
MNJNDX immunogenetics *antibodies*
MNJNG managing *controlling*

Letters aren't doubled for single sounds: to find alley use **L** not **LL**. Use **Y** and **W** as hard sounds only: to find yellow use **YL**. (Br)=British spelling or usage. * See dictionary.

MNJNK immunogenic *antibodies*
MNJNS manginess *shabbiness*
MNJNS monogynous *one wife*
MNJNSS monogenesis *single ancestor*
MNJNTK monogenetic *single ancestor*
MNJNTKS immunogenetics *antibodies*
MNJNTX immunogenetics *antibodies*
MNJR manager *director*
MNJR manger *crib*
MNJR mangier *shabby*
MNJR menagerie *zoo*
MNJRL managerial (adj) *supervisory* managerially (adv)
MNJRYL managerial (adj) *supervisory* managerially (adv)
MNJST mangiest *shabby*
MNJTS meningitis *brain disease*
MNJYR mangier *shabby*
MNJYST mangiest *shabby*
MNK maniac *lunatic*
MNK manic *frenzy*
MNK manqué *unfulfilled*
MNK mink *animal* mink (or) minks
MNK Monaco *country*
MNK monk *friar*
MNK monkey (n) *ape* (v) *tamper, fool* monkeys
MNK Munich *city*
MNKD manicotti *pasta*
MNKDLDN monocotyledon *plant*
MNKDLDNS monocotyledonous *plant*
MNKDPRSV manic-depressive *psychology*
MNKHD monkhood *friar*
MNKK monocoque *construction*
MNKL manacle *chain* manacled manacling
MNKL maniacal (adj) *crazy*

maniacally (adv)
MNKL monachal *monk*
MNKL monocle *eyeglass*
MNKLCHR monoculture *one type*
MNKLCHRL monocultural *one type*
MNKLD monocled *eyeglass*
MNKLNL monoclonal *one cell*
MNKLR monocular *one eye*
MNKLTR monoculture *one type*
MNKLTRL monocultural *one type*
MNKM Minicam (*trademark*) *camera*
MNKMPDR minicomputer *processor*
MNKMPTR minicomputer *processor*
MNKMPYDR minicomputer *processor*
MNKMPYTR minicomputer *processor*
MNKN Maine coon *cat*
MNKN manikin (or) mannikin *dwarf*
MNKN mankind *humans*
MNKN mannequin *model*
MNKND mankind *humans*
MNKPD monkeypod *tree*
MNKR manicure (v) *clip, trim* manicured manicuring
MNKR manicure (n) *nail treatment*
MNKR moniker *name*
MNKR monkery *friar* monkeries
MNKRC monocracy *rule by one* monocracies
MNKRD monochord *music*
MNKRDK monocratic *rule by one*
MNKRL Monte Carlo *city*
MNKRM monochrome *one color*
MNKRMDK monochromatic *one color*
MNKRMDKL monochromatically *one*

color
MNKRMDR monochromator *color*
MNKRMTK monochromatic *one color*
MNKRMTKL monochromatically *one color*
MNKRMTR monochromator *color*
MNKRMTZM monochromatism *one color*
MNKRNCH monkey wrench *tool*
MNKRS monocracy *rule by one* monocracies
MNKRST manicurist *nail groomer*
MNKRT monocrat *ruler*
MNKRTK monocratic *rule by one*
MNKS Manx *of the Isle of Man, cat*
MNKS minx *girl* minxes
MNKSD monoxide *chemical*
MNKSDL minoxidil *hair growth drug*
MNKSH monkish *friar*
MNKSHN monkeyshine *prank*
MNKT manicotti *pasta*
MNKTLDN monocotyledon *plant*
MNKTLDNS monocotyledonous *plant*
MNKWL minke whale *mammal*
MNKYLR monocular *one eye*
MNKYR manicure (v) *clip, trim* manicured manicuring
MNKYR manicure (n) *nail treatment*
MNKYRST manicurist *nail groomer*
MNL mainly *principally*
MNL manila *hemp, paper*
MNL Manila *city*
MNL manille *trump*
MNL manly *masculine* manlier manliest

Use letters that best describe the sounds you hear and omit the vowels. Use **S** or **K** instead of **C**: to find circle use **SRKL**. Use **J** to find joy, **JM** to find gem and **G** to find go.

MNL mantel *fireplace*
MNL mantle *cloak* mantled mantling
MNL manual (adj) *by hand* manually (adv)
MNL meanly *humbly, badly*
MNL menial (adj) *servant* menially (adv)
MNL mental (adj) *of the mind* mentally (adv)
MNLDR moonlighter *worker*
MNLFRM moniliform *jointed*
MNLG immunology *antibodies*
MNLG monologue *speech*
MNLGST monologuist (or) monologist *speaker*
MNLJ immunology *antibodies*
MNLJK immunologic (or) immunological (adj) *antibodies* immunologically (adv)
MNLJKL immunological (or) immunologic (adj) *antibodies* immunologically (adv)
MNLJST monologuist (or) monologist *speaker*
MNLN main line (n) *highway, vein*
MNLN mainland *continent*
MNLN mainline (v) *inject* (adj) *mainstream*
MNLND mainland *continent*
MNLNDR moneylender *pawnbroker*
MNLNS manliness *masculine*
MNLPS mantelpiece *fireplace*
MNLR manlier *masculine*
MNLR minelayer *weapons*
MNLS mindless *heedless*
MNLS Mona Lisa *painting*
MNLSL mindlessly *heedlessly*
MNLSNS mindlessness *heedless*
MNLST manliest *masculine*
MNLT moonlight (v) *hold a second job* moonlighted

moonlighting
MNLT moonlight (n) *illumination*
MNLT moonlit *lit by the moon*
MNLTH monolith *column*
MNLTHK monolithic *huge, single unit*
MNLTR moonlighter *worker*
MNLYR manlier *masculine*
MNLYR minelayer *weapons*
MNLYST manliest *masculine*
MNLZ Mona Lisa *painting*
MNM ammonium *ammonia*
MNM minim *fluid unit*
MNM minima (pl) *least minimum*
MNM omentum *fold* omenta (or) omentums
MNMD man-made *artificial*
MNMDLST monometallist *currency*
MNMDLZM monometallism *currency*
MNMDR manometer *device*
MNMDR monometer *verse*
MNMKR moneymaker *profitable*
MNML minimal (adj) *least* minimally (adv)
MNML monomial *math, name*
MNMLKLR monomolecular *atoms*
MNMLKYLR monomolecular *atoms*
MNMLQLR monomolecular *atoms*
MNMLST minimalist *simplicity*
MNMLZM minimalism *simplicity*
MNMM minimum *least bit* minima (or) minimums
MNMN moneyman *financier*
MNMN monomania *single idea*
MNMNKL monomaniacal (adj) *single idea* monomaniacally (adv)
MNMNL monumental (adj) *great* monumentally (adv)
MNMNT amendment

improving
MNMNT monument *memorial*
MNMNTL monumental (adj) *great* monumentally (adv)
MNMNY monomania *single idea*
MNMNYKL monomaniacal (adj) *single idea* monomaniacally (adv)
MNMR monomer *chemical*
MNMRKT money market *finance*
MNMTLST monometallist *currency*
MNMTLZM monometallism *currency*
MNMTR manometer *device*
MNMTR monometer *verse*
MNMYL monomial *math, name*
MNMZ minimize *reduce* minimized minimizing (Br) minimise
MNMZR minimizer *reducer* (Br) minimiser
MNN amnion *membrane* amnions (or) amnia
MNN meaning *intent*
MNN mining *ore*
MNN Minoan *of Crete*
MNND minuend *number*
MNNDR monandry *marriage* monandries
MNNFL meaningful (adj) *significant* meaningfully (adv)
MNNG meaning *intent*
MNNG mining *ore*
MNNG mounting *mound*
MNNGFL meaningful (adj) *significant* meaningfully (adv)
MNNGKS meninx *membrane* meninges
MNNGLS meaningless *insignificant*
MNNGX meninx *membrane* meninges
MNNGZ meninges (pl) *membrane* meninx
MNNJDS meningitis *brain*

Letters aren't doubled for single sounds: to find alley use **L** not **LL**. Use **Y** and **W** as hard sounds only: to find yellow use **YL**. (Br)=British spelling or usage. * See dictionary.

disease
MNNJTS meningitis *brain disease*
MNNJZ meninges (pl) *membrane* meninx
MNNKLDD mononucleated *cell*
MNNKLR mononuclear *cell*
MNNKLSS mononucleosis *disease*
MNNKLTD mononucleated *cell*
MNNKLYDD mononucleated *cell*
MNNKLYR mononuclear *cell*
MNNKLYSS mononucleosis *disease*
MNNKLYTD mononucleated *cell*
MNNKS meninx *membrane* meninges
MNNKYLR mononuclear *cell*
MNNLS meaningless *insignificant*
MNNQLDD mononucleated *cell*
MNNQLR mononuclear *cell*
MNNQLSS mononucleosis *disease*
MNNQLTD mononucleated *cell*
MNNS eminence *prominence*
MNNS immanence *inbred* immanency
MNNS imminence *danger* imminency
MNNSCHRDD monounsaturated *fat*
MNNSCHRT monounsaturate *fat*
MNNSCHRTD monounsaturated *fat*
MNNSS amanuensis *copyist* amanuenses
MNNSTRT monounsaturate *fat*
MNNSTRTD monounsaturated *fat*
MNNT eminent *prominent*
MNNT immanent *inbred*
MNNT imminent *happening*

soon
MNNT Mennonite *Anabaptist*
MNNTL eminently *prominent*
MNNTL imminently *happening soon*
MNNTS eminence *prominence*
MNNTS immanence *inbred* immanency
MNNTS imminence *danger* imminency
MNNX meninx *membrane* meninges
MNPDL monopodial (adj) *offshoots* monopodially (adv)
MNPDNS omnipotence *power*
MNPDNT omnipotent *powerful*
MNPDNTL omnipotently *powerful*
MNPDNTS omnipotence *power*
MNPDYL monopodial (adj) *offshoots* monopodially (adv)
MNPL maniple *sash, legion*
MNPL monopole *electrical charge*
MNPL monopoly *domination* monopolies
MNPLBL manipulable *controllable*
MNPLD monoploid *haploid*
MNPLDR manipulator *controller*
MNPLDV manipulative *controlling*
MNPLDVL manipulatively *controlling*
MNPLDVNS manipulativeness *control*
MNPLN monoplane *airplane*
MNPLR manipular *legion, control*
MNPLS Minneapolis *city*
MNPLSDK monopolistic *complete control*
MNPLSDKL monopolistically *complete control*

MNPLSHN manipulation *control*
MNPLST monopolist *complete control*
MNPLSTK monopolistic *complete control*
MNPLSTKL monopolistically *complete control*
MNPLT manipulate *control, change* manipulated manipulating
MNPLTR manipulator *controller*
MNPLTV manipulative *controlling*
MNPLTVL manipulatively *controlling*
MNPLTVNS manipulativeness *control*
MNPLZ monopolize *control completely* monopolized monopolizing (Br) monopolise
MNPLZR monopolizer *control completely* (Br) monopoliser
MNPLZSHN monopolization *complete control* (Br) monopolisation
MNPR manpower *human effort*
MNPRSNT omnipresent *everywhere*
MNPRZNS omnipresence *everywhere*
MNPRZNT omnipresent *everywhere*
MNPRZNTS omnipresence *everywhere*
MNPTNS omnipotence *power*
MNPTNT omnipotent *powerful*
MNPTNTL omnipotently *powerful*
MNPTNTS omnipotence *power*
MNPWR manpower *human effort*
MNPYLBL manipulable

Use letters that best describe the sounds you hear and omit the vowels. Use **S** or **K** instead of **C**: to find circle use **SRKL**. Use **J** to find joy, **JM** to find gem and **G** to find go.

controllable
MNPYLDR manipulator *controller*
MNPYLDV manipulative *controlling*
MNPYLDVL manipulatively *controlling*
MNPYLDVNS manipulativeness *control*
MNPYLR manipular *legion, control*
MNPYLSHN manipulation *control*
MNPYLT manipulate *control, change* manipulated manipulating
MNPYLTR manipulator *controller*
MNPYLTV manipulative *controlling*
MNPYLTVL manipulatively *controlling*
MNPYLTVNS manipulativeness *control*
MNPZ menopause *menstruation*
MNQLR monocular *one eye*
MNQR manicure *(v) clip, trim* manicured manicuring
MNQR manicure *(n) nail treatment*
MNQRST manicurist *nail groomer*
MNR almoner *beggar*
MNR amenorrhea *menses*
MNR man-hour *job time*
MNR manner *bearing, method*
MNR manor *house*
MNR manta ray *animal*
MNR manure *feces*
MNR menhir *tower*
MNR menorah *candles*
MNR meunière *cooking*
MNR miner *digger*
MNR minor *lesser, underage*
MNR minter *maker*
MNR Monterey *US city*
MNR Monterrey *Mexican city*
MNRD mannered *behavior*

MNRD minority *fewer* minorities
MNRDR mind reader *sixth sense*
MNRDR money order *check*
MNRFKCHR manufacture *produce* manufactured manufacturing
MNRG menorrhagia *large flow*
MNRGY menorrhagia *large flow*
MNRJ menorrhagia *large flow*
MNRJK Monterey Jack *cheese*
MNRJY menorrhagia *large flow*
MNRK amenorrheic *menses*
MNRK menarche *menstruation*
MNRK monarch *ruler*
MNRK monarchy *royal rule* monarchies
MNRKKL monarchical *ruling*
MNRKL menarcheal *menstruation*
MNRKL monarchal (or) monarchial *ruler*
MNRKYL menarcheal *menstruation*
MNRKYL monarchial (or) monarchal *ruler*
MNRKZM monarchism *royal rule*
MNRL mannerly *polite*
MNRL manorial *house*
MNRL mineral *metal*
MNRL monaural *sound*
MNRL monorail *train*
MNRLG mineralogy *science*
MNRLG minor league *sports*
MNRLJ mineralogy *science*
MNRLJKL mineralogical (adj) *inorganic* mineralogically (adv)
MNRLJST mineralogist *scientist*
MNRLNS mannerliness *politeness*
MNRLWDR mineral water

carbonated water
MNRLWTR mineral water *carbonated water*
MNRLZ mineralize *make into ore* mineralized mineralizing (Br) mineralise
MNRLZR mineralizer *make into ore* (Br) mineraliser
MNRLZSHN mineralization *make into ore* (Br) mineralisation
MNRM monorhyme *poem*
MNRN monuron *herbicide*
MNRNJ omnirange *radio*
MNRS manners *behavior*
MNRSH menorrhagia *large flow*
MNRT minaret *dome*
MNRT minority *fewer* minorities
MNRY amenorrhea *menses*
MNRYK amenorrheic *menses*
MNRYL manorial *house*
MNRZ manners *behavior*
MNRZ moonrise *time*
MNRZH menorrhagia *large flow*
MNRZM mannerism *pose*
MNS immense *huge*
MNS immunize *exempt, resist* immunized immunizing
MNS mains *(Br) utilities*
MNS manse *house*
MNS mantis *insect* mantises (or) mantes
MNS meanness *humbleness, malice*
MNS means *resources*
MNS menace *(v) endanger* menaced menacing
MNS menace *(n) danger, threat*
MNS menisci (pl) *curve* meniscus
MNS mince *(v) chop, prance* minced mincing
MNS mince *(n-Br) hamburger*
MNS minus *less*

Letters aren't doubled for single sounds: to find alley use **L** not **LL**. Use **Y** and **W** as hard sounds only: to find yellow use **YL**. (Br)=British spelling or usage. * See dictionary.

MNS ominous *threatening*
MNSBL municipal (adj) *government* municipally (adv)
MNSD amino acid *protein*
MNSD amnesty *pardon* amnesties
MNSD immensity *hugeness* immensities
MNSD Minnesota *US State*
MNSD moonseed *plant*
MNSDD many-sided *various aspects*
MNSDK monastic *monk*
MNSDK monistic *unity*
MNSDKL monastically *monk*
MNSDMGLDMT monosodium glutamate *flavor enhancer*
MNSDMGLTMT monosodium glutamate *flavor enhancer*
MNSDR aminoaciduria *excess protein*
MNSDR minister *(n) director (v) tend*
MNSDR ministry *clergy, agency* ministries
MNSDR monastery *monk* monasteries
MNSDR monster *ogre*
MNSDR Muenster *cheese*
MNSDRNS monstrance *vessel*
MNSDRNTS monstrance *vessel*
MNSDRY aminoaciduria *excess protein*
MNSDSZM monasticism *monk*
MNSDYR aminoaciduria *excess protein*
MNSDYRY aminoaciduria *excess protein*
MNSH amentia *retardation*
MNSH amnesia *no memory*
MNSH manège *horse*
MNSH mannish *masculine*
MNSH ménage *household*
MNSH mensch *respected one*
MNSH minutia *details* minutiae

MNSHK amnesiac (or) amnesic *no memory*
MNSHL moon shell *snail*
MNSHN ammoniation *add ammonia*
MNSHN ammunition *bullet*
MNSHN emanation *emittance*
MNSHN mansion *house*
MNSHN mention *(n) citation (v) cite*
MNSHN monition *warning*
MNSHN moonshine *illegal liquor*
MNSHN munition *armaments*
MNSHNBL mentionable *spoken*
MNSHNR moonshiner *illegal liquor*
MNSHNS munitions *armaments*
MNSHNS omniscience *knowledge*
MNSHNT omniscient *knowledge*
MNSHNTS omniscience *knowledge*
MNSHNZ munitions *armaments*
MNSHR menagerie *zoo*
MNSHRBL immensurable *beyond measure*
MNSHRBL mensurable *measurable*
MNSHRSHN mensuration *measurement*
MNSHT mainsheet *rope*
MNSHT moonshot *space flight*
MNSHTRW ménage à trois *three lovers*
MNSHTW ménage à trois *three lovers*
MNSHYK amnesiac (or) amnesic *no memory*
MNSK amnesic (or) amnesiac *no memory*
MNSK menisci (pl) *curve* meniscus
MNSK Minsk *city*
MNSK Montesquieu *philosopher*

MNSKL minuscule *small, letter*
MNSKP moonscape *lunar surface*
MNSKRD monosaccharide *sugar*
MNSKRP manuscript *document*
MNSKRPT manuscript *document*
MNSKRT miniskirt *attire*
MNSKS meniscus *curve* menisci
MNSKY Montesquieu *philosopher*
MNSKYL minuscule *small, letter*
MNSL immensely *hugely*
MNSL mainsail *ship*
MNSL Monticello *building*
MNSL ominously *threat*
MNSLBK monosyllabic *one syllable*
MNSLBKL monosyllabically *one syllable*
MNSLBL monosyllable *one syllable*
MNSLBSD monosyllabicity *one syllable*
MNSLBST monosyllabicity *one syllable*
MNSLDR manslaughter *killing*
MNSLTR manslaughter *killing*
MNSMT mincemeat *meat, pie*
MNSN mincing *dainty*
MNSN monsoon *rain*
MNSNG mincing *dainty*
MNSNGL menacingly *threaten*
MNSNGR minnesinger *poet*
MNSNL menacingly *threaten*
MNSNL monsoonal *rain*
MNSNPDK monosynaptic *nerve*
MNSNPDKL monosynaptically *nerve*
MNSNPTK monosynaptic *nerve*
MNSNPTKL

Use letters that best describe the sounds you hear and omit the vowels. Use **S** or **K** instead of **C**: to find circle use **SRKL**. Use **J** to find joy, **JM** to find gem and **G** to find go.

monosynaptically *nerve*

MNSNR monseigneur
French title messeigneurs

MNSNR monsignor *church
title* monsignors (or)
monsignori

MNSNS immenseness
hugeness

MNSNS ominousness *threat*

MNSNTSS amniocentesis
fetal sex test
amnioceteses

MNSNYR monseigneur
French title messeigneurs

MNSNYR monsignor *church
title* monsignors (or)
monsignori

MNSPBS mons pubis
mound montes pubis

MNSPDR emancipator
freedom

MNSPL maniple *steward*

MNSPLD municipality
government municipalities

MNSPLT municipality
government municipalities

MNSPLZ municipalize
govern municipalized
municipalizing

MNSPRDD mean-spirited
evil

MNSPRNG mainspring
mechanism, motive

MNSPRSHN
immunosuppression
against antibodies

MNSPRSNT
immunosuppressant
against antibodies

MNSPRSV
immunosuppressive
against antibodies

MNSPRTD mean-spirited
evil

MNSPSHN emancipation
freedom

MNSPSHNST
emancipationist *freedom*

MNSPT emancipate *free*
emancipated
emancipating

MNSPTR emancipator

freedom

MNSPYBS mons pubis
mound montes pubis

MNSQ Montesquieu
philosopher

MNSQL minuscule *small,
letter*

MNSR mincer *chopper,
prancer*

MNSR Montessori *education*

MNSRBL immensurable
beyond measure

MNSRBL mensurable
measurable

MNSRD mansard *roof*

MNSRSHN mensuration
measurement

MNSRVNT manservant *valet*
menservants

MNSRZ miniseries *TV
episodes*

MNSSDM immune system
resistance

MNSSTM immune system
resistance

MNST amnesty *pardon*
amnesties

MNST immensity *hugeness*
immensities

MNST mainstay *support*

MNST mind-set *opinion*

MNST Minnesota *US State*

MNST monist *unity*

MNST moonset *horizon*

MNSTK monastic *monk*

MNSTK monistic *unity*

MNSTKL monastically *monk*

MNSTN moonstone *gem*

MNSTR minister *(n) director
(v) tend*

MNSTR ministry *clergy,
agency* ministries

MNSTR minster *church*

MNSTR monastery *monk*
monasteries

MNSTR monster *ogre*

MNSTR Muenster *cheese*

MNSTRK moonstruck
dreamy

MNSTRL menstrual
menstruation

MNSTRL ministerial (adj)

legal order ministerially
(adv)

MNSTRL minstrel *musician*

MNSTRM mainstream *(n)
central current (v)* place in
regular classes

MNSTRN minestrone *soup*

MNSTRNS monstrance
vessel

MNSTRNT ministrant
director

MNSTRNTS monstrance
vessel

MNSTRS monstrous
gigantic, abnormal

MNSTRSD monstrosity *freak*
monstrosities

MNSTRSHN menstruation
monthly cycle

MNSTRSHN ministration
tending

MNSTRST monstrosity *freak*
monstrosities

MNSTRT menstruate
discharge blood
menstruated
menstruating

MNSTRWL menstrual
menstruation

MNSTRWSHN
menstruation *monthly
cycle*

MNSTRWT menstruate
discharge blood
menstruated
menstruating

MNSTRYL ministerial (adj)
legal order ministerially
(adv)

MNSTSZM monasticism
monk

MNSTT ministate *nation*

MNSVNRS mons veneris
mound montes veneris

MNSWPR minesweeper
warship

MNSWTD mansuetude
tameness

MNSWTYD mansuetude
tameness

MNSZ man-size (or) man-
sized *large*

Letters aren't doubled for single sounds: to find alley use **L** not **LL**. Use **Y** and **W** as hard
sounds only: to find yellow use **YL**. (Br)=British spelling or usage. * See dictionary.

MNSZ menses *monthly flow*
MNSZD man-sized (or) man-size *large*
MNT amanita *fungus*
MNT amenity *comfort* amenities
MNT ammoniate *add ammonia* ammoniated ammoniating
MNT Ammonite *Semite*
MNT ammonite *extinct animal*
MNT amount *quantity*
MNT emanate *emit* emanated emanating
MNT imminent *happening soon*
MNT immunity *exemption, resistance* immunities
MNT manatee *animal*
MNT manta *shawl*
MNT manteau *cloak*
MNT mayn't *(contr) may not*
MNT meant *(v-past) mean*
MNT menta (pl) *plate* mentum
MNT mint *(n) plant (v) make coins, create (adj) like new*
MNT minuet *music*
MNT minute *(n) 60 seconds (adj) tiny*
MNT monte *game*
MNT mount *(n) mountain, support, horse (v) climb, frame, launch**
MNT Mounty *police* Mounties
MNT omenta (pl) *fold* omentum
MNTB Manitoba *province*
MNTBNGK mountebank *pretender*
MNTBNK mountebank *pretender*
MNTCHL Monticello *building*
MNTCZ menses *monthly flow*
MNTDL montadale *sheep*
MNTGMR Montgomery *city*
MNTH month *calendar*
MNTHL menthol *mint*

MNTHL monthly *once a month* monthlies
MNTHLDD mentholated *mint*
MNTHLNG monthlong *calendar*
MNTHLTD mentholated *mint*
MNTHRP immunotherapy *treatment*
MNTHRPDK immunotherapeutic *treatment*
MNTHRPTK immunotherapeutic *treatment*
MNTHRPYDK immunotherapeutic *treatment*
MNTHRPYTK immunotherapeutic *treatment*
MNTHSDK monotheistic *one god*
MNTHST monotheist *one god*
MNTHSTK monotheistic *one god*
MNTHYSDK monotheistic *one god*
MNTHYST monotheist *one god*
MNTHYSTK monotheistic *one god*
MNTHYZM monotheism *one god*
MNTHZM monotheism *one god*
MNTJ mintage *coins*
MNTJK muntjac *animal*
MNTJLP mint julep *drink*
MNTK ammonitic *ammonia*
MNTK amniotic *womb*
MNTK mantic *prophetic*
MNTKR manticore *animal*
MNTKRL Monte Carlo *city*
MNTL imminently *happening soon*
MNTL mantel *fireplace*
MNTL mantilla *scarf*
MNTL mantle *cloak* mantled mantling

MNTL mental (adj) *of the mind* mentally (adv)
MNTL minutely *tiny bits*
MNTLD amontillado *wine* amontillados
MNTLD mentality *thought* mentalities
MNTLPS mantelpiece *fireplace*
MNTLRD man-tailored *masculine*
MNTLT mantelet (or) mantlet *cape*
MNTLT mentality *thought* mentalities
MNTM mean time *solar time*
MNTM meantime *during*
MNTM mentum *plate* menta
MNTM omentum *fold* omenta (or) omentums
MNTMK monatomic *one atom*
MNTMKNL Mount McKinley *mountain*
MNTMN minuteman *soldier* minutemen
MNTN amanitin *toxin*
MNTN maintain *keep up*
MNTN man-eating *eats humans*
MNTN monotone *one sound*
MNTN monotony *dullness*
MNTN Montaigne *essayist*
MNTN Montana *US State*
MNTN mountain *huge hill*
MNTN mounting *mound*
MNTNBL maintainable *keep up*
MNTNG man-eating *eats humans*
MNTNG mounting *mound*
MNTNGT mountain goat *animal*
MNTNK monotonic *one sound*
MNTNKL monotonically *one sound*
MNTNLN mountain lion *animal*
MNTNLYN mountain lion *animal*
MNTNNS maintenance

Use letters that best describe the sounds you hear and omit the vowels. Use **S** or **K** instead of **C**: to find circle use **SRKL**. Use **J** to find joy, **JM** to find gem and **G** to find go.

upkeep
MNTNNTS maintenance
upkeep
MNTNR maintainer *keep up*
MNTNR mountaineer
climber
MNTNS monotonous *dull*
MNTNS mountainous *huge*
MNTNSD monotonicity *one sound*
MNTNSD mountainside
huge hill
MNTNSH mountain ash *tree*
MNTNSL monotonously
dully
MNTNSL mountainously
huge
MNTNSNS
monotonousness *dullness*
MNTNSNS
mountainousness *huge*
MNTNST monotonicity *one sound*
MNTNSTTS Mountain
States *region*
MNTNTP mountaintop
summit
MNTNYRD montagnard
(often capitalized)
Vietnamese
MNTP maintop *platform*
MNTP monotype *impression*
MNTPK monotypic *one species*
MNTR man-eater *eats humans*
MNTR manta ray *animal*
MNTR mantra *meditate*
MNTR mentor *model*
MNTR minatory *threatening*
MNTR miniature *tiny*
MNTR minter *maker*
MNTR monetary *money*
MNTR monitor (*n*) *device, watcher* (*v*) *watch*
MNTR monitory *warning*
MNTR Monterey *US city*
MNTR Monterrey *Mexican city*
MNTRJK Monterey Jack
cheese
MNTRK mantric *meditate*

MNTRL monetarily *money*
MNTRL Montreal *city*
MNTRM monotreme
mammal
MNTRMZ man-at-arms
soldier men-at-arms
MNTRYL Montreal *city*
MNTRZ miniaturize *make small* miniaturized
miniaturizing
MNTRZSHN miniaturization
made small
MNTS immense *huge*
MNTS manse *house*
MNTS mantis *insect*
mantises (or) mantes
MNTS mantissa *logarithm*
MNTS mince (*v*) *chop, prance*
minced mincing
MNTS mince (*n-Br*)
hamburger
MNTS minutes *notes*
MNTSD immensity *hugeness*
immensities
MNTSDRNS monstrance
vessel
MNTSDRNTS monstrance
vessel
MNTSH amentia *retardation*
MNTSH mensch *respected one*
MNTSH montage *jumble*
montaged montaging
MNTSHN mentation *thought*
MNTSHRBL immensurable
beyond measure
MNTSHRBL mensurable
able to measure
MNTSK Montesquieu
philosopher
MNTSKY Montesquieu
philosopher
MNTSL immensely *hugely*
MNTSL Monticello *building*
MNTSMT mincemeat *meat, pie*
MNTSN mincing *dainty*
MNTSNG mincing *dainty*
MNTSNS immenseness
hugeness
MNTSNTHLNZ Mount St.
Helens *mountain*

MNTSPBS montes pubis
(pl) *mound* mons pubis
MNTSPYBS montes pubis
(pl) *mound* mons pubis
MNTSQ Montesquieu
philosopher
MNTSR mincer *chopper, prancer*
MNTSR Montessori
education
MNTSRBL immensurable
beyond measure
MNTSRBL mensurable *able to measure*
MNTSRSHN mensuration
measurement
MNTST immensity *hugeness*
immensities
MNTSTRNS monstrance
vessel
MNTSTRNTS monstrance
vessel
MNTSZ menses *monthly flow*
MNTVD Montevideo *city*
MNTVDY Montevideo *city*
MNTVRST Mount Everest
mountain
MNTY mantilla *scarf*
MNTYD amontillado *wine*
amontillados
MNTYR miniature *tiny*
MNTYRZ miniaturize *make small* miniaturized
miniaturizing
MNTYRZSHN
miniaturization *made small*
MNTZ monetize *coin money*
monetized monetizing
MNTZH montage *jumble*
montaged montaging
MNTZM Montezuma *Aztec emperor*
MNTZMSRVNJ
Montezuma's revenge
illness
MNTZPBS montes pubis
(pl) *mound* mons pubis
MNTZPYBS montes pubis
(pl) *mound* mons pubis
MNTZVNRS montes veneris
(pl) *mound* mons veneris

Letters aren't doubled for single sounds: to find alley use **L** not **LL**. Use **Y** and **W** as hard
sounds only: to find yellow use **YL**. (Br)=British spelling or usage. * See dictionary.

MNVD Montevideo *city*
MNVDY Montevideo *city*
MNVLNT monovalent *chemistry*
MNVN minivan *vehicle*
MNVR maneuver *(n) movement, trick (v) guide, scheme* (Br) manoeuvre
MNVR miniver *fur*
MNVR omnivore *food*
MNVRBL maneuverable *adroit*
MNVRBLD maneuverability *movable*
MNVRBLT maneuverability *movable*
MNVRS omnivorous *food*
MNVRST Mount Everest *mountain*
MNVWR man-of-war *ship* men-of-war
MNWL manual (adj) *by hand* manually (adv)
MNWL meanwhile *during*
MNWN Minoan *of Crete*
MNWND minuend *number*
MNWNSCHRDD monounsaturated *fat*
MNWNSCHRT monounsaturate *fat*
MNWNSCHRTD monounsaturated *fat*
MNWNSS amanuensis *copyist* amanuenses
MNWNSTRT monounsaturate *fat*
MNWNSTRTD monounsaturated *fat*
MNWR man-hour *job time*
MNWR man-of-war *ship* men-of-war
MNWRT moneywort *plant*
MNWSD amino acid *protein*
MNWSDR aminoaciduria *excess protein*
MNWSDRY aminoaciduria *excess protein*
MNWSDYR aminoaciduria *excess protein*
MNWSDYRY aminoaciduria *excess protein*

MNWT minuet *music*
MNX Manx *of the Isle of Man, cat*
MNX minx *girl* minxes
MNXD monoxide *chemical*
MNXDL minoxidil *hair growth drug*
MNY ammonia *chemical*
MNY amnia (pl) *membrane* amnion
MNY mania *madness*
MNY menu *food list* menus
MNYBRM manubrium *breastbone* manubria
MNYBRYM manubrium *breastbone* manubria
MNYCHR miniature *tiny*
MNYCHRZ miniaturize *make small* miniaturized miniaturizing
MNYCHRZSHN miniaturization *made small*
MNYDK amniotic *womb*
MNYDRVN menu-driven *computer*
MNYFKCHR manufacture *produce* manufactured manufacturing
MNYFKCHRR manufacturer *producer*
MNYFKDR manufactory *factory* manufactories
MNYFKSHR manufacture *produce* manufactured manufacturing
MNYFKSHRR manufacturer *producer*
MNYFKTR manufactory *factory* manufactories
MNYFKTR manufacture *produce* manufactured manufacturing
MNYFKTRR manufacturer *producer*
MNYFKTYR manufacture *produce* manufactured manufacturing
MNYK maniac *lunatic*
MNYKL maniacal (adj) *crazy* maniacally (adv)
MNYL manual (adj) *by hand* manually (adv)

MNYL menial (adj) *servant* menially (adv)
MNYM ammonium *ammonia*
MNYMNL monumental (adj) *great* monumentally (adv)
MNYMNT monument *memorial*
MNYMNTL monumental (adj) *great* monumentally (adv)
MNYN amnion *membrane* amnions (or) amnia
MNYN mañana *tomorrow*
MNYN mignon *small*
MNYN minion *helper*
MNYN minyan *quorum* minyanim (or) minyans
MNYND minuend *number*
MNYNM minyanim (pl) *quorum* minyan
MNYNSS amanuensis *copyist* amanuenses
MNYNT mignonette *plant*
MNYPLS Minneapolis *city*
MNYR manure *feces*
MNYR meunière *cooking*
MNYRDR money order *check*
MNYRN monuron *herbicide*
MNYSH minutia *details* minutiae
MNYSHN ammoniation *add ammonia*
MNYSKRP manuscript *document*
MNYSKRPT manuscript *document*
MNYSNTSS amniocentesis *fetal sex test* amniocenteses
MNYT ammoniate *add ammonia* ammoniated ammoniating
MNYT minuet *music*
MNYT minute *tiny*
MNYTK amniotic *womb*
MNYTL minutely *tiny bits*
MNYTR miniature *tiny*
MNYTRZ miniaturize *make small* miniaturized miniaturizing
MNYTRZSHN

Use letters that best describe the sounds you hear and omit the vowels. Use **S** or **K** instead of **C**: to find circle use **SRKL**. Use **J** to find joy, **JM** to find gem and **G** to find go.

miniaturization *made small*

MNYTYR miniature *tiny*

MNYTYRZ miniaturize *make small* miniaturized miniaturizing

MNYTYRZSHN miniaturization *made small*

MNYVR maneuver (*n*) *movement, trick* (*v*) *guide, scheme* (Br) manoeuvre

MNYVRBL maneuverable *adroit*

MNYVRBLD maneuverability *movable*

MNYVRBLT maneuverability *movable*

MNYWL manual (adj) *by hand* manually (adv)

MNYWND minuend *number*

MNYWNSS amanuensis *copyist* amanuenses

MNYWT minuet *music*

MNZ amends *recompense*

MNZ amnesia *no memory*

MNZ immunize *exempt, resist* immunized immunizing

MNZ mains (Br) *utilities*

MNZ mayonnaise *sauce*

MNZ means *resources*

MNZ mind's eye *imagination*

MNZGDK monozygotic *one egg*

MNZGTK monozygotic *one egg*

MNZH amnesia *no memory*

MNZH manège *horse*

MNZH ménage *household*

MNZHK amnesiac (or) amnesic *no memory*

MNZHR menagerie *zoo*

MNZHTRW ménage à trois *three lovers*

MNZHTW ménage à trois *three lovers*

MNZHYK amnesiac (or) amnesic *no memory*

MNZK amnesiac (or) amnesic *no memory*

MNZM monism *unity*

MNZM Montezuma *Aztec emperor*

MNZMSRVNJ Montezuma's revenge *illness*

MNZNGR minnesinger *poet*

MNZNT monzonite *rock*

MNZPBS mons pubis *mound* montes pubis

MNZPYBS mons pubis *mound* montes pubis

MNZSHN immunization *exempt, resist*

MNZVNRS mons veneris *mound* montes veneris

MNZWR menswear *clothing*

MNZY amnesia *no memory*

MNZYK amnesiac (or) amnesic *no memory*

MP amp *electricity*

MP imp *scamp*

MP map (*v*) *assign, plan, locate** mapped mapping

MP map (*n*) *representation*

MP mop (*v*) *wipe up* mopped mopping

MP mop (*n*) *implement, hair*

MP mope *sulk* moped moping

MP myope *person*

MP myopia *vision*

MP oompah *rhythm*

MP ump *umpire*

MPBL mappable *able to survey*

MPCH impeach *accuse, remove*

MPCHBL impeachable *remove*

MPCHMNT impeachment *removal*

MPCHS impetuous *impulsive*

MPCHSD impetuosity *impulsive* impetuosities

MPCHSL impetuously *impulsive*

MPCHSNS impetuousness *impulsive*

MPCHST impetuosity *impulsive* impetuosities

MPCHWS impetuous *impulsive*

MPCHWSD impetuosity *impulsive* impetuosities

MPCHWSL impetuously *impulsive*

MPCHWSNS impetuousness *impulsive*

MPCHWST impetuosity *impulsive* impetuosities

MPD impede *barrier* impeded impeding

MPD impiety *disrespect* impieties

MPD moped *motorbike*

MPDBL imputable *credited to*

MPDBLD imputability *credit*

MPDBLT imputability *credit*

MPDMNT impediment *barrier*

MPDMNT impedimenta *barriers*

MPDNS impedance *barrier*

MPDNS impotence *helpless, sterile* impotency

MPDNS impudence *boldness*

MPDNT impotent *helpless, sterile*

MPDNT impudent *bold*

MPDNTL impotently *helpless, sterile*

MPDNTL impudently *bold*

MPDNTS impedance *barrier*

MPDNTS impotence *helpless, sterile* impotency

MPDNTS impudence *boldness*

MPDR impeder *barrier*

MPDS impetus *incentive*

MPDT mapped out *planned*

MPFLS omphalos *hub*

MPFLSKPSS omphaloskepsis *meditation*

MPJ mpg (abbr) *miles per gallon*

MPK impact *force*

MPK myopic *vision*

MPKBL impeccable (adj) *flawless* impeccably (adv)

MPKBLD impeccability *flawless*

MPKBLT impeccability *flawless*

MPKDD impacted *anchored*

Letters aren't doubled for single sounds: to find alley use **L** not **LL**. Use **Y** and **W** as hard sounds only: to find yellow use **YL**. (Br)=British spelling or usage. * See dictionary.

MPKL myopically *vision*
MPKNS impecunious *poor*
MPKNSD impecuniosity
poverty
MPKNSL impecuniously
poor
MPKNSNS
impecuniousness *poor*
MPKNST impecuniosity
poverty
MPKNYS impecunious *poor*
MPKNYSD impecuniosity
poverty
MPKNYSL impecuniously
poor
MPKNYSNS
impecuniousness *poor*
MPKNYST impecuniosity
poverty
MPKSHN impaction
anchored
MPKT impact *force*
MPKTD impacted *anchored*
MPKYNS impecunious *poor*
MPKYNSD impecuniosity
poverty
MPKYNSL impecuniously
poor
MPKYNSNS
impecuniousness *poor*
MPKYNST impecuniosity
poverty
MPKYNYS impecunious
poor
MPKYNYSD impecuniosity
poverty
MPKYNYSL impecuniously
poor
MPKYNYSNS
impecuniousness *poor*
MPKYNYST impecuniosity
poverty
MPL ample *plenty* ampler
amplest
MPL amply *plentifully*
MPL ampoule (or) ampule
injection
MPL ampulla *flask* ampullae
MPL employ *hire, use*
MPL employee *worker*
MPL impale *pierce* impaled
impaling

MPL impel *move* impelled
impelling
MPL imply *suggest* implied
implying implies
MPL maple *tree*
MPL maypole *May Day*
MPLBL employable *hire, use*
MPLD implode *burst inward*
imploded imploding
MPLDKL impolitical (or)
impolitic (adj) *reckless*
impolitically (or)
impoliticly (adv)
MPLDN amplidyne *generator*
MPLF amplify *expand*
amplified amplifying
amplifies
MPLFD amplified *expanded*
MPLFKSHN amplification
expansion
MPLFR amplifier *expander*
MPLFYR amplifier *expander*
MPLKBL implacable (adj)
changeless implacably
(adv)
MPLKBLD implacability
changeless
MPLKBLT implacability
changeless
MPLKDV implicative
suggestion
MPLKDVL implicatively
suggestion
MPLKDVNS
implicativeness
suggestion
MPLKSHN implication
suggestion
MPLKT implicate *involve,*
imply implicated
implicating
MPLKTV implicative
suggestion
MPLKTVL implicatively
suggestion
MPLKTVNS implicativeness
suggestion
MPLMNR implementer (or)
implementor *accomplisher*
MPLMNT employment
work, use
MPLMNT implement (*n*) *tool*

(*v*) *carry out, equip*
MPLMNTR implementer (or)
implementor *accomplisher*
MPLMNTSHN
implementation
accomplishment
MPLN emplane *get on board*
MPLNBL implantable *insert*
MPLNR implanter *insert*
MPLNS ampleness *plenty*
MPLNT implant *insert*
MPLNTBL implantable
insert
MPLNTR implanter *insert*
MPLNTSHN implantation
insert
MPLPBL impalpable (adj)
hard to see or feel
impalpably (adv)
MPLPBLD impalpability
hard to see or feel
MPLPBLT impalpability *hard*
to see or feel
MPLR ampler *plentiful*
MPLR employer *boss*
MPLR impaler *pierce*
MPLR impeller *rotor*
MPLR implore *beg* implored
imploring
MPLRNGL imploringly *beg*
MPLS emplace *put*
emplaced emplacing
MPLS impulse (*v*) *motivate*
impulsed impulsing
MPLS impulse (*n*) *motive*
MPLSBL implausible (adj)
improbable implausibly
(adv)
MPLSBLD implausibility
improbable
MPLSBLT implausibility
improbable
MPLSHN implosion *inrush*
MPLSHN impulsion *force,*
motive
MPLSMNT emplacement
location
MPLST amplest *plentiful*
MPLST implicit *implied*
MPLSTL implicitly *implied*
MPLSTNS implicitness
implied

Use letters that best describe the sounds you hear and omit the vowels. Use **S** or **K** instead of **C**: to find circle use **SRKL**. Use **J** to find joy, **JM** to find gem and **G** to find go.

MPLSV implosive *inrush*
MPLSV impulsive *unplanned*
MPLSVL impulsively *unplanned*
MPLSVNS impulsiveness *unplanned*
MPLT impolite *rude*
MPLTD amplitude *fullness*
MPLTK impolitic (or) impolitical (adj) *reckless* impolitically (or) impoliticly (adv)
MPLTKL impolitical (or) impolitic (adj) *reckless* impolitically (or) impoliticly (adv)
MPLTL impolitely *rude*
MPLTNS impoliteness *rude*
MPLTYD amplitude *fullness*
MPLY employee *worker*
MPLYBL employable *hire, use*
MPLYR employer *boss*
MPLZBL implausible (adj) *improbable* implausibly (adv)
MPLZBLD implausibility *improbable*
MPLZBLT implausibility *improbable*
MPLZHN implosion *inrush*
MPLZV implosive *inrush*
MPMKR mapmaker *cartographer*
MPN impugn *attack*
MPN mapping *survey*
MPNBL impugnable *attack*
MPND empanada *food*
MPND impend *menace*
MPND impound *confine*
MPND impunity *exemption*
MPNDMNT impoundment *confine*
MPNDN impending *about to happen*
MPNDNG impending *about to happen*
MPNDNT impendent *approaching*
MPNDRBL imponderable (adj, n) *beyond thought* imponderably (adv)

MPNDRBLD imponderability *beyond thought*
MPNDRBLT imponderability *beyond thought*
MPNG mapping *survey*
MPNJ empennage *tail*
MPNJ impinge *trespass* impinged impinging
MPNJMNT impingement *trespassing*
MPNL impanel *enroll*
MPNMNT impoundment *confine*
MPNR impugner *attack*
MPNT impunity *exemption*
MPNTNT impenitent *not sorry*
MPNTNTL impenitently *not sorry*
MPNTRBL impenetrable (adj) *closed* impenetrably (adv)
MPNTRBLD impenetrability *closed*
MPNTRBLT impenetrability *closed*
MPP maypop *plant*
MPP mop up (v) *wipe, clear* mopped up mopping up
MPP mop-up (n) *conclusion*
MPQNS impecunious *poor*
MPQNSD impecuniosity *poverty*
MPQNSL impecuniously *poor*
MPQNSNS impecuniousness *poor*
MPQNST impecuniosity *poverty*
MPQNYS impecunious *poor*
MPQNYSD impecuniosity *poverty*
MPQNYSL impecuniously *poor*
MPQNYSNS impecuniousness *poor*
MPQNYST impecuniosity *poverty*
MPR ampere *electricity*
MPR empery *empire* emperies

MPR empire *realm*
MPR empower *enable*
MPR impair *harm*
MPR impure *foul*
MPR mapper *surveyor*
MPR moper *sulk*
MPR mopper *wiper*
MPR umpire *referee* umpired umpiring
MPRBBL improbable (adj) *unlikely* improbably (adv)
MPRBBLD improbability *unlikely* improbabilities
MPRBBLT improbability *unlikely* improbabilities
MPRBMT meprobamate *tranquilizer*
MPRCHN importune (v) *beg* importuned importuning
MPRCHN importune (n) *trouble*
MPRCHND importunity *trouble* importunities
MPRCHNT importunate *troublesome*
MPRCHNT importunity *trouble* importunities
MPRCHNTL importunately *troublesome*
MPRCHNTNS importunateness *trouble*
MPRD impurity *dirt* impurities
MPRDBL impartible (adj) *undivided* impartibly (adv)
MPRDBL importable *bring in*
MPRDNNT impertinent *insolent*
MPRDNNTL impertinently *insolent*
MPRDNS importance *value*
MPRDNS imprudence *rashness*
MPRDNT important *valuable*
MPRDNT imprudent *rash*
MPRDNTL importantly *valuable*
MPRDNTL imprudently *rash*
MPRDNTS importance *value*
MPRDNTS imprudence

Letters aren't doubled for single sounds: to find alley use **L** not **LL**. Use **Y** and **W** as hard sounds only: to find yellow use **YL**. (Br)=British spelling or usage. * See dictionary.

rashness

MPRDR importer *bring in*

MPRDV imperative *(adj)*
masterful, necessary (n)
rule

MPRDVL imperatively
masterful, necessary

MPRDVNS imperativeness
masterful, necessary

MPRFK imperfect *(adj)*
defective (n) verb

MPRFKDV imperfective
verb

MPRFKL imperfectly *flaw*

MPRFKNS imperfectness
flaw

MPRFKSHN imperfection
flaw

MPRFKT imperfect *(adj)*
defective (n) verb

MPRFKTL imperfectly *flaw*

MPRFKTNS imperfectness
flaw

MPRFKTV imperfective *verb*

MPRFRT imperforate *no*
holes

MPRGNBL impregnable
(adj) solid, dense
impregnably *(adv)*

MPRGNBLD impregnability
solid, dense

MPRGNBLT impregnability
solid, dense

MPRGNDR impregnator
fertilize, soak

MPRGNSHN impregnation
fertilize, soak

MPRGNT impregnate
fertilize, soak impregnated
impregnating

MPRGNTR impregnator
fertilize, soak

MPRJ amperage *electricity*

MPRKDGL impractical *(adj)*
idealistic impractically
(adv)

MPRKDKBL impracticable
(adj) impossible
impracticably *(adv)*

MPRKDKBLD
impracticability *impossible*
impracticabilities

MPRKDKBLT
impracticability *impossible*
impracticabilities

MPRKDKLD impracticality
idealistic

MPRKDKLT impracticality
idealistic

MPRKL empirical *(adj)*
observation empirically
(adv)

MPRKSHN imprecation
curse

MPRKT imprecate *curse*
imprecated imprecating

MPRKTKBL impracticable
(adj) impossible
impracticably *(adv)*

MPRKTKBLD
impracticability *impossible*
impracticabilities

MPRKTKBLT
impracticability *impossible*
impracticabilities

MPRKTKL impractical *(adj)*
idealistic impractically
(adv)

MPRKTKLD impracticality
idealistic

MPRKTKLT impracticality
idealistic

MPRKTR imprecatory *curse*

MPRL empyreal *heavens*

MPRL imperial *(adj) royal*
imperially *(adv)*

MPRL imperil *endanger*
imperiled (or) imperilled
imperiling (or) imperilling

MPRL impurely *foul*

MPRLSDK imperialistic
domination

MPRLSDKL imperialistically
domination

MPRLSTK imperialistic
domination

MPRLSTKL imperialistically
domination

MPRLZM imperialism
domination

MPRM emporium *store*
emporiums

MPRM imperium *control*

MPRMBL impermeable *no*

passage

MPRMBLD impermeability
no passage

MPRMBLT impermeability
no passage

MPRMCHR imprimatur
approval

MPRMN imipramine *drug*

MPRMNNS impermanence
temporary impermanency

MPRMNNT impermanent
temporary

MPRMNNTS
impermanence *temporary*
impermanency

MPRMNT empowerment
enable

MPRMNT impairment *harm*

MPRMNT impermanent
temporary

MPRMPT impromptu
improvised

MPRMSBL impermissable
(adj) not allowed
impermissably *(adv)*

MPRMT impromptu
improvised

MPRMTR imprimatur
approval

MPRMTYR imprimatur
approval

MPRMYBL impermeable *no*
passage

MPRMYBLD impermeability
no passage

MPRMYBLT impermeability
no passage

MPRN empyrean *heavens*

MPRNNG imprinting
learning

MPRNS impureness *foul*

MPRNT imprint *(v) impress*
(n) mark, name

MPRNTNG imprinting
learning

MPRPR improper *incorrect*

MPRPRD impropriety
misbehavior improprieties

MPRPRL improperly
incorrect

MPRPRT impropriety
misbehavior improprieties

Use letters that best describe the sounds you hear and omit the vowels. Use **S** or **K** instead of **C**: to find circle use **SRKL**. Use **J** to find joy, **JM** to find gem and **G** to find go.

MPRPRYD impropriety *misbehavior* improprieties

MPRPRYT impropriety *misbehavior* improprieties

MPRR emperor *ruler*

MPRR impairer *harm*

MPRS empress *royal title* empresses

MPRS imperious *domineering*

MPRS impress (v) *influence, force* (n) *stamp*

MPRSBL impressible *influence, force*

MPRSBLD impressibility *influence, force*

MPRSBLT impressibility *influence, force*

MPRSHBL imperishable (adj) *no decay* imperishably (adv)

MPRSHL impartial (adj) *fair* impartially (adv)

MPRSHLD impartiality *fairness*

MPRSHLT impartiality *fairness*

MPRSHN impression *idea, effect, copy**

MPRSHNBL impressionable *influence*

MPRSHNBLD impressionability *influence*

MPRSHNBLT impressionability *influence*

MPRSHNSDK impressionistic (or) impressionist *art, music*

MPRSHNST impressionist (or) impressionistic *art, music*

MPRSHNSTK impressionistic (or) impressionist *art, music*

MPRSHNZM impressionism *art, music*

MPRSHYLD impartiality *fairness*

MPRSHYLT impartiality *fairness*

MPRSL imperiously *domineering*

MPRSMNT impressment *seizing*

MPRSN ampersand *symbol* (&)

MPRSND ampersand *symbol* (&)

MPRSNDR impersonator *mimic*

MPRSNL impersonal (adj) *indefinite, unemotional* impersonally (adv)

MPRSNLD impersonality *indefinite, unemotional*

MPRSNLT impersonality *indefinite, unemotional*

MPRSNLZ impersonalize *make indefinite, unemotional* impersonalized impersonalizing (Br) impersonalise

MPRSNLZSHN impersonalization *indefinite, unemotional* (Br) impersonalisation

MPRSNS imperiousness *domineering*

MPRSNSHN impersonation *mimic*

MPRSNT impersonate *mimic* impersonated impersonating

MPRSNTR impersonator *mimic*

MPRSPDBL imperceptible (adj) *subtle* imperceptibly (adv)

MPRSPDBLD imperceptibility *subtle*

MPRSPDBLT imperceptibility *subtle*

MPRSPDV imperceptive *not aware*

MPRSPDVNS imperceptiveness *not aware*

MPRSPTBL imperceptible (adj) *subtle* imperceptibly (adv)

MPRSPTBLD

imperceptibility *subtle*

MPRSPTBLT imperceptibility *subtle*

MPRSPTV imperceptive *not aware*

MPRSPTVNS imperceptiveness *not aware*

MPRSR impresario *director* impresarios

MPRSRY impresario *director* impresarios

MPRSS imprecise *vague*

MPRSSHN imprecision *vagueness*

MPRSSL imprecisely *vague*

MPRSSNS impreciseness *vagueness*

MPRSST empiricist *observation*

MPRSV impressive *moving*

MPRSVL impressively *moving*

MPRSVNS impressiveness *moving*

MPRSZHN imprecision *vagueness*

MPRSZM empiricism *observation*

MPRT impart *give out*

MPRT import (v) *bring in* (n) *significance, goods*

MPRT impurity *dirt* impurities

MPRTBL impartible (adj) *undivided* impartibly (adv)

MPRTBL importable *bring in*

MPRTMNT impartment *give out*

MPRTN importune (v) *beg* importuned importuning

MPRTN importune (n) *trouble*

MPRTND importunity *trouble* importunities

MPRTNNS impertinence *insolence* impertinency

MPRTNNT impertinent *insolent*

MPRTNNTL impertinently *insolent*

MPRTNNTS impertinence *insolence* impertinency
MPRTNS importance *value*
MPRTNT important *valuable*
MPRTNT importunate *troublesome*
MPRTNT importunity *trouble* importunities
MPRTNTL importantly *valuable*
MPRTNTL importunately *troublesome*
MPRTNTNS importunateness *troublesome*
MPRTNTS importance *value*
MPRTR imperator *emperor*
MPRTR importer *bring in*
MPRTRBBL imperturbable (adj) *calm* imperturbably (adv)
MPRTRBBLD imperturbability *calmness*
MPRTRBBLT imperturbability *calmness*
MPRTRL imperatorial *emperor*
MPRTRYL imperatorial *emperor*
MPRTSHN impartation *give out*
MPRTSHN importation *bring in*
MPRTV imperative *(adj) masterful, necessary (n) rule*
MPRTVL imperatively *masterful, necessary*
MPRTVNS imperativeness *masterful, necessary*
MPRTYN importune *(v) beg* importuned importuning
MPRTYN importune *(n) trouble*
MPRTYND importunity *trouble* importunities
MPRTYNT importunate *troublesome*
MPRTYNT importunity *trouble* importunities
MPRTYNTL importunately *troublesome*

MPRTYNTNS importunateness *troublesome*
MPRV improve *better* improved improving
MPRVBL improvable *better*
MPRVDNS improvidence *no planning*
MPRVDNT improvident *no planning*
MPRVDNTL improvidently *no planning*
MPRVDNTS improvidence *no planning*
MPRVMNT improvement *better*
MPRVR improver *better*
MPRVS impervious *safe*
MPRVSL imperviously *safe*
MPRVSNS imperviousness *safe*
MPRVYS impervious *safe*
MPRVYSL imperviously *safe*
MPRVYSNS imperviousness *safe*
MPRVZ improvise *invent* improvised improvising
MPRVZR improviser (or) improvisor *inventor*
MPRVZSHN improvisation *invention*
MPRVZSHNL improvisational (adj) *invented* improvisationally (adv)
MPRYL empyreal *heavens*
MPRYL imperial (adj) *royal* imperially (adv)
MPRYLSDK imperialistic *domination*
MPRYLSDKL imperialistically *domination*
MPRYLSTK imperialistic *domination*
MPRYLSTKL imperialistically *domination*
MPRYLZM imperialism *domination*
MPRYM emporium *store* emporiums

MPRYM imperium *control*
MPRYN empyrean *heavens*
MPRYS imperious *domineering*
MPRYSL imperiously *domineering*
MPRYSNS imperiousness *domineering*
MPRZMNT imprisonment *confine*
MPRZN imprison *confine*
MPRZNMNT imprisonment *confine*
MPRZV impressive *moving*
MPS impasse *barrier*
MPS impious *disrespectful*
MPSBL impassable (adj) *cannot cross* impassably (adv)
MPSBL impassible (adj) *without feeling* impassibly (adv)
MPSBL impossible *difficult, unable to occur*
MPSBL impossibly *unbelievably*
MPSBLD impassability *cannot cross*
MPSBLD impassibility *without feeling*
MPSBLD impossibility *unable to occur* impossibilities
MPSBLT impassability *cannot cross*
MPSBLT impassibility *without feeling*
MPSBLT impossibility *unable to occur* impossibilities
MPSCHR imposture *fraud*
MPSD impasto *pigment* impastos
MPSDR impostor *false identity*
MPSH impish *mischievous*
MPSHN impassion *arouse*
MPSHND impassioned *intense*
MPSHNS impatience *anxiety*
MPSHNS impatiens *flower*

Use letters that best describe the sounds you hear and omit the vowels. Use **S** or **K** instead of **C**: to find circle use **SRKL**. Use **J** to find joy, **JM** to find gem and **G** to find go.

MPSHNT impatient *anxious*
MPSHNTL impatiently *anxious*
MPSHNTS impatience *anxiety*
MPSHNTS impatiens *flower*
MPSL impiously *disrespectfully*
MPSLN ampicillin *drug*
MPSN Maupassant (Guy de) *writer*
MPSNT Maupassant (Guy de) *writer*
MPST impasto *pigment* impastos
MPST impost *tax, arch*
MPSTD impastoed *pigment*
MPSTR impostor *false identity*
MPSTR imposture *fraud*
MPSTYR imposture *fraud*
MPSV impassive *no feeling*
MPSVD impassivity *no feeling*
MPSVL impassively *no feeling*
MPSVNS impassiveness *no feeling*
MPSVT impassivity *no feeling*
MPT amputee *one without limb(s)*
MPT empty *(v)* drain, discharge emptied emptying empties
MPT empty *(adj) void* emptier emptiest
MPT impiety *disrespect* impieties
MPT impute *credit* imputed imputing
MPT map out *route*
MPT moppet *child*
MPT Muppet *(trademark) puppet*
MPTBL imputable *credited to*
MPTBLD imputability *credit*
MPTBLT imputability *credit*
MPTDV imputative *credited to*
MPTG impetigo *rash*
MPTH empathy

understanding
MPTH myopathy *muscle disorder*
MPTHDD empty-headed *stupid*
MPTHDK empathetic *understanding*
MPTHK empathic *understanding*
MPTHK myopathic *muscle disorder*
MPTHKL empathically *understanding*
MPTHNDD empty-handed *nothing to show*
MPTHTK empathetic *understanding*
MPTHZ empathize *understand* empathized empathizing *(Br)* empathise
MPTJNS impetiginous *rash*
MPTL emptily *void*
MPTN umpteen *many*
MPTNS emptiness *void*
MPTNS impedance *barrier*
MPTNS impotence *helpless, sterile* impotency
MPTNT impotent *helpless, sterile*
MPTNTH umpteenth *many*
MPTNTL impotently *helpless, sterile*
MPTNTS impedance *barrier*
MPTNTS impotence *helpless, sterile* impotency
MPTR emptier *void*
MPTR impeder *barrier*
MPTS impetuous *impulsive*
MPTS impetus *incentive*
MPTSD impetuosity *impulsive* impetuosities
MPTSHN amputation *cut off limb*
MPTSHN imputation *credit*
MPTSL impetuously *impulsive*
MPTSNS impetuousness *impulsive*
MPTST emptiest *void*
MPTST impetuosity *impulsive* impetuosities

MPTT amputate *cut off* amputated amputating
MPTT mapped out *planned*
MPTTV imputative *credited to*
MPTWS impetuous *impulsive*
MPTWSL impetuously *impulsive*
MPTWSNS impetuousness *impulsive*
MPTYR emptier *void*
MPTYS impetuous *impulsive*
MPTYSD impetuosity *impulsive* impetuosities
MPTYSL impetuously *impulsive*
MPTYSNS impetuousness *impulsive*
MPTYST emptiest *void*
MPTYST impetuosity *impulsive* impetuosities
MPTYWS impetuous *impulsive*
MPTYWSD impetuosity *impulsive* impetuosities
MPTYWSL impetuously *impulsive*
MPTYWSNS impetuousness *impulsive*
MPTYWST impetuosity *impulsive* impetuosities
MPVRSH impoverish *make poor*
MPVRSHD impoverished *poor*
MPVRSHMNT impoverishment *poverty*
MPVRSHR impoverisher *make poor*
MPVRSHT impoverished *poor*
MPWR empower *enable*
MPWRMNT empowerment *enable*
MPWSNS impuissance *weakness*
MPWSNT impuissant *weak*
MPWSNTS impuissance *weakness*
MPY myopia *vision*
MPYD impiety *disrespect*

Letters aren't doubled for single sounds: to find alley use **L** not **LL**. Use **Y** and **W** as hard sounds only: to find yellow use **YL**. (Br)=British spelling or usage. * See dictionary.

impieties
MPYDBL imputable *credited to*
MPYDBLD imputability *credit*
MPYDBLT imputability *credit*
MPYDNS impudence *boldness*
MPYDNT impudent *bold*
MPYDNTL impudently *bold*
MPYDNTS impudence *boldness*
MPYL ampoule (or) ampule *injection*
MPYL ampulla *flask* ampullae
MPYN impugn *attack*
MPYNBL impugnable *attack*
MPYND impunity *exemption*
MPYNR impugner *attack*
MPYNT impunity *exemption*
MPYR impure *foul*
MPYR umpire *referee* umpired umpiring
MPYRD impurity *dirt* impurities
MPYRL impurely *foul*
MPYRNS impureness *foul*
MPYRT impurity *dirt* impurities
MPYS impious *disrespectful*
MPYSL impiously *disrespectfully*
MPYSNS impuissance *weakness*
MPYSNT impuissant *weak*
MPYSNTS impuissance *weakness*
MPYT amputee *one without limb(s)*
MPYT impiety *disrespect* impieties
MPYT impute *credit* imputed imputing
MPYTBL imputable *credited to*
MPYTBLD imputability *credit*
MPYTBLT imputability *credit*
MPYTDV imputative *credited to*

MPYTSHN amputation *cut off limb*
MPYTSHN imputation *credit*
MPYTT amputate *cut off* amputated amputating
MPYTTV imputative *credited to*
MPYWSNS impuissance *weakness*
MPYWSNT impuissant *weak*
MPYWSNTS impuissance *weakness*
MPZ impose *set, pass off, force into* imposed imposing
MPZN imposing *grand*
MPZNG imposing *grand*
MPZR imposer *set, pass off, force into*
MPZSHN imposition *tax, burden, deception*
MQL macula *spot* maculae
MQL macule *spot*
MQLC immaculacy *clean*
MQLDD maculated (or) maculate *spotted*
MQLS immaculacy *clean*
MQLSHN maculation *spots*
MQLT immaculate *clean*
MQLT maculate (or) maculated *spotted*
MQLTD maculated (or) maculate *spotted*
MQLTL immaculately *clean*
MQRL mercurial (adj) *changing* mercurially (adv)
MQRYL mercurial (adj) *changing* mercurially (adv)
MR amour *lover*
MR emery *sander* emeries
MR emir *Arab ruler*
MR emmer *wheat*
MR Imari *porcelain*
MR immure *imprison* immured immuring
MR Maori *New Zealand native* Maori (or) Maoris
MR mar *damage* marred marring
MR mare *horse* mares
MR mare *dark area* maria
MR marrow *bone*

MR marry *wed* married marrying marries
MR mayor *city leader*
MR mere *slight* merest
MR merry *jolly* merrier merriest
MR mire (v) *entangle, dirty* mired miring
MR mire (n) *mud*
MR mirror *reflection*
MR moiré (or) moire *pattern*
MR moor (n) *land* (v) *fasten*
MR Moor *Berber*
MR mor *humus*
MR mora *verse* morae (or) moras
MR more *additional*
MR morrow *tomorrow*
MR mower *cutter*
MR murre *bird*
MR murrey *berry*
MR myrrh *aromatic resin*
MR omer *weight*
MRB marabou *bird, silk*
MRBD morbid *unwholesome*
MRBDD morbidity *unwholesome, disease*
MRBDT morbidity *unwholesome, disease*
MRBL marble (n) *limestone*
MRBL marble (v) *mottle* marbled marbling
MRBL marbly *like limestone*
MRBLD marbled *mottled*
MRBLN marbling *coloration*
MRBLNG marbling *coloration*
MRBLZ marbleize *mottle* marbleized marbleizing (Br) marbleise
MRBLZ marbles *wits, game*
MRBN marrowbone *knee*
MRBN moribund *death* moribundity
MRBND moribund *death*
MRBNDD moribundity *death*
MRBNDT moribundity *death*
MRC mercy *pity* mercies
MRCBL amerciable *punishable*
MRCFL merciful *kindhearted*
MRCFL mercifully

fortunately
MRCH March *month*
MRCH march *stride*
marches
MRCH mariachi *music*
MRCHNDS merchandise
(n) wares
MRCHNDZ merchandise *(v)*
sell merchandised
merchandising
MRCHNDZN
merchandising *promotion*
MRCHNDZNG
merchandising *promotion*
MRCHNDZR merchandiser
seller
MRCHNT merchant *trader*
MRCHR marcher *strider*
MRCHR mortuary *burial*
mortuaries
MRCHWR mortuary *burial*
mortuaries
MRCLS merciless *pitiless*
MRCM americium *element*
MRCYBL amerciable
punishable
MRCYM americium *element*
MRCZ murices (or) murexes
(pl) *mollusk* murex
MRD amaretto *liqueur*
amaretti
MRD amoretto *cupid*
amoretti (or) amorettos
MRD emeriti (pl) *title*
emeritus
MRD maraud *search*
MRD married *person wed*
marrieds
MRD murid *rodent*
MRD myriad *many*
MRDF mortify *shame, deaden*
mortified mortifying
mortifies
MRDFKSHN mortification
denial, shame
MRDGR Mardi Gras *festival*
MRDK amaurotic *blindness*
MRDK muriatic *acid*
MRDL immortal (adj)
undying immortally (adv)
MRDL marital (adj) *marriage*
maritally (adv)

MRDL mortal *(n) human*
being
MRDL mortal (adj) *sure to die*
mortally (adv)
MRDL myrtle *tree*
MRDLZ immortalize *no*
death immortalized
immortalizing
(Br) immortalise
MRDLZR immortalizer *no*
death
(Br) immortaliser
MRDLZSHN
immortalization *no death*
(Br) immortalisation
MRDN meridian *circle,*
longitude
MRDNC mordancy
harshness
MRDNS mordancy *harshness*
MRDNT mordant *harsh*
MRDNT mordent *music*
MRDNTC mordancy
harshness
MRDNTS mordancy
harshness
MRDR marauder *searcher*
MRDR martyr *(n) victim (v)*
inflict pain
MRDR mirador *window*
MRDR mortar *(n) cement,*
cannon, cup (v) plaster
MRDR murder *kill*
MRDRBRD mortarboard *cap*
MRDRDM martyrdom *death*
MRDRLS mortarless *cement*
MRDRR murderer *killer*
MRDRS murderess *killer (f)*
MRDRS murderous
treacherous
MRDRZSHN martyrization
victimization
MRDS emeritus *title* emeriti
MRDS mortise *dovetail*
mortised mortising
MRDYN meridian *circle,*
longitude
MRDZSHN amortization
reduction
MRF morphia *morphine*
MRF morpho *butterfly*
morphos

MRFBD Murphy bed
furniture
MRFFNMKS
morphophonemics
language
MRFFNMX
morphophonemics
language
MRFJN morphogen *chemical*
MRFJNDK morphogenetic
cell growth
MRFJNSS morphogenesis
cell growth
MRFJNTK morphogenetic
cell growth
MRFLG morphology
structure
MRFLJ morphology
structure
MRFLJKL morphological
(adj) *structure*
morphologically (adv)
MRFLJST morphologist
structure
MRFM morpheme *word part*
MRFMK morphemic *word*
part
MRFMKL morphemically
word part
MRFMKS morphemics
language
MRFMTR morphometry
measurement
MRFMTRK morphometric
measurement
MRFMX morphemics
language
MRFN morphine *sedative*
MRFNZM morphinism
addiction
MRFS amorphous *shapeless*
MRFS Morpheus *Greek god*
MRFSL amorphously
shapeless
MRFSL Murphy's Law
observation
MRFSNS amorphousness
shapelessness
MRFY morphia *morphine*
MRFYS Morpheus *Greek god*
MRFZL Murphy's Law
observation

Letters aren't doubled for single sounds: to find alley use **L** not **LL**. Use **Y** and **W** as hard
sounds only: to find yellow use **YL**. (Br)=British spelling or usage. * See dictionary.

MRG margay *cat*
MRG morgue *crypt*
MRGJ mortgage *pledge* mortgaged mortgaging
MRGJ mortgagee *receiver*
MRGJR mortgagor *pledger*
MRGL marigold *flower*
MRGLD marigold *flower*
MRGN morgan *measurement*
MRGN Morgan *horse*
MRGNDK morganatic *marriage*
MRGNDKL morganatically *marriage*
MRGNSR merganser *duck*
MRGNTK morganatic *marriage*
MRGNTKL morganatically *marriage*
MRGNZR merganser *duck*
MRGRD margarita *cocktail*
MRGRN merry-go-round *ride*
MRGRND merry-go-round *ride*
MRGRT margarita *cocktail*
MRGRT marguerite *daisy*
MRGRV margrave *governor*
MRJ emerge *come out* emerged emerging
MRJ immerge *plunge into* immerged immerging
MRJ marriage *wedlock*
MRJ merge *combine* merged merging
MRJ mirage *vision*
MRJ moorage *pier*
MRJBL marriageable *wedlock*
MRJBLD marriageability *wedlock*
MRJBLT marriageability *wedlock*
MRJN emerging *coming out*
MRJN margin *(v)* border *(n)* edge, excess
MRJNC emergency *critical* need emergencies
MRJNG emerging *coming out*
MRJNL marginal (adj) *at the border* marginally (adv)

MRJNLZ marginalize *make unimportant* marginalized marginalizing
MRJNLZSHN marginalization *make unimportant*
MRJNS emergence *coming out*
MRJNS emergency *critical need* emergencies
MRJNS mergence *combination*
MRJNT emergent *coming out*
MRJNT marginate *put aside* marginated marginating
MRJNTC emergency *critical need* emergencies
MRJNTS emergence *coming out*
MRJNTS emergency *critical need* emergencies
MRJNTS mergence *combination*
MRJR merger *union*
MRJRM marjoram *herb*
MRJRN margarine *food*
MRK America *continent (North or South), USA*
MRK maraca *music*
MRK mark *(n) spot, German money, goal (v) label, notice, grade**
MRK markka *Finnish money* markkaa
MRK marque *brand*
MRK marquee *box office, tent*
MRK marquise *gem, canopy* marquises
MRK Morocco *country*
MRK morocco *leather*
MRK murk *gloom*
MRK murky *gloomy* murkier murkiest
MRKC marchese *nobleman* marchesi
MRKCN Marxian *of Marx*
MRKCYN Marxian *of Marx*
MRKD marcato *music*
MRKDBL marketable *fit for sale*
MRKDBLD marketability *fit*

for sale
MRKDBLT marketability *fit for sale*
MRKDL markedly *noticeably*
MRKDN markdown (n) *discount* mark down (v)
MRKDNG marketing *selling*
MRKDNS markedness *noticed*
MRKDR Mercator *map*
MRKL miracle *supernatural event*
MRKL murkily *gloomy*
MRKLS miraculous *mystical*
MRKLSL miraculously *mystically*
MRKLSNS miraculousness *mystical*
MRKM Omar Khayyám *poet*
MRKN American *of America*
MRKN Americana *American objects*
MRKN marking *spot*
MRKNG marking *spot*
MRKNS Americanese *language*
MRKNS murkiness *gloom*
MRKNSM American Samoa *islands*
MRKNSM Americanism *trait*
MRKNSMW American Samoa *islands*
MRKNST Americanist *historian* (Br) Americanisation
MRKNTL mercantile *trade*
MRKNTLSDK mercantilistic *trade*
MRKNTLST mercantilist *trader*
MRKNTLSTK mercantilistic *trade*
MRKNTLZM mercantilism *trade*
MRKNZ Americanese *language*
MRKNZ Americanize *make American* Americanized Americanizing (Br) Americanise
MRKNZM Americanism

trait
MRKNZSHN
  Americanization *made*
  American
  (Br) Americanisation
MRKP markup (n) *profit*
  mark up (v)
MRKR marker *pen*
MRKR Mercury *planet, god*
MRKR mercury *element*
MRKR murkier *gloomy*
MRKRL mercurial (adj)
  changing mercurially (adv)
MRKRYL mercurial (adj)
  changing mercurially (adv)
MRKS marchese *nobleman*
  marchesi
MRKS Marx (Karl)
  philosopher
MRKS murex *mollusk*
  murices (or) murexes
MRKSH Marrakesh *city*
MRKSKP America's Cup
  yacht race
MRKSMN marksman
  shooter marksmen
MRKSMNSHP
  marksmanship *shooting*
MRKSN Marxian *of Marx*
MRKSS Marquesas *islands*
MRKSST Marxist *philosopher*
MRKST marcasite *mineral*
MRKST marquisette *fabric*
MRKST murkiest *gloomy*
MRKSWMN markswoman
  shooter markswomen
MRKSYN Marxian *of Marx*
MRKSZM Marxism
  philosophy
MRKT marcato *music*
MRKT marked *spotted,*
  identified
MRKT market *store*
MRKT meerkat *animal*
MRKTBL marketable *fit for*
  sale
MRKTBLD marketability *fit*
  for sale
MRKTBLT marketability *fit*
  for sale
MRKTN marketing *selling*
MRKTNG marketing *selling*

MRKTPLS marketplace
  trade area
MRKTR marketeer *sales*
  specialist
MRKTR marketer *seller*
MRKTR marquetry *wood*
  craft
MRKTR Mercator *map*
MRKWS marquess (or)
  marquis *nobleman*
  marquesses (or)
  marquises (or) marquis
MRKWST marquessate (or)
  marquisate *nobleman*
MRKWST marquisette *fabric*
MRKWZT marquessate (or)
  marquisate *nobleman*
MRKWZT marquisette *fabric*
MRKYLS miraculous
  mystical
MRKYLSL miraculously
  mystically
MRKYLSNS
  miraculousness *mystical*
MRKYM Omar Khayyám
  poet
MRKYR Mercury *planet, god*
MRKYR mercury *element*
MRKYR murkier *gloomy*
MRKYRL mercurial (adj)
  changing mercurially (adv)
MRKYRYL mercurial (adj)
  changing mercurially (adv)
MRKYST murkiest *gloomy*
MRKZ marchesa
  noblewoman marchese
MRKZ marchese *nobleman*
  marchesi
MRKZ marquise *gem, canopy*
  marquises
MRKZKP America's Cup
  yacht race
MRKZS Marquesas *islands*
MRKZT marcasite *mineral*
MRKZT marquisette *fabric*
MRL Amarillo *city*
MRL amoral (adj) *beyond*
  morals amorally (adv)
MRL emerald *gem*
MRL immoral (adj) *no*
  principles immorally (adv)
MRL marl *clay*

MRL marly *like clay*
MRL mayoral *city official*
MRL merely *only*
MRL merlot *wine*
MRL merrily *jolly*
MRL moral (n) *lesson*
MRL moral (adj) *proper*
  morally (adv)
MRL morale *enthusiasm*
MRL moray eel *animal*
MRL morel *fungus*
MRL morello *cherry* morellos
MRL mural *painting*
MRLD amorality *beyond*
  morals
MRLD emerald *gem*
MRLD immorality *no*
  principles
MRLD morality *virtue*
MRLN marlin *fish*
MRLN marline *rope*
MRLN Maryland *US State*
MRLN Merlin *magician*
MRLN merlin *bird*
MRLN merlon *battlement*
MRLN moorland *wasteland*
MRLND Maryland *US State*
MRLND moorland *wasteland*
MRLNSPK marlinespike *tool*
MRLS amaryllis *plant*
MRLS more or less
  approximately
MRLSDK moralistic *proper*
MRLSDKL moralistically
  properly
MRLSM amoralism *beyond*
  morals
MRLSM immoralism *no*
  principles
MRLSM moralism *virtue*
MRLST moralist *philosopher*
MRLST muralist *painter*
MRLSTK moralistic *proper*
MRLSTKL moralistically
  properly
MRLT amorality *beyond*
  morals
MRLT immorality *no*
  principles immoralities
MRLT mayoralty *city official*
  mayoralties
MRLT morality *virtue*

Letters aren't doubled for single sounds: to find alley use **L** not **LL**. Use **Y** and **W** as hard
sounds only: to find yellow use **YL**. (Br)=British spelling or usage. * See dictionary.

moralities

MRLZ moralize *improve or explain ethics* moralized moralizing (Br) moralise

MRLZM amoralism *beyond morals*

MRLZM immoralism *no principles*

MRLZM moralism *virtue*

MRLZR moralizer *ethics* (Br) moraliser

MRLZSHN moralization *ethics* (Br) moralisation

MRMB marimba *xylophone*

MRMBST marimbist *musician*

MRMD mermaid *sea creature*

MRMDN myrmidon *follower*

MRMKFL myrmecophile *ants*

MRMKFLS myrmecophilous *ants*

MRMKLG myrmecology *ants*

MRMKLJ myrmecology *ants*

MRMKLJKL myrmecological *ants*

MRMKLJST myrmecologist *ants*

MRMKN merrymaking *fun*

MRMKNG merrymaking *fun*

MRMKR merrymaker *reveler*

MRMLD marmalade *jelly*

MRMN Mormon *Latter-Day Saint*

MRMNT immurement *prison*

MRMNT merriment *fun*

MRMR murmur *mutter*

MRMRR murmurer *mutterer*

MRMRS murmurous *low sounds*

MRMST marmoset *monkey*

MRMT marmot *rodent*

MRN marina *boats*

MRN marine *(adj) ocean (n) soldier*

MRN maroon *(n) color, slave (v) isolate*

MRN marron *nut*

MRN merino *wool* merinos

MRN mooring *pier*

MRN moraine *glacier*

MRN moreen *glossy fabric*

MRN morn *morning*

MRN Mornay *sauce*

MRN moron *idiot*

MRN mourn *grieve*

MRN murine *rodent*

MRN murrain *plague*

MRND marinade *sauce*

MRNDN Amerindian *American Indian*

MRNDR merry-andrew *clown*

MRNDYN Amerindian *American Indian*

MRNFL mournful (adj) *grieving* mournfully (adv)

MRNG marengo *sauce*

MRNG merengue *dance*

MRNG meringue *dessert*

MRNG mooring *pier*

MRNGG marengo *sauce*

MRNGG merengue *dance*

MRNK morainic *glacier*

MRNK moronic *idiotic*

MRNKR Marine Corps *US Armed Forces*

MRNL morainal *glacier*

MRNN morning *before noon*

MRNN mourning *grieving*

MRNNDV mourning dove *bird*

MRNNG morning *before noon*

MRNNG mourning *grieving*

MRNNGDV mourning dove *bird*

MRNR marinara *sauce*

MRNR mariner *seaman*

MRNR meunière *cooking*

MRNR mourner *griever*

MRNS merriness *fun*

MRNSHN marination *soaking*

MRNT marinate *soak* marinated marinating

MRNT marionette *puppet*

MRNTH amaranth *herb*

MRNTHN amaranthine *undying, herbal*

MRNYR meunière *cooking*

MRPD myriapod *insect*

MRQLS miraculous *mystical*

MRQLSL miraculously *mystically*

MRQLSNS miraculousness *mystical*

MRQR Mercury *planet, god*

MRQR mercury *element*

MRQRL mercurial (adj) *changing* mercurially (adv)

MRQRYL mercurial (adj) *changing* mercurially (adv)

MRQS marquess (or) marquis *nobleman* marquesses (or) marquises (or) marquis

MRQST marquessate (or) marquisate *nobleman*

MRQST marquisette *fabric*

MRQZT marquessate (or) marquisate *nobleman*

MRQZT marquisette *fabric*

MRR merrier *jolly*

MRR mirror *reflection*

MRRLS more or less *approximately*

MRS amerce *punish* amerced amercing

MRS amorous *loving*

MRS immerse *plunge into* immersed immersing

MRS Marseilles *city*

MRS mayoress *city official (f)*

MRS mercy *pity* mercies

MRS morass (n) *marsh* morassy (adj)

MRS morceau *music* morceaux

MRS morose *sad*

MRS morris *dance*

MRSBL amerciable *punishable*

MRSBL immersible *submerge*

MRSCHR morris chair *seat*

MRSD morosity *sadness*

MRSDK amoristic *loving*

MRSDK meristic *separate*

MRSDK myristic *fatty acid*

MRSDKL meristically *separately*

MRSDM meristem *plant*

Use letters that best describe the sounds you hear and omit the vowels. Use **S** or **K** instead of **C**: to find circle use **SRKL**. Use **J** to find joy, **JM** to find gem and **G** to find go.

tissue
MRSFL merciful *kindhearted*
MRSFL mercifully
fortunately
MRSH marsh *swamp*
marshes
MRSH marshy *swampy*
marshier marshiest
MRSH mirage *vision*
MRSH Moorish *of Moors*
MRSHBL amerciable
punishable
MRSHGS marsh gas
methane
MRSHL marshal *(v) enlist*
(n) rank
MRSHL martial (adj) *war*
martially (adv)
MRSHL martial law *military*
law
MRSHLN marshland *swamp*
MRSHLND marshland
swamp
MRSHLRTS martial arts
self-defense
MRSHM americium *element*
MRSHM meerschaum *clay*
MRSHML marshmallow
herb, confection
MRSHN Amerasian *Asian-*
American
MRSHN emersion *come out*
MRSHN immersion *plunge*
MRSHN maraschino *cherry*
maraschinos
MRSHN martian *(often*
capitalized) of Mars
MRSHNS marchioness *title*
MRSHNS marshiness
swamp
MRSHR marshier *swampy*
MRSHS Mauritius *island*
MRSHST marshiest *swampy*
MRSHYM americium
element
MRSHYR marshier *swampy*
MRSHYST marshiest
swampy
MRSKD Morse code
transmission
MRSKN maraschino *cherry*
maraschinos

MRSKPN mascarpone
cheese
MRSL amorously *lovingly*
MRSL marcel *wave*
marcelled marcelling
MRSL Marsala *city, wine*
MRSL morosely *sadly*
MRSL morsel *(n) bite*
MRSL morsel *(v) divide*
morseled (or) morselled
morseling (or) morselling
MRSLS merciless *pitiless*
MRSM americium *element*
MRSMNT amercement
punishment
MRSNR mercenary *(n)*
soldier (adj) greedy
mercenaries
MRSNS amorousness
lovingness
MRSNS moroseness *sadness*
MRSNST mare's nest
illusion mare's nests (or)
mares' nests
MRSP marsupia (pl) *pouch*
marsupium
MRSPL marsupial *mammal*
MRSPM marsupium *pouch*
marsupia
MRSPY marsupia (pl) *pouch*
marsupium
MRSPYL marsupial *mammal*
MRSPYM marsupium *pouch*
marsupia
MRSR mercery *(Br) fabric*
shop merceries
MRSRZ mercerize *yarn*
treatment mercerized
mercerizing
(Br) mercerise
MRSRZSHN mercerization
yarn treatment
(Br) mercerisation
MRSS amaurosis *blindness*
amauroses
MRST amorist *lover*
MRST merest *slight*
MRST merriest *jolliest*
MRST morosity *sadness*
MRSTK amoristic *loving*
MRSTK meristic *separate*
MRSTK myristic *fatty acid*

MRSTKL meristically
separately
MRSTL mare's tail *plant*
mare's tails (or) mares'
tails
MRSTM meristem *plant*
tissue
MRSYBL amerciable
punishable
MRSYM americium *element*
MRSZ murices (or) murexes
(pl) *mollusk* murex
MRT amaretto *liqueur*
amaretti
MRT amoretto *cupid*
amorettos (or) amoretti
MRT emeriti (pl) *title*
emeritus
MRT emirate *Arab state*
MRT mart *store*
MRT merit *(n) honor (v) earn*
MRTF mortify *shame, deaden*
mortified mortifying
mortifies
MRTFKSHN mortification
denial, shame
MRTGR Mardi Gras *festival*
MRTH mirth *gaiety*
MRTHFL mirthful (adj) *gay*
mirthfully (adv)
MRTHFLNS mirthfulness
gaiety
MRTHLD Merthiolate
(trademark) antiseptic
MRTHLS mirthless *no joy*
MRTHLSL mirthlessly *no joy*
MRTHLT Merthiolate
(trademark) antiseptic
MRTHN marathon *race*
MRTHNR marathoner *racer*
MRTHYLD Merthiolate
(trademark) antiseptic
MRTHYLT Merthiolate
(trademark) antiseptic
MRTHZVNYRD Martha's
Vineyard *island*
MRTK amaurotic *blindness*
MRTK muriatic *acid*
MRTKRC meritocracy
leadership meritocracies
MRTKRS meritocracy
leadership meritocracies

MRTL immortal (adj) undying immortally (adv)

MRTL marital (adj) *marriage* maritally (adv)

MRTL mortal (n) *human being*

MRTL mortal (adj) *sure to die* mortally (adv)

MRTL myrtle *tree*

MRTLD immortality *no death*

MRTLD mortality *death*

MRTLT immortality *no death*

MRTLT mortality *death*

MRTLZ immortalize *no death* immortalized immortalizing (Br) immortalise

MRTLZR immortalizer *no death* (Br) immortaliser

MRTLZSHN immortalization *no death* (Br) immortalisation

MRTM maritime *sea*

MRTMN mortmain *property*

MRTN marten *animal* marten (or) martens

MRTN martin *bird*

MRTN martini *drink*

MRTN Mauritania *country*

MRTNGL martingale *horse device*

MRTNK Martinique *island*

MRTNT martinet *dictator*

MRTNY Mauritania *country*

MRTR martyr (n) *victim* (v) *inflict pain*

MRTR moratoria (pl) *delay* moratorium

MRTR mortar (n) *cement, cannon, cup* (v) *plaster*

MRTR mortuary *burial* mortuaries

MRTRBRD mortarboard *cap*

MRTRDM martyrdom *death*

MRTRLS mortarless *cement*

MRTRM moratorium *delay* moratoriums (or) moratoria

MRTRS meritorious *deserving*

MRTRSHS meretricious

flashy

MRTRY moratoria (pl) *delay* moratorium

MRTRYM moratorium *delay* moratoriums (or) moratoria

MRTRYS meritorious *deserving*

MRTRZSHN martyrization *victimization*

MRTS emeritus *title* emeriti

MRTS mortise *dovetail* mortised mortising

MRTSHN mortician *undertaker*

MRTSPN marzipan *candy*

MRTWR mortuary *burial* mortuaries

MRTZ amortize *reduce* amortized amortizing

MRTZBL amortizable *reducing*

MRTZSHN amortization *reduction*

MRVL marvel *wonder* marveled (or) marvelled marveling (or) marvelling

MRVLS marvelous (or) marvellous *astonishing*

MRVLSL marvelously *astonishing*

MRVLSNS marvelousness *astonishing*

MRVR moreover *besides*

MRWD merry widow *corset*

MRWN marijuana *hemp*

MRX Marx (Karl) *philosopher*

MRX murex *mollusk* murices (or) murexes

MRXMN marksman *shooter* marksmen

MRXMNSHP marksmanship *shooting*

MRXN Marxian *of Marx*

MRXST Marxist *philosopher*

MRXWMN markswoman *shooter* markswomen

MRXYN Marxian *of Marx*

MRXZM Marxism *philosophy*

MRY Amarillo *city*

MRYCH mariachi *music*

MRYD myriad *many*

MRYDK muriatic *acid*

MRYL moray eel *animal*

MRYNT marionette *puppet*

MRYPD myriapod *insect*

MRYR merrier *jolly*

MRYST merriest *jolliest*

MRYTK muriatic *acid*

MRZ Mars *planet, Roman god*

MRZ mores *customs*

MRZH mirage *vision*

MRZHN Amerasian *Asian-American*

MRZHN emersion *come out*

MRZHN immersion *plunge*

MRZMK marasmic *underfed*

MRZMS marasmus *undernourishment*

MRZNST mare's nest *illusion* mare's nests (or) mares' nests

MRZPN marzipan *candy*

MRZTL mare's tail *plant* mare's tails (or) mares' tails

MS amass *gather*

MS amice *vestment*

MS amici (pl) *law* amicus

MS amiss *wrong*

MS emcee *host* emceed emceeing

MS mace *staff*

MS Mace (*trademark*) *chemical*

MS maize *corn*

MS Masai *African tribe* Masai (or) Masais

MS mass (n) *collection, bulk* (v) *assemble* (adj) *average* masses

MS Mass (n) *ceremony*

MS massé *billiards*

MS mesa *flatland*

MS mess (n) *food* (v) *dirty* messes

MS messiah *leader*

MS messy *dirty* messier messiest

MS mews *stables*

MS miss (n) *failure* (v) *omit, avoid, fail** misses

MS Miss *title* (f) Misses

MS missy *young girl*

Use letters that best describe the sounds you hear and omit the vowels. Use **S** or **K** instead of **C**: to find circle use **SRKL**. Use **J** to find joy, **JM** to find gem and **G** to find go.

MS moose *large animal*
moose
MS moss *plant* mosses
MS mossy *with moss*
mossier mossiest
MS most *more than half*
MS mouse *(n) small animal,*
device mice
MS mousse *dessert, foam*
moussed moussing
MS mousy (or) mousey
timid, grayish brown
mousier mousiest
MS muss *mess*
MS mussy *messy* mussier
mussiest
MS must-see *good viewing*
MSBGTN misbegotten
illegitimate
MSBHV misbehave *act badly*
misbehaved misbehaving
MSBHVR misbehavior *bad*
conduct
MSBHVYR misbehavior *bad*
conduct
(Br) misbehaviour
MSBK mossback *fish, fogy*
MSBL immiscible *no mix*
MSBL miscible *mix*
MSBL omissible *omit*
MSBLD immiscibility *no mix*
MSBLD miscibility *mix*
MSBLF misbelief *false notion*
MSBLT immiscibility *no mix*
MSBLT miscibility *mix*
MSBLV misbelieve *believe*
falsely misbelieved
misbelieving
MSBLVR misbeliever *heretic*
MSCHF mischief *irritant*
MSCHFS mischievous
harmful, playful
MSCHNS mischance *bad*
luck
MSCHNTS mischance *bad*
luck
MSCHR moisture *dampness*
MSCHRZ moisturize *dampen*
moisturized moisturizing
(Br) moisturise
MSCHRZR moisturizer
dampen

(Br) moisturiser
MSCHSTS Massachusetts
US State
MSCHVS mischievous
harmful, playful
MSCHVYS mischievous
harmful, playful
MSCHZTS Massachusetts
US State
MSD misty *blurry* mistier
mistiest
MSD musty *stale* mustier
mustiest
MSDD masted *with mast(s)*
MSDD mastoid *bone*
MSDD misdeed *error*
MSDF mastiff *dog*
MSDF mystify *bewilder*
mystified mystifying
mystifies
MSDFKSHN mystification
occult
MSDGFRN mastigophoran
protozoa
MSDGNS misdiagnose
wrong conclusion
misdiagnosed
misdiagnosing
MSDGNSS misdiagnosis
wrong conclusion
MSDK mastic *resin*
MSDK mystic *occult*
MSDK mystique *mystery*
MSDKDR masticator *chew*
MSDKL mystical (adj) *occult*
mystically (adv)
MSDKSHN mastication
chewing
MSDKT masticate *chew*
masticated masticating
MSDKTR masticator *chew*
MSDKTR masticatory *(adj)*
chewing (n) substance
masticatories
MSDL misdeal *cards*
misdealt misdealing
MSDL misdial *telephone*
MSDL mistily *blurry*
MSDL mustily *stale*
MSDMNR misdemeanor
misdeed
MSDNG Mao Tse-tung

Chinese leader
MSDNN Macedonian *of*
Macedonia
MSDNS mistiness *blurriness*
MSDNS mustiness *staleness*
MSDNYN Macedonian *of*
Macedonia
MSDR master *(n) teacher,*
ruler, model (v) overcome
(adj) principal, skilled*
MSDR mastery *skill,*
command
MSDR mister *sprayer*
MSDR Mister (or) Mr. *title*
Messrs
MSDR mistier *blurry*
MSDR muster *(v) gather (n)*
sample, inspection
MSDR mustier *stale*
MSDR mystery *puzzle*
mysteries
MSDRBDR masturbator
erotic stimulation
MSDRBSHN masturbation
erotic stimulation
MSDRBT masturbate *self-*
stimulate masturbated
masturbating
MSDRBTR masturbator
erotic stimulation
MSDRBTR masturbatory
erotic stimulation
MSDRD mustard *herb*
MSDRFL masterful (adj)
skilled masterfully (adv)
MSDRK misdirect *wrong*
direction
MSDRKSHN misdirection
wrong direction
MSDRKT misdirect *wrong*
direction
MSDRL masterly *skilled*
MSDRL mistral *wind*
MSDRLNS masterliness
skill
MSDRM mesoderm *germ*
layer
MSDRML mesodermal *germ*
layer
MSDRMN mastermind *(v)*
plan (n) planner
MSDRMND mastermind *(v)*

Letters aren't doubled for single sounds: to find alley use **L** not **LL**. Use **Y** and **W** as hard
sounds only: to find yellow use **YL**. (Br)=British spelling or usage. * See dictionary.

plan (n) planner

MSDRPS masterpiece *great work*

MSDRS misaddress *wrong address*

MSDRS mistress *lady* mistresses

MSDRSTRK masterstroke *great move*

MSDRWRK masterwork *great achievement*

MSDS myositis *soreness*

MSDST mistiest *blurry*

MSDST mustiest *stale*

MSDSZM mysticism *occult belief*

MSDT misdate *wrong day* misdated misdating

MSDVNCHR misadventure *mishap*

MSDVNTR misadventure *mishap*

MSDVZ misadvise *counsel badly* misadvised misadvising

MSDYGNS misdiagnose *wrong conclusion* misdiagnosed misdiagnosing

MSDYGNSS misdiagnosis *wrong conclusion*

MSDYL misdial *telephone*

MSDYR mistier *blurry*

MSDYR mustier *stale*

MSDYST mistiest *blurry*

MSDYST mustiest *stale*

MSDZN mycetozoan *slime mold*

MSDZWN mycetozoan *slime mold*

MSF massif *mountain*

MSF myself *of me*

MSFDK mesophytic *plant*

MSFL mesophyll *leaf layer*

MSFL misfile *wrong folder* misfiled misfiling

MSFR misfire *gun failure* misfired misfiring

MSFRCHN misfortune *trouble*

MSFRTN misfortune *trouble*

MSFT mesophyte *plant*

MSFT misfit *not conforming*

MSFTK mesophytic *plant*

MSFYL misfile *wrong folder* misfiled misfiling

MSFYR misfire *gun failure* misfired misfiring

MSFZNS misfeasance *trespass*

MSFZNTS misfeasance *trespass*

MSGD misguide *misdirect* misguided misguiding

MSGDD misguided *misdirected*

MSGDNS misguidance *bad direction*

MSGDNTS misguidance *bad direction*

MSGL mesoglea (or) mesogloea *gelatin*

MSGM misogamy *hatred of marriage*

MSGMST misogamist *marriage hater*

MSGVN misgiving *doubt*

MSGVNG misgiving *doubt*

MSGVRN misgovern *rule badly*

MSGVRNMNT misgovernment *bad ruling*

MSH Amish *religion*

MSH enmesh *snare*

MSH mash *crush* mashes

MSH mesh (v) *entangle* (n) *net* meshes

MSH mush (n) *soft substance* (v) *move over snow* mushes

MSH mushy *soft* mushier mushiest

MSHD machete *large knife*

MSHG meshuga (or) meshugge *fool*

MSHGN Michigan *US State*

MSHGNR meshuggener *fool*

MSHL mess hall *dining area*

MSHL mushily *softly*

MSHMNT enmeshment *snare*

MSHMSH mishmash *jumble*

MSHN emission *outflow*

MSHN emotion *mood*

MSHN machine (v) *tool* machined machining

MSHN machine (n) *mechanism*

MSHN mission *goal*

MSHN motion *movement*

MSHN omission *left out*

MSHNBL machinable *tool*

MSHNBLD machinability *tool*

MSHNBLT machinability *tool*

MSHNDL mishandle *treat badly* mishandled mishandling

MSHNDR machinator *schemer*

MSHNG mah-jongg (or) mahjong *game*

MSHNGN machine gun (n) *weapon* machine-gun (adj, v)

MSHNL emotional (adj) *moody* emotionally (adv)

MSHNLD emotionality *feelings*

MSHNLN Maginot Line *defense*

MSHNLS emotionless *no feelings*

MSHNLS motionless *no movement*

MSHNLSL emotionlessly *no feelings*

MSHNLSM emotionalism *feelings*

MSHNLSNS emotionlessness *no feelings*

MSHNLST emotionalist *feelings*

MSHNLT emotionality *feelings*

MSHNLZ emotionalize *arouse feelings* emotionalized emotionalizing

MSHNLZM emotionalism *feelings*

MSHNR machinery *working parts* machineries

Use letters that best describe the sounds you hear and omit the vowels. Use **S** or **K** instead of **C**: to find circle use **SRKL**. Use **J** to find joy, **JM** to find gem and **G** to find go.

MSHNR missionary *religion* missionaries
MSHNR missioner *religion*
MSHNS mushiness *softness*
MSHNSHN machination *plot*
MSHNST machinist *worker*
MSHNT machinate *plot* machinated machinating
MSHNTL machine tool *shaper*
MSHNTR machinator *schemer*
MSHNZ missionize *religion* missionized missionizing
MSHP mishap *accident*
MSHP misshape *twisted*
MSHPN misshapen *twisted*
MSHR masher *tool, flirt*
MSHR measure *(v) regulate, govern, allot** measured measuring
MSHR measure *(n) portion, tune, comparison**
MSHR mishear *misunderstand* misheard mishearing
MSHR Monsieur *title*
MSHR musher *sled travel*
MSHR mushier *soft*
MSHRBL immeasurable (adj) *beyond count* immeasurably (adv)
MSHRBL measurable (adj) *able to count* measurably (adv)
MSHRBLD measurability *portion*
MSHRBLT measurability *portion*
MSHRD measured *calculated*
MSHRLS measureless *unlimited*
MSHRM mushroom *(n) fungus (v) grow*
MSHRMNT measurement *size*
MSHRR measurer *allot, regulate*
MSHSH maxixe *dance* maxixes

MSHSHN emaciation *thinness*
MSHST mot juste *right word* mots justes
MSHST mushiest *soft*
MSHT emaciate *make thin* emaciated emaciating
MSHT machete *large knife*
MSHT meshed *knit*
MSHT mishit *hit badly* mishit mishitting
MSHWRK meshwork *network*
MSHYR mushier *soft*
MSHYSHN emaciation *thinness*
MSHYST mushiest *soft*
MSHYT emaciate *make thin* emaciated emaciating
MSJ massage *rub* massaged massaging
MSJ message *note* messaged messaging
MSJJ misjudge *mistake* misjudged misjudging
MSJJMNT misjudgment *mistake*
MSJN misogyny *hatred of women*
MSJNSDK misogynistic *woman hater*
MSJNSHN miscegenation *mixed races*
MSJNST misogynist *woman hater*
MSJNSTK misogynistic *woman hater*
MSJR massager *one who rubs*
MSK mask *cover*
MSK masque *drama*
MSK miscue *mistake* miscued miscuing
MSK Moscow *city*
MSK mosque *temple*
MSK moussaka *food*
MSK musk *odor*
MSK muskie (or) musky *fish* muskies
MSK musky *odorous* muskier muskiest
MSKD masked *covered*

MSKD mosquito *insect* mosquitoes
MSKD muscadet *wine*
MSKDM mastectomy *breast surgery* mastectomies
MSKDN muscadine *grape*
MSKDR mosquito *insect* mosquitoes
MSKG muskeg *bog*
MSKL mescal *cactus*
MSKLCHR musculature *muscles*
MSKLDR emasculator *weakener*
MSKLKLSHN miscalculation *wrong figures*
MSKLKLT miscalculate *figure wrongly* miscalculated miscalculating
MSKLKYLSHN miscalculation *wrong figures*
MSKLKYLT miscalculate *figure wrongly* miscalculated miscalculating
MSKLN masculine *male*
MSKLN mescaline *drug*
MSKLND masculinity *maleness*
MSKLNJ muskellunge *fish* muskellunge
MSKLNT masculinity *maleness*
MSKLNZ masculinize *make male* masculinized masculinizing (Br) masculinise
MSKLNZSHN masculinization *male* (Br) masculinisation
MSKLQLSHN miscalculation *wrong figures*
MSKLQLT miscalculate *figure wrongly* miscalculated miscalculating
MSKLR muscular *husky, strong*

Letters aren't doubled for single sounds: to find alley use **L** not **LL**. Use **Y** and **W** as hard sounds only: to find yellow use **YL**. (Br)=British spelling or usage. * See dictionary.

MSKLRD muscularity *strength*

MSKLRDSTRF muscular dystrophy *disease*

MSKLRL muscularly *strength*

MSKLRT muscularity *strength*

MSKLSHN emasculation *weakness*

MSKLT emasculate *weaken* emasculated emasculating

MSKLTR emasculator *weakener*

MSKLTR musculature *muscles*

MSKLTYR musculature *muscles*

MSKMLN muskmelon *fruit*

MSKMNKSHN miscommunication *unclear speech*

MSKMYNKSHN miscommunication *unclear speech*

MSKNCV misconceive *misunderstand* misconceived misconceiving

MSKNDK misconduct *wrongdoing*

MSKNDKT misconduct *wrongdoing*

MSKNGTP masking tape *adhesive*

MSKNSPSHN misconception *misunderstanding*

MSKNSTR misconstrue *misunderstand* misconstrued misconstruing

MSKNSTRKSHN misconstruction *badly made*

MSKNSV misconceive *misunderstand* misconceived misconceiving

MSKNT miscount *wrong number*

MSKNTP masking tape *adhesive*

MSKR mascara *makeup*

MSKR masker *cover*

MSKR massacre *kill* massacred massacring

MSKR miscarry *expel a fetus, fail* miscarried miscarrying miscarries

MSKR muskier *odor*

MSKRD masquerade *disguise* masqueraded masquerading

MSKRDR masquerader *disguiser*

MSKRJ miscarriage *failure, expulsion*

MSKRNT miscreant *unbelieving*

MSKRP mesocarp *middle layer*

MSKRPN mascarpone *cheese*

MSKRR massacrer *killer*

MSKRT muskrat *animal* muskrat (or) muskrats

MSKRTR masquerader *disguiser*

MSKRYNT miscreant *unbelieving*

MSKSDK masochistic *pain loving*

MSKSDKL masochistically *pain loving*

MSKST masochist *pain lover*

MSKST miscast *role*

MSKST muskiest *odor*

MSKSTK masochistic *pain loving*

MSKSTKL masochistically *pain loving*

MSKSTN M-16 *weapon*

MSKT mascot *symbol*

MSKT masked *covered*

MSKT mesquite *plant, charcoal*

MSKT mess kit *food*

MSKT miscount *wrong number*

MSKT mosquito *insect* mosquitoes

MSKT muscat *grape*

MSKT musket *gun*

MSKTL muscatel *wine*

MSKTM mastectomy *breast surgery* mastectomies

MSKTR mosquito *insect* mosquitoes

MSKTR musketeer *soldier*

MSKTR musketry *guns*

MSKVT Muscovite *Moscow native*

MSKVT muscovite *mineral*

MSKWSH musquash *rodent*

MSKWT misquote *repeat wrongly* misquoted misquoting

MSKWTSHN misquotation *repeat wrongly*

MSKY miscue *mistake* miscued miscuing

MSKYLCHR musculature *muscles*

MSKYLDR emasculator *weakener*

MSKYLN masculine *male*

MSKYLND masculinity *maleness*

MSKYLNT masculinity *maleness*

MSKYLNZ masculinize *make male* masculinized masculinizing (Br) masculinise

MSKYLNZSHN masculinization *male* (Br) masculinisation

MSKYLR muscular *husky, strong*

MSKYLRD muscularity *strength*

MSKYLRDSTRF muscular dystrophy *disease*

MSKYLRL muscularly *strength*

MSKYLRT muscularity *strength*

MSKYLSHN emasculation *weakness*

MSKYLT emasculate *weaken* emasculated emasculating

MSKYLTR emasculator *weakener*

Use letters that best describe the sounds you hear and omit the vowels. Use **S** or **K** instead of **C**: to find circle use **SRKL**. Use **J** to find joy, **JM** to find gem and **G** to find go.

MSKYLTR musculature *muscles*
MSKYLTYR musculature *muscles*
MSKYR muskier *odor*
MSKYST muskiest *odor*
MSKZM masochism *pleasure in pain*
MSL mausolea (pl) *tomb* mausoleum
MSL mesial (adj) *middle* mesially (adv)
MSL messily *dirty*
MSL micelle *molecule*
MSL misally *mismatch* misallied misallying misallies
MSL mislay *misplace* mislaid mislaying
MSL missal *book*
MSL missile *dart, weapon*
MSL moistly *damply*
MSL mostly *more than half*
MSL mousily *timid, grayish brown*
MSL muesli *cereal*
MSL muscle *(n) strength (v) push* muscled muscling
MSL muscle *(n) sinew*
MSL mussel *sea animal*
MSL mycelia (pl) *fungus* mycelium
MSLBL mislabel *wrong name*
MSLBN muscle-bound *rigid*
MSLBND muscle-bound *rigid*
MSLD mislead *deceive* misled misleading
MSLD muscled *strong, forced*
MSLF myself *of me*
MSLJ mucilage *gum*
MSLJNS mucilaginous *gummy*
MSLM mausoleum *tomb* mausoleums (or) mausolea
MSLM Muslim *Islamic*
MSLM mycelium *fungus* mycelia
MSLN messaline *silk fabric*
MSLN misalign *mismatch*

MSLN miscellanea *collection*
MSLN miscellany *writings* miscellanies
MSLN mousseline *cotton fabric*
MSLN muslin *fabric*
MSLNMNT misalignment *mismatch*
MSLNS misalliance *mismatch*
MSLNS miscellaneous *various*
MSLNTS misalliance *mismatch*
MSLNY miscellanea *collection*
MSLNYS miscellaneous *various*
MSLR micellar *molecule*
MSLT mistletoe *plant*
MSLTHK Mesolithic *geologic age*
MSLY mausolea (pl) *tomb* mausoleum
MSLY mycelia (pl) *fungus* mycelium
MSLYM mausoleum *tomb* mausoleums (or) mausolea
MSLYM mycelium *fungus* mycelia
MSLYNS misalliance *mismatch*
MSLYNTS misalliance *mismatch*
MSM misaim *bad shot*
MSMCH mismatch *poor pairing* mismatches
MSMNJ mismanage *direct badly* mismanaged mismanaging
MSMNJMNT mismanagement *bad direction*
MSMNT amassment *gathering*
MSMPL misemploy *use wrongly*
MSMR mesomere *middle part*
MSMRF mesomorph *body type*

MSMRKT mass-market *retail outlets*
MSMT messmate *partner*
MSN Mason *fraternal organization*
MSN mason *stone worker*
MSN meson *particle*
MSN missing *absent*
MSN moisten *dampen*
MSN myosin *muscle*
MSND missend *send wrongly* missent missending
MSNDRSTD misunderstood *(v-past) misunderstand*
MSNDRSTN misunderstand *interpret wrongly* misunderstood misunderstanding
MSNDRSTND misunderstand *interpret wrongly* misunderstood misunderstanding
MSNDRSTNDN misunderstanding *wrong interpretation*
MSNDRSTNDNG misunderstanding *wrong interpretation*
MSNFRM misinform *tell badly*
MSNFRMD misinformed *wrong knowledge*
MSNFRMSHN misinformation *untruth*
MSNG missing *absent*
MSNJR messenger *dispatch bearer*
MSNK Masonic *of Masons*
MSNK mesonic *particle*
MSNK messianic *crusading*
MSNKM mesenchyme *cells*
MSNM misname *miscall* misnamed misnaming
MSNMR misnomer *wrong name*
MSNN Mycenaean *of Mycenae*
MSNR masonry *stonework* masonries
MSNS messiness *dirt*
MSNS moistness *dampness*

Letters aren't doubled for single sounds: to find alley use **L** not **LL**. Use **Y** and **W** as hard sounds only: to find yellow use **YL**. (Br)=British spelling or usage. * See dictionary.

MSNS mousiness *timid, grayish brown*

MSNT maisonette *house*

MSNT Masonite *(trademark) fiberboard*

MSNT mustn't *(contr) must not*

MSNTHRP misanthrope *skeptic*

MSNTHRP misanthropy *skepticism*

MSNTHRPK misanthropic *skeptical*

MSNTHRPKL misanthropically *skeptically*

MSNTR mesentery *membrane* mesenteries

MSNTRN mesenteron *food canal*

MSNTRPRT misinterpret *understand wrongly*

MSNTRPRTSHN misinterpretation *understand wrongly*

MSNYN Mycenaean *of Mycenae*

MSNZM messianism *belief in savior*

MSPK misspeak *speak badly* misspoke misspeaking misspoken

MSPL misapply *apply badly* misapplied misapplying misapplies

MSPL misplay *play badly*

MSPL misspell *spell badly*

MSPLJK mesopelagic *depth*

MSPLKSHN misapplication *apply badly*

MSPLN misspelling *incorrect spelling*

MSPLNG misspelling *incorrect spelling*

MSPLS misplace *mislay* misplaced misplacing

MSPLSMNT misplacement *mislay*

MSPN misspend *waste* misspent misspending

MSPND misspend *waste* misspent misspending

MSPRDS mass-produce *machinery*

MSPRDYS mass-produce *machinery*

MSPRHN misapprehend *misunderstand*

MSPRHND misapprehend *misunderstand*

MSPRHNSHN misapprehension *misunderstanding*

MSPRNNCSHN mispronunciation *say wrongly*

MSPRNNCYSHN mispronunciation *say wrongly*

MSPRNNS mispronounce *say wrongly* mispronounced mispronouncing

MSPRNNSSHN mispronunciation *say wrongly*

MSPRNNSYSHN mispronunciation *say wrongly*

MSPRNNTCSHN mispronunciation *say wrongly*

MSPRNNTCYSHN mispronunciation *say wrongly*

MSPRNNTS mispronounce *say wrongly* mispronounced mispronouncing

MSPRNNTSSHN mispronunciation *say wrongly*

MSPRNNTSYSHN mispronunciation *say wrongly*

MSPRNT misprint *print badly*

MSPRPRSHN misappropriation *theft*

MSPRPRT misappropriate *steal* misappropriated misappropriating

MSPRPRYSHN misappropriation *theft*

MSPRPRYT misappropriate *steal* misappropriated misappropriating

MSPRSHN misprision *misunderstanding*

MSPRZHN misprision *misunderstanding*

MSPZ mesopause *atmosphere*

MSQ miscue *mistake* miscued miscuing

MSQLCHR musculature *muscles*

MSQLDR emasculator *weakener*

MSQLN masculine *male*

MSQLND masculinity *maleness*

MSQLNT masculinity *maleness*

MSQLNZ masculinize *make male* masculinized masculinizing (Br) masculinise

MSQLNZSHN masculinization *male* (Br) masculinisation

MSQLR muscular *husky, strong*

MSQLRD muscularity *strength*

MSQLRDSTRF muscular dystrophy *disease*

MSQLRL muscularly *strength*

MSQLRT muscularity *strength*

MSQLSHN emasculation *weakness*

MSQLT emasculate *weaken* emasculated emasculating

MSQLTR emasculator *weakener*

MSQLTR musculature *muscles*

MSQLTYR musculature *muscles*

MSQSH musquash *rodent*

MSQT misquote *repeat wrongly* misquoted misquoting

Use letters that best describe the sounds you hear and omit the vowels. Use **S** or **K** instead of **C**: to find circle use **SRKL**. Use **J** to find joy, **JM** to find gem and **G** to find go.

MSQTSHN misquotation *repeat wrongly*
MSR amasser *gatherer*
MSR emissary *agent* emissaries
MSR masseur *massager (m)*
MSR messier *dirty*
MSR mossier *with moss*
MSR mouser *cat*
MSR mousier *timid, grayish brown*
MSR mussier *messy*
MSRD misread *misinterpret* misread misreading
MSRDR macerator *waste away*
MSRL misrule *lawlessness* misruled misruling
MSRPRZNT misrepresent *deceive*
MSRPRZNTSHN misrepresentation *deception*
MSRSHN maceration *wasting*
MSRT macerate *waste away* macerated macerating
MSRT miswrite *write badly* miswrote miswriting miswritten
MSRTN miswritten *write badly*
MSRTR macerator *waste away*
MSRZ masseuse *massager (f)*
MSS emesis *vomit* emeses
MSS masseuse *massager (f)*
MSS meiosis *reduction*
MSS missus (or) missis *wife (Mrs.)*
MSS misuse *(n) poor usage*
MSS tmesis *word*
MSSDMT misestimate *guess wrongly* misestimated misestimating
MSSFR mesosphere *atmosphere*
MSSG massasauga *snake*
MSSH massage *rub* massaged massaging
MSSHN emaciation *thinness*

MSSHP misshape *twisted*
MSSHPN misshapen *twisted*
MSSHR massager *one who rubs*
MSSJ misusage *use badly*
MSSKLN mesocyclone *tornado*
MSSM mesosome *bacteria*
MSSP Mississippi *US State, river*
MSSR mosasaur *dinosaur*
MSST messiest *dirty*
MSST mossiest *with moss*
MSST mousiest *timid, grayish brown*
MSST mussiest *messy*
MSSTMT misestimate *guess wrongly* misestimated misestimating
MST amassed *gathered*
MST emaciate *make thin* emaciated emaciating
MST Maoist *follower of Mao*
MST masked *covered*
MST mast *ship*
MST missed *(v-past) miss*
MST mist *spray*
MST misty *blurry* mistier mistiest
MST moist *damp*
MST most *more than half*
MST must *(v) have to (n) essential, mold, grapes*
MST musty *stale* mustier mustiest
MSTC must-see *good viewing*
MSTD masted *with mast(s)*
MSTD masthead *sailboat, newspaper*
MSTD mastoid *bone*
MSTDK mastitic *breast infection*
MSTDN mastodon *extinct mammal*
MSTDS mastitis *breast infection*
MSTF mastiff *dog*
MSTF mystify *bewilder* mystified mystifying mystifies
MSTFGS mycetophagous

fungus
MSTFKSHN mystification *occult*
MSTFNGL mystifyingly *bewildering*
MSTFNL mystifyingly *bewildering*
MSTFR mystifier *bewilder*
MSTFYNGL mystifyingly *bewildering*
MSTFYNL mystifyingly *bewildering*
MSTFYR mystifier *bewilder*
MSTGFRN mastigophoran *protozoa*
MSTGG mystagogue *cultist*
MSTGG mystagogy *cults*
MSTGJ mystagogy *cults*
MSTHD masthead *sailboat, newspaper*
MSTHL mesothelia (pl) *lining* mesothelium
MSTHLM mesothelium *lining* mesothelia
MSTHLY mesothelia (pl) *lining* mesothelium
MSTHLYM mesothelium *lining* mesothelia
MSTHN myasthenia *muscles*
MSTHNY myasthenia *muscles*
MSTHRKS mesothorax *middle segment*
MSTHRX mesothorax *middle segment*
MSTK mastic *resin*
MSTK mistake *error* mistook mistaking mistaken
MSTK mystic *occult*
MSTK mystique *mystery*
MSTKDM mastectomy *breast surgery* mastectomies
MSTKDR masticator *chew*
MSTKL mystical (adj) *occult* mystically (adv)
MSTKN mistaken *wrong*
MSTKNL mistakenly *wrongly*
MSTKR mistaker *confused one*

Letters aren't doubled for single sounds: to find alley use **L** not **LL**. Use **Y** and **W** as hard sounds only: to find yellow use **YL**. (Br)=British spelling or usage. * See dictionary.

MSTKSHN mastication *chewing*

MSTKT masticate *chew* masticated masticating

MSTKTM mastectomy *breast surgery* mastectomies

MSTKTR masticator *chew*

MSTKTR masticatory *(adj) chewing (n) substance* masticatories

MSTL mistily *blurry*

MSTL moistly *damply*

MSTL mostly *more than half*

MSTL mustily *stale*

MSTM mistime *wrong time* mistimed mistiming

MSTM mycetoma *tumor* mycetomas (or) mycetomata

MSTMD mistimed *wrong time*

MSTMD mycetomata (pl) *tumor* mycetoma

MSTMT mycetomata (pl) *tumor* mycetoma

MSTNG Mao Tse-tung *Chinese leader*

MSTNG mustang *horse*

MSTNS mistiness *blurriness*

MSTNS moistness *dampness*

MSTNS mustiness *staleness*

MSTP misstep *blunder* misstepped misstepping

MSTR maestro *conductor, teacher* maestros (or) maestri

MSTR master *(n) teacher, ruler, model (v) overcome (adj) principal, skilled**

MSTR mastery *skill, command*

MSTR mister *spray*

MSTR Mister (or) Mr. *title* Messrs

MSTR mistier *blurry*

MSTR moisture *dampness*

MSTR muster *(v) gather (n) sample, inspection*

MSTR mustier *stale*

MSTR mystery *puzzle* mysteries

MSTRBDR masturbator *erotic stimulation*

MSTRBSHN masturbation *erotic stimulation*

MSTRBT masturbate *self-stimulate* masturbated masturbating

MSTRBTR masturbator *erotic stimulation*

MSTRBTR masturbatory *erotic stimulation*

MSTRD mustard *herb*

MSTRDM Amsterdam *city*

MSTRFL masterful (adj) *skilled* masterfully (adv)

MSTRL masterly *skilled*

MSTRL mistral *wind*

MSTRL mistrial *law*

MSTRLNS masterliness *skill*

MSTRMN mastermind *(v) plan (n) planner*

MSTRMND mastermind *(v) plan (n) planner*

MSTRP mousetrap *device*

MSTRPS masterpiece *great work*

MSTRS mistress *lady* mistresses

MSTRS mysterious *puzzling*

MSTRSL mysteriously *puzzling*

MSTRST mistrust *doubt*

MSTRSTRK masterstroke *great move*

MSTRT mistreat *abuse*

MSTRTMNT mistreatment *abuse*

MSTRWRK masterwork *great achievement*

MSTRYL mistrial *law*

MSTRYS mysterious *puzzling*

MSTRYSL mysteriously *puzzling*

MSTRZ moisturize *dampen* moisturized moisturizing (Br) moisturise

MSTRZR moisturizer *dampen* (Br) moisturiser

MSTS maestoso *majestic*

MSTS must-see *good*

viewing

MSTS myositis *soreness*

MSTSH mustache *lip hair*

MSTSH mustachio *large mustache* mustachios

MSTSHD mustached *lip hair*

MSTSHD mustachioed *large mustache*

MSTSHT mustached *lip hair*

MSTSHY mustachio *large mustache* mustachios

MSTSHYD mustachioed *large mustache*

MSTST mistiest *blurry*

MSTST mustiest *stale*

MSTSZM mysticism *occult belief*

MSTT misstate *speak in error* misstated misstating

MSTTK mastitic *breast infection*

MSTTMNT misstatement *error*

MSTTS mastitis *breast infection*

MSTYR mistier *blurry*

MSTYR mustier *stale*

MSTYST mistiest *blurry*

MSTYST mustiest *stale*

MSTZ maestoso *majestic*

MSTZ mestiza (f) *mixed race* mestizas

MSTZ mestizo (m) *mixed race* mestizos

MSTZN mycetozoan *slime mold*

MSTZWN mycetozoan *slime mold*

MSV massive *huge*

MSV missive *letter*

MSV misvalue *estimate wrongly* misvalued misvaluing

MSVL massively *hugely*

MSVL misvalue *estimate wrongly* misvalued misvaluing

MSVLY misvalue *estimate wrongly* misvalued misvaluing

MSVNS massiveness

Use letters that best describe the sounds you hear and omit the vowels. Use **S** or **K** instead of **C**: to find circle use **SRKL**. Use **J** to find joy, **JM** to find gem and **G** to find go.

hugeness
MSVR mess over *abuse*
MSVY misvalue *estimate wrongly* misvalued misvaluing
MSWJ messuage *premise*
MSWR masseur *massager (m)*
MSXTN M-16 *weapon*
MSY messiah *leader*
MSY Monsieur *title*
MSYL mesial (adj) *middle* mesially (adv)
MSYNK messianic *crusading*
MSYNZM messianism *belief in savior*
MSYR messier *dirty*
MSYR Monsieur *title*
MSYR mossier *with moss*
MSYR mousier *timid, grayish brown*
MSYR mussier *messy*
MSYS misuse (n) *poor usage*
MSYSHN emaciation *thinness*
MSYSJ misusage *use badly*
MSYST messiest *dirty*
MSYST mossiest *with moss*
MSYST mousiest *timid, grayish brown*
MSYST mussiest *messy*
MSYT emaciate *make thin* emaciated emaciating
MSYZ misuse (v) *use badly* misused misusing
MSYZR misuser *use badly*
MSZ masseuse *massager (f)*
MSZ missus (or) missis *wife (Mrs.)*
MSZ misuse (v) *use badly* misused misusing
MSZH massage *rub* massaged massaging
MSZHR massager *one who rubs*
MSZK Mesozoic *geologic era*
MSZR misuser *use badly*
MSZR mosasaur *dinosaur*
MSZWK Mesozoic *geologic era*
MT amity *friendship* amities
MT amount *quantity*

MT emit *give off* emitted emitting
MT emote *overact* emoted emoting
MT empty (v) *drain, discharge* emptied emptying empties
MT empty (adj) *void* emptier emptiest
MT mat (v) *pack down, tangle* matted matting
MT mat (n) *floor pad, fabric*
MT mate (v) *couple* mated mating
MT mate (n) *associate*
MT maté (or) mate *tree*
MT matey (Br) *friendly*
MT matte (adj) *dull* (n) *metal, film*
MT meat *flesh*
MT meaty *like flesh* meatier meatiest
MT media *voiced stop, muscle* mediae
MT media *news* medias
MT media (pl) *middle, material* medium
MT meet *come upon* met meeting
MT mete *measure* meted meting
MT métier (or) metier *work*
MT middy *blouse, sailor* middies
MT midi *mid-calf*
MT might (n) *strength* (v-past) *may*
MT mighty *powerful* mightier mightiest
MT mite *insect*
MT mitt *glove*
MT moat *ditch*
MT moiety *half* moieties
MT moot *debatable*
MT mot *joke* mots
MT mote *speck*
MT motte *hill*
MT motto *slogan* mottoes
MT mount (n) *mountain, support, horse* (v) *climb, frame, launch**
MT Mounty *police* Mounties

MT muddy *dirty* muddier muddiest
MT mute (v) *silence, melt, defecate* muted muting
MT mute (adj) *silent* muter mutest
MT mute (n) *silent one, muffler*
MT mutt *dog*
MT omit *leave out* omitted omitting
MTBL imitable *copied*
MTBL immutable (adj) *no change* immutably (adv)
MTBL meatball *food*
MTBL mutable (adj) *able to change* mutably (adv)
MTBLD immutability *no change*
MTBLD mutability *change*
MTBLK metabolic *cell chemistry*
MTBLKL metabolically *cell chemistry*
MTBLT immutability *no change*
MTBLT mutability *change*
MTBLZ metabolize *process food* metabolized metabolizing
MTBLZBL metabolizable *cell chemistry*
MTBLZM metabolism *cell chemistry*
MTBNGK mountebank *pretender*
MTBNK mountebank *pretender*
MTD ommatidia (pl) *eye* ommatidium
MTDK amitotic *simple cell division*
MTDKL amitotically *simple cell division*
MTDM ommatidium *eye* ommatidia
MTDR imitator *copier*
MTDR matador *bullfighter*
MTDR mediator *judge*
MTDV imitative *copy*
MTDVL imitatively *copy*
MTDVNS imitativeness *copy*

Letters aren't doubled for single sounds: to find alley use **L** not **LL**. Use **Y** and **W** as hard sounds only: to find yellow use **YL**. (Br)=British spelling or usage. * See dictionary.

MTDY ommatidia (pl) *eye*
ommatidium

MTDYM ommatidium *eye*
ommatidia

MTF modify *limit, change*
modified modifying
modifies

MTF motif *theme*

MTFK motific *theme*

MTFKSHN modification
change

MTFR metaphor *symbol*

MTFR modifier *word*

MTFRK metaphoric (or)
metaphorical (adj)
symbolic metaphorically
(adv)

MTFRKL metaphorically
(adv) *symbolic* metaphoric
(or) metaphorical (adj)

MTFRZ metaphrase
translation

MTFYR modifier *word*

MTFZ metaphase *growth*

MTFZKL metaphysical (adj)
supernatural
metaphysically (adv)

MTFZKS metaphysics
philosophy

MTFZSHN metaphysician
philosopher

MTFZX metaphysics
philosophy

MTGBL immitigable (adj) *no
relief* immitagably (adv)

MTGDR mitigator *reliever*

MTGDV mitigative *relief*

MTGNSS metagenesis *sex
alternation*

MTGSHN mitigation *relief*

MTGT mitigate *relieve*
mitigated mitigating

MTGTR mitigator *reliever*

MTGTR mitigatory *relieving*

MTGTV mitigative *relief*

MTH math *arithmetic*

MTH moth *insect* moths

MTH mothy *with moths*

MTH mouth *(n) opening (v)
talk* mouths

MTH mouthy *loud* mouthier
mouthiest

MTH myth *legend, fantasy*

MTH mythoi (pl) *legend*
mythos

MTHBL mothball *pesticide*

MTHD meathead *fool*

MTHD method *system*

MTHD mouthed *of the mouth*

MTHDD empty-headed
stupid

MTHDKL methodical (adj)
systematic methodically
(adv)

MTHDKLNS
methodicalness
systematic

MTHDLG methodology
procedures methodologies

MTHDLJ methodology
procedures methodologies

MTHDLJKL methodological
(adj) *ordered*
methodologically (adv)

MTHDLJST methodologist
procedures

MTHDN methadone *drug*

MTHDRN Methedrine
(trademark) drug

MTHDST Methodist *religion*

MTHDZ methodize *order*
methodized methodizing
(Br) methodise

MTHFL mouthful *food, speech*

MTHK mythic (or) mythical
(adj) *legendary* mythically
(adv)

MTHKL mythical (or) mythic
(adj) *legendary* mythically
(adv)

MTHKWLN methaqualone
sedative

MTHL methyl *chemical*

MTHLD Merthiolate
(trademark) antiseptic

MTHLG mythology *legends*
mythologies

MTHLJ mythology *legends*
mythologies

MTHLJKL mythological
(adj) *legendary*
mythologically (adv)

MTHLJR mythologer *create
legends*

MTHLJST mythologist
create legends

MTHLJZ mythologize *create
legends* mythologized
mythologizing

MTHLJZR mythologizer
create legends

MTHLK mothlike *like a moth*

MTHLKHL methyl alcohol
methanol

MTHLKWLN methaqualone
sedative

MTHLLKHL methyl alcohol
methanol

MTHLMN methylamine *gas*

MTHLN methylene *chemical*

MTHLQLN methaqualone
sedative

MTHLT Merthiolate
(trademark) antiseptic

MTHLT methylate *add
methyl* methylated
methylating

MTHLZNTHN
methylxanthine *chemical*

MTHMDKL mathematical
(adj) *arithmetic*
mathematically (adv)

MTHMDKS mathematics
arithmetic

MTHMDX mathematics
arithmetic

MTHMFDMN
methamphetamine *drug*

MTHMFTMN
methamphetamine *drug*

MTHMN mythomania *liar*

MTHMNK mythomaniac *liar*

MTHMNY mythomania *liar*

MTHMNYK mythomaniac
liar

MTHMTKL mathematical
(adj) *arithmetic*
mathematically (adv)

MTHMTKS mathematics
arithmetic

MTHMTSHN mathematician
arithmetic

MTHMTX mathematics
arithmetic

MTHMTZ mathematize
make arithmetic

Use letters that best describe the sounds you hear and omit the vowels. Use **S** or **K**
instead of **C**: to find circle use **SRKL**. Use **J** to find joy, **JM** to find gem and **G** to find go.

mathematized
mathematizing
MTHN methane *gas*
MTHN mouthing *talk or speech*
MTHNDD empty-handed *nothing to show*
MTHNFDMN methamphetamine *drug*
MTHNFTMN methamphetamine *drug*
MTHNG mouthing *talk or speech*
MTHNL methanol *alcohol*
MTHP mythopoeia *create myths*
MTHPK mythopoeic *create myths*
MTHPRF mothproof *pesticide*
MTHPRFR mothproofer *pesticide*
MTHPRT mouthpart *attachment*
MTHPS mouthpiece *device, spokesman*
MTHPY mythopoeia *create myths*
MTHPYK mythopoeic *create myths*
MTHQLN methaqualone *sedative*
MTHR mother *birth*
MTHR mouther *talker*
MTHR mouthier *talkative*
MTHRBRD motherboard *computer*
MTHRHD motherhood *give birth*
MTHRL motherly *caring*
MTHRLD mother lode *ore*
MTHRLN motherland *country*
MTHRLND motherland *country*
MTHRLNS motherliness *care*
MTHRNCHR Mother Nature *natural laws*
MTHRNL mother-in-law *relative* mothers-in-law
MTHRNTR Mother Nature

natural laws
MTHRTNG mother tongue *language*
MTHRVPRL mother-of-pearl *shell*
MTHRZNL mothers-in-law (pl) *relatives* mother-in-law
MTHS maths (*Br*) *arithmetic*
MTHS mythos *mythology* mythoi
MTHSL Methuselah *old man*
MTHST amethyst *gem*
MTHST mouthiest *talkative*
MTHSTN amethystine *gem*
MTHT mouthed *of the mouth*
MTHTMTH mouth-to-mouth *rescue*
MTHTN moth-eaten *with holes, outmoded*
MTHWDRN mouthwatering *appealing*
MTHWDRNG mouthwatering *appealing*
MTHWSH mouthwash *antiseptic* mouthwashes
MTHWTRN mouthwatering *appealing*
MTHWTRNG mouthwatering *appealing*
MTHYLD Merthiolate (*trademark*) *antiseptic*
MTHYLT Merthiolate (*trademark*) *antiseptic*
MTHYR mouthier *talkative*
MTHYST mouthiest *talkative*
MTHZL Methuselah *old man*
MTJNSS metagenesis *sex alternation*
MTK emetic *vomit*
MTK mattock *tool*
MTK medic *corpsman, herb*
MTK medico *physician* medicos
MTK meiotic *reduction*
MTKBL medicable *curable*
MTKD medicaid (*often capitalized*) *insurance*
MTKL emetically *vomit*
MTKL medical (adj) *doctor* medically (adv)
MTKL meiotically *reduction*

MTKLS meticulous *careful*
MTKLSL meticulously *carefully*
MTKLSNS meticulousness *extreme care*
MTKM modicum *small portion*
MTKNDR mitochondria (pl) *cell* mitochondrion
MTKNDRN mitochondrion *cell* mitochondria
MTKNDRY mitochondria (pl) *cell* mitochondrion
MTKNDRYN mitochondrion *cell* mitochondria
MTKR medicare (*often capitalized*) *insurance*
MTKR mediocre *ordinary*
MTKRD mediocrity *ordinariness* mediocrities
MTKRMDK metachromatic *stain*
MTKRMTK metachromatic *stain*
MTKRPL metacarpal *hand or foot*
MTKRPS metacarpus *hand or foot*
MTKRS motocross *race*
MTKRT mediocrity *ordinariness* mediocrities
MTKS meat-ax *cleaver*
MTKSHN medication *substance*
MTKT medicate *give medicine* medicated medicating
MTKYLS meticulous *careful*
MTKYLSL meticulously *carefully*
MTKYLSNS meticulousness *extreme care*
MTL emptily *void*
MTL immotile *not moving*
MTL medal *award*
MTL meddle *interfere* meddled meddling
MTL medial (adj) *average* medially (adv)
MTL metal *iron, gold, etc.*
MTL mettle *courage*

MTL middle *center*
MTL mightily *powerfully*
MTL model *shape, fashion*
modeled (or) modelled
modeling (or) modelling
MTL motel *inn*
MTL motile *moving*
MTL motley *variety*
MTL mottle *spot* mottled
mottling
MTL muddily *wet dirt*
MTL muddle *confuse*
muddled muddling
MTL mutual (adj) *shared*
mutually (adv)
MTLBR middlebrow *slightly
educated*
MTLD metalloid *like metal*
MTLD motility *movement*
MTLD mutuality *sharing*
MTLDD muddle-headed
confused
MTLDR mutilator *destroyer,
cutter*
MTLF meat loaf *food*
MTLFN metallophone *music*
MTLFRS metalliferous *with
metal*
MTLGRN middle ground
standpoint
MTLGRND middle ground
standpoint
MTLHDD muddle-headed
confused
MTLJ middle age *age 40-60*
MTLJD middle-aged *age 40-
60*
MTLJS Middle Ages *500-
1500 AD*
MTLJZ Middle Ages *500-
1500 AD*
MTLK metallic *hard, harsh*
MTLKL metallically *hard,
harsh*
MTLKLS middle-class (adj)
neither rich nor poor
middle class (n)
MTLMN middleman *dealer*
middlemen
MTLNG middling *halfway*
MTLNGGWSDK
metalinguistic *language*

MTLNGGWSTK
metalinguistic *language*
MTLNGWSDK
metalinguistic *language*
MTLNGWSTK
metalinguistic *language*
MTLR meddler *interferer*
MTLR middle ear *cavity*
MTLR middler *student*
MTLR modeler *shaper*
MTLR mottler *spot*
MTLRG metallurgy *metal
science*
MTLRJ metallurgy *metal
science*
MTLRJKL metallurgical
(adj) *metal science*
metallurgically (adv)
MTLRJST metallurgist *metal
scientist*
MTLS middle C *music*
MTLSHN mutilation
destruction
MTLSKL middle school
grades 5-8 or 6-8
MTLSM meddlesome
interfering
MTLSM mettlesome *spirited*
MTLST medalist (or)
medallist *award winner*
MTLST Middle East *region*
MTLT motility *movement*
MTLT mutilate *cut up*
mutilated mutilating
mutilation
MTLT mutuality *sharing*
MTLTHR muddle through
achieve slowly
MTLTR mutilator *destroyer,
cutter*
MTLVNR Medal of Honor
award
MTLVTHRD middle-of-the-
road *neutral*
MTLWR metalware *utensils*
MTLWRK metalwork *art
object*
MTLWRKNG metalworking
shaping metal
MTLWST Middle West
region
MTLWT middleweight *160*

or *165 pounds*
MTLZ metallize *add metal*
metallized metallizing
MTLZ mutualize *share*
mutualized mutualizing
MTLZM mutualism *sharing*
MTM medium (adj) *average*
(n) *environment*
MTM myotome *muscle*
MTMKNL Mount McKinley
mountain
MTMPSKSS
metempsychosis
reincarnation
MTMR metamere *segment*
MTMRFK metamorphic
changed
MTMRFKL metamorphically
changed
MTMRFS metamorphose
change metamorphosed
metamorphosing
MTMRFSS metamorphosis
change metamorphoses
MTMRFZ metamorphose
change metamorphosed
metamorphosing
MTMRFZM metamorphism
change
MTMRK metameric
segmented
MTMS mittimus *warrant*
MTMSKSS
metempsychosis
reincarnation
MTN amyotonia *loss of
muscle tone*
MTN emetine *vomiting*
MTN matin *prayer*
MTN matinee *afternoon
movie*
MTN matting *pad, tangle*
MTN median *center*
MTN meeting *assembly,
connection*
MTN midtown *city*
MTN mitten *glove*
MTN mountain *huge hill*
MTN mounting *mound*
MTN mouton *fur*
MTN mutiny *rebellion*
mutinies

Use letters that best describe the sounds you hear and omit the vowels. Use **S** or **K**
instead of **C**: to find circle use **SRKL**. Use **J** to find joy, **JM** to find gem and **G** to find go.

MTN mutton *meat*
MTN myotonia *spasm*
MTN umpteen *many*
MTNCHPS muttonchops *whiskers*
MTNFR metanephroi (pl) *kidney* metanephros
MTNFRS metanephros *kidney* metanephroi
MTNFSH muttonfish *snapper*
MTNG madding *vexing*
MTNG matting *pad, tangle*
MTNG meeting *assembly, connection*
MTNG mounting *mound*
MTNGHS meetinghouse *building*
MTNGT mountain goat *animal*
MTNHS meetinghouse *building*
MTNK myotonic *spasm*
MTNL matinal *early*
MTNLN mountain lion *animal*
MTNLYN mountain lion *animal*
MTNM metonym *figure of speech*
MTNM metonymy *figure of speech* metonymies
MTNMK metonymic *figure of speech*
MTNR mountaineer *climber*
MTNR mutineer *rebel*
MTNRN motoneuron *nerve*
MTNS emittance *energy*
MTNS emptiness *void*
MTNS immittance *electricity*
MTNS mateyness *(Br) friendship*
MTNS matins *prayer* (Br) mattins
MTNS meetinghouse *building*
MTNS mightiness *power*
MTNS mountainous *huge*
MTNS muddiness *wet dirt*
MTNS mutinous *rebellious*
MTNSD mountainside *huge hill*
MTNSFLN metencephalon

brain
MTNSH mountain ash *tree*
MTNSL mountainously *huge*
MTNSNS mountainousness *huge*
MTNSTTS Mountain States *region*
MTNT mediant *scale tone*
MTNT mutant *changed one*
MTNTH umpteenth *many*
MTNTP mountaintop *summit*
MTNTS emittance *energy*
MTNTS immittance *electricity*
MTNY amyotonia *loss of muscle tone*
MTNY myotonia *spasm*
MTNYRN motoneuron *nerve*
MTPKN meatpacking *food industry*
MTPKNG meatpacking *food industry*
MTQLS meticulous *careful*
MTQLSL meticulously *carefully*
MTQLSNS meticulousness *extreme care*
MTR amateur *not professional*
MTR amatory *loving*
MTR ammeter *ampere gauge*
MTR emitter *give off*
MTR emptier *void*
MTR immature *not ripe*
MTR madder *angry, crazy, herb, color*
MTR mater *mother*
MTR matter *subject, substance, care**
MTR mature *ripen, age* matured maturing
MTR meatier *fleshy, substantial*
MTR meteor *asteroid*
MTR meter *(n) measure, device (v) measure* (Br) metre
MTR metro *city* metros
MTR mightier *powerful*
MTR miter *(n) hat, joint (v) join*

(Br) mitre
MTR miter (or) mitre *joint*
MTR motor *engine*
MTR muddier *wet dirt*
MTR muter *silent*
MTR mutter *mumble*
MTR ohmmeter *ohm measurer*
MTRBK motorbike *vehicle*
MTRBKS miter box (or) mitre box *handsaw guide* miter boxes (or) mitre boxes
MTRBS motor bus *vehicle*
MTRBT motorboat *boat*
MTRBX miter box (or) mitre box *handsaw guide* miter boxes (or) mitre boxes
MTRCZ matrices (pl) *mold, math* matrix
MTRD immaturity *unripe*
MTRD maître d' (or) maitre d' *waiter* maître d's (or) maitre d's
MTRD maturity *ripeness*
MTRD meteoroid *comet*
MTRD moderato *tempo*
MTRDR made-to-order *custom made*
MTRDR moderator *speaker*
MTRDTL maître d'hotel *headwaiter* maîtres d'hotel
MTRHM motor home *mobile home*
MTRJ metrorrhagia *bleeding*
MTRJY metrorrhagia *bleeding*
MTRK amtrac (or) amtrack *vehicle*
MTRK Amtrak *railroad*
MTRK meteoric *fast*
MTRK metric (or) metrical *measure*
MTRKD motorcade *parade*
MTRKL metrical (or) metric (adj) *measurement* metrically (adv)
MTRKLNT matriculant *enrollee*
MTRKLSHN matriculation *enrollment*
MTRKLT matriculate *enroll*

Letters aren't doubled for single sounds: to find **alley** use **L** not **LL**. Use **Y** and **W** as hard sounds only: to find **yellow** use **YL**. (Br)=British spelling or usage. * See dictionary.

matriculated
matriculating
MTRKR motorcar *vehicle*
MTRKRS motocross *race*
MTRKRT motor court *motel*
MTRKS matrix *mold,*
material, array* matrices
(or) matrixes
MTRKSSTM metric system
measure
MTRKTN metric ton *measure*
MTRKYLNT matriculant
enrollee
MTRKYLSHN matriculation
enrollment
MTRKYLT matriculate *enroll*
matriculated
matriculating
MTRL immaterial
unimportant
MTRL immaturely *unripe*
MTRL material *(n) matter,*
cloth
MTRL material (adj) *physical*
materially (adv)
MTRL materially *physically*
MTRL materiel *equipment*
MTRL mitral *valve, joint*
MTRLG meteorology
weather
MTRLG metrology *measures*
MTRLJ meteorology *weather*
MTRLJ metrology *measures*
MTRLJK meteorologic (or)
meteorological (adj)
weather meteorologically
(adv)
MTRLJKL meteorological
(or) meteorologic (adj)
weather meteorologically
(adv)
MTRLJST meteorologist
weather forecaster
MTRLSDK materialistic
physical matter
MTRLST materialist *physical*
matter
MTRLSTK materialistic
physical matter
MTRLZ immaterialize
disappear immaterialized
immaterializing

(Br) immaterialise
MTRLZ materialize *appear*
materialized materializing
(Br) materialise
MTRLZM immaterialism *not*
physical
MTRLZM materialism
physical matter
MTRLZR materializer
sorcerer
(Br) materialiser
MTRLZSHN materialization
ghost
(Br) materialisation
MTRM midterm *exam*
MTRMD meter maid *parking*
tickets
MTRMN matrimony
marriage
MTRMN motorman *driver*
motormen
MTRMNL matrimonial (adj)
marriage matrimonially
(adv)
MTRMNYL matrimonial
(adj) *marriage*
matrimonially (adv)
MTRMTH motormouth *talk*
MTRN matron *woman*
MTRN modern *(adj) up-to-*
date (n) type, stylish one
MTRND maternity *motherly*
MTRNL maternal (adj)
mother maternally (adv)
MTRNL matronly *womanly*
MTRNM metronome *timing*
device
MTRNMK matronymic *name*
MTRNS modernize *update*
modernized modernizing
(Br) modernise
MTRNSDK modernistic *up-*
to-date
MTRNSSHN modernization
updating
(Br) modernisation
MTRNST modernist
philosopher
MTRNSTK modernistic *up-*
to-date
MTRNT maternity *motherly*
MTRNVNR matron of honor

wedding
(Br) matron of honour
MTRNZ modernize *update*
modernized modernizing
(Br) modernise
MTRNZM modernism
philosophy
MTRNZSHN modernization
updating
(Br) modernisation
MTRP ametropia *poor vision*
MTRPDLN amitriptyline
antidepressant
MTRPK ametropic *poor*
vision
MTRPL motor pool *vehicles*
MTRPLDN metropolitan *city*
MTRPLS metropolis *city*
MTRPLTN metropolitan *city*
MTRPTLN amitriptyline
antidepressant
MTRPY ametropia *poor*
vision
MTRQLNT matriculant
enrollee
MTRQLSHN matriculation
enrollment
MTRQLT matriculate *enroll*
matriculated
matriculating
MTRRJ metrorrhagia
bleeding
MTRRJY metrorrhagia
bleeding
MTRRK matriarch *female*
ruler
MTRRK matriarchy *female*
rule matriarchies
MTRRKL matriarchal *female*
ruler
MTRRSH metrorrhagia
bleeding
MTRRSHY metrorrhagia
bleeding
MTRRZH metrorrhagia
bleeding
MTRRZHY metrorrhagia
bleeding
MTRS mattress *bed*
mattresses
MTRSD matricide *murder of*
mother

Use letters that best describe the sounds you hear and omit the vowels. Use **S** or **K** instead of **C**: to find circle use **SRKL**. Use **J** to find joy, **JM** to find gem and **G** to find go.

MTRSH amateurish *incompetent*

MTRSH metrorrhagia *bleeding*

MTRSHL amateurishly *incompetently*

MTRSHN maturation *ripeness*

MTRSHN moderation *less intensity*

MTRSHNS amateurishness *incompetence*

MTRSHY metrorrhagia *bleeding*

MTRSKDR motor scooter *vehicle*

MTRSKL motorcycle *vehicle*

MTRSKLST motorcyclist *driver*

MTRSKTR motor scooter *vehicle*

MTRST motorist *driver*

MTRSZ matrices (pl) *mold, math* matrix

MTRSZ metricize *make metric* metricized metricizing

MTRT immaturity *unripe*

MTRT maturate *ripen* maturated maturating

MTRT maturity *ripeness*

MTRT meteorite *small asteroid*

MTRT moderate *(v)* preside, *lessen* moderated moderating

MTRT moderato *tempo*

MTRTL moderately *calm, ordinary*

MTRTNS moderateness *calmness, mediocrity*

MTRTR moderator *speaker*

MTRTRK motortruck *vehicle*

MTRVFK matter-of-fact *straightforward*

MTRVFKT matter-of-fact *straightforward*

MTRW motorway *road*

MTRX matrix *mold, material, array** matrices (or) matrixes

MTRYL immaterial

unimportant

MTRYL material *(n) matter, cloth*

MTRYL material (adj) *physical* materially (adv)

MTRYL materially *physically*

MTRYL materiel *equipment*

MTRYLSDK materialistic *physical matter*

MTRYLST materialist *physical matter*

MTRYLSTK materialistic *physical matter*

MTRYLZ immaterialize *disappear* immaterialized immaterializing

MTRYLZ materialize *appear* materialized materializing (Br) materialise

MTRYLZM immaterialism *not physical*

MTRYLZM materialism *physical matter*

MTRYLZR materializer *sorcerer* (Br) materialiser

MTRYLZSHN materialization *ghost* (Br) materialisation

MTRYRK matriarch *female ruler*

MTRYRK matriarchy *female rule* matriarchies

MTRYRKL matriarchal *female ruler*

MTRZ motorize *engine* motorized motorizing (Br) motorise

MTRZH metrorrhagia *bleeding*

MTRZHY metrorrhagia *bleeding*

MTRZM amateurism *incompetence*

MTRZSHN motorization *engine* (Br) motorisation

MTS Matisse *painter*

MTS matzo (or) matzoh *food* matzoth (or)matzos (or) matzohs

MTS meatus *body passage*

meatuses (or) meatus

MTS métis *mixed race* (pl) métis

MTS mezzo *singer* mezzos

MTSD miticide *insecticide*

MTSDNG Mao Tse-tung *Chinese leader*

MTSDSS metastasis *spread* metastases

MTSDSZ metastasize *spread* metastasized metastasizing

MTSHN imitation *copy*

MTSHN mediation *judgement*

MTSHN mutation *change*

MTSKLG metapsychology *mental structure*

MTSKLJ metapsychology *mental structure*

MTSN medicine *drug*

MTSNBL medicine ball *exercises*

MTSNMN medicine man *healer*

MTSNR metacenter *buoyancy*

MTSNSH medicine show *entertainment*

MTSNTHLNZ Mount St. Helens *mountain*

MTSNTR metacenter *buoyancy*

MTSRL mozzarella *cheese*

MTSRT Mozart *composer*

MTSS amitosis *simple cell division*

MTSS mitosis *cell division* mitoses

MTSSPRN mezzo-soprano *singer*

MTST emptiest *void*

MTST maddest *angry, crazy*

MTST meatiest *fleshy, substantial*

MTST mightiest *powerful*

MTST muddiest *wet dirt*

MTST mutest *silent*

MTSTNG Mao Tse-tung *Chinese leader*

MTSTNT mezzotint *engraving*

Letters aren't doubled for single sounds: to find alley use **L** not **LL**. Use **Y** and **W** as hard sounds only: to find yellow use **YL**. (Br)=British spelling or usage. * See dictionary.

MTSTSS metastasis *spread* metastases

MTSTSZ metastasize *spread* metastasized metastasizing

MTSV mitzvah *commandment* mitzvoth (or) mitzvahs

MTSVCH mezza voce *voice*

MTSVTH mitzvoth (pl) *commandment* mitzvah

MTT imitate *copy* imitated imitating

MTT mediate *judge* mediated mediating

MTT motet *music*

MTT mutate *change* mutated mutating

MTTDR meditator *thinker, non thinker*

MTTDV meditative *contemplating*

MTTDVL meditatively *contemplation*

MTTDVNS meditativeness *contemplation*

MTTHRKS metathorax *rear segment*

MTTHRX metathorax *rear segment*

MTTHSS metathesis *transposition* metatheses

MTTK amitotic *simple cell division*

MTTKL amitotically *simple cell division*

MTTR imitator *copier*

MTTR mediator *judge*

MTTRKS mediatrix *judge (f)*

MTTRNN Mediterranean *sea, region*

MTTRNYN Mediterranean *sea, region*

MTTRSL metatarsal *bone*

MTTRSS metatarsus *bone*

MTTRX mediatrix *judge (f)*

MTTSHN meditation *contemplation*

MTTT meditate *contemplate* meditated meditating

MTTTR meditator *thinker*

MTTTV meditative

contemplating

MTTTVL meditatively *contemplation*

MTTTVNS meditativeness *contemplation*

MTTV imitative *copy*

MTTVL imitatively *copy*

MTTVNS imitativeness *copy*

MTV amative *loving*

MTV emotive *feelings*

MTV motive *reason, music*

MTVDR motivator *driver*

MTVK motivic *reason, music*

MTVL amatively *loving*

MTVL emotively *feelings*

MTVLS motiveless *unplanned*

MTVNS amativeness *loving*

MTVRST Mount Everest *mountain*

MTVSHN motivation *stimulus*

MTVT motivate *compel* motivated motivating

MTVTR motivator *driver*

MTWL mutual (adj) *shared* mutually (adv)

MTWLD mutuality *sharing*

MTWLT mutuality *sharing*

MTWLZ mutualize *share* mutualized mutualizing

MTWLZM mutualism *sharing*

MTX meat-ax *cleaver*

MTY media *voiced stop, muscle* mediae

MTY media (pl) *middle, material* medium

MTY métier (or) metier *work*

MTYDR mediator *judge*

MTYKR mediocre *ordinary*

MTYKRD mediocrity *ordinariness* mediocrities

MTYKRT mediocrity *ordinariness* mediocrities

MTYL medial (adj) *average* medially (adv)

MTYM medium *(adj) average (n) environment*

MTYN median *center*

MTYNT mediant *scale tone*

MTYR amateur *not*

professional

MTYR emptier *void*

MTYR immature *unripe*

MTYR mature *ripen, age* matured maturing

MTYR meatier *fleshy, substantial*

MTYR meteor *asteroid*

MTYR mightier *powerful*

MTYR muddier *wet dirt*

MTYRD immaturity *unripe*

MTYRD maturity *ripeness*

MTYRD meteoroid *comet*

MTYRK meteoric *fast*

MTYRL immaturely *unripe*

MTYRLG meteorology *weather*

MTYRLJ meteorology *weather*

MTYRLJK meteorologic (or) meteorological (adj) *weather* meteorologically (adv)

MTYRLJKL meteorological (or) meteorologic (adj) *weather* meteorologically (adv)

MTYRLJST meteorologist *weather forecaster*

MTYRSH amateurish *incompetent*

MTYRSHL amateurishly *incompetently*

MTYRSHN maturation *ripeness*

MTYRSHNS amateurishness *incompetence*

MTYRT immaturity *unripe*

MTYRT maturate *ripen* maturated maturating

MTYRT maturity *ripeness*

MTYRT meteorite *small asteroid*

MTYRZM amateurism *incompetence*

MTYSHN mediation *judgement*

MTYST emptiest *void*

MTYST meatiest *fleshy, substantial*

MTYST mightiest *powerful*

Use letters that best describe the sounds you hear and omit the vowels. Use **S** or **K** instead of **C**: to find circle use **SRKL**. Use **J** to find joy, **JM** to find gem and **G** to find go.

MTYST muddiest *wet dirt*
MTYT mediate *judge* mediated mediating
MTYTR mediator *judge*
MTZ matzo (or) matzoh *food* matzoth (or)matzos (or) matzohs
MTZLM metaxylem *plant cell*
MTZN metazoan *animal*
MTZRL mozzarella *cheese*
MTZRT Mozart *composer*
MTZWN metazoan *animal*
MV mauve *color*
MV move (v) *drive, persuade, stir* moved moving*
MV move (n) *maneuver, change*
MV movie *film*
MVBL immovable (adj) *not moving* immovably (adv)
MVBL movable (or) moveable (adj) *change position* movably (adv)
MVBLD immovability *not moving*
MVBLD movability *change position*
MVBLT immovability *not moving*
MVBLT movability *change position*
MVDM moviedom *films*
MVGR moviegoer *watcher*
MVGWR moviegoer *watcher*
MVL Moviola *(trademark) film*
MVMKNG moviemaking *films*
MVMKR moviemaker *films*
MVMNT movement *change position*
MVN maven (or) mavin *expert*
MVN moving *in motion, emotional*
MVNG moving *in motion, emotional*
MVNGL movingly *in motion, emotional*
MVNL movingly *in motion, emotional*

MVNR maid of honor *wedding* (Br) maid of honour
MVR mover *change position, transfer*
MVRK maverick *independent one*
MVS mavis *bird*
MVYL Moviola *(trademark) film*
MW armoire *furniture*
MW Maui *island*
MW moa *bird*
MW moue *pout*
MWN M-1 *weapon*
MWN muon *particle*
MWR armoire *furniture*
MWR Maori *New Zealand native* Maori (or) Maoris
MWR moiré (or) moire *pattern*
MWR mower *cutter*
MWST Maoist *follower of Mao*
MWT émeute *uprising* émeutes
MWZM Maoism *philosophy*
MWZN muezzin *crier*
MX Amex (abbr) *American Express*
MX immix *combine*
MX max *maximum*
MX maxi *length* maxis
MX mix (n) *blend* (v) *blend, confuse, participate* mixes
MX moxie *pep, expertise*
MXBL mixable *blend*
MXCHR immixture *combination*
MXCHR mixture *blend*
MXD mixed *blended*
MXDM myxedema *disease*
MXDMDS myxedematous *disease*
MXDMTS myxedematous *disease*
MXDP mixed-up *confused*
MXK Mexico *country*
MXKN Mexican *of Mexico*
MXL maxilla *jaw* maxillae (or) maxillas
MXLFSHL maxillofacial *face*

MXLPD maxilliped *appendage*
MXLR maxillary *jaw*
MXM maxim *truth*
MXM maxima (pl) *upper limit* maximum
MXM myxoma *tumor* myxomas (or) myxomata
MXMCT myxomycete *slime mold*
MXMD myxomata (pl) *tumor* myxoma
MXML maximal (adj) *upper limit* maximally (adv)
MXMM maximum *upper limit* maxima (or) maximums
MXMST myxomycete *slime mold*
MXMT myxomata (pl) *tumor* myxoma
MXMTS myxomatous *tumor*
MXMTSS myxomatosis *virus*
MXMZ maximize *make the most of* maximized maximizing (Br) maximise
MXMZR maximizer *make the most of* (Br) maximiser
MXMZSHN maximization *make the most of* (Br) maximisation
MXP mix-up (n) *confusion, fight*
MXR mixer *blender, meeting, beverage*
MXSLN amoxicillin *drug* (Br) amoxycillin
MXT max out (slang) *extend to the limit*
MXT mixed *blended*
MXTP mixed-up *confused*
MXTR immixture *combination*
MXTR mixture *blend*
MXTYR immixture *combination*
MXVRL myxoviral *influenza*
MXVRS myxovirus *influenza*
MXWL maxwell *flux*

Letters aren't doubled for single sounds: to find alley use **L** not **LL**. Use **Y** and **W** as hard sounds only: to find yellow use **YL**. (Br)=British spelling or usage. * See dictionary.

MY emu *bird*
MY maillot *clothing*
MY maya *illusion*
MY Maya *Indian* Maya (or) Mayas
MY mayo *mayonnaise*
MY meow *cat sound*
MY mew *(n) gull, meow, abode (v) meow, confine*
MYBL amiable (adj) *friendly* amiably (adv)
MYBLD amiability *friendliness*
MYBLNS amiableness *friendliness*
MYBLST myoblast *muscle cell*
MYBLT amiability *friendliness*
MYCHL mutual (adj) *shared* mutually (adv)
MYCHLD mutuality *sharing*
MYCHLT mutuality *sharing*
MYCHLZ mutualize *share* mutualized mutualizing
MYCHLZM mutualism *sharing*
MYCHWL mutual (adj) *shared* mutually (adv)
MYCHWLD mutuality *sharing*
MYCHWLT mutuality *sharing*
MYCHWLZ mutualize *share* mutualized mutualizing
MYCHWLZM mutualism *sharing*
MYDBL immutable (adj) *no change* immutably (adv)
MYDBL mutable (adj) *able to change* mutably (adv)
MYDBLD immutability *no change*
MYDBLD mutability *change*
MYDBLT immutability *no change*
MYDBLT mutability *change*
MYDK meiotic *reduction*
MYDKL meiotically *reduction*
MYDLDR mutilator *destroyer, cutter*

MYDLSHN mutilation *destruction*
MYDLT mutilate *cut up* mutilated mutilating mutilation
MYDLTR mutilator *destroyer, cutter*
MYDN mutiny *rebellion* mutinies
MYDNR mutineer *rebel*
MYDNS mutinous *rebellious*
MYDNT mutant *changed one*
MYDR muter *silent*
MYDS meatus *body passage* meatuses (or) meatus
MYDST mutest *silent*
MYFBRL myofibril *muscle*
MYFLMNT myofilament *muscle*
MYGLBN myoglobin *blood*
MYGNK myogenic *heart rhythm*
MYJNK myogenic *heart rhythm*
MYK umiak *boat*
MYKD mucoid *slimy*
MYKLP mea culpa *fault*
MYKRDDS myocarditis *inflammation*
MYKRDL myocardial *heart*
MYKRDM myocardium *heart*
MYKRDTS myocarditis *inflammation*
MYKRDYL myocardial *heart*
MYKRDYM myocardium *heart*
MYKS mucosa *membrane* mucosae (or) mucosas
MYKS mucous (adj) *slimy*
MYKS mucus (n) *nasal secretion*
MYL mewl *meow*
MYL mildly *gently*
MYL mile *5,280 feet*
MYL moil *work, swirl*
MYL mule *animal, shoe*
MYL muley *hornless*
MYLBLST myeloblast *cell*
MYLD mulatto *mixed race* mulattoes (or) mulattos
MYLD myeloid *bone marrow*

MYLDDS myelitides (pl) *inflammation* myelitis
MYLDDZ myelitides (pl) *inflammation* myelitis
MYLDL mildly *gently*
MYLDNS mildness *gentleness*
MYLDR emulator *copier*
MYLDR mule deer *animal*
MYLDS myelitis *inflammation* myelitides
MYLG myology *muscles*
MYLGNS myelogenous *bone marrow*
MYLJ mileage *distance*
MYLJ myology *muscles*
MYLJNS myelogenous *bone marrow*
MYLK majolica *pottery*
MYLM myeloma *tumor*
MYLMDS myelomatous *tumor*
MYLMTS myelomatous *tumor*
MYLN myelin *nerve sheath*
MYLNDD myelinated *nerve sheath*
MYLNK myelinic *nerve sheath*
MYLNS mildness *gentleness*
MYLNTD myelinated *nerve sheath*
MYLPST milepost *distance marker*
MYLPTH myelopathy *disease*
MYLPTHK myelopathic *disease*
MYLR miler *racer*
MYLS emulous *copy*
MYLSDK myelocytic *cell*
MYLSH mulish *stubborn*
MYLSHL mulishly *stubbornly*
MYLSHN emulation *copy*
MYLSHNS mulishness *stubbornness*
MYLSKNR mule skinner *herder*
MYLSL emulously *copy*
MYLSNS emulousness *copy*
MYLSPRR miles per hour *speed*
MYLSPRWR miles per hour

Use letters that best describe the sounds you hear and omit the vowels. Use **S** or **K** instead of **C**: to find circle use **SRKL**. Use **J** to find joy, **JM** to find gem and **G** to find go.

speed
MYLST myelocyte *cell*
MYLSTK myelocytic *cell*
MYLSTN milestone *achievement*
MYLT amulet *charm*
MYLT emulate *copy* emulated emulating
MYLT mulatto *mixed race* mulattoes (or) mulattos
MYLTDS myelitides (pl) *inflammation* myelitis
MYLTR emulator *copier*
MYLTR muleteer *herder*
MYLTS myelitis *inflammation* myelitides
MYM Miami *city*
MYM myoma *tumor* myomas (or) myomata
MYMD myomata (pl) *tumor* myoma
MYMT myomata (pl) *tumor* myoma
MYN immune *exempt, resistant*
MYN Mayan *Yucatan*
MYN million *1,000,000*
MYN mullion *window*
MYN muon *particle*
MYND immunity *exemption, resistance* immunities
MYNDFSHNC immunodeficiency *no antibodies*
MYNDFSHNS immunodeficiency *no antibodies*
MYNDFSHNTC immunodeficiency *no antibodies*
MYNDFSHNTS immunodeficiency *no antibodies*
MYNDR meander *(n) path (v) wander*
MYNDRS meanderous *intricate*
MYNFSNS munificence *generosity*
MYNFSNT munificent *generous*
MYNFSNTL munificently

generously
MYNFSNTS munificence *generosity*
MYNGNK immunogenic *antibodies*
MYNJN immunogen *antibody*
MYNJNDKS immunogenetics *antibodies*
MYNJNDX immunogenetics *antibodies*
MYNJNK immunogenic *antibodies*
MYNJNTKS immunogenetics *antibodies*
MYNJNTX immunogenetics *antibodies*
MYNK Munich *city*
MYNLG immunology *antibodies*
MYNLJ immunology *antibodies*
MYNLJK immunologic (or) immunological (adj) *antibodies* immunologically (adv)
MYNLJKL immunological (or) immunologic (adj) *antibodies* immunologically (adv)
MYNR millionaire *wealth*
MYNRS millionairess *wealth*
MYNS immunize *exempt, resist* immunized immunizing
MYNSHN ammunition *bullet*
MYNSHN munition *armaments*
MYNSHNS munitions *armaments*
MYNSHNZ munitions *armaments*
MYNSPL municipal (adj) *government* municipally (adv)
MYNSPLD municipality *government* municipalities
MYNSPLT municipality *government* municipalities
MYNSPLZ municipalize

govern municipalized municipalizing
MYNSPRSHN immunosuppression *against antibodies*
MYNSPRSNT immunosuppressant *against antibodies*
MYNSPRSV immunosuppressive *against antibodies*
MYNSSDM immune system *resistance*
MYNSSTM immune system *resistance*
MYNT immunity *exemption, resistance* immunities
MYNT mayn't *(contr) may not*
MYNTH millionth *1,000,000*
MYNTHRP immunotherapy *treatment*
MYNTHRPDK immunotherapeutic *treatment*
MYNTHRPTK immunotherapeutic *treatment*
MYNTHRPYDK immunotherapeutic *treatment*
MYNTHRPYTK immunotherapeutic *treatment*
MYNZ immunize *exempt, resist* immunized immunizing
MYNZ mayonnaise *sauce*
MYNZSHN immunization *exempt, resist*
MYP myope *person*
MYP myopia *vision*
MYPK myopic *vision*
MYPKL myopically *vision*
MYPTH myopathy *muscle disorder*
MYPTHK myopathic *muscle disorder*
MYPY myopia *vision*
MYR immure *imprison* immured immuring
MYR mayor *city official*

Letters aren't doubled for single sounds: to find alley use **L** not **LL**. Use **Y** and **W** as hard sounds only: to find yellow use **YL**. (Br)=British spelling or usage. * See dictionary.

MYR mire *(v)* *entangle, dirty* mired miring
MYR mire *(n)* *mud*
MYRCZ murices (or) murexes (pl) *mollusk* murex
MYRD murid *rodent*
MYRDK muriatic *acid*
MYRK Majorca *island*
MYRKS murex *mollusk* murices (or) murexes
MYRL mayoral *city official*
MYRL mural *painting*
MYRLST muralist *painter*
MYRLT mayoralty *city official* mayoralties
MYRMNT immurement *prison*
MYRN murine *rodent*
MYRS mayoress *city official (f)*
MYRSZ murices (or) murexes (pl) *mollusk* murex
MYRTK muriatic *acid*
MYRX murex *mollusk* murices (or) murexes
MYRYDK muriatic *acid*
MYRYTK muriatic *acid*
MYS mews *stables*
MYSDS myositis *soreness*
MYSL muesli *cereal*
MYSLJ mucilage *gum*
MYSLJNS mucilaginous *gummy*
MYSN myosin *muscle*
MYSS meiosis *reduction*
MYSTHN myasthenia *muscles*
MYSTHNY myasthenia *muscles*
MYSTR maestro *conductor, teacher* maestros (or) maestri
MYSTS myositis *soreness*
MYT moiety *half* moieties
MYT mute *(adj) silent* muter mutest
MYT mute *(v) silence, melt, defecate* muted muting
MYT mute *(n) silent one, muffler*

MYTBL immutable (adj) *no change* immutably (adv)
MYTBL mutable (adj) *able to change* mutably (adv)
MYTBLD immutability *no change*
MYTBLD mutability *change*
MYTBLT immutability *no change*
MYTBLT mutability *change*
MYTK meiotic *reduction*
MYTKL meiotically *reduction*
MYTLDR mutilator *destroyer, cutter*
MYTLSHN mutilation *destruction*
MYTLT mutilate *cut up* mutilated mutilating mulilator
MYTLTR mutilator *destroyer, cutter*
MYTM myotome *muscle*
MYTN amyotonia *loss of muscle tone*
MYTN mutiny *rebellion* mutinies
MYTN myotonia *spasm*
MYTNK myotonic *spasm*
MYTNR mutineer *rebel*
MYTNS mutinous *rebellious*
MYTNT mutant *changed one*
MYTNY amyotonia *loss of muscle tone*
MYTNY myotonia *spasm*
MYTR muter *silent*
MYTS meatus *body passage* meatuses (or) meatus
MYTSHN mutation *change*
MYTST mutest *silent*
MYTT mutate *change* mutated mutating
MYWN muon *particle*
MYZ amuse *entertain* amused amusing
MYZ mews *stables*
MYZ muse *(v) ponder* mused musing
MYZ muse *(n) dream, poet, (capitalized) Greek myth*
MYZK music *tune*
MYZK Muzak *(trademark) music*

MYZKL musical (adj) *melodic* (n) *theater* musically (adv)
MYZKL musicale *(n) entertainment*
MYZKLD musicality *melody*
MYZKLG musicology *research*
MYZKLJ musicology *research*
MYZKLJST musicologist *researcher*
MYZKLT musicality *melody*
MYZL muesli *cereal*
MYZLG museology *museum*
MYZLJ museology *museum*
MYZLJST museologist *museum*
MYZM miasma *fog* miasmas (or) miasmata
MYZM museum *gallery*
MYZMD miasmata (pl) *fog* miasma
MYZMDK miasmatic *foggy*
MYZMK miasmic *foggy*
MYZMKL miasmically *foggy*
MYZML miasmal *foggy*
MYZMNT amusement *entertainment*
MYZMT miasmata (pl) *fog* miasma
MYZMTK miasmatic *foggy*
MYZN amusing *funny*
MYZN muezzin *crier*
MYZN musing *daydreaming*
MYZNG amusing *funny*
MYZNG musing *daydreaming*
MYZNGL amusingly *funny*
MYZR amuser *entertainer*
MYZSHN musician *instrumentalist*
MYZT musette *bagpipe*
MYZYLG museology *museum*
MYZYLJ museology *museum*
MYZYLJST museologist *museum*
MYZYM museum *gallery*
MZ alms *charity*
MZ amaze *astound* amazed

Use letters that best describe the sounds you hear and omit the vowels. Use **S** or **K** instead of **C**: to find circle use **SRKL**. Use **J** to find joy, **JM** to find gem and **G** to find go.

amazing

MZ amuse *entertain* amused amusing

MZ maize *corn*

MZ maze *puzzle*

MZ mazy *confusing*

MZ mews *stables*

MZ meze *food* mezes

MZ mezzo *singer* mezzos

MZ mosey *wander*

MZ mouse *(v) hunt for mice* moused mousing

MZ Ms. *title* Mses. (or) Mss.

MZ muse *(v) meditate* mused musing

MZ muse *(n) dream, poet, (capitalized) Greek myth*

MZ muzzy *dull, confused* muzzier muzziest

MZDL amazedly *with surprise*

MZDRM mesoderm *germ layer*

MZDRML mesodermal *germ layer*

MZFDK mesophytic *plant*

MZFL mesophyll *leaf layer*

MZFT mesophyte *plant*

MZFTK mesophytic *plant*

MZGL mesoglea (or) mesogloea *gelatin*

MZHNG mah-jongg (or) mahjong *game*

MZHNLN Maginot Line *defense*

MZHR measure *(v) regulate, govern, allot** measured measuring

MZHR measure *(n) portion, tune, comparison**

MZHR Monsieur *title*

MZHRBL immeasurable *(adj) beyond count* immeasurably *(adv)*

MZHRBL measurable *(adj) able to count* measurably *(adv)*

MZHRBLD measurability *portion*

MZHRBLT measurability *portion*

MZHRD measured

calculated

MZHRLS measureless *unlimited*

MZHRMNT measurement *size*

MZHRR measurer *allot, regulate*

MZHST mot juste *right word* mots justes

MZK mosaic *pattern* mosaicked mosaicking

MZK music *tune*

MZK Muzak *(trademark) music*

MZKL musical *(adj) melodic (n) theater* musically *(adv)*

MZKL musicale *(n) entertainment*

MZKLD musicality *melody*

MZKLG musicology *research*

MZKLJ musicology *research*

MZKLJST musicologist *researcher*

MZKLT musicality *melody*

MZKRP mesocarp *middle layer*

MZKSDK masochistic *pain loving*

MZKSDKL masochistically *pain loving*

MZKST masochist *pain lover*

MZKSTK masochistic *pain loving*

MZKSTKL masochistically *pain loving*

MZKZM masochism *pleasure in pain*

MZL mausolea *(pl) tomb* mausoleum

MZL measly *small* measlier measliest

MZL mesial *(adj) middle* mesially *(adv)*

MZL mizzle *rain* mizzled mizzling

MZL muesli *cereal*

MZL muzzily *dull, confused*

MZL muzzle *(v) gag* muzzled muzzling

MZL muzzle *(n) mouth, restraint*

MZLG museology *museum*

MZLJ museology *museum*

MZLJST museologist *museum*

MZLM mausoleum *tomb* mausoleums (or) mausolea

MZLM Muslim *Islamic*

MZLN muslin *fabric*

MZLNS mésalliance *marriage*

MZLNTS mesalliance *marriage*

MZLR measlier *small*

MZLR muzzler *silencer*

MZLS measles *disease*

MZLST measliest *small*

MZLTHK Mesolithic *geologic age*

MZLY mausolea *(pl) tomb* mausoleum

MZLYM mausoleum *tomb* mausoleums (or) mausolea

MZLYNS mesalliance *marriage*

MZLYNTS mesalliance *marriage*

MZLYR measlier *small*

MZLYST measliest *small*

MZLZ measles *disease*

MZM Maoism *philosophy*

MZM miasma *fog* miasmas (or) miasmata

MZM museum *gallery*

MZMBK Mozambique *country*

MZMD miasmata *(pl) fog* miasma

MZMDK miasmatic *foggy*

MZMK miasmic *foggy*

MZMKL miasmically *foggy*

MZML miasmal *foggy*

MZMNT amazement *surprise*

MZMNT amusement *entertainment*

MZMR mesomere *middle part*

MZMRF mesomorph *body type*

MZMRK mesmeric *fascinating*

Letters aren't doubled for single sounds: to find alley use **L** not **LL**. Use **Y** and **W** as hard sounds only: to find yellow use **YL**. (Br)=British spelling or usage. * See dictionary.

MZMRKL mesmerically *fascinating*

MZMRZ mesmerize *hypnotize* mesmerized mesmerizing (Br) mesmerise

MZMRZM mesmerism *hypnotism*

MZMRZR mesmerizer *hypnotizer* (Br) mesmeriser

MZMT miasmata (pl) *fog* miasma

MZMTK miasmatic *foggy*

MZN amazing *surprising*

MZN Amazon *river, woman*

MZN amusing *funny*

MZN meson *particle*

MZN mizzen *sail*

MZN muezzin *crier*

MZN musing *daydreaming*

MZNCN mise-en-scène *background* mise-en-scènes

MZNG amazing *surprising*

MZNG amusing *funny*

MZNG musing *daydreaming*

MZNGL amazingly *surprisingly*

MZNGL amusingly *funny*

MZNK mesonic *particle*

MZNKM mesenchyme *cells*

MZNL amazingly *surprisingly*

MZNMST mizzenmast *ship*

MZNN Amazonian *river, woman*

MZNN mezzanine *balcony*

MZNS muzziness *dull, confused*

MZNSN mise-en-scène *background* mise-en-scènes

MZNT maisonette *house*

MZNTHRP misanthrope *skeptic*

MZNTHRP misanthropy *skepticism*

MZNTHRPK misanthropic *skeptical*

MZNTHRPKL misanthropically

skeptically

MZNTR mesentery *membrane* mesenteries

MZNTRN mesenteron *food canal*

MZNYN Amazonian *river, woman*

MZPLJK mesopelagic *depth*

MZPZ mesopause *atmosphere*

MZR amuser *entertainer*

MZR maser *emitter*

MZR mazer *bowl*

MZR miser *stingy one*

MZR misery *woe* miseries

MZR Missouri *US State, river*

MZR Monsieur *title*

MZR mouser *cat*

MZR muzzier *dull, confused*

MZRBL miserable (adj) *wretched* miserably (adv)

MZRD mazard *face*

MZRD mazzard *cherry*

MZRK mazurka *dance*

MZRN mezereon *shrub*

MZRT Mozart *composer*

MZRYN mezereon *shrub*

MZSFR mesosphere *atmosphere*

MZSHN musician *instrumentalist*

MZSKLN mesocyclone *tornado*

MZSM mesosome *bacteria*

MZSPRN mezzo-soprano *singer*

MZSR mosasaur *dinosaur*

MZST muzziest *dull, confused*

MZT musette *bagpipe*

MZTHL mesothelia (pl) *lining* mesothelium

MZTHLM mesothelium *lining* mesothelia

MZTHLY mesothelia (pl) *lining* mesothelium

MZTHLYM mesothelium *lining* mesothelia

MZTHRKS mesothorax *middle segment*

MZTHRX mesothorax *middle segment*

MZTNT mezzotint *engraving*

MZVCH mezza voce *voice*

MZY Monsieur *title*

MZYK mosaic *pattern* mosaicked mosaicking

MZYL mesial (adj) *middle* mesially (adv)

MZYLG museology *museum*

MZYLJ museology *museum*

MZYLJST museologist *museum*

MZYM museum *gallery*

MZYR Monsieur *title*

MZYR muzzier *dull, confused*

MZYST muzziest *dull, confused*

MZZ mezuzah (or) mezuza *scroll* mezuzahs (or) mezuzas (or) mezuzot

MZZ missus (or) missis *wife* (Mrs.)

MZZ Moses *prophet*

MZZ Mrs. *married title*

MZZK Mesozoic *geologic era*

MZZR mosasaur *dinosaur*

MZZT mezuzot (pl) *scroll* mezuzah (or) mezuza

MZZWK Mesozoic *geologic era*

N

N aeon (or) eon *1 billion years*

N Ainu *Japan* Ainu (or) Ainus

N an *indefinite article*

N ana *quantity, collection* ana (or) anas

N and *also*

N anew *afresh*

N ani *bird*

N anna *money*

N annoy *bother*

N ante *money* anted anteing

Use letters that best describe the sounds you hear and omit the vowels. Use **S** or **K** instead of **C**: to find circle use **SRKL**. Use **J** to find joy, **JM** to find gem and **G** to find go.

N anti *opposed* antis
N any *(adj, pron, adv) every, all, at all**
N end *finish*
N gnaw *chew*
N gnu *antelope* gnu (or) gnus
N in *(prep) inside of (adj) stylish*
N inn *hotel*
N ion *particle*
N Ionia *ancient region*
N knee *(n) leg joint*
N knee *(v) kick* kneed kneeing
N knew *(v-past) know*
N know *perceive* knew known knowing
N nah (or) nay *no*
N née (or) nee *family name*
N neigh *horse*
N new *unused, modern, unfamiliar**
N nigh *near*
N no *negative, none* noes (or) nos
N now *this moment*
N nu *Greek letter*
N on *(prep) on top of (adv) active (n) position (adj) planned, (Br) possible**
N own *possess, control*
NB knob *lump, handle*
NB knobby *lumpy*
NB nab *catch* nabbed nabbing
NB neb *beak, snout*
NB nib *point*
NB nob *head*
NB nub *small lump, gist*
NB nubby *small lumps* nubbier nubbiest
NBB nabob *governor*
NBBTST Anabaptist *Protestant*
NBBTZD unbaptized *religion*
NBBTZM anabaptism *doctrine*
NBD antibody *immunity* antibodies
NBD anybody *a person*
NBD knobbed *with lumps*

NBD nobody *no person* nobodies
NBD unbowed *not bent*
NBDBL unbeatable (adj) *best* unbeatably (adv)
NBDD unabated *full force*
NBDK antibiotic *drug*
NBDK antibiotic *medicine*
NBDN unbidden *not asked*
NBJDD unbudgeted *not planned*
NBJKSHNBL unobjectionable *accepted*
NBJTD unbudgeted *not planned*
NBKL unbuckle *unfasten* unbuckled unbuckling
NBKMN unbecoming *not attractive*
NBKMNG unbecoming *not attractive*
NBKTRL antibacterial *combating germs*
NBKTRYL antibacterial *combating germs*
NBL enable *give power* enabled enabling
NBL ennoble *elevate* ennobled ennobling
NBL knobbly *small lumps*
NBL knowable *understandable*
NBL nebula *galaxy* nebulae
NBL nibble *eat* nibbled nibbling
NBL nobble *(Br) cheat* nobbled nobbling
NBL noble *lofty, moral* nobler noblest
NBL nobly *lofty, moral*
NBL nubble *small lump*
NBL nubile *marriage age*
NBL unable *not able*
NBL unknowable *beyond understanding*
NBLCHD unbleached *natural*
NBLCHT unbleached *natural*
NBLD inability *unfitness*
NBLD nobility *upper class*
NBLDD unbelted *no belt*

NBLF unbelief *doubt*
NBLK anabolic *steroid*
NBLK unblock *open*
NBLKSTRD anabolic steroid *muscle drug*
NBLM antebellum *before war*
NBLMN nobleman *upper class* noblemen
NBLMSHD unblemished *no marks*
NBLMSHT unblemished *no marks*
NBLNGKN unblinking *no emotion*
NBLNGKNG unblinking *no emotion*
NBLNKN unblinking *no emotion*
NBLNKNG unblinking *no emotion*
NBLNS nobleness *lofty, moral*
NBLNS unbalance *tilt*
NBLNST unbalanced *not adjusted, tilted, crazy*
NBLNTS unbalance *tilt*
NBLPRZ Nobel Prize *award*
NBLR enabler *helper*
NBLR nebular *galaxy*
NBLR nobler *loftier*
NBLS nebulous *vague*
NBLSBLJ noblesse oblige *duty*
NBLSBLSH noblesse oblige *duty*
NBLSBLZH noblesse oblige *duty*
NBLSD nebulosity *vagueness* nebulosities
NBLSDK antiballistic *intercepting*
NBLSL nebulously *vaguely*
NBLSNS nebulousness *vagueness*
NBLST nebulosity *vagueness* nebulosities
NBLST noblest *loftiest*
NBLST unblessed *evil*
NBLSTK antiballistic *intercepting*
NBLT inability *unfitness*
NBLT nobility *upper class*

Letters aren't doubled for single sounds: to find alley use **L** not **LL**. Use **Y** and **W** as hard sounds only: to find yellow use **YL**. (Br)=British spelling or usage. * See dictionary.

NBLT unbolt *open*
NBLT unbuilt *not made*
NBLTD unbelted *no belt*
NBLVBL unbelievable (adj)
improbable unbelievably
(adv)
NBLVN unbelieving *doubting*
NBLVNG unbelieving
doubting
NBLVR unbeliever *doubter*
NBLWMN noblewoman *rank*
noblewomen
NBLXTRD anabolic steroid
muscle drug
NBLZ nebulize *reduce to*
spray nebulized
nebulizing
NBLZM anabolism
metabolism
NBLZR nebulizer *reduce to*
spray
NBLZSHN nebulization
reduce to spray
NBN inbound *entering*
NBN nubbin *small lump*
NBN unbound *free*
NBND inbound *entering*
NBND unbend *straighten*
unbent unbending
NBND unbound *free*
NBNDBL unbendable
straight
NBNDD unbounded *free*
NBNDN unbending *straight*
NBNDNG unbending
straight
NBNNST unbeknownst
unknown
NBNS nubbiness *small*
lumps
NBPTST Anabaptist
Protestant
NBPTZD unbaptized *religion*
NBPTZM anabaptism
doctrine
NBR neighbor *(n) fellow man*
(adj) near (v) adjoin
(Br) neighbour
NBR nubbier *small lumps*
NBRBL unbearable (adj)
awful unbearably (adv)
NBRD inboard *boat motor*

NBRD inbred *(v-past)*
inherited
NBRD inbreed *mate* inbred
inbreeding
NBRD inebriety *drunkenness*
NBRD onboard *on a vehicle*
NBRDD inebriated *drunk*
NBRDL unbridle *set free*
unbridled unbridling
NBRDLD unbridled *no*
restraint
NBRDN inbreeding *mating*
NBRDND unburdened
relieved
NBRDNG inbreeding *mating*
NBRG Newburg (or)
Newburgh *sauce*
NBRHD neighborhood
vicinity
(Br) neighbourhood
NBRJD unabridged *complete*
NBRJT unabridged *complete*
NBRKBL unbreakable *tough*
NBRKN unbroken *whole*
NBRL neighborly *friendly*
(Br) neighbourly
NBRLNS neighborliness
friendliness
(Br) neighbourliness
NBRN inborn *inherited*
NBRN newborn *infant*
newborn (or) newborns
NBRN unborn *fetus*
NBRNR no-brainer *simple*
choice
NBRNT inebriant *intoxicant*
NBRSHN antiabortion
against pregnancy
termination
NBRSHN inebriation
drunkenness
NBRSHT en brochette
skewer
NBRSK Nebraska *US State*
NBRT inebriate *get drunk*
inebriated inebriating
NBRT inebriety *drunkenness*
NBRTD inebriated *drunk*
NBRTHBL unbreathable *bad*
air
NBRYD inebriety
drunkenness

NBRYDD inebriated *drunk*
NBRYNT inebriant *intoxicant*
NBRYSHN inebriation
drunkenness
NBRYT inebriate *get drunk*
inebriated inebriating
NBRYT inebriety
drunkenness
NBRYTD inebriated *drunk*
NBS nibs *title*
NBSH nebbish *meek one*
NBSHN inhibition
obstruction
NBSHT unabashed *no*
apology
NBSNC in absentia *gone*
NBSNCH in absentia *gone*
NBSNG antibusing *against*
school busing
NBSNS in absentia *gone*
NBSNSH in absentia *gone*
NBSS anabasis *advance*
anabases
NBST nubbiest *small lumps*
NBST unbiased *no prejudice*
NBTBL unbeatable (adj) *best*
unbeatably (adv)
NBTD unabated *full force*
NBTK antibiotic *drug*
NBTK antibiotic *medicine*
NBTN unbeaten *undefeated*
NBTN unbutton *open*
NBTNBL unobtainable *out*
of reach
NBTND unbuttoned *open*
NBTRSV unobtrusive
unnoticeable
NBTRSVL unobtrusively
unnoticeable
NBTRSVNS
unobtrusiveness
unnoticeable
NBTRZV unobtrusive
unnoticeable
NBTRZVL unobtrusively
unnoticeable
NBTRZVNS
unobtrusiveness
unnoticeable
NBYDK antibiotic *drug*
NBYL nebula *galaxy* nebulae
NBYLR nebular *galaxy*

Use letters that best describe the sounds you hear and omit the vowels. Use **S** or **K** instead of **C**: to find circle use **SRKL**. Use **J** to find joy, **JM** to find gem and **G** to find go.

NBYLS nebulous *vague*
NBYLSD nebulosity
vagueness nebulosities
NBYLSL nebulously *vaguely*
NBYLSNS nebulousness
vagueness
NBYLST nebulosity
vagueness nebulosities
NBYLZ nebulize *reduce to*
spray nebulized
nebulizing
NBYLZR nebulizer *reduce to*
spray
NBYLZSHN nebulization
reduce to spray
NBYR nubbier *small lumps*
NBYST nubbiest *small*
lumps
NBYST unbiased *no*
prejudice
NBYTK antibiotic *drug*
NBZ nibs *title*
NBZM unbosom *disclose*
NC antsy *nervous*
NC nausea *sickness*
NCD aniseed *anise*
NCD antecede *precede*
anteceded anteceding
NCDD unseeded *not sown,*
not ranked
NCDNS antecedence
priority
NCDNT antecedent *prior*
NCDNTS antecedence
priority
NCH inch *(n) 2.54 cm (v)*
move slowly inches
NCH nacho *food* nachos
NCH niche *(n) nook, small*
area
NCH niche *(v) put away*
niched niching
NCH Nietzsche *philosopher*
NCH notch *dent* notches
NCHD notched *dented*
NCHKT unchecked *not*
monitored
NCHLD enchilada *food*
NCHLT enchilada *food*
NCHMBR antechamber
lobby
NCHN enchain *handcuff*

NCHN unchain *free*
NCHND enchanted *charmed*
NCHND unchained *free*
NCHNJBL unchangeable
(adj) same unchangeably
(adv)
NCHNJD unchanged *same*
NCHNJN unchanging *same*
NCHNJNG unchanging
same
NCHNNG enchanting
charming
NCHNNGL enchantingly
charming
NCHNR enchanter *charmer*
NCHNT ancient *old*
NCHNT enchant *charm*
NCHNTD enchanted
charmed
NCHNTL anciently *long ago*
NCHNTMNT enchantment
charm
NCHNTNG enchanting
charming
NCHNTNGL enchantingly
charming
NCHNTNS ancientness *old*
age
NCHNTR enchanter *charmer*
NCHNTRS enchantress
charmer (f) enchantresses
NCHR nature *principle,*
*creation, type**
NCHRDBL uncharitable
(adj) severe uncharitably
(adv)
NCHRDD uncharted *no map*
NCHRFL neutrophil *(or)*
neutrophilic *stain*
NCHRFLK neutrophilic *(or)*
neutrophil *stain*
NCHRL au naturel *nude,*
natural
NCHRL natural *(adj) innate,*
normal naturally *(adv)*
NCHRL neutral *(adj)*
middling neutrally *(adv)*
NCHRL unnatural *(adj)*
irregular, contrary
unnaturally
NCHRLD neutrality *middle*
NCHRLNS unnaturalness

irregular, contrary
NCHRLS naturalize *make*
common, citizenship
naturalized naturalizing
(Br) naturalise
NCHRLSDK naturalistic
realistic
NCHRLSDKL
naturalistically *realistic*
NCHRLSSHN naturalization
make common, citizenship
(Br) naturalisation
NCHRLST naturalist *realist*
NCHRLSTK naturalistic
realistic
NCHRLSTKL naturalistically
realistic
NCHRLT neutrality *middle*
NCHRLZ naturalize *make*
common, citizenship
naturalized naturalizing
(Br) naturalise
NCHRLZ neutralize *cancel*
neutralized neutralizing
(Br) neutralise
NCHRLZM naturalism
realism
NCHRLZSHN naturalization
make common, citizenship
(Br) naturalisation
NCHRLZSHN neutralization
cancellation
(Br) neutralisation
NCHRN neutrino *particle*
without mass neutrinos
NCHRTBL uncharitable
(adj) severe uncharitably
(adv)
NCHRTD uncharted *no map*
NCHS enchase *ornament,*
inlay
NCHST unchaste *immodest*
NCHT notched *dented*
NCHV anchovy *fish*
anchovies *(or)* anchovy
NCHWRM inchworm *insect*
NCKN aniseikonia *vision*
NCKNK aniseikonic *vision*
NCKNY aniseikonia *vision*
NCL uncial *writing*
NCL unseal *open*
NCLD unsealed *open*

Letters aren't doubled for single sounds: to find alley use **L** not **LL**. Use **Y** and **W** as hard
sounds only: to find yellow use **YL**. (Br)=British spelling or usage. * See dictionary.

NCM inseam *sewing*
NCM unseam *separate*
NCML unseemly *inappropriate*
NCMLNS unseemliness *inappropriate*
NCN encaenia *ceremony*
NCN Nicene *church*
NCN unseen *invisible*
NCNS nescience *ignorance*
NCNT enceinte *pregnant*
NCNT nescient *ignorant*
NCNTS nescience *ignorance*
NCNY encaenia *ceremony*
NCRM antiserum *antibody drug*
NCS nauseous *sick*
NCSN unceasing *continuous*
NCSNG unceasing *continuous*
NCT nauseate *make sick* nauseated nauseating
NCT unseat *remove*
NCTD unseeded *not sown, not ranked*
NCY nausea *sickness*
NCYL uncial *writing*
NCYNS nescience *ignorance*
NCYNT enceinte *pregnant*
NCYNT nescient *ignorant*
NCYNTS nescience *ignorance*
NCYS nauseous *sick*
NCYT nauseate *make sick* nauseated nauseating
NCZN unceasing *continuous*
NCZNBL unseasonable (adj) *bad timing* unseasonably (adv)
NCZND unseasoned *inexperienced*
NCZNG unceasing *continuous*
ND Aeneid *poem*
ND and *also*
ND andouille *food*
ND annato *dye*
ND annuity *yearly money* annuities
ND anode *electrode*
ND end *finish*
ND endow *provide*

ND endue *provide* endued enduing
ND ennead *nine*
ND gnatty *with gnats*
ND India *country*
ND knead *press on*
ND knotty *tangled* knottier knottiest
ND naiad *nymph* naiads (or) naiades
ND NATO (abbr) North Atlantic Treaty Organization
ND natty *neat* nattier nattiest
ND naughty *wicked* naughtier naughtiest
ND need (v) *require* (n) *lack, poverty*
ND needy *poor* needier neediest
ND nidi (pl) *nest* nidus
ND nightie (or) nighty *garment* nighties
ND ninety *number (90)* nineties
ND nod *head motion* nodded nodding
ND noddy *oaf, bird*
ND node *lump*
ND nude *naked* nuder nudest
ND nutty *like nuts, silly* nuttier nuttiest
ND Oneida *Native American* Oneida (or) Oneidas
ND undo *reverse* undid undoing undone undoes
ND undue *excessive*
ND unity *oneness* unities
NDBDBL indubitable (adj) *no doubt* indubitably (adv)
NDBDBL undebatable (adj) *no discussion* undebatably (adv)
NDBDBLD indubitability *no doubt*
NDBDBLT indubitability *no doubt*
NDBL inaudible (adj) *no sound* inaudibly (adv)
NDBL inedible *not for eating*
NDBL notable (adj)

remarkable notably (adv)
NDBLD notability *importance*
NDBLT notability *importance*
NDBRNGK nudibranch *mollusk* nudibranchs
NDBRNK nudibranch *mollusk* nudibranchs
NDBTBL indubitable (adj) *no doubt* indubitably (adv)
NDBTBL undebatable (adj) *no discussion* undebatably (adv)
NDBTBLD indubitability *no doubt*
NDBTBLT indubitability *no doubt*
NDCHN Indochina *peninsula*
NDCHNZ Indochinese *of Indochina*
NDCZ indices (pl) (n) *pointer, list, number* index
NDD indeed *truly*
NDD knotted *tangled*
NDD noted *well known*
NDD nudity *bareness*
NDD unaided *without help*
NDD undead *living*
NDD united *combined*
NDD unneeded *not required*
NDDBL indictable *accuse*
NDDD indebted *owing*
NDDD undoubted *certain*
NDDD unedited *not revised*
NDDDL undoubtedly *certain*
NDDKNGDM United Kingdom *country*
NDDNKL endodontically *dentistry*
NDDNKS endodontics *dentistry*
NDDNSHNZ United Nations *international group*
NDDNST endodontist *dentist*
NDDNTKL endodontically *dentistry*
NDDNTKS endodontics *dentistry*
NDDNTST endodontist *dentist*
NDDNTX endodontics *dentistry*

Use letters that best describe the sounds you hear and omit the vowels. Use **S** or **K** instead of **C**: to find circle use **SRKL**. Use **J** to find joy, **JM** to find gem and **G** to find go.

NDDNX endodontics *dentistry*

NDDRM endoderm *inner layer*

NDDRML endodermal *inner layer*

NDDRMS endodermis *inner layer*

NDDSTTS United States *country*

NDF nod off *doze*

NDF notify *inform* notified notifying notifies

NDFBL notifiable *inform*

NDFDD undefeated *never beaten*

NDFDGBL indefatigable (adj) *untiring* indefatibably (adv)

NDFDK endophytic *plant*

NDFGS nidifugous *nest*

NDFKDBL indefectible (adj) *lasting* indefectibly (adv)

NDFKSHN nidification *nest*

NDFKSHN notification *message*

NDFKTBL indefectible (adj) *lasting* indefectibly (adv)

NDFL needful (adj) *necessary* needfully (adv)

NDFLNS needfulness *necessity*

NDFNBL indefinable (adj) *cannot describe* indefinably (adv)

NDFND undefined *no meaning*

NDFNSBL indefensible (adj) *inexcusable* indefensibly (adv)

NDFNT indefinite *vague*

NDFNTL indefinitely *vague, time*

NDFNTSBL indefensible (adj) *inexcusable* indefensibly (adv)

NDFRNS indifference *uncaring*

NDFRNT indifferent *uncaring*

NDFRNTS indifference *uncaring*

NDFT endophyte *plant*

NDFTD undefeated *never beaten*

NDFTGBL indefatigable (adj) *untiring* indefatigably (adv)

NDFTK endophytic *plant*

NDFYBL notifiable *inform*

NDFYGS nidifugous *nest*

NDFZBL indefeasible (adj) *cannot annul* indefeasibly (adv)

NDG indigo *blue* indigos (or) indigoes

NDGM endogamy *marriage*

NDGMS endogamous *marriage*

NDGND indignity *insult* indignities

NDGNFD undignified *no esteem*

NDGNK endogenic *from within*

NDGNNT indignant *insulted*

NDGNS endogenous *from within*

NDGNSHN indignation *anger*

NDGNSL endogenously *from within*

NDGNST undiagnosed *not identified*

NDGNT indignant *insulted*

NDGNT indignity *insult* indignities

NDGNZD undiagnosed *not identified*

NDGRD nitty-gritty *basics*

NDGRT nitty-gritty *basics*

NDJKBL ineducable *cannot learn*

NDJKBLD ineducability *cannot learn*

NDJKBLT ineducability *cannot learn*

NDJKDD uneducated *no schooling*

NDJKTD uneducated *no schooling*

NDJNK endogenic *from within*

NDJNS endogenous *from within*

NDJNS indigence *poverty*

NDJNS indigenous *native*

NDJNSL endogenously *from within*

NDJNT indigent *needy*

NDJNTS indigence *poverty*

NDJSCHN indigestion *heartburn*

NDJSDBL indigestible *not absorbed*

NDJSDBLD indigestibility *not absorbed*

NDJSDBLT indigestibility *not absorbed*

NDJSDD undigested *food*

NDJSTBL indigestible *not absorbed*

NDJSTBLD indigestibility *not absorbed*

NDJSTBLT indigestibility *not absorbed*

NDJSTD undigested *food*

NDK anodic *electrode*

NDK induct *initiate*

NDK noetic *intellect*

NDKD inductee *initiation*

NDKDD uneducated *no schooling*

NDKDR indicator *sign*

NDKDR inductor *initiator*

NDKDV indicative *verb, sign*

NDKDV inductive *initiation, inference*

NDKL anodically *electrode*

NDKL nautical (adj) *ship* nautically (adv)

NDKLML nautical mile *distance*

NDKLNBL indeclinable *no inflection*

NDKLRD undeclared *unspoken*

NDKLS nidicolous *nest*

NDKNT indicant *pointer*

NDKRD endocardia (pl) *heart* endocardium

NDKRD notochord *spine*

NDKRDL endocardial *heart*

NDKRDL notochordal *spine*

NDKRDM endocardium *heart* endocardia

NDKRDY endocardia (pl)
heart endocardium

NDKRDYL endocardial
heart

NDKRDYM endocardium
heart endocardia

NDKRM indecorum *bad taste*

NDKRN endocrine *gland*

NDKRNLG endocrinology
glands

NDKRNLJ endocrinology
glands

NDKRNLJK endocrinologic
(or) endocrinological
glands

NDKRNLJKL
endocrinological (or)
endocrinologic *glands*

NDKRNLJST
endocrinologist *gland
specialist*

NDKRP endocarp *fruit*

NDKRS indecorous *bad taste*

NDKS index *(n) pointer, list,
number* indexes (or)
indices

NDKS index *(v) list*

NDKSHN indication *sign*

NDKSHN induction
initiation, inference

NDKT indicate *signal*
indicated indicating

NDKT induct *initiate*

NDKT inductee *initiation*

NDKTD uneducated *no
schooling*

NDKTNS inductance
initiation

NDKTNTS inductance
initiation

NDKTR indicator *sign*

NDKTR inductor *initiator*

NDKTRNDR indoctrinator
instructor

NDKTRNSHN
indoctrination *instruction*

NDKTRNT indoctrinate
instruct indoctrinated
indoctrinating

NDKTRNTR indoctrinator
instructor

NDKTV indicative *verb, sign*

NDKTV inductive *initiation,
inference*

NDKWC inadequacy *lack*
inadequacies

NDKWS inadequacy *lack*
inadequacies

NDKWT inadequate *lacking*

NDKWTL inadequately
lacking

NDKWTNS inadequateness
lack

NDL anodal *electrode*

NDL indole *chemical*

NDL inutile *useless*

NDL know-it-all *smart one*

NDL natal *birth*

NDL nattily *neatly*

NDL naughtily *wickedly*

NDL nautili *(pl) animal*
nautilus

NDL needle *(v) tease, sew*
needled needling

NDL needle *(n) sewing tool,
stylus*

NDL nettle *(v) irritate, sting*
nettled nettling

NDL nettle *(n) plant*

NDL New Deal *government
program*

NDL New Delhi *city*

NDL nodal *(adj) lumpy*
nodally *(adv)*

NDL noddle *head*

NDL nodule *lump*

NDL noodle *(n) food, head*

NDL noodle *(v) improvise*
noodled noodling

NDL nudely *barely*

NDL nuttily *like nuts, silly*

NDL unduly *overly*

NDLBL indelible *(adj) lasting*
indelibly *(adv)*

NDLBLD indelibility *lasting*

NDLBLT indelibility *lasting*

NDLD nautiloid *animal*

NDLD nodality *lump*
nodalities

NDLDRDD unadulterated
pure

NDLDRTD unadulterated
pure

NDLF endleaf *paper*

endleaves

NDLJ indulge *pamper, yield*
indulged indulging

NDLJNS indulgence
forgiveness, weakness

NDLJNT indulgent
permissive

NDLJNTS indulgence
forgiveness, weakness

NDLJR indulger *pamper,
yield*

NDLKC indelicacy *improper*

NDLKS indelicacy *improper*

NDLKT indelicate *improper*

NDLNS indolence *laziness*

NDLNT indolent *lazy*

NDLNT undulant *wavy*

NDLNTL indolently *lazily*

NDLNTS indolence *laziness*

NDLPNT needlepoint
embroidery

NDLR needler *tease, sew*

NDLR nodular *lumpy*

NDLS endless *forever*

NDLS nautilus *animal*
nautiluses (or) nautili

NDLS needless *useless*

NDLSHN Andalusian *of
Spain*

NDLSHN undulation *wave*

NDLSL endlessly *forever*

NDLSL needlessly *useless*

NDLSM nettlesome
irritating

NDLSN Andalusian *of Spain*

NDLSNS endlessness
forever

NDLSNS needlessness
useless

NDLST andalusite *mineral*

NDLSYN Andalusian *of
Spain*

NDLT indult *privilege*

NDLT nodality *lump*
nodalities

NDLT undulate *wave*
undulated undulating

NDLTR undulatory *waves*

NDLTRDD unadulterated
pure

NDLTRTD unadulterated
pure

NDLVRD undelivered *not arrived*

NDLWRK needlework *sewing*

NDM anatomy *analysis, structure* anatomies

NDM indium *element*

NDM notum *thorax* nota

NDMB endamoeba *parasite*

NDMD undimmed *bright*

NDMDBL indomitable (adj) *unconquerable* indomitably (adv)

NDMK endemic *native*

NDMKL endemically *native*

NDMKRDK antidemocratic *against democracy*

NDMKRDK undemocratic *no vote*

NDMKRDKL undemocratically *no vote*

NDMKRTK antidemocratic *against democracy*

NDMKRTK undemocratic *no vote*

NDMKRTKL undemocratically *no vote*

NDMM neodymium *element*

NDMN anno Domini *after Christ (abbr) A.D.*

NDMND indemnity *security, exemption* indemnities

NDMNDNG undemanding *easy*

NDMNF indemnify *pay, secure* indemnified indemnifying indemnifies

NDMNFKSHN indemnification *compensation*

NDMNFR indemnifier *compensation*

NDMNFYR indemnifier *compensation*

NDMNSHNL unidimensional *one aspect*

NDMNSHNLD unidimensionality *one aspect*

NDMNSHNLT unidimensionality *one aspect*

NDMNSTRDV undemonstrative *no emotion*

NDMNSTRTV undemonstrative *no emotion*

NDMNT endowment *gift*

NDMNT indemnity *security, exemption* indemnities

NDMNTSHNL unidimensional *one aspect*

NDMNTSHNLD unidimensionality *one aspect*

NDMNTSHNLT unidimensionality *one aspect*

NDMRF endomorph *fat body*

NDMRF endomorphy *fat body*

NDMRFK endomorphic *fat body*

NDMRFZM endomorphism *math*

NDMSBL inadmissible (adj) *no entry* inadmissibly (adv)

NDMSD endemicity *native*

NDMST anatomist *body structure*

NDMST endemicity *native*

NDMST endmost *last*

NDMTBL indomitable (adj) *unconquerable* indomitably (adv)

NDMTR endometria (pl) *uterus* endometrium

NDMTRDS endometritis *uterus*

NDMTRM endometrium *uterus* endometria

NDMTRSS endometriosis *uterus*

NDMTRTS endometritis *uterus*

NDMTRY endometria (pl) *uterus* endometrium

NDMTRYDS endometritis *uterus*

NDMTRYM endometrium *uterus* endometria

NDMTRYSS endometriosis *uterus*

NDMTRYTS endometritis *uterus*

NDMYM neodymium *element*

NDMZ anatomize *analyze* anatomized anatomizing (Br) anatomise

NDMZM endemism *native*

NDN Andean *of the Andes*

NDN anodyne *(adj) innocuous (n) drug*

NDN ending *finish*

NDN Indian *of India*

NDN Indiana *US State*

NDN indign *unworthy*

NDN undine *water nymph*

NDN undoing *ruin*

NDN undone *not finished*

NDN undying *lasting*

NDNBL undeniable (adj) *true* undeniably (adv)

NDNCHN indention *space*

NDNCHR indenture *(v) bind* indentured indenturing

NDNCHR indenture *(n) contract, dent*

NDNCHRD indentured *documented*

NDND undaunted *fearless*

NDNFD unidentified *not known*

NDNG ending *finish*

NDNG knitting *weaving*

NDNG netting *snare, web*

NDNG undoing *ruin*

NDNG undying *lasting*

NDNJR endanger *imperil*

NDNJRD endangered *threatened*

NDNJRMNT endangerment *peril*

NDNK nudnick (or) nudnik *nuisance*

NDNPLS Indianapolis *city*

NDNS knottiness *tangles*

NDNS nattiness *neatness*

NDNS naughtiness *wickedness*

NDNS neediness *poverty*

NDNS nudeness *nakedness*

NDNS nuttiness *like nuts,*

---

silly

NDNSH Indonesia *country*

NDNSHN indention *space*

NDNSHN Indian Ocean *body of water*

NDNSHN Indonesian *of Indonesia*

NDNT andante *music*

NDNT annuitant *heir*

NDNT endnote *postscript*

NDNT indent *(v) margin,* (Br) *draw on (n) certificate*

NDNT needn't *(contr) need not*

NDNTD undaunted *fearless*

NDNTFD unidentified *not known*

NDNTN andantino *music* andantinos

NDNTR indenture *(v) bind* indentured indenturing

NDNTRD indentured *documented*

NDNTSHN indentation *notch*

NDNTSHR indenture *(v) bind* indentured indenturing

NDNTSHR indenture *(n) contract, dent*

NDNTSHRD indentured *documented*

NDNYBL undeniable (adj) *true* undeniably (adv)

NDNZ Indonesia *country*

NDNZH Indonesia *country*

NDNZHN Indonesian *of Indonesia*

NDNZN Indonesian *of Indonesia*

NDNZY Indonesia *country*

NDNZYN Indonesian *of Indonesia*

NDP knee-deep *knee-high*

NDPLMDK undiplomatic *heavy-handed*

NDPLMDKL undiplomatically *heavy-handedly*

NDPLMTK undiplomatic *heavy-handed*

NDPLMTKL undiplomatically *heavy-*

handedly

NDPLZM endoplasm *inner part*

NDPLZMK endoplasmic *inner part*

NDPNDBL undependable *not reliable*

NDPNDNS independence *freedom*

NDPNDNT independent *free*

NDPNDNTS independence *freedom*

NDPNT endpoint (or) end point *terminal*

NDPPR endpaper *book cover*

NDPRSNT antidepressant *drug*

NDPTH in-depth *thorough*

NDQC inadequacy *lack* inadequacies

NDQS inadequacy *lack* inadequacies

NDQT inadequate *lacking*

NDQTL inadequately *lacking*

NDQTNS inadequateness *lack*

NDR and/or *both or either*

NDR Andorra *country*

NDR anteater *animal*

NDR endear *love*

NDR endure *outlast, suffer* endured enduring

NDR enduro *race* enduros

NDR in utero *uterus*

NDR indoor *sheltered*

NDR knitter *weaver*

NDR knotter *tangler*

NDR knottier *tangles*

NDR nadir *low point*

NDR natter *chatter*

NDR nattier *neater*

NDR naughtier *wicked*

NDR needier *poor*

NDR neuter *(v) castrate (adj) neutral (n) gender, worker, animal*

NDR niter *chemical* (Br) *nitre*

NDR nitery *club* niteries

NDR notary *certifier* notaries

NDR nutter *(Br) nut*

NDR under *beneath*

NDRBD underbid *low offer* underbid underbidding

NDRBD underbody *frame* underbodies

NDRBDR underbidder *low offer*

NDRBL endurable (adj) *bearable* endurably (adv)

NDRBL underbelly *low side* underbellies

NDRBL unutterable (adj) *beyond words* unutterably (adv)

NDRBRSH underbrush *shrubbery*

NDRBTR underbidder *low offer*

NDRC endorsee *approver*

NDRC undersea *ocean*

NDRCHRJ undercharge *too little money* undercharged undercharging

NDRCHV underachieve *no accomplishment*

NDRCHVR underachiever *no accomplishment*

NDRD android *robot*

NDRD notoriety *fame* notorieties

NDRDD indurated *hard*

NDRDD underrated *valued less*

NDRDG underdog *loser, victim*

NDRDJKDD undereducated *little schooling*

NDRDJKTD undereducated *little schooling*

NDRDKDD undereducated *little schooling*

NDRDKTD undereducated *little schooling*

NDRDLZ underutilize *partly use* underutilized underutilizing (Br) underutilise

NDRDN underdone *rare*

NDRDR underwriter *guarantee*

NDRDRRZ underdrawers *underwear*

NDRDRZ underdrawers

Use letters that best describe the sounds you hear and omit the vowels. Use **S** or **K** instead of **C**: to find circle use **SRKL**. Use **J** to find joy, **JM** to find gem and **G** to find go.

underwear
NDRDT andradite *garnet*
NDRDV indurative *harden*
NDRDVLPD
underdeveloped
inadequate, immature, not industrialized
NDRDVLPT
underdeveloped
inadequate, immature, not industrialized
NDRDYKDD
undereducated *little schooling*
NDRDYKTD undereducated *little schooling*
NDRFD underfeed
malnourish underfed underfeeding
NDRFN endorphin *brain protein*
NDRFT underfoot *ground level, in the way*
NDRG antidrug *no drugs*
NDRG undergo *endure* undergoes underwent undergone undergoing
NDRGLZ underglaze *coating*
NDRGN androgyne *male and female*
NDRGN undergone *endured*
NDRGRD undergird *support*
NDRGRD undergrad *student*
NDRGRJT undergraduate *student*
NDRGRJWT undergraduate *student*
NDRGRMNT undergarment *underwear*
NDRGRN underground *below surface, secret*
NDRGRND underground *below surface, secret*
NDRGRTH undergrowth *shrubbery*
NDRHN underhand *throw*
NDRHND underhand *throw*
NDRHNDD underhanded *throw, evasive*
NDRHNG underhung *hanging*
NDRJ underage *too young*

NDRJKDD undereducated *little schooling*
NDRJKTD undereducated *little schooling*
NDRJN androgen *hormone*
NDRJN androgyne *male and female*
NDRJN androgyny *male and female*
NDRJNK androgenic *hormonal*
NDRJNS androgynous *male and female*
NDRK indirect *roundabout*
NDRK underact *no emotion*
NDRKDD undirected *not guided*
NDRKDNG undercoating *paint*
NDRKL indirectly *roundabout*
NDRKLS underclass *disadvantaged*
NDRKLSMN
underclassman *freshman or sophomore* underclassmen
NDRKLTHN underclothing *underwear*
NDRKLTHNG underclothing *underwear*
NDRKLTHS underclothes *underwear*
NDRKLTHZ underclothes *underwear*
NDRKLZ underclothes *underwear*
NDRKNS indirectness *roundabout*
NDRKNT undercount *too few*
NDRKRD undercard *program*
NDRKRJ undercarriage *support*
NDRKRNT undercurrent *hidden pull*
NDRKSHN indirection *aimlessness*
NDRKSHNL unidirectional (adj) *one way* unidirectionally (adv)

NDRKSPSHR
underexposure *not revealed, not well lit*
NDRKSPZ underexpose *not revealed, not well lit* underexposed underexposing
NDRKSPZD underexposed *not revealed, not well lit*
NDRKSPZHR
underexposure *not revealed, not well lit*
NDRKT indirect *roundabout*
NDRKT underact *no emotion*
NDRKT undercoat *paint*
NDRKT undercount *too few*
NDRKT undercut *cheat*
NDRKTD undirected *not guided*
NDRKTL indirectly *roundabout*
NDRKTN undercoating *paint*
NDRKTNG undercoating *paint*
NDRKTNS indirectness *roundabout*
NDRKVR undercover *covert*
NDRL underlay *support* underlaid underlaying
NDRL underlie *support* underlay underlain underlying
NDRLD underlaid *beneath*
NDRLN underlain *(v-past) underlie*
NDRLN underline *writing* underlined underlining
NDRLN underling *subordinate*
NDRLN underlying *beneath*
NDRLNG underling *subordinate*
NDRLNG underlying *beneath*
NDRLP underlip *lower lip*
NDRLYN underlying *beneath*
NDRLYNG underlying *beneath*
NDRM underarm *armpit*
NDRMD Andromeda *myth, stars*
NDRMD andromeda *shrub*

Letters aren't doubled for single sounds: to find alley use **L** not **LL**. Use **Y** and **W** as hard sounds only: to find yellow use **YL**. (Br)=British spelling or usage. * See dictionary.

NDRMFSZ underemphasize
  little attention
  underemphasized
  underemphasizing
  (Br) underemphasised
NDRMN undermine *weaken*
  undermined undermining
NDRMND undermanned
  lacking staff
NDRMNT endearment *love*
NDRMPLD underemployed
  less work
NDRMST undermost *lowest*
NDRN andiron *hearth*
NDRN cnidarian *jellyfish*
NDRN enduring *lasting*
NDRN underrun *below*
  estimate underran
  underrunning
NDRND unadorned *plain*
NDRNFSZ underemphasize
  little attention
  underemphasized
  underemphasizing
  (Br) underemphasised
NDRNG enduring *lasting*
NDRNGKBL undrinkable
  polluted
NDRNGL endearingly
  lovingly
NDRNKBL undrinkable
  polluted
NDRNL endearingly *lovingly*
NDRNRSHMNT
  undernourishment
  nutrition
NDRNRSHT
  undernourished *nutrition*
NDRNS endurance
  persistence
NDRNSHRD underinsured
  insurance
NDRNT knight-errant
  traveler knights-errant
NDRNTH underneath *below*
NDRNTS endurance
  persistence
NDRP underpay *pay less*
  underpaid underpaying
NDRPBLK notary public
  certifier notaries public
  (or) notary publics

NDRPBLSZD
  underpublicized *not made*
  known
  (Br) underpublicised
NDRPD underpaid *wages*
NDRPL underplay *play down*
NDRPN Indo-European
  language
NDRPN underpin *support*
  underpinned
  underpinning
NDRPNN underpinning
  support
NDRPNNG underpinning
  support
NDRPNS underpants
  underwear
NDRPNTN underpainting
  base coat
NDRPNTNG underpainting
  base coat
NDRPNTS underpants
  underwear
NDRPPLDD
  underpopulated *fewer*
  than normal
NDRPPLTD underpopulated
  fewer than normal
NDRPPYLDD
  underpopulated *fewer*
  than normal
NDRPPYLTD
  underpopulated *fewer*
  than normal
NDRPRDKSHN
  underproduction *less than*
  needed
NDRPRF underproof *less*
  alcohol
NDRPRPRD underprepared
  not ready
NDRPRS underprice *low*
  price underpriced
  underpricing
NDRPRSHDD
  underappreciated *taken*
  for granted
NDRPRSHTD
  underappreciated *taken*
  for granted
NDRPRSHYDD
  underappreciated *taken*

  for granted
NDRPRSHYTD
  underappreciated *taken*
  for granted
NDRPRSND
  underrepresented *stand*
  for another
NDRPRSNTD
  underrepresented *stand*
  for another
NDRPRSNTSHN
  underrepresentation
  stand for another
NDRPRT underpart *beneath*
NDRPRT underreport *low*
  estimate
NDRPRVLJD
  underprivileged
  disadvantaged
NDRPRZND
  underrepresented *stand*
  for another
NDRPRZNTD
  underrepresented *stand*
  for another
NDRPRZNTSHN
  underrepresentation
  stand for another
NDRPS underpass *roadway*
  underpasses
NDRPYN Indo-European
  language
NDRRM underarm *armpit*
NDRS endorse *approve*
  endorsed endorsing
NDRS endorsee *approver*
NDRS undersea *ocean*
NDRS undress *disrobe*
NDRSBL endorsable
  approvable
NDRSD underside *beneath*
NDRSD underused *partly*
  utilized
NDRSDMDD
  underestimated *underrate*
NDRSDMSHN
  underestimation *underrate*
NDRSDMT underestimate
  underrate underestimated
  underestimating
NDRSDMTD
  underestimated *underrate*

Use letters that best describe the sounds you hear and omit the vowels. Use **S** or **K**
instead of **C**: to find circle use **SRKL**. Use **J** to find joy, **JM** to find gem and **G** to find go.

NDRSHN induration *harden*
NDRSHRT undershirt
underwear
NDRSHT undershoot *too
low* undershot
undershooting
NDRSKR underscore
underline underscored
underscoring
NDRSKRT underskirt
petticoat
NDRSKRTR undersecretary
subordinate
undersecretaries
NDRSKST undersexed *little
desire*
NDRSL undersell *cheaper*
undersold underselling
NDRSLNG underslung *low*
NDRSMNT endorsement
approval
NDRSND undersigned
signature
NDRSNTRK androcentric
masculine
NDRST undressed *nude*
NDRSTD understood *known*
NDRSTD understudy *theater*
understudied
understudying
understudies
NDRSTDD understated *not
obvious*
NDRSTFT understaffed *few
workers*
NDRSTMDD
underestimated *underrate*
NDRSTMSHN
underestimation
underrate
NDRSTMT underestimate
underrate underestimated
underestimating
NDRSTMTD
underestimated *underrate*
NDRSTN understand
comprehend understood
understanding
NDRSTND understand
comprehend understood
understanding
NDRSTNDBL

understandable (adj)
comprehend
understandably (adv)
NDRSTNDN understanding
*(n) comprehension (adj)
sympathetic*
NDRSTNDNG
understanding *(n)
comprehension (adj)
sympathetic*
NDRSTR understeer *turn*
NDRSTR understory *plants*
NDRSTT understate *reduce*
understated understating
NDRSTTD understated *not
obvious*
NDRSTTMNT
understatement *restraint*
NDRSXT undersexed *little
desire*
NDRSZD undersized *small*
NDRT indurate *harden*
indurated indurating
NDRT notoriety *fame*
notorieties
NDRT underrate *less valued*
underrated underrating
NDRT undertow *ocean*
NDRT underwrite *guarantee*
underwrote underwriting
underwritten
NDRTD indurated *hard*
NDRTD underrated *valued
less*
NDRTHKNR under-the-
counter *illegal*
NDRTHKNTR under-the-
counter *illegal*
NDRTHKTR under-the-
counter *illegal*
NDRTHTBL under-the-table
illegal
NDRTK undertake *attempt*
undertook undertaking
undertaken
NDRTKN undertaking
enterprise
NDRTKNG undertaking
enterprise
NDRTKR undertaker *burial*
NDRTLZ underutilize *partly
use* underutilized

underutilizing
(Br) underutilise
NDRTN undertone *whisper*
NDRTN underwritten
guaranteed
NDRTR underwriter
guarantee
NDRTV indurative *harden*
NDRVL undervalue *below
worth* undervalued
undervaluing
NDRVLSHN undervaluation
below worth
NDRVLWSHN
undervaluation *below
worth*
NDRVLY undervalue *below
worth* undervalued
undervaluing
NDRVLYSHN
undervaluation *below
worth*
NDRVLYWSHN
undervaluation *below
worth*
NDRW under way (adv)
moving underway (adj)
NDRWD underwood
shrubbery
NDRWDR underwater
submerged
NDRWLM underwhelm *fail
to impress*
NDRWNG underwing
beneath, moth
NDRWNT underwent *(v-
past) undergo*
NDRWR underwear *garment*
NDRWRL underworld *hell,
crime*
NDRWRLD underworld *hell,
crime*
NDRWT underweight *too
light*
NDRWTR underwater
submerged
NDRXPSHR underexposure
not revealed, not well lit
NDRXPZ underexpose *not
revealed, not well lit*
underexposed
underexposing

Letters aren't doubled for single sounds: to find alley use **L** not **LL**. Use **Y** and **W** as hard sounds only: to find yellow use **YL**. (Br)=British spelling or usage. * See dictionary.

NDRXPZD underexposed *not revealed, not well lit*
NDRXPZHR underexposure *not revealed, not well lit*
NDRYD notoriety *fame* notorieties
NDRYDLZ underutilize *partly use* underutilized underutilizing (Br) underutilise
NDRYN cnidarian *jellyfish*
NDRYT notoriety *fame* notorieties
NDRYTLZ underutilize *partly use* underutilized underutilizing (Br) underutilise
NDRYZD underused *partly utilized*
NDRZ indoors *sheltered*
NDRZ notarize *signature* notarized notarizing
NDRZD underused *partly utilized*
NDRZSHN notarization *signature*
NDS Andes *mountains*
NDS induce *persuade* induced inducing
NDS nidus *nest* nidi (or) niduses
NDS no dice *never*
NDS notice *(v) heed, discern* noticed noticing
NDS notice *(n) alert*
NDSBL inducible *cause, infer*
NDSBL noticeable (adj) *clear* noticeably (adv)
NDSBL unnoticeable *not seen*
NDSBLD inducibility *cause, infer*
NDSBLT inducibility *cause, infer*
NDSDD undecided *not resolved*
NDSDK andesitic *rock*
NDSFRBL indecipherable *cannot decode*
NDSGSD undisguised *open*
NDSGZD undisguised *open*
NDSH indicia *markings*

NDSHY indicia *markings*
NDSKLDL endoskeletal *internal framework*
NDSKLDN endoskeleton *internal framework*
NDSKLTL endoskeletal *internal framework*
NDSKLTN endoskeleton *internal framework*
NDSKLZD undisclosed *secret*
NDSKP endoscope *examination device*
NDSKPK endoscopic *examination device*
NDSKPKL endoscopically *examination device*
NDSKRBBL indescribable (adj) *no description* indescribably (adv)
NDSKRMNT indiscriminate *random*
NDSKRMNTL indiscriminately *random*
NDSKRMNTNS indiscriminateness *random*
NDSKRSHN indiscretion *impolite*
NDSKRT indiscreet *impolite*
NDSKRTL indiscreetly · *impolite*
NDSKRTNS indiscreetness *impolite*
NDSL indocile *stubborn*
NDSLBL indissoluble (adj) *permanent* indissolubly (adv)
NDSLBLD indissolubility *permanent*
NDSLBLT indissolubility *permanent*
NDSLD indocility *stubbornness*
NDSLT indocility *stubbornness*
NDSLYBL indissoluble (adj) *permanent* indissolubly (adv)
NDSLYBLD indissolubility *permanent*
NDSLYBLT indissolubility

permanent
NDSMBDK endosymbiotic *live within*
NDSMBNT endosymbiont *live within*
NDSMBSS endosymbiosis *live within*
NDSMBTK endosymbiotic *live within*
NDSMBYDK endosymbiotic *live within*
NDSMBYNT endosymbiont *live within*
NDSMBYSS endosymbiosis *live within*
NDSMBYTK endosymbiotic *live within*
NDSMNT inducement *persuasion*
NDSNC indecency *offensiveness* indecencies
NDSNDD undescended *retained above*
NDSNS indecency *offensiveness* indecencies
NDSNT indecent *offensive*
NDSNTC indecency *offensiveness* indecencies
NDSNTL indecently *offensive*
NDSNTS indecency *offensiveness* indecencies
NDSPDBL indisputable (adj) *unquestionable* indisputably (adv)
NDSPDD undisputed *no argument*
NDSPLND undisciplined *no self-control*
NDSPNSBL indispensable (adj) *necessary* indispensably (adv)
NDSPNSBLD indispensability *necessary*
NDSPNSBLT indispensability *necessary*
NDSPR endospore *bacteria*
NDSPRM endosperm *seed*
NDSPTBL indisputable (adj) *unquestionable* indisputably (adv)
NDSPTD undisputed *no argument*

Use letters that best describe the sounds you hear and omit the vowels. Use **S** or **K** instead of **C**: to find circle use **SRKL**. Use **J** to find joy, **JM** to find gem and **G** to find go.

NDSPYDBL indisputable (adj) *unquestionable* indisputably (adv)

NDSPYDD undisputed *no argument*

NDSPYTBL indisputable (adj) *unquestionable* indisputably (adv)

NDSPYTD undisputed *no argument*

NDSPZ indispose *make unfit* indisposed indisposing

NDSPZD indisposed *ill, averse*

NDSPZSHN indisposition *ill, averse*

NDSR inducer *persuader*

NDSRNBL indiscernible (adj) *vague* indiscernibly (adv)

NDSSHN indecision *no resolution*

NDSSV indecisive *no resolution*

NDSSVL indecisively *no resolution*

NDSSVNS indecisiveness *no resolution*

NDST andesite *rock*

NDST knottiest *tangles*

NDST nattiest *neatest*

NDST naughtiest *wicked*

NDST neediest *poor*

NDST nudist *naked one*

NDST unnoticed *not seen*

NDSTK andesitic *rock*

NDSTNGGWSHBL indistinguishable (adj) *unclear* indistinguishably (adv)

NDSTNGK indistinct *vague*

NDSTNGKDV indistinctive *vague*

NDSTNGKT indistinct *vague*

NDSTNGKTV indistinctive *vague*

NDSTNGWSHBL indistinguishable (adj) *unclear* indistinguishably (adv)

NDSTNK indistinct *vague*

NDSTNKDV indistinctive

vague

NDSTNKT indistinct *vague*

NDSTNKTV indistinctive *vague*

NDSTR industry *effort, manufacturing* industries

NDSTRBD undisturbed *serene*

NDSTRKDBL indestructible (adj) *cannot ruin* indestructibly (adv)

NDSTRKDBLD indestructibility *cannot ruin*

NDSTRKDBLT indestructibility *cannot ruin*

NDSTRKTBL indestructible (adj) *cannot ruin* indestructibly (adv)

NDSTRKTBLD indestructibility *cannot ruin*

NDSTRKTBLT indestructibility *cannot ruin*

NDSTRL industrial (adj) *business, heavy-duty* industrially (adv)

NDSTRLST industrialist *businessman*

NDSTRLZ industrialize *manufacture* industrialized industrializing (Br) industrialise

NDSTRLZM industrialism *business*

NDSTRLZSHN industrialization *machines* (Br) industrialisation

NDSTRS industrious *busy*

NDSTRYL industrial (adj) *business, heavy-duty* industrially (adv)

NDSTRYLST industrialist *businessman*

NDSTRYLZ industrialize *manufacture* industrialized industrializing (Br) industrialise

NDSTRYLZM industrialism *business*

NDSTRYLZSHN industrialization *machines* (Br) industrialisation

NDSTRYS industrious *busy*

NDSTSS endocytosis *cell*

NDSTTK endocytotic *cell*

NDSZ indices (pl) (n) *pointer, list, number* index

NDSZHN indecision *no resolution*

NDT andouillette *sausage*

NDT antidote *counteract poison*

NDT indict *accuse*

NDT indite *compose* indited inditing

NDT nudity *bareness*

NDTBL indictable *accuse*

NDTD indebted *owing*

NDTD undoubted *certain*

NDTD unedited *not revised*

NDTDL undoubtedly *certain*

NDTHL endothelia (pl) *inner layer* endothelium

NDTHLL endothelial *inner layer*

NDTHLM endothelium *inner layer* endothelia

NDTHLY endothelia (pl) *inner layer* endothelium

NDTHLYL endothelial *inner layer*

NDTHLYM endothelium *inner layer* endothelia

NDTHRM endotherm *warm-blooded*

NDTHRM endothermy *warm-blooded*

NDTHRMK endothermic *warm-blooded*

NDTKDBL undetectable *not noticed*

NDTKTBL undetectable *not noticed*

NDTMNT indictment *accusation*

NDTR natatory (or) natatorial *swimming*

NDTRD undeterred *free*

NDTRFK endotrophic *between cells*

NDTRL natatorial (or)

Letters aren't doubled for single sounds: to find alley use **L** not **LL**. Use **Y** and **W** as hard sounds only: to find yellow use **YL**. (Br)=British spelling or usage. * See dictionary.

natatory *swimming*
NDTRM natatorium *pool*
NDTRMNBL indeterminable
(adj) *vague* indeterminably
(adv)
NDTRMNC indeterminacy
vagueness
NDTRMND undetermined
unknown
NDTRMNS indeterminacy
vagueness
NDTRMNSHN
indetermination *vagueness*
NDTRMNST indeterminist
unpredictable
NDTRMNT indeterminate
vague
NDTRMNZM indeterminism
unpredictable
NDTRYL natatorial (or)
natatory *swimming*
NDTRYM natatorium *pool*
NDV endive *lettuce*
NDV native *originating in*
NDV unitive *joining*
NDVDD undivided *whole*
NDVDJL individual (adj)
separate (n) person
individually (adv)
NDVDJLD individuality
personality individualities
NDVDJLSDK individualistic
independent
NDVDJLST individualist
each person
NDVDJLSTK individualistic
independent
NDVDJLT individuality
personality individualities
NDVDJLZ individualize
personalize individualized
individualizing
(Br) individualise
NDVDJLZM individualism
each person
NDVDJLZSHN
individualization *one
person*
(Br) individualisation
NDVDJSHN individuation
contrast
NDVDJT individuate *separate*

individuated individuating
NDVDJWLD individuality
personality individualities
NDVDJWLSDK
individualistic *independent*
NDVDJWLST individualist
each person
NDVDJWLSTK
individualistic *independent*
NDVDJWLT individuality
personality individualities
NDVDJWLZ individualize
personalize individualized
individualizing
(Br) individualise
NDVDJWLZM individualism
each person
NDVDJWLZSHN
individualization *one
person*
(Br) individualisation
NDVDJWSHN individuation
contrast
NDVDJWT individuate
separate individuated
individuating
NDVDL individual (adj)
separate (n) person
individually (adv)
NDVDLSDK individualistic
independent
NDVDLST individualist *each
person*
NDVDLSTK individualistic
independent
NDVDWL individual (adj)
separate (n) person
individually (adv)
NDVDWLSDK
individualistic *independent*
NDVDWLST individualist
each person
NDVDWLSTK individualistic
independent
NDVDYL individual (adj)
separate (n) person
individually (adv)
NDVDYWL individual (adj)
separate (n) person
individually (adv)
NDVJL individual (adj)
separate (n) person

individually (adv)
NDVJLD individuality
personality individualities
NDVJLSDK individualistic
independent
NDVJLST individualist *each
person*
NDVJLSTK individualistic
independent
NDVJLT individuality
personality individualities
NDVJLZ individualize
personalize individualized
individualizing
(Br) individualise
NDVJLZM individualism
each person
NDVJLZSHN
individualization *one
person*
(Br) individualisation
NDVJSHN individuation
contrast
NDVJT individuate *separate*
individuated individuating
NDVJWL individual (adj)
separate (n) person
individually (adv)
NDVJWLD individuality
personality individualities
NDVJWLSDK individualistic
independent
NDVJWLST individualist
each person
NDVJWLSTK individualistic
independent
NDVJWLT individuality
personality individualities
NDVJWLZ individualize
personalize individualized
individualizing
(Br) individualise
NDVJWLZM individualism
each person
NDVJWLZSHN
individualization *one
person*
(Br) individualisation
NDVJWSHN individuation
contrast
NDVJWT individuate
separate individuated

Use letters that best describe the sounds you hear and omit the vowels. Use **S** or **K** instead of **C**: to find circle use **SRKL**. Use **J** to find joy, **JM** to find gem and **G** to find go.

individuating
NDVLPD undeveloped *not exposed, uncultivated*
NDVLPT undeveloped *not exposed, uncultivated*
NDVMRKN Native American *American Indian*
NDVR endeavor *attempt* (Br) endeavour
NDVRDNS inadvertence *oversight* inadvertency
NDVRDNT inadvertent *unintentional*
NDVRDNTL inadvertently *unintentional*
NDVRDNTS inadvertence *oversight* inadvertency
NDVRTNS inadvertence *oversight* inadvertency
NDVRTNT inadvertent *unintentional*
NDVRTNTL inadvertently *unintentional*
NDVRTNTS inadvertence *oversight* inadvertency
NDVRTZD unadvertised *no commercials*
NDVSBL indivisible (adj) *cannot split* indivisibly (adv)
NDVST nativist *first inhabitants*
NDVSTK nativistic *first inhabitants*
NDVZBL inadvisable *not recommended*
NDVZBL indivisible (adj) *cannot split* indivisibly (adv)
NDVZBLD inadvisability *not recommended*
NDVZBLD indivisibility *wholeness*
NDVZBLT inadvisability *not recommended*
NDVZBLT indivisibility *wholeness*
NDVZD unadvised *reckless*
NDVZDL unadvisedly *recklessly*
NDVZM nativism *first inhabitants*

NDW andouille *food*
NDWL indwell *exist within*
NDWLN indwelling *inner force*
NDWLNG indwelling *inner force*
NDWLR indweller *exist within*
NDWN undoing *ruin*
NDWNG undoing *ruin*
NDWT andouillette *sausage*
NDWYT andouillette *sausage*
NDWZ endways *on end*
NDWZ endwise *on end*
NDX index *(n)* pointer, list, number indexes (or) indices
NDX index *(v)* list
NDY endue *provide* endued enduing
NDY India *country*
NDY undue *excessive*
NDYBDBL indubitable (adj) *no doubt* indubitably (adv)
NDYBDBLD indubitability *no doubt*
NDYBDBLT indubitability *no doubt*
NDYBTBL indubitable (adj) *no doubt* indubitably (adv)
NDYBTBLD indubitability *no doubt*
NDYBTBLT indubitability *no doubt*
NDYGNST undiagnosed *not identified*
NDYGNZD undiagnosed *not identified*
NDYKDD uneducated *no schooling*
NDYKTD uneducated *no schooling*
NDYL nodule *lump*
NDYL unduly *overly*
NDYLNT undulant *wavy*
NDYLR nodular *lumpy*
NDYLSHN undulation *wave*
NDYLT undulate *wave* undulated undulating
NDYLTR undulatory *waves*
NDYM indium *element*
NDYN Andean *of the Andes*

NDYN Indian *of India*
NDYN Indiana *US State*
NDYN undying *lasting*
NDYNG undying *lasting*
NDYNPLS Indianapolis *city*
NDYNSHN Indian Ocean *body of water*
NDYR endure *outlast, suffer* endured enduring
NDYR enduro *race* enduros
NDYR knottier *tangles*
NDYR nattier *neater*
NDYR naughtier *wicked*
NDYR needier *poor*
NDYRBL endurable (adj) *bearable* endurably (adv)
NDYRDD indurated *hard*
NDYRDV indurative *harden*
NDYRN andiron *hearth*
NDYRN enduring *lasting*
NDYRNG enduring *lasting*
NDYRNS endurance *persistence*
NDYRNTS endurance *persistence*
NDYRPN Indo-European *language*
NDYRPYN Indo-European *language*
NDYRSHN induration *harden*
NDYRT indurate *harden* indurated indurating
NDYRTD indurated *hard*
NDYRTV indurative *harden*
NDYS induce *persuade* induced inducing
NDYSBL inducible *cause, infer*
NDYSMNT inducement *persuasion*
NDYSR inducer *persuader*
NDYST knottiest *tangles*
NDYST nattiest *neatest*
NDYST naughtiest *wicked*
NDYST neediest *poor*
NDYT andouillette *sausage*
NDYWL nodule *lump*
NDYZR end user *consumer*
NDZ Andes *mountains*
NDZ anodize *coat* anodized anodizing

Letters aren't doubled for single sounds: to find alley use **L** not **LL**. Use **Y** and **W** as hard sounds only: to find yellow use **YL**. (Br)=British spelling or usage. * See dictionary.

NDZ anti-AIDS *serum*

NDZ nowadays *present time*

NDZ undies *underwear*

NDZM nudism *naked*

NDZR end user *consumer*

NDZRBL undesirable (adj) *not wanted* undesirably (adv)

NDZRD undesired *not wanted*

NDZRVD undeserved *not worthy*

NDZSHN anodization *coating*

NF enough *no more needed*

NF info *information*

NF knife *(v) slice, cut* knifed knifing

NF knife *(n) blade* knives

NF nephew *relative*

NF unify *unite* unified unifying unifies

NFB amphibia *animals*

NFBL amphibole *mineral*

NFBL amphiboly *phrase* amphibolies

NFBL enfeeble *weaken* enfeebled enfeebling

NFBL ineffable (adj) *unspeakable* ineffably (adv)

NFBL unifiable *join*

NFBLD ineffability *unspeakable*

NFBLG amphibology *phrase* amphibologies

NFBLJ amphibology *phrase* amphibologies

NFBLMNT enfeeblement *weaken*

NFBLT amphibolite *mineral*

NFBLT ineffability *unspeakable*

NFBN amphibian *water and land*

NFBS amphibious *water and land*

NFBSL amphibiously *water and land*

NFBSNS amphibiousness *water and land*

NFBY amphibia *animals*

NFBYN amphibian *water and land*

NFBYS amphibious *water and land*

NFBYSL amphibiously *water and land*

NFBYSNS amphibiousness *water and land*

NFCHDD infatuated *in love* infatuated infatuating

NFCHSHN infatuation *love*

NFCHT infatuate *love* infatuated infatuating

NFCHTD infatuated *in love* infatuated infatuating

NFCHWDD infatuated *in love* infatuated infatuating

NFCHWSHN infatuation *love*

NFCHWT infatuate *love* infatuated infatuating

NFCHWTD infatuated *in love* infatuated infatuating

NFCM emphysema *lung disease*

NFCMK emphysemic *lung disease*

NFCZ emphases (pl) *stress* emphasis

NFD nifty *marvelous* niftier niftiest

NFD unified *joined*

NFDD unfitted *not suited*

NFDK emphatic *forceful*

NFDKL emphatically *forceful*

NFDL infidel *disbeliever*

NFDLD infidelity *disloyalty* infidelities

NFDLT infidelity *disloyalty* infidelities

NFDMN amphetamine *stimulant*

NFDN infighting *rivalry*

NFDNG infighting *rivalry*

NFDNG unfitting *improper*

NFDR infighter *rivalry*

NFDRD unfettered *free*

NFJT knife-edged *sharp*

NFK infect *contaminate*

NFKC inefficacy *powerlessness* inefficacies

NFKCHL ineffectual (adj) *useless* ineffectually (adv)

NFKCHWL ineffectual (adj)

useless ineffectually (adv)

NFKDD unaffected *genuine*

NFKDR infector *germ spreader*

NFKDV ineffective *not working*

NFKDV infective *able to infect*

NFKDVL ineffectively *not working*

NFKDVNS ineffectiveness *not working*

NFKS inefficacy *powerlessness* inefficacies

NFKS infix *implant*

NFKSHL ineffectual (adj) *useless* ineffectually (adv)

NFKSHN infection *contamination*

NFKSHN unification *joined*

NFKSHS inefficacious *powerless*

NFKSHS infectious *contagious*

NFKSHSL inefficaciously *powerless*

NFKSHSL infectiously *contagious*

NFKSHSNS inefficaciousness *powerlessness*

NFKSHSNS infectiousness *contagious*

NFKSHWL ineffectual (adj) *useless* ineffectually (adv)

NFKST unfocused *unclear*

NFKT infect *contaminate*

NFKTD unaffected *genuine*

NFKTL ineffectual (adj) *useless* ineffectually (adv)

NFKTR infector *germ spreader*

NFKTV ineffective *not working*

NFKTV infective *able to infect*

NFKTVL ineffectively *not working*

NFKTVNS ineffectiveness *not working*

NFKTWL ineffectual (adj) *useless* ineffectually (adv)

NFL enfold *wrap*

Use letters that best describe the sounds you hear and omit the vowels. Use **S** or **K** instead of **C**: to find circle use **SRKL**. Use **J** to find joy, **JM** to find gem and **G** to find go.

NFL infield *sports*
NFL inflow *current*
NFL neophilia *newness*
NFL oenophile *wine lover*
NFL unfold *open*
NFLBL infallible (adj) *certain* infallibly (adv)
NFLBLD infallibility *certainty*
NFLBLT infallibility *certainty*
NFLD enfilade *gunfire* enfiladed enfilading
NFLD enfold *wrap*
NFLD infield *sports*
NFLD unfold *open*
NFLDBL inflatable *puff up*
NFLDD inflated *expanded*
NFLDD unaffiliated *no connection*
NFLDR infielder *sportsman*
NFLDR inflator (or) inflater *expand*
NFLDRD unfiltered *not strained*
NFLDRNG unfaltering *steady*
NFLDRNG unflattering *unfavorable*
NFLFLD unfulfilled *incomplete*
NFLGN unflagging *tireless*
NFLGNG unflagging *tireless*
NFLK inflict *cause*
NFLK neophiliac *newness*
NFLKCZ anaphylaxes (pl) *shock* anaphylaxis
NFLKDBL inflectable *emphasize*
NFLKDK anaphylactic *shock*
NFLKDKL anaphylactically *shock*
NFLKDR inflicter (or) inflictor *cause*
NFLKDV inflective *emphasize*
NFLKS influx *flow in* influxes
NFLKSBL inflexible (adj) *stiff, settled* inflexibly (adv)
NFLKSBLD inflexibility *stiff, settled*
NFLKSBLT inflexibility *stiff, settled*
NFLKSHN inflection *emphasis* (Br) inflexion

NFLKSHN infliction *imposition*
NFLKSS anaphylaxis *shock* anaphylaxes
NFLKSZ anaphylaxes (pl) *shock* anaphylaxis
NFLKT inflect *emphasize*
NFLKT inflict *cause*
NFLKTBL inflectable *emphasize*
NFLKTD anaphylactoid *shock*
NFLKTK anaphylactic *shock*
NFLKTKL anaphylactically *shock*
NFLKTR inflicter (or) inflictor *cause*
NFLKTV inflective *emphasize*
NFLKZZ anaphylaxes (pl) *shock* anaphylaxis
NFLM inflame *arouse strong emotion* inflamed inflaming
NFLMBL inflammable (adj) *excitable, easily ignitable* inflammably (adv)
NFLMDR nephelometer *cloudiness*
NFLMR inflamer *arouse strong emotion*
NFLMSHN inflammation *redness, swelling*
NFLMTR inflammatory *arouse strong emotion*
NFLMTR nephelometer *cloudiness*
NFLN anopheline *mosquito*
NFLN nepheline *mineral*
NFLN unfailing *constant*
NFLNCHL influential (adj) *powerful* influentially (adv)
NFLNCHN unflinching *steadfast*
NFLNCHNG unflinching *steadfast*
NFLNDK nephelinitic *rock*
NFLNG unfailing *constant*
NFLNG unfeeling *numb*
NFLNS influence *power* influenced influencing
NFLNSHL influential (adj) *powerful* influentially (adv)

NFLNT nephelinite *rock*
NFLNTK nephelinitic *rock*
NFLNTS influence *power* influenced influencing
NFLNZ influenza *disease*
NFLPBL unflappable (adj) *self-control* unflappably (adv)
NFLPBLD unflappability *self-control*
NFLPBLT unflappability *self-control*
NFLRSNS inflorescence *flower*
NFLRSNTS inflorescence *flower*
NFLSD infelicity *unhappy* infelicities
NFLSDS infelicitous *unhappy*
NFLSHN inflation *expansion*
NFLSHNR inflationary *expansion*
NFLST infelicity *unhappy* infelicities
NFLSTS infelicitous *unhappy*
NFLT in-flight *airplane*
NFLT inflate *expand* inflated inflating
NFLT no-fault *blameless*
NFLTBL inflatable *puff up*
NFLTD inflated *expanded*
NFLTD unaffiliated *no connection*
NFLTR inflator (or) inflater *expand*
NFLTRD unfiltered *not strained*
NFLTRDR infiltrator *one that enters*
NFLTRN unfaltering *steady*
NFLTRNG unfaltering *steady*
NFLTRNG unflattering *unfavorable*
NFLTRSHN infiltration *entrance into*
NFLTRT infiltrate *enter* infiltrated infiltrating
NFLTRTR infiltrator *one that enters*
NFLWNCHL influential (adj) *powerful* influentially (adv)

Letters aren't doubled for single sounds: to find alley use **L** not **LL**. Use **Y** and **W** as hard sounds only: to find yellow use **YL**. (Br)=British spelling or usage. * See dictionary.

NFLWNS influence *power* influenced influencing

NFLWNSHL influential (adj) *powerful* influentially (adv)

NFLWNTS influence *power* influenced influencing

NFLWNZ influenza *disease*

NFLX influx *flow in* influxes

NFLXBL inflexible (adj) *stiff, settled* inflexibly (adv)

NFLXBLD inflexibility *stiff, settled*

NFLXBLT inflexibility *stiff, settled*

NFLXS anaphylaxis *shock* anaphylaxes

NFLXZ anaphylaxes (pl) *shock* anaphylaxis

NFLYDD unaffiliated *no connection*

NFLYK neophiliac *newness*

NFLYTD unaffiliated *no connection*

NFLZ anopheles *mosquito*

NFM infamy *disgrace* infamies

NFMLR unfamiliar *strange*

NFMLRD unfamiliarity *strangeness*

NFMLRT unfamiliarity *strangeness*

NFMLYR unfamiliar *strange*

NFMLYRD unfamiliarity *strangeness*

NFMLYRT unfamiliarity *strangeness*

NFMRSHL infomercial *advertisement*

NFMS infamous *disgraceful*

NFMSL infamously *disgraceful*

NFMYR unfamiliar *strange*

NFMYRD unfamiliarity *strangeness*

NFMYRT unfamiliarity *strangeness*

NFNC infancy *childhood* infancies

NFND infinity *eternity* infinities

NFND unfeigned *natural*

NFNDD unfounded

groundless

NFNDLN Newfoundland *island*

NFNDLND Newfoundland *island*

NFNDV infinitive *verb*

NFNGGL antifungal *fungus prevention*

NFNGGLD newfangled *novel*

NFNGL antifungal *fungus prevention*

NFNGLD newfangled *novel*

NFNL antiphonal *alternate singing*

NFNLN Newfoundland *island*

NFNLND Newfoundland *island*

NFNS infancy *childhood* infancies

NFNSD infanticide *kill a baby*

NFNSDL infanticidal *kill a baby*

NFNSHT unfinished *in progress*

NFNSV inoffensive *no harm*

NFNT infant *baby*

NFNT infinite *eternal*

NFNT infinity *eternity* infinities

NFNTC infancy *childhood* infancies

NFNTD infinitude *eternity*

NFNTL infantile *immature*

NFNTLPRLSS infantile paralysis *polio*

NFNTLZM infantilism *immaturity*

NFNTR infantry *soldiers* infantries

NFNTRBL enfant terrible *brat* enfants terribles

NFNTRMN infantryman *soldier* infantrymen

NFNTS infancy *childhood* infancies

NFNTSD infanticide *kill a baby*

NFNTSDL infanticidal *kill a baby*

NFNTSML infinitesimal (adj) *small* infinitesimally (adv)

NFNTSV inoffensive *no harm*

NFNTV infinitive *verb*

NFNTYD infinitude *eternity*

NFPNT knifepoint, at *threat*

NFR amphora *jar* amphorae (or) amphoras

NFR anaphor *phrase* anaphors

NFR anaphora *repetition*

NFR infer *assume* inferred inferring

NFR unfair *cheating*

NFR unifier *make whole*

NFRBL inferable *assumed*

NFRCBL unforeseeable *surprise*

NFRCHNT unfortunate *regrettable*

NFRCHNTL unfortunately *regrettably*

NFRCN unforeseen *surprise*

NFRCYBL unforeseeable *surprise*

NFRD unafraid *fearless*

NFRDBL unaffordable *too expensive*

NFRDDZ nephritides (pl) *kidney* nephritis

NFRDK nephritic *kidney*

NFRDK nephrotic *disease*

NFRDL infertile *not productive*

NFRDL nephridial *excretion*

NFRDLZD unfertilized *not fruitful*

NFRDM nephridium *excretion*

NFRDN neo-Freudian *psychology*

NFRDS nephritis *kidney* nephritides

NFRDSHK anaphrodisiac *inhibitor*

NFRDSHYK anaphrodisiac *inhibitor*

NFRDYL nephridial *excretion*

NFRDYM nephridium *excretion*

NFRDYN neo-Freudian *psychology*

NFRDZHK anaphrodisiac *inhibitor*

NFRDZHYK anaphrodisiac *inhibitor*

NFRDZK anaphrodisiac *inhibitor*

NFRDZYK anaphrodisiac *inhibitor*

NFRGDBL unforgettable (adj) *memorable* unforgettably (adv)

NFRGTBL unforgettable (adj) *memorable* unforgettably (adv)

NFRGVBL unforgivable *no amends*

NFRGVNG unforgiving *no amends, harsh*

NFRK anaphoric *repetitive*

NFRK infract *violate*

NFRK nephric *kidney*

NFRK unfrock *priest*

NFRKCHS anfractuous *tortuous*

NFRKCHWS anfractuous *tortuous*

NFRKDD infarcted *dead area*

NFRKDM nephrectomy *kidney* nephrectomies

NFRKL anaphorically *repetitively*

NFRKSHN infarction *dead area*

NFRKSHN infraction *violation*

NFRKSHS anfractuous *tortuous*

NFRKSHWS anfractuous *tortuous*

NFRKT infarct *dead area*

NFRKT infract *violate*

NFRKTD infarcted *dead area*

NFRKTM nephrectomy *kidney* nephrectomies

NFRKTS anfractuous *tortuous*

NFRKTWS anfractuous *tortuous*

NFRKWNC infrequency *seldom* infrequence

NFRKWND unfrequented *rarely visited*

NFRKWNS infrequency *seldom* infrequence

NFRKWNT infrequent *seldom*

NFRKWNTC infrequency *seldom* infrequence

NFRKWNTD unfrequented *rarely visited*

NFRKWNTL infrequently *seldom*

NFRKWNTS infrequency *seldom* infrequence

NFRL unfairly *cheating*

NFRL unfurl *unfold*

NFRLG nephrology *kidney*

NFRLJ nephrology *kidney*

NFRLJST nephrologist *kidney*

NFRLS no-frills *simple*

NFRLZ no-frills *simple*

NFRM infirm *ill*

NFRM inform *tell*

NFRM uniform *(n) garment (adj) same*

NFRMD infirmity *illness* infirmities

NFRMD informed *educated*

NFRMD unformed *shapeless*

NFRMD uniformity *sameness* uniformities

NFRMDL informedly *educated*

NFRMDV informative *instructive*

NFRML informal (adj) *casual* informally (adv)

NFRMLD informality *casual* informalities

NFRMLT informality *casual* informalities

NFRMNT informant *informer*

NFRMR infirmary *hospital* infirmaries

NFRMR informer *tell*

NFRMSHN information *data*

NFRMT infirmity *illness* infirmities

NFRMT uniformity *sameness* uniformities

NFRMTV informative *instructive*

NFRN inferno *heat, hell*

infernos

NFRN nephron *kidney*

NFRNCHL inferential (adj) *suggestion* inferentially (adv)

NFRNCHZ enfranchise *political privilege* enfranchised enfranchising

NFRNCHZMNT enfranchisement *political privilege*

NFRNDL unfriendly *ill will*

NFRNDLNS unfriendliness *ill will*

NFRNJ infringe *invade* infringed infringing

NFRNJBL infrangible (adj) *unbreakable* infrangibly (adv)

NFRNJBLD infrangibility *unbreakable*

NFRNJBLT infrangibility *unbreakable*

NFRNJMNT infringement *invasion*

NFRNJR infringer *invader*

NFRNL infernal (adj) *hellish* infernally (adv)

NFRNL unfriendly *ill will*

NFRNLNS unfriendliness *ill will*

NFRNS inference *suggestion*

NFRNS unfairness *cheating*

NFRNSHD unfurnished *no furniture*

NFRNSHL inferential (adj) *suggestion* inferentially (adv)

NFRNSHT unfurnished *no furniture*

NFRNTS inference *suggestion*

NFRPTH nephropathy *kidney* nephropathies

NFRPTHK nephropathic *kidney*

NFRQNC infrequency *seldom* infrequence

NFRQND unfrequented *rarely visited*

NFRQNS infrequency

seldom infrequence
NFRQNT infrequent *seldom*
NFRQNTC infrequency
seldom infrequence
NFRQNTD unfrequented
rarely visited
NFRQNTL infrequently
seldom
NFRQNTS infrequency
seldom infrequence
NFRR inferior *beneath*
NFRR inferrer *judge*
NFRRD inferiority *beneath*
NFRRD infrared *color*
NFRRT inferiority *beneath*
NFRS enforce *compel*
agreement enforced
enforcing
NFRS nefarious *evil*
NFRSBL enforceable *compel*
agreement
NFRSBL unforeseeable
surprise
NFRSBLD enforceability
compel agreement
NFRSBLT enforceability
compel agreement
NFRSHN infuriation *anger*
NFRSL nefariously *evil*
NFRSMNT enforcement
compel agreement
NFRSN unforeseen *surprise*
NFRSNK infrasonic *sound*
NFRSR enforcer *compel*
agreement
NFRSS nephrosis *disease*
NFRST no-frost *refrigerator*
NFRST unforced *not*
compelled
NFRSTM nephrostome
opening
NFRSTRKCHR
infrastructure *framework*
NFRSTRKSHR
infrastructure *framework*
NFRSTRKTR infrastructure
framework
NFRSYBL unforeseeable
surprise
NFRT infuriate *anger*
infuriated infuriating
NFRT nephrite *kidney*

NFRTDZ nephritides (pl)
kidney nephritis
NFRTFL unfruitful (adj)
barren unfruitfully (adv)
NFRTFLNS unfruitfulness
barren
NFRTK nephritic *kidney*
NFRTK nephrotic *disease*
NFRTKSK nephrotoxic
poison
NFRTKSSD nephrotoxicity
poison
NFRTKSST nephrotoxicity
poison
NFRTL infertile *not*
productive
NFRTLD infertility *not*
productive
NFRTLT infertility *not*
productive
NFRTLZD unfertilized *not*
fruitful
NFRTNT unfortunate
regrettable
NFRTNTL unfortunately
regrettably
NFRTS nephritis *kidney*
nephritides
NFRTXK nephrotoxic *poison*
NFRTXSD nephrotoxicity
poison
NFRTXST nephrotoxicity
poison
NFRYR inferior *beneath*
NFRYRD inferiority *beneath*
NFRYRT inferiority *beneath*
NFRYS nefarious *evil*
NFRYSHN infuriation *anger*
NFRYSL nefariously *evil*
NFRYT infuriate *anger*
infuriated infuriating
NFRZ antifreeze *water*
additive
NFRZN unfrozen *thaw*
NFSBL ineffaceable (adj)
unbreakable ineffaceably
(adv)
NFSBLD ineffaceability
unbreakable
NFSBLT ineffaceability
unbreakable
NFSHL unofficial (adj) *not*

authorized unofficially
(adv)
NFSHN infusion *introduction*
NFSHN new-fashioned
modern
NFSHNBL unfashionable
(adj) *not stylish*
unfashionably (adv)
NFSHNBLNS
unfashionableness *not*
stylish
NFSHNC inefficiency *waste,*
unqualified inefficiencies
NFSHND new-fashioned
modern
NFSHNS inefficiency *waste,*
unqualified inefficiencies
NFSHNT inefficient *waste,*
unqualified
NFSHNTC inefficiency
waste, unqualified
inefficiencies
NFSHNTL inefficiently *waste,*
unqualified
NFSHNTS inefficiency
waste, unqualified
inefficiencies
NFSHST antifascist *against*
fascism
NFSHTL Neufchâtel *cheese*
NFSKP nephoscope *clouds*
NFSM emphysema *lung*
disease
NFSMK emphysemic *lung*
disease
NFSN unfasten *loosen*
NFSS emphasis *stress*
emphases
NFST infest *spread*
NFSTSHN infestation *spread*
NFSZ emphases (pl) *stress*
emphasis
NFSZ emphasize *stress*
emphasized emphasizing
(Br) emphasise
NFT neophyte *beginner*
NFT nifty *marvelous* niftier
niftiest
NFT unfit *not suited*
NFTD unfitted *not suited*
NFTDD infatuated *in love*
infatuated infatuating

Use letters that best describe the sounds you hear and omit the vowels. Use **S** or **K** instead of **C**: to find circle use **SRKL**. Use **J** to find joy, **JM** to find gem and **G** to find go.

NFTH naphtha *petroleum*
NFTHDR amphitheater *arena*
(Br) amphitheatre
NFTHFL unfaithful (adj) *disloyal* unfaithfully (adv)
NFTHLN naphthalene *petroleum*
NFTHMBL unfathomable *unknown*
NFTHN naphthene *wax*
NFTHTR amphitheater *arena* (Br) amphitheatre
NFTHYDR amphitheater *arena* (Br) amphitheatre
NFTHYTR amphitheater *arena* (Br) amphitheatre
NFTK emphatic *forceful*
NFTKL emphatically *forceful*
NFTMN amphetamine *stimulant*
NFTN infighting *rivalry*
NFTN unfitting *improper*
NFTNG infighting *rivalry*
NFTNG unfitting *improper*
NFTNMNT infotainment *documentary*
NFTR infighter *rivalry*
NFTRD unfettered *free*
NFTRK amphoteric *part of both*
NFTSHN infatuation *love*
NFTT infatuate *love* infatuated infatuating
NFTTD infatuated *in love* infatuated infatuating
NFTWDD infatuated *in love* infatuated infatuating
NFTWSHN infatuation *love*
NFTWT infatuate *love* infatuated infatuating
NFTWTD infatuated *in love* infatuated infatuating
NFVRBL unfavorable (adj) *negative* unfavorably (adv)
NFX infix *implant*
NFY nephew *relative*
NFYBL unifiable *join*
NFYR unifier *make whole*
NFYRSHN infuriation *anger*

NFYRT infuriate *anger* infuriated infuriating
NFYRYSHN infuriation *anger*
NFYRYT infuriate *anger* infuriated infuriating
NFYSHN infusion *introduction*
NFYZ infuse *introduce, inspire* infused infusing
NFYZBL infusible *cannot merge*
NFYZHN infusion *introduction*
NFYZR infuser *introduce, inspire*
NFZ anaphase *cell division*
NFZ infuse *introduce, inspire* infused infusing
NFZBL infeasible *not practical*
NFZBL infusible *cannot merge*
NFZD unfazed *undaunted*
NFZHN infusion *introduction*
NFZK anaphasic *cell division*
NFZM emphysema *lung disease*
NFZMK emphysemic *lung disease*
NFZR infuser *introduce, inspire*
NG awing *astounding*
NG nag *(v) annoy* nagged nagging
NG nag *(n) horse*
NG Nagoya *city*
NG nog *eggnog*
NGCHS unctuous *oily*
NGCHWS unctuous *oily*
NGD no-good *without value*
NGDL ungodly *wicked*
NGDLNS ungodliness *wicked*
NGDR negator *denyer*
NGDV negative *(adj) opposite, number, loss (n) refusal, drawback, image**
NGDVL negatively *opposite, number, loss**
NGDVNS negativeness *refusal, drawback, image**
NGDVSDK negativistic

doubtful
NGDVST negativist *doubter*
NGDVSTK negativistic *doubtful*
NGDVZM negativism *doubt*
NGF engulf *overwhelm*
NGFMNT engulfment *overwhelming*
NGGL angle *(v) fish, slant* angled angling
NGGL angle *(n) viewpoint, corner*
NGGL Anglo *English*
NGGL Angola *country*
NGGLFB Anglophobe *fearer of England*
NGGLFB Anglophobia *fear of England*
NGGLFBY Anglophobia *fear of England*
NGGLFL Anglophile (or) Anglophilic *England lover*
NGGLFL Anglophilia *love of England*
NGGLFLK Anglophiliac *England lover*
NGGLFLK Anglophilic (or) Anglophile *England lover*
NGGLFLY Anglophilia *love of England*
NGGLFLYK Anglophiliac *England lover*
NGGLFN anglophone *language*
NGGLKN Anglican *Protestant*
NGGLKNSM Anglicanism *Protestant*
NGGLKNZM Anglicanism *Protestant*
NGGLKTHLK Anglo-Catholic *English Catholic*
NGGLMRKN Anglo-American *English-American*
NGGLN angling *fishing*
NGGLN England *country*
NGGLND England *country*
NGGLNG angling *fishing*
NGGLR angler *fisherman, slanter*
NGGLR angular *with angles,*

Letters aren't doubled for single sounds: to find alley use **L** not **LL**. Use **Y** and **W** as hard sounds only: to find yellow use **YL**. (Br)=British spelling or usage. * See dictionary.

stiff

NGGLRD angularity *with angles, stiffness* angularities

NGGLRFSH anglerfish *fish*

NGGLRL angularly *with angles, stiff*

NGGLRN angle iron *joiner*

NGGLRT angularity *with angles, stiffness* angularities

NGGLSH English *of England*

NGGLSHCHNL English Channel *body of water*

NGGLSHMN Englishman *of England* Englishmen

NGGLSHN angulation *with angles, stiffness*

NGGLSHWMN Englishwoman *of England* Englishwomen

NGGLSKSN Anglo-Saxon *Germanic*

NGGLST anglesite *mineral*

NGGLSXN Anglo-Saxon *Germanic*

NGGLSZ anglicize *(often capitalized) make English* anglicized anglicizing

NGGLT ungulate *hoofs*

NGGLWMRKN Anglo-American *English-American*

NGGLWRM angleworm *earthworm*

NGGLYRN angle iron *joiner*

NGGR anger *ire*

NGGR angora *fur*

NGGR Angora *cat, goat, rabbit*

NGGR angry *wrathful* angrier angriest

NGGRF angiography *heart x-ray*

NGGRFK angiographic *heart x-ray*

NGGRL angrily *wrathfully*

NGGRM angiogram *heart x-ray*

NGGRR angrier *wrathful*

NGGRST angriest *wrathful*

NGGRYR angrier *wrathful*

NGGRYST angriest *wrathful*

NGGS Angus *cattle*

NGGT ingot *metal bar*

NGGWL Anguilla *island*

NGGWL ungual *nail, claw*

NGGWNL inguinal *groin*

NGGWNT unguent *ointment*

NGGWS unguis *claw* ungues

NGGWSH anguish *torment*

NGGWSHD anguished *tormented*

NGGWSHT anguished *tormented*

NGGYLR angular *with angles, stiff*

NGGYLRD angularity *with angles, stiffness* angularities

NGGYLRL angularly *with angles, stiff*

NGGYLRT angularity *with angles, stiffness* angularities

NGGYLSHN angulation *with angles, stiffness*

NGGYLT ungulate *hoofs*

NGHD Naugahyde *(trademark) fabric*

NGJ anagoge (or) anagogy *meaning* anagoges (or) anagogies

NGJ engage *bind, hire, promise** engaged engaging

NGJ engagé *(adj) supportive*

NGJD engaged *betrothed, occupied*

NGJK anagogic (or) anagogical (adj) *meaningful* anagogically (adv)

NGJKL anagogical (or) anagogic (adj) *meaningful* anagogically (adv)

NGJMNT engagement *pledge, encounter*

NGJN engaging *attractive*

NGJNG engaging *attractive*

NGJNGL engagingly *attractive*

NGJNL engagingly *attractive*

NGK ankh *cross*

NGK Inca *Quechuan*

NGK ink *pen*

NGK inky *black*

NGKB incubi (pl) *nightmare* incubus

NGKBDR incubator *hatch, baby care*

NGKBLT inkblot *smear*

NGKBS incubus *nightmare* incubi

NGKBSHN incubation *hatch*

NGKBT incubate *hatch* incubated incubating

NGKBTR incubator *hatch, baby care*

NGKCHS unctuous *oily*

NGKCHWS unctuous *oily*

NGKGN oncogene *cancer*

NGKGNK oncogenic *tumor*

NGKGNSS oncogenesis *tumor*

NGKHRN inkhorn *bottle*

NGKJN oncogene *cancer*

NGKJNK oncogenic *tumor*

NGKJNSD oncogenicity *tumor*

NGKJNSS oncogenesis *tumor*

NGKJNST oncogenicity *tumor*

NGKL ankle *foot joint*

NGKL uncle *family*

NGKLBN anklebone *talus*

NGKLDK ankylotic *stiff*

NGKLG oncology *tumor*

NGKLJ oncology *tumor*

NGKLJKL oncological *tumor*

NGKLJST oncologist *tumor*

NGKLMNT inclement *stormy*

NGKLN inkling *clue*

NGKLNG inkling *clue*

NGKLNMDR inclinometer *tilt*

NGKLNMTR inclinometer *tilt*

NGKLNSHN inclination *tendency*

NGKLSM Uncle Sam *government*

Use letters that best describe the sounds you hear and omit the vowels. Use **S** or **K** instead of **C**: to find circle use **SRKL**. Use **J** to find joy, **JM** to find gem and **G** to find go.

NGKLSR ankylosaur *dinosaur*

NGKLSRS ankylosaurus *dinosaur*

NGKLSS ankylosis *stiffness* ankyloses

NGKLT anklet *sock*

NGKLTK ankylotic *stiff*

NGKNBL incunabula (pl) *early work* incunabulum

NGKNBLM incunabulum *early work* incunabula

NGKNBYL incunabula (pl) *early work* incunabulum

NGKNBYLM incunabulum *early work* incunabula

NGKNS inkiness *black*

NGKR anchor *hold in place*

NGKR Ankara *city*

NGKR encore *reappear* encored encoring

NGKRDK anchoritic *cloistered*

NGKRDKL anchoritically *cloistered*

NGKRJ Anchorage *city*

NGKRJ anchorage *ship*

NGKRLS anchorless *not held in place*

NGKRMN anchorman *last one, moderator* anchormen

NGKRMNL incremental (adj) *increase* incrementally (adv)

NGKRMNT increment *increase*

NGKRMNTL incremental (adj) *increase* incrementally (adv)

NGKRN inkhorn *bottle*

NGKRPRSN anchorperson *last one, moderator*

NGKRT anchorite *hermit*

NGKRT ankerite *mineral*

NGKRTK anchoritic *cloistered*

NGKRTKL anchoritically *cloistered*

NGKRWMN anchorwoman *last one, moderator* anchorwomen

NGKSHN unction *salve*

NGKSHNT ancient *old*

NGKSHNTL anciently *long ago*

NGKSHNTNS ancientness *old age*

NGKSHS anxious *concerned*

NGKSHS unctuous *oily*

NGKSHSL anxiously *with concern*

NGKSHSNS anxiousness *with concern*

NGKSHWS unctuous *oily*

NGKSRKSS onchocerciasis *disease* onchocerciases

NGKSRKYSS onchocerciasis *disease* onchocerciases

NGKST angst *anxiety*

NGKSTRM angstrom *unit of length*

NGKWR enquiry *investigation* enquiries

NGKWR inquiry *investigation* inquiries

NGKWYR enquiry *investigation* enquiries

NGKWYR inquiry *investigation* inquiries

NGKWZDR inquisitor *examiner*

NGKWZDV inquisitive *curious*

NGKWZSHN inquisition *examination*

NGKWZTR inquisitor *examiner*

NGKWZTRL inquisitorial (adj) *examiner* inquisitorially (adv)

NGKWZTRYL inquisitorial (adj) *examiner* inquisitorially (adv)

NGKWZTV inquisitive *curious*

NGKYB incubi (pl) *nightmare* incubus

NGKYBDR incubator *hatch, baby care*

NGKYBS incubus *nightmare* incubi

NGKYBSHN incubation *hatch*

NGKYBT incubate *hatch* incubated incubating

NGKYBTR incubator *hatch, baby care*

NGKYNBL incunabula (pl) *early work* incunabulum

NGKYNBLM incunabulum *early work* incunabula

NGKYNBYL incunabula (pl) *early work* incunabulum

NGKYNBYLM incunabulum *early work* incunabula

NGKZD anxiety *concern* anxieties

NGKZT anxiety *concern* anxieties

NGKZYD anxiety *concern* anxieties

NGKZYT anxiety *concern* anxieties

NGL angle (v) *fish, slant* angled angling

NGL angle (n) *viewpoint, corner*

NGL Anglo *English*

NGL Angola *country*

NGL niggle *complain* niggled niggling

NGL niggle (Br) *complaint*

NGLD unglued *not stuck*

NGLF anaglyph *ornament*

NGLF engulf *overwhelm*

NGLFB Anglophobe *fearer of England*

NGLFB Anglophobia *fear of England*

NGLFBY Anglophobia *fear of England*

NGLFK anaglyphic *ornament*

NGLFL Anglophile (or) Anglophilic *England lover*

NGLFL Anglophilia *love of England*

NGLFLK Anglophiliac *England lover*

NGLFLK Anglophilic (or) Anglophile *England lover*

NGLFLY Anglophilia *love of England*

NGLFLYK Anglophiliac *England lover*

NGLFMNT engulfment

overwhelming
NGLFN anglophone *language*
NGLJ negligee *nightgown*
NGLJBL negligible (adj) *trifling* negligibly (adv)
NGLJBLD negligibility *trifling*
NGLJBLT negligibility *trifling*
NGLJNS negligence *carelessness*
NGLJNT negligent *careless*
NGLJNTL negligently *careless*
NGLJNTS negligence *carelessness*
NGLK neglect *ignore, forget*
NGLKDR neglecter *ignore, forget*
NGLKFL neglectful (adj) *careless* neglectfully (adv)
NGLKFLNS neglectfulness *carelessness*
NGLKN Anglican *Protestant*
NGLKNSM Anglicanism *Protestant*
NGLKNZM Anglicanism *Protestant*
NGLKT neglect *ignore, forget*
NGLKTFL neglectful (adj) *careless* neglectfully (adv)
NGLKTFLNS neglectfulness *carelessness*
NGLKTHLK Anglo-Catholic *English Catholic*
NGLKTR neglecter *ignore, forget*
NGLMRKN Anglo-American *English-American*
NGLN angling *fishing*
NGLN England *country*
NGLN niggling *annoying*
NGLND England *country*
NGLNG angling *fishing*
NGLNG niggling *annoying*
NGLR angler *fisherman, slanter*
NGLR angular *with angles, stiff*
NGLR niggler *complainer*
NGLRD angularity *with*

angles, stiffness angularities
NGLRFSH anglerfish *fish*
NGLRL angularly *with angles, stiff*
NGLRN angle iron *joiner*
NGLRS inglorious *shameful*
NGLRT angularity *with angles, stiffness* angularities
NGLRYS inglorious *shameful*
NGLSH English *of England*
NGLSH negligee *nightgown*
NGLSHCHNL English Channel *body of water*
NGLSHMN Englishman *of England* Englishmen
NGLSHN angulation *with angles, stiffness*
NGLSHWMN Englishwoman *of England* Englishwomen
NGLSKSN Anglo-Saxon *Germanic*
NGLST anglesite *mineral*
NGLSXN Anglo-Saxon *Germanic*
NGLSZ anglicize *(often capitalized) make English* anglicized anglicizing
NGLT ungulate *hoofs*
NGLWMRKN Anglo-American *English-American*
NGLWRM angleworm *earthworm*
NGLYRN angle iron *joiner*
NGLZH negligee *nightgown*
NGM angioma *tumor*
NGM enigma *mystery*
NGMDK enigmatic *mysterious*
NGMDKL enigmatically *mysteriously*
NGMDS angiomatous *tumor*
NGMTK enigmatic *mysterious*
NGMTKL enigmatically *mysteriously*
NGMTS angiomatous *tumor*
NGN Neogene *rocks*
NGN New Guinea *island*

NGN noggin *head*
NGN nogging *masonry*
NGN ongoing *continuing*
NGNG nogging *masonry*
NGNG ongoing *continuing*
NGNL ungainly *clumsy*
NGNLNS ungainliness *clumsy*
NGNS ingenious *clever*
NGNSL ingeniously *clever*
NGNSNS ingeniousness *clever*
NGNYS ingenious *clever*
NGNYSL ingeniously *clever*
NGNYSNS ingeniousness *clever*
NGPLSD angioplasty *vein balloon* angioplasties
NGPLST angioplasty *vein balloon* angioplasties
NGQB incubi (pl) *nightmare* incubus
NGQBDR incubator *hatch, baby care*
NGQBS incubus *nightmare* incubi
NGQBSHN incubation *hatch*
NGQBT incubate *hatch* incubated incubating
NGQBTR incubator *hatch, baby care*
NGQNBL incunabula (pl) *early work* incunabulum
NGQNBLM incunabulum *early work* incunabula
NGQNBYL incunabula (pl) *early work* incunabulum
NGQNBYLM incunabulum *early work* incunabula
NGQR enquiry *investigation* enquiries
NGQR inquiry *investigation* inquiries
NGQYR enquiry *investigation* enquiries
NGQYR inquiry *investigation* inquiries
NGQZDR inquisitor *examiner*
NGQZDV inquisitive *curious*
NGQZSHN inquisition *examination*

Use letters that best describe the sounds you hear and omit the vowels. Use **S** or **K** instead of **C**: to find circle use **SRKL**. Use **J** to find joy, **JM** to find gem and **G** to find go.

NGQZTR inquisitor *examiner*
NGQZTRL inquisitorial (adj) *examiner* inquisitorially (adv)
NGQZTRYL inquisitorial (adj) *examiner* inquisitorially (adv)
NGQZTV inquisitive *curious*
NGR anger *ire*
NGR Angora *cat, goat, rabbit*
NGR angora *fur*
NGR angry *wrathful* angrier angriest
NGR Honegger *composer*
NGR Negro *race* Negroes
NGR Nigeria *country*
NGRD en garde *challenge*
NGRD negroid *(often capitalized) race*
NGRD niggard *tightwad*
NGRDD integrated *combined*
NGRDD unguarded *free*
NGRDL engirdle *circle*
NGRDL niggardly *stingy*
NGRDNT ingredient *element*
NGRDR inaugurator *beginner*
NGRDR integrator *combiner*
NGRDTD ingratitude *not thankful*
NGRDTYD ingratitude *not thankful*
NGRDYNT ingredient *element*
NGRFB negrophobe *(often capitalized) hater or fearer of Negroes*
NGRFB negrophobia *(often capitalized) hatred or fear of Negroes*
NGRFBY negrophobia *(often capitalized) hatred or fear of Negroes*
NGRFLS Niagara Falls *waterfall*
NGRFLZ Niagara Falls *waterfall*
NGRJ engorge *fill* engorged engorging
NGRJMNT engorgement *fill*
NGRJTSHN ingurgitation *guzzle*

NGRJTT ingurgitate *guzzle* ingurgitated ingurgitating
NGRL angrily *wrathfully*
NGRL inaugural *election*
NGRM anagram *word game* anagrammed anagramming
NGRM engram *memory*
NGRMDK anagrammatic *word game*
NGRMDKL anagrammatically *word game*
NGRMDKL ungrammatical *incorrect speech*
NGRMTK anagrammatic *word game*
NGRMTKL anagrammatically *word game*
NGRMTKL ungrammatical *incorrect speech*
NGRMTZ anagrammatize *word game* anagrammatized anagrammatizing
NGRMTZSHN anagrammatization *word game*
NGRN engrain *instill*
NGRN ingrain *introduce*
NGRN ingrown *imbedded*
NGRND ingrained *deep-seated*
NGRP in-group *clique*
NGRR angrier *wrathful*
NGRS engross *copy, absorb* engrossed engrossing
NGRS ingress *entry*
NGRS Negress *black woman*
NGRSHDNG ingratiating *pleasing*
NGRSHN inauguration *beginning*
NGRSHN ingression *entrance*
NGRSHN integration *combination*
NGRSHS ungracious *rude*
NGRSHSL ungraciously *rude*
NGRSHSNS

ungraciousness *rudeness*
NGRSHT ingratiate *gain favor* ingratiated ingratiating
NGRSHTN ingratiating *pleasing*
NGRSHTNG ingratiating *pleasing*
NGRSHYDNG ingratiating *pleasing*
NGRSHYT ingratiate *gain favor* ingratiated ingratiating
NGRSHYTN ingratiating *pleasing*
NGRSHYTNG ingratiating *pleasing*
NGRSMNT engrossment *preoccupation*
NGRSN engrossing *absorbing*
NGRSNG engrossing *absorbing*
NGRSNGL engrossingly *absorbing*
NGRSNL engrossingly *absorbing*
NGRST angriest *wrathful*
NGRSV ingressive *entrance*
NGRT inaugurate *begin* inaugurated inaugurating
NGRT ingrate *not thankful*
NGRT integrate *combine* integrated integrating
NGRTD integrated *combined*
NGRTFL ungrateful (adj) *thankless* ungratefully (adv)
NGRTFLNS ungratefulness *thankless*
NGRTR inaugurator *beginner*
NGRTR integrator *combiner*
NGRTTD ingratitude *not thankful*
NGRTTYD ingratitude *not thankful*
NGRV engrave *cut* engraved engraving
NGRVD antigravity *weightless*
NGRVN engraving *impression*

Letters aren't doubled for single sounds: to find alley use **L** not **LL**. Use **Y** and **W** as hard sounds only: to find yellow use **YL**. (Br)=British spelling or usage. * See dictionary.

NGRVNG engraving *impression*
NGRVR engraver *cutter*
NGRVT antigravity *weightless*
NGRY Nigeria *country*
NGRYR angrier *wrathful*
NGRYST angriest *wrathful*
NGS Angus *cattle*
NGS negus *king, beverage*
NGSH engagé *(adj) supportive*
NGSHBL negotiable (adj) *deal, discuss, cross* negotiably (adv)
NGSHBLD negotiability *deal, discuss, cross*
NGSHBLT negotiability *deal, discuss, cross*
NGSHDR negotiator *deal, discuss, cross*
NGSHN negation *repeal*
NGSHNT ancient *old*
NGSHNTNS ancientness *old age*
NGSHS anxious *concerned*
NGSHS unctuous *oily*
NGSHSHN negotiation *deal, discuss, cross*
NGSHSL anxiously *with concern*
NGSHSNS anxiousness *with concern*
NGSHT negotiate *deal, discuss, cross* negotiated negotiating
NGSHTR negotiator *deal, discuss, cross*
NGSHWS unctuous *oily*
NGSHYDR negotiator *deal, discuss, cross*
NGSHYSHN negotiation *deal, discuss, cross*
NGSHYT negotiate *deal, discuss, cross* negotiated negotiating
NGSHYTR negotiator *deal, discuss, cross*
NGSK Nagasaki *city*
NGSKYZBL inexcusable (adj) *cannot forgive* inexcusably (adv)

NGSKZBL inexcusable (adj) *cannot forgive* inexcusably (adv)
NGSPLKBL inexplicable (adj) *no explanation* inexplicably (adv)
NGSPLKBLD inexplicability *no explanation*
NGSPLKBLT inexplicability *no explanation*
NGSPRM angiosperm *plant*
NGSPRMS angiospermous *plant*
NGSQZBL inexcusable (adj) *cannot forgive* inexcusably (adv)
NGST angst *anxiety*
NGSTRM angstrom *unit of length*
NGT ingot *metal bar*
NGT negate *repeal* negated negating
NGT nougat *candy*
NGT nugget *chunk*
NGTHK neo-Gothic *style*
NGTR negator *denyer*
NGTR negatory *(slang) no*
NGTR nugatory *vain*
NGTS unctuous *oily*
NGTV negative *(adj) opposite, number, loss (n) refusal, drawback, image**
NGTVD negativity *denial*
NGTVL negatively *opposite, number, loss**
NGTVNS negativeness *refusal, drawback, image**
NGTVSDK negativistic *doubtful*
NGTVST negativist *doubter*
NGTVSTK negativistic *doubtful*
NGTVT negativity *denial*
NGTVZM negativism *doubt*
NGTWS unctuous *oily*
NGVRMNT antigovernment *against rulers*
NGVRNBL ungovernable *unruly*
NGVRNMNT antigovernment *against rulers*

NGWL Anguilla *island*
NGWL ungual *nail, claw*
NGWN ongoing *continuing*
NGWNG ongoing *continuing*
NGWNL inguinal *groin*
NGWNT unguent *ointment*
NGWS unguis *claw* ungues
NGWSH anguish *torment*
NGWSHD anguished *tormented*
NGWSHT anguished *tormented*
NGXT angst *anxiety*
NGXTRM angstrom *unit of length*
NGY Nagoya *city*
NGYGRF angiography *heart x-ray*
NGYGRFK angiographic *heart x-ray*
NGYGRM angiogram *heart x-ray*
NGYLR angular *with angles, stiff*
NGYLRD angularity *with angles, stiffness* angularities
NGYLRL angularly *with angles, stiff*
NGYLRT angularity *with angles, stiffness* angularities
NGYLSHN angulation *with angles, stiffness*
NGYLT ungulate *hoofs*
NGYM angioma *tumor*
NGYMDS angiomatous *tumor*
NGYMTS angiomatous *tumor*
NGYPLSD angioplasty *vein balloon* angioplasties
NGYPLST angioplasty *vein balloon* angioplasties
NGYRDR inaugurator *beginner*
NGYRL inaugural *election*
NGYRSHN inauguration *beginning*
NGYRT inaugurate *begin* inaugurated inaugurating
NGYRTR inaugurator

Use letters that best describe the sounds you hear and omit the vowels. Use **S** or **K** instead of **C**: to find circle use **SRKL**. Use **J** to find joy, **JM** to find gem and **G** to find go.

beginner
NGYSPRM angiosperm *plant*
NGYSPRMS angiospermous *plant*
NGZD anxiety *concern* anxieties
NGZH engagé *(adj) supportive*
NGZK inexact *inaccurate*
NGZKDTD inexactitude *inaccurate*
NGZKT inexact *inaccurate*
NGZKTTD inexactitude *inaccurate*
NGZMND unexamined *thoughtless*
NGZRBL inexorable (adj) *relentless* inexorably (adv)
NGZRBLD inexorability *relentless*
NGZRBLT inexorability *relentless*
NGZRSZD unexercised *not used*
NGZSDBL inexhaustible (adj) *cannot use up or tire* inexhaustibly (adv)
NGZSDNT inexistent *not real*
NGZSTBL inexhaustible (adj) *cannot use up or tire* inexhaustibly (adv)
NGZSTNT inexistent *not real*
NGZT anxiety *concern* anxieties
NGZYD anxiety *concern* anxieties
NGZYT anxiety *concern* anxieties
NH anyhow *anyway*
NH knee-high *to the knees*
NH know-how *knowledge*
NH nohow *(slang) anyway*
NHBDBL inhabitable *okay to occupy*
NHBDD inhabited *occupied*
NHBDNT inhabitant *resident*
NHBDR inhibitor *obstruction*
NHBDV inhibitive *obstructing*
NHBRDZ New Hebrides *island*

NHBSHN inhibition *obstruction*
NHBT inhabit *live in*
NHBT inhibit *prevent*
NHBTBL inhabitable *okay to occupy*
NHBTD inhabited *occupied*
NHBTNT inhabitant *resident*
NHBTR inhibitor *obstruction*
NHBTR inhibitory *preventive*
NHBTSHN inhabitation *residence*
NHBTV inhibitive *obstructing*
NHCH unhitch *free*
NHDN anhedonia *no pleasure*
NHDNY anhedonia *no pleasure*
NHDR no-hitter *baseball*
NHDRD anhydride *no water*
NHDRS anhydrous *no water*
NHDRT anhydrite *mineral*
NHK unhook *unclasp*
NHL inhale *breathe* inhaled inhaling
NHL kneehole *desk*
NHL unholy *wicked*
NHLD unhallowed *unholy*
NHLDSBRD no-holds-barred *unrestricted*
NHLDZBRD no-holds-barred *unrestricted*
NHLNS unholiness *wicked*
NHLNT inhalant *respiration*
NHLR inhaler *device*
NHLSDK nihilistic *destructive*
NHLSHN inhalation *respiration*
NHLSM unwholesome *unsound*
NHLSML unwholesomely *unsound*
NHLST nihilist *destroyer*
NHLSTK nihilistic *destructive*
NHLTH unhealthy *sickly, risky*
NHLTHFL unhealthful *sickening*
NHLTHL unhealthily *sickening*
NHLTHNS unhealthiness

sickness
NHLZM nihilism *philosophy*
NHM Anaheim *city*
NHM inhume *bury* inhumed inhuming
NHMN inhuman *savage, cold*
NHMN inhumane *unkind*
NHMND inhumanity *cruelty* inhumanities
NHMNT inhumanity *cruelty* inhumanities
NHMPSHR New Hampshire *US State*
NHMSHN inhumation *bury*
NHMSHR New Hampshire *US State*
NHN unhand *let go*
NHND unhand *let go*
NHND unhandy *awkward*
NHNDL unhandily *awkward*
NHNDNS unhandiness *awkward*
NHNG anhinga *bird*
NHNGG anhinga *bird*
NHNJ unhinge *disrupt, unfasten* unhinged unhinging
NHNS enhance *increase* enhanced enhancing
NHNSMNT enhancement *increase*
NHNSR enhancer *increaser*
NHNTS enhance *increase* enhanced enhancing
NHNTSMNT enhancement *increase*
NHNTSR enhancer *increaser*
NHP unhappy *sad*
NHPNS unhappiness *sadness*
NHR antihero *betrayer*
NHR inhere *make part of* inhered inhering
NHRD unheard *silent*
NHRD unhurried *slow*
NHRDBL inheritable *legacy*
NHRDBLD inheritability *legacy*
NHRDBLT inheritability *legacy*
NHRDNS inheritance *legacy*
NHRDNTS inheritance

legacy
NHRDR inheritor *heir*
NHRDV unheard-of *unknown*
NHRMNK enharmonic *musical notes*
NHRMNK inharmonic *not musical*
NHRMNKL enharmonically *musical notes*
NHRMNS inharmonious *not musical*
NHRMNYS inharmonious *not musical*
NHRNS inherence *fundamental*
NHRNS unharness *divest*
NHRNT inherent *fundamental*
NHRNTS inherence *fundamental*
NHRS unhorse *get down* unhorsed unhorsing
NHRT inherit *legacy*
NHRT unhurt *not harmed*
NHRTBL inheritable *legacy*
NHRTBLD inheritability *legacy*
NHRTBLT inheritability *legacy*
NHRTNS inheritance *legacy*
NHRTNTS inheritance *legacy*
NHRTR inheritor *heir*
NHS in-house *within a facility*
NHSDMN antihistamine *allergy drug*
NHSPDBL inhospitable (adj) *not friendly* inhospitably (adv)
NHSPTBL inhospitable (adj) *not friendly* inhospitably (adv)
NHSPTLD inhospitality *not friendly*
NHSPTLT inhospitality *not friendly*
NHSTMN antihistamine *allergy drug*
NHT no-hit *baseball*
NHTR no-hitter *baseball*

NHWR anywhere *any place*
NHWR nowhere *in no place*
NHYM inhume *bury* inhumed inhuming
NHYMN inhuman *savage, cold*
NHYMN inhumane *unkind*
NHYMND inhumanity *cruelty* inhumanities
NHYMNT inhumanity *cruelty* inhumanities
NHYMSHN inhumation *bury*
NHZTDNG unhesitating *not checked*
NHZTTN unhesitating *not checked*
NHZTTNG unhesitating *not checked*
NJ enjoy *appreciate*
NJ Nietzsche *philosopher*
NJ nudge *tap* nudged nudging
NJBL enjoyable (adj) *appreciated* enjoyably (adv)
NJDSHS injudicious *unwise*
NJGRF angiography *heart x-ray*
NJGRFK angiographic *heart x-ray*
NJGRM angiogram *heart x-ray*
NJK inject *force into*
NJKBL ineducable *cannot learn*
NJKBLD ineducability *cannot learn*
NJKBLT ineducability *cannot learn*
NJKDD uneducated *no schooling*
NJKDR injector *force into*
NJKSHN injection *force into, shot*
NJKT inject *force into*
NJKTD uneducated *no schooling*
NJKTR injector *force into*
NJL angel *heavenly being*
NJL nodule *lump*
NJLDST angel dust *drug*
NJLFSH angelfish *fish*

NJLHR angel-hair *pasta*
NJLK angelic (or) angelical (adj) *cherubic* angelically (adv)
NJLK angelica *herb*
NJLKL angelical (or) angelic (adj) *cherubic* angelically (adv)
NJLNT undulant *wavy*
NJLR nodular *lumpy*
NJLSHN undulation *wave*
NJLT undulate *wave* undulated undulating
NJLTR undulatory *waves*
NJM angioma *tumor*
NJMDS angiomatous *tumor*
NJMNT enjambment (or) enjambement *run-on*
NJMNT enjoyment *pleasure*
NJMTS angiomatous *tumor*
NJN angina *heart*
NJN antigen *enzyme*
NJN engine *motor*
NJN enjoin *forbid*
NJN ingénue (or) ingenue *girl*
NJN Neogene *rocks*
NJND ingenuity *cleverness* ingenuities
NJNDR engender *beget*
NJNGDV injunctive *court order*
NJNGKDV injunctive *court order*
NJNGKSHN injunction *court order*
NJNGKTV injunctive *court order*
NJNGSHN injunction *court order*
NJNGTV injunctive *court order*
NJNKDV injunctive *court order*
NJNKSHN injunction *court order*
NJNKTV injunctive *court order*
NJNR engineer *(n) designer* *(v) contrive, guide*
NJNR enginery *motor*
NJNRN engineering *design*

Use letters that best describe the sounds you hear and omit the vowels. Use **S** or **K** instead of **C**: to find circle use **SRKL**. Use **J** to find joy, **JM** to find gem and **G** to find go.

NJNRNG engineering *design*
NJNS ingenious *clever*
NJNSL ingeniously *clever*
NJNSNS ingeniousness *clever*
NJNT ingenuity *cleverness* ingenuities
NJNWD ingenuity *cleverness* ingenuities
NJNWS ingenuous *artless*
NJNWT ingenuity *cleverness* ingenuities
NJNY ingénue (or) ingenue *girl*
NJNYD ingenuity *cleverness* ingenuities
NJNYS ingenious *clever*
NJNYS ingenuous *artless*
NJNYSL ingeniously *clever*
NJNYSNS ingeniousness *clever*
NJNYT ingenuity *cleverness* ingenuities
NJNYWD ingenuity *cleverness* ingenuities
NJNYWS ingenuous *artless*
NJNYWT ingenuity *cleverness* ingenuities
NJPLSD angioplasty *vein* balloon angioplasties
NJPLST angioplasty *vein* balloon angioplasties
NJR injure *harm* injured injuring
NJR injury *(n) damage, wrong* injuries
NJR Niger *river*
NJR Nigeria *country*
NJR onager *catapult*
NJRK knee-jerk (adj) *involuntary action* knee jerk (n)
NJRR injurer *harm*
NJRS injurious *harmful*
NJRY Nigeria *country*
NJRYS injurious *harmful*
NJRZ New Jersey *US State*
NJSCHN ingestion *eat*
NJSDS injustice *wrong*
NJSDV ingestive *eat*
NJSPRM angiosperm *plant*
NJSPRMS angiospermous

plant
NJST ingest *eat*
NJST unjust *unfair*
NJSTS injustice *wrong*
NJSTV ingestive *eat*
NJWL nodule *lump*
NJYBL enjoyable (adj) *appreciated* enjoyably (adv)
NJYGRF angiography *heart x-ray*
NJYGRFK angiographic *heart x-ray*
NJYGRM angiogram *heart x-ray*
NJYM angioma *tumor*
NJYMDS angiomatous *tumor*
NJYMTS angiomatous *tumor*
NJYPLSD angioplasty *vein* balloon angioplasties
NJYPLST angioplasty *vein* balloon angioplasties
NJYSPRM angiosperm *plant*
NJYSPRMS angiospermous *plant*
NK aeonic (or) aeonian *long-lasting*
NK ankh *cross*
NK antic *caper*
NK enoki *mushroom*
NK eunuch *neutered male* eunuches
NK ewe-neck *(n) animal defect*
NK gnocchi *dumpling*
NK Inca *Quechuan*
NK ink *pen*
NK inky *black*
NK ionic *atom*
NK Ionic *Greek*
NK knack *talent*
NK knock *hit*
NK neck *(v) kiss (n) body part, slender end*
NK nick *notch, mar*
NK nock *notch*
NK nook *cranny*
NK nuke *bomb, microwave* nuked nuking

NK unique *one and only*
NKB incubi (pl) *nightmare* incubus
NKBDR incubator *hatch, baby care*
NKBK knock back *swallow*
NKBLT inkblot *smear*
NKBS incubus *nightmare* incubi
NKBSHN incubation *hatch*
NKBT incubate *hatch* incubated incubating
NKBT knockabout *boisterous*
NKBTR incubator *hatch, baby care*
NKC anoxia *lack of oxygen*
NKC nixie *mail* nixies
NKCHD noctuid *moth*
NKCHS unctuous *oily*
NKCHWD noctuid *moth*
NKCHWS unctuous *oily*
NKCM anoxemia *lack of oxygen*
NKCMK anoxemic *lack of oxygen*
NKCMY anoxemia *lack of oxygen*
NKCY anoxia *lack of oxygen*
NKD encode *scramble* encoded encoding
NKD eunuchoid *intersexual*
NKD ewe-necked *(adj) animal defect*
NKD naked *bare*
NKD naked eye *without lens*
NKDDJ anecdotage *story*
NKDDL anecdotal (adj) *story* anecdotally (adv)
NKDDLSM anecdotalism *story*
NKDDLST anecdotalist (or) anecdotist *story teller*
NKDDLZM anecdotalism *story*
NKDDST anecdotist (or) anecdotalist *story teller*
NKDK enokidake *mushroom*
NKDL nakedly *barely*
NKDLP nyctalopia *night blindness*
NKDLPY nyctalopia *night blindness*

Letters aren't doubled for single sounds: to find alley use **L** not **LL**. Use **Y** and **W** as hard sounds only: to find yellow use **YL**. (Br)=British spelling or usage. * See dictionary.

NKDMK antiacademic *against schooling*

NKDN knock down *(v) fell, earn*

NKDN knockdown *(n) blow (adj) forceful*

NKDNS nakedness *bareness*

NKDR nectar *juice*

NKDRN nectarine *fruit*

NKDT anecdote *story*

NKDTJ anecdotage *story*

NKDTL anecdotal (adj) *story* anecdotally (adv)

NKDTLSM anecdotalism *story*

NKDTLST anecdotalist (or) anecdotist *story teller*

NKDTLZM anecdotalism *story*

NKDTST anecdotist (or) anecdotalist *story teller*

NKDTT nictitate *wink* nictitated nictitating

NKDV inactive *idle*

NKDV inchoative *beginning*

NKDVSHN inactivation *stop*

NKDVT inactivate *stop* inactivated inactivating

NKF knock off *(v) stop, rob, copy*

NKF knockoff *(n) copy*

NKFLN enkephalin *brain receptor*

NKGLNT anticoagulant *blood thinner*

NKGN oncogene *cancer*

NKGND incognito *disguise* incognitos

NKGNK oncogenic *tumor*

NKGNSS oncogenesis *tumor*

NKGNT incognito *disguise* incognitos

NKGNZNS incognizance *unaware*

NKGNZNT incognizant *unaware*

NKGNZNTS incognizance *unaware*

NKGYLNT anticoagulant *blood thinner*

NKHRN inkhorn *bottle*

NKHRNS incoherence *inconsistency, confusion*

NKHRNT incoherent *inconsistent, confusing*

NKHRNTL incoherently *inconsistent, confusing*

NKHRNTS incoherence *inconsistency, confusion*

NKJDNT incogitant *thoughtless*

NKJN oncogene *cancer*

NKJNK oncogenic *tumor*

NKJNSD oncogenicity *tumor*

NKJNSS oncogenesis *tumor*

NKJNST oncogenicity *tumor*

NKJTNT incogitant *thoughtless*

NKK anechoic *no echoes*

NKK uncock *trigger*

NKKD uncooked *raw*

NKKT uncooked *raw*

NKL ankle *foot joint*

NKL inocula (pl) *antigen* inoculum

NKL knuckle *finger joint* knuckled knuckling

NKL nickel *mineral, money*

NKL nuclei (pl) *center* nucleus

NKL uncle *family*

NKL uncoil *unbend*

NKL uncool *agitated, not stylish*

NKL uniquely *one and only*

NKLBL knuckle ball *baseball*

NKLBN anklebone *talus*

NKLBN knucklebone *bone*

NKLD include *embrace, involve* included including

NKLD nucleoid *DNA*

NKLD nuclide *atom*

NKLD unclad *naked*

NKLDD unclouded *clear*

NKLDFR uncalled-for *not required*

NKLDK ankylotic *stiff*

NKLDK nuclidic *atom*

NKLDN knuckle down *apply strength*

NKLDN New Caledonia *island*

NKLDN nickelodeon *jukebox*

NKLDNY New Caledonia *island*

NKLDR inoculator *infuse*

NKLDR nucleator *cluster*

NKLDRD uncluttered *neat*

NKLDSDR knuckle-duster *weapon*

NKLDSTR knuckle-duster *weapon*

NKLDYN nickelodeon *jukebox*

NKLFL nucleophile *substance*

NKLFLK nucleophilic *atomic*

NKLFLSD nucleophilicity *atomic*

NKLFLST nucleophilicity *atomic*

NKLFRS nickeliferous *mineral*

NKLG oncology *tumor*

NKLG unclog *clear* unclogged unclogging

NKLHD knucklehead *dumbbell*

NKLHDD knuckleheaded *dumbbell*

NKLJ oncology *tumor*

NKLJKL oncological *tumor*

NKLJST oncologist *tumor*

NKLKDR inculcator *implant*

NKLKLBL incalculable (adj) *uncertain* incalculably (adv)

NKLKLDD uncalculated *not figured*

NKLKLTD uncalculated *not figured*

NKLKSD nucleic acid *DNA, RNA*

NKLKSHN inculcation *implant*

NKLKT inculcate *implant* inculcated inculcating

NKLKTR inculcator *implant*

NKLKYLBL incalculable (adj) *uncertain* incalculably (adv)

NKLKYLDD uncalculated

not figured
NKLKYLTD uncalculated
not figured
NKLLS nucleolus *cell*
NKLM inoculum *infusion*
inocula
NKLMD unclaimed *no owner*
NKLMDK anticlimactic *not important*
NKLMKDK anticlimactic *not important*
NKLMKS anticlimax *not important*
NKLMKTK anticlimactic *not important*
NKLMNC inclemency *stormy*
NKLMNS inclemency *stormy*
NKLMNT inclement *stormy*
NKLMNTC inclemency *stormy*
NKLMNTS inclemency *stormy*
NKLMP unclamp *loosen*
NKLMTK anticlimactic *not important*
NKLMX anticlimax *not important*
NKLN incline *tilt, influence* inclined inclining
NKLN inkling *clue*
NKLN neckline *collar*
NKLN nuclein *protein, acid*
NKLN nucleon *particle*
NKLN unclean *dirty*
NKLNBL inclinable *tendency*
NKLNCH unclench *relax*
NKLND inclined *tendency, slope*
NKLNDM nickel-and-dime *(adj) small-time*
NKLNDM nickel-and-dime *(v) weaken slowly* nickeled-and-dimed (or) nickel-and-dimed nickeling-and-diming (or) nickel-and-diming
NKLNDR knuckle under *submit*
NKLNG inkling *clue*
NKLNK nucleonic *particle*

NKLNKS nucleonics *science*
NKLNL neocolonial *politics*
NKLNL uncleanly *dirty*
NKLNLNS uncleanliness *dirty*
NKLNLZM neocolonialism *politics*
NKLNMDR inclinometer *tilt*
NKLNMTR inclinometer *tilt*
NKLNN inclining *tilt, influence*
NKLNNG inclining *tilt, influence*
NKLNR incliner *tilt, influence*
NKLNSHN inclination *tendency*
NKLNT inoculant *antigen*
NKLNX nucleonics *science*
NKLNYL neocolonial *politics*
NKLNYLZM neocolonialism *politics*
NKLPBL inculpable *blameless*
NKLPLZM nucleoplasm *sap*
NKLPLZMK nucleoplasmic *sap*
NKLPRTN nucleoprotein *gene*
NKLPSHN inculpation *accusation*
NKLPT inculpate *accuse* inculpated inculpating
NKLPTR inculpatory *accusing*
NKLQLBL incalculable (adj) *uncertain* incalculably (adv)
NKLQLDD uncalculated *not figured*
NKLQLTD uncalculated *not figured*
NKLR knuckler *knuckleball*
NKLR nuclear *atomic, central*
NKLR unclear *blurry*
NKLRD uncolored *no stain* (Br) uncoloured
NKLS necklace *jewelry*
NKLS Nicholas *Saint, tsar*
NKLS nuclease *enzyme*
NKLS nucleus *center* nuclei
NKLSFD unclassified *not secret, not rated*

NKLSHN inclusion *embrace, involve*
NKLSHN inoculation *infusion*
NKLSHN nucleation *cluster*
NKLSHR enclosure *confine, surround*
NKLSK neoclassic (or) neoclassical *style*
NKLSKL neoclassical (or) neoclassic *style*
NKLSM Uncle Sam *government*
NKLSNS incalescence *warming*
NKLSNT incalescent *warming*
NKLSNTHSS nucleosynthesis *chemistry*
NKLSNTS incalescence *warming*
NKLSP enclasp *embrace*
NKLSP unclasp *open*
NKLSR ankylosaur *dinosaur*
NKLSRS ankylosaurus *dinosaur*
NKLSS ankylosis *stiffness* ankyloses
NKLSV inclusive *broad*
NKLT anklet *sock*
NKLT inoculate *infuse* inoculated inoculating
NKLT niccolite *mineral*
NKLT nucleate *cluster* nucleated nucleating
NKLTD nucleotide *acid*
NKLTH unclothe *strip* unclothed unclothing
NKLTK ankylotic *stiff*
NKLTK nuclidic *atom*
NKLTR inoculator *infuse*
NKLTR nucleator *cluster*
NKLTRD uncluttered *neat*
NKLV enclave *ethnic area*
NKLY nuclei (pl) *center* nucleus
NKLYD nucleoid *DNA*
NKLYDR nucleator *cluster*
NKLYFL nucleophile *substance*
NKLYFLK nucleophilic *atomic*

Letters aren't doubled for single sounds: to find alley use **L** not **LL**. Use **Y** and **W** as hard sounds only: to find yellow use **YL**. (Br)=British spelling or usage. * See dictionary.

NKLYFLSD nucleophilicity *atomic*

NKLYFLST nucleophilicity *atomic*

NKLYKSD nucleic acid *DNA, RNA*

NKLYLS nucleolus *cell*

NKLYN nuclein *protein, acid*

NKLYN nucleon *particle*

NKLYNK nucleonic *particle*

NKLYNKS nucleonics *science*

NKLYNX nucleonics *science*

NKLYPLZM nucleoplasm *sap*

NKLYPLZMK nucleoplasmic *sap*

NKLYPRTN nucleoprotein *gene*

NKLYR nuclear *atomic, central*

NKLYS nuclease *enzyme*

NKLYS nucleus *center* nuclei

NKLYSHN nucleation *cluster*

NKLYSNTHSS nucleosynthesis *chemistry*

NKLYT nucleate *cluster* nucleated nucleating

NKLYTD nucleotide *acid*

NKLYTR nucleator *cluster*

NKLYZ nuclease *enzyme*

NKLZ enclose *confine, surround* enclosed enclosing

NKLZ nuclease *enzyme*

NKLZHN inclusion *embrace, involve*

NKLZHR enclosure *confine, surround*

NKLZV inclusive *broad*

NKM encomia (pl) *praise* encomium

NKM income *money*

NKMBNC incumbency *occupancy* incumbencies

NKMBNS incumbency *occupancy* incumbencies

NKMBNT incumbent *occupant*

NKMBNTC incumbency *occupancy* incumbencies

NKMBNTS incumbency *occupancy* incumbencies

NKMBR encumber *burden*

NKMBRNS encumbrance *burden*

NKMBRNTS encumbrance *burden*

NKMBSDBL incombustible *cannot burn*

NKMBSTBL incombustible *cannot burn*

NKMD incommode *disturb* incommoded incommoding

NKMD uncombed *tangled*

NKMDBL incommutable (adj) *unchangeable* incommutably (adv)

NKMDD uncommitted *not promised*

NKMDS incommodious *inconvenient*

NKMDSL incommodiously *inconvenient*

NKMDSNS incommodiousness *inconvenient*

NKMDYS incommodious *inconvenient*

NKMDYSL incommodiously *inconvenient*

NKMDYSNS incommodiousness *inconvenient*

NKMFRDBL uncomfortable (adj) *uneasy* uncomfortably (adv)

NKMFRTBL uncomfortable (adj) *uneasy* uncomfortably (adv)

NKMM encomium *praise* encomiums (or) encomia

NKMN incoming *arriving*

NKMN oncoming *approaching*

NKMN uncommon *rare*

NKMNG incoming *arriving*

NKMNG oncoming *approaching*

NKMNKBL incommunicable (adj) *silent* incommunicably (adv)

NKMNKD incommunicado *solitary*

NKMNKDV uncommunicative *quiet*

NKMNKT incommunicado *solitary*

NKMNKTV uncommunicative *quiet*

NKMNSHRBL incommensurable (adj) *cannot compare* incommensurably (adv)

NKMNSHRT incommensurate *inadequate*

NKMNSRBL incommensurable (adj) *cannot compare* incommensurably (adv)

NKMNSRT incommensurate *inadequate*

NKMNST anticommunist *against communism*

NKMNT enactment *make law, act out*

NKMP encamp *set up tent*

NKMP unkempt *messy*

NKMPDBL incompatible (adj) *discord* incompatibly (adv)

NKMPDBL incomputable (adj) *large* incomputably (adv)

NKMPDBLD incompatibility *discord* incompatibilities

NKMPDBLT incompatibility *discord* incompatibilities

NKMPDDV anticompetitive *against competition*

NKMPDNS incompetence *without skill* incompetency

NKMPDNT incompetent *without skill*

NKMPDNTS incompetence *without skill* incompetency

NKMPDTV anticompetitive *against competition*

NKMPLKDD uncomplicated *simple*

NKMPLKTD uncomplicated

simple
NKMPLMNR
uncomplimentary
belittling
NKMPLMNTR
uncomplimentary
belittling
NKMPLNN uncomplaining
patient
NKMPLNNG uncomplaining
patient
NKMPLNT incompliant *not*
submissive
NKMPLT incomplete
unfinished
NKMPLTL incompletely
unfinished
NKMPLTNS
incompleteness
unfinished
NKMPLYNT incompliant *not*
submissive
NKMPMNT encampment
tents
NKMPND unaccompanied
alone
NKMPRBL incomparable
(adj) *matchless*
incomparably (adv)
NKMPRBLD
incomparability *matchless*
NKMPRBLT incomparability
matchless
NKMPRHNDN
uncomprehending *no*
understanding
NKMPRHNDNG
uncomprehending *no*
understanding
NKMPRHNSBL
incomprehensible (adj)
vague incomprehensibly
(adv)
NKMPRHNSBLD
incomprehensibility
vagueness
NKMPRHNSBLT
incomprehensibility
vagueness
NKMPRMZN
uncompromising
unbending

NKMPRMZNG
uncompromising
unbending
NKMPRSBL incompressible
cannot squeeze
NKMPS encompass *envelop,*
include encompasses
NKMPSMNT
encompassment *envelop,*
include
NKMPT unkempt *messy*
NKMPTBL incompatible
(adj) *discord* incompatibly
(adv)
NKMPTBL incomputable
(adj) *large* incomputably
(adv)
NKMPTBLD incompatibility
discord incompatibilities
NKMPTBLT incompatibility
discord incompatibilities
NKMPTDV anticompetitive
against competition
NKMPTNS incompetence
without skill
incompetency
NKMPTNT incompetent
without skill
NKMPTNTS incompetence
without skill
incompetency
NKMPTTV anticompetitive
against competition
NKMPYDBL incomputable
(adj) *large* incomputably
(adv)
NKMPYTBL incomputable
(adj) *large* incomputably
(adv)
NKMR newcomer *arrival*
NKMRL unicameral (adj) *one*
chamber unicamerally
(adv)
NKMST encomiast *praise*
NKMSTK encomiastic *praise*
NKMTBL incommutable
(adj) *unchangeable*
incommutably (adv)
NKMTD uncommitted *not*
promised
NKMY encomia (pl) *praise*
encomium

NKMYDBL incommutable
(adj) *unchangeable*
incommutably (adv)
NKMYM encomium *praise*
encomiums (or) encomia
NKMYNKBL
incommunicable (adj)
silent incommunicably
(adv)
NKMYNKD incommunicado
solitary
NKMYNKDV
uncommunicative *quiet*
NKMYNKT incommunicado
solitary
NKMYNKTV
uncommunicative *quiet*
NKMYNST anticommunist
against communism
NKMYST encomiast *praise*
NKMYSTK encomiastic
praise
NKMYTBL incommutable
(adj) *unchangeable*
incommutably (adv)
NKN necking *kissing*
NKN uncanny *weird*
NKN unkind *mean*
NKNBL incunabula (pl) *early*
work incunabulum
NKNBL unaccountable (adj)
strange, not responsible
unaccountably (adv)
NKNBL uncountable *many*
NKNBLM incunabulum *early*
work incunabula
NKNBYL incunabula (pl)
early work incunabulum
NKNBYLM incunabulum
early work incunabula
NKNCHNBL
unconscionable (adj)
unreasonable
unconscionably (adv)
NKNCHS unconscious *not*
aware
NKNCLD unconcealed *open*
NKNCVBL inconceivable
(adj) *unbelievable*
inconceivably (adv)
NKND anaconda *snake*
NKND knock-kneed *leg*

shape
NKND unaccounted unexplained
NKND uncounted *many*
NKND unkind *mean*
NKNDL enkindle *flame* enkindled enkindling
NKNDL unkindly *mean*
NKNDLNS unkindliness *meanness*
NKNDNS unkindness *meanness*
NKNDS incandesce *glow* incandesced incandescing
NKNDSHNL unconditional (adj) *absolute* unconditionally (adv)
NKNDSNS incandescence *glow*
NKNDSNT incandescent *glowing*
NKNDSNTS incandescence *glow*
NKNDT incondite *crude*
NKNFRMD inconformity *opposition* inconformities
NKNFRMD unconfirmed *not proven*
NKNFRMT inconformity *opposition* inconformities
NKNG necking *kissing*
NKNGGRD incongruity *not the same* incongruities
NKNGGRNT incongruent *not the same*
NKNGGRS incongruous *not expected*
NKNGGRT incongruity *not the same* incongruities
NKNGGRWD incongruity *not the same* incongruities
NKNGGRWNT incongruent *not the same*
NKNGGRWS incongruous *not expected*
NKNGGRWT incongruity *not the same* incongruities
NKNGKRBL unconquerable *strong*
NKNGNL uncongenial *rude*
NKNGNYL uncongenial

rude
NKNGRD incongruity *not the same* incongruities
NKNGRNT incongruent *not the same*
NKNGRS incongruous *not expected*
NKNGRT incongruity *not the same* incongruities
NKNGRWD incongruity *not the same* incongruities
NKNGRWNT incongruent *not the same*
NKNGRWS incongruous *not expected*
NKNGRWT incongruity *not the same* incongruities
NKNJNL uncongenial *rude*
NKNJNYL uncongenial *rude*
NKNK knickknack *ornament*
NKNKDD unconnected *not joined*
NKNKLSV inconclusive *no result*
NKNKLSVL inconclusively *no result*
NKNKLSVNS inconclusiveness *no result*
NKNKLZV inconclusive *no result*
NKNKLZVL inconclusively *no result*
NKNKLZVNS inconclusiveness *no result*
NKNKRBL unconquerable *strong*
NKNKTD unconnected *not joined*
NKNL uncannily *weird*
NKNL unkindly *mean*
NKNLNS unkindliness *meanness*
NKNM nickname *(n) name*
NKNM nickname *(v) name* nicknamed nicknaming
NKNMK uneconomic (or) uneconomical *wasteful*
NKNMKL uneconomical (or) uneconomic *wasteful*
NKNNS uncanniness *weird*

NKNR encounter *meet*
NKNS inkiness *black*
NKNS uniqueness *one and only*
NKNS unkindness *meanness*
NKNSDRBL inconsiderable (adj) *trivial* inconsiderably (adv)
NKNSDRSHN inconsideration *thoughtless*
NKNSDRT inconsiderate *thoughtless*
NKNSDRTL inconsiderately *thoughtless*
NKNSHNBL unconscionable (adj) *unreasonable* unconscionably (adv)
NKNSHS unconscious *not aware*
NKNSKWNCHL inconsequential (adj) *illogical, irrelevant* inconsequentially (adv)
NKNSKWNS inconsequence *illogical, irrelevant*
NKNSKWNSHL inconsequential (adj) *illogical, irrelevant* inconsequentially (adv)
NKNSKWNT inconsequent *illogical, irrelevant*
NKNSKWNTS inconsequence *illogical, irrelevant*
NKNSLBL inconsolable (adj) *sad* inconsolably (adv)
NKNSLD unconcealed *open*
NKNSMBL inconsumable (adj) *cannot eat* inconsumably (adv)
NKNSNNS inconsonance *disagreement*
NKNSNNT inconsonant *discordant*
NKNSNNTS inconsonance *disagreement*
NKNSPKS inconspicuous *not noticeable*

Use letters that best describe the sounds you hear and omit the vowels. Use **S** or **K** instead of **C**: to find circle use **SRKL**. Use **J** to find joy, **JM** to find gem and **G** to find go.

NKNSPKSL
inconspicuously *not noticeable*

NKNSPKSNS
inconspicuousness *not noticeable*

NKNSPKWS inconspicuous *not noticeable*

NKNSPKWSL
inconspicuously *not noticeable*

NKNSPKWSNS
inconspicuousness *not noticeable*

NKNSPKYS inconspicuous *not noticeable*

NKNSPKYSL
inconspicuously *not noticeable*

NKNSPKYSNS
inconspicuousness *not noticeable*

NKNSPKYWS
inconspicuous *not noticeable*

NKNSPKYWSL
inconspicuously *not noticeable*

NKNSPKYWSNS
inconspicuousness *not noticeable*

NKNSPQS inconspicuous *not noticeable*

NKNSPQSL
inconspicuously *not noticeable*

NKNSPQSNS
inconspicuousness *not noticeable*

NKNSPQWS inconspicuous *not noticeable*

NKNSPQWSL
inconspicuously *not noticeable*

NKNSPQWSNS
inconspicuousness *not noticeable*

NKNSQNCHL
inconsequential (adj)
illogical, irrelevant
inconsequentially (adv)

NKNSQNS inconsequence

illogical, irrelevant

NKNSQNSHL
inconsequential (adj)
illogical, irrelevant
inconsequentially (adv)

NKNSQNT inconsequent
illogical, irrelevant

NKNSQNTS inconsequence
illogical, irrelevant

NKNSRN unconcern
indifference

NKNSRND unconcerned
indifferent

NKNSRVDV
neoconservative *politics*

NKNSRVTV
neoconservative *politics*

NKNSSDNC inconsistency
unlikeliness
inconsistencies

NKNSSDNS inconsistency
unlikeliness
inconsistencies

NKNSSDNT inconsistent
unlikely

NKNSSDNTC inconsistency
unlikeliness
inconsistencies

NKNSSDNTL inconsistently
unlikely

NKNSSDNTS inconsistency
unlikeliness
inconsistencies

NKNSSTNC inconsistency
unlikeliness
inconsistencies

NKNSSTNS inconsistency
unlikeliness
inconsistencies

NKNSSTNT inconsistent
unlikely

NKNSSTNTC inconsistency
unlikeliness
inconsistencies

NKNSSTNTL inconsistently
unlikely

NKNSSTNTS inconsistency
unlikeliness
inconsistencies

NKNSTNC inconstancy
fickle

NKNSTNS inconstancy

fickle

NKNSTNT inconstant *fickle*

NKNSTNTC inconstancy
fickle

NKNSTNTL inconstantly
fickle

NKNSTNTS inconstancy
fickle

NKNSTRKDD
unconstructed *not shaped*

NKNSTRKTD
unconstructed *not shaped*

NKNSTTSHNL
unconstitutional (adj) *not lawful* unconstitutionally (adv)

NKNSTTYSHNL
unconstitutional (adj) *not lawful* unconstitutionally (adv)

NKNSVBL inconceivable
(adj) *unbelievable*
inconceivably (adv)

NKNSYMBL inconsumable
(adj) *cannot eat*
inconsumably (adv)

NKNT no-account *trifling*

NKNTBL unaccountable
(adj) *strange, not responsible* unaccountably (adv)

NKNTBL uncountable *many*

NKNTD unaccounted
unexplained

NKNTD uncounted *many*

NKNTNNS incontinence
unrestrained incontinency

NKNTNNT incontinent
unrestrained

NKNTNNTL incontinently
unrestrained

NKNTNNTS incontinence
unrestrained incontinency

NKNTNT incontinent
unrestrained

NKNTNTL incontinently
unrestrained

NKNTR encounter *meet*

NKNTRLBL uncontrollable
(adj) *wild* uncontrollably
(adv)

NKNTRLBLD

Letters aren't doubled for single sounds: to find alley use **L** not **LL**. Use **Y** and **W** as hard sounds only: to find yellow use **YL**. (Br)=British spelling or usage. * See dictionary.

NKNTRLBLT
uncontrollability *wildness*

NKNTRLD uncontrolled
wild

NKNTRVRDBL
incontrovertible (adj) *no dispute* incontrovertibly (adv)

NKNTRVRTBL
incontrovertible (adj) *no dispute* incontrovertibly (adv)

NKNTSDBL incontestable (adj) *no dispute* incontestably (adv)

NKNTSDD uncontested *no fight*

NKNTSHN incantation *spell*

NKNTSTBL incontestable (adj) *no dispute* incontestably (adv)

NKNTSTD uncontested *no fight*

NKNVLSNT anticonvulsant *prevents convulsions*

NKNVNCHNL
unconventional (adj) *not ordinary* unconventionally (adv)

NKNVNNS inconvenience *trouble* inconvenienced inconveniencing

NKNVNNT inconvenient *untimely*

NKNVNNTL inconveniently *untimely*

NKNVNNTS inconvenience *trouble* inconvenienced inconveniencing

NKNVNSHNL
unconventional (adj) *not ordinary* unconventionally (adv)

NKNVNSN unconvincing *not probable*

NKNVNSNG unconvincing *not probable*

NKNVNST unconvinced *doubtful*

NKNVNTSN unconvincing *not probable*

NKNVNTSNG unconvincing *not probable*

NKNVNYNS inconvenience *trouble* inconvenienced inconveniencing

NKNVNYNT inconvenient *untimely*

NKNVNYNTL
inconveniently *untimely*

NKNVNYNTS
inconvenience *trouble* inconvenienced inconveniencing

NKNVRDBL inconvertible (adj) *no exchange* inconvertibly (adv)

NKNVRTBL inconvertible (adj) *no exchange* inconvertibly (adv)

NKP kneecap *bone*

NKP knock up *(vulgar) impregnate*

NKP uncap *open* uncapped uncapping

NKP unkempt *messy*

NKPBL incapable (adj) *untrained* incapably (adv)

NKPBLD incapability *untrained*

NKPBLT incapability *untrained*

NKPD unoccupied *empty, no job*

NKPL uncouple *disconnect* uncoupled uncoupling

NKPLR uncoupler *disconnect*

NKPR innkeeper *hotel*

NKPRDV uncooperative *not helpful*

NKPRTV uncooperative *not helpful*

NKPSD incapacity *disability* incapacities

NKPSLDD encapsulated *enclose, summarize*

NKPSLSHN encapsulation *enclose, summarize*

NKPSLT encapsulate *enclose, summarize* encapsulated encapsulating

NKPSLTD encapsulated
enclose, summarize

NKPST incapacity *disability* incapacities

NKPSTSHN incapacitation *disability*

NKPSTT incapacitate *disable* incapacitated incapacitating

NKPSYLDD encapsulated *enclose, summarize*

NKPSYLSHN encapsulation *enclose, summarize*

NKPSYLT encapsulate *enclose, summarize* encapsulated encapsulating

NKPSYLTD encapsulated *enclose, summarize*

NKPT unkempt *messy*

NKR anchor *hold in place*

NKR Ankara *city*

NKR encore *reappear* encored encoring

NKR incur *become liable* incurred incurring

NKR knacker *(Br) buyer*

NKR knocker *door*

NKR nacre *shell*

NKRBKR Knickerbocker *New York*

NKRBKRZ knickerbockers *trousers*

NKRBL incurable (adj) *no remedy* incurably (adv)

NKRBLD incurability *no remedy*

NKRBLT incurability *no remedy*

NKRBRDD uncorroborated *not proven*

NKRBRTD uncorroborated *not proven*

NKRC inaccuracy *error* inaccuracies

NKRCH encroach *trespass*

NKRCHF neckerchief *scarf* neckerchiefs

NKRCHMNT encroachment *trespass*

NKRCHR encroacher *trespasser*

NKRD enchiridia (pl)

Use letters that best describe the sounds you hear and omit the vowels. Use **S** or **K** instead of **C**: to find circle use **SRKL**. Use **J** to find joy, **JM** to find gem and **G** to find go.

handbook enchiridion
NKRD una corda *piano*
NKRDBL incredible (adj) *improbable* incredibly (adv)
NKRDBLD incredibility *improbable*
NKRDBLT incredibility *improbable*
NKRDD uncrowded *spacious*
NKRDDD unaccredited *not certified*
NKRDDD uncredited *no acclaim*
NKRDFR uncared-for *ignored*
NKRDK anchoritic *cloistered*
NKRDK necrotic *dead*
NKRDKL anchoritically *cloistered*
NKRDKL neocortical *brain*
NKRDKL uncritical (adj) *accepting* uncritically (adv)
NKRDLD incredulity *disbelief*
NKRDLS incredulous *questioning*
NKRDLSL incredulously *questioning*
NKRDLT incredulity *disbelief*
NKRDN enchiridion *handbook* enchiridia
NKRDNDD uncoordinated *disjointed, spastic*
NKRDNSHN incoordination *no control*
NKRDNTD uncoordinated *disjointed, spastic*
NKRDTD unaccredited *not certified*
NKRDTD uncredited *no acclaim*
NKRDY enchiridia (pl) *handbook* enchiridion
NKRDYLD incredulity *disbelief*
NKRDYLS incredulous *questioning*
NKRDYLSL incredulously *questioning*
NKRDYLT incredulity *disbelief*
NKRDYN enchiridion *handbook* enchiridia

NKRFGS necrophagous *eating corpses*
NKRFL necrophilia *corpse*
NKRFLK necrophiliac *corpse lover*
NKRFLK necrophilic *corpse*
NKRFLSM necrophilism *corpse*
NKRFLY necrophilia *corpse*
NKRFLYK necrophiliac *corpse lover*
NKRFLZM necrophilism *corpse*
NKRGW Nicaragua *country*
NKRJ Anchorage *city*
NKRJ anchorage *ship*
NKRJ encourage *support* encouraged encouraging
NKRJBL incorrigible (adj) *unruly* incorrigibly (adv)
NKRJBLD incorrigibility *unruly*
NKRJBLT incorrigibility *unruly*
NKRJLD incredulity *disbelief*
NKRJLS incredulous *questioning*
NKRJLSL incredulously *questioning*
NKRJLT incredulity *disbelief*
NKRJMNT encouragement *support*
NKRJN encouraging *supporting*
NKRJNG encouraging *supporting*
NKRJR encourager *supporter*
NKRK incorrect *wrong*
NKRK uncork *open*
NKRKT incorrect *wrong*
NKRKT uncorked *open*
NKRL uncurl *straighten*
NKRLG necrology *death* necrologies
NKRLJ necrology *death* necrologies
NKRLJKL necrological *death*
NKRLJST necrologist *death*
NKRLS anchorless *not held in place*

NKRM anticrime *crime preventing*
NKRMN anchorman *last one, moderator* anchormen
NKRMNC necromancy *magic*
NKRMNL incremental (adj) *increase* incrementally (adv)
NKRMNS necromancy *magic*
NKRMNSHN incrimination *show fault*
NKRMNSR necromancer *magician*
NKRMNT increment *increase*
NKRMNT incriminate *accuse* incriminated incriminating
NKRMNTC necromancy *magic*
NKRMNTL incremental (adj) *increase* incrementally (adv)
NKRMNTR incriminatory *show fault*
NKRMNTS necromancy *magic*
NKRMNTSR necromancer *magician*
NKRN einkorn *wheat*
NKRN inkhorn *bottle*
NKRN uncaring *mean*
NKRN unicorn *animal*
NKRNG uncaring *mean*
NKRNSHN incarnation *embodiment*
NKRNSM anachronism *not chronological, from the past*
NKRNT incarnate *embody* incarnated incarnating
NKRNZM anachronism *not chronological, from the past*
NKRP encrypt *code*
NKRPC necropsy *autopsy* necropsied necropsying necropsies
NKRPDBL incorruptible (adj) *honest* incorruptibly (adv)
NKRPDBLD incorruptibility *honest*

Letters aren't doubled for single sounds: to find alley use **L** not **LL**. Use **Y** and **W** as hard sounds only: to find yellow use **YL**. (Br)=British spelling or usage. * See dictionary.

NKRPDBLT incorruptibility
honest
NKRPLS necropolis
cemetery
NKRPRD incorporeity *no
body*
NKRPRDD incorporated
united
NKRPRDR incorporator
unite
NKRPRL incorporeal (adj)
no body incorporeally
(adv)
NKRPRSHN incorporation
unity
NKRPRSN anchorperson
last one, moderator
NKRPRT incorporate *unite*
incorporated
incorporating
NKRPRT incorporeity *no
body*
NKRPRTD incorporated
united
NKRPRTR incorporator
unite
NKRPRYD incorporeity *no
body*
NKRPRYL incorporeal (adj)
no body incorporeally
(adv)
NKRPRYT incorporeity *no
body*
NKRPS necropsy *autopsy*
necropsied necropsying
necropsies
NKRPSHN encryption *code*
NKRPT encrypt *code*
NKRPT incorrupt *honest*
NKRPTBL incorruptible
(adj) *honest* incorruptibly
(adv)
NKRPTBLD incorruptibility
honest
NKRPTBLT incorruptibility
honest
NKRS inaccuracy *error*
inaccuracies
NKRS increase *add to*
increased increasing
NKRS incurious *indifferent*
NKRS knickers *trousers*

NKRS nacreous *shell*
NKRSBL incoercible *cannot
force*
NKRSBL increasable *add to*
NKRSCHN unchristian *other
faith*
NKRSD incuriosity
indifference
NKRSHN incursion *raid*
NKRSND unchristened *no
baptism*
NKRSNGL increasingly *more*
NKRSNL increasingly *more*
NKRSR increaser *add to*
NKRSRSHN incarceration
imprison
NKRSRT incarcerate
imprison incarcerated
incarcerating
NKRSS necrosis *death*
necroses
NKRST Antichrist *false
messiah*
NKRST encrust *harden*
NKRST incuriosity
indifference
NKRSTSHN incrustation
coating
NKRT anchorite *hermit*
NKRT ankerite *mineral*
NKRT inaccurate *faulty*
NKRTK anchoritic *cloistered*
NKRTK necrotic *dead*
NKRTKL anchoritically
cloistered
NKRTKL neocortical *brain*
NKRTKL uncritical (adj)
accepting uncritically (adv)
NKRTKS neocortex *brain*
NKRTL inaccurately *faulty*
NKRTX neocortex *brain*
NKRTZN necrotizing *dying*
NKRTZNG necrotizing *dying*
NKRV incurve *bend*
NKRVCHR incurvature *bend*
NKRVSHN incurvation *bend*
NKRVT incurvate *bend*
incurvated incurvating
NKRVTR incurvature *bend*
NKRWMN anchorwoman
last one, moderator
anchorwomen

NKRYS incurious *indifferent*
NKRYS nacreous *shell*
NKRYSD incuriosity
indifference
NKRYST incuriosity
indifference
NKRZ knickers *trousers*
NKRZHN incursion *raid*
NKS annex *join* annexes
(Br) annexe
NKS anoxia *lack of oxygen*
NKS encase *cover* encased
encasing
NKS innocuous *harmless*
NKS next *following*
NKS Nicosia *city*
NKS nix *no, nothing, veto*
NKS nixie *mail* nixies
NKS nocuous *harmful*
NKS onyx *quartz*
NKSDK encaustic *paint*
NKSDMD unaccustomed
not used to
NKSDNT antioxidant
chemical
NKSDR next door (adv)
adjacent next-door (adj)
NKSHN inaction *idleness*
NKSHN unction *salve*
NKSHNT ancient *old*
NKSHNTL anciently *long
ago*
NKSHNTNS ancientness *old
age*
NKSHS anxious *concerned*
NKSHS noxious *harmful*
NKSHS unctuous *oily*
NKSHSL anxiously *with
concern*
NKSHSL noxiously
harmfully
NKSHSNS anxiousness
with concern
NKSHSNS noxiousness
harm
NKSHWS unctuous *oily*
NKSK anoxic *lack of oxygen*
NKSKYZBL inexcusable
(adj) *cannot forgive*
inexcusably (adv)
NKSKZBL inexcusable (adj)
cannot forgive inexcusably

Use letters that best describe the sounds you hear and omit the vowels. Use **S** or **K** instead of **C**: to find circle use **SRKL**. Use **J** to find joy, **JM** to find gem and **G** to find go.

(adv)
NKSL nocuously *harmful*
NKSM anoxemia *lack of oxygen*
NKSMK anoxemic *lack of oxygen*
NKSMND unexamined *thoughtless*
NKSMNT encasement *cover*
NKSMY anoxemia *lack of oxygen*
NKSND unaccented *no emphasis*
NKSNTD unaccented *no emphasis*
NKSPBL inexpiable (adj) *unforgiven* inexpiably (adv)
NKSPDBL unacceptable (adj) *reject* unacceptably (adv)
NKSPDNC inexpediency *unwise* inexpedience
NKSPDNS inexpediency *unwise* inexpedience
NKSPDNT inexpedient *unwise*
NKSPDNTC inexpediency *unwise* inexpedience
NKSPDNTS inexpediency *unwise* inexpedience
NKSPDYNC inexpediency *unwise* inexpedience
NKSPDYNS inexpediency *unwise* inexpedience
NKSPDYNT inexpedient *unwise*
NKSPDYNTC inexpediency *unwise* inexpedience
NKSPDYNTS inexpediency *unwise* inexpedience
NKSPGNBL inexpugnable (adj) *stable* inexpugnably (adv)
NKSPKDD unexpected *surprise*
NKSPKDDL unexpectedly *surprise*
NKSPKDDNS unexpectedness *surprise*
NKSPKTD unexpected *surprise*

NKSPKTDL unexpectedly *surprise*
NKSPKTDNS unexpectedness *surprise*
NKSPLKBL inexplicable (adj) *no explanation* inexplicably (adv)
NKSPLKBLD inexplicability *no explanation*
NKSPLKBLT inexplicability *no explanation*
NKSPLNBL unexplainable (adj) *mysterious* unexplainably (adv)
NKSPLND unexplained *mysterious*
NKSPLRD unexplored *unknown*
NKSPNBL inexpugnable (adj) *stable* inexpugnably (adv)
NKSPNJBL inexpungible *cannot erase*
NKSPNSV inexpensive *low cost*
NKSPNSVL inexpensively *low cost*
NKSPRNS inexperience *no knowledge*
NKSPRNSD inexperienced *no knowledge*
NKSPRNST inexperienced *no knowledge*
NKSPRNTS inexperience *no knowledge*
NKSPRSBL inexpressible (adj) *no description* inexpressibly (adv)
NKSPRSBLD inexpressibility *no description*
NKSPRSBLT inexpressibility *no description*
NKSPRSV inexpressive *no expression*
NKSPRT inexpert *unskilled*
NKSPRTL inexpertly *unskilled*
NKSPRYNS inexperience *no knowledge*
NKSPRYNSD

inexperienced *no knowledge*
NKSPRYNST inexperienced *no knowledge*
NKSPRYNTS inexperience *no knowledge*
NKSPSHNBL unexceptionable (adj) *beyond reproach* unexceptionably (adv)
NKSPSHNBLNS unexceptionableness *beyond reproach*
NKSPSHNL unexceptional *commonplace*
NKSPTBL unacceptable (adj) *reject* unacceptably (adv)
NKSPYBL inexpiable (adj) *unforgiven* inexpiably (adv)
NKSPYNBL inexpugnable (adj) *stable* inexpugnably (adv)
NKSQZBL inexcusable (adj) *cannot forgive* inexcusably (adv)
NKSRBL inexorable (adj) *relentless* inexorably (adv)
NKSRBLD inexorability *relentless*
NKSRBLT inexorability *relentless*
NKSRKSS onchocerciasis *disease* onchocerciases
NKSRKYSS onchocerciasis *disease* onchocerciases
NKSRSZD unexercised *not used*
NKSS nexus *link, focus* nexuses (or) nexus
NKSSBL inaccessible (adj) *no passage* inaccessibly (adv)
NKSSBLD inaccessibility *no passage*
NKSSBLT inaccessibility *no passage*
NKSSHN annexation *joint*
NKSSHNL annexational *joint*
NKSSHNST annexationist

Letters aren't doubled for single sounds: to find alley use **L** not **LL**. Use **Y** and **W** as hard sounds only: to find yellow use **YL**. (Br)=British spelling or usage. * See dictionary.

joiner
NKST next *following*
NKST next to *beside*
NKSTK encaustic *paint*
NKSTMD unaccustomed *not used to*
NKSTNGGWSHBL inextinguishable (adj) *unquenchable* inextinguishably (adv)
NKSTNGWSHBL inextinguishable (adj) *unquenchable* inextinguishably (adv)
NKSTNS in extenso *full length*
NKSTR next door (adv) *adjacent* next-door (adj)
NKSTRKBL inextricable (adj) *tangle* inextricably (adv)
NKSVL Knoxville *city*
NKSY anoxia *lack of oxygen*
NKSY Nicosia *city*
NKT enact *make law, act out*
NKT ewe-necked *(adj) animal defect*
NKT inchoate *formless*
NKT knock out *(v) defeat, exhaust, produce*
NKT knockout *(n) defeat, sensation*
NKT necktie *attire*
NKT no-account *trifling*
NKT uncut *rough*
NKTBL unaccountable (adj) *strange, not responsible* unaccountably (adv)
NKTBL uncountable *many*
NKTD noctuid *moth*
NKTD unaccounted *unexplained*
NKTD uncounted *many*
NKTH uncouth *no manners*
NKTHL uncouthly *no manners*
NKTHNS uncouthness *no manners*
NKTL inchoately *formless*
NKTLP nyctalopia *night blindness*
NKTLPY nyctalopia *night*

blindness
NKTMBLST noctambulist *sleepwalker*
NKTMBYLST noctambulist *sleepwalker*
NKTMNT enactment *make law, act out*
NKTN nicotine *drug*
NKTNKSD nicotinic acid *drug*
NKTNS inchoateness *formless*
NKTR encounter *meet*
NKTR nectar *juice*
NKTRN nectarine *fruit*
NKTRN nocturne *night*
NKTRNL nocturnal (adj) *night* nocturnally (adv)
NKTS unctuous *oily*
NKTTT nictitate *wink* nictitated nictitating
NKTV inactive *idle*
NKTV inchoative *beginning*
NKTVD inactivity *idleness*
NKTVSHN inactivation *stop*
NKTVT inactivate *stop* inactivated inactivating
NKTVT inactivity *idleness*
NKTWD noctuid *moth*
NKTWS unctuous *oily*
NKVR uncover *reveal*
NKVRD uncovered *revealed*
NKWD inequity *unfairness* inequities
NKWD iniquity *sin* iniquities
NKWDBL inequitable (adj) *unfair* inequitably (adv)
NKWDD antiquated *old*
NKWDS iniquitous *sinful*
NKWDV inchoative *beginning*
NKWGLNT anticoagulant *blood thinner*
NKWGYLNT anticoagulant *blood thinner*
NKWK anechoic *no echoes*
NKWL unequal (adj) *not alike, unjust* unequally (adv)
NKWLD inequality *not equal* inequalities
NKWLD unequaled (or)

unequalled *without parallel*
NKWLFD unqualified *complete, unfit*
NKWLT inequality *not equal* inequalities
NKWNCHBL unquenchable *thirsty*
NKWND unacquainted *stranger*
NKWNTD unacquainted *stranger*
NKWPRDV uncooperative *not helpful*
NKWPRTV uncooperative *not helpful*
NKWR antiquary *old items* antiquaries
NKWR enquire *ask* enquired enquiring
NKWR enquiry *investigation* enquiries
NKWR inquire *ask* inquired inquiring
NKWR inquiry *investigation* inquiries
NKWR neckwear *scarf, tie*
NKWRDNDD uncoordinated *disjointed, spastic*
NKWRDNSHN incoordination *no control*
NKWRDNTD uncoordinated *disjointed, spastic*
NKWRN antiquarian *collector of old items*
NKWRR inquirer *ask*
NKWRSBL incoercible *cannot force*
NKWRST knockwurst (or) knackwurst *sausage*
NKWRYN antiquarian *collector of old items*
NKWS innocuous *harmless*
NKWS nocuous *harmful*
NKWSCHNBL unquestionable (adj) *no argument* unquestionably (adv)
NKWSCHND unquestioned *no argument*
NKWSCHNN unquestioning

Use letters that best describe the sounds you hear and omit the vowels. Use **S** or **K** instead of **C**: to find circle use **SRKL**. Use **J** to find joy, **JM** to find gem and **G** to find go.

no argument
NKWSCHNNG
unquestioning *no argument*
NKWSL nocuously *harmful*
NKWST inquest *inquiry*
NKWT antiquate *make old* antiquated antiquating
NKWT inchoate *formless*
NKWT inequity *unfairness* inequities
NKWT iniquity *sin* iniquities
NKWT unquote *end quote*
NKWTBL inequitable (adj) *unfair* inequitably (adv)
NKWTD antiquated *old*
NKWTD inquietude *disturbed*
NKWTL inchoately *formless*
NKWTNS inchoateness *formless*
NKWTS iniquitous *sinful*
NKWTV inchoative *beginning*
NKWVKBL unequivocably *clearly*
NKWVKL unequivocal (adj) *clear* unequivocally (adv)
NKWYR enquire *ask* enquired enquiring
NKWYR enquiry *investigation* enquiries
NKWYR inquire *ask* inquired inquiring
NKWYR inquiry *investigation* inquiries
NKWYRR inquirer *ask*
NKWYTD inquietude *disturbed*
NKWYTYD inquietude *disturbed*
NKWZDR inquisitor *examiner*
NKWZDV inquisitive *curious*
NKWZSHN inquisition *examination*
NKWZTR inquisitor *examiner*
NKWZTRL inquisitorial (adj) *examiner* inquisitorially (adv)
NKWZTRYL inquisitorial

(adj) *examiner* inquisitorially (adv)
NKWZTV inquisitive *curious*
NKYB incubi (pl) *nightmare* incubus
NKYBDR incubator *hatch, baby care*
NKYBS incubus *nightmare* incubi
NKYBSHN incubation *hatch*
NKYBT incubate *hatch* incubated incubating
NKYBTR incubator *hatch, baby care*
NKYL inocula (pl) *antigen* inoculum
NKYL nuclei (pl) *center* nucleus
NKYL uncoil *unbend*
NKYLDR inoculator *infuse*
NKYLM inoculum *infusion* inocula
NKYLNT inoculant *antigen*
NKYLR nuclear *atomic, central*
NKYLSHN inoculation *infusion*
NKYLSHN nucleation *cluster*
NKYLT inoculate *infuse* inoculated inoculating
NKYLT nucleate *cluster* nucleated nucleating
NKYLTR inoculator *infuse*
NKYLYSHN nucleation *cluster*
NKYLYT nucleate *cluster* nucleated nucleating
NKYLZ nuclease *enzyme*
NKYNBL incunabula (pl) *early work* incunabulum
NKYNBLM incunabulum *early work* incunabula
NKYNBYL incunabula (pl) *early work* incunabulum
NKYNBYLM incunabulum *early work* incunabula
NKYPD unoccupied *empty, no job*
NKYRBL incurable (adj) *no remedy* incurably (adv)
NKYRBLD incurability *no*

remedy
NKYRBLT incurability *no remedy*
NKYRC inaccuracy *error* inaccuracies
NKYRS inaccuracy *error* inaccuracies
NKYRS incurious *indifferent*
NKYRSD incuriosity *indifference*
NKYRST incuriosity *indifference*
NKYRT inaccurate *faulty*
NKYRTL inaccurately *faulty*
NKYRYS incurious *indifferent*
NKYRYSD incuriosity *indifference*
NKYRYST incuriosity *indifference*
NKYS innocuous *harmless*
NKYS nocuous *harmful*
NKYSL nocuously *harmful*
NKYWS innocuous *harmless*
NKYWS nocuous *harmful*
NKYWSL nocuously *harmful*
NKZD anxiety *concern* anxieties
NKZK anoxic *lack of oxygen*
NKZK inexact *inaccurate*
NKZKDTD inexactitude *inaccurate*
NKZKT inexact *inaccurate*
NKZKTTD inexactitude *inaccurate*
NKZMND unexamined *thoughtless*
NKZSDBL inexhaustible (adj) *cannot use up or tire* inexhaustibly (adv)
NKZSDNT inexistent *not real*
NKZSHN annexation *joint*
NKZSHNL annexational *joint*
NKZSHNST annexationist *joiner*
NKZSTBL inexhaustible (adj) *cannot use up or tire* inexhaustibly (adv)
NKZSTNT inexistent *not real*
NKZT anxiety *concern*

Letters aren't doubled for single sounds: to find alley use **L** not **LL**. Use **Y** and **W** as hard sounds only: to find yellow use **YL**. (Br)=British spelling or usage. * See dictionary.

anxieties
NKZYD anxiety *concern*
anxieties
NKZYT anxiety *concern*
anxieties
NL anal (adj) *rectum,
meticulous* anally (adv)
NL anile *senile*
NL anneal *tempered*
NL annual (adj) *yearly*
annually (adv)
NL annul *cancel* annulled
annulling
NL anole *lizard*
NL enisle *isolate*
NL enol *chemical*
NL in-law *relative*
NL inlay *set in* inlaid inlaying
NL kneel *on knees* knelt (or)
kneeled kneeling
NL knell *ringing*
NL knoll *hill*
NL know-all *(Br) know-it-all*
NL nail *pin*
NL newly *recently*
NL niello *alloy* nielli (or)
niellos
NL nil *zero*
NL Nile *river*
NL noel *(often capitalized)
Christmas*
NL noil *short fiber*
NL nolo *no further*
NL null *void*
NL nyala *antelope* nyalas (or)
nyala
NL only *(adv) sole, merely
(conj) except, but*
NLBDR nail-biter *contest*
NLBR antilabor *against
unions*
(Br) antilabour
NLBRL neoliberal
progressive
NLBRLZM neoliberalism
progressive
NLBTR nail-biter *contest*
NLCH unlatch *open*
NLCZ analyses (pl)
examination analysis
NLD anality *psychology*
analities

NLD annelid *worm*
NLD inlaid *set in*
NLD kneeled (or) knelt *(v-
past) kneel*
NLD no-load *no commission*
NLD nullity *nothingness*
nullities
NLD unlade *discharge cargo*
unladed unlading
unladen
NLD unload *deliver, relieve*
NLDBL ineludible
unavoidable
NLDD unleaded *printing, gas*
NLDK analytic (or) analytical
examined analytically
(adv)
NLDKL analytical (or)
analytic (adj) *examined*
analytically (adv)
NLDKS analytics *logic*
NLDLK unladylike *awkward*
NLDN annelidan *worm*
NLDN enlighten *give insight*
NLDN nail down *secure*
NLDND enlightened *wise*
NLDNMNT enlightenment
wisdom
NLDR annihilator *destroyer*
NLDRBL unalterable (adj)
no change unalterably
(adv)
NLDRD unaltered *no change*
NLDRD unlettered *illiterate*
NLDRL unilateral (adj) *one-
sided* unilaterally (adv)
NLDX analytics *logic*
NLF antilife *antagonistic*
NLF endleaf *paper*
endleaves
NLF nullify *void* nullified
nullifying nullifies
NLFBDK analphabetic
illiterate
NLFBTK analphabetic
illiterate
NLFBTSM analphabetism
illiterate
NLFBTZM analphabetism
illiterate
NLFKSHN nullification *made
void*

NLFL nail file *tool*
NLFL unlawful (adj) *not legal*
unlawfully (adv)
NLFR nullifier *voiding*
NLFYL nail file *tool*
NLFYR nullifier *voiding*
NLG analog *similarity*
(Br) analogue
NLG analogy *comparison*
analogies
NLG enology (or) oenology
wine
NLGHD Naugahyde
(trademark) fabric
NLGNS inelegance *bad taste*
NLGNT inelegant *bad taste*
NLGNTL inelegantly *bad
taste*
NLGNTS inelegance *bad
taste*
NLGS analogous *similar*
NLGSH analgesia *no pain*
NLGSK analgesic *no pain*
NLGSL analogously
similarly
NLGSNS analogousness
similarity
NLGZ analgesia *no pain*
NLGZH analgesia *no pain*
NLGZK analgesic *no pain*
NLHKCM unnilhexium
element
NLHKCYM unnilhexium
element
NLHKSM unnilhexium
element
NLHKSYM unnilhexium
element
NLHXM unnilhexium *element*
NLHXYM unnilhexium
element
NLJ analogy *comparison*
analogies
NLJ enology (or) oenology
wine
NLJ knowledge *information*
NLJBL ineligible *not qualified*
NLJBL knowledgeable (adj)
smart knowledgeably
(adv)
NLJBLD ineligibility
unacceptable

Use letters that best describe the sounds you hear and omit the vowels. Use **S** or **K**
instead of **C**: to find circle use **SRKL**. Use **J** to find joy, **JM** to find gem and **G** to find go.

NLJBLT ineligibility *unacceptable*

NLJKL analogical (adj) *similar* analogically (adv)

NLJKL enological *wine*

NLJKL ontological (adj) *existence* ontologically (adv)

NLJS analogous *similar*

NLJSDK neologistic *word*

NLJSH analgesia *no pain*

NLJSK analgesic *no pain*

NLJSL analogously *similarly*

NLJSNS analogousness *similarity*

NLJST analogist *comparer*

NLJST enologist *winemaker*

NLJSTK neologistic *word*

NLJZ analgesia *no pain*

NLJZ analogize *compare* analogized analogizing

NLJZH analgesia *no pain*

NLJZK analgesic *no pain*

NLJZM neologism *word*

NLK antilock *brakes*

NLK intellect *wisdom*

NLK unlike *different*

NLK unlock *open*

NLK unlucky *unfortunate*

NLKCHL intellectual (adj) *reasoning (n) thinker* intellectually (adv)

NLKCHLZ intellectualize *think* intellectualized intellectualizing

NLKCHLZR intellectualizer *thinker*

NLKCHWL intellectual (adj) *reasoning (n) thinker* intellectually (adv)

NLKCHWLZ intellectualize *think* intellectualized intellectualizing

NLKCHWLZR intellectualizer *thinker*

NLKDBL ineluctable (adj) *unavoidable* ineluctably (adv)

NLKDFR unlooked-for *unexpected*

NLKL unlikely *improbable*

NLKL unluckily *unfortunate*

NLKLHD unlikelihood *improbability*

NLKLNS unlikeliness *improbability*

NLKNS unlikeness *difference*

NLKNS unluckiness *misfortune*

NLKNTNDR nolo contendere *no contest*

NLKR onlooker *spectator*

NLKS analects *selections*

NLKSHL intellectual (adj) *reasoning (n) thinker* intellectually (adv)

NLKSHLZ intellectualize *think* intellectualized intellectualizing

NLKSHLZR intellectualizer *thinker*

NLKSHN intellection *thought*

NLKSHWL intellectual (adj) *reasoning (n) thinker* intellectually (adv)

NLKSHWLZ intellectualize *think* intellectualized intellectualizing

NLKSHWLZR intellectualizer *thinker*

NLKSN naloxone *drug*

NLKT intellect *wisdom*

NLKTBL ineluctable (adj) *unavoidable* ineluctably (adv)

NLKTFR unlooked-for *unexpected*

NLKTL intellectual (adj) *reasoning (n) thinker* intellectually (adv)

NLKTLZ intellectualize *think* intellectualized intellectualizing

NLKTLZR intellectualizer *thinker*

NLKTS analects *selections*

NLKTWL intellectual (adj) *reasoning (n) thinker* intellectually (adv)

NLKTWLZ intellectualize *think* intellectualized intellectualizing

NLKTWLZR intellectualizer *thinker*

NLKWDM unnilquadium *element*

NLKWDYM unnilquadium *element*

NLM analemma *scale*

NLMDD unlimited *no restrictions*

NLMDK analemmatic *scale*

NLMNT annulment *dissolution*

NLMTD unlimited *no restrictions*

NLMTK analemmatic *scale*

NLN aniline *dye*

NLN inland *not coastal*

NLN inulin *chemical*

NLN nylon *fiber*

NLN on-line *connected*

NLNBL inalienable (adj) *permanent* inalienably (adv)

NLNBLD inalienability *permanent*

NLNBLT inalienability *permanent*

NLND inland *not coastal*

NLND unlined *no lines*

NLNDRD unlaundered *dirty*

NLNDVD null and void *worthless*

NLNGGS anilingus (or) anilinctus *mouth and anus*

NLNGKTS anilinctus (or) anilingus *mouth and anus*

NLNGS anilingus (or) anilinctus *mouth and anus*

NLNKTS anilinctus (or) anilingus *mouth and anus*

NLNS nylons *stockings*

NLNVD null and void *worthless*

NLNZ nylons *stockings*

NLP antelope *animal* antelope (or) antelopes

NLPDK analeptic *drug*

NLPNM unnilpentium *element*

NLPNTM unnilpentium *element*

NLPNTYM unnilpentium *element*

NLPNYM unnilpentium

Letters aren't doubled for single sounds: to find alley use **L** not **LL**. Use **Y** and **W** as hard sounds only: to find yellow use **YL**. (Br)=British spelling or usage. * See dictionary.

element

NLPRS nol-pros *discontinue*
nol-prossed nol-prossing

NLPRS nulliparous *no offspring*

NLPTK analeptic *drug*

NLQDM unnilquadium *element*

NLQDYM unnilquadium *element*

NLR annular *ring*

NLR inlayer *set in*

NLR kneeler *person, board*

NLR nailer *hitter*

NLRFN nalorphine *drug*

NLRJ enlarge *expand* enlarged enlarging

NLRJMNT enlargement *expansion*

NLRJNK antiallergenic *not allergy promoting*

NLRJR enlarger *expander*

NLRN unlearn *forget*

NLRND unlearned *ignorant*

NLS analyze *study* analyzed analyzing (Br) analyse

NLS annulus *ring* annuli

NLS endless *forever*

NLS enlace *tangle* enlaced enlacing

NLS unlace *loosen* unlaced unlacing

NLS unless *except if*

NLS unloose *set free* unloosed unloosing

NLSBL analyzable *able to be studied*

NLSBLD analyzability *able to be studied*

NLSBLT analyzability *able to be studied*

NLSDD enlisted *rank*

NLSDD unlisted *not on roster*

NLSDK anelastic *not flexible*

NLSDK annalistic *chronicle*

NLSDK inelastic *inflexible*

NLSDK nihilistic *destructive*

NLSH unlash *untie*

NLSH unleash *let loose*

NLSHN annihilation *destruction*

NLSHN annulation *rings*

NLSL endlessly *forever*

NLSMNT enlacement *tangle*

NLSMNT enlistment *military*

NLSN nelson *wrestling hold*

NLSN unloosen *set free*

NLSNS endlessness *forever*

NLSNST unlicensed *not certified*

NLSR analyzer *studier*

NLSS analysis *examination* analyses

NLST analyst *examiner*

NLST annalist *chronicle*

NLST enlist *enroll, attract*

NLST nihilist *destroyer*

NLSTD enlisted *rank*

NLSTD unlisted *not on roster*

NLSTK anelastic *stress and strain*

NLSTK annalistic *chronicle*

NLSTK inelastic *inflexible*

NLSTK nihilistic *destructive*

NLSTMNT enlistment *military*

NLSTSD anelasticity *stress and strain*

NLSTSD inelasticity *inflexible*

NLSTST anelasticity *stress and strain*

NLSTST inelasticity *inflexible*

NLSZ analyses (pl) *examination* analysis

NLT anality *psychology* analities

NLT annihilate *destroy* annihilated annihilating

NLT annulate *ringed*

NLT inlet *cove*

NLT knelt *(v-past) kneel*

NLT nullity *nothingness* nullities

NLTH neolith *tool*

NLTHK Neolithic *Stone Age*

NLTK analytic (or) analytical *examined* analytically (adv)

NLTKL analytical (or) analytic (adj) *examined* analytically (adv)

NLTKS analytics *logic*

NLTN enlighten *give insight*

NLTND enlightened *wise*

NLTNMNT enlightenment *wisdom*

NLTR annihilator *destroyer*

NLTRBL unalterable (adj) *no change* unalterably (adv)

NLTRD unaltered *no change*

NLTRD unlettered *illiterate*

NLTRL unilateral (adj) *one-sided* unilaterally (adv)

NLTX analytics *logic*

NLVBL unlivable *unsuitable for living*

NLVBL unlovable *unpleasant*

NLVD unloved *no affection*

NLVL unlovely *ugly*

NLVN enliven *give life*

NLVND unleavened *no yeast*

NLWD newlywed *marriage*

NLX analects *selections*

NLXN naloxone *drug*

NLYNBL inalienable (adj) *permanent* inalienably (adv)

NLYNBLD inalienability *permanent*

NLYNBLT inalienability *permanent*

NLYR inlayer *set in*

NLZ analyze *study* analyzed analyzing (Br) analyse

NLZ annals *records*

NLZBL analyzable *able to be studied*

NLZBLD analyzability *able to be studied*

NLZBLT analyzability *able to be studied*

NLZM nihilism *philosophy*

NLZR analyzer *studier*

NLZSHN analyzation *study of*

NM anemia *disease* (Br) anaemia

NM anima *soul*

NM anomie *lawless*

NM enema *douche* enemas

NM enemy *foe* enemies

NM gnome *dwarf*

Use letters that best describe the sounds you hear and omit the vowels. Use **S** or **K** instead of **C**: to find circle use **SRKL**. Use **J** to find joy, **JM** to find gem and **G** to find go.

NM Nam *Vietnam*
NM name *(v)* call, choose
named naming
NM name *(n)* title, reputation
NM neem *tree*
NM neume *symbol*
NM noma *gangrene*
NM numb *no feeling*
NM pneum- (or) pneumo-
(comb form) air, lung
NM pneuma *spirit*
NMB Namibia *country*
NMB nimbi (pl) *cloud nimbus*
NMBGS unambiguous *clear*
NMBGWS unambiguous
clear
NMBGYS unambiguous
clear
NMBGYWS unambiguous
clear
NMBL nameable *identifiable*
NMBL nimble *spry* nimbler
nimblest
NMBL nimbly *spryly*
NMBLNS nimbleness
spryness
NMBLR nimbler *spry*
NMBLST nimblest *spry*
NMBPMB namby-pamby
weak
NMBR number *arithmetic,
many*
NMBRD unnumbered *many,
no numbers*
NMBRLS numberless *many*
NMBRWN number one *first*
NMBRZ Numbers *Bible*
NMBS nimbus *cloud* nimbi
(or) nimbuses
NMBSHS unambitious *no
drive*
NMBSTRDS nimbostratus
cloud
NMBSTRTS nimbostratus
cloud
NMBVLNT unambivalent
clear-cut
NMBY Namibia *country*
NMC intimacy *private*
intimacies
NMCHK nunchaku *weapon*
NMD enmity *hatred* enmities

NMD nomad *wanderer*
NMD unmade *messy, undone*
NMD unnamed *anonymous*
NMDBL inimitable (adj)
matchless inimitably (adv)
NMDD animated *alive*
NMDDD unmediated *no
agreement*
NMDFR pneumatophore *sac*
NMDGDD unmitigated *no
relief*
NMDGTD unmitigated *no
relief*
NMDK nematic *crystal*
NMDK neumatic *symbol*
NMDK nomadic *wandering*
NMDK pneumatic
compressed air
NMDKL pneumatically *air*
NMDLDK pneumatolytic
minerals
NMDLJKL nematological
worms
NMDLTK pneumatolytic
minerals
NMDP onomatopoeia *sound
word*
NMDPDK onomatopoetic
(or) onomatopoeic (adj)
sound word
onomatopoetically (or)
onomatopoeically (adv)
NMDPK onomatopoeic (or)
onomatopoetic (adj)
sound word
onomatopoeically (or)
onomatopoetically (adv)
NMDPLM nom de plume
pen name noms de plume
NMDPTK onomatopoetic
(or) onomatopoeic (adj)
sound word
onomatopoetically (or)
onomatopoeically (adv)
NMDPWDK onomatopoetic
(or) onomatopoeic (adj)
sound word
onomatopoetically (or)
onomatopoeically (adv)
NMDPWTK onomatopoetic
(or) onomatopoeic (adj)
sound word

onomatopoetically (or)
onomatopoeically (adv)
NMDPY onomatopoeia
sound word
NMDPYK onomatopoeic
(or) onomatopoetic (adj)
sound word
onomatopoeically (or)
onomatopoetically (adv)
NMDR animator *life-giver,
cartoonist*
NMDR antimatter *physics*
NMDRN antimodern *against
newness*
NMDRPN name-dropping
famous friends
NMDRPNG name-dropping
famous friends
NMDRPR name-dropper
famous friends
NMDSD nematocide (or)
nematicide *worm killer*
NMDSST nematocyst
stinger
NMDTD unmediated *no
agreement*
NMDVRSHN animadversion
remark
NMDVRT animadvert *remark*
NMDVRZHN animadversion
remark
NMDYDD unmediated *no
agreement*
NMDYTD unmediated *no
agreement*
NMF nymph *girl*
NMF nympho *sexual desire*
numphos
NMFL nemophila *plant*
NMFL nymphal *girlish*
NMFLD nymphalid *butterfly*
NMFMN nymphomania
sexual desire
NMFMNK nymphomaniac
sexual desire
NMFMNY nymphomania
sexual desire
NMFMNYK nymphomaniac
sexual desire
NMFT nymphet *girl*
NMGNDK antimagnetic *no
attraction*

Letters aren't doubled for single sounds: to find alley use **L** not **LL**. Use **Y** and **W** as hard
sounds only: to find yellow use **YL**. (Br)=British spelling or usage. * See dictionary.

NMGNTK antimagnetic *no attraction*

NMGRF pneumograph *breathing*

NMJNBL unimaginable (adj) *beyond thought* unimaginably (adv)

NMJNDV unimaginative *no creativity*

NMJNTV unimaginative *no creativity*

NMK anemic *insipid* (Br) anaemic

NMK anomic *lacking ideals*

NMK gnomic *dwarf*

NMK unmake *take apart* unmade unmaking

NMKKS pneumococcus *bacteria* pneumococci

NMKL anemically *insipidly* (Br) anaemically

NMKL inimical (adj) *unfriendly* inimically (adv)

NMKLN name-calling *insulting*

NMKLNG name-calling *insulting*

NMKNSS pneumoconiosis *black lung* pneumoconioses

NMKNYSS pneumoconiosis *black lung* pneumoconioses

NMKRBL antimicrobial *germs*

NMKRBYL antimicrobial *germs*

NMKSK New Mexico *US State*

NMKSR antimacassar *cover*

NML animal *(n) fauna, creature (adj) carnal*

NML anomaly *deviation* anomalies

NML enamel *lacquer* enameled (or) enamelled enameling (or) enamelling

NML namely *by name*

NML numbly *no feeling*

NMLD animality *vitality*

NMLD unmold *remove*

NMLG entomology *insects*

NMLJ entomology *insects*

NMLJKL entomological (adj) *insects* entomologically (adv)

NMLJST entomologist *insects*

NMLK animallike *like an animal*

NMLNDD unmyelinated *no coating*

NMLNTD unmyelinated *no coating*

NMLR enameler *lacquer*

NMLR nummular *lesions*

NMLS anomalous *deviant*

NMLS nameless *unknown*

NMLSL anomalously *deviantly*

NMLSM animalism *vitality*

NMLSNS anomalousness *deviation*

NMLST enamelist *lacquer*

NMLT animality *vitality*

NMLTR antimilitary *against weaponry*

NMLWR enamelware *metal*

NMLZ animalize *make animal* animalized animalizing

NMLZM animalism *vitality*

NMLZSHN animalization *make animal*

NMMDR anemometer *wind gauge*

NMMRM in memoriam *memorial*

NMMRYM in memoriam *memorial*

NMMTR anemometer *wind gauge*

NMMTR anemometry *wind science*

NMN anemone *flower, sea creature*

NMN gnomon *sundial*

NMN new moon *lunar phase*

NMN nominee *person named*

NMN noumena (pl) *without senses* noumenon

NMN numen *force* numina

NMN pneumonia *disease*

NMN unman *upset* unmanned unmanning

NMNBL unamenable *not friendly*

NMNCHNBL unmentionable (adj) unspeakable (n) *underwear*

NMNCZ anamneses (pl) *memory* anamnesis

NMND unmanned *automatic*

NMNDFL unmindful *careless*

NMNDR nominator *proposer*

NMNDS pneumonitis *lungs*

NMNDV nominative *grammar, name*

NMNFL unmindful *careless*

NMNJBL unmanageable (adj) *wild* unmanageably (adv)

NMNK mnemonic *memory*

NMNK pneumonic *lungs*

NMNKL mnemonically *memory*

NMNKLCHR nomenclature *list, name*

NMNKLTR nomenclature *list, name*

NMNKS mnemonics *memory*

NMNL antimonial *element*

NMNL nominal (adj) *name, trifling* nominally (adv)

NMNL unmanly *cowardly*

NMNLNS unmanliness *cowardly*

NMNLST nominalist *theorist*

NMNLZM nominalism *theory*

NMNN noumenon *without senses* noumena

NMNN unmeaning *senseless*

NMNNG unmeaning *senseless*

NMNRKST antimonarchist *against royalty*

NMNRL unmannerly *rude*

NMNRLNS unmannerliness *rudeness*

NMNS numbness *no feeling*

NMNS numinous *mysterious*

NMNSDK anamnestic *recalled*

NMNSHN nomination *proposal*

NMNSHNBL unmentionable

Use letters that best describe the sounds you hear and omit the vowels. Use **S** or **K** instead of **C**: to find circle use **SRKL**. Use **J** to find joy, **JM** to find gem and **G** to find go.

(adj) unspeakable (n)
underwear

NMNSLN no-man's-land
barren area

NMNSLND no-man's-land
barren area

NMNSNS numinousness
mystery

NMNSS anamnesis *memory*
anamneses

NMNSTK anamnestic
recalled

NMNSZ anamneses (pl)
memory anamnesis

NMNT nominate *name,*
propose nominated
nominating

NMNTR nominator *proposer*

NMNTS pneumonitis *lungs*

NMNTSHNBL
unmentionable *(adj)*
unspeakable (n) underwear

NMNTV nominative
grammar, name

NMNX mnemonics *memory*

NMNY pneumonia *disease*

NMNYL antimonial *element*

NMNZLN no-man's-land
barren area

NMNZLND no-man's-land
barren area

NMPCHBL unimpeachable
(adj) *beyond reproach*
unimpeachably (adv)

NMPDD unimpeded *not*
blocked

NMPLBL unemployable
unable to work

NMPLD unemployed *not*
working

NMPLMNT unemployment
not working

NMPLT nameplate
identification

NMPLYBL unemployable
unable to work

NMPN Phnom Penh *city*

NMPRD unimpaired
unbroken

NMPRDNT unimportant
minor

NMPRST unimpressed *not*

affected

NMPRTNT unimportant
minor

NMPRVD unimproved *not*
made better

NMPTD unimpeded *not*
blocked

NMR anymore *further*

NMR enamor *fascinate*
enamored enamoring
(Br) enamour

NMR namer *signifier*

NMR unmoor *cast off*

NMRBL enumerable
countable

NMRBL innumerable (adj)
countless innumerably
(adv)

NMRBL numerable *many*

NMRBLD enumerability
count

NMRBLT enumerability
count

NMRC innumeracy
ignorance of mathematics

NMRC numeracy *numbers*

NMRD enamored *fascinated*

NMRD inamorata *lover (f)*

NMRD unmarried *no spouse*

NMRDR enumerator *census*
taker

NMRDR numerator *number*

NMRDV enumerative *count*

NMRFK anamorphic
distorted

NMRK numeric *number*

NMRKDBL unmarketable
no sale

NMRKL numerical (adj)
numbers numberically
(adv)

NMRKN un-American *not*
patriotic

NMRKT unmarked *clean*

NMRKTBL unmarketable *no*
sale

NMRL numeral (adj) *number*
numerally (adv)

NMRL unmoral *beyond ethics*

NMRLD unmorality *beyond*
ethics

NMRLG numerology

numbers

NMRLJ numerology
numbers

NMRLJST numerologist
numbers

NMRLT unmorality *beyond*
ethics

NMRS innumeracy *ignorance*
of mathematics

NMRS innumerous *countless*

NMRS numeracy *numbers*

NMRS numerous *many*

NMRSFL unmerciful (adj)
cruel, extreme unmercifully
(adv)

NMRSHN enumeration
count

NMRSHN numeration
number system

NMRSL numerously *many*

NMRSNS numerousness
many

NMRT enumerate *count*
enumerated enumerating

NMRT inamorata *lover (f)*

NMRT innumerate *ignorant*
of mathematics

NMRT numerate *count*
numerated numerating

NMRTR enumerator *census*
taker

NMRTR numerator *number*

NMRTV enumerative *count*

NMS animus *spirit*

NMS en masse *together*

NMS intimacy *private*
intimacies

NMSD animosity *ill will*
animosities

NMSDK animistic *spiritual*

NMSH enmesh *snare*

NMSHMNT enmeshment
snare

NMSHN animation *liveliness,*
cartoon

NMSHN intimation
confidence

NMSHNL unemotional (adj)
no feelings unemotionally
(adv)

NMSK namesake *same name*

NMSK unmask *expose*

Letters aren't doubled for single sounds: to find alley use **L** not **LL**. Use **Y** and **W** as hard
sounds only: to find yellow use **YL**. (Br)=British spelling or usage. * See dictionary.

NMSKL numskull *idiot*
NMSL antimissile *interceptor*
NMSN Mnemosyne *Greek goddess*
NMSN neomycin *drug*
NMSS nemesis *opponent* nemeses
NMST animist *spirit*
NMST animosity *ill will* animosities
NMST endmost *last*
NMST inmost *center*
NMSTK animistic *spiritual*
NMSTKBL unmistakable (adj) *clear* unmistakably (adv)
NMT animate *(v) quicken* animated animating
NMT animate *(adj) alive*
NMT enmity *hatred* enmities
NMT inmate *prison*
NMT intimate *(v) suggest, announce* intimated intimating
NMT intimate *(adj) essential, close*
NMT unmeet *improper*
NMT unmet *not achieved*
NMTBL inimitable (adj) *matchless* inimitably (adv)
NMTD animated *alive*
NMTD nematode *worm*
NMTFR pneumatophore *sac*
NMTG name tag *identification*
NMTGDD unmitigated *no relief*
NMTGTD unmitigated *no relief*
NMTHRKS pneumothorax *lungs*
NMTHRX pneumothorax *lungs*
NMTK nematic *crystal*
NMTK neumatic *symbol*
NMTK nomadic *wandering*
NMTK pneumatic *compressed air*
NMTKL pneumatically *air*
NMTLDK pneumatolytic *minerals*
NMTLG nematology *worms*

NMTLG pneumatology *spirits*
NMTLJ nematology *worms*
NMTLJ pneumatology *spirits*
NMTLJKL nematological *worms*
NMTLJST nematologist *worms*
NMTLTK pneumatolytic *minerals*
NMTP onomatopoeia *sound word*
NMTPDK onomatopoetic (or) onomatopoeic (adj) *sound word* onomatopoetically (or) onomatopoeically (adv)
NMTPK onomatopoeic (or) onomatopoetic (adj) *sound word* onomatopoeically (or) onomatopoetically (adv)
NMTPTK onomatopoetic (or) onomatopoeic (adj) *sound word* onomatopoetically (or) onomatopoeically (adv)
NMTPWDK onomatopoetic (or) onomatopoeic (adj) *sound word* onomatopoetically (or) onomatopoeically (adv)
NMTPWTK onomatopoetic (or) onomatopoeic (adj) *sound word* onomatopoetically (or) onomatopoeically (adv)
NMTPY onomatopoeia *sound word*
NMTPYK onomatopoeic (or) onomatopoetic (adj) *sound word* onomatopoeically (or) onomatopoetically (adv)
NMTR animator *life-giver, cartoonist*
NMTR antimatter *physics*
NMTSD nematocide (or) nematicide *worm killer*
NMTSST nematocyst *stinger*

NMVD unmoved *no emotion, fixed*
NMXK New Mexico *US State*
NMY anemia *disease* (Br) anaemic
NMYLNDD unmyelinated *no coating*
NMYLNTD unmyelinated *no coating*
NMYLR nummular *lesions*
NMZDPLM noms de plume (pl) *pen name* nom de plume
NMZM animism *spirit*
NMZMDK numismatic *money*
NMZMDKL numismatically *money*
NMZMDKS numismatics *money*
NMZMDX numismatics *money*
NMZMTK numismatic *money*
NMZMTKL numismatically *money*
NMZMTKS numismatics *money*
NMZMTST numismatist *money*
NMZMTX numismatics *money*
NMZN Mnemosyne *Greek goddess*
NN aeonian (or) aeonic *long-lasting*
NN anion *negative ion*
NN anon *soon, again*
NN awning *shade*
NN inane *silly*
NN inning *sports*
NN Ionian *of Ionia*
NN known *(v-past) know*
NN nan *bread*
NN nana *grandmother*
NN nanny *nursemaid* nannies
NN nene *goose*
NN neon *gas*
NN nine *number (9)*
NN ninety *number (90)*

Use letters that best describe the sounds you hear and omit the vowels. Use **S** or **K** instead of **C**: to find circle use **SRKL**. Use **J** to find joy, **JM** to find gem and **G** to find go.

nineties
NN ninny *fool* ninnies
NN no-no *forbidden* no-no's (or) no-nos
NN non- *not*
NN none *not any*
NN noon *midday*
NN noun *word*
NN nun *religious sister*
NN onion *vegetable*
NN uh-uh *(interj) disagreement*
NN union *merger, labor group*
NN unknowing *ignorant*
NN unknown *undiscovered*
NNBJKDV nonobjective *subjective*
NNBJKTV nonobjective *subjective*
NNBLF nonbelief *doubt*
NNBLVR nonbeliever *doubter*
NNBNDNG nonbinding *loose*
NNBRKBL nonbreakable *permanent, tough*
NNBRSV nonabrasive *not rough*
NNC nuncio *pope* nuncios
NNCBL enunciable *pronounce*
NNCCHR nunciature *mission, office*
NNCDR annunciator *announcer*
NNCDR enunciator *pronounce*
NNCHK nunchaku *weapon*
NNCSHN annunciation *(often capitalized) announcement*
NNCSHN enunciation *pronounce*
NNCT annunciate *announce* annunciated annunciating
NNCT enunciate *pronounce* enunciated enunciating
NNCTR annunciator *announcer*
NNCTR enunciator *pronounce*
NNCTR nunciature *mission,*

office
NNCY nuncio *pope* nuncios
NNCYBL enunciable *pronounce*
NNCYCHR nunciature *mission, office*
NNCYDR annunciator *announcer*
NNCYDR enunciator *pronounce*
NNCYSHN annunciation *(often capitalized) announcement*
NNCYSHN enunciation *pronounce*
NNCYT annunciate *announce* annunciated annunciating
NNCYT enunciate *pronounce* enunciated enunciating
NNCYTR annunciator *announcer*
NNCYTR enunciator *pronounce*
NNCYTR nunciature *mission, office*
NND inanity *empty, silly* inanities
NND innuendo *hint* innuendos (or) innuendoes
NND ninety *number (90)* nineties
NND noonday *midday*
NND united *combined*
NNDDR inundator *overwhelm*
NNDFRBL nondeferable *no delay*
NNDG Onondaga *Native American*
NNDGRDBL nondegradable *permanent*
NNDGRTBL nondegradable *permanent*
NNDKNGDM United Kingdom *country*
NNDL neonatal *newborn*
NNDMNCHNL nondimensional *no facets*
NNDMNSHNL nondimensional *no facets*

NNDN nandina *shrub*
NNDN unending *eternal*
NNDNG unending *eternal*
NNDNKL nonidentical *not the same*
NNDNMNSHNL nondenominational *religion*
NNDNSHNS United Nations *international group*
NNDNTKL nonidentical *not the same*
NNDPTV nonadaptive *no change*
NNDR nondairy *no milk*
NNDRKSHNL nondirectional *no path*
NNDRTHL Neanderthal *caveman*
NNDRTL Neanderthal *caveman*
NNDSHN inundation *overwhelm*
NNDSKLSHR nondisclosure *silence*
NNDSKLZHR nondisclosure *silence*
NNDSKRP nondescript *plain*
NNDSKRPT nondescript *plain*
NNDSTRLZD unindustrialized *no industry* (Br) uninustrialised
NNDSTRYLZD unindustrialized *no industry* (Br) uninustrialised
NNDSTTS United States *country*
NNDT inundate *overwhelm* inundated inundating
NNDTCHBL nondetachable *connected*
NNDTD unindicted *not summoned*
NNDTR inundator *overwhelm*
NNDTR inundatory *overwhelming*
NNDTV nonadditive *number*

Letters aren't doubled for single sounds: to find alley use **L** not **LL**. Use **Y** and **W** as hard sounds only: to find yellow use **YL**. (Br)=British spelling or usage. * See dictionary.

NNDV nonnative *not originating in*

NNFDL nonfatal *not deadly*

NNFKSHN nonfiction *true*

NNFKSHNL nonfictional *true*

NNFL ninefold *nine times*

NNFLD ninefold *nine times*

NNFLMBL nonflammable *cannot burn*

NNFLMTR anti-inflammatory *remove swelling*

NNFLSHNR anti-inflationary *no growth*

NNFMN nymphomania *sexual desire*

NNFMNK nymphomaniac *sexual desire*

NNFMNY nymphomania *sexual desire*

NNFMNYK nymphomaniac *sexual desire*

NNFNDK nonphonetic *not as it sounds*

NNFNMK nonphonemic *not sounded*

NNFNTK nonphonetic *not as it sounds*

NNFRFCHR nonforfeiture *cannot give back*

NNFRFDBL nonforfeitable *cannot give back*

NNFRFTBL nonforfeitable *cannot give back*

NNFRFTR nonforfeiture *cannot give back*

NNFRFTYR nonforfeiture *cannot give back*

NNFRMD uninformed *ignorant*

NNFRMDV uninformative *no news*

NNFRMTV uninformative *no news*

NNFRS nonferrous *no iron*

NNFRSBL unenforceable *cannot uphold*

NNFT nonfat *without fat*

NNFTL nonfatal *not deadly*

NNFZNS nonfeasance *failure*

NNFZNTS nonfeasance *failure*

NNG annoying *bothersome*

NNG awning *shade*

NNG inning *sports*

NNG unknowing *ignorant*

NNGDV nonnegative *positive*

NNGGLN New England *region*

NNGGLND New England *region*

NNGKMPP nincompoop *fool*

NNGKRD unanchored *adrift*

NNGL annoyingly *bothersome*

NNGL knowingly *with knowledge*

NNGL unknowingly *no knowledge*

NNGLN New England *region*

NNGLND New England *region*

NNGRC nongreasy *not oily*

NNGRD non grata *unwelcome*

NNGRM nanogram *weight*

NNGRS nongreasy *not oily*

NNGRSHN nonaggression *no fighting*

NNGRT non grata *unwelcome*

NNGS innings *sports*

NNGSHBL nonnegotiable *no discussion, no passage*

NNGT nanny goat *animal*

NNGTV nonnegative *positive*

NNGZ innings *sports*

NNGZSDNS nonexistence *no life*

NNGZSDNTS nonexistence *no life*

NNGZSTNS nonexistence *no life*

NNGZSTNT nonexistent *not living*

NNGZSTNTS nonexistence *not living*

NNGZT antianxiety *calming*

NNGZYT antianxiety *calming*

NNHBDBL uninhabitable *unfit for life*

NNHBDD uninhabited *not lived in*

NNHBDD uninhibited *informal*

NNHBTBL uninhabitable *unfit for life*

NNHBTD uninhabited *not lived in*

NNHBTD uninhibited *informal*

NNHMGNS nonhomogeneous *not blended*

NNHMGNYS nonhomogeneous *not blended*

NNHMJNS nonhomogeneous *not blended*

NNHMJNYS nonhomogeneous *not blended*

NNHMN nonhuman *not human*

NNHPNN nonhappening *failed occurrence*

NNHPNNG nonhappening *failed occurrence*

NNHYMN nonhuman *not human*

NNHZRDS nonhazardous *not dangerous*

NNJ ninja *martial arts* ninja

NNJ nonage *minority*

NNJDSHL nonjudicial *no court*

NNJJMNL nonjudgmental *no judgment*

NNJJMNTL nonjudgmental *no judgment*

NNJK Union Jack *flag*

NNJNRN nonagenarian *age 90-99*

NNJNRYN nonagenarian *age 90-99*

NNJRD uninjured *no harm*

NNJSNT nonadjacent *apart*

NNK antiknock *prevent noise*

NNKLR antinuclear *no cell reaction, against nuclear power*

NNKLR nonnuclear *no*

Use letters that best describe the sounds you hear and omit the vowels. Use **S** or **K** instead of **C**: to find circle use **SRKL**. Use **J** to find joy, **JM** to find gem and **G** to find go.

atomic reaction
NNKLRK noncaloric *no food value*
NNKLYR antinuclear *no cell reaction, against nuclear power*
NNKLYR nonnuclear *no atomic reaction*
NNKMBDNT noncombatant *civilian*
NNKMBDV noncombative *civilian*
NNKMBRD unencumbered *free*
NNKMBTNT noncombatant *civilian*
NNKMBTV noncombative *civilian*
NNKMDL noncommittal (adj) *no indication* noncommittally (adv)
NNKMPLNS noncompliance *not conforming*
NNKMPLNTS noncompliance *not conforming*
NNKMPLYNS noncompliance *not conforming*
NNKMPLYNTS noncompliance *not conforming*
NNKMPP nincompoop *fool*
NNKMPSMNS non compos mentis *mentally ill*
NNKMPSMNTS non compos mentis *mentally ill*
NNKMRSHL noncommercial *no advertisement*
NNKMSHND noncommissioned *rank*
NNKMTL noncommittal (adj) *no indication* noncommittally (adv)
NNKN nankeen *fabric*
NNKNDKDR nonconductor *no movement*
NNKNDKTR nonconductor *no movement*

NNKNFRMD nonconformity *individuality*
NNKNFRMST nonconformist *individual*
NNKNFRMT nonconformity *individuality*
NNKNFRNTSHNL nonconfrontational *no fighting*
NNKNTJS noncontagious *no spread*
NNKPDV nuncupative *oral*
NNKPRDV noncooperative *disobedience*
NNKPRSHN noncooperation *disobedience*
NNKPRTV noncooperative *disobedience*
NNKPTV nuncupative *oral*
NNKRD unanchored *adrift*
NNKRDDD nonaccredited *no credentials*
NNKRDKL noncritical *no faultfinding*
NNKRDT noncredit *school*
NNKRDTD nonaccredited *no credentials*
NNKRSV noncorrosive *no rust*
NNKRTKL noncritical *no faultfinding*
NNKSHN nonaction *no movement*
NNKSPDNS nonacceptance *denial*
NNKSPDNTS nonacceptance *denial*
NNKSPTNS nonacceptance *denial*
NNKSPTNTS nonacceptance *denial*
NNKSSDNS nonexistence *not living*
NNKSSDNTS nonexistence *not living*
NNKSSTNS nonexistence *not living*
NNKSSTNT nonexistent *not living*
NNKSSTNTS nonexistence *not living*

NNKWNFBL nonquantifiable *no measure*
NNKWNFYBL nonquantifiable *no measure*
NNKWNTDV nonquantitative *no measure*
NNKWNTFBL nonquantifiable *no measure*
NNKWNTFYBL nonquantifiable *no measure*
NNKWNTTDV nonquantitative *no measure*
NNKWNTTTV nonquantitative *no measure*
NNKWNTTV nonquantitative *no measure*
NNKWPRDV noncooperative *disobedience*
NNKWPRSHN noncooperation *disobedience*
NNKWPRTV noncooperative *disobedient*
NNKWS nonaqueous *no water*
NNKWYS nonaqueous *no water*
NNKYLR antinuclear *no cell reaction, against nuclear power*
NNKYPDV nuncupative *oral*
NNKYPTV nuncupative *oral*
NNL inanely *silly*
NNL knowingly *with knowledge*
NNL unknowingly *no knowledge*
NNLKHLK nonalcoholic *without alcohol*
NNLN nonillion *number*
NNLND nonaligned *no allies*
NNLNR nonlinear *crooked*

Letters aren't doubled for single sounds: to find alley use **L** not **LL**. Use **Y** and **W** as hard sounds only: to find yellow use **YL**. (Br)=British spelling or usage. * See dictionary.

NNLNYR nonlinear *crooked*

NNLTHL nonlethal *not deadly*

NNLTND unenlightened *ignorant*

NNLVN nonliving *dead*

NNLVNG nonliving *dead*

NNLYN nonillion *number*

NNM anonym *false name*

NNM antonym *opposite* antonymy

NNMD anonymity *not named* anonymities

NNMD unanimity *agreement*

NNMDL nonmotile *not moving*

NNMDR nanometer *length*

NNMDRZD nonmotorized *no engine* (Br) nonmotorised

NNMK antonymic *opposite*

NNMLGNNT nonmalignant *safe*

NNMS anonymous *not named*

NNMS unanimous *agreement*

NNMSL anonymously *not named*

NNMSL unanimously *agreement*

NNMSNS anonymousness *not named*

NNMT anonymity *not named* anonymities

NNMT inanimate *lifeless*

NNMT unanimity *agreement*

NNMTL inanimately *lifeless*

NNMTL nonmotile *not moving*

NNMTNS inanimateness *lifeless*

NNMTR nanometer *length*

NNMTRZD nonmotorized *no engine* (Br) nonmotorised

NNN antiunion *against organized labor*

NNN ninon *fabric*

NNN unknown *undiscovered*

NNND nonentity *not material* nonentities

NNNDNG nonending *eternal*

NNNFLSHNR noninflationary *no increase*

NNNGJMNT nonengagement *no encounter*

NNNN nonunion *no trade union*

NNNRFRNS noninterference *no meddling*

NNNRFRNTS noninterference *no meddling*

NNNRVNCHN nonintervention *no meddling*

NNNRVNSHN nonintervention *no meddling*

NNNSNS no-nonsense *sensible*

NNNSNTS no-nonsense *sensible*

NNNST unannounced *no notification*

NNNT nonentity *not material* nonentities

NNNTD nonentity *not material* nonentities

NNNTRFRNS noninterference *no meddling*

NNNTRFRNTS noninterference *no meddling*

NNNTRSV nonintrusive *no entry*

NNNTRVNCHN nonintervention *no meddling*

NNNTRVNSHN nonintervention *no meddling*

NNNTT nonentity *not material* nonentities

NNNVLVMNT noninvolvement *no attachment*

NNNVRSL nonuniversal *not everywhere*

NNNYN nonunion *no trade union*

NNPLDKL nonpolitical (adj) *not associated with* nonpolitically (adv)

NNPLNGKTN nannoplankton *plants*

NNPLNKTN nannoplankton *plants*

NNPLR nonpolar *molecule*

NNPLS nonplus *puzzle* nonplussed nonplussing

NNPLST non placet *vote*

NNPLST nonplused *puzzled*

NNPLTKL nonpolitical (adj) *not associated with* nonpolitically (adv)

NNPMNT nonpayment *debt*

NNPNG nonpaying *volunteer*

NNPNZ ninepins *bowling*

NNPRDKDV nonproductive *inactive*

NNPRDKTV nonproductive *inactive*

NNPRDZN nonpartisan *no party*

NNPRFRMNS nonperformance *no action*

NNPRFRMNTS nonperformance *no action*

NNPRFSHNL nonprofessional (adj) *amateur* nonprofessionally (adv)

NNPRFT nonprofit *charity*

NNPRKDSNG nonpracticing *inactive*

NNPRKTSN nonpracticing *inactive*

NNPRKTSNG nonpracticing *inactive*

NNPRL nonpareil *candy, no equal*

NNPRLFRSHN nonproliferation *no spread*

NNPRLL nonparallel *not in line with*

NNPRS nonporous *no openings*

NNPRSHBL nonperishable *no decay*

NNPRSHNL nonoperational *broken*

NNPRSKWDR non

Use letters that best describe the sounds you hear and omit the vowels. Use **S** or **K** instead of **C**: to find circle use **SRKL**. Use **J** to find joy, **JM** to find gem and **G** to find go.

prosequitur *judgment*
NNPRSKWTR non prosequitur *judgment*
NNPRSN nonperson *no status*
NNPRSQDR non prosequitur *judgment*
NNPRSQTR non prosequitur *judgment*
NNPRTSPDNG nonparticipating *inactive*
NNPRTSPSHN nonparticipation *inaction*
NNPRTSPTN nonparticipating *inactive*
NNPRTSPTNG nonparticipating *inactive*
NNPRTZN nonpartisan *no party*
NNPYNG nonpaying *volunteer*
NNPZNS nonpoisonous *not deadly*
NNQLR antinuclear *no cell reaction, against nuclear power*
NNQLR nonnuclear *no atomic reaction*
NNQNFBL nonquantifiable *no measure*
NNQNFYBL nonquantifiable *no measure*
NNQNTDV nonquantitative *no measure*
NNQNTFBL nonquantifiable *no measure*
NNQNTFYBL nonquantifiable *no measure*
NNQNTTDV nonquantitative *no measure*
NNQNTTTV nonquantitative *no measure*
NNQNTTV nonquantitative *no measure*
NNQPDV nuncupative *oral*
NNQPTV nuncupative *oral*
NNQS nonaqueous *no water*
NNQYS nonaqueous *no water*
NNR anointer *apply oil, designate*

NNR nunnery *cloister* nunneries
NNRBN nonurban *not of the city*
NNRCHD unenriched *plain*
NNRCHT unenriched *plain*
NNRFLBL nonrefillable *filled only once*
NNRFNDBL nonrefundable *no money back*
NNRGLDD nonregulated *not controlled*
NNRGLTD nonregulated *not controlled*
NNRGYLDD nonregulated *not controlled*
NNRGYLTD nonregulated *not controlled*
NNRJD nonrigid *formless*
NNRKRN nonrecurring *one time only*
NNRKRNG nonrecurring *one time only*
NNRKRNT nonrecurrent *one time only*
NNRNBL nonrenewable *one time only*
NNRNL nonrenewal *one time only*
NNRNWBL nonrenewable *one time only*
NNRNWL nonrenewal *one time only*
NNRPDD uninterrupted *no breaks*
NNRPRSNTSHNL nonrepresentational *not objective*
NNRPRZNTSHNL nonrepresentational *not objective*
NNRPTD uninterrupted *no breaks*
NNRSHL nonracial (adj) *not ethnic* nonracially (adv)
NNRSKLBL nonrecyclable *not reused*
NNRSPNSV nonresponsive *no answer*
NNRSPNTSV nonresponsive *no answer*
NNRSTD uninterested *bored*

NNRSTN uninteresting *boring*
NNRSTNG uninteresting *boring*
NNRSTRKDD nonrestricted *no limits*
NNRSTRKDV nonrestrictive *no limits*
NNRSTRKTD nonrestricted *no limits*
NNRSTRKTV nonrestrictive *no limits*
NNRTRNBL nonreturnable *no return*
NNRTTNG nonirritating *not annoying*
NNRYZBL nonreusable *use once only*
NNRZBL nonreusable *use once only*
NNRZDNS nonresidence *not home* nonresidency
NNRZDNT nonresident *not home*
NNRZDNTS nonresidence *not home* nonresidency
NNRZSDNS nonresistance *submission*
NNRZSDNT nonresistant *submissive*
NNRZSDNTS nonresistance *submission*
NNRZSTNS nonresistance *submission*
NNRZSTNT nonresistant *submissive*
NNRZSTNTS nonresistance *submission*
NNS announce *herald* announced announcing
NNS annoyance *bother*
NNS antinoise *against noise*
NNS enounce *pronounce clearly* enounced enouncing
NNS inaneness *silly*
NNS nance *(vulgar) effeminate male*
NNS nonce *moment*
NNS nonuse *no usage*
NNS nowness *present time*
NNS nuncio *pope* nuncios

Letters aren't doubled for single sounds: to find alley use **L** not **LL**. Use **Y** and **W** as hard sounds only: to find yellow use **YL**. (Br)=British spelling or usage. * See dictionary.

NNSBJKDV nonsubjective *objective*

NNSBJKTV nonsubjective *objective*

NNSBL enunciable *pronounce*

NNSCH nonesuch *no equal*

NNSCHR nunciature *mission, office*

NNSDK onanistic *masturbation*

NNSDR annunciator *announcer*

NNSDR enunciator *pronounce*

NNSFL anencephaly *no brain* anencephalies

NNSFLK anencephalic *no brain*

NNSGRGDD nonsegregated *integrated*

NNSGRGTD nonsegregated *integrated*

NNSHDLD nonscheduled *no regular time*

NNSHDWLD nonscheduled *no regular time*

NNSHDYLD nonscheduled *no regular time*

NNSHJLD nonscheduled *no regular time*

NNSHJWLD nonscheduled *no regular time*

NNSHLNS nonchalance *coolness*

NNSHLNT nonchalant *cool*

NNSHLNTS nonchalance *coolness*

NNSHNL nonnational *no country*

NNSHRBL uninsurable *risky*

NNSHRD uninsured *no insurance*

NNSK nainsook *fabric*

NNSKD nonskid *sticky*

NNSKDLD nonscheduled *no regular time*

NNSKDWLD nonscheduled *no regular time*

NNSKDYLD nonscheduled *no regular time*

NNSKDYWLD

NNSCHEDULED *no regular time*

NNSKJLD nonscheduled *no regular time*

NNSKJWLD nonscheduled *no regular time*

NNSKN nanosecond *time*

NNSKN onionskin *paper*

NNSKND nanosecond *time*

NNSKNT nanosecond *time*

NNSKTRN nonsectarian *no special group*

NNSKWDR non sequitur *error*

NNSKWTR non sequitur *error*

NNSLBK nonsyllabic *language*

NNSLDD uninsulated *no padding*

NNSLKDV nonselective *not choosy*

NNSLKTV nonselective *not choosy*

NNSLLR noncellular *no cells*

NNSLP nonslip *sticky*

NNSLTD uninsulated *no padding*

NNSLYLR noncellular *no cells*

NNSMDRKL nonsymmetrical *uneven*

NNSMKN nonsmoking *no smoking*

NNSMKNG nonsmoking *no smoking*

NNSMKR nonsmoker *no smoking*

NNSMNT announcement *notification*

NNSMTRKL nonsymmetrical *uneven*

NNSNCHL nonessential *not needed*

NNSNS nonsense *no meaning, no value*

NNSNSHL nonessential *not needed*

NNSNSKL nonsensical (adj) *no meaning, no value* nonsensically (adv)

NNSNTS nonsense *no meaning, no value*

NNSNTSKL nonsensical (adj) *no meaning, no value* nonsensically (adv)

NNSPKN nonspeaking *mute*

NNSPKNG nonspeaking *mute*

NNSPRD uninspired *no motivation*

NNSPRT nonsupport *no maintenance*

NNSPYRD uninspired *no motivation*

NNSQDR non sequitur *error*

NNSQTR non sequitur *error*

NNSR announcer *notifier*

NNSRBL unanswerable (adj) *no question* unanswerably (adv)

NNSRD unanswered *no question*

NNSRJKL nonsurgical *no incision*

NNSSDMK nonsystemic *localized*

NNSSHL nonsocial *no interaction*

NNSSHN annunciation *(often capitalized) announcement*

NNSSHN enunciation *pronounce*

NNSSTMK nonsystemic *localized*

NNST annunciate *announce* annunciated annunciating

NNST enunciate *pronounce* enunciated enunciating

NNST unionist *labor*

NNSTHTZD unanesthetized *awake*

NNSTK nonstick *slippery*

NNSTK onanistic *masturbation*

NNSTNDRD nonstandard *unusual*

NNSTP nonstop *constant*

NNSTR annunciator *announcer*

NNSTR enunciator *pronounce*

Use letters that best describe the sounds you hear and omit the vowels. Use **S** or **K** instead of **C**: to find circle use **SRKL**. Use **J** to find joy, **JM** to find gem and **G** to find go.

NNSTR nunciature *mission, office*

NNSTRDR nonstarter *no initiative*

NNSTRTR nonstarter *no initiative*

NNSY nuncio *pope nuncios*

NNSYBL enunciable *pronounce*

NNSYCHR nunciature *mission, office*

NNSYDR annunciator *announcer*

NNSYDR enunciator *pronounce*

NNSYSHN annunciation *(often capitalized) announcement*

NNSYSHN enunciation *pronounce*

NNSYT annunciate *announce* annunciated annunciating

NNSYT enunciate *pronounce* enunciated enunciating

NNSYTR annunciator *announcer*

NNSYTR enunciator *pronounce*

NNSYTR nunciature *mission, office*

NNT anent *about*

NNT anoint *apply oil, designate*

NNT inanity *empty, silly* inanities

NNT neonate *newborn*

NNT ninety *number (90)* nineties

NNTC nuncio *pope nuncios*

NNTCBL enunciable *pronounce*

NNTCCHR nunciature *mission, office*

NNTCDR enunciator *pronounce*

NNTCSHN enunciation *pronounce*

NNTCT enunciate *pronounce* enunciated enunciating

NNTCTR enunciator *pronounce*

NNTCTR nunciature *mission, office*

NNTCY nuncio *pope nuncios*

NNTCYBL enunciable *pronounce*

NNTCYCHR nunciature *mission, office*

NNTCYDR enunciator *pronounce*

NNTCYSHN enunciation *pronounce*

NNTCYT enunciate *pronounce* enunciated enunciating

NNTCYTR enunciator *pronounce*

NNTCYTR nunciature *mission, office*

NNTD noontide *midday*

NNTH ninetieth *of number 90*

NNTH ninth *of number 9* ninths

NNTHLS nonetheless *nevertheless*

NNTHN know-nothing *stupid one*

NNTHNG know-nothing *stupid one*

NNTHNGKNG nonthinking *no thought*

NNTHNKNG nonthinking *no thought*

NNTHRPDK nontherapeutic *not curative*

NNTHRPTK nontherapeutic *not curative*

NNTHRPYDK nontherapeutic *not curative*

NNTHRPYTK nontherapeutic *not curative*

NNTHRTNN nonthreatening *safe*

NNTHRTNNG nonthreatening *safe*

NNTHZSTK unenthusiastic *indifferent*

NNTHZYSTK unenthusiastic *indifferent*

NNTK nunatak *mountain*

NNTKNKL nontechnical *no mechanism*

NNTKSBL nontaxable *no duty*

NNTKSK nontoxic *safe*

NNTKT Nantucket *city*

NNTL neonatal *newborn*

NNTLG neonatology *newborn*

NNTLJ neonatology *newborn*

NNTLJBL unintelligible (adj) *cannot decode* unintelligibly (adv)

NNTLJNT unintelligent *stupid*

NNTLJST neonatologist *newborn*

NNTLKCHL anti-intellectual *against learning*

NNTLKCHWL anti-intellectual *against learning*

NNTLKSHL anti-intellectual *against learning*

NNTLKSHWL anti-intellectual *against learning*

NNTLTRN nonutilitarian *not useful*

NNTLTRYN nonutilitarian *not useful*

NNTM noontime *midday*

NNTMNT anointment *apply oil, designate*

NNTN nineteen *number (19)*

NNTNDD unintended *accidental*

NNTNRD nontenured *no job security*

NNTNSHNL unintentional (adj) *accidental* unintentionally (adv)

NNTNTH nineteenth *of number 19*

NNTNYRD nontenured *no job security*

NNTPKL nontypical *unusual*

NNTPN nonutopian *no ideal*

NNTPYN nonutopian *no ideal*

NNTR anointer *apply oil, designate*

Letters aren't doubled for single sounds: to find alley use **L** not **LL**. Use **Y** and **W** as hard sounds only: to find yellow use **YL**. (Br)=British spelling or usage. * See dictionary.

NNTRDSHNL nontraditional *different*

NNTRP non troppo *music*

NNTRPDD uninterrupted *no breaks*

NNTRPTD uninterrupted *no breaks*

NNTRSFRBL nontransferable *no movement*

NNTRSTD uninterested *bored*

NNTRSTN uninteresting *boring*

NNTRSTNG uninteresting *boring*

NNTS announce *herald* announced announcing

NNTS annoyance *bother*

NNTS enounce *pronounce clearly* enounced enouncing

NNTS nance *(vulgar) effeminate male*

NNTS neo-Nazi *fascist*

NNTS nonce *moment*

NNTS nuncio *pope* nuncios

NNTSBL enunciable *pronounce*

NNTSCHR nunciature *mission, office*

NNTSDR enunciator *pronounce*

NNTSMNT announcement *notification*

NNTSPDD unanticipated *unexpected*

NNTSPTD unanticipated *unexpected*

NNTSR announcer *notifier*

NNTSRBL unanswerable (adj) *no question* unanswerably (adv)

NNTSRD unanswered *no question*

NNTSSHN enunciation *pronounce*

NNTST enunciate *pronounce* enunciated enunciating

NNTSTR enunciator *pronounce*

NNTSTR nunciature *mission, office*

NNTSY nuncio *pope* nuncios

NNTSYBL enunciable *pronounce*

NNTSYCHR nunciature *mission, office*

NNTSYDR enunciator *pronounce*

NNTSYSHN enunciation *pronounce*

NNTSYT enunciate *pronounce* enunciated enunciating

NNTSYTR enunciator *pronounce*

NNTSYTR nunciature *mission, office*

NNTTH ninetieth *of number* 90

NNTV nonnative *not originating in*

NNTXBL nontaxable *no duty*

NNTXK nontoxic *safe*

NNTYTH ninetieth *of number* 90

NNTZ neo-Nazi *fascist*

NNVBL nonviable *not living*

NNVBL unenviable *not desired*

NNVDD uninvited *not asked*

NNVDNG nonvoting *no vote*

NNVDR nonvoter *no vote*

NNVKL nonvocal *mute*

NNVLNS nonviolence *no fighting*

NNVLNT nonviolent *no fighting*

NNVLNTS nonviolence *no fighting*

NNVNT nonevent *failed occurrence*

NNVRBL nonverbal (adj) *no speech* nonverbally (adv)

NNVSKS nonviscous *gummy*

NNVTD uninvited *not asked*

NNVTNG nonvoting *no vote*

NNVTR nonvoter *no vote*

NNVYBL nonviable *not living*

NNVYBL unenviable *not desired*

NNVYLNS nonviolence *no fighting*

NNVYLNT nonviolent *no fighting*

NNVYLNTS nonviolence *no fighting*

NNWRKN nonworking *idle*

NNWRKNG nonworking *idle*

NNWT nonwhite *racial*

NNXPDNS nonacceptance *denial*

NNXPDNTS nonacceptance *denial*

NNXPTNS nonacceptance *denial*

NNXPTNTS nonacceptance *denial*

NNXSDNS nonexistence *not living*

NNXSDNTS nonexistence *not living*

NNXSTNS nonexistence *not living*

NNXSTNT nonexistent *not living*

NNXSTNTS nonexistence *not living*

NNYKLR antinuclear *no cell reaction, against nuclear power*

NNYKLR nonnuclear *no atomic reaction*

NNYKLYR antinuclear *no cell reaction, against nuclear power*

NNYKLYR nonnuclear *no atomic reaction*

NNYKYLR antinuclear *no cell reaction, against nuclear power*

NNYKYLR nonnuclear *no atomic reaction*

NNYLN nonyellowing *clear*

NNYLNG nonyellowing *clear*

NNYLWN nonyellowing *clear*

NNYLWNG nonyellowing *clear*

NNYN antiunion *against organized labor*

NNYN nonillion *number*

NNYNN nonunion *no trade union*

Use letters that best describe the sounds you hear and omit the vowels. Use **S** or **K** instead of **C**: to find circle use **SRKL**. Use **J** to find joy, **JM** to find gem and **G** to find go.

NNYNVRSL nonuniversal *not everywhere*

NNYNYN nonunion *no trade union*

NNYQLR antinuclear *no cell reaction, against nuclear power*

NNYQLR nonnuclear *no atomic reaction*

NNYS nonuse *no usage*

NNYTH ninetieth *of number 90*

NNYTLTRN nonutilitarian *not useful*

NNYTLTRYN nonutilitarian *not useful*

NNYTPN nonutopian *no ideal*

NNYTPYN nonutopian *no ideal*

NNZ antinoise *against noise*

NNZ neo-Nazi *fascist*

NNZ unionize *unite unionized unionizing (Br) unionise*

NNZM onanism *masturbation*

NNZM unionism *labor*

NNZSHN unionization *labor (Br) unionisation*

NNZT antianxiety *calming*

NNZYT antianxiety *calming*

NP inept *awkward*

NP knap *(Br) snap* knapped knapping

NP knap *(Br) summit*

NP nap *sleep, surface* napped napping

NP nape *neck*

NP nappe *sheet*

NP nappy *(Br) diaper, dish, ale* nappies

NP nappy *kinky* nappier nappiest

NP neap *tide*

NP nip *bite, sip* nipped nipping

NP nipa *palm tree*

NP nippy *cold* nippier nippiest

NP nope *no*

NPBLSHBL unpublishable

not printed

NPBLSHT unpublished *not printed*

NPCHL nuptial *marriage*

NPCHLD nuptiality *marriage rate*

NPCHLT nuptiality *marriage rate*

NPCHWL nuptial *marriage*

NPCHWLD nuptiality *marriage rate*

NPCHWLT nuptiality *marriage rate*

NPD antipode *opposite pole* antipodes

NPD in petto *secretly*

NPD unpaid *debt*

NPDL antipodal *germ cell*

NPDTD inaptitude *inability*

NPDTD ineptitude *lacking ability*

NPDTYD inaptitude *inability*

NPDTYD ineptitude *lacking ability*

NPFRM napiform *tapered*

NPK unpack *remove*

NPKN napkin *towel*

NPL imply *suggest* implied implying implies

NPL inaptly *unsuitable*

NPL ineptly *awkwardly*

NPL nauplii (pl) *larva* nauplius

NPL Nepal *country*

NPL Nepali *of Nepal* Nepali

NPL nippily *chilly*

NPL nipple *teat*

NPL nopal *cactus*

NPL unaptly *unable*

NPLBL unappealable *no recourse*

NPLD aneuploid *chromosomes*

NPLD implode *burst inward* imploded imploding

NPLD nippled *teats*

NPLD unpeeled *covered*

NPLDBL unpalatable *distasteful*

NPLDBLD unpalatability *distaste*

NPLDBLT unpalatability

distaste

NPLDN Neapolitan *of Naples*

NPLG unplug *disconnect, clear* unplugged unplugging

NPLJDK unapologetic *not sorry*

NPLJTK unapologetic *not sorry*

NPLK antiplaque *prevent tartar*

NPLKBL inapplicable (adj) *pointless* inapplicably (adv)

NPLKBLD inapplicability *pointless*

NPLKBLT inapplicability *pointless*

NPLM napalm *bomb*

NPLMD unplumbed *untested*

NPLN enplane *board*

NPLN Napoleon *emperor*

NPLN napoleon *pastry*

NPLN unappealing *distasteful*

NPLND unplanned *surprise*

NPLNG unappealing *distasteful*

NPLR implore *beg* implored imploring

NPLRNGL imploringly *beg*

NPLRZD unpolarized *random*

NPLS Annapolis *city*

NPLS anyplace *any location*

NPLS nauplius *larva* nauplii

NPLSDK anaplastic *cell reversion*

NPLSDK neoplastic *tumor*

NPLSH anaplasia *cell reversion*

NPLSH neoplasia *tumor*

NPLSHN antipollution *prevent filth*

NPLSHN implosion *inrush*

NPLSHT unpolished *raw*

NPLSM neoplasm *tumor*

NPLSMSS anaplasmosis *disease* anaplasmoses

NPLST unplaced *not rated*

NPLSTK anaplastic *cell reversion*

Letters aren't doubled for single sounds: to find **alley** use **L** not **LL**. Use **Y** and **W** as hard sounds only: to find **yellow** use **YL**. (Br)=British spelling or usage. * See dictionary.

NPLSTK neoplastic *tumor*
NPLSV implosive *inrush*
NPLT impolite *rude*
NPLTBL unpalatable
  distasteful
NPLTBLD unpalatability
  distaste
NPLTBLT unpalatability
  distaste
NPLTN Neapolitan *of Naples*
NPLY nauplii (pl) *larva*
  nauplius
NPLYN Napoleon *emperor*
NPLYN napoleon *pastry*
NPLYS nauplius *larva* nauplii
NPLZ Naples *city*
NPLZH anaplasia *cell*
  reversion
NPLZH neoplasia *tumor*
NPLZHN implosion *inrush*
NPLZM neoplasm *tumor*
NPLZMSS anaplasmosis
  disease anaplasmoses
NPLZNT unpleasant *angry*
NPLZNTL unpleasantly
  angry
NPLZNTNS unpleasantness
  anger
NPLZV implosive *inrush*
NPM napalm *bomb*
NPN kneepan *kneecap*
NPN nipping *chilling*
NPN unpin *unfasten*
  unpinned unpinning
NPND impound *confine*
NPND unopened *closed*
NPND unpainted *no coating*
NPNDMNT impoundment
  confine
NPNDTK nip and tuck *very*
  close
NPNG nipping *chilling*
NPNLT antepenult *syllable*
NPNLTMT antepenultimate
  syllable
NPNMNT impoundment
  confine
NPNS inaptness *unsuitable*
NPNS ineptness *lacking*
  ability
NPNS nippiness *cold*
NPNS unaptness *inability*

NPNT endpoint (or) end
  point *terminal*
NPNTD unpainted *no*
  coating
NPNTH nepenthe *drug*
NPNTHN nepenthean *drug*
NPNTHYN nepenthean *drug*
NPNTK nip and tuck *very*
  close
NPNZ Nipponese *Japanese*
  Nipponese
NPPLD unpeopled *no*
  humans
NPPLR unpopular *not*
  favored
NPPR endpaper *book cover*
NPPYLR unpopular *not*
  favored
NPR napery *linen*
NPR nappier *kinky*
NPR nipper *(Br) child*
NPR nippier *cold*
NPR no-par *stock*
NPRBL inoperable *no*
  surgery
NPRCHBL unapproachable
  (adj) *reserved*
  unapproachably (adv)
NPRD unpaired *no mate*
NPRDK antipyretic *fever*
  reducer
NPRDKDBL unpredictable
  (adj) *impulsive*
  unpredictably (adv)
NPRDKDBLD
  unpredictability
  impulsiveness
NPRDKDBLT
  unpredictability
  impulsiveness
NPRDKDV unproductive *no*
  effect
NPRDKL antiparticle *atomic*
NPRDKTBL unpredictable
  (adj) *impulsive*
  unpredictably (adv)
NPRDKTBLD
  unpredictability
  impulsiveness
NPRDKTBLT
  unpredictability
  impulsiveness

NPRDKTV unproductive *no*
  effect
NPRDNBL unpardonable
  unforgiven
NPRDV inoperative *not*
  working
NPRFDBL unprofitable (adj)
  no gain unprofitably (adv)
NPRFSHNL unprofessional
  (adj) *amateurish*
  unprofessionally (adv)
NPRFST unprofessed
  unspoken
NPRFTBL unprofitable (adj)
  no gain unprofitably (adv)
NPRGRMBL
  unprogrammable
  computer
NPRJDST unprejudiced *no*
  bias
NPRLLD unparalleled
  distinctive
NPRLMNTR
  unparliamentary
  autocratic
NPRMSNG unpromising
  unlikely
NPRN inpouring *flow in*
NPRN neoprene *rubber*
NPRNBL unprintable *unfit*
NPRNG inpouring *flow in*
NPRNNSBL
  unpronounceable *hard to*
  say
NPRNNTSBL
  unpronounceable *hard to*
  say
NPRNSPLD unprincipled
  immoral
NPRNTBL unprintable *unfit*
NPRNTSPLD unprincipled
  immoral
NPRPRD unprepared *not*
  ready
NPRPRT inappropriate
  unsuitable
NPRPRTL inappropriately
  unsuitable
NPRPRTNS
  inappropriateness
  unsuitable
NPRPRYT inappropriate

Use letters that best describe the sounds you hear and omit the vowels. Use **S** or **K** instead of **C**: to find circle use **SRKL**. Use **J** to find joy, **JM** to find gem and **G** to find go.

unsuitable
NPRPRYTL inappropriately
unsuitable
NPRPRYTNS
inappropriateness
unsuitable
NPRPSHS unpropitious
unlucky
NPRPTH naprapathy
treatment
NPRPZSNG
unprepossessing
unattractive
NPRSDND unprecedented
first
NPRSDNTD unprecedented
first
NPRSHBL inappreciable
(adj) *small* inappreciably
(adv)
NPRSHDD unappreciated
no thanks
NPRSHDV inappreciative
not thankful
NPRSHDVL inappreciatively
not thankful
NPRSHTD unappreciated
no thanks
NPRSHTV inappreciative
not thankful
NPRSHTVL inappreciatively
not thankful
NPRSHYDD unappreciated
no thanks
NPRSHYTD unappreciated
no thanks
NPRSN ampersand *symbol*
(&)
NPRSN unperson *not*
recognized
NPRSND ampersand *symbol*
(&)
NPRSNL antipersonnel
weapon
NPRSPRNT antiperspirant
prevents perspiration
NPRTD antiapartheid
against racism
NPRTK antipyretic *fever*
reducer
NPRTKDD unprotected *no*
shield

NPRTKL antiparticle *atomic*
NPRTKTD unprotected *no*
shield
NPRTN inopportune
inconvenient
NPRTNCHS unpretentious
modest
NPRTNCHSL
unpretentiously *modest*
NPRTNCHSNS
unpretentiousness
modesty
NPRTNSHS unpretentious
modest
NPRTNSHSL
unpretentiously *modest*
NPRTNSHSNS
unpretentiousness
modesty
NPRTNTSHS unpretentious
modest
NPRTNTSHSL
unpretentiously *modest*
NPRTNTSHSNS
unpretentiousness
modesty
NPRTRBD unperturbed
calm
NPRTV inoperative *not*
working
NPRTYN inopportune
inconvenient
NPRVBL unprovable *no*
proof
NPRVD unproved *no proof*
NPRVKD unprovoked *no*
stimulus
NPRVKT unprovoked *no*
stimulus
NPRVN unproven *no proof*
NPRZDND unprecedented
first
NPRZDNTD unprecedented
first
NPSD antipasto *food*
NPSDK anapestic *verse*
NPSHL nuptial *marriage*
NPSHLD nuptiality *marriage*
rate
NPSHLT nuptiality *marriage*
rate
NPSHNT inpatient *hospital*

NPSHWL nuptial *marriage*
NPSHWLD nuptiality
marriage rate
NPSHWLT nuptiality
marriage rate
NPSK knapsack *bag*
NPSN en passant *in passing*
NPSNT en passant *in*
passing
NPST anapest *verse*
NPST antipasto *food*
NPST nappiest *kinky*
NPST nippiest *cold*
NPSTK anapestic *verse*
NPT in petto *secretly*
NPT inapt *unsuitable*
NPT inept *awkward*
NPT input (v) *enter* inputted
(or) input inputting
NPT input (n) *data, advice,*
entry
NPT unapt *unable*
NPTH naphtha *petroleum*
NPTHDK antipathetic *hostile*
NPTHDKL antipathetically
hostilely
NPTHLN naphthalene
petroleum
NPTHN naphthene *wax*
NPTHTK antipathetic *hostile*
NPTHTKL antipathetically
hostilely
NPTL inaptly *unsuitable*
NPTL ineptly *awkwardly*
NPTL unaptly *unable*
NPTN Neptune *Roman god,*
planet
NPTNM neptunium *element*
NPTNS inappentence *no*
hunger
NPTNS inaptness *unsuitable*
NPTNS ineptness *lacking*
ability
NPTNS unaptness *inability*
NPTNTS inappentence *no*
hunger
NPTNYM neptunium
element
NPTRDK unpatriotic *not*
nationalistic
NPTRTK unpatriotic *not*
nationalistic

Letters aren't doubled for single sounds: to find alley use **L** not **LL**. Use **Y** and **W** as hard
sounds only: to find yellow use **YL**. (Br)=British spelling or usage. * See dictionary.

NPTRYDK unpatriotic *not nationalistic*

NPTRYTK unpatriotic *not nationalistic*

NPTSDK nepotistic *favoritism*

NPTSM nepotism *favoritism*

NPTSTK nepotistic *favoritism*

NPTTD inaptitude *inability*

NPTTD ineptitude *lacking ability*

NPTTYD inaptitude *inability*

NPTTYD ineptitude *lacking ability*

NPTYN Neptune *Roman god, planet*

NPTYNM neptunium *element*

NPTYNYM neptunium *element*

NPTZM nepotism *favoritism*

NPVD unpaved *no asphalt*

NPVRD antipoverty *prevent poverty*

NPVRT antipoverty *prevent poverty*

NPWD knapweed *plant*

NPYR nappier *kinky*

NPYR nippier *cold*

NPYST nappiest *kinky*

NPYST nippiest *cold*

NPZD unopposed *no resistance*

NQB incubi (pl) *nightmare* incubus

NQBDR incubator *hatch, baby care*

NQBS incubus *nightmare* incubi

NQBSHN incubation *hatch*

NQBT incubate *hatch* incubated incubating

NQBTR incubator *hatch, baby care*

NQD inequity *unfairness* inequities

NQD iniquity *sin* iniquities

NQDBL inequitable (adj) *unfair* inequitably (adv)

NQDD antiquated *old*

NQDS iniquitous *sinful*

NQL inocula (pl) *antigen* inoculum

NQL nuclei (pl) *center* nucleus

NQL unequal (adj) *not alike, unjust* unequally (adv)

NQLD inequality *not equal* inequalities

NQLD nucleoid *DNA*

NQLD unequaled (or) unequalled *without parallel*

NQLDR inoculator *infuse*

NQLDR nucleator *cluster*

NQLFD unqualified *complete, unfit*

NQLFL nucleophile *substance*

NQLFLK nucleophilic *atomic*

NQLFLSD nucleophilicity *atomic*

NQLFLST nucleophilicity *atomic*

NQLM inoculum *infusion* inocula

NQLN nuclein *protein, acid*

NQLN nucleon *particle*

NQLNK nucleonic *particle*

NQLNKS nucleonics *science*

NQLNT inoculant *antigen*

NQLNX nucleonics *science*

NQLPLSM nucleoplasm *sap*

NQLPLSMK nucleoplasmic *sap*

NQLPLZM nucleoplasm *sap*

NQLPLZMK nucleoplasmic *sap*

NQLPRTN nucleoprotein *gene*

NQLR nuclear *atomic, central*

NQLS nucleus *center* nuclei

NQLSHN inoculation *infusion*

NQLSHN nucleation *cluster*

NQLSNTHSS nucleosynthesis *chemistry*

NQLT inequality *not equal* inequalities

NQLT inoculate *infuse* inoculated inoculating

NQLT nucleate *cluster* nucleated nucleating

NQLTD nucleotide *acid*

NQLTR inoculator *infuse*

NQLTR nucleator *cluster*

NQLYSHN nucleation *cluster*

NQLYT nucleate *cluster* nucleated nucleating

NQLZ nuclease *enzyme*

NQNBL incunabula (pl) *early work* incunabulum

NQNBLM incunabulum *early work* incunabula

NQNBYL incunabula (pl) *early work* incunabulum

NQNBYLM incunabulum *early work* incunabula

NQNCHBL unquenchable *thirsty*

NQND unacquainted *stranger*

NQNTD unacquainted *stranger*

NQPD unoccupied *empty, no job*

NQR antiquary *old items* antiquaries

NQR enquire *ask* enquired enquiring

NQR enquiry *investigation* enquiries

NQR inquire *ask* inquired inquiring

NQR inquiry *investigation* inquiries

NQR neckwear *scarf, tie*

NQRBL incurable (adj) *no remedy* incurably (adv)

NQRBLD incurability *no remedy*

NQRBLT incurability *no remedy*

NQRC inaccuracy *error* inaccuracies

NQRN antiquarian *collector of old items*

NQRR inquirer *ask*

NQRS inaccuracy *error* inaccuracies

NQRS incurious *indifferent*

NQRSD incuriosity *indifference*

NQRST incuriosity *indifference*

NQRST knockwurst (or)

Use letters that best describe the sounds you hear and omit the vowels. Use **S** or **K** instead of **C**: to find circle use **SRKL**. Use **J** to find joy, **JM** to find gem and **G** to find go.

knackwurst *sausage*
NQRT inaccurate *faulty*
NQRTL inaccurately *faulty*
NQRYN antiquarian *collector of old items*
NQRYS incurious *indifferent*
NQRYSD incuriosity *indifference*
NQRYST incuriosity *indifference*
NQS innocuous *harmless*
NQS nocuous *harmful*
NQSCHNBL unquestionable (adj) *no argument* unquestionably (adv)
NQSCHND unquestioned *no argument*
NQSCHNN unquestioning *no argument*
NQSCHNNG unquestioning *no argument*
NQSL nocuously *harmful*
NQST inquest *inquiry*
NQT antiquate *make old* antiquated antiquating
NQT inequity *unfairness* inequities
NQT iniquity *sin iniquities*
NQT unquote *end quote*
NQTBL inequitable (adj) *unfair* inequitably (adv)
NQTD antiquated *old*
NQTD inquietude *disturbed*
NQTS iniquitous *sinful*
NQTYD inquietude *disturbed*
NQVKBL unequivocably *clearly*
NQVKL unequivocal (adj) *clear* unequivocally (adv)
NQWS innocuous *harmless*
NQWS nocuous *harmful*
NQWSL nocuously *harmful*
NQYR enquire *ask* enquired enquiring
NQYR enquiry *investigation* enquiries
NQYR inquire *ask* inquired inquiring
NQYR inquiry *investigation* inquiries
NQYRR inquirer *ask*

NQYTD inquietude *disturbed*
NQYTYD inquietude *disturbed*
NQZDR inquisitor *examiner*
NQZDV inquisitive *curious*
NQZSHN inquisition *examination*
NQZTR inquisitor *examiner*
NQZTRL inquisitorial (adj) *examiner* inquisitorially (adv)
NQZTRYL inquisitorial (adj) *examiner* inquisitorially (adv)
NQZTV inquisitive *curious*
NR annoyer *botherer*
NR anuria *urine*
NR enter *go into*
NR gnawer *chew*
NR honor *respect* (Br) honour
NR honoree *respected one* (Br) honouree
NR inner *inside*
NR inter- *between*
NR inure *accustom* inured inuring
NR knur *knob*
NR narrow *(adj) not wide, petty (v) decrease*
NR nary *not any*
NR ne'er *never*
NR near *close to*
NR Nehru *Indian leader*
NR nor *neither*
NR nori *sushi*
NR owner *possessor*
NR unary *single*
NRB anaerobe *no oxygen*
NRB Nairobi *city*
NRB nearby *close to*
NRBK anaerobic *no oxygen*
NRBKL anaerobically *no oxygen*
NRBL honorable (adj) *respect, renown* honorably (adv) (Br) honourable, honourably
NRBLSDM neuroblastoma *nerve cell* neuroblastomas (or) neuroblastomata

NRBLSDMD neuroblastomata (pl) *nerve cell* neuroblastoma
NRBLSDMT neuroblastomata (pl) *nerve cell* neuroblastoma
NRBLSTM neuroblastoma *nerve cell* neuroblastomas (or) neuroblastomata
NRBLSTMD neuroblastomata (pl) *nerve cell* neuroblastoma
NRBN narrowband *frequency*
NRBND narrowband *frequency*
NRBNGK interbank *between banks*
NRBNK interbank *between banks*
NRBR Ann Arbor *city*
NRBR near beer *liquor*
NRBRD interbreed *crossbreed* interbred interbreeding
NRBRNCH interbranch *between branches*
NRBZ antirabies *prevent hydrophobia*
NRC inter se *among themselves*
NRCD intercede *negotiate* interceded interceding
NRCDR interceder *negotiator*
NRCH enrich *improve* enriches
NRCHBL unreachable *too far*
NRCHMNT enrichment *improvement*
NRCHNJ interchange *exchange*
NRCHNJBL interchangeable (adj) *substitution* interchangeably (adv)
NRCHR nurture *(n) training, food*
NRCHR nurture *(v) foster, care* nurtured nurturing
NRCHRCH interchurch *between churches*

Letters aren't doubled for single sounds: to find alley use **L** not **LL**. Use **Y** and **W** as hard sounds only: to find yellow use **YL**. (Br)=British spelling or usage. * See dictionary.

NRCHRNS nurturance *care*
NRCHRNT nurturant *care*
NRCHRNTS nurturance *care*
NRCHRR nurturer *carer*
NRCHS unrighteous *wicked*
NRCHSL unrighteously *wicked*
NRCHSNS unrighteousness *wickedness*
NRCZ neuroses (pl) *psychology* neurosis
NRD aneroid *liquid*
NRD inroad *path*
NRD nerd *misfit* nerdy
NRD nereid *worm*
NRD Nereid *sea nymph*
NRD unread *unexamined*
NRD unready *unprepared*
NRDD unrated *no ranking*
NRDDZ neuritides (pl) *nerve* neuritis
NRDK Antarctic *ocean, region*
NRDK Antarctica *continent*
NRDK enuretic *urine*
NRDK interdict *forbid*
NRDK neritic *seacoast*
NRDK neurotic *psychology*
NRDK Nordic *Scandinavian*
NRDKBL ineradicable (adj) *permanent* ineradicably (adv)
NRDKDR introductory *first step*
NRDKL neurotically *psychology*
NRDKSHN interdiction *prohibition*
NRDKSHN introduction *presentation, insertion*
NRDKT interdict *forbid*
NRDKTR introductory *first step*
NRDL unriddle *explain*
NRDMD unredeemed *no savior*
NRDNL interdental (adj) *between teeth* interdentally (adv)
NRDNMNSHNL interdenominational *between faiths*

NRDNT inordinate *excessive*
NRDNTL inordinately *excessive*
NRDNTL interdental (adj) *between teeth* interdentally (adv)
NRDPNDNS interdependence *mutual reliance*
NRDPNDNT interdependent *mutual reliance*
NRDPNDNTS interdependence *mutual reliance*
NRDPRTMNL interdepartmental (adj) *between departments* interdepartmentally (adv)
NRDPRTMNTL interdepartmental (adj) *between departments* interdepartmentally (adv)
NRDR narrator *story teller*
NRDRML intradermal (adj) *within skin* intradermally (adv)
NRDRN intrauterine *in the uterus*
NRDS enteritis *intestines*
NRDS introduce *present, insert* introduced introducing
NRDS neuritis *nerve problems* neutitides
NRDSH nerdish *misfit*
NRDSPLNR interdisciplinary *between fields*
NRDV narrative *story*
NRDWL ne'er-do-well *failure*
NRDYS introduce *present, insert* introduced introducing
NRDZ innards *viscera*
NRFBRL neurofibril *protein*
NRFBRLR neurofibrillary *protein*
NRFBRM neurofibroma *mass*
NRFBRMTSS neurofibromatosis *disease*

NRFK honorific *title*
NRFK Norfolk *city*
NRFKLT interfaculty *between faculties*
NRFL interfile *arrange* interfiled interfiling
NRFLD unruffled *serene*
NRFR interfere *obstruct* interfered interfering
NRFRK Norfolk *city*
NRFRMKLG neuropharmacology *nerve drugs*
NRFRMKLJ neuropharmacology *nerve drugs*
NRFRMKLJKL neuropharmacological *nerve drugs*
NRFRMKLJST neuropharmacologist *nerve drugs*
NRFRN interferon *protein*
NRFRNS interference *obstruction*
NRFRNTS interference *obstruction*
NRFRR interferer *obstruct*
NRFS in-your-face *bold*
NRFS interface (*n*) *boundary*
NRFS interface (*v*) *communicate* interfaced interfacing
NRFS interoffice *between offices*
NRFSHL interfacial *bordering*
NRFSN interfacing *fabric*
NRFSNG interfacing *fabric*
NRFTH interfaith *between faiths*
NRFYL interfile *arrange* interfiled interfiling
NRFYZ interfuse *blend* interfused interfusing
NRFZ interfuse *blend* interfused interfusing
NRFZ interphase *cell division*
NRFZLG neurophysiology *nerve structure*
NRFZLJ neurophysiology

Use letters that best describe the sounds you hear and omit the vowels. Use **S** or **K** instead of **C**: to find circle use **SRKL**. Use **J** to find joy, **JM** to find gem and **G** to find go.

nerve structure
NRFZLJKL
neurophysiological *nerve structure*
NRFZLJST
neurophysiologist *nerve structure*
NRFZYLG neurophysiology *nerve structure*
NRFZYLJ neurophysiology *nerve structure*
NRFZYLJKL
neurophysiological *nerve structure*
NRFZYLJST
neurophysiologist *nerve structure*
NRG energy *power* energies
NRGBL unarguable (adj) *no question* unarguably (adv)
NRGDR interrogator *questioner*
NRGDV interrogative *question*
NRGL neuroglia *tissue*
NRGLDD unregulated *not overseen*
NRGLKDK intergalactic *between galaxies*
NRGLKDK intragalactic *within a galaxy*
NRGLKTK intergalactic *between galaxies*
NRGLKTK intragalactic *within a galaxy*
NRGLSHL interglacial *warm period*
NRGLTD unregulated *not overseen*
NRGLY neuroglia *tissue*
NRGNK inorganic *mineral*
NRGNK intragenic *within a gene*
NRGNK neurogenic *nerves*
NRGNKL neurogenically *nerves*
NRGNST Narraganset (or) Narragansett *Native American*
NRGNZD unorganized *unclear, messy* (Br) unorganised

NRGRD honor guard *military* (Br) honour guard
NRGRD intergrade *merge* intergraded intergrading
NRGTR interrogator *questioner*
NRGTR interrogatory *question* interrogatories
NRGTV interrogative *question*
NRGVRMNTL
intergovernmental *between governments*
NRGVRNMNTL
intergovernmental *between governments*
NRGWBL unarguable (adj) *no question* unarguably (adv)
NRGYBL unarguable (adj) *no question* unarguably (adv)
NRGYLDD unregulated *not overseen*
NRGYLTD unregulated *not overseen*
NRGYWBL unarguable (adj) *no question* unarguably (adv)
NRHPFCL
neurohypophyseal (or) neurohypophysial *pituitary*
NRHPFCYL
neurohypophyseal (or) neurohypophysial *pituitary*
NRHPFSL
neurohypophyseal (or) neurohypophysial *pituitary*
NRHPFSS neurohypophysis *pituitary*
NRHPFZL
neurohypophyseal (or) neurohypophysial *pituitary*
NRHRST unrehearsed *spontaneous*
NRHWL narwhal *whale*
NRJ energy *power* energies

NRJ enrage *anger* enraged enraging
NRJDK energetic *vitality*
NRJDKL energetically *vitality*
NRJK interject *introduce*
NRJK introject *incorporate*
NRJKSHN interjection *utterance*
NRJKSHN introjection *incorporation*
NRJKT interject *introduce*
NRJKT introject *incorporate*
NRJNC interagency *between agencies*
NRJNK intragenic *within a gene*
NRJNK neurogenic *nerves*
NRJNKL neurogenically *nerves*
NRJNL interregional *between areas*
NRJNL unoriginal *not fresh*
NRJNRSHNL
intergenerational *between ages*
NRJNRT unregenerate *stubborn*
NRJNRTL unregenerately *stubborn*
NRJNS interagency *between agencies*
NRJNTC interagency *between agencies*
NRJNTS interagency *between agencies*
NRJSDRD unregistered *not enrolled*
NRJSTRD unregistered *not enrolled*
NRJTK energetic *vitality*
NRJTKL energetically *vitality*
NRJZ energize *apply voltage, make active* energized energizing (Br) energise
NRJZR energizer *apply voltage, make active* (Br) energiser
NRK anarch *revolt leader*
NRK anarchy *no order*

Letters aren't doubled for single sounds: to find alley use **L** not **LL**. Use **Y** and **W** as hard sounds only: to find yellow use **YL**. (Br)=British spelling or usage. * See dictionary.

NRK anorak *coat*
NRK anuric *urine*
NRK interact *share*
NRK narc *(slang) drug policeman*
NRK nark *(v) (Br) annoy, (n) squealer*
NRK Newark *city*
NRK oneiric *dreams*
NRKC anorexia *not eating*
NRKCNRVS anorexia nervosa *not eating*
NRKCY anorexia *not eating*
NRKCYNRVS anorexia nervosa *not eating*
NRKCZ narcoses (pl) *stupor narcosis*
NRKDK anorectic *not eating*
NRKDK Antarctic *ocean, region*
NRKDK Antarctica *continent*
NRKDK narcotic *(n) drug (adj) dulling*
NRKDV interactive *two-way*
NRKDV neuroactive *stimulus*
NRKGNZD unrecognized *unknown* (Br) unrecognised
NRKK anarchic *without order*
NRKKL anarchically *without order*
NRKL oneirically *dreams*
NRKLB interclub *between clubs*
NRKLCHRL intercultural (adj) *between cultures* interculturally (adv)
NRKLJT intercollegiate *between colleges*
NRKLPC narcolepsy *sleep narcolepsies*
NRKLPDK narcoleptic *sleeper*
NRKLPS narcolepsy *sleep narcolepsies*
NRKLPTK narcoleptic *sleeper*
NRKLS interclass *between classes*
NRKLTRL intercultural (adj)

between cultures interculturally (adv)
NRKM intercom *communications*
NRKMNKSHN intercommunication *two-way speech*
NRKMNKT intercommunicate *exchange*
NRKMPN intercompany *between companies*
NRKMPN intracompany *within a company*
NRKMSTR neurochemistry *nerves*
NRKMYNKSHN intercommunication *two-way speech*
NRKMYNKT intercommunicate *exchange*
NRKNK interconnect *join*
NRKNKSHN interconnection *joint* (Br) interconnexion
NRKNKT interconnect *join*
NRKNNNL intercontinental *between continents*
NRKNNNTL intercontinental *between continents*
NRKNSTRKDD unreconstructed *no belief*
NRKNSTRKTD unreconstructed *no belief*
NRKNT intercounty *between counties*
NRKNTNNL intercontinental *between continents*
NRKNTNNTL intercontinental *between continents*
NRKNTR intercountry *between countries*
NRKNZD unrecognized *unknown* (Br) unrecognised
NRKRDKL intercortical *between outer layers*
NRKRF antiaircraft *defensive*
NRKRFT antiaircraft *defensive*

NRKRNL intracranial (adj) *inside the head* intracranially (adv)
NRKRNYL intracranial (adj) *inside the head* intracranially (adv)
NRKRP intercrop *alternate crops*
NRKRS intercourse *connection*
NRKRS intercross *breeding*
NRKRTKL intercortical *between outer layers*
NRKS anorexia *not eating*
NRKSDK anarchistic *without order*
NRKSDNG narrowcasting *transmission*
NRKSHN interaction *share*
NRKSK anorexic *not eating*
NRKSM anarchism *without order*
NRKSNRVS anorexia nervosa *not eating*
NRKSS narcosis *stupor narcoses*
NRKST anarchist *rebel*
NRKSTK anarchistic *without order*
NRKSTL intercoastal *between shores*
NRKSTL intercostal *between ribs*
NRKSTN narrowcasting *transmission*
NRKSTNG narrowcasting *transmission*
NRKSY anorexia *not eating*
NRKSYNRVS anorexia nervosa *not eating*
NRKSZ narcoses (pl) *stupor narcosis*
NRKT interact *share*
NRKT intercounty *between counties*
NRKTK anorectic *not eating*
NRKTK Antarctic *ocean, region*
NRKTK Antarctica *continent*
NRKTK narcotic *(n) drug (adj) dulling*
NRKTV interactive *two-way*

Use letters that best describe the sounds you hear and omit the vowels. Use **S** or **K** instead of **C**: to find circle use **SRKL**. Use **J** to find joy, **JM** to find gem and **G** to find go.

NRKTV neuroactive *stimulus*
NRKTZ narcotize *soothe* narcotized narcotizing
NRKWDD unrequited *not returned*
NRKWTD unrequited *not returned*
NRKZ anorexia *not eating*
NRKZK anorexic *not eating*
NRKZM anarchism *without order*
NRKZNRVS anorexia nervosa *not eating*
NRKZY anorexia *not eating*
NRKZYNRVS anorexia nervosa *not eating*
NRL enroll (or) enrol *sign up* enrolled enrolling
NRL enrollee *member*
NRL enteral (adj) *intestines* enterally (adv)
NRL gnarl *twist*
NRL gnarly *(slang) great, awful*
NRL honor roll *list* (Br) honour roll
NRL knurl *knob, knot, ridge*
NRL knurly *knobby*
NRL narrowly *barely*
NRL nearly *almost*
NRL neural (adj) *nerve* neurally (adv)
NRL neurula *embryo* neurulae (or) neurulas
NRL unreal *fantasy*
NRL unreel *unwind*
NRL unroll *unwind*
NRL unruly *willful*
NRLBL unreliable *not dependable*
NRLD gnarled *twisted*
NRLD interlude *interval*
NRLD knurled *knobby*
NRLDD interrelated *connected*
NRLDD unrelated *separate*
NRLG neuralgia *pain*
NRLG neurology *nerve science*
NRLGY neuralgia *pain*
NRLJ neuralgia *pain*
NRLJ neurology *nerve*

science
NRLJK neuralgic *painful*
NRLJKL neurological (or) neurologic (adj) *nerves* neurologically (adv)
NRLJS interreligious *between religions*
NRLJST neurologist *nerves*
NRLK interlock *unite*
NRLKDR interlocutor *speaker*
NRLKN interleukin *immunity*
NRLKTR interlocutor *speaker*
NRLKTR interlocutory *pronouncement*
NRLKYDR interlocutor *speaker*
NRLKYTR interlocutor *speaker*
NRLKYTR interlocutory *pronouncement*
NRLMNT enrollment *sign up*
NRLN interline *between lines*
NRLND interisland *between islands*
NRLNGK interlink *join*
NRLNK interlink *join*
NRLNN interlining *fabric*
NRLNNG interlining *fabric*
NRLNNG unrelenting *stern, constant*
NRLNR interlinear *between lines*
NRLNR interliner *transport*
NRLNR interlunar *moon phases*
NRLNS New Orleans *city*
NRLNS unruliness *willfulness*
NRLNTN unrelenting *stern, constant*
NRLNTNG unrelenting *stern, constant*
NRLNYR interlinear *between lines*
NRLNZ New Orleans *city*
NRLP interlope *intrude* interloped interloping interloper
NRLPDK neuroleptic *tranquilizer*
NRLPR interloper *intruder*

NRLPTK neuroleptic *tranquilizer*
NRLQDR interlocutor *speaker*
NRLQTR interlocutor *speaker*
NRLQTR interlocutory *pronouncement*
NRLRD interlard *mix in*
NRLS interlace *weave* interlaced interlacing
NRLSDK unrealistic *fantasy*
NRLSDKL unrealistically *fantasy*
NRLSHN interrelation *connection*
NRLSHN neurulation *embryo* (Br) neutraliser
NRLSHNSHP interrelationship *connection*
NRLSTK unrealistic *fantasy*
NRLSTKL unrealistically *fantasy*
NRLT inner light *soul*
NRLT interrelate *connect* interrelated interrelating
NRLTD interrelated *connected*
NRLTD unrelated *separate*
NRLV interleave *layer* interleaved interleaving
NRLY inter alia *among others*
NRLYBL unreliable *not dependable*
NRLYNS New Orleans *city*
NRLYNZ New Orleans *city*
NRM anteroom *lobby*
NRM interim *interval*
NRM neuroma *tumor* neuromas (or) neuromata
NRM norm *normal*
NRMD enormity *huge size* enormities
NRMD neuromata (pl) *tumor* neuroma
NRMD unarmed *without weapon*
NRMD unrhymed *poetry*
NRMDK antirheumatic *prevent rheumatism*
NRMDNG unremitting *constant*

Letters aren't doubled for single sounds: to find alley use **L** not **LL**. Use **Y** and **W** as hard sounds only: to find yellow use **YL**. (Br)=British spelling or usage. * See dictionary.

NRMDNS intermittence *occasional* intermittency

NRMDNT intermittent *occasional*

NRMDNTS intermittence *occasional* intermittency

NRMDR intermediary *go-between* intermediaries

NRMDR intermitter *discontinue*

NRMDT intermediate *middle*

NRMDTL intermediately *middle*

NRMDV normative *standards*

NRMDVL normatively *standards*

NRMDVNS normativeness *standards*

NRMDYR intermediary *go-between* intermediaries

NRMDYT intermediate *middle*

NRMDYTL intermediately *middle*

NRMDZ intermezzo *interlude* intermezzi (or) intermezzos

NRMKS intermix *blend*

NRMKSCHR intermixture *blend*

NRMKSTR intermixture *blend*

NRML normal (adj, n) *average, regular* normally (adv)

NRMLC normalcy *regular state*

NRMLD normality *regular state*

NRMLKLR intramolecular *within a molecule*

NRMLKYLR intramolecular *within a molecule*

NRMLQLR intramolecular *within a molecule*

NRMLS normalcy *regular state*

NRMLS normalize *make regular* normalized normalizing (Br) normalise

NRMLSSHN normalization

make regular (Br) normalisation

NRMLT normality *regular state*

NRMLZ normalize *make regular* normalized normalizing (Br) normalise

NRMLZSHN normalization *make regular* (Br) normalisation

NRMN Norman *of Normandy*

NRMND Normandy *region*

NRMNDD narrow-minded *prejudiced*

NRMNDDL narrow-mindedly *prejudiced*

NRMNDDNS narrow-mindedness *prejudice*

NRMNGGL intermingle *mix* intermingled intermingling

NRMNGL intermingle *mix* intermingled intermingling

NRMNT inurement *accustom*

NRMP on-ramp *highway*

NRMR intermarry *wed within a group* intermarried intermarrying intermarries

NRMRJ intermarriage *between groups*

NRMRKBL unremarkable (adj) *unnoticed* unremarkably (adv)

NRMRKD unremarked *unnoticed*

NRMRKN inter-American *between Americas*

NRMRKT unremarked *unnoticed*

NRMRL intramural (adj) *within an organization* intramurally (adv)

NRMS enormous *huge*

NRMS near miss *close call*

NRMSH intermesh *interlock*

NRMSHN intermission *interval*

NRMSKLR intramuscular *within a muscle*

NRMSKYLR intramuscular *within a muscle*

NRMSL enormously *hugely*

NRMSNS enormousness *huge size*

NRMSQLR intramuscular *within a muscle*

NRMST innermost *inward*

NRMT enormity *huge size* enormities

NRMT intermit *discontinue* intermitted intermitting

NRMT neuromata (pl) *tumor* neuroma

NRMTK antirheumatic *prevent rheumatism*

NRMTNG unremitting *constant*

NRMTNS intermittence *occasional* intermittency

NRMTNT intermittent *occasional*

NRMTNTS intermittence *occasional* intermittency

NRMTR intermitter *discontinue*

NRMTS intermezzo *interlude* intermezzi (or) intermezzos

NRMTV normative *standards*

NRMTVL normatively *standards*

NRMTVNS normativeness *standards*

NRMVBL unremovable *affixed*

NRMX intermix *blend*

NRMXCHR intermixture *blend*

NRMXTR intermixture *blend*

NRMYRL intramural (adj) *within an organization* intramurally (adv)

NRN anuran *amphibian*

NRN neuron *cell*

NRN unerring *correct*

NRNC inerrancy *no error*

NRNCN internecine *within a group, deadly*

NRND internode *between joints*

NRND unearned *not merited*

Use letters that best describe the sounds you hear and omit the vowels. Use **S** or **K** instead of **C**: to find circle use **SRKL**. Use **J** to find joy, **JM** to find gem and **G** to find go.

NRND unround *pronounce*
NRNDKRN neuroendocrine *hormone*
NRNDSTR interindustry *between industries*
NRNG unerring *correct*
NRNL neuronal *cell*
NRNS inerrancy *no error*
NRNS narrowness *not wide*
NRNSHNL international (adj) *between countries* internationally (adv)
NRNSHNL internationale *labor union*
NRNSHNLDTLN international date line *180th meridian*
NRNSHNLZ internationalize *involve many nations* internationalized internationalizing (Br) internationalise
NRNSHNLZM internationalism *cooperation policy*
NRNSHNLZSHN internationalization *many nations* (Br) internationalisation
NRNSN internecine *within a group, deadly*
NRNT inerrant *no error*
NRNT internet *computer net*
NRNTC inerrancy *no error*
NRNTS inerrancy *no error*
NRNZL intranasal (adj) *within a nose* intranasally (adv)
NRP enwrap *cover*
NRP interrupt *break in*
NRP unripe *immature*
NRP unwrap *uncover*
NRPCHR enrapture *delight* enraptured enrapturing
NRPDR interrupter *breaker*
NRPDRN neuropteran *insect*
NRPDRS neuropterous *insect*
NRPL interplay *interaction*
NRPL Interpol *police*
NRPLD interplead *law*
NRPLNTR interplanetary

between planets
NRPNNT unrepentant *no remorse*
NRPNS unripeness *immature*
NRPNT unrepentant *no remorse*
NRPNTNT unrepentant *no remorse*
NRPNTRT interpenetrate *fill* interpenetrated interpenetrating
NRPRBL interoperable *between systems*
NRPRBLD interoperability *between systems*
NRPRBLT interoperability *between systems*
NRPRD interparty *between parties*
NRPRSNL interpersonal (adj) *between people* interpersonally (adv)
NRPRSNL intrapersonal *within oneself*
NRPRT interparty *between parties*
NRPRZ enterprise *initiative, business*
NRPRZN enterprising *independent*
NRPRZNG enterprising *independent*
NRPRZR enterpriser *producer, organizer*
NRPSHN interruption *break*
NRPSHR enrapture *delight* enraptured enrapturing
NRPT enrapt *delighted*
NRPT interrupt *break in*
NRPTH neuropathy *degeneration*
NRPTHK neuropathic *degeneration*
NRPTHKL neuropathically *degeneration*
NRPTHLG neuropathology *nerve disease*
NRPTHLJ neuropathology *nerve disease*
NRPTHLJK neuropathologic (or)

neuropathological *nerve disease*
NRPTHLJKL neuropathological (or) neuropathologic *nerve disease*
NRPTHLJST neuropathologist *nerve disease*
NRPTR enrapture *delight* enraptured enrapturing
NRPTR interrupter *breaker*
NRPTRN neuropteran *insect*
NRPTRS neuropterous *insect*
NRPZ interpose *interrupt* interposed interposing
NRPZR interposer *interrupter*
NRPZSHN interposition *interruption*
NRQDD unrequited *not returned*
NRQTD unrequited *not returned*
NRR honoraria (pl) *payment* honorarium
NRR honorary *commemorative, unpaid*
NRR honorer *respecter* (Br) honourer
NRR inner ear *hearing*
NRRL honorarily *commemorative, unpaid*
NRRM honorarium *payment* honoraria (or) honorariums
NRRY honoraria (pl) *payment* honorarium
NRRYM honorarium *payment* honoraria (or) honorariums
NRS inter se *among themselves*
NRS nares *nostril*
NRS Norse *Scandinavian*
NRS nurse *(v) attend, rear, suck** nursed nursing
NRS nurse *(n) carer*
NRS onerous *troublesome*
NRSC narcissi (pl) *plant* narcissus

Letters aren't doubled for single sounds: to find alley use **L** not **LL**. Use **Y** and **W** as hard sounds only: to find yellow use **YL**. (Br)=British spelling or usage. * See dictionary.

NRSD inner city (n) *urban* inner-city (adj)

NRSD intercede *negotiate* interceded interceding

NRSD nearside *close by*

NRSDD interested *concerned*

NRSDD nearsighted *vision*

NRSDDL nearsightedly *vision*

NRSDDNS nearsightedness *vision*

NRSDR interceder *negotiator*

NRSDR nor'easter *wind*

NRSH inertia *stillness*

NRSH inrush *flow in*

NRSH nourish *feed*

NRSH onrush *onset*

NRSHL inertial (adj) *stillness* inertially (adv)

NRSHL interracial (adj) *between races* interracially (adv)

NRSHMNT nourishment *food*

NRSHN interocean *between oceans*

NRSHN narration *story*

NRSHN nourishing *nutritious*

NRSHN onrushing *onset*

NRSHNG nourishing *nutritious*

NRSHNG onrushing *onset*

NRSHP ownership *possession*

NRSHR nearshore *coast*

NRSHR nourisher *feeder*

NRSHTL Neufchâtel *cheese*

NRSK intersect *cross*

NRSKK intrapsychic *within the mind*

NRSKKL intrapsychically *within the mind*

NRSKLG neuropsychology *mental*

NRSKLJ neuropsychology *mental*

NRSKLJKL neuropsychological *mental*

NRSKLJST neuropsychologist *mental*

NRSKLSDK interscholastic *between schools*

NRSKLSTK interscholastic *between schools*

NRSKSHL intersexual (adj) *between sexes* intersexually (adv)

NRSKSHLD intersexuality *between sexes*

NRSKSHLT intersexuality *between sexes*

NRSKSHN intersection *crossing*

NRSKSHWL intersexual (adj) *between sexes* intersexually (adv)

NRSKSHWLD intersexuality *between sexes*

NRSKSHWLT intersexuality *between sexes*

NRSKT intersect *cross*

NRSKTR neuropsychiatry *mental*

NRSKTRK neuropsychiatric *mental*

NRSKTRST neuropsychiatrist *mental*

NRSKYTR neuropsychiatry *mental*

NRSKYTRK neuropsychiatric *mental*

NRSKYTRST neuropsychiatrist *mental*

NRSL innersole *shoe*

NRSL onerously *troublesome*

NRSLLR intercellular *between cells*

NRSLNG nursling *baby*

NRSLVD unresolved *not settled*

NRSLYLR intercellular *between cells*

NRSM aneurysm *dilation*

NRSMD nursemaid *babysitter*

NRSMDWF nurse-midwife *birth*

NRSMDWFR nurse-midwifery *birth*

NRSML aneurysmal *dilation*

NRSN nursing *profession*

NRSNG nursing *profession*

NRSNGHM nursing home *hospital*

NRSNHM nursing home *hospital*

NRSNS neuroscience *nerves*

NRSNS onerousness *troublesome*

NRSNSR neurosensory *nerves*

NRSNTS neuroscience *nerves*

NRSNTSR neurosensory *nerves*

NRSP intercept (v) seize (n) *code, signal*

NRSPDR interceptor *seize*

NRSPNSV unresponsive *silent*

NRSPNTSV unresponsive *silent*

NRSPR neurospora *fungus*

NRSPRNG innerspring *mattress*

NRSPRS intersperse *insert* interspersed interspersing

NRSPRSHN interspersion *insert*

NRSPRZHN interspersion *insert*

NRSPS inner space *inside*

NRSPS interspace *place between* interspaced interspacing

NRSPSHN interception *seizure*

NRSPT intercept (v) seize (n) *code, signal*

NRSPTR interceptor *seize*

NRSR nursery *bedroom, plants, school* nurseries

NRSRJKL neurosurgical *brain*

NRSRJN neurosurgeon *brain*

NRSRJR neurosurgery *brain*

NRSRMN nurseryman *plants* nurserymen

NRSRRM nursery rhyme *poem*

NRSRSKL nursery school *toddlers*

Use letters that best describe the sounds you hear and omit the vowels. Use **S** or **K** instead of **C**: to find circle use **SRKL**. Use **J** to find joy, **JM** to find gem and **G** to find go.

NRSS enuresis *urine*
NRSS narcissi (pl) *plant* narcissus
NRSS neurosis *psychology* neuroses
NRSSHN intercession *prayer*
NRSSHN intersession *between terms*
NRSSS narcissus *flower* narcissi (or) narcissuses (or) narcissus
NRSSSDK narcissistic *self-love*
NRSSST narcissist *self-love*
NRSSSTK narcissistic *self-love*
NRSSTK narcissistic *self-love*
NRSSTM honor system *trust* (Br) honour system
NRSSZM narcissism *self-love*
NRST inner city (n) *urban* inner-city (adj)
NRST intercity *between cities*
NRST interest (v) *engage attention* (n) *concern, company, benefit**
NRST Near East *Mediterranean region*
NRST unrest *turmoil*
NRSTCZ interstices (pl) *gap* interstice
NRSTD interested *concerned*
NRSTD nearsighted *vision*
NRSTDL nearsightedly *vision*
NRSTDNS nearsightedness *vision*
NRSTHN neurasthenia *mental disorder*
NRSTHNK neurasthenic *mental disorder*
NRSTHNKL neurasthenically *mental disorder*
NRSTHNY neurasthenia *mental disorder*
NRSTLR interstellar *between stars*

NRSTN interesting *fascinating*
NRSTNG interesting *fascinating*
NRSTR nor'easter *wind*
NRSTRKDD unrestricted *open*
NRSTRKTD unrestricted *open*
NRSTRND unrestrained *free*
NRSTRNDL unrestrainedly *free*
NRSTRNDNS unrestrainedness *freedom*
NRSTRNT unrestraint *freedom*
NRSTS interstice *gap*
NRSTSHL interstitial (adj) *between* interstitially (adv)
NRSTSZ interstices (pl) *gap* interstice
NRSTT interstate *between states*
NRSTT intrastate *within a state*
NRSVD unresolved *not settled*
NRSYNS neuroscience *nerves*
NRSYNTS neuroscience *nerves*
NRSZ neuroses (pl) *psychology* neurosis
NRT en route *on the way*
NRT in-wrought *decorated*
NRT inert *stillness*
NRT narrate *tell* narrated narrating
NRTB inner tube *tire*
NRTCHD unretouched *natural*
NRTCHT unretouched *natural*
NRTD unrated *no ranking*
NRTDL intertidal (adj) *above low tide* intertidally (adv)
NRTDZ neuritides (pl) *nerve* neuritis
NRTH north *direction*
NRTH unearth *uncover*
NRTHBN northbound *direction*

NRTHBND northbound *direction*
NRTHC North Sea *body of water*
NRTHDKD North Dakota *US State*
NRTHDKS neoorthodox *new truth* neoorthodoxy
NRTHDKS unorthodox *different* unorthodoxy
NRTHDKT North Dakota *US State*
NRTHDX neoorthodox *new truth* neoorthodoxy
NRTHDX unorthodox *different* unorthodoxy
NRTHKR North Korea *country*
NRTHKRLN North Carolina *US State*
NRTHKRY North Korea *country*
NRTHL unearthly *supernatural*
NRTHLN northland *country*
NRTHLND northland *country*
NRTHLNS unearthliness *supernatural*
NRTHMRK North America *continent*
NRTHMRKN North American *of North America*
NRTHNG northing *direction*
NRTHPL North Pole *region*
NRTHR norther *wind*
NRTHRDK antiarthritic *combating arthritis*
NRTHRL northerly *direction*
NRTHRN northern *direction*
NRTHRNLTS northern lights *aurora borealis*
NRTHRNR northerner *of the north*
NRTHRTK antiarthritic *combating arthritis*
NRTHS North Sea *body of water*
NRTHSDR northeaster *wind*
NRTHSDRL northeasterly *direction*

Letters aren't doubled for single sounds: to find alley use **L** not **LL**. Use **Y** and **W** as hard sounds only: to find yellow use **YL**. (Br)=British spelling or usage. * See dictionary.

NRTHSDRN northeastern *region*

NRTHSLP North Slope *region*

NRTHST northeast *direction*

NRTHSTR North Star *polestar*

NRTHSTR northeaster *wind*

NRTHSTRL northeasterly *direction*

NRTHSTRN northeastern *region*

NRTHWRD northward *direction*

NRTHWRDS northwards *direction*

NRTHWRDZ northwards *direction*

NRTHWSDR northwester *wind*

NRTHWSDRL northwesterly *direction*

NRTHWSDRN northwestern *direction*

NRTHWST northwest *direction*

NRTHWSTR northwester *wind*

NRTHWSTRL northwesterly *direction*

NRTHWSTRN northwestern *direction*

NRTK Antarctic *ocean, region*

NRTK Antarctica *continent*

NRTK enuretic *urine*

NRTK neritic *seacoast*

NRTK neurotic *psychology*

NRTK Nordic *Scandinavian*

NRTKL neurotically *psychology*

NRTKLC inarticulacy *unspoken*

NRTKLDD unarticulated *unspoken*

NRTKLS inarticulacy *unspoken*

NRTKLT inarticulate *unspoken*

NRTKLTD unarticulated *unspoken*

NRTKSK neurotoxic *poison*

NRTKSN neurotoxin *poison*

NRTKYLC inarticulacy *unspoken*

NRTKYLDD unarticulated *unspoken*

NRTKYLS inarticulacy *unspoken*

NRTKYLT inarticulate *unspoken*

NRTKYLTD unarticulated *unspoken*

NRTL unriddle *explain*

NRTN entertain *amuse, consider*

NRTN unwritten *not on paper*

NRTNMNT entertainment *amusement*

NRTNN entertaining *amusing*

NRTNNG entertaining *amusing*

NRTNR entertainer *amuser*

NRTQLC inarticulacy *unspoken*

NRTQLDD unarticulated *unspoken*

NRTQLS inarticulacy *unspoken*

NRTQLT inarticulate *unspoken*

NRTQLTD unarticulated *unspoken*

NRTR narrator *story teller*

NRTR nurture *(n) training, food*

NRTRBL intertribal (adj) *between tribes* intertribally (adv)

NRTRN intrauterine *in the uterus*

NRTRNS nurturance *care*

NRTRNSMDR neurotransmitter *synapse*

NRTRNSMTR neurotransmitter *synapse*

NRTRNT nurturant *care*

NRTRNTS nurturance *care*

NRTRNZMDR neurotransmitter *synapse*

NRTRNZMSHN neurotransmission *synapse*

NRTRNZMTR neurotransmitter *synapse*

NRTRR nurturer *carer*

NRTS enteritis *intestines*

NRTS nerts *(slang) nuts*

NRTS neuritis *nerve problems* neuritides

NRTV narrative *story*

NRTWN intertwine *weave* intertwined intertwining

NRTWNMNT intertwinement *tangle*

NRTXK neurotoxic *poison*

NRTXN neurotoxin *poison*

NRTYB inner tube *tire*

NRV interview *(n) consultation (v) consult*

NRV nerve *(v) give strength* nerved nerving

NRV nerve *(n) sinew, strength, gall**

NRV nervy *bold* nervier nerviest

NRV unnerve *upset* unnerved unnerving

NRV unreeve *withdraw* unreeved unreeving

NRVD nerved *veined, strong*

NRVGS nerve gas *weapon*

NRVL interval *space between*

NRVL unravel *come apart*

NRVLD unrivaled (or) unrivalled *supreme*

NRVN intervene *come between* intervened intervening

NRVN nirvana *bliss*

NRVNCHN intervention *come between*

NRVNCHNZM interventionism *come between*

NRVNGL unnervingly *upset*

NRVNK nirvanic *blissful*

NRVNL unnervingly *upset*

NRVNR intervenor (or) intervener *come between*

NRVNS intravenous *in the vein*

NRVNSHN intervention *come between*

NRVNSHNZM interventionism *come*

Use letters that best describe the sounds you hear and omit the vowels. Use **S** or **K** instead of **C**: to find circle use **SRKL**. Use **J** to find joy, **JM** to find gem and **G** to find go.

between

NRVR nervier *bolder*

NRVRKN nerve-racking (or) nerve-wracking *exhausting*

NRVRKNG nerve-racking (or) nerve-wracking *exhausting*

NRVS nervous *jumpy, timid*

NRVSBRKDN nervous breakdown *mental*

NRVSHN enervation *remove strength*

NRVSHN innervation *supply nerves*

NRVSKLR intravascular *in the vein*

NRVSKYLR intravascular *in the vein*

NRVSL nervously *jumpy, timid*

NRVSNS nervousnous *jumpy, timid*

NRVSQLR intravascular *in the vein*

NRVSSDM nervous system *nerves*

NRVSSTM nervous system *nerves*

NRVST nerviest *boldest*

NRVT enervate *remove strength* enervated enervating

NRVT innervate *supply nerves* innervated innervating

NRVW interviewee *person evaluated*

NRVWR interviewer *reporter*

NRVY interview *(n) consultation (v) consult*

NRVYR interviewer *reporter*

NRVYR nervier *bolder*

NRVYST nerviest *boldest*

NRVYW interviewee *person evaluated*

NRVYWR interviewer *reporter*

NRW Norway *country*

NRWGN Norwegian *of Norway*

NRWJN Norwegian *of*

Norway

NRWKDV neuroactive *stimulus*

NRWKTV neuroactive *stimulus*

NRWL narwhal *whale*

NRWNDKRN neuroendocrine *hormone*

NRWRDD unrewarded *no prize*

NRWRDN unrewarding *in vain*

NRWRDNG unrewarding *in vain*

NRWSDR nor'wester *wind*

NRWSTR nor'wester *wind*

NRWV interweave *mix* interwove interweaving interwoven

NRWVN interwoven *mixed*

NRX anorexia *not eating*

NRXK anorexic *not eating*

NRXNRVS anorexia nervosa *not eating*

NRXY anorexia *not eating*

NRXYNRVS anorexia nervosa *not eating*

NRY anuria *urine*

NRYD Nereid *sea nymph*

NRYD nereid *worm*

NRYDRN intrauterine *in the uterus*

NRYLSDK unrealistic *fantasy*

NRYLSDKL unrealistically *fantasy*

NRYLSTK unrealistic *fantasy*

NRYLSTKL unrealistically *fantasy*

NRYTRN intrauterine *in the uterus*

NRZ nares *nostril*

NRZLVD unresolved *not settled*

NRZM aneurysm *dilation*

NRZML aneurysmal *dilation*

NRZNBL unreasonable (adj) *ridiculous* unreasonably (adv)

NRZNL intrazonal *soil*

NRZNN unreasoning *ridiculous*

NRZNNG unreasoning *ridiculous*

NRZRV unreserve *frankness*

NRZRVD unreserved *entire, frank*

NRZVD unresolved *not settled*

NS Aeneas *Greek hero*

NS anise *plant*

NS antsy *nervous*

NS anus *rectum* anuses

NS ensue *follow* ensued ensuing

NS gneiss *rock*

NS NASA *(abbr) National Aeronatics and Space Administration*

NS Nassau *city*

NS nice *pleasing* nicer nicest

NS Nice *city*

NS niece *relative*

NS nisei *(often capitalized) Japanese* nisei

NS noose *bind* noosed noosing

NS nous *reason*

NS onus *stigma*

NS ounce *weight*

NS unsay *retract* unsaid unsaying

NS unsew *take apart*

NSBL insoluble *cannot dissolve or explain*

NSBL unusable *useless*

NSBLD insolubility *cannot dissolve or explain*

NSBLT insolubility *cannot dissolve or explain*

NSBRD insobriety *drunk*

NSBRDNSHN insubordination *disobedience*

NSBRDNT insubordinate *disobedient*

NSBRT insobriety *drunk*

NSBRYD insobriety *drunk*

NSBRYT insobriety *drunk*

NSBSTNCHL insubstantial *flimsy*

NSBSTNSHL insubstantial *flimsy*

NSCBLD unsociability

unfriendly
NSCBLT unsociability
unfriendly
NSCHRDD unsaturated *not absorbed*
NSCHRTD unsaturated *not absorbed*
NSCNS insouciance *unconcern*
NSCNT insouciant *casual*
NSCNTS insouciance *unconcern*
NSCYBLD unsociability *unfriendly*
NSCYBLT unsociability *unfriendly*
NSCYNS insouciance *unconcern*
NSCYNT insouciant *casual*
NSCYNTS insouciance *unconcern*
NSD Agnus Dei *prayer*
NSD aniseed *anise*
NSD antacid *neutralizer*
NSD antecede *precede* anteceded anteceding
NSD gneissoid *rock*
NSD honesty *truth*
NSD inside *within*
NSD ionicity *atoms*
NSD nasty *mean, obscene* nastier nastiest
NSD nicety *pleasantry* niceties
NSD onside *sports*
NSD unsaid *silent*
NSD unused *new*
NSDBL unsuitable (adj) *improper* unsuitably (adv)
NSDBLD unsuitability *improper*
NSDBLT unsuitability *improper*
NSDD unseeded *not sown, not ranked*
NSDD unsuited *improper*
NSDK gnostic *believer*
NSDK nostoc *algae*
NSDL nastily *mean, indecent*
NSDL unsaddle *horse*
NSDL unsettle *disturb* unsettled unsettling

NSDL unsubtle (adj) *bold* unsubtly (adv)
NSDLD unsettled *disturbed*
NSDLMNT unsettlement *disturbance*
NSDM oncidium *orchid*
NSDNL incidental (adj, n) *by chance* incidentally (adv)
NSDNS antecedence *priority*
NSDNS incidence *occurrence*
NSDNS nastiness *meanness, indecency*
NSDNT antecedent *prior*
NSDNT incident *occurrence*
NSDNTL incidental (adj) *by chance* incidentally (adv)
NSDNTS antecedence *priority*
NSDNTS incidence *occurrence*
NSDR inciter *urge, assist*
NSDR insider *member*
NSDR nester *squatter*
NSDRL nostril *nose*
NSDRM nostrum *remedy*
NSDRSHM nasturtium *flower*
NSDS insidious *treacherous, subtle*
NSDSL insidiously *treacherous, subtle*
NSDSZM gnosticism *belief*
NSDYM oncidium *orchid*
NSDYS insidious *treacherous, subtle*
NSDYSL insidiously *treacherous, subtle*
NSF UNICEF *fund*
NSF unsafe *dangerous*
NSFKNCHS unself-conscious *natural*
NSFKNSHS unself-conscious *natural*
NSFL encephala (pl) *brain* encephalon
NSFLDDZ encephalitides (pl) *brain inflammation* encephalitis
NSFLDK antisyphilitic *prevent syphilis*
NSFLDS encephalitis *brain*

inflammation encephalitides
NSFLGRF encephalograph *brain test*
NSFLGRF encephalography *brain test*
NSFLGRM encephalogram *brain test*
NSFLN encephalon *brain* encephala
NSFLPTH encephalopathy *brain disease*
NSFLPTHK encephalopathic *brain disease*
NSFLTDZ encephalitides (pl) *brain inflammation* encephalitis
NSFLTK antisyphilitic *prevent syphilis*
NSFLTS encephalitis *brain inflammation* encephalitides
NSFR encipher *write*
NSFR ensphere *circle*
NSFR insofar *extent*
NSFR ionosphere *atmosphere*
NSFR noosphere *evolution*
NSFRBL insufferable (adj) *unbearable* insufferably (adv)
NSFRMNT encipherment *writing*
NSFRR encipherer *writer*
NSFSDKDD unsophisticated *simple*
NSFSDKSHN unsophistication *simplicity*
NSFSDKTD unsophisticated *simple*
NSFSHNC insufficiency *lack* insufficiencies
NSFSHNS insufficiency *lack* insufficiencies
NSFSHNT insufficient *lacking*
NSFSHNTC insufficiency *lack* insufficiencies
NSFSHNTS insufficiency *lack* insufficiencies

Use letters that best describe the sounds you hear and omit the vowels. Use **S** or **K** instead of **C**: to find circle use **SRKL**. Use **J** to find joy, **JM** to find gem and **G** to find go.

NSFSTKDD unsophisticated *simple*

NSFSTKSHN unsophistication *simplicity*

NSFSTKTD unsophisticated *simple*

NSGN insignia *badge* insignia (or) insignias

NSGNFKNS insignificance *unimportant* insignificancy

NSGNFKNT insignificant *unimportant*

NSGNFKNTS insignificance *unimportant* insignificancy

NSGNY insignia *badge* insignia (or) insignias

NSGRGDD unsegregated *mixed*

NSGRGTD unsegregated *mixed*

NSH gnash *grind*

NSH nausea *sickness*

NSH niche *(v) put away* niched niching

NSH niche *(n) nook, small area*

NSH no-show *absent person*

NSH nosh *snack*

NSHD unshod *no shoes*

NSHDR initiator *starter*

NSHDV initiative *(adj) preliminary (n) enterprise*

NSHKBL unshakable (adj) *steady* unshakably (adv)

NSHKL unshackle *free* unshackled unshackling

NSHKN unshaken *steady*

NSHL initial *(v) approve* initialed (or) initialled initialing (or) initialling

NSHL initial *(adj) first (n) first letter* initially (adv)

NSHL uncial *writing*

NSHL unusual (adj) *rare* unusually (adv)

NSHLNS unusualness *rarity*

NSHLZ initialize *set to start* initialized initializing

NSHLZSHN initialization *set to start*

NSHMD unashamed *no guilt*

NSHMN unassuming *humble*

NSHMNG unassuming *humble*

NSHN enation *outgrowth*

NSHN ingénue (or) ingenue *girl*

NSHN nation *country*

NSHN notion *idea*

NSHNHD nationhood *country*

NSHNL national (adj) *country* nationally (adv)

NSHNL notional (adj) *imaginary* notionally (adv)

NSHNLD nationality *birth country* nationalities

NSHNLD notionality *imagination*

NSHNLGRD National Guard *militia*

NSHNLSDK nationalistic *country*

NSHNLSDKL nationalistically *country*

NSHNLSTK nationalistic *country*

NSHNLSTKL nationalistically *country*

NSHNLT nationality *birth country* nationalities

NSHNLT notionality *imagination*

NSHNLZ nationalize *government control* nationalized nationalizing (Br) nationalise

NSHNLZM nationalism *country*

NSHNLZR nationalizer *government control* (Br) nationaliser

NSHNLZSHN nationalization *government control* (Br) nationalisation

NSHNS nescience *ignorance*

NSHNSTT nation-state *country*

NSHNT ancient *old*

NSHNT nescient *ignorant*

NSHNTL anciently *long ago*

NSHNTNS ancientness *old age*

NSHNTS nescience *ignorance*

NSHNWD nationwide *coast-to-coast*

NSHP unship *unload, detatch* unshipped unshipping

NSHPD unshaped *natural*

NSHPT unshaped *natural*

NSHR ensure *make certain* ensured ensuring

NSHR inshore *near the coast*

NSHR insure *make certain* insured insuring

NSHR onshore *coastal, domestic*

NSHR unsure *not certain*

NSHRBL insurable *insurance*

NSHRD enshroud *cover*

NSHRD insured *policy*

NSHRN enshrine *preserve as sacred* enshrined enshrining

NSHRN enshrinee *Hall of Famer*

NSHRNMNT enshrinement *preservation*

NSHRNS insurance *protection*

NSHRNTS insurance *protection*

NSHRR insurer *underwriter*

NSHS nauseous *sick*

NSHSHN initiation *rite*

NSHT initiate *(v) begin* initiated initiating

NSHT initiate *(n) novice*

NSHT nauseate *make sick* nauseated nauseating

NSHTH ensheathe *cover* ensheathed ensheathing

NSHTH unsheathe *uncover* unsheathed unsheathing

NSHTL Neufchâtel *cheese*

NSHTR initiator *starter*

NSHTR initiatory *starting*

NSHTV initiative *(adj) preliminary (n) enterprise*

NSHVL Nashville *city*

NSHVN unshaven *bearded*
NSHWL unusual (adj) *rare*
  unusually (adv)
NSHWLNS unusualness
  rarity
NSHY nausea *sickness*
NSHYDR initiator *starter*
NSHYNS nescience
  ignorance
NSHYNT nescient *ignorant*
NSHYNTS nescience
  ignorance
NSHYSHN initiation *rite*
NSHYT initiate *(v) begin*
  initiated initiating
NSHYT initiate *(n) novice*
NSHYT nauseate *make sick*
  nauseated nauseating
NSHYTR initiator *starter*
NSHYTR initiatory *starting*
NSK gneissic *rock*
NSK insect *bug*
NSK kneesock *stocking*
NSK UNESCO *United
  Nations Educational,
  Scientific and Cultural
  Organization*
NSKDJLD unscheduled *not
  planned*
NSKDJWLD unscheduled
  not planned
NSKDK antipsychotic
  calming
NSKDLD unscheduled *not
  planned*
NSKDSD insecticide *kill
  bugs*
NSKDSDL insecticidal (adj)
  kill bugs insecticidally
  (adv)
NSKDVR insectivore *bug-
  eating*
NSKDWLD unscheduled
  not planned
NSKDYLD unscheduled *not
  planned*
NSKDYWLD unscheduled
  not planned
NSKJLD unscheduled *not
  planned*
NSKL unicycle *one wheel*
NSKLD unschooled *no*

education, *natural*
NSKLD unskilled *no ability*
NSKLFL unskillful (adj) *no
  ability* unskillfully (adv)
NSKLFLNS unskillfulness
  no ability
NSKLKL encyclical *papal
  letter*
NSKLPD encyclopedia
  reference books
NSKLPDK encyclopedic
  comprehensive
NSKLPDST encyclopedist
  writer
NSKLPDY encyclopedia
  reference books
NSKLPT encyclopedia
  reference books
NSKLPTK encyclopedic
  comprehensive
NSKLPTST encyclopedist
  writer
NSKLPTY encyclopedia
  reference books
NSKLST unicyclist *one wheel*
NSKLT inosculate *join*
  inosculated inosculating
NSKN aniseikonia *vision*
NSKNK aniseikonic *vision*
NSKNS ensconce *shelter,
  situate* ensconced
  ensconcing
NSKNTS ensconce *shelter,
  situate* ensconced
  ensconcing
NSKNY aniseikonia *vision*
NSKPBL inescapable (adj)
  sure to happen
  inescapably (adv)
NSKR insecure *fearful*
NSKR unscrew *open*
NSKRB inscribe *write*
  inscribed inscribing
NSKRBD inscribed *written*
NSKRBR inscriber *writer*
NSKRD insecurity *fear*
  insecurities
NSKRDBL inscrutable (adj)
  mysterious inscrutably
  (adv)
NSKRDBLD inscrutability
  mysterious

NSKRDBLT inscrutability
  mysterious
NSKRL insecurely *fearful*
NSKRMBL unscramble
  separate, restore
  unscrambled
  unscrambling
NSKRMBLR unscrambler
  separate, restore
NSKRN on-screen *film*
NSKRPDD unscripted
  spontaneous
NSKRPLS unscrupulous *no
  ethics*
NSKRPLSL unscrupulously
  no ethics
NSKRPLSNS
  unscrupulousness *no
  ethics*
NSKRPSHN inscription
  writing
NSKRPTD unscripted
  spontaneous
NSKRPYLS unscrupulous
  no ethics
NSKRPYLSL
  unscrupulously *no ethics*
NSKRPYLSNS
  unscrupulousness *no
  ethics*
NSKRT insecurity *fear*
  insecurities
NSKRTBL inscrutable (adj)
  mysterious inscrutably
  (adv)
NSKRTBLD inscrutability
  mysterious
NSKRTBLT inscrutability
  mysterious
NSKS unisex *one sex*
NSKS unsex *no gender*
NSKSHL unisexual *one sex*
NSKSHLD unisexuality *one
  sex*
NSKSHLT unisexuality *one
  sex*
NSKSHWL unisexual *one sex*
NSKSHWLD unisexuality
  one sex
NSKSHWLT unisexuality *one
  sex*
NSKSSFL unsuccessful

Use letters that best describe the sounds you hear and omit the vowels. Use **S** or **K** instead of **C**: to find circle use **SRKL**. Use **J** to find joy, **JM** to find gem and **G** to find go.

(adj) *failure*
unsuccessfully (adv)
NSKT insect *bug*
NSKT unasked *no question*
NSKTHD unscathed *not injured*
NSKTK antipsychotic *calming*
NSKTSD insecticide *kill bugs*
NSKTSDL insecticidal (adj) *kill bugs* insecticidally (adv)
NSKTVR insectivore *bug-eating*
NSKTVRS insectivorous *bug-eating*
NSKYLT inosculate *join* inosculated inosculating
NSKYR insecure *fearful*
NSKYRD insecurity *fear* insecurities
NSKYRL insecurely *fearful*
NSKYRT insecurity *fear* insecurities
NSL ancilla *aid* ancillae
NSL ensile *prepare fodder* ensiled ensiling
NSL ensoul *give soul*
NSL honestly *truthful*
NSL insole *shoe*
NSL nacelle *aircraft*
NSL nestle *cuddle* nestled nestling
NSL nicely *pleasantly*
NSL uncial *writing*
NSL unseal *open*
NSLBL insoluble *cannot dissolve or explain*
NSLBL unassailable (adj) *certain* unassailably (adv)
NSLBL unsalable *no sale*
NSLBLD insolubility *cannot dissolve or explain*
NSLBLT insolubility *cannot dissolve or explain*
NSLBRDD uncelebrated *unsung*
NSLBRS insalubrious *unwholesome*
NSLBRTD uncelebrated *unsung*

NSLBRYS insalubrious *unwholesome*
NSLD unsealed *open*
NSLD unsoiled *clean*
NSLD unsold *no sale*
NSLDD unsalted *no salt*
NSLDR insulator *protector*
NSLFKNCHS unself-conscious *natural*
NSLFKNSHS unself-conscious *natural*
NSLFSH unselfish *generous*
NSLFSHL unselfishly *generous*
NSLFSHNS unselfishness *generous*
NSLKBL unslakable *thirsty*
NSLKDD unselected *offhand*
NSLKTD unselected *offhand*
NSLLR unicellular *one cell*
NSLN insulin *hormone*
NSLN nestling *bird*
NSLNG nestling *bird*
NSLNG unsling *release*
NSLNS insolence *sassiness*
NSLNT insolent *impudent*
NSLNTS insolence *sassiness*
NSLR ancillary *extra*
NSLR insular *isolated*
NSLRD insularity *isolation*
NSLRT insularity *isolation*
NSLS nucellus *ovule*
NSLSDD unsolicited *not requested*
NSLSHN insolation *sunstroke, sunshine*
NSLSHN insulation *isolation, material*
NSLSTD unsolicited *not requested*
NSLT insulate *isolate* insulated insulating
NSLT insult *affront*
NSLT onslaught *onrush*
NSLTD unsalted *no salt*
NSLTR insulator *protector*
NSLV enslave *oppress* enslaved enslaving
NSLVBL insolvable *unexplained*
NSLVMNT enslavement *oppression*

NSLVNC insolvency *no money* insolvencies
NSLVNS insolvency *no money* insolvencies
NSLVNT insolvent *no money*
NSLVNTC insolvency *no money* insolvencies
NSLVNTS insolvency *no money* insolvencies
NSLVR antislavery *against bondage*
NSLVR enslaver *oppressor*
NSLYBL insoluble *cannot dissolve or explain*
NSLYBLD insolubility *cannot dissolve or explain*
NSLYBLT insolubility *cannot dissolve or explain*
NSLYLR unicellular *one cell*
NSM anosmia *not smelling*
NSM inseam *sewing*
NSM noisome *loud*
NSM unseam *separate*
NSMBL ensemble *group*
NSMBLD unassembled *in pieces*
NSMCH insomuch *in that*
NSMDK anti-Semitic *against Jews*
NSMDZM anti-Semitism *against Jews*
NSMKNG antismoking *against smoking*
NSML unseemly *inappropriate*
NSMLNS unseemliness *inappropriate*
NSMN insomnia *no sleep*
NSMN unassuming *humble*
NSMNDR inseminator *implant*
NSMNG unassuming *humble*
NSMNK insomniac *no sleep*
NSMNSHN insemination *implant*
NSMNT inseminate *implant* inseminated inseminating
NSMNTR inseminator *implant*
NSMNY insomnia *no sleep*
NSMNYK insomniac *no sleep*

Letters aren't doubled for single sounds: to find alley use **L** not **LL**. Use **Y** and **W** as hard sounds only: to find yellow use **YL**. (Br)=British spelling or usage. * See dictionary.

NSMPTHDK unsympathetic *unkind*

NSMPTHTK unsympathetic *unkind*

NSMT anti-Semite *against Jews*

NSMTK anti-Semitic *against Jews*

NSMTRK antisymmetric *equal*

NSMTRKL unsymmetrical (adj) *imbalanced* unsymmetrically (adv)

NSMTZM anti-Semitism *against Jews*

NSMY anosmia *not smelling*

NSN encaenia *ceremony*

NSN ensign *rank*

NSN insane *crazy*

NSN niacin *vitamin B*

NSN Nicene *church*

NSN unison *as one*

NSN unseen *invisible*

NSN unsound *faulty*

NSNC nascency *birth* nascencies

NSNCHL inessential *not necessary*

NSNCHL unessential *not necessary*

NSND insanity *craziness* insanities

NSND unsigned *no signature*

NSND unsound *faulty*

NSNDL unsoundly *faulty*

NSNDNS unsoundness *faulty*

NSNDR incendiary (n) *agitator* (adj) *fire* incendiaries

NSNDR insinuator *one who hints*

NSNDTS ins and outs *oddities, process*

NSNDYR incendiary (n) *agitator* (adj) *fire* incendiaries

NSNG unsung *no praise*

NSNGKBL unsinkable *floating*

NSNKBL unsinkable *floating*

NSNL nice-nelly *prudish*

NSNL unsoundly *faulty*

NSNMD niacinamide *vitamin B*

NSNP unsnap *unfasten* unsnapped unsnapping

NSNR ensnare *catch* ensnared ensnaring

NSNRDR incinerator *burning tool*

NSNRL ensnarl *tangle*

NSNRL unsnarl *disentangle*

NSNRSHN incineration *burn*

NSNRT incinerate *burn* incinerated incinerating

NSNRTR incinerator *burning tool*

NSNS incense (v) *perfume, arouse* incensed incensing

NSNS incense (n) *scent*

NSNS innocence *no guilt*

NSNS nascence *birth*

NSNS nascency *birth* nascencies

NSNS nescience *ignorance*

NSNS niceness *pleasant*

NSNS nuisance *bother*

NSNS unsoundness *faulty*

NSNSBL insensible (adj) *unconscious* insensibly (adv)

NSNSBLD insensibility *unconscious*

NSNSBLT insensibility *unconscious*

NSNSDV insensitive *no feeling*

NSNSHL inessential *not necessary*

NSNSHL unessential *not necessary*

NSNSHN insinuation *sly remark*

NSNSHNT insentient *unconscious*

NSNSHYNT insentient *unconscious*

NSNSR insincere *dishonest*

NSNSRD insincerity *dishonesty*

NSNSRT insincerity *dishonesty*

NSNST insensate *foolish*

NSNSTV insensitive *no feeling*

NSNSTVD insensitivity *no feeling*

NSNSTVT insensitivity *no feeling*

NSNT enceinte *pregnant*

NSNT innocent *not guilty*

NSNT insanity *craziness* insanities

NSNT insinuate *hint* insinuated insinuating

NSNT nascent *emerging*

NSNT nescient *ignorant*

NSNT nocent *harmful*

NSNTC nascency *birth* nascencies

NSNTD unscented *no aroma*

NSNTFK unscientific *no method*

NSNTFKL unscientifically *no method*

NSNTL innocently *not guilty*

NSNTN insinuating *hinting*

NSNTNG insinuating *hinting*

NSNTR insanitary *contaminated*

NSNTR insinuator *one who hints*

NSNTR unsanitary *dirty*

NSNTS incense (v) *perfume, arouse* incensed incensing

NSNTS incense (n) *scent*

NSNTS innocence *no guilt*

NSNTS ins and outs *oddities, process*

NSNTS nascence *birth*

NSNTS nascency *birth* nascencies

NSNTS nescience *ignorance*

NSNTS nuisance *bother*

NSNTSBL insensible (adj) *unconscious* insensibly (adv)

NSNTSBLD insensibility *unconscious*

NSNTSBLT insensibility *unconscious*

NSNTSDV insensitive *no feeling*

Use letters that best describe the sounds you hear and omit the vowels. Use **S** or **K** instead of **C**: to find circle use **SRKL**. Use **J** to find joy, **JM** to find gem and **G** to find go.

NSNTSHL unessential *not necessary*

NSNTSTV insensitive *no feeling*

NSNTSTVD insensitivity *no feeling*

NSNTSTVT insensitivity *no feeling*

NSNTV incentive *motive*

NSNV incentive *motive*

NSNWDR insinuator *one who hints*

NSNWSHN insinuation *sly remark*

NSNWT insinuate *hint* insinuated insinuating

NSNWTN insinuating *hinting*

NSNWTNG insinuating *hinting*

NSNWTR insinuator *one who hints*

NSNY encaenia *ceremony*

NSNYDR insinuator *one who hints*

NSNYSHN insinuation *sly remark*

NSNYT insinuate *hint* insinuated insinuating

NSNYTN insinuating *hinting*

NSNYTNG insinuating *hinting*

NSNYTR insinuator *one who hints*

NSNYWDR insinuator *one who hints*

NSNYWSHN insinuation *sly remark*

NSNYWT insinuate *hint* insinuated insinuating

NSNYWTN insinuating *hinting*

NSNYWTNG insinuating *hinting*

NSNYWTR insinuator *one who hints*

NSPD insipid *dull*

NSPDD insipidity *boring*

NSPDD unspotted *without blemish*

NSPDK antiseptic *kill germs*

NSPDT insipidity *boring*

NSPDV inceptive *origin*

NSPK inspect *examine*

NSPK newspeak *words*

NSPKBL unspeakable (adj) *no words* unspeakably (adv)

NSPKDR inspector *examiner*

NSPKN unspoken *silent*

NSPKSHN inspection *examination*

NSPKT inspect *examine*

NSPKTR inspector *examiner*

NSPLD unspoiled *pure*

NSPNS incipience *beginning* incipiency

NSPNT incipient *emerging*

NSPNTS incipience *beginning* incipiency

NSPR inspire *influence, breathe* inspired inspiring

NSPRBL inseparable (adj) *cannot divide* inseparably (adv)

NSPRBL insuperable (adj) *cannot overcome* insuperably (adv)

NSPRBLD inseparability *cannot divide*

NSPRBLT inseparability *cannot divide*

NSPRD inspired *outstanding*

NSPRDBL insupportable (adj) *cannot justify* insupportably (adv)

NSPRN inspiring *encouraging*

NSPRN unsparing *generous, ruthless*

NSPRNG inspiring *encouraging*

NSPRNG unsparing *generous, ruthless*

NSPRNG unsprung *no springs*

NSPRNGL unsparingly *generous, ruthless*

NSPRNL unsparingly *generous, ruthless*

NSPRR inspirer *influence, breathe*

NSPRSBL insuppressible *cannot hold back*

NSPRSHN inspiration *influence, breath*

NSPRSHNL inspirational (adj) *influence, breath* inspirationally (adv)

NSPRT inspirit *encourage*

NSPRTBL insupportable (adj) *cannot justify* insupportably (adv)

NSPRTR inspiratory *influence, breath*

NSPRTSMNLK unsportsmanlike *bad competitor*

NSPRZNG unsurprising *unexpected*

NSPRZNGL unsurprisingly *unexpected*

NSPSDR inspissator *thickener*

NSPSHN inception *origin*

NSPSHS inauspicious *unfavorable*

NSPSS antisepsis *kill germs*

NSPST inspissate *thicken* inspissated inspissating

NSPSTR inspissator *thickener*

NSPTD unspotted *without blemish*

NSPTK antiseptic *kill germs*

NSPTV inceptive *origin*

NSPYLD unspoiled *pure*

NSPYNS incipience *beginning* incipiency

NSPYNT incipient *emerging*

NSPYNTS incipience *beginning* incipiency

NSPYR inspire *influence, breathe* inspired inspiring

NSPYRD inspired *outstanding*

NSPYRN inspiring *encouraging*

NSPYRNG inspiring *encouraging*

NSPYRR inspirer *influence, breathe*

NSPZMDK antispasmodic *prevent spasms*

NSQLT inosculate *join* inosculated inosculating

Letters aren't doubled for single sounds: to find alley use **L** not **LL**. Use **Y** and **W** as hard sounds only: to find yellow use **YL**. (Br)=British spelling or usage. * See dictionary.

NSQR insecure *fearful*
NSQRD insecurity *fear* insecurities
NSQRL insecurely *fearful*
NSQRT insecurity *fear* insecurities
NSR answer *reply* answered answering
NSR naysayer *doubter*
NSR nicer *pleasant*
NSRBL answerable *responsible*
NSRDN uncertain *not sure*
NSRDND uncertainty *doubt* uncertainties
NSRDNT uncertainty *doubt* uncertainties
NSRDTD incertitude *uncertainty*
NSRDTYD incertitude *uncertainty*
NSRDV unassertive *modest*
NSRJNS insurgence *revolt* insurgency
NSRJNT insurgent *rebel*
NSRJNTS insurgence *revolt* insurgency
NSRKL encircle *surround* encircled encircling
NSRKLDD uncirculated *private*
NSRKLMNT encirclement *surround*
NSRKLTD uncirculated *private*
NSRKMSZD uncircumcised *foreskin*
NSRKSHN insurrection *rebellion*
NSRKYLDD uncirculated *private*
NSRKYLTD uncirculated *private*
NSRM antiserum *antibody* drug
NSRMNBL insurmountable (adj) *cannot overcome* insurmountably (adv)
NSRMNS unceremonious *informal*
NSRMNSL unceremoniously *informal*

NSRMNSNS unceremoniousness *informal*
NSRMNTBL insurmountable (adj) *cannot overcome* insurmountably (adv)
NSRMNYS unceremonious *informal*
NSRMNYSL unceremoniously *informal*
NSRMNYSNS unceremoniousness *informal*
NSRMTBL insurmountable (adj) *cannot overcome* insurmountably (adv)
NSRN anserine *goose*
NSRNG answering *responding*
NSRPRZNG unsurprising *unexpected*
NSRPRZNGL unsurprisingly *unexpected*
NSRQLDD uncirculated *private*
NSRQLTD uncirculated *private*
NSRR answerer *responder*
NSRSHN insertion *attachment*
NSRT insert (*v*) introduce (*n*) *attachment*
NSRTN uncertain *not sure*
NSRTND uncertainty *doubt* uncertainties
NSRTNT uncertainty *doubt* uncertainties
NSRTTD incertitude *uncertainty*
NSRTTYD incertitude *uncertainty*
NSRTV unassertive *modest*
NSRVS in-service *during work*
NSS enosis *union*
NSS gnosis *knowledge*
NSS nauseous *sick*
NSS nisus *endeavor* nisus
NSSBLD unsociability *unfriendly*
NSSCHS incestuous *sex*

NSSCHWS incestuous *sex*
NSSD necessity *requirement* necessities
NSSDD unassisted *no help*
NSSDR ancestor *forefather*
NSSDR ancestry *heritage*
NSSDRL ancestral (adj) *inherited* ancestrally (adv)
NSSDS necessitous *required*
NSSHBL insatiable (adj) *never satisfied* insatiably (adv)
NSSHBL unsociable (adj) *unfriendly* unsociably (adv)
NSSHBLD insatiability *no satisfaction*
NSSHBLD unsociability *unfriendly*
NSSHBLNS unsociableness *unfriendly*
NSSHBLT insatiability *no satisfaction*
NSSHBLT unsociability *unfriendly*
NSSHL antisocial (adj) *hostile* antisocially (adv)
NSSHN incision *cut*
NSSHNS insouciance *unconcern*
NSSHNTS insouciance *unconcern*
NSSHT insatiate *never satisfied*
NSSHYT insatiate *never satisfied*
NSSN unceasing *continuous*
NSSNG unceasing *continuous*
NSSNS insouciance *unconcern*
NSSNT incessant *constant*
NSSNT insouciant *casual*
NSSNTL incessantly *constant*
NSSNTS insouciance *unconcern*
NSSPDBL insusceptible (adj) *not liable* insusceptibly (adv)
NSSPDBLD insusceptibility *not liable*

Use letters that best describe the sounds you hear and omit the vowels. Use **S** or **K** instead of **C**: to find circle use **SRKL**. Use **J** to find joy, **JM** to find gem and **G** to find go.

NSSPDBLT insusceptibility *not liable*

NSSPKDNG unsuspecting *trusting*

NSSPKTN unsuspecting *trusting*

NSSPKTNG unsuspecting *trusting*

NSSPTBL insusceptible (adj) *not liable* insusceptibly (adv)

NSSPTBLD insusceptibility *not liable*

NSSPTBLT insusceptibility *not liable*

NSSR antecessor *ancestor*

NSSR necessary *required*

NSSR unnecessary *not needed*

NSSRL necessarily *unavoidably*

NSSRL unnecessarily *not needed*

NSST encyst *enclose*

NSST incest *sex*

NSST insist *demand*

NSST necessity *requirement* necessities

NSST nicest *pleasant*

NSSTD unassisted *no help*

NSSTMNT encystment *sac*

NSSTNS insistence *urgency* insistency

NSSTNT insistent *urgent*

NSSTNTS insistence *urgency* insistency

NSSTR ancestor *forefather*

NSSTR ancestry *heritage*

NSSTRL ancestral (adj) *inherited* ancestrally (adv)

NSSTS incestuous *sex*

NSSTS necessitous *required*

NSSTSHN necessitation *requirement*

NSSTT necessitate *require* necessitated necessitating

NSSTWS incestuous *sex*

NSSTYS incestuous *sex*

NSSTYWS incestuous *sex*

NSSV incisive *direct*

NSSYBLD unsociability

unfriendly

NSSYNS insouciance *unconcern*

NSSYNT insouciant *casual*

NSSYNTS insouciance *unconcern*

NST anisette *liqueur*

NST honest *truthful*

NST honesty *truth*

NST incite *arouse* incited inciting

NST inset (v) *place inside* inset (or) insetted insetting

NST inset (n) *channel, map*

NST insight *understanding*

NST ionicity *atoms*

NST nasty *mean, obscene* nastier nastiest

NST nauseate *make sick* nauseated nauseating

NST nest (n) *home, group* (v) *settle in, group*

NST nicety *pleasantry* niceties

NST on-site *local*

NST onset *beginning, attack*

NST unasked *no question*

NST unseat *remove*

NST unsought *not searched for*

NST unused *new*

NSTBL unstable (adj) *not steady* unstably (adv)

NSTBL unsuitable (adj) *improper* unsuitably (adv)

NSTBLD instability *not steady* instabilities

NSTBLD unsuitability *improper*

NSTBLNS unstableness *not steady*

NSTBLSHMNT antiestablishment *against rulers*

NSTBLT instability *not steady* instabilities

NSTBLT unsuitability *improper*

NSTD instead *in place of*

NSTD unseeded *not sown, not ranked*

NSTD unsteady *wavering*

NSTD unsuited *improper*

NSTDD unstated *silent*

NSTDD unstudied *unplanned*

NSTDL unsteadily *wavering*

NSTDN nystatin *antibiotic*

NSTDNS unsteadiness *wavering*

NSTDV instead of *in place of*

NSTFL insightful (adj) *understanding* insightfully (adv)

NSTG nest egg *savings*

NSTGDR instigator *provoke*

NSTGMDK anastigmatic *lens*

NSTGMK nystagmic *eye movement*

NSTGMN neostigmine *drug*

NSTGMS nystagmus *eye movement*

NSTGMTK anastigmatic *lens*

NSTGSHN instigation *provoke*

NSTGT instigate *provoke* instigated instigating

NSTGTR instigator *provoke*

NSTHDK anesthetic *painkiller* (Br) anaesthetic

NSTHDKL anesthetically *painkiller* (Br) anaesthetic

NSTHSH anesthesia *painkiller* (Br) anaesthesia

NSTHTK anesthetic *painkiller* (Br) anaesthetic

NSTHTKL anesthetically *painkiller* (Br) anaesthetic

NSTHTST anesthetist *painkiller*

NSTHTZ anesthetize *kill pain* anesthetized anesthetizing

NSTHZ anesthesia *painkiller* (Br) anaesthesia

NSTHZH anesthesia

Letters aren't doubled for single sounds: to find alley use **L** not **LL**. Use **Y** and **W** as hard sounds only: to find yellow use **YL**. (Br)=British spelling or usage. * See dictionary.

painkiller
(Br) anaesthesia

NSTHZLJST
anesthesiologist *painkiller*
(Br) anaesthesia

NSTHZY anesthesia
painkiller
(Br) anaesthesia

NSTHZYLJST
anesthesiologist *painkiller*
(Br) anaesthesia

NSTK gnostic *believer*

NSTK nostoc *algae*

NSTK unstick *release*
unstuck unsticking

NSTK unstuck *disarray*

NSTL honestly *truthful*

NSTL install *set up*

NSTL instill *put in*

NSTL nastily *mean, indecent*

NSTL unsaddle *horse*

NSTL unsettle *disturb*
unsettled unsettling

NSTL unsightly *ugly*

NSTL unsubtle (adj) *bold*
unsubtly (adv)

NSTLD unsettled *disturbed*

NSTLG nostalgia *yearning*

NSTLGY nostalgia *yearning*

NSTLJ nostalgia *yearning*

NSTLJK nostalgic *yearning*

NSTLJY nostalgia *yearning*

NSTLMNT installment *set
up, part*

NSTLMNT unsettlement
disturbance

NSTLMNTPLN installment
plan *payment*

NSTLNG nestling *bird*

NSTLNS unsightliness *ugly*

NSTLR installer *set up*

NSTLSHN installation *set up*

NSTMBL inestimable (adj)
valuable inestimably (adv)

NSTMNT incitement *arousal*

NSTN Einstein *physicist*

NSTN neuston *organism*

NSTN newsstand *market*

NSTND newsstand *market*

NSTNGDV instinctive
automatic

NSTNGK instinct *response*

NSTNGKDV instinctive
automatic

NSTNGKT instinct *response*

NSTNGKTV instinctive
automatic

NSTNGT instinct *response*

NSTNGTV instinctive
automatic

NSTNK instinct *response*

NSTNKDV instinctive
automatic

NSTNKT instinct *response*

NSTNKTV instinctive
automatic

NSTNS instance *example*

NSTNS nastiness *meanness,
indecency*

NSTNSHT instantiate
represent

NSTNSHYT instantiate
represent

NSTNT instant *moment*

NSTNTL instantly *without
delay*

NSTNTNG unstinting
generous

NSTNTNS instantaneous
momentary

NSTNTNYS instantaneous
momentary

NSTNTS instance *example*

NSTP instep *foot*

NSTP unstep *remove*
unstepped unstepping

NSTP unstop *open*
unstopped unstopping

NSTPBL unstoppable (adj)
relentless unstoppably
(adv)

NSTR inciter *urge, assist*

NSTR nester *squatter*

NSTRDD unsaturated *not
absorbed*

NSTRF anastrophe *word
inversion*

NSTRK instruct *teach*

NSTRKCHRD unstructured
not organized

NSTRKDR instructor *teacher*

NSTRKDV instructive
teaching

NSTRKSHN instruction

teaching

NSTRKSHNL instructional
teaching

NSTRKSHRD unstructured
not organized

NSTRKT instruct *teach*

NSTRKTR instructor *teacher*

NSTRKTRD unstructured
not organized

NSTRKTV instructive
teaching

NSTRL nostril *nose*

NSTRM nostrum *remedy*

NSTRMNL instrumental
(adj) *helpful, music*
instrumentally (adv)

NSTRMNLST
instrumentalist *musician*

NSTRMNT instrument *tool*

NSTRMNTL instrumental
(adj) *helpful, music*
instrumentally (adv)

NSTRMNTLD
instrumentality *means*
instrumentalities

NSTRMNTLST
instrumentalist *musician*

NSTRMNTLT
instrumentality *means*
instrumentalities

NSTRMNTSHN
instrumentation *music,
tools*

NSTRNG unstring *loosen*
unstrung unstringing

NSTRP unstrap *loosen*
unstrapped unstrapping

NSTRS anestrus (n) *without
sex* anestrous (adj)

NSTRSHM nasturtium
flower

NSTRST unstressed *no
tension, no emphasis*

NSTRTD unsaturated *not
absorbed*

NSTSFKDR unsatisfactory
unacceptable

NSTSFKDRL
unsatisfactorily
unacceptable

NSTSFKDRNS
unsatisfactoriness

Use letters that best describe the sounds you hear and omit the vowels. Use **S** or **K**
instead of **C**: to find circle use **SRKL**. Use **J** to find joy, **JM** to find gem and **G** to find go.

unacceptable
NSTSFKTR unsatisfactory
unacceptable
NSTSFKTRL
unsatisfactorily
unacceptable
NSTSFKTRNS
unsatisfactoriness
unacceptable
NSTSZM gnosticism *belief*
NSTT antistat *electricity*
NSTT instate *bestow, install*
instated instating
NSTTD unstated *silent*
NSTTDR instituter (or)
institutor *organizer*
NSTTN nystatin *antibiotic*
NSTTSHN institution
organization
NSTTSHNL institutional
(adj) *organization*
institutionally (adv)
NSTTSHNLZ institutionalize
incorporate, commit
institutionalized
institutionalizing
(Br) institutionalise
NSTTT institute *organize*
instituted instituting
NSTTT institute *organization*
NSTTTR instituter (or)
institutor *organizer*
NSTTYDR instituter (or)
institutor *organizer*
NSTTYSHN institution
organization
NSTTYSHNL institutional
(adj) *organization*
institutionally (adv)
NSTTYSHNLZ
institutionalize
incorporate, commit
institutionalized
institutionalizing
(Br) institutionalise
NSTTYT institute *organize*
instituted instituting
NSTTYT institute
organization
NSTTYTR instituter (or)
institutor *organizer*
NSVBL insolvable

unexplained
NSVD unsaved *no
redemption*
NSVL uncivil (adj) *rude*
uncivilly (adv)
NSVLD incivility *rudeness*
NSVLT incivility *rudeness*
NSVLZD uncivilized *wild*
(Br) uncivilised
NSVNC insolvency *no money*
insolvencies
NSVNS insolvency *no money*
insolvencies
NSVNT insolvent *no money*
NSVNTC insolvency *no
money* insolvencies
NSVNTS insolvency *no
money* insolvencies
NSVR unsavory *distasteful*
NSWRVNG unswerving
steady
NSWT en suite *connected
room*
NSWTND unsweetened *no
sugar*
NSX unisex *one sex*
NSX unsex *no gender*
NSY ensue *follow* ensued
ensuing
NSYBL insoluble *cannot
dissolve or explain*
NSYBLD insolubility *cannot
dissolve or explain*
NSYBLT insolubility *cannot
dissolve or explain*
NSYL uncial *writing*
NSYLD unsoiled *clean*
NSYLDR insulator *protector*
NSYLR insular *isolated*
NSYLR unicellular *one cell*
NSYLRD insularity *isolation*
NSYLRT insularity *isolation*
NSYLSHN insulation
isolation, material
NSYLT insulate *isolate*
insulated insulating
NSYLTR insulator *protector*
NSYNS nescience *ignorance*
NSYNT enceinte *pregnant*
NSYNT nescient *ignorant*
NSYNTFK unscientific *no
method*

NSYNTFKL unscientifically
no method
NSYNTS nescience
ignorance
NSYPRBL insuperable (adj)
cannot overcome
insuperably (adv)
NSYR naysayer *doubter*
NSYS nauseous *sick*
NSYT nauseate *make sick*
nauseated nauseating
NSZ Anasazi *Native
American* Anasazi
NSZ incise *carve* incised
incising
NSZD incised *carve*
NSZHN incision *cut*
NSZN unceasing *continuous*
NSZNBL unseasonable (adj)
bad timing unseasonably
(adv)
NSZND unseasoned
inexperienced
NSZNG unceasing
continuous
NSZR incisor *tooth*
NT ain't *(slang-contr) am not,
are not, is not**
NT annato *dye*
NT annuity *yearly money*
annuities
NT ant *crawling insect*
NT anta *wall* antas (or)
antae
NT ante *money* anted
anteing
NT anti *opposed*
NT aunt *relative*
NT endnote *postscript*
NT entity *being* entities
NT gnat *flying insect*
NT gnatty *with gnats*
NT innate *inborn*
NT into *(prep) within, against*
NT knight *feudal rank*
NT knit *weave* knit (or)
knitted knitting
NT knot *tangle* knotted
knotting
NT knotty *tangled* knottier
knottiest
NT knout *whip*

Letters aren't doubled for single sounds: to find alley use **L** not **LL**. Use **Y** and **W** as hard sounds only: to find yellow use **YL**. (Br)=British spelling or usage. * See dictionary.

NT NATO *(abbr) North Atlantic Treaty Organization*

NT natty *neat* nattier nattiest

NT naught *nothing*

NT naughty *wicked* naughtier naughtiest

NT neat *orderly, clean*

NT net *(v) enmesh, yield* netted netting

NT net *(n) mesh, profit (adj) basic*

NT newt *salamander*

NT nidi (pl) *nest* nidus

NT night *after dark*

NT nightie (or) nighty *garment* nighties

NT ninety *number (90)* nineties

NT nit *insect egg*

NT noddy *oaf, bird*

NT not *negative*

NT nota (pl) *thorax* notum

NT note *(v) notice, remark* noted noting

NT note *(n) sound, memo, notice**

NT nut *(v) seek food* nutted nutting

NT nut *(n) food, screw, lump**

NT nutty *like nuts, silly* nuttier nuttiest

NT onto *upon*

NT unit *one, group, quantity**

NT unite *join* united uniting

NT unity *oneness* unities

NT unknit *unravel* unknitted unknitting

NT untie *loosen* untied untying (or) untieing

NT unto *toward*

NTBD antibody *immunity* antibodies

NTBDK antibiotic *drug*

NTBDK antibiotic *medicine*

NTBK antitobacco *against smoking*

NTBK notebook *writing*

NTBKTRL antibacterial *combating germs*

NTBKTRYL antibacterial *combating germs*

NTBL notable *(adj) remarkable* notably *(adv)*

NTBLCHR entablature *column*

NTBLD notability *importance*

NTBLDNS night blindness *vision*

NTBLM antebellum *before war*

NTBLMNG night-blooming *flower after dark*

NTBLNS night blindness *vision*

NTBLSDK antiballistic *intercepting*

NTBLSTK antiballistic *intercepting*

NTBLT notability *importance*

NTBLTR entablature *column*

NTBN nota bene *mark*

NTBRN nut-brown *color*

NTBRSHN antiabortion *against pregnancy termination*

NTBSHN intubation *insert tube*

NTBSNG antibusing *against school busing*

NTBTK antibiotic *drug*

NTBTK antibiotic *medicine*

NTBYDK antibiotic *drug*

NTBYTK antibiotic *drug*

NTC antsy *nervous*

NTCD antecede *precede* anteceded anteceding

NTCDNS antecedence *priority*

NTCDNT antecedent *prior*

NTCDNTS antecedence *priority*

NTCHBL untouchable *beyond reach, caste*

NTCHD unattached *free*

NTCHMBR antechamber *lobby*

NTCHNT ancient *old*

NTCHNTL anciently *long ago*

NTCHT unattached *free*

NTCHT untouched *ignored*

NTCL uncial *writing*

NTCRM antiserum *antibody*

drug

NTCYL uncial *writing*

NTD in toto *entirely*

NTD knotted *tangled*

NTD nitid *bright*

NTD noted *well known*

NTD united *combined*

NTD unneeded *not required*

NTD untidy *messy*

NTDKNGDM United Kingdom *country*

NTDL entitle *authorize* entitled entitling

NTDL untidily *messily*

NTDLD untitled *no name*

NTDLMNT entitlement *authorization*

NTDLVN antediluvian *before flood*

NTDLVYN antediluvian *before flood*

NTDMKRDK antidemocratic *against democracy*

NTDMKRTK antidemocratic *against democracy*

NTDNS untidiness *mess*

NTDNSHNZ United Nations *international group*

NTDPRSNT antidepressant *drug*

NTDR annotator *commentator*

NTDR anteater *animal*

NTDRD untutored *no school*

NTDRG antidrug *no drugs*

NTDRS nightdress *garment*

NTDSTTS United States *country*

NTDT antedate *precede*

NTDT antidote *counteract poison*

NTDV annotative *noted*

NTDV intuitive *insightful*

NTDVL intuitively *insightful*

NTDVNS intuitiveness *insight*

NTDZ anti-AIDS *serum*

NTF notify *inform* notified notifying notifies

NTFBL notifiable *inform*

NTFGS nidifugous *nest*

NTFKSHN nidification *nest*

NTFKSHN notification *message*

NTFL nightfall *dark*

NTFN antiphony *alternate singing* antiphonies

NTFNGGL antifungal *fungus prevention*

NTFNGL antifungal *fungus prevention*

NTFNL antiphonal *alternate singing*

NTFRPRFT not-for-profit *charity*

NTFRZ antifreeze *water additive*

NTFSHST antifascist *against fascism*

NTFYBL notifiable *inform*

NTG Antigua *island*

NTGL intaglio *carving* intaglios

NTGL nutgall *swelling*

NTGLY intaglio *carving* intaglios

NTGMNT integument *cover*

NTGN nightgown *garment*

NTGNSDK antagonistic *adversarial*

NTGNSDKL antagonistically *adversarial*

NTGNSM antagonism *adversarial*

NTGNST antagonist *adversary*

NTGNSTK antagonistic *adversarial*

NTGNSTKL antagonistically *adversarial*

NTGNZ antagonize *provoke* antagonized antagonizing

NTGNZM antagonism *enmity*

NTGNZM antagonism *adversarial*

NTGRBL integrable *combine*

NTGRD integrity *honor*

NTGRD nitty-gritty *basics*

NTGRDD integrated *combined*

NTGRDR integrator

combiner

NTGRL integral (adj) *essential* integrally (adv)

NTGRSHN integration *combination*

NTGRT integrate *combine* integrated integrating

NTGRT integrity *honor*

NTGRT nitty-gritty *basics*

NTGRTD integrated *combined*

NTGRTR integrator *combiner*

NTGRVD antigravity *weightless*

NTGRVT antigravity *weightless*

NTGVRMNT antigovernment *against rulers*

NTGVRNMNT antigovernment *against rulers*

NTGW Antigua *island*

NTGYMNT integument *cover*

NTH nth *utmost*

NTHCH nuthatch *bird*

NTHD aunthood *relative*

NTHD knighthood *honor*

NTHDKL antithetical (adj) *contrasting* antithetically (adv)

NTHDV unthought-of *unexpected*

NTHFLT anthophyllite *mineral*

NTHJB on-the-job *training*

NTHK gnathic (or) gnathal *jaw*

NTHK nighthawk *bird*

NTHKL unethical *not moral*

NTHL anthill *mound*

NTHL gnathal (or) gnathic *jaw*

NTHL knothole *wood*

NTHLG anthology *collection* anthologies

NTHLJ anthology *collection* anthologies

NTHLJKL anthological *collection*

NTHLJST anthologist

collector

NTHLJZ anthologize *collect* anthologized anthologizing

NTHLJZR anthologizer *collector*

NTHM anathema *curse*

NTHM anthem *song*

NTHMTZ anathematize *curse* anathematized anathematizing

NTHN anything *any*

NTHN nothing *none*

NTHNG anything *any*

NTHNG nothing *none*

NTHNGKBL unthinkable *improbable*

NTHNGKN unthinking *heedless*

NTHNGKNG unthinking *heedless*

NTHNGNS nothingness *emptiness*

NTHNK inauthentic *not genuine*

NTHNKBL unthinkable *improbable*

NTHNKN unthinking *heedless*

NTHNKNG unthinking *heedless*

NTHNS nothingness *emptiness*

NTHNTK inauthentic *not genuine*

NTHNTSD inauthenticity *not genuine*

NTHNTST inauthenticity *not genuine*

NTHR another *not this*

NTHR anther *flower part*

NTHR antihero *betrayer*

NTHR neither *not either*

NTHR nether *lower*

NTHRCN anthracene *coal tar*

NTHRD antiauthority *rebellious*

NTHRD antithyroid *gland*

NTHRDM antheridium *flower part*

NTHRDYM antheridium *flower part*

NTHRKS anthrax *disease*

NTHRL antheral *flower part*

NTHRL enthrall (or) enthral *delight* enthralled enthralling

NTHRLMNT enthrallment *delight*

NTHRLNDS Netherlands (the) *country*

NTHRLNDZ Netherlands (the) *country*

NTHRLNS Netherlands (the) *country*

NTHRLNZ Netherlands (the) *country*

NTHRM anthurium *plant*

NTHRMST nethermost *lowest*

NTHRN enthrone *elevate* enthroned enthroning

NTHRNMNT enthronement *elevation*

NTHRPD anthropoid *ape*

NTHRPFG anthropophagi (pl) *(n)* cannibal anthropophagus

NTHRPFG anthropophagy *cannibalism*

NTHRPFGS anthropophagous *(adj)* man-eating

NTHRPFGS anthropophagus *(n)* cannibal anthropophagi

NTHRPFJ anthropophagi (pl) *(n)* cannibal anthropophagus

NTHRPFJ anthropophagy *cannibalism*

NTHRPJNK anthropogenic *human influence*

NTHRPK anthropic (or) anthropical *human*

NTHRPKL anthropical (or) anthropic *human*

NTHRPLG anthropology *science of humans*

NTHRPLJ anthropology *science of humans*

NTHRPLJKL anthropological (adj) *science of humans*

anthropologically (adv)

NTHRPLJST anthropologist *scientist*

NTHRPMRF anthropomorph *human figure*

NTHRPMRFK anthropomorphic *like a human*

NTHRPMRFKL anthropomorphically *like a human*

NTHRPMRFST anthropomorphist *humanizer*

NTHRPMRFZ anthropomorphize *humanization* anthropomorphized anthropomorphizing

NTHRPMRFZM anthropomorphism *humanization*

NTHRPMRFZSHN anthropomorphization *humanization*

NTHRPPTHSM anthropopathism *humanization*

NTHRPPTHZM anthropopathism *humanization*

NTHRPSNTRK anthropocentric *human-centered*

NTHRPSNTRKL anthropocentrically *human-centered*

NTHRPSNTRSM anthropocentrism *human-centered*

NTHRPSNTRST anthropocentricity *human-centered*

NTHRPSNTRZM anthropocentrism *human-centered*

NTHRSDK anthracitic *hard coal*

NTHRSN anthracene *coal tar*

NTHRST anthracite *hard*

coal

NTHRSTK anthracitic *hard coal*

NTHRT antiauthority *rebellious*

NTHRWRLD netherworld *underworld*

NTHRX anthrax *disease*

NTHRYM anthurium *plant*

NTHRZD unauthorized *no approval* (Br) unauthorised

NTHS enthuse *show passion* enthused enthusing

NTHS nuthouse *asylum*

NTHSDMN antihistamine *allergy drug*

NTHSS anthesis *opening*

NTHSTMN antihistamine *allergy drug*

NTHTKL antithetical (adj) *contrasting* antithetically (adv)

NTHTV unthought-of *unexpected*

NTHYS enthuse *show passion* enthused enthusing

NTHYZ enthuse *show passion* enthused enthusing

NTHYZSDK enthusiastic *passionate*

NTHYZSDKL enthusiastically *passionately*

NTHYZSM enthusiasm *passion*

NTHYZST enthusiast *passionate one*

NTHYZSTK enthusiastic *passionate*

NTHYZSTKL enthusiastically *passionately*

NTHYZYSDK enthusiastic *passionate*

NTHYZYSDKL enthusiastically *passionately*

NTHYZYSM enthusiasm *passion*

Use letters that best describe the sounds you hear and omit the vowels. Use **S** or **K** instead of **C**: to find circle use **SRKL**. Use **J** to find joy, **JM** to find gem and **G** to find go.

NTHYZYST enthusiast *passionate one*

NTHYZYSTK enthusiastic *passionate*

NTHYZYSTKL enthusiastically *passionately*

NTHYZYZM enthusiasm *passion*

NTHYZZM enthusiasm *passion*

NTHZ enthuse *show passion* enthused enthusing

NTHZN anthozoan *animal*

NTHZSDK enthusiastic *passionate*

NTHZSDKL enthusiastically *passionately*

NTHZSM enthusiasm *passion*

NTHZST enthusiast *passionate one*

NTHZSTK enthusiastic *passionate*

NTHZSTKL enthusiastically *passionately*

NTHZWN anthozoan *animal*

NTHZYSDK enthusiastic *passionate*

NTHZYSDKL enthusiastically *passionately*

NTHZYSM enthusiasm *passion*

NTHZYST enthusiast *passionate one*

NTHZYSTK enthusiastic *passionate*

NTHZYSTKL enthusiastically *passionately*

NTHZYZM enthusiasm *passion*

NTHZZM enthusiasm *passion*

NTJN antigen *enzyme*

NTJN ontogeny *development*

NTJNDK ontogenetic *development*

NTJNDKL ontogenetically *development*

NTJNSS ontogenesis

development

NTJNTK ontogenetic *development*

NTJNTKL ontogenetically *development*

NTJR integer *number*

NTJR nightjar *bird*

NTK anodic *electrode*

NTK antic *caper*

NTK Antioch *city*

NTK antique *old* antiqued antiquing

NTK intact *whole*

NTK intake *flow into*

NTK nighthawk *bird*

NTK noetic *intellect*

NTKDMK antiacademic *against schooling*

NTKGLNT anticoagulant *blood thinner*

NTKGYLNT anticoagulant *blood thinner*

NTKL anodically *electrode*

NTKL nautical (adj) *ship* nautically (adv)

NTKLB nightclub *entertainment*

NTKLBR nightclubber *entertainment*

NTKLMDK anticlimactic *not important*

NTKLMKDK anticlimactic *not important*

NTKLMKS anticlimax *not important*

NTKLMKTK anticlimactic *not important*

NTKLML nautical mile *distance*

NTKLMTK anticlimactic *not important*

NTKLMX anticlimax *not important*

NTKLS nidicolous *nest*

NTKMNST anticommunist *against communism*

NTKMPDDV anticompetitive *against competition*

NTKMPDTV anticompetitive *against competition*

NTKMPTDV anticompetitive

against competition

NTKMPTTV anticompetitive *against competition*

NTKMYNST anticommunist *against communism*

NTKNVLSNT anticonvulsant *prevents convulsions*

NTKP nightcap *hat, drink, contest*

NTKRD notochord *spine*

NTKRDL notochordal *spine*

NTKRKR nutcracker *implement*

NTKRLR night crawler *worm*

NTKRM anticrime *crime preventing*

NTKRST Antichrist *false messiah*

NTKS nutcase *crazy one*

NTKSDNT antioxidant *chemical*

NTKSK antitoxic *neutralize poison*

NTKSKDD intoxicated *drunk*

NTKSKNT intoxicant *alcohol, drug*

NTKSKSHN intoxication *drunkenness*

NTKSKT intoxicate *stupefy, elate* intoxicated intoxicating

NTKSKTD intoxicated *drunk*

NTKSN antitoxin *neutralize poison*

NTKT intact *whole*

NTKWD antiquity *ancient times, relic* antiquities

NTKWDD antiquated *old*

NTKWGLNT anticoagulant *blood thinner*

NTKWGYLNT anticoagulant *blood thinner*

NTKWR antiquary *old items* antiquaries ·

NTKWRN antiquarian *collector of old items*

NTKWRYN antiquarian *collector of old items*

NTKWT antiquate *make old*

Letters aren't doubled for single sounds: to find alley use **L** not **LL**. Use **Y** and **W** as hard sounds only: to find yellow use **YL**. (Br)=British spelling or usage. * See dictionary.

antiquated antiquating

NTKWT antiquity *ancient times, relic* antiquities

NTKWTD antiquated *old*

NTL entail *involve, restrict*

NTL intaglio *carving* intaglios

NTL inutile *useless*

NTL knightly *of knights*

NTL knothole *wood*

NTL know-it-all *smart one*

NTL natal *birth*

NTL nattily *neatly*

NTL naughtily *wickedly*

NTL nautili (pl) *animal* nautilus

NTL needle *(v) tease, sew* needled needling

NTL needle *(n) sewing tool, stylus*

NTL nettle *(v) irritate, sting* nettled nettling

NTL nettle *(n) plant*

NTL night owl *late hours*

NTL nightly *every night*

NTL noddle *head*

NTL noodle *(n) food, head*

NTL noodle *(v) improvise* noodled noodling

NTL nuttily *like nuts, silly*

NTL until *before*

NTL untold *unspoken*

NTLBR antilabor *against unions* (Br) antilabour

NTLCH night latch *lock*

NTLD natality *birthrate*

NTLD nautiloid *animal*

NTLD untold *unspoken*

NTLF antilife *antagonistic*

NTLF nightlife *activity*

NTLG ontology *existence*

NTLJ ontology *existence*

NTLJBL intelligible (adj) *understandable* intelligibly (adv)

NTLJBLD intelligibility *understand*

NTLJBLT intelligibility *understand*

NTLJKL ontological (adj) *existence* ontologically

(adv)

NTLJNS intelligence *mental ability*

NTLJNS intelligentsia *educated ones*

NTLJNSY intelligentsia *educated ones*

NTLJNT intelligent *clever, rational*

NTLJNTS intelligence *mental ability*

NTLJNTS intelligentsia *educated ones*

NTLJNTSY intelligentsia *educated ones*

NTLJST ontologist *existence*

NTLK antilock *brakes*

NTLK entelechy *cause* entelechies

NTLK intellect *wisdom*

NTLK nutlike *small and hard*

NTLKCHL intellectual (adj) *reasoning (n) thinker* intellectually (adv)

NTLKCHLZ intellectualize *think* intellectualized intellectualizing

NTLKCHLZR intellectualizer *thinker*

NTLKCHWL intellectual (adj) *reasoning (n) thinker* intellectually (adv)

NTLKCHWLZ intellectualize *think* intellectualized intellectualizing

NTLKCHWLZR intellectualizer *thinker*

NTLKSHL intellectual (adj) *reasoning (n) thinker* intellectually (adv)

NTLKSHLZ intellectualize *think* intellectualized intellectualizing

NTLKSHLZR intellectualizer *thinker*

NTLKSHN intellection *thought*

NTLKSHWL intellectual (adj) *reasoning (n) thinker* intellectually (adv)

NTLKSHWLZ intellectualize *think* intellectualized

intellectualizing

NTLKSHWLZR intellectualizer *thinker*

NTLKT intellect *wisdom*

NTLKTL intellectual (adj) *reasoning (n) thinker* intellectually (adv)

NTLKTLZ intellectualize *think* intellectualized intellectualizing

NTLKTLZR intellectualizer *thinker*

NTLKTWL intellectual (adj) *reasoning (n) thinker* intellectually (adv)

NTLKTWLZ intellectualize *think* intellectualized intellectualizing

NTLKTWLZR intellectualizer *thinker*

NTLMNT entailment *involvement, restriction*

NTLN ant lion *flying insect*

NTLNG nightlong *all night*

NTLP antelope *animal* antelope (or) antelopes

NTLPNT needlepoint *embroidery*

NTLR antler *head projection*

NTLR entailer *involve, restrict*

NTLR needler *tease, sew*

NTLRBL intolerable (adj) *unbearable* intolerably (adv)

NTLRJNK antiallergenic *not allergy promoting*

NTLRNS intolerance *sensitivity, prejudice*

NTLRNT intolerant *sensitive, prejudiced*

NTLRNTL intolerantly *sensitive, prejudiced*

NTLRNTS intolerance *sensitivity, prejudice*

NTLS nautilus *animal* nautiluses (or) nautili

NTLSM nettlesome *irritating*

NTLT natality *birthrate*

NTLT night-light *illumination*

NTLT nutlet *small nut*

Use letters that best describe the sounds you hear and omit the vowels. Use **S** or **K** instead of **C**: to find circle use **SRKL**. Use **J** to find joy, **JM** to find gem and **G** to find go.

NTLWRK needlework *sewing*

NTLY intaglio *carving* intaglios

NTLYN ant lion *flying insect*

NTM anatomy *analysis, structure* anatomies

NTM anytime *no special time*

NTM entomb *bury*

NTM nighttime *after dark*

NTM notum *thorax* nota

NTMC intimacy *private* intimacies

NTMD untamed *wild*

NTMDDR intimidator *bully*

NTMDR antimatter *physics*

NTMDRN antimodern *against newness*

NTMDSHN intimidation *bullying*

NTMDT intimidate *bully* intimidated intimidating

NTMDTR intimidator *bully*

NTMG nutmeg *spice*

NTMGNDK antimagnetic *no attraction*

NTMGNTK antimagnetic *no attraction*

NTMK anatomic (or) anatomical (adj) *body structure* anatomically (adv)

NTMKL anatomical (or) anatomic (adj) *body structure* anatomically (adv)

NTMKRBL antimicrobial *germs*

NTMKRBYL antimicrobial *germs*

NTMKSR antimacassar *cover*

NTML untimely *premature*

NTMLG entomology *insects*

NTMLJ entomology *insects*

NTMLJKL entomological (adj) *insects* entomologically (adv)

NTMLJST entomologist *insects*

NTMLNS untimeliness *premature*

NTMLTR antimilitary *against weaponry*

NTMN antimony *element*

NTMNL antimonial *element*

NTMNRKST antimonarchist *against royalty*

NTMNT entombment *burial*

NTMNT ointment *salve*

NTMNYL antimonial *element*

NTMPRNS intemperance *alcohol*

NTMPRNTS intemperance *alcohol*

NTMPRT intemperate *alcohol*

NTMR nightmare *bad dream*

NTMRDM ante meridiem *before noon*

NTMRDN ante meridiem *before noon*

NTMRDYM ante meridiem *before noon*

NTMRDYN ante meridiem *before noon*

NTMRSH nightmarish *frightening*

NTMRSHL nightmarishly *frightening*

NTMS intimacy *private* intimacies

NTMSHN intimation *confidence*

NTMSL antimissile *interceptor*

NTMSNS intumescence *swelling*

NTMSNT intumescent *swollen*

NTMSNTS intumescence *swelling*

NTMST anatomist *body structure*

NTMT intimate (v) *suggest, announce* intimated intimating

NTMT intimate *(adj) essential, close*

NTMTR antimatter *physics*

NTMZ anatomize *analyze* anatomized anatomizing (Br) anatomise

NTN antenna *sensor*

antennas (radio and TV) antennae (biology)

NTN intend *plan, mean*

NTN intone *voice* intoned intoning

NTN knitting *weaving*

NTN neaten *tidy*

NTN neoteny *larva*

NTN netting *snare, web*

NTN newton *unit of force*

NTN uneaten *not consumed*

NTNBL unattainable *beyond reach*

NTNBL untenable *no defense*

NTNBLD untenability *no defense*

NTNBLT untenability *no defense*

NTNCHN inattention *disregard*

NTNCHN intention *purpose*

NTNCHNL intentional (adj) *on purpose* intentionally (adv)

NTND intend *plan, mean*

NTNDD intended *marriage*

NTNDD unattended *not watched*

NTNDN intending *planning*

NTNDNG intending *planning*

NTNDNT intendant *official*

NTNFLMTR anti-inflammatory *remove swelling*

NTNFLSHNR anti-inflationary *no growth*

NTNG knitting *weaving*

NTNG netting *snare, web*

NTNGGL entangle *knot* entangled entangling

NTNGGL nightingale *bird*

NTNGGL untangle *straighten out* untangled untangling

NTNGGLMNT entanglement *knot*

NTNGGLR entangler *knot*

NTNGKSHN intinction *dipping*

NTNGL entangle *knot* entangled entangling

NTNGL nightingale *bird*

NTNGL untangle *straighten*

Letters aren't doubled for single sounds: to find alley use **L** not **LL**. Use **Y** and **W** as hard sounds only: to find yellow use **YL**. (Br)=British spelling or usage. * See dictionary.

out untangled untangling
NTNGLMNT entanglement *knot*
NTNGLR entangler *knot*
NTNGZT antianxiety *calming*
NTNGZYT antianxiety *calming*
NTNJBL intangible (n, adj) *abstract* intangibly (adv)
NTNJBLD intangibility *abstraction*
NTNJBLT intangibility *abstraction*
NTNK antiknock *prevent noise*
NTNKLR antinuclear *no cell reaction, against nuclear power*
NTNKLYR antinuclear *no cell reaction, against nuclear power*
NTNKSHN intinction *dipping*
NTNKYLR antinuclear *no cell reaction, against nuclear power*
NTNL antennule *small antenna*
NTNLR antennular *small antenna*
NTNM antinomy *opposition* antinomies
NTNM antonym *opposite* antonymy
NTNMK antonymic *opposite*
NTNMS antonymous *opposite*
NTNN antiunion *against organized labor*
NTNN Newtonian *of Newton*
NTNPSHL antenuptial *before marriage*
NTNPSHWL antenuptial *before marriage*
NTNQLR antinuclear *no cell reaction, against nuclear power*
NTNR intoner *speaker*
NTNS antinoise *against noise*
NTNS intense *extreme*
NTNS knottiness *tangles*
NTNS nattiness *neatness*
NTNS naughtiness

wickedness
NTNS nuttiness *like nuts, silly*
NTNSD intensity *extreme degree* intensities
NTNSF intensify *sharpen* intensified intensifying intensifies
NTNSFKSHN intensification *sharpen*
NTNSFR intensifier *sharpener*
NTNSHN inattention *disregard*
NTNSHN intention *purpose*
NTNSHN intonation *speech*
NTNSHNL intentional (adj) *on purpose* intentionally (adv)
NTNSHNL intonational *speech*
NTNSL intensely *extreme*
NTNSNS intenseness *extreme*
NTNST intensity *extreme degree* intensities
NTNSV intensive *concentrated*
NTNSVL intensively *concentrated*
NTNSVNS intensiveness *concentrated*
NTNT annuitant *heir*
NTNT entente *agree*
NTNT intent *purpose*
NTNT natant *swimming*
NTNTLKCHL anti-intellectual *against learning*
NTNTLKCHWL anti-intellectual *against learning*
NTNTLKSHL anti-intellectual *against learning*
NTNTLKSHWL anti-intellectual *against learning*
NTNTS intense *extreme*
NTNTSD intensity *extreme degree* intensities
NTNTSF intensify *sharpen*

intensified intensifying intensifies
NTNTSFKSHN intensification *sharpen*
NTNTSFYR intensifier *sharpener*
NTNTSL intensely *extreme*
NTNTSNS intenseness *extreme*
NTNTST intensity *extreme degree* intensities
NTNTSV intensive *concentrated*
NTNTSVL intensively *concentrated*
NTNTSVNS intensiveness *concentrated*
NTNTV inattentive *disregard*
NTNV inattentive *disregard*
NTNYKLR antinuclear *no cell reaction, against nuclear power*
NTNYKLYR antinuclear *no cell reaction, against nuclear power*
NTNYKYLR antinuclear *no cell reaction, against nuclear power*
NTNYL antennule *small antenna*
NTNYLR antennular *small antenna*
NTNYN antiunion *against organized labor*
NTNYN Newtonian *of Newton*
NTNYQLR antinuclear *no cell reaction, against nuclear power*
NTNZ antinoise *against noise*
NTNZT antianxiety *calming*
NTNZYT antianxiety *calming*
NTP neotype *specimen*
NTPD antipode *opposite pole* antipodes
NTPD notepad *paper*
NTPDL antipodal *germ cell*
NTPK nitpick *criticise*
NTPK nitpicky *critical*
NTPK nutpick *tool*
NTPKN nit-picking *criticism*
NTPKNG nit-picking

Use letters that best describe the sounds you hear and omit the vowels. Use **S** or **K** instead of **C**: to find circle use **SRKL**. Use **J** to find joy, **JM** to find gem and **G** to find go.

criticism
NTPKR nitpicker *criticise*
NTPLK antiplaque *prevent tartar*
NTPLSHN antipollution *prevent filth*
NTPNLT antepenult *syllable*
NTPNLTMT antepenultimate *syllable*
NTPPR notepaper *memo pad*
NTPRDK antipyretic *fever reducer*
NTPRDKL antiparticle *atomic*
NTPRSNL antipersonnel *weapon*
NTPRSPRNT antiperspirant *prevents perspiration*
NTPRTD antiapartheid *against racism*
NTPRTK antipyretic *fever reducer*
NTPRTKL antiparticle *atomic*
NTPRZ enterprise *initiative, business*
NTPRZN enterprising *independent*
NTPRZNG enterprising *independent*
NTPRZR enterpriser *producer, organizer*
NTPSD antipasto *food*
NTPST antipasto *food*
NTPT untapped *not used*
NTPTH antipathy *hostility* antipathies
NTPTHDK antipathetic *hostile*
NTPTHDKL antipathetically *hostilely*
NTPTHTK antipathetic *hostile*
NTPTHTKL antipathetically *hostilely*
NTPVRD antipoverty *prevent poverty*
NTPVRT antipoverty *prevent poverty*
NTQD antiquity *ancient times, relic* antiquities
NTQDD antiquated *old*

NTQR antiquary *old items* antiquaries
NTQRN antiquarian *collector of old items*
NTQRYN antiquarian *collector of old items*
NTQT antiquate *make old* antiquated antiquating
NTQT antiquity *ancient times, relic* antiquities
NTQTD antiquated *old*
NTR anteater *animal*
NTR antra (pl) *sinus* antrum
NTR enter *go into*
NTR entire *whole*
NTR entrée (or) entree *menu, entrance*
NTR entry *doorway, note* entries
NTR in utero *uterus*
NTR inter- *between*
NTR inter *bury* interred interring
NTR knitter *weaver*
NTR knotter *tangler*
NTR knottier *tangles*
NTR nadir *low point*
NTR natter *chatter*
NTR nattier *neater*
NTR nature *principle, creation, type**
NTR naughtier *wicked*
NTR neuter *(v)* castrate *(adj)* neutral *(n)* gender, worker, animal
NTR niter *chemical* (Br) nitre
NTR nitery *club* niteries
NTR nitro *nitroglycerin* nitros
NTR notary *certifier* notaries
NTR nutria *rodent*
NTR nutter *(Br) nut*
NTR Ontario *city*
NTR unitary *whole*
NTR untrue *false*
NTRBL unutterable (adj) *beyond words* unutterably (adv)
NTRBLD untroubled *calm*
NTRBNGK interbank *between banks*
NTRBNK interbank *between*

banks
NTRBRD interbreed *crossbreed* interbred interbreeding
NTRBRNCH interbranch *between branches*
NTRBZ antirabies *prevent hydrophobia*
NTRC inter se *among themselves*
NTRCD intercede *negotiate* interceded interceding
NTRCDR interceder *negotiator*
NTRCHNJ interchange *exchange*
NTRCHNJBL interchangeable (adj) *substitution* interchangeably (adv)
NTRCHRCH interchurch *between churches*
NTRCL enterocoele (or) enterocoel *intestines*
NTRCLK enterocoelic *intestines*
NTRCLS enterocoelous *intestines*
NTRD entirety *whole* entireties
NTRD entreaty *plea* entreaties
NTRD interred *(v-past)* inter
NTRD intrude *enter by force* intruded intruding
NTRD notoriety *fame* notorieties
NTRD untoward *unfavorable*
NTRD untried *new*
NTRD untrod (or) untrodden *not traveled*
NTRDK Antarctic *ocean, region*
NTRDK Antarctica *continent*
NTRDK interdict *forbid*
NTRDKDR introductory *first step*
NTRDKSHN interdiction *prohibition*
NTRDKSHN introduction *presentation, insertion*
NTRDKT interdict *forbid*

Letters aren't doubled for single sounds: to find alley use **L** not **LL**. Use **Y** and **W** as hard sounds only: to find yellow use **YL**. (Br)=British spelling or usage. * See dictionary.

NTRDKTR introductory *first step*

NTRDL untowardly *unfavorably*

NTRDN untrodden (or) untrod *not traveled*

NTRDNL interdental (adj) *between teeth* interdentally (adv)

NTRDNMNSHNL interdenominational *between faiths*

NTRDNTL interdental (adj) *between teeth* interdentally (adv)

NTRDPNDNS interdependence *mutual reliance*

NTRDPNDNT interdependent *mutual reliance*

NTRDPNDNTS interdependence *mutual reliance*

NTRDPRTMNL interdepartmental (adj) *between departments* interdepartmentally (adv)

NTRDPRTMNTL interdepartmental (adj) *between departments* interdepartmentally (adv)

NTRDR intruder *enter by force*

NTRDR night rider *terrorist*

NTRDRML intradermal (adj) *within skin* intradermally (adv)

NTRDRN intrauterine *in the uterus*

NTRDS enteritis *intestines*

NTRDS intrados *curve* intrados (or) intradoses

NTRDS introduce *present, insert* introduced introducing

NTRDSPLNR interdisciplinary *between fields*

NTRDV nutritive *nourishing*

NTRDYS introduce *present, insert* introduced

introducing

NTRFKLT interfaculty *between faculties*

NTRFKSHN nitrification *oxidation*

NTRFL interfile *arrange* interfiled interfiling

NTRFL neutrophil (or) neutrophilic *stain*

NTRFLK neutrophilic (or) neutrophil *stain*

NTRFR interfere *obstruct* interfered interfering

NTRFR nitrifier *bacteria*

NTRFRN interferon *protein*

NTRFRNS interference *obstruction*

NTRFRNTS interference *obstruction*

NTRFRR interferer *obstruct*

NTRFS interface (*v*) *communicate* interfaced interfacing

NTRFS interface (*n*) *boundary*

NTRFS interoffice *between offices*

NTRFSHL interfacial *bordering*

NTRFSN interfacing *fabric*

NTRFSNG interfacing *fabric*

NTRFTH interfaith *between faiths*

NTRFYL interfile *arrange* interfiled interfiling

NTRFYR nitrifier *bacteria*

NTRFYZ interfuse *blend* interfused interfusing

NTRFZ interfuse *blend* interfused interfusing

NTRFZ interphase *cell division*

NTRG interrogee *questioned one*

NTRG intrigue *scheme* intrigued intriguing

NTRGD interrogatee *questioned one*

NTRGDR interrogator *questioner*

NTRGDV interrogative *question*

NTRGLKDK intergalactic *between galaxies*

NTRGLKDK intragalactic *within a galaxy*

NTRGLKTK intergalactic *between galaxies*

NTRGLKTK intragalactic *within a galaxy*

NTRGLSHL interglacial *warm period*

NTRGLSRN nitroglycerin (or) nitroglycerine *explosive*

NTRGN intriguing *fascinating*

NTRGNG intriguing *fascinating*

NTRGNK intragenic *within a gene*

NTRGRD intergrade *merge* intergraded intergrading

NTRGRSHN introgression *entry*

NTRGRSNT introgressant *entry*

NTRGRSV introgressive *entry*

NTRGSHN interrogation *question*

NTRGSHNL interrogational *question*

NTRGT interrogate *question* interrogated interrogating

NTRGT interrogatee *questioned one*

NTRGTR interrogator *questioner*

NTRGTR interrogatory *question* interrogatories

NTRGTV interrogative *question*

NTRGVRMNTL intergovernmental *between governments*

NTRGVRNMNTL intergovernmental *between governments*

NTRJ entourage *attendants*

NTRJK interject *introduce*

NTRJK introject *incorporate*

NTRJKSHN interjection *utterance*

NTRJKSHN introjection

Use letters that best describe the sounds you hear and omit the vowels. Use **S** or **K** instead of **C**: to find circle use **SRKL**. Use **J** to find joy, **JM** to find gem and **G** to find go.

incorporation
NTRJKT interject *introduce*
NTRJKT introject *incorporate*
NTRJN nitrogen *element*
NTRJNC interagency *between agencies*
NTRJNK intragenic *within a gene*
NTRJNL interregional *between areas*
NTRJNRSHNL intergenerational *between ages*
NTRJNS interagency *between agencies*
NTRJNS nitrogenase *enzyme*
NTRJNTC interagency *between agencies*
NTRJNTS interagency *between agencies*
NTRJNZ nitrogenase *enzyme*
NTRK enteric *intestines*
NTRK interact *share*
NTRK neoteric *modern*
NTRK nitric *nitrogen*
NTRKC intricacy *trickiness* intricacies
NTRKDBL intractable (adj) *unruly* intractably (adv)
NTRKDK Antarctic *ocean, region*
NTRKDK Antarctica *continent*
NTRKDV interactive *two-way*
NTRKDV unattractive *ugly*
NTRKDVL unattractively *ugly*
NTRKDVNS unattractiveness *ugliness*
NTRKKL enterococcal *intestines*
NTRKKS enterococcus *intestines* enterococci
NTRKLB interclub *between clubs*
NTRKLCHRL intercultural (adj) *between cultures* interculturally (adv)
NTRKLJT intercollegiate

between colleges
NTRKLS interclass *between classes*
NTRKLTRL intercultural (adj) *between cultures* interculturally (adv)
NTRKM intercom *communications*
NTRKMNKSHN intercommunication *two-way speech*
NTRKMNKT intercommunicate *exchange*
NTRKMPN intercompany *between companies*
NTRKMPN intracompany *within a company*
NTRKMYNKSHN intercommunication *two-way speech*
NTRKMYNKT intercommunicate *exchange*
NTRKNK interconnect *join*
NTRKNKSHN interconnection *joint* (Br) interconnexion
NTRKNKT interconnect *join*
NTRKNNNL intercontinental *between continents*
NTRKNNNTL intercontinental *between continents*
NTRKNT intercounty *between counties*
NTRKNTNNL intercontinental *between continents*
NTRKNTNNTL intercontinental *between continents*
NTRKNTR intercountry *between countries*
NTRKRDKL intercortical *between outer layers*
NTRKRF antiaircraft *defensive*
NTRKRFT antiaircraft *defensive*
NTRKRNL intracranial (adj) *inside the head*

intracranially (adv)
NTRKRNYL intracranial (adj) *inside the head* intracranially (adv)
NTRKRP intercrop *alternate crops*
NTRKRS intercourse *connection*
NTRKRS intercross *breeding*
NTRKRTKL intercortical *between outer layers*
NTRKS intricacy *trickiness* intricacies
NTRKSHN interaction *share*
NTRKSTL intercoastal *between shores*
NTRKSTL intercostal *between ribs*
NTRKT entr'acte *intermission*
NTRKT interact *share*
NTRKT intercounty *between counties*
NTRKT intricate *tricky*
NTRKTBL intractable (adj) *unruly* intractably (adv)
NTRKTK Antarctic *ocean, region*
NTRKTK Antarctica *continent*
NTRKTL intricately *tricky*
NTRKTNS intricateness *trickiness*
NTRKTV interactive *two-way*
NTRKTV unattractive *ugly*
NTRKTVL unattractively *ugly*
NTRKTVNS unattractiveness *ugliness*
NTRL antral *sinus*
NTRL au naturel *nude, natural*
NTRL enteral (adj) *intestines* enterally (adv)
NTRL entirely *completely*
NTRL inter alia *among others*
NTRL natural (adj) *innate, normal* naturally (adv)
NTRL neutral (adj) *middling* neutrally (adv)
NTRL nitrile *cyanide*
NTRL notarial (adj) *signature*

notarially (adv)
NTRL unnatural (adj) *irregular, contrary* unnaturally
NTRL untruly *false*
NTRLD interlude *interval*
NTRLD neutrality *middle*
NTRLDD interrelated *connected*
NTRLJS interreligious *between religions*
NTRLK interlock *unite*
NTRLKDR interlocutor *speaker*
NTRLKN interleukin *immunity*
NTRLKTR interlocutor *speaker*
NTRLKTR interlocutory *pronouncement*
NTRLKYDR interlocutor *speaker*
NTRLKYTR interlocutor *speaker*
NTRLKYTR interlocutory *pronouncement*
NTRLN interline *between lines*
NTRLND interisland *between islands*
NTRLNGK interlink *join*
NTRLNK interlink *join*
NTRLNN interlining *fabric*
NTRLNNG interlining *fabric*
NTRLNR interlinear *between lines*
NTRLNR interliner *transport*
NTRLNR interlunar *moon phases*
NTRLNS unnaturalness *irregular, contrary*
NTRLNYR interlinear *between lines*
NTRLP interlope *intrude* interloped interloping interloper
NTRLPR interloper *intruder*
NTRLQDR interlocutor *speaker*
NTRLQTR interlocutor *speaker*
NTRLQTR interlocutory

pronouncement
NTRLRD interlard *mix in*
NTRLS entrails *intestines*
NTRLS interlace *weave* interlaced interlacing
NTRLS naturalize *make common, citizenship* naturalized naturalizing (Br) naturalise
NTRLSDK naturalistic *realistic*
NTRLSDKL naturalistically *realistic*
NTRLSHN interrelation *connection*
NTRLSHNSHP interrelationship *connection*
NTRLSSHN naturalization *make common, citizenship* (Br) naturalisation
NTRLST naturalist *realist*
NTRLSTKL naturalistically *realistic*
NTRLT interrelate *connect* interrelated interrelating
NTRLT neutrality *middle*
NTRLTD interrelated *connected*
NTRLV interleave *layer* interleaved interleaving
NTRLVL entry-level *lowest level*
NTRLY inter alia *among others*
NTRLZ entrails *intestines*
NTRLZ naturalize *make common, citizenship* naturalized naturalizing (Br) naturalise
NTRLZ neutralize *cancel* neutralized neutralizing (Br) neutralise
NTRLZM naturalism *realism*
NTRLZR neutralizer *canceller* (Br) neutraliser
NTRLZSHN naturalization *make common, citizenship* (Br) naturalisation
NTRLZSHN neutralization *cancellation*

(Br) neutralisation
NTRM anteroom *lobby*
NTRM antrum *sinus* antra
NTRM entremets *dessert*
NTRM interim *interval*
NTRMDK antirheumatic *prevent rheumatism*
NTRMDNS intermittence *occasional* intermittency
NTRMDNT intermittent *occasional*
NTRMDNTS intermittence *occasional* intermittency
NTRMDR intermediary *go-between* intermediaries
NTRMDR intermitter *discontinue*
NTRMDT intermediate *middle*
NTRMDTL intermediately *middle*
NTRMDYR intermediary *go-between* intermediaries
NTRMDYT intermediate *middle*
NTRMDYTL intermediately *middle*
NTRMDZ intermezzo *interlude* intermezzi (or) intermezzos
NTRMKS intermix *blend*
NTRMKSCHR intermixture *blend*
NTRMKSTR intermixture *blend*
NTRMLKLR intramolecular *within a molecule*
NTRMLKYLR intramolecular *within a molecule*
NTRMLQLR intramolecular *within a molecule*
NTRMNBL interminable (adj) *without end* interminably (adv)
NTRMNGGL intermingle *mix* intermingled intermingling
NTRMNGL intermingle *mix* intermingled intermingling
NTRMNT interment *burial*

Use letters that best describe the sounds you hear and omit the vowels. Use **S** or **K** instead of **C**: to find circle use **SRKL**. Use **J** to find joy, **JM** to find gem and **G** to find go.

NTRMNT nutriment *food*
NTRMP no-trump *cards*
NTRMR intermarry *wed within a group*
intermarried
intermarrying
intermarries
NTRMRJ intermarriage *between groups*
NTRMRKN inter-American *between Americas*
NTRMRL intramural (adj) *within an organization*
intramurally (adv)
NTRMSH intermesh *interlock*
NTRMSHN intermission *interval*
NTRMSHN intromission *insertion*
NTRMSKLR intramuscular *within a muscle*
NTRMSKYLR intramuscular *within a muscle*
NTRMSQLR intramuscular *within a muscle*
NTRMT intermit *discontinue* intermitted intermitting
NTRMT intromit *insert* intromitted intromitting
NTRMTK antirheumatic *prevent rheumatism*
NTRMTNS intermittence *occasional* intermittency
NTRMTNT intermittent *occasional*
NTRMTNTS intermittence *occasional* intermittency
NTRMTR intermitter *discontinue*
NTRMTS intermezzo *interlude* intermezzi (or) intermezzos
NTRMX intermix *blend*
NTRMXCHR intermixture *blend*
NTRMXTR intermixture *blend*
NTRMYRL intramural (adj) *within an organization* intramurally (adv)
NTRN enteron *intestines*

NTRN entrain *board*
NTRN intern (v) *detain* (n) *trainee*
NTRN internee *prisoner*
NTRN intron *genetic code*
NTRN neutrino *particle without mass* neutrinos
NTRN neutron *particle with mass*
NTRN Unitarian *religion*
NTRN untiring *constant*
NTRNCH entrench *cut into, invade*
NTRNCHMNT entrenchment *cut into, invade*
NTRNCN internecine *within a group, deadly*
NTRND internode *between joints*
NTRND untrained *not taught*
NTRNDSTR interindustry *between industries*
NTRNG untiring *constant*
NTRNL internal (adj) *inside* internally (adv)
NTRNLZ internalize *incorporate within* internalized internalizing (Br) internalise
NTRNMNT entrainment *board*
NTRNR entrainer *board*
NTRNS entireness *whole*
NTRNS entrance (v) *charm* entranced entrancing
NTRNS entrance (n) *doorway*
NTRNSDV intransitive *no object*
NTRNSDVL intransitively *no object*
NTRNSDVNS intransitiveness *no object*
NTRNSHNL international (adj) *between countries* internationally (adv)
NTRNSHNL internationale *labor union*
NTRNSHNLDTLN international date line *180th meridian*

NTRNSHNLZ internationalize *involve many nations*
internationalized
internationalizing
(Br) internationalise
NTRNSHNLZM internationalism *cooperation policy*
NTRNSHNLZSHN internationalization *many nations*
(Br) internationalisation
NTRNSHP internship *trainee*
NTRNSJNS intransigence *no compromise*
NTRNSJNT intransigent *no compromise*
NTRNSJNTL intransigently *no compromise*
NTRNSJNTS intransigence *no compromise*
NTRNSK intrinsic *essential*
NTRNSKL intrinsically *essential*
NTRNSMNT entrancement *charm*
NTRNSN internecine *within a group, deadly*
NTRNST internist *doctor*
NTRNSTV intransitive *no object*
NTRNSTVD intransitivity *no object*
NTRNSTVL intransitively *no object*
NTRNSTVNS intransitiveness *no object*
NTRNSTVT intransitivity *no object*
NTRNSW entranceway *door*
NTRNT entrant *contestant*
NTRNT internet *computer net*
NTRNT knight-errant *traveler* knights-errant
NTRNT nutrient *food*
NTRNTS entrance (v) *charm* entranced entrancing
NTRNTS entrance (n) *doorway*
NTRNTSMNT entrancement *charm*

Letters aren't doubled for single sounds: to find alley use **L** not **LL**. Use **Y** and **W** as hard sounds only: to find yellow use **YL**. (Br)=British spelling or usage. * See dictionary.

NTRNTSW entranceway *door*

NTRNZDV intransitive *no object*

NTRNZDVL intransitively *no object*

NTRNZDVNS intransitiveness *no object*

NTRNZJNS intransigence *no compromise*

NTRNZJNT intransigent *no compromise*

NTRNZJNTL intransigently *no compromise*

NTRNZJNTS intransigence *no compromise*

NTRNZK intrinsic *essential*

NTRNZKL intrinsically *essential*

NTRNZL intranasal (adj) *within a nose* intranasally (adv)

NTRNZTV intransitive *no object*

NTRNZTVD intransitivity *no object*

NTRNZTVL intransitively *no object*

NTRNZTVNS intransitiveness *no object*

NTRNZTVT intransitivity *no object*

NTRP entrap *snare*

NTRP entrepôt *trade center*

NTRP entropy *chaos* entropies

NTRP interrupt *break in*

NTRPBLK notary public *certifier* notaries public (or) notary publics

NTRPD intrepid *fearless*

NTRPDD intrepidity *no fear*

NTRPDL intrepidly *no fear*

NTRPDNS intrepidness *no fear*

NTRPDR interrupter *breaker*

NTRPDT intrepidity *no fear*

NTRPK entropic *chaos*

NTRPKL entropically *chaos*

NTRPKL Neotropical *region*

NTRPKS neotropics *region*

NTRPL interplay *interaction*

NTRPL Interpol *police*

NTRPLD interplead *law*

NTRPLDR interpolater *introducer*

NTRPLNTR interplanetary *between planets*

NTRPLSHN interpolation *introduction*

NTRPLT interpolate *introducer* interpolated interpolating

NTRPLTR interpolater *introducer*

NTRPMNT entrapment *snare*

NTRPNR entrepreneur *business*

NTRPNRL entrepreneurial (adj) *business* entrepreneurially (adv)

NTRPNRSHP entrepreneurship *business*

NTRPNRYL entrepreneurial (adj) *business* entrepreneurially (adv)

NTRPNTRT interpenetrate *fill* interpenetrated interpenetrating

NTRPNYR entrepreneur *business*

NTRPNYRL entrepreneurial (adj) *business* entrepreneurially (adv)

NTRPNYRSHP entrepreneurship *business*

NTRPNYRYL entrepreneurial (adj) *business* entrepreneurially (adv)

NTRPRBL interoperable *between systems*

NTRPRBLD interoperability *between systems*

NTRPRBLT interoperability *between systems*

NTRPRD interparty *between parties*

NTRPRDBL interpretable *explainable*

NTRPRDBLD interpretability *explainable*

NTRPRDBLT interpretability *explainable*

NTRPRDR interpreter *explainer*

NTRPRDV interpretive *adaptive*

NTRPRNR entrepreneur *business*

NTRPRNR intrapreneur *business*

NTRPRNRL entrepreneurial (adj) *business* entrepreneurially (adv)

NTRPRNRSHP entrepreneurship *business*

NTRPRNRYL entrepreneurial (adj) *business* entrepreneurially (adv)

NTRPRNYR entrepreneur *business*

NTRPRNYR intrapreneur *business*

NTRPRNYRL entrepreneurial (adj) *business* entrepreneurially (adv)

NTRPRNYRSHP entrepreneurship *business*

NTRPRNYRYL entrepreneurial (adj) *business* entrepreneurially (adv)

NTRPRSNL interpersonal (adj) *between people* interpersonally (adv)

NTRPRSNL intrapersonal (adj) *within oneself* intrapersonally (adv)

NTRPRT interparty *between parties*

NTRPRT interpret *explain*

NTRPRTBL interpretable *explainable*

NTRPRTBLD interpretability *explainable*

NTRPRTBLT interpretability *explainable*

NTRPRTR interpreter *explainer*

NTRPRTSHN interpretation *explanation*

NTRPRTV interpretive

adaptive
NTRPRZ enterprise
initiative, business
NTRPRZN enterprising
independent
NTRPRZNG enterprising
independent
NTRPRZR enterpriser
producer, organizer
NTRPSHN interruption *break*
NTRPT interrupt *break in*
NTRPT intrepid *fearless*
NTRPTH enteropathy
intestines
NTRPTL intrepidly *no fear*
NTRPTNS intrepidness *no fear*
NTRPTR interrupter *breaker*
NTRPX neotropics *region*
NTRPZ interpose *interrupt*
interposed interposing
NTRPZR interposer
interrupter
NTRPZSHN interposition
interruption
NTRR anterior *front*
NTRR interior *inside*
NTRRDKRDR interior
decorator *designer*
NTRRDKRTR interior
decorator *designer*
NTRRL anteriorly *front*
NTRRST antiterrorist *against fearful coercion*
NTRS inter se *among themselves*
NTRS nitrous *nitrogen*
NTRS notorious *famous*
NTRSBL untraceable *no trail*
NTRSD intercede *negotiate*
interceded interceding
NTRSDD interested
concerned
NTRSDM enterostomy
intestines enterostomies
NTRSDML enterostomal
intestines
NTRSDR interceder
negotiator
NTRSH entourage
attendants

NTRSH entrechat *leap*
NTRSHL interracial (adj)
between races interracially
(adv)
NTRSHN interocean *between oceans*
NTRSHN intrusion *entrance*
NTRSHN nutrition *food*
NTRSHNL nutritional (adj)
food nutritionally (adv)
NTRSHNST nutritionist *food*
NTRSHS nutritious *healthful*
NTRSHSL nutritiously
healthfully
NTRSHSNS nutritiousness
health
NTRSK intersect *cross*
NTRSKK intrapsychic
within the mind
NTRSKKL intrapsychically
within the mind
NTRSKLSDK
interscholastic *between schools*
NTRSKLSTK interscholastic
between schools
NTRSKSHL intersexual (adj)
between sexes intersexually
(adv)
NTRSKSHLD intersexuality
between sexes
NTRSKSHLT intersexuality
between sexes
NTRSKSHN intersection
crossing
NTRSKSHWL intersexual
(adj) *between sexes*
intersexually (adv)
NTRSKSHWLD
intersexuality *between sexes*
NTRSKSHWLT
intersexuality *between sexes*
NTRSKT intersect *cross*
NTRSL enterocoele (or)
enterocoel *intestines*
NTRSL notoriously *famous*
NTRSLK enterocoelic
intestines
NTRSLLR intercellular
between cells

NTRSLLR intracellular
within a cell
NTRSLLRL intracellularly
within a cell
NTRSLR intracellular *within a cell*
NTRSLRL intracellularly
within a cell
NTRSLS enterocoelous
intestines
NTRSLYLR intercellular
between cells
NTRSLYLR intracellular
within a cell
NTRSLYLRL intracellularly
within a cell
NTRSMN nitrosamine
cancer-causing
NTRSMNT entrustment
commitment
NTRSP intercept (v) seize (n)
code, signal
NTRSPDR interceptor *seize*
NTRSPK introspect *look inside*
NTRSPKDV introspective
look inside
NTRSPKDVL
introspectively *look inside*
NTRSPKDVNS
introspectiveness *look inside*
NTRSPKSHN introspection
look inside
NTRSPKSHNZM
introspectionism
psychology
NTRSPKT introspect *look inside*
NTRSPKTV introspective
look inside
NTRSPKTVL introspectively
look inside
NTRSPKTVNS
introspectiveness *look inside*
NTRSPRS intersperse *insert*
interspersed
interspersing
NTRSPRSHN interspersion
insert
NTRSPRZHN interspersion

---

insert

NTRSPS interspace *place between* interspaced interspacing

NTRSPSFK intraspecific *one species*

NTRSPSHN interception *seizure*

NTRSPT intercept *(v) seize (n) code, signal*

NTRSPTR interceptor *seize*

NTRSRBRL intracerebral (adj) *brain* intracerebrally (adv)

NTRSSHN intercession *prayer*

NTRSSHN intersession *between terms*

NTRST antitrust *against monopolies*

NTRST entrust *commit*

NTRST intercity *between cities*

NTRST interest *(v) engage attention (n) concern, company, benefit**

NTRSTCZ interstices (pl) *gap* interstice

NTRSTD interested *concerned*

NTRSTLR interstellar *between stars*

NTRSTM enterostomy *intestines* enterostomies

NTRSTML enterostomal *intestines*

NTRSTMNT entrustment *commitment*

NTRSTN interesting *fascinating*

NTRSTNG interesting *fascinating*

NTRSTS interstice *gap*

NTRSTSHL interstitial (adj) *between* interstitially (adv)

NTRSTSZ interstices (pl) *gap* interstice

NTRSTT interstate *between states*

NTRSTT intrastate *within a state*

NTRSV intrusive *invasive*

NTRSVL intrusively *invasively*

NTRSVNS intrusiveness *invasion*

NTRSYLR intracellular *within a cell*

NTRSYLRL intracellularly *within a cell*

NTRT entirety *whole* entireties

NTRT entreat *plead*

NTRT entreaty *plea* entreaties

NTRT introit *(often capitalized) prayer*

NTRT nitrate *nitric acid*

NTRT nitrite *nitrous acid*

NTRT notoriety *fame* notorieties

NTRTDL intertidal (adj) *above low tide* intertidally (adv)

NTRTH untruth *lie*

NTRTHFL untruthful (adj) *false* untruthfully (adv)

NTRTHFLNS untruthfulness *falsity*

NTRTHRDK antiarthritic *combating arthritis*

NTRTHRTK antiarthritic *combating arthritis*

NTRTK Antarctic *ocean, region*

NTRTK Antarctica *continent*

NTRTMNT entreatment *plea*

NTRTN entertain *amuse, consider*

NTRTNGL entreatingly *plead*

NTRTNMNT entertainment *amusement*

NTRTNN entertaining *amusing*

NTRTNNG entertaining *amusing*

NTRTNR entertainer *amuser*

NTRTRBL intertribal (adj) *between tribes* intertribally (adv)

NTRTRN intrauterine *in the uterus*

NTRTS enteritis *intestines*

NTRTV nutritive *nourishing*

NTRTWN intertwine *weave* intertwined intertwining

NTRTWNMNT intertwinement *tangle*

NTRV interview *(n) consultation (v) consult*

NTRVL interval *space between*

NTRVLD untraveled *no trails*

NTRVN intervene *come between* intervened intervening

NTRVNCHN intervention *come between*

NTRVNCHNZM interventionism *come between*

NTRVNR intervenor (or) intervener *come between*

NTRVNS intravenous *in the vein*

NTRVNSHN intervention *come between*

NTRVNSHNZM interventionism *come between*

NTRVRSHN introversion *turned inward*

NTRVRSV introversive *turned inward*

NTRVRSVL introversively *turned inward*

NTRVRT introvert *(v) turn inward (n) shy one*

NTRVRZHN introversion *turned inward*

NTRVRZV introversive *turned inward*

NTRVRZVL introversively *turned inward*

NTRVSKLR intravascular *in the vein*

NTRVSKYLR intravascular *in the vein*

NTRVSQLR intravascular *in the vein*

NTRVW interviewee *person evaluated*

NTRVWR interviewer *reporter*

NTRVY interview *(n) consultation (v) consult*

NTRVYR interviewer *reporter*

Use letters that best describe the sounds you hear and omit the vowels. Use **S** or **K** instead of **C**: to find circle use **SRKL**. Use **J** to find joy, **JM** to find gem and **G** to find go.

NTRVYW interviewee *person evaluated*
NTRVYWR interviewer *reporter*
NTRW entryway *passage*
NTRWV interweave *mix* interwove interweaving interwoven
NTRWVN interwoven *mixed*
NTRY nutria *rodent*
NTRY Ontario *city*
NTRYD notoriety *fame* notorieties
NTRYDRN intrauterine *in the uterus*
NTRYL notarial (adj) *signature* notarially (adv)
NTRYN Unitarian *religion*
NTRYNT nutrient *food*
NTRYR anterior *front*
NTRYR interior *inside*
NTRYRDKRDR interior decorator *designer*
NTRYRDKRTR interior decorator *designer*
NTRYRL anteriorly *front*
NTRYS notorious *famous*
NTRYSL notoriously *famous*
NTRYT notoriety *fame* notorieties
NTRYTRN intrauterine *in the uterus*
NTRZ notarize *signature* notarized notarizing
NTRZH entourage *attendants*
NTRZHN intrusion *entrance*
NTRZNL intrazonal *soil*
NTRZSHN notarization *signature*
NTRZV intrusive *invasive*
NTRZVL intrusively *invasively*
NTRZVNS intrusiveness *invasion*
NTS antsy *nervous*
NTS entice *tempt* enticed enticing
NTS Nazi *fascist*
NTS nidus *nest* nidi (or) niduses
NTS notice (v) *see* noticed

noticing
NTS notice (n) *alert*
NTS nuts *crazy, keen*
NTS ounce *weight*
NTSBL noticeable (adj) *clear* noticeably (adv)
NTSBL unnoticeable *not seen*
NTSCH Nietzsche *philosopher*
NTSD antacid *neutralizer*
NTSD antecede *precede* anteceded anteceding
NTSD nightside *not in daylight*
NTSDD untested *not tried*
NTSDMNT New Testament *bible*
NTSDN intestine (n) *food canal* (adj) *internal*
NTSDNL intestinal (adj) *food canal* intestinally (adv)
NTSDNS antecedence *priority*
NTSDNT antecedent *prior*
NTSDNTS antecedence *priority*
NTSFDL neat's-foot oil *tanning*
NTSFDYL neat's-foot oil *tanning*
NTSFLDK antisyphilitic *prevent syphilis*
NTSFLTK antisyphilitic *prevent syphilis*
NTSFTL neat's-foot oil *tanning*
NTSFTYL neat's-foot oil *tanning*
NTSHD nightshade *belladonna*
NTSHL nutshell *nut covering, brief statement*
NTSHL uncial *writing*
NTSHN annotation *comment*
NTSHN intuition *feeling*
NTSHN natation *swimming*
NTSHN notation *note*
NTSHN nutation *wobble*
NTSHNL notational *note*
NTSHNT ancient *old*
NTSHRT nightshirt *garment*

NTSJ nutsedge *grass*
NTSK netsuke *fastener* netsuke (or) netsukes
NTSKDK antipsychotic *calming*
NTSKL night school *education*
NTSKP nightscope *lens*
NTSKTK antipsychotic *calming*
NTSL Aunt Sally *object of criticism* Aunt Sallies
NTSL night soil *human feces*
NTSL uncial *writing*
NTSLN insulin *hormone*
NTSLVR antislavery *against bondage*
NTSMDK anti-Semitic *against Jews*
NTSMDZM anti-Semitism *against Jews*
NTSMKNG antismoking *against smoking*
NTSMNT enticement *temptation*
NTSMT anti-Semite *against Jews*
NTSMTK anti-Semitic *against Jews*
NTSMTRK antisymmetric *equal*
NTSMTZM anti-Semitism *against Jews*
NTSNGL enticingly *tempting*
NTSNL enticingly *tempting*
NTSNL intestinal (adj) *food canal* intestinally (adv)
NTSPDK antiseptic *kill germs*
NTSPDR anticipator *foresee, expect*
NTSPSHN anticipation *expectation*
NTSPSS antisepsis *kill germs*
NTSPT anticipate *foresee, expect* anticipated anticipating
NTSPT nightspot *club*
NTSPTK antiseptic *kill germs*
NTSPTR anticipator *foresee,*

Letters aren't doubled for single sounds: to find alley use **L** not **LL**. Use **Y** and **W** as hard sounds only: to find yellow use **YL**. (Br)=British spelling or usage. * See dictionary.

expect
NTSPTR anticipatory *foreseeable*
NTSPZMDK antispasmodic *prevent spasms*
NTSR answer *reply* answered answering
NTSRBL answerable *responsible*
NTSRM antiserum *antibody drug*
NTSRN anserine *goose*
NTSRNG answering *responding*
NTSRR answerer *responder*
NTSS entasis *convexity* entases
NTSSHL antisocial (adj) *hostile* antisocially (adv)
NTSSR antecessor *ancestor*
NTST knottiest *tangles*
NTST nattiest *neatest*
NTST naughtiest *wicked*
NTST unnoticed *not seen*
NTSTBLSHMNT antiestablishment *against rulers*
NTSTC intestacy *no will*
NTSTD untested *not tried*
NTSTK nightstick *club*
NTSTMNT New Testament *bible*
NTSTN intestine *(n) food canal (adj) internal*
NTSTN nightstand *table*
NTSTND nightstand *table*
NTSTNL intestinal (adj) *food canal* intestinally (adv)
NTSTRF antistrophy *repetition*
NTSTRFK antistrophic *repetition*
NTSTRFKL antistrophically *repetition*
NTSTS intestacy *no will*
NTSTT antistat *electricity*
NTSTT intestate *no will*
NTSV antitussive *cough*
NTSYL night soil *human feces*
NTSYL uncial *writing*
NTSZM Nazism (or) Naziism

fascism
NTT annotate *comment, note* annotated annotating
NTT entity *being* entities
NTT in toto *entirely*
NTT intuit *feel*
NTT nutate *wobble* nutated nutating
NTT uintaite *asphalt*
NTT untaught *natural, ignorant*
NTTBK antitobacco *against smoking*
NTTHDKL antithetical (adj) *contrasting* antithetically (adv)
NTTHR untether *untie*
NTTHRD antiauthority *rebellious*
NTTHRD antithyroid *gland*
NTTHRT antiauthority *rebellious*
NTTHSS antithesis *contrast* antitheses
NTTHTKL antithetical (adj) *contrasting* antithetically (adv)
NTTKSK antitoxic *neutralize poison*
NTTKSN antitoxin *neutralize poison*
NTTL entitle *authorize* entitled entitling
NTTLD untitled *no name*
NTTLMNT entitlement *authorization*
NTTR annotator *commentator*
NTTR anteater *animal*
NTTR natatory (or) natatorial *swimming*
NTTRD untutored *no school*
NTTRL natatorial (or) natatory *swimming*
NTTRM natatorium *pool*
NTTRRST antiterrorist *against fearful coercion*
NTTRST antitrust *against monopolies*
NTTRYL natatorial (or) natatory *swimming*
NTTRYM natatorium *pool*

NTTSV antitussive *cough*
NTTV annotative *noted*
NTTV intuitive *insightful*
NTTVL intuitively *insightful*
NTTVNS intuitiveness *insight*
NTTXK antitoxic *neutralize poison*
NTTXN antitoxin *neutralize poison*
NTV native *originating in*
NTV unitive *joining*
NTVD nativity *birth* nativities
NTVMRKN Native American *American Indian*
NTVND net-veined *circulation*
NTVNM antivenin *snakebite treatment*
NTVNN antivenin *snakebite treatment*
NTVRL antiviral *virus killing*
NTVST nativist *first inhabitants*
NTVSTK nativistic *first inhabitants*
NTVT nativity *birth* nativities
NTVZM nativism *first inhabitants*
NTWDV intuitive *insightful*
NTWDVL intuitively *insightful*
NTWDVNS intuitiveness *insight*
NTWKR nightwalker *prostitute*
NTWN entwine *tangle* entwined entwining
NTWN untwine *untangle* untwined untwining
NTWNGD net-winged *circulation*
NTWR antiwar *peaceful*
NTWR knitwear *clothing*
NTWRD untoward *unfavorable*
NTWRDL untowardly *unfavorably*
NTWRK network *fabric, system*
NTWRKNG networking *influence*

Use letters that best describe the sounds you hear and omit the vowels. Use **S** or **K** instead of **C**: to find circle use **SRKL**. Use **J** to find joy, **JM** to find gem and **G** to find go.

NTWRTH noteworthy *excellent*

NTWRTHL noteworthily *excellent*

NTWRTHNS noteworthiness *excellence*

NTWSHN intuition *feeling*

NTWST entwist *tangle*

NTWT antiwhite *racist*

NTWT intuit *feel*

NTWT nitwit *idiot*

NTWTHSTNDN notwithstanding *despite, however*

NTWTHSTNDNG notwithstanding *despite, however*

NTWTV intuitive *insightful*

NTWTVL intuitively *insightful*

NTWTVNS intuitiveness *insight*

NTXDNT antioxidant *chemical*

NTXK antitoxic *neutralize poison*

NTXKDD intoxicated *drunk*

NTXKNT intoxicant *alcohol, drug*

NTXKSHN intoxication *drunkenness*

NTXKT intoxicate *stupefy, elate intoxicated intoxicating*

NTXKTD intoxicated *drunk*

NTXN antitoxin *neutralize poison*

NTYBRSHN antiabortion *against pregnancy termination*

NTYBSHN intubation *insert tube*

NTYDRD untutored *no school*

NTYDV intuitive *insightful*

NTYDVL intuitively *insightful*

NTYDVNS intuitiveness *insight*

NTYDZ anti-AIDS *serum*

NTYK Antioch *city*

NTYKDMK antiacademic *against schooling*

NTYKSDNT antioxidant *chemical*

NTYLRJNK antiallergenic *not allergy promoting*

NTYMSNS intumescence *swelling*

NTYMSNT intumescent *swollen*

NTYMSNTS intumescence *swelling*

NTYNFLMTR anti-inflammatory *remove swelling*

NTYNFLSHNR anti-inflationary *no growth*

NTYNGZT antianxiety *calming*

NTYNGZYT antianxiety *calming*

NTYNN antiunion *against organized labor*

NTYNTLKCHL anti-intellectual *against learning*

NTYNTLKCHWL anti-intellectual *against learning*

NTYNTLKSHL anti-intellectual *against learning*

NTYNTLKSHWL anti-intellectual *against learning*

NTYNYN antiunion *against organized labor*

NTYNZT antianxiety *calming*

NTYNZYT antianxiety *calming*

NTYPRTD antiapartheid *against racism*

NTYR entire *whole*

NTYR knottier *tangles*

NTYR nattier *neater*

NTYR naughtier *wicked*

NTYRD entirety *whole entireties*

NTYRKRF antiaircraft *defensive*

NTYRKRFT antiaircraft *defensive*

NTYRL entirely *completely*

NTYRN untiring *constant*

NTYRNG untiring *constant*

NTYRNS entireness *whole*

NTYRT entirety *whole entireties*

NTYRTHRDK antiarthritic *combating arthritis*

NTYRTHRTK antiarthritic *combating arthritis*

NTYSHN intuition *feeling*

NTYST knottiest *tangles*

NTYST nattiest *neatest*

NTYST naughtiest *wicked*

NTYSTBLSHMNT antiestablishment *against rulers*

NTYT intuit *feel*

NTYT uintaite *asphalt*

NTYTHRD antiauthority *rebellious*

NTYTHRT antiauthority *rebellious*

NTYTRD untutored *no school*

NTYTV intuitive *insightful*

NTYTVL intuitively *insightful*

NTYTVNS intuitiveness *insight*

NTYWDV intuitive *insightful*

NTYWDVL intuitively *insightful*

NTYWDVNS intuitiveness *insight*

NTYWSHN intuition *feeling*

NTYWT intuit *feel*

NTYWTV intuitive *insightful*

NTYWTVL intuitively *insightful*

NTYWTVNS intuitiveness *insight*

NTYXDNT antioxidant *chemical*

NTZ Nazi *fascist*

NTZ unitize *divide unitized unitizing*

NTZZM Nazism (or) Naziism *fascism*

NV envoi (or) envoy *summary*

NV envoy *messenger*

NV envy *resent envied envying envies*

NV inveigh *protest*

NV knave *rogue*

Letters aren't doubled for single sounds: to find alley use **L** not **LL**. Use **Y** and **W** as hard sounds only: to find yellow use **YL**. (Br)=British spelling or usage. * See dictionary.

NV naïve (or) naive *simple* naiver naivest

NV nave *church, wheel*

NV navy *(often capitalized)* ships navies

NV névé *snow*

NV nevi (pl) *birthmark* nevus

NV nouveau *new*

NV nova *star* novas (or) novae

NVBL enviable (adj) *desirable* enviably (adv)

NVD invade *trespass* invaded invading

NVD navaid *beacon*

NVD Nevada *US State*

NVDBL inevitable (adj) *sure to happen* inevitably (adv)

NVDBL unavoidable (adj) *certain* unavoidably (adv)

NVDBLD inevitability *sure to happen* inevitabilities

NVDBLT inevitability *sure to happen* inevitabilities

NVDNG inviting *tempting*

NVDNGL invitingly *tempting*

NVDR innovator *inventor*

NVDR invader *trespasser*

NVDRT inveterate *steadfast*

NVDRTL inveterately *steadfast*

NVDS invidious *insulting*

NVDSL invidiously *insulting*

NVDSNS invidiousness *insult*

NVDV innovative *new*

NVDYS invidious *insulting*

NVDYSL invidiously *insulting*

NVDYSNS invidiousness *insult*

NVGBL navigable (adj) *ship passage* navigably (adv)

NVGBLD navigability *ship passage*

NVGBLT navigability *ship passage*

NVGDR navigator *steer, sail*

NVGL inveigle *lure* inveigled inveigling

NVGLR inveigler *lure*

NVGRDR invigorator

stimulator

NVGRDV invigorative *stimulating*

NVGRSHN invigoration *stimulation*

NVGRT invigorate *stimulate* invigorated invigorating

NVGRTR invigorator *stimulator*

NVGRTV invigorative *stimulating*

NVGSHN navigation *ship traffic*

NVGT navigate *steer, sail* navigated navigating

NVGTR navigator *steer, sail*

NVH Navajo *Native American* Navajo (or) Navajos

NVJNSHN invagination *enclosure*

NVJNT invaginate *enclose* invaginated invaginating

NVK invoke *solicit* invoked invoking

NVKDV invective *insult*

NVKL univocal (adj) *one meaning* univocally (adv)

NVKL unvocal *quiet*

NVKN Novocain *(trademark) drug*

NVKN novocaine *pain killer*

NVKR invoker *solicitor*

NVKSHN invocation *prayer*

NVKSHNL invocational *prayer*

NVKTR invocatory *prayer*

NVKTV invective *insult*

NVL anvil *block*

NVL naïvely (or) naively *simply*

NVL naval *ships*

NVL navel *belly button*

NVL nouvelle *new*

NVL novel *new, book*

NVL novella *short book* novellas (or) novelle

NVL unveil *uncover*

NVLBL invaluable (adj) *priceless* invaluably (adv)

NVLBL inviolable (adj) *protected* inviolably (adv)

NVLBL unavailable *out of*

reach

NVLBLD inviolability *protected*

NVLBLT inviolability *protected*

NVLD invalid (adj) *not true, sickly* (n) *disabled one*

NVLD novelty *new item* novelties

NVLD unvalued *not prized*

NVLD unveiled *open*

NVLDD invalidity *cancelation, illness* invalidities

NVLDDR invalidator *canceler*

NVLDSHN invalidation *cancelation*

NVLDT invalidate *cancel* invalidated invalidating

NVLDT invalidity *cancelation, illness* invalidities

NVLDTR invalidator *canceler*

NVLNG unavailing *useless*

NVLNRBL invulnerable (adj) *protected* invulnerably (adv)

NVLNRBLD invulnerability *protection*

NVLNRBLT invulnerability *protection*

NVLNT univalent *chemistry*

NVLNTR involuntary *no choice*

NVLNTRL involuntarily *no choice*

NVLNTRNS involuntariness *no choice*

NVLP envelop (v) *enclose*

NVLP envelope (n) *letter wrapper*

NVLPMNT envelopment *enclosure*

NVLRNJ navel orange *fruit*

NVLSDK novelistic *invented*

NVLSDKL novelistically *invented*

NVLSHN involution *complexity, curve*

NVLST novelist *writer*

NVLSTK novelistic *invented*

NVLSTKL novelistically *invented*

NVLT inviolate *pure*

Use letters that best describe the sounds you hear and omit the vowels. Use **S** or **K** instead of **C**: to find circle use **SRKL**. Use **J** to find joy, **JM** to find gem and **G** to find go.

NVLT involute *(v) disappear* involuted involuting

NVLT involute *(adj) curled (n) curve*

NVLT novelette *short book*

NVLT novelty *new item* novelties

NVLTL inviolately *pure*

NVLTNS inviolateness *purity*

NVLTR anovulatory *menses*

NVLV involve *include* involved involving

NVLV univalve *shellfish*

NVLVD involved *complex*

NVLVMNT involvement *inclusion*

NVLVR involver *includer*

NVLWBL invaluable (adj) *priceless* invaluably (adv)

NVLYBL invaluable (adj) *priceless* invaluably (adv)

NVLYD unvalued *not prized*

NVLYWBL invaluable (adj) *priceless* invaluably (adv)

NVLZ novelize *convert to a novel* novelized novelizing

NVLZSHN novelization *invention*

NVMBR November *month*

NVN novena *prayer*

NVN uneven *odd, irregular, rough*

NVNCHN invention *creation*

NVNGL envyingly *resentment*

NVNL envyingly *resentment*

NVNM antivenin *snakebite treatment*

NVNM envenom *poison*

NVNMZSHN envenomization *poison*

NVNN antivenin *snakebite treatment*

NVNR inventor *creator*

NVNS naiveness *simplicity*

NVNSBL invincible (adj) *strong* invincibly (adv)

NVNSBLD invincibility *strength*

NVNSBLNS invincibleness *strength*

NVNSBLT invincibility

strength

NVNSHN invention *creation*

NVNT invent *create*

NVNTFL uneventful (adj) *boring* uneventfully (adv0

NVNTR inventor *creator*

NVNTR inventory *list* inventoried inventorying inventories

NVNTSBL invincible (adj) *strong* invincibly (adv)

NVNTSBLD invincibility *strength*

NVNTSBLNS invincibleness *strength*

NVNTSBLT invincibility *strength*

NVNTV inventive *creative*

NVNV inventive *creative*

NVR knavery *mischief*

NVR naiver *simpler*

NVR never *at no time*

NVRBL invariable (adj) *constant* invariably (adv)

NVRBLD invariability *constant*

NVRBLT invariability *constant*

NVRDBL invertible *reversible*

NVRDBRT invertebrate *no spine*

NVRDR inverter *electricity*

NVRL antiviral *virus killing*

NVRMN never mind *much less*

NVRMND never mind *much less*

NVRMNL environmental (adj) *background* environmentally (adv)

NVRMNLST environmentalist *control pollution*

NVRMNLZM environmentalism *control pollution*

NVRMNT environment *background*

NVRMNTL environmental (adj) *background* environmentally (adv)

NVRMNTLST

environmentalist *control pollution*

NVRMNTLZM environmentalism *control pollution*

NVRMR nevermore *not ever again*

NVRNMNL environmental (adj) *background* environmentally (adv)

NVRNMNLST environmentalist *control pollution*

NVRNMNLZM environmentalism *control pollution*

NVRNMNT environment *background*

NVRNMNTL environmental (adj) *background* environmentally (adv)

NVRNMNTLST environmentalist *control pollution*

NVRNMNTLZM environmentalism *control pollution*

NVRNS environs *vicinity*

NVRNS invariance *no change*

NVRNSHD unvarnished *no polish*

NVRNSHT unvarnished *no polish*

NVRNTS invariance *no change*

NVRNVRLN never-never land *ideal place*

NVRNVRLND never-never land *ideal place*

NVRNZ environs *vicinity*

NVRS inverse *opposite*

NVRS universe *whole, cosmos*

NVRSD university *school* universities

NVRSH nouveau riche *newly rich* nouveaux riches

NVRSHN inversion *reversal, change, weather**

NVRSL inversely *opposite*

NVRSL universal (adj)

Letters aren't doubled for single sounds: to find alley use **L** not **LL**. Use **Y** and **W** as hard sounds only: to find yellow use **YL**. (Br)=British spelling or usage. * See dictionary.

everywhere, versatile
universally (adv)

NVRSLD universality
everywhere, clever

NVRSLNS universalness
everywhere, clever

NVRSLSDK universalistic
whole

NVRSLSTK universalistic
whole

NVRSLT universality
everywhere, clever

NVRSLZ universalize
generalize universalized
universalizing

NVRSLZSHN
universalization
generalization

NVRSR anniversary annual
date anniversaries

NVRST university school
universities

NVRT invert reverse

NVRTBL invertible reversible

NVRTBRT invertebrate no
spine

NVRTHLS nevertheless
however

NVRTR inverter electricity

NVRYBL invariable (adj)
constant invariably (adv)

NVRYBLD invariability
constant

NVRYBLT invariability
constant

NVRYNS invariance no
change

NVRYNTS invariance no
change

NVRZHN inversion reversal,
change, weather*

NVS envious jealous

NVS invoice bill invoiced
invoicing

NVS nevus birthmark nevi

NVS novice beginner

NVSDCHR investiture
establishment

NVSDGDR investigator
observer

NVSDGDV investigative
studious

NVSDGSHN investigation
study

NVSDGT investigate study
investigated investigating

NVSDGTR investigator
observer

NVSDGTR investigatory
observation

NVSDGTV investigative
studious

NVSDR investor pledge
money

NVSDTR investiture
establishment

NVSH knavish dishonest

NVSHN envision imagine

NVSHN innovation invention

NVSHN invasion forcible
entry

NVSHT novitiate beginning,
house

NVSHYT novitiate beginning,
house

NVSKSH Nova Scotia
province

NVSL enviously jealously

NVSMNT investment
envelope, money

NVSNS enviousness
jealousy

NVST invest grant control,
clothe, commit*

NVST naivest simplest

NVST unvoiced quiet

NVSTCHR investiture
establishment

NVSTGDR investigator
observer

NVSTGDV investigative
studious

NVSTGSHN investigation
study

NVSTGT investigate study
investigated investigating

NVSTGTR investigator
observer

NVSTGTR investigatory
observation

NVSTGTV investigative
studious

NVSTMNT investment
envelope, money

NVSTR investor pledge
money

NVSTTR investiture
establishment

NVSV invasive agressive

NVT innovate invent
innovated innovating

NVT invite ask, welcome
invited inviting

NVT invitee person asked

NVT naiveté innocence
(Br) naivety

NVTBL inevitable (adj) sure
to happen inevitably (adv)

NVTBLD inevitability sure to
happen inevitabilities

NVTBLT inevitability sure to
happen inevitabilities

NVTN inviting tempting

NVTNG inviting tempting

NVTNGL invitingly tempting

NVTR in vitro outside the
body

NVTR innovator inventor

NVTRT inveterate steadfast

NVTRTL inveterately
steadfast

NVTSHN invitation request

NVTV innovative new

NVV in vivo inside the body

NVV involve include involved
involving

NVVD involved complex

NVVMNT involvement
inclusion

NVVR involver includer

NVYBL enviable (adj)
desirable enviably (adv)

NVYLBL inviolable (adj)
protected inviolably (adv)

NVYLBLD inviolability
protected

NVYLBLT inviolability
protected

NVYLT inviolate pure

NVYLTL inviolately pure

NVYLTNS inviolateness
purity

NVYLTR anovulatory menses

NVYNGL envyingly
resentment

NVYNL envyingly resentment

Use letters that best describe the sounds you hear and omit the vowels. Use **S** or **K** instead of **C**: to find circle use **SRKL**. Use **J** to find joy, **JM** to find gem and **G** to find go.

NVYRMNL environmental (adj) *background* environmentally (adv)

NVYRMNLST environmentalist *control pollution*

NVYRMNLZM environmentalism *control pollution*

NVYRMNT environment *background*

NVYRMNTL environmental (adj) *background* environmentally (adv)

NVYRMNTLST environmentalist *control pollution*

NVYRMNTLZM environmentalism *control pollution*

NVYRNMNL environmental (adj) *background* environmentally (adv)

NVYRNMNLST environmentalist *control pollution*

NVYRNMNLZM environmentalism *control pollution*

NVYRNMNT environment *background*

NVYRNMNTL environmental (adj) *background* environmentally (adv)

NVYRNMNTLZM environmentalism *control pollution*

NVYRNS environs *vicinity*

NVYRNZ environs *vicinity*

NVYS envious *jealous*

NVYSL enviously *jealously*

NVYSNS enviousness *jealousy*

NVZ knives (pl) *blade* knife

NVZBL invisible (adj) *unseen* invisibly (adv)

NVZBLD invisibility *unseen*

NVZBLT invisibility *unseen*

NVZHN envision *imagine*

NVZHN invasion *forcible entry*

NVZJ envisage *imagine* envisaged envisaging

NVZV invasive *agressive*

NW anyway *in any case*

NW ennui *boredom*

NW noir *crime fiction film*

NWBL knowable *understandable*

NWBL unknowable *beyond understanding*

NWCHBL unwatchable *bad viewing*

NWD annuity *yearly money* annuities

NWD unwed *unmarried*

NWDD unweighted *no emphasis*

NWDK noetic *intellect*

NWDL know-it-all *smart one*

NWDNG unwitting *unaware*

NWDNGL unwittingly *unaware*

NWDNT annuitant *heir*

NWDZ nowadays *present time*

NWKNT no-account *trifling*

NWKST unwaxed *no polish*

NWKT no-account *trifling*

NWL annual (adj) *yearly* annually (adv)

NWL know-all *(Br) know-it-all*

NWL newel *staircase*

NWL noel *(often capitalized) Christmas*

NWL unwell *sick*

NWLD unwieldy *clumsy*

NWLKM unwelcome *no guest*

NWLN unwilling *hesitant*

NWLNG unwilling *hesitant*

NWLNGL unwillingly *hesitantly*

NWLNGNS unwillingness *hesitancy*

NWLNL unwillingly *hesitantly*

NWLNS unwillingness *hesitancy*

NWN anyone *any person*

NWN no one *no person*

NWN unknowing *ignorant*

NWN unwind *uncoil* unwound unwinding

NWND innuendo *hint* innuendos (or) innuendoes

NWND unwanted *not desired*

NWND unwind *uncoil* unwound unwinding

NWND unwonted *rare*

NWNDL unwontedly *rare*

NWNDNS unwontedness *rare*

NWNG unknowing *ignorant*

NWNGGLN New England *region*

NWNGGLND New England *region*

NWNGL knowingly *with knowledge*

NWNGL unknowingly *no knowledge*

NWNGLN New England *region*

NWNGLND New England *region*

NWNL knowingly *with knowledge*

NWNL unknowingly *no knowledge*

NWNS nuance *delicacy*

NWNTD unwanted *not desired*

NWNTD unwonted *rare*

NWNTDL unwontedly *rare*

NWNTDNS unwontedness *rare*

NWNTS nuance *delicacy*

NWR antiwar *peaceful*

NWR anywhere *any place*

NWR gnawer *chew*

NWR noir *crime fiction film*

NWR nowhere *no place*

NWR unaware *not sensing*

NWR unwary *heedless*

NWRD inward (or) inwards *inside*

NWRD onward *forward*

NWRD unwearied *fresh*

NWRDL inwardly *inside*

NWRDS inwards (or) inward *inside*

NWRDZ inwards (or) inward

Letters aren't doubled for single sounds: to find alley use **L** not **LL**. Use **Y** and **W** as hard sounds only: to find yellow use **YL**. (Br)=British spelling or usage. * See dictionary.

inside
NWRK Newark *city*
NWRKBL unworkable *not useful*
NWRL New World *America*
NWRL unwarily *heedless*
NWRL unworldly *spiritual*
NWRLD New World *America*
NWRLDL unworldly *spiritual*
NWRLDLNS unworldliness *spiritual*
NWRLNS New Orleans *city*
NWRLNZ New Orleans *city*
NWRLYNS New Orleans *city*
NWRLYNZ New Orleans *city*
NWRN unworn *new*
NWRNBL unwarrantable (adj) *not justified* unwarrantably (adv)
NWRND unwarranted *not justified*
NWRNDBL unwarrantable (adj) *not justified* unwarrantably (adv)
NWRNS unwariness *heedless*
NWRNTBL unwarrantable (adj) *not justified* unwarrantably (adv)
NWRNTD unwarranted *not justified*
NWRSH noirish *crime fiction*
NWRTH unworthy *unmerited*
NWRTHL unworthily *unmerited*
NWRTHNS unworthiness *unmerited*
NWRZ unawares *not sensing*
NWSFR noosphere *evolution*
NWSHD unwashed *dirty*
NWSHT unwashed *dirty*
NWT annuity *yearly money* annuities
NWT antiwhite *racist*
NWT unweight *shift sides*
NWTD unweighted *no emphasis*
NWTK noetic *intellect*
NWTL know-it-all *smart one*
NWTNG unwitting *unaware*
NWTNGL unwittingly

unaware
NWTNL unwittingly *unaware*
NWTNT annuitant *heir*
NWV inweave *knit* inwove inweaving inwoven
NWV new wave (n) *fad* new-wave (adj)
NWV unweave *unravel* unwove unweaving unwoven
NWVN inwoven *knitted in*
NWVN unwoven *unraveled*
NWVRN unwavering *steady*
NWVRNG unwavering *steady*
NWXT unwaxed *no polish*
NWZ anywise *anyway*
NWZ endways *on end*
NWZ endwise *on end*
NWZ nowise *in no way*
NWZ unwise *not smart*
NX annex *join* annexes (Br) annexe
NX anoxia *lack of oxygen*
NX next *following*
NX nix *no, nothing, veto*
NX nixie *mail* nixies
NX onyx *quartz*
NXDNT antioxidant *chemical*
NXDR next door (adv) *adjacent* next-door (adj)
NXK anoxic *lack of oxygen*
NXK inexact *inaccurate*
NXKDTD inexactitude *inaccurate*
NXKT inexact *inaccurate*
NXKTTD inexactitude *inaccurate*
NXKYZBL inexcusable (adj) *cannot forgive* inexcusably (adv)
NXKZBL inexcusable (adj) *cannot forgive* inexcusably (adv)
NXM anoxemia *lack of oxygen*
NXMK anoxemic *lack of oxygen*
NXMND unexamined *thoughtless*
NXMY anoxemia *lack of oxygen*

NXND unaccented *no emphasis*
NXNTD unaccented *no emphasis*
NXPBL inexpiable (adj) *unforgiven* inexpiably (adv)
NXPDBL unacceptable (adj) *reject* unacceptably (adv)
NXPDNC inexpediency *unwise* inexpedience
NXPDNS inexpediency *unwise* inexpedience
NXPDNT inexpedient *unwise*
NXPDNTC inexpediency *unwise* inexpedience
NXPDNTS inexpediency *unwise* inexpedience
NXPDYNC inexpediency *unwise* inexpedience
NXPDYNS inexpediency *unwise* inexpedience
NXPDYNT inexpedient *unwise*
NXPDYNTC inexpediency *unwise* inexpedience
NXPDYNTS inexpediency *unwise* inexpedience
NXPGNBL inexpugnable (adj) *stable* inexpugnably (adv)
NXPKDD unexpected *surprise*
NXPKDDL unexpectedly *surprise*
NXPKDDNS unexpectedness *surprise*
NXPKTD unexpected *surprise*
NXPKTDL unexpectedly *surprise*
NXPKTDNS unexpectedness *surprise*
NXPLKBL inexplicable (adj) *no explanation* inexplicably (adv)
NXPLKBLD inexplicability *no explanation*
NXPLKBLT inexplicability *no explanation*
NXPLNBL unexplainable

Use letters that best describe the sounds you hear and omit the vowels. Use **S** or **K** instead of **C**: to find circle use **SRKL**. Use **J** to find joy, **JM** to find gem and **G** to find go.

(adj) *mysterious* unexplainably (adv)

NXPLND unexplained *mysterious*

NXPLRD unexplored *unknown*

NXPNBL inexpugnable (adj) *stable* inexpugnably (adv)

NXPNJBL inexpungible *cannot erase*

NXPNSV inexpensive *low cost*

NXPNSVL inexpensively *low cost*

NXPRNS inexperience *no knowledge*

NXPRNSD inexperienced *no knowledge*

NXPRNST inexperienced *no knowledge*

NXPRNTS inexperience *no knowledge*

NXPRSBL inexpressible (adj) *no description* inexpressibly (adv)

NXPRSBLD inexpressibility *no description*

NXPRSBLT inexpressibility *no description*

NXPRSV inexpressive *no expression*

NXPRT inexpert *unskilled*

NXPRTL inexpertly *unskilled*

NXPRYNS inexperience *no knowledge*

NXPRYNSD inexperienced *no knowledge*

NXPRYNST inexperienced *no knowledge*

NXPRYNTS inexperience *no knowledge*

NXPSHNBL unexceptionable (adj) *beyond reproach* unexceptionably (adv)

NXPSHNBLNS unexceptionableness *beyond reproach*

NXPSHNL unexceptional *commonplace*

NXPTBL unacceptable (adj) *reject* unacceptably (adv)

NXPYBL inexpiable (adj) *unforgiven* inexpiably (adv)

NXPYNBL inexpugnable (adj) *stable* inexpugnably (adv)

NXQZBL inexcusable (adj) *cannot forgive* inexcusably (adv)

NXRBL inexorable (adj) *relentless* inexorably (adv)

NXRBLD inexorability *relentless*

NXRBLT inexorability *relentless*

NXRSZD unexercised *not used*

NXS nexus *link, focus* nexuses (or) nexus

NXSBL inaccessible (adj) *no passage* inaccessibly (adv)

NXSBLD inaccessibility *no passage*

NXSBLT inaccessibility *no passage*

NXSDBL inexhaustible (adj) *cannot use up or tire* inexhaustibly (adv)

NXSDNT inexistent *not real*

NXSHN annexation *joint*

NXSHNL annexational *joint*

NXSHNST annexationist *joiner*

NXSTBL inexhaustible (adj) *cannot use up or tire* inexhaustibly (adv)

NXSTNT inexistent *not real*

NXT next *following*

NXT next to *beside*

NXTNGGWSHBL inextinguishable (adj) *unquenchable* inextinguishably (adv)

NXTNGWSHBL inextinguishable (adj) *unquenchable* inextinguishably (adv)

NXTNS in extenso *full length*

NXTR next door (adv) *adjacent* next-door (adj)

NXTRKBL inextricable (adj)

tangle inextricably (adv)

NXVL Knoxville *city*

NXY anoxia *lack of oxygen*

NY anew *fresh*

NY gnu *antelope* gnu (or) gnus

NY Ionia *ancient region*

NY knew *(v-past) know*

NY new *unused, modern, unfamiliar**

NY nu *Greek letter*

NYBL nubile *marriage age*

NYBRG Newburg (or) Newburgh *sauce*

NYBRN newborn *infant* newborn (or) newborns

NYBRSHN antiabortion *against pregnancy termination*

NYCHRL neutral (adj) *middling* neutrally (adv)

NYD Aeneid *poem*

NYD annuity *yearly money* annuities

NYD naiad *nymph* naiads (or) naiades

NYD nude *naked* nuder nudest

NYDBRNGK nudibranch *mollusk* nudibranchs

NYDBRNK nudibranch *mollusk* nudibranchs

NYDD nudity *bareness*

NYDL inutile *useless*

NYDL New Deal *government program*

NYDL New Delhi *city*

NYDL nudely *barely*

NYDMM neodymium *element*

NYDMYM neodymium *element*

NYDNS nudeness *nakedness*

NYDNT annuitant *heir*

NYDR in utero *uterus*

NYDR neuter *(v) castrate (adj) neutral (n) gender, worker, animal*

NYDST nudist *naked one*

NYDT nudity *bareness*

NYDZ anti-AIDS *serum*

NYDZM nudism *naked*

Letters aren't doubled for single sounds: to find alley use **L** not **LL**. Use **Y** and **W** as hard sounds only: to find yellow use **YL**. (Br)=British spelling or usage. * See dictionary.

NYFL neophilia *newness*
NYFLK neophiliac *newness*
NYFLYK neophiliac *newness*
NYFNDLN Newfoundland *island*
NYFNDLND Newfoundland *island*
NYFNGGLD newfangled *novel*
NYFNGLD newfangled *novel*
NYFNLN Newfoundland *island*
NYFNLND Newfoundland *island*
NYFRDN neo-Freudian *psychology*
NYFRDYN neo-Freudian *psychology*
NYFSHN new-fashioned *modern*
NYFSHND new-fashioned *modern*
NYFSHTL Neufchâtel *cheese*
NYFT neophyte *beginner*
NYGN Neogene *rocks*
NYGN New Guinea *island*
NYGRFLS Niagara Falls *waterfall*
NYGRFLZ Niagara Falls *waterfall*
NYGTHK neo-Gothic *style*
NYGTR nugatory *vain*
NYHBRDZ New Hebrides *island*
NYHMPSHR New Hampshire *US State*
NYHMSHR New Hampshire *US State*
NYJN Neogene *rocks*
NYJRZ New Jersey *US State*
NYK gnocchi *dumpling*
NYK nuke *bomb, microwave* nuked nuking
NYKDMK antiacademic *against schooling*
NYKL nuclei (pl) *center* nucleus
NYKLD nucleoid *DNA*
NYKLD nuclide *atom*
NYKLDK nuclidic *atom*
NYKLDN New Caledonia

island
NYKLDNY New Caledonia *island*
NYKLDR nucleator *cluster*
NYKLFL nucleophile *substance*
NYKLFLK nucleophilic *atomic*
NYKLKSD nucleic acid *DNA, RNA*
NYKLLS nucleolus *cell*
NYKLN nuclein *protein, acid*
NYKLN nucleon *particle*
NYKLNK nucleonic *particle*
NYKLNKS nucleonics *science*
NYKLNL neocolonial *politics*
NYKLNLZM neocolonialism *politics*
NYKLNX nucleonics *science*
NYKLNYL neocolonial *politics*
NYKLNYLZM neocolonialism *politics*
NYKLPLZM nucleoplasm *sap*
NYKLPLZMK nucleoplasmic *sap*
NYKLPRTN nucleoprotein *gene*
NYKLR nuclear *atomic, central*
NYKLS nucleus *center* nuclei
NYKLSHN nucleation *cluster*
NYKLSK neoclassic (or) neoclassical *style*
NYKLSKL neoclassical (or) neoclassic *style*
NYKLSNTHSS nucleosynthesis *chemistry*
NYKLT nucleate *cluster* nucleated nucleating
NYKLTD nucleotide *acid*
NYKLTK nuclidic *atom*
NYKLTR nucleator *cluster*
NYKLY nuclei (pl) *center* nucleus
NYKLYD nucleoid *DNA*
NYKLYDR nucleator *cluster*
NYKLYFL nucleophile

substance
NYKLYFLK nucleophilic *atomic*
NYKLYFLSD nucleophilicity *atomic*
NYKLYFLST nucleophilicity *atomic*
NYKLYKSD nucleic acid *DNA, RNA*
NYKLYLS nucleolus *cell*
NYKLYN nuclein *protein, acid*
NYKLYN nucleon *particle*
NYKLYNK nucleonic *particle*
NYKLYNKS nucleonics *science*
NYKLYNX nucleonics *science*
NYKLYPLZM nucleoplasm *sap*
NYKLYPLZMK nucleoplasmic *sap*
NYKLYPRTN nucleoprotein *gene*
NYKLYR nuclear *atomic, central*
NYKLYS nuclease *enzyme*
NYKLYS nucleus *center* nuclei
NYKLYSHN nucleation *cluster*
NYKLYSNTHSS nucleosynthesis *chemistry*
NYKLYT nucleate *cluster* nucleated nucleating
NYKLYTD nucleotide *acid*
NYKLYTR nucleator *cluster*
NYKLYZ nuclease *enzyme*
NYKMR newcomer *arrival*
NYKNSRVDV neoconservative *politics*
NYKNSRVTV neoconservative *politics*
NYKRDKL neocortical *brain*
NYKRTKL neocortical *brain*
NYKRTKS neocortex *brain*
NYKRTX neocortex *brain*
NYKSDNT antioxidant *chemical*
NYL annual (adj) *yearly* annually (adv)
NYL enisle *isolate*

Use letters that best describe the sounds you hear and omit the vowels. Use **S** or **K** instead of **C**: to find circle use **SRKL**. Use **J** to find joy, **JM** to find gem and **G** to find go.

NYL newel *staircase*
NYL newly *recently*
NYL niello *alloy* nielli (or) niellos
NYL Nile *river*
NYL noil *short fiber*
NYL nyala *animal* nyalas (or) nyala
NYLBRL neoliberal *progressive*
NYLBRLZM neoliberalism *progressive*
NYLDN unyielding *tough*
NYLDNG unyielding *tough*
NYLDR annihilator *destroyer*
NYLJSDK neologistic *word*
NYLJSTK neologistic *word*
NYLJZM neologism *word*
NYLN inulin *chemical*
NYLR annular *ring*
NYLRJNK antiallergenic *not allergy promoting*
NYLS annulus *ring* annuli
NYLSDK nihilistic *destructive*
NYLSHN annihilation *destruction*
NYLSHN annulation *rings*
NYLST nihilist *destroyer*
NYLSTK nihilistic *destructive*
NYLT annihilate *destroy* annihilated annihilating
NYLT annulate *ringed*
NYLTH neolith *tool*
NYLTHK Neolithic *Stone Age*
NYLTR annihilator *destroyer*
NYLWD newlywed *marriage*
NYLZM nihilism *philosophy*
NYM neume *symbol*
NYM pneuma *spirit*
NYMDK neumatic *symbol*
NYMDK pneumatic *compressed air*
NYMDKL pneumatically *air*
NYMGRF pneumograph *breathing*
NYMKKS pneumococcus *bacteria* pneumococci
NYMKNSS pneumoconiosis *black lung* pneumoconioses
NYMKNYSS pneumoconiosis *black*

lung pneumoconioses
NYMKSK New Mexico *US State*
NYMN new moon *lunar phase*
NYMN numen *force* numina
NYMN pneumonia *disease*
NYMNDS pneumonitis *lungs*
NYMNK pneumonic *lungs*
NYMNS numinous *mysterious*
NYMNSNS numinousness *mystery*
NYMNTS pneumonitis *lungs*
NYMNY pneumonia *disease*
NYMRBL enumerable *countable*
NYMRBL innumerable (adj) *countless* innumerably (adv)
NYMRBL numerable *many*
NYMRBLD enumerability *count*
NYMRBLT enumerability *count*
NYMRC innumeracy *ignorance of mathematics*
NYMRC numeracy *numbers*
NYMRDR enumerator *census taker*
NYMRDR numerator *number*
NYMRDV enumerative *count*
NYMRK numeric *number*
NYMRKL numerical (adj) *numbers* numerically (adv)
NYMRL numeral (adj) *number* numerally (adv)
NYMRLG numerology *numbers*
NYMRLJ numerology *numbers*
NYMRLJST numerologist *numbers*
NYMRS innumeracy *ignorance of mathematics*
NYMRS innumerous *countless*
NYMRS numeracy *numbers*
NYMRS numerous *many*

NYMRSHN enumeration *count*
NYMRSHN numeration *number system*
NYMRSL numerously *many*
NYMRSNS numerousness *many*
NYMRT enumerate *count* enumerated enumerating
NYMRT innumerate *ignorant of mathematics*
NYMRT numerate *count* numerated numerating
NYMRTR enumerator *census taker*
NYMRTR numerator *number*
NYMRTV enumerative *count*
NYMSN neomycin *drug*
NYMTHRKS pneumothorax *lungs*
NYMTHRX pneumothorax *lungs*
NYMTK neumatic *symbol*
NYMTK pneumatic *compressed air*
NYMTKL pneumatically *air*
NYMTLG pneumatology *spirits*
NYMTLJ pneumatology *spirits*
NYMXSK New Mexico *US State*
NYMZMDK numismatic *money*
NYMZMDKL numismatically *money*
NYMZMDKS numismatics *money*
NYMZMDX numismatics *money*
NYMZMTK numismatic *money*
NYMZMTKL numismatically *money*
NYMZMTKS numismatics *money*
NYMZMTST numismatist *money*
NYMZMTX numismatics *money*
NYN aeonian (or) aeonic *long-lasting*

Letters aren't doubled for single sounds: to find alley use **L** not **LL**. Use **Y** and **W** as hard sounds only: to find yellow use **YL**. (Br)=British spelling or usage. * See dictionary.

NYN anion *negative ion*
NYN annoying *bothersome*
NYN neon *gas*
NYN onion *vegetable*
NYN union *merger, labor group*
NYND innuendo *hint* innuendos (or) innuendoes
NYNDL neonatal *newborn*
NYNDRTHL Neanderthal *caveman*
NYNDRTL Neanderthal *caveman*
NYNFLMTR anti-inflammatory *remove swelling*
NYNFLSHNR anti-inflationary *no growth*
NYNG annoying *bothersome*
NYNGGLN New England *region*
NYNGGLND New England *region*
NYNGL annoyingly *bothersome*
NYNGZT antianxiety *calming*
NYNGZYT antianxiety *calming*
NYNJK Union Jack *flag*
NYNN antiunion *against organized labor*
NYNS annoyance *bother*
NYNSKN onionskin *paper*
NYNST unionist *labor*
NYNT neonate *newborn*
NYNTL neonatal *newborn*
NYNTLG neonatology *newborn*
NYNTLJ neonatology *newborn*
NYNTLJST neonatologist *newborn*
NYNTLKCHL anti-intellectual *against learning*
NYNTLKCHWL anti-intellectual *against learning*
NYNTLKSHL anti-intellectual *against learning*

NYNTLKSHWL anti-intellectual *against learning*
NYNTS annoyance *bother*
NYNTS neo-Nazi *fascist*
NYNTZ neo-Nazi *fascist*
NYNYN antiunion *against organized labor*
NYNZ unionize *unite* unionized unionizing (Br) unionise
NYNZM unionism *labor*
NYNZSHN unionization *labor* (Br) unionisation
NYNZT antianxiety *calming*
NYNZYT antianxiety *calming*
NYPLD aneuploid *chromosomes*
NYPLDN Neapolitan *of Naples*
NYPLSDK neoplastic *tumor*
NYPLSH neoplasia *tumor*
NYPLSM neoplasm *tumor*
NYPLSTK neoplastic *tumor*
NYPLTN Neapolitan *of Naples*
NYPLZH neoplasia *tumor*
NYPLZM neoplasm *tumor*
NYPRN neoprene *rubber*
NYPRTD antiapartheid *against racism*
NYR annoyer *botherer*
NYR anuria *urine*
NYR inure *accustom* inured inuring
NYRBLSDM neuroblastoma *nerve cell* neuroblastomas (or) neuroblastomata
NYRBLSDMD neuroblastomata (pl) *nerve cell* neuroblastoma
NYRBLSDMT neuroblastomata (pl) *nerve cell* neuroblastoma
NYRBLSTM neuroblastoma *nerve cell* neuroblastomas (or) neuroblastomata
NYRBLSTMD neuroblastomata (pl) *nerve cell* neuroblastoma

NYRBLSTMT neuroblastomata (pl) *nerve cell* neuroblastoma
NYRCZ neuroses (pl) *psychology* neurosis
NYRDDZ neuritides (pl) *nerve* neuritis
NYRDK enuretic *urine*
NYRDK neurotic *psychology*
NYRDKL neurotically *psychology*
NYRDS neuritis *nerve problems* neutitides
NYRFBRL neurofibril *protein*
NYRFBRLR neurofibrillary *protein*
NYRFBRM neurofibroma *mass*
NYRFBRMTSS neurofibromatosis *disease*
NYRFRMKLG neuropharmacology *nerve drugs*
NYRFRMKLJ neuropharmacology *nerve drugs*
NYRFRMKLJKL neuropharmacological *nerve drugs*
NYRFRMKLJST neuropharmacologist *nerve drugs*
NYRFS in-your-face *agressive*
NYRFZLG neurophysiology *nerve structure*
NYRFZLJ neurophysiology *nerve structure*
NYRFZLJKL neurophysiological *nerve structure*
NYRFZLJST neurophysiologist *nerve structure*
NYRFZYLG neurophysiology *nerve structure*
NYRFZYLJ neurophysiology *nerve structure*
NYRFZYLJKL neurophysiological *nerve*

structure
NYRFZYLJST
neurophysiologist *nerve*
structure
NYRGL neuroglia *tissue*
NYRGLY neuroglia *tissue*
NYRGNK neurogenic *nerves*
NYRGNKL neurogenically
nerves
NYRHPFCL
neurohypophyseal (or)
neurohypophysial
pituitary
NYRHPFCYL
neurohypophyseal (or)
neurohypophysial
pituitary
NYRHPFSL
neurohypophyseal (or)
neurohypophysial
pituitary
NYRHPFSS
neurohypophysis
pituitary
NYRHPFSYL
neurohypophyseal (or)
neurohypophysial
pituitary
NYRHPFZL
neurohypophyseal (or)
neurohypophysial
pituitary
NYRHPFZYL
neurohypophyseal (or)
neurohypophysial
pituitary
NYRJNK neurogenic *nerves*
NYRJNKL neurogenically
nerves
NYRK anuric *urine*
NYRK New York *US State,*
city
NYRK Newark *city*
NYRKDV neuroactive
stimulus
NYRKMSTR
neurochemistry *nerves*
NYRKRF antiaircraft
defensive
NYRKRFT antiaircraft
defensive
NYRKTV neuroactive

stimulus
NYRL neural (adj) *nerve*
neurally (adv)
NYRL neurula *embryo*
neurulae (or) neurulas
NYRLG neurology *nerve*
science
NYRLJ neuralgia *pain*
NYRLJ neurology *nerve*
science
NYRLJK neuralgic *painful*
NYRLJKL neurological (or)
neurologic (adj) *nerves*
neurologically (adv)
NYRLJST neurologist *nerves*
NYRLNS New Orleans *city*
NYRLNZ New Orleans *city*
NYRLPDK neuroleptic
tranquilizer
NYRLPTK neuroleptic
tranquilizer
NYRLSHN neurulation
embryo
(Br) neutraliser
NYRM neuroma *tumor*
neuromas (or) neuromata
NYRMD neuromata (pl)
tumor neuroma
NYRMNT inurement
accustom
NYRMT neuromata (pl)
tumor neuroma
NYRN anuran *amphibian*
NYRN neuron *cell*
NYRNDKRN
neuroendocrine *hormone*
NYRNL neuronal *cell*
NYRPDRN neuropteran
insect
NYRPDRS neuropterous
insect
NYRPTH neuropathy
degeneration
NYRPTHK neuropathic
degeneration
NYRPTHKL neuropathically
degeneration
NYRPTHLG neuropathology
nerve disease
NYRPTHLJ neuropathology
nerve disease
NYRPTHLJK

neuropathologic (or)
neuropathological *nerve*
disease
NYRPTHLJKL
neuropathological (or)
neuropathologic *nerve*
disease
NYRPTHLJST
neuropathologist *nerve*
disease
NYRPTRN neuropteran
insect
NYRPTRS neuropterous
insect
NYRSKLG
neuropsychology *mental*
NYRSKLJ neuropsychology
mental
NYRSKLJKL
neuropsychological
mental
NYRSKLJST
neuropsychologist *mental*
NYRSKTR neuropsychiatry
mental
NYRSKTRK
neuropsychiatric *mental*
NYRSKTRST
neuropsychiatrist *mental*
NYRSKYTR
neuropsychiatry *mental*
NYRSKYTRK
neuropsychiatric *mental*
NYRSKYTRST
neuropsychiatrist *mental*
NYRSM aneurysm *dilation*
NYRSML aneurysmal
dilation
NYRSNS neuroscience
nerves
NYRSNSR neurosensory
nerves
NYRSNTS neuroscience
nerves
NYRSNTSR neurosensory
nerves
NYRSPR neurospora *fungus*
NYRSRJKL neurosurgical
brain
NYRSRJN neurosurgeon
brain
NYRSRJR neurosurgery

brain
NYRSS enuresis *urine*
NYRSS neurosis *psychology*
neuroses
NYRSTHN neurasthenia
mental disorder
NYRSTHNK neurasthenic
mental disorder
NYRSTHNKL
neurasthenically *mental*
disorder
NYRSTHNY neurasthenia
mental disorder
NYRSYNS neuroscience
nerves
NYRSYNTS neuroscience
nerves
NYRSZ neuroses (pl)
psychology neurosis
NYRTDZ neuritides (pl)
nerve neuritis
NYRTHDKS neoorthodox
new truth neoorthodoxy
NYRTHDX neoorthodox
new truth neoorthodoxy
NYRTHRDK antiarthritic
combating arthritis
NYRTHRTK antiarthritic
combating arthritis
NYRTK enuretic *urine*
NYRTK neurotic *psychology*
NYRTKL neurotically
psychology
NYRTKSK neurotoxic *poison*
NYRTKSN neurotoxin *poison*
NYRTRNSMDR
neurotransmitter *synapse*
NYRTRNSMTR
neurotransmitter *synapse*
NYRTRNZMDR
neurotransmitter *synapse*
NYRTRNZMSHN
neurotransmission
synapse
NYRTRNZMTR
neurotransmitter *synapse*
NYRTS neuritis *nerve*
problems neutitides
NYRTXK neurotoxic *poison*
NYRTXN neurotoxin *poison*
NYRWKDV neuroactive
stimulus

NYRWKTV neuroactive
stimulus
NYRWNDKRN
neuroendocrine *hormone*
NYRY anuria *urine*
NYRZM aneurysm *dilation*
NYRZML aneurysmal
dilation
NYS Aeneas *Greek hero*
NYSD Agnus Dei *prayer*
NYSHL unusual (adj) *rare*
unusually (adv)
NYSHLNS unusualness
rarity
NYSHTL Neufchâtel *cheese*
NYSHWL unusual (adj) *rare*
unusually (adv)
NYSHWLNS unusualness
rarity
NYSLS nucellus *ovule*
NYSN niacin *vitamin B*
NYSNMD niacinamide
vitamin B
NYSNS nuisance *bother*
NYSNTS nuisance *bother*
NYSPK newspeak *words*
NYST unused *new*
NYSTBLSHMNT
antiestablishment *against*
rulers
NYSTGMN neostigmine
drug
NYSTN neuston *organism*
NYT annuity *yearly money*
annuities
NYT newt *salamander*
NYTHRD antiauthority
rebellious
NYTHRT antiauthority
rebellious
NYTL inutile *useless*
NYTN neoteny *larva*
NYTN newton *unit of force*
NYTNN Newtonian *of*
Newton
NYTNT annuitant *heir*
NYTNYN Newtonian *of*
Newton
NYTP neotype *specimen*
NYTR in utero *uterus*
NYTR neuter *(v)* castrate
(adj) neutral *(n)* gender,

worker, animal
NYTR nutria *rodent*
NYTRDV nutritive *nourishing*
NYTRFL neutrophil (or)
neutrophilic *stain*
NYTRFLK neutrophilic (or)
neutrophil *stain*
NYTRK neoteric *modern*
NYTRL neutral (adj)
middling neutrally (adv)
NYTRLD neutrality *middle*
NYTRLSSHN neutralization
cancellation
(Br) neutralisation
NYTRLT neutrality *middle*
NYTRLZ neutralize *cancel*
neutralized neutralizing
(Br) neutralise
NYTRLZR neutralizer
canceller
(Br) neutraliser
NYTRLZSHN neutralization
cancellation
(Br) neutralisation
NYTRMNT nutriment *food*
NYTRN neutrino *particle*
without mass neutrinos
NYTRN neutron *particle with*
mass
NYTRNT nutrient *food*
NYTRPKL Neotropical
region
NYTRPKS neotropics *region*
NYTRPX neotropics *region*
NYTRSHN nutrition *food*
NYTRSHNL nutritional (adj)
food nutritionally (adv)
NYTRSHNST nutritionist
food
NYTRSHS nutritious
healthful
NYTRSHSL nutritiously
healthfully
NYTRSHSNS nutritiousness
health
NYTRTV nutritive *nourishing*
NYTRY nutria *rodent*
NYTRYNT nutrient *food*
NYTSDMNT New
Testament *bible*
NYTSHN nutation *wobble*
NYTSTMNT New Testament

Use letters that best describe the sounds you hear and omit the vowels. Use **S** or **K**
instead of **C**: to find circle use **SRKL**. Use **J** to find joy, **JM** to find gem and **G** to find go.

bible

NYTT nutate *wobble* nutated nutating

NYV naïve (or) naive *simple* naiver naivest

NYV nouveau *new*

NYVL naïvely (or) naively *simply*

NYVNS naiveness *simplicity*

NYVR naiver *simpler*

NYVRSH nouveau riche *newly rich* nouveaux riches

NYVST naivest *simplest*

NYVT naiveté *innocence* (Br) naivety

NYW ennui *boredom*

NYWD annuity *yearly money* annuities

NYWDNT annuitant *heir*

NYWL annual (adj) *yearly* annually (adv)

NYWL newel *staircase*

NYWND innuendo *hint* innuendos (or) innuendoes

NYWNGGLN New England *region*

NYWNGGLND New England *region*

NYWNGLN New England *region*

NYWNGLND New England *region*

NYWNS nuance *delicacy*

NYWNTS nuance *delicacy*

NYWRK Newark *city*

NYWRL New World *America*

NYWRLD New World *America*

NYWRLNS New Orleans *city*

NYWRLNZ New Orleans *city*

NYWRLYNS New Orleans *city*

NYWRLYNZ New Orleans *city*

NYWT annuity *yearly money* annuities

NYWTNT annuitant *heir*

NYWV new wave (n) *fad*

new-wave (adj)

NYXDNT antioxidant *chemical*

NYYRK New York *US State, city*

NYZ news *information*

NYZ newsy *chatty* newsier newsiest

NYZB newsboy *delivery*

NYZBL unusable *useless*

NYZBRK newsbreak *event*

NYZD unused *new*

NYZDLR newsdealer *seller*

NYZHL unusual (adj) *rare* unusually (adv)

NYZHLNS unusualness *rarity*

NYZHN newshound *journalist*

NYZHND newshound *journalist*

NYZHWL unusual (adj) *rare* unusually (adv)

NYZHWLNS unusualness *rarity*

NYZJNC news agency *media*

NYZJNS news agency *media*

NYZJNT newsagent *(Br) newsdealer*

NYZJNTC news agency *media*

NYZJNTS news agency *media*

NYZKSDR newscaster *broadcaster*

NYZKST newscast *broadcast*

NYZKSTR newscaster *broadcaster*

NYZLDR newsletter *leaflet*

NYZLN New Zealand *country*

NYZLND New Zealand *country*

NYZLTR newsletter *leaflet*

NYZMGZN newsmagazine *publication*

NYZMN newsman *reporter* newsmen

NYZPPR newspaper *publication, newsprint*

NYZPPRMN newspaperman *employee, owner* newspapermen

NYZPPRWMN newspaperwoman *employee, owner* newspaperwomen

NYZPRNT newsprint *paper*

NYZPRSN newsperson *reporter*

NYZR end user *consumer*

NYZR newsier *chatty*

NYZRL newsreel *film*

NYZRM newsroom *office*

NYZST newsiest *chatty*

NYZSTN newsstand *market*

NYZSTND newsstand *market*

NYZWMN newswoman *reporter* newswomen

NYZWRTH newsworthy *of interest*

NYZWRTHNS newsworthiness *of interest*

NYZYR newsier *chatty*

NYZYST newsiest *chatty*

NZ ionize *convert* ionized ionizing (Br) ionise

NZ nausea *sickness*

NZ Nazi *fascist*

NZ news *information*

NZ newsy *chatty* newsier newsiest

NZ noise (v) *spread rumors* noised noising

NZ noise (n) *sound*

NZ noisy *loud* noisier noisiest

NZ nose (v) *pry, smell* nosed nosing

NZ nose (n) *sense organ, aroma*

NZ nosy (or) nosey *prying* nosier nosiest

NZ unease *tension*

NZ uneasy *tense*

NZB newsboy *delivery*

NZBL unusable *useless*

NZBLD nosebleed *blood*

NZBN noseband *headstall*

Letters aren't doubled for single sounds: to find alley use **L** not **LL**. Use **Y** and **W** as hard sounds only: to find yellow use **YL**. (Br)=British spelling or usage. * See dictionary.

NZBND noseband *headstall*
NZBRK newsbreak *event*
NZD anxiety *concern*
anxieties
NZDK enzootic *native*
NZDLR newsdealer *seller*
NZDV nosedive (n) *plunge*
nose-dive (v)
NZFRNGKS nasopharynx
throat
NZFRNGL nasopharyngeal
throat
NZFRNGS nasopharynx
throat
NZFRNGX nasopharynx
throat
NZFRNGYL
nasopharyngeal *throat*
NZFRNJL nasopharyngeal
throat
NZFRNJYL nasopharyngeal
throat
NZFRNKS nasopharynx
throat
NZFRNX nasopharynx
throat
NZG nosegay *posy*
NZGRD noseguard *football*
NZH nausea *sickness*
NZHL unusual (adj) *rare*
unusually (adv)
NZHLNS unusualness *rarity*
NZHN ingénue (or) ingenue
girl
NZHN newshound *journalist*
NZHND newshound
journalist
NZHNY ingénue (or)
ingenue *girl*
NZHS nauseous *sick*
NZHT nauseate *make sick*
nauseated nauseating
NZHWL nosewheel *airplane*
NZHWL unusual (adj) *rare*
unusually (adv)
NZHWLNS unusualness
rarity
NZHYT nauseate *make sick*
nauseated nauseating
NZJB nose job *surgery*
NZJNC news agency *media*
NZJNS news agency *media*

NZJNT newsagent *(Br)*
newsdealer
NZJNTC news agency
media
NZJNTS news agency
media
NZK Anzac *Australia/New
Zealand*
NZKN nose cone *missile*
NZKSDR newscaster
broadcaster
NZKST newscast *broadcast*
NZKSTR newscaster
broadcaster
NZL nasal (adj) *nose* nasally
(adv)
NZL noisily *loud*
NZL nosily *prying*
NZL nozzle *spray*
NZL nuzzle *cuddle* nuzzled
nuzzling
NZL uneasily *difficult*
NZLD nasality *nose*
NZLDR newsletter *leaflet*
NZLN New Zealand *country*
NZLND New Zealand
country
NZLS noiseless *silent*
NZLT nasality *nose*
NZLTR newsletter *leaflet*
NZLZ nasalize *sound*
nasalized nasalizing
NZLZSHN nasalization
sound
NZM anosmia *not smelling*
NZM enzyme *chemical*
NZMCHZ inasmuch as
insofar
NZMDK enzymatic *chemical*
NZMDKL enzymatically
chemical
NZMGZN newsmagazine
publication
NZMK anosmic *not smelling*
NZMKR noisemaker *rattle,
horn*
NZMLG enzymology
enzymes
NZMLJ enzymology
enzymes
NZMLJST enzymologist
enzymes

NZMN newsman *reporter*
newsmen
NZMTK enzymatic *chemical*
NZMTKL enzymatically
chemical
NZMY anosmia *not smelling*
NZN newshound *journalist*
NZN unison *as one*
NZND newshound *journalist*
NZNDTS ins and outs
oddities, process
NZNS noisiness *loud*
NZNS nosiness *prying*
NZNS uneasiness *tension*
NZNTS ins and outs
oddities, process
NZP unzip *open* unzipped
unzipping
NZPPR newspaper
publication, newsprint
NZPPRMN newspaperman
employee, owner
newspapermen
NZPPRWMN
newspaperwoman
employee, owner
newspaperwomen
NZPRNT newsprint *paper*
NZPRSN newsperson
reporter
NZPS nosepiece *lens*
NZR end user *consumer*
NZR newsier *chatty*
NZR noisier *loud*
NZR nosier *prying*
NZRL newsreel *film*
NZRM newsroom *office*
NZRN Nazarene *of Nazareth,
Christian*
NZS nauseous *sick*
NZSHN ionization *atoms*
(Br) ionisation
NZSM noisome *loud*
NZST newsiest *chatty*
NZST noisiest *loud*
NZST nosiest *prying*
NZSTN newsstand *market*
NZSTND newsstand *market*
NZT anxiety *concern*
anxieties
NZT nauseate *make sick*
nauseated nauseating

Use letters that best describe the sounds you hear and omit the vowels. Use **S** or **K** instead of **C**: to find circle use **SRKL**. Use **J** to find joy, **JM** to find gem and **G** to find go.

NZT nose out *investigate*
NZTK enzootic *native*
NZWDK enzootic *native*
NZWL nosewheel *airplane*
NZWMN newswoman *reporter* newswomen
NZWRTH newsworthy *of interest*
NZWRTHNS newsworthiness *of interest*
NZWTK enzootic *native*
NZY nausea *sickness*
NZYD anxiety *concern* anxieties
NZYR newsier *chatty*
NZYR noisier *loud*
NZYR nosier *prying*
NZYS nauseous *sick*
NZYST newsiest *chatty*
NZYST noisiest *loud*
NZYST nosiest *prying*
NZYT anxiety *concern* anxieties
NZYT nauseate *make sick* nauseated nauseating
NZZM Nazism (or) Naziism *fascism*

P

P ape *(v) mimic* aped aping
P ape *(n) animal*
P apt *likely*
P épée (or) epee *sword*
P opah *fish*
P pa *father*
P paella *food*
P pas *dance step* pas
P paw *(n) foot (v) grab*
P pay *(v) give money* paid paying
P pay *(n) wage (adj) fee*
P payee *receiver*

P pe *Hebrew letter*
P pea *vegetable* peas
P pee *(v-vulgar) urinate* peed peeing
P pee *(n) alphabet letter, (vulgar) urine, (Br) penny*
P pew *bench*
P pi *Greek letter, mathematics* pis
P pie *pastry*
P poi *taro root* poi (or) pois
P up *above*
PB pooh-bah *(often capitalized) title*
PB pub *saloon*
PBK payback *repay*
PBK pubic *pelvis*
PBL epiboly *growth* epibolies
PBL payable *owed*
PBL pebble *(n) stone, surface*
PBL pebble *(v) pave, grain* pebbled pebbling
PBL pebbly *stony, grainy*
PBLD piebald *spotted*
PBLK epibolic *growth*
PBLK public *(adj) open, general, social (n) populace*
PBLKL publicly *openly*
PBLKN publican *taxes*
PBLKNS publicness *open*
PBLKSHN publication *writing*
PBLM pablum *bland*
PBLM pabulum *nutrient*
PBLSD publicity *attention*
PBLSH publish *print*
PBLSHBL publishable *printing*
PBLSHN publishing *printing*
PBLSHNG publishing *printing*
PBLSHR publisher *printing*
PBLSST publicist *writer*
PBLST epiblast *outer layer*
PBLST publicity *attention*
PBLSZ publicize *draw attention* publicized publicizing (Br) publicise
PBN pea bean *vegetable*
PBRD puberty *sexuality*

PBRD upbraid *scold*
PBRDL pubertal (or) puberal *sexuality*
PBRK pibroch *bagpipe*
PBRL puberal (or) pubertal *sexuality*
PBRNGN upbringing *training*
PBRNGNG upbringing *training*
PBRT puberty *sexuality*
PBRTL pubertal (or) puberal *sexuality*
PBS pubis *bone* pubes
PBSNS pubescense *hair*
PBSNT pubescent *hair*
PBSNTS pubescense *hair*
PBT upbeat *cheerful*
PBYLM pabulum *nutrient*
PBZ pubes *hair* pubes
PC pussy *cat* pussies
PC pussy *with pus* pussier pussiest
PCH Apache *Native American* Apache (or) Apaches
PCH patch *(n) area, cover, scrap (v) mend, connect* patches
PCH patchy *spotty* patchier patchiest
PCH peach *fruit* peaches
PCH peachy *dandy* peachier peachiest
PCH pitch *(n) tar, slope, field** pitches
PCH pitch *(v) erect, toss, slope* pitches
PCH pitchy *tar, black*
PCH poach *boil, steal*
PCH pooch *dog* pooches
PCH pouch *bag* pouches
PCH pouchy *baggy* pouchier pouchiest
PCH pusch *overthrow*
PCHBLK pitch-black *color*
PCHBLN pitchblende *mineral*
PCHBLND pitchblende *mineral*
PCHD pouched *with pocket*
PCHDRK pitch-dark *no*

Letters aren't doubled for single sounds: to find alley use **L** not **LL**. Use **Y** and **W** as hard sounds only: to find yellow use **YL**. (Br)=British spelling or usage. * See dictionary.

moon
PCHFRK pitchfork *tool*
PCHK paycheck *salary*
PCHK upchuck *vomit*
PCHL patchily *spotty*
PCHL patchouli *plant*
PCHLNS petulance
peevishness petulancy
PCHLNT petulant *peevish*
PCHLNTS petulance
peevishness petulancy
PCHLS patulous *spreading*
PCHMN pitchman *seller*
pitchmen
PCHN pitch in *help*
PCHN Puccini *composer*
PCHNS patchiness *in spots*
PCHPN pitch pine *tree*
PCHPP pitch pipe *music*
PCHR aperture *hole*
PCHR patchier *spotty*
PCHR peachier *dandy*
PCHR picture (v) *imagine*
pictured picturing
PCHR picture (n) *image*
PCHR pitcher *container,*
thrower
PCHR poacher *thief*
PCHR pouchier *baggy*
PCHRBK picture-book
beautiful
PCHRD pochard *duck*
PCHRFL pitcherful *container*
PCHRPRFK picture-perfect
flawless
PCHRPRFKT picture-
perfect *flawless*
PCHRSK picturesque
distinctive
PCHRSKL picturesquely
distinctively
PCHRSKNS
picturesqueness
distinctiveness
PCHST patchiest *spotty*
PCHST peachiest *dandy*
PCHST pouchiest *baggy*
PCHST puschist *overthrower*
PCHT pitchout (n) *baseball*
pitch out (v)
PCHT poached *boiled*
PCHT pouched *with pocket*

PCHWRK patchwork
hodgepodge
PCHYR patchier *spotty*
PCHYR peachier *dandy*
PCHYR pouchier *baggy*
PCHYST patchiest *spotty*
PCHYST peachiest *dandy*
PCHYST pouchiest *baggy*
PCHZ pachisi *game*
PCHZ Parcheesi *(trademark)*
game
PCN epicene *bisexual*
PCN piscina *basin*
PCN piscine *fish*
PCNZM epicenism
bisexuality
PCS piceous *like tar*
PCS Pisces *zodiac sign*
PCYS piceous *like tar*
PCZ apices (pl) *summit* apex
PCZ Pisces *zodiac sign*
PD epode *poem*
PD op-ed *editorial*
PD opioid *narcotic*
PD pad (n) *mat, protection,*
*foot**
PD pad (v) *walk, muffle,*
increase padded padding
PD paddy *rice* paddies
PD paid (v-past) *pay*
PD patio *porch* patios
PD patty *round mass* patties
PD payday *salary*
PD peaty *mossy*
PD petty *trivial, small-minded*
pettier pettiest
PD peyote *cactus*
PD pie-eyed *drunk*
PD pied *multi-colored*
PD pietà *(often capitalized)*
statue
PD piety *devotion* pieties
PD pita *plant, bread*
PD pity *feel sorry* pitied
pitying pities
PD pod *container* podded
podding
PD podia (pl) *dais* podium
PD potty (n) *toilet* potties
PD potty (adj) (Br) *trivial,*
crazy pottier pottiest
PD pouty *sulky*

PD putto *boy* putti
PD putty *cement* putties
PD uppity *snobbish*
PDBL pitiable (adj) *sorrowful*
pitiably (adv)
PDBL potable *drinkable*
PDBL POW *prisoner of war*
POWs
PDBLY POW *prisoner of war*
POWs
PDBY POW *prisoner of war*
POWs
PDD pitted *no seeds*
PDD potted *in a container*
PDDV putative *assumed*
PDF put off *delay, leave*
PDFGNG pettifogging
quibbling
PDFGR pettifogger *shyster*
PDFGR pettifoggery
quibbling
PDFL pedophile *molester*
PDFL pedophilia *child*
molestation
PDFL pitiful (adj) *pathetic*
pitifully (adv)
PDFLK pedophiliac (or)
pedophilic *child*
molestation
PDFLY pedophilia *child*
molestation
PDFLYK pedophiliac (or)
pedophilic *child*
molestation
PDFR petit four *cake* petit
fours (or) petits fours
PDFSR petty officer *rank*
PDGG pedagogue *teacher*
PDGG pedagogy *teaching*
PDGJ pedagogy *teaching*
PDGJKL pedagogical (adj)
teaching pedagogically
(adv)
PDGJKS pedagogics
teaching
PDGJX pedagogics *teaching*
PDGN Patagonia *region*
PDGNK paedogenic (or)
paedogenetic (adj)
reproduction
paedogenetically (adv)
PDGNSS paedogenesis

reproduction
PDGNY Patagonia *region*
PDGR pedigree *ancestors*
PDGR podagra *gout*
PDGRD pedigreed *ancestors*
PDJ pottage *stew*
PDJNDK paedogenetic (or) paedogenic (adj) *reproduction* paedogenetically (adv)
PDJNDK pedogenetic *soil*
PDJNK paedogenic (or) paedogenetic (adj) *reproduction* paedogenetically (adv)
PDJNSS paedogenesis *reproduction*
PDJNSS pedogenesis *soil*
PDJNTK paedogenetic (or) paedogenic (adj) *reproduction* paedogenetically (adv)
PDJNTK pedogenetic *soil*
PDJR petit jury *trial*
PDK optic *eye*
PDK paddock *enclosure*
PDK poetic *verse*
PDKB pedicab *tricycle*
PDKK pat-a-cake (or) patty-cake *game*
PDKL optical (adj) *eye* optically (adv)
PDKL pedicle *stalk, attachment*
PDKL pedocal *soil*
PDKL poetically *verse*
PDKLS pediculous *lousy*
PDKLSS pediculosis *lice*
PDKLT pediculate *fish*
PDKR pedicure *foot care*
PDKRST pedicurist *foot care*
PDKS optics *light*
PDKT petticoat *skirt*
PDKYLS pediculous *lousy*
PDKYLSS pediculosis *lice*
PDKYLT pediculate *fish*
PDKYR pedicure *foot care*
PDKYRST pedicurist *foot care*
PDL paddle (*n*) *oar, hitting implement*
PDL paddle (*v*) *propel, beat*

paddled paddling
PDL pedal (*n*) *lever* (adj) *foot,* (*v*) *ride*
PDL pedalo (*Br*) *paddleboat* pedalos
PDL peddle *sell* peddled peddling
PDL petal *flower*
PDL petiole *stem*
PDL pettily *small-minded*
PDL piddle *squander, urinate* piddled piddling
PDL poodle *dog*
PDL puddle (*v*) *muddy, wet* puddled puddling
PDL puddle (*n*) *pool*
PDLBL paddleball *game*
PDLBRD paddleboard *surf*
PDLBT paddleboat *vehicle*
PDLFR pedalfer *soil*
PDLFSH paddlefish *fish*
PDLG pedology *soil*
PDLHWL paddle wheel *boat*
PDLJ pedology *soil*
PDLJKL pedological *soil*
PDLJST pedologist *soil*
PDLK padlock *lock*
PDLK petallike *flower*
PDLL petiolule *stem*
PDLN puddling *iron*
PDLNG puddling *iron*
PDLNT pedal-note *low tone*
PDLR peddler *seller*
PDLR petiolar *stalk*
PDLRSN petit larceny *crime*
PDLS pitiless *not sad*
PDLT petiolate *stalk*
PDLWL paddle wheel *boat*
PDLWLR paddle wheeler *boat*
PDM epitome *example*
PDM optima (pl) *best* optimum
PDM podium *dais* podiums (or) podia
PDMDR pedometer *distance*
PDMK epidemic (*adj*) *prevalent* (*n*) *disease*
PDMKL epidemically (*adj*) *prevalent*
PDML optimal (adj) *best* optimally (adv)

PDML petit mal *epilepsy*
PDMLG epidemiology *disease*
PDMLJ epidemiology *disease*
PDMLJKL epidemiological (adj) *disease* epidemiologically (adv)
PDMLJST epidemiologist *disease*
PDMM optimum *best* optima
PDMNL pedimental *roof, slope*
PDMNT pediment *roof, slope*
PDMNT piedmont *mountain*
PDMNTL pedimental *roof, slope*
PDMRFK paedomorphic *juvenile*
PDMRFZM paedomorphism *juvenile*
PDMSD epidemicity (*adj*) *prevalence*
PDMSDK optimistic *positive*
PDMSDKL optimistically *positively*
PDMST epidemicity (*adj*) *prevalence*
PDMST optimist *positive*
PDMSTK optimistic *positive*
PDMSTKL optimistically *positively*
PDMTR pedometer *distance*
PDMYLG epidemiology *disease*
PDMYLJ epidemiology *disease*
PDMYLJKL epidemiological (adj) *disease* epidemiologically (adv)
PDMYLJST epidemiologist *disease*
PDMZ epitomize *represent* epitomized epitomizing (Br) epitomise
PDMZ optimize *make the best* optimized optimizing (Br) optimise
PDMZM optimism *positive*
PDN opt in *choose to*
PDN padding *matting, excess*
PDN pudding *food*

Letters aren't doubled for single sounds: to find alley use **L** not **LL**. Use **Y** and **W** as hard sounds only: to find yellow use **YL**. (Br)=British spelling or usage. * See dictionary.

PDN put in *enter*
PDN put on *(v) dress, pretend, apply**
PDN put-on *(adj) pretended (n) parody*
PDNC appetency *desire* appetencies
PDNC pudency *modesty*
PDND pudenda *(pl) genitals* pudendum
PDNDL pudendal *genitals*
PDNDM pudendum *genitals* pudenda
PDNG padding *matting, excess*
PDNG petting *caressing*
PDNG pitting *remove pits*
PDNG pudding *food*
PDNGKL peduncle *stalk*
PDNGKLDD pedunculated *attached*
PDNGKLR peduncular *stalk*
PDNGKLTD pedunculated *attached*
PDNGKYLDD pedunculated *attached*
PDNGKYLR peduncular *stalk*
PDNGKYLTD pedunculated *attached*
PDNGQLDD pedunculated *attached*
PDNGQLR peduncular *stalk*
PDNGQLTD pedunculated *attached*
PDNK pedantic *narrow*
PDNKL pedantically *narrowly*
PDNKL peduncle *stalk*
PDNKLDD pedunculated *attached*
PDNKLR peduncular *stalk*
PDNKLTD pedunculated *attached*
PDNKYLDD pedunculated *attached*
PDNKYLR peduncular *stalk*
PDNKYLTD pedunculated *attached*
PDNQLDD pedunculated *attached*
PDNQLR peduncular *stalk*

PDNQLTD pedunculated *attached*
PDNS appetency *desire* appetencies
PDNS pettiness *small-mindedness*
PDNS pittance *small amount*
PDNS pudency *modesty*
PDNT pedant *teacher*
PDNTC appetency *desire* appetencies
PDNTC pudency *modesty*
PDNTK pedantic *narrow*
PDNTKL pedantically *narrowly*
PDNTR pedantry *narrowness* pedantries
PDNTS appetency *desire* appetencies
PDNTS pittance *small amount*
PDNTS pudency *modesty*
PDP put up *(v) build, accommodate, can**
PDP put-up *(adj) arranged*
PDPN pattypan *vegetable*
PDPN put-upon *imposed*
PDPNT petit point *embroidery*
PDQLS pediculous *lousy*
PDQLSS pediculosis *lice*
PDQLT pediculate *fish*
PDQR pedicure *foot care*
PDQRST pedicurist *foot care*
PDR padre *father*
PDR pater *(Br) father*
PDR patter *talk*
PDR peter *(v) diminish (n-slang) penis*
PDR pewter *metal*
PDR pitier *concern*
PDR potter *(n) pottery maker (v) putter*
PDR pottery *clayware* potteries
PDR pouter *bird, sulker*
PDR powder *talc*
PDR powdery *fine and soft*
PDR putter *(n) golf (v) tinker*
PDRDT petered out *gone*
PDRF updraft *wind*
PDRFT updraft *wind*

PDRHRN powder horn *flask*
PDRKG powder keg *explosive*
PDRL epidural *outside membrane*
PDRLK powderlike *fine and soft*
PDRLS powderless *no dust*
PDRM powder room *bathroom*
PDRMD epidermoid *outer layer*
PDRML epidermal *outer layer*
PDRMS epidermis *outer layer*
PDRN padrone *master* padrones *(or)* padroni
PDRN pattern *(v) shape (n) design*
PDRNLS patternless *no design*
PDRNMKR patternmaker *designer*
PDRNN patterning *design*
PDRNNG patterning *design*
PDRNSDR paternoster *(often capitalized) Lord's prayer*
PDRNSTR paternoster *(often capitalized) Lord's prayer*
PDRPF powder-puff (adj) *women* powder puff (n)
PDRSDK pederastic *boy love*
PDRST pederast *boy love* pederasty
PDRSTK pederastic *boy love*
PDRT pay dirt *good discovery*
PDRT puttyroot *orchid*
PDS piteous *pity*
PDS poetess *writer (f)*
PDSDL pedestal (n) *base, column*
PDSH pettish *fretful*
PDSL pedicel *stalk, attachment*
PDSL piteously *pity*
PDSLT pedicellate *stalk, attachment*
PDSNS piteousness *pity*

Use letters that best describe the sounds you hear and omit the vowels. Use **S** or **K** instead of **C**: to find circle use **SRKL**. Use **J** to find joy, **JM** to find gem and **G** to find go.

PDSRS apatosaurus *dinosaur*

PDSTL pedestal *(v) put above* pedestaled (or) pedestalled pedestaling (or) pedestalling

PDSTL pedestal *(n) base, column*

PDSTRN pedestrian *(adj) on foot, common (n) walker*

PDSTRYN pedestrian *(adj) on foot, common (n) walker*

PDSZ poeticize *write verse* poeticized poeticizing

PDSZM poeticism *verse*

PDT opt out *choose not to*

PDT put out *(v) extinguish, annoy, have sex**

PDT putout *(n) baseball*

PDT update *modernize* updated updating

PDTD aptitude *ability*

PDTDNL aptitudinal (adj) *ability* aptitudinally (adv)

PDTR podiatry *feet*

PDTRK pediatric *children* (Br) paediatric

PDTRK podiatric *foot*

PDTRKS pediatrics *children* (Br) paediatrics

PDTRSHN pediatrician *doctor of children* (Br) paediatrician

PDTRST podiatrist *feet*

PDTRX pediatrics *children* (Br) paediatrics

PDTV optative *wish*

PDTV putative *assumed*

PDTYD aptitude *ability*

PDTYDNL aptitudinal (adj) *ability* aptitudinally (adv)

PDVR put over *(v) delay, trick*

PDWGN paddy wagon *police*

PDX optics *light*

PDY patio *porch* patios

PDY podia (pl) *dais* podium

PDYBL pitiable (adj) *sorrowful* pitiably (adv)

PDYL petiole *stem*

PDYLL petiolule *stem*

PDYLR petiolar *stalk*

PDYLT petiolate *stalk*

PDYM podium *dais* podiums (or) podia

PDYR pitier *concern*

PDYRL epidural *outside membrane*

PDYS piteous *pity*

PDYSL piteously *pity*

PDYSNS piteousness *pity*

PDYTR podiatry *feet*

PDYTRK pediatric *children* (Br) paediatric

PDYTRK podiatric *foot*

PDYTRKS pediatrics *children* (Br) paediatrics

PDYTRSHN pediatrician *doctor of children* (Br) paediatrician

PDYTRST podiatrist *feet*

PDYTRX pediatrics *children* (Br) paediatrics

PDZ poetize *write verse* poetized poetizing

PF payoff *money*

PF poof *(interj) magic* poof

PF pouf *fluffy part*

PF puff *(v) pant, swell up, waft (n) whiff, swelling, pad**

PF puffy *swollen*

PFBL puffball *fungus*

PFCL apophyseal *projecting part*

PFCYL apophyseal *projecting part*

PFD poufed (or) pouffed *puffed up*

PFDK epiphytic *air plant*

PFDKL epiphytically *air plant*

PFDR poofter *(Br-slang) homosexual*

PFDR puff adder *snake*

PFL peafowl *bird*

PFL piffle *trivial talk* piffled piffling

PFLD upfield *goal*

PFLN piffling *trivial*

PFLNG piffling *trivial*

PFLT apophylite *mineral*

PFN epifauna *animals*

PFN epiphany *(often capitalized) divine appearance* epiphanies

PFN pay phone *telephone*

PFN puffin *bird*

PFNG pfennig *money* pfennig

PFNK pfennig *money* pfennig

PFNMNL epiphenomenal (adj) *derivative* epiphenomenally (adv)

PFNMNLZM epiphenomenalism *derivation*

PFNMNN epiphenomenon *derivation* epiphenomena

PFNS puffiness *swelling*

PFR prefer *choose* preferred preferring

PFR puffer *fish*

PFR puffery *praise*

PFRBL preferable (adj) *chosen* preferably (adv)

PFRM epiphragm *membrane*

PFRMNT preferment *choice*

PFRNT up-front (adj) *frank* up front (adv)

PFRR preferer *chooser*

PFSL apophyseal *projecting part*

PFSS apophysis *projecting part* apophyses

PFSS epiphysis *bone, pineal gland* epiphyses

PFST pie-faced *round*

PFSYL apophyseal *projecting part*

PFT epiphyte *air plant*

PFT poofter *(Br-slang) homosexual*

PFT poufed (or) pouffed *puffed up*

PFTK epiphytic *air plant*

PFTKL epiphytically *air plant*

PFTR poofter *(Br-slang) homosexual*

PFTR puff adder *snake*

PFZL apophyseal *projecting part*

Letters aren't doubled for single sounds: to find alley use **L** not **LL**. Use **Y** and **W** as hard sounds only: to find yellow use **YL**. (Br)=British spelling or usage. * See dictionary.

PFZL epiphyseal *bone, pineal gland*

PFZYL apophyseal *projecting part*

PFZYL epiphyseal *bone, pineal gland*

PG apogee *orbit*

PG peg *(v) restrict, identify, hustle* pegged pegging

PG peg *(n) wooden pin, (Br) clothespin, drink*

PG pig *(v) overeat, mess up* pigged pigging

PG pig *(n) animal*

PG piggy *like a pig* piggier piggiest piggies

PG pogy *fish* pogies

PG pudgy *overweight* pudgier pudgiest (Br) podgy

PG pug *(v) knead* pugged pugging

PG pug *(n) dog, bun*

PGBK piggyback *carry*

PGBRD Peg-Board *(trademark) display*

PGBT pigboat *submarine*

PGD pagoda *temple*

PGFSH pigfish *fish*

PGHDD pigheaded *stubborn*

PGHDDNS pigheadedness *stubbornness*

PGL epigeal (or) epigean *surface*

PGLDL epiglottal *throat*

PGLDS epiglottis *throat*

PGLG peg leg *wooden*

PGLT piglet *swine*

PGLTL epiglottal *throat*

PGLTS epiglottis *throat*

PGM apogamy *unfertilized*

PGM pygmy *small one* pygmies

PGMD pygmoid *small*

PGMNT pigment *color*

PGMNTSHN pigmentation *color*

PGMS apogamous *unfertilized*

PGN apogean *orbit*

PGN epigean (or) epigeal *surface*

PGN epigone *disciple*

PGN pagan *heathen*

PGN piggin *pail*

PGNFRN pogonophoran *worm*

PGNL pignoli (or) pignolia *pine nut*

PGNS epigonous *disciple*

PGNS pudginess *overweight (Br) podginess*

PGNSD pugnacity *aggression*

PGNSH paganish *heathen*

PGNSHS pugnacious *aggressive*

PGNSHSL pugnaciously *aggressively*

PGNSHSNS pugnaciousness *aggressiveness*

PGNST pugnacity *aggression*

PGNZ paganize *become heathen* paganized paganizing

PGNZ pug nose *(n) face* pug-nosed (adj)

PGNZD pug-nosed *(adj) face* pug nose (n)

PGNZM paganism *heathen*

PGNZR paganizer *heathen*

PGPG Pago Pago *town*

PGPN pigpen *sty*

PGR piggery *sty* piggeries

PGR piggier *like a pig*

PGR pudgier *overweight (Br) podgier*

PGRD upgrade *(v) improve* upgraded upgrading

PGRD upgrade *(n) increase*

PGRF epigraph *inscription*

PGRF epigraphy *inscription*

PGRFK epigraphic *inscription*

PGRFKL epigraphically *inscription*

PGRFST epigraphist *inscription*

PGRM epigram *witty saying*

PGRM pogrom *massacre*

PGRMDK epigrammatic *witty saying*

PGRMDKL

epigrammatically *witty saying*

PGRMTK epigrammatic *witty saying*

PGRMTKL

epigrammatically *witty saying*

PGRMTST epigrammatist *witty saying*

PGRMTZ epigrammatize *express wit* epigrammatized epigrammatizing

PGRMTZR epigrammatizer *witty saying*

PGRN pea green *color*

PGRN pig iron *mineral*

PGRSHN progression *advancement*

PGRSV progressive *advancing*

PGRSVL progressively *advancing*

PGRSVNS progressiveness *advance*

PGRSVZM progressivism *advancement*

PGSH piggish *like a pig*

PGSHL piggishly *like a pig*

PGSHNS piggishness *like a pig*

PGSKN pigskin *leather, football*

PGSS Pegasus *horse*

PGST piggiest *like a pig*

PGST pigsty *pen* pigsties

PGST pudgiest *overweight (Br) podgiest*

PGSTK pogo stick *toy*

PGT pagoda *temple*

PGT pig out *(v) overeat* pigged out pigging out

PGT pig-out *(n) feast*

PGTL pigtail *hairdo*

PGYL epigeal (or) epigean *surface*

PGYN apogean *orbit*

PGYN epigean (or) epigeal *surface*

PGYR piggier *like a pig*

PGYR pudgier *overweight (Br) podgier*

Use letters that best describe the sounds you hear and omit the vowels. Use **S** or **K** instead of **C**: to find circle use **SRKL**. Use **J** to find joy, **JM** to find gem and **G** to find go.

PGYRN pig iron *mineral*
PGYST piggiest *like a pig*
PGYST pudgiest *overweight*
(Br) podgiest
PHL uphill *ascent*
PHL uphold *support* upheld
upholding
PHLD uphold *support*
upheld upholding
PHLSTR upholster *cover*
PHLSTR upholstery *covering*
upholsteries
PHLSTRR upholsterer
coverer
PHN peahen *bird*
PHVL upheaval *change*
PJ apogee *orbit*
PJ page (*n*) *book, aide*
PJ page (*v*) *summon, turn*
pages paged paging
PJ Piaget *psychologist*
PJ pudgy *overweight* pudgier
pudgiest
(Br) podgy
PJB pageboy *haircut*
PJD pygidia (pl) *rump*
pygidium
PJDM pygidium *rump*
pygidia
PJDY pygidia (pl) *rump*
pygidium
PJDYM pygidium *rump*
pygidia
PJKT pea jacket *coat*
PJL epigeal (or) epigean
surface
PJLSDK pugilistic *boxing*
PJLST pugilist *boxer*
PJLSTK pugilistic *boxing*
PJLZM pugilism *boxing*
PJM pajama *garment*
pajamas
(Br) pyjama
PJN apogean *orbit*
PJN epigean (or) epigeal
surface
PJN epigyny *flower*
PJN pidgin *language*
PJN pigeon *bird*
PJNDK epigenetic
development
PJNDKL epigenetically

development
PJNHL pigeonhole (*v*)
classify pigeonholed
pigeonholing
PJNHL pigeonhole (*n*)
recess, category
PJNNGGLSH Pidgin
English *language*
PJNNGLSH Pidgin English
language
PJNS epigynous *flower*
PJNS pudginess *overweight*
(Br) podginess
PJNSHN pagination *number*
pages
PJNSS epigenesis
development
PJNT pageant *contest*
PJNT paginate *number pages*
paginated paginating
PJNT pigeonite *mineral*
PJNTD pigeon-toed *feet*
PJNTK epigenetic
development
PJNTKL epigenetically
development
PJNTR pageantry *display*
PJNWNG pigeonwing *dance*
PJNZ pidginize *simplify*
pidginized pidginizing
PJR pager *beeper*
PJR pudgier *overweight*
(Br) podgier
PJRDV pejorative *belittling*
PJRTV pejorative *belittling*
PJS paduasoy *fabric*
PJST pudgiest *overweight*
(Br) podgiest
PJWS paduasoy *fabric*
PJYL epigeal (or) epigean
surface
PJYN apogean *orbit*
PJYN epigean (or) epigeal
surface
PJYR pudgier *overweight*
(Br) podgier
PJYST pudgiest *overweight*
(Br) podgiest
PJZ pj's (abbr) *pajamas*
PK apeak *vertical*
PK epic (*n*) *tale* (adj) *heroic*
PK epoch *time period*

PK opaque *milky*
PK OPEC (abbr)
Organization of Petroleum
Exporting Countries
PK PAC (abbr) *Political*
Action Committee
PK paca *rodent*
PK pack (*v*) *fill, carry, possess*
(*n*) *bundle, clique, paste**
PK pact *agreement*
PK pawky (Br) *shrewd*
PK peak *high point*
PK peaky *sickly*
PK pec *muscle*
PK peck (*n*) *measure* (*v*)
pierce, nag
PK pecky *decayed*
PK peek *look*
PK pekoe *tea*
PK pic (slang) *movie or photo*
pics (or) pix
PK pica *type*
PK pick (*v*) *choose, probe,*
pluck (*n*) *choice, tool, comb**
PK picky *particular* pickier
pickiest
PK picot *lace*
PK pike (*n*) *fish, spear, hill,*
road pike (or) pikes
PK pike (*v*) *pierce, leave*
piked piking
PK pique (*v*) *arouse* piqued
piquing
PK pique (*n*) *resentment*
PK piqué (or) pique *fabric*
PK piquet *game*
PK pock *pit*
PK poco *somewhat*
PK poke *jab* poked poking
PK pokey *jail* pokeys
PK poky (or) pokey *slow*
pokier pokiest pokiness
PK polka *dance*
PK puck *hockey*
PK puke *vomit* puked
puking
PK pukka *genuine*
PKB peekaboo *tiny look*
PKBK pocket book (or)
pocketbook *purse, book*
PKBR pokeberry *plant*
PKC epoxy *glue* epoxied (or)

Letters aren't doubled for single sounds: to find alley use **L** not **LL**. Use **Y** and **W** as hard
sounds only: to find yellow use **YL**. (Br)=British spelling or usage. * See dictionary.

epoxyed epoxying

PKC pixie (or) pixy *fairie* pixies

PKC pyxie *shrub*

PKCHR picture (*v*) *imagine* pictured picturing

PKCHR picture (*n*) *image*

PKCHRBK picture-book *beautiful*

PKCHRPRFK picture-perfect *flawless*

PKCHRPRFKT picture-perfect *flawless*

PKCHRSK picturesque *distinctive*

PKCHRSKL picturesquely *distinctively*

PKCHRSKNS picturesqueness *distinctiveness*

PKD peaked *sickly*

PKDGRF pictograph *drawing*

PKDGRFK pictographic *drawing*

PKDK pectic *plant gel*

PKDKL epicuticle *waxy layer*

PKDL epicotyl *seedling*

PKDL peccadillo *offense* peccadilloes (or) peccadillos

PKDL Piccadilly *London square*

PKDN pectin *plant gel*

PKDNS peakedness *pointed, sickly*

PKDNSHS pectinaceous *plant gel*

PKDNT pectinate *teeth*

PKDR picador *bullfight* picadors

PKDRL pectoral *muscle*

PKDRM pachyderm *animal*

PKDRMDS pachydermatous *thick-skinned*

PKDRMTS pachydermatous *thick-skinned*

PKDT polka dot (n) *spot* polka-dot (or) polka-dotted (adj)

PKF pick off (v) *catch* pickoff (n)

PKGRM picogram *weight*

PKHRS packhorse *animal*

PKJ package *parcel* packaged packaging

PKJR packager *parcel*

PKK ipecac (or) ipecacuanha *vomit*

PKK peacock *bird* peahen (f) peafowl (m,f)

PKKS panchax *fish*

PKKS pickax *tool* pickaxes

PKKWN ipecacuanha (or) ipecac *vomit*

PKL apical (adj) *on the tip* apically (adv)

PKL epical (adj) *heroic* epically (adv)

PKL epochal *time period*

PKL opaquely *milky*

PKL piccolo *music* piccolos

PKL pickle *brine* pickled pickling

PKL pokily *slow*

PKLCHR apiculture *bee keeping*

PKLCHRL apicultural *bee keeping*

PKLCHRST apiculturist *bee keeper*

PKLD pickled *drunk, preserved*

PKLDR peculator *cheater*

PKLKS epicalyx *flower*

PKLL piccalilli *relish*

PKLN picoline *solvent*

PKLPDK apocalyptic *prophetic*

PKLPDKL apocalyptically *prophetically*

PKLPS apocalypse *catastrophe*

PKLPTK apocalyptic *prophetic*

PKLPTKL apocalyptically *prophetically*

PKLR peculiar *strange*

PKLRD peculiarity *oddity* peculiarities

PKLRT peculiarity *oddity* peculiarities

PKLSHN peculation *cheating*

PKLT apiculate *pointed*

PKLT peculate *cheat* peculated peculating

PKLTHRM poikilotherm *cold-blooded*

PKLTR apiculture *bee keeping*

PKLTR peculator *cheater*

PKLTRL apicultural *bee keeping*

PKLTRST apiculturist *bee keeper*

PKLX epicalyx *flower*

PKLYR peculiar *strange*

PKLYRD peculiarity *oddity* peculiarities

PKLYRT peculiarity *oddity* peculiarities

PKMN upcoming *approaching*

PKMNG upcoming *approaching*

PKMP pick-me-up (n) *bracer*

PKMRK pockmark *hole*

PKMYP pick-me-up (n) *bracer*

PKN packing *material*

PKN pecan *nut*

PKN picayune (*n*) *money* (adj) *trivial*

PKN puccoon *plant*

PKNC piquancy *spicy*

PKND pycnidia (pl) *fungus* pycnidium

PKNDL pycnidial *fungus*

PKNDM pycnidium *fungus* pycnidia

PKNDSHVL pick-and-shovel *difficult*

PKNDY pycnidia (pl) *fungus* pycnidium

PKNDYL pycnidial *fungus*

PKNDYM pycnidium *fungus* pycnidia

PKNG packing *material*

PKNGND pycnogonid *sea spider*

PKNGRDR pecking order *society*

PKNGS pickings *scraps*

PKNK picnic (*v*) *eat outside* picnicked picnicking

Use letters that best describe the sounds you hear and omit the vowels. Use **S** or **K** instead of **C**: to find circle use **SRKL**. Use **J** to find joy, **JM** to find gem and **G** to find go.

PKNK picnic *(n) outing, easy task, ham*
PKNK picnicky *eat outside*
PKNKR picnicker *eater*
PKNMDR pycnometer *density*
PKNMTR pycnometer *density*
PKNR pecuniary *money*
PKNRDR pecking order *society*
PKNS opaqueness *milky*
PKNS Pekingese (or) Pekinese *dog, language*
PKNS piquancy *spicy*
PKNS pokiness *slow*
PKNSH picayunish *unimportant*
PKNSHVL pick-and-shovel *difficult*
PKNT peccant *faulty*
PKNT piquant *spicy*
PKNTC piquancy *spicy*
PKNTHK epicanthic *eyelid*
PKNTR up-country *outlying*
PKNTS piquancy *spicy*
PKNYR pecuniary *money*
PKNZ Pekingese (or) Pekinese *dog, language*
PKNZ pickings *scraps*
PKP apocope *letters*
PKP pick up *(v) collect, learn, perceive**
PKP pickup *(n) quickening, reception, truck**
PKP upkeep *maintain*
PKPC Poughkeepsie *city*
PKPKT pickpocket *thief*
PKPS Poughkeepsie *city*
PKQN ipecacuanha (or) ipecac *vomit*
PKR epicure *gourmet*
PKR packer *loader*
PKR peccary *animal* peccaries
PKR pecker *(vulgar) penis*
PKR pecker *(Br) courage*
PKR picaro *rascal* picaros
PKR picker *choose, tool, music**
PKR pickier *particular*
PKR piker *tightwad*

PKR poker *card game, prod*
PKR pucker *(v) tighten (n) wrinkle*
PKRD epicardia (pl) *heart* epicardium
PKRDL epicardial *heart*
PKRDM epicardium *heart* epicardia
PKRDY epicardia (pl) *heart* epicardium
PKRDYL epicardial *heart*
PKRDYM epicardium *heart* epicardia
PKRF apocrypha *writings*
PKRFL apocryphal (adj) *writings* apocryphally (adv)
PKRK picric *acid*
PKRL pickerel *fish* pickerel (or) pickerels
PKRN apocrine *gland*
PKRN epicurean *gourmet*
PKRN pecorino *cheese*
PKRN picaroon (or) pickaroon *rascal*
PKRS packhorse *animal*
PKRSDNDR procrastinator *delayer*
PKRSDNSHN procrastination *delay*
PKRSDNT procrastinate *delay* procrastinated procrastinating
PKRSDNTR procrastinator *delayer*
PKRSK picaresque *rascal*
PKRSTNDR procrastinator *delayer*
PKRSTNSHN procrastination *delay*
PKRSTNT procrastinate *delay* procrastinated procrastinating
PKRSTNTR procrastinator *delayer*
PKRT pack rat *rodent, hoarder*
PKRTKSN picrotoxin *remedy*
PKRTXN picrotoxin *remedy*
PKRWD peckerwood *(vulgar) Southerner*
PKRYN epicurean *gourmet*

PKS apex *top* apexes (or) apices
PKS epoxy *glue* epoxied (or) epoxyed epoxying
PKS pax *tablet, peace*
PKS Pecos *city*
PKS Picasso *artist*
PKS pixie (or) pixy *fairie* pixies
PKS pox *blemish* pox (or) poxes
PKS pyx *container*
PKS pyxie *shrub*
PKSDL packsaddle *load support*
PKSDZ pyxides (pl) *fruit* pyxis
PKSH peckish *(Br) hungry, grouchy*
PKSH puckish *whimsical*
PKSHR picture *(v) imagine* pictured picturing
PKSHR picture *(n) image*
PKSHRBK picture-book *beautiful*
PKSHRPRFK picture-perfect *flawless*
PKSHRPRFKT picture-perfect *flawless*
PKSHRSK picturesque *distinctive*
PKSHRSKL picturesquely *distinctively*
PKSHRSKNS picturesqueness *distinctiveness*
PKSK packsack *knapsack*
PKSL pixel *dot*
PKSLDD pixilated (or) pixillated *amusing*
PKSLSHN pixilation *amusement*
PKSLTD pixilated (or) pixillated *amusing*
PKSN pocosin *swamp*
PKSNDR pachysandra *plant*
PKSPK Pikes Peak *mountain*
PKSS pyxis *fruit* pyxides
PKST pickiest *particular*
PKSTL packsaddle *load support*

Letters aren't doubled for single sounds: to find alley use **L** not **LL**. Use **Y** and **W** as hard sounds only: to find yellow use **YL**. (Br)=British spelling or usage. * See dictionary.

PKSTN Pakistan *country*
PKSTN Pakistani *of Pakistan*
PKT packed *loaded*
PKT packet *package*
PKT pact *agreement*
PKT peacoat *garment*
PKT peaked *pointed*
PKT pick out *choose*
PKT picket *fence, protest*
PKT picotee *flower*
PKT piquet *game*
PKT pocket *pouch*
PKTBK pocket book (or)
   pocketbook *purse, book*
PKTBT picketboat *patrol*
PKTFL pocketful *amount*
PKTGRF pictograph
   drawing
PKTGRF pictography
   drawing
PKTGRFK pictographic
   drawing
PKTHRD packthread *twine*
PKTK pectic *plant gel*
PKTKL epicuticle *waxy layer*
PKTKLR epicuticular *waxy
   layer*
PKTKYLR epicuticular *waxy
   layer*
PKTL epicotyl *seedling*
PKTLN picket line *strike*
PKTN pachytene *cell
   division*
PKTN pectin *plant gel*
PKTNF pocketknife *tool*
   pocketknives
PKTNSHS pectinaceous
   plant gel
PKTNT pectinate *teeth*
PKTQLR epicuticular *waxy
   layer*
PKTR picture (v) *imagine*
   pictured picturing
PKTRBK picture-book
   beautiful
PKTRL pectoral *muscle*
PKTRL pictorial (adj) *images
   (n) magazine* pictorially
   (adv)
PKTRLZ pictorialize
   illustrate pictorialized
   pictorializing

PKTRPRFK picture-perfect
   flawless
PKTRPRFKT picture-
   perfect *flawless*
PKTRSK picturesque
   distinctive
PKTRSKL picturesquely
   distinctively
PKTRSKNS
   picturesqueness
   distinctiveness
PKTRYL pictorial (adj)
   images (n) magazine
   pictorially (adv)
PKTRYLZ pictorialize
   illustrate pictorialized
   pictorializing
PKTSZ pocket-size *small*
PKVR pick over *examine*
PKWD pokeweed *plant*
PKWNC piquancy *spicy*
PKWNS piquancy *spicy*
PKWNT piquant *spicy*
PKWNTC piquancy *spicy*
PKWNTS piquancy *spicy*
PKX panchax *fish*
PKX pickax *tool* pickaxes
PKYDKL epicuticle *waxy
   layer*
PKYLDR peculator *cheater*
PKYLR peculiar *strange*
PKYLRD peculiarity *oddity*
   peculiarities
PKYLRT peculiarity *oddity*
   peculiarities
PKYLSHN peculation
   cheating
PKYLT apiculate *pointed*
PKYLT peculate *cheat*
   peculated peculating
PKYLTR peculator *cheater*
PKYLYR peculiar *strange*
PKYLYRD peculiarity *oddity*
   peculiarities
PKYLYRT peculiarity *oddity*
   peculiarities
PKYN picayune (n) *money
   (adj) trivial*
PKYNR pecuniary *money*
PKYNSH picayunish
   unimportant
PKYNYR pecuniary *money*

PKYR epicure *gourmet*
PKYR pickier *particular*
PKYRN epicurean *gourmet*
PKYRYN epicurean *gourmet*
PKYST pickiest *particular*
PKYTKL epicuticle *waxy
   layer*
PKYTKLR epicuticular *waxy
   layer*
PKYTKYLR epicuticular
   waxy layer
PKYTQLR epicuticular *waxy
   layer*
PL Apollo *Greek god*
PL appall *disgust*
PL appeal (v) *accuse, request
   (n) entreaty, attraction*
PL apple *fruit*
PL apply *put on* applied
   applying applies
PL aptly *suitably* apt
PL opal *gem*
PL paella *food*
PL pail *bucket*
PL pal *befriend* palled palling
PL pale (v) *become whiter,
   fence* paled paling
PL pale (adj) *pallid, dim* paler
   palest
PL pale (n) *area*
PL palea *plants* paleae
PL palely *pallid, dim*
PL pall (n) *cloth, cover* (v)
   wane, drape
PL pallia (pl) *cloth, brain,
   mantle* pallium
PL pally *friendly*
PL pawl *tool*
PL payola *bribe*
PL peal *ring*
PL peel (v) *remove cover* (n)
   rind, utensil
PL pilau (or) pilaf (or) pilaff
   rice
PL pile *heap* piled piling
PL pilea (pl) *bird head* pileum
PL pili (pl) *hair* pilus
PL pill *medicine, ball, tiresome
   one**
PL pillow *headrest*
PL play (v) *amuse, perform,
   pretend (n) fun, drama,*

Use letters that best describe the sounds you hear and omit the vowels. Use **S** or **K** instead of **C**: to find circle use **SRKL**. Use **J** to find joy, **JM** to find gem and **G** to find go.

movement*
PL plea *beg*
PL plié *ballet*
PL plow (or) plough (n) *tool*
(v) *furrow, proceed steadily*
PL ploy *tactic*
PL ply (n) *layer* (v) *twist*
plied plying plies
PL Pole *Polish person*
PL pole (v) *propel* poled
poling
PL pole (n) *rod, opposite end,*
length*
PL polio *disease*
PL poll (n) *total votes, head*
(v) *shear, vote*
PL pollee *voter*
PL polo *sport, shirt*
PL poly *fabric* polys
PL pool (n) *water, game* (v)
combine
PL pule *whine* puled puling
PL pull (v) *tug, root, commit*
(n) *attraction**
PL pulley *wheel* pulleys
PL uphill *ascent*
PL uphold *support* upheld
upholding
PLB playboy *lover*
PLB plebe *freshman*
PLBDR apple butter *fruit*
spread
PLBK playback (n) *recording*
play back (v)
PLBK playbook *strategy*
PLBK plow back (v) *profits*
plowback (n)
PLBK pullback (n) *retreat*
pull back (v)
PLBKS pillbox *hat, vial, guns*
pillboxes
PLBL appealable *law*
PLBL playbill *theater*
PLBL pliable *bendable*
PLBLD appealability *law*
PLBLD pliability *bendability*
PLBLT appealability *law*
PLBLT pliability *bendability*
PLBN plebeian *common*
PLBPL play-by-play *sports*
PLBRGN plea bargain (n)
settlement plea-bargain (v)

PLBRGNNG plea
bargaining (n) *settlement*
PLBRR pallbearer *funeral*
PLBST plebiscite *vote*
PLBSTR plebiscitary *vote*
PLBTR apple butter *fruit*
spread
PLBX pillbox *hat, vial, guns*
pillboxes
PLBYN plebeian *common*
PLBZ plebs *populace* plebes
PLC policy *plan* policies
PLCB placebo *inert drug,*
soother placebos
PLCH Appalachia *region*
PLCHLDR policyholder
insurance
PLCHN Appalachian *of*
Appalachia
PLCHRD pilchard *fish*
PLCHY Appalachia *region*
PLCHYN Appalachian *of*
Appalachia
PLCN Paleocene *geologic*
age
PLCN Pliocene *epoch*
PLCZ pollices (pl) *thumb*
pollex
PLD applaud *clapping*
PLD applied *put on*
PLD pallid *pale*
PLD payload *cargo*
PLD pelota *game*
PLD plaid *pattern*
PLD plead *beg* pleaded (or)
pled pleading
PLD plod *slow pace* plodded
plodding
PLD ploidy *number*
PLD Pluto *planet*
PLD polity *political form*
polities
PLD polled *without horns*
PLD uphold *support* upheld
upholding
PLD upload *data*
PLDBL applaudable (adj)
clapping applaudably
(adv)
PLDBL palatable (adj) *tasty*
palatably (adv)
PLDBL pleadable *beg*

PLDBLD palatability *tasty*
PLDBLT palatability *tasty*
PLDD epauletted *ornament*
PLDD pileated *crested*
PLDJ pilotage *guiding,*
wages
PLDJ plottage *area*
PLDK politico *politician*
politicos
PLDKL apolitical (adj) *not*
political apolitically (adv)
PLDKL political (adj)
government politically
(adv)
PLDKLZ politicalize *create*
followers politicalized
politicalizing
PLDKRDK plutocratic
wealthy ruler
PLDKRT plutocrat *wealthy*
ruler
PLDKRTK plutocratic
wealthy ruler
PLDL palatal *mouth*
PLDL paludal *marshy*
PLDLZ palatalize *pronounce*
palatalized palatalizing
PLDLZSHN palatalization
pronunciation
PLDM palladium *safeguard,*
element
PLDN paladin *leader*
PLDN pleading *law*
PLDNG plaiting *braid*
PLDNG plating *metal cover*
PLDNG pleading *law*
PLDNGL pleadingly *beg*
PLDNGL ploddingly *slow*
PLDNS pallidness *paleness*
PLDNT pollutant *filth*
PLDPS platypus *animal*
platypuses
PLDR applauder *clapper*
PLDR palliator *moderator*
PLDR palter *trick*
PLDR plaiter *braider*
PLDR platter *plate*
PLDR pleader *beggar*
PLDR pleater *folder*
PLDR plodder *slow one*
PLDR plotter *plan, map*
PLDR polder *land*

Letters aren't doubled for single sounds: to find alley use **L** not **LL**. Use **Y** and **W** as hard
sounds only: to find yellow use **YL**. (Br)=British spelling or usage. * See dictionary.

PLDR polluter *make filthy*
PLDRGST poltergeist *ghost*
PLDRN platyrrhine *monkey*
PLDRR poulterer *fowl seller*
PLDRS palladrous *element*
PLDS pyelitis *pelvis*
PLDSHR plat du jour *dish*
plats du jour
PLDT plaudit *applause*
PLDT played out *spent*
PLDTD platitude *dull, trite*
remark
PLDTDNS platitudinous
speak tritely
PLDTDNZ platitudinize
speak tritely platitudinized
platitudinizing
PLDTYD platitude *dull, trite*
remark
PLDTYDNS platitudinous
trite
PLDTYDNZ platitudinize
speak tritely platitudinized
platitudinizing
PLDV palliative *moderating*
PLDV pollutive *filthy*
PLDYM palladium *safeguard,*
element
PLDZ Pleiades *Greek myth*
PLDZHR plat du jour *dish*
plats du jour
PLDZSHN palletization *load,*
store
(Br) palletisation
PLF pelf *riches*
PLF pilaf (or) pilaff (or) pilau
rice
PLF play-off (n) *tournament*
play off (v)
PLF uplift *raise*
PLFG polyphagia *appetite*
PLFG polyphagy *many foods*
PLFGS polyphagous *many*
foods
PLFGY polyphagia *appetite*
PLFJ polyphagia *appetite*
PLFJ polyphagy *many foods*
PLFJY polyphagia *appetite*
PLFL pailful *bucket*
PLFL playful (adj) *sportive*
playfully (adv)
PLFLDK polyphyletic

ancestors
PLFLDKL polyphyletically
ancestors
PLFLNS playfulness
sportiveness
PLFLTK polyphyletic
ancestors
PLFLTKL polyphyletically
ancestors
PLFN polyphone *many*
sounds
PLFN polyphony *many*
sounds
PLFNK polyphonic (or)
polyphonous *many*
sounds
PLFNS polyphonous (or)
polyphonic *many sounds*
PLFR pilfer *steal*
PLFRJ pilferage *stealing*
PLFRR pilferer *thief*
PLFRSHN proliferation
multiplication
PLFRT proliferate *multiply*
proliferated proliferating
PLFS paleface *Caucasian*
PLFT uplift *raise*
PLFZ polyphase *many stages*
PLFZK polyphasic *many*
stages
PLG apology *defense, regret*
apologies
PLG epilogue *ending*
PLG plague (n) *disease*
PLG plague (v) *distress*
plagued plaguing
PLG plug (n) *stopper, core,*
lure*
PLG plug (v) *stop up, shoot,*
work plugged plugging
PLGGL plug-ugly
unattractive
PLGLT polyglot *mixture*
PLGM polygamy *many mates*
PLGMS polygamous *many*
mates
PLGMST polygamist *many*
mates
PLGN plug-in (adj, n)
electricity plug in (v)
PLGN polygon *shape*
PLGNL polygonal (adj) *many*

sided polygonally (adv)
PLGR pellagra *disease*
PLGR plaguer *troublemaker*
PLGR playgoer *theater*
PLGR plugger *stopper,*
worker, shooter
PLGRF paleography *ancient*
writings
PLGRF polygraph *lie*
detector
PLGRFK paleographic (or)
paleographical (adj)
ancient writings
paleographically (adv)
PLGRFK polygraphic *lie*
detector
PLGRFKL paleographical
(or) paleographic (adj)
ancient writings
paleographically (adv)
PLGRFR polygrapher *lie*
detector
PLGRFST polygraphist *lie*
detector
PLGRM pilgrim *wayfarer*
PLGRMJ pilgrimage *journey*
PLGRN playground
recreation
PLGRND playground
recreation
PLGRS pellagrous *disease*
PLGWR playgoer *theater*
PLHDRL polyhedral *shape*
PLHDRN polyhedron *solid*
polyhedrons (or)
polyhedra
PLHK play hooky *absent*
PLHS playhouse *theater,*
small house
PLJ apology *defense, regret*
apologies
PLJ pelage *hair*
PLJ pillage *ruin* pillaged
pillaging
PLJ pledge *promise* pledged
pledging
PLJ pledgee *promised one*
PLJDK apologetic *sorry*
PLJDKL apologetically *sorry*
PLJDKS apologetics
discourse
PLJDX apologetics *discourse*

Use letters that best describe the sounds you hear and omit the vowels. Use **S** or **K** instead of **C**: to find circle use **SRKL**. Use **J** to find joy, **JM** to find gem and **G** to find go.

PLJK applejack *beverage*
PLJK pelagic *oceanic*
PLJN polygyny *many wives*
PLJNS polygynous *many wives*
PLJR pillager *ruiner*
PLJR pledger (or) pledgor *promise maker*
PLJRST plagiarist *literary theft*
PLJRSTK plagiaristic *literary theft*
PLJRZ plagiarize *steal words* plagiarized plagiarizing (Br) plagiarise
PLJRZM plagiarism *literary theft*
PLJST apologist *defender*
PLJTK apologetic *sorry*
PLJTKL apologetically *sorry*
PLJTKS apologetics *discourse*
PLJTX apologetics *discourse*
PLJZ apologize *express regret* apologized apologizing (Br) apologise
PLJZR apologizer *sorry one* (Br) apologiser
PLK appliqué *(v) overlay* appliquéd appliquéing
PLK appliqué *(n) decoration*
PLK palooka *boxer, oaf*
PLK pealike *small and round*
PLK plaque *teeth, award*
PLK plica *fold* plicae
PLK pluck *pick*
PLK plucky *brave* pluckier pluckiest
PLK polka *dance*
PLK pollack (or) pollock *fish* pollack (or) pollock
PLK pulque *drink*
PLKBL applicable *suitable*
PLKBL placable (adj) *soothing* placably (adv)
PLKBLD applicability *suitability*
PLKBLD placability *soothe*
PLKBLT applicability *suitability*
PLKBLT placability *soothe*

PLKCGLS Plexiglas *(trademark) plastic*
PLKD placoid *scale*
PLKDR applicator *tool*
PLKDR placater *soother*
PLKDT polka dot (n) *spot* polka-dot (or) polka-dotted (adj)
PLKDV applicative *applied*
PLKDV placative *soothe*
PLKL pellicle *membrane*
PLKL pluckily *brave*
PLKLNK polyclinic *medicine*
PLKN pelican *bird*
PLKNS pluckiness *bravery*
PLKNT applicant *person*
PLKPDRN plecopteran *fly*
PLKPTRN plecopteran *fly*
PLKR pluckier *brave*
PLKRBNT polycarbonate *plastic*
PLKRD placard *poster*
PLKRM polychrome (adj, v) *many colors* polychromy (n)
PLKRMDK polychromatic *many colors*
PLKRMTK polychromatic *many colors*
PLKRT applecart *plan*
PLKRTD pulchritude *beauty*
PLKRTDNS pulchritudinous *beautiful*
PLKRTYD pulchritude *beauty*
PLKRTYDNS pulchritudinous *beautiful*
PLKS pillowcase *bed linen*
PLKS poleax *tool* poleaxes
PLKS pollex *thumb* pollices
PLKS Pollux *star*
PLKSGLS Plexiglas *(trademark) plastic*
PLKSHN application *use*
PLKSHN placation *soothe*
PLKSR pelycosaur *dinosaur*
PLKSS plexus *network* plexuses
PLKST pluckiest *brave*
PLKT placate *soothe* placated placating
PLKT placket *slit*

PLKT plicate *fanlike*
PLKT polecat *animal* polecats (or) polecat
PLKT polychaete *worm*
PLKTR applicator *tool*
PLKTR applicatory *put to use*
PLKTR placater *soother*
PLKTR placatory *soothing*
PLKTRM plectrum *pick* plectra (or) plectrums
PLKTV applicative *applied*
PLKTV placative *soothe*
PLKYR pluckier *brave*
PLKYST pluckiest *brave*
PLL pallial *mantle, brain*
PLLSHN pullulation *swarm*
PLLST playlist *recordings*
PLLT pullulate *breed* pullulated pullulating
PLLTHK Paleolithic *Stone Age*
PLM aplomb *confidence*
PLM pallium *cloth, brain, mantle* pallia (or) palliums
PLM palm *tree, hand*
PLM pileum *bird head* pilea
PLM plum *fruit*
PLM plumb *(n) lead weight (adv) absolutely (v) measure, plumbing*
PLM plume *feather* plumed pluming
PLM plummy *choice* plummier plummiest
PLM plumy *downy* plumier plumiest
PLMBB plumb bob *weight*
PLMD palmed *hand*
PLMD palmetto *tree* palmettos (or) palmettoes
PLMD plumed *feathered*
PLMDR pulmotor *lungs*
PLMJ plumage *feathers*
PLMJD plumaged *feathers*
PLMK polemic *controversy*
PLMKL polemical (adj) *controversial* polemically (adv)
PLMKR playmaker *sports*
PLML pell-mell *fast*

Letters aren't doubled for single sounds: to find alley use **L** not **LL**. Use **Y** and **W** as hard sounds only: to find yellow use **YL**. (Br)=British spelling or usage. * See dictionary.

PLML plumule *bud*
PLMLDS poliomyelitis *disease*
PLMLK plumlike *fruity*
PLMLTS poliomyelitis *disease*
PLMN palimony *money*
PLMN palomino *horse* palominos
PLMN plowman *farmer* plowmen
PLMN plumbing *pipes*
PLMNG plumbing *pipes*
PLMNK pulmonic *lungs*
PLMNR pulmonary *lungs*
PLMNT pulmonate *lungs*
PLMP plump *(adj) ample (v) sink, support (n) fall (adv) directly*
PLMPL plumply *amply*
PLMPNS plumpness *ample*
PLMPSST palimpsest *layers*
PLMR palmar *hand*
PLMR palmary *best*
PLMR palmer *pilgrim*
PLMR palmier *many trees*
PLMR palmyra *tree*
PLMR plumber *pipe fixer*
PLMR plumeria *flower*
PLMR plumier *feather*
PLMR polymer *chemical*
PLMRF polymorph *many forms*
PLMRFK polymorphic *many forms*
PLMRFS polymorphous *many forms*
PLMRFZM polymorphism *many forms*
PLMRK polymeric *chemical*
PLMRY plumeria *flower*
PLMRZ polymerase *enzyme*
PLMRZ polymerize *combine* polymerized polymerizing (Br) polymerise
PLMRZM polymerism *chemical*
PLMRZSHN polymerization *combine* (Br) polymerisation
PLMS plumose *feathers*
PLMSHN palmation *like a hand*
PLMSL plimsoll *(Br) shoe*
PLMSND Palm Sunday *religion*
PLMSST palimpsest *layers*
PLMSST polemicist *arguer*
PLMST palmiest *many trees*
PLMST palmist *fortune teller*
PLMST plumiest *feathery*
PLMST polemist *arguer*
PLMSTR palmistry *fortune telling*
PLMSZ polemicize *argue* polemicized polemicizing
PLMT palmate *like a hand*
PLMT palmetto *tree* palmettos (or) palmettoes
PLMT pelmet *curtain*
PLMT playmate *friend*
PLMT plummet *fall*
PLMTH polymath *learned one*
PLMTH polymathy *vast learning*
PLMTHK polymathic *learned one*
PLMTR pulmotor *lungs*
PLMYL plumule *bud*
PLMYLDS poliomyelitis *disease*
PLMYLTS poliomyelitis *disease*
PLMYR palmier *many trees*
PLMYR plumier *feather*
PLMYST palmiest *many trees*
PLMYST plumiest *feathery*
PLMZ polemize *argue* polemized polemizing
PLN aplenty *enough*
PLN appalling *awful*
PLN appealing *attractive*
PLN opaline *gem*
PLN paling *fence*
PLN peeling *rind*
PLN piling *structure*
PLN plain *(adj) clear, simple (n) region*
PLN plan *scheme* planned planning
PLN plane *airplane, level, tool* planed planing
PLN plena *(pl) full* plenum
PLN plenty *more than enough*
PLN Poland *country*
PLN polenta *food*
PLN pollen *plant dust*
PLN Pollyanna *optimist*
PLN polynya *puddle* polynyas
PLN pylon *structure*
PLN upland *plateau*
PLNBL plantable *sow, settle, conceal*
PLNC pliancy *bendability*
PLNCHT planchet *disk*
PLND Poland *country*
PLND upland *plateau*
PLNDR plunder *steal*
PLNDR pollinator *pollen spreader*
PLNDR polyandry *many husbands*
PLNDRM palindrome *same both ways*
PLNDRMK palindromic *same both ways*
PLNDRMST palindromist *same both ways*
PLNDRR plunderer *stealer*
PLNDRS polyandrous *many husbands*
PLNF plaintiff *brings legal action*
PLNFL plentiful *(adj) more than enough* plentifully *(adv)*
PLNFRDK pyelonephritic *kidney*
PLNFRDS pyelonephritis *kidney*
PLNFRTK pyelonephritic *kidney*
PLNFRTS pyelonephritis *kidney*
PLNG appalling *awful*
PLNG appealing *attractive*
PLNG paling *fence*
PLNG peeling *rind*
PLNG piling *structure*
PLNGDN plankton *tiny organisms*
PLNGK plank *(n) board (v)*

Use letters that best describe the sounds you hear and omit the vowels. Use **S** or **K** instead of **C**: to find circle use **SRKL**. Use **J** to find joy, **JM** to find gem and **G** to find go.

set down
PLNGK plunk *plop*
PLNGK uplink *connect*
PLNGKDN plankton *tiny organisms*
PLNGKN palanquin *vehicle*
PLNGKN planking *boards*
PLNGKNG planking *boards*
PLNGKTN plankton *tiny organisms*
PLNGKWN palanquin *vehicle*
PLNGL appallingly *awfully*
PLNGL appealingly *attractively*
PLNGQN palanquin *vehicle*
PLNGRD plantigrade *walking*
PLNGTN plankton *tiny organisms*
PLNJ plunge *dive* plunged plunging
PLNJNC plangency *loud*
PLNJNS plangency *loud*
PLNJNT plangent *loud*
PLNJNTC plangency *loud*
PLNJNTS plangency *loud*
PLNJR plunger *piston, diver*
PLNK plank *(n) board (v) set down*
PLNK plunk *plop*
PLNK uplink *connect*
PLNKDN plankton *tiny organisms*
PLNKLTHZ plainclothes *police*
PLNKLZ plainclothes *police*
PLNKN palanquin *vehicle*
PLNKN planking *boards*
PLNKNG planking *boards*
PLNKTN plankton *tiny organisms*
PLNKWN palanquin *vehicle*
PLNL appealingly *attractively*
PLNL plainly *(adv) clearly, simply*
PLNL planula *larva* planulae
PLNLD planeload *airplane*
PLNM plenum *full* plenums (or) plena
PLNM pollinium *pollen mass*

pollinia
PLNM polonium *element*
PLNMDR planimeter *measurer*
PLNML polynomial *math*
PLNMS polyonymous *many names*
PLNMTR planimeter *measurer*
PLNMTRK planimetric *measured*
PLNMYL polynomial *math*
PLNN planning *plotting*
PLNNG planning *plotting*
PLNPTNCHR plenipotentiary *powerful one*
PLNPTNSHR plenipotentiary *powerful one*
PLNQN palanquin *vehicle*
PLNR planar *plane*
PLNR planner *schemer*
PLNR plantar *foot*
PLNR planter *farmer, container*
PLNR plenary *full*
PLNS appliance *tool*
PLNS opulence *more than enough*
PLNS paleness *pallid, dim*
PLNS plainness *simplicity*
PLNS plenteous *ample*
PLNS pliancy *bendability*
PLNSCHRDD polyunsaturated *fat*
PLNSCHRTD polyunsaturated *fat*
PLNSDK pleonastic *excessive*
PLNSDKL pleonastically *excessively*
PLNSFR planisphere *star map*
PLNSH planish *hammer*
PLNSH Polynesia *islands*
PLNSHN pollination *flower*
PLNSHN Polynesian *Hawaii*
PLNSHT planchette *writing*
PLNSNG plainsong *chant*
PLNSPKN plainspoken *frank*

PLNSPKNS plainspokenness *frankness*
PLNSS pollinosis (or) pollenosis *allergy*
PLNSTK pleonastic *excessive*
PLNSTKL pleonastically *excessively*
PLNSTRDD polyunsaturated *fat*
PLNSTRTD polyunsaturated *fat*
PLNT aplenty *enough*
PLNT appellant *appeal*
PLNT opulent *more than enough*
PLNT plaint *complaint*
PLNT planet *world*
PLNT plant *(n) flora, factory (v) sow, settle, conceal*
PLNT plenty *more than enough*
PLNT pliant *bendable*
PLNT polenta *food*
PLNT pollinate *flower* pollinated pollinating
PLNTBL plantable *sow, settle, conceal*
PLNTC pliancy *bendability*
PLNTD planetoid *asteroid*
PLNTD plenitude *more than enough*
PLNTDNS plenitudinous *more than enough*
PLNTF plaintiff *brings legal action*
PLNTGRD plantigrade *walking*
PLNTH plinth *base*
PLNTH polyantha *rose*
PLNTH polyanthi (pl) *primrose* polyanthus
PLNTHS polyanthus *primrose* polyanthuses (or) polyanthi
PLNTL opulently *more than enough*
PLNTLG paleontology *fossils*
PLNTLG planetology *planets*
PLNTLJ paleontology *fossils*

Letters aren't doubled for single sounds: to find alley use **L** not **LL**. Use **Y** and **W** as hard sounds only: to find yellow use **YL**. (Br)=British spelling or usage. * See dictionary.

PLNTLJ planetology *planets*
PLNTLJK paleontologic (or) paleontological *fossils*
PLNTLJKL paleontological (or) paleontologic *fossils*
PLNTLJKL planetological *planets*
PLNTLJST paleontologist *fossils*
PLNTLJST planetologist *planets*
PLNTN plantain *fruit*
PLNTN planting *crop*
PLNTNG planting *crop*
PLNTR planetaria (pl) *observatory* planetarium
PLNTR planetary *worlds*
PLNTR plantar *foot*
PLNTR planter *farmer, container*
PLNTR pollinator *pollen spreader*
PLNTRM planetarium *observatory* planetariums (or) planetaria
PLNTRY planetaria (pl) *observatory* planetarium
PLNTRYM planetarium *observatory* planetariums (or) planetaria
PLNTS appliance *tool*
PLNTS opulence *more than enough*
PLNTS plenteous *ample*
PLNTS pliancy *bendability*
PLNTSHN plantation *farm*
PLNTSML planetesimal *solar system*
PLNTV plaintive *sad*
PLNTVL plaintively *sadly*
PLNTVNS plaintiveness *sadness*
PLNTWD planetwide *international*
PLNTYD plenitude *more than enough*
PLNTYDNS plenitudinous *more than enough*
PLNTYS plenteous *ample*
PLNV plaintive *sad*
PLNVL plaintively *sadly*
PLNVNS plaintiveness

sadness
PLNY polynya *puddle* polynyas
PLNYL planula *larva* planulae
PLNYM pollinium *pollen mass* pollinia
PLNYM polonium *element*
PLNYS plenteous *ample*
PLNZ polonaise *garment, dance*
PLNZH Polynesia *islands*
PLNZHN Polynesian *Hawaii*
PLNZM pleonasm *excess*
PLNZMN plainsman *dweller* plainsmen
PLNZR pollenizer *plant*
PLP palpi (pl) *mouth* palpus
PLP pileup *mass*
PLP plop *fall heavily* plopped plopping
PLP polyp *jellyfish, lump*
PLP pull-up (n) *raise* pull up (v)
PLP pulp *soft mass*
PLP pulpy *mushy*
PLPBL palpable (adj) *touchable* palpably (adv)
PLPBLD palpability *touchable*
PLPBLT palpability *touchable*
PLPC epilepsy *convulsions* epilepsies
PLPD polypody *fern* polypodies
PLPDD epileptoid *convulsions*
PLPDK epileptic *convulsions*
PLPLD polyploid *chromosome* polyploidy
PLPLKC apoplexy *stroke*
PLPLKS apoplexy *stroke*
PLPLX apoplexy *stroke*
PLPN Pilipino *language*
PLPN playpen *crib*
PLPN polypnea *panting*
PLPNS pulpiness *soft mass*
PLPNSHN Peloponnesian *Greek*
PLPNY polypnea *panting*
PLPNZHN Peloponnesian *Greek*

PLPNZN Peloponnesian *Greek*
PLPPTD polypeptide *amino acid*
PLPRFK pluperfect *verb, complete*
PLPRFKT pluperfect *verb, complete*
PLPRPLN polypropylene *plastic*
PLPS epilepsy *convulsions* epilepsies
PLPS palpus *mouth* palpi
PLPSHN palpation *examination*
PLPT palpate *examine* palpated palpating
PLPT pulpit *sermon*
PLPTD epileptoid *convulsions*
PLPTK epileptic *convulsions*
PLPTNT palpitant *throbbing*
PLPTSHN palpitation *throb*
PLPTT palpitate *throb* palpitated palpitating
PLPWD pulpwood *paper*
PLR appealer *request, accuse*
PLR applier *tool, person*
PLR paler *less color*
PLR pallor *pale face*
PLR peeler *tool, crab, log*
PLR pillar *post*
PLR pillory (v) *punish* pilloried pillorying pillories
PLR pillory (n) *device* pillories
PLR player *amusement*
PLR pleura *lung* pleurae (or) pleuras
PLR polar *north, south*
PLR poller *voter*
PLR polyuria *urine*
PLR pylori (pl) *valve* pylorus
PLRBR polar bear *animal*
PLRC pleurisy *lungs*
PLRD polarity *opposite* polarities
PLRD Polaroid *(trademark) camera*
PLRD pollard *tree*
PLRDK pleuritic *lungs*

Use letters that best describe the sounds you hear and omit the vowels. Use **S** or **K** instead of **C**: to find circle use **SRKL**. Use **J** to find joy, **JM** to find gem and **G** to find go.

PLRDNG playwriting *theater*
PLRK pyloric *valve*
PLRL pleural *lungs*
PLRL plural *more than one*
PLRLD plurality *biggest share,* numerous **pluralities**
PLRLSDK pluralistic *many kinds*
PLRLSDKL pluralistically *many kinds*
PLRLSTK pluralistic *many kinds*
PLRLSTKL pluralistically *many kinds*
PLRLT plurality *biggest share,* numerous **pluralities**
PLRLZ pluralize *more than one* pluralized pluralizing
PLRLZM pluralism *many kinds*
PLRLZSHN pluralization *more than one*
PLRM playroom *amusement*
PLRM poolroom *billiards*
PLRMDR polarimeter *device*
PLRMTR polarimeter *device*
PLRMTR polarimetry *science*
PLRN pelerine *cape*
PLRNMN pleuropneumonia *disease*
PLRNMNY pleuropneumonia *disease*
PLRNYMN pleuropneumonia *disease*
PLRNYMNY pleuropneumonia *disease*
PLRS pelorus *compass*
PLRS pleurisy *lungs*
PLRS pylorus *valve* pylori
PLRSKP polariscope *device*
PLRSKPK polariscopic *device*
PLRT playwright *writer*
PLRT polarity *opposite* polarities
PLRTHM polyrhythm *music*
PLRTHMK polyrhythmic *music*
PLRTHN polyurethane *foam*
PLRTK pleuritic *lungs*
PLRTNG playwriting *theater*
PLRY polyuria *urine*

PLRZ pliers *tool*
PLRZ polarize *light, oppose* polarized polarizing (Br) polarise
PLRZSHN polarization *light, opposition* (Br) polarisation
PLS Appaloosa *horse*
PLS applause *clapping*
PLS palace *mansion*
PLS palliasse *mattress*
PLS pelisse *cloak*
PLS pilose *hair*
PLS pilus *hair* pili
PLS place *(v) set, rank, identify** placed placing
PLS place *(n) space, position, status**
PLS plissé *(or)* plisse *texture*
PLS plus *addition* pluses
PLS police *(v) patrol* policed policing
PLS police *(n) patrolman* police
PLS policy *plan* policies
PLS pulse *throb* pulsed pulsing
PLSB placebo *inert drug, soother* placebos
PLSBL placeable *set, rank, identify**
PLSD palisade *fence* palisaded palisading
PLSD pellucid *clear*
PLSD pilosity *hairiness*
PLSD placid *calm*
PLSD poolside *swimming*
PLSDCN plasticine *(trademark) clay*
PLSDD placidity *calmness*
PLSDK plastic *(adj) pliable (n) synthetic*
PLSDKL plastically *pliable*
PLSDKNM aplastic anemia *blood disease*
PLSDKNMY aplastic anemia *blood disease*
PLSDL placidly *calm*
PLSDNS placidness *calmness*
PLSDR pilaster *column*
PLSDR plaster *coating*

PLSDR polyester *fabric*
PLSDR pulsator *throb*
PLSDRBRD plasterboard *walls*
PLSDRD plastered *drunk*
PLSDRR plasterer *worker*
PLSDRS polyestrous *reproduction*
PLSDRWRK plasterwork *coating*
PLSDSN plasticine *(trademark) clay*
PLSDSZ plasticize *make pliable, coat* plasticized plasticizing
PLSDSZR plasticizer *make pliable, coat*
PLSDT placidity *calmness*
PLSH Appalachia *region*
PLSH palish *less color*
PLSH plush *luxurious*
PLSH plushy *luxury* plushier plushiest
PLSH polish *(n) shine, culture (v) rub, perfect* polishes
PLSH Polish *of Poland*
PLSHL palatial *(adj) grand* palatially *(adv)*
PLSHLDR placeholder *marker*
PLSHLDR policyholder *insurance*
PLSHN Appalachian *of Appalachia*
PLSHN appellation *name*
PLSHN epilation *hair removal*
PLSHN palliation *moderation*
PLSHN plosion *explosion*
PLSHN pollution *filth*
PLSHNS plushiness *luxury*
PLSHR pleasure *delight* pleasured pleasuring
PLSHR plowshare *tool*
PLSHR plushier *luxurious*
PLSHRBL pleasurable *(adj) pleasant* pleasurably *(adv)*
PLSHRBLD pleasurability *pleasant*
PLSHRBLNS pleasurableness *pleasant*

Letters aren't doubled for single sounds: to find alley use **L** not **LL**. Use **Y** and **W** as hard sounds only: to find yellow use **YL**. (Br)=British spelling or usage. * See dictionary.

PLSHRBLT pleasurability *pleasant*
PLSHRT polo shirt *garment*
PLSHST plushiest *luxurious*
PLSHY Appalachia *region*
PLSHYN Appalachian *of Appalachia*
PLSHYR plushier *luxurious*
PLSHYST plushiest *luxurious*
PLSKK placekick *football*
PLSKRD polysaccharide *carbohydrate*
PLSLBK polysyllabic *word*
PLSLBKL polysyllabically *word*
PLSLBL polysyllable *word*
PLSLDR placeholder *marker*
PLSLFD polysulfide *chemical*
PLSMN policeman *patrol policemen*
PLSMNT placement *assignment*
PLSMT place mat *table*
PLSN Paleocene *geologic age*
PLSN placenta *womb placentas (or) placentae*
PLSN Pliocene *epoch*
PLSNPDK polysynaptic *nerve*
PLSNPDKL polysynaptically *nerve*
PLSNPTK polysynaptic *nerve*
PLSNPTKL polysynaptically *nerve*
PLSNS opalescence *colorful*
PLSNT opalescent *colorful*
PLSNT placenta *womb placentas (or) placentae*
PLSNT pulsant *throbbing*
PLSNTRK polycentric *many centers*
PLSNTRZM polycentrism *many centers*
PLSNTS opalescence *colorful*
PLSPD pelecypod *animal*
PLSR placer *glacier*
PLSR pulsar *star*
PLSRBT polysorbate *emulsifier*

PLSS applesauce *cooked pulp*
PLSSHN pulsation *throb*
PLSSR plesiosaur *dinosaur*
PLST palest *less color*
PLST pilosity *hairiness*
PLST poloist *sport*
PLST pulsate *throb* pulsated pulsating
PLSTCN plasticine *(trademark) clay*
PLSTCN Pleistocene *epoch*
PLSTD plastid *cell*
PLSTK plastic *(adj) pliable (n) synthetic*
PLSTK plasticky *pliable*
PLSTKL plastically *pliable*
PLSTKNM aplastic anemia *blood disease*
PLSTKNMY aplastic anemia *blood disease*
PLSTN Palestine *country*
PLSTR palaestra *gymnasium palestrae*
PLSTR pilaster *column*
PLSTR plaster *coating*
PLSTR polestar *north star*
PLSTR pollster *questioner*
PLSTR polyester *fabric*
PLSTR pulsator *throb*
PLSTR upholster *cover*
PLSTR upholstery *covering* upholsteries
PLSTRBRD plasterboard *walls*
PLSTRD plastered *drunk*
PLSTRN plastron *pad, dickey*
PLSTRN polystyrene *plastic*
PLSTRR plasterer *worker*
PLSTRR upholsterer *coverer*
PLSTRS polyestrous *reproduction*
PLSTRWRK plasterwork *coating*
PLSTSD plasticity *pliability*
PLSTSN plasticine *(trademark) clay*
PLSTSN Pleistocene *epoch*
PLSTST plasticity *pliability*
PLSTSZ plasticize *make pliable, coat* plasticized plasticizing

PLSTSZR plasticizer *make pliable, coat*
PLSTSZSHN plasticization *pliability*
PLSV plosive *stop*
PLSWMN policewoman *patrol* policewomen
PLSYSR plesiosaur *dinosaur*
PLSZ pollices (pl) *thumb* pollex
PLT appellate *appeal*
PLT epaulet *shoulder ornament*
PLT palate *mouth*
PLT palette *board, color*
PLT pallet *bed, tool, platform*
PLT palliate *abate* palliated palliating
PLT pellet *tiny mass*
PLT pelota *game*
PLT pelt *(n) skin (v) hurl*
PLT pilot *guide*
PLT plait *braid*
PLT plat *map* platted platting
PLT plate *(v) cover* plated plating
PLT plate *(n) dish, metal, denture**
PLT plateau *tableland* plateaus (or) plateaux
PLT play out *finish, unreel*
PLT pleat *fold*
PLT plight *(v) pledge (n) pledge, predicament*
PLT plot *plan, map* plotted plotting
PLT Pluto *planet*
PLT polite *mannerly* politer politest
PLT polity *political form* polities
PLT pollute *make filthy* polluted polluting
PLT poult *turkey*
PLT pullet *fowl*
PLT pullout *(n) leave* pull out *(v)*
PLTBL palatable *(adj) tasty* palatably *(adv)*
PLTBL pleadable *beg*
PLTBLD palatability *tasty*
PLTBLT palatability *tasty*

Use letters that best describe the sounds you hear and omit the vowels. Use **S** or **K** instead of **C**: to find circle use **SRKL**. Use **J** to find joy, **JM** to find gem and **G** to find go.

PLTBR politburo *legislature*
PLTBYR politburo *legislature*
PLTD epauletted *ornament*
PLTD pileated *crested*
PLTFL plateful *dish*
PLTFRM platform *plan, structure*
PLTHLN polyethylene *plastic*
PLTHNG plaything *toy*
PLTHR plethora *excess*
PLTHRK plethoric *excessive*
PLTHS pilothouse *ship*
PLTHSDK polytheistic *many gods*
PLTHSDKL polytheistically *many gods*
PLTHST polytheist *many gods*
PLTHSTK polytheistic *many gods*
PLTHSTKL polytheistically *many gods*
PLTHYSDK polytheistic *many gods*
PLTHYSDKL polytheistically *many gods*
PLTHYST polytheist *many gods*
PLTHYSTK polytheistic *many gods*
PLTHYSTKL polytheistically *many gods*
PLTHYZM polytheism *many gods*
PLTHZM polytheism *many gods*
PLTHZMGRF
  plethysmograph *blood pressure* plethysmography
PLTHZMGRM
  plethysmogram *blood pressure*
PLTJ pilotage *guiding, wages*
PLTJ plottage *area*
PLTK politic *(adj) expedient*
PLTK politick *(v) campaign*
PLTK politico *politician* politicos
PLTKL apolitical (adj) *not political* apolitically (adv)
PLTKL political (adj) *government* politically

(adv)
PLTKLZ politicalize *create followers* politicalized politicalizing
PLTKNK polytechnic *applied arts*
PLTKR politicker *campaigner*
PLTKRC plutocracy *rule by wealthy* plutocracies
PLTKRDK plutocratic *wealthy ruler*
PLTKRS plutocracy *rule by wealthy* plutocracies
PLTKRT appellate court *appeal*
PLTKRT plutocrat *wealthy ruler*
PLTKRTK plutocratic *wealthy ruler*
PLTKS politics *art of governing*
PLTKS poll tax *levy* poll taxes
PLTKTNKS plate tectonics *geology*
PLTKTNX plate tectonics *geology*
PLTL palatal *mouth*
PLTL paludal *marshy*
PLTLT pilot light *flame*
PLTLT platelet *blood*
PLTLZ palatalize *pronounce* palatalized palatalizing
PLTLZSHN palatalization *pronunciation*
PLTM playtime *time for fun*
PLTMKR platemaker *printing*
PLTN palatine *(adj) palace, mouth (n) officer, cape, bone*
PLTN platen *roller*
PLTN plating *metal cover*
PLTN platoon *soldiers*
PLTN pluton *rock*
PLTNFL plentiful (adj) *more than enough* plentifully (adv)
PLTNG plaiting *braid*
PLTNG plating *metal cover*
PLTNG pleading *law*
PLTNGL pleadingly *beg*
PLTNGL ploddingly *slow*

PLTNK platonic *(often capitalized) Plato, friendly*
PLTNK plutonic *rock*
PLTNKL platonically *(often capitalized) Plato, friendly*
PLTNM platinum *element*
PLTNM plutonium *element*
PLTNT pollutant *filth*
PLTNYM plutonium *element*
PLTPS platypus *animal* platypuses
PLTR palliator *moderator*
PLTR palter *trick*
PLTR paltry *trifling* paltrier paltriest
PLTR pellitory *plant*
PLTR plaiter *braider*
PLTR plater *cover, horse*
PLTR platter *plate*
PLTR pleader *beggar*
PLTR pleater *folder*
PLTR plodder *slow one*
PLTR plotter *plan, map*
PLTR polluter *make filthy*
PLTR poultry *fowl*
PLTRGST poltergeist *ghost*
PLTRN platyrrhine *monkey*
PLTRN poltroon *coward*
PLTRNR poltroonery *cowardice*
PLTRNS paltriness *trifling*
PLTRR paltrier *trifling*
PLTRR poulterer *fowl seller*
PLTRST paltriest *trifling*
PLTRYR paltrier *trifling*
PLTRYST paltriest *trifling*
PLTS palazzo *building* palazzi
PLTS palletize *load, store* palletized palletizing (Br) palletise
PLTS pelletize *make small* pelletized pelletizing (Br) pelletise
PLTS poultice *medication* poulticed poulticing
PLTS pyelitis *pelvis*
PLTSHN politician *person running for office*
PLTSHR plat du jour *dish* plats du jour
PLTSR pelletizer *make small*

Letters aren't doubled for single sounds: to find alley use **L** not **LL**. Use **Y** and **W** as hard sounds only: to find yellow use **YL**. (Br)=British spelling or usage. * See dictionary.

(Br) pelletiser
PLTSR Pulitzer *journalist*
PLTSZ politicize *create followers* politicized politicizing (Br) politicise
PLTSZSHN politicization *create followers* (Br) politicisation
PLTTD platitude *dull, trite remark*
PLTTDNS platitudinous *trite*
PLTTYD platitude *dull, trite remark*
PLTTYDNS platitudinous *trite*
PLTTYDNZ platitudinize *speak tritely* platitudinized platitudinizing
PLTV appellative *name*
PLTV palliative *moderating*
PLTV pollutive *filthy*
PLTX politics *art of governing*
PLTX poll tax *levy* poll taxes
PLTZ palazzo *building* palazzi
PLTZ palletize *load, store* palletized palletizing (Br) palletise
PLTZ pelletize *make small* pelletized pelletizing (Br) pelletise
PLTZHR plat du jour *dish* plats du jour
PLTZR pelletizer *make small* (Br) pelletiser
PLTZR Pulitzer *journalist*
PLTZSHN palletization *load, store* (Br) palletisation
PLV Pahlavi *Iranian language*
PLVK pelvic *skeleton*
PLVL pluvial *rain*
PLVL pulvilli (pl) *adhesive* pulvillus
PLVLDR pole-vaulter *leap*
PLVLNT polyvalent *chemistry*
PLVLS pulvillus *adhesive* pulvilli
PLVLT pole vault *leap*
PLVLTR pole-vaulter *leap*

PLVNL polyvinyl *plastic*
PLVR palaver *talk*
PLVR plover *bird* plover (or) plovers
PLVR pull over *(v) steering*
PLVR pullover *(n) shirt*
PLVRLNT pulverulent *crumbly*
PLVRYLNT pulverulent *crumbly*
PLVRZ pulverize *demolish* pulverized pulverizing (Br) pulverise
PLVRZBL pulverizable *demolish* (Br) pulverisable
PLVRZSHN pulverization *demolish* (Br) pulverisation
PLVS pelvis *skeleton* pelvises (or) pelves
PLVS pluvious *rainy*
PLVYL pluvial *rain*
PLVYS pluvious *rainy*
PLVZ pelves (pl) *skeleton* pelvis
PLWBL plowable *land*
PLWD plywood *lumber*
PLWG pollywog (or) polliwog *tadpole*
PLWR playwear *clothing*
PLWR plower *plowman*
PLWST poloist *sport*
PLX poleax *tool* poleaxes
PLX pollex *thumb* pollices
PLX Pollux *star*
PLXGLS Plexiglas *(trademark) plastic*
PLXS plexus *network* plexuses
PLY palea *plants* paleae
PLY pallia (pl) *cloth, brain, mantle* pallium
PLY pilea (pl) *bird head* pileum
PLY plié *ballet*
PLY polio *disease*
PLYBL pliable *bendable*
PLYBLD pliability *bendability*
PLYBLT pliability *bendability*
PLYCN Paleocene *geologic age*

PLYCN Pliocene *epoch*
PLYDD pileated *crested*
PLYDL paludal *marshy*
PLYDR palliator *moderator*
PLYDV palliative *moderating*
PLYDZ Pleiades *Greek myth*
PLYF play-off (n) *tournament* play off (v)
PLYGRF paleography *ancient writings*
PLYGRFK paleographic (or) paleographical (adj) *ancient writings* paleographically (adv)
PLYGRFKL paleographical (or) paleographic (adj) *ancient writings* paleographically (adv)
PLYL pallial *mantle, brain*
PLYLSHN pullulation *swarm*
PLYLT pullulate *breed* pullulated pullulating
PLYLTHK Paleolithic *Stone Age*
PLYM pallium *cloth, brain, mantle* pallia (or) palliums
PLYM pileum *bird head* pilea
PLYMLDS poliomyelitis *disease*
PLYMLTS poliomyelitis *disease*
PLYMYLDS poliomyelitis *disease*
PLYMYLTS poliomyelitis *disease*
PLYN pillion *saddle*
PLYN Pollyanna *optimist*
PLYNC pliancy *bendability*
PLYNDR polyandry *many husbands*
PLYNDRS polyandrous *many husbands*
PLYNMS polyonymous *many names*
PLYNS appliance *tool*
PLYNS pliancy *bendability*
PLYNSCHRDD polyunsaturated *fat*
PLYNSCHRTD polyunsaturated *fat*
PLYNSDK pleonastic *excessive*

Use letters that best describe the sounds you hear and omit the vowels. Use **S** or **K** instead of **C**: to find circle use **SRKL**. Use **J** to find joy, **JM** to find gem and **G** to find go.

PLYNSDKL pleonastically *excessively*
PLYNSTK pleonastic *excessive*
PLYNSTKL pleonastically *excessively*
PLYNT pliant *bendable*
PLYNTC pliancy *bendability*
PLYNTH polyantha *rose*
PLYNTH polyanthi (pl) *primrose* polyanthus
PLYNTHS polyanthus *primrose* polyanthuses (or) polyanthi
PLYNTLG paleontology *fossils*
PLYNTLJ paleontology *fossils*
PLYNTLJK paleontologic (or) paleontological *fossils*
PLYNTLJKL paleontological (or) paleontologic *fossils*
PLYNTLJST paleontologist *fossils*
PLYNTS appliance *tool*
PLYNTS pliancy *bendability*
PLYNZM pleonasm *excess*
PLYR applier *tool, person*
PLYR player *gamesman*
PLYR polyuria *urine*
PLYRTHN polyurethane *foam*
PLYRY polyuria *urine*
PLYRZ pliers *tool*
PLYS palliasse *mattress*
PLYSDR polyester *fabric*
PLYSDRS polyestrous *reproduction*
PLYSHN palliation *moderation*
PLYSN Paleocene *geologic age*
PLYSN Pliocene *epoch*
PLYSTR polyester *fabric*
PLYSTRS polyestrous *reproduction*
PLYT palliate *moderate* palliated palliating
PLYT play out *finish, unreel*
PLYTD pileated *crested*
PLYTHLN polyethylene *plastic*

PLYTL paludal *marshy*
PLYTR palliator *moderator*
PLYTV palliative *moderating*
PLYZK Paleozoic *geological age*
PLYZWK Paleozoic *geological age*
PLZ applause *clapping*
PLZ palazzo *building* palazzi
PLZ palsy *(v) shaking* palsied palsying palsies
PLZ palsy *(n) paralysis, tremor* palsies
PLZ piles *ailment*
PLZ plaza *area*
PLZ please *gratify* pleased pleasing
PLZBL plausible (adj) *believable* plausibly (adv)
PLZBLD plausibility *believable* plausibilities
PLZBLT plausibility *believable* plausibilities
PLZD palsied *shaking*
PLZHN plosion *explosion*
PLZHR pleasure *delight* pleasured pleasuring
PLZHRBL pleasurable (adj) *pleasant* pleasurably (adv)
PLZHRBLD pleasurability *pleasant*
PLZHRBLNS pleasurableness *pleasant*
PLZHRBLT pleasurability *pleasant*
PLZK Paleozoic *geological age*
PLZM plasm *fluid*
PLZM plasma *blood, particles*
PLZMD plasmid *DNA*
PLZMDK plasmatic *blood, particles*
PLZMDM plasmodium *parasite* plasmodia
PLZMDY plasmodia (pl) *parasite* plasmodium
PLZMDYM plasmodium *parasite* plasmodia
PLZMFRSS plasmapheresis *blood*
PLZMLDK plasmolytic *shrinking*

PLZMLSS plasmolysis *shrinking*
PLZMLTK plasmolytic *shrinking*
PLZMLZ plasmolyze *shrink*
PLZMTK plasmatic *blood, particles*
PLZN pleasing *agreeable*
PLZNG pleasing *agreeable*
PLZNGL pleasingly *agreeably*
PLZNGNS pleasingness *agreeableness*
PLZNR pilsner (or) pilsener *beer*
PLZNS pleasance *delight*
PLZNT pleasant *agreeable*
PLZNTL pleasantly *agreeably*
PLZNTNS pleasantness *agreeableness*
PLZNTR pleasantry *banter* pleasantries
PLZNTS pleasance *delight*
PLZV plosive *stop*
PLZWK Paleozoic *geological age*
PLZWLZ palsy-walsy *friendly*
PM opium *narcotic*
PM p.m. (or) P.M. *afternoon*
PM palm *tree, hand*
PM palmy *with palms* palmier palmiest
PM Pima *Native American* Pimas (or) Pima
PM poem *verse*
PM pome *fruit*
PM puma *animal* pumas
PMD palmed *hand*
PMD palmetto *tree* palmettos (or) palmettoes
PMD pomade *hair cream*
PMFLT pamphlet *leaflet*
PMFLTR pamphleteer *writer*
PMGRNT pomegranate *fruit*
PMKN pemmican *food*
PMKN pumpkin *vegetable*
PMKNCD pumpkinseed *fish*
PMKNSD pumpkinseed *fish*
PMKTN pima cotton *cloth*

Letters aren't doubled for single sounds: to find alley use **L** not **LL**. Use **Y** and **W** as hard sounds only: to find yellow use **YL**. (Br)=British spelling or usage. * See dictionary.

PML pomelo *grapefruit* pomelos

PML pommel (v) *pound* pommeled (or) pommelled pommeling (or) pommelling

PML pommel (n) *knob*

PML pummel *pound* pummeled pummeling

PMLG pomology *fruit*

PMLHRS pommel horse *gymnast*

PMLJ pomology *fruit*

PMLJKL pomological *fruit*

PMLJST pomologist *fruit*

PMN ape-man *half human* ape-men

PMN pimento *allspice* pimentos (or) pimento

PMN pimiento *pepper* pimientos

PMNDR pomander *scent*

PMNT payment *money*

PMNT pimento *allspice* pimentos (or) pimento

PMNT pimiento *pepper* pimientos

PMP pampa *grassy plain* pampas

PMP pimp *solicitor*

PMP pomp *display*

PMP Pompeii *city*

PMP pump (v) *draw fluid, exert* (n) *device, shoe*

PMPDR pompadour *hairdo*

PMPKN pumpkin *vegetable*

PMPKNCD pumpkinseed *fish*

PMPKNSD pumpkinseed *fish*

PMPL pimple *blemish*

PMPL pimply *blemished*

PMPLD pimpled *blemished*

PMPLT pamphlet *leaflet*

PMPLTR pamphleteer *writer*

PMPM pom-pom *cheerleading, gun*

PMPM pompon *flower*

PMPN pampean *grassy*

PMPN pompano *fish* pompano (or) pompanos

PMPN pompon *flower*

PMPR pamper *indulge*

PMPR pumper *fire truck*

PMPRNKL pumpernickel *bread*

PMPRNL pimpernel *herb*

PMPRR pamperer *indulge*

PMPS pompous *proud*

PMPSD pomposity *pride* pomposities

PMPSL pompously *proudly*

PMPSNS pompousness *pride*

PMPST pomposity *pride* pomposities

PMPYN pampean *grassy*

PMR palmar *hand*

PMR palmary *best*

PMR palmer *pilgrim*

PMR palmier *many trees*

PMRKT upmarket *upscale*

PMS pomace *pulp*

PMS pumice *rock*

PMSDR paymaster *money*

PMSHN palmation *like a hand*

PMSHS pomaceous *apples*

PMSHS pumiceous *rock*

PMSND Palm Sunday *religion*

PMST palmiest *many trees*

PMST palmist *fortune teller*

PMST pumicite *rock*

PMST utmost *farthest, best*

PMSTR palmistry *fortune telling*

PMSTR paymaster *money*

PMT palmate *like a hand*

PMT palmetto *tree* palmettos (or) palmettoes

PMYN pimiento *pepper* pimientos

PMYNT pimiento *pepper* pimientos

PMYR palmier *many trees*

PMYST palmiest *many trees*

PN apian *bees*

PN apnea *breath* (Br) apnoea

PN append *attach*

PN appointee *person named*

PN eupnea *respiration*

PN open (adj) *not closed, vacant, frank* (n) *public, contest,* (v) *give access, reveal, expand**

PN opine *express opinion* opined opining

PN oppugn *fight*

PN paean *song*

PN paeon *verse*

PN pain *hurt*

PN pan (v) *wash, criticize, yield* panned panning

PN pan (n) *basin, pot, criticism*

PN pane *glass, section*

PN panne *fabric*

PN pantie (or) panty *underwear* panties

PN pawn *chess, loan*

PN Pawnee *Native American* Pawnee (or) Pawnees

PN peen *hammer*

PN pen (v) *write, enclose* penned penning

PN pen (n) *enclosure, writing tool, swan**

PN penne *pasta* penne

PN penny *coin* pennies (or) pence

PN peon *unskilled laborer* peons (or) peones

PN peony *flower* peonies

PN piano *music* pianos

PN pin (v) *fasten, hold down* pinned pinning

PN pin (n) *fastener, peg*

PN pine (v) *yearn* pined pining

PN pine (n) *tree, lumber*

PN pinna *leaf, feather* pinnae (or) pinnas

PN pinny *pinafore* pinnies

PN pinto *horse, bean* pintos

PN pointy *sharp* pointier pointiest

PN pone *corn mush*

PN pony *horse* ponies

PN pound *weight, hit*

PN puisne *rank*

PN pun *joke* punned punning

PN punny *joke* punnier

Use letters that best describe the sounds you hear and omit the vowels. Use **S** or **K** instead of **C**: to find circle use **SRKL**. Use **J** to find joy, **JM** to find gem and **G** to find go.

punniest

PN puny *small* punier
puniest

PN upon *on top of*

PNBL pinball *game*

PNBN pinbone *hip*

PNBRKR pawnbroker *lender*

PNBSKT Penobscot *Native American* Penobscot (or) Penobscots

PNC panacea *remedy*

PNCH paunch *belly* paunches

PNCH paunchy *fat* paunchier paunchiest

PNCH penuche *candy*

PNCH pinch *(n) small amount, arrest (v) squeeze* pinches

PNCH poncho *cape* ponchos

PNCH punch *hit, beverage* punches

PNCH punchy *dazed* punchier punchiest

PNCHBK pinchbeck *alloy*

PNCHBL punch bowl *container*

PNCHBL punchball *baseball*

PNCHBRD punchboard *prizes*

PNCHD pancetta *meat*

PNCHDR pinch-hitter *baseball*

PNCHDRNGK punch-drunk *dazed*

PNCHDRNK punch-drunk *dazed*

PNCHHDR pinch-hitter *baseball*

PNCHHT pinch-hit *baseball* pinch-hit pinch-hitting

PNCHHTR pinch-hitter *baseball*

PNCHN pension *retirement*

PNCHN punch in *time clock*

PNCHN puncheon *tool*

PNCHNBL pensionable *retiree*

PNCHNR pensionary *hireling* pensionaries

PNCHNR pensioner *retiree*

PNCHNS paunchiness *fat*

PNCHNT penchant *liking*

PNCHP punch up *(v) fortify*

PNCHP punch-up *(Br) fistfight*

PNCHR paunchier *fat*

PNCHR pincher *claw*

PNCHR pinscher *dog*

PNCHR puncher *hitter*

PNCHR punchier *dazed*

PNCHR puncture *pierce* punctured puncturing

PNCHST paunchiest *fat*

PNCHST punchiest *dazed*

PNCHT pancetta *meat*

PNCHT pinch-hit *baseball* pinch-hit pinch-hitting

PNCHT punch out (v) *fight, time clock* punch-out (n)

PNCHT punctuate *mark* punctuated punctuating

PNCHTR pinch-hitter *baseball*

PNCHYR paunchier *fat*

PNCHYR punchier *dazed*

PNCHYST paunchiest *fat*

PNCHYST punchiest *dazed*

PNCN poinciana *tree*

PNCY panacea *remedy*

PNCYN poinciana *tree*

PNCZN open season *time*

PND append *add to*

PND open-eyed *awake*

PND pained *hurting*

PND panda *animal*

PND pandy *(Br) punishment* pandied pandying pandies

PND paned *glass, section*

PND piñata (or) pinata *candy*

PND pointed *sharp*

PND pond *water*

PND pound *weight, hit*

PND upend *overturn*

PNDCZ appendices (pl) *attachment* appendix

PNDD pandowdy *dessert* pandowdies

PNDFLSH pound-foolish *unwise*

PNDJ appendage *part, limb*

PNDJ poundage *weight*

PNDKDM appendectomy

medical operation
appendectomies
(Br) appendicectomy

PNDKLR appendicular *limb*

PNDKMN up-and-coming *gaining*

PNDKMNG up-and-coming *gaining*

PNDKS appendix *attachment* appendixes (or) appendices

PNDKT pandect *laws*

PNDKTM appendectomy
medical operation
appendectomies
(Br) appendicectomy

PNDKYLR appendicular *limb*

PNDL peanut oil *fatty liquid*

PNDLM pendulum *swing*

PNDLR pendular *swinging*

PNDLS pendulous *hanging, swinging*

PNDMK pandemic *widespread*

PNDMNM pandemonium *tumult*

PNDMNYM pandemonium *tumult*

PNDN pending *awaiting*

PNDN up-and-down (adj) *motion* up and down (adv)

PNDNG pending *awaiting*

PNDNT appendant *associated*

PNDNT pendant *ornament*

PNDNT pendent *jutting*

PNDQLR appendicular *limb*

PNDR open door (n) *accessible* open-door (adj)

PNDR pander *satisfy*

PNDR Pandora *myth*

PNDR ponder *think*

PNDR pounder *tool, gun, weight*

PNDRBL ponderable *thinkable*

PNDRR ponderer *thinker*

PNDRS ponderosa *pine*

PNDRS ponderous *heavy*

PNDRSBKS Pandora's box

myth

PNDRSBX Pandora's box
myth

PNDRSL ponderously *heavy*

PNDRSNS ponderousness
heavy

PNDRZBKS Pandora's box
myth

PNDRZBX Pandora's box
myth

PNDSDS appendicitis
intestinal pain

PNDSKDM
appendicectomy *(Br)*
medical operation

PNDSKTM
appendicectomy *(Br)*
medical operation

PNDSTS appendicitis
intestinal pain

PNDSZ appendices (pl)
attachment appendix

PNDT pundit *teacher*

PNDTR punditry *teaching*

PNDV punitive *penalty*

PNDX appendix *attachment*
appendixes (or)
appendices

PNDYL peanut oil *fatty*
liquid

PNDYLM pendulum *swing*

PNDYLR pendular *swinging*

PNDYLS pendulous
hanging, swinging

PNF pawn off *give away*

PNF penknife *tool* penknives

PNF pontiff *pope*

PNFL painful (adj) *hurt*
painfully (adv)

PNFL panful *amount*

PNFL pinfold *pen*

PNFLD pinfold *pen*

PNFLSH pound-foolish
unwise

PNFR panfry *cook* panfried
panfrying panfries

PNFR pinafore *apron*

PNFRN epinephrine
hormone

PNFSH panfish *sunfish*

PNFSH pinfish *grunt*

PNFTHR pinfeather *bird*

PNG pang *spasm*

PNG Pangaea *original land*
mass

PNG ping *sound*

PNG pongee *silk*

PNGCHDR punctuator
marker

PNGCHL punctual (adj) *on*
time punctually (adv)

PNGCHLD punctuality *on*
time

PNGCHLT punctuality *on*
time

PNGCHR puncture *pierce*
punctured puncturing

PNGCHSHN punctuation
mark

PNGCHT punctuate *mark*
punctuated punctuating

PNGCHTR punctuator
marker

PNGCHWDR punctuator
marker

PNGCHWL punctual (adj)
on time punctually (adv)

PNGCHWLD punctuality *on*
time

PNGCHWLT punctuality *on*
time

PNGCHWSHN punctuation
mark

PNGCHWT punctuate *mark*
punctuated punctuating

PNGCHWTR punctuator
marker

PNGGL pangola *grass*

PNGGLN pangolin *mammal*

PNGGPNGG Pago Pago
town

PNGGWN penguin *bird*

PNGJD pongid *ape*

PNGK pink *color*

PNGK pinkeye *ailment*

PNGK pinko *politics* pinkos

PNGK pinky (or) pinkie
finger pinkies

PNGK punk (n) *hoodlum,*
tinder (adj) inferior, style

PNGK punkah *fan*

PNGK punkie *insect* punkies

PNGKCHDR punctuator
marker

PNGKCHL punctual (adj) *on*
time punctually (adv)

PNGKCHLD punctuality *on*
time

PNGKCHLT punctuality *on*
time

PNGKCHR puncture *pierce*
punctured puncturing

PNGKCHSHN punctuation
mark

PNGKCHT punctuate *mark*
punctuated punctuating

PNGKCHTR punctuator
marker

PNGKCHWDR punctuator
marker

PNGKCHWL punctual (adj)
on time punctually (adv)

PNGKCHWLD punctuality
on time

PNGKCHWLT punctuality
on time

PNGKCHWSHN
punctuation *mark*

PNGKCHWT punctuate
mark punctuated
punctuating

PNGKCHWTR punctuator
marker

PNGKN pinking *shears*

PNGKNG pinking *shears*

PNGKR punker *style*

PNGKRDK pancreatic *gland*

PNGKRS pancreas *gland*

PNGKRTDS pancreatitis
gland pancreatitides

PNGKRTK pancreatic *gland*

PNGKRTTS pancreatitis
gland pancreatitides

PNGKRYDK pancreatic
gland

PNGKRYS pancreas *gland*

PNGKRYTDS pancreatitis
gland pancreatitides

PNGKRYTK pancreatic
gland

PNGKRYTTS pancreatitis
gland pancreatitides

PNGKSH pinkish *color*

PNGKSH punkish *poor, rock*
and roll

PNGKSHDR punctuator

Use letters that best describe the sounds you hear and omit the vowels. Use **S** or **K** instead of **C**: to find circle use **SRKL**. Use **J** to find joy, **JM** to find gem and **G** to find go.

PNGKSHL punctual (adj) *on time* punctually (adv)
PNGKSHLD punctuality *on time*
PNGKSHLT punctuality *on time*
PNGKSHR puncture *pierce* punctured puncturing
PNGKSHSHN punctuation *mark*
PNGKSHT punctuate *mark* punctuated punctuating
PNGKSHTR punctuator *marker*
PNGKSHWDR punctuator *marker*
PNGKSHWL punctual (adj) *on time* punctually (adv)
PNGKSHWLD punctuality *on time*
PNGKSHWLT punctuality *on time*
PNGKSHWSHN punctuation *mark*
PNGKSHWT punctuate *mark* punctuated punctuating
PNGKSHWTR punctuator *marker*
PNGKSLP pink slip (n) *job termination* pink-slip (v)
PNGKTL punctilio *details* punctilios
PNGKTL punctual (adj) *on time* punctually (adv)
PNGKTLS punctilious *careful*
PNGKTLSL punctiliously *careful*
PNGKTLSNS punctiliousness *careful*
PNGKTLY punctilio *details* punctilios
PNGKTLYS punctilious *careful*
PNGKTLYSL punctiliously *careful*
PNGKTLYSNS punctiliousness *careful*
PNGKTSHN punctation *dots*
PNGKTT punctate *dots*

PNGKTWL punctual (adj) *on time* punctually (adv)
PNGL pangola *grass*
PNGLN pangolin *mammal*
PNGN pentagon *five sides*
PNGPNG Pago Pago *town*
PNGPNG ping-pong *sport*
PNGRF pantograph *device*
PNGRFK pantographic *device*
PNGRK panegyric *praise*
PNGRKL panegyrical (adj) *praise* panegyrically (adv)
PNGRM pentagram *symbol*
PNGRST panegyrist *praiser*
PNGSHDR punctuator *marker*
PNGSHL punctual (adj) *on time* punctually (adv)
PNGSHLD punctuality *on time*
PNGSHLT punctuality *on time*
PNGSHR puncture *pierce* punctured puncturing
PNGSHSHN punctuation *mark*
PNGSHT punctuate *mark* punctuated punctuating
PNGSHTR punctuator *marker*
PNGSHWDR punctuator *marker*
PNGSHWL punctual (adj) *on time* punctually (adv)
PNGSHWLD punctuality *on time*
PNGSHWLT punctuality *on time*
PNGSHWSHN punctuation *mark*
PNGSHWT punctuate *mark* punctuated punctuating
PNGSHWTR punctuator *marker*
PNGTDR punctuator *marker*
PNGTL punctual (adj) *on time* punctually (adv)
PNGTLD punctuality *on time*
PNGTLT punctuality *on time*
PNGTR puncture *pierce* punctured puncturing

PNGTSHN punctuation *mark*
PNGTT punctuate *mark* punctuated punctuating
PNGTTR punctuator *marker*
PNGTWDR punctuator *marker*
PNGTWL punctual (adj) *on time* punctually (adv)
PNGTWLD punctuality *on time*
PNGTWLT punctuality *on time*
PNGTWSHN punctuation *mark*
PNGTWT punctuate *mark* punctuated punctuating
PNGTWTR punctuator *marker*
PNGWN penguin *bird*
PNGXLP pink slip (n) *job termination* pink-slip (v)
PNGY Pangaea *original land mass*
PNHD pinhead *idiot*
PNHD pointy-head *intellectual*
PNHDD pinheaded *idiotic*
PNHDD pointy-headed *intellectual*
PNHDDNS pinheadedness *idiocy*
PNHL pinhole *small hole*
PNHLDR penholder *stand*
PNHMR Oppenheimer *physicist*
PNHNDD openhanded *generous*
PNHNDL panhandle *(v)* beg panhandled panhandling
PNHNDL panhandle *(n) territory*
PNHNDLR panhandler *beggar*
PNHNLR panhandler *beggar*
PNHRDD openhearted *frank*
PNHRTD openhearted *frank*
PNHRTH open-hearth *steelmaking*
PNHS open house *social affair*
PNHS penthouse *dwelling*

Letters aren't doubled for single sounds: to find alley use **L** not **LL**. Use **Y** and **W** as hard sounds only: to find yellow use **YL**. (Br)=British spelling or usage. * See dictionary.

PNHWL pinwheel *toy*
PNHZ panty hose *stockings*
PNJ Pangaea *original land mass*
PNJ peonage *labor*
PNJ pongee *silk*
PNJD pongid *ape*
PNJLM pendulum *swing*
PNJLR pendular *swinging*
PNJLS pendulous *hanging, swinging*
PNJNC pungency *acrid*
PNJNS pungency *acrid*
PNJNT pungent *acrid*
PNJNTC pungency *acrid*
PNJNTS pungency *acrid*
PNJRK panegyric *praise*
PNJRKL panegyrical (adj) *praise* panegyrically (adv)
PNJRST panegyrist *praiser*
PNJY Pangaea *original land mass*
PNK apneic *breath*
PNK eupneic *respiration*
PNK panic *fear* panicked panicking
PNK panicky *fearful*
PNK pink *color*
PNK pinkeye *ailment*
PNK pinko *politics* pinkos
PNK pinky (or) pinkie *finger* pinkies
PNK Pontiac *city*
PNK punk (*n*) *hoodlum,* tinder (*adj*) *inferior, style*
PNK punkah *fan*
PNK punkie *insect* punkies
PNKCHDR punctuator *marker*
PNKCHL punctual (adj) *on time* punctually (adv)
PNKCHLD punctuality *on time*
PNKCHLT punctuality *on time*
PNKCHR puncture *pierce* punctured puncturing
PNKCHSHN punctuation *mark*
PNKCHT punctuate *mark* punctuated punctuating
PNKCHTR punctuator

marker
PNKCHWDR punctuator *marker*
PNKCHWL punctual (adj) *on time* punctually (adv)
PNKCHWLD punctuality *on time*
PNKCHWLT punctuality *on time*
PNKCHWSHN punctuation *mark*
PNKCHWT punctuate *mark* punctuated punctuating
PNKCHWTR punctuator *marker*
PNKK pancake *food*
PNKL panicle *flower*
PNKL pentacle *star*
PNKL pinnacle *summit* pinnacled pinnacling
PNKL pinochle *game*
PNKLD piña colada *drink*
PNKLR painkiller *drug*
PNKLT piña colada *drink*
PNKM panicum *grass*
PNKMN up-and-coming *gaining*
PNKMNG up-and-coming *gaining*
PNKN pannikin *cup*
PNKN pinecone *pine tree*
PNKN pinking *shears*
PNKNG pinking *shears*
PNKR punker *style*
PNKRDK pancreatic *gland*
PNKRL pin curl *hair*
PNKRMDK panchromatic *all colors*
PNKRMTK panchromatic *all colors*
PNKRS pancreas *gland*
PNKRS pennycress *herb*
PNKRTDS pancreatitis *gland* pancreatitides
PNKRTK pancreatic *gland*
PNKRTTS pancreatitis *gland* pancreatitides
PNKRYDK pancreatic *gland*
PNKRYS pancreas *gland*
PNKRYTDS pancreatitis *gland* pancreatitides
PNKRYTK pancreatic *gland*

PNKRYTTS pancreatitis *gland* pancreatitides
PNKSH pinkish *color*
PNKSH punkish *poor, rock and roll*
PNKSHDR punctuator *marker*
PNKSHL punctual (adj) *on time* punctually (adv)
PNKSHLD punctuality *on time*
PNKSHLT punctuality *on time*
PNKSHN pincushion *sewing*
PNKSHR puncture *pierce* punctured puncturing
PNKSHSHN punctuation *mark*
PNKSHT punctuate *mark* punctuated punctuating
PNKSHTR punctuator *marker*
PNKSHWDR punctuator *marker*
PNKSHWL punctual (adj) *on time* punctually (adv)
PNKSHWLD punctuality *on time*
PNKSHWLT punctuality *on time*
PNKSHWSHN punctuation *mark*
PNKSHWT punctuate *mark* punctuated punctuating
PNKSHWTR punctuator *marker*
PNKSLP pink slip (n) *job termination* pink-slip (v)
PNKST Pentecost *Holy Ghost*
PNKSTL Pentecostal *Christian*
PNKSTRKN panic-stricken *fearful*
PNKTDR punctuator *marker*
PNKTL punctilio *details* punctilios
PNKTL punctual (adj) *on time* punctually (adv)
PNKTLD punctuality *on time*
PNKTLS punctilious *careful*
PNKTLSL punctiliously

Use letters that best describe the sounds you hear and omit the vowels. Use **S** or **K** instead of **C**: to find circle use **SRKL**. Use **J** to find joy, **JM** to find gem and **G** to find go.

careful
PNKTLSNS punctiliousness
careful
PNKTLT punctuality *on time*
PNKTLY punctilio *details*
punctilios
PNKTLYS punctilious *careful*
PNKTLYSL punctiliously
careful
PNKTLYSNS
punctiliousness *careful*
PNKTR puncture *pierce*
punctured puncturing
PNKTSHN punctation *dots*
PNKTSHN punctuation
mark
PNKTT punctate *dots*
PNKTT punctuate *mark*
punctuated punctuating
PNKTTR punctuator *marker*
PNKTWDR punctuator
marker
PNKTWL punctual (adj) *on
time* punctually (adv)
PNKTWLD punctuality *on
time*
PNKTWLT punctuality *on
time*
PNKTWSHN punctuation
mark
PNKTWT punctuate *mark*
punctuated punctuating
PNKTWTR punctuator
marker
PNL openly *frank*
PNL panel (v) *board* paneled
(or) panelled paneling (or)
panelling
PNL panel (n) *group, section,
wood*
PNL penal (adj) *law* penally
(adv)
PNL pignoli (or) pignolia
pine nut
PNL pineal *gland*
PNL punily *small*
PNLD penalty *loss, hardship*
penalties
PNLDMT penultimate *next
to last*
PNLDMTL penultimately
next to last

PNLG penology *prison*
PNLJ penology *prison*
PNLJKL penological *prison*
PNLJST penologist *prison*
PNLKPN panleukopenia *cat
disease*
PNLKPNY panleukopenia
cat disease
PNLN paneling *boards*
PNLN pantaloon (or)
pantalone *britches*
PNLNG paneling *boards*
PNLS painless *no hurt*
PNLS penalize *punish*
penalized penalizing
(Br) penalise
PNLS penniless *no money*
PNLST panelist *advisor*
PNLT penalty *loss, hardship*
penalties
PNLT penlight *illumination*
PNLT penult *next to last*
PNLTMT penultimate *next to
last*
PNLTMTL penultimately
next to last
PNLY pignoli (or) pignolia
pine nut
PNLZ penalize *punish*
penalized penalizing
(Br) penalise
PNLZSHN penalization
punishment
(Br) penalisation
PNM eponym *honoree*
PNM eponymy *honor*
eponymies
PNM Panama *country, hat*
PNM pen name *alias*
PNMBR penumbra *shade*
penumbrae (or)
penumbras
PNMK eponymic *honoree*
PNMKNL Panama Canal
waterway
PNMM pantomime *express
mutely* pantomimed
pantomiming
PNMMK pantomimic *express
mutely*
PNMMST pantomimist
express mutely

PNMN pantomime *express
mutely* pantomimed
pantomiming
PNMN penman *scribe*
penmen
PNMNDD open-minded
receptive
PNMNN Panamanian *of
Panama*
PNMNSHP penmanship
writing
PNMNT appointment
position, meeting
PNMNYN Panamanian *of
Panama*
PNMPN Phnom Penh *city*
PNMRKN Pan-American
North & South America
PNMS eponymous *honor*
PNMTHD openmouthed
amazement
PNMTHT openmouthed
amazement
PNN opening *beginning,
breach, chance**
PNN opinion *idea*
PNN pennon *streamer*
PNN penny ante (n) *poker*
penny-ante (adj)
PNN pinion (n) *wing, gear* (v)
bind
PNN piñon (or) pinyon *pine
nut* piñons (or) pinyons
(or) piñones
PNND open-end *not closed*
PNNDD open-ended *not
closed*
PNNDD opinionated
bullheaded
PNNDSHT open-and-shut
obvious
PNNDV opinionative
bullheaded
PNNDVL opinionatively
bullheaded
PNNDVNS opinionativeness
bullheaded
PNNG opening *beginning,
breach, chance**
PNNG painting *art*
PNNS penance *remedy*
PNNS puniness *small*

Letters aren't doubled for single sounds: to find alley use **L** not **LL**. Use **Y** and **W** as hard
sounds only: to find yellow use **YL**. (Br)=British spelling or usage. * See dictionary.

PNNSHL peninsula *land*
PNNSHLR peninsular *land*
PNNSHT open-and-shut *obvious*
PNNSL peninsula *land*
PNNSLR peninsular *land*
PNNSLR peninsular *land*
PNNSYL peninsula *land*
PNNSYLR peninsular *land*
PNNT opponent *against*
PNNT pennant *flag*
PNNT penny ante(n) *poker* penny-ante (adj)
PNNTD opinionated *bullheaded*
PNNTS penance *remedy*
PNNTV opinionative *bullheaded*
PNNTVL opinionatively *bullheaded*
PNNTVNS opinionativeness *bullheaded*
PNNW pinot noir *wine*
PNNWR pinot noir *wine*
PNNZ Apennines *mountains*
PNP open up *talk freely*
PNP pinup *picture*
PNPD pinniped *flippers*
PNPDK panoptic *wide view*
PNPL panoply *armor, display* panoplies
PNPL pineapple *fruit*
PNPLD panoplied *armor, display*
PNPNCHN penny-pinching *miserly*
PNPNCHNG penny-pinching *miserly*
PNPNCHR penny-pincher *miser*
PNPNT pinpoint *(v) locate* (adj) *precise* (n) *tiny point*
PNPP panpipe *music*
PNPRK pinprick *puncture*
PNPTK panoptic *wide view*
PNR eye-opener *surprise*
PNR open air (n) *without walls* open-air (adj)
PNR opener *device, start*
PNR oppugner *fighter*
PNR painter *artist*
PNR pannier *basket, hoop*

PNR pawner (or) pawnor *loaner*
PNR penury *poverty*
PNR pinery *trees* pineries
PNR pioneer *(v) originate* (n) *initiato* (adj) *original*
PNR pointer *indicator, dog, tip*
PNR pointier *sharp*
PNR punier *small*
PNR punnier *joke*
PNRL pennyroyal *mint*
PNRM panorama *wide view*
PNRMK panoramic *wide view*
PNRMKL panoramically *wide view*
PNRS penurious *stingy*
PNRSL penuriously *stingy*
PNRSNS penuriousness *stingy*
PNRYL pennyroyal *mint*
PNRYS penurious *stingy*
PNRYSL penuriously *stingy*
PNRYSNS penuriousness *stingy*
PNS aptness *suitability*
PNS openness *frankness*
PNS panacea *remedy*
PNS pants *trousers*
PNS pence (pl) *money* penny
PNS penis *sex organ* penes (or) penises
PNS ponce *(Br-slang) procurer*
PNS pounce *attack* pounced pouncing
PNSD poinsettia *plant*
PNSDR pinsetter *bowling*
PNSDY poinsettia *plant*
PNSH opuntia *cactus*
PNSH panache *tuft, verve*
PNSH punish *penalize*
PNSHBL punishable *penalize*
PNSHBLD punishability *penalize*
PNSHBLT punishability *penalize*
PNSHD Upanishad *philosophy*
PNSHMNT punishment

penalty
PNSHN pension *retirement*
PNSHNBL pensionable *retiree*
PNSHNR pensionary *hireling* pensionaries
PNSHNR pensioner *retiree*
PNSHP pawnshop *lending*
PNSHR pinscher *dog*
PNSHR puncture *pierce* punctured puncturing
PNSHR punisher *penalizer*
PNSHY opuntia *cactus*
PNSKSHL pansexual *many forms*
PNSKSHLD pansexuality *many forms*
PNSKSHLT pansexuality *many forms*
PNSKSHWL pansexual *many forms*
PNSKSHWLD pansexuality *many forms*
PNSKSHWLT pansexuality *many forms*
PNSL pencil *(n) marking tool*
PNSL pencil *(v) write* penciled (or) pencilled penciling (or) pencilling
PNSL penicillia (pl) *fungus* penicillium
PNSL peninsula *land*
PNSLM penicillium *fungus* penicillia
PNSLN penicillin *antibiotic*
PNSLVN Pennsylvania *US State*
PNSLVNY Pennsylvania *US State*
PNSLY penicillia (pl) *fungus* penicillium
PNSLYM penicillium *fungus* penicillia
PNSM pianissimo *softly*
PNSN pince-nez *eyeglass* pince-nez
PNSN poinciana *tree*
PNSNK pine snake *animal*
PNSP pinesap *resin*
PNSR pincer *tongs*
PNSR pinscher *dog*
PNSSM open sesame

Use letters that best describe the sounds you hear and omit the vowels. Use **S** or **K** instead of **C**: to find circle use **SRKL**. Use **J** to find joy, **JM** to find gem and **G** to find go.

command
PNST pantsuit *clothing*
PNST pianist *musician*
PNST poinsettia *flower*
PNST pointiest *sharp*
PNST puniest *small*
PNST punniest *joke*
PNSTK penstock *pipe*
PNSTKN painstaking *careful*
PNSTKNG painstaking
careful
PNSTR pinsetter *bowling*
PNSTR punster *joker*
PNSTRP pinstripe *thin line*
PNSTRPD pinstriped *thin
line*
PNSTRPT pinstriped *thin
line*
PNSTY poinsettia *flower*
PNSV pensive *dreamy*
PNSVL pensively *dreamy*
PNSVNS pensiveness
dreamy
PNSY panacea *remedy*
PNSYN poinciana *tree*
PNSZN open season *time*
PNT appoint *name*
PNT appointee *person named*
PNT paint *(n) fluid coating
(v) coat*
PNT pan out *succeed*
PNT pant *breath*
PNT pantie (or) panty
underwear panties
PNT peanut *legume*
PNT pennant *flag*
PNT pennate *feather*
PNT pent *confined*
PNT piñata (or) pinata *candy*
PNT pine nut *pignoli*
PNT pint *measurement*
PNT pinto *horse, bean* pintos
PNT point *(v) indicate (n)
item, purpose, tip**
PNT pointy *sharp* pointier
pointiest
PNT punnet *(Br) basket*
PNT punt *kick, (Br) gamble*
PNT punty *rod* punties
PNTBDR peanut butter *food*
PNTBLNGK point-blank
direct

PNTBLNK point-blank *direct*
PNTBRSH paintbrush *tool,
plant* paintbrushes
PNTBTR peanut butter *food*
PNTCN poinciana *tree*
PNTCYN poinciana *tree*
PNTD pentad *five*
PNTD pointed *sharp*
PNTDRS pantdress *garment*
PNTF pontiff *pope*
PNTFKDR pontificator
speaker
PNTFKL pontifical (adj) *pope*
pontifically (adv)
PNTFKSHN pontification
speech
PNTFKT pontificate *speak*
pontificated pontificating
PNTFKTR pontificator
speaker
PNTGN pentagon *five sides*
PNTGNL pentagonal (adj)
five sides pentagonally
(adv)
PNTGRF pantograph *device*
PNTGRFK pantographic
device
PNTGRM pentagram *symbol*
PNTHD pointy-head
intellectual
PNTHDD pointy-headed
intellectual
PNTHDK epenthetic *sound
insertion*
PNTHDRL pentahedral *five
faces*
PNTHDRN pentahedron *five
faces*
PNTHN pantheon *temple*
PNTHR panther *animal*
PNTHS penthouse *dwelling*
PNTHSDK pantheistic *many
gods*
PNTHSDKL pantheistically
many gods
PNTHSK pie-in-the-sky
unrealistic
PNTHSS epenthesis *sound
insertion* epentheses
PNTHST pantheist *many
gods*
PNTHSTK pantheistic *many

gods*
PNTHSTKL pantheistically
many gods
PNTHTK epenthetic *sound
insertion*
PNTHYN pantheon *temple*
PNTHYSDK pantheistic
many gods
PNTHYSDKL
pantheistically *many gods*
PNTHYST pantheist *many
gods*
PNTHYSTK pantheistic
many gods
PNTHYSTKL pantheistically
many gods
PNTHYZM pantheism *many
gods*
PNTHZ panty hose *stockings*
PNTHZM pantheism *many
gods*
PNTK Pentateuch *scripture*
PNTK Pontiac *city*
PNTKL pentacle *star*
PNTKST Pentecost *Holy
Ghost*
PNTKSTL Pentecostal
Christian
PNTL panatela *cigar*
PNTL peanut oil *fatty liquid*
PNTL pintail *duck* pintail (or)
pintails
PNTL pintle *pivot*
PNTL pointelle *design*
PNTL ponytail *hairdo*
PNTLN pantaloon (or)
pantalone *britches*
PNTLS pointless *senseless*
PNTLST pointillist *color dots*
PNTLTS pantalets (or)
pantalettes *trousers*
PNTLZM pointillism *color
dots*
PNTMDR pentameter *verse*
PNTMM pantomime *express
mutely* pantomimed
pantomiming
PNTMMK pantomimic
express mutely
PNTMMST pantomimist
express mutely
PNTMN pantomime *express*

Letters aren't doubled for single sounds: to find alley use **L** not **LL**. Use **Y** and **W** as hard
sounds only: to find yellow use **YL**. (Br)=British spelling or usage. * See dictionary.

mutely pantomimed pantomiming

PNTMNT appointment *position, meeting*

PNTMTR pentameter *verse*

PNTN painting *art*

PNTN pontoon *float*

PNTNCHL penitential (adj) *regretful* penitentially (adv)

PNTNCHR penitentiary *bishop, prison* penitentiaries

PNTNG painting *art*

PNTNK pentatonic *five tones*

PNTNS penitence *regret*

PNTNSHL penitential (adj) *regretful* penitentially (adv)

PNTNSHR penitentiary *bishop, prison* penitentiaries

PNTNT penitent *regretful*

PNTNTCHL penitential (adj) *regretful* penitentially (adv)

PNTNTCHR penitentiary *bishop, prison* penitentiaries

PNTNTS penitence *regret*

PNTNTSHL penitential (adj) *regretful* penitentially (adv)

PNTNTSHR penitentiary *bishop, prison* penitentiaries

PNTPLD pentaploid *genes*

PNTR painter *artist*

PNTR pantry *cupboard* pantries

PNTR pine tar *substance*

PNTR pointer *indicator, dog, tip*

PNTR pointier *sharp*

PNTR punter *kicker, (Br) gambler*

PNTRBL penetrable (adj) *enter* penetrably (adv)

PNTRBLD penetrability *enter*

PNTRBLT penetrability *enter*

PNTRDNG penetrating

perceptive

PNTRDV penetrative *acute*

PNTRL penetralia *private parts*

PNTRLY penetralia *private parts*

PNTRMDR penetrometer *consistency*

PNTRMN pantryman *food worker* pantrymen

PNTRMTR penetrometer *consistency*

PNTRSHN penetration *entry*

PNTRT penetrate *enter* penetrated penetrating

PNTRTN penetrating *perceptive*

PNTRTNG penetrating *perceptive*

PNTRTV penetrative *acute*

PNTS pants *trousers*

PNTS peanuts *very little*

PNTS penance *remedy*

PNTS pence (pl) *money* penny

PNTS penthouse *dwelling*

PNTS ponce (*Br-slang*) *procurer*

PNTS pounce *attack* pounced pouncing

PNTSD poinsettia *flower*

PNTSDY poinsettia *flower*

PNTSH opuntia *cactus*

PNTSHY opuntia *cactus*

PNTSL pencil (n) *writing tool*

PNTSL pencil (v) *write* penciled (or) pencilled penciling (or) pencilling

PNTSN pince-nez *eyeglass* pince-nez

PNTSN poinciana *tree*

PNTSR pincer *tongs*

PNTST pantsuit *clothing*

PNTST poinsettia *flower*

PNTST pointiest *sharp*

PNTSTY poinsettia *flower*

PNTSV pensive *dreamy*

PNTSVL pensively *dreamy*

PNTSYN poinciana *tree*

PNTSZ pint-size (or) pint-sized *small*

PNTSZD pint-sized (or) pint-size *small*

PNTT potentate *ruler*

PNTTHLN pentathlon *contest*

PNTTHLT pentathlete *contestant*

PNTTK Pentateuch *scripture*

PNTTNK pentatonic *five tones*

PNTTYK Pentateuch *scripture*

PNTV appointive *made by naming*

PNTV punitive *penalty*

PNTVLNT pentavalent *chemistry*

PNTWST pantywaist *sissy*

PNTYK Pentateuch *scripture*

PNTYK Pontiac *city*

PNTYL peanut oil *fatty liquid*

PNTYR pointier *sharp*

PNTYST pointiest *sharp*

PNTYST pointillist *color dots*

PNTYZM pointillism *color dots*

PNTZ pontes (pl) *brain* pons

PNV appointive *made by naming*

PNVLNT pentavalent *chemistry*

PNVZ penknives (pl) *tool* penknife

PNW peignoir *garment*

PNWD pinewood *lumber*

PNWL pinwale *fabric*

PNWL pinwheel *toy*

PNWR peignoir *garment*

PNWRK openwork *perforated*

PNWRM pinworm *insect*

PNWRT pennywort *plant*

PNWRTH pennyworth *bargain*

PNWSL pennywhistle *flute*

PNWST pantywaist *sissy*

PNWT pennyweight *weight*

PNWZ penny-wise *thrifty*

PNXLP pink slip (n) *job termination* pink-slip (v)

PNXTRKN panic-stricken

Use letters that best describe the sounds you hear and omit the vowels. Use **S** or **K** instead of **C**: to find circle use **SRKL**. Use **J** to find joy, **JM** to find gem and **G** to find go.

fearful
PNY apnea _breath_
(Br) apnoea
PNY eupnea _respiration_
PNYD piñata (or) pinata
candy
PNYK apneic _breath_
PNYK eupneic _respiration_
PNYK Pontiac _city_
PNYKLD piña colada _drink_
PNYKLT piña colada _drink_
PNYL pignoli (or) pignolia
pine nut
PNYL pineal _gland_
PNYLY pignoli (or) pignolia
pine nut
PNYN opinion _idea_
PNYN penny ante(n) _poker_
penny-ante (adj)
PNYN pinion (n) _wing, gear_
(v) _bind_
PNYN piñon (or) pinyon _pine
nut_ piñons (or) pinyons
(or) piñones
PNYNC poignancy _emotional_
PNYNDD opinionated
bullheaded
PNYNDV opinionative
bullheaded
PNYNDVL opinionatively
bullheaded
PNYNDVNS
opinionativeness
bullheaded
PNYNS poignancy _emotional_
PNYNT penny ante(n) _poker_
penny-ante (adj)
PNYNT poignant _emotional_
PNYNTC poignancy
emotional
PNYNTD opinionated
bullheaded
PNYNTL poignantly
emotionally
PNYNTS poignancy
emotional
PNYNTV opinionative
bullheaded
PNYNTVL opinionatively
bullheaded
PNYNTVNS
opinionativeness

bullheaded
PNYP pony up _pay money_
ponied up ponying up
ponies up
PNYR pannier _basket, hoop_
PNYR penury _poverty_
PNYR pointier _sharp_
PNYR punier _small_
PNYR punnier _joke_
PNYRD poniard (n) _dagger_
(v) _pierce_
PNYRS penurious _stingy_
PNYRSL penuriously _stingy_
PNYRSNS penuriousness
stingy
PNYRYS penurious _stingy_
PNYRYSL penuriously
stingy
PNYRYSNS penuriousness
stingy
PNYST pointiest _sharp_
PNYST puniest _small_
PNYST punniest _joke_
PNYT piñata (or) pinata
candy
PNZ pansy _flower_ pansies
PNZ panties _underwear_
PNZ pons _brain_ pontes
PNZM pianism _piano_
PNZNDLZ pins and needles
tingling
PNZNDNDLZ pins and
needles _tingling_
PNZR panzer _tank_
PP pap _soft food, nipple_
PP papa _father_
PP papaw _fruit_
PP papaya _fruit_
PP pappi (pl) _tuft_ pappus
PP pappy _father_ pappies
PP Papua _city_
PP pay up _settle debt_
PP peep (n) _bird sound_ (v)
glimpse
PP pep (v) _energize_ pepped
pepping
PP pep (n) _energy_
PP pepo _gourd_ pepos
PP peppy _energetic_ peppier
peppiest
PP pip (v) _peep, defeat_
pipped pipping

PP pip (n) _ailment, spot, seed_
PP pipe (n) _tube, voice, smoke_
PP pipe (v) _speak, trim,
transport_ piped piping
PP pooh-pooh _doubt_
PP poop (n-slang)
information, excrement (v-
slang) _fatigue, excrete_
PP pop (v) _burst_ popped
popping
PP pop (n) _father_ (adj)
popular, sudden
PP pop eye (n) _startled_ pop-
eyed (adj)
PP pope (often capitalized)
Catholic leader
PP poppa _papa_
PP poppy _flower_ poppies
PP pup _dog birth_ pupped
pupping
PP pup _dog_
PP pupa _insect_ pupae (or)
pupas
PP puppy _dog_ puppies
PPC papacy _pope_ papacies
PPCD poppy seed _seed_
PPD pop-eyed (adj) _startled_
pop eye (n)
PPDK eupeptic _cheerful_
PPDK peptic _digestive_
PPDK poop deck _ship_
PPDN pipe down _quiet_
PPDRM pipe dream _fantasy_
PPFDR pipe fitter _pipes_
PPFL pipeful _smoke_
PPFSH pipefish _fish_
PPFTR pipe fitter _pipes_
PPG Papago _Native
American_ Papago (or)
Papagos
PPGN popgun _weapon_
PPHD poppyhead _finial_
PPHD puppyhood _dog_
PPHL peephole _opening_
PPJ pipage (or) pipeage
pipes
PPKDR pipe cutter _machine_
PPKK poppycock _nonsense_
PPKN pipkin _pot_
PPKRN popcorn _food_
PPKTR pipe cutter _machine_
PPL papal (adj) _pope_ papally

Letters aren't doubled for single sounds: to find alley use **L** not **LL**. Use **Y** and **W** as hard
sounds only: to find yellow use **YL**. (Br)=British spelling or usage. * See dictionary.

(adv)
PPL papilla *nipple* papillae
PPL papule *pimple*
PPL peephole *opening*
PPL people (v) *populate* peopled peopling
PPL people (pl) (n) *humans*
PPL pep pill *drug*
PPL pepla (pl) *jacket part* peplum
PPL pupil *student, eye*
PPLJ pupillage *student*
PPLK puppylike *dog*
PPLKC apoplexy *stroke*
PPLKDK apoplectic *greatly excited*
PPLKDKL apoplectically *greatly excited*
PPLKS apoplexy *stroke*
PPLKTK apoplectic *greatly excited*
PPLKTKL apoplectically *greatly excited*
PPLM papilloma *tumor* papillomas (or) papillomata
PPLM peplum *jacket part* pepla
PPLMD papillomata (pl) *tumor* papilloma
PPLMT papillomata (pl) *tumor* papilloma
PPLN pipeline *tube*
PPLN poplin *fabric*
PPLNT pieplant *rhubarb*
PPLR papillary *nipple*
PPLR papular *pimple*
PPLR poplar *tree*
PPLR popular *liked*
PPLR pupillary *eye*
PPLRD popularity *approval*
PPLRT popularity *approval*
PPLRZ popularize *make accepted* popularized popularizing (Br) popularise
PPLRZSHN popularization *make accepted* (Br) popularisation
PPLS papillose *nipple*
PPLS populace *population*
PPLS populous *numerous*

PPLSHN population *inhabitants*
PPLSL populously *numerous*
PPLSNS populousness *numerous*
PPLST populist *common cause*
PPLT papillate *nipple*
PPLT populate *inhabit* populated populating
PPLX apoplexy *stroke*
PPN eye-popping *startling*
PPN papain *tenderizer*
PPN piping (adj) *very hot* (n) *border*
PPN pippin *apple, admired one*
PPNG eye-popping *startling*
PPNG piping (adj) *very hot* (n) *border*
PPNJ popinjay *strutter*
PPNS peppiness *energy*
PPP pipe up *speak out*
PPP pop-up (n) *pop fly*
PPR eyepopper *surprise*
PPR paper (n) *thin sheet, document* (v) *cover, fold*
PPR papery *thin and stiff*
PPR papyri (pl) *reed* papyrus
PPR pauper *poor one*
PPR peeper *eye, frog, voyeur*
PPR pepper (n) *vegetable, spice* (v) *sprinkle*
PPR peppery *spicy*
PPR peppier *more energy*
PPR piper *music*
PPR popery *Catholicism*
PPR popper *popping device*
PPR potpourri *collection*
PPRB paperboy *deliverer*
PPRBK paperback *book*
PPRBKS pepperbox *shaker, pistol*
PPRBN paperbound *book*
PPRBND paperbound *book*
PPRBRD paperboard *cardboard*
PPRBX pepperbox *shaker, pistol*
PPRDD purported *assumed*
PPRGN pipe organ *music*
PPRGRS peppergrass *cress*

PPRHNGR paperhanger *wallpaper*
PPRK paprika *pepper*
PPRKDR paper cutter *trimmer*
PPRKLP paper clip *fastener*
PPRKRN peppercorn *berry*
PPRKTR paper cutter *trimmer*
PPRL pep rally *sports* pep rallies
PPRLS paperless *no paper*
PPRM peperomia *herb*
PPRMN paper money *currency*
PPRMNT peppermint *plant*
PPRMSH papier-mâché *molding material*
PPRMY peperomia *herb*
PPRN pepperoni *meat*
PPRNCH pipe wrench *tool*
PPRNF paper knife *cutter*
PPRNS paperiness *like paper*
PPRNS pepperiness *spiciness*
PPRS papyrus *reed* papyri (or) papyruses
PPRT purport (n) *gist* (v) *claim*
PPRTD purported *assumed*
PPRTHN paper-thin *width*
PPRTR peppertree *evergreen*
PPRTRL paper trail *documentation*
PPRTRN paper-train *discipline*
PPRTS paparazzo *photographer* paparazzi
PPRTZ paparazzo *photographer* paparazzi
PPRV pay-per-view *TV*
PPRVY pay-per-view *TV*
PPRWRK paperwork *clerical*
PPRWT paperweight *heavy object*
PPRZ paparazzo *photographer* paparazzi
PPRZ pauperize *make poor* pauperized pauperizing
PPRZM pauperism *poor*
PPS papacy *pope* papacies

Use letters that best describe the sounds you hear and omit the vowels. Use **S** or **K** instead of **C**: to find circle use **SRKL**. Use **J** to find joy, **JM** to find gem and **G** to find go.

PPS papoose *baby*
PPS pappus *tuft* pappi
PPSD poppy seed *seed*
PPSH peep show *striptease*
PPSH popish *Catholic*
PPSH puppyish *dog*
PPSHN pupation
development
PPSKL Popsicle *(trademark)*
ice treat
PPSKWK pip-squeak *small*
PPSMR Pap smear *test*
PPSN pepsin *digestive*
PPSQK pip-squeak *small*
PPSSW pipsissewa *herb*
PPST papist *Catholic*
PPST peep sight *gun*
PPST peppiest *energetic*
PPSTN pipestone *rock*
PPT paupiette *food*
PPT pipette *tube*
PPT pipit *bird*
PPT poppet *oar, beam*
PPT pupate *develop* pupated
pupating
PPT puppet *toy*
PPTD peptide *protein*
PPTDK peptidic *protein*
PPTK eupeptic *cheerful*
PPTK pep talk
encouragement
PPTK peptic *digestive*
PPTN peptone *protein*
PPTNT pup tent *shelter*
PPTP pop-top *can*
PPTR papeterie *stationery*
PPTR puppeteer *animator*
PPTR puppetry *art*
puppetries
PPTST Pap test *examination*
PPVR popover *food*
PPVRN papaverine *opium*
PPW Papua *city*
PPY papaya *fruit*
PPY Papua *city*
PPYL papule *pimple*
PPYLR papular *pimple*
PPYLR popular *liked*
PPYLRD popularity *approval*
PPYLRT popularity *approval*
PPYLRZ popularize *make*
accepted popularized

popularizing
(Br) popularise
PPYLRZSHN popularization
make accepted
(Br) popularisation
PPYLS populace *population*
PPYLS populous *numerous*
PPYLSHN population
inhabitants
PPYLSL populously
numerous
PPYLSNS populousness
numerous
PPYLST populist *common*
cause
PPYLT populate *inhabit*
populated populating
PPYMSH papier-mâché
molding material
PPYN papain *tenderizer*
PPYR peppier *more energy*
PPYSH puppyish *dog*
PPYST peppiest *energetic*
PPYT papillote *wrapper*
PPYT paupiette *food*
PPYW Papua *city*
PQD pokeweed *plant*
PQDKL epicuticle *waxy*
layer
PQLDR peculator *cheater*
PQLR peculiar *strange*
PQLRD peculiarity *oddity*
peculiarities
PQLRT peculiarity *oddity*
peculiarities
PQLSHN peculation
cheating
PQLT apiculate *pointed*
PQLT peculate *cheat*
peculated peculating
PQLTR peculator *cheater*
PQLYR peculiar *strange*
PQLYRD peculiarity *oddity*
peculiarities
PQLYRT peculiarity *oddity*
peculiarities
PQNC piquancy *spicy*
PQNR pecuniary *money*
PQNS piquancy *spicy*
PQNT piquant *spicy*
PQNTC piquancy *spicy*
PQNTS piquancy *spicy*

PQNYR pecuniary *money*
PQR epicure *gourmet*
PQRN epicurean *gourmet*
PQRYN epicurean *gourmet*
PQTKL epicuticle *waxy layer*
PQTKLR epicuticular *waxy*
layer
PQTKYLR epicuticular *waxy*
layer
PQTQLR epicuticular *waxy*
layer
PR aper *mimic*
PR apiary *bees* apiaries
PR appear *view*
PR après *after*
PR au pair *babysitter* au
pairs
PR opera *music*
PR opera (pl) *work* opus
PR pair *two*
PR par (v) *golf* parred
parring
PR par (n) *value, norm* (adj)
normal
PR pare *trim* pared paring
PR pariah *outcast*
PR parr *salmon* parr
PR parry *ward off* parried
parrying parries
PR payer *giver*
PR pear *fruit*
PR peer (n) *an equal* (v) *look*
PR per (prep) *as* (adv) *each*
PR perry *juice*
PR Peru *country*
PR pier *structure*
PR Pierre *city*
PR poor *needy*
PR pore (v) *ponder* pored
poring
PR pore (n) *tiny opening*
PR pour *flow*
PR power *force*
PR pray *ask*
PR prey (n) *victim* prey
PR prey (v) *raid, devour*
preyed preying
PR pro *professional, not*
against pros
PR prow *ship's bow*
PR pry *snoop, force* pried
prying pries

Letters aren't doubled for single sounds: to find alley use **L** not **LL**. Use **Y** and **W** as hard
sounds only: to find yellow use **YL**. (Br)=British spelling or usage. * See dictionary.

PR pure *clean, perfect* purer purest

PR purée (or) puree *whip* pureed pureeing

PR purr *cat sound, contented murmur*

PR pyorrhea *gum disease*

PR pyre *funeral*

PR pyuria *pus in urine*

PR upper *higher*

PRB probe *(v) search* probed probing

PRB probe *(n) device*

PRBBL probable (adj) *likely* probably (adv)

PRBBLD probability *likelihood* probabilities

PRBBLSDK probabilistic *likely*

PRBBLST probabilist *likely*

PRBBLSTK probabilistic *likely*

PRBBLT probability *likelihood* probabilities

PRBBLZM probabilism *likely*

PRBD probity *honesty*

PRBDV probative *proof*

PRBDV prohibitive *restraining*

PRBF opéra bouffe *comedy*

PRBGL porbeagle *shark*

PRBK prebake *cook*

PRBKL parbuckle *hoist*

PRBL operable (adj) *use, surgery* operably (adv)

PRBL parable *story*

PRBL parabola *curve*

PRBL parboil *cook*

PRBL pourable *flow*

PRBL probable (adj) *likely* probably (adv)

PRBLD operability *use, surgery*

PRBLD paraboloid *curved*

PRBLD pure-blood (or) pure-blooded (adj) *breeding* pureblood (n)

PRBLDD pure-blooded (or) pure-blood (adj) *breeding* pureblood (n)

PRBLK parabolic *curved*

PRBLKL parabolically *curved*

PRBLM problem *mystery, difficulty*

PRBLMDK problematic (or) problematical (adj) *doubtful* problematically (adv)

PRBLMDKL problematical (or) problematic (adj) *doubtful* problematically (adv)

PRBLMTK problematic (or) problematical (adj) *doubtful* problematically (adv)

PRBLMTKL problematical (or) problematic (adj) *doubtful* problematically (adv)

PRBLT operability *use, surgery*

PRBN prebend *salary*

PRBND prebend *salary*

PRBNDR prebendary *salary* prebendaries

PRBRD purebred *breeding*

PRBRM opprobrium *disgrace*

PRBRS opprobrious *shameful*

PRBRSHN proabortion *legal abortion*

PRBRYM opprobrium *disgrace*

PRBRYS opprobrious *shameful*

PRBSDN proboscidean (or) proboscidian *elephant*

PRBSDYN proboscidean (or) proboscidian *elephant*

PRBSHN approbation *praise*

PRBSHN probation *test period*

PRBSHN prohibition *forbidding*

PRBSHNL probational (adj) *test period* probationally (adv)

PRBSHNR probationary *test period*

PRBSHNR probationer

tester

PRBSHNST prohibitionist *no alcohol*

PRBSKS proboscis *snout* proboscises

PRBSS proboscis *snout* proboscises

PRBT approbate *approve* approbated approbating

PRBT powerboat *ship*

PRBT probate *inheritance* probated probating

PRBT probity *honesty*

PRBT prohibit *forbid*

PRBTR approbatory *approved*

PRBTR prohibitory *forbidding*

PRBTV probative *proof*

PRBTV prohibitive *restraining*

PRBYL parboil *cook*

PRC piracy *robbery* piracies

PRC précis *summary* (pl) précis

PRC pricey *expensive*

PRC prissy *prim* prissier prissiest

PRC pursy *puckered* pursier pursiest

PRCD precede *come before* preceded preceding

PRCD proceed *advance*

PRCDN preceding *come before*

PRCDNG preceding *come before*

PRCDNGS proceedings *events*

PRCDNGZ proceedings *events*

PRCDNS precedence *come before*

PRCDNT precedent *come before*

PRCDNTS precedence *come before*

PRCDR procedure *way of doing*

PRCDRL procedural (adj) *orderly* procedurally (adv)

PRCDS proceeds *money*

Use letters that best describe the sounds you hear and omit the vowels. Use **S** or **K** instead of **C**: to find circle use **SRKL**. Use **J** to find joy, **JM** to find gem and **G** to find go.

PRCDYR procedure *way of doing*

PRCDYRL procedural (adj) *orderly* procedurally (adv)

PRCDZ proceeds *money*

PRCH approach *near*

PRCH parch *dry*

PRCH perch *(n) fish, resting place* perch *(or)* perches

PRCH perch *(v) alight*

PRCH porch *house* porches

PRCH preach *sermon*

PRCH preachy *like a sermon* preachier preachiest

PRCHBL approachable *able to come near*

PRCHBLD approachability *nearness*

PRCHBLT approachability *nearness*

PRCHD parched *thirsty*

PRCHGL Portugal *country*

PRCHGZ Portuguese *of Portugal*

PRCHK apparatchik *party member*

PRCHL preachily *like a sermon*

PRCHLK portulaca *plant*

PRCHMNT parchment *paper*

PRCHN porcino *mushroom* porcini

PRCHNS perchance *perhaps*

PRCHNS preachiness *like a sermon*

PRCHNTS perchance *perhaps*

PRCHR aperture *hole*

PRCHR preacher *sermon*

PRCHR preachier *like a sermon*

PRCHRN Percheron *horse*

PRCHRNT parturient *birth*

PRCHRSHN parturition *birth*

PRCHRYNT parturient *birth*

PRCHS pro-choice *for abortion*

PRCHS purchase *(v) buy* purchased purchasing

PRCHS purchase *(n) advantage, buy*

PRCHSBL purchasable *buy*

PRCHSR pro-choicer *for abortion*

PRCHSR purchaser *buyer*

PRCHST preachiest *like a sermon*

PRCHT parched *thirsty*

PRCHYR preachier *like a sermon*

PRCHYST preachiest *like a sermon*

PRCHZ pachisi *game*

PRCHZ Parcheesi *(trademark) game*

PRCJR procedure *way of doing*

PRCJRL procedural (adj) *orderly* procedurally (adv)

PRCN porcine *swine*

PRCN purse seine *net*

PRCNM proscenium *stage*

PRCNS prescience *foresight*

PRCNTS prescience *foresight*

PRCNYM proscenium *stage*

PRCR prissier *prim*

PRCR pursier *puckered*

PRCST prissiest *prim*

PRCST pursiest *puckered*

PRCV apperceive *understand* apperceived apperceiving

PRCV perceive *notice* perceived perceiving

PRCVBL perceivable (adj) *noticed* perceivably (adv)

PRCVR perceiver *notice*

PRCYNS prescience *foresight*

PRCYNTS prescience *foresight*

PRCYR prissier *prim*

PRCYR pursier *puckered*

PRCYST prissiest *prim*

PRCYST pursiest *puckered*

PRCZ pareses (pl) *paralysis* paresis

PRD operetta *music*

PRD parade *display* paraded parading

PRD parity *equality* parities

PRD parody *imitation*

parodied parodying parodies

PRD party *(v) revel* partied partying parties

PRD party *(n) group, festival* parties

PRD perdu (or) perdue *hidden*

PRD peridot *gem*

PRD period *punctuation, time*

PRD pretty *(v) make attractive* prettied prettying pretties

PRD pretty *(adj) beauty* prettier prettiest

PRD pretty *(adv) somewhat*

PRD pretty *(n) lingerie* pretties

PRD pride *conceit* prided priding

PRD prie-dieu *bench* prie-dieux

PRD prod *(v) urge, poke* prodded prodding

PRD prod *(n) stick*

PRD protea *flower*

PRD proud *arrogant*

PRD prude *moralist*

PRD purdah *seclusion*

PRD purity *spotless*

PRDBL partible *divide*

PRDBL portable (adj) *move about* portably (adv)

PRDBLD portability *move about*

PRDBLT portability *move about*

PRDCS predecease *die before* predeceased predeceasing

PRDD parotid *gland*

PRDDK peridotic *gem*

PRDDR predator *preying*

PRDDT peridotite *rock*

PRDDV partitive *division*

PRDF prettify *beautify* prettified prettifying prettifies

PRDFL prideful (adj) *arrogant* pridefully (adv)

PRDFL proudful *arrogant*

Letters aren't doubled for single sounds: to find alley use **L** not **LL**. Use **Y** and **W** as hard sounds only: to find yellow use **YL**. (Br)=British spelling or usage. * See dictionary.

PRDFLM protophloem *cells*
PRDFLNS pridefulness
arrogance
PRDFLWM protophloem
cells
PRDG prodigy *omen, talent*
prodigies
PRDGL prodigal (adj)
reckless prodigally (adv)
PRDGLD prodigality
recklessness
PRDGLT prodigality
recklessness
PRDHRDD proudhearted
haughty
PRDHRTD proudhearted
haughty
PRDHSTR protohistory
humans
PRDJ portage *(n) cargo*
PRDJ portage *(v) carry*
portaged portaging
PRDJ prodigy *omen, talent*
prodigies
PRDJ protégé (m) *student*
protégée (f)
PRDJS prodigious *enormous*
PRDJSCHN predigestion
eating
PRDJSL prodigiously
enormous
PRDJSNS prodigiousness
enormous
PRDJST predigest *eating*
PRDK aperiodic *irregular*
PRDK operatic *music*
PRDK periodic *occasional*
PRDK portico *porch*
porticoes (or) porticos
PRDK predict *foretell*
PRDK product *number,*
result
PRDK pyretic *fever*
PRDKBL predicable *logic*
PRDKDBL predictable (adj)
foretell predictably (adv)
PRDKDR predictor *foretell*
PRDKDV predicative *logic,*
verb
PRDKDV predictive *foretell*
PRDKDV productive *busy*
PRDKL aperiodically

irregularly
PRDKL particle *small bit*
PRDKL periodical *(n)*
magazine (adj) *occasional*
periodically (adv)
PRDKL protocol *record,*
etiquette
PRDKLBRD particleboard
bonded wood
PRDKLR parti-color (or)
parti-colored *patchy*
(Br) parti-colour
PRDKLRD parti-colored (or)
parti-color *patchy*
(Br) parti-coloured
PRDKMNT predicament
condition
PRDKS paradox
contradiction paradoxes
PRDKSHN predication
sermon
PRDKSHN prediction
forecast
PRDKSHN production
output
PRDKSKL paradoxical (adj)
contradictory
paradoxically(adv)
PRDKSKLD paradoxicality
contradictory
PRDKSKLT paradoxicality
contradictory
PRDKT predicate *(v) preach,*
base predicated
predicating
PRDKT predicate *(n) logic,*
verb
PRDKT predict *foretell*
PRDKT product *number,*
result
PRDKTBL predictable (adj)
foretell predictably (adv)
PRDKTR predicatory *preach*
PRDKTR predictor *foretell*
PRDKTRL predoctoral *study*
PRDKTV predicative *logic,*
verb
PRDKTV predictive *foretell*
PRDKTV productive *busy*
PRDKTVD productivity *yield*
PRDKTVT productivity *yield*
PRDL parietal *wall, visitation*

PRDL portal *doorway*
PRDL prattle *talk* prattled
prattling
PRDL predial *land*
PRDL prettily *beauty*
PRDL proudly *arrogant*
PRDLDK proteolytic *protein*
PRDLKSHN predilection
preference
PRDLN party line *telephone,*
policies
PRDLSS proteolysis *protein*
PRDLTK proteolytic *protein*
PRDM paradigm *pattern*
PRDM per diem *daily, fee*
PRDM protium *atom*
PRDMDK paradigmatic
pattern
PRDMDKL paradigmatically
pattern
PRDMN protamine *protein*
PRDMNNS predominance
prevailing
PRDMNNT predominant
prevailing
PRDMNNTS predominance
prevailing
PRDMNSHN predomination
prevailing
PRDMNT portamento *voice*
PRDMNT predominate
prevail predominated
predominating
PRDMTK paradigmatic
pattern
PRDMTKL paradigmatically
pattern
PRDN pardon *forgive*
PRDN predawn *before*
daylight
PRDN protean *versatile*
PRDN puritan *moralist*
PRDN pyridine *solvent*
PRDNBL pardonable (adj)
excusable pardonably
(adv)
PRDNCHL prudential (adj)
wise prudentially (adv)
PRDNDS peritonitis
abdomen
PRDNG parting *departure*
PRDNGL pratingly *talk*

Use letters that best describe the sounds you hear and omit the vowels. Use **S** or **K** instead of **C**: to find circle use **SRKL**. Use **J** to find joy, **JM** to find gem and **G** to find go.

PRDNKS periodontics *gums*
PRDNL periodontal (adj)
gums periodontally (adv)
PRDNNS appurtenance
attachment
PRDNNS pertinence
suitability
PRDNNT appurtenant
attached
PRDNNT pertinent *suitable*
PRDNNTS appurtenance
attachment
PRDNNTS pertinence
suitability
PRDNR partner *(n) colleague
(v) join with*
PRDNRSHP partnership
relationship
PRDNS prettiness *beauty*
PRDNS prudence *wisdom*
PRDNSHL prudential (adj)
wise prudentially (adv)
PRDNT pertinent *suitable*
PRDNT prudent *wise*
PRDNTCHL prudential (adj)
wise prudentially (adv)
PRDNTKS periodontics
gums
PRDNTL periodontal (adj)
gums periodontally (adv)
PRDNTS peritonitis *abdomen*
PRDNTS pertinence
suitability
PRDNTS prudence *wisdom*
PRDNTSHL prudential (adj)
wise prudentially (adv)
PRDNTX periodontics *gums*
PRDNX periodontics *gums*
PRDNZM puritanism
moralism
PRDPLST protoplast *cell*
PRDPLZM protoplasm *cells*
PRDPPR party pooper
refuser
PRDR operator *telephone,
fraud, performer**
PRDR parader *show-off*
PRDR perdure *last* perdured
perduring
PRDR porter *carry, clean*
PRDR praetor *official*
PRDR prater *talker*

PRDR prettier *beauty*
PRDR prie-dieu *bench* prie-
dieux
PRDR prudery *moralist*
pruderies
PRDRBL perdurable (adj)
lasting perdurably (adv)
PRDRBSHN perturbation
disturbance
PRDRHS porterhouse *steak*
PRDRJ porterage *fee*
PRDRK Puerto Rico
commonwealth
PRDRNCHRL preternatural
(adj) *psychic*
preternaturally (adv)
PRDRNTRL preternatural
(adj) *psychic*
preternaturally (adv)
PRDS apparatus *device*
apparatuses (or)
apparatus
PRDS paradise *heaven*
PRDS produce *(v) make,
bear* produced producing
PRDS produce *(n) fruit,
vegetable*
PRDS protease *enzyme*
PRDS proteus *bacteria*
PRDS Proteus *Greek god*
PRDSBL producible *makable*
PRDSD aperiodicity
irregularity
PRDSD periodicity *timing*
PRDSD predacity *prey*
PRDSDNT Protestant
religion
PRDSH protégé (m) *student*
protégée (f)
PRDSH prudish *priggish*
PRDSHL prudishly *priggish*
PRDSHN perdition *hell*
PRDSHN predation *plunder*
PRDSHNS prudishness
priggish
PRDSHS predaceous (or)
predacious *prey*
PRDSHSNS
predaceousness *prey*
PRDSK paradisaic *heavenly*
PRDSKL paradisaical (adj)
heavenly paradisaically

(adv)
PRDSL paradisial *heavenly*
PRDSPL participial (adj)
verb and adjective
participially (adv)
PRDSPL participle *verb*
PRDSPYL participial (adj)
verb and adjective
participially (adv)
PRDSPZ predispose *incline*
predisposed
predisposing
PRDSPZSHN
predisposition *inclination*
PRDSR producer *maker*
PRDSS predecease *die
before* predeceased
predeceasing
PRDSSR predecessor
ancestor
PRDST aperiodicity
irregularity
PRDST parodist *comic*
PRDST periodicity *timing*
PRDST predacity *prey*
PRDST prettiest *beauty*
PRDSTN predestine *fate*
predestined predestining
PRDSTNSHN
predestination *fate*
PRDSTNT Protestant
religion
PRDSTSHN protestation
dissent
PRDSYK paradisaic
heavenly
PRDSYKL paradisaical (adj)
heavenly paradisaically
(adv)
PRDSYL paradisial *heavenly*
PRDT peridot *gem*
PRDT predate *come before*
predated predating
PRDTK peridotic *gem*
PRDTP prototype *model*
PRDTPKL prototypical (adj)
model prototypically (adv)
PRDTPL prototypal *model*
PRDTR predator *preying*
PRDTR predatory *preying*
PRDTRMN predetermine
decide in advance

Letters aren't doubled for single sounds: to find alley use **L** not **LL**. Use **Y** and **W** as hard
sounds only: to find yellow use **YL**. (Br)=British spelling or usage. * See dictionary.

predetermined predetermining

PRDTRMNR predeterminer *decide in advance*

PRDTRMNSHN predetermination *decided in advance*

PRDTT peridotite *rock*

PRDTV partitive *division*

PRDV operative *working*

PRDV power dive (n) *airplane* power-dive (v)

PRDVNCHR peradventure *chance*

PRDVNSHR peradventure *chance*

PRDVNTR peradventure *chance*

PRDVSPCH part of speech *word*

PRDX paradox *contradiction* paradoxes

PRDXKL paradoxical (adj) *contradictory* paradoxically(adv)

PRDXKLD paradoxicality *contradictory*

PRDXKLT paradoxicality *contradictory*

PRDY perdu (or) perdue *hidden*

PRDY prie-dieu *bench* prie-dieux

PRDY protea *flower*

PRDYL predial *land*

PRDYLDK proteolytic *protein*

PRDYLSS proteolysis *protein*

PRDYLTK proteolytic *protein*

PRDYM per diem *daily, fee*

PRDYM protium *atom*

PRDYN protean *versatile*

PRDYR perdure *last* perdured perduring

PRDYR prettier *beauty*

PRDYR prie-dieu *bench* prie-dieux

PRDYRBL perdurable (adj) *lasting* perdurably (adv)

PRDYS produce (v) *make, bear* produced producing

PRDYS produce (n) *fruit, vegetables*

PRDYS protease *enzyme*

PRDYS Proteus *Greek god*

PRDYS proteus *bacteria*

PRDYSBL producible *makable*

PRDYSR producer *maker*

PRDYST prettiest *beauty*

PRDYZ protease *enzyme*

PRDZ protease *enzyme*

PRDZ protozoa (pl) *animal* protozoan

PRDZH protégé (m) *student* protégée (f)

PRDZK paradisaic *heavenly*

PRDZKL paradisaical (adj) *heavenly* paradisaically (adv)

PRDZL paradisial *heavenly*

PRDZL protozoal *animal*

PRDZLG protozoology *science*

PRDZLJ protozoology *science*

PRDZLJST protozoologist *scientist*

PRDZN partisan *follower*

PRDZN protozoan *animal* protozoa

PRDZNSHP partisanship *follower*

PRDZW protozoa (pl) *animal* protozoan

PRDZWL protozoal *animal*

PRDZWLG protozoology *science*

PRDZWLJ protozoology *science*

PRDZWLJST protozoologist *scientist*

PRDZWN protozoan *animal* protozoa

PRDZYK paradisaic *heavenly*

PRDZYKL paradisaical (adj) *heavenly* paradisaically (adv)

PRDZYL paradisial *heavenly*

PRF pair off *couple*

PRF paraph *signature*

PRF parfait *food*

PRF proof *evidence, check for errors*

PRF purify *cleanse* purified purifying purifies

PRFB prefab *construction*

PRFBRKSHN prefabrication *construction*

PRFBRKT prefabricate *construct* prefabricated prefabricating

PRFC prophecy (n) *prediction* prophecies

PRFD perfidy *treachery* perfidies

PRFDBL profitable (adj) *advantageous* profitably (adv)

PRFDBLD profitability *gain*

PRFDBLNS profitableness *gain*

PRFDBLT profitability *gain*

PRFDK prophetic *predictive*

PRFDKL prophetically *predictive*

PRFDRL profiterole *food*

PRFDS perfidious *faithless*

PRFDS prophetess *foreteller* (f)

PRFDSL perfidiously *faithless*

PRFDSNS perfidiousness *faithless*

PRFDYS perfidious *faithless*

PRFDYSL perfidiously *faithless*

PRFDYSNS perfidiousness *faithless*

PRFGR prefigure *imagine* prefigured prefiguring

PRFGRDV prefigurative *imagination*

PRFGRDVL prefiguratively *imagination*

PRFGRMNT prefigurement *imagination*

PRFGRSHN prefiguration *imagination*

PRFGRTV prefigurative *imagination*

PRFGRTVL prefiguratively *imagination*

PRFGYR prefigure *imagine*

Use letters that best describe the sounds you hear and omit the vowels. Use **S** or **K** instead of **C**: to find circle use **SRKL**. Use **J** to find joy, **JM** to find gem and **G** to find go.

prefigured prefiguring
PRFGYRDV prefigurative *imagination*
PRFGYRDVL prefiguratively *imagination*
PRFGYRMNT prefigurement *imagination*
PRFGYRSHN prefiguration *imagination*
PRFGYRTV prefigurative *imagination*
PRFGYRTVL prefiguratively *imagination*
PRFJ prophage *bacteria*
PRFK perfect *(adj) ideal, whole (v) improve (n) verb*
PRFK prefect *person*
PRFKCHR prefecture *residence*
PRFKD perfecta *bet*
PRFKD perfecto *cigar* perfectos
PRFKDBL perfectible *improvement*
PRFKDBLD perfectibility *improvement*
PRFKDBLT perfectibility *improvement*
PRFKDR purificator *cleansing*
PRFKDV perfective *complete*
PRFKL parfocal *(adj) lens* parfocally *(adv)*
PRFKL perfectly *quite*
PRFKS prefix *first part* prefixes
PRFKS prefocus *lens*
PRFKS prix fixe *meal*
PRFKSHN perfection *no flaws*
PRFKSHN purification *cleansing*
PRFKSHNST perfectionist *no flaws*
PRFKSHNZM perfectionism *no flaws*
PRFKSHR prefecture *residence*
PRFKT perfect *(adj) ideal, whole (v) improve (n) verb*
PRFKT perfecta *bet*
PRFKT perfecto *cigar*

perfectos
PRFKT prefect *person*
PRFKTBL perfectible *improvement*
PRFKTBLD perfectibility *improvement*
PRFKTBLT perfectibility *improvement*
PRFKTL perfectly *quite*
PRFKTR prefecture *residence*
PRFKTR purificator *cleansing*
PRFKTR purificatory *cleansing*
PRFKTV perfective *complete*
PRFKTVT perfectivity *complete*
PRFL powerful *(adj) mighty* powerfully *(adv)*
PRFL profile *outline* profiled profiling
PRFL purfle *ornament* purfled purfling
PRFLGC profligacy *extravagance*
PRFLGS profligacy *extravagance*
PRFLGT profligate *extravagant*
PRFLKCZ prophylaxes (pl) *preventive* prophylaxis
PRFLKDK prophylactic *preventive*
PRFLKDKL prophylactically *preventive*
PRFLKSS prophylaxis *preventive* prophylaxes
PRFLKSZ prophylaxes (pl) *preventive* prophylaxis
PRFLKTK prophylactic *preventive*
PRFLKTKL prophylactically *preventive*
PRFLT perfoliate *leaf*
PRFLT preflight *airplane*
PRFLT pyrophyllite *mineral*
PRFLXS prophylaxis *preventive* prophylaxes
PRFLXZ prophylaxes (pl) *preventive* prophylaxis
PRFLYT perfoliate *leaf*

PRFM perfume *scent* perfumed perfuming
PRFMR perfumer *scent*
PRFN paraffin *wax*
PRFN profane *corrupt* profaned profaning
PRFN profound *complete, deep*
PRFND profanity *irreverence* profanities
PRFND profound *complete, deep*
PRFNDD profundity *depth* profundities
PRFNDL profoundly *complete, deep*
PRFNDNS profoundness *complete, deep*
PRFNDT profundity *depth* profundities
PRFNGDR perfunctory *mechanical*
PRFNGKDR perfunctory *mechanical*
PRFNGKTR perfunctory *mechanical*
PRFNGKTRL perfunctorily *mechanical*
PRFNGTR perfunctory *mechanical*
PRFNGTRL perfunctorily *mechanical*
PRFNKDR perfunctory *mechanical*
PRFNKTR perfunctory *mechanical*
PRFNKTRL perfunctorily *mechanical*
PRFNL paraphernalia *accessory*
PRFNL profoundly *complete, deep*
PRFNLY paraphernalia *accessory*
PRFNR profaner *corrupter*
PRFNS profoundness *complete, deep*
PRFNSHN profanation *corruption*
PRFNT profanity *irreverence* profanities
PRFR periphery *edge*

Letters aren't doubled for single sounds: to find alley use **L** not **LL**. Use **Y** and **W** as hard sounds only: to find yellow use **YL**. (Br)=British spelling or usage. * See dictionary.

peripheries

PRFR porphyry *rock*
porphyries

PRFR prefer *choose*
preferred preferring

PRFR proffer *offer*

PRFR purifier *cleanser*

PRFRBL preferable (adj)
chosen preferably (adv)

PRFRCZ periphrases (pl)
expression periphrasis

PRFRD proofread *edit*
proofread proofreading

PRFRDD perforated *with*
holes

PRFRDK porphyritic *crystals*

PRFRDR perforator *make*
holes

PRFRDR proofreader *editor*

PRFRK pyrophoric *sparks*

PRFRL peripheral (adj) *edge*
peripherally (adv)

PRFRM perform *act out,*
effect, fulfill

PRFRM pro forma *formality*

PRFRM pyriform *pear-shaped*

PRFRMBL performable *act*
out

PRFRMBLD performability
act out

PRFRMBLT performability
act out

PRFRMN performing *art*

PRFRMNG performing *art*

PRFRMNS performance
feat, behavior, ability

PRFRMNT preferment
choice

PRFRMNTS performance
feat, behavior, ability

PRFRMR performer *act out,*
effect, fulfill

PRFRNCHL preferential
(adj) *choice* preferentially
(adv)

PRFRNL paraphernalia
accessory

PRFRNL prefrontal *front*
part

PRFRNLY paraphernalia
accessory

PRFRNS preference *choice*

PRFRNSHL preferential
(adj) *choice* preferentially
(adv)

PRFRNTL prefrontal *front*
part

PRFRNTS preference *choice*

PRFRR preferer *chooser*

PRFRS perforce *by force*

PRFRSDK paraphrastic
quote

PRFRSDK periphrastic
expression

PRFRSDKL paraphrastically
quote

PRFRSDKL periphrastically
expression

PRFRSHN perforation *hole*

PRFRSS periphrasis
expression periphrases

PRFRSTK paraphrastic
quote

PRFRSTK periphrastic
expression

PRFRSTKL paraphrastically
quote

PRFRSTKL periphrastically
expression

PRFRSZ periphrases (pl)
expression periphrasis

PRFRT perforate *make holes*
perforated perforating

PRFRTD perforated *with*
holes

PRFRTK porphyritic *crystals*

PRFRTR perforator *make*
holes

PRFRVD perfervid *passionate*

PRFRZ paraphrase *quote*
paraphrased
paraphrasing

PRFRZBL paraphrasable
quote

PRFRZN prefrozen *freeze*

PRFRZZ periphrases (pl)
expression periphrasis

PRFS preface *introduce*
prefaced prefacing

PRFS profess *state*

PRFS profuse *bountiful*

PRFS prophecy *(n)*
prediction prophecies

PRFS prophesy *(v) predict*

prophesied prophesying

PRFSDL professedly
claimed

PRFSH prophage *bacteria*

PRFSHN perfusion *injection*

PRFSHN profession
statement, calling

PRFSHN profusion *excess*

PRFSHNC proficiency *skill*
proficiencies

PRFSHNL professional (adj)
businesslike professionally
(adv)

PRFSHNLZM
professionalism
businesslike

PRFSHNS proficiency *skill*
proficiencies

PRFSHNST perfusionist
surgery

PRFSHNT proficient *skilled*

PRFSHNTC proficiency *skill*
proficiencies

PRFSHNTL proficiently
skillfully

PRFSHNTS proficiency *skill*
proficiencies

PRFSL profusely *bountiful*

PRFSNS profuseness
bounty

PRFSR prefacer *introducer*

PRFSR professor *teacher*

PRFSR prophesier *foreteller*

PRFSRL professorial (adj)
teacher professorially
(adv)

PRFSRSHP professorship
office

PRFSRT professorate *office*

PRFSRT professoriat
teachers

PRFSRYL professorial (adj)
teacher professorially
(adv)

PRFSRYT professoriat
teachers

PRFST professed *claimed*

PRFSYR prophesier
foreteller

PRFT profit *gain*

PRFT prophet *predictor*

PRFTBL profitable (adj)

Use letters that best describe the sounds you hear and omit the vowels. Use **S** or **K** instead of **C**: to find circle use **SRKL**. Use **J** to find joy, **JM** to find gem and **G** to find go.

advantageous profitably (adv)

PRFTBLD profitability *gain*

PRFTBLNS profitableness *gain*

PRFTBLT profitability *gain*

PRFTK prophetic *predictive*

PRFTKL prophetically *predictive*

PRFTLS profitless *no gain*

PRFTR prefatory *introduce*

PRFTR profiteer *seller*

PRFTRL profiterole *food*

PRFTS prophetess *foreteller (f)*

PRFX prefix *first part* prefixes

PRFX prix fixe *meal*

PRFYM perfume *scent* perfumed perfuming

PRFYMR perfumer *scent*

PRFYR purifier *cleanser*

PRFYS profuse *bountiful*

PRFYSHN perfusion *injection*

PRFYSHN profusion *excess*

PRFYSHNST perfusionist *surgery*

PRFYSL profusely *bountiful*

PRFYSNS profuseness *bounty*

PRFYZ perfuse *inject* perfused perfusing

PRFYZHN perfusion *injection*

PRFYZHN profusion *excess*

PRFYZHNST perfusionist *surgery*

PRFZ perfuse *inject* perfused perfusing

PRFZ prophase *cell division*

PRFZH prophage *bacteria*

PRFZHN perfusion *injection*

PRFZHN profusion *excess*

PRFZHNST perfusionist *surgery*

PRG perigee *orbit*

PRG pirogue *boat*

PRG porgy *fish* porgies

PRG Prague *city*

PRG prig *prude*

PRGDV prerogative *option*

PRGDV purgative *remover*

PRGL pergola *trellis*

PRGLDD proglottid *worm*

PRGLTD proglottid *worm*

PRGM pregame *sports*

PRGMDK pragmatic *practical*

PRGMDKL pragmatically *practically*

PRGMTK pragmatic *practical*

PRGMTKL pragmatically *practically*

PRGMTSDK pragmatistic *practicality*

PRGMTST pragmatist *practicality*

PRGMTSTK pragmatistic *practicality*

PRGMTZM pragmatism *practicality*

PRGN paragon *(n) model (v) match*

PRGNBL pregnable *capture*

PRGNBLT pregnability *capture*

PRGNC pregnancy *childbirth* pregnancies

PRGNCZ prognoses (pl) *forecast* prognosis

PRGNK pyrogenic *fever*

PRGNNC pregnancy *childbirth* pregnancies

PRGNNS pregnancy *childbirth* pregnancies

PRGNNT pregnant *childbirth*

PRGNNTC pregnancy *childbirth* pregnancies

PRGNNTS pregnancy *childbirth* pregnancies

PRGNS pregnancy *childbirth* pregnancies

PRGNSDK prognostic *prophecy*

PRGNSDKDR prognosticator *prediction*

PRGNSDKSHN prognostication *prediction*

PRGNSDKT prognosticate *predict* prognosticated prognosticating

PRGNSDKTR

prognosticator *prediction*

PRGNSS paragenesis *minerals*

PRGNSS prognosis *forecast* prognoses

PRGNSTK prognostic *prophecy*

PRGNSTKDR prognosticator *prediction*

PRGNSTKDV prognosticative *prediction*

PRGNSTKSHN prognostication *prediction*

PRGNSTKT prognosticate *predict* prognosticated prognosticating

PRGNSTKTR prognosticator *prediction*

PRGNSTKTV prognosticative *prediction*

PRGNSZ prognoses (pl) *forecast* prognosis

PRGNT pregnant *childbirth*

PRGNTC pregnancy *childbirth* pregnancies

PRGNTHS prognathous *jaws*

PRGNTS pregnancy *childbirth* pregnancies

PRGR operagoer *audience*

PRGR priggery *prude*

PRGRF paragraph *writing*

PRGRK paregoric *opium*

PRGRM program *(v) arrange, predetermine* programmed (or) programed programming (or) programing (Br) programme

PRGRM program *(n) outline* (Br) programme

PRGRMBL programmable *arrange, predetermine*

PRGRMBLD programmability *arrange, predetermine*

PRGRMBLT programmability *arrange, predetermine*

PRGRMDK programmatic *arranged*

PRGRMN programming

plan
PRGRMNG programming
plan
PRGRMR programmer
arranger
PRGRMTK programmatic
arranged
PRGRN peregrine *(adj)*
wandering (n) falcon
PRGRNSHN peregrination
travel
PRGRNT peregrinate *cross*
peregrinated
peregrinating
PRGRP peer group *equals*
PRGRS progress *advance*
PRGRSHN progression
advancement
PRGRSV progressive
advancing
PRGRSVL progressively
advancing
PRGRSVNS
progressiveness *advance*
PRGRSVZM progressivism
advancement
PRGSH priggish *prude*
PRGSHN purgation *clearing*
PRGSHNS priggishness
prude
PRGTR purgatory *suffering*
PRGTRL purgatorial
cleansing
PRGTRYL purgatorial
cleansing
PRGTV prerogative *option*
PRGTV purgative *remover*
PRGW Paraguay *country*
PRGWR operagoer *audience*
PRGZSDNS preexistence
live before
PRGZSDNT preexistent *live*
before
PRGZSDNTS preexistence
live before
PRGZST preexist *live before*
PRGZSTNS preexistence
live before
PRGZSTNT preexistent *live*
before
PRGZSTNTS preexistence
live before

PRH aparejo *packsaddle*
aparejos
PRHBDV prohibitive
restraining
PRHBSHN prohibition
forbidding
PRHBSHNST prohibitionist
no alcohol
PRHBT prohibit *forbid*
PRHBTR prohibitory
forbidding
PRHBTV prohibitive
restraining
PRHL parhelia (pl) *sun spot*
parhelion
PRHL perihelia (pl) *orbit*
parhelion
PRHLL perihelial *orbit*
PRHLN parhelion *sun spot*
parhelia
PRHLN perihelion *orbit*
perihelia
PRHLY parhelia (pl) *sun spot*
parhelion
PRHLY perihelia (pl) *orbit*
parhelion
PRHLYL perihelial *orbit*
PRHLYN parhelion *sun spot*
parhelia
PRHLYN perihelion *orbit*
perihelia
PRHMN prehuman *ancient*
PRHN apprehend *seize,*
understand
PRHN upper hand *advantage*
PRHNCHN apprehension
conception, arrest,
foreboding
PRHND apprehend *seize,*
understand
PRHND upper hand
advantage
PRHNSBL apprehensible
(adj) seize, understand
apprehensibly (adv)
PRHNSHN apprehension
conception, arrest,
foreboding
PRHNSHN prehension *grasp*
PRHNSL prehensile
grasping
PRHNSV apprehensive

conception, arrest,
foreboding
PRHNSVL apprehensively
conception, arrest,
foreboding
PRHNSVNS
apprehensiveness
conception, arrest,
foreboding
PRHNTSBL apprehensible
(adj) seize, understand
apprehensibly (adv)
PRHNTSL prehensile
grasping
PRHNTSV apprehensive
conception, arrest,
foreboding
PRHNTSVL apprehensively
conception, arrest,
foreboding
PRHNTSVNS
apprehensiveness
conception, arrest,
foreboding
PRHPS perhaps *maybe*
PRHS poorhouse *poverty*
PRHS powerhouse *strong*
one
PRHSTR prehistory *ancient*
PRHSTRK prehistoric
ancient
PRHYMN prehuman *ancient*
PRJ peerage *equal rank*
PRJ perigee *orbit*
PRJ porridge *cereal*
PRJ purge *clear* purged
purging
PRJDS prejudice *damage,*
bias *prejudicing*
prejudiced
PRJDSD prejudiced *biased*
PRJDSHL prejudicial (adj)
biased prejudicially (adv)
PRJDST prejudiced *biased*
PRJDV purgative *remover*
PRJJ prejudge *decide*
prejudged prejudging
PRJJMNT prejudgment
decision
PRJJR prejudger *decider*
PRJK project *(v) thrust,*
*estimate, display (n) plan**

Use letters that best describe the sounds you hear and omit the vowels. Use **S** or **K**
instead of **C**: to find circle use **SRKL**. Use **J** to find joy, **JM** to find gem and **G** to find go.

PRK

PRJKDR projector *picture device*

PRJKDV projective *geometry*

PRJKSHN projection *bulge, display*

PRJKSHNL projectional *bulge, display*

PRJKSHNST projectionist *film, maps*

PRJKT project (v) *thrust, estimate, display* (n) *plan**

PRJKTL projectile *missile*

PRJKTR projector *picture device*

PRJKTV projective *geometry*

PRJN perigyny *flower*

PRJN progeny *offspring* progenies

PRJN pyrogen *fever*

PRJNDK paragenetic *minerals*

PRJNDKL paragenetically *minerals*

PRJNDR progenitor *forefather*

PRJNK pyrogenic *fever*

PRJNS perigynous *flower*

PRJNSD pyrogenicity *fever*

PRJNSS paragenesis *minerals*

PRJNST pyrogenicity *fever*

PRJNTK paragenetic *minerals*

PRJNTKL paragenetically *minerals*

PRJNTR progenitor *forefather*

PRJR perdure *last* perdured perduring

PRJR perjure *lie* perjured perjuring

PRJR perjury *lying* perjuries

PRJR purger *cleanser*

PRJRBL perdurable (adj) *lasting* perdurably (adv)

PRJRR perjurer *liar*

PRJRS perjurious *liar*

PRJRYS perjurious *liar*

PRJSTN progestin *hormone*

PRJSTRN progesterone *hormone*

PRJSTSHNL progestational

ovulation

PRJT parget *plaster* pargeted (or) pargetted pargeting (or) pargetting

PRJTV purgative *remover*

PRK eparchy *diocese* eparchies

PRK park (n) *land* (v) *stop and stay*

PRK parka *jacket*

PRK parquet *floor*

PRK perique *tobacco*

PRK perk (v) *percolate, improve* (n) *benefit*

PRK perky (adj) *jaunty* perkier perkiest perkiness

PRK peruke *wig*

PRK pork *meat*

PRK porky *fat* porkier porkiest

PRK porky *porcupine* porkies

PRK prick (n) *pointed tool* (v) *pierce*

PRK pyric *burning*

PRK pyrrhic *poem*

PRKC apraxia *movement*

PRKC prexy (slang) *president* prexies

PRKC proxy *substitute* proxies

PRKC pyrexia *fever*

PRKCL preaxial *front*

PRKCL pyrexial *fever*

PRKCM proximo *next month*

PRKCMK proxemic *separation*

PRKCN pyroxene *mineral*

PRKCY apraxia *movement*

PRKCY pyrexia *fever*

PRKCYL preaxial *front*

PRKCYL pyrexial *fever*

PRKCZ praxes (pl) *action* praxis

PRKDK apractic (or) apraxic *movement*

PRKDKBL practicable (adj) *possible* practicably (adv)

PRKDKBLD practicability *possibility*

PRKDKBLNS practicableness

possibility

PRKDKBLT practicability *possibility*

PRKDKL practical (adj) *possible, useful* practically (adv)

PRKDKLD practicality *possibility, usefulness* practicalities

PRKDKLNS practicalness *possibility, usefulness*

PRKDKLT practicality *possibility, usefulness* practicalities

PRKDKM practicum *study*

PRKDLJK proctologic (or) proctological *anus*

PRKDLJKL proctological (or) proctologic *anus*

PRKDR proctor *supervisor*

PRKDS practice (n) *habit, business*

PRKDS practice (or) practise (v) *apply, do often* practiced (or) practised practicing (or) practising

PRKDSKP proctoscope *device*

PRKDSKPK proctoscopic *anus*

PRKDSR practicer *apply, do often*

PRKDV proactive *anticipate*

PRKFV Prokofiev *composer*

PRKFYF Prokofiev *composer*

PRKFYV Prokofiev *composer*

PRKGNDV precognitive *clairvoyance*

PRKGNSHN precognition *clairvoyance*

PRKGNTV precognitive *clairvoyance*

PRKK precook *heat*

PRKL opercula (pl) *lid* operculum

PRKL parochial (adj) *church-related* parochially (adv)

PRKL percale *fabric*

PRKL prickle *sting* prickled prickling

PRKL prickly *tingling, troublesome* pricklier

Letters aren't doubled for single sounds: to find alley use **L** not **LL**. Use **Y** and **W** as hard sounds only: to find yellow use **YL**. (Br)=British spelling or usage. * See dictionary.

prickliest
PRKLD preclude *rule out* precluded precluding
PRKLDD operculated (or) operculate *lidded*
PRKLDR percolator *coffeepot*
PRKLKLS precalculus *math*
PRKLKYLS precalculus *math*
PRKLM operculum *lid* opercula
PRKLM proclaim *declare*
PRKLMBN pre-Columbian *Columbus*
PRKLMBYN pre-Columbian *Columbus*
PRKLMR proclaimer *declarer*
PRKLMSHN proclamation *declaration*
PRKLN parkland *territory*
PRKLN percaline *fabric*
PRKLND parkland *territory*
PRKLNS prickliness *tingling, troublesome*
PRKLQLS precalculus *math*
PRKLR opercular *lid*
PRKLR pricklier *tingling, troublesome*
PRKLRT perchlorate *chemical*
PRKLS upper-class (adj) *elite* upper class (n)
PRKLSHN percolation *seep, bubble*
PRKLSHN preclusion *rule out*
PRKLSMN upperclassman *junior or senior* upperclassmen
PRKLST prickliest *tingling, troublesome*
PRKLSV preclusive *rule out*
PRKLT operculate (or) operculated *lidded*
PRKLT percolate *seep, bubble* percolated percolating
PRKLTD operculated (or) operculate *lidded*
PRKLTR percolator *coffeepot*
PRKLVD proclivity *leaning* proclivities

PRKLVT proclivity *leaning* proclivities
PRKLYR pricklier *tingling, troublesome*
PRKLYST prickliest *tingling, troublesome*
PRKLZHN preclusion *rule out*
PRKLZM parochialism *church-related*
PRKLZV preclusive *rule out*
PRKMBM procambium *plant*
PRKMBNT procumbent *lying*
PRKMBYM procambium *plant*
PRKN procaine *anesthetic*
PRKNCHS preconscious *psychology*
PRKNCV preconceive *prejudice* preconceived preconceiving
PRKNCVD preconceived *prejudiced*
PRKNDR perichondria (pl) *tissue* perichondrium
PRKNDRGRDN prekindergarten *school*
PRKNDRGRTN prekindergarten *school*
PRKNDRM perichondrium *tissue* perichondria
PRKNDRY perichondria (pl) *tissue* perichondrium
PRKNDRYM perichondrium *tissue* perichondria
PRKNDSHN precondition *requirement*
PRKNS perkiness *jauntiness*
PRKNS Preakness *race*
PRKNSHS preconscious *psychology*
PRKNSL precancel *stamps*
PRKNSL proconsul *diplomat*
PRKNSLR proconsular *diplomatic*
PRKNSLSHP proconsulship *diplomatic*
PRKNSLT proconsulate *diplomatic*
PRKNSNZDZZ Parkinson's

disease *tremors*
PRKNSNZL Parkinson's law *work*
PRKNSPSHN preconception *prejudice*
PRKNSRS precancerous *disease*
PRKNSV preconceive *prejudice* preconceived preconceiving
PRKNSVD preconceived *prejudiced*
PRKNTH pyracantha *shrub*
PRKNTSL precancel *stamps*
PRKNTSL proconsul *diplomat*
PRKNTSLR proconsular *diplomatic*
PRKNTSLSHP proconsulship *diplomatic*
PRKNTSLT proconsulate *diplomatic*
PRKNTSRS precancerous *disease*
PRKP pericope *book*
PRKP porkpie *hat*
PRKP preoccupy *concern* preoccupied preoccupying preoccupies
PRKPD per capita *each one*
PRKPD preoccupied *concerned*
PRKPN porcupine *animal*
PRKPNC preoccupancy *possession*
PRKPNS preoccupancy *possession*
PRKPNTC preoccupancy *possession*
PRKPNTS preoccupancy *possession*
PRKPSHN preoccupation *concern*
PRKPT per capita *each one*
PRKR perikarya (pl) *cell body* perikaryon
PRKR perkier *jauntier*
PRKR porker *pig*
PRKR porkier *fatter*
PRKR pricker *pointed tool*
PRKR procure *obtain*

Use letters that best describe the sounds you hear and omit the vowels. Use **S** or **K** instead of **C**: to find circle use **SRKL**. Use **J** to find joy, **JM** to find gem and **G** to find go.

procured procuring
PRKRBL procurable *obtainable*
PRKRD pericardia (pl) *heart sac* pericardium
PRKRDDS pericarditis *heart*
PRKRDK prokaryotic *cell*
PRKRDL pericardial *heart sac*
PRKRDM pericardium *heart sac* pericardia
PRKRDR procreator *reproduction*
PRKRDR procurator *obtainer*
PRKRDTS pericarditis *heart*
PRKRDY pericardia (pl) *heart sac* pericardium
PRKRDYL pericardial *heart sac*
PRKRDYM pericardium *heart sac* pericardia
PRKRL perikaryal *cell body*
PRKRMNT procurement *obtaining*
PRKRN perikaryon *cell body* perikarya
PRKRNT procreant *reproducing*
PRKRP pericarp *plant*
PRKRPDK procryptic *concealment*
PRKRPTK procryptic *concealment*
PRKRR procurer *obtainer*
PRKRS precarious *dangerous*
PRKRSCHN pre-Christian *Christ*
PRKRSDNDR procrastinator *delayer*
PRKRSDNSHN procrastination *delay*
PRKRSDNT procrastinate *delay* procrastinated procrastinating
PRKRSDNTR procrastinator *delayer*
PRKRSHN procreation *reproduction*
PRKRSHN procuration *obtaining*

PRKRSL precariously *dangerous*
PRKRSMS preChristmas *holiday*
PRKRSNS precariousness *danger*
PRKRSR precursor *forerunner*
PRKRSR precursory *preceding*
PRKRSTMS preChristmas *holiday*
PRKRSTNDR procrastinator *delayer*
PRKRSTNSHN procrastination *delay*
PRKRSTNT procrastinate *delay* procrastinated procrastinating
PRKRSTNTR procrastinator *delayer*
PRKRT procreate *beget* procreated procreating
PRKRT prokaryote *cell*
PRKRTK prokaryotic *cell*
PRKRTR procreator *reproduction*
PRKRTR procurator *obtainer*
PRKRY perikarya (pl) *cell body* perikaryon
PRKRYDK prokaryotic *cell*
PRKRYDR procreator *reproduction*
PRKRYL perikaryal *cell body*
PRKRYN perikaryon *cell body* perikarya
PRKRYNT procreant *reproducing*
PRKRYS precarious *dangerous*
PRKRYSHN procreation *reproduction*
PRKRYSL precariously *dangerous*
PRKRYSNS precariousness *danger*
PRKRYT procreate *beget* procreated procreating
PRKRYT prokaryote *cell*
PRKRYTK prokaryotic *cell*
PRKRYTR procreator *reproduction*

PRKS apraxia *movement*
PRKS percuss *tap*
PRKS perks *benefits*
PRKS prexy *(slang) president* prexies
PRKS proxy *substitute* proxies
PRKS Pyrex *(trademark) glassware*
PRKS pyrexia *fever*
PRKS uppercase (adj, n) *script* upper case (n)
PRKSD peroxide *bleach* peroxided peroxiding
PRKSD precocity *early maturity*
PRKSHN percussion *drum*
PRKSHN precaution *safeguard*
PRKSHNR precautionary *safeguard*
PRKSHNST percussionist *drummer*
PRKSHS precocious *early maturity*
PRKSHSL precociously *early maturity*
PRKSHSNS precociousness *early maturity*
PRKSK apraxic (or) apractic *movement*
PRKSK pyrexic *fever*
PRKSL preaxial *front*
PRKSL pyrexial *fever*
PRKSLN pyroxylin *coating*
PRKSLNS par excellence *best*
PRKSLNTS par excellence *best*
PRKSM proximo *next month*
PRKSMD proximity *nearness*
PRKSMDV approximative *near*
PRKSMK proxemic *separation*
PRKSML proximal (adj) *near* proximally (adv)
PRKSMSHN approximation *near*
PRKSMT approximate *(v) come close* approximated

Letters aren't doubled for single sounds: to find alley use **L** not **LL**. Use **Y** and **W** as hard sounds only: to find yellow use **YL**. (Br)=British spelling or usage. * See dictionary.

approximating
PRKSMT approximate *(adj)*
near
PRKSMT proximate *nearby*
PRKSMT proximity *nearness*
PRKSMTL approximately
nearly
PRKSMTL proximately
nearby
PRKSMTNS proximateness
nearness
PRKSMTV approximative
near
PRKSN pyroxene *mineral*
PRKSNT pyroxenite *rock*
PRKSS praxis *action* praxes
PRKST perkiest *jauntiest*
PRKST porkiest *fattest*
PRKST precocity *early*
maturity
PRKSV percussive *impact*
PRKSY apraxia *movement*
PRKSY pyrexia *fever*
PRKSYL preaxial *front*
PRKSYL pyrexial *fever*
PRKSZ praxes (pl) *action*
praxis
PRKSZM paroxysm *outburst*
PRKSZML paroxysmal
outburst
PRKT apricot *fruit*
PRKT parakeet *bird*
PRKT precut *cut beforehand*
PRKT pricket *spike*
PRKT uppercut *punch*
PRKTK apractic (or) apraxic
movement
PRKTKBL practicable (adj)
possible practicably (adv)
PRKTKBLD practicability
possibility
PRKTKBLNS
practicableness
possibility
PRKTKBLT practicability
possibility
PRKTKL practical (adj)
possible, useful practically
(adv)
PRKTKLD practicality
possibility, usefulness
practicalities

PRKTKLNS practicalness
possibility, usefulness
PRKTKLT practicality
possibility, usefulness
practicalities
PRKTKM practicum *study*
PRKTLG proctology *anus*
PRKTLJ proctology *anus*
PRKTLJK proctologic (or)
proctological *anus*
PRKTLJKL proctological
(or) proctologic *anus*
PRKTLJST proctologist
anus
PRKTR parquetry *wood*
parquetries
PRKTR precatory *wish*
PRKTR proctor *supervisor*
PRKTRL proctorial
supervisory
PRKTRYL proctorial
supervisory
PRKTS practice *(n) habit,*
business
PRKTS practice (or)
practise *(v) apply, do often*
practiced (or) practised
practicing (or) practising
PRKTSHNR practitioner
profession
PRKTSKP proctoscope
device
PRKTSKPK proctoscopic
anus
PRKTSR practicer *apply, do*
often
PRKTV proactive *anticipate*
PRKW parkway *road*
PRKWT paraquat *herbicide*
PRKWZT perquisite *benefit*
PRKYL opercula (pl) *lid*
operculum
PRKYL parochial (adj)
church-related parochially
(adv)
PRKYLDD operculated (or)
operculate *lidded*
PRKYLM operculum *lid*
opercula
PRKYLR opercular *lid*
PRKYLT operculate (or)
operculated *lidded*

PRKYLTD operculated (or)
operculate *lidded*
PRKYLZM parochialism
church-related
PRKYP preoccupy *concern*
preoccupied
preoccupying
preoccupies
PRKYPD preoccupied
concerned
PRKYPN porcupine *animal*
PRKYPNC preoccupancy
possession
PRKYPNS preoccupancy
possession
PRKYPNTC preoccupancy
possession
PRKYPNTS preoccupancy
possession
PRKYPSHN preoccupation
concern
PRKYR perkier *jauntier*
PRKYR porkier *fatter*
PRKYR procure *obtain*
procured procuring
PRKYRBL procurable
obtainable
PRKYRDR procurator
obtainer
PRKYRMNT procurement
obtaining
PRKYRR procurer *obtainer*
PRKYRSHN procuration
obtaining
PRKYRTR procurator
obtainer
PRKYST perkiest *jauntiest*
PRKYST porkiest *fattest*
PRKZSDNS preexistence
live before
PRKZSDNT preexistent *live*
before
PRKZSDNTS preexistence
live before
PRKZST preexist *live before*
PRKZSTNS preexistence
live before
PRKZSTNT preexistent *live*
before
PRKZSTNTS preexistence
live before
PRL apparel *dress* appareled

Use letters that best describe the sounds you hear and omit the vowels. Use **S** or **K** instead of **C**: to find circle use **SRKL**. Use **J** to find joy, **JM** to find gem and **G** to find go.

(or) apparelled appareling
(or) apparelling
PRL April *month*
PRL parlay *(n)* bet *(v)*
increase, bet
PRL parley *conference*
parleys
PRL parole *release* paroled
paroling
PRL parolee *felon*
PRL payroll *salary*
PRL pearl *gem*
PRL pearly *opaque and shiny*
pearlier pearliest
PRL peril *(n)* risk *(v)*
endanger
PRL poorly *badly*
PRL prowl *sneak*
PRL puerile (adj) *silly*
puerilely (adv)
PRL purely *simply*
PRL purl *knit, swirl*
PRL purlieu *neighborhood*
PRL pyrola *wintergreen*
PRL pyrrole *chemical*
PRLC prelacy *clergy*
PRLCHR prelature *clergy*
PRLD prelude *introduce,*
open preluded preluding
PRLD puerility *silliness*
PRLD pyrallid *moth*
PRLDHD paraldehyde *drug*
PRLDK paralytic *no*
movement
PRLDK pyrolytic *heat*
PRLDKL paralytically *no*
movement
PRLDRT preliterate *language*
PRLF pro-life *against*
abortion
PRLFK prolific *fruitful*
PRLFKC prolificacy *fruitful*
PRLFKL prolifically *fruitful*
PRLFKNS prolificness
fruitful
PRLFKS prolificacy *fruitful*
PRLFLZD April Fools' Day
1st of April
PRLFR pro-lifer *against*
abortion
PRLFRSHN proliferation
multiplication

PRLFRT proliferate *multiply*
proliferated proliferating
PRLG prologue *preface*
PRLGL paralegal *law*
PRLJZ prologize (or)
prologuize *speak*
prologized (or)
prologuized prologizing
(or) prologuizing
PRLJZM paralogism *false*
argument
PRLK pyrrolic *chemical*
PRLKDK parallactic
direction
PRLKDR prolocutor
spokesman
PRLKS parallax *direction*
PRLKS prolix *wordy*
PRLKSD prolixity *wordy*
PRLKSHN preelection
voting
PRLKST prolixity *wordy*
PRLKTK parallactic *direction*
PRLKTR prolocutor
spokesman
PRLKYDR prolocutor
spokesman
PRLKYTR prolocutor
spokesman
PRLL parallel *side by side,*
similar
PRLLGRM parallelogram
shape
PRLLZM parallelism *side by*
side, similar
PRLMF perilymph *ear*
PRLMNR preliminary
introductory preliminaries
PRLMNT parliament *(often*
capitalized) council
PRLMNTR parliamentary
council
PRLMNTRN
parliamentarian *(often*
capitalized) council
PRLMNTRYN
parliamentarian *(often*
capitalized) council
PRLMPF perilymph *ear*
PRLN perilune *orbit*
PRLN praline *candy*
PRLN purlin *roof*

PRLN purloin *steal*
PRLNCH prelaunch *rocket*
PRLND parlando (or)
parlante *tempo*
PRLNG prolong *extend*
PRLNGGWJ paralanguage
tone of voice
PRLNGGWSTKS
paralinguistics *tone of*
voice
PRLNGGWSTX
paralinguistics *tone of*
voice
PRLNGSHN prolongation
extension
PRLNGWJ paralanguage
tone of voice
PRLNGWSTKS
paralinguistics *tone of*
voice
PRLNGWSTX
paralinguistics *tone of*
voice
PRLNS parlance *speech*
PRLNS purulence *pus*
PRLNT parlante (or)
parlando *tempo*
PRLNT purulent *pus*
PRLNTS parlance *speech*
PRLNTS purulence *pus*
PRLPCZ prolepses (pl)
anticipation prolepsis
PRLPDK proleptic
anticipation
PRLPS prolapse *fall*
prolapsed prolapsing
PRLPSS prolepsis
anticipation prolepses
PRLPSZ prolepses (pl)
anticipation prolepsis
PRLPTK proleptic
anticipation
PRLQDR prolocutor
spokesman
PRLQTR prolocutor
spokesman
PRLR parlor *room*
(Br) parlour
PRLR pearlier *opaque and*
shiny
PRLR prowler *sneak*
PRLS peerless *without equal*

Letters aren't doubled for single sounds: to find alley use **L** not **LL**. Use **Y** and **W** as hard
sounds only: to find yellow use **YL**. (Br)=British spelling or usage. * See dictionary.

PRLS perilous *dangerous*
PRLS powerless *weak*
PRLS prelacy *clergy*
PRLSHN prolusion *introduction*
PRLSL perilously *dangerous*
PRLSL powerlessly *weak*
PRLSNS pearlescence *opaque and shiny*
PRLSNS perilousness *danger*
PRLSNS powerlessness *weakness*
PRLSNT pearlescent *opaque and shiny*
PRLSNTS pearlescence *opaque and shiny*
PRLSS paralysis *no movement* paralyses
PRLSS pyrolysis *heat*
PRLST pearliest *opaque and shiny*
PRLT pearlite *alloy*
PRLT prelate *clergy*
PRLT puerility *silliness*
PRLTK paralytic *no movement*
PRLTK pyrolytic *heat*
PRLTKL paralytically *no movement*
PRLTR prelature *clergy*
PRLTRN proletarian *worker*
PRLTRT preliterate *language*
PRLTRT proletariat *working class*
PRLTRYN proletarian *worker*
PRLTRYT proletariat *working class*
PRLTYR prelature *clergy*
PRLX parallax *direction*
PRLX prolix *wordy*
PRLXD prolixity *wordy*
PRLXT prolixity *wordy*
PRLY purlieu *neighborhood*
PRLYR pearlier *opaque and shiny*
PRLYST pearliest *opaque and shiny*
PRLZ paralyze *no movement* paralyzed paralyzing (Br) paralyse
PRLZ pyrolyze *heat*

pyrolyzed pyrolyzing
PRLZD pearlized *opaque and shiny*
PRLZHN prolusion *introduction*
PRLZM puerilism *childishness*
PRLZNGL paralyzingly *no movement* (Br) paralyse
PRLZNL paralyzingly *no movement* (Br) paralyse
PRLZR paralyzer *no movement* (Br) paralyse
PRLZR pyrolyzer *heater*
PRM pram *boat, (Br) baby carriage*
PRM preemie *baby*
PRM prim *neat* primmed primming primmer primmest
PRM prime *(v) prepare* primed priming
PRM prime *(n) youth, number, time (adj) basic, first**
PRM primo *best, first* primos
PRM prom *dance*
PRM promo *(abbr) promotion* promos
PRM Purim *feast*
PRMBL permeable *penetrate*
PRMBL preamble *introduction*
PRMBLD permeability *penetration*
PRMBLDR perambulator *stroller*
PRMBLSHN perambulation *stroll*
PRMBLT perambulate *stroll* perambulated perambulating
PRMBLT permeability *penetration*
PRMBLTR perambulator *stroller*
PRMBYLDR perambulator *stroller*
PRMBYLSHN

perambulation *stroll*
PRMBYLT perambulate *stroll* perambulated perambulating
PRMBYLTR perambulator *stroller*
PRMC paramecia (pl) *animal* paramecium
PRMC primacy *first*
PRMCHL pari-mutuel *wager*
PRMCHR premature *too soon*
PRMCHRD prematurity *too soon*
PRMCHRL prematurely *too soon*
PRMCHRT prematurity *too soon*
PRMCHWL pari-mutuel *wager*
PRMCM paramecium *animal* paramecia
PRMCS premises *land*
PRMCY paramecia (pl) *animal* paramecium
PRMCYM paramecium *animal* paramecia
PRMCZ premises *land*
PRMD premed *medicine*
PRMD pyramid *shape*
PRMDBL promotable *advance*
PRMDBLD promotability *advancement*
PRMDBLT promotability *advancement*
PRMDK paramedic *medical aide*
PRMDKL paramedical *medical aide*
PRMDKL premedical *student*
PRMDKL pyramidical *shape*
PRMDL pyramidal (adj) *shape* pyramidally (adv)
PRMDN prima donna *star*
PRMDR parameter *math, limit*
PRMDR perimeter *edge, margin*
PRMDR permitter *one allowing*

Use letters that best describe the sounds you hear and omit the vowels. Use **S** or **K** instead of **C**: to find circle use **SRKL**. Use **J** to find joy, **JM** to find gem and **G** to find go.

PRMDR preemptor *seize first*

PRMDR promoter *sports*

PRMDR pyrometer *temperature*

PRMDRN premodern *style*

PRMDTDD premeditated *planned before*

PRMDTDV premeditative *planned before*

PRMDTSHN premeditation *planned before*

PRMDTT premeditate *plan before* premeditated premeditating

PRMDTTD premeditated *planned before*

PRMDTTV premeditative *planned before*

PRMDV preemptive *seize first*

PRMDV primitive *original, crude*

PRMDVL primitively *original, crude*

PRMDVNS primitiveness *original, crude*

PRMDVZM primitivism *original, crude*

PRMFRST permafrost *ice*

PRMFSH prima facie *view*

PRMJNCHR primogeniture *firstborn*

PRMJNDR primogenitor *ancestor*

PRMJNTR primogenitor *ancestor*

PRMJNTR primogeniture *firstborn*

PRMJNTYR primogeniture *firstborn*

PRMKS premix *stir*

PRML primal *basic*

PRMLD primality *number*

PRMLGDR promulgator *declarer*

PRMLGSHN promulgation *declaration*

PRMLGT promulgate *declare* promulgated promulgating

PRMLGTR promulgator *declarer*

PRMLR premolar *tooth*

PRMLT primality *number*

PRMLTR paramilitary *armed force*

PRMM premium *(n) reward (adj) quality*

PRMN priming *explosive*

PRMN pyromania *fire urge*

PRMNC pyromancy *foretelling*

PRMND promenade *square dance* promenaded promenading

PRMNG priming *explosive*

PRMNK pyromaniac *fire urge*

PRMNKL pyromaniacal *fire urge*

PRMNNC permanency *everlasting* permanencies

PRMNNS permanence *everlasting*

PRMNNS permanency *everlasting* permanencies

PRMNNS preeminence *superiority*

PRMNNS prominence *projection*

PRMNNT permanent *(adj) everlasting (n) hair curl*

PRMNNT preeminent *superior*

PRMNNT prominent *noticeable*

PRMNNTC permanency *everlasting* permanencies

PRMNNTL permanently *everlasting*

PRMNNTS permanence *everlasting*

PRMNNTS permanency *everlasting* permanencies

PRMNNTS preeminence *superiority*

PRMNNTS prominence *projection*

PRMNS primness *neatness*

PRMNS pyromancy *foretelling*

PRMNSH paramnesia *memory disorder*

PRMNSHN premonition *warning*

PRMNSTRL premenstrual (adj) *before menstruation* premenstrually (adv)

PRMNSTRWL premenstrual (adj) *before menstruation* premenstrually (adv)

PRMNT paramount *supreme*

PRMNT prominent *noticeable*

PRMNTC paramountcy *supremacy*

PRMNTC pyromancy *foretelling*

PRMNTL paramountly *supremely*

PRMNTR premonitory *warning*

PRMNTR promontory *cliff* promontories

PRMNTRL premonitorily *warning*

PRMNTS paramountcy *supremacy*

PRMNTS prominence *projection*

PRMNTS pyromancy *foretelling*

PRMNY pyromania *fire urge*

PRMNYK pyromaniac *fire urge*

PRMNYKL pyromaniacal *fire urge*

PRMNZH paramnesia *memory disorder*

PRMP preamp *amplifier*

PRMP primp *vanity*

PRMP prompt *(adj) quick (n,v) cue*

PRMPBK promptbook *play*

PRMPDR peremptory *masterful*

PRMPDR preemptor *seize first*

PRMPDRL peremptorily *masterful*

PRMPDRNS peremptoriness *masterful*

PRMPDV preemptive *seize first*

PRMPL promptly *quickly*

PRMPLFR preamplifier

stereo
PRMPLFYR preamplifier
stereo
PRMPLMNT
preemployment *job*
PRMPSHN preemption *seize
first*
PRMPT preempt *seize first,
prevent*
PRMPT prompt *(adj) quick
(n,v) cue*
PRMPTBK promptbook
play
PRMPTL promptly *quickly*
PRMPTR peremptory
masterful
PRMPTR preemptor *seize
first*
PRMPTR prompter *reminder*
PRMPTRL peremptorily
masterful
PRMPTRNS
peremptoriness *masterful*
PRMPTV preemptive *seize
first*
PRMR paramour *lover*
PRMR premier *(n) chief (adj)
primary*
PRMR premiere *(v) first
showing* premiered
premiering
PRMR primary *chief, first*
primaries
PRMR primer *book, device*
PRMR primero *game*
PRMR primmer *neater*
PRMRD primordia *(pl)
primitive* primordium
PRMRDL premarital *before
marriage*
PRMRDL primordial *(adj)
primitive* primordially
(adv)
PRMRDM primordium
primitive primordia
PRMRDN prime meridian
longitude
PRMRDY primordia *(pl)
primitive* primordium
PRMRDYL primordial *(adj)
primitive* primordially
(adv)

PRMRDYM primordium
primitive primordia
PRMRDYN prime meridian
longitude
PRMRFT pyromorphite
mineral
PRMRL primarily *chief, first*
PRMRT prime rate *interest*
PRMRTL premarital *before
marriage*
PRMRZ primrose *plant*
PRMS paramecia *(pl) animal*
paramecium
PRMS premise *(v) propose*
premised premising
PRMS premise *(n)
assumption*
PRMS primacy *first*
PRMS primus *bishop*
PRMS promise *pledge*
promised promising
PRMSBL permissible *(adj)
allowed* permissibly *(adv)*
PRMSBLD permissibility
allowed
PRMSBLT permissibility
allowed
PRMSH paramecia *(pl)
animal* paramecium
PRMSH perimysia *(pl)
muscle* perimysium
PRMSHL primatial *apes*
PRMSHM paramecium
animal paramecia
PRMSHM perimysium
muscle perimysia
PRMSHN Parmesan *cheese*
PRMSHN permeation
penetration
PRMSHN permission
allowance
PRMSHN preemption *seize
first*
PRMSHN promotion
advance, marketing
PRMSHNL promotional
advance, marketing
PRMSHR premeasure *share*
PRMSHY paramecia *(pl)
animal* paramecium
PRMSHYM paramecium
animal paramecia

PRMSKD promiscuity
mingling promiscuities
PRMSKS promiscuous
casual
PRMSKSL promiscuously
casually
PRMSKSNS
promiscuousness
casualness
PRMSKT promiscuity
mingling promiscuities
PRMSKWD promiscuity
mingling promiscuities
PRMSKWS promiscuous
casual
PRMSKWSL promiscuously
casually
PRMSKWSNS
promiscuousness
casualness
PRMSKWT promiscuity
mingling promiscuities
PRMSKYD promiscuity
mingling promiscuities
PRMSKYS promiscuous
casual
PRMSKYSL promiscuously
casually
PRMSKYSNS
promiscuousness
casualness
PRMSKYT promiscuity
mingling promiscuities
PRMSKYWD promiscuity
mingling promiscuities
PRMSKYWS promiscuous
casual
PRMSKYWSL
promiscuously *casually*
PRMSKYWSNS
promiscuousness
casualness
PRMSKYWT promiscuity
mingling promiscuities
PRMSM paramecium *animal*
paramecia
PRMSN Parmesan *cheese*
PRMSN promising *likely*
PRMSN puromycin
antibiotic
PRMSNG promising *likely*
PRMSQD promiscuity

Use letters that best describe the sounds you hear and omit the vowels. Use **S** or **K**
instead of **C**: to find circle use **SRKL**. Use **J** to find joy, **JM** to find gem and **G** to find go.

mingling promiscuities
PRMSQS promiscuous *casual*
PRMSQSL promiscuously *casually*
PRMSQSNS promiscuousness *casualness*
PRMSQT promiscuity *mingling* promiscuities
PRMSQWD promiscuity *mingling* promiscuities
PRMSQWS promiscuous *casual*
PRMSQWSL promiscuously *casually*
PRMSQWSNS promiscuousness *casualness*
PRMSQWT promiscuity *mingling* promiscuities
PRMSR promissory *assurance*
PRMSS premises *land*
PRMST primmest *neatest*
PRMST uppermost *top*
PRMSV permissive *easy-going*
PRMSVL permissively *easy-going*
PRMSVNS permissiveness *easy-going*
PRMSY paramecia (pl) *animal* paramecium
PRMSYM paramecium *animal* paramecia
PRMSZ premises *land*
PRMT paramount *supreme*
PRMT permeate *penetrate* permeated permeating
PRMT permit *allow* permitted permitting
PRMT permittee *one allowed*
PRMT permute *change* permuted permuting
PRMT preempt *seize first, prevent*
PRMT primate *animal*
PRMT promote *advance* promoted promoting
PRMT prompt *(adj) quick (n,v) cue*

PRMTBK promptbook *play*
PRMTBL promotable *advance*
PRMTBLD promotability *advancement*
PRMTBLT promotability *advancement*
PRMTC paramountcy *supremacy*
PRMTH poor mouth (n) *plead poverty* poor-mouth (v)
PRMTHM promethium *element*
PRMTHN Promethean *original*
PRMTHS Prometheus *Greek myth*
PRMTHYM promethium *element*
PRMTHYN Promethean *original*
PRMTHYS Prometheus *Greek myth*
PRMTK paramedic *medical aide*
PRMTKL paramedical *medical aide*
PRMTL paramountly *supremely*
PRMTLG primatology *apes*
PRMTLJ primatology *apes*
PRMTLJKL primatological *apes*
PRMTLJST primatologist *apes*
PRMTR parameter *math, limit*
PRMTR perimeter *edge, margin*
PRMTR permitter *one allowing*
PRMTR preemptor *seize first*
PRMTR premature *too soon*
PRMTR promoter *sports*
PRMTR prompter *reminder*
PRMTR pyrometer *temperature* pyrometry
PRMTRD prematurity *too soon*
PRMTRK parametric *math, limit*

PRMTRK pyrometric *temperature*
PRMTRKL parametrically *math, limit*
PRMTRKL pyrometrically *temperature*
PRMTRL prematurely *too soon*
PRMTRT prematurity *too soon*
PRMTS paramountcy *supremacy*
PRMTSHN permutation *change*
PRMTSHNL permutational *change*
PRMTV preemptive *seize first*
PRMTV primitive *original, crude*
PRMTVL primitively *original, crude*
PRMTVNS primitiveness *original, crude*
PRMTVZM primitivism *original, crude*
PRMTWL pari-mutuel *wager*
PRMTYR premature *too soon*
PRMTYRD prematurity *too soon*
PRMTYRL prematurely *too soon*
PRMTYRT prematurity *too soon*
PRMTYWL pari-mutuel *wager*
PRMVL primeval (adj) *primitive* primevally (adv)
PRMX premix *stir*
PRMYBL permeable *penetrate*
PRMYBLD permeability *penetration*
PRMYBLT permeability *penetration*
PRMYCHL pari-mutuel *wager*
PRMYCHWL pari-mutuel *wager*
PRMYM premium *(n) reward (adj) quality*
PRMYR premier *(n) chief*

Letters aren't doubled for single sounds: to find alley use **L** not **LL**. Use **Y** and **W** as hard sounds only: to find yellow use **YL**. (Br)=British spelling or usage. * See dictionary.

(adj) primary
PRMYR premiere *(v) first showing* premiered premiering
PRMYSHN permeation *penetration*
PRMYT permeate *penetrate* permeated permeating
PRMYT permute *change* permuted permuting
PRMYTL pari-mutuel *wager*
PRMYTSHN permutation *change*
PRMYTSHNL permutational *change*
PRMYTWL pari-mutuel *wager*
PRMYTYL pari-mutuel *wager*
PRMYTYWL pari-mutuel *wager*
PRMZ perimysia *(pl) muscle* perimysium
PRMZH perimysia *(pl) muscle* perimysium
PRMZHM perimysium *muscle* perimysia
PRMZHN Parmesan *cheese*
PRMZHR premeasure *share*
PRMZM perimysium *muscle* perimysia
PRMZN Parmesan *cheese*
PRMZY perimysia *(pl) muscle* perimysium
PRMZYM perimysium *muscle* perimysia
PRN apiarian *bees*
PRN apron *garment, area*
PRN epergne *centerpiece*
PRN operon *gene*
PRN paranoia *fear*
PRN parian *porcelain*
PRN paring *cutting*
PRN pereion (or) pereon *thorax*
PRN perinea *(pl) anus* perineum
PRN perron *stairway*
PRN piranha *fish*
PRN porn (or) porno *pornography*
PRN prawn *shrimp*

PRN preen *primp*
PRN prone *(adj, adv) likely, face down, prostrate*
PRN pronto *quickly*
PRN prune *(v) trim (n) dried fruit* pruned pruning
PRN prying *curious*
PRNBL printable *write, copy*
PRNBLD printability *write, copy*
PRNBLT printability *write, copy*
PRND operand *data*
PRND paranoid *fearful*
PRND pyrenoid *protein*
PRNDL perinatal (adj) *birth* perinatally (adv)
PRNDL prenatal (adj) *before birth* prenatally (adv)
PRNDR pronator *muscle*
PRNFRK pronephric *renal*
PRNFRS pronephros *renal organ*
PRNG paring *cutting*
PRNG prong *fork*
PRNG prying *curious*
PRNGD pronged *forked*
PRNGHRN pronghorn *animal*
PRNGK prank *trick*
PRNGKM parenchyma *plant tissue*
PRNGKMDS parenchymatous *plant tissue*
PRNGKML parenchymal *plant tissue*
PRNGKMTS parenchymatous *plant tissue*
PRNGKSDR prankster *tricks*
PRNGKSH prankish *tricky*
PRNGKSHL prankishly *tricky*
PRNGKSHNS prankishness *trickiness*
PRNGKSTR prankster *tricks*
PRNGMNS praying mantis *insect*
PRNGMNTS praying mantis *insect*
PRNGRF pornography *erotic*

material
PRNGRFK pornographic *erotic material*
PRNGRFKL pornographically *erotic material*
PRNGRFR pornographer *erotic material*
PRNGRL preinaugural *induction*
PRNGXDR prankster *tricks*
PRNGXTR prankster *tricks*
PRNGYRL preinaugural *induction*
PRNHD parenthood *family*
PRNJ parentage *origin*
PRNJR porringer *bowl*
PRNK paranoiac *fearful*
PRNK perionychia (pl) *fingernail* perionychium
PRNK prank *trick*
PRNKL paranoiacally *fearful*
PRNKM parenchyma *plant tissue*
PRNKM perionychium *fingernail* perionychia
PRNKMDS parenchymatous *plant tissue*
PRNKML parenchymal *plant tissue*
PRNKMTS parenchymatous *plant tissue*
PRNKSDR prankster *tricks*
PRNKSH prankish *tricky*
PRNKSHL prankishly *tricky*
PRNKSHNS prankishness *trickiness*
PRNKSTR prankster *tricks*
PRNKY perionychia (pl) *fingernail* perionychium
PRNKYM perionychium *fingernail* perionychia
PRNL parental (adj) *father and mother* parentally (adv)
PRNL perennial (adj) *continual* perennially (adv)
PRNL perineal *anus*
PRNL peroneal *fibula*
PRNL prunella *fabric*
PRNM paronym *word*

Use letters that best describe the sounds you hear and omit the vowels. Use **S** or **K** instead of **C**: to find circle use **SRKL**. Use **J** to find joy, **JM** to find gem and **G** to find go.

PRNM per annum *per year*
PRNM perineum *anus* perinea
PRNMF paranymph *bridesmaid*
PRNMNL pronominal (adj) *pronoun* pronomially (adv)
PRNMNS praying mantis *insect*
PRNMNTS praying mantis *insect*
PRNMS paronymous *word*
PRNMSH paronomasia *pun*
PRNMZH paronomasia *pun*
PRNN pronoun *word*
PRNN pyronine *dye*
PRNNCSHN pronunciation *speech*
PRNNCYSHN pronunciation *speech*
PRNNFLK pyroninophylic *dye*
PRNNG printing *copier*
PRNNS pronounce *speak* pronounced pronouncing
PRNNSBL pronounceable *clear*
PRNNSMNT pronouncement *declaration*
PRNNSSHN pronunciation *speech*
PRNNST pronounced *decided, easily noticed*
PRNNSYSHN pronunciation *speech*
PRNNTS pronounce *speak* pronounced pronouncing
PRNNTSBL pronounceable *clear*
PRNNTSMNT pronouncement *declaration*
PRNNTST pronounced *decided, easily noticed*
PRNPCHL prenuptial *before a wedding*
PRNPCHWL prenuptial *before a wedding*
PRNPSHL prenuptial *before a wedding*
PRNPSHWL prenuptial *before a wedding*

PRNR perineuria (pl) *nerves* perineurium
PRNR prawner *boat*
PRNR printer *copier*
PRNRLMNT preenrollment *sign up*
PRNRM perineurium *nerves* perineuria
PRNRML paranormal (adj) *supernatural* paranormally (adv)
PRNRMLD paranormality *supernatural*
PRNRMLT paranormality *supernatural*
PRNRY perineuria (pl) *nerves* perineurium
PRNRYM perineurium *nerves* perineuria
PRNS appearance *look*
PRNS apprentice (v) *study* apprenticed apprenticing
PRNS apprentice (n) *student*
PRNS poorness *poverty*
PRNS prance *dance* pranced prancing
PRNS prince *royalty*
PRNS proneness *likely, flat*
PRNS pronounce *speak* pronounced pronouncing
PRNS prurience *lewdness* pruriency
PRNS pureness *spotless, chaste*
PRNSBL pronounceable *clear*
PRNSDM princedom *royalty*
PRNSHN pronation *rotation*
PRNSHP apprenticeship *beginning*
PRNSHS pernicious *deadly*
PRNSHSL perniciously *deadly*
PRNSHSNS perniciousness *deadliness*
PRNSKNSRT prince consort *royalty* princes consort
PRNSL princely *royal* princelier princeliest
PRNSLNG princeling *royalty*

PRNSLNS princeliness *royalty*
PRNSLR princelier *royalty*
PRNSLST princeliest *royalty*
PRNSLYR princelier *royalty*
PRNSLYST princeliest *royalty*
PRNSMNT pronouncement *declaration*
PRNSPL principal *chief*
PRNSPL principally *chiefly*
PRNSPL principle *rule*
PRNSPLD principality *territory* principalities
PRNSPLD principled *code of conduct*
PRNSPLT principality *territory* principalities
PRNSR prancer *dancer*
PRNSS princess *royal* princesses
PRNSSHP apprenticeship *beginning*
PRNST pronounced *decided, easily noticed*
PRNT apparent *obvious*
PRNT operant *effective*
PRNT parent *father, mother*
PRNT print *write, copy*
PRNT printout *computer*
PRNT pronate *rotate* pronated pronating
PRNT pronto *quickly*
PRNT prurient *lewd*
PRNTBL printable *write, copy*
PRNTBLD printability *write, copy*
PRNTBLT printability *write, copy*
PRNTCSHN pronunciation *speech*
PRNTCYSHN pronunciation *speech*
PRNTH perianth *flower*
PRNTHD parenthood *family*
PRNTHDKL parenthetical (adj) *brackets, straying* parenthetically (adv)
PRNTHSS parenthesis *brackets, digression* parentheses

Letters aren't doubled for single sounds: to find alley use **L** not **LL**. Use **Y** and **W** as hard sounds only: to find yellow use **YL**. (Br)=British spelling or usage. * See dictionary.

PRNTHSZ parenthesize *bracket, stray* parenthesized parenthesizing

PRNTHTKL parenthetical (adj) *brackets, straying* parenthetically (adv)

PRNTJ parentage *origin*

PRNTL apparently *obviously*

PRNTL parental (adj) *father and mother* parentally (adv)

PRNTL perinatal (adj) *birth* perinatally (adv)

PRNTL prenatal (adj) *before birth* prenatally (adv)

PRNTN printing *copier*

PRNTNG printing *copier*

PRNTR printer *copier*

PRNTR pronator *muscle*

PRNTRL parenteral (adj) *intestine* parenterally (adv)

PRNTS appearance *look*

PRNTS apprentice *(v) study* apprenticed apprenticing

PRNTS apprentice *(n) student*

PRNTS prance *dance* pranced prancing

PRNTS prince *royalty*

PRNTS pronounce *speak* pronounced pronouncing

PRNTS prurience *lewdness* pruriency

PRNTSBL pronounceable *clear*

PRNTSDM princedom *royalty*

PRNTSHP apprenticeship *beginning*

PRNTSKNSRT prince consort *royalty* princes consort

PRNTSL princely *royal* princelier princeliest

PRNTSLNG princeling *royalty*

PRNTSLNS princeliness *royalty*

PRNTSLR princelier *royalty*

PRNTSLST princeliest *royalty*

PRNTSLYR princelier *royalty*

PRNTSLYST princeliest *royalty*

PRNTSMNT pronouncement *declaration*

PRNTSPL principal *chief*

PRNTSPL principally *chiefly*

PRNTSPL principle *rule*

PRNTSPLD principality *territory* principalities

PRNTSPLD principled *code of conduct*

PRNTSPLT principality *territory* principalities

PRNTSR prancer *dancer*

PRNTSS princess *royal* princesses

PRNTSSHN pronunciation *speech*

PRNTSSHP apprenticeship *beginning*

PRNTST pronounced *decided, easily noticed*

PRNTSYSHN pronunciation *speech*

PRNTT printout *computer*

PRNXDR prankster *tricks*

PRNXTR prankster *tricks*

PRNY paranoia *fear*

PRNY perinea (pl) *anus* perineum

PRNYK paranoiac *fearful*

PRNYKL paranoiacally *fearful*

PRNYL perennial (adj) *continual* perennially (adv)

PRNYL perineal *anus*

PRNYL peroneal *fibula*

PRNYM perineum *anus* perinea

PRNYR perineuria (pl) *nerves* perineurium

PRNYRM perineurium *nerves* perineuria

PRNYRY perineuria (pl) *nerves* perineurium

PRNYRYM perineurium *nerves* perineuria

PRNZ Pyrenees *mountains*

PRP apropos *relevant*

PRP prep *prepare* prepped prepping

PRP prepay *advance money* prepaid prepaying

PRP preppy (or) preppie *college* preppies

PRP prop *(v) lean, support* propped propping

PRP prop *(n) theater, propeller*

PRP pyrope *garnet*

PRPBRD prepuberty *child*

PRPBRT prepuberty *child*

PRPBSNS prepubescence *child*

PRPBSNT prepubescent *child*

PRPBSNTS prepubescence *child*

PRPCHD perpetuity *eternity* perpetuities

PRPCHDR perpetuator *continuer*

PRPCHL perpetual (adj) *continual* perpetually (adv)

PRPCHSHN perpetuation *continuance*

PRPCHT perpetuate *continue* perpetuated perpetuating

PRPCHT perpetuity *eternity* perpetuities

PRPCHTR perpetuator *continuer*

PRPCHWD perpetuity *eternity* perpetuities

PRPCHWDR perpetuator *continuer*

PRPCHWL perpetual (adj) *continual* perpetually (adv)

PRPCHWSHN perpetuation *continuance*

PRPCHWT perpetuate *continue* perpetuated perpetuating

PRPCHWT perpetuity *eternity* perpetuities

PRPCHWTR perpetuator *continuer*

PRPD prepaid *money*

Use letters that best describe the sounds you hear and omit the vowels. Use **S** or **K** instead of **C**: to find circle use **SRKL**. Use **J** to find joy, **JM** to find gem and **G** to find go.

PRPDS peripatus *worm*
PRPGBL propagable *increase*
PRPGDR propagator *increaser*
PRPGDV propagative *increase*
PRPGND propaganda *misinformation*
PRPGNDST propagandist *misinformer*
PRPGNDZ propagandize *misinform* propagandized propagandizing
PRPGSHN propagation *increase*
PRPGT propagate *increase* propagated propagating
PRPGTR propagator *increaser*
PRPGTV propagative *increase*
PRPK priapic *manly*
PRPKJ prepackage *wrap* prepackaged prepackaging
PRPL preppily *college*
PRPL propel *move* propelled propelling
PRPL propyl *chemical*
PRPL purple *color* purpled purpling purpler purplest
PRPL purply *color*
PRPLG paraplegia *legs*
PRPLGY paraplegia *legs*
PRPLHRT Purple Heart *medal*
PRPLHRT purpleheart *wood*
PRPLJ paraplegia *legs*
PRPLJK paraplegic *legs*
PRPLJY paraplegia *legs*
PRPLKS perplex *puzzle*
PRPLKSD perplexity *puzzlement* perplexities
PRPLKST perplexed *puzzled*
PRPLKST perplexity *puzzlement* perplexities
PRPLN propylene *chemical*
PRPLNT propellant *gas*
PRPLR propeller *fan*
PRPLR purpler *color*

PRPLS propolis *wax*
PRPLSH purplish *color*
PRPLSHN propulsion *move forward*
PRPLST purplest *color*
PRPLSV propulsive *move forward*
PRPLX perplex *puzzle*
PRPLXD perplexity *puzzlement* perplexities
PRPLXT perplexed *puzzled*
PRPLXT perplexity *puzzlement* perplexities
PRPMNT prepayment *advance money*
PRPN propane *fuel*
PRPN propound *discuss*
PRPND perpend *ponder*
PRPND propound *discuss*
PRPNDKLR perpendicular *vertical*
PRPNDKLRD perpendicularity *vertical*
PRPNDKLRL perpendicularly *vertical*
PRPNDKLRT perpendicularity *vertical*
PRPNDKYLR perpendicular *vertical*
PRPNDKYLRD perpendicularity *vertical*
PRPNDKYLRL perpendicularly *vertical*
PRPNDKYLRT perpendicularity *vertical*
PRPNDQLR perpendicular *vertical*
PRPNDQLRD perpendicularity *vertical*
PRPNDQLRL perpendicularly *vertical*
PRPNDQLRT perpendicularity *vertical*
PRPNDRNS preponderance *majority*
PRPNDRNT preponderant *dominant*
PRPNDRNTL preponderantly *dominant*
PRPNDRNTS preponderance *majority*
PRPNDRT preponderate

dominate preponderated preponderating
PRPNDRTL preponderately *dominate*
PRPNGKWD propinquity *nearness*
PRPNGKWT propinquity *nearness*
PRPNGQD propinquity *nearness*
PRPNGQT propinquity *nearness*
PRPNKWD propinquity *nearness*
PRPNKWT propinquity *nearness*
PRPNNT proponent *advocate*
PRPNQD propinquity *nearness*
PRPNQT propinquity *nearness*
PRPNS preppiness *college*
PRPNSD propensity *leaning* propensities
PRPNST propensity *leaning* propensities
PRPNT propionate *chemical*
PRPNT proponent *advocate*
PRPNTSD propensity *leaning* propensities
PRPNTST propensity *leaning* propensities
PRPR prepare *get ready* prepared preparing
PRPR proper *correct, (Br) absolute*
PRPR puerperia (pl) *childbirth* puerperium
PRPRBL appropriable *take*
PRPRD property *land* properties
PRPRD propriety *dignity* proprieties
PRPRDD propertied *with land*
PRPRDD purported *assumed*
PRPRDDL purportedly *assumed*
PRPRDL preparedly *get ready*
PRPRDNS preparedness

Letters aren't doubled for single sounds: to find alley use **L** not **LL**. Use **Y** and **W** as hard sounds only: to find yellow use **YL**. (Br)=British spelling or usage. * See dictionary.

get ready

PRPRDR appropriator *taker*

PRPRDR proprietor *owner*

PRPRDRS proprietress *owner (f)* proprietresses

PRPRDRSHP proprietorship *ownership*

PRPRDV appropriative *taken or set aside*

PRPRDV preoperative *surgery*

PRPRDV preparative *readiness*

PRPRFSHNL paraprofessional *aide*

PRPRL properly *correctly, throughly, (Br) utterly*

PRPRM puerperium *childbirth* puerperia

PRPRNLL propranolol *beta blocker*

PRPRNS properness *correctness*

PRPRNT preprint *paper*

PRPRR preparer *get ready*

PRPRSHN appropriation *amount set aside*

PRPRSHN preparation *readiness*

PRPRSHN proportion *balance, share*

PRPRSHNL proportional (adj) *balance, share* proportionally (adv)

PRPRSHNLD proportionality *balance, share*

PRPRSHNLT proportionality *balance, share*

PRPRSHNT proportionate *balance, share* proportionated proportionating

PRPRT appropriate *(v) take* appropriated appropriating

PRPRT appropriate *(adj) suitable*

PRPRT property *land* properties

PRPRT propriety *dignity* proprieties

PRPRT purport *(n) gist (v) claim*

PRPRTD propertied *with land*

PRPRTD purported *assumed*

PRPRTDL purportedly *assumed*

PRPRTL appropriately *suitably*

PRPRTNS appropriateness *suitableness*

PRPRTR appropriator *taker*

PRPRTR preparatory *readiness*

PRPRTR proprietary *ownership* proprietaries

PRPRTR proprietor *owner*

PRPRTRL proprietorial *ownership*

PRPRTRS proprietress *owner (f)* proprietresses

PRPRTRSHP proprietorship *ownership*

PRPRTRYL proprietorial *ownership*

PRPRTV appropriative *taken or set aside*

PRPRTV preoperative *surgery*

PRPRTV preparative *readiness*

PRPRV preapprove *okay* preapproved preapproving

PRPRY puerperia (pl) *childbirth* puerperium

PRPRYBL appropriable *take*

PRPRYD propriety *dignity* proprieties

PRPRYDR appropriator *taker*

PRPRYDR proprietor *owner*

PRPRYDRS proprietress *owner (f)* proprietresses

PRPRYDRSHP proprietorship *ownership*

PRPRYDV appropriative *taken or set aside*

PRPRYM puerperium *childbirth* puerperia

PRPRYSHN appropriation *amount set aside*

PRPRYT appropriate *(v)* take appropriated appropriating

PRPRYT appropriate *(adj) suitable*

PRPRYT propriety *dignity* proprieties

PRPRYTL appropriately *suitably*

PRPRYTNS appropriateness *suitableness*

PRPRYTR appropriator *taker*

PRPRYTR proprietary *ownership* proprietaries

PRPRYTR proprietor *owner*

PRPRYTRL proprietorial *ownership*

PRPRYTRS proprietress *owner (f)* proprietresses

PRPRYTRSHP proprietorship *ownership*

PRPRYTRYL proprietorial *ownership*

PRPRYTV appropriative *taken or set aside*

PRPS pari passu *pace*

PRPS porpoise *animal*

PRPS prepuce *skin*

PRPS purpose *intention*

PRPSDRS preposterous *absurd*

PRPSDRSL preposterously *absurd*

PRPSDRSNS preposterousness *absurdity*

PRPSFL purposeful (adj) *intentional* purposefully (adv)

PRPSFLNS purposefulness *intentional*

PRPSHDR propitiator *calmer*

PRPSHS propitious *favorable*

PRPSHSHN propitiation *calmness*

PRPSHSL propitiously *favorable*

PRPSHSNS propitiousness *favor*

PRPSHT propitiate *calm*

---

propitiated propitiating
PRPSHTR propitiator *calmer*
PRPSHTR propitiatory
calming
PRPSHYDR propitiator
calmer
PRPSHYSHN propitiation
calmness
PRPSHYT propitiate *calm*
propitiated propitiating
PRPSHYTR propitiator
calmer
PRPSHYTR propitiatory
calming
PRPSL purposely
intentionally
PRPSLS purposeless *no*
intent
PRPSLSL purposelessly *no*
intent
PRPSLSNS
purposelessness *no*
intent
PRPSTRS preposterous
absurd
PRPSTRSL preposterously
absurd
PRPSTRSNS
preposterousness
absurdity
PRPSV purposive
intentional
PRPSVL purposively
intentional
PRPSVNS purposiveness
intentional
PRPT parapet *wall*
PRPT peripateia *plot change*
PRPTD perpetuity *eternity*
perpetuities
PRPTDK peripatetic
wandering
PRPTDKL peripatetically
wandering
PRPTDR perpetuator
continuer
PRPTL perpetual (adj)
continual perpetually
(adv)
PRPTRDR perpetrator
committer
PRPTRSHN perpetration

committal
PRPTRT perpetrate *commit*
perpetrated perpetrating
PRPTRTR perpetrator
committer
PRPTS peripatus *worm*
PRPTSHN perpetuation
continuance
PRPTT perpetuate *continue*
perpetuated perpetuating
PRPTT perpetuity *eternity*
perpetuities
PRPTTK peripatetic
wandering
PRPTTKL peripatetically
wandering
PRPTTR perpetuator
continuer
PRPTWD perpetuity *eternity*
perpetuities
PRPTWDR perpetuator
continuer
PRPTWL perpetual (adj)
continual perpetually
(adv)
PRPTWSHN perpetuation
continuance
PRPTWT perpetuate
continue perpetuated
perpetuating
PRPTWT perpetuity *eternity*
perpetuities
PRPTWTR perpetuator
continuer
PRPTY peripateia *plot*
change
PRPTYD perpetuity *eternity*
perpetuities
PRPTYT perpetuity *eternity*
perpetuities
PRPTYWD perpetuity
eternity perpetuities
PRPTYWT perpetuity
eternity perpetuities
PRPYBRD prepuberty *child*
PRPYBRT prepuberty *child*
PRPYBSNS prepubescence
child
PRPYBSNT prepubescent
child
PRPYBSNTS
prepubescence *child*

PRPYNT propionate
chemical
PRPYS prepuce *skin*
PRPZ propose *offer*
proposed proposing
PRPZL proposal *offer*
PRPZR proposer *offerer*
PRPZS prepossess
influence
PRPZSHN preposition
relational word
PRPZSHN prepossession
prejudice
PRPZSHN proposition *plan*
PRPZSHNL prepositional
(adj) *relational word*
prepositionally (adv)
PRPZSHNL propositional
plan
PRPZSN prepossessing
influence
PRPZSNG prepossessing
influence
PRQ parkway *road*
PRQL opercula (pl) *lid*
operculum
PRQL parochial (adj) *church-*
related parochially (adv)
PRQLDD operculated (or)
operculate *lidded*
PRQLM operculum *lid*
opercula
PRQLR opercular *lid*
PRQLT operculate (or)
operculated *lidded*
PRQLTD operculated (or)
operculate *lidded*
PRQLZM parochialism
church-related
PRQP preoccupy *concern*
preoccupied
preoccupying
preoccupies
PRQPD preoccupied
concerned
PRQPN porcupine *animal*
PRQPNC preoccupancy
possession
PRQPNS preoccupancy
possession
PRQPNTC preoccupancy
possession

PRQPNTS preoccupancy *possession*

PRQPSHN preoccupation *concern*

PRQR procure *obtain* procured procuring

PRQRBL procurable *obtainable*

PRQRDR procurator *obtainer*

PRQRMNT procurement *obtaining*

PRQRR procurer *obtainer*

PRQRSHN procuration *obtaining*

PRQRTR procurator *obtainer*

PRQT paraquat *herbicide*

PRQZT perquisite *benefit*

PRR a priori *reasoning*

PRR apriori *deduce*

PRR parure *set*

PRR pourer *container*

PRR prairie *land*

PRR prayer *request*

PRR prier *nosy one*

PRR prior *previous*

PRR priory *monastery* priories

PRR uproar *noise*

PRRD priority *preference* priorities

PRRD pro rata *share*

PRRDG prairie dog *rodent*

PRRDN preordain *decree*

PRRDNMNT preordainment *decree*

PRRDNSHN preordination *decree*

PRRFL prayerful (adj) *devout* prayerfully (adv)

PRRFLNS prayerfulness *devotion*

PRRG prorogue *suspend* prorogued proroguing

PRRGDV prerogative *option*

PRRGSHN prorogation *suspension*

PRRGTV prerogative *option*

PRRJRT pyrargyrite *mineral*

PRRKRD prerecord *tape*

PRRKWZT prerequisite *necessity*

PRRNJ prearrange *set up* prearranged prearranging

PRRNJMNT prearrangement *set up*

PRRNS prurience *lewdness* pruriency

PRRNT prurient *lewd*

PRRNTS prurience *lewdness* pruriency

PRRQZT prerequisite *necessity*

PRRS prioress *nun*

PRRS uproarious *loud*

PRRSHN peroration *speech*

PRRSHN proration *division*

PRRSHP priorship *religion*

PRRT perorate *speech* perorated perorating

PRRT priority *preference* priorities

PRRT pro rata *share*

PRRT prorate *divide* prorated prorating

PRRTZ prioritize *rate* prioritized prioritizing

PRRYNS prurience *lewdness* pruriency

PRRYNT prurient *lewd*

PRRYNTS prurience *lewdness* pruriency

PRRYS uproarious *loud*

PRS aperçu *outline* aperçus

PRS operose *tiresome*

PRS oppress *burden*

PRS Paris *city*

PRS parous *with offspring*

PRS parse *grammar* parsed parsing

PRS peeress *equal rank (f)*

PRS per se *exactly*

PRS perse *blue*

PRS pierce *stab* pierced piercing

PRS piracy *robbery* piracies

PRS porous *with holes*

PRS précis *summary* (pl) précis

PRS press (n) *news* (v) *push* presses

PRS price *cost* priced pricing

PRS pricey *expensive*

PRS prissy *prim* prissier prissiest

PRS prowess *ability*

PRS purse (v) *pucker* pursed pursing

PRS purse (n) *wallet*

PRS pursue *chase* pursued pursuing

PRS pursy *puckered* pursier pursiest

PRSBDR presbyter *church*

PRSBKS press box *reporters* press boxes

PRSBP presbyopia *vision*

PRSBPK presbyopic *vision*

PRSBPY presbyopia *vision*

PRSBRD pressboard *ironing*

PRSBTR presbyter *church*

PRSBTR presbytery *church* presbyteries

PRSBTRN Presbyterian *church*

PRSBTRYN Presbyterian *church*

PRSBX press box *reporters* press boxes

PRSBYP presbyopia *vision*

PRSBYPK presbyopic *vision*

PRSBYPY presbyopia *vision*

PRSD parricide *kill a parent*

PRSD porosity *with holes* porosities

PRSD precede *come before* preceded preceding

PRSD presidio *fort* presidios

PRSD proceed *advance*

PRSD prosody *verse* prosodies

PRSDK parasitic *using*

PRSDK puristic *traditional*

PRSDKL parasitically *using*

PRSDKL puristically *traditional*

PRSDL parricidal *kill a parent*

PRSDM presidium *committee* presidia (or) presidiums

PRSDN preceding *come before*

Use letters that best describe the sounds you hear and omit the vowels. Use **S** or **K** instead of **C**: to find circle use **SRKL**. Use **J** to find joy, **JM** to find gem and **G** to find go.

PRSDN pristine *pure*
PRSDNG preceding *come before*
PRSDNGS proceedings *events*
PRSDNGZ proceedings *events*
PRSDNS precedence *come before*
PRSDNT precedent *come before*
PRSDNTS precedence *come before*
PRSDR procedure *way of doing*
PRSDRL procedural (adj) *orderly* procedurally (adv)
PRSDRS proestrus *menstruation*
PRSDS priestess *clergy (f)* priestesses
PRSDS proceeds *money*
PRSDTSHN prostitution *debasement*
PRSDTT prostitute *whore* prostituted prostituting
PRSDTYSHN prostitution *debasement*
PRSDTYT prostitute *whore* prostituted prostituting
PRSDY presidio *fort* presidios
PRSDYM presidium *committee* presidia (or) presidiums
PRSDYR procedure *way of doing*
PRSDYRL procedural (adj) *orderly* procedurally (adv)
PRSDZ proceeds *money*
PRSDZM parasitism *using*
PRSFKSN price-fixing *fraud*
PRSFKSNG price-fixing *fraud*
PRSFLJ persiflage *talk*
PRSFLSH persiflage *talk*
PRSFLZH persiflage *talk*
PRSFN Persephone *myth*
PRSFXN price-fixing *fraud*
PRSFXNG price-fixing *fraud*
PRSGNF presignify *foretell* presignified presignifying

presignifies
PRSH parish *church district* parishes
PRSH perish *die*
PRSH poorish *poverty*
PRSH Portia *heroine*
PRSHBL appreciable (adj) *noticeable* appreciably (adv)
PRSHBL perishable *decay*
PRSHBLD perishability *decay*
PRSHBLT perishability *decay*
PRSHD prosciutto *meat* prosciutti
PRSHDR appreciator *value*
PRSHDST parachutist *jumper*
PRSHDV appreciative *value*
PRSHK piroshki (or) pirozhki *food*
PRSHL partial (adj) *piece, biased* partially (adv)
PRSHLD partiality *bias* partialities
PRSHLT partiality *bias* partialities
PRSHM protium *atom*
PRSHN apparition *ghost*
PRSHN apportion *divide*
PRSHN operation *function, surgery*
PRSHN oppression *burden*
PRSHN Parisian *of Paris*
PRSHN Persian *of Persia*
PRSHN portion *share*
PRSHNBL apportionable *able to be divided*
PRSHNGF Persian Gulf *body of water*
PRSHNGLF Persian Gulf *body of water*
PRSHNL apparitional *ghost*
PRSHNL operational (adj) *working* operationally (adv)
PRSHNLS portionless *no share*
PRSHNMNT apportionment *divided part*
PRSHNR parishioner *church member*

PRSHNS prescience *foresight*
PRSHNTS prescience *foresight*
PRSHPT pear-shaped *oval*
PRSHR pressure *force* pressured pressuring
PRSHRLS pressureless *no force*
PRSHRNGK preshrink *fabric* preshrank preshrunk
PRSHRNK preshrink *fabric* preshrank preshrunk
PRSHRZ pressurize *add force* pressurized pressurizing (Br) pressurise
PRSHRZR pressurizer *add force* (Br) pressuriser
PRSHS precious *(adj) valuable, refined (adv) very*
PRSHSD preciosity *refinement* preciosities
PRSHSHN appreciation *value*
PRSHSL preciously *refined*
PRSHSNS preciousness *refinement*
PRSHST preciosity *refinement* preciosities
PRSHT appreciate *value* appreciated appreciating
PRSHT parachute *airplane* parachuted parachuting
PRSHT prosciutto *meat* prosciutti
PRSHTR appreciator *value*
PRSHTST parachutist *jumper*
PRSHTV appreciative *value*
PRSHYDR appreciator *value*
PRSHYDV appreciative *value*
PRSHYLD partiality *bias* partialities
PRSHYLT partiality *bias* partialities
PRSHYM protium *atom*
PRSHYNS prescience *foresight*
PRSHYNTS prescience

Letters aren't doubled for single sounds: to find alley use **L** not **LL**. Use **Y** and **W** as hard sounds only: to find yellow use **YL**. (Br)=British spelling or usage. * See dictionary.

foresight
PRSHYSD preciosity
refinement preciosities
PRSHYSHN appreciation
value
PRSHYST preciosity
refinement preciosities
PRSHYT appreciate *value*
appreciated appreciating
PRSHYTR appreciator *value*
PRSHYTV appreciative
value
PRSJ presage *predict*
presaged presaging
PRSJNT press agent *news*
PRSJR procedure *way of*
doing
PRSJRL procedural (adj)
orderly procedurally (adv)
PRSK après-ski *social*
PRSK parsec *3.26 light years*
PRSK presoak *rinse*
PRSK prosaic *prose, ordinary*
PRSKDBL prosecutable
legal suit
PRSKDNG price-cutting *sale*
PRSKDR persecutor *abuser*
PRSKDR price-cutter *sale*
PRSKDR prosecutor *lawyer*
PRSKL pericycle *plants*
PRSKL preschool
kindergarden
PRSKL prosaically *prose,*
ordinary
PRSKLG parapsychology
extra sensory perception
PRSKLJ parapsychology
extra sensory perception
PRSKLJKL
parapsychological *extra*
sensory perception
PRSKLJST
parapsychologist *extra*
sensory perception
PRSKLK pericyclic *plants*
PRSKLR preschooler
kindergarden
PRSKP periscope *lens*
PRSKPK periscopic *lens*
PRSKRB prescribe *order*
prescribed prescribing
PRSKRB proscribe *forbid*

proscribed proscribing
PRSKRPDV prescriptive
usage
PRSKRPDV proscriptive
forbidden
PRSKRPSHN prescription
title, medicine
PRSKRPSHN proscription
forbid
PRSKRPTV prescriptive
usage
PRSKRPTV proscriptive
forbidden
PRSKSHN persecution
abuse
PRSKSHN prosecution *law*
PRSKT persecute *abuse*
persecuted persecuting
PRSKT persecutee *one*
abused
PRSKT press kit *promotions*
PRSKT prosecute *legal suit*
prosecuted prosecuting
PRSKTBL prosecutable
legal suit
PRSKTN price-cutting *sale*
PRSKTNG price-cutting *sale*
PRSKTR persecutor *abuser*
PRSKTR price-cutter *sale*
PRSKTR prosecutor *lawyer*
PRSKYDBL prosecutable
legal suit
PRSKYDR persecutor
abuser
PRSKYDR prosecutor
lawyer
PRSKYSHN persecution
abuse
PRSKYSHN prosecution
law
PRSKYT persecute *abuse*
persecuted persecuting
PRSKYT persecutee *one*
abused
PRSKYT prosecute *legal*
suit prosecuted
prosecuting
PRSKYTBL prosecutable
legal suit
PRSKYTR persecutor
abuser
PRSKYTR prosecutor

lawyer
PRSL operosely *tiresome*
PRSL parasol *umbrella*
PRSL parcel *portion, package*
parceled (or) parcelled
parceling (or) parcelling
PRSL parsley *herb*
PRSL porously *with holes*
PRSL presell *market* presold
preselling
PRSL priestly *clergy*
PRSL prissily *prim*
PRSLD parsleyed *herb*
PRSLKSHN preselection
choice
PRSLKT preselect *choose*
PRSLN parasailing *sport*
PRSLN porcelain *ceramic*
PRSLN purslane *herb*
PRSLNG parasailing *sport*
PRSLNLZ porcelainize *make*
glassy porcelainized
porcelainizing
PRSLNS porcelaneous (or)
porcellaneous *glassy*
PRSLNS priestliness *clergy*
PRSLNYS porcelaneous (or)
porcellaneous *glassy*
PRSLPST parcel post *mail*
PRSLS priceless *valuable*
PRSLT proselyte *recruit*
PRSLTZ proselytize *recruit*
proselytized proselytizing
(Br) proselytise
PRSLTZM proselytism
recruiting
PRSLTZR proselytizer
recruiter
(Br) proselytiser
PRSLTZSHN proselytization
recruiting
(Br) proselytisation
PRSMBLD preassembled
constructed
PRSMN parsimony *thrift*
PRSMN persimmon *fruit*
PRSMN pressman *printing*
pressmen
PRSMNS parsimonious
thrifty
PRSMNSL parsimoniously
thrifty

Use letters that best describe the sounds you hear and omit the vowels. Use **S** or **K** instead of **C**: to find circle use **SRKL**. Use **J** to find joy, **JM** to find gem and **G** to find go.

PRSMNYS parsimonious *thrifty*
PRSMNYSL parsimoniously *thrifty*
PRSMPTHDK parasympathetic *nervous system*
PRSMPTHTK parasympathetic *nervous system*
PRSMRK pressmark *(Br) book*
PRSN parson *clergy*
PRSN person *human*
PRSN persona *character* personae (or) personas
PRSN piercing *sharp*
PRSN porcine *swine*
PRSN preassign *denote*
PRSN pressing *important*
PRSN purse seine *net*
PRSNBL personable *attractive*
PRSNBLNS personableness *attractiveness*
PRSNDR personator *representer*
PRSNF personify *embody* personified personifying personifies
PRSNFKSHN personification *characterization*
PRSNFR personifier *characterization*
PRSNFYR personifier *characterization*
PRSNG piercing *sharp*
PRSNG pressing *important*
PRSNGK precinct *territory*
PRSNGKT precinct *territory*
PRSNGRD persona grata *welcome one*
PRSNGRT persona grata *welcome one*
PRSNJ parsonage *house*
PRSNJ percentage *proportion*
PRSNJ personage *human*
PRSNK precinct *territory*
PRSNKD persnickety *finicky*

PRSNKDNS persnicketiness *finicky*
PRSNKT persnickety *finicky*
PRSNKT precinct *territory*
PRSNKTNS persnicketiness *finicky*
PRSNL personal *(n) ad, foul*
PRSNL personal (adj) *private* personally (adv)
PRSNL personnel *people*
PRSNLD personality *disposition* personalities
PRSNLT personality *disposition* personalities
PRSNLZ personalize *individualize* personalized personalizing (Br) personalise
PRSNLZSHN personalization *individualize* (Br) personalisation
PRSNM proscenium *stage*
PRSNNNGRD persona non grata *unwelcome one*
PRSNNNGRT persona non grata *unwelcome one*
PRSNP parsnip *vegetable*
PRSNR parcenary *heir*
PRSNR parcener *heir*
PRSNS operoseness *tiresome*
PRSNS porousness *with holes*
PRSNS prescience *foresight*
PRSNS prissiness *prim*
PRSNS pursuance *following*
PRSNSHN personation *represent*
PRSNSR precensor *suppress*
PRSNT percent *proportion*
PRSNT personate *represent* personated personating
PRSNT pursuant *following*
PRSNTHDK parasynthetic *words*
PRSNTHSS parasynthesis *words*
PRSNTHTK parasynthetic *words*
PRSNTJ percentage *proportion*

PRSNTL percentile *proportion*
PRSNTMNT presentiment *hunch*
PRSNTR personator *representer*
PRSNTS prescience *foresight*
PRSNTS pursuance *following*
PRSNTSR precensor *suppress*
PRSNYM proscenium *stage*
PRSP praecipe *legal writ*
PRSP precept *rule*
PRSPCHL perceptual (adj) *sensory* perceptually (adv)
PRSPCHWL perceptual (adj) *sensory* perceptually (adv)
PRSPDBL perceptible (adj) *sensed* perceptibly (adv)
PRSPDBL precipitable *condense*
PRSPDNC precipitancy *haste*
PRSPDNS precipitance *haste*
PRSPDNS precipitancy *haste*
PRSPDNT precipitant *condenser*
PRSPDNTC precipitancy *haste*
PRSPDNTL precipitantly *condenser*
PRSPDNTNS precipitantness *condenser*
PRSPDNTS precipitance *haste*
PRSPDNTS precipitancy *haste*
PRSPDR preceptor *teacher*
PRSPDS precipitous *steep*
PRSPDSL precipitously *steep*
PRSPDSNS precipitousness *steep*
PRSPDV apperceptive *understand*
PRSPDV perceptive *aware*
PRSPDVNS perceptiveness

Letters aren't doubled for single sounds: to find alley use **L** not **LL**. Use **Y** and **W** as hard sounds only: to find yellow use **YL**. (Br)=British spelling or usage. * See dictionary.

awareness
PRSPK prospect *(v)* explore
(n) outlook
PRSPKD perspicuity
clearness
PRSPKDR prospector
explorer
PRSPKDS prospectus
description prospectuses
PRSPKDV perspective *view*
PRSPKDV prospective
expected
PRSPKS perspicuous *clear*
PRSPKSD perspicacity
shrewdness
PRSPKSHS perspicacious
shrewd
PRSPKSHSNS
perspicaciousness
shrewdness
PRSPKST perspicacity
shrewdness
PRSPKT perspicuity
clearness
PRSPKT prospect *(v)*
explore *(n)* outlook
PRSPKTR prospector
explorer
PRSPKTS prospectus
description prospectuses
PRSPKTV perspective *view*
PRSPKTV prospective
expected
PRSPKWD perspicuity
clearness
PRSPKWS perspicuous
clear
PRSPKWT perspicuity
clearness
PRSPKYD perspicuity
clearness
PRSPKYS perspicuous *clear*
PRSPKYT perspicuity
clearness
PRSPKYWD perspicuity
clearness
PRSPKYWS perspicuous
clear
PRSPKYWT perspicuity
clearness
PRSPNT percipient *observer*
PRSPNTS percipience

awareness
PRSPQD perspicuity
clearness
PRSPQS perspicuous *clear*
PRSPQT perspicuity
clearness
PRSPQWD perspicuity
clearness
PRSPQWS perspicuous
clear
PRSPQWT perspicuity
clearness
PRSPR perspire *sweat*
perspired perspiring
PRSPR prosper *live well*
PRSPRD prosperity *success*
PRSPRS prosperous
successful
PRSPRSHN perspiration
sweat
PRSPRSL prosperously
success
PRSPRSNS
prosperousness *success*
PRSPRT prosperity *success*
PRSPRTR perspiratory
sweat
PRSPS precipice *cliff*
PRSPS presuppose *guess*
presupposed
presupposing
PRSPSHL perceptual (adj)
sensory perceptually (adv)
PRSPSHN apperception
understand
PRSPSHN perception *view*
PRSPSHWL perceptual
(adj) *sensory* perceptually
(adv)
PRSPT percept *senses*
PRSPT precept *rule*
PRSPTBL perceptible (adj)
sensed perceptibly (adv)
PRSPTBL precipitable
condense
PRSPTDR precipitator
condense, hasten
PRSPTDV precipitative
condense, hasten
PRSPTL perceptual (adj)
sensory perceptually (adv)
PRSPTNC precipitancy

haste
PRSPTNS precipitance
haste
PRSPTNS precipitancy
haste
PRSPTNT precipitant
condenser
PRSPTNTC precipitancy
haste
PRSPTNTL precipitantly
condenser
PRSPTNTNS
precipitantness *condenser*
PRSPTNTS precipitance
haste
PRSPTNTS precipitancy
haste
PRSPTR preceptor *teacher*
PRSPTS precipitous *steep*
PRSPTSHN precipitation
haste, weather
PRSPTSL precipitously
steep
PRSPTSNS precipitousness
steep
PRSPTT precipitate
condense, hasten
precipitated precipitating
PRSPTTR precipitator
condense, hasten
PRSPTTV precipitative
condense, hasten
PRSPTV apperceptive
understand
PRSPTV perceptive *aware*
PRSPTVNS perceptiveness
awareness
PRSPTWL perceptual (adj)
sensory perceptually (adv)
PRSPYNT percipient
observer
PRSPYNTS percipience
awareness
PRSPYR perspire *sweat*
perspired perspiring
PRSPZ presuppose *guess*
presupposed
presupposing
PRSPZSHN presupposition
guess
PRSQDBL prosecutable
legal suit

Use letters that best describe the sounds you hear and omit the vowels. Use **S** or **K** instead of **C**: to find circle use **SRKL**. Use **J** to find joy, **JM** to find gem and **G** to find go.

PRSQDR persecutor *abuser*
PRSQDR prosecutor *lawyer*
PRSQSHN persecution *abuse*
PRSQSHN prosecution *law*
PRSQT persecute *abuse* persecuted persecuting
PRSQT persecutee *one abused*
PRSQT prosecute *legal suit* prosecuted prosecuting
PRSQTBL prosecutable *legal suit*
PRSQTR persecutor *abuser*
PRSQTR prosecutor *lawyer*
PRSR oppressor *bully*
PRSR parser *computers*
PRSR presser *pusher*
PRSR pressor *blood*
PRSR prissier *prim*
PRSR purser *money*
PRSR pursier *puckered*
PRSR pursuer *chaser*
PRSRM pressroom *printing*
PRSRN pressrun *production*
PRSRPD prosauropod *dinosaur*
PRSRT presort *divide up*
PRSRVR persevere *persist* persevered persevering
PRSRVRNS perseverance *persistence*
PRSRVRNTS perseverance *persistence*
PRSS paresis *paralysis* pareses
PRSS precise *exact*
PRSS process (v) *prepare, prosecute* (n) *procedure* (adj) *treated* processes
PRSS pyrosis *heartburn*
PRSSBL processible (or) processable *prepare, prosecute*
PRSSBLD processibility (or) processability *prepare, prosecute*
PRSSBLT processibility (or) processability *prepare, prosecute*
PRSSDNC persistency *determination*

PRSSDNS persistence *determination*
PRSSDNS persistency *determination*
PRSSDNT persistent *determined*
PRSSDNTC persistency *determination*
PRSSDNTS persistence *determination*
PRSSDNTS persistency *determination*
PRSSHN precession *going before*
PRSSHN precisian *moralist*
PRSSHN precision *exactness*
PRSSHN procession *parade*
PRSSHNL precessional *going before*
PRSSHNL processional *parade*
PRSSL precisely *exact*
PRSSNS preciseness *exact*
PRSSR processor *preparer, computer*
PRSST persist *continue*
PRSST prissiest *prim*
PRSST prosaist *prose, ordinary*
PRSST pursiest *puckered*
PRSSTNC persistency *determination*
PRSSTNS persistence *determination*
PRSSTNS persistency *determination*
PRSSTNT persistent *determined*
PRSSTNTC persistency *determination*
PRSSTNTS persistence *determination*
PRSSTNTS persistency *determination*
PRST apiarist *beekeeper*
PRST parasite *user*
PRST periostea (pl) *bone* periosteum
PRST pierced *with holes*
PRST porosity *with holes* porosities
PRST preset *set beforehand*

PRST presto *magic*
PRST priced *cost*
PRST priest *clergy*
PRST Proust *writer*
PRST purist *traditionalist*
PRST pursuit *work, chase*
PRSTBLSH preestablish *creation*
PRSTD priesthood *clergy*
PRSTDJTDR prestidigitator *magician*
PRSTDJTSHN prestidigitation *magic*
PRSTDJTTR prestidigitator *magician*
PRSTDK prostatic *gland*
PRSTG price tag *cost*
PRSTGLNDN prostaglandin *fatty acid*
PRSTHCZ prostheses (pl) *device* prosthesis
PRSTHD priesthood *clergy*
PRSTHDK prosthetic *device, protein*
PRSTHDKS prosthetics *device*
PRSTHDNKS prosthodontics *teeth*
PRSTHDNST prosthodontist *teeth*
PRSTHDNTKS prosthodontics *teeth*
PRSTHDNTST prosthodontist *teeth*
PRSTHDNTX prosthodontics *teeth*
PRSTHDNX prosthodontics *teeth*
PRSTHDX prosthetics *device*
PRSTHSH paresthesia *tingling*
PRSTHSS prosthesis *device* prostheses
PRSTHSZ prostheses (pl) *device* prosthesis
PRSTHTK prosthetic *device, protein*
PRSTHTKS prosthetics *device*
PRSTHTST prosthetist *designer*

Letters aren't doubled for single sounds: to find alley use **L** not **LL**. Use **Y** and **W** as hard sounds only: to find yellow use **YL**. (Br)=British spelling or usage. * See dictionary.

PRSTHTX prosthetics *device*
PRSTHZH paresthesia *tingling*
PRSTJ prestige *influence*
PRSTJS prestigious *influencial*
PRSTJSL prestigiously *influencial*
PRSTJSNS prestigiousness *influence*
PRSTK parasitic *using*
PRSTK puristic *traditional*
PRSTKL parasitically *using*
PRSTKL puristically *traditional*
PRSTL parricidal *kill a parent*
PRSTL periosteal *bone*
PRSTL peristyle *pillar*
PRSTL priestly *clergy*
PRSTLDK peristaltic *contraction*
PRSTLG parasitology *science*
PRSTLJ parasitology *science*
PRSTLNS priestliness *clergy*
PRSTLSS peristalsis *contraction* peristalses
PRSTLTK peristaltic *contraction*
PRSTM periosteum *bone* periostea
PRSTM peristome *mouth*
PRSTN pristine *pure*
PRSTRK perestroika *reform*
PRSTRS prestress *add tension*
PRSTRS proestrus *menstruation*
PRSTRSHN prostration *collapse*
PRSTRT prostate *gland*
PRSTRT prostrate *lie flat* prostrated prostrating
PRSTS priestess *clergy (f)* priestesses
PRSTSH prestige *influence*
PRSTSM prestissimo *faster*
PRSTSS parasitosis *disease* parasitoses
PRSTT prostate *gland*
PRSTTDR prostitutor *whore*

PRSTTDS prostatitis *inflammation*
PRSTTK prostatic *gland*
PRSTTSHN prostitution *debasement*
PRSTTT prostitute *whore* prostituted prostituting
PRSTTTR prostitutor *whore*
PRSTTTS prostatitis *inflammation*
PRSTTYSHN prostitution *debasement*
PRSTTYT prostitute *whore* prostituted prostituting
PRSTY periostea (pl) *bone* periosteum
PRSTYL periosteal *bone*
PRSTYM periosteum *bone* periostea
PRSTZH prestige *influence*
PRSTZM parasitism *using*
PRSV apperceive *understand* apperceived apperceiving
PRSV appraisive *estimate*
PRSV oppressive *harsh*
PRSV perceive *notice* perceived perceiving
PRSVBL perceivable (adj) *noticed* perceivably (adv)
PRSVL oppressively *harshly*
PRSVNS oppressiveness *harshness*
PRSVNT pursuivant *follower*
PRSVR perceiver *notice*
PRSVR persevere *persist* persevered persevering
PRSVRNS perseverance *persistence*
PRSVRNTS perseverance *persistence*
PRSWD persuade *move, urge* persuaded persuading
PRSWDBL persuadable *move, urge*
PRSWDR persuader *move, urge*
PRSWNS pursuance *following*
PRSWNT pursuant *following*
PRSWNTS pursuance

following
PRSWR pursuer *chaser*
PRSWRK presswork *printing*
PRSWSBL persuasible *move, urge*
PRSWSBLD persuasibility *move, urge*
PRSWSBLT persuasibility *move, urge*
PRSWSHN persuasion *move, urge*
PRSWSV persuasive *move, urge*
PRSWZBL persuasible *move, urge*
PRSWZBLD persuasibility *move, urge*
PRSWZBLT persuasibility *move, urge*
PRSWZHN persuasion *move, urge*
PRSWZV persuasive *move, urge*
PRSY pursue *chase* pursued pursuing
PRSYK prosaic *prose, ordinary*
PRSYKL prosaically *prose, ordinary*
PRSYNS prescience *foresight*
PRSYNTS prescience *foresight*
PRSYR prissier *prim*
PRSYR pursier *puckered*
PRSYR pursuer *chaser*
PRSYST prissiest *prim*
PRSYST prosaist *prose, ordinary*
PRSYST pursiest *puckered*
PRSYT pursuit *work, chase*
PRSYWR pursuer *chaser*
PRSYZM prosaism *prose, ordinary*
PRSZ pareses (pl) *paralysis* paresis
PRSZ précis (pl) *summaries* précis
PRSZHN precisian *moralist*
PRSZHN precision *exactness*
PRSZM prosaism *prose,*

Use letters that best describe the sounds you hear and omit the vowels. Use **S** or **K** instead of **C**: to find circle use **SRKL**. Use **J** to find joy, **JM** to find gem and **G** to find go.

ordinary
PRT apart *separate*
PRT aport *left side*
PRT op art *artwork*
PRT operate *function,*
surgery operated
operating
PRT operetta *music*
PRT parity *equality* parities
PRT parrot *bird, repeat*
PRT part *(n) portion, member*
*(v) divide, die, separate**
PRT party *(v) revel* partied
partying parties
PRT party *(n) group, festival*
parties
PRT pert *lively*
PRT pirate *(v) steal* pirated
pirating
PRT pirate *(n) thief*
PRT pirouette *turn*
pirouetted pirouetting
PRT port *wine, pier, left*
PRT prate *talk* prated
prating
PRT pretty *(adj) beauty*
prettier prettiest
PRT pretty *(v) make attractive*
prettied prettying pretties
PRT pretty *(adv) somewhat*
PRT pretty *(n) lingerie*
pretties
PRT protea *flower*
PRT purity *spotless*
PRT pyrite *mineral*
PRT upright *vertical*
PRT uproot *dig up*
PRTBL partible *divide*
PRTBL portable *(adj) move*
about portably *(adv)*
PRTBLD portability *move*
about
PRTBLT portability *move*
about
PRTBRNS protuberance
projection
PRTBRNTS protuberance
projection
PRTCHK apparatchik *party*
member
PRTD apartheid *racial*
segregation

PRTD parotid *gland*
PRTDV partitive *division*
PRTF aperitif *liqueur*
PRTF prettify *beautify*
prettified prettifying
prettifies
PRTFD paratyphoid *fever*
PRTFL portfolio *folder*
portfolios
PRTFL pratfall *mishap*
PRTFLM protophloem *cells*
PRTFLWM protophloem
cells
PRTFLY portfolio *folder*
portfolios
PRTFRM apart from
separated
PRTGL Portugal *country*
PRTGNST protagonist
leader
PRTGZ Portuguese *of*
Portugal
PRTHC perithecia (pl)
fungus perithecium
PRTHCM perithecium
fungus perithecia
PRTHCY perithecia (pl)
fungus perithecium
PRTHCYM perithecium
fungus perithecia
PRTHD apartheid *racial*
segregation
PRTHL porthole *window*
PRTHNJNDK
parthenogenetic
reproduction
PRTHNJNDKL
parthenogenetically
reproduction
PRTHNJNSS
parthenogenesis
reproduction
PRTHNJNTK
parthenogenetic
reproduction
PRTHNJNTKL
parthenogenetically
reproduction
PRTHNN Parthenon
building
PRTHNTR prothonotary
clerk prothonotaries

PRTHRD parathyroid *gland*
PRTHRD pyrethroid
insecticide
PRTHRKS prothorax *insect*
PRTHRM pyrethrum *flower*
PRTHRN pyrethrin
insecticide
PRTHRX prothorax *insect*
PRTHS perithecia (pl)
fungus perithecium
PRTHSH perithecia (pl)
fungus perithecium
PRTHSHM perithecium
fungus perithecia
PRTHSHY perithecia (pl)
fungus perithecium
PRTHSHYM perithecium
fungus perithecia
PRTHSM perithecium
fungus perithecia
PRTHSTR protohistory
humans
PRTHSY perithecia (pl)
fungus perithecium
PRTHSYM perithecium
fungus perithecia
PRTHT apartheid *racial*
segregation
PRTJ portage *(n) cargo*
PRTJ portage *(v) carry*
portaged portaging
PRTJ protégé (m) *student*
protégée (f)
PRTK operatic *music*
PRTK partake *share* partook
partaking partaken
PRTK portico *porch*
porticoes (or) porticos
PRTK protect *defend*
PRTK pyretic *fever*
PRTKDNT protectant
defender
PRTKDR protector *defender*
PRTKDR protectory
orphanage protectories
PRTKDRT protectorate
government
PRTKDV protective
defensive
PRTKDVL protectively
defensive
PRTKDVNS protectiveness

Letters aren't doubled for single sounds: to find alley use **L** not **LL**. Use **Y** and **W** as hard
sounds only: to find yellow use **YL**. (Br)=British spelling or usage. * See dictionary.

defensive
PRTKL particle *small bit*
PRTKL particulate *small pieces*
PRTKL protocol *record, etiquette*
PRTKLBRD particleboard *bonded wood*
PRTKLR parti-color (or) parti-colored *patchy* (Br) parti-colour
PRTKLR particular *(adj) exacting, special (n) item*
PRTKLRD parti-colored (or) parti-color *patchy* (Br) parti-coloured
PRTKLRD particularity *detail* particularities
PRTKLRL particularly *especially*
PRTKLRT particularity *detail* particularities
PRTKLRZ particularize *detail* particularized particularizing (Br) particularise
PRTKLRZSHN particularization *detail* (Br) particularisation
PRTKLS portcullis *grate*
PRTKNK pyrotechnic *fireworks*
PRTKNKL pyrotechnically *fireworks*
PRTKNKS pyrotechnics *fireworks*
PRTKNX pyrotechnics *fireworks*
PRTKS pretext *motive*
PRTKSHN protection *defense*
PRTKSHNST protectionist *restricter*
PRTKSHNZM protectionism *restriction*
PRTKSS parataxis *placement*
PRTKST pretext *motive*
PRTKT protect *defend*
PRTKTNT protectant *defender*
PRTKTR protector *defender*
PRTKTR protectory

orphanage protectories
PRTKTRT protectorate *government*
PRTKTV protective *defensive*
PRTKTVL protectively *defensive*
PRTKTVNS protectiveness *defensive*
PRTKYLR particular *(adj) exacting, special (n) item*
PRTKYLRD particularity *detail* particularities
PRTKYLRL particularly *especially*
PRTKYLRT particularity *detail* particularities
PRTKYLRZ particularize *detail* particularized particularizing (Br) particularise
PRTKYLRZSHN particularization *detail* (Br) particularisation
PRTKYLT particulate *small pieces*
PRTL parietal *wall, visitation*
PRTL pertly *lively*
PRTL portal *doorway*
PRTL porthole *window*
PRTL portly *stout* portlier portliest
PRTL prattle *talk* prattled prattling
PRTL prettily *beauty*
PRTLDK proteolytic *protein*
PRTLK portulaca *plant*
PRTLN party line *telephone, policies*
PRTLN Portland *city*
PRTLND Portland *city*
PRTLNS portliness *stoutness*
PRTLR portlier *stout*
PRTLSS proteolysis *protein*
PRTLST portliest *stout*
PRTLTK proteolytic *protein*
PRTLYR portlier *stout*
PRTLYST portliest *stout*
PRTM part-time *less than full-time*
PRTM pro tem *temporary* pro tempore
PRTM protium *atom*

PRTMN protamine *protein*
PRTMNT apartment *abode*
PRTMNT portamento *voice*
PRTMNT portmanteau *(n) suitcase, word,(adj) combination* portmanteaus (or) portmanteaux
PRTMPR pro tempore *temporary* pro tem
PRTMR part-timer *less than full-time*
PRTN appertain *relate*
PRTN opportune *advantage*
PRTN parting *departure*
PRTN peritonea (pl) *membrane* peritoneum
PRTN pertain *relate*
PRTN portend *indicate*
PRTN preteen *before age 13*
PRTN pretend *act*
PRTN protean *versatile*
PRTN protein *amino acid*
PRTN proton *atom*
PRTN puritan *moralist*
PRTNCHN pretension *ambition*
PRTNCHS pretentious *showy*
PRTND opportunity *advantage* opportunities
PRTND portend *indicate*
PRTND pretend *act*
PRTNDD pretended *false*
PRTNDR pretender *claimant, hypocrite*
PRTNDS peritonitis *abdomen*
PRTNG parting *departure*
PRTNGKL pratincole *bird*
PRTNGL pratingly *talk*
PRTNJR preteen-ager *before age 13*
PRTNK protonic *atom*
PRTNKL pratincole *bird*
PRTNKL puritanical (adj) *moralistic* puritanically (adv)
PRTNL opportunely *advantage*
PRTNM peritoneum *membrane* peritoneums (or) peritonea

Use letters that best describe the sounds you hear and omit the vowels. Use **S** or **K** instead of **C**: to find circle use **SRKL**. Use **J** to find joy, **JM** to find gem and **G** to find go.

PRTNNS appurtenance *attachment*
PRTNNS pertinence *suitability*
PRTNNS purtenance *pluck*
PRTNNT appurtenant *attached*
PRTNNT pertinent *suitable*
PRTNNTS appurtenance *attachment*
PRTNNTS pertinence *suitability*
PRTNNTS purtenance *pluck*
PRTNR partner *(n) colleague (v) join with*
PRTNR proteinuria *urine*
PRTNRSHP partnership *relationship*
PRTNRY proteinuria *urine*
PRTNS opportuneness *advantage*
PRTNS pertness *liveliness*
PRTNS pretense (or) pretence *claim, pretext*
PRTNS prettiness *beauty*
PRTNSD pertinacity *stubbornness*
PRTNSDK opportunistic *advantage*
PRTNSDKL opportunistically *advantage*
PRTNSHN pretension *ambition*
PRTNSHS pertinacious *stubborn*
PRTNSHS pretentious *showy*
PRTNSHS proteinaceous *with protein*
PRTNSHSL pertinaciously *stubborn*
PRTNSHSNS pertinaciousness *stubborn*
PRTNST opportunist *advantage*
PRTNST pertinacity *stubbornness*
PRTNSTK opportunistic *advantage*
PRTNSTKL

opportunistically *advantage*
PRTNT appurtenant *attached*
PRTNT opportunity *advantage* opportunities
PRTNT pertinent *suitable*
PRTNT portent *omen*
PRTNT protonate *atom* protonated protonating
PRTNTS peritonitis *abdomen*
PRTNTS pertinence *suitability*
PRTNTS portentous *threatening*
PRTNTS pretense (or) pretence *claim, pretext*
PRTNTSHN pretension *ambition*
PRTNTSHS pretentious *showy*
PRTNY peritonea (pl) *membrane* peritoneum
PRTNYM peritoneum *membrane* peritoneums (or) peritonea
PRTNYR proteinuria *urine*
PRTNYRY proteinuria *urine*
PRTNZM opportunism *advantage*
PRTNZM puritanism *moralism*
PRTPLST protoplast *cell*
PRTPLZM protoplasm *cells*
PRTPPR party pooper *refuser*
PRTPRT pret-a-porter *clothing*
PRTQLR particular *(adj) exacting, special (n) item*
PRTQLRD particularity *detail* particularities
PRTQLRL particularly *especially*
PRTQLRT particularity *detail* particularities
PRTQLRZ particularize *detail* particularized particularizing (Br) particularise
PRTQLRZSHN particularization *detail* (Br) particularisation

PRTQLT particulate *small pieces*
PRTR aperture *hole*
PRTR operator *telephone, fraud, performer**
PRTR parterre *garden*
PRTR porter *carry, clean*
PRTR portiere *curtain*
PRTR portray *act*
PRTR praetor *official*
PRTR prater *talker*
PRTR Pretoria *city*
PRTR prettier *beauty*
PRTRB perturb *disturb*
PRTRBBL perturbable *disturb*
PRTRBSHN perturbation *disturbance*
PRTRCHR portraiture *picture*
PRTRD protrude *stick out* protruded protruding
PRTRHS porterhouse *steak*
PRTRJ partridge *bird* partridge (or) partridges
PRTRJ porterage *fee*
PRTRK protract *extend*
PRTRK Puerto Rico *commonwealth*
PRTRKDD protracted *extended*
PRTRKDL protractile *extension*
PRTRKDR protractor *angles*
PRTRKDV protractive *extensive*
PRTRKSHN protraction *extension*
PRTRKT protract *extend*
PRTRKTD protracted *extended*
PRTRKTL protractile *extension*
PRTRKTR protractor *angles*
PRTRKTV protractive *extensive*
PRTRL portrayal *portrait*
PRTRL pretrial *law*
PRTRM preterm *premature*
PRTRMSHN pretermission *omission*
PRTRMT pretermit *omit,*

suspend pretermitted
pretermitting
PRTRNCHRL preternatural
(adj) *psychic*
preternaturally (adv)
PRTRNT parturient *birth*
PRTRNTRL preternatural
(adj) *psychic*
preternaturally (adv)
PRTRPR paratrooper
parachute
PRTRPS paratroops
parachute
PRTRR portrayer *depict*
PRTRS portress *carry, clean*
(f)
PRTRSHN parturition *birth*
PRTRSHN protrusion
projection
PRTRSV protrusive
prominent
PRTRT portrait *picture*
PRTRTR portraiture *picture*
PRTRTST portraitist *artist*
PRTRTYR portraiture *picture*
PRTRY Pretoria *city*
PRTRYL portrayal *portrait*
PRTRYL pretrial *law*
PRTRYNT parturient *birth*
PRTRYR portrayer *depict*
PRTRZV protrusive
prominent
PRTS apparatus *device*
apparatuses (or)
apparatus
PRTS protease *enzyme*
PRTS protest *dissent*
PRTS Proteus *Greek god*
PRTS proteus *bacteria*
PRTSDNT Protestant
religion
PRTSDR protester (or)
protestor *dissenter*
PRTSH portage (*v*) *carry*
portaged portaging
PRTSH portage (*n*) *cargo*
PRTSH protégé (m) *student*
protégée (f)
PRTSHN partition *division*
PRTSHNR partitioner
division
PRTSL pretzel *food*

PRTSMTH Portsmouth *city*
PRTSPDR participator
sharer
PRTSPDV participative
sharing
PRTSPL participial (adj) *verb
and adjective* participially
(adv)
PRTSPL participle *verb*
PRTSPNT participant *sharer*
PRTSPSHN participation
share
PRTSPT participate *share*
participated participating
PRTSPTR participator
sharer
PRTSPTR participatory
sharing
PRTSPTV participative
sharing
PRTSPYL participial (adj)
verb and adjective
participially (adv)
PRTSS parotisis *mumps*
PRTSS pertussis *cough*
PRTSS protasis *introduction,
clause* protases
PRTST pretest *try out*
PRTST prettiest *beauty*
PRTST protest *dissent*
PRTST protist *algae*
PRTSTN protistan *algae*
PRTSTNT Protestant
religion
PRTSTR protester (or)
protestor *dissenter*
PRTSTSHN protestation
dissent
PRTT apartheid *racial
segregation*
PRTT partite *divided*
PRTT pyrrhotite *mineral*
PRTTP prototype *model*
PRTTPKL prototypical (adj)
model prototypically (adv)
PRTTPL prototypal *model*
PRTTV partitive *division*
PRTV operative *working*
PRTVL operatively *working*
PRTVNS operativeness
working
PRTVSPCH part of speech

word
PRTX pretext *motive*
PRTXS parataxis *placement*
PRTXT pretext *motive*
PRTY protea *flower*
PRTYBRNS protuberance
projection
PRTYBRNTS protuberance
projection
PRTYGL Portugal *country*
PRTYGZ Portuguese *of
Portugal*
PRTYLDK proteolytic
protein
PRTYLSS proteolysis
protein
PRTYLTK proteolytic *protein*
PRTYM protium *atom*
PRTYN opportune *advantage*
PRTYN protean *versatile*
PRTYND opportunity
advantage opportunities
PRTYNL opportunely
advantage
PRTYNS opportuneness
advantage
PRTYNSDK opportunistic
advantage
PRTYNSDKL
opportunistically
advantage
PRTYNST opportunist
advantage
PRTYNSTK opportunistic
advantage
PRTYNSTKL
opportunistically
advantage
PRTYNT opportunity
advantage opportunities
PRTYNZM opportunism
advantage
PRTYR aperture *hole*
PRTYR portiere *curtain*
PRTYR prettier *beauty*
PRTYRNT parturient *birth*
PRTYRSHN parturition *birth*
PRTYRYNT parturient *birth*
PRTYS protease *enzyme*
PRTYS Proteus *Greek god*
PRTYS proteus *bacteria*
PRTYST prettiest *beauty*

Use letters that best describe the sounds you hear and omit the vowels. Use **S** or **K** instead of **C**: to find circle use **SRKL**. Use **J** to find joy, **JM** to find gem and **G** to find go.

PRTYZ protease *enzyme*
PRTZ protease *enzyme*
PRTZ protozoa (pl) *animal* protozoan
PRTZH portage *(v) carry* portaged portaging
PRTZH portage *(n) cargo*
PRTZH protégé *(m) student* protégée (f)
PRTZL pretzel *food*
PRTZL protozoal *animal*
PRTZLG protozoology *science*
PRTZLJ protozoology *science*
PRTZLJST protozoologist *scientist*
PRTZN partisan *follower*
PRTZN protozoan *animal* protozoa
PRTZNSHP partisanship *follower*
PRTZW protozoa (pl) *animal* protozoan
PRTZWL protozoal *animal*
PRTZWLG protozoology *science*
PRTZWLJ protozoology *science*
PRTZWLJST protozoologist *scientist*
PRTZWN protozoan *animal* protozoa
PRV approve *okay* approved approving
PRV pareve *food*
PRV preview *survey*
PRV privy *private* privies
PRV prove *certify* proved (or) proven proving
PRV purvey *supply*
PRV purview *range*
PRVBL approvable (adj) *okay* approvably (adv)
PRVBL provable (adj) *certify* provably (adv)
PRVBLNS provableness *certify*
PRVC privacy *seclusion* privacies
PRVD approved *okay*
PRVD pervade *spread*

pervaded pervading
PRVD private eye *detective*
PRVD provide *give* provided providing
PRVDD provided *on condition*
PRVDN providing *in case*
PRVDNCHL providential (adj) *lucky* providentially (adv)
PRVDNG providing *in case*
PRVDNS providence *guidance*
PRVDNSHL providential (adj) *lucky* providentially (adv)
PRVDNT provident *cautious*
PRVDNTS providence *guidance*
PRVDR pervader *spreader*
PRVDR provider *breadwinner*
PRVDV privative *lack, word*
PRVK provoke *incite* provoked provoking
PRVKDV provocative *stimulating*
PRVKDVL provocatively *stimulating*
PRVKDVNS provocativeness *stimulation*
PRVKN provoking *annoying*
PRVKNG provoking *annoying*
PRVKR provoker *inciter*
PRVKSHN provocation *incitement*
PRVKTR provocateur *inciter*
PRVKTV provocative *stimulating*
PRVKTVL provocatively *stimulating*
PRVKTVNS provocativeness *stimulation*
PRVKTYR provocateur *inciter*
PRVL approval *okay*
PRVL prevail *win*
PRVLJ privilege *giving advantage* privileged

privileging
PRVLJD privileged *having an advantage*
PRVLN provolone *cheese*
PRVLNS prevalence *dominance*
PRVLNT prevalent *dominant*
PRVLNTS prevalence *dominance*
PRVN parvenu *upstart* parvenus
PRVN proven *tested*
PRVNBL preventable *avoidable, stoppable*
PRVNCHL provincial *(n) local (adj) simple*
PRVNCHLST provincialist *local*
PRVNCHLZM provincialism *local, simple*
PRVNCHN prevention *avoidance*
PRVNDR provender *food*
PRVNDV preventative *avoidable, stoppable*
PRVNGL approvingly *okay*
PRVNL approvingly *okay*
PRVNNS provenance *source*
PRVNNS provenience *source*
PRVNNT prevenient *before*
PRVNNTS provenance *source*
PRVNNTS provenience *source*
PRVNS province *territory*
PRVNS purveyance *supply*
PRVNSHL provincial *(n) local (adj) simple*
PRVNSHLST provincialist *local*
PRVNSHLZM provincialism *local, simple*
PRVNSHN prevention *avoidance*
PRVNSL Provençal (or) Provençale *France*
PRVNT prevent *avoid, stop*
PRVNTBL preventable *avoidable, stoppable*
PRVNTRKLS proventriculus *stomach*
PRVNTRKYLS

Letters aren't doubled for single sounds: to find alley use **L** not **LL**. Use **Y** and **W** as hard sounds only: to find yellow use **YL**. (Br)=British spelling or usage. * See dictionary.

proventriculus *stomach*
PRVNTRQLS proventriculus
stomach
PRVNTS province *territory*
PRVNTS purveyance *supply*
PRVNTTV preventative
avoidable, stoppable
PRVNTV preventative
avoidable, stoppable
PRVNTV preventive
avoidance
PRVNV preventive *avoidance*
PRVNY parvenu *upstart*
parvenus
PRVNYNS provenience
source
PRVNYNT prevenient *before*
PRVNYNTS provenience
source
PRVR prover *tester*
PRVR purveyor *supplier*
PRVR upriver *direction*
PRVRB proverb *adage*
PRVRBL preverbal *before*
speech
PRVRBL proverbial (adj)
adage proverbially (adv)
PRVRBS Proverbs *Bible*
PRVRBYL proverbial (adj)
adage proverbially (adv)
PRVRBZ Proverbs *Bible*
PRVRKDR prevaricator *liar*
PRVRKSHN prevarication
lie
PRVRKT prevaricate *lie*
prevaricated
prevaricating
PRVRKTR prevaricator *liar*
PRVRS perverse *corrupt,*
contrary
PRVRSD perversity *corrupt,*
contrary perversities
PRVRSHN perversion
corrupt, contrary
PRVRST perversity *corrupt,*
contrary perversities
PRVRSV perversive
corrupting
PRVRT pervert *corrupt one*
PRVRZHN perversion
corrupt, contrary
PRVS parvis *court*

PRVS pervious *open*
PRVS previous *before*
PRVS privacy *seclusion*
privacies
PRVSHN pervasion *spread*
PRVSHN prevision *forecast*
PRVSHN privation *lack*
PRVSHN provision *(n) stock*
(v) supply
PRVSHNL provisional (adj)
temporary provisionally
(adv)
PRVSHNR provisioner
supplier
PRVSL previously *before*
PRVST provost *officer*
PRVSV pervasive *spreading*
PRVT private *secluded*
PRVT private eye *detective*
PRVT privet *shrub*
PRVTR privateer *ship*
PRVTV privative *lack, word*
PRVTZ privatize *private*
control privatized
privatizing
(Br) privatise
PRVTZM privatism *personal*
PRVTZSHN privatization
private control
(Br) privatisation
PRVVRS parvovirus *disease*
PRVY preview *survey*
PRVY purview *range*
PRVYNS purveyance *supply*
PRVYNTS purveyance
supply
PRVYR purveyor *supplier*
PRVYS pervious *open*
PRVYS previous *before*
PRVYSL previously *before*
PRVZ proviso *condition*
provisos (or) provisoes
PRVZHN pervasion *spread*
PRVZHN prevision *forecast*
PRVZHN provision *(n) stock*
(v) supply
PRVZHNL provisional (adj)
temporary provisionally
(adv)
PRVZHNR provisioner
supplier
PRVZR provisory *conditional*

PRVZV pervasive *spreading*
PRWBDV prohibitive
restraining
PRWBRSHN proabortion
legal abortion
PRWBSHN prohibition
forbidding
PRWBSHNST prohibitionist
no alcohol
PRWBT prohibit *forbid*
PRWBTR prohibitory
forbidden
PRWBTV prohibitive
restraining
PRWKDV proactive
anticipate
PRWKTV proactive
anticipate
PRWLR prowler *sneak*
PRWNGKL periwinkle *plant,*
color, mollusk
PRWNKL periwinkle *plant,*
color, mollusk
PRWR prewar *conflict*
PRWS prowess *ability*
PRWSDRS proestrus
menstruation
PRWSTRS proestrus
menstruation
PRWT pirouette *turn*
pirouetted pirouetting
PRX apraxia *movement*
PRX perks *benefits*
PRX prexy *(slang) president*
prexies
PRX proxy *substitute* proxies
PRX Pyrex *(trademark)*
glassware
PRX pyrexia *fever*
PRXD peroxide *bleach*
peroxided peroxiding
PRXK apraxic (or) apractic
movement
PRXK pyrexic *fever*
PRXL preaxial *front*
PRXL pyrexial *fever*
PRXLN pyroxylin *coating*
PRXLNS par excellence *best*
PRXLNTS par excellence
best
PRXM proximo *next month*
PRXMD proximity *nearness*

Use letters that best describe the sounds you hear and omit the vowels. Use **S** or **K** instead of **C**: to find circle use **SRKL**. Use **J** to find joy, **JM** to find gem and **G** to find go.

PRXMDV approximative *near*

PRXMK proxemic *separation*

PRXML proximal (adj) *near* proximally (adv)

PRXMSHN approximation *near*

PRXMT approximate *(v) come close* approximated approximating

PRXMT approximate *(adj) near*

PRXMT proximate *nearby*

PRXMT proximity *nearness*

PRXMTL approximately *nearly*

PRXMTL proximately *nearby*

PRXMTNS proximateness *nearness*

PRXMTV approximative *near*

PRXN pyroxene *mineral*

PRXNT pyroxenite *rock*

PRXS praxis *action* praxes

PRXSDNS preexistence *live before*

PRXSDNT preexistent *live before*

PRXSDNTS preexistence *live before*

PRXST preexist *live before*

PRXSTNS preexistence *live before*

PRXSTNT preexistent *live before*

PRXSTNTS preexistence *live before*

PRXY apraxia *movement*

PRXY pyrexia *fever*

PRXYL preaxial *front*

PRXYL pyrexial *fever*

PRXZ praxes (pl) *action* praxis

PRXZM paroxysm *outburst*

PRXZML paroxysmal *outburst*

PRY pariah *outcast*

PRY pyorrhea *gum disease*

PRY pyuria *pus in urine*

PRYD period *punctuation, time*

PRYDK aperiodic *irregular*

PRYDK periodic *occasional*

PRYDKL aperiodically *irregularly*

PRYDKL periodical *(n) magazine (adj) occasional*

PRYDKL periodical (adj) *occasional (n) magazine* periodically (adv)

PRYDL parietal *wall, visitation*

PRYDNKS periodontics *gums*

PRYDNL periodontal (adj) *gums* periodontally (adv)

PRYDNTKS periodontics *gums*

PRYDNTL periodontal (adj) *gums* periodontally (adv)

PRYDNTX periodontics *gums*

PRYDNX periodontics *gums*

PRYDSD aperiodicity *irregularity*

PRYDSD periodicity *timing*

PRYDST aperiodicity *irregularity*

PRYDST periodicity *timing*

PRYGZSDNS preexistence *live before*

PRYGZSDNT preexistent *live before*

PRYGZSDNTS preexistence *live before*

PRYGZST preexist *live before*

PRYGZSTNS preexistence *live before*

PRYGZSTNT preexistent *live before*

PRYGZSTNTS preexistence *live before*

PRYKCL preaxial *front*

PRYKCYL preaxial *front*

PRYKP preoccupy *concern* preoccupied preoccupying preoccupies

PRYKPD preoccupied *concerned*

PRYKPNC preoccupancy *possession*

PRYKPNS preoccupancy

possession

PRYKPNTC preoccupancy *possession*

PRYKPNTS preoccupancy *possession*

PRYKPSHN preoccupation *concern*

PRYKSL preaxial *front*

PRYKSYL preaxial *front*

PRYKYP preoccupy *concern* preoccupied preoccupying preoccupies

PRYKYPD preoccupied *concerned*

PRYKYPNC preoccupancy *possession*

PRYKYPNS preoccupancy *possession*

PRYKYPNTC preoccupancy *possession*

PRYKYPNTS preoccupancy *possession*

PRYKYPSHN preoccupation *concern*

PRYKZSDNS preexistence *live before*

PRYKZSDNT preexistent *live before*

PRYKZSDNTS preexistence *live before*

PRYKZST preexist *live before*

PRYKZSTNS preexistence *live before*

PRYKZSTNT preexistent *live before*

PRYKZSTNTS preexistence *live before*

PRYLKSHN preelection *voting*

PRYLNT purulent *pus*

PRYMBL preamble *introduction*

PRYMDR preemptor *seize first*

PRYMDV preemptive *seize first*

PRYMNNS preeminence *superiority*

PRYMNNT preeminent *superior*

Letters aren't doubled for single sounds: to find alley use **L** not **LL**. Use **Y** and **W** as hard sounds only: to find yellow use **YL**. (Br)=British spelling or usage. * See dictionary.

PRYMNNTS preeminence *superiority*
PRYMP preamp *amplifier*
PRYMPDR preemptor *seize first*
PRYMPDV preemptive *seize first*
PRYMPLFR preamplifier *stereo*
PRYMPLFYR preamplifier *stereo*
PRYMPLMNT preemployment *job*
PRYMPSHN preemption *seize first*
PRYMPT preempt *seize first, prevent*
PRYMPTR preemptor *seize first*
PRYMPTV preemptive *seize first*
PRYMSHN preemption *seize first*
PRYMT preempt *seize first, prevent*
PRYMTR preemptor *seize first*
PRYMTV preemptive *seize first*
PRYN apiarian *bees*
PRYN parian *porcelain*
PRYN pereion (or) pereon *thorax*
PRYN prying *curious*
PRYNG prying *curious*
PRYNGMNS praying mantis *insect*
PRYNGMNTS praying mantis *insect*
PRYNGRL preinaugural *induction*
PRYNGYRL preinaugural *induction*
PRYNK perionychia (pl) *fingernail* perionychium
PRYNKM perionychium *fingernail* perionychia
PRYNKY perionychia (pl) *fingernail* perionychium
PRYNKYM perionychium *fingernail* perionychia
PRYNRLMNT preenrollment

sign up
PRYNT prurient *lewd*
PRYNTH perianth *flower*
PRYPK priapic *manly*
PRYPRDV preoperative *surgery*
PRYPRTV preoperative *surgery*
PRYPRV preapprove *okay* preapproved preapproving
PRYQP preoccupy *concern* preoccupied preoccupying preoccupies
PRYQPD preoccupied *concerned*
PRYQPNC preoccupancy *possession*
PRYQPNS preoccupancy *possession*
PRYQPNTC preoccupancy *possession*
PRYQPNTS preoccupancy *possession*
PRYQPSHN preoccupation *concern*
PRYR a priori *reasoning*
PRYR apriori *deduce*
PRYR prayer *request*
PRYR prier *nosy one*
PRYR prior *previous*
PRYR priory *monestary* priories
PRYRD priority *preference* priorities
PRYRDN preordain *decree*
PRYRDNMNT preordainment *decree*
PRYRDNSHN preordination *decree*
PRYRFL prayerful (adj) *devout* prayerfully (adv)
PRYRFLNS prayerfulness *devotion*
PRYRNJ prearrange *set up* prearranged prearranging
PRYRNJMNT prearrangement *set up*
PRYRS prioress *nun*
PRYRSHP priorship *religion*
PRYRT priority *preference*

priorities
PRYRTZ prioritize *rate* prioritized prioritizing
PRYSMBLD preassembled *constructed*
PRYSN preassign *denote*
PRYST periostea (pl) *bone* periosteum
PRYSTBLSH preestablish *creation*
PRYSTL periosteal *bone*
PRYSTM periosteum *bone* periostea
PRYSTY periostea (pl) *bone* periosteum
PRYSTYL periosteal *bone*
PRYSTYM periosteum *bone* periostea
PRYTL parietal *wall, visitation*
PRYXL preaxial *front*
PRYXSDNS preexistence *live before*
PRYXSDNT preexistent *live before*
PRYXSDNTS preexistence *live before*
PRYXSTNS preexistence *live before*
PRYXSTNT preexistent *live before*
PRYXSTNTS preexistence *live before*
PRYXYL preaxial *front*
PRZ appraise *estimate* appraised appraising
PRZ appraisee *rated one*
PRZ apprise *inform* apprised apprising
PRZ apprize *value* apprized apprizing
PRZ apyrase *enzyme*
PRZ peruse *read* perused perusing
PRZ praise (v) *glorify* praised praising
PRZ praise (n) *approval, worship*
PRZ prez (slang) *president* prezes
PRZ prize *award* prized prizing

Use letters that best describe the sounds you hear and omit the vowels. Use **S** or **K** instead of **C**: to find circle use **SRKL**. Use **J** to find joy, **JM** to find gem and **G** to find go.

PRZ prose *writing*
PRZ prosy *dull* prosier prosiest
PRZBDR presbyter *church*
PRZBP presbyopia *vision*
PRZBPK presbyopic *vision*
PRZBPY presbyopia *vision*
PRZBTR presbyter *church*
PRZBTR presbytery *church* presbyteries
PRZBTRN Presbyterian *church*
PRZBTRYN Presbyterian *church*
PRZBYP presbyopia *vision*
PRZBYPK presbyopic *vision*
PRZBYPY presbyopia *vision*
PRZD preside *direct* presided presiding
PRZD presidio *fort* presidios
PRZDM presidium *committee* presidia (or) presidiums
PRZDNC presidency *office* presidencies
PRZDNCHL presidential (adj) *leader* presidentially (adv)
PRZDNLK president-elect *leader*
PRZDNLKT president-elect *leader*
PRZDNS presidency *office* presidencies
PRZDNSHL presidential (adj) *leader* presidentially (adv)
PRZDNT president *leader*
PRZDNTC presidency *office* presidencies
PRZDNTLK president-elect *leader*
PRZDNTLKT president-elect *leader*
PRZDNTS presidency *office* presidencies
PRZDR presider *occupier*
PRZDY presidio *fort* presidios
PRZDYM presidium *committee* presidia (or)

presidiums
PRZFDN prizefighting *boxing*
PRZFDNG prizefighting *boxing*
PRZFDR prizefighter *boxing*
PRZFT prizefight *boxing*
PRZFTN prizefighting *boxing*
PRZFTNG prizefighting *boxing*
PRZFTR prizefighter *boxing*
PRZHN Parisian *of Paris*
PRZHN Persian *of Persia*
PRZHNGF Persian Gulf *body of water*
PRZHNGLF Persian Gulf *body of water*
PRZK prosaic *prose, ordinary*
PRZKL prosaically *prose, ordinary*
PRZL appraisal *rating*
PRZL perusal *reading*
PRZL prosily *dull*
PRZM presume *dare, imply* presumed presuming
PRZM prism *light*
PRZM purism *words*
PRZMBL presumable (adj) *implied* presumably (adv)
PRZMCHS presumptuous *pushy*
PRZMCHWS presumptuous *pushy*
PRZMDK prismatic *light*
PRZMDV presumptive *probable*
PRZMNT appraisement *estimation*
PRZMPCHS presumptuous *pushy*
PRZMPCHWS presumptuous *pushy*
PRZMPDV presumptive *probable*
PRZMPSHN presumption *audacity*
PRZMPSHS presumptuous *pushy*
PRZMPSHWS presumptuous *pushy*
PRZMPTV presumptive

probable
PRZMSHN presumption *audacity*
PRZMSHS presumptuous *pushy*
PRZMSHWS presumptuous *pushy*
PRZMTK prismatic *light*
PRZMTS presumptuous *pushy*
PRZMTV presumptive *probable*
PRZMTWS presumptuous *pushy*
PRZN Parisian *of Paris*
PRZN prison *jail*
PRZN uprising *revolt*
PRZNBL presentable (adj) *show* presentably (adv)
PRZNBLD presentability *show*
PRZNBLNS presentableness *show*
PRZNBLT presentability *show*
PRZND present-day *now*
PRZNG uprising *revolt*
PRZNGL appraisingly *estimate*
PRZNR presenter *giver*
PRZNR prisoner *jailed one*
PRZNS presence *nearness, bearing*
PRZNS prosiness *dullness*
PRZNT present (n) *gift, now* (v) *give, perform* (adj) *now, verb**
PRZNT presentee *receiver*
PRZNTBL presentable (adj) *show* presentably (adv)
PRZNTBLD presentability *show*
PRZNTBLNS presentableness *show*
PRZNTBLT presentability *show*
PRZNTD present-day *now*
PRZNTL presently *now*
PRZNTMNT presentiment *hunch*
PRZNTMNT presentment *statement*

Letters aren't doubled for single sounds: to find alley use **L** not **LL**. Use **Y** and **W** as hard sounds only: to find yellow use **YL**. (Br)=British spelling or usage. * See dictionary.

PRZNTR presenter *giver*
PRZNTS presence *nearness, bearing*
PRZNTSHN presentation *show, gift*
PRZPMTS presumptuous *pushy*
PRZPMTWS presumptuous *pushy*
PRZR appraiser *rater*
PRZR peruser *reader*
PRZR praiser *glorifier*
PRZR prosier *duller*
PRZRV preserve *(v) protect, can* preserved preserving
PRZRV preserve *(n) jam, park*
PRZRVBL preservable *protection, canning*
PRZRVDV preservative *protection, canning*
PRZRVR preserver *protecter*
PRZRVSHN preservation *protection, canning*
PRZRVTV preservative *protection, canning*
PRZSDNT persistent *determined*
PRZST prosaist *prose, ordinary*
PRZST prosiest *dullest*
PRZSTNT persistent *determined*
PRZV appraisive *estimate*
PRZWNN prizewinning *award*
PRZWNNG prizewinning *award*
PRZWNR prizewinner *award*
PRZWRTH praiseworthy *admirable*
PRZWRTHL praiseworthily *admirable*
PRZWRTHNS praiseworthiness *admirable*
PRZYK prosaic *prose, ordinary*
PRZYKL prosaically *prose, ordinary*
PRZYM presume *dare, imply* presumed presuming

PRZYMBL presumable (adj) *implied* presumably (adv)
PRZYR prosier *duller*
PRZYST prosaist *prose, ordinary*
PRZYST prosiest *dullest*
PRZYZM prosaism *prose, ordinary*
PRZZM prosaism *prose, ordinary*
PS apace *swiftly*
PS apiece *each*
PS apse *church area*
PS eyepiece *lens*
PS oops *(interj) mistake*
PS opts *chooses*
PS opus *work* opera
PS pace *(v) stride* paced pacing
PS pace *(n) speed, gait*
PS pase *matador*
PS paseo *walk* paseos
PS pass *(v) move ahead, depart, occur* (n) road, realization, effort,** passes
PS passé *outmoded*
PS PC *(abbr) personal computer*
PS peace *serenity*
PS peso *money* pesos
PS piece *portion* pieced piecing
PS pious *holy*
PS piss *(n-vulgar) urine (v-vulgar) urinate, (Br) drunk*
PS posse *group*
PS puce *dark red*
PS pus *cellular debris*
PS puss *cat, face* pusses
PS pussy *cat* pussies
PS pussy *with pus* pussier pussiest
PSBG postbag *(Br) mail*
PSBK passbook *bank*
PSBKS postbox *mail* postboxes
PSBL passable (adj) *fair, open* passably (adv)
PSBL passible *suffering*
PSBL peaceable (adj) *serene* peaceably (adv)
PSBL possible (adj)

attainable possibly (adv)
PSBLD possibility *attainable goal* possibilities
PSBLT possibility *attainable goal* possibilities
PSBRD pasteboard *cardboard, sham*
PSBX postbox *mail* postboxes
PSCHL pustule *pimple*
PSCHLDD pustulated *pimples*
PSCHLDR postulator *claim*
PSCHLNC postulancy *probation* postulancies
PSCHLNS postulancy *probation* postulancies
PSCHLNT postulant *probation*
PSCHLNT pustulant *pimple*
PSCHLNTC postulancy *probation* postulancies
PSCHLNTS postulancy *probation* postulancies
PSCHLR pustular *pimples*
PSCHLSHN postulation *claim*
PSCHLT postulate *claim* postulated postulating
PSCHLTD pustulated *pimples*
PSCHLTR postulator *claim*
PSCHMS posthumous *after death*
PSCHMSL posthumously *after death*
PSCHMSNS posthumousness *after death*
PSCHR pasture *(v) graze* pastured pasturing
PSCHR pasture *(n) field*
PSCHR posture *position* postured posturing
PSCHRL postural *position*
PSCHRLN pastureland *field*
PSCHRLND pastureland *field*
PSCHRR posturer *position*
PSCHRZ pasteurize *sterilize* pasteurized pasteurizing (Br) pasteurise

---

Use letters that best describe the sounds you hear and omit the vowels. Use **S** or **K** instead of **C**: to find circle use **SRKL**. Use **J** to find joy, **JM** to find gem and **G** to find go.

PSCHRZSHN
pasteurization *sterilization*
(Br) pasteurisation
PSD episode *event*
PSD opacity *milky* opacities
PSD pasta *noodles*
PSD pasty *like glue* pastier
pastiest
PSD paucity *few*
PSD peseta *money*
PSD pesto *sauce*
PSD upside *positive*
PSDBT post-obit *after death*
PSDC apostasy *defection*
apostasies
PSDCH pasticcio *imitation*
pasticci
PSDCHY pasticcio *imitation*
pasticci
PSDJ postage *stamps*
PSDK episodic *occasional*
PSDK postdoc *after PhD.*
PSDKDRL postdoctoral
after PhD.
PSDKL episodically
occasionally
PSDKTRL postdoctoral
after PhD.
PSDL apsidal *orbit*
PSDL pesthole *disease*
PSDL pestle *(v) crush*
pestled pestling
PSDL pestle *(n) tool*
PSDL pistil *plant*
PSDL pistol *firearm*
PSDL pistole *coin*
PSDL postal *(adj) mail,*
(slang) crazy
PSDLNCHL pestilential *(adj)*
deadly pestilentially *(adv)*
PSDLNS pestilence *plague*
PSDLNSHL pestilential *(adj)*
deadly pestilentially *(adv)*
PSDLNT pestilent *deadly*
PSDLNTS pestilence *plague*
PSDLR epistolary *book*
epistolaries
PSDLVN postdiluvian *after*
flood
PSDLVYN postdiluvian *after*
flood
PSDLWP pistol-whip *beat*

pistol-whipped pistol-
whipping
PSDMLG epistemology
knowledge
PSDMLJ epistemology
knowledge
PSDN Pasadena *city*
PSDN pastina *noodle*
PSDN piston *engine*
PSDN Poseidon *Greek god*
PSDN upside down *(adv)*
inverted upside-down
(adj)
PSDNBR Epstein-Barr *virus*
PSDNS pastiness *like glue*
PSDR pacesetter *example*
PSDR pastier *glue*
PSDR pastor *clergy*
PSDR pastry *food* pastries
PSDR pester *bother*
PSDR poster *picture*
PSDRL pastoral *(adj)*
livestock pastorally *(adv)*
PSDRM pastrami *meat*
PSDRN pastern *foot*
PSDRT pastorate *parson*
PSDRZSTNS pièce de
résistance *showpiece*
pieces de resistance
PSDRZSTNTS pièce de
résistance *showpiece*
pieces de resistance
PSDS apostasy *defection*
apostasies
PSDS pastis *liqueur*
PSDSD pesticide *pest killer*
PSDST pastiest *glue*
PSDT apostate *defector*
PSDT postdate *after today*
postdated postdating
PSDTZ apostatize *defect*
apostatized apostatizing
(Br) apostatise
PSDYR pastier *glue*
PSDYST pastiest *glue*
PSDZ apsides *(pl) orbit*
apsis
PSDZ pasties *striptease*
PSF pacify *soothe* pacified
pacifying pacifies
PSF pass off *deceive*
PSF pie safe *container*

PSF piss off *(v-vulgar)* make
angry, (vulgar command)
leave
PSFBL pacifiable *soothe*
PSFK pacific *peaceful*
PSFK Pacific *ocean*
PSFK specific *particular*
PSFKD ipso facto *by that*
fact
PSFKL pacifically *peaceful*
PSFKL specifically
particularly
PSFKSHN Pacific Ocean
body of water
PSFKSHN pacification
soothing
PSFKT ipso facto *by that*
fact
PSFL pass-fail *school*
PSFL peaceful *(adj) serene*
peacefully *(adj)*
PSFR pacifier *soother*
PSFRN peace offering *gift*
PSFRNG peace offering *gift*
PSFSR peace officer
policeman
PSFST pacifist *no war*
PSFYBL pacifiable *soothe*
PSFYR pacifier *soother*
PSFZM pacifism *no war*
PSGD spaghetti *food*
PSGDZ piece goods *cloth*
PSGRJT postgraduate
school
PSGRJWT postgraduate
school
PSGT spaghetti *food*
PSH apish *imitative*
PSH pasha *officer*
PSH Peugeot *(trademark) car*
PSH Piaget *psychologist*
PSH posh *costly*
PSH push *shove, urge*
PSH pushy *aggressive*
pushier pushiest
PSH uppish *snob*
PSHBK push-bike *(Br)*
bicycle
PSHBL pushball *game*
PSHBRM push broom *brush*
PSHBTN push-button *(adj)*
automatic push button *(n)*

Letters aren't doubled for single sounds: to find alley use **L** not **LL**. Use **Y** and **W** as hard
sounds only: to find yellow use **YL**. (Br)=British spelling or usage. * See dictionary.

PSHCHR pushchair *stroller*
PSHDN pushdown *data*
PSHDR peashooter *blowgun*
PSHF push off *leave*
PSHFT upshift *gears*
PSHKRT pushcart *wheelbarrow*
PSHL apishly *imitative*
PSHL poshly *costly*
PSHL pushily *aggressive*
PSHN option *choice*
PSHN passion *ardor*
PSHN potion *mixture*
PSHN push on *continue*
PSHN pushing *nearly*
PSHNFLR passionflower *herb*
PSHNFLWR passionflower *herb*
PSHNFRT passion fruit *food*
PSHNG pushing *nearly*
PSHNL optional (adj) *choice* optionally (adv)
PSHNLD optionality *choice*
PSHNLS passionless *no ardor*
PSHNLT optionality *choice*
PSHNS apishness *imitative*
PSHNS patience *wait*
PSHNS poshness *wealth*
PSHNS pushiness *aggressive*
PSHNT passionate *ardor*
PSHNT patient *(adj) unhurried (n) medical*
PSHNTL passionately *ardor*
PSHNTS patience *wait*
PSHP push-up *(n) exercise*
PSHPL push-pull *current*
PSHPN pushpin *tack*
PSHR pusher *one who urges or shoves, drug dealer*
PSHR pushier *aggressive*
PSHST pushiest *aggressive*
PSHT Pashto *language*
PSHT upshot *result*
PSHTR peashooter *blowgun*
PSHVR pushover *easily fooled or beaten*
PSHYR pushier *aggressive*
PSHYST pushiest *aggressive*
PSJ passage *path, death, phrase**

PSJW passageway *path*
PSJWRK passagework *music*
PSK Pasch *Easter*
PSK passkey *lock*
PSK pesky *annoying* peskier peskiest
PSKD postcode *ZIP code*
PSKD spaghetti *food*
PSKDL postcoital *after mating*
PSKL epicycle *orbit*
PSKL opuscula (pl) *work* opusculum
PSKL opuscule *work*
PSKL PASCAL *computer*
PSKL paschal *Easter*
PSKL upscale *expensive*
PSKLCHR pisciculture *fish*
PSKLD epicycloid *orbit*
PSKLDL epicycloidal *orbit*
PSKLJT postcollegiate *after college*
PSKLK epicyclic *orbit*
PSKLM opusculum *work* opuscula
PSKLNL postcolonial *history*
PSKLNYL postcolonial *history*
PSKLTR pisciculture *fish*
PSKMNN post-communion *Mass*
PSKMNYN post-communion *Mass*
PSKMYNN post-communion *Mass*
PSKMYNYN post-communion *Mass*
PSKNDR postsecondary *college*
PSKNS peskiness *annoying*
PSKPC episcopacy *bishops* episcopacies
PSKPL episcopal *(often capitalized) church, bishop*
PSKPLN Episcopalian *church*
PSKPLYN Episcopalian *church*
PSKPN peacekeeping *enforcement*

PSKPNG peacekeeping *enforcement*
PSKPR peacekeeper *enforcer*
PSKPS episcopacy *bishops* episcopacies
PSKPT episcopate *bishop*
PSKR peace corps *workers*
PSKR peskier *annoying*
PSKRB prescribe *order* prescribed prescribing
PSKRB proscribe *forbid* proscribed proscribing
PSKRD postcard *mail*
PSKRNL postcranial (adj) *head* postcranially (adv)
PSKRNYL postcranial (adj) *head* postcranially (adv)
PSKRP postscript *letter*
PSKRPDV prescriptive *usage*
PSKRPDV proscriptive *forbidden*
PSKRPSHN prescription *title, medicine*
PSKRPSHN proscription *forbid*
PSKRPT postscript *letter*
PSKRPTV prescriptive *usage*
PSKRPTV proscriptive *forbidden*
PSKST peskiest *annoying*
PSKT spaghetti *food*
PSKTL postcoital *after mating*
PSKTR piscatory *fish*
PSKTRL piscatorial *fish*
PSKTRYL piscatorial *fish*
PSKWDL postcoital *after mating*
PSKWND pasquinade *satire* pasquinaded pasquinading
PSKWTL postcoital *after sex*
PSKYL opuscula (pl) *work* opusculum
PSKYL opuscule *work*
PSKYLM opusculum *work* opuscula
PSKYR peskier *annoying*
PSKYST peskiest *annoying*
PSL apostle *follower*

Use letters that best describe the sounds you hear and omit the vowels. Use **S** or **K** instead of **C**: to find circle use **SRKL**. Use **J** to find joy, **JM** to find gem and **G** to find go.

PSL epistle *letter*
PSL pas seul *dance*
PSL passel *many*
PSL pestle (v) crush pestled pestling
PSL pestle (n) tool
PSLDRL ipsilateral (adj) same side ipsilaterally (adv)
PSLDRT postliterate *media*
PSLN epsilon *5th Greek letter*
PSLN upsilon *20th Greek letter, particle*
PSLNMD pusillanimity *cowardice*
PSLNMS pusillanimous *cowardly*
PSLNMT pusillanimity *cowardice*
PSLTRL ipsilateral (adj) *same side* ipsilaterally (adv)
PSLTRT postliterate *media*
PSM opossum (or) possum *animal* opossums (or) possums
PSM possum *animal*
PSMDRN postmodern *traditional*
PSMDRNST postmodernist *traditional*
PSMDRNZM postmodernism *tradition*
PSMKN peacemaking *soothing*
PSMKNG peacemaking *soothing*
PSMKR pacemaker *device, example*
PSMKR peacemaker *soother*
PSML piecemeal *gradually*
PSMLNYL postmillennial *1000 years*
PSMN postman *mail* postmen
PSMNPZL postmenopausal *after menstruation*
PSMNTR passementerie *braid*
PSMRDL postmarital *after wedding*
PSMRDM post meridiem *after noon*

PSMRDM postmortem *autopsy*
PSMRDYM post meridiem *after noon*
PSMRK postmark *mail*
PSMRTL postmarital *after wedding*
PSMRTM postmortem *autopsy*
PSMSDK pessimistic *hopeless*
PSMSDKL pessimistically *hopelessly*
PSMSDR postmaster *mail*
PSMSLTS Epsom salts *purging*
PSMST pessimist *hopeless one*
PSMSTK pessimistic *hopeless*
PSMSTKL pessimistically *hopelessly*
PSMSTR postmaster *mail*
PSMSTRS postmistress *mail* postmistresses
PSMZM pessimism *hopelessness*
PSN opsin *protein*
PSN passing (adj) slight (adv) greatly (n) death
PSN peace sign *gesture*
PSN piscina *basin*
PSN piscine *fish*
PSNDL postnatal (adj) birth postnatally (adv)
PSNDNS ups and downs *fate*
PSNDNZ ups and downs *fate*
PSNG passing (adj) slight (adv) greatly (n) death
PSNJR passenger *traveler*
PSNN opsonin *antibody*
PSNPCHL postnuptial *after mating*
PSNPCHWL postnuptial *after mating*
PSNPSHL postnuptial *after mating*
PSNPSHWL postnuptial *after mating*
PSNR epicenter *focus*

PSNSLTS Epsom salts *purging*
PSNT passant *gait*
PSNT pissant (vulgar) *insignificant one*
PSNT puissant *powerful*
PSNTL postnatal (adj) birth postnatally (adv)
PSNTR epicenter *focus*
PSNZL postnasal *sinus*
PSNZM epicenism *bisexuality*
PSP pea soup *food, fog*
PSPBRD postpuberty *adult*
PSPBRT postpuberty *adult*
PSPBSNT postpubescent *adult*
PSPD postpaid *mail*
PSPN postpone *defer* postponed postponing
PSPNBL postponable *defer*
PSPNMNT postponement *defer*
PSPP peace pipe *smoking device*
PSPRDKSHN postproduction *film*
PSPRNG upspring *spring up* upsprang (or) upsprung upspringing
PSPRT passe-partout *key*
PSPRT passport *document*
PSPYBRD postpuberty *adult*
PSPYBRT postpuberty *adult*
PSPYBSNT postpubescent *adult*
PSQL opuscula (pl) work opusculum
PSQL opuscule *work*
PSQLM opusculum *work* opuscula
PSQND pasquinade *satire* pasquinaded pasquinading
PSR pacer *horse*
PSR pas seul *dance*
PSR pessary *device* pessaries
PSRB passer-by *stranger* passers-by

Letters aren't doubled for single sounds: to find alley use **L** not **LL**. Use **Y** and **W** as hard sounds only: to find yellow use **YL**. (Br)=British spelling or usage. * See dictionary.

PSRJ upsurge *rise*
PSRJKL postsurgical *surgery*
PSRN passerine *bird*
PSRSB passers-by (pl) *stranger* passer-by
PSRZB passers-by (pl) *stranger* passer-by
PSS apsis *orbit* apsides
PSS piceous *like tar*
PSS Pisces *zodiac sign*
PST opacity *milky* opacities
PST opposite *reverse*
PST pass out *faint*
PST passed *went by*
PST past *before now*
PST pasta *noodles*
PST paste *glue, defeat* pasted pasting
PST pasty *like glue* pastier pastiest
PST paucity *few*
PST peseta *money*
PST pesto *sauce*
PST pissed *(vulgar) angry, (Br) drunk*
PST posset *beverage*
PST post *(v) mail, score, inform (n) pole, mail*
PST pursuit *work, chase*
PST upset *disturb, tip over* upset upsetting
PSTBG postbag *(Br) mail*
PSTBKS postbox *mail* postboxes
PSTBRD pasteboard *cardboard, sham*
PSTBT post-obit *after death*
PSTBX postbox *mail* postboxes
PSTC apostasy *defection* apostasies
PSTCH pasticcio *imitation* pasticci
PSTCHY pasticcio *imitation* pasticci
PSTDK postdoc *after PhD.*
PSTDKTRL postdoctoral *after PhD.*
PSTDLVN postdiluvian *after flood*
PSTDLVYN postdiluvian

after flood
PSTDT postdate *after today* postdated postdating
PSTFR post-free *(Br) postpaid*
PSTFRS pestiferous *troublesome*
PSTFS post office *mail*
PSTGRJT postgraduate *school*
PSTGRJWT postgraduate *school*
PSTHL pesthole *disease*
PSTHL posthole *pole*
PSTHPNDK posthypnotic *after trance*
PSTHPNTK posthypnotic *after trance*
PSTHR pass-through *price*
PSTHRN post horn *music*
PSTHRS post-horse *mail*
PSTHST posthaste *hurry*
PSTJ postage *stamps*
PSTJ upstage *theater* upstaged upstaging
PSTK postdoc *after PhD.*
PSTKCL postaxial *side*
PSTKCYL postaxial *side*
PSTKCZ epistaxes (pl) *nosebleed* epistaxis
PSTKD postcode *ZIP code*
PSTKDL postcoital *after sex*
PSTKDRL postdoctoral *after PhD.*
PSTKLJT postcollegiate *after college*
PSTKLNL postcolonial *history*
PSTKLNYL postcolonial *history*
PSTKMNN post-communion *Mass*
PSTKMNYN post-communion *Mass*
PSTKMYNN post-communion *Mass*
PSTKMYNYN post-communion *Mass*
PSTKRD postcard *mail*
PSTKRNL postcranial (adj) *head* postcranially (adv)
PSTKRNYL postcranial (adj)

head postcranially (adv)
PSTKSL postaxial *side*
PSTKSS epistaxis *nosebleed* epistaxes
PSTKSYL postaxial *side*
PSTKSZ epistaxes (pl) *nosebleed* epistaxis
PSTKTL postcoital *after sex*
PSTKTRL postdoctoral *after PhD.*
PSTKWDL postcoital *after sex*
PSTKWTL postcoital *after sex*
PSTL apsidal *orbit*
PSTL pastel *color*
PSTL pastille *scent*
PSTL pesthole *disease*
PSTL pestle *(v) crush* pestled pestling
PSTL pestle *(n) tool*
PSTL pistil *plant*
PSTL pistol *firearm*
PSTL pistole *coin*
PSTL postal *(adj) mail, (slang) crazy*
PSTL posthole *pole*
PSTL pustule *pimple*
PSTLDD pustulated *pimples*
PSTLDR postulator *claim*
PSTLDRT postliterate *media*
PSTLK apostolic *papal*
PSTLN postilion (or) postillion *rider*
PSTLNC postulancy *probation* postulancies
PSTLNCHL pestilential (adj) *deadly* pestilentially (adv)
PSTLNS pestilence *plague*
PSTLNS postulancy *probation* postulancies
PSTLNSHL pestilential (adj) *deadly* pestilentially (adv)
PSTLNT pestilent *deadly*
PSTLNT postulant *probation*
PSTLNT pustulant *pimple*
PSTLNTC postulancy *probation* postulancies
PSTLNTS pestilence *plague*
PSTLNTS postulancy *probation* postulancies
PSTLR epistolary *book*

Use letters that best describe the sounds you hear and omit the vowels. Use **S** or **K** instead of **C**: to find circle use **SRKL**. Use **J** to find joy, **JM** to find gem and **G** to find go.

epistolaries
PSTLR pistoleer *armed one*
PSTLR pustular *pimples*
PSTLSHN postulation *claim*
PSTLST pastelist (or)
pastellist *artist*
PSTLT apostolate *mission*
PSTLT postulate *claim*
postulated postulating
PSTLTD pustulated *pimples*
PSTLTR postulator *claim*
PSTLTRT postliterate *media*
PSTLVN postdiluvian *after flood*
PSTLVYN postdiluvian *after flood*
PSTLWP pistol-whip *beat*
pistol-whipped pistol-whipping
PSTLYN postilion (or)
postillion *rider*
PSTM pastime *hobby*
PSTM peacetime *no war*
PSTM post time *race*
PSTMDRN postmodern
traditional
PSTMDRNST
postmodernist *traditional*
PSTMDRNZM
postmodernism *tradition*
PSTMK epistemic *knowledge*
PSTMKL epistemically
knowledge
PSTMLG epistemology
knowledge
PSTMLJ epistemology
knowledge
PSTMLNYL postmillennial
1000 years
PSTMN postman *mail*
postmen
PSTMNPZL
postmenopausal *after menstruation*
PSTMRDL postmarital *after wedding*
PSTMRDM post meridiem
after noon
PSTMRDM postmortem
autopsy
PSTMRDYM post meridiem
after noon

PSTMRK postmark *mail*
PSTMRTL postmarital *after wedding*
PSTMRTM postmortem
autopsy
PSTMS posthumous *after death*
PSTMSDR postmaster *mail*
PSTMSL posthumously
after death
PSTMSNS
posthumousness *after death*
PSTMSTR postmaster *mail*
PSTMSTRS postmistress
mail postmistresses
PSTN pastina *noodle*
PSTN piston *engine*
PSTN posting *assignment, public notice*
PSTNBR Epstein-Barr *virus*
PSTNDL postnatal (adj)
birth postnatally (adv)
PSTNDN upstanding
upright
PSTNDNG upstanding
upright
PSTNFKSHN postinfection
disease
PSTNG posting *assignment, public notice*
PSTNGRL postinaugural
after induction
PSTNGYRL postinaugural
after induction
PSTNPCHL postnuptial
after mating
PSTNPCHWL postnuptial
after mating
PSTNPSHL postnuptial *after mating*
PSTNPSHWL postnuptial
after mating
PSTNS past tense *verb*
PSTNS pastiness *like glue*
PSTNTL postnatal (adj) *birth*
postnatally (adv)
PSTNZL postnasal *sinus*
PSTPBRD postpuberty
adult
PSTPBRT postpuberty *adult*
PSTPBSNT postpubescent

adult
PSTPD postpaid *mail*
PSTPN postpone *defer*
postponed postponing
PSTPNBL postponable *defer*
PSTPNMNT postponement
defer
PSTPRDKSHN
postproduction *film*
PSTPRDV postoperative
after surgery
PSTPRTV postoperative
after surgery
PSTPYBRD postpuberty
adult
PSTPYBRT postpuberty
adult
PSTPYBSNT
postpubescent *adult*
PSTR pacesetter *example*
PSTR Pasteur *chemist*
PSTR pastier *glue*
PSTR pastor *clergy*
PSTR pastry *food* pastries
PSTR pasture (v) *graze*
pastured pasturing
PSTR pasture (n) *field*
PSTR pester *bother*
PSTR poster *picture*
PSTR posture *position*
postured posturing
PSTRD posterity *offspring*
PSTRF apostrophe *mark*
PSTRF epistrophe *word repetition*
PSTRFK apostrophic
personified
PSTRFZ apostrophize
personify apostrophized
apostrophizing
(Br) apostrophise
PSTRK upstroke *swing*
PSTRL pastoral (adj)
livestock pastorally (adv)
PSTRL postural *position*
PSTRLN pastureland *field*
PSTRLND pastureland *field*
PSTRM pastrami *meat*
PSTRM upstream *river*
PSTRMDK post-traumatic
psychology
PSTRMTK post-traumatic

psychology
PSTRN pastern *foot*
PSTRN post horn *music*
PSTRR a posteriori
reasoning
PSTRR posterior *rear*
PSTRR posturer *position*
PSTRRD posteriority *rear*
PSTRRT posteriority *rear*
PSTRS post-horse *mail*
PSTRT pastorate *parson*
PSTRT posterity *offspring*
PSTRT upstart *riser*
PSTRYR a posteriori
reasoning
PSTRYR posterior *rear*
PSTRYRD posteriority *rear*
PSTRYRT posteriority *rear*
PSTRZ pasteurize *sterilize*
pasteurized pasteurizing
(Br) pasteurise
PSTRZ upstairs *upper story*
PSTRZSHN pasteurization
sterilization
(Br) pasteurisation
PSTS apostasy *defection*
apostasies
PSTS pasties *striptease*
PSTS pastis *liqueur*
PSTSD pesticide *pest killer*
PSTSH pastiche *hodgepodge*
PSTSH pistachio *tree, nut*
pistachios
PSTSH postiche *wig*
PSTSHY pistachio *tree, nut*
pistachios
PSTSKNDR postsecondary
college
PSTSKRP postscript *letter*
PSTSKRPT postscript *letter*
PSTSRJKL postsurgical
surgery
PSTSS epistasis *suppression*
epistases
PSTST pastiest *glue*
PSTST posttest *exam*
PSTT apostate *defector*
PSTT upstate *northern*
PSTTZ apostatize *defect*
apostatized apostatizing
(Br) apostatise
PSTWMN postwoman *mail*

postwomen
PSTWR postwar *conflict*
PSTXL postaxial *side*
PSTXS epistaxis *nosebleed*
epistaxes
PSTXYL postaxial *side*
PSTXZ epistaxes (pl)
nosebleed epistaxis
PSTYL pustule *pimple*
PSTYLDD pustulated
pimples
PSTYLDR postulator *claim*
PSTYLNC postulancy
probation postulancies
PSTYLNS postulancy
probation postulancies
PSTYLNT postulant
probation
PSTYLNT pustulant *pimple*
PSTYLNTC postulancy
probation postulancies
PSTYLNTS postulancy
probation postulancies
PSTYLR pustular *pimples*
PSTYLSHN postulation
claim
PSTYLT postulate *claim*
postulated postulating
PSTYLTD pustulated
pimples
PSTYLTR postulator *claim*
PSTYMS posthumous *after*
death
PSTYMSL posthumously
after death
PSTYMSNS
posthumousness *after*
death
PSTYN postilion (or)
postillion *rider*
PSTYR Pasteur *chemist*
PSTYR pastier *glue*
PSTYR pasture (v) *graze*
pastured pasturing
PSTYR pasture (n) *field*
PSTYR posture *position*
postured posturing
PSTYRL postural *position*
PSTYRR posturer *position*
PSTYRZ pasteurize *sterilize*
pasteurized pasteurizing
(Br) pasteurise

PSTYRZSHN pasteurization
sterilization
(Br) pasteurisation
PSTYST pastiest *glue*
PSTZ pasties *striptease*
PSV passive *inactive*
PSVD passivity *inactivity*
PSVNS passiveness
inactivity
PSVR pass over *ignore*
PSVR Passover *holiday*
PSVT passivity *inactivity*
PSVZM passivism *inactivity*
PSW pissoir *urinal*
PSW postwar *conflict*
PSWMN postwoman *mail*
postwomen
PSWNG upswing *increase*
PSWP upsweep *push up*
upswept upsweeping
PSWP upswept *push up*
PSWPT upswept *push up*
PSWR pissoir *urinal*
PSWRD password *code*
PSWRK piecework *labor*
PSWRKR pieceworker
laborer
PSWZ piecewise *intervals*
PSY paseo *walk* paseos
PSYDN Poseidon *Greek god*
PSYS piceous *like tar*
PSYT pursuit *work, chase*
PSZ apices (pl) *summit* apex
PSZ Pisces *zodiac sign*
PT apt *likely*
PT opiate *narcotic*
PT opt *choose*
PT paddy *rice* paddies
PT Paiute *Native American*
PT pat (v) *tap* patted patting
PT pat (n) *tap, small amount*
PT pate *head*
PT pâté *food*
PT patio *porch* patios
PT patty *round mass* patties
PT payout *money*
PT peat *moss*
PT peaty *mossy*
PT pet (v) *fondle* petted
petting
PT pet (n) *favored one, tame*
animal

Use letters that best describe the sounds you hear and omit the vowels. Use **S** or **K** instead of **C**: to find circle use **SRKL**. Use **J** to find joy, **JM** to find gem and **G** to find go.

PT petty *trivial, small-minded* pettier pettiest

PT peyote *cactus*

PT pietà *(often capitalized) statue*

PT piety *devotion* pieties

PT pit *(v) bury, scar, remove seed* pitted pitting

PT pit *(n) hole, worst, seed*

PT pita *plant, bread*

PT pity *feel sorry* pitied pitying pities

PT poet *writer*

PT pot *vessel* potted potting

PT potto *monkey* pottos

PT potty *(n) toilet* potties

PT potty *(adj) (Br) trivial, crazy* pottier pottiest

PT pout *(v) sulk (n) fish, expression*

PT pouty *sulky*

PT put *place* put putting

PT putt *golf*

PT puttee *legging*

PT putto *boy* putti

PT putty *cement* putties

PT uppity *snobbish*

PTBL pit bull *dog*

PTBL pitiable (adj) *sorrowful* pitiably (adv)

PTBL potable *drinkable*

PTBL potbelly *abdomen, stove* potbellies

PTBL potboil *poor work*

PTBLD potbellied *rounded*

PTBLR potboiler *poor work*

PTBRNS protuberance *projection*

PTBRNTS protuberance *projection*

PTBT PT boat *ship*

PTBYL potboil *poor work*

PTC patsy *fool* patsies

PTD pitted *no seeds*

PTD potato *vegetable* potatoes

PTD pothead *(slang) marijuana smoker*

PTD potted *in a container*

PTDFWGR pate de foie gras *food* pates de foie gras

PTDN put down *(v) stop, humiliate, consume**

PTDN put-down *(n) remark*

PTDT up-to-date *modern*

PTDV optative *wish*

PTDV putative *assumed*

PTDVL optatively *wish*

PTF epitaph *words on tombstone*

PTF put off *delay, leave*

PTFGNG pettifogging *quibbling*

PTFGR pettifogger *shyster*

PTFGR pettifoggery *quibbling*

PTFK epitaphic *tombstone*

PTFL epitaphial *tombstone*

PTFL pedophile *molester*

PTFL pedophilia *child molestation*

PTFL pitfall *problem*

PTFL pitiful (adj) *pathetic* pitifully (adv)

PTFL potful *container*

PTFLK pedophiliac (or) pedophilic *child molestation*

PTFLY pedophilia *child molestation*

PTFLYK pedophiliac (or) pedophilic *child molestation*

PTFR petit four *cake* petit fours (or) petits fours

PTFSR petty officer *rank*

PTFYL epitaphial *tombstone*

PTGG pedagogue *teacher*

PTGG pedagogy *teaching*

PTGJ pedagogy *teaching*

PTGJKL pedagogical (adj) *teaching* pedagogically (adv)

PTGJKS pedagogics *teaching*

PTGJX pedagogics *teaching*

PTGN Patagonia *region*

PTGNY Patagonia *region*

PTGR pedigree *ancestors*

PTGRD pedigreed *ancestors*

PTH apathy *indifference*

PTH path *road* paths

PTH pith *center part*

PTH pithy *to the point* pithier pithiest

PTHD pothead *(slang) marijuana smoker*

PTHDK apathetic *indifferent*

PTHDK epithetic (or) epithetical *name*

PTHDK pathetic *sad*

PTHDKL apathetically *indifferently*

PTHDKL epithetical (or) epithetic *name*

PTHDKL pathetically *sad*

PTHFNDNG pathfinding *scouting*

PTHFNDR pathfinder *scout*

PTHGNK pathogenic *disease*

PTHGNMNK pathognomonic *disease*

PTHGRN Pythagorean *theory*

PTHGRS Pythagoras *mathematician*

PTHGRYN Pythagorean *theory*

PTHJN pathogen *disease*

PTHJNDK pathogenetic *disease*

PTHJNK pathogenic *disease*

PTHJNSS pathogenesis *disease*

PTHJNTK pathogenetic *disease*

PTHK pothook *hanger*

PTHKNTHRPN pithecanthropine *ancestor*

PTHKR apothecary *pharmacy* apothecaries

PTHL epithelia (pl) *tissue* epithelium

PTHL pithily *to the point*

PTHL pothole *road*

PTHLD epithelioid *tissue*

PTHLDR pot holder *cloth*

PTHLG pathology *disease* pathologies

PTHLJ pathology *disease* pathologies

PTHLJKL pathological (adj) *disease* pathologically (adv)

PTHLJST pathologist

Letters aren't doubled for single sounds: to find alley use **L** not **LL**. Use **Y** and **W** as hard sounds only: to find yellow use **YL**. (Br)=British spelling or usage. * See dictionary.

disease
PTHLL epithelial *tissue*
PTHLM epithelioma *tumor*
PTHLM epithelium *tissue*
epithelia
PTHLM ophthalmia
inflammation
PTHLMK ophthalmic *eye*
PTHLMLG ophthalmology
eye
PTHLMLJ ophthalmology
eye
PTHLMLJK ophthalmologic
(or) ophthalmological
(adj) *eye*
ophthalmologically (adv)
PTHLMLJKL
ophthalmological (or)
ophthalmologic (adj) *eye*
ophthalmologically (adv)
PTHLMLJST
ophthalmologist *eye*
PTHLMSKP
ophthalmoscope
instrument
PTHLMSKPK
ophthalmoscopic
instrument
PTHLMY ophthalmia
inflammation
PTHLS pathless *no road*
PTHLY epithelia (pl) *tissue*
epithelium
PTHLYD epithelioid *tissue*
PTHLYL epithelial *tissue*
PTHLYM epithelioma *tumor*
PTHLYM epithelium *tissue*
epithelia
PTHM apothegm *wise saying*
PTHMLG ophthalmology
eye
PTHMLJ ophthalmology *eye*
PTHMLJK ophthalmologic
(or) ophthalmological
(adj) *eye*
ophthalmologically (adv)
PTHMLJKL
ophthalmological (or)
ophthalmologic (adj) *eye*
ophthalmologically (adv)
PTHMLJST
ophthalmologist *eye*

PTHMSKP ophthalmoscope
instrument
PTHMSKPK
ophthalmoscopic
instrument
PTHN python *snake*
PTHNK pythonic *prophet (f)*
PTHNMNK pathognomonic
disease
PTHNS pithiness *to the point*
PTHNS pythoness *prophet
(f)*
PTHR pithier *to the point*
PTHR pother *commotion*
PTHRB potherb *seasoning*
PTHRST upthrust *elevate*
PTHS pathos *pity*
PTHST pithiest *to the point*
PTHT epithet *name*
PTHTK apathetic *indifferent*
PTHTK epithetic (or)
epithetical *name*
PTHTK pathetic *sad*
PTHTKL apathetically
indifferently
PTHTKL epithetical (or)
epithetic *name*
PTHTKL pathetically *sad*
PTHW pathway *course*
PTHYR pithier *to the point*
PTHYST pithiest *to the point*
PTJ potage *creamy soup*
PTJ pottage *stew*
PTJNDK pedogenetic *soil*
PTJNSS pedogenesis *soil*
PTJNTK pedogenetic *soil*
PTJR petit jury *trial*
PTK optic *lens*
PTK paddock *enclosure*
PTK petechia *blood spot*
petechiae
PTK poetic *verse*
PTK pothook *hanger*
PTK uptake *understanding,
flue*
PTK uptick *rise*
PTKB pedicab *tricycle*
PTKK pat-a-cake (or) patty-
cake *game*
PTKK petcock *valve*
PTKL optical (adj) *lens*
optically (adv)

PTKL pedicle *stalk,
attachment*
PTKL poetically *verse*
PTKR pedicure *foot care*
PTKRNLN Pitcairn Island
land mass
PTKRNLND Pitcairn Island
land mass
PTKRST pedicurist *foot care*
PTKS optics *light*
PTKT petticoat *skirt*
PTKY petechia *blood spot*
petechiae
PTKYR pedicure *foot care*
PTKYRST pedicurist *foot
care*
PTL aptly *suitably* apt
PTL paddle *(n) oar, hitting
implement*
PTL partly *somewhat*
PTL patella *kneecap* patellae
(or) patellas
PTL pedal *(n) lever (adj) foot
(v) ride*
PTL peddle *sell* peddled
peddling
PTL petal *flower*
PTL petiole *stem*
PTL pettily *small-minded*
PTL piddle *squander, urinate*
piddled piddling
PTL pothole *road*
PTL puddle *(v) muddy, wet*
puddled puddling
PTL puddle *(n) pool*
PTLBL paddleball *game*
PTLBRD paddleboard *surf*
PTLBT paddleboat *vehicle*
PTLCH potlatch *feast*
PTLD petalled *flower*
PTLDR pot holder *cloth*
PTLFRM patelliform *disk-
shaped*
PTLFSH paddlefish *fish*
PTLG putlog *timber*
PTLJKL pedological *soil*
PTLK petallike *flower*
PTLK potluck *whatever food*
PTLL petiolule *stem*
PTLM Ptolemy *astronomer,
king*
PTLNG puddling *iron*

Use letters that best describe the sounds you hear and omit the vowels. Use **S** or **K** instead of **C**: to find circle use **SRKL**. Use **J** to find joy, **JM** to find gem and **G** to find go.

PTLNS petulance
peevishness petulancy
PTLNT pedal-note *low tone*
PTLNT petulant *peevish*
PTLNTS petulance
peevishness petulancy
PTLR patellar *kneecap*
PTLR petiolar *stalk*
PTLRSN petit larceny *crime*
PTLS patulous *spreading*
PTLS pitiless *not sad*
PTLT petiolate *stalk*
PTLWL paddle wheel *boat*
PTLWLR paddle wheeler
boat
PTM epitome *example*
PTM optima (pl) *best*
optimum
PTM uptime *connected*
PTMDR potometer *water*
PTML optimal (adj) *best*
optimally (adv)
PTML petit mal *epilepsy*
PTMM optimum *best* optima
PTMNL pedimental *roof,*
slope
PTMNT pediment *roof, slope*
PTMNTL pedimental *roof,*
slope
PTMP up-tempo *fast*
PTMRK pockmark *hole*
PTMS peat moss *turf*
PTMSDK optimistic *positive*
PTMSDKL optimistically
positively
PTMST optimist *positive*
PTMSTK optimistic *positive*
PTMSTKL optimistically
positively
PTMTR optometry *eyes*
PTMTR potometer *water*
PTMTRST optometrist *eyes*
PTMZ epitomize *represent*
epitomized epitomizing
(Br) epitomise
PTMZ optimize *make the best*
optimized optimizing
(Br) optimise
PTMZM optimism *positive*
PTN opt in *choose to*
PTN paten *plate*
PTN patina *shine or natural*

finish patinas (or) patinae
PTN patten *shoe*
PTN petunia *flower*
PTN piton *spike*
PTN poteen *whiskey*
PTN put in *enter*
PTN put on (v) *dress,*
*pretend, apply**
PTN put-on (adj) *pretended*
(n) *parody*
PTN uptown *city*
PTNBL patentable *original*
PTNBLD patentability
original
PTNBLT patentability
original
PTNC appetency *desire*
appetencies
PTNC patency *obvious*
PTNC potency *strength*
potencies
PTNCHL potential (adj, n)
possible potentially (adv)
PTNCHLD potentiality
possibility potentialities
PTNCHLT potentiality
possibility potentialities
PTNCHYLD potentiality
possibility potentialities
PTNCHYLT potentiality
possibility potentialities
PTNG padding *matting,*
excess
PTNG petting *caressing*
PTNG pitting *remove pits*
PTNG pudding *food*
PTNL patently *obvious*
PTNLTHR patent leather
glossy
PTNS appetency *desire*
appetencies
PTNS aptness *suitability*
PTNS patency *obvious*
PTNS pettiness *small-*
mindedness
PTNS pittance *tiny amount*
PTNS potency *strength*
potencies
PTNSHL potential (adj)
possible potentially (adv)
PTNSHLD potentiality
possibility potentialities

PTNSHLT potentiality
possibility potentialities
PTNSHYLD potentiality
possibility potentialities
PTNSHYLT potentiality
possibility potentialities
PTNT patent (n) *right,*
leather (v) *originate*
PTNT patentee *originator*
PTNT patinate *shine*
patinated patinating
PTNT potent *strong*
PTNTBL patentable *original*
PTNTBLD patentability
original
PTNTBLT patentability
original
PTNTC appetency *desire*
appetencies
PTNTC patency *obvious*
PTNTC potency *strength*
potencies
PTNTD patented *originated*
PTNTL patently *obvious*
PTNTLTHR patent leather
glossy
PTNTR patentor *grantor*
PTNTS appetency *desire*
appetencies
PTNTS patency *obvious*
PTNTS pittance *tiny amount*
PTNTS potency *strength*
potencies
PTNTT potentate *ruler*
PTNY petunia *flower*
PTP potpie *food*
PTP put up (v) *build,*
*accommodate, can**
PTP put-up (adj) *arranged*
PTPN pattypan *vegetable*
PTPN put-upon *imposed*
PTPNT petit point
embroidery
PTPR potpourri *collection*
PTQR pedicure *foot care*
PTQRST pedicurist *foot care*
PTR aperture *hole*
PTR pater (Br) *father*
PTR patter *talk, tap*
PTR peter (v) *diminish* (n-
slang) *penis*
PTR pettier *small-minded*

Letters aren't doubled for single sounds: to find alley use **L** not **LL**. Use **Y** and **W** as hard
sounds only: to find yellow use **YL**. (Br)=British spelling or usage. * See dictionary.

PTR pewter *metal*
PTR pitier *concern*
PTR poetry *verse*
PTR potter (*n*) *pottery maker*
(*v*) *putter*
PTR pottery *clayware*
potteries
PTR pouter *bird, sulker*
PTR putter (*n*) *golf* (*v*) *tinker*
PTRB potherb *seasoning*
PTRD petard *explosive*
PTRD protrude *stick out*
protruded protruding
PTRD putrid *foul*
PTRDD putridity *foulness*
PTRDK patriotic *nationalist*
PTRDKL patriotically
nationalist
PTRDL putridly *foul*
PTRDLR petrodollar *oil*
PTRDSH petri dish *bacteria*
PTRDT petered out *gone*
PTRDT putridity *foulness*
PTRF petrify *harden, deaden*
petrified petrifies
PTRF putrefy *rot* putrefied
putrefying putrifies
PTRFKDV putrefactive
rotting
PTRFKSHN petrifaction (or)
petrification *hardness*
PTRFKSHN putrefaction *rot*
PTRFKTV putrefactive
rotting
PTRGLF petroglyph *writing*
on a rock
PTRGNSS petrogenesis
rocks
PTRGRF petrography *rocks*
PTRGRFKL petrographical
(adj) *rocks*
petrographically (adv)
PTRGRFR petrographer
rocks
PTRKMKL petrochemical
oil
PTRKMSDR petrochemistry
oil
PTRKMSTR petrochemistry
oil
PTRKS apteryx *kiwi*
PTRL patrol *watch* patrolled

patrolling
PTRL petrale *flounder*
PTRL petrel *bird*
PTRL petrol *gasoline*
PTRLDM petrolatum *salve*
PTRLG petrology *rocks*
PTRLJ petrology *rocks*
PTRLJK petrologic (or)
petrological (adj) *rocks*
petrologically (adv)
PTRLJKL petrological (or)
petrologic (adj) *rocks*
petrologically (adv)
PTRLJST petrologist *rocks*
PTRLKR patrol car *police*
PTRLM petroleum *oil*
PTRLMN patrolman *police*
patrolmen
PTRLNL patrilineal *male line*
PTRLNYL patrilineal *male*
line
PTRLTM petrolatum *salve*
PTRLWGN patrol wagon
police
PTRLWMN patrolwoman
police patrolwomen
PTRLYM petroleum *oil*
PTRMN patrimony *heritage*
PTRMNL patrimonial
heritage
PTRMNYL patrimonial
heritage
PTRN patron *advisor*
PTRN pattern (*v*) *shape* (*n*)
design
PTRN upturn *rise*
PTRND paternity *father*
PTRNJ patronage *influence*
PTRNL paternal (adj) *father*
paternally (adv)
PTRNL petronel *gun*
PTRNLS patternless *no*
design
PTRNLSDK paternalistic
controlling
PTRNLSDKL
paternalistically
controlling
PTRNLST paternalist
controller
PTRNLSTK paternalistic
controlling

PTRNLSTKL
paternalistically
controlling
PTRNLZM paternalism
control
PTRNMK patronymic *name*
PTRNMKR patternmaker
designer
PTRNN patterning *design*
PTRNNG patterning *design*
PTRNSDR paternoster
(*often capitalized*) *Lord's*
prayer
PTRNSNT patron saint
angel
PTRNSTR paternoster
(*often capitalized*) *Lord's*
prayer
PTRNT paternity *father*
PTRNZ patronize *support,*
treat coolly patronized
patronizing
(Br) patronise
PTRNZSHN patronization
support, treat coolly
(Br) patronisation
PTRRK patriarch *father*
PTRRK patriarchy *rule by*
men patriarchies
PTRRKL patriarchal *father*
PTRS petrous *ear*
PTRSD patricide *father*
murder
PTRSDK pederastic *boy love*
PTRSHN patrician *aristocrat*
PTRSHN protrusion
projection
PTRSL petrosal *ear*
PTRSNS putrescence *rot*
PTRSNT putrescent *rotting*
PTRSNTS putrescence *rot*
PTRST pederast *boy love*
pederasty
PTRSTK pederastic *boy love*
PTRSV protrusive *prominent*
PTRT patriot *nationalist*
PTRT puttyroot *orchid*
PTRTK patriotic *nationalist*
PTRTKL patriotically
nationalist
PTRTZM patriotism
nationalism

Use letters that best describe the sounds you hear and omit the vowels. Use **S** or **K** instead of **C**: to find circle use **SRKL**. Use **J** to find joy, **JM** to find gem and **G** to find go.

PTRX apteryx *kiwi*
PTRYDK patriotic *nationalist*
PTRYDKL patriotically *nationalist*
PTRYRK patriarch *father*
PTRYRK patriarchy *rule by men* patriarchies
PTRYRKL patriarchal *father*
PTRYT patriot *nationalist*
PTRYTK patriotic *nationalist*
PTRYTKL patriotically *nationalist*
PTRYTZM patriotism *nationalism*
PTRZHN protrusion *projection*
PTRZV protrusive *prominent*
PTS opts *chooses*
PTS patsy *fool* patsies
PTS piteous *pity*
PTS pizza *food*
PTS poetess *writer (f)*
PTSBRG Pittsburgh *city*
PTSDK pietistic *devoted*
PTSDKL pietistically *devoted*
PTSDL pedestal *(n) column*
PTSH pettish *fretful*
PTSH potage *creamy soup*
PTSHN optician *eyes*
PTSHN petition *request*
PTSHN potation *drink*
PTSHNR petitioner *request*
PTSHRD potsherd *piece*
PTSHT potshot *attack* potshot potshotting
PTSK potassic *chemical*
PTSKD pizzicato *plucking* pizzicati
PTSKT pizzicato *plucking* pizzicati
PTSL pedicel *stalk, attachment*
PTSL piteously *pity*
PTSM potassium *chemical*
PTSNS piteousness *pity*
PTSR patisserie *bakery*
PTSR pizzeria *pizza*
PTSRS apatosaurus *dinosaur*
PTSRY pizzeria *pizza*
PTSS epitasis *theater* epitases

PTST pettiest *small-minded*
PTST pietist *devoted*
PTSTK pietistic *devoted*
PTSTKL pietistically *devoted*
PTSTP pit stop *rest*
PTSYM potassium *chemical*
PTSZ poeticize *write verse* poeticized poeticizing
PTSZM poeticism *verse*
PTT apatite *mineral*
PTT appetite *desire*
PTT opt out *choose not to*
PTT petit *small (legal)*
PTT petite *small (size)*
PTT potato *vegetable* potatoes
PTT put out *(v) extinguish, annoy, have sex**
PTT putout *(n) baseball*
PTT uptight *tense*
PTTD aptitude *ability*
PTTDNL aptitudinal (adj) *ability* aptitudinally (adv)
PTTHMNT up-to-the-minute *modern*
PTTR pituitary *gland* pituitaries
PTTV optative *wish*
PTTV putative *assumed*
PTTVL optatively *wish*
PTTYD aptitude *ability*
PTTYDNL aptitudinal (adj) *ability* aptitudinally (adv)
PTVR put over *(v) delay, trick*
PTW patois *jargon* patois
PTWGN paddy wagon *police*
PTWTR pituitary *gland* pituitaries
PTWZ patois (pl) *jargon* patois
PTX optics *light*
PTY patio *porch* patios
PTYBL pitiable (adj) *sorrowful* pitiably (adv)
PTYBRNS protuberance *projection*
PTYBRNTS protuberance *projection*
PTYL petiole *stem*
PTYLL petiolule *stem*
PTYLNS petulance

peevishness petulancy
PTYLNT petulant *peevish*
PTYLNTS petulance *peevishness* petulancy
PTYLR petiolar *stalk*
PTYLT petiolate *stalk*
PTYN petunia *flower*
PTYNY petunia *flower*
PTYR aperture *hole*
PTYR pettier *small-minded*
PTYR pitier *concern*
PTYS piteous *pity*
PTYSL piteously *pity*
PTYSNS piteousness *pity*
PTYST pettiest *small-minded*
PTYTR pituitary *gland* pituitaries
PTYWTR pituitary *gland* pituitaries
PTZ pizza *food*
PTZ poetize *write verse* poetized poetizing
PTZH potage *creamy soup*
PTZKD pizzicato *plucking* pizzicati
PTZKT pizzicato *plucking* pizzicati
PTZM pietism *devotion*
PTZN appetizing *appealing* (Br) appetising
PTZNG appetizing *appealing* (Br) appetising
PTZNGL appetizingly *in an appealing manner* (Br) appetisingly
PTZR appetizer *food* (Br) appetiser
PTZR patzer *chess*
PTZR pizzeria *pizza*
PTZRY pizzeria *pizza*
PV pave *smooth* paved paving
PV pavé *jewelry*
PV peeve *annoy* peeved peeving
PVDL pivotal (adj) *crucial* pivotally (adv)
PVL upheaval *change*
PVLV pavlova *dessert*
PVLYN pavilion *tent*
PVMNT pavement *sidewalk*
PVN pavane *dance*

Letters aren't doubled for single sounds: to find alley use **L** not **LL**. Use **Y** and **W** as hard sounds only: to find yellow use **YL**. (Br)=British spelling or usage. * See dictionary.

PVN paving *pavement*
PVNG paving *pavement*
PVR paver *smoother*
PVRD poverty *poor*
poverties
PVRT poverty *poor*
PVRTSTRKN poverty-
stricken *poor*
PVSH peevish *fretful*
PVT pivot *turn*
PVTL pivotal (adj) *crucial*
pivotally (adv)
PVYN pavilion *tent*
PW peewee *small*
PW pewee *bird*
PW poi *taro root* poi (or) pois
PW powwow *gathering*
PWBL pueblo *town* pueblos
PWDK poetic *verse*
PWDKL poetically *verse*
PWDS poetess *writer (f)*
PWDSZ poeticize *write verse*
poeticized poeticizing
PWDSZM poeticism *verse*
PWDZ poetize *write verse*
poetized poetizing
PWM poem *verse*
PWN upwind *direction*
PWND upwind *direction*
PWNT pointe *ballet*
PWNTLST pointillist *color
dots*
PWNTLZM pointillism *color
dots*
PWNTYST pointillist *color
dots*
PWNTYZM pointillism *color
dots*
PWR power *force*
PWRBT powerboat *ship*
PWRD upward (or) upwards
higher
PWRDRK Puerto Rico
commonwealth
PWRDS upwards (or)
upward *higher*
PWRDV power dive (n)
airplane power-dive (v)
PWRDZ upwards (or)
upward *higher*
PWRFL powerful (adj)
mighty powerfully (adv)

PWRHS powerhouse *strong
one*
PWRLS powerless *weak*
PWRLSL powerlessly *weak*
PWRLSNS powerlessness
weakness
PWRTRK Puerto Rico
commonwealth
PWSNS puissance *power*
PWSNT puissant *powerful*
PWSNTS puissance *power*
PWT peewit *bird*
PWT poet *writer*
PWT pointe *ballet*
PWTK poetic *verse*
PWTKL poetically *verse*
PWTR poetry *verse*
PWTS poetess *writer (f)*
PWTSZ poeticize *write verse*
poeticized poeticizing
PWTSZM poeticism *verse*
PWTZ poetize *write verse*
poetized poetizing
PWW powwow *gathering*
PX apex *top* apexes (or)
apices
PX epoxy *glue* epoxied (or)
epoxyed epoxying
PX pax *tablet, peace*
PX pixie (or) pixy *fairie*
pixies
PX pox *blemish* pox (or)
poxes
PX pyx *container*
PX pyxie *shrub*
PXDL packsaddle *load
support*
PXDZ pyxides (pl) *fruit*
pyxis
PXK packsack *knapsack*
PXL pixel *dot*
PXLDD pixilated (or)
pixillated *amusing*
PXLSHN pixilation
amusement
PXLTD pixilated (or)
pixillated *amusing*
PXPK Pikes Peak *mountain*
PXS pyxis *fruit* pyxides
PXTL packsaddle *load
support*
PY paella *food*

PY payee *receiver*
PY pew *bench*
PYBK pubic *pelvis*
PYBL payable *owed*
PYBRD puberty *sexuality*
PYBRDL pubertal (or)
puberal *sexuality*
PYBRL puberal (or) pubertal
sexuality
PYBRT puberty *sexuality*
PYBRTL pubertal (or)
puberal *sexuality*
PYBS pubis *bone* pubes
PYBSNS pubescense *hair*
PYBSNT pubescent *hair*
PYBSNTS pubescense *hair*
PYBZ pubes *hair* pubes
PYD opioid *narcotic*
PYD peyote *cactus*
PYD pie-eyed *drunk*
PYD pietà *(often capitalized)
statue*
PYD piety *devotion* pieties
PYDBL POW *prisoner of war*
POWs
PYDBLY POW *prisoner of
war* POWs
PYDDV putative *assumed*
PYDNC pudency *modesty*
PYDND pudenda (pl)
genitals pudendum
PYDNDL pudendal *genitals*
PYDNDM pudendum
genitals pudenda
PYDNS pudency *modesty*
PYDNTC pudency *modesty*
PYDNTS pudency *modesty*
PYDR pewter *metal*
PYDTV putative *assumed*
PYF payoff *money*
PYJ Piaget *psychologist*
PYJLSDK pugilistic *boxing*
PYJLST pugilist *boxer*
PYJLSTK pugilistic *boxing*
PYJLZM pugilism *boxing*
PYK puke *vomit* puked
puking
PYL payola *bribe*
PYL pile *heap* piled piling
PYL pule *whine* puled puling
PYLDS pyelitis *pelvis*
PYLN piling *structure*

Use letters that best describe the sounds you hear and omit the vowels. Use **S** or **K** instead of **C**: to find circle use **SRKL**. Use **J** to find joy, **JM** to find gem and **G** to find go.

PYLNFRDK pyelonephritic *kidney*
PYLNFRDS pyelonephritis *kidney*
PYLNFRTK pyelonephritic *kidney*
PYLNFRTS pyelonephritis *kidney*
PYLNG piling *structure*
PYLNS opulence *more than enough*
PYLNT opulent *more than enough*
PYLNTL opulently *more than enough*
PYLNTS opulence *more than enough*
PYLP pileup *mass*
PYLTS pyelitis *pelvis*
PYLTSR Pulitzer *journalist*
PYLTZR Pulitzer *journalist*
PYLZ piles *ailment*
PYM opium *narcotic*
PYM puma *animal* pumas
PYMS pumice *rock*
PYMSHS pumiceous *rock*
PYMST pumicite *rock*
PYN apian *bees*
PYN oppugn *fight*
PYN paean *song*
PYN paeon *verse*
PYN peon *unskilled laborer* peons (or) peones
PYN peony *flower* peonies
PYN piano *music* pianos
PYN puisne *rank*
PYN puny *small* punier puniest
PYNDV punitive *penalty*
PYNJ peonage *labor*
PYNL punily *small*
PYNNS puniness *small*
PYNR oppugner *fighter*
PYNR pioneer *(v)* originate *(n)* initiator *(adj)* original
PYNR punier *small*
PYNSM pianissimo *softly*
PYNST pianist *musician*
PYNST puniest *small*
PYNTHSK pie-in-the-sky *unrealistic*
PYNTV punitive *penalty*

PYNYR punier *small*
PYNYST puniest *small*
PYNZM pianism *piano*
PYP pay up *settle debt*
PYP pupa *insect* pupae (or) pupas
PYPL pupil *student, eye*
PYPLJ pupillage *student*
PYPLR pupillary *eye*
PYPSHN pupation *development*
PYPT pupate *develop* pupated pupating
PYR apiary *bees* apiaries
PYR paillard *beef*
PYR payer *giver*
PYR Pierre *city*
PYR pure *clean, perfect* purer purest
PYR purée (or) puree *whip* pureed pureeing
PYR pyorrhea *gum disease*
PYR pyre *funeral*
PYR pyuria *pus in urine*
PYRBLD pure-blood (or) pure-blooded (adj) *breeding* pureblood (n)
PYRBLDD pure-blooded (or) pure-blood (adj) *breeding* pureblood (n)
PYRBRD purebred *breeding*
PYRD purity *spotless*
PYRDN puritan *moralist*
PYRDNZM puritanism *moralism*
PYRF purify *cleanse* purified purifying purifies
PYRFKDR purificator *cleansing*
PYRFKSHN purification *cleansing*
PYRFKTR purificator *cleansing*
PYRFKTR purificatory *cleansing*
PYRFR purifier *cleanser*
PYRFYR purifier *cleanser*
PYRL puerile (adj) *silly* puerilely (adv)
PYRL purely *simply*
PYRLD puerility *silliness*
PYRLNS purulence *pus*

PYRLNT purulent *pus*
PYRLNTS purulence *pus*
PYRLT puerility *silliness*
PYRLZM puerilism *childishness*
PYRM Purim *feast*
PYRMSN puromycin *antibiotic*
PYRN apiarian *bees*
PYRNS prurience *lewdness* pruriency
PYRNS pureness *spotless, chaste*
PYRNT prurient *lewd*
PYRNTS prurience *lewdness* pruriency
PYRPR puerperia (pl) *childbirth* puerperium
PYRPRM puerperium *childbirth* puerperia
PYRPRY puerperia (pl) *childbirth* puerperium
PYRPRYM puerperium *childbirth* puerperia
PYRSDK puristic *traditional*
PYRSDKL puristically *traditional*
PYRST apiarist *beekeeper*
PYRST purist *traditionalist*
PYRSTK puristic *traditional*
PYRSTKL puristically *traditional*
PYRT purity *spotless*
PYRTN puritan *moralist*
PYRTNKL puritanical (adj) *moralistic* puritanically (adv)
PYRTNZM puritanism *moralism*
PYRY pyorrhea *gum disease*
PYRY pyuria *pus in urine*
PYRYLNS purulence *pus*
PYRYLNT purulent *pus*
PYRYLNTS purulence *pus*
PYRYN apiarian *bees*
PYRYNT prurient *lewd*
PYRZM purism *words*
PYS pious *holy*
PYS puce *dark red*
PYSDRZSTNS pièce de résistance *showpiece* pieces de resistance

---

Letters aren't doubled for single sounds: to find alley use **L** not **LL**. Use **Y** and **W** as hard sounds only: to find yellow use **YL**. (Br)=British spelling or usage. * See dictionary.

PYSDRZSTNTS pièce de résistance *showpiece* pieces de resistance

PYSH Peugeot *(trademark) car*

PYSH Piaget *psychologist*

PYSLNMD pusillanimity *cowardice*

PYSLNMS pusillanimous *cowardly*

PYSLNMT pusillanimity *cowardice*

PYSNS puissance *power*

PYSNT puissant *powerful*

PYSNTS puissance *power*

PYT opiate *narcotic*

PYT Paiute *Native American*

PYT payout *money*

PYT peyote *cactus*

PYT pietà *(often capitalized) statue*

PYT piety *devotion* pieties

PYTDV putative *assumed*

PYTR pewter *metal*

PYTRD putrid *foul*

PYTRDD putridity *foulness*

PYTRDL putridly *foul*

PYTRDT putridity *foulness*

PYTRF putrefy *rot* putrefied putrefying putrifies

PYTRFKDV putrefactive *rotting*

PYTRFKSHN putrefaction *rot*

PYTRFKTV putrefactive *rotting*

PYTRSNS putrescence *rot*

PYTRSNT putrescent *rotting*

PYTRSNTS putrescence *rot*

PYTS piazza *square, porch* piazzas (or) piazze

PYTSDK pietistic *devoted*

PYTSDKL pietistically *devoted*

PYTST pietist *devoted*

PYTSTK pietistic *devoted*

PYTSTKL pietistically *devoted*

PYTTV putative *assumed*

PYTZ piazza *square, porch* piazzas (or) piazze

PYTZM pietism *devotion*

PYWSNS puissance *power*

PYWSNT puissant *powerful*

PYWSNTS puissance *power*

PYZ piazza *square, porch* piazzas (or) piazze

PYZG pay-as-you-go *no credit*

PYZH Peugeot *(trademark) car*

PYZH Piaget *psychologist*

PYZYG pay-as-you-go *no credit*

PZ appease *satisfy* appeased appeasing

PZ appose *place nearby* apposed apposing

PZ oppose *resist* opposed opposing

PZ pas *dance step* pas

PZ pause *wait* paused pausing

PZ piazza *square, porch* piazzas (or) piazze

PZ poise *balance* poised poising

PZ pose *(v) offer, model* posed posing

PZ pose *(n) posture*

PZ posy *flower* posies

PZBL appeasable *satisfy*

PZBL opposable *other side*

PZBLD opposability *resist*

PZBLT opposability *resist*

PZD opposed *against*

PZD poised *balanced, ready*

PZDK epizootic *disease*

PZDM episiotomy *enlargement*

PZDV appositive *grammar*

PZDV positive *plus, good*

PZDVL positively *plus, good*

PZDVNS positiveness *plus, good*

PZDVSDK positivistic *hopeful*

PZDVSDKL positivistically *hopefully*

PZDVST positivist *one who hopes*

PZDVSTK positivistic *hopeful*

PZDVSTKL positivistically *hopefully*

PZDVZM positivism *hope*

PZG pay-as-you-go *no credit*

PZH Peugeot *(trademark) car*

PZH Piaget *psychologist*

PZK epizoic *parasite*

PZL paisley *design*

PZL puzzle *mystery* puzzled puzzling

PZLMNT puzzlement *mystery*

PZLN puzzling *mysterious*

PZLNG puzzling *mysterious*

PZLR puzzler *mystery*

PZMNT appeasement *satisfaction*

PZN poison *toxin*

PZNDKYZ p's and q's *manners*

PZNDQZ p's and q's *manners*

PZNDR peasantry *workers*

PZNK poison oak *plant*

PZNKYZ p's and q's *manners*

PZNPL poison pill *finance*

PZNPN poison-pen *letter*

PZNQZ p's and q's *manners*

PZNS poisonous *toxic*

PZNT peasant *worker*

PZNTR peasantry *workers*

PZNV poison ivy *plant*

PZNWD poisonwood *tree*

PZPDK aposiopetic *incomplete thought*

PZPSS aposiopesis *incomplete thought* aposiopeses

PZPTK aposiopetic *incomplete thought*

PZR appeaser *satisfier*

PZR opposer *other side*

PZR poser *question*

PZR poseur *pretender*

PZRV preserve *(v) protect,* can preserved preserving

PZRV preserve *(n) jam, park*

PZRVDV preservative *protection, canning*

PZRVR preserver *protecter*

Use letters that best describe the sounds you hear and omit the vowels. Use **S** or **K** instead of **C**: to find circle use **SRKL**. Use **J** to find joy, **JM** to find gem and **G** to find go.

PZRVTV preservative *protection, canning*
PZS possess *own*
PZSD possessed *calm, crazy*
PZSDL possessedly *calm, crazy*
PZSDNS possessedness *calm, crazy*
PZSHN apposition *grammar*
PZSHN opposition *reverse*
PZSHN position *place, rank*
PZSHN possession *ownership*
PZSHNL oppositional *reverse*
PZSHNL positional *place*
PZSHNL possessional *ownership*
PZSHNLS possessionless *no ownership*
PZSHNST oppositionist *reverse*
PZSR possessor *owner*
PZSR possessory *ownership*
PZST possessed *calm, crazy*
PZSV possessive *ownership, grammar*
PZSVL possessively *ownership*
PZSVNS possessiveness *ownership*
PZT apposite *relevant*
PZT opposite *reverse*
PZT posit *fix, suggest*
PZTK epizootic *disease*
PZTM episiotomy *enlargement*
PZTRN positron *particle*
PZTV appositive *grammar*
PZTV positive *plus, good*
PZTVL positively *plus, good*
PZTVNS positiveness *plus, good*
PZTVSDK positivistic *hopeful*
PZTVSDKL positivistically *hopefully*
PZTVST positivist *one who hopes*
PZTVSTK positivistic *hopeful*
PZTVSTKL positivistically *hopefully*

PZTVZM positivism *hope*
PZWDK epizootic *disease*
PZWK epizoic *parasite*
PZWTK epizootic *disease*
PZYDM episiotomy *enlargement*
PZYG pay-as-you-go *no credit*
PZYPDK aposiopetic *incomplete thought*
PZYPSS aposiopesis *incomplete thought* aposiopeses
PZYPTK aposiopetic *incomplete thought*
PZYR poseur *pretender*
PZYTM episiotomy *enlargement*
PZZ pizzazz (or) pizazz *glamour*

Q aqua *water, color* aquas (pl, color) aquae (pl, water)
Q cue *(v) prompt, line up* cued cuing (or) cueing
Q cue *(n) hint, line, rod*
Q ecu *(often capitalized) European Currency Unit* ecus
Q IQ *(abbr) intelligence quotient*
Q Kauai *island*
Q q *alphabet letter* q's (or) qs
Q qua *who*
Q quay (or) quai *pier*
Q queue *(v) line up* queued queuing
Q queue *(n) line, braid*
QB Cuba *country*
QB cube *block, math, steak* cubed cubing
QB cubé (or) cube *shrub*

QBB cubeb *pepper*
QBD cuboid *bone, shape*
QBDL cuboidal *shape*
QBJ cubage *volume*
QBK cubic *shape*
QBK Quebec *province*
QBKL cubical (adj) *shape* cubically (adv)
QBKL cubicle *room*
QBL cue ball *billiards*
QBL equable (adj) *steady* equably (adv)
QBL quibble *argue* quibbled quibbling
QBLD equability *steadiness*
QBLR quibbler *arguer*
QBLT equability *steadiness*
QBR cuber *block, math*
QBRT cube root *math*
QBSDK cubistic *art*
QBST cubist *artist*
QBSTK cube steak *meat*
QBSTK cubistic *art*
QBT cubit *length*
QBZM cubism *art*
QCH kwacha *money* kwacha
QD acuity *sharpness* acuities
QD cutie (or) cutey *pretty one* cuties (or) cuteys
QD equid *horse family*
QD equity *law, value* equities
QD kudo *award, praise* kudos
QD quad *(n) square, BTUs* (adj) four
QD quad *(v) typeset* quadded quadding
QD quid *money, wad*
QD quod *(Br-slang) prison*
QD quota *share*
QDBL equitable (adj) *fair* equitably (adv)
QDBL quotable *repeat*
QDBLD equitability *fairness*
QDBLD quotability *repeat*
QDBLNS equitableness *fairness*
QDBLT equitability *fairness*
QDBLT quotability *repeat*
QDK aquatic *in water*
QDK aqueduct *waterway*
QDKL aquatically *in water*

Letters aren't doubled for single sounds: to find alley use **L** not **LL**. Use **Y** and **W** as hard sounds only: to find yellow use **YL**. (Br)=British spelling or usage. * See dictionary.

QDKL cuticle *skin*
QDKS aquatics *water sports*
QDKT aqueduct *waterway*
QDL acquittal *discharge*
QDLBT quodlibet *dispute, miscellany*
QDNNGK quidnunc *busybody*
QDNNK quidnunc *busybody*
QDNS acquittance *receipt*
QDNS quittance *payment*
QDNTS acquittance *receipt*
QDNTS quittance *payment*
QDPRKW quid pro quo *deal, even exchange*
QDR acquitter *behave, set free*
QDR cuadrilla *bullfight*
QDR cuter *prettier*
QDR Ecuador *country*
QDR equator *midway between poles*
QDR quitter *defeatist*
QDR quittor *disease*
QDRCHR quadrature *stars, math*
QDRDK quadratic *math*
QDRFNK quadraphonic *four channels*
QDRK quadric *math*
QDRL cuadrilla *bullfight*
QDRL quadrille *game, dance, square*
QDRLDRL quadrilateral *4 sides*
QDRLTRL quadrilateral *4 sides*
QDRLYN quadrillion *number*
QDRLYNTH quadrillionth *number*
QDRMNS quadrumanous *primate*
QDRMVRT quadrumvirate *group of 4*
QDRN quadroon *ancestry*
QDRNGGL quadrangle *square*
QDRNGGLR quadrangular *square*
QDRNGGYLR quadrangular *square*
QDRNGL quadrangle *square*

QDRNGLR quadrangular *square*
QDRNGYLR quadrangular *square*
QDRNL quadrennial (adj) *4 years* quadrennially (adv)
QDRNM quadrennium *4 years* quadrenniums (or) quadrennia
QDRNR quaternary *4 units* quaternaries
QDRNT quadrant *area*
QDRNYL quadrennial (adj) *4 years* quadrennially (adv)
QDRNYM quadrennium *4 years* quadrenniums (or) quadrennia
QDRPD quadruped *4 feet*
QDRPL quadruple *times 4* quadrupled quadrupling
QDRPLG quadriplegia *paralysis*
QDRPLGY quadriplegia *paralysis*
QDRPLJ quadriplegia *paralysis*
QDRPLJK quadriplegic *paralysis*
QDRPLJY quadriplegia *paralysis*
QDRPLKSHN quadruplication *4 copies*
QDRPLKT quadruplicate *4 copies* quadruplicated quadruplicating
QDRPLT quadruplet *4 offspring*
QDRPRTT quadripartite *4 parts*
QDRSNTNR quatercentenary *400 years*
QDRSPS quadriceps *muscle*
QDRT quadrat *rectangle*
QDRT quadrate *square*
QDRTK quadratic *math*
QDRTR quadrature *stars, math*
QDRTYR quadrature *stars, math*
QDRVL quadrivial *4 roads*
QDRVLNT quadrivalent

genes
QDRVYL quadrivial *4 roads*
QDRY cuadrilla *bullfight*
QDRYN quadrillion *number*
QDRYNTH quadrillionth *number*
QDS cutis *skin* cutes (or) cutises
QDS quietus *death*
QDSDNT equidistant *equal distance*
QDST cutest *prettiest*
QDSTNT equidistant *equal distance*
QDX aquatics *water sports*
QF coif *hairdo* coiffed (or) coifed coiffing (or) coifing
QF quaff *drink*
QF quiff *(Br) forelock*
QFR aquifer *rock*
QFR coiffeur *hairdresser*
QFR coiffure *hairstyle*
QFR quaffer *drinker*
QFRD coiffured *hairstyle*
QFYR coiffeur *hairdresser*
QFYR coiffure *hairstyle*
QFYRD coiffured *hairstyle*
QFYZ coiffeuse *hairdresser (f)*
QFZ coiffeuse *hairdresser (f)*
QG quag *marsh*
QG quagga *animal*
QGMR quagmire *bog, crisis*
QHG quahog *clam*
QJ quayage *fee, piers*
QK cuke *cucumber*
QK quack *(v,n) duck sound (n, adj) fraud*
QK quake *shake* quaked quaking
QK quick *(adj) fast, living (n) sensitive area, heart*
QK quickie *fast motion*
QKBRD quick bread *food*
QKD aquacade *water exhibition*
QKFRZ quick-freeze *chill* quick-froze quick-freezing quick-frozen
QKL quickly *fast*
QKLCHR aquaculture *farming*

Use letters that best describe the sounds you hear and omit the vowels. Use **S** or **K** instead of **C**: to find circle use **SRKL**. Use **J** to find joy, **JM** to find gem and **G** to find go.

QKLCHRL aquacultural *farming*
QKLCHRST aquaculturist *farmer*
QKLM quicklime *lime*
QKLM quitclaim *deed*
QKLTR aquaculture *farming*
QKLTRL aquacultural *farming*
QKLTRST aquaculturist *farmer*
QKMBR cucumber *vegetable*
QKN quicken *revive*
QKNS quickness *fast*
QKR quackery *pretense* quackeries
QKR Quaker *Religious Society of Friends*
QKSDK quixotic *impractical*
QKSDKL quixotical (adj) *impractical* quixotically (adv)
QKSLVR quicksilver *mercury*
QKSN quicksand *trap*
QKSND quicksand *trap*
QKST quickset *(Br) plants*
QKST quixote *politeness*
QKSTK quixotic *impractical*
QKSTKL quixotical (adj) *impractical* quixotically (adv)
QKSTP quickstep *march*
QKSTZM quixotism *politeness*
QKTM quick time *march*
QKTMPRD quick-tempered *anger*
QKWDD quick-witted *intelligent*
QKWDDNS quick-wittedness *intelligence*
QKWTD quick-witted *intelligent*
QKWTDNS quick-wittedness *intelligence*
QKZDK quixotic *impractical*
QKZDKL quixotical (adj) *impractical* quixotically (adv)
QKZT quixote *politeness*
QKZTK quixotic *impractical*
QKZTKL quixotical (adj)

impractical quixotically (adv)
QL equal *(v) make the same* equaled (or) equalled equaling (or) equalling
QL equally *(adv) same*
QL oculi (pl) *window oculus*
QL quail *(n) bird (v) cower*
QL quale *universal* qualia
QL qualia (pl) *universal* quale
QL quell *stop*
QL quill *feather*
QLBK quillback *fish*
QLBR equilibria (pl) *balance* equilibrium
QLBRDR equilibrator *balance*
QLBRM equilibrium *balance* equilibriums (or) equilibria
QLBRNT equilibrant *balance*
QLBRSHN equilibration *balance*
QLBRST equilibrist *balance*
QLBRSTK equilibristic *balance*
QLBRT equilibrate *balance* equilibrated equilibrating
QLBRTR equilibrator *balance*
QLBRY equilibria (pl) *balance* eqiilibrium
QLBRYM equilibrium *balance* equilibriums (or) equilibria
QLD equality *sameness* equalities
QLD Quaalude *(trademark) drug*
QLD quality *nature, grade* qualities
QLDRL equilateral *equal sides*
QLF qualify *certify, modify* qualified qualifying qualifies
QLFBL qualifiable *eligible*
QLFD qualified *eligible*
QLFKSHN qualification *eligibility*
QLFR qualifier *eligible*
QLFYBL qualifiable *eligible*
QLFYR qualifier *eligible*

QLKS culex *mosquito*
QLLMPR Kuala Lumpur *city*
QLM qualm *doubt, fear*
QLMDR oculomotor *nerve*
QLMSH qualmish *sick*
QLMSHL qualmishly *sick*
QLMSHNS qualmishness *sick*
QLMTR oculomotor *nerve*
QLN aquiline *eagle-like*
QLND aquilinity *eagles*
QLNG Aqua-Lung *(trademark) scuba gear*
QLNR culinary *cooking*
QLNRL culinarily *cooking*
QLNRN culinarian *chef*
QLNRYN culinarian *chef*
QLNT aquilinity *eagles*
QLR ocular *eyepiece*
QLR queller *stopper*
QLRST ocularist *glass eye*
QLS oculus *window oculi*
QLST oculist *eye doctor*
QLT culet *armor*
QLT equality *sameness* equalities
QLT quality *nature, grade* qualities
QLT quilt *(n) coverlet, (v) sew*
QLTDV qualitative *characteristic*
QLTN quilting *fabric, sewing*
QLTNG quilting *fabric, sewing*
QLTRL equilateral *equal sides*
QLTS culottes *skirt*
QLTTV qualitative *characteristic*
QLX culex *mosquito*
QLY qualia (pl) *universal* quale
QLZ equalize *make equal, tie the score* equalized equalizing (Br) equalise
QLZR equalizer *makes equal, ties the score* (Br) equaliser
QLZSHN equalization *made equal, tied score* (Br) equalisation
QM qualm *doubt, fear*

Letters aren't doubled for single sounds: to find alley use **L** not **LL**. Use **Y** and **W** as hard sounds only: to find yellow use **YL**. (Br)=British spelling or usage. * See dictionary.

QMLDR accumulator *gatherer*

QMLDV accumulative *gathered*

QMLDV cumulative *additional*

QMLNMBS cumulonimbus *cloud*

QMLS cumulous *cloudlike*

QMLS cumulus *cloud*

QMLSHN accumulation *gathering*

QMLSHN cumulation *mass*

QMLT accumulate *gather* accumulated accumulating

QMLT cumulate *amass* cumulated cumulating

QMLTR accumulator *gatherer*

QMLTV accumulative *gathered*

QMLTV cumulative *additional*

QMN acumen *keenness*

QMN cumin *spice*

QMNKL ecumenical (adj) *church* ecumenically (adv) (Br) oecumenical

QMNKS ecumenics *church*

QMNST ecumenist *church*

QMNT acuminate *tapered*

QMNX ecumenics *church*

QMNZM ecumenism *church*

QMRN aquamarine *color*

QMSH qualmish *sick*

QMSHL qualmishly *sick*

QMSHNS qualmishness *sick*

QMYLDR accumulator *gatherer*

QMYLDV accumulative *gathered*

QMYLDV cumulative *additional*

QMYLNMBS cumulonimbus *cloud*

QMYLS cumulous *cloudlike*

QMYLS cumulus *cloud*

QMYLSHN accumulation *gathering*

QMYLSHN cumulation *mass*

QMYLT accumulate *gather* accumulated accumulating

QMYLT cumulate *amass* cumulated cumulating

QMYLTR accumulator *gatherer*

QMYLTV accumulative *gathered*

QMYLTV cumulative *additional*

QN equine *horse*

QN quean *prostitute*

QN queen *(n) ruler (v) dominate, chess*

QN quoin *wedge*

QNCH quench *put out, cool, relieve*

QNCHBL quenchable *put out, cool, relieve*

QNCHLS quenchless *no relief, no end*

QNCHR quencher *put out, cool, relieve*

QND quantity *amount* quantities

QNDM quondam *former*

QNDN quinidine *drug*

QNDR quandary *doubt* quandaries

QNDSLYN quindecillion *number*

QNDSYN quindecillion *number*

QNFBL quantifiable *count*

QNFKSHN quantification *count*

QNFKSHNL quantificational (adj) *count* quantificationally (adv)

QNFR quantifier *count*

QNFRM cuneiform *wedge*

QNFYBL quantifiable *count*

QNFYR quantifier *count*

QNGGLR equiangular *same angles*

QNGGYLR equiangular *same angles*

QNGLR equiangular *same angles*

QNGYLR equiangular *same angles*

QNKS equinox *equal day and night*

QNKSHL equinoctial *equal day and night*

QNKWNL quinquennial (adj) *5 years* quinquennially (adv)

QNKWNYL quinquennial (adj) *5 years* quinquennially (adv)

QNL queenly *regal* queenlier queenliest

QNL quenelle *dumpling*

QNL quiniela (or) quinella *bet*

QNLNS queenliness *regal*

QNLR queenlier *regal*

QNLST queenliest *regal*

QNLYR queenlier *regal*

QNLYST queenliest *regal*

QNM quantum *amount, large* quanta

QNMD equanimity *balance* equanimities

QNMT equanimity *balance* equanimities

QNN quinine *alkaloid*

QNN quinone *benzene derivative*

QNNS acquaintance *familiarity, person*

QNNSHP acquaintanceship *familiarity*

QNNTS acquaintance *familiarity, person*

QNQNL quinquennial (adj) *5 years* quinquennially (adv)

QNQNYL quinquennial (adj) *5 years* quinquennially (adv)

QNS acquaintance *familiarity, person*

QNS Aquinas (Thomas) *Catholic saint*

QNS quince *fruit*

QNSD queenside *chess*

QNSHP acquaintanceship *familiarity*

QNSHP queenship *rank*

QNSNCHL quintessential (adj) *pure form* quintessentially (adv)

QNSNSHL quintessential

Use letters that best describe the sounds you hear and omit the vowels. Use **S** or **K** instead of **C**: to find circle use **SRKL**. Use **J** to find joy, **JM** to find gem and **G** to find go.

(adj) *pure form*
quintessentially (adv)
QNSNTNL quincentennial
500 years
QNSNTNR quincentenary
500 years
QNSNTNYL quincentennial
500 years
QNSTHT Quonset hut
(trademark) shelter
QNSZ queen-size *large*
QNT acquaint *introduce,*
inform
QNT aquanaut *diver*
QNT cuneate *triangular*
QNT quaint *odd, old-*
fashioned
QNT quanta (pl) *amount,*
large quantum
QNT quantity *amount*
quantities
QNT quint *5 offspring*
QNTD quantity *amount*
quantities
QNTDV quantitative *amount*
QNTFBL quantifiable *count*
QNTFKSHN quantification
count
QNTFKSHNL
quantificational (adj)
count quantificationally
(adv)
QNTFR quantifier *count*
QNTFYBL quantifiable *count*
QNTFYR quantifier *count*
QNTL quaintly *oddly*
QNTL quantal *choices*
QNTL quintal *weight*
QNTLYN quintillion *number*
QNTLYNTH quintillionth
number
QNTM quantum *amount,*
large quanta
QNTN quintain *target*
QNTNS acquaintance
familiarity, person
QNTNS quaintness *oddness*
QNTNSHP
acquaintanceship
familiarity
QNTNTS acquaintance
familiarity, person

QNTPL quintuple *5 times*
quintupled quintupling
QNTPLKT quintuplicate *5*
copies quintuplicated
quintuplicating
QNTPLT quintuplet *5*
offspring
QNTS acquaintance
familiarity, person
QNTS quince *fruit*
QNTSNCHL quintessential
(adj) *pure form*
quintessentially (adv)
QNTSNS quintessence *pure*
form
QNTSNSHL quintessential
(adj) *pure form*
quintessentially (adv)
QNTSNTS quintessence
pure form
QNTT quantity *amount*
quantities
QNTT quintet *set of 5*
QNTTDV quantitative
amount
QNTTTV quantitative
amount
QNTTV quantitative *amount*
QNTYN quintillion *number*
QNTYNTH quintillionth
number
QNTYPL quintuple *5 times*
quintupled quintupling
QNTYPLKT quintuplicate *5*
copies quintuplicated
quintuplicating
QNTYPLT quintuplet *5*
offspring
QNTZ quantize *divide*
quantized quantizing
QNTZR quantizer *divider*
QNTZSHN quantization
division
QNX equinox *equal day and*
night
QNYFRM cuneiform *wedge*
QNYL quiniela (or) quinella
bet
QNYT cuneate *triangular*
QNZ kwanza *money*
kwanzas (or) kwanza
QNZ quinsy *abscess*

QNZSHN quantization
division
QNZTHT Quonset hut
(trademark) shelter
QP equip *furnish* equipped
equipping
QP Kewpie *(trademark) doll*
QP occupy *fill, reside*
occupied occupying
occupies
QP quip *remark* quipped
quipping
QPD Cupid *Roman god of*
love
QPDD cupidity *desire*
cupidities
QPDT cupidity *desire*
cupidities
QPJ equipage *carriage*
QPL cupel *strainer* cupelled
(or) cupeled cupelling (or)
cupeling
QPL cupola *roof*
QPL cupule *cup-shaped*
QPLD cupolaed *roof*
QPLN aquaplane *airplane*
(Br) hydroplane
QPLNS equipollence *equal*
force
QPLNT equipollent *equal*
force
QPLNTS equipollence *equal*
force
QPLR cupeler *refiner*
QPLSHN cupellation
refinement
QPMNT equipment
belongings
QPN coupon *ticket*
QPNCHR acupuncture
Chinese therapy
QPNGCHR acupuncture
Chinese therapy
QPNGKCHR acupuncture
Chinese therapy
QPNGKSHR acupuncture
Chinese therapy
QPNGSHR acupuncture
Chinese therapy
QPNKCHR acupuncture
Chinese therapy
QPNKSHR acupuncture

Letters aren't doubled for single sounds: to find alley use **L** not **LL**. Use **Y** and **W** as hard
sounds only: to find yellow use **YL**. (Br)=British spelling or usage. * See dictionary.

Chinese therapy
QPNS occupancy *residents* occupancies
QPNSHR acupuncture *Chinese therapy*
QPNT occupant *resident*
QPNTS occupancy *residents* occupancies
QPR quipper *remarker*
QPRFRS cupriferous *copper*
QPRS cuprous *copper*
QPRSHR acupressure *massage*
QPRT cuprite *copper*
QPSHN occupation *job, seizure*
QPSHNL occupational (adj) *job, seizure* occupationally (adv)
QPSTR quipster *remarker*
QPYL cupule *cup-shaped*
QPZ equipoise *counterbalance*
QR acquire *gain* acquired acquiring
QR aquaria (pl) *fish tank* aquarium
QR choir *singing*
QR cure (v) *heal, prepare* cured curing
QR curé *priest*
QR cure (n) *remedy*
QR curia *law court* curiae
QR curie *radioactivity*
QR Curie *scientist*
QR curio *curiosity* curios
QR equerry *horse caretaker* equerries
QR kauri *tree*
QR quarry (v) *dig* quarried quarrying quarries
QR quarry (n) *stone, prey, pane* quarries
QR queer (adj) *odd, homosexual* (v) *spoil*
QR query *ask* queried querying queries
QR quire *paper*
QRB choirboy *singer*
QRBL acquirable *able to be gained*
QRBL curable (adj) *heal,*

prepare curably (adv)
QRC accuracy *correctness* accuracies
QRC curacy *office* curacies
QRCTN quercetin *pigment*
QRD acquired *gained*
QRD awkward *clumsy*
QRD quarto *music* quartos
QRDL awkwardly *clumsily*
QRDNS awkwardness *clumsiness*
QRDR curator *caretaker*
QRDR quarter (v) *divide, lodge* (n) *one fourth, area, money**
QRDRBK quarterback *football*
QRDRDK quarterdeck *ship*
QRDRFNL quarterfinal *exam*
QRDRHRS quarter horse *animal*
QRDRL quarterly *4 times per year* quarterlies
QRDRMSDR quartermaster *provider*
QRDRMSTR quartermaster *provider*
QRDRN quartering *right angle*
QRDRNG quartering *right angle*
QRDRSN quartersawn *boards*
QRDRSTF quarterstaff *weapon*
QRDV curative *healing*
QRK quark *particle*
QRK quirk *twist, trait*
QRKL quirkily *twist, trait*
QRKNS quirkiness *twist, trait*
QRKSH quirkish *twist, trait*
QRL aquarelle *watercolor*
QRL cure-all *remedy*
QRL quarrel *fight* quarreled (or) quarrelled quarreling (or) quarrelling
QRL queerly *odd, homosexual*
QRLF choir loft *gallery*
QRLFT choir loft *gallery*
QRLR quarreler (or) quarreller *fighter*

QRLS querulous *peevish*
QRLSL querulously *peevishly*
QRLSM quarrelsome *hostile*
QRLSNS querulousness *peevishness*
QRLST aquarellist *artist*
QRM aquarium *fish tank* aquariums (or) aquaria
QRM curium *element*
QRM quorum *majority*
QRMN quarryman *worker* quarrymen
QRMNT acquirement *gain*
QRMSDR choirmaster *director*
QRMSTR choirmaster *director*
QRN quern *grinder*
QRNS queerness *odd, homosexual*
QRNTN quarantine *separate* quarantined quarantining
QRR curare *poison*
QRR curer *healer*
QRR quarrier *worker*
QRS accuracy *correctness* accuracies
QRS Aquarius *zodiac sign*
QRS cuirass *armor*
QRS Curacao *island*
QRS curacao *liqueur*
QRS curacy *office* curacies
QRS curassow *bird*
QRS curious *inquisitive, strange*
QRSD curiosity *interest, curio* curiosities
QRSH queerish *odd, homosexual*
QRSL curiously *strangely*
QRSNS curiousness *inquisitive, odd*
QRST aquarist *fish tank*
QRST curiosity *interest, curio* curiosities
QRST querist *question*
QRSTN quercetin *pigment*
QRSTRN quercitron *bark, dye*
QRT accurate *correct*
QRT curate *organize and*

Use letters that best describe the sounds you hear and omit the vowels. Use **S** or **K** instead of **C**: to find circle use **SRKL**. Use **J** to find joy, **JM** to find gem and **G** to find go.

oversee curated curating
QRT curette *scoop* curetted curetting
QRT quart *measure*
QRT quarto *music* quartos
QRT quirt *whip*
QRTJ curettage *scraping*
QRTL accurately *correctly*
QRTL quartile *4 parts*
QRTN quartan *4 days, fever*
QRTNS accurateness *correctness*
QRTR curator *caretaker*
QRTR quarter *(v) divide, lodge (n) one fourth, area, money**
QRTRBK quarterback *football*
QRTRDK quarterdeck *ship*
QRTRFNL quarterfinal *exam*
QRTRHRS quarter horse *animal*
QRTRL quarterly *4 times per year* quarterlies
QRTRMSDR quartermaster *provider*
QRTRMSTR quartermaster *provider*
QRTRN quartering *right angle*
QRTRNG quartering *right angle*
QRTRSN quartersawn *boards*
QRTRSTF quarterstaff *weapon*
QRTS quartz *rock*
QRTSS quartzose *rock*
QRTST quartzite *rock*
QRTT quartet *group of 4*
QRTV curative *healing*
QRTZS quartzose *rock*
QRY aquaria (pl) *fish tank* aquarium
QRY curia *law court*
QRY curio *curiosity* curios
QRYLS querulous *peevish*
QRYLSL querulously *peevishly*
QRYLSNS querulousness *peevishness*
QRYM aquarium *fish tank*

aquariums (or) aquaria
QRYM curium *element*
QRYR quarrier *worker*
QRYS Aquarius *zodiac sign*
QRYS curious *inquisitive, strange*
QRYSD curiosity *interest, curio* curiosities
QRYSL curiously *strangely*
QRYSNS curiousness *inquisitive, odd*
QRYST curiosity *interest, curio* curiosities
QS acquiesce *agree* acquiesced acquiescing
QS aqueous *water*
QS quasi *somewhat*
QSCHN question *(n) inquiry, issue (v) ask*
QSCHNBL questionable (adj) *doubtful* questionably (adv)
QSCHNBLNS questionableness *doubt*
QSCHNR questioner *inquirer*
QSCHNR questionnaire *survey*
QSD cuesta *hill*
QSD quayside *pier*
QSDM equisetum *plant* equisetums (or) equiseta
QSH quash *suppress*
QSH quassia *drug*
QSHN equation *math*
QSHNT quotient *number*
QSHRKR kwashiorkor *disease*
QSHYRKR kwashiorkor *disease*
QSK cusec *unit of flow*
QSNS acquiescence *agreement*
QSNS quiescence *inactivity*
QSNT acquiescent *agreeable*
QSNT quiescent *inactive*
QSNTL acquiescently *agreeably*
QSNTS acquiescence *agreement*
QSNTS quiescence *inactivity*

QSR quasar *star*
QST cuesta *hill*
QST quest *search*
QSTM equisetum *plant* equisetums (or) equiseta
QSTRN equestrian (m or f) *horseback rider* equestrienne (f)
QSTRYN equestrian (m or f) *horseback rider* equestrienne (f)
QT acquit *discharge* acquitted acquitting
QT acuity *sharpness* acuities
QT acute *sharp* acuter acutest
QT cute *pretty* cuter cutest
QT cutie (or) cutey *pretty one* cuties (or) cuteys
QT equate *make equal* equated equating
QT equity *law, value* equities
QT quiet *still*
QT quit *stop, give up* quit quitting
QT quite *fully, rather*
QT quoit *ring*
QT quota *share*
QT quote *repeat* quoted quoting
QTBL equitable (adj) *fair* equitably (adv)
QTBL quotable *repeat*
QTBLD equitability *fairness*
QTBLD quotability *repeat*
QTBLNS equitableness *fairness*
QTBLT equitability *fairness*
QTBLT quotability *repeat*
QTC cutesy *obnoxious* cutesier cutesiest
QTCR cutesier *obnoxious*
QTCST cutesiest *obnoxious*
QTCYR cutesier *obnoxious*
QTCYST cutesiest *obnoxious*
QTD quietude *rest*
QTDN quotidian *common*
QTDYN quotidian *common*
QTH quoth *said*
QTK aquatic *in water*
QTKL aquatically *in water*
QTKL cuticle *skin*

Letters aren't doubled for single sounds: to find alley use **L** not **LL**. Use **Y** and **W** as hard sounds only: to find yellow use **YL**. (Br)=British spelling or usage. * See dictionary.

QTKLM quitclaim *deed*
QTKLR cuticular *skin*
QTKS aquatics *water sports*
QTKYLR cuticular *skin*
QTL acquittal *discharge*
QTL acutely *sharply*
QTL quietly *still*
QTN cutin *waxy layer*
QTN quieten *still*
QTNS acquittance *receipt*
QTNS acuteness *sharpness*
QTNS cutaneous *skin*
QTNS cuteness *pretty*
QTNS quietness *stillness*
QTNS quittance *payment*
QTNT aquatint *etching method*
QTNTS acquittance *receipt*
QTNTS quittance *payment*
QTNYS cutaneous *skin*
QTP Q-Tip *(trademark) swab*
QTQLR cuticular *skin*
QTR acquitter *behave, set free*
QTR acuter *sharper*
QTR cuter *prettier*
QTR equator *midway between poles*
QTR quitter *defeatist*
QTR quittor *disease*
QTRL equatorial *midway between poles*
QTRLGN Equatorial Guinea *country*
QTRN quatrain *verse*
QTRNN quaternion *4 parts*
QTRNR quaternary *4 units* quaternaries
QTRNYN quaternion *4 parts*
QTRSNTNR quatercentenary *400 years*
QTRYL equatorial *midway between poles*
QTRYLGN Equatorial Guinea *country*
QTS cutesy *obnoxious* cutesier cutesiest
QTS cutis *skin* cutes (or) cutises
QTS quietus *death*
QTS quits *even terms*
QTSHN equitation *horseback riding*
QTSHN quotation *repeat*
QTSLKDL Quetzalcoatl *Aztec god*
QTSLKTL Quetzalcoatl *Aztec god*
QTSLKWDL Quetzalcoatl *Aztec god*
QTSLKWTL Quetzalcoatl *Aztec god*
QTSR cutesier *obnoxious*
QTSST cutesiest *obnoxious*
QTST acutest *sharpest*
QTST cutest *prettiest*
QTSYR cutesier *obnoxious*
QTSYST cutesiest *obnoxious*
QTX aquatics *water sports*
QTYD quietude *rest*
QTZ cutes (pl) *skin* cutis
QTZ cutesy *obnoxious* cutesier cutesiest
QTZM quietism *religion*
QTZR cutesier *obnoxious*
QTZST cutesiest *obnoxious*
QTZYR cutesier *obnoxious*
QTZYST cutesiest *obnoxious*
QVD aqua vitae *liquor*
QVK equivoque *pun*
QVKDR equivocator *liar*
QVKL equivocal (adj) *questionable* equivocally (adv)
QVKSHN equivocation *lie*
QVKT equivocate *lie* equivocated equivocating
QVKTR equivocator *liar*
QVLNS equivalence *same value* equivalency
QVLNT equivalent *same value*
QVLNTL equivalently *same value*
QVLNTS equivalence *same value* equivalency
QVR quaver *tremble, trill*
QVR quavery *tremble, trill*
QVR quiver (v) *shake* (n) *arrow holder*
QVRNGL quaveringly *tremble, trill*
QVT aqua vitae *liquor*
QVT cuvette *test tube*
QWD acuity *sharpness* acuities
QWT acuity *sharpness* acuities
QXDK quixotic *impractical*
QXDKL quixotical (adj) *impractical* quixotically (adv)
QXLVR quicksilver *mercury*
QXN quicksand *trap*
QXND quicksand *trap*
QXT quickset (Br) *plants*
QXT quixote *politeness*
QXTK quixotic *impractical*
QXTKL quixotical (adj) *impractical* quixotically (adv)
QXTP quickstep *march*
QXTZM quixotism *politeness*
QYJ quayage *fee, piers*
QYR acquire *gain* acquired acquiring
QYR choir *singing*
QYR quire *paper*
QYRB choirboy *singer*
QYRBL acquirable *able to be gained*
QYRD acquired *gained*
QYRLF choir loft *gallery*
QYRLFT choir loft *gallery*
QYRMNT acquirement *gain*
QYRMSDR choirmaster *director*
QYRMSTR choirmaster *director*
QYS acquiesce *agree* acquiesced acquiescing
QYS aqueous *water*
QYSNS acquiescence *agreement*
QYSNS quiescence *inactivity*
QYSNT acquiescent *agreeable*
QYSNT quiescent *inactive*
QYSNTL acquiescently *agreeably*
QYSNTS acquiescence *agreement*
QYSNTS quiescence *inactivity*

Use letters that best describe the sounds you hear and omit the vowels. Use **S** or **K** instead of **C**: to find circle use **SRKL**. Use **J** to find joy, **JM** to find gem and **G** to find go.

QYT quiet *still*
QYTD quietude *rest*
QYTL quietly *still*
QYTN quieten *still*
QYTNS quietness *stillness*
QYTYD quietude *rest*
QYTZM quietism *religion*
QZ accuse *blame* accused accusing
QZ quasi *somewhat*
QZ queasy *nauseated* queasier queasiest
QZ quiz *test* quizzed quizzing quizzes
QZD accused *defendant* accused
QZDM equisetum *plant* equisetums (or) equiseta
QZDV accusative *blaming*
QZDV acquisitive *covetous*
QZHN equation *math*
QZJDSHL quasi-judicial (adj) *law* quasi-judicially (adv)
QZKL quizzical (adj) *puzzled* quizzically (adv)
QZL accusal *blame*
QZLJSLDV quasi-legislative *law*
QZLJSLTV quasi-legislative *law*
QZLN quisling *traitor*
QZLNG quisling *traitor*
QZMD Quasimodo *Low Sunday, fictional character, poet*
QZMSDR quizmaster *tester*
QZMSTR quizmaster *tester*
QZMT Quasimodo *Low Sunday, fictional character, poet*
QZN cuisine *food*
QZNGL accusingly *with blame*
QZNS queasiness *sickened*
QZPRDK quasiperiodic *unpredictable*
QZPRDKL quasiparticle *vibration*
QZPRDSD quasiperiodicity *unpredictable*
QZPRDST quasiperiodicity

unpredictable
QZPRTKL quasiparticle *vibration*
QZPRYDK quasiperiodic *unpredictable*
QZPRYDSD quasiperiodicity *unpredictable*
QZPRYDST quasiperiodicity *unpredictable*
QZR accuser *blamer*
QZR quasar *star*
QZR queasier *sickened*
QZR quizzer *tester*
QZSHN accusation *blame*
QZSHN acquisition *gain*
QZSHNL acquisitional *gained*
QZST queasiest *sickened*
QZT accused *defendant* accused
QZTM equisetum *plant* equisetums (or) equiseta
QZTR accusatory *blaming*
QZTR acquisitor *gainer*
QZTRL accusatorial (adj) *blaming* accusatorially (adv)
QZTRYL accusatorial (adj) *blaming* accusatorially (adv)
QZTV accusative *blaming*
QZTV acquisitive *covetous*
QZTVL acquisitively *covetously*
QZTVNS acquisitiveness *covetousness*
QZYR queasier *sickened*
QZYST queasiest *sickened*

R

R aerie *nest*
R aero *aircraft*
R aery *heavenly* aerier aeriest
R air (v) *ventilate, broadcast, express* (n) *wind, tune, pose**
R airy *lofty, proud, windy* airier airiest
R ar *alphabet letter (R)*
R are *exist*
R area *space*
R aria *song*
R array *display*
R arrow *weapon*
R aura *halo*
R awry *twisted*
R ear *hearing*
R eerie *weird* eerier eeriest
R era *time*
R ere *before*
R Erie *city, lake*
R err (v) *be mistaken*
R error *mistake*
R euro *money, animal* euros
R ewer *pitcher*
R eyer *watcher*
R heir *inheritor*
R hour *60 minutes*
R IRA *Irish Republican Army*
R ire *anger* ired iring
R o'er (contr) *over*
R oar *boat*
R or *either*
R ore *mineral* ore
R our *not your*
R Ra *deity*
R rah (interj) *cheer*
R raw *uncooked, vulgar* rawer rawest
R ray (n) *light, fish* (v) *radiate*
R re (n) *musical tone* (prep) *regarding*
R rhea *bird*
R rho *Greek letter*
R Rio (abbr) *Rio de Janeiro*
R roe *fish eggs* roe (or) roes
R Rouault *artist*
R roué *sensual man*
R rouille *sauce*
R roux *sauce* roux
R row (n) *line, brawl* (v) *use*

Letters aren't doubled for single sounds: to find alley use **L** not **LL**. Use **Y** and **W** as hard sounds only: to find yellow use **YL**. (Br)=British spelling or usage. * See dictionary.

oars

R rue *regret* rued ruing

R rye *grain*

R uraei (pl) *symbol* uraeus

R urea *urine*

R wry *(adj) twisted, humorous* wryer wryest

R wry *(v) twist* wried wrying wries

R you're *(contr) you are*

RB aerobe *organism*

RB Arab *middle Eastern*

RB Arabia *peninsula*

RB herb *plant*

RB orb *sphere*

RB rabbi *priest*

RB rib *(v) tease, ridge* ribbed ribbing

RB rib *(n) bone, ridge*

RB rob *steal* robbed robbing

RB robe *clothes* robed robing

RB rub *(v) touch, annoy* rubbed rubbing

RB rub *(n) difficulty*

RB rube *oaf*

RB ruby *gem, red* rubies

RBBTZ rebaptize *initiate* rebaptized rebaptizing

RBD rabato *collar* rabatos

RBD rabid *rabies, furious*

RBD rubato *tempo* rubatos

RBDD rabidity *rabies, furious*

RBDK aerobatic *flying*

RBDK robotic *machine*

RBDKS aerobatics *flying feats*

RBDL orbital *circle*

RBDL rabidly *rabies, furious*

RBDL rebuttal *opposition*

RBDM rhabdom (or) rhabdome *rod*

RBDM rubidium *element*

RBDMR rhabdomere *eye*

RBDN rubdown *massage*

RBDNS rabidness *rabies, furious*

RBDR arbiter *negotiator*

RBDR orbiter *spacecraft*

RBDR rabbiter *hunter*

RBDR rebutter *opposer*

RBDS arbutus *plant*

RBDSL rhabdocoele *worm*

RBDT rabidity *rabies, furious*

RBDX aerobatics *flying feats*

RBDYM rubidium *element*

RBF rebuff *refusal*

RBFLVN riboflavin *vitamin B*

RBFLVNSS ariboflavinosis *disease*

RBFSHNT rubefacient *redness*

RBG air bag *safety device*

RBJ herbage *plant*

RBK aerobic *with oxygen*

RBK Arabic *of Arabia*

RBK arabica *shrub*

RBK Auerbach *writer*

RBK rebec (or) rebeck *instrument*

RBK rebuke *scold* rebuked rebuking

RBK rhebok *antelope*

RBK roebuck *deer*

RBKJ rib cage *skeleton*

RBKL aerobically *with oxygen*

RBKLR orbicular *circular*

RBKLRL orbicularly *circularly*

RBKN rubicund *reddish*

RBKND rubicund *reddish*

RBKS aerobics *exercises*

RBKYLR orbicular *circular*

RBKYLRL orbicularly *circularly*

RBL air ball *missed shot*

RBL arable *cropland*

RBL herbal *plant*

RBL rabble *mob* rabbled rabbling

RBL Rabelais *satirist*

RBL rebel *(v) oppose, resist* rebelled rebelling

RBL rebel *(n) opposer (adj) dissident*

RBL roble *tree*

RBL rubble *fragments*

RBL rubella *German measles*

RBL rubeola *measles*

RBL ruble *money*

RBLD arability *cropland*

RBLD rebuild *erect again* rebuilt rebuilding

RBLD ribald *crude*

RBLDR ribaldry *crudeness* ribaldries

RBLK herblike *plant*

RBLMNT rabblement *disturbance*

RBLN rebellion *uprising*

RBLNS rebalance *equal weight* rebalanced rebalancing

RBLNTS rebalance *equal weight* rebalanced rebalancing

RBLRZN rabble-rousing *disturbing*

RBLRZNG rabble-rousing *disturbing*

RBLRZR rabble-rouser *disturber*

RBLS Rabelais *satirist*

RBLS rebellious *resisting*

RBLSHN Rabelaisian *extravagant*

RBLST herbalist *healer*

RBLT arability *cropland*

RBLT rebuilt *(v-past) rebuild*

RBLT rubellite *gem*

RBLTDR rehabilitator *restore*

RBLTDV rehabilitative *restore*

RBLTNT rehabilitant *restored one*

RBLTSHN rehabilitation *restoration*

RBLTT rehabilitate *restore* rehabilitated rehabilitating

RBLTTR rehabilitator *restore*

RBLTTV rehabilitative *restore*

RBLYN rebellion *uprising*

RBLYS rebellious *resisting*

RBLYSL rebelliously *resisting*

RBLYSNS rebelliousness *resistance*

RBLZ Rabelais *satirist*

RBLZHN Rabelaisian *extravagant*

RBLZN Rabelaisian *extravagant*

RBLZYN Rabelaisian *extravagant*

Use letters that best describe the sounds you hear and omit the vowels. Use **S** or **K** instead of **C**: to find circle use **SRKL**. Use **J** to find joy, **JM** to find gem and **G** to find go.

RBM erbium *element*
RBN Arabian *of Arabia*
RBN rebound *bounce off*
RBN Reuben *artist, sandwich*
RBN ribbing *teasing, ridge*
RBN ribbon *strip*
RBN robin *bird*
RBN rubbing *image*
RBN urban *city*
RBN urbane *poised*
RBNC Arabian Sea *body of water*
RBND rawboned *lean*
RBND rebound *bounce off*
RBND urbanity *good manners* urbanities
RBNFSH ribbonfish *animal*
RBNG ribbing *teasing, ridge*
RBNG rubbing *image*
RBNK rabbinic (or) rabbinical (adj) *Jewish* rabbinically (adv)
RBNKL rabbinical (or) rabbinic (adj) *Jewish* rabbinically (adv)
RBNKLK ribonucleic *genes*
RBNKLSD ribonucleoside *genes*
RBNKLTD ribonucleotide *genes*
RBNKLYK ribonucleic *genes*
RBNKLYSD ribonucleoside *genes*
RBNKLYTD ribonucleotide *genes*
RBNKLYZ ribonuclease *genes*
RBNKLZ ribonuclease *genes*
RBNS Arabian Sea *body of water*
RBNSDK urbanistic *planner*
RBNSDKL urbanistically *planner*
RBNST urbanist *planner*
RBNSTK urbanistic *planner*
RBNSTKL urbanistically *planner*
RBNT urbanite *city dweller*
RBNT urbanity *good manners* urbanities
RBNYKLK ribonucleic *genes*
RBNYKLSD ribonucleoside

RBNYKLTD ribonucleotide *genes*
RBNYKLYK ribonucleic *genes*
RBNYKLYSD ribonucleoside *genes*
RBNYKLYTD ribonucleotide *genes*
RBNYKLYZ ribonuclease *genes*
RBNYKLZ ribonuclease *genes*
RBNZ urbanize *city growth* urbanized urbanizing (Br) urbanise
RBNZM urbanism *city*
RBNZSHN urbanization *city growth* (Br) urbanisation
RBPTZ rebaptize *initiate* rebaptized rebaptizing
RBQLR orbicular *circular*
RBQLRL orbicularly *circularly*
RBR arbor *tree, shaft* (Br) arbour
RBR herbaria (pl) *plant collection* herbarium
RBR raw bar *shellfish*
RBR rebar *concrete*
RBR rebore *drill again* rebored reboring
RBR robber *thief*
RBR robbery *crime* robberies
RBR rubber *latex*
RBR rubbery *elastic*
RBRB rhubarb *vegetable*
RBRBN rubber band *holder*
RBRBND rubber band *holder*
RBRD Arbor Day *holiday*
RBRD arboreta (pl) *plantation* arboretum
RBRDKST rebroadcast *airing*
RBRDM arboretum *plantation* arboretums (or) arboreta
RBRK air brake *stop*
RBRK rubric *title*

RBRK rubric (or) rubrical (adj) *titled* rubrically (adv)
RBRKDR rubricator *commentator*
RBRKL rubrical (or) rubric (adj) *titled* rubrically (adv)
RBRKLCHR arboriculture *tree cultivation*
RBRKLCHRL arboricultural *tree cultivation*
RBRKLTR arboriculture *tree cultivation*
RBRKLTRL arboricultural *tree cultivation*
RBRKSHN rubrication *comment*
RBRKT rubricate *comment* rubricated rubricating
RBRKTR rubricator *commentator*
RBRL arboreal (adj) *tree* arboreally (adv)
RBRM herbarium *plant collection* herbaria
RBRN airborne *flight*
RBRN reborn *given another birth*
RBRNK rubberneck *gawk*
RBRS arboreous *tree*
RBRSH airbrush *atomizer* airbrushes
RBRSNS arborescence *like a tree*
RBRSNT arborescent *like a tree*
RBRSNTS arborescence *like a tree*
RBRST airburst *bomb*
RBRST arborist *tree specialist*
RBRSTMP rubber stamp (n) *imprint* rubber-stamp (v, adj)
RBRT arboreta (pl) *plantation* arboretum
RBRTH rebirth *new life*
RBRTM arboretum *plantation* arboretums (or) arboreta
RBRVT arborvitae *cypress*
RBRY herbaria (pl) *plant collection* herbarium

Letters aren't doubled for single sounds: to find alley use **L** not **LL**. Use **Y** and **W** as hard sounds only: to find yellow use **YL**. (Br)=British spelling or usage. * See dictionary.

RBRYL arboreal (adj) *tree*
arboreally (adv)
RBRYM herbarium *plant*
collection herbaria
RBRYS arboreous *tree*
RBRZ arborize *branch*
arborized arborizing
RBRZD rubberized *latex*
RBS air base *airport*
RBS airbus *airplane*
RBS Erebus *Greek myth*
RBS rebus *monkey*
RBS rubious *red*
RBS rubus *plant* rubus
RBSCHS robustious *loud*
RBSCHSL robustiously *loud*
RBSCHSNS robustiousness
loud
RBSD herbicide *kill plants*
RBSD robusta *coffee*
RBSDL herbicidal (adj) *kill
plants* herbicidally (adv)
RBSH rubbish *trash*
RBSH rubbishy *trashy*
RBSHR rubbisher *trash man*
RBSHS herbaceous *plant*
RBSK arabesque *art style,
position*
RBSPR Robespierre
revolutionary
RBSPYR Robespierre
revolutionary
RBST robust *healthy*
RBST robusta *coffee*
RBT airboat *vehicle*
RBT orbit *circle*
RBT rabato *collar* rabatos
RBT rabbett *joint*
RBT rabbit *animal* rabbit (or)
rabbits
RBT rarebit *food*
RBT rebait *fishing*
RBT rebate *money* rebated
rebating
RBT reboot *computer*
RBT rebut *refute* rebutted
rebutting
RBT robot *machine*
RBT rowboat *oars*
RBT rubato *tempo* rubatos
RBTBRSH rabbitbrush *plant*
RBTHRT rubythroat

hummingbird
RBTK aerobatic *flying*
RBTK robotic *mechanical*
RBTKS aerobatics *flying
feats*
RBTL orbital *circle*
RBTL rebuttal *opposition*
RBTPNCH rabbit punch
boxing rabbit punches
RBTR arbiter *negotiator*
RBTR orbiter *spacecraft*
RBTR rabbiter *hunter*
RBTR rabbitry *animals*
RBTR rebutter *opposer*
RBTRBL arbitrable
negotiable
RBTRDR arbitrator *judge*
RBTRJ arbitrage *profit by
trading* arbitraged
arbitraging
RBTRJR arbitrageur (or)
arbitrager *trader*
RBTRL arbitral *not
determined*
RBTRR arbitrary *random*
RBTRRL arbitrarily *randomly*
RBTRRNS arbitrariness
randomness
RBTRSH arbitrage *profit by
trading* arbitraged
arbitraging
RBTRSHN arbitration
judgement
RBTRSHR arbitrageur (or)
arbitrager *trader*
RBTRT arbitrate *judge*
arbitrated arbitrating
RBTRTR arbitrator *judge*
RBTRZ rabbit ears *antenna*
RBTRZH arbitrage *profit by
trading* arbitraged
arbitraging
RBTRZHR arbitrageur (or)
arbitrager *trader*
RBTS arbutus *plant*
RBTX aerobatics *flying feats*
RBTZ robotize *mechanize*
robotized robotizing
RBVR herbivore *eat plants*
RBVRS herbivorous *eat
plants*
RBX aerobics *exercises*

RBY Arabia *peninsula*
RBYDS arbutus *plant*
RBYK rebuke *scold* rebuked
rebuking
RBYL rubeola *measles*
RBYM erbium *element*
RBYN Arabian *of Arabia*
RBYN rebellion *uprising*
RBYNC Arabian Sea *body of
water*
RBYNS Arabian Sea *body of
water*
RBYS rebellious *resisting*
RBYS rubious *red*
RBYSL rebelliously *resisting*
RBYSNS rebelliousness
resistance
RBYTS arbutus *plant*
RBZ rabies *disease*
RBZ rebozo *scarf* rebozos
RBZ ribes *shrub* ribes
RC racy *indecent, sporty*
racier raciest
RCD recede *retreat* receded
receding
RCD reseda *color*
RCD reseed *plant*
RCH arch *curve* arches
RCH orache (or) orach *herb*
RCH reach *attain, stretch*
reaches
RCH retch *vomit*
RCH Rh *blood*
RCH rich *wealthy, lush* riches
RCH roach *(n) insect, fish,
hair (v) brush up* roaches
RCH wretch *miserable one*
RCHBSHP archbishop
clergy
RCHD wretched *miserable*
RCHDCSN archdiocesan
archbishop territory
RCHDCZ archdiocese
archbishop territory
RCHDK archduke *prince*
RCHDKL archducal *princely*
RCHDKN archdeacon *clergy*
RCHDSS archdiocese
archbishop territory
RCHDSSN archdiocesan
archbishop territory
RCHDSZ archdiocese

Use letters that best describe the sounds you hear and omit the vowels. Use **S** or **K** instead of **C**: to find circle use **SRKL**. Use **J** to find joy, **JM** to find gem and **G** to find go.

archbishop territory
RCHDYCSN archdiocesan *archbishop territory*
RCHDYCZ archdiocese *archbishop territory*
RCHDYK archduke *prince*
RCHDYKL archducal *princely*
RCHDYSS archdiocese *archbishop territory*
RCHDYSSN archdiocesan *archbishop territory*
RCHDYSZ archdiocese *archbishop territory*
RCHFKDR Rh factor *blood*
RCHFKTR Rh factor *blood*
RCHK recheck *examine*
RCHL richly *abundantly*
RCHL ritual *ceremony*
RCHLSDK ritualistic *ceremony*
RCHLSDKL ritualistically *ceremony*
RCHLSTK ritualistic *ceremony*
RCHLSTKL ritualistically *ceremony*
RCHLZ ritualize *ceremony* ritualized ritualizing
RCHLZM ritualism *ceremony*
RCHMN Richmond *city*
RCHMND Richmond *city*
RCHN richen *add wealth*
RCHN urchin *child*
RCHNL rechannel *direction*
RCHNM archenemy *main foe* archenemies
RCHNS richness *wealth, lush*
RCHR archer *bow and arrow user*
RCHR archery *bow and arrow*
RCHRD orchard *trees*
RCHRFSH archerfish *fish*
RCHRJ recharge *renew* recharged recharging
RCHRJBL rechargeable *renewable*
RCHRJR recharger *renew*
RCHS righteous *moral*
RCHSDR Rochester *city*

RCHSL righteously *morally*
RCHSNS righteousness *morals*
RCHSTR Rochester *city*
RCHT ratchet *tool*
RCHT rochet *robe*
RCHTP archetype *example*
RCHTPL archetypal (adj) *example* archetypally (adv)
RCHW archway *passage*
RCHWL ritual *ceremony*
RCHWLSDK ritualistic *ceremony*
RCHWLSDKL ritualistically *ceremony*
RCHWLSTK ritualistic *ceremony*
RCHWLSTKL ritualistically *ceremony*
RCHWLZ ritualize *ceremony* ritualized ritualizing
RCHWLZM ritualism *ceremony*
RCHZ riches *wealth*
RCL reseal *close tightly*
RCLBL resealable *close tightly*
RCM raceme *flower*
RCMK racemic *mixture*
RCMZ racemize *mix*
RCMZSHN racemization *mix*
RCN arsine *poisonous gas*
RCNS raciness *indecent, sporty*
RCR racier *indecent, sporty*
RCST raciest *indecent, sporty*
RCT receipt *received, payment token*
RCV receive *get, greet* received receiving
RCVBL receivable *debt*
RCVR receiver *get, greet*
RCVRSHP receivership *debt*
RCYR racier *indecent, sporty*
RCYST raciest *indecent, sporty*
RCZ arses (pl) *verse* arsis
RD air raid *alarm*
RD aired *spoke*
RD aorta *blood vessel* aortas

(or) aortae
RD arid *dry*
RD arietta *song*
RD arty *artistic* artier artiest
RD eared *with ears*
RD Erato *Greek Muse*
RD erode *crumble* eroded eroding
RD errata (pl) *list* erratum
RD oread *nymph*
RD rad *energy*
RD radii (pl) *circle* radius
RD radio *wireless* radios
RD raid *attack*
RD ratty *tangled, shabby, irritable* rattier rattiest
RD read (v) *take in words, predict, understand** read reading
RD read (adv) *informed*
RD ready (v) *prepare* readied readying readies
RD ready (adj) *prepared* readier readiest
RD red *color* redder reddest
RD red-eye *flight, whiskey*
RD redeye *gravy*
RD redo *do again* redid redoing redone redoes
RD reed *stalk*
RD reedy *with stalks* reedier reediest
RD retia (pl) *plexus* rete
RD riata *lariat*
RD rid *free from* ridded ridding
RD ride *travel* rode riding ridden
RD righty *right-handed* righties
RD road *highway*
RD roadie *entertainment*
RD rod *stick, gun*
RD rode (v-past) *ride*
RD rodeo *cowboy event* rodeos
RD rood *cross*
RD rooty *soil*
RD roti *bread*
RD rowdy *rough and loud* rowdies rowdier rowdiest
RD rudd *fish*

Letters aren't doubled for single sounds: to find alley use **L** not **LL**. Use **Y** and **W** as hard sounds only: to find yellow use **YL**. (Br)=British spelling or usage. * See dictionary.

RD ruddy *reddish* ruddier
ruddiest

RD rude *impolite* ruder
rudest

RD rutty *grooved* ruttier
ruttiest

RD urd *legume*

RD Urdu *language*

RDBD redbud *tree*

RDBD roadbed *street*

RDBF oeil-de-boeuf *eye*
oeils-de-boeuf

RDBG rutabaga *vegetable*

RDBGR rutabaga *vegetable*

RDBK rudbeckia *herb*

RDBKY rudbeckia *herb*

RDBL irritable (adj) *grouchy*
irritably (adv)

RDBL ratable (or) rateable
(adj) *rank* ratably (adv)

RDBL readable (adj) *reading*
readably (adv)

RDBL redouble *intensify*
redoubled redoubling

RDBL ridable (or) rideable
travel

RDBL writable *inscribe*

RDBLD irritability *grouchy*
irritabilities

RDBLD readability *reading*

RDBLD roadability *driving*

RDBLDD red-blooded
vigorous

RDBLK roadblock *blockade*

RDBLNS irritableness
grouchy

RDBLT irritability *grouchy*
irritabilities

RDBLT readability *reading*

RDBLT roadability *driving*

RDBRD redbird *bird*

RDBRK redbrick
construction

RDBRST redbreast *bird, fish*

RDBT red-bait *communism*

RDC Red Sea *body of water*

RDCH radicchio *lettuce*

RDCHK artichoke *vegetable*

RDCHY radicchio *lettuce*

RDCZ radices (or) radixes
(pl) *number* radix

RDD aridity *dryness*

RDD redid *(v-past)* redo

RDD reeded *decorated*

RDD ridotto *festival* ridottos

RDDBL redoubtable
defensive

RDDKSHN rededication
devotion

RDDKT rededicate *devote*
rededicated rededicating

RDDM rhytidome *bark*

RDDNDRN rhododendron
shrub

RDDNS rootedness *planted*

RDDR irradiator *x-ray*

RDDR radiator *cooler*

RDDV irradiative *x-ray*

RDF ratafia *liqueur*

RDF ratify *approve* ratified
ratifying ratifies

RDF write off *(v) reduce,*
dismiss

RDF write-off *(n) reduction*

RDFD radiophoto *picture*

RDFK artifact *object*
(Br) artefact

RDFKSHN ratification
approval

RDFKT artifact *object*
(Br) artefact

RDFN radiophone *telephone*

RDFR ratifier *approver*

RDFR rotifer *animal*

RDFS artifice *trick*

RDFSH redfish *fish*

RDFSHL artificial (adj)
imitation artificially (adv)

RDFSHLD artificiality
imitation

RDFSHLT artificiality
imitation

RDFSHYLD artificiality
imitation

RDFSHYLT artificiality
imitation

RDFSR artificer *tricker*

RDFT radiophoto *picture*

RDFY ratafia *liqueur*

RDFYR ratifier *approver*

RDG red dog *(n, v) blitz*

RDGNK erotogenic *sex*

RDGRF radiograph *X-ray*

RDGRF radiography *X-ray*

RDGRFK radiographic X-
ray

RDGRFKL radiographically
X-*ray*

RDGRM radiogram *message*

RDGRVR rotogravure
pictures

RDGRVYR rotogravure
pictures

RDHD redhead *hair*

RDHDD redheaded *hair*

RDHG road hog *driver*

RDHNDD red-handed *guilty*

RDHS roadhouse *nightclub,*
inn

RDHT red-hot *heat*

RDJKSHN reeducation
teaching

RDJKT reeducate *teach*
reeducated reeducating

RDJNK erotogenic *sex*

RDJNR Rio de Janeiro *city*

RDK arctic *(often capitalized)*
ocean, region

RDK erotic *sexy*

RDK erotica *sexy art*

RDK erratic *irregular*

RDK iridic *iris*

RDK radicchio *lettuce*

RDK redact *edit*

RDK uratic *urine*

RDKBL eradicable *destroy*

RDKDR eradicator *destroyer*

RDKDR redactor *editor*

RDKDV radioactive *atomic*

RDKDV reductive *simplified*

RDKL article *thing*

RDKL erotically *sexy*

RDKL erratical (or) erratic
(adj) *irregular* erratically
(adv)

RDKL radical *(n) root*

RDKL radical (adj) *extreme*
radically (adv)

RDKL radicle *seed*

RDKL reticule *bag*

RDKL ridicule *mock* ridiculed
ridiculing

RDKL roadkill *dead animal*

RDKLR radicular *nerve*

RDKLR ridiculer *mocker*

RDKLS ridiculous *absurd*

RDKLSL ridiculously *absurd*

RDKLSNS ridiculousness *absurd*

RDKLZ radicalize *make extreme* radicalized radicalizing (Br) radicalise

RDKLZM radicalism *extreme*

RDKR urticaria *itching*

RDKRBN radiocarbon *carbon 14*

RDKRDR redecorator *beautifier*

RDKRL urticarial *itching*

RDKRPT red carpet (n) *welcome* red-carpet (adj)

RDKRS Red Cross *emblem*

RDKRSHN redecoration *beautification*

RDKRST rhodochrosite *mineral*

RDKRT redecorate *beautify* redecorated redecorating

RDKRTR redecorator *beautifier*

RDKRY urticaria *itching*

RDKRYL urticarial *itching*

RDKS radix *number* radices (or) radixes

RDKS redux *brought back*

RDKSHN Arctic Ocean *body of water*

RDKSHN eradication *destruction*

RDKSHN redaction *edit*

RDKSHN reduction *lessen, simplify*

RDKSHN reeducation *teaching*

RDKSHNST reductionist *simplifier*

RDKSHNZM reductionism *simplify*

RDKT eradicate *destroy* eradicated eradicating

RDKT redact *edit*

RDKT redcoat *soldier*

RDKT reeducate *teach* reeducated reeducating

RDKT urticate *itch* urticated urticating

RDKTR eradicator *destroyer*

RDKTR redactor *editor*

RDKTV radioactive *atomic*

RDKTV reductive *simplified*

RDKTVD radioactivity *atomic*

RDKTVT radioactivity *atomic*

RDKY radicchio *lettuce*

RDKYL reticule *bag*

RDKYL ridicule *mock* ridiculed ridiculing

RDKYLR radicular *nerve*

RDKYLR ridiculer *mocker*

RDKYLS ridiculous *absurd*

RDKYLSL ridiculously *absurd*

RDKYLSNS ridiculousness *absurd*

RDL Airedale *dog*

RDL artily *artistic*

RDL ordeal *trial*

RDL raddle (v) *weave, paint* raddled raddling

RDL raddle (n) *pigment*

RDL radial (adj) *like rays* radially (adv)

RDL radula *mouth* radulae

RDL ratel *weasel*

RDL rattle (v) *shake, noise* rattled rattling

RDL rattle (n) *toy, noise*

RDL rattly *noisy*

RDL raw deal *swindle*

RDL readily *easily*

RDL readily *promptly, willingly, easily*

RDL redial *phone again*

RDL riddle *question, permeate* riddled riddling

RDL rowdily *roughly*

RDL ruddily *reddish*

RDL ruddle *redden* ruddled ruddling

RDL rudely *impolite*

RDL rutile *mineral*

RDL urodele *amphibian*

RDLBRN rattlebrain *thoughtless one*

RDLBRND rattlebrained *thoughtless*

RDLD raddled *confused, worn*

RDLDK radiolytic *breakdown*

RDLDR red-letter *special*

RDLG iridology *eye study* iridologies

RDLG radiology *X-ray*

RDLJ iridology *eye study* iridologies

RDLJ radiology *X-ray*

RDLJK radiologic (or) radiological (adj) *X-ray* radiologically (adv)

RDLJKL radiological (or) radiologic (adj) *X-ray* radiologically (adv)

RDLJST iridologist *eye study*

RDLJST radiologist *X-ray*

RDLN ortolan *bird*

RDLN rattling (adj) *lively* (adv) *very*

RDLN redline *speed*

RDLN Rhode Island *US State*

RDLN Ritalin (trademark) *drug*

RDLND Rhode Island *US State*

RDLNG rattling (adj) *lively* (adv) *very*

RDLNS redolence *fragrance*

RDLNT redolent *scented*

RDLNT rutilant *red glow*

RDLNTS redolence *fragrance*

RDLR Eurodollar *currency*

RDLR rattler *snake, toy*

RDLRT red alert *danger*

RDLSNK rattlesnake *reptile*

RDLSS radiolysis *breakdown*

RDLTK radiolytic *breakdown*

RDLTR red-letter *special*

RDLTRP rattletrap *old car*

RDLZ reutilize *use again* reutilized reutilizing (Br) reutilise

RDM erratum *error* errata

RDM iridium *metallic element*

RDM radium *element*

RDM radome *cover*

RDM redeem *save*

RDM rhodium *element*

RDMBL irredeemable (adj) *cannot save* irredeemably (adv)

Letters aren't doubled for single sounds: to find alley use **L** not **LL**. Use **Y** and **W** as hard sounds only: to find yellow use **YL**. (Br)=British spelling or usage. * See dictionary.

RDMBL redeemable (adj)
save redeemably (adv)
RDMD ready-made (or)
readymade (n)
commonplace ready-made
(adj)
RDMDR radiometer *device*
RDMDV redemptive *saving*
RDMMDK radiomimetic *like*
X-rays
RDMMTK radiomimetic *like*
X-rays
RDMN redeeming *offsetting*
RDMN rhodamine *dye*
RDMN rodman *surveyor*
RDMNG redeeming
offsetting
RDMNL rudimental
fundamental
RDMNT rudiment
fundamental part
RDMNTD rodomontade
rant
RDMNTHN rhadamanthine
strict
RDMNTL rudimental
fundamental
RDMNTR rudimentary
fundamental
RDMNTRL rudimentarily
fundamental
RDMNTRNS
rudimentariness
fundamental
RDMP road map *atlas*
RDMPDV redemptive *saving*
RDMPSHN redemption
saving
RDMPTR redemptory *saving*
RDMPTV redemptive *saving*
RDMR redeemer *saver*
RDMSHN redemption
saving
RDMTR radiometer *device*
RDMTR redemptory *saving*
RDMTRK radiometric *device*
RDMTV redemptive *saving*
RDN aerodyne *aircraft*
RDN ordain *appoint*
RDN radian *measurement*
RDN radon *gas*
RDN reading *indication*

RDN redden *blush*
RDN redone *(v-past)* redo
RDN redound *rebound*
RDN reeding *milling*
RDN ridden *travelled*
RDN riding *vehicle, district*
RDN right on (or) right-on
agreement
RDN Rodin *sculptor*
RDN rotten *decayed*
RDN write down *(v) record*
write-down (n)
RDN write in (v) *ballot* write-
in (n, adj)
RDN write-down *(n)*
reduction
RDNC ardency *passion*
RDND redound *rebound*
RDNDNC redundancy
repetition redundancies
RDNDNS redundancy
repetition redundancies
RDNDNT redundant
repetitious
RDNDNTC redundancy
repetition redundancies
RDNDNTS redundancy
repetition redundancies
RDNG rating *rank*
RDNG reading *indication*
RDNG reeding *milling*
RDNG riding *vehicle, district*
RDNG writing *lettering,*
record
RDNGGLD right-angled (or)
right-angle (adj) 90
degrees right angle (n)
RDNGK red ink *deficit*
RDNGL right-angle (or)
right-angled (adj) 90
degrees right angle (n)
RDNGLD right-angled (or)
right-angle (adj) 90
degrees right angle (n)
RDNK red ink *deficit*
RDNK redneck *rube*
RDNL ordinal *order*
RDNL read-only *computer*
RDNL rottenly *decay*
RDNMK aerodynamic *air*
motion
RDNMKL aerodynamically

air motion
RDNMKS aerodynamics *air*
motion
RDNMNT ordainment
appointment
RDNMSST aerodynamicist
air motion scientist
RDNMX aerodynamics *air*
motion
RDNNS ordinance *law*
RDNNS ordnance *supplies*
RDNNS ordonnance
arrangement
RDNNTS ordinance *law*
RDNNTS ordnance *supplies*
RDNNTS ordonnance
arrangement
RDNR ordainer *appointer*
RDNR ordinary *(n)*
clergyman, judge, (Br) meal
(adj) *expected, common*
ordinaries
RDNR ordinary (adj) *common*
RDNRL ordinarily *commonly*
RDNRNS ordinariness
common
RDNS ardency *passion*
RDNS aridness *dryness*
RDNS artiness *artistic*
RDNS irradiance *x-ray*
RDNS radiance *glow*
RDNS readiness *preparation*
RDNS readiness *promptness,*
willingness
RDNS redness *color*
RDNS reediness *full of stalks*
RDNS riddance *loss*
RDNS rottenness *decay*
RDNS rowdiness *roughness*
RDNS ruddiness *redness*
RDNS rudeness *impolite*
RDNSD rodenticide *kills*
rodents
RDNSHN ordination
appointment
RDNSTN rottenstone *polish*
RDNT ardent *passionate*
RDNT irritant *annoyance*
RDNT ordinate *axis*
RDNT radiant *glowing*
RDNT red ant *insect*
RDNT rhodonite *mineral*

Use letters that best describe the sounds you hear and omit the vowels. Use **S** or **K**
instead of **C**: to find circle use **SRKL**. Use **J** to find joy, **JM** to find gem and **G** to find go.

RDNT rodent *animal*
RDNTC ardency *passion*
RDNTS ardency *passion*
RDNTS irradiance *x-ray*
RDNTS radiance *glow*
RDNTS riddance *loss*
RDNTSD rodenticide *kills rodents*
RDP write up (v) *report* write-up (n)
RDPK radiopaque *no X-ray*
RDPL redeploy *relocate*
RDPLKDV reduplicative *copy*
RDPLKSHN reduplication *copy*
RDPLKT reduplicate *copy* reduplicated reduplicating
RDPLKTV reduplicative *copy*
RDPLMNT redeployment *relocation*
RDPLN rataplan *beat*
RDPNSL red-pencil *censor*
RDPNTSL red-pencil *censor*
RDPSN rhodopsin *pigment*
RDQL reticule *bag*
RDQL ridicule *mock* ridiculed ridiculing
RDQLR radicular *nerve*
RDQLR ridiculer *mocker*
RDQLS ridiculous *absurd*
RDQLSL ridiculously *absurd*
RDQLSNS ridiculousness *absurd*
RDR aerator *add oxygen*
RDR air-dry *wind*
RDR air-to-air *missile*
RDR ardor *passion* (Br) ardour
RDR artery *blood vessel* arteries
RDR artier *artistic*
RDR orator *speaker*
RDR order (v) *demand, arrange* (n) *group, class, command**
RDR ordure *waste matter*
RDR radar *locator*
RDR raider *attacker*
RDR rater *ranking*

RDR ratter *cat, dog*
RDR rattier *tangled, shabby, irritable*
RDR reader *book, person*
RDR redder *color*
RDR redear *fish*
RDR redraw *describe* redrew redrawn
RDR rhodora *plant*
RDR rider *traveller*
RDR rioter *reveler*
RDR rooter *root, supporter*
RDR rotary *wheel* rotaries
RDR Rotary *club*
RDR rotor *blade*
RDR router *machine, horse*
RDR rowdier *rough*
RDR rudder *steering*
RDR ruddier *reddish*
RDR ruder *impolite*
RDR ruttier *grooved*
RDR ureter *duct*
RDR writer *inscriber*
RDRDM Rotterdam *city*
RDRF redraft *write*
RDRFT redraft *write*
RDRK redirect *change course*
RDRK rhetoric *language*
RDRKRFT rotorcraft *vehicle* rotorcraft
RDRKT redirect *change course*
RDRL orderly (n) *soldier* orderlies
RDRL orderly (adj, adv) *tidy*
RDRL ruderal *vegetation*
RDRLNS orderliness *neatness*
RDRLS riderless *no traveller*
RDRM aerodrome (Br) *airfield*
RDRM airdrome *airport* (Br) aerodrome
RDRM eardrum *hearing*
RDRM ready room *pilots*
RDRM red drum *fish*
RDRN redrawn (v-past) *redraw*
RDRN wrought iron *metal*
RDRNR roadrunner *bird*
RDRP airdrop *parachute*
RDRP eardrop *medicine*

RDRS redress *remedy*
RDRSHN reiteration *repeat*
RDRSHN rhetorician *orator*
RDRSHP readership *persons*
RDRSHP ridership *vehicles*
RDRSKP radarscope *screen*
RDRT redroot *herb*
RDRT reiterate *repeat* reiterated reiterating
RDRV hors d'oeuvre *appetizer* hors d'oeuvres
RDRZ Reuters *news*
RDS arduous *difficult*
RDS artist *craftsman*
RDS Eurydice *myth*
RDS iritis *eye*
RDS radius *circle* radii
RDS Red Sea *body of water*
RDS reduce *lessen* reduced reducing
RDS riotous *disorderly*
RDS roadhouse *nightclub, inn*
RDSBL irreducible (adj) *cannot simplify* irreducibly (adv)
RDSBL reducible (adj) *simplify* reducibly (adv)
RDSBLD irreducibility *cannot simplify*
RDSBLD reducibility *simplify*
RDSBLT irreducibility *cannot simplify*
RDSBLT reducibility *simplify*
RDSD raticide *rat killer*
RDSD roadside *street*
RDSDR roadster *car*
RDSH radish *vegetable* radishes
RDSH reddish *color*
RDSH Rhodesia *region*
RDSH road show *entertainment*
RDSH ruttish *lustful*
RDSHFT redshift *gravity*
RDSHN erudition *learning*
RDSHN irradiation *x-ray*
RDSHN radiation *energy*
RDSHNGK redshank *bird*
RDSHNK redshank *bird*
RDSHNR Rio de Janeiro

Letters aren't doubled for single sounds: to find alley use **L** not **LL**. Use **Y** and **W** as hard sounds only: to find yellow use **YL**. (Br)=British spelling or usage. * See dictionary.

city
RDSHRT redshirt *athlete*
RDSKVR rediscover *find*
RDSKVR rediscovery *thing found*
RDSL riotously *disorderly*
RDSN artisan *craftsman*
RDSND radiosonde *transmitter*
RDSNPR red snapper *fish*
RDSNS iridescence *shine*
RDSNS reticence *restraint reticency*
RDSNS riotousness *disorderly*
RDSNT iridescent *shiny*
RDSNT red cent *penny*
RDSNT reticent *silent*
RDSNTL iridescently *shiny*
RDSNTS iridescence *shine*
RDSNTS reticence *restraint reticency*
RDSR reducer *lessen*
RDST artiest *artistic*
RDST artist *craftsman*
RDST rattiest *tangled, shabby, irritable*
RDST reddest *color*
RDST rowdiest *rough*
RDST ruddiest *reddish*
RDST rudest *impolite*
RDST ruttiest *grooved*
RDSTP radioisotope *atom*
RDSTR artistry *skill, craft*
RDSTR roadster *car*
RDSTRBSHN redistribution *allocation*
RDSTRBT redistribute *allocate* redistributed redistributing
RDSTRBYSHN redistribution *allocation*
RDSTRBYT redistribute *allocate* redistributed redistributing
RDSTRK redistrict *divide area*
RDSTRKT redistrict *divide area*
RDSTRT redstart *bird*
RDSZ eroticize *make sexy* eroticized eroticizing

RDSZ radices (or) radixes (pl) *number* radix
RDSZM eroticism *sexiness*
RDSZM erraticism *irregularity*
RDT aridity *dryness*
RDT erudite *educated*
RDT irradiate *x-ray* irradiated irradiating
RDT radiate *glow* radiated radiating
RDT ratatouille *stew*
RDT readout (n) *information* read out (v)
RDT redoubt *defense*
RDT redout *red vision*
RDT reedit *correct*
RDT ridotto *festival* ridottos
RDT write out *inscribe*
RDTBL redoubtable *defensive*
RDTD red tide *algae*
RDTHRP radiotherapy X-*rays*
RDTHRPST radiotherapist X-*rays*
RDTL red-tailed *feathers*
RDTLD red-tailed *feathers*
RDTLFN radiotelephone *wireless*
RDTLGRF radiotelegraph *wireless*
RDTLR rototiller *plow*
RDTP red tape *paperwork*
RDTP redtop *grass*
RDTR irradiator *x-ray*
RDTR radiator *cooler*
RDTT rat-a-tat (or) rat-a-tat-tat *sound*
RDTV irradiative *x-ray*
RDTW ratatouille *stew*
RDTWR ready-to-wear *manufactured*
RDVD redivide *carve up*
RDVLP redevelop *build again*
RDVLPMNT redevelopment *modernization*
RDVLPR redeveloper *builder*
RDVRK aardvark *anteater*
RDVW right-of-way *yield*

rights-of-way
RDW right away *soon*
RDW right-of-way *yield* rights-of-way
RDW roadway *street*
RDWD redwood *tree*
RDWF aardwolf *hyena* aardwolves
RDWKDV radioactive *atomic*
RDWKTV radioactive *atomic*
RDWKTVD radioactivity *atomic*
RDWKTVT radioactivity *atomic*
RDWLF aardwolf *hyena* aardwolves
RDWNG redwing *bird*
RDWNGD red-winged *feathers*
RDWRK roadwork *construction*
RDWRTH roadworthy *driving*
RDWRTHNS roadworthiness *driving*
RDWS arduous *difficult*
RDWSL arduously *difficult*
RDWSTP radioisotope *atom*
RDWV radio wave *wireless*
RDX radix *number* radices (or) radixes
RDX redux *brought back*
RDY radii (pl) *circle* radius
RDY radio *wireless* radios
RDY retia (pl) *plexus* rete
RDY rodeo *cowboy event* rodeos
RDYDR irradiator *x-ray*
RDYDR radiator *cooler*
RDYDV irradiative *x-ray*
RDYFD radiophoto *picture*
RDYFN radiophone *telephone*
RDYFT radiophoto *picture*
RDYGRF radiograph *X-ray*
RDYGRF radiography *X-ray*
RDYGRFK radiographic X-*ray*
RDYGRFKL radiographically *X-ray*
RDYGRM radiogram *message*

Use letters that best describe the sounds you hear and omit the vowels. Use **S** or **K** instead of **C**: to find circle use **SRKL**. Use **J** to find joy, **JM** to find gem and **G** to find go.

RDYKDV radioactive *atomic*
RDYKRBN radiocarbon *carbon 14*
RDYKSHN reeducation *teaching*
RDYKT reeducate *teach* reeducated reeducating
RDYKTV radioactive *atomic*
RDYKTVD radioactivity *atomic*
RDYKTVT radioactivity *atomic*
RDYL radial (adj) *like rays* radially (adv)
RDYL radula *mouth* radulae
RDYL redial *phone again*
RDYLDK radiolytic *breakdown*
RDYLG radiology *X-ray*
RDYLJ radiology *X-ray*
RDYLJK radiologic (or) radiological (adj) *X-ray* radiologically (adv)
RDYLJKL radiological (or) radiologic (adj) *X-ray* radiologically (adv)
RDYLJST radiologist *X-ray*
RDYLSS radiolysis *breakdown*
RDYLTK radiolytic *breakdown*
RDYM iridium *metallic element*
RDYM radium *element*
RDYM rhodium *element*
RDYMDR radiometer *device*
RDYMMDK radiomimetic *like X-rays*
RDYMMTK radiomimetic *like X-rays*
RDYMTR radiometer *device*
RDYMTRK radiometric *device*
RDYN radian *measurement*
RDYNS irradiance *x-ray*
RDYNS radiance *glow*
RDYNT radiant *glowing*
RDYNTS irradiance *x-ray*
RDYNTS radiance *glow*
RDYPK radiopaque *no X-ray*
RDYPLKDV reduplicative *copy*
RDYPLKSHN reduplication *copy*
RDYPLKT reduplicate *copy* reduplicated reduplicating
RDYPLKTV reduplicative *copy*
RDYR artier *artistic*
RDYR ordure *waste matter*
RDYR rattier *tangled, shabby, irritable*
RDYR rowdier *rough*
RDYR ruddier *reddish*
RDYR ruttier *grooved*
RDYRN wrought iron *metal*
RDYS arduous *difficult*
RDYS radius *circle* radii
RDYS reduce *lessen* reduced reducing
RDYSBL irreducible (adj) *cannot simplify* irreducibly (adv)
RDYSBL reducible (adj) *simplify* reducibly (adv)
RDYSBLD irreducibility *cannot simplify*
RDYSBLD reducibility *simplify*
RDYSBLT irreducibility *cannot simplify* .
RDYSBLT reducibility *simplify*
RDYSHN irradiation *x-ray*
RDYSHN radiation *energy*
RDYSND radiosonde *transmitter*
RDYSR reducer *lessen*
RDYST artiest *artistic*
RDYST rattiest *tangled, shabby, irritable*
RDYST rowdiest *rough*
RDYST ruddiest *reddish*
RDYST ruttiest *grooved*
RDYSTP radioisotope *atom*
RDYT irradiate *x-ray* irradiated irradiating
RDYT radiate *glow* radiated radiating
RDYTHRP radiotherapy *X-rays*
RDYTHRPST radiotherapist

X-rays
RDYTLFN radiotelephone *wireless*
RDYTLGRF radiotelegraph *wireless*
RDYTR irradiator *x-ray*
RDYTR radiator *cooler*
RDYTV irradiative *x-ray*
RDYWKDV radioactive *atomic*
RDYWKTV radioactive *atomic*
RDYWKTVD radioactivity *atomic*
RDYWKTVT radioactivity *atomic*
RDYWS arduous *difficult*
RDYWSL arduously *difficult*
RDYWSTP radioisotope *atom*
RDYWV radio wave *wireless*
RDYZM rowdyism *roughness*
RDZ irides (pl) *eye, flower* iris
RDZ redoes *does again*
RDZ Rhodes *island*
RDZH Rhodesia *region*
RDZHNR Rio de Janeiro *city*
RDZM rowdyism *roughness*
RDZN artisan *craftsman*
RDZN redesign *plan again*
RDZNS reticence *restraint* reticency
RDZNT reticent *silent*
RDZNTS reticence *restraint* reticency
RDZSHN erotization *make sexy*
RF raffia *palm, fiber*
RF raphe *ridge*
RF reef (n) *sail, coral* (v) *sail*
RF reify *make real* reified reifying reifies
RF rife *widespread*
RF riff *music, skim*
RF rift *separation*
RF roof *top*
RF rough *not smooth, tough* rougher roughest
RF ruff (n) *collar, fringe, bird, fish* (v) *trump**
RFDBL irrefutable (adj)

Letters aren't doubled for single sounds: to find alley use **L** not **LL**. Use **Y** and **W** as hard sounds only: to find yellow use **YL**. (Br)=British spelling or usage. * See dictionary.

cannot *deny* irrefutably (adv)

RFDBL refutable (adj) *deny* refutably (adv)

RFDBLD irrefutability *cannot deny*

RFDBLD refutability *deny*

RFDBLT irrefutability *cannot deny*

RFDBLT refutability *deny*

RFDR rafter *beam, logger*

RFDR refuter *deny*

RFDR rough-dry *not ironed*

RFG refugee *fleeing*

RFGBL irrefragable (adj) *no argument* irrefragably (adv)

RFGBLD irrefragability *no argument*

RFGBLT irrefragability *no argument*

RFGR refigure *count* refigured refiguring

RFGYR refigure *count* refigured refiguring

RFH rough-hew *chop* rough-hewed rough-hewing rough-hewn

RFHN rough-hewn *chopped* rough-hewn

RFHS roughhouse (n) *tough play*

RFHY rough-hew *chop* rough-hewed rough-hewing rough-hewn

RFHYN rough-hewn *chopped* rough-hewn

RFHZ roughhouse (v) *fight* roughhoused roughhousing

RFJ refuge *safe place*

RFJ refugee *fleeing*

RFJ roughage *fiber*

RFK orphic *mystic*

RFKDR refectory *dining hall* refectories

RFKL orphically *mystically*

RFKS refocus *adjust again*

RFKSHN refection *food*

RFKSHN reification *make real*

RFKST roughcast *plaster*

roughcast roughcasting

RFKTR refectory *dining hall* refectories

RFL air rifle *gun*

RFL airfield *airport* (Br) aerodrome

RFL airflow *wind*

RFL airfoil *airplane* (Br) aerofoil

RFL earful *sound*

RFL ireful *angry*

RFL raffle *lottery* raffled raffling

RFL Raphael *artist*

RFL refile *sort* refiled refiling

RFL refill *replenish*

RFL refuel *add fuel*

RFL riffle *shuffle* riffled riffling

RFL rifle (v) *search* rifled rifling

RFL rifle (n) *gun*

RFL roughly *crude, close*

RFL rueful (adj) *sorry* ruefully (adv)

RFL ruffle (v) *disturb* ruffled ruffling

RFL ruffle (n) *fringe*

RFLBL refillable *replenish*

RFLBRD riflebird *bird*

RFLD airfield *airport* (Br) aerodrome

RFLJNS refulgence *brilliance*

RFLJNT refulgent *brilliant*

RFLJNTS refulgence *brilliance*

RFLK reflect *mirror, think*

RFLKDR reflector *mirror*

RFLKDV reflective *mirror, thinking*

RFLKS reflex (n) *response* (adj) *bent, unconscious* reflexes

RFLKS reflux *flow back*

RFLKSHN reflection *mirror, thinking* (Br) reflexion

RFLKSLG reflexology *behavior*

RFLKSLJ reflexology *behavior*

RFLKSV irreflexive *math*

RFLKSV reflexive *grammar, behavior*

RFLKSVD reflexivity *mirror, grammar, behavior*

RFLKSVL reflexively *mirror, grammar, behavior*

RFLKSVNS reflexiveness *mirror, grammar, behavior*

RFLKSVT reflexivity *mirror, grammar, behavior*

RFLKT reflect *mirror, think*

RFLKTR reflector *mirror*

RFLKTV reflective *mirror, thinking*

RFLM oriflamme *symbol*

RFLMN rifleman *shooter* riflemen

RFLN roofline *building*

RFLNS ruefulness *sorrow*

RFLNT refluent *flow back*

RFLP earflap *cap*

RFLR riflery *shooting*

RFLS roofless *no cover*

RFLSHN reflation *price increase*

RFLWNT refluent *flow back*

RFLX reflex (n) *response* (adj) *bent, unconscious* reflexes

RFLX reflux *flow back*

RFLXLG reflexology *behavior*

RFLXLJ reflexology *behavior*

RFLXV irreflexive *math*

RFLXV reflexive *grammar, behavior*

RFLXVD reflexivity *mirror, grammar, behavior*

RFLXVL reflexively *mirror, grammar, behavior*

RFLXVNS reflexiveness *mirror, grammar, behavior*

RFLXVT reflexivity *mirror, grammar, behavior*

RFN earphone *listen*

RFN orphan *no parents*

RFN refine *purify* refined refining

RFN refund *money*

RFN roofing *material*

RFN roughen *not smooth, tough*

Use letters that best describe the sounds you hear and omit the vowels. Use **S** or **K** instead of **C**: to find circle use **SRKL**. Use **J** to find joy, **JM** to find gem and **G** to find go.

RFN ruffian *bully*
RFND refined *pure, proper*
RFND refund *money*
RFNDRD rough-and-ready *productive*
RFNG roofing *material*
RFNJ orphanage *institution*
RFNK roughneck *rowdy one*
RFNMNT refinement *pure, proper*
RFNNS refinance *loans* refinanced refinancing
RFNNTS refinance *loans* refinanced refinancing
RFNR refiner *purifier*
RFNR refinery *purifying factory* refineries
RFNRD rough-and-ready *productive*
RFNS raffinose *sugar*
RFNS roughness *not smooth, tough*
RFNSH refinish *new surface* refinishes
RFNSHR refinisher *new surface*
RFNTMBL rough-and-tumble *fighting*
RFNZ raffinose *sugar*
RFR airfare *fee*
RFR airy-fairy *(Br) delicate*
RFR orphrey *embroidery* orphreys
RFR reefer *coat, ship, marijuana*
RFR refer *direct, relate, classify** referred referring
RFR referee *judge* refereed refereeing
RFR refry *cook again* refried refrying refries
RFR reoffer *offer again*
RFR roofer *roof maker*
RFR rougher *not smooth, tough*
RFRBL referable *direct, relate, classify**
RFRBSH refurbish *remodel*
RFRBSHMNT refurbishment *remodel*
RFRBSHR refurbisher *remodel*

RFRD refried *cooked again*
RFRDR roughrider (or) Rough Rider *cavalry*
RFRF riffraff *rubbish*
RFRJRDR refrigerator *cooler*
RFRJRNT refrigerant *coolant*
RFRJRSHN refrigeration *coolant*
RFRJRT refrigerate *cool* refrigerated refrigerating
RFRJRTR refrigerator *cooler*
RFRK refract *distort*
RFRKDL refractile *distorted*
RFRKDR refractor *telescope*
RFRKDR refractory *(adj) unruly (n) material* refractories
RFRKDV refractive *distortion*
RFRKSHN refraction *distortion*
RFRKT refract *distort*
RFRKTL refractile *distorted*
RFRKTR refractor *telescope*
RFRKTR refractory *(adj) unruly (n) material* refractories
RFRKTV refractive *distortion*
RFRKTVD refractivity *distortion*
RFRKTVT refractivity *distortion*
RFRL referral *direction, guarantee*
RFRM airframe *structure*
RFRM reaffirm *assert*
RFRM reform *make better*
RFRMBL irreformable *uncontrollable*
RFRMBL reformable *make better*
RFRMBLD irreformability *uncontrollable*
RFRMBLT irreformability *uncontrollable*
RFRMD reformed *changed*
RFRMDV reformative *structure*
RFRMLSHN reformulation *develop, prepare*
RFRMLT reformulate *develop, prepare*

reformulated reformulating
RFRMR reformer *changer*
RFRMSHN reaffirmation *consent*
RFRMSHN reformation *restructure*
RFRMT reformat *set up again* reformatted reformatting
RFRMTR reformatory *youth prison* reformatories
RFRMTV reformative *structure*
RFRMYLSHN reformulation *develop, prepare*
RFRMYLT reformulate *develop, prepare* reformulated reformulating
RFRN refrain *(v) curb (n) verse*
RFRNCHL referential *(adj) symbol* referentially *(adv)*
RFRND referenda *(pl) vote* referendum
RFRNDM referendum *vote* referenda (or) referendums
RFRNGKS oropharynx *mouth*
RFRNGL oropharyngeal *mouth*
RFRNGX oropharynx *mouth*
RFRNGYL oropharyngeal *mouth*
RFRNJBL refrangible *distortion*
RFRNJBLD refrangibility *distortion*
RFRNJBLT refrangibility *distortion*
RFRNJL oropharyngeal *mouth*
RFRNJYL oropharyngeal *mouth*
RFRNKS oropharynx *mouth*
RFRNMNT refrainment *curb*
RFRNS reference *(v) quote* referenced referencing
RFRNS reference *(n) mention, fact book, relation**

Letters aren't doubled for single sounds: to find alley use **L** not **LL**. Use **Y** and **W** as hard sounds only: to find yellow use **YL**. (Br)=British spelling or usage. * See dictionary.

RFRNSH refurnish *new furniture*
RFRNSHL referential (adj) *symbol* referentially (adv)
RFRNT referent *symbol*
RFRNTS reference *(v) quote* referenced referencing
RFRNTS reference *(n) mention, fact book, relation**
RFRNTSHL referential (adj) *symbol* referentially (adv)
RFRNX oropharynx *mouth*
RFRR referrer *direction, guarantee*
RFRS air force *military*
RFRS auriferous *gold*
RFRSH refresh *renew*
RFRSHMNT refreshment *stimulation*
RFRSHN refreshing *stimulating*
RFRSHNG refreshing *stimulating*
RFRSHR refresher *reminder*
RFRST reforest *trees*
RFRSTSHN reforestation *trees*
RFRSWN Air Force One *airplane*
RFRT airfreight *transport*
RFRTR roughrider (or) Rough Rider *cavalry*
RFRZ refreeze *ice* refroze refreezing
RFRZ rephrase *other words* rephrased rephrasing
RFRZN refrozen *ice*
RFS orifice *opening*
RFS refuse *(n) trash*
RFS roughhouse *(n) tough play*
RFS rufous *reddish*
RFSH oarfish *fish*
RFSH raffish *crude*
RFSH refuge *safe place*
RFSHD roughshod *brutal force*
RFSHL raffishly *crude*
RFSHN refashion *create*
RFSHNS raffishness *crude*
RFSL refusal *denial*
RFSNT rufescent *reddish*

RFST roughest *not smooth, tough*
RFT raft *boat, many*
RFT refit *modify* refitted refitting
RFT refute *deny* refuted refuting
RFT rift *separation*
RFTBL irrefutable (adj) *cannot deny* irrefutably (adv)
RFTBL refutable (adj) *deny* refutably (adv)
RFTBLD irrefutability *cannot deny*
RFTBLD refutability *deny*
RFTBLT irrefutability *cannot deny*
RFTBLT refutability *deny*
RFTP rooftop *building*
RFTR rafter *beam, logger*
RFTR refuter *deny*
RFTSHN refutation *denial*
RFY raffia *palm, fiber*
RFYDBL irrefutable (adj) *cannot deny* irrefutably (adv)
RFYDBL refutable (adj) *deny* refutably (adv)
RFYDBLD irrefutability *cannot deny*
RFYDBLD refutability *deny*
RFYDBLT irrefutability *cannot deny*
RFYDBLT refutability *deny*
RFYDR refuter *deny*
RFYG refugee *fleeing*
RFYJ refuge *safe place*
RFYJ refugee *fleeing*
RFYL airfoil *airplane* (Br) aerofoil
RFYL Raphael *artist*
RFYL refile *sort* refiled refiling
RFYL refuel *add fuel*
RFYN ruffian *bully*
RFYS refuse *(n) trash*
RFYSH refuge *safe place*
RFYT refute *deny* refuted refuting
RFYTBL irrefutable (adj) *cannot deny* irrefutably

(adv)
RFYTBL refutable (adj) *deny* refutably (adv)
RFYTBLD irrefutability *cannot deny*
RFYTBLD refutability *deny*
RFYTBLT irrefutability *cannot deny*
RFYTBLT refutability *deny*
RFYTR refuter *deny*
RFYTSHN refutation *denial*
RFYZ refuse *(v) decline (n) trash* refused refusing
RFYZH refuge *safe place*
RFYZL refusal *denial*
RFZ refuse *(v) decline (n) trash* refused refusing
RFZ roughhouse *(v) fight* roughhoused roughhousing
RFZH refuge *safe place*
RFZL refusal *denial*
RG argot *jargon*
RG argue *discuss* argued arguing
RG erg *unit of work*
RG ergo *therefore*
RG orgy *wild party* orgies
RG rag *(v) tease* ragged ragging
RG rag *(n) old clothing, music, newspaper**
RG raga *music*
RG ragout *stew*
RG reggae *music*
RG ridgy *crested*
RG rig *(v) equip, fix* rigged rigging
RG rig *(n) ship, dress*
RG rogue *(v) weed out* rogued roguing
RG rogue *(n) scamp*
RG rug *carpet*
RG ruga *fold* rugae
RG rugae (pl) *fold* ruga
RGB rugby *sport*
RGBL arguable (adj) *debatable* arguably (adv)
RGC argosy *ship* argosies
RGD ragged *torn* raggedy
RGD regatta *boat race*
RGD rugged *rough*

Use letters that best describe the sounds you hear and omit the vowels. Use **S** or **K** instead of **C**: to find circle use **SRKL**. Use **J** to find joy, **JM** to find gem and **G** to find go.

RGDN rigadoon (or) rigaudon *dance*

RGDR irrigator *water*

RGDV ergative *language*

RGF argufy *wrangle* argufied argufying argufies

RGFR argufier *wrangler*

RGFYR argufier *wrangler*

RGL argali *animal*

RGL argil *clay*

RGL argol *wine*

RGL argyle *pattern*

RGL arugula *herb*

RGL regal (adj) *royal* regally (adv)

RGL regale *feast* regaled regaling

RGL regalia *finery*

RGL rugola *herb*

RGL wriggle *squirm* wriggled wriggling

RGL wriggly *squirmy*

RGLD regality *splendor* regalities

RGLDR regulator *controller*

RGLDV regulative *law, control*

RGLN raglan *sleeve*

RGLR irregular *abnormal, uneven*

RGLR regular *normal, even*

RGLR wriggler *squirmer*

RGLRD irregularity *abnormal, uneven* irregularities

RGLRD regularity *normal, even* regularities

RGLRL regularly *manner, timing*

RGLRT irregularity *abnormal, uneven* irregularities

RGLRT regularity *normal, even* regularities

RGLRZ regularize *make normal* regularized regularizing

RGLRZSHN regularization *normal, even*

RGLS hourglass *timepiece* hourglasses

RGLS orgulous *proud*

RGLS rugulose *wrinkles*

RGLSHN regulation *law, control*

RGLT regality *splendor* regalities

RGLT regulate *control* regulated regulating

RGLTR regulator *controller*

RGLTR regulatory *controlling*

RGLTV regulative *law, control*

RGLY regalia *finery*

RGM origami *paper art*

RGM regime *pattern, government*

RGMDR ergometer *work measure*

RGMFN ragamuffin *child*

RGMN argumenta (pl) *disagreement* argumentum

RGMN ragman *trash*

RGMNDV argumentative *quarrelsome*

RGMNM argumentum *dispute* argumenta

RGMNT argument *disagreement*

RGMNT argumenta (pl) *disagreement* argumentum

RGMNTM argumentum *dispute* argumenta

RGMNTSHN argumentation *debate*

RGMNTTV argumentative *quarrelsome*

RGMNTV argumentative *quarrelsome*

RGMRL rigmarole (or) rigamarole *nonsense*

RGMTR ergometer *work measure*

RGMTRK ergometric *work measure*

RGN air gun *BB gun*

RGN argon *gas*

RGN oregano *herb*

RGN Oregon *US State*

RGN organ *music, body*

RGN orgone *energy*

RGN regain *take back*

RGN rigging *ropes*

RGND organdy *fabric*

organdies

RGNG rigging *ropes*

RGNK organic *living, natural*

RGNK orogenic *mountains*

RGNKL organically *living, natural*

RGNL organelle *cell part*

RGNLG organology *organ study*

RGNLJ organology *organ study*

RGNMK ergonomic *design*

RGNMKL ergonomically *design*

RGNMKS ergonomics *design*

RGNMST ergonomist *design*

RGNMX ergonomics *design*

RGNN organon *knowledge*

RGNS arrogance *conceit*

RGNS erogenous *sex*

RGNSHN reignition *flame*

RGNSS orogenesis *mountains*

RGNST organist *music*

RGNT argonaut *sailor*

RGNT arrogant *haughty*

RGNT reignite *flame* reignited reigniting

RGNTS arrogance *conceit*

RGNZ organize *arrange* organized organizing (Br) organise

RGNZ organza *fabric*

RGNZBL organizable *order* (Br) organisable

RGNZM organism *complex whole*

RGNZN organzine *yarn*

RGNZR organizer *arranger* (Br) organiser

RGNZSHN organization *association* (Br) organisation

RGPKR ragpicker *trash*

RGR arguer *disputer*

RGR regrow *grow again* regrew regrowing regrown

RGR rigger *ropes*

RGR rigor *severity* (Br) rigour

Letters aren't doubled for single sounds: to find alley use **L** not **LL**. Use **Y** and **W** as hard sounds only: to find yellow use **YL**. (Br)=British spelling or usage. * See dictionary.

RGR roguery *mischief* rogueries

RGR rugger *rugby*

RGRD regard (n) *attention, gaze, esteem* (v) *respect, heed**

RGRDBL regrettable (adj) *sorrow* regrettably (adv)

RGRDFL regardful (adj) *attentive* regardfully (adv)

RGRDLS irregardless (*non-standard adv*) *anyway*

RGRDLS regardless (*preferred-adv*) *anyway*

RGRDLS regardless (*adj*) *careless*

RGRDLSL regardlessly *careless*

RGRDLSNS regardlessness *careless*

RGRDN regarding *concerning*

RGRDNG regarding *concerning*

RGRDS regards *greetings*

RGRF orography *mountains*

RGRFK orographic *mountains*

RGRJTSHN regurgitation *vomit*

RGRJTT regurgitate *vomit* regurgitated regurgitating

RGRM aerogram (or) aerogramme (*Br*) *airmail*

RGRMRDS rigor mortis *death*

RGRMRTS rigor mortis *death*

RGRN regrown *grow again*

RGRND Rio Grande *river*

RGRP regroup *reorganize*

RGRS regress *go back*

RGRS rigorous *harsh* (Br) rigourous

RGRS ryegrass *plant*

RGRSHN regression *go back*

RGRSL rigorously *harsh* (Br) rigourously

RGRSNS rigorousness *harsh* (Br) rigourousness

RGRST rigorist *inflexible*

(Br) rigourist

RGRSV regressive *go back, decrease*

RGRSVD regressivity *go back, decrease*

RGRSVL regressively *go back, decrease*

RGRSVNS regressiveness *go back, decrease*

RGRSVT regressivity *go back, decrease*

RGRT regret *sorrow* regretted regretting

RGRTBL regrettable (adj) *sorrow* regrettably (adv)

RGRTFL regretful (adj) *sorrowful* regretfully (adv)

RGRZM rigorism *inflexibility* (Br) rigourism

RGS argosy *ship* argosies

RGS rugose *wrinkled*

RGSD rugosity *wrinkles*

RGSDK ergastic *byproduct*

RGSDK orgiastic *frenzied*

RGSDRL ergosterol *vitamin D*

RGSH roguish *mischievous*

RGSHL roguishly *mischievous*

RGSHN arrogation *assumption*

RGSHN irrigation *water*

RGSHNS roguishness *mischief*

RGST rugosity *wrinkles*

RGSTK ergastic *byproduct*

RGSTK orgiastic *frenzied*

RGSTRL ergosterol *vitamin D*

RGT argot *jargon*

RGT arrogate *assume* arrogated arrogating

RGT ergot *fungus*

RGT irrigate *water* irrigated irrigating

RGT regatta *boat race*

RGTG ragtag *unkempt*

RGTM ragtime *music*

RGTN rigatoni *pasta*

RGTP ragtop *car*

RGTR irrigator *water*

RGTV ergative *language*

RGTZD ergotized *poison*

RGTZM ergotism *poison*

RGW Uruguay *country*

RGWBL arguable (adj) *debatable* arguably (adv)

RGWD ragweed *plant*

RGWR arguer *disputer*

RGY argue *discuss* argued arguing

RGYBL arguable (adj) *debatable* arguably (adv)

RGYF argufy *wrangle* argufied argufying argufies

RGYFR argufier *wrangler*

RGYFYR argufier *wrangler*

RGYL arugula *herb*

RGYLDR regulator *controller*

RGYLDV regulative *law, control*

RGYLR irregular *abnormal, uneven*

RGYLR regular *normal, even*

RGYLRD irregularity *abnormal, uneven* irregularities

RGYLRD regularity *normal, even* regularities

RGYLRL regularly *manner, timing*

RGYLRT irregularity *abnormal, uneven* irregularities

RGYLRT regularity *normal, even* regularities

RGYLRZ regularize *make normal* regularized regularizing

RGYLRZSHN regularization *normal, even*

RGYLS orgulous *proud*

RGYLS rugulose *wrinkles*

RGYLSHN regulation *law, control*

RGYLT regulate *control* regulated regulating

RGYLTR regulator *controller*

RGYLTR regulatory *controlling*

RGYLTV regulative *law, control*

RGYMN argumenta (pl)

Use letters that best describe the sounds you hear and omit the vowels. Use **S** or **K** instead of **C**: to find circle use **SRKL**. Use **J** to find joy, **JM** to find gem and **G** to find go.

disagreement argumentum
RGYMNDV argumentative *quarrelsome*
RGYMNM argumentum *dispute* argumenta
RGYMNT argument *disagreement*
RGYMNT argumenta (pl) *disagreement* argumentum
RGYMNTM argumentum *dispute* argumenta
RGYMNTSHN argumentation *debate*
RGYMNTTV argumentative *quarrelsome*
RGYMNTV argumentative *quarrelsome*
RGYR arguer *disputer*
RGYSDK orgiastic *frenzied*
RGYSTK orgiastic *frenzied*
RGYWBL arguable (adj) *debatable* arguably (adv)
RGYWR arguer *disputer*
RGZM orgasm *climax*
RGZMK orgasmic *climactic*
RGZMN reexamine *test* reexamined reexamining
RGZMNSHN reexamination *test*
RH rioja *wine*
RHBLTDR rehabilitator *restore*
RHBLTDV rehabilitative *restore*
RHBLTNT rehabilitant *restored one*
RHBLTSHN rehabilitation *restoration*
RHBLTT rehabilitate *restore* rehabilitated rehabilitating
RHBLTTR rehabilitator *restore*
RHBLTTV rehabilitative *restore*
RHD airhead *foolish one*
RHD arrowhead *weapon*
RHD rawhide *leather*
RHDD airheaded *foolish*
RHL airhole *vent*
RHNG rehang *suspend* rehung rehanging

RHR rehire *employ* rehired rehiring
RHRS rehearse *practice* rehearsed rehearsing
RHRSL rehearsal *recital*
RHRSR rehearser *practicer*
RHSH rehash *repeat*
RHT reheat *cook again*
RHYR rehire *employ* rehired rehiring
RHZ rehouse *shelter* rehoused rehousing
RJ orgy *wild party* orgies
RJ rage (v) *fight* raged raging
RJ rage (n) *anger, fashion*
RJ raj *rule*
RJ raja (or) rajah *ruler*
RJ ridge *crest* ridged ridging
RJ ridgy *crested*
RJ rouge (v) *redden* rouged rouging
RJ rouge (n) *cosmetic*
RJ rugae (pl) *fold* ruga
RJ urge (v) *entreat, force* urged urging
RJ urge (n) *desire, impulse*
RJD rigid *unbending*
RJDD rigidity *unbending* rigidities
RJDF rigidify *make unbending* rigidified rigidifying rigidifies
RJDL rigidly *unbending*
RJDNS rigidness *unbending*
RJDT rigidity *unbending* rigidities
RJK reject (v) *refuse, repulse* (n) *substandard*
RJKSHN reeducation *teaching*
RJKSHN rejection *refused*
RJKT reeducate *teach* reeducated reeducating
RJKT reject (v) *refuse, repulse* (n) substandard*
RJL radula *mouth* radulae
RJL Rigel *star*
RJLN ridgeline *crest*
RJM regime *pattern, government*
RJMN regimen *plan, rule*

RJMNL regimental *organized*
RJMNT regiment (n) *army* (v) *organize*
RJMNTL regimental *organized*
RJMNTSHN regimentation *organization*
RJN origin *source*
RJN orogeny *mountains*
RJN raging *wild*
RJN region *area*
RJN rejoin *meet, answer*
RJNC regency *royal* regencies
RJNC urgency *importance* urgencies
RJNDK orogenetic *mountains*
RJNDL urogenital *urine*
RJNDR originator *creator*
RJNDR rejoinder *reply*
RJNG raging *wild*
RJNK orogenic *mountains*
RJNL original (adj) *first* originally (adv)
RJNL regional (adj) *area* regionally (adv)
RJNLD originality *freshness*
RJNLST regionalist *area*
RJNLT originality *freshness*
RJNLZN regionalism *area*
RJNRC regeneracy *creation*
RJNRDR regenerator *creator*
RJNRDV regenerative *creation*
RJNRS regeneracy *creation*
RJNRSHN regeneration *creation*
RJNRT regenerate *create* regenerated regenerating
RJNRTR regenerator *creator*
RJNRTV regenerative *creation*
RJNS erogenous *sex*
RJNS regency *royal* regencies
RJNS urgency *importance* urgencies
RJNSHN origination *source*
RJNSS orogenesis *mountains*
RJNT argent *silver*

Letters aren't doubled for single sounds: to find alley use **L** not **LL**. Use **Y** and **W** as hard sounds only: to find yellow use **YL**. (Br)=British spelling or usage. * See dictionary.

RJNT originate *begin, spring*
originated originating
RJNT reagent *substance*
RJNT regent *ruler*
RJNT urgent *important*
RJNTC regency *royal*
regencies
RJNTC urgency *importance*
urgencies
RJNTK orogenetic
mountains
RJNTL urgently *important*
RJNTL urogenital *urine*
RJNTN Argentina *country*
RJNTN Argentine *of*
Argentina
RJNTN argentine *silvery*
RJNTNN Argentinean *of*
Argentina
RJNTNYN Argentinean *of*
Argentina
RJNTR originator *creator*
RJNTS regency *royal*
regencies
RJNTS urgency *importance*
urgencies
RJPL ridgepole *tent*
RJR ordure *waste matter*
RJR roger *understood*
RJS arduous *difficult*
RJS rejoice *celebrate* rejoiced
rejoicing
RJSD regicide *king murder*
RJSDK orgiastic *frenzied*
RJSDR register *(n) record,*
music, grille (v) percieve,
*achieve, enroll**
RJSMNT readjustment *set*
properly
RJSN rejoicing *celebration*
RJSNG rejoicing *celebration*
RJSR régisseur (or)
regisseur *director*
RJST readjust *set properly*
RJSTK orgiastic *frenzied*
RJSTMNT readjustment *set*
properly
RJSTR register *(n) record,*
music, grille (v) percieve,
*achieve, enroll**
RJSTR registry *listing*
registries

RJSTRBL registrable *(v)*
*percieve, achieve, enroll**
RJSTRNT registrant *enrollee*
RJSTRR registrar *recorder*
RJSTRSHN registration
enrollment
RJVNDR rejuvenator *renew*
RJVNSHN rejuvenation
renew
RJVNSNS rejuvenescence
make young
RJVNSNT rejuvenescent
make young
RJVNSNTS rejuvenescence
make young
RJVNT rejuvenate *renew*
rejuvenated rejuvenating
RJVNTR rejuvenator *renew*
RJWS arduous *difficult*
RJWSL arduously *difficult*
RJYSDK orgiastic *frenzied*
RJYSTK orgiastic *frenzied*
RK arc *curve* arced arcing
RK areca *palm*
RK ark *boat, box*
RK auric *gold*
RK earache *pain*
RK erica *shrub*
RK eureka *(interj) discovery*
RK Iraq *country*
RK Iraqi *of Iraq*
RK irk *annoy*
RK orca *whale*
RK rack *(n) frame, antlers (v)*
torture, strain
RK rake *(v) scratch, glance,*
*sweep** raked raking
RK rake *(n) tool, slope,*
*libertine**
RK raki *liqueur*
RK react *respond*
RK reek *smell*
RK Reich *German*
RK rekey *typing*
RK rickey *drink* rickeys
RK roc *bird*
RK rocaille *rococo*
RK rock *(n) stone, music (v)*
music, shake
RK rocky *rough, wobbly*
rockier rockiest
RK rook *(v) trick (n) bird,*

chess piece
RK rookie *beginner*
RK rooky *birds*
RK roque *game*
RK ruck *fold, jumble*
RK uric *urine*
RK wrack *ruin, torture*
RK wreak *inflict*
RK wreck *(v) destroy (n)*
remains
RKBDM rock bottom (n)
deepest part rock-bottom
(adj)
RKBL rockabilly *music*
RKBN rockbound *rocky*
RKBND rockbound *rocky*
RKBTM rock bottom (n)
deepest part rock-bottom
(adj)
RKD arcade *passage*
RKD arcadia *scene*
RKD area code *telephone*
zone
RKD ericoid *shrub*
RKD orchid *flower*
RKD recta (pl) *anus* rectum
RKD recto *right-hand* rectos
RKD rickety *unstable*
RKD ricotta *cheese*
RKDBL erectable *upright*
RKDF rectify *correct* rectified
rectifying rectifies
RKDFBL rectifiable (adj)
correction rectifiably (adv)
RKDFKSHN rectification
correction
RKDFR rectifier *correction*
RKDFYBL rectifiable (adj)
correction rectifiably (adv)
RKDFYR rectifier *correction*
RKDK arctic *(often*
capitalized) ocean, region
RKDKSHN Arctic Ocean
body of water
RKDL erectile *upright*
RKDL rectal (adj) *anus*
rectally (adv)
RKDLNR rectilinear *straight*
RKDLNYR rectilinear
straight
RKDM rectum *anus* rectums
(or) recta

Use letters that best describe the sounds you hear and omit the vowels. Use **S** or **K** instead of **C**: to find circle use **SRKL**. Use **J** to find joy, **JM** to find gem and **G** to find go.

RKDN arcadian *pastoral*
RKDNT reactant *chemistry*
RKDNTS reactance *circuit*
RKDR erector *builder*
RKDR reactor *device*
RKDR rector *clergy*
RKDR rectory *house* rectories
RKDR Richter *seismologist, scale*
RKDSHS orchidaceous *orchid*
RKDTD rectitude *straight*
RKDTYD rectitude *straight*
RKDV reactive *responsive*
RKDVSHN reactivation *start again*
RKDVT reactivate *start again* reactivated reactivating
RKDY arcadia *scene*
RKDYN arcadian *pastoral*
RKFL rockfall *landslide*
RKFRD Roquefort *(trademark) cheese*
RKFRT Roquefort *(trademark) cheese*
RKFSH rockfish *animal*
RKGN archegonia (pl) *sex organ* archegonium
RKGNM archegonium *sex organ* archegonia
RKGNSHN recognition *notice*
RKGNY archegonia (pl) *sex organ* archegonium
RKGNYM archegonium *sex organ* archegonia
RKGNZ recognize *realize, admit* recognized recognizing (Br) recognise
RKGNZBL recognizable (adj) *realize, admit* recognizably (adv)
RKGNZNS recognizance *pledge*
RKGNZNTS recognizance *pledge*
RKHN rock hound *geology*
RKHND rock hound *geology*
RKHPR rockhopper *penguin*
RKJ wreckage *remains*

RKK archaic *old-fashioned*
RKK rococo *showy*
RKKL archaically *old-fashioned*
RKL auricle *heart, ear-shaped*
RKL oracle *foreteller*
RKL recall *remember, bring back*
RKL recoil *draw back*
RKLBRSHN recalibration *set accuracy*
RKLBRT recalibrate *set accuracy* recalibrated recalibrating
RKLG archaeology (or) archeology *relics*
RKLJ archaeology (or) archeology *relics*
RKLJKL archaeological (adj) *relics* archaeologically (adv)
RKLJST archaeologist *relics*
RKLK re-collect *gather again*
RKLK recollect *remember*
RKLKLSHN recalculation *figuring*
RKLKLT recalculate *figure* recalculated recalculating
RKLKSHN recollection *remembrance*
RKLKT re-collect *gather again*
RKLKT recollect *remember*
RKLKYLSHN recalculation *figuring*
RKLKYLT recalculate *figure* recalculated recalculating
RKLM reclaim *tame, rescue*
RKLMBL irreclaimable (adj) *cannot use again* irreclaimably (adv)
RKLMBL reclaimable *tame, rescue*
RKLMSHN reclamation *recovery*
RKLN recline *lie back* reclined reclining
RKLN rockling *fish*
RKLNG rockling *fish*
RKLNR recliner *chair*
RKLQLSHN recalculation *figuring*

RKLQLT recalculate *figure* recalculated recalculating
RKLR auricular *hearing*
RKLR oracular *domineering*
RKLR recolor *tint* (Br) recolour
RKLRD oracularity *domination*
RKLRL oracularly *domineering*
RKLRT oracularity *domination*
RKLS reckless *careless*
RKLS recluse *solitary*
RKLSF reclassify *sort* reclassified reclassifying reclassifies
RKLSHN reclusion *solitary*
RKLSL recklessly *carelessly*
RKLSNS recklessness *carelessness*
RKLSTRNS recalcitrance *resistance*
RKLSTRNT recalcitrant *resistant*
RKLSTRNTS recalcitrance *resistance*
RKLSV reclusive *solitary*
RKLT auriculate *ear-shaped*
RKLT raclette *cheese*
RKLZ recluse *solitary*
RKLZBL reclosable *seal*
RKLZHN reclusion *solitary*
RKLZV reclusive *solitary*
RKM recamier *couch*
RKMBN recombine *mix* recombined recombining
RKMBNC recumbency *rest* recumbencies
RKMBNNT recombinant *gene*
RKMBNS recumbency *rest* recumbencies
RKMBNT recumbent *resting*
RKMBNTC recumbency *rest* recumbencies
RKMBNTS recumbency *rest* recumbencies
RKMDL recommittal *deposit*
RKMDZ Archimedes *mathematician*
RKMN recommend *favor*

Letters aren't doubled for single sounds: to find alley use **L** not **LL**. Use **Y** and **W** as hard sounds only: to find yellow use **YL**. (Br)=British spelling or usage. * See dictionary.

RKMND recommend *favor*
RKMNDSHN
  recommendation *favor*
RKMNNF Rachmaninoff
  composer
RKMPNS recompense *pay*
  recompensed
  recompensing
RKMPNTS recompense *pay*
  recompensed
  recompensing
RKMPZ recompose
  rearrange recomposed
  recomposing
RKMT recommit *deposit with*
  recommitted
  recommitting
RKMTL recommittal *deposit*
RKMTMNT recommitment
  deposit
RKMY recamier *couch*
RKN arcana (pl) *mystery*
  arcanum
RKN arcane *secret*
RKN Archean (or) Archaean
  geologic age
RKN raccoon *animal*
  raccoon (or) raccoons
RKN racon *beacon*
RKN reckon *figure*
RKN recoin *mint again*
RKN rocking *swaying*
RKNBR wrecking bar *tool*
RKND arachnid *spider*
RKND arachnoid *spidery*
RKNDL rekindle *ignite again*
  rekindled rekindling
RKNDPNYN rack and
  pinion *steering*
RKNDR reconnoiter (or)
  reconnoitre *survey*
  reconnoitered (or)
  reconnoitred
  reconnoitering (or)
  reconnoitring
RKNDRL rock and roll (or)
  rock'n'roll *music*
RKNDSHN air-condition
  cool
RKNDSHN recondition *fix*
RKNDSHND air-
  conditioned *cooled*

RKNDSHNG air-
  conditioning *cooling*
RKNDSHNN air-
  conditioning *cooling*
RKNDSHNNG air-
  conditioning *cooling*
RKNDSHNR air conditioner
  air cooler
RKNDT recondite *concealed*
RKNFGR reconfigure *set up*
  reconfigured
  reconfiguring
RKNFGYR reconfigure *set
  up* reconfigured
  reconfiguring
RKNFRM reconfirm *verify*
RKNG rocking *swaying*
RKNGBR wrecking bar *tool*
RKNJL archangel *chief angel*
RKNK reconnect *attach*
RKNK urocanic *acid*
RKNKSHN reconnection
  attachment
RKNKT reconnect *attach*
RKNL Erie Canal *waterway*
RKNLZ recanalize *flow*
  recanalized recanalizing
RKNLZSHN recanalization
  flow
RKNM arcanum *mystery*
  arcana
RKNN reckoning *account*
RKNNG reckoning *account*
RKNPNYN rack and pinion
  steering
RKNRL rock and roll (or)
  rock'n'roll *music*
RKNS Arkansas *US State*
RKNS rockiness *rough,
  wobbly*
RKNS urokinase *enzyme*
RKNSDR reconsider *weigh*
RKNSHN recognition *notice*
RKNSKRT reconsecrate
  declare sacred
  reconsecrated
  reconsecrating
RKNSL reconcile *adapt,
  settle* reconciled
  reconciling
RKNSLBL irreconcilable
  (adj) *cannot adapt*

irreconcilably (adv)
RKNSLBL reconcilable (adj)
  adapt, settle reconcilably
  (adv)
RKNSLBLD irreconcilability
  cannot adapt
RKNSLBLD reconcilability
  adapt, settle
RKNSLBLT irreconcilability
  cannot adapt
RKNSLBLT reconcilability
  adapt, settle
RKNSLMNT reconcilement
  adapt, settle
RKNSLR reconciler *adapt,
  settle*
RKNSLSHN reconciliation
  adapt, settle
RKNSLTR reconciliatory
  adapt, settle
RKNSLYSHN reconciliation
  adapt, settle
RKNSLYTR reconciliatory
  adapt, settle
RKNSNS reconnaissance
  survey
RKNSNTS reconnaissance
  survey
RKNSTRK reconstruct *build*
RKNSTRKDV
  reconstructive *creative*
RKNSTRKSHN
  reconstruction *creation*
RKNSTRKSHNST
  reconstructionist *creation*
RKNSTRKSHNZM
  reconstructionism
  creation
RKNSTRKT reconstruct
  build
RKNSTRKTV reconstructive
  creative
RKNT recant *revoke*
RKNT recount *recite, number*
RKNTK recontact *connect
  with*
RKNTKT recontact *connect
  with*
RKNTR raconteur *storyteller*
RKNTR reconnoiter (or)
  reconnoitre *survey*
  reconnoitered (or)

Use letters that best describe the sounds you hear and omit the vowels. Use **S** or **K** instead of **C**: to find circle use **SRKL**. Use **J** to find joy, **JM** to find gem and **G** to find go.

reconnoitred
reconnoitering (or)
reconnoitring
RKNTR recontour *shape again*
RKNTRN archenteron *(n) gut*
RKNTYR raconteur *storyteller*
RKNV reconvey *send*
RKNVN reconvene *assemble* reconvened reconvening
RKNVNS reconveyance *send*
RKNVNTS reconveyance *send*
RKNVRSHN reconversion *alteration*
RKNVRT reconvert *change*
RKNVRZHN reconversion *alteration*
RKNVYNS reconveyance *send*
RKNVYNTS reconveyance *send*
RKNZ recognize *realize,* admit recognized recognizing (Br) recognise
RKNZ urokinase *enzyme*
RKNZBL recognizable (adj) *realize,* admit recognizably (adv)
RKNZNS reconnaissance *survey*
RKNZNTS reconnaissance *survey*
RKP rack up *gain*
RKP recap *repeat* recapped recapping
RKP recopy *duplicate* recopied recopying recopies
RKP recoup *regain*
RKPBL recappable *repeat*
RKPBL recoupable *regain*
RKPCHLSHN recapitulation *sum up*
RKPCHLT recapitulate *sum up* recapitulated recapitulating
RKPCHR recapture *take*

recaptured recapturing
RKPDLZ recapitalize *corporate structure* recapitalized recapitalizing (Br) recapitalise
RKPDLZSHN recapitalization *corporate structure* (Br) recapitalisation
RKPLG archipelago *island* archipelagoes (or) archipelagos
RKPLJK archipelagic *island*
RKPMNT recoupment *regain*
RKPR rockhopper *penguin*
RKPRDV recuperative *get well*
RKPRSHN recuperation *get well*
RKPRT recuperate *get well* recuperated recuperating
RKPRTV recuperative *get well*
RKPTLSHN recapitulation *sum up*
RKPTLT recapitulate *sum up* recapitulated recapitulating
RKPTLZ recapitalize *corporate structure* recapitalized recapitalizing (Br) recapitalise
RKPTLZSHN recapitalization *corporate structure* (Br) recapitalisation
RKPTR recapture *take* recaptured recapturing
RKPTRKS archaeopteryx *dinosaur*
RKPTRX archaeopteryx *dinosaur*
RKPTYLSHN recapitulation *sum up*
RKPTYLT recapitulate *sum up* recapitulated recapitulating
RKR aircrew *flight crew*
RKR araucaria *tree*

RKR raker *sweeper*
RKR recur *happen again* recurred recurring
RKR rocker *chair, musician*
RKR rockery *(Br) garden* rockeries
RKR rockier *rough, wobbly*
RKR rookery *nest* rookeries
RKR wrecker *vehicle, destroyer*
RKRD record *(n) document, music (v) write, tape, register**
RKRDBL recordable *write, tape, register**
RKRDN recording *tape, disc*
RKRDNG recording *tape, disc*
RKRDR recorder *judge, music*
RKRDS recrudesce *break out* recrudesced recrudescing
RKRDSHN recordation *document*
RKRDSNS recrudescence *break out*
RKRDSNTS recrudescence *break out*
RKRDST recordist *tape, disc*
RKRF aircraft *airplane*
RKRFT aircraft *airplane*
RKRK recork *cap*
RKRK rickrack (or) ricrac *fringe*
RKRM urochrome *pigment*
RKRMNSHN recrimination *accusation*
RKRMNT recriminate *accuse* recriminated recriminating
RKRMNTR recriminatory *accusation*
RKRNS recurrence *happen again*
RKRNT rack-rent (v) *payment* rack rent (n)
RKRNT recreant *coward*
RKRNT recurrent *happen again*
RKRNTS recurrence *happen again*

Letters aren't doubled for single sounds: to find alley use **L** not **LL**. Use **Y** and **W** as hard sounds only: to find yellow use **YL**. (Br)=British spelling or usage. * See dictionary.

RKRS recourse *help*
RKRS recross *cross again*
RKRSHN recreation *play, thing made*
RKRSHN recursion *return*
RKRSHNL recreational *play*
RKRSHNST recreationist *play*
RKRSV recursive *return*
RKRT recreate *play, make* recreated recreating
RKRT recruit *(v) enlist (n) enlistee*
RKRT Urquhart *writer*
RKRTNG recording *tape, disc*
RKRTR recorder *judge, music*
RKRTST recordist *tape, disc*
RKRVD recurved *bent*
RKRVT recurvate *bent*
RKRY araucaria *tree*
RKRYNT recreant *coward*
RKRYSHN recreation *play, thing made*
RKRYSHNL recreational *play*
RKRYSHNST recreationist *play*
RKRYT recreate *play, make* recreated recreating
RKRZ rockrose *herb*
RKRZBL wrecker's ball *demolisher*
RKRZHN recursion *return*
RKS aurochs *ox* aurochs
RKS oryx *antelope* oryx (or) oryxes
RKS raucous *loud*
RKS recuse *refuse* recused recusing
RKS rex *animal* rexes (or) rex
RKS ruckus *disturbance*
RKSCHNJ reexchange *trade* reexchanged reexchanging
RKSDRL orchestral (adj) *music* orchestrally (adv)
RKSH rakish *like a rascal, streamlined*
RKSH ricksha (or) rickshaw

vehicle
RKSH ricochet *bounce* ricocheted (or) ricochetted ricocheting (or) ricochetting
RKSHFT rockshaft *cylinder*
RKSHL rakishly *rascal*
RKSHN air-cushion (adj) *pillow*
RKSHN erection *upright*
RKSHN reaction *response*
RKSHN ruction *disturbance*
RKSHNR reactionary *ultraconservative* reactionaries
RKSHNS rakishness *rogue*
RKSHS ericaceous *shrub*
RKSHT ricochet *bounce* ricocheted (or) ricochetted ricocheting (or) ricochetting
RKSK rucksack *knapsack*
RKSLT rock salt *mineral*
RKSM irksome *tiresome*
RKSMN reexamine *test* reexamined reexamining
RKSMNSHN reexamination *test*
RKSNT recusant *refuser*
RKSPLR reexplore *investigate* reexplored reexploring
RKSPR archesporia (pl) *cell* archesporium
RKSPRM archesporium *cell* archesporia
RKSPRNS reexperience *undergo, live* reexperienced reexperiencing
RKSPRNTS reexperience *undergo, live* reexperienced reexperiencing
RKSPRS air express *mail*
RKSPRY archesporia (pl) *cell* archesporium
RKSPRYM archesporium *cell* archesporia
RKSPRYNS reexperience *undergo, live* reexperienced

reexperiencing
RKSPRYNTS reexperience *undergo, live* reexperienced reexperiencing
RKST archaist *old-fashioned*
RKST recast *throw, remodel* recast recasting
RKST rockiest *rough, wobbly*
RKSTK archaistic *old-fashioned*
RKSTR orchestra *music*
RKSTRDR orchestrator *composer*
RKSTRL orchestral (adj) *music* orchestrally (adv)
RKSTRSHN orchestration *composition*
RKSTRT orchestrate *compose* orchestrated orchestrating
RKSTRTR orchestrator *composer*
RKT erect *upright*
RKT eruct *belch*
RKT racket *paddle, noise* (Br) racquet
RKT react *respond*
RKT recount *recite, number*
RKT recta (pl) *anus* rectum
RKT recto *right-hand* rectos
RKT recut *carve, edit* recut recutting
RKT rickety *unstable*
RKT ricotta *cheese*
RKT rocket *missile, plant*
RKTBL erectable *upright*
RKTBL racquetball *sport*
RKTF rectify *correct* rectified rectifying rectifies
RKTFBL rectifiable (adj) *correction* rectifiably (adv)
RKTFKSHN rectification *correction*
RKTFR rectifier *correction*
RKTFYBL rectifiable (adj) *correction* rectifiably (adv)
RKTFYR rectifier *correction*
RKTK architect *designer*
RKTK arctic *(often capitalized) ocean, region*
RKTKCHR architecture

Use letters that best describe the sounds you hear and omit the vowels. Use **S** or **K** instead of **C**: to find circle use **SRKL**. Use **J** to find joy, **JM** to find gem and **G** to find go.

building, form
RKTKCHRL architectural (adj) *building* architecturally (adv)
RKTKSHN Arctic Ocean *body of water*
RKTKSHR architecture *building, form*
RKTKSHRL architectural (adj) *building* architecturally (adv)
RKTKT architect *designer*
RKTKTR architecture *building, form*
RKTKTRL architectural (adj) *building* architecturally (adv)
RKTL erectile *upright*
RKTL rectal (adj) *anus* rectally (adv)
RKTLD erectility *upright*
RKTLNR rectilinear *straight*
RKTLNYR rectilinear *straight*
RKTLT erectility *upright*
RKTM rectum *anus* rectums (or) recta
RKTNGGL rectangle *shape*
RKTNGGLR rectangular *shape*
RKTNGGYLR rectangular *shape*
RKTNGL rectangle *shape*
RKTNGLR rectangular *shape*
RKTNGYLR rectangular *shape*
RKTNT reactant *chemistry*
RKTNTS reactance *circuit*
RKTP archetype *example*
RKTPL archetypal (adj) *example* archetypally (adv)
RKTR erector *builder*
RKTR racketeer *criminal*
RKTR reactor *responder, device*
RKTR rector *clergy*
RKTR rectory *house* rectories
RKTR Richter *seismologist, scale*
RKTR rocketeer *astronaut*
RKTR rocketry *science*

RKTS rickets *disease*
RKTS rickettsia *bacteria* rickettsias (or) rickettsiae
RKTSHN eructation *belch*
RKTSL rickettsial *disease*
RKTSY rickettsia *bacteria* rickettsias (or) rickettsiae
RKTSYL rickettsial *disease*
RKTTD rectitude *straight*
RKTTYD rectitude *straight*
RKTV reactive *responsive*
RKTVD reactivity *response*
RKTVSHN reactivation *start again*
RKTVT reactivate *start again* reactivated reactivating
RKTVT reactivity *response*
RKV archive *record*
RKVL archival *records*
RKVR recover *get well, regain*
RKVR recovery *get well, regain* recoveries
RKVRBL irrecoverable (adj) *cannot get back* irrecoverably (adv)
RKVRBL recoverable *get well, regain*
RKVRBLD recoverability *get well, regain*
RKVRBLT recoverability *get well, regain*
RKVRR recoverer *get well, regain*
RKVS archives *records*
RKVST archivist *record keeper*
RKVZ archives *records*
RKW Iroquois *Native Americans* Iroquois
RKW rockaway *carriage*
RKWD rockweed *algae*
RKWDL requital *repayment*
RKWDR requiter *repay*
RKWM requiem *mass for the dead*
RKWNT reacquaint *meet*
RKWP reequip *prepare, furnish* reequipt reequipping
RKWR require *demand* required requiring

RKWRD required *needed*
RKWRMNT requirement *need*
RKWSKT requiescat *prayer*
RKWST request *(v)* ask *(n)* demand
RKWT requite *repay* requited requiting
RKWTL requital *repayment*
RKWTR requiter *repay*
RKWYM requiem *mass for the dead*
RKWYR require *demand* required requiring
RKWYRD required *needed*
RKWYRMNT requirement *need*
RKWYSKT requiescat *prayer*
RKWZ Iroquois *Native Americans* Iroquois
RKWZSHN requisition *demand*
RKWZT requisite *necessary thing*
RKYK archaic *old-fashioned*
RKYKL archaically *old-fashioned*
RKYL recoil *draw back*
RKYLG archaeology (or) archeology *relics*
RKYLJ archaeology (or) archeology *relics*
RKYLJKL archaeological (adj) *relics* archaeologically (adv)
RKYLJST archaeologist *relics*
RKYLR auricular *hearing*
RKYLR oracular *domineering*
RKYLRD oracularity *domination*
RKYLRL oracularly *domineering*
RKYLRT oracularity *domination*
RKYLT auriculate *ear-shaped*
RKYN Archean (or) Archaean *geologic age*
RKYPRDV recuperative *get well*
RKYPRSHN recuperation

get well
RKYPRT recuperate *get well* recuperated recuperating
RKYPRTV recuperative *get well*
RKYPTRKS archaeopteryx *dinosaur*
RKYPTRX archaeopteryx *dinosaur*
RKYR rockier *rough, wobbly*
RKYST archaist *old-fashioned*
RKYST rockiest *rough, wobbly*
RKYSTK archaistic *old-fashioned*
RKYVK Reykjavik *city*
RKYZ recuse *refuse* recused recusing
RKYZBL irrecusable (adj) *no exception* irrecusably (adv)
RKYZM archaism *old-fashioned*
RKYZNT recusant *refuser*
RKZ recuse *refuse* recused recusing
RKZ Rockies *Rocky Mountains*
RKZBL irrecusable (adj) *no exception* irrecusably (adv)
RKZM archaism *old-fashioned*
RKZMN reexamine *test* reexamined reexamining
RKZMNSHN reexamination *test*
RKZNT recusant *refuser*
RL aerial (n) *antenna*
RL aerial (adj) *(adj) air, thin, fanciful** aerially (adv)
RL aerily *heavenly*
RL airily *lofty, proud, windy*
RL areal (adj) *field* areally (adv)
RL areola *ring* areolae (or) areolas
RL aril *seed*
RL aryl *hydrocarbon*
RL aural (adj) *hearing* aurally (adv)
RL aureole (or) aureola *halo*
RL earl *title*

RL early *primitive, sooner* earlier earliest
RL eerily *weirdly*
RL hourly *every 60 minutes*
RL oral (adj) *mouth, verbal* orally (adv)
RL oriel *window*
RL oriole *bird*
RL rail (n) *bar, bird* (v) *scold* rails
RL rale *breath*
RL Raleigh *city*
RL rally (v) *revive* rallied rallying rallies
RL rally (n) *meeting* rallies
RL rawly *uncooked, naked, coarse*
RL real *actual*
RL really *truly*
RL reel (v) *whirl,*(n) *device*
RL relay *send, race*
RL rely *depend* relied relying relies
RL rial (or) riyal *Middle East money*
RL rile *upset* riled riling
RL rill (n) *brook, valley* (v) *flow*
RL roil *stir up*
RL roily *turbulent*
RL role *actor's part*
RL roll (n) *list, food, movement* (v) *move, toss*
RL rouleau *small roll* rouleaux
RL rowel (v) *trouble* roweled (or) rowelled roweling (or) rowelling
RL rowel (n) *tool*
RL royal (adj) *regal* royally (adv)
RL rule (v) *control, line* ruled ruling
RL rule (n) *guide, law, measure*
RL urial *sheep*
RL wryly *twisted*
RLB earlobe *part of ear*
RLBK rollback (n) *reduce* roll back (v)
RLBL relabel *name again* relabeled (or) relabelled

relabeling (or) relabelling
RLBL reliable (adj) *dependable* reliably (adv)
RLBLD reliability *dependability*
RLBLT reliability *dependability*
RLBR roll bar *car*
RLBRD early bird *first*
RLBRD railbird *bird*
RLD orality *mouth, verbal*
RLD railhead *trains*
RLD reality *facts* realities
RLD realty *land*
RLD reload *fill again*
RLD roulade *singing, meat*
RLD royalty *monarchy* royalties
RLDBL relatable *tell, connect*
RLDD related *connected*
RLDK rhyolitic *lava*
RLDR realtor *land agent*
RLDRL reel-to-reel *tape*
RLDV irrelative *does not apply*
RLDV relative *kin, comparison*
RLDVL irrelatively *does not apply*
RLDVL relatively *somewhat*
RLDVZM relativism *comparison*
RLF airlift *transport*
RLF real-life (adj) *actual*
RLF reel off *recite*
RLF relief *aid, sculpture*
RLF rolf (*often capitalized*) *massage*
RLF roll-off *bowling*
RLFNG Rolfing *massage*
RLFR rolfer (*often capitalized*) *massage*
RLFT airlift *transport*
RLG urology *urine*
RLGSHN relegation *banish, assign*
RLGT relegate *banish, assign* relegated relegating
RLHD railhead *trains*
RLJ urology *urine*
RLJK urologic *urine*
RLJN religion *faith*

Use letters that best describe the sounds you hear and omit the vowels. Use **S** or **K** instead of **C**: to find circle use **SRKL**. Use **J** to find joy, **JM** to find gem and **G** to find go.

RLJS irreligious *not devoted*
RLJS religious *devoted*
RLJSL irreligiously *not devoted*
RLJSL religiously *devotedly*
RLJSNS religiousness *devotion*
RLJST urologist *urine*
RLK air lock *door*
RLK earlock *hair*
RLK oarlock *boat*
RLK reelect *choose again*
RLK relic *memento*
RLK relock *key*
RLK rollick *romp*
RLKL roll call *list*
RLKN rollicking *romp*
RLKNG rollicking *romp*
RLKR railcar *trains*
RLKS relax *rest, adjust*
RLKSD relaxed *informal, at ease*
RLKSHN reallocation *distribution*
RLKSHN reelection *choosen again*
RLKSHN relocation *move*
RLKSN relaxin *hormone*
RLKSNT relaxant *less tense*
RLKSSHN relaxation *less tense, recreation*
RLKST relaxed *informal, at ease*
RLKSTR roller-coaster (adj) *amusement* roller coaster (n)
RLKT reallocate *distribute* reallocated reallocating
RLKT reelect *choose again*
RLKT relocate *move* relocated relocating
RLKT relocatee *mover*
RLKTNS reluctance *hesitance, magnets*
RLKTNT reluctant *hesitant*
RLKTNTS reluctance *hesitance, magnets*
RLKWR reliquary *shrine* reliquaries
RLM heirloom *antique*
RLM realm *region*
RLN air lane *flight path*

RLN air line *straight line*
RLN airline *transportation*
RLN Ireland *country*
RLN Orlon *(trademark) fabric*
RLN railing *bannister*
RLN realign *straighten*
RLN ruling *judgement, controlling*
RLNCH relaunch *initiate, take off*
RLND Ireland *country*
RLNG hour-long *60 minutes*
RLNG railing *bannister*
RLNG ruling *judgement, controlling*
RLNGKWSH relinquish *surrender*
RLNGKWSHMNT relinquishment *surrender*
RLNGQSH relinquish *surrender*
RLNGQSHMNT relinquishment *surrender*
RLNK roll-neck *collar*
RLNKWSH relinquish *surrender*
RLNKWSHMNT relinquishment *surrender*
RLNMNT realignment *straightening*
RLNQSH relinquish *surrender*
RLNQSHMNT relinquishment *surrender*
RLNR airliner *airplane*
RLNS earliness *promptness*
RLNS reliance *dependability*
RLNT relent *soften*
RLNT reliant *dependable*
RLNTLS relentless *harsh*
RLNTLSL relentlessly *harsh*
RLNTLSNS relentlessness *harsh*
RLNTS reliance *dependability*
RLP orlop *deck*
RLP roll up *collect, arrive*
RLPL role-play *act*
RLPL roly-poly *round roly-polies*
RLPLTK realpolitik *practicality*

RLPS relapse *(v) fall back, worsen* relapsed relapsing
RLPS relapse *(n) worsening*
RLQR reliquary *shrine* reliquaries
RLR areolar *ring*
RLR earlier *sooner*
RLR raillery *jest* railleries
RLR roller *round device*
RLR ruler *controller*
RLRD railroad *trains*
RLRKSTR roller-coaster (adj) *amusement* roller coaster (n)
RLRNGK roller rink *skate*
RLRNK roller rink *skate*
RLRSKT roller skate *shoe wheels*
RLS airless *no air*
RLS release *set free* released releasing
RLSDK realistic *lifelike, factual*
RLSDKL realistically *lifelike, factual*
RLSH relish *(n) flavor, delight, condiment (v) enjoy* relishes
RLSHN relation *account, kinship, reference**
RLSHNL relational (adj) *connected* relationally (adv)
RLSHNSHP relationship *kinship*
RLSKT roller skate *shoe wheels*
RLSNT relucent *shining*
RLSPLDR rail-splitter *trains*
RLSPLTR rail-splitter *trains*
RLST aerialist *trapeze*
RLST earliest *soonest*
RLST realist *facts*
RLST royalist *monarchy*
RLSTK realistic *lifelike, factual*
RLSTKL realistically *lifelike, factual*
RLSTT real estate *land*
RLT areolate *ring*
RLT arillate *seed*
RLT orality *mouth, verbal*

Letters aren't doubled for single sounds: to find alley use **L** not **LL**. Use **Y** and **W** as hard sounds only: to find yellow use **YL**. (Br)=British spelling or usage. * See dictionary.

RLT reality *facts* realities
RLT realty *land*
RLT relate *tell, connect* related relating
RLT relight *fire, illumination* relit relighting
RLT rhyolite *lava*
RLT rialto *marketplace* rialtos
RLT roll out (v) *bring forward* rollout (n)
RLT Rouault *artist*
RLT roulette *game wheel*
RLT royalty *monarchy* royalties
RLT rule out *exclude, prevent*
RLTBL relatable *tell, connect*
RLTD related *connected*
RLTH urolith *calculus*
RLTK rhyolitic *lava*
RLTP rolltop *desk*
RLTR realtor *land agent*
RLTRL reel-to-reel *tape*
RLTS rillettes *meat*
RLTV irrelative *does not apply*
RLTV relative *kin, comparison*
RLTVD relativity *comparison, theory* relativities
RLTVL irrelatively *does not apply*
RLTVL relatively *somewhat*
RLTVT relativity *comparison, theory* relativities
RLTVZM relativism *comparison*
RLV relieve *ease* relieved relieving
RLV relive *live again* relived reliving
RLVBL relievable (adj) *ease* relievably (adv)
RLVD relieved *eased*
RLVNS irrelevance *does not apply* irrelevancy
RLVNS relevance *related* relevancy
RLVNT irrelevant *does not apply*
RLVNT relevant *related*
RLVNTL relevantly *related*
RLVNTS irrelevance *does not apply* irrelevancy
RLVNTS relevance *related*

relevancy
RLVR reliever *ease, baseball*
RLW railway *trains*
RLW rollaway *portable*
RLWD earlywood *springwood*
RLWRLD real-world (adj) *actual*
RLX relax *rest, adjust*
RLXD relaxed *informal, at ease*
RLXN relaxin *hormone*
RLXNT relaxant *less tense*
RLXSHN relaxation *less tense, recreation*
RLXT relaxed *informal, at ease*
RLYBL reliable (adj) *dependable* reliably (adv)
RLYBLD reliability *dependability*
RLYBLT reliability *dependability*
RLYNS reliance *dependability*
RLYNT reliant *dependable*
RLYNTS reliance *dependability*
RLYR earlier *sooner*
RLYST earliest *soonest*
RLYTS rillettes *meat*
RLZ realize *understand* realized realizing
RLZBL realizable *accomplish*
RLZM oralism *teaching*
RLZM realism *facts, lifelike*
RLZM royalism *monarchy*
RLZSHN realization *understanding*
RM arm (n) *limb, weapon* (v) *equip, prepare*
RM army *military* armies
RM aroma *scent*
RM arum *plant*
RM eye rhyme *verse*
RM RAM (abbr) *Random-access memory*
RM ram (v) *push* rammed ramming
RM ram (n) *male sheep*
RM ramie *fiber*
RM ream (v) *bore* (n) *paper*
RM rem *radiation* rems

RM REM *Rapid Eye Movement*
RM rheum *mucous*
RM rheumy *like mucous*
RM rhomb *shape* rhombs
RM rhumb *compass* rhumbs
RM rhyme *poem* rhymed rhyming
RM rim *edge* rimmed rimming
RM rime *frost* rimed riming
RM rimy *frosty*
RM roam *wander*
RM ROM *computer*
RM Rome *city*
RM Romeo *lover* Romeos
RM room (n) *place* (v) *occupy*
RM roomy *large* roomier roomiest
RM rum *liquor*
RM rummy *drunkard, game* rummies
RM uremia *illness*
RMB rhomb *shape* rhombs
RMB rhombi (pl) *shape* rhombus
RMB rhumb *compass* rhumbs
RMB Rimbaud *poet*
RMB rumba *dance*
RMBD rhomboid *shape*
RMBD rhomboidei (pl) *muscle* rhomboideus
RMBD Rimbaud *poet*
RMBDL rhomboidal *shape*
RMBDS rhomboideus *muscle* rhomboidei
RMBDY rhomboidei (pl) *muscle* rhomboideus
RMBDYS rhomboideus *muscle* rhomboidei
RMBK rhombic *shape*
RMBL airmobile *vehicle*
RMBL ramble *roam, talk* rambled rambling
RMBL rumble (v) *growl* rumbled rumbling
RMBL rumble (n) *fight, sound*
RMBL rumbly *rattling*
RMBLR rambler *roamer*
RMBN armband *sleeve*

Use letters that best describe the sounds you hear and omit the vowels. Use **S** or **K** instead of **C**: to find circle use **SRKL**. Use **J** to find joy, **JM** to find gem and **G** to find go.

RMBND armband *sleeve*

RMBNGCHS rambunctious *unruly*

RMBNGCHSL rambunctiously *unruly*

RMBNGCHSNS rambunctiousness *unruly*

RMBNGKCHS rambunctious *unruly*

RMBNGKCHSL rambunctiously *unruly*

RMBNGKCHSNS rambunctiousness *unruly*

RMBNGKSHS rambunctious *unruly*

RMBNGKSHSL rambunctiously *unruly*

RMBNGKSHSNS rambunctiousness *unruly*

RMBNGSHS rambunctious *unruly*

RMBNGSHSL rambunctiously *unruly*

RMBNGSHSNS rambunctiousness *unruly*

RMBNKCHS rambunctious *unruly*

RMBNKCHSL rambunctiously *unruly*

RMBNKCHSNS rambunctiousness *unruly*

RMBNKSHS rambunctious *unruly*

RMBNKSHSL rambunctiously *unruly*

RMBNKSHSNS rambunctiousness *unruly*

RMBRNT Rembrandt *artist*

RMBRS reimburse *pay* reimbursed reimbursing

RMBRSBL reimbursable *payment*

RMBRSMNT reimbursement *payment*

RMBS rhombus *shape* rhombuses (or) rhombi

RMCH rematch *contest* rematches

RMCHR armature *device*

RMCHR armchair *seat*

RMD armada *group*

RMD armed *weapons, limbs*

RMD remade *create again*

RMD remedy *cure* remedied remedying remedies

RMD remuda *herd*

RMD rimmed *edged*

RMDBL irremediable (adj) *cannot correct* irremediably (adv)

RMDBL remediable *correction*

RMDBL remittable *relax, pay*

RMDFRSS armed forces *military*

RMDK aromatic *fragrant*

RMDK eremitic (or) eremitical *withdrawn*

RMDK rheumatic *joints*

RMDKL aromatically *fragrantly*

RMDKL eremitical (or) eremitic *withdrawn*

RMDKL rheumatically *joints*

RMDL armadillo *animal* armadillos

RMDL remedial (adj) *corrective* remedially (adv)

RMDL remittal *relax, pay*

RMDL remodel *shape, design*

RMDN Ramadan *holy day*

RMDNS remittance *money*

RMDNT remittent *disease*

RMDNTS remittance *money*

RMDR remoter *secluded*

RMDSHN remediation *correction*

RMDSN aeromedicine *flying*

RMDST remotest *secluded*

RMDT remediate *correct* remediated remediating

RMDY armadillo *animal* armadillos

RMDYBL irremediable (adj) *cannot correct* irremediably (adv)

RMDYBL remediable *correction*

RMDYL remedial (adj) *corrective* remedially (adv)

RMDYSHN remediation *correction*

RMDYT remediate *correct* remediated remediating

RMF earmuff *warmer*

RMF ramify *split* ramified ramifying ramifies

RMFKSHN ramification *outgrowth*

RMFL armful *load* armfuls (or) armsful

RMFL roomful *crowd*

RMFRSS armed forces *military*

RMFSZ reemphasize *stress* reemphasized reemphasizing (Br) reemphasise

RMGDN Armageddon *final battle*

RMGTN Armageddon *final battle*

RMGZ remiges (pl) *feather* remex

RMHL armhole *opening*

RMJ rummage *search* rummaged rummaging

RMJR rummager *searcher*

RMJT ramjet *engine*

RMJZ remiges (pl) *feather* remex

RMK Aramaic *language*

RMK remake *create again* remade remaking

RMK rumaki *food*

RMK uremic *illness*

RMKN ramekin *dish*

RMKNKS aeromechanics *gas equilibrium*

RMKNX aeromechanics *gas equilibrium*

RMKS remex *feather* remiges

RMKS remix *mingle again*

RML airmail *postage* (Br) aerogram (or) aerogramme

RML ormolu *decoration*

RMLD armload *amount*

RMLD remold *form*

RMLDL romeldale *sheep*

RMLK armlock *hammerlock*

RMLN rhumb line *compass*

RMLS rimless *no edge*

RMLT armlet *band*

RMMBR remember *bring to*

Letters aren't doubled for single sounds: to find alley use **L** not **LL**. Use **Y** and **W** as hard sounds only: to find yellow use **YL**. (Br)=British spelling or usage. * See dictionary.

mind

RMMBRBL rememberable
bring to mind

RMMBRNS remembrance
memory

RMMBRNTS remembrance
memory

RMMNT armament weapon

RMN airman pilot airmen

RMN Aramaean Syrian

RMN Armenia country

RMN ermine animal ermines
(or) ermine

RMN remain continue

RMN remand send back

RMN remind remember

RMN romaine lettuce

RMN Roman of Rome

RMN Romania country

RMN rumen stomach rumina
(or) rumens

RMND remand send back

RMND remind remember

RMNDR remainder left over

RMNDR reminder hint

RMNDR ruminator musing,
chew

RMNDV ruminative musing,
chew

RMNFKCHR remanufacture
production
remanufactured
remanufacturing

RMNFKSHR remanufacture
production
remanufactured
remanufacturing

RMNFKTR remanufacture
production
remanufactured
remanufacturing

RMNK Armagnac brandy

RMNK romantic love

RMNKL roman à clef book
romans à clef

RMNKL romantically love

RMNKLF roman à clef book
romans à clef

RMNMRL Roman numeral
number

RMNN Armenian of Armenia

RMNN Romanian of

Romania

RMNNS remanence magnets

RMNNT remanent magnets

RMNNT remnant leftover

RMNNT ruminant cud,
ponder

RMNNTS remanence
magnets

RMNRDR remunerator one
who pays

RMNRDV remunerative
profitable

RMNRDVL remuneratively
profitable

RMNRDVNS
remunerativeness
profitable

RMNRSHN remuneration
pay

RMNRT remunerate pay
remunerated
remunerating

RMNRTR remunerator one
who pays

RMNRTV remunerative
profitable

RMNRTVL remuneratively
profitable

RMNRTVNS
remunerativeness
profitable

RMNS remains corpse,
leftovers

RMNS reminisce recall
reminisced reminiscing

RMNS rhamnose sugar

RMNS romance love
romanced romancing

RMNS roominess space

RMNSHN rumination
musing, chew

RMNSHP airmanship
piloting skill

RMNSK Romanesque of
Rome

RMNSNS reminiscence
recall

RMNSNT reminiscent
suggestive

RMNSNTL reminiscently
suggestive

RMNSNTS reminiscence

recall

RMNSR reminiscer
remember

RMNSTRDR remonstrator
protester

RMNSTRDV remonstrative
protesting

RMNSTRNS remonstrance
protest

RMNSTRNT remonstrant
protester

RMNSTRNTS
remonstrance protest

RMNSTRSHN
remonstration protest

RMNSTRT remonstrate
protest remonstrated
remonstrating

RMNSTRTR remonstrator
protester

RMNSTRTV remonstrative
protesting

RMNSZ romanticize make
ideal romanticized
romanticizing
(Br) romanticise

RMNSZM romanticism love

RMNT army ant insect

RMNT raiment finery

RMNT remint coin

RMNT remnant leftover

RMNT remount (v) revert,
hang (n) new horse

RMNT ruminate ponder, chew
ruminated ruminating

RMNTK romantic love

RMNTKL romantically love

RMNTR ruminator musing,
chew

RMNTS romance love
romanced romancing

RMNTSZ romanticize make
ideal romanticized
romanticizing
(Br) romanticise

RMNTSZM romanticism
love

RMNTV ruminative musing,
chew

RMNY Armenia country

RMNY Romania country

RMNYFKCHR

Use letters that best describe the sounds you hear and omit the vowels. Use **S** or **K**
instead of **C**: to find circle use **SRKL**. Use **J** to find joy, **JM** to find gem and **G** to find go.

remanufacture *production*
remanufactured
remanufacturing
RMNYFKSHR
remanufacture *production*
remanufactured
remanufacturing
RMNYFKTR remanufacture
production
remanufactured
remanufacturing
RMNYK Armagnac *brandy*
RMNYMRL Roman numeral
number
RMNYN Armenian *of*
Armenia
RMNYN Romanian *of*
Romania
RMNZ remains *corpse,*
leftovers
RMNZ rhamnose *sugar*
RMNZ Romanize *make*
Roman Romanized
Romanizing
(Br) romanise
RMNZKL romans à clef (pl)
book roman à clef
RMNZKLF romans à clef
(pl) *book* roman à clef
RMP ramp *incline*
RMP remap *map again*
remapped remapping
RMP romp *(v) play, win (n)*
carefree play
RMP rump *buttocks*
RMPGS rampageous *riotous*
RMPGSL rampageously
riotous
RMPGSNS
rampageousness *riotous*
RMPGYS rampageous
riotous
RMPGYSL rampageously
riotous
RMPGYSNS
rampageousness *riotous*
RMPJ rampage *riot*
rampaged rampaging
RMPJS rampageous *riotous*
RMPJSL rampageously
riotous
RMPJSNS

rampageousness *riotous*
RMPK rampike *tree*
RMPL reemploy *hire*
RMPL rumple *tousle*
rumpled rumpling
RMPLMNT reemployment
hiring
RMPNC rampancy *stance,*
widespread, wildness
RMPNS rampancy *stance,*
widespread, wildness
RMPNT rampant *stance,*
widespread, wildness
RMPNTC rampancy *stance,*
widespread, wildness
RMPNTL rampantly *stance,*
widespread, wildness
RMPNTS rampancy *stance,*
widespread, wildness
RMPR romper *player,*
garment
RMPRT rampart *barrier*
RMPT armpit *body area*
RMPZ reimpose *burden*
reimposed reimposing
RMPZSHN reimposition *tax,*
burden
RMR armoire *furniture*
RMR armor *protection*
(Br) armour
RMR armory *weapons*
armories
(Br) armoury
RMR reamer *borer*
RMR remarry *wed again*
remarried remarrying
remarries
RMR remora *fish* remoras
RMR rhymer *poet*
RMR roamer *wanderer*
RMR roomer *lodger*
RMR roomier *larger*
RMR rumor *gossip*
(Br) rumour
RMRD armored *protected*
(Br) armoured
RMRD ramrod *firearm, boss*
RMRJ reemerge *come out*
reemerged reemerging
RMRJ remarriage *wed again*
RMRJNS reemergence *come*
out

RMRJNT reemergent *come*
out
RMRJNTS reemergence
come out
RMRK earmark *designate*
RMRK remark *respond*
RMRK remarque *sketch*
RMRK rimrock *outcrop*
RMRKBL remarkable (adj)
uncommon remarkably
(adv)
RMRKT earmarked
designated
RMRKT remarket *sell*
RMRLS armorless
defenseless
(Br) armourless
RMRMNGGR rumormonger
gossip
(Br) rumour
RMRMNGR rumormonger
gossip
(Br) rumour
RMRR armorer *protector*
(Br) armourer
RMRS remorse *guilt*
RMRSFL remorseful (adj)
guilty remorsefully (adv)
RMRSFLNS remorsefulness
guilt
RMRSLN arm wrestling *test*
of strength
RMRSLNG arm wrestling
test of strength
RMRSLS remorseless
merciless
RMRSLSL remorselessly
merciless
RMRSLSNS
remorselessness
merciless
RMRST armrest *support*
RMS air mass *atmosphere* air
masses
RMS remiss *careless*
RMSBL irremissible *not*
forgiven
RMSBL remissible *forgiven*
RMSDR remaster *recordings*
RMSHKL ramshackle
rickety
RMSHKLD ramshackled

Letters aren't doubled for single sounds: to find alley use **L** not **LL**. Use **Y** and **W** as hard
sounds only: to find yellow use **YL**. (Br)=British spelling or usage. * See dictionary.

rickety
RMSHN remission *relief, postponement*
RMSHR remeasure *allot* remeasured remeasuring
RMSHRN ramshorn *snail*
RMSK ransack *plunder, search*
RMSKKRSKV Rimsky-Korsakov *composer*
RMSRN ramshorn *snail*
RMST roomiest *largest*
RMSTR remaster *recordings*
RMSTR rhymester *poet*
RMSTS armistice *truce*
RMT eremite *hermit*
RMT ramet *clone*
RMT remit *relax, pay* remitted remitting
RMT remote *(adj) secluded (n) remote control* remoter remotest
RMT remount *(v) revert, hang (n) new horse*
RMT roomette *small room*
RMT roommate *person*
RMTBL remittable *relax, pay*
RMTD rheumatoid *arthritis*
RMTHRP aromatherapy *massage*
RMTHRPST aromatherapist *massage*
RMTK aromatic *fragrant*
RMTK eremitic (or) eremitical *withdrawn*
RMTK rheumatic *joints*
RMTKL aromatically *fragrantly*
RMTKL eremitical (or) eremitic *withdrawn*
RMTKL rheumatically *joints*
RMTKNTRL remote control *device*
RMTL remittal *relax, pay*
RMTLG rheumatology *science*
RMTLJ rheumatology *science*
RMTLJST rheumatologist *doctor*
RMTNS remittance *money*
RMTNT remittent *disease*

RMTNTS remittance *money*
RMTR armature *device*
RMTR remoter *secluded*
RMTRS air mattress *inflatable bed*
RMTST remotest *secluded*
RMTWSTN arm-twisting *pressure*
RMTWSTNG arm-twisting *pressure*
RMTZ aromatize *flavor* aromatized aromatizing
RMTZM rheumatism *arthritis*
RMV remove *take away* removed removing
RMVBL irremovable (adj) *cannot move* irremovably (adv)
RMVBL removable (adj) *take away* removably (adv)
RMVD removed *distance*
RMVL removal *take away*
RMVR remover *take away*
RMW armoire *furniture*
RMWR armoire *furniture*
RMWRM armyworm *moth*
RMX remex *feather* remiges
RMX remix *mingle again*
RMY Romeo *lover* Romeos
RMY uremia *illness*
RMYD remuda *herd*
RMYK Aramaic *language*
RMYN Aramaean *Syrian*
RMYNRDR remunerator *one who pays*
RMYNRDV remunerative *profitable*
RMYNRDVL remuneratively *profitable*
RMYNRDVNS remunerativeness *profitable*
RMYNRSHN remuneration *pay*
RMYNRT remunerate *pay* remunerated remunerating
RMYNRTR remunerator *one who pays*
RMYNRTV remunerative *profitable*

RMYNRTVL remuneratively *profitable*
RMYNRTVNS remunerativeness *profitable*
RMYNT army ant *insect*
RMYR roomier *larger*
RMYST roomiest *largest*
RMZ remise *deed* remised remising
RMZHR remeasure *allot* remeasured remeasuring
RMZLNGKTH arm's length *distance*
RMZLNGTH arm's length *distance*
RMZLNKTH arm's length *distance*
RMZLNTH arm's length *distance*
RN airing *exposure*
RN arena *theater*
RN Arian *doctrine*
RN around *near*
RN arraign *call*
RN Aryan *Indo-European*
RN earing *rope*
RN earn *work for*
RN erne *bird*
RN errand *mission*
RN Iran *country*
RN iron *(n) metal, pressing device (v) press*
RN irony *sarcasm* ironies
RN Orion *constellation*
RN rain *(n) precipitation (v) fall, pour*
RN rainy *wet* rainier rainiest
RN rand *money* rand
RN rani (or) ranee *queen*
RN rayon *fabric*
RN reign *rule*
RN rein *strap*
RN renew *start again*
RN Reno *city*
RN Rhine *region*
RN rhino *animal, money* rhino (or) rhinos
RN rind *peel*
RN roan *color*
RN round *circle*
RN rowan *tree*

Use letters that best describe the sounds you hear and omit the vowels. Use **S** or **K** instead of **C**: to find circle use **SRKL**. Use **J** to find joy, **JM** to find gem and **G** to find go.

RN rowen *aftermath*
RN ruin *destroy*
RN run *(v) gallop, circulate, operate** ran running
RN run *(n) race, ravel, sequence**
RN rune *alphabet*
RN runny *drippy*
RN urine *liquid waste*
RN urn *vase*
RN wren *bird*
RNB rainbow *prism*
RNBK runback *football*
RNBL renewable (adj) *start again* renewably (adv)
RNBN ironbound *rugged*
RNBND ironbound *rugged*
RNBR rowanberry *tree* rowanberries
RNBRD rainbird *bird*
RNBRK ironbark *tree*
RNBT runabout *stray, vehicle*
RNC errancy *mistake* errancies
RNCH ranch *farm* ranches
RNCH rancho *small ranch* ranchos
RNCH raunch *lewdness*
RNCH raunchy *lewd* raunchier raunchiest
RNCH wrench *(n) tool (v) twist* wrenches
RNCHK rain check *ticket*
RNCHL raunchily *lewd*
RNCHN roentgen *X-ray*
RNCHNGL wrenchingly *twisted*
RNCHNL wrenchingly *twisted*
RNCHNS raunchiness *lewdness*
RNCHR rancher *farmer*
RNCHR ranchero *farmer, farm* rancheros
RNCHR raunchier *lewd*
RNCHST raunchiest *lewd*
RNCHYR raunchier *lewd*
RNCHYST raunchiest *lewd*
RND around *near*
RND errand *mission*
RND oriented *directed*
RND rand *money* rand

RND randy *lustful*
RND reendow *give*
RND rend *tear, split* rent rending
RND renowned *famous*
RND rind *peel*
RND rondeau *poem* rondeaux
RND rondo *music* rondos
RND round *circle*
RND Rwanda *country*
RNDBT roundabout *(adj) indirect, circuitous (n) detour, (Br) traffic circle*
RNDD reunited *together*
RNDD rounded *curved*
RNDHS roundhouse *trains*
RNDK aeronautic *flying*
RNDKL aeronautical (adj) *flying* aeronautically (adv)
RNDKS aeronautics *flying*
RNDL rondel (or) rondelle *verse*
RNDL roundel *curve*
RNDL roundelay *song*
RNDL rundle *ladder*
RNDM random *haphazard*
RNDMKSS random-access *in any order*
RNDML randomly *in any order*
RNDMNS randomness *in any order*
RNDMXS random-access *in any order*
RNDMZ randomize *in any order* randomized randomizing
RNDMZR randomizer *in any order*
RNDMZSHN randomization *in any order*
RNDN run down *(v) chase, ridicule*
RNDN run-down *(adj) worn out*
RNDN rundown *(n) baseball, summary*
RNDNT renitent *opposed*
RNDP round up *(v) gather up* roundup (n)
RNDR reindeer *animal*

RNDR render *give, make*
RNDR rounder *game, bum*
RNDRBL renderable *give, make*
RNDRBN round-robin *statement, series*
RNDRP raindrop *water*
RNDRPST rinderpest *disease*
RNDRR renderer *give, make*
RNDS rhinitis *nose*
RNDSHLDRD round-shouldered *stooped*
RNDSHN rendition *surrender, interpretation*
RNDSM ransom *(v) rescue (n) payment*
RNDSMR ransomer *rescuer*
RNDT reindict *accuse* reindicted reindicting
RNDTHKLK round-the-clock *constant*
RNDTMNT reindictment *accusation*
RNDTRP round-trip *travel*
RNDV rendezvous *(v) meet (n) meeting* rendezvoused rendezvousing
RNDVZ rendezvous (pl) *meeting* rendezvous
RNDWD roundwood *timber*
RNDWRM roundworm *worm*
RNDX aeronautics *flying*
RNF reunify *come together* reunified reunifying reunifies
RNF run off *(v) copy, drive away, steal*
RNF runoff *(n) race, stream*
RNFKSHN reunification *come together*
RNFL rainfall *precipitation*
RNFLSHN reinflation *made larger*
RNFLT reinflate *make larger* reinflated reinflating
RNFRS reinforce *strengthen* reinforced reinforcing
RNFRSMNT reinforcement *added strength*
RNFRSR reinforcer *strengthener*

Letters aren't doubled for single sounds: to find alley use **L** not **LL**. Use **Y** and **W** as hard sounds only: to find yellow use **YL**. (Br)=British spelling or usage. * See dictionary.

RNFRST rain forest *woodland*
RNFSZ reemphasize *stress* reemphasized reemphasizing (Br) reemphasise
RNG airing *exposure*
RNG earing *rope*
RNG earring *jewelry*
RNG O-ring *gasket*
RNG orangy (or) orangey *(adj) color, taste*
RNG rangy *tall* rangier rangiest
RNG renege *deny, cancel* reneged reneging
RNG ring *(v) sound* rang rung ringing
RNG ring *(n) circle, sound*
RNG ring *(v) encircle* ringed ringing
RNG rung *(n) crossbar, (v-past)* ring
RNG wring *twist* wrung wringing
RNG wrong *(adj) improper, sinful, incorrect* wronger wrongest
RNG wrong *(adv) incorrectly*
RNG wrong *(v) harm (n) injustice*
RNGD renegade *outlaw*
RNGD ringed *encircled*
RNGD wronged *harmed*
RNGDN wrongdoing *sin*
RNGDNG wrongdoing *sin*
RNGDR wrongdoer *sinner*
RNGDWN wrongdoing *sin*
RNGDWNG wrongdoing *sin*
RNGDWR wrongdoer *sinner*
RNGFL wrongful (adj) *unjust* wrongfully (adv)
RNGFLNS wrongfulness *injustice*
RNGG eryngo *plant* eryngoes (or) eryngos
RNGGL wrangle *argue* wrangled wrangling
RNGGLR wrangler *arguer, cowboy*
RNGGN Rangoon *city*
RNGHDD wrongheaded

incorrect
RNGHDDL wrongheadedly *incorrect*
RNGHDDNS wrongheadedness *incorrect*
RNGJ rain gauge *device*
RNGJ reengage *bind* reengaged reengaging
RNGJMNT reengagement *binding*
RNGK rank *(n) position (adj) foul, flagrant (v) arrange*
RNGK rhonchi (pl) *snore* rhonchus
RNGK rink *ice*
RNGKDNGK rinky-dink *(slang) small*
RNGKL rankle *irritate* rankled rankling
RNGKL wrinkle *crease* wrinkled wrinkling
RNGKL wrinkly *creased*
RNGKM aerenchyma *tissue*
RNGKN Rankine *physicist*
RNGKN ranking *foremost*
RNGKNDFL rank and file *(n) personnel*
RNGKNDFL rank-and-file *(adj) enlisted*
RNGKNDFLR rank and filer *member*
RNGKNFL rank and file *(n) personnel*
RNGKNFL rank-and-file *(adj) enlisted*
RNGKNFLR rank and filer *member*
RNGKNG ranking *foremost*
RNGKNS rankness *foulness*
RNGKR rancor *ill will* (Br) rancour
RNGKR ranker *officer*
RNGKRS rancorous *ill will* (Br) rancourous
RNGKRSL rancorously *ill will* (Br) rancourous
RNGKS rhonchus *snore* rhonchi
RNGL wrangle *argue* wrangled wrangling

RNGL wrongly *improper*
RNGLDR ringleader *gang head*
RNGLR wrangler *arguer, cowboy*
RNGLT ringlet *curl*
RNGLTR ringleader *gang head*
RNGMSDR ringmaster *circus*
RNGMSTR ringmaster *circus*
RNGN Rangoon *city*
RNGN ringing *sound*
RNGNG ringing *sound*
RNGNK ringneck *animal*
RNGNKD ring-necked *feathers*
RNGNKT ring-necked *feathers*
RNGNS ranginess *tall*
RNGNS wrongness *improper*
RNGP ring up *phone, sell, win*
RNGR rangier *tall*
RNGR reneger *deny, cancel*
RNGR ringer *bell, fake*
RNGR wringer *squeezer*
RNGRF renograph *X-ray* renography
RNGRM renogram *X-ray*
RNGRT reintegrate *combine* reintegrated reintegrating
RNGSD ringside *seating*
RNGSHBL renegotiable *adjustable*
RNGSHSHN renegotiation *adjustment*
RNGSHT renegotiate *adjust* renegotiated renegotiating
RNGSHYSHN renegotiation *adjustment*
RNGSHYT renegotiate *adjust* renegotiated renegotiating
RNGST rangiest *tall*
RNGTL ringtail *raccoon*
RNGTLD ring-tailed *color, shape*
RNGTN orangutan *ape*
RNGTNG orangutan *ape*

Use letters that best describe the sounds you hear and omit the vowels. Use **S** or **K** instead of **C**: to find circle use **SRKL**. Use **J** to find joy, **JM** to find gem and **G** to find go.

RNGTS ringtoss *game*
RNGWRM ringworm *fungus*
RNGYR rangier *tall*
RNGYST rangiest *tall*
RNHBT reinhabit *dwell*
RNHS roundhouse *trains*
RNJ arrange *place* arranged arranging
RNJ Iron Age *prehistoric*
RNJ orange *(n) color, fruit*
RNJ orangy (or) orangey *(adj) color, taste*
RNJ range *(v) classify, graze, extend** ranged ranging
RNJ range *(n) land, stove, scope**
RNJ rangy *tall* rangier rangiest
RNJD orangeade *beverage*
RNJLN rangeland *grazing*
RNJLND rangeland *grazing*
RNJMN Orangeman *Irish Protestant*
RNJMNT arrangement *placement*
RNJN rendzina *soil*
RNJN roentgen *X-ray*
RNJNDL urinogenital *urine*
RNJNR reengineer *reshape*
RNJNS ranginess *tall*
RNJNTL urinogenital *urine*
RNJR arranger *planner*
RNJR ranger *officer*
RNJR rangier *tall*
RNJR reinjure *(v) hurt again* reinjured reinjuring
RNJR reinjury *(n) hurt*
RNJSH orangish *color*
RNJST rangiest *tall*
RNJWD orangewood *tree*
RNJYR rangier *tall*
RNJYST rangiest *tall*
RNK arnica *herb*
RNK irenic *peaceful* (Br) eirenic
RNK ironic (or) ironical *sarcastic* ironically (adv)
RNK Orinoco *city*
RNK rank *(n) position (adj) foul, flagrant (v) arrange*
RNK rhonchi (pl) *snore* rhonchus

RNK rink *ice*
RNK Roanoke *city*
RNK wryneck *woodpecker*
RNKDNK rinky-dink *(slang) small*
RNKL irenically *peacefully* (Br) eirenically
RNKL ironical (or) ironic *sarcastic* ironically (adv)
RNKL rankle *irritate* rankled rankling
RNKL wrinkle *crease* wrinkled wrinkling
RNKL wrinkly *creased*
RNKLD ironclad *(adj) firm (n) ship*
RNKM aerenchyma *tissue*
RNKN Rankine *physicist*
RNKN ranking *foremost*
RNKNDFL rank and file *(n) personnel*
RNKNDFL rank-and-file *(adj) enlisted*
RNKNDFLR rank and filer *member*
RNKNFL rank and file *(n) personnel*
RNKNFL rank-and-file *(adj) enlisted*
RNKNFLR rank and filer *member*
RNKNG ranking *foremost*
RNKNS rankness *foulness*
RNKNTR reencounter *meeting*
RNKR rancor *ill will* (Br) rancour
RNKR ranker *officer*
RNKR rent-a-car *vehicle*
RNKRNSHN reincarnation *born again*
RNKRNT reincarnate *born again* reincarnated reincarnating
RNKRPRT reincorporate *combine* reincorporated reincorporating
RNKRS rancorous *ill will* (Br) rancourous
RNKRSL rancorously *ill will* (Br) rancourous
RNKRTN Iron Curtain

communism
RNKS rhonchus *snore* rhonchi
RNKT raincoat *garment*
RNKTR reencounter *meeting*
RNL oriental (adj) *(often capitalized) eastern* orientally (adv)
RNL ranula *cyst*
RNL renal *kidney*
RNL renewal *begin again*
RNL rental *lease*
RNL rhinal *nose*
RNL runnel *streamlet*
RNL uranyl *chemical*
RNL urinal *toilet*
RNLN Rhineland *region*
RNLND Rhineland *region*
RNLNG iron lung *device*
RNLS runless *no score*
RNLSMNT reenlistment *sign up again*
RNLSS urinalysis *test* urinalyses
RNLST reenlist *sign up again*
RNLSTMNT reenlistment *sign up again*
RNLT runlet *stream*
RNM aeronomy *atmosphere*
RNM rename *label again* renamed renaming
RNM rhenium *element*
RNM uranium *element*
RNMBR renumber *count*
RNMK aeronomic (or) aeronomical *atmosphere*
RNMKL aeronomical (or) aeronomic *atmospheric*
RNMKR rainmaker *cloud seeder, moneymaker*
RNMNGGR ironmonger *(Br) iron making* ironmongery
RNMNGR ironmonger *(Br) iron making* ironmongery
RNMNL ornamental (adj) *decorative* ornamentally (adv)
RNMNT arraignment *call*
RNMNT ornament *decoration*
RNMNT renominate *name* renominated renominating

Letters aren't doubled for single sounds: to find alley use **L** not **LL**. Use **Y** and **W** as hard sounds only: to find yellow use **YL**. (Br)=British spelling or usage. * See dictionary.

RNMNTL ornamental (adj) *decorative* ornamentally (adv)

RNMNTSHN ornamentation *decoration*

RNMSHN reanimation *pep*

RNMST aeronomist *scientist*

RNMT reanimate *pep up* reanimated reanimating

RNN Iranian *of Iran*

RNN ironing *pressing, clothes*

RNN rennin *enzyme*

RNN renown *fame*

RNN reunion *come together*

RNN run in *(v) insert, arrest*

RNN run on *(v) talk, continue*

RNN run-in *(n) quarrel, insert*

RNN run-on *(adj, n) lengthy*

RNN running *race*

RNNBK running back *sports*

RNNBRD running board *car*

RNNCDV renunciative *denial*

RNNCSHN renunciation *denial*

RNNCTR renunciatory *denial*

RNNCTV renunciative *denial*

RNNCYDV renunciative *denial*

RNNCYSHN renunciation *denial*

RNNCYTR renunciatory *denial*

RNNCYTV renunciative *denial*

RNND renowned *famous*

RNNDG running dog *hireling*

RNNG ironing *pressing, clothes*

RNNG ranting *scolding*

RNNG running *race*

RNNGBK running back *sports*

RNNGBRD running board *car*

RNNGDG running dog *hireling*

RNNGKL ranunculi *(pl) buttercup* ranunculus

RNNGKLS ranunculus *buttercup* ranunculuses

(or) ranunculi

RNNGKYL ranunculi *(pl) buttercup* ranunculus

RNNGKYLS ranunculus *buttercup* ranunculuses (or) ranunculi

RNNGMT running mate *election*

RNNGQL ranunculi *(pl) buttercup* ranunculus

RNNGQLS ranunculus *buttercup* ranunculuses (or) ranunculi

RNNGS earnings *pay*

RNNKL ranunculi *(pl) buttercup* ranunculus

RNNKLS ranunculus *buttercup* ranunculuses (or) ranunculi

RNNKYL ranunculi *(pl) buttercup* ranunculus

RNNKYLS ranunculus *buttercup* ranunculuses (or) ranunculi

RNNMT running mate *election*

RNNQL ranunculi *(pl) buttercup* ranunculus

RNNQLS ranunculus *buttercup* ranunculuses (or) ranunculi

RNNS earnings *pay*

RNNS renounce *refuse, resign* renounced renouncing

RNNSDV renunciative *denial*

RNNSFLK rhinencephalic *brain*

RNNSFLN rhinencephalon *brain*

RNNSMNT renouncement *refusal, resignation*

RNNSSHN renunciation *denial*

RNNSTR renunciatory *denial*

RNNSTV renunciative *denial*

RNNSYDV renunciative *denial*

RNNSYSHN renunciation *denial*

RNNSYTR renunciatory *denial*

RNNSYTV renunciative *denial*

RNNT uraninite *mineral*

RNNTS renounce *refuse, resign* renounced renouncing

RNNTSMNT renouncement *refusal, resignation*

RNNZ earnings *pay*

RNP run up *(v) increase, achieve*

RNP run-up *(n) increase*

RNPLSD rhinoplasty *nose job*

RNPLST rhinoplasty *nose job*

RNPRF rainproof *dry*

RNR earner *worker*

RNR ornery *irritable* ornerier orneriest

RNR rainier *wet*

RNR reenter *enter again*

RNR renter *lease*

RNR runner *racer, messenger, vine**

RNR urinary *urine*

RNRBN round-robin *statement, series*

RNRJZ reenergize *strengthen* reenergized reenergizing (Br) reenergise

RNRL reenroll *sign up again*

RNRN runaround (the) *delay*

RNRND runaround (the) *delay*

RNRNS orneriness *irritability*

RNRP runner-up *second place* runners-up

RNRR ornerier *irritable*

RNRST orneriest *irritable*

RNRYR ornerier *irritable*

RNRYST orneriest *irritable*

RNRZP runners-up *(pl) second place* runner-up

RNS airiness *lofty, proud, windy*

RNS eeriness *weirdness*

RNS errancy *mistake* errancies

RNS erroneous *wrong*

RNS rawness *naked, crude,*

uncooked

RNS rinse *wash* rinsed rinsing

RNS ruinous *destructive*

RNS Uranus *planet*

RNS urinous *liquid waste*

RNS wryness *twist*

RNSD ironside *strong one*

RNSD rancid *offensive*

RNSDNS rancidness *offensive*

RNSHLDRD round-shouldered *stooped*

RNSHN roentgen *X-ray*

RNSHN ruination *damage*

RNSHN urination *discharge urine*

RNSHR reinsure *insure again* reinsured reinsuring

RNSHRNS reinsurance *insure again*

RNSHRNTS reinsurance *insure again*

RNSHS arenaceous *sandy*

RNSK ransack *plunder, search*

RNSKP rhinoscopy *examination*

RNSL earnestly *sincere*

RNSL erroneously *wrong*

RNSL ruinously *destructive*

RNSM ransom *(v) rescue (n) payment*

RNSMR ransomer *rescuer*

RNSNS earnestness *sincerity*

RNSNS erroneousness *wrong*

RNSNS renaissance *(often capitalized) revival*

RNSNS renascence *new life*

RNSNS ruinousness *destruction*

RNSNT renascent *new life*

RNSNTS renaissance *(often capitalized) revival*

RNSNTS renascence *new life*

RNSPK reinspect *examine*

RNSPKT reinspect *examine*

RNSPT rainspout *gutter*

RNSRS rhinoceros *animal*

rhinoceroses (or) rhinoceros (or) rhinoceri

RNSRSHN reinsertion *place inside*

RNSRT reinsert *place inside*

RNST earnest *sincere*

RNST rainiest *wet*

RNSTL earnestly *sincere*

RNSTL reinstall *put in*

RNSTN ironstone *rock*

RNSTN rhinestone *glass*

RNSTNS earnestness *sincere*

RNSTRM rainstorm *weather*

RNSTT reinstate *restore* reinstated reinstating

RNSTTT reinstitute *establish again* reinstituted reinstituting

RNT aeronaut *flyer*

RNT aren't *(contr) are not*

RNT arrant *out-and-out*

RNT errant *roving, mistaken*

RNT iron out *smooth, resolve*

RNT orient *(n) (often capitalized) east (v) position*

RNT ornate *elaborate*

RNT rant *scold*

RNT reknit *weave again* reknitted reknitting

RNT rennet *enzyme*

RNT rent *(v) lease (v-past) rend (n) payment*

RNT rentier *property owner*

RNT reunite *come together* reunited reuniting

RNT ruinate *damage* ruinated ruinating

RNT run out *expire, complete, expel**

RNT runt *small*

RNT urinate *discharge urine* urinated urinating

RNTC errancy *mistake* errancies

RNTCHN roentgen *X-ray*

RNTD oriented *directed*

RNTD reunited *together*

RNTGN roentgen *X-ray*

RNTGRT reintegrate *combine* reintegrated reintegrating

RNTHK ornithic *birds*

RNTHKLK round-the-clock *constant*

RNTHLG ornithology *birds*

RNTHLJ ornithology *birds*

RNTHLJKL ornithological (adj) *birds* ornithologically (adv)

RNTHLJST ornithologist *birds*

RNTHML run-of-the-mill *average*

RNTHPD ornithopod *dinosaur*

RNTHPDR ornithopter *aircraft*

RNTHPTR ornithopter *aircraft*

RNTHR run through *(v) pierce, do quickly*

RNTHR run-through *(n) rehearsal*

RNTHSKN ornithischian *dinosaur*

RNTHSKYN ornithischian *dinosaur*

RNTHSS ornithosis *disease* ornithoses

RNTJN roentgen *X-ray*

RNTK aeronautic *flying*

RNTKL aeronautical (adj) *flying* aeronautically (adv)

RNTKR rent-a-car *vehicle*

RNTKS aeronautics *flying*

RNTL oriental (adj) *(often capitalized) eastern* orientally (adv)

RNTL ornately *elaborately*

RNTL rental *lease*

RNTN ranting *scolding*

RNTNC renitency *opposition*

RNTNG ranting *scolding*

RNTNGL rantingly *scold*

RNTNL rantingly *scold*

RNTNS ornateness *elaboration*

RNTNS renitency *opposition*

RNTNT renitent *opposed*

RNTNTC renitency *opposition*

RNTNTS renitency *opposition*

Letters aren't doubled for single sounds: to find alley use **L** not **LL**. Use **Y** and **W** as hard sounds only: to find yellow use **YL**. (Br)=British spelling or usage. * See dictionary.

RNTR ranter *scolder*
RNTR reenter *enter again*
RNTR reentry *enter again*
RNTR reinter *bury again* reinterred reinterring
RNTR renter *lease*
RNTRDS reintroduce *insert, make known* reintroduced reintroducing
RNTRDYS reintroduce *insert, make known* reintroduced reintroducing
RNTRNG orienteering *race*
RNTRP round-trip *travel*
RNTRPRT reinterpret *figure out*
RNTS errancy *mistake* errancies
RNTS rhinitis *nose*
RNTS rinse *wash* rinsed rinsing
RNTSHN orientation *adjustment*
RNTSHN roentgen *X-ray*
RNTSHNL orientational (adj) *adjustment* orientationally (adv)
RNTSM ransom (v) *rescue* (n) *payment*
RNTSMR ransomer *rescuer*
RNTT orientate *position, face east* orientated orientating
RNTX aeronautics *flying*
RNTY rentier *property owner*
RNVDR renovator *restore*
RNVDV renovative *restoration*
RNVGRSHN reinvigoration *make lively*
RNVGRT reinvigorate *make lively* reinvigorated reinvigorating
RNVNT reinvent *make*
RNVR run over (v) *overflow, exceed, collide**
RNVR run-over (adj) *extending*
RNVR runover (n) *extra*
RNVRS rhinovirus *common cold*
RNVSHN renovation

restoration
RNVSKLR renovascular *kidneys*
RNVSKYLR renovascular *kidneys*
RNVSQLR renovascular *kidneys*
RNVST reinvest *put money in*
RNVT renovate *restore* renovated renovating
RNVTHML run-of-the-mill *average*
RNVTR renovator *restore*
RNVTV renovative *restoration*
RNW Renoir *artist*
RNW runaway (n) *fugitive* (adj) *successful, uncontrolled, fugitive*
RNW runway *ramp*
RNWBL renewable (adj) *start again* renewably (adv)
RNWD ironwood *tree*
RNWD roundwood *timber*
RNWDR rainwater *precipitation*
RNWL renewal *begin again*
RNWR ironware *articles*
RNWR rainwear *clothing*
RNWR Renoir *artist*
RNWRK ironwork *product*
RNWRKR ironworker *producer*
RNWRM roundworm *worm*
RNWTR rainwater *precipitation*
RNY renew *start again*
RNYBL renewable (adj) *start again* renewably (adv)
RNYL ranula *cyst*
RNYL renewal *begin again*
RNYM rhenium *element*
RNYM uranium *element*
RNYN Iranian *of Iran*
RNYN reunion *come together*
RNYR rainier *wet*
RNYS erroneous *wrong*
RNYSL erroneously *wrong*
RNYSNS erroneousness *wrong*

RNYST rainiest *wet*
RNYWBL renewable (adj) *start again* renewably (adv)
RNYWL renewal *begin again*
RNZ ironize *sarcasm* ironized ironizing
RNZNS renaissance (*often capitalized*) *revival*
RNZNTS renaissance (*often capitalized*) *revival*
RP Europa *Greek myth*
RP Europe *continent*
RP irrupt *pour in*
RP rap (n) *music, prison*
RP rap (v) *hit, talk* rapped rapping
RP rape (v) *violate* raped raping
RP rape (n) *herb*
RP rappee *snuff*
RP reap *harvest*
RP rep (abbr) *repetition, reputation, representative**
RP rep (or) repp *fabric*
RP repay *pay back* repaid repaying
RP rip (v) *tear apart, attack* ripped ripping
RP rip (n) *current, cut*
RP ripe *mature* riper ripest
RP rope (v) *tie, lure* roped roping
RP rope (n) *cord*
RP rupee *money*
RP wrap *cover* wrapped wrapping
RPBLK republic *government*
RPBLKN republican *government*
RPBLKNZ republicanize *government* republicanized republicanizing
RPBLKNZM republicanism *government*
RPBLKSHN republication *put out again*
RPBLSH republish *put out again*
RPBLSHR republisher *copier*
RPCD rapeseed *oil*

Use letters that best describe the sounds you hear and omit the vowels. Use **S** or **K** instead of **C**: to find circle use **SRKL**. Use **J** to find joy, **JM** to find gem and **G** to find go.

RPCHR rapture *ecstasy* raptured rapturing
RPCHR rupture *burst* ruptured rupturing
RPCHRS rapturous *ecstatic*
RPCHRSL rapturously *ecstatic*
RPCHRSNS rapturousness *ecstatic*
RPD rapid *(adj) quick (n) current*
RPD ripped *(slang) drunk, stoned*
RPD uropod *appendage*
RPDBL eruptible *burst*
RPDBL repeatable *do again*
RPDBL reputable (adj) *esteemed* reputably (adv)
RPDBLD repeatability *do again*
RPDBLD reputability *esteem*
RPDBLT repeatability *do again*
RPDBLT reputability *esteem*
RPDD rapidity *speed*
RPDD repeated *done again*
RPDD reputed *believed*
RPDDL repeatedly *done again*
RPDDL reputedly *supposedly*
RPDDV repetitive *repeat*
RPDDVL repetitively *repeat*
RPDDVNS repetitiveness *repeat*
RPDFR rapid-fire *shots, quick*
RPDFYR rapid-fire *shots, quick*
RPDL rapidly *quickly*
RPDL reptile *animal*
RPDNG repeating *done again and again*
RPDNS rapidness *quickness*
RPDNSR ropedancer *acrobat*
RPDNTSR ropedancer *acrobat*
RPDR raptor *bird of prey*
RPDR repeater *speak again, watch, firearm***
RPDS Euripides *dramatist*
RPDSHN repudiation *reject, decline*

RPDT rapidity *speed*
RPDT repudiate *reject, decline* repudiated repudiating
RPDTV repetitive *repeat*
RPDTVL repetitively *repeat*
RPDTVNS repetitiveness *repeat*
RPDV eruptive *burst*
RPDV irruptive *pour in*
RPDYSHN repudiation *reject, decline*
RPDYT repudiate *reject, decline* repudiated repudiating
RPDZ Euripides *dramatist*
RPF rip off (v) *cheat* rip-off (n)
RPGL uropygial *gland*
RPGM uropygium *rump*
RPGNNS repugnance *dislike*
RPGNNT repugnant *dislike*
RPGNNTL repugnantly *dislike*
RPGNNTS repugnance *dislike* repugnancy
RPGNT repugnant *dislike*
RPGNTL repugnantly *dislike*
RPGNTS repugnance *dislike*
RPGYL uropygial *gland*
RPGYM uropygium *rump*
RPH Arapaho *Native American*
RPJ arpeggio *chord* arpeggios
RPJL uropygial *gland*
RPJM uropygium *rump*
RPJY arpeggio *chord* arpeggios
RPJYL uropygial *gland*
RPJYM uropygium *rump*
RPK ear pick *device*
RPKJ repackage *change* repackaged repackaging
RPKJR repackager *changer*
RPKRD rip cord *parachute*
RPKSHN repercussion *effect*
RPKT air pocket *down current*
RPL airplay *broadcast*
RPL rappel *descend*

rappelled rappelling
RPL reapply *put on, enlist* reapplied reapplying reapplies
RPL repeal *cancel*
RPL repel *drive back* repelled repelling
RPL replay *repeat*
RPL reply *answer* replied replying replies
RPL repoll *count again*
RPL ripple *wave* rippled rippling
RPLBL irrepealable *cannot repeal*
RPLBL repealable *cancel*
RPLDR repleader *law*
RPLG earplug *insert*
RPLK replica *copy*
RPLKBL replicable *copy*
RPLKDV replicative *copy*
RPLKSHN reapplication *put on, enlist*
RPLKSHN replication *copy*
RPLKT replicate *copy* replicated replicating
RPLKTV replicative *copy*
RPLN airplane *aircraft* (Br) aeroplane
RPLNC repellency *repulsive*
RPLNS repellency *repulsive*
RPLNSH replenish *fill again*
RPLNSHBL replenishable *fill again*
RPLNSHMNT replenishment *fill again*
RPLNSHR replenisher *fill again*
RPLNT repellent *repulsive*
RPLNT replant *sow again*
RPLNTC repellency *repulsive*
RPLNTL repellently *repulsive*
RPLNTS repellency *repulsive*
RPLNTSHN replantation *sow again*
RPLR repealer *canceler*
RPLR repeller *resister*
RPLRZSHN repolarization *magnetism* (Br) repolarisation

Letters aren't doubled for single sounds: to find alley use **L** not **LL**. Use **Y** and **W** as hard sounds only: to find yellow use **YL**. (Br)=British spelling or usage. * See dictionary.

RPLS replace *put back, substitute* replaced replacing

RPLS repulse *repel* repulsed repulsing

RPLSBL irreplaceable (adj) *no substitute* irreplaceably (adv)

RPLSBL replaceable *substitute*

RPLSBLD irreplaceability *no substitute*

RPLSBLNS irreplaceableness *no substitute*

RPLSBLT irreplaceability *no substitute*

RPLSDR reupholster *cover*

RPLSHN repletion *fullness*

RPLSHN repulsion *aversion*

RPLSMNT replacement *substitute*

RPLSR replacer *substitute*

RPLSTR reupholster *cover*

RPLSV repulsive *disgusting*

RPLSVL repulsively *disgusting*

RPLSVNS repulsiveness *disgust*

RPLT replete *full*

RPLTNS repleteness *fullness*

RPLVN replevin *recovery*

RPM europium *element*

RPM rpm *(abbr) revolutions per minute*

RPMP air pump *device*

RPN European *of Europe*

RPN orpine *herb*

RPN rapine *loot*

RPN rapini *broccoli*

RPN repine *long for*

RPN repugn *oppose*

RPN ripen *mature*

RPN wrapping *cover*

RPNG wrapping *cover*

RPNNS repentance *regret*

RPNNT repentant *regretful*

RPNNTL repentantly *regretful*

RPNNTS repentance *regret*

RPNR repiner *long for*

RPNS ripeness *maturity*

RPNT reappoint *name*

RPNT repent *regret*

RPNT repentant *regretful*

RPNTMNT reappointment *naming*

RPNTNS repentance *regret*

RPNTNT repentant *regretful*

RPNTNTL repentantly *regretful*

RPNTNTS repentance *regret*

RPNTS repentance *regret*

RPP wrap up (v) *end* wrap-up (n)

RPPLT repopulate *birth* repopulated repopulating

RPPYLT repopulate *birth* repopulated repopulating

RPR airpower *military strength*

RPR raper *violator*

RPR rapier *sword*

RPR rapparee *bandit*

RPR rapper *knocker, musician*

RPR rapport *easy to talk*

RPR reaper *gatherer*

RPR reappear *show up again*

RPR repair *mend*

RPR repower *engine*

RPR repro *copy* repros

RPR riper *mature*

RPR ripper *cutter, perfection*

RPR wrapper *cover*

RPRBDV reprobative *critical*

RPRBL irreparable (adj) *cannot repair* irreparably (adv)

RPRBL repairable *mend*

RPRBL reparable *mend*

RPRBSHN reprobation *criticism*

RPRBT reprobate (v) *criticize* reprobated reprobating

RPRBT reprobate (n) *wrongdoer (adj) depraved*

RPRBTR reprobatory *critical*

RPRBTV reprobative *critical*

RPRC air piracy *hijacking*

RPRCH reproach *blame, rebuke* reproaches

RPRCHBL irreproachable

(adj) *no rebuke* irreproachably (adv)

RPRCHBL reproachable *blame, rebuke*

RPRCHBLNS irreproachableness *no rebuke*

RPRCHFL reproachful (adj) *blameful, rebuking* reproachfully (adv)

RPRCHFLNS reproachfulness *blame, rebuke*

RPRCHMN rapprochement *cordiality*

RPRCHMNT rapprochement *cordiality*

RPRCHR reproacher *blame, rebuke*

RPRCHS repurchase *buy* repurchased repurchasing

RPRDDL reportedly *supposedly*

RPRDJ reportage *news*

RPRDKDV reproductive *copy, birth*

RPRDKSHN reproduction *copy, birth*

RPRDKTV reproductive *copy, birth*

RPRDR reporter *news*

RPRDS reproduce *copy, give birth* reproduced reproducing

RPRDSBL reproducible (adj) *copy, give birth* reproducibly (adv)

RPRDSR reproducer *copy, give birth*

RPRDYS reproduce *copy, give birth* reproduced reproducing

RPRDYSBL reproducible (adj) *copy, give birth* reproducibly (adv)

RPRDYSR reproducer *copy, give birth*

RPRF reproof *scolding*

RPRGRF reprography *copy*

RPRGRFK reprographic *copy*

Use letters that best describe the sounds you hear and omit the vowels. Use **S** or **K** instead of **C**: to find circle use **SRKL**. Use **J** to find joy, **JM** to find gem and **G** to find go.

RPRGRFR reprographer *copier*

RPRGRM reprogram *revise* reprogrammed reprogramming

RPRGRMBL reprogrammable *revise*

RPRHN reprehend *criticize*

RPRHNCHN reprehension *scolding*

RPRHND reprehend *criticize*

RPRHNSBL reprehensible (adj) *guilty* reprehensibly (adv)

RPRHNSBLD reprehensibility *guilt*

RPRHNSBLNS reprehensibleness *guilty*

RPRHNSBLT reprehensibility *guilt*

RPRHNSHN reprehension *scolding*

RPRHNSV reprehensive *scolding*

RPRHNTSBL reprehensible (adj) *guilty* reprehensibly (adv)

RPRHNTSBLD reprehensibility *guilt*

RPRHNTSBLNS reprehensibleness *guilt*

RPRHNTSBLT reprehensibility *guilt*

RPRK airpark *airport*

RPRKSHN repercussion *effect*

RPRMN repairman *mender* repairmen

RPRMN reprimand (v) *reprove* (n) *reproof*

RPRMND reprimand (v) *reprove* (n) *reproof*

RPRN riparian *waterway*

RPRN wraparound *encircle*

RPRND wraparound *encircle*

RPRNR reprinter *copier*

RPRNS reappearance *show up again*

RPRNT reprint *copy again*

RPRNTR reprinter *copier*

RPRNTS reappearance *show up again*

RPRR repairer *mend*

RPRRN rip-roaring *noisy*

RPRRNG rip-roaring *noisy*

RPRS air piracy *hijacking*

RPRS repress *restrain* represses

RPRSBL irrepressible (adj) *cannot stop* irrepressibly (adv)

RPRSBL repressible *restrain*

RPRSHMN rapprochement *cordiality*

RPRSHMNT rapprochement *cordiality*

RPRSHN reapportion *divide*

RPRSHN reparation *payback*

RPRSHN repression *restraint*

RPRSHNMNT reapportionment *division*

RPRSHNST repressionist *restrainer*

RPRSHR air pressure *atmosphere*

RPRSR repressor *restrainer*

RPRSS reprocess *treatment*

RPRST repressed *restrained*

RPRSV repressive *restraint*

RPRSVL repressively *restraint*

RPRSVNS repressiveness *restraint*

RPRT airport *flights*

RPRT repartee *wit*

RPRT report (v) *relate*,(n) *account, noise*

RPRTBL reportable *news*

RPRTDL reportedly *supposedly*

RPRTJ reportage *news*

RPRTR rapporteur *reporter*

RPRTR repertory *company* repertories

RPRTR reporter *news*

RPRTSH reportage *news*

RPRTSHN repartition *distribution*

RPRTV reparative *payback*

RPRTW repertoire *list, supply*

RPRTWR repertoire *list, supply*

RPRTZH reportage *news*

RPRV reprieve *delay* reprieved reprieving

RPRV reprove *scold* reproved reproving

RPRVNGL reprovingly *scolding*

RPRVR reprover *scolder*

RPRYN riparian *waterway*

RPRZ reappraise *value* reappraised reappraising

RPRZ reprise *repeat* reprised reprising

RPRZL reappraisal *value*

RPRZL reprisal *payback*

RPRZNBL representable *depict, symbolize*

RPRZNDV representative (n) *example, delegate* (adj) *likeness, stand for another*

RPRZNDVL representatively *likeness*

RPRZNDVNS representativeness *likeness*

RPRZNT represent *depict, symbolize*

RPRZNTBL representable *depict, symbolize*

RPRZNTDV representative (n) *example, delegate* (adj) *likeness, stand for another*

RPRZNTDVL representatively *likeness*

RPRZNTDVNS representativeness *likeness*

RPRZNTSHN representation *likeness, stand for another*

RPRZNTSHNL representational (adj) *likeness, stand for another* representationally (adv)

RPRZNTTV representative (n) *example, delegate* (adj) *likeness, stand for another*

RPRZNTTVD representativity *likeness*

RPRZNTTVL representatively *likeness*

RPRZNTTVNS

Letters aren't doubled for single sounds: to find alley use **L** not **LL**. Use **Y** and **W** as hard sounds only: to find yellow use **YL**. (Br)=British spelling or usage. * See dictionary.

representativeness
likeness

RPRZNTTVT
representativity *likeness*

RPRZNTV representative
(n) example, delegate (adj)
likeness, stand for another

RPRZNTVD representativity
likeness

RPRZNTVL representatively
likeness

RPRZNTVNS
representativeness
likeness

RPRZNTVT representativity
likeness

RPS earpiece *earphone,*
glasses

RPS repass *go by again*

RPS repast *food*

RPS repoussé *pattern*

RPS ripsaw *tool*

RPSD rapacity *greed*

RPSD rapeseed *oil*

RPSD rhapsody *bliss*
rhapsodies

RPSDK rhapsodic *blissful*

RPSDKL rhapsodically
blissfully

RPSDST rhapsodist *blissful*
one

RPSDZ rhapsodize *speak,*
write rhapsodized
rhapsodizing

RPSH arpeggio *chord*
arpeggios

RPSHJ repechage *rowing*

RPSHL rapaciously *greedy*

RPSHN eruption *burst*

RPSHN irruption *pour in*

RPSHR rupture *burst*
ruptured rupturing

RPSHS rapacious *greedy*

RPSHSH repechage *rowing*

RPSHSNS rapaciousness
greed

RPSHY arpeggio *chord*
arpeggios

RPSHZH repechage *rowing*

RPSKLN rapscallion *rascal*

RPSKLYN rapscallion *rascal*

RPSKYN rapscallion *rascal*

RPSNRDNG ripsnorting
extraordinary

RPSNRDR ripsnorter
extraordinary thing

RPSNRTN ripsnorting
extraordinary

RPSNRTNG ripsnorting
extraordinary

RPSNRTR ripsnorter
extraordinary thing

RPST airpost *mail*

RPST rapacity *greed*

RPST rapist *violator*

RPST repast *food*

RPST ripest *mature*

RPST riposte *retort* riposted
riposting

RPSTP ripstop *fabric*

RPT erupt *burst*

RPT irrupt *pour in*

RPT rapt *enchanted*

RPT repeat *do again*

RPT repot *plant again*
repotted repotting

RPT repute *(v) consider*
reputed reputing

RPT repute *(n) status*

RPT ripped *(slang) drunk,*
stoned

RPTBL eruptible *burst*

RPTBL repeatable *do again*

RPTBL reputable (adj)
esteemed reputably (adv)

RPTBLD repeatability *do*
again

RPTBLD reputability *esteem*

RPTBLT repeatability *do*
again

RPTBLT reputability *esteem*

RPTD repeated *done again*

RPTD reputed *believed*

RPTD riptide *dangerous*
current

RPTDL repeatedly *done*
again

RPTDL reputedly *supposedly*

RPTDV repetitive *repeat*

RPTDVL repetitively *repeat*

RPTDVNS repetitiveness
repeat

RPTL reptile *animal*

RPTLN reptilian *animal*

RPTLYN reptilian *animal*

RPTN repeating *done again*
and again

RPTNG repeating *done again*
and again

RPTR raptor *bird of prey*

RPTR rapture *ecstasy*
raptured rapturing

RPTR repeater *speak again,*
watch, firearm*

RPTR repertory *company*
repertories

RPTR rupture *burst* ruptured
rupturing

RPTRL raptorial *bird of prey*

RPTRS rapturous *ecstatic*

RPTRSHN repatriation
return to country

RPTRSL rapturously *ecstatic*

RPTRSNS rapturousness
ecstatic

RPTRT repatriate *return to*
country repatriated
repatriating

RPTRYL raptorial *bird of*
prey

RPTRYSHN repatriation
return to country

RPTRYT repatriate *return to*
country repatriated
repatriating

RPTSHN repetition *repeat*

RPTSHN reputation *good*
name

RPTSHS repetitious *repeat*

RPTSHSL repetitiously
repeat

RPTSHSNS repetitiousness
repeat

RPTTV repetitive *repeat*

RPTTVL repetitively *repeat*

RPTTVNS repetitiveness
repeat

RPTV eruptive *burst*

RPTV irruptive *pour in*

RPTW repertoire *list, supply*

RPTWR repertoire *list,*
supply

RPTYN reptilian *animal*

RPW ropeway *cable*

RPWK ropewalk *acrobat*

RPWKR ropewalker *acrobat*

Use letters that best describe the sounds you hear and omit the vowels. Use **S** or **K**
instead of **C**: to find circle use **SRKL**. Use **J** to find joy, **JM** to find gem and **G** to find go.

RPWR airpower *military strength*
RPWR repower *engine*
RPYDBL reputable (adj) *esteemed* reputably (adv)
RPYDBLD reputability *esteem*
RPYDBLT reputability *esteem*
RPYDD reputed *believed*
RPYDDL reputedly *supposedly*
RPYDSHN repudiation *reject, decline*
RPYDT repudiate *reject, decline* repudiated repudiating
RPYDYSHN repudiation *reject, decline*
RPYDYT repudiate *reject, decline* repudiated repudiating
RPYM europium *element*
RPYM rpm *(abbr) revolutions per minute*
RPYN European *of Europe*
RPYN repugn *oppose*
RPYR rapier *sword*
RPYT repute *(v) consider* reputed reputing
RPYT repute *(n) status*
RPYTBL reputable (adj) *esteemed* reputably (adv)
RPYTBLD reputability *esteem*
RPYTBLT reputability *esteem*
RPYTD reputed *believed*
RPYTDL reputedly *supposedly*
RPYTSHN reputation *good name*
RPZ repose *rest* reposed reposing
RPZ repoussé *pattern*
RPZFL reposeful (adj) *relaxing* reposefully (adv)
RPZFLNS reposefulness *relaxation*
RPZH arpeggio *chord* arpeggios
RPZHY arpeggio *chord* arpeggios

RPZS repossess *take back*
RPZSHN reposition *store, replace, revise*
RPZSHN repossession *taken back*
RPZSR repossessor *take back*
RPZT reposit *store, replace*
RPZTR repository *container* repositories
RQ Iroquois *Native Americans* Iroquois
RQD rockweed *algae*
RQDL requital *repayment*
RQDR requiter *repay*
RQLR auricular *hearing*
RQLR oracular *domineering*
RQLRD oracularity *domination*
RQLRL oracularly *domineering*
RQLRT oracularity *domination*
RQLT auriculate *ear-shaped*
RQM requiem *mass for the dead*
RQNT reacquaint *meet*
RQP reequip *prepare, furnish* reequipt reequipping
RQPRDV recuperative *get well*
RQPRSHN recuperation *get well*
RQPRT recuperate *get well* recuperated recuperating
RQPRTV recuperative *get well*
RQR require *demand* required requiring
RQRD required *needed*
RQRMNT requirement *need*
RQSKT requiescat *prayer*
RQST request *(v) ask (n) demand*
RQT requite *repay* requited requiting
RQTL requital *repayment*
RQTR requiter *repay*
RQYM requiem *mass for the dead*
RQYR require *demand* required requiring

RQYRD required *needed*
RQYRMNT requirement *need*
RQYSKT requiescat *prayer*
RQZ Iroquois *Native Americans* Iroquois
RQZ recuse *refuse* recused recusing
RQZBL irrecusable (adj) *no exception* irrecusably (adv)
RQZNT recusant *refuser*
RQZSHN requisition *demand*
RQZT requisite *necessary thing*
RR aerier *heavenly*
RR airer *frame*
RR airier *lofty, proud, windy*
RR aurora *light* auroras (or) aurorae
RR Aurora *Roman goddess*
RR eerier *weirder*
RR error *mistake*
RR orrery *apparatus* orreries
RR rah-rah (adj) *spirit*
RR rare *scarce, raw* rarer rarest
RR rawer *uncooked, vulgar*
RR rear *back end*
RR roar *(n) sound (v) make noise*
RRBK roorback *falsehood*
RRBRLS aurora borealis *northern lights*
RRBRYLS aurora borealis *northern lights*
RRBT rarebit *food*
RRD rarity *unusual* rarities
RRD reread *read again* reread rereading
RRDR reorder *(v) arrange, call for (n) duplicate*
RRDS reredos *screen*
RRF rarefy *refine* rarefied rarefying rarefies
RRFD rarefied *high*
RRFKSHN rarefaction *refinement*
RRFKSHNL rarefactional *refinement*
RRGLT reregulate *control* reregulated reregulating
RRGNZ reorganize *arrange*

Letters aren't doubled for single sounds: to find alley use **L** not **LL**. Use **Y** and **W** as hard sounds only: to find yellow use **YL**. (Br)=British spelling or usage. * See dictionary.

reorganized reorganizing (Br) reorganise

RRGNZR reorganizer *arranger* (Br) reorganiser

RRGNZSHN reorganization *arrangement* (Br) reorganisation

RRGRD rearguard (adj) *resistance* rear guard (n)

RRGYLT reregulate *control* reregulated reregulating

RRJ arrearage *overdue*

RRKRD rerecord *write, tape*

RRL auroral *light*

RRL rarely *hardly ever*

RRL rural *country*

RRLS rerelease *send out* rereleased rereleasing

RRM rearm *weapons*

RRMMNT rearmament *weapons*

RRN aurorean *light*

RRN raring *eager*

RRN rerun (v) *repeat* (n) reran rerunning

RRN roaring *extremely*

RRND rear end (n) *buttocks*

RRND rear-end (v) *crash*

RRNG raring *eager*

RRNG roaring *extremely*

RRNGTWNTS Roaring '20s *1920-1929*

RRNGTWNTZ Roaring '20s *1920-1929*

RRNGTWNZ Roaring '20s *1920-1929*

RRNJ rearrange *straighten* rearranged rearranging

RRNJMNT rearrangement *straightening*

RRNTWNTS Roaring '20s *1920-1929*

RRNTWNTZ Roaring '20s *1920-1929*

RRNTWNZ Roaring '20s *1920-1929*

RRP rewrap *enclose* rewrapped rewrapping

RRR roarer *shouter, horse*

RRS arrears *debt*

RRSH raree-show *peep show*

RRSHK Rorschach *inkblot test*

RRST rearrest *law*

RRT arrowroot *plant*

RRT rarity *unusual* rarities

RRT reroute *detour* rerouted rerouting

RRT rewrite *edit* rewrote rewriting rewritten

RRVS rara avis *rarity* rara avises (or) rara aves

RRWRD rearward *toward the back*

RRYN aurorean *light*

RRZ arrears *debt*

RS Aires *zodiac sign*

RS arioso *music* ariosos (or) ariosi

RS arose *got up*

RS arras *tapestry* arras

RS arse (Br) *ass*

RS erase *cancel* erased erasing

RS Eros *Greek god*

RS erose *uneven*

RS heiress *inheritor* (f)

RS iris *eye, flower* irises (or) irides

RS orris *plant*

RS race (v) *gallop, hurry* raced racing

RS race (n) *contest, ancestry*

RS racy *indecent, sporty* racier raciest

RS reissue *put out again* reissued reissuing

RS rhus *plant* rhuses (or) rhus

RS rice *cereal grass*

RS Rousseau *artist, writer*

RS ruse *trick*

RS uraeus *symbol* uraei

RS urease *enzyme*

RS wrasse *fish* wrasses

RSBL erasable *cancel*

RSBL irascible (adj) *angry* irascibly (adv)

RSBLD irascibility *anger*

RSBLNS irascibleness *anger*

RSBLT erasability *cancel*

RSBLT irascibility *anger*

RSBMT resubmit *send in*

again resubmitted resubmitting

RSBN wristband *strap*

RSBND wristband *strap*

RSBRD ricebird *bobolink*

RSD arrestee *person stopped*

RSD recede *retreat* receded receding

RSD reseda *color*

RSD reseed *plant*

RSD rusty *corroded, slow* rustier rustiest

RSDBT roustabout *worker*

RSDD oersted *magnetism*

RSDK aoristic *verb*

RSDK eristic *argumentative*

RSDK rustic *rural*

RSDKDR rusticator *live in the country*

RSDKL aoristically *verb*

RSDKL eristically *argumentative*

RSDKL rustically *rural*

RSDKRDK aristocratic *elite*

RSDKRT aristocrat *nobleman*

RSDKRTK aristocratic *elite*

RSDKSHN rustication *live in the country*

RSDKT rusticate *live in the country* rusticated rusticating

RSDKTR rusticator *live in the country*

RSDL recital *exhibition*

RSDL resettle *colonize, clear, resolve** resettled resettling

RSDL rustily *corroded, slow, surly*

RSDLM rostellum *beak*

RSDLMNT resettlement *colony*

RSDN arresting *impressive*

RSDNG arresting *impressive*

RSDNG resting *inactive*

RSDNS rustiness *corroded, slow, surly*

RSDR arrester (or) arrestor *stopper*

RSDR rester *relaxer*

RSDR roaster *cooker*

Use letters that best describe the sounds you hear and omit the vowels. Use **S** or **K** instead of **C**: to find circle use **SRKL**. Use **J** to find joy, **JM** to find gem and **G** to find go.

RSDR roister *carouse*
RSDR rooster *fowl*
RSDR roster *list of names*
RSDR rouster *worker*
RSDR rustier *corroded, slow, surly*
RSDRL rostral *snout, stage*
RSDRM rostrum *stage* rostra (or) rostrums
RSDRR roisterer *carouser*
RSDRS roisterous *carousing*
RSDRSHN restoration *renewal*
RSDRSL roisterously *carousing*
RSDSD rusticity *simplicity*
RSDST rusticity *simplicity*
RSDST rustiest *corroded, slow, surly*
RSDTSHN restitution *pay back*
RSDTYSHN restitution *pay back*
RSDV restive *contrary*
RSDVSDK recidivistic *relapse*
RSDVST recidivist *relapse*
RSDVSTK recidivistic *relapse*
RSDVZM recidivism *relapse*
RSDYR rustier *corroded, slow, surly*
RSDYST rustiest *corroded, slow, surly*
RSF ourself *myself* ourselves
RSFL restful (adj) *relaxing* restfully (adv)
RSFLNS restfulness *relaxation*
RSH Irish *of Ireland*
RSH orgeat *syrup*
RSH raj *rule*
RSH raja (or) rajah *ruler*
RSH rash (n) *blemish* (adj) *daring* rashes
RSH ratio *proportion* ratios
RSH reissue *put out again* reissued reissuing
RSH reshoe *horse* reshoed reshoeing
RSH rouge (v) *redden* rouged rouging

RSH rouge (n) *cosmetic*
RSH ruche (or) ruching *fabric*
RSH rush (v) *hurry, charge* (n) *hurry, attack, feeling** rushes
RSH rushee *fraternity*
RSH Russia *country*
RSHC Irish Sea *body of water*
RSHF réchauffé *rehash, dish*
RSHFL reshuffle *reorganize* reshuffled reshuffling
RSHK Rorschach *inkblot test*
RSHL racial (adj) *ancestry* racially (adv)
RSHL rashly *daring*
RSHL Richelieu *statesman*
RSHL urushiol *irritant*
RSHLSDK racialistic *ancestry*
RSHLST racialist *ancestry*
RSHLSTK racialistic *ancestry*
RSHLT rushlight *candle*
RSHLY Richelieu *statesman*
RSHLZM racialism *ancestry*
RSHM regime *pattern, government*
RSHMN Irishman *of Ireland* Irishmen
RSHN aeration *add oxygen*
RSHN erosion *worn away*
RSHN Eurasian *European and Asian*
RSHN oration *speech*
RSHN ration *portion*
RSHN ruching (or) ruche *fabric*
RSHN rushing *football*
RSHN Russian *of Russia*
RSHNG ruching (or) ruche *fabric*
RSHNG rushing *football*
RSHNL irrational (adj) *not reasoning* irrationally (adv)
RSHNL rational (adj) *reasonable* rationally (adv)
RSHNL rationale *basis*
RSHNLD irrationality *not reasonable*
RSHNLD rationality *reason*

rationalities
RSHNLSDK rationalistic (or) rationalist *reason*
RSHNLSDKL rationalistically *reason*
RSHNLST rationalist (n) *reasoner*
RSHNLST rationalist (or) rationalistic *reason*
RSHNLSTK rationalistic (or) rationalist *reason*
RSHNLSTKL rationalistically *reason*
RSHNLT irrationality *not reasonable*
RSHNLT rationality *reason* rationalities
RSHNLZ rationalize *reason* rationalized rationalizing (Br) rationalise
RSHNLZM rationalism *reason*
RSHNLZR rationalizer *reasoner* (Br) rationaliser
RSHNLZSHN rationalization *reason* (Br) rationalisation
RSHNRLT Russian roulette *gun game*
RSHNS rashness *daring*
RSHP airship *blimp*
RSHP reshape *shape again* reshaped reshaping
RSHR eraser *rub-out device*
RSHR erasure *cancellation*
RSHR rasher *bacon*
RSHR reassure *comfort* reassured reassuring
RSHR rush hour (n) *peak time* rush-hour (adj)
RSHR rusher *football*
RSHRNS reassurance *comfort*
RSHRNTS reassurance *comfort*
RSHRS racehorse *animal*
RSHRSH recherché *rare*
RSHS Irish Sea *body of water*
RSHSDR Irish setter *dog*
RSHSHN Rosh Hashana *Jewish new year*

Letters aren't doubled for single sounds: to find alley use **L** not **LL**. Use **Y** and **W** as hard sounds only: to find yellow use **YL**. (Br)=British spelling or usage. * See dictionary.

RSHSNDR ratiocinator *reasoner*

RSHSNSHN ratiocination *reason*

RSHSNT ratiocinate *reason* ratiocinated ratiocinating

RSHSNTR ratiocinator *reasoner*

RSHSR régisseur (or) regisseur *director*

RSHSTR Irish setter *dog*

RSHT earshot *hearing range*

RSHT orgeat *syrup*

RSHT wrist shot *hit*

RSHTRR Irish terrier *dog*

RSHTRYR Irish terrier *dog*

RSHWMN Irishwoman *of Ireland* Irishwomen

RSHWR rush hour (n) *peak time* rush-hour (adj)

RSHY ratio *proportion* ratios

RSHYL urushiol *irritant*

RSHYSNDR ratiocinator *reasoner*

RSHYSNSHN ratiocination *reason*

RSHYSNT ratiocinate *reason* ratiocinated ratiocinating

RSHYSNTR ratiocinator *reasoner*

RSK air sac *lungs*

RSK airsick *nauseous*

RSK rescue *save* rescued rescuing

RSK risk *danger*

RSK risky *dangerous* riskier riskiest

RSK risque *sexy*

RSK rusk *bread*

RSKBL rescuable *save*

RSKDBL resectable *removal*

RSKDBLD resectability *removal*

RSKDBLT resectability *removal*

RSKDJL reschedule *plan* rescheduled rescheduling

RSKDJWL reschedule *plan* rescheduled rescheduling

RSKJL reschedule *plan* rescheduled rescheduling

RSKJWL reschedule *plan* rescheduled rescheduling

RSKL rascal (n) *rogue*

RSKL rascal (adj) *dishonest* rascally (adv)

RSKL recycle *use again* recycled recycling

RSKL rescale *adjust again* rescaled rescaling

RSKLB recyclable *use again*

RSKLD rascality *mischief* rascalities

RSKLD recycled *used again*

RSKLR recycler *use again*

RSKLT rascality *mischief* rascalities

RSKNS airsickness *nausea*

RSKR airscrew (Br) *propeller*

RSKR rescuer *savior*

RSKR riskier *dangerous*

RSKRS racecourse *track*

RSKRSHN Rosicrucian *religion*

RSKSHN resection *removal*

RSKST riskiest *dangerous*

RSKT resect *remove*

RSKTBL resectable *removal*

RSKTBLD resectability *removal*

RSKTBLT resectability *removal*

RSKWBL rescuable *save*

RSKWR rescuer *savior*

RSKY rescue *save* rescued rescuing

RSKYBL rescuable *save*

RSKYR rescuer *savior*

RSKYR riskier *dangerous*

RSKYST riskiest *dangerous*

RSKYWBL rescuable *save*

RSKYWR rescuer *savior*

RSL aerosol *mist*

RSL racily *indecent, sporty*

RSL resale *for selling again*

RSL reseal *close tightly*

RSL resell *market again* resold reselling

RSL resole *shoe* resoled resoling

RSL rustle *sound, steal* rustled rustling

RSL uracil *genes*

RSL wrestle *grapple* wrestled wrestling

RSLBL irresoluble (adj) *cannot solve* irresolubly (adv)

RSLBL resalable *fit for sale*

RSLBL resealable *close tightly*

RSLBL resoluble (adj) *break up, decide* resolubly (adv)

RSLF ourself *myself* ourselves

RSLK wristlock *wrestling*

RSLN wrestling *grappling*

RSLNG Riesling *grape, wine*

RSLNG wrestling *grappling*

RSLR rustler *thief*

RSLR wrestler *grappler*

RSLS restless *fidgety*

RSLSHN resolution *courage, document*

RSLSL restlessly *fidgety*

RSLSNS restlessness *fidgety*

RSLT irresolute *uncertain*

RSLT resolute *firm*

RSLT wristlet *bracelet*

RSLVZ ourselves *us* ourself

RSLYBL resoluble (adj) *break up, decide* resolubly (adv)

RSLZ aerosolize *disperse as mist* aerosolized aerosolizing

RSM raceme *flower*

RSMBL reassemble (v) *gather, construct*

RSMBL reassembly (n) *construction*

RSMBLJ reassemblage *gathering*

RSMK racemic *mixture*

RSMZ racemize *mix*

RSMZSHN racemization *mix*

RSN arsine *poisonous gas*

RSN arson *fire*

RSN racing *sport*

RSN reassign *appoint*

RSN resend *transmit again*

Use letters that best describe the sounds you hear and omit the vowels. Use **S** or **K** instead of **C**: to find circle use **SRKL**. Use **J** to find joy, **JM** to find gem and **G** to find go.

resent resending
RSN ursine *of bears*
RSNC recency *up-to-date*
RSNCHN recension *text*
RSND rescind *revoke*
RSND resend *transmit again*
resent resending
RSNDMNT rescindment
repeal, void
RSNDR rescinder *revoker*
RSNDRM Reye's syndrome
disease
RSNG racing *sport*
RSNK arsenic *poison*
RSNL arsenal *weapons*
RSNMNT reassignment
appointment
RSNMNT rescindment
repeal, void
RSNS arsonous *fire*
RSNS raciness *indecent,*
sporty
RSNS recency *up-to-date*
RSNSHN recension *text*
RSNST arsonist *fire*
RSNT arsenate *arsenic*
RSNT recent *of late*
RSNTC recency *up-to-date*
RSNTL recently *of late*
RSNTS recency *up-to-date*
RSP rasp *grate*
RSP raspy *grating*
RSP recipe *formula*
RSPD airspeed *velocity*
RSPDKL receptacle
container
RSPDR receptor *receiver*
RSPDV receptive *open*
RSPDVL receptively *open*
RSPDVNS receptiveness
openness
RSPK respect *regard*
RSPKDBL respectable (adj)
proper respectably (adv)
RSPKDBLD respectability
proper
RSPKDBLT respectability
proper
RSPKDD respected
esteemed
RSPKDR respecter *regard*
RSPKDV irrespective

regardless
RSPKDV respective
particular
RSPKFL respectful (adj)
regard respectfully (adv)
RSPKFLNS respectfulness
regard
RSPKT respect *regard*
RSPKTBL respectable (adj)
proper respectably (adv)
RSPKTBLD respectability
proper
RSPKTBLT respectability
proper
RSPKTD respected *esteemed*
RSPKTFL respectful (adj)
regard respectfully (adv)
RSPKTFLNS respectfulness
regard
RSPKTR respecter *regard*
RSPKTV irrespective
regardless
RSPKTV respective
particular
RSPL respell *phonetics*
RSPL resupply *provide*
resupplied resupplying
resupplies
RSPLDNG earsplitting *loud*
RSPLNDNS resplendence
brilliance
RSPLNDNT resplendent
brilliant
RSPLNDNTS resplendence
brilliance
RSPLNG respelling
phonetics
RSPLTN earsplitting *loud*
RSPLTNG earsplitting *loud*
RSPN respond *answer*
RSPN wrist pin *stud*
RSPND respond *answer*
RSPNDNT respondent
answer
RSPNDR responder
answerer
RSPNGL raspingly *gratingly*
RSPNL raspingly *gratingly*
RSPNS recipience *receive*
RSPNS response *answer*
RSPNSBL irresponsible
(adj) *not liable*

irresponsibly (adv)
RSPNSBL responsible (adj)
caring responsibly (adv)
RSPNSBLD irresponsibility
not liable
RSPNSBLD responsibility
caring responsibilities
RSPNSBLNS
irresponsibleness *not*
liable
RSPNSBLT irresponsibility
not liable
RSPNSBLT responsibility
caring responsibilities
RSPNSV responsive *answer*
RSPNSVL responsively
answer
RSPNSVNS responsiveness
answer
RSPNT recipient *receiver*
RSPNTS recipience *receive*
RSPNTS response *answer*
RSPNTSBL irresponsible
(adj) *not liable*
irresponsibly (adv)
RSPNTSBL responsible
(adj) *caring* responsibly
(adv)
RSPNTSBLD
irresponsibility *not liable*
RSPNTSBLD responsibility
caring responsibilities
RSPNTSBLNS
irresponsibleness *not*
liable
RSPNTSBLT irresponsibility
not liable
RSPNTSBLT responsibility
caring responsibilities
RSPNTSV responsive
answer
RSPNTSVL responsively
answer
RSPNTSVNS
responsiveness *answer*
RSPR rasper *grater*
RSPR respire *breathe*
respired respiring
RSPRBL respirable *breath*
RSPRDR respirator *breath*
RSPRF rustproof *no rust*
RSPRKDR reciprocator

return in kind
RSPRKL reciprocal (adj) *opposite* reciprocally (adv)
RSPRKSHN reciprocation *return in kind*
RSPRKT reciprocate *return in kind* reciprocated reciprocating
RSPRKTR reciprocator *return in kind*
RSPRMDR respirometer *breathing*
RSPRMTR respirometer *breathing*
RSPRSD reciprocity *return in kind* reciprocities
RSPRSHN respiration *breath*
RSPRST reciprocity *return in kind* reciprocities
RSPRTR respirator *breath*
RSPRTR respiratory *breathing*
RSPS aerospace *atmospheric*
RSPS airspace *boundary*
RSPSHN reception *receive, welcome*
RSPSHNST receptionist *receive, welcome*
RSPT respite *short rest*
RSPTKL receptacle *container*
RSPTR receptor *receiver*
RSPTV receptive *open*
RSPTVD receptivity *openness*
RSPTVL receptively *open*
RSPTVNS receptiveness *openness*
RSPTVT receptivity *openness*
RSPYNS recipience *receive*
RSPYNT recipient *receiver*
RSPYNTS recipience *receive*
RSPYR respire *breathe* respired respiring
RSQ rescue *save* rescued rescuing
RSQBL rescuable *save*
RSQR rescuer *savior*
RSQWBL rescuable *save*
RSQWR rescuer *savior*
RSR eraser *rub-out device*

RSR racer *runner, snake*
RSR racier *indecent, sporty*
RSR ricer *utensil*
RSRCH research *inquiry*
RSRCHBL researchable *inquiry*
RSRCHR researcher *inquirer*
RSRCHST researchist *inquirer*
RSRDF recertify *confirm* recertified recertifying recertifies
RSRFS resurface *appear* resurfaced resurfacing
RSRFSR resurfacer *appear*
RSRJ resurge *rise* resurged resurging
RSRJNS resurgence *rise*
RSRJNT resurgent *rising*
RSRJNTS resurgence *rise*
RSRKLT recirculate *flow* recirculated recirculating
RSRKYLT recirculate *flow* recirculated recirculating
RSRM rest room *toilet*
RSRQLT recirculate *flow* recirculated recirculating
RSRS racehorse *animal*
RSRS resource *supply*
RSRSFL resourceful (adj) *capable* resourcefully (adv)
RSRSFLNS resourcefulness *capability*
RSRT orrisroot *plant*
RSRTF recertify *confirm* recertified recertifying recertifies
RSS arsis *verse* arses
RSS reassess *weigh*
RSS recess *alcove, break* recesses
RSS rhesus *monkey*
RSSDBL irresistible (adj) *cannot refrain* irresistibly (adv)
RSSDBLD irresistibility *cannot refrain*
RSSDBLT irresistibility *cannot refrain*
RSSHN recession *withdrawal*

RSSHN recision *cancellation*
RSSHN rescission *repeal, void*
RSSHNL recessional *hymn*
RSSHT wrist shot *hit*
RSSMNT reassessment *weighing*
RSST raciest *indecent, sporty*
RSST racist *prejudice*
RSSTBL irresistible (adj) *cannot refrain* irresistibly (adv)
RSSTBLD irresistibility *cannot refrain*
RSSTBLT irresistibility *cannot refrain*
RSSTDR resuscitator *breathing*
RSSTSHN resuscitation *revival*
RSSTT resuscitate *revive* resuscitated resuscitating
RSSTTR resuscitator *breathing*
RSSV recessive *withdrawn, gene*
RSSVL recessively *withdrawn, gene*
RSSVNS recessiveness *withdrawn, gene*
RST aeriest *heavenly*
RST airiest *lofty, proud, windy*
RST aorist *verb*
RST arista *bristle* aristae (or) aristas
RST arrest *stop*
RST arrestee *person stopped*
RST eeriest *weirdest*
RST rawest *uncooked, vulgar*
RST receipt *received, payment token*
RST recite *speak* recited reciting
RST reset *set again* reset resetting
RST rest (v) *relax* (n) *remainder, repose, silence*
RST risotto *food* risottos
RST roast *heat*
RST roost *perch*

Use letters that best describe the sounds you hear and omit the vowels. Use **S** or **K** instead of **C**: to find circle use **SRKL**. Use **J** to find joy, **JM** to find gem and **G** to find go.

RST roust *action*
RST russet *color*
RST rust *(v)* corrode *(n)* corrosion
RST rusty *corroded, slow* rustier rustiest
RST wrest *pull*
RST wrist *joint*
RSTBLSH reestablish *create again*
RSTBN wristband *strap*
RSTBND wristband *strap*
RSTBT roustabout *worker*
RSTD oersted *magnetism*
RSTDKS aerostatics *equilibrium*
RSTDL Aristotle *philosopher*
RSTDLN Aristotelian *of Aristotle*
RSTDLYN Aristotelian *of Aristotle*
RSTDV recitative *speech*
RSTDX aerostatics *equilibrium*
RSTFL restful (adj) *relaxing* restfully (adv)
RSTFLNS restfulness *relaxation*
RSTFNS Aristophanes *dramatist*
RSTFNZ Aristophanes *dramatist*
RSTFRN Rastafarian *religion*
RSTFRYN Rastafarian *religion*
RSTHWL erstwhile *former*
RSTK aoristic *verb*
RSTK eristic *argumentative*
RSTK restock *replace goods*
RSTK rustic *rural*
RSTKDR rusticator *live in the country*
RSTKL aoristically *verb*
RSTKL eristically *argumentative*
RSTKL rustically *rural*
RSTKRC aristocracy *upper class* aristocracies
RSTKRDK aristocratic *elite*
RSTKRS aristocracy *upper class* aristocracies

RSTKRT aristocrat *nobleman*
RSTKRTK aristocratic *elite*
RSTKSHN rustication *live in the country*
RSTKT rusticate *live in the country* rusticated rusticating
RSTKTR rusticator *live in the country*
RSTL recital *exhibition*
RSTL resettle *colonize, clear, resolve** resettled resettlling
RSTL rustily *corroded, slow, surly*
RSTL urostyle *bone*
RSTLK wristlock *wrestling*
RSTLM rostellum *beak*
RSTLMNT resettlement *colony*
RSTLS restless *fidgety*
RSTLSL restlessly *fidgety*
RSTLSNS restlessness *fidgety*
RSTLT wristlet *bracelet*
RSTN arresting *impressive*
RSTN resting *inactive*
RSTNG arresting *impressive*
RSTNG resting *inactive*
RSTNS rustiness *corroded, slow, surly*
RSTPN wrist pin *stud*
RSTPRF rustproof *no rust*
RSTR arrester (or) arrestor *stopper*
RSTR rester *relaxer*
RSTR restore *renew* restored restoring
RSTR roaster *cooker*
RSTR roister *carouse*
RSTR rooster *fowl*
RSTR roster *list of names*
RSTR rouster *worker*
RSTR rustier *corroded, slow, surly*
RSTRBL restorable *renewable*
RSTRCHR restructure *remake* restructured restructuring
RSTRDV restorative *renewal*
RSTRK air strike *military*

action
RSTRK racetrack *arena*
RSTRK restrict *limit*
RSTRKCHR restructure *remake* restructured restructuring
RSTRKDD restricted *limited*
RSTRKDV restrictive *limiting*
RSTRKSHN restriction *limitation*
RSTRKSHR restructure *remake* restructured restructuring
RSTRKT restrict *limit*
RSTRKTD restricted *limited*
RSTRKTR restructure *remake* restructured restructuring
RSTRKTV restrictive *limiting*
RSTRL rostral *snout, stage*
RSTRM airstream *airflow*
RSTRM rest room *toilet*
RSTRM rostrum *stage* rostra (or) rostrums
RSTRN restrain *hold back*
RSTRND restrained *held back*
RSTRNT restaurant *eatery*
RSTRNT restraint *control*
RSTRNTR restaurateur *proprietor*
RSTRNTYR restaurateur *proprietor*
RSTRP airstrip *airport*
RSTRR roisterer *carouser*
RSTRS roisterous *carousing*
RSTRSHN restoration *renewal*
RSTRSL roisterously *carousing*
RSTRT restart *begin again*
RSTRTV restorative *renewal*
RSTS ersatz *substitute*
RSTSD rusticity *simplicity*
RSTSHN recitation *read, repeat*
RSTSHT wrist shot *hit*
RSTST rusticity *simplicity*
RSTST rustiest *corroded, slow, surly*

Letters aren't doubled for single sounds: to find alley use **L** not **LL**. Use **Y** and **W** as hard sounds only: to find yellow use **YL**. (Br)=British spelling or usage. * See dictionary.

RSTT aerostat *aircraft*

RSTT restate *echo* restated restating

RSTT rheostat *current*

RSTTKS aerostatics *equilibrium*

RSTTL Aristotle *philosopher*

RSTTLN Aristotelian *of Aristotle*

RSTTLYN Aristotelian *of Aristotle*

RSTTMNT restatement *echo*

RSTTSHN restitution *pay back*

RSTTV recitative *speech*

RSTTX aerostatics *equilibrium*

RSTTYSHN restitution *pay back*

RSTV restive *contrary*

RSTWCH wristwatch *timepiece*

RSTWL erstwhile *former*

RSTYR rustier *corroded, slow, surly*

RSTYST rustiest *corroded, slow, surly*

RSV erosive *worn away*

RSV receive *get, greet* received receiving

RSVBL receivable *debt*

RSVLT Roosevelt *US president*

RSVR receiver *get, greet*

RSVRSHP receivership *debt*

RSVZ ourselves *us* ourself

RSW raceway *track*

RSWCH wristwatch *timepiece*

RSWL Roswell *city*

RSY reissue *put out again* reissued reissuing

RSYR racier *indecent, sporty*

RSYST raciest *indecent, sporty*

RSZ arses (pl) *verse* arsis

RSZHN recision *cancellation*

RSZHN rescission *repeal, void*

RSZM racism *prejudice*

RT aerate *add oxygen* aerated aerating

RT air right *property*

RT aorta *blood vessel* aortas (or) aortae

RT arête *ridge*

RT arietta *song*

RT aright *correctly*

RT art *skill, craft*

RT arty *artistic* artier artiest

RT Erato *Greek Muse*

RT errata (pl) *list* erratum

RT irate *angry*

RT ort *scrap*

RT rat *(v) betray, hunt* rats ratted ratting

RT rat *(n) animal*

RT rate *rank, value* rated rating

RT ratty *tangled, shabby, irritable* rattier rattiest

RT ret *soak* retted retting

RT rete *plexus* retia

RT retia (pl) *plexus* rete

RT retie *knot again* retied retying (or) retieing

RT riata *lariat*

RT right *(adj) correct, side (n) entitlement, side (adv) straight, truth (v) avenge, justify**

RT righty *right-handed* righties

RT rillettes *meat*

RT riot *disturbance*

RT rite *religion*

RT root *(n) plant part, basis (v) cheer, plant*

RT rooty *soil*

RT rot *decay* rotted rotting rotten

RT rote *mechanical memory*

RT roti *bread*

RT rout *uncover, defeat, (Br) bellow**

RT route *line of travel* routed routing

RT ruddy *reddish* ruddier ruddiest

RT rut *groove, sex* rutted rutting

RT rutty *grooved* ruttier ruttiest

RT urate *urine*

RT wright *craftsman*

RT writ *court order*

RT write *inscribe* wrote writing written

RT wrote *(v-past) write*

RT wrought *created, excited*

RTBG ratbag *(Aus) freaky*

RTBG rutabaga *vegetable*

RTBGR rutabaga *vegetable*

RTBL irritable (adj) *grouchy* irritably (adv)

RTBL ratable (or) rateable (adj) *rank* ratably (adv)

RTBL retable *altar*

RTBL writable *inscribe*

RTBLD irritability *grouchy* irritabilities

RTBLD roadability *driving*

RTBLNS irritableness *grouchy*

RTBLT irritability *grouchy* irritabilities

RTBLT roadability *driving*

RTBR root beer *beverage*

RTC artsy *artistic*

RTC ROTC (abbr) *Reserve Officers Training Corps*

RTCH reattach *connect*

RTCH retouch *improve*

RTCHK artichoke *vegetable*

RTCHMNT reattachment *connection*

RTCHR retoucher *improver*

RTD red tide *algae*

RTDBL rotatable *turning*

RTDD irritated *inflamed*

RTDK art deco *1920s and 1930s style*

RTDM rhytidome *bark*

RTDN write down *(v) record* write-down (n)

RTDN write-down *(n) reduction*

RTDNS rootedness *planted*

RTDR rotator *muscle* rotators (or) rotatores

RTDV irritative *annoying*

RTDV rotative *spin*

RTF ratafia *liqueur*

RTF ratify *approve* ratified ratifying ratifies

RTF write off *(v) reduce,*

Use letters that best describe the sounds you hear and omit the vowels. Use **S** or **K** instead of **C**: to find circle use **SRKL**. Use **J** to find joy, **JM** to find gem and **G** to find go.

dismiss
RTF write-off *(n) reduction*
RTFK artifact *object*
(Br) *artefact*
RTFKSHN ratification
approval
RTFKT artifact *object*
(Br) *artefact*
RTFL artful (adj) *sly* artfully
(adv)
RTFLNS artfulness *slyness*
RTFNGK rat fink *(slang)*
informer
RTFNK rat fink *(slang)*
informer
RTFR ratifier *approver*
RTFR rotifer *animal*
RTFS artifice *trick*
RTFSH ratfish *fish*
RTFSHL artificial (adj)
imitation artificially (adv)
RTFSHLD artificiality
imitation
RTFSHLT artificiality
imitation
RTFSHYLD artificiality
imitation
RTFSHYLT artificiality
imitation
RTFSR artificer *tricker*
RTFY ratafia *liqueur*
RTFYR ratifier *approver*
RTG retag *price again*
retagged retagging
RTGNK erotogenic *sex*
RTGRVR rotogravure
pictures
RTGRVYR rotogravure
pictures
RTGT rotgut *liquor*
RTH earth *(often capitalized)*
planet, soil
RTH earthy *natural* earthier
earthiest
RTH ruth *sorrow*
RTH wraith *ghost* wraiths
RTH wrath *anger*
RTH wreath *flowers*
RTH wreathe *decorate*
wreathed wreathing
RTH writhe *squirm* writhed
writhing

RTHBN earthbound
unimaginative
RTHBND earthbound
unimaginative
RTHBRN earthborn *mortal*
RTHDK orthotic *support*
RTHDKC orthodoxy *belief*
orthodoxies
RTHDKS orthodox
conventional
RTHDKS orthodoxy *belief*
orthodoxies
RTHDNCH orthodontia *teeth*
RTHDNK orthodontic (adj)
teeth orthodontically (adv)
RTHDNKS orthodontics
teeth
RTHDNSH orthodontia *teeth*
RTHDNST orthodontist *teeth*
RTHDNTK orthodontic (adj)
teeth orthodontically (adv)
RTHDNTKS orthodontics
teeth
RTHDNTSH orthodontia
teeth
RTHDNTST orthodontist
teeth
RTHDX orthodox
conventional
RTHDX orthodoxy *belief*
orthodoxies
RTHFL ruthful (adj) *sorry*
ruthfully (adv)
RTHFL wrathful (adj) *angry*
wrathfully (adv)
RTHFLNS ruthfulness
sorrow
RTHFLNS wrathfulness
anger
RTHGNL orthogonal (adj)
angles orthogonally (adv)
RTHGNSS orthogenesis
variation
RTHGRF orthography
spelling
RTHGRFK orthographic
spelling
RTHGRFKL
orthographically *spelling*
RTHJNDK orthogenetic
variation
RTHJNDKL

orthogenetically *variation*
RTHJNSS orthogenesis
variation
RTHJNTK orthogenetic
variation
RTHJNTKL orthogenetically
variation
RTHKN orthicon *camera*
RTHKWK earthquake
upheaval
RTHL earthily *natural*
RTHL earthly *world, possible*
RTHL roothold *grip*
RTHLD roothold *grip*
RTHLK wraithlike *ghostly*
RTHLNG earthling *of the
earth*
RTHLNS earthliness
ordinary
RTHLS ruthless *cruel*
RTHLSL ruthlessly *cruel*
RTHLSNS ruthlessness
cruelty
RTHLT earthlight *reflection*
RTHM arrhythmia *heart
condition*
RTHM erythema *redness*
RTHM eurythmy (or)
eurhythmy *dance*
RTHM rhythm *beat, meter,
pattern*
RTHMDK arithmetic (or)
arithmetical (adj) *by
number* arithmetically
(adv)
RTHMDKL arithmetical (or)
arithmetic (adj) *by number*
arithmetically (adv)
RTHMDS erythematous
redness
RTHMK arrhythmic *irregular
beat*
RTHMK rhythmic (or)
rhythmical (adj) *beat,
meter, pattern* rhythmically
(adv)
RTHMKL rhythmical (or)
rhythmic (adj) *beat, meter,
pattern* rhythmically (adv)
RTHMKS eurythmics (or)
eurhythmics *dance*
RTHMLKLR orthomolecular

mental illness

RTHMLKYLR orthomolecular *mental illness*

RTHMLQLR orthomolecular *mental illness*

RTHMSD rhythmicity *beat, meter, pattern*

RTHMST rhythmicity *beat, meter, pattern*

RTHMST rhythmist *beat, meter, pattern*

RTHMTHR earth mother *nurturer*

RTHMTK arithmetic *(n) mathematics*

RTHMTK arithmetic (or) arithmetical (adj) *by number* arithmetically (adv)

RTHMTKL arithmetical (or) arithmetic (adj) *by number* arithmetically (adv)

RTHMTS erythematous *redness*

RTHMTSHN arithmetician *calculator*

RTHMVN earthmoving *machine*

RTHMVNG earthmoving *machine*

RTHMVR earthmover *machine*

RTHMX eurythmics (or) eurhythmics *dance*

RTHMY arrhythmia *heart condition*

RTHN earthen *clay*

RTHN right-hand *side*

RTHN urethane (or) urethan *plastic*

RTHND right-hand *side*

RTHNDD right-handed *side*

RTHNDR right-hander *side*

RTHNGK rethink *consider again* rethought rethinking

RTHNK rethink *consider again* rethought rethinking

RTHNM ruthenium *element*

RTHNS earthiness

naturalness

RTHNWR earthenware *pottery*

RTHNYM ruthenium *element*

RTHPD arthropod *animal*

RTHPDK orthopedic *skeleton*

RTHPDKL orthopedically *skeleton*

RTHPDKS orthopedics *skeleton*

RTHPDR orthoptera *insect*

RTHPDRD orthopteroid *insect*

RTHPDRN orthopteran *insect*

RTHPDRST orthopterist *insect*

RTHPDST orthopedist *skeleton*

RTHPDX orthopedics *skeleton*

RTHPTK orthopedic *skeleton*

RTHPTKL orthopedically *skeleton*

RTHPTKS orthopedics *skeleton*

RTHPTR orthoptera *insect*

RTHPTRD orthopteroid *insect*

RTHPTRN orthopteran *insect*

RTHPTRST orthopterist *insect*

RTHPTST orthopedist *skeleton*

RTHPTX orthopedics *skeleton*

RTHQK earthquake *upheaval*

RTHR earthier *natural*

RTHR rather *instead of*

RTHR urethra *canal* urethras (or) urethrae

RTHRBLST erythroblast *red blood cell*

RTHRBLSTSS erythroblastosis *Rh disease* erythroblastoses

RTHRCZ arthroses (pl) *joint disease* arthrosis

RTHRD erythroid *red blood cell*

RTHRD rethread *needle*

RTHRDK arthritic *joint swelling*

RTHRDKL arthritically *joint swelling*

RTHRDS arthritis *joint swelling* arthritides

RTHRDS urethritis *illness*

RTHRL urethral *canal*

RTHRMSN erythromycin *antibiotic*

RTHRPD arthropod *animal*

RTHRSDK erythrocytic *red blood cell*

RTHRSKP arthroscope *surgery*

RTHRSKP arthroscopy *surgery*

RTHRSKP urethroscope *viewer*

RTHRSKPK arthroscopic *surgery*

RTHRSS arthrosis *joint disease* arthroses

RTHRST erythrocyte *red blood cell*

RTHRSTK erythrocytic *red blood cell*

RTHRSZ arthroses (pl) *joint disease* arthrosis

RTHRTDZ arthritides (pl) *joint swelling* arthritis

RTHRTK arthritic *joint swelling*

RTHRTKL arthritically *joint swelling*

RTHRTS arthritis *joint swelling* arthritides

RTHRTS urethritis *illness*

RTHRZM erythrism *redness*

RTHSHDRN earth-shattering *important*

RTHSHDRNG earth-shattering *important*

RTHSHKN earthshaking *important*

RTHSHKNG earthshaking *important*

RTHSHN earthshine *reflection*

RTHSHTRN earth-shattering *important*

Use letters that best describe the sounds you hear and omit the vowels. Use **S** or **K** instead of **C**: to find circle use **SRKL**. Use **J** to find joy, **JM** to find gem and **G** to find go.

RTHSHTRNG earth-
  shattering *important*
RTHSKLR rathskeller *tavern*
RTHSKP arthroscope
  surgery
RTHSKP arthroscopy
  surgery
RTHSKPK arthroscopic
  surgery
RTHSKPK orthoscopic
  image
RTHSKTR orthopsychiatry
  youth
RTHSKTRK
  orthopsychiatric *youth*
RTHSKTRST
  orthopsychiatrist *youth*
RTHSKYTR orthopsychiatry
  youth
RTHSKYTRK
  orthopsychiatric *youth*
RTHSKYTRST
  orthopsychiatrist *youth*
RTHSNR orthocenter
  intersection
RTHSNTR orthocenter
  intersection
RTHST earthiest *natural*
RTHSTR earthstar *fungus*
RTHSTSHN earth station
  transmitter
RTHT rethought *considered*
RTHTK orthotic *support*
RTHTN earth tone *color*
RTHWRD earthward
  direction
RTHWRK earthwork
  embankment
RTHWRM earthworm
  animal
RTHYR earthier *natural*
RTHYST earthiest *natural*
RTJNK erotogenic *sex*
RTK arctic *(often capitalized)*
  ocean, region
RTK erotic *sexy*
RTK erotica *sexy art*
RTK erratic *irregular*
RTK iridic *iris*
RTK retake *recapture* retook
  retaking retaken
RTK uratic *urine*

RTKL article *thing*
RTKL erotically *sexy*
RTKL erratical (adj) *irregular*
  erratically (adv)
RTKL reticule *bag*
RTKL ridicule *mock* ridiculed
  ridiculing
RTKLD Oort cloud *comets*
RTKLDD articulated *hinged*
RTKLDR articulator
  pronunciation, jointed
RTKLM reticulum *stomach*
RTKLR articular *joint*
RTKLR reticular *network*
RTKLR ridiculer *mocker*
RTKLSHN articulation
  pronunciation, jointed
RTKLSHN reticulation
  network
RTKLST reticulocyte *blood*
RTKLT articulate *pronounce,*
  jointed articulated
  articulating
RTKLT reticulate *network*
  reticulated reticulating
RTKLTD articulated *hinged*
RTKLTL articulately
  pronunciation, jointed
RTKLTNS articulateness
  pronunciation, jointed
RTKLTR articulator
  pronunciation, jointed
RTKLTR articulatory
  pronunciation, jointed
RTKR urticaria *itching*
RTKRL urticarial *itching*
RTKRY urticaria *itching*
RTKRYL urticarial *itching*
RTKS urtext *original*
RTKSHN Arctic Ocean *body*
  of water
RTKST urtext *original*
RTKT urticate *itch* urticated
  urticating
RTKYL reticule *bag*
RTKYL ridicule *mock*
  ridiculed ridiculing
RTKYLDD articulated
  hinged
RTKYLDR articulator
  pronunciation, jointed
RTKYLM reticulum *stomach*

RTKYLR articular *joint*
RTKYLR reticular *network*
RTKYLR ridiculer *mocker*
RTKYLSHN articulation
  pronunciation, jointed
RTKYLSHN reticulation
  network
RTKYLST reticulocyte *blood*
RTKYLT articulate
  pronounce, jointed
  articulated articulating
RTKYLT reticulate *network*
  reticulated reticulating
RTKYLTD articulated *hinged*
RTKYLTL articulately
  pronunciation, jointed
RTKYLTNS articulateness
  pronunciation, jointed
RTKYLTR articulator
  pronunciation, jointed
RTKYLTR articulatory
  pronunciation, jointed
RTL artily *artistic*
RTL irately *angry*
RTL raddle *(v) weave, paint*
  raddled raddling
RTL raddle *(n) pigment*
RTL rat-tail *file*
RTL ratel *weasel*
RTL rattail *horse*
RTL rattle *(v) shake, noise*
  rattled rattling
RTL rattle *(n) toy, noise*
RTL rattly *noisy*
RTL red-tailed *feathers*
RTL retail *sell*
RTL retell *speak again* retold
  retelling
RTL retool *equip*
RTL riddle *question, permeate*
  riddled riddling
RTL rightly *correctly*
RTL ritual *ceremony*
RTL ruddily *reddish*
RTL ruddle *redden* ruddled
  ruddling
RTL rutile *mineral*
RTLBRN rattlebrain
  thoughtless one
RTLBRND rattlebrained
  thoughtless
RTLD raddled *confused,*

worn
RTLD red-tailed *feathers*
RTLD roothold *grip*
RTLDV retaliative *revenge*
RTLF right-to-life (adj) *no abortion*
RTLFR right-to-lifer (n) *no abortion*
RTLN ortolan *bird*
RTLN ratline *rope*
RTLN rattling *(adj) lively (adv) very*
RTLN retailing *selling*
RTLN Ritalin *(trademark) drug*
RTLNG rattling *(adj) lively (adv) very*
RTLNG retailing *selling*
RTLNT rutilant *red glow*
RTLR artillery *weapons artilleries*
RTLR rattler *snake, toy*
RTLR retailer *seller*
RTLRMN artilleryman *weapons artillerymen*
RTLRST artillerist *weapons*
RTLS artless *natural*
RTLS artless *without beauty*
RTLS rootless *no roots*
RTLSDK ritualistic *ceremony*
RTLSDKL ritualistically *ceremony*
RTLSHN retaliation *revenge*
RTLSL artlessly *naturally*
RTLSNK rattlesnake *reptile*
RTLSNS artlessness *naturalness*
RTLSTK ritualistic *ceremony*
RTLSTKL ritualistically *ceremony*
RTLT retaliate *repay* retaliated retaliating
RTLT rootlet *root*
RTLTR retaliatory *revenge*
RTLTRP rattletrap *old car*
RTLTV retaliative *revenge*
RTLYDV retaliative *revenge*
RTLYSHN retaliation *revenge*
RTLYT retaliate *repay* retaliated retaliating
RTLYTR retaliatory *revenge*
RTLYTV retaliative *revenge*

RTLZ reutilize *use again* reutilized reutilizing (Br) reutilise
RTLZ ritualize *ceremony* ritualized ritualizing
RTLZM ritualism *ceremony*
RTM airtime *broadcast*
RTM erratum *error* errata
RTMDR ratemeter *counter*
RTMN rhodamine *dye*
RTMNDD right-minded *truth*
RTMP reattempt *try*
RTMPT reattempt *try*
RTMT reattempt *try*
RTMTR ratemeter *counter*
RTN ratiné (or) ratine *fabric*
RTN rating *rank*
RTN ratoon *root*
RTN rattan *wicker*
RTN ratton *rat*
RTN retain *keep*
RTN retina *eye* retinas (or) retinae
RTN retinue *attendants*
RTN rhatany *plant*
RTN ridden *travelled*
RTN right on (or) right-on *agreement*
RTN right-hand *side*
RTN rotten *decayed*
RTN rotund *round*
RTN routine *(n) pattern (adj) ordinary*
RTN write in (v) *ballot* write-in (n, adj)
RTN writing *lettering, record*
RTN written *inscribed*
RTND orotund *pompous*
RTND retinoid *vitamin A*
RTND right-hand *side*
RTND rotund *round*
RTND rotunda *room*
RTNDD orotundity *pompous*
RTNDD right-handed *side*
RTNDL rotundly *round*
RTNDNS rotundness *round*
RTNDR right-hander *side*
RTNDS retinitis *eye*
RTNDT orotundity *pompous*
RTNG rating *rank*
RTNG writing *lettering,*

record
RTNGGLD right-angled (or) right-angle (adj) 90 *degrees* right angle (n)
RTNGL right-angle (or) right-angled (adj) 90 *degrees* right angle (n)
RTNGLD right-angled (or) right-angle (adj) 90 *degrees* right angle (n)
RTNL retinal *eye*
RTNL retinol *vitamin A*
RTNL retinula *eye* retinulae
RTNL rottenly *decay*
RTNPTH retinopathy *blindness*
RTNR retainer *servant, fee*
RTNS artiness *artistic*
RTNS irateness *angry*
RTNS riddance *loss*
RTNS rightness *correctness*
RTNS rottenness *decay*
RTNS rotundness *round*
RTNS ruddiness *redness*
RTNSHN retention *holding back*
RTNSKP retinoscopy *eye test*
RTNSTN rottenstone *polish*
RTNT irritant *annoyance*
RTNTS retinitis *eye*
RTNTS riddance *loss*
RTNTV retentive *holding back*
RTNTVD retentivity *magnetism*
RTNTVL retentively *holding*
RTNTVNS retentiveness *holding*
RTNTVT retentivity *magnetism*
RTNV art nouveau *late 19th century style*
RTNV retentive *holding back*
RTNVL retentively *holding*
RTNVNS retentiveness *holding*
RTNY retinue *attendants*
RTNYL retinula *eye* retinulae
RTNZ routinize *make ordinary* routinized routinizing

Use letters that best describe the sounds you hear and omit the vowels. Use **S** or **K** instead of **C**: to find circle use **SRKL**. Use **J** to find joy, **JM** to find gem and **G** to find go.

RTP red tape *paperwork*
RTP redtop *grass*
RTP write up (v) *report* write-up (n)
RTPLN rataplan *beat*
RTPR ratepayer *consumer, (Br) taxpayer*
RTPYR ratepayer *consumer, (Br) taxpayer*
RTQL reticule *bag*
RTQL ridicule *mock* ridiculed ridiculing
RTQLDD articulated *hinged*
RTQLDR articulator *pronunciation, jointed*
RTQLM reticulum *stomach*
RTQLR articular *joint*
RTQLR reticular *network*
RTQLR ridiculer *mocker*
RTQLSHN articulation *pronunciation, jointed*
RTQLSHN reticulation *network*
RTQLST reticulocyte *blood*
RTQLT articulate *pronounce, jointed* articulated articulating
RTQLT reticulate *network* reticulated reticulating
RTQLTD articulated *hinged*
RTQLTL articulately *pronunciation, jointed*
RTQLTNS articulateness *pronunciation, jointed*
RTQLTR articulator *pronunciation, jointed*
RTQLTR articulatory *pronunciation, jointed*
RTR aerator *add oxygen*
RTR air-to-air *missile*
RTR artery *blood vessel* arteries
RTR artier *artistic*
RTR orator *speaker*
RTR oratorio *chorus* oratorios
RTR oratory *prayer* oratories
RTR rater *ranking*
RTR ratter *cat, dog*
RTR rattier *tangled, shabby, irritable*
RTR redder *color*

RTR retire *stop work, sleep* retired retiring
RTR retiree *former worker*
RTR retry *attempt again* retried retrying retries
RTR rioter *reveler*
RTR rooter *root, supporter*
RTR Rotary *club*
RTR rotary *wheel* rotaries
RTR rotor *blade*
RTR router *machine, horse*
RTR rudder *steering*
RTR ruddier *reddish*
RTR ruttier *grooved*
RTR ureter *duct*
RTR writer *inscriber*
RTRBDV retributive *payment*
RTRBSHN retribution *payment*
RTRBTV retributive *payment*
RTRBYDV retributive *payment*
RTRBYSHN retribution *payment*
RTRBYTV retributive *payment*
RTRCD retrocede *give back* retroceded retroceding
RTRD retard *slow*
RTRD retread *(n) tire (v) make new*
RTRDD retarded *slow*
RTRDK retrodict *infer*
RTRDKT retrodict *infer*
RTRDM Rotterdam *city*
RTRDND ritardando *tempo*
RTRDNT retardant *slow down*
RTRDSHN retardation *slowness*
RTRDT retardate *person*
RTRFLKS retroflex *bent*
RTRFLKSHN retroflexion (or) retroflection *bend*
RTRFLX retroflex *bent*
RTRFR retrofire *ignition* retrofired retrofiring
RTRFT retrofit *install parts*
RTRFYR retrofire *ignition* retrofired retrofiring
RTRGRD retrograde *backward*

RTRGRDSHN retrogradation *backward*
RTRGRM arteriogram *x-ray*
RTRGRS retrogress *revert*
RTRGRSHN retrogression *reversion*
RTRK retract *take back*
RTRK rhetoric *language*
RTRKDBL retractable *take back*
RTRKDL retractile *take back*
RTRKDR retractor *take back*
RTRKDV retroactive *prior time*
RTRKL oratorical (adj) *speech* oratorically (adv)
RTRKL rhetorical (adj) *language* rhetorically (adv)
RTRKRFT rotorcraft *vehicle* rotorcraft
RTRKSHN retraction *take back*
RTRKSHN retroaction *reaction*
RTRKT retract *take back*
RTRKTBL retractable *take back*
RTRKTL retractile *take back*
RTRKTR retractor *take back*
RTRKTV retroactive *prior time*
RTRL arterial (adj) *blood* arterially (adv)
RTRL arteriole *blood vessel*
RTRL retrial *law*
RTRLR arteriolar *blood*
RTRMNT retirement *no work*
RTRN retrain *teach*
RTRN return *(v, adj) give back, go back (n) recurrence, statement*
RTRN returnee *one going back*
RTRN Rotarian *club member*
RTRN wrought iron *metal*
RTRNBL retrainable *teach*
RTRNBL returnable *give back*
RTRNCH retrench *shorten*
RTRNZMT retransmit *send again* retransmitted retransmitting

Letters aren't doubled for single sounds: to find alley use **L** not **LL**. Use **Y** and **W** as hard sounds only: to find yellow use **YL**. (Br)=British spelling or usage. * See dictionary.

RTRP rattrap *snare, shack*
RTRRKT retro-rocket *spacecraft*
RTRS rat race *confusion, boring routine*
RTRS retrace *follow* retraced retracing
RTRS retroussé *turned up*
RTRSBL retraceable *follow*
RTRSD retrocede *give back* retroceded retroceding
RTRSHN reiteration *repeat*
RTRSHN rhetorician *language*
RTRSKLRSS arteriosclerosis *disease*
RTRSPK retrospect *review*
RTRSPKSHN retrospection *review*
RTRSPKT retrospect *review*
RTRSSHN retrocession *give back*
RTRT reiterate *repeat* reiterated reiterating
RTRT retort *answer*
RTRT retreat *(v)* go back *(n) refuge, withdrawal*
RTRV retrieve *regain, bring back* retrieved retrieving
RTRVBL irretrievable *(adj) gone* irretrievably *(adv)*
RTRVBL retrievable *regain*
RTRVBLD irretrievability *gone*
RTRVBLD retrievability *regain*
RTRVBLT irretrievability *gone*
RTRVBLT retrievability *regain*
RTRVL retrieval *regain*
RTRVR retriever *dog*
RTRVRS retrovirus *disease*
RTRVRSHN retroversion *bend*
RTRVRZHN retroversion *bend*
RTRWKDV retroactive *prior time*
RTRWKSHN retroaction *reaction*
RTRWKTV retroactive *prior*

time
RTRY oratorio *chorus* oratorios
RTRYGRM arteriogram *x-ray*
RTRYL arterial *(adj) blood* arterially *(adv)*
RTRYL arteriole *blood vessel*
RTRYL retrial *law*
RTRYLR arteriolar *blood*
RTRYN Rotarian *club member*
RTRYSKLRSS arteriosclerosis *disease*
RTRZ Reuters *news*
RTS artist *craftsman*
RTS artsy *artistic*
RTS iritis *eye*
RTS retuse *rounded*
RTS rillettes *meat*
RTS riotous *disorderly*
RTS ritzy *stylish* ritzier ritziest
RTS ROTC *(abbr) Reserve Officers Training Corps*
RTSD raticide *rat killer*
RTSDK artistic *skillful*
RTSDKL artistically *skillfully*
RTSH reddish *color*
RTSH ruttish *lustful*
RTSHN artesian *well*
RTSHN irritation *annoyance*
RTSHN rotation *revolve*
RTSHNL irrotational *not revolving*
RTSHNL rotational *revolving*
RTSKLR rathskeller *tavern*
RTSL riotously *disorderly*
RTSN artisan *craftsman*
RTSN retsina *wine*
RTSNDR ratiocinator *reasoner*
RTSNS reticence *restraint* reticency
RTSNS riotousness *disorderly*
RTSNSHN ratiocination *reason*
RTSNT ratiocinate *reason* ratiocinated ratiocinating
RTSNT reticent *silent*
RTSNTR ratiocinator

reasoner
RTSNTS reticence *restraint* reticency
RTSR ritzier *stylish*
RTSR rotisserie *grill*
RTSST eroticist *sex*
RTSST ritziest *stylish*
RTST artiest *artistic*
RTST artist *craftsman*
RTST artiste *entertainer*
RTST rattiest *tangled, shabby, irritable*
RTST reddest *color*
RTST retest *examination*
RTST ruddiest *reddish*
RTST ruttiest *grooved*
RTSTK artistic *skillful*
RTSTK rootstock *plant*
RTSTKL artistically *skillfully*
RTSTR artistry *skill, craft*
RTSYR ritzier *stylish*
RTSYST ritziest *stylish*
RTSZ eroticize *make sexy* eroticized eroticizing
RTSZM eroticism *sexiness*
RTSZM erraticism *irregularity*
RTT airtight *sealed*
RTT irritate *annoy* irritated irritating
RTT ratatouille *stew*
RTT ratite *bird*
RTT rotate *turn* rotated rotating
RTT write out *inscribe*
RTTBL rotatable *turning*
RTTD irritated *inflamed*
RTTR rotator *muscle* rotators (or) rotatores
RTTV irritative *annoying*
RTTV rotative *spin*
RTTW ratatouille *stew*
RTVW right-of-way *yield* rights-of-way
RTW right away *soon*
RTW right-of-way *yield* rights-of-way
RTWL right whale *animal*
RTWL ritual *ceremony*
RTWLR rottweiler *dog*
RTWLSDK ritualistic *ceremony*

Use letters that best describe the sounds you hear and omit the vowels. Use **S** or **K** instead of **C**: to find circle use **SRKL**. Use **J** to find joy, **JM** to find gem and **G** to find go.

RTWLSDKL ritualistically *ceremony*

RTWLSTK ritualistic *ceremony*

RTWLSTKL ritualistically *ceremony*

RTWLZ ritualize *ceremony* ritualized ritualizing

RTWLZM ritualism *ceremony*

RTWNG right wing (n) *conservative* right-wing (adj)

RTWNGR right-winger *reactionary*

RTWRD rightward *to the right*

RTWRK artwork *creation*

RTWRK right-to-work (adj) *labor*

RTX urtext *original*

RTXT urtext *original*

RTY retia (pl) *plexus* rete

RTYR artier *artistic*

RTYR rattier *tangled, shabby, irritable*

RTYR retire *stop work, sleep* retired retiring

RTYR ruddier *reddish*

RTYR ruttier *grooved*

RTYRMNT retirement *no work*

RTYRN wrought iron *metal*

RTYSNDR ratiocinator *reasoner*

RTYSNSHN ratiocination *reason*

RTYSNT ratiocinate *reason* ratiocinated ratiocinating

RTYSNTR ratiocinator *reasoner*

RTYST artiest *artistic*

RTYST rattiest *tangled, shabby, irritable*

RTYST ruddiest *reddish*

RTYST ruttiest *grooved*

RTZ erotize *make sexy* erotized erotizing

RTZ ritzy *stylish* ritzier ritziest

RTZ ROTC (abbr) *Reserve Officers Training Corps*

RTZHN artesian *well*

RTZHNWL artesian well *water*

RTZN artisan *craftsman*

RTZN retsina *wine*

RTZNS reticence *restraint* reticency

RTZNT reticent *silent*

RTZNTS reticence *restraint* reticency

RTZR ritzier *stylish*

RTZSHN erotization *make sexy*

RTZST ritziest *stylish*

RTZYR ritzier *stylish*

RTZYST ritziest *stylish*

RV arrive *reach* arrived arriving

RV au revoir *farewell*

RV rave (v) *speak wildly* raved raving

RV rave (n) *approval, party*

RV reeve (v) *fasten* rove (or) reeved reeving

RV reeve (n) *agent*

RV rev *increase quickly* revved revving

RV review (v) *look over, criticize* (n) *inspection, evaluation*

RV revue *show*

RV rive *tear apart* rived riven riving

RV rove *wander* roved roving

RVBL reviewable *look over, criticize*

RVDLZ revitalize *give life* revitalized revitalizing (Br) revitalise

RVDLZSHN revitalization *new life* (Br) revitalisation

RVDN riveting *fascinating*

RVDNG riveting *fascinating*

RVDR riveter *fastener*

RVJ ravage *damage* ravaged ravaging

RVJMNT ravagement *damage*

RVJR ravager *damager*

RVJTT revegetate *plants*

RVK revoke *take back* revoked revoking

RVKBL irrevocable (adj) *cannot cancel* irrevocably (adv)

RVKBL revocable *take back*

RVKBLD irrevocability *cannot cancel*

RVKBLT irrevocability *cannot cancel*

RVKSHN revocation *take back*

RVL arrival *reach, attain*

RVL ravel *tangle, fray* raveled (or) ravelled raveling (or) ravelling

RVL ravioli *food* ravioli

RVL reveal *make known*

RVL reveille *bugle sound*

RVL revel *delight*

RVL revile *denounce* reviled reviling

RVL rival *foe*

RVLDSHN revalidation *certify*

RVLDT revalidate *certify* revalidated revalidating

RVLMNT ravelment *undo, fray*

RVLMNT revealment *disclosure*

RVLN raveling (or) ravelling *fray*

RVLN revealing *open*

RVLNG raveling (or) ravelling *fray*

RVLNG revealing *open*

RVLNT irrelevant *does not apply*

RVLR raveler *tangle, fray*

RVLR reveler (or) reveller *celebrant*

RVLR revelry *merrymaking*

RVLR reviler *denounce*

RVLR rivalry *competition* rivalries

RVLRS rivalrous *competitive*

RVLSHN reevaluation *weighing*

RVLSHN revelation *disclosure*

RVLSHN revolution *cycle, rebellion*

RVLSHN revulsion *disgust*

RVLSHNR revolutionary *rebellion, new* revolutionaries
RVLSHNZ revolutionize *change, overthrow* revolutionized revolutionizing (Br) revolutionise
RVLT reevaluate *weigh* reevaluated reevaluating
RVLT revolt *(v)* rebel *(n) rebellion*
RVLT rivulet *stream*
RVLTN revolting *awful*
RVLTNG revolting *awful*
RVLTR revelatory *disclosure*
RVLV revolve *rotate* revolved revolving
RVLVBL revolvable *rotate*
RVLVN revolving *rotating*
RVLVNG revolving *rotating*
RVLVR revolver *gun, rotater*
RVLWSHN reevaluation *weighing*
RVLWT reevaluate *weigh* reevaluated reevaluating
RVLYSHN reevaluation *weighing*
RVLYT reevaluate *weigh* reevaluated reevaluating
RVLYWSHN reevaluation *weighing*
RVLYWT reevaluate *weigh* reevaluated reevaluating
RVMP revamp *remake*
RVN raven *(n) bird (v) devour*
RVN ravine *ditch*
RVN raving *(n) wild talk (adj) ravishing*
RVN revenue *money*
RVN roving *wandering*
RVNG raving *(n) wild talk (adj) ravishing*
RVNG roving *wandering*
RVNJ revenge *get even* revenged revenging
RVNJFL revengeful *(adj) get even* revengefully *(adv)*
RVNJFLNS revengefulness *get even*
RVNJR revenger *get even*
RVNR revenuer *taxes*

RVNS irrelevance *does not apply* irrelevancy
RVNS ravenous *hungry*
RVNSH revanche *revenge*
RVNSHST revanchist *revenge*
RVNSL ravenously *hungry*
RVNSNS ravenousness *hunger*
RVNTS irrelevance *does not apply* irrelevancy
RVNWR revenuer *taxes*
RVNY revenue *money*
RVNYWR revenuer *taxes*
RVR arriver *destination*
RVR raver *madman*
RVR revere *honor* revered revering
RVR reverie *daydream*
RVR reviewer *critic*
RVR river *stream*
RVR riviera *resort*
RVR riviere *necklace*
RVR rover *wanderer*
RVRB reverb *echo*
RVRBD riverbed *water*
RVRBNGK riverbank *ledge*
RVRBNK riverbank *ledge*
RVRBRDV reverberative *echo*
RVRBRNT reverberant *echoes*
RVRBRSHN reverberation *echo*
RVRBRT reverberate *echo* reverberated reverberating
RVRBRTR reverberatory *echo*
RVRBRTV reverberative *echo*
RVRBT riverboat *ship*
RVRD revered *honored*
RVRDBL revertible *return*
RVRDNT revertant *transformed*
RVRDR reverter *return*
RVRFRNT riverfront *shoreline*
RVRN reverend *title*
RVRN riverine *stream*
RVRNCHL reverential *(adj)*

awed reverentially *(adv)*
RVRND reverend *title*
RVRNS irreverence *disrespect*
RVRNS reverence *awe* reverenced reverencing
RVRNSHL reverential *(adj) awed* reverentially *(adv)*
RVRNT irreverent *disrespect*
RVRNT reverent *in awe* reverent
RVRNTL reverently *in awe*
RVRNTS irreverence *disrespect*
RVRNTS reverence *awe* reverenced reverencing
RVRS reverse *opposite* reversed reversing
RVRSBL irreversible *(adj) no opposite side* irreversibly *(adv)*
RVRSBL reversible *(adj) opposite* reversibly *(adv)*
RVRSBLD irreversibility *no opposite side*
RVRSBLD reversibility *opposite*
RVRSBLT irreversibility *no opposite side*
RVRSBLT reversibility *opposite*
RVRSD riverside *stream*
RVRSHN reversion *return*
RVRSHNR reversionary *returning*
RVRSL reversal *change*
RVRT revert *return*
RVRTBL revertible *return*
RVRTNT revertant *transformed*
RVRTR reverter *return*
RVRZ revers *lapel*
RVRZHN reversion *return*
RVRZHNR reversionary *returning*
RVSH ravish *rape*
RVSH revanche *revenge*
RVSHMNT ravishment *rape*
RVSHN ravishing *lovely*
RVSHN revision *change*
RVSHNG ravishing *lovely*
RVSHNR revisionary *change*

Use letters that best describe the sounds you hear and omit the vowels. Use **S** or **K** instead of **C**: to find circle use **SRKL**. Use **J** to find joy, **JM** to find gem and **G** to find go.

RVSHR ravisher *rapist*
RVSHST revanchist *revenge*
RVST revest *reinvest*
RVT revet *embankment*
revetted revetting
RVT rivet *(n) bolt (v) fasten*
RVTLZ revitalize *give life*
revitalized revitalizing
(Br) revitalise
RVTLZSHN revitalization
new life
(Br) revitalisation
RVTMNT revetment
embankment
RVTN riveting *fascinating*
RVTNG riveting *fascinating*
RVTR riveter *fastener*
RVV revive *restore* revived
reviving
RVV revolve *rotate* revolved
revolving
RVVBL revivable *give life*
RVVBL revolvable *rotate*
RVVF revivify *give life*
revivified revivifying
revivifies
RVVL revival *renewal*
RVVLST revivalist *clergyman*
RVVLZM revivalism *religion*
RVVN revolving *rotating*
RVVNG revolving *rotating*
RVVR revolver *gun, rotater*
RVW au revoir *farewell*
RVWBL reviewable *look over,*
criticize
RVWR au revoir *farewell*
RVWR reviewer *critic*
RVY review *(v) look over,*
criticize (n) inspection,
evaluation
RVY revue *show*
RVYBL reviewable *look over,*
criticize
RVYL ravioli *food ravioli*
RVYLT rivulet *stream*
RVYR reviewer *critic*
RVYR riviera *resort*
RVYR riviere *necklace*
RVYWBL reviewable *look*
over, criticize
RVYWR reviewer *critic*
RVZ revise *change* revised

revising
RVZBL revisable *change*
RVZD revised *changed*
RVZHN revision *change*
RVZHNR revisionary *change*
RVZL revisal *change*
RVZR reviser (or) revisor
changer
RVZR revisory *change*
RVZT revisit *return*
RW airway *passage*
RW areaway *basement*
RW reweigh *scale*
RW Rouault *artist*
RW roué *sensual man*
RW rouille *sauce*
RWD arrowwood *shrub*
RWG earwig *(v) annoy*
earwigged earwigging
RWG earwig *(n) insect*
RWK reawake *rouse*
RWKN reawaken *rouse*
RWKNN reawakening
arousal
RWKNNG reawakening
arousal
RWKNS earwitness *reporter*
RWKS earwax *substance*
RWL rowel *(v) trouble*
roweled (or) rowelled
roweling (or) rowelling
RWL rowel *(n) tool*
RWLF rauwolfia *plant*
RWLFY rauwolfia *plant*
RWLT Rouault *artist*
RWN rewind *coil again*
rewound rewinding
RWN rowan *tree*
RWN rowen *aftermath*
RWN ruin *destroy*
RWNBR rowanberry *tree*
rowanberries
RWND rewind *coil again*
rewound rewinding
RWND Rwanda *country*
RWNK Roanoke *city*
RWNS ruinous *destructive*
RWNSHN ruination *damage*
RWNSL ruinously *destructive*
RWNSNS ruinousness
destruction
RWNT ruinate *damage*

ruinated ruinating
RWR rewire *electricity*
rewired rewiring
RWRD reward *payment*
RWRD reword *edit*
RWRDN rewarding
satisfying
RWRDNG rewarding
satisfying
RWRK rework *mend*
RWRM arrowworm *organism*
RWRM rewarm *heat again*
RWRTH airworthy *fit for*
flight
RWRTHNS airworthiness *fit*
for flight
RWSH rewash *cleanse again*
RWT rewet *moisten* rewet
rewetting
RWTNS earwitness *reporter*
RWV airwave *transmission*
medium
RWV reweave *patch hole*
rewove (or) reweaved
reweaving rewoven
RWVN rewoven *repaired*
RWVZ airwaves *transmission*
mediums
RWX earwax *substance*
RWYR rewire *electricity*
rewired rewiring
RX aurochs *ox* aurochs
RX oryx *antelope* oryx (or)
oryxes
RX rex *animal* rexes (or) rex
RXCHNJ reexchange *trade*
reexchanged
reexchanging
RXMN reexamine *test*
reexamined reexamining
RXMNSHN reexamination
test
RXPLR reexplore *investigate*
reexplored reexploring
RXPRNS reexperience
undergo, live
reexperienced
reexperiencing
RXPRNTS reexperience
undergo, live
reexperienced
reexperiencing

Letters aren't doubled for single sounds: to find alley use **L** not **LL**. Use **Y** and **W** as hard sounds only: to find yellow use **YL**. (Br)=British spelling or usage. * See dictionary.

RXPRS air express *mail*
RXPRYNS reexperience *undergo, live* reexperienced reexperiencing
RXPRYNTS reexperience *undergo, live* reexperienced reexperiencing
RY area *space*
RY aria *song*
RY arroyo *gully* arroyos
RY rhea *bird*
RY Rio *(abbr) Rio de Janeiro*
RY rya *rug*
RY uraei (pl) *symbol* uraeus
RY urea *urine*
RYD arietta *song*
RYD oread *nymph*
RYD riata *lariat*
RYDJKSHN reeducation *teaching*
RYDJKT reeducate *teach* reeducated reeducating
RYDJNR Rio de Janeiro *city*
RYDKSHN reeducation *teaching*
RYDKT reeducate *teach* reeducated reeducating
RYDLZ reutilize *use again* reutilized reutilizing (Br) reutilise
RYDR rioter *person*
RYDRSHN reiteration *repeat*
RYDRT reiterate *repeat* reiterated reiterating
RYDS riotous *disorderly*
RYDSHN erudition *learning*
RYDSHNR Rio de Janeiro *city*
RYDSL riotously *disorderly*
RYDSNS riotousness *disorderly*
RYDT erudite *educated*
RYDT reedit *correct*
RYDYKSHN reeducation *teaching*
RYDYKT reeducate *teach* reeducated reeducating
RYDZHNR Rio de Janeiro *city*
RYF reify *make real* reified

reifying reifies
RYFKSHN reification *make real*
RYFR reoffer *offer again*
RYFRM reaffirm *assert*
RYFRMSHN reaffirmation *consent*
RYGNSHN reignition *flame*
RYGNT reignite *flame* reignited reigniting
RYGRND Rio Grande *river*
RYGZMN reexamine *test* reexamined reexamining
RYGZMNSHN reexamination *test*
RYH rioja *wine*
RYJKSHN reeducation *teaching*
RYJKT reeducate *teach* reeducated reeducating
RYJNT reagent *substance*
RYJSMNT readjustment *set properly*
RYJST readjust *set properly*
RYJSTMNT readjustment *set properly*
RYK react *respond*
RYKD area code *telephone zone*
RYKDNS reactance *circuit*
RYKDNT reactant *chemistry*
RYKDNTS reactance *circuit*
RYKDR reactor *responder, device*
RYKDV reactive *responsive*
RYKDVSHN reactivation *start again*
RYKDVT reactivate *start again* reactivated reactivating
RYKSCHNJ reexchange *trade* reexchanged reexchanging
RYKSHN reaction *response*
RYKSHNR reactionary *ultraconservative* reactionaries
RYKSMN reexamine *test* reexamined reexamining
RYKSMNSHN reexamination *test*
RYKSPLR reexplore

investigate reexplored reexploring
RYKSPRNS reexperience *undergo, live* reexperienced reexperiencing
RYKSPRNTS reexperience *undergo, live* reexperienced reexperiencing
RYKSPRYNS reexperience *undergo, live* reexperienced reexperiencing
RYKSPRYNTS reexperience *undergo, live* reexperienced reexperiencing
RYKT react *respond*
RYKTNS reactance *circuit*
RYKTNT reactant *chemistry*
RYKTNTS reactance *circuit*
RYKTR reactor *responder, device*
RYKTV reactive *responsive*
RYKTVD reactivity *response*
RYKTVSHN reactivation *start again*
RYKTVT reactivate *start again* reactivated reactivating
RYKTVT reactivity *response*
RYKWNT reacquaint *meet*
RYKWP reequip *prepare, furnish* reequipt reequipping
RYKZMN reexamine *test* reexamined reexamining
RYKZMNSHN reexamination *test*
RYL aerial *(n) antenna*
RYL aerial (adj) *(adj) air, thin, fanciful** aerially (adv)
RYL areal (adj) *field* areally (adv)
RYL areola *ring* areolae (or) areolas
RYL aureole (or) aureola *halo*
RYL oriel *window*
RYL oriole *bird*
RYL real *actual*

Use letters that best describe the sounds you hear and omit the vowels. Use **S** or **K** instead of **C**: to find circle use **SRKL**. Use **J** to find joy, **JM** to find gem and **G** to find go.

RYL really *truly*
RYL rial (or) riyal *money*
RYL rile *upset* riled riling
RYL roil *stir up*
RYL roily *turbulent*
RYL royal (adj) *regal* royally (adv)
RYL urial *sheep*
RYLD reality *facts* realities
RYLD realty *land*
RYLD royalty *monarchy* royalties
RYLDK rhyolitic *lava*
RYLDR realtor *land agent*
RYLK reelect *choose again*
RYLKSHN reallocation *distribution*
RYLKSHN reelection *choosen again*
RYLKT reallocate *distribute* reallocated reallocating
RYLKT reelect *choose again*
RYLN realign *straighten*
RYLNMNT realignment *straightening*
RYLR areolar *ring*
RYLSDK realistic *lifelike, factual*
RYLSDKL realistically *lifelike, factual*
RYLST aerialist *trapeze*
RYLST realist *facts*
RYLST royalist *monarchy*
RYLSTK realistic *lifelike, factual*
RYLSTKL realistically *lifelike, factual*
RYLT areolate *ring*
RYLT reality *facts* realities
RYLT realty *land*
RYLT rhyolite *lava*
RYLT rialto *marketplace* rialtos
RYLT royalty *monarchy* royalties
RYLTK rhyolitic *lava*
RYLTR realtor *land agent*
RYLZ realize *understand* realized realizing
RYLZBL realizable *accomplish*
RYLZM realism *facts, lifelike*

RYLZM royalism *monarchy*
RYLZSHN realization *understanding*
RYMBRS reimburse *pay* reimbursed reimbursing
RYMBRSBL reimbursable *payment*
RYMBRSMNT reimbursement *payment*
RYMFSZ reemphasize *stress* reemphasized reemphasizing (Br) reemphasise
RYMPL reemploy *hire*
RYMPLMNT reemployment *hiring*
RYMPZ reimpose *burden* reimposed reimposing
RYMPZSHN reimposition *tax, burden*
RYMRJ reemerge *come out* reemerged reemerging
RYMRJNS reemergence *come out*
RYMRJNT reemergent *come out*
RYMRJNTS reemergence *come out*
RYN Arian *doctrine*
RYN Aryan *Indo-European*
RYN Orion *constellation*
RYN rayon *fabric*
RYND oriented *directed*
RYND reendow *give*
RYNDD reunited *together*
RYNDT reindict *accuse* reindicted reindicting
RYNDTMNT reindictment *accusation*
RYNF reunify *come together* reunified reunifying reunifies
RYNFKSHN reunification *come together*
RYNFLSHN reinflation *made larger*
RYNFLT reinflate *make larger* reinflated reinflating
RYNFRS reinforce *strengthen* reinforced reinforcing
RYNFRSMNT reinforcement

added strength
RYNFRSR reinforcer *strengthener*
RYNFSZ reemphasize *stress* reemphasized reemphasizing (Br) reemphasise
RYNGJ reengage *bind* reengaged reengaging
RYNGJMNT reengagement *binding*
RYNGRT reintegrate *combine* reintegrated reintegrating
RYNHBT reinhabit *dwell*
RYNJNR reengineer *reshape*
RYNJR reinjure (v) *hurt again* reinjured reinjuring
RYNJR reinjury (n) *hurt*
RYNKNTR reencounter *meeting*
RYNKRNSHN reincarnation *born again*
RYNKRNT reincarnate *born again* reincarnated reincarnating
RYNKRPRT reincorporate *combine* reincorporated reincorporating
RYNKTR reencounter *meeting*
RYNL oriental (adj) *(often capitalized) eastern* orientally (adv)
RYNLSMNT reenlistment *sign up again*
RYNLST reenlist *sign up again*
RYNLSTMNT reenlistment *sign up again*
RYNMSHN reanimation *pep*
RYNMT reanimate *pep up* reanimated reanimating
RYNN reunion *come together*
RYNRJZ reenergize *strengthen* reenergized reenergizing (Br) reenergise
RYNRL reenroll *sign up again*
RYNSHR reinsure *insure again* reinsured reinsuring

Letters aren't doubled for single sounds: to find alley use **L** not **LL**. Use **Y** and **W** as hard sounds only: to find yellow use **YL**. (Br)=British spelling or usage. * See dictionary.

RYNSHRNS reinsurance
insure again
RYNSHRNTS reinsurance
insure again
RYNSPK reinspect *examine*
RYNSPKT reinspect *examine*
RYNSRSHN reinsertion
place inside
RYNSRT reinsert *place inside*
RYNSTL reinstall *put in*
RYNSTT reinstate *restore*
reinstated reinstating
RYNSTTT reinstitute
establish again reinstituted
reinstituting
RYNT orient *(n) (often*
capitalized) east (v) position
RYNT reunite *come together*
reunited reuniting
RYNTD oriented *directed*
RYNTD reunited *together*
RYNTGRT reintegrate
combine reintegrated
reintegrating
RYNTL oriental (adj) *(often*
capitalized) eastern
orientally (adv)
RYNTR reinter *bury again*
reinterred reinterring
RYNTRDS reintroduce
insert, make known
reintroduced
reintroducing
RYNTRDYS reintroduce
insert, make known
reintroduced
reintroducing
RYNTRNG orienteering *race*
RYNTRPRT reinterpret
figure out
RYNTSHN orientation
adjustment
RYNTSHNL orientational
(adj) *adjustment*
orientationally (adv)
RYNTT orientate *position,*
face east orientated
orientating
RYNVGRSHN reinvigoration
make lively
RYNVGRT reinvigorate *make*
lively reinvigorated

reinvigorating
RYNVNT reinvent *make*
RYNVST reinvest *put money*
in
RYNYN reunion *come*
together
RYPL reapply *put on, enlist*
reapplied reapplying
reapplies
RYPLKSHN reapplication
put on, enlist
RYPLSDR reupholster *cover*
RYPLSTR reupholster *cover*
RYPNT reappoint *name*
RYPNTMNT reappointment
naming
RYPR reappear *show up*
again
RYPRNS reappearance
show up again
RYPRNTS reappearance
show up again
RYPRSHN reapportion
divide
RYPRSHNMNT
reapportionment *division*
RYPRZ reappraise *value*
reappraised reappraising
RYPRZL reappraisal *value*
RYQNT reacquaint *meet*
RYQP reequip *prepare,*
furnish reequipt
reequipping
RYR aerier *heavenly*
RYR airier *lofty, proud, windy*
RYR eerier *weirder*
RYRDR reorder *(v) arrange,*
call for (n) duplicate
RYRGNZ reorganize *arrange*
reorganized reorganizing
(Br) reorganise
RYRGNZR reorganizer
arranger
(Br) reorganiser
RYRGNZSHN
reorganization
arrangement
(Br) reorganisation
RYRM rearm *weapons*
RYRMMNT rearmament
weapons
RYRNJ rearrange *straighten*

rearranged rearranging
RYRNJMNT rearrangement
straightening
RYRST rearrest *law*
RYS arioso *music* ariosos
(or) ariosi
RYS uraeus *symbol* uraei
RYS urease *enzyme*
RYSH reissue *put out again*
reissued reissuing
RYSHR reassure *comfort*
reassured reassuring
RYSHRNS reassurance
comfort
RYSHRNTS reassurance
comfort
RYSMBL reassemble *(v)*
gather, construct
RYSMBL reassembly *(n)*
construction
RYSMBLJ reassemblage
gathering
RYSN reassign *appoint*
RYSNMNT reassignment
appointment
RYSS reassess *weigh*
RYSSMNT reassessment
weighing
RYST aeriest *heavenly*
RYST airiest *lofty, proud,*
windy
RYST eeriest *weirdest*
RYSTBLSH reestablish
create again
RYSTT rheostat *current*
RYT arietta *song*
RYT riata *lariat*
RYT rillettes *meat*
RYT riot *disturbance*
RYTCH reattach *connect*
RYTCHMNT reattachment
connection
RYTLZ reutilize *use again*
reutilized reutilizing
(Br) reutilise
RYTMP reattempt *try*
RYTMPT reattempt *try*
RYTMT reattempt *try*
RYTR rioter *person*
RYTRSHN reiteration *repeat*
RYTRT reiterate *repeat*
reiterated reiterating

Use letters that best describe the sounds you hear and omit the vowels. Use **S** or **K** instead of **C**: to find circle use **SRKL**. Use **J** to find joy, **JM** to find gem and **G** to find go.

RYTS rillettes *meat*
RYTS riotous *disorderly*
RYTSL riotously *disorderly*
RYTSNS riotousness *disorderly*
RYVLSHN reevaluation *weighing*
RYVLT reevaluate *weigh* reevaluated reevaluating
RYVLWSHN reevaluation *weighing*
RYVLWT reevaluate *weigh* reevaluated reevaluating
RYVLYWSHN reevaluation *weighing*
RYVLYWT reevaluate *weigh* reevaluated reevaluating
RYW areaway *basement*
RYWK reawake *rouse*
RYWKN reawaken *rouse*
RYWKNN reawakening *arousal*
RYWKNNG reawakening *arousal*
RYXCHNJ reexchange *trade* reexchanged reexchanging
RYXMN reexamine *test* reexamined reexamining
RYXMNSHN reexamination *test*
RYXPLR reexplore *investigate* reexplored reexploring
RYXPRNS reexperience *undergo, live* reexperienced reexperiencing
RYXPRNTS reexperience *undergo, live* reexperienced reexperiencing
RYXPRYNS reexperience *undergo, live* reexperienced reexperiencing
RYXPRYNTS reexperience *undergo, live* reexperienced reexperiencing
RYZ reuse *use again* reused reusing

RYZ urease *enzyme*
RYZBL reusable (adj) *use again* reusably (adv)
RYZBLD reusability *use again*
RYZBLT reusability *use again*
RZ Aires *zodiac sign*
RZ Ares *Greek god*
RZ Aries *constellation*
RZ arise *get up* arose arising arisen
RZ arouse *waken* aroused arousing
RZ orzo *pasta*
RZ ours *not yours*
RZ raise *lift* raised raising
RZ rays (pl) *sunlight* ray
RZ raze *demolish* razed razing
RZ razz *tease*
RZ reuse *use again* reused reusing
RZ rise (v) *ascend, happen, result** rose rising risen
RZ rise (n) *hill, (Br) raise, reaction**
RZ rose *flower, color*
RZ rosé *wine*
RZ rosy *pink, optimistic* rosier rosiest
RZ rouse *awaken, spur* roused rousing
RZ roux (pl) *sauce* roux
RZ ruse *trick*
RZ urease *enzyme*
RZBD rosebud *flower*
RZBL irresoluble (adj) *cannot solve* irresolubly (adv)
RZBL resoluble (adj) *break up, decide* resolubly (adv)
RZBL reusable (adj) *use again* reusably (adv)
RZBL risible *laughter*
RZBLD reusability *use again*
RZBLD risibility *laughter* risibilities
RZBLT reusability *use again*
RZBLT risibility *laughter* risibilities
RZBR rasbora *fish*
RZBR raspberry *fruit*

raspberries
RZBSH rosebush *shrub* rosebushes
RZD raised *elevated*
RZD reside *live* resided residing
RZD residua (pl) *remainder* residuum
RZD residue *remainder*
RZD rhizoid *root*
RZDJ residua (pl) *remainder* residuum
RZDJL residual (adj) *remainder* residually (adv)
RZDJM residuum *remainder* residua
RZDJR residuary *remainder*
RZDJW residua (pl) *remainder* residuum
RZDJWL residual (adj) *remainder* residually (adv)
RZDJWM residuum *remainder* residua
RZDJWR residuary *remainder*
RZDL residual (adj) *remainder* residually (adv)
RZDM residuum *remainder* residua
RZDM rhizotomy *roots*
RZDNC residency *study* residencies
RZDNCHL residential (adj) *home* residentially (adv)
RZDNS residence *home*
RZDNS residency *study* residencies
RZDNSHL residential (adj) *home* residentially (adv)
RZDNT resident (adj) *living here* (n) *inhabitant*
RZDNTC residency *study* residencies
RZDNTS residence *home*
RZDNTS residency *study* residencies
RZDR resider *inhabitant*
RZDR residuary *remainder*
RZDSTN Rosetta stone *hieroglyphics*
RZDW residua (pl) *remainder* residuum

RZD

RZDWL residual (adj) *remainder* residually (adv)

RZDWM residuum *remainder* residua

RZDWR residuary *remainder*

RZDY residue *remainder*

RZGNSHN resignation *surrender*

RZH orgeat *syrup*

RZH raj *rule*

RZH raja (or) rajah *ruler*

RZH rouge *(v)* redden rouged rouging

RZH rouge *(n)* cosmetic

RZHM regime *pattern, government*

RZHN erosion *worn away*

RZHN Eurasian *European and Asian*

RZHR erasure *cancellation*

RZHSR régisseur (or) regisseur *director*

RZHT orgeat *syrup*

RZJ residua (pl) *remainder* residuum

RZJ residue *remainder*

RZJL residual (adj) *remainder* residually (adv)

RZJM residuum *remainder* residua

RZJR residuary *remainder*

RZJW residua (pl) *remainder* residuum

RZJWL residual (adj) *remainder* residually (adv)

RZJWM residuum *remainder* residua

RZJWR residuary *remainder*

RZJYM residuum *remainder* residua

RZJYWM residuum *remainder* residua

RZKLRD rose-colored *pink* (Br) rose-coloured

RZKRSHN Rosicrucian *religion*

RZL arousal *awakening*

RZL resile *spring back* resiled resiling

RZL roseola *rash*

RZL rosily *pink, cheerful*

RZLBL irresoluble (adj)

cannot solve irresolubly (adv)

RZLBL resoluble (adj) *break up, decide* resolubly (adv)

RZLDNT resultant *outcome*

RZLDZL razzle-dazzle *display*

RZLNG Riesling *grape, wine*

RZLNS resilience *strength* resiliency

RZLNT resilient *strong*

RZLNTS resilience *strength* resiliency

RZLR roseolar *rash*

RZLSHN irresolution *uncertain*

RZLSHN resolution *courage, document*

RZLT irresolute *uncertain*

RZLT resolute *firm*

RZLT result *outcome*

RZLTL irresolutely *uncertain*

RZLTNS irresoluteness *uncertain*

RZLTNT resultant *outcome*

RZLV resolve *break up, decide* resolved resolving

RZLVBL resolvable *break up, decide*

RZLVNT resolvent *analysis*

RZLYBL irresoluble (adj) *cannot solve* irresolubly (adv)

RZLYBL resoluble (adj) *break up, decide* resolubly (adv)

RZLYNS resilience *strength* resiliency

RZLYNT resilient *strong*

RZLYNTS resilience *strength* resiliency

RZM resume *begin again* resumed resuming

RZM résumé (or) resumé (or) resume *job summary*

RZM rhizome *root*

RZMBL resemble *be alike* resembled resembling

RZMBLNS resemblance *likeness*

RZMBLNTS resemblance *likeness*

RZMDS rhizomatous *roots*

RZMK rhizomic *roots*

RZMN oarsman *boat* oarsmen

RZMNSHP oarsmanship *rowing*

RZMPSHN resumption *begin again*

RZMR rosemary *herb* rosemaries

RZMSHN resumption *begin again*

RZMTS rhizomatous *roots*

RZMTZ razzmatazz *display, zing* (Br) razzamatazz

RZN Arizona *US State*

RZN raisin *fruit*

RZN reason *thinking*

RZN resign *quit*

RZN resin *sap*

RZN resound *echo*

RZN rezone *boundary* rezoned rezoning

RZN risen *(v-pp)* rise

RZN rising *up*

RZN rosin *pine resin*

RZN rousing *spirited*

RZNBL reasonable (adj) *fair* reasonably (adv)

RZNBLNS reasonableness *fairness*

RZND resigned *quit, submitting*

RZND resound *echo*

RZNDL resignedly *submission*

RZNDN resounding *loud, emphatic*

RZNDNG resounding *loud, emphatic*

RZNDNS resignedness *submission*

RZNDR resonator *echo*

RZNDTR raison d'être *reason*

RZNG rising *up*

RZNG rousing *spirited*

RZNN reasoning *thinking*

RZNNG reasoning *thinking*

RZNNS resonance *vibration*

RZNNT resonant *echo*

RZNNTS resonance

Use letters that best describe the sounds you hear and omit the vowels. Use **S** or **K** instead of **C**: to find circle use **SRKL**. Use **J** to find joy, **JM** to find gem and **G** to find go.

vibration

RZNR resigner *quit, submit*

RZNS resinous *sap*

RZNS rosiness *pink, cheerfulness*

RZNT resent *ill will*

RZNT resilient *strong*

RZNT resinate *flavor* resinated resinating

RZNT resonate *echo* resonated resonating

RZNTFL resentful (adj) *ill will* resentfully (adv)

RZNTFLNS resentfulness *ill will*

RZNTMNT resentment *ill will*

RZNTR resonator *echo*

RZNTS resonance *vibration*

RZNWD rosinweed *plant*

RZPD rhizopod *protozoa*

RZPLN rhizoplane *roots*

RZPS rhizopus *fungus*

RZR razer *demolisher*

RZR razor *blade*

RZR riser *stair*

RZR rosary *prayers* rosaries

RZR rosier *pink, cheerful*

RZRB resorb *suck in*

RZRBK razorback *hog*

RZRBL razorbill *bird*

RZRBSHN resorption *suck in*

RZRK resurrect *raise*

RZRKSHN resurrection *rising*

RZRKSHNST resurrectionist *body snatcher, riser*

RZRKT resurrect *raise*

RZRN rosarian *roses*

RZRPSHN resorption *suck in*

RZRS resource *supply*

RZRSFL resourceful (adj) *capable* resourcefully (adv)

RZRSFLNS resourcefulness *capability*

RZRT resort (n) *spa, recourse* (v) *use*

RZRV reserve (v) *keep, defer* reserved reserving

RZRV reserve (n) *land, caution, substitute**

RZRVD reserved *set aside for, silent*

RZRVDL reservedly *silent*

RZRVR reservoir *lake, supply*

RZRVSHN reservation *arrangement, doubt, area*

RZRVSHNST reservationist *arranger*

RZRVST reservist *military*

RZRVW reservoir *lake, supply*

RZRVWR reservoir *lake, supply*

RZRYN rosarian *roses*

RZSDBL irresistible (adj) *cannot refrain* irresistibly (adv)

RZSDBL resistible (adj) *refrain, oppose* resistibly (adv)

RZSDBLD irresistibility *cannot refrain*

RZSDBLD resistibility *refrain, oppose*

RZSDBLT irresistibility *cannot refrain*

RZSDBLT resistibility *refrain, oppose*

RZSDNS resistance *refrain, oppose*

RZSDNTS resistance *refrain, oppose*

RZSDR resister *refrain, oppose*

RZSDR resistor *electrical part*

RZSDV resistive *refrain, oppose*

RZSFR rhizosphere *soil*

RZSHS rosaceous *roses*

RZSNDRM Reye's syndrome *disease*

RZST resist *refrain, oppose*

RZST rosiest *pink, cheerful*

RZSTBL irresistible (adj) *cannot refrain* irresistibly (adv)

RZSTBL resistible (adj) *refrain, oppose* resistibly (adv)

RZSTBLD irresistibility *cannot refrain*

RZSTBLD resistibility *refrain, oppose*

RZSTBLT irresistibility *cannot refrain*

RZSTBLT resistibility *refrain, oppose*

RZSTNS resistance *refrain, oppose*

RZSTNT resistant *refrain, oppose*

RZSTNTS resistance *refrain, oppose*

RZSTR resister *refrain, oppose*

RZSTR resistor *electrical part*

RZSTV resistive *refrain, oppose*

RZSTVD resistivity *refrain, oppose*

RZSTVT resistivity *refrain, oppose*

RZT risotto *food* risottos

RZT roseate *rosy*

RZT rosette *ornament*

RZTL roseately *rosy*

RZTM rhizotomy *roots*

RZTS ersatz *substitute*

RZTSTN Rosetta stone *hieroglyphics*

RZV erosive *worn away*

RZV resolve *break up, decide* resolved resolving

RZVBL resolvable *break up, decide*

RZVLT Roosevelt *US president*

RZVNT resolvent *analysis*

RZVR reservoir *lake, supply*

RZVWR reservoir *lake, supply*

RZWD rosewood *tree*

RZWL Roswell *city*

RZWMN oarswoman *rowing* oarswomen

RZYBL irresoluble (adj) *cannot solve* irresolubly (adv)

RZYBL resoluble (adj) *break up, decide* resolubly (adv)

RZYL resile *spring back*

Letters aren't doubled for single sounds: to find alley use **L** not **LL**. Use **Y** and **W** as hard sounds only: to find yellow use **YL**. (Br)=British spelling or usage. * See dictionary.

resiled resiling
RZYL roseola *rash*
RZYLR roseolar *rash*
RZYM resume *begin again* resumed resuming
RZYNS resilience *strength* resiliency
RZYNT resilient *strong*
RZYNTS resilience *strength* resiliency
RZYR rosier *pink, cheerful*
RZYST rosiest *pink, cheerful*
RZYT roseate *rosy*
RZYTL roseately *rosy*

S

S ace *card, single shot* aced acing
S aecia (pl) *fungus* aecium
S asci (pl) *spore* ascus
S ass *buttocks, fool* asses (Br) *arse*
S assay *analysis*
S Aussie *of Australia*
S cee *letter C*
S essay (n) *prose, trial* (v) *attempt*
S ice *frozen water* iced icing
S icy *frozen* icier iciest
S Issei *Japanese immigrant* Issei
S issue (n) *matter, child, publishing**
S issue (v) *emerge, result, provide* issued issuing
S os *bone* ossa
S os *mouth* ora
S saw (v-past) *see* (n) *tool, proverb*
S saw (v) *cut* sawed (or) sawn sawing
S say (v) *speak* said saying
S say (n) *statement* says

S sea *ocean*
S see (v) *view, understand, escort** saw seen seeing
S see (n) *authority*
S sew *stitch* sewed sewing sewn
S sigh *breathing*
S Sioux *Native American* Sioux
S so *musical tone, thus, true**
S sou *money* sous
S sough *sound*
S sous *assistant*
S sow (v) *reap* sowed sowing sown
S sow (n) *pig* (f)
S soy *bean*
S sue *seek justice* sued suing
S us *you and me*
S use (n) *purpose*
SB CB (abbr) *citizens band (radio)*
SB ceiba *tree*
SB sabot *shoe*
SB Seabee *Navy*
SB sib *relative*
SB sob *cry* sobbed sobbing
SB sub (v) *substitute* subbed subbing
SB sub (n) *boat, food, substitute*
SBCHSR subchaser *ship*
SBCLN subceiling *roof*
SBCLNG subceiling *roof*
SBD seabed *ocean*
SBD subdue *calm* subdued subduing
SBD subhead *title*
SBD subito *music*
SBDBTNT subdebutante *girl*
SBDBYTNT subdebutante *girl*
SBDD subdued *calm*
SBDK sub judice *in court*
SBDKL sabbatical *rest*
SBDKN subdeacon *cleric*
SBDKSHN subduction *descent*
SBDL sabadilla *plant*
SBDMNNT subdominant *influence*

SBDMNT subdominant *influence*
SBDNG iceboating *sailing*
SBDR subduer *calm*
SBDRFJ subterfuge *tricks*
SBDRFSH subterfuge *tricks*
SBDRFYJ subterfuge *tricks*
SBDRFYSH subterfuge *tricks*
SBDRFYZH subterfuge *tricks*
SBDRFZH subterfuge *tricks*
SBDRL subdural *between layers*
SBDRML subdermal (adj) *skin* subdermally (adv)
SBDSHN subaudition *between the lines*
SBDVD subdivide *separate* subdivided subdividing
SBDVDBL subdividable *separate*
SBDVDR subdivider*separator*
SBDVLPMNT subdevelopment *housing*
SBDVSHN subdivision *category, land*
SBDVZHN subdivision *category, land*
SBDY sabadilla *plant*
SBDY subdue *calm* subdued subduing
SBDYR subduer *calm*
SBDYRL subdural *between layers*
SBFL subfield *division*
SBFLD subfield *division*
SBFLM subphylum *category*
SBFLR subfloor *base*
SBFML subfamily *group* subfamilies
SBFRZN subfreezing *icy*
SBFRZNG subfreezing *icy*
SBG seabag *luggage*
SBG sow bug *insect*
SBGM subgum *food*
SBGRP subgroup *part*
SBHD subhead *title*
SBHMD subhumid *moisture*
SBHMN subhuman *animal*
SBHYMD subhumid

Use letters that best describe the sounds you hear and omit the vowels. Use **S** or **K** instead of **C**: to find circle use **SRKL**. Use **J** to find joy, **JM** to find gem and **G** to find go.

moisture
SBHYMN subhuman *animal*
SBJDS sub judice *in court*
SBJGDR subjugator
  conquerer
SBJGSHN subjugation
  control
SBJGT subjugate *conquer*
  subjugated subjugating
SBJGTR subjugator
  conquerer
SBJK subject *(v) control,*
  force to endure (n) citizen,
  motive, word (adj) liable
SBJKDV subjective
  grammar, personal, illusory
SBJKDVZM subjectivism
  feeling
SBJKSHN subjection
  dominion
SBJKT subject *(v) control,*
  force to endure (n) citizen,
  motive, word (adj) liable
SBJKTV subjective
  grammar, personal, illusory
SBJKTVD subjectivity
  grammar, personal, illusory
SBJKTVT subjectivity
  grammar, personal, illusory
SBJKTVZ subjectivize *make*
  personal
SBJKTVZM subjectivism
  feeling
SBJN subjoin *append*
SBJNC subagency
  department
SBJNGKDV subjunctive
  verb
SBJNGKSHN subjunction
  join
SBJNGKTV subjunctive
  verb
SBJNKDV subjunctive *verb*
SBJNKSHN subjunction
  join
SBJNKTV subjunctive *verb*
SBJNRSHN subgeneration
  creation
SBJNS subagency
  department
SBJNS subgenus *type*
SBJNT subagent *employee*

SBJNTC subagency
  department
SBJNTS subagency
  department
SBJSNC subjacency *below*
SBJSNS subjacency *below*
SBJSNT subjacent *below*
SBJSNTC subjacency *below*
SBJSNTL subjacently *below*
SBJSNTS subjacency *below*
SBK osso buco *food*
SBK sawbuck *(slang) $10*
  bill
SBKBNT subcabinet
  government
SBKDGR subcategory *part*
  subcategories
SBKDS subcutis *skin*
SBKLCHR subculture *group*
SBKLMKS subclimax *stable*
SBKLMX subclimax *stable*
SBKLNKL subclinical (adj)
  not detected subclinically
  (adv)
SBKLS subclass *category*
  subclasses
SBKLSFKSHN
  subclassification *division*
SBKLTR subculture *group*
SBKLVN subclavian
  collarbone
SBKLVYN subclavian
  collarbone
SBKMD subcommittee
  group
SBKMPK subcompact
  vehicle
SBKMPKT subcompact
  vehicle
SBKMT subcommittee
  group
SBKNCHS subconscious
  mind
SBKNGDM subkingdom
  category
SBKNNNT subcontinent
  land mass
SBKNSHS subconscious
  mind
SBKNTNNT subcontinent
  land mass
SBKNTRK subcontract

third party
SBKNTRKDR
  subcontractor *third party*
SBKNTRKT subcontract
  third party
SBKNTRKTR
  subcontractor *third party*
SBKRDKL subcortical *brain*
SBKRDKL subcritical
  insufficient
SBKRTKL subcortical *brain*
SBKRTKL subcritical
  insufficient
SBKS icebox *freezer*
  iceboxes
SBKS soapbox *crate*
  soapboxes
SBKT subacute *tapered*
SBKTGR subcategory *part*
  subcategories
SBKTNS subcutaneous *skin*
SBKTNYS subcutaneous
  skin
SBKTS subcutis *skin*
SBKWS subaqueous *water*
SBKWYS subaqueous *water*
SBKYDS subcutis *skin*
SBKYT subacute *tapered*
SBKYTNS subcutaneous
  skin
SBKYTNYS subcutaneous
  skin
SBKYTS subcutis *skin*
SBL issuable (adj) *open*
  issuably (adv)
SBL sable *(n) animal, color*
  (adj) dark sables
SBL sayable *spoken*
SBL sibyl *fortune teller*
SBL sowbelly *pork*
  sowbellies
SBL suable (adj) *legal action*
  suably (adv)
SBLD suability *law*
SBLDRC subliteracy *poor*
  writing
SBLDRL sublittoral *under*
  water
SBLDRS subliteracy *poor*
  writing
SBLDRT subliterate *poor*
  writing

Letters aren't doubled for single sounds: to find alley use **L** not **LL**. Use **Y** and **W** as hard
sounds only: to find yellow use **YL**. (Br)=British spelling or usage. * See dictionary.

SBLK sibylic (or) sibyllic *fortune teller*

SBLKSSHN subluxation *dislocation*

SBLM sublime *improve* sublimed subliming

SBLM sublime *splendid* sublimer sublimest

SBLMBL sublimable *improvement*

SBLMD sublimity *improvement* sublimities

SBLML sublimely *splendid*

SBLMNL subliminal (adj) *unconscious* subliminally (adv)

SBLMNS sublimeness *splendor*

SBLMR sublimer *splendid*

SBLMSHN sublimation *improvement*

SBLMST sublimest *splendid*

SBLMT sublimate *improve* sublimated sublimating

SBLMT sublimity *improvement* sublimities

SBLN sibling *brother or sister*

SBLN sibylline *fortune teller*

SBLNG sibling *brother or sister*

SBLNGGWL sublingual *tongue*

SBLNGWL sublingual *tongue*

SBLNR sublunary *earth*

SBLNS sibilance *"s" or "sh" sound*

SBLNT sibilant *"s" or "sh" sound*

SBLNTS sibilance *"s" or "sh" sound*

SBLPN subalpine *foothills*

SBLS sublease *rent* subleased subleasing

SBLSHN sibilation *hiss*

SBLSNS sublicense *certify*

SBLSNTS sublicense *certify*

SBLT sibilate *hiss* sibilated sibilating

SBLT suability *law*

SBLT sublet *rent* sublet subletting

SBLT subulate *tapering*

SBLTHL sublethal (adj) *not deadly* sublethally (adv)

SBLTNNT sublieutenant *rank*

SBLTNT sublieutenant *rank*

SBLTRC subliteracy *poor writing*

SBLTRL sublittoral *under water*

SBLTRN subaltern *subordinate*

SBLTRS subliteracy *poor writing*

SBLTRT subliterate *poor writing*

SBLXSHN subluxation *dislocation*

SBM sebum *fat*

SBMDL submittal *presentation, surrender*

SBMKRSKPK submicroscopic *tiny*

SBMKS submucosa *tissue*

SBMKSL submucosal *tissue*

SBMLDPL submultiple *number*

SBMLTPL submultiple *number*

SBMNCHR subminiature *tiny*

SBMNDBLR submandibular *jaw*

SBMNDBYLR submandibular *jaw*

SBMNTR subminiature *tiny*

SBMNTYR subminiature *tiny*

SBMNYCHR subminiature *tiny*

SBMNYTR subminiature *tiny*

SBMNYTYR subminiature *tiny*

SBMRJ submerge *put under water, suppress* submerged submerging

SBMRJBL submergible *put under water, suppress*

SBMRJNL submarginal *edge, less*

SBMRJNS submergence *put under water, suppress*

SBMRJNTS submergence *put under water, suppress*

SBMRN submarine *(v) attack* submarined submarining

SBMRN submarine *(n) ship*

SBMRNR submariner *sailor*

SBMRS submerse *put under water* submersed submersing

SBMRSBL submersible *put under water*

SBMRSHN submersion *put under water*

SBMRZHN submersion *put under water*

SBMSHN submission *presentation, surrender*

SBMSHNGN submachine gun *weapon*

SBMSV submissive *yielding*

SBMSVL submissively *yielding*

SBMSVNS submissiveness *yielding*

SBMT submit *present, yield* submitted submitting

SBMTL submittal *presentation, surrender*

SBMYKS submucosa *tissue*

SBMYKSL submucosal *tissue*

SBMZV submissive *yielding*

SBMZVL submissively *yielding*

SBMZVNS submissiveness *yielding*

SBN eastbound *direction*

SBN icebound *frozen*

SBN sabin *acoustics*

SBN soybean *plant*

SBND eastbound *direction*

SBND icebound *frozen*

SBNDCZ subindices (pl) *division* subindex

SBNDKS subindex *division* subindices

SBNDSZ subindices (pl) *division* subindex

SBNDX subindex *division* subindices

Use letters that best describe the sounds you hear and omit the vowels. Use **S** or **K** instead of **C**: to find circle use **SRKL**. Use **J** to find joy, **JM** to find gem and **G** to find go.

SBNRML subnormal (adj) *low, small* subnormally (adv)

SBNRMLD subnormality *low, small* subnormalities

SBNRMLT subnormality *low, small* subnormalities

SBNS sawbones *(slang) surgeon* sawbones (or) sawboneses

SBNTR subentry *note* subentries

SBNZ sawbones *(slang) surgeon* sawbones (or) sawboneses

SBPKL subapical *top*

SBPLR subpolar *cold region*

SBPLT subplot *fiction, land*

SBPN subpoena *summon* subpoenaed subpoenaing

SBPR subpar *below average*

SBPRFSHNL subprofessional *employee*

SBPRGRF subparagraph *writing*

SBPRGRM subprogram *computer*

SBPRNSPL subprincipal *assistant*

SBQDS subcutis *skin*

SBQS subaqueous *water*

SBQT subacute *tapered*

SBQTNS subcutaneous *skin*

SBQTNYS subcutaneous *skin*

SBQTS subcutis *skin*

SBQYS subaqueous *water*

SBR ciboria (pl) *chalice* ciborium

SBR isobar *line, atom*

SBR saber (or) sabre *sword* sabered (or) sabred sabering (or) sabring

SBR seborrhea *disease*

SBR Siberia *region*

SBR soapberry *plant* soapberries

SBR sober *not drunk, serious*

SBRB suburb *outside city*

SBRB suburbia *outside city*

SBRBDL suborbital *eye, flight*

SBRBN suburban *outside city*

SBRBNT suburbanite *outside city*

SBRBNZ suburbanize *residential* suburbanized suburbanizing (Br) suburbanise

SBRBNZSHN suburbanization *residential* (Br) suburbanisation

SBRBTL suborbital *eye, flight*

SBRBY suburbia *outside city*

SBRD seabird *bird*

SBRD seaboard *coast*

SBRD sobriety *no drugs*

SBRDK subarctic *polar*

SBRDK sybaritic *lustful*

SBRDKL sybaritically *lustfully*

SBRDNDV subordinative *inferior*

SBRDNSHN subordination *inferiority*

SBRDNT subordinate *(v) make inferior* subordinated subordinating

SBRDNT subordinate *(n) less value*

SBRDNTV subordinative *inferior*

SBRDR suborder *category*

SBRDZM sybaritism *lust*

SBRG cyborg *robot*

SBRG iceberg *floe*

SBRGSHN subrogation *substitute*

SBRGT subrogate *substitute* subrogated subrogating

SBRJN subregion *area*

SBRJNL subregional *area*

SBRK isobaric *line, pressure, atom*

SBRK seborrheic *disease*

SBRK sobriquet *nickname*

SBRKDK subarctic *polar*

SBRKR icebreaker *ship, game*

SBRKT sobriquet *nickname*

SBRKTK subarctic *polar*

SBRL subaerial (adj) *surface* subaerially (adv)

SBRM ciborium *chalice* ciboria

SBRMTRKS sabermetrics *baseball*

SBRMTRSHN sabermetrician *baseball*

SBRMTRX sabermetrics *baseball*

SBRN seaborne *ocean*

SBRN Siberian *of Siberia*

SBRN sobering *serious*

SBRN suberin *cork*

SBRN suborn *perjury*

SBRNDKS cybernetics *control systems*

SBRNDX cybernetics *control systems*

SBRNG sobering *serious*

SBRNR suborner *perjury*

SBRNSHN subornation *inducement*

SBRNTKS cybernetics *control systems*

SBRNTX cybernetics *control systems*

SBRPNGK cyberpunk *computer hacker*

SBRPNK cyberpunk *computer hacker*

SBRPSHN subreption *falsehood*

SBRPTSHS subreptitious *falsehood*

SBRSDD sobersided *solemn*

SBRSDZ sobersides *solemn*

SBRSPS cyberspace *computers*

SBRT sobriety *no drugs*

SBRT soubrette *maid*

SBRT sybarite *lustful one*

SBRTK subarctic *polar*

SBRTK sybaritic *lustful*

SBRTKL sybaritically *lustfully*

SBRTN subroutine *computer*

SBRTTH saber-toothed *tiger*

SBRTTHD saber-toothed

Letters aren't doubled for single sounds: to find alley use **L** not **LL**. Use **Y** and **W** as hard sounds only: to find yellow use **YL**. (Br)=British spelling or usage. * See dictionary.

tiger
SBRTTHT saber-toothed
tiger
SBRTZM sybaritism *lust*
SBRY ciboria (pl) *chalice*
ciborium
SBRY seborrhea *disease*
SBRY Siberia *region*
SBRYD sobriety *no drugs*
SBRYK seborrheic *disease*
SBRYL subaerial (adj)
surface subaerially (adv)
SBRYM ciborium *chalice*
SBRYN Siberian *of Siberia*
SBRYT sobriety *no drugs*
SBRZ sea breeze *wind*
SBRZ sub rosa (adv) *secret*
sub-rosa (adj)
SBRZSHN suberization *cork*
SBS sea bass *fish*
SBS subbase *molding*
SBSD subside *sink*
subsided subsiding
SBSD subsidy *payment*
subsidies
SBSDNS subsidence
sinking
SBSDNTS subsidence
sinking
SBSDR subsidiary *secondary*
subsidiaries
SBSDS asbestos *mineral*
SBSDYR subsidiary
secondary subsidiaries
SBSDZ subsidize *pay*
subsidized subsidizing
(Br) subsidise
SBSDZR subsidizer *payer*
(Br) subsidiser
SBSDZSHN subsidization
payment
(Br) subsidisation
SBSHNK suboceanic *sea*
bottom
SBSHRN sub-Saharan
desert
SBSHS sebaceous *fatty*
SBSHYNK suboceanic *sea*
bottom
SBSK sebacic *acid*
SBSKL subscale *small*
SBSKRB subscribe *attest,*

agree subscribed
subscribing
SBSKRBR subscriber *attest,*
agree
SBSKRP subscript *symbol*
SBSKRPSHN subscription
signature, pledge
SBSKRPT subscript *symbol*
SBSKSHN subsection
division
SBSKWNS subsequence
following
SBSKWNT subsequent
following
SBSKWNTL subsequently
following
SBSKWNTS subsequence
following
SBSL subsoil *earth*
SBSLLR subcellular *small*
SBSLN subceiling *roof*
SBSLNG subceiling *roof*
SBSLR subcellular *small*
SBSLYLR subcellular *small*
SBSM subsume *enclose*
subsumed subsuming
SBSMBL subassembly *part*
subassemblies
SBSMNT subbasement
cellar
SBSNK subsonic *speed*
SBSNTRL subcentral (adj)
center subcentrally (adv)
SBSPCS subspecies
category
SBSPCZ subspecies
category
SBSPS subspace *universe*
SBSPSHS subspecies
category
SBSPSHZ subspecies
category
SBSPSS subspecies
category
SBSPSZ subspecies
category
SBSQNS subsequence
following
SBSQNT subsequent
following
SBSQNTL subsequently
following

SBSQNTS subsequence
following
SBSRFS subsurface
underground
SBSRVNS subservience
slavery subserviency
SBSRVNT subservient
beneath
SBSRVNTL subserviently
beneath
SBSRVNTS subservience
slavery subserviency
SBSRVYNS subservience
slavery subserviency
SBSRVYNT subservient
beneath
SBSRVYNTL subserviently
beneath
SBSRVYNTS subservience
slavery subserviency
SBSSDM subsystem *group*
SBSSDNS subsistence *life*
support
SBSSDNT subsistent *life*
support
SBSSDNTS subsistence *life*
support
SBSSDR sob sister
sentimental one
SBSST subsist *live*
SBSSTM subsystem *group*
SBSSTNS subsistence *life*
support
SBSSTNT subsistent *life*
support
SBSSTNTS subsistence *life*
support
SBSSTR sob sister
sentimental one
SBST subset *category*
SBSTDV substitutive
replacement
SBSTJ substage *microscope*
SBSTNCHL substantial (adj)
real, sturdy, ample
substantially (adv)
SBSTNCHLD substantiality
real, sturdy, ample
substantialities
SBSTNCHLT substantiality
real, sturdy, ample
substantialities

Use letters that best describe the sounds you hear and omit the vowels. Use **S** or **K** instead of **C**: to find circle use **SRKL**. Use **J** to find joy, **JM** to find gem and **G** to find go.

SBSTNCHSHN
substantiation
confirmation
SBSTNCHT substantiate
confirm substantiated
substantiating
SBSTNCHYLD
substantiality *real, sturdy,*
ample substantialities
SBSTNCHYLT substantiality
real, sturdy, ample
substantialities
SBSTNCHYSHN
substantiation
confirmation
SBSTNCHYT substantiate
confirm substantiated
substantiating
SBSTNDRD substandard
below normal
SBSTNS substance *essence,*
material
SBSTNSHL substantial (adj)
real, sturdy, ample
substantially (adv)
SBSTNSHLD substantiality
real, sturdy, ample
substantialities
SBSTNSHLT substantiality
real, sturdy, ample
substantialities
SBSTNSHSHN
substantiation
confirmation
SBSTNSHT substantiate
confirm substantiated
substantiating
SBSTNSHYLD
substantiality *real, sturdy,*
ample substantialities
SBSTNSHYLT substantiality
real, sturdy, ample
substantialities
SBSTNSHYSHN
substantiation
confirmation
SBSTNSHYT substantiate
confirm substantiated
substantiating
SBSTNTS substance
essence, material
SBSTNTV substantive *(n)*

noun (adj) enduring,
grammar, large amount
SBSTNTVL substantival
noun
SBSTR sob story *tearjerker*
sob stories
SBSTRD substrata (pl)
foundation substratum
SBSTRDM substratum
foundation substrata
SBSTRKCHR substructure
support
SBSTRKCHRL
substructural (adj)
support substructurally
(adv)
SBSTRKSHR substructure
support
SBSTRKSHRL
substructural (adj)
support substructurally
(adv)
SBSTRKTR substructure
support
SBSTRKTRL substructural
(adj) *support*
substructurally (adv)
SBSTRT substrata (pl)
foundation substratum
SBSTRT substrate
foundation
SBSTRTM substratum
foundation substrata
SBSTS asbestos *mineral*
SBSTSHN substation *branch*
SBSTSHN substitution
replacement
SBSTSHNL substitutional
(adj) *replacement*
substitutionally (adv)
SBSTSS asbestosis *disease*
asbestoses
SBSTT substitute *replace*
substituted substituting
SBSTTDBL substitutable
replacement
SBSTTDBLD substitutability
replacement
SBSTTDBLT substitutability
replacement
SBSTTDV substitutive
replacement

SBSTTSHN substitution
replacement
SBSTTSHNL substitutional
(adj) *replacement*
substitutionally (adv)
SBSTTT substitute *replace*
substituted substituting
SBSTTTBL substitutable
replacement
SBSTTTBLD substitutability
replacement
SBSTTTBLT substitutability
replacement
SBSTTTV substitutive
replacement
SBSTTYDBL substitutable
replacement
SBSTTYDBLD
substitutability
replacement
SBSTTYDBLT
substitutability
replacement
SBSTTYDV substitutive
replacement
SBSTTYSHN substitution
replacement
SBSTTYSHNL
substitutional (adj)
replacement
substitutionally (adv)
SBSTTYT substitute *replace*
substituted substituting
SBSTTYTBL substitutable
replacement
SBSTTYTBLD
substitutability
replacement
SBSTTYTBLT
substitutability
replacement
SBSTTYTV substitutive
replacement
SBSYL subsoil *earth*
SBSYLR subcellular *small*
SBSYM subsume *enclose*
subsumed subsuming
SBT iceboat *ship*
SBT sabbat *witches*
SBT sabot *shoe*
SBT subito *music*
SBTDL subtitle *name*

Letters aren't doubled for single sounds: to find alley use **L** not **LL**. Use **Y** and **W** as hard
sounds only: to find yellow use **YL**. (Br)=British spelling or usage. * See dictionary.

subtitled subtitling
SBTDL subtotal *number*
SBTH Sabbath *holy day*
SBTJ sabotage *destruction*
sabotaged sabotaging
SBTKL sabbatical *rest*
SBTKS subtext *meaning*
SBTKSCHL subtextual
meaning
SBTKSCHWL subtextual
meaning
SBTKST subtext *meaning*
SBTKSTL subtextual
meaning
SBTKSTWL subtextual
meaning
SBTKSTYL subtextual
meaning
SBTKSTYWL subtextual
meaning
SBTL subtile *foxiness*
subtiler subtilest
SBTL subtilely *foxiness*
SBTLNS subtileness
foxiness
SBTLR subtiler *foxiness*
SBTLST subtilest *foxiness*
SBTMK subatomic *particles*
SBTN subteen *child*
SBTN subtend *measure,*
occupy
SBTND subtend *measure,*
occupy
SBTNG iceboating *sailing*
SBTNK subtonic *music*
SBTNNC subtenancy
renting
SBTNNS subtenancy
renting
SBTNNT subtenant *renting*
SBTNNTC subtenancy
renting
SBTNNTS subtenancy
renting
SBTNT subtenant *renting*
SBTNTC subtenancy
renting
SBTNTS subtenancy *renting*
SBTP subtype *category*
SBTPK subtopic *theme*
SBTR saboteur *destroyer*
SBTRFJ subterfuge *tricks*

SBTRFSH subterfuge *tricks*
SBTRFYJ subterfuge *tricks*
SBTRFYSH subterfuge
tricks
SBTRFYZH subterfuge
tricks
SBTRFZH subterfuge *tricks*
SBTRHN subtrahend
number
SBTRHND subtrahend
number
SBTRK subtract *take away*
SBTRKDV subtractive *take*
away
SBTRKSHN subtraction *take*
away
SBTRKT subtract *take away*
SBTRKTV subtractive *take*
away
SBTRMNL subterminal *near*
the end
SBTRNN subterranean
underground
SBTRNYN subterranean
underground
SBTRPKL subtropical
weather
SBTRPKS subtropics *region*
SBTRPX subtropics *region*
SBTSH sabotage *destruction*
sabotaged sabotaging
SBTTL subtitle *name*
subtitled subtitling
SBTTL subtotal *number*
SBTX subtext *meaning*
SBTXCHL subtextual
meaning
SBTXCHWL subtextual
meaning
SBTXT subtext *meaning*
SBTXTL subtextual *meaning*
SBTXTWL subtextual
meaning
SBTXTYL subtextual
meaning
SBTXTYWL subtextual
meaning
SBTZH sabotage *destruction*
sabotaged sabotaging
SBVKL subvocal *whisper*
SBVKLZSHN
subvocalization *whisper*

(Br) subvocalisation
SBVNCHN subvention
support
SBVNSHN subvention
support
SBVRSHN subversion
overthrow
SBVRSHNR subversionary
overthrow
SBVRSV subversive
undermining
SBVRSVL subversively
undermining
SBVRSVNS subversiveness
undermining
SBVRT subvert *undermine*
SBVRZHN subversion
overthrow
SBVRZHNR subversionary
overthrow
SBVRZV subversive
undermining
SBVRZVL subversively
undermining
SBVRZVNS subversiveness
undermining
SBW subway *passage,*
railway
SBX icebox *freezer* iceboxes
SBX soapbox *crate*
soapboxes
SBYDK sub judice *in court*
SBYLT subulate *tapering*
SBZR subzero *freezing*
SC sassy *impudent, lively*
sassier sassiest
SC saucy *bold, gravy, smart*
saucier sauciest
SC sissy *timid, effeminate*
sissies
SC sycee *money*
SCD secede *pull out*
seceded seceding
SCDR seceder *pull out*
SCDV associative *related*
SCGRM sociogram *chart*
SCH eschew *shun*
SCH seiche *wave*
SCH such *so much, type*
SCHDBL escheatable *no*
heirs
SCHDD situated *located*

Use letters that best describe the sounds you hear and omit the vowels. Use **S** or **K** instead of **C**: to find circle use **SRKL**. Use **J** to find joy, **JM** to find gem and **G** to find go.

SCHL eschewal *rejection*
SCHL satchel *bag*
SCHLFL satchelful *bag*
SCHM sachem *chief*
SCHMK sachemic *chief*
SCHN Szechuan (or) Szechwan *Chinese*
SCHNC East China Sea *body of water*
SCHNDSCH such and such *not named*
SCHNG souchong *tea*
SCHNS East China Sea *body of water*
SCHNSCH such and such *not named*
SCHR estuary *delta area* estuaries
SCHR oyster *animal*
SCHR side chair *furniture*
SCHR suture *stitch* sutured suturing
SCHRBD oyster bed *ocean*
SCHRBL saturable *soak*
SCHRDD saturated *soaked*
SCHRDR saturator *soaked*
SCHRKCHR oystercatcher *bird*
SCHRKRB oyster crab *animal*
SCHRL estuarial *delta area*
SCHRN estuarine *delta area*
SCHRNG oystering *gather oysters*
SCHRNT saturant *soak*
SCHRSHN saturation *soaking*
SCHRT saturate *soak* saturated saturating
SCHRTD saturated *soaked*
SCHRTR saturator *soaked*
SCHRYL estuarial *delta area*
SCHSHN situation *site, status, problem*
SCHSHNL situational *site, status, problem*
SCHST ice chest *cooler*
SCHT escheat *no heirs*
SCHT situate *locate* situated situating
SCHTBL escheatable *no heirs*

SCHTD situated *located*
SCHWDD situated *located*
SCHWL eschewal *rejection*
SCHWN Szechuan (or) Szechwan *Chinese*
SCHWR estuary *delta area* estuaries
SCHWRL estuarial *delta area*
SCHWRN estuarine *delta area*
SCHWRYL estuarial *delta area*
SCHWSHN situation *site, status, problem*
SCHWSHNL situational *site, status, problem*
SCHWT situate *locate* situated situating
SCHWTD situated *located*
SCKLCHRL sociocultural (adj) *groups* socioculturally (adv)
SCKLTRL sociocultural (adj) *groups* socioculturally (adv)
SCKNMK socioeconomic *money*
SCLG sociology *group study*
SCLJ sociology *group study*
SCLJKL sociological (adj) *group study* sociologically (adv)
SCLJST sociologist *group study*
SCLN caecilian *animal*
SCLNGGWSDK sociolinguistic *language*
SCLNGGWSTK sociolinguistic *language*
SCLNGSDK sociolinguistic *language*
SCLNGSTK sociolinguistic *language*
SCLNGWSDK sociolinguistic *language*
SCLNGWSTK sociolinguistic *language*
SCLYN caecilian *animal*
SCMTR sociometry *group study*
SCMTRK sociometric *group study*

SCNS sauciness *bold, gravy, smart*
SCPLDKL sociopolitical *groups and politics*
SCPLTKL sociopolitical *groups and politics*
SCPTH sociopath *mental illness*
SCR sassier *impudent, lively*
SCR saucier *bold, gravy, smart*
SCSHN association *group*
SCSKSHL sociosexual *gender*
SCSKSHWL sociosexual *gender*
SCST sassiest *impudent, lively*
SCST sauciest *bold, gravy, smart*
SCSXL sociosexual *gender*
SCSXWL sociosexual *gender*
SCT associate *(v) join* associated associating
SCT associate *(n) partner, degree (adj) connected*
SCTV associative *related*
SCWKNMK socioeconomic *money*
SCYDV associative *related*
SCYGRM sociogram *chart*
SCYKLCHRL sociocultural (adj) *groups* socioculturally (adv)
SCYKNMK socioeconomic *money*
SCYLG sociology *group study*
SCYLJ sociology *group study*
SCYLJKL sociological (adj) *group study* sociologically (adv)
SCYLJST sociologist *group study*
SCYLNGGWSDK sociolinguistic *language*
SCYLNGGWSTK sociolinguistic *language*
SCYLNGSDK sociolinguistic *language*

Letters aren't doubled for single sounds: to find alley use **L** not **LL**. Use **Y** and **W** as hard sounds only: to find yellow use **YL**. (Br)=British spelling or usage. * See dictionary.

SCYLNGSTK sociolinguistic *language*

SCYLNGWSDK sociolinguistic *language*

SCYLNGWSTK sociolinguistic *language*

SCYMTR sociometry *group study*

SCYMTRK sociometric *group study*

SCYPLDKL sociopolitical *groups and politics*

SCYPLTKL sociopolitical *groups and politics*

SCYPTH sociopath *mental illness*

SCYR sassier *impudent, lively*

SCYR saucier *bold, gravy, smart*

SCYSHN association *group*

SCYSKSHL sociosexual *gender*

SCYSKSHWL sociosexual *gender*

SCYST sassiest *impudent, lively*

SCYST sauciest *bold, gravy, smart*

SCYT associate (v) *join* associated associating

SCYT associate (n) *partner,* degree (adj) *connected*

SCYTV associative *related*

SCYWKNMK socioeconomic *money*

SD acedia *apathy*

SD acid *chemical*

SD aside *comment, next to*

SD C.O.D. (abbr) *cash on delivery*

SD cede *grant, give up* ceded ceding

SD city *town* cities

SD ostia (pl) *mouth* ostium

SD pseudo *false*

SD sad *sorrow* sadder saddest

SD said (v-past) *say*

SD seed (n) *embryo, ranking* (v) *plant* seed (or) seeds

SD seedy *run-down* seedier

seediest

SD side (v) *agree* sided siding

SD side (n) *surface, slope, part**

SD sod *grass* sodded sodding

SD soda *drink, sodium*

SD sooty *black* sootier sootiest

SDBD seedbed *soil*

SDBL citable *quote, summon*

SDBL suitable (adj) *fit* suitably (adv)

SDBLD suitability *fitness*

SDBLST osteoblast *cell*

SDBLT suitability *fitness*

SDBN sideband *frequency*

SDBND sideband *frequency*

SDBR sidebar *story*

SDBRD sideboard *furniture*

SDBRNS sideburns *facial hair*

SDBRNZ sideburns *facial hair*

SDBSD side-by-side (adj) *adjacent* side by side (adv)

SDBSDR sodbuster *farmer*

SDBSTR sodbuster *farmer*

SDC acey-deucey *card game*

SDCHR side chair *furniture*

SDCL pseudocoel *sac*

SDCLMT pseudocoelomate *sac*

SDCN psittacine *parrots*

SDD acidity *like acid* acidities

SDD assiduity *diligence* assiduities

SDD cited *quote, summon*

SDD sighted *not blind*

SDDL citadel *fortress*

SDDV sedative *relaxer*

SDF acetify *sour* acetifies acetified acetifying

SDF acidify *make acid* acidifies acidified acidifying

SDF citify *urbanize* citified citifying citifies

SDF sawed-off *short*

SDF set off (v) *leave*

SDF setoff (n) *decoration*

SDFD acidified *made acid*

SDFD citified *urbanized*

SDFK side effect *result*

SDFKSHN acetification *sour*

SDFKSHN acidification *making acid*

SDFKT side effect *result*

SDFL acidophil *acid stain*

SDFLK acidophilic *acid staining*

SDFLK cytophilic *cell affinity*

SDFLS acidophilus *milk*

SDFNTN soda fountain *ice cream*

SDFR acidifier *maker of acid*

SDFTN soda fountain *ice cream*

SDFYR acidifier *maker of acid*

SDGLNS side-glance *look*

SDGLNTS side-glance *look*

SDGNK osteogenic *bone*

SDGNSS osteogenesis *bone*

SDHD acidhead *LSD user*

SDHRS side horse *pommel horse*

SDJNK osteogenic *bone*

SDJNSS osteogenesis *bone*

SDJRK soda jerk *ice cream*

SDK acetic *acid*

SDK acidic *acid*

SDK ascetic *severe*

SDK sciatic *nerve*

SDK sciatica *pain*

SDK sea duck *bird*

SDKDK psittacotic *disease*

SDKDRS seductress *enticer* (f) seductresses

SDKDV seductive *enticing*

SDKK seedcake *food*

SDKK sidekick *buddy*

SDKL ascetically *severely*

SDKN cytokine *immunity*

SDKNDK cytokinetic *cell division*

SDKNN cytokinin *plant growth*

SDKNSS cytokinesis *cell division*

SDKNTK cytokinetic *cell*

Use letters that best describe the sounds you hear and omit the vowels. Use **S** or **K** instead of **C**: to find circle use **SRKL**. Use **J** to find joy, **JM** to find gem and **G** to find go.

division
SDKR sidecar *motorcycle*
SDKSD acetic acid *vinegar*
SDKSHN seduction
enticement
SDKSS psittacosis *disease*
SDKTK psittacotic *disease*
SDKTRS seductress *enticer*
(f) seductresses
SDKTV seductive *enticing*
SDL acetal *aldehyde*
SDL acetyl *acid*
SDL acidly *bitterly*
SDL cedilla *mark*
SDL ostiole *pore*
SDL saddle *horse* saddled
saddling
SDL saw-whet owl *bird*
SDL Seattle *city*
SDL sedilia *seats*
SDL seedily *run-down*
SDL seidel *mug*
SDL settle *(v) fix, adjust*
settled settling
SDL settle *(n) bench*
SDL sidle *move sideways*
sidled sidling
SDL sootily *black*
SDL subtle *slight, refined,*
crafty subtler subtlest
SDL subtly *slightly*
SDLB saddlebow *front*
SDLBG saddlebag *pouch*
SDLBRD saddlebred *horse*
SDLD sedulity *diligence*
SDLD sodality *brotherhood*
sodalities
SDLD subtlety *slight, refined,*
crafty subtleties
SDLDK cytolytic *cell death*
SDLDV acetylative *with*
acetyl
SDLHRN saddle horn
pommel
SDLHRS saddle horse
riding
SDLKLN acetylcholine
neurotransmitter
SDLKLNSTRS
acetylcholinesterase
enzyme
SDLKLNSTRZ

acetylcholinesterase
enzyme
SDLKLTH saddlecloth *horse*
SDLMNT settlement *village,*
agreement
SDLN acetylene *gas*
SDLN seedling *plant*
SDLN sideline *(n) border,*
extra job
SDLN sideline *(v) remove*
SDLNG seedling *plant*
SDLNG sidelong *slanting*
SDLNS subtleness *slight,*
refined, crafty
SDLNT acidulent *harsh*
SDLR saddler *merchant*
SDLR saddlery *business*
saddleries
SDLR settler *pioneer*
SDLR subtler *slight, refined,*
crafty
SDLRN saddle horn *pommel*
SDLRS saddle horse *riding*
SDLS acidulous *harsh*
SDLS sedulous *diligent*
SDLSHN acetylation *adding*
acetyl
SDLSHN acidulation *making*
acid
SDLSLY sedulously *diligent*
SDLSNS sedulousness
diligence
SDLSR saddle sore *blister*
SDLST sodalist *brother*
SDLST subtlest *slight,*
refined, crafty
SDLT acetylate *chemical*
acetylated acetylating
SDLT acidulate *make acid*
acidulated acidulating
SDLT satellite *orbiter*
SDLT sedulity *diligence*
SDLT sidelight *illumination*
SDLT sodality *brotherhood*
sodalities
SDLT subtlety *slight, refined,*
crafty subtleties
SDLTK cytolytic *cell death*
SDLTR saddletree *frame*
SDLTV acetylative *with*
acetyl
SDLY sedilia *seats*

SDM ostium *mouth* ostia
SDM sedum *herb*
SDM sodium *element*
SDM sodomy *sex*
SDMBL estimable *valuation*
SDMD acetamide *chemical*
SDMDK sodomitic (or)
sodomitical *sex*
SDMDKL sodomitical (or)
sodomitic *sex*
SDMDR estimator *appraiser*
SDMDV estimative *appraise,*
conclude
SDMN sideman *band*
SDMNFN acetaminophen
pain reliever
SDMNT sediment *deposit*
SDMNTLG sedimentology
deposit
SDMNTLJ sedimentology
deposit
SDMNTLJKL
sedimentological (adj)
deposit sedimentologically
(adv)
SDMNTLJST
sedimentologist *deposit*
SDMNTR sedimentary
deposits
SDMNTSHN sedimentation
deposits
SDMRF pseudomorph
mineral
SDMRFK pseudomorphic
mineral
SDMRFS pseudomorphous
mineral
SDMRFZM
pseudomorphism *mineral*
SDMSHN estimation
opinion, honor
SDMSKSDK
sadomasochistic *pain*
SDMSKST sadomasochist
pain
SDMSKSTK
sadomasochistic *pain*
SDMSKZM
sadomasochism *pain*
SDMST sodomist *sex*
SDMT estimate *(v) appraise,*
conclude estimated

Letters aren't doubled for single sounds: to find alley use **L** not **LL**. Use **Y** and **W** as hard
sounds only: to find yellow use **YL**. (Br)=British spelling or usage. * See dictionary.

estimating
SDMT estimate (n)
   calculation
SDMTK sodomitic (or)
   sodomitical sex
SDMTKL sodomitical (or)
   sodomitic sex
SDMTR estimator appraiser
SDMTV estimative appraise,
   conclude
SDMVPRLMP sodium-
   vapor lamp lamp
SDMZ sodomize sex
   sodomized sodomizing
SDN sadden sorrow
SDN sedan vehicle
SDN set-in (n, adj) insert set
   in (v)
SDN siding track, walls
SDN sit-down meal, no work
SDN sit-in (n) protest sit in (v)
SDN sodden (adj) soggy (v)
   soak
SDN Sudan country
SDN sudden abrupt
SDN Sydney city
SDNG seating chairs
SDNG setting place
SDNG siding track, walls
SDNG sitting meal
SDNG suiting fabric
SDNL soddenly soggy
SDNL suddenly abruptly
SDNM pseudonym false
   name
SDNMD pseudonymity pen
   name
SDNMS pseudonymous pen
   name
SDNMSL pseudonymously
   pen name
SDNMSNS
   pseudonymousness pen
   name
SDNMT pseudonymity pen
   name
SDNS acidness bitterness
SDNS seediness run-down
SDNS soddenness soggy
SDNS sootiness black
SDNS suddenness
   abruptness

SDNTR sedentary settled,
   attached
SDNTSHN ostentation
   display
SDNTSHS ostentatious
   showy
SDNZ Sudanese of Sudan
SDP set up (v) build, frame,
   harden
SDP setup (n) makeup, plan
SDP sit up (v) rise, stay
   awake
SDP sit-up (n) exercise
SDPD pseudopod foot
SDPD seedpod sac
SDPDL pseudopodal (or)
   pseudopodial foot
SDPDYL pseudopodial (or)
   pseudopodal foot
SDPLSD osteoplasty
   surgery
SDPLSDK osteoplastic
   surgery
SDPLST osteoplasty surgery
SDPLSTK osteoplastic
   surgery
SDPLZM cytoplasm cells
SDPLZMK cytoplasmic cells
SDPLZMKL cytoplasmically
   cells
SDPP soda pop beverage
SDPRDK osteoporotic
   disease
SDPRSS osteoporosis
   disease osteoporoses
SDPRTK osteoporotic
   disease
SDPS sidepiece wall
SDPTH osteopath doctor
SDPTH osteopathy bone
SDPTHK osteopathic bone
SDPTHKL osteopathically
   bone
SDR aster flower
SDR cedar tree
SDR ceder yielder
SDR cider apples
   (Br) cyder
SDR Easter feast day
SDR ester fragrance
SDR Esther biblical woman
SDR ouster expulsion

SDR oyster animal
SDR sadder sorrow
SDR satyr deity, lecher,
   butterfly
SDR seater sitting space
SDR seder (often capitalized)
   feast
SDR seeder planter
SDR seedier run-down
SDR setter dog
SDR siddur book siddurim
SDR sitter baby-sitter
SDR solder (v) weld (n) alloy
SDR sootier blacker
SDR suitor pursue, sue, woo
SDRB Saudi Arabia country
SDRBD oyster bed ocean
SDRBRD cedarbird
   waxwing
SDRBY Saudi Arabia
   country
SDRD asteroid tiny planet
SDRD Saturday weekend day
SDRD side road street
SDRFK sudorific sweat
SDRFRS sudoriferous sweat
SDRK acid rock music
SDRK asterisk star
SDRKCHR oystercatcher
   bird
SDRKRB oyster crab animal
SDRKS asterisk star
SDRL easterly direction
SDRL estrual menstruation
   (Br) oestrual
SDRL sidereal stars
SDRM siddurim (pl) book
   siddur
SDRM side arm (n) weapon
SDRM side drum music
SDRM sidearm (adj) pitch
SDRN acid rain precipitation
SDRN eastern direction
SDRN sadiron press
SDRN Saturn planet
SDRNG oystering gather
   oysters
SDRNL saturnalia orgy
SDRNLN saturnalian orgy
SDRNLY saturnalia orgy
SDRNLYN saturnalian orgy
SDRNN saturnine sullen

Use letters that best describe the sounds you hear and omit the vowels. Use **S** or **K**
instead of **C**: to find circle use **SRKL**. Use **J** to find joy, **JM** to find gem and **G** to find go.

SDRNT sederunt *sitting*
SDRNZM saturnism *lead poisoning*
SDRPR eavesdropper *listener*
SDRS esterase *enzyme*
SDRS estrous (adj) *ovulation* estrus (n) (Br) oestrous, oestrus
SDRS satirize *ridicule* satirized satirizing (Br) satirise
SDRS side-dress (v) *fertilizer* side dress (n)
SDRSK asterisk *star*
SDRSN side-dressing *fertilizer*
SDRSNG side-dressing *fertilizer*
SDRSS satyriasis *sex urge*
SDRST satirist *ridiculer*
SDRSZ ostracize *exclude* ostracized ostracizing (Br) ostracise
SDRSZM ostracism *exclusion*
SDRT siderite *ore, meteorite*
SDRTHRDS osteoarthritis *disease*
SDRTHRTS osteoarthritis *disease*
SDRWD cedarwood *lumber*
SDRWL estrual *menstruation* (Br) oestrual
SDRWS estrous (adj) *ovulation* estrus (n) (Br) oestrous, oestrus
SDRX asterisk *star*
SDRYL sidereal *stars*
SDRYSS satyriasis *sex urge*
SDRZ esterase *enzyme*
SDRZ satirize *ridicule* satirized satirizing (Br) satirise
SDS AC/DC (n) *electricity* (n-slang) *bisexual*
SDS acetous *sour*
SDS acey-deucey *card game*
SDS assiduous *diligent*
SDS seduce *entice* seduced seducing
SDS situs *place*

SDS suds *foam*
SDSD set-aside *portion*
SDSDK sadistic *pain*
SDSDKL sadistically *pain*
SDSDL sidesaddle *riding*
SDSF satisfy *fulfill, pay* satisfied satisfying satisfies
SDSFBL satisfiable *fulfilling, payable*
SDSFD satisfied *fulfilled, paid*
SDSFKDR satisfactory *fulfilling*
SDSFKDRNS satisfactoriness *fulfillment*
SDSFKSHN satisfaction *contentment, payment*
SDSFKTR satisfactory *fulfilling*
SDSFKTRL satisfactorily *fulfilling*
SDSFKTRNS satisfactoriness *fulfillment*
SDSFYBL satisfiable *fulfilling, payable*
SDSH side dish *food*
SDSH sideshow *entertainment*
SDSH sottish *drunk, stupid*
SDSHN sedation *relaxation*
SDSHN sedition *rebellion*
SDSHS seditious *rebellious*
SDSHSL seditiously *rebelliously*
SDSHSNS seditiousness *rebelliousness*
SDSKN side-scan *sonar*
SDSL assiduously *diligently*
SDSL pseudocoel *sac*
SDSLMT pseudocoelomate *sac*
SDSLP sideslip *slide*
SDSMNT seducement *enticement*
SDSN citizen *resident*
SDSN cytosine *gene*
SDSN psittacine *parrots*
SDSNR citizenry *residents* citizenries

SDSNS assiduousness *diligence*
SDSNS pseudoscience *unproven*
SDSNSHP citizenship *community membership*
SDSNTFK pseudoscientific *unproven*
SDSNTS pseudoscience *unproven*
SDSNTST pseudoscientist *unproven*
SDSPLDNG sidesplitting *funny*
SDSPLTN sidesplitting *funny*
SDSPLTNG sidesplitting *funny*
SDSPN sidespin *rotation*
SDSR seducer *enticer*
SDSRKM osteosarcoma *cancer*
SDSS acidosis *reduced alkalinity*
SDSSS pseudocyesis *pregnancy*
SDST osteocyte *bone*
SDST saddest *sorrow*
SDST sadist *pain*
SDST sawdust *wood*
SDST seediest *run-down*
SDST sootiest *blackest*
SDSTK sadistic *pain*
SDSTKL sadistically *pain*
SDSTL sidesaddle *riding*
SDSTP sidestep (v) *avoid* side step (n)
SDSTRDL side-straddle *jumping jack*
SDSTRK sidestroke *swimming*
SDSTRM sidestream *smoke*
SDSTRT side street *road*
SDSTRTL side-straddle *jumping jack*
SDSTT city-state *territory*
SDSWP sideswipe *scrape* sideswiped sideswiping
SDSYNS pseudoscience *unproven*
SDSYNTFK pseudoscientific

Letters aren't doubled for single sounds: to find alley use **L** not **LL**. Use **Y** and **W** as hard sounds only: to find yellow use **YL**. (Br)=British spelling or usage. * See dictionary.

unproven

SDSYNTS pseudoscience
unproven

SDSYNTST pseudoscientist
unproven

SDSZM asceticism *severity*

SDT acidity *like acid* acidities

SDT assiduity *diligence*
assiduities

SDT sedate *quiet* sedated
sedating

SDT set out *(v) describe,*
leave

SDT setout *(n) display*

SDT sit out *refrain*

SDTBL side table *furniture*

SDTK acidotic *reduced*
alkalinity

SDTKSK cytotoxic *kill cells*

SDTKSN cytotoxin *cell killer*

SDTM seedtime *season*

SDTR sudatory *sweat room*
sudatories

SDTRK sidetrack *(n) wall*
diversion (v) deflect

SDTRM sudatorium *sweat*
room

SDTRYM sudatorium *sweat*
room

SDTST acid test *severe test*

SDTV sedative *relaxer*

SDTXK cytotoxic *kill cells*

SDTXN cytotoxin *kill cells*

SDVCH sotto voce *music*

SDWD assiduity *diligence*
assiduities

SDWD citywide *area*

SDWDR soda water
beverage

SDWK sidewalk *pavement*

SDWL side-wheel *boat*

SDWL sidewall *tire*

SDWLR side-wheeler *boat*

SDWNDR sidewinder *snake,*
punch

SDWS assiduous *diligent*

SDWSKRD side-whiskered
facial hair

SDWSKRS side-whiskers
facial hair

SDWSL assiduously
diligently

SDWSNS assiduousness
diligence

SDWT assiduity *diligence*
assiduities

SDWTR soda water *beverage*

SDWZ sideways *diagonal*

SDWZ sidewise *diagonal*

SDY acedia *apathy*

SDY ostia (pl) *mouth* ostium

SDYBLST osteoblast *cell*

SDYC acey-deucey *card*
game

SDYD assiduity *diligence*
assiduities

SDYGNK osteogenic *bone*

SDYGNSS osteogenesis
bone

SDYJNK osteogenic *bone*

SDYJNSS osteogenesis
bone

SDYL ostiole *pore*

SDYLD sedulity *diligence*

SDYLNT acidulent *harsh*

SDYLS acidulous *harsh*

SDYLS sedulous *diligent*

SDYLSHN acidulation
making acid

SDYLSL sedulously *diligent*

SDYLSNS sedulousness
diligence

SDYLT acidulate *make acid*
acidulated acidulating

SDYLT sedulity *diligence*

SDYM ostium *mouth* ostia

SDYM sodium *element*

SDYMVPRLMP sodium-
vapor lamp *lamp*

SDYPLSD osteoplasty
surgery

SDYPLSDK osteoplastic
surgery

SDYPLST osteoplasty
surgery

SDYPLSTK osteoplastic
surgery

SDYPRDK osteoporotic
disease

SDYPRSS osteoporosis
disease osteoporoses

SDYPRTK osteoporotic
disease

SDYPTH osteopath *doctor*

SDYPTH osteopathy *bone*

SDYPTHK osteopathic *bone*

SDYPTHKL osteopathically
bone

SDYR seedier *run-down*

SDYR sootier *blacker*

SDYRB Saudi Arabia
country

SDYRBY Saudi Arabia
country

SDYRN sadiron *press*

SDYS acey-deucey *card*
game

SDYS assiduous *diligent*

SDYS seduce *entice*
seduced seducing

SDYSL assiduously
diligently

SDYSMNT seducement
enticement

SDYSNS assiduousness
diligence

SDYSR seducer *enticer*

SDYSRKM osteosarcoma
cancer

SDYST osteocyte *bone*

SDYST seediest *run-down*

SDYST sootiest *blackest*

SDYT assiduity *diligence*
assiduities

SDYWD assiduity *diligence*
assiduities

SDYWS assiduous *diligent*

SDYWSL assiduously
diligently

SDYWSNS assiduousness
diligence

SDYWT assiduity *diligence*
assiduities

SDZ suds *foam*

SDZ sudsy *foamy* sudsier
sudsiest

SDZM sadism *pain*

SDZN citizen *resident*

SDZN cytosine *gene*

SDZNR citizenry *residents*
citizenries

SDZNSHP citizenship
community membership

SDZR sudsier *foamy*

SDZST sudsiest *foamy*

SDZYR sudsier *foamy*

SDZYST sudsiest *foamy*

SF ossify *become hard*
ossified ossifying ossifies

SF safe *(adj) secure* safer
safest

SF safe *(n) vault*

SF Sappho *poet*

SF sci-fi *science fiction*

SF self *person* selves

SF sift *separate*

SF sofa *couch*

SF soft *not hard, mild,
sluggish**

SF sough *noise*

SF Sufi *mystic*

SFBD sofa bed *couch*

SFBK softback *book*

SFBL softball *sport*

SFBLD soft-boiled *mushy*

SFBND softbound *book*

SFBS self-abuse
masturbation, reproach

SFBSMNT self-abasement
disapproval

SFBYLD soft-boiled *mushy*

SFBYS self-abuse
masturbation, reproach

SFCKN self-seeking *selfish*

SFCKNG self-seeking *selfish*

SFCLN self-sealing *closure*

SFCLNG self-sealing *closure*

SFD safety *(n) security*
safeties

SFD safety *(v) protect*
safetied safetying
safeties

SFD seafood *food*

SFD softy (or) softie
sentimental one softies

SFDBLT safety belt *seatbelt*

SFDCT self-deceit *dishonest*

SFDD asafetida (or)
asafoetida *resin*

SFDFDNG self-defeating
harmful

SFDFNS self-defense
protection

SFDFNTS self-defense
protection

SFDFTN self-defeating
harmful

SFDFTNG self-defeating

harmful

SFDHSV self-adhesive *glue*

SFDJKDD self-educated *no
schooling*

SFDJKTD self-educated *no
schooling*

SFDL asphodel *herb*

SFDL isophotal *light*

SFDNGZ siftings *material*

SFDNL self-denial *restraint*

SFDNT safety net *security*

SFDNYL self-denial *restraint*

SFDNZ siftings *material*

SFDPN safety pin *fastener*

SFDPRKDNG self-
deprecating *belittle*

SFDPRKTN self-
deprecating *belittle*

SFDPRKTNG self-
deprecating *belittle*

SFDPST safe-deposit
storage

SFDPZT safe-deposit
storage

SFDR sifter *separator*

SFDRKDD self-directed
independent

SFDRKTD self-directed
independent

SFDRNGK soft drink
beverage

SFDRNK soft drink *beverage*

SFDRST self-addressed
mail

SFDRVN self-driven
ambitious

SFDSPLN self-discipline
regulation

SFDST self-deceit *dishonest*

SFDSTRKDN self-
destructing *ruin*

SFDSTRKDNG self-
destructing *ruin*

SFDSTRKDV self-
destructive *ruinous*

SFDSTRKTN self-
destructing *ruin*

SFDSTRKTNG self-
destructing *ruin*

SFDSTRKTV self-
destructive *ruinous*

SFDT self-doubt *question*

SFDTRMNSHN self-
determination *choice*

SFDVLV safety valve *vent*

SFDVV safety valve *vent*

SFFSN self-effacing *modest*

SFFSNG self-effacing
modest

SFG esophagi (pl) *throat*
esophagus
(Br) oesophagi

SFGMGRF sphygmograph
pulse

SFGMMNMDR
sphygmomanometer
blood pressure

SFGMMNMTR
sphygmomanometer
blood pressure

SFGMMNMTR
sphygmomanometry
blood pressure

SFGNM sphagnum *moss*

SFGNS sphagnous *mossy*

SFGRD safeguard *defend*

SFGS esophagus *throat*
esophagi
(Br) oesophagus

SFGVRND self-governed
control

SFGVRNN self-governing
control

SFGVRNNG self-governing
control

SFHD selfhood *personality*

SFHLN self-healing *get well*

SFHLNG self-healing *get
well*

SFHLP self-help
independence

SFHPNSS self-hypnosis
trance

SFHRDD softhearted *kind*

SFHRTD softhearted *kind*

SFHT self-hate *loathing*

SFJ esophagi (pl) *throat*
esophagus
(Br) oesophagi

SFJKDD self-educated *no
schooling*

SFJKTD self-educated *no
schooling*

SFK sapphic *verse*

SFK sifaka *animal*
SFK Suffolk *city, county*
SFK Sufic *mystic*
SFKC asphyxia *no oxygen*
SFKCDR asphyxiator *no oxygen*
SFKCSHN asphyxiation *no oxygen*
SFKCT asphyxiate *no oxygen* asphyxiated asphyxiating
SFKCTR asphyxiator *no oxygen*
SFKCY asphyxia *no oxygen*
SFKCYDR asphyxiator *no oxygen*
SFKCYSHN asphyxiation *no oxygen*
SFKCYT asphyxiate *no oxygen* asphyxiated asphyxiating
SFKCYTR asphyxiator *no oxygen*
SFKDV suffocative *no air*
SFKLZ Sophocles *dramatist*
SFKNCHS self-conscious *shy*
SFKNDK safe-conduct *protection*
SFKNDKT safe-conduct *protection*
SFKNFDNS self-confidence *certainty*
SFKNFDNT self-confident *certain*
SFKNFDNTS self-confidence *certainty*
SFKNFST self-confessed *admitted*
SFKNSHS self-conscious *shy*
SFKNTMP self-contempt *hatred*
SFKNTMPT self-contempt *hatred*
SFKNTND self-contained *independent, reserved*
SFKNTND self-contented *happy*
SFKNTNTD self-contented *happy*
SFKNTRL self-control

restraint
SFKNTRLD self-controlled restrained
SFKPN safekeeping *security*
SFKPNG safekeeping *security*
SFKR soft-core *sex*
SFKRDKL self-critical *find fault*
SFKRDSZM self-criticism *find fault*
SFKRKN safecracking *thieving*
SFKRKNG safecracking *thieving*
SFKRKR safecracker *thief*
SFKRTKL self-critical *find fault*
SFKRTSZM self-criticism *find fault*
SFKS asphyxia *no oxygen*
SFKS soft-focus *lens*
SFKS suffix *ending* suffixes
SFKSDR asphyxiator *no oxygen*
SFKSHLZ self-actualize *realize potential* self-actualized self-actualizing
SFKSHLZSHN self-actualization *realize potential*
SFKSHN ossification *become hard*
SFKSHN suffocation *no air*
SFKSHWLZ self-actualize *realize potential* self-actualized self-actualizing
SFKSHWLZSHN self-actualization *realize potential*
SFKSPLNTR self-explanatory *understood*
SFKSPRSHN self-expression *personality*
SFKSSHN asphyxiation *no oxygen*
SFKSSHN suffixation *ending*
SFKST asphyxiate *no oxygen* asphyxiated asphyxiating

SFKSTR asphyxiator *no oxygen*
SFKSY asphyxia *no oxygen*
SFKSYDR asphyxiator *no oxygen*
SFKSYSHN asphyxiation *no oxygen*
SFKSYT asphyxiate *no oxygen* asphyxiated asphyxiating
SFKSYTR asphyxiator *no oxygen*
SFKT suffocate *block air* suffocated suffocating
SFKTN self-acting *automatic*
SFKTNG self-acting *automatic*
SFKTNGL suffocatingly *blocked air*
SFKTNL suffocatingly *blocked air*
SFKTV suffocative *no air*
SFKVR softcover *book*
SFKZSHN suffixation *ending*
SFL ice field *glacier*
SFL ice floe *iceberg*
SFL icefall *waterfall*
SFL sawfly *insect* sawflies
SFL soufflé *food*
SFL useful (adj) *serviceable* usefully (adv)
SFLD ice field *glacier*
SFLD souffléed *puffed*
SFLDK syphilitic *disease*
SFLDN self-loading *pack, start*
SFLDNG self-loading *pack, start*
SFLFLMNT self-fulfillment *success*
SFLFLN self-fulfilling *expected, independent*
SFLFLNG self-fulfilling *expected, independent*
SFLG psephology *elections*
SFLJ psephology *elections*
SFLJKL psephological *elections*
SFLJST psephologist *elections*
SFLK cephalic *head*
SFLN soft-land *landing*

Use letters that best describe the sounds you hear and omit the vowels. Use **S** or **K** instead of **C**: to find circle use **SRKL**. Use **J** to find joy, **JM** to find gem and **G** to find go.

SFLN soft-line *flexible*
SFLND soft-land *landing*
SFLNS usefulness *service*
SFLP self-help *independence*
SFLPD cephalopod *mollusk*
SFLR safflower *herb*
SFLRT sphalerite *ore*
SFLS acephalous *no head*
SFLS selfless *generous*
SFLS Sioux Falls *city*
SFLS syphilis *disease*
SFLT asphalt *coal substance*
SFLT safelight *darkroom*
SFLTHRKS cephalothorax *united head and thorax*
SFLTHRX cephalothorax *united head and thorax*
SFLTK syphilitic *disease*
SFLV self-love *conceit*
SFLWR safflower *herb*
SFLZ Sioux Falls *city*
SFLZSHN cephalization *head*
SFMD self-made *effort*
SFMDVDD self-motivated *driven*
SFMDVTD self-motivated *driven*
SFMJ self-image *esteem*
SFMPLD self-employed *work*
SFMPRDNS self-importance *conceit*
SFMPRDNT self-important *conceited*
SFMPRDNTS self-importance *conceit*
SFMPRTNS self-importance *conceit*
SFMPRTNT self-important *conceited*
SFMPRTNTS self-importance *conceit*
SFMPRVMNT self-improvement *betterment*
SFMPZD self-imposed *established*
SFMR sophomore *second year*
SFMRK sophomoric *immature*
SFMTVDD self-motivated

driven
SFMTVTD self-motivated *driven*
SFN siphon *(n) tube (v) draw off*
SFN soften *melt*
SFN sphene *mineral*
SFND sphenoid (or) sphenoidal *wedge*
SFNDL sphenoidal (or) sphenoid *wedge*
SFNDLJNS self-indulgence *enjoyment*
SFNDLJNT self-indulgent *enjoyment*
SFNDLJNTS self-indulgence *enjoyment*
SFNDST self-induced *influenced*
SFNDYST self-induced *influenced*
SFNFLKDD self-inflicted *harm*
SFNFLKTD self-inflicted *harm*
SFNGDR sphincter *muscle*
SFNGDRK sphincteric *muscle*
SFNGKDR sphincter *muscle*
SFNGKDRK sphincteric *muscle*
SFNGKS sphinx *Egyptian image, hawkmoth, (capitalized) monster* sphinxes (or) sphinges
SFNGKTR sphincter *muscle*
SFNGKTRK sphincteric *muscle*
SFNGTR sphincter *muscle*
SFNGTRK sphincteric *muscle*
SFNGX sphinx *Egyptian image, hawkmoth, (capitalized) monster* sphinxes (or) sphinges
SFNGZ sphinges (pl) *Egyptian image, hawkmoth, (capitalized) monster* sphinx
SFNJD sphingid *hawkmoth*
SFNJZ sphinges (pl) *Egyptian image, hawkmoth,*

(capitalized) monster sphinx
SFNKDR sphincter *muscle*
SFNKDRK sphincteric *muscle*
SFNKRMNTN self-incriminating *guilt*
SFNKRMNTNG self-incriminating *guilt*
SFNKS sphinx *Egyptian image, hawkmoth, (capitalized) monster* sphinxes (or) sphinges
SFNKTR sphincter *muscle*
SFNKTRK sphincteric *muscle*
SFNPSD sphenopsid *plant*
SFNR softener *make smooth*
SFNRST self-interest *advantage*
SFNS saphenous *vein*
SFNSHRNS self-insurance *savings*
SFNSHRNTS self-insurance *savings*
SFNTRST self-interest *advantage*
SFNX sphinx *Egyptian image, hawkmoth, (capitalized) monster* sphinxes (or) sphinges
SFPD self-pity *feel sorry*
SFPDL soft-pedal (v) *de-emphasize* soft pedal (n)
SFPND self-appointed *named*
SFPNTD self-appointed *named*
SFPRKLMD self-proclaimed *declared*
SFPRPLD self-propelled *movement*
SFPRTKSHN self-protection *defense*
SFPRTRT self-portrait *picture*
SFPRZRVSHN self-preservation *protect*
SFPT self-pity *feel sorry*
SFPZSHN self-possession *calm*
SFPZST self-possessed

calm

SFR cipher *code, zero* ciphered ciphering (Br) cypher

SFR safari *jungle*

SFR safer *secure*

SFR sapphire *gem*

SFR sphere *ball* sphered sphering

SFR sphery *round*

SFR suffer *endure pain*

SFRBL sufferable (adj) *endure pain* sufferably (adv)

SFRCHS self-righteous *narrow-minded*

SFRD spheroid *round*

SFRDL spheroidal (adj) *round* spheroidally (adv)

SFRDLZSHN self-fertilization *reproduction*

SFRGLDNG self-regulating *automatic*

SFRGLTN self-regulating *automatic*

SFRGLTNG self-regulating *automatic*

SFRGYLDNG self-regulating *automatic*

SFRGYLTN self-regulating *automatic*

SFRGYLTNG self-regulating *automatic*

SFRJ suffrage *vote*

SFRJST suffragist *vote*

SFRJT suffragette *voter*

SFRK aspheric (or) aspherical *not round*

SFRKCHR usufructuary *user*

SFRKCHWR usufructuary *user*

SFRKL aspherical (or) aspheric *not round*

SFRKL spherical (adj) *round* spherically (adv)

SFRKS sferics *atmosphere*

SFRKT usufruct *right*

SFRKTR usufructuary *user*

SFRKTWR usufructuary *user*

SFRL safrole *perfume*

SFRL spheral *round*

SFRL spherule *globe*

SFRLNS self-reliance *confidence*

SFRLNT self-reliant *confident*

SFRLNTS self-reliance *confidence*

SFRLT spherulite *crystal*

SFRLYNS self-reliance *confidence*

SFRLYNT self-reliant *confident*

SFRLYNTS self-reliance *confidence*

SFRLZSHN self-realization *understanding*

SFRMDR spherometer *curvature*

SFRMTR spherometer *curvature*

SFRN saffron *spice*

SFRN seafaring *ocean*

SFRN suffering *pain*

SFRNG seafaring *ocean*

SFRNG suffering *pain*

SFRNL self-renewal *restore*

SFRNN safranine (or) safranin *dye*

SFRNS sufferance *pain*

SFRNT seafront *shoreline*

SFRNTS sufferance *pain*

SFRNWL self-renewal *restore*

SFRPLST spheroplast *cell*

SFRPRCH self-reproach *blame*

SFRR seafarer *sailor*

SFRR sufferer *pain*

SFRSPK self-respect *regard*

SFRSPKT self-respect *regard*

SFRSTRNT self-restraint *hold back*

SFRTLZSHN self-fertilization *reproduction*

SFRTSND sforzando *chord* sforzandos (or) sforzandi

SFRTZND sforzando *chord* sforzandos (or) sforzandi

SFRX sferics *atmosphere*

SFRYL spherule *globe*

SFRYLT spherulite *crystal*

SFRYLZSHN self-realization *understanding*

SFRZN self-rising *flour*

SFRZNG self-rising *flour*

SFS suffice *satisfy* sufficed sufficing

SFS suffuse *fill* suffused suffusing

SFSDK sophistic (or) sophistical *thinking*

SFSDKDD sophisticated *complex, refined*

SFSDKDDL sophisticatedly *complex, refined*

SFSDKL sophistical (or) sophistic (adj) *thinking* sophistically (adv)

SFSDKSHN sophistication *complex, refined*

SFSDKT sophisticate *change, make complex* sophisticated sophisticating

SFSDKTD sophisticated *complex, refined*

SFSDKTDL sophisticatedly *complex, refined*

SFSDR sophistry *reasoning*

SFSDSFD self-satisfied *smug*

SFSDSFKSHN self-satisfaction *smugness*

SFSFSHNT self-sufficient *independent*

SFSH sawfish *fish*

SFSH selfish *greedy*

SFSH soft-shoe *dance*

SFSHL soft-shell (or) soft-shelled (adj) *outer cover* softshell (n)

SFSHLD soft-shelled (or) soft-shell (adj) *outer cover* softshell (n)

SFSHN suffusion *fill*

SFSHNC sufficiency *enough*

SFSHNS sufficiency *enough*

SFSHNT sufficient *enough*

SFSHNTC sufficiency *enough*

SFSHNTL sufficiently *enough*

SFSHNTS sufficiency

Use letters that best describe the sounds you hear and omit the vowels. Use **S** or **K** instead of **C**: to find circle use **SRKL**. Use **J** to find joy, **JM** to find gem and **G** to find go.

enough
SFSHRD self-assured *confident*
SFSHRNS self-assurance *confidence*
SFSHRNTS self-assurance *confidence*
SFSKN self-seeking *selfish*
SFSKNG self-seeking *selfish*
SFSKRFS self-sacrifice *offering, loss*
SFSKRFSN self-sacrificing *offering, loss*
SFSKRFSNG self-sacrificing *offering, loss*
SFSL soft sell *market*
SFSLN self-sealing *closure*
SFSLNG self-sealing *closure*
SFSM selfsame *identical*
SFSNRD self-centered *proud, vain*
SFSNTRD self-centered *proud, vain*
SFSP soft-soap (v) *flatter* soft soap (n)
SFSPKN soft-spoken *mannerly*
SFSPRT self-support *independence*
SFSPT soft spot *weakness*
SFSR sufficer *satisfy*
SFSRDV self-assertive *aggressive*
SFSRTV self-assertive *aggressive*
SFSRVN self-serving *selfish*
SFSRVNG self-serving *selfish*
SFSRVS self-service *do-it-yourself*
SFSSTNN self-sustaining *maintain*
SFSSTNNG self-sustaining *maintain*
SFST safest *secure*
SFST sophist *thinker*
SFSTK sophistic (or) sophistical *thinking*
SFSTKDD sophisticated *complex, refined*
SFSTKDDL sophisticatedly *complex, refined*

SFSTKL sophistical (or) sophistic (adj) *thinking* sophistically (adv)
SFSTKSHN sophistication *complex, refined*
SFSTKT sophisticate *change, make complex* sophisticated sophisticating
SFSTKTD sophisticated *complex, refined*
SFSTKTDL sophisticatedly *complex, refined*
SFSTLD self-styled *supposed*
SFSTM scyphistoma *larva* scyphistomae
SFSTM self-esteem *confidence*
SFSTR sophistry *reasoning*
SFSTRDR self-starter *initiative*
SFSTRTR self-starter *initiative*
SFSTSFD self-satisfied *smug*
SFSTSFKSHN self-satisfaction *smugness*
SFSTYLD self-styled *supposed*
SFSV suffusive *filled*
SFT isophote *light*
SFT safety (n) *security* safeties
SFT safety (v) *protect* safetied safetying safeties
SFT self-hate *loathing*
SFT sift *separate*
SFT soffit *arch*
SFT soft *not hard, mild, sluggish**
SFT softy (or) softie *sentimental one* softies
SFTBK softback *book*
SFTBL softball *sport*
SFTBLD soft-boiled *mushy*
SFTBLT safety belt *seatbelt*
SFTBND softbound *book*
SFTBYLD soft-boiled *mushy*
SFTCH soft touch *fool*
SFTD asafetida (or) asafoetida *resin*

SFTD softhead *fool*
SFTDD softheaded *foolish*
SFTDPST safe-deposit *storage*
SFTDPZT safe-deposit *storage*
SFTDRNGK soft drink *beverage*
SFTDRNK soft drink *beverage*
SFTFKS soft-focus *lens*
SFTHD softhead *fool*
SFTHDD softheaded *foolish*
SFTHRDD softhearted *kind*
SFTHRTD softhearted *kind*
SFTKR soft-core *sex*
SFTKVR softcover *book*
SFTL isophotal *light*
SFTLN soft-land *landing*
SFTLN soft-line *flexible*
SFTLND soft-land *landing*
SFTNGZ siftings *material*
SFTNT safety net *security*
SFTNZ siftings *material*
SFTPLD soft-pedal (v) *de-emphasize* soft pedal (n)
SFTPN safety pin *fastener*
SFTR sifter *separator*
SFTRCHR self-torture *pain*
SFTRDD softhearted *kind*
SFTRTD softhearted *kind*
SFTRTR self-torture *pain*
SFTSH soft-shoe *dance*
SFTSHL soft-shell (or) soft-shelled (adj) *outer cover* softshell (n)
SFTSHLD soft-shelled (or) soft-shell (adj) *outer cover* softshell (n)
SFTSL soft sell *market*
SFTSP soft-soap (v) *flatter* soft soap (n)
SFTSPKN soft-spoken *mannerly*
SFTSPT soft spot *weakness*
SFTT self-taught *no teacher*
SFTVLV safety valve *vent*
SFTVV safety valve *vent*
SFTWD softwood *pine*
SFTWR software *computer*
SFVDNT self-evident *obvious*

Letters aren't doubled for single sounds: to find alley use **L** not **LL**. Use **Y** and **W** as hard sounds only: to find yellow use **YL**. (Br)=British spelling or usage. * See dictionary.

SFWD softwood *pine*
SFWLD self-willed *stubborn*
SFWNDN self-winding *coil*
SFWNDNG self-winding *coil*
SFWR self-aware *conscious*
SFWR software *computer*
SFWRNS self-awareness *consciousness*
SFX asphyxia *no oxygen*
SFX suffix *ending* suffixes
SFXDR asphyxiator *no oxygen*
SFXPLNTR self-explanatory *understood*
SFXPRSHN self-expression *personality*
SFXSHN asphyxiation *no oxygen*
SFXSHN suffixation *ending*
SFXT asphyxiate *no oxygen* asphyxiated asphyxiating
SFXTR asphyxiator *no oxygen*
SFXY asphyxia *no oxygen*
SFXYDR asphyxiator *no oxygen*
SFXYSHN asphyxiation *no oxygen*
SFXYT asphyxiate *no oxygen* asphyxiated asphyxiating
SFXYTR asphyxiator *no oxygen*
SFYR sapphire *gem*
SFYS suffuse *fill* suffused suffusing
SFYSHN suffusion *fill*
SFYSV suffusive *filled*
SFYZ suffuse *fill* suffused suffusing
SFYZHN suffusion *fill*
SFYZV suffusive *filled*
SFZ suffuse *fill* suffused suffusing
SFZHN suffusion *fill*
SFZM sophism *philosophy*
SFZM Sufism *mysticism*
SFZN scyphozoan *jellyfish*
SFZV suffusive *filled*
SFZWN scyphozoan *jellyfish*
SG sag *bend* sagged sagging
SG saga *story*

SG sago *starch* sagos
SG sego *lily*
SG soggy *wet* soggier soggiest
SGCS eisegeses (pl) *interpretation* eisegesis
SGCZ eisegeses (pl) *interpretation* eisegesis
SGD seguidilla *dance*
SGDL seguidilla *dance*
SGDLY seguidilla *dance*
SGDY seguidilla *dance*
SGFRD Siegfried *hero*
SGJSCHN suggestion *hint, trance*
SGJSDBL suggestible *hint, trance*
SGJSDBLD suggestibility *hint, trance*
SGJSDBLT suggestibility *hint, trance*
SGJSDV suggestive *hint, trance*
SGJST suggest *hint*
SGJSTBL suggestible *hint, trance*
SGJSTBLD suggestibility *hint, trance*
SGJSTBLT suggestibility *hint, trance*
SGJSTV suggestive *hint, trance*
SGL sea gull *bird*
SGL soggily *wet*
SGM isogamy *cell*
SGM sigma *Greek letter*
SGMD sigmoid *curved*
SGMDL sigmoidally *curved*
SGMDSKP sigmoidoscopy *colon exam*
SGMND segmented *divided*
SGMNL segmental (adj) *partial* segmentally (adv)
SGMNT segment *part*
SGMNTD segmented *divided*
SGMNTL segmental (adj) *partial* segmentally (adv)
SGMNTR segmentary *partial*
SGMNTSHN segmentation *part*

SGMR sagamore *chief*
SGMS isogamous *cell*
SGMT isogamete *cell*
SGN isogony *growth*
SGN Saigon *city*
SGN seagoing *ocean*
SGNCHR signature *name*
SGNF signify *mean, matter* signified signifying signifies
SGNFKNS significance *importance*
SGNFKNT significant *important*
SGNFKNTL significantly *important*
SGNFKNTS significance *importance*
SGNFKSHN signification *signs, consequence*
SGNFN signifying *goading*
SGNFNG signifying *goading*
SGNFR signifier *symbol*
SGNFYN signifying *goading*
SGNFYNG signifying *goading*
SGNFYR signifier *symbol*
SGNG seagoing *ocean*
SGNK isogenic *genes*
SGNK isogonic *growth*
SGNL signal (v) *notify* signaled (or) signalled signaling (or) signalling
SGNL signal (n) *sign, impulse* (adj) *great*
SGNLMN signalman *signs* signalmen
SGNLZ signalize *indicate* signalized signalizing (Br) signalise
SGNS Cygnus *star*
SGNS sogginess *wet*
SGNSHN assignation *allotment*
SGNT cygnet *swan*
SGNT signet *seal*
SGNTR signatory *signer* signatories
SGNTR signature *name*
SGR cigar *smoke*
SGR saguaro *cactus* saguaros

Use letters that best describe the sounds you hear and omit the vowels. Use **S** or **K** instead of **C**: to find circle use **SRKL**. Use **J** to find joy, **JM** to find gem and **G** to find go.

SGR sauger *fish*
SGR soggier *wet*
SGRFD sgraffito *decoration* sgraffiti
SGRFT sgraffito *decoration* sgraffiti
SGRGDD segregated *separate*
SGRGSHN segregation *separation*
SGRGSHNST segregationist *separation*
SGRGT segregate *separate* segregated segregating
SGRGTD segregated *separate*
SGRM isogram *map*
SGRS saw grass *plant*
SGRT cigarette *smoke*
SGSD sagacity *shrewdness*
SGSHS sagacious *shrewd*
SGSHSL sagaciously *shrewd*
SGSHSNS sagaciousness *shrewd*
SGSS eisegesis *interpretation* eisegeses
SGST sagacity *shrewdness*
SGST soggiest *wet*
SGSZ eisegeses (pl) *interpretation* eisegesis
SGW segue *transition* segued segueing
SGWN seagoing *ocean*
SGWNG seagoing *ocean*
SGWR saguaro *cactus* saguaros
SGYR soggier *wet*
SGYST soggiest *wet*
SH aecia (pl) *fungus* aecium
SH ash *tree, dust* ashes
SH ashy *dusty* ashier ashiest
SH Asia *continent*
SH au jus *in juice*
SH eschew *shun*
SH ice show *entertainment*
SH issue (v) *emerge, result, provide* issued issuing
SH issue (n) *matter, child, publishing**
SH shah *(often capitalized) king*

SH shaw *thicket, (Br) stem*
SH she *(pron) female*
SH shea *tree*
SH shh (or) shhh *(interj) silence*
SH shoe (v) *cover feet* shod shoeing
SH shoe (n) *foot cover, box*
SH shoo *send away*
SH show (v) *declare, demonstrate, display** showed showing shown
SH show (n) *display, pretense*
SH showy *flashy* showier showiest
SH shy (v) *show distaste or fright* shied shying shies
SH shy (adj) *timid, short* shier (or) shyer shiest (or) shyest
SH shy (n) *jump, fling* shies
SHB jabot *collar*
SHB sahib *master*
SHB shabby *messy, mean* shabbier shabbiest
SHBL Chablis *wine*
SHBL issuable (adj) *open* issuably (adv)
SHBL shabbily *messy, mean*
SHBL shoebill *bird*
SHBL show bill *advertising poster*
SHBLK shoeblack *polisher*
SHBLTH shibboleth *truism*
SHBNG shebang *everything*
SHBNS shabbiness *messy, mean*
SHBR jabiru *bird*
SHBR shabbier *messy, mean*
SHBST shabbiest *messy, mean*
SHBT showboat (n) *ship* (v) *get attention*
SHBYR shabbier *messy, mean*
SHBYST shabbiest *messy, mean*
SHBZ showbiz *theater*
SHBZNS show business *theater*
SHD eye shadow *makeup*
SHD eyeshade *visor*

SHD shade (v) *darken, surpass, slant** shaded shading
SHD shade (n) *color, ghost, shelter**
SHD shadow *darkness, trace*
SHD shadowy *vague*
SHD shady *shameful* shadier shadiest
SHD she'd (contr) *she had, she would*
SHD shed (v) *cast off* shed shedding
SHD shed (n) *building*
SHD shittah *tree* shittahs (or) shittim
SHD shod (v-past) *shoe*
SHD shoddy *bad quality* shoddier shoddiest
SHD should (v-past) *shall*
SHD shut-eye *sleep*
SHDF shut off (v) *stop* shutoff (n)
SHDJL schedule (n) *timetable*
SHDJL schedule (v) *assign time* scheduled scheduling
SHDJWL schedule (n) *timetable*
SHDJWL schedule (v) *assign time* scheduled scheduling
SHDK Asiatic *of Asia*
SHDK shaddock *fruit*
SHDK shtick *bit*
SHDL isohyetal *rainfall*
SHDL schedule (v) *assign time* scheduled scheduling
SHDL schedule (n) *timetable*
SHDL shadily *shamefully*
SHDL shoddily *bad quality*
SHDL shuttle (v) *move back and forth* shuttled shuttling
SHDL shuttle (n) *transport*
SHDLKK shuttlecock (n) *badminton* (v) *bandy*
SHDM shittim (pl) *tree* shittah
SHDMWD shittimwood *tree*

Letters aren't doubled for single sounds: to find alley use **L** not **LL**. Use **Y** and **W** as hard sounds only: to find yellow use **YL**. (Br)=British spelling or usage. * See dictionary.

SHDN shading *darkening*
SHDN shotten *herring*
SHDN shouldn't *(contr)*
should not
SHDN showdown *conflict*
SHDN shut down (v) *close*
shutdown (n)
SHDN shut-in (n, adj) *confine*
shut in (v)
SHDNG shading *darkening*
SHDNG sheeting *material*
SHDNS shadiness
shamefulness
SHDNS shoddiness *bad*
quality
SHDNT shouldn't *(contr)*
should not
SHDP shoot up *inject*
SHDR shadier *shameful*
SHDR shatter (v) *smash* (n)
fragment
SHDR shedder *cast off*
SHDR shoddier *bad quality*
SHDR shooter *revolver,*
marble, drink
SHDR shudder *shiver*
SHDR shutter *cover*
SHDRBG shutterbug
photographer
SHDRPRF shatterproof
unbreakable
SHDRV chef d'oeuvre
masterpiece chefs
d'oeuvre
SHDSPR jeu d'esprit *joke*
jeux d'esprit
SHDST chutist *parachute*
SHDST shadiest *shameful*
SHDST shoddiest *bad*
quality
SHDT shoot-out *fight*
SHDT shut out (v) *exclude*
SHDT shutout (n) *no score*
SHDTL shtetl *town* shtetlach
SHDTLK shtetlach (pl) *town*
shtetl
SHDVR chef d'oeuvre
masterpiece chefs
d'oeuvre
SHDW shadowy *vague*
SHDWL schedule (v) *assign*
time scheduled

scheduling
SHDWL schedule (n)
timetable
SHDYL schedule (v) *assign*
time scheduled
scheduling
SHDYL schedule (n)
timetable
SHDYR shadier *shameful*
SHDYR shoddier *bad quality*
SHDYST shadiest *shameful*
SHDYST shoddiest *bad*
quality
SHDYWL schedule (v)
assign time scheduled
scheduling
SHDYWL schedule (n)
timetable
SHF chef *cook*
SHF shaft *tunnel, rod* shafts
(or) shaves
SHF sheaf *bundle* sheaves
SHF shelf *flat projection*
shelves
SHF show off (v) *exhibit*
SHF show-off (n)
exhibitionist show-offy
(adj)
SHFD shifty *tricky* shiftier
shiftiest
SHFDL shiftily *tricky*
SHFDNS shiftiness *tricky*
SHFDR shiftier *tricky*
SHFDST shiftiest *tricky*
SHFDYR shiftier *tricky*
SHFDYST shiftiest *tricky*
SHFL shoofly *rocker, pie*
SHFL shuffle *jumble, step*
shuffled shuffling
SHFLBRD shuffleboard
game
SHFLF shelf life *storage time*
SHFLK shelflike *flat*
projection
SHFLS shiftless *lazy*
SHFLSL shiftlessly *lazy*
SHFLSNS shiftlessness *lazy*
SHFN chiffon (n) *fabric* (adj)
whipped
SHFND chiffonade *garnish*
SHFNR chiffonier *chest*
SHFR chauffeur *driver*

chauffeured chauffering
SHFR shofar *trumpet*
shofroth
SHFRB chifforobe *furniture*
SHFRTH shofroth (pl)
trumpet shofar
SHFT shaft *tunnel, rod*
shafts (or) shaves
SHFT shift (v) *change*
position (n) *garment, work,*
gear*
SHFT shifty *tricky* shiftier
shiftiest
SHFTL shiftily *tricky*
SHFTLS shiftless *lazy*
SHFTLSL shiftlessly *lazy*
SHFTLSNS shiftlessness
lazy
SHFTNS shiftiness *tricky*
SHFTR shiftier *tricky*
SHFTS Auschwitz *city,*
prison
SHFTST shiftiest *tricky*
SHFTYR shiftier *tricky*
SHFTYST shiftiest *tricky*
SHFYR chauffeur *driver*
chauffeured chauffering
SHG gigot *meat* gigots
SHG gigue *dance*
SHG shag (v) *chase, dance,*
roughen shagged
shagging
SHG shag (n) *fiber, nap*
SHG shaggy *untidy*
shaggier shaggiest
SHG shoji *screen* shoji
SHGBRK shagbark *tree*
SHGL Chagall *artist*
SHGL shaggily *untidy*
SHGL shigella *bacteria*
shigellae
SHGLSS shigellosis
dysentery shigelloses
SHGMN shaggymane
mushroom
SHGN shogun *ruler*
SHGNS shagginess *untidy*
SHGR shaggier *untidy*
SHGR sugar *sweetener*
SHGR sugary *sweet*
SHGRBR sugarberry *fruit*
sugarberries

Use letters that best describe the sounds you hear and omit the vowels. Use **S** or **K**
instead of **C**: to find circle use **SRKL**. Use **J** to find joy, **JM** to find gem and **G** to find go.

SHGRHS sugarhouse *refinery*
SHGRKN sugarcane *grass*
SHGRKT sugarcoat *make sweet*
SHGRL showgirl *entertainer*
SHGRLF sugarloaf *cone, hill*
SHGRN chagrin *distress* chagrined chagrining
SHGRPLM sugarplum *candy*
SHGST shaggiest *untidy*
SHGT gigot *meat* gigots
SHGWRND jaguarundi *wildcat*
SHGYR shaggier *untidy*
SHGYST shaggiest *untidy*
SHHRN shoehorn *device*
SHHRZD Scheherazade *story teller*
SHJ shoji *screen* shoji
SHJL schedule *(v) assign time* scheduled scheduling
SHJL schedule *(n) timetable*
SHJWL schedule *(v) assign time* scheduled scheduling
SHJWL schedule *(n) timetable*
SHK chic *stylish*
SHK ice hockey *sport*
SHK shack *house*
SHK shake *(v) agitate, clasp hands, upset* shook shaking shaken
SHK shake *(n) tremble, beverage, shingle**
SHK shaky *wobbly, uncertain* shakier shakiest
SHK sheikh (or) sheik *Arab chief*
SHK shock *(n) surprise, disturbance, mass (adj) bushy (v) disturb*
SHK shook *bundle, shock*
SHK shuck *(n) husk (v) remove*
SHKBL shakable (or) shakeable *agitate*
SHKBL shockable *surprise*
SHKBSRBR shock absorber *no bumps*

SHKBZRBR shock absorber *no bumps*
SHKDM sheikhdom (or) sheikdom *region*
SHKDN shake down *(v) settle, extort*
SHKDN shakedown *(n) extortion, bed, search**
SHKG Chicago *city*
SHKL chicly *stylish*
SHKL shackle *chain* shackled shackling
SHKL shakily *wobbly, uncertain*
SHKL shekel *money*
SHKMR jacamar *bird*
SHKN ash can *waste*
SHKN chaconne *dance*
SHKN chicane *trick* chicaned chicaning
SHKN shocking *surprising*
SHKNG shocking *surprising*
SHKNR chicanery *trickery* chicaneries
SHKNS chicness *style*
SHKNS shakiness *wobbly, uncertain*
SHKNZ Ashkenazi *Jew*
SHKP shake-up (n) *reorganize* shake up (v)
SHKP shook-up *disturbed*
SHKPRF shockproof *resistant*
SHKR chakra *energy*
SHKR shaker *dispenser*
SHKR shakier *wobbly, uncertain*
SHKR shocker *surprise*
SHKS shiksa (or) shikse *non-Jew*
SHKS showcase *display* showcased showcasing
SHKS shucks *(interj) disappointment*
SHKSPR Shakespeare *dramatist*
SHKSPRN Shakespearean *of Shakespeare*
SHKSPRYN Shakespearean *of Shakespeare*
SHKST shakiest *wobbly, uncertain*

SHKT shakeout *culling*
SHKTHRP shock therapy *treatment*
SHKTRPS shock troops *military*
SHKTRTMNT shock treatment *treatment*
SHKWV shock wave *reaction*
SHKYR shakier *wobbly, uncertain*
SHKYST shakiest *wobbly, uncertain*
SHL asshole *(vulgar) idiot*
SHL chalet *house*
SHL challis *fabric* challises
SHL eschewal *rejection*
SHL gelée *cosmetic*
SHL joual *language*
SHL shale *rock*
SHL shaley *rocky*
SHL shall *intend to should*
SHL shallow *not deep*
SHL shawl *cape*
SHL she'll *(contr) she will, she shall*
SHL sheila *girl*
SHL shell *(n) hard cover, projectile, blouse (v) uncover, bombard**
SHL shelly *with shells* shellier shelliest
SHL shill *decoy*
SHL shoal *shallow, group*
SHL shul *synagogue*
SHL shyly *bashful*
SHL usual (adj) *typical* usually (adv)
SHLBK shellback *sailor*
SHLBN shell bean *vegetable*
SHLD sheltie (or) shelty *pony, dog* shelties
SHLD shield *protection*
SHLDK shelduck *bird*
SHLDR shelter *protection*
SHLDR shoulder *(n) arm joint (v) carry*
SHLDRK sheldrake *bird*
SHLF shelf *flat projection* shelves
SHLFL shelfful *contents*
SHLFLF shelf life *storage*

Letters aren't doubled for single sounds: to find alley use **L** not **LL**. Use **Y** and **W** as hard sounds only: to find yellow use **YL**. (Br)=British spelling or usage. * See dictionary.

time
SHLFLK shelflike *flat projection*
SHLFS shelf ice *ocean*
SHLFSH shellfish *animal*
SHLGM shell game *fraud*
SHLK schlock *inferior*
SHLK shellac *lacquer* shellacked shellacking
SHLK shylock *loan shark*
SHLL shillelagh *cudgel*
SHLM shalom *greeting*
SHLML schlemiel *chump*
SHLN echelon *formation*
SHLN julienne *slice* julienned julienning
SHLN shalloon *fabric*
SHLNG schilling *Austrian money*
SHLNG shilling *British money*
SHLP schlepp (or) schlep *haul*
SHLP shallop *boat*
SHLPRF shellproof *resist bombs*
SHLR ashlar *stone*
SHLR schiller *luster*
SHLR sheller *remove, collect*
SHLR shellier *more shells*
SHLRN schlieren *rocks*
SHLS Aeschylus *dramatist*
SHLS challis *fabric* challises
SHLS shoelace *string*
SHLS shoeless *barefoot*
SHLSHK shell shock *combat stress*
SHLSHKD shell-shocked *combat stress*
SHLSHKT shell-shocked *combat stress*
SHLSHL shilly-shally *hesitate* shilly-shallied shilly-shallying shilly-shallies
SHLST shelliest *most shells*
SHLT scheelite *mineral*
SHLT shallot *onion*
SHLT shell out *pay*
SHLT sheltie (or) shelty *pony, dog* shelties
SHLTR shelter *protection*
SHLV shelve *place on shelf,*

put aside shelved shelving
SHLVN shelving *slope, flat projection*
SHLVNG shelving *slope, flat projection*
SHLVZ shelves (pl) *flat projection* shelf
SHLWRK shellwork *shell art*
SHLYN julienne *slice* julienned julienning
SHLYR shellier *more shells*
SHLYST shelliest *most shells*
SHM aecium *fungus* aecia
SHM assume *suppose* assumed assuming
SHM chamois *antelope, leather* chamois
SHM schmo (or) schmoe *(slang) jerk* schmoes
SHM sham *fake* shammed shamming
SHM shame *(v) disgrace* shamed shaming
SHM shame *(n) pity*
SHM shawm *music*
SHM shim *wedge* shimmed shimming
SHM shimmy *dance, vibrate* shimmied shimmying shimmies
SHM shinny *(v) climb* shinnied shinnying shinnies
SHM show-me *proof*
SHMBL assumable (adj) *received, supposed* assumably (adv)
SHMBL shamble *shuffle* shambled shambling
SHMBLS shambles *wreckage*
SHMBLZ shambles *wreckage*
SHMBR chambray *fabric*
SHMD ashamed *disgraced*
SHMDL ashamedly *disgraced*
SHMFL shameful (adj) *indecent* shamefully (adv)
SHMFLNS shamefulness *indecency*
SHMFST shamefaced

bashful, disgraced
SHMK schmuck *(slang) jerk*
SHMK sumac *plant*
SHMKR shoemaker *cobbler*
SHMLN chameleon *animal, easily changed*
SHMLNK chameleonic *animal, easily changed*
SHMLS shameless *disgraceful*
SHMLSL shamelessly *disgraceful*
SHMLSNS shamelessness *disgrace*
SHMLTS schmaltz *sentimental* schmaltzy
SHMLTZ schmaltz *sentimental* schmaltzy
SHMLYN chameleon *animal, easily changed*
SHMLYNK chameleonic *animal, easily changed*
SHMN assuming *pretentious*
SHMN shaman *wise one* shamans
SHMN showman *entertainer* showmen
SHMNDFR chemin de fer *card game*
SHMNG assuming *pretentious*
SHMNK shamanic *religion*
SHMNSDK shamanistic *religion*
SHMNST shamanist *religion*
SHMNSTK shamanistic *religion*
SHMNZM shamanism *religion*
SHMP shampoo *hair wash* shampoos
SHMPN champagne *beverage*
SHMPN champaign *field*
SHMPN Champaign *city (IL)*
SHMPNYN champignon *mushroom*
SHMR chimere *robe*
SHMR schmear (or) schmeer *whole*
SHMR shimmer *shine*

Use letters that best describe the sounds you hear and omit the vowels. Use **S** or **K** instead of **C:** to find circle use **SRKL**. Use **J** to find joy, **JM** to find gem and **G** to find go.

SHMR shimmery *shiny*
SHMRK shamrock *clover*
SHMS chemise *clothing*
SHMS shamus *detective*
SHMZ chemise *clothing*
SHMZ schmooze (or) shmooze *chat* schmoozed (or) shmoozed schmoozing (or) shmoozing
SHN ashen *pale*
SHN Asian *of Asia*
SHN chaîne *ballet*
SHN Cheyenne *Native American* Cheyenne (or) Cheyennes
SHN ocean *sea*
SHN scena *song*
SHN shanty *hut* shanties
SHN Shawnee *Native American* Shawnee (or) Shawnees
SHN sheen *gloss*
SHN shin *(v) climb* shinned shinning
SHN shin *(n) leg*
SHN shine *(v) glisten* shone (or) shined shining
SHN shine *(n) luster, liking*
SHN shinny *(v) climb* shinnied shinnying shinnies
SHN shinny *game*
SHN shiny *glistening* shinier shiniest
SHN shoe-in *sure thing*
SHN shoo-in *easy winner*
SHN shown *(v-past) show*
SHN shun *avoid* shunned shunning
SHNBN shinbone *leg*
SHND shandy *drink* shandies
SHND shindy *party* shindys (or) shindies
SHNDG shindig *party*
SHNDGF shandygaff *drink*
SHNDL chandelle *climbing turn*
SHNDLR chandelier *ornate light*
SHNDRM gendarme *police*

SHNFRNT oceanfront shoreline
SHNGGL shingle *(v) overlap, lay roofing* shingled shingling
SHNGGL shingle *(n) roofing, sign, gravel**
SHNGGLZ shingles *pain*
SHNGGRL Shangri-la *paradise*
SHNGH Shanghai *city*
SHNGH shanghai *abduct* shanghaied shanghaiing
SHNGK shank *(v) hit badly (n) leg, stem*
SHNGKR chancre *syphilis*
SHNGKRD chancroid *syphilis*
SHNGKRS chancrous *syphilis*
SHNGKSHK Chiang Kai-shek *Chinese president*
SHNGL shingle *(n) roofing, sign, gravel**
SHNGL shingle *(v) overlap, lay roofing* shingled shingling
SHNGLZ shingles *pain*
SHNGN oceangoing *sea*
SHNGNG oceangoing *sea*
SHNGRF oceanography *sea*
SHNGRFK oceanographic *sea*
SHNGRFR oceanographer *sea*
SHNGRL Shangri-la *paradise*
SHNGWN oceangoing *sea*
SHNGWNG oceangoing *sea*
SHNK Chinook *people, wind*
SHNK oceanic *sea*
SHNK schnook *(slang) fool*
SHNK shank *(v) hit badly (n) leg, stem*
SHNKR chancre *syphilis*
SHNKRD chancroid *syphilis*
SHNKRS chancrous *syphilis*
SHNKSHK Chiang Kai-shek *Chinese president*
SHNL chenille *fabric*
SHNLF shinleaf *plant* shinleafs
SHNLG oceanology *sea*

SHNLJ oceanology *sea*
SHNLJST oceanologist *sea*
SHNN shining *bright*
SHNNG shining *bright*
SHNNGN shenanigan *mischief*
SHNNS shininess *glisten*
SHNPK shunpike *road*
SHNPRVKTR agent provocateur *sympathizer* agents provocateurs
SHNPS schnapps *liquor* schnapps
SHNR genre *category*
SHNR oceanaria (pl) *aquarium* oceanarium
SHNR shiner *black eye*
SHNR shinier *glistening*
SHNR shinnery *trees* shinneries
SHNRM oceanarium *aquarium* oceanariums (or) oceanaria
SHNRR schnorrer *beggar*
SHNRY oceanaria (pl) *aquarium* oceanarium
SHNRYM oceanarium *aquarium* oceanariums (or) oceanaria
SHNS issuance *emerge, emit*
SHNS shyness *bashful*
SHNSKW je ne sais quoi *mystery*
SHNSN chanson *song* chansons
SHNSNR chansonnier *singer*
SHNSNY chansonnier *singer*
SHNSNYR chansonnier *singer*
SHNSQ je ne sais quoi *mystery*
SHNST shiniest *glistening*
SHNT chantey (or) chanty *song* chanteys (or) chanties
SHNT shanty *hut* shanties
SHNT shunt *(v) switch (n) passage*
SHNTKLR chanticleer *rooster*
SHNTN shantytown *huts*

Letters aren't doubled for single sounds: to find alley use **L** not **LL**. Use **Y** and **W** as hard sounds only: to find yellow use **YL**. (Br)=British spelling or usage. * See dictionary.

SHNTNG shantung *fabric*
SHNTRL chanterelle *mushroom*
SHNTS issuance *emerge, emit*
SHNTSL schnitzel *meat*
SHNTTN shantytown *huts*
SHNTYZ chanteuse *singer (f)*
SHNTZ chanteuse *singer (f)*
SHNTZL schnitzel *meat*
SHNWSR chinoiserie *style*
SHNWZR chinoiserie *style*
SHNYN chignon *hairdo*
SHNYR shinier *glistening*
SHNYST shiniest *glistening*
SHNZL schnozzle *(slang) nose*
SHNZR schnauzer *dog*
SHP chapeau *hat* chapeaus (or) chapeaux
SHP shape *form* shaped shaping
SHP sheep *animal* sheep
SHP ship *(v) transport* shipped shipping
SHP ship *(n) boat*
SHP shop *market* shopped shopping
SHP show up *arrive, expose*
SHPBL shapable (or) shapeable *form*
SHPBL shippable *transport*
SHPBLDN shipbuilding *make boats*
SHPBLDNG shipbuilding *make boats*
SHPBLDR shipbuilder *make boats*
SHPBR sheepberry *plant* sheepberries
SHPBRD shipboard *boat*
SHPDG sheepdog *animal*
SHPDP sheep-dip *insecticide*
SHPFDR shipfitter *make boats, plumber*
SHPFTR shipfitter *make boats, plumber*
SHPHRDN sheepherding *tend sheep*
SHPHRDNG sheepherding *tend sheep*

SHPHRDR sheepherder *tend sheep*
SHPK shoepac (or) shoepack *boot*
SHPKPR shopkeeper *manager*
SHPKT sheepcote *(Br) shelter*
SHPL shapely *good form* shapelier shapeliest
SHPLD shipload *amount*
SHPLFDR shoplifter *thief*
SHPLFTR shoplifter *thief*
SHPLR shapelier *good form*
SHPLS shapeless *without form*
SHPLS showplace *display*
SHPLSL shapelessly *without form*
SHPLSNS shapelessness *without form*
SHPLST shapeliest *good form*
SHPLYR shapelier *good form*
SHPLYST shapeliest *good form*
SHPMNT shipment *cargo*
SHPMT shipmate *sailor*
SHPN Chopin *composer*
SHPN shipping *boats, dept.*
SHPN shopping *market*
SHPNG shipping *boats, dept.*
SHPNG shopping *market*
SHPNR shipowner *boats*
SHPP shape up *(v) improve*
SHPP shape-up *(n) hiring*
SHPR shipper *transporter*
SHPR shopper *buyer*
SHPRD shepherd *tend sheep, guide, dog*
SHPRDN sheepherding *tend sheep*
SHPRDNG sheepherding *tend sheep*
SHPRDR sheepherder *tend sheep*
SHPRDS shepherdess *tend sheep (f)*
SHPRK shipwreck *boat*
SHPRL chaparral *thicket*
SHPRN chaperon (or) chaperone *companion*

chaperoned chaperoning
SHPRT shipwright *carpenter*
SHPS chaps *leggings, fellows*
SHPS showpiece *display*
SHPSD sheepshead *fish*
SHPSD shipside *dock*
SHPSH sheepish *embarrassed*
SHPSHD sheepshead *fish*
SHPSHFDR shape-shifter *change forms*
SHPSHFTR shape-shifter *change forms*
SHPSHNGK sheepshank *knot*
SHPSHNK sheepshank *knot*
SHPSHP shipshape *tidy*
SHPSHRN sheepshearing *clip fur*
SHPSHRNG sheepshearing *clip fur*
SHPSHRR sheepshearer *clip fur*
SHPSKN sheepskin *leather, diploma*
SHPTK shoptalk *jargon*
SHPWND shopwindow *display*
SHPWRM shipworm *clam*
SHPWRN shopworn *stale*
SHPYRD shipyard *construction*
SHQV shock wave *reaction*
SHR ashore *on land*
SHR assure *certify* assured assuring
SHR azure *blue*
SHR Escher *artist*
SHR giro *fund transfer*
SHR issuer *emerge, emit*
SHR osier *tree*
SHR ossuary *burial* ossuaries
SHR Sahara *desert*
SHR share *(v) divide* shared sharing
SHR share *(n) piece, stock*
SHR shear *cut, clip* sheared (or) shorn shearing
SHR sheer *(adj) transparent (v) swerve (adv) complete (n) fabric**

Use letters that best describe the sounds you hear and omit the vowels. Use **S** or **K** instead of **C**: to find circle use **SRKL**. Use **J** to find joy, **JM** to find gem and **G** to find go.

SHR sherry *wine* sherries
SHR shier (or) shyer *bashful*
SHR shire *town*
SHR shirr *gather, bake*
SHR shore *(v) prop up* shored shoring
SHR shore *(n) land*
SHR shower *(n) spray,rain, party (v) rain, give*
SHR shrew *animal, scolding*
SHR sure *certain* surer surest
SHR usher *theater*
SHR usury *high interest rate* usuries
SHRB shrub *plant, beverage*
SHRBL shareable (or) sharable *divided*
SHRBN charabanc *(Br) bus*
SHRBNG charabanc *(Br) bus*
SHRBNGK charabanc *(Br) bus*
SHRBNK charabanc *(Br) bus*
SHRBR shrubbery *plants* shrubberies
SHRBRD shorebird *animal*
SHRBRT sherbet *ice cream*
SHRBT sherbet *ice cream*
SHRD assured *confident*
SHRD charade *pretense*
SHRD shard *piece*
SHRD sheared *cut, clip*
SHRD shorty (or) shortie *small one* shorties
SHRD showerhead *bath*
SHRD shred *(v) tear up* shredded shredding
SHRD shred *(n) scrap*
SHRD shrewd *smart*
SHRD shroud *cover*
SHRD surety *guarantee* sureties
SHRDJ shortage *lack*
SHRDL assuredly *confidently*
SHRDN chardonnay *wine*
SHRDNG shirting *fabric*
SHRDNR jardinière (or) jardiniere *stand, food*
SHRDNYR jardinière (or) jardiniere *stand, food*

SHRDR shorthair *fur*
SHRDRDR short-order *cook*
SHRDRN shorthorn *cattle*
SHRDZ charades *game*
SHRF sharif *nobleman*
SHRF sheriff *police*
SHRFDD surefooted *no stumbling*
SHRFDDL surefootedly *no stumbling*
SHRFDDNS surefootedness *no stumbling*
SHRFR surefire *certain*
SHRFRNT shorefront *coast*
SHRFTD surefooted *no stumbling*
SHRFTDL surefootedly *no stumbling*
SHRFTDNS surefootedness *no stumbling*
SHRFYR surefire *certain*
SHRG shrug *uncertainty movement* shrugged shrugging
SHRGTT shergottite *meteorite*
SHRHD showerhead *bath*
SHRHLDR shareholder *stocks*
SHRHNDD sure-handed *capable*
SHRJDFR chargé d'affaires *diplomat* chargés d'affaires
SHRK Chirac *French prime minister*
SHRK shark *animal, crafty one*
SHRK shirk *avoid*
SHRK shriek *yell*
SHRK shrike *bird*
SHRK sirocco *wind* siroccos
SHRKK shortcake *dessert*
SHRKLK sharklike *animal*
SHRKR shirker *avoider*
SHRKRPR sharecropper *farmer*
SHRKSKN sharkskin *leather, fabric*
SHRL schorl *gemstone*
SHRL shrill *noisy* shrilly

SHRL surely *certainly*
SHRLDN charlatan *faker*
SHRLDR shareholder *stocks*
SHRLK sherlock *detective*
SHRLK shrewlike *animal, scolding*
SHRLMN Charlemagne *emperor*
SHRLN shearling *lamb*
SHRLN shoreline *coast*
SHRLNG shearling *lamb*
SHRLNGK Sri Lanka *country*
SHRLNK Sri Lanka *country*
SHRLNS shrillness *noise*
SHRLT Charlotte *city*
SHRLTN charlatan *faker*
SHRLTRS charlotte russe *dessert*
SHRM ashram *guru*
SHRM showroom *display area*
SHRMP shrimp *animal, small one* shrimps (or) shrimp
SHRMPR shrimper *fisherman*
SHRN Acheron *river*
SHRN shirring *gather*
SHRN shoehorn *device*
SHRN shoring *brace*
SHRN shorn *(v-past) shear*
SHRN shrine *altar* shrined shrining
SHRNF sure enough *(adv) genuine* sure-enough *(adj)*
SHRNG shirring *gather*
SHRNG shoring *brace*
SHRNG showring *animals*
SHRNGK shrank *(v-past) shrink*
SHRNGK shrink *(v) become smaller* shrank shrunk (or) shrunken shrinking
SHRNGK shrink *(n) psychiatrist*
SHRNGK shrunk *shrink*
SHRNGKBL shrinkable *become smaller*
SHRNGKJ shrinkage *become smaller*
SHRNGKRP shrink-wrap

---

cover shrink-wrapped shrink-wrapping

SHRNK shrank (v-past) shrink

SHRNK shrink (v) become smaller shrank shrunk (or) shrunken shrinking

SHRNK shrink (n) psychiatrist

SHRNK shrunk shrink

SHRNKBL shrinkable become smaller

SHRNKJ shrinkage become smaller

SHRNKRP shrink-wrap cover shrink-wrapped shrink-wrapping

SHRNR Shriner Mason

SHRNS assurance certification

SHRNS sureness certainty

SHRNTS assurance certification

SHRP shar-pei dog sharpeis

SHRP sharp keen, severe, distinct*

SHRP sharpie (or) sharpy boat, person sharpies

SHRPD sharp-eyed vision

SHRPL sharply keen, severe, distinct*

SHRPN sharpen hone

SHRPN shear pin clip

SHRPNL shrapnel bomb shrapnel

SHRPNR sharpener honer

SHRPNS sharpness keen, severe, distinct*

SHRPNZD sharp-nosed face

SHRPR sharper cheater

SHRPSDD sharp-sighted vision

SHRPSHDNG sharpshooting good aim

SHRPSHDR sharpshooter good aim

SHRPSHND sharp-shinned hawk

SHRPSHTN sharpshooting good aim

SHRPSHTNG

sharpshooting good aim

SHRPSHTR sharpshooter good aim

SHRPST sharp-set eager

SHRPSTD sharp-sighted vision

SHRPTNGD sharp-tongued harsh

SHRPWDD sharp-witted acute mind

SHRPWTD sharp-witted acute mind

SHRR assurer (or) assuror certifier

SHRR surer certain

SHRR usurer lender

SHRS sawhorse support

SHRS sea horse animal

SHRS usurious high interest rate

SHRSD shoreside coast

SHRSHDFR chargé d'affaires diplomat chargés d'affaires

SHRST surest certain

SHRT azurite mineral

SHRT cheroot cigar

SHRT shirt clothing

SHRT short small

SHRT shorty (or) shortie small one shorties

SHRT surety guarantee sureties

SHRT usherette theater

SHRTBRD shortbread cookie

SHRTCHNJ shortchange cheat shortchanged shortchanging

SHRTCHNJR shortchanger cheater

SHRTDRS shirtdress clothing

SHRTFL shortfall failure

SHRTFRNT shirtfront clothing

SHRTHL short-haul transport

SHRTHN shorthand writing

SHRTHND shorthand writing

SHRTHNDD shorthanded labor

SHRTHR shorthair fur

SHRTHRN shorthorn cattle

SHRTJ shortage lack

SHRTKK shortcake dessert

SHRTKMN shortcoming lack

SHRTKMNG shortcoming lack

SHRTKT shortcut (v) bypass shortcut shortcutting

SHRTKT shortcut (n) route

SHRTL shirttail clothing

SHRTL short-haul transport

SHRTL shortly soon

SHRTLST shortlist (n) choice short-list (v)

SHRTLVD short-lived lifespan

SHRTMKR shirtmaker tailor

SHRTMPRD short-tempered grouchy

SHRTN shirting fabric

SHRTN shorten cut off

SHRTN shorthand writing

SHRTND shorthand writing

SHRTNG shirting fabric

SHRTNN shortening fat

SHRTNNG shortening fat

SHRTNS shortness briefness

SHRTR shorthair fur

SHRTRBS short ribs meat

SHRTRD short-eared ears

SHRTRDR short-order cook

SHRTRN short run (n) brief time short-run (adj)

SHRTRN shorthorn cattle

SHRTRNJ short-range soon, near

SHRTRS chartreuse color

SHRTRS shirtdress clothing

SHRTRZ chartreuse color

SHRTSDD shortsighted nearsighted

SHRTSDDL shortsightedly nearsighted

SHRTSDDNS

shortsightedness nearsighted

SHRTSLV shirtsleeve arm cover

SHRTSPKN short-spoken curt

Use letters that best describe the sounds you hear and omit the vowels. Use **S** or **K** instead of **C**: to find circle use **SRKL**. Use **J** to find joy, **JM** to find gem and **G** to find go.

SHRTSRKT short-circuit (v) *bypass*

SHRTSTD shortsighted *nearsighted*

SHRTSTDL shortsightedly *nearsighted*

SHRTSTDNS shortsightedness *nearsighted*

SHRTSTP short-stop *etching*

SHRTSTP shortstop *baseball*

SHRTSTR short story *book* short stories

SHRTWNDD short-winded *out of breath, brief*

SHRTWST shirtwaist *clothing*

SHRTWT short weight (n) *light* short-weight (v)

SHRTWV shortwave *radio*

SHRV shrive *reconcile* shrived (or) shrove shriving shriven

SHRVL shrieval *(Br) sheriff*

SHRVL shrivel *dwindle* shriveled (or) shrivelled shriveling (or) shrivelling

SHRVLD shrievalty *(Br) sheriff*

SHRVLT shrievalty *(Br) sheriff*

SHRVN shriven *(v-past) shrive*

SHRWDR shearwater *bird*

SHRWR shareware *computer*

SHRWRD shoreward *coast*

SHRWTR shearwater *bird*

SHRYS usurious *high interest rate*

SHRZ shears *scissors*

SHRZHDFR chargé d'affaires *diplomat* chargés d'affaires

SHS ashes *fire dust* ash

SHS au jus *in juice*

SHS chassé *dance* chasséd chasséing

SHS chassis *frame* chassis

SHS icehouse *freezer*

SHS otiose *vain*

SHS schuss *ski*

SHSD otiosity *in vain*

SHSDR shyster *no scruples*

SHSDSM schistosome *worm*

SHSDSML schistosomal *worm*

SHSDSMSS schistosomiasis *disease* schistosomiases

SHSDSMYSS schistosomiasis *disease* schistosomiases

SHSH chichi *stylish*

SHSH shush *quiet*

SHSHKBB shish kebab *food*

SHSL otiosely *vainly*

SHSN jacana *bird*

SHSPR aeciospore *fungus*

SHSR chasseur *hunter, footman*

SHSS chassis *frame* chassis

SHST otiosity *in vain*

SHST schist *rock*

SHST shiest (or) shyest *bashful*

SHSTPN showstopping *exceptional*

SHSTPNG showstopping *exceptional*

SHSTPR showstopper *exceptional*

SHSTR shyster *no scruples*

SHSTRNG shoestring *cord, little money*

SHSTS schistose *rocky*

SHSTSD schistosity *rocky*

SHSTSM schistosome *worm*

SHSTSML schistosomal *worm*

SHSTSMSS schistosomiasis *disease* schistosomiases

SHSTSMYSS schistosomiasis *disease* schistosomiases

SHSTST schistosity *rocky*

SHSZ chassis *frame* chassis

SHT as yet *until now*

SHT chateau *house*

SHT chute *slide* chuted chuting

SHT eyeshot *view*

SHT isohyet *rainfall*

SHT jeté *ballet*

SHT sheet *(n) paper, cloth (v) shroud, flow (adj) rolled**

SHT Shiite *Muslim*

SHT shit *(v-vulgar) defecate* shit (or) shat shitting

SHT shit *(n) worthless, nonsense*

SHT shittah *tree* shittahs (or) shittim

SHT shoat *pig*

SHT shoddy *bad quality* shoddier shoddiest

SHT shoot *(v) gun, play, wreck* shot shooting

SHT shoot *(n) film, branch*

SHT shot *gun, finished, try**

SHT shout *yell*

SHT shut *close* shut shutting

SHT shut-eye *sleep*

SHTBN sheet bend *hitch*

SHTBND sheet bend *hitch*

SHTBRN chateaubriand *food*

SHTBRND chateaubriand *food*

SHTBRYN chateaubriand *food*

SHTBRYND chateaubriand *food*

SHTDN shut down (v) *close* shutdown (n)

SHTF shut off (v) *stop* shutoff (n)

SHTGN shotgun *(n) weapon (adj) coerced, hit-or-miss*

SHTH sheath *case, dress* sheaths

SHTH sheathe *cover* sheathed sheathing

SHTHN sheathing *cover*

SHTHNG sheathing *cover*

SHTK Asiatic *of Asia*

SHTK shaddock *fruit*

SHTK shiitake *mushroom*

SHTK shtick *bit*

SHTL isohyetal *rainfall*

SHTL shoddily *bad quality*

SHTL shuttle *(v) move back and forth* shuttled

shuttling
SHTL shuttle (n) transport
SHTLKK shuttlecock (n) badminton (v) bandy
SHTLN Shetland pony, dog
SHTLND Shetland pony, dog
SHTM shittim (pl) tree shittah
SHTMWD shittimwood tree
SHTN shotten herring
SHTN shut-in (n, adj) confine shut in (v)
SHTNG sheeting material
SHTNS shoddiness bad quality
SHTP shoot up inject
SHTPDR shot-putter sports
SHTPT shot put sport
SHTPTR shot-putter sports
SHTR ashtray receptacle
SHTR shatter (v) smash (n) fragment
SHTR shedder cast off
SHTR shoddier bad quality
SHTR shoe tree shoes
SHTR shooter revolver, marble, drink
SHTR shudder shiver
SHTR shutter cover
SHTRBG shutterbug photographer
SHTRDL strudel pastry
SHTRK Sheetrock (trademark) plasterboard
SHTRM short-term brief time
SHTRPRF shatterproof unbreakable
SHTRSL streusel cake topping
SHTRZL streusel cake topping
SHTS shih tzu dog shih tzus
SHTSH schottische dance
SHTST chutist parachute
SHTST shoddiest bad quality
SHTT shoot-out fight
SHTT shut out (v) exclude
SHTT shutout (n) no score
SHTTGRT Stuttgart city
SHTTL shtetl town shtetlach
SHTTLK shtetlach (pl) town shtetl

SHTWTS Auschwitz city, prison
SHTYR shoddier bad quality
SHTYST shoddiest bad quality
SHTZ shiatsu massage
SHTZ shih tzu dog shih tzus
SHV Chevy Chevrolet Chevies
SHV shave slice, cut off hair shaved shaving shaven
SHV sheave bind sheaved sheaving
SHV shiv (slang) knife
SHV Shiva Hindu deity
SHV shove push shoved shoving
SHVL à cheval astride
SHVL Asheville city
SHVL chevalier noble
SHVL shovel (v) dig shoveled (or) shovelled shoveling (or) shovelling
SHVL shovel (n) scoop
SHVLFL shovelful scoop shovelfuls
SHVLNZ shovelnose fish
SHVLR chevalier noble
SHVLR chivalry gallantry
SHVLR shoveler (or) shoveller scooper
SHVLRK chivalric valiant
SHVLRS chivalrous valiant
SHVLRSL chivalrously valiantly
SHVLRSNS chivalrousness valiant
SHVLY chevalier noble
SHVLYR chevalier noble
SHVN shaving slice
SHVNG shaving slice
SHVNSDK chauvinistic superior
SHVNSDKL chauvinistically superior
SHVNST chauvinist superiority
SHVNSTK chauvinistic superior
SHVNSTKL chauvinistically superior
SHVNZM chauvinism

superiority
SHVR shaver razor, boy
SHVR shiver (v) shake, shatter (n) piece, tremble
SHVR shivery breakable, trembling
SHVR shover pusher
SHVRN chevron V-shaped
SHVS shaves (pl) tunnel, rod shaft
SHVT cheviot sheep
SHVTS Auschwitz city, prison
SHVYT cheviot sheep
SHVZ shaves (pl) tunnel, rod shaft
SHVZ sheaves (pl) bundle sheaf
SHVZ shelves (pl) flat projection shelf
SHW schwa vowel
SHW showy flashy showier showiest
SHWBL issuable (adj) open issuably (adv)
SHWDVVR joie de vivre enjoyment
SHWF show off (v) exhibit
SHWF show-off (n) exhibitionist show-offy (adj)
SHWL eschewal rejection
SHWL joual language
SHWL showily flashy
SHWL usual (adj) typical usually (adv)
SHWN shoo-in easy winner
SHWN showing display, performance
SHWNG showing display, performance
SHWNS issuance emerge, emit
SHWNS showiness flashy
SHWNTS issuance emerge, emit
SHWP show up arrive, expose
SHWR issuer emerge, emit
SHWR ossuary burial ossuaries
SHWR shower (n) spray, rain,

Use letters that best describe the sounds you hear and omit the vowels. Use **S** or **K** instead of **C**: to find circle use **SRKL**. Use **J** to find joy, **JM** to find gem and **G** to find go.

party (v) rain, give
SHWR showier *flashy*
SHWRD showerhead *bath*
SHWRHD showerhead *bath*
SHWRN shoehorn *device*
SHWST showiest *flashy*
SHWTS Auschwitz *city, prison*
SHWYR showier *flashy*
SHWYST showiest *flashy*
SHX shiksa (or) shikse *non-Jew*
SHX shucks *(interj) disappointment*
SHXPR Shakespeare *dramatist*
SHXPRN Shakespearean *of Shakespeare*
SHXPRYN Shakespearean *of Shakespeare*
SHY aecia (pl) *fungus* aecium
SHY issue *(v)* emerge, result, provide issued issuing
SHY issue *(n) matter, child, publishing**
SHYDK Asiatic *of Asia*
SHYDL isohyetal *rainfall*
SHYM aecium *fungus* aecia
SHYN Cheyenne *Native American* Cheyenne (or) Cheyennes
SHYNK oceanic *sea*
SHYR shier (or) shyer *bashful*
SHYR shire *town*
SHYS otiose *vain*
SHYSD otiosity *in vain*
SHYSL otiosely *vainly*
SHYSPR aeciospore *fungus*
SHYST otiosity *in vain*
SHYST shiest (or) shyest *bashful*
SHYT as yet *until now*
SHYT isohyet *rainfall*
SHYT Shiite *Muslim*
SHYTK Asiatic *of Asia*
SHYTL isohyetal *rainfall*
SHYTZ shiatsu *massage*
SHZ ashes *fire dust* ash
SHZ chaise *carriage, chair*
SHZ chose *thing*

SHZLNG chaise longue *chair* chaise longues
SHZLNJ chaise longue *chair* chaise longues
SHZM schism *division*
SHZMDK schismatic *division*
SHZMTK schismatic *division*
SHZMTZ schismatize *divide* schismatized schismatizing
SJ assuage *ease* assuaged assuaging
SJ ice age *(often capitalized) era*
SJ Osage *Native American* Osages (or) Osage
SJ sage *(adj) wise* sager sagest
SJ sage *(n) wise one, herb*
SJ sedge *plant* sedgy
SJ sewage *waste*
SJ siege *capture*
SJ usage *practice*
SJBRSH sagebrush *shrub*
SJD assiduity *diligence* assiduities
SJDL sagital (adj) *median* sagitally (adv)
SJL sigil *seal, sign*
SJLD sedulity *diligence*
SJLNT acidulent *harsh*
SJLS acidulous *harsh*
SJLS sedulous *diligent*
SJLSHN acidulation *making acid*
SJLSLY sedulously *diligent*
SJLSNS sedulousness *diligence*
SJLT acidulate *make acid* acidulated acidulating
SJLT sedulity *diligence*
SJNK isogenic *genes*
SJR sager *wiser*
SJRN sojourn *stay*
SJRNR sojourner *resident*
SJS assiduous *diligent*
SJSCHN suggestion *hint, trance*
SJSDBL suggestible *hint, trance*

SJSDBLD suggestibility *hint, trance*
SJSDBLT suggestibility *hint, trance*
SJSDV suggestive *hint, trance*
SJSL assiduously *diligently*
SJSNS assiduousness *diligence*
SJSS eisegesis *interpretation* eisegeses
SJST sagest *wisest*
SJST suggest *hint*
SJSTBL suggestible *hint, trance*
SJSTBLD suggestibility *hint, trance*
SJSTBLT suggestibility *hint, trance*
SJSTV suggestive *hint, trance*
SJT assiduity *diligence* assiduities
SJTL sagital (adj) *median* sagitally (adv)
SJTRS Sagittarius *zodiac sign*
SJTRYS Sagittarius *zodiac sign*
SJTT sagittate *arrow*
SJWD assiduity *diligence* assiduities
SJWS assiduous *diligent*
SJWSL assiduously *diligently*
SJWSNS assiduousness *diligence*
SJWT assiduity *diligence* assiduities
SK acequia *canal*
SK asci (pl) *spore* ascus
SK ASCII *computer language*
SK ask *request* asked asking
SK askew *tilted*
SK ceca (pl) *pouch* cecum
SK ice hockey *sport*
SK ischia (pl) *pelvis* ischium (Br) ischaemia
SK Osaka *city*
SK psych *outguess* psyched psyching
SK Psyche *Greek myth*

Letters aren't doubled for single sounds: to find alley use **L** not **LL**. Use **Y** and **W** as hard sounds only: to find yellow use **YL**. (Br)=British spelling or usage. * See dictionary.

SK psyche *soul, mind*
SK psycho *(slang) crazy one* psychos
SK sac *pouch*
SK SAC *(abbr) Strategic Air Command*
SK sack *(n) bag, bed (v) dismiss, tackle*
SK sacque *jacket*
SK sake *purpose*
SK sake (or) saki *wine*
SK scow *boat*
SK sec *dry*
SK secco *dry, short*
SK sect *group*
SK seek *look for* sought seeking
SK Seiko *(trademark) watch*
SK sequoia *tree*
SK Sequoya (or) Sequoyah (or) Sequoia *Cherokee scholar*
SK sic *(v) attack* sicced siccing
SK sic *(adv) copy exactly*
SK sick *ill*
SK sickie *ill person* sickies
SK sicko *deviant person* sickos
SK Sikh *Indian*
SK ska *music*
SK skew *twist*
SK ski *(v) glide* skied skiing
SK ski *(n) snow* skis
SK skua *bird*
SK sky *(n) heaven* skies
SK sky *(v-Br) flip, hit* skied (or) skyed skying skies
SK skyey *of heaven*
SK soak *drench*
SK sock *(v) hit (n) foot cover* socks
SK sockeye *salmon*
SK socko *outstanding*
SK suck *draw in*
SKB scab *crust* scabbed scabbing
SKB scabby *crusty* scabbier scabbiest
SKB scuba *dive*
SKB sick bay *clinic*
SKB succuba *demon*

succubae
SKB succubi (pl) *demon* succubus
SKBB skibob *vehicle*
SKBBL psychobabble *jargon*
SKBBLR psychobabbler *jargon*
SKBBN skibobbing *gliding*
SKBBNG skibobbing *gliding*
SKBBR skibobber *glider*
SKBD sickbed *recline*
SKBK skewback *arch*
SKBKS skybox *sports*
SKBL skewbald *white patches*
SKBL skiable *glide*
SKBLD skewbald *white patches*
SKBR scabbier *crusty*
SKBRD scabbard *sheath*
SKBRS scabrous *rough*
SKBRSL scabrously *rough*
SKBRSNS scabrousness *rough*
SKBS scabies *mange* scabies
SKBS scabious *(n) herb (adj) scabby*
SKBS succubus *demon* succubi
SKBST scabbiest *crusty*
SKBX skybox *sports*
SKBYR scabbier *crusty*
SKBYS scabious *(n) herb (adj) scabby*
SKBYST scabbiest *crusty*
SKBZ scabies *mange* scabies
SKC sexy *tempting* sexier sexiest
SKCD succeed *prevail, accomplish*
SKCDN succedanea (pl) *substitute* succedaneum
SKCDNM succedaneum *substitute* succedaneums (or) succedanea
SKCDNT succedent *following*
SKCDNY succedanea (pl) *substitute* succedaneum

SKCDNYM succedaneum *substitute* succedaneums (or) succedanea
SKCH scotch *(v) end (n) whiskey*
SKCH scutch *(v) separate (n) hammer*
SKCH sketch *(v) draw (n) drawing, outline, scene* sketches
SKCH sketchy *slight* sketchier sketchiest
SKCHBK sketchbook *drawing*
SKCHL sketchily *slight*
SKCHN escutcheon *shield*
SKCHNS sketchiness *slight*
SKCHR scutcher *separator*
SKCHR sketchier *slight*
SKCHRSH Scotch-Irish *bloodline*
SKCHST sketchiest *slight*
SKCHTP Scotch tape *(trademark) adhesive*
SKCHYR sketchier *slight*
SKCHYST sketchiest *slight*
SKCNS sexiness *temptation*
SKCR sexier *tempting*
SKCST sexiest *tempting*
SKCYR sexier *tempting*
SKCYST sexiest *tempting*
SKCZ psychoses (pl) *abnormality* psychosis
SKD cicada *insect* cicadas
SKD cycad *plant*
SKD escudo *coin* escudos
SKD saccade *eye movement*
SKD Scottie *dog, person*
SKD scud *rush* scudded scudding
SKD skewed *twisted*
SKD skid *(v) slip, haul* skidded skidding
SKD skid *(n) support, slip, pallet*
SKD skiddoo (or) skidoo *depart*
SKDD cycadeoid *plant*
SKDDL skedaddle *scram* skedaddled skedaddling
SKDFT cycadophyte *plant*
SKDJL schedule *(n)*

timetable

SKDJL schedule *(v)* assign
time scheduled
scheduling

SKDJWL schedule *(n)*
timetable

SKDJWL schedule *(v)*
assign time scheduled
scheduling

SKDK psychotic *abnormal*

SKDKL psychotically
abnormally

SKDL psychedelia
hallucinate

SKDL schedule *(v)* assign
time scheduled
scheduling

SKDL schedule *(n) timetable*

SKDL scuttle *(v) scrap,*
scurry scuttled scuttling

SKDL scuttle *(n) hole, pail*

SKDL sectile *cut*

SKDL skittle *game, pin*

SKDLBT scuttlebutt *cask,*
rumor

SKDLDD scutellated (or)
scutellate *plated*

SKDLJKL scatological
excrement

SKDLJR sockdolager (or)
sockdologer *final stroke*

SKDLK psychedelic
hallucinate

SKDLKL psychedelically
hallucinate

SKDLT scutellate (or)
scutellated *plated*

SKDLTD scutellated (or)
scutellate *plated*

SKDLY psychedelia
hallucinate

SKDMD scotomata (pl)
blind spot scotoma

SKDMMDK
psychotomimetic *make*
insane

SKDMMTK
psychotomimetic *make*
insane

SKDMT scotomata (pl) *blind*
spot scotoma

SKDN socked in *foggy*

SKDNG scouting *search,*
youth organization

SKDNG skating *sport*

SKDNMK psychodynamic
motivation

SKDNMKL
psychodynamically
motivation

SKDNMKS
psychodynamics
motivation

SKDNMX psychodynamics
motivation

SKDR ice skater *glide*

SKDR mosquito *insect*
mosquitoes

SKDR scatter *sprinkle*

SKDR scooter *vehicle*

SKDR scoter *duck* scoters
(or) scoter

SKDR scouter *searcher,*
leader

SKDR scutter *scamper*

SKDR sector *(n) area (v)*
divide

SKDR skater *glider*

SKDR skeeter *boat, shooter*

SKDR skid row *district*

SKDR skidder *tractor*

SKDR skitter *twitch* skittery

SKDRBRN scatterbrain
heedless one

SKDRBRND scatterbrained
heedless

SKDRG scatter rug *carpet*

SKDRGN scattergun
shotgun

SKDRL escadrille *squad*

SKDRM psychodrama
acting out

SKDRMDK psychodramatic
acting out

SKDRMTK psychodramatic
acting out

SKDRN scattering *sprinkling*

SKDRNG scattering
sprinkling

SKDRR scatterer *sprinkler*

SKDSH Scottish *of Scotland*

SKDSH skittish *nervous*

SKDSHL skittishly *nervous*

SKDSHNS skittishness

nervous

SKDTL skedaddle *scram*
skedaddled skedaddling

SKDVN skydiving *parachute*

SKDVNG skydiving
parachute

SKDVR sky diver *parachute*

SKDWL schedule *(v)* assign
time scheduled
scheduling

SKDWL schedule *(n)*
timetable

SKDYD cycadeoid *plant*

SKDYL schedule *(v)* assign
time scheduled
scheduling

SKDYL schedule *(n)*
timetable

SKDYWL schedule *(v)*
assign time scheduled
scheduling

SKDYWL schedule *(n)*
timetable

SKDZ scads *(slang) lots*

SKDZ skids *(slang) getting*
worse

SKF scoff *mock*

SKF scuff *scrape*

SKF skiff *boat*

SKFD scaphoid *bone*

SKFL sackful *bag*

SKFL scaffold *support*

SKFL scofflaw *violator*

SKFL scuffle *struggle*
scuffled scuffling

SKFL skiffle *jazz*

SKFLD scaffold *support*

SKFLDN scaffolding *support*

SKFLDNG scaffolding
support

SKFNC sycophancy *flattery*

SKFNK sycophantic
flattering

SKFNKL sycophantically
flattering

SKFNS sycophancy *flattery*

SKFNT sycophant *flatterer*

SKFNTC sycophancy
flattery

SKFNTK sycophantic
flattering

SKFNTKL sycophantically

flattering
SKFNTL sycophantly
flattering
SKFNTS sycophancy
flattery
SKFNTSH sycophantish
flattering
SKFNTSHL sycophantishly
flattering
SKFNTZM sycophantism
flattery
SKFR scoffer *mocker*
SKFRMKLG
psychopharmacology
drugs
SKFRMKLJ
psychopharmacology
drugs
SKFRMKLJKL
psychopharmacological
drugs
SKFRMKLJST
psychopharmacologist
drugs
SKFZKL psychophysical
(adj) *body and mind*
psychophysically (adv)
SKFZKS psychophysics
body and mind
SKFZLG psychophysiology
body and mind
SKFZLJ psychophysiology
body and mind
SKFZLJKL
psychophysiological *body
and mind*
SKFZLJST
psychophysiologist *body
and mind*
SKFZSST psychophysicist
body and mind
SKFZX psychophysics *body
and mind*
SKFZYLG
psychophysiology *body
and mind*
SKFZYLJ
psychophysiology *body
and mind*
SKFZYLJKL
psychophysiological *body
and mind*

SKFZYLJST
psychophysiologist *body
and mind*
SKG skeg *keel*
SKGNK psychogenic *mental*
SKGNKL psychogenically
mental
SKGRF psychograph
biography
SKH sky-high (adv) *very
much, apart* (adj) *exorbitant*
SKHK skyhook *shot, crane*
SKJK skyjack *airplane*
SKJKR skyjacker *airplane*
SKJL schedule (v) *assign
time* scheduled
scheduling
SKJL schedule (n) *timetable*
SKJMP ski jump *hill*
SKJNDK psychogenetic
development
SKJNK psychogenic *mental*
SKJNKL psychogenically
mental
SKJNSS psychogenesis
development
SKJNTK psychogenetic
development
SKJRN skijoring *sport*
SKJRNG skijoring *sport*
SKJWL schedule (v) *assign
time* scheduled
scheduling
SKJWL schedule (n)
timetable
SKK psychic *supernatural*
SKK skyhook *shot, crane*
SKK sukiyaki *food*
SKKL psychically
supernatural
SKKL Schuylkill *river*
SKKNDK psychokinetic
movement
SKKNSS psychokinesis
movement
SKKNTK psychokinetic
movement
SKKP skycap *porter*
SKL cecal (adj) *pouch*
cecally (adv)
SKL cycle *ride, time* cycled
cycling

SKL ice-cold *freezing*
SKL icicle *frozen water*
SKL ischial *pelvis*
(Br) ischaemia
SKL ossicle *bone*
SKL saccule *pouch*
SKL sacculi (pl) *pouch*
sacculus
SKL scald *burn*
SKL scale (v) *weigh, climb,
fish* scaled scaling
SKL scale (n) *weigh, fish,
music**
SKL scall *skin sore*
SKL scaly *flaky, poor* scalier
scaliest
SKL school *education*
SKL scold *punish*
SKL scowl *frown*
SKL scull (v) *row* (n) *boat*
SKL sick call *illness*
SKL sickle (n) *cutter* (adj)
crescent
SKL sickle (v) *cut, bend*
sickled sickling
SKL sickly *ill*
SKL skill *ability*
SKL skoal *toast to health*
SKL skull *head*
SKL socle *pedestal*
SKL suckle *nurse* suckled
suckling
SKLB schoolboy *student*
SKLBG schoolbag *carrier*
SKLBK schoolbook *text*
SKLBL scalable *climbable*
SKLCHLDRN
schoolchildren *students*
SKLCZ scolices (pl)
tapeworm scolex
SKLD cichlid *fish*
SKLD cycloid *curve, moods*
SKLD escalade *climb*
SKLD ice-cold *freezing*
SKLD scald *burn*
SKLD scold *punish*
SKLD seclude *isolate*
secluded secluding
SKLD skilled *with ability*
SKLD so-called *named*
SKLDD sacculated *pouches*
SKLDD secluded *private*

Use letters that best describe the sounds you hear and omit the vowels. Use **S** or **K**
instead of **C**: to find circle use **SRKL**. Use **J** to find joy, **JM** to find gem and **G** to find go.

SKLDGR skulduggery (or) skullduggery *trick* skulduggeries (or) skullduggeries

SKLDK scoliotic *curve*

SKLDL skeletal (adj) *bones* skeletally (adv)

SKLDN scalding *hot*

SKLDN scale-down *reduce*

SKLDN scolding *reproof*

SKLDN skeleton *bones*

SKLDNG scalding *hot*

SKLDNG scolding *reproof*

SKLDNK skeleton key *lock*

SKLDR escalator *moving stairs*

SKLDR skelter *scurry*

SKLF sclaff *golf*

SKLF ski lift *conveyor*

SKLFL skillful (adj) *proficient* skillfully (adv) (Br) skilful, skilfully

SKLFLNS skillfulness *proficiency* (Br) skilfulness

SKLFT ski lift *conveyor*

SKLG psychology *mental* psychologies

SKLGRL schoolgirl *student*

SKLHS schoolhouse *building*

SKLJ psychology *mental* psychologies

SKLJ school-age *approx. 6-18 years old*

SKLJKL psychological (adj) *mental* psychologically (adv)

SKLJST psychologist *mental*

SKLJZ psychologize *interpret* psychologized psychologizing (Br) psychologise

SKLK acyclic *not recurring*

SKLK cyclic (or) cyclical *recurring*

SKLK saclike *pouch*

SKLK skulk *(v) lurk (n) foxes*

SKLKD schoolkid *student*

SKLKL cyclical (or) cyclic (adj) *recurring* cyclically (adv)

SKLKL Schuylkill *river*

SKLKP skullcap *hat*

SKLKS scolex *tapeworm* scolices

SKLKT scilicet *namely*

SKLL scagliola *marble*

SKLM osculum *opening*

SKLM scholium *comment* scholia (or) scholiums

SKLM sicklemia *illness*

SKLMDR cyclometer *distance register*

SKLMM schoolma'am (or) schoolmarm *teacher*

SKLMN cyclamen *primrose*

SKLMP C-clamp *tool*

SKLMRM schoolmarm (or) schoolma'am *teacher*

SKLMSDR schoolmaster *teacher*

SKLMSTR schoolmaster *teacher*

SKLMT cyclamate *sweetener*

SKLMT schoolmate *student*

SKLMTR cyclometer *distance register*

SKLMY sicklemia *illness*

SKLN cyclone *tornado*

SKLN scalene *triangle*

SKLN scallion *onion*

SKLN schooling *education*

SKLN scullion *servant*

SKLN skyline *horizon*

SKLN suckling *nursing*

SKLNG schooling *education*

SKLNG skilling *money* (Scandinavia) (Br) skilfulness

SKLNG suckling *nursing*

SKLNGWSDKS psycholinguistics *speech*

SKLNGWSDX psycholinguistics *speech*

SKLNGWSTKS psycholinguistics *speech*

SKLNGWSTX psycholinguistics *speech*

SKLNK cyclonic *tornado*

SKLNKL cyclonically *tornado*

SKLNS sickliness *illness*

SKLNS succulence *juicy*

SKLNT esculent *edible*

SKLNT succulent *juicy*

SKLNTL succulently *juicy*

SKLNTS succulence *juicy*

SKLP scale-up *increase*

SKLP scallop *(n) mollusk, border, slice (v) cook, cut arcs*

SKLP scalp *(n) hair (v) remove hair, resell*

SKLP sculpt *mold*

SKLP skelp *(Br) slap*

SKLPCHR sculpture *mold* sculptured sculpturing

SKLPCHRL sculptural (adj) *molded* sculpturally (adv)

SKLPCHRSK sculpturesque *molded*

SKLPD cyclopedia *encyclopedia*

SKLPDR sculptor *artist*

SKLPDY cyclopedia *encyclopedia*

SKLPL scalpel *knife*

SKLPN cyclopean *one-eyed*

SKLPN scallopini (or) scaloppine *veal*

SKLPNDR scolopendra *insect*

SKLPR scalper *reseller*

SKLPS Cyclops *one-eyed giant* Cyclopes

SKLPSHR sculpture *mold* sculptured sculpturing

SKLPSHRL sculptural (adj) *molded* sculpturally (adv)

SKLPSHRSK sculpturesque *molded*

SKLPT sculpt *mold*

SKLPTR sculptor *artist*

SKLPTR sculpture *mold* sculptured sculpturing

SKLPTRL sculptural (adj) *molded* sculpturally (adv)

SKLPTRS sculptress *artist (f)*

SKLPTRSK sculpturesque *molded*

SKLPYN cyclopean *one-eyed*

SKLR acicular *needle*

SKLR cycler *rider, timer*

Letters aren't doubled for single sounds: to find alley use **L** not **LL**. Use **Y** and **W** as hard sounds only: to find yellow use **YL**. (Br)=British spelling or usage. * See dictionary.

SKLR ossicular *bone*
SKLR saccular *pouch*
SKLR scalar *(adj) scaled (n) number*
SKLR scalare *fish*
SKLR scaler *dental tool*
SKLR scalier *flaky, poor*
SKLR scholar *education*
SKLR sclera *eye*
SKLR scullery *kitchen* sculleries
SKLR secular *(adj) not religious*
SKLR secular *(n) layman* seculars (or) secular
SKLRDK sclerotic *hard*
SKLRDN sclerotin *protein*
SKLRDRM scleroderma *disease*
SKLRDZSHN sclerotization *hardening*
SKLRFRM scalariform *ladder*
SKLRFRML scalariformly *ladder*
SKLRK skylark *(n) bird (v) frolic*
SKLRL scholarly *education*
SKLRL scleral *eye*
SKLRM cyclorama *display*
SKLRM schoolroom *class*
SKLRMDR sclerometer *hardness*
SKLRMTR sclerometer *hardness*
SKLRNGKM sclerenchyma *cells*
SKLRNGKMTS sclerenchymatous *cells*
SKLRNKM sclerenchyma *cells*
SKLRNKMTS sclerenchymatous *cells*
SKLRS secularize *remove religion* secularized securalizing (Br) secularise
SKLRSH sclerotia (pl) *mass* sclerotium
SKLRSHL sclerotial *massed*
SKLRSHM sclerotium *mass* sclerotia

SKLRSHP scholarship *education*
SKLRSHY sclerotia (pl) *mass* sclerotium
SKLRSHYM sclerotium *mass* sclerotia
SKLRSS sclerosis *hardening*
SKLRST secularist *no religion*
SKLRT sclerite *plate*
SKLRTK sclerotic *hard*
SKLRTN sclerotin *protein*
SKLRTZD sclerotized *hardened*
SKLRTZSHN sclerotization *hardening*
SKLRZ secularize *remove religion* secularized securalizing (Br) secularise
SKLRZM secularism *no religion*
SKLS sacculus *pouch* sacculi
SKLS schoolhouse *building*
SKLS skill-less (or) skilless *no ability*
SKLSD cyclicity *recurrence*
SKLSDK scholastic *education*
SKLSDKL scholastically *education*
SKLSDSZM scholasticism *education*
SKLSHN escalation *increase*
SKLSHN osculation *kiss*
SKLSHN sacculation *pouches*
SKLSHN seclusion *privacy*
SKLSL sickle cell (n) *blood* sickle-cell (adj)
SKLSNS skill-lessness (or) skillessness *no ability*
SKLSS scoliosis *curve* scolioses
SKLST cyclicity *recurrence*
SKLST cyclist *rider*
SKLST scaliest *flaky, poor*
SKLST scholiast *speaker*
SKLST scolecite *mineral*
SKLSTK scholastic *education*

SKLSTKL scholastically *education*
SKLSTKT scholasticate *education*
SKLSTSZM scholasticism *education*
SKLSV seclusive *private*
SKLSVL seclusively *private*
SKLSVNS seclusiveness *private*
SKLSZ scolices (pl) *tapeworm* scolex
SKLT escalate *increase* escalated escalating
SKLT osculate *kiss* osculated osculating
SKLT skillet *frying pan*
SKLT skylight *roof hole*
SKLTCHR schoolteacher *education*
SKLTD sacculated *pouches*
SKLTH sackcloth *fabric*
SKLTK scoliotic *curve*
SKLTL skeletal (adj) *bones* skeletally (adv)
SKLTM schooltime *education*
SKLTN skeleton *bones*
SKLTNK skeleton key *lock*
SKLTNZ skeletonize *reduce* skeletonized skeletonizing (Br) skeletonise
SKLTR escalator *moving stairs*
SKLTR skelter *scurry*
SKLTRN cyclotron *ion accelerator*
SKLTSHN auscultation *listening*
SKLTT auscultate *listen* ausculated ausculating
SKLTTR auscultatory *listening*
SKLVR acyclovir *drug*
SKLWG scalawag *scamp*
SKLWRK schoolwork *education*
SKLX scolex *tapeworm* scolices
SKLYDK scoliotic *curve*
SKLYL scagliola *marble*
SKLYM scholium *comment*

Use letters that best describe the sounds you hear and omit the vowels. Use **S** or **K** instead of **C**: to find circle use **SRKL**. Use **J** to find joy, **JM** to find gem and **G** to find go.

scholia (or) scholiums
SKLYN scallion *onion*
SKLYN scullion *servant*
SKLYR scalier *flaky, poor*
SKLYR schoolyear *term*
SKLYSS scoliosis *curve*
scolioses
SKLYST scaliest *flaky, poor*
SKLYST scholiast *speaker*
SKLYTK scoliotic *curve*
SKLZHN seclusion *privacy*
SKLZV seclusive *private*
SKLZVL seclusively *private*
SKLZVNS seclusiveness
private
SKM cecum *pouch* ceca
SKM Eskimo *Alaskan native*
Eskimo (or) Eskimos
SKM ischemia *anemia*
(Br) ischaemia
SKM ischium *pelvis* ischia
(Br) ischaemia
SKM scam *swindle*
SKM schema *outline*
schemata
SKM scheme *plan* schemed
scheming
SKM scum *slimy film*
scummed scumming
SKM scummy *dirty*
SKM skim *(v) remove top
layer, glance* skimmed
skimming
SKM skim *(n) layer (adj) milk*
SKM succumb *give in* .
SKMBG scumbag *(slang)
dirty one*
SKMBL scumble *color*
scumbled scumbling
SKMBL skimobile *vehicle*
SKMBRD scombroid *fish*
SKMCT ascomycete *fungus*
SKMCTS ascomycetous
fungus
SKMD schemata (pl) *outline*
schema
SKMDK schematic *outline*
SKMDKL schematically
outline
SKMDR psychomotor
activity
SKMDZSHN

schematization *plan*
SKMFRNS circumference
perimeter
SKMFRNTS circumference
perimeter
SKMK ischemic *anemia*
(Br) ischaemia
SKMN scammony *plant*
scammonies
SKMN scheming *tricky*
SKMN skimming *part
removed*
SKMN sycamine *tree*
SKMNG scheming *tricky*
SKMNG skimming *part
removed*
SKMP scamp *rascal*
SKMP scampi *shrimp*
scampi
SKMP skimp *shorten*
SKMP skimpy *smallish*
skimpier skimpiest
SKMPFRNS circumference
perimeter
SKMPFRNTS
circumference *perimeter*
SKMPL skimpily *smallish*
SKMPNS skimpiness
smallish
SKMPR scamper *run*
SKMPR skimpier *smallish*
SKMPST skimpiest *smallish*
SKMPYR skimpier *smallish*
SKMPYST skimpiest
smallish
SKMR skimmer *hat, bird,
scoop**
SKMR sycamore *tree*
SKMST ascomycete *fungus*
SKMSTS ascomycetous
fungus
SKMT schemata (pl) *outline*
schema
SKMTK schematic *outline*
SKMTKL schematically
outline
SKMTR psychometry
divination
SKMTR psychomotor
activity
SKMTRSHN
psychometrician *tests*

SKMTZ schematize *plan*
schematized
schematizing
SKMTZM schematism *plan*
SKMTZSHN schematization
plan
SKMY ischemia *anemia*
(Br) ischaemia
SKN sacking *fabric*
SKN scan *look* scanned
scanning
SKN scanty *skimpy* scantier
scantiest
SKN scone *pastry*
SKN second *(n) time,
ranking (v) support, (Br)
release*
SKN sicken *make ill*
SKN skein (or) skean (or)
skeane *yarn, birds*
SKN skin *(v) peel, scrape*
skinned skinning
SKN skin *(n) outer covering*
SKN skinny *slender* skinnier
skinniest
SKN suck in *dupe*
SKN syconia (pl) *fig*
syconium
SKNBL scannable *readable*
SKNBST second-best (adj)
runner-up second best
(n, adv)
SKND second *(n) time,
ranking (v) support, (Br)
release*
SKND secondo *lower part*
secondi
SKND skinned *complexion*
SKNDBST second-best
(adj) *runner-up* second
best (n, adv)
SKNDGR second-degree
burn, murder
SKNDGS second-guess (n)
question
SKNDHN second hand *(n)
go-between, clock*
SKNDHN secondhand *(adj)
used (adv) indirectly*
SKNDHND second hand *(n)
go-between, clock*
SKNDHND secondhand

Letters aren't doubled for single sounds: to find alley use **L** not **LL**. Use **Y** and **W** as hard
sounds only: to find yellow use **YL**. (Br)=British spelling or usage. * See dictionary.

(adj) used (adv) indirectly
SKNDKLS second-class *(adj) commonplace* second class (n)
SKNDL scandal *disgrace*
SKNDLMNGGR scandalmonger *gossip*
SKNDLMNGR scandalmonger *gossip*
SKNDLS scandalize *disgrace* scandalized scandalizing (Br) scandalise
SKNDLS scandalous *shocking*
SKNDLZ scandalize *disgrace* scandalized scandalizing (Br) scandalise
SKNDM scandium *element*
SKNDNT scandent *climbing*
SKNDNV Scandinavia *peninsula*
SKNDNVN Scandinavian *of Scandinavia*
SKNDNVY Scandinavia *peninsula*
SKNDNVYN Scandinavian *of Scandinavia*
SKNDP skin-deep *shallow*
SKNDP skinny-dip *swim nude*
SKNDPR skinny-dipper *swim nude*
SKNDR secondary *less important, intermediate* secondaries
SKNDRL scoundrel (adj,n) *rascal* scoundrelly (adv)
SKNDRL secondarily *less important*
SKNDRT second-rate *commonplace*
SKNDSTR second-story (adj) *building* second story (n)
SKNDSTRNG second-string *reserve*
SKNDV skin-dive (v) *underwater* skin diving (n)
SKNDVN skin diving (n) *underwater* skin-dive (v)
SKNDVNG skin diving (n) *underwater* skin-dive (v)

SKNDVR skin diver *underwater*
SKNDYM scandium *element*
SKNFLNT skinflint *miser*
SKNG sacking *fabric*
SKNG skiing *gliding*
SKNGK skink (n) *lizard* (v) *pour*
SKNGK skunk (n) *animal* (v) *defeat, cheat* skunks
SKNGKR skinker *bartender*
SKNGL scungilli *conch*
SKNGS second-guess (n) *question*
SKNHD skinhead *extremist*
SKNHN second hand (n) *go-between, clock*
SKNHN secondhand (adj) *used (adv) indirectly*
SKNHND second hand (n) *go-between, clock*
SKNHND secondhand (adj) *used (adv) indirectly*
SKNJL scungilli *conch*
SKNK skink (n) *lizard* (v) *pour*
SKNK skunk (n) *animal* (v) *defeat, cheat*
SKNKDD Schenectady *city*
SKNKLS second-clas (adj) *commonplace* second class (n)
SKNKR skinker *bartender*
SKNKTD Schenectady *city*
SKNL scantily *skimpy*
SKNLDK psychoanalytic *mental*
SKNLDKL psychoanalytically *mental*
SKNLSS psychoanalysis *treatment*
SKNLST psychoanalyst *doctor*
SKNLTK psychoanalytic *mental*
SKNLTKL psychoanalytically *mental*
SKNLZ psychoanalyze *mental treatment* psychoanalyzed psychoanalyzing
SKNM syconium *fig* syconia

SKNN sickening *disgusting*
SKNNG sickening *disgusting*
SKNNGL sickeningly *disgusting*
SKNNL sickeningly *disgusting*
SKNNS scantiness *skimpy*
SKNNS skinniness *slender*
SKNPP skin-pop *injection*
SKNPPR skin-popper *injection*
SKNR scanner *tracer*
SKNR scantier *skimpy*
SKNR schooner *boat*
SKNR skinner *remove skin*
SKNR skinnier *slender*
SKNRDK psychoneurotic *emotional*
SKNRSS psychoneurosis *emotion*
SKNRT second-rate *commonplace*
SKNRTK psychoneurotic *emotional*
SKNS askance *sideways*
SKNS sconce *bracket*
SKNS sickness *illness*
SKNS skewness *twist*
SKNSHN scansion *verse*
SKNST scantiest *skimpy*
SKNST skinniest *slender*
SKNSTR second-story (adj) *building* second story (n)
SKNSTRNG second-string *reserve*
SKNT scant *skimpy*
SKNT scanty *meager* scantier scantiest
SKNT secant *line*
SKNT second (n) *time, ranking* (v) *support,* (Br) *release*
SKNTBST second-best (adj) *runner-up* second best (n, adv)
SKNTGS second-guess (n) *question*
SKNTHN second hand (n) *go-between, clock*
SKNTHN secondhand (adj) *used (adv) indirectly*
SKNTHND second hand (n)

Use letters that best describe the sounds you hear and omit the vowels. Use **S** or **K** instead of **C**: to find circle use **SRKL**. Use **J** to find joy, **JM** to find gem and **G** to find go.

go-between, clock
SKNTHND secondhand (adj) used (adv) indirectly
SKNTKLS second-class (adj) commonplace second class (n)
SKNTL scantily skimpy
SKNTL scantly skimpy
SKNTLN scantling frame, minimum
SKNTLNG scantling frame, minimum
SKNTNS scantiness skimpy
SKNTNS scantness skimpy
SKNTR scantier skimpy
SKNTRT second-rate commonplace
SKNTS askance sideways
SKNTS sconce bracket
SKNTSHN scansion verse
SKNTST scantiest skimpy
SKNTST skin test allergy
SKNTSTR second-story (adj) building second story (n)
SKNTSTRNG second-string reserve
SKNTT skintight fitted
SKNTYR scantier skimpy
SKNTYST scantiest skimpy
SKNY syconia (pl) fig syconium
SKNYM syconium fig syconia
SKNYR scantier skimpy
SKNYR skinnier slender
SKNYRDK psychoneurotic emotional
SKNYRSS psychoneurosis emotion
SKNYRTK psychoneurotic emotional
SKNYST scantiest skimpy
SKNYST skinniest slender
SKP escape flee escaped escaping
SKP escapee runaway
SKP ice cap glacier
SKP scape shaft, view
SKP scaup duck scaup (or) scaups
SKP scoop shovel

SKP scope (v) look at scoped scoping
SKP scope (n) range, viewer
SKP scup fish scup
SKP skep beehive
SKP skip (v) omit, leap, depart* skipped skipping
SKP skip (n) step, captain
SKPD escapade adventure
SKPDK skeptic doubter
SKPDKL skeptical (adj) doubt skeptically (adv)
SKPDSZM skepticism doubt
SKPFL scoopful shovel
SKPGRS scapegrace rascal
SKPGT scapegoat blame
SKPJK skipjack fish skipjacks (or) skipjack
SKPL scapula bone scapulae (or) scapulas
SKPLMN scopolamine poison
SKPLR scapular cloth square, feather, shoulders
SKPMNT escapement vent
SKPR scupper (n) drain (v-Br) end
SKPR skipper (n) insect, leader (v) lead
SKPRNNG scuppernong grape
SKPS scapose shaft
SKPSS skepsis doubt
SKPST escapist diversions
SKPTH psychopath deranged one
SKPTH psychopathy dysfunction
SKPTHK psychopathic deranged
SKPTHLG psychopathology dysfunction
SKPTHLJ psychopathology dysfunction
SKPTHLJKL psychopathological (adj) dysfunctional psychopathologically (adv)
SKPTHLJST psychopathologist dysfunction

SKPTK skeptic doubter
SKPTKL skeptical (adj) doubt skeptically (adv)
SKPTSZM skepticism doubt
SKPYL scapula bone scapulae (or) scapulas
SKPYLR scapular cloth square, feather, shoulders
SKPZM escapism diversions
SKR eschar scab
SKR Escher artist
SKR escrow held in trust
SKR esker glacier
SKR Oscar award
SKR sacra (pl) bone sacrum
SKR saker falcon
SKR scar mark scarred scarring
SKR scare frighten scared scaring
SKR scarry marked
SKR scary alarming scarier scariest
SKR score (v) count, notch, acquire* scored scoring
SKR score (n) count, topic, music*
SKR scoria slag scoriae
SKR scour search, clean
SKR scree rocks
SKR screw twist
SKR screwy zany screwier screwiest
SKR scurry hurry scurried scurrying scurries
SKR secure (v) make safe, effect, ensure* secured securing
SKR secure (adj) safe, dependable securer securest
SKR seeker searcher
SKR skerry reef skerries
SKR skewer (n) rod (v) pierce, criticize
SKR skier glider
SKR skirr (v) flee, skim (n) roar
SKR soaker drench
SKR soccer sport
SKR succor help (Br) succour

Letters aren't doubled for single sounds: to find alley use **L** not **LL**. Use **Y** and **W** as hard sounds only: to find yellow use **YL**. (Br)=British spelling or usage. * See dictionary.

SKR sucker *candy, dupe*
SKR sucre *money*
SKRB ascribe *relate to* ascribed ascribing
SKRB scarab *beetle*
SKRB scribe *write, mark* scribed scribing
SKRB scrub *(v) wash, cancel* scrubbed scrubbing
SKRB scrub *(n) stunted, inferior*
SKRB scrubby *stunted, shabby* scrubbier scrubbiest
SKRBBL ascribable *relating to*
SKRBD ascribed *related to*
SKRBDK scorbutic *disease*
SKRBK ascorbic *acid*
SKRBK scrapbook *collection*
SKRBK scrub oak *tree*
SKRBKSD ascorbic acid *vitamin C*
SKRBL scrabble *scrawl, scribble* scrabbled scrabbling
SKRBL Scrabble *(trademark) game*
SKRBL scrabbly *scrubby*
SKRBL screwball *zany*
SKRBL scribal *writer*
SKRBL scribble *write* scribbled scribbling
SKRBLN scrubland *dry area*
SKRBLND scrubland *dry area*
SKRBLR scribbler *write*
SKRBNRS scrub nurse *hospital*
SKRBPN scrub pine *tree*
SKRBR scriber *tool*
SKRBR scrubber *wash, rub*
SKRBR scrubbier *stunted, shabby*
SKRBRD scoreboard *count*
SKRBST scrubbiest *stunted, shabby*
SKRBTK scorbutic *disease*
SKRBWMN scrubwoman *cleaner* scrubwomen
SKRBYDK scorbutic *disease*
SKRBYR scrubbier *stunted,*

shabby
SKRBYST scrubbiest *stunted, shabby*
SKRBYTK scorbutic *disease*
SKRC secrecy *hiding* secrecies
SKRCH scorch *burn*
SKRCH scratch *scrape* scratches
SKRCH scratchy *prickly* scratchier scratchiest
SKRCH screech *noise* screeches
SKRCH screechy *noisy*
SKRCHL scratchily *prickly*
SKRCHL screech owl *bird*
SKRCHNS scratchiness *prickly*
SKRCHR scorcher *hot, fast*
SKRCHR scratchier *prickly*
SKRCHST scratchiest *prickly*
SKRCHWL screech owl *bird*
SKRCHYR scratchier *prickly*
SKRCHYST scratchiest *prickly*
SKRD ascarid *worm*
SKRD saccharide *sugar*
SKRD sacred *holy*
SKRD scared *fearful*
SKRD screed *speech, tool*
SKRD scrod *fish*
SKRD scrota *(pl) testes* scrotum
SKRD secured *safe, locked*
SKRD security *safety* securities
SKRDBL scrutable *understandable*
SKRDK escharotic *scab*
SKRDK Socratic *of Socrates*
SKRDKT scaredy-cat *fearful person*
SKRDL saccharoidal *sugar*
SKRDM scrotum *testes* scrota (or) scrotums
SKRDN scrutiny *study* scrutinies
SKRDNG skirting *border*
SKRDNG skywriting *airplane*
SKRDNS scrutinize *examine* scrutinized scrutinizing

(Br) scrutinise
SKRDNZ scrutinize *examine* scrutinized scrutinizing (Br) scrutinise
SKRDR secretor *blood*
SKRDR skywriter *airplane*
SKRDRVR screwdriver *tool*
SKRDV secretive *silent*
SKRDVL secretively *silent*
SKRDVNS secretiveness *silence*
SKRDZ Socrates *philosopher*
SKRF scarf *joint* scarfs
SKRF scarf *cloth* scarves (or) scarfs
SKRF scarify *cut, frighten* scarified scarifying scarifies
SKRF scruff *neck*
SKRF scruffy *shaggy* scruffier scruffiest
SKRF scurf *remains* scurfy
SKRFKSHN saccharification *sugar*
SKRFKSHN scarification *cut, frighten*
SKRFL scrofula *neck*
SKRFL scruffily *shaggy*
SKRFLK psychrophilic *cold*
SKRFLS scrofulous *diseased*
SKRFNS scruffiness *shaggy*
SKRFR scruffier *shaggy*
SKRFS sacrifice *offer, give up* sacrificed sacrificing
SKRFSHL sacrificial *(adj) offer, give up* sacrificially *(adv)*
SKRFSKN scarfskin *cuticle*
SKRFST scruffiest *shaggy*
SKRFYL scrofula *neck*
SKRFYLS scrofulous *diseased*
SKRFYR scruffier *shaggy*
SKRFYST scruffiest *shaggy*
SKRG escargot *snail* escargots
SKRG scrag *(v) choke* scragged scragging
SKRG scrag *(n) neck*
SKRG scraggy *rough* scraggier scraggiest
SKRGL scraggly *scrawny,*

unkempt scragglier
scraggliest
SKRGLR scragglier *scrawny,*
unkempt
SKRGLST scraggliest
scrawny, unkempt
SKRGLYR scragglier
scrawny, unkempt
SKRGLYST scraggliest
scrawny, unkempt
SKRGR scraggier *rough*
SKRGST scraggiest *rough*
SKRGYR scraggier *rough*
SKRGYST scraggiest *rough*
SKRHD scarehead *headline*
SKRJ scourge *whip*
scourged scourging
SKRJ scrooge *(often*
capitalized) miser
SKRKPR scorekeeper
counter
SKRKR scarecrow *crops*
SKRKRD scorecard *count*
SKRKT skyrocket *(v)*
catapult (n) rocket
SKRL escarole *lettuce*
SKRL sacral *holy, near*
sacrum
SKRL scarily *alarming*
SKRL scrawl *write*
SKRL scroll *roll, paper, curve*
SKRL scurrile (or) scurril
obscene
SKRL skirl *tone*
SKRLD scurrility *obscenity*
scurrilities
SKRLJ sacrilege *sin*
SKRLJS sacrilegious *sinful*
SKRLJSL sacrilegiously
sinfully
SKRLJSNS
sacrilegiousness *sin*
SKRLK sacroiliac *spine*
SKRLR scrawler *writer*
SKRLS scoreless *no points*
SKRLS scurrilous *obscene*
SKRLSL scurrilously *obscene*
SKRLSNS scurrilousness
obscenity
SKRLT scarlet *red*
SKRLT scurrility *obscenity*
scurrilities

SKRLTN scarlatina *disease*
SKRLWRK scrollwork *design*
SKRLYK sacroiliac *spine*
SKRM ice cream (n) *dessert*
ice-cream (adj)
SKRM sacrum *bone* sacra
SKRM scram *leave*
scrammed scramming
SKRM scream *yell*
SKRM scrim *fabric*
SKRM sickroom *clinic*
SKRMBL scramble *(v)*
hurry, jumble scrambled
scrambling
SKRMBL scramble *(n)*
jumble
SKRMBLR scrambler
transmission, hurry
SKRMCH scaramouch (or)
scaramouche *rascal*
SKRMCHS scrumptious
delicious
SKRMCZ saccharomyces
yeast
SKRMDR psychrometer
dryness
SKRMDR saccharimeter
sugar
SKRMDR saccharometer
hydrometer
SKRMJ scrimmage *battle,*
football scrimmaged
scrimmaging
SKRMN Sacramento *city*
SKRMN screaming *extreme*
SKRMNG screaming
extreme
SKRMNGGR scaremonger
alarmist
SKRMNGR scaremonger
alarmist
SKRMNL sacramental (adj)
rite sacramentally (adv)
SKRMNLST sacramentalist
rite
SKRMNLZM
sacramentalism *rite*
SKRMNT sacrament *rite*
SKRMNT Sacramento *city*
SKRMNT securement *safe,*
locked
SKRMNTL sacramental

(adj) *rite* sacramentally
(adv)
SKRMNTLST
sacramentalist *rite*
SKRMNTLZM
sacramentalism *rite*
SKRMP scrimp *economize*
SKRMP scrimpy *economical*
SKRMPCHS scrumptious
delicious
SKRMPSHS scrumptious
delicious
SKRMR screamer *yell, bird*
SKRMSH scaramouch (or)
scaramouche *rascal*
SKRMSH scrimshaw
carving
SKRMSH skirmish (n) *fight*
(v) *search* skirmishes
SKRMSHNDR
scrimshander *carver*
SKRMSHR skirmisher *fight,*
search
SKRMSHS scrumptious
delicious
SKRMSZ saccharomyces
yeast
SKRMTR psychrometer
dryness
SKRMTR saccharimeter
sugar
SKRMTR saccharometer
hydrometer
SKRMTRK psychrometric
dryness
SKRN isochron (or)
isochrone *time line*
SKRN saccharin *(n)*
sweetener
SKRN saccharine *(adj) sweet*
SKRN scorn *contempt*
SKRN scrawny *thin*
scrawnier scrawniest
SKRN screen *(n) wire mesh,*
protector, display (v) guard,
*film, hide**
SKRNCH scrunch *crush*
SKRNFL scornful (adj)
contempt scornfully (adv)
SKRNFLNS scornfulness
contempt
SKRNG scroungy *(slang)*

Letters aren't doubled for single sounds: to find alley use **L** not **LL**. Use **Y** and **W** as hard
sounds only: to find yellow use **YL**. (Br)=British spelling or usage. * See dictionary.

ragged scroungier scroungiest

SKRNGR scroungier *ragged*

SKRNGST scroungiest *ragged*

SKRNGYR scroungier *ragged*

SKRNGYST scroungiest *ragged*

SKRNJ scrounge *search, steal* scrounged scrounging

SKRNJ scroungy *(slang) ragged* scroungier scroungiest

SKRNJR scrounger *searcher*

SKRNJR scroungier *ragged*

SKRNJST scroungiest *ragged*

SKRNJYR scroungier *ragged*

SKRNJYST scroungiest *ragged*

SKRNL isochronal (adj) *time* isochronally (adv)

SKRNN screening *movies*

SKRNNG screening *movies*

SKRNNS scrawniness *thin*

SKRNPL screenplay *script*

SKRNR scorner *contempt*

SKRNR scrawnier *thin*

SKRNRDR screenwriter *script*

SKRNRTR screenwriter *script*

SKRNS isochronous *time*

SKRNS screwiness *zany*

SKRNSL isochronously *time*

SKRNST scrawniest *thin*

SKRNTST screen-test (v) *movies* screen test (n)

SKRNYR scrawnier *thin*

SKRNYST scrawniest *thin*

SKRNZM isochronism *time*

SKRP scare up *find*

SKRP scarp *cliff*

SKRP Scorpio *zodiac sign*

SKRP scrap *junk, fight* scrapped scrapping

SKRP scrape *(v) rub, collect* scraped scraping

SKRP scrape *(n) fight*

SKRP scrappy *feisty* scrappier scrappiest

SKRP screwup (n) *error* screw up (v)

SKRP scrip *money*

SKRP script *text*

SKRPBK scrapbook *collection*

SKRPCHR scripture *bible*

SKRPCHRL scriptural (adj) *biblical* scripturally (adv)

SKRPDV ascriptive *relating to*

SKRPHP scrap heap *junk*

SKRPK scrapbook *collection*

SKRPL scrapple *food*

SKRPL scruple *ethics* scrupled scrupling

SKRPLS scrupulous *careful*

SKRPLSL scrupulously *careful*

SKRPLSNS scrupulousness *careful*

SKRPMNT escarpment *cliff*

SKRPN scorpion *spider*

SKRPNS scrappiness *feisty*

SKRPP scrap heap *junk*

SKRPR scarper *(Br) flee*

SKRPR scraper *tool*

SKRPR scrapper *fighter*

SKRPR scrappier *feisty*

SKRPRDR scriptwriter *playwrite*

SKRPRTR scriptwriter *playwrite*

SKRPSHN ascription *relationship*

SKRPSHR scripture *bible*

SKRPSHRL scriptural (adj) *biblical* scripturally (adv)

SKRPST scrappiest *feisty*

SKRPT scrip *money*

SKRPT script *text*

SKRPTR scripture *bible*

SKRPTRDR scriptwriter *playwrite*

SKRPTRL scriptural (adj) *biblical* scripturally (adv)

SKRPTRTR scriptwriter *playwrite*

SKRPTSHR scripture *bible*

SKRPTSHRL scriptural (adj)

biblical scripturally (adv)

SKRPTV ascriptive *relating to*

SKRPY Scorpio *star sign*

SKRPYLS scrupulous *careful*

SKRPYLSL scrupulously *careful*

SKRPYLSNS scrupulousness *careful*

SKRPYN scorpion *spider*

SKRPYR scrappier *feisty*

SKRPYST scrappiest *feisty*

SKRR sacraria (pl) *sanctuary* sacrarium

SKRR scarier *alarming*

SKRR scorer *points*

SKRR screwier *zany*

SKRR securer *safe, locked*

SKRR succorer *helper* (Br) succourer

SKRRM sacrarium *sanctuary* sacraria

SKRRY sacraria (pl) *sanctuary* sacrarium

SKRRYM sacrarium *sanctuary* sacraria

SKRS saccharase *sweet*

SKRS scarce *rare* scarcer scarcest

SKRS scarious *texture*

SKRS secrecy *hiding* secrecies

SKRS Siqueiros *artist*

SKRS sucrase *invertase*

SKRS sucrose *sugar*

SKRSD sacristy *room* sacristies

SKRSD scarcity *lack* scarcities

SKRSDN sacristan *church*

SKRSHN secretion *concealment, elimination*

SKRSHS scoriaceous *slag*

SKRSL scarcely *barely*

SKRSNGK sacrosanct *sacred*

SKRSNGKT sacrosanct *sacred*

SKRSNGKTD sacrosanctity *sacred*

SKRSNGKTT sacrosanctity

Use letters that best describe the sounds you hear and omit the vowels. Use **S** or **K** instead of **C**: to find circle use **SRKL**. Use **J** to find joy, **JM** to find gem and **G** to find go.

sacred
SKRSNGTD sacrosanctity
sacred
SKRSNGTT sacrosanctity
sacred
SKRSNK sacrosanct *sacred*
SKRSNKT sacrosanct
sacred
SKRSNKTD sacrosanctity
sacred
SKRSNKTT sacrosanctity
sacred
SKRSNS scarceness *rarity*
SKRSS ascariasis *disease*
ascariases
SKRST sacristy *room*
sacristies
SKRST scarcity *lack*
scarcities
SKRST scariest *alarming*
SKRST screwiest *zany*
SKRST securest *safe, locked*
SKRSTN sacristan *church*
SKRT escort *companion*
SKRT scrota (pl) *testes*
scrotum
SKRT secret *hidden*
SKRT secrete *hide, form and*
give off secreted
secreting
SKRT security *safety*
securities
SKRT skirt *(n) garment (v) go*
around
SKRT skywrite *airplane*
skywrote skywriting
skywritten
SKRTBL scrutable
understandable
SKRTBLT secret ballot *vote*
SKRTK escharotic *scab*
SKRTK Socratic *of Socrates*
SKRTM scrotum *testes*
scrota (or) scrotums
SKRTN scrutiny *study*
scrutinies
SKRTN secretin *hormone*
SKRTN skywriting *airplane*
SKRTNG skirting *border*
SKRTNG skywriting *airplane*
SKRTNS scrutinize *examine*
scrutinized scrutinizing

(Br) scrutinise
SKRTNZ scrutinize *examine*
scrutinized scrutinizing
(Br) scrutinise
SKRTR secretary *clerk, desk*
secretaries
SKRTR secretor *blood*
SKRTR secretory *form and*
give off
SKRTR skywriter *airplane*
SKRTRL secretarial *clerk,*
desk
SKRTRT secretariat
administration
SKRTRYL secretarial *clerk,*
desk
SKRTRYT secretariat
administration
SKRTS scherzo *music*
scherzos (or) scherzi
SKRTSND scherzando
tempo scherzandos
SKRTSRVS secret service
(often capitalized)
Presidential guard
SKRTV secretive *silent*
SKRTVL secretively *silent*
SKRTVNS secretiveness
silence
SKRTWR escritoire *desk*
SKRTZ Socrates *philosopher*
SKRV scurvy *disease*
SKRVL scurvily *despicable*
SKRVNS scurviness
contempt
SKRVS scarves (pl) *cloth*
scarf
SKRVZ scarves (pl) *cloth*
scarf
SKRW screwy *zany* screwier
screwiest
SKRWLK sacroiliac *spine*
SKRWLYK sacroiliac *spine*
SKRWNS screwiness *zany*
SKRWP screwup (n) *error*
screw up (v)
SKRWR screwier *zany*
SKRWRM screwworm
blowfly
SKRWST screwiest *zany*
SKRWYR screwier *zany*
SKRWYST screwiest *zany*

SKRY scoria *slag* scoriae
SKRYR scarier *alarming*
SKRYR screwier *zany*
SKRYS scarious *texture*
SKRYSHS scoriaceous *slag*
SKRYSS ascariasis *disease*
ascariases
SKRYST scariest *alarming*
SKRYST screwiest *zany*
SKRZ saccharase *sweet*
SKS ascus *spore* asci
SKS ice ax *tool* ice axes
SKS sax *saxophone*
SKS scouse *food, dialect*
SKS sex *gender*
SKS sexy *tempting* sexier
sexiest
SKS six *number (6)* sixes
SKS sox (pl) *stocking* sock
SKSD sixty *number (60)*
sixties
SKSD succeed *prevail,*
accomplish
SKSDN succedanea (pl)
substitute succedaneum
SKSDNM succedaneum
substitute succedaneums
(or) succedanea
SKSDNT sextant *distances*
SKSDNT succedent
following
SKSDNY succedanea (pl)
substitute succedaneum
SKSDNYM succedaneum
substitute succedaneums
(or) succedanea
SKSDSH sixtyish *like or*
nearly 60
SKSDTH sixtieth *of number*
60
SKSDYSH sixtyish *like or*
nearly 60
SKSDYTH sixtieth *of number*
60
SKSFL sixfold *times 6*
SKSFLD sixfold *times 6*
SKSFN saxophone *music*
SKSFNK saxophonic *music*
SKSFNST saxophonist
musician
SKSGN six-gun *weapon*
SKSH scotia *molding*

SKSH sickish *ill*
SKSHDR six-shooter *weapon*
SKSHL asexual *no gender*
SKSHL sexual (adj) *gender* sexually (adv)
SKSHL sickishly *ill*
SKSHLD sexuality *gender*
SKSHLT sexuality *gender*
SKSHLZ sexualize *gender* sexualized sexualizing
SKSHN section *piece*
SKSHN succession *follow*
SKSHN suction *draw in*
SKSHNL sectional (n, adj) *pieces* sectionally (adv)
SKSHNLZM sectionalism *regions*
SKSHNS sickishness *ill*
SKSHRN saxhorn *music*
SKSHTR six-shooter *weapon*
SKSHWL asexual *no gender*
SKSHWL sexual (adj) *gender* sexually (adv)
SKSHWLD sexuality *gender*
SKSHWLT sexuality *gender*
SKSHWLZ sexualize *gender* sexualized sexualizing
SKSJNRN sexagenarian *age 60-69*
SKSJNRYN sexagenarian *age 60-69*
SKSKRPR skyscraper *building*
SKSKSHL psychosexual (adj) *sex* psychosexually (adv)
SKSKSHLD psychosexuality *sex*
SKSKSHLT psychosexuality *sex*
SKSKSHWL psychosexual (adj) *sex* psychosexually (adv)
SKSKSHWLD psychosexuality *sex*
SKSKSHWLT psychosexuality *sex*
SKSL sexily *tempting*
SKSLG sexology *sex study*
SKSLJ sexology *sex study*
SKSLJST sexologist *sex*

study
SKSLS sexless *no gender*
SKSMBL sex symbol *idol*
SKSMDK psychosomatic *mental*
SKSMDKL psychosomatically *mental*
SKSMTK psychosomatic *mental*
SKSMTKL psychosomatically *mental*
SKSN cycasin *chemical*
SKSN Saxon *person*
SKSN saxony *fabric* saxonies
SKSNGK succinct *brief*
SKSNGKL succinctly *briefly*
SKSNGKNS succinctness *brief*
SKSNGKT succinct *brief*
SKSNGKTL succinctly *briefly*
SKSNGKTNS succinctness *brief*
SKSNGT succinct *brief*
SKSNGTL succinctly *briefly*
SKSNGTNS succinctness *brief*
SKSNK succinct *brief*
SKSNKL succinctly *briefly*
SKSNKNS succinctness *brief*
SKSNKT succinct *brief*
SKSNKTL succinctly *briefly*
SKSNKTNS succinctness *brief*
SKSNS sexiness *temptation*
SKSNTHSS psychosynthesis *body and mind*
SKSPK six-pack *group of 6*
SKSPLTSHN sexploitation *misuse sex*
SKSPN sixpenny *money*
SKSPNS sixpence *money*
SKSPNTS sixpence *money*
SKSPT sexpot *arousing one (f)*
SKSR Scouser *Liverpool*
SKSR sexier *tempting*
SKSRJKL psychosurgical *brain*

SKSRJN psychosurgeon *brain*
SKSRJR psychosurgery *brain*
SKSRN saxhorn *music*
SKSS psychosis *dysfunction* psychoses
SKSS success *achievement* successes
SKSS sycosis *hair*
SKSSFL successful (adj) *favorable* successfully (adv)
SKSSHL psychosocial (adj) *interactions* psychosocially (adv)
SKSSHN succession *follow*
SKSSHNL successional (adj) *following* successionally (adv)
SKSSR successor *follower*
SKSSSHN succession *follow*
SKSST sexiest *tempting*
SKSSV successive *in order*
SKSSVNS successiveness *in order*
SKST seacoast *shoreline*
SKST sixty *number (60)* sixties
SKSTH sixth *of number 6*
SKSTHN psychasthenia *neurosis*
SKSTHNK psychasthenic *neurosis*
SKSTHNY psychasthenia *neurosis*
SKSTLN sextillion *number*
SKSTLYN sextillion *number*
SKSTN sexton *clergy*
SKSTN sixteen *number (16)*
SKSTNT sextant *distances*
SKSTNTH sixteenth *of number 16*
SKSTPL sextuple *times 6* sextupled sextupling
SKSTPLT sextuplet *6 offspring*
SKSTSH sixtyish *like or nearly 60*
SKSTT sextet *group of 6*
SKSTTH sixtieth *of number*

Use letters that best describe the sounds you hear and omit the vowels. Use **S** or **K** instead of **C**: to find circle use **SRKL**. Use **J** to find joy, **JM** to find gem and **G** to find go.

60
SKSTYN sextillion *number*
SKSTYPL sextuple *times 6* sextupled sextupling
SKSTYPLT sextuplet *6 offspring*
SKSTYSH sixtyish *like or nearly 60*
SKSTYTH sixtieth *of number 60*
SKSV successive *in order*
SKSYR sexier *tempting*
SKSYST sexiest *tempting*
SKSZ psychoses (pl) *abnormality* psychosis
SKSZM sexism *gender bias*
SKT ascot *scarf*
SKT cicada *insect* cicadas
SKT eye socket *face*
SKT ice skate *(n) boot*
SKT ice-skate (v) *glide* ice-skated ice-skating
SKT psych-out *outguess*
SKT saccate *pouch*
SKT sack coat *garment*
SKT scat (v) *leave, sing* scatted scatting
SKT scat (n) *feces, jazz*
SKT scoot *hurry*
SKT Scot *of Scotland*
SKT Scottie *dog, person*
SKT scout (n) *searcher, youth* (v) *explore, mock*
SKT scute *scale*
SKT sect *group*
SKT skat *game*
SKT skate (v) *glide* skated skating
SKT skate (n) *shoe attachment, ray, horse*
SKT skeet *trapshoot*
SKT skit *sketch*
SKT socket *cavity*
SKTBRD skateboard *vehicle*
SKTFR scot-free *no penalty*
SKTGT scapegoat *blame*
SKTH scathe (v) *scorch* scathed scathing
SKTH scathe (n) *injury*
SKTHLS scatheless *no harm*
SKTHN scathing *severe*
SKTHNG scathing *severe*

SKTHRP psychotherapy *treatment* psychotherapies
SKTHRPDK psychotherapeutic *treatment*
SKTHRPDKL psychotherapeutically *treatment*
SKTHRPST psychotherapist *doctor*
SKTHRPTK psychotherapeutic *treatment*
SKTHRPTKL psychotherapeutically *treatment*
SKTHRPYDK psychotherapeutic *treatment*
SKTHRPYDKL psychotherapeutically *treatment*
SKTHRPYTK psychotherapeutic *treatment*
SKTHRPYTKL psychotherapeutically *treatment*
SKTK psychotic *abnormal*
SKTKL psychotically *abnormally*
SKTL scutella (pl) *plate* scutellum
SKTL scuttle (v) *scrap, scurry* scuttled scuttling
SKTL scuttle (n) *hole, pail*
SKTL sectile *cut*
SKTL skittle *game, pin*
SKTLBT scuttlebutt *cask, rumor*
SKTLDD scutellated (or) scutellate *plated*
SKTLG eschatology *end of the world* eschatologies
SKTLG scatology *waste matter*
SKTLJ eschatology *end of the world* eschatologies
SKTLJ scatology *waste matter*
SKTLJKL eschatological

(adj) *end of the world* eschatologically (adv)
SKTLJKL scatological *excrement*
SKTLM scutellum *plate* scutella
SKTLN Scotland *country*
SKTLND Scotland *country*
SKTLNDYRD Scotland Yard *police*
SKTLNYRD Scotland Yard *police*
SKTLR scutellar *plated*
SKTLT scutellate (or) scutellated *plated*
SKTLTD scutellated (or) scutellate *plated*
SKTM scotoma *blind spot* scotomas (or) scotomata
SKTMD scotomata (pl) *blind spot* scotoma
SKTMMDK psychotomimetic *make insane*
SKTMMTK psychotomimetic *make insane*
SKTMSDR scoutmaster *youth leader*
SKTMSTR scoutmaster *youth leader*
SKTMT scotomata (pl) *blind spot* scotoma
SKTN sacaton *grass*
SKTN scouting *search, youth organization*
SKTN skating *sport*
SKTN socked in *foggy*
SKTNG scouting *search, youth organization*
SKTNG skating *sport*
SKTPK scotopic *blind spot*
SKTR ice skater *glide*
SKTR mosquito *insect* mosquitoes
SKTR psychiatry *mental*
SKTR scatter *sprinkle*
SKTR scooter *vehicle*
SKTR scoter *duck* scoters (or) scoter
SKTR scouter *searcher, leader*
SKTR scutter *scamper*

Letters aren't doubled for single sounds: to find **alley** use **L** not **LL**. Use **Y** and **W** as hard sounds only: to find **yellow** use **YL**. (Br)=British spelling or usage. * See dictionary.

SKTR secateur *(Br) shears*
SKTR secretary *clerk, desk*
secretaries
SKTR sector *(n) area (v)*
divide
SKTR skater *glider*
SKTR skeeter *boat, shooter*
SKTR skidder *tractor*
SKTR skitter *twitch* skittery
SKTRBRN scatterbrain
heedless one
SKTRBRND scatterbrained
heedless
SKTRCS cicatrices (pl) *scar*
cicatrix
SKTRCZ cicatrices (pl) *scar*
cicatrix
SKTRG scatter rug *carpet*
SKTRGN scattergun
shotgun
SKTRK psychiatric *mental*
SKTRKL psychiatrically
mental
SKTRKS cicatrix *scar*
cicatrices
SKTRN scattering *sprinkling*
SKTRN sectarian *(adj)*
narrow-minded *(n)*
obstinate one
SKTRNG scattering
sprinkling
SKTRPK psychotropic *mind*
SKTRR scatterer *sprinkler*
SKTRST psychiatrist *mental*
SKTRSZ cicatrices (pl) *scar*
cicatrix
SKTRX cicatrix *scar*
cicatrices
SKTRYN sectarian *(adj)*
narrow-minded *(n)*
obstinate one
SKTRZSHN cicatrization
scarring
SKTS schizo *person* schizos
SKTS schizy (or) schizzy
psychotic
SKTSD schizoid *split*
SKTSFRN schizophrene
psychotic
SKTSFRN schizophrenia
psychosis
SKTSFRNK schizophrenic

psychotic
SKTSFRNKL
schizophrenically
psychotic
SKTSFRNY schizophrenia
psychosis
SKTSH Scottish *of Scotland*
SKTSH skittish *nervous*
SKTSH succotash *vegetables*
SKTSHL skittishly *nervous*
SKTSHNS skittishness
nervous
SKTZ schizo *person* schizos
SKTZ schizy (or) schizzy
psychotic
SKTZD schizoid *split*
SKTZFRN schizophrene
psychotic
SKTZFRN schizophrenia
psychosis
SKTZFRNK schizophrenic
psychotic
SKTZFRNKL
schizophrenically
psychotic
SKTZFRNY schizophrenia
psychosis
SKV skive *pare* skived
skiving
SKV skivvy *(Br) servant*
skivvies
SKVNJ scavenge *rescue,*
clean scavenged
scavenging
SKVNJR scavenger *rescuer,*
cleaner
SKVR skiver *leather*
SKVS Skivvies *underwear*
(trademark)
SKVZ Skivvies *underwear*
(trademark)
SKW acequia *canal*
SKW sequoia *tree*
SKW Sequoya (or)
Sequoyah (or) Sequoia
Cherokee scholar
SKW skua *bird*
SKW skyway *airspace*
SKW sock away *save*
SKW squaw *Native*
American woman
SKWB squab *bird* squabs

SKWB squib *(v) ridicule, fire,*
kick squibbed squibbing
SKWB squib *(n) satire,*
firecracker
SKWB usquebaugh *whiskey*
SKWBL squabble *quarrel*
squabbled squabbling
SKWBLR squabbler *quarrel*
SKWD squad *group*
SKWD squatty *short and fat*
squattier squattiest
SKWD squid *mollusk* squid
(or) squids
SKWDKR squad car *police*
SKWDR sequitur
consequence
SKWDR squatter *settler*
SKWDR squattier *short and*
fat
SKWDRN squadron *group*
SKWDST squattiest *short*
and fat
SKWDYR squattier *short and*
fat
SKWDYST squattiest *short*
and fat
SKWFSH squawfish *fish*
SKWG squeegee *wipe*
squeeggeed
squeegeeing
SKWGL squiggle *wiggle*
squiggled squiggling
SKWGL squiggly *wiggly*
SKWJ squeegee *wipe*
squeeggeed
squeegeeing
SKWK squawk *loud cry*
SKWK squeak *shrill noise*
SKWK squeaky *shrill*
SKWKR squeaker *contest*
SKWL scowl *frown*
SKWL sequel *subsequent*
SKWL squall *wind, scream*
SKWL squally *gusty*
squallier squalliest
SKWL squeal *shrill cry*
SKWL squill *herb*
SKWL squilla *crayfish*
squillas (or) squillae
SKWLCH squelch *crush*
SKWLCHR squelcher
crusher

Use letters that best describe the sounds you hear and omit the vowels. Use **S** or **K** instead of **C**: to find circle use **SRKL**. Use **J** to find joy, **JM** to find gem and **G** to find go.

SKWLD squalid *dirty*
SKWLDL squalidly *dirty*
SKWLDNS squalidness *dirty*
SKWLN squalene *chemical*
SKWLN squall line *storm*
SKWLR squallier *windier*
SKWLR squalor *filth*
SKWLR squealer *shrill cry*
SKWLST squalliest *windier*
SKWLYR squallier *windier*
SKWLYST squalliest *windier*
SKWM squama *scale* squamae
SKWMLS squamulose *lobes*
SKWMS squamous *scaly*
SKWMSH squeamish *queasy*
SKWMSHN squamation *scales*
SKWMSL squamosal *bone*
SKWMT squamate *scaly*
SKWMYLS squamulose *lobes*
SKWN sequin *ornament*
SKWN squinty *eyes*
SKWNCH squinch *(v) squint (n) support*
SKWNCHL sequential (adj) *in order* sequentially (adv)
SKWND sequined (or) sequinned *ornaments*
SKWND squint-eyed *cross-eyed*
SKWNDR squander *scatter, lose*
SKWNLDK psychoanalytic *mental*
SKWNLDKL psychoanalytically *mental*
SKWNLSS psychoanalysis *treatment*
SKWNLST psychoanalyst *doctor*
SKWNLTK psychoanalytic *mental*
SKWNLTKL psychoanalytically *mental*
SKWNLZ psychoanalyze *mental treatment* psychoanalyzed psychoanalyzing

SKWNS sequence *order* sequenced sequencing
SKWNSHL sequential (adj) *in order* sequentially (adv)
SKWNT squint *eyes, variation* squinty
SKWNT squinty *eyes*
SKWNTD squint-eyed *cross-eyed*
SKWNTS sequence *order* sequenced sequencing
SKWNTYD squint-eyed *cross-eyed*
SKWR esquire *rank*
SKWR scour *search, clean*
SKWR skewer *(n) rod (v) pierce, criticize*
SKWR skiwear *clothing*
SKWR square *(adj) shape, even* squarer squarest
SKWR square *(v) settle up, shape, number** squared squaring
SKWR square *(n) block, number, conventional one**
SKWR square *(adv) honest, direct*
SKWR squire *(v) escort* squired squiring
SKWR squire *(n) rank*
SKWRD skyward *up*
SKWRDNS square dance *(n) dancing* square-dance *(v)*
SKWRDNSNG square dancing *dancing*
SKWRDNSR square dancer *dancing*
SKWRDNTS square dance *(n) dancing* square-dance *(v)*
SKWRDNTSNG square dancing *dancing*
SKWRDNTSR square dancer *dancing*
SKWRDR squirter *spray*
SKWRGD square-rigged *sails*
SKWRGR square-rigger *sails*
SKWRL squarely *directly*
SKWRL squirrel *(v) store up*

squirreled (or) squirrelled squirreling (or) squirrelling
SKWRL squirrel *(n) animal*
SKWRM squirm *fidget*
SKWRM squirmy *fidgety*
SKWRNS squareness *shape, conventional, fair*
SKWRNT square knot *join cords*
SKWRRK squirearchy *aristocrats* squirearchies
SKWRS Siqueiros *artist*
SKWRSH squarish *blocky*
SKWRSHLDRD square-shouldered *straight*
SKWRT square root *number*
SKWRT squirt *spray*
SKWRTD square-toed *old-fashioned*
SKWRTR squirter *spray*
SKWSDR sequester *separate*
SKWSH squash *(v) crush (n) vegetable, game* squashes (or) squash
SKWSH squashy *soft* squashier squashiest
SKWSH squish *(v) squelch*
SKWSH squishy *soft and damp* squishier squishiest
SKWSHL squashily *soft*
SKWSHNS squashiness *soft*
SKWSHNS squishiness *soft and damp*
SKWSHR squashier *soft*
SKWSHR squishier *soft and damp*
SKWSHS sequacious *servile*
SKWSHST squashiest *soft*
SKWSHST squishiest *soft and damp*
SKWSHYR squashier *soft*
SKWSHYR squishier *soft and damp*
SKWSHYST squashiest *soft*
SKWSHYST squishiest *soft and damp*
SKWST sacahuiste (or) sacahuista *grass*
SKWSTR sequester *separate*
SKWSTRM sequestrum *bone* sequestrums

Letters aren't doubled for single sounds: to find alley use **L** not **LL**. Use **Y** and **W** as hard sounds only: to find yellow use **YL**. (Br)=British spelling or usage. * See dictionary.

SKWSTRSHN
sequestration *custody*
SKWT squat *(v)* crouch
squatted squatting
SKWT squat *(adj)* short
squatter squattest
SKWT squat *(v, n)* pose,
posture *(n-slang)* nothing
SKWT squatty *short and fat*
squattier squattiest
SKWTR sequitur
consequence
SKWTR squatter *settler*
SKWTR squattier *short and
fat*
SKWTST squattiest *short
and fat*
SKWTYR squattier *short and
fat*
SKWTYST squattiest *short
and fat*
SKWY acequia *canal*
SKWY sequoia *tree*
SKWY Sequoya (or)
Sequoyah (or) Sequoia
Cherokee scholar
SKWYR esquire *rank*
SKWYR squire *(v)* escort
squired squiring
SKWYR squire *(n)* rank
SKWYRRK squirearchy
aristocrats squirearchies
SKWZ squeeze *exert
pressure* squeezed
squeezing
SKWZBL squeezable (adj)
exert pressure squeezably
(adv)
SKWZBLD squeezability
exert pressure
SKWZBLT squeezability
exert pressure
SKWZPL squeeze play
baseball, extortion
SKWZR squeezer *extractor*
SKY acequia *canal*
SKY askew *tilted*
SKY eschew *shun*
SKY ischia (pl) *pelvis*
ischium
(Br) ischaemia
SKY sequoia *tree*

SKY Sequoya (or)
Sequoyah (or) Sequoia
Cherokee scholar
SKY skew *twist*
SKY skua *bird*
SKY skyey *of heaven*
SKYB succuba *demon*
succubae
SKYB succubi (pl) *demon*
succubus
SKYBK skewback *arch*
SKYBL skewbald *white
patches*
SKYBL skiable *glide*
SKYBLD skewbald *white
patches*
SKYBS succubus *demon*
succubi
SKYD escudo *coin* escudos
SKYD skewed *twisted*
SKYK skyhook *shot, crane*
SKYK sukiyaki *food*
SKYL ischial *pelvis*
(Br) ischaemia
SKYL saccule *pouch*
SKYL sacculi (pl) *pouch*
sacculus
SKYLDD sacculated *pouches*
SKYLDR escalator *moving
stairs*
SKYLM osculum *opening*
SKYLNS succulence *juicy*
SKYLNT esculent *edible*
SKYLNT succulent *juicy*
SKYLNTL succulently *juicy*
SKYLNTS succulence *juicy*
SKYLR acicular *needle*
SKYLR ossicular *bone*
SKYLR saccular *pouch*
SKYLR secular *(adj)* not
religious
SKYLR secular *(n)* layman
seculars (or) secular
SKYLRS secularize *remove
religion* secularized
secularizing
(Br) secularise
SKYLRST secularist *no
religion*
SKYLRZ secularize *remove
religion* secularized
secularizing

(Br) secularise
SKYLRZM secularism *no
religion*
SKYLS sacculus *pouch*
sacculi
SKYLSHN escalation
increase
SKYLSHN osculation *kiss*
SKYLSHN sacculation
pouches
SKYLT escalate *increase*
escalated escalating
SKYLT osculate *kiss*
osculated osculating
SKYLTD sacculated *pouches*
SKYLTR escalator *moving
stairs*
SKYM ischium *pelvis* ischia
(Br) ischaemia
SKYN scallion *onion*
SKYN scullion *servant*
SKYNG skiing *gliding*
SKYNS skewness *twist*
SKYR secure *(v)* make safe,
effect, ensure* secured
securing
SKYR secure *(adj)* safe,
dependable securer
securest
SKYR skewer *(n)* rod *(v)*
pierce, criticize
SKYR skier *glider*
SKYRD secured *safe, locked*
SKYRD security *safety*
securities
SKYRMNT securement *safe,
locked*
SKYRR securer *safe, locked*
SKYRST securest *safe,
locked*
SKYRT security *safety*
securities
SKYTR psychiatry *mental*
SKYTRK psychiatric *mental*
SKYTRKL psychiatrically
mental
SKYTRST psychiatrist
mental
SKYW skua *bird*
SKYWR skewer *(n)* rod *(v)*
pierce, criticize
SKZ scuzzy *(slang)* dirty

Use letters that best describe the sounds you hear and omit the vowels. Use **S** or **K**
instead of **C**: to find circle use **SRKL**. Use **J** to find joy, **JM** to find gem and **G** to find go.

SKZ skies (pl) *(n) air above sky*

SKZ skis (pl) *(n) snow* ski

SKZD schizoid *split*

SKZFRN schizophrene *psychotic*

SKZFRN schizophrenia *psychosis*

SKZFRNK schizophrenic *psychotic*

SKZFRNKL schizophrenically *psychotic*

SKZFRNY schizophrenia *psychosis*

SKZM schism *division*

SKZMDK schismatic *division*

SKZMTK schismatic *division*

SKZMTZ schismatize *divide* schismatized schismatizing

SKZN cycasin *chemical*

SL acyl *chemical*

SL assail *attack*

SL cel *cartoon*

SL cell *room, unit*

SL cilia (pl) *cell hair* cilium

SL icily *frigid*

SL istle *fiber*

SL ocelli (pl) *eye* ocellus

SL Oslo *city*

SL psylla *plant lice*

SL sail *(n) fabric, cruise (v) travel*

SL sale *sell*

SL sallow *(n) tree (adj) color*

SL sally *leap* sallied sallying sallies

SL scilla *herb*

SL Scylla *Greek myth*

SL seal *(n) animal, emblem, closure (v) secure*

SL sell *market* sold selling

SL Seoul *city*

SL sill *framework*

SL silly *stupid, giddy* sillier silliest

SL silo *storehouse* silos

SL slaw *food*

SL slay *kill* slew slain

slaying

SL sleigh *snow*

SL slew *(v) pivot (n) large number*

SL sloe *fruit*

SL slough *(n) swamp (v) slog*

SL slow *(adj) dull, not fast (v) delay*

SL slue *skid*

SL sly *clever* slier (or) slyer sliest (or) slyest

SL soil *(n) earth (v) get dirty*

SL sol *money, musical tone, fluid* soles

SL Sol *sun god*

SL sola (pl) *soil* solum

SL sole *(adj) only (n) foot, fish*

SL solei (pl) *muscle* soleus

SL solely *only*

SL solo *(n) music* solos (or) soli

SL solo *(v) perform alone* soloed soloing

SL solo *(adj, adv) alone*

SL soul *spirit*

SL sully *dirty* sullied sullying sullies

SLB slab *(v) cover thickly* slabbed slabbing

SLB slab *(n) thick slice*

SLB slob *messy one*

SLB slobby *messy*

SLB slub *(v) twist* slubbed slubbing

SLB slub *(n) yarn*

SLB syllabi (pl) *outline* syllabus

SLBB syllabub *drink*

SLBC celibacy *no sex*

SLBF syllabify *divide words* syllabified syllabifying syllabifies

SLBFKSHN syllabification *divide words*

SLBK syllabic *word part*

SLBKSHN syllabication *divide words*

SLBKT syllabicate *divide words* syllabicated syllabicating

SLBL assailable *attack*

SLBL isolable *alone*

SLBL sailable *seaworthy*

SLBL salable (or) saleable *marketable*

SLBL sellable *market*

SLBL soluble *dissolve, explain*

SLBL syllable *(v) number, arrange* syllabled syllabling

SLBL syllable *(n) word part*

SLBLD solubility *dissolve*

SLBLT solubility *dissolve*

SLBLZ solubilize *dissolve* solubilized solubilizing (Br) solubilise

SLBR isallobar *line*

SLBR slabber *drool*

SLBR slobber *drool*

SLBR syllabary *wordbook* syllabaries

SLBRD celebrity *fame* celebrities

SLBRD sailboard *sport*

SLBRD salubrity *health*

SLBRDD celebrated *famous*

SLBRDR celebrator *party, rite*

SLBRN soilborne *transmission*

SLBRNT celebrant *priest*

SLBRR slobberer *drool*

SLBRS salubrious *healthful*

SLBRSHN celebration *happy time*

SLBRSL salubriously *healthful*

SLBRSNS salubriousness *healthful*

SLBRT celebrate *extol, party* celebrated celebrating

SLBRT celebrity *fame* celebrities

SLBRT salubrity *health*

SLBRTD celebrated *famous*

SLBRTHR soul brother *black male*

SLBRTR celebrator *party, rite*

SLBRTR celebratory *notable*

SLBRYS salubrious *healthful*

SLBRYSL salubriously

---

healthful

SLBRYSNS salubriousness
healthful

SLBS celibacy *no sex*

SLBS syllabus *outline* syllabi
(or) syllabuses

SLBSDD slab-sided *walls,
lank*

SLBSH slobbish *messy*

SLBT celibate *no sex*

SLBT sailboat *ship*

SLBTS slyboots *clever one*

SLC Selassie (Haile) *emperor*

SLC sulci (pl) *ditch* sulcus

SLCH slouch *droop, lout*

SLCH slouchy *droopy*
slouchier slouchiest

SLCHL slouchily *droopy*

SLCHNS slouchiness *droopy*

SLCHR sloucher *droop, lout*

SLCHR slouchier *droopy*

SLCHST slouchiest *droopy*

SLCHYR slouchier *droopy*

SLCHYST slouchiest *droopy*

SLCS Celsius *thermometer*

SLCYS Celsius *thermometer*

SLD celled *organism*

SLD psyllid *plant lice*

SLD salad *food, mixture*

SLD salty *brine, crude* saltier
saltiest

SLD sild *fish* sild (or) silds

SLD sled *vehicle* sledded
sledding

SLD slide *glide* slid sliding

SLD sloe-eyed *slanted*

SLD slutty *immoral*

SLD sold *(v-past)* sell

SLD solid *(adj) firm, prudent
(n) hard shape*

SLDD isolated *separate*

SLDD solidity *firmness*
solidities

SLDF solidify *make hard*
solidified solidifying
solidifies

SLDFKSHN solidification
make hard

SLDG sled dog *animal*

SLDK Celtic *Indo-European*

SLDLKN solid-looking
substantial

SLDLKNG solid-looking
substantial

SLDM seldom *infrequent*

SLDN celadon *color*

SLDN sledding *sport*

SLDN sliding *gliding*

SLDN slowdown *gradual
stop*

SLDNG slating *stone*

SLDNG sledding *sport*

SLDNG sliding *gliding*

SLDR assaulter *attack*

SLDR isolator *separate*

SLDR oscillator *vibrator*

SLDR Psalter *book*

SLDR psaltery *zither*
psalteries

SLDR saluter *greeter*

SLDR slater *scheduler, insect*

SLDR slaughter *kill*

SLDR slider *pitch*

SLDRD solidarity *unity*

SLDRHS slaughterhouse
butchery

SLDRL slide rule *math*

SLDRN slattern *prostitute*

SLDRNL slatternly *untidy*

SLDRNLNS slatternliness
untidy

SLDRR slaughterer *killer*

SLDRS slaughterous
murderous

SLDRT solidarity *unity*

SLDSH sluttish *prostitute*

SLDSHL sluttishly *prostitute*

SLDSHNS sluttishness
prostitute

SLDSTT solid-state *physics*

SLDT sold-out *tickets*

SLDT solidity *firmness*
solidities

SLDTR salutatory *welcome*
salutatories

SLDTRN salutatorian
student

SLDTRYN salutatorian
student

SLDV assaultive *attack*

SLDVL assaultively *attack*

SLDVNS assaultiveness
attack

SLF self *person* selves

SLF sell-off *(n) sale* sell off
(v)

SLF slough *(n) dead skin (v)
shed*

SLF sol-fa *scale*

SLF sulfa *drug*

SLF sulfur *element*
(Br) sulphur

SLF sylph *female*

SLFBS self-abuse
masturbation, reproach

SLFBSMNT self-abasement
disapproval

SLFBYS self-abuse
masturbation, reproach

SLFCKN self-seeking *selfish*

SLFCKNG self-seeking
selfish

SLFCLN self-sealing *closure*

SLFCLNG self-sealing
closure

SLFD selfhood *personality*

SLFD soul food *southern*

SLFD sulfide *compound*
(Br) sulphide

SLFD sylphid *female*

SLFDCT self-deceit
dishonest

SLFDD slow-footed
plodding

SLFDFDNG self-defeating
harmful

SLFDFNS self-defense
protection

SLFDFNTS self-defense
protection

SLFDFTN self-defeating
harmful

SLFDFTNG self-defeating
harmful

SLFDHSV self-adhesive
glue

SLFDJKDD self-educated
no schooling

SLFDJKTD self-educated
no schooling

SLFDK psilophytic *plant*

SLFDK sulfitic *salt or ester*

SLFDNL self-denial *restraint*

SLFDNYL self-denial
restraint

SLFDPRKDNG self-

deprecating *belittle*
SLFDPRKTN self-deprecating *belittle*
SLFDPRKTNG self-deprecating *belittle*
SLFDRKDD self-directed *independent*
SLFDRKTD self-directed *independent*
SLFDRST self-addressed *mail*
SLFDRVN self-driven *ambitious*
SLFDSPLN self-discipline *regulation*
SLFDST self-deceit *dishonest*
SLFDSTRKDN self-destructing *ruin*
SLFDSTRKDNG self-destructing *ruin*
SLFDSTRKDV self-destructive *ruinous*
SLFDSTRKTN self-destructing *ruin*
SLFDSTRKTNG self-destructing *ruin*
SLFDSTRKTV self-destructive *ruinous*
SLFDT self-doubt *question*
SLFDTRMNSHN self-determination *choice*
SLFFSN self-effacing *modest*
SLFFSNG self-effacing *modest*
SLFG solfeggio *singing*
SLFGVRND self-governed *control*
SLFGVRNN self-governing *control*
SLFGVRNNG self-governing *control*
SLFGY solfeggio *singing*
SLFHD selfhood *personality*
SLFHLN self-healing *get well*
SLFHLNG self-healing *get well*
SLFHLP self-help *independence*
SLFHPNSS self-hypnosis *trance*

SLFHT self-hate *loathing*
SLFJ solfeggio *singing*
SLFJKDD self-educated *no schooling*
SLFJKTD self-educated *no schooling*
SLFJY solfeggio *singing*
SLFKNCHS self-conscious *shy*
SLFKNFDNS self-confidence *certainty*
SLFKNFDNT self-confident *certain*
SLFKNFDNTS self-confidence *certainty*
SLFKNFST self-confessed *admitted*
SLFKNSHS self-conscious *shy*
SLFKNTMP self-contempt *hatred*
SLFKNTMPT self-contempt *hatred*
SLFKNTND self-contained *independent, reserved*
SLFKNTND self-contented *happy*
SLFKNTNTD self-contented *happy*
SLFKNTRL self-control *restraint*
SLFKNTRLD self-controlled *restrained*
SLFKRDKL self-critical *find fault*
SLFKRDSZM self-criticism *find fault*
SLFKRTKL self-critical *find fault*
SLFKRTSZM self-criticism *find fault*
SLFKSHLZ self-actualize *realize potential* self-actualized self-actualizing
SLFKSHLZSHN self-actualization *realize potential*
SLFKSHWLZ self-actualize *realize potential* self-actualized self-actualizing

SLFKSHWLZSHN self-actualization *realize potential*
SLFKSPLNTR self-explanatory *understood*
SLFKSPRSHN self-expression *personality*
SLFKTLZ self-actualize *realize potential* self-actualized self-actualizing
SLFKTLZSHN self-actualization *realize potential*
SLFKTN self-acting *automatic*
SLFKTNG self-acting *automatic*
SLFKTWLZ self-actualize *realize potential* self-actualized self-actualizing
SLFKTWLZSHN self-actualization *realize potential*
SLFL soulful (adj) *emotion* soulfully (adv)
SLFLDN self-loading *pack, start*
SLFLDNG self-loading *pack, start*
SLFLFLMNT self-fulfillment *success*
SLFLFLN self-fulfilling *expected, independent*
SLFLFLNG self-fulfilling *expected, independent*
SLFLK sylphlike *female*
SLFLKSHN solifluction *creeping*
SLFLN self-healing *get well*
SLFLNG self-healing *get well*
SLFLNS soulfulness *emotion*
SLFLP self-help *independence*
SLFLS selfless *generous*
SLFLV self-love *conceit*
SLFMD self-made *effort*
SLFMDVDD self-motivated *driven*
SLFMDVTD self-motivated

Letters aren't doubled for single sounds: to find alley use **L** not **LL**. Use **Y** and **W** as hard sounds only: to find yellow use **YL**. (Br)=British spelling or usage. * See dictionary.

driven
SLFMJ self-image *esteem*
SLFMPLD self-employed *work*
SLFMPRDNS self-importance *conceit*
SLFMPRDNT self-important *conceited*
SLFMPRDNTS self-importance *conceit*
SLFMPRTNS self-importance *conceit*
SLFMPRTNT self-important *conceited*
SLFMPRTNTS self-importance *conceit*
SLFMPRVMNT self-improvement *betterment*
SLFMPZD self-imposed *established*
SLFMTVDD self-motivated *driven*
SLFMTVTD self-motivated *driven*
SLFN cellophane *film*
SLFNDLJNS self-indulgence *enjoyment*
SLFNDLJNT self-indulgent *enjoyment*
SLFNDLJNTS self-indulgence *enjoyment*
SLFNDST self-induced *influenced*
SLFNDYST self-induced *influenced*
SLFNFLKDD self-inflicted *harm*
SLFNFLKTD self-inflicted *harm*
SLFNKRMNTN self-incriminating *guilt*
SLFNKRMNTNG self-incriminating *guilt*
SLFNRST self-interest *advantage*
SLFNSHRNS self-insurance *savings*
SLFNSHRNTS self-insurance *savings*
SLFNTRST self-interest *advantage*
SLFPD self-pity *feel sorry*

SLFPND self-appointed *named*
SLFPNTD self-appointed *named*
SLFPRKLMD self-proclaimed *declared*
SLFPRPLD self-propelled *movement*
SLFPRTKSHN self-protection *defense*
SLFPRTRT self-portrait *picture*
SLFPRZRVSHN self-preservation *protect*
SLFPT self-pity *feel sorry*
SLFPZSHN self-possession *calm*
SLFPZST self-possessed *calm*
SLFR sulfa *drug*
SLFR sulfur *element* (Br) sulphur
SLFRCHS self-righteous *narrow-minded*
SLFRDLZSHN self-fertilization *reproduction*
SLFRGLDNG self-regulating *automatic*
SLFRGLTN self-regulating *automatic*
SLFRGLTNG self-regulating *automatic*
SLFRGYLDNG self-regulating *automatic*
SLFRGYLTN self-regulating *automatic*
SLFRGYLTNG self-regulating *automatic*
SLFRK sulfuric *chemical* (Br) sulphuric
SLFRLNS self-reliance *confidence*
SLFRLNT self-reliant *confident*
SLFRLNTS self-reliance *confidence*
SLFRLYNS self-reliance *confidence*
SLFRLYNT self-reliant *confident*
SLFRLYNTS self-reliance *confidence*

SLFRLZSHN self-realization *understanding*
SLFRNL self-renewal *restore*
SLFRNWL self-renewal *restore*
SLFRPRCH self-reproach *blame*
SLFRS sulfurize *add sulfur* sulfurized sulfurizing (Br) sulphurise
SLFRS sulfurous *with sulfur, profane* (Br) sulphureous
SLFRSL sulfurously *with sulfur, profane* (Br) sulphureously
SLFRSNS sulfurousness *with sulfur, profane* (Br) sulphureousness
SLFRSPK self-respect *regard*
SLFRSPKT self-respect *regard*
SLFRSTRNT self-restraint *hold back*
SLFRTLZSHN self-fertilization *reproduction*
SLFRYLZSHN self-realization *understanding*
SLFRZ sulfurize *add sulfur* sulfurized sulfurizing (Br) sulphurise
SLFRZN self-rising *flour*
SLFRZNG self-rising *flour*
SLFSDSFD self-satisfied *smug*
SLFSDSFKSHN self-satisfaction *smugness*
SLFSFSHNT self-sufficient *independent*
SLFSH sailfish *fish*
SLFSH selfish *greedy*
SLFSH solfège *singing*
SLFSHRD self-assured *confident*
SLFSHRNS self-assurance *confidence*
SLFSHRNTS self-assurance *confidence*
SLFSKN self-seeking *selfish*
SLFSKNG self-seeking *selfish*

Use letters that best describe the sounds you hear and omit the vowels. Use **S** or **K** instead of **C**: to find circle use **SRKL**. Use **J** to find joy, **JM** to find gem and **G** to find go.

SLFSKRFS self-sacrifice *offering, loss*

SLFSKRFSN self-sacrificing *offering, loss*

SLFSKRFSNG self-sacrificing *offering, loss*

SLFSLN self-sealing *closure*

SLFSLNG self-sealing *closure*

SLFSM selfsame *identical*

SLFSNRD self-centered *proud, vain*

SLFSNTRD self-centered *proud, vain*

SLFSPRT self-support *independence*

SLFSRDV self-assertive *aggressive*

SLFSRTV self-assertive *aggressive*

SLFSRVN self-serving *selfish*

SLFSRVNG self-serving *selfish*

SLFSRVS self-service *do-it-yourself*

SLFSSTNN self-sustaining *maintain*

SLFSSTNNG self-sustaining *maintain*

SLFSTLD self-styled *supposed*

SLFSTM self-esteem *confidence*

SLFSTRDR self-starter *initiative*

SLFSTRTR self-starter *initiative*

SLFSTSFD self-satisfied *smug*

SLFSTSFKSHN self-satisfaction *smugness*

SLFSTYLD self-styled *supposed*

SLFT psilophyte *plant*

SLFT self-hate *loathing*

SLFT sulfate *add acid* sulfated sulfating (Br) sulphate

SLFT sulfite *salt or ester*

SLFTD slow-footed *plodding*

SLFTK psilophytic *plant*

SLFTK sulfitic *salt or ester*

SLFTR solfatara *volcano*

SLFTRCHR self-torture *pain*

SLFTT self-taught *no teacher*

SLFVDNT self-evident *obvious*

SLFWLD self-willed *stubborn*

SLFWNDN self-winding *coil*

SLFWNDNG self-winding *coil*

SLFWR self-aware *conscious*

SLFWRNS self-awareness *consciousness*

SLFXPLNTR self-explanatory *understood*

SLFXPRSHN self-expression *personality*

SLFYRK sulfuric *chemical* (Br) sulphuric

SLFZH solfège *singing*

SLG sawlog *lumber*

SLG slag *residue*

SLG slog *walk slowly* slogged slogging

SLG sludgy *muddy*

SLG slug *(v) punch, drink, typeset* slugged slugging

SLG slug *(n) bullet, animal, type**

SLGBD slugabed *slow one*

SLGFST slugfest *fight*

SLGN slogan *phrase*

SLGNR sloganeer *phrases*

SLGNZ sloganize *phrase* sloganized sloganizing

SLGR slugger *hitter*

SLGRD sluggard *lazy one*

SLGRF oscillograph *device*

SLGRF oscillography *science*

SLGRFK oscillographic *science*

SLGRFKL oscillographically *science*

SLGS sea legs *walking*

SLGSH sluggish *slow*

SLGZ sea legs *walking*

SLJ silage *fodder*

SLJ sledge *sleigh, hammer* sledged sledging

SLJ sludge *mud*

SLJ sludgy *muddy*

SLJ soilage *dirt*

SLJHMR sledgehammer *(n) tool (v) hit (adj) heavy-handed*

SLJN sloe gin *liquor*

SLJNL selaginella *moss*

SLJR soldier *military*

SLJR soldiery *military*

SLJRN soldiering *military*

SLJRNG soldiering *military*

SLJSDK syllogistic *logic*

SLJSDKL syllogistically *logic*

SLJST syllogist *logician*

SLJSTK syllogistic *logic*

SLJSTKL syllogistically *logic*

SLJZ syllogize *reason* syllogized syllogizing

SLJZM syllogism *logic*

SLK celiac *cavity*

SLK salchow *skating*

SLK saluki *dog*

SLK select *choose, excellent*

SLK silica *sand*

SLK silique *seed capsule*

SLK silk *fabric*

SLK silky *soft and smooth* silkier silkiest

SLK slack *loose, extra part*

SLK slake *quench* slaked slaking

SLK sleek *slick*

SLK slick *(adj) slippery, clever (n) tool, magazine*

SLK sulci *(pl) ditch* sulcus

SLK sulk *pout*

SLK sulky *(n) cart (adj) sullen* sulkies

SLKD selectee *chosen one*

SLKDBL selectable *chosen, excellent*

SLKDK silicotic *diseased*

SLKDR selector *chooser*

SLKDV selective *specific*

SLKDVL selectively *specific*

SLKDVNS selectiveness *specific*

SLKL silkily *soft and smooth*

SLKL slackly *slow*

SLKL sleekly *slick*

SLKL sulkily *sullen*

SLKLTH sailcloth *canvas*

Letters aren't doubled for single sounds: to find alley use **L** not **LL**. Use **Y** and **W** as hard sounds only: to find yellow use **YL**. (Br)=British spelling or usage. * See dictionary.

SLKMN selectman *administrator*
SLKN selachian *fish*
SLKN silicon *element*
SLKN silicone *compound*
SLKN silken *soft*
SLKN slacken *slow*
SLKN sleeken *slick*
SLKNS silkiness *soft and smooth*
SLKNS slackness *slowness*
SLKNS sleekness *slick*
SLKNS sulkiness *sullen*
SLKNTH coelacanth *fish*
SLKR silkier *soft and smooth*
SLKR slacker *idler, looser*
SLKR slicker *raincoat, swindler*
SLKS silex *silica*
SLKS sulcus *ditch* sulci
SLKSHN selection *choice*
SLKSKRN silk screen (n) *stencil* silk-screen (v)
SLKSN siloxane *chemical*
SLKSS silicosis *disease*
SLKST silkiest *soft and smooth*
SLKSTKN silk stocking (n) *wealthy* silk-stocking (adj)
SLKSTKNG silk stocking (n) *wealthy* silk-stocking (adj)
SLKT select *choose, excellent*
SLKT selectee *chosen one*
SLKT silicate *salt*
SLKT sulcate *ditch*
SLKTBL selectable *chosen, excellent*
SLKTK silicotic *diseased*
SLKTMN selectman *administrator*
SLKTR selector *chooser*
SLKTV selective *specific*
SLKTVD selectivity *specific*
SLKTVL selectively *specific*
SLKTVNS selectiveness *specific*
SLKTVT selectivity *specific*
SLKV salchow *skating*
SLKWD silkweed *milkweed*
SLKWRM silkworm *moth larva*
SLKYN selachian *fish*

SLKYR silkier *soft and smooth*
SLKYST silkiest *soft and smooth*
SLL salal *shrub*
SLL slowly *not fast*
SLL slyly *clever*
SLLD celluloid *film*
SLLDS cellulitis *inflammation*
SLLKW soliloquy *talk to oneself* soliloquies
SLLKWS soliloquize *talk to oneself* soliloquized soliloquizing (Br) soliloquise
SLLKWST soliloquist *talk to oneself*
SLLKWZ soliloquize *talk to oneself* soliloquized soliloquizing (Br) soliloquise
SLLM slalom *zigzag*
SLLQ soliloquy *talk to oneself* soliloquies
SLLQS soliloquize *talk to oneself* soliloquized soliloquizing (Br) soliloquise
SLLQST soliloquist *talk to oneself*
SLLQZ soliloquize *talk to oneself* soliloquized soliloquizing (Br) soliloquise
SLLR acellular *no cells*
SLLR cellular *cells, telephone*
SLLRD cellularity *cells, telephone*
SLLRT cellularity *cells, telephone*
SLLS cellulose *cell wall*
SLLT cellulite *fat*
SLLTS cellulitis *inflammation*
SLM asylum *refuge*
SLM cilium *cell hair* cilia
SLM coelom *space* coeloms (or) coelomata
SLM Islam *religion*
SLM psalm *song*
SLM psyllium *laxative*
SLM salaam *greeting*

SLM salami *meat*
SLM Salem *city*
SLM salmi *stew*
SLM slam *hit, shut* slammed slamming
SLM slim *thin* slimmed slimming slimmer slimmest
SLM slime (v) *smear* slimed sliming
SLM slime (n) *wet mud*
SLM slimy *sticky, vile* slimier slimiest
SLM slum (v) *low-class interaction* slummed slumming
SLM slum (n) *poor area*
SLM slummy *rundown* slummier slummiest
SLM solemn *serious*
SLM solum *soil* sola (or) solums
SLMBD Islamabad *city*
SLMBK psalmbook *songs*
SLMBL slimeball *odious one*
SLMBNG slam-bang (slang) *loud*
SLMBR slumber *sleep*
SLMBRS slumberous (or) slumbrous *sleepy*
SLMD coelomata (pl) *space* coelom
SLMD psalmody *book*
SLMGLN slumgullion *stew*
SLMGLYN slumgullion *stew*
SLMGND salmagundi *salad*
SLMGYN slumgullion *stew*
SLMJM slim-jim *slender, tool*
SLMK coelomic *with space*
SLMK Islamic *of Islam*
SLML slimily *sticky, vile*
SLML slimly *thin*
SLMLRD slumlord *landlord*
SLMN salmon *fish* salmon
SLMNBR salmonberry *raspberry* salmonberries
SLMNC Solomon Sea *body of water*
SLMND salmonid (or) salmonoid *fish*
SLMND solemnity *event* solemnities

Use letters that best describe the sounds you hear and omit the vowels. Use **S** or **K** instead of **C**: to find circle use **SRKL**. Use **J** to find joy, **JM** to find gem and **G** to find go.

SLMNDR salamander *animal*

SLMNF solemnify *make serious* solemnified solemnifying solemnifies

SLMNL salmonella *poison* salmonellae (or) salmonellas (or) salmonella

SLMNS sliminess *sticky, vile*

SLMNS slimness *thin*

SLMNS Solomon Sea *body of water*

SLMNSDKS slimnastics *exercise*

SLMNSDX slimnastics *exercise*

SLMNSTKS slimnastics *exercise*

SLMNSTX slimnastics *exercise*

SLMNT sillimanite *mineral*

SLMNT solemnity *event* solemnities

SLMNZ solemnize *honor* solemnized solemnizing

SLMNZSHN solemnization *honor*

SLMP slump *decline, droop*

SLMR slammer *(slang) jail*

SLMR slimier *sticky, vile*

SLMR slimmer *thin*

SLMR slummier *rundown*

SLMSHN slow-motion *replay*

SLMST psalmist *writer*

SLMST slimiest *sticky, vile*

SLMST slimmest *thin*

SLMST slummiest *rundown*

SLMT acoelomate *one cavity*

SLMT coelomata (pl) *space* coelom

SLMT coelomate *with space*

SLMT soul mate *friend*

SLMYR slimier *sticky, vile*

SLMYR slummier *rundown*

SLMYST slimiest *sticky, vile*

SLMYST slummiest *rundown*

SLMZSHN solmization *music*

SLN ceiling *cover*

SLN Iceland *country*

SLN sailing *navigation*

SLN saline *salt*

SLN salon *room, gallery*

SLN saloon *tavern*

SLN sea lion *animal*

SLN sea-lane *route*

SLN sileni (pl) *deity* silenus

SLN slain *(v-past) slay*

SLN solon *lawgiver*

SLN sullen *pouty*

SLNC saliency *highlight* saliencies

SLND Iceland *country*

SLND salinity *salt*

SLND selenide *compound*

SLND solenoid *magnet*

SLNDK Icelandic *of Iceland*

SLNDL solenoidal *magnet*

SLNDN celandine *herb*

SLNDR cylinder *tube*

SLNDR Icelander *of Iceland*

SLNDR slander *libel*

SLNDR slender *thin*

SLNDRKL cylindrical (adj) *tube* cylindrically (adv)

SLNDRS slanderous *libel*

SLNDRSL slanderously *libel*

SLNDRSNS slanderousness *libel*

SLNDRZ slenderize *make thin* slenderized slenderizing

SLNG ceiling *cover*

SLNG sailing *navigation*

SLNG slang *jargon*

SLNG slangy *jargon*

SLNG sling *(v) throw* slung slinging

SLNG sling *(n) support, throwing device*

SLNG so long *goodbye*

SLNGK slink *(v) creep* slunk slinking

SLNGK slinky *sleek* slinkier slinkiest

SLNGKL slinkily *sleek*

SLNGKNS slinkiness *sleek*

SLNGKR slinkier *sleek*

SLNGKST slinkiest *sleek*

SLNGKYR slinkier *sleek*

SLNGKYST slinkiest *sleek*

SLNGL slangily *jargon*

SLNGNS slanginess *jargon*

SLNGSHT slingshot *weapon*

SLNGZ so long as *provided*

SLNK slink *(n) premature one*

SLNK slink *(v) creep* slunk slinking

SLNK slinky *sleek* slinkier slinkiest

SLNKL slinkily *sleek*

SLNKNS slinkiness *sleek*

SLNKR slinkier *sleek*

SLNKST slinkiest *sleek*

SLNKYR slinkier *sleek*

SLNKYST slinkiest *sleek*

SLNL sullenly *pouty*

SLNM selenium *element*

SLNM solanum *herb*

SLNMDR salinometer *salt*

SLNMTR salinometer *salt*

SLNN solanine *chemical*

SLNS salience *highlight*

SLNS saliency *highlight* saliencies

SLNS salinize *salt* salinized salinizing

SLNS sallowness *color*

SLNS silence *quiet* silenced silencing

SLNS silenus *deity* sileni

SLNS silliness *stupid, giddy*

SLNS slowness *not fast*

SLNS slyness *clever*

SLNS sullenness *pouting*

SLNSHS solanaceous *plant*

SLNSR silencer *quiet*

SLNT aslant *tilt*

SLNT assailant *attacker*

SLNT salient *noticeable*

SLNT salinity *salt*

SLNT sealant *glue*

SLNT selenate *salt*

SLNT selenite *gypsum*

SLNT silent *quiet*

SLNT slant *tilt*

SLNT slanty *tilted*

SLNTC saliency *highlight* saliencies

SLNTL saliently *noticeable*

SLNTL silently *quiet*

SLNTNS silentness *quiet*

SLNTR cilantro *herb*

Letters aren't doubled for single sounds: to find alley use **L** not **LL**. Use **Y** and **W** as hard sounds only: to find yellow use **YL**. (Br)=British spelling or usage. * See dictionary.

SLNTR coelentera (pl) *cavity* coelenteron

SLNTRN coelenteron *cavity* coelentera

SLNTRT coelenterate *animal*

SLNTS salience *highlight*

SLNTS saliency *highlight* saliencies

SLNTS silence *quiet* silenced silencing

SLNTSR silencer *quiet*

SLNTWZ slantwise *diagonal*

SLNYM selenium *element*

SLNZ salinize *salt* salinized salinizing

SLNZSHN salinization *salt*

SLP asleep *not awake*

SLP aslope *tilted*

SLP salep *starch*

SLP salp *fish*

SLP slap *hit* slapped slapping

SLP sleep *slumber* slept sleeping

SLP sleepy *tired* sleepier sleepiest

SLP slip (v) *slide* slipped slipping

SLP slip (n) *garment, ship, twig*

SLP sloop *boat*

SLP slop (v) *spill, tramp, feed* slopped slopping

SLP slop (n) *swill, clothing*

SLP slope *incline* sloped sloping

SLP sloppy *messy* sloppier sloppiest

SLPCH slow-pitch *softball*

SLPDK sylleptic *modifying*

SLPDSH slapdash *slipshod*

SLPFRM slip form (n) *construction* slipform (v)

SLPGLSS salpiglossis *herb*

SLPHD sleepyhead *tired one*

SLPHP slaphappy *carefree*

SLPJ slippage *loss*

SLPJ sloppy joe *food*

SLPJK slapjack *game*

SLPK slowpoke *sluggish one*

SLPKS slipcase *container*

SLPKVR slipcover *furniture*

SLPL sleepily *tired*

SLPL sloppily *messy*

SLPLN sailplane *glider*

SLPLS sleepless *no slumber*

SLPLSL sleeplessly *no slumber*

SLPLSNS sleeplessness *no slumber*

SLPLT soleplate *construction*

SLPN sleep-in (adj) *slumber* sleep in (v)

SLPN slip-on *cover*

SLPNBG sleeping bag *bedding*

SLPNGBG sleeping bag *bedding*

SLPNGKR sleeping car *train*

SLPNGPL sleeping pill *drug*

SLPNJDS salpingitis *inflammation*

SLPNJTS salpingitis *inflammation*

SLPNKR sleeping car *train*

SLPNPL sleeping pill *drug*

SLPNS sleepiness *tired*

SLPNS sloppiness *messy*

SLPNT slipknot *noose*

SLPP slap-up (Br) *super*

SLPP slipup (n) *mistake* slip up (v)

SLPR sleeper *slumberer, unexpected hit*

SLPR sleepier *tired*

SLPR slipper *shoe*

SLPR slippery *slick* slipperier slipperiest

SLPR sloppier *messy*

SLPRNS slipperiness *slick*

SLPRR slipperier *slick*

SLPRST slipperiest *slick*

SLPRYR slipperier *slick*

SLPRYST slipperiest *slick*

SLPSHD slipshod *careless*

SLPSHT slap shot *hockey*

SLPSHT slip-sheet (v) *printing* slip sheet (n)

SLPSL slipsole *shoe*

SLPSS syllepsis *modifier* syllepses

SLPSSDK solipsistic *self*

SLPSSDKL solipsistically *self*

SLPSST solipsist *self*

SLPSSTK solipsistic *self*

SLPSSTKL solipsistically *self*

SLPST sleepiest *tired*

SLPST sloppiest *messy*

SLPSTCH slip stitch *sewing*

SLPSTK slapstick *comedy, hitter*

SLPSTRM slipstream *fluid flow*

SLPSZM solipsism *self*

SLPT slept (v-past) *sleep*

SLPTK sylleptic *modifying*

SLPVR slipover *garment*

SLPW slipway *ship*

SLPWK sleepwalk *dreaming*

SLPWKR sleepwalker *dreaming*

SLPWRK slopwork *cheap*

SLPYR sleepier *tired*

SLPYR sloppier *messy*

SLPYST sleepiest *tired*

SLPYST sloppiest *messy*

SLQD silkweed *milkweed*

SLQRM silkworm *moth larva*

SLR celery *vegetable* celeries

SLR cellar *basement*

SLR ciliary *cell hair*

SLR hostler *works with horses, trains*

SLR ocellar *eye*

SLR sailer *boat type*

SLR sailor *seaman*

SLR salary *wages* salaries

SLR sealer *glue*

SLR seller *marketer*

SLR sillier *stupid, giddy*

SLR slayer *killer*

SLR slier (or) slyer *clever*

SLR slur *blur, insult* slurred slurring

SLR slurry *mush* slurried slurrying slurries

SLR soilure *stain*

SLR solar *sun*

SLR solaria (pl) *sun room* solarium

SLRD celerity *speed*

SLRD salaried *wages*

Use letters that best describe the sounds you hear and omit the vowels. Use **S** or **K** instead of **C**: to find circle use **SRKL**. Use **J** to find joy, **JM** to find gem and **G** to find go.

SLRDS saleratus *leavening*
SLRJ cellarage *basement*
SLRK celeriac *root*
SLRM saleroom *(Br) display area*
SLRM solarium *sun room* solaria
SLRP slurp *suck*
SLRPLKSS solar plexus *abdomen*
SLRPLXS solar plexus *abdomen*
SLRR cellarer *provider*
SLRSL solar cell *battery*
SLRSSDM solar system *planets*
SLRSSTM solar system *planets*
SLRT celerity *speed*
SLRT cellarette (or) cellaret *cabinet*
SLRTS saleratus *leavening*
SLRY solaria (pl) *sun room* solarium
SLRYK celeriac *root*
SLRYM solarium *sun room* solaria
SLRYT salariat *wages*
SLRZ solarize *expose to light* solarized solarizing
SLRZSHN solarization *exposure*
SLS ocellus *eye* ocelli
SLS salsa *sauce*
SLS Selassie (Haile) *emperor*
SLS slice *cut* sliced slicing
SLS sluice *drain* sluiced sluicing
SLS soilless *no dirt*
SLS solace *comfort* solaced solacing
SLS soleus *muscle* solei
SLS solus *alone*
SLS sulci (pl) *ditch* sulcus
SLS useless *senseless*
SLSBN psilocybin *drug*
SLSBR Salisbury *physician, steak*
SLSCHL celestial (adj) *heavenly* celestially (adv)
SLSD celesta (or) celeste

music
SLSDK sciolistic *smart*
SLSDNT solicitant *one who asks*
SLSDR solicitor *ask, lawyer*
SLSDS solicitous *concerned, eager*
SLSDSL solicitously *concerned*
SLSDSNS solicitousness *concern*
SLSF salsify *herb*
SLSF silicify *silicon* silicified silicifying silicifies
SLSGRL salesgirl *seller*
SLSH sallowish *color*
SLSH slash *(v) cut (n) slit, swamp* slashes
SLSH slosh *splash*
SLSH slush *ice and water* slushes
SLSH slushy *icy, trashy* slushier slushiest
SLSH solatia (pl) *payment* solatium
SLSHFN slush fund *money*
SLSHFND slush fund *money*
SLSHM solatium *payment* solatia
SLSHN acylation *acyl addition*
SLSHN isolation *separation*
SLSHN oscillation *movement*
SLSHN solution *answer, liquid*
SLSHNG slashing *pelting, swamp*
SLSHNS slushiness *icy, trashy*
SLSHNST isolationist *separation*
SLSHNZM isolationism *separation*
SLSHR slushier *icy, trashy*
SLSHS salacious *lustful*
SLSHS siliceous (or) silicious *silica*
SLSHSL salaciously *lustfully*
SLSHSNS salaciousness *lust*
SLSHST slushiest *icy, trashy*

SLSHYR slushier *icy, trashy*
SLSHYST slushiest *icy, trashy*
SLSK silicic *silicon*
SLSKLRK salesclerk *seller*
SLSKN sealskin *fur*
SLSKP oscilloscope *current*
SLSKPK oscilloscopic *current*
SLSL uselessly *senselessly*
SLSLD saleslady *seller* salesladies
SLSLK salicylic *acid*
SLSLP sales slip *receipt*
SLSLT salicylate *acid*
SLSMN salesman *seller* salesmen
SLSMNSHP salesmanship *selling*
SLSN salicin *chemical*
SLSN selsyn *motor*
SLSNS uselessness *senselessness*
SLSPPL salespeople *sellers*
SLSPRSN salesperson *seller*
SLSRCHN soul-searching *conscience*
SLSRCHNG soul-searching *conscience*
SLSRM salesroom *display area*
SLSS Celsius *thermometer*
SLSSDK solecistic *blundering*
SLSST solecist *blunderer*
SLSSTK solecistic *blundering*
SLST celesta (or) celeste *music*
SLST scilicet *namely*
SLST sciolist *smarty*
SLST silliest *stupid, giddy*
SLST sliest (or) slyest *clever*
SLST solicit *ask for*
SLSTD solicitude *concern*
SLSTK sciolistic *smart*
SLSTKS sales tax *payment*
SLSTL celestial (adj) *heavenly* celestially (adv)
SLSTNT solicitant *one who asks*
SLSTR solicitor *ask, lawyer*

Letters aren't doubled for single sounds: to find **alley** use **L** not **LL**. Use **Y** and **W** as hard sounds only: to find **yellow** use **YL**. (Br)=British spelling or usage. * See dictionary.

SLSTS solicitous *concerned, eager*
SLSTS solstice *sun*
SLSTSHL solstitial *sun*
SLSTSHN solicitation *request*
SLSTSL solicitously *concerned*
SLSTSNS solicitousness *concern*
SLSTX sales tax *payment*
SLSTYD solicitude *concern*
SLSTYL celestial (adj) *heavenly* celestially (adv)
SLSW sluiceway *channel*
SLSWMN saleswoman *seller* saleswomen
SLSYS Celsius *thermometer*
SLSZM solecism *blunder*
SLT acylate *add acyl* acylated acylating
SLT assault *attack*
SLT Celt *Indo-European*
SLT celt *chisel*
SLT ciliate *cell hair*
SLT isolate *separate* isolated isolating
SLT ocelot *animal*
SLT oscillate *vibrate* oscillated oscillating
SLT SALT (abbr) *Strategic Arms Limitation Talks*
SLT salt *brine*
SLT salty *brine, crude* saltier saltiest
SLT salute *greet* saluted saluting
SLT sellout (n) *tickets* sell out (v)
SLT silhouette *outline* silhouetted silhouetting
SLT silt *mud* silty
SLT slat (v) *hurl, hit* slatted slatting
SLT slat (n) *wood strip*
SLT slate (n) *rock, gray color* (v) *schedule, cover with slate,* (Br) *criticize* slated slating
SLT slate (n) *rock, record, list**
SLT sleet *ice*

SLT sleight *skill*
SLT slight (adj) *meager, thin* (v) *neglect*
SLT slit *cut* slit slitting
SLT slot *notch* slotted slotting
SLT slut *prostitute*
SLT slutty *immoral*
SLT solute *dissolved*
SLTBK slotback *football*
SLTBKS saltbox *dwelling* saltboxes
SLTBSH saltbush *plant*
SLTBX saltbox *dwelling* saltboxes
SLTD isolated *separate*
SLTD solitude *alone*
SLTDRN solitudarian *recluse*
SLTDRYN solitudarian *recluse*
SLTH sleuth *detective*
SLTH sloth *animal, laziness*
SLTHFL slothful (adj) *lazy* slothfully (adv)
SLTHFLNS slothfulness *laziness*
SLTHR slather *squander*
SLTHR slither *slide*
SLTHR slithery *slippery*
SLTK Celtic *Indo-European*
SLTL saltily *brine, crude*
SLTL slightly *barely*
SLTLKSD Salt Lake City *city*
SLTLKST Salt Lake City *city*
SLTLS saltless *no brine, dull*
SLTMBK saltimbocca *food*
SLTN saltine *cracker*
SLTN sultan *ruler*
SLTN sultana *raisin, wife*
SLTNDPPR salt-and-pepper *black-and-white*
SLTNG slating *stone*
SLTNG sledding *sport*
SLTNK sultanic *ruler*
SLTNPPR salt-and-pepper *black-and-white*
SLTNS saltiness *taste, crude*
SLTNS slightness *frailty*
SLTNT sultanate *realm*
SLTPDR saltpeter *chemical*
SLTPN salt pan *pit*

SLTPTR saltpeter *chemical*
SLTR assaulter *attack*
SLTR isolator *separate*
SLTR oscillator *vibrator*
SLTR oscillatory *moving*
SLTR Psalter *book*
SLTR psaltery *zither* psalteries
SLTR salutary *healthful*
SLTR saluter *greeter*
SLTR slater *schedule, insect*
SLTR slaughter *kill*
SLTR solitaire *gem, game*
SLTR solitary *alone* solitaries
SLTR sultry *hot, sexy* sultrier sultriest
SLTRHS slaughterhouse *butchery*
SLTRL saltarello *dance* saltarellos
SLTRL salutarily *health*
SLTRL sultrily *hot, sexy*
SLTRN slattern *prostitute*
SLTRNL slatternly *untidy*
SLTRNLNS slatternliness *untidy*
SLTRNS salutariness *health*
SLTRNS sultriness *hot, sexy*
SLTRR slaughterer *killer*
SLTRR sultrier *hot, sexy*
SLTRS slaughterous *murderous*
SLTRST sultriest *hot, sexy*
SLTRYR sultrier *hot, sexy*
SLTRYST sultriest *hot, sexy*
SLTSH sluttish *prostitute*
SLTSHKR saltshaker *container*
SLTSHL sluttishly *prostitute*
SLTSHN saltation *dance*
SLTSHN salutation *greeting*
SLTSHN siltation *mud*
SLTSHNL salutational *greeting*
SLTSHNS sluttishness *prostitute*
SLTSLR saltcellar *container*
SLTSR seltzer *water*
SLTSTN siltstone *rock*
SLTTR saltatory *leaping*
SLTTR salutatory *welcome* salutatories

Use letters that best describe the sounds you hear and omit the vowels. Use **S** or **K** instead of **C**: to find circle use **SRKL**. Use **J** to find joy, **JM** to find gem and **G** to find go.

SLTTRL saltatorial *leaping*
SLTTRN salutatorian *student*
SLTTRYL saltatorial *leaping*
SLTTRYN salutatorian *student*
SLTV assaultive *attack*
SLTVL assaultively *attack*
SLTVNS assaultiveness *attack*
SLTWDR saltwater *ocean*
SLTWRKS saltworks *factory*
SLTWRT saltwort *shrub*
SLTWRX saltworks *factory*
SLTWTR saltwater *ocean*
SLTYD solitude *alone*
SLTYDRN solitudarian *recluse*
SLTYDRYN solitudarian *recluse*
SLTZR seltzer *water*
SLV saliva *spittle*
SLV salve *remedy* salved salving
SLV salvia *plant*
SLV salvo *shot* salvos (or) salvoes
SLV silva *trees*
SLV Slav *Slavic*
SLV slave *(v) toil* slaved slaving
SLV slave *(n) servant*
SLV slavey *drudge* slaveys
SLV sleeve *shirt, cover* sleeved sleeving
SLV solve *explain* solved solving
SLVBL salvable *save*
SLVBL solvable *explain*
SLVBLD solvability *explain*
SLVBLT solvability *explain*
SLVDK sylvatic *wild animals*
SLVDRVR slave driver *supervisor*
SLVFK salvific *redeeming*
SLVHLDR slaveholder *owner*
SLVJ salvage *save* salvaged salvaging
SLVJ selvage (or) selvedge *fabric*
SLVJBL salvageable *save*
SLVJR salvager *saver*

SLVK Slavic *language*
SLVK Slovak *Slavic*
SLVKLCHR silviculture *forests*
SLVKLCHRL silvicultural *(adj) forests* silviculturally *(adv)*
SLVKLCHRST silviculturist *forests*
SLVKLTR silviculture *forests*
SLVKLTRL silvicultural *(adj) forests* silviculturally *(adv)*
SLVKLTRST silviculturist *forests*
SLVKN Slovakian *Slavic*
SLVKYN Slovakian *Slavic*
SLVL sea level *altitude*
SLVLDR slaveholder *owner*
SLVLS sleeveless *no shirt, cover*
SLVLSS solvolysis *chemistry*
SLVLT sleevelet *arm cover*
SLVN sloven *unkempt*
SLVN sylvan *woods*
SLVNC solvency *pay debts, dissolve*
SLVNL slovenly *unkempt*
SLVNLNS slovenliness *unkempt*
SLVNS solvency *pay debts, dissolve*
SLVNT solvent *able, liquid*
SLVNT sylvanite *mineral*
SLVNTC solvency *pay debts, dissolve*
SLVNTS solvency *pay debts, dissolve*
SLVR salivary *spittle*
SLVR salver *tray*
SLVR silver *(n) element, flatware (adj) white sheen, 25th year (v) coat with silver*
SLVR silvery *shiny*
SLVR slaver *person, ship, saliva*
SLVR slavery *bondage*
SLVR sliver *splinter*
SLVR solver *answer*
SLVRBK silverback *gorilla*
SLVRBR silverberry *shrub* silverberries

SLVRFSH silverfish *insect, fish*
SLVRN silvern *like silver*
SLVRNS silveriness *shine*
SLVRPLDD silver-plated *coated*
SLVRPLT silver plate *flatware*
SLVRPLTD silver-plated *coated*
SLVRPNT silverpoint *drawing*
SLVRSDZ silversides *fish*
SLVRSMTH silversmith *craftsman*
SLVRTNGD silver-tongued *persuasive*
SLVRWD silverweed *plant*
SLVRWR silverware *flatware*
SLVSH slavish *copying, serving*
SLVSHN salvation *deliverance*
SLVSHNST salvationist *deliverance*
SLVSHNZM salvationism *deliverance*
SLVT salivate *drool* salivated salivating
SLVT solvate *chemistry*
SLVT sylvite *mineral*
SLVTK sylvatic *wild animals*
SLVVTS slivovitz *brandy*
SLVY salvia *plant*
SLVZ selves (pl) *persons* self
SLWD sloe-eyed *slanted*
SLWDD slow-witted *dull*
SLWDST silhouettist *outline*
SLWRM slowworm *lizard*
SLWSH sallowish *color*
SLWST soloist *performer*
SLWT silhouette *outline* silhouetted silhouetting
SLWTD slow-witted *dull*
SLWTST silhouettist *outline*
SLX silex *silica*
SLXN siloxane *chemical*
SLY cilia (pl) *cell hair* cilium
SLY solei (pl) *muscle* soleus
SLYBL soluble *dissolve, explain*
SLYBLD solubility *dissolve*

SLYBLT solubility *dissolve*
SLYBLZ solubilize *dissolve*
solubilized solubilizing
(Br) solubilise
SLYK celiac *cavity*
SLYLD celluloid *film*
SLYLDS cellulitis
inflammation
SLYLR acellular *no cells*
SLYLR cellular *cells,*
telephone
SLYLRD cellularity *cells,*
telephone
SLYLRT cellularity *cells,*
telephone
SLYLS cellulose *cell wall*
SLYLT cellulite *fat*
SLYLTS cellulitis
inflammation
SLYM cilium *cell hair* cilia
SLYM psyllium *laxative*
SLYN sea lion *animal*
SLYNC saliency *highlight*
saliencies
SLYNS salience *highlight*
SLYNS saliency *highlight*
saliencies
SLYNT salient *noticeable*
SLYNTC saliency *highlight*
saliencies
SLYNTL saliently *noticeable*
SLYNTS salience *highlight*
SLYNTS saliency *highlight*
saliencies
SLYR ciliary *cell hair*
SLYR sillier *stupid, giddy*
SLYR slayer *killer*
SLYR slier (or) slyer *clever*
SLYS soleus *muscle* solei
SLYST silliest *stupid, giddy*
SLYST sliest (or) slyest
clever
SLYT ciliate *cell hair*
SLYT solute *dissolved*
SLYTR salutary *healthful*
SLYTRL salutarily *health*
SLYTRNS salutariness
health
SLYTSHN salutation *greeting*
SLYTSHNL salutational
greeting

SLZ sleaze *poor quality*
SLZ sleazy *poor quality*
sleazier sleaziest
SLZBG sleazebag *(slang)*
low character
SLZBL sleazeball *(slang) low*
character
SLZBR Salisbury *physician,*
steak
SLZGRL salesgirl *seller*
SLZKLRK salesclerk *seller*
SLZL sleazily *poor quality*
SLZLD saleslady *seller*
salesladies
SLZM sciolism *learning*
SLZMN salesman *seller*
salesmen
SLZMNSHP salesmanship
selling
SLZNS sleaziness *poor*
quality
SLZPPL salespeople *sellers*
SLZPRSN salesperson *seller*
SLZR sleazier *poor quality*
SLZRM salesroom *display*
area
SLZST sleaziest *poor quality*
SLZTKS sales tax *payment*
SLZTX sales tax *payment*
SLZWMN saleswoman *seller*
saleswomen
SLZYR sleazier *poor quality*
SLZYST sleaziest *poor*
quality
SM aecium *fungus* aecia
SM assume *suppose*
assumed assuming
SM awesome *extraordinary*
SM cyma *molding*
SM cyme *flower*
SM psalm *song*
SM SAM *(abbr) surface-to-air*
missile
SM same *alike*
SM Samoa *islands*
SM seam *sew*
SM seamy *wicked* seamier
seamiest
SM seem *appear*
SM seme *sign*
SM smew *bird*
SM soma *cell body* somata

(or) somas
SM soma *intoxicant*
SM some *part*
SM sum *add, recount*
summed summing
SM summa *treatise* summae
SM sumo *wrestling*
SMB samba *dance*
SMB sambo *judo*
SMBD somebody *person*
SMBDK symbiotic
cooperation
SMBDKL symbiotically
cooperation
SMBK psalmbook *songs*
SMBL assemble *gather,*
construct assembled
assembling
SMBL assembly *gathering*
assemblies
SMBL assumable (adj)
received, supposed
assumably (adv)
SMBL cymbal *music*
SMBL summable *add*
SMBL symbol *(n) sign*
SMBL symbol *(v) represent*
symboled (or) symbolled
symboling (or) symbolling
SMBLG symbology *meaning*
symbologies
SMBLJ assemblage *group*
SMBLJ symbology *meaning*
symbologies
SMBLK symbolic
representing
SMBLKL symbolically
representing
SMBLLN assembly line
production
SMBLMN assemblyman
group member
assemblymen
SMBLNS semblance
likeness
SMBLNTS semblance
likeness
SMBLR assembler *converter*
SMBLSDK symbolistic
representative
SMBLST cymbalist *musician*
SMBLST symbolist *signs,*

Use letters that best describe the sounds you hear and omit the vowels. Use **S** or **K** instead of **C**: to find circle use **SRKL**. Use **J** to find joy, **JM** to find gem and **G** to find go.

metaphysics

SMBLSTK symbolistic
representative

SMBLWMN
assemblywoman *group
member* assemblywomen

SMBLZ symbolize *represent*
symbolized symbolizing
(Br) symbolise

SMBLZM symbolism
representation

SMBLZR symbolizer
represent
(Br) symboliser

SMBNT symbiont
cooperation

SMBR somber (or) sombre
gloomy

SMBRR sombrero *hat*
sombreros

SMBRV semibreve *whole
note*

SMBSS symbiosis
cooperation symbioses

SMBT symbiote *companion*

SMBTK symbiotic
cooperation

SMBTKL symbiotically
cooperation

SMBYDK symbiotic
cooperation

SMBYDKL symbiotically
cooperation

SMBYNT symbiont
cooperation

SMBYSS symbiosis
cooperation symbioses

SMBYT symbiote *companion*

SMBYTK symbiotic
cooperation

SMBYTKL symbiotically
cooperation

SMCH smooch *kiss, smear*
smooches

SMCHR sumptuary *limited*

SMCHS sumptuous
magnificent

SMCHSL sumptuously
magnificent

SMCHSNS sumptuousness
magnificence

SMCHWR sumptuary

limited

SMCHWS sumptuous
magnificent

SMCHWSL sumptuously
magnificent

SMCHWSNS
sumptuousness
magnificence

SMCKRT semisecret *not
announced*

SMD psalmody *song*

SMD Samoyed *Siberia, dog*

SMD smutty *fungus, soot,
indecency* smuttier
smuttiest

SMD somata (pl) *cell body*
soma

SMD someday *future*

SMDK semiotic *symbols*

SMDK Semitic *Jew*

SMDK somatic *cell body*

SMDKL somatically *cell body*

SMDKMNR
semidocumentary *film*

SMDKMNTR
semidocumentary *film*

SMDKYMNR
semidocumentary *film*

SMDKYMNTR
semidocumentary *film*

SMDL smuttily *fungus, soot,
indecency*

SMDL submittal
presentation, surrender

SMDLJKL somatological
evolution

SMDM semidome *roof*

SMDM symptom *sign*

SMDMDK semiautomatic
partly mechanized

SMDMDKL
asymptomatically *no
signs*

SMDMDR semidiameter
radius

SMDMNNT semidominant
genes

SMDMNT semidominant
genes

SMDMSDKDD
semidomesticated
tameness

SMDMSDKTD
semidomesticated
tameness

SMDMSTKDD
semidomesticated
tameness

SMDMSTKSHN
semidomestication
tameness

SMDMSTKTD
semidomesticated
tameness

SMDMTK semiautomatic
partly mechanized

SMDMTKL
asymptomatically *no
signs*

SMDMTR semidiameter
radius

SMDNS smuttiness *fungus,
soot, indecency*

SMDPLR somatopleure
tissue

SMDQMNR
semidocumentary *film*

SMDQMNTR
semidocumentary *film*

SMDR semidry *damp*

SMDR smatter *speak, dabble*

SMDR smiter *hit, captivate*

SMDR smuttier *fungus, soot,
indecency*

SMDRK isometric *exercise*

SMDRKL isometrically
exercise

SMDRKNS semidarkness
twilight

SMDRKS isometrics *exercise*

SMDRN smattering *scant bit*

SMDRNG smattering *scant
bit*

SMDRNL semidiurnal *twice
a day*

SMDRX isometrics *exercise*

SMDSNSR somatosensory
beyond senses

SMDSNTSR
somatosensory *beyond
senses*

SMDSST semioticist
symbols

SMDST smuttiest *fungus,*

Letters aren't doubled for single sounds: to find alley use **L** not **LL**. Use **Y** and **W** as hard
sounds only: to find yellow use **YL**. (Br)=British spelling or usage. * See dictionary.

soot, *indecency*

SMDTCHD semidetached
residences

SMDTCHT semidetached
residences

SMDTP somatotype *body
shape*

SMDTRPK somatotropic
hormone

SMDTRPN somatotropin
hormone

SMDV assumptive *taken for
granted*

SMDVN semidivine *godly*

SMDWRF semidwarf
undersize

SMDYMDR semidiameter
radius

SMDYMTR semidiameter
radius

SMDYR smuttier *fungus,
soot, indecency*

SMDYRNL semidiurnal
twice a day

SMDYST smuttiest *fungus,
soot, indecency*

SMFDD semifitted *shaped*

SMFLD semifluid *sticky*

SMFLKSBL semiflexible
bending

SMFLWD semifluid *sticky*

SMFLXBL semiflexible
bending

SMFN symphony *music*
symphonies

SMFNK symphonic *music*
symphonically

SMFNL semifinal *competition*

SMFNLST semifinalist
competitor

SMFNST symphonist *music*

SMFR samphire *plant*

SMFR semaphore *signal*
semaphored
semaphoring

SMFRML semiformal *attire*

SMFSHL semiofficial (adj)
authorized semiofficially
(adv)

SMFSS symphysis *bone*
symphyses

SMFTD semifitted *shaped*

SMG smog *polluted air*

SMG smoggy *polluted*
smoggier smoggiest

SMG smudgy *blur*

SMG smug *self-satisfied*
smugger smuggest

SMGL smuggle *illegal
transport* smuggled
smuggling

SMGL smugly *self-satisfied*

SMGLR smuggler *illegal
transport*

SMGLS semigloss *shine*

SMGM smegma *pus*

SMGNS smudginess *blur*

SMGNS smugness *self-
satisfaction*

SMGR smoggier *polluted*

SMGR smugger *self-satisfied*

SMGRP semigroup *math*

SMGST smoggiest *polluted*

SMGST smuggest *self-
satisfied*

SMGYR smoggier *polluted*

SMGYST smoggiest *polluted*

SMH somehow *means*

SMHWR somewhere *place*

SMHWT somewhat *slightly*

SMJ smudge *blur* smudged
smudging

SMJ smudgy *blur*

SMJL smudgily *blur*

SMJN smidgen *tiny bit*

SMJNS smudginess *blur*

SMK smack (v) hit, kiss (adv)
directly (n) taste, kiss, ship*

SMK smock (n) apron (v)
embroider

SMK smoke *fire, cigarette*
smoked smoking

SMK smoky *with fumes*
smokier smokiest

SMK sumac *plant*

SMKBL smokable (or)
smokeable *smoke*

SMKDB smack-dab *exactly*

SMKDK smectic *crystal*

SMKHS smokehouse *meat*

SMKJK smokejack *chimney*

SMKL smokily *with fumes*

SMKLN semicolon
punctuation

SMKLNL semicolonial
dependent

SMKLNYL semicolonial
dependent

SMKLS smokeless *no smoke*

SMKLSK semiclassic *music*

SMKLSKL semiclassical
music

SMKMLD summa cum
laude *distinction*

SMKMRSHL
semicommercial *products*

SMKN smacking *brisk*

SMKN smocking *embroidery*

SMKNCHS semiconscious
responsive

SMKNDKR
semiconductor *electricity*

SMKNDKTR semiconductor
electricity

SMKNG smacking *brisk*

SMKNG smocking
embroidery

SMKNS smokiness *with
fumes*

SMKNSHS semiconscious
responsive

SMKNSRVDV
semiconservative
reproduction

SMKNSRVTV
semiconservative
reproduction

SMKR smacker (slang)
dollar

SMKR smoker *person,
gathering*

SMKR smokier *with fumes*

SMKRSTLN semicrystalline
crystals

SMKS smokehouse *meat*

SMKSKRN smoke screen
obscurity

SMKST smokiest *with fumes*

SMKSTK smokestack
chimney

SMKT smoke out *drive out*

SMKTK smectic *crystal*

SMKWDK semiaquatic
water

SMKWNTDV
semiquantitative *precision*

Use letters that best describe the sounds you hear and omit the vowels. Use **S** or **K**
instead of **C**: to find circle use **SRKL**. Use **J** to find joy, **JM** to find gem and **G** to find go.

SMKWNTTDV semiquantitative *precision*

SMKWNTTTV semiquantitative *precision*

SMKWTK semiaquatic *water*

SMKWVR semiquaver *note*

SMKYR smokier *with fumes*

SMKYST smokiest *with fumes*

SMKZ Smokies *Smoky Mountains*

SML awesomely *extraordinary*

SML sawmill *lumber*

SML seemly *attractive, fit* seemlier seemliest

SML simile *figure of speech*

SML small *little*

SML smell *(v) perceive, stink* smelled (or) smelt smelling

SML smell *(n) odor*

SML smelly *stinky* smellier smelliest

SML smile *grin* smiled smiling

SML smiley *grinning*

SML Somali *of Somalia*

SML Somalia *country*

SML sommelier *wine* sommeliers

SMLBL assimilable *taken in*

SMLBLD assimilability *taken in*

SMLBLT assimilability *taken in*

SMLDD simulated *imitation*

SMLDR assimilator *take in*

SMLDR simulator *imitator*

SMLDR smelter (or) smeltery *furnace*

SMLDR smolder (or) smoulder *burn*

SMLDRT semiliterate *language*

SMLDV assimilative *taken in*

SMLFR small-fry *minor*

SMLG semiology *signs*

SMLGRTHMK semilogarithmic *math*

SMLJ semiology *signs*

SMLJKL semiological (adj) *signs* semiologically (adv)

SMLJNDR semilegendary *myth*

SMLJST semiologist *signs*

SMLK ice milk *dessert*

SMLKLMS small-claims *court*

SMLKR simulacra (pl) *trace, image* simulacrum

SMLKRM simulacrum *trace, image* simulacra

SMLKST simulcast *broadcast*

SMLKWD semiliquid *viscous*

SMLMNDD small-minded *petty*

SMLMNDDL small-mindedly *petty*

SMLMNDDNS small-mindedness *petty*

SMLMTH smallmouth *bass*

SMLN cymling *squash*

SMLN semolina *wheat*

SMLNG cymling *squash*

SMLNGL smilingly *grinning*

SMLNL smilingly *grinning*

SMLNR semilunar *crescent*

SMLNS seemliness *attractive, fit*

SMLNS smallness *little*

SMLNTSDN small intestine *digestion*

SMLNTSTN small intestine *digestion*

SMLPKS smallpox *disease*

SMLPX smallpox *disease*

SMLQD semiliquid *viscous*

SMLR seemlier *attractive, fit*

SMLR similar *alike*

SMLR smeller *nose*

SMLR smellier *stinky*

SMLR smiler *grinner*

SMLRD similarity *alike* similarities

SMLRM small arm *weapon*

SMLRT similarity *alike* similarities

SMLRZ small hours *after midnight*

SMLS seamless *smooth*

SMLSDRS semilustrous *shiny*

SMLSH smallish *tinier*

SMLSHN assimilation *taken in*

SMLSHN simulation *imitation*

SMLSKL small-scale *tiny*

SMLSKRN small screen *TV*

SMLSL seamlessly *smooth*

SMLSNS seamlessness *smooth*

SMLSRD smallsword *fencing*

SMLST seemliest *attractive, fit*

SMLST smelliest *stinky*

SMLSTF small stuff *rope*

SMLSTRS semilustrous *shiny*

SMLSWRD smallsword *fencing*

SMLT assimilate *take in* assimilated assimilating

SMLT simulate *imitate* simulated simulating

SMLT smalt *blue*

SMLT smalto *mosaic* smalti

SMLT smelt *(n) fish* smelts (or) smelt

SMLT smelt *(v) refine (v-past)* smell

SMLT smolt *salmon*

SMLTD similitude *likeness*

SMLTD simulated *imitation*

SMLTHL semilethal *deadly*

SMLTK small talk *chitchat*

SMLTM small-time *petty*

SMLTND simultaneity *same time*

SMLTNS simultaneous *same time*

SMLTNSL simultaneously *same time*

SMLTNSNS simultaneousness *same time*

SMLTNT simultaneity *same time*

SMLTNYD simultaneity *same time*

SMLTNYS simultaneous *same time*

SMLTNYSL simultaneously

Letters aren't doubled for single sounds: to find alley use **L** not **LL**. Use **Y** and **W** as hard sounds only: to find yellow use **YL**. (Br)=British spelling or usage. * See dictionary.

same time

SMLTNYSNS
simultaneousness *same time*

SMLTNYT simultaneity *same time*

SMLTR assimilator *take in*

SMLTR simulator *imitator*

SMLTR smelter (or) smeltery *furnace*

SMLTRT semiliterate *language*

SMLTT smaltite *mineral*

SMLTV assimilative *taken in*

SMLTYD similitude *likeness*

SMLWRZ small hours *after midnight*

SMLY Somalia *country*

SMLY sommelier *wine* sommeliers

SMLYR seemlier *attractive, fit*

SMLYR smellier *stinky*

SMLYST seemliest *attractive, fit*

SMLYST smelliest *stinky*

SMM sememe *sign*

SMM simoom (or) simoon *dry wind*

SMMDL semimetal *element*

SMMK sememic *sign*

SMMKR semimicro *size*

SMMNSDK semimonastic *monk*

SMMNSTK semimonastic *monk*

SMMNTHL semimonthly *twice a month* semimonthlies

SMMPRKL semiempirical *observation*

SMMST semimoist *damp*

SMMT semimatte *luster*

SMMTL semimetal *element*

SMMTLK semimetallic *element*

SMN assuming *pretentious*

SMN iceman *deliverer* icemen

SMN isthmian *inhabitant*

SMN saimin *soup*

SMN salmon *fish* salmon

SMN seaman *sailor* seamen

SMN seeming *evident*

SMN semen *sperm*

SMN simian *ape*

SMN simony *church*

SMN simoon (or) simoom *dry wind*

SMN summon *call*

SMNBR salmonberry *raspberry* salmonberries

SMNCHR subminiature *tiny*

SMNCHRL seminatural *modified*

SMND salmonid (or) salmonoid *fish*

SMND seminude *undressed*

SMNDD seminudity *undressed*

SMNDPNDNT semi-independent *partly reliant*

SMNDT seminudity *undressed*

SMNFRS seminiferous *seed*

SMNFRS somniferous *sleep*

SMNFSHNT somnifacient *hypnotic*

SMNG assuming *pretentious*

SMNG seeming *evident*

SMNGP summing-up *recount* summings-up

SMNK semantic *language*

SMNK simoniac *church*

SMNKL semantically *language*

SMNKL simoniacal (adj) *church* simoniacally (adv)

SMNKS semantics *language*

SMNL salmonella *poison* salmonellae (or) salmonellas (or) salmonella

SMNL semiannual (adj) *twice a year* semiannually (adv)

SMNL seminal (adj) *creative, seed* seminally (adv)

SMNL Seminole *Native American*

SMNL simnel *bun, (Br) cake*

SMNLNS somnolence *sleep*

SMNLNT somnolent *sleep*

SMNLNTS somnolence

sleep

SMNMBLNT
somnambulant *sleep walking*

SMNMBLST somnambulist *sleep walking*

SMNMBLT somnambulate *sleep walking* somnambulated somnambulating

SMNMBLZM
somnambulism *sleep walking*

SMNMBYLNT
somnambulant *sleep walking*

SMNMBYLST
somnambulist *sleep walking*

SMNMBYLT somnambulate *sleep walking* somnambulated somnambulating

SMNMBYLZM
somnambulism *sleep walking*

SMNMD seminomad *wanderer*

SMNP summing-up *recount* summings-up

SMNPR simon-pure *untainted*

SMNPYR simon-pure *untainted*

SMNR seminar *class*

SMNR seminary *school* seminaries

SMNRN seminarian *student*

SMNRYN seminarian *student*

SMNS awesomeness *extraordinary*

SMNS sameness *alike*

SMNS seaminess *wickedness*

SMNS summons *citation* summonses

SMNSHP seamanship *sailing*

SMNSST semanticist *language*

SMNT cement *(n) concrete (v) unite*

Use letters that best describe the sounds you hear and omit the vowels. Use **S** or **K** instead of **C**: to find circle use **SRKL**. Use **J** to find joy, **JM** to find gem and **G** to find go.

SMNTK semantic *language*

SMNTK semi-antique *50-100 years old*

SMNTKL semantically *language*

SMNTKS semantics *language*

SMNTR cementer *concrete, unify*

SMNTR subminiature *tiny*

SMNTRL seminatural *modified*

SMNTSHN cementation *concrete, unity*

SMNTSHS cementitious *concrete*

SMNTSST semanticist *language*

SMNTX semantics *language*

SMNTYR subminiature *tiny*

SMNWL semiannual (adj) *twice a year* semiannually (adv)

SMNX semantics *language*

SMNYK simoniac *church*

SMNYKL simoniacal (adj) *church* simoniacally (adv)

SMNYL semiannual (adj) *twice a year* semiannually (adv)

SMNYTR subminiature *tiny*

SMNYTYR subminiature *tiny*

SMNYWL semiannual (adj) *twice a year* semiannually (adv)

SMNZ siemens *electricity* siemens

SMNZ simonize *wax* simonized simonizing

SMNZ summons *citation* summonses

SMP samp *food*

SMP simp *idiot*

SMP sum-up (n) *total, conclude* sum up (v)

SMP sump *low area, (Br) oil pan*

SMPBLK semipublic *availability*

SMPCHR sumptuary *limited*

SMPCHS sumptuous *magnificent*

SMPCHSL sumptuously *magnificent*

SMPCHSNS sumptuousness *magnificence*

SMPCHWR sumptuary *limited*

SMPCHWS sumptuous *magnificent*

SMPCHWSL sumptuously *magnificent*

SMPCHWSNS sumptuousness *magnificence*

SMPDK simpatico *agreeable*

SMPDL sympodial *axis*

SMPDM symptom *sign*

SMPDMDK asymptomatic *no signs*

SMPDMDK symptomatic *suggestive*

SMPDMDKL asymptomatically *no signs*

SMPDMDKL symptomatically *suggestively*

SMPDMTK asymptomatic *no signs*

SMPDMTK symptomatic *suggestive*

SMPDMTKL asymptomatically *no signs*

SMPDMTKL symptomatically *suggestively*

SMPDR sumpter *animal*

SMPDV assumptive *taken for granted*

SMPDYL sympodial *axis*

SMPK semiopaque *cloudy*

SMPL sample (*v*) *test* sampled sampling

SMPL sample (*n*) *specimen*

SMPL simple *easy, plain, foolish* simpler simplest

SMPL simply *easily, clearly, really*

SMPLCZ simplices (pl) *word, space* simplex

SMPLDKL semipolitical *power*

SMPLDN simpleton *fool*

SMPLF simplify *make easy* simplified simplifying simplifies

SMPLFKSHN simplification *make easy*

SMPLFR simplifier *make easy*

SMPLFYR simplifier *make easy*

SMPLKS simplex *word, space* simplexes (or) simplices (or) simplicia

SMPLMDD semipalmated *webbed*

SMPLMNDD simpleminded *foolish*

SMPLMTD semipalmated *webbed*

SMPLN sampling *test group*

SMPLNG sampling *test group*

SMPLR sampler *needlework*

SMPLR simpler *easier*

SMPLS semplice *music*

SMPLS someplace *location*

SMPLSD simplicity *ease, innocence*

SMPLSDK simplistic *falsely easy*

SMPLSDKL simplistically *falsely easy*

SMPLSH simplicia (pl) *word, space* simplex

SMPLSHL simplicial (adj) *word, space* simplicially (adv)

SMPLST simplest *easiest*

SMPLST simplicity *ease, innocence*

SMPLSTK simplistic *falsely easy*

SMPLSTKL simplistically *falsely easy*

SMPLSZ simplices (pl) *word, space* simplex

SMPLTKL semipolitical *power*

SMPLTN simpleton *fool*

SMPLX simplex *word, space* simplexes (or) simplices

Letters aren't doubled for single sounds: to find alley use **L** not **LL**. Use **Y** and **W** as hard sounds only: to find yellow use **YL**. (Br)=British spelling or usage. * See dictionary.

(or) simplicia
SMPLZM simplism *falsely easy*
SMPMP sump pump *suction*
SMPN sampan *boat*
SMPPLR semipopular *liked*
SMPPYLR semipopular *liked*
SMPR semipro *part-time paid*
SMPR sempre *music*
SMPR simper *whine, smirk*
SMPRFSHNL semiprofessional (adj) *part-time paid* semiprofessionally (adv)
SMPRMBL semipermeable *pass through*
SMPRMNNT semipermanent *lasting*
SMPRMYBL semipermeable *pass through*
SMPRNGRF semipornography *lewdness*
SMPRNGRFK semipornographic *lewd*
SMPRSDK semiparasitic *plant*
SMPRSHS semiprecious *value*
SMPRSLN semiporcelain *ceramic*
SMPRST semiparasite *plant*
SMPRSTK semiparasitic *plant*
SMPRVT semiprivate *secluded*
SMPRVVM sempervivum *herb*
SMPSDL semipostal *stamp*
SMPSHN assumption *arising, arrogance*
SMPSHR sumptuary *limited*
SMPSHS sumptuous *magnificent*
SMPSHSL sumptuously *magnificent*
SMPSHSNS sumptuousness *magnificence*

SMPSHWR sumptuary *limited*
SMPSHWS sumptuous *magnificent*
SMPSHWSL sumptuously *magnificent*
SMPSHWSNS sumptuousness *magnificence*
SMPSN Samson *Biblical strong man*
SMPSTL semipostal *stamp*
SMPTDK asymptotic *curved*
SMPTDKL asymptotically *curved*
SMPTH sympathy *attraction, pity* sympathies
SMPTHDK sympathetic *approval, compassion, interdependence**
SMPTHDKL sympathetically *approval, compassion, interdependence**
SMPTHN sympathin *chemical*
SMPTHTK sympathetic *approval, compassion, interdependence**
SMPTHTKL sympathetically *approval, compassion, interdependence**
SMPTHZ sympathize *share grief* sympathized sympathizing (Br) sympathise
SMPTHZR sympathizer *share grief* (Br) sympathiser
SMPTK simpatico *agreeable*
SMPTM symptom *sign*
SMPTMDK asymptomatic *no signs*
SMPTMDK symptomatic *suggestive*
SMPTMDKL asymptomatically *no signs*
SMPTMDKL symptomatically *suggestively*
SMPTMLS symptomless *no signs*

SMPTMTK asymptomatic *no signs*
SMPTMTK symptomatic *suggestive*
SMPTMTKL asymptomatically *no signs*
SMPTMTKL symptomatically *suggestively*
SMPTMTLG symptomatology *disease signs*
SMPTMTLJ symptomatology *disease signs*
SMPTMTLJK symptomatologic (or) symptomatological (adj) *disease signs* symptomatologically (adv)
SMPTMTLJKL symptomatological (or) symptomatologic (adj) *disease signs* symptomatologically (adv)
SMPTR sumpter *animal*
SMPTR sumptuary *limited*
SMPTRND sempiternity *forever*
SMPTRNL sempiternal (adj) *forever* sempiternally (adv)
SMPTRNT sempiternity *forever*
SMPTS sumptuous *magnificent*
SMPTSL sumptuously *magnificent*
SMPTSNS sumptuousness *magnificence*
SMPTT asymptote *curve*
SMPTTK asymptotic *curved*
SMPTTKL asymptotically *curved*
SMPTV assumptive *taken for granted*
SMPTWR sumptuary *limited*
SMPTWS sumptuous *magnificent*

Use letters that best describe the sounds you hear and omit the vowels. Use **S** or **K** instead of **C**: to find circle use **SRKL**. Use **J** to find joy, **JM** to find gem and **G** to find go.

SMPTWSL sumptuously *magnificent*

SMPTWSNS sumptuousness *magnificence*

SMPZ symposia (pl) *discussion* symposium

SMPZM symposium *discussion* symposia (or) symposiums

SMPZRK symposiarch *leader*

SMPZST symposiast *attendee*

SMPZY symposia (pl) *discussion* symposium

SMPZYM symposium *discussion* symposia (or) symposiums

SMPZYRK symposiarch *leader*

SMPZYST symposiast *attendee*

SMQDK semiaquatic *water*

SMQNTDV semiquantitative *precision*

SMQNTTDV semiquantitative *precision*

SMQNTTV semiquantitative *precision*

SMQTK semiaquatic *water*

SMQVR semiquaver *note*

SMR isomer *compound*

SMR samara *fruit*

SMR Samaria *ancient city*

SMR samurai *warrior* samurai

SMR seamier *wicked*

SMR simmer *boil*

SMR smear *(v) wipe, sully (n) spot, accusation*

SMR smeary *smudged*

SMR summary *brief account* summaries

SMR summer *season*

SMR summery *warm*

SMRBRL semiarboreal *trees*

SMRBRYL semiarboreal *trees*

SMRCH smirch *dirty*

SMRD semiarid *dry*

SMRD smarty (or) smartie

smart aleck smarties

SMRDLK smart aleck (n) *objectionable* smart-aleck (adj)

SMRDLK smart-alecky *objectionable*

SMRDN Samaritan *helper*

SMRDPNS smarty-pants *obnoxious one*

SMRDPNTS smarty-pants *obnoxious one*

SMRDS smart-ass *objectionable*

SMRF isomorph *identical*

SMRFK isomorphic *identical*

SMRFKL isomorphically *identical*

SMRFS isomorphous *identical*

SMRFZM isomorphism *identical*

SMRGDT smaragdite *mineral*

SMRGSBRD smorgasbord *buffet*

SMRHS summerhouse *residence*

SMRJ submerge *put under water, suppress* submerged submerging

SMRJBL submergible *put under water, suppress*

SMRJD semirigid *flexible*

SMRJNS submergence *put under water, suppress*

SMRJNTS submergence *put under water, suppress*

SMRK isomeric *chemical*

SMRK semierect *tilted*

SMRK smirk *grin*

SMRKT semierect *tilted*

SMRL summarily *briefly*

SMRLJS semireligious *church*

SMRLNG summerlong *seasonal*

SMRM smarm *smugness, sleaze*

SMRM smarmy *smug, sleazy*

SMRML smarmily *smug, sleazy*

SMRMNS smarminess

smug, sleazy

SMRN submarine *(v) attack* submarined submarining

SMRNR submariner *sailor*

SMRRL semirural *country*

SMRS submerse *put under water* submersed submersing

SMRSBL submersible *put under water*

SMRSHN submersion *put under water*

SMRSKT samarskite *mineral*

SMRSLT somersault *leap*

SMRST somersault *leap*

SMRT smart *intelligent, stylish, brisk*

SMRT smarty (or) smartie *smart aleck* smarties

SMRTL smartly *intelligent, stylish, brisk*

SMRTLK smart aleck (n) *objectionable* smart-aleck (adj)

SMRTLK smart-alecky *objectionable*

SMRTM summertime *season*

SMRTN Samaritan *helper*

SMRTN smarten *get wise*

SMRTNS smartness *intelligent, stylish, brisk*

SMRTPNS smarty-pants *obnoxious one*

SMRTPNTS smarty-pants *obnoxious one*

SMRTRD semiretired *part-time*

SMRTRMNT semiretirement *part-time*

SMRTS smart-ass *objectionable*

SMRTWD smartweed *plant*

SMRTYRD semiretired *part-time*

SMRTYRMNT semiretirement *part-time*

SMRWD summerwood *tree ring*

SMRY Samaria *city*

SMRZ isomerase *enzyme*

SMRZ summarize *make brief*

---

summarized
summarizing
(Br) summarise
SMRZBL summarizable
make brief
(Br) summarisable
SMRZHN submersion *put
under water*
SMRZM isomerism
chemistry
SMRZR summarizer *make
brief*
(Br) summariser
SMRZSHN summarization
make brief
(Br) summarisation
SMS cymose *flower*
SMS isthmus *strip of land*
isthmuses
SMSBMRSBL
semisubmersible *platform*
SMSDNTR semisedentary
movement
SMSDR semester *school*
SMSF semisoft *not hard*
SMSFT semisoft *not hard*
SMSH cymatia (pl) *molding*
cymatium
SMSH smash *hit* smashes
SMSHD smashed *drunk,
broken*
SMSHM cymatium *molding*
cymatia
SMSHN assumption *arising,
arrogance*
SMSHN smashing *fabulous*
SMSHN submission
presentation, surrender
SMSHN summation *account,
total*
SMSHNG smashing *fabulous*
SMSHNGL smashingly
fabulous
SMSHNGN submachine
gun *weapon*
SMSHNL smashingly
fabulous
SMSHNL summational
account, total
SMSHP smashup *crash*
SMSHR smasher *hitter*
SMSHR sumptuary *limited*

SMSHRB semishrubby
plants
SMSHS sumptuous
magnificent
SMSHSL sumptuously
magnificent
SMSHSNS sumptuousness
magnificence
SMSHT smashed *drunk,
broken*
SMSHWR sumptuary *limited*
SMSHWS sumptuous
magnificent
SMSHWSL sumptuously
magnificent
SMSHWSNS
sumptuousness
magnificence
SMSKLD semiskilled *labor*
SMSKRD semisacred
religion
SMSKRT semisecret *not
announced*
SMSLD semisolid *sticky*
SMSLNDRKL
semicylindrical *roundness*
SMSN samisen *music*
SMSN Samson *Biblical
strong man*
SMSNTHDK semisynthetic
man-made
SMSNTHTK semisynthetic
man-made
SMSR samsara *cycle*
SMSRKL semicircle *arc*
SMSRKLR semicircular *arc*
SMSRKYLR semicircular
arc
SMSRQLR semicircular *arc*
SMSS osmosis *absorption*
SMSS semiosis *signing
process*
SMST psalmist *writer*
SMST seamiest *wicked*
SMSTR semester *school*
SMSTRS seamstress *sewing*
seamstresses
SMSV submissive *yielding*
SMSVL submissively
yielding
SMSVLZD semicivilized
wildness

SMSVNS submissiveness
yielding
SMSWT semisweet *sugar*
SMT samite *fabric*
SMT Semite *Jew*
SMT smite *hit, captivate*
smote smiting smitten
SMT smut (v) *taint* smutted
smutting
SMT smut (n) *fungus, soot,
indecency*
SMT smutty *fungus, soot,
indecency* smuttier
smuttiest
SMT somata (pl) *cell body*
soma
SMT submit *present, yield*
submitted submitting
SMT summit *peak*
SMTDK asymptotic *curved*
SMTDKL asymptotically
curved
SMTH smith *metal worker*
SMTH smithy *workshop,
blacksmith* smithies
SMTH smooth *even, clear*
SMTH smoothy (or)
smoothie *drink*
smoothies
SMTHBR smoothbore *gun*
SMTHL smoothly *even, clear*
SMTHN smoothen *even,
clear*
SMTHN something *item*
SMTHNG something *item*
SMTHNS smoothness *even,
clear*
SMTHR smother (v) *deprive
of air* (n) *smoke*
SMTHRNZ smithereens *tiny
bits*
SMTHTNGD smooth-
tongued *ingratiating*
SMTK semiotic *symbols*
SMTK Semitic *Jew*
SMTK somatic *cell body*
SMTKL somatically *cell body*
SMTL smuttily *fungus, soot,
indecency*
SMTL submittal *presentation,
surrender*
SMTLG somatology

Use letters that best describe the sounds you hear and omit the vowels. Use **S** or **K**
instead of **C**: to find circle use **SRKL**. Use **J** to find joy, **JM** to find gem and **G** to find go.

evolution

SMTLJ somatology *evolution*

SMTLJKL somatological *evolution*

SMTM sometime *indefinite time*

SMTM symptom *sign*

SMTMDK asymptomatic *no signs*

SMTMDK semiautomatic *partly mechanized*

SMTMDK symptomatic *suggestive*

SMTMDKL asymptomatically *no signs*

SMTMDKL symptomatically *suggestively*

SMTMLS symptomless *no signs*

SMTMTK asymptomatic *no signs*

SMTMTK semiautomatic *partly mechanized*

SMTMTK symptomatic *suggestive*

SMTMTKL asymptomatically *no signs*

SMTMTKL symptomatically *suggestively*

SMTMTLG symptomatology *disease signs*

SMTMTLJ symptomatology *disease signs*

SMTMTLJK symptomatologic (or) symptomatological (adj) *disease signs* symptomatologically (adv)

SMTMTLJKL symptomatological (or) symptomatologic (adj) *disease signs* symptomatologically (adv)

SMTMZ sometimes *occasionally*

SMTN semitone *music*

SMTN smitten *hit, captivated*

SMTNK semitonic *music*

SMTNKL semitonically *music*

SMTNL semitonal (adj) *music* semitonally (adv)

SMTNMS semiautonomous *independence*

SMTNS smuttiness *fungus, soot, indecency*

SMTPLR somatopleure *tissue*

SMTR asymmetry *irregular shape*

SMTR cemetery *tomb* cemeteries

SMTR isometry *mapping* isometries

SMTR scimitar *sword*

SMTR smatter *speak, dabble*

SMTR smiter *hit, captivate*

SMTR smuttier *fungus, soot, indecency*

SMTR summiteer *attendee*

SMTR summitry *conference*

SMTR sumptuary *limited*

SMTR symmetry *balance* symmetries

SMTRK asymmetric (or) asymmetrical (adj) *irregular shape* asymmetrically (adv)

SMTRK isometric *exercise*

SMTRK symmetric (or) symmetrical (adj) *balanced* symmetrically (adv)

SMTRKL asymmetrical (or) asymmetric (adj) *irregular shape* asymmetrically (adv)

SMTRKL isometrically *exercise*

SMTRKL symmetrical (or) symmetric (adj) *balanced* symmetrically (adv)

SMTRKS isometrics *exercise*

SMTRLR semitrailer *truck*

SMTRN smattering *scant bit*

SMTRNG smattering *scant bit*

SMTRNZLSNT semitranslucent *clearness*

SMTRNZPRNT semitransparent *clearness*

SMTRPKL semitropical *climate*

SMTRSCHL semiterrestrial *land*

SMTRSHTRL semiterrestrial *land*

SMTRSHTRYL semiterrestrial *land*

SMTRSTRL semiterrestrial *land*

SMTRSTRYL semiterrestrial *land*

SMTRX isometrics *exercise*

SMTRZ symmetrize *balance* symmetrized symmetrizing

SMTRZSHN symmetrization *balance*

SMTS sumptuous *magnificent*

SMTSHN semiotician *symbols*

SMTSL sumptuously *magnificent*

SMTSNS sumptuousness *magnificence*

SMTSNSR somatosensory *beyond senses*

SMTSNTSR somatosensory *beyond senses*

SMTSST semioticist *symbols*

SMTST Semitist *Jews*

SMTST smuttiest *fungus, soot, indecency*

SMTT asymptote *curve*

SMTTK asymptotic *curved*

SMTTKL asymptotically *curved*

SMTTP somatotype *body shape*

SMTTRPK somatotropic *hormone*

SMTTRPN somatotropin *hormone*

SMTV assumptive *taken for granted*

SMTWR sumptuary *limited*

SMTWS sumptuous *magnificent*

SMTWSL sumptuously

Letters aren't doubled for single sounds: to find alley use **L** not **LL**. Use **Y** and **W** as hard sounds only: to find yellow use **YL**. (Br)=British spelling or usage. * See dictionary.

magnificent

SMTWSNS sumptuousness
magnificence

SMTYR smuttier *fungus,
soot, indecency*

SMTYST smuttiest *fungus,
soot, indecency*

SMTZM Semitism *Jews*

SMVL semivowel *sound*

SMVR samovar *urn*

SMVWL semivowel *sound*

SMW Samoa *islands*

SMW someway *in some
manner*

SMWKL semiweekly *twice a
week* semiweeklies

SMWN someone *person*

SMWR somewhere *place*

SMWRKS semiworks
manufacturing

SMWRX semiworks
manufacturing

SMWT somewhat *slightly*

SMY smew *bird*

SMYD Samoyed *Siberia, dog*

SMYDK semiotic *symbols*

SMYDMDK semiautomatic
partly mechanized

SMYDMTK semiautomatic
partly mechanized

SMYDSST semioticist
symbols

SMYFSHL semiofficial (adj)
authorized semiofficially
(adv)

SMYKWDK semiaquatic
water

SMYKWTK semiaquatic
water

SMYLDD simulated
imitation

SMYLDR simulator *imitator*

SMYLG semiology *signs*

SMYLJ semiology *signs*

SMYLJKL semiological (adj)
signs semiologically (adv)

SMYLJST semiologist *signs*

SMYLKR simulacra (pl)
trace, image simulacrum

SMYLKRM simulacrum
trace, image simulacra

SMYLSHN simulation

imitation

SMYLT simulate *imitate*
simulated simulating

SMYLTD simulated *imitation*

SMYLTR simulator *imitator*

SMYMPRKL semiempirical
observation

SMYN isthmian *inhabitant*

SMYN simian *ape*

SMYNDPNDNT semi-
independent *partly reliant*

SMYNTK semi-antique *50-
100 years old*

SMYNWL semiannual (adj)
twice a year semiannually
(adv)

SMYNYL semiannual (adj)
twice a year semiannually
(adv)

SMYNYWL semiannual (adj)
twice a year semiannually
(adv)

SMYPK semiopaque *cloudy*

SMYQDK semiaquatic *water*

SMYQTK semiaquatic *water*

SMYR seamier *wicked*

SMYRBRL semiarboreal
trees

SMYRBRYL semiarboreal
trees

SMYRD semiarid *dry*

SMYRK semierect *tilted*

SMYRKT semierect *tilted*

SMYRL semiyearly *twice a
year*

SMYSS semiosis *signing
process*

SMYST seamiest *wicked*

SMYTK semiotic *symbols*

SMYTMDK semiautomatic
partly mechanized

SMYTMTK semiautomatic
partly mechanized

SMYTNMS
semiautonomous
independence

SMYTSHN semiotician
symbols

SMYTSST semioticist
symbols

SMZ Siamese *of Thailand*

SMZV submissive *yielding*

SMZVL submissively
yielding

SMZVNS submissiveness
yielding

SN acini (pl) *sac* acinus

SN asana *posture*

SN ascend *rise*

SN assign *allot*

SN assignee *person*

SN cine *movie*

SN cyan *color*

SN eosin *dye*

SN Essene *monk*

SN icing *frosting, hockey*

SN oscine *bird*

SN ossein *collagen*

SN sain *(Br) bless*

SN sand *beach*

SN sane *not crazy* saner
sanest

SN sang *sing*

SN Santa *Santa Claus*

SN sauna *steam bath*

SN sawney *(Br) fool*

SN saying *proverb*

SN scene *view, stage*

SN scion *heir, plant shoot*

SN seeing *inasmuch as*

SN seen *(v-past) see*

SN segno *divided* segnos

SN seine *net* seined seining

SN Seine *river*

SN sen *money (Malay)*

SN send *convey, delight,
dismiss** sent sending

SN sene *money (Samoa)*
sene

SN senna *plant*

SN sewing *stitch*

SN sewn *stitched*

SN sienna *pigment*

SN sign *(n) symbol, omen,
symptom (v) write name,
indicate**

SN sin *offense* sinned sinning

SN sine *mathematics*

SN snow *ice*

SN son *male child*

SN sonny *boy*

SN soon *promptly*

SN sound *(n) noise, inlet
(adv) thorough (adj) solid,*

Use letters that best describe the sounds you hear and omit the vowels. Use **S** or **K**
instead of **C**: to find circle use **SRKL**. Use **J** to find joy, **JM** to find gem and **G** to find go.

hard, healthy (v) voice,
*measure depth**

SN sown *(v-past)* sow

SN sun *(v) bask* sunned
sunning

SN sun *(n) star*

SN sunn *hemp*

SN Sunni *Islam*

SN sunny *sunshine* sunnier
sunniest

SN usnea *lichen*

SNB snob *haughty one*

SNB snub *ignore, blunt*
snubbed snubbing

SNB sonobuoy *transmitter*

SNB sunbow *arch*

SNBDK cenobitic *monastic*

SNBG sandbag *(n) container*
(v) hit, coerce, misrepresent

SNBKD sunbaked *cooked*

SNBKS sandbox *play area*
sandboxes

SNBKS sound box *speaker*
sound boxes

SNBKT sunbaked *cooked*

SNBL assignable *allot*

SNBL snowball *(n) sphere (v)*
enlarge

SNBLK sunblock *sunscreen*

SNBLN snow-blind *reflection*

SNBLND snow-blind
reflection

SNBLST sandblast *smoothe*

SNBLT snowbelt *cold region*

SNBLT Sun Belt *region*

SNBM sunbeam *light ray*

SNBN snap bean *vegetable*

SNBN snowbound *shut in*

SNBND sanbenito *coat*
sanbenitos

SNBND snowbound *shut in*

SNBNGK snowbank *mound*

SNBNK snowbank *mound*

SNBNT sanbenito *coat*
sanbenitos

SNBNT sunbonnet *hat*

SNBNZD snub-nosed *blunt*

SNBR cinnabar *pigment*

SNBR sandbar *reef*

SNBR sandbur *thistle*

SNBR snobbery *haughtiness*
snobberies

SNBR snowberry *plant*
snowberries

SNBRD signboard *poster*

SNBRD snowbird *junco*

SNBRD snowboard *ski*

SNBRD sunbird *animal*

SNBRN sunburn *redden*
sunburned (or) sunburnt
sunburning

SNBRNRD Saint Bernard
dog

SNBRR sound barrier *speed*

SNBRST sunburst *flash,*
design

SNBRYR sound barrier
speed

SNBSH snobbish *haughty*

SNBSHL snobbishly
haughty

SNBSHNS snobbishness
haughty

SNBT cenobite *monk*

SNBT sound bite *phrase*

SNBTH sunbath *sun*
exposure

SNBTH sunbathe *tan*
sunbathed sunbathing

SNBTHR sunbather *tan*

SNBTK cenobitic *monastic*

SNBX sandbox *play area*
sandboxes

SNBX sound box *speaker*
sound boxes

SNBZM snobbism *haughty*

SNCH cinch *girth, easy*
cinches

SNCH snatch *grab*

SNCH snitch *steal, tattle*
snitches

SNCHL essential *(n)*
necessity

SNCHL essential (adj)
necessary essentially (adv)

SNCHL sensual (adj) *sexual*
sensually (adv)

SNCHLD sensuality *flesh*

SNCHLNS essentialness
nature, need

SNCHLST essentialist *basic*
skills

SNCHLT sensuality *flesh*

SNCHN ascension *rise*

SNCHNT sentient *aware*

SNCHR century *100 years,*
cricket score centuries

SNCHR cincture *belt*

SNCHR snitcher *tattler*

SNCHRN centurion *officer*

SNCHRYN centurion *officer*

SNCHS sensuous *flesh*
appeal

SNCHSL sensuously *flesh*
appeal

SNCHSNS sensuousness
flesh appeal

SNCHWL sensual (adj)
sexual sensually (adv)

SNCHWLD sensuality *flesh*

SNCHWLT sensuality *flesh*

SNCHWS sensuous *flesh*
appeal

SNCHWSL sensuously *flesh*
appeal

SNCHWSNS sensuousness
flesh appeal

SNCR sincere *true* sincerer
sincerest

SNCRL sincerely *honest*

SNCRNS sincereness
honesty

SNCRR sincerer *true*

SNCRST sincerest *true*

SND ascend *rise*

SND cyanide *poison*

SND sainted *pious*

SND sand *beach*

SND sandhi *sound*

SND sandy *beach* sandier
sandiest

SND sanity *mental health*

SND scend *wave*

SND scented *odor*

SND send *convey, delight,*
*dismiss** sent sending

SND signed *numbers*

SND snide *sarcastic, false*

SND snood *cap*

SND snooty *snobbish*
snootier snootiest

SND snotty *spiteful, mucus*
snottier snottiest

SND sonata *music*

SND sound *(n) noise, inlet*
(adv) thorough (adj) solid,

Letters aren't doubled for single sounds: to find alley use **L** not **LL**. Use **Y** and **W** as hard
sounds only: to find yellow use **YL**. (Br)=British spelling or usage. * See dictionary.

hard, healthy (v) voice, measure depth*

SND sundae *ice cream*
SND Sunday *weekday*
SND sundew *herb*
SND synod *council*
SNDBG sandbag *(n) container (v) hit, coerce, misrepresent*
SNDBKS sandbox *play area* sandboxes
SNDBKS sound box *speaker* sound boxes
SNDBL ascendable *(or)* ascendible *rise*
SNDBL soundable *noise*
SNDBLST sandblast *smoothe*
SNDBR sandbar *reef*
SNDBR sandbur *thistle*
SNDBRR sound barrier *speed*
SNDBRYR sound barrier *speed*
SNDBT sound bite *phrase*
SNDBX sandbox *play area* sandboxes
SNDBX sound box *speaker* sound boxes
SNDD asyndeta *(pl) not connected* asyndeton
SNDDK syndetic *connective*
SNDDKL syndetically *connective*
SNDDN asyndeton *not connected* asyndetons *(or)* asyndeta
SNDF send-off *departure*
SNDF sound off *speak*
SNDFKS sound effects *noises*
SNDFL sand flea *jumping insect*
SNDFL sand fly *flying insect*
SNDFX sound effects *noises*
SNDG San Diego *city*
SNDG sandhog *tunnels*
SNDHG sandhog *tunnels*
SNDHL sandhill *crane*
SNDK cyanotic *discoloration*
SNDK Sinitic *Chinese*
SNDK syenitic *rock*

SNDK syndic *magistrate*
SNDK synodic *(or)* synodical *conjunction*
SNDKDL syndactyly *webbing*
SNDKDR syndicator *seller*
SNDKL syndical *magistrate*
SNDKL synodical *(or)* synodic *conjunction*
SNDKLST syndicalist *rule by workers*
SNDKLZM syndicalism *rule by workers*
SNDKSHN syndication *association*
SNDKST sand-cast *mold*
SNDKT syndicate *(v) sell* syndicated syndicating
SNDKT syndicate *(n) association*
SNDKTL syndactyly *webbing*
SNDKTR syndicator *seller*
SNDL sandal *shoe*
SNDL sandhill *crane*
SNDL snidely *sarcastic, false*
SNDL snootily *aloof*
SNDL soundly *thorough*
SNDL sundial *timepiece*
SNDLK soundalike *similar*
SNDLR sand dollar *sea creature*
SNDLS soundless *silent*
SNDLSL soundlessly *silent*
SNDLSNS soundlessness *silence*
SNDLT sandlot *sports*
SNDLWD sandalwood *tree*
SNDMN sandman *sleep*
SNDMN soundman *music*
SNDMNG Santo Domingo *city*
SNDMNGG Santo Domingo *city*
SNDN ascending *rising*
SNDN sounding *(adj) loud (n) depth, sampling*
SNDN sundown *sunset*
SNDNBRD sounding board *pulpit*
SNDNC ascendancy *supremacy*
SNDNG ascending *rising*

SNDNG sounding *(adj) loud (n) depth, sampling*
SNDNGBRD sounding board *pulpit*
SNDNGL soundingly *loudly*
SNDNL soundingly *loudly*
SNDNR sundowner *(Br) drink, (Aus) hobo*
SNDNS ascendance *supremacy*
SNDNS ascendancy *supremacy*
SNDNS sandiness *beach*
SNDNS snideness *sarcastic, false*
SNDNS snootiness *aloof*
SNDNS snottiness *spiteful, mucus*
SNDNS soundness *healthy, valid, hard*
SNDNT ascendant *rising, position*
SNDNTC ascendancy *supremacy*
SNDNTL ascendantly *rising, position*
SNDNTS ascendance *supremacy*
SNDNTS ascendancy *supremacy*
SNDP send-up *(n) imitation* send up *(v)*
SNDPL sandpile *play area*
SNDPPR sandpaper *rasp*
SNDPPR sandpiper *bird*
SNDPRF soundproof *no noise*
SNDPT sandpit *(Br) sandbox*
SNDPYL sandpile *play area*
SNDR ascender *climber*
SNDR asunder *separate*
SNDR cinder *ash*
SNDR sander *machine*
SNDR sandier *beach*
SNDR senator *lawmaker*
SNDR sender *deliver, transmit, dismiss**
SNDR snootier *aloof*
SNDR snottier *spiteful, mucus*
SNDR sounder *depth device*
SNDR sunder *separate*

Use letters that best describe the sounds you hear and omit the vowels. Use **S** or **K** instead of **C**: to find circle use **SRKL**. Use **J** to find joy, **JM** to find gem and **G** to find go.

SNDR sundry *various* sundries
SNDRF snowdrift *mound*
SNDRFT snowdrift *mound*
SNDRK sandarac *resin*
SNDRL Cinderella *fairy tale*
SNDRLN sanderling *bird*
SNDRLNG sanderling *bird*
SNDRM syndrome *pattern*
SNDRP snowdrop *herb*
SNDRPS sundrops *herb*
SNDRS sundress *garment*
SNDS so-and-so *no name* so-and-sos (or) so-and-so's
SNDSH sandshoe *tennis shoe*
SNDSKL Sunday school *religion*
SNDSP sandsoap *cleaner*
SNDSPR sandspur *thistle*
SNDST sandiest *beach*
SNDST snootiest *aloof*
SNDST snottiest *spiteful, mucus*
SNDSTJ soundstage *movies*
SNDSTN sandstone *rock*
SNDSTRM sandstorm *dessert*
SNDT asyndeta (pl) *not connected* asyndeton
SNDTK syndetic *connective*
SNDTKL syndetically *connective*
SNDTN asyndeton *not connected* asyndetons (or) asyndeta
SNDTRK sound track *music*
SNDTRP sand trap *golf*
SNDV sanative *cure*
SNDWCH sandwich *food*
SNDWRM sandworm *bait*
SNDWRT sandwort *herb*
SNDY sundew *herb*
SNDYG San Diego *city*
SNDYL sundial *timepiece*
SNDYR sandier *beach*
SNDYR snootier *aloof*
SNDYR snottier *spiteful, mucus*
SNDYST sandiest *beach*
SNDYST snootiest *aloof*

SNDYST snottiest *spiteful, mucus*
SNDZMSS syndesmosis *connection* syndesmoses
SNF Santa Fe *city*
SNF sign off *end, approve*
SNF snafu *confusion*
SNF sniff *smell*
SNF sniffy *haughty* sniffier sniffiest
SNF snuff *(n) tobacco (v) extinguish, sniff*
SNFBKS snuffbox *container* snuffboxes
SNFBX snuffbox *container* snuffboxes
SNFDR snifter *sip, goblet*
SNFL centerfold *magazine*
SNFL sand flea *jumping insect*
SNFL sand fly *flying insect*
SNFL sinful (adj) *wrong* sinfully (adv)
SNFL snaffle *(v) cheat* snaffled snaffling
SNFL snaffle *(n) bridle bit*
SNFL sniffily *arrogant*
SNFL sniffle *nose* sniffled sniffling
SNFL snowfall *precipitation*
SNFL snuffle *snivel* snuffled snuffling
SNFLD centerfold *magazine*
SNFLD snowfield *glacier*
SNFLK eosinophilic *dye, blood*
SNFLK snowflake *precipitation*
SNFLNS sinfulness *wrongdoing*
SNFLR sniffler *nose*
SNFLR sunflower *plant*
SNFLWR sunflower *plant*
SNFN sainfoin *herb*
SNFN sinfonia *overture sinfonie*
SNFN symphony *music* symphonies
SNFND sinfonietta *orchestra*
SNFNK symphonic *music* symphonically
SNFNS sniffiness *arrogance*

SNFNST symphonist *music*
SNFNT sinfonietta *orchestra*
SNFNY sinfonia *overture sinfonie*
SNFNYD sinfonietta *orchestra*
SNFNYT sinfonietta *orchestra*
SNFR sniffer *nose*
SNFR sniffier *arrogant*
SNFR snuffer *extinguish*
SNFRNSSK San Francisco *city*
SNFRW sangfroid *calmness*
SNFRZD Sanforized *(trademark) shrunk*
SNFSH sniffish *arrogant*
SNFSH sunfish *animal*
SNFSHL sniffishly *arrogantly*
SNFSHNS sniffishness *arrogance*
SNFSS symphysis *bone* symphyses
SNFST sniffiest *arrogant*
SNFTR snifter *sip, goblet*
SNFW sangfroid *calmness*
SNFYR sniffier *arrogant*
SNFYST sniffiest *arrogant*
SNG icing *frosting, hockey*
SNG sang *sing*
SNG saying *proverb*
SNG seeing *inasmuch as*
SNG senega *root*
SNG sewing *stitch*
SNG sing *music* sang singing sung
SNG snag *(v) tear, grab, snare* snagged snagging
SNG snag *(n) obstacle, tangle*
SNG snaggy *tangled*
SNG snug *(adj) cozy* snugger snuggest
SNG snug *(v) fit closely* snugged snugging
SNG song *melody*
SNG sung *(v-past) sing*
SNGBK songbook *music*
SNGBRD songbird *animal*
SNGCHR cincture *belt*
SNGCHR sanctuary *shelter* sanctuaries
SNGCHWR sanctuary

Letters aren't doubled for single sounds: to find alley use **L** not **LL**. Use **Y** and **W** as hard sounds only: to find yellow use **YL**. (Br)=British spelling or usage. * See dictionary.

shelter sanctuaries

SNGDD sanctity *holiness* sanctities

SNGDM sanctum *holy place* sanctums

SNGDMN sanctimony *too pious* sanctimonies

SNGDMNS sanctimonious *too pious*

SNGDMNYS sanctimonious *too pious*

SNGDT sanctity *holiness* sanctities

SNGFL songful (adj) *music* songfully (adv)

SNGFLNS songfulness *music*

SNGFST songfest *music*

SNGFW sangfroid *calmness*

SNGG synagogue (or) synagog *church*

SNGGL single (v) *select, score* singled singling

SNGGL single (adj) *lone, uniform, unbroken**

SNGGL singly *alone*

SNGGL synagogal *church*

SNGGLBLND single-blind *experiment*

SNGGLBRSDD single-breasted *garment*

SNGGLBRSTD single-breasted *garment*

SNGGLFL single file *line*

SNGGLFT single-foot *rack* single-foots

SNGGLFZ single-phase *circuit*

SNGGLHNDD single-handed *alone*

SNGGLHNDR single-hander *sailor*

SNGGLHRDD single-hearted *sincere*

SNGGLHRTD single-hearted *sincere*

SNGGLKSHN single-action *gun*

SNGGLMNDD single-minded *focused*

SNGGLNS singleness *individual*

SNGGLNTR single entry *bookkeeping*

SNGGLNZ single-lens *camera*

SNGGLR singular *separate, strange*

SNGGLRD singularity *peculiarity* singularities

SNGGLRT singularity *peculiarity* singularities

SNGGLRZ singularize *make individual* singularized singularizing

SNGGLRZSHN singularization *make individual*

SNGGLSPS single-space *type* single-spaced single-spacing

SNGGLT singlet *undershirt, atom*

SNGGLTN singleton *one*

SNGGLTRK single-track *limited range*

SNGGLVLD single-valued *number*

SNGGLVLYD single-valued *number*

SNGGM syngamy *union*

SNGGR sangria *drink*

SNGGRY sangria *drink*

SNGGWN sanguine *ruddy, confident*

SNGGWNR sanguinaria *bloodroot*

SNGGWNR sanguinary *bloody*

SNGGWNRL sanguinarily *bloody*

SNGGWNRY sanguinaria *bloodroot*

SNGGWNS sanguineous *blood*

SNGGWNYS sanguineous *blood*

SNGGYLR singular *separate, strange*

SNGGYLRD singularity *peculiarity* singularities

SNGGYLRT singularity *peculiarity* singularities

SNGGYLRZ singularize

make individual singularized singularizing

SNGGYLRZSHN singularization *make individual*

SNGK sank *under water*

SNGK sink (v) *fall, penetrate, invest** sank sunk sinking

SNGK sink (n) *tub, pool*

SNGK sync *same time* synced syncing

SNGKBL sinkable *fall, penetrate, invest**

SNGKCHR cincture *belt*

SNGKCHR sanctuary *shelter* sanctuaries

SNGKCHWR sanctuary *shelter* sanctuaries

SNGKDD sanctity *holiness* sanctities

SNGKDM sanctum *holy place* sanctums

SNGKDMN sanctimony *too pious* sanctimonies

SNGKDMNS sanctimonious *too pious*

SNGKDMNYS sanctimonious *too pious*

SNGKDT sanctity *holiness* sanctities

SNGKFL cinquefoil *herb, design*

SNGKFYL cinquefoil *herb, design*

SNGKHL sinkhole *pit*

SNGKL sinkhole *pit*

SNGKN cinquain *poem*

SNGKN sunken *fallen*

SNGKP syncope *faint*

SNGKPDD syncopated *cut short*

SNGKPDV syncopative *modified*

SNGKPL syncopal *faint*

SNGKPSHN syncopation *rhythm, dance*

SNGKPT syncopate *cut short* syncopated syncopating

SNGKPTD syncopated *cut short*

SNGKPTV syncopative

Use letters that best describe the sounds you hear and omit the vowels. Use **S** or **K** instead of **C**: to find circle use **SRKL**. Use **J** to find joy, **JM** to find gem and **G** to find go.

modified
SNGKR sinker *weight, doughnut, pitch*
SNGKRMSH synchromesh *gears*
SNGKRN asynchrony (or) asynchronism *different*
SNGKRN synchrony *same time* synchronies
SNGKRND synchroneity *same time*
SNGKRNK synchronic *descriptive*
SNGKRNKL synchronical (adj) *descriptive* synchronically (adv)
SNGKRNS asynchronous *different*
SNGKRNS synchronous *same time*
SNGKRNSL synchronously *same time*
SNGKRNSNS synchronousness *same time*
SNGKRNST synchronicity *same time*
SNGKRNSTK synchronistic *simultaneous*
SNGKRNT synchroneity *same time*
SNGKRNYD synchroneity *same time*
SNGKRNYT synchroneity *same time*
SNGKRNZ synchronize *same time* synchronized synchronizing (Br) synchronise
SNGKRNZM asynchronism (or) asynchrony *different*
SNGKRNZM synchronism *simultaneous*
SNGKRNZSHN synchronization *simultaneous* (Br) synchronisation
SNGKRSKP synchroscope *simultaneous*
SNGKRTRN synchrotron *particles*
SNGKRTZ syncretize *merge*

syncretized syncretizing (Br) syncretise
SNGKRTZM syncretism *merging*
SNGKSHN sanction *approve*
SNGKSHR sanctuary *shelter* sanctuaries
SNGKSHWR sanctuary *shelter* sanctuaries
SNGKTD sanctity *holiness* sanctities
SNGKTF sanctify *bless* sanctified sanctifying sanctifies
SNGKTFKSHN sanctification *bless*
SNGKTFYR sanctifier *holy spirit*
SNGKTM sanctum *holy place* sanctums
SNGKTMN sanctimony *too pious* sanctimonies
SNGKTMNS sanctimonious *too pious*
SNGKTMNYS sanctimonious *too pious*
SNGKTR cincture *belt*
SNGKTT sanctity *holiness* sanctities
SNGL Senegal *country, river*
SNGL single *(v) select, score* singled singling
SNGL single *(adj) lone, uniform, unbroken**
SNGL singly *alone*
SNGL sniggle *catch eels* sniggled sniggling
SNGL snuggle *cuddle* snuggled snuggling
SNGL snugly *cozy*
SNGLBLND single-blind *experiment*
SNGLBRSDD single-breasted *garment*
SNGLBRSTD single-breasted *garment*
SNGLFL single file *line*
SNGLFT single-foot *rack* single-foots
SNGLFZ single-phase *circuit*
SNGLHNDD single-handed

alone
SNGLHNDR single-hander *sailor*
SNGLHRDD single-hearted *sincere*
SNGLHRTD single-hearted *sincere*
SNGLKSHN single-action *gun*
SNGLMNDD single-minded *focused*
SNGLNS singleness *individual*
SNGLNTR single entry *bookkeeping*
SNGLNZ single-lens *camera*
SNGLR singular *separate, strange*
SNGLRD singularity *peculiarity* singularities
SNGLRT singularity *peculiarity* singularities
SNGLRZ singularize *make individual* singularized singularizing
SNGLRZSHN singularization *make individual*
SNGLSPS single-space *type* single-spaced single-spacing
SNGLSS sunglasses *lenses*
SNGLSZ sunglasses *lenses*
SNGLT singlet *undershirt, atom*
SNGLTN singleton *one*
SNGLTRK single-track *limited range*
SNGLTTH snaggletooth *dental*
SNGLTTHD snaggletoothed *dental*
SNGLTTHT snaggletoothed *dental*
SNGLVLD single-valued *number*
SNGLVLYD single-valued *number*
SNGM syngamy *union*
SNGMSHN sewing machine *stitcher*
SNGN singing *voiced music*

Letters aren't doubled for single sounds: to find alley use **L** not **LL**. Use **Y** and **W** as hard sounds only: to find yellow use **YL**. (Br)=British spelling or usage. * See dictionary.

SNGNG singing *voiced music*
SNGNS snugness *coziness*
SNGPR Singapore *island*
SNGR sangria *drink*
SNGR singer *song*
SNGR snigger *snicker*
SNGR snuggery *(Br) room* snuggeries
SNGRD centigrade *temperature*
SNGRDR songwriter *music*
SNGRF scenography *theater*
SNGRF sonography *ultrasound*
SNGRFK scenographic *theater*
SNGRFR scenographer *theater*
SNGRM centigram *weight*
SNGRM sonogram *ultrasound*
SNGRTR songwriter *music*
SNGRY sangria *drink*
SNGS snow goose *bird* snow geese
SNGSHN sanction *approve*
SNGSHR sanctuary *shelter* sanctuaries
SNGSHWR sanctuary *shelter* sanctuaries
SNGSNG singsong *(n) rhythm, (Br) songfest (adj) monotonous*
SNGSPL singspiel *music*
SNGSTR songster *singer*
SNGSTRS songstress *singer*
SNGTD sanctity *holiness* sanctities
SNGTF sanctify *bless* sanctified sanctifying sanctifies
SNGTFYR sanctifier *holy spirit*
SNGTM sanctum *holy place* sanctums
SNGTMN sanctimony *too pious* sanctimonies
SNGTMNS sanctimonious *too pious*
SNGTMNYS sanctimonious *too pious*
SNGTR sanctuary *shelter* sanctuaries

SNGTT sanctity *holiness* sanctities
SNGTWR sanctuary *shelter* sanctuaries
SNGWN sanguine *ruddy, confident*
SNGWNR sanguinaria *bloodroot*
SNGWNR sanguinary *bloody*
SNGWNRL sanguinarily *bloody*
SNGWNRY sanguinaria *bloodroot*
SNGWNS sanguineous *blood*
SNGWNYS sanguineous *blood*
SNGYLR singular *separate, strange*
SNGYLRD singularity *peculiarity* singularities
SNGYLRT singularity *peculiarity* singularities
SNGYLRZ singularize *make individual* singularized singularizing
SNGYLRZSHN singularization *make individual*
SNHG sandhog *tunnels*
SNHWT snow-white *color*
SNHZ San Jose *city*
SNJ signage *signal, mark*
SNJ singe *burn* singed singeing
SNJB snow job *deception*
SNJN cyanogen *gas*
SNJNK syngeneic *identical*
SNJNYK syngeneic *identical*
SNJNZWRT Saint-John's-wort *herb*
SNK cyanic *acid*
SNK cynic *doubter*
SNK sank *under water*
SNK scenic *pretty view*
SNK Seneca *Native American* Seneca (or) Senecas
SNK sink *(v) fall, penetrate, invest** sank sunk sinking
SNK sink *(n) tub, pool*

SNK snack *food*
SNK snake *(v) wind* snaked snaking
SNK snake *(n) animal*
SNK snaky *winding*
SNK sneak *lurk* sneaked (or) snuck sneaking
SNK sneaky *stealthy* sneakier sneakiest
SNK snick *nick, click*
SNK snook *fish, gesture* snook (or) snooks
SNK sonic *sound*
SNKBL sinkable *fall, penetrate, invest**
SNKBM sonic boom *sound*
SNKBR snack bar *food*
SNKBRD snakebird *bird*
SNKBT snakebit (or) snakebitten *unlucky*
SNKBT snakebite *bite of a snake*
SNKBTN snakebitten (or) snakebit *unlucky*
SNKCHR cincture *belt*
SNKCHR sanctuary *shelter* sanctuaries
SNKCHWR sanctuary *shelter* sanctuaries
SNKDD sanctity *holiness* sanctities
SNKDK synecdoche *figure of speech*
SNKDKK synecdochic *figure of speech*
SNKDKKL synecdochical *(adj) figure of speech* synecdochically (adv)
SNKDM sanctum *holy place* sanctums
SNKDMN sanctimony *too pious* sanctimonies
SNKDMNS sanctimonious *too pious*
SNKDMNYS sanctimonious *too pious*
SNKDNS snake dance (n) *ceremony* snake-dance (v)
SNKDNTS snake dance (n) *ceremony* snake-dance (v)
SNKDT sanctity *holiness* sanctities

Use letters that best describe the sounds you hear and omit the vowels. Use **S** or **K** instead of **C**: to find circle use **SRKL**. Use **J** to find joy, **JM** to find gem and **G** to find go.

SNKDTD senectitude *senior*
SNKDTYD senectitude *senior*
SNKFL cinquefoil *herb, design*
SNKFYL cinquefoil *herb, design*
SNKHL sinkhole *pit*
SNKL cenacle *retreat house*
SNKL cynical (adj) *doubtful* cynically (adv)
SNKL scenically *pretty view*
SNKL snake oil *potion*
SNKL snakily *winding*
SNKL sneakily *stealthy*
SNKLG synecology *communities*
SNKLJ synecology *communities*
SNKLJKL synecological *communities*
SNKLN syncline *trough*
SNKLNL synclinal *incline*
SNKLZ Santa Claus *Christmas*
SNKN cinquain *poem*
SNKN sneaking *mean, sly*
SNKN sunken *fallen*
SNKNG sneaking *mean, sly*
SNKNS sneakiness *stealthy*
SNKP syncope *faint*
SNKPDD syncopated *cut short*
SNKPDV syncopative *modified*
SNKPL syncopal *faint*
SNKPSHN syncopation *rhythm, dance*
SNKPT snowcapped *white*
SNKPT syncopate *cut short* syncopated syncopating
SNKPTD syncopated *cut short*
SNKPTV syncopative *modified*
SNKR sinecure *position*
SNKR sinker *weight, doughnut, pitch*
SNKR sneaker *shoe, lurker*
SNKR sneakier *stealthy*
SNKR snicker *laugh*
SNKR snooker *(n) game (v)*

trick
SNKRMSH synchromesh *gears*
SNKRN asynchrony (or) asynchronism *different*
SNKRN synchrony *same time* synchronies
SNKRN synkaryon *nucleus*
SNKRND synchroneity *same time*
SNKRNK synchronic *descriptive*
SNKRNKL synchronical (adj) *descriptive* synchronically (adv)
SNKRNS asynchronous *different*
SNKRNS synchronous *same time*
SNKRNSL synchronously *same time*
SNKRNSNS synchronousness *same time*
SNKRNST synchronicity *same time*
SNKRNSTK synchronistic *simultaneous*
SNKRNT synchroneity *same time*
SNKRNYD synchroneity *same time*
SNKRNYT synchroneity *same time*
SNKRNZ synchronize *same time* synchronized synchronizing (Br) synchronise
SNKRNZM asynchronism (or) asynchrony *different*
SNKRNZM synchronism *simultaneous*
SNKRNZSHN synchronization *simultaneous* (Br) synchronisation
SNKRSKP synchroscope *simultaneous*
SNKRSN snickersnee *knife*
SNKRT snakeroot *plant*
SNKRTRN synchrotron *particles*

SNKRTZ syncretize *merge* syncretized syncretizing (Br) syncretise
SNKRTZM syncretism *merging*
SNKRV sine curve *mathematics*
SNKRYN synkaryon *nucleus*
SNKSHN sanction *approve*
SNKSHN sonication *sound*
SNKSHR sanctuary *shelter* sanctuaries
SNKSHWR sanctuary *shelter* sanctuaries
SNKSKN snakeskin *leather*
SNKST sand-cast *mold*
SNKST sneakiest *stealthy*
SNKT sonicate *sound* sonicated sonicating
SNKTD sanctity *holiness* sanctities
SNKTF sanctify *bless* sanctified sanctifying sanctifies
SNKTFKSHN sanctification *bless*
SNKTFR sanctifier *holy spirit*
SNKTFYR sanctifier *holy spirit*
SNKTM sanctum *holy place* sanctums
SNKTMN sanctimony *too pious* sanctimonies
SNKTMNS sanctimonious *too pious*
SNKTMNYS sanctimonious *too pious*
SNKTR cincture *belt*
SNKTR sanctuary *shelter* sanctuaries
SNKTT sanctity *holiness* sanctities
SNKTTD senectitude *senior*
SNKTTYD senectitude *senior*
SNKTWR sanctuary *shelter* sanctuaries
SNKWD snakeweed *plant*
SNKWNN sine qua non *essential*
SNKYL snake oil *potion*

SNKYR sinecure *position*
SNKYR sneakier *stealthy*
SNKYST sneakiest *stealthy*
SNL senile *confused*
SNL snail *animal*
SNL snell *fishing*
SNL soundly *thorough*
SNL sunnily *bright*
SNLD senility *confusion*
SNLDR centiliter *measure*
SNLDR scintillator *sparkler*
SNLF synaloepha (or)
synalepha *vowel sounds*
SNLG sinologue *China*
SNLG sinology *China*
SNLGSDR snollygoster *ogre*
SNLGSTR snollygoster *ogre*
SNLJ sinology *China*
SNLJST sinologist *China*
SNLMDR scintillometer *flash*
SNLMP sunlamp *light*
SNLMTR scintillometer *flash*
SNLN santolina *shrub*
SNLN snow line *margin*
SNLPRD snow leopard
animal
SNLPST snail-paced *slowly*
SNLS sinless *no wrong*
SNLS soundless *silent*
SNLS sunless *dark*
SNLSHN scintillation *flash*
SNLSL sinlessly *no wrong*
SNLSL soundlessly *silent*
SNLSNS sinlessness *no wrong*
SNLSNS soundlessness
silence
SNLT sandlot *sports*
SNLT scintillate *sparkle*
scintillated scintillating
SNLT senility *confusion*
SNLT sunlight *daytime*
SNLT sunlit *bright*
SNLTN scintillating *witty*
SNLTNG scintillating *witty*
SNLTR centiliter *measure*
SNLTR scintillator *sparkler*
SNLZPS snail's pace *slowly*
SNM cinema *movie*
SNM tsunami *wave*
tsunamis
SNMBL snowmobile *vehicle*

SNMBLN snowmobiling
sport
SNMBLNG snowmobiling
sport
SNMD cyanamide *chemical*
SNMDK cinematic *film*
SNMDR centimeter *measure*
SNMKN snowmaking
artificial
SNMKNG snowmaking
artificial
SNMKR snowmaker *device*
SNMN cinnamon *spice*
SNMN sandman *sleep*
SNMN snowman *sculpture*
SNMN soundman *music*
SNMNL sentimental (adj)
emotional sentimentally
(adv)
SNMNLST sentimentalist
emotions
SNMNLZ sentimentalize
emotionalize
sentimentalized
sentimentalizing
(Br) sentimentalise
SNMNLZM sentimentalism
emotions
SNMNLZSHN
sentimentalization
emotions
(Br) sentimentalise
SNMNT assignment *work*
SNMNT sentiment *emotion,*
opinion
SNMNTL sentimental (adj)
emotional sentimentally
(adv)
SNMNTLD sentimentality
emotions sentimentalities
SNMNTLST sentimentalist
emotions
SNMNTLT sentimentality
emotions sentimentalities
SNMNTLZ sentimentalize
emotionalize
sentimentalized
sentimentalizing
(Br) sentimentalise
SNMNTLZM
sentimentalism *emotions*
SNMNTLZSHN

sentimentalization
emotions
(Br) sentimentalise
SNMRN San Marino *country*
SNMSHN sewing machine
stitcher
SNMTGRF cinematography
photography
SNMTGRFR
cinematographer
cameraman
SNMTK cinematheque
theater
SNMTK cinematic *film*
SNMTR centimeter *measure*
SNMVRT cinema verité
realistic
SNN asinine *foolish*
SNN cyanine *dye*
SNN Santa Ana *wind*
SNN sign in *register*
SNN sign on *start*
SNND asininity *foolishness*
SNNL asininely *foolishly*
SNNL son-in-law *relative*
sons-in-law
SNNM synonym *same*
meaning
SNNM synonymy *sameness*
synonymies
SNNMD synonymity *same*
meaning
SNNMK synonymic *same*
meaning
SNNMS synonymous *same*
meaning
SNNMSL synonymously
same meaning
SNNMT synonymity *same*
meaning
SNNS assonance *sound alike*
SNNS sentence (v) *punish*
sentenced sentencing
SNNS sentence (n) *words,*
judgement
SNNS sunniness *brightness*
SNNT asininity *foolishness*
SNNT assonant *sound alike*
SNNT sonant *voiced*
SNNTN San Antonio *city*
SNNTNY San Antonio *city*
SNNTS assonance *sound*

Use letters that best describe the sounds you hear and omit the vowels. Use **S** or **K**
instead of **C**: to find circle use **SRKL**. Use **J** to find joy, **JM** to find gem and **G** to find go.

alike

SNNTS sentence (v) punish sentenced sentencing

SNNTS sentence (n) words, judgement

SNP sannup married man

SNP sign up (v) enroll sign-up (adj)

SNP snap (v) break, toss, retort snapped snapping

SNP snap (n) instant, cookie, clasp

SNP snap pea green bean

SNP snappy quick, stylish snappier snappiest

SNP snip cut snipped snipping

SNP snipe (v) shoot sniped sniping

SNP snipe (n) bird snipes (or) snipe

SNP snippy rude snippier snippiest

SNP snoop pry

SNP snoopy prying

SNP snow pea edible pod

SNP sunup dawn

SNPBK snapback (n) rebound snap back (v)

SNPBN snap bean vegetable

SNPBRM snap-brim hat

SNPD centipede insect

SNPD snippety rude

SNPDK synaptic nerves

SNPDK synoptic whole view

SNPDKL synaptically nerves

SNPDL sympodial axis

SNPDRGN snapdragon flower

SNPDYL sympodial axis

SNPK snowpack accumulation

SNPL sandpile play area

SNPL snappily quick, stylish

SNPL snippily rude

SNPL snoopily prying

SNPL snowplow machine

SNPN snap bean vegetable

SNPN snap-on fastener

SNPNS snappiness quick, stylish

SNPPR sandpaper rasp

SNPPR sandpiper bird

SNPR snapper turtle, fish snappers (or) snapper

SNPR snappier quick, stylish

SNPR sniper shooter

SNPR snippier rude

SNPR snooper pryer

SNPRBK snapper-back football

SNPRCH sunporch room

SNPRF soundproof no noise

SNPRM snap-brim hat

SNPS centerpiece core, decoration

SNPS synapse nerves synapsed synapsing

SNPSD synapsid reptile

SNPSH snappish curt

SNPSHDR snapshooter camera

SNPSHL snappishly curt

SNPSHNS snappishness curt

SNPSHT snapshot camera

SNPSHTR snapshooter camera

SNPSS asynapsis no pairing asynapses

SNPSS synapsis pairing synapses

SNPSS synopsis outline, verb synopses

SNPST signpost signal, mark

SNPST snappiest quick, stylish

SNPST snippiest rude

SNPSZ synopsize summarize synopsized synopsizing

SNPT sandpit (Br) sandbox

SNPT snippet tiny amount

SNPT snippety rude

SNPTH sympathy attraction, pity sympathies

SNPTHDK sympathetic approval, compassion, interdependence*

SNPTHDKL sympathetically approval, compassion, interdependence*

SNPTHTK sympathetic approval, compassion, interdependence*

SNPTHTKL sympathetically approval, compassion, interdependence*

SNPTHZ sympathize share grief sympathized sympathizing (Br) sympathise

SNPTHZR sympathizer share grief (Br) sympathiser

SNPTK synaptic nerves

SNPTK synoptic whole view

SNPTKL synaptically nerves

SNPYL sandpile play area

SNPYR snappier quick, stylish

SNPYR snippier rude

SNPYST snappiest quick, stylish

SNPYST snippiest rude

SNPZ symposia (pl) discussion symposium

SNPZM symposium discussion symposia (or) symposiums

SNPZRK symposiarch leader

SNPZST symposiast attendee

SNPZY symposia (pl) discussion symposium

SNPZYM symposium discussion symposia (or) symposiums

SNPZYRK symposiarch leader

SNPZYST symposiast attendee

SNQD snakeweed plant

SNQNN sine qua non essential

SNQR sinecure position

SNR assentor (or) assenter one who agrees

SNR assigner (or) assignor allot

SNR center middle, focus centered centering (Br) centre

SNR coenuri (pl) tapeworm coenurus

Letters aren't doubled for single sounds: to find alley use **L** not **LL**. Use **Y** and **W** as hard sounds only: to find yellow use **YL**. (Br)=British spelling or usage. * See dictionary.

SNR saner *not crazy*
SNR saunter *stroll*
SNR scenario *plot* scenarios
SNR scenery *view* sceneries
SNR seigneur *lord*
SNR seigneury *estate* seigneuries
SNR seigniory (or) seignory *territory* seigniories (or) seignories
SNR seiner *boat, person*
SNR senary *six*
SNR senior *superior, eldest*
SNR senor (or) señor *Spanish man* senors (or) señores
SNR señora (or) senora *Spanish woman* senoras
SNR signor *Italian man* signors (or) signori
SNR signora *Italian woman* signoras (or) signore
SNR sinner *scamp*
SNR snare *trap* snared snaring
SNR sneer *scoff*
SNR snore *sleep* snored snoring
SNR sonar *radar*
SNR sooner *prompt, willing*
SNR Sooner *Oklahoma*
SNR sunnier *brighter*
SNRBRD centerboard *keel*
SNRD centered *middle, stable*
SNRD seniority *position, superior*
SNRD senorita (or) señorita *Spanish girl* senoritas
SNRD sonority *loudness* sonorities
SNRDRM snare drum *music*
SNRF sunroof *vehicle*
SNRFL center field *baseball*
SNRFL centerfold *magazine*
SNRFLD center field *baseball*
SNRFLD centerfold *magazine*
SNRFLDR center fielder *baseball*
SNRG synergy *interaction*
SNRJ seigniorage (or)

seignorage *revenue*
SNRJ synergy *interaction*
SNRJD synergid *cells*
SNRJDK synergetic *cooperation*
SNRJK synergic *cooperation*
SNRJKL synergically *cooperation*
SNRJSDK synergistic *interacting*
SNRJSDKL synergistically *interacting*
SNRJST synergist *enhancer*
SNRJSTK synergistic *interacting*
SNRJSTKL synergistically *interacting*
SNRJTK synergetic *cooperation*
SNRJZM synergism *interaction*
SNRK snarky *snappish*
SNRKL snorkel *(n)* air tube *(v)* swim
SNRKLR snorkeler *swimmer*
SNRL snarl *growl, tangle* snarly
SNRLN centerline *middle*
SNRLR snarler *growl, tangle*
SNRM sunroom *porch*
SNRN signorina *Italian girl* signorinas (or) signorine
SNRPS centerpiece *core, decoration*
SNRR cineraria *plant*
SNRR cinerary *cremation*
SNRR saunterer *stroller*
SNRR snarer *trapper*
SNRR sneerer *scoffer*
SNRR snorer *sleeper*
SNRRM cinerarium *cremation*
SNRRY cineraria *plant*
SNRRYM cinerarium *cremation*
SNRS coenurus *tapeworm* coenuri
SNRS sonorous *loudness*
SNRSL sonorously *loudness*
SNRSNS sonorousness *loudness*
SNRSS syneresis *contraction*

SNRST scenarist *writer*
SNRSTJ center stage *theater*
SNRT seniority *position, superior*
SNRT senorita (or) señorita *Spanish girl* senoritas
SNRT snort *(v)* sniffle, inhale *(n)* sound, sip
SNRT sonority *loudness* sonorities
SNRTHRSS synarthrosis *bones* synarthroses
SNRY scenario *plot* scenarios
SNRZ sunrise *dawn*
SNS acinous *(adj)* with sacs
SNS acinus *(n)* sac acini
SNS cense *incense* censed censing
SNS essence *nature, odor, entity**
SNS iciness *frigid*
SNS sans *without*
SNS sansei *Japanese* sansei
SNS science *nature study*
SNS seance *spirits*
SNS sense *(v)* perceive sensed sensing
SNS sense *(n)* wisdom, perception, meaning*
SNS since *subsequently*
SNS sinuous *winding, complex*
SNS sinus *cavity* sinuses
SNS so-and-so *no name* so-and-sos (or) so-and-so's
SNS soundness *health, valid, hard*
SNSBL sensible *(adj)* sane, aware sensibly *(adv)*
SNSBLD sensibility *emotion* sensibilities
SNSBLNS sensibleness *sane, aware*
SNSBLT sensibility *emotion* sensibilities
SNSD sinuosity *waves* sinuosities
SNSD sinusoid *sine wave, passage*
SNSDK coenocytic

Use letters that best describe the sounds you hear and omit the vowels. Use **S** or **K** instead of **C**: to find circle use **SRKL**. Use **J** to find joy, **JM** to find gem and **G** to find go.

protoplasm
SNSDL sinusoidal (adj) *sine wave* sinusoidally (adv)
SNSDP sunny-side up *egg*
SNSDR sinister *evil*
SNSDRL sinistral *left-handed*
SNSDS sinusitis *inflammation*
SNSDV sensitive *aware, liable*
SNSH sandshoe *tennis shoe*
SNSH senecio *plant senecios*
SNSH snowshoe *walking frame* snowshoed snowshoeing
SNSHD sunshade *protection*
SNSHL essential *(n) necessity*
SNSHL essential (adj) *necessary* essentially (adv)
SNSHL sensual (adj) *sexual* sensually (adv)
SNSHLD essentiality *nature, need*
SNSHLD sensuality *flesh*
SNSHLNS essentialness *nature, need*
SNSHLST essentialist *basic skills*
SNSHLT essentiality *nature, need*
SNSHLT sensuality *flesh*
SNSHN ascension *rise*
SNSHN assignation *allotment*
SNSHN sunshine *light*
SNSHNS sentience *awareness*
SNSHNT sentient *aware*
SNSHNTS sentience *awareness*
SNSHP sonship *relationship*
SNSHR censure *blame* censured censuring
SNSHR cynosure *focal point*
SNSHRBL censurable *blame*
SNSHRR censurer *blamer*
SNSHS sensuous *flesh appeal*
SNSHSNS sensuousness *flesh appeal*

SNSHWL sensual (adj) *sexual* sensually (adv)
SNSHWLD sensuality *flesh*
SNSHWLT sensuality *flesh*
SNSHWS sensuous *flesh appeal*
SNSHWSL sensuously *flesh appeal*
SNSHWSNS sensuousness *flesh appeal*
SNSHY senecio *plant senecios*
SNSHYLD essentiality *nature, need*
SNSHYLT essentiality *nature, need*
SNSHYNS sentience *awareness*
SNSHYNT sentient *aware*
SNSHYNTS sentience *awareness*
SNSKRN sunscreen *lotion*
SNSKRT Sanskrit *language*
SNSL sinuously *winding, complex*
SNSLD snowslide *avalanche*
SNSLS senseless *stupid, numb*
SNSLVDR San Salvador *city*
SNSM sinsemilla *marijuana*
SNSML sinsemilla *marijuana*
SNSMY sinsemilla *marijuana*
SNSND Cincinnati *city*
SNSNS senescence *growth*
SNSNS sinuousness *winding, complex*
SNSNT Cincinnati *city*
SNSNT senescent *growth*
SNSNTS senescence *growth*
SNSP sandsoap *cleaner*
SNSPR sandspur *thistle*
SNSPSHZ cenospecies *related*
SNSPT sunspot *dark area*
SNSR censer *incense*
SNSR censor *suppress* censored censoring
SNSR sensor *detector*
SNSR sensory *feeling*
SNSR sincere *true* sincerer sincerest

SNSRD censored *suppressed*
SNSRD sincerity *honesty*
SNSRF sans serif (or) sanserif *type*
SNSRL sensorial (adj) *feeling* sensorially (adv)
SNSRL sincerely *honest*
SNSRNS sincereness *honesty*
SNSRR sincerer *true*
SNSRS censorious *critical*
SNSRSHP censorship *suppression*
SNSRSL censoriously *critically*
SNSRSNS censoriousness *criticism*
SNSRST sincerest *true*
SNSRT sincerity *honesty*
SNSRYL sensorial (adj) *feeling* sensorially (adv)
SNSRYS censorious *critical*
SNSRYSL censoriously *critically*
SNSRYSNS censoriousness *criticism*
SNSS census *count*
SNSS cyanosis *discoloration*
SNSSH syncytia (pl) *cell mass* syncytium
SNSSHM syncytium *cell mass* syncytia
SNSSHN sensation *feeling*
SNSSHNL sensational (adj) *feelings, great* sensationally (adv)
SNSSHNLSDK sensationalistic *intense reactions*
SNSSHNLST sensationalist *intense reactions*
SNSSHNLSTK sensationalistic *intense reactions*
SNSSHNLZ sensationalize *make intense* sensationalized sensationalizing (Br) sensationalise
SNSSHNLZM sensationalism *intense reactions*

Letters aren't doubled for single sounds: to find alley use **L** not **LL**. Use **Y** and **W** as hard sounds only: to find yellow use **YL**. (Br)=British spelling or usage. * See dictionary.

SNSSHY syncytia (pl) *cell mass* syncytium

SNSSHYM syncytium *cell mass* syncytia

SNST coenocyte *protoplasm*

SNST sanest *not crazy*

SNST sensate *feeling*

SNST sinuosity *waves* sinuosities

SNST snowsuit *garment*

SNST sunniest *brightest*

SNST sunset *dusk*

SNST sunsuit *garment*

SNSTHDK synesthetic *sensation*

SNSTHSH synesthesia *sensation*

SNSTHTK synesthetic *sensation*

SNSTHZH synesthesia *sensation*

SNSTJ soundstage *movies*

SNSTK coenocytic *protoplasm*

SNSTN sandstone *rock*

SNSTR sinister *evil*

SNSTRK sunstroke *illness*

SNSTRK sunstruck *touched by sun*

SNSTRL sinistral *left-handed*

SNSTRM sandstorm *dessert*

SNSTRM snowstorm *snow and wind*

SNSTS sensitize *make receptive* sensitized sensitizing (Br) sensitise

SNSTS sinusitis *inflammation*

SNSTSS synostosis *bones* synostoses

SNSTV sensitive *aware, liable*

SNSTVD sensitivity *awareness, feeling* sensitivities

SNSTVL sensitively *aware, liable*

SNSTVT sensitivity *awareness, feeling* sensitivities

SNSTZ sensitize *make receptive* sensitized

sensitizing (Br) sensitise

SNSTZSHN sensitization *make receptive* (Br) sensitisation

SNSZ sinicize *make Chinese* sinicized sinicizing

SNSZM cynicism *doubt*

SNT ascent *rise*

SNT assent *agree*

SNT cent *penny*

SNT saint *(often capitalized) holy one*

SNT sanity *mental health*

SNT Santa *Santa Claus*

SNT santo *image* santos

SNT scent *odor*

SNT senate *legislature*

SNT sennet *signal*

SNT sennit *braid*

SNT sent *(v-past) send*

SNT sinuate *wavy*

SNT snit *irritation*

SNT snoot *(n) snob (v) look down on*

SNT snooty *snobbish* snootier snootiest

SNT snot *mucus, spiteful one*

SNT snotty *spiteful, mucus* snottier snottiest

SNT snout *nose*

SNT sonata *music*

SNT sonnet *poem*

SNT syenite *rock*

SNTBRNRD Saint Bernard *dog*

SNTCHL sensual (adj) *sexual* sensually (adv)

SNTCHLD sensuality *flesh*

SNTCHLT sensuality *flesh*

SNTCHNT sentient *aware*

SNTCHS sensuous *flesh appeal*

SNTCHSL sensuously *flesh appeal*

SNTCHSNS sensuousness *flesh appeal*

SNTCHWL sensual (adj) *sexual* sensually (adv)

SNTCHWLD sensuality *flesh*

SNTCHWLT sensuality *flesh*

SNTCHWS sensuous *flesh*

appeal

SNTCHWSL sensuously *flesh appeal*

SNTCHWSNS sensuousness *flesh appeal*

SNTD sainted *pious*

SNTD scented *odor*

SNTDMNG Santo Domingo *city*

SNTDMNGG Santo Domingo *city*

SNTF cenotaph *tomb*

SNTF Santa Fe *city*

SNTFK scientific *observant*

SNTFKL scientifically *observantly*

SNTGRD centigrade *temperature*

SNTGRF scintigraphy *X-ray*

SNTGRFK scintigraphic *X-ray*

SNTGRM centigram *weight*

SNTH snath (or) snathe *handle*

SNTHD sainthood *holiness*

SNTHDK synthetic *reasoning, imitation*

SNTHDKL synthetically *reasoning, imitation*

SNTHSS synthesis *combination* syntheses

SNTHSZ synthesize *combine* synthesized synthesizing

SNTHSZR synthesizer *combiner, music*

SNTHTK synthetic *reasoning, imitation*

SNTHTKL synthetically *reasoning, imitation*

SNTHTS synthetase *enzyme*

SNTHTZ synthetase *enzyme*

SNTJNZWRT Saint-John's-wort *herb*

SNTK cyanotic *discoloration*

SNTK Sinitic *Chinese*

SNTK syenitic *rock*

SNTK synodic (or) synodical *conjunction*

SNTKDK syntactic (or) syntactical (adj) *arrangement* syntactically (adv)

Use letters that best describe the sounds you hear and omit the vowels. Use **S** or **K** instead of **C**: to find circle use **SRKL**. Use **J** to find joy, **JM** to find gem and **G** to find go.

SNTKDKL syntactical (or) syntactic (adj) *arrangement* syntactically (adv)

SNTKDKS syntactics *arrangement*

SNTKDX syntactics *arrangement*

SNTKL synodical (or) synodic *conjunction*

SNTKLZ Santa Claus *Christmas*

SNTKR Saint Croix *river, island*

SNTKS syntax *arrangement*

SNTKTK syntactic (or) syntactical (adj) *arrangement* syntactically (adv)

SNTKTKL syntactical (or) syntactic (adj) *arrangement* syntactically (adv)

SNTKTKS syntactics *arrangement*

SNTKTX syntactics *arrangement*

SNTL saintly *holy* saintlier saintliest

SNTL scintilla *tiny bit*

SNTL snootily *aloof*

SNTLDR centiliter *measure*

SNTLDR scintillator *sparkler*

SNTLMDR scintillometer *flash*

SNTLMTR scintillometer *flash*

SNTLN centillion *number*

SNTLN santolina *shrub*

SNTLNS saintliness *holiness*

SNTLNT scintillant *sparkling*

SNTLNTL scintillantly *sparkling*

SNTLR saintlier *holy*

SNTLSHN scintillation *flash*

SNTLST saintliest *holy*

SNTLT scintillate *sparkle* scintillated scintillating

SNTLTN scintillating *witty*

SNTLTNG scintillating *witty*

SNTLTR centiliter *measure*

SNTLTR scintillator *sparkler*

SNTLYN centillion *number*

SNTLYR saintlier *holy*

SNTLYST saintliest *holy*

SNTMDR centimeter *measure*

SNTMNL sentimental (adj) *emotional* sentimentally (adv)

SNTMNLST sentimentalist *emotions*

SNTMNLZ sentimentalize *emotionalize* sentimentalized sentimentalizing (Br) sentimentalise

SNTMNLZM sentimentalism *emotions*

SNTMNLZSHN sentimentalization *emotions* (Br) sentimentalise

SNTMNT sentiment *emotion, opinion*

SNTMNTL sentimental (adj) *emotional* sentimentally (adv)

SNTMNTLD sentimentality *emotions* sentimentalities

SNTMNTLST sentimentalist *emotions*

SNTMNTLT sentimentality *emotions* sentimentalities

SNTMNTLZ sentimentalize *emotionalize* sentimentalized sentimentalizing (Br) sentimentalise

SNTMNTLZM sentimentalism *emotions*

SNTMNTLZSHN sentimentalization *emotions* (Br) sentimentalise

SNTMTR centimeter *measure*

SNTN Santa Ana *wind*

SNTN sonatina *music*

SNTN suntan *darken skin*

SNTNCHL sentential *words, logic*

SNTNCHS sententious *pithy*

SNTNCHSL sententiously *pithy*

SNTNCHSNS sententiousness *pithy*

SNTND suntanned *darken skin*

SNTNL centennial *100 years*

SNTNL sentinel *guard*

SNTNN santonin *poison*

SNTNR centenary *100 years*

SNTNRN centenarian *100 years old*

SNTNRYN centenarian *100 years old*

SNTNS sentence (v) *punish* sentenced sentencing

SNTNS sentence (n) *judgement, words*

SNTNS snootiness *aloof*

SNTNS snottiness *spiteful, mucus*

SNTNSH sententia *proverb* sententiae

SNTNSHL sentential *words, logic*

SNTNSHS sententious *pithy*

SNTNSHSL sententiously *pithy*

SNTNSHSNS sententiousness *pithy*

SNTNSHY sententia *proverb* sententiae

SNTNT sentient *aware*

SNTNTCHL sentential *words, logic*

SNTNTCHS sententious *pithy*

SNTNTCHSL sententiously *pithy*

SNTNTCHSNS sententiousness *pithy*

SNTNTS sentence (v) *punish* sentenced sentencing

SNTNTS sentence (n) *judgement, words*

SNTNTS sentience *awareness*

SNTNTSH sententia *proverb* sententiae

SNTNTSHL sentential *words, logic*

SNTNTSHS sententious

Letters aren't doubled for single sounds: to find alley use **L** not **LL**. Use **Y** and **W** as hard sounds only: to find yellow use **YL**. (Br)=British spelling or usage. * See dictionary.

SNTNTSHSL sententiously *pithy*

SNTNTSHSNS sententiousness *pithy*

SNTNTSHY sententia *proverb* sententiae

SNTNYL centennial *100 years*

SNTPD centipede *insect*

SNTR assentor (or) assenter *one who agrees*

SNTR centaur *monster*

SNTR center *middle, focus* centered centering (Br) centre

SNTR centra (pl) *center* centrum

SNTR century *100 years, cricket score* centuries

SNTR sanatoria (pl) *rest* sanatorium

SNTR sanitaria (pl) *health* sanitarium

SNTR sanitary *clean*

SNTR santir (or) santour *music*

SNTR saunter *stroll*

SNTR senator *lawmaker*

SNTR sentry *guard* sentries

SNTR sinter *heat*

SNTR snootier *aloof*

SNTR snottier *spiteful, mucus*

SNTR sonneteer *poet*

SNTRBRD centerboard *keel*

SNTRD centered *middle, stable*

SNTRD centroid *center of mass*

SNTRFGL centrifugal *away from center*

SNTRFJ centrifuge *separator* centrifuged centrifuging

SNTRFKL centrifugal *away from center*

SNTRFL center field *baseball*

SNTRFL centerfold *magazine*

SNTRFLD center field *baseball*

SNTRFLD centerfold

magazine

SNTRFLDR center fielder *baseball*

SNTRFSH centrifuge *separator* centrifuged centrifuging

SNTRFYGL centrifugal *away from center*

SNTRFYJ centrifuge *separator* centrifuged centrifuging

SNTRFYKL centrifugal *away from center*

SNTRFYSH centrifuge *separator* centrifuged centrifuging

SNTRFYZH centrifuge *separator* centrifuged centrifuging

SNTRFZH centrifuge *separator* centrifuged centrifuging

SNTRK acentric *no center*

SNTRK centric *center*

SNTRK sound track *music*

SNTRKL centrically *center*

SNTRL central (adj) *center* centrally (adv)

SNTRL centriole *cell*

SNTRL sanitarily *clean*

SNTRL senatorial *senate*

SNTRLD centrality *middle*

SNTRLN centerline *middle*

SNTRLST centralist *power center*

SNTRLT centrality *middle*

SNTRLZ centralize *consolidate* centralized centralizing (Br) centralise

SNTRLZM centralism *power center*

SNTRLZR centralizer *consolidater* (Br) centraliser

SNTRLZSHN centralization *consolidation* (Br) centralisation

SNTRM centrum *center* centrums (or) centra

SNTRM sanatorium *rest* sanatoriums (or)

sanatoria

SNTRM sanitarium *health* sanitariums (or) sanitaria

SNTRN centurion *officer*

SNTRN senatorian *senate*

SNTRP sand trap *golf*

SNTRPDL centripetal *toward the center*

SNTRPK isentropic *chaos*

SNTRPKL isentropically *chaos*

SNTRPS centerpiece *core, decoration*

SNTRPTL centripetal *toward the center*

SNTRR saunterer *stroller*

SNTRSD centricity *center* centricities

SNTRST centricity *center* centricities

SNTRST centrist *moderate*

SNTRSTJ center stage *theater*

SNTRY sanatoria (pl) *rest* sanatorium

SNTRY sanitaria (pl) *health* sanitarium

SNTRYL centriole *cell*

SNTRYL senatorial *senate*

SNTRYM sanatorium *rest* sanatoriums (or) sanatoria

SNTRYM sanitarium *health* sanitariums (or) sanitaria

SNTRYN centurion *officer*

SNTRYN senatorian *senate*

SNTRZM centrism *moderation*

SNTS essence *nature, odor, entity**

SNTS science *nature study*

SNTS seance *spirits*

SNTS sense (v) *perceive* sensed sensing

SNTS sense (n) *wisdom, perception, meaning**

SNTS since *subsequently*

SNTSBL sensible (adj) *sane, aware* sensibly (adv)

SNTSBLD sensibility *emotion* sensibilities

SNTSBLNS sensibleness

Use letters that best describe the sounds you hear and omit the vowels. Use **S** or **K** instead of **C**: to find circle use **SRKL**. Use **J** to find joy, **JM** to find gem and **G** to find go.

sane, aware
SNTSBLT sensibility *emotion* sensibilities
SNTSDV sensitive *aware, liable*
SNTSDVL sensitively *aware, liable*
SNTSHL sensual (adj) *sexual* sensually (adv)
SNTSHLD sensuality *flesh*
SNTSHLT sensuality *flesh*
SNTSHN assentation *agreement*
SNTSHN sanitation *cleanliness*
SNTSHNT sentient *aware*
SNTSHNTS sentience *awareness*
SNTSHR censure *blame* censured censuring
SNTSHRBL censurable *blame*
SNTSHRR censurer *blamer*
SNTSHS sensuous *flesh appeal*
SNTSHSL sensuously *flesh appeal*
SNTSHSNS sensuousness *flesh appeal*
SNTSHWL sensual (adj) *sexual* sensually (adv)
SNTSHWLD sensuality *flesh*
SNTSHWLT sensuality *flesh*
SNTSHWS sensuous *flesh appeal*
SNTSHWSL sensuously *flesh appeal*
SNTSHWSNS sensuousness *flesh appeal*
SNTSHYNT sentient *aware*
SNTSHYNTS sentience *awareness*
SNTSLS senseless *stupid, numb*
SNTSM sinsemilla *marijuana*
SNTSML centesimal *hundredth*
SNTSML sinsemilla *marijuana*
SNTSMY sinsemilla *marijuana*
SNTSR censer *incense*

SNTSR censor *suppress* censored censoring
SNTSR sensor *detector*
SNTSR sensory *feeling*
SNTSRD censored *suppressed*
SNTSRL sensorial (adj) *feeling* sensorially (adv)
SNTSRS censorious *critical*
SNTSRSHP censorship *suppression*
SNTSRSL censoriously *critically*
SNTSRSNS censoriousness *criticism*
SNTSRYL sensorial (adj) *feeling* sensorially (adv)
SNTSRYS censorious *critical*
SNTSRYSL censoriously *critically*
SNTSRYSNS censoriousness *criticism*
SNTSS census *count*
SNTST scientist *student of nature*
SNTST snootiest *aloof*
SNTST snottiest *spiteful, mucus*
SNTSTS sensitize *make receptive* sensitized sensitizing (Br) sensitise
SNTSTV sensitive *aware, liable*
SNTSTVD sensitivity *awareness, feeling* sensitivities
SNTSTVL sensitively *aware, liable*
SNTSTVT sensitivity *awareness, feeling* sensitivities
SNTSTZ sensitize *make receptive* sensitized sensitizing (Br) sensitise
SNTSTZSHN sensitization *make receptive* (Br) sensitisation
SNTV sanative *cure*
SNTX syntax *arrangement*

SNTYN centillion *number*
SNTYNS sentience *awareness*
SNTYNT sentient *aware*
SNTYNTS sentience *awareness*
SNTYR snootier *aloof*
SNTYR snottier *spiteful, mucus*
SNTYRN centurion *officer*
SNTYRYN centurion *officer*
SNTYST snootiest *aloof*
SNTYST snottiest *spiteful, mucus*
SNTZ sanitize *clean* sanitized sanitizing
SNTZM scientism *nature study*
SNV synovia *fluid*
SNVBCH son of a bitch *(vulgar interj)* surprise, bastard sons of bitches
SNVDS synovitis *inflammation*
SNVGN son of a gun *(interj)* surprise, person sons of guns
SNVL snivel *runny nose, cry* sniveled (or) snivelled sniveling (or) snivelling
SNVL synovial *lubricating*
SNVLR sniveler *runny nose, cry*
SNVTS synovitis *inflammation*
SNVY synovia *fluid*
SNVYL synovial *lubricating*
SNW snowy *with snow, white* snowier snowiest
SNWCH sandwich *food*
SNWN San Juan *city*
SNWRD sunward (or) sunwards *direction*
SNWRDZ sunwards (or) sunward *direction*
SNWRM sandworm *bait*
SNWRT sandwort *herb*
SNWS sinuous *winding, complex*
SNWSD sinuosity *waves* sinuosities
SNWSL sinuously *winding,*

Letters aren't doubled for single sounds: to find alley use **L** not **LL**. Use **Y** and **W** as hard sounds only: to find yellow use **YL**. (Br)=British spelling or usage. * See dictionary.

complex

SNWSNS sinuousness *winding, complex*

SNWST sinuosity *waves* sinuosities

SNWT sinuate *wavy*

SNWT snow-white *color*

SNY segno *divided* segnos

SNY sinew *strength*

SNY sinewy *stringy*

SNY usnea *lichen*

SNYR coenuri (pl) *tapeworm* coenurus

SNYR seigneur *lord*

SNYR seigneury *estate* seigneuries

SNYR seigniory (or) seignory *territory* seigniories (or) seignories

SNYR senior *superior, eldest*

SNYR senor (or) señor *Spanish man* senors (or) señores

SNYR señora (or) senora *Spanish woman* senoras

SNYR signor *Italian man* signors (or) signori

SNYR signora *Italian woman* signoras (or) signore

SNYR sunnier *brighter*

SNYRD seniority *position, superior*

SNYRD senorita (or) señorita *Spanish girl* senoritas

SNYRJ seigniorage (or) seignorage *revenue*

SNYRN signorina *Italian girl* signorinas (or) signorine

SNYRS coenurus *tapeworm* coenuri

SNYRT seniority *position, superior*

SNYRT senorita (or) señorita *Spanish girl* senoritas

SNYS sannyasi (or) sannyasin *holy man*

SNYS sinuous *winding, complex*

SNYSD sinuosity *waves* sinuosities

SNYSL sinuously *winding, complex*

SNYSN sannyasin (or) sannyasi *holy man*

SNYSNS sinuousness *winding, complex*

SNYST sinuosity *waves* sinuosities

SNYST sunniest *brightest*

SNYT sinuate *wavy*

SNYW sinewy *stringy*

SNYWS sinuous *winding, complex*

SNYWSD sinuosity *waves* sinuosities

SNYWSL sinuously *winding, complex*

SNYWSNS sinuousness *winding, complex*

SNYWST sinuosity *waves* sinuosities

SNYWT sinuate *wavy*

SNZ as soon as *when*

SNZ San Jose *city*

SNZ sans *without*

SNZ snazzy *fancy* snazzier snazziest

SNZ sneeze *nasal reflex* sneezed sneezing

SNZ sneezy *nasal reflex*

SNZ snooze *sleep* snoozed snoozing

SNZK Cenozoic *geologic era*

SNZKLT sansculotte *radical*

SNZKYLT sansculotte *radical*

SNZQLT sansculotte *radical*

SNZR snazzier *fancy*

SNZSRF sans serif (or) sanserif *type*

SNZSS synizesis *contraction*

SNZST snazziest *fancy*

SNZWK Cenozoic *geologic era*

SNZYR snazzier *fancy*

SNZYST snazziest *fancy*

SP Aesop *fables*

SP asp *snake*

SP espy *glimpse* espied espying espies

SP sap (v) *weaken* sapped sapping

SP sap (n) *plant juice, fool*

SP sappy *juicy, silly* sappier sappiest

SP seep *ooze*

SP sepia *brown*

SP sepoy *Indian soldier*

SP sew up *mend, complete, assure*

SP sip *drink* sipped sipping

SP soap (n) *cleanser* (v) *wash*

SP soapy *lathered* soapier soapiest

SP sop (v) *soak* sopped sopping

SP sop (n) *food, gift*

SP soppy *wet, mawkish* soppier soppiest

SP soup *food*

SP soupy *liquid* soupier soupiest

SP spa *resort, tub*

SP spay *remove ovaries* spayed spaying

SP spew *vomit, exude* spewed spewing

SP spy *watch* spied spying spies

SP sup *eat* supped supping

SPBKS soapbox *crate* soapboxes

SPBR soapberry *plant* soapberries

SPBX soapbox *crate* soapboxes

SPC spacey *dazed* spacier spaciest

SPC spicy *flavorful, racy* spicier spiciest

SPCH speech *talk* speeches

SPCHF speechify *talk* speechified speechifying speechifies

SPCHKK spatchcock *chicken*

SPCHL spatula *flat tool*

SPCHLS speechless *silent*

SPCHLSL speechlessly *silent*

SPCHLSNS speechlessness *silence*

SPCHLT spatulate *flat*

SPCHRDR speechwriter

Use letters that best describe the sounds you hear and omit the vowels. Use **S** or **K** instead of **C**: to find circle use **SRKL**. Use **J** to find joy, **JM** to find gem and **G** to find go.

writing
SPCHRTR speechwriter *writing*
SPCNS spiciness *flavor, racy*
SPCR spacier *dazed*
SPCR spicier *flavor, racy*
SPCSHN speciation *form species*
SPCST spaciest *dazed*
SPCST spiciest *flavor, racy*
SPCT speciate *form species*
SPCYR spacier *dazed*
SPCYR spicier *flavor, racy*
SPCYSHN speciation *form species*
SPCYST spaciest *dazed*
SPCYST spiciest *flavor, racy*
SPCYT speciate *form species*
SPCZ species *type*
SPD saphead *fool*
SPD sapid *flavorful*
SPD sapodilla *tree*
SPD septa (pl) *membrane* septum
SPD spade *shovel* spaded spading
SPD spayed *removed ovaries*
SPD sped *(v-past) speed*
SPD speed *(n) rate of motion*
SPD speed *(v) go fast* sped (or) speeded speeding
SPD speedo *speedometer* speedos
SPD speedy *fast* speedier speediest
SPD spotty *marked, seldom* spottier spottiest
SPD spud *(v) dig* spudded spudding
SPD spud *(n) potato, tool*
SPD sputa (pl) *saliva* sputum
SPDBL speedball *game, fast one, (slang) drug*
SPDBL spottable *marked, stain, see*
SPDBMP speed bump *ridge*
SPDBT speedboat *water craft*
SPDCM septicemia *infection*
SPDCMY septicemia *infection*
SPDCZ spadices (pl) *flower*

spadix
SPDD sapidity *flavor*
SPDD spotted *mark, stain, see*
SPDD spouted *pipe, spurt*
SPDFL spadeful *shovel*
SPDFRK speed freak *drugs*
SPDFSH spadefish *fish*
SPDJR soup du jour *food*
SPDK aseptic *no germs*
SPDK septic *putrid*
SPDKL aseptically *no germs*
SPDKS spadix *flower* spadices
SPDL sapodilla *tree*
SPDL septal *membrane*
SPDL speedily *fast*
SPDL spittle *saliva*
SPDL spottily *marked, seldom*
SPDLBG spittlebug *insect*
SPDM septum *membrane* septa
SPDM sputum *saliva* sputa
SPDMDR speedometer *speedometer*
SPDMTR speedometer *speedometer*
SPDN speeding *swiftness*
SPDNG speeding *swiftness*
SPDNGMJ spitting image *duplicate*
SPDNS speediness *quickness*
SPDNS spottiness *marked, seldom*
SPDP speedup *acceleration*
SPDR scepter *staff* (Br) sceptre
SPDR spatter *splash*
SPDR speeder *one going fast*
SPDR speedier *faster*
SPDR spider *insect*
SPDR spidery *fine lines, insect*
SPDR spitter *one that spits, pitch*
SPDR spotter *mark, stain, see*
SPDR spottier *marked, seldom*
SPDR spouter *spurt, declaim*
SPDR sputter *spit, squirt*

SPDRDK spatterdock *flower*
SPDRDN speed-reading *quickness*
SPDRDNG speed-reading *quickness*
SPDRL espadrille *sandal*
SPDRLK spiderlike *insect*
SPDRR sputterer *spit, squirt*
SPDRSH spiderish *insect*
SPDRWB spiderweb *thread*
SPDRWRT spiderwort *plant*
SPDSDL septicidal *seeds*
SPDSDR aspidistra *plant*
SPDSHR soup du jour *food*
SPDSM septicemia *infection*
SPDSMY septicemia *infection*
SPDST speediest *fastest*
SPDST spottiest *marked, seldom*
SPDSTR aspidistra *plant*
SPDSTR speedster *racer*
SPDSZ spadices (pl) *flower* spadix
SPDT sapidity *flavor*
SPDT septate *membrane*
SPDTRP speed trap *swiftness*
SPDW speedway *road, racecourse*
SPDWRK spadework *digging*
SPDX spadix *flower* spadices
SPDY sapodilla *tree*
SPDYR speedier *faster*
SPDYR spottier *marked, seldom*
SPDYST speediest *fastest*
SPDYST spottiest *marked, seldom*
SPDZHR soup du jour *food*
SPF spiffy *smart* spiffier spiffiest
SPF spoof *hoax* spoofy
SPFL spiffily *smart*
SPFNS spiffiness *smart*
SPFR spiffier *smart*
SPFR spoofery *hoax*
SPFST spiffiest *smart*
SPFYR spiffier *smart*
SPFYST spiffiest *smart*

Letters aren't doubled for single sounds: to find alley use **L** not **LL**. Use **Y** and **W** as hard sounds only: to find yellow use **YL**. (Br)=British spelling or usage. * See dictionary.

SPGD spaghetti *food*

SPGLS spyglass *telescope* spyglasses

SPGT spaghetti *food*

SPGT spigot *faucet*

SPGTN spaghettini *food*

SPHD saphead *fool*

SPJ seepage *ooze*

SPK aspect *appearance, phase*

SPK aspic *food*

SPK ice pack *glacier*

SPK ice pick *tool*

SPK isopach *geology*

SPK sepuku *suicide*

SPK speak *talk* spoke speaking spoken

SPK spec *write specifications* specced (or) spec'd speccing

SPK speck *spot*

SPK spica *bandage* spicae

SPK spike *(v) pierce, disable, add alcohol** spiked spiking

SPK spike *(n) nail, peak*

SPK spiky *pointy* spikier spikiest

SPK spoke *wheel*

SPK spook *(n) ghost, spy (v) scare*

SPK spooky *eerie* spookier spookiest

SPKBL speakable *talk*

SPKD spiccato *music* spiccatos

SPKD spiked *pointed, impure*

SPKDKL spectacle *exhibit*

SPKDKLD spectacled *with glasses*

SPKDKLZ spectacles *glasses*

SPKDR specter (or) spectre *ghost*

SPKDRGRF spectrograph *radiation*

SPKDRGRM spectrogram *diagram*

SPKDRL spectral (adj) *ghostly* spectrally (adv)

SPKDRM spectrum *range, light* spectra (or)

spectrums

SPKL spackle *plastic paste* spackled spackling

SPKL speckle *spot* speckled speckling

SPKL specula (pl) *device, chart, color patch* speculum

SPKL spicule *spike*

SPKL spikily *pointy*

SPKL spookily *eerie*

SPKLDR speculator *think, risk*

SPKLDV speculative *theory, risk*

SPKLM speculum *device, chart, color patch* specula

SPKLR specular *mirror*

SPKLR spicular *spike*

SPKLSHN speculation *theory, risk*

SPKLSHN spiculation *spike*

SPKLT speculate *think, risk* speculated speculating

SPKLTR speculator *think, risk*

SPKLTV speculative *theory, risk*

SPKN speaking *language*

SPKN Spokane *city*

SPKN spoken *voiced*

SPKNDSPN spick-and-span (or) spic-and-span *clean*

SPKNG speaking *language*

SPKNS spikiness *pointy*

SPKNS spookiness *eerie*

SPKNSPN spick-and-span (or) spic-and-span *clean*

SPKP speak up *talk*

SPKR speaker *talker, stereo part*

SPKR spikier *pointy*

SPKR spookery *ghosts* spookeries

SPKR spookier *eerie*

SPKRFN speakerphone *telephone*

SPKS specs *eyeglasses, specifications*

SPKSHV spokeshave *planing*

SPKSMN spokesman *representative* spokesmen

SPKSPRSN spokesperson *representative*

SPKST spikiest *pointy*

SPKST spookiest *eerie*

SPKSWMN spokeswoman *representative* spokeswomen

SPKT aspect *appearance, phase*

SPKT speak-out (n) *talk* speak out (v)

SPKT spicate *spiky*

SPKT spiccato *music* spiccatos

SPKT spigot *faucet*

SPKT spiked *pointed, impure*

SPKT spooked *scared*

SPKTDR spectator *watcher*

SPKTKL spectacle *exhibit*

SPKTKLD spectacled *with glasses*

SPKTKLR spectacular (adj) *sensational* spectacularly (adv)

SPKTKLZ spectacles *glasses*

SPKTKYLR spectacular (adj) *sensational* spectacularly (adv)

SPKTQLR spectacular (adj) *sensational* spectacularly (adv)

SPKTR specter (or) spectre *ghost*

SPKTR spectra (pl) *range, light* spectrum

SPKTRGRF spectrograph *radiation*

SPKTRGRM spectrogram *diagram*

SPKTRL spectral (adj) *ghostly* spectrally (adv)

SPKTRM spectrum *range, light* spectra (or) spectrums

SPKTRMDR spectrometer *light measure*

SPKTRMTR spectrometer *light measure*

SPKTRSKP spectroscope

Use letters that best describe the sounds you hear and omit the vowels. Use **S** or **K** instead of **C**: to find circle use **SRKL**. Use **J** to find joy, **JM** to find gem and **G** to find go.

electromagnetics
SPKTRSKP spectroscopy
electromagnetics
SPKTT spectate *watch*
spectated spectating
SPKTTR spectator *watcher*
SPKYL specula (pl) *device,
chart, color patch*
speculum
SPKYL spicule *spike*
SPKYLDR speculator *think,
risk*
SPKYLDV speculative
theory, risk
SPKYLM speculum *device,
chart, color patch* specula
SPKYLR specular *mirror*
SPKYLR spicular *spike*
SPKYLSHN speculation
theory, risk
SPKYLSHN spiculation
spike
SPKYLT speculate *think,
risk* speculated
speculating
SPKYLTR speculator *think,
risk*
SPKYLTV speculative
theory, risk
SPKYR spikier *pointy*
SPKYR spookier *eerie*
SPKYST spikiest *pointy*
SPKYST spookiest *eerie*
SPKZ speakeasy *bar*
speakeasies
SPL espial *observation*
SPL sepal *flower*
SPL soapily *lathered*
SPL spall *(n) stone (v) break
up*
SPL spell *(v) words, relieve*
spelled (or) spelt (Br)
spelling
SPL spell *(n) trance, time*
SPL spiel *sales talk*
SPL spill *run out, tell*
SPL splay *spread*
SPL spoil *damage*
SPL spool *(n) thread (v) coil*
SPL supple *elastic* suppler
supplest
SPL supple (v) *make soft*

suppled suppling
SPL supplely (or) supply
(adj) *elastic*
SPL supply *provision*
supplied supplying
supplies
SPLBL spallable *break up*
SPLBN spellbound *charmed*
SPLBND spellbind *charm*
spellbound spellbinding
SPLBND spellbound
charmed
SPLBNDN spellbinding
charming
SPLBNDNG spellbinding
charming
SPLBNDR spellbinder
charmer
SPLCH splotch *spot*
splotches
SPLCH splotchy *spotted*
SPLCHR sepulture *burial*
SPLD sepaloid *leaf*
SPLDNG splitting *division*
SPLDR splatter *splash*
SPLDR splutter *stammer*
spluttery
SPLDR spoliator *plunder*
SPLDV suppletive *words*
SPLFDD splayfooted *flatfoot*
SPLFT splayfoot *flatfoot*
SPLFTD splayfooted *flatfoot*
SPLJ spillage *excess*
SPLJ spoilage *damage*
SPLJK supplejack *vine*
SPLKNT supplicant *beggar*
SPLKR sepulchre (or)
sepulcher *tomb*
SPLKRL sepulchral *tomb*
SPLKSHN supplication
begging
SPLKT supplicate *beg*
supplicated supplicating
SPLKTR supplicatory
begging
SPLLG speleology *caves*
SPLLJ speleology *caves*
SPLLJKL speleological
caves
SPLLJST speleologist *caves*
SPLMNL supplemental
additional

SPLMNR supplementary
additional
SPLMNR supplementer
adder
SPLMNT supplement
addition
SPLMNTL supplemental
additional
SPLMNTR supplementary
additional
SPLMNTR supplementer
adder
SPLMNTSHN
supplementation *addition*
SPLN sapling *tree*
SPLN seaplane *airplane*
SPLN spelling *words*
SPLN spleen *organ*
SPLN spleeny *peevish*
SPLN splenii (pl) *muscle*
splenius
SPLN spline *strip, key,
function*
SPLNB spelling bee *contest*
SPLND esplanade *roadway*
SPLNDD splendid *glorious*
SPLNDDL splendidly
glorious
SPLNDDNS splendidness
glorious
SPLNDFRS splendiferous
glorious
SPLNDK splenetic *spiteful*
SPLNDKL splenetically
spiteful
SPLNDNT splendent *glossy*
SPLNDR splendor
magnificence
(Br) splendour
SPLNDRS splendorous
magnificent
(Br) splendourous
SPLNFL spleenful *spite*
SPLNG sapling *tree*
SPLNG spelling *words*
SPLNGB spelling bee
contest
SPLNGKN spelunking *caves*
SPLNGKNG spelunking
caves
SPLNGKNK splanchnic
visceral

Letters aren't doubled for single sounds: to find alley use **L** not **LL**. Use **Y** and **W** as hard
sounds only: to find yellow use **YL**. (Br)=British spelling or usage. * See dictionary.

SPLNGKR spelunker *caves*
SPLNK splenic *spleen*.
SPLNKDM splenectomy *spleen* splenectomies
SPLNKN spelunking *caves*
SPLNKNG spelunking *caves*
SPLNKNK splanchnic *visceral*
SPLNKR spelunker *caves*
SPLNKTM splenectomy *spleen* splenectomies
SPLNMGL splenomegaly *spleen* splenomegalies
SPLNR splinter *(n)* sliver *(v) split*
SPLNS splenius *muscle* splenii
SPLNS suppleness *elasticity*
SPLNS suppliance *begging*
SPLNT ice plant *fig marigold*
SPLNT splint *support, strip*
SPLNT supplant *replace*
SPLNT suppliant *beggar*
SPLNTK splenetic *spiteful*
SPLNTKL splenetically *spiteful*
SPLNTL suppliantly *begging*
SPLNTR splinter *(n)* sliver *(v) split*
SPLNTS suppliance *begging*
SPLNWRT spleenwort *fern*
SPLNY splenii (pl) *muscle* splenius
SPLNYS splenius *muscle* splenii
SPLR espalier *trellis*
SPLR speller *book, one who spells*
SPLR spoiler *damage*
SPLR subpolar *cold region*
SPLR suppler *elastic*
SPLR supplier *provision*
SPLRJ splurge *indulge* splurged splurging
SPLS splice *join* spliced splicing
SPLSH splash *scatter* splashes
SPLSH splashy *showy* splashier splashiest
SPLSHBRD splashboard *dashboard*

SPLSHDN splashdown *landing*
SPLSHL splashily *showy*
SPLSHN spallation *ejection*
SPLSHN spoliation *plunder*
SPLSHN suppletion *words*
SPLSHNS splashiness *showy*
SPLSHR splasher *scatter*
SPLSHR splashier *showy*
SPLSHST splashiest *showy*
SPLSHYR splashier *showy*
SPLSHYST splashiest *showy*
SPLSPRT spoilsport *damager*
SPLST supplest *elastic*
SPLT spelt (Br) *(v-past)* spell
SPLT splat *noise, chair*
SPLT split *divide* split splitting
SPLT spoliate *plunder* spoliated spoliating
SPLT subplot *fiction, land*
SPLTH isopleth *graph*
SPLTLVL split-level *house*
SPLTN splitting *division*
SPLTNG splitting *division*
SPLTR sepulture *burial*
SPLTR splatter *splash*
SPLTR splutter *stammer* spluttery
SPLTR spoliator *plunder*
SPLTS splits *legs spread*
SPLTV suppletive *words*
SPLVR spillover *excess*
SPLW spillway *passage*
SPLYDR spoliator *plunder*
SPLYLG speleology *caves*
SPLYLJ speleology *caves*
SPLYLJKL speleological *caves*
SPLYLJST speleologist *caves*
SPLYNS suppliance *begging*
SPLYNT suppliant *beggar*
SPLYNTL suppliantly *begging*
SPLYNTS suppliance *begging*
SPLYR espalier *trellis*
SPLYR supplier *provision*

SPLYSHN spoliation *plunder*
SPLYT spoliate *plunder* spoliated spoliating
SPLYTR spoliator *plunder*
SPM Spam *(trademark) food*
SPM spume *foam* spumed spuming
SPM spumy *foamy*
SPMN spumoni (or) spumone *ice cream*
SPMS spumous *foamy*
SPN Aspen *city*
SPN aspen *tree*
SPN sopping *wet*
SPN Spain *country*
SPN span *bridge* spanned spanning
SPN spawn *birth*
SPN spend *use up, pay out* spent spending
SPN spin *twirl, ride* spun spinning
SPN spine *back, thorn*
SPN spiny *thorny* spinier spiniest
SPN spoon *(n)* utensil *(v) neck*
SPN spoony *foolish* spoonier spooniest
SPN subpoena *summon* subpoenaed subpoenaing
SPN supine *face up*
SPNBFD spina bifida *disease*
SPNBL spoonbill *bird*
SPNBLD spoon-billed *snout*
SPNCH spinach *vegetable*
SPND spend *use up, pay out* spent spending
SPND spondee *verse*
SPNDBL spendable *use up, pay out*
SPNDK spondaic *verse*
SPNDKS spandex *elastic*
SPNDL spindle *(v)* grow, spike spindled spindling
SPNDL spindle *(n)* pin, newel, axle
SPNDL spindly *flimsy* spindlier spindliest
SPNDLR spindlier *flimsy*
SPNDLST spindliest *flimsy*

Use letters that best describe the sounds you hear and omit the vowels. Use **S** or **K** instead of **C**: to find circle use **SRKL**. Use **J** to find joy, **JM** to find gem and **G** to find go.

SPNDLYR spindlier *flimsy*
SPNDLYST spindliest *flimsy*
SPNDR spender *use up, pay out*
SPNDRFT spindrift *spray*
SPNDRL spandrel *arch*
SPNDTHRF spendthrift *waster*
SPNDTHRFT spendthrift *waster*
SPNDX spandex *elastic*
SPNDYK spondaic *verse*
SPNF saponify *soap* saponified saponifying saponifies
SPNF spin-off (n) *by-product* spin off (v)
SPNFBL saponifiable *soap*
SPNFD spoon-feed *easy consumption* spoon-fed spoon-feeding
SPNFKS spinifex *grass*
SPNFKSHN saponification *soap*
SPNFL spoonful *measure* spoonfuls
SPNFR saponifier *soap*
SPNFX spinifex *grass*
SPNFYBL saponifiable *soap*
SPNFYR saponifier *soap*
SPNG sopping *wet*
SPNG spongy *soft with holes* spongier spongiest
SPNGGL spangle *sparkle* spangled spangling
SPNGGLSH Spanglish *Spanish and English*
SPNGK spank *punish*
SPNGK spunk *energy*
SPNGK spunky *daring* spunkier spunkiest
SPNGKL spunkily *daring*
SPNGKN spanking *punishment*
SPNGKNG spanking *punishment*
SPNGKNS spunkiness *daring*
SPNGKR spanker *hitter*
SPNGKR spunkier *daring*
SPNGKST spunkiest *daring*
SPNGKYR spunkier *daring*

SPNGKYST spunkiest *daring*
SPNGL spangle *sparkle* spangled spangling
SPNGLSH Spanglish *Spanish and English*
SPNGNS sponginess *soft with holes*
SPNGR spongier *soft with holes*
SPNGST spongiest *soft with holes*
SPNGYR spongier *soft with holes*
SPNGYST spongiest *soft with holes*
SPNJ espionage *spying*
SPNJ sponge *soak* sponged sponging
SPNJ spongy *soft with holes* spongier spongiest
SPNJBTH sponge bath *wash*
SPNJKK sponge cake *dessert*
SPNJN spongin *protein*
SPNJNS sponginess *soft with holes*
SPNJR sponger *parasite*
SPNJR spongier *soft with holes*
SPNJST spongiest *soft with holes*
SPNJWR spongeware *pottery*
SPNJYR spongier *soft with holes*
SPNJYST spongiest *soft with holes*
SPNK spank *punish*
SPNK spunk *energy*
SPNK spunky *plucky* spunkier spunkiest
SPNKL spunkily *daring*
SPNKN spanking *punishment*
SPNKNG spanking *punishment*
SPNKNS spunkiness *daring*
SPNKPD spanakopita (or) spanokopita *food*
SPNKPT spanakopita (or)

spanokopita *food*
SPNKR spanker *hitter*
SPNKR spinnaker *sail*
SPNKR spunkier *daring*
SPNKST spunkiest *daring*
SPNKYR spunkier *daring*
SPNKYST spunkiest *daring*
SPNL spaniel *dog*
SPNL spinal (adj) *backbone* spinally (adv)
SPNL spindly *flimsy* spindlier spindliest
SPNL spinel (or) spinelle *mineral*
SPNL spinule *thorn*
SPNL supinely *face up*
SPNLR spindlier *flimsy*
SPNLS spineless *no backbone, no thorns*
SPNLS spinulose *thorny*
SPNLST spindliest *flimsy*
SPNLYR spindlier *flimsy*
SPNLYST spindliest *flimsy*
SPNN spinning *fishing, yarn*
SPNNG spinning *fishing, yarn*
SPNR spanner *tool*
SPNR spinier *thorny*
SPNR spinner *lure, dial*
SPNR spinor *math*
SPNR spoonier *foolish*
SPNRD Spaniard *of Spain*
SPNRT spinneret (or) spinnerette *filament*
SPNRZM spoonerism *words*
SPNS sapience *wisdom*
SPNS sappiness *juicy, silly*
SPNS soapiness *lathered*
SPNS soppiness *wet*
SPNS spinose *spiny*
SPNS spinous *spines*
SPNS supineness *face up*
SPNSD spinosity *spines*
SPNSH espionage *spying*
SPNSH Spanish *of Spain*
SPNSHS saponaceous *soap*
SPNSHSNS saponaceousness *soap*
SPNSN sponson *projection*
SPNSR spencer *sail, jacket*
SPNSR sponsor (n) *responsible one* (v) *advertise*

SPNSRL sponsorial *responsible*
SPNSRSHP sponsorship *responsibility*
SPNSRYL sponsorial *responsible*
SPNST spiniest *thorny*
SPNST spinosity *spines*
SPNST spooniest *foolish*
SPNSTR spinster *unmarried*
SPNSTRHD spinsterhood *unmarried*
SPNSTRL spinsterly *unmarried*
SPNSTRSH spinsterish *unmarried*
SPNT ice point *temperature*
SPNT sapient *wise*
SPNT spent *exhausted*
SPNT spinet *piano*
SPNT spinout (n) *skid* spin out (v)
SPNT supinate *lay backward* supinated supinating
SPNTHRF spendthrift *waster*
SPNTHRFT spendthrift *waster*
SPNTN spontoon *pike*
SPNTND spontaneity *naturalness* spontaneities
SPNTNS spontaneous *natural*
SPNTNSL spontaneously *natural*
SPNTNSNS spontaneousness *natural*
SPNTNT spontaneity *naturalness* spontaneities
SPNTNYD spontaneity *naturalness* spontaneities
SPNTNYS spontaneous *natural*
SPNTNYSL spontaneously *natural*
SPNTNYSNS spontaneousness *natural*
SPNTNYT spontaneity *naturalness* spontaneities
SPNTS sapience *wisdom*
SPNTSN sponson *projection*
SPNTSR spencer *sail, jacket*

SPNTSR sponsor (n) *responsible one* (v) *advertise*
SPNTSRL sponsorial *responsible*
SPNTSRSHP sponsorship *responsibility*
SPNTSRYL sponsorial *responsible*
SPNYL spaniel *dog*
SPNYL spinule *thorn*
SPNYLS spinulose *thorny*
SPNYR spinier *thorny*
SPNYR spoonier *foolish*
SPNYRD Spaniard *of Spain*
SPNYST spiniest *thorny*
SPNYST spooniest *foolish*
SPNZH espionage *spying*
SPP sopaipilla (or) sopapilla *food*
SPPL sopaipilla (or) sopapilla *food*
SPPR soap opera *drama*
SPPY sopaipilla (or) sopapilla *food*
SPQL specula (pl) *device, chart, color patch* speculum
SPQL spicule *spike*
SPQLDR speculator *think, risk*
SPQLDV speculative *theory, risk*
SPQLM speculum *device, chart, color patch* specula
SPQLR specular *mirror*
SPQLR spicular *spike*
SPQLSHN speculation *theory, risk*
SPQLSHN spiculation *spike*
SPQLT speculate *think, risk* speculated speculating
SPQLTR speculator *think, risk*
SPQLTV speculative *theory, risk*
SPR aspire *desire* aspired aspiring
SPR esprit *spirit*
SPR oospore *zygote*
SPR osprey *hawk* ospreys
SPR sappier *juicy, silly*
SPR sea power *navy*

SPR soaper *drama*
SPR soapier *lathered*
SPR soppier *wetter*
SPR soupier *liquid*
SPR spar (n) *pole*
SPR spar (v) *fight* sparred sparring
SPR spare (n) *extra*
SPR spare (adj) *scarce* sparer sparest
SPR spare (v) *refrain from* spared sparing
SPR sparrow *small bird*
SPR spear (v) *pierce* (n) *lance, sprout* (adj) *male*
SPR spier *spy*
SPR spire *steeple* spired spiring
SPR spirea (or) spiraea *plant*
SPR spoor *track*
SPR spore *seed* spored sporing
SPR spray (n) *mist, flowers* (v) *disperse*
SPR spree *binge*
SPR sprue *mold, disease*
SPR spry *nimble* sprier (or) spryer spriest (or) spryest
SPR spur (v) *urge* spurred spurring
SPR spur (n) *spike*
SPR spurrey (or) spurry *herb* spurreys (or) spurries
SPR subpar *below average*
SPR super (n-abbrv) *supervisor, superintendent*
SPR super (adv) *extremely* (adj) *great*
SPR supper *meal*
SPRB superb *splendid*
SPRBL separable (adj) *divide, divorce, part* separably (adv)
SPRBL Super Bowl *football*
SPRBL superable *overcome*
SPRBL Superball (trademark) *toy*
SPRBL superbly *very well*
SPRBLD separability *divide, divorce, part*
SPRBLT separability *divide, divorce, part*

Use letters that best describe the sounds you hear and omit the vowels. Use **S** or **K** instead of **C**: to find circle use **SRKL**. Use **J** to find joy, **JM** to find gem and **G** to find go.

SPRBNDNS
superabundance *excess*

SPRBNDNT superabundant
excessive

SPRBNDNTS
superabundance *excess*

SPRBNS superbness
excellence

SPRBZ spareribs *meat*

SPRC sprucy *piney* sprucier
spruciest

SPRCD supersede *replace*
superseded superseding

SPRCDR superseder
replacer

SPRCDR supersedure
replacement

SPRCDYR supersedure
replacement

SPRCH superrich *wealth*

SPRCHL spiritual *(n) song*

SPRCHL spiritual (adj)
sacred spiritually *(adv)*

SPRCHLD spirituality *soul*
spiritualities

SPRCHLNS spiritualness
soul

SPRCHLSDK spiritualistic
soul

SPRCHLSTK spiritualistic
soul

SPRCHLT spirituality *soul*
spiritualities

SPRCHLZ spiritualize *soul*
spiritualized spiritualizing

SPRCHLZM spiritualism
soul

SPRCHLZSHN
spiritualization *soul*

SPRCHRJ supercharge
pressurize supercharged
supercharging

SPRCHRJR supercharger
pressurizer

SPRCHS spirituous *alcohol*

SPRCHVR superachiever
success

SPRCHWL spiritual *(n) song*

SPRCHWL spiritual (adj)
sacred spiritually *(adv)*

SPRCHWLD spirituality *soul*
spiritualities

SPRCHWLNS spiritualness
soul

SPRCHWLSDK spiritualistic
soul

SPRCHWLSTK spiritualistic
soul

SPRCHWLT spirituality *soul*
spiritualities

SPRCHWLZ spiritualize *soul*
spiritualized spiritualizing

SPRCHWLZM spiritualism
soul

SPRCHWLZSHN
spiritualization *soul*

SPRCHWS spirituous
alcohol

SPRCJR supersedure
replacement

SPRCKRT supersecret
hidden

SPRD asperity *severity*
asperities

SPRD spearhead *(v) lead (n)*
point

SPRD sporty *sporting style*
sportier sportiest

SPRD spread *(v) wipe,*
widen, separate* spread
spreading

SPRD spread *(n) ranch,*
feast, gap*

SPRDBL supportable
sustain

SPRDD spirited *lively, brave*

SPRDDL spiritedly *lively,*
brave

SPRDDNS spiritedness
lively, brave

SPRDGL spread eagle *(n)*
pose

SPRDGL spread-eagle *(v)*
sprawl (adj) bombastic

SPRDK sporadic *occasional*

SPRDKL sporadically
occasional

SPRDKR esprit de corps
spirit

SPRDL spraddle *sprawl*
spraddled spraddling

SPRDLKS superdeluxe *fine*

SPRDLX superdeluxe *fine*

SPRDLY sportily *sporting*

style

SPRDN Spartan *of Sparta,*
disciplined

SPRDNG sporting *games*

SPRDNGL sportingly *games*

SPRDNS sportiness
sporting style

SPRDPR super-duper
(slang) fabulous

SPRDR aspirator *suction*
device

SPRDR separator *divider*

SPRDR sportier *sporting*
style

SPRDR spreader *wipe,*
widen, scatter

SPRDR supporter *hold up,*
advocate, comfort

SPRDS spiritous *soul*

SPRDSHT spreadsheet
accounting

SPRDST separatist *apart*

SPRDST spiritist *soul*

SPRDST sportiest *sporting*
style

SPRDV separative *divide*

SPRDV sportive *playful*

SPRDV supportive *hold up,*
advocate, comfort

SPRDVL sportively *playful*

SPRDVNS sportiveness
playfulness

SPRDVNS supportiveness
hold up, advocate, comfort

SPRDYR sportier *sporting*
style

SPRDYST sportiest *sporting*
style

SPRDZM separatism *apart*

SPRDZM spiritism *soul*

SPRFDK saprophytic *decay-*
eating

SPRFDK sporophytic *spore*
plant

SPRFDKL saprophytically
decay-eating

SPRFGS saprophagous
decay

SPRFK soporific *sleep*

SPRFL sporophyll *leaf*

SPRFLD superfluity *excess*
superfluities

Letters aren't doubled for single sounds: to find alley use **L** not **LL**. Use **Y** and **W** as hard
sounds only: to find yellow use **YL**. (Br)=British spelling or usage. * See dictionary.

SPRFLS superfluous *extra*

SPRFLSL superfluously *extra*

SPRFLSNS superfluousness *extra*

SPRFLT superfluity *excess* superfluities

SPRFLWD superfluity *excess* superfluities

SPRFLWS superfluous *extra*

SPRFLWSL superfluously *extra*

SPRFLWSNS superfluousness *extra*

SPRFLWT superfluity *excess* superfluities

SPRFN superfine *texture, grade*

SPRFND superfund *toxic waste*

SPRFR sporophore *seeds*

SPRFRS soporiferous *sleep*

SPRFRSNS soporiferousness *sleep*

SPRFSH spearfish *fish*

SPRFSHL superficial (adj) *shallow* superficially (adv)

SPRFSHLD superficiality *shallowness* superficialities

SPRFSHLT superficiality *shallowness* superficialities

SPRFSHNL subprofessional *employee*

SPRFSHYLD superficiality *shallowness* superficialities

SPRFSHYLT superficiality *shallowness* superficialities

SPRFST superfast *quick*

SPRFT saprophyte *decay-eater*

SPRFT sporophyte *spore plant*

SPRFTK saprophytic *decay-eating*

SPRFTK sporophytic *spore plant*

SPRFTKL saprophytically *decay-eating*

SPRG sprig *(v) plant, nail* sprigged sprigging

SPRG sprig *(n) twig*

SPRG superego *psychology*

SPRGL superglue *adhesive*

SPRGN asparagine *amino acid*

SPRGN speargun *weapon*

SPRGN sporogonia (pl) *seeds* sporogonium

SPRGN sporogony *seeds*

SPRGN supergene *heredity*

SPRGNK saprogenic *decay*

SPRGNK sporogenic *seeds*

SPRGNK sporogonic *seeds*

SPRGNM sporogonium *seeds* sporogonia

SPRGNS sporogenous *seeds*

SPRGNSS sporogenesis *seeds*

SPRGNY sporogonia (pl) *seeds* sporogonium

SPRGNYM sporogonium *seeds* sporogonia

SPRGRF subparagraph *writing*

SPRGRM subprogram *computer*

SPRGRP supergroup *rock and roll*

SPRGS asparagus *vegetable* asparagus

SPRHD spearhead *(v) lead (n) point*

SPRHDRDN superheterodyne *radio*

SPRHLKS superhelix *DNA coil*

SPRHLX superhelix *DNA coil*

SPRHMN superhuman *divine*

SPRHR superhero *superman*

SPRHT superheat *vaporize*

SPRHTD superheated *vaporized*

SPRHTRDN superheterodyne *radio*

SPRHW superhighway *road*

SPRHYMN superhuman *divine*

SPRJ spurge *plant*

SPRJL aspergilla (pl) *holy water* aspergillum

SPRJL aspergilli (pl) *fungi* aspergillus

SPRJLM aspergillum *container* aspergilla (or) aspergillums

SPRJLS aspergillus *fungus* aspergilli

SPRJN asparagine *amino acid*

SPRJN supergene *heredity*

SPRJNC superagency *government* superagencies

SPRJNK saprogenic *decay*

SPRJNK sporogenic *seeds*

SPRJNS sporogenous *seeds*

SPRJNS superagency *government* superagencies

SPRJNSS sporogenesis *seeds*

SPRJNTC superagency *government* superagencies

SPRJNTS superagency *government* superagencies

SPRJR spirogyra *algae*

SPRJSNT superjacent *above or upon*

SPRK spark *(v) fire, woo (n) flash, lover*

SPRKDL spirochetal *bacteria*

SPRKL sparkle *twinkle* sparkled sparkling

SPRKL sparkly *twinkly*

SPRKL spiracle *vent*

SPRKL supercool *freeze*

SPRKLDR supercollider *atoms*

SPRKLN sparkling *bubbly*

SPRKLNG sparkling *bubbly*

SPRKLR sparkler *fireworks*

SPRKLSL supercolossal *huge*

SPRKLSTR supercluster *galaxies*

SPRKMPDR supercomputer *mainframe*

SPRKMPDTV supercompetitive *try to win*

SPRKMPTR supercomputer *mainframe*

Use letters that best describe the sounds you hear and omit the vowels. Use **S** or **K** instead of **C**: to find circle use **SRKL**. Use **J** to find joy, **JM** to find gem and **G** to find go.

SPRKMPTTV supercompetitive *try to win*

SPRKMPYDR supercomputer *mainframe*

SPRKMPYTR supercomputer *mainframe*

SPRKNDKDR superconductor *electricity*

SPRKNDKDV superconductive *electricity*

SPRKNDKTR superconductor *electricity*

SPRKNDKTV superconductive *electricity*

SPRKNDKTVT superconductivity *electricity*

SPRKNFDNT superconfident *assured*

SPRKNSRVDV superconservative *traditional*

SPRKNSRVTV superconservative *traditional*

SPRKPLG spark plug *engine*

SPRKR sparker *lover*

SPRKRDKL supercritical *temperature*

SPRKRG supercargo *ship*

SPRKRP sporocarp *seeds*

SPRKRTKL supercritical *temperature*

SPRKSHS supercautious *careful*

SPRKT spirochete *bacteria*

SPRKT sprocket *tool*

SPRKTL spirochetal *bacteria*

SPRL spiral *(v) wind around* spiraled (or) spiralled spiraling (or) spiralling

SPRL spiral (adj, n) *coil* spirally (adv)

SPRL spirilla (pl) *bacteria* spirillum

SPRL sprawl *spread*

SPRL spryly *nimbly*

SPRL superalloy *metal*

SPRLDV sporulative *seed*

SPRLDV superlative *extreme*

SPRLDVL superlatively *extreme*

SPRLK sparrowlike *tiny*

SPRLM spirillum *bacteria* spirilla

SPRLMNL supraliminal *conscious*

SPRLNR superliner *ship*

SPRLRJ superlarge *huge*

SPRLSHN sporulation *seed*

SPRLT sperrylite *mineral*

SPRLT sporulate *seed* sporulated sporulating

SPRLT superlight *no weight*

SPRLTV sporulative *seed*

SPRLTV superlative *extreme*

SPRLTVL superlatively *extreme*

SPRLVSHN superelevation *height*

SPRLZM superrealism *natural*

SPRM sperm *semen* sperm (or) sperms

SPRM supreme *foremost*

SPRM supremo *chief* supremos

SPRMC supremacy *power* supremacies

SPRMDD spermatid *cell*

SPRMDFR spermatophore *packet*

SPRMDFT spermatophyte *plant*

SPRMDGN spermatogonia (pl) *cell* spermatogonium

SPRMDGNK spermatogenic *transformation*

SPRMDGNM spermatogonium *cell* spermatogonia

SPRMDGNSS spermatogenesis *transformation*

SPRMDGNY spermatogonia (pl) *cell* spermatogonium

SPRMDGNYM

spermatogonium *cell* spermatogonia

SPRMDJNK spermatogenic *transformation*

SPRMDJNSS spermatogenesis *transformation*

SPRMDK spermatic *semen*

SPRMDL supermodel *fashion*

SPRMDR spirometer *breathing*

SPRMDRN supermodern *new*

SPRMDST spermatocyte *cell*

SPRMDZ spermatozoa (pl) *male cell* spermatozoon

SPRMDZD spermatozoid *male cell*

SPRMDZN spermatozoon *male cell* spermatozoa

SPRMDZW spermatozoa (pl) *male cell* spermatozoon

SPRMDZWD spermatozoid *male cell*

SPRMDZWN spermatozoon *male cell* spermatozoa

SPRMFL spermophile *squirrel*

SPRMGNSS spermiogenesis *transformation*

SPRMHWL sperm whale *animal*

SPRMJNSS spermiogenesis *transformation*

SPRML supremely *foremost*

SPRMN superman *superior one* supermen

SPRMNS supremeness *ultimate*

SPRMNT spearmint *plant*

SPRMPZ superimpose *put on top* superimposed superimposing

SPRMPZBL superimposable *put on top*

SPRMPZSHN

superimposition *put on top*

SPRMRKT supermarket *store*

SPRMS supremacy *power* supremacies

SPRMSD spermaceti *whale oil*

SPRMSD spermicide *semen killer*

SPRMSDL spermicidal *semen killer*

SPRMSH spermatia (pl) *cell* spermatium

SPRMSHM spermatium *cell* spermatia

SPRMSHY spermatia (pl) *cell* spermatium

SPRMSHYM spermatium *cell* spermatia

SPRMSST supremacist *racist*

SPRMST spermaceti *whale oil*

SPRMSTL spermicidal *semen killer*

SPRMTD spermatid *cell*

SPRMTFR spermatophore *packet*

SPRMTFT spermatophyte *plant*

SPRMTGN spermatogonia (pl) *cell* spermatogonium

SPRMTGNK spermatogenic *transformation*

SPRMTGNM spermatogonium *cell* spermatogonia

SPRMTGNSS spermatogenesis *transformation*

SPRMTGNY spermatogonia (pl) *cell* spermatogonium

SPRMTGNYM spermatogonium *cell* spermatogonia

SPRMTHK spermatheca *sac*

SPRMTJNK spermatogenic *transformation*

SPRMTJNSS spermatogenesis *transformation*

SPRMTK spermatic *semen*

SPRMTR spirometer *breathing*

SPRMTR spirometry *breathing*

SPRMTRK spirometric *breathing*

SPRMTST spermatocyte *cell*

SPRMTZ spermatozoa (pl) *male cell* spermatozoon

SPRMTZD spermatozoid *male cell*

SPRMTZN spermatozoon *male cell* spermatozoa

SPRMTZW spermatozoa (pl) *male cell* spermatozoon

SPRMTZWD spermatozoid *male cell*

SPRMTZWN spermatozoon *male cell* spermatozoa

SPRMWL sperm whale *animal*

SPRMYGNSS spermiogenesis *transformation*

SPRMYJNSS spermiogenesis *transformation*

SPRN aspirin *drug* aspirin (or) aspirins

SPRN cyprian *prostitute*

SPRN Cyprian *of Cyprus*

SPRN soprano *voice* sopranos

SPRN sparing *scarce*

SPRN sporran *pouch*

SPRN sprain *injury*

SPRN spurn *(v) decline (n) rejection*

SPRNCHRL supernatural (adj) *spirit* supernaturally (adv)

SPRNCHRLNS supernaturalness *spirit*

SPRNCHRLSDK supernaturalistic *spirit*

SPRNCHRLST supernaturalist *spirit*

SPRNCHRLSTK supernaturalistic *spirit*

SPRND cyprinid *fish*

SPRNDS superinduce *bring on*

SPRNDYS superinduce *bring on*

SPRNG sparing *scarce*

SPRNG sporangia (pl) *seed* sporangium

SPRNG spring *(n) season, water, bounce**

SPRNG spring *(v) water, leap, issue* sprang (or) sprung springing

SPRNG springy *elastic* springier springiest

SPRNG sprung *(v-past) spring*

SPRNGBK springbok *gazelle* springbok (or) springboks

SPRNGBRD springboard *diving, departure point*

SPRNGFL Springfield *city*

SPRNGFLD Springfield *city*

SPRNGFR sporangiophore *stalk*

SPRNGFRM springform *pan*

SPRNGHD springhead *fountainhead*

SPRNGHS springhouse *cooler*

SPRNGKL sprinkle *scatter* sprinkled sprinkling

SPRNGKLN sprinkling *scattering*

SPRNGKLNG sprinkling *scattering*

SPRNGKLR sprinkler *spray*

SPRNGL sparingly *scarcely*

SPRNGL sporangial *seed*

SPRNGLD spring-load *tension*

SPRNGM sporangium *seed* sporangia

SPRNGN springing *arch*

SPRNGNG springing *arch*

SPRNGNS springiness *elastic*

SPRNGR springer *arch, spaniel, cow*

SPRNGR springier *elastic*

SPRNGST springiest *elastic*

Use letters that best describe the sounds you hear and omit the vowels. Use **S** or **K** instead of **C**: to find circle use **SRKL**. Use **J** to find joy, **JM** to find gem and **G** to find go.

SPRNGTD spring tide *ocean*
SPRNGTL springtail *insect*
SPRNGTM springtime
season
SPRNGY sporangia (pl) *seed*
sporangium
SPRNGYFR
sporangiophore *stalk*
SPRNGYL sporangial *seed*
SPRNGYM sporangium *seed*
sporangia
SPRNGYR springier *elastic*
SPRNGYST springiest
elastic
SPRNJ sporangia (pl) *seed*
sporangium
SPRNJ springe *snare*
SPRNJFR sporangiophore
stalk
SPRNJL sporangial *seed*
SPRNJM sporangium *seed*
sporangia
SPRNJY sporangia (pl) *seed*
sporangium
SPRNJYFR sporangiophore
stalk
SPRNJYL sporangial *seed*
SPRNJYM sporangium *seed*
sporangia
SPRNKL sprinkle *scatter*
sprinkled sprinkling
SPRNKLN sprinkling
scattering
SPRNKLNG sprinkling
scattering
SPRNKLR sprinkler *spray*
SPRNL sparingly *scarcely*
SPRNL supernal (adj)
heavenly supernally (adv)
SPRNMRR supernumerary
many supernumeraries
SPRNN sopranino *music*
sopraninos
SPRNR sprinter *racer*
SPRNR spurner *decliner*
SPRNRML supernormal
beyond human
SPRNRMLD supernormality
beyond human
SPRNRMLT supernormality
beyond human
SPRNS esperance *hope*

SPRNS spryness *nimbleness*
SPRNSHN superannuation
retirement
SPRNSPL subprincipal
assistant
SPRNT aspirant *seeker*
SPRNT spirant *speech*
SPRNT sprint *race*
SPRNT superannuate *retire*
superannuated
superannuating
SPRNTN superintend *direct*
SPRNTND superintend
direct
SPRNTNDNC
superintendency
authority
superintendencies
SPRNTNDNS
superintendence
authority
SPRNTNDNS
superintendency
authority
superintendencies
SPRNTNDNT
superintendent *director*
SPRNTNDNTC
superintendency
authority
superintendencies
SPRNTNDNTS
superintendence
authority
SPRNTNDNTS
superintendency
authority
superintendencies
SPRNTR sprinter *racer*
SPRNTRL supernatural (adj)
spirit supernaturally (adv)
SPRNTRLNS
supernaturalness *spirit*
SPRNTRLST
supernaturalist *spirit*
SPRNTRLSTK
supernaturalistic *spirit*
SPRNTS esperance *hope*
SPRNWSHN
superannuation *retirement*
SPRNWT superannuate
retire superannuated

superannuating
SPRNYMRR
supernumerary *many*
supernumeraries
SPRNYSHN
superannuation *retirement*
SPRNYT superannuate
retire superannuated
superannuating
SPRNYWSHN
superannuation *retirement*
SPRNYWT superannuate
retire superannuated
superannuating
SPRPDM cypripedium
orchid
SPRPDYM cypripedium
orchid
SPRPL isopropyl *alkyl*
SPRPR superpower *nation*
SPRPWR superpower
nation
SPRPZ superpose *lay over*
superposed superposing
SPRR aspirer *seeker*
SPRR sparer *scarcer*
SPRR sprier (or) spryer
nimble
SPRR superior *better*
SPRRD superiority *better*
superiorities
SPRRGSHN supererogation
excess
SPRRGTR supererogatory
excessive
SPRRNL suprarenal *kidneys*
SPRRT superiority *better*
superiorities
SPRS asperse *slander*
aspersed aspersing
SPRS cypress *tree*
SPRS Cyprus *island*
SPRS espresso *coffee*
SPRS sparse *scarce* sparser
sparsest
SPRS spruce (v) *neaten*
spruced sprucing
SPRS spruce (adj) *neat*
sprucer sprucest
SPRS spruce (n) *tree*
SPRS sprucy *piney* sprucier
spruciest

Letters aren't doubled for single sounds: to find alley use **L** not **LL**. Use **Y** and **W** as hard
sounds only: to find yellow use **YL**. (Br)=British spelling or usage. * See dictionary.

SPRS spurious *false*
SPRS superrace *people*
SPRS suppress *subdue*
SPRSBL suppressible
subdue
SPRSBLD suppressibility
subdue
SPRSBLT suppressibility
subdue
SPRSCHRDD
supersaturated *wet*
SPRSCHRSHN
supersaturation *wetness*
SPRSCHRT supersaturate
wet supersaturated
supersaturating
SPRSCHRTD
supersaturated *wet*
SPRSD sparsity *scarceness*
sparsities
SPRSD sporicide *spore killer*
SPRSD supersede *replace*
superseded superseding
SPRSDL sporicidal *spore*
killer
SPRSDR superseder
replacer
SPRSDR supersedure
replacement
SPRSDYR supersedure
replacement
SPRSF supersafe *security*
SPRSFT supersoft *silky*
SPRSHN aspersion *slander*
SPRSHN aspiration
ambition, breath
SPRSHN separation *divide,*
divorce, part
SPRSHN suppression
subdue
SPRSHN suppuration *pus*
SPRSJR supersedure
replacement
SPRSKRB superscribe
address superscribed
superscribing
SPRSKRP superscript
symbol
SPRSKRPSHN
superscription *address*
SPRSKRPT superscript
symbol

SPRSKRT supersecret
hidden
SPRSL sparsely *scarcely*
SPRSL sprucely *neat*
SPRSLS supercilious *proud*
SPRSLSL superciliously
proud
SPRSLSNS
superciliousness *pride*
SPRSLTH supersleuth *spy*
SPRSLYS supercilious *proud*
SPRSLYSL superciliously
proud
SPRSLYSNS
superciliousness *pride*
SPRSMTH supersmooth
elegant
SPRSNK supersonic *speed*
SPRSNKL supersonically
speed
SPRSNR supercenter *store*
SPRSNS sparseness *scarce*
SPRSNS spruceness *neat*
SPRSNSBL supersensible
spiritual
SPRSNSDV supersensitive
feeling
SPRSNSR supersensory
feeling
SPRSNSTV supersensitive
feeling
SPRSNSTVD
supersensitivity *feeling*
SPRSNSTVT
supersensitivity *feeling*
SPRSNT suppressant
subdue
SPRSNTR supercenter *store*
SPRSNTSBL supersensible
spiritual
SPRSNTSDV supersensitive
feeling
SPRSNTSR supersensory
feeling
SPRSNTSTV supersensitive
feeling
SPRSNTSTVD
supersensitivity *feeling*
SPRSNTSTVT
supersensitivity *feeling*
SPRSR sparser *scarcer*
SPRSR suppressor *subdue*

SPRSST sparsest *scarcest*
SPRSST sporocyst *sac*
SPRST sparest *scarcest*
SPRST sparsity *scarceness*
sparsities
SPRST spriest (or) spryest
nimble
SPRSTR superstar *famous*
one
SPRSTRDD supersaturated
wet
SPRSTRDM superstardom
fame
SPRSTRKCHR
superstructure *above*
basement or deck
SPRSTRKSHR
superstructure *above*
basement or deck
SPRSTRKTR
superstructure *above*
basement or deck
SPRSTRNG superstrong
tough
SPRSTRSHN
supersaturation *wetness*
SPRSTRT supersaturate
wet supersaturated
supersaturating
SPRSTRTD supersaturated
wet
SPRSTSHN superstation
broadcasting
SPRSTSHN superstition
irrational belief
SPRSTSHS superstitious
irrational belief
SPRSTT superstate *nation*
SPRSV suppressive *subdue*
SPRSWT supersweet
cloying
SPRSZ supersize *large*
SPRSZD supersized *large*
SPRT asperity *severity*
asperities
SPRT aspirate *(v)* *breathe*
aspirated aspirating
SPRT aspirate *(n)* *sound*
SPRT seaport *ships*
SPRT separate *divide,*
divorce, part separated
separating

Use letters that best describe the sounds you hear and omit the vowels. Use **S** or **K** instead of **C**: to find circle use **SRKL**. Use **J** to find joy, **JM** to find gem and **G** to find go.

SPRT spirit (n) soul, distillate, courage (v) animate, carry off*

SPRT sport game

SPRT sporty sporting style sportier sportiest

SPRT sprat herring

SPRT sprit pole

SPRT sprite elf

SPRT sprout (v) grow (n) shoot

SPRT spurt (v) spout (n) jet, moment

SPRT support sustain

SPRT suppurate pus suppurated suppurating

SPRTBL supportable sustain

SPRTD spirited lively, brave

SPRTDL spiritedly lively, brave

SPRTDNS spiritedness lively, brave

SPRTF sportif sporty

SPRTFL sportful (adj) playful sportfully (adv)

SPRTFLNS sportfulness playful

SPRTFSHN sportfishing rod and reel

SPRTFSHNG sportfishing rod and reel

SPRTHK superthick dense

SPRTHLT superathlete sports

SPRTHN superthin filmy

SPRTK sporadic occasional

SPRTKL sporadically occasional

SPRTL spiritual (n) song

SPRTL sportily sporting style

SPRTL spraddle sprawl spraddled spraddling

SPRTL sprightly lively sprightlier sprightliest

SPRTLD spirituality soul spiritualities

SPRTLNS spiritualness soul

SPRTLNS sprightliness lively

SPRTLR sprightlier lively

SPRTLSDK spiritualistic soul

SPRTLST sprightliest lively

SPRTLSTK spiritualistic soul

SPRTLT spirituality soul spiritualities

SPRTLYR sprightlier lively

SPRTLYST sprightliest lively

SPRTLZ spiritualize soul spiritualized spiritualizing

SPRTLZM spiritualism soul

SPRTLZSHN spiritualization soul

SPRTM aspartame sweetener

SPRTN Spartan of Sparta, disciplined

SPRTN sporting games

SPRTNG sporting games

SPRTNGKR supertanker ship

SPRTNGL sportingly games

SPRTNKR supertanker ship

SPRTNL sportingly games

SPRTNS sportiness sporting style

SPRTR aspirator suction device

SPRTR separator divider

SPRTR sportier sporting style

SPRTR supporter hold up, advocate, comfort

SPRTS spiritous soul

SPRTS spirituous alcohol

SPRTS spritz spray

SPRTSKR sports car vehicle

SPRTSKST sportscast broadcast

SPRTSL spritsail boat

SPRTSMN sportsman game player sportsmen

SPRTSMNSHP sportsmanship good conduct

SPRTSR spritzer sprayer

SPRTST separatist apart

SPRTST spiritist soul

SPRTST sportiest sporting style

SPRTSWMN sportswoman games sportswomen

SPRTSWR sportswear clothing

SPRTT supertight sealed

SPRTV separative divide

SPRTV sportive playful

SPRTV supportive hold up, advocate, comfort

SPRTVL sportively playful

SPRTVNS sportiveness playfulness

SPRTVNS supportiveness hold up, advocate, comfort

SPRTWL spiritual (n) song

SPRTWLD spirituality soul spiritualities

SPRTWLNS spiritualness soul

SPRTWLSDK spiritualistic soul

SPRTWLSTK spiritualistic soul

SPRTWLT spirituality soul spiritualities

SPRTWLZ spiritualize soul spiritualized spiritualizing

SPRTWLZM spiritualism soul

SPRTWLZSHN spiritualization soul

SPRTWS spirituous alcohol

SPRTYR sportier sporting style

SPRTYST sportiest sporting style

SPRTZ spritz spray

SPRTZM separatism apart

SPRTZM spiritism soul

SPRTZR spritzer sprayer

SPRVN supervene follow supervened supervening

SPRVNCHN supervention following

SPRVNSHN supervention following

SPRVNTSHN supervention following

SPRVSHN supervision direction

SPRVZ supervise oversee supervised supervising

SPRVZHN supervision direction

SPRVZR supervisor overseer

Letters aren't doubled for single sounds: to find alley use **L** not **LL**. Use **Y** and **W** as hard sounds only: to find yellow use **YL**. (Br)=British spelling or usage. * See dictionary.

SPRVZR supervisory *overseeing*
SPRWD superwide *trailer*
SPRWMN superwoman *exceptional one* superwomen
SPRWPN superweapon *war*
SPRY spirea (or) spiraea *plant*
SPRYLDV sporulative *seed*
SPRYLSHN sporulation *seed*
SPRYLT sporulate *seed* sporulated sporulating
SPRYLTV sporulative *seed*
SPRYLZM superrealism *natural*
SPRYN cyprian *prostitute*
SPRYN Cyprian *of Cyprus*
SPRYR sprier (or) spryer *nimble*
SPRYR superior *better*
SPRYRD superiority *better* superiorities
SPRYRT superiority *better* superiorities
SPRYS spurious *false*
SPRYST spriest (or) spryest *nimble*
SPRZ surprise *astonish* surprised surprising
SPRZHN aspersion *slander*
SPRZL surprisal *astonishment*
SPRZN sporozoan *parasite*
SPRZN surprising *astonishing*
SPRZNG surprising *astonishing*
SPRZNGL surprisingly *astonishing*
SPRZNL surprisingly *astonishing*
SPRZT sporozoite *parasite*
SPRZV suppressive *subdue*
SPRZWN sporozoan *parasite*
SPRZWT sporozoite *parasite*
SPS auspice *omen, support* auspices
SPS espouse *adopt, marry* espoused espousing
SPS space *(v) arrange* spaced spacing
SPS space *(n) distance, area*
SPS spacey *dazed* spacier spaciest
SPS spice *flavor* spiced spicing
SPS spicy *flavorful, racy* spicier spiciest
SPS spouse *marriage*
SPSBSH spicebush *shrub*
SPSDK spastic *twitching*
SPSDKL spastically *twitching*
SPSDS soapsuds *lather*
SPSDT spaced-out (or) spaced *dazed*
SPSDZ soapsuds *lather*
SPSF specify *detail* specified specifying specifies
SPSFBL specifiable *detail*
SPSFK specific *particular*
SPSFKL specifically *particularly*
SPSFKSHN specification *detail*
SPSFLT spaceflight *travel*
SPSFSD specificity *detail*
SPSFST specificity *detail*
SPSFYBL specifiable *detail*
SPSHDL space shuttle *vehicle*
SPSHL especial (adj) *particular* especially (adv)
SPSHL spatial (adj) *space* spatially (adv)
SPSHL special (adj) *unequaled* specially (adv)
SPSHLD spatiality *space*
SPSHLD speciality *quality, aptitude* specialities
SPSHLD specialty *best* specialties
SPSHLDLVR special delivery *mail*
SPSHLNS specialness *distinctive*
SPSHLS specialize *make particular* specialized specializing (Br) specialise
SPSHLST specialist *adept*
one, rank
SPSHLT spatiality *space*
SPSHLT speciality *quality, aptitude* specialities
SPSHLT specialty *best* specialties
SPSHLZ specialize *make particular* specialized specializing (Br) specialise
SPSHLZM specialism *specialty*
SPSHLZSHN specialization *make particular* (Br) specialisation
SPSHP spaceship *rocket*
SPSHS auspicious *favorable*
SPSHS spacious *large*
SPSHS specious *deceptive*
SPSHSHN speciation *form species*
SPSHSL spaciously *large*
SPSHSL speciously *deceptive*
SPSHSNS spaciousness *large*
SPSHSNS speciousness *deception*
SPSHT speciate *form species*
SPSHTL space shuttle *vehicle*
SPSHYLD spatiality *space*
SPSHYLD speciality *quality, aptitude* specialities
SPSHYLD specialty *best* specialties
SPSHYLT spatiality *space*
SPSHYLT speciality *quality, aptitude* specialities
SPSHYLT specialty *best* specialties
SPSHYSHN speciation *form species*
SPSHYT speciate *form species*
SPSHZ species *type*
SPSJ space age (n) *modern* space-age (adj)
SPSKDT space cadet *forgetful one*
SPSKR sapsucker *bird*
SPSKRF spacecraft *rocket*

Use letters that best describe the sounds you hear and omit the vowels. Use **S** or **K** instead of **C**: to find circle use **SRKL**. Use **J** to find joy, **JM** to find gem and **G** to find go.

SPSKRFT spacecraft *rocket*

SPSL espousal *betrothal, belief*

SPSL spicily *flavor, racy*

SPSL spousal *marriage*

SPSMN spaceman *astronaut* spacemen

SPSMN specimen *sample*

SPSN soupçon *trace*

SPSN spacing *distance*

SPSNG spacing *distance*

SPSNS spiciness *flavor, racy*

SPSPN soupspoon *ladle*

SPSPRT spaceport *launching*

SPSR espouser *marry, adopt*

SPSR spacier *dazed*

SPSR spicier *flavor, racy*

SPSRTN spessartine (or) spessartite *gemstone*

SPSRTT spessartite (or) spessartine *gemstone*

SPSS asepsis *no germs*

SPSS auspices *support*

SPSS sepsis *decay* sepses

SPSSHDL space shuttle *vehicle*

SPSSHN speciation *form species*

SPSSHTL space shuttle *vehicle*

SPSST spaciest *dazed*

SPSST spiciest *flavor, racy*

SPST sappiest *juicy, silly*

SPST soapiest *lathered*

SPST soppiest *wettest*

SPST soupiest *liquid*

SPST space suit *astronaut*

SPST spaced (or) spaced-out *dazed*

SPST speciate *form species*

SPSTK spastic *twitching*

SPSTKL spastically *twitching*

SPSTM space-time *continuum*

SPSTN soapstone *rock*

SPSTR suppository *anal insertion* suppositories

SPSTSHN space station *orbiter*

SPSTT spaced-out (or)

spaced *dazed*

SPSWK space walk *astronaut*

SPSYR spacier *dazed*

SPSYR spicier *flavor, racy*

SPSYSHN speciation *form species*

SPSYST spaciest *dazed*

SPSYST spiciest *flavor, racy*

SPSYT speciate *form species*

SPSZ auspices *support*

SPSZ species *type*

SPT eyespot *color, fungus*

SPT septa (pl) *membrane* septum

SPT spat *quarrel* spatted spatting

SPT spat *(v-past)* spit *(n) fight, shoe cover*

SPT spate *flood*

SPT spit *(v) eject* spit (or) spat spitting

SPT spit *(v) impale* spitted spitting

SPT spit *(n) saliva, rod, land*

SPT spite *(v) annoy, shame* spited spiting

SPT spite *(n) revenge*

SPT spot *mark, stain, see** spotted spotting

SPT spotty *marked, infrequent* spottier spottiest

SPT spout *pipe, spurt*

SPT sputa (pl) *saliva* sputum

SPTBL spitball *baseball*

SPTBL spottable *marked, stain, see*

SPTCHK spot-check *sample*

SPTCM septicemia *infection*

SPTCMY septicemia *infection*

SPTD spotted *mark, stain, see*

SPTD spouted *pipe, spurt*

SPTFL spiteful (adj) *revengeful* spitefully (adv)

SPTFLNS spitefulness *revenge*

SPTFR spitfire *emotional*

SPTFYR spitfire *emotional*

SPTH spathe *seed*

SPTJNRN septuagenarian *age 70-79*

SPTJNRYN septuagenarian *age 70-79*

SPTK aseptic *no germs*

SPTK septic *putrid*

SPTKL aseptically *no germs*

SPTKRL spit curl *hair*

SPTL septal *membrane*

SPTL spatula *flat tool*

SPTL spittle *saliva*

SPTL spottily *marked, seldom*

SPTLBG spittlebug *insect*

SPTLN septillion *number*

SPTLS spotless *pure*

SPTLSL spotlessly *pure*

SPTLSNS spotlessness *pure*

SPTLT spatulate *flat*

SPTLT spotlight *illumination* spotlighted (or) spotlit spotlighting

SPTLYN septillion *number*

SPTM septum *membrane* septa

SPTM sputum *saliva* sputa

SPTMBR September *month*

SPTN spittoon *cuspidor*

SPTNGMJ spitting image *duplicate*

SPTNK sputnik *spacecraft*

SPTNL septennial (adj) *7 years* septenially (adv)

SPTNMJ spitting image *duplicate*

SPTNS spottiness *marked, seldom*

SPTR scepter *staff* (Br) sceptre

SPTR spatter *splash*

SPTR spitter *one that spits, pitch*

SPTR spotter *mark, stain, see*

SPTR spottier *marked, seldom*

SPTR spouter *spurt, declaim*

SPTR sputter *spit, squirt*

SPTRDK spatterdock *flower*

SPTRR sputterer *spit, squirt*

SPTS spitz *dog*

SPTSDL septicidal *seeds*

SPTSM septicemia *infection*

Letters aren't doubled for single sounds: to find alley use **L** not **LL**. Use **Y** and **W** as hard sounds only: to find yellow use **YL**. (Br)=British spelling or usage. * See dictionary.

SPTSMY septicemia *infection*
SPTST spottiest *marked, seldom*
SPTT septate *membrane*
SPTT septet *group of 7*
SPTWJNRN septuagenarian *age 70-79*
SPTWJNRYN septuagenarian *age 70-79*
SPTYN septillion *number*
SPTYR spottier *marked, seldom*
SPTYST spottiest *marked, seldom*
SPTZ spitz *dog*
SPV spiv *(Br) slacker*
SPWD sapwood *tree*
SPWR sea power *navy*
SPX specs *eyeglasses, specifications*
SPY sepia *brown*
SPY spew *vomit, exude* spewed spewing
SPYD sputa (pl) *saliva* sputum
SPYDM sputum *saliva* sputa
SPYL espial *observation*
SPYL spoil *damage*
SPYLJ spoilage *damage*
SPYLR spoiler *damage*
SPYLSPRT spoilsport *damager*
SPYM spume *foam* spumed spuming
SPYM spumy *foamy*
SPYMS spumous *foamy*
SPYNJ espionage *spying*
SPYNS sapience *wisdom*
SPYNSH espionage *spying*
SPYNT sapient *wise*
SPYNTS sapience *wisdom*
SPYNZH espionage *spying*
SPYR sappier *juicy, silly*
SPYR soapier *lathered*
SPYR soppier *wetter*
SPYR soupier *liquid*
SPYR spier *spy*
SPYR spire *steeple* spired spiring
SPYRS spurious *false*
SPYRSHN suppuration *pus*

SPYRT suppurate *pus* suppurated suppurating
SPYRYS spurious *false*
SPYST sappiest *juicy, silly*
SPYST soapiest *lathered*
SPYST soppiest *wettest*
SPYST soupiest *liquid*
SPYT sputa (pl) *saliva* sputum
SPYTM sputum *saliva* sputa
SPZ espouse *marry, adopt* espoused espousing
SPZ spaz *(slang) klutz* spazzes
SPZ spouse *marriage*
SPZ suppose *assume* supposed supposing
SPZBL supposable (adj) *conceivable* supposably (adv)
SPZD supposed *alleged*
SPZDL supposedly *allegedly*
SPZL espousal *betrothal, belief*
SPZL spousal *marriage*
SPZM spasm *twitch*
SPZMDK spasmodic *twitch*
SPZMDKL spasmodically *twitch*
SPZMTK spasmodic *twitch*
SPZMTKL spasmodically *twitch*
SPZN supposing *assuming*
SPZNG supposing *assuming*
SPZR espouser *marry, adopt*
SPZSHN supposition *assumption*
SPZTR suppository *anal insertion* suppositories
SPZTSHS supposititious *false*
SQ acequia *canal*
SQ askew *tilted*
SQ eschew *shun*
SQ sequoia *tree*
SQ Sequoya (or) Sequoyah (or) Sequoia *Cherokee scholar*
SQ skew *twist*
SQ skua *bird*
SQ squaw *Native American woman*

SQB squab *bird* squabs
SQB squib (v) *ridicule, fire, kick* squibbed squibbing
SQB squib (n) *satire, firecracker*
SQB succuba *demon* succubae
SQB succubi (pl) *demon* succubus
SQB usquebaugh *whiskey*
SQBK skewback *arch*
SQBL skewbald *white patches*
SQBL squabble *quarrel* squabbled squabbling
SQBLD skewbald *white patches*
SQBLR squabbler *quarrel*
SQBS succubus *demon* succubi
SQD escudo *coin* escudos
SQD skewed *twisted*
SQD squad *group*
SQD squatty *short and fat* squattier squattiest
SQD squid *mollusk* squid (or) squids
SQDKR squad car *police*
SQDR sequitur *consequence*
SQDR squatter *settler*
SQDR squattier *short and fat*
SQDRN squadron *group*
SQDST squattiest *short and fat*
SQDYR squattier *short and fat*
SQDYST squattiest *short and fat*
SQFSH squawfish *fish*
SQG squeegee *wipe* squeeggeed squeegeeing
SQGL squiggle *wiggle* squiggled squiggling
SQGL squiggly *wiggly*
SQJ squeegee *wipe* squeeggeed squeegeeing
SQK squawk *loud cry*
SQK squeak *shrill noise*
SQK squeaky *shrill*
SQKR squeaker *contest*

Use letters that best describe the sounds you hear and omit the vowels. Use **S** or **K** instead of **C**: to find circle use **SRKL**. Use **J** to find joy, **JM** to find gem and **G** to find go.

SQL eschewal *rejection*
SQL saccule *pouch*
SQL sacculi (pl) *pouch* sacculus
SQL sequel *subsequent*
SQL squall *wind, scream*
SQL squally *gusty* squallier squalliest
SQL squeal *shrill cry*
SQL squill *herb*
SQL squilla *crayfish* squillas (or) squillae
SQLCH squelch *crush*
SQLCHR squelcher *crusher*
SQLD squalid *dirty*
SQLDD sacculated *pouches*
SQLDL squalidly *dirty*
SQLDNS squalidness *dirty*
SQLDR escalator *moving* stairs
SQLM osculum *opening*
SQLN squalene *chemical*
SQLN squall line *storm*
SQLNS succulence *juicy*
SQLNT esculent *edible*
SQLNT succulent *juicy*
SQLNTL succulently *juicy*
SQLNTS succulence *juicy*
SQLR acicular *needle*
SQLR ossicular *bone*
SQLR saccular *pouch*
SQLR secular *(adj) not religious*
SQLR secular *(n) layman* seculars (or) secular
SQLR squallier *windier*
SQLR squalor *filth*
SQLR squealer *shrill cry*
SQLRS secularize *remove religion* secularized secularizing (Br) secularise
SQLRST secularist *no religion*
SQLRZ secularize *remove religion* secularized secularizing (Br) secularise
SQLRZM secularism *no religion*
SQLS sacculus *pouch* sacculi

SQLSHN escalation *increase*
SQLSHN osculation *kiss*
SQLSHN sacculation *pouches*
SQLST squalliest *windier*
SQLT escalate *increase* escalated escalating
SQLT osculate *kiss* osculated osculating
SQLTD sacculated *pouches*
SQLTR escalator *moving* stairs
SQLYR squallier *windier*
SQLYST squalliest *windier*
SQM squama *scale* squamae
SQMLS squamulose *lobes*
SQMS squamous *scaly*
SQMSH squeamish *queasy*
SQMSHN squamation *scales*
SQMSL squamosal *bone*
SQMT squamate *scaly*
SQMYLS squamulose *lobes*
SQN sequin *ornament*
SQN squinty *eyes*
SQNCH squinch *(v) squint (n) support*
SQNCHL sequential *(adj) in order* sequentially *(adv)*
SQND sequined (or) sequinned *ornaments*
SQND squint-eyed *cross-eyed*
SQNDR squander *scatter, lose*
SQNS sequence *order* sequenced sequencing
SQNS skewness *twist*
SQNSHL sequential *(adj) in order* sequentially *(adv)*
SQNT squint *eyes, variation* squinty
SQNT squinty *eyes*
SQNTD squint-eyed *cross-eyed*
SQNTS sequence *order* sequenced sequencing
SQNTYD squint-eyed *cross-eyed*
SQR esquire *rank*
SQR secure *(v) make safe, effect, ensure** secured

securing
SQR secure *(adj) safe, dependable* securer securest
SQR skewer *(n) rod (v) pierce, criticize*
SQR square *(adj) shape, even* squarer squarest
SQR square *(v) settle up, shape, number** squared squaring
SQR square *(n) block, number, conventional one**
SQR square *(adv) honest, direct*
SQR squire *(v) escort* squired squiring
SQR squire *(n) rank*
SQRD secured *safe, locked*
SQRD security *safety* securities
SQRDNS square dance (n) *dancing* square-dance (v)
SQRDNSNG square dancing *dancing*
SQRDNSR square dancer *dancing*
SQRDNTS square dance (n) *dancing* square-dance (v)
SQRDNTSNG square dancing *dancing*
SQRDNTSR square dancer *dancing*
SQRDR squirter *spray*
SQRGD square-rigged *sails*
SQRGR square-rigger *sails*
SQRL squarely *directly*
SQRL squirrel *(v) store up* squirreled (or) squirrelled squirreling (or) squirrelling
SQRL squirrel *(n) animal*
SQRM squirm *fidget*
SQRM squirmy *fidgety*
SQRMNT securement *safe, locked*
SQRNS squareness *shape, conventional, fair*
SQRNT square knot *join cords*
SQRR securer *safe, locked*
SQRRK squirearchy

Letters aren't doubled for single sounds: to find alley use **L** not **LL**. Use **Y** and **W** as hard sounds only: to find yellow use **YL**. (Br)=British spelling or usage. * See dictionary.

aristocrats squirearchies
SQRS Siqueiros *artist*
SQRSH squarish *blocky*
SQRSHLDRD square-shouldered *straight*
SQRST securest *safe, locked*
SQRT security *safety* securities
SQRT square root *number*
SQRT squirt *spray*
SQRTD square-toed *old-fashioned*
SQRTR squirter *spray*
SQSDR sequester *separate*
SQSH squash *(v) crush (n) vegetable, game* squashes (or) squash
SQSH squashy *soft* squashier squashiest
SQSH squish *(v) squelch*
SQSH squishy *soft and damp* squishier squishiest
SQSHL squashily *soft*
SQSHNS squashiness *soft*
SQSHNS squishiness *soft and damp*
SQSHR squashier *soft*
SQSHR squishier *soft and damp*
SQSHS sequacious *servile*
SQSHST squashiest *soft*
SQSHST squishiest *soft and damp*
SQSHYR squashier *soft*
SQSHYR squishier *soft and damp*
SQSHYST squashiest *soft*
SQSHYST squishiest *soft and damp*
SQSTR sequester *separate*
SQSTRM sequestrum *bone* sequestrums
SQSTRSHN sequestration *custody*
SQT squat *(v) crouch* squatted squatting
SQT squat *(adj) short* squatter squattest
SQT squat *(v) pose (n) a posture, (slang) nothing*
SQT squatty *short and fat* squattier squattiest

SQTR sequitur *consequence*
SQTR squatter *settler*
SQTR squattier *short and fat*
SQTST squattiest *short and fat*
SQTYR squattier *short and fat*
SQTYST squattiest *short and fat*
SQW skua *bird*
SQWR skewer *(n) rod (v) pierce, criticize*
SQY acequia *canal*
SQY sequoia *tree*
SQY Sequoya (or) Sequoyah (or) Sequoia *Cherokee scholar*
SQYR esquire *rank*
SQYR squire *(v) escort* squired squiring
SQYR squire *(n) rank*
SQYRRK squirearchy *aristocrats* squirearchies
SQZ squeeze *exert pressure* squeezed squeezing
SQZBL squeezable (adj) *exert pressure* squeezably (adv)
SQZBLD squeezability *exert pressure*
SQZBLT squeezability *exert pressure*
SQZPL squeeze play *baseball, extortion*
SQZR squeezer *extractor*
SR assayer *estimator*
SR cere *wrap* cered cering
SR cere *(n) nodule*
SR cero *fish* cero (or) ceros
SR ciré (or) cire *fabric*
SR cirri (pl) *arm, cloud* cirrus
SR essayer *tester*
SR eyesore *mess*
SR icier *frozen*
SR issuer *emerge, emit*
SR ossuary *burial* ossuaries
SR sari *dress*
SR saury *fish* sauries
SR sear *burn*
SR seer *prophet* seers (or) seer
SR sera (pl) *drug* serum

SR sere *(adj) dry (n) ecology*
SR serow *animal*
SR sewer *pipe, stitcher*
SR sierra *mountains, fish*
SR sir *man*
SR sire *(v) beget* sired siring
SR sire *(n) father*
SR soar *fly*
SR sora *bird*
SR sore *pain, anger* sorer sorest
SR sori (pl) *spore* sorus
SR sorrow *sadness*
SR sorry *sad, bad* sorrier sorriest
SR sour *flavor*
SR sower *planter*
SR surah *fabric*
SR surra *disease*
SR surrey *carriage* surreys
SR Syria *country*
SR usury *high interest rate* usuries
SRB acerb *sour*
SRB Serb *of Serbia*
SRB sorb *take up*
SRB sorbet *sherbet*
SRBBL sorbable *take up*
SRBBLD sorbability *take up*
SRBBLT sorbability *take up*
SRBD acerbity *acidity* acerbities
SRBDL sorbitol *alcohol*
SRBK acerbic *acid*
SRBKL acerbically *acidly*
SRBKRSHN Serbo-Croatian *person, language*
SRBKRWSHN Serbo-Croatian *person, language*
SRBL cerebella (pl) *brain* cerebellum
SRBL sour ball *candy*
SRBLM cerebellum *brain* cerebellums (or) cerebella
SRBLPLZ cerebral palsy *disease*
SRBNT sorbent *absorb*
SRBR cerebra (pl) *brain* cerebrum
SRBRL cerebral (adj) *intellectual* cerebrally

Use letters that best describe the sounds you hear and omit the vowels. Use **S** or **K** instead of **C**: to find circle use **SRKL**. Use **J** to find joy, **JM** to find gem and **G** to find go.

(adv)

SRBRLPLZ cerebral palsy *disease*

SRBRM cerebrum *brain* cerebrums (or) cerebra

SRBRSPNL cerebrospinal *brain and spine*

SRBRT cerebrate *think* cerebrated cerebrating

SRBRTN sauerbraten *food*

SRBS surbase *molding*

SRBT acerbate *vex* acerbated acerbating

SRBT acerbity *acidity* acerbities

SRBT sorbate *chemical*

SRBT sorbet *sherbet*

SRBTL sorbitol *alcohol*

SRC cerci (pl) *sensor* cercus

SRC Circe *Greek myth*

SRCH search *look for* searches

SRCHBL searchable *look for*

SRCHLT searchlight *illumination*

SRCHN sea urchin *sea animal*

SRCHNGL searchingly *look for*

SRCHNL searchingly *look for*

SRCHR searcher *look for*

SRCHRJ surcharge *extra cost* surcharged surcharging

SRCS surcease *stop* surceased surceasing

SRCZ surcease *stop* surceased surceasing

SRD sard *mineral*

SRD Saturday *weekend day*

SRD serried *crowded*

SRD sorehead *angry one*

SRD sort of *rather*

SRD sortie *attack*

SRD sourdough *bread*

SRD surd *irrational, silent*

SRD sword *weapon*

SRDBL sortable *arrange*

SRDD assorted *varied*

SRDD serrated *notched*

SRDD sordid *filthy*

SRDDL assertedly *allegedly*

SRDF certify *confirm, license* certified certifying

SRDFBL certifiable (adj) *assured* certifiably (adv)

SRDFD certified *authorized*

SRDFDML certified mail *proof of delivery*

SRDFKSHN certification *license*

SRDFR certifier *confirm, license*

SRDFSH swordfish *animal*

SRDFYBL certifiable (adj) *assured* certifiably (adv)

SRDFYR certifier *confirm, license*

SRDK cirrhotic *liver disease*

SRDK psoriatic *disease*

SRDN certain *sure*

SRDN sardine *fish*

SRDN sordino *mute* sordini

SRDND certainty *sureness* certainties

SRDNK sardonic *mocking*

SRDNKL sardonically *mocking*

SRDNKS sardonyx *quartz*

SRDNL certainly *surely*

SRDNSZM sardonicism *mocking*

SRDNT certainty *sureness* certainties

SRDNX sardonyx *quartz*

SRDPL swordplay *fencing*

SRDR sorter *arranger*

SRDTD certitude *certainty*

SRDTL swordtail *fish*

SRDTYD certitude *certainty*

SRDV assertive *aggressive*

SRDV sort of *rather*

SRDVL assertively *agressively*

SRDVNS assertiveness *agressiveness*

SRDZ sorites *logic* sorites

SRDZMN swordsman *fencing* swordsmen

SRDZMNSHP swordsmanship *fencing*

SRF seraph *angel* seraphim

SRF serf *slave*

SRF serif *type*

SRF surf *waves*

SRFBRD surfbird *animal*

SRFBRD surfboard *water sport*

SRFBT surfboat *big waves*

SRFDM serfdom *slavery*

SRFKDNT surfactant *detergent*

SRFKSDN surf casting *fishing*

SRFKSDNG surf casting *fishing*

SRFKSDR surf caster *fishing*

SRFKSTN surf casting *fishing*

SRFKSTNG surf casting *fishing*

SRFKSTR surf caster *fishing*

SRFKTNT surfactant *detergent*

SRFL sorrowful (adj) *sadness* sorrowfully (adv)

SRFLNS sorrowfulness *sadness*

SRFM seraphim (pl) *angel* seraph

SRFN seraphim (pl) *angel* seraph

SRFN surfing *wave sport*

SRFNG surfing *wave sport*

SRFNTRF surf and turf *meal*

SRFPRCH surfperch *fish*

SRFR surfer *sportsman*

SRFRZNBZ surfer's knobs *knees*

SRFS surface (v) *make smooth, show up* surfaced surfacing

SRFS surface (n) *external* (adj) *superficial*

SRFSH surf fish *perch*

SRFSHS scire facias *law*

SRFSN surfacing *material*

SRFSNG surfacing *material*

SRFSTR surface-to-air *missile*

SRFSTWR surface-to-air *missile*

SRFT surfeit *excess*

Letters aren't doubled for single sounds: to find alley use **L** not **LL**. Use **Y** and **W** as hard sounds only: to find yellow use **YL**. (Br)=British spelling or usage. * See dictionary.

SRG sorgo *grass, syrup*
SRGC surrogacy *mother*
SRGM sorghum *grass, syrup*
SRGRF serigraph *silk-screen*
SRGRF serigraphy *silk-screen*
SRGRFR serigrapher *silk-screen*
SRGS sargasso *seaweed* sargassos
SRGS surrogacy *mother*
SRGSM sargassum *seaweed*
SRGT surrogate *substitute* surrogated surrogating
SRHD sorehead *angry one*
SRJ sarge *sargeant*
SRJ serge *fabric*
SRJ sewerage *waste*
SRJ surge *swell* surged surging
SRJKDV surjective *onto*
SRJKL surgical (adj) *operation* surgically (adv)
SRJKSHN surjection *onto*
SRJKTV surjective *onto*
SRJN serging *carpet*
SRJN surgeon *doctor*
SRJNC sergeancy *rank*
SRJNFSH surgeonfish *animal*
SRJNG serging *carpet*
SRJNS sergeancy *rank*
SRJNT assurgent *rising*
SRJNT sergeant *rank*
SRJNTC sergeancy *rank*
SRJNTS sergeancy *rank*
SRJR surgery *operation* surgeries
SRK circa *about*
SRK cirque *valley*
SRK serac *ice*
SRK sirocco *wind* siroccos·
SRKD sarcoid *disease*
SRKDN circadian *cycle*
SRKDS circuitous *winding*
SRKDSL circuitously *winding*
SRKDSNS circuitousness *winding*
SRKDSS sarcoidosis *disease* sarcoidoses
SRKDYN circadian *cycle*

SRKFG sarcophagi (pl) *coffin* sarcophagus
SRKFGS sarcophagus *coffin* sarcophagi
SRKFJ sarcophagi (pl) *coffin* sarcophagus
SRKL circle (v) *enclose, revolve around* circled circling
SRKL circle (n) *ring, orbit*
SRKLCHR sericulture *silk*
SRKLCHRL sericultural *silk*
SRKLCHRST sericulturist *silk*
SRKLDR circulator *move in a circle*
SRKLDV circulative *flowing*
SRKLM sarcolemma *muscles*
SRKLML sarcolemmal *muscles*
SRKLR circler *enclose, revolve around*
SRKLR circular *round*
SRKLRZ circularize *publicize* circularized circularizing (Br) circularise
SRKLSHN circulation *flow*
SRKLT circlet *ornament*
SRKLT circulate *move in a circle* circulated circulating
SRKLTR circulator *move in a circle*
SRKLTR circulatory *blood*
SRKLTR sericulture *silk*
SRKLTRL sericultural *silk*
SRKLTRST sericulturist *silk*
SRKLTV circulative *flowing*
SRKM sarcoma *tumor* sarcomas
SRKM succumb *yield*
SRKMD sarcomata (pl) *tumor* sarcoma
SRKMFRNS circumference *perimeter*
SRKMFRNTS circumference *perimeter*
SRKMK seriocomic *serious and comic*
SRKMLKSHN circumlocution *wordiness*

SRKMLKYSHN circumlocution *wordiness*
SRKMLQSHN circumlocution *wordiness*
SRKMMBLT circumambulate *walk in circles* circumambulated circumambulating
SRKMMBNT circumambient *encompassing*
SRKMMBYLT circumambulate *walk in circles* circumambulated circumambulating
SRKMMBYNT circumambient *encompassing*
SRKMNVGDR circumnavigator *go around*
SRKMNVGSHN circumnavigation *go around*
SRKMNVGT circumnavigate *go around* circumnavigated circumnavigating
SRKMNVGTR circumnavigator *go around*
SRKMPFRNS circumference *perimeter*
SRKMPFRNTS circumference *perimeter*
SRKMR sarcomere *muscle*
SRKMSKRB circumscribe *limit*
SRKMSKRPSHN circumscription *limit*
SRKMSPK circumspect *cautious*
SRKMSPKT circumspect *cautious*
SRKMSSHN circumcision *cut sex organ*
SRKMSTNCHL circumstantial (adj) *incidental* circumstantially (adv)
SRKMSTNS circumstance *occurrence*

Use letters that best describe the sounds you hear and omit the vowels. Use **S** or **K** instead of **C**: to find circle use **SRKL**. Use **J** to find joy, **JM** to find gem and **G** to find go.

SRKMSTNSHL circumstantial (adj) *incidental* circumstantially (adv)
SRKMSTNTS circumstance *occurrence*
SRKMSZ circumcise *cut sex organ* circumcised circumcising
SRKMSZHN circumcision *cut sex organ*
SRKMSZR circumciser *cut sex organ*
SRKMT sarcomata (pl) *tumor* sarcoma
SRKMTCZ sarcomatoses (pl) *tumor* sarcomatosis
SRKMTS sarcomatous *tumor*
SRKMTSS sarcomatosis *tumor* sarcomatoses
SRKMTSZ sarcomatoses (pl) *tumor* sarcomatosis
SRKMVNCHN circumvention *get around*
SRKMVNSHN circumvention *get around*
SRKMVNT circumvent *get around*
SRKPLZM sarcoplasm *muscle*
SRKPLZMK sarcoplasmic *muscle*
SRKRM sour cream *milk product*
SRKRT sauerkraut *food*
SRKS cercus *sensor* cerci
SRKS circus *entertainment* circuses
SRKS Syracuse *city*
SRKSDK sarcastic *irony*
SRKSDKL sarcastically *irony*
SRKSM sarcosome *muscle*
SRKSML sarcosomal *muscle*
SRKSTK sarcastic *irony*
SRKSTKL sarcastically *irony*
SRKT circuit *route, electricity*
SRKTBRKR circuit breaker *electricity*

SRKTR circuitry *electricity* circuitries
SRKTS circuitous *winding*
SRKTSL circuitously *winding*
SRKTSNS circuitousness *winding*
SRKWDS circuitous *winding*
SRKWDSL circuitously *winding*
SRKWDSNS circuitousness *winding*
SRKWTS circuitous *winding*
SRKWTSL circuitously *winding*
SRKWTSNS circuitousness *winding*
SRKYDS circuitous *winding*
SRKYDSL circuitously *winding*
SRKYDSNS circuitousness *winding*
SRKYLDR circulator *move in a circle*
SRKYLDV circulative *flowing*
SRKYLR circular *round*
SRKYLRZ circularize *publicize* circularized circularizing (Br) circularise
SRKYLSHN circulation *flow*
SRKYLT circulate *move in a circle* circulated circulating
SRKYLTR circulator *move in a circle*
SRKYLTR circulatory *blood*
SRKYLTV circulative *flowing*
SRKYS Syracuse *city*
SRKYTS circuitous *winding*
SRKYTSL circuitously *winding*
SRKYTSNS circuitousness *winding*
SRKYWDS circuitous *winding*
SRKYWDSL circuitously *winding*
SRKYWDSNS circuitousness *winding*
SRKYWTS circuitous

winding
SRKYWTSL circuitously *winding*
SRKYWTSNS circuitousness *winding*
SRKYZ Syracuse *city*
SRKZ Syracuse *city*
SRKZM sarcasm *irony*
SRL acerola *shrub*
SRL cereal *grain*
SRL saurel *fish*
SRL seraglio *harem* seraglios
SRL seral *ecology*
SRL serial *series*
SRL sorely *very*
SRL sorrel *color, horse, plant*
SRL sorrily *sad, bad*
SRL surly *rude* surlier surliest
SRL surreal (adj) *dreamlike* surreally (adv)
SRLG serology *serum*
SRLJ serology *serum*
SRLJK serologic (or) serological (adj) *serum* serologically (adv)
SRLJKL serological (or) serologic (adj) *serum* serologically (adv)
SRLJST serologist *serum*
SRLKTH cerecloth *body wrap*
SRLN cerulean *sky blue*
SRLN Sierra Leone *country*
SRLN sirloin *meat*
SRLNGK Sri Lanka *country*
SRLNK Sri Lanka *country*
SRLNS surliness *rudeness*
SRLR surlier *rude*
SRLSDK surrealistic *dreamlike*
SRLSDKL surrealistically *dreamlike*
SRLST serialist *writer*
SRLST surliest *rude*
SRLST surrealist *artist*
SRLSTK surrealistic *dreamlike*
SRLSTKL surrealistically *dreamlike*
SRLY seraglio *harem*

Letters aren't doubled for single sounds: to find alley use **L** not **LL**. Use **Y** and **W** as hard sounds only: to find yellow use **YL**. (Br)=British spelling or usage. * See dictionary.

seraglios
SRLYN cerulean *sky blue*
SRLYN Sierra Leone *country*
SRLYR surlier *rude*
SRLYST surliest *rude*
SRLZ serialize *arrange*
serialized serializing
(Br) serialise
SRLZM serialism *music*
SRLZM surrealism *fantasy*
SRM cerium *element*
SRM serum *drug* serums
(or) sera
SRMK ceramic *pottery*
SRMN ceremony *ritual*
ceremonies
SRMN cerumen *earwax*
SRMN sermon *speech*
SRMNBL surmountable
overcome
SRMNL ceremonial (adj)
ritual ceremonially (adv)
SRMNS ceremonious *ritual*
SRMNS ceruminous *earwax*
SRMNSL ceremoniously
ritual
SRMNSNS
ceremoniousness *ritual*
SRMNT cerement *shroud*
SRMNT sermonette *speech*
SRMNT surmount *overcome*
SRMNTBL surmountable
overcome
SRMNYL ceremonial (adj)
ritual ceremonially (adv)
SRMNYS ceremonious
ritual
SRMNYSL ceremoniously
ritual
SRMNYSNS
ceremoniousness *ritual*
SRMNZ sermonize *lecture*
sermonized sermonizing
SRMS surmise *guess*
surmised surmising
SRMSH sour mash *whiskey*
SRMT surmount *overcome*
SRMTBL surmountable
overcome
SRMZ surmise *guess*
surmised surmising
SRN saran *resin*

SRN sarin *chemical*
SRN saurian *reptile*
SRN serene *calm*
SRN serrano *pepper*
serranos
SRN sierran (*often*
capitalized) *mountains*
SRN siren (*n*) *temptress,*
alarm, amphibian (adj)
enticing
SRN soaring *flying*
SRN surround (*v*) *encircle* (*n*)
border
SRND serenade (*v*) *sing* (*n*)
song serenaded
serenading
SRND serenity *calmness*
SRND serranid *fish*
SRND surround (*v*) *encircle*
(*n*) *border*
SRNDBRJRK Cyrano de
Bergerac *poet*
SRNDBRSHRK Cyrano de
Bergerac *poet*
SRNDBRZHRK Cyrano de
Bergerac *poet*
SRNDNGS surroundings
environment
SRNDNGZ surroundings
environment
SRNDNS surroundings
environment
SRNDNZ surroundings
environment
SRNDPD serendipity *luck*
SRNDPDS serendipitous
lucky
SRNDPDSL serendipitously
lucky
SRNDPT serendipity *luck*
SRNDPTS serendipitous
lucky
SRNDPTSL serendipitously
lucky
SRNDR surrender *give up*
SRNG sarong *dress*
SRNG soaring *flying*
SRNG syringa *plant*
SRNGD Serengeti *plain*
SRNGG syringa *plant*
SRNGT Serengeti *plain*
SRNJ syringe *inject, irrigate*

syringed syringing
SRNL serenely *calm*
SRNM Surinam *country*
SRNM surname *family name*
or last name
SRNN sirenian *mammal*
SRNS sereneness *calmness*
SRNS soreness *pain*
SRNS sorriness *sad, bad*
SRNT serenity *calmness*
SRNYN sirenian *mammal*
SRP serape *cloak*
SRP syrup *thick fluid*
SRP usurp *seize*
SRPD sauropod *dinosaur*
SRPDV sorptive *absorb*
SRPJNS serpiginous
creeping
SRPLNT supplant *replace*
SRPLS surplice (*n*) *cloak*
(*adj*) *neckline*
SRPLS surplus *excess*
SRPLSJ surplusage *excess*
SRPNT serpent *snake*
SRPNTN serpentine
winding
SRPR usurper *seize*
SRPRZ surprise *astonish*
surprised surprising
SRPRZL surprisal
astonishment
SRPRZN surprising
astonishing
SRPRZNG surprising
astonishing
SRPRZNGL surprisingly
astonishing
SRPRZNL surprisingly
astonishing
SRPS sourpuss *grouch*
sourpusses
SRPS surpass *exceed*
SRPSBL surpassable *exceed*
SRPSHN sorption *absorb*
SRPSHN usurpation *seizure*
SRPSN surpassing
exceeding
SRPSNG surpassing
exceeding
SRPTSHS surreptitious
secret
SRPTSHSL surreptitiously

secret
SRPTV sorptive *absorb*
SRQDS circuitous *winding*
SRQDSL circuitously
winding
SRQDSNS circuitousness
winding
SRQLDR circulator *move in a circle*
SRQLDV circulative *flowing*
SRQLR circular *round*
SRQLRZ circularize
publicize circularized
circularizing
(Br) circularise
SRQLSHN circulation *flow*
SRQLT circulate *move in a circle* circulated
circulating
SRQLTR circulator *move in a circle*
SRQLTR circulatory *blood*
SRQLTV circulative *flowing*
SRQS Syracuse *city*
SRQTS circuitous *winding*
SRQTSL circuitously
winding
SRQTSNS circuitousness
winding
SRQWDS circuitous
winding
SRQWDSL circuitously
winding
SRQWDSNS circuitousness
winding
SRQWTS circuitous *winding*
SRQWTSL circuitously
winding
SRQWTSNS circuitousness
winding
SRQZ Syracuse *city*
SRR sorer *painful*
SRR sorrier *sad, bad*
SRRD sorority *women's club*
sororities
SRRL sororal *sisterly*
SRRT sororate *marriage*
SRRT sorority *women's club*
sororities
SRS cerci (pl) *sensor* cercus
SRS cereus *cactus*
SRS Circe *Greek myth*

SRS cirrus *arm, cloud* cirri
SRS scirrhous *tumor*
SRS serious *solemn, earnest*
SRS serosa *membrane*
SRS serous *watery*
SRS sorus *spore* sori
SRS source *origin*
SRSBK sourcebook *history*
SRSHN assertion *declaration*
SRSHN serration *notched*
SRSHS sericeous *hairy*
SRSKN saurischian *dinosaur*
SRSKR seersucker *fabric*
SRSKYN saurischian
dinosaur
SRSL seriously *earnest, severe*
SRSMKRD sursum corda
(often capitalized) worship
SRSMNDD serious-minded
solemn, earnest
SRSN sericin *protein*
SRSNS seriousness *solemn, earnest*
SRSNT sarcenet *fabric*
SRSPRL sarsaparilla *root*
SRSR sorcery *magic*
SRSRR sorcerer *wizard*
SRSRS sorceress *wizard (f)*
sorceresses
SRSS cirrhosis *liver disease*
cirrhoses
SRSS psoriasis *disease*
SRSS surcease *stop*
surceased surceasing
SRST sorest *painful*
SRST sorriest *sad, bad*
SRSZ surcease *stop*
surceased surceasing
SRT assert *declare*
SRT assort *classify*
SRT cerate *salve*
SRT seriate *arrange* seriated
seriating
(Br) serialise
SRT serrate *notch* serrated
serrating
SRT sort (v) *arrange* (n) *type*
SRT sort of *rather*
SRT sortie *attack*
SRTBL sortable *arrange*
SRTD assorted *varied*

SRTD serrated *notched*
SRTD sordid *filthy*
SRTDL assertedly *allegedly*
SRTF certify *confirm, license*
certified certifying
SRTFBL certifiable (adj)
assured certifiably (adv)
SRTFD certified *authorized*
SRTFDML certified mail
proof of delivery
SRTFKSHN certification
license
SRTFKT certificate (v)
authorize certificated
certificating
SRTFKT certificate (n)
document
SRTFKTR certificatory
authorized
SRTFR certifier *confirm, license*
SRTFYBL certifiable (adj)
assured certifiably (adv)
SRTFYR certifier *confirm, license*
SRTK cirrhotic *liver disease*
SRTK psoriatic *disease*
SRTKS surtax *extra fee*
surtaxes
SRTLJ sortilege *sorcery*
SRTMNT assortment *variety*
SRTN ascertain *learn*
SRTN certain *sure*
SRTNBL ascertainable
knowable
SRTND certainty *sureness*
certainties
SRTNL certainly *surely*
SRTNL serotinal *summer*
SRTNMNT ascertainment
discovery
SRTNN serotonin *chemical*
SRTNS serotinous *late seeding*
SRTNT certainty *sureness*
certainties
SRTP serotype *antigens*
SRTR sartorii (pl) *muscle*
sartorius
SRTR sorter *arranger*
SRTRL sartorial (adj)
clothing sartorially (adv)

Letters aren't doubled for single sounds: to find alley use **L** not **LL**. Use **Y** and **W** as hard sounds only: to find yellow use **YL**. (Br)=British spelling or usage. * See dictionary.

SRTRS sartorius *muscle* sartorii

SRTRY sartorii (pl) *muscle* sartorius

SRTRYL sartorial (adj) *clothing* sartorially (adv)

SRTRYS sartorius *muscle* sartorii

SRTSHN sortition *cast lots*

SRTTD certitude *certainty*

SRTTYD certitude *certainty*

SRTV assertive *agressive*

SRTV sort of *rather*

SRTVL assertively *agressively*

SRTVNS assertiveness *agressiveness*

SRTX surtax *extra fee* surtaxes

SRTZ sorites *logic* sorites

SRV serve *work for, bring, gratify** served serving

SRV survey *(n) poll (v) collect data* surveys

SRVCZ cervices (pl) *neck* cervix

SRVDR servitor *servant (m)*

SRVKL cervical *neck*

SRVKS cervix *neck* cervices (or) cervixes

SRVL serval *wildcat*

SRVL servile (adj) *slave* servilely (adv)

SRVL surveil *watch* surveilled surveilling

SRVLD servility *slavery*

SRVLNS servileness *slavery*

SRVLNS surveillance *watch*

SRVLNT surveillant *watcher*

SRVLNTS surveillance *watch*

SRVLT servility *slavery*

SRVMDR servomotor *power device*

SRVMKNZM servomechanism *power device*

SRVMTR servomotor *power device*

SRVN cervine *deer*

SRVN serving *helping*

SRVN surveying *land*

SRVNG serving *helping*

SRVNG surveying *land*

SRVNHD servanthood *service*

SRVNT servant *aide*

SRVNT sirvente (or) sirventes *song* sirventes

SRVNTHD servanthood *service*

SRVNTS Cervantes *writer*

SRVNTZ Cervantes *writer*

SRVR server *assistant*

SRVR surveyor *land*

SRVS service *(v) repair, mate* serviced servicing

SRVS service *(n) help, meeting, mating**

SRVSBL serviceable (adj) *useful* serviceably (adv)

SRVSBLD serviceability *usefulness*

SRVSBLT serviceability *usefulness*

SRVSDS cervicitis *inflammation*

SRVSMN serviceman *armed forces* servicemen

SRVSTS cervicitis *inflammation*

SRVSZ cervices (pl) *neck* cervix

SRVT serviette *(Br) napkin*

SRVTD servitude *slavery*

SRVTR servitor *servant (m)*

SRVTYD servitude *slavery*

SRVV survive *stay alive* survived surviving

SRVVBL survivable *stay alive*

SRVVBLD survivability *stay alive*

SRVVBLT survivability *stay alive*

SRVVL survival *stay alive*

SRVVLST survivalist *stay alive*

SRVVR survivor *stay alive*

SRVVRSHP survivorship *stay alive, legal right*

SRVX cervix *neck* cervices (or) cervixes

SRVYN surveying *land*

SRVYNG surveying *land*

SRVYR surveyor *land*

SRVYT serviette *(Br) napkin*

SRWD sourwood *tree*

SRY Syria *country*

SRYDK psoriatic *disease*

SRYKMK seriocomic *serious and comic*

SRYL cereal *grain*

SRYL serial *series*

SRYLSDK surrealistic *dreamlike*

SRYLSDKL surrealistically *dreamlike*

SRYLST serialist *writer*

SRYLST surrealist *artist*

SRYLSTK surrealistic *dreamlike*

SRYLSTKL surrealistically *dreamlike*

SRYLZ serialize *arrange* serialized serializing (Br) serialise

SRYLZM serialism *music*

SRYLZM surrealism *fantasy*

SRYM cerium *element*

SRYN saurian *reptile*

SRYR sorrier *sad, bad*

SRYS cereus *cactus*

SRYS serious *solemn, earnest*

SRYSL seriously *earnest, severe*

SRYSMNDD serious-minded *solemn, earnest*

SRYSNS seriousness *solemn, earnest*

SRYSS psoriasis *disease*

SRYST sorriest *sad, bad*

SRYT seriate *arrange* seriated seriating (Br) serialise

SRYTK psoriatic *disease*

SRZ Ceres *Roman goddess*

SRZ series *set, group* series

SRZ serosa *membrane*

SRZL serosal *membrane*

SS assess *estimate*

SS cease *stop* ceased ceasing

SS Isis *Egyptian goddess*

SS oasis *water* oases

SS osseous *bony*

Use letters that best describe the sounds you hear and omit the vowels. Use **S** or **K** instead of **C**: to find circle use **SRKL**. Use **J** to find joy, **JM** to find gem and **G** to find go.

SS sass *rude talk*
SS sassy *impudent, lively*
sassier sassiest
SS sauce *(v) season, sass*
sauced saucing
SS sauce *(n) gravy, liquor*
SS saucy *bold, gravy, smart*
saucier sauciest
SS say-so *authorization*
SS seesaw *(v) move up and*
down (n) plank
SS sis *sister*
SS sissy *timid, effeminate*
sissies
SS so-so *average*
SS SOS *call for help*
SS souse *drench, binge*
soused sousing
SS sycee *money*
SSBKS saucebox *sassy one*
SSBL assessable *estimable*
SSBT sauceboat *container*
SSBX saucebox *sassy one*
SSD cesta *basket*
SSD cesti *(pl) belt, glove*
cestus
SSD psocid *insect*
SSD seaside *coastal area*
SSD secede *pull out*
seceded seceding
SSD siesta *nap*
SSD Sioux City *city*
SSD society *group* societies
SSD suicide *kill oneself*
suicided suiciding
SSDD cestode *tapeworm*
SSDDS cystitis *bladder*
SSDK cystic *sac*
SSDKFBRSS cystic fibrosis
disease
SSDL societal *(adj) group*
societally *(adv)*
SSDL suicidal *(adj) kill*
oneself suicidally *(adv)*
SSDM system *group, order,*
method
SSDMDK systematic *orderly*
SSDMDKL systematically
orderly
SSDMDZSHN
systematization *order*
(Br) systematisation

SSDMK systemic *common*
SSDMLS systemless *no*
order
SSDMTK systematic *orderly*
SSDMTKL systematically
orderly
SSDMTZ systematize *order*
systematized
systematizing
(Br) systematise
SSDMTZR systematizer
order
(Br) systematiser
SSDMTZSHN
systematization *order*
(Br) systematisation
SSDMZ systemize *order*
systemized systemizing
SSDMZSHN
systematization *order*
(Br) systematisation
SSDN cysteine *amino acid*
SSDN cystine *amino acid*
SSDNNS sustenance
nourishment, support
SSDNNTS sustenance
nourishment, support
SSDNTS sustenance
nourishment, support
SSDR seceder *pull out*
SSDR sister *sibling*
SSDRHD sisterhood *society*
SSDRL sisterly *friendly*
SSDRN cistern *reservoir*
SSDRNL sister-in-law
relative sisters-in-law
SSDS cestus *belt* cesti
SSDSKP cystoscope
instrument
SSDSKPK cystoscopic
instrument
SSDTS cystitis *bladder*
SSDV associative *related*
SSFD sissified *timid,*
effeminate
SSFN Sisyphean (or)
Sisyphian *very difficult*
SSFN sousaphone *music*
SSFR cease-fire *no shooting*
SSFRS sassafras *plant*
SSFS Sisyphus *Greek myth*
SSFYN Sisyphean (or)

Sisyphian *very difficult*
SSFYR cease-fire *no*
shooting
SSG syzygy *in line* syzygies
SSGRM sociogram *chart*
SSH ice show *entertainment*
SSH sachet *scented bag*
SSH sash *band, door, window*
sashes
SSH sashay *strut*
SSH seiche *wave*
SSH sushi *food*
SSHBL satiable *satisfy*
SSHBL sociable (adj)
friendly sociably (adv)
SSHBLD sociability
neighborly
SSHBLNS sociableness
friendliness
SSHBLT sociability
neighborly
SSHDV associative *related*
SSHGRM sociogram *chart*
SSHKLCHRL sociocultural
(adj) *groups*
socioculturally (adv)
SSHKNMK socioeconomic
money
SSHL asocial *not friendly*
SSHL seashell *mollusk*
SSHL social (adj) *friendly,*
group socially (adv)
SSHLD sociality *mingling*
socialities
SSHLG sociology *group*
study
SSHLJ sociology *group*
study
SSHLJKL sociological (adj)
group study sociologically
(adv)
SSHLJST sociologist *group*
study
SSHLNGGWSDK
sociolinguistic *language*
SSHLNGGWSTK
sociolinguistic *language*
SSHLNGSDK
sociolinguistic *language*
SSHLNGSTK sociolinguistic
language
SSHLNGWSDK

Letters aren't doubled for single sounds: to find alley use **L** not **LL**. Use **Y** and **W** as hard
sounds only: to find yellow use **YL**. (Br)=British spelling or usage. * See dictionary.

sociolinguistic *language*
SSHLNGWSTK
sociolinguistic *language*
SSHLS socialize *mingle*
socialized socializing
(Br) socialise
SSHLSDK socialistic *state ownership*
SSHLSDKL socialistically *state ownership*
SSHLSKRD social security *entitlement*
SSHLSKRT social security *entitlement*
SSHLSKYRD social security *entitlement*
SSHLSKYRT social security *entitlement*
SSHLSQRD social security *entitlement*
SSHLSQRT social security *entitlement*
SSHLST socialist *state ownership*
SSHLSTK socialistic *state ownership*
SSHLSTKL socialistically *state ownership*
SSHLT socialite *prominent person*
SSHLT sociality *mingling* socialities
SSHLZ Seychelles *islands*
SSHLZ socialize *mingle* socialized socializing (Br) socialise
SSHLZM socialism *state ownership*
SSHLZSHN socialization *mingling* (Br) socialisation
SSHM sashimi *food*
SSHMTR sociometry *group study*
SSHMTRK sociometric *group study*
SSHN cession *yielding*
SSHN scission *cutting*
SSHN secession *pull out*
SSHN session *meeting*
SSHN Szechuan (or) Szechwan *Chinese*

SSHNG souchong *tea*
SSHPLDKL sociopolitical *groups and politics*
SSHPLTKL sociopolitical *groups and politics*
SSHPTH sociopath *mental illness*
SSHR caesura *pause* caesuras
SSHR seashore *beach*
SSHR seizure *grasp, spasm*
SSHRL caesural *pause*
SSHSHN association *group*
SSHSHN satiation *satisfy*
SSHSKSHL sociosexual *gender*
SSHSKSHWL sociosexual *gender*
SSHSXL sociosexual *gender*
SSHSXWL sociosexual *gender*
SSHT associate *(v) join* associated associating
SSHT associate *(n) partner, degree (adj) connected*
SSHT satiate *satisfy* satiated satiating
SSHTV associative *related*
SSHWKNMK socioeconomic *money*
SSHWN Szechuan (or) Szechwan *Chinese*
SSHYDV associative *related*
SSHYGRM sociogram *chart*
SSHYKLCHRL sociocultural (adj) *groups* socioculturally (adv)
SSHYKNMK socioeconomic *money*
SSHYLD sociality *mingling* socialities
SSHYLG sociology *group study*
SSHYLJ sociology *group study*
SSHYLJKL sociological (adj) *group study* sociologically (adv)
SSHYLJST sociologist *group study*
SSHYLNGGWSDK sociolinguistic *language*

SSHYLNGGWSTK sociolinguistic *language*
SSHYLNGSDK sociolinguistic *language*
SSHYLNGSTK sociolinguistic *language*
SSHYLNGWSDK sociolinguistic *language*
SSHYLNGWSTK sociolinguistic *language*
SSHYLT sociality *mingling* socialities
SSHYMTR sociometry *group study*
SSHYMTRK sociometric *group study*
SSHYPLDKL sociopolitical *groups and politics*
SSHYPLTKL sociopolitical *groups and politics*
SSHYPTH sociopath *mental illness*
SSHYSHN association *group*
SSHYSHN satiation *satisfy*
SSHYSKSHL sociosexual *gender*
SSHYSKSHWL sociosexual *gender*
SSHYT associate *(v) join* associated associating
SSHYT associate *(n) partner, degree (adj) connected*
SSHYT satiate *satisfy* satiated satiating
SSHYTV associative *related*
SSHYWKNMK socioeconomic *money*
SSJ sausage *meat*
SSJ syzygy *in line* syzygies
SSK seasick *nausea*
SSKCHWN Saskatchewan *river, province*
SSKLCHRL sociocultural (adj) *groups* socioculturally (adv)
SSKLTRL sociocultural (adj) *groups* socioculturally (adv)
SSKN siskin *bird*
SSKNMK socioeconomic

Use letters that best describe the sounds you hear and omit the vowels. Use **S** or **K** instead of **C**: to find circle use **SRKL**. Use **J** to find joy, **JM** to find gem and **G** to find go.

money
SSKNS seasickness *nausea*
SSKP seascape *view*
SSKT Sea Scout *youth*
SSKTN saskatoon *fruit*
SSKWCH Sasquatch *creature*
SSKWPDLN sesquipedalian *long words*
SSKWPDLYN sesquipedalian *long words*
SSKWRT sea squirt *sea animal*
SSKWSNTNL sesquicentennial *150 years*
SSKWSNTNR sesquicentenary *150 years*
SSKWSNTNYL sesquicentennial *150 years*
SSL saucily *bold, gravy, smart*
SSL scissile *cut*
SSL sessile *attached*
SSL Sicily *island*
SSL sisal *plant*
SSLG sea slug *sea animal*
SSLG sociology *group study*
SSLJ sociology *group study*
SSLJKL sociological (adj) *group study* sociologically (adv)
SSLJST sociologist *group study*
SSLK suslik *squirrel, color*
SSLN caecilian *animal*
SSLN Sicilian *of Sicily*
SSLNGGWSDK sociolinguistic *language*
SSLNGGWSTK sociolinguistic *language*
SSLNGSDK sociolinguistic *language*
SSLNGSTK sociolinguistic *language*
SSLNGWSDK sociolinguistic *language*
SSLNGWSTK sociolinguistic *language*

SSLS ceaseless *constant*
SSLSL ceaselessly *constantly*
SSLSNS ceaselessness *without pause*
SSLYN caecilian *animal*
SSLYN Sicilian *of Sicily*
SSLZ isosceles *triangle*
SSM sesame *seed*
SSMD sesamoid *bone*
SSMNT assessment *estimation*
SSMTR sociometry *group study*
SSMTRK sociometric *group study*
SSN assassin *killer*
SSNDR assassinator *killer*
SSNDSST cease and desist *stop*
SSNGK succinct *brief*
SSNGKL succinctly *briefly*
SSNGKNS succinctness *brief*
SSNGKT succinct *brief*
SSNGKTL succinctly *briefly*
SSNGKTNS succinctness *brief*
SSNGT succinct *brief*
SSNGTL succinctly *briefly*
SSNGTNS succinctness *brief*
SSNK sea snake *serpent*
SSNK succinct *brief*
SSNKL succinctly *briefly*
SSNKNS succinctness *brief*
SSNKT succinct *brief*
SSNKTL succinctly *briefly*
SSNKTNS succinctness *brief*
SSNS sauciness *bold, gravy, smart*
SSNSHN assassination *murder*
SSNT assassinate *kill* assassinated assassinating
SSNTR assassinator *killer*
SSP sysop *computer*
SSPDBL susceptible (adj) *prone to* susceptibly (adv)
SSPDBLD susceptibility

prone to susceptibilities
SSPDBLT susceptibility *prone to* susceptibilities
SSPDV susceptive *prone to*
SSPK suspect *(v) distrust, (n) criminal (adj) doubtful*
SSPKT suspect *(v) distrust, (n) criminal (adj) doubtful*
SSPL cesspool *sewage*
SSPLDKL sociopolitical *groups and politics*
SSPLTKL sociopolitical *groups and politics*
SSPN saucepan *pot*
SSPN suspend *hang, defer*
SSPNCHN suspension *hang, delay*
SSPND suspend *hang, defer*
SSPNDRS suspenders *trouser support*
SSPNDRZ suspenders *trouser support*
SSPNS suspense *anxiety*
SSPNSFL suspenseful (adj) *anxious* suspensefully (adv)
SSPNSFLNS suspensefulness *anxiety*
SSPNSHN suspension *hang, delay*
SSPNSR suspensor *cells*
SSPNSR suspensory *(adj) doubtful*
SSPNSR suspensory *(n) supporter* suspensories
SSPNSV suspensive *deferred, anxious*
SSPNTCHN suspension *hang, delay*
SSPNTS suspense *anxiety*
SSPNTSFL suspenseful (adj) *anxious* suspensefully (adv)
SSPNTSFLNS suspensefulness *anxiety*
SSPNTSHN suspension *hang, delay*
SSPNTSR suspensor *cells*
SSPNTSR suspensory *(adj) indecisive*
SSPNTSR suspensory *(n) supporter* suspensories

Letters aren't doubled for single sounds: to find alley use **L** not **LL**. Use **Y** and **W** as hard sounds only: to find yellow use **YL**. (Br)=British spelling or usage. * See dictionary.

SSPNTSV suspensive *deferred, anxious*
SSPR aeciospore *fungus*
SSPR suspire *sigh* suspired suspiring
SSPRL sarsaparilla *root*
SSPRSHN suspiration *sigh*
SSPSHN suspicion *mistrust*
SSPSHS suspicious *questionable*
SSPSHSL suspiciously *questionable*
SSPSHSNS suspiciousness *questionable*
SSPT cesspit *sewage*
SSPTBL susceptible (adj) *prone to* susceptibly (adv)
SSPTBLD susceptibility *prone to* susceptibilities
SSPTBLT susceptibility *prone to* susceptibilities
SSPTH sociopath *mental illness*
SSPTS caespitose *tufts*
SSPTV susceptive *prone to*
SSPTVD susceptivity *prone to* susceptivities
SSPTVT susceptivity *prone to* susceptivities
SSPTZ caespitose *tufts*
SSQCH Sasquatch *creature*
SSQPDLN sesquipedalian *long words*
SSQPDLYN sesquipedalian *long words*
SSQRT sea squirt *sea animal*
SSQSNTNL sesquicentennial *150 years*
SSQSNTNR sesquicentenary *150 years*
SSQSNTNYL sesquicentennial *150 years*
SSR accessory *adjunct* accessories
SSR assessor *valuer*
SSR Cicero *Roman ruler*
SSR sassier *impudent, lively*
SSR saucer *plate*
SSR saucier *bold, gravy, smart*
SSRDDL sacerdotal (adj) *priestly* sacerdotally (adv)
SSRDDLST sacerdotalist *priest*
SSRDDLZM sacerdotalism *priest*
SSRDTL sacerdotal (adj) *priestly* sacerdotally (adv)
SSRDTLST sacerdotalist *priest*
SSRDTLZM sacerdotalism *priest*
SSRN Caesarean *birth*
SSRN cicerone *guide* ciceroni
SSRNSKSHN Caesarean section *birth*
SSRNT susurrant *whisper*
SSRPNT sea serpent *creature*
SSRS susurrus (n) *whisper* susurrous (adj)
SSRSHN susurration *whisper*
SSRYN Caesarean *birth*
SSRYNSKSHN Caesarean section *birth*
SSRZ accessorize *add supplement(s)* accessorized accessorizing (Br) accessorise
SSSHN association *group*
SSSHN cessation *stop*
SSSHN secession *pull out*
SSSHNST secessionist *pull out*
SSSKSHL sociosexual *gender*
SSSKSHWL sociosexual *gender*
SSST sassiest *impudent, lively*
SSST sauciest *bold, gravy, smart*
SSSXL sociosexual *gender*
SSSXWL sociosexual *gender*
SST assist *help*
SST associate (v) *join* associated associating
SST associate (n) *partner, degree* (adj) connected
SST cesta *basket*
SST cesti (pl) *belt, glove* cestus
SST cyst *sac*
SST essayist *writer*
SST iciest *frozen*
SST oocyst *cell*
SST siesta *nap*
SST Sioux City *city*
SST society *group* societies
SSTD cestode *tapeworm*
SSTDS cystitis *bladder*
SSTK cystic *sac*
SSTKFBRSS cystic fibrosis *disease*
SSTL societal (adj) *group* societally (adv)
SSTL systole *contraction*
SSTLDK systaltic *pulsing*
SSTLK systolic *pulsing*
SSTLTK systaltic *pulsing*
SSTM system *group, order, method*
SSTMDK systematic *orderly*
SSTMDKL systematically *orderly*
SSTMDKS systematics *classification*
SSTMDX systematics *classification*
SSTMDZSHN systematization *order* (Br) systematisation
SSTMK systemic *common*
SSTMLS systemless *no order*
SSTMTK systematic *orderly*
SSTMTKL systematically *orderly*
SSTMTKS systematics *classification*
SSTMTX systematics *classification*
SSTMTZ systematize *order* systematized systematizing (Br) systematise
SSTMTZR systematizer *order* (Br) systematiser
SSTMTZSHN

Use letters that best describe the sounds you hear and omit the vowels. Use **S** or **K** instead of **C**: to find circle use **SRKL**. Use **J** to find joy, **JM** to find gem and **G** to find go.

systematization *order*
(Br) systematisation
SSTMZ systemize *order*
systemized systemizing
SSTMZSHN
systematization *order*
(Br) systematisation
SSTN cysteine *amino acid*
SSTN cystine *amino acid*
SSTN sestina *verse*
SSTN sustain *nourish,*
support, confirm
SSTNBL sustainable
nourish, support, confirm
SSTNBLD sustainability
nourish, support, confirm
SSTNBLT sustainability
nourish, support, confirm
SSTND sostenuto *music*
SSTNNS sustenance
nourishment, support
SSTNNTS sustenance
nourishment, support
SSTNR sustainer *nourish,*
support, confirm
SSTNS assistance *help*
SSTNT assistant *helper*
SSTNT sostenuto *music*
SSTNTDV sustentative
support
SSTNTS assistance *help*
SSTNTS sustenance
nourishment, support
SSTNTSHN sustentation
support
SSTNTTV sustentative
support
SSTR sea star *starfish*
SSTR sister *sibling*
SSTRHD sisterhood *society*
SSTRL sisterly *friendly*
SSTRN cistern *reservoir*
SSTRN seastrand *seashore*
SSTRND seastrand *seashore*
SSTRNL sister-in-law
relative sisters-in-law
SSTS cestus *belt* cesti
SSTSKP cystoscope
instrument
SSTSKPK cystoscopic
instrument
SSTT sestet *six lines*

SSTTS cystitis *bladder*
SSTV associative *related*
SSWKNMK socioeconomic
money
SSYD society *group*
societies
SSYDL societal (adj) *group*
societally (adv)
SSYDV associative *related*
SSYGRM sociogram *chart*
SSYKLCHRL sociocultural
(adj) *groups*
socioculturally (adv)
SSYKNMK socioeconomic
money
SSYLG sociology *group*
study
SSYLJ sociology *group*
study
SSYLJKL sociological (adj)
group study sociologically
(adv)
SSYLJST sociologist *group*
study
SSYLNGGWSDK
sociolinguistic *language*
SSYLNGGWSTK
sociolinguistic *language*
SSYLNGSDK
sociolinguistic *language*
SSYLNGSTK sociolinguistic
language
SSYLNGWSDK
sociolinguistic *language*
SSYLNGWSTK
sociolinguistic *language*
SSYMTR sociometry *group*
study
SSYMTRK sociometric
group study
SSYN Sicilian *of Sicily*
SSYPLDKL sociopolitical
groups and politics
SSYPLTKL sociopolitical
groups and politics
SSYPTH sociopath *mental*
illness
SSYR sassier *impudent,*
lively
SSYR saucier *bold, gravy,*
smart
SSYSHN association *group*

SSYSKSHL sociosexual
gender
SSYSKSHWL sociosexual
gender
SSYST sassiest *impudent,*
lively
SSYST sauciest *bold, gravy,*
smart
SSYT associate (v) *join*
associated associating
SSYT associate (n) *partner,*
degree (adj) *connected*
SSYT society *group*
societies
SSYTL societal (adj) *group*
societally (adv)
SSYTV associative *related*
SSYWKNMK
socioeconomic *money*
ST asked (v-past) *ask*
ST asset *property*
ST cite *quote, summon* cited
citing
ST city *town* cities
ST east *direction*
ST East *region*
ST eyesight *vision*
ST ice-out *thaw*
ST oast *oven*
ST oocyte *egg*
ST ostia (pl) *mouth* ostium
ST oust *eject*
ST sate *fill* sated sating
ST sauté *cook* sautéed (or)
sautéd sautéing
ST seat *chair*
ST set (v) *put, fix, arrange*
set setting
ST set (n) *group, bent, score**
ST set to (v) *begin*
ST set-to (n) *debate, fight*
set-tos
ST seta *bristle* setae
ST settee *sofa*
ST sight *vision*
ST sit (v) *rest* sat sitting
ST sit (n) *fit, seat*
ST site (v) *locate* sited siting
ST site (n) *area*
ST soot *carbon*
ST sooty *black* sootier
sootiest

Letters aren't doubled for single sounds: to find alley use **L** not **LL**. Use **Y** and **W** as hard
sounds only: to find yellow use **YL**. (Br)=British spelling or usage. * See dictionary.

ST sot *drunkard*

ST sought *(v-past) seek*

ST stay *(v) remain, secure, sustain (n) halting, support*

ST stew *(n) food (v) cook, worry*

ST stoa *porch*

ST stow *store, load*

ST sty *(n) pigpen* sties

ST sty *(v) pen* stied *(or)* styed stying sties

ST sty *(or)* stye *(n) eyelid sore* sties *(or)* styes

ST suet *fat*

ST suit *set, clothes*

ST suite *set, group, music**

ST suttee *widow*

STB stab *(v) pierce* stabbed stabbing

STB stab *(n) try, thrust*

STB stub *(v) grub up, put out* stubbed stubbing

STB stub *(n) remnant*

STB stubby *short and thick* stubbier stubbiest

STBK setback (n) *reverse, delay* set back (v)

STBL acetabula (pl) *sucker, hipbone* acetabulum

STBL citable *quote, summon*

STBL side table *furniture*

STBL stabile *(n) sculpture (adj) stable*

STBL stable *(n, v) barn* stabled stabling

STBL stable *(adj) firm, even* stabler stablest

STBL stably *firmly*

STBL stubble *growth*

STBL stubbly *with growth*

STBL suitable (adj) *fit* suitably (adv)

STBLD stability *firm, even* stabilities

STBLD stubbled *with growth*

STBLD suitability *fitness*

STBLM acetabulum *sucker, hipbone* acetabulums (or) acetabula

STBLMT stablemate *animal*

STBLN stabling *barn*

STBLNG stabling *barn*

STBLNS stableness *firm*

STBLR acetabular *sucker, hipbone*

STBLR stabler *firm*

STBLSH establish *set up, prove*

STBLSHBL establishable *set up, prove*

STBLSHD established *set up, proven*

STBLSHMNT establishment *business, social order*

STBLSHMNTRN establishmentarian *social order*

STBLSHMNTRNZM establishmentarianism *social order*

STBLSHR establisher *set up, prove*

STBLSHT established *set up, proven*

STBLST osteoblast *cell*

STBLST stablest *firm*

STBLT seat belt *restraint*

STBLT stability *firm, even* stabilities

STBLT suitability *fitness*

STBLZ stabilize *make firm* stabilized stabilizing

STBLZR stabilizer *make firm*

STBLZSHN stabilization *make firm*

STBN eastbound *direction*

STBND eastbound *direction*

STBNT stibnite *mineral*

STBR stabber *thrust*

STBR stubbier *short and thick*

STBRN stubborn *mulish*

STBRNL stubbornly *mulishly*

STBRNS stubbornness *mulishness*

STBST stubbiest *short and thick*

STBYL acetabula (pl) *sucker, hipbone* acetabulum

STBYLM acetabulum *sucker, hipbone* acetabulums (or) acetabula

STBYLR acetabular *sucker, hipbone*

STBYR stubbier *short and thick*

STBYST stubbiest *short and thick*

STC sightsee *tour* sightsaw sightseeing

STCH statue *sculpture*

STCH stitch *sew* stitches

STCHNC East China Sea *body of water*

STCHNS East China Sea *body of water*

STCHR statuary *sculpture* statuaries

STCHR stature *height*

STCHR stitcher *sewer*

STCHR stitchery *sewing*

STCHSK statuesque *shapely*

STCHT statuette *sculpture*

STCHT statute *law*

STCHTR statutory *legal*

STCHTRL statutorily *legal*

STCHWR statuary *sculpture* statuaries

STCHWRT stitchwort *plant*

STCHWSK statuesque *shapely*

STCHWT statuette *sculpture*

STCN psittacine *parrots*

STCN sight-seeing (adj, n) *touring* sightseeing (v)

STCN sightseeing

STCNG sight-seeing (adj, n) *touring* sightseeing (v)

STCNG sightseeing

STCR sightseer *tourist*

STCYN sight-seeing (adj, n) *touring* sightseeing (v)

STCYNG sight-seeing (adj, n) *touring* sightseeing (v)

STCYR sightseer *tourist*

STCZ stases (pl) *slowing* stasis

STD cited *quote, summon*

STD satiety *fullness*

STD sighted *not blind*

STD stadia *survey*

STD stadia (pl) *arena* stadium

STD staid *sober*

STD stead *advantage*

Use letters that best describe the sounds you hear and omit the vowels. Use **S** or **K** instead of **C**: to find circle use **SRKL**. Use **J** to find joy, **JM** to find gem and **G** to find go.

STD steady (v) make firm steadied steadying steadies

STD steady (adj) fixed, uniform, dependable* steadier steadiest steadily steadiness

STD steed horse

STD stood (v-past) stand

STD stud (v) nail, decorate studded studding

STD stud (n) horse, guy, timber*

STD studio workroom studios

STD study (v) consider studied studying studies

STD study (n) room, consideration studies

STDBK studbook breeding

STDBL statable (or) stateable report

STDD stated spoken

STDD studied thoughtful

STDFS steadfast faithful

STDFST steadfast faithful

STDHL study hall classroom

STDHRS studhorse stallion

STDK ecstatic overjoyed

STDK static (adj) stationary, electrostatic (n) noise, opposition

STDK staticky noisy

STDKL ecstatically overjoyed

STDKL statical (adj) not moving, electrostatic statically (adv)

STDKS statics mechanics

STDL citadel fortress

STDL staidly sober

STDL steadily continuous

STDM stadium arena stadia (or) stadiums

STDN sit-down meal, no work

STDN studding wall

STDNG studding wall

STDNGSL studding sail ship

STDNS staidness sober

STDNS steadiness continuous movement or strength

STDNT student learner

STDPKR stud poker game

STDR stator machine part

STDR steadier firmer

STDR stutter speech

STDRR stutterer speech

STDS statice plant

STDS status condition, rank statuses

STDS studious careful

STDSKW status quo state of affairs

STDSM statism central control

STDSQ status quo state of affairs

STDSST statocyst balance

STDST statist central control

STDST steadiest firmest

STDSTSHN statistician mathematician

STDV stative condition

STDX statics mechanics

STDY stadia survey

STDY stadia (pl) arena stadium

STDY studio workroom studios

STDYM stadium arena stadia (or) stadiums

STDYR steadier firmer

STDYS studious careful

STDYST steadiest firmest

STDZM statism central control

STF acetify sour acetifies acetified acetifying

STF acidify make acid acidifies acidified acidifying

STF citify urbanize citified citifying cities

STF set off (v) leave

STF setoff (n) decoration

STF staff rod, music, personnel*

STF staph infection

STF stiff (adj) rigid (n) corpse, fellow (adv) severely (v) cheat

STF stuff (v) pack (n) materials

STF stuffy airless, haughty stuffier stuffiest

STFD citified urbanized

STFKSHN acetification sour

STFKSHN acidification making acid

STFKT certificate (v) authorize certificated certificating

STFKT certificate (n) document

STFL stifle muffle, deter stifled stifling

STFL stuffily airless, snobbish

STFLK cytophilic cell affinity

STFLKK staphylococci (pl) bacteria staphylococcus

STFLKKL staphylococcal bacteria

STFLKKS staphylococci (pl) bacteria staphylococcus

STFLKKS staphylococcus bacteria staphylococci

STFLKKSK staphylococcic bacteria

STFLKXK staphylococcic bacteria

STFLNGL stiflingly suffocating

STFLR stifler muffle, deter

STFN stiffen make rigid

STFN stuffing food, material

STFNBKS stuffing box no leaks

STFNBX stuffing box no leaks

STFNG stuffing food, material

STFNGBKS stuffing box no leaks

STFNGBX stuffing box no leaks

STFNKT stiff-necked haughty

STFNR stiffener starch

STFNS stuffiness airless, snobbish

STFR staffer worker

STFR stuffer one that stuffs

STFR stuffier airless, snobbish

STFRM stiff-arm ward off

STFSHRT stuffed shirt pompous one

Letters aren't doubled for single sounds: to find alley use **L** not **LL**. Use **Y** and **W** as hard sounds only: to find yellow use **YL**. (Br)=British spelling or usage. * See dictionary.

STFSRJNT staff sergeant *rank*

STFST stuffiest *airless, snobbish*

STFTSHRT stuffed shirt *pompous one*

STFYR stuffier *airless, snobbish*

STFYST stuffiest *airless, snobbish*

STG stag *(n) deer (adj) male* stags (or) stag

STG staggy *male*

STG stagy *theatrical* stagier stagiest

STG stodgy *heavy, drab* stodgier stodgiest

STG stogie (or) stogy *cigar* stogies

STGFLSHN stagflation *economics*

STGHND staghound *dog*

STGHRN staghorn *antlers*

STGM stigma *stain* stigmata (or) stigmas

STGMD stigmata (pl) *stain* stigma

STGMDK astigmatic *vision*

STGMDK stigmatic *stain*

STGMDKLY stigmatically *stain*

STGMDZSHN stigmatization *stain*

STGMT stigmata (pl) *stain* stigma

STGMTK astigmatic *vision*

STGMTK stigmatic *stain*

STGMTKL stigmatically *stain*

STGMTST stigmatist *stained one*

STGMTZ stigmatize *stain* stigmatized stigmatizing

STGMTZM astigmatism *vision*

STGMTZSHN stigmatization *stain*

STGN stygian *gloomy*

STGNK osteogenic *bone*

STGNNC stagnancy *stale*

STGNNS stagnancy *stale*

STGNNT stagnant *stale*

STGNNTC stagnancy *stale*

STGNNTL stagnantly *stale*

STGNNTS stagnancy *stale*

STGNS staginess *theatrical*

STGNS stodginess *heavy, drab*

STGNSHN stagnation *staleness*

STGNSS osteogenesis *bone*

STGNT stagnate *get stale* stagnated stagnating

STGR stagger *totter* staggered staggering

STGR stagier *theatrical*

STGR stodgier *heavy, drab*

STGRBSH staggerbush *plant*

STGRN staggering *overwhelming*

STGRNG staggering *overwhelming*

STGRNGL staggeringly *overwhelming*

STGRNL staggeringly *overwhelming*

STGRR staggerer *totterer*

STGSR stegosaur *dinosaur*

STGSRS stegosaurus *dinosaur*

STGST stagiest *theatrical*

STGST stodgiest *heavy, drab*

STGYN stygian *gloomy*

STGYR stagier *theatrical*

STGYR stodgier *heavy, drab*

STGYST stagiest *theatrical*

STGYST stodgiest *heavy, drab*

STH saithe *fish* saithe

STH scythe *(v) cut* scythed scything

STH scythe *(n) cutter*

STH seethe *churn* seethed seething

STH sooth *truth*

STH soothe *comfort* soothed soothing

STH south *direction*

STH South *region*

STHBN southbound *direction*

STHBND southbound *direction*

STHCHNC South China Sea *body of water*

STHCHNS South China Sea *body of water*

STHDK aesthetic (or) aesthetical *artistic*

STHDKD South Dakota *US State*

STHDKL aesthetical (or) aesthetic (adj) *artistic* aesthetically (adv)

STHDKS aesthetics *philosophy of beauty*

STHDKT South Dakota *US State*

STHDSZ aestheticize *make beautiful* aestheticized aestheticizing

STHDSZM aestheticism *beauty*

STHDX aesthetics *philosophy of beauty*

STHFRK South Africa *country*

STHKR South Korea *country*

STHKRLN South Carolina *US State*

STHKRY South Korea *country*

STHLN southland *(often capitalized) region*

STHLND southland *(often capitalized) region*

STHMN isthmian *inhabitant*

STHMRK South America *continent*

STHMS isthmus *strip of land* isthmuses

STHN asthenia *weakness*

STHN seething *hot, churning*

STHN soothing *comforting*

STHN southern *direction*

STHN southing *direction*

STHNG seething *hot, churning*

STHNG soothing *comforting*

STHNG southing *direction*

STHNGL soothingly *comforting*

STHNGNS soothingness *comforting*

Use letters that best describe the sounds you hear and omit the vowels. Use **S** or **K** instead of **C**: to find circle use **SRKL**. Use **J** to find joy, **JM** to find gem and **G** to find go.

STHNK asthenic *weak*

STHNL soothingly *comforting*

STHNMST southernmost *south edge*

STHNR Southerner *South resident*

STHNS soothingness *comforting*

STHNWD southernwood *shrub*

STHNY asthenia *weakness*

STHP southpaw *left-handed*

STHPL South Pole *region*

STHR see-through *transparent*

STHRL southerly *direction* southerlies

STHRM isotherm *temperature*

STHRML isothermal *temperature*

STHRN southern *direction*

STHRNMST southernmost *south edge*

STHRNR Southerner *South resident*

STHRNWD southernwood *shrub*

STHS soothsay *predict*

STHSDR southeaster *wind*

STHSDRL southeasterly *direction*

STHSDRN southeastern *direction*

STHSN soothsaying *predict*

STHSNG soothsaying *predict*

STHSR soothsayer *predict*

STHST southeast *direction*

STHST Southeast *region*

STHSTHST south-southeast *direction*

STHSTHWST south-southwest *direction*

STHSTR southeaster *wind*

STHSTRL southeasterly *direction*

STHSTRN southeastern *direction*

STHSTWRD southeastward *direction*

STHSWRD southeastward *direction*

STHSYN soothsaying *predict*

STHSYNG soothsaying *predict*

STHSYR soothsayer *predict*

STHT aesthete *beauty lover*

STHTK aesthetic (or) aesthetical *artistic*

STHTKL aesthetical (or) aesthetic (adj) *artistic* aesthetically (adv)

STHTKS aesthetics *philosophy of beauty*

STHTSHN aesthetician *artist*

STHTSZ aestheticize *make beautiful* aestheticized aestheticizing

STHTSZM aestheticism *beauty*

STHTX aesthetics *philosophy of beauty*

STHWRD southward *direction*

STHWSDR southwester *wind*

STHWSDRL southwesterly *direction*

STHWSDRN southwestern *direction*

STHWST southwest *direction*

STHWST Southwest *region*

STHWSTR southwester *wind*

STHWSTRL southwesterly *direction*

STHWSTRN southwestern *direction*

STHWSTWRD southwestward *direction*

STJ stage (n) *step, carriage, theatre*

STJ stage (v) *create for effect* staged staging

STJ stagy *theatrical* stagier stagiest

STJ stodge (Br) *fill up* stodged stodging

STJ stodgy *heavy, drab*

stodgier stodgiest

STJ stooge *puppet* stooged stooging

STJ stowage *cargo*

STJFRT stage fright *nervousness*

STJHN stagehand *theater*

STJHND stagehand *theater*

STJKCH stagecoach *vehicle* stagecoaches

STJKRF stagecraft *theater*

STJKRFT stagecraft *theater*

STJL stagily *theatrical*

STJL stodgily *heavy, drab*

STJN staging *scaffolding, theater, troops**

STJN stygian *gloomy*

STJNG staging *scaffolding, theater, troops**

STJNK osteogenic *bone*

STJNS staginess *theatrical*

STJNS stodginess *heavy, drab*

STJNSS osteogenesis *bone*

STJR stagier *theatrical*

STJR stodgier *heavy, drab*

STJST stagiest *theatrical*

STJST stodgiest *heavy, drab*

STJSTRK stagestruck *acting*

STJYN stygian *gloomy*

STJYR stagier *theatrical*

STJYR stodgier *heavy, drab*

STJYST stagiest *theatrical*

STJYST stodgiest *heavy, drab*

STK acetic *acid*

STK ascetic *severe*

STK eyestalk *vision*

STK isotach *wind speed*

STK sciatic *nerve*

STK sciatica *pain*

STK stack *pile*

STK stake (n) *share, post*

STK stake (v) *bet, mark limits, back* staked staking

STK stalk (n) *plant* (v) *pursue*

STK steak *meat*

STK stick (v) *adhere, stump, balk** stuck sticking

STK stick (n) *wood, club, stop**

STK sticky *adhesive, muggy, difficult* stickier stickiest

STK stock *(v)* supply *(n) animals, soup, finance (adj) standard, goods**

STK stocky *hefty* stockier stockiest

STK stoic (or) stoical *impassive*

STK stoke *feed, stir, fuel* stoked stoking

STK stucco *plaster* stuccos (or) stuccoes

STK stuck *(v-past) stick*

STKBL stackable *pile*

STKBL stickball *game*

STKBRDR stockbreeder *livestock*

STKBRKN stockbroking *finance*

STKBRKNG stockbroking *finance*

STKBRKR stockbroker *finance*

STKBRKRJ stockbrokerage *finance*

STKCD stickseed *herb*

STKD staccato *disjointed*

STKD stockade *prison* stockaded stockading

STKD stoked *exhilarated*

STKD stuccoed *plaster*

STKDK psittacotic *disease*

STKFSH stockfish *dried fish*

STKHL stokehold *boiler room*

STKHLD stokehold *boiler room*

STKHLDR stakeholder *bets*

STKHLDR stockholder *stocks*

STKHLM Stockholm *city*

STKHM Stockholm *city*

STKJBR stockjobber *finance*

STKKSCHNJ stock exchange *finance*

STKL ascetically *severely*

STKL stickle *scruple* stickled stickling

STKL stockily *hefty*

STKL stoical (or) stoic (adj) *impassive* stoically (adv)

STKL stokehold *boiler room*

STKLBK stickleback *fish*

STKLD stokehold *boiler room*

STKLDR stakeholder *bets*

STKLDR stockholder *stocks*

STKLR stickler *exactness, puzzle*

STKM sitcom *comedy*

STKM stickum *glue*

STKMN stickman *games*

STKMN stockman *livestock* stockmen

STKMRKT stock market *finance*

STKMTH stichomythia *dispute*

STKMTHK stichomythic *dispute*

STKMTHY stichomythia *dispute*

STKMTR stoichiometry *chemistry*

STKMTRK stoichiometric *chemistry*

STKMTRKL stoichiometrically *chemistry*

STKN cytokine *immunity*

STKN eustachian *ear tube*

STKN stocking *socks*

STKNDK cytokinetic *cell division*

STKNG stocking *socks*

STKNGHRS stalking-horse *masked purpose*

STKNHRS stalking-horse *masked purpose*

STKNN cytokinin *plant growth*

STKNS stickiness *adhesion, difficulty*

STKNS stockiness *hefty*

STKNSS cytokinesis *cell division*

STKNT stockinette (or) stockinet *fabric*

STKNTHMD stick-in-the-mud *no fun*

STKNTK cytokinetic *cell division*

STKNTRD stock-in-trade

equipment

STKP stick up *(v) protrude*

STKP stickup *(n) robbery*

STKP stuck-up *conceited*

STKPL stockpile *(v) gather* stockpiled stockpiling

STKPL stockpile *(n) supply*

STKPLR stockpiler *gatherer*

STKPN stickpin *necktie*

STKPR stockkeeper *herdsman*

STKPSHN stock option *contract*

STKPT stockpot *soup*

STKPYL stockpile *(v) gather* stockpiled stockpiling

STKPYL stockpile *(n) supply*

STKPYLR stockpiler *gatherer*

STKR stacker *pile*

STKR sticker *tag*

STKR stickier *adhesive, difficulty*

STKR stock car *automobile*

STKR stockier *hefty*

STKR stoker *furnace*

STKRM stockroom *storage*

STKS suitcase *luggage*

STKSD acetic acid *vinegar*

STKSD stickseed *herb*

STKSDK stochastic *random*

STKSHF stick shift *vehicle*

STKSHFT stick shift *vehicle*

STKSHN stiction *force*

STKSS psittacosis *disease*

STKST stickiest *adhesive, difficult*

STKST stockiest *hefty*

STKSTK stochastic *random*

STKSTL stock-still *no movement*

STKT staccato *disjointed*

STKT stakeout (n) *watch* stake out (v)

STKT stoked *exhilarated*

STKTDVNS stick-to-itiveness *persistence*

STKTK psittacotic *disease*

STKTK stocktake *inventory*

STKTKN stocktaking *inventory*

STKTKNG stocktaking

Use letters that best describe the sounds you hear and omit the vowels. Use **S** or **K** instead of **C**: to find circle use **SRKL**. Use **J** to find joy, **JM** to find gem and **G** to find go.

inventory

STKTT sticktight *flower*

STKTTVNS stick-to-itiveness *persistence*

STKTWDVNS stick-to-itiveness *persistence*

STKTWTVNS stick-to-itiveness *persistence*

STKWRK stuccowork *plaster*

STKXCHNJ stock exchange *finance*

STKYMTR stoichiometry *chemistry*

STKYMTRK stoichiometric *chemistry*

STKYMTRKL stoichiometrically *chemistry*

STKYN eustachian *ear tube*

STKYR stickier *adhesive, difficult*

STKYR stockier *hefty*

STKYRD stockyard *animals in a pen*

STKYST stickiest *adhesive, difficult*

STKYST stockiest *hefty*

STL acetal *aldehyde*

STL acetyl *acid*

STL eustele *plant stem*

STL ostiole *pore*

STL saddle *horse* saddled saddling

STL saw-whet owl *bird*

STL Seattle *city*

STL settle *(v) fix, adjust* settled settling

STL settle *(n) bench*

STL sightly *attractive*

STL sootily *black*

STL sotol *plant*

STL stale *(v) urinate, age* staled staling

STL stale *(adj) old* staler stalest

STL stall *(n) barn, no lift (v) hesitate*

STL steal *(v) rob, sneak* stole stealing stolen

STL steal *(n) bargain*

STL steel *(n) metal (v)*

strengthen

STL steelie *marble*

STL steely *hard and cold* steelier steeliest

STL stela *(or)* stele *pillar* stelae

STL stile *stair*

STL still *(adj) calm (adv) yet (n) distillery (v) distill, calm**

STL stilly *quietly*

STL stole *(v-past) steal (n) scarf*

STL stool *chair, feces, stump**

STL stoolie *spy*

STL style *manner, fashion* styled styling

STL styli *(pl) pen* stylus

STL subtle *slight, refined, crafty* subtler subtlest

STL subtly *slightly*

STLB saddlebow *front*

STLBG saddlebag *pouch*

STLBK stylebook *fashion*

STLBRD saddlebred *horse*

STLBRN stillborn *dead fetus*

STLBRTH stillbirth *dead fetus*

STLBSTRL stilbestrol *chemical*

STLBT stilbite *mineral*

STLD stiletto *dagger* stilettos *(or)* stilettoes

STLD stolid *unemotional*

STLD styloid *pointed*

STLD subtlety *slight, refined, crafty* subtleties

STLDD stilted *haughty*

STLDDL stiltedly *haughty*

STLDDNS stiltedness *haughtiness*

STLDHD acetaldehyde *chemical*

STLDK cytolytic *cell death*

STLDL stolidly *unemotional*

STLDT stolidity *unemotional*

STLDV acetylative *with acetyl*

STLF still life *picture* still lifes

STLFD stall-feed *fatten* stall-fed stall-feeding

STLFRM styliform *bristly*

STLG cetology *whale study*

STLG cytology *cell study*

STLG stalag *prison*

STLGMT stalagmite *cave (floor)*

STLGTT stalactite *cave (top)*

STLHD steelhead *trout* steelhead

STLHRN saddle horn *pommel*

STLHRS saddle horse *riding*

STLJ cetology *whale study*

STLJ cytology *cell study*

STLJST cetologist *whale study*

STLKLN acetylcholine *neurotransmitter*

STLKLNSTRS acetylcholinesterase *enzyme*

STLKLNSTRZ acetylcholinesterase *enzyme*

STLKLTH saddlecloth *horse*

STLKMT stalagmite *cave (floor)*

STLKTDK stalactitic *cave (top)*

STLKTT stalactite *cave (top)*

STLKTTK stalactitic *cave (top)*

STLMKN steelmaking *manufacture*

STLMKNG steelmaking *manufacture*

STLMKR steelmaker *manufacture*

STLMNT settlement *village, agreement*

STLMT stalemate *deadlock* stalemated stalemating

STLN acetylene *gas*

STLN Stalin *Russian leader*

STLN stolen *(v-past) steal*

STLN stollen *bread*

STLN stolon *branch*

STLNFRS stoloniferous *branches*

STLNS sightliness *attractive*

STLNS subtleness *slight, refined, crafty*

STLNZM Stalinism *politics*

Letters aren't doubled for single sounds: to find alley use **L** not **LL**. Use **Y** and **W** as hard sounds only: to find yellow use **YL**. (Br)=British spelling or usage. * See dictionary.

STLPJN stool pigeon *decoy, spy*
STLR hostler *works with horses, trains*
STLR saddler *merchant*
STLR saddlery *business* saddleries
STLR settler *pioneer*
STLR staler *older*
STLR steelier *hard and cold*
STLR stellar *star*
STLR stylar *ovary*
STLR styler *artist*
STLR subtler *slight, refined, crafty*
STLR sutler *storekeeper*
STLRM stillroom *pantry*
STLRN saddle horn *pommel*
STLRS saddle horse *riding*
STLS sightless *blind*
STLS styleless *no fashion*
STLS stylus *pen* styli
STLSDK stylistic *designed*
STLSDKL stylistically *design*
STLSH stylish *fashion*
STLSHL stylishly *fashion*
STLSHN acetylation *adding acetyl*
STLSHNS stylishness *fashion*
STLSL sightlessly *blind*
STLSLSLKSD acetylsalicylic acid *acid salt*
STLSLSLT acetylsalicylate *acid salt*
STLSNS sightlessness *blind*
STLSR saddle sore *blister*
STLSS cytolysis *cell death*
STLST stalest *oldest*
STLST steeliest *hard and cold*
STLST stylist *artist*
STLST subtlest *slight, refined, crafty*
STLSTK stylistic *designed*
STLSTKL stylistically *design*
STLT acetylate *chemical* acetylated acetylating
STLT satellite *orbiter*
STLT stellate *star-shaped*
STLT stiletto *dagger* stilettos

(or) stilettoes
STLT stilt *pole, bird*
STLT stylet *probe*
STLT subtlety *slight, refined, crafty* subtleties
STLTD stilted *haughty*
STLTDL stiltedly *haughty*
STLTDNS stiltedness *haughtiness*
STLTF stultify *dull* stultified stultifying stultifies
STLTFKSHN stultification *dullness*
STLTH stealth *sneak*
STLTH stealthy *sneaky* stealthier stealthiest
STLTHL stealthily *sneaky*
STLTHNS stealthiness *sneaky*
STLTHR stealthier *sneaky*
STLTHST stealthiest *sneaky*
STLTHYR stealthier *sneaky*
STLTHYST stealthiest *sneaky*
STLTK cytolytic *cell death*
STLTN Stilton *cheese*
STLTR saddletree *frame*
STLTRP steel-trap (adj) *snare* steel trap (n)
STLTV acetylative *with acetyl*
STLWL steel wool *scour*
STLWRK steelwork *manufacture*
STLWRKR steelworker *manufacture*
STLWRT stalwart *strong*
STLWRTL stalwartly *strong*
STLWRTNS stalwartness *strength*
STLYN stallion *horse, stud*
STLYR steelier *hard and cold*
STLYRD steelyard *balance*
STLYST steeliest *hard and cold*
STLZ stylize *design* stylized stylizing (Br) stylise
STLZSHN stylization *design* (Br) stylisation
STM esteem *respect*
STM ostium *mouth* ostia

STM seedtime *season*
STM sodomy *sex*
STM steam (v) *boil* (n) *vapor*
STM steamy *humid* steamier steamiest
STM stem (v) *go against, spring, stop** stemmed stemming
STM stem (n) *stalk, ship's bow, dam**
STM stemma *insect eye* stemmata
STM stoma *opening* stomata
STM stymie *obstruct* stymied stymieing
STMBL estimable *valuation*
STMBL Istanbul *city*
STMBL stumble *trip up* stumbled stumbling
STMBLBM stumblebum *bad boxer*
STMBLNBLK stumbling block *obstacle*
STMBLNGBLK stumbling block *obstacle*
STMBLR stumbler *blunderer*
STMBR sawtimber *lumber*
STMBT steamboat *ship*
STMD acetamide *chemical*
STMD steamed *angry, cooked*
STMDK sodomitic (or) sodomitical *sex*
STMDKL sodomitical (or) sodomitic *sex*
STMDPD stomatopod *crustacean*
STMDR estimator *appraiser*
STMDV estimative *appraise, conclude*
STMFDR steamfitter *plumber*
STMFTR steamfitter *plumber*
STMK stomach *belly, pride*
STMKK stomachache *pain*
STMKK stomachic *digestion*
STMKR stomacher *waist*
STML steamily *hot*
STML stimuli (pl) *incentive* stimulus
STMLDR stimulator *arouser*

Use letters that best describe the sounds you hear and omit the vowels. Use **S** or **K** instead of **C**: to find circle use **SRKL**. Use **J** to find joy, **JM** to find gem and **G** to find go.

STMLDV stimulative *arousing*
STMLNBLK stumbling block *obstacle*
STMLNGBLK stumbling block *obstacle*
STMLNT stimulant *drug*
STMLS stemless *no stalk*
STMLS stimulus *incentive* stimuli
STMLSHN stimulation *arousal*
STMLT stimulate *arouse* stimulated stimulating
STMLTR stimulator *arouser*
STMLTV stimulative *arousing*
STMN stamen *flower* stamens
STMN stamina *strength*
STMNFN acetaminophen *pain reliever*
STMNS steaminess *hot*
STMNT staminate *flower*
STMP stamp *(n) postage (v) pound*
STMP stomp *foot pounding*
STMP stump *(n) tree, stub (v) confuse, trim, travel*
STMP stumpy *stubby*
STMPD stampede *(v) flee* stampeded stampeding
STMPD stampede *(n) rush*
STMPDR stampeder *cause of flight*
STMPJ stumpage *timber*
STMPNGGRN stamping ground *territory*
STMPNGGRND stamping ground *territory*
STMPNGRN stamping ground *territory*
STMPNGRND stamping ground *territory*
STMPR stamper *pounder*
STMR stammer *stutter*
STMR steamer *ship, cooker*
STMR steamier *hot*
STMRL steamroll (or) steamroller *push over*
STMRLR steamroller (or) steamroll *push over*

STMRR stammerer *stutter*
STMSHN estimation *opinion, honor*
STMSHP steamship *boat*
STMSHVL steam shovel *machine*
STMST sodomist *sex*
STMST steamiest *hot*
STMT estimate *(v) appraise, conclude* estimated estimating
STMT estimate *(n) calculation*
STMT stemmata (pl) *insect eye* stemma
STMT stomata (pl) *opening* stoma
STMT stomate *opening*
STMTDS stomatitis *disease* stomatitides (or) stomatitises
STMTK sodomitic (or) sodomitical *sex*
STMTKL sodomitical (or) sodomitic *sex*
STMTL stomatal *opening*
STMTPD stomatopod *crustacean*
STMTR estimator *appraiser*
STMTTDZ stomatitides (pl) *disease* stomatitis
STMTTS stomatitis *disease* stomatitides (or) stomatitises
STMTV estimative *appraise, conclude*
STMWNDN stem-winding *watch*
STMWNDNG stem-winding *watch*
STMWNDR stem-winder *watch*
STMWR stemware *wine glass*
STMYL stimuli (pl) *incentive* stimulus
STMYLDR stimulator *arouser*
STMYLDV stimulative *arousing*
STMYLNT stimulant *drug*
STMYLS stimulus *incentive*

stimuli
STMYLSHN stimulation *arousal*
STMYLT stimulate *arouse* stimulated stimulating
STMYLTR stimulator *arouser*
STMYLTV stimulative *arousing*
STMYR steamier *hot*
STMYST steamiest *hot*
STMZ sodomize *sex* sodomized sodomizing
STN acetone *chemical*
STN astound *baffle*
STN Austin *city*
STN easting *direction*
STN Satan *devil*
STN sateen *cotton fabric*
STN satin *silk fabric*
STN satiny *shiny*
STN seating *chairs*
STN set-in *(n, adj) insert* set in (v)
STN setting *place*
STN sit-in *(n) protest* sit in (v)
STN sitting *meal*
STN soutane *garment*
STN stain *mark*
STN stand *(v) support upright, remain, bear** stood standing
STN stand *(n) stop, stay, platform**
STN stein *mug*
STN Sten *gun*
STN steno *secretary* stenos
STN stone *(v) hurl rocks, sharpen* stoned stoning
STN stone *(n) rock (adj) utterly (adj) absolute*
STN stony *rocky, insensitive* stonier stoniest
STN stun *daze* stunned stunning
STNB stand by *(v) defend, wait*
STNB standby *(n, adj, adv) substitute* standbys
STNBL Istanbul *city*
STNBL stainable *mark*
STNBLN stone-blind *no sight*

STNBLND stone-blind *no sight*

STNCH stanch *stop up*

STNCH staunch *firm*

STNCH stench *bad odor* stenches

STNCH stenchy *bad odor*

STNCHFL stenchful *bad odor*

STNCHL staunchly *firmly*

STNCHN stanchion *support, harness*

STNCHNS staunchness *firmness*

STNCHT stonechat *bird*

STND astound *baffle*

STND stand *(v) support upright, remain, bear** stood standing

STND stand *(n) stop, stay, platform**

STND standee *occupant*

STND stoned *drunk, high*

STNDB stand by *(v) defend, wait*

STNDB standby *(n, adj, adv) substitute* standbys

STNDF stand off *(v) stall, repel*

STNDF standoff *(n, adj) tied, hold apart*

STNDF stone-deaf *no hearing*

STNDFSH standoffish *reserved*

STNDFSHL standoffishly *reserved*

STNDFSHNS standoffishness *reserved*

STNDGLS stained glass *decoration*

STNDK stenotic *narrowing*

STNDN astounding *awesome*

STNDN stand in (v) *substitute* stand-in (n)

STNDN stand-down (n) *relax, withdraw* stand down (v)

STNDN standing *(adj) erect, stale (n) position*

STNDNG astounding *awesome*

STNDNG standing *(adj) erect, stale (n) position*

STNDNGL astoundingly *awesomely*

STNDNL astoundingly *awesomely*

STNDP stand up (v) *erect* stand-up (n, adj)

STNDPNT standpoint *position*

STNDPP standpipe *reservoir*

STNDPT stand pat (v) *resist* standpat (adj)

STNDRD standard *(n) gauge, banner (adj) regular*

STNDRDBRD standardbred *horse*

STNDRDBRR standard-bearer *flag*

STNDRDZ standardize *agree* standardized standardizing (Br) standardise

STNDRDZSHN standardization *agreement* (Br) standardisation

STNDSTL standstill *stop*

STNDT stand out (v) *project, resist*

STNDT standout *(n) excellent one*

STNFSH stonefish *animal*

STNFST stone-faced *no emotion*

STNG easting *direction*

STNG seating *chairs*

STNG setting *place*

STNG sitting *meal*

STNG sting *(v) prick, cheat* stung stinging

STNG sting *(n) sharp pain, trap*

STNG stingy *tightfisted* stingier stingiest

STNG stung *(v-past) sting*

STNG suiting *fabric*

STNGK stank *(v-past) stink (n-Br) pond, dam*

STNGK stink *bad odor* stank (or) stunk stinking

STNGK stinky *smelly*

STNGKBG stinkbug *insect*

STNGKBM stink bomb *weapon*

STNGKHRN stinkhorn *fungus*

STNGKN stinking *odor, extremely*

STNGKNG stinking *bad odor, extremely*

STNGKPT stinkpot *weapon, mean one*

STNGKR stinker *odor, difficulty*

STNGKRD stinkard *mean one*

STNGKRN stinkhorn *fungus*

STNGKWD stinkweed *plant*

STNGKWD stinkwood *tree*

STNGLS stained glass *decoration*

STNGNS stinginess *tightfisted*

STNGQD stinkweed *plant*

STNGQD stinkwood *tree*

STNGR stinger *poison organ, cocktail, remark*

STNGR stingier *tightfisted*

STNGR stingray *animal*

STNGRF stenography *secretary*

STNGRFK stenographic *secretary*

STNGRFKL stenographically *secretary*

STNGRFR stenographer *secretary*

STNGRN stone-ground *milling*

STNGRND stone-ground *milling*

STNGST stingiest *tightfisted*

STNGYR stingier *tightfisted*

STNGYST stingiest *tightfisted*

STNHP stanhope *buggy*

STNHRDD stonyhearted *cruel*

STNHRTD stonyhearted *cruel*

STNJ stingy *tightfisted* stingier stingiest

STNJ Stone Age *prehistory*

STNJL stingily *tightfisted*

Use letters that best describe the sounds you hear and omit the vowels. Use **S** or **K** instead of **C**: to find circle use **SRKL**. Use **J** to find joy, **JM** to find gem and **G** to find go.

STNJNS stinginess *tightfisted*
STNJR stingier *tightfisted*
STNJST stingiest *tightfisted*
STNJYR stingier *tightfisted*
STNJYST stingiest *tightfisted*
STNK acetonic *chemical*
STNK isotonic *tension*
STNK satanic *devil*
STNK stank *(v-past) stink (n-Br) pond, dam*
STNK stannic *tin*
STNK stink *bad odor* stank (or) stunk *stinking*
STNK stinky *smelly*
STNKBG stinkbug *insect*
STNKBM stink bomb *weapon*
STNKDR stonecutter *quarry*
STNKHRN stinkhorn *fungus*
STNKL isotonically *tension*
STNKL satanically *devil*
STNKLD stone-cold *absolutely*
STNKN stinking *bad odor, extremely*
STNKNG stinking *bad odor, extremely*
STNKPT stinkpot *weapon, mean one*
STNKR stinker *odor, difficulty*
STNKRD stinkard *mean one*
STNKRN stinkhorn *fungus*
STNKTR stonecutter *quarry*
STNKWD stinkweed *plant*
STNKWD stinkwood *tree*
STNL stonily *rocky, insensitive*
STNLS stainless *no discoloration*
STNLSL stainlessly *no discoloration*
STNLSNS stainlessness *no discoloration*
STNLSTL stainless steel *no rust*
STNMSN stonemason *builder*
STNN Estonian *of Estonia*
STNN stanine *scores*

STNN stunning *shocking*
STNNG stunning *shocking*
STNNS stoniness *rocky, insensitive*
STNP stanhope *buggy*
STNPNT standpoint *position*
STNPP standpipe *reservoir*
STNPRF stainproof *no discoloration*
STNPT stand pat (v) *resist* standpat (adj)
STNQD stinkweed *plant*
STNQD stinkwood *tree*
STNR stainer *discolorer*
STNR stannery *tin working* stanneries
STNR stonier *rocky, insensitive*
STNR stunner *shocker*
STNS sootiness *black*
STNS stance *posture*
STNS stannous *tin*
STNSBL ostensible (adj) *apparent* ostensibly (adv)
STNSD isotonicity *tension*
STNSH astonish *surprise*
STNSHMNT astonishment *surprise*
STNSHN astonishing *surprising*
STNSHN stanchion *support, harness*
STNSHNG astonishing *surprising*
STNSHNGL astonishingly *surprisingly*
STNSHNL astonishingly *surprisingly*
STNSL stencil *cutout* stenciled (or) stencilled stenciling (or) stencilling
STNSL studding sail *boat*
STNSLR stenciler (or) stenciller *cutout*
STNSS stenosis *narrowing* stenoses
STNST isotonicity *tension*
STNST satanist *devil*
STNST stoniest *rocky, insensitive*
STNSTL standstill *stop*
STNSV ostensive *apparent*

STNSVL ostensively *apparently*
STNT satinet *fabric*
STNT stannite *mineral*
STNT stint (n) *task, bird* (v) *restrict*
STNT stunt (v) *hinder growth* (n) *feat*
STNTK stenotic *narrowing*
STNTMN stuntman *movies* stuntmen
STNTP stenotype *writing* stenotypy
STNTPK stenotopic *narrow range*
STNTPST stenotypist *writing*
STNTR stentor *loud voice*
STNTR stinter *restrict*
STNTRN stentorian *loud voice*
STNTRYN stentorian *loud voice*
STNTS stance *posture*
STNTSBL ostensible (adj) *apparent* ostensibly (adv)
STNTSHN ostentation *display*
STNTSHS ostentatious *showy*
STNTSL stencil *cutout* stenciled (or) stencilled stenciling (or) stencilling
STNTSL studding sail *boat*
STNTSLR stenciler (or) stenciller *cutout*
STNTSV ostensive *apparent*
STNTSVL ostensively *apparently*
STNTWMN stuntwoman *movies* stuntwomen
STNWD satinwood *tree*
STNWL stone wall (n) *fence, block*
STNWL stonewall (v) *evade*
STNWR stoneware *ceramic*
STNWRK stonework *masonry*
STNWRT stonewort *algae*
STNWSHD stonewashed *softened*
STNWSHT stonewashed

Letters aren't doubled for single sounds: to find alley use **L** not **LL**. Use **Y** and **W** as hard sounds only: to find yellow use **YL**. (Br)=British spelling or usage. * See dictionary.

softened
STNYN Estonian *of Estonia*
STNYR stonier *rocky, insensitive*
STNYST stoniest *rocky, insensitive*
STNZ stanza *poem*
STNZK stanzaic *poem*
STNZM satanism *devil*
STNZYK stanzaic *poem*
STP estop *prohibit* estopped estopping
STP isotope *atom*
STP set up *(v) build, frame, harden*
STP setup *(n) makeup, plan*
STP sit up *(v) rise, stay awake*
STP sit-up *(n) exercise*
STP steep *(adj) high, tilted (v) soak*
STP step *(v) walk* stepped stepping
STP step *(n) stair, stride, interval**
STP steppe *arid land*
STP stipe *stem*
STP stoop *(v) bend (n) porch, bend*
STP stop *block, halt, end* stopped stopping
STP stope *mine*
STP stoup *container*
STP stupa *shrine*
STP stupe *hot compress, dolt*
STPBRTHR stepbrother *relative*
STPCHL stepchild *relative* stepchildren
STPCHLD stepchild *relative* stepchildren
STPCHLDRN stepchildren (pl) *relative* stepchild
STPD stupid *dull, dense*
STPDD stupidity *dull, dense* stupidities
STPDDR stepdaughter *relative*
STPDK styptic *stop bleeding*
STPDL stapedial *ear*
STPDL stupidly *dull, dense*
STPDN step down (v)

decrease step-down (adj)
STPDNS stupidness *dull, dense*
STPDP stepped-up *strengthened*
STPDT stupidity *dull, dense* stupidities
STPDTR stepdaughter *relative*
STPDYL stapedial *ear*
STPDZ stapedes (pl) *ear* stapes
STPDZ stipites (pl) *stalk* stipes
STPF stupefy *astound, make stupid* stupefied stupefying stupefies
STPFKSHN stupefaction *stupid, astounded*
STPFML stepfamily *relatives* stepfamilies
STPFTHR stepfather *relative*
STPGP stopgap *makeshift*
STPJ stoppage *halt*
STPK isotopic *atom*
STPKK stopcock *plug*
STPKL isotopically *atom*
STPL estoppel *prohibition*
STPL stapelia *herb*
STPL staple *(v) fasten* stapled stapling
STPL staple *(n) fastener, source (adj) principal*
STPL steeple *church*
STPL stipple *speckle* stippled stippling
STPL stipule *leaf*
STPL stopple *plug* stoppled stoppling
STPLBSH steeplebush *plant*
STPLCHS steeplechase *race*
STPLCHSR steeplechaser *racer*
STPLDR stepladder *riser*
STPLDR stipulator *contractor*
STPLJK steeplejack *smokestacks*
STPLR stapler *fastener*
STPLR stippler *speckle*
STPLR stipular *with stalk*
STPLSD osteoplasty *surgery*

STPLSDK osteoplastic *surgery*
STPLSHN stipulation *contract*
STPLST osteoplasty *surgery*
STPLSTK osteoplastic *surgery*
STPLT stipulate *(v) contract* stipulated stipulating
STPLT stipulate *(adj) with stalk*
STPLT stoplight *traffic*
STPLTR stepladder *riser*
STPLTR stipulator *contractor*
STPLTR stipulatory *contractual*
STPLY stapelia *herb*
STPLZM cytoplasm *cell*
STPLZMK cytoplasmic *cell*
STPLZMKL cytoplasmically *cell*
STPMTHR stepmother *relative*
STPN estopping *prohibiting*
STPN steepen *increase slope*
STPN step in *(v) intervene*
STPN step-in *(n) clothing*
STPN stewpan *pot*
STPN stipend *money*
STPND stipend *money*
STPNDG stop-and-go *slow*
STPNDR stipendiary *wages* stipendiaries
STPNDS stupendous *amazing*
STPNDSL stupendously *amazing*
STPNDSNS stupendousness *greatness*
STPNDYR stipendiary *wages* stipendiaries
STPNG estopping *prohibiting*
STPNG stop-and-go *slow*
STPNGSTN stepping-stone *advance*
STPNSTN stepping-stone *advance*
STPP step-up (adj) *increase* step up (v)
STPR stepper *dancer*
STPR stopper *plug*

Use letters that best describe the sounds you hear and omit the vowels. Use **S** or **K** instead of **C**: to find circle use **SRKL**. Use **J** to find joy, **JM** to find gem and **G** to find go.

STPR stupor *daze*
STPRDK osteoporotic *disease*
STPRNT stepparent *relative*
STPRSS osteoporosis *disease* osteoporoses
STPRTK osteoporotic *disease*
STPSN steapsin *pancreas*
STPSN stepson *relative*
STPSN stop sign *traffic*
STPSSDR stepsister *relative*
STPSSTR stepsister *relative*
STPT stop out *withdraw*
STPTH osteopath *doctor*
STPTH osteopathy *bone*
STPTHK osteopathic *bone*
STPTHKL osteopathically *bone*
STPTK styptic *stop bleeding*
STPTP stepped-up *strengthened*
STPTZ stipites (pl) *stalk* stipes
STPVR stopover *rest*
STPWCH stopwatch *timing* stopwatches
STPWZ stepwise *like stairs*
STPYL stipule *leaf*
STPYLDR stipulator *contractor*
STPYLR stipular *with stalk*
STPYLSHN stipulation *contract*
STPYLT stipulate *(v) contract* stipulated stipulating
STPYLT stipulate *(adj) with stalk*
STPYLTR stipulator *contractor*
STPYLTR stipulatory *contractual*
STPZ stapes *ear* stapes (or) stapedes
STPZ stipes *stalk* stipites
STR aster *flower*
STR astir *move about*
STR astray *lost*
STR austere *severe*
STR Australia *continent*
STR Austria *country*

STR Easter *feast day*
STR ester *fragrance*
STR Esther *biblical woman*
STR estuary *delta area* estuaries
STR ouster *expulsion*
STR oyster *animal*
STR sadder *sorrow*
STR satire *wit*
STR satori *bliss*
STR satyr *deity, lecher, butterfly*
STR seater *sitting space*
STR setter *dog*
STR siddur *book* siddurim
STR sitar *music*
STR sitter *baby-sitter*
STR sootier *blacker*
STR stair *step*
STR star *(v) headline* starred starring
STR star *(n) sun*
STR stare *look at* stared staring
STR starry *many stars* starrier starriest
STR stayer *supporter*
STR steer *(n) cow (v) guide*
STR stereo *sound*
STR stir *(v) mix, disturb, move* stirred stirring
STR stir *(n) activity, (slang) prison*
STR store *(v) keep* stored storing
STR store *(n) business, supply*
STR story *tale, level* stories
STR straw *grain, tube, color**
STR stray *wander*
STR strew *spread* strewed (or) strewn strewing
STR stria *stripe* striae
STR suitor *pursue, sue, woo*
STR sutra *scripture*
STR suture *stitch* sutured suturing
STRB strobe *flash*
STRBD oyster bed *ocean*
STRBK storybook *tales*
STRBL saturable *soak*
STRBL storable *holding*

STRBL strobila *budding* strobilae
STRBL strobili (pl) *bud* strobilus
STRBLG astrobiology *star science*
STRBLJ astrobiology *star science*
STRBLJST astrobiologist *star scientist*
STRBLS strobilus *bud* strobili
STRBLSHN strobilation *budding*
STRBLT strobe light *flash*
STRBR strawberry *fruit* strawberries
STRBRD starboard *right side*
STRBRD storyboard *sketches*
STRBS straw boss *supervisor*
STRBSKP stroboscope *cycles*
STRBSKPK stroboscopic *cycles*
STRBT store-bought *not handmade*
STRBYLG astrobiology *star science*
STRBYLJ astrobiology *star science*
STRBYLJST astrobiologist *star scientist*
STRBZMK strabismic *squint*
STRBZMS strabismus *squint*
STRC citrusy *like fruit*
STRCH ostrich *bird* ostriches
STRCH starch *stiffener*
STRCH starchy *stiff* starchier starchiest
STRCH stretch *(v) expand (n) extent, walk, elastic* stretches
STRCH stretchy *elastic*
STRCHL starchily *stiffly*
STRCHMBR star-chamber *secret*
STRCHMRKS stretch

Letters aren't doubled for single sounds: to find alley use **L** not **LL**. Use **Y** and **W** as hard sounds only: to find yellow use **YL**. (Br)=British spelling or usage. * See dictionary.

marks *skin*

STRCHMRX stretch marks *skin*

STRCHNS starchiness *stiffness*

STRCHR starchier *stiffer*

STRCHR stretcher *carrier*

STRCHST starchiest *stiffest*

STRCHT stretch-out *work without pay*

STRCHYR starchier *stiffer*

STRCHYST starchiest *stiffest*

STRD asteroid *tiny planet*

STRD astride *legs apart*

STRD austerity *severity* austerities

STRD Saturday *weekend day*

STRD satyrid *butterfly*

STRD sight-read *music* sight-read sight-reading

STRD starry-eyed *visionary*

STRD steroid *hormone*

STRD steward *manager*

STRD storeyed (or) storied *floors*

STRD storied *famous*

STRD strata (pl) *layers* stratum

STRD strati (pl) *cloud* stratus

STRD stretto *music* stretti (or) strettos

STRD stride *step* strode striding stridden

STRD strode *(v-past)* stride

STRD stroud *fabric*

STRD sturdy *strong* sturdier sturdiest

STRDD saturated *soaked*

STRDF stratify *layer* stratified stratifying stratifies

STRDFKSHN stratification *layers*

STRDFRM stratiform *layered*

STRDG strategy *plan* strategies

STRDGRFK stratigraphic *geology*

STRDJ straightedge *ruler*

STRDJ strategy *plan* strategies

STRDJBRLDR Strait of Gibralter *body of water*

STRDJBRLTR Strait of Gibralter *body of water*

STRDJL strigil *wiper*

STRDJLS stridulous *shrill noise*

STRDJLSHN stridulation *shrill noise*

STRDJLSL stridulously *shrill noise*

STRDJLT stridulate *shrill noise* stridulated stridulating

STRDJLTR stridulatory *shrill noise*

STRDJM stratagem *trick*

STRDJST strategist *planner*

STRDKMLS stratocumulus *cloud*

STRDKMYLS stratocumulus *cloud*

STRDKYMLS stratocumulus *cloud*

STRDKYMYLS stratocumulus *cloud*

STRDL astraddle *both sides*

STRDL startle *surprise* startled startling

STRDL steroidal *hormone*

STRDL straddle *be on both sides* straddled straddling

STRDL strudel *pastry*

STRDL sturdily *strong*

STRDLNG startling *surprise*

STRDLR straddler *be on both sides*

STRDLS stridulous *shrill noise*

STRDLSHN stridulation *shrill noise* .

STRDLSL stridulously *shrill noise*

STRDLT stridulate *shrill noise* stridulated stridulating

STRDLTR stridulatory *shrill noise*

STRDM astrodome *arena*

STRDM stardom *fame*

STRDM stratum *layer* strata

STRDNS stridence *loudness*

stridency

STRDNS sturdiness *strong*

STRDNT strident *loud*

STRDNTL stridently *loud*

STRDNTS stridence *loudness* stridency

STRDQMLS stratocumulus *cloud*

STRDQMYLS stratocumulus *cloud*

STRDR saturator *soaked*

STRDR starter *motor, initiator*

STRDR stertor *snoring*

STRDR straight-arrow *direct person*

STRDR stridor *noise*

STRDR strutter *show off*

STRDR sturdier *strong*

STRDRM straight-arm *ward off*

STRDRS stertorous *snoring*

STRDRSL stertorously *snoring*

STRDS stewardess *manager (f)* stewardesses

STRDS stratus *cloud* strati

STRDSFR stratosphere *atmosphere*

STRDSFRK stratospheric *atmosphere*

STRDST stardust *magic*

STRDST sturdiest *strong*

STRDT straight-out *blunt*

STRDVJBRLDR Strait of Gibralter *body of water*

STRDVJBRLTR Strait of Gibralter *body of water*

STRDVRS Stradivarius *violin maker*

STRDVRYS Stradivarius *violin maker*

STRDW straightaway *(adj, adv) immediate (n) road*

STRDW straightway *immediately*

STRDYLS stridulous *shrill noise*

STRDYLSHN stridulation *shrill noise*

STRDYLSL stridulously *shrill noise*

Use letters that best describe the sounds you hear and omit the vowels. Use **S** or **K** instead of **C**: to find circle use **SRKL**. Use **J** to find joy, **JM** to find gem and **G** to find go.

STRDYLT stridulate *shrill noise* stridulated stridulating

STRDYLTR stridulatory *shrill noise*

STRDYR sturdier *strong*

STRDYST sturdiest *strong*

STRF strafe *machine-gun* strafed strafing

STRF strife *conflict*

STRF strophe *stanza*

STRFK strophic *stanza*

STRFLR starflower *plant*

STRFLR strawflower *herb*

STRFLWR starflower *plant*

STRFLWR strawflower *herb*

STRFM Styrofoam *(trademark) plastic*

STRFN stereophony *separate sound*

STRFNK stereophonic *separate sound*

STRFNKL stereophonically *separate sound*

STRFR stir-fry *cook*

STRFRNT storefront *display*

STRFRT star fruit *fruit*

STRFSH starfish *animal*

STRFZKL astrophysical (adj) *star behavior* astrophysically (adv)

STRFZKS astrophysics *star behavior*

STRFZSST astrophysicist *star behavior*

STRFZX astrophysics *star behavior*

STRGL straggle *stray* straggled straggling

STRGL straggly *spread out* stragglier straggliest

STRGL struggle *fight* struggled struggling

STRGLR straggler *stray*

STRGLR stragglier *spread out*

STRGLR struggler *fighter*

STRGLST straggliest *spread out*

STRGLYR stragglier *spread out*

STRGLYST straggliest

spread out

STRGM sterigma *stalk* sterigmata

STRGMD sterigmata (pl) *stalk* sterigma

STRGMT sterigmata (pl) *stalk* sterigma

STRGNF stroganoff *stew*

STRGNK estrogenic *sexual heat* (Br) oestrogenic

STRGNKL estrogenically *sexual heat* (Br) oestrogenically

STRGRF stereograph *3-D picture*

STRGRF stereography *3-D science*

STRGRFK stereographic *3-D picture*

STRGRM stereogram *diagram*

STRGS strigose *bristles*

STRGZ stargaze *watch heavens* stargazed stargazing

STRGZN stargazing *watch heavens*

STRGZNG stargazing *watch heavens*

STRGZR stargazer *watch heavens*

STRHS storehouse *building*

STRHT strawhat *summer theater*

STRJ ostrich *bird* ostriches

STRJ steerage *aim*

STRJ storage *safekeeping*

STRJL strigil *wiper*

STRJLS stridulous *shrill noise*

STRJLSHN stridulation *shrill noise*

STRJLSL stridulously *shrill noise*

STRJLT stridulate *shrill noise* stridulated stridulating

STRJLTR stridulatory *shrill noise*

STRJN estrogen *hormone* (Br) oestrogen

STRJN sturgeon *fish*

STRJNK estrogenic *sexual heat* (Br) oestrogenic

STRJNKL estrogenically *sexual heat* (Br) oestrogenically

STRJW steerageway *motion*

STRK asterisk *star*

STRK awestruck *full of wonder*

STRK citric *fruit*

STRK esoteric *private*

STRK esoterica *private items*

STRK ostraca (pl) *fragment* ostracon

STRK satiric (or) satirical (adj) *sarcastic* satirically (adv)

STRK satyric *deity, lecher, butterfly*

STRK stark *absolute, bare, harsh*

STRK stearic *acid*

STRK steric *space*

STRK stirk *cow*

STRK stork *bird*

STRK streak *stripe, speed, run*

STRK streaky *lined, nervous* streakier streakiest

STRK strict *exact*

STRK strike (v) *hit, delete, labor** struck striking

STRK strike (n) *labor, attack, baseball**

STRK stroke *rub, swing, mark* stroked stroking

STRK struck *(v-past)* strike

STRKBN strikebound *labor*

STRKBND strikebound *labor*

STRKBRKN strikebreaking *anti-union tactic*

STRKBRKNG strikebreaking *anti-union tactic*

STRKBRKR strikebreaker *replacement*

STRKCHR oystercatcher *bird*

STRKCHR stricture *restraint*

Letters aren't doubled for single sounds: to find alley use **L** not **LL**. Use **Y** and **W** as hard sounds only: to find yellow use **YL**. (Br)=British spelling or usage. * See dictionary.

STRKCHR structure (v) form structured structuring

STRKCHR structure (n) building, arrangement

STRKCHRD structured formed, set up

STRKCHRL structural (adj) physical structurally (adv)

STRKCHRLST structuralist science methods

STRKCHRLZ structuralize organize structuralized structuralizing

STRKCHRLZM structuralism science methods

STRKCHRLZSHN structuralization organization

STRKD ostracod animal

STRKD streaked lined, upset

STRKJR structure (v) form structured structuring

STRKJR structure (n) building, arrangement

STRKJRD structured formed, set up

STRKJRL structural (adj) physical structurally (adv)

STRKJRLST structuralist science methods

STRKJRLZ structuralize organize structuralized structuralizing

STRKJRLZM structuralism science methods

STRKJRLZSHN structuralization organization

STRKL esoterically privately

STRKL satirical (or) satiric (adj) sarcastic satirically (adv)

STRKL sterically space

STRKL strickle tool

STRKL strictly exact

STRKN astrakhan cloth

STRKN ostracon fragment ostraca

STRKN streaking hair color

STRKN stricken wounded,

(v-past) strike

STRKN striking noticeable

STRKNG streaking hair color

STRKNG striking noticeable

STRKNN strychnine poison

STRKNS streakiness lined, nervous

STRKNS strictness exact

STRKPR storekeeper seller

STRKR streaker naked runner

STRKR streakier lined, nervous

STRKR striker hammer, worker

STRKR stroker caress, persuade

STRKRB oyster crab animal

STRKRST star-crossed ill-fated

STRKRZ stir-crazy (slang) distress

STRKS asterisk star

STRKS staircase steps

STRKS storax sap

STRKSBL storksbill plant

STRKSD citric acid fruit acid

STRKSHR stricture restraint

STRKSHR structure (n) building, arrangement

STRKSHR structure (v) form structured structuring

STRKSHRD structured formed, set up

STRKSHRL structural (adj) physical structurally (adv)

STRKSHRLST structuralist science methods

STRKSHRLZ structuralize organize structuralized structuralizing

STRKSHRLZM structuralism science methods

STRKSHRLZSHN structuralization organization

STRKST streakiest lined, nervous

STRKT streaked lined, upset

STRKT strict exact

STRKT strike out (v) erase,

fail, embark*

STRKT strikeout (n) baseball

STRKTL strictly exact

STRKTNS strictness exact

STRKTR stricture restraint

STRKTR structure (n) building, arrangement

STRKTR structure (v) form structured structuring

STRKTRD structured formed, set up

STRKTRL structural (adj) physical structurally (adv)

STRKTRLST structuralist science methods

STRKTRLZ structuralize organize structuralized structuralizing

STRKTRLZM structuralism science methods

STRKTRLZSHN structuralization organization

STRKVR strikeover typing

STRKYR streakier lined, nervous

STRKYST streakiest lined, nervous

STRKZN strike zone baseball

STRL astral (adj) stars astrally (adv)

STRL austerely severely

STRL austral (often capitalized) southern australes

STRL Australia continent

STRL citral chemical

STRL easterly direction

STRL estriol hormone (Br) oestriol

STRL estrual menstruation (Br) oestrual

STRL estuarial delta area

STRL sterile (adj) no germs, lifeless sterilely (adv)

STRL sterol alcohol

STRL stroll walk

STRLB astrolabe device

STRLD sterility no germs, lifeless

STRLG astrology horoscope

STRLG soteriology salvation

Use letters that best describe the sounds you hear and omit the vowels. Use **S** or **K** instead of **C**: to find circle use **SRKL**. Use **J** to find joy, **JM** to find gem and **G** to find go.

STRLJ astrology *horoscope*
STRLJ soteriology *salvation*
STRLJKL astrological (adj) *horoscope* astrologically (adv)
STRLJKL soteriological *salvation*
STRLJR astrologer *horoscope*
STRLN Australian *of Australia*
STRLN starling *bird*
STRLN sterling *silver, pure*
STRLN story line *plot*
STRLNG starling *bird*
STRLNG sterling *silver, pure*
STRLR stroller *actor, carriage, walker*
STRLS starless *no stars*
STRLSH Australasia *region*
STRLT starlet *celebrity*
STRLT starlight *light from stars*
STRLT starlit *lit by stars*
STRLT sterility *no germs, lifeless*
STRLY Australia *continent*
STRLYN Australian *of Australia*
STRLZ sterilize *no germs, lifeless* sterilized sterilizing
STRLZH Australasia *region*
STRLZR sterilizer *no germs, lifeless*
STRLZSHN sterilization *no germs, lifeless*
STRM ice storm *freezing weather*
STRM siddurim (pl) *book* siddur
STRM storeroom *storage area*
STRM storm (n) *bad weather* (v) *rage, blow*
STRM stormy *violent* stormier stormiest
STRM stream *water flow*
STRM strum *play music* strummed strumming
STRM struma *goiter* strumae (or) strumas
STRMBD streambed

channel
STRMBN stormbound *cut off*
STRMBND stormbound *cut off*
STRMDLDK stromatolitic *fossil*
STRMDLT stromatolite *fossil*
STRMDLTK stromatolitic *fossil*
STRMDR storm door *protection*
STRML stormily *violently*
STRMLN streamline *shape, update* streamlined streamlining
STRMLND streamlined *shaped*
STRMN streaming *flowing*
STRMNG streaming *flowing*
STRMNS storminess *violence*
STRMPT strumpet *prostitute*
STRMR stormier *violent*
STRMR streamer *paper*
STRMR strummer *musician*
STRMSLR storm cellar *basement*
STRMST stormiest *violent*
STRMTLDK stromatolitic *fossil*
STRMTLT stromatolite *fossil*
STRMTLTK stromatolitic *fossil*
STRMTR astrometry *star measurement*
STRMYR stormier *violent*
STRMYST stormiest *violent*
STRN astern *behind*
STRN Australian *of Australia*
STRN Austrian *of Austria*
STRN citrine *stone*
STRN citron *fruit*
STRN eastern *direction*
STRN estuarine *delta area*
STRN eyestrain *vision*
STRN Saturn *planet*
STRN sauterne (or) sauternes *wine*
STRN stearin *chemical*
STRN stern (n) *boat rear* (adj) *severe*

STRN sterna (pl) *bone* sternum
STRN stirring *exciting*
STRN strain (n) *breed, tune* (v) *exert, filter*
STRN strand (v) *leave* (n) *coastal area, thread*
STRN strewn (v-past) *strew*
STRN styrene *rubber*
STRND saturniid *moth*
STRND strained *difficult*
STRND strand (v) *leave* (n) *coastal area, rope*
STRNDD stranded *threads*
STRNDKL astronautical (adj) *space travel* astronautically (adv)
STRNDKS astronautics *space travel*
STRNDX astronautics *space travel*
STRNG oystering *gather oysters*
STRNG stirring *exciting*
STRNG string (n) *thread, line*
STRNG string (v) *tune, extend, fool** strung stringing
STRNG stringy *wiry* stringier stringiest
STRNG strong *robust*
STRNG strung (v-past) *string*
STRNGBKS strongbox *safe* strongboxes
STRNGBN string bean *vegetable*
STRNGBRK stringybark *eucalyptus*
STRNGBS string bass *music*
STRNGBX strongbox *safe* strongboxes
STRNGGL strangle *choke, suppress* strangled strangling
STRNGGLHL stranglehold *choke*
STRNGGLHLD stranglehold *choke*
STRNGGLR strangler *choker*
STRNGGLSHN strangulation *choking*

Letters aren't doubled for single sounds: to find alley use **L** not **LL**. Use **Y** and **W** as hard sounds only: to find yellow use **YL**. (Br)=British spelling or usage. * See dictionary.

STRNGGLT strangulate *choke* strangulated strangulating

STRNGGYLSHN strangulation *choking*

STRNGGYLT strangulate *choke* strangulated strangulating

STRNGHL stronghold *fort*

STRNGHLD stronghold *fort*

STRNGHLT stringhalt *lameness*

STRNGHWL steering wheel *guide*

STRNGKRS stringcourse *design*

STRNGKTH strength *power*

STRNGKTHN strengthen *make strong*

STRNGL strangle *choke, suppress* strangled strangling

STRNGL strongly *intensity, power*

STRNGLHL stranglehold *choke*

STRNGLHLD stranglehold *choke*

STRNGLR strangler *choker*

STRNGLSHN strangulation *choking*

STRNGLT strangulate *choke* strangulated strangulating

STRNGMN strongman *controller*

STRNGMNDD strong-minded *independent*

STRNGNS stringiness *wiry*

STRNGPS stringpiece *timber*

STRNGR stringer *wire, timber, reporter**

STRNGR stringier *wiry*

STRNGRM strong-arm (v, adj) *bully*

STRNGST stringiest *wiry*

STRNGT string tie *neckwear*

STRNGT strung out *drugs*

STRNGTH strength *power*

STRNGTHN strengthen *make strong*

STRNGWL steering wheel *guide*

STRNGYLSHN strangulation *choking*

STRNGYLT strangulate *choke* strangulated strangulating

STRNGYR stringier *wiry*

STRNGYST stringiest *wiry*

STRNHWL steering wheel *guide*

STRNHWLR stern-wheeler *boat*

STRNJ estrange *alienate* estranged estranging

STRNJ strange *odd, unknown* stranger strangest

STRNJL strangely *oddly*

STRNJL strongyle *worm*

STRNJMNT estrangement *alienation*

STRNJNC astringency *pucker*

STRNJNC stringency *tightness*

STRNJND stringendo *tempo*

STRNJNS astringency *pucker*

STRNJNS strangeness *oddness*

STRNJNS stringency *tightness*

STRNJNT astxringent *pucker*

STRNJNT stringent *tight*

STRNJNTC astringency *pucker*

STRNJNTC stringency *tightness*

STRNJNTL astringently *puckered*

STRNJNTL stringently *tight*

STRNJNTS astringency *pucker*

STRNJNTS stringency *tightness*

STRNJR estranger *alienator*

STRNJR stranger *(n) unfamiliar one (adj) odder*

STRNJST strangest *oddest*

STRNKTH strength *power*

STRNKTHN strengthen *make strong*

STRNL citronella *grass, oil*

STRNL saturnalia *orgy*

STRNL sternal *sternum*

STRNL sternly *harshly*

STRNLN saturnalian *orgy*

STRNLY saturnalia *orgy*

STRNLYN saturnalian *orgy*

STRNM astronomy *star observation*

STRNM sternum *bone* sternums (or) sterna

STRNMKL astronomical *very high*

STRNMKL astronomical (adj) *stars, enormous* astronomically (adv)

STRNMR astronomer *star observer*

STRNMST sternmost *rear end*

STRNN saturnine *sullen*

STRNR strainer *sieve, tightener*

STRNS austereness *severeness*

STRNS sternness *severity*

STRNS strenuous *powerful*

STRNSD strenuosity *zeal*

STRNSHM strontium *element*

STRNSHYM strontium *element*

STRNSL strenuously *powerfully*

STRNSNS strenuousness *power*

STRNST strenuosity *zeal*

STRNT astronaut *space traveller*

STRNT saturant *soak*

STRNT sternite *insect part*

STRNTH strength *power*

STRNTHN strengthen *make strong*

STRNTKL astronautical (adj) *space travel* astronautically (adv)

STRNTKS astronautics *space travel*

STRNTM strontium *element*

Use letters that best describe the sounds you hear and omit the vowels. Use **S** or **K** instead of **C**: to find circle use **SRKL**. Use **J** to find joy, **JM** to find gem and **G** to find go.

STRNTSHM strontium *element*

STRNTSHN sternutation *sneezing*

STRNTSHYM strontium *element*

STRNTX astronautics *space travel*

STRNTYM strontium *element*

STRNWL steering wheel *guide*

STRNWLR stern-wheeler *boat*

STRNWS strenuous *powerful*

STRNWSD strenuosity *zeal*

STRNWSL strenuously *powerfully*

STRNWSNS strenuousness *power*

STRNWST strenuosity *zeal*

STRNYD saturniid *moth*

STRNYS strenuous *powerful*

STRNYSD strenuosity *zeal*

STRNYSL strenuously *powerfully*

STRNYSNS strenuousness *power*

STRNYST strenuosity *zeal*

STRNYTSHN sternutation *sneezing*

STRNYWS strenuous *powerful*

STRNYWSD strenuosity *zeal*

STRNYWSL strenuously *powerfully*

STRNYWSNS strenuousness *power*

STRNYWST strenuosity *zeal*

STRNZM saturnism *lead poisoning*

STRP isotropy *same value*

STRP satrap *ruler*

STRP satrapy *territory* satrapies

STRP stirrup *saddle*

STRP strap (v) *attach, bind, beat* strapped strapping

STRP strap (n) *belt*

STRP strep *throat*

STRP strip (v) *remove, peel* stripped stripping

STRP strip (n) *narrow band*

STRP stripe *line* striped striping

STRP stripy *streaked* stripier stripiest

STRP strop (v) *sharpen* stropped stropping

STRP strop (n) *razor strap*

STRP stroppy (Br) *touchy*

STRPD strappado *torture*

STRPDKKL streptococcal *bacteria*

STRPDKKS streptococcus *bacteria* streptococci

STRPDKN stereopticon *projector*

STRPDMCT streptomycete *fungus*

STRPDMSN streptomycin *antibiotic*

STRPDMST streptomycete *fungus*

STRPDN stripped-down *simple*

STRPK isotropic *same value*

STRPKP stirrup cup *vessel*

STRPKRPN strip-cropping *planting*

STRPKRPNG strip-cropping *planting*

STRPLN stripling *youth*

STRPLNG stripling *youth*

STRPLS strapless *garment*

STRPMN strip-mine (v) *coal* strip mine (n)

STRPN strapping *sturdy*

STRPNG strapping *sturdy*

STRPR strapper *big one*

STRPR striper *fish*

STRPR stripper *remover*

STRPS stirps *family* stirpes

STRPSS stereopsis *vision*

STRPT strappado *torture*

STRPTHRT strep throat *illness*

STRPTKKL streptococcal *bacteria*

STRPTKKS streptococcus *bacteria* streptococci

STRPTKN stereopticon *projector*

STRPTMCT streptomycete *fungus*

STRPTMSN streptomycin *antibiotic*

STRPTMST streptomycete *fungus*

STRPTZ striptease *dance*

STRPTZR stripteaser *dancer*

STRR starer *look at*

STRR starrier *more stars*

STRR stirrer *exciter*

STRR strayer *wanderer*

STRS citrus *fruit* citrus (or) citruses

STRS citrusy *like fruit*

STRS esterase *enzyme*

STRS estrous (adj) *ovulation* estrus (n) (Br) oestrous, oestrus

STRS satirize *ridicule* satirized satirizing (Br) satirise

STRS storehouse *building*

STRS Straus *French composer*

STRS Strauss *philosopher, German composer*

STRS stress (n) *force, strain* (v) *emphasize* stresses

STRSDK astrocytic *cell*

STRSDT stressed-out *anxious*

STRSFL stressful (adj) *strain* stressfully (adv)

STRSHN saturation *soaking*

STRSHN striation *stripe*

STRSK asterisk *star*

STRSKP stereoscope *optical device*

STRSKP stereoscopy *optical science*

STRSKPK stereoscopic *optical device*

STRSKPKL stereoscopically *optical device*

STRSL streusel *cake topping*

STRSLS stressless *no strain*

STRSPNGGLD star-spangled *many stars*

STRSPNGLD star-spangled *many stars*

Letters aren't doubled for single sounds: to find alley use **L** not **LL**. Use **Y** and **W** as hard sounds only: to find yellow use **YL**. (Br)=British spelling or usage. * See dictionary.

STR

STRSR stressor *stimulus*

STRSS satyriasis *sex urge*

STRST astrocyte *cell*

STRST satirist *ridiculer*

STRST sitarist *music*

STRST starriest *many stars*

STRSTK astrocytic *cell*

STRSTM astrocytoma *tumor*

STRSTT stressed-out *anxious*

STRSZ ostracize *exclude* ostracized ostracizing (Br) ostracise

STRSZM esotericism *privacy*

STRSZM ostracism *exclusion*

STRT austerity *severity* austerities

STRT citrate *fruit acid*

STRT saturate *soak* saturated saturating

STRT start *(v) begin (n) spasm, beginning*

STRT stearate *chemical*

STRT straight *not bent, honest, correct**

STRT strait *(n) isthmus (adj) tight, difficult*

STRT strata *(pl) layers* stratum

STRT strati *(pl) cloud* stratus

STRT street *road*

STRT stretto *music* stretti *(or)* strettos

STRT striate *stripe* striated striating

STRT strut *swagger* strutted strutting

STRTD Eastertide *feast period*

STRTD saturated *soaked*

STRTF stratify *layer* stratified stratifying stratifies

STRTFKSHN stratification *layers*

STRTFRD straightforward *direct*

STRTFRDNS straightforwardness *direct*

STRTFRM stratiform *layered*

STRTFRWRD straightforward *direct*

STRTFRWRDNS straightforwardness *direct*

STRTFS straight face *(n) no emotion*

STRTFST straight-faced *(adj) (adj) no emotion*

STRTG strategy *plan* strategies

STRTGRF stratigraphy *geology*

STRTGRFK stratigraphic *geology*

STRTH strath *valley*

STRTHRDS osteoarthritis *disease*

STRTHRTS osteoarthritis *disease*

STRTJ straightedge *ruler*

STRTJ strategy *plan* strategies

STRTJBRLDR Strait of Gibralter *body of water*

STRTJBRLTR Strait of Gibralter *body of water*

STRTJK strategic *planned* strategically *(adv)*

STRTJKL strategical *(adj) planned* strategically *(adv)*

STRTJKT straitjacket *restriction*

STRTJM stratagem *trick*

STRTJST strategist *planner*

STRTKMLS stratocumulus *cloud*

STRTKMYLS stratocumulus *cloud*

STRTKR streetcar *trolley*

STRTKRC stratocracy *military rule*

STRTKRS stratocracy *military rule*

STRTKYMLS stratocumulus *cloud*

STRTKYMYLS stratocumulus *cloud*

STRTL astraddle *both sides*

STRTL startle *surprise* startled startling

STRTL straddle *be on both sides* straddled straddling

STRTL straitly *tight, difficult*

STRTLN startling *surprise*

STRTLN straight-line *direct*

STRTLNG startling *surprise*

STRTLR storyteller *reciter, liar*

STRTLR straddler *be on both sides*

STRTLST straitlaced *(or)* straightlaced *strict*

STRTLT streetlight *illumination*

STRTM stratum *layer* strata

STRTMN straight man *comedy* straight men

STRTN straighten *correct*

STRTN straiten *confine*

STRTNR straightener *unbend*

STRTNS straitness *tight, difficult*

STRTP stereotype *model* stereotyped stereotyping

STRTP stereotypy *repetition* stereotypies

STRTPD stereotyped *commonplace*

STRTPKL stereotypical *(adj) commonplace* stereotypically *(adv)*

STRTPT stereotyped *commonplace*

STRTQMLS stratocumulus *cloud*

STRTQMYLS stratocumulus *cloud*

STRTR saturator *soaked*

STRTR starter *motor, initiator*

STRTR stertor *snoring*

STRTR straight-arrow *direct person*

STRTR strutter *show off*

STRTRF Astro Turf *(trademark) carpet*

STRTRM straight-arm *ward off*

STRTRS stertorous *snoring*

STRTRSL stertorously *snoring*

STRTRZR straight razor

Use letters that best describe the sounds you hear and omit the vowels. Use **S** or **K** instead of **C**: to find circle use **SRKL**. Use **J** to find joy, **JM** to find gem and **G** to find go.

cutter
STRTS stratus *cloud* strati
STRTSFR stratosphere *atmosphere*
STRTSFRK stratospheric *atmosphere*
STRTSKP streetscape *view*
STRTSMRT street-smart *wise*
STRTT straight-out *blunt*
STRTVJBRLDR Strait of Gibralter *body of water*
STRTVJBRLTR Strait of Gibralter *body of water*
STRTVRS Stradivarius *violin maker*
STRTVRYS Stradivarius *violin maker*
STRTW straightaway *(adj, adv) immediate (n) road*
STRTW straightway *immediately*
STRTWKN streetwalking *prostitution*
STRTWKNG streetwalking *prostitution*
STRTWKR streetwalker *prostitute*
STRTWZ streetwise *smart*
STRV starve *no food* starved starving
STRV strive *attempt* strove (or) strived striving striven
STRV strove *(v-past)* strive
STRVLNG starveling *thin one*
STRVSHN starvation *no food*
STRVT straw vote *poll*
STRW stairway *steps*
STRWD storewide *most merchandise*
STRWL estrual *menstruation* (Br) oestrual
STRWL stairwell *steps*
STRWS estrous *(adj) ovulation* estrus *(n)* (Br) oestrous, oestrus
STRX asterisk *star*
STRX storax *sap*
STRY Australia *continent*
STRY Austria *country*

STRY stereo *sound*
STRY stria *stripe* striae
STRYD starry-eyed *visionary*
STRYFN stereophony *separate sound*
STRYFNK stereophonic *separate sound*
STRYFNKL stereophonically *separate sound*
STRYGRF stereograph *3-D picture*
STRYGRF stereography *3-D science*
STRYGRFK stereographic *3-D picture*
STRYGRM stereogram *diagram*
STRYL estriol *hormone* (Br) oestriol
STRYL estuarial *delta area*
STRYLG soteriology *salvation*
STRYLJ soteriology *salvation*
STRYLJKL soteriological *salvation*
STRYN Australian *of Australia*
STRYN Austrian *of Austria*
STRYPDKN stereopticon *projector*
STRYPSS stereopsis *vision*
STRYPTKN stereopticon *projector*
STRYR starrier *more stars*
STRYR strayer *wanderer*
STRYSHN striation *stripe*
STRYSKP stereoscope *optical device*
STRYSKP stereoscopy *optical science*
STRYSKPK stereoscopic *optical device*
STRYSKPKL stereoscopically *optical device*
STRYSS satyriasis *sex urge*
STRYST starriest *many stars*
STRYT striate *stripe* striated striating

STRYTP stereotype *model* stereotyped stereotyping
STRYTP stereotypy *repetition* stereotypies
STRYTPD stereotyped *commonplace*
STRYTPKL stereotypical *(adj) commonplace* stereotypically (adv)
STRYTPT stereotyped *commonplace*
STRZ esterase *enzyme*
STRZ satirize *ridicule* satirized satirizing (Br) satirise
STRZL streusel *cake topping*
STRZM asterism *constellation*
STRZMN steersman *helmsman* steersmen
STRZNBRZ Stars and Bars *Confederate flag*
STRZNDBRZ Stars and Bars *Confederate flag*
STRZNDSTRPS Stars and Stripes *US flag*
STRZNSTRPS Stars and Stripes *US flag*
STS acetous *sour*
STS setose *bristly*
STS sightsee *tour* sightsaw sightseeing
STS situs *place*
STS stoss *glacier*
STSBTH sitz bath *tub*
STSD set-aside *portion*
STSF satisfy *fulfill, pay* satisfied satisfying satisfies
STSFBL satisfiable *fulfilling, payable*
STSFD satisfied *fulfilled, paid*
STSFKDR satisfactory *fulfilling*
STSFKDRNS satisfactoriness *fulfillment*
STSFKSHN satisfaction *contentment, payment*
STSFKTR satisfactory *fulfilling*

Letters aren't doubled for single sounds: to find alley use **L** not **LL**. Use **Y** and **W** as hard sounds only: to find yellow use **YL**. (Br)=British spelling or usage. * See dictionary.

STSFKTRL satisfactorily *fulfilling*

STSFKTRNS satisfactoriness *fulfillment*

STSFL tsetse fly *insect* tsetse flies

STSFYBL satisfiable *fulfilling, payable*

STSH sottish *drunk, stupid*

STSH soutache *braid*

STSH stash *hide* stashes

STSHN cetacean *animal*

STSHN citation *mention, summons*

STSHN eustachian *ear tube*

STSHN situation *site, status, problem*

STSHN station *place*

STSHNL situational *site, status, problem*

STSHNL stational *church*

STSHNMSTR stationmaster *railroad*

STSHNR stationary *immobile*

STSHNR stationer *paper seller*

STSHNR stationery *writing paper*

STSHNRFRNT stationary front *weather*

STSHNWGN station wagon *vehicle*

STSHS cetaceous *marine animal*

STSHS setaceous *bristly*

STSHYN eustachian *ear tube*

STSKR setscrew *hardware*

STSL staysail *boat*

STSM satsuma *tree*

STSN citizen *resident*

STSN cytosine *gene*

STSN psittacine *parrots*

STSN sight-seeing (adj, n) *touring* sightseeing (v)

STSN sightseeing

STSNG sight-seeing (adj, n) *touring* sightseeing (v)

STSNG sightseeing

STSNR citizenry *residents* citizenries

STSNSHP citizenship

community membership

STSR sightseer *tourist*

STSRKM osteosarcoma *cancer*

STSS stasis *slowing* stases

STST acid test *severe test*

STST osteocyte *bone*

STST saddest *sorrow*

STST sootiest *blackest*

STSTT city-state *territory*

STSYN sight-seeing (adj, n) *touring* sightseeing (v)

STSYNG sight-seeing (adj, n) *touring* sightseeing (v)

STSYR sightseer *tourist*

STSZ stases (pl) *slowing* stasis

STSZM asceticism *severity*

STSZM stoicism *impassivity*

STT acetate *cellulose material*

STT astute *smart*

STT estate *property*

STT satiety *fullness*

STT set out (v) *describe, leave*

STT setout (n) *display*

STT sit out *refrain*

STT situate *locate* situated situating

STT stat *statistic*

STT state (v) *declare* stated stating

STT state (n) *condition, governed area*

STT statue *sculpture*

STT statute *law*

STT stet *retain* stetted stetting

STT stoat *animal*

STT stout (adj) *strong, fat, bold (n) ale, large size*

STTBL statable (or) stateable *report*

STTD situated *located*

STTD stated *spoken*

STTGRT Stuttgart *city*

STTH saw-toothed *teeth*

STTH sawtooth *teeth*

STTHD statehood *government*

STTHRDD stouthearted *brave*

STTHRDDL stoutheartedly *brave*

STTHRDDNS stoutheartedness *bravery*

STTHRTD stouthearted *brave*

STTHRTDL stoutheartedly *brave*

STTHRTDNS stoutheartedness *bravery*

STTHS statehouse *government*

STTHSKP stethoscope *listening device*

STTHSKPK stethoscopic *listening device*

STTHT saw-toothed *teeth*

STTK ecstatic *overjoyed*

STTK static (adj) *stationary, electrostatic (n) noise, opposition*

STTK staticky *noisy*

STTKL ecstatically *overjoyed*

STTKL statical (adj) *not moving, electrostatic* statically (adv)

STTKS statics *mechanics*

STTKSK cytotoxic *kill cells*

STTKSN cytotoxin *kill cells*

STTL astutely *wisely*

STTL stately *grand* statelier stateliest

STTLNS stateliness *grand*

STTLR statelier *grand*

STTLS stateless *no nation*

STTLSNS statelessness *no nation*

STTLST stateliest *grand*

STTLYR statelier *grand*

STTLYST stateliest *grand*

STTMNT statement *remark*

STTN stouten *make strong*

STTNG studding *wall*

STTNGSL studding sail *ship*

STTNS astuteness *wisdom*

STTR stator *machine part*

STTR statuary *sculpture* statuaries

STTR stature *height*

STTR statutory *legal*

STTR stutter *speech*

STTRL statutorily *legal*

Use letters that best describe the sounds you hear and omit the vowels. Use **S** or **K** instead of **C**: to find circle use **SRKL**. Use **J** to find joy, **JM** to find gem and **G** to find go.

STTRM stateroom *cabin*
STTRR stutterer *speech*
STTS statice *plant*
STTS status *condition, rank* statuses
STTSD stateside *continental US*
STTSDK statistic *estimate*
STTSDKL statistical (adj) *estimated* statistically (adv)
STTSDKS statistics *mathematics*
STTSDX statistics *mathematics*
STTSK statuesque *shapely*
STTSKW status quo *state of affairs*
STTSM statism *central control*
STTSMN statesman *politician* statesmen
STTSMNL statesmanly *politician*
STTSMNLK statesmanlike *politician*
STTSMNSHP statesmanship *politician*
STTSQ status quo *state of affairs*
STTSST statocyst *balance*
STTST statist *central control*
STTSTK statistic *estimate*
STTSTKL statistical (adj) *estimated* statistically (adv)
STTSTKS statistics *mathematics*
STTSTSHN statistician *mathematician*
STTSTX statistics *mathematics*
STTT statuette *sculpture*
STTT steatite *soapstone*
STTV stative *condition*
STTWD statewide *within state boundary*
STTWR statuary *sculpture* statuaries
STTWSK statuesque *shapely*
STTWT statuette *sculpture*
STTX statics *mechanics*

STTXK cytotoxic *kill cells*
STTXN cytotoxin *kill cells*
STTZM statism *central control*
STV stave *(v) puncture* staved (or) stove staving
STV stave *(n) wood strip*
STV steeve *incline* steeved steeving
STV stove *heater, (Br) greenhouse*
STVCH sotto voce *music*
STVDR stevedore *load or unload ships* stevedored stevedoring
STVPP stovepipe *chimney, hat*
STVZ staves (pl) *stick* staff
STVZKR stavesacre *plant*
STW stoa *porch*
STW stow away *(v) hide* stowaway (n)
STWD citywide *area*
STWJ stowage *cargo*
STWK stoic (or) stoical *impassive*
STWKL stoical (or) stoic (adj) *impassive* stoically (adv)
STWR estuary *delta area* estuaries
STWRD eastward *direction*
STWRD steward *manager*
STWRDS stewardess *manager (f)* stewardesses
STWRL estuarial *delta area*
STWRN estuarine *delta area*
STWRTHRDS osteoarthritis *disease*
STWRTHRTS osteoarthritis *disease*
STWRYL estuarial *delta area*
STWSHN situation *site, status, problem*
STWSHNL situational *site, status, problem*
STWSZM stoicism *impassivity*
STWT situate *locate* situated situating
STWTD situated *located*
STWW stow away *(v) hide*

stowaway (n)
STY ostia (pl) *mouth* ostium
STY stew *(n) food (v) cook, worry*
STYBLST osteoblast *cell*
STYD satiety *fullness*
STYD studio *workroom* studios
STYDNT student *learner*
STYDS studious *careful*
STYDY studio *workroom* studios
STYDYS studious *careful*
STYGNK osteogenic *bone*
STYGNSS osteogenesis *bone*
STYJNK osteogenic *bone*
STYJNSS osteogenesis *bone*
STYL ostiole *pore*
STYL stile *stair*
STYL style *manner, fashion* styled styling
STYL styli (pl) *pen* stylus
STYLBK stylebook *fashion*
STYLD styloid *pointed*
STYLFRM styliform *bristly*
STYLR styler *artist*
STYLS styleless *no fashion*
STYLS stylus *pen* styli
STYLSDK stylistic *designed*
STYLSDKL stylistically *design*
STYLSH stylish *fashion*
STYLSHL stylishly *fashion*
STYLSHNS stylishness *fashion*
STYLST stylist *artist*
STYLSTK stylistic *designed*
STYLSTKL stylistically *design*
STYLT stylet *probe*
STYLZ stylize *design* stylized stylizing (Br) stylise
STYLZSHN stylization *design* (Br) stylisation
STYM ostium *pore* ostia
STYN stallion *horse, stud*
STYP stoop *(v) bend (n) porch, bend*

Letters aren't doubled for single sounds: to find alley use **L** not **LL**. Use **Y** and **W** as hard sounds only: to find yellow use **YL**. (Br)=British spelling or usage. * See dictionary.

STYP stupe *hot compress, dolt*

STYPD stupid *dull, dense*

STYPDD stupidity *dull, dense* stupidities

STYPDL stupidly *dull, dense*

STYPDNS stupidness *dull, dense*

STYPDT stupidity *dull, dense* stupidities

STYPF stupefy *astound, make stupid* stupefied stupefying stupefies

STYPFKSHN stupefaction *stupid, astounded*

STYPLSD osteoplasty *surgery*

STYPLSDK osteoplastic *surgery*

STYPLST osteoplasty *surgery*

STYPLSTK osteoplastic *surgery*

STYPN stewpan *pot*

STYPNDS stupendous *amazing*

STYPNDSL stupendously *amazing*

STYPNDSNS stupendousness *greatness*

STYPR stupor *daze*

STYPRDK osteoporotic *disease*

STYPRSS osteoporosis *disease* osteoporoses

STYPRTK osteoporotic *disease*

STYPSN steapsin *pancreas*

STYPTH osteopath *doctor*

STYPTH osteopathy *bone*

STYPTHK osteopathic *bone*

STYPTHKL osteopathically *bone*

STYR sootier *blacker*

STYR stayer *supporter*

STYRD steward *manager*

STYRDS stewardess *manager (f)* stewardesses

STYRTHRDS osteoarthritis *disease*

STYRTHRTS osteoarthritis *disease*

STYSRKM osteosarcoma *cancer*

STYST osteocyte *bone*

STYST sootiest *blackest*

STYT astute *smart*

STYT satiety *fullness*

STYT statute *law*

STYTL astutely *wisely*

STYTNS astuteness *wisdom*

STYTR statutory *legal*

STYTRL statutorily *legal*

STYTT steatite *soapstone*

STYWRD steward *manager*

STYWRDS stewardess *manager (f)* stewardesses

STYWRTHRDS osteoarthritis *disease*

STYWRTHRTS osteoarthritis *disease*

STZBTH sitz bath *tub*

STZN citizen *resident*

STZN cytosine *gene*

STZNR citizenry *residents* citizenries

STZNSHP citizenship *community membership*

SV civvy *clothing* civvies

SV salve *remedy* salved salving

SV save *(v) rescue, preserve* saved saving

SV save *(prep, conj) except*

SV savvy *understand* savvied savvying savvies

SV sieve *sift* sieved sieving

SV solve *explain* solved solving

SVBL savable (or) saveable *redeem, keep*

SVBL solvable *explain*

SVBLD solvability *explain*

SVBLT solvability *explain*

SVBN sieva bean *vegetable*

SVCH seviche *food*

SVJ savage *(n) wild one (adj) fierce*

SVJL savagely *fierce*

SVJNS savageness *fierce*

SVJPN Sea of Japan *body of water*

SVJR savagery *fierceness* savageries

SVK civic *civil*

SVKS civics *social science*

SVL civil (adj) *polite* civilly (adv)

SVL civil law *justice*

SVL save-all *receptacle*

SVL saveloy *(Br) sausage*

SVLD civility *manners* civilities

SVLDFNS civil defense *protection*

SVLDFNTS civil defense *protection*

SVLK souvlakia (or) souvlaki *food*

SVLN civilian *non-military*

SVLRTS civil rights *liberties*

SVLSRVS civil service *government*

SVLSS solvolysis *chemistry*

SVLT civility *manners* civilities

SVLT svelte *shapely*

SVLTL sveltely *shapely*

SVLTNS svelteness *shapely*

SVLYN civilian *non-military*

SVLZ civilize *socially refine* civilized civilizing (Br) civilise

SVLZD civilized *cultivated* (Br) civilised

SVLZR civilizer *social refiner* (Br) civiliser

SVLZSHN civilization *culture* (Br) civilisation

SVN savanna *grassland*

SVN Savannah *city, river*

SVN savin *tree*

SVN saving *(prep, conj) except (n) deliverance*

SVN seven *number (7)*

SVNC solvency *pay debts, dissolve*

SVNCS seven seas *oceans*

SVNCZ seven seas *oceans*

SVND seventy *number (70)* seventies

SVNDTH seventieth *of number 70*

SVNDYTH seventieth *of number 70*

SVNFL sevenfold *times seven*

Use letters that best describe the sounds you hear and omit the vowels. Use **S** or **K** instead of **C**: to find circle use **SRKL**. Use **J** to find joy, **JM** to find gem and **G** to find go.

SVNFLD sevenfold *times seven*

SVNG saving *(prep, conj)* except *(n) deliverance*

SVNGL Svengali *hypnotist*

SVNGZ savings *money*

SVNNBLNGK sauvignon blanc *wine*

SVNNBLNK sauvignon blanc *wine*

SVNP seven-up *game*

SVNR souvenir *memento*

SVNS solvency *pay debts, dissolve*

SVNSZ seven seas *oceans*

SVNT savant *scholar*

SVNT seventy *number (70) seventies*

SVNT solvent *able, liquid*

SVNTC solvency *pay debts, dissolve*

SVNTH seventh *of number 7*

SVNTN seventeen *number (17)*

SVNTNTH seventeenth *of number 17*

SVNTS solvency *pay debts, dissolve*

SVNTTH seventieth *of number 70*

SVNTYTH seventieth *of number 70*

SVNYNBLNGK sauvignon blanc *wine*

SVNYNBLNK sauvignon blanc *wine*

SVNZ savings *money*

SVR saver *money in bank*

SVR savior (or) saviour *redeemer*

SVR savor *taste* (Br) savour

SVR savory *(adj) tasty* (Br) savoury

SVR savory *(adj) appetizing (n) herb, (Br) dessert savories* (Br) savoury

SVR sever *cut*

SVR severe *harsh* severer severest

SVR solver *answer*

SVRBL severable *able to be cut*

SVRBLD severability *cut*

SVRBLT severability *cut*

SVRD severity *harshness*

SVRL savorily *taste*

SVRL several *many*

SVRL severally *separately*

SVRL severely *harshly*

SVRLT severalty *separateness*

SVRN savarin *cake*

SVRN sovereign *ruler*

SVRND sovereignty *power sovereignties*

SVRNS savoriness *taste*

SVRNS severance *separation*

SVRNS severeness *harshness*

SVRNT sovereignty *power sovereignties*

SVRNTS severance *separation*

SVRSHN asseveration *division*

SVRT asseverate *divide* asseverated asseverating

SVRT severity *harshness*

SVSH seviche *food*

SVT civet *animal*

SVT savate *boxing*

SVT soviet *(often capitalized) council*

SVTNN Soviet Union *former country*

SVTNYN Soviet Union *former country*

SVTYNYN Soviet Union *former country*

SVWFR savoir faire *tact*

SVWRFR savoir faire *tact*

SVX civics *social science*

SVYR savior (or) saviour *redeemer*

SVYRD Savoyard *theater*

SVYT soviet *(often capitalized) council*

SVYTNN Soviet Union *former country*

SVYTYNN Soviet Union *former country*

SVYTYNYN Soviet Union *former country*

SW seaway *route*

SW sway *(n) power (v) swing*

SWB swab *wipe* swabbed swabbing

SWB swabbie *(slang) sailor* swabbies

SWBK swayback *bent backbone*

SWBK zwieback *cookie*

SWBKT swaybacked *bent backbone*

SWBL issuable *(adj) open* issuably *(adv)*

SWBL suable *(adj) legal action* suably *(adv)*

SWBLD suability *law*

SWBLT suability *law*

SWBR swabber *wipe*

SWCH swatch *cloth piece* swatches

SWCH switch *change, punish* switches

SWCHBK switchback *zigzag*

SWCHBLD switchblade *knife*

SWCHBRD switchboard *telephone*

SWCHDR switch-hitter *baseball*

SWCHHDR switch-hitter *baseball*

SWCHHT switch-hit *baseball*

SWCHHTR switch-hitter *baseball*

SWCHMN switchman *railroad* switchmen

SWCHR switcheroo *reverse* switcheroos

SWCHT switch-hit *baseball*

SWCHTR switch-hitter *baseball*

SWCHYRD switchyard *railroad*

SWD seaweed *plant*

SWD suede *leather*

SWD sweaty *damp* sweatier sweatiest

SWD Swede *of Sweden*

SWD sweetie *loved one*

SWDD sweated *labor*

SWDL saw-whet owl *bird*

SWDL swaddle *wrap*

Letters aren't doubled for single sounds: to find alley use **L** not **LL**. Use **Y** and **W** as hard sounds only: to find yellow use **YL**. (Br)=British spelling or usage. * See dictionary.

swaddled swaddling
SWDN Sweden *country*
SWDN swidden *cropland*
SWDNS sweatiness *wetness*
SWDR seawater *ocean*
SWDR swatter *paddle*
SWDR sweater *clothing*
SWDR sweatier *wet*
SWDRT sweetheart *loved one*
SWDRVST sweater-vest *clothing*
SWDSH Swedish *of Sweden*
SWDSH sweetish *like sugar*
SWDST sweatiest *wet*
SWDYR sweatier *wet*
SWDYST sweatiest *wet*
SWDZN soi-disant *so-called*
SWF swift *(adj, adv) fast (n) lizard, bird, reel*
SWFL swiftly *fast*
SWFNS swiftness *speed*
SWFT swift *(adj, adv) fast (n) lizard, bird, reel*
SWFTL swiftly *fast*
SWFTNS swiftness *speed*
SWG swag *(v) sway* swagged swagging
SWG swag *(n) loot, cluster, pack*
SWG swig *drink* swigged swigging
SWGMN swagman *(Aus) drifter*
SWGR swagger *prance, brag, bully*
SWHL Swahili *Bantu* Swahili (or) Swahilis
SWJ assuage *ease* assuaged assuaging
SWJ sewage *waste*
SWJ swage *shape* swaged swaging
SWJMNT assuagement *relief*
SWKRT sauerkraut *food*
SWL seawall *levee*
SWL sei whale *animal*
SWL swale *land*
SWL swallow *(v) eat (n) bird*
SWL swell *(v) expand* swelled swelling swollen

SWL swell *(n) wave (interj) great*
SWL swill *(n) garbage (v) guzzle*
SWLDR swelter *sweat*
SWLDRN sweltering *hot*
SWLDRNG sweltering *hot*
SWLFSH swellfish *puffer*
SWLHD swellhead *conceited*
SWLHDD swellheaded *conceited*
SWLHDDNS swellheadedness *conceit*
SWLN swelling *enlargement*
SWLN swollen *enlarged*
SWLNG swelling *enlargement*
SWLTL swallowtail *butterfly*
SWLTLD swallow-tailed *butterfly*
SWLTR swelter *sweat*
SWLTRN sweltering *hot*
SWLTRNG sweltering *hot*
SWM swam *(v-past)* swim
SWM swami *guru*
SWM swim *move in water* swam swum swimming
SWMBL swimmable *can move in water*
SWMN swimming *water sport*
SWMNG swimming *water sport*
SWMNGL swimmingly *very well*
SWMNL swimmingly *very well*
SWMP swamp *marsh*
SWMP swampy *marshy* swampier swampiest
SWMPLN swampland *marsh*
SWMPLND swampland *marsh*
SWMPNS swampiness *marshy*
SWMPR swamper *marsh dweller, helper*
SWMPR swampier *marshy*
SWMPST swampiest *marshy*
SWMPYR swampier *marshy*
SWMPYST swampiest

marshy
SWMR swimmer *move in water*
SWMRT swimmeret *appendage*
SWMST swimsuit *garment*
SWMWR swimwear *garment*
SWN sewing *stitch*
SWN Suwannee *river*
SWN swain *shepherd*
SWN swan *(n) bird* swans
SWN swan *(v) dally, swear* swanned swanning
SWN swine *pig*
SWN swoon *faint*
SWNDL swindle *cheat* swindled swindling
SWNDLR swindler *cheater*
SWNDV swan dive *plunge*
SWNG sewing *stitch*
SWNG swing *sway, sweep, arc* swung swinging
SWNG swingy *swaying* swingier swingiest
SWNG swung *(v-past) swing*
SWNGK swank *elegant*
SWNGK swanky *elegant* swankier swankiest
SWNGKL swankily *elegant*
SWNGKNS swankiness *elegance*
SWNGKR swankier *elegant*
SWNGKST swankiest *elegant*
SWNGKYR swankier *elegant*
SWNGKYST swankiest *elegant*
SWNGMN swingman *two positions*
SWNGMSHN sewing machine *stitcher*
SWNGN swinging *lively*
SWNGNG swinging *lively*
SWNGR swinger *lively one*
SWNGR swingier *swaying*
SWNGSHFT swing shift *work*
SWNGST swingiest *swaying*
SWNGYR swingier *swaying*
SWNGYST swingiest *swaying*
SWNHRD swineherd *pig*

Use letters that best describe the sounds you hear and omit the vowels. Use **S** or **K** instead of **C**: to find circle use **SRKL**. Use **J** to find joy, **JM** to find gem and **G** to find go.

tender
SWNK swank *elegant*
SWNK swanky *elegant*
swankier swankiest
SWNKL swankily *elegant*
SWNKNS swankiness
elegance
SWNKR swankier *elegant*
SWNKST swankiest *elegant*
SWNKYR swankier *elegant*
SWNKYST swankiest
elegant
SWNLR swindler *cheater*
SWNMSHN sewing
machine *stitcher*
SWNS issuance *emerge, emit*
SWNSDN swansdown
feathers, fabric
SWNSH swinish *piggy*
SWNSKN swanskin *feathers,*
fabric
SWNSNG swan song
farewell
SWNT suint *sweat*
SWNTS issuance *emerge,*
emit
SWNY soigné *sleek*
SWNZDN swansdown
feathers, fabric
SWP sew up *mend, complete,*
assure
SWP swap *trade* swapped
swapping
(Br) swop
SWP sweep *(v) brush,*
destroy, win all* swept
sweeping
SWP sweep *(n) broom,*
victory, scope*
SWP swept *(v-past) sweep*
SWP swipe *hit, remark, steal*
swiped swiping
SWP swoop *sweep, carry off*
SWPBK swept-back *wings*
SWPN sweeping *wide curve*
SWPNG sweeping *wide*
curve
SWPR swapper *trader*
SWPR sweeper *broom*
SWPSTKS sweepstakes
contest
SWPSTX sweepstakes

contest
SWPT swept *(v-past) sweep*
SWPTBK swept-back *wings*
SWR issuer *emerge, emit*
SWR ossuary *burial*
ossuaries
SWR sewer *waste pipe,*
stitcher
SWR soirée (or) soiree *party*
SWR sour *flavor*
SWR sower *planter*
SWR swear *oath* swore
swearing sworn
SWRBL sour ball *candy*
SWRBRTN sauerbraten *food*
SWRD eastward *direction*
SWRD seaward *toward the*
sea
SWRD sourdough *bread*
SWRD sward *grass*
SWRF swarf *fragments*
SWRJ sewerage *waste*
SWRKRM sour cream *milk*
product
SWRKRT sauerkraut *food*
SWRL swirl *whirl*
SWRL swirly *whirling*
swirlier swirliest
SWRLR swirlier *whirling*
SWRLST swirliest *whirling*
SWRLYR swirlier *whirling*
SWRLYST swirliest *whirling*
SWRM aswarm *crowded*
SWRM swarm *crowd*
SWRMSH sour mash
whiskey
SWRN swear in *oath*
SWRN sworn *(v-past) swear*
SWRPS sourpuss *grouch*
sourpusses
SWRR swearer *oath*
SWRTH seaworthy *afloat*
SWRTH swarthy *dark*
swarthier swarthiest
SWRTHNS seaworthiness
afloat
SWRTHNS swarthiness *dark*
SWRTHR swarthier *dark*
SWRTHST swarthiest *dark*
SWRTHYR swarthier *dark*
SWRTHYST swarthiest *dark*
SWRV swerve *veer* swerved

swerving
SWRWD sourwood *tree*
SWRWRD swearword
profanity
SWS SOS *call for help*
SWS swiss *fabric, cheese*
SWS Swiss *of Switzerland*
SWSD suicide *kill oneself*
suicided suiciding
SWSDK swastika *symbol*
SWSDL suicidal (adj) *kill*
oneself suicidally (adv)
SWSDR sou'wester *wind*
SWSH assuage *ease*
assuaged assuaging
SWSH swash *(v,n) swagger*
swashes
SWSH swish *(n) hiss, sweep,*
basketball (adj) smart
swishes
SWSH swishy *hissing, girlish*
swishier swishiest
SWSHBKL swashbuckle
dare swashbuckled
swashbuckling
SWSHBKLN swashbuckling
daring
SWSHBKLNG
swashbuckling *daring*
SWSHBKLR swashbuckler
daring one
SWSHMNT assuagement
relief
SWSHN suasion *influence*
SWSHR swishier *hissing,*
girlish
SWSHST swishiest *hissing,*
girlish
SWSHYR swishier *hissing,*
girlish
SWSHYST swishiest *hissing,*
girlish
SWSTK swastika *symbol*
SWSTR sou'wester *wind*
SWSV assuasive *relief*
SWT suet *fat*
SWT suite *set, group, music**
SWT swat *hit* swatted
swatting
SWT sweat *(v) perspire,*
worry sweat (or) sweated
sweating

Letters aren't doubled for single sounds: to find alley use **L** not **LL**. Use **Y** and **W** as hard
sounds only: to find yellow use **YL**. (Br)=British spelling or usage. * See dictionary.

SWT sweat (n) work, perspiration

SWT sweaty damp sweatier sweatiest

SWT sweet sugary, agreeable, skillful

SWT sweetie loved one

SWTBKS sweatbox prison

SWTBN sweatband hat liner, head band

SWTBND sweatband hat liner, head band

SWTBRD sweetbread food

SWTBRR sweetbrier rose

SWTBRYR sweetbrier rose

SWTBX sweatbox prison

SWTD sweated labor

SWTH swath strip

SWTH swathe bandage swathed swathing

SWTHR swather harvest

SWTHRT sweetheart loved one

SWTK sweet-talk (v) flattery sweet talk (n)

SWTL saw-whet owl bird

SWTL swaddle wrap swaddled swaddling

SWTMT sweetmeat candy

SWTN sweeten add sugar, increase

SWTNDSR sweet-and-sour taste

SWTNDSWR sweet-and-sour taste

SWTNN sweetening sugar, increase

SWTNNG sweetening sugar, increase

SWTNR sweetener sugar, increase

SWTNS sweatiness wetness

SWTNSR sweet-and-sour taste

SWTNSWR sweet-and-sour taste

SWTP sweet pea vegetable

SWTPNTS sweatpants trousers

SWTPPR sweet pepper vegetable

SWTPTD sweet potato vegetable

SWTPTT sweet potato vegetable

SWTR seawater ocean

SWTR swatter paddle

SWTR sweater clothing

SWTR sweatier wet

SWTRT sweetheart loved one

SWTRVST sweater-vest clothing

SWTSH Swedish of Sweden

SWTSH sweetish like sugar

SWTSHP sweatshop factory

SWTSHP sweetshop candy store

SWTSHRT sweatshirt garment

SWTSP sweetsop sugar apple

SWTSPT sweet spot hitting

SWTSRLN Switzerland country

SWTSRLND Switzerland country

SWTST sweat suit garment

SWTST sweatiest wet

SWTTH sweet tooth craving

SWTTTH sweet tooth craving

SWTYR sweatier wet

SWTYST sweatiest wet

SWTZRLN Switzerland country

SWTZRLND Switzerland country

SWV Soave wine

SWV suave smooth

SWVD suavity smoothness

SWVL suavely smoothly

SWVL swivel twist swiveled (or) swivelled swiveling (or) swivelling

SWVNS suaveness smoothness

SWVT suavity smoothness

SWZH assuage ease assuaged assuaging

SWZHMNT assuagement relief

SWZHN suasion influence

SWZL swizzle mix, drink swizzled swizzling

SWZLN Swaziland country

SWZLND Swaziland country

SWZLR swizzler stirrer

SWZLSTK swizzle stick stirrer

SWZV assuasive relief

SX ice ax tool ice axes

SX sax saxophone

SX sex gender

SX sexy tempting sexier sexiest

SX six number (6) sixes

SX sox (pl) stocking sock

SXD sixty number (60) sixties

SXDNT sextant distances

SXDSH sixtyish like or nearly 60

SXDTH sixtieth of number 60

SXDYSH sixtyish like or nearly 60

SXDYTH sixtieth of number 60

SXFL sixfold times 6

SXFLD sixfold times 6

SXFN saxophone music

SXFNK saxophonic music

SXFNST saxophonist musician

SXGN six-gun weapon

SXHRN saxhorn music

SXJNRN sexagenarian age 60-69

SXJNRYN sexagenarian age 60-69

SXL sexily tempting

SXL sexual (adj) gender sexually (adv)

SXLD sexuality gender

SXLG sexology sex study

SXLJ sexology sex study

SXLJST sexologist sex study

SXLS sexless no gender

SXLT sexuality gender

SXLZ sexualize gender sexualized sexualizing

SXMBL sex symbol idol

SXN Saxon person

SXN saxony fabric saxonies

SXNS sexiness temptation

SXPK six-pack group of 6

Use letters that best describe the sounds you hear and omit the vowels. Use **S** or **K** instead of **C**: to find circle use **SRKL**. Use **J** to find joy, **JM** to find gem and **G** to find go.

SXPLTSHN sexploitation *misuse sex*
SXPN sixpenny *money*
SXPNS sixpence *money*
SXPNTS sixpence *money*
SXPT sexpot *arousing one (f)*
SXR sexier *tempting*
SXRN saxhorn *music*
SXSHDR six-shooter *weapon*
SXSHTR six-shooter *weapon*
SXSMBL sex symbol *idol*
SXST sexiest *tempting*
SXT sixty *number (60)* sixties
SXTH sixth *of number 6*
SXTLN sextillion *number*
SXTLYN sextillion *number*
SXTN sexton *clergy*
SXTN sixteen *number (16)*
SXTNT sextant *distances*
SXTNTH sixteenth *of number 16*
SXTPL sextuple *times 6* sextupled sextupling
SXTPLT sextuplet *6 offspring*
SXTSH sixtyish *like or nearly 60*
SXTT sextet *group of 6*
SXTTH sixtieth *of number 60*
SXTYN sextillion *number*
SXTYPL sextuple *times 6* sextupled sextupling
SXTYPLT sextuplet *6 offspring*
SXTYSH sixtyish *like or nearly 60*
SXTYTH sixtieth *of number 60*
SXWL sexual (adj) *gender* sexually (adv)
SXWLD sexuality *gender*
SXWLT sexuality *gender*
SXWLZ sexualize *gender* sexualized sexualizing
SXYR sexier *tempting*
SXYST sexiest *tempting*
SXZM sexism *gender bias*
SY aecia (pl) *fungus* aecium
SY issue *(v) emerge, result, provide* issued issuing
SY issue *(n) matter, child, publishing**

SY sue *seek justice* sued suing
SYBL issuable (adj) *open* issuably (adv)
SYBL sayable *spoken*
SYBL soluble *dissolve, explain*
SYBLD solubility *dissolve*
SYBLT solubility *dissolve*
SYBLZ solubilize *dissolve* solubilized solubilizing (Br) solubilise
SYBN soybean *plant*
SYD sayyid *lord*
SYDBL suitable (adj) *fit* suitably (adv)
SYDBLD suitability *fitness*
SYDBLT suitability *fitness*
SYDK sciatic *nerve*
SYDK sciatica *pain*
SYDL Seattle *city*
SYDNG suiting *fabric*
SYDR suitor *pursue, sue, woo*
SYL soil *(n) earth (v) get dirty*
SYLBRN soilborne *transmission*
SYLJ soilage *dirt*
SYLR soilure *stain*
SYLS soilless *no dirt*
SYLSDK sciolistic *smart*
SYLST sciolist *smarty*
SYLSTK sciolistic *smart*
SYLYR soilure *stain*
SYLZM sciolism *learning*
SYM aecium *fungus* aecia
SYM assume *suppose* assumed assuming
SYMBL assumable (adj) *received, supposed* assumably (adv)
SYMN assuming *pretentious*
SYMNG assuming *pretentious*
SYMZ Siamese *of Thailand*
SYN cyan *color*
SYN ossein *collagen*
SYN saying *proverb*
SYN scion *heir, plant shoot*
SYN seeing *inasmuch as*
SYN sienna *pigment*
SYND cyanide *poison*

SYNDK cyanotic *discoloration*
SYNDK syenitic *rock*
SYNG saying *proverb*
SYNG seeing *inasmuch as*
SYNJN cyanogen *gas*
SYNK cyanic *acid*
SYNMD cyanamide *chemical*
SYNN cyanine *dye*
SYNS science *nature study*
SYNS seance *spirits*
SYNSS cyanosis *discoloration*
SYNT syenite *rock*
SYNTFK scientific *observant*
SYNTFKL scientifically *observantly*
SYNTK cyanotic *discoloration*
SYNTK syenitic *rock*
SYNTS science *nature study*
SYNTS seance *spirits*
SYNTST scientist *student of nature*
SYNTZM scientism *nature study*
SYR assayer *estimator*
SYR essayer *tester*
SYR icier *frozen*
SYR issuer *emerge, emit*
SYR ossuary *burial* ossuaries
SYR sawyer *cutter, insect, tree*
SYR seer *prophet* seers (or) seer
SYR sewer *waste pipe*
SYR sierra *mountains, fish*
SYR sire *(v) beget* sired siring
SYR sire *(n) father*
SYRCHN sea urchin *sea animal*
SYRLN Sierra Leone *country*
SYRLYN Sierra Leone *country*
SYRN sierran *(often capitalized) mountains*
SYS osseous *bony*
SYSD siesta *nap*
SYSD suicide *kill oneself*

Letters aren't doubled for single sounds: to find alley use **L** not **LL**. Use **Y** and **W** as hard sounds only: to find yellow use **YL**. (Br)=British spelling or usage. * See dictionary.

suicided suiciding
SYSDL suicidal (adj) *kill oneself* suicidally (adv)
SYSPR aeciospore *fungus*
SYST essayist *writer*
SYST iciest *frozen*
SYST siesta *nap*
SYT suet *fat*
SYT suit *set, clothes*
SYTBL suitable (adj) *fit* suitably (adv)
SYTBLD suitability *fitness*
SYTBLT suitability *fitness*
SYTK sciatic *nerve*
SYTK sciatica *pain*
SYTKS suitcase *luggage*
SYTL Seattle *city*
SYTNG suiting *fabric*
SYTR suitor *pursue, sue, woo*
SYWBL issuable (adj) *open* issuably (adv)
SYWNS issuance *emerge, emit*
SYWNTS issuance *emerge, emit*
SYWR issuer *emerge, emit*
SYWR ossuary *burial* ossuaries
SYWR sewer *waste pipe*
SYWSD suicide *kill oneself* suicided suiciding
SYWSDL suicidal (adj) *kill oneself* suicidally (adv)
SYWT suet *fat*
SZ assize *session*
SZ cease *stop* ceased ceasing
SZ oases (pl) *water* oasis
SZ says *speaks*
SZ seize *grasp* seized seizing
SZ size (v) *compare, stiffen* sized sizing
SZ size (n) *bigness, glue*
SZ Sousa *composer*
SZBL sizable (or) sizeable (adj) *large* sizably (adv)
SZBLNS sizableness *large*
SZFN sousaphone *music*
SZFR cease-fire *no shooting*
SZFYR cease-fire *no shooting*

SZG syzygy *in line* syzygies
SZHN scission *cutting*
SZHR caesura *pause* caesuras
SZHR seizure *grasp, spasm*
SZHRL caesural *pause*
SZJ syzygy *in line* syzygies
SZL sisal *plant*
SZL sizzle *fry* sizzled sizzling
SZLD sozzled *drunk*
SZLR sizzler *scorcher*
SZLS ceaseless *constant*
SZLSL ceaselessly *constantly*
SZLSNS ceaselessness *without pause*
SZM cesium *element* (Br) caesium
SZM isozyme *enzyme*
SZM schism *division*
SZMDK schismatic *division*
SZMGRF seismograph *earthquake*
SZMGRF seismography *earthquake*
SZMGRFR seismographer *earthquake*
SZMGRM seismogram *earthquake*
SZMK seismic *earthquake*
SZMKL seismically *earthquake*
SZMLG seismology *earthquake*
SZMLJ seismology *earthquake*
SZMLJKL seismological *earthquake*
SZMLJST seismologist *earthquake*
SZMMDR seismometer *earthquake*
SZMMTR seismometer *earthquake*
SZMMTR seismometry *earthquake*
SZMSD seismicity *earthquake*
SZMST seismicity *earthquake*
SZMTK schismatic *division*

SZMTZ schismatize *divide* schismatized schismatizing
SZN Cézanne *artist*
SZN season (v) *spice* (n) *time of year*
SZN seizing *rope*
SZN sizing *glue, measurement*
SZNBL seasonable (adj) *well-timed* seasonably (adv)
SZNBLNS seasonableness *good timing*
SZNDSST cease and desist *stop*
SZNG seizing *rope*
SZNG sizing *glue, measurement*
SZNL seasonal (adj) *time of year* seasonally (adv)
SZNLD seasonality *time of year*
SZNLS seasonless *any time*
SZNLT seasonality *time of year*
SZNN seasoning *spices*
SZNNG seasoning *spices*
SZNR seasoner *spices*
SZR Caesar *Roman ruler*
SZR caesura *pause* caesuras
SZR scissor *cutter* scissors
SZRK Sazerac (trademark) *liquor*
SZRL caesural *pause*
SZRN Caesarean *birth*
SZRN suzerain *overlord*
SZRNSKSHN Caesarean section *birth*
SZRNT suzerainty *realm*
SZRS scissors *cutting tool*
SZRYN Caesarean *birth*
SZRYNSKSHN Caesarean section *birth*
SZRZ scissors *cutting tool*
SZYM cesium *element* (Br) caesium
SZYR caesura *pause* caesuras (or) caesurae
SZYRL caesural *pause*

Use letters that best describe the sounds you hear and omit the vowels. Use **S** or **K** instead of **C**: to find circle use **SRKL**. Use **J** to find joy, **JM** to find gem and **G** to find go.

T

T at *(prep) denotes place, time, manner**
T ate *(v-past) eat*
T aught *all, zero*
T auto *car* autos
T e.t.a. *(abbr) estimated time of arrival*
T eat *ingest, corrode* ate eating eaten
T eight *number (8)*
T eighty *number (80)* eighties
T eta *Greek letter*
T etui *small case* etuis
T eye-to-eye *agreement*
T iota *tiny bit*
T it *that thing*
T oat *grain*
T ought *should*
T out *(adv) not in (v) eject (prep) outward (adj) external, absent**
T out of *depleted, beyond*
T taille *land tax*
T Tao *philosophy*
T tau *Greek letter*
T taw *Hebrew letter, marble*
T tea *beverage*
T tee *(v) golf* teed teeing
T tee *(n) alphabet letter, holder, shape*
T Thai *of Thailand* Thai (or) Thais
T ti *musical tone, tree*
T tie *knot, link* tied tying
T to *(prep) until, purpose, direction**
T toe *foot* toed toeing
T toea *money* toea
T too *also, excessively*
T tow *(v, n) pull (n) fiber*
T toy *(n) plaything (v) play*

(adj) small
T two *number (2)* twos
T Utah *US State*
T Ute *Native American*
TB attaboy *(interj) approval*
TB tab *(v) designate, space* tabbed tabbing
TB tab *(n) flap, bill, space*
TB tabby *(n) cat, cement (adj) striped* tabbies
TB taboo *banned* taboos
TB tibia *bone* tibiae
TB toby *mug*
TB tub *bathe* tubbed tubbing
TB tuba *horn* tubas
TB tubby *fat* tubbier tubbiest
TB tube *pipe, tire, TV*
TBBL tubbable *bathe*
TBD out-of-body *spiritual*
TBD outbid *offer more* outbid outbidding
TBFL tubful *vat*
TBFR two-by-four *size*
TBG tea bag *pouch*
TBGN toboggan *sled*
TBGRF autobiography *personal history* autobiographies
TBGRFK autobiographic *of oneself*
TBGRFKL autobiographical *(adj) of oneself* autobiographically (adv)
TBGRFR autobiographer *writer*
TBK outback *rural area*
TBK tieback *curtain*
TBK tobacco *plant* tobaccos
TBKNST tobacconist *dealer*
TBL addable (or) addible *sum*
TBL eatable *food*
TBL edible *fit to eat*
TBL T-ball *sport*
TBL T-bill *treasury note*
TBL tabbouleh *food*
TBL tabla *drum*
TBL table *(n) furniture, list*
TBL table *(v) remove from agenda, (Br) place on*

agenda tabled tabling
TBL tableau *picture* tableaux
TBL tea ball *strainer*
TBL tubal *tube*
TBL tubule *pipe*
TBLCHR tablature *music*
TBLD edibility *fit to eat*
TBLD tabloid *(adj) compressed (n) newspaper*
TBLDN outbuilding *shed*
TBLDNG outbuilding *shed*
TBLDR tabulator *counter*
TBLDT table d'hôte *meal*
TBLFL tableful *amount*
TBLGSHN tubal ligation *surgery*
TBLHP table-hop *socialize* table-hopped table-hopping
TBLKLTH tablecloth *cover*
TBLMT tablemate *companion*
TBLN tableland *plateau*
TBLND tableland *plateau*
TBLR tabular *columns, flat*
TBLR tubular *pipe*
TBLRS tabula rasa *blank slate* tabulae rasae
TBLRZ tabula rasa *blank slate* tabulae rasae
TBLS tubeless *pneumatic*
TBLSHN tabulation *count*
TBLSPN tablespoon *measure*
TBLSPNFL tablespoonful *measure* tablespoonfuls
TBLT edibility *fit to eat*
TBLT tablet *pad, pill*
TBLT tabulate *count* tabulated tabulating
TBLTNS table tennis *sport*
TBLTP tabletop *flat area*
TBLTR tablature *music*
TBLTR tabulator *counter*
TBLTYR tablature *music*
TBLWN table wine *beverage*
TBLWR tableware *utensils*
TBN autobahn *highway*
TBN outbound *going away*
TBN T-bone *steak*
TBN tubing *pipe*
TBND outbound *going away*

Letters aren't doubled for single sounds: to find alley use **L** not **LL**. Use **Y** and **W** as hard sounds only: to find yellow use **YL**. (Br)=British spelling or usage. * See dictionary.

TBND tabanid *horsefly*
TBNG tubing *pipe*
TBR T-bar *ski lift*
TBR tabor *drum*
(Br) tabour
TBR teaberry *plant*
teaberries
TBR tubbier *fat*
TBR tuber *bulb*
TBRD outboard *motor*
TBRD outbreed *unrelated*
mates outbred
outbreeding
TBRD tabard *tunic*
TBRK outbreak *increase,*
revolt
TBRKL tubercle *lump*
TBRKLN tuberculin *test*
TBRKLR tubercular *disease*
TBRKLS tuberculous
diseased
TBRKLSS tuberculosis
disease tuberculoses
TBRKR tiebreaker *score*
TBRKYLN tuberculin *test*
TBRKYLR tubercular *disease*
TBRKYLS tuberculous
diseased
TBRKYLSS tuberculosis
disease tuberculoses
TBRNKL tabernacle *tent,*
box
TBRQLN tuberculin *test*
TBRQLR tubercular *disease*
TBRQLS tuberculous
diseased
TBRQLSS tuberculosis
disease tuberculoses
TBRS tuberous *lumpy*
TBRSD tuberosity *lump*
tuberosities
TBRST outburst *shout*
TBRST tuberosity *lump*
tuberosities
TBRT taboret (or) tabouret
stool
TBRZ tuberose *herb*
TBSK Tabasco (*trademark*)
sauce
TBST tubaist (or) tubist
musician
TBST tubbiest *fat*

TBT to boot *added*
TBT towboat *ship*
TBT two-bit *cheap*
TBTN Tibetan *of Tibet*
TBTS two bits *25 cents*
TBY tibia *bone* tibiae
TBYGRF autobiography
personal history
autobiographies
TBYGRFK autobiographic
of oneself
TBYGRFKL
autobiographical (adj) *of*
oneself autobiographically
(adv)
TBYGRFR autobiographer
writer
TBYL tubule *pipe*
TBYLDR tabulator *counter*
TBYLR tabular *columns, flat*
TBYLR tubular *pipe*
TBYLRS tabula rasa *blank*
slate tabulae rasae
TBYLRZ tabula rasa *blank*
slate tabulae rasae
TBYLSHN tabulation *count*
TBYLT tabulate *count*
tabulated tabulating
TBYLTR tabulator *counter*
TBYR tubbier *fat*
TBYST tubbiest *fat*
TBZ tabes *disease* tabes
TCH attach *join to*
TCH tai chi (or) t'ai chi
martial arts
TCH teach *educate* taught
teaching
TCH tetchy *peevish* tetchier
tetchiest
TCH touch (v) *feel, affect,*
concern (n) *feel, hint,*
defect* touches
TCH touchy *sensitive*
touchier touchiest
TCHBK touchback *football*
TCHBL attachable *join to*
TCHBL teachable *educate*
TCHBL touchable *feel*
TCHD attached *joined to*
TCHD touched *grateful,*
crazy
TCHDN touchdown *football*

TCHFL touchy-feely
emotions
TCHHL touchhole *vent*
TCHL tetchily *peevish*
TCHL touchhole *vent*
TCHLR titular *known as*
TCHMNT attachment
seizure, fidelity
TCHN teach-in *seminar*
TCHN teaching *education*
TCHN touching *moving,*
concerning
TCHNDG touch and go
(adj) *uncertain*
TCHNDG touch-and-go (n)
landing
TCHNG teaching *education*
TCHNG touch and go (adj)
uncertain
TCHNG touch-and-go (n)
landing
TCHNG touching *moving,*
concerning
TCHNS tetchiness *peevish*
TCHNS touchiness
sensitivity
TCHP touch-up (n) *fix* touch
up (v)
TCHR teacher *educator*
TCHR tetchier *peevish*
TCHR toucher *feeler*
TCHR touchier *sensitive*
TCHST tetchiest *peevish*
TCHST touchiest *sensitive*
TCHSTN touchstone *flint,*
standard
TCHT attached *joined to*
TCHT touched *grateful,*
crazy
TCHTP touch-type (v)
typing
TCHWD touchwood *punk*
TCHYR tetchier *peevish*
TCHYR touchier *sensitive*
TCHYST tetchiest *peevish*
TCHYST touchiest *sensitive*
TD e.t.d. (abbr) *estimated*
time of departure
TD étude *music*
TD outdo (v) *best* outdid
outdone outdoing
outdoes

Use letters that best describe the sounds you hear and omit the vowels. Use **S** or **K** instead of **C**: to find circle use **SRKL**. Use **J** to find joy, **JM** to find gem and **G** to find go.

TD tad *boy, bit*
TD tatty *shabby* tattier tattiest
TD teddy *bear, chemise* teddies
TD teiid *lizard*
TD tide *(n) ocean*
TD tide *(v) surge* tided tiding
TD tidy *(v) make neat* tidied tidying tidies
TD tidy *(adj) fair, neat* tidier tidyiest
TD tidy *(n) box, napkin* tidies
TD tie-dye *fabric* tie-dyed tie-dyeing
TD to-do *fuss* to-dos
TD toad *frog*
TD toady *flatter* toadied toadying toadies
TD tod *(Br) clump*
TD today *now*
TD toddy *drink* toddies
TD toed *foot*
TD tutti *music*
TDBR teddy bear *toy*
TDBT tidbit *morsel*
TDD outdid *bested*
TDDD outdated *not current*
TDF auto-da-fé *burn* autos-da-fé
TDF teed off *angry*
TDFRD tutti-frutti *fruits*
TDFRT tutti-frutti *fruits*
TDFSH toadfish *animal*
TDL tattle *gossip* tattled tattling
TDL tidal (adj) *ocean* tidally (adv)
TDL tiddly *(Br) drunk*
TDL title *name, rank* titled titling
TDL tittle *mark*
TDL toddle *totter* toddled toddling
TDL tootle *sound* tootled tootling
TDL total *(v) add up, wreck* totaled (or) totalled totaling (or) totalling
TDL total *(n, adj, adv) entire*
TDL totally *completely*
TDLD titled *rank, name*

TDLDNG titillating *suggestive*
TDLDV titillative *suggestive*
TDLHLDR titleholder *champion*
TDLJ tutelage *teach*
TDLJKL tautological (adj) *repetitious* tautologically (adv)
TDLN tideland *shore*
TDLND tideland *shore*
TDLR tattler *informer*
TDLR tiddler *(Br) fish*
TDLR toddler *child*
TDLR tutelary *guardian* tutelaries
TDLSHN titillation *arousal*
TDLT titillate *arouse* titillated titillating
TDLTDL tittle-tattle *gossip* tittle-tattled tittle-tattling
TDLTL tattletale *informer*
TDLTN titillating *suggestive*
TDLTNG titillating *suggestive*
TDLTTL tittle-tattle *gossip* tittle-tattled tittle-tattling
TDLTV titillative *suggestive*
TDLWNGKS tiddlywinks *game*
TDLWNGX tiddlywinks *game*
TDLWNKS tiddlywinks *game*
TDLWNX tiddlywinks *game*
TDLWV tidal wave *ocean*
TDLZ totalize *add up* totalized totalizing
TDLZDR totalizator (or) totalisator *wager*
TDLZTR totalizator (or) totalisator *wager*
TDM autotomy *division*
TDM Te Deum *hymn* Te Deums
TDM tedium *boredom*
TDM totem *pole*
TDMNCHNL two-dimensional *flat*
TDMNCHNLD two-dimensionality *flatness*
TDMNCHNLT two-dimensionality *flatness*
TDMNSHNL two-dimensional *flat*
TDMNSHNLD two-

dimensionality *flatness*
TDMNSHNLT two-dimensionality *flatness*
TDMR tautomer *isomer*
TDMRK tidemark *high water*
TDMRZM tautomerism *isomer*
TDMS autotomous *division*
TDMZ autotomize *divide* autotomized autotomizing
TDN outdone *bested*
TDN tie-down *rope*
TDNG tatting *lace*
TDNGS tidings (pl) *news* tiding
TDNM tautonym *name*
TDNS tattiness *shabby*
TDNS toe dance (n) *ballet* toe-dance (v)
TDNSN thé dansant *tea dance* thés dansants
TDNSN toe dancing *ballet*
TDNSNG toe dancing *ballet*
TDNSR toe dancer *ballet*
TDNTS toe dance (n) *ballet* toe-dance (v)
TDNTSN toe dancing *ballet*
TDNTSNG toe dancing *ballet*
TDNTSR toe dancer *ballet*
TDPL tadpole *frog*
TDPTNC totipotency *cloning*
TDPTNS totipotency *cloning*
TDPTNT totipotent *cloning*
TDPTNTC totipotency *cloning*
TDPTNTS totipotency *cloning*
TDR outdoor *open air*
TDR outdraw *attract, gun* outdrew outdrawn outdrawing
TDR tatter *shred, rag*
TDR tattier *shabby*
TDR tawdry *gaudy* tawdrier tawdriest
TDR teeter *(n) seesaw (v) wobble*
TDR tetter *disease*
TDR titer *concentration*
TDR titter *giggle*

Letters aren't doubled for single sounds: to find alley use **L** not **LL**. Use **Y** and **W** as hard sounds only: to find yellow use **YL**. (Br)=British spelling or usage. * See dictionary.

TDR totter *sway*
TDR tottery *infirm*
TDR touter *praiser*
TDR Tudor *royalty*
TDR tutor *teacher*
TDR two-door (adj) *vehicle*
TDRBRD teeterboard *seesaw*
TDRD tattered *torn*
TDRDMLN tatterdemalion
  ragged one
TDRDMLYN tatterdemalion
  ragged one
TDRL tawdrily *gaudy*
TDRN outdrawn *attract, gun*
TDRN tottering *unsteady*
TDRNG tottering *unsteady*
TDRNS tawdriness *gaudy*
TDRR tawdrier *gaudy*
TDRR titterer *giggler*
TDRS outdress *clothing*
TDRSHP tutorship *teaching*
TDRSL tattersall *pattern*
TDRST tawdriest *gaudy*
TDRTDR teeter-totter *seesaw*
TDRTTR teeter-totter *seesaw*
TDRYR tawdrier *gaudy*
TDRYST tawdriest *gaudy*
TDRZ out-of-doors *open air*
TDRZ outdoors *open air*
TDRZ outdoorsy *like open air*
TDS tedious *tiresome*
TDSL tediously *tiresome*
TDSNS tediousness *tiresome*
TDST tattiest *shabby*
TDSTL toadstool *fungus*
TDSTN toadstone *charm*
TDSTNS outdistance *go
  farther* outdistanced
  outdistancing
TDSTNTS outdistance *go
  farther* outdistanced
  outdistancing
TDT out-of-date *obsolete*
TDT toe-to-toe *fight*
TDTD outdated *not current*
TDTT tête-à-tête *private*
TDV additive *ingredient*
TDVT titivate *smarten*
  titivated titivating
TDW tideway *channel*
TDWDR tidewater *coastal*
TDWTR tidewater *coastal*

TDYM Te Deum *hymn* Te
  Deums
TDYM tedium *boredom*
TDYR tattier *shabby*
TDYS tedious *tiresome*
TDYSL tediously *tiresome*
TDYSNS tediousness
  tiresome
TDYST tattiest *shabby*
TDYZM toadyism *flattery*
TDZ outdoes *bests*
TDZM toadyism *flattery*
TF étouffée *stew*
TF taffy *chewy candy* taffies
TF tee off *golf* teed off
  teeing off
TF teff *grain*
TF tiff *quarrel*
TF toff *(Br) dandy*
TF toffee (or) toffy *butter
  candy* toffees (or) toffies
TF tofu *food*
TF tophi (pl) *gout* tophus
TF tough *strong*
TF toughie *thug* toughies
TF tufa *porous rock*
TF tuff *volcanic rock*
TF tuft *clump*
TFD taffeta *fabric*
TFD typhoid *disease*
TFDFVR typhoid fever
  disease
TFDMR Typhoid Mary
  carrier Typhoid Marys
TFDR outfitter *equipment,
  dress*
TFKS outfox *outsmart*
TFL eightfold *eight times*
TFL outfall *sewer*
TFL outfield *baseball*
TFL outflow *stream out*
TFL toughly *strong, mean*
TFL twofold *two times*
TFLD eightfold *eight times*
TFLD outfield *baseball*
TFLD twofold *two times*
TFLDR outfielder *baseball*
TFLN Teflon *(trademark) no
  sticking*
TFLNGK outflank *get around*
TFLNK outflank *get around*
TFLSL typhlosole *fold*

TFMNDD tough-minded
  realistic
TFN tiffany *fabric* tiffanies
TFN tiffin *(Br) lunch*
TFN toughen *make strong*
TFN typhoon *storm*
TFNM taphonomy *fossil*
TFNMK taphonomic *fossil*
TFNMST taphonomist *fossil*
TFNS toughness *strong,
  mean*
TFR tephra *ash*
TFR twofer *two for one*
TFRL taffrail *ship*
TFS outface *defy* outfaced
  outfacing
TFS tophus *gout* tophi
TFS typhus *disease*
TFSD two-faced *false*
TFSDD two-fisted *energetic*
TFSHS tufaceous *porous
  rock*
TFSHS tuffaceous *volcanic
  rock*
TFST two-faced *false*
TFSTD two-fisted *energetic*
TFT outfit *equip, dress*
  outfitted outfitting
TFT taffeta *fabric*
TFT toft *homestead*
TFT tuffet *seat*
TFT tuft *clump*
TFTR outfitter *equipment,
  dress*
TFX outfox *outsmart*
TFZ two-phase *stages*
TG outgo *outlet* outgoes
  outgoing
TG tag *label, touch* tagged
  tagging
TG tog *dress up* togged
  togging
TG toga *garment*
TG Togo *country*
TG togue *fish*
TG tug *pull* tugged tugging
TGBT tugboat *ship*
TGFWR tug-of-war *struggle*
TGL toggle *pin, switch*
  toggled toggling
TGLBLT toggle bolt
  hardware

Use letters that best describe the sounds you hear and omit the vowels. Use **S** or **K**
instead of **C**: to find circle use **SRKL**. Use **J** to find joy, **JM** to find gem and **G** to find go.

TGLNG tagalong *follow*
TGLSWCH toggle switch *electricity*
TGLTL tagliatelle *noodle*
TGLYTL tagliatelle *noodle*
TGM autogamy *self-fertilization*
TGMN tegmen *cover* tegmina
TGMN tegmenta (pl) *cover* tegmentum
TGMNL tegmental *cover*
TGMNM tegmentum *cover* tegmenta
TGMNT tegmenta (pl) *cover* tegmentum
TGMNT tegument *cover*
TGMNTL tegmental *cover*
TGMNTM tegmentum *cover* tegmenta
TGMS autogamous *self-fertilized*
TGN outgoing *leaving, sociable*
TGN outgun *more firepower*
TGNG outgoing *leaving, sociable*
TGR outgrow *grow too fast* outgrew outgrown
TGR tiger *animal*
TGR tigereye (or) tiger's-eye *stone*
TGR toggery *clothing*
TGR tugger *puller*
TGRF autograph *signature*
TGRFK autographic *self-written*
TGRLL tiger lily *flower* tiger lilies
TGRMTH tiger moth *insect*
TGRN outgrown *grow too fast*
TGRS outgross *more money*
TGRS tigress *animal*
TGRS Tigris *river*
TGRTH outgrowth *by-product*
TGRZ tiger's-eye (or) tigereye *stone*
TGS outguess *outwit*
TGSGLP Tegucigalpa *city*
TGTHR together *same time,*

combined, organized*
TGTHRNS togetherness *in one place*
TGWN outgoing *leaving, sociable*
TGWNG outgoing *leaving, sociable*
TGWR tug-of-war *struggle*
TGYMNT tegument *cover*
TGZ togs *clothing*
TH edh *phonetic letter*
TH eighth *of number 8* eighths
TH oath *vow* oaths
TH thaw *melt*
TH the *definite article**
TH thee *(archaic) you*
TH thew *strength*
TH they *others*
TH thigh *leg*
TH thou *(archaic) you*
TH though *while, however, even if**
TH thy *(archaic) your*
TH towhee *bird*
TH youth *immature one* youths
THBN thighbone *leg*
THCH thatch *straw cover* thatches
THCHR thatcher *straw cover*
THD Tahiti *island*
THD theta *Greek letter*
THD they'd *(contr) they had, they would*
THD thud *thump* thudded thudding
THD towhead *blond, sandbar*
THDC theodicy *God and evil* theodicies
THDK thetic *poetry*
THDKL thetically *poetry*
THDLT theodolite *surveying*
THDR theater (or) theatre *stage*
THDRGR theatergoer *audience*
THDRGWR theatergoer *audience*
THDS theodicy *God and evil* theodicies
THDT thought-out (adj)

considered thought out (v)
THDW thataway *direction*
THF thief *steal* thieves
THFL youthful (adj) *immature* youthfully (adv)
THFLNS youthfulness *immaturity*
THFN theophany *vision of God* theophanies
THFNK theophanic *vision of God*
THFT theft *steal*
THG thug *gangster*
THGN theogony *origin of gods* theogonies
THGR thuggery *gangster*
THGSH thuggish *gangster*
THK ethic *principle*
THK ootheca *egg case* oothecae
THK theca *skin* thecae
THK thick *dense*
THKD thickhead *stupid one*
THKDD thicketed *trees*
THKDD thickheaded *stupid*
THKHD thickhead *stupid one*
THKHDD thickheaded *stupid*
THKL ethical (adj) *principled* ethically (adv)
THKL thecal *skin*
THKLD ethicality *principles*
THKLNS ethicalness *principles*
THKLT ethicality *principles*
THKN thicken *make dense*
THKNN thickening *make dense*
THKNNG thickening *make dense*
THKNR thickener *make dense*
THKNS thickness *density*
THKRC theocracy *divine rule* theocracies
THKRDK theocratic *divine ruler*
THKRDKL theocratically *divine ruler*
THKRS theocracy *divine rule* theocracies
THKRT theocrat *divine ruler*

Letters aren't doubled for single sounds: to find alley use **L** not **LL**. Use **Y** and **W** as hard sounds only: to find yellow use **YL**. (Br)=British spelling or usage. * See dictionary.

THKRTK theocratic *divine ruler*

THKRTKL theocratically *divine ruler*

THKS ethics *principles*

THKSKND thick-skinned *tough*

THKST thickset *stocky*

THKT thicket *trees* thickety

THKTD thicketed *trees*

THKWDD thick-witted *stupid*

THKWTD thick-witted *stupid*

THL ethyl *chemical*

THL they'll *(contr) they will, they shall*

THL thole *(v) tolerate* tholed tholing

THL thole *(n) oar pin*

THL toehold *grasp*

THLCN thylacine *animal*

THLD thalloid *plant*

THLD toehold *grasp*

THLDK athletic *active*

THLDKL athletically *actively*

THLDKS athletics *sports*

THLDMD thalidomide *drug*

THLDSZM athleticism *activity*

THLDX athletics *sports*

THLFDK thallophytic *plant*

THLFT thallophyte *plant*

THLFTK thallophytic *plant*

THLG ethology *behavior*

THLG hidalgo *(often capitalized) nobleman* hidalgos

THLG theologue *religion*

THLG theology *religion* theologies

THLJ ethology *behavior*

THLJ theology *religion* theologies

THLJKL ethological *behavior*

THLJKL theological *(adj) religious* theologically *(adv)*

THLJN theologian *study of God*

THLJST ethologist *behavior*

THLJZ theologize *religion*

theologized theologizing *(Br)* theologise

THLJZR theologizer *religion (Br)* theologiser

THLK phthalic *acid*

THLKD thylakoid *photosynthesis*

THLM thalami (pl) *brain* thalamus

THLM thallium *element*

THLMK thalamic *brain*

THLMS thalamus *brain* thalami

THLN ethylene *chemical*

THLPN tholepin *oar holder*

THLS thallus *plant* thalli *(or)* thalluses

THLSK thalassic *inland seas*

THLSKRC thalassocracy *maritime rule*

THLSKRS thalassocracy *maritime rule*

THLSM thalassemia *anemia (Br)* thalassaemia

THLSMK thalassemic *anemic*

THLSMY thalassemia *anemia (Br)* thalassaemia

THLSN thylacine *animal*

THLSNN phthalocyanine *dye*

THLSYNN phthalocyanine *dye*

THLT athlete *sportsman*

THLTK athletic *active*

THLTKL athletically *actively*

THLTKS athletics *sports*

THLTSFT athlete's foot *fungus*

THLTSZM athleticism *activity*

THLTX athletics *sports*

THLYM thallium *element*

THM at home *(n) reception*

THM at-home *(adj) in the house*

THM them *those*

THM theme *topic*

THM thumb *(n) hand digit (v) turn pages, hitchhike*

THM thyme *herb* thymy *(or)*

thymey

THMBL thimble *sewing, lining*

THMBLBR thimbleberry *fruit* thimbleberries

THMBLFL thimbleful *amount*

THMDK thematic *word stem*

THMHL thumbhole *opening*

THMK thymic *gland*

THMKDM thymectomy *surgery* thymectomies

THMKTM thymectomy *surgery* thymectomies

THML thumbhole *opening*

THML thymol *antiseptic*

THMMDR thermometer *heat measure*

THMMTR thermometer *heat measure*

THMN thiamine *vitamin B1*

THMN thymine *DNA base*

THMNDKS thumb index (n) *book notches*

THMNDX thumb index (n) *book notches*

THMNL thumbnail *fingernail*

THMP thump *knock*

THMPN thumping *great*

THMPNG thumping *great*

THMPR thumper *knocker*

THMPRNT thumbprint *fingerprint*

THMS thymus *gland*

THMSDN thumbs-down *rejection*

THMSKR thumbscrew *hardware, torture*

THMSLVZ themselves *those ones*

THMSN thymosin *protein*

THMSNG theme song *music*

THMSP thumbs-up *approval*

THMST thymocyte *cell*

THMTK thematic *word stem*

THMTK thumbtack *nail*

THMTRG thaumaturgy *magic*

THMTRJ thaumaturge *magician*

THMTRJ thaumaturgy *magic*

THMTRJST thaumaturgist

Use letters that best describe the sounds you hear and omit the vowels. Use **S** or **K** instead of **C**: to find circle use **SRKL**. Use **J** to find joy, **JM** to find gem and **G** to find go.

magician

THMWL thumbwheel *control*

THMZDN thumbs-down *rejection*

THMZP thumbs-up *approval*

THN ethane *fuel*

THN ethene *hydrocarbon*

THN tahini *sesame paste*

THN than *comparison*

THN thane *baron*

THN then *at that time, besides, consequence*

THN thin *slim, weak, scarce* thinned thinning thinner thinnest

THN thine *(archaic) yours*

THNBTN ethnobotany *plant lore*

THNBTNST ethnobotanist *plant lore*

THNDD two-handed *both hands*

THNDR thunder *roar*

THNDRBLT thunderbolt *lightning*

THNDRBRD thunderbird *myth*

THNDRD thunderhead *cloud*

THNDRHD thunderhead *cloud*

THNDRKLD thundercloud *storm*

THNDRKLP thunderclap *loud noise*

THNDRN thundering *intense*

THNDRNG thundering *intense*

THNDRS thunderous *loud*

THNDRSHR thundershower *storm*

THNDRSHWR thundershower *storm*

THNDRSTRK thunderstruck *silenced*

THNDRSTRKN thunderstricken *silenced*

THNDRSTRM thunderstorm *weather*

THNG thing *object*

THNG thong *strip, sandal*

THNGK thank *gratitude*

THNGK think *reason, realize,*

reflect* thought thinking

THNGKBL thinkable (adj) *conceivable* thinkably (adv)

THNGKFL thankful (adj) *grateful* thankfully (adv)

THNGKFLNS thankfulness *grateful*

THNGKLS thankless *ungrateful*

THNGKN thinking *reason, realize, reflect**

THNGKNG thinking *reason, realize, reflect**

THNGKR thinker *reason, realize, reflect**

THNGKS thanks *gratitude*

THNGKSGVN thanksgiving *gratitude*

THNGKSGVNG thanksgiving *gratitude*

THNGKTNGK think tank *research*

THNGKY thank-you *gratitude*

THNGMBB thingamabob *gadget*

THNGMJG thingamajig *gadget*

THNGNTSLF thing-in-itself *independent*

THNGQ thank-you *gratitude*

THNGRF ethnography *cultures*

THNGX thanks *gratitude*

THNGXGVN thanksgiving *gratitude*

THNGXGVNG thanksgiving *gratitude*

THNHSTR ethnohistory *cultures*

THNHSTRK ethnohistoric (or) ethnohistorical *cultures*

THNHSTRKL ethnohistorical (or) ethnohistoric *cultures*

THNHSTRN ethnohistorian *cultures*

THNHSTRYN ethnohistorian *cultures*

THNK authentic *real*

THNK chthonic *infernal*

THNK ethnic *culture*

THNK thank *gratitude*

THNK think *reason, realize, reflect* thought thinking*

THNKBL thinkable (adj) *conceivable* thinkably (adv)

THNKDR authenticator *confirmer*

THNKFL thankful (adj) *grateful* thankfully (adv)

THNKFLNS thankfulness *grateful*

THNKKLNZN ethnic cleansing *murder*

THNKKLNZNG ethnic cleansing *murder*

THNKL authentically *really*

THNKL ethnical (adj) *cultural* ethnically (adv)

THNKLNZN ethnic cleansing *murder*

THNKLNZNG ethnic cleansing *murder*

THNKLS thankless *ungrateful*

THNKN thinking *reason, realize, reflect**

THNKNG thinking *reason, realize, reflect**

THNKR thinker *reason, realize, reflect**

THNKS euthenics *living conditions*

THNKS thanks *gratitude*

THNKSGVN thanksgiving *gratitude*

THNKSGVNG thanksgiving *gratitude*

THNKSHN authentication *confirmation*

THNKT authenticate *confirm* authenticated authenticating

THNKTNK think tank *research*

THNKTR authenticator *confirmer*

THNKY thank-you *gratitude*

THNL ethanol *alcohol*

THNLG ethnology *cultures*

THNLJ ethnology *cultures*

THNLJKL ethnological

Letters aren't doubled for single sounds: to find alley use **L** not **LL**. Use **Y** and **W** as hard sounds only: to find yellow use **YL**. (Br)=British spelling or usage. * See dictionary.

cultures

THNM athenaeum (or) atheneum *school, library*

THNM theonomy *rule by God*

THNMS theonomous *rule by God*

THNQ thank-you *gratitude*

THNR thenar *thumb*

THNR thinner *skinny*

THNS thence *from there*

THNSD ethnicity *culture*

THNSFRTH thenceforth *from then on*

THNSH euthanasia *merciful death*

THNSK euthanasic *merciful death*

THNSKND thin-skinned *sensitive*

THNSNTRK ethnocentric *race superiority*

THNSNTRKL ethnocentrical *race superiority*

THNSNTRSD ethnocentricity *race superiority*

THNSNTRST ethnocentricity *race superiority*

THNSNTRZM ethnocentrism *race superiority*

THNST ethnicity *culture*

THNST euthenist *living conditions*

THNST thinnest *skinny*

THNTK authentic *real*

THNTKDR authenticator *confirmer*

THNTKL authentically *really*

THNTKSHN authentication *confirmation*

THNTKT authenticate *confirm* authenticated authenticating

THNTKTR authenticator *confirmer*

THNTLG thanatology *death*

THNTLJ thanatology *death*

THNTLJKL thanatological *death*

THNTLJST thanatologist *death*

THNTS Thanatos *death instinct*

THNTS thence *from there*

THNTSD authenticity *genuineness*

THNTSFRTH thenceforth *from then on*

THNTST authenticity *genuineness*

THNTZ euthanatize *kill with mercy* euthanatized euthanatizing

THNX euthenics *living conditions*

THNX thanks *gratitude*

THNXGVN thanksgiving *gratitude*

THNXGVNG thanksgiving *gratitude*

THNYM athenaeum (or) atheneum *school, library*

THNZ Athens *city*

THNZ euthanize *kill with mercy* euthanized euthanizing

THNZH euthanasia *merciful death*

THNZK euthanasic *merciful death*

THP Ethiopia *country*

THPNDK autohypnotic *self-induced trance*

THPNSS autohypnosis *self-induced trance*

THPNTK autohypnotic *self-induced trance*

THPY Ethiopia *country*

THQDD thick-witted *stupid*

THQTD thick-witted *stupid*

THR author *writer*

THR either *choice*

THR ether *gas*

THR other *second, different, additional**

THR their *of them*

THR theory *idea* theories

THR there *that place*

THR they're *(contr) they are*

THR Thoreau *writer*

THR thoria *chemical*

THR thorough *complete*

THR three *number (3)*

THR threw *(v-past) throw*

THR throe *pang*

THR through *finished, end-to-end*

THR throw *(v) toss, roll, hurl* threw throwing thrown

THR throw *(n) toss, risk, scarf**

THRB thereby *in that manner*

THRB throb *pulse* throbbed throbbing

THRBGR three-bagger *triple*

THRBK throw back *(v) delay, reflect*

THRBK throwback *(n) reversion*

THRBL thurible *incense*

THRBRD thoroughbred *horse*

THRBTS thereabouts *near that place*

THRCZ arthroses *(pl) joint disease* arthrosis

THRCZ thoraces *(pl) chest* thorax

THRD 3-D *three-dimensional*

THRD authority *power* authorities

THRD euthyroid *gland*

THRD third *of number 3*

THRD thirty *number (30)* thirties

THRD thread *(n) string (v) pass through or between*

THRD thready *stringy*

THRD throaty *hoarse* throatier throatiest

THRD thyroid *gland*

THRDBR threadbare *shabby*

THRDBS third base *baseball*

THRDD throated *neck*

THRDDS thyroiditis *inflammation*

THRDFN threadfin *fish*

THRDFR theretofore *until then*

THRDGR third degree *(n) questioning*

Use letters that best describe the sounds you hear and omit the vowels. Use **S** or **K** instead of **C**: to find circle use **SRKL**. Use **J** to find joy, **JM** to find gem and **G** to find go.

THRDGR third-degree (adj) burn

THRDK arthritic joint swelling

THRDKDM thyroidectomy surgery thyroidectomies

THRDKL arthritically joint swelling

THRDKL theoretical (adj) assumed theoretically (adv)

THRDKLS third class (n) cheaper third-class (adj)

THRDKR three-decker warship

THRDKTM thyroidectomy surgery thyroidectomies

THRDL throatily hoarse

THRDL throttle (v) choke, slow throttled throttling

THRDL throttle (n) throat, valve

THRDL thyroidal gland

THRDLK threadlike stringy

THRDMNCHNL three-dimensional lifelike

THRDMNSHNL three-dimensional lifelike

THRDNS threadiness stringy

THRDNS throatiness hoarse

THRDR threader device

THRDR throatier hoarse

THRDRL third rail subway

THRDRT third-rate cheap, shoddy

THRDS arthritis joint swelling arthritides

THRDST throatiest hoarse

THRDSTT third estate commons

THRDT thirty-eight gun

THRDT thirty-two gun

THRDTH thirtieth of number 30

THRDTHR thirty-three record

THRDTHRD thirty-thirty gun

THRDTHRT thirty-thirty gun

THRDTS thyroiditis inflammation

THRDWRLD third world

(often capitalized) underdeveloped

THRDWRM threadworm animal

THRDYR throatier hoarse

THRDYST throatiest hoarse

THRDYT thirty-eight gun

THRDYTH thirtieth of number 30

THRF thrift plant, savings

THRF throw off get rid of, emit, mislead

THRFD thrifty sparing thriftier thriftiest

THRFDL thriftily sparing

THRFDNS thriftiness sparing

THRFDR thereafter from then on

THRFDR thriftier sparing

THRFDST thriftiest sparing

THRFDYR thriftier sparing

THRFDYST thriftiest sparing

THRFL threefold triple

THRFLD threefold triple

THRFR therefore because

THRFR thoroughfare road

THRFR thurifer alter boy

THRFRM therefrom from that place

THRFT thrift plant, savings

THRFT thrifty sparing thriftier thriftiest

THRFTL thriftily sparing

THRFTNS thriftiness sparing

THRFTR thereafter from then on

THRFTR thriftier sparing

THRFTST thriftiest sparing

THRFTYR thriftier sparing

THRFTYST thriftiest sparing

THRGLBLN thyroglobulin protein

THRGLBYLN thyroglobulin protein

THRGN thoroughgoing complete

THRGNG thoroughgoing complete

THRGWN thoroughgoing complete

THRGWNG thoroughgoing

complete

THRHNDD three-handed 3 players

THRHWLR three-wheeler tricycle

THRJNK atherogenic fat in arteries

THRJNSS atherogenesis fat in arteries

THRK theriaca antidote

THRKCZ thoraces (pl) chest thorax

THRKL theriacal antidote

THRKLR three-color printing (Br) three-colour

THRKRDMN three-card monte gambling

THRKRDMNT three-card monte gambling

THRKRDR three-quarter length

THRKRTR three-quarter length

THRKS thorax chest thoraxes (or) thoraces

THRKSK thoracic chest

THRKSKL thoracically chest

THRKSN thyroxine (or) thyroxin hormone

THRKSZ thoraces (pl) chest thorax

THRKWRDR three-quarter length

THRKWRTR three-quarter length

THRL ethereal (adj) airy ethereally (adv)

THRL thoroughly completely

THRL thrall bondage

THRL thrill excite

THRL thurl cow's hip

THRLD ethereality airiness

THRLDM thralldom (or) thraldom bondage

THRLGD three-legged 3 supports

THRLNGL thrillingly excitement

THRLR thriller drama

THRLT ethereality airiness

THRLZ etherealize make

Letters aren't doubled for single sounds: to find alley use **L** not **LL**. Use **Y** and **W** as hard sounds only: to find yellow use **YL**. (Br)=British spelling or usage. * See dictionary.

indefinite etherealized
etherealizing
THRM atheroma *fat in arteries*
THRM theorem *idea*
THRM therm *heat*
THRM thorium *element*
THRM thrum *fringe*
thrummed thrumming
THRMB thrombi (pl) *blood clot* thrombus
THRMBCZ thromboses (pl) *blood clot* thrombosis
THRMBLTK thrombolytic *no blood clots*
THRMBN thrombin *enzyme*
THRMBS thrombus *blood clot* thrombi
THRMBSDK thrombocytic *blood*
THRMBSS thrombosis *blood clot* thromboses
THRMBST thrombocyte *blood*
THRMBSTK thrombocytic *blood*
THRMBSZ thromboses (pl) *blood clot* thrombosis
THRMDNMK
thermodynamic *heat*
THRMDNMKL
thermodynamically *heat*
THRMDNMKS
thermodynamics *heat*
THRMDNMX
thermodynamics *heat*
THRMDS atheromatous *fat in arteries*
THRMFK theriomorphic *animal form*
THRMFL thermophile *growth in heat*
THRMFLK thermophilic *growth in heat*
THRMGRF thermograph *heat measure*
THRMGRF thermography *heat measure*
THRMGRFK thermographic *heat measure*
THRMGRFKL
thermographically *heat*

measure
THRMGRM thermogram *heat measure*
THRMK thermic *heat*
THRMKL thermically *heat*
THRMKMKL
thermochemical *heat*
THRMKMSTR
thermochemistry *heat*
THRML thermal (adj) *heat* thermally (adv)
THRMLKTRK
thermoelectric *heat*
THRMLKTRSD
thermoelectricity *heat*
THRMLKTRST
thermoelectricity *heat*
THRMLMT three-mile limit *territory*
THRMLZ thermalize *heat* thermalized thermalizing
THRMLZSHN
thermalization *heat*
THRMMDR thermometer *heat measure*
THRMMTR thermometer *heat measure*
THRMNK thermionic *particles*
THRMNKLR thermonuclear *atomic*
THRMNKLYR
thermonuclear *atomic*
THRMNKS thermionics *particles*
THRMNKYLR
thermonuclear *atomic*
THRMNQLR thermonuclear *atomic*
THRMNX thermionics *particles*
THRMNYKLR
thermonuclear *atomic*
THRMNYKLYR
thermonuclear *atomic*
THRMPL thermopile *generator*
THRMPLSDK thermoplastic *soft and hard*
THRMPLSTK thermoplastic *soft and hard*
THRMRGLDR

thermoregulator
temperature
THRMRGLSHN
thermoregulation
temperature
THRMRGLT thermoregulate
temperature
THRMRGLTR
thermoregulator
temperature
THRMRGLTR
thermoregulatory
temperature
THRMRGYLDR
thermoregulator
temperature
THRMRGYLSHN
thermoregulation
temperature
THRMRGYLT
thermoregulate
temperature
THRMRGYLTR
thermoregulator
temperature
THRMRGYLTR
thermoregulatory
temperature
THRMS thermos *bottle*
THRMSDR thermistor
electricity
THRMSFR thermosphere
atmosphere
THRMSKP thermoscope
temperature
THRMSTDK thermostatic
heat regulator
THRMSTDKL
thermostatically *heat regulator*
THRMSTR thermistor
electricity
THRMSTT thermostat *heat regulator*
THRMSTTK thermostatic
heat regulator
THRMSTTKL
thermostatically *heat regulator*
THRMT thermite *incendiary*
THRMTRPK thermotropic
heat response

THRMTRPZM thermotropism *heat response*

THRMTS atheromatous *fat in arteries*

THRMWLKTRK thermoelectric *heat*

THRMWLKTRSD thermoelectricity *heat*

THRMWLKTRST thermoelectricity *heat*

THRMYNK thermionic *particles*

THRMYNKS thermionics *particles*

THRMYNX thermionics *particles*

THRN eutherian *placental mammals*

THRN Tehran *city*

THRN therein *inside*

THRN thereon *upon*

THRN thorn *spike*

THRN thorny *spiny* thornier thorniest

THRN throne *chair* throned throning

THRN throw in (v) *toss, join* throw-in (n)

THRN thrown *(v-past) throw*

THRNBK thornback *ray*

THRNBSH thornbush *shrub*

THRND thorned *spiny*

THRND threnody *sad song* threnodies

THRNDK threnodic *sad song*

THRNDR thereunder *beneath*

THRNDST threnodist *sad song*

THRNFDR thereinafter *following*

THRNFTR thereinafter *following*

THRNG throng *crowd*

THRNLS thornless *smooth*

THRNN threonine *amino acid*

THRNNS thorniness *spines*

THRNPL thorn apple *hawthorn*

THRNR thornier *spiny*

THRNS otherness *difference*

THRNS thoroughness *completeness*

THRNST thorniest *spiny*

THRNT thorianite *mineral*

THRNTK threnodic *sad song*

THRNYR thornier *spiny*

THRNYST thorniest *spiny*

THRP therapy *treatment* therapies

THRP throw up *vomit*

THRPD arthropod *animal*

THRPD theropod *dinosaur*

THRPDK therapeutic *healing*

THRPDKL therapeutically *healing*

THRPDKS therapeutics *healing*

THRPDX therapeutics *healing*

THRPN thereupon *therefore*

THRPN threepenny *poor*

THRPNS threepence *money* threepence (or) threepences

THRPNT three-point *landing*

THRPNTS threepence *money* threepence (or) threepences

THRPS three-piece *suit*

THRPSD therapsid *reptile*

THRPST therapist *treatment*

THRPT throughput *output*

THRPTK therapeutic *healing*

THRPTKL therapeutically *healing*

THRPTKS therapeutics *healing*

THRPTX therapeutics *healing*

THRPYDK therapeutic *healing*

THRPYDKL therapeutically *healing*

THRPYDKS therapeutics *healing*

THRPYDX therapeutics *healing*

THRPYTK therapeutic *healing*

THRPYTKL therapeutically *healing*

THRPYTKS therapeutics *healing*

THRPYTX therapeutics *healing*

THRQRDR three-quarter *length*

THRQRTR three-quarter *length*

THRR either-or *choice*

THRRG throw rug *carpet*

THRRNG three-ring *circus*

THRRS three R's *reading, writing, arithmetic*

THRRZ three R's *reading, writing, arithmetic*

THRS authoress *writer (f)*

THRS thrice *three times*

THRS thyrse *flower*

THRS thyrsi (pl) *staff* thyrsus

THRSD thirsty *craving* thirstier thirstiest

THRSD Thursday *weekday*

THRSDL thirstily *craving*

THRSDNS thirstiness *craving*

THRSDR thirstier *craving*

THRSDR thruster *pusher*

THRSDR thyristor *semiconductor*

THRSDST thirstiest *craving*

THRSDYR thirstier *craving*

THRSDYST thirstiest *craving*

THRSH thrash *separate, whip* thrashes

THRSH thresh *grain* threshes

THRSH thrush *bird, disease* thrushes

THRSHHL threshold *doorway*

THRSHHLD threshold *doorway*

THRSHL threshold *doorway*

THRSHLD threshold *doorway*

THRSHN Thracian *language*

THRSHN thrashing *(slang) whipping*

THRSHNG thrashing *(slang) whipping*

THRSHP authorship *written*

---

by

THRSHR thrasher *bird, separator, whipper*
THRSHR thresher *reaper*
THRSK thoracic *chest*
THRSKL thoracically *chest*
THRSKLRSS atherosclerosis *fat in arteries*
THRSKP arthroscope *surgery*
THRSKP arthroscopy *surgery*
THRSKPK arthroscopic *surgery*
THRSKR threescore *sixty*
THRSL throstle *bird*
THRSM threesome *group of 3*
THRSS arthrosis *joint disease* arthroses
THRSS thyrsus *staff* thyrsi
THRST athirst *eager*
THRST athrocyte *waste cell*
THRST theorist *speculator*
THRST thirst *craving*
THRST thirsty *craving* thirstier thirstiest
THRST thrust *push* thrust thrusting
THRSTL thirstily *craving*
THRSTNS thirstiness *craving*
THRSTR thirstier *craving*
THRSTR thruster *pusher*
THRSTR thyristor *semiconductor*
THRSTST thirstiest *craving*
THRSTYR thirstier *craving*
THRSTYST thirstiest *craving*
THRSZ arthroses (pl) *joint disease* arthrosis
THRSZ thoraces (pl) *chest* thorax
THRT authority *power* authorities
THRT thereat *at that place*
THRT thereto *to that*
THRT thirty *number (30)* thirties
THRT threat *danger*
THRT throat *neck*

THRT throaty *hoarse* throatier throatiest
THRT throughout *everywhere*
THRT throw out *remove, display, confuse**
THRTD three-toed *foot*
THRTD throated *neck*
THRTDV authoritative *official*
THRTDZ arthritides (pl) *joint swelling* arthritis
THRTFR theretofore *until then*
THRTK arthritic *joint swelling*
THRTKL arthritically *joint swelling*
THRTKL theoretical (adj) *assumed* theoretically (adv)
THRTL throatily *hoarse*
THRTL throttle (v) *choke, slow* throttled throttling
THRTL throttle (n) *throat, valve*
THRTLCH throatlatch *halter*
THRTN thirteen *number (13)*
THRTN threaten *terrify, warn*
THRTND threatened *nearly extinct*
THRTNNGL threateningly *terrifying*
THRTNNL threateningly *terrifying*
THRTNS throatiness *hoarse*
THRTNTH thirteenth *of number 13*
THRTR throatier *hoarse*
THRTRN authoritarian *dictatorial*
THRTRNZM authoritarianism *dictatorship*
THRTRPK thyrotropic *thyroid*
THRTRPN thyrotropin *hormone*
THRTRYN authoritarian *dictatorial*
THRTRYNZM authoritarianism

dictatorship
THRTS arthritis *joint swelling* arthritides
THRTSHN theoretician *speculator*
THRTST throatiest *hoarse*
THRTT thirty-eight *gun*
THRTT thirty-two *gun*
THRTTH thirtieth *of number 30*
THRTTHR thirty-three *record*
THRTTHRD thirty-thirty *gun*
THRTTHRT thirty-thirty *gun*
THRTTV authoritative *official*
THRTYR throatier *hoarse*
THRTYST throatiest *hoarse*
THRTYT thirty-eight *gun*
THRTYTH thirtieth *of number 30*
THRV thereof *of that*
THRV thrive *flourish* throve (or) thrived thriving thriven
THRVN thriving *successful*
THRVNG thriving *successful*
THRVR thriver *flourish*
THRVR throw over *reject*
THRW three-way *three parts*
THRW throwaway *disposable, casual*
THRW thruway *highway*
THRWF throw off *get rid of, emit, mislead*
THRWLR three-wheeler *tricycle*
THRWN throw in (v) *toss, join* throw-in (n)
THRWP throw up *vomit*
THRWRLD otherworld *beyond death*
THRWRLDL otherworldly *strange*
THRWT throughout *everywhere*
THRWT throw out *remove, display, confuse**
THRWTH therewith *with that*
THRWVR throw over *reject*
THRWW throwaway *disposable, casual*
THRWZ otherwise *or else*

Use letters that best describe the sounds you hear and omit the vowels. Use **S** or **K** instead of **C**: to find circle use **SRKL**. Use **J** to find joy, **JM** to find gem and **G** to find go.

THRX thorax *chest* thoraxes (or) thoraces
THRXK thoracic *chest*
THRXKL thoracically *chest*
THRXN thyroxine (or) thyroxin *hormone*
THRXZ thoraces (pl) *chest* thorax
THRY thoria *chemical*
THRYK theriaca *antidote*
THRYKL theriacal *antidote*
THRYL ethereal (adj) *airy* ethereally (adv)
THRYLD ethereality *airiness*
THRYLT ethereality *airiness*
THRYLZ etherealize *make indefinite* etherealized etherealizing
THRYM thorium *element*
THRYMFK theriomorphic *animal form*
THRYN eutherian *placental mammals*
THRYNN threonine *amino acid*
THRYNT thorianite *mineral*
THRYRS three R's *reading, writing, arithmetic*
THRZ authorize *empower* authorized authorizing (Br) authorise
THRZ etherize *numb* etherized etherizing
THRZ theirs *not yours*
THRZ theorize *speculate* theorized theorizing (Br) theorise
THRZ there's *(contr) there is*
THRZ throes *struggle*
THRZD Thursday *weekday*
THRZN Thorazine *(trademark) drug*
THRZR etherizer *numb*
THRZSHN authorization *sanction* (Br) authorisation
THRZSHN etherization *numb*
THS ethos *beliefs*
THS outhouse *toilet*
THS teahouse *restaurant*
THS this *(pron, adj) near or present one (adv) indicates extent** these

THS thus *so*
THSDK atheistic (or) atheistical (adj) *no God* atheistically (adv)
THSDK theistic *belief in God*
THSDKL atheistical (or) atheistic (adj) *no God* atheistically (adv)
THSDKL theistically *belief in God*
THSF theosophy *mystical insight* theosophies
THSF thyself *(archaic) yourself*
THSFKL theosophical (adj) *mystic* theosophically (adv)
THSFST theosophist *mystic*
THSHN ethician *principles*
THSHN Tahitian *of Tahiti*
THSKP arthroscope *surgery*
THSKP arthroscopy *surgery*
THSKPK arthroscopic *surgery*
THSL thistle *plant*
THSL thistly *prickly*
THSL thusly *as such*
THSLDN thistledown *flower*
THSLF thyself *(archaic) yourself*
THSLTB thistle tube *funnel*
THSMN isthmian *inhabitant*
THSMS isthmus *strip of land* isthmuses
THSMYN isthmian *inhabitant*
THSN thousand *number*
THSND thousand *number*
THSNDFL thousandfold *number*
THSNDFLD thousandfold *number*
THSNDLGR thousand-legger *millipede*
THSNLGR thousand-legger *millipede*
THSNTRK theocentric *God*
THSNTRSD theocentricity *God*
THSNTRST theocentricity

God
THSNTRZM theocentrism *God*
THSPN thespian *(often capitalized) dramatic*
THSPYN thespian *(often capitalized) dramatic*
THSR thesauri (pl) *synonyms* thesaurus
THSRS thesaurus *synonyms* thesauri (or) thesauruses
THSS phthisis *tuberculosis* phthises
THSS thesis *verse, argument* theses
THSST ethicist *principles*
THST atheist *no God*
THST theist *belief in God*
THSTK atheistic (or) atheistical (adj) *no God* atheistically (adv)
THSTK theistic *belief in God*
THSTKL atheistical (or) atheistic (adj) *no God* atheistically (adv)
THSTKL theistically *belief in God*
THT Tahiti *island*
THT that *(conj, adj, pron, adv)** those
THT theta *Greek letter*
THT thought *(v-past) think*
THTFL thoughtful (adj) *considerate* thoughtfully (adv)
THTFLNS thoughtfulness *consideration*
THTHR thither *tere*
THTHRT thitherto *until then*
THTK thetic *poetry*
THTKL thetically *poetry*
THTLS thoughtless *reckless*
THTLSL thoughtlessly *reckless*
THTLSNS thoughtlessness *reckless*
THTR theater (or) theatre *stage*
THTRGR theatergoer *audience*
THTRGWR theatergoer *audience*

Letters aren't doubled for single sounds: to find alley use **L** not **LL**. Use **Y** and **W** as hard sounds only: to find yellow use **YL**. (Br)=British spelling or usage. * See dictionary.

THTRKL theatrical (adj) *dramatic* theatrically (adv)

THTRKLD theatricality *drama*

THTRKLT theatricality *drama*

THTRKLZ theatricalize *dramatize* theatricalized theatricalizing

THTRKLZSHN theatricalization *drama*

THTRKS theatrics *dramatics*

THTRX theatrics *dramatics*

THTT thought-out (adj) *considered* thought out (v)

THTW thataway *direction*

THV they've *(contr) they have*

THV thieve *steal* thieved thieving

THVR thievery *stealing* thieveries

THVSH thievish *steal*

THVSHL thievishly *steal*

THVSHNS thievishness *stealing*

THVZ thieves (pl) *steal* thief

THWK thwack *hit*

THWN Tijuana *city*

THWRT athwart *across*

THWRT thwart *prevent*

THWRTSHP athwartship *side to side*

THX ethics *principles*

THXKND thick-skinned *tough*

THXT thickset *stocky*

THY thew *strength*

THYDC theodicy *God and evil* theodicies

THYDLT theodolite *surveying*

THYDR theater (or) theatre *stage*

THYDRGR theatergoer *audience*

THYDRGWR theatergoer *audience*

THYDS theodicy *God and evil* theodicies

THYFN theophany *vision of God* theophanies

THYFNK theophanic *vision*

of God

THYGN theogony *origin of gods* theogonies

THYKRC theocracy *divine rule* theocracies

THYKRDK theocratic *divine ruler*

THYKRDKL theocratically *divine ruler*

THYKRS theocracy *divine rule* theocracies

THYKRT theocrat *divine ruler*

THYKRTK theocratic *divine ruler*

THYKRTKL theocratically *divine ruler*

THYLG theologue *religion*

THYLG theology *religion* theologies

THYLJ theology *religion* theologies

THYLJKL theological (adj) *religious* theologically (adv)

THYLJN theologian *study of God*

THYLJZ theologize *religion* theologized theologizing (Br) theologise

THYLJZR theologizer *religion* (Br) theologiser

THYMN thiamine *vitamin B1*

THYNM theonomy *rule by God*

THYNMS theonomous *rule by God*

THYP Ethiopia *country*

THYPY Ethiopia *country*

THYR theory *idea* theories

THYRDKL theoretical (adj) *assumed* theoretically (adv)

THYRM theorem *idea*

THYRST theorist *speculator*

THYRTKL theoretical (adj) *assumed* theoretically (adv)

THYRTSHN theoretician *speculator*

THYRZ theorize *speculate*

theorized theorizing (Br) theorise

THYSDK atheistic (or) atheistical (adj) *no God* atheistically (adv)

THYSDK theistic *belief in God*

THYSDKL atheistical (or) atheistic (adj) *no God* atheistically (adv)

THYSDKL theistically *belief in God*

THYSF theosophy *mystical insight* theosophies

THYSFKL theosophical (adj) *mystic* theosophically (adv)

THYSFST theosophist *mystic*

THYSNTRK theocentric *God*

THYSNTRSD theocentricity *God*

THYSNTRST theocentricity *God*

THYSNTRZM theocentrism *God*

THYST atheist *no God*

THYST theist *belief in God*

THYSTK atheistic (or) atheistical (adj) *no God* atheistically (adv)

THYSTK theistic *belief in God*

THYSTKL atheistical (or) atheistic (adj) *no God* atheistically (adv)

THYSTKL theistically *belief in God*

THYTR theater (or) theatre *stage*

THYTRGR theatergoer *audience*

THYTRGWR theatergoer *audience*

THYTRKL theatrical (adj) *dramatic* theatrically (adv)

THYTRKLD theatricality *drama*

THYTRKLT theatricality *drama*

THYTRKLZ theatricalize *dramatize* theatricalized

Use letters that best describe the sounds you hear and omit the vowels. Use **S** or **K** instead of **C**: to find circle use **SRKL**. Use **J** to find joy, **JM** to find gem and **G** to find go.

theatricalizing
THYTRKLZSHN
theatricalization *drama*
THYTRKS theatrics
dramatics
THYTRX theatrics *dramatics*
THYZM atheism *no God*
THYZM theism *belief in God*
THZ these (pl) *(pron, adj)*
*near or present ones** this
THZ those (pl) *(adj)* specified
*ones** that
THZBN thespian *(often
capitalized) dramatic*
THZBYN thespian *(often
capitalized) dramatic*
THZM atheism *no God*
THZM theism *belief in God*
THZN thousand *number*
THZND thousand *number*
THZNDFL thousandfold
number
THZNDFLD thousandfold
number
THZNDLGR thousand-
legger *millipede*
THZNDTH thousandth *one
of 1,000*
THZNFL thousandfold
number
THZNFLD thousandfold
number
THZNLGR thousand-legger
millipede
THZNTH thousandth *one of
1,000*
TJ êtagère (or) etagere
furniture
TJ outage *loss, interruption*
TJ tai chi (or) t'ai chi *martial
arts*
TJ towage *pulling*
TJD two-edged *sharpened*
TJMHL Taj Mahal *tomb*
TJMP outjump *leap*
TJNK autogenic *from within*
TJNS autogenous *from
within*
TJNSL autogenously *from
within*
TJT two-edged *sharpened*
TK addict *one who needs*

TK attack *assault, spasm*
TK attic *upper room*
TK etic *no structure*
TK outtake *vent, unused film*
TK outtalk *verbalize*
TK tack *(v) attach, turn (n)
nail, course*
TK tacky *sticky, shabby*
tackier tackiest
TK taco *food tacos*
TK tact *diplomacy*
TK take *(v) sieze, delight,
select** took taking taken
TK take *(n) income, haul,
outlook**
TK talk *speak*
TK talkie *movie*
TK teak *tree*
TK tic *spasm*
TK tick *(n) insect, mark,
second (v) mark time*
TK Tokay *wine*
TK toke *(slang) puff* toked
toking
TK Tokyo *city*
TK took *(v-past) take*
TK toque *small hat, chef's hat*
TK tuck *(v) fold, eat (n) fold*
TK tuque *stocking hat*
TK tyke *child*
TK Utica *city*
TKBK take back *retrieve*
TKBK talk back *sass*
TKBRD tackboard *display*
TKC ataxia *confusion*
TKC taxi *(n) vehicle* taxis
TKC taxi *(v) drive slowly*
taxied taxiing (or) taxying
taxis (or) taxies
TKCD tuxedo *formal attire*
tuxedos (or) tuxedoes
TKCDRM taxidermy *stuff
animals*
TKCDRMST taxidermist
stuff animals
TKCHL tactual (adj) *touch*
tactually (adv)
TKCHRJ take-charge
forceful
TKCHWL tactual (adj) *touch*
tactually (adv)
TKCKB taxicab *vehicle*

TKCM taxeme *grammar*
TKCM toxemia *illness*
TKCMDR taximeter *fare*
TKCMK taxemic *grammar*
TKCMN taximan *(Br) cab
driver*
TKCMTR taximeter *fare*
TKCMY toxemia *illness*
TKCSTN taxi stand *parking
area*
TKCSTND taxi stand
parking area
TKCW taxiway *airport*
TKCY ataxia *confusion*
TKCZ taxes (pl) *reflex* taxis
TKD ticked *flecked, angry*
TKD toccata *music*
TKDD addicted *habitual need*
TKDD eutectoid *melting
point*
TKDK eutectic *melting point*
TKDK tactic *maneuver*
TKDKL tactical (adj) *combat*
tactically (adv)
TKDKS tactics *maneuver*
TKDL tactile *touch*
TKDL tactilely *touch*
TKDL teakettle *pot*
TKDLDK autocatalytic
reactive
TKDLDKL autocatalytically
reactively
TKDLR tic douloureux
spasm
TKDLTK autocatalytic
reactive
TKDLTKL autocatalytically
reactively
TKDM tectum *roof* tecta
TKDN takedown (adj, n)
remove, lower take down
(v)
TKDV talkative *fluent*
TKDVL talkatively *fluently*
TKDVNS talkativeness
fluency
TKDX tactics *maneuver*
TKF take off *(v) remove, fly,
depart*
TKF takeoff (n, adj)
caricature, ascent
TKF tick off *anger*

Letters aren't doubled for single sounds: to find alley use **L** not **LL**. Use **Y** and **W** as hard
sounds only: to find yellow use **YL**. (Br)=British spelling or usage. * See dictionary.

TKFL tactful (adj) *diplomatic* tactfully (adv)

TKFLNS tactfulness *diplomacy*

TKFRL tocopherol *chemical*

TKH takahe *bird*

TKH tuckahoe *plant*

TKHM take-home *income*

TKK oatcake *flat cake*

TKK outkick *boot*

TKK tea cake *pastry*

TKKRD tachycardia *heartbeat*

TKKRDY tachycardia *heartbeat*

TKL tackle *(v) wrestle* tackled tackling

TKL tackle *(n) equipment, rope, football*

TKL tequila *liquor*

TKL tickle *laugh* tickled tickling

TKLR tickler *laugh, file*

TKLS outclass *best*

TKLS tactless *insensitive*

TKLSH ticklish *touchy*

TKLSHL ticklishly *touchy*

TKLSHNS ticklishness *touchy*

TKLSL tactlessly *insensitive*

TKLSNS tactlessness *insensitive*

TKLV autoclave *pressure device*

TKM outcome *result*

TKM Tacoma *city*

TKM take-home *income*

TKMDR tachometer *rpm gauge*

TKMTR tachometer *rpm gauge*

TKN tachyon *particle*

TKN take in *(v) furl, shelter, dupe**

TKN take on *undertake, hire*

TKN take-in *(n) deception*

TKN takin *animal*

TKN ticking *fabric*

TKN token *symbol*

TKN toucan *bird*

TKN tycoon *magnate*

TKNBBL technobabble *jargon*

TKND tachinid *fly*

TKNFB technophobia *hate technology*

TKNFBY technophobia *hate technology*

TKNFL technophile *love technology*

TKNG ticking *fabric*

TKNGS takings *receipts*

TKNGT talking-to *lecture*

TKNK technic *technology*

TKNK technique *skill*

TKNKL technical (adj) *scientific, legal* technically (adv)

TKNKLD technicality *detail* technicalities

TKNKLR Technicolor *(trademark) film*

TKNKLT technicality *detail* technicalities

TKNKRC technocracy *rule by specialists* technocracies

TKNKRDK technocratic *rule by specialists*

TKNKRS technocracy *rule by specialists* technocracies

TKNKRT technocrat *rule by specialists*

TKNKRTK technocratic *rule by specialists*

TKNLG technology *applied knowledge* technologies

TKNLJ technology *applied knowledge* technologies

TKNLJKL technological (adj) *scientific* technologically (adv)

TKNLJST technologist *scientist*

TKNLJZ technologize *apply knowledge* technologized technologizing

TKNS tackiness *sticky, shabby*

TKNS takings *receipts*

TKNSHM technitium *element*

TKNSHN technician *specialist*

TKNSHYM technitium *element*

TKNT taconite *iron*

TKNT talking-to *lecture*

TKNTRNK technetronic *shaped by technology*

TKNZ takings *receipts*

TKNZM tokenism *symbolic effort*

TKP take-up (n) *lift, absorb, occupy** take up (v)

TKP talk up *advocate*

TKP teacup *dish*

TKPFL teacupful *amount*

TKPNT tuck-point *mortar*

TKR attacker *assaulter*

TKR outcry *clamor* outcries

TKR tackier *sticky, shabby*

TKR taker *seizer*

TKR talker *speaker*

TKR ticker *watch, machine, heart*

TKR tucker (v) *tire out* (n) *food, lace*

TKRBG tucker-bag *(Aus) knapsack*

TKRC autocracy *dictatorship* autocracies

TKRDK autocratic *dictatorial*

TKRDKL autocratically *dictatorially*

TKRP outcrop (n) *rock* (v) *appear*

TKRPN outcropping *rock*

TKRPNG outcropping *rock*

TKRS autocracy *dictatorship* autocracies

TKRS autocross *race*

TKRT autocrat *dictator*

TKRT out-of-court *law*

TKRT tea cart *table*

TKRT tucker out *exhaust* tuckered out tuckering out

TKRTHM tachyarrythmia *heartbeat*

TKRTHMY tachyarrythmia *heartbeat*

TKRTK autocratic *dictatorial*

TKRTKL autocratically *dictatorially*

TKRTP ticker tape *paper*

Use letters that best describe the sounds you hear and omit the vowels. Use **S** or **K** instead of **C**: to find circle use **SRKL**. Use **J** to find joy, **JM** to find gem and **G** to find go.

TKS addax *animal* addaxes
TKS ataxia *confusion*
TKS tax *levy, demand* taxes
TKS taxa (pl) *group* taxon
TKS taxi *(n) vehicle* taxis
TKS taxi *(v) drive slowly*
    taxied taxiing (or) taxying
    taxis (or) taxies
TKS text *writings*
TKS tux *(abbr) tuxedo* tuxes
TKSBK textbook *school*
TKSBL taxable *levy*
TKSBLD taxability *levy*
TKSBLT taxability *levy*
TKSCHL textual (adj)
    writings textually (adv)
TKSCHR texture *substance,*
    pattern
TKSCHRD textured
    substance, pattern
TKSCHRL textural (adj)
    substance, pattern
    texturally (adv)
TKSCHWL textual (adj)
    writings textually (adv)
TKSD toxoid *immunization*
TKSD tuxedo *formal attire*
    tuxedos (or) tuxedoes
TKSDL textile *cloth*
TKSDRM taxidermy *stuff*
    animals
TKSDRMST taxidermist
    stuff animals
TKSDSKP tachistoscope
    brief look
TKSDSKPK tachistoscopic
    brief look
TKSDSKPKL
    tachistoscopically *brief*
    look
TKSFL toxophily *archery*
TKSFLT toxophilite *archery*
TKSFN toxaphene
    insecticide
TKSGNK toxigenic *poison*
TKSGZMP tax-exempt *no*
    levy
TKSGZMPT tax-exempt *no*
    levy
TKSH talk show *discussion*
TKSHP tuckshop *(Br) eatery*
TKSJNK toxigenic *poison*

TKSK ataxic *confused*
TKSK toxic *poison*
TKSKB taxicab *vehicle*
TKSKCZ toxicoses (pl)
    illness toxicosis
TKSKLG toxicology *poison*
TKSKLJ toxicology *poison*
TKSKLJKL toxicological
    (adj) *poison* toxicologically
    (adv)
TKSKLJST toxicologist
    poison
TKSKNT toxicant *poison*
TKSKSMP tax-exempt *no*
    levy
TKSKSMPT tax-exempt *no*
    levy
TKSKSS toxicosis *illness*
    toxicoses
TKSKSZ toxicoses (pl)
    illness toxicosis
TKSKZMP tax-exempt *no*
    levy
TKSKZMPT tax-exempt *no*
    levy
TKSM taxeme *grammar*
TKSM toxemia *illness*
TKSMDR taximeter *fare*
TKSMK taxemic *grammar*
TKSMKS Tex-Mex *Mexican-*
    American
TKSMN taximan *(Br) cab*
    driver
TKSMTR taximeter *fare*
TKSMX Tex-Mex *Mexican-*
    American
TKSMY toxemia *illness*
TKSN taxing *stressful*
TKSN taxon *classification*
    taxa
TKSN tocsin *alarm*
TKSN toxin *poison*
TKSNG taxing *stressful*
TKSNGL taxingly *stressful*
TKSNL taxingly *stressful*
TKSNM taxonomy
    classification
TKSNMK taxonomic
    classification
TKSNMKL taxonomically
    classification
TKSNMST taxonomist

classification
TKSPLZM toxoplasma
    disease
TKSPLZMCZ
    toxoplasmoses (pl)
    disease toxoplasmosis
TKSPLZMK toxoplasmic
    disease
TKSPLZMSS
    toxoplasmosis *disease*
    toxoplasmoses
TKSPLZMSZ
    toxoplasmoses (pl)
    disease toxoplasmosis
TKSPN taxpaying *levy*
TKSPNG taxpaying *levy*
TKSPR taxpayer *citizen*
TKSPYN taxpaying *levy*
TKSPYNG taxpaying *levy*
TKSPYR taxpayer *citizen*
TKSR taxer *levy*
TKSRKN Texarkana *city*
TKSS taxis *reflex* taxes
TKSS taxus *tree* taxus
TKSS Texas *US State*
TKSSD toxicity *poison*
TKSSHN taxation *levy*
TKSSST toxicity *poison*
TKSSTN taxi stand *parking*
    area
TKSSTND taxi stand
    parking area
TKST outcast *expelled one*
TKST tackiest *sticky, shabby*
TKST text *writings*
TKSTBK textbook *school*
TKSTL textile *cloth*
TKSTL textual (adj) *writings*
    textually (adv)
TKSTR texture *substance,*
    pattern
TKSTRD textured *substance,*
    pattern
TKSTRL textural (adj)
    substance, pattern
    texturally (adv)
TKSTSKP tachistoscope
    brief look
TKSTSKPK tachistoscopic
    brief look
TKSTSKPKL
    tachistoscopically *brief*

Letters aren't doubled for single sounds: to find alley use **L** not **LL**. Use **Y** and **W** as hard
sounds only: to find yellow use **YL**. (Br)=British spelling or usage. * See dictionary.

look
TKSTWL textual (adj)
 writings textually (adv)
TKSW taxiway *airport*
TKSXMP tax-exempt *no*
 levy
TKSXMPT tax-exempt *no*
 levy
TKSY ataxia *confusion*
TKSZ taxes (pl) *reflex* taxis
TKT addict *one who needs*
TKT etiquette *manners*
TKT tacet *music*
TKT tact *diplomacy*
TKT takeout (n) *remove* take-
 out (adj), take out (v)
TKT ticked *flecked, angry*
TKT ticket *permit, tag*
TKT toccata *music*
TKTD addicted *habitual need*
TKTD eutectoid *melting*
 point
TKTFL tactful (adj)
 diplomatic tactfully (adv)
TKTFLNS tactfulness
 diplomacy
TKTHN autochthon
 originating where found
 authocthons (or)
 authocthones
TKTHN talkathon *discussion*
TKTHNS autochthonous
 originating where found
TKTK eutectic *melting point*
TKTK tactic *maneuver*
TKTK ticktack (or) tictac
 sound
TKTK ticktock *clock*
TKTK ticky-tacky *sleazy*
TKTKL tactical (adj) *combat*
 tactically (adv)
TKTKS tactics *maneuver*
TKTKT ticktacktoe (or) tic-
 tac-toe *game*
TKTL tactile *touch*
TKTL tactilely *touch*
TKTL tactual (adj) *touch*
 tactually (adv)
TKTL teakettle *pot*
TKTLD tactility *touch*
TKTLDK autocatalytic
 reactive

TKTLDKL autocatalytically
 reactively
TKTLS tactless *insensitive*
TKTLSL tactlessly
 insensitive
TKTLSNS tactlessness
 insensitive
TKTLSS autocatalysis
 reaction autocatalyses
TKTLT tactility *touch*
TKTLTK autocatalytic
 reactive
TKTLTKL autocatalytically
 reactively
TKTM tectum *roof* tecta
TKTNK tectonic *geology*
TKTNKL tectonically *geology*
TKTNKS tectonics *geology*
TKTNX tectonics *geology*
TKTR haute couture *fashion*
TKTSHN tactician *maneuver*
TKTT tektite *meteor*
TKTV talkative *fluent*
TKTVL talkatively *fluently*
TKTVNS talkativeness
 fluency
TKTWL tactual (adj) *touch*
 tactually (adv)
TKTX tactics *maneuver*
TKTYR haute couture
 fashion
TKVL Tocqueville *writer*
TKVR takeover (n) *control*
 take over (v)
TKW take-away *(Br)* take-out
TKWD teakwood *tree*
TKWKW tu quoque *you too*
TKWND tae kwon do *karate*
TKWQ tu quoque *you too*
TKWZN haute cuisine *food*
TKY Tokyo *city*
TKYN tachyon *particle*
TKYR tackier *sticky, shabby*
TKYRTHM tachyarrythmia
 heartbeat
TKYRTHMY tachyarrythmia
 heartbeat
TKYST tackiest *sticky,*
 shabby
TKZN haute cuisine *food*
TL addle *spoil* addled
 addling

TL at all *in any way*
TL atoll *island*
TL ayatollah *religious leader*
TL et alia *and others*
TL it'll *(contr)* it will, it shall
TL Italy *country*
TL outlaw *bandit*
TL outlay *spend* outlaid
 outlaying
TL tael *weight*
TL tail *(n) appendage, follower,*
 rear (v) follow
TL taille *land tax*
TL tala *money* tala
TL tale *story*
TL tali (pl) *bone* talus
TL tall *high*
TL tallow *fat* tallowy
TL tally *count* tallied tallying
 tallies
TL teal *duck, color*
TL tele (or) telly *(Br)*
 television teles (or) tellys
TL telia (pl) *fungus* telium
TL tell *narrate* told telling
TL til *herb*
TL tile *ceramic square* tiled
 tiling
TL till *plow, money, until*
TL toil *work*
TL tole *metal*
TL toll *tax*
TL toll (or) tole *attract* tolled
 (or) toled tolling (or)
 toling
TL tool *(n) instrument (v)*
 drive
TL towel *dry*
TL tule *plant*
TL tulle *net*
TL utile *useful*
 (Br) utilisable
TLB tallboy *chest*
TLBK tailback *football*
TLBKS toolbox *chest*
 toolboxes
TLBL tillable *plow*
TLBN tailbone *coccyx*
TLBRR talebearer *tattletale*
TLBTH tollbooth *payment*
TLBX toolbox *chest*
 toolboxes

Use letters that best describe the sounds you hear and omit the vowels. Use **S** or **K** instead of **C**: to find circle use **SRKL**. Use **J** to find joy, **JM** to find gem and **G** to find go.

TLD out loud *verbal*
TLD tailed *with tail*
TLD tilde *mark*
TLD told *(v-past) tell*
TLD utility *fitness, service* utilities
TLDK autolytic *self-destructive*
TLDK tholeiitic *rock*
TLDL atlatl *dart gun*
TLF tell off *scold, assign duty*
TLFD telephoto *lens* telephotos
TLFN tail fin *vehicle design*
TLFN telephone *(v) call (n) device* telephoned telephoning
TLFN telephony *voice communication*
TLFNK telephonic *calling device*
TLFNR telephoner *caller*
TLFNST telephonist *(Br) operator*
TLFSH tilefish *animal*
TLFT telephoto *lens* telephotos
TLFTGRF telephotography *lens*
TLFZ telophase *cell division*
TLG etiology *cause* etiologies
TLGDR tailgater *follow closely*
TLGRF telegraph *(v) use signal device (n) device*
TLGRF telegraphy *communication*
TLGRFK telegraphic *brief, signal*
TLGRFR telegrapher *message sender*
TLGRFST telegraphist *message sender*
TLGRFZ telegraphese *language*
TLGRM telegram *(v) use signal device (n) dispatch* telegrammed telegramming
TLGS autologous *same source*

TLGT tailgate *follow closely* tailgated tailgating
TLGT tollgate *payment*
TLGTR tailgater *follow closely*
TLH tallyho *call, coach* tallyhos
TLHC Tallahassee *city*
TLHLDR toolholder *cutting bits*
TLHS Tallahassee *city*
TLHS Toll House *(trademark) cookie*
TLHS tollhouse *payment*
TLHS toolhouse *shed*
TLJ etiology *cause* etiologies
TLJ tallage *tax*
TLJ tillage *crops*
TLJK etiologic *cause*
TLJNK telegenic *attractive*
TLJST etiologist *cause*
TLK italic *font style*
TLK outlook *view*
TLK taillike *like a tail*
TLK talc *powder*
TLK telic *goal*
TLKL telically *goal*
TLKL toll call *long-distance*
TLKM talcum *powder*
TLKMDR telecommuter *work at home*
TLKMNKSHN telecommunication *broadcasting*
TLKMT telecommute *work at home* telecommuted telecommuting
TLKMTR telecommuter *work at home*
TLKMYDR telecommuter *work at home*
TLKMYNKSHN telecommunication *broadcasting*
TLKMYT telecommute *work at home* telecommuted telecommuting
TLKMYTR telecommuter *work at home*
TLKNDK telekinetic *movement*
TLKNDKL telekinetically

movement
TLKNFRNSNG teleconferencing *communication*
TLKNFRNTSNG teleconferencing *communication*
TLKNSS telekinesis *movement*
TLKNTK telekinetic *movement*
TLKNTKL telekinetically *movement*
TLKPR Telecopier *(trademark) duplicator*
TLKPYR Telecopier *(trademark) duplicator*
TLKRS telecourse *study*
TLKS italics *font style*
TLKS telex *(v) use message device (n) device*
TLKST telecast *broadcast* telecast telecasting
TLKSTR telecaster *broadcaster*
TLKT tailcoat *garment*
TLL tell-all *reveal secrets*
TLLG teleology *design*
TLLJ teleology *design*
TLLJKL teleological (adj) *design* teleologically (adv)
TLLJST teleologist *design*
TLM Ptolemy *astronomer, king*
TLM telium *fungus* telia
TLMD Talmud *instruction*
TLMDR telemeter *distance*
TLMKN toolmaking *machinist*
TLMKNG toolmaking *machinist*
TLMKR toolmaker *machinist*
TLMN tallyman *accounts*
TLMN Tuolumne *river*
TLMRK telemark *skiing*
TLMRKDNG telemarketing *telephone sales*
TLMRKDR telemarketer *telephone sales*
TLMRKTN telemarketing *telephone sales*
TLMRKTNG telemarketing

Letters aren't doubled for single sounds: to find alley use **L** not **LL**. Use **Y** and **W** as hard sounds only: to find yellow use **YL**. (Br)=British spelling or usage. * See dictionary.

telephone sales
TLMRKTR telemarketer
telephone sales
TLMTR telemeter distance
TLMTR telemetry distance
TLMTRK telemetric distance
TLMTRKL telemetrically
distance
TLN Atlanta city
TLN Italian of Italy
TLN outline sketch outlined
outlining
TLN outlying remote
TLN ptyalin saliva
TLN tail end last one
TLN tailing leavings
TLN talon claw
TLN telling valid
TLN Thailand country
TLN tie-line phone
TLN tiling tiles
TLN toluene solvent
TLN toweling fabric
TLN towline rope
TLND tail end last one
TLND taloned claws
TLND Thailand country
TLNDR outlander foreigner
TLNDR tailender last one
TLNDR Uitlander foreigner
TLNDSH outlandish strange
TLNG outlying remote
TLNG tailing leavings
TLNG telling valid
TLNG tiling tiles
TLNG toweling fabric
TLNK Atlantic (the) body of
water
TLNKSD Atlantic City city
TLNKSHN Atlantic Ocean
body of water
TLNKST Atlantic City city
TLNL Tylenol (trademark)
drug
TLNS Atlantis mythical island
TLNS tallness height
TLNSFLK telencephalic
brain
TLNSFLN telencephalon
brain
TLNT Atlanta city
TLNT talent skill

TLNTD talented skilled
TLNTK Atlantic (the) body of
water
TLNTKSD Atlantic City city
TLNTKSHN Atlantic Ocean
body of water
TLNTKST Atlantic City city
TLNTLS talentless no skills
TLNTS Atlantis mythical
island
TLNTZ atlantes (pl) map
atlas
TLP tulip flower
TLPL teleplay theater on TV
TLPLN tailplane stabilizer
TLPP tailpipe outlet
TLPRMPDR TelePrompTer
(trademark) script
TLPRMPTR TelePrompTer
(trademark) script
TLPRMTR TelePrompTer
(trademark) script
TLPRNR teleprinter writing
device
TLPRNTR teleprinter
writing device
TLPRSSN teleprocessing
computer
TLPRSSNG teleprocessing
computer
TLPRT teleport transfer
TLPRTSHN teleportation
movement
TLPS tailpiece end, music
device
TLPTH telepath mind reader
TLPTH telepathy mind
reading
TLPTHK telepathic mind
reader
TLPTHKL telepathically
mind reader
TLPWD tulipwood tree
TLPZ talipes clubfoot
TLR atelier studio
TLR outlawry banditry
TLR outlier remote one
TLR tailor clothing
TLR taler coin
TLR teller bank
TLR tiller farmer, steering
TLR toiler worker

TLRBL tolerable (adj)
passable, good tolerably
(adv)
TLRBLD tolerability passable,
goodness
TLRBLT tolerability passable,
goodness
TLRBRD tailorbird animal
TLRD tailored fitted
TLRD telluride compound
TLRD toll road highway
TLRDR tolerator endure,
allow
TLRK telluric earth
TLRM tellurium element
TLRM toolroom workshop
TLRM tularemia disease
TLRMD tailor-made fitted
TLRMK tularemic disease
TLRMY tularemia disease
TLRN tailoring fitting
TLRNG tailoring fitting
TLRNGGLG otolaryngology
ear, nose and throat
TLRNGGLJ otolaryngology
ear, nose and throat
TLRNGGLJKL
otolaryngological ear, nose
and throat
TLRNGGLJST
otolaryngologist ear, nose
and throat
TLRNGLG otolaryngology
ear, nose and throat
TLRNGLJ otolaryngology
ear, nose and throat
TLRNGLJKL
otolaryngological ear, nose
and throat
TLRNGLJST
otolaryngologist ear, nose
and throat
TLRNS tolerance endure,
allow
TLRNT tolerant endure, allow
TLRNTL tolerantly endure,
allow
TLRNTS tolerance endure,
allow
TLRS tailrace water
TLRSHN toleration endure,
allow

Use letters that best describe the sounds you hear and omit the vowels. Use **S** or **K**
instead of **C**: to find circle use **SRKL**. Use **J** to find joy, **JM** to find gem and **G** to find go.

TLRT tolerate *endure, allow* tolerated tolerating

TLRTR tolerator *endure, allow*

TLRTV tolerative *endure, allow*

TLRYM tellurium *element*

TLS atlas *map* atlantes

TLS Atlas *Greek myth*

TLS tailless *no tail*

TLS talus *bone* tali

TLS telos *end*

TLS toeless *no toes*

TLS tollhouse *payment*

TLS Tulsa *city*

TLS utilize *use* utilized utilizing (Br) utilise

TLSH tallish *high*

TLSHD toolshed *storage*

TLSHN etiolation *whiten*

TLSKP telescope *(v) collapse or extend* telescoped telescoping

TLSKP telescope *(n) enlarger*

TLSKPK telescopic *enlarging*

TLSKPKL telescopically *enlarging*

TLSLD tailslide *airplane*

TLSLTRK Toulouse-Lautrec *artist*

TLSM toilsome *exhausting*

TLSMN talisman *charm* talismans

TLSPN tailspin *airplane*

TLSS autolysis *breakdown*

TLSS telesis *progress* teleses

TLST outlast *prevail*

TLSZ italicize *type* italicized italicizing (Br) italicise

TLT atilt *slanted*

TLT etiolate *whiten* etiolated etiolating

TLT outlet *vent, market*

TLT taillight *signal*

TLT tholeiite *rock*

TLT tilt *slant, combat*

TLT toilet *bathroom*

TLT towelette *small towel*

TLT utility *fitness, service* utilities

TLTH otolith *ear*

TLTH tallith *shawl*

TLTHK otolithic *ear*

TLTHN telethon *fundraiser*

TLTK autolytic *self-destructive*

TLTK tholeiitic *rock*

TLTKSS telotaxis *response*

TLTKST teletext *messages*

TLTL atlatl *dart gun*

TLTL tagliatelle *noodle*

TLTL telltale *obvious*

TLTLN tale-telling *stories*

TLTLNG tale-telling *stories*

TLTLR tale-teller *stories*

TLTMDR tiltmeter *slant*

TLTMTR tiltmeter *slant*

TLTP Teletype *(trademark) write*

TLTPPR toilet paper *bathroom*

TLTPRDR teletypewriter *printing*

TLTPRTR teletypewriter *printing*

TLTPSDR Teletypesetter *(trademark) printing*

TLTPSTR Teletypesetter *(trademark) printing*

TLTR toiletry *cleanser* toiletries

TLTRDR tilt-rotor *aircraft*

TLTRN utilitarian *useful*

TLTRNZM utilitarianism *usefulness*

TLTRTR tilt-rotor *aircraft*

TLTRYN utilitarian *useful*

TLTRYNZM utilitarianism *usefulness*

TLTWDR toilet water *perfume*

TLTWTR toilet water *perfume*

TLTXS telotaxis *response*

TLTXT teletext *messages*

TLTYRD tiltyard *arena*

TLV outlive *live longer* outlived outliving

TLV teleview *watch TV*

TLVNJLST televangelist

religion

TLVNJLZM televangelism *religion*

TLVR televiewer *watch TV*

TLVSHN television *broadcasting*

TLVV Tel Aviv *city*

TLVWR televiewer *watch TV*

TLVY teleview *watch TV*

TLVYR televiewer *watch TV*

TLVYWR televiewer *watch TV*

TLVZ televise *broadcast* televised televising

TLVZHN television *broadcasting*

TLW tollway *highway*

TLWDR tailwater *drainage*

TLWN tailwind *air*

TLWN toluene *solvent*

TLWND tailwind *air*

TLWRN toilworn *tired*

TLWTR tailwater *drainage*

TLX italics *font style*

TLX telex *(v) use message device (n) device*

TLY atelier *studio*

TLY et alia *and others*

TLY hotelier *innkeeper*

TLY telia (pl) *fungus* telium

TLYDK tholeiitic *rock*

TLYLG teleology *design*

TLYLJ teleology *design*

TLYLJKL teleological (adj) *design* teleologically (adv)

TLYLJST teleologist *design*

TLYM telium *fungus* telia

TLYN Italian *of Italy*

TLYN outlying *remote*

TLYN toluene *solvent*

TLYNG outlying *remote*

TLYR atelier *studio*

TLYR hotelier *innkeeper*

TLYR outlier *remote one*

TLYRD telluride *compound*

TLYRK telluric *earth*

TLYT tholeiite *rock*

TLYTK tholeiitic *rock*

TLYTL tagliatelle *noodle*

TLYWN toluene *solvent*

TLZ autolyze *self-destruct* autolyzed autolyzing

Letters aren't doubled for single sounds: to find alley use **L** not **LL**. Use **Y** and **W** as hard sounds only: to find yellow use **YL**. (Br)=British spelling or usage. * See dictionary.

(Br) autolyse

TLZ utilize *use* utilized utilizing (Br) utilise

TLZBL utilizable *useful* (Br) utilisable

TLZM ptyalism *saliva*

TLZMN talesman *jury* talesmen

TLZMN talisman *charm* talismans

TLZR utilizer *user* (Br) utiliser

TLZSHN utilization *use* (Br) utilisation

TM atemoya *fruit*

TM atom *particle*

TM atomy *mite* atomies

TM autumn *Fall season*

TM etyma (pl) *word* etymon

TM item *article*

TM tam *hat*

TM tame *(v) subdue* tamed taming

TM tame *(adj) not wild* tamer tamest

TM team *group*

TM teem *plentiful*

TM thyme *herb* thymy (or) thymey

TM time *(v) schedule, record* timed timing

TM time *(n) duration, season, rhythm**

TM tomb *grave*

TM tome *book*

TM tummy *belly* tummies

TMB tomboy *boyish*

TMBK tombac *alloy*

TMBKT Timbuktu (or) Tombouctou *city*

TMBL automobile *car*

TMBL tamable (or) tameable *subdue*

TMBL tambala *money* tambala (or) tambalas

TMBL timbal *drum*

TMBL timbale *food*

TMBL tumble *roll, drop* tumbled tumbling

TMBL tymbal *membrane*

TMBLBG tumblebug *insect*

TMBLDN tumble-down *falling apart*

TMBLDR tumble dry *clothes*

TMBLN tumbling *gymnastics*

TMBLNG tumbling *gymnastics*

TMBLR temblor *earthquake*

TMBLR tumbler *glass, acrobat*

TMBLWD tumbleweed *plant*

TMBM atom bomb *nuclear weapon*

TMBM time bomb *weapon*

TMBR tambour *drum, embroidery*

TMBR tamboura (or) tambura *lute*

TMBR timber *wood*

TMBR timbre *sound*

TMBRD timbered *wooded*

TMBRHCH timber hitch *knot*

TMBRL timbral *sound*

TMBRL timbrel *drum*

TMBRL tumbrel (or) tumbril *vehicle*

TMBRLN timberland *woods*

TMBRLN timberline *altitude*

TMBRLND timberland *woods*

TMBRMN timberman *logger* timbermen

TMBRN tambourine *drum*

TMBRWF timber wolf *animal*

TMBRWLF timber wolf *animal*

TMBRWRK timberwork *construction*

TMBYSH tomboyish *male*

TMCH outmatch *prevail*

TMCHT outmatched *bested*

TMD automata (pl) *robot* automaton

TMD timed *clocked*

TMD timid *shy*

TMD tomato *food* tomatoes

TMD tumid *swollen*

TMDBL temptable *lure*

TMDD automated *mechanized*

TMDD outmoded *obsolete*

TMDD timidity *shyness*

TMDK automatic *mechanical*

TMDKL automatically *mechanically*

TMDL timidly *shy*

TMDNS timidness *shy*

TMDRLS timed-release (or) time-release *scheduled*

TMDT timidity *shyness*

TMDV automotive *car*

TMDW tomatoey *taste*

TMFKSHN tumefaction *swelling*

TMFL tomfool *blockhead*

TMFLR tomfoolery *playfulness*

TMFRM time frame *period*

TMGN tommy-gun (v) *machine gun* tommy gun (n)

TMGRF tomography *X-ray*

TMGRFK tomographic *X-ray*

TMGRM tomogram *X-ray*

TMHK tomahawk *ax*

TMK atomic *of atoms*

TMKBM atomic bomb *nuclear weapon*

TMKD tomcod *fish*

TMKLK atomic clock *precise clock*

TMKLK time clock *job timer*

TMKLR time killer *diversion*

TMKNMBR atomic number *chemistry*

TMKNRG atomic energy *nuclear reactor*

TMKNRJ atomic energy *nuclear reactor*

TMKNSMN time-consuming *wasteful*

TMKNSMNG time-consuming *wasteful*

TMKPN timekeeping *counting*

TMKPNG timekeeping *counting*

TMKPR timekeeper *counter*

TMKR automaker *car producer*

TMKRD time card *wages*

TMKT tomcat *animal*

Use letters that best describe the sounds you hear and omit the vowels. Use **S** or **K** instead of **C**: to find circle use **SRKL**. Use **J** to find joy, **JM** to find gem and **G** to find go.

TMKWT atomic weight *mass*
TML oatmeal *cereal food*
TML tamale *food*
TML timely *convenient* timelier timeliest
TML tomalley *liver* tomalleys
TMLCHS tumultuous *disorderly*
TMLCHSL tumultuously *disorderly*
TMLCHSNS tumultuousness *disorderly*
TMLCHWS tumultuous *disorderly*
TMLCHWSL tumultuously *disorderly*
TMLCHWSNS tumultuousness *disorderly*
TMLG etymology *word source* etymologies
TMLJ etymology *word source* etymologies
TMLJKL etymological (adj) *word source* etymologically (adv)
TMLJST etymologist *word source*
TMLJZ etymologize *word source* etymologized etymologizing (Br) etomologise
TMLK time lock *closure*
TMLN time line *schedule*
TMLNS timeliness *convenient*
TMLPS time-lapse *photography*
TMLR timelier *convenient*
TMLS timeless *eternal*
TMLS tumulus *mound*
TMLSL timelessly *eternal*
TMLSNS timelessness *eternal*
TMLST timeliest *convenient*
TMLT tumult *disorder*
TMLTS tumultuous *disorderly*
TMLTSL tumultuously *disorderly*

TMLTSNS tumultuousness *disorderly*
TMLTWS tumultuous *disorderly*
TMLTWSL tumultuously *disorderly*
TMLTWSNS tumultuousness *disorderly*
TMLYR timelier *convenient*
TMLYST timeliest *convenient*
TMN atman *soul*
TMN autoimmune *disease-fighting*
TMN etymon *word* etyma
TMN ottoman *footstool*
TMN Ottoman *Empire*
TMN ptomaine *poison*
TMN teeming *plentiful*
TMN timing *best moment, stopwatch*
TMND tamandua *anteater*
TMNDHF time and a half *wages*
TMNDW tamandua *anteater*
TMNG teeming *plentiful*
TMNG timing *best moment, stopwatch*
TMNHF time and a half *wages*
TMNJ tamandua *anteater*
TMNJW tamandua *anteater*
TMNL autumnal (adj) *seasonal* autumnally (adv)
TMNM tomentum *hair* tomenta
TMNRD time-honored *traditional*
TMNT autoimmunity *disease-fighting*
TMNT tomenta (pl) *hair* tomentum
TMNTM tomentum *hair* tomenta
TMNTS tomentose *hairy*
TMNVR outmaneuver *better scheme* (Br) outmanoeuver
TMNYVR outmaneuver *better scheme* (Br) outmanoeuver
TMP a tempo *music*

TMP attempt *try*
TMP tamp *pack*
TMP temp (abbr) *temporary, temperature*
TMP tempeh *food*
TMP tempo *rhythm* tempi (or) tempos
TMP tempt *lure*
TMP tump (n) *mound* (v) *overturn*
TMPCHS tempestuous *stormy*
TMPCHSL tempestuously *stormy*
TMPCHSNS tempestuousness *storminess*
TMPCHWS tempestuous *stormy*
TMPCHWSL tempestuously *stormy*
TMPCHWSNS tempestuousness *storminess*
TMPDBL attemptable *try*
TMPDBL temptable *lure*
TMPL temple *church, forehead*
TMPLN tumpline *sling*
TMPLT template *pattern*
TMPN tampion *gun*
TMPN tampon *plug*
TMPN timpani *drum*
TMPN tympan *padding*
TMPN tympana (pl) *ear, arch* tympanum
TMPN tympany *wordiness* tympanies
TMPNK tympanic *ear, arch*
TMPNM tympanum *ear, arch* tympana
TMPNST timpanist *drummer*
TMPR tamper *interfere*
TMPR temper *emotion, modify*
TMPR tempera *painting*
TMPR tempura *food*
TMPRCHR temperature *degree of heat*
TMPRD tempered *moderated*
TMPRL atemporal (adj) *without time* atemporally

Letters aren't doubled for single sounds: to find alley use **L** not **LL**. Use **Y** and **W** as hard sounds only: to find yellow use **YL**. (Br)=British spelling or usage. * See dictionary.

(adv)

TMPRL temporal (adj) *time, forehead, civil* temporally (adv)

TMPRLD temporality *time, forehead, civil* temporalities

TMPRLT temporality *time, forehead, civil* temporalities

TMPRMNL temperamental (adj) *moody* termperamentally (adv)

TMPRMNT temperament *character*

TMPRMNTL temperamental (adj) *moody* termperamentally (adv)

TMPRNS temperance *moderation*

TMPRNTS temperance *moderation*

TMPRPRF tamperproof *no interference*

TMPRR tamperer *interferer*

TMPRR temporary *limited time*

TMPRRL temporarily *limited time*

TMPRRNS temporariness *limited time*

TMPRT temperate *moderate*

TMPRTL temperately *moderate*

TMPRTNS temperateness *moderation*

TMPRTR temperature *degree of heat*

TMPRTYR temperature *degree of heat*

TMPRZ temporize *adjust* temporized temporizing (Br) temporise

TMPRZR temporizer *adjuster* (Br) temporiser

TMPRZSHN temporization *adjustment* (Br) temporisation

TMPS timepiece *clock*

TMPSCHS tempestuous *stormy*

TMPSCHSL tempestuously *stormy*

TMPSCHSNS tempestuousness *storminess*

TMPSCHWS tempestuous *stormy*

TMPSCHWSL tempestuously *stormy*

TMPSCHWSNS tempestuousness *storminess*

TMPST tempest *storm*

TMPSTS tempestuous *stormy*

TMPSTSL tempestuously *stormy*

TMPSTSNS tempestuousness *storminess*

TMPSTWS tempestuous *stormy*

TMPSTWSL tempestuously *stormy*

TMPSTWSNS tempestuousness *storminess*

TMPT attempt *try*

TMPT tempt *lure*

TMPTBL attemptable *try*

TMPTBL temptable *lure*

TMPTN tempting *luring*

TMPTNG tempting *luring*

TMPTNGL temptingly *luring*

TMPTNL temptingly *luring*

TMPTR tempter *one who lures*

TMPTRS temptress *one who lures (f)*

TMPTS tempestuous *stormy*

TMPTSHN temptation *lure*

TMPTSL tempestuously *stormy*

TMPTSNS tempestuousness *storminess*

TMPTWS tempestuous *stormy*

TMPTWSL tempestuously *stormy*

TMPTWSNS tempestuousness

storminess

TMPYN tampion *gun*

TMR tamarau *buffalo*

TMR tamari *sauce*

TMR tamer *subdue*

TMR timer *clock, person*

TMR tomorrow *next day*

TMR tumor *growth* (Br) tumour

TMRD temerity *daring* temerities

TMRFZM automorphism *similarity*

TMRK tamarack *tree*

TMRL tamarillo *shrub*

TMRL tumoral *growth* (Br) tumoural

TMRLK tumorlike *growth* (Br) tumourlike

TMRLS time-release (or) timed-release *scheduled*

TMRN tamarin *animal*

TMRND tamarind *tree*

TMRRS temerarious *daring*

TMRRSL temerariously *daring*

TMRRSNS temerariousness *daring*

TMRRYS temerarious *daring*

TMRRYSL temerariously *daring*

TMRRYSNS temerariousness *daring*

TMRS timorous *fearful*

TMRS tumorous *growths* (Br) tumourous

TMRSK tamarisk *shrub*

TMRSL timorously *fearful*

TMRSNS timorousness *fearful*

TMRT temerity *daring* temerities

TMRT tommyrot *nonsense*

TMS Thames *river*

TMS times *multiply*

TMS utmost *farthest, best*

TMSFR atmosphere *air mass*

TMSFRK atmospheric *air mass*

TMSFRKL atmospherically *air mass*

Use letters that best describe the sounds you hear and omit the vowels. Use **S** or **K** instead of **C**: to find circle use **SRKL**. Use **J** to find joy, **JM** to find gem and **G** to find go.

TMSFRKS atmospherics *air mass*

TMSFRX atmospherics *air mass*

TMSHN automation *mechanization*

TMSHN time machine *past and future*

TMSHNR tam-o'-shanter *hat*

TMSHNTR tam-o'-shanter *hat*

TMSHRN time-sharing *joint usage*

TMSHRNG time-sharing *joint usage*

TMSHT time sheet *wages*

TMSKWR Times Square *New York City area*

TMSNS tumescence *swelling*

TMSNT tumescent *swollen*

TMSNTS tumescence *swelling*

TMSQR Times Square *New York City area*

TMSRVN timeserving *pleasing*

TMSRVNG timeserving *pleasing*

TMSRVR timeserver *pleaser*

TMSS tmesis *word*

TMST outmost *remote*

TMST tamest *subdue*

TMST utmost *farthest, best*

TMSTN tombstone *grave*

TMSTR teamster *driver*

TMSTRZ Teamsters *union*

TMSVN timesaving *hastening*

TMSVNG timesaving *hastening*

TMSVR time-saver *quickener*

TMT Automat *(trademark) cafeteria*

TMT automata (pl) *robot* automaton

TMT automate *mechanize* automated automating

TMT teammate *group member*

TMT tempt *lure*

TMT time-out *rest*

TMT tomatillo *fruit* tomatillos

TMT tomato *food* tomatoes

TMTBL temptable *lure*

TMTBL timetable (n) *agenda* time-table (v)

TMTD automated *mechanized*

TMTH timothy *grass*

TMTK automatic *mechanical*

TMTKL automatically *mechanically*

TMTL tomatillo *fruit* tomatillos

TMTLY tomatillo *fruit* tomatillos

TMTM tom-tom *drum*

TMTN automaton *robot* automatons (or) automata

TMTN tempting *luring*

TMTNG tempting *luring*

TMTNGL temptingly *luring*

TMTNL temptingly *luring*

TMTR tempter *one who lures*

TMTRL time trial *race*

TMTRS temptress *one who lures (f)*

TMTRYL time trial *race*

TMTSDD time-tested *proven*

TMTSHN temptation *lure*

TMTSTD time-tested *proven*

TMTT tomtit *bird*

TMTV automotive *car*

TMTW tomatoey *taste*

TMTY tomatillo *fruit* tomatillos

TMWRK teamwork *cooperation*

TMWRK timework *job*

TMWRKR timeworker *employee*

TMWRN timeworn *old*

TMWRP time warp *postponement*

TMY atemoya *fruit*

TMYLS tumulus *mound*

TMYN autoimmune *disease-fighting*

TMYNT autoimmunity *disease-fighting*

TMZ atomize *spray* atomized atomizing (Br) atomise

TMZ itemize *list* itemized itemizing (Br) itemise

TMZ Thames *river*

TMZ times *multiply*

TMZN time zone *region*

TMZR atomizer *sprayer* (Br) atomiser

TMZSHN itemization *list* (Br) itemisation

TN atone *make amends* atoned atoning

TN atony *no muscle tone*

TN attain *reach, gain*

TN attend (v) *look after, heed, be present**

TN attune *harmonize* attuned attuning

TN eaten (v-past) *eat*

TN eating *food*

TN eighteen *number (18)*

TN oaten *grain*

TN oughtn't (contr) *ought not*

TN outing *trip, disclosure*

TN taenia *tapeworm* taeniae (or) taenias

TN tan (v) *whip, leather, sun* tanned tanning

TN tan (adj, n) *color* tanner tannest

TN tawny *brown* tawnier tawniest tawnies

TN teen *adolescent*

TN teeny *small* teenier teeniest

TN ten *number (10)*

TN tend *care, listen, direct**

TN tie in (v) *connection* tie-in (n)

TN tin (v) *can* tinned tinning

TN tin (n) *element, container*

TN tine *fork*

TN tinea *ringworm*

TN tinny *cheap* tinnier tinniest

TN tiny *small* tinier tiniest

TN toe-in *wheel position*

TN ton *weight* tons

TN tone (v) *sound, soften,*

Letters aren't doubled for single sounds: to find alley use **L** not **LL**. Use **Y** and **W** as hard sounds only: to find yellow use **YL**. (Br)=British spelling or usage. * See dictionary.

blend toned toning

TN tone (n) *sound, style, health*

TN tonne *metric weight*

TN tonneau *rear seat* tonneaus

TN tony *stylish* tonier toniest

TN Tony *award*

TN toon *tree*

TN town *city*

TN tun *cask*

TN tuna *fish* tuna (or) tunas

TN tune (v) *adjust* tuned tuning

TN tune (n) *melody, approach*

TNBL attainable *reach, gain*

TNBL tenable (adj) *logical* tenably (adv)

TNBL tunable (adj) *harmony* tunably (adv)

TNBLD attainability *gain, reach*

TNBLD tenability *logic*

TNBLT attainability *gain, reach*

TNBLT tenability *logic*

TNBPR teenybopper *adolescent*

TNBRFK tenebrific *gloomy*

TNBRS tenebrous *gloomy*

TNBRST tenebrist *artist*

TNBRZM tenebrism *art style*

TNC teensy *small* teensier teensiest

TNC Tennessee *US State*

TNCHN attention *heed*

TNCHN tension *stress*

TNCHR tincture *color* tinctured tincturing

TNCR teensier *small*

TNCST teensiest *small*

TNCWNC teensy-weensy *small*

TNCYR teensier *small*

TNCYST teensiest *small*

TND attend (v) *look after, heed, be present**

TND ctenoid *toothed*

TND tend *care, listen, direct**

TND tenuity *slenderness*

TND tenuto *music*

TND toned *strong, tinted*

TNDD two-handed *both hands*

TNDF tone-deaf *not musical*

TNDFR to and fro (adv) *back and forth* to-and-fro (n, adj)

TNDK tonetic *language*

TNDKL tonetically *language*

TNDM tandem *two in line*

TNDN tendon *sinew*

TNDNC tendency *bias* tendencies

TNDNCHS tendentious *biased* (Br) tendencious

TNDNCHSL tendentiously *biased* (Br) tendenciously

TNDNCHSNS tendentiousness *bias* (Br) tendenciousness

TNDNDS tendinitis (or) tendonitis *inflammation*

TNDNS attendance *presence*

TNDNS tendency *bias* tendencies

TNDNS tendinous *sinewy*

TNDNSHS tendentious *biased* (Br) tendencious

TNDNSHSL tendentiously *biased* (Br) tendenciously

TNDNSHSNS tendentiousness *bias* (Br) tendenciousness

TNDNT attendant *aide*

TNDNTC tendency *bias* tendencies

TNDNTS attendance *presence*

TNDNTS tendency *bias* tendencies

TNDNTS tendinitis (or) tendonitis *inflammation*

TNDR attainder *loss*

TNDR attenuator *reducer*

TNDR tandoor *oven*

TNDR tandoori *baked*

TNDR tender (adj) *soft, gentle* (v) *offer,* (n) *attendant*

TNDR tinder *fire*

TNDR tundra *arctic plain*

TNDRBKS tinderbox *fire* tinderboxes

TNDRBX tinderbox *fire* tinderboxes

TNDRFT tenderfoot *beginner* tenderfeet

TNDRHRDD tenderhearted *sympathetic*

TNDRHRTD tenderhearted *sympathetic*

TNDRL tenderly *gently*

TNDRLN tenderloin *meat*

TNDRMNDD tender-minded *idealistic*

TNDRNS tenderness *gentleness*

TNDRZ tenderize *make soft* tenderized tenderizing

TNDRZR tenderizer *make soft*

TNDRZSHN tenderization *make soft*

TNDS tinnitus *hearing*

TNDT out-and-out *complete*

TNDV tentative *uncertain*

TNDVL tentatively *uncertain*

TNDVNS tentativeness *uncertainty*

TNFL tenfold *times ten*

TNFL tinfoil *aluminum wrap*

TNFL tuneful (adj) *musical* tunefully (adv)

TNFLD tenfold *times ten*

TNFLNS tunefulness *musical*

TNFR ctenophore *comb jelly*

TNFR to and fro (adv) *back and forth* to-and-fro (n, adj)

TNFRN ctenophoran *comb jelly*

TNFSH tunafish *fish*

TNFYL tinfoil *aluminum wrap*

TNG eating *food*

TNG outing *trip, disclosure*

TNG tang *taste, sound*

TNG tango *dance* tangos

TNG tangy *tasty* tangier tangiest

TNG ting *sound*

TNG Tonga *islands*

Use letters that best describe the sounds you hear and omit the vowels. Use **S** or **K** instead of **C**: to find circle use **SRKL**. Use **J** to find joy, **JM** to find gem and **G** to find go.

TNG tongue (v) lick, join boards tongued tonguing

TNG tongue (n) taste organ, language, pin*

TNG tung tree

TNGCHR tincture color tinctured tincturing

TNGG tango dance tangos

TNGG Tonga islands

TNGGL tangle knot tangled tangling

TNGGL tangly knotted

TNGGL tingle prickle tingled tingling

TNGGL tingly prickly

TNGGLD tangled knot

TNGGLMNT tanglement knot

TNGGN Tongan of Tonga

TNGGRM tangram puzzle

TNGK tank (n) receptacle, vehicle (v) lose, store

TNGK tanka poem

TNGKCHR tincture color tinctured tincturing

TNGKFL tankful amount

TNGKJ tankage storage, fertilizer

TNGKL tinkle sound, urinate tinkled tinkling

TNGKL tinkly sound

TNGKR tank car rail transport

TNGKR tanker ship

TNGKR tinker repair

TNGKRD tankard mug

TNGKRR tinkerer repairman

TNGKSHR tincture color tinctured tincturing

TNGKT tanked (slang) drunk

TNGKT tinct color

TNGKTRL tinctorial (adj) color tinctorially (adv)

TNGKTRYL tinctorial (adj) color tinctorially (adv)

TNGL tangle knot tangled tangling

TNGL tangly knotted

TNGL tingle prickle tingled tingling

TNGL tingly prickly

TNGLD tangled knot

TNGLK tonguelike flap

TNGLMNT tanglement knot

TNGLNHT ten-gallon hat cowboy

TNGLS tongueless mute

TNGLSHN tongue-lashing scolding

TNGLSHNG tongue-lashing scolding

TNGN Tongan of Tonga

TNGNCHK tongue-in-cheek ironic

TNGR tangier taste

TNGRM tangram puzzle

TNGST tangiest taste

TNGSTN tungsten element

TNGT tanked (slang) drunk

TNGT tongue-tie no speech

TNGTD tongue-tied no speech

TNGTR tincture color tinctured tincturing

TNGTRL tinctorial (adj) color tinctorially (adv)

TNGTRYL tinctorial (adj) color tinctorially (adv)

TNGYR tangier taste

TNGYST tangiest taste

TNGZ tongs grasp

TNHL town hall building

TNHRN tinhorn pretender

TNHS town house residence

TNJ tannage leather

TNJ teenage (or) teenaged age 13-19

TNJ tinge trace tinged tingeing (or) tinging

TNJ tonnage weight

TNJBL tangible (adj) perceptible tangibly (adv)

TNJBLD tangibility perceptible tangibilities

TNJBLNS tangibleness perceptible

TNJBLT tangibility perceptible tangibilities

TNJD teenaged (or) teenage age 13-19

TNJL tangelo fruit tangelos

TNJNC tangency digression

TNJNCHL tangential (adj) digressing tangentially

(adv)

TNJNS tangency digression

TNJNSHL tangential (adj) digressing tangentially (adv)

TNJNT tangent digression

TNJNTC tangency digression

TNJNTS tangency digression

TNJR tanager bird

TNJR teenager age 13-19

TNJRN tangerine fruit

TNK atonic without accent

TNK tank (n) receptacle, vehicle (v) lose, store

TNK tanka poem

TNK tannic acid

TNK tonic (n) drug, beverage, sound (adj) refreshing, speech

TNK tunic garment

TNK tunica membrane tunicae

TNKCHR tincture color tinctured tincturing

TNKFL tankful amount

TNKJ tankage storage, fertilizer

TNKL tentacle arm

TNKL tinkle sound, urinate tinkled tinkling

TNKL tinkly sound

TNKL tunicle garment

TNKLR tone color music (Br) tone colour

TNKN tin can container

TNKR tank car rail transport

TNKR tanker ship

TNKR tinker repair

TNKR town car vehicle

TNKRD tankard mug

TNKRR tinkerer repairman

TNKSHR tincture color tinctured tincturing

TNKSLF tonic sol-fa music

TNKT tanked (slang) drunk

TNKT tinct color

TNKT tunicate outer layer

TNKTR tincture color tinctured tincturing

TNKTRL tinctorial (adj) color tinctorially (adv)

Letters aren't doubled for single sounds: to find alley use **L** not **LL**. Use **Y** and **W** as hard sounds only: to find yellow use **YL**. (Br)=British spelling or usage. * See dictionary.

TNKTRYL tinctorial (adj) *color* tinctorially (adv)

TNL atonal *disharmonic*

TNL tineal *ringworm*

TNL tinnily *cheap*

TNL toenail *foot*

TNL tonal (adj) *sound* tonally (adv)

TNL town hall *building*

TNL tunnel *burrow* tunneled (or) tunnelled tunneling (or) tunnelling

TNLD tonality *arrangement* tonalities

TNLK tunnellike *tube*

TNLM tantalum *element* (Br) tantalising

TNLR tunneler *burrow*

TNLS toneless *weak*

TNLS tuneless *no music*

TNLSL tonelessly *weak*

TNLSNS tonelessness *weak*

TNLT tonality *arrangement* tonalities

TNLZ tantalize *tease* tantalized tantalizing (Br) tantalise

TNLZ tin lizzie *car*

TNLZNG tantalizing *desired* (Br) tantalising

TNLZNGL tantalizingly *desired* (Br) tantalising

TNLZR tantalizer *teaser* (Br) tantaliser

TNM autonomy *self-government* autonomies

TNM toneme *speech*

TNMBR outnumber *exceed*

TNMDR tonometer *pitch, pressure*

TNMK autonomic *involuntary*

TNMK tonemic *speech*

TNMKL autonomically *involuntarily*

TNMNT atonement *amends*

TNMNT attainment *accomplishment*

TNMNT attunement *harmony*

TNMNT tantamount *equal*

TNMNT tenement *building*

TNMS autonomous *free*

TNMT tantamount *equal*

TNMTR tonometer *pitch, pressure*

TNMTR tonometry *pitch, pressure*

TNN tannin *astringent*

TNN tanning *leather, spanking*

TNN tenon *dovetail*

TNNC tenancy *residence* tenancies

TNNFRK tuning fork *music*

TNNG tanning *leather, spanking*

TNNGFRK tuning fork *music*

TNNS tawniness *brown*

TNNS tenancy *residence* tenancies

TNNS tininess *smallness*

TNNS tinniness *cheap*

TNNT tenant *renter*

TNNT tenet *doctrine*

TNNTC tenancy *residence* tenancies

TNNTR tenantry *residence* tenantries

TNNTS tenancy *residence* tenancies

TNP tune-up *adjust*

TNPLST tonoplast *membrane*

TNPLT tinplate (n) *coating* tin-plate (v)

TNPN tenpenny *ten cents*

TNPNZ tenpins *bowling*

TNR itinerary *tour outline* itineraries

TNR tanner *leather, color, (Br) money*

TNR tannery *leather factory* tanneries

TNR tawnier *brown*

TNR teenier *small*

TNR tenor *voice, meaning* (Br) tenour

TNR tenure *grasp, status*

TNR tin ear *tone deaf*

TNR tinier *smaller*

TNR tinner *tinsmith*

TNR tinnier *cheap*

TNR toner *copying solution, cosmetic*

TNR tonier *stylish*

TNR tuner *adjuster, radio*

TNRBL tenurable *grasp, status*

TNRD tenured *teaching*

TNRL tenurial (adj) *grasp, status* tenurially (adv)

TNRM tonearm *record player*

TNRN tinhorn *pretender*

TNRNC itinerancy *traveling*

TNRNS itinerancy *traveling*

TNRNT itinerant *traveling*

TNRNTC itinerancy *traveling*

TNRNTS itinerancy *traveling*

TNRR itinerary *tour outline* itineraries

TNRSHN itineration *travel*

TNRT itinerate *travel* itinerated itinerating

TNRTRK tenure-track *teaching*

TNRYL tenurial (adj) *grasp, status* tenurially (adv)

TNS teensy *small* teensier teensiest

TNS Tennessee *US State*

TNS tennis *sport*

TNS tense (n) *verb*

TNS tense (v) *tighten* tensed tensing

TNS tense (adj) *tight* tenser tensest

TNS tenuous *thin*

TNS tetanus *disease*

TNS town house *residence*

TNS Tunis *city*

TNSD tenacity *courage*

TNSD tensity *tightness* tensities

TNSD tonicity *vigor*

TNSFK townsfolk *people*

TNSH tannish *brown*

TNSH tennis shoe *footwear*

TNSH Tunisia *country*

TNSHN attention *heed*

TNSHN attenuation *reduction*

TNSHN tension *stress*

TNSHP township *government*

Use letters that best describe the sounds you hear and omit the vowels. Use **S** or **K** instead of **C**: to find circle use **SRKL**. Use **J** to find joy, **JM** to find gem and **G** to find go.

TNT

TNSHR tincture *color* tinctured tincturing
TNSHR tonsure *shave* tonsured tonsuring
TNSHS tenacious *strong, persistent*
TNSHSL tenaciously *strong, persistent*
TNSHSNS tenaciousness *strong, persistent*
TNSKP townscape *view*
TNSL tensely *tightly*
TNSL tensile *flexible*
TNSL tinsel *shiny thread*
TNSL tonsil *throat*
TNSL utensil *implement*
TNSLD tensility *flexibility*
TNSLDS tonsillitis *illness*
TNSLKDM tonsillectomy *surgery* tonsillectomies
TNSLKTM tonsillectomy *surgery* tonsillectomies
TNSLR tonsillar *throat*
TNSLT tensility *flexibility*
TNSLTS tonsillitis *illness*
TNSMN townsman *resident* townsmen
TNSMTH tinsmith *tin worker*
TNSMTH tunesmith *song writer*
TNSNS tenseness *tightness*
TNSNTSTR ten-cent store *five-and-ten*
TNSPPL townspeople *residents*
TNSR teensier *small*
TNSR tenser *tighter*
TNSR tensor *muscle, vector*
TNSRL tonsorial *barber*
TNSRYL tonsorial *barber*
TNSS taeniasis *tapeworm*
TNSST teensiest *small*
TNSST tensest *tightest*
TNST tannest *color*
TNST tawniest *brown*
TNST teeniest *small*
TNST tenacity *courage*
TNST tennist *tennis player*
TNST tensity *tightness* tensities
TNST tiniest *smallest*
TNST tinniest *cheap*

TNST tonicity *vigor*
TNST toniest *stylish*
TNSV tensive *tight*
TNSWMN townswoman *resident* townswomen
TNSWNS teensy-weensy *small*
TNSYR teensier *small*
TNSYST teensiest *small*
TNT attenuate *reduce* attenuated attenuating
TNT oughtn't *(contr) ought not*
TNT out-and-out *complete*
TNT taint *stain*
TNT tannate *chemical*
TNT taunt *reproach*
TNT tenant *renter*
TNT tenet *doctrine*
TNT tent *fabric shelter*
TNT tenuity *slenderness*
TNT tenuto *music*
TNT tint *dye*
TNT tonette *flute*
TNT tonight *this evening*
TNT tune out *ignore*
TNTBD autoantibody *cell* autoantibodies
TNTBT autoantibody *cell* autoantibodies
TNTC teensy *small* teensier teensiest
TNTCHR tincture *color* tinctured tincturing
TNTCR teensier *small*
TNTCST teensiest *small*
TNTCWNC teensy-weensy *small*
TNTCWNTC teensy-weensy *small*
TNTCYR teensier *small*
TNTCYST teensiest *small*
TNTDV tentative *uncertain*
TNTDVL tentatively *uncertain*
TNTDVNS tentativeness *uncertainty*
TNTH eighteenth *of number 18*
TNTH tenth *of number 10*
TNTK tonetic *language*
TNTKL tentacle *arm*

TNTKL tonetically *language*
TNTKLR tentacular *arms*
TNTKSKSHN autointoxication *self-poisoning*
TNTKYLR tentacular *arms*
TNTLK tentlike *canopy*
TNTLM tantalum *element* (Br) tantalising
TNTLZ tantalize *tease* tantalized tantalizing (Br) tantalise
TNTLZNG tantalizing *desired* (Br) tantalising
TNTLZNGL tantalizingly *desired* (Br) tantalising
TNTLZR tantalizer *teaser* (Br) tantaliser
TNTMNT tantamount *equal*
TNTMT tantamount *equal*
TNTN tontine *finance*
TNTNBLSHN tintinnabulation *ringing*
TNTNBYLSHN tintinnabulation *ringing*
TNTNGL tauntingly *teasing*
TNTNL tauntingly *teasing*
TNTP tintype *photography*
TNTQLR tentacular *arms*
TNTR attenuator *reducer*
TNTR tantara *fanfare*
TNTR tantra *rituals*
TNTR taunter *teaser*
TNTR tenter *frame*
TNTRHK tenterhook *nail*
TNTRK tantric *rituals*
TNTRM tantrum *temper*
TNTS teensy *small* teensier teensiest
TNTS tense *(n) verb*
TNTS tense *(v) tighten* tensed tensing
TNTS tense *(adj) tight* tenser tensest
TNTS tinnitus *hearing*
TNTSD tensity *tightness* tensities
TNTSHN tension *stress*
TNTSHR tincture *color* tinctured tincturing
TNTSL tensely *tightly*

Letters aren't doubled for single sounds: to find alley use **L** not **LL**. Use **Y** and **W** as hard sounds only: to find yellow use **YL**. (Br)=British spelling or usage. * See dictionary.

TNTSL tensile *flexible*
TNTSL tinsel *shiny thread*
TNTSL tonsil *throat*
TNTSL utensil *implement*
TNTSLD tensility *flexibility*
TNTSLDS tonsillitis *illness*
TNTSLKDM tonsillectomy *surgery* tonsillectomies
TNTSLKTM tonsillectomy *surgery* tonsillectomies
TNTSLR tonsillar *throat*
TNTSLT tensility *flexibility*
TNTSLTS tonsillitis *illness*
TNTSNS tenseness *tightness*
TNTSR teensier *small*
TNTSR tenser *tighter*
TNTSR tensor *muscle, vector*
TNTSST teensiest *small*
TNTSST tensest *tightest*
TNTST tensity *tightness* tensities
TNTSV tensive *tight*
TNTSWNS teensy-weensy *small*
TNTSWNTS teensy-weensy *small*
TNTSYR teensier *small*
TNTSYST teensiest *small*
TNTTV tentative *uncertain*
TNTTVL tentatively *uncertain*
TNTTVNS tentativeness *uncertainty*
TNTV attentive *observant*
TNTV tantivy *gallop* tantivies
TNTV tentative *uncertain*
TNTVL tentatively *uncertain*
TNTVNS tentativeness *uncertainty*
TNTXKSHN autointoxication *self-poisoning*
TNV attentive *observant*
TNWD tenuity *slenderness*
TNWDR attenuator *reducer*
TNWN teeny-weeny *small*
TNWR tinware *utinsils*
TNWRK tinwork *crafts*
TNWS tenuous *thin*
TNWSHN attenuation *reduction*

TNWT attenuate *reduce* attenuated attenuating
TNWT tenuity *slenderness*
TNWTR attenuator *reducer*
TNXLF tonic sol-fa *music*
TNY taenia *tapeworm* taeniae (or) taenias
TNY tinea *ringworm*
TNYD tenuity *slenderness*
TNYDR attenuator *reducer*
TNYL tineal *ringworm*
TNYR tawnier *brown*
TNYR teenier *small*
TNYR tenure *grasp, status*
TNYR tinier *smaller*
TNYR tinnier *cheap*
TNYR tonier *stylish*
TNYRBL tenurable *grasp, status*
TNYRD tenured *teaching*
TNYRL tenurial (adj) *grasp, status* tenurially (adv)
TNYRTRK tenure-track *teaching*
TNYRYL tenurial (adj) *grasp, status* tenurially (adv)
TNYS tenuous *thin*
TNYSHN attenuation *reduction*
TNYSS taeniasis *tapeworm*
TNYST tawniest *brown*
TNYST teeniest *small*
TNYST tiniest *smallest*
TNYST tinniest *cheap*
TNYST toniest *stylish*
TNYT attenuate *reduce* attenuated attenuating
TNYT tenuity *slenderness*
TNYTR attenuator *reducer*
TNYWD tenuity *slenderness*
TNYWDR attenuator *reducer*
TNYWS tenuous *thin*
TNYWSHN attenuation *reduction*
TNYWT attenuate *reduce* attenuated attenuating
TNYWT tenuity *slenderness*
TNYWTR attenuator *reducer*
TNZ teens *age 13-19*
TNZ tennies *shoes*
TNZH Tunisia *country*
TNZMN townsman *resident*

townsmen
TNZMS tenesmus *painful urge*
TNZN Tanzania *country*
TNZNT tanzanite *mineral*
TNZNY Tanzania *country*
TNZPPL townspeople *residents*
TNZWMN townswoman *resident* townswomen
TP atop *on*
TP atopy *allergy*
TP Taipei *city*
TP tap (v) *hit, listen, draw out** tapped tapping
TP tap (n) *faucet, wiretap, hit*
TP tapa *food, cloth*
TP tape *record, fasten* taped taping
TP taupe *color*
TP teapoy *table*
TP tepee *tent*
TP tie up (v) *rope, stop* tie-up (n)
TP tip *tilt, advice, gratuity** tipped tipping
TP top (n) *toy, garment, pinnacle (adj) best**
TP top (v) *cover, pinch, excel** topped topping
TP tope (n) *shark, mound*
TP tope (v) *drink* toped toping
TP topi *animal* topi (or) topis
TP topoi (pl) *theme* topos
TP toupee *wig*
TP type *sort, keyboard, prefigure* typed typing
TP typo *error* typos
TP utopia *ideal*
TPBL typeable *sort, keyboard, prefigure*
TPBT top boot *shoe*
TPC autopsy *cadaver* autopsies
TPC tipsy *drunk* tipsier tipsiest
TPCNS tipsiness *drunk*
TPCR tipsier *drunker*
TPCST tipsiest *drunkest*
TPCYR tipsier *drunker*
TPCYST tipsiest *drunkest*

Use letters that best describe the sounds you hear and omit the vowels. Use **S** or **K** instead of **C**: to find circle use **SRKL**. Use **J** to find joy, **JM** to find gem and **G** to find go.

TPD tapeta (pl) *cell layer* tapetum

TPD tepid *lukewarm*

TPDD tepidity *lukewarm*

TPDG top dog *chief*

TPDK tape deck *recording*

TPDL tepidly *lukewarm*

TPDLR top dollar *money*

TPDM tapetum *cell layer* tapeta

TPDNS tap dance (n) *footwork* tap-dance (v)

TPDNS tepidness *lukewarm*

TPDNSNG tap dancing *footwork*

TPDNSR tap dancer *footwork*

TPDNTS tap dance (n) *footwork* tap-dance (v)

TPDNTSNG tap dancing *footwork*

TPDNTSR tap dancer *footwork*

TPDRR top drawer (n) *peak* top-drawer (adj)

TPDRS top-dress *scatter*

TPDRSN topdressing *soil*

TPDRSNG topdressing *soil*

TPDT tapped out *no money*

TPDT tepidity *lukewarm*

TPF tip-off (n, v) *hint*

TPF typify *represent* typified typifying typifies

TPFKSHN typification *representation*

TPFLT topflight *best*

TPFS typeface *printing*

TPGLNT topgallant *sail*

TPGN top gun *leader*

TPGRF topography *map*

TPGRF typograph *letterpress* typography

TPGRFK topographic *map*

TPGRFK typographic (or) typographical (adj) *printing* typographically (adv)

TPGRFKL topographical (adj) *map* topographically (adv)

TPGRFKL typographical (or) typographic (adj) *printing*

typographically (adv)

TPGRFR topographer *map*

TPGRFR typographer *printing*

TPHL taphole *vent*

TPHT top hat *formal*

TPHV top-heavy *unbalanced*

TPK atopic *allergy*

TPK tapioca *food*

TPK topic *subject*

TPK typic *symbolic*

TPKK topkick *rank*

TPKL atypical (adj) *irregular* atypically (adv)

TPKL topical (adj) *local, subject* topically (adv)

TPKL typical (adj) *regular* typically (adv)

TPKLD topicality *local, subject* topicalities

TPKLD typicality *regularity*

TPKLNS typicalness *regularity*

TPKLT topicality *local, subject* topicalities

TPKLT typicality *regularity*

TPKRS topcross *breed*

TPKRT tipcart *wagon*

TPKST typecast *stereotype* typecast typecasting

TPKT out-of-pocket *expense*

TPKT topcoat *garment*

TPL outplay *play better*

TPL taphole *vent*

TPL tipple *drink* tippled tippling

TPL topple *overthrow, fall* toppled toppling

TPL tupelo *tree* tupelos

TPL two-ply *two layers*

TPL typal *type*

TPLFD toplofty *haughty*

TPLFDNS toploftiness *haughty*

TPLFT toplofty *haughty*

TPLFTNS toploftiness *haughty*

TPLG topology *math* topologies

TPLG typology *categories* typologies

TPLJ topology *math*

topologies

TPLJ typology *categories* typologies

TPLJKL topological (adj) *math* topologically (adv)

TPLJKL typological (adj) *categories* typologically (adv)

TPLJST topologist *math*

TPLJST typologist *categories*

TPLR tippler *drunkard*

TPLS topless *no shirt*

TPLSMNT outplacement *employment*

TPLT autopilot *guidance system*

TPLT toeplate *shoe*

TPMN topminnow *fish*

TPMSHR tape measure *length*

TPMST topmast *ship*

TPMST topmost *highest*

TPMZHR tape measure *length*

TPN taipan *businessman, snake*

TPN tap-in *golf*

TPN tapping *decreasing*

TPN tiepin *necktie*

TPN tip-in (n) *basketball* tip in (v)

TPN topping (n) *decoration* (adj) *highest*

TPN twopenny *money* twopennies

TPN utopian *ideal*

TPNCH outpunch *hit better*

TPNCH top-notch *best*

TPNG tapping *decreasing*

TPNG topping (n) *decoration* (adj) *highest*

TPNM toponymy *place-name*

TPNMK toponymic *place-name*

TPNMST toponymist *place-name*

TPNS tuppence *twopence*

TPNS twopence *money* twopence (or) twopences

TPNT outpoint *sail, win*

TPNT topknot *hairdo*

TPNTS tuppence *twopence*

Letters aren't doubled for single sounds: to find **alley** use **L** not **LL**. Use **Y** and **W** as hard sounds only: to find **yellow** use **YL**. (Br)=British spelling or usage. * See dictionary.

TPNTS twopence *money* twopence (or) twopences

TPNZM utopianism *idealism*

TPP top up (v) *(Br) fill* top-up (n)

TPR outpour *flow out*

TPR taper *(v) decrease (n)* candle, decrease

TPR tapir *animal* tapir (or) tapirs

TPR tapper *one that taps*

TPR tipper *giver*

TPR toper *drunk*

TPR topiary *shrub* topiaries

TPR topper *coat, hat, remark*

TPRD two-party *politics*

TPRDN typewritten *(v-past)* typewrite

TPRDR typewriter *keyboard*

TPRF taper off *decrease*

TPRKRD tape-record *sound copy*

TPRKRDR tape recorder *sound copy*

TPRM taproom *bar*

TPRN outpouring *flow out*

TPRNG outpouring *flow out*

TPRSTK taperstick *candle holder*

TPRT taproot *plant*

TPRT tea party *social* tea parties

TPRT two-party *politics*

TPRT typewrite *keyboard* typewrote typewriting typewritten

TPRTN typewritten *(v-past)* typewrite

TPRTR typewriter *keyboard*

TPS autopsy *cadaver* autopsies

TPS outpace *go faster* outpaced outpacing

TPS taps *music*

TPS tipsy *drunk* tipsier tipsiest

TPS toepiece *cover*

TPS topos *theme* topoi

TPS tops *best*

TPS two-piece *in two parts*

TPSD topside *upper level*

TPSDNG typesetting

printing

TPSDR tipster *hinter*

TPSDR typesetter *printing*

TPSHLF top-shelf *best*

TPSHNT outpatient *hospital*

TPSKRP typescript *manuscript*

TPSKRPT typescript *manuscript*

TPSKRT top secret *confidential*

TPSL tipsily *drunk*

TPSL topsail *ship*

TPSL topsoil *land*

TPSNS tipsiness *drunk*

TPSPN topspin *motion*

TPSR tipsier *drunker*

TPSST tipsiest *drunkest*

TPST outpost *remote branch, fort*

TPST typeset *printing* typeset typesetting

TPST typist *keyboard*

TPST utopist *idealist*

TPSTCH topstitch *sewing*

TPSTN typesetting *printing*

TPSTNG typesetting *printing*

TPSTR tapestry *fabric* tapestries

TPSTR tipster *hinter*

TPSTR typesetter *printing*

TPSTRV topsy-turvy *upside down*

TPSTRVNS topsy-turviness *upside down*

TPSYL topsoil *land*

TPSYR tipsier *drunker*

TPSYST tipsiest *drunkest*

TPT output *result* outputted outputting

TPT tapeta (pl) *cell layer* tapetum

TPT tappet *lever*

TPT teapot *vessel*

TPT tippet *cape*

TPT tiptoe *walk softly* tiptoed tiptoeing

TPT top hat *formal*

TPTH towpath *lane*

TPTM tapetum *cell layer* tapeta

TPTP tip-top *highest, best*

TPTT tapped out *no money*

TPV top-heavy *unbalanced*

TPWDR tap water *faucet*

TPWRK topwork *grafting*

TPWRM tapeworm *animal*

TPWTR tap water *faucet*

TPY utopia *ideal*

TPYK tapioca *food*

TPYN utopian *ideal*

TPYNZM utopianism *idealism*

TPYR topiary *shrub* topiaries

TPZ topaz *mineral*

TPZM utopism *idealism*

TQD teakwood *tree*

TQKW tu quoque *you too*

TQND tae kwon do *karate*

TQQ tu quoque *you too*

TQZN haute cuisine *food*

TR adder *snake*

TR atria (pl) *hall, heart* atrium

TR attar *oil*

TR attire *dress* attired attiring

TR auteur *film direction*

TR eater *one who eats*

TR eatery *diner*

TR hauteur *arrogance*

TR oater *western*

TR otter *aquatic animal* otters

TR outer *external*

TR outré *bizarre*

TR tahr *goatlike animal*

TR tar *(n) black substance, sailor*

TR tar *(v) defile, smear* tarred tarring

TR tare *(n) weed, weight*

TR tare *(v) weigh* tared taring

TR taro *plant* taros

TR tarot *cards*

TR tarry *(adj) like tar*

TR tarry *(v) delay* tarried tarrying tarries

TR tear *(v) cry* teared tearing

TR tear *(v) rip, speed* tore tearing torn

TR tear *(n) rip, droplet, hurry**

Use letters that best describe the sounds you hear and omit the vowels. Use **S** or **K** instead of **C**: to find circle use **SRKL**. Use **J** to find joy, **JM** to find gem and **G** to find go.

TR teary *crying* tearier teariest
TR terai *hat*
TR terra *earth*
TR terror *fear*
TR terry *fabric* terries
TR tiara *crown*
TR tier *one that ties, level*
TR tire *(n) wheel* (Br) tyre
TR tire *(v) wear out* tired tiring
TR tor *hill*
TR Torah *scripture*
TR tori (pl) *ridge* torus
TR torii *gateway* torii
TR Tory *loyalist* Tories
TR tour *travel*
TR tower *(v) height (n) structure*
TR tray *holder*
TR tree *(v) corner* treed treeing
TR tree *(n) plant, diagram*
TR trey *three spot, card* treys
TR trio *group of three*
TR troy *weight*
TR true *(v) level* trued trueing
TR true *(adj) honest, straight* truer truest
TR true *(n, adv) real*
TR try *attempt, sample* tried trying tries
TR tyro *novice* tyros
TR udder *teat*
TR uteri (pl) *womb* uterus
TR utter *(v) speak (adj) total*
TRB tribe *group*
TRB turbo *super-charged* turbos
TRB turbot *fish* turbot
TRBCHRJD turbocharged *super-charged*
TRBCHRJR turbocharger *super-charged*
TRBD turbid *muddy*
TRBDBL attributable *credited to*
TRBDD trabeated *beams*
TRBDL turbidly *muddy*
TRBDNS turbidness *muddy*

TRBDR troubadour *poet*
TRBDT turbidite *sediment*
TRBDT turbidity *muddiness*
TRBDV attributive *joined*
TRBDVL attributively *joined, explained*
TRBFN turbofan *jet*
TRBJNRDR turbogenerator *electricity*
TRBJNRTR turbogenerator *electricity*
TRBJT turbojet *airplane*
TRBKL trabecula *bar, fold* trabeculae
TRBKYL trabecula *bar, fold* trabeculae
TRBL tearable *rip*
TRBL terrible (adj) *very bad* terribly (adv)
TRBL treble *triple, soprano* trebled trebling
TRBL triable *trial*
TRBL tribal (adj) *group* tribally (adv)
TRBL trouble *(v) worry, disturb* troubled troubling
TRBL trouble *(n) ailment, pains, drawback*
TRBL true-blue (adj) *loyal* true blue (n)
TRBL utterable *speech*
TRBLD troubled *worried*
TRBLG tribology *friction*
TRBLJ tribology *friction*
TRBLJKL tribological *friction*
TRBLJST tribologist *friction*
TRBLKLF treble clef *music*
TRBLMKR troublemaker *disturber*
TRBLN tourbillion *whirlwind*
TRBLN troubling *worrisome*
TRBLNG troubling *worrisome*
TRBLNS terribleness *very bad*
TRBLNS turbulence *commotion*
TRBLNT turbulent *agitated*
TRBLNTS turbulence *commotion*
TRBLR troubler *disturber*

TRBLSHDR troubleshooter *investigator*
TRBLSHN tribulation *distress*
TRBLSHT troubleshoot *investigate*
TRBLSHTR troubleshooter *investigator*
TRBLSM troublesome *difficult*
TRBLSML troublesomely *difficult*
TRBLSMNS troublesomeness *difficulty*
TRBLYN tourbillion *whirlwind*
TRBLZM tribalism *group*
TRBM terbium *element*
TRBM ytterbium *element*
TRBN tribune *defender*
TRBN turban *headdress*
TRBN turbine *engine*
TRBND turbaned (or) turbanned *headdress*
TRBNGKS Outer Banks *islands*
TRBNGX Outer Banks *islands*
TRBNKS Outer Banks *islands*
TRBNL tribunal *court*
TRBNT tribunate *term of office*
TRBNT turbinate *(adj) cone (n) plate*
TRBNTH terebinth *tree*
TRBNX Outer Banks *islands*
TRBPRP turboprop *airplane*
TRBQL trabecula *bar, fold* trabeculae
TRBRK tribrach *verse*
TRBRKK tribrachic *verse*
TRBRN trueborn *ancestry*
TRBSH tarboosh *hat*
TRBSHN attribution *characteristic*
TRBT attribute *(v) explain, account for* attributed attributing
TRBT attribute *(n) trait*
TRBT tribute *respect*

Letters aren't doubled for single sounds: to find alley use **L** not **LL**. Use **Y** and **W** as hard sounds only: to find yellow use **YL**. (Br)=British spelling or usage. * See dictionary.

TRBT turbot *fish* turbot
TRBTBL attributable *credited to*
TRBTD trabeated *beams*
TRBTR tributary *payment, stream* tributaries
TRBTV attributive *joined*
TRBTVL attributively *joined, explained*
TRBYDBL attributable *credited to*
TRBYDD trabeated *beams*
TRBYDV attributive *joined*
TRBYDVL attributively *joined, explained*
TRBYLNS turbulence *commotion*
TRBYLNT turbulent *agitated*
TRBYLNTS turbulence *commotion*
TRBYLSHN tribulation *distress*
TRBYM terbium *element*
TRBYM ytterbium *element*
TRBYN tourbillion *whirlwind*
TRBYN tribune *defender*
TRBYNL tribunal *court*
TRBYNT tribunate *term of office*
TRBYSHN attribution *characteristic*
TRBYT attribute *(v) explain, account for* attributed attributing
TRBYT attribute *(n) trait*
TRBYT tribute *respect*
TRBYTBL attributable *credited to*
TRBYTD trabeated *beams*
TRBYTR tributary *payment, stream* tributaries
TRBYTV attributive *joined*
TRBYTVL attributively *joined, explained*
TRBZMN tribesman *group member* tribesmen
TRCH outreach *extend*
TRCH torch *fire, (Br) flashlight* torches
TRCH torchy *love song* torchier torchiest
TRCHBRR torchbearer *front*
runner
TRCHLT torchlight *lamp*
TRCHNT trecento *14th century*
TRCHR torchier *love song*
TRCHR torture *torment* tortured torturing
TRCHR treachery *treason* treacheries
TRCHRS torturous *painful*
TRCHRS treacherous *faithless, hazardous*
TRCHRSHN trituration *powder*
TRCHRSL torturously *painful*
TRCHRSL treacherously *faithless, hazardous*
TRCHRSNS treacherousness *faithless, hazardous*
TRCHRT triturate *crush* triturated triturating
TRCHS tortuous *twisted*
TRCHSD tortuosity *bend* tortuosities
TRCHSL tortuously *twisted*
TRCHSNG torch song *music*
TRCHSNS tortuousness *twisted*
TRCHST torchiest *love song*
TRCHST tortuosity *bend* tortuosities
TRCHWD torchwood *tree*
TRCHWS tortuous *twisted*
TRCHWSD tortuosity *bend* tortuosities
TRCHWSL tortuously *twisted*
TRCHWSNS tortuousness *twisted*
TRCHWST tortuosity *bend* tortuosities
TRCHYR torchier *love song*
TRCHYST torchiest *love song*
TRCR tarsier *animal*
TRCYR tarsier *animal*
TRD outride *ride better* outrode outriding outridden
TRD tardo *slow*
TRD tardy *late* tardier tardiest
TRD tarty *lewd*
TRD tiered *layered*
TRD tirade *speech*
TRD tired *weary, trite*
TRD toroid *shape*
TRD torrid *hot*
TRD toward (or) towards *(prep) direction (adj) soon*
TRD trade *(v) swap* traded trading
TRD trade *(n) skill*
TRD tread *(v) step, swim* trod treading trodden (or) trod
TRD tread *(n) step, tire pattern*
TRD treaty *pact* treaties
TRD treed *with trees, up a tree*
TRD triad *trinity*
TRD tried *(v-past) try*
TRD triode *tube*
TRD turd *(vulgar) feces*
TRDBK trade book *general reading*
TRDBL tradable *swap*
TRDBL treatable *care for, act upon*
TRDBLT treatability *care for, act upon*
TRDD torridity *hot*
TRDD turreted *tower*
TRDF trade-off (n) *exchange* trade off (v)
TRDFRNS Tour de France *race*
TRDFRNTS Tour de France *race*
TRDFRS tour de force *feat* tours de force
TRDFT pteridophyte *fern*
TRDGNK teratogenic *malformations*
TRDGNSD teratogenicity *malformations*
TRDGNST teratogenicity *malformations*
TRDJN teratogen *malformations*
TRDJNK teratogenic *malformations*

Use letters that best describe the sounds you hear and omit the vowels. Use **S** or **K** instead of **C**: to find circle use **SRKL**. Use **J** to find joy, **JM** to find gem and **G** to find go.

TRDJNSD teratogenicity *malformations*
TRDJNST teratogenicity *malformations*
TRDK autoerotic *self-stimulating*
TRDK triadic *trinity*
TRDKDL pterodactyl *dinosaur*
TRDKL triadically *trinity*
TRDKS toreutics *embossing*
TRDKTL pterodactyl *dinosaur*
TRDL tardily *late*
TRDL toroidal *shape*
TRDL torridly *hot*
TRDL towardly *favorable*
TRDL treadle *pedal* treadled treadling
TRDL turtle *animal*
TRDLBK turtleback *convex*
TRDLDV turtledove *pigeon*
TRDLFWG Tierra del Fuego *island*
TRDLG pteridology *ferns*
TRDLJ pteridology *ferns*
TRDLJK teratologic (or) teratological *abnormal*
TRDLJKL teratological (or) teratologic *abnormal*
TRDLJST pteridologist *ferns*
TRDLNK turtleneck *shirt*
TRDM tritium *isotope*
TRDML treadmill *boring*
TRDMNCHNL tridimensional *3 dimensions*
TRDMNSHNL tridimensional *3 dimensions*
TRDMRK trademark *name*
TRDN pteridine *pigment*
TRDN teardown (n) *disassemble* tear down (v)
TRDN trade down *barter*
TRDN trade in (v) *exchange* trade-in (n)
TRDN trodden *(v-past)* tread
TRDNM trade name *trademark*
TRDNN trade union *labor*
TRDNS tardiness *late*

TRDNS torridness *heat*
TRDNT trident *3 points*
TRDNYN trade union *labor*
TRDP tart up *dress up*
TRDP trade up *exchange*
TRDR outrider *forerunner*
TRDR tardier *late*
TRDR tartar *crust, sediment, person (capitalized)*
TRDR toreador *bullfight*
TRDR trader *dealer*
TRDR traitor *betrayer*
TRDR treater *care for, act upon**
TRDR triter *overused*
TRDR trotter *horse*
TRDRL tendril *stem*
TRDRLD tendriled (or) tendrilled *stems*
TRDRLS tendrilous *stems*
TRDRP teardrop *crying, gem, shape*
TRDRS traitorous *betrayal*
TRDRS traitress (or) traitoress *betrayer (f)*
TRDRSL traitorously *betrayal*
TRDRSS tartar sauce (or) tartare sauce *seasoning*
TRDRT trade route *path*
TRDS tortoise *animal*
TRDS traduce *belittle* traduced traducing
TRDS treatise *argument*
TRDSH tartish *saucy*
TRDSHL tortoiseshell *turtle, butterfly, pattern*
TRDSHN tradition *custom*
TRDSHNL traditional (adj) *customary* traditionally (adv)
TRDSHNLSDK traditionalistic *custom*
TRDSHNLST traditionalist *custom*
TRDSHNLSTK traditionalistic *custom*
TRDSHNLZ traditionalize *custom* traditionalized traditionalizing
TRDSHNLZM traditionalism *custom*

TRDSKL trade school *education*
TRDSKRT trade secret *formula*
TRDSMNT traducement *belittling*
TRDSPRM pteridosperm *fern*
TRDSR traducer *belittler*
TRDSSHL tortoiseshell *turtle, butterfly, pattern*
TRDST tardiest *late*
TRDST tritest *overused*
TRDSZM autoeroticism (or) autoerotism *self-stimulation*
TRDT torridity *hot*
TRDV iterative *repetition*
TRDWND trade wind *breeze*
TRDX toreutics *embossing*
TRDYM tritium *isotope*
TRDYNYN trade union *labor*
TRDYR tardier *late*
TRDYS traduce *belittle* traduced traducing
TRDYSMNT traducement *belittling*
TRDYSR traducer *belittler*
TRDYST tardiest *late*
TRDZ towards (or) toward *(prep) direction*
TRDZ treatise *argument*
TRDZM autoerotism (or) autoeroticism *self-stimulation*
TRDZMN tradesman *dealer* tradesmen
TRF atrophy *waste away* atrophied atrophying atrophies
TRF eutrophy *mineral enrichment*
TRF tariff *tax*
TRF terrify *frighten* terrified terrifying terrifies
TRF trophy *award* trophies
TRF trough *trench* troughs
TRF turf *earth* turfs
TRFBLST trophoblast *embryo*
TRFK atrophic *waste away*
TRFK eutrophic *mineral*

Letters aren't doubled for single sounds: to find alley use **L** not **LL**. Use **Y** and **W** as hard sounds only: to find yellow use **YL**. (Br)=British spelling or usage. * See dictionary.

enrichment
TRFK terrific *fabulous*
TRFK traffic *trade, movement* trafficked trafficking
TRFK trophic *nutrition*
TRFKD trifecta *wager*
TRFKL terrifically *fabulously*
TRFKL trifocal *three lenses*
TRFKL trophically *nutrition*
TRFKLT traffic light *vehicles*
TRFKR trafficker *trader*
TRFKSHN eutrophication *mineral enrichment*
TRFKT trifecta *wager*
TRFL tearful (adj) *crying* tearfully (adv)
TRFL trefoil *clover*
TRFL trifle (v) *dally* trifled trifling
TRFL trifle (n) *sweet* (adj) *slight*
TRFL truffle *fungus, candy*
TRFL turophile *cheese*
TRFLD truffled *fungus*
TRFLKSS trophalaxis *food exchange*
TRFLLT trifoliolate *3 leaves*
TRFLM trifolium *clover*
TRFLN trifling *unimportant*
TRFLNG trifling *unimportant*
TRFLNS tearfulness *crying*
TRFLT trifoliate *3 leaves*
TRFLXS trophalaxis *food exchange*
TRFLYLT trifoliolate *3 leaves*
TRFLYM trifolium *clover*
TRFLYT trifoliate *3 leaves*
TRFN terrifying *scary*
TRFN trephine *scalpel*
TRFNG terrifying *scary*
TRFNSHN trephination *skull hole*
TRFR troffer *lighting*
TRFRG tree frog *animal*
TRFRKSHN trifurcation *3 branches*
TRFRKT trifurcate *3 branches*
TRFRM terra firma *earth*
TRFRM tree farm *crop*
TRFRM triform *3 natures*
TRFTHNG triphthong *3*

sounds
TRFYL trefoil *clover*
TRFYN terrifying *scary*
TRFYNG terrifying *scary*
TRFZT trophozoite *protozoan*
TRFZWT trophozoite *protozoan*
TRG terga (pl) *dorsal part* tergum
TRG trig *math*
TRGD pterygoid *skull*
TRGDBL targetable *goal, signal*
TRGLDT troglodyte *primitive man*
TRGLF triglyph *tablet*
TRGLFK triglyphic (or) triglyphical *tablet*
TRGLFKL triglyphical (or) triglyphic *tablet*
TRGLSRD triglyceride *chemical*
TRGM tergum *dorsal part* terga
TRGN tarragon *spice*
TRGN trigon *threefold*
TRGNL trigonal (adj) *threefold* trigonally (adv)
TRGNMTR trigonometry *math*
TRGNMTRK trigonometric *math*
TRGNS terrigenous *sediment*
TRGR outrigger *boat*
TRGR trigger (n) *lever* (v) *activate*
TRGRD triggered *lever*
TRGRFSH triggerfish *animal*
TRGRHP trigger-happy *gunfire*
TRGRMN triggerman *gunman*
TRGS tear gas (n) *weapon* teargas (v)
TRGT target *goal, signal*
TRGTBL targetable *goal, signal*
TRHBRD trihybrid *genes*
TRHDRL trihedral *3 faces*
TRHL Tarheel *North Carolinian*

TRHPR treehopper *insect*
TRHRDD truehearted *loyal*
TRHRTD truehearted *loyal*
TRHS tree house *structure*
TRJ outrage *anger* outraged outraging
TRJ treillage *trellis*
TRJ triage *priority*
TRJ trudge *slog* trudged trudging
TRJD tragedy *disaster* tragedies
TRJD turgid *swollen*
TRJDN tragedian (m) *actor* tragedienne (f)
TRJDYN tragedian (m) *actor* tragedienne (f)
TRJK tragic *disastrous*
TRJK traject *transfer*
TRJKDR trajectory *pathway* trajectories
TRJKL tragically *disastrous*
TRJKMD tragicomedy *theater* tragicomedies
TRJKMK tragicomic *theater*
TRJKNTH tragacanth *gum*
TRJKSHN trajection *transference*
TRJKT traject *transfer*
TRJKTR trajectory *pathway* trajectories
TRJM triduum *prayer*
TRJMNL trigeminal *nerve*
TRJN Trojan *of Troy*
TRJNHRS Trojan horse *spy vehicle*
TRJNRS Trojan horse *spy vehicle*
TRJNS terrigenous *sediment*
TRJRKN tear-jerking *sad*
TRJRKNG tear-jerking *sad*
TRJRKR tearjerker *sad story*
TRJS outrageous *fantastic*
TRJSNS turgescence *swelling*
TRJSNT turgescent *swollen*
TRJSNTS turgescence *swelling*
TRJT trijet *airplane*
TRJVRSDR tergiversator *evader*
TRJVRSSHN tergiversation

Use letters that best describe the sounds you hear and omit the vowels. Use **S** or **K** instead of **C**: to find circle use **SRKL**. Use **J** to find joy, **JM** to find gem and **G** to find go.

evasion
TRJVRST tergiversate *evade*
tergiversated
tergiversating
TRJVRSTR tergiversator
evader
TRJWM triduum *prayer*
TRK attract *lure*
TRK autarky *independence*
TRK tarok *cards*
TRK teriyaki *food*
TRK toric *shape*
TRK torque *rotation* torqued
torquing
TRK touraco *bird* touracos
TRK trachea *trunk* tracheae
TRK track *(v) follow (n) path*
TRK tract *land, pamphlet*
TRK trek *travel* trekked
trekking
TRK trick *(n) prank (v) fool*
TRK tricky *deceptive* trickier
trickiest
TRK tricot *fabric*
TRK trike *tricycle*
TRK troche *tablet*
TRK trochee *poetry*
TRK troika *sled, rule by three*
TRK truck *(n) vehicle (v)*
transport, barter
TRK Turk *of Turkey*
TRK turkey *bird, fool* turkeys
TRK Turkey *country*
TRKBL trackball *computer*
TRKCL triaxial *3 main lines*
TRKCYL triaxial *3 main lines*
TRKD terra-cotta *clay*
TRKD tracheid *cell*
TRKDBL tractable (adj)
obedient tractably (adv)
TRKDBLD tractability
obedience
TRKDBLT tractability
obedience
TRKDD tracheated (or)
tracheate *trunk*
TRKDK ataractic (or)
ataraxic *tranquilizer*
TRKDK trachytic *rock*
TRKDM tracheotomy
surgery tracheotomies
TRKDM trichotomy *3 parts*

trichotomies
TRKDMS trichotomous *3 parts*
TRKDNC attractancy
allurement
TRKDNS attractancy
allurement
TRKDNT attractant
allurement
TRKDNTC attractancy
allurement
TRKDNTS attractancy
allurement
TRKDR attractor *lure*
TRKDR tractor *machine*
TRKDS tracheitis *illness*
TRKDT tractate *report*
TRKDV attractive *alluring*
TRKDV tractive *hold*
TRKDVL attractively
alluringly
TRKDVNS attractiveness
alluring
TRKFRM truck farm
vegetables
TRKFT tracheophyte *plant*
TRKGN trichogyne *tube*
TRKJ trackage *railway*
TRKJ truckage *payment*
TRKJN trichogyne *tube*
TRKK autarkic *independent*
TRKK trochaic *poetry*
TRKKL autarkical
independent
TRKL tracheole *insect*
TRKL treacle *syrup*
TRKL treacly *sweet*
TRKL trickily *deceptive*
TRKL trickle *flow* trickled
trickling
TRKL trochlea *pulley*
TRKL truckle *yield* truckled
truckling
TRKLD triclad *flatworm*
(Br) tricolour
TRKLD truckload *weight*
TRKLDN trickle-down *flow*
TRKLG trichology
hairdressing
TRKLJ trichology
hairdressing
TRKLJST trichologist

hairdresser
TRKLN tracklaying *(v)*
railway (adj) vehicle
TRKLN truckline
transportation
TRKLNG tracklaying *(v)*
railway (adj) vehicle
TRKLNK triclinic *3 axes*
(Br) tricolour
TRKLNS truculence *cruelty*
truculency
TRKLNT truculent *cruel*
TRKLNTL truculently *cruel*
TRKLNTS truculence
cruelty truculency
TRKLR tracheolar *insect*
TRKLR tricolor *3 colors*
(Br) tricolour
TRKLR trochlear *pulley,*
nerve
TRKLRD tricolored *3 colors,*
French
(Br) tricolour
TRKLS terricolous *ground*
TRKLT tricolette *fabric*
(Br) tricolour
TRKLY trochlea *pulley*
TRKLYN tracklaying *(v)*
railway (adj) vehicle
TRKLYNG tracklaying *(v)*
railway (adj) vehicle
TRKLYR trochlear *pulley,*
nerve
TRKM trachoma *disease*
TRKM trichome *hair*
TRKMN trackman *racer*
trackmen
TRKMNSS trichomoniasis
disease trichomoniases
TRKMNYSS trichomoniasis
disease trichomoniases
TRKN tracking *assigning*
TRKN trichina *worm*
trichinae
TRKN trucking
transportation
TRKNDFLD track-and-field
sports
TRKNFLD track-and-field
sports
TRKNG tracking *assigning*
TRKNG trucking

Letters aren't doubled for single sounds: to find alley use **L** not **LL**. Use **Y** and **W** as hard
sounds only: to find yellow use **YL**. (Br)=British spelling or usage. * See dictionary.

transportation
TRKNR trochanter *femur*
TRKNS trichinous *wormy*
TRKNS trickiness *deception*
TRKNSS trichinosis *disease*
TRKNTR trochanter *femur*
TRKNZ trichinize *infest*
trichinized trichinizing
TRKR tracheary *plant vessel*
TRKR tracker *follower*
TRKR trekker *traveler*
TRKR tricker *deceiver*
TRKR trickery *deception*
TRKR trickier *deceptive*
TRKR trocar *surgery*
TRKR trucker *truck driver*
TRKRMDK trichromatic *3 colors*
TRKRMT trichromat *3 colors*
TRKRMTK trichromatic *3 colors*
TRKRMTZM trichromatism *3 colors*
TRKRN tricorn *3 horns, 3 corners*
TRKRN tricorne (or) tricorn *hat*
TRKRNRD tricornered *3 corners*
TRKRTRDR trick-or-treater *Halloween*
TRKRTRT trick or treat (n) *Halloween* trick-or-treat (v)
TRKRTRTR trick-or-treater *Halloween*
TRKS turquoise *mineral, color*
TRKSD trackside *area*
TRKSDM tracheostomy *surgery* tracheostomies
TRKSDR trickster *deceiver*
TRKSH Turkish *of Turkey*
TRKSHBTH Turkish bath *steam*
TRKSHN attraction *allure*
TRKSHN traction *hold*
TRKSHNL tractional *hold*
TRKSK ataraxic (or) ataraxic *tranquilizer*
TRKSL triaxial *3 main lines*
TRKSPD tricuspid *3 points,*

TRKSPT tricuspid *3 points, tooth*
TRKSS trichiasis *eyelid*
TRKSST trichocyst *stinger*
TRKST tracksuit *clothing*
TRKST trickiest *deceptive*
TRKSTM tracheostomy *surgery* tracheostomies
TRKSTP truck stop *eatery*
TRKSTR trickster *deceiver*
TRKSYL triaxial *3 main lines*
TRKT attract *lure*
TRKT terra-cotta *clay*
TRKT tracheate (or) tracheated *trunk*
TRKT trachyte *rock*
TRKT tracked *rail*
TRKT tract *land, pamphlet*
TRKT tricot *fabric*
TRKTBL tractable (adj) *obedient* tractably (adv)
TRKTBLD tractability *obedience*
TRKTBLT tractability *obedience*
TRKTD tracheated (or) tracheate *trunk*
TRKTDNTC attractancy *allurement*
TRKTDNTS attractancy *allurement*
TRKTHSN trichothecene *toxin*
TRKTK ataractic (or) ataraxic *tranquilizer*
TRKTK trachytic *rock*
TRKTM tracheotomy *surgery* tracheotomies
TRKTM trichotomy *3 parts* trichotomies
TRKTMS trichotomous *3 parts*
TRKTN tricotine *fabric*
TRKTNC attractancy *allurement*
TRKTNS attractancy *allurement*
TRKTNT attractant *allurement*
TRKTR attractor *lure*
TRKTR tractor *machine*

TRKTS tracheitis *illness*
TRKTT tractate *report*
TRKTV attractive *alluring*
TRKTV tractive *hold*
TRKTVL attractively *alluringly*
TRKTVNS attractiveness *alluring*
TRKW trackway *path*
TRKWS terraqueous *land and water*
TRKWTRS triquetrous *angles*
TRKWYS terraqueous *land and water*
TRKWZ turquoise *mineral, color*
TRKY trachea *trunk* tracheae
TRKYD tracheid *cell*
TRKYDD tracheated (or) tracheate *trunk*
TRKYDM tracheotomy *surgery* tracheotomies
TRKYDS tracheitis *illness*
TRKYFT tracheophyte *plant*
TRKYK trochaic *poetry*
TRKYL tracheole *insect*
TRKYLNS truculence *cruelty* truculency
TRKYLNT truculent *cruel*
TRKYLNTL truculently *cruel*
TRKYLNTS truculence *cruelty* truculency
TRKYLR tracheolar *insect*
TRKYR tracheary *plant vessel*
TRKYR trickier *deceptive*
TRKYSDM tracheostomy *surgery* tracheostomies
TRKYSS trichiasis *eyelid*
TRKYST trickiest *deceptive*
TRKYSTM tracheostomy *surgery* tracheostomies
TRKYT tracheate (or) tracheated *trunk*
TRKYTD tracheated (or) tracheate *trunk*
TRKYTM tracheotomy *surgery* tracheotomies
TRKYTS tracheitis *illness*
TRKZ turquoise *mineral,*

Use letters that best describe the sounds you hear and omit the vowels. Use **S** or **K** instead of **C**: to find circle use **SRKL**. Use **J** to find joy, **JM** to find gem and **G** to find go.

color
TRL pteryla *bird* pterylae
TRL torula *fungus* torulae
TRL trail *(v)* follow *(n)* path
TRL trawl *net*
TRL trial *test, law*
TRL trill *(n)* sound *(v)* twirl, quaver, trickle
TRL triol *chemical*
TRL troll *(v)* fish, ramble *(n)* lure, dwarf, giant
TRL trolley *streetcar* trolleys
TRL trowel *tool*
TRL trull *harlot*
TRL truly *honestly*
TRL utterly *completely*
TRLB trilby *(Br)* hat trilbies
TRLBLZN trailblazing *leading*
TRLBLZNG trailblazing *leading*
TRLBLZR trailblazer *leader*
TRLBRKR trailbreaker *leader*
TRLBT trilobite *animal*
TRLD trailhead *path*
TRLDRL trilateral *3 sides*
TRLDRL triliteral *3 letters*
TRLF true-life *actual*
TRLG trialogue *3-way conversation*
TRLG trilogy *3 works* trilogies
TRLHD trailhead *path*
TRLJ treillage *trellis*
TRLJ trilogy *3 works* trilogies
TRLK treelike *branches*
TRLM trillium *herb*
TRLMKS trail mix *food*
TRLMX trail mix *food*
TRLN tree line *altitude*
TRLN trillion *number (1,000,000,000)*
TRLNGGWL trilingual (adj) *3 languages* trilingually (adv)
TRLNGWL trilingual (adj) *3 languages* trilingually (adv)
TRLNR trilinear *3 lines*
TRLNYR trilinear *3 lines*
TRLP trollop *prostitute*
TRLR trailer *vehicle, film*
TRLR trawler *boat*
TRLRMN trawlerman *netter*

TRLS tireless *strong*
TRLS treeless *no trees*
TRLS trellis *frame*
TRLSD trailside *path*
TRLSH treillage *trellis*
TRLST trellised *framed*
TRLSWRK trelliswork *frame*
TRLT triolet *poem*
TRLT troilite *mineral*
TRLTN tarlatan *fabric*
TRLTRL trilateral *3 sides*
TRLTRL triliteral *3 letters*
TRLV truelove *sweetheart*
TRLYM trillium *herb*
TRLYN trillion *number (1,000,000,000)*
TRM atrium *hall, heart* atria
TRM tearoom *restaurant*
TRM term *(n)* time, word *(v)* name
TRM tram *(n)* wagon, *(Br)* streetcar
TRM tram *(v)* haul trammed tramming
TRM trauma *injury* traumas
TRM trim *(v)* cut, adjust trimmed trimming
TRM trim *(adj)* slim trimmer trimmest
TRM trim *(n)* haircut, decoration, condition
TRM yttrium *element*
TRMBL tremble *shake* trembled trembling
TRMBL trembly *shaky*
TRMBN trombone *music*
TRMBNST trombonist *musician*
TRMDK traumatic *harmful*
TRMDKL traumatically *harmful*
TRMDR trimotor *3 engines*
TRMF triumph *(n)* victory *(v)* prevail
TRMFL triumphal *victorious*
TRMFNT triumphant *victorious*
TRMFNTL triumphantly *victorious*
TRMGN ptarmigan *bird*
TRMGNT termagant *shrew*
TRMK tarmac *runway*

TRMKDM tarmacadam *pavement*
TRMKR tramcar *(Br)* streetcar
TRML trammel *(v)* catch, hinder trammeled (or) trammelled trammeling (or) trammelling
TRML trammel *(n)* net, restraint, compass
TRML tremolo *music* tremolos
TRML trimly *slim*
TRML trommel *sieve*
TRML turmoil *confusion*
TRMLN tourmaline *mineral*
TRMLN tramline *(Br)* rails
TRMLS termless *unending*
TRMLS tremulous *shaken*
TRMN termini (pl) *end* terminus
TRMN trimming *decoration*
TRMNBL terminable (adj) *end* terminably (adv)
TRMNDR terminator *line, ender*
TRMNDS tremendous *huge*
TRMNDSL tremendously *huge*
TRMNDSNS tremendousness *huge*
TRMNDV terminative *ending*
TRMNG trimming *decoration*
TRMNL terminal *(n)* end, station
TRMNL terminal (adj) *last, fatal* terminally (adv)
TRMNLG terminology *names* terminologies
TRMNLJ terminology *names* terminologies
TRMNLJKL terminological (adj) *names* terminologically (adv)
TRMNR tormentor *torturer*
TRMNS terminus *goal, tip* termini (or) terminuses
TRMNS trimness *slim*
TRMNSHN termination *conclusion*
TRMNSHNL terminational *conclusion*

Letters aren't doubled for single sounds: to find alley use **L** not **LL**. Use **Y** and **W** as hard sounds only: to find yellow use **YL**. (Br)=British spelling or usage. * See dictionary.

TRMNT terminate *end* terminated terminating

TRMNT torment *torture*

TRMNTHL trimonthly *every 3 months*

TRMNTL tormentil *plant*

TRMNTR terminator *line, ender*

TRMNTR tormentor *torturer*

TRMNTV terminative *ending*

TRMP tramp *(v) hike (n) hobo, prostitute*

TRMP tromp *stomp*

TRMP trump *(n) cards (v) outdo*

TRMPDP trumped-up *dishonest*

TRMPDR trumpeter *musician*

TRMPF triumph *(n) victor, (v) prevail*

TRMPFL triumphal *victorious*

TRMPFNT triumphant *victorious*

TRMPFNTL triumphantly *victorious*

TRMPL trample *walk on* trampled trampling

TRMPL trompe l'oeil *painting style*

TRMPLN trampoline *springboard*

TRMPLNR trampoliner *springboard*

TRMPLNST trampolinist *springboard*

TRMPR trumpery *nonsense*

TRMPT trumpet *music*

TRMPTP trumped-up *dishonest*

TRMPTR trumpeter *musician*

TRMR termer *elected one*

TRMR tremor *shake*

TRMR trimmer *cutter, slimmer*

TRMRFK trimorphic *3 forms*

TRMRK turmeric *herb*

TRMRN trimaran *sailboat*

TRMRS trimerous *in threes*

TRMSDR trimester *3 months*

TRMSN Terramycin *(trademark) drug*

TRMST outermost *external*

TRMST trimmest *slimmest*

TRMST uttermost *complete, extreme*

TRMSTR trimester *3 months*

TRMT termite *insect*

TRMTD trematode *flatworm*

TRMTK traumatic *harmful*

TRMTKL traumatically *harmful*

TRMTR termitaria (pl) *nest* termitarium

TRMTR trimeter *poetry*

TRMTR trimotor *3 engines*

TRMTRM termitarium *nest* termitaria

TRMTRY termitaria (pl) *nest* termitarium

TRMTRYM termitarium *nest* termitaria

TRMTS traumatize *injure* traumatized traumatizing *(Br)* traumatise

TRMTSM traumatism *injury*

TRMTZ traumatize *injure* traumatized traumatizing *(Br)* traumatise

TRMTZM traumatism *injury*

TRMTZSHN traumatization *injury* *(Br)* traumatisation

TRMVRT triumvirate *3 rulers*

TRMWL Trombe wall *building*

TRMYL turmoil *confusion*

TRMYLS tremulous *shaken*

TRN attorney *lawyer* attorneys

TRN outrun *run better, run faster* outran outrunning

TRN pterin *pigment*

TRN tarn *lake*

TRN tearing *violent, (Br) splendid*

TRN Tehran *city*

TRN tern *bird*

TRN terne *alloy*

TRN terrain *land*

TRN terrane *rock*

TRN terrene *(adj) ordinary*

(n) earth

TRN terrine *food*

TRN Toronto *city*

TRN touring *travel*

TRN tourney *contest* tourneys

TRN towering *excessive*

TRN train *(n) vehicle (v) teach*

TRN trainee *learner*

TRN trend *tendency, vogue*

TRN trine *three*

TRN triune *trinity*

TRN trona *mineral*

TRN trying *difficult*

TRN tureen *pot*

TRN turn *(v) rotate, change, apply (n) rotation, bend, change**

TRN tyranny *oppression* tyrannies

TRN U-turn *turn around*

TRN uterine *womb*

TRNBKL turnbuckle *tighten*

TRNBL trainable *teach*

TRNBL turnable *rotate*

TRNBLD trainability *learner*

TRNBLT trainability *learner*

TRNBT turnabout *reversal*

TRNC truancy *absence* truancies

TRNCH trench *(n) ditch (v) carve* trenches

TRNCHFT trench foot *disease*

TRNCHKT trench coat *garment*

TRNCHL tarantula *spider* tarantulas

TRNCHL torrential *(adj) flood* torrentially *(adv)*

TRNCHMTH trench mouth *disease*

TRNCHN truncheon *baton*

TRNCHNC trenchancy *clearness*

TRNCHNS trenchancy *clearness*

TRNCHNT trenchant *clear*

TRNCHNTC trenchancy *clearness*

TRNCHNTL trenchantly *clearly*

Use letters that best describe the sounds you hear and omit the vowels. Use **S** or **K** instead of **C**: to find circle use **SRKL**. Use **J** to find joy, **JM** to find gem and **G** to find go.

TRNCHNTS trenchancy *clearness*
TRNCHR trencher *platter*
TRNCHRMN trencherman *eater*
TRNCNS transience *temporary* transiency
TRNCNT transient *temporary*
TRNCNTS transience *temporary* transiency
TRNCVR transceiver *communications*
TRNCYNS transience *temporary* transiency
TRNCYNT transient *temporary*
TRNCYNTS transience *temporary* transiency
TRND eternity *forever* eternities
TRND tornado *whirlwind* tornadoes (or) tornados
TRND tournedos *beef* tournedos
TRND trend *tendency, vogue*
TRND trendy *stylish* trendier trendiest
TRND trinity *three in one* trinities
TRNDD Trinidad *island*
TRNDK tornadic *whirlwind*
TRNDKS Adirondacks *mountains*
TRNDL trendily *stylish*
TRNDL trundle *wheel, roll* trundled trundling
TRNDN pteranodon *dinosaur*
TRNDN turndown (adj, n) *reject* turn down (v)
TRNDN turned-on *hip*
TRNDNS trendiness *stylish*
TRNDR trendier *stylish*
TRNDS tournedos *beef* tournedos
TRNDSDR trendsetter *stylish*
TRNDST trendiest *stylish*
TRNDSTR trendsetter *stylish*
TRNDX Adirondacks

mountains
TRNDYR trendier *stylish*
TRNDYST trendiest *stylish*
TRNF turn off (v) *dismiss, deflect, bore**
TRNF turnoff (n) *exit*
TRNG tearing *violent, (Br) splendid*
TRNG touring *travel*
TRNG towering *excessive*
TRNG trying *difficult*
TRNGGL triangle *shape*
TRNGGLR triangular *3 sides*
TRNGGLSHN triangulation *3 sides*
TRNGGLT triangulate *3 sides* triangulated triangulating
TRNGGYLR triangular *3 sides*
TRNGGYLSHN triangulation *3 sides*
TRNGGYLT triangulate *3 sides* triangulated triangulating
TRNGK outrank *exceed*
TRNGK trunk *torso, stem, luggage**
TRNGKDD truncated *cut off*
TRNGKFSH trunkfish *animal*
TRNGKLN trunk line *channel*
TRNGKSHN truncation *cut off*
TRNGKT trinket *ornament*
TRNGKT truncate *cut off* truncated truncating
TRNGKTD truncated *cut off*
TRNGKWL tranquil (adj) *calm* tranquilly (adv)
TRNGKWLD tranquillity (or) tranquility *calmness*
TRNGKWLNS tranquilness *calm*
TRNGKWLT tranquillity (or) tranquility *calmness*
TRNGKWLZ tranquilize *relax* tranquilized tranquilizing
TRNGKWLZR tranquilizer *relaxer*
TRNGL triangle *shape*
TRNGLR triangular *3 sides*
TRNGLSHN triangulation *3*

sides
TRNGLT triangulate *3 sides* triangulated triangulating
TRNGNS transience *temporary* transiency
TRNGNT transient *temporary*
TRNGNTS transience *temporary* transiency
TRNGQL tranquil (adj) *calm* tranquilly (adv)
TRNGQLD tranquillity (or) tranquility *calmness*
TRNGQLNS tranquilness *calm*
TRNGQLT tranquillity (or) tranquility *calmness*
TRNGQLZ tranquilize *relax* tranquilized tranquilizing
TRNGQLZR tranquilizer *relaxer*
TRNGYLR triangular *3 sides*
TRNGYLSHN triangulation *3 sides*
TRNGYLT triangulate *3 sides* triangulated triangulating
TRNGYNS transience *temporary* transiency
TRNGYNT transient *temporary*
TRNGYNTS transience *temporary* transiency
TRNJNRL attorney general *government lawyer* attorneys general (or) attorney generals
TRNJNS transience *temporary* transiency
TRNJNT transient *temporary*
TRNJNTS transience *temporary* transiency
TRNJYNT transient *temporary*
TRNK outrank *exceed*
TRNK trunk *torso, stem, luggage**
TRNK turnkey (n) *prison* (adj) *ready* turnkeys
TRNKDD truncated *cut off*
TRNKFSH trunkfish *animal*
TRNKL tyrannical (adj) *oppressive* tyrannically

Letters aren't doubled for single sounds: to find alley use **L** not **LL**. Use **Y** and **W** as hard sounds only: to find yellow use **YL**. (Br)=British spelling or usage. * See dictionary.

(adv)

TRNKLN trunk line *channel*

TRNKSHN truncation *cut off*

TRNKT tourniquet *bleeding*

TRNKT trinket *ornament*

TRNKT truncate *cut off* truncated truncating

TRNKT turncoat *traitor*

TRNKTD truncated *cut off*

TRNKWL tranquil (adj) *calm* tranquilly (adv)

TRNKWLD tranquillity (or) tranquility *calmness*

TRNKWLNS tranquilness *calm*

TRNKWLT tranquillity (or) tranquility *calmness*

TRNKWLZ tranquilize *relax* tranquilized tranquilizing

TRNKWLZR tranquilizer *relaxer*

TRNL eternal (adj) *forever* eternally (adv)

TRNL tornillo *wood cutter* tornillos

TRNL treenail *peg*

TRNL triennial (n, adj) *three years* triennially (adv)

TRNL trinal *triple*

TRNLD trainload *railroad*

TRNLRNGGLG otorhinolaryngology *ear, nose and throat*

TRNLRNGGLJ otorhinolaryngology *ear, nose and throat*

TRNLRNGGLJKL otorhinolaryngological *ear, nose and throat*

TRNLRNGGLJST otorhinolaryngologist *ear, nose and throat*

TRNLRNGLG otorhinolaryngology *ear, nose and throat*

TRNLRNGLJ otorhinolaryngology *ear, nose and throat*

TRNLRNGLJKL otorhinolaryngological *ear, nose and throat*

TRNLRNGLJST

otorhinolaryngologist *ear, nose and throat*

TRNLZ eternalize *immortalize* eternalized eternalizing

TRNM triennium *three years* trienniums (or) triennia

TRNML trinomial *number*

TRNMN trainman *railroad* trainmen

TRNMNT tournament *contest*

TRNMYL trinomial *number*

TRNN training *education*

TRNN trunnion *pivot*

TRNN turn in *(v) hand over, put on, sleep*

TRNN turn on (v) *activate, get high* turn-on (n)

TRNN turn-in *(n) slant*

TRNN turning *direction, lathe*

TRNNG training *education*

TRNNG turning *direction, lathe*

TRNNGPNT turning point *change*

TRNNPNT turning point *change*

TRNP turn up *increase, appear*

TRNP turnip *vegetable*

TRNPK turnpike *road*

TRNPL trompe l'oeil *painting style*

TRNPLT terneplate *alloy*

TRNQL tranquil (adj) *calm* tranquilly (adv)

TRNQLD tranquillity (or) tranquility *calmness*

TRNQLNS tranquilness *calm*

TRNQLT tranquillity (or) tranquility *calmness*

TRNQLZ tranquilize *relax* tranquilized tranquilizing

TRNQLZR tranquilizer *relaxer*

TRNR ternary *three*

TRNR trainer *teacher*

TRNR turner *rotator*

TRNRN turnaround (n) *reverse* turn around (v)

TRNRND turnaround (n)

reverse turn around (v)

TRNS tarriance *delay*

TRNS trance *hypnotize* tranced trancing

TRNS trounce *defeat* trounced trouncing

TRNS truancy *absence* truancies

TRNS tyrannous *oppressive*

TRNS utterance *speech*

TRNSBSTNCHSHN transubstantiation *change form*

TRNSBSTNCHT transubstantiate *change form* transubstantiated transubstantiating

TRNSBSTNCHYSHN transubstantiation *change form*

TRNSBSTNCHYT transubstantiate *change form* transubstantiated transubstantiating

TRNSBSTNSHSHN transubstantiation *change form*

TRNSBSTNSHT transubstantiate *change form* transubstantiated transubstantiating

TRNSBSTNSHYSHN transubstantiation *change form*

TRNSBSTNSHYT transubstantiate *change form* transubstantiated transubstantiating

TRNSD transude *ooze out* transuded transuding

TRNSDKSHN transduction *conversion*

TRNSDR trendsetter *stylish*

TRNSDS transduce *convert*

TRNSDSHN transudation *ooze out*

TRNSDSR transducer *converter*

TRNSDT transudate *ooze out*

TRNSDV transitive *relationship*

TRNSDYS transduce

Use letters that best describe the sounds you hear and omit the vowels. Use **S** or **K** instead of **C**: to find circle use **SRKL**. Use **J** to find joy, **JM** to find gem and **G** to find go.

convert
TRNSDYSR transducer
converter
TRNSFGR transfigure
change form transfigured
transfiguring
TRNSFGRSHN
transfiguration *change in*
form
TRNSFGYR transfigure
change form transfigured
transfiguring
TRNSFGYRSHN
transfiguration *change in*
form
TRNSFKS transfix *pierce*
TRNSFKSHN transfixion
piercing
TRNSFNT transfinite
number
TRNSFR transfer *move*
transferred transferring
TRNSFR transferee *one*
moved
TRNSFRBL transferable
movable
TRNSFRBLD transferability
movable
TRNSFRBLT transferability
movable
TRNSFRL transferal *move*
TRNSFRM transform
convert, change
TRNSFRMDV
transformative *change*
TRNSFRMR transformer
converter
TRNSFRMSHN
transformation *change*
TRNSFRMSHNL
transformational (adj)
change transformationally
(adv)
TRNSFRMSHNLST
transformationalist
grammar
TRNSFRMTV
transformative *change*
TRNSFRN transferrin *blood*
TRNSFRNS transference
movement
TRNSFRNSHL

transferential *movement*
TRNSFRNTS transference
movement
TRNSFRNTSHL
transferential *movement*
TRNSFRR transferrer *mover*
TRNSFRZ transferase
enzyme
TRNSFSHN transfusion
transfer
TRNSFSHNL transfusional
transfer
TRNSFX transfix *pierce*
TRNSFYSHN transfusion
transfer
TRNSFYSHNL transfusional
transfer
TRNSFYZ transfuse
penetrate, transmit
transfused transfusing
TRNSFYZBL transfusible
(or) transfusable
penetrate, transmit
TRNSFYZHN transfusion
transfer
TRNSFYZHNL transfusional
transfer
TRNSFZ transfuse *penetrate,*
transmit transfused
transfusing
TRNSFZBL transfusible (or)
transfusable *penetrate,*
transmit
TRNSFZHN transfusion
transfer
TRNSFZHNL transfusional
transfer
TRNSGNK transgenic *genes*
TRNSGRS transgress *sin*
TRNSGRSHN transgression
sin
TRNSGRSR transgressor
sinner
TRNSGRSV transgressive
sinning
TRNSH tarnish *stain, film*
TRNSHBL tarnishable *stain,*
film
TRNSHL tarantula *spider*
tarantulas
TRNSHL torrential (adj) *flood*
torrentially (adv)

TRNSHMNS transhumance
livestock
TRNSHMNTS
transhumance *livestock*
TRNSHN tarnation
damnation
TRNSHN truncheon *baton*
TRNSHNS transience
temporary transiency
TRNSHNT transient
temporary
TRNSHNTS transience
temporary transiency
TRNSHP attorneyship
lawyer
TRNSHP transship *transfer*
transshipped
transshipping
TRNSHPMNT
transshipment *transfer*
TRNSHYMNS
transhumance *livestock*
TRNSHYMNTS
transhumance *livestock*
TRNSHYNS transience
temporary transiency
TRNSHYNT transient
temporary
TRNSHYNTS transience
temporary transiency
TRNSJNK transgenic *genes*
TRNSK transact *do*
TRNSK transect *divide*
TRNSK Transkei *region*
TRNSKCHL transsexual
change sex
TRNSKCHWL transsexual
change sex
TRNSKDR transactor
exchanger
TRNSKLCHRL transcultural
traditions
TRNSKLTRL transcultural
traditions
TRNSKNNNL
transcontinental *coast to*
coast
TRNSKNTNNL
transcontinental *coast to*
coast
TRNSKNTNNTL
transcontinental *coast to*

Letters aren't doubled for single sounds: to find alley use **L** not **LL**. Use **Y** and **W** as hard
sounds only: to find yellow use **YL**. (Br)=British spelling or usage. * See dictionary.

coast

TRNSKRB transcribe *record* transcribed transcribing

TRNSKRBR transcriber *recorder*

TRNSKRP transcript *copy*

TRNSKRPSHN transcription *copy*

TRNSKRPSHNL transcriptional (adj) *copy* transcriptionally (adv)

TRNSKRPSHNST transcriptionist *copier*

TRNSKRPT transcript *copy*

TRNSKSHL transsexual *change sex*

TRNSKSHLD transsexuality *change sex*

TRNSKSHLT transsexuality *change sex*

TRNSKSHN transaction *exchange*

TRNSKSHNL transactional *interactions*

TRNSKSHWL transsexual *change sex*

TRNSKSHWLD transsexuality *change sex*

TRNSKSHWLT transsexuality *change sex*

TRNSKSL transaxle *vehicle*

TRNSKT transact *do*

TRNSKT transect *divide*

TRNSKTR transactor *exchanger*

TRNSKZL transaxle *vehicle*

TRNSL turnsole *herb*

TRNSLDBL translatable *interpret, change*

TRNSLDR translator *interpret, change*

TRNSLDRSHN transliteration *spelling*

TRNSLDRT transliterate *spell* transliterated transliterating

TRNSLKSHN translocation *displacement*

TRNSLKT translocate *displace* translocated translocating

TRNSLSHN translation

interpret, change

TRNSLSNC translucence *clearness* translucency

TRNSLSNS translucence *clearness* translucency

TRNSLSNT translucent *clear*

TRNSLSNTC translucence *clearness* translucency

TRNSLSNTS translucence *clearness* translucency

TRNSLT translate *interpret, change* translated translating

TRNSLTBL translatable *interpret, change*

TRNSLTR translator *interpret, change*

TRNSLTRSHN transliteration *spelling*

TRNSLTRT transliterate *spell* transliterated transliterating

TRNSLVN Transylvania *region*

TRNSLVNY Transylvania *region*

TRNSM transom *crosspiece*

TRNSMDBL transmittable *send, conduct*

TRNSMDBL transmutable *convert*

TRNSMDL transmittal *conveyance*

TRNSMDNS transmittance *conveyance*

TRNSMDNTS transmittance *conveyance*

TRNSMDR transmitter *sender*

TRNSMGRDR transmigrator *movement* transmigratory

TRNSMGRF transmogrify *transform* transmogrified transmogrifying transmogrifies

TRNSMGRFKSHN transmogrification *change*

TRNSMGRSHN transmigration *movement*

TRNSMGRT transmigrate *move* transmigrated

transmigrating

TRNSMGRTR transmigrator *movement* transmigratory

TRNSMSBL transmissible *pass on*

TRNSMSHN transmission *broadcast, gears, movement*

TRNSMSV transmissive *broadcast, movement*

TRNSMSVD transmissivity *broadcast, movement*

TRNSMSVT transmissivity *broadcast, movement*

TRNSMT transmit *send, conduct* transmitted transmitting

TRNSMT transmute *convert* transmuted transmuting

TRNSMTBL transmittable *send, conduct*

TRNSMTBL transmutable *convert*

TRNSMTDV transmutative *conversion*

TRNSMTL transmittal *conveyance*

TRNSMTNS transmittance *conveyance*

TRNSMTNTS transmittance *conveyance*

TRNSMTR transmitter *sender*

TRNSMTSHN transmutation *conversion*

TRNSMTTV transmutative *conversion*

TRNSMYDBL transmutable *convert*

TRNSMYT transmute *convert* transmuted transmuting

TRNSMYTBL transmutable *convert*

TRNSMYTDV transmutative *conversion*

TRNSMYTSHN transmutation *conversion*

TRNSMYTTV transmutative *conversion*

TRNSN transcend *rise above, exceed*

TRNSND transcend *rise*

Use letters that best describe the sounds you hear and omit the vowels. Use **S** or **K** instead of **C**: to find circle use **SRKL**. Use **J** to find joy, **JM** to find gem and **G** to find go.

above, exceed
TRNSNDNL transcendental
(adj) *supernatural*
transcendentally (adv)
TRNSNDNLZM
transcendentalism
supernatural
TRNSNDNS transcendence
rise above, exceed
transcendency
TRNSNDNT transcendent
surpassing
TRNSNDNTL
transcendental (adj)
supernatural
transcendentally (adv)
TRNSNDNTLZM
transcendentalism
supernatural
TRNSNDNTS
transcendence *rise above,*
exceed transcendency
TRNSNK transonic *speed*
TRNSNS transience
temporary transiency
TRNSNSHNL transnational
beyond nations
TRNSNT transient *temporary*
TRNSNTS transience
temporary transiency
TRNSPDL transeptal *church*
TRNSPKS transpicuous
understood
TRNSPKYS transpicuous
understood
TRNSPLNT transplant
relocate
TRNSPLNTBL
transplantable *movable*
TRNSPLNTR transplanter
mover
TRNSPLNTSHN
transplantation *movement*
TRNSPLR transpolar *across*
poles
TRNSPNDR transponder
receiver
TRNSPQS transpicuous
understood
TRNSPR transpire *seep out,*
happen transpired
transpiring

TRNSPRDBL transportable
movable
TRNSPRDBLD
transportability *movable*
TRNSPRDBLT
transportability *movable*
TRNSPRDR transporter
mover
TRNSPRNC transparency
clearness transparencies
TRNSPRNS transparence
clearness
TRNSPRNS transparency
clearness transparencies
TRNSPRNT transparent
clear
TRNSPRNTC transparency
clearness transparencies
TRNSPRNTL transparently
clear
TRNSPRNTNS
transparentness *clear*
TRNSPRNTS transparence
clearness
TRNSPRNTS transparency
clearness transparencies
TRNSPRSHN transpiration
seep out
TRNSPRSNL transpersonal
beyond ego
TRNSPRT transport (v)
move (n) vehicle
TRNSPRTBL transportable
movable
TRNSPRTBLD
transportability *movable*
TRNSPRTBLT
transportability *movable*
TRNSPRTR transporter
mover
TRNSPRTSHN
transportation *vehicle*
TRNSPSFK transpacific
across the Pacific
TRNSPT transept *church*
TRNSPT turnspit *roast*
TRNSPTL transeptal *church*
TRNSPZ transpose *reverse*
transposed transposing
TRNSPZBL transposable
reverse
TRNSPZSHN transposition

reversal
TRNSR tyrannosaur
dinosaur
TRNSRS tyrannosaurus
dinosaur
TRNSSDR transistor
electricity
TRNSSDRZ transistorize
electricity transistorized
transistorizing
(Br) transistorise
TRNSSHN transition *change*
TRNSSHNK transoceanic
beyond oceans
TRNSSHNL transitional
(adj) *change* transitionally
(adv)
TRNSSHYNK transoceanic
beyond oceans
TRNSSTR transistor
electricity
TRNSSTRZ transistorize
electricity transistorized
transistorizing
(Br) transistorise
TRNSSTRZSHN
transistorization *electricity*
(Br) transistorisation
TRNST transit (n) *passage* (v)
travel
TRNSTL turnstile *gate*
TRNSTLNK transatlantic
ocean
TRNSTLNTK transatlantic
ocean
TRNSTN turnstone *bird*
TRNSTR transitory
temporary
TRNSTR trendsetter *stylish*
TRNSTRL transitorily
temporary
TRNSTRNS transitoriness
temporary
TRNSTV transitive
relationship
TRNSTVD transitivity
relationship
TRNSTVT transitivity
relationship
TRNSVL transvalue
reappraise transvalued
transvaluing

Letters aren't doubled for single sounds: to find alley use **L** not **LL**. Use **Y** and **W** as hard
sounds only: to find yellow use **YL**. (Br)=British spelling or usage. * See dictionary.

TRNSVLY transvalue *reappraise* transvalued transvaluing
TRNSVR transceiver *communications*
TRNSVRS transverse *crosswise*
TRNSVRSBL transversable *cross*
TRNSVRSL transversal *intersection*
TRNSVRSL transversely *crosswise*
TRNSVRZL transversal *intersection*
TRNSVSDT transvestite *cross-dresser*
TRNSVSTT transvestite *cross-dresser*
TRNSVSTZM transvestism *cross-dressing*
TRNSXL transaxle *vehicle*
TRNSXL transsexual *change sex*
TRNSXLD transsexuality *change sex*
TRNSXLT transsexuality *change sex*
TRNSXWL transsexual *change sex*
TRNSXWLD transsexuality *change sex*
TRNSXWLT transsexuality *change sex*
TRNSYD transude *ooze out* transuded transuding
TRNSYDSHN transudation *ooze out*
TRNSYDT transudate *ooze out*
TRNSYNS transience *temporary* transiency
TRNSYNT transient *temporary*
TRNSYNTS transience *temporary* transiency
TRNT eternity *forever* eternities
TRNT ternate *in threes*
TRNT Toronto *city*
TRNT torrent *flood*
TRNT trinity *three in one*

trinities
TRNT truant *absent*
TRNT turn out *(v)* evict, clean, end*
TRNT turnout *(n) number of people, road, dress, (Br) striker*
TRNT tyrant *dictator*
TRNTBL turntable *rotate*
TRNTC truancy *absence* truancies
TRNTCHL tarantula *spider* tarantulas
TRNTCVR transceiver *communications*
TRNTK tornadic *whirlwind*
TRNTL attorney-at-law *lawyer* attorneys-at-law
TRNTL tarantella *dance*
TRNTL tarantula *spider* tarantulas
TRNTRN trinitarian *three in one*
TRNTRYN trinitarian *three in one*
TRNTS tarriance *delay*
TRNTS trance *hypnotize* tranced trancing
TRNTS trounce *defeat* trounced trouncing
TRNTS truancy *absence* truancies
TRNTS utterance *speech*
TRNTSDKSHN transduction *conversion*
TRNTSDS transduce *convert*
TRNTSDSR transducer *converter*
TRNTSDV transitive *relationship*
TRNTSDYS transduce *convert*
TRNTSDYSR transducer *converter*
TRNTSFGR transfigure *change form* transfigured transfiguring
TRNTSFGRSHN transfiguration *change in form*
TRNTSFGYR transfigure

change form transfigured transfiguring
TRNTSFGYRSHN transfiguration *change in form*
TRNTSFKS transfix *pierce*
TRNTSFKSHN transfixion *piercing*
TRNTSFNT transfinite *number*
TRNTSFR transfer *move* transferred transferring
TRNTSFR transferee *one moved*
TRNTSFRBL transferable *movable*
TRNTSFRBLD transferability *movable*
TRNTSFRBLT transferability *movable*
TRNTSFRL transferal *move*
TRNTSFRM transform *convert, change*
TRNTSFRMDV transformative *change*
TRNTSFRMR transformer *converter*
TRNTSFRMSHN transformation *change*
TRNTSFRMSHNL transformational (adj) *change* transformationally (adv)
TRNTSFRMSHNLST transformationalist *grammar*
TRNTSFRMTV transformative *change*
TRNTSFRN transferrin *blood*
TRNTSFRNS transference *movement*
TRNTSFRNSHL transferential *movement*
TRNTSFRNTS transference *movement*
TRNTSFRNTSHL transferential *movement*
TRNTSFRR transferrer *mover*
TRNTSFRZ transferase *enzyme*
TRNTSFSHN transfusion

transfer
TRNTSFSHNL transfusional
transfer
TRNTSFX transfix *pierce*
TRNTSFYSHN transfusion
transfer
TRNTSFYSHNL
transfusional *transfer*
TRNTSFYZ transfuse
penetrate, transmit
transfused transfusing
TRNTSFYZBL transfusible
(or) transfusable
penetrate, transmit
TRNTSFYZHN transfusion
transfer
TRNTSFYZHNL
transfusional *transfer*
TRNTSFZ transfuse
penetrate, transmit
transfused transfusing
TRNTSFZBL transfusible
(or) transfusable
penetrate, transmit
TRNTSFZHN transfusion
transfer
TRNTSFZHNL transfusional
transfer
TRNTSGNK transgenic
genes
TRNTSGRS transgress *sin*
TRNTSGRSHN
transgression *sin*
TRNTSGRSR transgressor
sinner
TRNTSGRSV transgressive
sinning
TRNTSHL tarantula *spider*
tarantulas
TRNTSHL torrential (adj)
flood torrentially (adv)
TRNTSHMNS
transhumance *livestock*
TRNTSHMNTS
transhumance *livestock*
TRNTSHNT transient
temporary
TRNTSHYNT transient
temporary
TRNTSJNK transgenic
genes
TRNTSK transact *do*

TRNTSK transect *divide*
TRNTSKDR transactor
exchanger
TRNTSKNNNL
transcontinental *coast to
coast*
TRNTSKNTNNL
transcontinental *coast to
coast*
TRNTSKNTNNTL
transcontinental *coast to
coast*
TRNTSKRB transcribe
record transcribed
transcribing
TRNTSKRBR transcriber
recorder
TRNTSKRP transcript *copy*
TRNTSKRPSHN
transcription *copy*
TRNTSKRPSHNL
transcriptional (adj) *copy*
transcriptionally (adv)
TRNTSKRPSHNST
transcriptionist *copier*
TRNTSKRPT transcript *copy*
TRNTSKSHN transaction
exchange
TRNTSKSHNL
transactional *interactions*
TRNTSKSL transaxle *vehicle*
TRNTSKT transact *do*
TRNTSKT transect *divide*
TRNTSKTR transactor
exchanger
TRNTSLDBL translatable
interpret, change
TRNTSLDR translator
interpret, change
TRNTSLDRSHN
transliteration *spelling*
TRNTSLDRT transliterate
spell transliterated
transliterating
TRNTSLKSHN
translocation *displacement*
TRNTSLKT translocate
displace translocated
translocating
TRNTSLSHN translation
interpret, change
TRNTSLSNC translucence

clearness translucency
TRNTSLSNS translucence
clearness translucency
TRNTSLSNT translucent
clear
TRNTSLSNTC translucence
clearness translucency
TRNTSLSNTS translucence
clearness translucency
TRNTSLT translate *interpret,
change* translated
translating
TRNTSLTBL translatable
interpret, change
TRNTSLTR translator
interpret, change
TRNTSLTRSHN
transliteration *spelling*
TRNTSLTRT transliterate
spell transliterated
transliterating
TRNTSM transom *crosspiece*
TRNTSMDBL transmittable
send, conduct
TRNTSMDBL transmutable
convert
TRNTSMDL transmittal
conveyance
TRNTSMDNS transmittance
conveyance
TRNTSMDNTS
transmittance *conveyance*
TRNTSMDR transmitter
sender
TRNTSMGRDR
transmigrator *movement*
transmigratory
TRNTSMGRF transmogrify
transform transmogrified
transmogrifying
transmogrifies
TRNTSMGRFKSHN
transmogrification *change*
TRNTSMGRSHN
transmigration *movement*
TRNTSMGRT transmigrate
move transmigrated
transmigrating
TRNTSMGRTR
transmigrator *movement*
transmigratory
TRNTSMSBL transmissible

Letters aren't doubled for single sounds: to find alley use **L** not **LL**. Use **Y** and **W** as hard
sounds only: to find yellow use **YL**. (Br)=British spelling or usage. * See dictionary.

pass on
TRNTSMSHN transmission
broadcast, gears, movement
TRNTSMSV transmissive
broadcast, movement
TRNTSMSVD transmissivity
broadcast, movement
TRNTSMSVT transmissivity
broadcast, movement
TRNTSMT transmit *send,
conduct* transmitted
transmitting
TRNTSMT transmute
convert transmuted
transmuting
TRNTSMTBL transmittable
send, conduct
TRNTSMTBL transmutable
convert
TRNTSMTDV transmutative
conversion
TRNTSMTL transmittal
conveyance
TRNTSMTNS transmittance
conveyance
TRNTSMTNTS
transmittance *conveyance*
TRNTSMTR transmitter
sender
TRNTSMTSHN
transmutation *conversion*
TRNTSMTTV transmutative
conversion
TRNTSMYDBL
transmutable *convert*
TRNTSMYT transmute
convert transmuted
transmuting
TRNTSMYTBL
transmutable *convert*
TRNTSMYTDV
transmutative *conversion*
TRNTSMYTSHN
transmutation *conversion*
TRNTSMYTTV
transmutative *conversion*
TRNTSN transcend *rise
above, exceed*
TRNTSND transcend *rise
above, exceed*
TRNTSNDNL
transcendental (adj)

supernatural
transcendentally (adv)
TRNTSNDNLZM
transcendentalism
supernatural
TRNTSNDNS
transcendence *rise above,
exceed* transcendency
TRNTSNDNT transcendent
surpassing
TRNTSNDNTL
transcendental (adj)
supernatural
transcendentally (adv)
TRNTSNDNTLZM
transcendentalism
supernatural
TRNTSNDNTS
transcendence *rise above,
exceed* transcendency
TRNTSNK transonic *speed*
TRNTSNSHNL
transnational *beyond
nations*
TRNTSNT transient
temporary
TRNTSPDL transeptal
church
TRNTSPKS transpicuous
understood
TRNTSPLNT transplant
relocate
TRNTSPNDR transponder
receiver
TRNTSPR transpire *seep out,
happen* transpired
transpiring
TRNTSPRNC transparency
clearness transparencies
TRNTSPRNS transparence
clearness
TRNTSPRNS transparency
clearness transparencies
TRNTSPRNT transparent
clear
TRNTSPRNTC
transparency *clearness*
transparencies
TRNTSPRNTL transparently
clear
TRNTSPRNTNS
transparentness *clear*

TRNTSPRNTS
transparence *clearness*
TRNTSPRNTS
transparency *clearness*
transparencies
TRNTSPRSHN transpiration
seep out
TRNTSPRSNL
transpersonal *beyond ego*
TRNTSPSFK transpacific
across the Pacific
TRNTSPT transept *church*
TRNTSPTL transeptal
church
TRNTSSDR transistor
electricity
TRNTSSDRZ transistorize
electricity transistorized
transistorizing
(Br) transistorise
TRNTSSHN transition
change
TRNTSSHNK transoceanic
beyond oceans
TRNTSSHNL transitional
(adj) *change* transitionally
(adv)
TRNTSSHYNK
transoceanic *beyond
oceans*
TRNTSSTR transistor
electricity
TRNTSSTRZ transistorize
electricity transistorized
transistorizing
(Br) transistorise
TRNTSSTRZSHN
transistorization *electricity*
(Br) transistorisation
TRNTST transit *(n) passage
(v) travel*
TRNTSTLNK transatlantic
ocean
TRNTSTLNTK transatlantic
ocean
TRNTSTR transitory
temporary
TRNTSTRL transitorily
temporary
TRNTSTRNS transitoriness
temporary
TRNTSTV transitive

Use letters that best describe the sounds you hear and omit the vowels. Use **S** or **K** instead of **C**: to find circle use **SRKL**. Use **J** to find joy, **JM** to find gem and **G** to find go.

relationship
TRNTSTVD transitivity
relationship
TRNTSTVT transitivity
relationship
TRNTSVR transceiver
communications
TRNTSVRS transverse
crosswise
TRNTSXL transaxle vehicle
TRNTSYNT transient
temporary
TRNTZK transact do
TRNTZKT transact do
TRNVR turn over (v) rotate
TRNVR turnover (n, adj)
reversal, pastry,
reorganization
TRNY tornillo wood cutter
tornillos
TRNYL triennial (n, adj) three
years triennially (adv)
TRNYM triennium three years
trienniums (or) triennia
TRNYN trunnion pivot
TRNZ eternize immortalize
eternized eternizing
TRNZ tyrannize oppress
tyrannized tyrannizing
(Br) tyrannise
TRNZD transude ooze out
transuded transuding
TRNZDKSHN transduction
conversion
TRNZDS transduce convert
TRNZDSHN transudation
ooze out
TRNZDSR transducer
converter
TRNZDT transudate ooze out
TRNZDV transitive
relationship
TRNZDYS transduce
convert
TRNZDYSR transducer
converter
TRNZFGR transfigure
change form transfigured
transfiguring
TRNZFGRSHN
transfiguration change in
form

TRNZFGYR transfigure
change form transfigured
transfiguring
TRNZFGYRSHN
transfiguration change in
form
TRNZFKS transfix pierce
TRNZFKSHN transfixion
piercing
TRNZFNT transfinite
number
TRNZFR transfer move
transferred transferring
TRNZFR transferee one
moved
TRNZFRBL transferable
movable
TRNZFRBLD transferability
movable
TRNZFRBLT transferability
movable
TRNZFRL transferal move
TRNZFRM transform
convert, change
TRNZFRMDV
transformative change
TRNZFRMR transformer
converter
TRNZFRMSHN
transformation change
TRNZFRMSHNL
transformational (adj)
change transformationally
(adv)
TRNZFRMSHNLST
transformationalist
grammar
TRNZFRMTV
transformative change
TRNZFRN transferrin blood
TRNZFRNS transference
movement
TRNZFRNSHL
transferential movement
TRNZFRNTS transference
movement
TRNZFRNTSHL
transferential movement
TRNZFRR transferrer mover
TRNZFRZ transferase
enzyme
TRNZFSHN transfusion

transfer
TRNZFSHNL transfusional
transfer
TRNZFX transfix pierce
TRNZFYSHN transfusion
transfer
TRNZFYSHNL transfusional
transfer
TRNZFYZ transfuse
penetrate, transmit
transfused transfusing
TRNZFYZBL transfusible
(or) transfusable
penetrate, transmit
TRNZFYZHN transfusion
transfer
TRNZFYZHNL transfusional
transfer
TRNZFZ transfuse penetrate,
transmit transfused
transfusing
TRNZFZBL transfusible (or)
transfusable penetrate,
transmit
TRNZFZHN transfusion
transfer
TRNZFZHNL transfusional
transfer
TRNZGNK transgenic genes
TRNZGRS transgress sin
TRNZGRSHN transgression
sin
TRNZGRSR transgressor
sinner
TRNZGRSV transgressive
sinning
TRNZHMNS transhumance
livestock
TRNZHMNTS
transhumance livestock
TRNZHNS transience
temporary transiency
TRNZHNT transient
temporary
TRNZHNTS transience
temporary transiency
TRNZHYMNS
transhumance livestock
TRNZHYMNTS
transhumance livestock
TRNZHYNS transience
temporary transiency

TRNZHYNT transient
temporary
TRNZHYNTS transience
temporary transiency
TRNZJNK transgenic *genes*
TRNZK transact *do*
TRNZKDR transactor
exchanger
TRNZKLCHRL transcultural
traditions
TRNZKLTRL transcultural
traditions
TRNZKNNNL
transcontinental *coast to coast*
TRNZKNNTL
transcontinental *coast to coast*
TRNZKNTNNL
transcontinental *coast to coast*
TRNZKNTNNTL
transcontinental *coast to coast*
TRNZKSHN transaction
exchange
TRNZKSHNL transactional
interactions
TRNZKSL transaxle *vehicle*
TRNZKT transact *do*
TRNZKTNS transcutaneous
skin puncture
TRNZKTNYS
transcutaneous *skin puncture*
TRNZKTR transactor
exchanger
TRNZKYTNS
transcutaneous *skin puncture*
TRNZKYTNYS
transcutaneous *skin puncture*
TRNZKZL transaxle *vehicle*
TRNZLDBL translatable
interpret, change
TRNZLDR translator
interpret, change
TRNZLDRSHN
transliteration *spelling*
TRNZLDRT transliterate
spell transliterated

transliterating
TRNZLKSHN translocation
displacement
TRNZLKT translocate
displace
TRNZLSHN translation
interpret, change
TRNZLSNC translucence
clearness translucency
TRNZLSNS translucence
clearness translucency
TRNZLSNT translucent *clear*
TRNZLSNTC translucence
clearness translucency
TRNZLSNTS translucence
clearness translucency
TRNZLT translate *interpret,
change* translated
translating
TRNZLTBL translatable
interpret, change
TRNZLTR translator
interpret, change
TRNZLTRSHN
transliteration *spelling*
TRNZLTRT transliterate
spell transliterated
transliterating
TRNZMDBL transmittable
send, conduct
TRNZMDBL transmutable
convert
TRNZMDL transmittal
conveyance
TRNZMDNS transmittance
conveyance
TRNZMDNTS transmittance
conveyance
TRNZMDR transmitter
sender
TRNZMGRDR
transmigrator *movement*
transmigratory
TRNZMGRF transmogrify
transform transmogrified
transmogrifying
transmogrifies
TRNZMGRFKSHN
transmogrification *change*
TRNZMGRSHN
transmigration *movement*
TRNZMGRT transmigrate

move transmigrated
transmigrating
TRNZMGRTR transmigrator
movement transmigratory
TRNZMSBL transmissible
pass on
TRNZMSHN transmission
broadcast, gears, movement
TRNZMSV transmissive
broadcast, movement
TRNZMSVD transmissivity
broadcast, movement
TRNZMSVT transmissivity
broadcast, movement
TRNZMT transmit *send,
conduct* transmitted
transmitting
TRNZMT transmute *convert*
transmuted transmuting
TRNZMTBL transmittable
send, conduct
TRNZMTBL transmutable
convert
TRNZMTDV transmutative
conversion
TRNZMTL transmittal
conveyance
TRNZMTNS transmittance
conveyance
TRNZMTNTS transmittance
conveyance
TRNZMTR transmitter
sender
TRNZMTSHN
transmutation *conversion*
TRNZMTTV transmutative
conversion
TRNZMYDBL transmutable
convert
TRNZMYT transmute
convert transmuted
transmuting
TRNZMYTBL transmutable
convert
TRNZMYTDV transmutative
conversion
TRNZMYTSHN
transmutation *conversion*
TRNZMYTTV transmutative
conversion
TRNZNS transience
temporary transiency

Use letters that best describe the sounds you hear and omit the vowels. Use **S** or **K** instead of **C**: to find circle use **SRKL**. Use **J** to find joy, **JM** to find gem and **G** to find go.

TRNZNSHNL transnational *beyond nations*
TRNZNT transient *temporary*
TRNZNTS transience *temporary* transiency
TRNZPKS transpicuous *understood*
TRNZPLNT transplant *relocate*
TRNZPLNTBL transplantable *movable*
TRNZPLNTR transplanter *mover*
TRNZPLNTSHN transplantation *movement*
TRNZPLR transpolar *across poles*
TRNZPQS transpicuous *understood*
TRNZPR transpire *seep out, happen* transpired transpiring
TRNZPRDBL transportable *movable*
TRNZPRDBLD transportability *movable*
TRNZPRDBLT transportability *movable*
TRNZPRDR transporter *mover*
TRNZPRNC transparency *clearness* transparencies
TRNZPRNS transparence *clearness*
TRNZPRNS transparency *clearness* transparencies
TRNZPRNT transparent *clear*
TRNZPRNTC transparency *clearness* transparencies
TRNZPRNTL transparently *clear*
TRNZPRNTNS transparentness *clear*
TRNZPRNTS transparence *clearness*
TRNZPRNTS transparency *clearness* transparencies
TRNZPRSHN transpiration *seep out*
TRNZPRSNL transpersonal *beyond ego*

TRNZPRTBL transportable *movable*
TRNZPRTBLD transportability *movable*
TRNZPRTBLT transportability *movable*
TRNZPRTR transporter *mover*
TRNZPRTSHN transportation *vehicle*
TRNZPSFK transpacific *across the Pacific*
TRNZPZSHN transposition *reversal*
TRNZQTNS transcutaneous *skin puncture*
TRNZQTNYS transcutaneous *skin puncture*
TRNZR tyrannizer *oppress* (Br) tyranniser
TRNZSDR transistor *electricity*
TRNZSDRZ transistorize *electricity* transistorized transistorizing (Br) transistorise
TRNZSDRZSHN transistorization *electricity* (Br) transistorisation
TRNZSHN transition *change*
TRNZSHNK transoceanic *beyond oceans*
TRNZSHNL transitional (adj) *change* transitionally (adv)
TRNZSHYNK transoceanic *beyond oceans*
TRNZSTR transistor *electricity*
TRNZSTRNS transitoriness *temporary*
TRNZSTRZ transistorize *electricity* transistorized transistorizing (Br) transistorise
TRNZSTRZSHN transistorization *electricity* (Br) transistorisation
TRNZT transit (n) *passage* (v) *travel*
TRNZTLNK transatlantic

ocean
TRNZTLNTK transatlantic *ocean*
TRNZTR transitory *temporary*
TRNZTRL transitorily *temporary*
TRNZTV transitive *relationship*
TRNZTVD transitivity *relationship*
TRNZTVT transitivity *relationship*
TRNZVL transvalue *reappraise* transvalued transvaluing
TRNZVLSHN transvaluation *reappraisal*
TRNZVLWSHN transvaluation *reappraisal*
TRNZVLY transvalue *reappraise* transvalued transvaluing
TRNZVLYSHN transvaluation *reappraisal*
TRNZVLYWSHN transvaluation *reappraisal*
TRNZVRS transverse *crosswise*
TRNZVRSBL transversable *cross*
TRNZVRSL transversal *intersection*
TRNZVRSL transversely *crosswise*
TRNZVSDT transvestite *cross-dresser*
TRNZVSTT transvestite *cross-dresser*
TRNZVSTZM transvestism *cross-dressing*
TRNZXL transaxle *vehicle*
TRNZYD transude *ooze out* transuded transuding
TRNZYDSHN transudation *ooze out*
TRNZYDT transudate *ooze out*
TRNZYNS transience *temporary* transiency
TRNZYNT transient *temporary*

Letters aren't doubled for single sounds: to find alley use **L** not **LL**. Use **Y** and **W** as hard sounds only: to find yellow use **YL**. (Br)=British spelling or usage. * See dictionary.

TRNZYNTS transience *temporary* transiency

TRP tarp *cover, sailor*

TRP tear up *rip*

TRP towrope *pull*

TRP trap *snare* trapped trapping

TRP trip *(n) journey*

TRP trip *(v) stumble, get high* tripped tripping

TRP tripe *trash*

TRP trippy *drugs*

TRP troop *(n) soldiers (v) walk*

TRP trope *word*

TRP troupe *theater* trouped trouping

TRPD pteropod *mollusk*

TRPD torpedo *submarine* torpedoed torpedoing torpedoes

TRPD torpid *tired*

TRPD trepid *fearful*

TRPD tripod *three legged*

TRPDD torpidity *tiredness*

TRPDK triptych *trilogy*

TRPDK tryptic *enzyme*

TRPDMN tryptamine *chemical*

TRPDNT trepidant *fearful*

TRPDR trapdoor (n) *opening* trap-door (adj)

TRPDSHN trepidation *fear*

TRPDT torpidity *tiredness*

TRPHMR trip-hammer *machine*

TRPK tropic *latitude, reaction*

TRPKBRD tropic bird *animal*

TRPKL tropical (adj) *near equator* tropically (adv)

TRPKLZ tropicalize *adapt for heat* tropicalized tropicalizing

TRPKS tropics *region*

TRPKVKNSR tropic of Cancer *latitude*

TRPKVKPRKRN tropic of Capricorn *latitude*

TRPL triple *three times, baseball* tripled tripling

TRPL triply *(adv) three times*

TRPL Tripoli *city*

TRPL tripoli *dirt*

TRPLD triploid *genes*

TRPLDKR triple-decker *3 layers*

TRPLHDR triple-header *3 games*

TRPLJKL tropological (adj) *moral* tropologically (adv)

TRPLJMP triple jump *track and field*

TRPLKRN Triple Crown *title*

TRPLKS triplex *3 floors, 3 sections*

TRPLKSHN triplication *3 copies*

TRPLKT triplicate *3 copies* triplicated triplicating

TRPLN tarpaulin *cover, sailor*

TRPLN terreplein *platform*

TRPLN trapline *series of traps*

TRPLN triplane *airplane*

TRPLPL triple play *baseball*

TRPLSD triplicity *3 copies, horoscope* triplicities

TRPLSK triple sec *liqueur*

TRPLSPS triple-space *3 lines* triple-spaced triple-spacing

TRPLST triplicity *3 copies, horoscope* triplicities

TRPLT triplet *one of three*

TRPLTHRT triple threat (n) *3 skills* triple-threat (adj)

TRPLTL tripletail *fish*

TRPLX triplex *3 floors, 3 sections*

TRPMR trip-hammer *machine*

TRPN atropine *drug*

TRPN tarpon *fish* tarpon (or) tarpons

TRPN terpene *hydrocarbon*

TRPN terrapin *turtle*

TRPN trepan *bore, tool* trepanned trepanning

TRPN truepenny *honest one*

TRPNGZ trappings *signs*

TRPNM treponema *bacteria* treponemata (or) treponemas

TRPNMD treponemata (pl) *bacteria* treponema

TRPNMT treponemata (pl) *bacteria* treponema

TRPNS trappings *signs*

TRPNSM trypanosome *organism*

TRPNT trapunto *quilt* trapuntos

TRPNT tripinnate *3 parts*

TRPNTN turpentine *solvent*

TRPNZ trappings *signs*

TRPNZM trypanosome *organism*

TRPR torpor *tiredness*

TRPR trapper *snare*

TRPR tripper *tourist*

TRPR trooper *soldier*

TRPR trouper *actor*

TRPRDT tripartite *3 parts*

TRPRTT tripartite *3 parts*

TRPS traipse *walk* traipsed traipsing

TRPS traps *luggage*

TRPSFR troposphere *atmosphere*

TRPSHDNG trapshooting *clay pigeons*

TRPSHDR trapshooter *clay pigeons*

TRPSHP troopship *boat*

TRPSHTN trapshooting *clay pigeons*

TRPSHTNG trapshooting *clay pigeons*

TRPSHTR trapshooter *clay pigeons*

TRPSKR Terpsichore *Muse*

TRPSKRN terpsichorean *dancing*

TRPSKRYN terpsichorean *dancing*

TRPSN trypsin *enzyme*

TRPSNJN trypsinogen *secretion*

TRPST Trappist *monk*

TRPT try-pot *whaler*

TRPTD turpitude *corruption*

TRPTFN tryptophan *amino acid*

TRPTHNG triphthong *3 sounds*

Use letters that best describe the sounds you hear and omit the vowels. Use **S** or **K** instead of **C**: to find circle use **SRKL**. Use **J** to find joy, **JM** to find gem and **G** to find go.

TRPTK triptych *trilogy*
TRPTK tryptic *enzyme*
TRPTMN tryptamine *chemical*
TRPTYD turpitude *corruption*
TRPWR trip wire *trigger*
TRPWYR trip wire *trigger*
TRPX tropics *region*
TRPZ trapeze *acrobat*
TRPZ trapezia (pl) *shape* trapezium
TRPZD trapezoid *shape*
TRPZM trapezium *shape* trapeziums (or) trapezia
TRPZM tropism *response*
TRPZY trapezia (pl) *shape* trapezium
TRPZYM trapezium *shape* trapeziums (or) trapezia
TRQ trackway *path*
TRQLNS truculence *cruelty* truculency
TRQLNT truculent *cruel*
TRQLNTL truculently *cruel*
TRQLNTS truculence *cruelty* truculency
TRQS terraqueous *land and water*
TRQTRS triquetrous *angles*
TRQYS terraqueous *land and water*
TRQZ turquoise *mineral, color*
TRR tearer *ripper*
TRR tearier *crying*
TRR terraria (pl) *enclosure* terrarium
TRR terrier *dog*
TRR terror *fear*
TRR torero *bullfight* toreros
TRR trier *attempter, tube*
TRR truer *honest, straight*
TRRK triarchy *3 rulers* triarchies
TRRM terrarium *enclosure* terraria (or) terrariums
TRRM trireme *boat*
TRRSDK terroristic *threat of violence*
TRRST terrorist *threat of violence*

TRRSTK terroristic *threat of violence*
TRRY terraria (pl) *enclosure* terrarium
TRRYM terrarium *enclosure* terraria (or) terrariums
TRRZ terrorize *threaten violence* terrorized terrorizing (Br) terrorise
TRRZM terrorism *threat of violence*
TRRZSHN terrorization *threat of violence* (Br) terrorisation
TRS outrace *run faster*
TRS tarsi (pl) *ankle* tarsus
TRS Taurus *zodiac sign*
TRS terce *canon*
TRS terrace *porch, row* terraced terracing
TRS terse *brief* terser tersest
TRS tierce *cards*
TRS torso *trunk* torsos (or) torsi
TRS torus *ridge* tori
TRS trace (v) *copy, follow* traced tracing
TRS trace (n) *track, sign, strap**
TRS tress *hair* tresses
TRS trice (v) *lash* triced tricing
TRS trice (n) *instant*
TRS trousseau *wardrobe* trousseaux (or) trousseaus
TRS truce *cease-fire* truced trucing
TRS truss *support* trusses
TRS uterus *womb* uteri
TRSBL traceable (adj) *tracking* traceably (adv)
TRSBLD traceability *tracking*
TRSBLT traceability *tracking*
TRSBSDR trustbuster *no monopoly*
TRSBSTR trustbuster *no monopoly*
TRSCHL terrestrial (adj) *earth* terrestrially (adv)

TRSD atrocity *wickedness* atrocities
TRSD torsade *cord*
TRSD touristy *for travelers*
TRSD trustee *agent* trusteed trusteeing
TRSD trusty (adj) *loyal* trustier trustiest
TRSD trusty (n) *prisoner* trusties
TRSD turista *sickness*
TRSDK touristic *travel*
TRSDNS trustiness *reliability*
TRSDR trustier *loyal*
TRSDSHP trusteeship *control*
TRSDST trustiest *loyal*
TRSDYR trustier *loyal*
TRSDYST trustiest *loyal*
TRSFL tristful (adj) *sad* tristfully (adv)
TRSFL trustful (adj) *honest* trustfully (adv)
TRSFLNS tristfulness *sadness*
TRSFLNS trustfulness *honesty*
TRSFN trust fund *money*
TRSFND trust fund *money*
TRSH atresia *absence, closure*
TRSH trash (n) *garbage* (v) *destroy*
TRSH trashy *like garbage* trashier trashiest
TRSH treillage *trellis*
TRSH triage *priority*
TRSH troche *tablet*
TRSHFSH trash fish *not edible*
TRSHM tritium *isotope*
TRSHMN trashman *garbage*
TRSHN attrition *loss*
TRSHN iteration *repetition*
TRSHN tertian *48 hours*
TRSHN torchon *lace*
TRSHN torsion *twist*
TRSHNL torsional (adj) *twisted* torsionally (adv)
TRSHNS trashiness *garbage*
TRSHR tertiary (n) *monk, rocks* tertiaries

TRSHR tertiary *(adj) third, rocks, chemicals**

TRSHR torchère *lamp*

TRSHR trashier *garbage*

TRSHR treasure *prize* treasured treasuring

TRSHR treasury *money* treasuries

TRSHRBL treasurable *precious*

TRSHRHS treasure-house *collection*

TRSHRR treasurer *money*

TRSHRTRV treasure trove *discovery*

TRSHS atrocious *terrible*

TRSHS tortious *law*

TRSHSL atrociously *terribly*

TRSHSL tortiously *law*

TRSHSNS atrociousness *barbarism*

TRSHST trashiest *garbage*

TRSHT tear sheet *publication*

TRSHTRL terrestrial (adj) *earth* terrestrially (adv)

TRSHTRYL terrestrial (adj) *earth* terrestrially (adv)

TRSHYM tritium *isotope*

TRSHYR tertiary *(n) monk, rocks* tertiaries

TRSHYR tertiary *(adj) third, rocks, chemicals**

TRSHYR trashier *garbage*

TRSHYST trashiest *garbage*

TRSK Triassic *dinosaur age*

TRSK trisect *divide in three*

TRSKDKFB triskaidekaphobia *fear of 13*

TRSKDKFBY triskaidekaphobia *fear of 13*

TRSKL tricycle *vehicle*

TRSKL triskele (or) triskelion *3 branches*

TRSKLK tricyclic *chemical*

TRSKLN triskelion (or) triskele *3 branches*

TRSKLYN triskelion (or) triskele *3 branches*

TRSKRD trisaccharide *sugar*

TRSKT trisect *divide in three*

TRSKWR try square *tool*

TRSKYN triskelion (or) triskele *3 branches*

TRSL tarsal *bone, cartilage*

TRSL tersely *briefly*

TRSL trestle *support*

TRSL trysail *boat*

TRSLBK trisyllabic *3 syllables*

TRSLBL trisyllable *3 syllables*

TRSLFD trisulfide *chemical*

TRSLWRK trestlework *support*

TRSM tiresome *slow*

TRSMS trismus *lockjaw*

TRSN tracing *copy*

TRSN trussing *framework*

TRSN tyrosine *amino acid*

TRSNG tracing *copy*

TRSNG trussing *framework*

TRSNS terseness *briefness*

TRSNS tyrosinase *enzyme*

TRSNTNL tercentennial *300 years*

TRSNTNR tercentenary *300 years* tercentenaries

TRSNTNYL tercentennial *300 years*

TRSNZ tyrosinase *enzyme*

TRSPS outer space *universe*

TRSPS trespass *sin, invade* trespasses

TRSPS triceps *muscles*

TRSPSR trespasser *sin, invade*

TRSQR try square *tool*

TRSR pterosaur *dinosaur*

TRSR tarsier *animal*

TRSR terser *brief*

TRSR tracer *copy, find*

TRSR tracery *ornament* traceries

TRSR trusser *binder*

TRSRTPS triceratops *dinosaur* triceratops

TRSS tarsus *ankle* tarsi

TRSST tersest *brief*

TRST atrocity *wickedness* atrocities

TRST auteurist *film direction*

TRST teariest *crying*

TRST tercet *sonnet*

TRST terrorist *threat of violence*

TRST tourist *traveler*

TRST touristy *for travelers*

TRST triste *sad*

TRST truest *honest, straight*

TRST trust *reliance, fund*

TRST trustee *agent* trusteed trusteeing

TRST trusty *(n) prisoner* trusties

TRST trusty *(adj) loyal* trustier trustiest

TRST tryst *meeting*

TRST turista *sickness*

TRSTBSDR trustbuster *no monopoly*

TRSTBSTR trustbuster *no monopoly*

TRSTFL tristful (adj) *sad* tristfully (adv)

TRSTFL trustful (adj) *honest* trustfully (adv)

TRSTFLNS tristfulness *sadness*

TRSTFLNS trustfulness *honesty*

TRSTFN trust fund *money*

TRSTFND trust fund *money*

TRSTK touristic *travel*

TRSTL terrestrial (adj) *earth* terrestrially (adv)

TRSTN tearstain *streak*

TRSTND tearstained *streaked*

TRSTNS trustiness *reliability*

TRSTR trustier *loyal*

TRSTRL terrestrial (adj) *earth* terrestrially (adv)

TRSTRYL terrestrial (adj) *earth* terrestrially (adv)

TRSTSHP trusteeship *control*

TRSTST trustiest *loyal*

TRSTT triacetate *fabric*

TRSTT tristate *three states*

TRSTWRTH trustworthy *reliable*

Use letters that best describe the sounds you hear and omit the vowels. Use **S** or **K** instead of **C**: to find circle use **SRKL**. Use **J** to find joy, **JM** to find gem and **G** to find go.

TRSTWRTHL trustworthily
  reliable
TRSTWRTHNS
  trustworthiness *reliability*
TRSTYL terrestrial (adj)
  earth terrestrially (adv)
TRSTYR trustier *loyal*
TRSTYST trustiest *loyal*
TRSTZ tristeza *disease*
TRSWRTH trustworthy
  reliable
TRSWRTHL trustworthily
  reliable
TRSWRTHNS
  trustworthiness *reliability*
TRSYR tarsier *animal*
TRT iterate *repeat* iterated
  iterating
TRT outright *complete*
TRT tart *(adj) sour (n) pie,*
  lewd woman
TRT tarty *lewd*
TRT terete *rounded*
TRT terret *harness*
TRT tort *injury*
TRT torte *cake* torten (or)
  tortes
TRT tortilla *food*
TRT trait *feature*
TRT treat *(v) deal with,*
  delight, handle (n) delight
TRT treaty *pact* treaties
TRT trite *overused* triter
  tritest
TRT trot *(v) hurry* trotted
  trotting
TRT trot *(n) gait, line*
TRT trout *fish* trout
TRT tryout (n) *test* try out (v)
TRT turret *tower*
TRTBL treatable *care for, act*
  upon
TRTBLT treatability *care for,*
  act upon
TRTD tree toad *animal*
TRTD turreted *tower*
TRTGNK teratogenic
  malformations
TRTGNSD teratogenicity
  malformations
TRTGNST teratogenicity
  malformations

TRTH troth *betrothal*
TRTH trough *trench* troughs
TRTH truth *fact* truths
TRTHFL truthful (adj) *honest*
  truthfully (adv)
TRTHFLNS truthfulness
  honesty
TRTHLN triathlon *sport*
TRTHLT triathlete *sports*
TRTHRSN tyrothricin
  antibiotic
TRTHYZM tritheism *3 Gods*
TRTHZM tritheism *3 Gods*
TRTJN teratogen
  malformations
TRTJNK teratogenic
  malformations
TRTJNSD teratogenicity
  malformations
TRTJNST teratogenicity
  malformations
TRTK autoerotic *self-*
  stimulating
TRTK triadic *trinity*
TRTKL triadically *trinity*
TRTKS toreutics *embossing*
TRTL tritely *overused*
TRTL turtle *animal*
TRTLBK turtleback *convex*
TRTLDV turtledove *pigeon*
TRTLG teratology
  abnormalities
TRTLJ teratology
  abnormalities
TRTLJK teratologic (or)
  teratological *abnormal*
TRTLJKL teratological (or)
  teratologic *abnormal*
TRTLJST teratologist
  abnormalities
TRTLN tortellini *pasta*
TRTLN trotline *fishing*
TRTLNK turtleneck *shirt*
TRTLT tartlet *pie*
TRTM teratoma *tumor*
TRTM tritium *isotope*
TRTM tritoma *herb*
TRTMNT treatment *handling*
TRTN tartan *plaid*
TRTN torten (pl) *cake* torte
TRTN tortoni *ice cream*
TRTN triton *shellfish, god*

  (often capitalized)
TRTN tritone *music*
TRTNS tartness *taste*
TRTNS triteness *overused*
TRTP tart up *dress up*
TRTP treetop *top of tree*
TRTPRCH trout-perch *fish*
TRTR tartar *crust, sediment,*
  person (capitalized)
TRTR tartare *steak*
TRTR territory *region*
  territories
TRTR torture *torment*
  tortured torturing
TRTR traitor *betrayer*
TRTR trattoria *cafe* trattorias
  (or) trattorie
TRTR treater *care for, act*
  *upon**
TRTR triter *overused*
TRTR trotter *horse*
TRTRL territorial (adj)
  regional territorially (adv)
TRTRLD territoriality *region*
TRTRLST territorialist *region*
TRTRLT territoriality *region*
TRTRLZ territorialize *make*
  regions territorialized
  territorializing
TRTRLZM territorialism
  region
TRTRS torturous *painful*
TRTRS traitorous *betrayal*
TRTRS traitress (or)
  traitoress *betrayer (f)*
TRTRSD tortricid *moth*
TRTRSHN trituration *powder*
TRTRSL torturously *painful*
TRTRSL traitorously *betrayal*
TRTRSS tartar sauce (or)
  tartare sauce *seasoning*
TRTRT tartrate *acid*
TRTRT triturate *crush*
  triturated triturating
TRTRY trattoria *cafe*
  trattorias (or) trattorie
TRTRYL territorial (adj)
  regional territorially (adv)
TRTRYLD territoriality *region*
TRTRYLST territorialist
  region
TRTRYLT territoriality *region*

Letters aren't doubled for single sounds: to find alley use **L** not **LL**. Use **Y** and **W** as hard
sounds only: to find yellow use **YL**. (Br)=British spelling or usage. * See dictionary.

TRTRYLZ territorialize *make regions* territorialized territorializing

TRTRYLZM territorialism *region*

TRTS terrazzo *flooring*

TRTS tortoise *turtle*

TRTS tortuous *twisted*

TRTS treatise *argument*

TRTSD tortuosity *bend* tortuosities

TRTSH tartish *saucy*

TRTSHL tortoiseshell *turtle, butterfly, pattern*

TRTSK Trotsky *philosopher*

TRTSKT Trotskyite *revolutionary*

TRTSKYT Trotskyite *revolutionary*

TRTSKYZM Trotskyism *revolution*

TRTSKZM Trotskyism *revolution*

TRTSL tortuously *twisted*

TRTSNDRM Tourette's syndrome *disease*

TRTSNS tortuousness *twisted*

TRTSRM terza rima *verse*

TRTSSHL tortoiseshell *turtle, butterfly, pattern*

TRTST tortuosity *bend* tortuosities

TRTST tritest *overused*

TRTSZM autoeroticism (or) autoerotism *self-stimulation*

TRTV iterative *repetition*

TRTWS tortuous *twisted*

TRTWSD tortuosity *bend* tortuosities

TRTWSL tortuously *twisted*

TRTWSNS tortuousness *twisted*

TRTWST tortuosity *bend* tortuosities

TRTX toreutics *embossing*

TRTY tortilla *food*

TRTYM tritium *isotope*

TRTZ terrazzo *flooring*

TRTZ treatise *argument*

TRTZM autoerotism (or)

autoeroticism *self-stimulation*

TRV travois *sled* travois

TRV trivia *trifles*

TRV trove *treasure*

TRVL travail *labor*

TRVL travel *journey* traveled (or) travelled traveling (or) travelling

TRVL trivial (adj) *worthless* trivially (adv)

TRVLD traveled (or) travelled *journey*

TRVLD triviality *trifle* trivialities

TRVLG travelogue (or) travelog *lecture, film*

TRVLN traveling (or) travelling *journey*

TRVLNG traveling (or) travelling *journey*

TRVLNT trivalent *chemistry*

TRVLR traveler (or) traveller *journey*

TRVLRSCHK traveler's check *money*

TRVLRZCHK traveler's check *money*

TRVLT triviality *trifle* trivialities

TRVLZ trivialize *make ordinary* trivialized trivializing (Br) trivialise

TRVLZSHN trivialization *make ordinary* (Br) trivialisation

TRVNTRKLR atrioventricular *heart*

TRVNTRKYLR atrioventricular *heart*

TRVNTRQLR atrioventricular *heart*

TRVR trover *recovery*

TRVRS traverse (n) *crosspiece, zigzag* (v) *cross, swivel* (adj) *across* traversed traversing

TRVRSBL traversable *cross, swivel*

TRVRSL traversal *cross, swivel*

TRVRSR traverser *cross, swivel*

TRVRTN travertine *mineral*

TRVSD travesty *imitation* travestied travestying travesties

TRVST travesty *imitation* travestied travestying travesties

TRVT trivet *stand*

TRVW travois *sled* travois

TRVY trivia *trifles*

TRVYL trivial (adj) *worthless* trivially (adv)

TRVYLD triviality *trifle* trivialities

TRVYLT triviality *trifle* trivialities

TRVYLZ trivialize *make ordinary* trivialized trivializing (Br) trivialise

TRVYLZSHN trivialization *make ordinary* (Br) trivialisation

TRW tearaway (Br) *reckless teen*

TRWKL triweekly *3 per week* triweeklies

TRWL trowel *tool*

TRWLT troilite *mineral*

TRWNC truancy *absence* truancies

TRWNS truancy *absence* truancies

TRWNT truant *absent*

TRWNTC truancy *absence* truancies

TRWNTS truancy *absence* truancies

TRWR outerwear *clothing*

TRWR truer *honest, straight*

TRWST truest *honest, straight*

TRWT terawatt *power*

TRWZM truism *truth*

TRXD trackside *area*

TRXDR trickster *deceiver*

TRXK ataraxic (or) ataractic *tranquilizer*

TRXL triaxial *3 main lines*

TRXT tracksuit *clothing*

Use letters that best describe the sounds you hear and omit the vowels. Use **S** or **K** instead of **C**: to find circle use **SRKL**. Use **J** to find joy, **JM** to find gem and **G** to find go.

TRXTP truck stop *eatery*	**TRYNGGLSHN** triangulation *3 sides*	**TRYVNTRKLR** atrioventricular *heart*
TRXTR trickster *deceiver*		**TRYVNTRKYLR** atrioventricular *heart*
TRXYL triaxial *3 main lines*	**TRYNGGLT** triangulate *3 sides* triangulated triangulating	**TRYVNTRQLR** atrioventricular *heart*
TRY atria (pl) *hall, heart* atrium	**TRYNGGYLR** triangular *3 sides*	**TRYXL** triaxial *3 main lines*
TRY trio *group of three*	**TRYNGGYLSHN** triangulation *3 sides*	**TRYXYL** triaxial *3 main lines*
TRYBL triable *trial*		**TRYZH** treillage *trellis*
TRYD triad *trinity*	**TRYNGGYLT** triangulate *3 sides* triangulated triangulating	**TRYZH** triage *priority*
TRYD triode *electron tube*		**TRZ** tea rose *flower*
TRYDK triadic *trinity*	**TRYNGL** triangle *shape*	**TRZ** terrazzo *flooring*
TRYDKL triadically *trinity*	**TRYNGLR** triangular *3 sides*	**TRZ** terrorize *threaten violence* terrorized terrorizing (Br) terrorise
TRYDR toreador *bullfight*	**TRYNGLSHN** triangulation *3 sides*	
TRYJ treillage *trellis*		
TRYJ triage *priority*	**TRYNGLT** triangulate *3 sides* triangulated triangulating	**TRZH** atresia *absence, closure*
TRYK teriyaki *food*		**TRZH** treillage *trellis*
TRYKSL triaxial *3 main lines*	**TRYNGYLR** triangular *3 sides*	**TRZH** triage *priority*
TRYKSYL triaxial *3 main lines*	**TRYNGYLSHN** triangulation *3 sides*	**TRZHR** treasure *prize* treasured treasuring
TRYL torula *fungus* torulae		**TRZHR** treasury *money* treasuries
TRYL trial *test, law*	**TRYNGYLT** triangulate *3 sides* triangulated triangulating	
TRYL triol *chemical*		**TRZHRBL** treasurable *precious*
TRYLG trialogue *3-way conversation*	**TRYNL** triennial (n, adj) *three years* triennially (adv)	**TRZHRHS** treasure-house *collection*
TRYLT triolet *poem*	**TRYNM** triennium *three years* trienniums (or) triennia	**TRZHRR** treasurer *money*
TRYM atrium *hall, heart* atria	**TRYNS** tarriance *delay*	**TRZHRTRV** treasure trove *discovery*
TRYM yttrium *element*	**TRYNTS** tarriance *delay*	**TRZM** terrorism *threat of violence*
TRYMF triumph *(n) victory (v) prevail*	**TRYNYL** triennial (n, adj) *three years* triennially (adv)	**TRZM** tourism *travel*
TRYMFL triumphal *victorious*	**TRYNYM** triennium *three years* trienniums (or) triennia	**TRZM** truism *truth*
TRYMFNT triumphant *victorious*		**TRZMS** trismus *lockjaw*
TRYMFNTL triumphantly *victorious*	**TRYR** tearier *crying*	**TRZN** atrazine *drug*
TRYMPF triumph *(n) victory (v) prevail*	**TRYR** terrier *dog*	**TRZN** treason *disloyalty*
TRYMPFL triumphal *victorious*	**TRYR** trier *attempter, tube*	**TRZNBL** treasonable (adj) *disloyal* treasonably (adv)
TRYMPFNT triumphant *victorious*	**TRYRK** triarchy *3 rulers* triarchies	**TRZNS** treasonous *disloyal*
TRYMPFNTL triumphantly *victorious*	**TRYSH** treillage *trellis*	**TRZR** trouser *pants*
TRYMVRT triumvirate *3 rulers*	**TRYSH** triage *priority*	**TRZRM** terza rima *verse*
TRYN trillion *number (1,000,000,000)*	**TRYSK** Triassic *dinosaur age*	**TRZRS** trousers *pants*
TRYN triune *trinity*	**TRYST** teariest *crying*	**TRZRZ** trousers *pants*
TRYN trying *difficult*	**TRYSTT** triacetate *fabric*	**TRZSHN** terrorization *threat of violence* (Br) terrorisation
TRYNG trying *difficult*	**TRYT** tryout (n) *test* try out (v)	**TS** it's *(contr) it is*
TRYNGGL triangle *shape*	**TRYTHLN** triathlon *sport*	**TS** its *belonging to it*
TRYNGGLR triangular *3 sides*	**TRYTHLT** triathlete *sports*	**TS** otiose *vain*
	TRYTK triadic *trinity*	**TS** outhouse *toilet*
	TRYTKL triadically *trinity*	**TS** tights *stockings*

Letters aren't doubled for single sounds: to find alley use **L** not **LL**. Use **Y** and **W** as hard sounds only: to find yellow use **YL**. (Br)=British spelling or usage. * See dictionary.

TS tissue *paper, cells, network*
TS toss *throw* tosses
TS tussah (or) tussore *fabric*
TSBB Addis Ababa *city*
TSBD taste bud *tongue*
TSD otiosity *in vain*
TSD outside *beyond, outer area*
TSD testee *person examined*
TSD testy *angry* testier testiest
TSD toasty *browned, warm* toastier toastiest
TSD Tuesday *weekday*
TSDBL testable *evaluation*
TSDBLD testability *evaluation*
TSDBLT testability *evaluation*
TSDC testacy *will* testacies
TSDD tested *qualified*
TSDD two-sided *two faces*
TSDDR testator *will*
TSDF autos-da-fé (pl) *burn* auto-da-fé
TSDF testify *give evidence* testified testifying testifies
TSDFR testifier *witness*
TSDFYR testifier *witness*
TSDK autistic *self-absorbed*
TSDK zaddik *Jewish leader* zaddikim
TSDKL autistically *self-absorbed*
TSDKL testicle *male gland*
TSDKM zaddikim (pl) *Jewish leader* zaddik
TSDL tastily *flavor*
TSDL testily *angry*
TSDMN testimony *evidence* testimonies
TSDMNL testimonial *evidence, tribute*
TSDMNR testamentary *Bible, will, proof*
TSDMNT testament *Bible, will, proof*
TSDMNTR testamentary *Bible, will, proof*
TSDMNYL testimonial *evidence, tribute*

TSDNS tastiness *flavor*
TSDNS testiness *anger*
TSDR attester *verifier*
TSDR et cetera *and so forth*
TSDR etcetera *odds and ends*
TSDR outsider *alien*
TSDR taster *tongue*
TSDR tastier *flavor*
TSDR testier *angrier*
TSDR toaster *heater*
TSDR toastier *warmer*
TSDR two-suiter *luggage*
TSDRV test-drive *evaluate* test-drove test-driving test-driven
TSDS testacy *will* testacies
TSDS testis *male gland* testes
TSDSDRN testosterone *hormone*
TSDST tastiest *flavor*
TSDST testiest *angriest*
TSDST toastiest *warmest*
TSDSTRN testosterone *hormone*
TSDT testate *will*
TSDTRKS testatrix *will (f)*
TSDTRX testatrix *will (f)*
TSDYR tastier *flavor*
TSDYR testier *angrier*
TSDYR toastier *warmer*
TSDYST tastiest *flavor*
TSDYST testiest *angriest*
TSDYST toastiest *warmest*
TSDZ testes (pl) *male gland* testis
TSFL tasteful (adj) *flavorful, preferred* tastefully (adv)
TSFL test-fly *evaluate* test-flew test-flying test-flown test-flies
TSFL tsetse fly *insect* tsetse flies
TSFLNS tastefulness *flavor, preference*
TSGJSCHN autosuggestion *hypnosis*
TSH attaché *diplomat*
TSH étagère (or) etagere *furniture*
TSH tissue *paper, cells, network*

TSH touché *(interj) good hit*
TSH tusche *ink*
TSH tush *(n-slang) buttocks, (interj) reproach*
TSHKS attaché case *briefcase*
TSHLR tissular *cells*
TSHMHL Taj Mahal *tomb*
TSHN outshine *brighter* outshone outshining
TSHN titian *brown*
TSHN Titian *artist*
TSHN tuition *fee*
TSHP tea shop *store*
TSHRT T-shirt *garment*
TSHS autoecious *in one place*
TSHSL autoeciously *in one place*
TSHST tachist *painter*
TSHT outshoot *aim, go beyond* outshot outshooting
TSHZM tachism *painting*
TSJSCHN autosuggestion *hypnosis*
TSK task *job*
TSK tusk *tooth*
TSK tussock *tuft*
TSKD zucchetto *skullcap* zucchettos
TSKFRS task force *group*
TSKMSDR taskmaster *supervisor*
TSKMSTR taskmaster *supervisor*
TSKN Tuscan *of Tuscany*
TSKNN Toscanini *conductor*
TSKR outscore *better score* outscored outscoring
TSKR tusker *elephant*
TSKRTS outskirts *border*
TSKS Tay-Sachs *disease*
TSKT zucchetto *skullcap* zucchettos
TSKWR T square *ruler*
TSL otiosely *vainly*
TSL outsell *sell more* outsold outselling
TSL outsole *shoe*
TSL T cell *immunity*
TSL tassel *fringe* tasseled

Use letters that best describe the sounds you hear and omit the vowels. Use **S** or **K** instead of **C**: to find circle use **SRKL**. Use **J** to find joy, **JM** to find gem and **G** to find go.

(or) tasselled tasseling
(or) tasselling
TSL tesla *magnetics*
TSL tousle *rumple* tousled tousling
TSL tussle *wrestle* tussled tussling
TSLDD tessellated *mosaic*
TSLF itself *its own nature*
TSLS tasteless *no flavor, rude*
TSLSHN tessellation *mosaic*
TSLSL tastelessly *no flavor, rudely*
TSLSNS tastelessness *no flavor, rudeness*
TSLT tessellate *mosaic* tessellated tessellating
TSLTD tessellated *mosaic*
TSM autism *self-absorption*
TSM twosome *couple*
TSMRT outsmart *outwit*
TSMSDR taskmaster *supervisor*
TSMSDR toastmaster *speaker*
TSMSTR taskmaster *supervisor*
TSMSTR toastmaster *speaker*
TSN Tucson *city*
TSNDR zander *fish* zander (or) zanders
TSNM tsunami *wave* tsunamis
TSP toss-up (n) *even chance*
TSPKN outspoken *frank*
TSPKNL outspokenly *frank*
TSPKNS outspokenness *frankness*
TSPN teaspoon *utensil*
TSPND outspend *money*
TSPNFL teaspoonful *measure* teaspoonfuls
TSPNT outspent *money*
TSPRD outspread *extended*
TSQR T square *ruler*
TSR czar *ruler*
TSR tessera *ticket, tile* tesserae
TSRK tesseract *cube*
TSRKT tesseract *cube*

TSRN czarina *wife of czar*
TSRSN outsourcing *subcontracting*
TSRSNG outsourcing *subcontracting*
TSRVS tea service *serving set*
TSRZM czarism *dictatorship*
TSS phthisis *tuberculosis* phthises
TSS ptosis *saliva* ptoses
TSST otocyst *organ*
TST attest *verify*
TST otiosity *in vain*
TST out-of-sight (slang) *superior*
TST outset *beginning*
TST outstay *stay longer*
TST tacet *music*
TST tacit *suggested*
TST Taoist *philosophy*
TST taste (v) *perceive, sample* tasted tasting
TST taste (n) *flavor, preference*
TST tea set *serving pieces*
TST test (n) *examination, proof, shell* (v) *try*
TST testee *person examined*
TST testy *angry* testier testiest
TST toast *bread, roast, poem*
TST toasty *browned, warm* toastier toastiest
TSTB test tube (n) *laboratory* test-tube (adj)
TSTBD taste bud *tongue*
TSTBL testable *evaluation*
TSTBLD testability *evaluation*
TSTBLT testability *evaluation*
TSTC testacy *will* testacies
TSTD tested *qualified*
TSTD tostada *food*
TSTD two-sided *two faces*
TSTDR testator *will*
TSTDRV test-drive *evaluate* test-drove test-driving test-driven
TSTF testify *give evidence* testified testifying testifies

TSTFL tasteful (adj) *flavorful, preferred* tastefully (adv)
TSTFL test-fly *evaluate* test-flew test-flying test-flown test-flies
TSTFLNS tastefulness *flavor, preference*
TSTFR testifier *witness*
TSTFYR testifier *witness*
TSTGST zeitgeist (often capitalized) *culture*
TSTK autistic *self-absorbed*
TSTK zaddik *Jewish leader* zaddikim
TSTKL autistically *self-absorbed*
TSTKL testicle *male gland*
TSTKLR testicular *male gland*
TSTKM zaddikim (pl) *Jewish leader* zaddik
TSTKYLR testicular *male gland*
TSTL tacitly *suggested*
TSTL tastily *flavor*
TSTL testily *angry*
TSTLS tasteless *no flavor, rude*
TSTLSL tastelessly *no flavor, rudely*
TSTLSNS tastelessness *no flavor, rudeness*
TSTMN testimony *evidence* testimonies
TSTMNL testimonial *evidence, tribute*
TSTMNR testamentary *Bible, will, proof*
TSTMNT testament *Bible, will, proof*
TSTMNTR testamentary *Bible, will, proof*
TSTMNYL testimonial *evidence, tribute*
TSTMSDR toastmaster *speaker*
TSTMSTR toastmaster *speaker*
TSTN testing *difficult*
TSTNDN outstanding *great*
TSTNDNG outstanding

Letters aren't doubled for single sounds: to find **alley** use **L** not **LL**. Use **Y** and **W** as hard sounds only: to find **yellow** use **YL**. (Br)=British spelling or usage. * See dictionary.

great

TSTNG testing *difficult*
TSTNS tacitness *suggestion*
TSTNS tastiness *flavor*
TSTNS testiness *irate*
TSTP two-step *dance*
TSTQLR testicular *male gland*
TSTR attester *verifier*
TSTR et cetera *and so forth*
TSTR etcetera *odds and ends*
TSTR outstare *look at longer* outstared outstaring
TSTR taster *tongue*
TSTR tastier *flavor*
TSTR tessitura *melody*
TSTR tester *examiner*
TSTR testier *angrier*
TSTR toaster *heater*
TSTR toastier *warmer*
TSTR two-suiter *luggage*
TSTRCH outstretch *extend*
TSTRD autostrada *highway* autostradas (or) autostrade
TSTRN taciturn *silent*
TSTRND taciturnity *silence*
TSTRNT taciturnity *silence*
TSTRP outstrip *exceed* outstripped outstripping
TSTS testacy *will* testacies
TSTS testis *male gland* testes
TSTSDRN testosterone *hormone*
TSTSFL tsetse fly *insect* tsetse flies
TSTSHN attestation *oath*
TSTSHN outstation *post*
TSTSHS testaceous *shell, brick*
TSTST tastiest *flavor*
TSTST testiest *angriest*
TSTST toastiest *warmest*
TSTSTRN testosterone *hormone*
TSTT testate *will*
TSTTR testator *will*
TSTTRKS testatrix *will (f)*
TSTTRX testatrix *will (f)*
TSTYB test tube (n) *laboratory* test-tube (adj)

TSTYR tastier *flavor*
TSTYR testier *angrier*
TSTYR toastier *warmer*
TSTYST tastiest *flavor*
TSTYST testiest *angriest*
TSTYST toastiest *warmest*
TSTZ testes (pl) *male gland* testis
TSV tussive *cough*
TSVTRN zwitterion *particle*
TSVTRYN zwitterion *particle*
TSX Tay-Sachs *disease*
TSY tissue *paper, cells, network*
TSZ outsize (or) outsized *large*
TSZD outsized (or) outsize *large*
TSZM autoecism *in one place*
TT tat *lace* tatted tatting
TT tattoo *skin marking, tap* tattoos
TT tatty *shabby* tattier tattiest
TT taught *(v-past)* teach
TT taut *tight*
TT teat *nipple*
TT teddy *bear, chemise* teddies
TT tight *snug, capable, drunk**
TT tit *bird, (vulgar) teat*
TT titi *monkey, tree*
TT toddy *drink* toddies
TT toot *(v) sound (n) spree, sound*
TT tot *(v) add* totted totting
TT tot *(n) child, sip*
TT tote *carry* toted toting
TT tout *praise*
TT tutee *student*
TT tutti *music*
TT tutu *skirt*
TTBG tote bag *pack*
TTBL tea table *furniture*
TTBR teddy bear *toy*
TTBRD tote board *racetrack*
TTC tootsy *foot* tootsies
TTD attitude *position, state of mind*
TTD two-toed *with two toes*
TTDL teetotal *no alcohol*
TTDLR teetotaler (or)

teetotaller *no alcohol*
TTDLST teetotalist *no alcohol*
TTDLZM teetotalism *no alcohol*
TTDNL attitudinal (adj) *position, state of mind* attitudinally (adv)
TTDNZ attitudinize *pose* attitudinized attitudinizing (Br) attitudinise
TTFRD tutti-frutti *fruits*
TTFRT tutti-frutti *fruits*
TTFRTT tit for tat (n) *revenge* tit-for-tat (adj)
TTFSDD tightfisted *miserly*
TTFSTD tightfisted *miserly*
TTG tautog *fish*
TTH eightieth *of number 80*
TTH eyetooth *canine tooth*
TTH teeth (pl) *dental tooth*
TTH teethe *grow teeth* teethed teething
TTH tithe *(v) give ten percent* tithed tithing
TTH tithe *(n) ten percent tax*
TTH tooth *dental* teeth
TTH toothy *many teeth, tasty* toothier toothiest
TTHBRSH toothbrush *scrubber* toothbrushes
TTHD toothed *with teeth*
TTHK toothache *pain*
TTHL toothily *more teeth, tasty*
TTHLS toothless *no teeth*
TTHN teething *cutting teeth*
TTHN tithing *administrators*
TTHNG teething *cutting teeth*
TTHNG tithing *administrators*
TTHNGK outthink *outwit* outthought outthinking
TTHNGRNG teething ring *biting toy*
TTHNK outthink *outwit* outthought outthinking
TTHNRNG teething ring *biting toy*
TTHPDR toothpowder *cleanser*

Use letters that best describe the sounds you hear and omit the vowels. Use **S** or **K** instead of **C**: to find circle use **SRKL**. Use **J** to find joy, **JM** to find gem and **G** to find go.

TTHPK toothpick *remove food*
TTHPST toothpaste *cleanser*
TTHR teether *tooth device*
TTHR tether *(v) fasten (n) rope*
TTHR toothier *more teeth, tasty*
TTHRBL tetherball *game*
TTHSM toothsome *tasty*
TTHSML toothsomely *tasty*
TTHSMNS toothsomeness *tasty*
TTHST toothiest *more teeth, tasty*
TTHT toothed *with teeth*
TTHW out-of-the-way *hidden*
TTHYR toothier *more teeth, tasty*
TTHYST toothiest *more teeth, tasty*
TTK tie tack (or) tie tac *pin*
TTL tattle *gossip* tattled tattling
TTL tautly *tightly*
TTL tea towel *cloth*
TTL tiddly *(Br) drunk*
TTL title *rank, name* titled titling
TTL tittle *mark*
TTL toddle *totter* toddled toddling
TTL tootle *sound* tootled tootling
TTL total *(v) add up, wreck* totaled (or) totalled totaling (or) totalling
TTL total *(n, adj, adv) entire*
TTL totally *completely*
TTLD titled *name, rank*
TTLD totality *whole* totalities
TTLDNG titillating *suggestive*
TTLDV titillative *suggestive*
TTLG tautology *repetition* tautologies
TTLGS tautologous *repetitious*
TTLGSL tautologously *repetitious*
TTLHLDR titleholder *champion*

TTLJ tautology *repetition* tautologies
TTLJ tutelage *teach*
TTLJKL tautological (adj) *repetitious* tautologically (adv)
TTLPT tight-lipped *silent*
TTLR tattler *informer*
TTLR titular *known as*
TTLR toddler *child*
TTLR tutelary *guardian* tutelaries
TTLSHN titillation *arousal*
TTLT titillate *arouse* titillated titillating
TTLT totality *whole* totalities
TTLTDL tittle-tattle *gossip* tittle-tattled tittle-tattling
TTLTL tattletale *informer*
TTLTN titillating *suggestive*
TTLTNG titillating *suggestive*
TTLTRN totalitarian *dictator*
TTLTRNZM totalitarianism *dictator*
TTLTRYN totalitarian *dictator*
TTLTRYNZM totalitarianism *dictator*
TTLTTL tittle-tattle *gossip* tittle-tattled tittle-tattling
TTLTV titillative *suggestive*
TTLWNGKS tiddlywinks *game*
TTLWNGX tiddlywinks *game*
TTLWNKS tiddlywinks *game*
TTLWNX tiddlywinks *game*
TTLZ totalize *add up* totalized totalizing
TTLZDR totalizator (or) totalisator *wager*
TTLZTR totalizator (or) totalisator *wager*
TTM autotomy *division*
TTM tatami *mat* tatami (or) tatamis
TTM teatime *afternoon*
TTM tee time *golf*
TTM totem *pole*
TTM two-time *cheat* two-timed two-timing
TTMK totemic *pole*
TTMR tautomer *isomer*

TTMR two-timer *cheater*
TTMRZM tautomerism *isomer*
TTMS autotomous *division*
TTMS titmouse *animal* titmice
TTMTHD tight-mouthed *silent*
TTMTHT tight-mouthed *silent*
TTMZ autotomize *divide* autotomized autotomizing
TTN tauten *tighten*
TTN tetany *spasm*
TTN Teuton *German*
TTN tight end *football*
TTN tighten *taut*
TTN titan *giant*
TTN two-tone *colored*
TTND tight end *football*
TTND two-toned *colored*
TTNG tatting *lace*
TTNK tetanic *disease*
TTNK Teutonic *German*
TTNK titanic *huge*
TTNKL titanically *huge*
TTNM tautonym *name*
TTNM titanium *element*
TTNR out-of-towner *foreigner*
TTNR tightener *taut*
TTNS tattiness *shabby*
TTNS tautness *tight*
TTNS tetanus *disease*
TTNS titaness *giant (f)*
TTNT tight-knit *close*
TTNYM titanium *element*
TTNZ teutonize *make German* teutonized teutonizing
TTNZM titanism *(often capitalized) revolt*
TTPTNC totipotency *cloning*
TTPTNS totipotency *cloning*
TTPTNT totipotent *cloning*
TTPTNTC totipotency *cloning*
TTPTNTS totipotency *cloning*
TTR tatter *shred, rag*
TTR tattier *shabby*

Letters aren't doubled for single sounds: to find alley use **L** not **LL**. Use **Y** and **W** as hard sounds only: to find yellow use **YL**. (Br)=British spelling or usage. * See dictionary.

TTR tattooer *skin marker*
TTR teeter *(n) seesaw (v) wobble*
TTR tetra *fish*
TTR tetter *disease*
TTR titer *concentration*
TTR titter *giggle*
TTR totter *sway*
TTR tottery *infirm*
TTR touter *praiser*
TTR tuatara *reptile*
TTR Tudor *royalty*
TTR tutor *teacher*
TTRBRD teeterboard *seesaw*
TTRD tattered *torn*
TTRD tetrad *group of four*
TTRDMLN tatterdemalion *ragged one*
TTRDMLYN tatterdemalion *ragged one*
TTRF autotroph *organism*
TTRF autotrophy *self-nourishment*
TTRFK autotrophic *self-nourishing*
TTRFKL autotrophically *self-nourishing*
TTRGNL tetragonal (adj) *crystal* tetragonally (adv)
TTRHDR tetrahedra (pl) *four sides* tetrahedron
TTRHDRL tetrahedral (adj) *four sides* tetrahedrally (adv)
TTRHDRN tetrahedron *four sides* tetrahedrons (or) tetrahedra
TTRK tetrarch *governor*
TTRK tetrarchy *four rulers* tetrarchies
TTRK tow truck *vehicle*
TTRKLRD tetrachloride *chemical*
TTRKN tetracaine *anesthetic*
TTRKRD tetrachord *four tones*
TTRL tetryl *explosive*
TTRL tutorial *lesson*
TTRLG tetralogy *four pieces* tetralogies
TTRLJ tetralogy *four pieces* tetralogies

TTRMDR tetrameter *verse*
TTRMR tetramer *four pieces*
TTRMRK tetrameric *four pieces*
TTRMRS tetramerous *four pieces*
TTRMTR tetrameter *verse*
TTRN tottering *unsteady*
TTRNG tottering *unsteady*
TTRP tightrope *acrobat*
TTRPD tetrapod *four feet*
TTRPLD tetraploid *genes*
TTRRK tetrarch *governor*
TTRRK tetrarchy *four rulers* tetrarchies
TTRSHN titration *dissolving*
TTRSHP tutorship *teaching*
TTRSKLN tetracycline *antibiotic*
TTRSL tattersall *pattern*
TTRT titrate *dissolve* titrated titrating
TTRTDR teeter-totter *seesaw*
TTRTTR teeter-totter *seesaw*
TTRYL tutorial *lesson*
TTRZN tetrazzini *food*
TTS tights *stockings*
TTS tootsy *foot* tootsies
TTSFL tsetse fly *insect* tsetse flies
TTST tattiest *shabby*
TTST tattooist *skin marker*
TTT toe-to-toe *fight*
TTT tut-tut *disapprove, disbelieve* tut-tutted tut-tutting
TTTL teetotal *no alcohol*
TTTLR teetotaler (or) teetotaller *no alcohol*
TTTLST teetotalist *no alcohol*
TTTLZM teetotalism *no alcohol*
TTTT tête-à-tête *private*
TTTT tut-tut *disapprove, disbelieve* tut-tutted tut-tutting
TTV additive *ingredient*
TTVD additivity *sum*
TTVT additivity *sum*
TTVT titivate *smarten* titivated titivating
TTWD tightwad *miser*

TTWL tea towel *cloth*
TTWR tattooer *skin marker*
TTWR tightwire *acrobatics*
TTWST tattooist *skin marker*
TTWYR tightwire *acrobatics*
TTYD attitude *position, state of mind*
TTYDNL attitudinal (adj) *position, state of mind* attitudinally (adv)
TTYDNZ attitudinize *pose* attitudinized attitudinizing (Br) attitudinise
TTYLR titular *known as*
TTYR tattier *shabby*
TTYST tattiest *shabby*
TTZFL tsetse fly *insect* tsetse flies
TV out of *depleted, beyond*
TV TV *(abbr) television* TVs
TVBD out-of-body *spiritual*
TVDRZ out-of-doors *open air*
TVDT out-of-date *obsolete*
TVKRT out-of-court *law*
TVPKT out-of-pocket *expense*
TVRN tavern *inn*
TVRNR taverner *innkeeper*
TVSDK atavistic *throwback*
TVSDKL atavistically *throwback*
TVST out-of-sight *(slang) superior*
TVSTK atavistic *throwback*
TVSTKL atavistically *throwback*
TVT outvote *get more votes* outvoted outvoting
TVTHW out-of-the-way *hidden*
TVTNR out-of-towner *foreigner*
TVZM atavism *throwback*
TW etui *small case* etuis
TW eye-to-eye *agreement*
TW Ottawa *Native American* Ottawas (or) Ottawa
TW outweigh *heavier*
TW towhee *bird*
TW two-way *both sides*

Use letters that best describe the sounds you hear and omit the vowels. Use **S** or **K** instead of **C**: to find circle use **SRKL**. Use **J** to find joy, **JM** to find gem and **G** to find go.

TWCH twitch *quiver* twitches
TWCH twitchy *jerky*
TWCHL twitchily *quivering*
TWD tweed *fabric*
TWD tweedy *informal* tweedier tweediest
TWDL twaddle *babble* twaddled twaddling
TWDL twiddle *rotate* twiddled twiddling
TWDLR twaddler *babbler*
TWDNS tweediness *informal*
TWDR tweedier *informal*
TWDR tweeter *stereo*
TWDR twitter *chirp, giggle, flutter*
TWDR twittery *giggle, flutter*
TWDST tweediest *informal*
TWDYR tweedier *informal*
TWDYST tweediest *informal*
TWG twig *(v) understand* twigged twigging
TWG twig *(n) branch*
TWG twiggy *branched*
TWGN tea wagon *table*
TWJ towage *pulling*
TWJD two-edged *sharpened*
TWJT two-edged *sharpened*
TWK tweak *pinch, adjust*
TWKS twixt (or) 'twixt *between*
TWKST twixt (or) 'twixt *between*
TWL toile *linen*
TWL towel *dry*
TWL twill *fabric*
TWLD twilled *fabric*
TWLFTH twelfth *of number 12*
TWLMN Tuolumne *river*
TWLN toweling *fabric*
TWLNG toweling *fabric*
TWLP Atahuallpa (or) Atahualpa *Inca king*
TWLR two-wheeler *bicycle*
TWLT toilette *fancy dress*
TWLT towelette *small towel*
TWLT twilight *dusk, dawn*
TWLTH twelfth *of number 12*
TWLV twelve *number (12)*
TWLVMNTH twelvemonth

year
TWMN autoimmune *disease-fighting*
TWMNT autoimmunity *disease-fighting*
TWMYN autoimmune *disease-fighting*
TWMYNT autoimmunity *disease-fighting*
TWN Taiwan *island*
TWN Tijuana *city*
TWN toe-in *wheel position*
TWN twain *two, pair*
TWN twenty *number (20)* twenties
TWN twin *couple* twinned twinning
TWN twine *cord* twined twining
TWNBR twinberry *plant*
TWNDD two-handed *both hands*
TWNFLR twinflower *plant*
TWNFLWR twinflower *plant*
TWNG twang *nasal*
TWNGKL twinkle *sparkle* twinkled twinkling
TWNGKLN twinkling *wink*
TWNGKLNG twinkling *wink*
TWNJ twinge *tweak, stab* twinged twinging
TWNKL twinkle *sparkle* twinkled twinkling
TWNKLN twinkling *wink*
TWNKLNG twinkling *wink*
TWNSZ twin-size *for one*
TWNT twenty *number (20)* twenties
TWNT twenty-two *gun*
TWNT twi-night *evening*
TWNTBD autoantibody *cell* autoantibodies
TWNTBT autoantibody *cell* autoantibodies
TWNTH twentieth *of number 20*
TWNTKSKSHN autointoxication *self-poisoning*
TWNTT twenty-two *gun*
TWNTTH twentieth *of number 20*

TWNTTWNT twenty-twenty *vision, gun*
TWNTWN twenty-one *game*
TWNTWN twenty-twenty *vision, gun*
TWNTXKSHN autointoxication *self-poisoning*
TWNTYTH twentieth *of number 20*
TWNWN twenty-one *game*
TWNYTH twentieth *of number 20*
TWR outwear *be sturdier* outwore outworn outwearing
TWR tower *(v) height (n) structure*
TWR tuyere *nozzle*
TWRD outward *outside*
TWRD toward (or) towards *(prep) direction (adj) soon*
TWRDK autoerotic *self-stimulating*
TWRDL outwardly *externally*
TWRDL towardly *favorable*
TWRDNS outwardness *external*
TWRDSZM autoeroticism (or) autoerotism *self-stimulation*
TWRDZ towards (or) toward *(prep) direction*
TWRDZM autoerotism (or) autoeroticism *self-stimulation*
TWRK outwork *work better, defense*
TWRKR autoworker *car maker*
TWRL twirl *spin*
TWRLR twirler *spinner*
TWRN outworn *(v-past) outwear*
TWRN towering *excessive*
TWRNG towering *excessive*
TWRP twerp *silly one*
TWRTK autoerotic *self-stimulating*
TWRTSZM autoeroticism (or) autoerotism *self-stimulation*

Letters aren't doubled for single sounds: to find alley use **L** not **LL**. Use **Y** and **W** as hard sounds only: to find yellow use **YL**. (Br)=British spelling or usage. * See dictionary.

TWRTZM autoerotism (or) autoeroticism *self-stimulation*

TWS twice *two times*

TWSBRN twice-born *born again*

TWSDR twister *tornado*

TWSHN tuition *fee*

TWSHS autoecious *in one place*

TWSHSL autoeciously *in one place*

TWST Taoist *philosophy*

TWST twist (v) *twine, sprain, distort* (n) *thread, dance, eccentricity**

TWSTD twisted *sick*

TWSTLD twice-told *repeated*

TWSTN twisting *trickery*

TWSTNG twisting *trickery*

TWSTR twister *tornado*

TWSZM autoecism *in one place*

TWT outwit *more clever* outwitted outwitting

TWT tweet *chirp*

TWT twit (n) *fool*

TWT twit (v) *tease* twitted twitting

TWTL twaddle *babble* twaddled twaddling

TWTL twiddle *rotate* twiddled twiddling

TWTLR twaddler *babbler*

TWTR tuatara *reptile*

TWTR tweeter *stereo*

TWTR twitter *chirp, giggle, flutter*

TWTR twittery *giggle, flutter*

TWX twixt (or) 'twixt *between*

TWXT twixt (or) 'twixt *between*

TWYR tuyere *nozzle*

TWZ 'twas (contr) *it was*

TWZ tweeze *pluck* tweezed tweezing

TWZM Taoism *philosophy*

TWZR tweezer *pluck* tweezers

TX addax *animal* addaxes

TX ataxia *confusion*

TX tax *levy, demand* taxes

TX taxa (pl) *group* taxon

TX taxi (n) *vehicle* taxis

TX taxi (v) *drive slowly* taxied taxiing (or) taxying taxis (or) taxies

TX text *writings*

TX tux (abbr) *tuxedo* tuxes

TXBK textbook *school*

TXBL taxable *levy*

TXBLD taxability *levy*

TXBLT taxability *levy*

TXCHL textual (adj) *writings* textually (adv)

TXCHR texture *substance, pattern*

TXCHRD textured *substance, pattern*

TXCHRL textural (adj) *substance, pattern* texturally (adv)

TXCHWL textual (adj) *writings* textually (adv)

TXD toxoid *immunization*

TXD tuxedo *formal attire* tuxedos (or) tuxedoes

TXDL textile *cloth*

TXDRM taxidermy *stuff animals*

TXDRMST taxidermist *stuff animals*

TXFL toxophily *archery*

TXFLT toxophilite *archery*

TXFN toxaphene *insecticide*

TXGNK toxigenic *poison*

TXGZMP tax-exempt *no levy*

TXGZMPT tax-exempt *no levy*

TXJNK toxigenic *poison*

TXK ataxic *confused*

TXK toxic *poison*

TXKB taxicab *vehicle*

TXKCZ toxicoses (pl) *illness* toxicosis

TXKLG toxicology *poison*

TXKLJ toxicology *poison*

TXKLJKL toxicological (adj) *poison* toxicologically (adv)

TXKLJST toxicologist *poison*

TXKNT toxicant *poison*

TXKSMP tax-exempt *no levy*

TXKSMPT tax-exempt *no levy*

TXKSS toxicosis *illness* toxicoses

TXKSZ toxicoses (pl) *illness* toxicosis

TXKZMP tax-exempt *no levy*

TXKZMPT tax-exempt *no levy*

TXM taxeme *grammar*

TXM toxemia *illness*

TXMDR taximeter *fare*

TXMK taxemic *grammar*

TXMKS Tex-Mex *Mexican-American*

TXMN taximan (Br) *cab driver*

TXMTR taximeter *fare*

TXMX Tex-Mex *Mexican-American*

TXMY toxemia *illness*

TXN taxing *stressful*

TXN taxon *classification* taxa

TXN tocsin *alarm*

TXN toxin *poison*

TXNG taxing *stressful*

TXNGL taxingly *stressful*

TXNL taxingly *stressful*

TXNM taxonomy *classification*

TXNMK taxonomic *classification*

TXNMKL taxonomically *classification*

TXNMST taxonomist *classification*

TXPLZM toxoplasma *disease*

TXPLZMCZ toxoplasmoses (pl) *disease* toxoplasmosis

TXPLZMK toxoplasmic *disease*

TXPLZMSS toxoplasmosis *disease* toxoplasmoses

TXPLZMSZ toxoplasmoses (pl) *disease* toxoplasmosis

TXPN taxpaying *levy*

TXPNG taxpaying *levy*

TXPR taxpayer *citizen*

TXPYN taxpaying *levy*

TXPYNG taxpaying *levy*

Use letters that best describe the sounds you hear and omit the vowels. Use **S** or **K** instead of **C**: to find circle use **SRKL**. Use **J** to find joy, **JM** to find gem and **G** to find go.

TXPYR taxpayer *citizen*
TXR taxer *levy*
TXRKN Texarkana *city*
TXS taxis *reflex* taxes
TXS taxus *tree* taxus
TXS Texas *US State*
TXSD toxicity *poison*
TXSHN taxation *levy*
TXST toxicity *poison*
TXSTN taxi stand *parking area*
TXSTND taxi stand *parking area*
TXT text *writings*
TXTBK textbook *school*
TXTL textile *cloth*
TXTL textual (adj) *writings* textually (adv)
TXTR texture *substance, pattern*
TXTRD textured *substance, pattern*
TXTRL textural (adj) *substance, pattern* texturally (adv)
TXTWL textual (adj) *writings* textually (adv)
TXW taxiway *airport*
TXXMP tax-exempt *no levy*
TXXMPT tax-exempt *no levy*
TXY ataxia *confusion*
TXZ taxes (pl) *reflex* taxis
TY taille *land tax*
TY toea *money* toea
TYB tuba *horn* tubas
TYB tube *pipe, tire, TV*
TYBL tubal *tube*
TYBL tubule *pipe*
TYBLGSHN tubal ligation *surgery*
TYBLR tubular *pipe*
TYBLS tubeless *pneumatic*
TYBN tubing *pipe*
TYBNG tubing *pipe*
TYBR tuber *bulb*
TYBRKL tubercle *lump*
TYBRKLN tuberculin *test*
TYBRKLR tubercular *disease*
TYBRKLS tuberculous *diseased*
TYBRKLSS tuberculosis *disease* tuberculoses

TYBRKYLN tuberculin *test*
TYBRKYLR tubercular *disease*
TYBRKYLS tuberculous *diseased*
TYBRKYLSS tuberculosis *disease* tuberculoses
TYBRQLN tuberculin *test*
TYBRQLR tubercular *disease*
TYBRQLS tuberculous *diseased*
TYBRQLSS tuberculosis *disease* tuberculoses
TYBRS tuberous *lumpy*
TYBRSD tuberosity *lump* tuberosities
TYBRST tuberosity *lump* tuberosities
TYBRZ tuberose *herb*
TYBST tubaist (or) tubist *musician*
TYBYL tubule *pipe*
TYBYLR tubular *pipe*
TYD étude *music*
TYD teiid *lizard*
TYDLJ tutelage *teach*
TYDLR tutelary *guardian* tutelaries
TYDR Tudor *royalty*
TYDR tutor *teacher*
TYDRSHP tutorship *teaching*
TYF tee off *golf* teed off teeing off
TYK tuque *hat*
TYKWKW tu quoque *you too*
TYKWQ tu quoque *you too*
TYL taille *land tax*
TYL tile *ceramic square* tiled tiling
TYL toil *work*
TYLFSH tilefish *animal*
TYLG etiology *cause* etiologies
TYLJ etiology *cause* etiologies
TYLJK etiologic *cause*
TYLJST etiologist *cause*
TYLN ptyalin *saliva*
TYLN tiling *tiles*
TYLNG tiling *tiles*
TYLP tulip *flower*

TYLPWD tulipwood *tree*
TYLR toiler *worker*
TYLRM tularemia *disease*
TYLRMK tularemic *disease*
TYLRMY tularemia *disease*
TYLSHN etiolation *whiten*
TYLSM toilsome *exhausting*
TYLT etiolate *whiten* etiolated etiolating
TYLWRN toilworn *tired*
TYLZM ptyalism *saliva*
TYMD tumid *swollen*
TYMFKSHN tumefaction *swelling*
TYMLCHS tumultuous *disorderly*
TYMLCHSL tumultuously *disorderly*
TYMLCHSNS tumultuousness *disorderly*
TYMLCHWS tumultuous *disorderly*
TYMLCHWSL tumultuously *disorderly*
TYMLCHWSNS tumultuousness *disorderly*
TYMLS tumulus *mound*
TYMLT tumult *disorder*
TYMR tumor *growth* (Br) tumour
TYMRL tumoral *growth* (Br) tumoural
TYMRLK tumorlike *growth* (Br) tumourlike
TYMRS tumorous *growths* (Br) tumourous
TYMSNS tumescence *swelling*
TYMSNT tumescent *swollen*
TYMSNTS tumescence *swelling*
TYMYLS tumulus *mound*
TYN attune *harmonize* attuned attuning
TYN tie in (v) *connection* tie-in (n)
TYN toyon *shrub*
TYN tuna *fish* tuna (or) tunas
TYN tune *(v) adjust* tuned tuning

Letters aren't doubled for single sounds: to find alley use **L** not **LL**. Use **Y** and **W** as hard sounds only: to find yellow use **YL**. (Br)=British spelling or usage. * See dictionary.

TYN tune *(n)* *melody, approach*
TYNBL tunable (adj) *harmony* tunably (adv)
TYNFL tuneful (adj) *musical* tunefully (adv)
TYNFLNS tunefulness *musical*
TYNK tunic *garment*
TYNK tunica *membrane* tunicae
TYNKL tunicle *garment*
TYNKT tunicate *outer layer*
TYNLS tuneless *no music*
TYNMNT attunement *harmony*
TYNNFRK tuning fork *music*
TYNNGFRK tuning fork *music*
TYNP tune-up *adjust*
TYNR tuner *adjuster, radio*
TYNS Tunis *city*
TYNSH Tunisia *country*
TYNSMTH tunesmith *song writer*
TYNT tune out *ignore*
TYNZH Tunisia *country*
TYP tie up (v) *rope, stop* tie-up (n)
TYPL tupelo *tree* tupelos
TYQKW tu quoque *you too*
TYQQ tu quoque *you too*
TYR auteur *film direction*
TYR hauteur *arrogance*
TYR tiara *crown*
TYR tier *one that ties, level*
TYR tire *(v) wear out* tired tiring
TYR tire *(n) wheel* (Br) tyre
TYRD tired *weary, trite*
TYRDLFWG Tierra del Fuego *island*
TYRFL turophile *cheese*
TYRLS tireless *strong*
TYRN tureen *pot*
TYRSM tiresome *slow*
TYRST auteurist *film direction*
TYS otiose *vain*
TYSD otiosity *in vain*
TYSD Tuesday *weekday*

TYSHN tuition *fee*
TYSL otiosely *vainly*
TYSST otocyst *organ*
TYST otiosity *in vain*
TYTH eightieth *of number 80*
TYTLJ tutelage *teach*
TYTLR tutelary *guardian* tutelaries
TYTNK Teutonic *German*
TYTNZ teutonize *make German* teutonized teutonizing
TYTR Tudor *royalty*
TYTR tutor *teacher*
TYTRL tutorial *lesson*
TYTRSHP tutorship *teaching*
TYTRYL tutorial *lesson*
TYWN Tijuana *city*
TYWSHN tuition *fee*
TYZD Tuesday *weekday*
TZ tawse *(Br) strap*
TZ tease *taunt* teased teasing
TZ 'tis *(contr) it is*
TZ tizzy *confusion* tizzies
TZD Tuesday *weekday*
TZDF autos-da-fé (pl) *burn* auto-da-fé
TZFL tsetse fly *insect* tsetse flies
TZH étagère (or) etagere *furniture*
TZHMHL Taj Mahal *tomb*
TZK phthisic *tuberculosis*
TZKL phthisical *tuberculosis*
TZL teasel *(v) nap cloth* teaseled (or) teaselled teaseling (or) teaselling
TZL teasel *(n) herb*
TZL tousle *rumple* tousled tousling
TZM autism *self-absorption*
TZM Taoism *philosophy*
TZMN Tasmania *island state*
TZMNC Tasman Sea *body of water*
TZMNS Tasman Sea *body of water*
TZMNY Tasmania *island state*
TZN tisane *infusion*
TZR teaser *taunter*

V

V avo *money* avos
V avow *assert*
V eve *evening*
V Eve *Biblical woman*
V I've *(contr) I have*
V ivy *vine* ivies
V of *(prep) denotes origin**
V ova *(pl) eggs* ovum
V uvea *eye*
V vee *alphabet letter (V)*
V via *by way of*
V vie *compete* vied vying
V view *vista, opinion*
V vow *(v) swear (n) oath*
V you've *(contr) you have*
VB vibe *vibration*
VBL viable (adj) *survivable* viably (adv)
VBL viewable *vision*
VBLD viability *survival*
VBLT viability *survival*
VBR vibrio *bacteria* vibrios
VBRD vibrato *music* vibratos
VBRDR vibrator *device*
VBRFN vibraphone *music*
VBRFNST vibraphonist *music*
VBRHRP vibraharp *music*
VBRHRPST vibraharpist *music*
VBRN vibrion *bacteria*
VBRNC vibrancy *energy* vibrance
VBRNM viburnum *shrub*
VBRNS vibrancy *energy* vibrance
VBRNT vibrant *energetic, bright*
VBRNTC vibrancy *energy* vibrance
VBRNTL vibrantly *energetic, bright*

Use letters that best describe the sounds you hear and omit the vowels. Use **S** or **K** instead of **C**: to find circle use **SRKL**. Use **J** to find joy, **JM** to find gem and **G** to find go.

VBRNTS vibrancy *energy* vibrance

VBRS vibrissa *whisker* vibrissae

VBRSHN vibration *quivering*

VBRSHNL vibrational *quivering*

VBRSHNLS vibrationless *still*

VBRSS vibriosis *abortion* vibrioses

VBRT vibrate *quiver* vibrated vibrating

VBRT vibrato *music* vibratos

VBRTL vibratile *quivering*

VBRTR vibrator *device*

VBRTR vibratory *quivering*

VBRY vibrio *bacteria* vibrios

VBRYN vibrion *bacteria*

VBRYSS vibriosis *abortion* vibrioses

VCH vetch *plant*

VCH vouch *certify*

VCHF VHF *(abbr) very high frequency*

VCHLN vetchling *plant*

VCHLNG vetchling *plant*

VCHR voucher *proof*

VCHSF vouchsafe *grant* vouchsafed vouchsafing

VCHSW vichyssoise *soup*

VCHSWZ vichyssoise *soup*

VD avid *eager*

VD avoid *shun*

VD evade *escape* evaded evading

VD ivied *vines, school*

VD ovoid *egg-shaped*

VD V-E Day *war*

VD Veda *Hindu*

VD veto *reject* vetoes

VD vide *example*

VD video *movie* videos

VD vita *résumé* vitae

VD vitta *stripe* vittae

VD void *(adj) empty, annul (n) space, lack*

VD voodoo *magic* voodoos

VDBL avoidable (adj) *shun* avoidably (adv)

VDBL evadable *escape*

VDBL evitable *avoidable*

VDBL voidable *empty, annul*

VDD avidity *eagerness*

VDD viduity *widow*

VDFL videophile *film lover*

VDFN videophone *TV telephone* videophoned videophoning

VDGRF videography *camera*

VDGRFR videographer *camera*

VDK oviduct *egg tube*

VDK vatic *foretelling*

VDK Vedic *scripture*

VDK viaduct *waterway*

VDK vodka *liquor*

VDKLCHR viticulture *grapes*

VDKLCHRL viticultural (adj) *grapes* viticulturally (adv)

VDKLCHRST viticulturist *grapes*

VDKLTR viticulture *grapes*

VDKLTRL viticultural (adj) *grapes* viticulturally (adv)

VDKLTRST viticulturist *grapes*

VDKN Vatican *Papal state*

VDKN vidicon *camera*

VDKST videocassette *tape*

VDKT oviduct *egg tube*

VDKT viaduct *waterway*

VDL avowedly *frankly*

VDL vedalia *ladybug*

VDL victual *(v) eat* victualed (or) victualled victualing (or) victualling

VDL victual *(n) food*

VDL vital (adj) *essential* vitally (adv)

VDLG vitiligo *white spots*

VDLJNSS vitellogenesis *yolk*

VDLKT videlicet *namely*

VDLN vitelline *yolk*

VDLR victualler (or) victualer *food provider*

VDLS vitellus *yolk*

VDLSDK vitalistic *self-determination*

VDLST videlicet *namely*

VDLST vitalist *self-determination*

VDLSTK vitalistic *self-determination*

VDLY vedalia *ladybug*

VDLZ vitalize *enliven* vitalized vitalizing

VDLZM vitalism *self-determinism*

VDLZSHN vitalization *liveliness*

VDMN vitamin *nutrient*

VDNCHL evidential (adj) *proof* evidentially (adv)

VDNCHR evidentiary *proof*

VDNR veterinary *animal doctor*

VDNRN veterinarian *animal doctor*

VDNRYN veterinarian *animal doctor*

VDNS avidness *eagerness*

VDNS avoidance *shun*

VDNS evidence *data, proof* evidenced evidencing

VDNSHL evidential (adj) *proof* evidentially (adv)

VDNSHR evidentiary *proof*

VDNT evident *obvious*

VDNT Vedanta *belief*

VDNTK Vedantic *Hindu*

VDNTL evidently *obviously*

VDNTS avoidance *shun*

VDNTS evidence *data, proof* evidenced evidencing

VDPRF veto-proof *no rejection*

VDR aviator *pilot*

VDR avoider *shun*

VDR evader *escape*

VDR vetoer *refuser*

VDR voider *empty, annul*

VDR votary *believer* votaries

VDR voter *election*

VDRN veteran *soldier*

VDRNR veterinary *animal doctor*

VDRNRN veterinarian *animal doctor*

VDRNRYN veterinarian *animal doctor*

VDRST votarist *believer*

VDS uveitis *inflammation*

VDS vadose *water*

VDT avidity *eagerness*

Letters aren't doubled for single sounds: to find alley use **L** not **LL**. Use **Y** and **W** as hard sounds only: to find yellow use **YL**. (Br)=British spelling or usage. * See dictionary.

VDT vedette *vigil*
VDT viduity *widow*
VDTKS videotex *text on TV*
VDTP videotape *camera* videotaped videotaping
VDTX videotex *text on TV*
VDV votive *prayer*
VDVL vaudeville *entertainment*
VDVL votively *prayer*
VDVLN vaudevillian *entertainment*
VDVLYN vaudevillian *entertainment*
VDVNS votiveness *prayer*
VDVYN vaudevillian *entertainment*
VDWD viduity *widow*
VDWR vetoer *refuser*
VDWT viduity *widow*
VDWZM voodooism *witchcraft*
VDY video *movie* videos
VDYDSK videodisc (or) videodisk *movie*
VDYFL videophile *film lover*
VDYFN videophone *TV telephone* videophoned videophoning
VDYGRF videography *camera*
VDYGRFR videographer *camera*
VDYKST videocassette *tape*
VDYTKS videotex *text on TV*
VDYTP videotape *camera* videotaped videotaping
VDYTX videotex *text on TV*
VDZM voodooism *witchcraft*
VFN avifauna *birds*
VFNDR viewfinder *camera*
VFNL avifaunal *birds*
VFRVSNS effervescence *bubbles*
VG vague *unclear* vaguer vaguest
VG Vega *star*
VG veggie *(slang) vegetable* (Br) veg
VG viga *rafter*
VG vogue *style*

VGBN vagabond *wanderer*
VGBND vagabond *wanderer*
VGDM vagatomy *surgery* vagatomies
VGL vagal (adj) *nerve* vagally (adv)
VGL vaguely *unclear*
VGN vegan *no meat or dairy*
VGNR Wagner *composer*
VGNRN Wagnerian *of Wagner*
VGNRYN Wagnerian *of Wagner*
VGNS vagueness *unclear*
VGNSM veganism *no meat or dairy*
VGNZM veganism *no meat or dairy*
VGR vagary *whim* vagaries
VGR vaguer *unclear*
VGR vigor *health* (Br) vigour
VGRNC vagrancy *wandering* vagrancies
VGRNS vagrancy *wandering* vagrancies
VGRNT vagrant *wanderer*
VGRNTC vagrancy *wandering* vagrancies
VGRNTS vagrancy *wandering* vagrancies
VGRS vagarious *changeable*
VGRS vigoroso *music*
VGRS vigorous *forceful* (Br) vigourous
VGRSH vigorish *fee*
VGRSL vigorously *forceful* (Br) vigourously
VGRSNS vigorousness *forcefulness* (Br) vigourousness
VGRYS vagarious *changeable*
VGSH voguish *stylish*
VGSHNS voguishness *style*
VGST vaguest *unclear*
VGTM vagatomy *surgery* vagatomies
VHKL vehicle *transportation*
VHKLR vehicular *transportation*
VHKYLR vehicular *transportation*

VHMNS vehemence *strength*
VHMNT vehement *strong*
VHMNTL vehemently *strongly*
VHMNTS vehemence *strength*
VHQLR vehicular *transportation*
VJ veejay *music videos*
VJ veggie *(slang) vegetable* (Br) veg
VJ voyage *journey* voyaged voyaging
VJD V-J Day *war*
VJDBL vegetable *plant*
VJDL vegetal *plant*
VJL vagile *free to move*
VJL vigil *watch, prayer*
VJLD vagility *free to move*
VJLN vigilante *crime punisher*
VJLNS vigilance *watchful*
VJLNT vigilant *watchful*
VJLNT vigilante *crime punisher*
VJLNTL vigilantly *watchful*
VJLNTS vigilance *watchful*
VJLNTZM vigilantism *crime punishment*
VJLT vagility *free to move*
VJN vagina *sex organ* vaginae (or) vaginas
VJNDS vaginitis *inflammation*
VJNL vaginal (adj) *genital* vaginally (adv)
VJNTS vaginitis *inflammation*
VJR voyager *traveller*
VJR voyageur *fur transport*
VJSML vigesimal *of number 20*
VJTBL vegetable *plant*
VJTDV vegetative *like plants*
VJTDVL vegetatively *like plants*
VJTDVNS vegetativeness *like plants*
VJTL vegetal *plant*
VJTRN vegetarian *no meat*
VJTRNZM vegetarianism *no meat*

Use letters that best describe the sounds you hear and omit the vowels. Use **S** or **K** instead of **C**: to find circle use **SRKL**. Use **J** to find joy, **JM** to find gem and **G** to find go.

VJTRYN vegetarian *no meat*
VJTRYNZM vegetarianism *no meat*
VJTSHN vegetation *plants*
VJTT vegetate *grow plants, be passive* vegetated vegetating
VJTTV vegetative *like plants*
VJTTVL vegetatively *like plants*
VJTTVNS vegetativeness *like plants*
VK evacuee *person removed*
VK evoke *conjure up* evoked evoking
VK vacua *(pl) emptiness* vacuum
VKBL evocable *inspire*
VKBL vocable *word*
VKBLR vocabular *(adj) of words*
VKBLR vocabulary *(n) words* vocabularies
VKBYLR vocabular *(adj) of words*
VKBYLR vocabulary *(n) words* vocabularies
VKCN vaccine *drug*
VKCN vaccinia *cowpox*
VKCNL vaccinial *cowpox*
VKCNY vaccinia *cowpox*
VKCNYL vaccinial *cowpox*
VKD avocado *fruit* avocados
VKD vacuity *emptiness* vacuities
VKDM victim *sacrifice, dupe*
VKDMLS victimless *no complaint*
VKDMZ victimize *cheat, sacrifice* victimized victimizing (Br) victimise
VKDMZR victimizer *cheat, sacrifice* (Br) victimiser
VKDMZSHN victimization *deception* (Br) victimisation
VKDR evictor *person expelling*
VKDR vector *direction*

VKDR victor *winner*
VKDR victory *win* victories
VKDV evacuative *empty, vacated*
VKDV evocative *conjuring up*
VKDV vocative *grammar*
VKDVL vocatively *grammar*
VKL vacuole *cavity*
VKL vehicle *transportation*
VKL vocal *(adj) voice* vocally *(adv)*
VKLK vocalic *vowels*
VKLKL vocalically *vowels*
VKLR vacuolar *cavity*
VKLSHN vacuolation *cavity*
VKLST vocalist *singer*
VKLZ vocalize *voice* vocalized vocalizing (Br) vocalise
VKLZM vocalism *voice, vowels*
VKLZR vocalizer *voice* (Br) vocaliser
VKLZSHN vocalization *voice* (Br) vocalisation
VKM vacuum *emptiness, cleaner* vacuums (or) vacua
VKMPKD vacuum-packed *remove air*
VKMPKT vacuum-packed *remove air*
VKN vicuña (or) vicuna *animal*
VKN Viking *Nordic*
VKNC vacancy *empty space* vacancies
VKNG Viking *Nordic*
VKNS vacancy *empty space* vacancies
VKNS vacantness *empty*
VKNS viscountess *title*
VKNT vacant *empty*
VKNT viscount *title*
VKNTC vacancy *empty space* vacancies
VKNTL vacantly *empty*
VKNTNS vacantness *empty*
VKNTS vacancy *empty space* vacancies
VKNTS viscountess *title*

VKNY vicuña (or) vicuna *animal*
VKR vaquero *cowboy* vaqueros
VKR vicar *clergy*
VKRJ vicarage *clergy*
VKRL vicarial *clergy*
VKRNS vicariance *breakup*
VKRNT vicariant *part*
VKRNTS vicariance *breakup*
VKRS of course *certainly*
VKRS vicarious *substitute*
VKRSHP vicarship *clergy*
VKRSL vicariously *substitute*
VKRSNS vicariousness *substitution*
VKRT vicariate *clergy*
VKRYL vicarial *clergy*
VKRYNS vicariance *breakup*
VKRYNT vicariant *part*
VKRYNTS vicariance *breakup*
VKRYS vicarious *substitute*
VKRYSL vicariously *substitute*
VKRYSNS vicariousness *substitution*
VKRYT vicariate *clergy*
VKS vacuous *empty*
VKS vex *annoy, puzzle*
VKSHN avocation *hobby*
VKSHN evacuation *empty, vacated*
VKSHN eviction *expulsion*
VKSHN evocation *calling forth*
VKSHN vacation *holiday*
VKSHN vocation *job*
VKSHNL avocational *(adj) hobby* avocationally *(adv)*
VKSHNL vocational *(adj) job* vocationally *(adv)*
VKSHNLST vocationalist *job*
VKSHNLZM vocationalism *job*
VKSL vacuously *empty*
VKSL vexilla *(pl) flag, feather* vexillum
VKSLLG vexillology *flags*
VKSLLJ vexillology *flags*
VKSLLJK vexillologic (or) vexillological *flags*

Letters aren't doubled for single sounds: to find alley use **L** not **LL**. Use **Y** and **W** as hard sounds only: to find yellow use **YL**. (Br)=British spelling or usage. * See dictionary.

VKSLLJKL vexillological (or) vexillologic *flags*
VKSLLJST vexillologist *flags*
VKSLM vexillum *flag, feather* vexilla
VKSN vaccine *drug*
VKSN vaccinia *cowpox*
VKSN vixen *fox, woman*
VKSNDR vaccinator *innoculator*
VKSNL vaccinal *protection*
VKSNL vaccinial *cowpox*
VKSNS vacuousness *empty*
VKSNSH vixenish *fox, woman*
VKSNSHN vaccination *innoculation*
VKSNT vaccinate *innoculate* vaccinated vaccinating
VKSNTR vaccinator *innoculator*
VKSNY vaccinia *cowpox*
VKSNYL vaccinial *cowpox*
VKSPPL vox populi *popular sentiment*
VKSPPYL vox populi *popular sentiment*
VKSSHN vexation *annoy, puzzle*
VKSSHS vexatious *annoy, puzzle*
VKSSHSL vexatiously *annoy, puzzle*
VKSSHSNS vexatiousness *annoy, puzzle*
VKT evacuate *empty, vacate* evacuated evacuating
VKT evict *expel*
VKT evictee *person expelled*
VKT vacate *annul, get out* vacated vacating
VKT vacuity *emptiness* vacuities
VKT viscount *title*
VKTM victim *sacrifice, dupe*
VKTMLS victimless *no complaint*
VKTMZ victimize *cheat, sacrifice* victimized victimizing (Br) victimise
VKTMZR victimizer *cheat,*

sacrifice
(Br) victimiser
VKTMZSHN victimization *deception* (Br) victimisation
VKTR evictor *person expelling*
VKTR evocator *summoner*
VKTR vector *direction*
VKTR victor *winner*
VKTR Victoria *city*
VKTR victoria *carriage*
VKTR victory *win* victories
VKTRL vectorial (adj) *direction* vectorially (adv)
VKTRL Victrola *(trademark) phonograph*
VKTRN Victorian *of Queen Victoria*
VKTRS victorious *winning*
VKTRSL victoriously *winning*
VKTRSNS victoriousness *winning*
VKTRYN Victorian *of Queen Victoria*
VKTRYS victorious *winning*
VKTRYSL victoriously *winning*
VKTRYSNS victoriousness *winning*
VKTS viscountess *title*
VKTV evacuative *empty, vacated*
VKTV evocative *conjuring up*
VKTV vocative *grammar*
VKTVL vocatively *grammar*
VKW evacuee *person removed*
VKW vacua (pl) *emptiness* vacuum
VKWD vacuity *emptiness* vacuities
VKWDV evacuative *empty, vacated*
VKWL vacuole *cavity*
VKWLR vacuolar *cavity*
VKWLSHN vacuolation *cavity*
VKWS vacuous *empty*
VKWSHN evacuation *empty, vacated*

VKWSL vacuously *empty*
VKWSNS vacuousness *empty*
VKWT evacuate *empty, vacate* evacuated evacuating
VKWT vacuity *emptiness* vacuities
VKWTV evacuative *empty, vacated*
VKY evacuee *person removed*
VKY vacua (pl) *emptiness* vacuum
VKYD vacuity *emptiness* vacuities
VKYL vacuole *cavity*
VKYLR vacuolar *cavity*
VKYLSHN vacuolation *cavity*
VKYM vacuum *emptiness, cleaner* vacuums (or) vacua
VKYMPKD vacuum-packed *remove air*
VKYMPKT vacuum-packed *remove air*
VKYN vicuña (or) vicuna *animal*
VKYNY vicuña (or) vicuna *animal*
VKYS vacuous *empty*
VKYSHN evacuation *empty, vacated*
VKYSL vacuously *empty*
VKYSNS vacuousness *empty*
VKYT evacuate *empty, vacate* evacuated evacuating
VKYT vacuity *emptiness* vacuities
VKYTV evacuative *empty, vacated*
VKYW evacuee *person removed*
VKYW vacua (pl) *emptiness* vacuum
VKYWD vacuity *emptiness* vacuities
VKYWDV evacuative *empty, vacated*
VKYWL vacuole *cavity*
VKYWLR vacuolar *cavity*

Use letters that best describe the sounds you hear and omit the vowels. Use **S** or **K** instead of **C**: to find circle use **SRKL**. Use **J** to find joy, **JM** to find gem and **G** to find go.

VKYWLSHN vacuolation *cavity*
VKYWS vacuous *empty*
VKYWSHN evacuation *empty, vacated*
VKYWSL vacuously *empty*
VKYWSNS vacuousness *empty*
VKYWT evacuate *empty, vacate* evacuated evacuating
VKYWT vacuity *emptiness* vacuities
VKYWTV evacuative *empty, vacated*
VL avail *assist*
VL avowal *acknowledgment*
VL evil *bad* eviler (or) eviller evilest (or) evillest
VL evil eye *glare*
VL evilly *with evil*
VL oval *shape*
VL ovolo *molding*
VL ovule *egg*
VL uveal *eye*
VL uvula *throat lobe* uvulas (or) uvulae
VL vail *lower*
VL vale *valley*
VL valet *servant*
VL valley *depression* valleys
VL value *(v)* rate, prize valued valuing
VL value *(n) worth, tint*
VL veal *meat*
VL veil *screen*
VL vela *(pl) soft palate* velum
VL vial *bottle*
VL vile *base, foul* viler vilest
VL vilely *base, foul*
VL vill *town*
VL villa *house*
VL viol *old violin*
VL viola *violin/cello, flower*
VL voilà (or) voila *(interj) there it is*
VL voile *fabric*
VL vole *animal, cards*
VL volley *(n) shot, burst* volleys
VL volley *(v) propel* volleyed volleying

VL vowel *letter*
VLBL available *usable, accessible*
VLBL valuable (adj) *worthy* valuably (adv)
VLBL violable (adj) *harm* violably (adv)
VLBL volleyball *sport*
VLBL voluble (adj) *talkative* volubly (adv)
VLBLD availability *usable, accessible*
VLBLD violability *harm*
VLBLD volubility *talkative*
VLBLNS volubleness *talkative*
VLBLT availability *usable, accessible*
VLBLT violability *harm*
VLBLT volubility *talkative*
VLCH veloce *music*
VLCHR vulture *bird, predator*
VLCHRN vulturine *predatory*
VLCHRS vulturous *predatory*
VLD valid *correct*
VLD valued *worthy*
VLD valuta *foreign exchange*
VLD veiled *dim*
VLD veld (or) veldt *grassland*
VLD velleity *wish* velleities
VLDD validity *correctness*
VLDD vaulted *arched*
VLDD voluted (or) volute *spiral*
VLDDD validated *confirmed*
VLDJ voltage *electricity*
VLDK villatic *rural*
VLDKDR valedictory *farewell* valedictories
VLDKSHN valediction *farewell*
VLDKTR valedictory *farewell* valedictories
VLDKTRN valedictorian *best student*
VLDKTRYN valedictorian *best student*
VLDL validly *correct*
VLDL volatile *lively, fickle*
VLDLNS volatileness *lively, fickle*
VLDLZ volatilize *vaporize*

volatilized volatilizing
VLDLZSHN volatilization *vaporize*
VLDMPR volt-ampere *electrical unit*
VLDNG vaulting *arched*
VLDR evaluator *rater*
VLDR evildoer *sinner*
VLDR valuator *appraiser*
VLDR vaulter *leaper*
VLDR violator *break, rape*
VLDRM velodrome *track*
VLDSHN validation *confirmation*
VLDT validate *confirm* validated validating
VLDT validity *correctness*
VLDTD validated *confirmed*
VLDV evaluative *rating*
VLDV violative *break, rape*
VLDV volitive *will*
VLDWR evildoer *sinner*
VLF vilify *belittle* vilified vilifying vilifies
VLFKSHN vilification *abuse*
VLFR vilifier *belittler*
VLFRM villiform *hair-like*
VLFS Oval Office *President*
VLFYR vilifier *belittler*
VLG Ivy League *college*
VLG Volga *river*
VLGR Ivy Leaguer *collegian*
VLGR vulgar *crude*
VLGRD vulgarity *crudeness* vulgarities
VLGRL vulgarly *crudely*
VLGRN vulgarian *crude one*
VLGRT vulgarity *crudeness* vulgarities
VLGRYN vulgarian *crude one*
VLGRZ vulgarize *make crude* vulgarized vulgarizing (Br) vulgarise
VLGRZM vulgarism *crudeness*
VLGRZR vulgarizer *make crude* (Br) vulgariser
VLGRZSHN vulgarization *make crude* (Br) vulgarisation
VLGS valgus *deformity*

Letters aren't doubled for single sounds: to find alley use **L** not **LL**. Use **Y** and **W** as hard sounds only: to find yellow use **YL**. (Br)=British spelling or usage. * See dictionary.

VLGS vulgus *verse*
VLGT vulgate *common speech, (capitalized) Latin Bible*
VLJ village *town*
VLJR villager *inhabitant*
VLKL vallecula *groove* valleculae
VLKLR vallecular *grooved*
VLKN volcano *lava vent* volcanoes (or) volcanos
VLKN Vulcan *Roman god*
VLKNK volcanic *lava vent*
VLKNKL volcanically *lava vent*
VLKNLG volcanology *lava vents*
VLKNLJ volcanology *lava vents*
VLKNLJK volcanologic *lava vent*
VLKNLJKL volcanological *lava vent*
VLKNLJST volcanologist *lava vents*
VLKNZ vulcanize *treat rubber* vulcanized vulcanizing (Br) vulcanise
VLKNZM volcanism *lava vent*
VLKNZR vulcanizer *treat rubber* (Br) vulcaniser
VLKNZSHN vulcanization *treat rubber* (Br) vulcanisation
VLKNZT vulcanizate *treat rubber* (Br) vulcanisate
VLKR Valkyrie *myth*
VLKR Velcro *(trademark) closure*
VLKYL vallecula *groove* valleculae
VLKYLR vallecular *grooved*
VLLS valueless *no worth*
VLM Valium *(trademark) drug*
VLM vellum *paper*
VLM velum *soft palate* vela
VLM volume *bulk, book*
VLMDR volumeter *bulk*

VLMN velamen *root* velamina
VLMNDD evil-minded *wicked*
VLMNS voluminous *full*
VLMNSD voluminosity *fullness*
VLMNSL voluminously *fullness*
VLMNSNS voluminousness *fullness*
VLMNST voluminosity *fullness*
VLMTR volumeter *bulk*
VLMTRK volumetric *bulk*
VLMTRKL volumetrically *bulk*
VLN valonia *acorns*
VLN villain *evil one (m)*
VLN villainy *evil* villainies
VLN villein *peasant*
VLN violin *music*
VLNCH avalanche *mass in motion*
VLNCHL violoncello *music*
VLNCHLST violoncellist *music*
VLNG veiling *fabric*
VLNL villanella *song*
VLNL villanelle *poem*
VLNRBL vulnerable (adj) *open to attack* vulnerably (adv)
VLNRBLD vulnerability *open to attack* vulnerabilities
VLNRBLT vulnerability *open to attack* vulnerabilities
VLNRR vulnerary *healing*
VLNS evilness *badness*
VLNS valance *drapery*
VLNS valence *chemistry*
VLNS vileness *base, foul*
VLNS villainess *evil one (f)*
VLNS villainous *(adj) evil*
VLNS violence *force*
VLNST valanced *draped*
VLNST violinist *musician*
VLNT valiant *heroic*
VLNT violent *forceful*
VLNT volant *flying, quick*
VLNT volante *music*
VLNTL violently *forceful*

VLNTN valentine *sweetheart*
VLNTR voluntary *(n) music, chooser (adj) free choice, no pay* voluntaries
VLNTR volunteer *free choice, no pay*
VLNTRL voluntarily *free choice, no pay*
VLNTRSDK voluntaristic *free choice, no pay*
VLNTRST voluntarist *free choice, no pay*
VLNTRSTK voluntaristic *free choice, no pay*
VLNTRZM voluntarism *free choice, no pay*
VLNTRZM volunteerism *free work*
VLNTS valance *drapery*
VLNTS valence *chemistry*
VLNTS violence *force*
VLNY valonia *acorns*
VLPCHR voluptuary *luxury* voluptuaries
VLPCHS voluptuous *sexy*
VLPCHSL voluptuously *sexy*
VLPCHSNS voluptuousness *sexy*
VLPCHWR voluptuary *luxury* voluptuaries
VLPCHWS voluptuous *sexy*
VLPCHWSL voluptuously *sexy*
VLPCHWSNS voluptuousness *sexy*
VLPLCHL valpolicella *wine*
VLPLN volplane *glide* volplaned volplaning
VLPN vilipend *ridicule*
VLPN vulpine *foxy*
VLPND vilipend *ridicule*
VLPSHR voluptuary *luxury* voluptuaries
VLPSHS voluptuous *sexy*
VLPSHSL voluptuously *sexy*
VLPSHSNS voluptuousness *sexy*
VLPSHWR voluptuary *luxury* voluptuaries
VLPSHWS voluptuous *sexy*
VLPSHWSL voluptuously *sexy*

Use letters that best describe the sounds you hear and omit the vowels. Use **S** or **K** instead of **C**: to find circle use **SRKL**. Use **J** to find joy, **JM** to find gem and **G** to find go.

VLPSHWSNS voluptuousness *sexy*
VLPTR voluptuary *luxury* voluptuaries
VLPTS voluptuous *sexy*
VLPTSL voluptuously *sexy*
VLPTSNS voluptuousness *sexy*
VLPTWR voluptuary *luxury* voluptuaries
VLPTWS voluptuous *sexy*
VLPTWSL voluptuously *sexy*
VLPTWSNS voluptuousness *sexy*
VLQL vallecula *groove* valleculae
VLQLR vallecular *grooved*
VLR uvular *throat lobe*
VLR valor *bravery* (Br) valour
VLR vealer *calf*
VLR velar *soft palate*
VLR velaria (pl) *awning* velarium
VLR velour *fabric* velours
VLR volar *palm, sole*
VLRM velarium *awning* velaria
VLRN valerian *herb*
VLRS valorous *brave* (Br) valourous
VLRY velaria (pl) *awning* velarium
VLRYM velarium *awning* velaria
VLRYN valerian *herb*
VLRZ valorize *boost* valorized valorizing (Br) valourize
VLRZSHN valorization *boost* (Br) valourization
VLS valise *suitcase*
VLS villous *hairy*
VLS villus *hair* villi
VLSD velocity *speed* velocities
VLSD villosity *hairs* villosities
VLSHN avulsion *separation*
VLSHN evaluation *rating*
VLSHN evolution *development*

VLSHN evulsion *extraction*
VLSHN ovulation *discharge egg*
VLSHN valuation *appraisal*
VLSHN violation *break, rape*
VLSHN volition *will*
VLSHNL valuational (adj) *appraisal* valuationally (adv)
VLSHNL volitional *willful*
VLSHNR evolutionary *development*
VLSHNRL evolutionarily *development*
VLSHNST evolutionist *development*
VLSHNZM evolutionism *development*
VLSHS violaceous *purple*
VLSMDR velocimeter *speed*
VLSMTR velocimeter *speed*
VLSPD velocipede *vehicle*
VLST velocity *speed* velocities
VLST villosity *hairs* villosities
VLST violist *musician*
VLT evaluate *rate* evaluated evaluating
VLT ovulate *discharge egg* ovulated ovulating
VLT valet *servant*
VLT vallate *raised edge*
VLT valuta *foreign exchange*
VLT vault (n) *safe, arch* (v) *leap*
VLT veld (or) veldt *grassland*
VLT velleity *wish* velleities
VLT velouté *sauce*
VLT violate *break, rape* violated violating
VLT violet *color, flower*
VLT volt *movement, electrical unit*
VLT volute *spiral*
VLTD vaulted *arched*
VLTD voluted (or) volute *spiral*
VLTDNR valetudinary *sick one* valetudinaries
VLTDNRN valetudinarian *sick one*
VLTDNRYN valetudinarian

sick one
VLTJ voltage *electricity*
VLTK villatic *rural*
VLTK voltaic *electricity*
VLTL volatile *lively, fickle*
VLTLD volatility *lively, fickle*
VLTLNS volatileness *lively, fickle*
VLTLT volatility *lively, fickle*
VLTLZ volatilize *vaporize* volatilized volatilizing
VLTLZSHN volatilization *vaporize*
VLTMDR voltmeter *circuitry*
VLTMPR volt-ampere *electrical unit*
VLTMTR voltmeter *circuitry*
VLTN vaulting *arched*
VLTN volutin *substance*
VLTNG vaulting *arched*
VLTR evaluator *rater*
VLTR valuator *appraiser*
VLTR vaulter *leaper*
VLTR violator *break, rape*
VLTR Voltaire *writer*
VLTR vulture *bird, predator*
VLTRN vulturine *predatory*
VLTRS vulturous *predatory*
VLTV evaluative *rating*
VLTV violative *break, rape*
VLTV volitive *will*
VLTYK voltaic *electricity*
VLV evolve *develop* evolved evolving
VLV valve *venting device*
VLV vol-au-vent *shell*
VLV volva *fungus*
VLV vulva *sex organs* vulvae
VLVBL evolvable *development*
VLVD velvety *soft*
VLVKS volvox *algae*
VLVL valvula *vent, fold* valvulae
VLVL vulval (or) vulvar *sex organs*
VLVLDS valvulitis *inflammation*
VLVLR valvular *vent, fold*
VLVLS volvulus *twist*
VLVLTS valvulitis *inflammation*

VLVMNT evolvement *development*
VLVN vol-au-vent *shell*
VLVNT vol-au-vent *shell*
VLVR vulvar (or) vulval *sex organs*
VLVT valvate *vented*
VLVT velvet *fabric, soft*
VLVT velvety *soft*
VLVTN velveteen *fabric*
VLVVJNDS vulvovaginitis *inflammation*
VLVVJNTS vulvovaginitis *inflammation*
VLVX volvox *algae*
VLVYL valvula *vent, fold* valvulae
VLVYLDS valvulitis *inflammation*
VLVYLR valvular *vent, fold*
VLVYLS volvulus *twist*
VLVYLTS valvulitis *inflammation*
VLWBL valuable (adj) *worthy* valuably (adv)
VLWDR evaluator *rater*
VLWDR valuator *appraiser*
VLWDV evaluative *rating*
VLWSHN evaluation *rating*
VLWSHN valuation *appraisal*
VLWSHNL valuational (adj) *appraisal* valuationally (adv)
VLWT evaluate *rate* evaluated evaluating
VLWTR evaluator *rater*
VLWTR valuator *appraiser*
VLWTV evaluative *rating*
VLY value (v) *rate, prize* valued valuing
VLY value (n) *worth, tint*
VLYBL valuable (adj) *worthy* valuably (adv)
VLYBL voluble (adj) *talkative* volubly (adv)
VLYBLD volubility *talkative*
VLYBLNS volubleness *talkative*
VLYBLT volubility *talkative*
VLYD valued *worthy*
VLYD velleity *wish* velleities
VLYDR evaluator *rater*

VLYDR valuator *appraiser*
VLYDV evaluative *rating*
VLYLS valueless *no worth*
VLYM Valium (trademark) *drug*
VLYM volume *bulk, book*
VLYMDR volumeter *bulk*
VLYMTR volumeter *bulk*
VLYMTRK volumetric *bulk*
VLYMTRKL volumetrically *bulk*
VLYNT valiant *heroic*
VLYSHN evaluation *rating*
VLYSHN evolution *development*
VLYSHN valuation *appraisal*
VLYSHNL valuational (adj) *appraisal* valuationally (adv)
VLYSHNR evolutionary *development*
VLYSHNRL evolutionarily *development*
VLYSHNST evolutionist *development*
VLYSHNZM evolutionism *development*
VLYT evaluate *rate* evaluated evaluating
VLYT velleity *wish* velleities
VLYTN volutin *substance*
VLYTR evaluator *rater*
VLYTR valuator *appraiser*
VLYTV evaluative *rating*
VLYWBL valuable (adj) *worthy* valuably (adv)
VLYWDR evaluator *rater*
VLYWDR valuator *appraiser*
VLYWDV evaluative *rating*
VLYWSHN evaluation *rating*
VLYWSHN valuation *appraisal*
VLYWSHNL valuational (adj) *appraisal* valuationally (adv)
VLYWT evaluate *rate* evaluated evaluating
VLYWTR evaluator *rater*
VLYWTR valuator *appraiser*
VLYWTV evaluative *rating*
VLZ vowelize *indicate sounds* vowelized vowelizing

VM ovum *egg* ova
VM vim *energy*
VMDR vomiter *disgorger*
VMDS vomitus *disgorged matter*
VMNS vehemence *strength*
VMNT vehement *strong*
VMNTL vehemently *strongly*
VMNTS vehemence *strength*
VMP vamp (n) *seducer, shoe, music* (v) *seduce, invent, patch*
VMPR vampire *blood sucker*
VMPRSH vampirish *blood sucker*
VMPRZM vampirism *blood sucker*
VMPSH vampish *alluring*
VMRNR weimaraner *dog*
VMS vamoose *depart* vamoosed vamoosing
VMSN viomycin *antibiotic*
VMT vomit *disgorge*
VMTR vomiter *disgorger*
VMTR vomitory *entrance* vomitories
VMTS vomitus *disgorged matter*
VN avenue *street*
VN avian *bird*
VN even (v) *level, steady* evened evening
VN even (adj) *level, steady* (adv) *exactly, quite, intensive**
VN oven *cook*
VN ovine *sheep*
VN vain *futile, conceited*
VN van (v) *transport* vanned vanning
VN van (n) *vehicle*
VN vane *blade, feather*
VN vaunty *proud*
VN vein *blood, streak*
VN veiny *streaked*
VN vend *sell*
VN venue *location*
VN Vienna *city*
VN vina *music*
VN vine (n) *plant*
VN vine (v) *twine* vined vining

Use letters that best describe the sounds you hear and omit the vowels. Use **S** or **K** instead of **C**: to find circle use **SRKL**. Use **J** to find joy, **JM** to find gem and **G** to find go.

VN vino *wine* vinos
VN viny *with vines* vinier viniest
VNBRD ovenbird *bird*
VNCHL eventual (adj) ultimate eventually (adv)
VNCHLD eventuality *possibility* eventualities
VNCHLT eventuality *possibility* eventualities
VNCHR venture *risk* ventured venturing
VNCHRR venturer *risk*
VNCHRS venturous *risky*
VNCHRSL venturously *risky*
VNCHRSM venturesome *risky*
VNCHRSML venturesomely *risky*
VNCHRSMNS venturesomeness *risky*
VNCHRSNS venturousness *risky*
VNCHT eventuate *result* eventuated eventuating
VNCHWL eventual (adj) ultimate eventually (adv)
VNCHWLD eventuality *possibility* eventualities
VNCHWLT eventuality *possibility* eventualities
VNCHWT eventuate *result* eventuated eventuating
VND vanity *conceit, futility* vanities
VND vaunted *praised*
VND veined *streaked*
VND vend *sell*
VND vendee *buyer*
VND vendue *auction*
VND viand *food*
VNDD vendetta *feud*
VNDK Vandyke *collar, beard*
VNDKBL vindicable *justify, avenge*
VNDKDR vindicator *defender*
VNDKDV vindictive *spiteful*
VNDKDVL vindictively *spiteful*
VNDKDVNS vindictiveness *spiteful*
VNDKSHN vindication

defense
VNDKT vindicate *justify, avenge* vindicated vindicating
VNDKTR vindicator *defender*
VNDKTR vindicatory *punishing*
VNDKTV vindictive *spiteful*
VNDKTVL vindictively *spiteful*
VNDKTVNS vindictiveness *spiteful*
VNDL vandal *destroyer*
VNDL vindaloo *food*
VNDLSDK vandalistic *destruction*
VNDLSTK vandalistic *destruction*
VNDLZ vandalize *destroy* vandalized vandalizing (Br) vandalise
VNDLZM vandalism *destruction*
VNDM vanadium *element*
VNDR vendor *seller*
VNDRKND wunderkind *smart child* wunderkinder
VNDRKNDR wunderkinder (pl) *smart child* wunderkint
VNDRKNT wunderkind *smart child* wunderkinder
VNDT vanadate *salt*
VNDT vendetta *feud*
VNDY vendue *auction*
VNDYM vanadium *element*
VNF vinify *make wine* vinified vinifying vinifies
VNFK ventifact *stone*
VNFKSHN vinification *make wine*
VNFKT ventifact *stone*
VNFR vinifera *grapes*
VNG van Gogh *artist*
VNG viewing *watching*
VNGF van Gogh *artist*
VNGK van Gogh *artist*
VNGK vinca *plant*
VNGKL vincula (pl) *link* vinculum
VNGKLM vinculum *link* vinculums (or) vincula
VNGKLR avuncular *uncle*

VNGKWSH vanquish *conquer*
VNGKWSHBL vanquishable *conquer*
VNGKWSHR vanquisher *conqueror*
VNGKYL vincula (pl) *link* vinculum
VNGKYLM vinculum *link* vinculums (or) vincula
VNGKYLR avuncular *uncle*
VNGKYLRD avuncularity *uncle*
VNGKYLRT avuncularity *uncle*
VNGLR vainglory *vanity*
VNGLRS vainglorious *boastful*
VNGLRYS vainglorious *boastful*
VNGQL vincula (pl) *link* vinculum
VNGQLM vinculum *link* vinculums (or) vincula
VNGQLR avuncular *uncle*
VNGQLRD avuncularity *uncle*
VNGQLRT avuncularity *uncle*
VNGQSH vanquish *conquer*
VNGQSHBL vanquishable *conquer*
VNGQSHR vanquisher *conqueror*
VNGR vinegar *sour liquid*
VNGR vinegary *sour*
VNGRD avant-garde *trendsetters*
VNGRD vanguard *forefront*
VNGRF venography *vein*
VNGRSH vinegarish *sour*
VNGRT vinaigrette *sauce*
VNHNDD evenhanded *fair*
VNJ avenge *pay back* avenged avenging
VNJ vantage *superiority*
VNJ vintage (n) *wine season* (adj) classic
VNJFL vengeful (adj) *revenge* vengefully (adv)
VNJFLNS vengefulness *revenge*

Letters aren't doubled for single sounds: to find alley use **L** not **LL**. Use **Y** and **W** as hard sounds only: to find yellow use **YL**. (Br)=British spelling or usage. * See dictionary.

VNJLKL evangelical (adj)
fundamentalist
evangelically (adv)
VNJLSDK evangelistic
religious zeal
VNJLSDKL evangelistically
religious zeal
VNJLST evangelist *preacher*
VNJLSTK evangelistic
religious zeal
VNJLSTKL evangelistically
religious zeal
VNJLZ evangelize *convert,*
preach evangelized
evangelizing
VNJLZM evangelism
religious zeal
VNJLZSHN evangelization
convert, preach
VNJNS vengeance *revenge*
VNJNTS vengeance *revenge*
VNJR avenger *punisher*
VNK V-neck *collar*
VNK vinca *plant*
VNKK van Gogh *artist*
VNKL vincula (pl) *link*
vinculum
VNKLCHR viniculture
winemaking
VNKLM vinculum *link*
vinculums (or) vincula
VNKLR avuncular *uncle*
VNKLR vernacular
expression
VNKLRD avuncularity *uncle*
VNKLRT avuncularity *uncle*
VNKLRZM vernacularism
idiom
VNKLTR viniculture
winemaking
VNKS avionics *space vehicles*
VNKV vena cava *heart*
venae cavae
VNKVR Vancouver *city*
VNKWSH vanquish *conquer*
VNKWSHBL vanquishable
conquer
VNKWSHR vanquisher
conqueror
VNKYL vincula (pl) *link*
vinculum
VNKYLM vinculum *link*

vinculums (or) vincula
VNKYLR avuncular *uncle*
VNKYLR vernacular
expression
VNKYLRD avuncularity
uncle
VNKYLRT avuncularity
uncle
VNKYLRZM vernacularism
idiom
VNL evenly *level*
VNL vainly *futile, conceited*
VNL vanilla *flavor bean*
VNL venal (adj) *corrupt*
venally (adv)
VNL venial (adj) *easily*
excused venially (adv)
VNL venule *vein*
VNL vinyl *plastic*
VNLD venality *corruption*
VNLDR ventilator *air out*
VNLN vanillin *flavor*
VNLNS venialness *easily*
excused
VNLSHN ventilation *air out*
VNLT veinlet *small vein*
VNLT venality *corruption*
VNLT ventilate *air out*
ventilated ventilating
VNLTR ventilator *air out*
VNM venom *poison*
VNMRNR weimaraner *dog*
VNMS venomous *poison,*
spite
VNMSL venomously *poison,*
spite
VNMSNS venomousness
poison, spite
VNN evening *dusk*
VNNG evening *dusk*
VNNG veining *pattern*
VNNGL vauntingly *praise*
VNNL vauntingly *praise*
VNPL vanpool *commute*
VNPLNG vanpooling
commute
VNPRF ovenproof *baking*
VNQL vincula (pl) *link*
vinculum
VNQLM vinculum *link*
vinculums (or) vincula
VNQLR avuncular *uncle*

VNQLR vernacular
expression
VNQLRD avuncularity *uncle*
VNQLRT avuncularity *uncle*
VNQLRZM vernacularism
idiom
VNQSH vanquish *conquer*
VNQSHBL vanquishable
conquer
VNQSHR vanquisher
conqueror
VNR vaunter *praiser*
VNR veneer *thin outer layer*
VNR venery *game*
VNR vinery *vine area* vineries
VNR vinier *more vines*
VNRBL venerable *old, sacred*
VNRBLD venerability *old,*
sacred
VNRBLNS venerableness
old, sacred
VNRBLT venerability *old,*
sacred
VNRDR venerator *respect*
VNRL venereal *disease*
VNRN vigneron *winegrower*
VNRNG veneering *thin outer*
layer
VNRSHN veneration *respect*
VNRT venerate *revere*
venerated venerating
VNRTR venerator *respect*
VNRYL venereal *disease*
VNS evanesce *vanish*
evanesced evanescing
VNS evenness *level*
VNS evince *show* evinced
evincing
VNS vainness *futile,*
conceited
VNS Venice *city*
VNS venous *vein*
VNS Venus *goddess, planet*
VNS vinous *wine*
VNSBL evincible *show*
VNSBL vincible *defeat*
VNSD vinosity *wine*
vinosities
VNSH vanish *disappear*
vanished vanishes
VNSHN venation *veins*
VNSHN venetian *(often*

capitalized) of Venice
VNSHN Venusian *of Venus*
VNSHR vanisher *disappear*
VNSHR venture *risk*
ventured venturing
VNSHRR venturer *risk*
VNSHRS venturous *risky*
VNSHRSL venturously *risky*
VNSHRSM venturesome
risky
VNSHRSML venturesomely
risky
VNSHRSMNS
venturesomeness *risky*
VNSHRSNS venturousness
risky
VNSHS vinaceous *wine*
VNSKSHN venesection
bloodletting
VNSL venously *vein*
VNSL vinously *wine*
VNSN venison *deer*
VNSNG evensong *prayer*
VNSNS evanescence
vanishing
VNSNT evanescent
vanishing
VNSNTS evanescence
vanishing
VNST viniest *vines*
VNST vinosity *wine*
vinosities
VNT event *occurrence*
VNT vanity *conceit, futility*
vanities
VNT vaunt *brag*
VNT vaunty *proud*
VNT vent *outlet*
VNT vignette *(v) describe*
vignetted vignetting
VNT vignette *(n) scene*
VNTD eventide *evening*
VNTD vaunted *praised*
VNTFK ventifact *stone*
VNTFKT ventifact *stone*
VNTFL eventful (adj) *busy*
eventfully (adv)
VNTFLNS eventfulness *busy*
VNTGRD avant-garde *trend-setters*
VNTJ vantage *superiority*
VNTJ ventage *opening*

VNTJ vintage *(n) wine season*
(adj) classic
VNTL eventual (adj) *ultimate*
eventually (adv)
VNTLD eventuality
possibility eventualities
VNTLDR ventilator *air out*
VNTLSHN ventilation *air out*
VNTLT eventuality *possibility*
eventualities
VNTLT ventilate *air out*
ventilated ventilating
VNTLTR ventilator *air out*
VNTNGL vauntingly *praise*
VNTNL vauntingly *praise*
VNTNR vintner *wine seller*
VNTR vaunter *praiser*
VNTR venter *offspring*
VNTR venture *risk* ventured
venturing
VNTR venturi *tube*
VNTRKL ventricle *cavity,*
heart
VNTRKL ventriculi (pl)
stomach ventriculus
VNTRKLR ventricular *cavity,*
heart
VNTRKLS ventriculus
stomach ventriculi
VNTRKS ventricose *swollen*
VNTRKYL ventriculi (pl)
stomach ventriculus
VNTRKYLR ventricular
cavity, heart
VNTRKYLS ventriculus
stomach
VNTRL ventral (adj) *belly*
ventrally (adv)
VNTRLDRL ventrolateral
side
VNTRLKL ventriloquial (adj)
throw voice ventriloquially
(adv)
VNTRLKW ventriloquy
throw voice
VNTRLKWL ventriloquial
(adj) *throw voice*
ventriloquially (adv)
VNTRLKWST ventriloquist
throw voice
VNTRLKWYL ventriloquial
(adj) *throw voice*

ventriloquially (adv)
VNTRLKWZ ventriloquize
throw voice ventriloquized
ventriloquizing
VNTRLKWZM
ventriloquism *throw voice*
VNTRLQ ventriloquy *throw*
voice
VNTRLQL ventriloquial (adj)
throw voice ventriloquially
(adv)
VNTRLQST ventriloquist
throw voice
VNTRLQYL ventriloquial
(adj) *throw voice*
ventriloquially (adv)
VNTRLQZ ventriloquize
throw voice ventriloquized
ventriloquizing
VNTRLQZM ventriloquism
throw voice
VNTRLTRL ventrolateral *side*
VNTRMDL ventromedial
side
VNTRMDYL ventromedial
side
VNTRQL ventriculi (pl)
stomach ventriculus
VNTRQLR ventricular *cavity,*
heart
VNTRQLS ventriculus
stomach
VNTRR venturer *risk*
VNTRS venturous *risky*
VNTRSL venturously *risky*
VNTRSM venturesome *risky*
VNTRSML venturesomely
risky
VNTRSMNS
venturesomeness *risky*
VNTRSNS venturousness
risky
VNTS evince *show* evinced
evincing
VNTSBL evincible *show*
VNTSBL vincible *defeat*
VNTSHR venture *risk*
ventured venturing
VNTSHRR venturer *risk*
VNTSHRS venturous *risky*
VNTSHRSL venturously
risky

Letters aren't doubled for single sounds: to find alley use **L** not **LL**. Use **Y** and **W** as hard
sounds only: to find yellow use **YL**. (Br)=British spelling or usage. * See dictionary.

VNTSHRSM venturesome
risky
VNTSHRSML
venturesomely *risky*
VNTSHRSMNS
venturesomeness *risky*
VNTSHRSNS
venturousness *risky*
VNTT eventuate *result*
eventuated eventuating
VNTWL eventual (adj)
ultimate eventually (adv)
VNTWLD eventuality
possibility eventualities
VNTWLT eventuality
possibility eventualities
VNTWT eventuate *result*
eventuated eventuating
VNTYR venture *risk*
ventured venturing
VNX avionics *space vehicles*
VNY avenue *street*
VNY venue *location*
VNYDR vignetter *describer*
VNYL venial (adj) *easily*
excused venially (adv)
VNYL venule *vein*
VNYLNS venialness *easily*
excused
VNYR vinier *more vines*
VNYRD vineyard *grapevines*
VNYRDST vineyardist
grapevines
VNYRN vigneron *winegrower*
VNYSHN Venusian *of Venus*
VNYST viniest *vines*
VNYT vignette *(v) describe*
vignetted vignetting
VNYT vignette *(n) scene*
VNYTR vignetter *describer*
VNYZHN Venusian *of Venus*
VNZHN Venusian *of Venus*
VNZL Venezuela *country*
VNZWL Venezuela *country*
VP veep *(slang) vice president*
VP VIP *(abbr) very important*
person VIPs
VPD vapid *dull*
VPDD vapidity *dullness*
vapidities
VPDL vapidly *dull*
VPDNS vapidness *dullness*

VPDT vapidity *dullness*
vapidities
VPNT viewpoint *opinion*
VPR vapor *(n) gas (v) emit,*
brag
(Br) vapour
VPR viper *snake*
VPRD vaporetto *boat*
vaporetti
VPRDD evaporated
disappeared
VPRDK evaporitic *rock*
VPRDR evaporator *disappear*
VPRDV evaporative
disappearing
VPRLK vapor lock *fuel*
(Br) vapour lock
VPRN viperine *deadly*
VPRNG vaporing *bragging*
(Br) vapouring
VPRR vaporer *emit, brag*
(Br) vapourer
VPRS oviparous *eggs*
VPRS vaporous *misty,*
gaseous
VPRS viperous *deadly*
VPRSH vaporish *gassy,*
nervous
(Br) vapourish
VPRSH viperish *deadly*
VPRSHN evaporation
disappearance
VPRSL vaporously *misty,*
gaseous
VPRSL viperously *deadly*
VPRSNS vaporousness
misty, gaseous
VPRT evaporate *disappear*
evaporated evaporating
VPRT evaporite *rock*
VPRT vaporetto *boat*
vaporetti
VPRTD evaporated
disappeared
VPRTK evaporitic *rock*
VPRTR evaporator *disappear*
VPRTV evaporative
disappearing
VPRWR vaporware *computer*
VPRZ vaporize *become mist*
vaporized vaporizing
(Br) vaporise

VPRZBL vaporizable *mist*
(Br) vaporisable
VPRZR vaporizer *atomizer*
(Br) vaporiser
VPRZSHN vaporization *mist*
(Br) vaporisation
VPZDR ovipositor *lay eggs*
VPZSHN oviposition *lay*
eggs
VPZSHNL ovipositional *lay*
eggs
VPZT oviposit *lay eggs*
VPZTR ovipositor *lay eggs*
VQ evacuee *person removed*
VQ vacua (pl) *emptiness*
vacuum
VQD vacuity *emptiness*
vacuities
VQDV evacuative *empty,*
vacated
VQL vacuole *cavity*
VQLR vacuolar *cavity*
VQLSHN vacuolation *cavity*
VQM vacuum *emptiness,*
cleaner vacuums (or)
vacua
VQMPKD vacuum-packed
remove air
VQMPKT vacuum-packed
remove air
VQN vicuña (or) vicuna
animal
VQNY vicuña (or) vicuna
animal
VQS vacuous *empty*
VQSHN evacuation *empty,*
vacated
VQSL vacuously *empty*
VQSNS vacuousness *empty*
VQT evacuate *empty, vacate*
evacuated evacuating
VQT vacuity *emptiness*
vacuities
VQTV evacuative *empty,*
vacated
VQW evacuee *person*
removed
VQW vacua (pl) *emptiness*
vacuum
VQWD vacuity *emptiness*
vacuities
VQWDV evacuative *empty,*

Use letters that best describe the sounds you hear and omit the vowels. Use **S** or **K** instead of **C**: to find circle use **SRKL**. Use **J** to find joy, **JM** to find gem and **G** to find go.

vacated
VQWL vacuole *cavity*
VQWLR vacuolar *cavity*
VQWLSHN vacuolation *cavity*
VQWS vacuous *empty*
VQWSHN evacuation *empty, vacated*
VQWSL vacuously *empty*
VQWSNS vacuousness *empty*
VQWT evacuate *empty, vacate* evacuated evacuating
VQWT vacuity *emptiness* vacuities
VQWTV evacuative *empty, vacated*
VR aver *affirm* averred averring
VR aviary *birds* aviaries
VR ever *always*
VR every *each*
VR ivory *tusk* ivories
VR oeuvre *body of work* oeuvres
VR ovary *female gland* ovaries
VR over *above, through, across**
VR overawe *stun* overawed overawing
VR vara *33.33 inches*
VR varia *miscellany*
VR vary *differ* varied varies
VR veer *turn*
VR veery *bird* veeries
VR very *(adv) truly, exceedingly*
VR very *(adj) true, absolute* verier veriest
VR vireo *bird* vireos
VRB overbuy *purchase more* overbought overbuying
VRB verb *word*
VRBD everybody *all persons*
VRBD overbid *offer more* overbid overbidding
VRBDM verbatim *word for word*
VRBDN verboten *forbidden*
VRBJ verbiage *words*

VRBK overbake *cook more*
VRBK overbook *reserve too many*
VRBL overbill *charge too much*
VRBL variable *(adj) changing* variably *(adv)*
VRBL verbal *(adj) speech* verbally *(adv)*
VRBLD overbuild *construction* overbuilt overbuilding
VRBLD variability *change*
VRBLMNG everblooming *flowering*
VRBLN overblown *inflated*
VRBLNS overbalance *tilt* overbalanced overbalancing
VRBLNS variableness *change*
VRBLNTS overbalance *tilt* overbalanced overbalancing
VRBLS overblouse *clothing*
VRBLST verbalist *explainer*
VRBLT overbuilt *(v-past) overbuild*
VRBLT variability *change*
VRBLZ verbalize *speak* verbalized verbalizing
VRBLZM verbalism *wording*
VRBLZR verbalizer *speaker*
VRBLZSHN verbalization *speech*
VRBN verbena *plant*
VRBNDNS overabundance *too much*
VRBNDNT overabundant *too much*
VRBNDNTS overabundance *too much*
VRBR overbear *domineer* overbore overborne overbearing
VRBRD overboard *in the water, to extremes*
VRBRDN overburden *weigh down, rock cover*
VRBRN overbearing *domineering*
VRBRNG overbearing

domineering
VRBS verbose *wordy*
VRBSD verbosity *wordy*
VRBSL verbosely *wordy*
VRBSNS verboseness *wordy*
VRBST verbosity *wordy*
VRBT overbite *teeth*
VRBT overbought *(v-past) overbuy*
VRBTM verbatim *word for word*
VRBTN verboten *forbidden*
VRBYJ verbiage *words*
VRC oversee *supervise* oversaw overseen overseeing
VRCH overreach *reach beyond*
VRCH virtue *morality*
VRCHL virtual *(adj) implied* virtually *(adv)*
VRCHLD virtuality *essence* virtualities
VRCHLS virtueless *no merit*
VRCHLT virtuality *essence* virtualities
VRCHR overture *proposal, prelude*
VRCHRJ overcharge *money* overcharged overcharging
VRCHS virtuosa *skilled one (f)* virtuosas
VRCHS virtuoso *skilled one (m)* virtuosos *(or)* virtuosi
VRCHS virtuous *sinless*
VRCHSD virtuosity *skill* virtuosities
VRCHSL virtuously *sinlessly*
VRCHSNS virtuousness *without sin*
VRCHST virtuosity *skill* virtuosities
VRCHV overachieve *exceed standards* overachieved overachieving
VRCHVMNT overachievement *exceed standards*
VRCHVR overachiever *exceed standards*

Letters aren't doubled for single sounds: to find alley use **L** not **LL**. Use **Y** and **W** as hard sounds only: to find yellow use **YL**. (Br)=British spelling or usage. * See dictionary.

VRCHWL virtual (adj) *implied* virtually (adv)
VRCHWLD virtuality *essence* virtualities
VRCHWLT virtuality *essence* virtualities
VRCHWS virtuosa *skilled one (f)* virtuosas
VRCHWS virtuoso *skilled one (m)* virtuosos (or) virtuosi
VRCHWS virtuous *sinless*
VRCHWSD virtuosity *skill* virtuosities
VRCHWSL virtuously *sinlessly*
VRCHWSNS virtuousness *without sin*
VRCHWST virtuosity *skill* virtuosities
VRCR overseer *supervisor*
VRCYR overseer *supervisor*
VRCZ overseas *abroad*
VRCZ varices (pl) *vein* varix
VRD everyday *commonplace, daily*
VRD overdo *do in excess* overdid overdone overdoing overdoes
VRD overdue *late*
VRD override *(v) trample, annul, overlap* overrode overriding overridden
VRD override *(n) commission*
VRD varied *diverse*
VRD varied *different*
VRD variety *diversity* varieties
VRD verity *truth* verities
VRD virid *green*
VRD viroid *disease*
VRDB overdub *sound*
VRDBL veritable (adj) *in fact* veritably (adv)
VRDBLNS veritableness *in fact*
VRDBR vertebra *spine* vertebrae (or) vertebras
VRDBRL vertebral *spine*
VRDBRT vertebrate *spine*
VRDCZ vertices (pl) *summit* vertex

VRDCZ vortices (pl) *whirlpool* vortex
VRDD overrated *too highly praised*
VRDD viridity *green*
VRDG vertigo *dizziness* vertigoes (or) vertigos
VRDGR verdigris *pigment*
VRDGRS verdigris *pigment*
VRDJKDD overeducated *schooling*
VRDJKTD overeducated *schooling*
VRDK verdict *judgment*
VRDKDD overeducated *schooling*
VRDKL veridical (adj) *truthful* veridically (adv)
VRDKL vertical (adj) *upright* vertically (adv)
VRDKL vortical (adj) *swirling* vortically (adv)
VRDKLD veridicality *truth*
VRDKLD verticality *upright*
VRDKLNS verticalness *upright*
VRDKLT veridicality *truth*
VRDKLT verticality *upright*
VRDKT verdict *judgment*
VRDKTD overeducated *schooling*
VRDL varietal *assortment*
VRDLZ overutilize *wear out* overutilized overutilizing (Br) overutilise
VRDLZSHN overutilization *wear out* (Br) overutilisation
VRDN overdone *(v-past)* overdo
VRDN verdin *bird*
VRDN viridian *green*
VRDNC verdancy *green*
VRDNS verdancy *green*
VRDNT verdant *green*
VRDNTC verdancy *green*
VRDNTL verdantly *green*
VRDNTS verdancy *green*
VRDPZ avoirdupois *weight*
VRDR overdraw *remove too much* overdrew overdrawn overdrawing

VRDR overeater *eat too much*
VRDR verdure *green*
VRDRF overdraft *check*
VRDRFT overdraft *check*
VRDRMDK overdramatic *emotional*
VRDRMTK overdramatic *emotional*
VRDRMTZ overdramatize *emote* overdramatized overdramatizing (Br) overdramatise
VRDRS overdress *clothing*
VRDRV overdrive *transmission*
VRDS overdose *drug* overdosed overdosing
VRDSL verticil *circle*
VRDSL vorticella *organism* vorticellae (or) vorticellas
VRDSLT verticillate *circled*
VRDSNT viridescent *greenish*
VRDSZ vertices (pl) *summit* vertex
VRDSZ vortices (pl) *whirlpool* vortex
VRDT viridity *green*
VRDVLP overdevelop *film*
VRDY overdue *late*
VRDYKDD overeducated *schooling*
VRDYKTD overeducated *schooling*
VRDYN viridian *green*
VRDYR verdure *green*
VRF verify *confirm* verified verifying verifies
VRFBL verifiable *prove*
VRFKSHN verification *proof*
VRFL overflow *spill*
VRFL overfly *airplane* overflies overflew overflown overflying
VRFLT overflight *aircraft*
VRFMLR overfamiliar *too chummy*
VRFMLRD overfamiliarity *too chummy*
VRFMLRT overfamiliarity *too chummy*
VRFMLYR overfamiliar *too*

Use letters that best describe the sounds you hear and omit the vowels. Use **S** or **K** instead of **C**: to find circle use **SRKL**. Use **J** to find joy, **JM** to find gem and **G** to find go.

chummy
VRFMLYRD overfamiliarity
too chummy
VRFMLYRT overfamiliarity
too chummy
VRFMYR overfamiliar *too
chummy*
VRFMYRD overfamiliarity
too chummy
VRFMYRT overfamiliarity
too chummy
VRFR verifier *confirmer*
VRFRDLZ overfertilize *crops*
overfertilized
overfertilizing
VRFRDLZSHN
overfertilization *crops*
VRFRTLZ overfertilize *crops*
overfertilized
overfertilizing
VRFRTLZSHN
overfertilization *crops*
VRFTG overfatigue *tired*
VRFYBL verifiable *prove*
VRFYR verifier *confirmer*
VRG virago *strong woman*
viragoes (or) viragos
VRG virga *wisp*
VRG Virgo *zodiac sign*
VRGDD variegated *many
colors*
VRGL virgule *diagonal*
VRGLDZ Everglades *swamp*
VRGLZ overglaze *apply
coating*
VRGR overeager *anxious*
VRGR overgrow *grow
excessively* overgrew
overgrown overgrowing
VRGRMNT overgarment
clothing
VRGRN evergreen *perennial*
VRGRN overgrown *weedy*
VRGRZ overgraze *eat grass*
VRGSHN variegation *many
colors*
VRGT variegate *dapple*
variegated variegating
VRGT virgate *(adj) rod-
shaped (n) land*
VRGTD variegated *many
colors*

VRGYL virgule *diagonal*
VRGZRSHN overexertion
work
VRGZRT overexert *work*
VRHD overhead *aloft*
VRHDD overheated *hot*
VRHL overhaul *repair*
VRHN overhand *stroke, stitch*
VRHND overhand *stroke,
stitch*
VRHNDD overhanded *stroke*
VRHNG overhang *project*
overhung overhanging
VRHR overhear *listen*
overheard overhearing
VRHRD overheard *listen*
VRHT overheat *hot*
VRHTD overheated *hot*
VRHWLM overwhelm *upset,
overpower*
VRHWLMN overwhelming
extreme
VRHWLMNG overwhelming
extreme
VRHWM overwhelm *upset,
overpower*
VRHWMN overwhelming
extreme
VRHWMNG overwhelming
extreme
VRHWR everywhere *all
places*
VRJ average *normal*
averaged averaging
VRJ overage *(n) surplus*
VRJ overage *(adj) too old*
VRJ verge *(v) border, sink*
verged verging
VRJ verge *brink, rod, (Br)
road*
VRJD overjoyed *happy*
VRJKDD overeducated
schooling
VRJKTD overeducated
schooling
VRJN virgin *untouched*
VRJN Virginia *US State*
VRJND virginity *maidenhood*
virginities
VRJNL virginal *(n) spinet*
VRJNL virginal (adj) *pure*
virginally (adv)

VRJNLNDZ Virgin Islands
land mass
VRJNLNZ Virgin Islands
land mass
VRJNRLZ overgeneralize
make vague
overgeneralized
overgeneralizing
(Br) overgeneralise
VRJNS viraginous *strong
woman*
VRJNT virginity *maidenhood*
virginities
VRJNY Virginia *US State*
VRJR verdure *green*
VRJR verger *(Br) attendant*
VRJS verjuice *acidity*
VRK verruca *wart* verrucae
VRKCL varicocele *veins*
(Br) varicoloured
VRKDV overactive *too busy*
VRKK overcook *food*
VRKL overcall *card bid*
VRKL overkill *too much*
VRKLRD varicolored *many
colors*
(Br) varicoloured
VRKM overcome *conquer*
overcame overcoming
VRKMPLKT overcomplicate
difficulty
VRKMPNSSHN
overcompensation
imbalance
VRKMPNST
overcompensate
imbalance
overcompensated
overcompensating
VRKMRSHLZ
overcommercialize
advertising
overcommercialized
overcommercializing
(Br) overcommercialise
VRKMT overcommit *oblige*
VRKNFDNS overconfidence
arrogance
VRKNFDNT overconfident
arrogant
VRKNFDNTS
overconfidence *arrogance*

Letters aren't doubled for single sounds: to find alley use **L** not **LL**. Use **Y** and **W** as hard
sounds only: to find yellow use **YL**. (Br)=British spelling or usage. * See dictionary.

VRKNSRND overconcerned *caring*
VRKPDLZ overcapitalize *excess money* overcapitalized overcapitalizing (Br) overcapitalise
VRKPDLZSHN overcapitalization *excess money* (Br) overcapitalisation
VRKPSD overcapacity *production*
VRKPST overcapacity *production*
VRKPTLZ overcapitalize *excess money* overcapitalized overcapitalizing (Br) overcapitalise
VRKPTLZSHN overcapitalization *excess money* (Br) overcapitalisation
VRKRD overcrowd *too many*
VRKRKT overcorrect *steering*
VRKRZ Veracruz *Mexican state, city*
VRKS varicose *swollen*
VRKS varix *(n) swollen vein* varices
VRKS verrucose *warty*
VRKSD varicosity *swollen* varicosities
VRKSHN overreaction *exaggerated response*
VRKSHS overcautious *careful*
VRKSL varicocele *veins* (Br) varicoloured
VRKSPLN overexplain *give reasons*
VRKSPND overexpand *increase*
VRKSPNSHN overexpansion *increase*
VRKSPNTSHN overexpansion *increase*
VRKSPSHR overexposure *film*
VRKSPZ overexpose *film*

overexposed overexposing
VRKSPZHR overexposure *film*
VRKST Ivory Coast *region*
VRKST overcast *weather* overcast overcasting
VRKST overexcite *thrill* overexcited overexciting
VRKST varicosity *swollen* varicosities
VRKSTN overextend *expand, commit*
VRKSTNCHN overextension *expand, commit*
VRKSTND overextend *expand, commit*
VRKSTNSHN overextension *expand, commit*
VRKT overact *emote*
VRKT overcoat *outerwear*
VRKT overreact *exaggerated response*
VRKTV overactive *too busy*
VRKWLFD overqualified *experience*
VRKZRSHN overexertion *work*
VRKZRT overexert *work*
VRL ovariole *egg*
VRL overall *total*
VRL overlay *superimpose* overlaid overlaying
VRL overlie *rest on* overlay overlain overlying
VRL overly *too much*
VRL overrule *reverse* overruled overruling
VRL variola *smallpox*
VRL verily *truly*
VRL viral *(adj) virus* virally *(adv)*
VRL virelay *poem*
VRL virile *(adj) manly* virilely *(adv)*
VRLD overload *excess quantity*
VRLD virility *manliness*
VRLDN overladen *overlap*
VRLFRS viruliferous *infected*
VRLG virology *virus*

VRLG vorlage *skiing*
VRLJ virology *virus*
VRLJK virologic (or) virological *(adj) virus* virologically *(adv)*
VRLJKL virological (or) virologic *(adj) virus* virologically *(adv)*
VRLJST virologist *virus*
VRLK overlook *(v) inspect, ignore (n) view*
VRLN overland *across land*
VRLND overland *across land*
VRLNG overlong *too long*
VRLNS overreliance *dependency*
VRLNS virulence *bitterness* virulency
VRLNT virulent *deadly*
VRLNTL virulently *deadly*
VRLNTS overreliance *dependency*
VRLNTS virulence *bitterness* virulency
VRLP overlap *cover* overlapped overlapping
VRLP overleap *jump* overleaped (or) overleapt overleaping
VRLRD overlord *ruler*
VRLRJ overlarge *big*
VRLS overalls *clothing*
VRLSTN everlasting *eternal*
VRLSTNG everlasting *eternal*
VRLT virility *manliness*
VRLYNS overreliance *dependency*
VRLYNTS overreliance *dependency*
VRLZ overalls *clothing*
VRLZM virilism *male*
VRM viremia *virus*
VRMBSHS overambitious *excessive goals*
VRMCH overmatch *defeat*
VRMCH overmuch *in excess*
VRMCHL vermicelli *pasta*
VRMDKT overmedicate *medicine* overmedicated overmedicating
VRMDR variometer *climb*

VRMFJ vermifuge *kill worms*
VRMFRM vermiform *worm-shaped*
VRMFSZ overemphasize *stress* overemphasized overemphasizing (Br) overemphasise
VRMFYJ vermifuge *kill worms*
VRMK viremic *virus*
VRMKLDD vermiculated (or) vermiculate *worm-eaten*
VRMKLR vermicular *worms*
VRMKLT vermiculate (or) vermiculated *worm-eaten*
VRMKLT vermiculite *mineral*
VRMKLTD vermiculated (or) vermiculate *worm-eaten*
VRMKYLDD vermiculated (or) vermiculate *worm-eaten*
VRMKYLR vermicular *worms*
VRMKYLT vermiculate (or) vermiculated *worm-eaten*
VRMKYLT vermiculite *mineral*
VRMKYLTD vermiculated (or) vermiculate *worm-eaten*
VRML vermeil *silver*
VRMLN vermilion *red*
VRMLYN vermilion *red*
VRMN everyman *(often capitalized) average man*
VRMN vermin *creatures* vermin
VRMNJ overmanage *direct* overmanaged overmanaging
VRMNS verminous *filthy*
VRMNT averment *affirmation*
VRMNT varmint *pest*
VRMNT Vermont *US State*
VRMQLDD vermiculated (or) vermiculate *worm-eaten*
VRMQLR vermicular *worms*
VRMQLT vermiculate (or) vermiculated *worm-eaten*

VRMQLT vermiculite *mineral*
VRMQLTD vermiculated (or) vermiculate *worm-eaten*
VRMR evermore *always*
VRMSD vermicide *kill worms*
VRMSHNL overemotional *sentiment*
VRMTH vermouth *wine*
VRMTR variometer *climb*
VRMY viremia *virus*
VRMYN vermilion *red*
VRN ovarian *egg*
VRN overrun *infest* overran overrunning
VRN virion *virus*
VRND veranda (or) verandah *porch*
VRNDLJ overindulge *spoil, gratify* overindulged overindulging
VRNDLJNS overindulgence *spoil, gratify*
VRNDLJNT overindulgent *spoil, gratify*
VRNDLJNTS overindulgence *spoil, gratify*
VRNFLT overinflate *blow up* overinflated overinflating
VRNFSZ overemphasize *stress* overemphasized overemphasizing (Br) overemphasise
VRNGKSHS overanxious *nervous*
VRNGSHS overanxious *nervous*
VRNK veronica *cloth, speedwell, cape*
VRNKLR vernacular *expression*
VRNKLRZM vernacularism *idiom*
VRNKSHS overanxious *nervous*
VRNKYLR vernacular *expression*
VRNKYLRZM vernacularism *idiom*
VRNL vernal (adj) *youthful* vernally (adv)

VRNLZ vernalize *flower* vernalized vernalizing
VRNLZSHN vernalization *fast flowering*
VRNQLR vernacular *expression*
VRNQLRZM vernacularism *idiom*
VRNR vernier *scale, engine*
VRNS overnice *too kind*
VRNS variance *difference*
VRNSH varnish *gloss* varnishes
VRNSHN vernation *bud leaves*
VRNSHR varnisher *glosser*
VRNSJ vernissage *preview*
VRNSSH vernissage *preview*
VRNSZH vernissage *preview*
VRNT overnight *sudden, all night*
VRNT variant *different*
VRNTS variance *difference*
VRNYR vernier *scale, engine*
VRP overpay *money* overpaid overpaying
VRP overripe *maturity*
VRPKJ overpackage *wrap* overpackaged overpackaging
VRPL overplay *exaggerate*
VRPLS everyplace *all places*
VRPMNT overpayment *money*
VRPPLSHN overpopulation *births*
VRPPLT overpopulate *births* overpopulated overpopulating
VRPPYLSHN overpopulation *births*
VRPPYLT overpopulate *births* overpopulated overpopulating
VRPR overpower *subdue*
VRPRDKSHN overproduction *manufacture*
VRPRDS overproduce *manufacture* overproduced overproducing

VRPRDYS overproduce *manufacture* overproduced overproducing

VRPRN overpowering *overwhelming*

VRPRNG overpowering *overwhelming*

VRPRNT overprint *printing*

VRPRS overprice *money*

VRPRSKRB overprescribe *medication*

VRPRTK overprotect *guard*

VRPRTKDV overprotective *guard*

VRPRTKSHN overprotection *guard*

VRPRTKT overprotect *guard*

VRPRTKTV overprotective *guard*

VRPS overpass *highway* overpasses

VRPSKRB overprescribe *medication*

VRPWR overpower *subdue*

VRPWRN overpowering *overwhelming*

VRPWRNG overpowering *overwhelming*

VRQLFD overqualified *experience*

VRRM overarm *overhand*

VRRM variorum *text*

VRS avarice *greed*

VRS averse *opposed*

VRS overissue *money* overissued overissuing

VRS oversee *supervise* oversaw overseen overseeing

VRS various *several*

VRS varus *knock-kneed*

VRS verrucae (pl) *wart* verruca

VRS Versailles *city*

VRS verse (v) *poetry, study* versed versing

VRS verse (n) *poem, Bible*

VRS verso *page* versos

VRS virus *organism*

VRSBSKRB oversubscribe *sign, support*

oversubscribed oversubscribing

VRSD varsity *team* varsities

VRSD veracity *truth* veracities

VRSD virucide (or) viricide *kill virus*

VRSD voracity *hunger*

VRSDK veristic *everyday*

VRSDL versatile (adj) *adaptable* versatilely (adv)

VRSDL virucidal (or) viricidal *kill virus*

VRSDLNS versatileness *adaptability*

VRSDMSHN overestimation *guess*

VRSDMT overestimate *guess* overestimated overestimating

VRSF versify *write poetry* versified versifying versifies

VRSFKSHN versification *poetry*

VRSFR versifier *poet*

VRSFYR versifier *poet*

VRSH overissue *money* overissued overissuing

VRSH overshoe *boot* overshoes

VRSHD overshadow *outweigh*

VRSHN aversion *dislike*

VRSHN eversion *inside out*

VRSHN variation *difference*

VRSHN version *account*

VRSHNL versional *account*

VRSHP viewership *audience*

VRSHRT overshirt *clothing*

VRSHS avaricious *greedy*

VRSHS veracious *honest*

VRSHS voracious *hungry*

VRSHSL veraciously *honestly*

VRSHSL voraciously *hungry*

VRSHSNS veraciousness *honesty*

VRSHSNS voraciousness *hunger*

VRSHT overshoot *pass* overshot overshooting

VRSKRT overskirt *clothing*

VRSKST oversexed *sex drive*

VRSL aversely *disinclined*

VRSL oversell *sell too much* oversold overselling

VRSL varicella *chicken pox*

VRSL variously *different*

VRSLD oversold *market*

VRSLP oversleep *awaken late* overslept oversleeping

VRSLPT overslept *awaken late*

VRSMLR verisimilar *probable*

VRSMLTD verisimilitude *probability*

VRSMLTDNS verisimilitudinous *probability*

VRSMLTYD verisimilitude *probability*

VRSMLTYDNS verisimilitudinous *probability*

VRSMPLF oversimplify *make too easy* oversimplified oversimplifying oversimplifies

VRSMPLFKSHN oversimplification *make easy*

VRSNS averseness *disinclined*

VRSNS variousness *difference*

VRSNS virescence *green*

VRSNSDV oversensitive *touchy*

VRSNSTV oversensitive *touchy*

VRSNSTVD oversensitivity *touchiness*

VRSNSTVT oversensitivity *touchiness*

VRSNT versant *knowledgeable*

VRSNT virescent *green*

VRSNTS virescence *green*

VRSPL oversupply *goods* oversupplied oversupplying

Use letters that best describe the sounds you hear and omit the vowels. Use **S** or **K** instead of **C**: to find circle use **SRKL**. Use **J** to find joy, **JM** to find gem and **G** to find go.

oversupplies

VRSPND overspend *money* overspent overspending

VRSPRD overspread *put on* overspread overspreading

VRSPSHLZ overspecialize *make specific* overspecialized overspecializing (Br) overspecialise

VRSPSHLZSHN overspecialization *make specific* (Br) overspecialisation

VRSR overseer *supervisor*

VRSS versus *against*

VRSSPSHS oversuspicious *wary*

VRST overset *upset* overset oversetting

VRST oversight *error, care*

VRST overstay *stay too long*

VRST varsity *team* varsities

VRST veracity *truth* veracities

VRST verist *everyday*

VRST voracity *hunger*

VRSTF overstaff *too many people*

VRSTF overstuff *material*

VRSTFT overstuffed *upholstery*

VRSTK overstock *goods*

VRSTK veristic *everyday*

VRSTL versatile (adj) *adaptable* versatilely (adv)

VRSTL virucidal (or) viricidal *kill virus*

VRSTLD versatility *adaptability*

VRSTLNS versatileness *adaptability*

VRSTLT versatility *adaptability*

VRSTMSHN overestimation *guess*

VRSTMT overestimate *guess* overestimated overestimating

VRSTP overstep *transgress* overstepped

overstepping

VRSTR oversteer *drive*

VRSTR varistor *voltage*

VRSTRCH overstretch *reach*

VRSTRNG overstrung *sensitive*

VRSTT overstate *exaggerate* overstated overstating

VRSTTMNT overstatement *exaggeration*

VRSV aversive *avoiding*

VRSWT oversweet *sugary*

VRSXT oversexed *sex drive*

VRSY overissue *money* overissued overissuing

VRSYR overseer *supervisor*

VRSZ overseas *abroad*

VRSZ oversize (or) oversized *too large*

VRSZ varices (pl) *vein* varix

VRSZD oversized (or) oversize *too large*

VRT avert *turn away*

VRT evert *inside out*

VRT overeat *food* overate overeaten overeating

VRT overrate *rank* overrated overrating

VRT overt *in the open*

VRT overwrite *elaborate* overwrote overwriting overwritten

VRT overwrought *strained*

VRT variety *diversity* varieties

VRT verité *realism in filming*

VRT verity *truth* verities

VRT virtu *arts*

VRT virtue *morality*

VRTBL veritable (adj) *in fact* veritably (adv)

VRTBLNS veritableness *in fact*

VRTBR vertebra *spine* vertebrae (or) vertebras

VRTBRL vertebral *spine*

VRTBRT vertebrate *spine*

VRTCZ vertices (pl) *summit* vertex

VRTCZ vortices (pl) *whirlpool* vortex

VRTD overrated *too highly*

praised

VRTG vertigo *dizziness* vertigoes (or) vertigos

VRTHHL over-the-hill *past prime*

VRTHKNR over-the-counter *public selling*

VRTHKNTR over-the-counter *public selling*

VRTHKTR over-the-counter *public selling*

VRTHNG everything *all things*

VRTHR over there *not here*

VRTHR overthrow *upset, defeat* overthrew overthrown overthrowing

VRTHTP over-the-top *gaudy*

VRTJNS vertiginous *dizziness*

VRTJNSL vertiginously *dizziness*

VRTK overtake *pass* overtook overtaking overtaken

VRTK overtalk *babble*

VRTKDV overtalkative *babble*

VRTKL veridical (adj) *truthful* veridically (adv)

VRTKL vertical (adj) *upright* vertically (adv)

VRTKL vortical (adj) *swirling* vortically (adv)

VRTKLD veridicality *truth*

VRTKLD verticality *upright*

VRTKLNS verticalness *upright*

VRTKLT veridicality *truth*

VRTKLT verticality *upright*

VRTKN overtaken *passed*

VRTKS overtax *levy, tire out*

VRTKS vertex *summit* vertices

VRTKS vortex *whirlpool* vortices

VRTKTV overtalkative *babble*

VRTL varietal *assortment*

VRTL virtual (adj) *implied* virtually (adv)

VRTLD virtuality *essence* virtualities

VRTLS virtueless *no merit*

VRTLT virtuality *essence*
virtualities

VRTLZ overutilize *wear out*
overutilized overutilizing
(Br) overutilise

VRTLZSHN overutilization
wear out
(Br) overutilisation

VRTM overtime *extra period*

VRTN overtone *music,*
suggestion

VRTR overeater *eat too much*

VRTR overture *proposal,*
prelude

VRTRN overturn *upset,*
destroy

VRTS virtuosa *skilled one (f)*
virtuosas

VRTS virtuoso *skilled one (m)*
virtuosos (or) virtuosi

VRTS virtuous *sinless*

VRTSD virtuosity *skill*
virtuosities

VRTSL verticil *circle*

VRTSL virtuously *sinlessly*

VRTSL vorticella *organism*
vorticellae (or) vorticellas

VRTSLT verticillate *circled*

VRTSNS virtuousness
without sin

VRTST virtuosity *skill*
virtuosities

VRTSZ vertices (pl) *summit*
vertex

VRTSZ vortices (pl)
whirlpool vortex

VRTWL virtual (adj) *implied*
virtually (adv)

VRTWLD virtuality *essence*
virtualities

VRTWLT virtuality *essence*
virtualities

VRTWS virtuosa *skilled one*
(f) virtuosas

VRTWS virtuoso *skilled one*
(m) virtuosos (or) virtuosi

VRTWS virtuous *sinless*

VRTWSD virtuosity *skill*
virtuosities

VRTWSL virtuously *sinlessly*

VRTWSNS virtuousness

without sin

VRTWST virtuosity *skill*
virtuosities

VRTX overtax *levy, tire out*

VRTX vertex *summit*
vertices

VRTX vortex *whirlpool*
vortices

VRTYR overture *proposal,*
prelude

VRV overview *summary*

VRV varve *layer*

VRV verve *energy*

VRVL overvalue *worth*
overvalued overvaluing

VRVLY overvalue *worth*
overvalued overvaluing

VRVN vervain *plant*

VRVS effervesce *bubble*
effervesced effervescing

VRVSNT effervescent
bubbles

VRVSNTS effervescence
bubbles

VRVT uvarovite *gemstone*

VRVY overview *summary*

VRWLM overwhelm *upset,*
overpower

VRWLMN overwhelming
extreme

VRWLMNG overwhelming
extreme

VRWM overwhelm *upset,*
overpower

VRWMN everywoman *(often*
capitalized) average woman

VRWMN overwhelming
extreme

VRWMNG overwhelming
extreme

VRWN everyone *all persons*

VRWNN overweening
arrogant

VRWNNG overweening
arrogant

VRWR everywhere *all places*

VRWR overwear *exhaust*
overwore overworn
overwearing

VRWRK overwork *labor*

VRWT overweight *fat*

VRWTH over with *finished*

VRX varix (*n*) *swollen vein*
varices

VRXPLN overexplain *give*
reasons

VRXPND overexpand
increase

VRXPNSHN overexpansion
increase

VRXPNTSHN
overexpansion *increase*

VRXPSHR overexposure
film

VRXPZ overexpose *film*
overexposed
overexposing

VRXPZHR overexposure
film

VRXRSHN overexertion
work

VRXRT overexert *work*

VRXT overexcite *thrill*
overexcited overexciting

VRXTN overextend *expand,*
commit

VRXTNCHN overextension
expand, commit

VRXTND overextend
expand, commit

VRXTNSHN overextension
expand, commit

VRY varia *miscellany*

VRY vireo *bird* vireos

VRYBL variable (adj)
changing variably (adv)

VRYBLD variability *change*

VRYBLNS variableness
change

VRYBLT variability *change*

VRYD variety *diversity*
varieties

VRYDL varietal *assortment*

VRYDLZ overutilize *wear out*
overutilized overutilizing
(Br) overutilise

VRYDLZSHN overutilization
wear out
(Br) overutilisation

VRYGT variegate *dapple*
variegated variegating

VRYKSHN overreaction
exaggerated response

VRYKT overreact

Use letters that best describe the sounds you hear and omit the vowels. Use **S** or **K** instead of **C**: to find circle use **SRKL**. Use **J** to find joy, **JM** to find gem and **G** to find go.

exaggerated response
VRYL ovariole *egg*
VRYL variola *smallpox*
VRYLNS virulence *bitterness*
   virulency
VRYLNT virulent *deadly*
VRYLNTL virulently *deadly*
VRYLNTS virulence
   bitterness virulency
VRYMDR variometer *climb*
VRYMTR variometer *climb*
VRYN ovarian *egg*
VRYN virion *virus*
VRYNS variance *difference*
VRYNT variant *different*
VRYNTS variance *difference*
VRYRM variorum *text*
VRYS various *several*
VRYSHN variation *difference*
VRYSL variously *different*
VRYSNS variousness
   difference
VRYT variety *diversity*
   varieties
VRYTL varietal *assortment*
VRYTLZ overutilize *wear out*
   overutilized overutilizing
   (Br) overutilise
VRYTLZSHN overutilization
   wear out
   (Br) overutilisation
VRYZ overuse *wear out*
   overused overusing
VRZ overuse *wear out*
   overused overusing
VRZHN aversion *dislike*
VRZHN eversion *inside out*
VRZHN version *account*
VRZHNL versional *account*
VRZLS overzealous
   passionate
VRZM verism *everyday*
VS vas *blood vessel* vasa
VS vase *flowers*
VS vice *wickedness, fault,*
   rank
VS vis *power* vires
VS visa *passport* visaed
   visaing
VS vise *clamp* vised vising
   (Br) vice
VS voice *(v) express* voiced

voicing
VS voice *(n) human*
   utterance, verb
VSBKS voice box *larynx*
VSBX voice box *larynx*
VSCHNSLR vice-chancellor
   title
VSCHNTSLR vice-
   chancellor *title*
VSCHR vesture *clothe*
   vestured vesturing
VSD ovicide *egg killer*
VSD vestee *dickey*
VSD viscid *sticky*
VSD vista *view*
VSDBL vestibule *entrance*
VSDBYL vestibule *entrance*
VSDD vested *guaranteed*
VSDD viscidity *sticky*
VSDFRNSH vasa deferentia
   (pl) *tube* vas deferens
VSDFRNTSH vasa
   deferentia (pl) *tube* vas
   deferens
VSDFRNZ vas deferens *tube*
   vasa deferentia
VSDJ vestige *trace*
VSDL vestal *sinless*
VSDL viscidly *sticky*
VSDMRL vice admiral *rank*
VSDR vestiary *closet*
VSDRP eavesdrop *listen*
VSDRPR eavesdropper
   listener
VSDT viscidity *sticky*
VSDYR vestiary *closet*
VSF vouchsafe *grant*
   vouchsafed vouchsafing
VSFRDR vociferator *shouter*
VSFRNT vociferant *shouting*
VSFRS vociferous *shouting*
VSFRSHN vociferation
   shouting
VSFRSL vociferously
   shouting
VSFRSNS vociferousness
   shouting
VSFRT vociferate *shout*
   vociferated vociferating
VSFRTR vociferator *shouter*
VSHDR vitiator *disgracer*
VSHL visual (adj) *sight*

visually (adv)
VSHL vizsla *dog*
VSHLD visual aid *picture*
VSHLZ visualize *imagine*
   visualized visualizing
   (Br) visualise
VSHLZR visualizer *imagine*
   (Br) visualiser
VSHLZSHN visualization
   mental image
   (Br) visualisation
VSHN aviation *airplane*
VSHN evasion *dodge*
VSHN ovation *applause*
VSHN Vishnu *Hindu deity*
VSHN vision *sight*
VSHND visioned *seen*
VSHNL visional (adj) *sight*
   visionally (adv)
VSHNLS visionless *blind*
VSHNR visionary *(adj)*
   imaginary (n) seer
   visionaries
VSHR voyageur *fur transport*
VSHS vicious *spiteful*
VSHSHN vitiation
   impairment
VSHSL viciously *spitefully*
VSHSNS viciousness *spite*
VSHSW vichyssoise *soup*
VSHSWZ vichyssoise *soup*
VSHT vitiate *impair* vitiated
   vitiating
VSHTR vitiator *disgracer*
VSHWL visual (adj) *sight*
   visually (adv)
VSHWLD visual aid *picture*
VSHWLZ visualize *imagine*
   visualized visualizing
   (Br) visualise
VSHWLZR visualizer
   imagine
   (Br) visualiser
VSHWLZSHN visualization
   mental image
   (Br) visualisation
VSHYDR vitiator *disgracer*
VSHYSHN vitiation
   impairment
VSHYT vitiate *impair* vitiated
   vitiating
VSHYTR vitiator *disgracer*

VSJ visage *face*
VSJD visaged *face*
VSKDM vasectomy *sterilization* vasectomies
VSKDMZ vasectomize *sterilize* vasectomized vasectomizing
VSKL vascula (pl) *box* vasculum
VSKL vesical *urinary*
VSKL vesicle *blister*
VSKLCHR vasculature *veins*
VSKLDDZ vasculitides (pl) *inflammation* vasculitis
VSKLDS vasculitis *inflammation* vasculitides
VSKLM vasculum *box* vascula
VSKLR vascular *vein*
VSKLR vesicular *blister*
VSKLRD vascularity *vein*
VSKLRD vesicularity *blister*
VSKLRT vascularity *vein*
VSKLRT vesicularity *blister*
VSKLRZSHN vascularization *vein*
VSKLSHN vesiculation *blister*
VSKLT vesiculate *blister* vesiculated vesiculating
VSKLTDZ vasculitides (pl) *inflammation* vasculitis
VSKLTR vasculature *veins*
VSKLTS vasculitis *inflammation* vasculitides
VSKLTYR vasculature *veins*
VSKMDR viscometer *stickiness*
VSKMTR viscometer *stickiness*
VSKMTR viscometry *stickiness*
VSKMTRK viscometric *stickiness*
VSKNS viscountess *title*
VSKNSL vice-consul *title*
VSKNT vesicant *blister*
VSKNT viscount *title*
VSKNTS viscountess *title*
VSKNTSL vice-consul *title*
VSKS viscose *fiber*
VSKS viscous *liquid*

VSKS viscus *organs* viscera
VSKSD viscosity *flow* viscosities
VSKSL viscously *liquid*
VSKSMDR viscosimeter *flow*
VSKSMTR viscosimeter *flow*
VSKSMTRK viscosimetric *flow*
VSKSNS viscousness *liquid*
VSKST viscosity *flow* viscosities
VSKT viscount *title*
VSKTM vasectomy *sterilization* vasectomies
VSKTMZ vasectomize *sterilize* vasectomized vasectomizing
VSKTS viscountess *title*
VSKWD vice squad *police*
VSKWS viscous *liquid*
VSKWSL viscously *liquid*
VSKWSNS viscousness *liquid*
VSKYL vascula (pl) *box* vasculum
VSKYLCHR vasculature *veins*
VSKYLDDZ vasculitides (pl) *inflammation* vasculitis
VSKYLDS vasculitis *inflammation* vasculitides
VSKYLM vasculum *box* vascula
VSKYLR vascular *vein*
VSKYLR vesicular *blister*
VSKYLRD vascularity *vein*
VSKYLRD vesicularity *blister*
VSKYLRT vascularity *vein*
VSKYLRT vesicularity *blister*
VSKYLRZSHN vascularization *vein*
VSKYLSHN vesiculation *blister*
VSKYLT vesiculate *blister* vesiculated vesiculating
VSKYLTDZ vasculitides (pl) *inflammation* vasculitis
VSKYLTR vasculature *veins*
VSKYLTS vasculitis

inflammation vasculitides
VSKYLTYR vasculature *veins*
VSKYS viscous *liquid*
VSKYSL viscously *liquid*
VSKYSNS viscousness *liquid*
VSKYWS viscous *liquid*
VSKYWSL viscously *liquid*
VSKYWSNS viscousness *liquid*
VSL vassal *servant*
VSL vastly *extremely*
VSL vessel *ship, container*
VSL vizsla *dog*
VSLDR vacillator *doubter*
VSLJ vassalage *servitude*
VSLK vaselike *vessel*
VSLN Vaseline *(trademark) jelly*
VSLS voiceless *silent*
VSLSHN vacillation *doubt*
VSLSNS voicelessness *silence*
VSLT vacillate *waver* vacillated vacillating
VSLTR vacillator *doubter*
VSML voice mail *message*
VSMNT vestment *garment*
VSND vicinity *neighborhood* vicinities
VSNL vicennial *every 20 years*
VSNL vicinal *local*
VSNS vastness *hugeness*
VSNT vicinity *neighborhood* vicinities
VSNYL vicennial *every 20 years*
VSPD vespid *wasp*
VSPKT vest-pocket *small*
VSPN vespine *wasp*
VSPR vesper *evening*
VSPRL vesperal *evening*
VSPRNT voiceprint *pattern*
VSPRTN vespertine *evening*
VSPRZ vespers *evening*
VSPRZDNC vice presidency *rank*
VSPRZDNCHL vice presidential *rank*
VSPRZDNS vice presidency

Use letters that best describe the sounds you hear and omit the vowels. Use **S** or **K** instead of **C**: to find circle use **SRKL**. Use **J** to find joy, **JM** to find gem and **G** to find go.

rank
VSPRZDNSHL vice presidential *rank*
VSPRZDNT vice president *rank*
VSPRZDNTC vice presidency *rank*
VSPRZDNTS vice presidency *rank*
VSPRZDNTSHL vice presidential *rank*
VSQD vice squad *police*
VSQL vascula (pl) *box* vasculum
VSQLCHR vasculature *veins*
VSQLDDZ vasculitides (pl) *inflammation* vasculitis
VSQLDS vasculitis *inflammation* vasculitides
VSQLM vasculum *box* vascula
VSQLR vascular *vein*
VSQLR vesicular *blister*
VSQLRD vascularity *vein*
VSQLRD vesicularity *blister*
VSQLRT vascularity *vein*
VSQLRT vesicularity *blister*
VSQLRZSHN vascularization *vein*
VSQLSHN vesiculation *blister*
VSQLT vesiculate *blister* vesiculated vesiculating
VSQLTDZ vasculitides (pl) *inflammation* vasculitis
VSQLTR vasculature *veins*
VSQLTS vasculitis *inflammation* vasculitides
VSQLTYR vasculature *veins*
VSQS viscous *liquid*
VSQSL viscously *liquid*
VSQSNS viscousness *liquid*
VSQWS viscous *liquid*
VSQWSL viscously *liquid*
VSQWSNS viscousness *liquid*
VSR VCR *(abbr) videocassette recorder*
VSR viceroy *title*
VSR viscera (pl) *organs* viscus
VSRGL viceregal *governor*

VSRJNT vice-regent *title*
VSRL visceral (adj) *deep, earthy* viscerally (adv)
VSRN vicereine *governor's wife*
VSRSHN evisceration *gut*
VSRT eviscerate *gut* eviscerated eviscerating
VSRYLD viceroyalty *office*
VSRYLT viceroyalty *office*
VSSTD vicissitude *change, chance*
VSSTDNS vicissitudinous *change, chance*
VSSTYD vicissitude *change, chance*
VSSTYDNS vicissitudinous *change, chance*
VST avast *(interj) stop*
VST Avesta *sacred book*
VST avocet *bird*
VST vast *big*
VST vest *(n) garment (v) grant*
VST vestee *dickey*
VST vista *view*
VST voiced *spoken*
VSTBL vestibule *entrance*
VSTBLR vestibular *entrance*
VSTBYL vestibule *entrance*
VSTBYLR vestibular *entrance*
VSTD vested *guaranteed*
VSTGL vestigial (adj) *trace* vestigially (adv)
VSTGYL vestigial (adj) *trace* vestigially (adv)
VSTJ vestige *trace*
VSTJL vestigial (adj) *trace* vestigially (adv)
VSTJYL vestigial (adj) *trace* vestigially (adv)
VSTL vastly *extremely*
VSTL vestal *sinless*
VSTMNT vestment *garment*
VSTNS vastness *hugeness*
VSTPKT vest-pocket *small*
VSTR vestiary *closet*
VSTR vestry *church room* vestries
VSTR vesture *clothe* vestured vesturing

VSTTD vastitude *hugeness*
VSTTYD vastitude *hugeness*
VSTYR vestiary *closet*
VSV evasive *puzzling, obscure*
VSV vis-à-vis *(n) escort (prep) in relation to (adv) together* vis-à-vis
VSVL evasively *puzzling, obscure*
VSVN vesuvian *cigar match*
VSVNS evasiveness *puzzling, obscure*
VSVR voice-over *narrator*
VSVRS vice versa *opposite*
VSVYN vesuvian *cigar match*
VSW voussoir *arch*
VSWR voussoir *arch*
VSYR VCR *(abbr) videocassette recorder*
VT ovate *egg-shaped*
VT V-8 *engine*
VT vat *tub* vatted vatting
VT vet *(v) evaluate* vetted vetting
VT vet *(n-abbr) veteran, veterinarian*
VT veto *reject* vetoes
VT vita *résumé* vitae
VT vitta *stripe* vittae
VT vote *ballot* voted voting
VTBL evitable *avoidable*
VTD vat dye (n) *tint*
VTDD vat-dyed (adj) *tinted*
VTGRD avant-garde *trend-setters*
VTK vatic *foretelling*
VTKLCHR viticulture *grapes*
VTKLCHRL viticultural (adj) *grapes* viticulturally (adv)
VTKLCHRST viticulturist *grapes*
VTKLTR viticulture *grapes*
VTKLTRL viticultural (adj) *grapes* viticulturally (adv)
VTKLTRST viticulturist *grapes*
VTKN Vatican *Papal state*
VTKNG Vietcong *communist* Vietcong
VTL victual *(n) food*
VTL victual *(v) eat* victualed

Letters aren't doubled for single sounds: to find alley use **L** not **LL**. Use **Y** and **W** as hard sounds only: to find yellow use **YL**. (Br)=British spelling or usage. * See dictionary.

(or) victualled victualing
(or) victualling

VTL vital (adj) *essential* vitally (adv)

VTLD vitality *lively* vitalities

VTLG vitiligo *white spots*

VTLJNSS vitellogenesis *yolk*

VTLN vitelline *yolk*

VTLR victualler (or) victualer *food provider*

VTLS vitellus *yolk*

VTLS voteless *no ballot*

VTLSDK vitalistic *self-determination*

VTLST vitalist *self-determination*

VTLSTK vitalistic *self-determination*

VTLT vitality *lively* vitalities

VTLZ vitalize *enliven* vitalized vitalizing

VTLZM vitalism *self-determinism*

VTLZSHN vitalization *liveliness*

VTMN vitamin *nutrient*

VTNM Vietnam *country*

VTNMZ Vietnamese *of Vietnam*

VTNR veterinary *animal doctor*

VTNRN veterinarian *animal doctor*

VTNRYN veterinarian *animal doctor*

VTPRDR vituperator *scolder*

VTPRDV vituperative *scolding*

VTPRF veto-proof *no rejection*

VTPRSHN vituperation *abuse* vituperate

VTPRT vituperate *scold* vituperated vituperating

VTPRTR vituperator *scolder*

VTPRTR vituperatory *scolding*

VTPRTV vituperative *scolding*

VTR avatar *perfect example*

VTR aviator *pilot*

VTR vetoer *refuser*

VTR votary *believer* votaries

VTR voter *election*

VTRCZ aviatrices (or) aviatrixes (pl) *pilot (f)* aviatrix

VTRF vitrify *make glassy* vitrified vitrifying vitrifies

VTRFBL vitrifiable *glassy*

VTRFKSHN vitrification *glassy*

VTRFYBL vitrifiable *glassy*

VTRKDM vitrectomy *surgery* vitrectomies

VTRKS aviatrix *pilot (f)* aviatrixes (or) aviatrices

VTRKTM vitrectomy *surgery* vitrectomies

VTRL vitriol *sulfate*

VTRLK vitriolic *caustic*

VTRN veteran *soldier*

VTRNR veterinary *animal doctor*

VTRNRN veterinarian *animal doctor*

VTRNRYN veterinarian *animal doctor*

VTRS vitreous *glassy*

VTRST votarist *believer*

VTRSZ aviatrices (or) aviatrixes (pl) *pilot (f)* aviatrix

VTRX aviatrix *pilot (f)* aviatrixes (or) aviatrices

VTRYL vitriol *sulfate*

VTRYLK vitriolic *caustic*

VTRYS vitreous *glassy*

VTS uveitis *inflammation*

VTV votive *prayer*

VTVL votively *prayer*

VTVNS votiveness *prayer*

VTWR vetoer *refuser*

VTYPRDR vituperator *scolder*

VTYPRDV vituperative *scolding*

VTYPRSHN vituperation *abuse* vituperate

VTYPRT vituperate *scold* vituperated vituperating

VTYPRTR vituperator *scolder*

VTYPRTR vituperatory

scolding

VTYPRTV vituperative *scolding*

VV evolve *develop* evolved evolving

VV viva *(interj) approval*

VVBL evolvable *development*

VVCH vivace *tempo*

VVD vivid *clear*

VVDL vividly *clearly*

VVDNS vividness *clearness*

VVF vivify *bring to life* vivified vivifying vivifies

VVFKSHN vivification *bring to life*

VVFR vivifier *bring to life*

VVFYR vivifier *bring to life*

VVMNT evolvement *development*

VVPRD viviparity *live young*

VVPRS ovoviviparous *eggs*

VVPRS viviparous *live young*

VVPRSL ovoviviparously *eggs*

VVPRSL viviparously *live young*

VVPRSNS ovoviviparousness *eggs*

VVPRT viviparity *live young*

VVR vivaria (pl) *animal pen* vivarium

VVR Vouvray *wine*

VVRD viverrid *animal*

VVRM vivarium *animal pen* vivaria (or) vivariums

VVRY vivaria (pl) *animal pen* vivarium

VVRYM vivarium *animal pen* vivaria (or) vivariums

VVSD vivacity *liveliness*

VVSHS vivacious *lively*

VVSHSL vivaciously *lively*

VVSHSNS vivaciousness *liveliness*

VVSK vivisect *surgery*

VVSKSHN vivisection *surgery*

VVSKT vivisect *surgery*

VVST vivacity *liveliness*

VVVCH viva voce *oral*

VVVS viva voce *oral*

VW au revior *farewell*

Use letters that best describe the sounds you hear and omit the vowels. Use **S** or **K** instead of **C**: to find circle use **SRKL**. Use **J** to find joy, **JM** to find gem and **G** to find go.

VWBL viewable *vision*
VWDL avowedly *frankly*
VWL avowal *acknowledgment*
VWL voilà (or) voila *(interj)* there it is
VWL vowel *letter*
VWLZ vowelize *indicate sounds* vowelized vowelizing
VWNG viewing *watching*
VWR viewer *watcher*
VWR voyeur *peeker*
VWRDPZ avoirdupois *weight*
VWRDR voir dire *test*
VWRSDK voyeuristic *peeking*
VWRSDKL voyeuristically *peeking*
VWRSHP viewership *audience*
VWRSTK voyeuristic *peeking*
VWRSTKL voyeuristically *peeking*
VWRZM voyeurism *peeking*
VWYJR voyageur *fur transport*
VWYR voyeur *peeker*
VWYRSDK voyeuristic *peeking*
VWYRSDKL voyeuristically *peeking*
VWYRSTK voyeuristic *peeking*
VWYRSTKL voyeuristically *peeking*
VWYRZM voyeurism *peeking*
VWYSHR voyageur *fur transport*
VWYZHR voyageur *fur transport*
VX vex *annoy, puzzle*
VXL vexilla (pl) *flag, feather* vexillum
VXLLG vexillology *flags*
VXLLJ vexillology *flags*
VXLLJK vexillologic (or) vexillological *flags*
VXLLJKL vexillological (or) vexillologic *flags*
VXLLJST vexillologist *flags*
VXLM vexillum *flag, feather*

vexilla
VXN vaccine *drug*
VXN vaccinia *cowpox*
VXN vixen *fox, woman*
VXNDR vaccinator *innoculator*
VXNL vaccinal *protection*
VXNL vaccinial *cowpox*
VXNSH vixenish *fox, woman*
VXNSHN vaccination *innoculation*
VXNT vaccinate *innoculate* vaccinated vaccinating
VXNTR vaccinator *innoculator*
VXNY vaccinia *cowpox*
VXNYL vaccinial *cowpox*
VXPPL vox populi *popular sentiment*
VXPPYL vox populi *popular sentiment*
VXSHN vexation *annoy, puzzle*
VXSHS vexatious *annoy, puzzle*
VXSHSL vexatiously *annoy, puzzle*
VXSHSNS vexatiousness *annoy, puzzle*
VY uvea *eye*
VY value (v) *rate, prize* valued valuing
VY value (n) *worth, tint*
VY via *by way of*
VY view *vista, opinion*
VYBL viable (adj) *survivable* viably (adv)
VYBL viewable *vision*
VYBLD viability *survival*
VYBLT viability *survival*
VYCHF VHF (abbr) *very high frequency*
VYD valued *worthy*
VYDK viaduct *waterway*
VYDKT viaduct *waterway*
VYDR aviator *pilot*
VYDS uveitis *inflammation*
VYFNDR viewfinder *camera*
VYJ voyage *journey* voyaged voyaging
VYJR voyager *traveller*
VYJR voyageur *fur transport*

VYKL vehicle *transportation*
VYL ovule *egg*
VYL uveal *eye*
VYL uvula *throat lobe* uvulas (or) uvulae
VYL vial *bottle*
VYL vile *base, foul* viler vilest
VYL vilely *base, foul*
VYL viol *old violin*
VYL viola *violin/cello, flower*
VYL voile *fabric*
VYLBL violable (adj) *harm* violably (adv)
VYLBLD violability *harm*
VYLBLT violability *harm*
VYLDR violator *break, rape*
VYLDV violative *break, rape*
VYLN violin *music*
VYLNCHL violoncello *music*
VYLNCHLST violoncellist *music*
VYLNS vileness *base, foul*
VYLNS violence *force*
VYLNST violinist *musician*
VYLNT violent *forceful*
VYLNTL violently *forceful*
VYLNTS violence *force*
VYLR uvular *throat lobe*
VYLS valueless *no worth*
VYLSHN ovulation *discharge egg*
VYLSHN violation *break, rape*
VYLSHS violaceous *purple*
VYLST violist *musician*
VYLT ovulate *discharge egg* ovulated ovulating
VYLT violate *break, rape* violated violating
VYLT violet *color, flower*
VYLTR violator *break, rape*
VYLTV violative *break, rape*
VYMNS vehemence *strength*
VYMNT vehement *strong*
VYMNTL vehemently *strongly*
VYMNTS vehemence *strength*
VYMSN viomycin *antibiotic*
VYN avian *bird*
VYN Vienna *city*
VYND viand *food*
VYNG viewing *watching*

Letters aren't doubled for single sounds: to find alley use **L** not **LL**. Use **Y** and **W** as hard sounds only: to find yellow use **YL**. (Br)=British spelling or usage. * See dictionary.

VYNKS avionics *space vehicles*
VYNT valiant *heroic*
VYNX avionics *space vehicles*
VYP VIP *(abbr) very important person* VIPs
VYPNT viewpoint *opinion*
VYR aviary *birds* aviaries
VYR viewer *watcher*
VYR voyeur *peeker*
VYRSDK voyeuristic *peeking*
VYRSDKL voyeuristically *peeking*
VYRSHP viewership *audience*
VYRSTK voyeuristic *peeking*
VYRSTKL voyeuristically *peeking*
VYRZM voyeurism *peeking*
VYSHN aviation *airplane*
VYSHR voyageur *fur transport*
VYT V-8 *engine*
VYTKNG Vietcong *communist* Vietcong
VYTNM Vietnam *country*
VYTNMZ Vietnamese *of Vietnam*
VYTR aviator *pilot*
VYTRCZ aviatrices (or) aviatrixes (pl) *pilot (f)* aviatrix
VYTRKS aviatrix *pilot (f)* aviatrixes (or) aviatrices
VYTRSZ aviatrices (or) aviatrixes (pl) *pilot (f)* aviatrix
VYTRX aviatrix *pilot (f)* aviatrixes (or) aviatrices
VYTS uveitis *inflammation*
VYWBL viewable *vision*
VYWNG viewing *watching*
VYWR viewer *watcher*
VYWRSHP viewership *audience*
VYZHR voyageur *fur transport*
VZ eaves *roof*
VZ vase *flowers*
VZ visa *passport* visaed visaing
VZBL visible (adj) *clear*

visibly (adv)
VZBLD visibility *clearness* visibilities
VZBLNS visibleness *clearness*
VZBLT visibility *clearness* visibilities
VZDBL visitable *inspect, call*
VZDLSHN vasodilation (or) vasodilatation *widening*
VZDLTSHN vasodilatation (or) vasodilation *widening*
VZDN visiting *invited*
VZDNG visiting *invited*
VZDNT visitant *visitor*
VZDR visitor *inspector, caller*
VZDRP eavesdrop *listen*
VZDRPR eavesdropper *listener*
VZHL visual (adj) *sight* visually (adv)
VZHL vizsla *dog*
VZHLD visual aid *picture*
VZHLZ visualize *imagine* visualized visualizing (Br) visualise
VZHLZR visualizer *imagine* (Br) visualiser
VZHLZSHN visualization *mental image* (Br) visualisation
VZHN evasion *dodge*
VZHN vision *sight*
VZHND visioned *seen*
VZHNL visional (adj) *sight* visionally (adv)
VZHNLS visionless *blind*
VZHNR visionary *(adj) imaginary (n) seer* visionaries
VZHR voyageur *fur transport*
VZHWL visual (adj) *sight* visually (adv)
VZHWLD visual aid *picture*
VZHWLZ visualize *imagine* visualized visualizing (Br) visualise
VZHWLZR visualizer *imagine* (Br) visualiser
VZHWLZSHN visualization *mental image*

(Br) visualisation
VZJ visage *face*
VZJD visaged *face*
VZKDM vasectomy *sterilization* vasectomies
VZKDMZ vasectomize *sterilize* vasectomized vasectomizing
VZKDV vasoactive *veins*
VZKNSTRKDR vasoconstrictor *narrowing*
VZKNSTRKDV vasoconstrictive *narrowing*
VZKNSTRKSHN vasoconstriction *veins*
VZKNSTRKTR vasoconstrictor *narrowing*
VZKNSTRKTV vasoconstrictive *narrowing*
VZKTM vasectomy *sterilization* vasectomies
VZKTMZ vasectomize *sterilize* vasectomized vasectomizing
VZKTV vasoactive *veins*
VZL vizsla *dog*
VZLK vaselike *vessel*
VZLN Vaseline *(trademark) jelly*
VZMDR vasomotor *veins*
VZMTR vasomotor *veins*
VZPRSN vasopressin *hormone*
VZPRSR vasopressor *squeezing*
VZR visor *eye shade*
VZR vizier *Muslim officer*
VZRD visored *eye shade*
VZRD vizard *disguise*
VZRL vizierial *Muslim officer*
VZRLS visorless *no eye shade*
VZRSHP viziership *region*
VZRT vizierate *region*
VZRYL vizierial *Muslim officer*
VZSPZM vasospasm *squeezing*
VZT visit *pay a call, chat*

Use letters that best describe the sounds you hear and omit the vowels. Use **S** or **K** instead of **C**: to find circle use **SRKL**. Use **J** to find joy, **JM** to find gem and **G** to find go.

VZTBL visitable *inspect, call*
VZTN visiting *invited*
VZTNG visiting *invited*
VZTNT visitant *spirit, bird*
VZTR visitor *inspector, caller*
VZTSHN visitation
  inspection, custody
VZTSN vasotocin *hormone*
VZV evasive *puzzling,*
  obscure
VZV vis-à-vis *(n) escort*
  (prep) in relation to (adv)
  together vis-à-vis
VZVGL vasovagal *nerve and*
  vein
VZVL evasively *puzzling,*
  obscure
VZVNS evasiveness
  puzzling, obscure
VZWKDV vasoactive *veins*
VZWKTV vasoactive *veins*

W

W away *distance*
W aweigh *anchor*
W Iowa *US State*
W ow *(interj) pain*
W way *route*
W we *I and others*
W wee *small*
W weigh *measure*
W whee *(interj) delight*
W whew *(interj) relief*
W whey *milk*
W whoa *stop*
W why *for what reason* whys
W woe *grief*
W woo *court* wooed wooing
W wow *(interj) wonder (v)*
  excite (n) hit, sound
W wye *alphabet letter (Y)*
W y *(n) fork, consonant letter*
WB web *(v) ensnare* webbed

webbing
WB web *(n) snare, network,*
  vane
WBFD webfed *printing*
WBFDD web-footed *fused*
  toes
WBFST web-offset *printing*
WBFT webfoot *fused toes*
WBFTD web-footed *fused*
  toes
WBGN woebegone *sorry*
WBL waybill *document*
WBL weighable *measure*
WBL wobble *waver* wobbled
  wobbling
WBL wobbly *wavering*
WBLNS wobbliness
  wavering
WBLR wobbler *waverer*
WBN webbing *tape*
WBNG webbing *tape*
WBPRS web press *printing*
WBR weber *magnetism*
WBSPNR web spinner
  spider
WBWRK webwork *network*
WBWRM webworm *insect*
WC wussy *(slang) wimpy*
WCH watch *(v) look (n)*
  timepiece watches
WCH which *what one*
WCH witch *sorceress* witches
WCHBL watchable *worthy*
WCHBN watchband *strap*
WCHBND watchband *strap*
WCHDG watchdog *guard*
WCHDKDR witch doctor
  healer
WCHDKTR witch doctor
  healer
WCHF UHF *(abbr) Ultra*
  High Frequency
WCHFL watchful *(adj)*
  observant watchfully *(adv)*
WCHFLNS watchfulness
  observant
WCHFR watch fire *signal*
WCHFYR watch fire *signal*
WCHHNT witch-hunt
  persecution
WCHHZL witch hazel *shrub*
WCHK woodchuck *animal*

WCHKP watch cap *navy*
WCHKRF witchcraft *magic*
WCHKRFT witchcraft *magic*
WCHKS watchcase *covering*
WCHMKLT whatchamacallit
  gizmo
WCHMKR watchmaker
  clocks
WCHMN watchman *guard*
  watchmen
WCHN witching *sorcery*
WCHNG witching *sorcery*
WCHNT watch night *prayer*
WCHNT witch-hunt
  persecution
WCHPR woodchopper
  lumberjack
WCHR watcher *observer*
WCHR witchery *sorcery*
  witcheries
WCHT watch out *observe*
WCHT Wichita *city*
WCHT woodchat *bird*
WCHTR watchtower *lookout*
WCHTWR watchtower
  lookout
WCHVR whichever *any*
WCHWD witchweed *plant*
WCHWRD watchword
  slogan
WCHZBRM witches'-broom
  growth
WCHZL witch hazel *shrub*
WCZ oases *(pl) water* oasis
WD oidia *(pl) fungus* oidium
WD wad *lump* wadded
  wadding
WD waddy *club* waddies
WD wade *walk in water*
  waded wading
WD wadi *gully* wadis
WD we'd *(contr) we would,*
  we had
WD wed *unite* wedded
  wedding
WD weed *plant*
WD weedy *overgrown*
  weedier weediest
WD weighty *heavy* weightier
  weightiest
WD whitey *(slang-often*
  capitalized) white person

Letters aren't doubled for single sounds: to find alley use **L** not **LL**. Use **Y** and **W** as hard sounds only: to find yellow use **YL**. (Br)=British spelling or usage. * See dictionary.

WD whydah *bird*
WD wide *broad* wider widest
WD widow *survivor*
WD witty *clever* wittier wittiest
WD wood *tree, golf club, forest*
WD woody *(adj) like wood* woodier woodiest
WD woody *(or)* woodie *(n) vehicle* woodies
WD would *(v-past) will*
WDB would-be *desire*
WDBD wide-body *jet* wide-bodies
WDBL wettable *moisture*
WDBLD wettability *moisture*
WDBLK woodblock (n) *printing* wood-block (adj)
WDBLT wettability *moisture*
WDBN woodbine *shrub*
WDBRN wood-boring *insect*
WDBRNG wood-boring *insect*
WDCHK woodchuck *animal*
WDCHPR woodchopper *lumberjack*
WDCHT woodchat *bird*
WDD weighted *heavy*
WDD wide-eyed *amazed*
WDD widowhood *survival*
WDD witted *smart*
WDD wooded *trees*
WDF what-if *question*
WDHD widowhood *survival*
WDJ wattage *power unit*
WDK white oak *tree*
WDK wood duck *bird*
WDKDNG woodcutting *lumberjack*
WDKDR woodcutter *lumberjack*
WDKK woodcock *bird* woodcocks (or) woodcock
WDKRF woodcraft *skill*
WDKRFT woodcraft *skill*
WDKRVN wood carving *ornament*
WDKRVNG wood carving *ornament*
WDKRVR wood-carver

whittler
WDKT woodcut *printing*
WDKTN woodcutting *lumberjack*
WDKTNG woodcutting *lumberjack*
WDKTR woodcutter *lumberjack*
WDL waddle *walk* waddled waddling
WDL wattle *(v) interweave* wattled wattling
WDL wattle *(n) tree, neck skin, thatch*
WDL weightily *heavily*
WDL wheedle *lure* wheedled wheedling
WDL whittle *carve* whittled whittling
WDL wittily *cleverly*
WDLFNT white elephant *animal, junk*
WDLK wedlock *marriage*
WDLKHL wood alcohol *methanol*
WDLN whittling *carving*
WDLN woodland *forest*
WDLND woodland *forest*
WDLNG whittling *carving*
WDLR whittler *carver*
WDLT woodlot *forest*
WDM oidium *fungus* oidia
WDMTH widemouthed *gaping*
WDMTHD widemouthed *gaping*
WDMTHT widemouthed *gaping*
WDN wadding *lump, plug*
WDN wasn't *(contr) was not*
WDN wedding *marriage*
WDN widen *broaden*
WDN wooden *stiff, wood*
WDN wouldn't *(contr) would not*
WDNG wadding *lump, plug*
WDNG wedding *marriage*
WDNG whiting *fish*
WDNGGL wide-angle *lens*
WDNGL wide-angle *lens*
WDNGL wittingly *knowingly*
WDNHD woodenhead

stupid
WDNHDD woodenheaded *stupid*
WDNMN wood anemone *plant*
WDNS weediness *overgrown*
WDNS weightiness *heaviness*
WDNS wittiness *cleverness*
WDNS woodiness *stiffness, of wood*
WDNT wasn't *(contr) was not*
WDNT wouldn't *(contr) would not*
WDNWR woodenware *utensils*
WDNZD Wednesday *weekday*
WDPC wood pussy *skunk*
WDPKR woodpecker *bird*
WDPL woodpile *firewood*
WDPLP wood pulp *cellulose*
WDPN wide-open *gaping*
WDPS wood pussy *skunk*
WDPYL woodpile *firewood*
WDR wader *bird, boot*
WDR waiter *server*
WDR water *liquid*
WDR watery *thin liquid, wishy-washy*
WDR watt-hour *power unit*
WDR weeder *tool*
WDR weedier *overgrown*
WDR weightier *heavier*
WDR wetter *moist*
WDR wheatear *bird*
WDR whetter *sharpener*
WDR wider *broad*
WDR widower *survivor*
WDR wittier *clever*
WDRB water boy *refreshments*
WDRBD water bed *sleep*
WDRBFL water buffalo *animal*
WDRBG water bag *container, womb*
WDRBG water bug *insect*
WDRBK waterbuck *antelope*
WDRBRD waterbird *swimmer, wader*
WDRBRN waterborne *via water*

Use letters that best describe the sounds you hear and omit the vowels. Use **S** or **K** instead of **C**: to find circle use **SRKL**. Use **J** to find joy, **JM** to find gem and **G** to find go.

WDRCHSNT water chestnut *vegetable*
WDRCHSTNT water chestnut *vegetable*
WDRF woodruff *herb*
WDRFL waterfall *rapids*
WDRFL waterfowl *bird* waterfowl
WDRFRNT waterfront *shoreline*
WDRFWL waterfowl *bird* waterfowl
WDRGJ water gauge *depth*
WDRGLS water glass *vessel* water glasses
WDRGT Watergate *scandal*
WDRHDR water heater *appliance*
WDRHL water hole *oasis*
WDRHTR water heater *appliance*
WDRHWL waterwheel *rotator*
WDRKLD water-cooled *engine*
WDRKLR watercolor *paint* (Br) watercolour
WDRKLR watercooler *drinks*
WDRKLZT water closet *bathroom*
WDRKRF watercraft *boat*
WDRKRFT watercraft *boat*
WDRKRS watercourse *channel*
WDRKRS watercress *plant*
WDRL waterloo *defeat* waterloos
WDRLG waterlog *drench* waterlogged waterlogging
WDRLL water lily *plant* water lilies
WDRLN water line (or) waterline *highest level*
WDRLS waterless *no water*
WDRLVL water level *instrument*
WDRMDR water meter *quantity*
WDRMKSN water moccasin *snake*

WDRML water mill *machinery*
WDRMLN watermelon *fruit*
WDRMN water main *pipe*
WDRMN waterman *boating* watermen
WDRMRK watermark *design*
WDRMTR water meter *quantity*
WDRNJN wide-ranging *everywhere*
WDRNJNG wide-ranging *everywhere*
WDRNMF water nymph *myth*
WDRNS wateriness *soggy, weak*
WDRPL water polo *sport*
WDRPLNT water-repellent *no penetration*
WDRPP water pipe *smoke*
WDRPR waterpower *machinery*
WDRPRF waterproof *no penetration*
WDRPRFN waterproofing *no penetration*
WDRPRFNG waterproofing *no penetration*
WDRPRFR waterproofer *no penetration*
WDRPSDL water pistol *squirt gun*
WDRPSTL water pistol *squirt gun*
WDRPWR waterpower *machinery*
WDRR waterer *sprinkler*
WDRS water ice *dessert*
WDRSD waterside *coastal*
WDRSFR water sapphire *gem*
WDRSH waterish *soggy, weak*
WDRSHD watershed *divide, turning point*
WDRSK water ski (n) *sport* water-ski (v)
WDRSK water-soak *drench*
WDRSK waterski *sport*
WDRSKL water cycle *weather*

WDRSKN waterskiing *sport*
WDRSKNG waterskiing *sport*
WDRSKP waterscape *view*
WDRSKR water-skier *sportsman*
WDRSKYN waterskiing *sport*
WDRSKYNG waterskiing *sport*
WDRSKYR water-skier *sportsman*
WDRSNK water snake *reptile*
WDRSPNL water spaniel *dog*
WDRSPNYL water spaniel *dog*
WDRSPT water spot *citrus disease*
WDRSPT waterspout *pipe, tornado*
WDRSTRDR water strider *insect*
WDRT water rat *animal*
WDRT water right *access*
WDRTBL water table *saturation*
WDRTHRSH waterthrush *bird*
WDRTKC water taxi *boat*
WDRTKS water taxi *boat*
WDRTR water tower *reservoir*
WDRTT watertight *no leaks*
WDRTWR water tower *reservoir*
WDRTX water taxi *boat*
WDRVPR water vapor *steam*
WDRW waterway *channel*
WDRWCH water witch *find water*
WDRWCHN water witching *find water*
WDRWCHNG water witching *find water*
WDRWCHR water witcher *find water*
WDRWD waterweed *plant*
WDRWGN water wagon *sprinkler*
WDRWL waterwheel *rotator*

Letters aren't doubled for single sounds: to find alley use **L** not **LL**. Use **Y** and **W** as hard sounds only: to find yellow use **YL**. (Br)=British spelling or usage. * See dictionary.

WDRWNGZ water wings *buoy*
WDRWRKS waterworks *fountain, supply system*
WDRWRN waterworn *smoothed*
WDRWRX waterworks *fountain, supply system*
WDRWV water wave *hairstyle*
WDRZSDNT water-resistant *no penetration*
WDRZSTNT water-resistant *no penetration*
WDSH wettish *moist*
WDSH white ash *tree*
WDSHD woodshed *storage*
WDSKRN wide-screen *picture*
WDSPK widow's peak *hairline*
WDSPRD widespread *everywhere*
WDST weediest *overgrown*
WDST weightiest *heavy*
WDST wettest *moist*
WDST widest *broad*
WDST wittiest *clever*
WDSTV woodstove *heater*
WDSWK widow's walk *platform*
WDSZM witticism *remark*
WDT whiteout *snow*
WDT wideout *receiver*
WDTH width *dimension*
WDTK wood tick *insect*
WDTR wood tar *leavings*
WDVR whatever *anything*
WDWD widowhood *survival*
WDWK wide-awake *alert*
WDWN woodwind *music*
WDWND woodwind *music*
WDWR watt-hour *power unit*
WDWR widower *survivor*
WDWRK woodwork *fittings*
WDWRKN woodworking *carving*
WDWRKNG woodworking *carving*
WDWRKR woodworker *carver*
WDWRM woodworm *larva*

WDY oidia (pl) *fungus* oidium
WDYM oidium *fungus* oidia
WDYR weedier *overgrown*
WDYR weightier *heavier*
WDYR wittier *clever*
WDYST weediest *overgrown*
WDYST weightiest *heavy*
WDYST wittiest *clever*
WDZ woods *forest*
WDZ woodsy *with trees*
WDZMN woodsman *trees* woodsmen
WDZPK widow's peak *hairline*
WDZWK widow's walk *platform*
WF WAF (abbr) *Women's Air Force*
WF waif *lost property, child*
WF whiff *puff*
WF wife *spouse* wives
WF wolf (n) *animal* (v) *devour* wolves
WF woof *weave*
WFBR wolfberry *plant* wolfberries
WFD wifty *ditsy*
WFDJ waftage *drifting*
WFDR wafter *drift*
WFHN wolfhound *dog*
WFHND wolfhound *dog*
WFL waffle (v) *flip-flop* waffled waffling
WFL waffle (n) *pastry, tripe*
WFL whiffle *air* whiffled whiffling
WFL wifely *domestic*
WFL Wiffle (trademark) *baseball*
WFL woeful *sorry*
WFLK wolflike *canine*
WFLNS wifeliness *domestic*
WFLRN waffle iron *utensil*
WFLTR whiffletree *harness*
WFLYRN waffle iron *utensil*
WFN wolfhound *dog*
WFND wolfhound *dog*
WFPK wolf pack *animals*
WFR wafer *thin cake*
WFR wolfer *hunter*
WFR woofer *speaker*

WFRM wolfram *tungsten*
WFRMT wolframite *mineral*
WFRNG wayfaring *traveling*
WFRR wayfarer *traveler*
WFSBN wolfsbane *herb*
WFT waft *drift*
WFT weft *thread*
WFT wifty *ditsy*
WFTJ waftage *drifting*
WFTR wafter *drift*
WG Ouija (trademark) *game*
WG wag *swing, gossip* wagged wagging
WG wedgie *shoe*
WG Whig *parliament*
WG wig (n) *hairpiece*
WG wig (v) *rebuke* wigged wigging
WG wog (vulgar) *foreigner*
WGBRD Ouija board *game*
WGD wigged *hairpiece*
WGDT wigged-out *crazy*
WGL waggle *move a part* waggled waggling
WGL waggly *swinging*
WGL wiggle *jiggle* wiggled wiggling
WGL wiggly *jiggly*
WGLR wiggler *larva, jiggler*
WGLT wiglet *hairpiece*
WGM Iwo Jima *island*
WGM oogamy *fertilization*
WGMS oogamous *fertilization*
WGN oogonia (pl) *germ cell* oogonium
WGN wagon *vehicle* (Br) waggon
WGN wigan *fabric*
WGNL oogonial *germ cell*
WGNM oogonium *germ cell* oogonia
WGNR Wagner *composer*
WGNR wagoner *driver*
WGNT wagonette *vehicle*
WGNY oogonia (pl) *germ cell* oogonium
WGNYL oogonial *germ cell*
WGNYM oogonium *germ cell* oogonia
WGR waggery *joke* waggeries

Use letters that best describe the sounds you hear and omit the vowels. Use **S** or **K** instead of **C**: to find circle use **SRKL**. Use **J** to find joy, **JM** to find gem and **G** to find go.

WGR Whiggery *parliament*
WGSH waggish *humorous*
WGSH Whiggish *parliament*
WGSHL waggishly *humorous*
WGSHNS waggishness *humorous*
WGTL wagtail *bird*
WGWG wigwag *signal* wigwagged wigwagging
WGWM wigwam *hut*
WH Oahu *island*
WH wahoo *tree, fish (interj) excitement* wahoos
WHN wahine *woman*
WJ Ouija *(trademark) game*
WJ wage *(v) engage in* waged waging
WJ wage *(v) payment*
WJ wedge *(v) cram* wedged wedging
WJ wedge *(n) tool*
WJ wedgie *shoe*
WJBRD Ouija board *game*
WJM Iwo Jima *island*
WJN wigeon (or) widgeon *duck* wigeon (or) wigeons (or) widgeon (or) widgeons
WJR wager *bet*
WJRNR wage earner *worker*
WJT widget *gadget*
WJWD Wedgwood *china*
WK awake *not sleeping* awoke awaking awoken (or) awaked
WK WAC *(abbr) Women's Army Corps*
WK wacko *crazy one* wackos
WK wacky *crazy* wackier wackiest
WK wake *(v) arouse* woke waking woken (or) waked
WK wake *(n) vigil, aftermath*
WK walk *(v) step, roam (n) pathway, vocation, gait**
WK weak *powerless*
WK week *seven days*
WK weka *bird*
WK whack *(v) strike, (Br) defeat (n) blow, portion*
WK wick *candle*

WK wok *pan*
WKBT walkabout *hike*
WKC waxy *smooth and white* waxier waxiest
WKCNS waxiness *smooth and white*
WKCR waxier *smooth and white*
WKCST waxiest *smooth and white*
WKCYR waxier *smooth and white*
WKCYST waxiest *smooth and white*
WKD weekday *Monday thru Friday*
WKD wicked *evil*
WKDL wickedly *evil*
WKDNS wickedness *evil*
WKDNT y-coordinate *math*
WKDT whacked-out *(slang) tired, (slang) drugged*
WKFL wakeful *(adj) sleepless* wakefully *(adv)*
WKFLNS wakefulness *sleeplessness*
WKFSH weakfish *animal*
WKHRDD weakhearted *no courage*
WKHRTD weakhearted *no courage*
WKL wackily *crazy*
WKL weakly *no power*
WKL weekly *once a week* weeklies
WKLN Wake Island *land mass*
WKLN weakling *no power*
WKLND Wake Island *land mass*
WKLNG weakling *no power*
WKLNG weeklong *seven days*
WKLS wakeless *unbroken*
WKM Joachim *violinist*
WKMN Walkman *(trademark) radio*
WKMNDD weak-minded *foolish*
WKMNDDNS weak-mindedness *foolish*
WKN awaken *arouse*

WKN awoken *aroused*
WKN waken *arouse*
WKN waking *not sleeping*
WKN walk-in *(adj, n) step into*
WKN walk-on *(n) acting role*
WKN walking *up and about*
WKN weaken *lose power*
WKN weekend *Saturday and Sunday*
WKN whacking *very*
WKN wicking *candle*
WKN woken *(v-past) wake*
WKND weak-kneed *timid*
WKND weekend *Saturday and Sunday*
WKNDR weekender *vacation, luggage*
WKNG waking *not sleeping*
WKNG walking *up and about*
WKNG whacking *very*
WKNG wicking *candle*
WKNGPPRZ walking papers *dismissal*
WKNGSTK walking stick *insect*
WKNN awakening *arousal*
WKNNG awakening *arousal*
WKNPPRZ walking papers *dismissal*
WKNR wakener *arouser*
WKNR weakener *power depleter*
WKNS eyewitness *observer*
WKNS wackiness *craziness*
WKNS weakness *fault*
WKNS witness *(v) observe (n) observer* witnesses
WKNSBKS witness-box *law*
WKNSBX witness-box *law*
WKNSTK walking stick *insect*
WKNSTN witness stand *law*
WKNSTND witness stand *law*
WKNT weeknight *Monday thru Friday*
WKP wake-up *arouse*
WKP wake-up *(adj) arouse* wake up *(v)*
WKP walk-up *(n, adj) apartment*

Letters aren't doubled for single sounds: to find alley use **L** not **LL**. Use **Y** and **W** as hard sounds only: to find yellow use **YL**. (Br)=British spelling or usage. * See dictionary.

WKP wickiup *hut*
WKR wackier *crazier*
WKR walker *stepper, shoe*
WKR weaker *less power*
WKR wicker *straw*
WKRBN wake-robin *flower*
WKRMSM Y chromosome *genes*
WKRWRK wickerwork *straw*
WKS wax (n) *substance* (v) *shine, increase, become* waxes
WKS waxy *smooth and white* waxier waxiest
WKSBL waxbill *bird*
WKSBN wax bean *vegetable*
WKSD weak side (n) *inferior* weakside (adj)
WKSN waxen *flexible, pale*
WKSN waxing *polish, remove* hair
WKSNG waxing *polish, remove hair*
WKSNS waxiness *smooth and white*
WKSPPR wax paper *wrap*
WKSR waxer *polisher*
WKSR waxier *smooth and white*
WKSS y-axis *math*
WKSST waxiest *smooth and white*
WKSSTR weak sister *ineffectual one*
WKST wackiest *craziest*
WKSTPPR waxed paper *wrap*
WKSWNG waxwing *bird*
WKSWRK waxwork *dummy*
WKSYR waxier *smooth and white*
WKSYST waxiest *smooth and white*
WKT walkout (n) *strike* walk out (v)
WKT wicket *gate, stump*
WKTHN walkathon *charity*
WKTHR walk-through (n) *rehearsal*
WKTK walkie-talkie *radio*
WKTT whacked-out *(slang)* tired, *(slang) drugged*

WKVR walkover *easy win*
WKW walkaway *victory*
WKW walkway *path*
WKWDNT y-coordinate *math*
WKYP wickiup *hut*
WKYR wackier *crazier*
WKYST wackiest *craziest*
WL awhile *time*
WL AWOL *(abbr) absent without leave*
WL owl *bird*
WL wail *lament*
WL wale *welt* waled waling
WL wall (n) *barrier, side* (v) *surround, immure*
WL wallah *occupation*
WL walleye *eye, fish*
WL wallow (v) *roll in, delight* (n) *mud*
WL waylay *ambush* waylaid waylaying
WL we'll *(contr) we will, we shall*
WL weal *good, ridge*
WL well (n) *water hole, source*
WL well (adv) *fine, right* better best
WL whale (n) *animal* whales (or) whale
WL whale (v) *hunt whales, thrash* whaled whaling
WL wheal *welt*
WL wheel *disk*
WL wheelie *stunt*
WL while (v) *pass time* whiled whiling
WL while (conj) *during*
WL wield *handle*
WL wild *untamed*
WL wile (v) *pass time* wiled wiling
WL wile (n) *trick*
WL will (v) *shall, intend, bequeath* (n) *volition, document**
WL willow *tree*
WL willowy *slim and graceful*
WL wily *crafty* wilier wiliest
WL wool *sheep hair*
WL woolly *like wool* woollier woolliest

WL you-all *all of you*
WLB wallaby *animal* wallabies
WLBHVD well-behaved *polite*
WLBLNST well-balanced *regulated*
WLBLVD well-beloved *adored*
WLBN well-being *contentment*
WLBN whalebone *baleen*
WLBNG well-being *contentment*
WLBR wheelbarrow *cart*
WLBR wild boar *pig*
WLBR woolly bear *caterpillar*
WLBRD wallboard *material*
WLBRD well-bred *cultured*
WLBRN wellborn *noble, rich*
WLBS wheelbase *length*
WLBT whaleboat *ship*
WLBYN well-being *contentment*
WLBYNG well-being *contentment*
WLCH Welsh *of Wales*
WLCH welsh (v) *withdraw*
WLCHR welsher *withdrawer*
WLCHR wheelchair *vehicle*
WLCHRBT Welsh rabbit *food*
WLCHRRBT Welsh rabbit *food*
WLD walleyed *staring*
WLD weald *forest*
WLD weld *join*
WLD wellhead *source*
WLD wheeled *movable*
WLD wield *handle*
WLD wieldy *easy to handle*
WLD wild *untamed*
WLD willed *deliberate*
WLD wold *meadow*
WLDBR wild boar *pig*
WLDBST wildebeest *animal* wildebeests
WLDD wild-eyed *extreme*
WLDFL wildfowl *bird*
WLDFLR wildflower *plant*
WLDFLWR wildflower *plant*

Use letters that best describe the sounds you hear and omit the vowels. Use **S** or **K** instead of **C**: to find circle use **SRKL**. Use **J** to find joy, **JM** to find gem and **G** to find go.

WLDFND well-defined *described*

WLDFR wildfire *burn, glow, plant disease*

WLDFYR wildfire *burn, glow, plant disease*

WLDGSCHS wild-goose chase *search*

WLDK well deck *ship*

WLDKDR wildcatter *driller, promoter, striker*

WLDKRD wild card *unknown factor*

WLDKT wildcat *(v) prospect* wildcatted wildcatting

WLDKT wildcat *(n) animal*

WLDKTR wildcatter *driller, promoter, striker*

WLDL wildly *extremely*

WLDLF wildlife *animals*

WLDLN wildland *uncultivated*

WLDLN wildling *uncultivated*

WLDLND wildland *uncultivated*

WLDLNG wildling *uncultivated*

WLDMNT weldment *unit*

WLDN well-done *cooked*

WLDN wilding *uncultivated*

WLDNG wilding *uncultivated*

WLDNS wildness *not tame*

WLDPCH wild pitch *baseball* wild pitches

WLDR welder *(or) weldor joiner*

WLDR welter *confusion*

WLDR wielder *handler*

WLDR wild rye *grain*

WLDRNS wilderness *remote area*

WLDRS wild rice *grain*

WLDRWT welterweight *136-147 pounds*

WLDS wilds *wilderness*

WLDSPZD well-disposed *friendly*

WLDTS wild oats *indiscretions*

WLDVLPT well-developed

WLDVZD well-advised *prudent*

WLDWL wall-to-wall *floor*

WLDWST Wild West *frontier*

WLDZ wilds *wilderness*

WLF well-off *prosperous*

WLF wildlife *animals*

WLF wolf *(n) animal (v) devour* wolves

WLFBR wolfberry *plant* wolfberries

WLFHN wolfhound *dog*

WLFHND wolfhound *dog*

WLFKST well-fixed *rich*

WLFL wailful *(adj) mournful* wailfully *(adv)*

WLFL willful *(or) wilful (adj) unruly* willfully *(adv)*

WLFLK wolflike *canine*

WLFLNS willfulness *unruly*

WLFLR wallflower *shy one*

WLFLR wildflower *plant*

WLFLWR wallflower *shy one*

WLFLWR wildflower *plant*

WLFN wolfhound *dog*

WLFND well-found *furnished*

WLFND wolfhound *dog*

WLFNDD well-founded *reasoned*

WLFNT wulfenite *mineral*

WLFPK wolf pack *animals*

WLFR welfare *prosperity, benefits*

WLFR wildfire *burn, glow, plant disease*

WLFR wolfer *hunter*

WLFRM wolfram *tungsten*

WLFRMT wolframite *mineral*

WLFRZM welfarism *social system*

WLFSBN wolfsbane *herb*

WLFSH wolffish *toothed fish*

WLFSH wolfish *like a wolf*

WLFSHL wolfishly *like a wolf*

WLFSHNS wolfishness *like a wolf*

WLFT wool fat *lanolin*

WLFVRD well-favored *handsome*

WLFXT well-fixed *rich*

WLFYR wildfire *burn, glow, plant disease*

WLG oology *bird's eggs*

WLGRMD well-groomed

neat

WLGRNDD well-grounded *foundation*

WLGSCHS wild-goose chase *search*

WLGTHR wool-gather *daydream*

WLGTHRN woolgathering *daydreaming*

WLGTHRNG woolgathering *daydreaming*

WLGTHRR woolgatherer *daydreamer*

WLHD wellhead *source*

WLHDD woolly-headed *vague*

WLHLD well-heeled *rich*

WLHNDLD well-handled *managed*

WLHRS wheelhorse *animal*

WLHS wheelhouse *ship*

WLJ oology *bird's eggs*

WLJST oologist *bird's eggs*

WLJSTD well-adjusted *balanced*

WLK wheel lock *gun*

WLK whelk *snail, pustule*

WLK wilco *roger*

WLKDR wildcatter *driller, promoter, striker*

WLKM welcome *(v) greet* welcomed welcoming

WLKM welcome *(n) reception (adj) received gladly*

WLKMR welcomer *greeter*

WLKNDSHND well-conditioned *sound*

WLKRD wild card *unknown factor*

WLKT wildcat *(v) prospect* wildcatted wildcatting

WLKT wildcat *(n) animal*

WLKTR wildcatter *driller, promoter, striker*

WLLD well-oiled *smooth*

WLM whelm *engulf*

WLMD well-made *sturdy*

WLMN wheelman *driver* wheelmen

WLMNN well-meaning *good*

WLMNNG well-meaning

Letters aren't doubled for single sounds: to find alley use **L** not **LL**. Use **Y** and **W** as hard sounds only: to find yellow use **YL**. (Br)=British spelling or usage. * See dictionary.

good
WLMNT well-meant *good*
WLN well-nigh *near*
WLN whaling *hunt whales*
WLN wheeling *riding*
WLN willing *voluntary*
WLN woolen (or) woollen *of wool*
WLNFRMD well-informed *knowledgeable*
WLNG whaling *hunt whales*
WLNG wheeling *riding*
WLNG willing *voluntary*
WLNGL willingly *voluntary*
WLNGNS willingness *voluntary*
WLNGTN Wellington *boot*
WLNGWL Wailing Wall *prayer*
WLNL willingly *voluntary*
WLNL willy-nilly *haphazard*
WLNN well-known *famous*
WLNS wildness *not tame*
WLNS wiliness *trickiness*
WLNS willingness *voluntary*
WLNS woolliness *like wool*
WLNT walnut *food*
WLNT well-knit *strong*
WLNTNCHND well-intentioned *good*
WLNTNSHND well-intentioned *good*
WLNWL Wailing Wall *prayer*
WLP wallop *hit*
WLP whelp *young one*
WLPL woolpack *wrapper*
WLPLG wall plug *electricity*
WLPLT wall plate *electricity*
WLPN walloping *large*
WLPND well-appointed *complete*
WLPNG walloping *large*
WLPNTD well-appointed *complete*
WLPPR wallpaper *decoration*
WLPR willpower *determination*
WLPRZRVD well-preserved *young looking*
WLPWR willpower *determination*
WLR wailer *cryer*

WLR waler *horse*
WLR wallaroo *animal* wallaroos
WLR whaler *hunter, ship*
WLR wheeler *vehicle*
WLR wild rye *grain*
WLR wilier *trickier*
WLR woollier *like wool*
WLRD well-read *informed*
WLRDLR wheeler-dealer *shrewd one*
WLRDRD well-ordered *arranged*
WLRNDD well-rounded *widespread*
WLRS walrus *animal* walrus (or) walruses
WLRS wild rice *grain*
WLRT wheelwright *make or fix wheels*
WLS waltz *dance* waltzes
WLS wilds *wilderness*
WLSDNT wollastonite *mineral*
WLSH owlish *like an owl*
WLSH Welsh *of Wales*
WLSH welsh *(v) withdraw*
WLSHD woolshed *shearing*
WLSHL owlishly *like an owl*
WLSHNS owlishness *like an owl*
WLSHR welsher *withdrawer*
WLSHRBT Welsh rabbit *food*
WLSHRRBT Welsh rabbit *food*
WLSK woolsack *cushion*
WLSKN woolskin *sheepskin*
WLSPKN well-spoken *courteous*
WLSPRNG wellspring *source*
WLSR waltzer *dancer*
WLST well-set *established*
WLST whilst *during*
WLST wiliest *trickiest*
WLST woolliest *like wool*
WLSTNT wollastonite *mineral*
WLSTPLR wool stapler *dealer*
WLSTRT Wall Street *US financial center*

WLT owlet *bird*
WLT wallet *purse*
WLT welt *seam, ridge*
WLT wilt *limp*
WLTD well-to-do *rich*
WLTH wealth *riches*
WLTH wealthy *rich* wealthier wealthiest
WLTHDV well-thought-of *good reputation*
WLTHL wealthily *riches*
WLTHNS wealthiness *riches*
WLTHR wealthier *richer*
WLTHST wealthiest *richest*
WLTHTV well-thought-of *good reputation*
WLTHWSP will-o'-the-wisp *goal*
WLTHYR wealthier *richer*
WLTHYST wealthiest *richest*
WLTKN well-taken *justifiable*
WLTMD well-timed *suitable*
WLTR welter *confusion*
WLTRND well-turned *shapely*
WLTRWT welterweight *136-147 pounds*
WLTS waltz *dance* waltzes
WLTSR waltzer *dancer*
WLTWL wall-to-wall *floor*
WLTZ waltz *dance* waltzes
WLTZR waltzer *dancer*
WLVRN wolverine *weasel* wolverines
WLVTHWSP will-o'-the-wisp *goal*
WLVZ wolves (pl) *more than one wolf* wolf
WLW williwaw *wind*
WLW willowy *slim and graceful*
WLWL Walla Walla *city*
WLWR willowware *dinnerware*
WLWRK wheelwork *gears*
WLWRN well-worn *trite*
WLWSHR well-wisher *congratulate*
WLWST Wild West *frontier*
WLYLD well-oiled *smooth*
WLYR wilier *trickier*
WLYR woollier *like wool*

Use letters that best describe the sounds you hear and omit the vowels. Use **S** or **K** instead of **C**: to find circle use **SRKL**. Use **J** to find joy, **JM** to find gem and **G** to find go.

WLYST wiliest *trickiest*
WLYST woolliest *like wool*
WLZ Wales *country*
WLZ wilds *wilderness*
WLZ willies (slang—
uneasiness) *uneasiness*
WLZ woollies *garments*
WLZMN wheelsman *driver*
wheelsmen
WM wham *(v) hit, sound*
whammed whamming
WM wham (or) whammo
(adv) abruptly
WM whammy *curse*
whammies
WM whim *impulse*
WM womb *uterus*
WMBL wamble *stagger*
wambled wambling
WMBL wimble *tool*
WMBLDN Wimbledon
borough
WMBLTN Wimbledon
borough
WMBT wombat *animal*
WMN woman *female* women
WMNFK womenfolk *females*
WMNG Wyoming *US State*
WMNHD womanhood
female
WMNKN womankind *females*
WMNKND womankind
females
WMNL womanly *female*
WMNLK womanlike *female*
WMNLNS womanliness
female
WMNSH womanish *female*
WMNSHL womanishly
female
WMNSHNS womanishness
female
WMNZ womanize *make
female, pursue females*
womanized womanizing
(Br) womanise
WMNZR womanizer *make
female, pursue females*
(Br) womaniser
WMP whomp *slap*
WMP wimp *coward*
WMP wimpy *cowardly*

WMPL wimple *veil* wimpled
wimpling
WMPM wampum *money*
WMPNS wimpiness
cowardly
WMPR whimper *whine*
WMPSH wimpish *cowardly*
WMPSHNS wimpishness
cowardly
WMR woomera *rod*
WMRNR weimaraner *dog*
WMZ whimsy *impulse*
whimsies
WMZKL whimsical (adj)
fanciful whimsically (adv)
WMZKLD whimsicality
fanciful
WMZKLNS whimsicalness
fanciful
WMZKLT whimsicality
fanciful
WN one *(n) number 1 (pron)
person (adj) single unit,
entity**
WN owing *due to*
WN wain *wagon*
WN wan *pale* wanned
wanning wanner wannest
WN wane *decrease* waned
waning
WN wean *detach*
WN weenie *nerd, hot dog,
(slang) penis*
WN weeny *small*
WN weigh-in (n) *measure*
weigh in (v)
WN when *what time*
WN whine *complain* whined
whining
WN whinny *neigh* whinnied
whinnies
WN whiny (or) whiney
complaining
WN wienie (or) wiener *hot
dog*
WN win *succeed* won winning
WN wine *drink* wined wining
WN winnow *separate*
WN wino *(slang) usually
drunk on wine* winos
WN winy *like wine* winier
winiest

WN won *(v-past)* win
WN wynn (or) wyn *runic
letter*
WN yuan *money* yuan
WNB wanna-be *aspirer*
WNBG windbag *talkative one*
WNBL winnable *can succeed*
WNBLN windblown *tilted*
WNBRK windbreak *shelter*
WNBRKR windbreaker
jacket
WNBRN windburn *redness*
WNBRND windburned
redness
WNCH wench *woman*
wenches
WNCH winch *hoist* winches
WNCHL windchill
temperature
WNCHM wind chime *music*
WNCHSTR Winchester *city*
WND wand *rod*
WND want ad *advertisement*
WND wend *travel*
WND wind *(n) air*
WND wind *(v) coil* wound
winding
WND window *opening*
WND windy *breezy* windier
windiest
WND wound *(n) injury (v)
hurt*
WND wound *(v-past)* wind
WNDBG windbag *talkative
one*
WNDBKS window box
plants window boxes
WNDBLN windblown *tilted*
WNDBRK windbreak *shelter*
WNDBRKR windbreaker
jacket
WNDBRN windburn *redness*
WNDBRND windburned
redness
WNDBX window box *plants*
window boxes
WNDCHL windchill
temperature
WNDCHM wind chime
music
WNDD winded *breathless*
WNDD windowed *with*

Letters aren't doubled for single sounds: to find alley use **L** not **LL**. Use **Y** and **W** as hard
sounds only: to find yellow use **YL**. (Br)=British spelling or usage. * See dictionary.

windows

WNDD wounded *injured*

WNDDRS window-dress *display*

WNDDRSN window dressing *display*

WNDDRSNG window dressing *display*

WNDDRSR window dresser *display*

WNDFL windfall *gain*

WNDHVR windhover *(Br) bird*

WNDJ windage *gun sight*

WNDJMNG windjamming *sailing*

WNDJMR windjammer *ship*

WNDL windily *breeze*

WNDLS windlass *winch* windlasses

WNDLS windless *no wind*

WNDLSL windlessly *no wind*

WNDML windmill *(n) machine (v) spin*

WNDN winding *(adj) spiral (n) coil*

WNDNG winding *(adj) spiral (n) coil*

WNDNS windiness *breeze*

WNDP wind up *(v) motion, end* wound up winding up

WNDP windup *(n) motion, end (adj) spring-wound*

WNDPN windowpane *glass*

WNDPP windpipe *trachea*

WNDPRF windproof *impenetrable*

WNDR one-nighter *single evening*

WNDR wander *stray*

WNDR winder *tool, step*

WNDR windier *breezy*

WNDR windrow *piled in a row*

WNDR wonder *marvel*

WNDRFL wonderful (adj) *marvelous* wonderfully (adv)

WNDRFLNS wonderfulness *marvelous*

WNDRKND wunderkind *smart child* wunderkinder

WNDRKNDR wunderkinder (pl) *smart child* wunderkint

WNDRKNT wunderkind *smart child* wunderkinder

WNDRLN wonderland *imagination*

WNDRLND wonderland *imagination*

WNDRLST wanderlust *desire to stray*

WNDRMNT wonderment *surprise*

WNDRN wandering *straying*

WNDRNG wandering *straying*

WNDRR wanderer *strayer*

WNDRS wondrous *extraordinary*

WNDRSL wondrously *extraordinary*

WNDRSNS wondrousness *extraordinary*

WNDRWRK wonderwork *accomplishment*

WNDRWRKN wonder-working *miracles*

WNDRWRKNG wonder-working *miracles*

WNDRWRKR wonder-worker *miracles*

WNDRZ wind rose *diagram*

WNDSHD window shade *curtain*

WNDSHL windshield *screen*

WNDSHLD windshield *screen*

WNDSHP window-shop *look over* window-shopped window-shopping

WNDSHPR window-shopper *looker*

WNDSHR wind shear *shift*

WNDSK wind sock *indicator*

WNDSKRN windscreen *(Br) windshield*

WNDSL windowsill *frame*

WNDSPRNT wind sprint *race*

WNDSRFN windsurfing *sailboard*

WNDSRFNG windsurfing *sailboard*

WNDSRFR Windsurfer *(trademark) sailboard*

WNDST windiest *breezy*

WNDSTRM windstorm *high winds*

WNDSWP windswept *blown*

WNDSWPT windswept *blown*

WNDT wind tee *vane*

WNDT wyandotte *fowl*

WNDTNL wind tunnel *air flow*

WNDVR windhover *(Br) bird*

WNDW windway *air pipe*

WNDWN one-to-one *paired*

WNDWRD windward *toward wind*

WNDYR windier *breezy*

WNDYST windiest *breezy*

WNF one-off *(Br) unique*

WNFL windfall *gain*

WNG awing *astounding*

WNG owing *due to*

WNG whang *(n) thong, (Br) chunk (v) beat*

WNG wing *(n) limb, flight, (Br) fender (v) fly, wound, improvise**

WNGBK wingback *football*

WNGCHR wing chair *furniture*

WNGD winged *with wings, swift*

WNGDNG wingding *party*

WNGFDD wing-footed *swift*

WNGFTD wing-footed *swift*

WNGGL wangle *finagle* wangled wangling

WNGK eyewink *blink*

WNGK wink *eye, moment*

WNGK wonk *(slang) nerd*

WNGK wonky *(Br) unsteady*

WNGKL winkle *(v) twinkle, (Br) evict* winkled winkling

WNGL wangle *finagle* wangled wangling

WNGLK winglike *flying*

WNGLS wineglass *vessel* wineglasses

Use letters that best describe the sounds you hear and omit the vowels. Use **S** or **K** instead of **C**: to find circle use **SRKL**. Use **J** to find joy, **JM** to find gem and **G** to find go.

WNGLS wingless *no wings*
WNGLT winglet *airfoil*
WNGMN wingman *pilot*
   wingmen
WNGNT wing nut *hardware*
WNGR winger *player*
WNGRR winegrower *planter*
WNGRWR winegrower
   planter
WNGSPN wingspan *width*
WNGSPRD wingspread
   width
WNGT owing to *because of*
WNGTP wing tip *shoe*
WNGVR wingover *movement*
WNHNDD one-handed
   using one hand
WNHRS one-horse *small*
WNJMNG windjamming
   sailing
WNJMR windjammer *ship*
WNK eyewink *blink*
WNK wink *eye, moment*
WNK wonk *(slang) nerd*
WNK wonky *(Br) unsteady*
WNKL winkle *(v) twinkle,*
   (Br) evict winkled
   winkling
WNL wanly *pale*
WNLN weanling *baby*
WNLNG weanling *baby*
WNLNR one-liner *joke*
WNLS windlass *winch*
   windlasses
WNLS windless *no wind*
WNLS winless *no victory*
WNLSL windlessly *no wind*
WNML windmill *(n) machine*
   (v) spin
WNMN one-man *individual*
WNMRNR weimaraner *dog*
WNN winning *(n) victory*
   (adj) delightful
WNNG wanting *lacking*
WNNG winning *(n) victory*
   (adj) delightful
WNNGL winningly *(n)*
   victory (adj) delightful
WNNL winningly *(n) victory*
   (adj) delightful
WNNWN one-on-one
   encounter

WNP one-up *outdo* one-
   upped one-upping
WNPG Winnipeg *river, city,*
   lake
WNPMNSHP one-
   upmanship *outdo*
WNPP windpipe *trachea*
WNPRF windproof
   impenetrable
WNPRS winepress *squeezer*
   winepresses
WNPS one-piece *undivided*
WNPSMNSHP one-
   upmanship *outdo*
WNR wanner *paler*
WNR weaner *detach*
WNR whiner *complainer*
WNR wiener (or) wienie *hot*
   dog
WNR windrow *piled in a row*
WNR winery *wine producer*
   wineries
WNR winier *like wine*
WNR winner *victor*
WNR winnower *separator*
WNR winter *season*
WNRBR winterberry *shrub*
   winterberries
WNRGRN wintergreen *herb*
WNRKL winter-kill *exposure*
   death
WNRR winterer *resident*
WNRT wainwright *wagons*
WNRTM wintertime *season*
WNRZ wind rose *diagram*
WNRZ winterize
   weatherproof winterized
   winterizing
WNRZSHN winterization
   weatherproof
WNS once *one time, formerly*
WNS oneness *unity*
WNS wanness *paleness*
WNS whence *what place*
WNS wince *shrink back*
   winced wincing
WNSDD one-sided *partial*
WNSF oneself *person*
WNSHL windshield *screen*
WNSHLD windshield *screen*
WNSHP wineshop *tavern*
WNSHR wind shear *shift*

WNSHT one-shot *single*
WNSK wind sock *indicator*
WNSKN wineskin *bag*
WNSKRN windscreen *(Br)*
   windshield
WNSKT wainscot *panel*
   wainscoted (or)
   wainscotted wainscoting
   (or) wainscotting
WNSKT wainscoting (or)
   wainscotting *panelling*
WNSLF oneself *person*
WNSLR wine cellar *storage*
WNSLR wine seller *merchant*
WNSM winsome *cheerful*
WNSML winsomely *cheerful*
WNSMNS winsomeness
   cheer
WNSP Winesap *apple*
WNSPRNT wind sprint *race*
WNSRFN windsurfing
   sailboard
WNSRFNG windsurfing
   sailboard
WNSRFR Windsurfer
   (trademark) sailboard
WNST wannest *palest*
WNST winiest *like wine*
WNSTP one-step *dance*
WNSTP one-stop *complete*
WNSTRM windstorm *high*
   winds
WNSVR once-over *survey*
WNSWP windswept *blown*
WNSWPT windswept *blown*
WNT one-night *single*
   evening
WNT one-two *punches*
WNT owing to *because of*
WNT want *desire*
WNT went *(v-past) go*
WNT wind tee *vane*
WNT won't *(contr) will not*
WNT wont *accustomed* wont
   (or) wonted wonting
WNTD want ad
   advertisement
WNTM onetime *former, once*
   only
WNTN wanting *lacking*
WNTN wanton *lewd*
WNTN wonton *dumpling*

Letters aren't doubled for single sounds: to find alley use **L** not **LL**. Use **Y** and **W** as hard
sounds only: to find yellow use **YL**. (Br)=British spelling or usage. * See dictionary.

WNTNG wanting *lacking*
WNTNL wantonly *lewd*
WNTNL wind tunnel *air flow*
WNTNS wantonness *lewd*
WNTR one-nighter *single evening*
WNTR winter *season*
WNTR wintry *cold* wintrier wintriest
WNTRBR winterberry *shrub* winterberries
WNTRGRN wintergreen *herb*
WNTRK one-track *narrow*
WNTRKL winter-kill *exposure death*
WNTRR winterer *resident*
WNTRR wintrier *colder*
WNTRST wintriest *coldest*
WNTRTM wintertime *season*
WNTRYR wintrier *colder*
WNTRYST wintriest *coldest*
WNTRZ winterize *weatherproof* winterized winterizing
WNTRZSHN winterization *weatherproof*
WNTS once *one time, formerly*
WNTS whence *what place*
WNTS wince *shrink back* winced wincing
WNTSVR once-over *survey*
WNTT uintaite *asphalt*
WNTWN one-to-one *paired*
WNTYT uintaite *asphalt*
WNTZ once *one time, formerly*
WNVR whenever *anytime*
WNW one-way *direction*
WNW windway *air pipe*
WNWR winnower *separator*
WNWRD windward *toward wind*
WNYR winier *like wine*
WNYST winiest *like wine*
WNZ winze *passage*
WNZD Wednesday *weekday*
WP weep *cry* wept weeping
WP weepy *teary*
WP whip *lash* whipped whipping
WP whippy *springy* whippier

whippiest
WP whoop *yell*
WP whoopee *(interj) exuberance*
WP whop *hit hard* whopped whopping
WP wipe *(v) rub off* wiped wiping
WP wipe *(n) jeer, blow, towel*
WPD wapiti *elk* wapiti (or) wapitis
WPDD whoop-de-do (or) whoop-de-doo *activity*
WPDT wiped out *(slang) drunk, (slang) tired*
WPHL weep hole *drain*
WPKRD whipcord *rope, fabric*
WPL weep hole *drain*
WPLSH whiplash *injury* whiplashes
WPLTR whippletree *harness*
WPN weapon *tool for injury*
WPN weeping *crying*
WPN whipping *beating, fabric, stitch*
WPN whopping *unbelievable*
WPNB whipping boy *blamed one*
WPNG weeping *crying*
WPNG whipping *beating, fabric, stitch*
WPNG whopping *unbelievable*
WPNGB whipping boy *blamed one*
WPNGKF whooping cough *disease*
WPNGKRN whooping crane *bird*
WPNGWL weeping willow *tree*
WPNKF whooping cough *disease*
WPNKRN whooping crane *bird*
WPNLS weaponless *no tool for injury*
WPNR weaponry *tools for injury*
WPNTK wapentake *shire*
WPNWL weeping willow

tree
WPR weeper *cry*
WPR whippier *springy*
WPR whooper *crane, one that yells*
WPR whopper *large thing, lie*
WPR wiper *tool, person*
WPRSNPR whippersnapper *insignificant one*
WPRWL whippoorwill *bird*
WPS whipsaw *(n) tool (v) victimize*
WPS whoops *(interj) mistake*
WPST whippiest *springy*
WPSTCH whipstitch *sewing* whipstitches
WPSTK whipstock *handle*
WPSTL whip stall *airplane*
WPT wapiti *elk* wapiti (or) wapitis
WPT wept *(v-past) weep*
WPT whipped *(slang) tired*
WPT whippet *dog*
WPT wipe out *(v) destroy* wipeout (n)
WPTT wiped out *(slang) drunk, (slang) tired*
WPWRM whipworm *parasite*
WPYR whippier *springy*
WPYST whippiest *springy*
WR aware *conscious*
WR ewer *pitcher*
WR hour *60 minutes*
WR our *not your*
WR war *fight* warred warring
WR ware *article for sale*
WR wary *careful* warier wariest
WR we're *(contr) we are*
WR wear *clothing, fray* wore wearing worn
WR weary *(v) tire* wearied wearying wearies
WR weary *(adj) tired* wearier weariest
WR weigher *measurer*
WR weir *dam*
WR were *(v-past) are*
WR where *what place*
WR wherry *boat* wherries
WR whir *revolve, sound* whirred whirring

WR wire *thread, telegraph* wired wiring

WR wiry *like wire* wirier wiriest

WR wooer *lover*

WR wore *(v-past) wear*

WR worry *fret* worried worrying worryies

WRB whereby *by what*

WRBB war baby *birth* war babies

WRBK Auerbach *writer*

WRBL warble *sing* warbled warbling

WRBL wearable *clothing, fray*

WRBLD wearability *clothing, fray*

WRBLR warbler *singer, bird*

WRBLT wearability *clothing, fray*

WRBRD war bride *marriage*

WRBTS whereabouts *what place*

WRCHS huaraches *sandals*

WRCHST war chest *fund*

WRCHSTR Worcester *porcelain*

WRCHZ huaraches *sandals*

WRD award *(n) prize (v) grant*

WRD ward *area, person*

WRD warty *with warts*

WRD weird *strange*

WRD weirdo (or) weirdie (or) weirdy *(slang) odd person* weirdos (or) wierdies

WRD word *language*

WRD wordy *many words* wordier wordiest

WRDBK wordbook *dictionary*

WRDBL awardable *conferable*

WRDFRWRD word-for-word *exact quote*

WRDJ wordage *language*

WRDL weirdly *strangely*

WRDL wordily *many words*

WRDLBNK World Bank *lender*

WRDLMNDD worldly-minded *materialistic*

WRDLS wordless *silent*

WRDLSL wordlessly *silent*

WRDLSNS wordlessness *silence*

WRDLWZ worldly-wise *sophisticated*

WRDN warden *prison*

WRDN wear down *erode*

WRDN wording *speech*

WRDNG wording *speech*

WRDNS war dance *ceremony*

WRDNS weirdness *strangeness*

WRDNS wordiness *many words*

WRDNTS war dance *ceremony*

WRDPL wordplay *wit*

WRDPRSSN word processing *computer*

WRDPRSSNG word processing *computer*

WRDPRSSR word processor *computer*

WRDR voir dire *test*

WRDR warder *guard*

WRDR wiredraw *stretch*

WRDR wordier *many words*

WRDRB wardrobe *clothing*

WRDRM wardroom *ship*

WRDRN wiredrawn *indirect*

WRDRS wardress *guard (f)*

WRDSMTH wordsmith *writer*

WRDST wordiest *many words*

WRDVMTH word-of-mouth (adj) *oral* word of mouth (n)

WRDYR wordier *many words*

WRDYST wordiest *many words*

WRF wharf *pier* wharves

WRFD wirephoto *picture*

WRFJ wharfage *pier*

WRFL weariful (adj) *tired* wearifully (adv)

WRFMSTR wharfmaster *manager*

WRFNGR wharfinger *manager*

WRFNJR wharfinger *manager*

WRFR warfare *fighting*

WRFR wherefore *why*

WRFRN warfarin *poison*

WRFT wirephoto *picture*

WRGJ wire gauge *measure*

WRGLS hourglass *timepiece* hourglasses

WRGM war game (n) *pretend to fight* war-game (v)

WRGRS wire grass *plant*

WRHD warhead *missile*

WRHR wirehair *animal*

WRHRD wirehaired *stiff coat*

WRHRS warhorse *animal, veteran*

WRHS warehouse *storage* warehoused warehousing

WRHSR warehouser *storage*

WRHZ warehouse *storage* warehoused warehousing

WRHZR warehouser *storage*

WRK work (n) *effort, result* (v) *labor, arrange, succeed**

WRKBG workbag *pack*

WRKBK workbook *manual*

WRKBKS workbox *materials*

WRKBL workable *practicality*

WRKBLD workability *practicality*

WRKBLNS workableness *practicality*

WRKBLT workability *practicality*

WRKBNCH workbench *tools* workbenches

WRKBSKT workbasket *needlework*

WRKBT workboat *commerce*

WRKBX workbox *materials*

WRKD workaday *ordinary*

WRKD workday *time period*

WRKDP worked up *excited*

WRKF work off *dispose of*

WRKFR workfare *welfare*

WRKFRS workforce *labor*

WRKHLK workaholic

Letters aren't doubled for single sounds: to find alley use **L** not **LL**. Use **Y** and **W** as hard sounds only: to find yellow use **YL**. (Br)=British spelling or usage. * See dictionary.

compulsive
WRKHLZM workaholism
compulsion
WRKHRS workhorse *hard worker*
WRKHS workhouse *prison*
WRKLB war club *weapon*
WRKLD workload *job*
WRKLS workless *no job*
WRKMN workman *laborer* workmen
WRKMNLK workmanlike skillful
WRKMNSHP workmanship skill
WRKMT workmate *(Br) worker*
WRKN working *(n) operation (adj) labor, adequate*
WRKNG working *(n) operation (adj) labor, adequate*
WRKNGKLS working-class *(adj) wages* working class *(n)*
WRKNGMN workingman *laborer*
WRKNGWMN workingwoman *laborer*
WRKNKLS working-class *(adj) wages* working class *(n)*
WRKNMN workingman *laborer*
WRKNWMN workingwoman *laborer*
WRKP work up *(v) rouse*
WRKP work-up *(n) spacing*
WRKP workup *(n) study*
WRKPLS workplace *office, factory*
WRKPPL workpeople *(Br) laborers*
WRKPS workpiece *article*
WRKR war cry *yell* war cries
WRKR worker *laborer*
WRKRM war crime *felony*
WRKRM workroom *workshop*
WRKRS workhorse *hard worker*
WRKS workhouse *prison*

WRKS works *(n) factory, production, everything**
WRKSHP workshop *room, program*
WRKSTD work-study *school*
WRKSTSHN workstation *area, computer*
WRKT work out *(v) solve, develop, exercise*
WRKT workout *(n, adj) exercise, test*
WRKTBL worktable *furniture*
WRKTHK work ethic *labor*
WRKVR work over *rework, beat up*
WRKWK workweek *job time*
WRL hourly *every 60 minutes*
WRL warily *carefully*
WRL wearily *tire*
WRL whirl *(n) bustle (v) rotate*
WRL whirly *rush, storm* whirlies
WRL whorl *swirl*
WRL world *planet*
WRLBDR world-beater *champion*
WRLBNGK World Bank *lender*
WRLBNK World Bank *lender*
WRLBRD whirlybird *helicopter*
WRLBTR world-beater *champion*
WRLD whorled *swirled*
WRLD world *planet*
WRLDBDR world-beater *champion*
WRLDBNGK World Bank *lender*
WRLDBNK World Bank *lender*
WRLDBTR world-beater *champion*
WRLDKLS world-class *(adj) best*
WRLDL worldly *earthly*
WRLDLNS worldliness *earthly*
WRLDPR world power *strong nation*

WRLDPWR world power *strong nation*
WRLDSFR world's fair *exposition*
WRLDSHKN world-shaking *important*
WRLDSHKNG world-shaking *important*
WRLDSRZ World Series *baseball*
WRLDV worldview *outlook*
WRLDVY worldview *outlook*
WRLDWD worldwide *entire planet*
WRLDWR world war *fight*
WRLDWR world-weary *bored*
WRLDWRT World War II *fight*
WRLDWRWN World War I *fight*
WRLDZFR world's fair *exposition*
WRLGG whirligig *spinner*
WRLK warlike *hostile*
WRLK warlock *witch (m)*
WRLKLS world-class *(adj) best*
WRLNG hour-long *60 minutes*
WRLPL whirlpool *vortex*
WRLPR world power *strong nation*
WRLPWR world power *strong nation*
WRLRD warlord *leader*
WRLS weariless *energetic*
WRLS wireless *telegraph*
WRLSHKN world-shaking *important*
WRLSHKNG world-shaking *important*
WRLSRZ World Series *baseball*
WRLWD worldwide *entire planet*
WRLWN whirlwind *rush, storm*
WRLWND whirlwind *rush, storm*
WRLWR world war *fight*
WRLWR world-weary *bored*

Use letters that best describe the sounds you hear and omit the vowels. Use **S** or **K** instead of **C**: to find circle use **SRKL**. Use **J** to find joy, **JM** to find gem and **G** to find go.

WRLWRT World War II *fight*
WRLWRWN World War I *fight*
WRM war room *military*
WRM wareroom *exhibit*
WRM warm *heat* warmer warmest
WRM worm *animal*
WRM wormy *with worms* wormier wormiest
WRMBLDD warm-blooded *temperature, fervent*
WRMDVR warmed-over *stale*
WRMFNS worm fence *barrier*
WRMFNTS worm fence *barrier*
WRMFRNT warm front *weather*
WRMGR worm gear *wheel*
WRMHL wormhole *passage*
WRMHRDD warmhearted *affectionate*
WRMHRTD warmhearted *affectionate*
WRMHWL worm wheel *gear*
WRML wormhole *passage*
WRMNGGR warmonger *agitator*
WRMNGGRN warmongering *agitating*
WRMNGGRNG warmongering *agitating*
WRMNGPN warming pan *pot*
WRMNGR warmonger *agitator*
WRMNGRN warmongering *agitating*
WRMNGRNG warmongering *agitating*
WRMNPN warming pan *pot*
WRMNS warmness *heat*
WRMNT worriment *concern*
WRMP warm up (v) *prepare* warm-up (n, adj)
WRMPTH warmth *heat*
WRMR warmer *heat*
WRMR wormer *drug*
WRMR wormier *more worms*
WRMSH warmish *heated*

WRMSNK worm snake *reptile*
WRMST warmest *heat*
WRMST wormiest *most worms*
WRMTH warmth *heat*
WRMTN worm-eaten *holes*
WRMWD wormwood *plant, bitterness*
WRMWL worm wheel *gear*
WRMYR wormier *more worms*
WRMYST wormiest *most worms*
WRN warn *alert*
WRN warren *nest, area*
WRN wearing *tiring*
WRN wherein *in which, how*
WRN wiring *wires*
WRN worn *(v-past) wear*
WRNDTR wear and tear *loss*
WRNFSR warrant officer *rank*
WRNG wearing *tiring*
WRNG wiring *wires*
WRNGL wearingly *tiring*
WRNL wearingly *tiring*
WRNN warning *alarm*
WRNNG warning *alarm*
WRNR warner *counsel*
WRNR warrantor *gives guarantee*
WRNR warrener *gamekeeper*
WRNS awareness *understanding*
WRNS wariness *care*
WRNS weariness *tiredness*
WRNS wiriness *like wire*
WRNT warrant *sanction*
WRNT warrantee *receives guarantee*
WRNT warranty *guarantee* warranties
WRNT weren't *(contr) were not*
WRNT worn-out *tired, used up*
WRNTFSR warrant officer *rank*
WRNTR warrantor *gives guarantee*
WRNTR wear and tear *loss*

WRP warp *(n) yarns, base, twist (v) deform, arrange*
WRPJ warpage *twist*
WRPLN warplane *airplane*
WRPLR wire-puller *tool*
WRPN whereupon *on which*
WRPNT war paint *makeup*
WRPTH warpath *anger*
WRR warier *careful*
WRR warrior *fighter*
WRR wearier *tired*
WRR wirer *person wiring*
WRR wirier *like wire*
WRR worrier *concern*
WRS Warsaw *city*
WRS worse *inferior, sicker*
WRSDD worsted *yarn*
WRSF ourself *myself* ourselves
WRSHP warship *boat*
WRSHP worship *respect* worshiped (or) worshipped worshiping (or) worshipping
WRSHPFL worshipful (adj) *respectful* worshipfully (adv)
WRSHPFLNS worshipfulness *respect*
WRSHPR worshiper (or) worshipper *respect*
WRSLF ourself *myself* ourselves
WRSLVZ ourselves *us* ourself
WRSM wearisome *tiring*
WRSM worrisome *fretful*
WRSN worsen *make bad*
WRSSTR Worcester *porcelain*
WRST wariest *careful*
WRST weariest *tiring*
WRST wiriest *like wire*
WRST worst *most evil, ill, or faulty*
WRST wurst *sausage*
WRSTD worsted *yarn*
WRSTKS worst-case *bad outcome*
WRSTR Worcester *porcelain*
WRSTRSHR Worcestershire *sauce*

Letters aren't doubled for single sounds: to find alley use **L** not **LL**. Use **Y** and **W** as hard sounds only: to find yellow use **YL**. (Br)=British spelling or usage. * See dictionary.

WRSTSHR Worcestershire *sauce*

WRSVZ ourselves *us* ourself

WRT wart *skin lesion*

WRT warty *with warts*

WRT wear out *tire, become useless*

WRT whereat *at which*

WRT whereto *to what end*

WRT wort *plant, liquid*

WRTG warthog *animal*

WRTH worth *value, merit*

WRTH worthy *valuable, meritorious* worthier worthiest

WRTHG warthog *animal*

WRTHHWL worthwhile *valuable*

WRTHL worthily *value, merit*

WRTHLS worthless *no value, no merit*

WRTHLSL worthlessly *no value, no merit*

WRTHLSNS worthlessness *no value, no merit*

WRTHNS worthiness *value, merit*

WRTHR worthier *value, merit*

WRTHST worthiest *value, merit*

WRTHWL worthwhile *valuable*

WRTHYR worthier *value, merit*

WRTHYST worthiest *value, merit*

WRTM wartime *fighting*

WRTP wiretap *listen* wiretapped wiretapping

WRTPR wiretapper *listener*

WRV whereof *of which, of whom*

WRVR wherever *anywhere*

WRWF werewolf *creature* werewolves

WRWLF werewolf *creature* werewolves

WRWRK wirework *mesh*

WRWRM wireworm *larva*

WRWRT worrywart *fretful one*

WRWTH wherewith *how*

WRWTHL wherewithal *how, resources*

WRX works *(n) factory, production, everything**

WRYR warier *careful*

WRYR warrior *fighter*

WRYR wearier *tired*

WRYR wirier *like wire*

WRYR worrier *concern*

WRYST wariest *careful*

WRYST weariest *tired*

WRYST wiriest *like wire*

WRZ ours *not yours*

WRZ whereas *although, since*

WRZ worries *concerns*

WRZN war zone *battlefield*

WS wuss *(slang) wimp* wusses

WS wussy *(slang) wimpy*

WSB wasabi *herb*

WSBN waistband *clothing*

WSBN westbound *direction*

WSBND waistband *clothing*

WSBND westbound *direction*

WSBSKT wastebasket *trashcan*

WSCH huisache *shrub*

WSD wayside *beside*

WSDD wasted *ravaged, high*

WSDN wasting *decay*

WSDNG wasting *decay*

WSDNG westing *direction*

WSDR waster *destroyer, consumer*

WSDRL westerly *direction* westerlies

WSDRN western *(adj) direction (n) film, book*

WSDRNR Westerner *of the West*

WSDRNZ westernize *change* westernized westernizing

WSDRNZSHN westernization *changeover* (Br) westernisation

WSFL wasteful (adj) *extravagant* wastefully (adv)

WSFL wistful (adj) *thoughtful* wistfully (adv)

WSFLNS wistfulness *thoughtfulness*

WSH awash *flooded*

WSH eyewash *eye cleaner*

WSH wash *(v) bathe (n) marsh, refuse, paint**

WSH whoosh *rush*

WSH wish *hope* wishes

WSHBL washable *suitable to wash*

WSHBL washbowl *sink*

WSHBLD washability *cleanse*

WSHBLT washability *cleanse*

WSHBN wishbone *clavicles, shape*

WSHBRD washboard *scrubber, ship*

WSHBZN washbasin *sink*

WSHDP washed-up *finished*

WSHDT washed-out *tired, faded*

WSHFL wishful (adj) *desirous* wishfully (adv)

WSHFLNS wishfulness *desire*

WSHKLTH washcloth *bathe*

WSHLST wish list *dreams*

WSHN washing *clean*

WSHNDWR wash-and-wear *fabric*

WSHNG washing *clean*

WSHNGDN Washington *city, US president*

WSHNGTN Washington *city, US president*

WSHNTN Washington *city, US president*

WSHNWR wash-and-wear *fabric*

WSHR washer *hardware, laundry*

WSHRG washrag *bath*

WSHRM washroom *lavatory*

WSHRMN washerman *laundry* washermen

WSHRWMN washerwoman *laundry* washerwomen

WSHS washhouse *laundry*

WSHSTN washstand *sink*

WSHSTND washstand *sink*

WSHT wash out *(v) clean, reject, fade*

Use letters that best describe the sounds you hear and omit the vowels. Use **S** or **K** instead of **C**: to find circle use **SRKL**. Use **J** to find joy, **JM** to find gem and **G** to find go.

WSHT washout *(n) failure, erosion*
WSHTB washtub *laundry*
WSHTP washed-up *finished*
WSHTR washateria *laundry*
WSHTRY washateria *laundry*
WSHTT washed-out *tired, faded*
WSHWSH wishy-washy *weak*
WSHWSHNS wishy-washiness *weakness*
WSK whisk *brush, mix*
WSK whiskey *liquor*
WSKBRM whisk broom *brush*
WSKNSN Wisconsin *US State*
WSKR whisker *hair*
WSKRD whiskered *hair*
WSKT waistcoat *garment*
WSL wassail *hot drink*
WSL whistle *shrill sound* whistled whistling
WSLBLR whistle-blower *informer*
WSLBLWR whistle-blower *informer*
WSLN waistline *body*
WSLN wasteland *barren area*
WSLN whistling *hissing*
WSLND wasteland *barren area*
WSLNG whistling *hissing*
WSLR whistler *bird, animal, signal*
WSLSTP whistle-stop *train station*
WSNRTHWST west-northwest *direction*
WSP wasp *insect*
WSP WASP *(abbr) white Anglo-Saxon Protestant*
WSP wisp *(n) frail thing (v) drift*
WSP wispy *frail*
WSPL wispily *frail*
WSPNS wispiness *frailty*
WSPNT West Point *military school*
WSPP waste pipe *sewer*

WSPPR wastepaper *discard*
WSPR oospore *zygote*
WSPR whisper *(v) speak softly (n) rumor, trace, soft speech*
WSPRN whispering *hiss, gossip*
WSPRNG whispering *hiss, gossip*
WSPRR whisperer *gossip*
WSPSH waspish *sulky, small-waisted*
WSPSH wispish *frail*
WSPSHL waspishly *sulky, small-waisted*
WSPSHNS waspishness *sulky, small-waisted*
WSPWSTD wasp-waisted *slender*
WSRMN Wassermann *bacteriologist, test*
WSS oasis *water* oases
WSST oocyst *cell*
WST oocyte *egg*
WST waist *torso*
WST waste *(v) squander, kill, ravage* wasted wasting
WST waste *(n) desert, scrap, sewage*
WST west *direction*
WST whist *(n) game (adj, v) silence*
WSTBN waistband *clothing*
WSTBN westbound *direction*
WSTBND waistband *clothing*
WSTBND westbound *direction*
WSTBSKT wastebasket *trashcan*
WSTD wasted *ravaged, high*
WSTFL wasteful (adj) *extravagant* wastefully (adv)
WSTFL wistful (adj) *thoughtful* wistfully (adv)
WSTFLNS wistfulness *thoughtfulness*
WSTHWST west-southwest *direction*
WSTJ wastage *loss*

WSTKT waistcoat *garment*
WSTLN waistline *body*
WSTLN wasteland *barren area*
WSTLND wasteland *barren area*
WSTM wisdom *insight*
WSTN wasting *decay*
WSTNG wasting *decay*
WSTNG westing *direction*
WSTNRTHWST west-northwest *direction*
WSTPNT West Point *military school*
WSTPP waste pipe *sewer*
WSTPPR wastepaper *discard*
WSTR waster *destroyer, consumer*
WSTR wester *direction*
WSTR wisteria (or) wistaria *plant*
WSTR Worcester *porcelain*
WSTRL wastrel *vagabond*
WSTRL westerly *direction* westerlies
WSTRN western (adj) *direction (n) film, book*
WSTRNR Westerner *of the West*
WSTRNSM Western Samoa *islands*
WSTRNSMW Western Samoa *islands*
WSTRNZ westernize *change* westernized westernizing
WSTRNZSHN westernization *changeover*
WSTRSHR Worcestershire *sauce*
WSTRY wisteria (or) wistaria *plant*
WSTSHN way station *stop*
WSTSHR Worcestershire *sauce*
WSTSTHWST west-southwest *direction*
WSTVRJN West Virginia *US State*
WSTVRJNY West Virginia *US State*
WSTWDR wastewater

Letters aren't doubled for single sounds: to find alley use **L** not **LL**. Use **Y** and **W** as hard sounds only: to find yellow use **YL**. (Br)=British spelling or usage. * See dictionary.

sewage

WSTWRD westward *direction*

WSTWTR wastewater *sewage*

WSVRJN West Virginia *US State*

WSVRJNY West Virginia *US State*

WSWDR wastewater *sewage*

WSWRD westward *direction*

WSWTR wastewater *sewage*

WSZ oases (pl) *water* oasis

WT await *wait for, be in store*

WT waddy *club* waddies

WT wadi *gully* wadis

WT wait *(v) remain, serve (n) time period, musician*

WT watt *power unit*

WT weight *poundage, importance*

WT weighty *heavy* weightier weightiest

WT wet *(v) moisten* wet (or) wetted wetting

WT wet *(adj) damp (Br) weak* wetter wettest

WT what *which thing*

WT wheat *grain*

WT whet *(v) sharpen* whetted whetting

WT whet *(n) time, goad, appetizer*

WT whit *particle*

WT white *color* whiter whitest

WT white-tie (adj) *formal* white tie (n)

WT whitey *(slang-often capitalized) white person*

WT wit *humor, acumen, thinker*

WT witty *clever* wittier wittiest

WTBK wetback *immigrant*

WTBL wettable *moisture*

WTBLD wettability *moisture*

WTBLNGKT wet blanket *no fun*

WTBLNKT wet blanket *no fun*

WTBLT wettability *moisture*

WTBN white bean *vegetable*

WTBR wet bar *liquor*

WTBRCH white birch *tree*

WTBRD white-bread *(adj) bland*

WTBRD whitebeard *old one*

WTBS white bass *fish*

WTBT whitebait *fish*

WTCBS white sea bass *fish*

WTCDR white cedar *tree*

WTD weighted *heavy*

WTD whited *bleached*

WTD witted *smart*

WTDD white-headed *old*

WTDN wet down *sprinkle*

WTF what-if *question*

WTFDD white-footed *mouse*

WTFL whitefly *insect* whiteflies

WTFLG white flag *surrender*

WTFLT white flight *racial bias*

WTFS whiteface *color, clown*

WTFSH whitefish *animal*

WTFST white-faced *face color*

WTFTD white-footed *mouse*

WTGDZ white goods *linens, appliances*

WTGL white gold *metal*

WTGLD white gold *metal*

WTGRB white grub *larva*

WTH width *dimension*

WTH with *beside*

WTH withy *(n) twig (adj) tough* withies

WTHD whitehead *pimple*

WTHDD white-headed *old*

WTHDR withdraw *remove, retreat, retract* withdrew withdrawing withdrawn

WTHDRL withdrawal *remove, retreat, retract*

WTHDRN withdrawn *loner*

WTHDRWL withdrawal *remove, retreat, retract*

WTHHL withhold *keep* withheld withholding

WTHHLD withhold *keep* withheld withholding

WTHK ootheca *egg case* oothecae

WTHL withal *besides*

WTHL withhold *keep* withheld withholding

WTHLD withhold *keep* withheld withholding

WTHN within *inside*

WTHNR white hunter *safari*

WTHNTR white hunter *safari*

WTHP white hope *contender*

WTHR weather *(n) wind, rain, etc. (v) bear up*

WTHR wether *sheep, goat*

WTHR whether *if*

WTHR whither *where*

WTHR wither *(v) dry up (n) horse*

WTHR wuther *bluster*

WTHRBLD weatherability *bear up*

WTHRBLT weatherability *bear up*

WTHRBN weather-bound *no travel*

WTHRBND weather-bound *no travel*

WTHRBR weather bureau *forecasts*

WTHRBRD weatherboard *siding*

WTHRBRDD weatherboarded *siding*

WTHRBRDN weatherboarding *siding*

WTHRBRDNG weatherboarding *siding*

WTHRBRND weather-burned *tanned*

WTHRBTN weather-beaten *worn*

WTHRBYR weather bureau *forecasts*

WTHRD weathered *worn*

WTHRD white-haired *old*

WTHRGLS weatherglass *barometer*

WTHRKK weathercock *vane*

WTHRKST weathercast *forecast*

WTHRKSTR weathercaster *forecaster*

WTHRL weatherly *sailing*

WTHRMN weatherman

forecaster weathermen
WTHRMP weather map *forecasts*
WTHRN weathering *wear out, bear up*
WTHRNG weathering *wear out, bear up*
WTHRNG withering *spoiling*
WTHRPRF weatherproof *no damage*
WTHRPRSN weatherperson *forecaster*
WTHRSTRP weather strip (n) *insulation*
WTHRSTRP weather-strip (v) *insulate* weather-stripped weather-stripping
WTHRSTRPN weather stripping (n) *insulation*
WTHRSTRPNG weather stripping (n) *insulation*
WTHRT witherite *mineral*
WTHRVN weather vane *wind*
WTHRWRN weatherworn *exposure*
WTHRWZ weather-wise *good forecasting*
WTHRZ weatherize *insulate* weatherized weatherizing
WTHRZ withers *horse* (Br) wither
WTHRZSHN weatherization *insulation*
WTHS White House *US president*
WTHSTD withstood (*v-past*) *withstand*
WTHSTN withstand *resist* withstood withstanding
WTHSTND withstand *resist* withstood withstanding
WTHT white heat *hot*
WTHT white-hot *earnest*
WTHT with-it *up-to-date*
WTHT without *lacking, outside*
WTJ wattage *power unit*
WTJRM wheat germ *kernel*
WTK white oak *tree*
WTK wood tick *insect*

WTKLR white-collar *worker*
WTKP whitecap *wave*
WTKRND white-crowned *sparrow*
WTL waddle *walk* waddled waddling
WTL wattle (n) *tree, neck skin, thatch*
WTL wattle (v) *interweave* wattled wattling
WTL weightily *heavy*
WTL wetly *moist*
WTL what all (*pron*) *whatnot*
WTL white lie *falsehood*
WTL whitely *color*
WTL whitetail *deer*
WTL whitlow *vegetable*
WTL whittle *carve* whittled whittling
WTL wittily *cleverly*
WTLF witloof *plant*
WTLFDN weight lifting *barbells*
WTLFDNG weight lifting *barbells*
WTLFDR weight lifter *barbells*
WTLFNT white elephant *animal, junk*
WTLFTN weight lifting *barbells*
WTLFTNG weight lifting *barbells*
WTLFTR weight lifter *barbells*
WTLN wetland *marsh*
WTLN whittling *carving*
WTLN witling *fool*
WTLND wetland *marsh*
WTLNG whittling *carving*
WTLNG witling *fool*
WTLR whittler *carver*
WTLS weightless *no weight*
WTLS witless *foolish*
WTLSL weightlessly *no weight*
WTLSL witlessly *foolishly*
WTLSNS weightlessness *no weight*
WTLSNS witlessness *foolishness*
WTLTNN white lightning

liquor
WTLTNNG white lightning *liquor*
WTLVRD white-livered *cowardly*
WTMDR wattmeter *electricity*
WTMTR wattmeter *electricity*
WTN wheaten *grain, color*
WTN whiten *bleach*
WTNG wadding *lump, plug*
WTNG whiting *fish*
WTNGL wittingly *knowingly*
WTNKL white-knuckle *nervous*
WTNN whitening *bleach*
WTNNG whitening *bleach*
WTNR whitener *bleach*
WTNRS wet nurse (n) *care* wet-nurse (v)
WTNS eyewitness *observer*
WTNS weightiness *heaviness*
WTNS wetness *moisture*
WTNS whiteness *pallor*
WTNS witness (v) *observe* (n) *observer* witnesses
WTNS wittiness *cleverness*
WTNSBKS witness-box *law*
WTNSBX witness-box *law*
WTNSTN witness stand *law*
WTNSTND witness stand *law*
WTNT whatnot *miscellany*
WTNT white knight *rescuer*
WTNZ white noise *background*
WTPN white pine *tree*
WTPPR white paper *report*
WTPRCH white perch *fish*
WTR wader *bird, boot*
WTR waiter *server*
WTR water *liquid*
WTR watery *thin liquid, wishy-washy*
WTR watt-hour *power unit*
WTR weightier *heavier*
WTR wetter *moist*
WTR wheatear *bird*
WTR whetter *sharpener*
WTR wittier *clever*
WTR wood tar *leavings*

Letters aren't doubled for single sounds: to find alley use **L** not **LL**. Use **Y** and **W** as hard sounds only: to find yellow use **YL**. (Br)=British spelling or usage. * See dictionary.

WTRB water boy
  refreshments
WTRBD water bed *sleep*
WTRBFL water buffalo
  animal
WTRBG water bag
  container, womb
WTRBG water bug *insect*
WTRBK waterbuck *antelope*
WTRBRD waterbird
  swimmer, wader
WTRBRN waterborne *via*
  water
WTRCHSNT water chestnut
  vegetable
WTRCHSTNT water
  chestnut *vegetable*
WTRD white-haired *old*
WTRFL waterfall *rapids*
WTRFL waterfowl *bird*
  waterfowl
WTRFRNT waterfront
  shoreline
WTRFWL waterfowl *bird*
  waterfowl
WTRGJ water gauge *depth*
WTRGLS water glass *vessel*
  water glasses
WTRGT Watergate *scandal*
WTRHDR water heater
  appliance
WTRHL water hole *oasis*
WTRHTR water heater
  appliance
WTRHWL waterwheel
  rotator
WTRKLD water-cooled
  engine
WTRKLR watercolor *paint*
  (Br) watercolour
WTRKLR watercooler *drinks*
WTRKLZT water closet
  bathroom
WTRKRF watercraft *boat*
WTRKRFT watercraft *boat*
WTRKRS watercourse
  channel
WTRKRS watercress *plant*
WTRL waterloo *defeat*
  waterloos
WTRLG waterlog *drench*
  waterlogged

waterlogging
WTRLL water lily *plant*
  water lilies
WTRLN water line (or)
  waterline *highest level*
WTRLS waterless *no water*
WTRLVL water level
  instrument
WTRM white room *clean area*
WTRMDR water meter
  quantity
WTRMKSN water moccasin
  snake
WTRML water mill
  machinery
WTRMLN watermelon *fruit*
WTRMN water main *pipe*
WTRMN waterman *boating*
  watermen
WTRMRK watermark *design*
WTRMTR water meter
  quantity
WTRNMF water nymph
  myth
WTRNS wateriness *soggy,*
  weak
WTRPL water polo *sport*
WTRPLNT water-repellent
  no penetration
WTRPP water pipe *smoke*
WTRPR waterpower
  machinery
WTRPRF waterproof *no*
  penetration
WTRPRFN waterproofing *no*
  penetration
WTRPRFNG waterproofing
  no penetration
WTRPRFR waterproofer *no*
  penetration
WTRPSDL water pistol
  squirt gun
WTRPSTL water pistol
  squirt gun
WTRPWR waterpower
  machinery
WTRRR waterer *sprinkler*
WTRS waitress *server (f)*
  waitresses
WTRS water ice *dessert*
WTRS white rice *grain*
WTRSD waterside *coastal*

WTRSFR water sapphire
  gem
WTRSH waterish *soggy,*
  weak
WTRSH white trash *poor*
  class
WTRSHD watershed *divide,*
  turning point
WTRSK water ski (n) *sport*
  water-ski (v)
WTRSK water-soak *drench*
WTRSK waterski *sport*
WTRSKL water cycle
  weather
WTRSKN waterskiing *sport*
WTRSKNG waterskiing
  sport
WTRSKP waterscape *view*
WTRSKR water-skier
  sportsman
WTRSKYN waterskiing *sport*
WTRSKYNG waterskiing
  sport
WTRSKYR water-skier
  sportsman
WTRSNK water snake
  reptile
WTRSPNL water spaniel
  dog
WTRSPNYL water spaniel
  dog
WTRSPT water spot *citrus*
  disease
WTRSPT waterspout *pipe,*
  tornado
WTRSTRDR water strider
  insect
WTRT water rat *animal*
WTRT water right *access*
WTRTBL water table
  saturation
WTRTHRSH waterthrush
  bird
WTRTKC water taxi *boat*
WTRTKS water taxi *boat*
WTRTR water tower
  reservoir
WTRTT watertight *no leaks*
WTRTWR water tower
  reservoir
WTRTX water taxi *boat*
WTRVPR water vapor *steam*

Use letters that best describe the sounds you hear and omit the vowels. Use **S** or **K** instead of **C**: to find circle use **SRKL**. Use **J** to find joy, **JM** to find gem and **G** to find go.

WTRW waterway *channel*

WTRWCH water witch *find water*

WTRWCHN water witching *find water*

WTRWCHNG water witching *find water*

WTRWCHR water witcher *find water*

WTRWD waterweed *plant*

WTRWGN water wagon *sprinkler*

WTRWL waterwheel *rotator*

WTRWNGZ water wings *buoy*

WTRWRKS waterworks *fountain, supply system*

WTRWRN waterworn *smoothed*

WTRWRX waterworks *fountain, supply system*

WTRWV water wave *hairstyle*

WTRZSDNT water-resistant *no penetration*

WTRZSTNT water-resistant *no penetration*

WTS wits *mental ability, sanity*

WTSBS white sea bass *fish*

WTSDR white cedar *tree*

WTSH wettish *moist*

WTSH white ash *tree*

WTSL white cell *blood*

WTSL white sale *discount*

WTSND Whitsunday *Pentecost*

WTSPS white space *no print*

WTSS whatsis (or) whatsit *gadget*

WTSS white sauce *food*

WTST weightiest *heavy*

WTST wet suit *attire*

WTST wettest *moist*

WTST whatsit (or) whatsis *gadget*

WTST wittiest *clever*

WTSTN whetstone *sharpener*

WTSVR whatsoever *anything*

WTSWVR whatsoever

anything

WTSZM witticism *remark*

WTT white-hot *earnest*

WTT whiteout *snow*

WTT wideout *receiver*

WTTHRT whitethroat *bird*

WTVR whatever *anything*

WTW white way *theater district*

WTWD whitewood *tree*

WTWDR white water (n) *foam* white-water (adj)

WTWL white whale *animal*

WTWL whitewall *tire*

WTWN white wine *drink*

WTWNG whitewing *uniform*

WTWR watt-hour *power unit*

WTWSH wet wash *bathe*

WTWSH whitewash (v) *gloss over* (n) *lime, defeat*

WTWSHNG whitewashing *lime*

WTWTR white water (n) *foam* white-water (adj)

WTYR weightier *heavier*

WTYR wittier *clever*

WTYST weightiest *heavy*

WTYST wittiest *clever*

WTZNFNDL white zinfandel *wine*

WV waive *give up* waived waiving

WV wave (v) *flutter, signal* waved waving

WV WAVE (abbr) *Women Accepted for Volunteer Emergency Service (US Navy)*

WV wave (n) *ocean swell, curve*

WV wavy *curving* wavier waviest

WV we've (contr) *we have*

WV weave (v) *interlace, sway* wove weaving woven (or) weaved

WV weave (n) *pattern*

WV wive *marry* wived wiving

WVBN wave band *radio*

WVBND wave band *radio*

WVD waved *curving*

WVFRM waveform *curving*

WVGD waveguide *light*

WVL wavily *curving*

WVL weevil *insect*

WVL weevily (or) weevilly *with weevils*

WVLNGKTH wavelength *measure*

WVLNGTH wavelength *measure*

WVLNKTH wavelength *measure*

WVLNTH wavelength *measure*

WVLT wavelet *ripple*

WVN woven (v-past) *weave*

WVNS waviness *curving*

WVR waiver *give up rights*

WVR waver (n) *person waving*

WVR waver (v) *sway, hesitate*

WVR wavier *curving*

WVR weaver *fabric maker*

WVRBRD weaverbird *animal*

WVRN wyvern *animal*

WVRNGL waveringly *sway, hesitate*

WVRNL waveringly *sway, hesitate*

WVRR waverer *sway, hesitate*

WVST waviest *curving*

WVYR wavier *curving*

WVYST waviest *curving*

WVZ wives (pl) *spouse* wife

WVZ wolves (pl) *more than one wolf* wolf

WWPDL wa-wa pedal *music*

WWPTL wa-wa pedal *music*

WWR wooer *lover*

WWRD wayward *contrary*

WWRDL waywardly *contrary*

WWRDNS waywardness *contrary*

WWRN wayworn *weary*

WX wax (n) *substance* (v) *shine, increase, become* waxes

WX waxy *smooth and white* waxier waxiest

WXBL waxbill *bird*

WXBN wax bean *vegetable*

WXN waxen *flexible, pale*

WXN waxing *polish, remove*

Letters aren't doubled for single sounds: to find alley use **L** not **LL**. Use **Y** and **W** as hard sounds only: to find yellow use **YL**. (Br)=British spelling or usage. * See dictionary.

hair

WXNG waxing *polish, remove hair*

WXNS waxiness *smooth and white*

WXPPR wax paper *wrap*

WXR waxer *polisher*

WXR waxier *smooth and white*

WXS y-axis *math*

WXST waxiest *smooth and white*

WXTPPR waxed paper *wrap*

WXWNG waxwing *bird*

WXWRK waxwork *dummy*

WXYR waxier *smooth and white*

WXYST waxiest *smooth and white*

WY whew *(interj) relief*

WYBL weighable *measure*

WYKSS y-axis *math*

WYL while *(v) pass time* whiled whiling

WYL while *(conj) during*

WYL wild *untamed*

WYL wile *(v) pass time* wiled wiling

WYL wile *(n) trick*

WYL wily *crafty* wilier wiliest

WYLBR wild boar *pig*

WYLD wild *untamed*

WYLDBR wild boar *pig*

WYLDD wild-eyed *extreme*

WYLDFL wildfowl *bird*

WYLDFLR wildflower *plant*

WYLDFLWR wildflower *plant*

WYLDFR wildfire *burn, glow, plant disease*

WYLDFYR wildfire *burn, glow, plant disease*

WYLDGSCHS wild-goose chase *search*

WYLDKDR wildcatter *driller, promoter, striker*

WYLDKRD wild card *unknown factor*

WYLDKT wildcat *(v) prospect* wildcatted wildcatting

WYLDKT wildcat *(n) animal*

WYLDKTR wildcatter *driller, promoter, striker*

WYLDL wildly *extremely*

WYLDLF wildlife *animals*

WYLDLN wildland *uncultivated*

WYLDLN wildling *uncultivated*

WYLDLND wildland *uncultivated*

WYLDLNG wildling *uncultivated*

WYLDN wilding *uncultivated*

WYLDNG wilding *uncultivated*

WYLDNS wildness *not tame*

WYLDPCH wild pitch *baseball* wild pitches

WYLDR wild rye *grain*

WYLDRS wild rice *grain*

WYLDS wilds *wilderness*

WYLDTS wild oats *indiscretions*

WYLDWST Wild West *frontier*

WYLDZ wilds *wilderness*

WYLF wildlife *animals*

WYLFLR wildflower *plant*

WYLFLWR wildflower *plant*

WYLFR wildfire *burn, glow, plant disease*

WYLFYR wildfire *burn, glow, plant disease*

WYLGSCHS wild-goose chase *search*

WYLKDR wildcatter *driller, promoter, striker*

WYLKRD wild card *unknown factor*

WYLKT wildcat *(v) prospect* wildcatted wildcatting

WYLKT wildcat *(n) animal*

WYLKTR wildcatter *driller, promoter, striker*

WYLN wildland *uncultivated*

WYLND wildland *uncultivated*

WYLNS wildness *not tame*

WYLR wild rye *grain*

WYLRS wild rice *grain*

WYLWST Wild West *frontier*

WYMNG Wyoming *US State*

WYN weigh-in *(n) measure* weigh in *(v)*

WYNDT wyandotte *fowl*

WYR weigher *measurer*

WYR wire *thread, telegraph* wired wiring

WYR wiry *like wire* wirier wiriest

WYRDR wiredraw *stretch*

WYRDRN wiredrawn *indirect*

WYRFD wirephoto *picture*

WYRFT wirephoto *picture*

WYRGJ wire gauge *measure*

WYRGRS wire grass *plant*

WYRHR wirehair *animal*

WYRHRD wirehaired *stiff coat*

WYRLS wireless *telegraph*

WYRN wiring *wires*

WYRNG wiring *wires*

WYRNS wiriness *like wire*

WYRPLR wire-puller *tool*

WYRR wirer *person wiring*

WYRR wirier *like wire*

WYRST wiriest *like wire*

WYRTP wiretap *listen* wiretapped wiretapping

WYRTPR wiretapper *listener*

WYRWRK wirework *mesh*

WYRWRM wireworm *larva*

WYRYR wirier *like wire*

WYRYST wiriest *like wire*

WYT way out *exit*

WYT way-out *(slang) groovy*

WYXS y-axis *math*

WZ was *(v-past) to be*

WZ ways *methods*

WZ wheeze *hiss* wheezed wheezing

WZ wheezy *hissing* wheezier wheeziest

WZ whiz *wizard* whizzes

WZ whiz *(or) whizz (v) hiss, fly* whizzed whizzing

WZ whiz *(or) whizz sound* whizzes

WZ wise *(adj) sage, sensible* wiser wisest

WZ wise *(v) learn, teach* wised wising

WZ wiz *wizard*

Use letters that best describe the sounds you hear and omit the vowels. Use **S** or **K** instead of **C**: to find circle use **SRKL**. Use **J** to find joy, **JM** to find gem and **G** to find go.

pardon excusably (adv)

XKZR excuser *pardon*

XKZTR excusatory *pardon*

XL axel *jump*

XL axial (adj) *axis* axially (adv)

XL axil *leaf*

XL axilla *armpit* axillae (or) axillas

XL axle *wheel*

XL excel *surpass* excelled excelling

XL exhale *breathe out* exhaled exhaling

XL exile *banish* exiled exiling

XLG axiology *ethics*

XLJ axiology *ethics*

XLJKL axiological (adj) *ethical* axiologically (adv)

XLK oxalic *acid*

XLNC excellency *title* excellencies

XLNS excellence *virtue, best quality*

XLNS excellency *title* excellencies

XLNT excellent *first-class*

XLNT exhalant (or) exhalent *outflow*

XLNTC excellency *title* excellencies

XLNTL excellently *first-class*

XLNTS excellence *virtue, best quality*

XLNTS excellency *title* excellencies

XLP oxlip *plant*

XLR auxiliary *help, extra* auxiliaries

XLR axillar *feather*

XLR axillary *feather* axillaries

XLRDNGL acceleratingly *increasingly*

XLRDR accelerator *speed device*

XLRDV accelerative *increased*

XLRDV exhilarative *stimulated*

XLRMDR accelerometer *speed measure*

XLRMTR accelerometer *speed measure*

XLRND accelerando *tempo* accelerandos

XLRNT accelerant *speed*

XLRNT exhilarant *enliven*

XLRSHN acceleration *speed*

XLRSHN exhilaration *stimulation*

XLRT accelerate *speed up* accelerated accelerating

XLRT exhilarate *enliven* exhilarated exhilarating

XLRTNGL acceleratingly *increasingly*

XLRTNL acceleratingly *increasingly*

XLRTR accelerator *speed device*

XLRTV accelerative *increased*

XLRTV exhilarative *stimulated*

XLS oxalis *plant*

XLSHN exhalation *outflow*

XLSHR excelsior *packaging*

XLSHYR excelsior *packaging*

XLSR excelsior *packaging*

XLSYR excelsior *packaging*

XLT exalt *praise*

XLT exult *rejoice*

XLT oxalate *acid salt*

XLTDL exaltedly *elevated*

XLTNC exultancy *rejoicing* exultance

XLTNS exultance *rejoicing* exultancy

XLTNT exultant *rejoicing*

XLTNTC exultancy *rejoicing* exultance

XLTNTS exultance *rejoicing* exultancy

XLTR exalter *praiser*

XLTSHN exaltation *praise*

XLTSHN exultation *rejoicing*

XLYR auxiliary *help, extra* auxiliaries

XM axiom *truth*

XM eczema *skin rash*

XM exam *test*

XM exhume *dig up* exhumed exhuming

XMDK axiomatic *self-evident*

XMDKL axiomatically *self-evidently*

XMDS eczematous *skin rash*

XMN examine *inspect, test* examined examining

XMN examinee *person tested*

XMNBL examinable *inspect, test*

XMNNT examinant *tester*

XMNR examiner *inspector, tester*

XMNSHN examination *inspection, test*

XMP exempt *free*

XMPL example *model, instance*

XMPLF exemplify *embody* exemplified exemplifying exemplifies

XMPLFKSHN exemplification *illustration*

XMPLGRSH exempli gratia *for example (e.g.)*

XMPLR exemplar *model*

XMPLR exemplary *model*

XMPLRL exemplarily *model*

XMPLRNS exemplariness *model*

XMPSHN exemption *freedom*

XMPT exempt *free*

XMR exhumer *dig up*

XMR oxymora (pl) *contradiction* oxymoron

XMRN oxymoron *contradiction* oxymora

XMRNK oxymoronic *contradictory*

XMRNKL oxymoronically *contradictory*

XMS Xmas *Christmas*

XMSHN exemption *freedom*

XMSHN exhumation *dig up*

XMT exempt *free*

XMTK axiomatic *self-evident*

XMTKL axiomatically *self-evidently*

XMTS eczematous *skin rash*

XN auxin *plant hormone*

XN axion *particle*

XN axon *neuron*

Letters aren't doubled for single sounds: to find **alley** use **L** not **LL**. Use **Y** and **W** as hard sounds only: to find **yellow** use **YL**. (Br)=British spelling or usage. * See dictionary.

XN exine *outer layer*
XN exon *protein*
XN oxen (pl) *animal ox*
XNCHL accentual *emphasis*
XNCHSHN accentuation
  emphasis
XNCHT accentuate
  emphasize accentuated
  accentuating
XNCHWL accentual
  emphasis
XNCHWSHN accentuation
  emphasis
XNCHWT accentuate
  emphasize accentuated
  accentuating
XNK auxinic *plant hormone*
XNM axoneme *cilium*
XNML axonemal *cilium*
XNMT exanimate *lifeless*
XNMTRK axonometric
  drawing
XNRDV exonerative
  forgiving
XNRSHN exoneration
  forgiveness
XNRSPT x-intercept *math*
XNRT exonerate *forgive*
  exonerated exonerating
XNRTV exonerative
  forgiving
XNSHL accentual *emphasis*
XNSHSHN accentuation
  emphasis
XNSHT accentuate
  emphasize accentuated
  accentuating
XNSHWL accentual
  emphasis
XNSHWSHN accentuation
  emphasis
XNSHWT accentuate
  emphasize accentuated
  accentuating
XNT accent *inflection,*
  emphasis
XNT exeunt *exit*
XNTL accentual *emphasis*
XNTLS accentless *without*
  emphasis, inflection
XNTRK eccentric *strange*
XNTRKL eccentrically

  strangely
XNTRSD eccentricity
  strangeness eccentricities
XNTRSPT x-intercept *math*
XNTRST eccentricity
  strangeness eccentricities
XNTSHL accentual *emphasis*
XNTSHN accentuation
  emphasis
XNTSHT accentuate
  emphasize accentuated
  accentuating
XNTSHWL accentual
  emphasis
XNTSHWT accentuate
  emphasize accentuated
  accentuating
XNTT accentuate *emphasize*
  accentuated
  accentuating
XNTWL accentual *emphasis*
XNTWSHN accentuation
  emphasis
XNTWT accentuate
  emphasize accentuated
  accentuating
XP accept *receive*
XP except *(prep) exclusion*
  (v) exclude, object (conj)
  unless, only
XPBL acceptable *receivable*
XPBL expiable *amends*
XPDBL acceptable (adj)
  adequate acceptably (adv)
XPDBLD acceptability
  adequacy
XPDBLT acceptability
  adequacy
XPDD accepted *approved*
XPDDR expediter *dispatcher*
XPDL occipital (adj) *bone*
  occipitally (adv)
XPDNC expediency
  suitability expedience
XPDNS acceptance
  receptiveness
XPDNS expedience
  suitability expediency
XPDNT acceptant *receptive*
XPDNT expedient *suitable*
XPDNTC expediency
  suitability expedience

XPDNTS acceptance
  receptiveness
XPDNTS expedience
  suitability expediency
XPDR accepter (or)
  acceptor *receiver*
XPDR accipiter *hawk*
XPDR expiator *atonement*
XPDSHN expedition
  journey, speed
XPDSHNR expeditionary
  journey
XPDSHS expeditious *fast*
XPDSHSL expeditiously *fast*
XPDSHSNS
  expeditiousness *speed*
XPDT expedite *speed up*
  expedited expediting
XPDTR expediter *dispatcher*
XPDV acceptive *adequate*
XPDYNC expediency
  suitability expedience
XPDYNS expedience
  suitability expediency
XPDYNT expedient *suitable*
XPDYNTC expediency
  suitability expedience
XPDYNTS expedience
  suitability expediency
XPK expect *look forward,*
  think, await
XPKDBL expectable (adj)
  look forward, think, await
  expectably (adv)
XPKDDL expectedly *look*
  forward, think, await
XPKDNC expectancy *look*
  forward, think, await
  expectancies
XPKDNS expectancy *look*
  forward, think, await
  expectancies
XPKDNT expectant *look*
  forward, think, await
XPKDNTC expectancy *look*
  forward, think, await
  expectancies
XPKDNTS expectancy *look*
  forward, think, await
  expectancies
XPKDRNT expectorant
  mucus

Use letters that best describe the sounds you hear and omit the vowels. Use **S** or **K** instead of **C**: to find circle use **SRKL**. Use **J** to find joy, **JM** to find gem and **G** to find go.

XPKDRSHN expectoration *spit*

XPKDRT expectorate *spit* expectorated expectorating

XPKT expect *look forward, think, await*

XPKTBL expectable (adj) *look forward, think, await* expectably (adv)

XPKTDL expectedly *look forward, think, await*

XPKTDV expectative *look forward, think, await*

XPKTNC expectancy *look forward, think, await* expectancies

XPKTNS expectancy *look forward, think, await* expectancies

XPKTNT expectant *look forward, think, await*

XPKTNTC expectancy *look forward, think, await* expectancies

XPKTNTS expectancy *look forward, think, await* expectancies

XPKTRNT expectorant *mucus*

XPKTRSHN expectoration *spit*

XPKTRT expectorate *spit* expectorated expectorating

XPKTSHN expectation *look forward, think, await*

XPKTTV expectative *look forward, think, await*

XPL expel *eject* expelled expelling

XPL expellee *ejected one*

XPLBL expellable *eject*

XPLD explode *burst* exploded exploding

XPLDBL exploitable *use*

XPLDD exploded *(adj) diagram*

XPLDR exploder *burst*

XPLDR exploiter *user*

XPLDV expletive *word*

XPLKBL explicable (adj)

explain explicably (adv)

XPLKDV explicative *explanation*

XPLKSHN explication *explanation*

XPLKT explicate *explain* explicated explicating

XPLKTR explicatory *explanation*

XPLKTV explicative *explanation*

XPLN explain *clarify*

XPLNBL explainable *clarify*

XPLNSHN explanation *clarification*

XPLNT explant *remove*

XPLNTR explanatory *clarify*

XPLNTRL explanatorily *clarify*

XPLNTSHN explantation *removal*

XPLR explore *investigate* explored exploring

XPLR explorer *investigator*

XPLRDV explorative *investigation*

XPLRR explorer *investigator*

XPLRSHN exploration *investigation*

XPLRTR exploratory *investigation*

XPLRTV explorative *investigation*

XPLSD explicit *specific*

XPLSHN explosion *burst*

XPLSHN expulsion *ejection*

XPLST explicit *specific*

XPLSTL explicitly *specifically*

XPLSTNS explicitness *specific*

XPLSV explosive *burst*

XPLSVL explosively *burst*

XPLSVNS explosiveness *burst*

XPLT exploit *(n) feat (v) use*

XPLTBL exploitable *use*

XPLTDV exploitative *use*

XPLTDVL exploitatively *use*

XPLTR expletory *word*

XPLTR exploiter *user*

XPLTSHN exploitation *use*

XPLTTV exploitative *use*

XPLTTVL exploitatively *use*

XPLTV expletive *word*

XPLZHN explosion *burst*

XPLZV explosive *burst*

XPLZVL explosively *burst*

XPLZVNS explosiveness *burst*

XPN expand *swell*

XPN expend *spend*

XPN expound *explain*

XPNCHN expansion *increase*

XPNCHNR expansionary *increase*

XPNCHNST expansionist *more territory*

XPNCHNZM expansionism *more territory*

XPND expand *swell*

XPND expend *spend*

XPND expound *explain*

XPNDBL expandable *swelling*

XPNDBL expendable *easy to replace*

XPNDBLD expandability *swelling*

XPNDBLD expendability *easy to replace*

XPNDBLT expandability *swelling*

XPNDBLT expendability *easy to replace*

XPNDCHR expenditure *expense*

XPNDD expanded *swelled*

XPNDR expander *increaser*

XPNDTR expenditure *expense*

XPNJ expunge *cancel, destroy* expunged expunging

XPNJR expunger *cancel, destroy*

XPNNCHL exponential (adj) *rapid increase* exponentially (adv)

XPNNSHL exponential (adj) *rapid increase* exponentially (adv)

XPNNT exponent *math symbol, example*

XPNS expanse *extent*

Letters aren't doubled for single sounds: to find alley use **L** not **LL**. Use **Y** and **W** as hard sounds only: to find yellow use **YL**. (Br)=British spelling or usage. * See dictionary.

XPNS expense *(v) charge* expensed expensing
XPNS expense *(n) cost*
XPNSBL expansible *increase*
XPNSBLD expansibility *increase*
XPNSBLT expansibility *increase*
XPNSHN expansion *increase*
XPNSHNR expansionary *increase*
XPNSHNST expansionist *more territory*
XPNSHNZM expansionism *more territory*
XPNSV expansive *sizable*
XPNSV expensive *costly*
XPNSVL expensively *costly*
XPNT excipient *inert base*
XPNTS expanse *extent*
XPNTS expense *(v) charge* expensed expensing
XPNTS expense *(n) cost*
XPNTSBL expansible *increase*
XPNTSBLD expansibility *increase*
XPNTSBLT expansibility *increase*
XPNTSV expansive *sizable*
XPNTSV expensive *costly*
XPNTSVL expensively *costly*
XPR expire *end, breathe out* expired expiring
XPR expiry *end, death* expiries
XPRDBL exportable *removal*
XPRDBLD exportability *removal*
XPRDBLT exportability *removal*
XPRDR exporter *wholesaler*
XPRGDR expurgator *cleanser*
XPRGSHN expurgation *cleansing*
XPRGT expurgate *cleanse* expurgated expurgating
XPRGTR expurgator *cleanser*
XPRMNL experimental (adj) *unproven* experimentally

(adv)
XPRMNLST experimentalist *tester*
XPRMNR experimenter *tester*
XPRMNT experiment *test*
XPRMNTL experimental (adj) *unproven* experimentally (adv)
XPRMNTLST experimentalist *tester*
XPRMNTR experimenter *tester*
XPRMNTSHN experimentation *testing*
XPRNCHL experiential (adj) *questionable* experientially (adv)
XPRNS experience *(v) undergo* experienced experiencing
XPRNS experience *(n) knowledge, life*
XPRNSD experienced *practiced*
XPRNSHL experiential (adj) *questionable* experientially (adv)
XPRNST experienced *practiced*
XPRNTS experience *(v) undergo* experienced experiencing
XPRNTS experience *(n) knowledge, life*
XPRPRDR expropriator *taker*
XPRPRSHN expropriation *taking*
XPRPRT expropriate *take* expropriated expropriating
XPRPRTR expropriator *taker*
XPRPRYDR expropriator *taker*
XPRPRYSHN expropriation *taking*
XPRPRYT expropriate *take* expropriated expropriating
XPRPRYTR expropriator

taker
XPRS espresso *coffee*
XPRS express *(v) state, squeeze (n) delivery (adj) explicit, fast*
XPRSBL expressible *state, squeeze*
XPRSHN expiration *end, breathe out*
XPRSHN expression *utterance, symbol*
XPRSHNLS expressionless *reserved*
XPRSHNSDK expressionistic *art*
XPRSHNSTK expressionistic *art*
XPRSHNZM expressionism *art*
XPRSJ expressage *fee*
XPRSL expressly *definitely*
XPRSMN expressman *delivery* expressmen
XPRSV expressive *show feeling*
XPRSVD expressivity *show feeling, affect* expressivities
XPRSVNS expressiveness *show feeling*
XPRSVT expressivity *show feeling, affect* expressivities
XPRSW expressway *highway*
XPRT ex parte *partisan*
XPRT expert (adj) *proficient (n) master*
XPRT export *(v) remove (n) commodity*
XPRTBL exportable *removal*
XPRTBLD exportability *removal*
XPRTBLT exportability *removal*
XPRTR expiratory *breathe out*
XPRTR exporter *wholesaler*
XPRTS expertise *skill*
XPRTSHN exportation *removal*
XPRTZ expertise *skill*

Use letters that best describe the sounds you hear and omit the vowels. Use **S** or **K** instead of **C**: to find circle use **SRKL**. Use **J** to find joy, **JM** to find gem and **G** to find go.

XPRYNCHL experiential (adj) *questionable* experientially (adv)
XPRYNS experience *(v)* *undergo* experienced experiencing
XPRYNS experience *(n)* *knowledge, life*
XPRYNSD experienced *practiced*
XPRYNSHL experiential (adj) *questionable* experientially (adv)
XPRYNST experienced *practiced*
XPRYNTS experience *(v)* *undergo* experienced experiencing
XPRYNTS experience *(n)* *knowledge, life*
XPSCHLSHN expostulation *discussion*
XPSCHLT expostulate *discuss*
XPSCHLTR expostulatory *discussion*
XPSFKD ex post facto *after the fact*
XPSFKT ex post facto *after the fact*
XPSHN exception *exclusion, objection*
XPSHN expiation *atonement*
XPSHNBL exceptionable (adj) *objection* exceptionably (adv)
XPSHNBLT exceptionability *objection*
XPSHNL exceptional (adj) *rare* exceptionally (adv)
XPSHR exposure *no protection*
XPSHSHN expatiation *wandering*
XPSHT expatiate *wander* expatiated expatiating
XPSHYSHN expatiation *wandering*
XPSHYT expatiate *wander* expatiated expatiating
XPSTFKD ex post facto *after the fact*

XPSTFKT ex post facto *after the fact*
XPSTLSHN expostulation *discussion*
XPSTLT expostulate *discuss*
XPSTLTR expostulatory *discussion*
XPT accept *receive*
XPT except (prep) *exclusion* (v) *exclude, object* (conj) *unless, only*
XPT expat *exile*
XPT expiate *make amends* expiated expiating
XPT occiput *skull* occiputs (or) occipita
XPTBL acceptable *receivable*
XPTBL acceptable (adj) *adequate* acceptably (adv)
XPTBLD acceptability *adequacy*
XPTBLT acceptability *adequacy*
XPTD accepted *approved*
XPTL occipital (adj) *bone* occipitally (adv)
XPTNGL acceptingly *approving*
XPTNGNS acceptingness *approval*
XPTNS acceptance *receptiveness*
XPTNT acceptant *receptive*
XPTNTS acceptance *receptiveness*
XPTR accepter (or) acceptor *receiver*
XPTR accipiter *hawk*
XPTR expiator *atonement*
XPTRN accipitrine *hawklike*
XPTRSHN expatriation *exile*
XPTRT expatriate *exile* expatriated expatriating
XPTRYSHN expatriation *exile*
XPTRYT expatriate *exile* expatriated expatriating
XPTSHN acceptation *approval*
XPTV acceptive *adequate*
XPYBL expiable *amends*
XPYDR expiator *atonement*

XPYNT excipient *inert base*
XPYR expire *end, breathe out* expired expiring
XPYSHN expiation *atonement*
XPYT expiate *make amends* expiated expiating
XPYTR expiator *atonement*
XPZ expose *(v)* *bare* exposed exposing
XPZ exposé (or) expose *(n)* *facts*
XPZD exposed *open*
XPZDR expositor *commentator*
XPZHR exposure *no protection*
XPZR exposer *displayer*
XPZSHN exposition *essay, display*
XPZTR expositor *commentator*
XPZTR expository *explaining*
XQDBL executable *kill, perform*
XQDNT executant *performer*
XQDR executor *administrator*
XQDV executive *law, manager*
XQS excuse *(n)* *reason*
XQSBL excusable (adj) *pardon* excusably (adv)
XQSHN execution *kill, perform*
XQSHNR executioner *killer*
XQST exquisite *perfect, acute*
XQSTL exquisitely *perfect, acute*
XQSTNS exquisiteness *perfect, acute*
XQSTR excusatory *pardon*
XQT execute *kill, perform* executed executing
XQTBL executable *kill, perform*
XQTNT executant *performer*
XQTR executor *administrator*
XQTR executory *administrative*

Letters aren't doubled for single sounds: to find alley use **L** not **LL**. Use **Y** and **W** as hard sounds only: to find yellow use **YL**. (Br)=British spelling or usage. * See dictionary.

XQTRCZ executrices (or) executrixes (pl) *administrator (f)* executrix

XQTRKS executrix *administrator (f)* executrices (or) executrixes

XQTRSZ executrices (or) executrixes (pl) *administrator (f)* executrix

XQTRX executrix *administrator (f)* executrices (or) executrixes

XQTV executive *law, manager*

XQZ excuse *(v) pardon* excused excusing

XQZBL excusable (adj) *pardon* excusably (adv)

XQZR excuser *pardon*

XQZT exquisite *perfect, acute*

XQZTL exquisitely *perfect, acute*

XQZTNS exquisiteness *perfect, acute*

XQZTR excusatory *pardon*

XR X ray (n) *radium* X-ray (adj) x-ray (v)

XRB exurb *outer suburb*

XRB exurbia *outer suburb*

XRBDNS exorbitance *excess*

XRBDNT exorbitant *excessive*

XRBDNTS exorbitance *excess*

XRBN exurban *outer suburb*

XRBNT exurbanite *outer suburb*

XRBTNS exorbitance *excess*

XRBTNT exorbitant *excessive*

XRBTNTS exorbitance *excess*

XRBY exurbia *outer suburb*

XRDD X-rated *offensive*

XRDSHN x-radiation *X rays*

XRDTR exhortatory *warning*

XRDYSHN x-radiation *X rays*

XRL uxorial *wife*

XRP excerpt *extract*

XRPDR excerptor (or) excerpter *extractor*

XRPT excerpt *extract*

XRPTR excerptor (or) excerpter *extractor*

XRS uxorious *love of wife*

XRSD uxoricide *wife murder*

XRSHN exertion *effort*

XRSKL Exercycle *(trademark) bicycle*

XRSL uxoriously *love of wife*

XRSNS uxoriousness *love of wife*

XRSS oxyuriasis *pinworms*

XRSST exorcist *expel evil*

XRSZ exercise *(v) exert, use* exercised exercising

XRSZ exercise *(n) use, exertion, drill*

XRSZ exorcise *expel evil* exorcised exercising

XRSZBL exercisable *exert, use*

XRSZM exorcism *expel evil*

XRSZR exerciser *machine*

XRT exert *put forth effort, wield*

XRT exhort *warn*

XRT oxheart *cherry*

XRTD X-rated *offensive*

XRTSHN exhortation *warning*

XRTTR exhortatory *warning*

XRTTV exhortative *warning*

XRYL uxorial *wife*

XRYS uxorious *love of wife*

XRYSL uxoriously *love of wife*

XRYSNS uxoriousness *love of wife*

XRYSS oxyuriasis *pinworms*

XS access *(n) onset, entry (v) get at* accesses

XS axis *line, partnership* axes

XS excess *overage* excesses

XSBL accessible (adj) *available* accessibly (adv)

XSBLD accessibility *availability*

XSBLNS accessibleness *availability*

XSBLT accessibility *availability*

XSCHN exhaustion *depletion*

XSDBL exhaustible *deplete, tired*

XSDBLD exhaustibility *deplete, tired*

XSDBLT exhaustibility *deplete, tired*

XSDV exhaustive *thorough*

XSFR exosphere *atmosphere*

XSHN accession *increase, approach*

XSHN excision *removal*

XSHNL accessional *increasing, approaching*

XSKLTL exoskeletal *outer frame*

XSKLTN exoskeleton *outer frame*

XSKSHN x-section *cross section*

XSLN oxacillin *antibiotic*

XSPR exospore *separate*

XSPRDDL exasperatedly *irritation*

XSPRDNGL exasperatingly *irritation*

XSPRDNL exasperatingly *irritation*

XSPRSHN exasperation *irritation*

XSPRT exasperate *irritate* exasperated exasperating

XSPRTDL exasperatedly *irritation*

XSPRTNGL exasperatingly *irritation*

XSPRTNL exasperatingly *irritation*

XSR accessory *adjunct* accessories

XSRBSHN exacerbation *make worse*

XSRBT exacerbate *make worse* exacerbated exacerbating

XSRL accessorial *supplementary*

XSRYL accessorial *supplementary*

XSRZ accessorize *add supplement(s)*

Use letters that best describe the sounds you hear and omit the vowels. Use **S** or **K** instead of **C**: to find circle use **SRKL**. Use **J** to find joy, **JM** to find gem and **G** to find go.

accessorized
accessorizing
(Br) accessorise

XST exhaust (v) deplete, tire
(n) vapor

XST exist live

XSTBL exhaustible deplete,
tired

XSTBLD exhaustibility
deplete, tired

XSTBLT exhaustibility
deplete, tired

XSTCZ exostoses (pl)
outgrowth exotosis

XSTNCHL existential (adj)
experience existentially
(adv)

XSTNCHLST existentialist
philosopher

XSTNCHLZM existentialism
philosophy

XSTNS existence life

XSTNSHL existential (adj)
experience existentially
(adv)

XSTNSHLST existentialist
philosopher

XSTNSHLZM existentialism
philosophy

XSTNT existent living

XSTNTS existence life

XSTSS exocytosis cell fusion
exocytoses

XSTSS exostosis outgrowth
exotoses

XSTSZ exostoses (pl)
outgrowth exotosis

XSTV exhaustive thorough

XSV excessive extreme

XSVL excessively extremely

XSVNS excessiveness
extremity

XT asked (v-past) ask

XT excite arouse excited
exciting

XT exit (v) leave (n)
departure, way out

XT x-height type

XTBL excitable arousal

XTBLD excitability arousal

XTBLNS excitableness
arousal

XTBLT excitability arousal

XTC ecstasy rapture
ecstasies

XTDK ecstatic overjoyed

XTDKL ecstatically overjoyed

XTDL excitedly aroused

XTK exotic foreign, unusual

XTK exotica unusual items

XTKL exotically foreign,
unusual

XTKNS exoticness foreign,
unusual

XTL extol glorify extolled
extolling

XTL oxtail meat

XTLMNT extolment
glorification

XTLR extoller glorifier

XTMNT excitement arousal

XTMPR extempore offhand

XTMPRNS extemporaneous
offhand

XTMPRNSL
extemporaneously
offhand

XTMPRNT extemporaneity
offhand

XTMPRNYS
extemporaneous offhand

XTMPRNYSL
extemporaneously
offhand

XTMPRNYT
extemporaneity offhand

XTMPRZ extemporize
compose extemporized
extemporizing
(Br) extemporise

XTMPRZR extemporizer
composer
(Br) extemporiser

XTMPRZSHN
extemporization
composition
(Br) extemporisation

XTN exciting stimulating

XTN extend unbend, increase
bulk, reach out*

XTNCHN extension unbend,
increase bulk

XTNCHNL extensional (adj)
comprehensive

extensionally (adv)

XTND extend unbend,
increase bulk, reach out*

XTNDBL extendable
unbend, increase bulk, reach
out*

XTNDBLD extendability
unbend, increase bulk, reach
out*

XTNDBLT extendability
unbend, increase bulk, reach
out*

XTNDD extended long,
intensive

XTNDNG extenuating
decreasing

XTNDR extender increaser

XTNDR extenuator one who
decreases

XTNG exciting stimulating

XTNG oxtongue plant

XTNGGWSH extinguish
quench, nullify

XTNGGWSHBL
extinguishable quench,
nullify

XTNGGWSHMNT
extinguishment quench,
nullify

XTNGGWSHR extinguisher
quench, nullify

XTNGK extinct not active,
not existing

XTNGKSHN extinction not
active, not existing

XTNGKT extinct not active,
not existing

XTNGT extinct not active,
not existing

XTNGWSH extinguish
quench, nullify

XTNGWSHBL
extinguishable quench,
nullify

XTNGWSHMNT
extinguishment quench,
nullify

XTNGWSHR extinguisher
quench, nullify

XTNK extinct not active, not
existing

XTNKSHN extinction not

Letters aren't doubled for single sounds: to find **alley** use **L** not **LL**. Use **Y** and **W** as hard
sounds only: to find **yellow** use **YL**. (Br)=British spelling or usage. * See dictionary.

active, not existing

XTNKT extinct *not active, not existing*

XTNSBL extensible *long, intensive*

XTNSBLD extensibility *increase*

XTNSBLT extensibility *increase*

XTNSHN extension *unbend, increase bulk*

XTNSHN extenuation *excuse*

XTNSHNL extensional (adj) *comprehensive* extensionally (adv)

XTNSL extensile *long, intensive*

XTNSMDR extensometer *device*

XTNSMTR extensometer *device*

XTNSR extensor *muscle*

XTNSV extensive *considerable*

XTNSVL extensively *considerably*

XTNSVNS extensiveness *large size*

XTNT excitant *arouser*

XTNT extant *existing*

XTNT extent *scope*

XTNT extenuate *decrease* extenuated extenuating

XTNT extinct *not active, not existing*

XTNTN extenuating *decreasing*

XTNTNG extenuating *decreasing*

XTNTR extenuator *one who decreases*

XTNTSBL extensible *long, intensive*

XTNTSBLD extensibility *increase*

XTNTSBLT extensibility *increase*

XTNTSL extensile *long, intensive*

XTNTSMDR extensometer *device*

XTNTSMTR extensometer

device

XTNTSR extensor *muscle*

XTNTSV extensive *considerable*

XTNTSVL extensively *considerably*

XTNTSVNS extensiveness *large size*

XTNWDNG extenuating *decreasing*

XTNWDR extenuator *one who decreases*

XTNWSHN extenuation *excuse*

XTNWT extenuate *decrease* extenuated extenuating

XTNWTN extenuating *decreasing*

XTNWTNG extenuating *decreasing*

XTNWTR extenuator *one who decreases*

XTNYDNG extenuating *decreasing*

XTNYDR extenuator *one who decreases*

XTNYSHN extenuation *excuse*

XTNYT extenuate *decrease* extenuated extenuating

XTNYTN extenuating *decreasing*

XTNYTNG extenuating *decreasing*

XTNYTR extenuator *one who decreases*

XTNYWDNG extenuating *decreasing*

XTNYWDR extenuator *one who decreases*

XTNYWSHN extenuation *excuse*

XTNYWT extenuate *decrease* extenuated extenuating

XTNYWTN extenuating *decreasing*

XTNYWTNG extenuating *decreasing*

XTNYWTR extenuator *one who decreases*

XTR et cetera *and so forth*

XTR etcetera *odds and ends*

XTR exciter *generator*

XTR excitor *nerve*

XTR extra *additional*

XTRD extrude *push out* extruded extruding

XTRDDBL extraditable *return for trial*

XTRDNR extraordinaire *special (used after the noun)*

XTRDNR extraordinary *special (used before the noun)*

XTRDNRL extraordinarily *exceptionally*

XTRDR extorter *obtain illegally*

XTRDR extruder *push out*

XTRDSHN extradition *return for trial*

XTRDT extradite *return for trial* extradited extraditing

XTRDTBL extraditable *return for trial*

XTRDV extortive *obtain illegally*

XTRF auxotroph *growth substance* auxotrophy

XTRFK auxotrophic *growth substance*

XTRJDSHL extrajudicial (adj) *private* extrajudicially (adv)

XTRK exoteric *external*

XTRK extract (v) *withdraw* (n) *excerpt*

XTRKBL extricable *disentangle*

XTRKDBL extractable *withdraw, excerpt*

XTRKDBLD extractability *withdraw, excerpt*

XTRKDBLT extractability *withdraw, excerpt*

XTRKDR extractor *withdraw, excerpt*

XTRKDV extractive *withdraw, excerpt*

XTRKL exoterically *external*

XTRKRKLR extracurricular *after school, sporting*

Use letters that best describe the sounds you hear and omit the vowels. Use **S** or **K** instead of **C**: to find circle use **SRKL**. Use **J** to find joy, **JM** to find gem and **G** to find go.

XTRKRKYLR
extracurricular *after school, sporting*

XTRKRQLR extracurricular *after school, sporting*

XTRKSHN extraction *lineage, thing withdrawn*

XTRKSHN extrication *disentangle*

XTRKT extract *(v) withdraw (n) excerpt*

XTRKT extricate *disentangle* extricated extricating

XTRKTBL extractable *withdraw, excerpt*

XTRKTBLD extractability *withdraw, excerpt*

XTRKTBLT extractability *withdraw, excerpt*

XTRKTR extractor *withdraw, excerpt*

XTRKTV extractive *withdraw, excerpt*

XTRLGL extralegal (adj) *private* extralegally (adv)

XTRM extreme *(adj) excessive (n) maximum*

XTRMD extremity *far point, limb* extremities

XTRML extremely *excessively*

XTRMNDR exterminator *destroyer*

XTRMNSHN extermination *destruction*

XTRMNT exterminate *destroy* exterminated exterminating

XTRMNTR exterminator *destroyer*

XTRMRDL extramarital *adulterous*

XTRMRL extramural (adj) *competition* extramurally (adv)

XTRMRTL extramarital *adulterous*

XTRMST extremist *beyond the norm*

XTRMT extremity *far point, limb* extremities

XTRMYRL extramural (adj)

competition extramurally (adv)

XTRMZM extremism *beyond the norm*

XTRNL external (adj) *outside* externally (adv)

XTRNLD externality *outside*

XTRNLT externality *outside*

XTRNLZ externalize *reason* externalized externalizing (Br) externalise

XTRNLZM externalism *outside*

XTRNLZSHN
externalization *outside* (Br) externalisation

XTRNS extraneous *outside*

XTRNSK extrinsic *external*

XTRNSKL extrinsically *externally*

XTRNSL extraneously *outside*

XTRNSNS extraneousness *outside*

XTRNYS extraneous *outside*

XTRNYSL extraneously *outside*

XTRNYSNS
extraneousness *outside*

XTRNZK extrinsic *external*

XTRNZKL extrinsically *externally*

XTRPDR extirpator *destroyer*

XTRPLDR extrapolator *infer*

XTRPLDV extrapolative *infer*

XTRPLSHN extrapolation *inferral*

XTRPLT extrapolate *infer* extrapolated extrapolating

XTRPLTR extrapolator *infer*

XTRPLTV extrapolative *infer*

XTRPSHN extirpation *destruction*

XTRPT extirpate *destroy* extirpated extirpating

XTRPTR extirpator *destroyer*

XTRR exterior *outside*

XTRRDNR extraordinaire *special (used after the noun)*

XTRRDNR extraordinary *special (used before the noun)*

XTRRDNRL extraordinarily *exceptionally*

XTRRZ exteriorize *make obvious* exteriorized exteriorizing (Br) exteriorise

XTRSHN extortion *obtain illegally*

XTRSHN extrusion *pushed out*

XTRSHNR extortioner *obtain illegally*

XTRSHNST extortionist *obtain illegally*

XTRSHNT extortionate *excessive*

XTRSNSR extrasensory *perceptive*

XTRSNTSR extrasensory *perceptive*

XTRSV extrusive *pushed out*

XTRT extort *obtain illegally*

XTRTR extorter *obtain illegally*

XTRTRSCHL extraterrestrial *alien*

XTRTRSTRL extraterrestrial *alien*

XTRTRSTRYL
extraterrestrial *alien*

XTRTRTRL extraterritorial *outside*

XTRTRTRLD
extraterritoriality *outside*

XTRTRTRLT
extraterritoriality *outside*

XTRTRTRYL extraterritorial *outside*

XTRTRTRYLD
extraterritoriality *outside*

XTRTRTRYLT
extraterritoriality *outside*

XTRTV extortive *obtain illegally*

XTRVGNS extravagance *excess* extravagancy

XTRVGNT extravagant *excessive*

XTRVGNTS extravagance

excess extravagancy
XTRVGNZ extravaganza
lavish show
XTRVHKLR extravehicular
outside of vehicle
XTRVHKYLR extravehicular
outside of vehicle
XTRVHQLR extravehicular
outside of vehicle
XTRVRSHN extroversion
(or) extraversion *outgoing*
XTRVRT extrovert *outgoing*
XTRVRZHN extroversion
(or) extraversion *outgoing*
XTRVSKLR extravascular
ouside of vein
XTRVSKYLR extravascular
ouside of vein
XTRVSQLR extravascular
outside of vein
XTRYR exterior *outside*
XTRYRZ exteriorize *make*
obvious exteriorized
exteriorizing
(Br) exteriorise
XTRZHN extrusion *pushed*
out
XTRZV extrusive *pushed out*
XTS ecstasy *rapture*
ecstasies
XTSHN excitation *arousal*
XTSK oxytocic *contraction*
XTSN oxytocin *hormone*
XTT x-ed out *deleted*
XTTK ecstatic *overjoyed*
XTTKL ecstatically *overjoyed*
XTTR excitatory *arousal*
XTTRSKLN oxytetracycline
antibiotic
XVR Xavier *Catholic saint*
XVYR Xavier *Catholic saint*
XXS x-axis *math*
XXSS x-axis *math*
XYD exude *ooze* exuded
exuding
XYDSHN exudation *material*
XYDT exudate *material*
XYL axial (adj) *axis* axially
(adv)
XYLG axiology *ethics*
XYLJ axiology *ethics*
XYLJKL axiological (adj)

ethical axiologically (adv)
XYM axiom *truth*
XYM exhume *dig up*
exhumed exhuming
XYMDK axiomatic *self-*
evident
XYMDKL axiomatically *self-*
evidently
XYMR exhumer *dig up*
XYMSHN exhumation *dig*
up
XYMTK axiomatic *self-*
evident
XYMTKL axiomatically *self-*
evidently
XYN axion *particle*
XYNT exeunt *exit*
XYRSS oxyuriasis *pinworms*
XYRYSS oxyuriasis
pinworms
XZ excise *(v)* remove, tax
excised excising
XZ excise *(n) tax*
XZBL excisable *remove, tax*
XZHN excision *removal*
XZJRDR exaggerator
overstatement
XZJRDV exaggerative
overstatement
XZJRSHN exaggeration
overstatement
XZJRT exaggerate *overstate*
exaggerated
exaggerating
XZJRTR exaggerator
overstatement
XZJRTV exaggerative
overstatement
XZK exact *(v)* demand *(adj)*
precise
XZKD exacta *wager*
XZKDN exacting *difficult*
XZKDNG exacting *difficult*
XZKDTD exactitude
precision
XZKDTYD exactitude
precision
XZKL exactly *precisely*
XZKT exact *(v)* demand *(adj)*
precise
XZKT exacta *wager*
XZKTL exactly *precisely*

XZKTN exacting *difficult*
XZKTNG exacting *difficult*
XZKTTD exactitude
precision
XZKTTYD exactitude
precision
XZLT exalt *praise*
XZLTDL exaltedly *elevated*
XZLTR exalter *praiser*
XZLTSHN exaltation *praise*
XZM exam *test*
XZMN examine *inspect, test*
examined examining
XZMN examinee *person*
tested
XZMNBL examinable
inspect, test
XZMNNT examinant *tester*
XZMNR examiner *inspector,*
tester
XZMNSHN examination
inspection, test
XZMPL example *model,*
instance
XZNMT exanimate *lifeless*
XZPM oxazepam
tranquilizer
XZRP excerpt *extract*
XZRPDR excerptor (or)
excerpter *extractor*
XZRPT excerpt *extract*
XZRPTR excerptor (or)
excerpter *extractor*
XZSPRDDL exasperatedly
irritation
XZSPRDNGL
exasperatingly *irritation*
XZSPRDNL exasperatingly
irritation
XZSPRSHN exasperation
irritation
XZSPRT exasperate *irritate*
exasperated
exasperating
XZSPRTDL exasperatedly
irritation
XZSPRTNGL
exasperatingly *irritation*
XZSPRTNL exasperatingly
irritation
XZSRBSHN exacerbation
make worse

Use letters that best describe the sounds you hear and omit the vowels. Use **S** or **K**
instead of **C**: to find circle use **SRKL**. Use **J** to find joy, **JM** to find gem and **G** to find go.

XZSRBT exacerbate *make worse* exacerbated exacerbating

Y

Y ewe *sheep*
Y lo *volcanic moon*
Y IOU *I owe you* IOUs
Y olla *pot* ollas
Y oyez *(interj) court cry* oyesses
Y u *alphabet letter* u's (or) us
Y yaw *weave*
Y ye *(archaic) you*
Y yea *yes*
Y yeah *yes (informal)*
Y yew *tree*
Y yo *(interj) hello*
Y you *(pron) not me*
YB yob (or) yobbo *(Br) lout* yobbos (or) yobboes
YBKWD ubiquity *widespread*
YBKWDS ubiquitous *widespread*
YBKWDSL ubiquitously *widespread*
YBKWDSNS ubiquitousness *widespread*
YBKWT ubiquity *widespread*
YBKWTS ubiquitous *widespread*
YBKWTSL ubiquitously *widespread*
YBKWTSNS ubiquitousness *widespread*
YBNG Ubangi *African*
YBNGG Ubangi *African*
YBQD ubiquity *widespread*
YBQDS ubiquitous *widespread*
YBQDSL ubiquitously *widespread*
YBQDSNS ubiquitousness *widespread*

YBQT ubiquity *widespread*
YBQTS ubiquitous *widespread*
YBQTSL ubiquitously *widespread*
YBQTSNS ubiquitousness *widespread*
YBR yabber *talk*
YBT U-boat *ship*
YCHF UHF *(abbr) Ultra High Frequency*
YCZ oyesses (pl) *(interj) court cry* oyez
YD iota *tiny bit*
YD IUD *(abbr) intrauterine device*
YD yautia *plant*
YD yeti *abominable snowman*
YD yod *Hebrew letter*
YD you'd *(contr) you would, you had*
YDD iodide *chemical*
YDGN yataghan *saber*
YDK Utica *city*
YDL utile *useful* (Br) utilisable
YDL yodel *sing* yodeled (or) yodelled yodeling (or) yodelling
YDLR yodeler *singer*
YDLS utilize *use* utilized utilizing (Br) utilise
YDLZ utilize *use* utilized utilizing (Br) utilise
YDLZBL utilizable *useful* (Br) utilisable
YDLZR utilizer *user* (Br) utiliser
YDLZSHN utilization *use* (Br) utilisation
YDN iodine *element*
YDNG yachting *boating*
YDR uteri (pl) *womb* uterus
YDRN uterine *womb*
YDRS uterus *womb* uteri
YDSH Yiddish *language*
YDT iodate *salt*
YDY yautia *plant*
YDZ iodize *with iodine*

iodized iodizing (Br) iodise
YF UFO *(abbr) Unidentified Flying Object* UFOs
YFDK euphotic *water plants*
YFMKS euphemics *improvement*
YFMSDK euphemistic *inoffensive expression*
YFMSDKL euphemistically *inoffensive expression*
YFMST euphemist *inoffensive expression*
YFMSTK euphemistic *inoffensive expression*
YFMSTKL euphemistically *inoffensive expression*
YFMX euphemics *improvement*
YFMZ euphemize *inoffensive expression* euphemized euphemizing (Br) euphemise
YFMZM euphemism *inoffensive expression*
YFMZR euphemizer *inoffensive expression* (Br) euphemiser
YFN euphony *sound* euphonies
YFNK euphonic *sound*
YFNKL euphonically *sound*
YFNM euphonium *music*
YFNS euphonious *sound*
YFNYM euphonium *music*
YFNYS euphonious *sound*
YFR euphoria *elation*
YFRB euphorbia *plant*
YFRBY euphorbia *plant*
YFRK euphoric *elated*
YFRKL euphorically *elated*
YFRNT euphoriant *drug*
YFRY euphoria *elation*
YFRYNT euphoriant *drug*
YFSDK euphuistic *elegant language*
YFSDKL euphuistically *elegant language*
YFST euphuist *elegant language*
YFSTK euphuistic *elegant language*

Letters aren't doubled for single sounds: to find alley use **L** not **LL**. Use **Y** and **W** as hard sounds only: to find yellow use **YL**. (Br)=British spelling or usage. * See dictionary.

YFSTKL euphuistically *elegant language*
YFTK euphotic *water plants*
YFWSDK euphuistic *elegant language*
YFWSDKL euphuistically *elegant language*
YFWST euphuist *elegant language*
YFWSTK euphuistic *elegant language*
YFWSTKL euphuistically *elegant language*
YFWZM euphuism *elegant language*
YFYSDK euphuistic *elegant language*
YFYSDKL euphuistically *elegant language*
YFYST euphuist *elegant language*
YFYSTK euphuistic *elegant language*
YFYSTKL euphuistically *elegant language*
YFYWSDK euphuistic *elegant language*
YFYWSDKL euphuistically *elegant language*
YFYWST euphuist *elegant language*
YFYWSTK euphuistic *elegant language*
YFYWSTKL euphuistically *elegant language*
YFYWZM euphuism *elegant language*
YFYZM euphuism *elegant language*
YG yagi *antenna*
YG yegg *robber*
YG yoga *philosophy*
YG yogi *person* yogis
YG yuga *Hindu age*
YGLN euglena *algae*
YGLND euglenoid *algae*
YGN Eugene *city*
YGND Uganda *country*
YGNK eugenic *breeding*
YGNKL eugenically *breeding*
YGNKS eugenics *breeding*
YGNSST eugenicist *breeding*

YGNST eugenist *breeding*
YGNX eugenics *breeding*
YGR jaeger *hunter, bird*
YGRT yogurt *food*
YGSLV Yugoslav *of Yugoslavia*
YGSLV Yugoslavia *country*
YGSLVY Yugoslavia *country*
YH yahoo *boor* yahoos
YH yoo-hoo *(interj)* call
YHMBN yohimbine *alkaloid*
YHNSBRG Johannesburg *city*
YHPS eohippus *primitive horse*
YJN Eugene *city*
YJNK eugenic *breeding*
YJNKL eugenically *breeding*
YJNKS eugenics *breeding*
YJNSST eugenicist *breeding*
YJNST eugenist *breeding*
YJNX eugenics *breeding*
YK uke *ukulele, music*
YK yak *(n) animal* yaks
YK yak *(v) talk* yakked yakking
YK Yaqui *Native American*
YK yech (or) yecch (interj—disgust) *(interj) disgust*
YK yoke *(v) join* yoked yoking
YK yoke *(n) frame, bondage*
YK yolk *egg*
YK yucca (or) yuca *cactus*
YK yuck *(interj) disgust*
YK yucky *distasteful*
YKHM Yokohama *city*
YKL yokel *gullible one*
YKLD Euclid *geometry*
YKLDN euclidean *(often capitalized) geometry*
YKLDYN euclidean *(often capitalized) geometry*
YKLL ukulele *music*
YKLPDS eucalyptus *tree* eucalypti (or) eucalyptuses
YKLPT eucalypt *tree*
YKLPTL eucalyptol *oil*
YKLPTS eucalyptus *tree* eucalypti (or) eucalyptuses

YKM Joachim *violinist*
YKN Yukon *city, territory*
YKR euchre *(v) cheat* euchred euchring
YKR euchre *(n) card game*
YKRDK eucritic *rock*
YKRDK eukaryotic *organism*
YKRN Ukraine *country*
YKRNN Ukrainian *of Ukraine*
YKRNYN Ukrainian *of Ukraine*
YKRST Eucharist *communion*
YKRT eucrite *rock*
YKRT eukaryote *organism*
YKRTK eucritic *rock*
YKRTK eukaryotic *organism*
YKRYDK eukaryotic *organism*
YKRYT eukaryote *organism*
YKRYTK eukaryotic *organism*
YKS Aeacus *Greek myth*
YKS ukase *edict*
YKTN Yucatan *peninsula*
YKTR yakitori *food*
YKZ ukase *edict*
YL aioli *sauce*
YL aisle *pathway*
YL isle *island*
YL oil *grease*
YL oily *greasy* oilier oiliest
YL y'all *(contr) you all*
YL yawl *boat*
YL yell *shout*
YL yellow *color*
YL you'll *(contr) you will*
YL you-all *all of you*
YL yowl *howl*
YL yule *Christmas*
YLBLD yellow-bellied *cowardly*
YLBRD oilbird *bird*
YLCD oilseed *crop*
YLD oiled *greased, drunk*
YLD yield *(v) submit, defer (n) product*
YLDG yellow-dog *mean*
YLDNG yielding *productive, flexible*
YLDR yielder *produce, surrender*

Use letters that best describe the sounds you hear and omit the vowels. Use **S** or **K** instead of **C**: to find circle use **SRKL**. Use **J** to find joy, **JM** to find gem and **G** to find go.

YLFL oil field *region*
YLFLD oil field *region*
YLFN yellowfin *tuna*
YLFVR yellow fever *disease*
YLG eulogy *praise* eulogies
YLG yule log *hearth*
YLHMR yellowhammer *bird*
YLJ eulogy *praise* eulogies
YLJK yellow jack *disease, fish*
YLJKT yellow jacket *wasp*
YLJSDK eulogistic *praise*
YLJSDKL eulogistically *praise*
YLJST eulogist *praiser*
YLJSTK eulogistic *praise*
YLJSTKL eulogistically *praise*
YLJZ eulogize *praise* eulogized eulogizing (Br) eulogise
YLJZR eulogizer *praiser* (Br) eulogiser
YLKLTH oilcloth *fabric*
YLKN eulachon *fish* eulachon (or) eulachons
YLKN oilcan *container*
YLKST ulexite *mineral*
YLLGS yellowlegs *bird*
YLM ulema (or) ulama *mullahs*
YLMN oilman *worker* oilmen
YLMR yellowhammer *bird*
YLN aeolian *wind sound*
YLN eolian *wind*
YLN uhlan *cavalry*
YLP yelp *squeal*
YLPJZ yellow pages *telephone book*
YLPLM oil palm *tree*
YLPM oil palm *tree*
YLPN oil pan *receptacle*
YLPN yellow pine *tree*
YLPR yelper *squealer*
YLPRCH yellow perch *fish*
YLPRL yellow peril *fear of Asia*
YLR oiler *person, ship, container*
YLR oilier *greasy*
YLS Aeolus *Greek myth*
YLSD oilseed *crop*

YLSH yellowish *color*
YLSKN oilskin *cloth*
YLST oiliest *greasy*
YLSTN oilstone *whetstone*
YLT Yalta *city*
YLTD yuletide *(often capitalized) Christmas*
YLTH eolith *flint*
YLTHK Eolithic *geologic age*
YLTHRT yellowthroat *bird*
YLTL yellowtail *fish*
YLVMN Isle of Man *island*
YLVWT Isle of Wight *island*
YLWD yellowwood *tree*
YLWL oil well *pump*
YLWMR yellowhammer *bird*
YLWR yellowware *pottery*
YLWSH yellowish *color*
YLXT ulexite *mineral*
YLYN aeolian *wind sound*
YLYN eolian *wind*
YLYR oilier *greasy*
YLYST oiliest *greasy*
YM A.M. (or) a.m. *(abbr)* ante meridiem *(before noon)*
YM iamb (or) iambus *poetry* iambs (or) iambuses
YM llama *animal*
YM yam *potato*
YM yummy *tasty* yummier yummiest
YMBK iambic *poetry*
YMBN yohimbine *alkaloid*
YMBS iambus (or) iamb *poetry* iambuses (or) iambs
YMK yarmulke *skullcap*
YMKPR Yom Kippur *holiday*
YMLK yarmulke *skullcap*
YMN Yemen *country*
YMN yeoman *assistant* yeomen
YMNL yeomanly *bravely*
YMNR yeomanry *middle class*
YMR yammer *whine, talk*
YMR yummier *tasty*
YMST yummiest *tasty*
YMYR yummier *tasty*
YMYST yummiest *tasty*
YN aeon (or) eon *1 billion years*

YN ion *particle*
YN Ionia *ancient region*
YN yawn *sleepiness, gape*
YN yean *birth*
YN yen *(v) desire* yenned yenning
YN yen *(n) money, desire* yen
YN yin *feminine*
YN yon *distant*
YN yuan *money* yuan
YND unity *oneness* unities
YNDD united *combined*
YNDDKNGDM United Kingdom *country*
YNDDNSHNS United Nations *international group*
YNDDSTTS United States *country*
YNDMNSHNL unidimensional *one aspect*
YNDMNSHNLD unidimensionality *one aspect*
YNDMNSHNLT unidimensionality *one aspect*
YNDMNTSHNL unidimensional *one aspect*
YNDMNTSHNLD unidimensionality *one aspect*
YNDMNTSHNLT unidimensionality *one aspect*
YNDR yonder *distance*
YNDRKSHNL unidirectional *one way*
YNDV unitive *joining*
YNF unify *unite* unified unifying unifies
YNFBL unifiable *join*
YNFD unified *joined*
YNFKSHN unification *joined*
YNFR unifier *make whole*
YNFRM uniform *(n) garment (adj) same*
YNFRMD uniformity *sameness* uniformities
YNFRMT uniformity *sameness* uniformities
YNFYBL unifiable *join*

Letters aren't doubled for single sounds: to find alley use **L** not **LL**. Use **Y** and **W** as hard sounds only: to find yellow use **YL**. (Br)=British spelling or usage. * See dictionary.

YNFYR unifier *make whole*
YNG Jung *psychologist*
YNG yang *masculine*
YNG yin *feminine*
YNG young *immature*
   younger youngest
YNGBR youngberry *fruit*
   youngberries
YNGGR younger *immature*
YNGGST youngest
   immature
YNGK yank *pull*
YNGK Yank (or) Yankee
   native of US
YNGKS Yangtze *river*
YNGLN youngling *immature*
   one
YNGLNG youngling
   immature one
YNGN Jungian *psychology*
YNGR younger *immature*
YNGS Yangtze *river*
YNGSH youngish *immature*
YNGST youngest *immature*
YNGSTR youngster
   immature one
YNGX Yangtze *river*
YNGYN Jungian *psychology*
YNK aeonic (or) aeonian
   long-lasting
YNK eunuch *neutered male*
   eunuches
YNK ewe-neck *(n) animal*
   defect
YNK ionic *particle*
YNK Ionic *Greek*
YNK unique *one and only*
YNK yank *pull*
YNK Yank (or) Yankee *native*
   of US
YNKD eunuchoid *intersexual*
YNKD ewe-necked *(adj)*
   animal defect
YNKL uniquely *one and only*
YNKMRL unicameral (adj)
   one chamber unicamerally
   (adv)
YNKNS uniqueness *one and*
   only
YNKRN unicorn *animal*
YNKS Yangtze *river*
YNKT ewe-necked *(adj)*

animal defect
YNLDRL unilateral (adj) *one-*
   sided unilaterally *(adv)*
YNLHKCM unnilhexium
   element
YNLHKCYM unnilhexium
   element
YNLHKSM unnilhexium
   element
YNLHKSYM unnilhexium
   element
YNLHXM unnilhexium
   element
YNLHXYM unnilhexium
   element
YNLKWDM unnilquadium
   element
YNLKWDYM unnilquadium
   element
YNLN yeanling *lamb, kid*
YNLNG yeanling *lamb, kid*
YNLPNM unnilpentium
   element
YNLPNTM unnilpentium
   element
YNLPNTYM unnilpentium
   element
YNLPNYM unnilpentium
   element
YNLQDM unnilquadium
   element
YNLQDYM unnilquadium
   element
YNLTRL unilateral (adj) *one-*
   sided unilaterally *(adv)*
YNN aeonian (or) aeonic
   long-lasting
YNN Ionian *of Ionia*
YNN union *merger, labor*
   group
YNN yawning *wide open*
YNND united *combined*
YNNDKNGDM United
   Kingdom *country*
YNNDNSHNS United
   Nations *international*
   group
YNNDSTTS United States
   country
YNNG yawning *wide open*
YNNJK Union Jack *flag*
YNNMD unanimity

agreement
YNNMS unanimous
   agreement
YNNMSL unanimously
   agreement
YNNMT unanimity *agreement*
YNNST unionist *labor*
YNNZ unionize *unite*
   unionized unionizing
   (Br) unionise
YNNZM unionism *labor*
YNNZSHN unionization
   labor
   (Br) unionisation
YNR unary *single*
YNR yawner *gaper, boring*
YNSD ionicity *atoms*
YNSF UNICEF *fund*
YNSFR ionosphere
   atmosphere
YNSH yen-shee *residue*
YNSK UNESCO *United*
   Nations Educational,
   Scientific and Cultural
   Organization
YNSKL unicycle *one wheel*
YNSKLST unicyclist *one*
   wheel
YNSKS unisex *one sex*
YNSKSHL unisexual *one sex*
YNSKSHWL unisexual *one*
   sex
YNSLLR unicellular *one cell*
YNSLYLR unicellular *one cell*
YNSN unison *as one*
YNST ionicity *atoms*
YNSX unisex *one sex*
YNSYLR unicellular *one cell*
YNT unit *one, group,*
   *quantity**
YNT unite *join* united uniting
YNT unity *oneness* unities
YNT yenta *gossip*
YNTD united *combined*
YNTDKNGDM United
   Kingdom *country*
YNTDNSHNS United
   Nations *international*
   group
YNTDSTTS United States
   country
YNTR unitary *whole*

Use letters that best describe the sounds you hear and omit the vowels. Use **S** or **K** instead of **C**: to find circle use **SRKL**. Use **J** to find joy, **JM** to find gem and **G** to find go.

YNTR yantra *icon*
YNTRN Unitarian *religion*
YNTRYN Unitarian *religion*
YNTT uintaite *asphalt*
YNTV unitive *joining*
YNTYT uintaite *asphalt*
YNTZ unitize *divide* unitized unitizing
YNVKL univocal (adj) *one meaning* univocally (adv)
YNVLNT univalent *chemistry*
YNVLV univalve *shellfish*
YNVRS universe *whole, cosmos*
YNVRSD university *school* universities
YNVRSL universal (adj) *everywhere, versatile* universally (adv)
YNVRSLD universality *everywhere, clever*
YNVRSLNS universalness *everywhere, clever*
YNVRSLSDK universalistic *whole*
YNVRSLSTK universalistic *whole*
YNVRSLT universality *everywhere, clever*
YNVRSLZ universalize *generalize* universalized universalizing
YNVRSLZSHN universalization *generalization*
YNVRST university *school* universities
YNX Yangtze *river*
YNY Ionia *ancient region*
YNYN aeonian (or) aeonic *long-lasting*
YNYN Ionian *of Ionia*
YNYN union *merger, labor group*
YNYNJK Union Jack *flag*
YNYNST unionist *labor*
YNYNZ unionize *unite* unionized unionizing (Br) unionise
YNYNZM unionism *labor*
YNYNZSHN unionization *labor*

(Br) unionisation
YNZ ionize *convert* ionized ionizing
(Br) ionise
YNZN unison *as one*
YNZSHN ionization *atoms*
(Br) ionisation
YP yap (v) *bark, talk* yapped yapping
YP yap (n) *yelp, (slang) mouth*
YP yawp (or) yaup *squawk*
YP yep (slang) *yes*
YP yip *bark* yipped yipping
YP yippee (interj) *joy*
YP yippie *political activist*
YP yup (slang) *yes*
YP yuppie *materialist*
YPN eupnea *respiration*
YPN yaupon *plant*
YPNK eupneic *respiration*
YPNR eye-opener *surprise*
YPNSHD Upanishad *philosophy*
YPNY eupnea *respiration*
YPNYK eupneic *respiration*
YPPDK eupeptic *cheerful*
YPPTK eupeptic *cheerful*
YPSLN upsilon *20th Greek letter, particle*
YR euro *money, animal* euros
YR ewer *pitcher*
YR eyer *watcher*
YR gyro *spinner, sandwich* gyros
YR IRA *Irish Republican Army*
YR ire *anger* ired iring
YR uraei (pl) *symbol* uraeus
YR urea *urine*
YR yarrow *herb*
YR year *January-December*
YR yore *long ago*
YR you're (contr) *you are*
YR your *of you*
YRBK yearbook *annual*
YRD aorta *blood vessel* aortas (or) aortae
YRD yard *outdoor area, length, mast*
YRDBRD yardbird *soldier*
YRDGDZ yard goods *fabrics*

YRDJ yardage *fabrics*
YRDK uratic *urine*
YRDL urodele *amphibian*
YRDLN yard line *football*
YRDLR Eurodollar *currency*
YRDMN yardman *laborer* yardmen
YRDMSTR yardmaster *railroad*
YRDR ureter *duct*
YRDRM yardarm *ship*
YRDS Eurydice *myth*
YRDSL yard sale *used goods*
YRDSTK yardstick *measure*
YRFL ireful *angry*
YRGW Uruguay *country*
YRJNDL urogenital *urine*
YRJNTL urogenital *urine*
YRK eureka (interj) *discovery*
YRK uric *urine*
YRK Yorkie *dog*
YRKNK urocanic *acid*
YRKNS urokinase *enzyme*
YRKNZ urokinase *enzyme*
YRKRM urochrome *pigment*
YRL yearly *annually*
YRLG urology *urine*
YRLJ urology *urine*
YRLJK urologic *urine*
YRLJST urologist *urine*
YRLN Ireland *country*
YRLN yearling *animal*
YRLND Ireland *country*
YRLNG yearling *animal*
YRLNG yearlong *all year*
YRLTH urolith *calculus*
YRM uremia *illness*
YRMK uremic *illness*
YRMY uremia *illness*
YRN iron (n) *metal, pressing device* (v) *press*
YRN irony *sarcasm* ironies
YRN urine *liquid waste*
YRN yarn *thread, tale*
YRN year-end *end of year*
YRN year-round *not seasonal*
YRN yearn *desire*
YRNBN ironbound *rugged*
YRNBND ironbound *rugged*
YRNBRK ironbark *tree*
YRND yarn-dye *pigment*
YRND year-end *end of year*

Letters aren't doubled for single sounds: to find alley use **L** not **LL**. Use **Y** and **W** as hard sounds only: to find yellow use **YL**. (Br)=British spelling or usage. * See dictionary.

YRND year-round *not seasonal*

YRNJ Iron Age *prehistoric*

YRNJNDL urinogenital *urine*

YRNJNTL urinogenital *urine*

YRNKLD ironclad *(adj) firm (n) ship*

YRNKRTN Iron Curtain *communism*

YRNL uranyl *chemical*

YRNL urinal *toilet*

YRNLNG iron lung *device*

YRNLSS urinalysis *test* urinalyses

YRNM uranium *element*

YRNMNGGR ironmonger *(Br) iron making* ironmongery

YRNMNGR ironmonger *(Br) iron making* ironmongery

YRNN ironing *pressing, clothes*

YRNN yearning *desire*

YRNNG ironing *pressing, clothes*

YRNNG yearning *desire*

YRNNT uraninite *mineral*

YRNR urinary *urine*

YRNS Uranus *planet*

YRNS urinous *liquid waste*

YRNSD ironside *strong one*

YRNSHN urination *discharge urine*

YRNSTN ironstone *rock*

YRNT iron out *smooth, resolve*

YRNT urinate *discharge urine* urinated urinating

YRNWD ironwood *tree*

YRNWR ironware *articles*

YRNWRK ironwork *product*

YRNWRKR ironworker *producer*

YRNYM uranium *element*

YRNZ ironize *sarcasm* ironized ironizing

YRP Europa *Greek myth*

YRP Europe *continent*

YRPD uropod *appendage*

YRPDS Euripides *dramatist*

YRPDZ Euripides *dramatist*

YRPGL uropygial *gland*

YRPGM uropygium *rump*

YRPGYL uropygial *gland*

YRPGYM uropygium *rump*

YRPJL uropygial *gland*

YRPJM uropygium *rump*

YRPJYL uropygial *gland*

YRPJYM uropygium *rump*

YRPM europium *element*

YRPN European *of Europe*

YRPYM europium *element*

YRPYN European *of Europe*

YRS uraeus *symbol* uraei

YRS urease *enzyme*

YRSDK aoristic *verb*

YRSDKL aoristically *verb*

YRSF yourself *one that is you* yourselves

YRSHL urushiol *irritant*

YRSHN Eurasian *European and Asian*

YRSHYL urushiol *irritant*

YRSL uracil *genes*

YRSLF yourself *one that is you* yourselves

YRSLVZ yourselves *those that are you*

YRST aorist *verb*

YRSTK aoristic *verb*

YRSTKL aoristically *verb*

YRSTL urostyle *bone*

YRSVZ yourselves *those that are you*

YRT aorta *blood vessel* aortas (or) aortae

YRT urate *urine*

YRT yurt *tent*

YRTHM eurythmy (or) eurhythmy *dance*

YRTHMKS eurythmics (or) eurhythmics *dance*

YRTHMX eurythmics (or) eurhythmics *dance*

YRTHN urethane (or) urethan *plastic*

YRTHR urethra *canal* urethras (or) urethrae

YRTHRDS urethritis *illness*

YRTHRL urethral *canal*

YRTHRSKP urethroscope *viewer*

YRTHRTS urethritis *illness*

YRTK uratic *urine*

YRTR ureter *duct*

YRY uraei (pl) *symbol* uraeus

YRY urea *urine*

YRYS uraeus *symbol* uraei

YRYS urease *enzyme*

YRYZ urease *enzyme*

YRZ urease *enzyme*

YRZ yours *not mine*

YRZHN Eurasian *European and Asian*

YS oyez *(interj) court cry* oyesses

YS use *(n) purpose*

YS yes *consent*

YSD yeasty *like yeast, frivolous* yeastier yeastiest

YSDRD yesterday *past*

YSDRYR yesteryear *past*

YSFL useful (adj) *serviceable* usefully (adv)

YSFLNS usefulness *service*

YSFRKCHWR usufructuary *user*

YSFRKT usufruct *right*

YSGNTM jus gentium *law*

YSGNTYM jus gentium *law*

YSHL usual (adj) *typical* usually (adv)

YSHMK yashmak *veil*

YSHRR usurer *lender*

YSHRS usurious *high interest rate*

YSHRYS usurious *high interest rate*

YSHV yeshiva *school* yeshivas (or) yeshivot

YSHVT yeshivot (pl) *school* yeshiva

YSHVTH yeshivot (pl) *school* yeshiva

YSHWL usual (adj) *typical* usually (adv)

YSJ usage *practice*

YSLS useless *senseless*

YSLSL uselessly *senselessly*

YSLSNS uselessness *senselessness*

YSMD Yosemite *park, river, falls*

YSMK yashmak *veil*

YSMN yes-man *agree*

Use letters that best describe the sounds you hear and omit the vowels. Use **S** or **K** instead of **C**: to find circle use **SRKL**. Use **J** to find joy, **JM** to find gem and **G** to find go.

YSMT Yosemite *park, river, falls*
YSN eosin *dye*
YSNFLK eosinophilic *dye, blood*
YSR usury *high interest rate* usuries
YSR yea-sayer *agreement*
YSRP usurp *seize*
YSRPR usurper *seize*
YSRPSHN usurpation *seizure*
YST yeast *fungus*
YST yeasty *like yeast, frivolous* yeastier yeastiest
YSTKN eustachian *ear tube*
YSTKYN eustachian *ear tube*
YSTL eustele *plant stem*
YSTR yeastier *like yeast, frivolous*
YSTRD yesterday *past*
YSTRYR yesteryear *past*
YSTSHN eustachian *ear tube*
YSTSHYN eustachian *ear tube*
YSTST yeastiest *like yeast, frivolous*
YSTYR yeastier *like yeast, frivolous*
YSTYST yeastiest *like yeast, frivolous*
YSYR yea-sayer *agreement*
YSZ oyesses (pl) *(interj) court cry* oyez
YT iota *tiny bit*
YT Utah *US State*
YT Ute *Native American*
YT yacht *boat*
YT yautia *plant*
YT yet *soon*
YT yeti *abominable snowman*
YTGN yataghan *saber*
YTH youth *immature one* youths
YTHFL youthful (adj) *immature* youthfully (adv)
YTHFLNS youthfulness *immaturity*
YTHNKS euthenics *living conditions*
YTHNSH euthanasia *merciful death*
YTHNSK euthanasic *merciful death*
YTHNST euthenist *living conditions*
YTHNTZ euthanatize *kill with mercy* euthanatized euthanatizing
YTHNX euthenics *living conditions*
YTHNZ euthanize *kill with mercy* euthanized euthanizing
YTHNZH euthanasia *merciful death*
YTHNZK euthanasic *merciful death*
YTHRD euthyroid *gland*
YTHRN eutherian *placental mammals*
YTHRYN eutherian *placental mammals*
YTK Utica *city*
YTKDD eutectoid *melting point*
YTKDK eutectic *melting point*
YTKTD eutectoid *melting point*
YTKTK eutectic *melting point*
YTL ayatollah *religious leader*
YTL utile *useful* (Br) utilisable
YTLD utility *fitness, service* utilities
YTLNDR Uitlander *foreigner*
YTLS utilize *use* utilized utilizing (Br) utilise
YTLT utility *fitness, service* utilities
YTLTRN utilitarian *useful*
YTLTRNZM utilitarianism *useful is good*
YTLTRYN utilitarian *useful*
YTLTRYNZM utilitarianism *useful is good*
YTLZ utilize *use* utilized utilizing (Br) utilise
YTLZBL utilizable *useful*

(Br) utilisable
YTLZR utilizer *user* (Br) utiliser
YTLZSHN utilization *use* (Br) utilisation
YTN yachting *boating*
YTNG yachting *boating*
YTNSL utensil *implement*
YTNTSL utensil *implement*
YTP utopia *ideal*
YTPN utopian *ideal*
YTPNZM utopianism *idealism*
YTPST utopist *idealist*
YTPY utopia *ideal*
YTPYN utopian *ideal*
YTPYNZM utopianism *idealism*
YTPZM utopism *idealism*
YTR uteri (pl) *womb* uterus
YTRF eutrophy *mineral enrichment*
YTRFK eutrophic *mineral enrichment*
YTRFKSHN eutrophication *mineral enrichment*
YTRN U-turn *turn around*
YTRN uterine *womb*
YTRS uterus *womb* uteri
YTS Yeats *poet*
YTSH Yiddish *language*
YTSMN yachtsman *sailor* yachtsmen
YTY yautia *plant*
YV uvea *eye*
YV you've *(contr) you have*
YVDS uveitis *inflammation*
YVL uveal *eye*
YVL uvula *throat lobe* uvulas (or) uvulae
YVLR uvular *throat lobe*
YVRVT uvarovite *gemstone*
YVTS uveitis *inflammation*
YVY uvea *eye*
YVYDS uveitis *inflammation*
YVYL uveal *eye*
YVYL uvula *throat lobe* uvulas (or) uvulae
YVYLR uvular *throat lobe*
YVYTS uveitis *inflammation*
YW Iowa *US State*
YWCHF UHF *(abbr)*

Letters aren't doubled for single sounds: to find alley use **L** not **LL**. Use **Y** and **W** as hard sounds only: to find yellow use **YL**. (Br)=British spelling or usage. * See dictionary.

friendliness *easy*

Ultrahigh Frequency

YWKM Joachim *violinist*
YWL you'll *(contr) you will*
YWL you-all *all of you*
YWMBN yohimbine *alkaloid*
YWN yuan *money* yuan
YWNTT uintaite *asphalt*
YWNTYT uintaite *asphalt*
YWR ewer *pitcher*
YWR you're *(contr) you are*
YY IOU *I owe you* IOUs
YY yo-yo *(n) toy* yo-yos
YY yo-yo *(v) fluctuate* yo-yoed yo-yoing
YZ oyez *(interj) court cry* oyesses
YZ use *(v) utilize* used using
YZ yaws *disease*
YZBL usable *(adj) convenient* usably *(adv)*
YZBLD usability *convenience*
YZBLT usability *convenience*
YZD used *not new*
YZFRKCHWR usufructuary *user*
YZFRKT usufruct *right*
YZFRKTR usufructuary *user*
YZFRKTWR usufructuary *user*
YZHL usual *(adj) typical* usually *(adv)*
YZHR usury *high interest rate* usuries
YZHRR usurer *lender*
YZHRS usurious *high interest rate*
YZHRYS usurious *high interest rate*
YZHWL usual *(adj) typical* usually *(adv)*
YZJ usage *practice*
YZNS usance *use, time*
YZNTS usance *use, time*
YZR user *utilizer*
YZR usury *high interest rate* usuries
YZRFRNDL user-friendly *easy*
YZRFRNDLNS user-friendliness *easy*
YZRFRNL user-friendly *easy*
YZRFRNLNS user-

YZRP usurp *seize*
YZRPR usurper *seize*
YZRPSHN usurpation *seizure*
YZRR usurer *lender*
YZRS usurious *high interest rate*
YZRYS usurious *high interest rate*

Z

Z as *(adv, conj, pron, prep) denotes comparison, sequence**
Z Aussie *of Australia*
Z azo *chemistry*
Z ease *(v) relieve* eased easing
Z ease *(n) naturalness, comfort*
Z easy *simple* easier easiest
Z is *exists*
Z Isaiah *prophet*
Z ooze *(v) slow flow* oozed oozing
Z ooze *(n) slime*
Z oozy *slimy* oozier ooziest
Z ouzo *liqueur*
Z use *(v) utilize* used using
Z uzi *(or)* Uzi *gun*
Z xi *Greek letter* xis
Z xu *money* xu
Z z *alphabet letter* z's *(or)* zs
Z zoo *animals* zoos
ZB zebu *animal*
ZBGLN zabaglione *dessert*
ZBGLYN zabaglione *dessert*
ZBK xebec *ship*
ZBL usable *(adj) convenient* usably *(adv)*
ZBLD usability *convenience*

ZBLN zabaglione *dessert*
ZBLT usability *convenience*
ZBLYN zabaglione *dessert*
ZBR zebra *animal* zebras
ZBRWD zebrawood *tree*
ZBSDS asbestos *mineral*
ZBSTS asbestos *mineral*
ZBSTSS asbestosis *disease* asbestoses
ZBY zebu *animal*
ZCHR easy chair *furniture*
ZD used *not new*
ZD zed *(Br) the letter Z*
ZD zeta *Greek letter*
ZD ziti *pasta*
ZD zooid *organism*
ZDG zydeco *music*
ZDK asdic *sonar*
ZDK zaddik *Jewish leader* zaddikim
ZDK zodiac *horoscope*
ZDK zydeco *music*
ZDKL zodiacal *horoscope*
ZDKM zaddikim *(pl) Jewish leader* zaddik
ZDL seidel *mug*
ZDRP eavesdrop *listen*
ZDRPR eavesdropper *listener*
ZDYK zodiac *horoscope*
ZDYKL zodiacal *horoscope*
ZF as if *that**
ZF Azov *(the Sea of) body of water*
ZFD xiphoid *breastbone*
ZFDG zaftig *plump*
ZFLK zoophilic *(or)* zoophilous *love of animals*
ZFLS zoophilous *(or)* zoophilic *love of animals*
ZFR as for *concerning*
ZFR zephyr *breeze, fabric*
ZFRKCHWR usufructuary *user*
ZFRKT usufruct *right*
ZFRKTR usufructuary *user*
ZFRKTWR usufructuary *user*
ZFSTRN xiphisterna *(pl) breastbone* xiphisternum
ZFSTRNM xiphisternum *breastbone* xiphisterna

Use letters that best describe the sounds you hear and omit the vowels. Use **S** or **K** instead of **C**: to find circle use **SRKL**. Use **J** to find joy, **JM** to find gem and **G** to find go.

ZFT zoophyte *animal*
ZFTG zaftig *plump*
ZG zag *turn, angle* zagged zagging
ZG zig *turn, angle* zigged zigging
ZGDKDL zygodactyl *toes*
ZGDKTL zygodactyl *toes*
ZGDKTLS zygodactylous *toes*
ZGGRF zoogeography *animals*
ZGGRFK zoogeographic (or) zoogeographical (adj) *animals* zoogeographically (adv)
ZGGRFR zoogeographer *animals*
ZGM zeugma *phrase*
ZGM zygoma *arch* zygomata
ZGMD zygomata (pl) *arch* zygoma
ZGMDK zygomatic *arch*
ZGMRF zygomorphy *order*
ZGMRFK zygomorphic *order*
ZGMT zygomata (pl) *arch* zygoma
ZGMTK zygomatic *arch*
ZGN easygoing *relaxed*
ZGNG easygoing *relaxed*
ZGNK zoogenic *animals*
ZGPFCZ zygapophyses (pl) *neural arch* zygapophysis
ZGPFSS zygapophysis *neural arch* zygapophyses
ZGPFSZ zygapophyses (pl) *neural arch* zygapophysis
ZGPFZZ zygapophyses (pl) *neural arch* zygapophysis
ZGRFD sgraffito *decoration* sgraffiti
ZGRFT sgraffito *decoration* sgraffiti
ZGRT ziggurat *pyramid*
ZGS azygos *anatomy*
ZGSPR zygospore *reproduction*
ZGT zygote *reproduction*
ZGTN zygotene *reproduction*
ZGWN easygoing *relaxed*

ZGWNG easygoing *relaxed*
ZGYGRF zoogeography *animals*
ZGYGRFK zoogeographic (or) zoogeographical (adj) *animals* zoogeographically (adv)
ZGYGRFR zoogeographer *animals*
ZGZG zigzag *turn, angle* zigzagged zigzagging
ZH Asia *continent*
ZH au jus *in juice*
ZHB jabot *collar*
ZHBR jabiru *bird*
ZHDK Asiatic *of Asia*
ZHDSPR jeu d'esprit *joke* jeux d'esprit
ZHG gigot *meat* gigots
ZHG gigue *dance*
ZHGT gigot *meat* gigots
ZHGWRND jaguarundi *wildcat*
ZHKMR jacamar *bird*
ZHL gelée *cosmetic*
ZHL joual *language*
ZHL usual (adj) *typical* usually (adv)
ZHLN julienne *slice* julienned julienning
ZHLYN julienne *slice* julienned julienning
ZHN Asian *of Asia*
ZHNDRM gendarme *police*
ZHNPRVKTR agent provocateur *sympathizer* agents provocateurs
ZHNR genre *category*
ZHNSKW je ne sais quoi *mystery*
ZHNSQ je ne sais quoi *mystery*
ZHR azure *blue*
ZHR giro *fund transfer*
ZHR osier *tree*
ZHR usury *high interest rate* usuries
ZHRDNR jardinière (or) jardiniere *stand, food*
ZHRDNYR jardinière (or) jardiniere *stand, food*
ZHRR usurer *lender*

ZHRS usurious *high interest rate*
ZHRT azurite *mineral*
ZHRYS usurious *high interest rate*
ZHS au jus *in juice*
ZHSN jacana *bird*
ZHT as yet *until now*
ZHT jeté *ballet*
ZHTK Asiatic *of Asia*
ZHWDVVR joie de vivre *enjoyment*
ZHWL joual *language*
ZHWL usual (adj) *typical* usually (adv)
ZHYDK Asiatic *of Asia*
ZHYT as yet *until now*
ZHYTK Asiatic *of Asia*
ZJ usage *practice*
ZJGRF zoogeography *animals*
ZJGRFK zoogeographic (or) zoogeographical (adj) *animals* zoogeographically (adv)
ZJGRFR zoogeographer *animals*
ZJNK zoogenic *animals*
ZJYGRF zoogeography *animals*
ZJYGRFK zoogeographic (or) zoogeographical (adj) *animals* zoogeographically (adv)
ZJYGRFR zoogeographer *animals*
ZK ASCII *computer language*
ZK azoic *before life*
ZK Isaac *biblical son*
ZKD zucchetto *skullcap* zucchettos
ZKL Ezekiel *prophet*
ZKN zucchini *vegetable* zucchini (or) zucchinis
ZKPR zookeeper *animals*
ZKRDNT z-coordinate *math*
ZKSS z-axis *math*
ZKT zucchetto *skullcap* zucchettos
ZKWRDNT z-coordinate *math*
ZKYL Ezekiel *prophet*

Letters aren't doubled for single sounds: to find alley use **L** not **LL**. Use **Y** and **W** as hard sounds only: to find yellow use **YL**. (Br)=British spelling or usage. * See dictionary.

ZL azalea *plant*
ZL azole *chemical*
ZL easel *stand*
ZL easily *simply*
ZL Oslo *city*
ZL ouzel *bird, dipper*
ZL zeal *eagerness*
ZL Zulu *African*
ZLCH zilch *nothing*
ZLD zloty *money* zlotys (or) zloty
ZLDK zeolitic *silicate*
ZLDN xylidine *amino*
ZLFGS xylophagous *wood-eating*
ZLFN xylophone *music*
ZLFNST xylophonist *musician*
ZLG zoology *animals*
ZLGRF xylograph *engraver*
ZLGRF xylography *engraving*
ZLGRFK xylographic *engraving*
ZLGRFKL xylographical *engraving*
ZLGRFR xylographer *engraver*
ZLJ zoology *animals*
ZLJKL zoological (adj) *animals* zoologically (adv)
ZLJST zoologist *animals*
ZLL xylol *hydrocarbon*
ZLM Islam *religion*
ZLM xylem *plant stem*
ZLMBD Islamabad *city*
ZLMK Islamic *of Islam*
ZLN xylan *plant sugar*
ZLN xylene *hydrocarbon*
ZLN zillion *large number*
ZLNGZ as long as *ever since*
ZLNR zillionaire *rich one*
ZLS xylose *sugar*
ZLS zealous *passionate*
ZLSL zealously *passionate*
ZLSNS zealousness *passion*
ZLT zealot *fanatic*
ZLT zeolite *silicate*
ZLT zloty *money* zlotys (or) zloty
ZLTK zeolitic *silicate*
ZLTL xylitol *alcohol*

ZLTR zealotry *fanaticism* zealotries
ZLTR zoolatry *animal worship*
ZLY azalea *plant*
ZLYN zillion *large number*
ZLYNR zillionaire *rich one*
ZM asthma *disease*
ZM ism *belief*
ZM zamia *plant*
ZM zoom *speed*
ZMB Zambia *country*
ZMB zombie *voodoo*
ZMBBW Zimbabwe *country*
ZMBF zombify *voodoo* zombified zombifying zombifies
ZMBFKSHN zombification *voodoo*
ZMBLK zombielike *voodoo*
ZMBY Zambia *country*
ZMBYZM zombiism *voodoo*
ZMBZM zombiism *voodoo*
ZMCZ zymoses (pl) *fermentation, infection, disease* zymosis
ZMDK asthmatic *breathing difficulty*
ZMDK osmotic *take into*
ZMDK zymotic *fermentation, infection, disease*
ZMDKL asthmatically *breathing difficulty*
ZMDKL osmotically *take into*
ZMDKL zymotically *fermentation, infection, disease*
ZMGRM zymogram *enzymes*
ZMJN zymogen *protein*
ZMLNZ zoom lens *camera*
ZMM osmium *mineral*
ZMMDR osmometer *pressure*
ZMMTR osmometer *pressure*
ZMND osmunda *plant*
ZMNT easement *land*
ZMRF zoomorph *deity*
ZMRFK zoomorphic *deity*
ZMRK easy mark *gullible one*
ZMS zymase *enzyme*

ZMSN zymosan *yeast*
ZMSS osmosis *absorption*
ZMSS zymosis *fermentation, infection, disease* zymoses
ZMSZ zymoses (pl) *fermentation, infection, disease* zymosis
ZMTH azimuth *arc*
ZMTHL azimuthal (adj) *arc* azimuthally (adv)
ZMTK asthmatic *breathing difficulty*
ZMTK osmotic *take into*
ZMTK zymotic *fermentation, infection, disease*
ZMTKL asthmatically *breathing difficulty*
ZMTKL osmotically *take into*
ZMTKL zymotically *fermentation, infection, disease*
ZMY zamia *plant*
ZMYM osmium *mineral*
ZMZ zymase *enzyme*
ZN ozone *oxygen*
ZN xenia *pollen*
ZN zany (n) *foolish one* zanies
ZN zany (adj) *foolish* zanier zaniest
ZN zayin *Hebrew letter*
ZN Zen *Buddhism*
ZN zinnia *flower*
ZN Zion *Israel*
ZN zone (v) *surround, partition* zoned zoning
ZN zone (n) *region*
ZN Zuni *Native American*
ZNBDK xenobiotic *chemical*
ZNBTK xenobiotic *chemical*
ZNBYDK xenobiotic *chemical*
ZNBYTK xenobiotic *chemical*
ZND Xanadu *heaven*
ZNDR zander *fish* zander (or) zanders
ZNDZ oohs and aahs (interj) *appreciation*
ZNDZ zounds (interj) *oath*
ZNFB xenophobe *fear of foreigners*

Use letters that best describe the sounds you hear and omit the vowels. Use **S** or **K** instead of **C**: to find circle use **SRKL**. Use **J** to find joy, **JM** to find gem and **G** to find go.

ZNFB xenophobia *fear of foreigners*

ZNFBK xenophobic *fear of foreigners*

ZNFBKL xenophobically *fear of foreigners*

ZNFBY xenophobia *fear of foreigners*

ZNFL xenophile *love of foreign*

ZNFNDL zinfandel *wine*

ZNG zing *(n) zest (v) speed, hit*

ZNG zingy *sharp* zingier zingiest

ZNGDT zonked-out *stupefied*

ZNGK zinc *metal* zinced (or) zincked zincing (or) zincking

ZNGK zonk *strike*

ZNGKT zincite *mineral*

ZNGKT zonked *stupefied*

ZNGKTT zonked-out *stupefied*

ZNGLS isinglass *gelatin*

ZNGNK xenogeneic *other species*

ZNGNYK xenogeneic *other species*

ZNGR zinger *surprise*

ZNGR zingier *sharper*

ZNGRF xenograft *tissue*

ZNGRFT xenograft *tissue*

ZNGST zingiest *sharpest*

ZNGT zonked *stupefied*

ZNGTT zonked-out *stupefied*

ZNGYR zingier *sharper*

ZNGYST zingiest *sharpest*

ZNHR Eisenhower *US president*

ZNHWR Eisenhower *US president*

ZNJNK xenogeneic *other species*

ZNJNYK xenogeneic *other species*

ZNK zinc *metal* zinced (or) zincked zincing (or) zincking

ZNK zonk *strike*

ZNKDT zonked-out *stupefied*

ZNKT zincite *mineral*

ZNKT zonked *stupefied*

ZNKTT zonked-out *stupefied*

ZNL azonal *immature soil*

ZNL zanily *foolishly*

ZNL zonal (adj) *mature soil, area* zonally (adv)

ZNLR ozone layer *atmosphere*

ZNLTH xenolith *rock*

ZNLTHK xenolithic *rock*

ZNLYR ozone layer *atmosphere*

ZNN xenon *element*

ZNNS zaniness *foolishness* zany

ZNR zanier *foolish*

ZNS easiness *simplicity*

ZNS usance *use, time*

ZNSFR ozonosphere *ozone layer*

ZNSHN ozonation *oxygen*

ZNSHN zonation *arrangement*

ZNST zaniest *foolish*

ZNST Zionist *Jew*

ZNT isn't *(contraction) is not*

ZNTH zenith *high point*

ZNTHFL xanthophyll *pigment*

ZNTHN xanthan *thickener*

ZNTHN xanthene *dye*

ZNTHN xanthine *uric acid*

ZNTHN xanthone *ketone*

ZNTHP Xanthippe (or) Xantippe *wife of Socrates, shrew*

ZNTHT xanthate *acid*

ZNTP Xantippe (or) Xanthippe *wife of Socrates, shrew*

ZNTRPK xenotropic *reproduction*

ZNTS usance *use, time*

ZNY xenia *pollen*

ZNY zinnia *flower*

ZNYR zanier *foolish*

ZNYST zaniest *foolish*

ZNZ oohs and aahs *(interj) appreciation*

ZNZ ozonize *add ozone* ozonized ozonizing

ZNZ zounds *(interj) oath*

ZNZM Zionism *Israel*

ZP zap *hit, irradiate* zapped zapping

ZP zip *speed, fasten* zipped zipping

ZP zippy *fast* zippier zippiest

ZPGN zip gun *weapon*

ZPKD ZIP Code (n) *address* zip-code (v)

ZPLN zeppelin *airship*

ZPLNGKDR zooplankter *animal*

ZPLNGKTN zooplankton *animals*

ZPLNGKTR zooplankter *animal*

ZPLNKDR zooplankter *animal*

ZPLNKTN zooplankton *animals*

ZPLNKTR zooplankter *animal*

ZPR zapper *hitter*

ZPR zipper *closure, fast one*

ZPR zippier *fast*

ZPST zippiest *fast*

ZPYR zippier *fast*

ZPYST zippiest *fast*

ZR czar *ruler*

ZR easier *simpler*

ZR oozier *slimy*

ZR tsar (or) tzar *ruler*

ZR user *utilizer*

ZR usury *high interest rate* usuries

ZR Zaire *country*

ZR zaire *money*

ZR zero *(n) number* zeros

ZR zero *(v) focus* zeroed zeroing

ZR zori *shoe* zori

ZRBJN Azerbaijan *region*

ZRBS zero-base (or) zero-based *budget*

ZRBSHN Azerbaijan *region*

ZRBST zero-based (or) zero-base *budget*

ZRBZHN Azerbaijan *region*

ZRD izzard *letter Z*

ZRDRM xeroderma *skin*

ZRFDK xerophytic *plant*

Letters aren't doubled for single sounds: to find alley use **L** not **LL**. Use **Y** and **W** as hard sounds only: to find yellow use **YL**. (Br)=British spelling or usage. * See dictionary.

ZRFL xerophile (or) xerophilous *(adj) dry*

ZRFL xerophily *(n) dryness*

ZRFLS xerophilous (or) xerophile *(adj) dry*

ZRFRNDL user-friendly *easy*

ZRFRNDLNS user-friendliness *easy*

ZRFRNL user-friendly *easy*

ZRFRNLNS user-friendliness *easy*

ZRFT xerophyte *plant*

ZRFTK xerophytic *plant*

ZRFTZM xerophytism *plant*

ZRFYL xerophile (or) xerophilous *(adj) dry*

ZRGRF xerography *copy*

ZRGRFK xerographic *copy*

ZRGRFKL xerographically *copy*

ZRK xeric *dry*

ZRK zerk *grease fitting*

ZRK Zurich *city*

ZRKN zircon *mineral*

ZRKN zirconia *crystal*

ZRKNM zirconium *element*

ZRKNY zirconia *crystal*

ZRKNYM zirconium *element*

ZRKS Ozarks *region*

ZRKS Xerox *(trademark) copier*

ZRL Israel *country*

ZRL Israeli *of Israel*

ZRLT Israelite *of Israel*

ZRN czarina *wife of czar*

ZRP usurp *seize*

ZRPR usurper *seize*

ZRPSHN usurpation *seizure*

ZRR usurer *lender*

ZRS usurious *high interest rate*

ZRSKP Xeriscape *(trademark) little water*

ZRSM zero-sum *gain/loss*

ZRSTRNZM Zoroastrianism *religion*

ZRSTRYNZM Zoroastrianism *religion*

ZRTH zeroth *number zero*

ZRWSTRNZM Zoroastrianism *religion*

ZRWSTRYNZM

ZRX Ozarks *region*

ZRX Xerox *(trademark) copier*

ZRYL Israel *country*

ZRYLT Israelite *of Israel*

ZRYS usurious *high interest rate*

ZRZ Azores *islands*

ZRZL zarzuela *operetta*

ZRZM czarism *dictatorship*

ZRZWL zarzuela *operetta*

ZS Xhosa *African*

ZS Zeus *Greek god*

ZS zoysia *grass*

ZSD zesty *enthusiastic, flavorful* zestier zestiest

ZSDR zestier *enthusiasm, flavor*

ZSDRL zoosterol *steroid*

ZSDST zestiest *enthusiasm, flavor*

ZSDYR zestier *enthusiasm, flavor*

ZSDYST zestiest *enthusiasm, flavor*

ZSFL zestful (adj) *enthusiasm, flavor* zestfully (adv)

ZSFLNS zestfulness *enthusiasm, flavor*

ZSH zoysia *grass*

ZSNZ as soon as *when*

ZSPR zoospore *reproduction*

ZSPRM azoospermia *no sperm*

ZSPRMY azoospermia *no sperm*

ZSPRNGM zoosporangium *spore case*

ZSPRNGYM zoosporangium *spore case*

ZSPRNJM zoosporangium *spore case*

ZSPRNJYM zoosporangium *spore case*

ZST easiest *simplest*

ZST ooziest *slimy*

ZST zest *enthusiasm, flavor*

ZST zesty *enthusiastic, flavorful* zestier zestiest

ZSTFL zestful (adj) *enthusiasm, flavor* zestfully (adv)

ZSTFLNS zestfulness *enthusiasm, flavor*

ZSTR zestier *enthusiasm, flavor*

ZSTR zoster *herpes*

ZSTRL zoosterol *steroid*

ZSTRT easy street *no worries*

ZSTST zestiest *enthusiasm, flavor*

ZSTYR zestier *enthusiasm, flavor*

ZSTYST zestiest *enthusiasm, flavor*

ZSY zoysia *grass*

ZT as to *concerning*

ZT zeta *Greek letter*

ZT zit *(slang) pimple*

ZT ziti *pasta*

ZTGST zeitgeist *(often capitalized) culture*

ZTH as though *as if*

ZTH azoth *mercury*

ZTHR zither *music*

ZTHRST zitherist *musician*

ZTK Aztec *Mexican*

ZTK zaddik *Jewish leader* zaddikim

ZTKM zaddikim (pl) *Jewish leader* zaddik

ZTKN Aztecan *Mexican*

ZTKNKL zootechnical *animals*

ZTKNKS zootechnics *animals*

ZTKNX zootechnics *animals*

ZTM azotemia *disease*

ZTMY azotemia *disease*

ZTR azoturia *horse disease*

ZTRY azoturia *horse disease*

ZTSDR zoot-suiter *clothing*

ZTST zoot suit *clothing*

ZTSTR zoot-suiter *clothing*

ZTYR azoturia *horse disease*

ZTYRY azoturia *horse disease*

ZV as of *since*

ZV Azov (the Sea of) *body of water*

ZVR Xavier *Catholic saint*

ZVYR Xavier *Catholic saint*

ZW zoea *crab* zoeae (or)

Use letters that best describe the sounds you hear and omit the vowels. Use **S** or **K** instead of **C**: to find circle use **SRKL**. Use **J** to find joy, **JM** to find gem and **G** to find go.

zoeas

ZW zowie *(interj) surprise*
ZWBK zwieback *cookie*
ZWD zooid *organism*
ZWFLK zoophilic (or)
zoophilous *love of animals*
ZWFLS zoophilous (or)
zoophilic *love of animals*
ZWFT zoophyte *animal*
ZWGGRF zoogeography
animals
ZWGGRFK zoogeographic
(or) zoogeographical (adj)
animals
zoogeographically (adv)
ZWGGRFR zoogeographer
animals
ZWGNK zoogenic *animals*
ZWGYGRF zoogeography
animals
ZWGYGRFK zoogeographic
(or) zoogeographical (adj)
animals
zoogeographically (adv)
ZWGYGRFR
zoogeographer *animals*
ZWJGRF zoogeography
animals
ZWJGRFK zoogeographic
(or) zoogeographical (adj)
animals
zoogeographically (adv)
ZWJGRFR zoogeographer
animals
ZWJNK zoogenic *animals*
ZWJYGRF zoogeography
animals
ZWJYGRFK zoogeographic
(or) zoogeographical (adj)
animals
zoogeographically (adv)
ZWJYGRFR zoogeographer
animals
ZWK azoic *before life*
ZWLG zoology *animals*
ZWLJ zoology *animals*
ZWLJKL zoological (adj)
animals zoologically (adv)
ZWLJST zoologist *animals*
ZWLTR zoolatry *animal
worship*
ZWLZ as well as *also*

ZWMRF zoomorph *deity*
ZWMRFK zoomorphic *deity*
ZWPLNGKDR zooplankter
animal
ZWPLNGKTN zooplankton
animals
ZWPLNGKTR zooplankter
animal
ZWPLNKDR zooplankter
animal
ZWPLNKTN zooplankton
animals
ZWPLNKTR zooplankter
animal
ZWSDRL zoosterol *steroid*
ZWSPR zoospore
reproduction
ZWSPRM azoospermia *no
sperm*
ZWSPRMY azoospermia *no
sperm*
ZWSPRNGM
zoosporangium *spore case*
ZWSPRNGYM
zoosporangium *spore case*
ZWSPRNJM
zoosporangium *spore case*
ZWSPRNJYM
zoosporangium *spore case*
ZWSTRL zoosterol *steroid*
ZWTKNKL zootechnical
animals
ZWTKNKS zootechnics
animals
ZWTKNX zootechnics
animals
ZWTRN zwitterion *particle*
ZWTRYN zwitterion *particle*
ZWY zoea *crab* zoeae (or)
zoeas
ZXS z-axis *math*
ZY Isaiah *prophet*
ZYKSS z-axis *math*
ZYLDK zeolitic *silicate*
ZYLT zeolite *silicate*
ZYLTK zeolitic *silicate*
ZYN zayin *Hebrew letter*
ZYN zillion *large number*
ZYN Zion *Israel*
ZYNR zillionaire *rich one*
ZYNST Zionist *Jew*
ZYNZM Zionism *Israel*

ZYR easier *simpler*
ZYR oozier *slimy*
ZYR zaire *money*
ZYR Zaire *country*
ZYS Zeus *Greek god*
ZYST easiest *simplest*
ZYST ooziest *slimy*
ZYT as yet *until now*
ZYXS z-axis *math*
ZZ as is *in this condition*
ZZ zoysia *grass*
ZZFL tsetse fly *insect* tsetse
flies
ZZH zoysia *grass*
ZZTH zizith *tassels*
ZZY zoysia *grass*

Letters aren't doubled for single sounds: to find alley use **L** not **LL**. Use **Y** and **W** as hard
sounds only: to find yellow use **YL**. (Br)=British spelling or usage. * See dictionary.